KEY TO PRONUNCIATIONS

s	see, miss	z	zeal, lazy, those
sh	shoe, push	zh	vision, measure
t	ten, bit		
th	thin, path	ə	occurs only in unaccented syllables and indicates the sound of
t̶h	that, other		a *in* alone
ŭ	up, love		e *in* system
ū	use, cute		i *in* easily
û	urge, burn		o *in* gallop
v	voice, live		u *in* circus
w	west, away		
y	yes, young		

ME SCALE

600 B.C.–A.D. 125

B.C.

600 Ezekiel
Babylonians sack Jerusalem
Exile in Babylon
Second Isaiah
Cyrus begins Persian Empire
Haggai and Zechariah
Second temple built

500

Nehemiah rebuilds Jerusalem

400 The Pentateuch accepted as Scripture (or 550?)

Alexander conquers East

300 Egypt rules Palestine

The Prophets accepted as Scripture

200 Syria rules Palestine

Maccabees
Hasmonean rulers

100

Romans conquer Palestine

Herod the Great

Third temple built

A.D.

Jesus' ministry

Paul's ministry, letters

Romans destroy Jerusalem

100 The Writings close OT Canon

Last NT books written

THE INTERPRETER'S DICTIONARY OF THE BIBLE

EDITORIAL BOARD

THE INTERPRETER'S DICTIONARY OF THE BIBLE

An Illustrated Encyclopedia

IDENTIFYING AND EXPLAINING ALL PROPER NAMES AND SIGNIFICANT TERMS AND SUBJECTS IN THE HOLY SCRIPTURES, INCLUDING THE APOCRYPHA

With Attention to Archaeological Discoveries and Researches into the Life and Faith of Ancient Times

מלאה הארץ דעה את־יהוה

The earth shall be full of the knowledge of the Lord—ISAIAH 11:9*c*

NASHVILLE *Abingdon Press* NEW YORK

ISBN 0-687-19272-2
Library of Congress Catalog Card Number: 62-9387

I

MANUFACTURED BY THE PARTHENON PRESS, AT NASHVILLE, TENNESSEE, UNITED STATES OF AMERICA

ABBREVIATIONS

א — Codex Sinaiticus
A — Codex Alexandrinus
AA — *Alttestamentliche Abhandlungen*
AAA — *Annals of Archaeology and Anthropology*
AASOR — *Annual of the American Schools of Oriental Research*
Ab. — Aboth
Add. Esth. — Additions to Esther
AFO — *Archiv für Orientforschung*
AJA — *American Journal of Archaeology*
AJSL — *American Journal of Semitic Languages and Literatures*
AJT — *American Journal of Theology*
Akkad. — Akkadian
Amer. Trans. — *The Complete Bible, an American Translation* (Smith and Goodspeed)
ANEP — J. B. Pritchard, ed., *The Ancient Near East in Pictures*
ANET — J. B. Pritchard, ed., *Ancient Near Eastern Texts*
AO — *Der alte Orient*
APAW — *Abhandlungen der Preussichen Akademie der Wissenschaften*
Apoc. — Apocrypha
Apocal. Bar. — Apocalypse of Baruch
Aq. — Aquila
'Ar. — 'Aruk
ARAB — D. D. Luckenbill, *Ancient Records of Assyria and Babylonia*
Arab. — Arabic
'Arak. — 'Arakin
Aram. — Aramaic
ARE — J. H. Breasted, *Ancient Records of Egypt*
ARN — Aboth d'Rabbi Nathan
art. — article
ARW — *Archiv für Religionswissenschaft*
ASAE — *Annales du service des antiquités de l'Égypte*
Asmp. Moses — Assumption of Moses
ASV — American Standard Version (1901)
AT — *Altes* or *Ancien Testament*
ATR — *Anglican Theological Review*
'A.Z. — 'Abodah Zarah

B — Codex Vaticanus
BA — *Biblical Archaeologist*
Bar. — Baruch
Barn. — The Epistle of Barnabas
BASOR — *Bulletin of the American Schools of Oriental Research*
B.B. — Baba Bathra
Bek. — Bekereth
Bel — Bel and the Dragon
Ber. — Berakoth
Bez. — Beẓah
B.K. — Baba Ḳamma
bk. — book
B.M. — Baba Meẓi'a
Bibl. — *Biblica*
Bibl. Stud. — *Biblische Studien*
Bik. — Bikkurim
BS — *Bibliotheca Sacra*
BW — *Biblical World*
BWANT — *Beiträge zur Wissenschaft vom Alten und Neuen Testament*
BWAT — *Beiträge zur Wissenschaft vom Alten Testament*
BZ — *Biblische Zeitschrift*
BZAW — *Beihefte zur Zeitschrift für die alttestamentliche Wissenschaft*
BZF — *Biblische Zeitfragen*

C — Codex Ephraemi Syri
ca. — *circa* (about)
CDC — Cairo Genizah Document of the Damascus Covenanters (The Zadokite Documents)
cf. — *confer* (compare)
ch. — chapter
Chr. — Chronicles
Clem. — Clement (I and II)
Clem. Misc. — Clement of Alexandria *Miscellanies*
Col. — Colossians
col. — column
Cor. — Corinthians
CSEL — *Corpus Scriptorum Ecclesiasticorum Latinorum*
D — Codex Bezae; Codex Claromontanus; Deuteronomist source
Dan. — Daniel
Dem. — Demai
Deut. — Deuteronomy
Did. — The Didache
div. — division
DSS — Dead Sea Scrolls

E — east; Elohist source
EB — Early Bronze Age
EB — *Études bibliques*
Eccl. — Ecclesiastes
Ecclus. — Ecclesiasticus
ed. — edited, edition, editor
e.g. — *exempli gratia* (for example)
Egyp. — Egyptian
EH — *Exegetisches Handbuch zum Alten Testament*
EI — Early Iron Age
Eph. — Ephesians
'Er. — 'Erubin
ERV — English Revised Version (1881-85)
Esd. — Esdras
esp. — especially
Esth. — Esther
ET — *Expository Times*
Ethio. — Ethiopian
Euseb. Hist. — Eusebius *History of the Christian Church*
Euseb. Onom. — Eusebius *Onomasticon*
Exod. — Exodus
Exp. — *The Expositor*
Ezek. — Ezekiel

fem. — feminine
fig. — figure (illustration)
FRLANT — *Forschungen zur Religion und Literatur des Alten und Neuen Testaments*

G — Greek
Gal. — Galatians
Gen. — Genesis
Giṭ. — Giṭṭin
Gordon — C. H. Gordon, *Ugaritic Manual*
Gr. — Greek
GSAI — *Giornale della società asiatica italiana*

GTT — *Gereformeerd theologisch Tijdschrift*

H — Hebrew; Holiness Code
Hab. — Habakkuk
Hag. — Haggai
Ḥag. — Ḥagigah
Ḥal. — Ḥallah
HAT — *Handbuch zum Alten Testament*
HDB — James Hastings, ed., *A Dictionary of the Bible*
Heb. — Hebrew; the Letter to the Hebrews
HERE — James Hastings, ed., *Encyclopedia of Religion and Ethics*
Herm. Mand. — The Shepherd of Hermas, Mandates
Herm. Sim. — The Shepherd of Hermas, Similitudes
Herm. Vis. — The Shepherd of Hermas, Visions
Hitt. — Hittite
HKAT — *Handkommentar zum Alten Testament*
Hor. — Horayoth
Hos. — Hosea
HS — *Die heilige Schrift des Alten Testaments*
HTR — *Harvard Theological Review*
HUCA — *Hebrew Union College Annual*

ICC — International Critical Commentary
i.e. — *id est* (that is)
IEJ — *Israel Exploration Journal*
Ign. Eph. — The Epistle of Ignatius to the Ephesians
Ign. Magn. — The Epistle of Ignatius to the Magnesians
Ign. Phila. — The Epistle of Ignatius to the Philadelphians
Ign. Polyc. — The Epistle of Ignatius to Polycarp
Ign. Rom. — The Epistle of Ignatius to the Romans
Ign. Smyr. — The Epistle of Ignatius to the Smyrnaeans
Ign. Trall. — The Epistle of Ignatius to the Trallians
intro. — introduction
Iren. Her. — Irenaeus *Against Heresies*
Iron — Iron Age
Isa. — Isaiah

J — Yahwist source
JA — *Journal asiatique*
JAOS — *Journal of the American Oriental Society*
Jas. — James
JBL — *Journal of Biblical Literature and Exegesis*
JBR — *Journal of Bible and Religion*
JEA — *Journal of Egyptian Archaeology*
Jer. — Jeremiah
JJGL — *Jahrbuch für jüdische Geschichte und Literatur*
JNES — *Journal of Near Eastern Studies*
Jos. Antiq. — Josephus *The Antiquities of the Jews*
Jos. Apion — Josephus *Against Apion*
Jos. Life — Josephus *Life*
Jos. War — Josephus *The Jewish War*
Josh. — Joshua
JPOS — *Journal of the Palestine Oriental Society*
JQR — *Jewish Quarterly Review*
JR — *Journal of Religion*
JRAS — *Journal of the Royal Asiatic Society*
JSOR — *Journal of the Society of Oriental Research*
J.T. — Jerusalem Talmud
Jth. — Judith
JTS — *Journal of Theological Studies*
Jub. — Jubilees
Judg. — Judges
Just. Apol. — Justin Martyr *Apology*
Just. Dial. — Justin Martyr *Dialogue with Trypho*

KAT — *Kommentar zum Alten Testament*
Kel. — Kelim
Ker. — Kerithoth
Keth. — Kethuboth
KHC — *Kurzer Hand-Kommentar zum Alten Testament*
Ḳid. — Ḳiddushin
Kil. — Kil'ayim
KJV — King James Version
KUB — *Keilschrifturkunden aus Boghazköi*

L — Lukan source
Lam. — Lamentations
Lat. — Latin
LB — Late Bronze Age
Lev. — Leviticus
LXX — Septuagint

M — Matthean source
M. — Mishna
Ma'as. — Ma'asroth
Ma'as Sh. — Ma'aser Sheni
Macc. — Maccabees
Mak. — Makkoth
Maksh. — Makshirin
Mal. — Malachi
Mart. Polyc. — *The Martyrdom of Polycarp*
masc. — masculine
Matt. — Matthew
MB — Middle Bronze Age
Meg. — Megillah
Me'il. — Me'ilah
Mek. — Mekilta
Men. — Menaḥoth
mg. — margin
MGWJ — *Monatsschrift für Geschichte und Wissenschaft des Judentums*
Mic. — Micah
Miḳ. — Miḳwa'oth
M.Ḳ. — Mo'ed Ḳaṭan
MS, MSS — manuscript, manuscripts
MT — Masoretic Text
MVAG — *Mitteilungen der vorderasiatisch-aegyptischen Gesellschaft*

N — north
n. — note
Nah. — Nahum
Naz. — Nazir
NE — northeast
Ned. — Nedarim
Neg. — Nega'im
Neh. — Nehemiah
NF — Neue Folge
Nid. — Niddah
NKZ — *Neue kirchliche Zeitschrift*
NS — Nova series
NT — New Testament
NTS — *New Testament Studies*
NTSt — *Nieuwe theologische Studien*
NTT — *Nieuw theologisch Tijdschrift*
Num. — Numbers
NW — northwest

Obad. — Obadiah
Ohol. — Oholoth
OL — Old Latin
OLZ — *Orientalistische Literaturzeitung*
'Or. — 'Orlah
OT — Old Testament

P — Priestly source
p., pp. — page, pages
Par. — Parah
PEQ — *Palestine Exploration Quarterly* (*Palestine Exploration Quarterly Fund*)
Pers. — Persian
Pes. — Pesaḥim
Pesiḳ. dRK — Pesiḳta di Rab Kahana
Pesiḳ. R. — Pesiḳtha Rabbathi
Pet. — Peter
Phil. — Philippians
Philem. — Philemon
Phoen. — Phoenicia
Pir. R. El. — Pirke di Rabbi Eliezer
PJ — *Palästina Jahrbuch*
pl. — plate (herein, color illustration)
Pliny Nat. Hist. — Pliny *Natural History*

Polyc. Phil. — The Epistle of Polycarp to the Philippians
Prayer Man. — The Prayer of Manasseh
Prov. — Proverbs
Ps., Pss. — Psalm, Psalms
PSBA — *Proceedings of the Society of Biblical Archaeology*
Pseudep. — Pseudepigrapha
Pss. Sol. — Psalms of Solomon
pt. — part
PTR — *Princeton Theological Review*

Q — *Quelle* ("Sayings" source in the gospels)
1QH — Thanksgiving Hymns
1QIs[a] — Isaiah Scroll (published by the American Schools of Oriental Research)
1QIs[b] — Isaiah Scroll (published by E. L. Sukenik, Hebrew University, Jerusalem, Israel)
1QM — War Scroll
1QpHab — Habakkuk Commentary
1QS — Manual of Discipline
1QSa — Rule of the Congregation

RB — *Revue biblique*
REJ — *Revue des études juives*
Rev. — Revelation
rev. — revised, revision, reviser
R. H. — Rosh Hashanah
RHPR — *Revue d'histoire et de philosophie religieuses*
RHR — *Revue de l'histoire des religions*
Rom. — Romans
RR — *Ricerche religiose*
RS — *Revue sémitique*
RSR — *Recherches de science religieuse*
RSV — Revised Standard Version (1946-52)
RTP — *Revue de théologie et de philosophie*

S — south
Sam. — Samuel
Samar. — Samaritan recension
Sanh. — Sanhedrin
SE — southeast
sec. — section
Shab. — Shabbath
Sheb. — Shebi'ith
Shebu. — Shebu'oth
Sheḳ. — Sheḳalim
SL — *Series Latina*
Song of S. — Song of Songs
Song Thr. Ch. — Song of the Three Children (or Young Men)
Soṭ. — Soṭah
SPAW — *Sitzungsberichte der Preussischen Akademie der Wissenschaften*
STZ — *Schweizerische theologische Zeitschrift*
Suk. — Sukkah
Sumer. — Sumerian
Sus. — Susanna
SW — southwest
SWP — *Survey of Western Palestine*
Symm. — Symmachus
Syr. — Syriac

Ta'an. — Ta'anith
Tac. Ann. — Tacitus *Annals*
Tac. Hist. — Tacitus *Histories*
Tam. — Tamid
Tanḥ. — Tanḥuma
Targ. — Targum
T.B. — Babylonian Talmud
TdbK. — Tanna debe Eliyahu
Tem. — Temurah
Ter. — Terumoth
Tert. Apol. — Tertullian *Apology*
Tert. Marcion — Tertullian *Against Marcion*
Tert. Presc. Her. — Tertullian *Prescriptions Against the Heretics*
Test. Asher — Testament of Asher
Test. Benj. — Testament of Benjamin
Test. Dan — Testament of Dan
Test. Gad — Testament of Gad
Test. Iss. — Testament of Issachar
Test. Joseph — Testament of Joseph
Test. Judah — Testament of Judah
Test. Levi — Testament of Levi
Test. Naph. — Testament of Naphtali
Test. Reuben — Testament of Reuben
Test. Simeon — Testament of Simeon
Test. Zeb. — Testament of Zebulun
Theod. — Theodotion
Theol. — *Theology*
Theol. Rundschau — *Theologische Rundschau*
Thess. — Thessalonians
Tim. — Timothy
Tit. — Titus
TLZ — *Theologische Literaturzeitung*
Tob. — Tobit
Ṭoh. — Ṭohoroth
Tosaf. — Tosafoth
Tosef. — Tosefta
TQ — *Theologische Quartalschrift*
trans. — translated, translation, translator
Tristram *NHB* — H. B. Tristram, *The Natural History of the Bible*
TSBA — *Transactions of the Society of Biblical Archaeology*
TSK — *Theologische Studien und Kritiken*
TT — *Theologisch Tijdschrift*
TU — *Texte und Untersuchungen zur Geschichte der altchristlichen Literatur*
TWNT — *Theologisches Wörterbuch zum Neuen Testament*
Ṭ.Y. — Ṭebul Yom

Ugar. — Ugaritic
'Uḳ. — 'Uḳẓin

vol. — volume
vs., vss. — verse, verses
VT — *Vetus Testamentum*
Vulg. — Vulgate

W — west
WC — Westminster Commentaries
Wisd. Sol. — Wisdom of Solomon
WZKM — *Wiener Zeitschrift für die Kunde des Morgenlandes*

Y — Yahweh
Yeb. — Yebamoth
Yom. — Yoma

ZA — *Zeitschrift für Assyriologie und verwandte Gebiete*
Zab. — Zabin
ZAW — *Zeitschrift für die alttestamentliche Wissenschaft*
ZDMG — *Zeitschrift der deutschen morgenländischen Gesellschaft*
ZDPV — *Zeitschrift des deutschen Palästina-Vereins*
Zeb. — Zebaḥim
Zech. — Zechariah
Zeph. — Zephaniah
ZNW — *Zeitschrift für die neutestamentliche Wissenschaft und die Kunde der älteren Kirche*
ZS — *Zeitschrift für Semitistik*
ZST — *Zeitschrift für systematische Theologie*
ZThK — *Zeitschrift für Theologie und Kirche*

K

KAB kăb [קב]; KJV CAB. A measure of capacity mentioned only in II Kings 6:25. According to Josephus and rabbinical sources it would be slightly larger than a quart. *See* WEIGHTS AND MEASURES § C4*j*.

KABZEEL kăb′zĭ əl [קבצאל, may God gather]. Alternately: JEKABZEEL jĭ— [יקבצאל] (Neh. 11:25). A city in the extreme SE part of Judah, near the border of Edom (Josh. 15:21). It was the native town of Benaiah, one of the chief officers of David and Solomon (II Sam. 23:20; I Chr. 11:22). It was one of the towns reoccupied by the Judeans after their return from the Babylonian exile. The site is unknown. S. COHEN

KADESH, KADESH-BARNEA kā′dĭsh, bär′nĭ ə [קדש, קדש ברנע; Καδὴς τοῦ Βαρνή]; KJV Apoc. CADES kā′dēz [Κῆδες, Κάδης] (I Macc. 11:63, 73); CADES-BARNE kā′dēz bär′nĭ [Καδὴς Βαρνή] (Jth. 5:14); KADES kā′dēz [Κάδης] (Jth. 1:9). Alternately: ENMISHPAT ĕn mĭsh′păt [עין משפט, spring of judgment] (Gen. 14:7); MERIBATH-KADESH mĕr′ə băth kā′dĭsh [מרבת קדש, (waters of) strife at Kadesh] (Deut. 32:51; Ezek. 47:19; 48:28); KJV MERIBAH-KADESH mĕr′ə bə— in Deut. 32:51. An oasis in the Wilderness of Zin, where the Israelites encamped for a lengthy period during their travels from Egypt to Canaan.

1. Name. The names Kadesh and Kedesh are used for cities that were ancient sanctuaries in the land of Canaan; the MT is usually careful to use the former in the cities of Judah and the latter for those in the N. The meaning of the word "Barnea," which is appended to this Kadesh to distinguish it from the others, is unknown; it may be a personal name, of similar formation to those of Bera and Birsha (Gen. 14:2).

2. Location. Kadesh-barnea is located just S of the Israelite border, not far from its W extremity at the river of Egypt (Wadi el-'Arish; Num. 34:4-5). Ezek. 47:19; 48:28 has the same location for Meribath-kadesh (KJV "waters of strife in Kadesh"). There are three springs, grouped closely together, which suit this locality: 'Ain el-Qudeirat, 'Ain Qedeis, and 'Ain Qoseimeh. The latter is entirely too small to have taken care of the Israelites (*see* AZMON). Trumbull made out a strong case for 'Ain Qedeis, which retains the Arabic form of the name, and for a long time was accepted by Bible scholars; but the investigations of Woolley and Lawrence have pronounced in favor of 'Ain el-Qudeirat, which is by far the largest of the three, the only one which flows all year, and is close to extensive land for pasturage. There are also the remains of an Israelite fortress maintained there between the tenth and eighth centuries B.C., located to guard the Israelite settlement. In any case, the Israelites who were encamped in the locality undoubtedly made use of all three springs. Fig. KAD 1.

Courtesy of Nelson Glueck

1. Wadi Qudeirat, with Khirbet Qudeirat (Kadesh-barnea?) back of the trees

3. History. The first reference to Kadesh-barnea is in Gen. 14:7, where it is mentioned together with its old name En-mishpat; it is described as being not far from EL-PARAN and the point farthest W that was reached by the raid of Chedorlaomer and his confederates. It is also spoken of as being near Beer-lahai-roi (Gen. 16:14), where both Abraham and Isaac frequently sojourned, and as both of them traveled through the Negeb, Kadesh-barnea was probably one of their watering places.

After Moses and the Israelites left Mount Sinai, they journeyed northwestward across the "great and terrible wilderness" (el-Tih) toward the hill country of the Amalekites and settled in Kadesh-barnea (Deut. 1:19-20). The corresponding passage in Num. 13:26 speaks of the location as the wilderness of PARAN, but it is evident that Kadesh is meant. It was from here that a company was sent out to spy out the land of Canaan; when their unfavorable report led to the divine decree that the entire generation would perish in the wilderness and only their children inherit the land promised by God, it was from Kadesh that the Israelites, rejecting the counsel of Moses, made a hasty attempt to force their way into the hill country of the Amorites and were beaten back with great slaughter. After this event, they remained in Kadesh "for many days" (Num. 13; 14; Deut. 1).

It is not certain how long this first sojourn in Kadesh lasted. The whole series of chapters from Num. 15 to 19 has no mention of any removal, and ch. 20 finds them still in Kadesh, so that it might be inferred from them that almost the entire period of the wilderness sojourn was spent there. But chs. 15–19 are all from the P document and represent an intrusion in the JE narrative; hence it is probable that they have misplaced some accounts of the journeys, which are summarized in Num. 33. This list of stations follows closely the account of the leaving Egypt, journey to Sinai and trip northwestward as far as Hazeroth, and the station before Kadesh, and gives a number of stations from that point on until the end of the wilderness wanderings, when Kadesh reoccurs just before the death of Aaron (vs. 36). The first sojourn at Kadesh-barnea is completely omitted; it is possible that the list is defective or that Kadesh is regarded as the same as RITHMAH. According to Deuteronomy, it was apparently not long after the abortive invasion that the Israelites left Kadesh, for it was thirty-eight years from that time that they reached the brook Zered (Deut. 2:14).

According to the account in Num. 20, it was at Kadesh that the people murmured because of lack of water; Moses brought forth a supply from the rock, but was punished for some lack of faith, not clearly defined, by being forbidden to enter the Promised Land. This argument (*m^e^rîbhâ*) gave rise to the name Meribath-kadesh. According to Num. 20:14-21 it was from Kadesh that Moses sent messengers to the king of Edom, requesting a passage through his country, which was refused; this account is repeated in Judg. 11:16-17. Deuteronomy, however, knows nothing of such an embassy and even indicates that the Israelites passed through the Seir territory of the Edomites (Deut. 2:4-8, 29) and gives no hint of any murmuring about water in a second trip to Kadesh, unless the statement that "the LORD was angry with me on your account" (Deut. 3:26) refers to this story. *See* EXODUS, ROUTE OF, § 2.

The final reference to Kadesh-barnea—or rather, to Meribath-Kadesh—is when Ezekiel makes it a part of the S border of his idealized land of Israel (Ezek. 47:19; 48:28). There are also indications that in some older accounts that have been preserved Kadesh was regarded as much nearer the mount of revelation than the later narratives have it. Thus, in one passage the voice of the Lord shakes the wilderness of Kadesh (Ps. 29:8); in the passage in Deut. 33:2, which describes the advance of God from his holy mountain and mentions, in turn, Sinai, Seir, and Mount Paran, the words "from the ten thousands of holy ones" (*mērîbh^e^bhôth qōdhesh*) are probably to be emended to *mēm^e^rîbhath qādhesh*, "from Meribath-Kadesh."

Bibliography. H. C. Trumbull, *Kadesh-Barnea* (1884); C. L. Woolley and T. E. Lawrence, *The Wilderness of Zin* (1914-15); W. F. Albright, *Recent Discoveries in Bible Lands* (1955), pp. 86-87.

S. COHEN

KADESH ON THE ORONTES ō rŏn'tēz [קדש; Amarna *Qidši, etc.*]. A town S of the Lake of Hums, where the famous battle between the Egyptians under Ramses II and the Hittites took place in 1288 B.C.; modern Tell Nebi Mend.

KADMIEL kăd'mĭ əl [קדמיאל, God is of old, *or* God goes before]. A Levite name connected with several aspects of postexilic reconstruction (Ezra 2:40; 3:9; Neh. 7:43; 9:4-5; 10:9; 12:8, 24).

KADMONITES kăd'mə nīts [קדמני, easterners] (Gen. 15:19). The Semitic people, nomadic or pastoral, who inhabited the Syro-Arabian Desert between Palestine-Syria and the Euphrates River.

Since the Hebrews, in orienting themselves with relation to the four directions, always faced the direction of sunrise, the East was called קדם, "front" or "before." The land of Qedem (Gen. 25:6; RSV "East Country"), to which Abram sent the sons of Keturah, who bear Arabian names, is believed to have been in the Syrian Desert, E of Byblos. The Kadmonites, associated with the nomadic Kenites and Kenizzites, are among those whose lands God gave to Abram and his descendants (Gen. 15:18-21). The name seems quite parallel to the more common designation, "sons of Qedem" (RSV "people of the east"), among whom were included Job (Job 1:3; cf. 18:20), the camel-riding Midianite kings (Judg. 8:10-12, 21, 26), and the wise men who bear names with Arabian associations (I Kings 4:30-31—H 5:10).

Bibliography. R. Kittel, *Geschichte des Volkes Israel* (1921), vol. I, p. 392, note 2; J. A. Montgomery, *Arabia and the Bible* (1934); W. F. Albright, "The Oracles of Balaam," *JBL*, LXIII (1944), 211.

R. A. BOWMAN

KAIN kān [קין (1 *below*), הקין (2 *below;* KJV CAIN)]. **1.** Singular collective form of the clan name equivalent to the KENITES. It occurs in Num. 24:22 (KJV THE KENITE) in the oracle of Balaam, and also in Judg. 4:11, where it is translated "the Kenites." The same word designates Cain, the son of Adam and Eve, and some scholars view Cain as the eponymous ancestor of the Kenites, but this is very doubtful.

G. M. LANDES

2. A city in the S of the hill country of Judah; identified with Khirbet Yaqin, SE of Hebron (Josh. 15:57). According to Arab tradition it was from a hill nearby that Abraham witnessed the destruction of Sodom and Gomorrah. As the name indicates, Kain was a settlement of the Kenites. It has been suggested by some scholars that the name of the city was not Kain, but Zanoah, and that the last word of vs. 56 should be read with the first word of vs. 57—i.e., "and Zanoah of Kain" (or "of the Kenites"), and also that "nine" instead of "ten" cities be read in vs. 57 (following the LXX). In Judg. 4:11, מקין (RSV "from the Kenites," but probably to be read "from Kain") should be translated: "And Heber the Kenite, a descendant of Hobab . . . left Kain" (lit., "was separated from Kain").

Bibliography. A. Alt, "Das Institut im Jahre 1925," *PJB*, (1926), 76-77; M. Noth, *Das Buch Josua* (2nd ed., 1953), pp. 92, 98.

S. COHEN

KAIWAN. *See* SAKKUTH AND KAIWAN.

KALLAI kăl'ī [קלי] (Neh. 12:20). A priest in the time of Joiakim.

KAMON kā'mən [קמון] (Judg. 10:5); KJV CAMON. A city of Gilead where the judge Jair died and was buried. It may be the same as the Kamoun (Καμοῦν) of Polybius which is mentioned after Pella. It has been identified as Qamm, a village *ca.* three miles N of Ṭaiyibeh, but Steuernagel's description of the place indicates no settlement earlier than Roman times, so this is a case of a name wandering. Another

possibility is the village of Qumeim, E-NE of Irbid.
S. COHEN

KANAH kā'nə [קנה, reed]. **1.** The brook Kanah (נחל קנה; KJV "river Kanah"), an important feature of the border between Ephraim and Manasseh. The N border of Ephraim extended from TAPPUAH westward along the brook Kanah, ending at the Mediterranean (Josh. 16:8). In defining the S border of Manasseh, similar information is reported, including the naming of the brook Kanah (Josh. 17:9), with the additional statement that some of the cities of Manasseh were S of the brook in Ephraim (see 16:9).

Most commentators identify the brook Kanah with the Wadi Qanah, which flows into the modern Yarkon before reaching the Mediterranean. It has been suggested that at the time of Joshua its lower course may have been different, discharging its waters into the Mediterranean N of modern Arsuf (Apollonia).

2. The city of Kanah (not to be confused with NT Cana), on the N border of the territory of Asher (Josh. 19:28). The ancient name is preserved in the modern Qana, located *ca.* six miles SE of Tyre.

Bibliography. W. F. Albright, "The Administrative Divisions of Israel and Judah," *JPOS,* V (1925), 30; D. Baly, *The Geography of the Bible* (1957), pp. 134, 136-37, 176; E. Danelius, "The Boundary of Ephraim and Manasseh in the Western Plain," *PEQ,* XC (1958), 32-43.
W. L. REED

KAREAH kə rē'ə [קרח, bald one]; KJV once CAREAH (II Kings 25:23). The father of Johanan, who was a Judean contemporary of Jeremiah and one of the captains of the forces in the open country who escaped deportation by Nebuchadnezzar (II Kings 25:23; Jer. 40:8 ff; 41:11 ff; 42:1, 8; 43:2 ff).
M. NEWMAN

KARKA kär'kə [הקרקע, the floor] (Josh. 15:3); KJV KARKAA kär'kĭ ə. A city on the S border of Judah, near Azmon. The site is unknown.
S. COHEN

KARKOR kär'kôr [קרקר] (Judg. 8:10-11). A place in E Gilead, somewhere up in the mountains, where Gideon for the second time surprised and defeated the Midianites. Its site is unknown. S. COHEN

KARNAIM kär nā'əm [קרנים, two horns *or* peaks] (Amos 6:13); KJV HORNS. A city in N Transjordan; same as ASHTEROTH-KARNAIM. Amos apparently makes a wordplay on the meaning of Karnaim ("horns") and Lo-debar ("a thing of nought").

KARTAH kär'tə [קרתה] (Josh. 21:34). A Levitical town in the territory allotted to Zebulun. Its location is unknown.

KARTAN kär'tăn [קרתן] (Josh. 21:32). A Levitical town in Naphtali; the same as KIRIATHAIM (I Chr. 6:76—H 6:61). It is perhaps to be identified with Khirbet el-Qureiyeh in Upper Galilee.

KATTATH kăt'ăth [קטת] (Josh. 19:15). A town in Zebulun; probably the same as KITRON in Judg. 1:30.

KEDAR kē'dər [קדר, mighty, *or* swarthy]. The second son of Ishmael (Gen. 25:13; I Chr. 1:29), and the eponym of an important Arab tribe. Some Arab genealogists trace the ancestry of the prophet Muḥammad through Kedar.

1. Biblical description
2. Associations
3. Location
4. History
   a. Relations with Assyria
   b. Relations with Babylonia
   c. Influence in the time of Geshem
5. Religion

Bibliography

1. Biblical description. The Kedarites were desert-dwellers (Isa. 42:11), living alone (Jer. 49:31) in tents (Ps. 120:5; Jer. 49:29), which were black in color (Song of S. 1:5; cf. black goat's-hair tents of modern Bedouin) and which had curtains (Jer. 49:29). Some Kedarites lived in unwalled villages, *ḥ^{a}ṣērîm* (Isa. 42:11; cf. Arabic *ḥaḍarīyah* of settled Arabs). They were herdsmen with flocks of sheep and goats (Isa. 60:7; Jer. 49:29, 32), which they brought as far as Tyre for sale (Ezek. 27:21), and camels (Jer. 49:29, 32). They "cut the corners" of their hair (Jer. 49:32; an Arab custom noted by Herodotus III.8; cf. shaving the head in Arabia today). They were ruled by princes who conducted trading enterprises (Ezek. 27:21; cf. the sheiks of the modern Bedouin). They were known for their fighters and particularly their archers (Isa. 21:17). Evidently the Kedarites occupied a position of power and "glory" in the ancient Near East (vs. 16).

2. Associations. In Gen. 25:13, Kedar is associated with eleven other Ishmaelite tribes, most of which can be located in N Arabia. In Jer. 49:28, Kedar is included among the "people of the east," who are elsewhere shown to have lived E of Syria-Palestine (Gen. 29:1; Judg. 6:3; Ezek. 25:4, 10; *see* EAST, PEOPLE OF THE). Arab tribes and places mentioned in connection with Kedar include Dedanites and Tema (Isa. 21:13-14), Sela (42:11), Midian, Ephah, Sheba, and Nebaioth (60:6-7), and Hazor (Jer. 49:28, 33).

3. Location. According to Gen. 25:18, Kedar and his brothers settled between Havilah (some place in Arabia) and Shur (E of Egypt and S of Palestine). Jer. 2:10 refers to Cyprus on the W and Kedar on the E. Isa. 21:13-16; Ezek. 27:21 imply that Kedar was in Arabia. According to the above indications, the territory of Kedar was E of Transjordan, and doubtless at least part of the tribe wandered in this area seeking pasture like modern Bedouin. In the fifth century B.C. there were also Kedarites on the E border of Egypt. *See* § 4*c below.*

4. History. ***a. Relations with Assyria.*** The Assyrian campaign records of the seventh century B.C. refer to the Kedarites (Assyrian *Qidri, Qadri*) in such a way as to indicate that by this time the name of this tribe was practically synonymous with Arabs. E.g., Hazail is called king of the Arabs by Esarhaddon and also king of Kedar by Ashurbanipal. This Hazail was defeated by Sennacherib of Assyria (704-681), who took Arab idols from Adumatu (biblical

Dumah). At the plea of Hazail, Esarhaddon (680-669) returned these images. Another king of Kedar, Ammuladi, attacked Palestine-Syria, but Ashurbanipal (668-633) defeated him. Kedarites were among the soldiers of Abiate, the leading Arab general in the wars against Ashurbanipal. The Arabs whom Ashurbanipal took captive are called Kedarites. It is noteworthy that these Kedarites were in league with the Nabaiateans (biblical Nebaioth, with whom Kedar is associated; *see* § 2 *above*). The tribute and booty taken by the Assyrians from Kedar include typical products of Arabia, as mentioned in the Bible: gold, precious stones, aromatic matter, camels, donkeys, sheep, goats, and cattle.

b. Relations with Babylonia. According to Jer. 49:28, Nebuchadnezzar (605-562) conquered Kedar, and this conquest of N Arabia is confirmed by a quotation of Berossus the Babylonian historian, preserved by Josephus (Apion I.xix). Nabonidus (555-539) occupied the important caravan centers, Tema and Adummu (biblical Dumah), which, as indicated above, had been controlled by Hazail, king of Kedar.

c. Influence in the time of Geshem. Geshem the Arabian was one who obstructed the work of Nehemiah in rebuilding the wall of Jerusalem (*ca.* 440 B.C. (Neh. 2:19; 6:1-2, 6). His importance is shown by the fact that a Lihyanite inscription at al-'Ula (biblical Dedan) is probably dated in his time.* From an Aramaic inscription of the fifth century B.C. from Tell el-Maskhutah in Egypt we learn that Geshem was king of Kedar and that there were Kedarites on the E border of Egypt, perhaps stationed there as guards by the Persians. According to these data, Kedarite influence in the later fifth century extended from Transjordan, to N Arabia, to the border of Egypt, the territory later controlled by the Nabateans. Fig. KED 2.

From *Journal of Near Eastern Studies*, published by the University of Chicago Press; copyright 1956 by the University of Chicago

2. Votive inscription (Aramaic) of "Qainu the son of Geshem, king of Kedar," on a fifth-century-B.C. silver bowl found at Tell el-Maskhuta in Egypt

5. Religion. Assyrian records tell of the shrine of Hazail king of Kedar, at Adumatu. The following gods had images there: Atarsamain (often mentioned as the chief goddess of the Arabs and identified by the Assyrians with Ishtar Dilbat), Dai, Nahai, Ruldaiu, Abirillu, and Atarquruma. The chief functionary of the shrine was a priestess of Atarsamain. A symbol of this goddess was a star of gold decorated with precious stones. Another name for this goddess was han-Ilat (originally meaning "the goddess"), attested in the Aramaic inscription mentioned above. According to the Babylonian Talmud (Ta'an. 5*b*), the Kedarites worshiped water—perhaps a reference to the veneration of sacred wells or of Ba'l, the spirit of underground water, in pre-Islamic Arabia.

Bibliography. al-Ṭabarī, *Ta'rīkh al-rusul w-al-mulūk* (ed. M. J. de Goeje; 1879-81); F.-M. Abel, *Géographie de la Palestine*, I (1933), 296; J. A. Montgomery, *Arabia and the Bible* (1934), pp. 45, 58, 62; A. L. Oppenheim, trans., the Babylonian and Assyrian Historical Texts, in J. B. Pritchard, ed., *ANET* (2nd ed., 1955); I. Rabinowitz, "Aramaic Inscriptions of the Fifth Century B.C.E. from a North-Arab Shrine in Egypt," *JNES*, XV (1956), 1-9; P. K. Hitti, *History of the Arabs* (6th ed., 1958), p. 42.

J. A. THOMPSON

KEDEMAH kĕd'ə mə [קדמה] (Gen. 25:15; I Chr. 1:31). A son of Ishmael, and the name of an Arabian tribe. It is apparently identical with NODAB. With the name cf. בני קדם (*bᵉnê qedhem*), "sons (people) of the East."

S. COHEN

KEDEMOTH kĕd'ə mŏth [קדמות]. A priestly city in Reuben, apparently situated on the Upper Arnon (Josh. 13:18; 21:37). It was from the wilderness nearby that Moses sent a message to Sihon, king of the Amorites, requesting a passage through his country (Deut. 2:26). It was one of the Levitical cities, assigned to the Merarites (Josh. 21:37; I Chr. 6:79—H 6:64). The city may be either Kasr ez-Za'feran or Khirbet er-Remeil, both of which are in that vicinity and were in existence at that time.

S. COHEN

KEDESH kē'dĕsh [קדש, sacred place, *or* sanctuary]; Apoc. KADESH kā'dĭsh [Κηδες, Κεδες] (I Macc. 11:63, 73); KJV Apoc. CADES kā'dēz. **1.** A town on the S border of Judah (Josh. 15:23); same as KADESH.

2. A Canaanite town in E Galilee, the king of which was defeated by Joshua (Josh. 12:22). It was allotted to Naphtali (19:32, 37) and hence called Kedesh in Naphtali (Judg. 4:6). It was also called Kedesh in Galilee, and was set apart as one of the cities of refuge and allotted to the Gershonite Levites as one of their residences (Josh. 20:7; 21:32). It is identified with Tell Qades, situated in the hills NW of Lake Huleh.

Kedesh in Naphtali was the home of Barak (Judg. 4:6) and where Deborah and Barak gathered their followers for the battle with Sisera (vss. 1-10). In its vicinity Heber the Kenite pitched his tent, in which Sisera met his death at the hands of Jael, Heber's wife (4:21; 5:24-27). Tiglath-pileser captured the town, along with others, in the reign of Pekah king of Israel, and exiled its inhabitants to Assyria (II Kings 15:29). Here too Jonathan Maccabeus defeated the army of Demetrius (I Macc. 11:63, 73). At the time of Josephus it belonged to the Phoenicians (War II.xviii.1; IV.ii.3).

3. According to I Chr. 6:72—6:67, a city in Issachar, allotted to the Gershonite Levites. In Josh. 21:28 this town is called Kishion (קִשְׁיוֹן; KJV "Kishon"). It has been suggested that "Kishion" should be changed to "Kishon." "Kedesh in Issachar" may have arisen from misreading "Kishon" for "Kedesh," a scribal error antedating the LXX. If Kedesh existed as a town, Abel proposes an identification with Tell Abū Qedeis, 2½ miles SE of Megiddo, and would combine with it the Kedesh of Judg. 4:11. It is doubtful, however, that the tribal claims of Issachar ever extended this far SW.

Bibliography. W. F. Albright, "The Topography of the Tribe of Issachar," *ZAW*, 44 (1926), 231; F.-M. Abel, *Géographie de la Palestine,* II (1938), 412, 415-16; W. F. Albright, "The List of Levitic Cities," *Louis Ginzberg Jubilee Volume* (English section; 1945), pp. 49 ff. J. L. Mihelic

KEDESH IN NAPHTALI năf'tə lī [קֶדֶשׁ נַפְתָּלִי] (Judg. 4:6); KJV KEDESH-NAPHTALI. A town in Galilee; the home of Barak son of Abinoam; same as Kedesh 2.

KEDRON kē'drən [Κεδρών] (I Macc. 15:39-41; 16:9); KJV CEDRON sē'drən. A town near Modin; identified with modern Qatra, and probably same as Gederah (Josh. 15:36). Kedron was fortified by Antiochus VII of Syria in order that he might attack Judea, in the time of Simon Maccabeus.

N. Turner

KEEPER. The translation of a number of Hebrew and Greek words, signifying:

a) A guard or watchman, especially over cattle, vineyards, and orchards; so also a herdsman. Such laborers are depicted on a shell from the third millennium B.C. at Tell El-Obeid. In Egypt the keepers of cattle were the lowest class, but in Israel theirs was an honorable profession* (Gen. 47:6; I Sam. 11:5; 21:7; I Chr. 27:29; etc.). As urbanization increased, however, the prestige of this class declined (I Kings 4:23; Eccl. 2:7). Uzziah, Hezekiah, and Josiah in Judah, as well as Mesha of Moab, were cattle raisers (II Kings 3:4 ff; II Cor. 26:10; 32:28-29; 35:7-9). Amos may have been a keeper of cattle (Amos 7:14).

Courtesy of Staatliche Museen, Berlin

3. A keeper feeding a temple herd; from a marble cylinder seal of the Uruk period (end of fourth millennium) containing details of pastoral life

Abel was a keeper of sheep and so a shepherd (Gen. 4:2). The term is used also for those who watch over vineyards (Song of S. 1:6; 8:11; Isa. 27:3) and orchards (Prov. 27:18), so a watchman (II Kings 17:9; Job 27:18; Jer. 31:6). Fig. KEE 3.

b) Similarly, the guard of a prison (Gen. 39:21, 23; Acts 5:23; 12:6). Sentinels were set to guard the tomb of Jesus (Matt. 27:65).

c) Symbolically, a person is to be a keeper of his tongue and lips (Pss. 34:13; 141:3). C. U. Wolf

KEHELATHAH kē'ə lā'thə [קְהֵלָתָה, assembly] (Num. 33:22-23). One of the stopping places of the Israelites after Hazeroth. The name is perhaps a doublet of Makheloth (Num. 33:25-26). The LXX has almost identical names for the two: Μακελλάθ (vss. 22-23) and Μακηλὼθ (vss. 25-26).

J. L. Mihelic

KEILAH kē ī'lə [קְעִילָה, קְעִלָה]. A fortified city of Judah in the Shephelah district of Libnah-Mareshah (Josh. 15:44; cf. I Chr. 4:19); identified with modern Khirbet Qila, 8½ miles NW of Hebron.

David rescued Keilah from a Philistine attack, but when Saul heard that David was at Keilah, he sent a detachment of troops to take David and his men. David, after consulting the oracle, decided that the gratitude of the citizenry did not extend to protecting him against Saul, so he withdrew again into the wilderness of Ziph (I Sam. 23:1-13). Keilah was occupied and rebuilt by Jewish returnees from the Exile (Neh. 3:17-18).

Qilti (Keilah), during the turbulent Amarna period in Palestine, seems to have been on the border of the territory of the prince of Jerusalem, Abdu-Heba, and the prince of Hebron, Shuwardata. Letters from each addressed to Akh-en-Aton of Egypt (*ca.* 1369-1353) complain of the other's "improper" occupation of Keilah at various times (*ANET* 487-89).

Keilah was one of a number of places at which the prophet Habakkuk was said to be buried.

V. R. Gold

KELAIAH kĭ lā'yə [קֵלָיָה, *perhaps* Y has dishonored] (Ezra 10:23; I Esd. 9:23); KJV Apoc. COLIUS kō lī'əs. One of the Levites compelled by Ezra to give up their foreign wives; identified with Kelita.

KELITA kĭ lī'tə [קְלִיטָא, *perhaps* adopted one, *more probably* crippled, dwarfed one; Apoc. Καλιτας]; KJV Apoc. CALITAS kə lī'təs (I Esd. 9:23, 48). A Levite who assisted in interpreting the law when it was read at the great assembly in the time of Ezra (Neh. 8:7; I Esd. 9:48) and who participated in the sealing of the covenant (Neh. 10:10—H 10:11). According to Ezra 10:23 (cf. I Esd. 9:23), Kelaiah, one of the Levites compelled by Ezra to give up their foreign wives, was also called Kelita (קֵלָיָה הוּא קְלִיטָא). Possibly this is a gloss which falsely identifies two different people. More likely it refers to one man with two different names. When he is introduced, both his real name and his nickname ("Cripple") are given, and subsequently he is alluded to by his nickname alone. M. Newman

KEMUEL kĕm'yōō əl [קמואל; *meaning obscure*]. **1.** The father of Aram, and the son of Nahor the brother of Abraham (Gen. 22:21).

2. A leader of the tribe of Ephraim, and its commissioner for the allotment of Canaan (Num. 34:24).

3. A Levite; father of Hashabiah, who is listed as a contemporary of King David (I Chr. 27:17).

B. T. DAHLBERG

KENAN kē'nən [קינן, *from* קין; *see* CAIN; LXX Καιναν] (Gen. 5:9-14; I Chr. 1:2); KJV CAINAN kā'nən in Genesis. Alternately: CAINAN [Καιναμ] (Luke 3:37). Son of Enosh (NT "Enos").

KENATH kē'năth [קנת]. A city in E Gilead which was taken by Nobah and given his own name (Num. 32:42). The old name seems to have persisted, for we later read that Kenath fell into the hands of Aram and Geshur (I Chr. 2:23). The site is probably Qanawat in el-Hauran, NE of es-Suweideh, a city of the Druses.

S. COHEN

KENAZ kē'năz [קנז]; KENIZZITE kĕn'ə zīt; KJV KENEZITE in Num. 32:12; Josh. 14:6, 14. **1.** Son of Eliphaz the first-born of Esau (Gen. 36:11; I Chr. 1:36); Edomite clan chief (Gen. 36:15, 42; I Chr. 1:53); eponymous ancestor of the Kenizzites. *See* 3 *below*.

2. The father of Othniel (Josh. 15:17; Judg. 1:13; 3:9, 11) and Seraiah (I Chr. 4:13).

3. Grandson of Caleb through Elah (I Chr. 4:15). The gentilic adjective "Kenizzites" refers once to a people whose land Yahweh gave to Abraham's descendants (Gen. 15:19) and three times to Caleb son of Jephunneh (Num. 32:12; Josh. 14:6, 14).

Kenizzites were a non-Israelite people who moved into the Negeb, apparently from the SE, before the main body of the Conquest. They were composed of the clans of the Calebites, who occupied Hebron (formerly called KIRIATH-ARBA; modern el-Khalil; Josh. 14:6-14; 15:52-54); the Othnielites, who occupied Debir (formerly KIRIATH-SEPHER; modern Tell Beit Mirsim[?]; Josh. 15:15-19; Judg. 1:11-15); and perhaps the Jerahmeelites, who must have occupied the southernmost hill country of the Negeb (I Sam. 27:10; 30:29). Later all these became politically related to the composite group generally termed Judah. They were also associated with Edomites and, most probably, with Kenites, from whom they would have learned copper and iron smithery (cf. I Chr. 4:13-14).

Bibliography. N. Glueck, "Ḳenites and Ḳenizzites," *PEQ*, LXXII (1940), 22-24.

L. HICKS

KENITES kĕn'īts, kē'nīts [קיני, הקיני, הקינים, belonging to the (copper) smiths; Arab. *qayn*, Aram. קיניא, smith]; KAIN [קין]. A nomadic or seminomadic tribe of smiths, who as early as the thirteenth century B.C. appear to have made their livelihood as metal craftsmen, inhabiting the rocky country S of Tell 'Arad on the W slopes of the mineral-rich Wadi 'Arabah above Tamar (Num. 24:21; Judg. 1:16). It is probable that they bore some resemblance to the modern Arab tribe, the Sleib, who ply their trade (somewhat like the gypsies, Arabic *Nawar*) as traveling smiths or tinkers, more or less following regular trade routes with their asses and tools, and who support themselves by means of their craftsmanship, supplemented by music and divination. The ancient Kenites, however, were probably more prosperous than the notoriously poor Sleib, and certainly more respected by the surrounding population. Nomadic tribes of metalworkers in the ancient Near East are known from the early second millennium B.C., at least if the famous party of Asiatics depicted on a tomb at Beni-hasan (nineteenth century B.C.) represents such a group, as their portrayal would seem to indicate. Although there is no positive evidence to relate the early biblical tradition concerning TUBAL-CAIN to the Kenites, such a connection is possible. Both copper and iron are known to have been mined at a very early date in the Jordan Valley and elsewhere in this region.

1. Earliest references
2. Connection with the Mosaic movement
3. Kenites and Amalekites
4. Kenites and David
5. Final disappearance
Bibliography

1. Earliest references. In the earliest biblical reference the Kenites appear at the head of a list of peoples living in Canaan whom God had promised Abram to dispossess in order to give the land to his descendants (Gen. 15:19). From the thirteenth century, or a little later, stems another early mention of the Kenites in the oracles of Balaam (Num. 24:21-22), where the perennial Kenite abodes are described as "set in the rock," doubtless referring to the region of the Wadi 'Arabah. There follows a curious passage in which the Kenites are consigned to destruction, one of the rare instances in biblical tradition when Kenites are viewed unfavorably. The historical basis for this judgment eludes us.

2. Connection with the Mosaic movement. Most often the Kenites are seen in close association with the Hebrews, or at least holding a recognized place in Israelite society. They may have introduced the arts of mining and metallurgy to the Israelites, and perhaps also to Edom. We are told, however, that at the time of Samuel the Israelites had no smiths of their own, since the Philistines had removed them (I Sam. 13:19-20). In Judg. 4:11 the Kenites are designated as the descendants of HOBAB (cf. also Judg. 1:16), although elsewhere Moses' father-in-law is termed a Midianite (Exod. 2:16-21; 18:1; *see* JETHRO; REUEL). The Kenites may have been living among the Midianites (*see* MIDIAN) at this time. Shortly thereafter, we learn that the Kenites entered Palestine in company with the tribe of Judah—a relationship which seems to be reaffirmed by I Sam. 15:6, where it is acknowledged that the Kenites "showed kindness" (or, more literally, "showed loyalty") to Israel during the Exodus. At any event, it is clear that these traveling craftsmen were associated with the Mosaic movement, and it has been suggested that Moses learned from his Kenite father-in-law how to fashion the copper serpent (Num. 21:8-9). Some scholars assert that Moses was introduced to Yahweh and his worship through Kenite mediation. Our present evidence does not support this, although the possibility cannot be ruled out. Still more tenuous is the hypothesis held by those who think the casuistic type of Mosaic legal tradition was borrowed from the Kenites.

3. Kenites and Amalekites. After reaching the Negeb near Arad in S Palestine, the Kenites apparently settled among the AMALEKITES (emending Judg. 1:16 to read העמלקי for העם, as most scholars suggest). In any case, we find the Kenites in close association with the Amalekites in the time of Saul (*ca.* 1020-1000 B.C.), when the latter warns them to depart from the doomed Amalekites if they wish to escape destruction (I Sam. 15:6). This does not necessarily mean that the Kenites "belonged" to Amalek, as sometimes maintained (notwithstanding the mention of the Kenites immediately following Amalek in the oracles of Balaam, Num. 24:20-22), any more than it means that they "belonged" to Midian or Judah at other times in their history. In the period of the judges, a nomadic branch of the Kenites, apparently under the leadership of Heber, lived in Galilee (Judg. 4:11; 5:24). The historical circumstances surrounding this movement are unknown. The fact that Kenites are mentioned in biblical tradition as living in various places in Palestine not only illustrates their nomadic character, but also suggests that they were not completely absorbed by any other people, but maintained a separate existence throughout most of their history. The Chronicler (I Chr. 2:55) designates as Kenite certain families of scribes who dwelt at Jabez in S Judah, tracing their ancestry from Hammath, father of the house of Rechab.

4. Kenites and David. The last mention of the Kenites in connection with the history of Israel is during the time of David before he became king over all Israel (*ca.* 1000). While David dwelt in the Philistine city of Gath, he made raids on some of the foes of Israel, but told Achish, king of Gath, that he was plundering enemies of the Philistines, among whom were clans living in the Negeb of the Kenites (I Sam. 27:10). Subsequently, he sent gifts of spoil to the "elders of Judah" and "to his kinsmen" (with the LXX), among whom are named those residing "in the cities of the Kenites" (I Sam. 30:29). Since all place names mentioned in this connection are well-known sites in the S Judean hill country, presumably the "cities of the Kenites" are also to be sought in this region. Possibly one of them was KAIN, listed in Josh. 15:57. It has been suggested that David was related to the Kenites through his marriages to Ahinoam and Abigail (I Sam. 25:42-43; cf. Josh. 15:55), but this is very doubtful.

5. Final disappearance. We hear no more of the Kenites in the later history of Israel. Presumably they disappeared or lost their identity during the early first millennium B.C. The relationship sometimes posited between the biblical Kenites and the early Islamic tribe Banu 'l-Qayn in the region between Teima and Hauran (sixth century A.D.) cannot be demonstrated.

Bibliography. F.-M. Abel, *Géographie de la Palestine* (1933), I, 273; H. Schmökel, "Jahwe und die Keniter," *JBL,* 52 (1933), 212-29; W. F. Albright, *Archaeology and the Religion of Israel* (3rd ed., 1953), pp. 98-99, 109, 200, 205, 210; M. Noth, *Geschichte Israels* (2nd ed., 1955), pp. 57-58, 75, 140, 166.

G. M. LANDES

KENIZZITE. *See* KENAZ.

KENOSIS kĭ nō'sĭs, kĕ— [κένωσις, emptying, depletion]. A term used in Christian theology from the third or fourth century on, to describe the idea expressed in Phil. 2:7, according to which the pre-existent Christ "emptied himself," "impoverished himself," or laid aside his equality with God, in order to become man. It is difficult to know exactly what Paul implied by this bold language. He can hardly have supposed that Christ entirely lost his divinity or his special relation to God the Father in assuming humanity; otherwise his incarnate life would have had no more significance than that of any other prophet or teacher. The point must therefore be that Christ voluntarily stripped himself of the insignia and prerogatives of deity. That in Paul's mind this is not a case of God's masquerading as man, but of Christ's suffering all the consequences of his humanity, is shown, not only by Phil. 2:8: "He humbled himself and became obedient unto death," but also by the statement that Christ was "crucified in weakness" (II Cor. 13:4) and the strong language regarding the Cross as a scandal or "stumbling block" (I Cor. 1:18-30). There is some reason to think that the passage Phil. 2:5-11 had as its source an early Christian hymn or proclamation of the gospel and thus is even older than the Pauline letters.

The word "kenosis" was originally used in patristic literature as a synonym for the INCARNATION to express the condescension of the Son of God (cf. II Cor. 8:9); it is employed in modern theology to describe a wider doctrine—namely, that Christ voluntarily gave up some or all of his divine attributes and submitted to all the conditions of human life, including the limitation of knowledge. While several parts of the NT furnish data to support this doctrine (*see* HUMANITY OF CHRIST), the Gospel of John appears to take a different position. It portrays the earthly Jesus as possessing miraculous power and knowledge and asserting his constant communion and full equality with the Father (see, e.g., John 1:14, 48; 5:19-24; 10:30; 11:41-42; 13:1-3). *See also* CHRIST; SON OF GOD.

Bibliography. Besides the commentaries of Beare, Dibelius, Lightfoot, Lohmeyer, and Vincent on Phil. 2:5-11, see E. Lohmeyer, *Kyrios Jesus: eine Untersuchung zu Phil. 2:5-11* (1928).

S. E. JOHNSON

KERAK, KHIRBET. *See* KHIRBET KERAK.

KERCHIEFS. *See* VEIL *f.*

KERE. *See* QERE.

KEREN-HAPPUCH kĕr'ən hăp'ək [קרן הפוך, horn of antimony (eye shadow); *i.e.*, a cosmetics case, a compact] (Job 42:14). The youngest of the daughters who were born to Job after the restoration of his fortunes.

KERIOTH kĕr'ĭ ŏth [הקריות, קריות, cities]; KJV KIRIOTH kĭr'ĭ ŏth in Amos 2:2. **1.** A city in the tableland of Moab (Jer. 48:24), apparently strongly fortified (Amos 2:2; also Jer. 48:41, if it refers to Kerioth [RSV "cities"]). Mesha of Moab (*see* MOABITE STONE) claims to have brought the chieftain of Ataroth before CHEMOSH in Kerioth, so apparently Kerioth contained a sanctuary of Chemosh.

Perhaps Kerioth is identical with AR, since Amos 2:2 seems to treat it as the capital of Moab.

E. D. GROHMAN

2. *See* KERIOTH-HEZRON.

KERIOTH-HEZRON kĕr'ĭ ŏth hĕz'rən [קריות חצרון] (Josh. 15:25); KJV KERIOTH AND HEZRON. A village of Judah in the Negeb district of Beer-sheba; usually identified with Khirbet el-Qaryatein, 4½ miles S of Maon. Some scholars, with the KJV, separate Kerioth from Hezron. *See* HAZOR.

V. R. GOLD

KEROS kĭr'ŏs [קירס] (Ezra 2:44). Head of a family of postexilic temple servants. *See* NETHINIM.

KERYGMA kĭ rĭg'mə [κηρύγμα]. The general term for PREACHING. *See also* GOSPEL, especially §§ 1*b-d*, 2*a*.

KETAB kē'tăb [Κητάβ]; KJV CETAB sē'tăb. Head of a family of temple servants who returned with Zerubbabel (I Esd. 5:30; omitted in the parallels Ezra 2:46; Neh. 7:48). *See* NETHINIM.

KETHIBH kə thēv' [כתיב, that which is written]. The authoritative consonantal MT, from which the QERE marginal readings show divergence. *See* TEXT, OT, § A3*a*.

KETTLE. The translation of דוד, a vessel in which the sacrifice might be boiled, in I Sam. 2:14; and of סיר, a vessel in which meat was cooked, in Mic. 3:3 RSV (KJV POT). *See* POTTERY § 3*a*.

KETURAH kĭ tŏŏr'ə [קטורה, incense, *or perhaps* the perfumed one]. The second wife of Abraham, who bore him six sons (Gen. 25:1-6 [J]; I Chr. 1:32-33).

It was presumably after Sarah's death that Keturah became Abraham's wife and gave birth to Zimran, Jokshan, Medan, Midian, Ishbak, and Shuah. Gen. 25:6 (cf. I Chr. 1:32) gives her a lesser status than that of wife by speaking of the sons of Abraham's "concubines" (evidently Keturah and Hagar), to whom he gave presents and whom he sent away to the "east country."

The Keturah tradition seems to reflect the belief of the Hebrews that they were related to these six Arab tribes who lived to the E and S of Palestine and whose eponymous ancestors were Keturah's sons. The Keturah tribes were indeed sons of Abraham, but, of course, through a subordinate wife. The number six suggests that they were organized into some kind of tribal amphictyony, concerning which we know nothing more. The most prominent of these six tribes elsewhere in the OT is MIDIAN.

M. NEWMAN

KEY [κλείς]. Literally, an instrument for locking or unlocking doors or gates; figuratively, that which controls entrance or exit. In the NT the word is used only as an eschatological symbol of authority and power delegated by God. As the Messiah, Jesus receives power to admit or exclude men from the kingdom of David (Rev. 3:7). As one who died and was

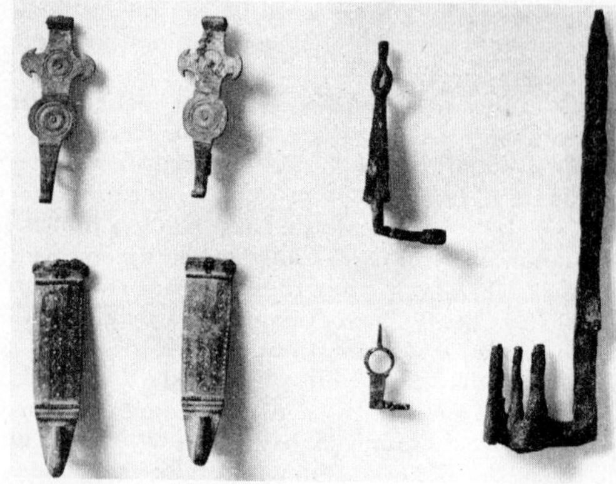

Courtesy of the Royal Ontario Museum, Toronto

4. Palestinian keys, bronze

raised, he has power over Death and Hades (1:18). The key is used to release plagues from the Abyss (20:1). The scribes are said to possess the key of knowledge, which enables men to enter the kingdom (Luke 11:52; cf. Matt. 23:13). Given to Peter and the church, the key conveys the power to bind and loose (Matt. 16:18-19). Open gates signify unrestricted access to God's forgiveness and community (Rev. 21:25; 22:14). For this symbolic usage, there are many antecedents in diverse Near Eastern traditions.

Fig. KEY 4.

Bibliography. P. S. Minear, *Christian Hope and the Second Coming* (1954), pp. 175-88; W. F. Arndt and F. W. Gingrich, *Greek-English Lexicon* (1957), pp. 434-35. P. S. MINEAR

KEYS, POWER OF. *See* POWER OF KEYS.

KEZIAH kĭ zī'ə [קציעה, cassia (cinnamon)] (Job 42:14); KJV KEZIA. The second of Job's daughters who were born to him when his fortunes were restored.

KEZIZ, VALLEY OF kē'zĭz. KJV translation of עמק קציץ (RSV EMEK-KEZIZ) in Josh. 18:21.

KHIRBET KERAK kĭr'bĕt kûr'äk [Arab. ruins of the fortress]. An important archaeological site on the S shore of the Sea of Galilee, W of the mouth of the Jordan River. Khirbet Kerak is strategically located near a ford of the Jordan, through which passes one of the routes linking Palestine with Damascus and the N, and along the principal N-S route in the Jordan Valley. The nearby intersection of these routes inevitably made the site an important center of trade.

The mound covers an area of nearly sixty acres, extending a distance of *ca.* 3/5 mile along the shore. Excavations were carried on from 1944-55 by B. Maisler (Mazar), M. Stekelis, M. Avi-Yonah, P. L. O. Guy, and recently by Bar-Adon. The site seems to have been more or less continuously occupied from the Late Chalcolithic (Esdraelon culture) through the EB III period. It is in the latter occupation that great quantities of Khirbet Kerak pottery—named after this site, in which it was first discovered—were found (*see* POTTERY). An enormous

From *Israel Exploration Journal*, vol. 2, no. 2, pl. 10

5. Foundation of a building of the Early Bronze Age at Khirbet Kerak. A Roman bath pipeline can be seen on the surface.

building, perhaps a granary, with eight large circular rooms was also found in this stratum.* The next occupation, MB I, is represented by houses and a potter's workshop. Several tombs of MB II have also been discovered on the mound. The site was unoccupied until the Persian period, and it is because of this occupational gap, which corresponds to the major OT period, that the site is not mentioned in the biblical narrative. During the Hellenistic period a new city was built, which was protected by strong fortifications and contained many fine houses with painted plaster walls. It is probably to be identified with Philoteria, a city named in honor of the sister of Ptolemy Philadelphus. The Roman period is represented by a fortress of the second-third centuries A.D., and a large bath, of the fourth-fifth centuries A.D. In the Talmud, Khirbet Kerak is called Beth-Yerah (house of the Moon [god]). Fig. KHI 5.

Bibliography. L. Sukenik, "The Ancient City of Philoteria (Beth-Yerah)," *JPOS*, 2 (1922), 101-9; W. F. Albright, "Bronze Age Mounds of Northern Palestine and the Hauran," *BASOR*, 19 (1925), 17; B. Maisler, M. Stekelis, and M. Avi-Yonah, "The Excavations at Beth-Yerah (Khirbet Kerak) 1944-1946," *IEJ*, 2 (1952), 142, 165-73, 218-29, 251-52. See also "Notes and News" in *IEJ* (1953-55).

G. W. VAN BEEK

KHIRBET QUMRAN kĭr'bĕt ko͝om'rän. The ruins of an Essene monastery which was the center of the community of the DEAD SEA SCROLLS. Khirbet Qumran is situated at the W coast of the Dead Sea, 8½ miles S of Jericho.

KIBROTH-HATTAAVAH kĭb'rōth hə tā'ə və [קברות התאוה, graves of craving *or* appetite] (Num. 11:34; 33:16; Deut. 9:22). The first stopping place of the Israelites after they left Sinai and before they came to Hazeroth. In their craving for flesh, the Israelites overindulged in eating quails, which a wind from the Lord had brought from the sea (Num. 11:31). As a result an epidemic broke out in which very many people died. The dead were buried on the spot, and these graves gave the place its name.

The place may perhaps be identified with Rueis el-Ebeirij, which is *ca.* a ten-hour journey by foot from Jebel Musa, the mountain generally identified with Sinai.

Bibliography. E. H. Palmer, *The Desert of the Exodus* (1872), pp. 212-14; R. Savignac, *RB*, X (1913), 433-38; F.-M. Abel, *Géographie de la Palestine*, II (1938), 214, 417.

J. L. MIHELIC

KIBZAIM kĭb zā'əm [קבצים]. A city in Ephraim, one of the forty-eight cities allotted to the Levites after the conquest of Canaan (Josh. 21:22). Its location is uncertain. The Chronicler's parallel list has at this point (I Chr. 6:68—H 6:53) the name Jokmeam, not to be confused with the Jokmeam of Zebulun in I Kings 4:12, which is to be equated with JOKNEAM, located at Tell Qeimun. It has been suggested that Jokmeam is not a corruption of Kibzaim, but that both cities occurred originally here, in the list of LEVITICAL CITIES.

Bibliography. W. F. Albright, "The List of Levitic Cities," *Louis Ginzberg Jubilee Volume* (English section; 1945), pp. 51-52, 67-68.

H. G. MAY

KID [גדי (*feminine* גדיה *in* Song of S. 1:8), *sometimes alone, but generally in* גדי עזים, kid of goats; *cf.* Akkad. *gadû*, Ugar. *gdy*, Arab. *jady;* for עזים (*plural of* עז), *see* GOAT; בני עזים (II Chr. 35:7), sons of goats; שה (Num. 15:11; *usually* "lamb"), *see* CATTLE; ἔριφος]; KJV KID OF GOATS [שעיר עזים, hairy one of goats (RSV *correctly* "goat," "male goat")]. A young goat. In the husbandry of ancient Israel a young male kid was the most expendable of the animals, being less valuable than either its mother or a young lamb, and it therefore served admirably as a small present or as the meat basis for a special meal (Gen. 27:9; 38:17; Judg. 6:19; 13:15; 15:1; I Sam. 10:3; 16:20; Luke 15:29). A year-old kid is suitable for the Passover (Exod. 12:5; cf. II Chr. 35:7); on general regulations for sacrifices involving kids, see Num. 15:11-16. In the picture of the future age of peace, marked by amity among even the animals, the kid is grouped with the leopard (Isa. 11:6).

The thrice-repeated injunction against boiling a kid in goat's milk, the milk commonly available in OT times (Exod. 23:19; 34:26; Deut. 14:21), has long been suspected of being directed against some popular Canaanite ritualistic practice. Maimonides (died 1204) suggested that the act was prohibited because "it is connected with idolatry . . . or . . . used on some festival of the heathen." This suspicion has received some confirmation from Ugaritic: in the drama "The Birth of the Gods" a kid is cooked in milk as part of a sacrificial meal to ensure good crops for the ensuing seven years. The biblical prohibition eventually came to serve as the scriptural basis for the Jewish dietary conventions about the separation of meat and milk in cooking and at meals.

See also UGARIT. W. S. MCCULLOUGH

KIDNAPING. *See* CRIMES AND PUNISHMENTS § C6*a*.

KIDNEYS [כליות; νεφροί]. Like most other words for parts of the physical body, the word "kidneys" has both a literal and a metaphorical sense. When the word is used for the human kidneys, usually with metaphorical overtones, the KJV translates "reins" (e.g., Jer. 12:2; Rev. 2:23); the RSV in these passages renders "mind," "heart," "soul," or "inward parts," except in Job 16:13 ("kidneys").

With the exception of Isa. 34:6, the kidneys of animals are mentioned only in connection with sacrificial regulations. In all the sacrifices other than the whole burnt offering (where no such distinction was possible), the kidneys, together with the fat attached to them, and certain other bits of fat, along with the CAUL of the liver, were the special parts to be burned upon the altar as a gift to Yahweh (Exod. 29:13; Lev. 3:4, 10, 15). Perhaps originally, because of their color and density, the kidneys may have been regarded as in a special sense the seat of life and consequently, along with the blood, the peculiar perquisite of the deity. Later this conception seems to have been at least partially rationalized by seeing in them the choicest part of the animal; a strange expression in Deut. 32:14 speaks of the choicest of the wheat as the "fat of kidneys" (cf. KJV and RSV).

The reasons which led to the attaching of special value to the kidneys in animal sacrifice may have led also to the view that they are an important center of psychic and moral life in man. In a number of passages, the "reins" (KJV) are associated with the HEART as constituting the innermost sanctuary of the human personality; God is able to examine even this and to know its secrets (Pss. 7:9; 26:2; Jer. 11:20; 17:10; 20:12; Rev. 2:23). Emotions are occasionally attributed to the "reins": grief or bitterness (Ps. 73:21 KJV), and joy (Prov. 23:16 KJV). More characteristic are the passages which seem to connect the kidneys with the moral life. This is suggested by the passages, mentioned above, which speak of God's examining or testing the reins and is made explicit in Ps. 16:7 KJV; Prov. 23:16 KJV, where it is said that the reins "instruct" a man and rejoice when the "lips speak right things." The passages are too few, however, for it to be possible to build upon them any theory that the Hebrews regarded moral judgment as the special function of the kidneys.

R. C. DENTAN

KIDRON, BROOK kĭd'rən [קדרון]; KJV CEDRON sē'drən [Κεδρών] in John 18:1. The name attached to a valley E of Jerusalem, dividing the E parts of the city from the Mount of Olives. The Arabic names given to its upper sections show no great consistency. In its lower course, the valley is called today Wadi en-Nār. On leaving the suburbs of Jerusalem, the brook of Kidron, which gives the valley its name, bears to the SE, winds through the wilderness of Judah, and drains into the Dead Sea, some ten miles from the mouth of the Jordan following the shore line. Fig. KID 6.

The Kidron is described as a נחל—viz., a valley down which a stream of water may flow intermittently. This term is rendered in the LXX and in the NT by χειμάρρος, and in the English versions by "brook." The actual bed of the valley in its suburban

Courtesy of Harriet-Louise H. Patterson

6. The Kidron Valley, with the so-called "Tomb of Absalom" at the left-center

portions is from ten to fifty feet above the primitive level, because of the accumulation of rubbish. No water runs in it except for a brief interval after heavy rainfalls. During the earlier period of the monarchy, however, the waters of the spring of GIHON* were allowed to flow freely in the Kidron, previously to being diverted by means of a tunnel to the pool of SILOAM. Fig. GIH 32.

Orchards and gardens were watered from the brook or from irrigation channels dug along the lower slopes of the valley beneath the city of David. These gardens are referred to in II Kings 23:4; Jer. 31:40 as the "fields" of the Kidron. The Davidic kings owned some property in the Kidron, which on account of this came to be known as the King's Valley (*see* SHAVEH, VALLEY OF). Absalom set up a monument for himself in the King's Valley (II Sam. 18:18), by which the domain of the Kidron is obviously meant. The exact location of the royal estate, however, is not known. Nehemiah's mention of the KING'S GARDEN, in connection with the Pool of Shelah, or Pool of the Aqueduct (Neh. 3:15), suggests that it extended at least as far as the junction of the valley with the TYROPOEON VALLEY, and perhaps occupied the lower tract of the Tyropoeon itself with its ancient reservoir. The irrigation of the Kidron gardens must have been drastically reduced when Hezekiah sealed off Gihon and the waterspouts of the old aqueduct, and blocked definitely the access to the city through the Tyropoeon, in prevision of the Assyrian invasion.

The Kidron is commonly regarded as the E boundary of Jerusalem. David crossed it as he fled his capital in the days of Absalom's rebellion (II Sam. 15:23); Shimei was assigned a forced residence in Jerusalem and forbidden ever to pass beyond the Kidron limit (I Kings 2:37).

The valley and the neighboring areas have been repeatedly the theater of the struggle between the religion of the Hebrew God, Yahweh, and foreign cults, like those practiced on the high places of the Mount of Corruption (*see* CORRUPTION, MOUNT OF) and of TOPHETH. The books of Kings and Chronicles record the destruction of idols and other illicit paraphernalia in the valley or in the fields of the Kidron by the pious monarchs Asa and Josiah (I Kings 15:13; II Kings 23:4, 6, 12; II Chr. 15:16; 29:16; 30:14).

The rocky slopes and scarps on the E side of the valley have been used for the burial of the dead until our days. Some of the rock-cut tombs among the houses and shanties of Selwan and the so-called Tomb of the Daughter of Pharaoh toward the N edge of the village go back to the pre-exilic monarchy. The four monuments surrounded today by the tombstones of a modern Jewish cemetery, opposite the SE corner of the temple area, may date from the third century B.C., in spite of their being identified fancifully as the tombs of Jehoshaphat, of Absalom, of James the Less (in reality the vault of the priestly family of the Benê Ḥĕzîr, according to the Hebrew inscription on the frieze), and of Zechariah (cf. Matt. 23:35). All these tombs have been looted, and have been used as shelters by Christian anchorites.

The Fourth Gospel mentions explicitly the Valley of Kidron, which Jesus crossed with his disciples after leaving the Upper Room, when they went to spend the night at Gethsemane (John 18:1). In this passage, the reading τοῦ Κεδρῶν is the only one true to the Hebrew usage, and must prevail over the numerous readings which have failed to recognize Kidron as a proper name and have read instead: τῶν Κέδρων, τοῦ Κέδρου, or even τῶν δένδρων.

The name of the Kidron occurs in a messianic passage of Jer. 31:40, which opened the way for all sorts of symbolic interpretations void of topographical significance. Thus some exegetes of the fourth century of the Christian era identified the Valley of Kidron with the Valley of Jehoshaphat or of Decision (*see* JEHOSHAPHAT, VALLEY OF; DECISION, VALLEY OF), the Valley of Baca (*see* BACA, VALLEY OF), or with the "rich valley" (RSV), the "fat valleys" (KJV), of Isa. 28:1, by reason of a confusion between the Hebrew גיא שמנים and NT Gethsemane. *See* map under JERUSALEM, and under OLIVES, MOUNT OF.

Bibliography. G. A. Smith, *Jerusalem,* I (1907), 39-41; H. Vincent and F.-M. Abel, *Jérusalem Nouvelle,* I–II (1914), 305; G. Dalman, *Jerusalem und sein Gelände* (1930), pp. 159-89; F.-M. Abel, *Géographie de la Palestine,* I (1933), 83-84, 400-401; J. Simons, *Jerusalem in the OT* (1952), pp. 9-10; H. Vincent, *Jérusalem de l'Ancien Testament,* I (1954), 327-42 (ancient tombs in the Kidron Valley). G. A. BARROIS

KILAN kī'lən [Κιλάν] (I Esd. 5:15); KJV CEILAN sē'lən. Head of a family who returned from captivity. J. C. SWAIM

KILN. A large oven or furnace used for processing various materials. In Hebrew תנור is used both for the small bread oven used in the home and for the large pottery kiln used in the factory. The potter's kiln gave the name "Tower of the Ovens" to a part of the fortifications of Jerusalem (Neh. 3:11). The firing of the kiln was the key trade secret in ancient ceramics, and therefore it did not enter into figurative language, as did the other phases of the potter's work.

In Nah. 3:14 the old translation of מלבן was "brickkiln," but the RSV correctly reads "brick mold." "Brick mold" should probably also be the translation in II Sam. 12:31, although the text is uncertain. Most Palestine brick was sun-dried, not kiln-fired. The glazed tile of Exod. 24:10, however, came out of the potter's kiln.

The smoking furnace of Gen. 19:28; Exod. 19:18 was probably a charcoal kiln, although by etymology it could be a smelting furnace. In later Israelite history such a smoking furnace could also have been a lime kiln.

For more details on kilns, *see* POTTERY. J. L. KELSO

KINAH kī'nə [קינה] (Josh. 15:22). A city in the extreme SE of Judah, near the boundary of Edom. The name indicates a settlement of the KENITES and may be preserved in that of the Wadi el-Qeini, S of Hebron. S. COHEN

KINDNESS. *See* LOVE IN THE OT; MERCY.

KINE. KJV plural of Cow.

***KING, KINGSHIP.** "King" is the designation applied to a male sovereign, who usually exercised power over an independent nation and had the right to transmit the royal power to his descendants. Kingship is the state, office, and dignity of a king and the power wielded by him.

1. Biblical terminology
2. Kingship in the ancient Near East
3. Beginnings of the Israelite kingship
4. Hereditary transmission of the Israelite kingship
5. Duties of the king
   a. Military defense
   b. Upholding justice
6. Execution of the royal power
   a. The law of the kings
   b. Royal officials
   c. Royal revenue
   d. Royal attributes
7. Religious aspects of the Israelite kingship
   a. The Lord as the king of Israel
   b. Enthronement of the king
   c. Divine kingship in the ancient Near East
   d. The problem of divine kingship in Israel
   e. The cultic functions of the king
   f. The king and the New Year festival

Bibliography

1. Biblical terminology. The OT uses the Hebrew noun מלך for "king" as the designation of a foreign king (e.g., Gen. 39:20) as well as an Israelite king (e.g., Gen. 36:31). Besides an earthly monarch, the Lord also received this title (e.g., I Sam. 12:12). The verb מלך, which means "to be or to become king, to reign," is also applied to foreign (e.g., Judg. 4:2) and Israelite (e.g., I Kings 16:22) monarchs, as well as to God (e.g., Exod. 15:18). The verb משל, meaning "rule, have dominion, reign," shows a similar width in applicability (cf. Judg. 8:23). The Israelite kings were also called PRINCE and "the LORD's anointed" (*see* MESSIAH [JEWISH]). The words מלוכה (e.g., I Sam. 14:47), ממלכה (e.g., Amos 7:13), ממלכות (e.g., I Sam. 15:28), and the late word מלכות (e.g., Num. 24:7) express royal power, reign, and sovereignty.

The NT applies the noun βασιλεύς, "king" (e.g., Matt. 1:6), and the verb βασιλεύειν, "to be king, to reign, rule" (e.g., Matt. 2:22). The Greek word βασιλεία is the LXX (e.g., Tob. 13:1) and NT (e.g., Luke 1:33) expression for "kingship."

2. Kingship in the ancient Near East. The monarchies of the ancient Near East represent three types. The first group was the petty kings of the Palestine cities who, in many cases, were of foreign origin and ruled, with the support of a military aristocracy, over the population of the city-state. The Egyptian and Mesopotamian kings of the biblical period represented a second type, whose kingship was regarded as a political order divinely ordained for the good of the empire. The third class of kingship might be seen in the kingship of the Transjordanian peoples, who were ethnically related to the Hebrews. There, the kingship had its roots in the military leadership of the native army and was, therefore, completely national in its characteristics.

3. Beginnings of the Israelite kingship. In the earliest times, the Israelites of the settled country were under the leadership of tribal or clan chieftains. Only occasionally did there appear charismatic leaders who rallied a number of the tribes into a united military enterprise for the deliverance of the hard-pressed Israelites. Deuteronomic systemizers of the Israelite history later called these heroes judges (*see* JUDGE). In premonarchic Israel there was no political, administrative, or military organization which would have embraced the whole of the people of Israel. The only tie effectively joining the people was their faith. They entered into a covenant with Yahweh and recognized him as their king (Deut. 33:5). Of course, this kingship of God meant, first of all, a religious recognition of his reign (*see* THEOCRACY) and carried the danger of total anarchy (Judg. 21:25). The first attempt to introduce a kingship in Israel is associated with GIDEON, who was offered the rule over the people of Israel (?) by the assembled warriors after the victory over the raiding Midianites (Judg. 8:22). Gideon's refusal of the offer clearly witnesses to the recognition of the Lord's kingship (vs. 23). The difficulty of interpretation becomes apparent when the fact is considered that, after Gideon's death, Abimelech claimed the kingship of Shechem as his rightful heritage (Judg. 9:1-3). In this light, the refusal of the royal power by Gideon appears puzzling, and there have been several attempts to eliminate the contradiction. The offered solutions of this enigma are: (*a*) to deny the historicity of Gideon's refusal of the kingship, (*b*) to interpret his words as a shrewd diplomatic rejection of the external signs of kingship and a silent acceptance of the royal power, or (*c*) to understand it as Gideon's oath pledging to preserve, undisturbed, the continuity of the theocracy during his rule. Whatever is the case, the kingship of Gideon and that of his son, Abimelech, were limited in importance and scope. The tribal kingship of Gideon and the city kingship of Abimelech were abortive attempts to establish a kingship in Israel.

The institution of the kingship in Israel was prepared by the slow settlement of the nomadic people and the embracement of a sedentary civilization. These changes meant a slow dissolution of the clan and tribal authorities and produced a need for greater political cohesion. However, the final impetus, and probably the most decisive one, came from the desperate political situation. In the time of Samuel, the Israelites were under a heavy Philistine yoke (I Sam. 13:19-21); some of the territories, which had escaped the Philistine overlordship, suffered repeatedly under other onslaughts brought about by the Transjordanian Ammonites (I Sam. 11:1-2) and the inroads of foraying nomads such as the Amalekites (14:48). Thus, the introduction of kingship was a historical necessity. The so-called antimonarchic source of the books of Samuel disclaimed this historical necessity of the institution of kingship (I Sam. 7:13-14), and stamped the people's wish to have a king as an apostasy and rejection of the Lord's kingship (I Sam. 8:7). To be sure, there was provision made to ensure the continuity of the theocracy, even if in mediated form, through the reign of an earthly vassal. Accordingly, Saul was selected and anointed by the Lord to be king over Israel (I Sam. 10) and to be the ruler and military leader of the nation (I Sam. 8:20; 10:1). Saul appeared to be a charismatic leader, and, in the matter of inspiration, he was clearly related to the judges (cf. I Sam. 11:6). His reign represents a transition between the type of tribal kingship, like that of Gideon, and the type of national monarchy. So Saul relied almost exclusively on the men of his own tribe, that of Benjamin (I Sam. 22:6-8), but claimed sway over all Israel.

4. Hereditary transmission of the Israelite kingship. In the beginning, there were no clearly defined provisions for the transmission of the royal power. The Israelite kingship, in its initial stage, preserved some of the charismatic aspects of the office of judge, and consequently it was dependent on a special divine designation as to who would be the king. Already in Saul's reign, the two principles of succession to the throne, the hereditary principle (I Sam. 20:31) and the charismatic principle (I Sam. 11:6; 16:13-14; 20:12-16), appeared to be in tension. At the time of the death of Saul, however, the two principles overtly clashed. Thus Judah accepted David's kingship (II Sam. 2:4), but the N and Transjordanian tribes that of Ish-bosheth, Saul's son (vss. 8-10). Probably a survival of the idea of charismatic kingship helped to facilitate the revolutions which led to the changing dynasties of the Northern Kingdom. *See*, e.g., JEHU 1.

Even though the hereditary character of the kingship was recognized, the right of primogeniture was not always statutorily established in the ancient Near East. Thus, in the Hittite Empire, King Telepinus (1525-1520 B.C.) regulated, relatively late, the succession to the throne. Esarhaddon of Assyria (681 B.C.) was installed as crown prince, though he had elder brothers. The same unsettled situation is revealed in Aram by the Hadad inscription, in the question: "Who among my sons will grasp the sceptre and will sit on my seat?" A similarity to these cases may be discovered in the case of Abimelech's claim to Gideon's throne (Judg. 9:2). In the struggle for the Davidic throne, between Solomon and Adonijah (I Kings 1–2), the right of the first-born and the right of the father to designate his heir conflicted. To be sure, the law of primogeniture could not have been unequivocally settled, even in family law in the earliest times, as the existence of the Deuteronomic law regulating the question of inheritance (Deut. 21:15-17) indicates. The fact that the names of the mothers of the kings of Judah are preserved (e.g., I Kings 14:21; 15:2, 10; 22:42) is indicative of the assumption that the maternal side of the king's forebears played some kind of role in the succession to the Davidic throne.

5. Duties of the king. The duties of the king were threefold: he was the military leader of the nation, the supreme judge, and, in the earliest period at least, an officiating priest.

a. Military defense. The king was the first military leader of the nation, and his duty was to lead the army and to fight the battles of the nation (I Sam. 8:20). Thus, kings led the army as Saul did in the war against the Amalekites (I Sam. 15:4-5), Ahab at Ramoth-gilead against the Syrians (I Kings 22:29-36), and Jehoram in the war against the Moabites (II Kings 3:6-12).

b. Upholding justice. The king's duties in the ancient Near East included the obligation to uphold the concept of justice within the nation; to support the rights of the widows and the poor, as is manifested by the Ugaritic legend of Keret. Also the kings of both Israelite kingdoms had the duty and power for adjudicating occasional disputed cases and for correcting legal injustice (II Sam. 12:1-6; 14:4-7; 15:2; I Kings 3:16-28). However, the king's legal function must not be interpreted as a kind of supreme tribunal, for the administering of justice was normally practiced by the elders (*see* ELDER) without any provision for further appeal (Deut. 19:12; 21:20).

6. Execution of the royal power. The limits of the royal power were defined by the laws of kingship; for the execution of his power, the king needed officials who helped him to secure the revenue necessary for the maintenance of the royal power.

a. The law of the kings. The premonarchic Israelite concept of kingship was seriously influenced by some bitter experiences of the Israelites with the kings of the numerous petty states of Canaan. So Jotham's fable taught that only useless fellows were willing to accept the dubious honor of kingship (Judg. 9:7-15). At the time of Samuel, there was opposition to the introduction of the kingship, and the despotic excesses of the kings are depicted as the "ways of the king" by some later author (I Sam. 8:10-18). But the power of the king was not completely unrestrained.

The elders made a covenant with the new king (II Sam. 5:3; II Kings 11:17). The rights and duties of kingship were codified and deposited in the central sanctuary (I Sam. 10:25), most likely during the anointment ceremony. The king was not exempt from the regulations of ancient civil laws and customs. Ahab resented, but accepted, the right of Naboth to keep his inheritance (I Kings 21:4). Kings acquired the property of their subjects by buying it, as did David the threshing floor of Araunah the Jebusite (II Sam. 24:24), and Omri bought the hill of Samaria for his capital to be built upon (I Kings 16:24). Undoubtedly, kings had the right to seize and appropriate the estate of a conspirator (II Sam. 16:4) or a person who "cursed God and the king" (I Kings 21:10).

The king was not the absolute lord of the life of his subjects. David did not have the power to take Bathsheba from Uriah or to kill Uriah overtly. Instead, he had to resort to cunning plots (II Sam. 11). Naboth was executed after due legal procedure, but the accusation was false and plotted by royal command (I Kings 21:8-14), for even Jezebel tried to preserve the appearance of legality. The severe denunciation of kings by prophets points also to the fact that the king was subject to laws. Nathan sternly rebuked David (II Sam. 12:1-15), and Elijah Ahab (I Kings 21:17-24), for their disregard of the law. The Deuteronomic law of the kingship (Deut. 17:14-20), which subjected the king to the law, was not complete innovation, but an extreme development of a prevalent practice. To be sure, the existence of the laws of kingship, which outlined and limited the royal power, did not deter the flagrant disregard for the law of some powerful rulers such as SOLOMON and MANASSEH.

b. Royal officials. The members of the royal entourage were those who "saw the king's face" (Esth. 1:14). The bodyguard, composed of foreign mercenaries, was in constant company of the king during military enterprises (II Sam. 15:18), and it played an important part in the coronation of Solomon (I Kings 1:38) and of Jehoash (II Kings 11:4). The commander of the bodyguard (II Sam. 8:18) and the commander of the army belonged to the royal court (I Sam. 14:50; II Sam. 8:16). There were the recorder, whose duty was possibly that of an "announcer" at the court (II Sam. 8:16; I Kings 4:3), the secretary (II Sam. 8:17; II Kings 18:18), and the chief administrator, who "was over the officers" of the twelve administrative districts (I Kings 4:5). There was also a man in charge of the palace (I Kings 4:6), who was a kind of major-domo over the royal household (I Kings 18:3; II Kings 18:18) and was called steward (Isa. 22:15). There were an overseer of the forced labor (II Sam. 20:24; I Kings 4:6), a "friend" of the king (II Sam. 15:37; I Kings 4:5; I Chr. 27:33), a counselor (II Sam. 15:12), and a keeper of the wardrobe (II Kings 22:14). There were also some minor officials in charge of the royal farms (I Chr. 27:25-31). Probably the Israelite court, like the Persian court, also had a cupbearer (Neh. 1:11).

Besides these secular officers, priests were attached to the royal court (II Sam. 8:17; 20:25; I Kings 4:4). Prophets were also associated with the court, as Nathan was with David's court (II Sam. 7:2; 12:25), and Gad, David's seer (I Sam. 22:5; II Sam. 24:10-25).

c. Royal revenue. Saul did not subject the people to taxation; he lived in the rustic simplicity of his paternal estate and kept court under the tamarisk tree (I Sam. 22:6). His followers brought him occasional gifts (I Sam. 10:27; 16:20). David had considerable spoil from his many wars (II Sam. 8:1-14), and thus there was no urgent need for taxation of the people. However, the census of the people, completed on David's command, was most likely preparatory to a system of taxation (II Sam. 24:1-9), but apparently the general taxation of the people was first introduced by Solomon. During the reign of Solomon, the territory of the N tribes was divided into twelve administrative and revenue districts (I Kings 4:7-19, 27-28), headed by twelve officers (vs. 7), whose duty it was, each in his turn, to provide for the royal household for one month of the year (vss. 7, 27-28). The same administrative and revenue districts remained in existence, even in the independent Northern Kingdom, as the ostraca of Samaria reveal. The tax was paid in kinds, with the delivery of a tenth of farm products and animals (I Sam. 8:15, 17) for the needs of the royal household (I Kings 4:28; cf. Amos 7:1). Occasionally, extraordinary taxes were levied in the land (II Kings 23:35).

The king also had his own estate. Apparently David already had large land holdings (I Chr. 27:25-31). Uzziah had large flocks and both farm lands and vineyards (II Chr. 26:10), and so had Hezekiah (32:27-29). The royal landholdings grew considerably at the expense and to the detriment of the people (Ezek. 45:8).

The bond service or *corvée* might be regarded as a royal revenue. This form of forced labor was already introduced under the reign of David; the name of the officer in charge of the *corvée* was included in the list of David's officers (II Sam. 20:24). Later, the same man, Adoniram, was also in charge of the *corvée* under the reign of Solomon (I Kings 4:6). This type of forced labor hardly burdened "all Israel" (I Kings 5:13), but only some of the descendants of the original inhabitants of the land who were kept in servitude (I Kings 9:20-22; cf. Josh. 9:3-21; Judg. 1:27-35).

Several of the most important trade routes of the Fertile Crescent passed through Israel, and Solomon secured an income from the road toll paid by the merchants (I Kings 10:15). He also had an extensive trade in horses and chariots (*see* MEGGIDO) which was apparently a monopoly (I Kings 10:28-29). The merchant fleet of Solomon took up trade connections with some Arabian and probably African ports (I Kings 9:26-28). An unsuccessful building of fleets is remembered from the time of Jehoshaphat of Judah (I Kings 22:47-49). The vivid interest of the kings in mercantile enterprise is also documented in the agreement of Ben-hadad of Syria and Ahab of Israel, which permitted Ahab to establish Israelite bazaars in Damascus (I Kings 20:34). The copper refineries of EZION-GEBER also contributed to the royal income.

d. Royal attributes. The attributes of the king symbolically expressed his power. The crown (II Sam. 1:10; II Kings 11:12; Pss. 89:39; 132:18), the scepter (Num. 24:17; Ps. 45:6), and the throne (II Sam. 14:9; I Kings 2:12) were royal attributes par excellence. However, these attributes also implied the consecrated character of the king. It is possible that the spear (I Sam. 22:6; II Sam. 1:6) and the armlet (II Sam. 1:10) served, in Saul's case, as symbols expressing the royal authority, but they did not become of foremost importance. The possession of the royal harem indicated the right of the seizure of the royal power (II Sam. 16:20-22; I Kings 2:19-23); yet the harem can hardly be regarded as an outright symbol of the royal authority. The palace (II Sam. 5:11-12; I Kings 7:1-12; 22:39), the royal sanctuary (II Sam. 7:1-2), the chariot (I Sam. 8:11; I Kings 1:5), were not attributes of the king, but their splendor served to enhance the glory of the monarch and indicate his power and riches.

7. Religious aspects of the Israelite kingship. In the ancient Near East, kingship was nowhere a purely secular institution. And in Israel, there were religious implications of the office of kingship.

a. The Lord as the King of Israel. The Lord was the original King of Israel. Unfortunately, the dating and the evaluation of the historicity of the biblical passages (e.g., Exod. 15:18; 19:6; Num. 23:21; Deut. 33:5; I Sam. 8:7; 12:12; Judg. 8:23) supporting this contention are often disputed. Some scholars think that all these evidences are too late and of no value. But there is sufficient evidence to substantiate the claim that the COVENANT of Israel with Yahweh was a royal covenant, and Israel pledged loyalty to him in a covenantal ceremony (cf. Josh. 24). Therefore, in some circles, the earthly kingship was thought of as an apostasy (I Sam. 8:7; Hos. 8:4). But even in circles favorable toward human kingship, the Lord's kingship over Israel was maintained as an article of faith. Earthly kingship was derived from divine authority, as the expressions "the LORD's anointed" (e.g., I Sam. 16:6; II Sam. 1:14) and "prince" (נגיד; e.g., I Sam. 9:16; 10:1; 13:14) seem to indicate. The king's role was that of a vassal of Yahweh.

b. Enthronement of the king. The fact that the Lord was recognized as the absolute ruler of Israel, who had appointed as his vassal the king, did not exclude, at least in the earliest period of the monarchy, the democratic acceptance of the king by the elders and chieftains (I Sam. 11:15; II Sam. 5:3; I Kings 12:1, 20). This democratic recognition appeared in the making of a covenant before the Lord (II Sam. 5:3; 3:21). How long this democratic side of the enthronement survived in the two kingdoms cannot be decided, for the details of the enthronement ritual are not available. The main elements, if not the order, of the enthronement ritual might be reconstructed from the detailed accounts of the enthronement of Solomon (I Kings 1:32-40) and Joash (II Kings 11:4-20).

The most essential part of the enthronement ceremony was the anointment of the king, and the less decisive components of the ritual surrounded this particular one. Solomon was brought on the mule of his father to the Gihon, accompanied by the foreign mercenaries. Probably a sacrifice was made at Gihon by Solomon (cf. I Kings 1:9), and then he was anointed by the priest Zadok (I Kings 1:38-39) and the prophet Nathan (vss. 34-35). After the anointment of the king, they blew the trumpet, and the people shouted: "Long live King Solomon!" Then, a festival procession accompanied the new king from the holy place to the throne, and he took his place and received the obeisance of the officials and the royal princes (I Kings 1:40, 53). The enthronement of Jehoash was composed of a coronation by the priest of the temple, the receiving of the "testimony," and the anointment. Those present clapped their hands and shouted: "Long live the king!" (II Kings 11:12). Afterward, the anointed king stood at the pillar (which most likely was one of the pillars of the temple), and the people rejoiced and blew the trumpets (II Kings 11:13-14). A covenant was made between the Lord and the king and the people (vs. 17). From the temple, accompanied by the bodyguards and the people, the king went to the royal palace and took his place upon the throne (vs. 19). Somewhere within this ceremony, the king received a new name, a throne name; this change of the king's name was already practiced in ancient Sumer. Thus, Eliakim's throne name became Jehoiakim (II Kings 23:34), and Mattaniah's regnal name became Zedekiah (24:17). Jedidiah was the private name of Solomon (II Sam. 12:25), and it is probable that Elhanan (*see* ELHANAN 1) was the original name of David.

c. Divine kingship in the ancient Near East. The kings were believed to be superhuman in the ancient Near East. In the Amarna Letters, the Canaanite vassals address their Egyptian sovereign as "my god," "my sun," "sun of the land," and "my breath." The Egyptian Pharaoh was regarded as the earthly manifestation of the gods Horus, Seth, and Osiris. The Egyptians believed that the king was the very son of the gods by his nature, for he was begotten by Re. Thus the king was the absolute lawgiver of his land, ruling by divine decrees. He did not merely uphold justice, but he was the very source of justice as the incarnation of the heavenly justice. As the god Osiris, the Pharaoh was also the giver of life, sustainer of fertility, and dispenser of abundant blessing. The Egyptian kings, being divine, were worshiped in their life and death.

The Mesopotamian concept of kingship was compatible with the divinity of the king. The early

Sumerians most often looked upon the king as one of the human beings—greater, to be sure, than other men, but still a man. The Sumerian king reigned in his god's stead as a viceregent. But the early Babylonian kings freely used the title "god." Their divinity, however, largely differed from that of the Pharaoh. The Babylonian king was a divine servant of the gods, chosen to maintain the reign of the gods. The relationship of the Babylonian king to the gods and goddesses was conceived as sonship by adoption and not by nature. The divine election endowed the king with "divine," superhuman qualities, but his divinity was "functional" rather than metaphysical. Therefore, the king, unlike the Egyptian Pharaohs, was never worshiped.

The Babylonian king was a "divine" intermediary between the gods and the people, and accordingly one of his main functions was to participate in the most important religious rites; especially in his role in the New Year festival, which was of crucial importance. In a ritual drama which re-enacted the creation myth, he helped the gods establish for a year the cosmic order. The ritual represented Marduk's initial imprisonment and humiliation by the forces of chaos and his subsequent victory over the chaos-dragon, Tiamat (*see* DEEP, THE). Occasionally the king took part in the rite of "sacred marriage," from which blessing and fertility stemmed forth for the land and the people. In the cultic drama of the New Year festival, the king, though representing the deity, was not regarded as identical with him.

The Hittites never recognized the living king as a god. Nevertheless, the divinity of the dead kings was an established belief. The king in the N Syrian states was not an offspring or son of the gods. Neither is there any evidence that the king was deified after his death.

In Canaan, as the Ugaritic documents indicate, kings of the legendary past like Keret were recognized as demigods. Keret's son was suckled by the goddess Asherah. King Keret himself was the "son" and "servant" of the highest god, El, and received immortality.

The prevalent variations in the Near Eastern concept of kingship militate against the contention that there was a general Near Eastern belief in the divinity of the kings.

d. The problem of divine kingship in Israel. The question of divine kingship in Israel must be viewed within the context of Israel's monotheism and the nonuniform estimate of kingship among the nations of the ancient Near East.

By the anointment, the king of Israel became sacrosanct (II Sam. 1:14, 16). David did not dare kill King Saul, who was at his mercy, and forbade Abishai to slay the Lord's anointed (I Sam. 26:9). After David cut off the skirt of Saul's robe, he was afraid, and "[his] heart smote him" (I Sam. 24:5). Whoever cursed the king deserved to be put to death (II Sam. 19:21-22; I Kings 21:10, 13). God and the king were equally to be feared and obeyed (Prov. 24:21). The king's unique position can be further illustrated by a comparison of his wisdom to that of the angel of God (II Sam. 14:17, 20; 19:27).

It was an article of faith in Judah that God made an everlasting covenant with David for the establishment of his dynasty (II Sam. 23:5; cf. 7:8-15; Ps. 89:19-37). The kings of Judah were heirs to the divine promise given in the dynastic oracle (II Sam. 7:5-16) that the Davidic king would be the "son" of God (vs. 14). This "divine sonship" of the king did not rest on divine procreation as in Egypt; the king of Judah remained David's descendant by nature (II Sam. 7:12). His sonship was expressed in terms of adoption, as the adoption formula "You are my son, today I have begotten you" (Ps. 2:7), suggests. The Davidic king could be called the first-born of God (Ps. 89:27). In the language of myth, a psalm tells that he was born from the womb of dawn (Ps. 110:3), and that he sat at the right hand of God (Ps. 110:1). In an exaggerated praise, he might have been called "god" (though there are difficulties with the rendering of this text), and his throne was regarded as divine (Ps. 45:6).

Because of such intimacy with God, the king embodied the Lord's blessing, which meant harmony and prosperity, peace and well-being, for the whole people. Therefore, the king was the life-sustaining breath (Lam. 4:20) and the protecting shield of the people (Ps. 89:18). Fertility was connected with him; abundance of grain and blossoming forth of the human race were equally among his works of "righteousness" (Ps. 72:3, 16). Accordingly, the king was called the "lamp of Israel" (II Sam. 21:17); his life, which was worth the lives of ten thousand heroes (II Sam. 18:3), had to be protected in the interest of the nation. Through adoption, the king became God's heir and could ask for universal dominion over the nations of the earth (Ps. 2:8), for the first wish of the king after his anointment was granted by God (cf. I Kings 3:5). He established divine justice in the world (Pss. 45:4, 7; 72:1-4) and destroyed his enemies (Pss. 2:9; 21:10-12; 45:5), who cringed before him as chastised slaves (Pss. 72:9; 110:1).

A mistaken evaluation of the evidence presented above led some scholars to maintain that the belief in the divinity of the Hebrew king was a deeply rooted conviction in ancient Israel and Judah. But this assumption can hardly stand close scrutiny.

Indubitably, a superior importance of the Israelite king as God's unique instrument must be maintained. The king's inviolable character cannot be denied either; there are, however, indications that inviolability was not an exclusive royal privilege but was shared also by the priests (I Sam. 22:17-18; I Kings 2:27). The threefold comparison of the king's wisdom to that of the angel of God (II Sam. 14:17, 20; 19:27) loses its implications when it is remembered that twice the speakers either tried to deceive the "omniscient" king or received a clear indication of the king's fallibility. The assumption is at hand that at least some of the exaggerated expressions must be accounted for as stylistic borrowings from the language of the royal courts of the great empires.

The kings apparently did not assume their own divinity, as the words of the king of Israel reveal: "Am I God, to kill and to make alive?" (II Kings 5:7; cf. 6:26-27). The sonship of Israel (Hos. 11:1) and the Israelites (Isa. 1:2) also is rooted in the thought of divine covenantal adoption and differs only in the degree of proximity from that of the king. To be sure, the king of the Davidic dynasty was a channel of blessing, but the source of the blessing was the Lord himself (Ps. 132:11-18). The king was not worshiped; on the contrary, the people entreated God in behalf of the king (Pss. 20:1-5; 72:15). The argument of silence also might be introduced rightly at this point: it is significant that the prophetic denunciations of the kings never censured the monarchs because of their claim upon divinity.

The king of Israel was close to God, but his proximity to the deity must not be interpreted as identity, metaphysical or functional. His intimacy with God qualified him as the Lord's vicegerent in Israel and in the world.

e. The cultic functions of the king. The king's importance in Israel's religion was enhanced by his association with the cult. As Melchizedek, king of Salem, was the priest of God Most High (Gen. 14:18), and as the kings of most of the ancient Near Eastern nations performed priestly functions, so the Israelite king, at least in the earliest period, exercised cultic functions. On important occasions the kings offered sacrifices to God, as did Saul (I Sam. 13:10; 14:35), David (II Sam. 6:13, 17; 24:25), and Solomon (I Kings 3:4, 15; 8:62; 9:25). Saul erected an altar to the Lord (I Sam. 14:33-34), as did David (II Sam. 24:21; cf. Ahaz' cultic role in II Kings 16:10-18). David's sons were priests (II Sam. 8:18); Absalom (II Sam. 15:12) and Adonijah (I Kings 1:9) offered sacrifices at sacred places. In the Northern Kingdom, Jeroboam officiated at the sacrifices (I Kings 12:32; 13:1; cf. II Kings 10:24).

The kings presented supplication for the nation on important occasions. Solomon (I Kings 8:22-53) and Hezekiah (II Kings 19:14-19) are examples. David danced in the ark procession clad in a linen ephod, which was priestly garment par excellence (II Sam. 6:14). Afterward, he blessed the people in the name of the Lord of hosts (II Sam. 6:18), and so did Solomon at the dedication of the temple (I Kings 8:14).

The king had authority over the priests and, at least to some extent, over the cult. He could punish the priests (I Sam. 22:11-18; I Kings 2:26-27), for the priests, in the beginning, were regarded as royal officials (II Sam. 8:17; 20:25). The king's duty extended not merely to the supervision of the cult, but he could even reform the cult, as the reforms of Asa (I Kings 15:12-15), Hezekiah (II Kings 18:1-7), and Josiah (II Kings 22:3–23:23) amply illustrate. Jehoash regulated the priestly income (II Kings 12:4-16). Noteworthy is the important part credited to David in the preparations for the building of the temple and in the musical aspects of the cult (I Chr. 22; 25). Though the historicity of the Chronicler's information can hardly be asserted, it manifestly shows the memory of an undisputed royal influence upon the cult.

The importance of the cultic role of the king, however, must not be overestimated, for it must be measured by the fact that, in the premonarchic period and probably even later, any paterfamilias had the right to offer sacrifices, establish a shrine, and appoint his own priests (Judg. 17:5, 10).

f. The king and the New Year festival. It is assumed in some schools of biblical scholarship that the most important cultic function of the reigning monarch of Judah was his participation in the ritual of the NEW YEAR festival. For lack of direct evidence concerning the pre-exilic New Year festival, the so-called "enthronement of the LORD" psalms (47; 93; 96–99) are utilized in the attempt to reconstruct the ritual. Similarly, the royal psalms (2; 18; 20–21; etc.) and the psalms of royal lamentations (3; 11–13; etc.; *see* PSALMS, BOOK OF) serve as elements in the reconstruction undertaken by scholars.

The so-called "myth-and-ritual school" of the history of religions endeavors to establish that myth and ritual stood in organic relationship within the religions of the ancient Near East. Thus the New Year ritual in Babylon is interpreted as a dramatic re-enactment of the creation myth (*see* § 7*c above*). There is sufficient evidence supporting the existence of a ritual drama of the same kind in Ugarit. The New Year ritual in Israel itself, it is claimed, complied with the general Near Eastern ritual pattern or was the result of the Israelite adaptation of a hypothetical Jebusite ritual of El Elyon, God Most High. *See* GOD, NAMES OF, § C2*b*.

The proposed reconstructions of the Israelite New Year ritual enlist several elements, but there are two constant motifs present: (*a*) a sham battle in sacramental re-enactment of God's struggle against and victory over the forces of chaos at the Creation; (*b*) a procession of the ark-throne (*see* ARK OF THE COVENANT) with the triumphant Creator enthroned as the giver and sustainer of life. Other elements of the ritual would be identified as the ritual humiliation and suffering of the king in the grip of "Death"; the monarch's ritual combat against his enemies, who were also the foes of the Lord; and the king's annual enthronement.

There are, however, several weighty objections to this reconstruction of the pre-exilic New Year ritual. The so-called "enthronement of the LORD" psalms are questioned as having any relevance to the observance of a New Year festival, and they are proposed to be designated as sabbath psalms. The ritual humiliation and cultic suffering of the king are also disputed on the ground that the psalms identified as "psalms of royal lamentations" can be construed with impressive cogency as laments of the suffering innocent wrongly accused. Similarly, it is proposed, the royal psalms might echo historical situations, and a ritual background is not necessary to their understanding (*see* PSALMS, BOOK OF). The paucity of incontestable data leaves any hypothesis on the pre-exilic New Year festival extremely vulnerable.

Whatever be the case in regard to the existence of the pre-exilic New Year ritual, this much can be convincingly established: that the king did not represent the Deity in the Israelite ritual. In the ritual combat it was the Lord who delivered the hard-pressed king (Ps. 18:43). The royal suffering must not be construed as re-enactment of a divine humiliation and imprisonment alien to Israel's faith. In the ritual, the king's role could have been the leading of the ark procession (Ps. 132:6-10) in a cultic commemoration of David's original ark procession, in which this ideal "anointed of the LORD" danced before the ark-throne of God (II Sam. 6:12-19). The king's function was essentially that of a priestly intermediary who represented the people in penitence and supplication before God in accord with his office as the "priest after the order of Melchizedek" (Ps. 110:4).

Bibliography. E. R. Goodenough, "Kingship in Early Israel," *JBL,* XLIII (1929), 169-205. H. Gressmann, *Der Messias* (1929). A. Alt, *Die Staatenbildung der Israeliten in Palästina, Verfassungsgeschichtliche Studien* (1930). A. Lods, "La Divinisation du Roi dans l'Orient Méditerranéen et ses Répercussions dans l'Ancien Israël," *RHPR* (1930), 209-21. C. R. North, "The OT Estimate of the Monarchy," *AJSL,* XLVIII (1931), 1-19; "The Religious Aspects of Hebrew Kingship," *ZAW,* L, N.F. IX (1932), 8-38. A. R. Johnson, "The Rôle of the King in the Jerusalem Cultus," *The Labyrinth: Further Studies in the Relation Between Myth and Ritual in the Ancient World* (ed. S. H. Hooke; 1935), pp. 71-111. I. Engnell, *Studies in Divine Kingship in the Ancient Near East* (1943). A. Bentzen, *Det sakrale kongedømme* (1945). N. H. Snaith, *The Jewish New Year Festival: Its Origin and Development* (1947). H. Frankfort, *Kingship and the Gods, A Study of Ancient Near Eastern Religion as the Integration of Society and Nature* (1948). C. J. Gadd, *Ideas of Divine Rule in the Ancient East* (1948). A. Alt, "Das Königtum in den Reichen Israel und Juda," *VT,* I (1951), 1-22. J. de Fraine, *L'aspect religieux de la royauté israélite; L'institution monarchique dans l'AT et dans les textes mésopotamiens* (1954). S. Mowinckel, *He That Cometh* (1954), pp. 21-95. A. Bentzen, *King and Messiah* (1955). A. R. Johnson, *Sacral Kingship in Ancient Israel* (1955). G. Widengren, *Sakrales Königtum im AT und im Judentum* (1955). J. H. Grønbaeck, "Kongens kultiske funktion i det forexilske Israel," *Dansk Teologisk Tidskrift,* XX (1956), 1-16. A. A. Koolhaas, *Theocratie en monarchie in Israel; Eenige opmerkingen over der verhouding van de theocratie en het israëlitische koningschap in het OT* (1957). G. Widengren, "King and Covenant," *Journal of Semitic Studies,* II (1957), 1-32. M. Noth, *Amt und Berufung im AT* (1958). A. Alt, *La Regalità Sacra/The Sacral Kingship* (NVMEN, Supplement IV; 1959), "V. Israel," pp. 281-366.

S. Szikszai

***KINGDOM OF GOD, OF HEAVEN** [ἡ βασιλεία τοῦ θεοῦ, τῶν οὐρανῶν]. These synonymous expressions (*see* §§ 1*b-c below*) represent an idea which is deeply rooted in the thought of the OT, and which constitutes the central theme of the teaching of Jesus as recorded in the Synoptic gospels. The basic meaning of the idea, in the Bible, is that of the kingly rule or sovereignty of God (*see* § 1 *below*), rather than that of the sphere, or realm, in which his rule operates. The latter meaning is, however, necessarily implied in the idea. The Bible regards the kingly rule of God under three different aspects: as an eternal fact, as manifested upon earth in its acceptance by men, and as a consummation to be hoped for in the future. In the last of these aspects, the idea is an eschatological one. It is this eschatological aspect that predominates in the teaching of Jesus on the kingdom of God, and modern discussions of Christian eschatology have largely centered around the question of the interpretation of his teaching on this subject.

1. Terminology and meaning
   - *a.* In the OT
   - *b.* In later Jewish literature
   - *c.* In the NT
2. The Jewish background
   - *a.* The preprophetic period
   - *b.* The influence of the prophets
   - *c.* The postexilic period
   - *d.* Rabbinic teaching
3. The teaching of Jesus
   - *a.* The imminence of the kingdom
   - *b.* The kingdom as present
   - *c.* The consummation of the kingdom
   - *d.* The kingdom and the Cross
   - *e.* The community of the kingdom
   - *f.* The discipline of the kingdom
4. The kingdom of God in the rest of the NT
   - *a.* Acts
   - *b.* Pauline letters
   - *c.* Johannine literature
   - *d.* Other books

Bibliography

1. Terminology and meaning. The purpose of this preliminary section is to survey briefly the use, in the biblical and related literature, of the term "kingdom of God" and its equivalents, and to consider the meaning of the terms.

a. In the OT. The actual phrase "kingdom of God" does not appear in the OT, except for one occurrence of the form "kingdom of the Lord" (*malkuth Yahweh*) in one of the latest books (I Chr. 28:5). The word "kingdom," however, is sometimes used in relation to God. "Thy kingdom" occurs in Pss. 45:6 ERV; 145:11, 13; and "his kingdom" in Pss. 103:19; 145:12 RSV mg. In I Chr. 17:14 "my kingdom" appears on the lips of "the Lord of hosts." In all the foregoing passages the Hebrew word is מלכות. In Obad. 21; Ps. 22:28 ERV, "the kingdom" is described as "the Lord's"; in each case the Hebrew word is מלוכה. The phrase "Thine is the kingdom, O Lord," is found in I Chr. 29:11; in this case the Hebrew is ממלכה. In the Aramaic portion of the book of Daniel "his kingdom" occurs in 4:3, 34; 7:27 ERV, while in Dan. 2:44 we read of the "God of heaven" setting up "a kingdom." In all these passages the Aramaic word is מלכותא. The different Hebrew and Aramaic words for "kingdom" mentioned above, when applied to God, all have, as their primary meaning, the idea of "kingship," "sovereignty," or "kingly rule."

b. In later Jewish literature. In the Apoc. the phrase "kingdom of God" (βασιλεία τοῦ θεοῦ) occurs once (Wisd. Sol. 10:10), and there are occasional references to "his [or thy] kingdom" (e.g., Tob. 13:1; Wisd. Sol. 6:4; Song Thr. Ch. 33). A similar usage is found in the Pseudep. (e.g., Enoch 41:1; 52:4; Pss. Sol. 5:18; 17:3, 30-34; Asmp. Moses 10:1). In later literature the phrases "kingdom of God" and (especially) "kingdom of heaven" occur more frequently, being used particularly by the Targ. writers (*see* Targum) who wished to avoid the thought that God in person should appear on earth. Thus, e.g., the Targ. on Isa. 40:9 substitutes for "Behold your God" the phrase: "The kingdom [Aramaic מלכותא] of your God has become manifest"; similar substitutions appear in the Targ. on Isa. 31:4; 52:7; Ezek. 7:7, 10; 11:24; Obad. 21; Mic. 4:7; Zech. 14:9. There is no difference in meaning between the forms "kingdom of God" and "kingdom of heaven" in this connection, since the word "heaven" was frequently used by the Jews as a reverent periphrasis for the divine name (*see* God, Names of). The term "kingdom" (Aramaic מלכותא) also appears, in relation to God, in Jewish prayers (e.g., the Kaddish prayer, which includes the petition: "May he establish his kingdom during your life"). As in the OT (*see* § 1*a above*), so in all this later literature, the meaning of "kingdom" is fundamentally that of "sovereignty" or "rule."

c. In the NT. The terms "kingdom of God" and "kingdom of heaven" occur very frequently in the

Synoptic gospels. The use of the latter form is, however, confined to the Gospel of Matthew, which, in keeping with its Jewish-Christian character (*see* MATTHEW, GOSPEL OF), regularly adopts the periphrasis "heaven" for "God" (*see* § 1*b above*). "Kingdom of God," however, appears in Matt. 12:28; 19:24; 21:31, 43. It is possible that Jesus himself sometimes used the periphrasis and spoke of the kingdom of heaven, but the evidence suggests that "kingdom of God" was the form of the expression normally used by him. Other equivalent expressions which occur in the Synoptics are: "thy kingdom" (Matt. 6:10; Luke 11:2); "his kingdom" (Matt. 6:33; Luke 12:31); "the kingdom" (Matt. 4:23; 8:12; 9:35; 13:19, 38; 24:14; 25:34; Luke 12:32); "the kingdom of their Father" (Matt. 13:43); "my Father's kingdom" (Matt. 26:29). In all the foregoing passages the kingdom is regarded as belonging to God. In a few passages the kingdom is spoken of as belonging to "the Son of man" (Matt. 13:41; 16:28), or to Jesus himself (Matt. 20:21; Luke 1:33; 22:29-30; 23:42 RSV mg.).

In the Fourth Gospel the term "kingdom of God" occurs twice (John 3:3, 5), and the phrase "my kingdom" appears on the lips of Jesus in John 18:36 ERV-ASV.

In Acts "kingdom of God" occurs six times (1:3; 8:12; 14:22; 19:8; 28:23, 31) and "the kingdom" twice (1:6; 20:25). In the Pauline letters "kingdom of God" is found in Rom. 14:17; I Cor. 4:20; 6:9-10; 15:50; Gal. 5:21; Col. 4:11; II Thess. 1:5. I Cor. 15:24 speaks of Christ's delivering "the kingdom to God the Father," and Eph. 5:5 has the phrase "the kingdom of Christ and of God." "His own kingdom" (i.e., God's) occurs in I Thess. 2:12, and "the kingdom of his beloved Son" in Col. 1:13. In the Pastoral letters "his kingdom" is used twice with reference to Christ (II Tim. 4:1, 18). In Hebrews "thy kingdom" occurs in connection with "the Son" in 1:8, and "a kingdom" is found in 12:28. In the Catholic letters "the kingdom" occurs in reference to God in Jas. 2:5, and II Pet. 1:11 refers to "the eternal kingdom of our Lord and Savior Jesus Christ." Finally, in Revelation we have references to the "tribulation and kingdom and patience which are in Jesus" (1:9 ERV-ASV), "the kingdom of our Lord and of his Christ" (11:15), and "the kingdom of our God" (12:10).

In every NT passage referred to above, the word for "kingdom" is βασιλεία. The primary meaning of this word, like that of its Hebrew and Aramaic counterparts (*see* §§ 1*a-b above*), is that of "kingship" or "rule," although its use is extended, to a greater degree than is the case with the Semitic words, to include the meaning of "realm" or "territory governed by a king." It must be remembered, however, that in the teaching of Jesus, and consequently in NT usage generally, the Greek βασιλεία represents the מלכותא of his native Aramaic, and must be understood accordingly.

2. The Jewish background. If the actual term "kingdom," in relation to God, is of comparatively rare occurrence in the OT (*see* § 1*a above*), the concept in which the idea of the kingdom of God is rooted—namely, the concept of God as king—is, nevertheless, everywhere present.

a. The preprophetic period. In the early period of Israelite religious history, the kingship of Yahweh over Israel, like that of other gods over their respective peoples (e.g., Chemosh over Moab and Milcom over Ammon—see I Kings 11:33), was regarded as something similar to human kingship. The sovereignty of each god was limited to the territory, and the subjects, of the nation that worshiped him. To leave the land of Israel was to leave the jurisdiction of the God of Israel, and to become unable to worship him (see II Kings 5:17-18, where Naaman the Syrian seeks to overcome this difficulty by transporting a quantity of earth from Yahweh's territory into that of Rimmon; cf. also I Sam. 26:19; Ps. 137:4). The god's sovereignty was also limited in the sense that his functions as king were fairly strictly defined; in the main, his functions were to provide help against the nation's enemies, counsel by oracles or soothsayers in matters of national difficulty, and a sentence of justice when a case was too hard for human decision. Yet a further limitation of the god's sovereignty was involved in the fact that his people and his land were as essential to him as he was to them, since the idea of a god without a land and a people to rule over was inconceivable. This meant that there was a limit to what a god could do with his people, since he could not destroy them or surrender them to a foreign power without disinheriting himself. In all these ways, the sovereignty of Yahweh over Israel was regarded as limited. Within such limitations, however, it was absolute: "You shall have no other gods before me" (Exod. 20:3).

b. The influence of the prophets. If the kingship of Yahweh over Israel was at first regarded in the same light as that of other gods over their peoples, the way in which the idea developed in Israel was very different from that which was the case elsewhere. This was primarily due to the work of the great prophets of the eighth and subsequent centuries B.C., the effect of which was to remove the above-mentioned limitations from the conception of Yahweh's sovereignty. The message of these prophets brought a new insight into the nature and character of Yahweh, and at the same time a realization that his sovereignty was universal and unrestricted in its scope. The insistence that Yahweh's essential nature was absolute holiness, righteousness, and love made impossible the restriction of his functions as king to those of a mere helper in time of need. He came to be seen as the ever-watchful guardian of justice and mercy in the relations of man to man, and the swift judge of all wrong and oppression. All human affairs, and all men's dealings with one another, must come under his jurisdiction. For the prophets, Yahweh was not so much the champion of Israel as the champion of righteousness; and the natural corollary of this development was the extension of his sovereignty to include other nations besides Israel. Thus Amos proclaimed that not only Israel but many other nations also were accountable to Yahweh for their transgressions (Amos 1–2), that the people of Israel were like the Ethiopians to him, and that, just as he had brought up Israel from the land of Egypt, so it was Yahweh who had also brought up the Philistines from Caphtor and the Syrians from Kir (Amos 9:7). Similar ideas appear in Isa. 5:26; Jer. 27:5-11.

The bitter experiences of the Babylonian exile, which the prophets regarded as the punishment of

Judah for her sins, gave added force to this spiritualizing and universalizing of the conception of Yahweh's kingship. In Deutero-Isaiah there appears the idea that Yahweh can use the mighty world powers, and the events of history outside Israel, to bring about the fulfilment of his own purposes. The rise of the Persian Empire is spoken of as his work, and CYRUS referred to as the "shepherd" and the "anointed" of Yahweh (Isa. 41:1-7; 44:24–45:25). The other gods cease to be regarded as rival deities and become mere nonentities.

> I am the LORD, and there is no other,
> besides me there is no God
> (Isa. 45:5).

This degradation of other deities involved not only the tribal and national gods, but also the whole host of nature and fertility gods and goddesses. Thus the sovereignty of Yahweh was seen to extend, not only over all the nations, but over the whole of nature as well (Job 38–41; Hos. 2:8). With the rise of this monotheistic faith, the relation between Yahweh and Israel could no longer be regarded as one of mutual dependence. Thus all limitations came to be removed from the idea of Yahweh's kingship, and it was seen to be, not a national and limited monarchy, but an ethical and universal reign. In this sense, God is eternally and universally king; his "kingdom is an everlasting kingdom," which "rules over all" (Pss. 145:13; 103:19).

c. The postexilic period. This new conception of Yahweh's kingship as eternal and universal, which we have seen to be the result of prophetic teaching, raised, however, new problems. The conviction that the whole world was subject to one God had to be reconciled with the hard facts of experience, for nothing was more obvious than that the rule of God was not universally recognized and obeyed, not even within Israel herself. The attempt to solve this problem led inevitably to the development of eschatology. True as it was that God was eternally king, there was clearly a sense in which his complete and absolute sovereignty was not yet manifested in this world. So there arose the conception of the rule of God as a hope for the future.

The beginnings of Jewish eschatology are to be found in the writings of the prophets themselves. Though they were primarily preachers to their own day, warning men of the just demands of God and of the inevitable consequences of behavior and policies that were at variance with his rule, the prophets nevertheless looked beyond the present and the immediate future to a great DAY OF THE LORD, when God would triumphantly intervene to establish his sovereignty finally and absolutely. In contrast to popular expectation, this day was not to be one of divine deliverance for Israel and vengeance on her enemies, but rather a day of judgment for Israel as for every other nation (Amos 5:18-20; Zeph. 1:14-18). And beyond this day of the Lord, the prophets saw the coming of a new and golden age of universal peace and harmony under the sovereign rule of God (Isa. 2:2-4; 11:6-9; Mic. 4:1-4). This eschatological expectation was developed in an apocalyptic direction in such postexilic writings as Joel; Isa. 24–27; Zech. 9–14, until it reached its fullest development in Daniel and the extracanonical apocalypses of the last two centuries B.C. and the first A.D. *See* APOCALYPTICISM.

Apocalyptic really arose out of the attempt to reconcile a faith in the sovereignty of a good God with the experience of evil and suffering in this world. The solution it offered to this problem involved a qualified dualism, which saw a spiritual kingdom of evil, headed by SATAN, at war with the kingdom, or rule, of God. This powerfully organized kingdom of evil, though it often appeared to be in the ascendant in this world, existed only by the permission of God, and would ultimately be overthrown. Indeed, the sufferings and disasters which were mounting with such rapidity, to the consternation of the faithful, were, to the apocalyptists, merely the signs of the approaching end.

The time and the nature of the final consummation of the reign of God are variously described in the different apocalypses. Some look for a golden age to be realized on earth, whereas others look only to the establishment of the eternal kingdom in heaven. Sometimes the kingdom is thought of as being established by the direct intervention of God without any mediator; thus, e.g., in Asmp. Moses 10:1:

> Then His kingdom shall appear throughout all His
> creation,
> And then Satan shall be no more,
> And sorrow shall depart with him.

At other times the coming of the kingdom is associated with the figure of a MESSIAH; thus, e.g., in Apocal. Bar. 73:

> It shall come to pass, when He [the Messiah] has
> brought low everything that is in the world,
> And has sat down in peace for the age on the throne
> of His kingdom,
> That joy shall then be revealed,
> And rest shall appear.

Of special importance for the background of the NT doctrine of the kingdom of God is the vision of Dan. 7, where the dominion of the successive world empires to which Israel was subject from the Exile onward, represented by the beasts, is seen to be taken away, and the kingdom given to the "saints of the Most High" (7:18, 22, 25, 27), represented by "one like a son of man" (7:13; *see* SON OF MAN), whose

> dominion is an everlasting dominion,
> which shall not pass away,
> and his kingdom one
> that shall not be destroyed
> (7:14).

Underneath all the differences of form which the conception takes in the apocalyptic writings, there lies, however, the common conviction that the reign of God is shortly to become effective over all the world. Such was the hope cherished by the faithful in Israel through all the vicissitudes of the centuries immediately preceding the Christian era. It finds expression in the prayer of the Kaddish, which pious Jews prayed in the first century A.D. as they do today, and which concludes with the petition: "May he establish his kingdom during your life and during your days, and during the life of all the house of Israel." The gospels themselves afford an occasional glimpse of such faithful souls who were "looking for the kingdom of God" (Mark 15:43; Luke 23:51; cf. Luke 2: 25, 38; 14:15; 17:20; 19:11).

It was to a people that cherished this eschatological hope that JOHN THE BAPTIST began to preach *ca.* A.D. 28-29. Matthew attributes to John the statement: "Repent, for the kingdom of heaven is at hand" (3:2). It is probable that the actual words of John have here been assimilated to those of Jesus at Matt. 4:17 (cf. Mark 1:15). Nevertheless, the burden of John's prophetic message was the announcement that the day of the Lord was imminent, and the appeal to men to repent in preparation for that day, and to signify their repentance by submitting to the rite of baptism. The new element in John's eschatology, as compared with that of the popular expectation, was that the Messiah would come, not so much as a national deliverer, but as the judge, whose "winnowing fork is in his hand, and he will clear his threshing floor and gather his wheat into the granary, but the chaff he will burn with unquenchable fire" (Matt. 3:12; Luke 3:17). Moreover, this judgment or "wrath to come" would fall upon Jews as well as Gentiles, unless they had prepared themselves by repentance and the bearing of fruit that befitted repentance; to be able to claim physical descent from Abraham would be no guarantee of escape (Matt. 3:7-10; Luke 3:7-9). In spite of this harsh element in his message, the preaching of John the Baptist met with a considerable response, and multitudes "were baptized by him in the river Jordan, confessing their sins" (Mark 1:5). It is thus evident that when the ministry of Jesus opened, the thought of the coming consummation of the reign of God was very much in men's minds.

*d. **Rabbinic teaching.*** While the rabbis who were contemporary with the beginning of the Christian era certainly shared the eschatological hope referred to *above* (*see* § 2*c*), they were equally concerned with another aspect of the idea of God's sovereignty. They thought of it as a divine discipline to be accepted by individuals by obedient submission to God's will. In the rabbinic literature (which belongs to a later date, but which probably embodies the teaching of a much earlier period), the kingdom of God (or heaven) is sometimes spoken of as something to be "taken upon" oneself. Thus Israel is said to have taken upon herself Yahweh's kingdom at Sinai. The proselyte who adopts the law thereby "takes upon himself the kingdom of heaven." And for the Jew, the daily recitation of the Shema (Deut. 6:4-5) is regarded as a continually repeated "taking upon oneself of the yoke of the kingdom of God." In this sense, of course, the kingdom of God (or heaven) is thought of as a reality that is present and effective wherever the rule of God is submitted to by perfect obedience to the law.

3. The teaching of Jesus. That the kingdom of God was the theme of Jesus' public preaching during the Galilean ministry, we are expressly told by the evangelists (Matt. 4:23; 9:35; Luke 8:1; 9:11; cf. Luke 4:43-44). An examination of his sayings and parables, as recorded in the Synoptic gospels, confirms that the idea of the kingdom occupied a central place in the whole of Jesus' thought and teaching. The term "kingdom of God," or one of its equivalents (*see* § 1*c above*), occurs frequently on his lips in each of the Synoptic sources (*see* SYNOPTIC PROBLEM). It is found in thirteen sayings in Mark, some thirteen in Q, some twenty-five in M, and some six in L. The accounts of the mission of the disciples reveal that the message which they were sent to proclaim also concerned the kingdom of God (Matt. 10:7; Luke 9:2; 10:9, 11). That the idea of the kingdom of God was a familiar one to the contemporaries of Jesus, is clear from what has been said about its place in apocalyptic and rabbinic thought (*see* § 2*c-d above*). Jesus himself was fully aware of the different ways in which, as we have seen, the idea of the kingdom of God could be conceived: the idea of God as eternally king (*see* § 2*b above*); the idea of the sovereignty of God as a present reality wherever individuals acknowledge it by obedient submission to his will (*see* § 2*d above*); and the idea of the kingdom as the object of the eschatological hope (*see* § 2*c above*). Each of these ideas is to some extent reflected in the teaching of Jesus, but the idea that predominates is the eschatological one. The main problem in connection with the interpretation of Jesus' eschatological teaching arises from the paradox that, whereas much of it envisages the kingdom of God as about to come into being in the near future, there are also sayings which clearly imply that the kingdom, in the eschatological sense, has already come in the person and ministry of Jesus himself. Attempts have been made to bring the teaching as a whole into one consistent pattern, either of futurist or of "realized" eschatology (*see* ESCHATOLOGY OF NT), but such attempts invariably involve a strained and unnatural exegesis of a number of the sayings. It is accordingly advisable to allow for the existence, in Jesus' thought, of both emphases, and to attempt to understand their relationship to one another.

*a. **The imminence of the kingdom.*** According to Mark 1:14-15, Jesus began his public ministry in Galilee with the proclamation: "The time is fulfilled, and the kingdom of God is at hand; repent, and believe in the gospel." Many scholars prefer the translation "has come" to "is at hand" for the Greek ἤγγικεν in this passage, and so include it among the sayings in which Jesus speaks of the kingdom as already present (*see* § 3*b below*). This interpretation depends upon the view that the Greek verb in question (ἐγγίζω) represents the Aramaic מטא, which means "to arrive." It is true that ἐγγίζω is sometimes used in the LXX to translate מטא and the Hebrew נגע, which also means "to arrive." Such cases, however, are exceptional; in the majority of its occurrences in the LXX, ἐγγίζω has its normal Greek meaning of "to draw near," and where it does mean "to reach, or arrive," the context makes it clear that such is, in fact, the meaning. Moreover, the usual meaning of ἐγγίζω in the NT is "to draw near." The idea that "the kingdom of God has come" could have been expressed much less ambiguously than by the use of the verb ἤγγικεν; indeed, it is so expressed by the use of ἔφθασεν in Matt. 12:28; Luke 11:20 (*see* § 3*b below*).

In view of these considerations, it is better to understand the words of Mark 1:15 as indicating the imminence, rather than the actual presence, of the kingdom of God. The same interpretation will naturally apply to the use of the same expression, ἤγγικεν ἡ βασιλεία τοῦ θεοῦ (τῶν οὐρανῶν), in the message delivered by Jesus to his disciples when sending them out on their mission (Matt. 10:7; Luke 10:9, 11). Thus Jesus opened his ministry with the proclamation that the eschatological event, the kingdom of God, was near, and later sent his disciples out to make the same proclamation.

The same emphasis on the kingdom of God as an event which is to take place in the near future is to be seen in the important saying: "Truly, I say to you; there are some standing here who will not taste death before they see the kingdom of God come with power" (Mark 9:1). Here again, there are some scholars who interpret the saying as implying the actual presence of the kingdom, the promise being that some of the bystanders would come to see, in the future, that the kingdom of God had already come in the person and ministry of Jesus. This, however, is a strained interpretation of the words, which in their natural sense point to the coming of the kingdom as an imminent future event. The words "with power" suggest a coming in a fuller and more final sense, in contrast with the coming of the kingdom that has already taken place (*see* § 3*b below*). The prophecy of Mark 9:1 is sometimes regarded as having been fulfilled in a historical event such as the Transfiguration, or the Resurrection, or the fall of Jerusalem, or the triumphant spread of Christianity throughout the Roman Empire. It is much more likely, however, that Jesus was here speaking of the final consummation of the kingdom of God. That the author of Matthew understood the saying in this sense is clear from the fact that he substitutes, for Mark's "kingdom of God come with power," the phrase "the Son of man coming in his kingdom" (Matt. 16:28); and this interpretation is confirmed by the fact that, in another saying recorded by Mark, Jesus uses the phrase "with great power" in a reference to the coming of the Son of man: "And then they will see the Son of man coming in clouds with great power and glory" (Mark 13:26). The coming of the kingdom of God "with power" (Mark 9:1) is thus to be identified with the PAROUSIA of the SON OF MAN, and as such is clearly a future event.

Another indication that Jesus thought of the kingdom of God as being established in the future is seen in his saying at the Last Supper: "Truly, I say to you, I shall not drink again of the fruit of the vine until that day when I drink it new in the kingdom of God" (Mark 14:25; cf. Luke 22:18, which is probably the L version of the same saying; Luke records also a similar saying, with reference to the Passover meal, in 22:16). Jesus is here thinking of the consummation of the kingdom of God, in terms of the messianic banquet (*see* MESSIAH), of which the Last Supper is an anticipation. The same thought appears later in Luke's account of the Supper, where Jesus, however, speaks of the kingdom as appointed for himself by the Father: "As my Father appointed a kingdom for me, so do I appoint for you that you may eat and drink at my table in my kingdom" (Luke 22:29-30). These sayings at the Last Supper reveal that the thought of the coming consummation of the kingdom of God was prominent in Jesus' mind as he faced his death, and suggest that he believed his death to be a necessary step toward that consummation (*see* § 3*d below*). The idea of the messianic banquet in the future, consummated kingdom of God is found again in a saying which belongs to the Q source: "I tell you, many will come from east and west and sit at table with Abraham, Isaac, and Jacob in the kingdom of heaven" (Matt. 8:11; cf. Luke 13:28-29). It is also implied in the parable of which variant forms appear in Matt. 22:1-14 (the marriage feast; note the introductory formula: "The kingdom of heaven may be compared to . . .") and Luke 14:16-24 (the great supper; note that here the parable is Jesus' reply to a man who said: "Blessed is he who shall eat bread in the kingdom of God!").

The imagery of a marriage feast is also a feature of the parable of the wise and foolish maidens (Matt. 25:1-13). The emphasis in this parable, however, is on the thought of an impending crisis, for which men are exhorted to be prepared. The introductory formula: "Then the kingdom of heaven shall be compared to . . ." (Matt. 25:1), connects this impending crisis with the kingdom. The same thought of an impending crisis of judgment appears in the following parable of the talents (Matt. 25:14-30); cf. the parable of the pounds (Luke 19:11-27), which is probably the L version of the same parable, and which is told to men who "supposed that the kingdom of God was to appear immediately" (Luke 19:11). The third parable of Matt. 25, that of the sheep and the goats (vss. 31-46), clearly points to a future judgment, at which "the King will say to those at his right hand, 'Come, O blessed of my Father, inherit the kingdom prepared for you from the foundation of the world' " (vs. 34). A number of other parables stress the need for preparedness in the face of an impending crisis; such are the servants of the absent householder (Mark 13:33-37; cf. Luke 12:35-38), the faithful and unfaithful servants (Matt. 24:45-51; Luke 12:42-46), and the thief at night (Matt. 24:43-44; Luke 12:39-40). In these, the crisis is pictured in terms of the parousia of the Son of man rather than of the coming of the kingdom of God as such, but as we have seen, no distinction need be drawn between these two different ways of speaking of the *eschaton.* All these parables of crisis or judgment may thus be understood as implying the expectation that the kingdom of God, in its full and final sense, was to come in the future—and in the near future at that, since the exhortations to his contemporaries to be watchful and prepared would be pointless unless Jesus thought of the coming as happening within their lifetime (cf. Mark 9:1, discussed above).

Another group of parables describe processes of growth. Four of these are specifically related to the kingdom of God; they are the seed growing secretly (Mark 4:26-29), the tares (Matt. 13:24-30), the mustard seed (Matt. 13:31-32; Mark 4:30-32; Luke 13:18-19), and the leaven (Matt. 13:33; Luke 13:20-21). Though it is not explicitly said to refer to the kingdom, the parable of the sower (Matt. 13:3-9; Mark 4:3-9; Luke 8:5-8) occurs in the same context in Mark and Matthew, and obviously belongs to the same group. While these parables may rightly be claimed to imply an actual presence of the kingdom (*see* § 3*b below*), the fact that in each case the process of growth culminates in a climax (the harvest, the full-grown tree, the leavening of the whole) suggests that the future consummation of the kingdom is also in mind. In the interpretation of the parable of the tares given in Matt. 13:36-43, we are expressly told that "the harvest is the close of the age," and that when it comes, "the righteous will shine like the sun in the kingdom of their Father." There are, however, good reasons for regarding this interpretation (and that of the closely similar parable of the dragnet in Matt. 13:47-50) as not belonging to the authentic teaching of Jesus.

Finally, we may mention what is perhaps the clearest indication of all that Jesus thought of the coming of the kingdom of God in terms of the future —namely, the petition which forms part of the prayer which he taught to his disciples: "Thy kingdom come" (Matt. 6:10; Luke 11:2).

b. The kingdom as present. This aspect of Jesus' teaching about the kingdom of God is seen most clearly in sayings in which he explains the significance of his own mighty works. Of special importance is the saying, which occurs in the Q version of the Beelzebul controversy: "If it is by the finger of God that I cast out demons, then the kingdom of God has come upon you" (Luke 11:20; cf. Matt. 12: 28). The verb here is ἔφθασεν, the aorist tense of φθάνω, which in Hellenistic Greek had almost entirely lost its classical meaning of "to anticipate, or precede," and normally meant "to arrive" (this is its clear meaning in four out of the five other occurrences of the verb in the NT). Moreover, φθάνω is used in the LXX to translate the Hebrew נגע and the Aramaic מטא, both of which mean "to arrive." The Aramaic underlying φθάνω in the saying of Jesus under consideration was probably מטא. The translation of ἔφθασεν by "has come" is thus undoubtedly correct, and attempts to explain it as an example of the familiar prophetic device of speaking of a future event as though it had already happened are hardly convincing. The saying is accordingly to be interpreted as meaning that Jesus' exorcisms are an indication that the kingdom, in a real sense, has already arrived. This interpretation is confirmed by the saying which follows in Q, and which is also found in the Markan version of the Beelzebul controversy: "How can one enter a strong man's house and plunder his goods, unless he first binds the strong man? Then indeed he may plunder his house" (Matt. 12:29; cf. Mark 3:27; Luke 11:21-22). Here the "strong man" clearly stands for SATAN; and it was a definite Jewish expectation that at the last day Satan would be bound. The actual plundering of Satan's house implied by Jesus' exorcisms is thus an indication that the *eschaton* is already in operation.

A similar interpretation of the significance of his mighty works appears in Jesus' reply to the question of John the Baptist: "Go and tell John what you have seen and heard: the blind receive their sight, the lame walk, lepers are cleansed, and the deaf hear, the dead are raised up, the poor have good news preached to them" (Luke 7:22; cf. Matt. 11:4-5). The actual term "kingdom of God" does not occur in this context, but Jesus refers to his miracles in language that clearly echoes the prophetic description of the messianic last days (cf. Isa. 29:18-19; 35:5-6; 61: 1). There are also other sayings which, though not specifically referring to the kingdom, suggest that the eschatological hope of Israel is finding fulfilment in the acts and words of Jesus. These are the declaration of blessedness upon the disciples (Matt. 13:16-17; Luke 10:23-24), and the reference to the "something greater" that "is here" (Matt. 12:41-42; Luke 11:31-32; cf. Matt. 12:6).

The actual presence of the kingdom is again implied in a Q saying which is found in widely different forms in Matt. 11:12-13; Luke 16:16. There is widespread agreement that neither evangelist has preserved the saying as a whole in its original form, but that Luke has preserved more accurately the reference to the law and the prophets, whereas Matthew's version of the rest of the saying is closer to the original (Luke having mitigated its harshness by introducing the idea of the good news being preached). Thus the original saying was probably something like this: "The law and the prophets were until John; since then the kingdom of God βιάζεται, and men of violence (βιασταί) take it by force (ἁρπάζουσιν αὐτήν)." The latter half of the saying is still ambiguous, since βιάζεται can be taken either as passive ("suffers violence") or as middle ("exercises its power"). Whichever of these interpretations is adopted, however, the saying clearly distinguishes between two periods, that of the law and the prophets on the one hand and that of the kingdom of God on the other, and makes the ministry of John the Baptist the dividing line between them. If the kingdom of God is suffering violence (whether at the hands of its enemies, as some think, or at the hands of enthusiasts who are eager to enter it at all costs, as others interpret βιασταὶ ἁρπάζουσιν αὐτήν), it must already be in existence. On the other hand, if it is exercising its power, it must equally clearly be already in existence.

Another saying, the meaning of which has been the subject of much discussion, but which on the whole seems to support the view that Jesus thought of the kingdom as present, is that which is found only in Luke 17:20-21. The first problem that arises here concerns the meaning of the Greek expression ἐντὸς ὑμῶν, which can be translated either "in the midst of you" (RSV) or "within you" (RSV mg.). The latter is the more natural meaning of the Greek phrase as such, but several considerations make it likely that the former is the correct interpretation in this context. The idea of the kingdom as an inward principle or disposition in men suits neither the context of this saying nor the general tenor of Jesus' teaching on the subject, and it must not be forgotten that he is addressing, not his own disciples, but certain Pharisees who asked "when the kingdom of God was coming" (vs. 20). Moreover, the ambiguity of the preposition was probably more marked in the Aramaic which Jesus spoke than is the case with the Greek ἐντός. If the translation: "The kingdom of God is in the midst of you," is adopted, it is possible to understand the statement as referring to a future coming of the kingdom; in this case, the reply to the Pharisees' question would mean that it is useless to try to predict the time of the kingdom's coming, since it will suddenly come to be in their midst, without previous warning. The more natural interpretation of Jesus' reply, however, is that it means that the kingdom is already "in the midst of" men, in his own person and ministry. It may be added that, if the reading "within you" is adopted, the saying still implies the actual presence of the kingdom, though in rather a different sense.

The parables of growth, although they point forward to a consummation that still lies in the future (*see* § 3*a above*), nevertheless imply that the kingdom is, in a real sense, already present. The present activity of Jesus, during his ministry, corresponds to the sowing of the seed, or the planting of the leaven in the meal, and the point of the parables is that the process of growth, or leavening, is a divine activity that will inevitably follow, until the climax or consummation is reached. The kingdom itself is likened to the act of sowing in the parables of the seed growing secretly (Mark 4:26) and the tares (Matt. 13:24), and to the mustard seed and leaven respectively in the parables of the mustard seed (Luke 13:18-19) and the leaven (Luke 13:20-21). Thus the process has already been set in motion, and is, in a real sense, a present manifestation of the kingdom.

These parables of growth point the way to the solution of the problem of reconciling the two divergent emphases which have been noted in the teaching of Jesus about the kingdom of God. There is no good reason to suppose that the two emphases belong to different periods of the ministry, and represent a development of his thought from the idea of the kingdom as imminent to that of it as actually present; as we have seen, the imminence of the kingdom was still in his mind at the close of his ministry (*see* § 3*a above*). The evidence suggests rather that he held both ideas in his mind, sometimes emphasizing the one and at other times the other. And in the parables of growth the relationship between the two ideas becomes clear. In the person and ministry of Jesus, the kingdom is already present germinally or in principle; the messianic age has been inaugurated. But it is not yet seen in its complete fulfilment, so that a consummation may still be looked for in the future; in the words of Mark 9:1, the kingdom is still to come "with power" (*see* § 3*a above*).

This means that the eschatology of Jesus was a radical departure from that of the Jewish apocalypses (*see* § 2*c above*). Instead of conceiving the *eschaton* as one cataclysmic, world-ending manifestation of divine power, he conceived it as a kind of "new era," bounded at its opening and close by decisive manifestations of divine power, and marked throughout by the constant operation of the same divine power. In his own coming, the powers of the "age to come" (*see* TIME) had invaded the "present age," and were now at work within it. This meant that God had begun to rule in the world in a fuller sense than was the case before; in other words, that the kingdom of God, in the eschatological sense, had been inaugurated. The eschatological process thus inaugurated would, however, be consummated in the future by a further decisive manifestation of divine power.

c. The consummation of the kingdom. Jesus expressly disclaimed any precise knowledge as to the time of the future consummation (Mark 13:32). Nevertheless, the evidence suggests that he expected it to take place in the near, rather than the distant, future (*see* § 3*a above*). It is true that there are clear indications that he envisaged an interval that was to elapse before history came to an end. He warned his disciples of the sufferings that awaited them (Mark 13:9-13); he predicted historical events like the fall of Jerusalem (Luke 19:41-44) and the destruction of the temple (Mark 13:2); his ethical teaching (*see* TEACHING OF JESUS) is clearly related to life in this imperfect world; and he commanded his disciples to continue the rite of the Last Supper after his death (I Cor. 11:24-25; cf. Luke 22:19-20 RSV mg:). It would seem, however, that the interval he envisaged was a comparatively short one—a fact which may be accounted for as an example of the foreshortening of the future that was characteristic of Hebrew prophecy. *See* PROPHET.

d. The kingdom and the Cross. There is no saying of Jesus in which he explicitly connects the coming of the kingdom of God with his own death. There is ample evidence, however, that he regarded his death and resurrection as the necessary fulfilment of his messianic mission (Mark 8:31; 9:12, 31; 10:33-34, 45; Luke 12:49-50; 13:32-33; 17:25). It is clear, therefore, that the Cross must be related to the conception of the kingdom. If the kingdom had already come during the ministry of Jesus (*see* § 3*b above*), it could not be said that the Cross was the condition of its coming. Nor, if the coming of the kingdom "with power" refers to the final consummation (*see* § 3*a above* on Mark 9:1), and if Jesus envisaged an interval between his death and that consummation (*see* § 3*c above*), can his death and resurrection be identified with the coming of the kingdom "with power." The fact that the thought of the coming consummation of the kingdom was present in Jesus' mind as he faced his death does suggest, however, that he regarded his death as a necessary step toward the consummation (*see* § 3*a above* on Mark 14:25). This means that the Cross was an essential element in that whole eschatological process which was inaugurated by the coming of Jesus (*see* § 3*b above*). The Cross, however, is not to be separated from the ministry which preceded it; as the inevitable fulfilment of that messianic ministry, it belongs with it as part of that decisive manifestation of divine power which inaugurated the eschatological process.

e. The community of the kingdom. The kingly rule, or sovereignty, of God, which is the basic meaning of the term "kingdom of God" (*see* § 1 *above*), cannot be conceived as operating *in vacuo*. Thus the idea necessarily implies the further idea of a realm or community in which the rule is exercised. The thought of such a community appears in much of Jesus' teaching about the kingdom. Those sayings which picture the kingdom in terms of the messianic banquet (*see* § 3*a above*) clearly imply a community, as do also the parables of the mustard seed (with its picture of the birds—a familiar symbol for the Gentile nations—nesting in the branches), the tares, and the dragnet (Matt. 13:31-32, 24-30, 36-43, 47-50). In these sayings and parables, the community is primarily that of the future, consummated kingdom (*see* § 3*a above*), though the parables may be said to imply that the community is already being brought into being in the present, and will continue to grow until the final consummation (*see* § 3*b above*).

In a number of sayings Jesus speaks of persons entering into the kingdom (Matt. 5:20; 7:21; 18:3; 21:31; 23:13; Mark 9:47; 10:15, 23-25). In most of these the future tenses used suggest that entry into the consummated kingdom is meant. The conditions upon which such entry may be obtained, however, are thought of as being fulfilled in the present; these are obedience to God's will (Matt. 7:21), the displaying of a righteousness that "exceeds that of the scribes and Pharisees" (Matt. 5:20; the nature of this superior righteousness is made clear in the antitheses which follow in vss. 21-48), the willingness to sacrifice any possession that might constitute a hindrance or stumbling block (Mark 9:47; 10:23-25), and above all the readiness to receive the kingdom in a spirit of childlike trust and humility (Mark 10:15; cf. Matt. 18:3). The saying in Mark 10:15 suggests that the kingdom may be received in the present as a gift from God. The same thought appears in Luke 12:32, where the kingdom is described as God's gift to the "little flock" of Jesus' disciples. The latter saying, which is peculiar to Luke, is closely linked in this gospel to the Q saying which urges the disciples to seek the kingdom in preference to all material benefits (Matt. 6:33; Luke 12:31). In the beatitudes, the kingdom is said to belong, presumably as a present possession, to the "poor" (Matt. 5:3; Luke 6:20; the term "poor" is here a synonym for "pious" or "saintly"—*see* POOR) and to "those who are persecuted for righteousness' sake" (Matt. 5:10); and in Mark 10:14 it is said to belong to those of a childlike spirit.

This evidence, taken as a whole, suggests that the kingdom, which has come in the person and the ministry of Jesus, may be received by individuals, as a gift of divine grace, in the present. So to receive it means humbly and loyally to submit to God's rule by obedience to the commandments of Jesus. This aspect of Jesus' teaching corresponds to the rabbinic idea of "taking upon oneself the yoke of the kingdom of God" (*see* § 2*d above;* cf. Jesus' reference to his "yoke" in Matt. 11:29-30). Those who receive the kingdom in this way constitute the present community of the kingdom of God, and to them is promised entrance, in the future, into the consummated kingdom.

Another group of sayings which clearly point to a community of the kingdom may be mentioned—namely, those which speak of comparative greatness or littleness within it. "He who is least in the kingdom of God" is said to be greater than John the Baptist (Matt. 11:11; Luke 7:28); that this saying has reference to the present community is likely, not only in view of the present tense, but also in view of the fact that Jesus would hardly have excluded John from the consummated kingdom, in which the patriarchs were to share (Matt. 8:11). In Matt. 18:1-4, the criterion of greatness in the kingdom is shown to be the possession of that spirit of childlike humility which is the main condition required for entry into it (cf. Mark 10:14-15). Matt. 5:19, which implies a quite different criterion of greatness and littleness in the kingdom, is widely believed to represent a piece of Jewish-Christian apologetic rather than the authentic teaching of Jesus.

It is in this idea of a community of those who have submitted to the rule of God made manifest in Jesus that the connection is to be found between the idea of the kingdom of God and that of the church (*see* CHURCH, IDEA OF). It is not the kingdom as such (as has often been supposed), but rather the community that is necessarily implied by it, that is to be identified with the church.

f. The discipline of the kingdom. The kingdom of God is a gift of divine grace offered to all who are willing and able to receive it (*see* § 3*e above*). To receive it, however, means to submit to a discipline that makes absolute demands upon a person's loyalty and devotion. The kingdom is the one thing of supreme value and importance for men, to be sought in precedence over all else (Matt. 6:33; Luke 12:31). The twin parables of the treasure and the pearl (Matt. 13:44-46) emphasize that it is well worth while for a man to surrender everything else that he possesses in order to gain the kingdom. The same insistence that no sacrifice is too great to make in order to secure entrance into the kingdom is seen in Mark 9:43-47, where "life" and the "kingdom of God" are clearly synonymous terms (*see* § 4*c below*). The service of the kingdom is to take precedence over even the most sacred and urgent of other duties (Matt. 8:21-22; Luke 9:59-60), and only those who seek it with single-minded interest and attention are "fit for the kingdom of God" (Luke 9:61-62). The ethical demands of the kingdom involve a standard of righteousness that exceeds even that of the Jewish law (Matt. 5:20). This standard of righteousness, which is set forth in the ethical teaching of Jesus (*see* TEACHING OF JESUS; SERMON ON THE MOUNT), constitutes a way of life to which those who belong to the present community of the kingdom of God are called; and their loyal pursuance of this way of life is the condition upon which they will receive entry, at the last, into the consummated kingdom (*see* § 3*e above*). The basis of this new way of life is to be seen in the twin commandments of love to God and love to one's neighbor (Mark 12:28-31). To acknowledge, as did the scribe, the supremacy of these commandments is to be "not far from the kingdom of God" (Mark 12:34); but actual entry into the kingdom depends, not upon any kind of formal acknowledgment, but upon active obedience (Matt. 7:21).

4. The kingdom of God in the rest of the NT. In view of the centrality of the idea of the kingdom of God in the teaching of Jesus as recorded in the Synoptic gospels (*see* § 3 *above*), it is surprising how comparatively rarely the term occurs in the other books of the NT. The subject of the church's preaching in the apostolic age was not so much the kingdom of God as such, but rather Christ himself. The difference, however, is merely one of terminology and of standpoint. Our study of the teaching of Jesus has revealed the close connection in which the idea of the kingdom stands to his own person and work. And the fact is that the early Christian preachers were less concerned with repeating the message of Jesus, in his terms, than with proclaiming the significance of Jesus himself as the crucified and risen Messiah (cf. I Cor. 1:23; 2:2; 15:3-4), who was shortly to return in glory (cf. I Thess. 1:10; II Thess. 1:7). The proclamation of the historical events of the life, death, and resurrection of Jesus corresponded to the announcement that the kingdom of God had already come, and the expectation of the PAROUSIA corresponded to Jesus' emphasis upon the future consummation of the kingdom. That the church did not lose touch with the actual terms of Jesus' own message, however, is proved by the fact that it preserved the message in the gospel tradition. It remains for us to review briefly such use as is made of the concept of the kingdom of God in the NT, outside the Synoptic gospels.

a. Acts. According to Acts 1:3, Jesus continued, during his postresurrection appearances to his disciples, to speak to them about the kingdom of God. That they were still slow to understand the true meaning of his teaching, and that they continued to think of the kingdom in nationalist terms, is indicated by their question: "Lord, will you at this time restore the kingdom to Israel?" (1:6). In 8:12, the content of Philip's preaching in Samaria is described as "good news about the kingdom of God and the name of Jesus Christ." A similar combination of "preaching the kingdom of God and teaching about the Lord Jesus Christ" is seen in the reference to Paul's witnessing in Rome (28:31; cf. 28:23—"testifying to the kingdom of God and trying to convince them about Jesus"). In 19:8, we are told that Paul, in the synagogue at Ephesus, "for three months spoke boldly, arguing and pleading about the kingdom of God"; and in 20:25, Paul himself addresses the Ephesian elders as "all you among whom I have gone about preaching the kingdom." Thus the evidence of Acts suggests that the idea of the kingdom of God was not entirely absent from the preaching of the apostles, and that it was closely related to preaching about Jesus Christ. The references mentioned above are all very general, and tell us nothing about the content of the apostles' preaching of the kingdom. There is, however, another reference, in 14:22, to Paul and Barnabas, in Lystra, Iconium, and Antioch, "strengthening the souls of the disciples, exhorting them to continue in the faith, and saying that through many tribulations we must enter the kingdom of God"; in this passage it is clearly the future, consummated kingdom that is in mind (*see* § 3*e above* on the sayings of Jesus concerning entrance into the kingdom).

b. Pauline letters. The evidence of Acts, so far as Paul's usage is concerned, is confirmed by the occurrence of the term "kingdom of God," or its equivalent, in a number of passages in the letters. The same double emphasis, on the kingdom as a present reality and as a future hope, as is found in the teaching of Jesus (*see* § 3 *above*), appears also in Paul's references to it. Passages which clearly refer to the present life of Christians in this world are Rom. 14:17; I Cor. 4:20, in both of which Paul is describing the kind of life which is to be lived by those who have submitted to the rule of God, and so are members of the present community of the kingdom (*see* § 3*e above*). It is a life in which what matters "is not eating and drinking, but righteousness and peace and joy in the Holy Ghost" (Rom. 14:17 ERV); and it is a life which "does not consist in talk but in power" (I Cor. 4:20). Thus Paul emphasizes both the blessings which belong to those who have received the kingdom and the moral demands which it makes upon them (*see* § 3*f above*). The moral demands of the kingdom are also stressed in a number of passages in which Paul gives lists of vices which preclude men from inheriting the kingdom of God (I Cor. 6:9-10; Gal. 5:21; Eph. 5:5). In each of these (in spite of the fact that the tense in Eph. 5:5 is present, and not future as in the others), the reference seems clearly to be to the inheritance of the future, consummated kingdom; cf. I Cor. 15:50 ("Flesh and blood cannot inherit the kingdom of God"), where the same expression is used in a context which even more clearly demands a future reference. II Thess. 1:5 ("that you may be made worthy of the kingdom of God, for which you are suffering") also seems to require a future reference; cf. Acts 14:22 (*see* § 4*a above*). In I Thess. 2:12, the linking of the idea of God's kingdom with that of his GLORY suggests that the future kingdom is in mind, though the words "to lead a life worthy of God" may indicate that the idea of the present kingdom is not excluded. Col. 4:11, in which Paul speaks of certain men as his "fellow workers for the kingdom of God," is a very general reference, which might be understood in terms of either the present or the future, but perhaps the preposition which is used (εἰς, "unto") makes the future the more likely.

In a few passages Paul speaks of the kingdom as Christ's. Eph. 5:5 ("kingdom of Christ and of God") suggests that he meant no clear distinction between the two phrases. I Cor. 15:24-28, however, seems to mean that he thought of Christ as ruling over the kingdom, in the capacity of vice-regent, during the interval before the final consummation, "when he delivers the kingdom to God the Father." This is confirmed by Col. 1:13, where the Father is said to have "delivered us from the dominion of darkness and transferred us to the kingdom of his beloved Son"; the reference here is clearly to the present status of Christians. It seems, therefore, that when Paul speaks of the kingdom of Christ, he is thinking of the present kingdom; this does not mean, however, that he does not occasionally use "kingdom of God" also in a present sense (*see above* on Rom. 14:17; I Cor. 4:20). There are two passages in II Timothy which speak of the kingdom as Christ's, and which refer to the future (4:1: "his appearing and his kingdom"; 4:18: "The Lord will . . . save me for his heavenly kingdom"). It is doubtful, however, whether these represent the genuine thought of Paul. *See* PASTORAL LETTERS.

c. Johannine literature. In the Fourth Gospel the term "kingdom of God" occurs twice in the words of Jesus to Nicodemus (John 3:3, 5). No distinction need be drawn between the idea of seeing the kingdom in the former reference and that of entering it in the latter. The two statements taken together mean that entrance into the kingdom is dependent upon the experience of REGENERATION. In general, however, this evangelist has reinterpreted the teaching of Jesus, so that instead of speaking of the kingdom of God he speaks of eternal life, or LIFE. In this connection, it is important to remember that even in Mark's Gospel the idea of the kingdom is sometimes equated with that of "life" or "eternal life" (*see* § 3*f above* on Mark 9:43-47; cf. also 10:17 with 10:23-25). The fact that "life" in Johannine thought is primarily a present possession of believers (cf. John 5:24; I John 3:14; 5:12) suggests that in John 3:3-5 the kingdom of God is thought of as present rather than future (in contrast to the Synoptic passages which speak of entrance into the kingdom; *see* § 3*e above*).

The word "king" is used of Jesus frequently in the Fourth Gospel (1:49; 6:15; 12:13, 15; 18:33, 37, 39; 19:3, 12, 14-15, 19, 21), and in 18:36 Jesus himself speaks of his "kingship" (ERV-ASV "kingdom"; the Greek is βασιλεία), which "is not of this world." This usage implies the idea of a spiritual sovereignty which Jesus is already exercising as Messiah.

The book of Revelation (*see* REVELATION, BOOK

OF), in keeping with its apocalyptic character, looks forward to the consummated kingdom of God. In 11:15 it is described as the "kingdom of our Lord and of his Christ" (cf. Eph. 5:5; *see* § 4*b above*), and in 12:10 the "kingdom of our God" is linked with the "authority of his Christ." These passages imply an eternal reign of God and Christ together, rather than the Pauline idea of a reign of Christ until the consummation "when he delivers the kingdom to God the Father" (*see* § 4*b above,* on I Cor. 15:24-28). In Rev. 1:9, John claims to share with his readers in "the tribulation and kingdom and patience which are in Jesus" (ERV-ASV); this passage seems to imply the idea of the kingdom as a fact of present experience.

d. Other books. In spite of its prevailing Platonism, the Letter to the Hebrews (*see* HEBREWS, LETTER TO THE) contains much eschatological thought. The last days are regarded as having arrived (cf. 1:2; 6:5; 9:26), but a future consummation is looked for (cf. 9:28; 10:25, 37). The idea of the kingdom of God as such, however, is not prominent, and appears only in two passages. In 12:28 it is described as a "kingdom that cannot be shaken," which is to be received by Christians; the context suggests that the receiving is thought of as taking place in the future, when the last day is ushered in by the shaking and removal of heaven and earth (12:25-27). The other reference to the kingdom is at 1:8, which quotes Ps. 45:6, interpreting it messianically; thus Christ is regarded as the messianic king, the scepter of whose kingdom is a righteous scepter.

The Letter of James contains one reference to "the kingdom" which God "has promised to those who love him" (2:5); the heirs of this kingdom are "those who are poor in the world," whom God has chosen "to be rich in faith" (cf. Matt. 5:3; Luke 6:20; *see* § 3*e above*). The future kingdom is meant (cf. Paul's references to inheriting the kingdom; *see* § 4*b above*), and the idea of a community is clearly implied.

Finally, in II Pet. 1:11 (*see* PETER, SECOND LETTER OF), there is a late, conventional reference to the future kingdom as the "eternal kingdom of our Lord and Savior Jesus Christ," into which Christians who are zealous to confirm their call and election, so that they never fall, are promised an entrance.

Bibliography. G. Dalman, *The Words of Jesus* (trans. D. M. Kay; 1902), pp. 91-147; A. Schweitzer, *The Quest of the Historical Jesus* (trans. W. Montgomery; 1910); G. Gloege, *Reich Gottes und Kirche im NT* (1929); T. W. Manson, *The Teaching of Jesus* (1931); E. F. Scott, *The Kingdom of God in the NT* (1931); C. H. Dodd, *The Parables of the Kingdom* (1935); F. C. Grant, *The Gospel of the Kingdom* (1940); C. J. Cadoux, *The Historic Mission of Jesus* (1941); R. Otto, *The Kingdom of God and the Son of Man* (trans. F. V. Filson and B. Lee-Woolf; new and rev. ed., 1943); T. W. Manson, *The Sayings of Jesus* (1949); R. H. Fuller, *The Mission and Achievement of Jesus* (1954); H. Roberts, *Jesus and the Kingdom of God* (1955); W. G. Kümmel, *Promise and Fulfilment* (trans. D. M. Barton; 1957).

O. E. EVANS

KINGDOM OF ISRAEL. *See* ISRAEL, HISTORY OF.

KINGDOM OF JUDAH. *See* ISRAEL, HISTORY OF.

***KINGS, I AND II** [מלכים]. The eleventh and twelfth books in the English Bible, and the fifth and sixth books of the Former Prophets in the Hebrew Bible. They report the events of the Solomonic monarchy and the divided kingdoms, from the anointment of Solomon to the exilic episode of the captive King Jehoiachin's admission to the court of Babylon as a guest of the royal table.

A. Title
B. Contents
  1. Solomon's ascension and reign
  2. The vicissitudes of the two kingdoms
  3. The surviving kingdom of Judah
C. Composition
  1. Framework
  2. The Deuteronomic outlook of the framework
  3. The sources mentioned
    a. The Book of the Acts of Solomon
    b. The Book of the Chronicles of the Kings of Israel
    c. The Book of the Chronicles of the Kings of Judah
  4. Other sources
    a. Davidic court narrative
    b. Elijah cycle
    c. Elisha cycle
    d. Ahab source
    e. Isaiah source
    f. A prophetic source
  5. The problem of a pre-Deuteronomic book of Kings
  6. The Deuteronomic edition
  7. The purpose of the Deuteronomic author
D. Text
Bibliography

A. *TITLE.* The title of the books in the Hebrew canon is I and II Kings. These two books were originally one, but the LXX first introduced the division and named them the third and fourth books of the "Kingdoms" (βασιλεῶν γ' and δ'), for the books of Samuel are the first and second books of the "Kingdoms." The English title "Kings" can be traced to Jerome, who preferred the name *Regum* ("Kings") in consonance with the Hebrew title as against the literal translation of the LXX title, *Regnorum* ("Kingdoms"). The division of the book into two books appeared in the Hebrew text first, in a MS in A.D. 1448, and was printed thus in the Bible of Felix Pratensis in 1517-18. The final Masora (*see* TEXT, OT) appears only at the end of II Kings and consonantly regards both books as one.

A Talmudic tradition which maintains that Jeremiah was the author of the books of Kings (B.B. 15*b*) appears to be without foundation, and merely mirrors a trend in later Judaism which tried to assign all the biblical books to prophetic authors.

B. *CONTENTS.* The contents of the books can be divided into three parts: (*a*) Solomon's ascension to the throne and his reign (I Kings 1–11); (*b*) the vicissitudes of the two kingdoms (I Kings 12–II Kings 17); and (*c*) the surviving kingdom of Judah (II Kings 18–25). *See* map "Palestine: I Kings 1–11, The Kingdom of Solomon," under SOLOMON.

1. Solomon's ascension and reign (I Kings 1-11). This narrative complex begins with the depiction of David's senility (I Kings 1:1-4). When Adonijah, the eldest son of David, was unexpectedly proclaimed king, Bathsheba, the mother of Solomon, and Nathan the prophet asked David to designate Solomon as the successor to the throne (vss. 5-27). David yielded to the entreaty and commanded Zadok the priest and Nathan the prophet to anoint Solomon to be king. Thus Solomon was anointed at Gihon in David's lifetime. When the news reached Adonijah and his followers, they scattered (vss. 28-53).

The dying King David charged Solomon to be pious (2:1-4) and gave him advice on how to consolidate his throne (vss. 5-12). Shortly after David's death, Solomon had his brother Adonijah killed (vss. 13-25). Abiathar the priest, one of the supporters of Adonijah's *coup d'état,* was banished to Anathoth (vss. 26-27), Joab was executed (vss. 28-35), and, in addition, Shimei was killed when he left Jerusalem on an errand in disregard of the royal prohibition (vss. 36-46).

At the high place of Gibeon, Solomon offered sacrifice to the LORD, who appeared to him in a dream and granted Solomon's request for wisdom (I Kings 3:1-15). The next episode illustrates Solomon's wisdom by his shrewd judgment in the suit of the two harlots (vss. 16-28).

Lists of Solomon's court officials (4:1-6) and provincial administrators (vss. 7-19) are followed by a depiction of the splendor of Solomon's court, his power (vss. 20-28), and his incomparable wisdom (vss. 29-34).

The preparation for the building of the temple and the treaty with Hiram of Tyre (ch. 5) precede the erection of the temple building (ch. 6). An account of the building of the royal palaces (7:1-12) is concluded by the report on the casting of the bronze pillars (vss. 13-22), the making of the bronze sea (vss. 23-26), and the making of other bronze vessels and objects (vss. 27-47). The listing of the temple furnishings closes with the report on the golden objects of the house of the Lord (vss. 48-51).

The dedication of the temple is related in considerable length. First, the ark of the Lord was brought into the temple (8:1-13). Then Solomon addressed himself to the people (vss. 14-21). His prayer (vss. 22-53), his blessing given to the people (vss. 54-61), and the ensuing sacrifices and feast (vss. 62-66) bring to a conclusion the dedication of the temple.

In a second vision, the Lord appeared to Solomon and warned him to remain faithful (9:1-9). There are reports on several issues of the Solomonic reign in ch. 9, such as the selling of twenty Galilean cities to Hiram of Tyre (vss. 10-14), the use of forced labor in the building activities (vss. 15-24), and Solomon's sacrifices and overseas commerce (vss. 25-28).

The narrative of the visit of the Queen of Sheba to Solomon's court (10:1-13) is followed by an enumeration of Solomon's splendors and commercial success (vss. 14-29).

Solomon's riches are also seen in the number of his wives and concubines, but the foreign wives led him astray to the worship of strange gods (11:1-13). As divine punishment for Solomon's apostasy, external and internal difficulties arose. Hadad of Edom returned from Egypt and revolted against Solomon (vss. 14-22), as did Rezon of Syria, who, after establishing his reign in Damascus, denied fealty to Solomon (vss. 23-25). In Israel itself, Jeroboam, an Ephraimite, started an abortive rebellion (vss. 26-40).

Finally, the death of Solomon is concisely reported (vss. 41-43).

2. The vicissitudes of the two kingdoms (I Kings 12–II Kings 17). After the death of Solomon, Rehoboam, his son and successor, entered into negotiations with the elders of the people at Shechem.

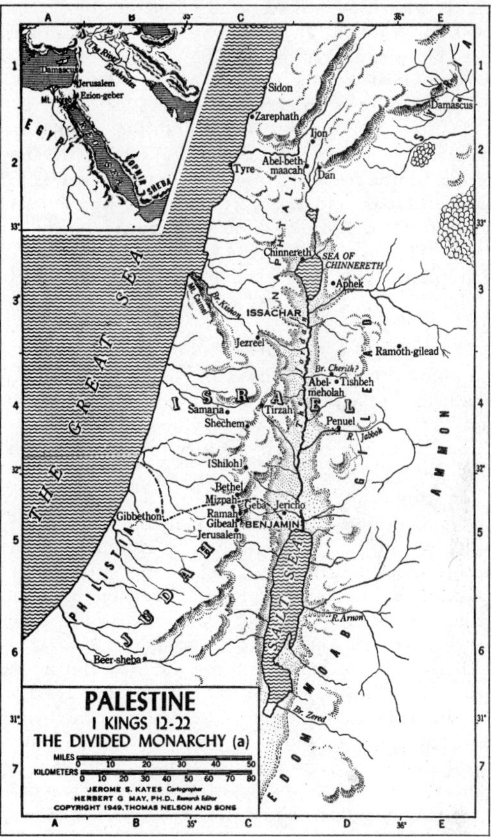

The ill-advised rigidity of Rehoboam led to the secession of the N tribes from Judah and Jeroboam's election to the throne of Israel (I Kings 12:1-20). An oracle averted the danger of civil war between the two kingdoms (vss. 21-24). Jeroboam consolidated his kingdom and devised the cult of Bethel and Dan (vss. 25-33).

An anonymous man of God from Judah foretold to Jeroboam the Josianic reform and the resulting destruction of the sanctuary of Bethel (13:1-10). This anonymous prophet was killed by a lion and buried in Bethel (vss. 11-34).

When her child was sick, the wife of Jeroboam visited Ahijah the prophet, who foretold the death of the child and condemned Jeroboam for his apostasy (14:1-16). After a short report on the child's death and that of Jeroboam (vss. 17-20), the chapter is concluded by an account of Rehoboam's reign in Judah, including the invasion of Judah by Shishak, king of Egypt (vss. 21-31).

The synchronistic accounts of the reign of Abijam of Judah (15:1-8) and the reign of his son, Asa (vss. 9-24), include Asa's cultic reforms (vss. 11-15) and his war against Baasha of Israel. In this war, his alliance with Syria secured victory for him (vss. 16-24). Nadab, the son of Jeroboam, reigned over Israel for two years but was assassinated by Baasha (vss. 25-32).

Baasha's reign (15:33–16:7) and that of his son, Elah (16:8-14), are shortly related. Zimri, who conspired against Elah and murdered him and the whole house of Baasha, could not reap the fruits of his conspiracy, for he was defeated by Omri in the ensuing civil war (vss. 15-22). Omri's reign over Israel and the founding and naming of Samaria as the capital are summarily related (vss. 23-28). A short introduction to Ahab's reign closes ch. 16 (vss. 29-34).

During the reign of Ahab, Elijah the prophet announced the coming of a drought (17:1). In the time of the famine resulting from the drought, he was fed by the ravens first (vss. 2-7), and later by the jar of meal and cruse of oil which were miraculously unspent. The jar and the cruse belonged to a widow of Zarephath (vss. 8-16). When the son of the widow suddenly died, Elijah resuscitated the child (vss. 17-24).

The prophet appeared before King Ahab to announce the end of the drought and to extend a challenge to the prophets of Baal (18:1-19). The contest between the prophets of Baal and Elijah on Mount Carmel brought victory to Elijah and the drought's end (vss. 20-46).

In spite of the vindication of the Lord's rule over the land, Elijah had to flee for his life through the wilderness of Judah to the mount of Horeb, where he received a new divine commission and further encouragement (19:1-18). Elijah, following the divine command, called Elisha, as his successor, into his service (vss. 19-21).

Ben-hadad of Syria besieged Samaria during the reign of Ahab of Israel, but Ahab succeeded in repelling the Syrian force (20:1-21). The next year, Ben-hadad attempted to repair the defeat by a new campaign, but Israel triumphed by crushing the Syrian army at Aphek (vss. 22-30) and even capturing Ben-hadad. The latter gladly accepted the peace dictates of Ahab in exchange for his freedom (vss. 31-34). The liberation of the Syrian king brought severe reprimand upon Ahab from an anonymous member of the prophetic guilds (vss. 35-43).

Naboth, an Israelite farmer, refused to sell his vineyard to Ahab, who ardently desired to possess it. In order to acquire the vineyard, Jezebel, the wife of Ahab, plotted the death of Naboth (21:1-14). Thus Ahab took possession of the coveted vineyard (vss. 15-16), but for this he was condemned by Elijah (vss. 17-29).

Ahab planned a military attack upon Syria and was encouraged by four hundred prophets (22:1-12). But when Micaiah the son of Imlah was summoned, he prophesied disaster (vss. 13-28). This prophecy was fulfilled, for even Ahab died in the battle (vss. 29-40). The account of the reign of Jehoshaphat of Judah (vss. 41-50) and the introduction to the reign of Ahaziah of Israel (vss. 51-53) close the first book of Kings.

The report on Ahaziah's reign is continued with the miracle of Elijah's calling fire from heaven upon the royal troops that were sent to capture him (II Kings 1).

When Elijah was taken up to heaven, Elisha, his disciple, became the heir of his spirit (2:1-18). After

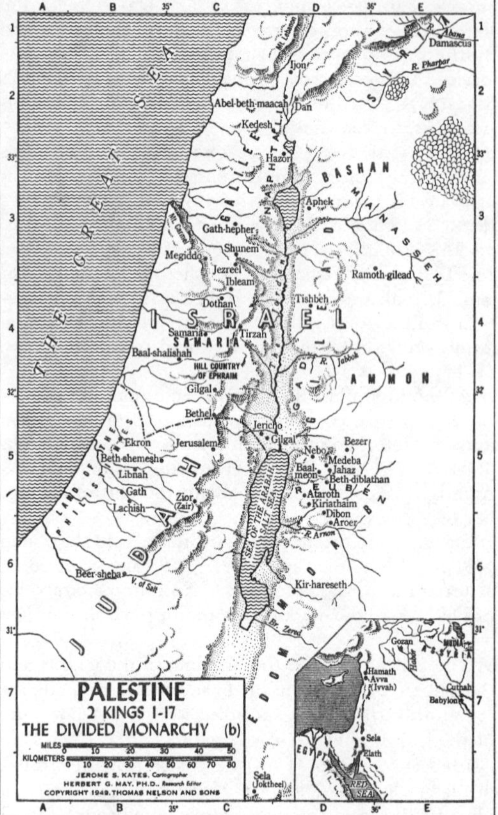

this, Elisha healed the water of Jericho (vss. 19-22). On one occasion, two bears killed some children who mocked the prophet (vss. 23-25).

Jehoram, son of Ahab, and Jehoshaphat of Judah went on a united military campaign against Moab and defeated the Moabites in accord with Elisha's prophecy (ch. 3).

A collection of miracle narratives centered around Elisha includes the miraculous filling of the vessels of a widow with oil (4:1-7), the resuscitation of the son of a woman of Shunem (vss. 8-37), the making harmless of the poisoned food of the prophets (vss. 38-41), and the feeding of a hundred men with twenty loaves and a sack of fresh grain (vss. 42-44).

Elisha also healed Naaman, the commander of the Syrian army, of his leprosy (5:1-19). The disease cleaved to Gehazi, Elisha's servant, as punishment for his greed and lies (vss. 20-27).

Elisha caused an axe head to float on the water of the Jordan (6:1-7), and he blinded a Syrian raiding party and thus helped to capture them (vss. 8-23). Ben-hadad again besieged Samaria, and the king of Israel blamed Elisha for this misfortune and for the ensuing famine in the city (vss. 24-31). The king even went so far as to want to take Elisha's life, but Elisha's insistence that the famine would end the next day saved his life (6:32–7:2). And, indeed, during the night the Syrian army left its encampment in flight, for the Lord caused them to hear the sound of chariots and horses, thus ending the siege and the famine (7:3-20).

In another episode, it is reported that the Shunammite woman spent a time in the land of the Philistines, but, upon her return, her estate was restored to her by the king (8:1-6). Elisha went to Damascus and foretold to Hazael that he would become the king of Syria (vss. 7-15). The reigns of Jehoram of Judah (vss. 16-24) and of his son Ahaziah (vss. 25-29) receive a summary treatment.

Jehu, the commander in chief of Joram of Israel's army, was anointed to be king by a disciple of Elisha (9:1-13). In the subsequent revolution, Jehu killed his king, Joram, and Ahaziah, the king of Judah (vss. 14-29). Jezebel, the queen dowager, was killed by her eunuchs, who joined Jehu's revolt (vss. 30-37).

During the ensuing events, the whole dynasty of Ahab (10:1-11) and forty-two Judean princes (vss. 12-14) were massacred. Jehonadab the Rechabite accompanied Jehu, and together they wiped out the Baal-worshipers of Israel (vss. 15-31). A short summary of Jehu's reign concludes ch. 10 (vss. 32-36).

After the death of Ahaziah of Judah, his mother, Athaliah, seized the throne of Jerusalem (11:1-3), but her reign was overthrown seven years later, and her grandson Jehoash was anointed king over Judah (vss. 4-21).

Jehoash, during his reign (12:1-3), regulated the use of the temple income (vss. 4-16). Jehoash paid tribute to Hazael of Syria (vss. 17-18); he was killed by conspirators in a palace revolt (vss. 19-21).

Reports on the kingship of Jehoahaz of Israel (13:1-9) and that of his son, Jehoash (vss. 10-13), precede Elisha's deathbed scene and his symbolic acts with the arrows (vss. 14-19). Nevertheless, Elisha's death did not mean the end of his miraculous power, for a dead man rose as soon as his corpse touched Elisha's bones (vss. 20-21). A short summary of Jehoash' victory over the Syrians closes the chapter (vss. 22-25).

Amaziah, the king of Judah, after consolidating his power, executed the murderers of his father (14:1-6). After his victory over the Edomites (vs. 7), Amaziah challenged Israel to war and was defeated by Jehoash of Israel (vss. 8-14). Short reports are included in this chapter concerning the death of Jehoash of Israel (vss. 15-16), the assassination of Amaziah (vss. 17-22), and the reign of Jeroboam II of Israel (vss. 23-29).

In similar fashion, summary notices appear on Azariah of Judah (15:1-7), Zechariah (vss. 8-12), Shallum (vss. 13-15), Menahem (vss. 16-22), Pekahiah (vss. 23-26), and Pekah (vss. 27-31), successive kings of Israel, and finally on Jotham of Judah (vss. 32-38).

The reign of Ahaz of Judah, which occupies the whole of ch. 16, included the Syro-Ephraimitic War, his visit to Tiglath-pileser in Damascus, and the building of a new altar in Jerusalem.

The end of Israel is narrated in ch. 17 by the presentation of the account of Hoshea's reign, the fall of Samaria (vss. 1-6), and a recapitulation of Israel's apostasy which brought the Lord's judgment on Samaria (vss. 7-23). In place of the exiled people of Israel, the Assyrians brought to Samaria a variety of people from the four corners of the empire, who became the Samaritans (vss. 24-41).

3. The surviving kingdom of Judah (II Kings 18-25). In connection with Hezekiah's reign, several

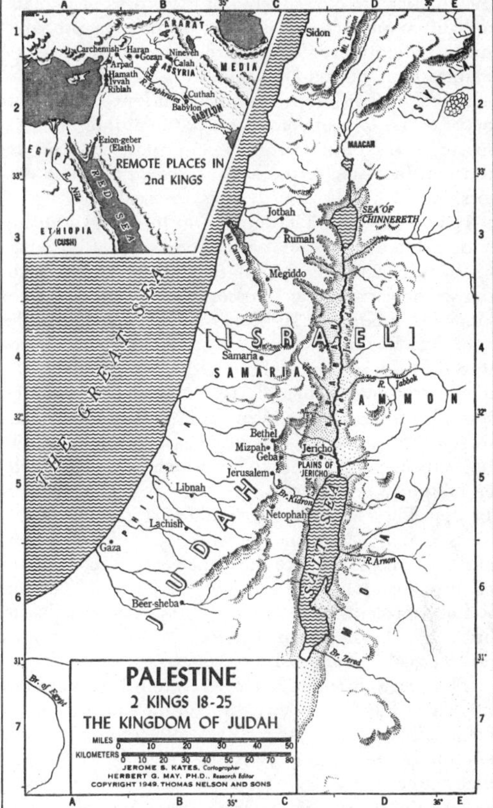

PALESTINE
2 KINGS 18-25
THE KINGDOM OF JUDAH

details are related: his reform of the cult (18:1-8), the fall of Samaria (vss. 9-12), and Sennacherib's expedition against Judah (18:13–19:37).

Hezekiah's sickness and recovery (20:1-11) and the embassy of Merodach-baladan to his court (vss. 12-21) are the themes of ch. 20.

The evil reigns of Manasseh (21:1-18) and his son, Amon (vss. 19-26), precede King Josiah, under whose reign the Book of the Law was found in the temple (ch. 22); after this discovery a reform was completed in accord with the regulations of the Book of the Law (23:1-25). Josiah's untimely death at Megiddo (23:26-30) was the prelude to the short reign of Jehoahaz (vss. 31-35) and that of Jehoiakim (23:36–24:7).

Jehoiachin's abortive reign, his surrender to Nebuchadnezzar, and his exile to Babylon follow in quick succession (24:8-17). The reign of Zedekiah, the last king of Judah, the siege of the city of Jerusalem (24:18–25:7), the fall of Jerusalem, the plundering and burning of the temple and the city (25:8-17), the execution of the leaders of the people (vss. 18-21), and Gedaliah's assassination by Ishmael (vss. 22-26) brought the fate of Judah to its end. A final hopeful note appears in the report that, in the thirty-seventh year of his exile, Jehoiachin was accepted as a guest of the royal table of Evil-merodach, king of Babylon (vss. 27-30).

C. *COMPOSITION.* The books of Kings show unmistakable traces of composition. Apparently, several distinct sources are present and joined by a stereotyped framework. Like ancient Near Eastern literature in general, so individual literary pieces of these books are most likely not the works of so many individual authors, but in each instance the probability of collective or corporate authorship must be maintained. The same is true in the case of the collection and edition of the independent sources. (If only for the sake of convenience, the author and editor will be mentioned in the singular, without the constant inclusion of the remark "or authors and editors.")

1. Framework. The reports on the kings of Israel and Judah are enclosed in a framework of introductory and concluding formulas. Though some parts of this framework appear in connection with the earliest kings (cf. I Kings 2:10-12; 11:41-43; 14:19-20), the complete formula does not appear until it is introduced in the case of Rehoboam (I Kings 14:21-31). The introductory formula is: "Now Rehoboam the son of Solomon reigned in Judah. Rehoboam was forty-one years old when he began to reign, and he reigned seventeen years in Jerusalem. . . . His mother's name was Naamah the Ammonitess" (I Kings 14:21). The concluding formula is stated in vss. 29-31 as follows: "Now the rest of the acts of Rehoboam, and all that he did, are they not written in the Book of the Chronicles of the Kings of Judah? . . . And Rehoboam slept with his fathers and was buried with his fathers in the city of David. . . . And Abijam his son reigned in his stead."

The same introductory and concluding formulas serve as a frame for the reports on the kings of Judah (cf. I Kings 15:1-8, 9-24; 22:41-50). The framework enclosing the reign of the kings of Israel differs in that neither the kings' ages at the time of their ascension to the throne nor their mothers' names are included in the formulas (cf. I Kings 15:25-32; 15:33–16:7; 16:8-14). The introductory or the concluding formula, or both, are missing in some cases—e.g., in the case of Joram and Ahaziah, who were killed in the Jehu revolution, the concluding formula is missing (II Kings 9:22-28). In Athaliah's case both opening and closing formulas are absent (II Kings 11).

For lack of an absolute chronological system, the author of the books used a synchronistic interrelating method for the establishment of the data of the kings of Israel and Judah. Thus in the introductory formula of a king, a reference to the other monarch is present —e.g.: "Now in the eighteenth year of King Jeroboam the son of Nebat, Abijam began to reign over Judah" (I Kings 15:1), or "Nadab the son of Jeroboam began to reign over Israel in the second year of Asa king of Judah" (vs. 25). This synchronization of the regnal years of the monarchs of the two kingdoms is, unfortunately, not always reliable. There are discrepancies between the synchronistic data and the absolute regnal years of the individual kings, and also the established dates of Babylonian and Assyrian history; e.g., the time elapsed from the revolution of Jehu to the fall of Samaria is 170 years according to the synchronistic system, 165 years if computed by the regnal years of Judah, and 143 years and 7 months according to the regnal years of Israel, when, in reality, only 121 years passed by in this period according to Assyrian documents. This inaccuracy in the chronology of the books led some scholars to the complete rejection of the synchronistic system and to a drastic revision of the regnal years. Contemporary scholarship, in general, is inclined to accept the essential validity of the synchronistic system, but nevertheless it recognizes also the presence of many inaccuracies which might be traced to errors in transmission, either of the documents used by the writer of the framework or of the completed books of Kings. Some scholars proposed that the chronology of the books is the result of the mingling of several chronological systems. *See* CHRONOLOGY OF THE OT.

2. The Deuteronomic outlook of the framework. Another characteristic feature of the framework is the judgment pronounced on the kings of Israel and Judah. These judgments clearly reveal a Deuteronomic point of view; e.g., Rehoboam is condemned in the statement: "Judah did what was evil in the sight of the LORD, and they provoked him to jealousy with their sins which they committed, more than all that their fathers had done. For they also built for themselves high places, and pillars, and Asherim on every high hill and under every green tree; and there were also male cult prostitutes in the land. They did according to all the abominations of the nations which the LORD drove out before the people of Israel" (I Kings 14:22-24). This condemnation of Rehoboam of Israel is in complete harmony with the Deuteronomic requirements of the unity and purity of the cult. In order to safeguard the purity of the cult, its centralization and the destruction of the high places, pillars, and Asherim were required by the Deuteronomist (cf. Deut. 12:1-3, 29-31).

The judgments pronounced on the kings of Judah are unqualifiedly appreciative only for Hezekiah (II Kings 18:3-7) and Josiah (II Kings 22:2), for these two kings abolished the sacrifices on the high places (as required by the Deuteronomic legislation) and made general reforms of the cult. The favorable decisions on Asa (I Kings 15:11-14), Jehoshaphat (I Kings 22:43), Jehoash (II Kings 12:2-3), Azariah (II Kings 15:3-4), and Jotham (II Kings 15:34-35) are limited in this manner: "He did what was right in the eyes of the LORD, according to all that his father Uzziah had done. Nevertheless the high places were not removed; the people still sacrificed and burned incense on the high places" (II Kings 15:34-35). All the other kings of Judah are summarily condemned with the stereotyped expression that they "did what was evil in the sight of the LORD" (cf. II Kings 8:18, 27; 21:2, 20). Nonetheless, the author thought that worship at the local high places was legitimate before the building of the temple (I Kings 3:2).

Besides the high places, the N shrines were especially denounced by the author as being contrary to the will of the Lord. There is even a report given on how Jeroboam, in his attempt to alienate the N tribes from the temple of Jerusalem, founded the shrines of Bethel and Dan (I Kings 12:26-33). The preservation of these N pilgrim shrines is constantly referred to as the "way of Jeroboam" or the "sin which he committed, making Israel to sin" (cf. I Kings 15:26, 34; 16:19). By application of this measure, all the kings of Israel, with the exception of Shallum, who reigned for only one month (II Kings 15:13-16), were condemned for not doing what was right in the eyes of the Lord (cf. I Kings 15:26, 34; 16:25). This general condemnation of the kings of Israel extended even to Zimri, who reigned for only seven days (I Kings 16:19), and upon Jehu, the great partisan of the Lord (II Kings 10:29-31). To be sure, in Jehu's case, as in also the cases of Jehoram (II Kings 3:2) and Hoshea (17:2), the criticism was somewhat meliorated.

Some of the kings were further denounced because of the worship of foreign gods, which is variably designated as either the "way of the kings of Israel" (II Kings 16:3), or the "way of the house of Ahab" (II Kings 8:27). For the worship of other gods, Ahab and his son Ahaziah of Israel (I Kings 16:31-33; 22:53) were condemned, as were Jehoram (II Kings 8:18), Ahaziah (8:27), Ahaz (16:2-4), Manasseh (21:2-9), and Amon (21:20-22), kings of Judah. In all these instances, the convictions of the Deuteronomic school can be discovered.

3. The sources mentioned. There are three sources mentioned by title in the books of Kings. These are: (*a*) the Book of the Acts of Solomon, (*b*) the Book of the Chronicles of the Kings of Israel, and (*c*) the Book of the Chronicles of the Kings of Judah.

a. The Book of the Acts of Solomon. At the end of the Solomon narrative complex, which occupies I Kings 3–11, there appears the reference: "Now the rest of the acts of Solomon, and all that he did, and his wisdom, are they not written in the book of the acts of Solomon?" (11:41). This reference offers sufficient information for a fair estimate of the nature of the lost Book of the Acts of Solomon. Because of the mention made of the "wisdom" of Solomon, one must assume that the original source included much legendary and folklore material. Into this class belong the Lord's appearance in Solomon's dream, Solomon's entreaty of the Lord for wisdom (I Kings 3:4-15), the well-known episode of the Solomonic judgment (vss. 16-28), and the visit of the Queen of Sheba, who "came to test him with hard questions" (10:1-10).

Besides the apparently legendary material on Solomon's wisdom, contemporary lists were utilized by the compiler of the source. Such lists are the list of Solomon's court officials (I Kings 4:1-6) and that of the provincial administrators (4:7-19, 27-28), both of which might originally have been deposits of the court archives. The description of the building and furnishing of the temple might have come from the temple archives (I Kings 6; 7:15-31). The description of Solomon's wisdom and splendor (I Kings 4: 20-26, 29-34), the account of his agreement with Hiram of Tyre (ch. 5), the details of Solomon's settlement of Hiram's claim for the services rendered (9:10-14), the report on the royal building activities and the use of forced labor (vss. 15-24), and the memories of Solomon's mercantile enterprise (9:26-28; 10:11-12) are based upon reliable ancient archival tradition.

Thus, the Book of the Acts of Solomon must be recognized as a late collection of archival material which included some legendary biographical information for the enhancement of the wisdom and glory of the king. So, sound and veracious historical reports and legends mingle in this composite work.

b. The Book of the Chronicles of the Kings of Israel. This source is repeatedly referred to in the closing formulas of the author. The first time this source is mentioned is in connection with Jeroboam I (I Kings 14:19), the last time in the concluding statement concerning Pekah's reign (II Kings 15:31); and altogether the book is mentioned seventeen times. The reports on Joram of Israel, the victim of the Jehu revolution, and Hoshea, the last king of Israel, are not concluded by this stereotyped reference. Some scholars assumed that the reference to the Book of the Chronicles of the Kings of Israel was missing in the concluding formula of the reign of Hoshea because Hoshea, having been the last monarch of Israel, was not included at all in this source. The case for this assumption is, in some degree, weakened by the fact that the reference is also missing in the case of Joram, whose predecessors and successors are definitely reported in this source.

The assumption was sometimes entertained that the Book of the Chronicles of the Kings of Israel and that of the kings of Judah were, in reality, a single historical work, and the difference is merely manifest in the two separate and inaccurate titles. This view, however, can hardly be maintained under critical scrutiny. The references to the source offer occasional glimpses of the real nature of the original Chronicles of the Kings of Israel. Thus, it is stated that the source incorporated an account on the "acts of Jeroboam, how he warred and how he reigned" (I Kings 14:19). This source included reports in Zimri's case on the "conspiracy which he made" (I Kings 16:20), in the case of Ahab on the "ivory house which he built, and all the cities that he built" (22:39), and in connection with Joash on the "might with which he fought against Amaziah king of Judah" (II Kings 13: 12). These references reveal the annalistic nature of the source, which most probably contained all the memorable events of the reign of every king and was preserved in the court archives. These annals were concluded shortly before Samaria's fall, *ca.* 724 B.C.

c. The Book of the Chronicles of the Kings of Judah. This source is mentioned first in the concluding formula attached to the account of the reign of Rehoboam (I Kings 14:29), last in that of Jehoiakim (II Kings 24:5), and fifteen times altogether. Again, there are reports on some of the Judean kings which do not contain any reference to these chronicles. The lack of reference in the case of the kings Ahaziah, Jehoahaz, Jehoiachin, and Zedekiah might be explained by the circumstances of their deaths, which prohibited the author's application of the stereotyped formula of the death and burial of the king (cf. I Kings 14:31). Thus, the author left out the whole concluding formula in the cases in question. The fact that the concluding formula of Jehoiakim points to this source (II Kings 24:5) militates against the assumption, maintained by some scholars, that the Book of the Chronicles of the Kings of Judah was completed with the account of the reign of Josiah. Allusions to Asa's building activities (I Kings 15:23), to the wars of Jehoshaphat (22:45), and to Hezekiah's building of a water reservoir and water conduit (II Kings 20:20) clearly establish the annalistic character of this source. These annals, like the Book of the Chronicles of the Kings of Israel, are court annals and were deposited in the royal archives of Jerusalem. The last pages of these Judean annals were written in *ca.* 590 B.C.

4. Other sources. Besides these three annalistic sources utilized and mentioned by the Deuteronomic author, there were also, manifestly, other sources upon which he had drawn. The fact that the author does not refer to the origin of some material does in no way justify the assumption that those pieces were interpolated by the later Deuteronomic editor. But the main theme of fidelity to the Lord in the unity and purity of the cult seems to join, so effectively, the different materials that their incorporation must have been completed by the Deuteronomic author. The Davidic court narrative; the Elijah, Elisha, Ahab, Isaiah sources; and some other prophetic narratives might be distinguished as sources unnamed but utilized by the author.

a. Davidic court narrative. I Kings 1-2 is the direct continuation of the Davidic court memoirs preserved in II Sam. 9-20 and represents the same outlook, distinctive stylistic ability, and proximity to the events related. It is a product of the second half of the tenth century B.C. *See* SAMUEL, I AND II, § C4*b*.

b. Elijah cycle. The Elijah stories embrace I Kings 17-19; 21; II Kings 1. The sequence of chs. 17-19; 21 in I Kings is interrupted by the story of the war of Ahab against the Syrians in ch. 20. The LXX and the Lucianic recension place the Ahab story (ch. 20) after the Naboth episode (ch. 21). This smoother order might have been the original sequence of the narratives. The Elijah cycle might be recognized as a N narrative complex. The lack of condemnation of the "calf worship" of Bethel and occasional telltale remarks (e.g., "Beer-sheba, which belongs to Judah" [I Kings 19:3]) help to establish that the Elijah stories originated in the N. The admiration paid to the prophet Elijah and the noticeable enhancement of the memories of his power and greatness are conceivably motivated by the disciples' pious and affectionate veneration of their master. The organ of the preservation and transmission of these Elijah stories was apparently the N prophetic guilds. The Elijah cycle is securely anchored in history, but nevertheless, its transformation into legends had started. The narratives in I Kings 17-19; 21 reveal high moral spirit, unyielding allegiance to the Lord, and profound theological sensitivity.

The narratives in I Kings 17-18 are joined by the link of the disastrous drought and the eventual coming of the rain. The resuscitation of the dead child of the widow of Zarephath (17:17-24) and the ordeal on Mount Carmel (ch. 18) fill the frame of the drought narrative. The account of the Horeb pilgrimage (I Kings 19) appears to be an independent narrative which originally served as introduction to the appointment of Elisha, Jehu, and Hazael as God's instruments of history. To be sure, the fulfilment of the divine command to anoint Hazael and Jehu (I Kings 19:15-16) is lacking, for apparently it was suppressed in favor of the version preserved in the Elisha cycle (II Kings 8-10). Only the call of Elisha into the service of Elijah (I Kings 19:19-21) corresponds with the divine command (vs. 16).

The great reverence of the narrator for the prophet does not hinder him in the consideration of many important problems. The focal questions of monotheism and complete allegiance to the only God (I Kings 18:21, 27, 36-39) gain expression in the narrative of the contest on Mount Carmel. The problems of the revelation of God (I Kings 19:9-13), the responsibilities of the prophetic office (vss. 14-17), and God's hidden work in history (vs. 18) occupy the foreground of the story of the pilgrimage to Horeb. The Naboth story (I Kings 21) represents an undoubtedly historical episode which throws light upon the tyranny of Ahab and Jezebel and documents the existence of inheritance laws sanctioned by custom. It is, however, more important that the Naboth story also reveals the ethical integrity, social responsibility, and unfailing courage of this Israelite prophet who intrepidly confronted the king with his wrongdoings and proclaimed a disastrous judgment upon the royal house. The same courageous attitude and single-mindedness of the prophet are vividly depicted in his encounter with the king, in which Elijah flung the accusation "troubler of Israel" back at King Ahab (18:17-19).

The story in II Kings 1 is unlike the rest of the Elijah stories and shows a measure of affinity with the Elisha cycle of legends. In spite of the crude and immoral thaumaturgical atmosphere of the narrative, there is a probably historical kernel preserved within this narrative. To this historical kernel belong the sickness of Ahaziah and his inquiry of BAAL-ZEBUB, the God of Ekron (1:2). Indubitably also, the condemnation of Ahaziah for inquiring of a strange god is completely consistent with Elijah's character (vss. 3-8). The story of the destruction of the hundred men by heavenly fire (vss. 9-16)—with the folk-tale motifs present—is a legendary overgrowth of the original narrative.

c. Elisha cycle. The Elisha stories, which occupy II Kings 2-13, represent a circle of tradition which was independent from that of the Elijah cycle. There is such a marked difference in literary expression and religious outlook that the common authorship of the Elijah and Elisha stories can hardly be entertained. The fact that some of the themes of the Elijah narratives appear in a new setting within the Elisha cycle, as is the case in the parallel stories of an unspent oil cruse (I Kings 17:8-16; II Kings 4:1-7) and the resuscitation of a dead child (I Kings 17:17-24; II Kings 4:18-37), seems to indicate that there was free interaction between the two traditions in the oral stage of their development. The motif of the transfer of Elijah's mantle to Elisha is common to both cycles of tradition (I Kings 19:19; II Kings 2:13-14). It is interesting to note that a special divine commission was given to Elijah on Mount Horeb to anoint Hazael of Syria and Jehu of Israel (I Kings 19:15-16), but the mission was completed only by Elisha (II Kings 8:7-15; 9:1-13). All these factors contribute to the recognition that the Elijah and Elisha cycles of tradition belong to the same general environment.

The Elisha narrative complex embraces a wide variety of literary pieces ranging from miracle narratives (e.g., II Kings 4:38-41) to the historical report (e.g., II Kings 9:1-10:27). The narratives which are centered around magical and thaumaturgical motifs must be classified as miracle narratives. Miracle narratives are the healing of the waters of Jericho (II Kings 2:19-22), the miracle of the jar of oil (4:1-7), the healing of the poisonous food (vss. 38-41), the feeding of the hundred men (vss. 42-44), and the miracle of the floating axe head (6:1-7.) On the other hand, the stories of the translation of Elijah, the transfer of the prophet's spirit (2:1-18), and the resuscitating power of Elisha's dead body (13:20-21) transcend the sphere of the magical and belong to the type of medieval miracle legends of the saints. As literature, all these stories are deeply rooted in folk tale; their aim is to glorify the prophet by the means of an emphasis on the prophetic power.

In all these legends and miracle stories, the prophet Elisha is surrounded by the prophetic schools of Bethel, Jericho, and Gilgal, and he seems to be their leader. It is justifiable to assume that these prophetic colleges represent the literary circle where the narratives originated and were reverently transmitted.

There are other narratives of the Elisha cycle which might be regarded as legends, for they reveal a less folkloristic element and a greater proximity to the historical happenings of the time. The story of the healing of Naaman (5:1-27) and the Shunammite stories (4:8-37; 8:1-6) belong to this class. They have in common that Elisha is in the company of his servant, Gehazi, and is not surrounded by the prophetic disciples, though his close relationship to the prophetic groups is implied (5:22). To be sure, no consecutive narrative can be reconstructed from these stories. Their common traits are outweighed by some discrepancies. It must be especially noted that in the second story of the Shunammite woman, Elisha seems to be dead (8:4-5), and Gehazi appears in the company of the king, but apparently he does not have the leprosy with which he was already smitten in Elisha's lifetime (5:27).

There are some other narratives within the Elisha cycle which present Elisha in the middle of political turmoil and military activity; these stories might be defined as historical narratives. These historical narratives include the stories on Elisha's role in Joram's war against Mesha king of Moab (3:4-27) and during the Syrian wars (6:8–7:20). The historical narratives presenting the Syrian wars (6:8–7:20) are in no way one literary piece. The narrative which relates how Elisha thwarted the surprise attacks of the Syrians by foretelling them to the king of Israel and how he blinded a Syrian raiding party (6:8-23), asserts that "the Syrians came no more on raids into the land of Israel" (vs. 23). Notwithstanding, the next verse commences with the narrative of Ben-hadad's siege of Samaria, the resulting famine in the city, and the miraculous deliverance of the city as it was foretold by Elisha (6:24–7:20). The loose connection between these historical narratives might be further illustrated with the relationship of Elisha toward the court. This relationship shifts, within these narratives, from definite friendliness (6:9, 21) to open animosity (3:13-14; 6:31-32). This unevenness of the narratives points to sharply fixed tradition preceding the written transmission of the stories.

If the historical narratives revealed a proximity in their relationship to historical events, the same might also be noted even more so in the case of the historical narratives of the anointment of Hazael by Elisha (8:7-15), the Jehu revolution (chs. 9–10), and the death of Elisha (13:14-19). In these narratives a historical core is viewed from the angle of prophetic tradition.

d. Ahab source. The Ahab narratives (I Kings 20; 22:1-38), which interrupt the continuity of the Elijah source, markedly differ from the latter in their portrayal of Ahab. These narratives show a vivid interest in the Syrian wars, and their emphatic enmity toward the Syrians (20:42) sets them apart from the Elijah and Elisha cycles. These Ahab narratives are interwoven with prophetic traditions of the Northern Kingdom which relate Ahab's controversy with an anonymous prophet (20:35-43) and with Micaiah the son of Imlah (22:5-28). Some scholars assume, on insufficient grounds, that this source was continued by II Kings 3:4-27; 6:8-23; 6:24–7:20, which seem to fit better the Elisha cycle. The Ahab source, as its apparent closeness to the Syrian wars of Ahab would indicate, must have been written in the late ninth or early eighth century B.C.

The Elijah, Elisha, and Ahab sources have in common a definite interest in the destiny of the Northern Kingdom and in the prophetic traditions of the N, and this is indicative of the N origin of these sources.

e. Isaiah source. Placed between the introductory and concluding formulas on Hezekiah's reign (II Kings 18:1-12; 20:20-21), a literary complex appears (18:13–20:19) which, because of its emphasized interest in the prophet Isaiah of Jerusalem, might be designated as the Isaiah source. This source was incorporated into the books of Kings from an independent collection of Isaiah legends. This complex is duplicated, with the exception of 18:14-16, in the biblical book of Isaiah (chs. 36–39). Biblical scholarship, in general, agrees that these Isaiah legends were transplanted from the books of Kings to the book of ISAIAH.

This source represents the coalescence of historical narratives and the prophetic legends. That the prophetic legends' influence was decisive in this process can easily be conceived if the matter-of-fact report on the events of Sennacherib's campaign against Judah (18:14-16) is compared with the two other versions of the same (18:17–19:8, 36-37; 19:9*b*-35). Apparently the report of Hezekiah's tribute paid to Sennacherib (18:14-16) is based upon a laconic record in the Book of the Chronicles of the Kings of Judah. The two other versions, which relate the miraculous deliverance of Jerusalem in accord with the encouraging prophecy of Isaiah (19:6-7, 20-34), bear the stamp of the prophetic legends. Also, the story of the sickness of Hezekiah and his recovery, together with the miraculous recessing of the shadow given as a sign for the divine promise delivered by Isaiah (20:1-11), has to be regarded as prophetic legend. The account of the visit of the embassy of Merodach-baladan (20:12-19) is based on historical memories; this account was revised by the second Deuteronomic editor, who was familiar with the events following the fall of Jerusalem. The whole complex of Isaiah legends originated in Jerusalem among Isaiah's disciples and was transmitted by the same prophetic circle and could have been put in written form around the middle of the seventh century B.C.

f. A prophetic source. There is one more source present in the books of Kings. This source contains independent prophetic legends which might still have been in the formative process of oral transmission when the Deuteronomic author incorporated them into his work—as their adaptation to the Deuteronomic ideas would indicate. The prophecies of Ahijah the Shilonite (I Kings 11:29-39; 14:1-18) and their fulfilment (12:15; 15:29) demonstrate perceivably the didactic tendencies of the Deuteronomic author. The same late outlook also characterizes the prophetic words of Shemaiah (I Kings 12:21-24). The story of the condemnation of the altar of Bethel by an anonymous prophet (I Kings 12:32–13:34), who even knows the name of Josiah (13:2), might be a faint reminiscence of Amos' denunciatory prophecies in Bethel (cf. Amos 7:10-16; 9:1). Or this story might be a late local tradition of Bethel (cf. II Kings 23:16-20) which was adapted to the Deuteronomic thoughts. Another prophecy of anonymous character condemns Manasseh and is acquainted with the fall of Jerusalem (II Kings 21:7-15); accordingly, its literary formulation must also be from the pen of the Deuteronomic editor.

5. The problem of a pre-Deuteronomic book of Kings. Some scholars propose that the Deuteronomic editor had utilized one already complete literary work into which he incorporated the annalistic accounts of the Book of the Acts of Solomon, the Chronicles of Judah, and that of Israel. Thus, the pre-Deuteronomic book of Kings would have embraced all the sources which are not referred to by title. This pre-Deuteronomic book of Kings would have been the continuation of the books of Samuel and would have consisted of several strata, which were the continuation of the strata apparent in the books of Samuel. The attempted separation of two (J and E) or three (L, J, and E) strata is not convincing. There are several proposed analyses of the assumed pre-Deuteronomic book which agree in only one aspect—that they take it for granted that the sources of the Pentateuch (or sources closely related to them) extend beyond the books of Samuel. Thus J is traced to I Kings 12 by one scholar, to II Kings 17:3-4 by another; similarly, E was supposed to be found in II Kings 22–23 or even in II Kings 25. Some scholars assume that a pre-Deuteronomic book was in existence, but, beyond the assertion of the possibility of the continuation of the sources of the books of Samuel, they do not attempt to demonstrate their thesis in an analysis.

The occasional traces of parallel traditions are not sufficient for the separation of continuous strata which would span the books. The discrepancies and parallel accounts can be explained as a mere accumulation of variants of the same tradition. To be sure, the possibility of the existence of a pre-Deuteronomic book of Kings cannot be disproved, but the assumption of its existence is in no way necessary for the understanding of the formation of the books of Kings.

6. The Deuteronomic edition. It has already been demonstrated (*see* § C2 *above*) that the author of the framework of the books of Kings is definitely under the influence of the Deuteronomic thought. It is also obvious that whoever wrote the framework is also responsible for the conception of the whole work, for the framework alone ensures the continuity of thought and purpose of the books. Thus, if the framework is Deuteronomic in thought, it is justifiable to speak of a Deuteronomic editor or author. There are, however, some discrepancies which can hardly be explained by the assumption of only one Deuteronomic editor. Thus, the prophecy in II Kings 22:20 does not reveal knowledge of the death of Josiah on the battlefield of Megiddo (23:29-30); the destruction of the temple is not known in I Kings 8:8; the Davidic dynasty was still on the throne at the writing of I Kings 9:21; 11:36; II Kings 8:19. These facts lead to the recognition that there was one Deuteronomic editor writing before the death of Josiah (609 B.C.). On the other hand, the existence of references to the destruction of the temple (I Kings 9:6-9), and to the Exile (I Kings 8:46-53; II Kings 21:11-15; 22:16-17), and the inclusion of the report on the fall of Jerusalem (II Kings 24:1–25:26), and of the exilic narrative of the favor shown to the captive King Jehoiachin by Evil-merodach (25:27-30), presuppose a second Deuteronomic editor. His activity is dated as *ca.* 550 B.C. by the last event reported (561 B.C.) and the lack of any reference to the fall of Babylon (539 B.C.).

Still, there was a solution proposed to explain the unevenness of the books of Kings and to maintain that only one editor was at work in the book. According to this theory, the only Deuteronomic editor of the book who would also be responsible for a great historical work embracing Deut. 1–II Kings 25 would be one who was writing during the Exile, and therefore all the references to the Exile are his work (I Kings 8:46-53; 9:6-9; etc.). Other passages, which are obviously unaware of the Exile (I Kings 8:8; 9:21; II Kings 8:19; etc.), would be accounted for by the editor's incorporation of unchanged older documents into his work. Accordingly, the role of the editor would have been, in part, a servile compilation of the sources and documents as the discrepancies would indicate. This solution cannot be rejected on a priori grounds, but the assumption of two Deuteronomic editors is able to eliminate the difficulties in a more satisfactory manner.

Nevertheless, even among those scholars who accept two Deuteronomic editors, agreement is not complete. So it was proposed that the first Deuteronomic editor wrote, not before, but after the death of Josiah, and his work was concluded with II Kings 23:28, and that the preceding verses (25*b*-27), which allude to the fall of Jerusalem and to the Exile, are the work of the second editor. This suggestion also maintains that the first Deuteronomic editor was so blinded by the Deuteronomic conviction that good deeds gain their earthly reward, that when Josiah, the Deuteronomic reformer and paragon of the Deuteronomic virtues (II Kings 23:25*a*), died on the battlefield, the editor disregarded the facts which contradicted his theology and wrote as if Josiah had died in peace (II Kings 22:20). The supporting evidences for this contention are in the introductory statement for Josiah (II Kings 22:1), which states the length of the king's reign as thirty-one years and reports judgment on the king's reign (vs. 2), and in the concluding reference to the Book of the Chronicles of the Kings of Judah (23:28). The evident difficulty of this theory is that a deliberate silence about the tragic end of Josiah is hardly compatible with the editor's unmistakable intention to appeal to his contemporaries, whom he could not have blinded to the contemporaneous events. It is much more plausible to assume that the first editor wrote before the death of Josiah, and that the "thirty-one years" of Josiah's reign (II Kings 22:1) was inserted into the introductory formula by the later editor. The concluding formula (23:28) itself would have originated in its entirety from the pen of the later editor, who also supplied an identical reference to the Book of the Chronicles of Judah in the case of Jehoiakim (II Kings 24:5), who died in 597 B.C.

The second Deuteronomic editor (*ca.* 550 B.C.) apparently wrote during the Exile, as his reference "beyond the River" (i.e., "beyond the Euphrates," in the Hebrew text of I Kings 4:24) to the Palestinian region reveals. When Jehoiachin, the exiled king of Judah, was admitted to the Babylonian court, this editor understood it as a sign of the returning divine favor. The second editor was confronted with the crux of the Deuteronomic theology (the untimely death of the pious King Josiah in 609 B.C.), but he thought to solve this crux by the assumption that the Lord's wrath was so fierce, "because of all the provocations with which Manasseh had provoked him" (II Kings 23:26), that not even the righteous reign and pious reforms of Josiah could quench his anger (vss. 27-28; cf. 24:1-4). The same thought is also expressed in the words of Huldah the prophetess (II Kings 22:15-20), which apparently were adapted by the second editor. The divine warning given to Solomon in I Kings 9:1-9 is written by the second editor, as can be recognized by the allusion to the destruction of the temple (vs. 8). The second editor maintains that Samaria deserved destruction because of the embracement of the Canaanitish idolatry (II Kings 17:7-18). This view is at variance with the first editor's conviction that Samaria was destroyed because of the calf-worship of Bethel (vss. 21-23).

7. The purpose of the Deuteronomic author. The first Deuteronomic editor of the books of Kings, who might rightly be called the Deuteronomic author, was motivated by the Deuteronomic theology of the unity and purity of worship which recognized only the Jerusalem temple as the sole, legitimate sanctuary of the Lord. Therefore, he condemned all the kings of Israel, for they all shared in the calf-worship, the "sin of Jeroboam the son of Nebat." Guided by the same theological outlook, he denounced those kings of Judah who did not destroy the local shrines, the high places. The author's advocacy of the unity of the worship, however, did not make him a cultic formalist. In his eyes, the cult was one expression of Israel's allegiance to the Lord which had to be manifest in the whole life of the holy people.

The Deuteronomic author did not conceive this literary work in the terms of secular historiography, but as a history of the Lord's dealings with his chosen people. The author's foremost interest in God's plan with his people explains the fact that such an important king (at least by secular standards) as Omri of Israel is handled in a mere six verses (I Kings 16:23-28). The author recognized the prophets as the Lord's spokesmen in history, and therefore he incorporated into these books bulks of prophetic narratives in the Elijah and Elisha cycles. Similarly, the Ahab source aroused the author's interest because of its prophetic implications, and not because of its merits as relatively objective historical narrative. Undoubtedly, the work of the Deuteronomic editor cannot be compared with any Western historical writing, secular or ecclesiastical, because the goal before the eyes of the author was not merely to report the events of the past, but to give an evaluation and criticism of the past as an admonition for contemporaries. This work, by retelling the apostasy and the ensuing trials and visitations of the holy people, called to repentance, conversion, and total commitment of the national existence in allegiance to the Lord. The work of the Deuteronomic author is like a long sermon using the history of the chosen people for illustration; as a matter of fact, the same admonishing, instructive, and edifying spirit permeates this historical work as the Deuteronomic sermons of Deut. 5–11.

D. *TEXT.* The books of Kings, as they are preserved in the MT, do not represent, in every detail, the best text. The LXX, which is often shorter than the MT, and the Lucianic recension of the LXX present, in places, more reliable variants, and they are essential to the reconstruction of the text. The discovery of fragments of the books of Kings in the Dead Sea region seems to support the theory of the existence of a Hebrew text which, on the whole, was closer to the LXX than to the MT, and which, in some cases, was superior to both.

Bibliography. Commentaries: I. Benziger, *KHC* (1899); R. Kittel, *HKAT* (1900); J. Skinner, *NCB* (1904); W. E. Barnes, *Cambridge Bible* (1911); J. A. Montgomery and H. S. Gehman, *ICC* (1951); N. H. Snaith, *IB* (1951).

Special studies: C. F. Burney, *Notes on the Hebrew Text of the Books of Kings* (1903); M. Noth, *Überlieferungsgeschichtliche Studien,* vol. I (1943); G. von Rad, *Studies in Deuteronomy* (1953); A. Jepsen, *Die Quellen des Königsbuches* (1956).

S. SZIKSZAI

KING'S GARDEN [גן המלך]. A royal estate near Jerusalem, mentioned (Neh. 3:15) in connection with the Pool of Shelah (*see* SHELAH, POOL OF), toward the junction of the Tyropoeon with the Kidron. *See* KIDRON, BROOK.

KING'S HIGHWAY [דרך המלך]. A road mentioned three times in the Bible, twice by this name; Moses promised the Edomites and Sihon that the Israelites would keep strictly to it in passing through their lands (Num. 20:17; 21:22; see also Deut. 2:27). These references are to a well-known highway which ran from Damascus to the Gulf of Aqabah along the length of E Palestine, passing through Bashan, Gilead, Ammon, Moab, and Edom and connecting with the roads that led across the Negeb toward the coastal route from Phoenicia to Egypt. Archaeological investigation has shown that there was a line of fortresses along it. The first ones were apparently destroyed by the raid of Chedorlaomer and his allies, who followed it and picked off one town after another (Gen. 14); the region was then uninhabited for about six hundred years, and then new fortresses were built by the invading peoples who resettled there. The road was used by the Nabataean traders; Trajan had it rebuilt after he conquered the latter people (A.D. 106), and it became known as Trajan's Road. The Arabic name, Tariq es-Sultani, has the same meaning as that of the Hebrew; the modern road in Jordan closely follows the original course, with modifications for automobile traffic.

Fig. KIN 7.

Courtesy of the Air Officer Commanding, Royal Air Force, Middle East; photo courtesy of the American Schools of Oriental Research

7. King's Highway; in the background it runs N across Brook Zered.

Bibliography. N. Glueck, *The Other Side of the Jordan* (1940), pp. 10-16. S. COHEN

KING'S POOL [ברכת המלך] (Neh. 2:14). Presumably the same as the Pool of Shelah (*see* SHELAH, POOL OF), a reservoir of the king's garden in Jerusalem. *See* JERUSALEM § 7*b*.

KING'S VALE, VALLEY [עמק המלך]; KJV KING'S DALE. *See* SHAVEH, VALLEY OF.

***KINSHIP.** *See* FAMILY; MARRIAGE.

KIR kĭr [קיר, Heb. wall, Moabite city]. **1.** A city of Moab, mentioned in connection with Ar in Isaiah's oracle against Moab (15:1). Kir is probably the same city as KIR-HARESETH, an ancient capital of Moab, located at Kerak, *ca.* seventeen miles S of the Arnon and eleven miles E of the Dead Sea.

E. D. GROHMAN

* **2.** A Mesopotamian locality (Isa. 22:6; cf. vs. 5) from which Arameans had migrated to Syria (Amos 9:7) and to which their descendants were exiled as a result of the Assyrian deportations (1:5)—e.g., at the hands of Tiglath-pileser during the reign of Ahaz (II Kings 16:9). Amos (9:7) knew of an exodus saga according to which God had brought the Arameans out of Kir to their promised land (probably Damascus), much like the exodus of Israel from Egypt (and of the Philistines from Caphtor). The tragedy of the forced return of the Arameans to Kir is paralleled by the aversion of the Hebrews to being sent back to Egypt (Deut. 17:16; 28:68). C. H. GORDON

KIR-HARESETH kĭr hăr'ə sĕth [קיר חרשת, Heb. wall of potsherds, Moabite city of potsherds] (II Kings 3:25; Isa. 16:7); KJV KIR-HARASETH in II Kings 3:25. Alternately: KIR-HERES —hĭr'ĭz [קיר חרש; LXX ταῖχος ὃ ἐνεκαίνισας *in* Isa. 16:11 *suggests* Kir-hadesheth, new city, *perhaps corrupted into* Kir-hareseth, wall of potsherds] (Isa. 16:11; Jer. 48:31, 36); KJV KIR-HARESH —hăr'ĕsh in Isa. 16:11. An ancient capital of Moab, located *ca.* seventeen miles S of the Arnon and eleven miles E of the Dead Sea. Modern Kerak is 3,110 feet above the Mediterranean, and so 4,400 feet above the Dead Sea, standing on a small plateau *ca.* 2,500 feet long. Except at one or two points, Kerak is isolated from the surrounding hills by valleys more than 300 feet deep. The neighboring hills overlook the city.

In the time of Elisha, while Mesha was king of Moab, the kings of Israel, Judah, and Edom attacked Moab from the S (II Kings 3:4 ff). After a miraculous victory by the allies, the Moabites fled and the allied armies pursued, destroying the land and besieging Kir-hareseth. To turn the tide of battle, Mesha sacrificed his oldest son as a burnt offering upon the wall. Thereupon "there came great wrath upon Israel," and the allied armies withdrew. Kir-hareseth, or Kir-heres, is mentioned twice in Isaiah's oracle against Moab (16:7, 11) and twice in Jeremiah's (48:31, 36). Also, KIR (1), mentioned in Isa. 15:1, is probably the same city.

A tunnel, a cul-de-sac *ca.* two hundred yards long, runs toward the citadel from the wadi below. It is probably an abortive water passage, begun but never finished by some Moabite king, the water source being found too weak or the work being interrupted. The account mentioned above of the siege against Kir-hareseth illustrates the need of the city for a good water supply. In 1924 great masses of distinctive Moabite pottery were found on the steep SE slopes of the hill, below the citadel. In addition, pottery of the Nabatean, Roman, Byzantine, and medieval Arabic periods has been found.

Courtesy of Denis Baly

8. Kir-hareseth (modern el-Kerak)

There are impressive remains at Kerak from later times. In *ca.* 1140 a castle was built by the Crusaders under King Fulco of Jerusalem. It fell into the hands of Saladin in 1188. Since the time of the Crusades, the Greek bishop of Petra has had his seat at Kerak. Fig. KIR 8.

Bibliography. W. F. Albright, "The Archaeological Results of an Expedition to Moab and the Dead Sea," *BASOR,* 14 (1924), 10-11; F.-M. Abel, *Géographie de la Palestine,* II (1938), 418-19. E. D. GROHMAN

KIRIATH kĭr'ĭ ăth [קרית, city of] (Josh. 18:28 RSV mg.); KJV KIRJATH kûr'jăth. *See* KIRIATH-JEARIM.

KIRIATHAIM kĭr'ĭ ə thā'əm [קריתים, קריתמה, two cities]; KJV alternately KIRJATHAIM kûr'jə thā'əm. **1.** A city of the Moabite tableland (Jer. 48:1, 23;

Ezek. 25:9), assigned to the tribe of Reuben (Num. 32:37; Josh. 13:19). It was in Moabite hands in Mesha's time, since he spoke of building Qaryaten (קריתן; *see* MOABITE STONE). Kiriathaim has frequently been identified with el-Qereiyat, 5½ miles W-NW of Dibon, but no remains have been found there earlier than the first century B.C.

Bibliography. F.-M. Abel, *Géographie de la Palestine,* II (1938), 419; N. Glueck, *Explorations in Eastern Palestine,* III, *AASOR,* XVIII-XIX (1937-39), 131.

2. A city of the tribe of Naphtali given to the Gershomites (I Chr. 6:76—H 6:61); probably identical with KARTAN in the parallel list in Josh. 21:32.

E. D. GROHMAN

KIRIATH-ARBA kĭr'ĭ ăth är'bə [קרית ארבע, city of four, tetrapolis]; KJV KIRJATH-ARBA kûr'jăth-är'bə. The ancient name of HEBRON, near which the cave of Machpelah, burial place of the patriarchs, was located (Gen. 23:2; 35:27). Caleb captured it from the Anakim, after whose great hero, Arba, the city was allegedly named (Josh. 14:15; cf. 15:13). It was the chief city of a hill-country district (15:54) and was both a city of refuge (20:7) and a Levitical city (of the Kohathite family; Josh. 21:11). The tradition of the ancient name of Hebron, Kiriath-arba, persisted throughout the biblical period, reappearing as a city in which returnees from the Exile settled (Neh. 11:25).

V. R. GOLD

KIRIATH-ARIM kĭr'ĭ ăth âr'ĭm [קרית ערים]; KJV KIRJATH-ARIM kûr'jăth âr'ĭm; KJV Apoc. KIRIATHIARIUS kĭr'ĭ ăth'ĭ âr'ĭ əs (I Esd. 5:19). A misspelling in Ezra 2:25 for KIRIATH-JEARIM.

KIRIATH-BAAL kĭr'ĭ ăth bā'əl, bāl [קרית בעל, city of Baal] (Josh. 15:60; 18:14); KJV KIRJATH-BAAL kûr'jăth bā'əl, bāl. Same as KIRIATH-JEARIM.

KIRIATH-HUZOTH kĭr'ĭ ăth hū'zŏth [קרית חצות, city of streets; LXX πόλεις ἐπαύλεων *suggests perhaps an original* קרית חצרות, city of courts] (Num. 22:39); KJV KIRJATH-HUZOTH kûr'jăth hū'zŏth. A Moabite city, the first place to which Balak took Balaam. It was apparently near the Arnon (vs. 36), not far from Bamoth-baal (vs. 41). Its precise location is uncertain.

E. D. GROHMAN

KIRIATHIARIUS. KJV Apoc. form of KIRIATH-ARIM.

KIRIATH-JEARIM kĭr'ĭ ăth jē'ə rĭm [קרית יערים, city of forests]; KJV KIRJATH-JEARIM kûr'jăth jē'ə rĭm. Also: BAALAH bā'ə lə [בעלה] (Josh. 15:9; I Chr. 13:6), KJV BAALE OF JUDAH bā'ə lĭ; BAALE-JUDAH [בעלי יהודה] (II Sam. 6:2), KJV BAALE OF JUDAH; KIRIATH-ARIM kĭr'ĭ ăth âr'ĭm [קרית ערים] (Ezra 2:25), KJV KIRJATH-ARIM kûr'jăth âr'ĭm; KIRIATH-BAAL kĭr'ĭ ăth bā'əl, bāl' [קרית בעל] (Josh. 15:60; 18:14), KJV KIRJATH-BAAL kûr'jăth bā'əl, bāl'. A city of Judah identified with Deir al-Azhar near the modern village of Qaryet el-'Inab or Abu Ghosh (after an early-nineteenth-century sheik who terrorized the countryside), *ca.* 8⅓ miles N of Jerusalem. Eusebius refers to Kiriath-jearim (Cariathiareim) twice, once as 9 and once as 10 (Roman) miles from Jerusalem on the road to Diospolis (Lydda, Lod). Peter the Deacon also places it 9 miles from Jerusalem.

Deir al-Azhar lies on a commanding hill just to the W of Abu Ghosh. Pottery from the Late Bronze and Early Iron periods, as well as later periods, can be picked up on the surface of the tell, which was well situated for defense and observation of the surrounding territory. Later, the city seems to have moved from the hill to the site of Abu Ghosh, perhaps during the Roman period, as indicated by the excavation in 1944 of the Crusader church at Abu Ghosh.

Kiriath-jearim first appears as a member of the Gibeonite confederacy of four strategically located fortress cities occupied by Hivites, possibly a non-Semitic people (e.g., Hittites or Hurrians; Josh. 9:17; cf. II Sam. 21:1-9). Its earlier name seems to have been Kiriath-Baal ("city of the god Baal"). In the description of Judah's N boundary it appears as Baalah, a shortened form of the name (Josh. 15:9-10). In the description of the Benjaminite borders, it appears as Kiriath-Baal (Josh. 15:60; 18:14). It was the boundary point where the E border of Dan, the W border of Benjamin, and the N border of Judah met. In the course of their northward migration, the Danites camped near Kiriath-jearim, a place always well supplied with water (Judg. 18:12).

After the Battle of Ebenezer (*ca.* 1050), the Philistines carried the captured ark of the covenant to Ashdod. After a series of unpleasant incidents, including the smashing of the cult statue of Dagon and a plague of boils, the Philistines' diviners suggested a device by which the cause might be determined. It turned out to be their possession of the ark. It was returned to Beth-shemesh, from which, after another untoward incident, it was sent on to Kiriath-jearim. Here it remained in a specially designated house, feared by both Philistines and Israelites, until David brought it to Jerusalem with great pomp and ceremony (I Sam. 5:1–7:2; II Sam. 6:1-15, where Kiriath-jearim is called Baale-judah; I Chr. 13:1-13; 15:1-29). In the royal administrative reorganization, it was assigned to the province of Jerusalem (Josh. 15:60; 18:28, where it appears as Kiriath [LXX Kiriath-jearim] and is attributed to the tribe of Benjamin, to whom it may originally have belonged, though by the time of the judges it was said to belong to Judah; cf. Judg. 18:12; I Chr. 2:50-53).

The ill-fated prophet Uriah, son of Shemaiah, a contemporary of Jeremiah, came from Kiriath-jearim (Jer. 26:20-23). Among those who returned from the Exile were people from Kiriath-jearim (Neh. 7:29; Ezra 2:25, where it appears as Kiriath-arim).

In the Roman period a fort was built over the ruins of Kiriath-jearim as a military post to guard the strategic Roman road between Jerusalem and the maritime plain. The garrison, consisting of a detachment of the Tenth Legion (*Fretensis*), whose headquarters were in Jerusalem, built a large reservoir near the spring at Qaryet el-'Inab—Abu Ghosh, whose walls were later used in the foundation of a medieval church. During the Byzantine period a basilica was built on Deir el-Azhar (Kiriath-jearim) commemorating the long stay of the ark of the covenant in Kiriath-jearim.

Bibliography. F. T. Cooke, "The Site of Kiriath-jearim," *AASOR,* V (1923-24), 105-20; R. de Vaux and A. M. Steve, *Fouilles à Qaryet El-'Enab Abû Ghôsh, Palestine* (1950).

V. R. GOLD

KIRIATH-SANNAH kĭr'ĭ ăth săn'ə [קרית סנה] (Josh. 15:49); KJV KIRJATH-SANNAH kûr'jăth—. Another name, perhaps a misspelling, for KIRIATH-SEPHER.

KIRIATH-SEPHER kĭr'ĭ ăth sē'fər [קרית ספר, city of the scribe] (Josh. 15:15-16; Judg. 1:11-12); KJV KIRJATH-SEPHER kûr'jăth—. The older name for DEBIR 2.

KIRIOTH. KJV form of KERIOTH in Amos 2:2.

KIRJATH. KJV form of Kiriath. *See* KIRIATH-JEARIM.

KIRJATHAIM. KJV alternate form of KIRIATHAIM.

KIRJATH-ARBA. KJV form of KIRIATH-ARBA.

KIRJATH-HUZOTH. KJV form of KIRIATH-HUZOTH.

KIRJATH-JEARIM. KJV form of KIRIATH-JEARIM.

KIRJATH-SANNAH. KJV form of KIRIATH-SANNAH.

KIRJATH-SEPHER. KJV form of KIRIATH-SEPHER.

KISH kĭsh [קיש; Κίς]; KJV CIS sĭs in Acts 13:21; CISAI sī'sī in Add. Esth. 11:2. **1.** A Benjaminite of Gibeah; the father of King Saul. According to I Sam. 9:1 he appears to have been the son of ABIEL (1), but was more probably the son of NER (cf. I Chr. 8:33).

Kish is described as a man of wealth, who possessed servants and asses (I Sam. 9:3). The representation of Saul that his family was the humblest of all the families of the tribe of Benjamin must be construed as an illustration of oriental modesty (I Sam. 9:21). Kish was doubtless present at the selection of the king at Mizpah, when the Matrites, a clan of the Benjaminites to which he belonged, obtained the lot. From this clan Saul was ultimately chosen king (I Sam. 10:20-24). No other details of the life of Kish are preserved except the notice of his sepulchre in Zela of Benjamin, where Saul and Jonathan were also interred (II Sam. 21:14).

2. A Benjaminite who is included among the sons (?) of Jeiel (I Chr. 8:30; 9:36). He should probably be distinguished from the Kish who was the father of Saul.

3. Son of Mahli, a Levite of the family of Merari. His sons married the daughters of his brother, Eleazar (I Chr. 23:21-22). His son Jerahmeel became the head of the family of Kish and gave his name to one of the courses into which the Levites were presumably divided (I Chr. 24:29).

4. Son of Abdi, a Levite of the family of the Merarites. He assisted in the cleansing of the temple in the reign of Hezekiah (II Chr. 29:12).

5. A Benjaminite who is described as an ancestor of Mordecai, the uncle of Esther (Esth. 2:5).

E. R. DALGLISH

KISHI kĭsh'ī [קישי, *possibly* gift] (I Chr. 6:44—H 6:29). Alternate name of KUSHAIAH.

Bibliography. M. Noth, *Die israelitischen Personennamen* (1928), p. 171, note 3.

KISHION kĭsh'ĭ ən [קשיון] (Josh. 19:20; 21:28); KJV KISHON kĭsh'ən in Josh. 21:28. A Levitical town in Issachar. The Chronicler's list reads "Kedesh" at this point (I Chr. 6:72—H 6:57), which is probably in error. Kishion is mentioned in the Thutmose III list (no. 37, spelled *Qsn*) of conquered towns. Its location is uncertain; two sites have been suggested: Tell el-Muqarqash and Tell el-'Ajjul (near En-dor).

Bibliography. W. F. Albright, "The Topography of the Tribe of Issachar," *ZAW,* N.F. 3 (1926), p. 231; F.-M. Abel, *Géographie de la Palestine,* II (1938), 422-23.

G. W. VAN BEEK

KISHON kī'shŏn, kĭsh'ŏn [קישון]; KJV alternately KISON kĭs'ən (Ps. 83:9—H 83:10). A river draining the W part of the Valley of Jezreel, or Plain of Esdraelon, and the Plain of Acco. The major sources of the Kishon, known in Arabic as Nahr el-Muqatta', are located at the E end of the Plain of Esdraelon. From the SE, Wadi en-Nusf, whose name changes downstream to Wadi Shemmah, flows northward from the vicinity of Jenin, S of Mount Gilboa.

Courtesy of Herbert G. May

9. The River Kishon

From the NE, Wadi Muweili, which rises from springs W of the foot of Mount Tabor, makes its way southwestward. The latter is joined by Wadi el-Mujahiyeh, which has its origin in the Galilean hills S of Nazareth. From the SW, the waters from several springs in the vicinity of Megiddo join and flow northeastward. The confluence of these sources takes place in the center of the plain, at a point *ca.* four miles NE of Megiddo. Other wadies, draining the Galilean hills on the N—including especially Wadi el-Khawajah—and the Carmel Range on the S, feed into the Kishon as it winds northwestward across the plain, roughly paralleling the Carmel Range. Most of these wadies are dry except during the winter, when water from heavy rains fills their courses and rushes down to collect in the Kishon. Fig. KIS 9.

In the Valley of Jezreel the Kishon is scarcely more than a brook, attaining a width of *ca.* twenty feet in the spring. Its width increases near the W end of the plain, and at Tell el-Qassis it is slightly more than thirty feet wide and *ca.* three or four feet deep in June. In spite of its relatively small size, it is a formidable geographical barrier during the rainy months of winter and early spring, when its bed is boggy and the plain on both sides is marshy. Fording is difficult at this time. By summer, however, its bed is usually dry. As it crosses the plain, the Kishon gradually descends from an elevation of *ca.* three hundred feet at its SE source near Jenin, to *ca.* eighty feet above sea level at the point where it leaves the plain. A slight rise of land in the center of the plain deflects the river to the N and largely determines its course.

The Kishon leaves the Valley of Jezreel and enters the Plain of Acco through a narrow pass formed by a jutting spur of the Galilean hills, which almost touches Mount Carmel a short distance NW of Tell el-Qassis. After entering the Plain of Acco, the Kishon hugs the foot of Mount Carmel to a point slightly W of Tell el-Harbaj (possibly HELKATH), where it changes course to the N, and empties into the Mediterranean Sea just S of the sand dunes along the coast. Its total length from its sources to the Sea is approximately twenty-three miles.

In the Plain of Acco, the Kishon receives the waters of a number of tributaries, chiefly the Wadi el-Melek from SW Galilee, and from several springs, especially those at el-Harbaj on the N, and at Jelameh and Yajur on the S. These sources supply enough water to make the Kishon a perennial stream for the remainder of its length, and it attains a width of *ca.* sixty-five feet in this plain.

The Kishon is chiefly remembered in the OT as the scene of the defeat of Sisera by Barak and Deborah. According to Judg. 4:7, 13, Sisera, the Canaanite captain residing at HAROSHETH of the Gentiles, led his forces and chariotry to do battle with Barak and Deborah of Israel at the Kishon. The exact place where this battle was fought is not known, but the poetic account—the Song of Deborah—states that it took place in the vicinity of Taanach, by the Waters of Megiddo—i.e., in the Valley of Jezreel, perhaps near the confluence of the streams which make up the Kishon (Judg. 5:19). The battle was apparently waged when the Kishon was in flood after a heavy rainstorm, with the result that Sisera's chariots became mired in the boggy plain, and his forces fled before Barak's lighter-armed troops (vs. 21). To later Israelites, the victory at the Kishon was evidence of God's providence, and the psalmist cites this victory among others in his petition for God's help against the enemies of Israel in his time (Ps. 83: 9—H 83:10). The Kishon is also mentioned in connection with the contest on Mount Carmel between the prophets of Baal and Elijah. Following Elijah's triumph, the discredited prophets of Baal were taken to the river and put to death there (I Kings 18:40).

Bibliography. C. R. Conder and H. H. Kitchener, *The Survey of Western Palestine,* I (1881), 265-67; F.-M. Abel, *Géographie de la Palestine,* I (1933), 158-59; D. Baly, *The Geography of the Bible* (1957). G. W. VAN BEEK

KISS. A touch of the lips to another person's lips, cheek, hands, feet, as a gesture of affection or homage, frequently in greeting or farewell, and usually without erotic meaning.

1. Terminology. The Hebrew verb is נשק substantive נשיקה; LXX and NT φιλέω and καταφιλέω substantive φίλημα. The Hebrew verb is used figuratively to mean "touch" in Ezek. 3:13; Ps. 85:10—H 85:11.

2. The familiar kiss. The seductive kiss of the "loose woman" in Prov. 7:13 and the romantic kisses of lovers in Song of S. 1:2; 8:1 are exceptional in biblical usage. Most commonly it is one member of a family who kisses another: a son his father (Jacob kisses Isaac in Gen. 27:26-27; Joseph kisses Jacob in Gen. 50:1); a son his parents (Elisha in I Kings 19: 20) or father-in-law (Moses kisses Jethro in Exod. 18:7); a man his son (David kisses Absalom in II Sam. 14:33) or children (Laban in Gen. 31:28, 55) or grandsons (Jacob kisses Ephraim and Manasseh in Gen. 48:10); a man his brothers (Esau kisses Jacob in Gen. 33:4; Joseph his brothers in Gen. 45:15; Moses kisses Aaron in Exod. 4:27); his cousin (Jacob kisses Rachel in Gen. 29:11) or nephew (Laban kisses Jacob in Gen. 29:13); or finally, a woman her daughters-in-law (Naomi kisses Ruth and Orpah in Ruth 1:9; cf. vs. 14).

Also beyond the circle of the family but without erotic overtones, one man may kiss another as FRIEND, genuinely so as David does Jonathan (I Sam. 20:41) and Barzillai (II Sam. 19:39—H 19:40) or in hypocrisy as Absalom the politician does (II Sam. 15: 5; cf. Prov. 27:6), or even in treacherous pretense (as Joab kisses Amasa in II Sam. 20:9).

It appears that biblical man acted out his feelings with less reserve than we; other demonstrative gestures usually attended the kiss. Kissing, one clutched and embraced the other (II Sam. 15:5; 20:9; Prov. 7:13; Gen. 29:13; 33:4; 48:10) and wept (Gen. 33:4), or merely wept (Gen. 29:11; 45:15; 50:1; I Sam. 20: 41; Ruth 1:9, 14). Sometimes one bowed deeply (Exod. 18:7; I Sam. 20:41; II Sam. 14:33; I Kings 19:18) or even groveled, "licking the dust of"—i.e., kissing—the other's feet (Isa. 49:23; cf. Mic. 7:17; Ps. 72:9; dubiously also Ps. 2:12).

3. The ceremonial kiss. The gestures do not seem always to have been an expression of genuine emotion; they were often a kind of ceremony. The biblical combination of kissing with weeping may be compared to the ceremonious weeping on similar (by no means always sorrowful) occasions also among other cultures. The obeisance, too, and "licking the dust" present an obvious ceremonial aspect; even so, for example, according to proud boasts of Sargon and Sennacherib, the kings of conquered peoples kissed their conquerors' feet in abject surrender. Related, though in different contexts, were the kiss which Samuel gave Saul as he anointed him (I Sam. 10:1) and the kisses which worshipers directed to the sundry objects of their reverence—Baal, an idol, the moon (I Kings 19:18; Hos. 13:2; Job 31:26-27).

Other occasions also suggest the ceremonial or conventional nature of the kiss. It is frequently associated with greeting, especially when persons meet after an extended absence (Gen. 29:11, 13; 33:4; 45: 15; Exod. 4:27; 18:7; II Sam. 20:9) or when they are about to part (Gen. 31:28, 55; Ruth 1:9, 14; I Sam. 20:41-42; II Sam. 19:39—H 19:40; I Kings 19:20), and when they part at the approach or occurrence of death (Gen. 27:26; 50:1). The kiss may be the prelude to a solemn blessing (Gen. 27:26-27; 31:55; II Sam. 19:39—H 19:40).

4. In the Apoc. OT examples of the kiss find parallels in the Apoc. Raguel weeps and speaks a blessing as he greets and kisses Tobit (Tob. 7:6-7); he also kisses and blesses his daughter when they part (10:12). The kissing of another's hand in Ecclus. 29:5 appears to be a beggar's gesture of servility.

5. In the NT. The NT material also largely parallels that of the OT. In the parable in Luke 15:20 the father embraces and kisses his returned son. The Ephesian elders weep and embrace Paul and kiss him as he sets sail (Acts 20:37). Both demonstrations have OT parallels. The homage of the sinful woman who, weeping, anoints and kisses the feet of Jesus (Luke 7:38, 45) is a touching counterpart to Isa. 49:23. The Judas kiss of Luke 22:47-48 is proverbial for betrayal, and it too has its OT equivalent in Joab's treachery to Amasa (II Sam. 20:9).

Several of the Pauline letters conclude: "Greet one another with a holy kiss" (φίλημα ἅγιον) or a "kiss of love" (φίλημα ἀγάπης; Rom. 16:16; I Cor. 16:20; II Cor. 13:12; I Thess. 5:26; I Pet. 5:14; cf. Luke 7:45), a ceremonious greeting comparable to the practice reflected in the OT.

The rabbinic period added the poetic thought that such a one as Moses died with the kiss of God upon his lips (*Midrash Deut. rabbah*, 11). S. H. Blank

KITCHEN [בית המבשלים, house of those who cook] (Ezek. 46:24); KJV PLACE OF THEM THAT BOIL. One of four small oblong subcourts at the corners of the outer court of Ezekiel's ideal temple. They were provided with hearths for boiling such sacrifices as the common people were allowed to eat (Ezek. 46:21-24). The sin, guilt, and cereal offerings were cooked in kitchens within the priests' chambers (vss. 19-20), so that their greater holiness would be protected from contact with unconsecrated persons. *See* Sacrifice and Offerings; Temple, Jerusalem.

L. E. Toombs

KITE [איה, *see* Falcon; דאה (Lev. 11:14; KJV VULTURE); דיה (Deut. 14:13, *though the word is absent from five* Heb. MSS, Samar., *and* LXX, *and* RSV *therefore omits it;* KJV VULTURE), *plural* דיות (Isa. 34:15; KJV VULTURES), *possibly* swift one, *from* דאה, to fly swiftly; *cf.* Ugar. *d'y*, to fly, *and diy(m)*, bird(s), *serving as a parallel to nšr(m)*, eagle(s); LXX γύψ, vulture (Lev. 11:14; *and seemingly also* Deut. 14:13); ἔλαφος, deer (Isa. 34:15); Vulg. *milvus*, kite; Targ. (Onq.) דיתא]. A medium-sized bird of prey, best described as the scavenger of the hawk family (Accipitridae), of the subfamily Milvinae of the genus Milvus. The common red kite (*Milvus milvus milvus*) is found in Palestine, as is the black-winged one (*Elanus caeruleus caeruleus*, of the genus Elanus, of the subfamily Elaninae). It is a reasonable supposition that דאה (*dā'â*) refers to the kites. As the latter eat not only refuse, but also various small birds and mammals, there is nothing improbable in the association of these birds with a deserted human habitation in Isa. 34:15. W. S. McCullough

KITHLISH. KJV form of Chitlish.

KITRON kĭt'rŏn [קטרון] (Judg. 1:30). A town in Zebulun, from which Israel could not expel the Canaanites; probably the same as Kattath. Its location is uncertain, although two sites, Tell Qurdaneh and Tell el-Far, have been suggested.

Bibliography. W. F. Albright, "Contributions to the Historical Geography of Palestine," *AASOR*, 2-3 (1923), 26-29; A. Alt, "Die Reise," *PJB*, 25 (1929), 40-42.

G. W. Van Beek

KITTIM kĭt'ĭm [כתים]; KJV alternately CHITTIM; KJV Apoc. CHETTIIM kĕ tī'əm, CITIMS sĭt'ĭmz. The Hebrew name for Cyprus, used by late writers for Greece and Rome.

Kittim was used at first in the OT for the island of Cyprus. The name itself, as was known to Josephus (Antiq. I.vi.1), derived from the name of the city-state of Kition (Latin Citium, present-day Larnaka) on the SE coast of the island. Kition was the important Phoenician establishment on Cyprus since the ninth-eighth century B.C., and Phoenician inscriptions found there refer to the city as כתי, *Kty*. Although there was still a large autochthonous population, the island was by the eighth century B.C. essentially Greek in population. This is acknowledged by the listing of Kittim as one of the sons of Yawan (Ionia, and by extension Greece), along with Elisha, an older name for Cyprus; Rhodes (Rodanim); and Tarshish (Gen. 10:4; I Chr. 1:7).

For the Israelite, Kittim was a land across the sea and associated with ships, as may be seen from the present state of a difficult line of the "Song of Balaam":

> Ships shall come from Kittim
> and shall afflict Asshur and Eber
> (Num. 24:24).

Cyprus served for a while as a haven for Tyrians and Sidonians fleeing from the Assyrians. However, under Sargon, a statue of whom was found at Kition, Assyrian rule spread to Cyprus. This rule was expanded and maintained under Sennacherib and Esarhaddon. The latter boasted that besides Tyre and Sidon, his control extended from Cyprus as far as Tarshish. The allusions to Kittim (Cyprus) in Isa. 23:1, 12 (vs. 13, too, if כתים is to be read for כשדים of the MT), are to this era, and vs. 12 may refer to the flight from Sennacherib of Luli of Sidon to Cyprus and Luli's death there.

To the Judean, Kittim was a familiar place. Jeremiah used Kedar for the E and the coasts of Kittim (Cyprus) for the W as geographical poles in pointing out the unique disloyalty of his countrymen to God (Jer. 2:10). After the fall of the Assyrian Empire the close ties of Phoenician Cyprus to its mother cities on the mainland remained. In his lamentation over Tyre, Ezekiel lists Kittim (Cyprus) as the source of pine used for the decks of Phoenician ships (Ezek. 27:6).

Since Cyprus was increasingly under Greek influence and maintained strong contact with the Greek mainlands during the period of Persian rule, it is not at all surprising that the name Kittim came to be used generally for areas beyond the seas. The extended use of Kittim may be seen in I Macc. 1:1, where Alexander the Great, identified as a Macedonian, is described as one "who came from the land of

Kittim" (Χεττιιμ). In I Macc. 8:5 Perseus, a Macedonian king, is called "King of the Kittim" (Κιτιέων βασιλέα; RSV "king of the Macedonians"). In a contemporary writer, Daniel, the use of Kittim is further extended and used for the Romans. The author of Dan. 11:30 meant by ובאו בו ציים כתים: "Roman ships shall come against him." As scholars have pointed out, he understood וצים מיד כתים וענו אשור וענו עבר (Num. 24:24) to mean: "Ships shall come forth from Kittim [the Romans] and shall afflict Asshur [the Seleucid Syrians], who in turn shall afflict Eber [the Hebrews]." For him this passage alluded to Rome's compelling Antiochus IV to withdraw completely from Egypt in 168 B.C., and to the subsequent persecution of the Jews by Antiochus. The LXX of Dan. 11:30 was aware of this meaning in translating כתים by Ῥωμαῖοι. There are also references to the Kittim in the Pseudep. The Kittim are mentioned in Jub. 24:28-29; 37:11. Some interpreters have understood these passages to refer to the Hittites, but this is due to the fact that Kittim is, at times, written Χεττιιμ, Χεττειν, etc. (Ezek. 27:6 LXX; I Macc. 1:1; etc.) in Greek and that this, when occurring in an unclear context, may be mistaken for Hittites (and may have been so understood by the translator of Jubilees into Ethiopic). In the Testament of Simeon, the Kittim are listed along with the Canaanites, the Amalekites, and the Philistines (Cappadocians = Caphtorim, as in the LXX) as enemies of the Jews and among those to be destroyed. In these texts the Seleucid Greeks seem to fit the needs of the passages best.

The Kittim are also to be found in the Dead Sea Scrolls. In the Habakkuk Commentary (1QpHab) the Chaldeans (כשדים) of the text are interpreted as the Kittim, spelled here as כתיאים. In this text we learn that the Kittim are swift in battle (2.12-14), come from afar from the isles of the sea, on their horses like an eagle (3.9-11). All fear them, and their plans are evil (3.4-5); they despise the fortresses of the nations, conquer and destroy them (4.5-9). They are merciless and do not pity anyone (6.3-5). They sacrifice to their insignia and weapons (6.3-5). The army of the Kittim will in the end take over the wealth of the last priests of Jerusalem (9.5-6). The description fits the Romans best, and the last two remarks concerning the Kittim make this identification highly probable. The Romans, according to Josephus, sacrificed to their standards. In the War of the Sons of Light and the Sons of Darkness (1QM), the Kittim (spelled here כתיים) are listed among the enemies of the "sons of light." Indeed, the purpose of the war is the disappearance of the Kittim (1.6). The day in which the Kittim will fall will be one of great battle (1.9-12). In the rest of this scroll there are references to a ruler of the Kittim (15.2) and to troops of the Kittim (11.11; 16.2, 5, 7-8; 17.14; 18.2; 19.10). The name gave the author occasion for an etymological pun: והכתיים יכתו, "and the Kittim will be smashed" (18.2), based, undoubtedly, on Jer. 46:5. The Kittim are not limited to a particular area, and some are established in Egypt (1.4 is an allusion to Roman forces in Egypt). A skilful identification of the Kittim with Assyria (כתיי אשור; 1.2) enabled the author to apply anti-Assyrian prophecies to the Kittim (1.6; 11.11; 18.2; 19.10). The identification of the Kittim in these works with the Seleucid Greeks, proposed by many scholars on the basis of the early publication of only a few columns of 1QM, was almost entirely abandoned with the publication of all of 1QM, in which the identification of the Kittim with the Romans is clear. This identification was bolstered by the publication of 4QpNah., where the line "by the hands of the Kings of Greece [יון] from Antiochus until the rise of the rulers of the Kittim [כתיאים]" (1.3) makes identification with the Romans positive. The identification of the Kittim of the Qumran texts with either opposition sectarians or the Seleucid Greeks is not warranted by the texts. The *Pesharim* and 1QM were among the latest texts of the Qumran sect, and for their writers the conquest of Judea by the Romans in 63 B.C. was a historical fact. Later tradition based on the usage which developed during this period referred various OT passages using כתים to the Romans: Num. 24:24 (Targ. Onq.; Vulg.); Ezek. 27:6 (Targ. Jon.; Vulg.); Dan 11:30 (LXX; Targ. Jon.; Vulg.).

Bibliography. R. H. Charles, *The Book of Jubilees* (1902), p. xxxi, section 9; J. A. Montgomery, *Daniel* (1927), pp. 455-56; G. Hill, *A History of Cyprus*, I (1940), 96-97; H. L. Ginsberg, *Studies in Daniel* (1948), p. 78; H. H. Rowley, "The Kittim and the Dead Sea Scrolls," *PEQ* (1956), pp. 92-109; Y. Yadin, *The Scroll of the War of the Sons of Light Against the Sons of Darkness* (Hebrew; 1957), pp. 21-24; F. M. Cross, Jr., *The Ancient Library of Qumran and Modern Biblical Studies* (1958), 92-93; R. North, " 'Kittim' War or 'Sectaries' Liturgy?" *Bibl.*, 39 (1958), 84-93.

J. C. GREENFIELD

KNEAD [לוש]; KNEADING BOWL, KNEADING-TROUGH [משארת]. The process of kneading consisted of mixing flour with water in a kneading-trough containing a small piece of the previous day's batch (cf. Gen. 18:6; I Sam. 28:24; II Sam. 13:8; Jer. 7:18; Hos. 7:4). The dough was then allowed to stand until it fermented. The bowl, or trough, could be made of wood, bronze, or earthenware. During the plagues the frogs invaded even the Egyptian kneading bowls (Exod. 8:3—H 7:28); the Israelites were careful to take their bowls with them when they fled from Egypt (12:34). The kneading-troughs are among the objects of Yahweh's blessing and cursing (Deut. 28:5, 17).

See also BAKING; BREAD § 1*b;* LEAVEN; VESSELS.

J. F. ROSS

KNEEL [ברך; Akkad. *birku;* γονυπετεῖν]; KNEE [ברך, *from* kneel; γόνυ]. The Hebrew word is the same root as that for "blessing," and this suggests that the blessing was received in the kneeling position (*see* BLESSINGS AND CURSES). Weakness in the knees was said to be caused by fear (Job 4:4; Isa. 35:3; Ezek. 7:17; 21:12; Dan. 5:6; Nah. 2:10; Heb. 12:12) or by fasting (Ps. 109:24) or by disease (Deut. 28:35). The knees were considered, as today, the seat of intimate affection, where Samson slept (Judg. 16:19; cf. II Kings 4:20) and where children were dandled (Isa. 66:12). "Upon the knees" is a figure of adoption, whereby a handmaid's child is recognized as a child of her mistress (Gen. 30:3); though the reference may originally have been to birth on the father's knees (cf. Gen. 50:23; Job 3:12). Children were sometimes placed "between the knees"—i.e., as near as possible to the seat of life—for blessing (cf. Gen. 48:12 and the euphemism "under the thigh" in Gen. 24:2, 9; 47:29). "Knee-deep" is a measurement of water in Ezekiel's temple river (Ezek. 47:4). In the NT "knee" occurs in phrases of obeisance and prayer (Mark 15:19 KJV; Luke 5:8; Rom. 11:4; 14:11; Eph. 3:14; Phil. 2:10).

"Kneeling" is expressed by the same verb (II Chr. 6:13; Matt. 17:14; etc.); or by "bow the knee," to drink (Judg. 7:5-6) or to worship and pray (Isa. 45: 23). There are variants such as "set upon the knees" (Dan. 10:10; cf. Luke 22:41; Acts 7:60; 9:40; 20:36; 21:5; etc.). Kneeling is the posture of (*a*) petition: Daniel (Dan. 6:10); the dying Stephen (Acts 7:60); Peter (Acts 9:40); Paul (Acts 20:36; Eph. 3:14); Elijah also prayed with his head between his knees (I Kings 18:42); (*b*) obeisance to a superior (cf. II Kings 1:13; Matt. 17:14; 27:29; Mark 1:40; 10:17; Luke 5:8); (*c*) worship. Like spreading the hands and prostration, kneeling was a posture of worship.

So Solomon (I Kings 8:54=II Chr. 6:13) and worshipers generally (I Kings 19:18; Isa. 45:23) knelt. Most instructive is Ps. 95:6, where kneeling succeeds prostration. Following the entry in 95:2, the prostration in vs. 6 shows that the worshiper has reached his station of worship, and the kneeling suggests that there was something for him to see, so he did not remain prostrate.

Bibliography. H. Bolkestein, "Theophrastos' Charakter der Deisidaimonia," *Religionsgeschichtliche Versuche und Vorarbeiten,* vol. XXI, no. 2 (1929), pp. 21-39; A. Delatte, "Le baiser, l'agenouillement et le prosternement de l'adoration chez les Grecs," *Académie royale de Belgique, Bulletin de la Classe des Lettres et des Sciences morales et politiques,* 5th Series, XXXVII (1951), 423-50. G. Henton Davies

KNIFE [מאכלת, *specific term for the slaughterer's knife* (Gen. 22:6; Judg. 19:29; Prov. 30:4); חרב, *normally* SWORD; שׂכין (Prov. 23:2), *probably* Aram. *loan word;* KJV מחלף (Ezra 1:9; RSV CENSER)]. A small single- or double-edged cutting instrument of flint, copper, bronze, or iron, used mainly for domestic purposes. *See* Weapons and Implements of War.

The knife resembles the dagger or short stabbing sword, but is smaller and more cheaply made, and usually has no ornamentation on blade or pommel. The ambiguity among these implements is reflected in the language of the OT, where the common Hebrew word for "sword" (חרב) is translated once in the RSV (Josh. 5:2) and three times in the KJV (Josh. 5:2; I Kings 18:28; Ezek. 5:1) by the English "knife."

Almost every archaeological expedition in Palestine has produced some knives. The "Canaanite" type of Flint knife, in use from *ca.* 3500 B.C. until replaced by metal, was *ca.* six inches long, with a double edge and a raised central ridge. Joshua was ordered to make flint knives (חרבות צרים) for the circumcision of the Israelites (Josh. 5:2-3). Since at this time the flint knife was not in ordinary domestic use, its employment in circumcision implies an ancient ritual to which an old form of knife was appropriate. The copper knife was used from the patriarchal period to the Early Monarchy. The most common form was a straight blade six to ten inches long, although knives with curved tips have also been found. The handles were sometimes made in one piece with the blade; and sometimes wooden handles, fastened to the blade by a tang or by rivets, were provided. When introduced, iron knives followed the same general pattern as their copper forerunners. The metal blades were cast in limestone molds. One such mold, designed to make a blade sixteen inches long, was found at Tell Beit Mirsim, and reminds one of the large knife used by the Levite for his gruesome task (Judg. 19:29), and by Abraham for the sacrifice of Isaac (Gen. 22:6).

The knife served many purposes in the ancient economy—e.g., pruning trees, killing and skinning animals, and slaughtering sacrifices. The knife might even be used as a razor, for there was apparently little difference in form between the two. Jehoiakim's Penknife (תער; Jer. 36:23) is the same word elsewhere translated "razor." The KJV includes twenty-nine knives among the temple furnishings (Ezra 1:9), but here the RSV reads "censers," following I Esd. 2:13. When comparison with a cutting edge is required, biblical metaphors almost invariably speak of the sword. Only once (Prov. 30:14) is "knife" used in this way, as a metaphor for rapaciousness.

Bibliography. W. F. Petrie, *Tools and Weapons* (1917), pp. 22-28; A. G. Barrois, *Manuel d'Archéologie Biblique,* I (1939), 384. K. Galling, *Biblisches Reallexikon* (1937), p. 378.

L. E. Toombs

KNOP. 1. KJV translation of כפתר (RSV Capital), a detail of the Lampstand in the tabernacle, in Exod. 25:31, 33-36; 37:17, 19-22. The translation "knop" was probably derived from the LXX σφαιρωτήρ (Vulg. *sphaerula*), a knob-shaped ornament.

2. KJV translation of פקעים (RSV Gourd) in I Kings 6:18; 7:24. E. M. Good

***KNOWLEDGE.** The verb "to know" is used in two different ways—viz., in a realistic sense, referring to individual objects with which we are familiar, and in a scientific sense, where knowledge is concerned with the general features or the "essence" of things. The former usage implies a personal relationship between knower and thing known; nevertheless, there is considerable difference between "objective" knowledge, in which the individual is primarily eager to apprehend the "whatness" of the object, and existential" knowledge, in which the individual apprehends the object merely as a factor by which his self-consciousness is affected in a specific way.

Knowledge in the OT is of the realistic and objective type under the two aspects. Failure to differentiate between the OT view of knowledge and scientific knowledge has often resulted in erroneous exegesis.

1. In the OT
   a. Knowledge in general
   b. Knowledge of God
   c. God's knowledge
2. In the intertestamental period
3. In the NT
   a. Common features
   b. John
   c. Paul
   d. Paul and Gnosticism

Bibliography

1. In the OT. ***a. Knowledge in general.*** The noun "knowledge" in the English versions of the OT is the rendering of a number of cognate words, such as דעת, מדע, דעה, and דע, all of which are derived from the verb ידע. The lexicons often render the latter by "to know from experience," which is appropriate in some instances—e.g., to know afflictions (I Kings 8:38), loss of children (Isa. 47:8), disease or grief (Isa. 53:3), or God's vengeance (Ezek. 25:14). However, the fact that ידע can be used to designate sexual intercourse—e.g., on the part of the husband (Gen. 4:1, 17, 25) and on the part of the woman (Num. 31:18, 35; Judg. 21:12)—points to the fact that for the Hebrews, "to know" does not simply mean to be aware of the existence or nature of a particular object. Knowledge implies also the awareness of the specific relationship in which the individual stands with that object, or of the significance the object has for him.

In accordance with the Hebrew view of man, in which the individual is considered as a differentiated totality rather than as a being composed of body and mind, knowledge is an activity in which the whole individual is engaged, not his mind only. The heart, which is sometimes mentioned as the organ of knowledge (see, e.g., Ps. 49:3; Prov. 2:2; 10:8; Isa. 6:10), is not being conceived of as a special noetic faculty, but rather the use of the term explains the fact that this kind of knowledge is always accompanied by an emotional reaction. The relation in which the object stands to the individual causes the latter to rejoice (e.g., Pss. 1:2; 19:7-10; 40:16) or to be grieved, to love it or to hate it (e.g., Pss. 34:8; 119:97, 103-4; Prov. 23:6). On account of the particular character of the object this reaction cannot be limited to mere sentiments. Full comprehension of the object manifests itself in action which corresponds to the relationship apprehended—e.g.:

> The ox knows its owner,
> and the ass its master's crib:
> but Israel does not know
> (Isa. 1:3).

Israel's lack of knowledge is not theoretical ignorance, but rather failure to practice the filial relationship in which they stand with God.

The "tree of the knowledge of good and evil" (Gen. 2:17) is not to provide scientific or theosophic knowledge, or a purely theoretical knowledge of moral values. Rather, as the forbidden tree it will disclose the difference between good and evil to the first couple through their very act of eating the fruit. It is through trespassing God's prohibition that one will "know" what the wrong is like—viz., a quality of one's own self in action.

The OT evinces no interest in the possible limitation of knowledge. There is an awareness of the fact that to know a person is more difficult than to know a thing, because a person must disclose his will in order to be adequately known (e.g., Prov. 25:3: "The mind of kings is unsearchable"). While the fact that man is unable to know the future is taken seriously (e.g., Ps. 39:6), the view is generally held that man is capable of knowing everything required for a meaningful and worth-while life. However, in a view similar to modern pragmatism it is held that the original encounter with the object does not immediately yield full and true knowledge. It is from partial ignorance (e.g., Deut. 11:2) through practical tests that the individual is taught what the true nature and significance of the object is and by what kind of reaction the individual will fully apprehend and comprehend it. That final stage of knowledge is called WISDOM. In order to shorten the way to full knowledge, the individual is advised to seek and heed the teaching of the wise men (e.g., Prov. 1:1-7; 5:1; 13:14; Eccl. 8:1). The fool, in turn, is the man who, instead of following the arduous road to wisdom, is satisfied with the primary impressions.

b. The knowledge of God. In the field of religion, "knowledge" is the principal term used to describe man's right relation to God. In numerous instances, where Christian usage would speak of "faith" and "to believe," the OT employs the phrase "to know God" (e.g., Judg. 2:10; Jer. 10:25; 31:34). The knowledge of God is thought of as originating in the same manner as all other knowledge—namely, by an encounter with God. However, unlike the pagan religions, in which people apprehend various aspects of the nature of the divine from the general features of this world, the OT derives the knowledge of God from those outstanding historical events in which God has evidenced or is showing the interest he takes in the subject (e.g., Exod. 9:29; Lev. 23:43; Deut. 4:32-39; Pss. 9:10; 59:13; 78:16; Hos. 2:19-20).

Since God does not enter into every man's experience directly, knowledge of God is dependent on the witness of those privileged persons to whom he has revealed himself—e.g., Abraham, Moses, Joshua, the judges, David, the prophets (*see* REVELATION). This does not mean, however, that for the majority of the people knowledge of God was confined to the acceptance of the witness of the "men of God." Rather, guided by their message, people are advised "to seek" God (e.g., Deut. 4:29; I Chr. 16:11; 28:9; II Chr. 7:14; Ezra 8:22; Pss. 9:10; 14:2; 119:2; Isa. 9:13; 51:1). This phrase does not denote the search for an unknown entity, but rather an effort of the will to comprehend the significance which God's dealing with his people has for the individual and for the nation, as well as the readiness to live the kind of life which is in accordance with this significance. The reciprocal character of man's knowledge of God comes out in the fact that the believer's life is considered as one in which God teaches man (e.g., Exod. 4:12; 33:13; I Kings 8:36; Pss. 25:4; 27:11; 86:11; 90:12; Isa. 28:9; 54:13; Jer. 31:34) or searches and tests him (e.g., Job, or the Servant of God; cf. also Ps. 139:1-2, 23; Jer. 12:3; 16:21; 17:10)—i.e., one in which by means of the experiences through which he is to pass, a man will become aware concretely of what it means to have a God (Prov. 4; cf. Deut. 8:5: "As a man disciplines his son, the LORD your God disciplines you"). The "FOOL" is therefore particularly the man who refuses to be taught and educated by God (Job 2:10; 30:8; Pss. 14:1; 53:1).

Thus knowledge of God implies a knowledge of oneself as related to God—e.g., as acknowledging one's transgression (Ps. 51:3), realizing the former and present benefits of God (Jer. 9:12*b* LXX; Ezek. 34:27-28), or assuming one's religious obligations (e.g., Isa. 1:3). Thus as grammatical object of "to know" one finds quite frequently "God's ways" or "precepts" instead of "God" (e.g., Pss. 25:4, 12; 119:104; cf. Hos. 6:3). Because knowledge of God is experience of the reality of God, not merely knowledge of propositions concerning God, it frightens man (e.g., Exod. 3:6; Job 27:34), and the fear of God (*see* FEAR) is an essential ingredient in the OT knowledge of God (e.g., Pss. 25:14; 111:10; Prov. 9:10). This fear is not a mere sentiment. It manifests itself in a way of life, in which man respects the majesty and power of God. Only the righteous man (*see* RIGHTEOUSNESS) can therefore be said truly to know God (e.g., Deut. 4:39; Jer. 22:15-16). This feature, more than any other, brings out the wide gulf which separates the Hebraic from the Greek view of knowledge. In the latter, knowledge itself is purely theoretical, and it is left to man's discretion whether or not he will derive rules for conduct from his insight, whereas in the OT the person who does not act in accordance with what God has done or plans to do has but a fragmentary knowledge, which, if not coupled with the fear of God, will eventually result in moral disintegration (e.g., Hos. 4:1).

The God of the OT is a God who wants to be known. While his revelations are limited to a few chosen ones, they are to be taught to all members of the nation (e.g., Deut. 4:9; 5:31; 6:7; Ps. 51:13), and the promise is extended to Israel that eventually all shall know God (Jer. 31:34; cf. Isa. 11:9). However, since the knowledge of God rests upon his self-disclosure, mankind will never be able to know more of God than God deigns to reveal (Prov. 25:2). Thus in a way God remains hidden (Isa. 45:15) and unsearchable (Job 37:5; 42:3; Prov. 25:1).

c. God's knowledge. In view of the personalistic character of the biblical religion, it is not surprising to find knowledge ascribed to God. There is nothing that could be hidden from God (e.g., Ps. 139:1-18). However, this knowledge of God is not, like the later concept of omniscience, a mere awareness of all that is and goes on in this world. God's knowledge is primarily knowledge of people, and like all knowledge, too, implies an interest taken in those whom he knows. Often the phrase designates acts of care, help, and succor (e.g., Job 31:6; Pss. 1:6; 50:11; 73:11; 103:13-14; 144:3; Nah. 1:7)—i.e., treating everyone according to his deserts (e.g., Jer. 17:9-10). This knowledge manifests itself especially in God's mighty deeds and judgments (e.g., Job 36:5). Thus in a special sense those known by God are his chosen ones (Jer. 1:5; Hos. 5:3; Amos 3:2; in the latter two passages the term has the sexual connotation), and in turn those whom God does not know, or knows from afar only (e.g., Ps. 138:6; cf. Matt. 25:12) are those whom God disregards or leaves devoid of support.

2. In the intertestamental period. The Jewish literature of the period between the end of the Exile and the days of Jesus evidences the continuation of the OT view of knowledge. However, since the rabbis are preoccupied with the knowledge of the law, they lose sight of the basic encounter with God, and as a result knowledge of the law of God is understood as the ability so to interpret the Torah that it yields practical juridical rules. In the DEAD SEA SCROLLS and in the Zadokite Document (*see* ZADOKITE FRAGMENTS), however, a new concept of knowledge appears, which is based upon a special illumination which the Spirit of God has imparted to certain individuals. This knowledge serves to apprehend the true sense of the Torah and to be aware of the stage reached by the eschatological process. This type of knowledge comes closest to the prophetic experience in the OT. However, whereas the prophet receives a divine message, the "Teacher of Righteousness" excels his contemporaries by the fact that he possesses a new noetic faculty, by which he is enabled spontaneously to grasp the exact meaning of the Torah.

3. In the NT. ***a. Common features.*** The writers of the NT continue the OT usage, and particularly in the Fourth Gospel knowledge of God and faith are practically synonymous. However, in view of the new level which has been reached in the realization of God's redemptive work, the knowledge of God, too, has been modified. True knowledge expresses itself in action (e.g., Luke 19:44; Acts 2:36; II Pet. 2:20-21; Rev. 2:23), but what matters is in the first place the right attitude, the purity of heart (Matt. 5:8) which engenders the action, not the action itself. Whereas in the OT the knowledge of God was focused upon his past deeds and thus upon his faithfulness, the NT looks primarily toward the goal which the Lord is about to realize and thus concentrates upon God's redemptive purpose. The subject matter of knowledge is often described as God's mystery or the mystery of the kingdom (*see* MYSTERY)—i.e., the disclosure of the fact that God is now entering upon the final act of the redemptive drama (e.g., Mark 4:11 and parallels; Rom. 11:25; 16:25; I Cor. 2:1; 15:51; Eph. 1:9; Col. 1:26-27; Rev. 10:7; cf. II Pet. 3:17). Thus the Christian's knowledge of God carries finality within it.

While in the NT the subject matter of knowledge can be described in OT fashion as that of the way of God (e.g., John 14:4; Acts 13:10; I Cor. 12:31; Heb. 3:10) or the will of the Lord (Col. 1:9), it is not so much the commanding will of God which is thereby designated as, rather, his redemptive purpose and his goal, which is Jesus (e.g., Acts 2:36). The only true knowledge of God is therefore the one which the Son has (Matt. 11:27). Thus the knowledge of God requires a special revelation which comes to man through the life and teachings of Jesus (John 1:14; 14:10). He is, as John describes him, the final "Word" of God. In order to know God, people must therefore listen to him (e.g., Mark 4:3, 9, 24; Eph. 1:13; 3:2; Phil. 4:9; Col. 1:23)—i.e., be willing to heed God's message. However, the communication of the revelation and the attention paid to it do not preclude misunderstandings (e.g., Jas. 1:3), nor does the communication immediately engender full knowledge of God, as is evidenced, e.g., by the disciples' lack of understanding (e.g., Matt. 15:10, 17; 16:9, 11; John 2:22; 6:60; 12:16; 14:20; cf. I John 5:13). The sublimity of the redemptive work of God transcends the natural limits of the human mind. God himself has to work the understanding of his revelation (e.g., Phil. 2:13; II Pet. 1:2; I John 5:20) by imparting his Holy Spirit to those who have accepted his revelation (I Cor. 2:10-12; I John 2:20; 3:24; cf. Luke 19:42, 44). The individual's views and experiences have therefore to be tested by God's word and commandment as evidenced in the work of Christ (e.g., I Cor. 14:37). Failing to teach that God is capable of revealing himself afresh, the scribes have taken away from the people the "key of knowledge" (Luke 11:52). *See* IGNORANCE.

b. John. Among the NT writers, John and Paul have given special thought to the problem of knowledge. John emphasizes particularly the fact that Jesus not only has perfect knowledge of God's purpose and nature (John 3:11; 4:22; 7:28-29; 8:14, 55; 10:15; 12:50; 13:3), because he is anxious not to do anything but the Father's will (5:30), but he also desires through his ministry to disclose the Father to all men (e.g., 14:1-17; 17:1-6). Though from the beginning mankind was offered an opportunity to know God (1:9), man's actual or "natural" knowledge of the divine revelation is useless and misleading, because of his sin (John 1:10; 8:54-55; I John 3:6). Even the Jews' knowledge of God remains, therefore, sheer ignorance, unless it leads to a love of Jesus in which his saving function is recognized (John 14:28; I John 3:16; 4:17). The first step of true knowledge consists in receiving Jesus' message; on this road his followers will be led to the full TRUTH (John 8:31-32).

However, this message consists in actions, which are signs, *semeia* (*see* SIGNS IN THE NT)—i.e., events in which the outward circumstances point toward the divine will of Christ embodied in them. Those only who are willing to believe that in his actions Jesus is doing the will of the Father, receive the LIGHT which enables them to discern the Son of God in his hiddenness. In Jesus one sees eventually God (John 14:17). Thus knowledge, which has reached this level, is not a mere acceptance of God's revelation, but rather an ontic relationship with God has been established therein. In turn, one has eternal LIFE in such knowledge (17:3). The believer is therefore certain that God, or Christ, abides in him (I John 3:24; cf. John 14:17) and transforms him into his likeness (I John 3:2; 4:2). The proof that one has attained to this knowledge is found in the assurance that Jesus came from God (John 16:30; 17:8), in readiness to follow his example (John 7:17; I John 2:3-5, 29), and consequently in the public profession of faith—i.e., the willingness to suffer for Christ's sake (e.g., John 7:12; I John 4:2; cf. 2:3; 3:24). Because Christ is present in the church through his Spirit, its message has the same effects as that of Jesus (I John 4:6). Even without personally seeing the works of Christ, one is able to believe by accepting the eyewitnesses' testimony (John 20:29-31).

The knowledge brought by Jesus is contrasted with that of the rabbis (John 7:28; 8:19; 9:24, 29), who from the knowledge of the commandments formed both their image of God and the aim of life. Jesus reminds his disciples that in him they know the goal and thus the way. What they ought to do is not told them in advance; they will learn it as they love Jesus and the Father who sent him (e.g., John 14:4-12; I John 5:2).

Certain writers have defined John's view of knowledge as belonging to Hellenistic mysticism. While John shares with Hellenism the individualistic concept of knowledge, he has this in common with Pharisaism. Thus no special outward influence needs to be postulated. Furthermore, even though John uses freely the terminology and thought-patterns of Hellenistic mysticism, he does so in order to present in an apologetic way what is a typically Hebraic concept of knowledge. He wants to show his contemporaries how their epistemology has to be modified to make sense religiously.

According to John, knowledge does not lead to a gradual merger of the knower's mind with that of God, but rather to a harmony of their wills in which God remains distinctly the authority to be recognized. Furthermore, the subject matter of true knowledge is shown to be, not God's eternal nature, but rather the divine love which at a very definite moment has entered into our lives (e.g., John 16:30: "now we know"; cf. 17:7)—i.e., God's dealing with us. The truth which liberates (8:32)—a typically Stoic expression—does not so much make a person indifferent toward social conditions as free from the fetters of unbelief and sin.

While John shares with Hellenistic epistemology the clear distinction of levels of knowledge, the development from the original apperception of the message to the union of the wills is not so much the result of the individual's efforts or of his possessing a special faculty of "higher" knowledge as of the intrinsic challenge of the message, or of it being the light or the truth.

Even the concept of the Logos, which seems to be so conspicuously Hellenistic, is understood as the Hebrew *dabar* (*see* WORD). Far from being the basis of a rational world, it interprets the universe as a divine communication destined to lead people to personal fellowship with God (I John 1:1-3). By means of the "Word" speaking within themselves, people are enabled to become aware of their relation to God and to make this relatedness articulate in acts of obedience to, and love of, God.

c. Paul. A somewhat different picture is offered in Paul's letters. Whereas for John it is the earthly ministry of Jesus, which through its signs (σημεῖα) forms the basis of the knowledge of God, for Paul it is primarily the experience of the risen Lord's operation in the life of his church (*see* CHURCH, LIFE AND ORGANIZATION OF). Thereby knowledge assumes a personal character, by means of which it is essentially differentiated from the knowledge of Gnosticism.

The Christian knowledge transcends all other knowledge, including that of the OT, by the fact that in Jesus Christ for the first time in the history of mankind the glory of God has been manifested in a human life (II Cor. 4:6). Hence there can be no true knowledge of God except in his manifestation in Christ (e.g., Gal. 4:9; Col. 2:2-3). Paul's view differs from John's in that John finds the divine manifestation in specific actions of Jesus, whereas Paul focuses his attention upon the moral and spiritual character of Jesus. In him the goal of God's "mystery"—i.e., of his saving purpose—becomes visible (I Cor. 2:7; Eph. 1:2-4; Col. 1:9; 3:23-24), and thus he determines our moral obligations (e.g., Eph. 5:5; Col. 3:16). Christ offers also the clue to all God's works in the universe (Col. 2:2-3; cf. I Cor. 1:24). Furthermore, since Christ fulfils a divine mission, knowledge of him implies awareness of the future eschatological events as well (Phil. 3:10-11; I Thess. 4:13-18; cf. I Cor. 15:35-57). Above all, however, knowledge of Christ is the realization of his saving significance (I Cor. 2:12-13; Phil. 1:9-10; Philem. 6). Thus he is the supreme value, and our whole scale of values has to be reappraised and orientated toward this fact (Phil. 3:8).

Though all men are capable of knowing God, the knowledge of Christ is given to those only in whom the HOLY SPIRIT operates (e.g., I Cor. 2:12-13; Eph. 3:4-5; Phil. 3:8). It is through the Holy Spirit that the believers are enabled to apprehend the manifestation of God in the earthly life of the man Jesus (I Cor. 2:10-13). This spiritual comprehension of God's revelation Paul contrasts with a religious knowledge κατὰ σάρκα—i.e., of a purely earthly character (I Cor. 3:1-3; II Cor. 5:16; cf. I Thess. 5:12)—in which God's work is related to innerworldly goals only. Such were, e.g., the Jewish eschatological and messianic expectations. Truly spiritual knowledge originates in the hearing of the message in which God's revelation in Christ is proclaimed (Rom. 10:17; I Cor. 8:1; Col. 1:6; I Thess. 4:9). Faithful acceptance of the "word of Christ" (Rom. 10:17; Eph. 1:13) or the "gospel" (e.g., Rom. 1:15; 10:16; I Cor. 1:17; II Cor. 4:3; Eph. 3:6; Col. 1:5) leads to spiritual experience, both of its reality and of its implications (Rom. 15:14; I Cor. 1:5; II Cor. 8:9; Gal. 2:9; Eph. 1:18). However, Paul points out that even the richest spiritual knowledge remains fragmentary here on earth (e.g., Rom. 11:34; I Cor. 13:12-13), both because of the limited range of our experience and because the Spirit of Christ has to operate upon an earthly mind. Progress in spiritual knowledge can, nevertheless, be accomplished by means of mental discipline and willingness to listen to God (I Cor. 1: 24-27).

Since spiritual knowledge is dependent upon verbal communications (e.g., Rom. 10:14; Eph. 4:21; cf. I Cor. 15:1), it can easily be mistaken for theological verity—i.e., propositions which are accepted on account of their intrinsic consistency (e.g., Rom. 3:19; 7:1; I Cor. 3:16; 5:6; 6:15; 8:4; Eph. 5:5). However, from the very beginning, spiritual knowledge points to its ontological basis—viz., the relation in which the believer stands to or "in" Christ (Eph. 1:18-19; Phil. 3:8-18)—and it is intended to lead to experience, e.g., of the crucifixion of our "old self" (Rom. 6:6), of Christ's love (Eph. 3:19), or of the power of his resurrection (Phil. 3:10) and the spiritual world in general (Phil. 3:8; Col. 2:2-3). Such progress of knowledge is the fruit, not of reasoning, but rather of a deepened insight of the heart (Eph. 1:17; cf. 3:19)—i.e., of intensive listening to the Holy Spirit, who together with the message comes to the audience as the intrinsic "intention" of the message. The level of spiritual knowledge is not due to one's possessing larger or smaller portions of the Spirit, because the Spirit is a person rather than an energy (e.g., I Cor. 12:11; I Thess. 4:8; cf. John 8:34), but to man's willingness to follow his promptings (e.g., I Thess. 5:19). It is this experience of the Spirit's reality in one's own life which in turn moves the believer to actions (Rom. 2:18; 6:22; I Cor. 3:16; 6:13-16; Gal. 5:22; Eph. 5:9; Col. 1:6) such as would not follow from speculative views.

Paul insists that God is a God who wants to be known (Rom. 16:25). His purpose in granting this kind of spiritual knowledge is to let man be formed into the likeness of Christ (Gal. 4:19; Col. 3:10; cf. Rom. 2:20; 8:28) and in this "metamorphosis" (Rom. 8:29; 12:2; Phil. 3:21) to have full knowledge (I Cor. 2:12; *see* IMAGE). By imparting such knowledge to man, God indicates that he takes man seriously and that he will arrange all things for our good (Rom. 8:26). In turn, this formative function of knowledge effects the kind of conduct in which the believer's relation to Christ becomes articulate (Rom. 6:17: "form of instruction"; II Tim. 1:13: "form of sound words"; cf. Rom. 2:20: "form of knowledge"). In all these instances, "form" is not a legal "standard" (so RSV) but rather a formative principle realizing itself from within the individual.

Developments in the church of Corinth made Paul aware of the fact that the experiential character of spiritual knowledge brings it into proximity to enthusiastic and ecstatic experiences which have nothing to do with faith (I Cor. 12–14). He was therefore anxious to indicate criteria by which genuine spiritual knowledge could be tested. First of all, it must be in agreement with the Lord, or the revelation of our Lord (e.g., Rom. 14:14; I Cor. 1:7; 4:4; 7:10; 9:1, 14; 10:9)—i.e., with the life and sayings of Jesus. He is the reliable and unshakable foundation of all knowledge (I Cor. 3:11). Secondly, there is the witness of the OT (e.g., I Cor. 1:11; 10:1-13; 14:37; 15:3-4; II Cor. 1:18), which is closely related to the Lord, because he is the Amen—i.e., the fulfilment of its promises (II Cor. 1:19-20). Thirdly, there is the agreement with God's manifestations in the universe (e.g., Rom. 1:21). Finally, there is the witness of the Spirit in our own experience, which is characterized by the fact that it confirms our deepest aspirations while at the same time overcoming our reluctance to follow them (e.g., Rom. 8:16, 26). The individual's willingness to accept all these tests is proof of his having a genuine spiritual knowledge.

A further test is the collective character of spiritual knowledge. It has entered into history through the witness and proclamation of the apostles (*see* APOSTLE), who were the ones to see the heavenly glory of the risen Lord (I Cor. 15:5-9) and who were commissioned to propagate the gospel (e.g., Rom. 15:14; I Cor. 9:1; 12:28; II Cor. 12:11; Gal. 1:1; Eph. 3:8, 10). The nucleus of spiritual knowledge is formed by the tradition (παράδοσις; *see* TRADITION, ORAL) of the church (Rom. 6:17; I Cor. 11:2, 23; 15:1, 3; Gal. 1:9, 12; Phil. 4:9; I Thess. 2:13; 4:1; II Thess. 2:15; 3:6). There is also a special spiritual gift of knowledge (γνῶσις; I Cor. 12:8; 13:2, 8; 14:6; II Cor. 6:6; 11:6) by which certain members of the church are enabled more distinctly than others to discern the implications and applications of its message. The test of the genuineness of such a charisma is to be found in genuine humility and love (e.g., I Cor. 8:1-2), which, far from boasting of such knowledge (Col. 1: 28; cf. I Cor. 1:29, 31), is anxious to let the other members of the church share in it (I Cor. 14:26).

Like the OT writers, Paul, too, in some passages uses the phrase "being known by God" (I Cor. 8:3; 13:12; Gal. 4:9). God knows the best way to the goal he has set himself, and thus manifests himself in actions which both disclose the futility of unenlightened wisdom (I Cor. 1:20; 3:20) and refute it effectively (I Cor. 1:25). God's "knowledge" is therefore not to be identified with his omniscience; rather, the term designates those special events in which the truth or the falsehood of people's attitude toward God is brought to the light. Thus whatever takes place in the redemption of mankind presupposes that it has been known beforehand by God (Rom. 8:29; 11:2; cf. I Pet. 1:20). This indicates that in all his works God acts with a purpose and thus uses those best fit for the specific end contemplated. This foreknowledge manifests itself in the election of his chosen people (Rom. 11:2) or of individual believers (Rom. 8:3, 29; 13:12; Gal. 4:29; II Tim. 2:19). As a manifesting activity the divine knowledge is seen in a man's love of God (I Cor. 8:3) as well as in his knowledge of God (I Cor. 8:3; 13:12; Gal. 4:9).

Consequently, the Christian knowledge of God is not the result of speculative insight, but rather is based upon the experience of being used by God for his saving work. Thus the egotistic tendency implied in man's desire for salvation is overcome in such knowledge by the awareness of God's redemptive action in and upon the individual. The believer knows from inner experience that he is Christ's, not his own (e.g., Rom. 14:7-8; I Cor. 3:21-23; II Cor. 10:7; Gal. 3:29). While substantially the believer's knowledge of God is his awareness of being known by God, man's knowledge here on earth never equals the divine knowledge, because of the fundamental difference between God's Spirit and the human mind. God's knowledge requires no mediation. He knows all things directly in himself (I Cor. 2:10-12). Far from ever erring in his ways, he arranges everything exactly in accordance with the nature of the people as well as with his ultimate goal (Rom. 11:33; I Cor. 1:20-21). Conversely, our knowledge remains fragmentary, because in this life we apprehend God only indirectly, as through a mirror, in our experience of our being known by him (I Cor. 13:12). Thus our "good works" are but symbols of our faith and not good in themselves. The reason for the limited character of man's knowledge of God is not found, as in the OT, in the limitations of man's wisdom, but rather in the mode of the givenness of God, and thus there is hope that though a creature, man will know God face to face—i.e., as he is—in the life to come. But since it is God in Christ who is apprehended in Christian knowledge, there is divine truth even in its provisional, earthly stage, and consequently the believer's actions and words bear adequate and effective witness to God's saving work (e.g., I Cor. 1:6-7, 25; 2:6; 3:1-3; 4:1-5; II Cor. 2:14-16; 3:5).

The believer's knowledge of God is radically contrasted by Paul with man's natural wisdom. God's will is known to all men as it manifests itself in the voice of conscience (Rom. 2:14-16). Yet the natural religious knowledge of the Gentiles is a perverted one, because on account of their sinfulness they interpret the data in the wrong way (Rom. 1:18). They transmute the transcendence of God into immanence (Rom. 1:23), and instead of relating their insights to God's ultimate goal, they interpret God as serving human ends (II Cor. 4:4). The wrongness of their religious knowledge can be seen most clearly in their lack of true reverence for the transcendence of God, their lack of gratitude for all that we possess, and their unwillingness to dedicate their lives to his service (e.g., Rom. 1:21-25). Thus no matter how bright and keen their intellect may be, their wisdom is futile (Rom. 1:21; Eph. 4:17), foolish (I Cor. 3:19), and blind (II Cor. 4:4; cf. I Cor. 1:20-21), and their moral standards serve to justify immoral practices (Rom. 1:28-32). Paul does not teach that man's reason is worthless, nor does he hold that the believer is privileged by having a special cognitive faculty for religion, but rather he contends that apart from faith all human knowledge operates in a wrong frame of reference. Man is never fully devoid of a knowledge of God, but the original datum is falsified as a result of his arbitrary arguments and speculations (II Cor. 10:5). Failing to see the consistency of God's operations, he sees the gospel as an absurdity (I Cor. 1:23). Since the unconverted man's thinking moves in a vicious circle, the cogency of logical arguments will not convince him; only God's Spirit is able to lead him to an acceptance of the truth (I Cor. 2:10-13; Eph. 1:17).

d. Paul and Gnosticism. A word should finally be said about Paul's relation to GNOSTICISM. While our survey has shown that Paul's mentality and concept of knowledge represents substantially the dynamic realism of the Hebraic type, it is certain that formally the Apostle, more than any other NT writer, shows the influence of Hellenistic thought. Quite apart from the fact that Paul employs terms and stylistic patterns of popular Hellenistic philosophy, the influence is most obvious in his insistence upon "systematic" thought. He wants to show how Christ is related to everything in the universe. He is not satisfied, e.g., with proclaiming the lordship of Christ, but is anxious also to show the exact place Christ occupies in relation to all other cosmic powers (e.g., Col. 1:15-20; cf. I Cor. 8:4-6). Similarly he discusses, e.g., man's place in the universe (e.g., Rom. 8:18-25), the place of Christian faith among the world's religions (Rom. 1–3), the diversity and the relative value of the various gifts of the Spirit (I Cor. 12–14), or the order of the final eschatological events (I Cor. 15:22-28). This is a procedure which has no parallel in other biblical writers. However, it is not truly Hellenistic, either. For Paul presents a comprehensive view of the concrete facts, whereas Hellenistic philosophy aims at a logical classification of the essences underlying the concrete facts.

However, when all is said about Hellenistic influences upon Paul's mind, we are still worlds apart from Gnosticism. While it is true that Paul has used oriental materials which have also been incorporated into the Gnostic systems, his thinking not only is not Gnostic but is opposed to it. For Gnostic mentality it is characteristic to believe that by an intellectual knowledge of the arrangement of the universe the initiate will be able to map out his own way of salvation. Paul, on the contrary, will say that the better we get to know Christ, the more deliberately we shall cling to him as our only salvation (Phil. 3:8). The knowledge itself is not valuable; separated from its object, it puffs up (I Cor. 8:1). Christians are enriched by the knowledge of Christ (e.g., I Cor. 1:5; Eph. 1:17; cf. Rom. 11:33), because thereby they are enabled in all spheres of existence to be "in Christ."

Furthermore, whereas the Gnostic knowledge is a faculty with practically unlimited applicability, Paul points out that Christ is the limit of all knowledge (Col. 2:3) and that he confounds our aberrations. Beyond what God has done in him, there is nothing that man is capable of knowing concerning salvation. Thereby not only a supreme value but also an ultimate goal has been introduced into the system of knowledge (e.g., Phil. 2:10-11; Col. 1:16). Teleology is completely absent from the Gnostic systems; they are built upon the principle of static values. Finally, while the Gnostic systems share with Paul the search for comprehensiveness, they do not, like Paul, start with the experience of a redeemer (e.g., Gal. 1:16, where, however contrary to the RSV, we should read "to reveal his son *in* me"; cf. 1:12; I Cor. 2:10). Rather, by means of an ontological analysis of the universe they finally attain to a supreme reality, out of which, in turn, the order and the "mechanics" of being are interpreted. As a result, in lieu of the basic conflict between sin and salvation, which is implied in Paul's original experience and which dominates his whole thinking, we find in Gnosticism merely gradual differences of being.

It is true that Paul, too, knows a special charisma of knowledge (*gnosis*) transcending the general knowledge that is given to all the believers through the Holy Spirit (e.g., I Cor. 8:1; 14:6). But whatever he may have meant thereby, it cannot be the esoteric knowledge of Gnosticism, given the fact that he fights so fiercely against false knowledge and philosophy (I Cor. 1:17, 20-25; Col. 2:8, 23), contrasting them with the "foolishness of the cross" (I Cor. 1:18, 23). The argument in I Cor. 8 suggests that this special knowledge is the ability to discern the comprehensive function of Christ in the universe (cf. also II Cor. 2:11). Unlike esoteric Gnostic knowledge, the "secret and hidden wisdom of God" (I Cor. 2:7) is therefore not to be kept secret, except for a few initiates, but rather to be proclaimed to all men (Rom. 1:14); cf. also the recurrent phrase "I do not want you to be ignorant" (e.g., Rom. 1:13; 11:25; I Cor. 10:1; 12:1; I Thess. 4:13) referring to spiritual mysteries. Finally, it would never have come to a Gnostic's mind to interpret lack of knowledge of the mysteries as the work of the Devil (II Cor. 4:4), but rather as a result of man's natural inability.

Bibliography. On the biblical view in general: E. La B. Cherbonnier, "Biblical Metaphysics and Christian Philosophy," *Theology Today,* IX (1952), 360-75; H. M. Feret, *Connaissance biblique de Dieu* (1955).

On the OT in general: E. Baumann, "ידע und seine Derivate. Eine sprachlich-exegetische Studie," *ZAW,* XXVIII (1908), 22-41, 110-43; W. Reiss, "Gott nicht kennen im Alten Testament," *ZAW,* XVII (1940-41), 70-98; J. Coppens, "La connaissance du Bien et du Mal et le Péché du Paradis," *Analecta Louvaniensia Biblica et Orientalia,* 2nd Series, Fasc. 3 (1948); G. J. Botterweck, "Gott erkennen," *Sprachgebrauch des Alten Testaments* (1951); T. Boman, *Das hebräische Denken im Vergleich mit dem griechischen* (2nd ed., 1952); C. Tresmontant, *Essai sur la pensée hébraïque* (1953); I. Engnell, " 'Knowledge' and 'Life' in the Creation Story," in M. Noth, ed., *Wisdom in Israel* (Supplement to *VT;* 1955).

On individual writers of the OT: S. Mowinckel, *Die Erkenntnis Gottes bei den alttestamentlichen Propheten* (1941); W. Zimmerli, *Erkenntnis Gottes nach Ezechiel, Abh. z. Th. ANT* (1954).

On the NT in general: P. Thomson, " 'Know' in the NT," *Exp.,* 9th Series, III (1925), 379-82; R. M. Pope, "Faith and Knowledge in Pauline and Johannine Thought," *ET,* XXXI (1929/30), 421-27; H. Schlier, "Über die Erkenntnis Gottes bei den Heiden," *Evangelische Theologie* (1935), pp. 9-26; F. C. Grant, *An Introduction to NT Thought* (1950), pp. 43-62; H. Schlier, "Kerygma und Sophia. Zur neutestamentlichen Grundlegung des Dogmas," *Evangelische Theologie,* X (1950), 481-507.

On individual writers of the NT: M. E. Lyman, *Knowledge of God in Johannine Thought* (1925); J. Huby, "De la connaissance de foi dans S. Jean," *RSR,* XXI (1931), 385-421; E. Prucker, *Gnosis Theou. Untersuchungen zur Bedeutung eines religiösen Begriffes beim Apostel Paulus und seiner Umwelt* (Cassiciacum IV; 1937); L. Cerfaux, " 'L'aveuglement de l'esprit' dans l'Évangile de saint Marc," *Museon,* LIX (1946), 267-79; M.-E. Boismard, "La connaissance de Dieu dans l'Alliance nouvelle d'après la première lettre de saint Jean," *RB,* LVI (1949), 365-91; J. Dupont, *Gnosis, La connaissance religieuse dans les épîtres de saint Paul* (1949); C. H. Dodd, *The Interpretation of the Fourth Gospel* (1953), pp. 151-69; W. Stählin, *Das johanneische Denken* (1954).

On Gnosticism: R. Reitzenstein, *Poimandres* (1904); W. Bousset, *Hauptprobleme der Gnosis* (1907); R. Bultmann, *Der Stil der Paulinischen Predigt und die kynisch-stoische Diatribe,* FRLANT, XIII (1910); A. Norden, *Agnostos Theos* (1913); A. Fridrichsen, "Gnosis," *Festschrift E. Lehman* (1927), pp. 85-109; R. Reitzenstein, *Die hellenistischen Mysterienreligionen nach ihren Grundgedanken und Wirkungen* (3rd ed., 1927); R. P. Casey, "Gnosis, Gnosticism and the NT," *The Background of the NT and Its Eschatology: Studies in Honor of C. H. Dodd* (1956).

O. A. PIPER

KOA kō'ə [קוע] (Ezek. 23:23). A gentilic mentioned in the sequence Babylonians, Chaldeans, Pekod, Shoa, and Koa. Since the Pekod clearly correspond to the Paqudai, living in S Babylonia, it has usually been suggested that Shoa refers to the Sūtu people and Koa correspondingly to the Guti, but it seems more likely to consider "Shoa" and "Koa" a rhyming locution, like "Krethi" and "Plethi," "Gog" and "Magog."

A. L. OPPENHEIM

KOHATH kō'hăth [קהת; LXX Κααθ]; **KOHATHITE** —hă thīt. Second son of LEVI (Gen. 46:11; Exod. 6:16; Num. 3:17; I Chr. 6:1—H 5:27; 6:16—H 6:1; 6:38—H 6:23; 23:6). He was the father of Amram, Izhar, Hebron, and Uzziel (Exod. 6:18; Num. 3:19; I Chr. 6:2—H 5:28; 6:18—H 6:3; 23:12), who became heads of Kohathite branches (Num. 3:27), and he died at the age of 133 (Exod. 6:18). Since Kohath was the grandfather of Aaron, Moses, and Miriam (Exod. 6:20; Num. 26:59; *see* AMRAM), the Kohathites (usually משפחת הקהתי or בני קהת, but twice בני הקהתים [II Chr. 20:19; 34:12], once בני הקהתי [Num. 4:34], and once just הקהתים [10:21]) were the most important of the Levitical families.

All information about Kohath as a person and the Kohathite families descended from him comes through either the priestly writer (*see* PENTATEUCH § A) or the Chronicler (*see* CHRONICLES, I AND II) and falls into the periods of the Exodus, the Conquest, the Monarchy, and the Restoration.

1. Exodus. When the TABERNACLE was constructed in the wilderness, the three chief Levitical families—Gershonites, Kohathites, and Merarites—were stationed around it and charged with its care and transit. Divided into four major families, the Kohathites numbered 8,600 males from one month upward (Num. 3:28) and 2,750 from thirty years old up to fifty, all who could "enter the service, to do the work in the tent of meeting" (4:1-3, 34-37). Their station was on the S side of the tabernacle; and their "charge" (משמרת) was the ark, table, lampstand, altars, sacred vessels, and screen (3:29-31). But the Kohathites were not to touch these "holy things" (הקדש)—or, at 4:4, "most holy things" (קדש הקדשים)—lest they die. Whenever the camp was moved, Aaron and his sons would cover the holy things and fit them with poles, by which the Kohathites could then carry them upon their shoulders (4:4-15, 17-20; 7:9; cf. 10:21).

2. Conquest. At the occupation of Palestine the Kohathites who were descendants of Aaron received by lot thirteen cities, with their pasture lands, from the tribes of Judah, Simeon, and Benjamin (Josh. 21:4, 9-19; I Chr. 6:54-60—H 6:39-45). The remaining Kohathite families received ten cities, including Shechem as a "city of refuge," from the tribes of Ephraim and Dan and the half-tribe of Manasseh (Josh. 21:5, 20-26; I Chr. 6:61, 66-70—H 6:46, 51-55). The Kohathite families possessed, therefore, significant territory in the hill country of S (Judah) and central (Ephraim) Palestine.

3. Monarchy. When David "prepared a place for the ark of God, and pitched a tent for it," he gathered 120 Kohathites, under Uriel as chief (I Chr. 15:5), to bring the ark up into Jerusalem. Then Heman was appointed to represent them in the "service of song in the house of the LORD" (6:33—H 6:19).

When JEHOSHAPHAT sought the Lord for the deliverance of Israel from Moab and Ammon, Levites of the Kohathite line functioned as sacred ministers (II Chr. 20:19).

In 725 B.C., when Hezekiah called upon the Levites to purify Judah's cultic practices, Mahath and Joel represented the Kohathites (II Chr. 29:12).

Similarly, when Josiah undertook to repair the temple in 621 B.C., the Kohathites Zechariah and Meshullam were among the supervising Levites (II Chr. 34:12). *See* JOSIAH.

4. Restoration. Upon the return from exile in Babylon, when ministers were appointed their tasks in the temple, some of the Kohathites "had charge of the showbread, to prepare it every Sabbath" (I Chr. 9:32). L. HICKS

KOHELETH. Hebrew title of ECCLESIASTES.

KOLA kō'lə [Χωλά, *also* Κωλα, Κειλα; *omitted in* Vulg.]; KJV COLA. A locality mentioned in Jth. 15:4. Possibly identical with HOLON in Josh. 15:51.

KOLAIAH kō lā'yə [קוליה, voice of Yahu]. **1.** Ancestor of some Benjaminites living in Jerusalem after the Exile (Neh. 11:7).

2. The father of the false prophet Ahab (Jer. 29:21).

KONA kō'nə [Κώνα *or* Κείλα]; KJV THE VILLAGES. A locality mentioned in Jth. 4:4; the location is unknown. Codex A and a later corrector of א understood κώμαι, "villages." P. WINTER

KOPH kōf [ק, *q* (*Qôph*)]. The nineteenth letter of the Hebrew ALPHABET as it is placed in the KJV at the head of the nineteenth section of the acrostic psalm, Ps. 119, where each verse of this section of the psalm begins with this letter.

KORAH kôr'ə [קרח, bald; Κορέ]; KORAHITES —īts [הקרחי, הקרחים, בני הקרחים]; SONS OF KORAH [בני קרח] (Exod. 6:24); KJV alternately: CORE kôr'ĭ (Jude 11); KORATHITES kôr'ə thīts (Num. 26:58); KORHITES kôr'hīts (Exod. 6:24; I Chr. 12:6; 26:1; II Chr. 20:19); SONS OF KORE kôr'ĭ (I Chr. 26:19).

1. A son of ESAU (Gen. 36:5, 14; I Chr. 1:35); chief of a clan of EDOM (Gen. 36:18).

2. A grandson of ESAU; son of ELIPHAZ; chief of a clan of EDOM (Gen. 36:16 [not listed in vss. 11-12; I Chr. 1:36]).

3. A leader of rebellion in the wilderness. The narrative in Num. 16 interweaves three revolts: a JE story of a revolt by laymen led by DATHAN and ABIRAM against the civil authority claimed by Moses (vss. 1*b*-2*a*, 12-15, 25-26, 27*b*-32*a*, 33-34), a P story of a revolt led by Korah (vss. 1*a*α, 2*b*-7*a*, 18-24, 35, 41-50); a later revision of Korah's revolt by a P redactor (vss. 1*a*β, 7*b*-11, 16-17, 35, 36-40). The first two stories originally were told independently of each other and subsequently were combined; the third worked over the material according to P perspectives existing in a time later than the first P writer. The two P versions are to be understood in the context of the struggles which occurred over religious leadership. In P, Korah led 250 leaders of the people in protesting against the Levites (represented by Moses and Aaron) as the only ones to discharge religious offices, since "all the congregation are holy, every one of them, and the LORD is among them" (vss. 1*a*α, 3). Moses invited Korah and those with him to a trial by ordeal: the next day they were to bring fire pans with incense, and Yahweh would choose who was holy and thus could come near Yahweh and perform religious offices (vss. 5-7*a*). The following day the glory of Yahweh appeared, and Yahweh ordered Moses and Aaron to separate themselves from the congregation, to escape the destruction about to come (vss. 18-24). Fire came from Yahweh and consumed the rebels (vs. 35). The next day the people spoke for Korah and his associates and protested the action of Moses and Aaron. The congregation assembled at the tent of meeting; the glory of Yahweh appeared again; Yahweh proposed instant destruction of the people; Moses and Aaron interceded; and Aaron, with his censer filled with incense and fire from the altar, stopped the plague (vss. 41-50). In this story Korah and the others protesting were non-Levites (cf. 27:3, where a Manassite has to make clear that he was not a follower of Korah). The issue was the prerogatives of the Levites in religious affairs. The story was an assertion of Levitical pre-eminence, and bears witness to the downfall of other groups. In the redactional material by a later P reviser, the struggle was within the tribe of Levi. Korah was a Levite (vs. 1*a*β) and led other Levites in a protest against the monopoly of the priesthood by Aaron, a protest which asserted the claim of all Levites to the priesthood (vss. 7*b*-11). The trial by ordeal (vss. 16-17) and the destruction by fire (vs. 35) were repeated from P. The censers of Korah and his company were hammered into a covering for the altar, as a warning that none but priests should come near to the altar of Yahweh (vss. 36-40). This later P redaction may indicate that at some time the Levites, who previously had had a higher status, were assigned a lower position relative to the priesthood (*see* PRIESTS AND LEVITES). The P story and the P redaction suggest that developments in the leadership of the cult occurred with considerable inner opposition. They further suggest that there was a time when Korah and those descended from him were important. The further identity of Korah in the P story is uncertain; in the P redaction Korah is identified as the son of IZHAR. *See* § 4 *below.*

4. A Levite, a descendant of IZHAR, of the family of KOHATH (Exod. 6:21; I Chr. 6:22, 37). The attempt to correlate passages where Korah and the Korahites appear encounters gaps and variations in the method of treatment. The Korahites were one of four or five families of Levite-priests located around HEBRON sometime between Deborah and David; the LXX lists them third and the MT fifth (Num. 26: 58*a*, an ancient genealogy, possibly redacted by addition of "Mahlites" and rearrangement). ASSIR; ELKANAH; and ABIASAPH are listed as the families of the Korahites in Exod. 6:24; these and other names are aligned vertically in the genealogical lists in I Chr. 6:22-23, 37. This Korah may be the figure of that name in the P redaction in Num. 16 (*see* § 3 *above;* Num. 26:11 states that "the sons of Korah did not die"). At some time the "sons of Korah" and ASAPH were the two great guilds of temple singers: the superscriptions of some Psalms indicate that they may have been taken from the hymnbook of the Korahite choir (Pss. 42; 44–49; 84–85; 87–88). The Korahites are named alongside the Kohathites as singers in II Chr. 20:19. In late arrangement the three guilds of temple singers were HEMAN; ASAPH; ETHAN (I Chr. 6:33-48, revised material reflecting late postexilic times)—Heman has replaced Korah. The Korahites were gatekeepers (I Chr. 9:19; 26:1, 19), and bakers of sacrificial cakes (9:31).

5. A son of HEBRON in a Calebite genealogy (I Chr. 2:43; *see* CALEB); possibly a geographical name: perhaps a town in Judah somewhere in the neighborhood of Hebron. In the latter case the five Korahites among those who joined David at ZIKLAG (12:6) may have been persons from this town. If they were Benjaminites, as stated in vs. 2, they may have been from another town of this name (site unknown). More probably I Chr. 12 is largely fictional exaggeration: it is unsupported by I Sam. 27, and it is unlikely that more than a few Benjaminites joined David.

Bibliography. M. Noth, *Die Israelitischen Personennamen* (1928), p. 227; K. Möhlenbrink, "Die levitischen Überlieferungen des ATs," *ZAW,* LII (1934), 188-89, 191-206, 230; A. C. Welch, *The Work of the Chronicler* (1939), pp. 96, 115; W. Rudolf, *Chronikbücher,* HAT (1955), pp. 174-75.

T. M. MAUCH

KORE kôr'ĭ [קוֹרֵא (I Chr. 9:19; II Chr. 31:14), קֹרֵא (I Chr. 26:1), partridge]. **1.** A Levite of the house of Korah (I Chr. 9:19; 26:1).

2. KJV form of KORAH 4 in I Chr. 26:19.

3. A Levite, son of Imnah; appointed to have charge of the freewill offerings in the reign of King Hezekiah (II Chr. 31:14). B. T. DAHLBERG

KOZ kŏz [קוֹץ, thorn]; KJV COZ. **1.** A descendant of Judah (I Chr. 4:8); perhaps an ancestor of the priestly house HAKKOZ.

2. KJV alternate form of HAKKOZ.

*__KUE__ kū'ĭ [קְוֵה; Akkad. *Que;* κουε; Vulg. *Coa*]. Probably an ancient name of CILICIA in Asia Minor, most likely E Cilicia.

The name is found in I Kings 10:28; II Chr. 1:16, but it seems not to have been understood by the Masoretes, while the LXX came closer to the meaning. The RSV has rendered מִקְוֵה as "from Kue," while the KJV has "linen yarn." Kue is mentioned as a country from which King Solomon imported horses. It is mentioned together with Mizraim, which does not here mean Egypt (as KJV-RSV), but probably Musri, a country in Asia Minor, like Kue. Cilicia is situated on the fertile coastal plain in the S part of Asia Minor, with the Taurus Mountains in the N and the W, and the Amanus Mountains as border against Syria in the E. Cilicia was famous for its horses, which were bred here in great numbers. In the annalistic reports of King Shalmaneser III of Assyria (858-824 B.C.) Kue is mentioned. The king of this country was one of Shalmaneser's opponents. King Tiglath-pileser III (744-727) received tribute from King Urik of Kue and King Urikki, as can be seen from building inscriptions and from slabs found in ancient Calah. A. S. KAPELRUD

KUSHAIAH ko͝o shā'yə [קוּשָׁיָהוּ] (I Chr. 15:17). A Merarite Levite, listed as one of the singers for the sanctuary in the reign of King David; called Kishi in I Chr. 6:44—H 6:29.

L. A symbol used by certain scholars to designate the hypothetical source of much of the material peculiar to Luke, exclusive of the infancy narrative and the passion story. The source is believed to have originated *ca.* A.D. 60(?), perhaps in Caesarea and either in oral or in written form, and to have been composed mainly of stories and parables (*see* Q for contrast) which breathe a spirit of sympathy for the poor and the outcast and the universalistic implications of God's love.

See also SYNOPTIC PROBLEM; LUKE, GOSPEL OF.

D. T. ROWLINGSON

LAADAH lā'ə də [לעדה, *perhaps* having a fat neck or throat; *cf.* Arab. *luṛdun*] (I Chr. 4:21). A descendant of Judah.

Bibliography. M. Noth, *Die israelitischen Personennamen* (1928), p. 227.

LAADAN. KJV form of LADAN.

LABAN (MAN) lā'bən [לבן, white; *apparently originally* Akkad.; *cf.* Aram. (Gen. Apocryphon XX.4); *cf. also personal name* לבלי *and place names* בולה *and* לבלון; *the frequent occurrence of the root* לבן *in* Gen. 30:25-43 *may reflect a popular etymology*].

1. Family and residence. Although the various sources are not consistent concerning Laban's family relationships, it is best to see him as Rebekah's brother, whose dominant personality eclipses the role of his father, Bethuel (Gen. 24:24, 29; 25:20; 28:5). He is clearly the father of Leah and Rachel (29:16). As the grandson of Nahor (29:5 probably indicates more general relationship, as does 24:48 · ["my master's kinsman"]), Laban lived in the "city of Nahor," which was in the vicinity of—if not identical with—the strategic metropolis Haran (27:43; 29:4; *see* NAHOR 3; HARAN 4). This area, also called PADDAN-ARAM (28:2), was the home of an Aramean family (note "Laban the Aramean" in 25:20[P]; 31:24[E]) related collaterally with the Israelites. *See* ARAM 1.

The story of Laban circles mainly around two figures: Abraham's trusted servant (ch. 24) and Jacob (chs. 29–31).

2. Laban and Abraham's steward. When Abraham sent his major-domo back "to my country and to my kindred" (24:4) to obtain a wife for Isaac, Laban was chiefly responsible for the betrothal of Rebekah. *See* ABRAHAM § C1*m;* ISAAC § 2*d.*

Laban is introduced as a man whose curiosity took him out to meet a stranger (24:29) and whose hospitality prompted him to bring the traveler into his home and care personally for him (vss. 31-32; cf. 29:13-14). Moreover, it is to Laban's credit that first to last, in this matter, he recognized the activity of God in the steward's mission (24:31, 50-51) and blessed his sister when she left (vs. 60).

However, the first word about Laban leaves the inescapable impression that his hospitality was motivated by self-interest (vs. 30). His expectation of personal gain was satisfied; for the visitor, having told of his master's prosperity (vs. 35), gave Rebekah's family lavish gifts (vs. 53; cf. also 30:27-30*a*). It may be, also, that the desire to share longer in this largess was partly responsible for Laban's reluctance to let his guest depart (24:55).

3. Laban and Jacob. After Jacob defrauded Esau (see JACOB SON OF ISAAC § C1), he fled to his uncle (27:41-44; cf. 27:46–28:5). Laban received him (29:13-14), agreed to give him Rachel in payment, but deceived him by making him take Leah first (vss. 15-27), then gave him the younger sister in exchange for further service (vss. 28-30). When Jacob wished to return to his "own home and country," Laban agreed with him on a satisfactory division of the flock, which had prospered under Jacob's care. When Laban sought by cleverness to hinder—if not defraud—Jacob in the bargain, he demonstrated the same self-interest which characterized his dealings with Abraham's servant (30:25-43).

Upon learning not only that Jacob had outwitted him in the deal but also that Rachel had stolen the "household gods" (התרפים in 31:19; אלהים in vs. 30; *see* TERAPHIM), Laban pursued and accosted them. At GILEAD (4), in Transjordan, the two kinsmen entered into a mutual nonaggression covenant, each swearing by the God of his fathers (ch. 31; *see* PATRIARCHS § 4). This Mizpah pact, now combined with other traditions, probably represents at its earliest level an actual agreement between Israelites and Arameans concerning the borderland separating them.

See also GALEED; MIZPAH 1.

Bibliography. S. R. Driver, *The Book of Genesis,* WC (12th ed., 1926), pp. 232-38, 268-72, 277-90. G. von Rad, *Das erste Buch Mose,* ATD, 3 (1952), 217-23; 4 (1953), 250-54, 260-73. F. M. T. Böhl, "Wortspiele im AT," *Opera Minora* (1953), pp. 21-22. *See also* the bibliography under JACOB.

L. HICKS

LABAN (PLACE). A place in the Sinai region, mentioned with Tophel, Hazeroth, and Dizahab (Deut. 1:1). Some have identified it with Libnah, the third stopping place after Hazeroth (Num. 33:20), but the location is unknown.

LABANA. KJV Apoc. form of LEBANAH.

LABOR. Physical or mental toil; usually the physical exertion necessary to subdue the land and supply the wants of the individual and society.

יגיע is the labor and toil which produces (Job 39:11, 16). In the return from Babylon, each man was to leave his own task and rebuild the walls of the city (Neh. 5:13). In the KJV "labor" is most frequently equivalent to the RSV "produce" or "wealth" (Isa. 45:14; cf. Ps. 128:2).

מעשה is anything which is done or made by man. It includes the work of farming, the labor of slaves, the creation of God, the worship of God-fearers, the skill of the craftsman, and the produce of manufacture. עמל emphasizes the sense of toil and hard labor which accompanies much of man's work. The Hebrew also uses מלאכה for "occupation" or "workmanship," עבודה for the labor of slaves and craftsmen, and פעלה for deeds of any kind.

The Greek κόπος is in the LXX for עמל and signifies "toil" and "manual labor." In the NT, however, it is used primarily of the travail and suffering of the righteous to accomplish the will of God (I Cor. 15:58; II Cor. 5:5). The general term for "work" or "business" of any kind is ἔργον. Again, in the NT this is seldom used of the physical labor of workmen, but more particularly of humanitarian deeds and the works of righteousness.

Probably all labor can be classified as follows: (*a*) that of the independent or self-employed, such as shepherd or farmer (*see* OCCUPATIONS); (*b*) that of craftsmen (*see* CRAFTS); (*c*) that of the hired laborer receiving a daily wage (*see* SERVANT); (*d*) that of the native and foreign-born slave (*see* SLAVERY).

God labored at the Creation (Gen. 1), and he continues to labor (Ps. 104:24; Isa. 28:29; etc.). Man was given work to perform in this creation (Gen. 2:15). Sin did not make labor necessary, but it made it less rewarding and subject to frustrations and problems (Gen. 3:19; *see* FALL). There was no exemption from labor by reason of sex. In the ancient Near East women were sometimes the beasts of burden. Men and women frequently performed the same tasks. Jesus worked (John 5:17). Paul also worked and he expected the Christians to work (Acts 18:3; I Thess. 4:11; II Thess. 3:10 ff). All the apostles were workmen before they were commissioned.

Manual labor was honored among the Hebrews, in contrast to the Greek and Roman emphasis on mental and spiritual activity. Human labor has a dignity all its own. Physical exertion, even with its accompanying sweat, was not looked down upon. Toil was honored (Prov. 10:16). Hard work by the wife (31:15) and by the craftsman (22:29) is praised. The lazy man should look to the ant for an example (6:6 ff). Six days of labor were as much a part of the covenant command as the one day of rest (Exod. 20:9-11). Idleness was the real curse (Eccl. 10:18). Labor was always blessed (Exod. 34:21; Ps. 127:1; Prov. 10:4; 21:5; Eccl. 5:11; Ecclus. 10:30; etc.). God rewards the honest laborer (Gen. 26:12; 39:5; Ps. 107:36-37; Eccl. 2:24; etc.).

Laborers were protected by law (Lev. 19:13; Deut. 24:14). Masters should be merciful to laborers, whether slave or free (Eph. 6:9; Philemon). A workman is worthy of his pay (Luke 10:7). Freeborn laborers were often associated in guilds, especially those engaged in crafts. Jacob labored in order to gain a wife (Gen. 31:40-41). Many workers had overseers (Ruth 2:5; I Sam. 11:5; Matt. 20:1; I Cor. 3:9; etc.).

Forced labor was practiced by the Egyptians and imitated by Solomon and his son (I Kings 11:28 ff). Objection to this type of labor is already indicated by the prophet Samuel (I Sam. 8:11-17). Yet Asa later followed this practice in Judah (I Kings 15:22). The *corvée* was used largely on special projects such as road building and the making of monumental palaces. The citizen may have been impressed only for the duration of the project and was not considered a slave. This type of labor was seldom used in agriculture. The Romans likewise could impress the citizens of occupied countries into special duty and labor (Matt. 5:41). But with the end in sight (*see* ESCHATOLOGY OF THE NT), such people were to be patient.

C. U. WOLF

LACCUNUS lə kū′nəs [Λακκοῦνος, *possibly from* כלל בניה (Ezra 10:30; *the final* ל *of the first word has been read as the first consonant of the second word, and the* ב *of the second word was read as a* כ] (I Esd. 9:31); KJV LACUNUS. One of the sons of Addi who put away their foreign wives and children in the time of Ezra.

C. T. FRITSCH

LACE [פתיל]. A twisted thread or CORD. Such a cord of purple was used to fasten the breastpiece to the rings of the ephod (Exod. 28:28; 39:21), and the golden plate to the turban for Aaron (Exod. 28:37; 39:31).

LACEDAEMONIANS lăs′ə dĭ mō′nĭ ənz [Λακεδαιμονίοι]. The inhabitants of Lacedaemon, or SPARTA, the capital of Laconia in S Greece—a name sometimes used of all Laconia (Homer *Iliad* II.581; Herodotus I.67). Friendly relationships with the Jews were established as early as *ca.* 270 B.C., perhaps growing out of the mutual friendship of the Jews and the Spartans with Egypt as well as out of their common conception of a community of law. That a Jewish colony existed in Sparta in the second century B.C. is suggested by the fact that Jason the high priest found asylum there in 168 (II Macc. 5:9). Diplomatic relations between Sparta and the Maccabean state were renewed in the time of Jonathan, as attested by the letter he wrote to the Spartans *ca.* 146 B.C. and recorded in I Macc. 12:6-18 (cf. Jos. Antiq. XIII.v.8). The authenticity of this and the other official letters in I Maccabees has been questioned frequently, but there is no doubt that there were declarations of friendship made at this time by the Romans and the Spartans with the Jews; and many scholars regard them as genuine state documents in complete or abridged form. Jonathan writes that earlier Areios I, king of Sparta (309-265), sent a letter of friendship to the high priest Onias I (320-290), a copy of which follows in vss. 20-23 (cf. Jos. Antiq. XII.iv.10). Mention is made of a blood relationship between the Spartans and the Jews, apparently a widely diffused legend in the East (cf. II Macc. 5:9, where the name Lacedaemonian appears). I Macc. 14:20-22 preserves an official letter from the Spartans to Jonathan's successor, Simon, which, though probably genuine, is set in an appendix to the original book, which may have consisted only of chs. 1–12. Finally, I Macc. 15:16-22 records a declaration of friendship between the Roman Senate and the Jews, written by the consul Lucius to the king of Egypt and addressed also to neighboring countries including the Spartans (vs. 23; cf. Jos. Antiq. XIV.viii.5).

Bibliography. W. Schubart, "Bemerkungen zum Stile hellenistischer Königsbriefe," *Archiv für Papyrusforschung,* VI (1920), 324-47; M. Ginsburg, "Sparta and Judaea," *Classical Philology,* XXIX (1934), 117-22; F.-M. Abel, *Les livres de Maccabées* (1949), pp. 231-33. E. W. SAUNDERS

***LACHISH** lā'kĭsh [לכיש] (Josh. 10:3, 31-33; 12:11; 15:39; II Kings 14:19; 18:14, 17; 19:8; II Chr. 11:9; 25:27; 32:9; Neh. 11:30; Isa. 36:2; Jer. 34:7; Mic. 1:13). A city of Judah lying midway between Jerusalem and Gaza.

1. Name and identification
2. Excavation and history
3. The fosse temple
4. Inscriptions
5. The Lachish Letters
Bibliography

1. Name and identification. Outside the OT the name of Lachish first appears prominently in the Akkadian correspondence of the Pharaoh Akh-en-Aton recovered from Tell el-Amarna. A single occurrence of *Ra-ki-ša* in the hieratic papyrus no. 1116 A of the Hermitage collection, a document contemporary with Thut-mose III, and of a "king of *La-ti-ša*(?)" named in a hieratic inscription on a pottery bowl (*see d* under § 4 *below*), are perhaps the only mentions of

Courtesy of the Trustees of the British Museum

1. Lachish attacked by Sennacherib (704-681 B.C.) and siege engines, which are protected by warriors who shoot from behind shields; from Quyunjiq (Nineveh)

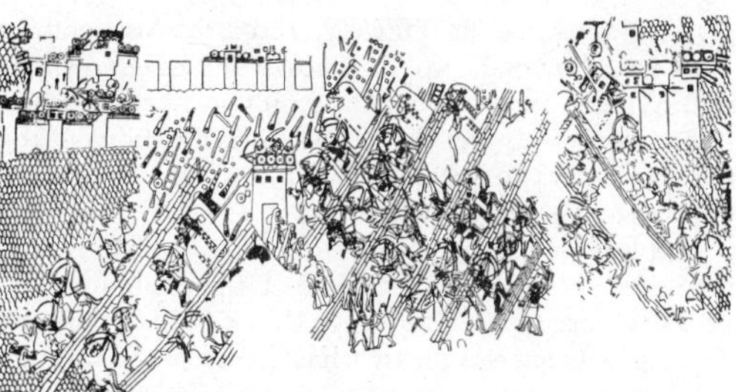

Copyright: By permission of the Trustees of the late Sir Henry S. Wellcome

2. A drawing from a bas relief from Sennacherib's palace at Nineveh, showing the siege of Lachish

Lachish in the Egyptian language, unless—against the probabilities—a place name *Lu-ga-za* in the Karnak lists of Thut-mose III refers to the same city. The Amarna correspondence contains five references to a city spelled alternatively *Lakisu* or *Lakišu;* and three of the letters actually emanate from individuals, named Iabni-ilu and Zimridi, who style themselves "man of Lachish." The same name, *Lakisu,* is given to a town depicted as surrendering after a siege in the wall reliefs of Sennacherib's palace at Nineveh (Figs. LAC 1-2). These Akkadian names assuredly refer to the same place as the OT Lachish.

Copyright: The Matson Photo Service

3. Lachish (modern Tell ed-Duweir)

It is the general belief that Lachish stood on the site known as Tell ed-Duweir (Fig. LAC 3), an imposing mound lying five miles by road to the SW of Beit Jibrin, the ancient Eleutheropolis. The identification rests on three considerations: Tell ed-Duweir is the most prominent Bronze and Iron Age site in the region indicated by Eusebius for the contemporary village of Lachish, "in the 7th mile from Eleutheropolis to Daroma"; excavation has revealed a striking resemblance between the Iron Age ruins at Tell ed-Duweir and the pictorial representation of Lachish at Nineveh; and the ascertained history of Tell ed-Duweir corresponds correctly with that of Lachish as inferred from literary sources.

2. Excavation and history. Tell ed-Duweir lies toward the lower W slopes of the Judean hill country. It rises from a valley in which settlement has been favored at all times by the presence of copious water near the surface. The surrounding ridges have yielded finds of worked flints giving evidence of human habitation as early as Upper Paleolithic times.

The tell and certain areas of the neighboring slopes were explored between 1932 and 1938 by the Wellcome-Marston Archaeological Research Expedition, directed by James L. Starkey, and after his death in 1938 by Charles H. Inge. Knowledge of the history of the site is derived from the results of these excavations, combined with the historical indications of the OT and the nonbiblical Akkadian and Assyrian documents named above.

Natural caves in the limestone slopes of the valley sheltered an open settlement in Upper Chalcolithic times (before *ca.* 3000 B.C.) and in the first phase of the Early Bronze Age; this has been traced over an area of nearly two hundred acres. The culture is characterized by sherds of pottery, stone mortars and querns, and a few stone maceheads and other implements of flint and bone. Marks in the soft limestone show that many of the caves were enlarged by their occupants, using stone adzes.

In the Early Bronze II period, *ca.* 2800 B.C., the settlement contracted and moved to the site of the present tell; the old cave dwellings then began to be used as tombs. We cannot follow subsequent urban developments in detail; until the Late Bronze Age they are known only from limited soundings in the flanks of the mound and by inference from the contents of cemeteries. For the Late Bronze Age (1600-1200 B.C.) the ruins of the fosse temple (*see* § 3 *below*) furnished some detailed evidence.

The city on its growing mound was first protected *ca.* 1700 B.C. by a fosse and a plaster-covered glacis rising to a height of *ca.* one hundred feet above the valley and presumably crowned by a brick wall. These defenses belonged to the period of Hyksos domination, and they had fallen into disuse early in the Late Bronze Age when a small temple was built on rubbish accumulated at the bottom of the fosse (*ca.* 1550 B.C.). This event corresponded in time with the renewal of Egyptian power in Asia; at an earlier stage Egyptian influence had already been active in Lachish, as shown by the presence of numerous scarabs, of Egyptian or foreign manufacture, dating from the Twelfth to the Twenty-second Dynasty. The Tell el-Amarna Letters (fourteenth century) reveal the Egyptian party in Lachish suffering the same embarrassments as their confrères in other Canaanite cities. In one letter written from Jerusalem the city is linked with Ashkelon and Gezer, and charged with having supplied the HABIRU with food and oil. In another it is reported that Zimridi's servants have conspired with the Habiru against him, and perhaps killed him. Confused as the situation is which the correspondence reveals, we can assume that the prosperity of the city and the interests of its rulers were always closely linked with the maintenance of Egyptian power.

Having been twice enlarged during this period, the fosse temple was finally destroyed by fire simultaneously with a general conflagration within the town, *ca.* 1200 B.C. The event reveals the decay of Egyptian power, and may be linked with the invasion of the hill country by Israel and the slaughter of King Japhia (Josh. 10:3-40).

Ca. 1000 B.C., perhaps by the initiative of David or Solomon, the city was reconstructed. Either then or soon afterward a massive stone platform was raised about the ruins of a Bronze Age building at the center of the mound to form the podium of a brickwork palace, of which all other trace has vanished. The same podium, however, successively enlarged in later centuries, served to support a citadel or governor's residence, which in one form or another, with only a break after Sennacherib's invasion of Judah, lasted throughout the history of Lachish.

II Chr. 11:9 tells us that Rehoboam fortified Lachish; and Asa probably strengthened it (14:7) shortly before 900 B.C. A great enlargement of the citadel may perhaps be attributed to Jehoshaphat, who set garrisons in the cities of Judah (ch. 17). To Lachish, King Amaziah of Judah fled for his life from a conspiracy against him in Jerusalem, and in Lachish nevertheless he lost it (ch. 25). The defenses of the city then consisted of an upper wall of brick following the edge of the mound and a lower wall or revetment of stone halfway down the slope. Both walls followed a roughly rectangular plan, and both were built with alternate recesses and projections. Outside the walls near the SW corner there stood a square outwork defending a roadway which led up the slope toward the gateway of the city. To the late eighth century may be attributed an enigmatic shaft which was found driven into the rock within the SE corner of the inner wall. Surrounded by funnel-shaped slopes of crushed chalk laid on a bed of rock chippings, this prodigious excavation, forming a hollow cube some fifty feet each way, was presumably intended for storing water within the city. It may well have been undertaken, like Hezekiah's tunnel in Jerusalem, for purposes of defense when Judah was threatened by Assyria (*see* WATER WORKS). The work was never finished. *Ca.* 700 B.C., Sennacherib captured Lachish and encamped there; the marks of a vast conflagration within the town, as well as arrowheads, slingshots, a spearhead, and an Assyrian bronze helmet crest found in a thick bed of ashes on the approach road, bear visible witness to his assault, which was also depicted in relief on the palace walls at Nineveh.

After Sennacherib's withdrawal reconstruction within the city was slow; but the defenses were restored and improved, possibly by Manasseh (II Chr. 33:11-14). A new stone wall replaced the upper line of brick, and the former outwork was incorporated as a bastion in the lower revetment. The entrance to the city was then contrived to pass through two gates, the outer one in the bastion facing S, the inner one on the line of the upper wall facing W. Thus an intruder must first approach the bastion with his unshielded right side exposed to missiles from the wall and then, having penetrated the outer gate, must turn to the right and advance uphill across an enclosed court to the inner gate.

Nebuchadrezzar captured Lachish in 588-586 B.C. (Jer. 34:7). Marks of a huge conflagration on the road leading up to the gate, and on the adjacent wall, show that the attackers relied largely on fire, for which felled olive trees not yet harvested supplied the fuel. An earlier layer of ashes within the city may have been a relic of the first campaign of Nebuchadrezzar against Jehoiakim in 597 B.C.

Between *ca.* 586 and 450 B.C., Lachish lay deserted. It revived for three centuries under the Persian and Hellenistic kings (Neh. 11:30). On the site of the old citadel a new residence was then built in N Syrian style, with suites of rooms opening through columned porches on a central court. Here, we may suppose, a Persian governor lived and worked. To the NE a smaller building was built some years later in a similar style. It had a broad flight of steps leading up from a central court into an antechamber, which gave access in turn to a small, square room or shrine. The orientation of this building and the discovery in it of a small limestone altar, with crude reliefs of a human hand and of a human figure in an act of adoration, suggested that the building was a solar temple, which the excavators attributed tentatively to the Seleucid period.

The city was finally deserted, never to be reoccupied, *ca.* 150 B.C.

3. The fosse temple. This deserves separate description, for it is one of the most informative relics of the Canaanite religion that have been recovered in Palestine. Like the Tophet at Jerusalem, it lay outside the city, in the disused fosse of the Middle Bronze Age. It was built of unhewn stones set in mud mortar, and in all its stages consisted essentially of a large cult room with varying subsidiary annexes. The cult room was seemingly open to all worshipers.

Built probably in the sixteenth century B.C., the cult room was initially a rectangle measuring thirty-three feet from N to S and half this width from E to W. It was entered by a door near the N end of the long W wall. A small, square room with an outside door adjoined the N wall; and another was connected with the cult room on the W. The roof of the cult room was carried by two wooden posts resting on stone bases aligned on the long axis of the room. The cult was focused on a low bench or offering table of clay, having three projections attached to its front, which was applied to the middle of the short S wall. Before it a large pottery jar was found sunk into the floor of the shrine; and this seemed to have replaced an earlier and smaller jar of which the bottom part was also found embedded nearby. A heap of other pottery vessels, mostly dipper flasks, lay on the ground beside one end of the bench.

This earliest temple, of which inevitably little remains, was demolished and replaced *ca.* 1450 B.C. by a much larger structure, in which the cult room was doubled in width while the N annex, rebuilt and enlarged, became an anteroom and the principal entrance to the shrine. The second annex was now suppressed, but a new room, connected with the cult room by a door, and having also an outside door, was attached to the S wall. The roof of the new cult room was carried by four, instead of two, posts.

In this second stage of the temple the offering table was enlarged and remade of rough stones instead of clay, and with only one projection in the middle of its front face. The W end of the table incorporated a small concealed cupboard facing to the side, which contained lamps. Several long benches built of mud bricks were provided at the same time against or parallel to the N, E, and W walls of the cult room. Large numbers of plain pottery bowls were found placed on or fallen beside these benches. Where in the first temple there had been a pottery jar, directly in front of the offering table, in the second there was a small hearth sunk in the floor and surrounded by a curb of clay and plaster.

Ca. 1350 B.C. or later the temple was again modified (Fig. TEM 44); its floor level was raised and its columns and roof rebuilt. Excavation has revealed the lines of ashes where its wooden crossbeams joined the tops of the columns to the side and end walls. A second room was added to the S end of the temple, making two rooms behind the cult room, each connected with it by a doorway. At this stage of the temple the offering table was rebuilt and transformed into a spacious white-plastered platform, partly recessed into the back wall and partly projecting from it. On it, in a mass of burnt debris, were found lying numerous delicate vessels, ornaments, and beads, of ivory, glass, faïence, and alabaster, among them scarabs of Amenophis III. At a late stage an altar of mud bricks had been built against the front of the platform; three steps against it on the W side illustrated the arrangement prohibited by Exod. 20:26. A new lamp cupboard was built against the S wall of the room W of the platform; and in front of this stood a tall, tubular pottery libation stand. Balancing this, on the E side of the platform was an earthenware bin with four handles. There was still a hearth before the platform. Three small cupboards or niches were built into the E wall of the cult room at this time, and a few extra benches were provided. Some thirty-five pottery bowls were found stored in one of the wall cupboards, and many more had fallen from the other two.

Vast quantities of pottery vessels, both plain and decorated, but with a predominance of shallow hemispherical bowls, were recovered from all the

4. The Duweir ewer (1350-1200 B.C.), with inscription beginning "A gift to . . ."); from a water color by B. Gaver

rooms; and the soil was full of the bones of birds, animals, and fish. The animals included sheep or goats, oxen, and gazelles or ibexes; they were all young, and nearly all the identifiable bones were right shoulder bones (cf. the priest's portion of the peace offering in Lev. 7:32). Before the cult platform among other pottery fragments was found an earthenware footbath (cf. Exod. 40:31). A violent conflagration had destroyed the temple *ca.* 1200 B.C. or a few years before. The ground outside the building was honeycombed with pits, in which it was clear that refuse from the temple had been thrown throughout its history—not only ashes, bones, and broken pots, but also whole vessels and more precious objects of bone, ivory, faïence, or metal.

No cult statue was found in the temple, but an ivory hand was recovered from one of the pits and a bronze statuette of a seated male deity out of context in the fosse.

Two inscribed pottery vessels were found in rubbish outside the temple, a ewer and a bowl. The former was decorated round the neck with wavy lines and squares in red paint, while on the shoulder was a zone of crudely stylized animals supporting an inscription of eleven letters and a mark composed of three dots (Fig. LAC 4). The ewer is attributed to the third stage of the temple and the second half of the thirteenth century. The letters closely resemble those scratched on the rocks of Serabit el-Khadim, and they are also recognizably akin to early Phoenician inscriptions of the tenth and later centuries; they are therefore to some extent a link between the two (*see* ALPHABET). Many different readings have been proposed, but most agree that the first word is to be read *mtn,* "gift," and the last *'lt,* "goddess."

The bowl is inscribed in black ink with eleven unintelligible letters or parts of letters.

The exact nature of the cult cannot be known. The many small bowls which were found in the precincts have been likened to the "gardens of Adonis," vessels containing quick-flowering anemones, with which country folk in Syria once celebrated the flowering and early death of spring. The cult shrine, too, in its enlarged final stage, with its cosmetic pots and trinkets, has been explained as a sacred marriage bed. These are possible explanations of some of the facts. We can be sure only that the cult room was open to all worshipers; that they brought with them innumerable pottery bowls and put them on the benches; that young animals were sacrificed and consumed; that the cult table received precious objects; and that fire burned in the hearth before it, lamps were lit, and libations poured. The debris of holy days was periodically removed and dumped in pits outside the temple.

4. Inscriptions. Lachish has produced more evidence of literacy during the Bronze and Iron Ages than any other town in Palestine. In chronological sequence the principal documents are:

a) A bronze dagger blade inscribed vertically with four signs (*ca.* 1600 B.C. or before). One sign, representing a human head, is fully pictographic, and may be read, if the language is Semitic, and the notation acrophonic, as *r* (*rosh*). No interpretation of the text is possible at present.

b) Five pieces of pottery inscribed with alphabetic signs of "Sinaitic" type (*ca.* 1350-1200 B.C.; *see* INSCRIPTIONS; ALPHABET): (i) censer lid with three unintelligible signs painted in red; (ii) bowl with eleven signs painted in white lime, of whch five seem to read in Semitic *bšlšt*—"for three"—and six are disputed; (iii and iv) ewer and bowl fragment (*see above*); (v) sherd with parts of four letters in black ink tentatively reading *l'wt,* perhaps after 1200 B.C.

c) Four-sided paste seal with name of Amenophis II (*ca.* 1450-1425) on one side and on another Ptah facing a row of eight unintelligible marks resembling North Semitic signs.

d) Egyptian (*ca.* 1200 B.C. or later): (i) fragment of a clay coffin painted with clear but unintelligible hieroglyphic signs in red; (ii) fragments of a pottery bowl inscribed in ink with a hieratic text seemingly concerned with taxation, and including the words "king (of) Latish(?)"; also two other small hieratic inscribed sherds.

e) Scratched on a limestone step in the stairs leading up to the citadel platform, the first five letters of the Hebrew alphabet, אבגדה, written in their traditional order (*ca.* 800 B.C.).

f) Fragment of a jar incised with six early Hebrew characters *btlmlk* "royal *bath,*" a measure of volume (*see* WEIGHTS AND MEASURES; *ca.* eighth century B.C.).

g) Seven seals or seal impressions with names inscribed in early Hebrew characters (eighth-sixth century B.C.). One reads "belonging to Gedaliah who is over the household"—perhaps identical with the Gedaliah son of Ahikam made governor of Judea by Nebuchadrezzar (II Kings 25:22; Fig. GED 16).

h) Stamped jar handles (eighth to early sixth century): (*i*) forty-eight with names of private persons, either owners or potters; (*ii*) *ca.* three hundred stamped *lmlk,* "belonging to the king," followed by one of the names Hebron, Ziph, Sokoh, or *Mmšt,* combined with a scarab or winged scroll symbol.

i) Early sixth-century ostraca. Twenty-one pot fragments inscribed with texts in black ink. All but two appear to have been letters, the most important being a group of eighteen texts recovered from a small room built in one of the towers of the outer city gate and opening on the courtyard of the bastion. *See* § 5 *below.*

j) Six three-quarter-spherical stone weights engraved with the words *nṣp* (one example), *pym* (two), or *bq'* (two; seventh-sixth century B.C.). The sixth weight is marked simply *b,* while others were found with numerical signs.

k) A stone altar incised with a three-line votive text in Aramaic script, beginning with the word *lbnt',* "incense" (*ca.* fifth-fourth century B.C.). The third line, containing the letters *lyh mr',* might be read: "To Yah(weh) Lord [of heaven]," by analogy with contemporary Aramaic texts from Elephantine.

5. The Lachish Letters. The eighteen texts mentioned under *i* in § 4 *above* lay on the floor of a room filled with ashes from the conflagration which had destroyed Lachish. Written in a Hebrew identical with the language of the latest pre-exilic books of the OT, during the last decade of the Judean kingdom (*ca.* 590 B.C.), their epigraphic and linguistic interest is surpassed only by their unique historical character.

The texts have been often translated, and their significance much discussed. The most interesting historically are the letters numbered 3, 4, and 6. Letter 3 gives the names of both writer and recipient: the former is Hoshaiah, a subordinate official in an outpost of Lachish; the latter Ya'osh, his superior in the city itself. Ya'osh is addressed also in the second and sixth letters; and the tone and substance of the whole series suggest that all belong to the same correspondence.

Copyright: The Matson Photo Service

5. The Lachish Letter No. 3

Letter 3 consists largely of exculpations by Hoshaiah evoked by some rebuke over a letter.* It ends with a report of various military movements, including a journey to Egypt by the captain Koniah son of Elnathan, and of a warning message brought by an unnamed prophet from Tobiah, a royal official, to Shallum son of Yaddu'a. Fig. LAC 5.

Letter 4 (Fig. INS 15) acknowledges orders, reports certain facts and actions, and ends: "We are looking for the signals of Lachish, according to all the indications my Lord has given, because we do not see Azekah."

Letter 6 comments on a letter from the king and on the demoralizing contents of letters received from princes in Jerusalem. The writer urges Ya'osh to protest in writing.

In sum, the Lachish Letters are a unique example of cursive script and epistolary style in Judah at the time of Jeremiah; and they are firsthand documents of the uneasy political and military situation reigning in Judah on the eve of Nebuchadrezzar's destruction of Jerusalem.

Bibliography. Publications of the Wellcome-Marston Archaeological Research Expedition to the Near East (1938-57), Lachish I: H. Torczyner, L. Harding, A. Lewis, and J. L. Starkey, *The Lachish Letters*. Lachish II: O. Tufnell, C. H. Inge, and L. Harding, *The Fosse Temple*. Lachish III: O. Tufnell, *The Iron Age*. Lachish IV: O. Tufnell, *The Bronze Age*.

R. W. HAMILTON

LACUNUS. KJV form of LACCUNUS.

LADAN lā'dən [לַעְדָּן, *perhaps* fleshy at the throat; *cf.* LAADAH]; KJV LAADAN lā'ə dən. **1.** An ancestor of Joshua (I Chr. 7:26).

2. A Gershonite Levite; eponymous ancestor of several father's houses (I Chr. 23:7-9; 26:21).

3. KJV form of DELAIAH in I Esd. 5:37.

B. T. DAHLBERG

LADDER [סֻלָּם] (Gen. 28:12). A series of steps made for ascent and descent. The steps may be of metal, rope, wood, stone, etc. In its one occurrence in the Bible the word symbolizes God's present care and man's ascending prayer (*see* JACOB).

The rock strata exposed naturally in the vicinity of Bethel suggests "flight of stairs" would be a more appropriate translation. Ladders are depicted on the Ur-Nammu stela showing the construction of a ziggurat. Egyptian friezes show ladders raised against walls for scaling in warfare already in the Fifth and

Courtesy of the Trustees of the British Museum

6. An Assyrian relief from Tell Halaf showing a man climbing a date palm by a ladder (ninth century B.C.)

Sixth Dynasties. Assyrians used siege ladders against Hamath, Lachish, etc. Ladders were also used in the siege of DATHEMA (I Macc. 5:30).

Fig. LAD 6.

See also STAIR; CARPENTER; WAR, METHODS OF.

C. U. WOLF

LADDER OF TYRE tīr. A prominent landmark, apparently a mountain *ca.* twelve miles N of Ptolemaïs (Acre), according to Jos. War II.x.2. Josephus says that, among the mountains of Galilee and Carmel, it was the "highest of all." This statement has led some to suggest that the Ladder of Tyre was the high ridge which bounds the plain of Acre on the N, rising to over a thousand feet; indeed, on the seaward side there are distinct steps formed by three mountains: Ras el-Abyad (the White Cape), Ras en-Naqura, and Ras el-Musheirifeh. From the S side, silhouetted against the sky, these mountains would give the impression of a huge ladder by which one might ascend into the land of Tyre. The W end of the ridge drops sheer into the sea, and there is no way around it; one must ascend into Phoenicia as by a ladder. The difficulty of this interpretation is that Josephus states that the Ladder is higher than Carmel, and yet Carmel rises to over eighteen hundred feet.

Whatever its precise position, the Ladder was the N border of the region over which SIMON MACCABEUS was made governor by Antiochus VI (I Macc. 11:59; *see* ANTIOCHUS 6).

Bibliography. W. M. Thomson, *The Land and the Book* (1901), pp. 302 ff. A. P. Stanley, *Sinai and Palestine* (1910), pp. 203 ff. F.-M. Abel, *Géographie de la Palestine* (1938), I, 301, 306; II, 135. N. TURNER

LAEL lā'əl [לאל, belonging to God] (Num. 3:24). A Gershonite Levite; the father of Eliasaph.

LAHAD lā'hăd [להד, *perhaps* slow, indolent; *cf.* Arab. *lahdun*] (I Chr. 4:2). A descendant of Judah.

Bibliography. M. Noth, *Die israelitischen Personennamen* (1928), p. 227.

LAHAI-ROI. KJV form of BEER-LAHAI-ROI.

LAHMAM lä'măm [לחמם] (Josh. 15:40). A village of Judah in the Shephelah district of Lachish; usually identified with modern Khirbet el-Lahm, 2½ miles S of Beit Jibrin (Eleutheropolis).

LAHMI lä'mī [לחמי] (I Chr. 20:5). Brother of Goliath the Gittite. He was slain by Elhanan the son of Jair. However, the text of II Sam. 21:19 reads: "Elhanan the son of Jair ['oregim' is admittedly a scribal error from the following line], the Bethlehemite, slew Goliath." The rendering of the words "the Bethlehemite" (בית־הלחמי את) as "Lahmi the brother of" (את־לחמי אחי) by the Chronicler is usually considered an attempt to harmonize I Sam. 17 and II Sam. 21:19. Older interpreters argued generally for the originality of I Chr. 20:5. E. R. DALGLISH

LAISH lā'ĭsh [ליש (1 *below*), lion; לישה (2-3 *below*)].
1. The father of Paltiel (Palti in I Sam. 25:44), to whom Saul gave his daughter Michal, the wife of the proscribed David. Ishbaal took her from Paltiel and returned her to David (I Sam. 25:44; II Sam. 3:15).

2. A Canaanite city in N Palestine (Judg. 18:7, 14, 27, 29); called Leshem in Josh. 19:47, and later known as Dan.

3. KJV form of LAISHAH.

LAISHAH lā'ə shə [לישה, lion] (Isa. 10:30); KJV LAISH. A village of Benjamin, NE of Jerusalem; listed between Gallim and Anathoth in Isaiah's visionary and poetic portrayal of a hostile army's village-by-village advance on Jerusalem from the N (Isa. 10:28-34). The site is possibly to be identified with modern el-Isawiyeh. W. H. MORTON

LAKE OF GENNESARET. *See* GENNESARET, LAKE OF; GALILEE, SEA OF.

LAKKUM lăk'əm [לקום] (Josh. 19:33). A border town in Naphtali. It is generally identified with Khirbet el-Mansurah, a site *ca.* three miles SW of Khirbet Kerak.

LAMA. *See* ELI, ELI, LAMA SABACHTHANI.

LAMB. In addition to its literal usage, the lamb is a frequent symbol in both the OT and the NT.

1. In the OT. Several Hebrew words are translated "lamb." By far the most common term is כבש ("male lamb") and the feminine form, כבשה; occasionally by metathesis—i.e., inversion—כשב and כשבה are used. In the priestly legislation of Exodus, Leviticus, and Numbers, these terms appear many times.

The term שה also denotes a youngster from the sheep (lit., "small cattle," צום; *see* SHEEP; SHEPHERD). Very infrequently (see I Sam. 7:9; Isa. 65:25) the terms טלה and טלאים (see Isa. 40:11) appear; and, finally, indicating probably a state of maturation between the he-lamb proper and the RAM (איל), the term כר (see, e.g., Jer. 51:40; Amos 6:4).

The lamb is the dominant sacrificial victim. It was, from the point of our earliest knowledge of the institution (Exod. 12:11-12), the central symbol and sacrifice in the PASSOVER. Morning and evening burnt offerings (Exod. 29:38-42); the first day of each (lunar) month (Num. 28:11); all seven days of Passover (Num. 28:16-19); the Feast of Weeks (Num. 28:26-27; *see* FEASTS AND FASTS); the Day of Atonement (Num. 29:7-8; but cf. Lev. 16, where the victims are rams, goats, and bulls); the Feast of Tabernacles (Num. 29:13 ff)—all these, together with sacrificial prescriptions for numerous eventualities (see, e.g., Lev. 3:6, 4:27, 32; 5:6), called for the sacrifice of lambs.

For the Israelites, as for other peoples, the lamb symbolized, among other things, innocence and gentleness. Nathan's parable to David, employed by the prophet in denunciation and conviction of the sin of the king in the Bathsheba affair, may then suggest the relative innocence of the woman, since she is analogous to the lamb (כבשה; II Sam. 12:3). As used figuratively of persons, the term could be calculated to summon the sympathetic emotions of concern and pity and compassion, as in the case of Second Isaiah's consoling words to exiled Israel about to be redeemed by Yahweh:

> He will feed his flock like a shepherd,
> he will gather the lambs [טלאים] in his arms,
> he will carry them in his bosom
> (Isa. 40:11).

Or in the same manner, Jeremiah, who refers to himself as a "gentle lamb" (11:19; but cf. Hebrew כבש ארופ; see Commentaries). With not altogether dissimilar connotations, Israelite prophetism describes the era of the consummation of Yahweh's purpose and reign with this remarkable figurative use of the lamb:

> The wolf shall dwell with the lamb [כבש],
> and the leopard shall lie down with the kid,
> and the calf and the lion and the fatling together,
> and a little child shall lead them
> (Isa. 11:6).

All the qualities of innocence, purity, and meekness, and possibly also a sense of efficaciousness, derived from the actual sacrificial system, are summoned with deepest poignancy in the figurative use of the lamb as applied to the Suffering Servant:

> He was oppressed, and he was afflicted,
> yet he opened not his mouth;
> like a lamb [שה] that is led to the slaughter,
> and like a sheep that before its shearers is dumb,
> so he opened not his mouth
> (Isa. 53:7; see also vss. 4-6).

2. In the NT. In the NT (ἀμνός, ἀρήν, and ἀρνίον), the term is used only figuratively. In Luke 10:3 the Seventy are sent forth "as lambs in the midst of wolves" (the only occurrence of ἀρήν; generally ἀρνός is used); in John 21:15, Jesus admonishes Peter: "Feed my lambs" (the diminutive form, ἀρνίον, from ἀρήν); and in Rev. 13:11 the Antichrist is seen as having "two horns like a lamb" (ἀρνίον). All other occurrences (ἀμνός in John 1:29, 36; Acts 8:32; I Pet. 1:19; and ἀρνίον, aside from John 21:15, only in Revelation, where the term appears, in addition to 13:11, some twenty-eight times in reference to Christ in chs. 5–22) are figurative allusions to the person and work of Jesus Christ. Although the exact significance of the term in Revelation has been a point of debate among scholars and interpreters, the Lamb here appears as Savior and as Ruler of the world; and, despite the difference in term, the word probably conveys the same essential character as is intended in the word ἀμνός.

Strong inferences out of the life and cultic practice of ancient Israel are surely present in these:

a) John the Baptist sees Jesus approaching and cries: "Behold, the Lamb of God, who takes away the sin of the world!" (John 1:29). The next day he declares of Jesus again: "Behold, the Lamb of God!"

b) Acts 8:32 quotes Isa. 53:7, imprecisely (cf. above):

> As a sheep led to the slaughter
> or a lamb before its shearer is dumb,
> so he opens not his mouth.

c) I Pet. 1:18-19 affirms: "You know that you were ransomed from the futile ways inherited from your fathers, not with perishable things such as silver or gold, but with the precious blood of Christ, like that of a lamb without blemish or spot."

d) The innocence and purity of the OT sacrificial lamb and the lamb's function in redeeming and restoring man's relationship with God are employed in the early church community in essential interpretation of Jesus Christ. B. D. Napier

LAME, LAMENESS [צלע; χωλός]. A physical condition in which a person experiences difficulty in walking, or finds himself unable to do so. Lameness may be congenital, if existing from birth; or acquired, if it is subsequently developed. Congenital lameness may be the result of mineral or vitamin deficiencies during the intra-uterine life of the fetus.

The lack of orthopedic knowledge in antiquity made cyllosis (clubfoot) a far more permanent malformation than at present. Some of the more frequently found forms of cyllosis were talipes equinus, in which the heel is permanently retracted from the ground, with the weight resting on the ball of the foot; talipes calcaneus, in which the heel projects downward to carry bodily weight; talipes valgus, a permanent outward eversion of the foot, and talipes equino-varus, an inversion of the feet in which only the outer borders rest on the ground.

Imperfectly formed lower limbs, or legs of unequal length, were apparently not unknown in early Israelite history (cf. Lev. 21:18), and such deformities were an impediment to the priesthood. The general incidence of lameness among the Hebrews is difficult to estimate for lack of proper data. However, the narrative of II Sam. 5:6, 8, would seem to suggest that during the early monarchy there were numerous lame and crippled persons among the inhabitants of the Jebusite stronghold of Jerusalem. Allusions to the physical deformity of lameness found their way into the realm of the proverb. Thus the sages of Israel could speak of a proverb in the mouth of a fool as being like the legs of a lame man (Prov. 26:7).

Courtesy of the Wellcome Historical Medical Museum, London

7. A lame man with an atrophied right leg (the result of infantile paralysis?), from an Egyptian stele of the Eighteenth Dynasty (1570-1310 B.C.)

To what extent lameness was due to malnutrition or deficiency diseases such as rickets can only be conjectured. More certain is the evidence which Egyptian monuments present for the existence of such afflictions as tuberculous spondylitis (inflammation of one or more of the spinal vertebrae, otherwise known as Pott's Disease). Two instances of these lesions have been depicted in figures carved on ancient Egyptian monuments, and dated *ca.* 2000 B.C. In one of these, the lower cervical and upper dorsal regions are involved, while the other indicates that the lesion was situated in the lumbar region.* If there was any degree of compression of the spinal cord in these or any other instances of Pott's Disease, there would be a corresponding amount of paraplegia, which would involve the extremities at the very least. While the existence of Pott's Disease still remains to be demonstrated clinically in Palestinian skeletons, there are good reasons for supposing that it did in fact exist there (cf. Lev. 21:20, where גבן and דק imply spinal kyphosis). Fig. LAM 7.

Another Egyptian monument has preserved with remarkable fidelity a picture of a Syrian settler who had been afflicted with anterior poliomyelitis (infantile paralysis). The portrait, dated *ca.* 1200 B.C., shows the man working at agricultural pursuits, carrying a long staff held in position across his body by his left forearm. His left leg is well developed, but the right leg is deformed, with the foot drawn up in a manner characteristic of infantile paralysis. The fact that this man is clearly depicted as a Syrian immigrant furnishes grounds for believing that poliomyelitis, with its attendant disabilities, was not uncommon in Bible lands generally.

It is not unreasonable to expect the lame to include those who suffered from bilateral congenital dislocation of the hip joint, because the pelvic socket was too shallow to accommodate the head of the femur properly. The consequent dislocation, if left untreated, would produce a characteristic waddling gait. In children and adults, hip-joint disease is most frequently tubercular in nature. If remedial measures are neglected, deformities of the pelvis and legs may follow, with a shortening of the latter. In any event, the hip joint may become ankylosed (immobile).

Specific pathology of the bones must also be included as an important cause of lameness. Osteoarthritis in elderly persons would inhibit movement, and in a chronic state would produce some deformity. *Osteitis deformans juvenilis,* in which the head and neck of the femur become flattened and shortened, may have afflicted Hebrew children. To what extent paraplegic conditions were responsible for lameness is again uncertain. However, ataxic paraplegia, resulting in progressive paralysis of the leg muscles, and senile paraplegia, with general weakness or actual developing paralysis of the lower extremities, should not be excluded from the larger picture of pathological conditions contributing to lameness.

Probably many persons became disabled through fractures of bones, particularly if a fragile condition of the bones, leading to spontaneous fractures (*osteopsathyrosis*), was present. While Egyptian physicians were proficient at reducing and splinting fractures, there is no indication that such procedures were undertaken in Israel (cf. Lev. 21:19).

A childhood accident at the hands of his nurse (II Sam. 4:4) occurred to Mephibosheth, the son of Jonathan. As a result, he was lame for the rest of his days. Apparently some form of treatment was applied locally for the disability, since he did not pause to dress (עשׁה; LXX ἐθεράπευσεν) his feet before meeting with David (II Sam. 19:24). The precise nature of the complaint from which he suffered is uncertain.

The healing of the lame formed part of the therapeutic activity of Jesus (Matt. 15:30; 21:14), although the references to those who were cured of their lameness are general in nature, and in consequence afford no proper indication of the actual ailment with which individuals were afflicted.

More fully documented are the accounts of the lame being healed through the ministry of the disciples in the early church. Peter and John were confronted by a congenitally lame man as they passed by the Gate Beautiful to enter the temple (Acts 3:2). His lameness was apparently due to weakness of the astragalus and metatarsus bones of the foot. Luke used the technical terms βάσις ("foot") and σφυρά ("ankles"), found alike in classical and medical writers from Hippocrates onward. The lameness may have been due to cyllosis, or to some congenital malformation such as *spina bifida,* although cases of the latter do not always survive adolescence. Another congenital cripple was healed by Paul at Lystra (Acts 14:8), and he too may have suffered from some form of cyllosis. R. K. HARRISON

LAMECH lā'mĭk [למך; Λαμεχ].

1. In the J tradition
2. In the P tradition
3. The Song of Lamech
4. Unity of meaning
5. In the NT
6. In apocryphal literature

Bibliography

1. In the J tradition. According to the Yahwist, Lamech was the son of Methushael, of the line of Cain, and the husband of Adah and Zillah (Gen. 4:18-24). Adah bore Jabal, the "father of those who dwell in tents and have cattle," and Jubal, the "father of all those who play the lyre and pipe." Zillah bore TUBAL-CAIN, the "forger of all instruments of bronze and iron," and his sister, Naamah. In line with the Yahwist's interest in etiologies, this genealogy accounts very briefly for the rise of nomads, musicians, and smiths (metalworkers). To Lamech also are attributed, at least by inference, the beginning of polygamy—or, more strictly, bigamy—and the ugly growth of human pride. *See* § 3 *below.*

2. In the P tradition. According to the Priestly source (*see* P), Lamech was the son of Methuselah, of the line of Seth, and the father of Noah (Gen. 5:25-28, 30-32; cf. I Chr. 1:3). He was 182 years old when Noah was born, then lived 595 years longer, having other children. He died at the age of 777 years. However, Gen. 5:29 is from J; and the Noah which it describes as mitigating the curse Yahweh had laid upon the ground because of man's sin (cf. 3:17-19) might not originally have been linked with the Flood.

3. The Song of Lamech. The Song (Gen. 4:23-24) is an ancient poem similar in mood to Judg. 15:

16; I Sam. 18:7 (*see* POETRY, HEBREW). If "Adah and Zillah" are not intrinsic parts of the Song (cf. Commentaries), it may originally have been unrelated to the genealogy; for the Song itself does not necessarily presuppose the manufacture of weapons by Tubal-cain, as has often been held. However, its reference to the wives of Lamech, Cain, and the increase of sin through man's pride and desire for almost limitless revenge now tie it closely to the Yahwist's epic.

4. Unity of meaning. Regardless of their original relationship, these three traditions are linked together in the present Genesis story and teach that although the human family (through Lamech) increased in sin as it advanced in civilization, it also (through Noah) received partial remission of the curse. Further, the occurrence of the number 7 serves as a unifying motif: Cain was to be avenged 7 times, Lamech 77; and Lamech lived 777 years.

5. In the NT. Lamech's genealogy as given in Luke 3:36 agrees with P (*see* § 2 *above*). Jesus' word about unlimited forgiveness (Matt. 18:22) may be a conscious reference to the Song of Lamech.

6. In apocryphal literature. In the Dead Sea Genesis Apocryphon, Lamech confronts his wife, Bat-Enosh ("Bêtênôs, the daughter of Bârâkî'îl," in Jubilees), with the suspicion that their son (Noah in Jubilees; Menachem in Jashar) is not his. Although she assures him that the child is indeed from him, not from a stranger or divine being (ולא מן כול עירין ולא מן כול בני שמין), for additional information Lamech hastens to his father, Methuselah, who in turn has recourse to Enoch, his father, from whom he is sure of learning the truth (II.1-26; the text breaks here). The book of JUBILEES supplies further information about such divine beings (especially the "Watchers" [4:15]; *see also* WATCHER) and Enoch's divinely revealed knowledge (4:17-19, 23).

Bibliography. N. Avigad and Y. Yadin, *A Genesis Apocryphon* (1956), pp. 16-19, 40.

L. HICKS

LAMED lä'mĭd (Heb. lä'mĕth) [ל, *l* (*Lāmedh*)]. The twelfth letter of the Hebrew ALPHABET as it is placed in the KJV at the head of the twelfth section of the acrostic psalm, Ps. 119, where each verse of this section of the psalm begins with this letter.

LAMENTATION. *See* MOURNING.

LAMENTATIONS, BOOK OF lăm'ən tā'shənz [איכה, O how! LXX Θρῆνοι, Dirges]. The OT book normally third among the Megilloth (*see* CANON OF THE OT). The LXX and Vulg. place it after the book of Jeremiah. The English versions enlarged the title to read "Lamentations of Jeremiah."

Lamentations consists of five poems imitative of the forms of individual lament and funeral celebration, four of which are acrostic in form. The meter is mixed, with a prevailing 3+2 pattern. The occasion for the poems was the destruction of Jerusalem in 586 B.C. The cruelty of the plundering enemy, the ravages of plague and famine, the helplessness of leaders, and the cessation of the temple cultus are described poignantly.

Tradition has regarded Jeremiah as the author, but without justification. The poems were probably composed during a period of years for the annual lament over Jerusalem's fall. One hand may be responsible for the first four poems. Events are seen through the eyes of Palestinian Jews who lived in the economically and spiritually depleted homeland between 586 and 538 B.C. The book is doubtless a liturgical collection from an originally larger assortment of commemorative laments. Catharsis of grief and despair is a primary aim of the poems. Animated by a prophetic spirit, the poet is moved by contrition at the judgment of Yahweh and by hope in the divine purposes in spite of Israel's historical nemesis.

1. Literary form
2. Occasion
3. Authorship
4. Liturgical use
5. Purpose
Bibliography

1. Literary form. Lamentations consists of five poems, of which four are ACROSTIC. The twenty-two letters of the Hebrew alphabet are given in succession throughout each poem, appearing at the beginning of each verse or strophe. Poems 1-3 have three lines to a stanza (except for an accidental four lines in 1:7; 2:19), whereas the fourth poem has but two lines to a strophe. The final poem is not acrostic, but is alphabetic in the sense that it contains twenty-two lines. Another variation is in the third chapter, where the acrostic device is used at the beginning of each line rather than strophe (thus there are three *'āleph* lines, three *bêth* lines, etc.). The dominant metric pattern is 3+2, with ample exceptions in 2+2, 2+3, and 3+3 form. The fifth poem is chiefly 3+3. *See* POETRY, HEBREW, § D.

In spite of the rather artificial form, Lamentations attains a remarkable emotional vitality. Although the poems lack the literary finesse associated with the elegiac tradition in English literature, they compare favorably with ancient Near Eastern laments, including other OT specimens. While one of the motivations for the acrostic form may have been to facilitate memory, another, and more cogent, reason was to express the completeness of grief and despair and the plenitude of faith and hope. There are parallels from later synagogue compositions (e.g., the *widui* or lists of sins and sinners in alphabetic form, and poems such as Yose ben Yose's seventh-century acrostic for the Day of Atonement). A regular Talmudic idiom speaks of keeping the Torah "from *'āleph* to *tāw*."

As to literary type, the poems are composite. Chs. 1–2; 4 have traits of the funeral song (e.g., II Sam. 1:17-27; *see* MOURNING). As Amos had earlier applied a funeral lament to Israel (5:1-2), so does the poet of Lamentations, although he pictures Jerusalem not as the corpse but as the sorrowing widow. The third poem is in individual lament style, seemingly the protest of a lone sufferer, although the context shows that Judah is personified in the manner of corporate personality. The interpretation is confirmed by the explicit national reference of individual imagery elsewhere in the book (e.g., 1:13-16). Thus the imagery and mood of individual lament and funeral dirge have been joined to a national catastrophe in order to convey its deeply personal and tragic import.

2. Occasion. The capture and destruction of Jerusalem by the Chaldeans (*see* CHALDEA) in 586 B.C. is background for all the poems, and the immediate subject of at least the first, second, and fourth. Dissenting opinions that find the occasion of lament in the pillage of the temple by Antiochus IV Epiphanes (*see* ANTIOCHUS 4) in 168 B.C. or the Roman Pompey in 63 B.C. are not convincing. While Lamentations offers no direct historical evidence (the only proper name is Edom [4:22]), it does correlate substantially and convincingly with the accounts of the last days of Judah found in the book of Kings and the book of Jeremiah. Among the relevant points of comparison are: siege (II Kings 25:1-2; Lam. 2:22; 3:5, 7), famine (II Kings 25:3; Jer. 37:21; Lam. 1:11, 19; 2:11-12, 19-20; 4:4-5, 9-10), flight of the king (II Kings 25:4-7; Lam. 1:3, 6; 2:2; 4:19-20), looting of the temple (II Kings 25:13-15; Lam. 1:10; 2:6-7), burning of the temple, palace, and important buildings (II Kings 25:8-9; Lam. 2:3-5; 4:11; 5:18), demolition of the city walls (II Kings 25:10; Lam. 2:7-9), slaughter of the leaders (II Kings 25:18-21; Jer. 39:6; Lam. 1:15; 2:2, 20; 4:16), exile of the inhabitants (II Kings 25:11-12; Lam. 1:1, 4-5, 18; 2:9, 14; 3:2, 19; 4:22; 5:2), expectation and collapse of foreign help (Jer. 27:1-11; 37:5-10; Lam. 4:17; 5:6), Judah's fickle political allies (II Kings 24:2; Jer. 40:14; Lam. 1:2, 8, 17, 19), and the provincial status of Judah (II Kings 25:22, 24-25; Lam. 1:1; 5:8-9).

3. Authorship. The traditional author is the prophet Jeremiah. His role is classically represented in Michelangelo's Sistine Chapel painting, where he sits in the brooding and melancholy posture of lament. The tradition can be traced back to the LXX preface: "And it came to pass after the captivity of Israel and the desolation of Jerusalem that Jeremiah sat mourning and he lamented this lament over Jerusalem and said . . . ." Whereupon the text of Lamentations follows. Furthermore, the LXX places the book after the book of Jeremiah. The Vulg. follows the same tradition. Even the Talmud claims Jeremianic authorship. Apparently the common source for the traditions was II Chr. 35:25: "Jeremiah also uttered a lament for Josiah; and all the singing men and singing women have spoken of Josiah in their laments to this day. They made these an ordinance in Israel; behold, they are written in the Laments." The Chronicler hardly refers to the book of Lamentations, since it contains no lament over Josiah but only brief reference to Zedekiah. But traditions have been set in motion with less justification, and it is likely that the careful distinction of Chronicles was overlooked by later readers.

Internal evidence indicates not an iota of support for the tradition. Jeremiah is never named or implied. There are, as a matter of fact, some fairly telling arguments against Jeremianic authorship. One wonders if so adamant a prophet could have closely and sympathetically identified himself with the city's reliance on foreign help and facile trust in the king (4:16, 19). It is difficult to imagine the prophet, who remained in Palestine only a few weeks after Jerusalem's capture, writing the fifth poem, with its ennui and lassitude induced by years of foreign occupation. It is unlikely that Jeremiah, who in the whole of his identified writings never resorts to extensive poetic formalities, should have undertaken the construction of acrostic poems. And finally, if the poems are by the prophet, it is difficult to know why they were not included in the book of Jeremiah, especially when we consider how many oracles of much later origin have been collected under his name.

With the surrender of the traditional theory, most scholars have assumed the activity of two or more poets. The third poem is frequently treated as a fifth- or fourth-century mosaic of psalm clichés. It is true that many differences may be pointed out among the poems, especially contrasting the first and third with the second and fourth. Yet the affinities, linguistic and ideological, are considerable. Diversities within the same poem as great as those between poems can be singled out, and yet few would ignore the acrostic unity of each of the poems and argue for composite authorship for any one chapter. Several literary types and images have been freely appropriated but not wholly assimilated, yet a single mood pervades the collection. All the poems are rooted in the same historical era—i.e., the period of the Palestinian "exile" (586-538 B.C.). Probably the first four poems, and possibly all five, come from the same poet. It is arguable that the nostalgia toward the king and enthusiasm for nobility (e.g., 1:6; 4:7-8) point to an origin in court circles, perhaps within the family of Shaphan (*see* SHAPHAN 1), whose members had been cordial toward Jeremiah (Jer. 26:24; 29:3; 36:10; 40:5). One difficulty with the hypothesis is that the ranks of the nobility were severely decimated by execution and deportation.

4. Liturgical use. The subtle differences between the poems, as well as the manifest repetitions, suggest that they were composed one at a time and not as parts of a greater whole. The fourfold repetition of the acrostic makes this almost conclusive. There is no dramatic progress. Any of the poems can stand alone. Lamentations is best thought of as a collection of laments to be sung on the annual fast days in remembrance of the fall of Jerusalem (cf. Jer. 41:4-5; Zech. 7:1-5). Probably these poems represent the selective sifting of many seasons. Out of a large number of compositions, long years of usage had endeared these to the community as most expressive of the chastened mood of Israel—both in its abysmal sorrow and in its unshakable faith. The final poem looks like a summary appended to the four acrostics, intended to round out the anthology and even bring it up to date.

The process of compilation was governed by a chiastic principle. Chs. 1 and 5 are summaries of the disaster, chs. 2 and 4 more explicit recitals of the details of death and devastation, while ch. 3 occupies the pivotal position in form (intensified acrostic; *see* § 1 *above*) and content (trust in the goodness of God toward Israel). The strophes which are important from the standpoint of theology are central in the poem's structure and, consequently, the crux of the entire collection (3:31-36). The effect of the compilation has been to make everything lead up to the third poem and then flow away from it, thereby putting the climax in the middle.

Catharsis of grief and dejection is the aim of lament liturgies. In Lamentations the acrostic, the quasi-dialogue structure, the iteration and savagery of expression, are best accounted for by liturgical use. Public recital of the poems on the appropriate memorial days, perhaps with various readers taking the parts of Zion, the groups of citizens, the onlookers, etc., must have been an effective outlet for the pent-up emotion of a people who had lost practically everything that belonged to their former mode of life. In orthodox Jewry, Lamentations has been read in the synagogue since *ca.* A.D. 70 to commemorate the fall of the city to the Romans and the dispersion of Israel. Christian interpretation has assigned the poems to the sufferings of Jesus Christ, with readings designated from Lamentations for Holy Week.

5. Purpose. The axis around which the thought of the book turns is the conflict between historical faith and historical actuality (*see* SUFFERING AND EVIL). Although this enigma is the age-old despair of religion, it took on peculiar urgency on account of the sharp reversal of Israel's historical destiny after 586 B.C. In substance, Lamentations asks: What is the meaning of the terrible calamities that have overtaken us between 608 and 586 B.C. (*see* ISRAEL, HISTORY OF)—i.e., from the untimely death of King JOSIAH through vassalage and rebellion, siege and famine, to the city's humiliation and the extinction of the state? Can these events really be understood as expressive of Yahweh's will? If so, what is our present role? Has Yahweh further plans with Israel? How are we to react to a God who has chastened his people without mercy? Lamentations reveals a deep sense of desertion by men and God, and confronts suffering as a threat to God's purposes in history and thus, inevitably, to the very life of faith.

There is a bitter realism in the book. No efforts have been spared to portray the carnage and destruction. The plight of the emaciated and dying children is etched in pathetic detail. Cannibalism, provoked by extreme hunger, and the slaughter of the priests in the temple, are cited by the poet as the ultimate denial of God's purpose with Israel. The poems throb with a spiritually desolating anguish. And yet almost the whole of the compilation is cast in the mold of prayer, as the poet lifts before God the appalling scene and thereby lays the basis for plaintive appeal. The essence of biblical PRAYER in its vigor and candor could not be better illustrated.

But alongside this "priestly" intercessory protest runs a profoundly "prophetic" stream of thought. Lamentations vindicates the prophetic word of doom. Jerusalem has fallen because of her sin; her fate, though extreme, was a deserved one. The poet counsels passivity toward the enemy and quiet trust in God. He exhibits an absolute loyalty to Yahwism, firmly rejecting all temptations to syncretism or polytheism of the sort that enticed other exilic Jews (e.g., Isa. 57; Jer. 44; Ezek. 8). The poet berates faithless prophets and priests, secure in his faith that the religion of Yahweh could continue independent of professional leadership. The book indicates a steady hope in God's covenant love. *See* LOVE IN THE OT.

Lamentations spans the death of Hebraism and the birth of Judaism. Concentrated in the third poem (especially in the climactic vss. 19-39) are several of the dominant convictions of that faith which was to spring phoenixlike from the ashes and rubble of political annihilation: responsibility for sin, the disciplinary value of suffering, the absolute justice and abiding love of God, the inscrutability of his ways, the unconquerable trust of the believer, the necessity of patience. God's further purposes with Israel are grounded solely in his love and mercy, unfathomable but dependable. With fervor, chastened and refined by suffering, Lamentations proclaims Israel's incredible faith and writes it indelibly into the liturgical practice of Judaism.

Bibliography. Commentaries: K. Budde, *KHC* (1898). M. Löhr, *HKAT* (2nd ed., 1907). A. S. Peake, Century Bible (1912). A. W. Streane, Cambridge Bible (1913). W. Rudolph, *KAT* (1939). M. Haller, *HAT* (1940). H. Wiesmann (1954). H.-J. Kraus, *Biblischer Kommentar AT* (1956). T. J. Meek, *IB* (1956).

Special studies: M. Löhr, "Der Sprachgebrauch des Buches der Klagelieder," *ZAW,* XIV (1894), 31-50; "Threni III und die jeremianische Autorschaft des Buches der Klagelieder," *ZAW,* XXIV (1904), 1-16. H. Jahnow, *Das hebräische Leichenlied im Rahmen der Völkerdichtung,* BZAW (1923). H. Wiesmann, "Der Zweck der Klagelieder des Jeremias," *Bibl.,* VII (1926), 412-28; "Das Leid im Buche der Klagelieder," *Zeitschrift für Aszese und Mystik,* IV (1929), 97-125; "Die literarische Art der Klagelieder," *TQ,* CX (1929), 381-428; "Der geschichtliche Hintergrund des Büchleins der Klagelieder," *BZ,* XXII (1934), 20-43. W. Rudolph, "Der Text der Klagelieder," *ZAW,* LVI (1938), 101-22. N. K. Gottwald, *Studies in the Book of Lamentations* (1954). E. Jannssen, *Juda in der Exilzeit* (1956). N. K. GOTTWALD

LAMP [מנורה (KJV CANDLESTICK), ניר (KJV *alternately* LIGHT; PLOWING), נר (KJV *alternately* CANDLE), KJV לפיד (RSV TORCH); λαμπάς (*alternately* TORCH), λύχνος (KJV *alternately* CANDLE; LIGHT)].

Lamps are mentioned many times in the OT, referring mostly to the lamps of the LAMPSTAND in the tabernacle and in the temple, but also used with symbolical meaning. The few passages where the lamp is mentioned as an object of daily use are styled in a way which shows how common it was (e.g., Prov. 31:18; Jer. 25:10). This is in agreement with the numberless lamps found in excavations.

Lamps of the OT period were made exclusively of pottery. In earliest times a saucer filled with olive

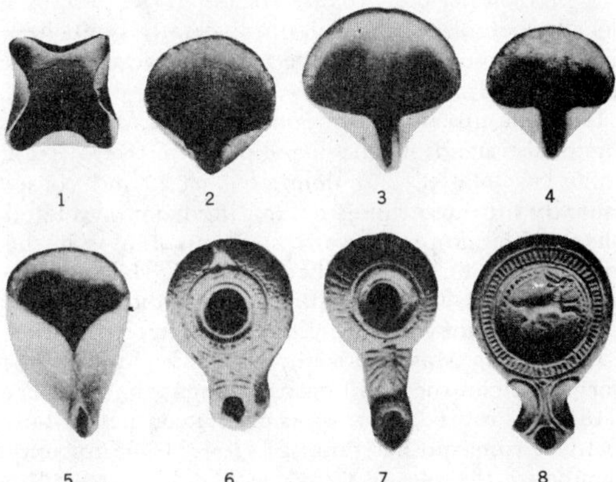

From *Atlas of the Bible* (Thomas Nelson & Sons Limited)

8. Oil lamps from various periods: 1-3 are from the three periods of the Bronze Age, 3000-2000 B.C., 2000-1600 B.C., 1600-1200 B.C.; 4-5, with a narrower lip, are Israelite types; 5 is fourth-century; 6, 7, and 8 are Hellenistic, Roman, and Byzantine respectively.

oil (cf. Exod. 27:20), on the rim of which rested a wick of twisted thread, was used. *Ca.* 2000 B.C. the first real lamps appeared: the saucers had the rims pinched in four places to form lips for holding the wick. From the Middle Bronze Age onward the lamp had a single lip (Fig. LAM 8). The lip became increasingly pinched, and in the Israelite period the lamp acquired a base. Seven-lipped lamps, such as those mentioned in Zech. 4:2, have also been found. Fig. LAM 11.

The first lamps in the temple may have been similar to the type described above (I Sam. 3:3), but several lamps were later joined on a common stem from which the seven-branched lampstand, the "menorah," developed. Fig. LAM 10.

Under the impact of Greek models introduced into Palestine in the fifth-fourth centuries B.C., the open saucer lamp was replaced in Hellenistic times by a covered, spouted model, which was wheel-made; the spout was formed from a lump of clay attached to the round body. The ascendancy of the covered lamp was interrupted only by archaic revivals like the Maccabean folded type and occasional remnants of an earlier age, but it had been universally adopted by 100 B.C. The spout gradually became shorter and was incorporated in the Roman period into the lamp itself; at the same time the molded lamp—made in two separate sections, upper and lower—was introduced. The round-bodied Roman lamp with a nozzle that projects only slightly was followed by molded lamps with a square end in which the wick hole was made; these in turn gave way to oval or pear-shaped types in late Roman and Byzantine times. Lamps in the Hellenistic Roman period were normally smaller and more delicate than their earlier counterparts. Fig. LAM 8.

The KJV translation "candle" is, of course, inaccurate. The small clay oil lamp was a commonplace, as its abundance on excavated sites, in tomb deposits, and in literary references indicates. Candles were not in use until after the biblical period.

The lamp, when taken together with "light" and "lampstand," had considerable symbolic power in the biblical period. Broadly speaking, the lamp is a localization of LIGHT, which universally symbolizes life, as opposed to death—the realm of darkness. This accounts in part for the nearly universal practice of placing lamps in tomb deposits. Light, and hence lamp, also stands for the divine presence (Rev. 21:23; 22:5; cf. John 8:12; I John 1:5; etc.), and consequently for those things emanating from or related thereto: the prophetic word is a lamp shining in the darkness (John 5:35 [cf. Ecclus. 48:1]; II Pet. 1:19; cf. Mark 4:21-22; Luke 8:16-17, where the context of this saying differs from the ethical interpretation given to it in Matt. 5:15-16); as a saving and transforming light, the lamp may represent the law (Ps. 119:105; Prov. 6:23) or works of righteousness (Matt. 5:15). From another point of view, the lamp may symbolize the eyes of God (Zech. 4:1-14, with the suggestion that the seven lamps on the Menorah are the seven planets; I Clem. 21:2), just as the woman lights a lamp to aid her eyes in searching for the lost coin (Luke 15:8); the eye may be depicted as the lamp of the body—i.e., the medium (or source?) of light. The lamp is a symbol of the lasting existence of the Davidic dynasty in I Kings 11:36; 15:4; II Kings 8:19; II Chr. 21:7. God is the lamp, lighting the darkness (II Sam. 22:29). The symbolism is sufficiently plastic to be utilized in a wide range of contexts, as this brief summary shows, although the root of the concept lies in the light-life equation, irrespective of whether it is understood transcendently or immanently.

Bibliography. K. Galling, "Die Beleuchtungsgeräte im israelitisch-jüdischen Kulturgebiet," *ZDPV,* 46 (1923), 1-50. C. A. Reisner, *et al., Harvard Excavations at Samaria,* I (1924), 317-25. J. Pedersen, *Israel,* I-II (1926), 448 ff, 464 ff. W. F. Albright, *Tell Beit Mirsim,* I, *AASOR,* XII (1932), 25, 42-43, 70-71, 86-87. K. Galling, *Biblisches Reallexikon* (1937), cols. 347 ff. F. W. Robins, *The Story of the Lamp* (1939). E. R. Goodenough, *Jewish Symbols in the Greco-Roman Period,* I (1953), 139 ff, 148; II (1953), 136-37; IV (1954), 77-98. C. Singer, *et al.*, eds., *A History of Technology,* I (1954), 235-37.

R. W. FUNK AND I. BEN-DOR

LAMPSTAND [מנורה, *menôrâ, from* נור, light; Aram. נברשתא (Dan. 5:5 *only*); λυχνία]; KJV (anachronistically) CANDLESTICK. A device for elevating a lamp so that its light will cover a large area; specifically, the sacred seven-branched lampstand of the temple and the tabernacle. *See* MENORAH.

1. Archaeological data
2. The menorah
3. The menorah as a symbol
4. History of the menorah

Bibliography

1. Archaeological data. The simplest method of elevating a lamp for better illumination is to set it in a niche in the wall or on a shelf jutting from a wall or a pillar, or to suspend it by a cord from the ceiling (cf. possibly Eccl. 12:6). If, however, the lamp is

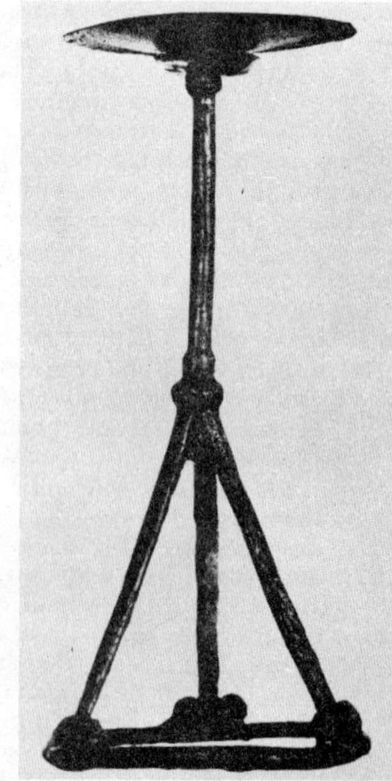

Courtesy of the Oriental Institute, the University of Chicago

9. Tripod or offering stand from Megiddo tombs (Late Bronze II)

placed on a stand, it is easier to tend, and the lighting is more efficient (Matt. 5:15). A great variety of stands have come from the excavation of Palestinian cities. Usually they are made of pottery and are roughly cylindrical in shape, with holes along the sides and painted designs on the exterior surface. The function these stands were intended to fill is not always clear, and the specimens actually found may be offering stands or supports for incense vessels, but the lampstand was probably of similar type. A variety of metallic stand from Megiddo and Beth-shan, consisting of a single upright shaft rising from a tripod base, has been suggested as illustrative of the lampstands of Solomon's temple.* Lamps with high bases were common in Iron Age Palestine (*see* LAMP), and it was only necessary to increase the height of the base in order to produce what was in effect a lamp and lampstand in one piece. A seven-spouted lamp of this kind was found at Tell Ta'annak, and provides an excellent archaeological illustration of the lampstand (RSV "lamp") which the Shunammite woman provided for Elisha's private chamber (II Kings 4:10). The lampstand of Zechariah's vision (Zech. 4:2, 11) was probably an elaborate example of the same type. *See* § 3 *below*. Fig. LAM 9.

2. The menorah. Lampstands in private houses or royal palaces are rarely mentioned in the Bible (II Kings 4:10; Luke 8:16), which is concerned almost exclusively with the sacred lampstands of the tabernacle and the temple. Indeed, the Hebrew word for "lampstand" (*m[e]nôrâ*) has been adopted as a technical term for the seven-branched lamp ("menorah"), and has become one of the best-known symbols of Judaism, found today in both synagogue and home. The single menorah which stood on the S side of the tabernacle opposite the table for the bread of the Presence (Exod. 26:35) is described in detail in Exod. 25:31-40; 37:17-24. It consisted of three main parts: the base, the shaft, and the branches. From a tripod base a vertical shaft arose, from either side of which sprang three branches, curving upward to the same height as the central shaft. Each branch and the shaft terminated in a cup, made in the form of an open almond flower, the extended petals of which held a lamp, so that support was provided for seven lamps in all. These were probably of the seven-spouted variety common in the Israelite period (Zech. 4:2).

10. Seven-branched candelabra of Herod's temple, from the arch of Titus at Rome

The branches and central shaft were decorated with the open-almond blossom motif, three to each branch and four on the central shaft. The insistence that the menorah was made by skilled craftsmen is understandable in view of the fact that it was made all in one piece out of *ca.* ninety-six pounds of gold (one talent), and that its complex decoration was of hammered work.

The lampstands of Solomon's temple are not described in detail, but we learn from I Kings 7:49 that there were ten of them placed before the inner sanctuary, five on the N and five on the S side. Additional lampstands of gold and silver were provided, probably for lighting the lesser rooms (I Chr. 28:15). In the second temple, built after the return from the Exile, the tabernacle practice of having only one menorah was restored (I Macc. 1:21; 4:49), and this was continued in Herod's temple, the menorah of which may be seen pictured with the other spoils taken from the temple on the triumphal arch of Titus in Rome. Figs. LAM 10; MUS 85.

3. The menorah as a symbol. The origin and early symbolic value of the sevenfold lamp is obscure. Its branched structure has suggested that it may be connected with the tree of life, a familiar symbol even in pre-Israelite Palestine. If this suggestion is true, the rounded tripod base may represent the world mountain from which the tree grows. Light and life are certainly related concepts in ancient thought. Seven is an almost universally sacred number, but the reason for its association with the sacred lamp is not clear. Zech. 4:10 interprets the seven lamps as the seven eyes of the Lord, "which range through the whole earth"—probably an oblique reference to the seven planets as the eyes of heaven.

Apart from a single reference to the tabernacle menorah in Heb. 9:2, and casual mention of household lampstands (Mark 4:21), lampstands in the NT are confined to the book of Revelation, where they have a symbolic function. The seven churches of Asia are represented by seven lampstands, among which "one like a son of man" (the Christ) walks (Rev. 1:12-20). The church at Ephesus is threatened with the removal of its lampstand if it fails to repent (Rev. 2:5).

4. History of the menorah. Since the description of the menorah in Exodus probably dates from postexilic times (fifth century B.C. or later), the actual appearance of the menorahs of the tabernacle and temple can only be reconstructed tentatively from archaeological data and some biblical allusions. The most important of the latter is Zech. 4:2, 11, where the lampstand consists of a large bowl, elevated on a stand, with seven lamps, each having seven spouts, ranged around its rim.* It is variously conjectured that the support for the bowl was a metal tripod, or a chalicelike stand resembling the tall-footed lamps referred to above. By the time of the second temple the more familiar seven-branched form had been adopted. Antigonus Mattathias (40-37 B.C.) used the menorah as a symbol on his coinage, but apart from this the menorah is not a common symbol until after the destruction of the temple in A.D. 70. After that time it rapidly became one of the most common of all Jewish symbols, appearing on buildings, in catacombs, and on small objects such as amulets and

From Kurt Galling, *Handbuch zum Alten Testament;* by permission of J. C. B. Mohr (Paul Siebeck), Tübingen

11. Suggested archaeological reconstruction of the lampstand in Zech. 4

lamps (*see* SYNAGOGUE). The basic form of the menorah in these representations remains the same as that described in the Exodus passage, although it is often much simplified and occasionally five, nine, or eleven branches are depicted. With the introduction of candles the lampstand became a candelabrum, thus providing a kind of historic justification for the translation "candlestick." Fig. LAM 11.

Bibliography. K. Galling, *Biblisches Reallexikon* (1937), p. 348; G. E. Wright, "Solomon's Temple Reconstructed," *BA,* vol. IV (1941); E. R. Goodenough, *Jewish Symbols in the Graeco-Roman Period* (1953). L. E. TOOMBS

LANCE. *See* WEAPONS AND IMPLEMENTS OF WAR § 3*d.*

LANCETS [רמח]. A textual error in I Kings 18:28 KJV (RSV correctly LANCES). *See* WEAPONS AND IMPLEMENTS OF WAR § 3*e.*

LAND CROCODILE [כח, *possibly* strong one; *cf.* כח, strength, power] (Lev. 11:30); KJV CHAMELEON. An old name for the "monitor," any of a family (Varanidae) of large, carnivorous lizards ranging from four to seven feet in length, of the genus Varanus. Two species are reported by Tristram as living in Palestine.

The context in Lev. 11 suggests that כח (*kôaḥ*) is a reptile and probably a lizard; the LXX and the Vulg. take the word as "chameleon," and the Peshitta as "mole." If the monitor is meant, the Hebrew word doubtless indicates that it was the largest and strongest lizard known in Israel.

W. S. MCCULLOUGH

LAND LAWS. Those laws in the Pentateuch pertaining to the allotment of land by tribes and the provision for its protection (Num. 27:5-11; 36:5-9; Deut. 19:14; 27:17). For sabbatical-year legislation on land (Exod. 23:10-11; Lev. 25), *see* JUBILEE.

See also LAW IN THE OT.

LANDMARK [גבול, גבולה, border]. In the ancient Near East stones were erected to mark the boundaries between fields, districts, and nations (Gen. 31:51-52). In Mesopotamia and Egypt these were often elaborately inscribed, and it may be assumed that Palestinian landmarks had at least a few words of identification. Naturally the removal of landmarks was a serious offense. It is specifically mentioned as a crime in Babylonian law and is prohibited in the Instruction of Amen-em-opet (*see* EGYPT) as well as in Greek and Roman law. The Code (*cf.* DEUTERONOMY) twice warns against the removal of landmarks (Deut. 19:14; 27:17). The offense was also used as a symbol of overturning ancient customs or laws (Prov. 22:28; 23:10; cf. Job 24:2; Philo *On the Special Laws* IV.149-50). Thus those who defect from the Qumran sect are called "removers of the landmark." *See* TRIBE § 2*f.* Fig. LAN 12.

Courtesy of the University Museum of the University of Pennsylvania

12. A boundary stone of Nebuchadnezzar I, from Nippur (twelfth century B.C.)

Bibliography. S. R. Driver, *Deuteronomy,* ICC (1895), pp. 234-35 (on Greek and Roman laws); P. S. Landersdorfer, *Die Kultur der Babylonier und Assyrer* (1913), p. 157 (on Babylonian laws); C. Rabin, *The Zadokite Documents* (1954), pp. 4, 20, 42 (on the Qumran material); J. B. Pritchard, ed., *ANET* (2nd ed., 1955), p. 422 (on Egyptian prohibition). J. F. Ross

LANE. The translation of ῥύμη in Luke 14:21 (STREET in Acts 9:11; 12:10). *See* CITY § B2*c*.

LANGUAGES OF THE ANCIENT NEAR EAST. Interest in the linguistic diversity of the ancient world appears in such biblical stories as the tower of BABEL and the day of PENTECOST. By counting the peoples enumerated in Gen. 10 the rabbis later figured at seventy-two the number of languages spoken in the ancient world. This number found wide acceptance among both Christians and Mohammedans. Of many peoples mentioned in the Bible we have no linguistic records whatever. At the same time, modern exploration has uncovered texts in the languages of peoples not identifiable in the Bible. Knowledge of such languages is necessarily derived from written documents; and as the art of writing arose in the Near East only *ca.* 3500 B.C., we can know nothing of these languages earlier than this date. The earliest WRITING was pictographic or ideographic. These ideograms became phonograms when a symbol stood for a sound and no longer for the meaning. In early writing symbols were used frequently both as ideograms and phonograms. Only at a later period did alphabets develop (*see* ALPHABET) out of these syllabic, ideographic systems.

Records in some languages of the ancient Near East are almost completely intelligible, others only partly intelligible, while others are still undeciphered. For some there is available an abundance of material, for others much less—perhaps only proper names, a few glosses, or texts too brief and obscure to permit of any sure interpretation. Any classification other than geographical is thus hardly practicable.

1. Mesopotamian group
2. Zaghros group
3. Anatolian group
4. Iranian group
5. Syro-Palestinian group
6. Aaegean group
7. Coastal languages of Asia Minor
8. Egypto-Berber group

1. Mesopotamian group. The art of writing would seem to have originated in S Mesopotamia, where the earliest intelligible texts are in Sumerian. The inhabitants of SUMER invented a pictographic script which, when it came to be written on clay instead of inscribed on harder material, developed the characteristic wedge-shaped signs known as the cuneiform script. In this we have Sumerian texts from *ca.* 3200 B.C. to Arsacid times. Sumerian is a non-Semitic, non–Indo-European language of an agglutinative type. There are two dialects, the *eme-ku* and the *eme-sal,* of which the former is the older. Early in the third millennium B.C. incoming Semitic speakers had become an important element in N and central Mesopotamia. From the Sumerians they learned the cuneiform script in which they wrote their own language. This is Akkadian, the first of the Semitic languages (*see* SEMITES) to appear in written form. Its main dialects are Babylonian and Assyrian. (*See* ASSYRIA AND BABYLONIA.) Between the fifteenth and thirteenth centuries, however, Akkadian became a lingua franca in much of the Near East, and was adopted by peoples of non-Semitic speech habits, giving rise to such dialectal forms of Akkadian as Cappadocian, Nuzi, Elamite, and the Mari dialect used by the Amorite invaders. Akkadian is known from inscriptions and tablets from *ca.* 2800 B.C. to A.D. 50. From Seleucid times come a few Akkadian texts in Greek transcription. So great was the prestige of Akkadian culture that neighboring peoples adopted the cuneiform script to write their own languages.

2. Zaghros group. From early times Mesopotamia has been subject to invasion by the hill peoples. From the Zaghros Mountains have come certain recognizable groups of invaders. The Guti from this region established a dynasty of Gutium between the fourth and fifth dynasties of Uruk. There are no connected texts in their language, but the names of the Gutian kings are non-Semitic and seem unrelated to any known language family. Of the later Kassites from the Zaghros, who held hegemony in Babylonia for hundreds of years, there are, besides names of gods and men, a number of glosses in Babylonian texts. The names of their overlords are Indo-European, but the glosses suggest that the common Kassite folk spoke a language akin to Elamitish. An even more important invasion was that of the Hurrians, the OT Horites, who from the fifteenth to the thirteenth century B.C. exercised considerable influence in the Near East, from the Zaghros to the Mediterranean and as far S as Egypt. The Mittani overlords of these Hurrians were of Indo-European speech, as appears from their names, the names of their gods, and their numerals. The Hurrian language, however, known from great numbers of cuneiform texts, is an agglutinative language unrelated to any known linguistic family.

To this group should be attached the Elamite languages (*see* ELAM), for which considerable material is available but which are not yet fully intelligible. The earliest inscriptions from Susa, the main city of Elam, are in a pictographic script which is possibly of Mesopotamian origin but which may be an independent development. Later the people of Susa adopted the cuneiform script which they used for writing an Elamite dialect of Akkadian but also for writing their own language. If the pictograph language is called Proto-Elamite, the earliest cuneiform texts, from *ca.* 2500 B.C., may be called Old Susian. The same language, but in a more developed form and a somewhat different style of cuneiform script, is used in texts from the sixteenth to the eighth century B.C., and may be called Neo-Susian. In the Achaemenid period a still later form of the language is used both for inscriptions on rock and on thousands of clay tablets, and is known as Elamitish. All attempts to relate these to other language families have failed.

3. Anatolian group. The cuneiform script spread also westward into Anatolia, where it was used to write Akkadian and also local languages. Perhaps through the Hurrians it came to the HITTITES, a people of Indo-European speech who had entered Asia Minor from the W and established a kingdom in the bend of the Halys River. In their inscriptions they call themselves Nesians, but they had superseded an older Khatti people, whose name, in the modified form "Hitti," is that by which they came to be known. Their own language is Indo-European of the *centum* type; but the language of the older people, now known as Proto-Khatti, appears to be unrelated to any known linguistic family. Inscriptions in a hieroglyphic script, not yet fully intelligible but thought to be associated with the Hittite Empire and so called hieroglyphic Hittite, though known to be younger than cuneiform Hittite, are possibly in the language of the Cilician kingdom of Kassuwatna. The Nesians were not the only Indo-European speakers to invade Asia Minor, for among the cuneiform texts are a few in Luwian and Palawi, which seem to be cognate dialects belonging to roughly the same period as the Hittite cuneiform texts.

A much later invasion of Indo-Europeans brought speakers of the *satem*-type Phrygian into central Anatolia. Its inscriptions belong to two groups: the Old Phrygian, which are of the seventh and sixth centuries B.C. and are written in an alphabet of the old W Greek type; and the Neo-Phrygian of the Roman period, written in the ordinary Greek alphabet. Phrygian seems still to have been spoken in that area till the fifth century A.D. A relatively small warrior group of similar origin moving farther E imposed their rule on the Urartean land, and their Indo-European speech spoken by their Urartean subjects developed into Armenian, which we know only as a Christian language, since it was not written till after the conversion of the country to Christianity. The original Urarteans had long been writing their language in cuneiform script. It was formerly called Vannic, because the earliest inscriptions came from near Lake Van, and some call it Kaldi. These inscriptions date from between 840 and 640 B.C. and are in a non-Semitic, non-Indo-European language. Unsuccessful attempts have been made to relate it to Hurrian and to the Caucasian languages.

4. Iranian group. To the N and the E of Elam were the lands of the MEDES and the Persians (*see* PERSIA). These speakers of Indo-European dialects came as invaders to settle among peoples of quite different speech habits. The earliest inscriptions are those of the Achaemenid rulers, Darius, Cyrus, Xerxes, Artaxerxes, etc., written in an alphabetized form of cuneiform script. This was the language of the Persians from Persis, and is known as Old Persian. Median is known only from person and place names and some glosses. It gave rise, however, to the Middle Iranian dialect of Arsacid Pahlavi used throughout the great Parthian Empire. Avestan, the language of the older Zoroastrian scriptures, possibly represents the old Bactrian tongue of the NE, from which area came also the Soghdian language. The tongue of the Scythians belongs to this Iranian group. It is represented by Ossetian, still spoken in the Caucasus. Avestan and Pahlavi are written in a script probably derived from Syriac.

5. Syro-Palestinian group. Both the Egyptian hieroglyphic script and the Mesopotamian cuneiform script were in early use in Syria and Palestine, and from both of them developed scripts for writing the local languages. The excavations at Ras Shamra in uncovering the ancient city of UGARIT revealed a whole literature written in an alphabetic script based on a selection of cuneiform signs. These Ugaritic texts come from the period 1500-1300 B.C. and are in a Semitic language. Phoenician is also a Semitic language. Its inscriptions range from the twelfth century B.C. to the sixth century A.D. and are in a characteristic alphabet developed by the Phoenicians out of earlier attempts at adapting Egyptian hieroglyphic signs to write Semitic. The form of the language used in the Phoenician colonies in North Africa is called Punic. It was still in use in the lifetime of Augustine. Excavations at Byblos have revealed another group of inscriptions written in a semihieroglyphic script based on Egyptian. This Byblian language would also seem to be Semitic. Far S in Sinai at Serabit al-Khadem has been found yet another script based on Egyptian, which links up with certain enigmatic inscriptions found elsewhere in Palestine, whose language when satisfactorily interpreted will probably also be found to be Semitic. The Canaanitish tongues, Hebrew, Aramaic, Samaritan, Moabite, Edomite, and Ammonite, are all Semitic. *See* HEBREW LANGUAGE; ARAMAIC LANGUAGE; EDOM; MOAB.

Here also should be mentioned the Arabian groups (*see* ARABIANS). Numerous inscriptions from the South Arabian kingdoms and from their N trade outposts reveal the Minaeo-Sabaean language from as early as the ninth century B.C. Certain North Arabian groups learned from them their distinctive alphabet, which they adapted to write their own Dedanite, Lihyanite, Thamudic, and Safaite dialects, which are the precursors of classical Arabic. The Arabians present on the day of Pentecost were doubtless Nabateans, whose language, written in a modification of the Aramaic script, continued in use up to Islamic times. All the Arabian dialects are Semitic.

6. Aegean group. In historical times Greek (*see* GREEK LANGUAGE), in various dialectal forms, was spoken in the Aegean, but these dialectal forms arose because it was Greek imposed upon peoples of other speech habits. Possibly there is evidence of some of these earlier languages in the Cretan and Cypriote inscriptions. The Minoan language of the Cretan hieroglyphic inscriptions is still undeciphered. Besides the hieroglyphs, however, two groups of linear inscriptions of Cretan origin are known, named Linear A and Linear B. Linear B has proved to be an archaic form of Achaean Greek. Some Cypriote inscriptions in a script closely resembling the Cretan are called Cypro-Minoan. The Cypriotes also used a purely syllabic script. The earlier inscriptions in this script, called Eteo-Cypriote, are still undeciphered, but later texts in the same script have proved to be in a dialect of Arcadian Greek. If the mysterious Phaistos disk turns out to be Philistine, it should doubtless be included here.

7. Coastal languages of Asia Minor. These are known mostly from proper names, but for a few we have some glosses, and for a lesser number some short inscriptions, partly in strange alphabetic scripts and later in the Greek script. Cilician, Pisidian,

Mysian, Isaurian, and Lycaonian are known only from a few glosses which tell little about the nature of the languages. Of Sideto-Pamphylian there are coin inscriptions from the fourth and third centuries B.C., and three undatable tomb inscriptions in Sidetan and Greek. Carian is known from proper names of a characteristic form, from some glosses, eighty graffiti, and three bilingual inscriptions of the seventh century B.C. from Egypt. Lydian is represented in inscriptions recovered from the excavations at Sardis and a bilingual Lydian-Aramaic text. The inscriptions date from the fifth and fourth centuries B.C. For Lycian there is also a body of inscriptional material, some in Greek letters but many in a strange script. Some are bilingual Greek-Lycian texts dating from the first century B.C. There is no certainty of linguistic connections of these coastal languages.

8. Egypto-Berber group. Almost as anciently attested as Sumerian is the old Egyptian language (*see* EGYPT) which also was at first written in pictograms, still familiar as the hieroglyphs on the Pharaonic monuments. A more cursive form of this writing for use on softer materials is the Hieratic script, and a still more cursive form, which appears *ca.* 700 B.C., is the Demotic script. The language underwent great changes during its history, so the language of Dynasties I–VIII (*ca.* 3000-2155) is called Old Egyptian, that of Dynasties IX–XVIII (2155-1350) Middle Egyptian, and that of Dynasties XIX–XXIV (1350-720) Late Egyptian. From then on till Roman times it, like the script, is referred to as Demotic. After the Christianization of Egypt the documents in a new alphabet based on Greek script are called Coptic, the four main dialects of which are Sahidic in Upper Egypt, Akhmimic and Fayyumic in Middle Egypt, and Bohairic in Lower Egypt.

Far up the Nile the Ethiopian rulers of Napata had adopted the Egyptian language for their inscriptions as early as the eighth century B.C. In the first century B.C., however, at the capital city of Meroe, the seat of that Candace whose eunuch appears in Acts 8:26-39, there had been developed from the hieroglyphs a system of signs for writing the local Meroitic language, inscriptions which, both in lapidary and in cursive, continue till late in the third century A.D. Though this script can be read, the inscriptions are still undeciphered. To the W of Egypt lies the area of the Berber languages, only one of which, Numidian, presents inscriptions of any age. It is written in a curious Libyan alphabet of uncertain origin, and the texts, which date from the second century A.D., are only partially intelligible.

Bibliography. General: E. Forrer, *Die acht Sprachen der Boghazkoi Inschriften* (1919). J. Friedrich, "Alt-kleinasiatische Sprachen," *Reallexikon der Vorgeschichte,* I (1924), 126-42; Kleinasiatische Sprachdenkmäler (1932). B. Hrozný, *Histoire de l'Asie antérieure* (1947). J. Friedrich, *Entzifferung verschollener Schriften und Sprachen* (1954).

On Sumerian: A. Deimel, *Sumerische Grammatik* (1939); *Sumerisches Lexikon* (1928—). A. Falkenstein, *Grammatik der Sprache Gudeas von Lagaš* (1949-50).

On Akkadian: C. Bezold, *Babylonisch-Assyrisches Glossar* (1926). R. Labat, *Manuel d'épigraphie akkadienne* (1926). W. von Soden, *Grundriss der akkadischen Grammatik* (1952). I. J. Gelb, *Old Akkadian Writing and Grammar* (1952); *Glossary of Old Akkadian* (1957).

On Kassite: K. Balkan, *Kassiterstudien: I. Die Sprache der Kassiten* (1954).

On Hurrian: J. Friedrich, *Kleine Beiträge zur churritischen Grammatik* (1939). E. A. Speiser, *Introduction to Hurrian* (1941).

On Proto-Elamite: V. Scheil, "Documents élamites en écriture proto-élamite," *Mémoires de la Délégation en Perse,* vol. VI (1905). C. Franck, *Zur Entzifferung der altelamischen Inschriften* (1912); *Die altelamischen Steininschriften* (1923). F. Bork, *Die Steininschriften von Susa* (1924).

On Elamitish: F. König, F. Bork, and G. Hüsing, *Corpus Inscriptionum Elamicarum* (1926—). F. Bork, "Elam. B. Sprache," *Reallexikon der Vorgeschichte,* III (1925), 70-83; "Elamische Studien," *MAOG,* vol. VII, no. 3 (1933), pp. 3-31. H. H. Paper, *The Phonology and Morphology of Royal Achaemenid Elamite* (1955).

On Khatti: H. Güterbock, "Chattische Texte," *Keilschrifturkunden aus Boghazkoi,* vol. XXVIII (1935).

On cuneiform Hittite: E. H. Sturtevant, *Comparative Grammar of the Hittite Language* (1923). J. Friedrich, *Hethitisches Elementarbuch* (2 vols.; 1940-46). F. Sommer, *Hethiter und Hethitisch* (1948). J. Friedrich, *Hethitisches Wörterbuch* (1952).

On hieroglyphic Hittite: B. Hrozný, *Les inscriptions hittites hiéroglyphes* (3 vols.; 1933-37). I. J. Gelb, *Hittite Hieroglyphs* (3 pts.; 1931-42); *Hittite Hieroglyphic Monuments* (1939). J. Friedrich, *Entzifferungsgeschichte der hethitischen Hieroglyphenschrift* (1939).

On Luwian: H. Otten, *Luvische Texte in Umschrift* (1953).

On Palawi: H. T. Bossert, *Ein hethitische Königssiegel* (1944).

On Phrygian: N. Jokl, "Phryger. A. Sprache," *Reallexikon der Vorgeschichte,* X (1928), 141-53.

On Armenian: A. Meillet, *Altarmenisches Elementarbuch* (1913).

On Urartean: C. F. Lehmann-Haupt, *Corpus Inscriptionum Chaldicarum* (1928—). J. Friedrich, *Einführung ins Urartäische* (1933). N. E. Vrouyr, *Inscriptions ourartéennes* (1952).

On Old Persian: R. G. Kent, *Old Persian Grammar, Texts, Lexicon* (1930). A. Meillet and E. Benveniste, *Grammaire du vieux-perse* (1931).

On Avestan: C. Bartholomae, *Altiranisches Wörterbuch* (1904). H. Reichelt, *Awestisches Elementarbuch* (1909).

On Pahlavi: H. S. Nyberg, *Hilfsbuch des Pehlevi* (2 vols.; 1928-31).

On Soghdian: R. Gauthiot and E. Benveniste, *Essai de Grammaire sogdienne* (2 vols.; 1923-29).

On Ugaritic: C. Gordon, *Ugaritic Manual* (2nd ed., 1955).

On Byblian: N. Dunand, *Byblia Grammata* (1945). E. Dhorme, "Déchiffrement des inscriptions pseudo-hiéroglyphes de Byblos," *Syria,* XXV (1948), 1-35.

On Serabit: W. F. Albright, "The Early Alphabetic Inscriptions from Sinai," *BASOR,* no. 110 (1948).

On Philistine: G. Ipsen, "Der Diskus von Phaestos," *Indogermanische Forschungen,* XLVII (1929), 1-41.

On Cretan: A. Evans, *Scripta Minoa* (1909). G. P. Carratelli, "Le iscrizioni preelleniche de Haghia Triada in Creta e della Grecia peninsolare," *Monumenti Antichi,* vol. XI, no. 4 (1945). B. Hrozný, *Les inscriptions crétoises* (1949). M. Ventris and J. Chadwick, *Documents in Mycenaean Greek* (1956).

On Cypriote: S. Casson, "The Cypriot Script of the Bronze Age," *Iraq,* VI (1939), 39-44. J. F. Daniel, "Prolegomena to the Cypro-Minoan Script," *AJA,* XLV (1941), 249-82.

On Lycian: J. Sundwall, *Die einheimischen Namen der Lykier* (1913). F. Kretschmer, "Die Stellung der lykischen Sprache," *Glotta,* XXVII (1939), 256-61; XXVIII (1940), 101-16.

On Carian: F. Bork, "Die Sprache der Karaer," *AFO,* VII (1931), 14-23.

On Lydian: E. Littmann, "Lydian Inscriptions," *Sardis,* vol. VI, no. 1 (1916). E. Deeters, "Lydia. Sprache und Schrift," in Pauly-Wissowa, XXVI (1927), 2153-61.

On hieroglyphic Egyptian: A. Erman, *Die Hieroglyphen* (1917). G. Möller, *Hieratische Paläograohie* (3 vols.; 1919). A. Erman and H. Grapow, *Ägyptisches Wörterbuch* (1921-53). H. Sottas and E. Drioton, *Introduction à l'étude des hiéroglyphes* (1922). F. Spiegelberg, *Demotische Grammatik* (1925). A. H. Gardiner, *Egyptian Grammar* (1927).

On Coptic: W E. Crum, *A Coptic Dictionary* (1939). G. Steindorff, *Lehrbuch der koptischen Grammatik* (1951).

On Meroitic: F. L. Griffiths, *Meroitic Inscriptions* (2 vols.; 1911-12); "Meroitic Studies," *JEA* (1916, 1917, 1925, 1929).

A. Jeffery

LANGUAGES OF THE BIBLE. The Bible, as every other scripture, reflects the linguistic environment in which its documents were written (*see* Languages of the Ancient Near East). Thus, though the OT is in the Hebrew Language and the NT in the Greek Language, there are names, words, phrases, from other languages in use in the environment of the biblical writers. There is frequent reference to this linguistic diversity. Ahasuerus had his edict written to every province in its own script and to every people in its own language (Esth. 3:12). Nehemiah found that where the Jews had taken wives from Ashdod, Ammon, and Moab, their children could not speak the language of Judah but spoke the language of each people (Neh. 13:23-24). Officials in besieged Jerusalem besought the Assyrian envoys to speak in Aramaic rather than in Hebrew (II Kings 18:26). The gospels tell that the inscription above the cross was in Greek, Latin, and Hebrew. Jews from the Diaspora who heard the apostolic preaching on the Day of Pentecost were amazed to hear the gospel proclaimed in their own native languages (Acts 2:6-7).

Whole chapters in Daniel and Ezra are in the official Aramaic of the chancelleries, while in the NT such familiar expressions as "Eloi, Eloi, lama sabach-thani," "Talitha cumi," and "Maranatha" are in the colloquial Aramaic of the day. *See* Aramaic Language.

When Pharaoh gave Joseph the name Zaphenath-paneah and the servants cried before him, "Abrek" (Gen. 41:43, 45), these represent Egyptian words.

Similarly when Daniel is given the name Belteshazzar (Dan. 1:7), and when the officers of the Assyrian king are called Tartan, Rabsaris, Rabshakeh (II Kings 18:17), these represent Babylonian and Assyrian words.

The musical instruments in Dan. 3—the "lyre," "trigon," "harp," and "bagpipe"—are Greek words.

The title "satrap" (Ezra 8:36; Esth. 3:12) and those translated "counselors," "treasurers," "justices," in Dan. 3:2-3, are Persian words.

In the NT "centurion" (Mark 15:39), "legion" (Luke 8:30), "praetorian" (Phil. 1:13), "denarii" (Matt. 18:28), are Latin words.

Place names in the Bible are from a variety of languages, and there are several words of uncertain meaning whose origin is unknown.

A. Jeffery

LANTERN. The translation of φανός, which is used in the Greek Bible only at John 18:3. The word comes from the common word φαίνω, which means "to appear" or "to shine." It is evident that it refers to some means of giving light, but even in its extra-biblical usages, which are rather rare, it has never been discovered in a context clear enough to enable us to gain an exact picture of it. It may have been a kind of torch, though the more common word for "torch," λαμπάς, is used along with it in John's passage. It is an open question as to whether John was trying to distinguish between two different kinds of lights or was employing the two words as synonyms.

S. A. Cartledge

*__LAODICEA__ lā ŏd′ə sē′ə, lā′ə də sē′ə [Λαοδικία *or* Λαοδίκεια]; LAODICEANS —ənz. A city in SW Asia Minor.

Laodicea is one of the cities in the Valley of the Lycus (modern Çürüksuçay), a tributary of the Maeander. It is located in the extreme SW of Phrygia and sometimes is considered as belonging to Caria—a geographical uncertainty also reflecting the mixed ethnic situation to be assumed for pre-Hellenistic times. The site occupied by Laodicea is an almost square plateau some hundred feet above the river valley, S of the river and the modern railroad station of Goncali. The flat hill of the city is protected by two smaller rivers, the ancient Asopus (Baspinar) and Caprus (Gümüşçay), both tributaries of the Lycus. To the S lie the high mountains Salbacus and Cadmus (the Babadağ and Akdağ Range).

The city was located on the ancient highway leading up from Ephesus through the Maeander and Lycus valleys to the E and ultimately to Syria (Strabo XIV.663). Colossae is ten miles to the E, while Hierapolis lies six miles to the N of Laodicea.

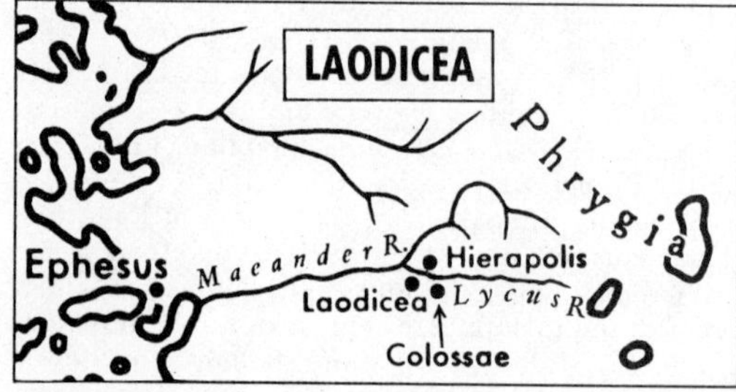

Pliny (Nat. Hist. V.105) gives the earlier names of Laodicea as Diospolis or Rhoas, the latter perhaps standing for a Phrygian village in this area. As a city, Laodicea was founded by the Seleucids, presumably *ca.* 250 B.C. by Antiochus II, who named it after his wife, Laodice. It was meant to be a Seleucid stronghold in the area, to which its location made it eminently suitable. Some inscriptions refer to the early Hellenistic history of the site, but not much is known in detail. In 190 B.C., Laodicea came under Pergamenian rule, which meant some decline for the city; but prosperity increased under the Romans after 133 B.C. (cf. Strabo XII.578), when the city was allowed to develop its economic and commercial potential. It was made the center of a judicial district (*conventus*) to which Hierapolis, and later also Cibyra, among other cities, belonged.

Although the region of the Lycus Valley is subject to earthquakes and Laodicea was hit several times, the reference by Tacitus to the earthquake of A.D. 60 shows that the city was prominent and wealthy enough to be reconstructed without financial aid from the Romans (Ann. XIV.27).

Laodicea's wealth was related to her fertile land and good grazing grounds for the sheep, whose raven-black wool (Strabo XII.578) made her famous. Special garments and carpets were woven in the city, and guilds of craftsmen (e.g., fullers and cloak-makers) are attested. In this industry Lacodicea was a prominent partner and competitor of the Ionian cities and its neighbors Colossae and Hierapolis.

The prosperity led to the development of financial operations and banking at Laodicea (Cicero *Ep. ad Fam.* III.5; cf. the boast in Rev. 3:17). Local benefactors increased the material prestige of the city—e.g., Hieron, who left the city two thousand talents, and the family of the orator Zenon, whose descendants were kings in various parts of Asia Minor (Strabo XII.578). The city struck its own coins from the second century B.C. on, with iconographic references to the local river gods and cults.

The population of the city included Greek-speaking Syrians, Romans, and Romanized natives, as well as a prominent and wealthy Jewish contingent. In 62 B.C., by order of the governor Flaccus, the annual contributions which the Jews were accustomed to send to Jerusalem were seized and sent to Rome; twenty pounds of gold were taken at Laodicea (Cicero *Pro Flacco* 68). The special rights of the Jews were abolished in A.D. 70.

The early history of Christianity and the church at Laodicea (Rev. 1:11; 3:14) is not much illuminated by local evidence. The association of the early Christian community in Laodicea with those in Colossae and Hierapolis (Col. 2:1; 4:13-16) reflects the joint religious development in the Lycus Valley. Laodicea emerged in the fourth century as the most prominent bishopric in Phrygia. In those days it was also the secular capital of W Phrygia and was called Metropolis of Asia.

The city suffered in the wars of Seljuks and Turks and was abandoned soon after the thirteenth century, to be succeeded by the modern town of Denizli; although the identification of the once famous city was never lost to memory.

Nowadays the ruins of Laodicea (Eski Hissar) occupy a large area strewn with architectural fragments. It is unexcavated, and the final identification of the various buildings will have to wait for archaeological confirmation. The lines of the ancient city walls can still be traced. The triple E gate (the "Syrian" gate) was dedicated to Vespasian, as proved by an inscription.

Some of the buildings are relatively well preserved. A stadium lies in the SW part of the site. It is of Roman shape with two semicircular ends, of *ca.* a thousand feet in length, and, like the E gate, dedicated to Vespasian (in A.D. 79). Gladiatorial combats are known to have been staged in Laodicea in the first century B.C. A large building near the stadium, probably of the Hadrianic period, may represent a gymnasium or baths. Its arches, piers, and colonnades are much dilapidated. Two theaters are in better preservation. The remains of an aqueduct and water tower have attracted the special attention of early travelers. Water, brought from springs near Denizli, was carried partly on arches of masonry but part of the way in stone barrel pipes, up and down the slopes. The necropolis of the town is on the N side, near the river, where many disturbed sarcophagi mark the site.

Courtesy of William Sanford La Sor

13. Ruins of a bridge at Laodicea

The general date of the ruins is Roman, presumably representing the state after the earthquake of A.D. 60 and the ostentatious material wealth alluded to by historians.

Fig. LAO 13.

Bibliography. W. M. Ramsay, *The Cities and Bishoprics of Phrygia* (1895), I, 32-83; *Monumenta Asiae Minoris Antiqua,* VI (1939), pp. x-xi, 1-14; D. Magie, *Roman Rule in Asia Minor* (1950), I, 127.

M. J. MELLINK

LAODICEANS, EPISTLE TO THE. A short letter purporting to have been written by Paul and occasioned solely by the reference in Col. 4:16 to the "letter from Laodicea." *See* APOCYPHA, NT.

The date of the composition is unknown. That it was in existence in the fourth century is evidenced by warnings against it by many of the fathers, notably Jerome. By the sixth century it was widely accepted as Pauline and is found in many Latin MSS of the NT. The two earliest occurrences are in the Pseudo-Augustine *Speculum* (a group of OL MSS edited by Mai) and the famous sixth-century Vulg. MS Fuldensis. From then until the fifteenth century its presence in Latin MSS is about as common as its absence. Its most common position is after Colossians, but in some MSS it stands after II Thessalonians, between Titus and Philemon, after Philemon, after Hebrews (a very common position), and at the end of the NT. Despite Jerome's stricture ("Some say also 'To the Laodiceans,' but we reject this"; *De Viris Illustribus* 5), it was regarded as authentic by Gregory the Great. To be sure, it was not canonical: the church had said that there were fourteen such letters by Paul. To Gregory this number was highly appropriate, for it suggested a combination of the Ten Commandments and the four gospels. Nonetheless, Gregory held, Paul actually wrote fifteen, and this, he clearly implied, was one of them. Haymo of Halberstadt (died A.D. 853), in commenting on Col. 4:16, remarks that the Apostle "directs the Laodicean epistle to be read to the Colossians because, though very short and not considered in the canon, it still has some use." The tenth-century Anglo-Saxon abbot of Cerne, Alfric, did not trouble himself with Gregory's nice distinction between "Pauline" and "canonical" but listed this writing as one of the fifteen which were "loud as thunder to faithful people." It is found not only in many Latin Bibles but also in many of the vernacular versions into which the Vulg. was translated—notably, in many editions of the pre-Luther German Bible. Although not translated by Wyclif or Purvey, it was added before the middle of the fifteenth century in two distinct English versions. After the sixteenth century its influence rapidly declined.

Although it exists only in Latin and has been widely regarded as originally composed in that language, its frequent Grecisms, its wide variation from both the diction of the OL and the Vulg. in the form in which its catena of excerpts from the Pauline letters occurs, and the occasional warnings against it by the Greek fathers combine to make the hypothesis of a Greek original far from unlikely. Both Theodore of Mopsuestia and Theodoret condemned it as spurious. The Second Council of Nicea (A.D. 787) gave warning: "Indeed a forged epistle of the divine apostle is extant, having a place in some copies of the Apostle, which our Fathers rejected as not his own." That this apocryphon is to be identified with the "Epistle to the Laodiceans" mentioned in the Muratorian Fragment (*ca.* A.D. 180) along with one "to the Alexandrians," as produced in the interests of the heresy of Marcion and which "cannot be received in the catholic church," has seemed to most scholars, despite Harnack's advocacy, quite impossible.

The writing itself is simply a cento of short, unconnected Pauline phrases lifted bodily from the canonical letters. Dependence upon Philippians is the heaviest, but there is also clear use of Galatians, I and II Timothy, and I and II Corinthians, while reminiscences of both II Peter and Matthew are probably to be seen. Unlike many pseudonymous writings, this trivial little forgery has no ax to grind, and it is devoid of any purpose, doctrinal or otherwise, save to fill the gap suggested by the reference in Col. 4:16, which word has intrigued readers in every age and has led to many speculations: (*a*) a letter from the Laodiceans to Paul; (*b*) a letter from Laodicea by Paul himself; (*c*) a letter to Laodicea by Paul or someone else.

The little letter—the Latin contains but 247 words—begins: "Paul, an apostle not of men or by man, but by Jesus Christ, unto the brethren that are at Laodicea"; expresses thanks for their perseverance in his (Christ's) works; warns them against heresy and those "who are filthy in lucre"; mentions his "bonds seen of all men," which he suffers in Christ, but wherein he rejoices and is glad; advises them that it is God who works in them; admonishes that their petitions be made openly to God; bids them do "what things are sound and true and sober and just and to be loved"; advises them that "the saints salute" them; and, of course, concludes: "And cause [this epistle] to be read unto those of Colossae, and [the epistle] of the Colossians [to be read] unto you."

One has but to read this utterly trivial and artificial congeries of disjointed phrases, lifted bodily from their earlier contexts and hitched together without rhyme or reason, to agree with Erasmus: "There is no argument which will more effectively convince that this is not by Paul than the epistle itself."

Bibliography. A convenient English translation of the epistle is given by M. R. James, *The Apocryphal NT* (1924), pp. 478-79. For a more detailed discussion, including a partial list of the MSS carrying it and a reconstruction of the conjectured Greek original, see J. B. Lightfoot, *Saint Paul's Epistles to the Colossians and Philemon* (9th ed., 1890), pp. 272-98. See also A. von Harnack, *Die apokryphen Briefe des Paulus an die Laodicensis und Korinther* (1905). M. S. ENSLIN

LAPIS LAZULI lăp'ĭs lăz'yo͝o lī. RSV mg. alternate rendering for SAPPHIRE in Job 28:6 and seven other passages. Lapis lazuli is a stone of rich azure blue, frequently showing spangles of iron pyrites. The sapphire of Theophrastus and Pliny was probably lapis lazuli. A few specimens of this stone have been discovered in Palestine. It was used more widely in Mesopotamia as a semiprecious stone, for seals, ornaments, inlay, and occasional small objects.

W. E. STAPLES

LAPPIDOTH lăp'ə dŏth [לַפִּידוֹת] (Judg. 4:4). The husband of Deborah the prophetess, whose home appears to have been in the vicinity between Ramah and Bethel.

LAPWING. KJV translation of דוּכִיפַת (RSV HOOPOE). While the lapwing (*Vanellus vanellus; Hoplopterus spinosus*) is known in Palestine in the summer (R. Lydekker, *Royal Natural History* [1895], IV, 480-84), it is probable that the bird designated is the hoopoe. W. S. MCCULLOUGH

LASEA lə sē'ə [ἡ Λασαία] (Acts 27:8). A city on the S coast of Crete.

The name of the city, which appears as Λασαία in the Common Text, is found as Λασσαία in Codex Sinaiticus (where a corrector has also changed it to Λαΐσσα), as Λασέα in Codex Vaticanus, as 'Αλάσσα in Codex Alexandrinus, and as *Thalassa* in the Vulg. The variant spellings suggest that the place was not well known, and it is not mentioned by ancient geographers. This need not be surprising, since even in Homer's time there were ninety cities on Crete (*Odyssey* XIX.174). In 1853 Captain T. A. B. Spratt, directing a Mediterranean survey, found ancient ruins on the shore near FAIR HAVENS, and these may well be identified with Lasea. Probably it was only a small coast town.

Bibliography. T. A. B. Spratt, *Travels and Researches in Crete* (1865), II, 7-8; Bürchner, "Lasaia," *Pauly-Wissowa, XII, i* (1924), col. 883. J. FINEGAN

LASHA lā'shə [לֶשַׁע] (Gen. 10:19). One of the (NE?) boundary points for the land of the Canaanites; the location is unknown. With good reason, Lasha has been compared with Laish-Dan (cf. Josh. 19:47; Judg 18:29). Jerome, following a Jewish tradition, places it at Callirrhoe, a ravine E of the Dead Sea, famous for its hot springs. Herod the Great visited it during his last illness. V. R. GOLD

LASHARON lă shâr'ən [לַשָּׁרוֹן] (Josh. 12:18). A city whose king was defeated by Joshua. Probably the word is not the name of a city, but was originally part of the phrase "Aphek belonging to Sharon," distinguishing this from other Apheks (cf. the LXX B reading: Σαρων, Saron). *See* SHARON. W. L. REED

LASHES, FORTY LESS ONE. *See* CRIMES AND PUNISHMENTS.

LAST DAY(S), LATTER DAYS. *See* ESCHATOLOGY OF THE NT.

LAST SUPPER, THE. The last meal of Jesus with his disciples, on the eve of his passion, as related by the Synoptic evangelists (Matt. 26:17-30; Mark 14: 12:26; Luke 22:7-38) and by Paul (I Cor. 11:23-26). The meal is mentioned also in the Gospel of John (13:2 ff), though without precise reference to any institution of the sacrament of the Lord's Supper. But the Fourth Evangelist treats of the sacrament in the discourse appended to the miracle of the feeding of the multitude (especially 6:51-56). *See also* AGAPE; LORD'S SUPPER.

Critical problems for the interpreter of the Last Supper accounts concern the occasion of the meal, the textual tradition of Jesus' words and their authenticity, and the meaning of his words and actions. These problems, of course, cannot be isolated from the larger questions raised by the literary, historical, and theological criticism of the gospels. But in this particular case, the problems have been so complicated by doctrinal controversy in the church that it is difficult for any interpreter to approach them without some degree of subjective or ecclesiastical bias.

1. The occasion of the Supper. The problem of the occasion of the Last Supper is involved in the broader question of the chronology of the Passion. All the evangelists and the unanimous tradition of the church agree that the Last Supper took place on Thursday evening before the crucifixion of Jesus, which occurred on a Friday. If one counts the day in the Jewish manner, from sunset to sunset, then the Synoptic gospels relate that the Supper and the Crucifixion occurred on the festival of the PASSOVER—i.e., on Nisan 15. By this reckoning, the Last Supper was a Passover meal. The Gospel of John, however, is explicit in stating that the Crucifixion occurred on the "preparation day" or eve of the Passover—i.e., Nisan 14—and that in the year of Jesus' death the Passover fell, not on Friday, but on the sabbath (18: 28; 19:14, 31). In this case, the Last Supper could not have been a Passover meal, since the paschal lambs would not have been slaughtered until Friday afternoon, at the time when Jesus was on the cross. With this Johannine tradition is commonly associated the connection made by Paul (I Cor. 5:7) between the death of Jesus and the sacrifice of the paschal lamb on the preparation day of the feast. Biblical critics have been sharply divided in their preferences for the Synoptic or the Johannine chronology, respectively. Similarly, in ecclesiastical usages, the Latin church, by its use of unleavened bread in the Eucharist, supports the Synoptics; the Greek church, by its use of leavened bread in the rite, adheres to the Johannine position.

Numerous theories have been offered to reconcile this discrepancy in chronology and harmonize the gospel traditions. The chronological notices of Mark, upon which Matthew and Luke appear to depend, are inherently contradictory—especially 14:12, where the "first day of Unleavened Bread" (Nisan 15) is erroneously identified with the day "when they sacrificed the Passover lamb" (Nisan 14). To some critics, this confusion is evidence that Mark's tradition of the Passion originally agreed with John's, and that Mark's identification of the Last Supper with the Passover (particularly by his insertion of the Preparation pericope, 14:12-16) is a later and less authentic interpretation. Others consider the text of Mark 14:12 to be merely the result of ignorance or of a faulty translation from Aramaic to Greek, and in no way to impair Mark's trustworthiness in identifying the Supper with the Passover. Even if the pericope recounting the preparation for the Supper were not an original part of Mark's basic source for the Passion, it may nonetheless represent an ancient and sound tradition. Some scholars have interpreted the saying of Jesus in Luke 22:15 to mean an "unfulfilled desire" to eat the Passover, thus bringing the special Lukan material into line with John. But others maintain that the phrase is a Semitism and expresses an "intense," rather than an "unfulfilled," wish of Jesus.

Several Jewish scholars have put forward the view that in the year of Jesus' death the Passover was observed on two consecutive days, because of different reckonings of its date by the Sadducees and the Pharisees respectively. But such a theory lacks incisive evidence in Jewish and rabbinic sources. The many efforts to solve the problem by recourse to astronomical calculations of the coincidence of the full moon of Nisan and the sabbath have all proved to be inconclusive. This is partly because of our ignorance of the precise method used by the Jews at that time in observing and calculating the date of the new moon, and partly because of uncertainties about the exact year, among several possibilities, of the death of Jesus. Hence the majority of scholars fall back upon a preference for one gospel tradition as over against another, on the basis of internal criticism of the passion narrative itself.

Opponents of the Passover interpretation of the Last Supper have marshaled a formidable series of objections to the Synoptic theory from the regulations for Passover observance known to have been operative in the time of Jesus. Many of these have to do with details of the passion narrative as a whole. Those that are specifically related to the Supper are: (*a*) the absence of any reference to the Passover lamb itself, the principal constituent of any Passover meal; (*b*) the use of the Greek word for ordinary bread (ἄρτος) instead of the technical term for unleavened bread (ἄζυμα); (*c*) the mention of only one, or at most two, cups of wine, whereas the Passover ritual provided for four cups. Further objection is made to the Synoptic dating on the grounds that the Lord's Supper as observed in the early church betrays none of the distinctive features of the Passover; and that, if the Passover meal had been the occasion of the institution of the Eucharist, one would have expected the rite to have been an annual rather than a weekly, or even daily, observance in the church.

None of these objections to the Synoptic interpretation is decisive. The evangelists' purpose was not to describe a Passover meal as such, but only to report those features that were distinctively marked by words or actions of Jesus, or were continued in the ritual of the church. It has been demonstrated that the word for ordinary, leavened bread was at times used also for unleavened bread in the OT and the Talmud, and by Greek writers such as Philo and Josephus. As to the observance of the Lord's Supper in the church—the eschatological outlook of the early Christians accounts for the frequency of the rite, as an anticipation or foretaste of the "Supper of the Lamb" in the age to come.

There are not wanting suggestions of other occasions for the Supper on the part of those who oppose the Passover interpretation. A theory that has found wide acceptance relates the words of Jesus at the Supper to the Jewish kiddush, a special form of blessing, or sanctification, said over a wine cup at the beginning of special holy days such as the sabbath and Passover. This theory suffers, however, from the total lack of evidence that the kiddush of the Passover, any more than the Passover meal itself, was ever anticipated and observed twenty-four hours in advance.

Another explanation has been the suggestion that Jesus and his disciples formed a *Chaburah,* or fellowship group, that from time to time enjoyed together formal religious meals. The evidence for such groups comes only from later rabbinic sources, and the meals of these groups were celebrated on special occasions such as weddings, funerals, circumcision, etc. There is no proof that they were religious associations of a more regular communal life and discipline. In any case, all meals of Jews, whether taken alone or in family or friendly groups, were religious, in the sense that formal benedictions offered to God over bread and wine were always said (though the use of wine was generally confined to special occasions of festivity or mourning). If the Last Supper was not a Passover, it was probably an ordinary meal of Jesus with his disciples, albeit specially dignified by Jesus for a particular purpose and intention. The use of a special wine "cup of blessing" at the conclusion of the meal at least testifies to the more solemn character of the occasion.

Courtesy of Verlag Herder Kg., Freiburg

14. A fresco of the Last Supper, from a catacomb of Callistus (*ca.* A.D. 200)

The question whether the Last Supper was a Passover meal or not may never be definitely settled in the light of our present sources of information. But at least it can be affirmed that the thoughts of the Passover season were in the mind and heart of Jesus and his disciples at the time (in the same way that a Christian today is likely to be mindful of the birth of his Lord already on the eve of Christmas Day). These paschal motifs, continued in the early oral tradition of the church's celebration of the Lord's Supper, may explain the differing ways in which the evangelists in their writing down of the gospel story interpret the occasion of the Last Supper. Fig. LAS 14.

2. The text. Only a few of the major problems of the textual tradition of the NT narratives of the Last Supper can be noted here. It is generally agreed that the accounts of Mark and Paul are equally primitive and independent of each other. Careful comparison of these two traditions affords a primary basis for establishing the authentic details of the occasion. The narrative of Matthew is largely dependent upon Mark; and its chief additions—notably the phrase "for the remission of sins"—are commonly ascribed to the influence of liturgical use or theological reflection. The Lukan version presents greater difficulties, for the text has come down to us in several recensions. Throughout his Passion narrative, Luke availed himself of a special source or sources in addition to Mark, and it is possible that he was also familiar with the Pauline tradition about the Supper. The simplest solution of the problem would be to take Luke 22:15-18 as derived from his special source, and 22:19-20 as based upon the Pauline tradition, with some Markan influence throughout the whole account. This full, or "long," version of Luke is supported by all Greek MSS except Codex Bezae (D), and also by most of the versions except the older Syr. (before the Peshitta) and some of the Old Latin texts.

The shorter text, contained in D and some Old Latin MSS, omits Luke 22:19*b*-20; whereas the older Syr. versions present the verses of the narrative in this order: 15-16, 19, 17-18. A number of scholars, including the translators of the RSV, accept the shorter version of Luke as original with its cup-bread rather than bread-cup order—a sequence also found in the Didache. The principal argument of those who accept this shorter version is the close textual similarity of vss. 19*b*-20 to I Cor. 11:24-25. They consider these verses, therefore, to be an interpolation. Those who object to this position rightly question how such an interpolation could have found its way into all Greek MSS save one, and into most of the versions. The longer version is also supported by such ancient witnesses as Marcion, Justin, and Tatian. It is much easier to explain the shorter text, and the Syr. variants, as corrections of the longer version, in order either to avoid a cup-bread sequence or to eliminate one of the two cups mentioned. The curious order of the longer version, if it be such, is probably the result of Luke's manner of treating his sources. In any case, the shorter text of Luke, in association with the Didache material, provides no justification for theories concerning a variant form of celebration of the Supper, whether by Jesus or by the early church.

More difficult is the problem posed by the command of Jesus: "Do this in remembrance of me," contained in the Pauline and longer Lukan narratives, but wanting in Mark and Matthew. A decision for or against the authenticity of the command cannot be made on grounds of the textual evidence alone, but rests in large measure upon one's view regarding the meaning that Jesus gave to the Supper and his intentions for his disciples. If Jesus anticipated the coming of the kingdom in climax to his own ministry and death, the command would not have any purpose. If, on the other hand, he expected a long interim between his earthly career and the final end of the age, the repetition of the Supper by his disciples, in remembrance of him, would be a bond uniting them "until he come."

3. The meaning of Jesus. There can be no question but that the Supper was in Jesus' mind an anticipation of the messianic banquet that he would share with his disciples in the coming kingdom. The imagery of the banquet was a common Jewish symbol for the life of the age to come (e.g., Ps. 23:5; Isa. 25:6 ff; 55:1 ff; 65:13; Zeph. 1:7; Enoch 62:14; Syr. Apocal. Bar. 29:3-8; cf. Mark 10:37, Luke 14:15;

Rev. 7:16-17; 19:9; 22:17). Jesus had appropriated this figure in his own teaching about the kingdom (Matt. 8:11; 22:2; 25:10; Luke 14:16; 22:29-30), and had applied it specifically in his ministry by eating with sinners, thereby indicating to them his offer of the divine acceptance and forgiveness—a significance that was not missed by his enemies (cf. Matt. 9:10-12; Mark 2:15-17; Luke 15:2). The feeding of the multitude was a messianic sign, recognized as such by the crowd (John 6:14-15). All the gospel accounts of the miracle show a close, textual assimilation of the narrative with the account of the Last Supper; and the discourse appended to the miracle in John 6 unmistakably draws out the relation of Christ as the "bread of God" with the Eucharist of the church and the resurrection to eternal life "at the last day" (cf. Mark 8:14-21). Moreover, the Jewish Passover celebrations in Jesus' day were vividly linked with the eschatological expectations of the final deliverance of God's people from bondage (see M. Pes. 10.6). A clear trace of this outlook is the midrash of Paul on the meaning of "unleavened bread" (I Cor. 5:7-8).

It is also clear that Jesus' words, identifying the bread and the cup at the Supper with his own flesh and blood, linked the elements in the most intimate way with his death. Later theological controversy has beclouded his meaning, in what precise way this identification should be defined. But the words unmistakably interpret the significance of his death as a vicarious sacrifice "for many"—i.e., a sacrifice universal in its scope. One cannot miss the allusion to the Suffering Servant (Isa. 53:10-12), or fail to recall his earlier saying of the Son of man, who came "to give his life as a ransom for many" (Mark 10:45 and parallels). It should be noted, too, that the separation of flesh and blood of sacrificial victims was essential in the OT cult. Whether the sacrifice of Jesus was comparable to the Passover victim or to a sin offering is debatable. But it is most probable that we are confronted here with a creative association of sacrificial types, in Jesus' own mind, of both a redemptive and an expiatory nature.

Both the eschatological and the sacrificial connotations of Jesus' words are linked in further creative unity by his reference to the "covenant." Such a term could only indicate on Jesus' part a deliberate act of fulfilment of the Old Covenant, established on Mount Sinai after the Passover deliverance from Egypt (Exod. 19:3 ff; 24:1 ff), and an inauguration of the New Covenant foretold by Jeremiah (31:31-34). Thus Jesus offered his disciples in the Supper a full participation in the atoning benefits of his own self-offering on the cross—deliverance from the bondage of this world, remission of sins, incorporation in the new people of God, an inner obedience of the heart to the will of God, and the joy and benediction of his presence and fellowship in the age to come. The words and actions of Jesus at the Last Supper testify more clearly than does any other place in the gospel tradition to the consciousness of Jesus of the uniqueness of his person and mission, both in continuity with the OT revelation and in fulfilment of the OT promise.

Seen in this perspective, the question of the authenticity of the command to repeat the Supper "in remembrance of me" becomes relatively unimportant. The repetition of the act is far more than a memorial of a past event. It looks forward to a future consummation "until he come." The question has been raised, however, whether the "remembrance of me" refers in any case to Jesus' disciples', or to God's, remembrance of him. If the latter interpretation is adopted, the Supper is a prayer of the messianic community—a remembrance before God—that God should remember his Messiah by bringing into existence his kingdom. To "do this"—i.e., to celebrate the Supper—is to realize the final consummation of God's redemptive purpose, whether viewed as accomplished in the death and resurrection of Jesus, or in his coming at the end of time. The Supper expresses the paradoxical character of the gospel witness in twofold dimension: to a kingdom that is both here and now and also yet to come.

Bibliography. In addition to the standard commentaries on the gospels and I Corinthians, one should consult, as an indispensable guide, J. Jeremias, *The Eucharistic Words of Jesus* (1955), with its copious bibliography. See also: H. Strack and P. Billerbeck, *Kommentar zum NT aus Talmud und Midrash*, II (1924), 812-53; W. O. E. Oesterley, *The Jewish Background of the Christian Liturgy* (1925); G. Dalman, *Jesus-Jeshua* (1929); F. J. Leenhardt, *Le Sacrement de la Sainte-Cène* (1948); T. Preiss, *Life in Christ* (1954), pp. 81-99. For further discussions of the problems, *see* bibliography under AGAPE; LORD'S SUPPER.

M. H. SHEPHERD, JR.

LASTHENES lăs′thə nēz [Λασθένης] (I Macc. 11:32). Governor of Coele-Syria in the days of Jonathan the Hasmonean. Josephus (Antiq. XIII.iv.3) calls him Lasthenes the Cretan, who brought mercenary soldiers to Demetrius. He had the title of honor, "kinsman."

When Jonathan and his government were recognized by Demetrius, he received a copy of a letter sent by Demetrius to Lasthenes, in which the Jews were extolled as friends. Promises were made to do them good because of their good will. The letter to Lasthenes delineated the boundaries of Judea and reaffirmed the cession of the three districts of Samaria to Judea. It also assured the exemption from taxes, and the tribute that had originally appertained to the Syrians was now bestowed upon the Jews. All who offered sacrifices to Jerusalem (excluding perhaps Samaritans and Hellenized Jews) were exempt from dues.

Bibliography. S. Tedesche and S. Zeitlin, *I Maccabees* (1950), pp. 43, 191-92.

S. B. HOENIG

LATCH. In Song of S. 5:4 for מן החר, "from the hole," the RSV has "to the latch," which is not a good translation. In the context it is probably a euphemism.

LATCHET. KJV translation of שרוך in Gen. 14:23; Isa. 5:27 (RSV SANDAL-THONG) and ἱμάς in Mark 1:7; Luke 3:16; John 1:27 (RSV THONG). "Latchet" is an archaism for a leather strap or thong by which sandals are tied. *See* SANDALS AND SHOES.

LATIN [Ῥωμαϊκός] (Luke 23:38 mg.; John 19:20). The language spoken by the Romans. It is stated that the title on the cross "was written in Hebrew, in Latin, and in Greek" (*see* INSCRIPTION ON THE CROSS). In Italy every educated Roman used Greek as well as Latin. In Palestine a knowledge of Latin was limited to those who were involved in legal, military, and official duties. B. M. Metzger

*LATIN VERSIONS, OLD. Beginning in the latter part of the second century A.D., anonymous translators made many translations of the Bible into vernacular Latin. Despite the popularity of Jerome's Latin Vulg., these other renderings continued to be used here and there throughout Europe until the late Middle Ages. *See* Versions, Ancient, § 3.

B. M. Metzger

LATTER RAIN. Alternate translation of מלקוש. *See* Spring Rain.

LATTICE [אשנב, חרכים, שבכה] (Judg. 5:28; II Kings 1:2; Prov. 7:6 [KJV CASEMENT]; Song of S. 2:9). A window covering through which one could look. *See* House; Window.

LAVER [כיור; λούτρον]. A fairly large vessel. In the OT the Hebrew word usually (cf. Zech. 12:6) refers to a metal basin or bowl used in rites of purification. Hence, in the NT the Greek term is related to the water of baptism (e.g., Eph. 5:26; Tit. 3:5; etc.).

1. In the tabernacle. The tabernacle laver (Exod. 30:18, 28; 31:9; 35:16; 38:8; 39:39; 40:7, 11, 30) was a copper-bronze basin for water which stood on a "foot" or base (Exod. 30:18); it was made "from the mirrors of the ministering women . . . of the tent" (Exod. 38:8; cf. I Sam. 2:22) and was located between the altar and the door of the tabernacle. The Levites were to cleanse themselves ritually "lest they die" (Exod. 30:20-21; Num. 8:7; *see* Bathing); the laver thus was intended to make holy the priests and, presumably, the sacrifices. Some ancient versions append to Num. 4:14 the provision that when transported, lavers and bases were to be wrapped in a purple cloth and protected by a blue skin covering.

2. In the Solomonic temple. In the temple (*see* Temple, Jerusalem) lavers included: (*a*) the molten sea (*see* Sea, Molten)* and (*b*) ten smaller but sizable bronze lavers or bowls, each supported by stands of artistic and exceptional workmanship (I Kings 7:27-39; II Chr. 4:6). Fig. SEA 34.

These ten bronze bowls held 40 baths each (*ca.* 243 gallons, weighing *ca.* a ton; I Kings 7:38). If the lavers were hemispherical, the diameters would have been *ca.* 5 feet (3.3 cubits).

The stands (I Kings 7:27-37) were "four cubits long, four cubits wide, and three cubits high." The lower part consisted of panels decorated with lions, oxen, and cherubim and framed in beveled borders with wreaths. The upper round-bowl support was within a "crown" which projected upward one cubit

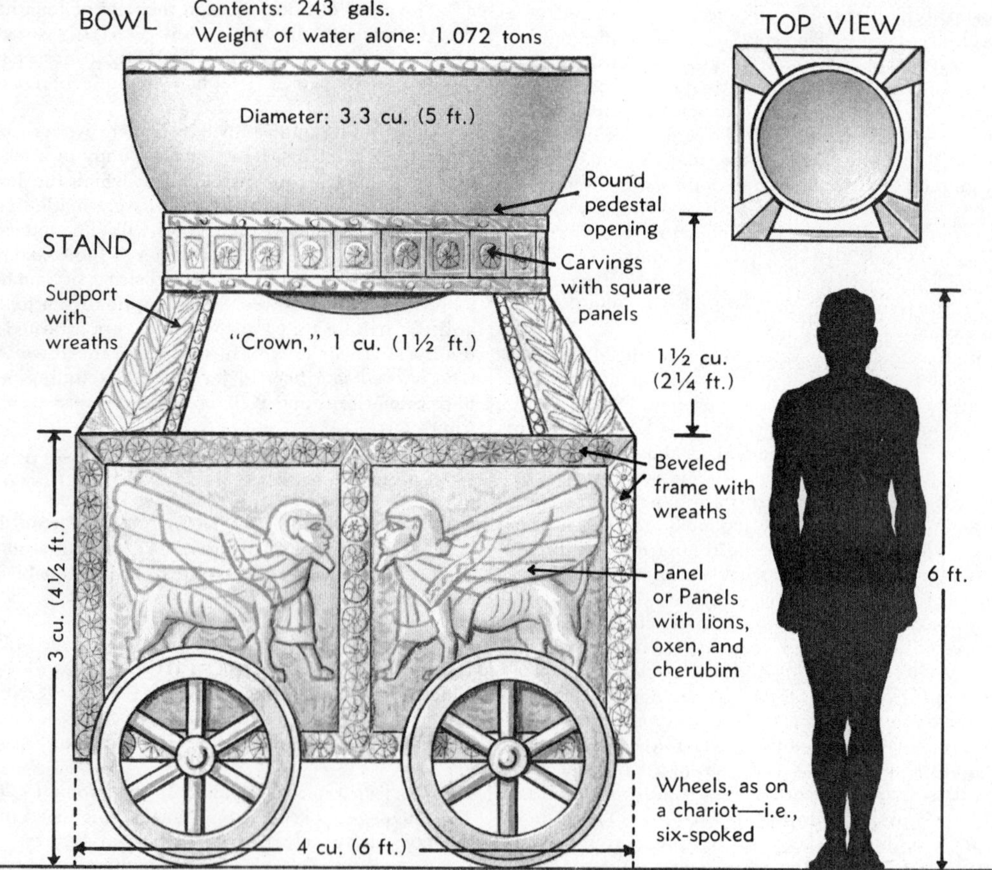

P. L. Garber

15. Drawing showing one of the ten lavers and bases of Solomon's temple

and had corner supports "with wreaths at the side of each." The cast bronze chariotlike (six-spoked) wheels were 1½ cubits high and turned on axles made "of one piece with the stand." Such detailed descriptions even with some archaeological parallels do not provide an exact picture of these technically remarkable castings. It is still more difficult to see how such stands of cast bronze and small wheels could carry the weight involved. The ten stands were sent as scrap metal to Assyria by King Ahaz (II Kings 16:17; cf. the "stands" of II Kings 25:13, 16; Jer. 52:17, 20).

II Chr. 4:6 states that the sacrificial offerings were purified by water from the ten bowls. Their height in comparison with a man's raises some question as to their practical usefulness for such purposes. The Ezekiel (40:48–43:17) description of the temple does not contain any reference to lavers. Fig. LAV 15.

3. In the NT. The NT employs the LXX word for "laver" (λούτρον) solely in metaphorical connection with baptism (Eph. 5:26; Tit. 3:5); the word is translated "washing."

Bibliography. G. Schumacher, *Tell El-Mutesellim* (1908), plate 38. H. Gressmann, *Altorientalische Texte Und Bilder Zum AT* (1909), II, 42, the Cyprus wheeled base. I. Benzinger, *Hebraesche Archaeologie* (3rd ed., 1927), plate xiv: 2, 3. C. Watzinger, *Denkmaeler Palestinas* (1933), pp. 105-6. For archaeological illustrations of lavers, see: *BA*, IV (1941), 29 (a drawing of a tripod base from Ras Shamra). W. F. Albright, *Archaeology and the Religion of Israel* (2nd ed., 1946), pp. 152-54. J. L. Kelso, *The Ceramic Vocabulary of the OT* (1948), p. 20. The most recent attempt at a restoration of the wilderness tabernacle laver was made by H. J. Soulen in a painting done as an illustration (p. 844) for G. E. Wright, "Bringing OT Times to Life," *The National Geographic Magazine*, vol. CXII (1957).

P. L. GARBER

***LAW IN THE OT.** Law has as its object the maintenance of life in community. Two aspects of law will inevitably be found in a community in which a legal tradition of complex character has developed: (*a*) the policies or general statements which provide the legal understandings of how life in community is to be maintained; and (*b*) the procedures by which these policies are to be put into effect and applied in specific instances.

The OT does not have different terms for these two aspects of law, but they are nonetheless easily recognized in the legal materials. The policies are closely related to the self-understanding of Israel as a covenant community under God. The procedural legislation also reveals at a number of points the extent to which the covenant relationship between God and Israel is intimately involved in actual judicial proceedings.

The time-honored distinction between the OT as a book of law and the NT as a book of divine grace is without grounds or justification. Divine grace and mercy are the presupposition of law in the OT; and the grace and love of God displayed in the NT events issue in the legal obligations of the New Covenant. Furthermore, the OT contains evidence of a long history of legal developments which must be assessed before the place of law is adequately understood. Paul's polemics against the law in Galatians and Romans are directed against an understanding of law which is by no means characteristic of the OT as a whole.

A. OT terms for law
   1. Law in biblical Hebrew
   2. Law in LXX Greek
B. Law in the pre-Mosaic period
C. Law in the period from Moses to the Exile
   1. Law and covenant
   2. The Ten Commandments
   3. The Covenant Code
   4. Law and the tribal confederacy
   5. Law and the kingship
   6. Law and the prophets
   7. The Deuteronomic legislation
D. The Exile and its significance for law
   1. The destruction of the temple
   2. Law and the priests
   3. The Holiness Code
   4. Other priestly legal materials
   5. Law and eschatology
      a. Law and the New Covenant
      b. Law and the restored community
      c. Law and worship
E. Law in the postexilic period
   1. Law as the dominant reality within Judaism
   2. Law and wisdom
   3. Obedience to the law and the hope of Israel
Bibliography

A. *OT TERMS FOR LAW.* The basic term for "law" in the OT would appear at first glance to be "Torah." In Judaism this term is used to designate the first five books of the OT, the Pentateuch. Its actual meaning, however, is not "law" but "instruction," "guidance," "direction." Torah is that which points the way for the faithful Israelite and for the community of Israel. Not merely the laws of the Pentateuch provide guidance; the entire story of God's dealings with mankind and with Israel points the way. The term "Torah" may therefore stand in the way of an adequate understanding of law in the OT, if it is given too prominent a place.

1. Law in biblical Hebrew. Apart from the term "Torah" (תורה), no single Hebrew word is widely translated "law." The most common designations for Israelite law are מצוה, "commandment" (Gen. 26:5; Exod. 15:26); דבר, "word" (Exod. 34:28; Deut. 4:13); חק and its cognate terms, "decree," "precept" (Amos 2:4); משפט, "judgment," "ordinance," "custom" (Exod. 21:1). In the postexilic period the term דת becomes rather prominent (Esth. 1:8). This is a loan word from Old Persian, with the meaning "order," "law," regulation." In the Aramaic portions of the OT, the same word is frequently used as a synonym for תורה (Dan. 6:5; Ezra 7:14).

In a few instances the terms חק and משפט are used as though they were intended to summarize two types of Israelite law (Exod. 15:25; Josh. 24:25; Ezra 7:10). In Exod. 24:3 the terms דבר and משפט (in the plural) may also point to a distinction between two types of law. It has been suggested that these two types may refer, respectively, to the "policy" and the "procedural" aspects of law mentioned above.

2. Law in LXX Greek. The LXX regularly translates the Hebrew word תורה by the Greek νόμος (Exod. 24:12). The same Greek term is also used less frequently to translate מצוה (Prov. 6:20), דבר (Ps. 119:57—G 118:57), חק (Josh. 24:25), משפט (Jer. 49:

12—G 29:12), and חֹק (Prov. 13:15). The Greek term ἐντολή ("commandment," "order," "decree") is more customarily used to render the Hebrew word מִצְוָה (Gen. 26:5), while πρόσταγμα ("order," "injunction") and δικαίωμα ("regulation," "requirement") often appear for חֹק and its cognate terms (Gen. 26:5; Exod. 18:16). The Greek δικαίωμα is more frequently found as the translation of מִשְׁפָּט (Exod. 21:1).

B. *LAW IN THE PRE-MOSAIC PERIOD.* Since all the materials in the Pentateuch date, in their present literary form, from the period following the exodus from Egypt, it is impossible to describe with any certainty the form and content of legal materials from the pre-Mosaic period. It is in order, however, to sketch tentatively those characteristic features of law which appear to antedate the Sinai covenant and the organization of the community of Israel into a twelve-tribe system. On the problems of literary composition of the Pentateuch, *see* PENTATEUCH. For the history of the pre-Mosaic period, *see* ISRAEL, HISTORY OF.

Legal and social customs reflected in the book of Genesis have appeared in a new light as a result of the recovery of comparable materials from the second millennium B.C. found in NW Mesopotamia (*see* MARI; NUZI; PATRIARCHS; ARCHAEOLOGY). A man whose wife had borne him no son might adopt a slave as his heir (Gen. 15:1-4; 24:1-2). Such an adopted son had his rights secured by law in the event that a natural son should later be born. A barren wife was expected to provide another wife to bear children to her husband; she is expressly prohibited from sending such children away (cf. Gen. 16:1-6; 21:8-14; 30:1-13). The possession of the household gods was an indication of the right to the inheritance of the first-born (Gen. 31:19, 30-35). Deathbed oaths also appear to have had a binding character in law, as indicated by a lawsuit among brothers about the ownership of a slave-wife of the dead father (Gen. 24:1-9).

These indications of a common legal and social tradition between the ancestors of the Israelites and the peoples of NW Mesopotamia make clear that the period prior to the Exodus was not without its laws and community regulations. The ancestors of the Israelites are not to be understood as wandering nomads without any sort of legal tradition apart from that which is suited to tribal life among such nomads. At the same time, however, the indications of a kind of tribal law in this period and in later epochs are not to be overlooked or ignored. One of the most basic features of Israelite law belongs to this period: the notion of tribal wholeness and the necessity for vengeance in the face of any weakening of tribal integrity.

Blood revenge is one of the most fundamental aspects of tribal law. It is concerned with the restoration of health (*shālôm*) when the tribal solidarity had been damaged by the loss of one of its members. Normally the family was responsible for the execution of blood vengeance (Judg. 8:18-21). No more than restoration of the wrong done was considered proper. The Song of Lamech (Gen. 4:23-24) probably represents the brutal and excessive aspects of blood vengeance, which are not condoned in the OT.

It is highly probable that in the pre-Mosaic era the tribal groups from which the community of Israel was to be formed had, therefore, a fairly well-developed system of legal procedures based on customs widely prevalent in the ancient Near East. Certain matters, such as blood vengeance, marriage and adoption procedures, and the like, were administered by the heads of families or tribal chieftains. Others, however, involved relations among several tribes. Treaties or covenants were made between tribes regulating boundaries and grazing rights (Gen. 31:43-54), or legitimizing intermarriage (Gen. 34). Such arrangements were sanctioned by an oath ceremony in which the parties to the covenant each pledged to uphold the agreement and invoked the curse of God (or the gods) against themselves if they should not remain faithful to the agreement.

Courtesy of the Falcon's Wing Press

16. The Ur-Nammu Law Code, the oldest law code as yet uncovered

In addition to these occasional connections between the laws and customs of the ancient world and those of early Israel, reference must be made to the several law collections which have been recovered from the ruins of ancient Near Eastern cities. The earliest collection of laws thus far discovered is that of the Sumerian king Ur-Nammu of the city of Ur, dated to *ca.* 2050 B.C.* Next in chronological order is that ascribed to the Amorite king Bilalama of the city of

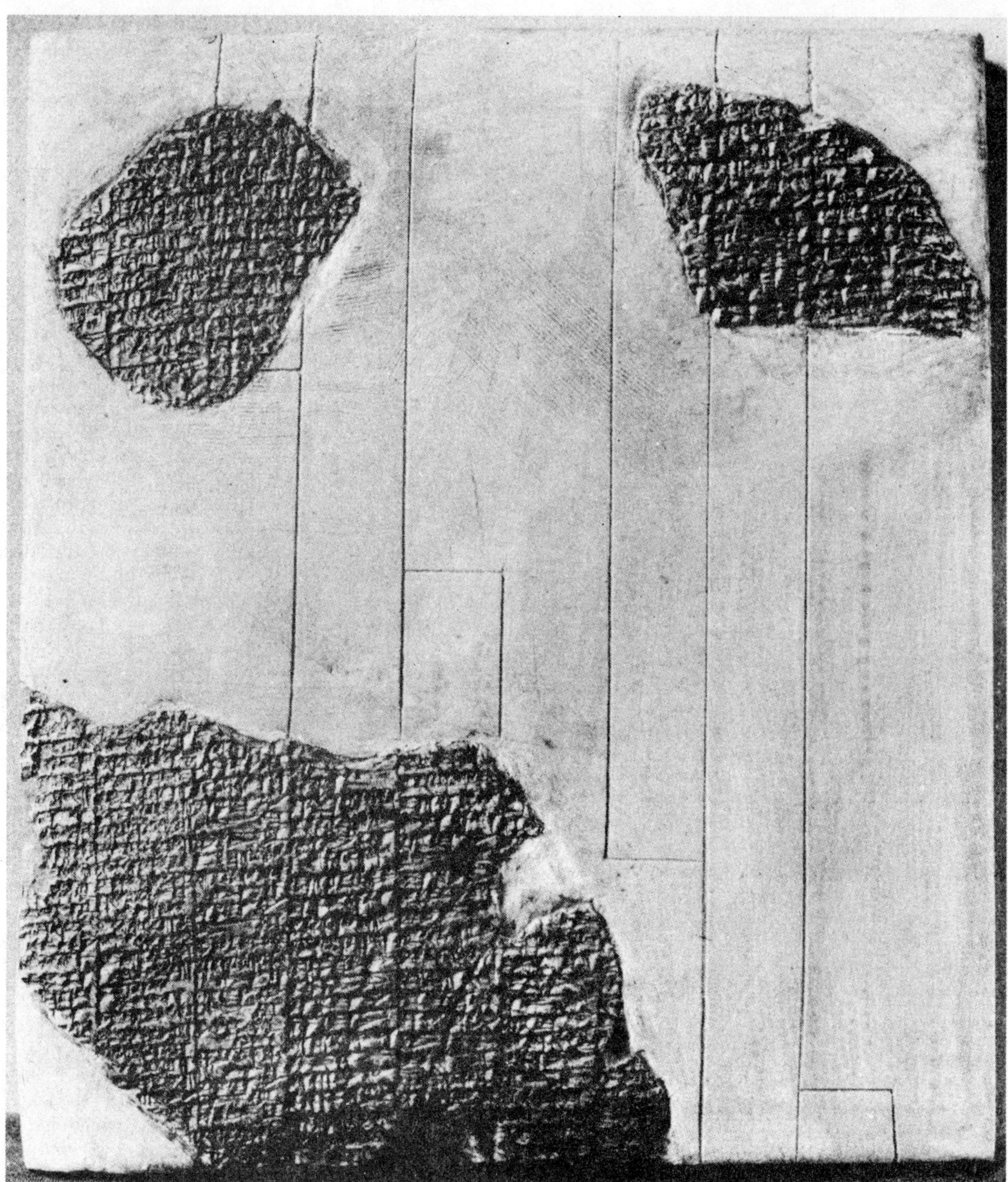

Courtesy of the Falcon's Wing Press

17. Cast of tablet reconstructed from three fragments of the Lipit-Ishtar Code

Eshnunna, from the last quarter of the twentieth century B.C. The third collection is from Lipit-Ishtar, ruler of the Sumero-Akkadian Dynasty from the city of Isin. This collection is dated to the first half of the nineteenth century B.C. Figs. LAW 16-17.

The most famous law collection of the ancient world is that of Hammurabi of Babylon.* The dates of Hammurabi's reign remain uncertain; most probably the collection of laws dates from the end of the eighteenth century B.C. The Hittite laws probably belong to the middle of the fifteenth century B.C., although they bear the marks of revision and thus antedate, perhaps by centuries, the time of their collection.* A group of Assyrian laws from the Middle Assyrian Empire are assigned to the fifteenth or fourteenth century B.C., although the law tablets themselves belong to the period of Tiglath-pileser I (twelfth century B.C.). A small body of Neo-Babylonian laws is also available, presumably from the end of the seventh century B.C. Figs. HAM 5; LAW 18-19.

The connections between Israelite and ancient Near Eastern law are undeniable, although the precise nature of such connections is difficult to determine. The form of the collections consists of a prologue, the laws, and an epilogue. This form is preserved in the Lipit-Ishtar and Hammurabi laws but is missing from the others. In the prologue the laws are traced to the action of the gods, who had appointed the king to rule over the land and had provided,

From *Atlas of the Bible* (Thomas Nelson & Sons Limited)

18. A section of the Code of Hammurabi. *See* Fig. HAM 5.

through these laws, for his wise and just rule. The contents of the laws reveals that, in each case, the affairs of highly complex societies are being regulated by the laws. Perhaps the most striking difference between these laws and those of Israel is the preponderance of laws dealing with property over those dealing with persons. In the OT, the opposite is so.

The epilogues affirm the faithfulness of the kings in upholding these divine laws and apply curses upon anyone who violates them or damages the tablets or the steles upon which they have been written. The form of the law collections is quite similar to that found in certain bodies of Israelite law. The contents also bear many marks of similarity; it is beyond question that these ancient laws, particularly those of early Mesopotamia, have been of considerable influence in the formation of the laws of the OT. *See* § C3 *below; see also* TEN COMMANDMENTS.

In the subsequent period, however, these regulations and customs are set in a new context by the exodus (*see* EXODUS, BOOK OF) from Egypt and Israel's growing awareness of what it meant to be a people of the one God, Yahweh.

C. *LAW IN THE PERIOD FROM MOSES TO THE EXILE.* The testimony of all biblical writers is unanimous in assigning to Moses a unique place in the promulgation of the divine law. In later times (Neh. 8:1) the "law of Moses" became a regular designation for the entire Pentateuch. Laws which actually developed centuries later were traced back to the events at Mount Sinai or to the plains of Moab, where God communicated with Moses face to face.

Although this judgment is historically erroneous, its theological meaning is clear. The act of divine redemption which brought forth a band of slaves from Egypt was the decisive moment in Israelite history. The covenant between God and Israel at the holy mountain (Exod. 19–24) provided the foundation for all Israelite law. Yahweh had called forth a people from the nations of mankind and had made this people his own. The people in turn had acknowledged that Yahweh was their God. With this acknowledgment of Yahweh's demonstrated power and mercy, the people were bound to the God who had delivered them. They were his people, and the totality of their life was at his command.

1. Law and covenant. Israelite law is, accordingly, covenant law. Law rests upon an understanding of the meaning of life in community. The meaning of Israel's life is provided by the saving action of God in her midst. God, who redeemed her, has a purpose for her. Through Israel, all the families of the earth are to receive blessing (Gen. 12:3). The covenant relationship thus issues in a distinctive type of Israelite law which is of fundamental importance. It is this type of law which sets forth the policy on the basis of which all procedural law is to be understood. *See above.*

The result of the Exodus upon Israelite law was that the legal tradition of the tribes was itself transformed and the distinctive type of law referred to above attained a dominant position. In the book of Exodus many evidences of both facts are present. The TEN COMMANDMENTS represent this distinctive type, and the Covenant Code (Exod. 20:22–23:33) represents the older legal tradition at one stage of its transformation.

2. The Ten Commandments. The Ten Commandments are found in the OT in two places (Exod. 20:2-17; Deut. 5:6-21). Although the variations in the two versions are slight (cf. Exod. 20:11 with Deut. 5:15; Exod. 20:17 with Deut. 5:21), even these slight differences make clear that the Ten Commandments have not been handed down without change from the time of Moses.

The Ten Commandments open with the self-identification of God: "I, Yahweh, am your God, who brought you out of the land of Egypt, out of the house of bondage" (Exod. 20:2; Deut. 5:6). The relationship between Yahweh and Israel which sets the condition of the act of lawgiving is one of divine redemption. God has acted to save, and he now calls this act to remembrance as the presupposition of the commandments to follow.

The commandments are to be understood as the stipulations of the covenant relationship. They are stated negatively, with only two exceptions (the sabbath command and the command to honor parents). These two exceptions have very probably undergone changes from negative commandments in the course of history. In its original form, the Ten Commandments probably consisted of very short sentences preceded by the strong negative particle, לא.

These stipulations indicate that the covenant God is in a position to specify unqualifiedly what the covenant conditions are. God commands and Israel is to obey. Nothing is promised as a result of obedience (apart from the probably late addition to the com-

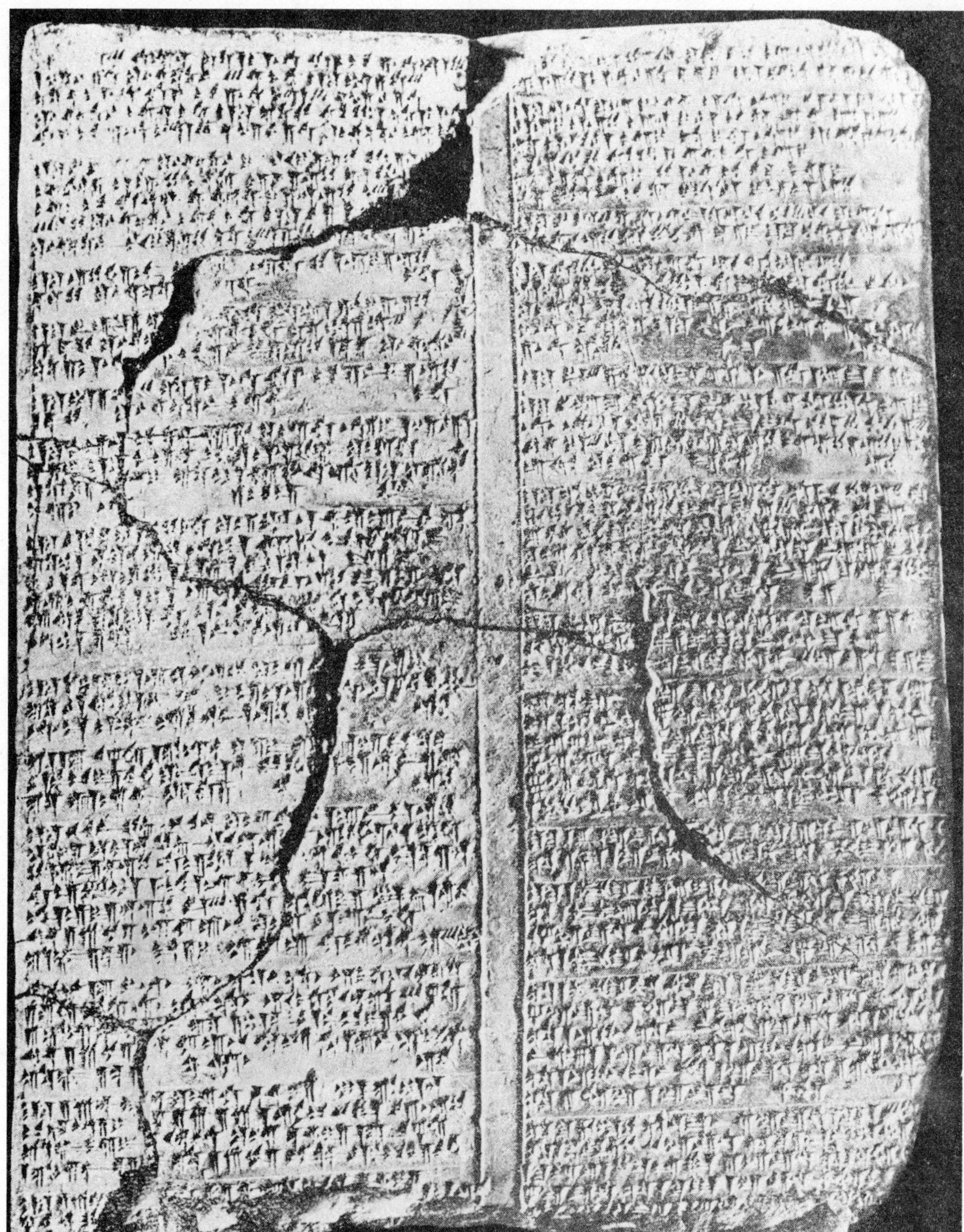

Courtesy of the Philosophical Library

19. Clay tablet with a cuneiform inscription, containing a Hittite code

mandment to honor parents). It is naturally understood that the keeping of the commandments means life and blessing (cf. Deut. 30:15-20), but the covenant relationship does not rest on a *quid pro quo* understanding. Israel is not commanded to keep these commandments in order that God may prosper her cause; she is called to obedience without qualification.

The Commandments are addressed to the individual Israelite ("you"); yet he is addressed as a member of the Israelite community. This is the law of the covenant community—the "neighbor" is the neighbor Israelite—but what is commanded applies to this community as a whole and to all its members.

Not a word appears in the Ten Commandments concerning the manner of upholding and enforcing this legislation. This is the policy statement on law which must then be made effective in procedure. Yet it is remarkable that one of the commandments (the law on covetousness) hardly allows for any kind of legal implementation. These commandments obviously intend to define negatively the very heart of the covenant relationship. They exclude those kinds of actions or intentions which are not in keeping with the nature of the bond between Israel and her God.

Such policy law, however, by virtue of its negative cast, is remarkably restricted in its content. The aim is certainly not to constrict the freedom of Israel or to make the community slavishly dependent upon the divine judgment in all matters. Legislation stated negatively actually provides the most extraordinary freedom in the covenant relationship. The history of Israelite law is evidence for the fact that this freedom has been put to full use. The Ten Commandments are often pointed to as the foundation of Western society. This they could not have become had they not been in the form of prohibitions of a categorical sort which then leave open the manner of their enforcement and allow for development within the whole field of positive legal procedures. *See* TEN COMMANDMENTS.

3. The Covenant Code. Immediately following upon the Ten Commandments in Exodus is a body of law of mixed character generally designated the Covenant Code or the Book of the Covenant (Exod. 20:22–23:33). This body of legal materials contains some laws stated in a form very similar to that of the Ten Commandments. The Covenant Code may be outlined as follows:

- I. Historical-theological prologue, 20:22 (the counterpart to Exod. 20:2)
- II. Laws on true Yahweh worship, 20:23-26
- III. Laws dealing with persons, 21:1-32
  - A. Slavery, vss. 1-11
  - B. Bodily injury, vss. 12-32
- IV. Property laws, 21:33–22:17—H 21:33–22:16
- V. Laws on maintenance of covenant, 22:18–23:19—H 22:17–23:19
  - A. Exclusive claim of Yahweh upon Israel, 22:18-20—H 22:17-19
  - B. Dealings with the stranger and the weak, 22:21-27—H 22:20-26
  - C. Maintenance of covenant holiness, 22:28-31—H 22:27-30
  - D. Dealings with the neighbor in general, 23:1-9
  - E. The sabbatical year; the sabbath; the festivals, 23:10-19
- VI. Epilogue containing warnings and promises, 23:20-33
  - A. God's protecting messenger or angel, vss. 20-21
  - B. Warnings and promises concerning entrance into the Land of Promise, vss. 22-33

Among these laws are some with the formal characteristics of the Ten Commandments—categorical prohibitions which do not specify how they are to be implemented (20:23; 23:1-2, 6; etc.). Another form of law quite similar to these categorical prohibitions is found in 21:12, 15-17; 22:19—H 22:18. These laws open with an active participle ("Whoever strikes, steals, curses," etc.) and close with the strong Hebrew expression, "he shall surely be put to death." Such laws probably belong to the same understanding of the relationship between God and Israel as outlined in connection with the Ten Commandments. *See* § C2 *above*.

Another entirely different form of law predominates in the Covenant Code, however. This is procedural law, consisting of precise specifications of how particular legal issues are to be dealt with. Such laws open with a specification of the general matter at law, introduced by the Hebrew particle כי, "When," or "When it should happen that . . . ." This is followed by a subordinate clause, introduced by the weaker Hebrew particle אם, "If," in which particular legal situations growing out of the general issue are covered. The following example illustrates the form of such laws: "When [כי] a man sells his daughter as a slave, she shall not go out as the male slaves do. If [אם] she does not please her master, who has designated her for himself, then he shall let her be redeemed; he shall have no right to sell her to a foreign people, since he has dealt faithlessly with her. If [אם] he designates her for his son, he shall deal with her as with a daughter. If [אם] he takes another wife to himself, he shall not diminish her food, her clothing, or her marital rights. And if [אם] he does not do these three things for her, she shall go out for nothing, without payment of money." (Exod. 21:7-11.)

The distinctions between this type of law and those dealt with above are obvious. The brief, categorical law, normally in the form of a prohibition, is entirely unlike this type of explicit, procedural law. The two types are often referred to, respectively, as apodictic (categorical) and casuistic (*see bibliography*). The casuistic or case-law type is the dominant form of law known from the ancient Near East. Several law collections from Mesopotamia and Asia Minor have been discovered by archaeologists. The best known of these is the Code of Hammurabi (seventeenth century B.C.), but older codes from Mesopotamia have also been discovered, as well as the Hittite Code from Asia Minor (middle of second millennium B.C.).

The use of the term "code" may, however, be misleading. These law collections are better understood as having resulted from the promulgation of a body of law at various times for the purpose of providing a general standard to guide the judges. They do not represent precise stipulations for the regulation of all legal matters. Rather, they serve as a collection of precedents, of guides for the legal authorities. No doubt, the ancient judges were in a position to exercise considerable freedom in the use of these legal guides.

Since the discovery and publication of the Hammurabi Code in 1902, it has been acknowledged that the Covenant Code is remarkably similar in content and form to the laws of ancient Mesopotamia. This judgment has been greatly strengthened by the comparison of the Covenant Code with the other law codes from Mesopotamia and Asia Minor. There can be no doubt that the laws of the OT (and the Covenant Code in particular) have been influenced by these non-Israelite laws, directly or indirectly. E.g., in the laws from the old Amorite city of Eshnunna in Mesopotamia (dated to the twentieth century B.C.) one law concerning the goring ox has its almost exact counterpart in Exod. 21:35: (*a*) "If an ox gores an(other) ox and causes (its) death, both ox owners shall divide (among themselves) the price of the live ox and also the equivalent of the dead ox" (Eshnunna Law 53; *see bibliography*). (*b*) "When one man's ox hurts another's so that it dies, then they shall sell the live ox and divide the price of it; and the dead beast also shall they divide" (Exod. 21:35). The examples of such near parallels could be multiplied.

The more remarkable fact, however, is that this common tradition of law which the early Israelites and the other peoples shared has been modified at many points in light of the Israelite understanding of the covenant relationship. The stringent laws against idolatry demonstrate that Yahweh alone is to be worshiped. The existence of other gods is probably not doubted, but Israel is reminded again and again that Yahweh alone is the God who has authority in her life and destiny.

In the midst of the case law, elements of the categorical type of law also appear. In the law on female slavery quoted above, the expression "since he has dealt faithlessly with her" (בבגדו־בה) is explicable on the basis of a covenant relationship which specifies what the true relationships between an Israelite and his neighbor are. Further, the requirement that a disliked slave-wife still be treated as a wife in every respect points to an understanding of the relationship between man and woman which has no counterpart in the other laws of the ancient world. The laws dealing with oxen have their parallels in several of the other law collections of Asia Minor and Mesopotamia. Yet the Israelite requirement that a goring ox be stoned and its flesh not be eaten (Exod. 21:28, 32) rests on the view that life belongs to God; even beasts must not take human life. Should they do so, they are acting in place of God (cf. Gen. 9:5).

The laws on SLAVERY are quite different from those of the neighboring peoples. Circumstances may force a man to sell his daughter into slavery, yet the daughter is and must be treated as a wife. The Hebrew slave (Exod. 21:2-6) may or may not be an Israelite in the full sense of the term. It appears probable that the term עברי ("Hebrew") refers rather to an outsider, one who stands outside the legal and covenantal community of Israel—although perhaps related to Israel by blood and historical background. It may be, however, that an Israelite, a full member of the covenant community, may be sold (or may sell himself) into slavery or bond service (Lev. 25:39). Yet all classes of slaves are to be given their freedom after a six-year period, unless they decide otherwise (Exod. 21:2-6).

Certain of these laws (e.g., 22:21-27—H 22:20-26; 23:1-12) show a remarkable concern for the weak and the oppressed. Once again, such legislation would seem to presuppose the experience of Israel at the Exodus, when God demonstrated his graciousness to a band of slaves in a foreign land.

The Covenant Code is generally dated, not to the wilderness period, but to the period after the entrance of the Israelites into Canaan (after 1200 B.C.). This may very well be correct. Yet it should be remembered that the ancestors of the Israelites had their own laws and customs prior to the Exodus (*see* § B *above*). Some legislation of the sort found in the Covenant Code might just as well be considered a part of the law proceedings brought by the patriarchs into Palestine centuries before the Exodus. The laws, indeed, presuppose a settled people engaged to some extent in agriculture and living in close relations with foreign peoples. It is doubtful that all the legislation contained in the code was a part of the pre-Mosaic legal tradition. There is no reason to deny that some of it may have antedated the Exodus.

Even so, it is the period following the Exodus and the Sinai events which saw the firm establishment of a body of customary law, as the necessities of a new mode of life developed.

4. Law and the tribal confederacy. The books of Genesis and Exodus indicate that already in pre-Mosaic times the Israelites consisted of twelve tribes, bound together by blood ties. Each tribe had as its head one of the twelve sons of Jacob. This twelve-tribe confederacy is much more a product of the period following upon the Exodus (Josh. 24; *see bibliography*). The entrance of the Israelites into Canaan under Joshua (*ca.* 1200 B.C.) was effected without opposition in the central hill country. The valley beside the old Canaanite city of Shechem became the gathering place for the Israelite tribes. It is highly probable, therefore, that in that region other Hebrew tribes and peoples who had not been involved in Egyptian slavery entered the covenant community under Joshua. The twelve-tribe confederacy may well have been in existence before this time, but it became an important legal entity only after the conquest of Canaan by Joshua had been effected.

This twelve-tribe system actually provides the basic communal and institutional structure for Israelite law. The law of Israel had its roots in the covenant relationship. This covenant relationship was regularly reaffirmed at the tribal center in a great tribal gathering (Deut. 27; 31:9-13; Josh. 8:30-35; 24), in connection with which the laws of Israel were read aloud and the people called upon to pledge renewed allegiance to the covenant God and his requirements.

It is noteworthy that the laws of Israel never became state law. They always maintained their relationship to the covenant God. Not even the greatest of Israel's kings were looked upon as lawgivers.

The Covenant Code has often been considered to be the law given by Joshua to the people at Shechem (Josh. 24:25). This may have been the case, although the apparent distinction between חק and משפט in Josh. 24:25 may rather point to two types of law—the categorical and the case law. Should this be true, then it may well be that the Ten Commandments in some form provided the covenant stipulation—the legal policy—and the Covenant Code (in an early form) the procedural law materials.

Distinction is often made between cultic, moral, and juridical types of law. Such a distinction may be useful in the present day, but it is not a distinction which ancient man knew or would recognize. The early priests were oracle givers (Deut. 33:8-10) and guardians of the sanctuaries. Their judgments would be sought on procedures for sacrifices, and in particular concerning the matter of clean and unclean offerings. Each worshiper in this period would make his own sacrifices, however (Judg. 6:19-24). It is not surprising, therefore, to find in the legal materials a mixture of cultic, ethical, and juridical legislation. The aim of all law was the maintenance of the wholeness and health of the covenant community. Cult, ethics, and jurisprudence were all involved in the health and holiness of the community.

5. Law and the kingship. The introduction of the institution of kingship (*see* KING) into the life of Israel (I Sam. 8–12; II Sam. 5:1-10) wrought considerable change in the legal practices of Israel. The loose tribal organization with its central gathering place was superseded by a monarchical system with a capital city, Jerusalem. The king soon came to exercise the function of a supreme court in legal matters (II Sam. 15:2-6). It is remarkable, however, that the king was not himself beyond the law or a law to himself (II Sam. 11–12); the covenant stipulations applied with equal force to him. Even more noteworthy is the fact that at no time in the life of Israel did a king set up his own law. The laws of Israel during the long period of the united and divided kingdoms were always understood to be those which Yahweh himself had disclosed to Moses on Sinai. Many changes in the legal system and practices came about, but all such changes were regarded, not as modifications introduced by the state, but as resting firmly upon the Mosaic tradition.

During the period of the kingship, many pressures were at work to bring about a centralization of the legal traditions under the kingship and the Jerusalem priesthood. It is highly probable that under David and Solomon much of the earlier legislation was gathered together and promulgated as a kind of constitution of the monarchical state. The present form of the Covenant Code (Exod. 20:22–23:33) may stem from the close of David's reign. Yet no collection of such laws was interpreted to be the law of the state; it was Yahweh's law, revealed to Moses.

Counterpressures were operative at the same time to preserve the force and efficacy of the law within the family, village, and town. The Israelites always seem to have maintained a dual attitude toward the kingship. It was instituted by Yahweh himself, but it came about as a consequence of the failure of Israel to be Yahweh's people (Judg. 8:22-23; I Sam. 8; 12). Such a view of kingship is not to be assigned merely to a late period of Israelite history; it belongs to the very essence of Israel's understanding of the covenant relationship between God and his people.

The attitude toward kingship is reflected in the attitude of the Israelites toward Jerusalem. The capital city was the seat of government and of worship. It was also an old Canaanite city into which David and his successors settled their troops, among whom were many foreigners. Jerusalem was not possessed by any of the Israelite tribes in the early period. After the conquest of the city by David (II Sam. 5:6-10), it was still considered to be a separate entity, distinct from the genuinely Israelite territory. The "men of Judah" are frequently contrasted with the "inhabitants of Jerusalem" (Isa. 5:3; Jer. 11:2; cf. "Judah and Jerusalem" in Isa. 1:1; 2:1; 3:1; etc.). The result of this attitude toward Jerusalem was that the law was never fully entrusted to a special class of interpreters directly related to and under the authority of the king. In the towns and villages, moreover, there was determined resistance to any kinds of innovations which were believed to be departures from the covenant law. It was from the towns and villages in particular that the prophetic movement of the eighth century stemmed; and from these areas the Deuteronomic legislation (*see* § 7 *below*) seems to have developed.

6. Law and the prophets. The prophets (*see* PROPHET) of Israel exercised many functions related to the law. Chief among these was the task of directing attention, in the name of Yahweh, to those breaches of the covenant stipulations which, if not repaired, would bring Yahweh's judgment upon Israel. Only occasionally do the prophets actually refer to the law. Hosea is quite explicit, however, in referring to the transgression of the law (8:1, 12). He also appears to refer to the prologue and the first commandment of the Ten Commandments (13:4). Amos describes many specific acts of injustice which document the failure of Israel to maintain the covenant relationship. In the judgment against Judah (Amos 2:4-5), reference is found to Yahweh's law (תורה) and his statutes (חקים). This passage may not be from Amos, however, but from a later period. The expression "for I will pass through the midst of you" (Amos 5:17) probably indicates the coming of Yahweh to punish Israel for violating the covenant requirements (cf. Gen. 15:17; Deut. 29:12—H 29:11; Jer. 34:18).

Isaiah refers to "testimony" (עדה) and "teaching" (תורה; 8:16; 30:8) which are written down for a later period. Such references suggest the collection of the oracles of the prophet, however, not the writing out of laws of an earlier period. In general, it may be said that the great prophets presuppose the existence of a legal tradition by which the covenant between Yahweh and the people of Israel is to be maintained. They attack the people for their violation of the covenant and its legal requirements. Particular terms are used to depict this covenant violation: Amos is concerned especially with injustice and unrighteousness; Hosea with infidelity and lack of knowledge of God; Isaiah with unbelief and violation of the holiness of Yahweh. Their concern is to call the people to repentance and to a reconsecration to the covenant stipulations. Although they refer only occasionally to the older legal materials, the latter provide the indispensable context for the strictures of the prophets against their generation.

7. The Deuteronomic legislation. The book of Deuteronomy is represented as a long speech given by Moses to the people of Israel in the plains of Moab, shortly before they are to cross over into the Land of Promise (Deut. 1:1-5). In this instance as in others, the OT writers are attributing to Moses a body of legislation which has a long history behind it, a history reaching far into the period following the death of Moses.

The culmination of the history of this legal collection must be seen as related to the great reform of JOSIAH of Judah in 622-621 B.C., as recorded in II Kings 22–23 (cf. II Chr. 34–35). Josiah's reform followed upon the discovery of a Book of the Law in the temple (II Kings 22:8-11), and was carried out in accordance with the provisions set forth in this book. The reform included the destruction of the places of worship outside the city of Jerusalem, the cleansing of the temple, and the centralization of worship in the Jerusalem temple.

While the contents of this Book of the Law are unknown, it may be assumed that they embodied much of what is now found in chs. 12–26 of the book of Deuteronomy. A comparison of the contents of these chapters with the steps taken in Josiah's reform reveals many apparent points of contact. It is not possible, however, to consider the Book of the Law found in the temple as the actual text of Deuteronomy as it now stands in the OT. The legislation in Deuteronomy has had a very long and complex history. The reform of Josiah was undoubtedly carried through in the spirit of the Deuteronomic legislation, but this legislation had developed, it appears, through centuries of teaching and preaching on the part of earlier Israelites, and in particular, the teaching Levites (*see* PRIESTS AND LEVITES) of the town and country areas of N Israel and Judah.

The materials in Deuteronomy of particular importance for the history and understanding of Israelite law are found in the following sections: (*a*) ch. 5—a second version of the Ten Commandments (*see* § C2 *above*); (*b*) chs. 12–26—the law collection itself; and (*c*) ch. 27—a curse ritual from the ancient ceremony of covenant renewal in the region of the city of Shechem. The entire book, however, expresses in the strongest way possible the significance of the divine law for the life of Israel. To love God and to keep his commandments—this is Israel's very life and blessing (Deut. 6:4-9; 30:19-20). To forsake God and to go after other gods—this is death, curse, and evil (Deut. 8:11-20; 28:15-68; 30:15-18; etc.).

The entire book is cast in the form of a series of sermons or homilies by Moses to the people. This fact provides the best clue to its origin and background. It is not priestly legislation or prophetic oracles; neither is it primarily historical reminiscence or interpretation. Rather, the Deuteronomic materials represent a body of teaching in sermonic style which had developed through the centuries, particularly in the towns and villages. Local priests and teaching Levites had probably been primarily responsible for its development. The aim was to give force and direct applicability to the ancient covenant law under changing conditions.

Of particular importance is the way in which the contemporaneity of subsequent generations with the community of the wilderness period is stressed. This law does not belong merely to a past epoch; God has constantly reaffirmed its relevance up to this day (cf. Deut. 5:2-3; 26:16-19; 29:10-15; 30:11-14; etc.). While the phrase "this day" purports to refer to the day of the gathering of Israel in the plains of Moab prior to the death of Moses, it is clear that much more is at stake. Each generation stands in the same relation to God as did that generation with whom God made his covenant at the holy mountain.

Within the legislation proper (chs. 12–26 and ch. 27) the same sermonic approach is discernible. The various forms of law noted in the Covenant Code and in the Ten Commandments appear again and again; but these are usually underscored through appeals to historical precedent, to the consequences of disobedience, and particularly to the love and grace of God for his people. Strictures against idolatry are especially prominent in the entire book. The exclusive claim of the covenant God upon Israel is stressed over and over. Yet the legislation discloses the remarkable adaptability of the teaching priests and Levites as social, economic, and political conditions have changed since the days of Moses. Tests of the authenticity of a prophetic message are provided (13:1-5; 18:21-22). The institution of the cities of refuge is amplified (4:41-43; 19:1-13). Provision is made for judicial appeal to the Levitical priests and judges of the central sanctuary (17:8-13), a provision which later is made to apply to Jerusalem only. The authority and limitations of kingship are prescribed (17:14-20). In these and in other instances the Deuteronomic legislation discloses how the older policy legislation of the covenant community could be made applicable to changing circumstances without losing its force as the direct command of the covenant God.

The strongly humanitarian tone and flavor of this legislation are unmistakable. The widow and the orphan, the poor and oppressed, are singled out for particular treatment. There are to be no poor within Israel, because of God's blessing upon his people; yet the Deuteronomists acknowledge almost in the same breath that the poor will never cease out of the land (Deut. 15:4, 11). The legislation prohibits the cutting down of fruit trees in time of warfare (20:19-20), the defilement of the land of Israel by various means (21:22-23; 22:9-10; 23:12-14), and in particular the defilement of the holy people. These regulations are designed to ensure that both land and people will correspond with the promise and intention of God for his people. They are measures to be taken to maintain the covenant relationship. Pollution of the land is considered a repudiation of its character as the Land of Promise. Corruption of the people would mean that God's holy people had profaned his covenant. Neglect or mistreatment of the poor and the oppressed, of the sojourner within the gate, or of the runaway slave, would mean that Israel had forgotten her own period of enslavement in Egypt; it would also mean that she had turned her back upon the purpose of God to make of her an example to all the nations, so that through her, God's blessing would go forth to all peoples.

Legislation concerning the holy war is found in ch. 20. It is probable that these stipulations had developed during the period of Israel's domination by foreign powers (the Assyrians in particular). Under the Assyrian overlordship, no Israelite standing army could be maintained. Such provisions as these in ch. 20, however, may have enabled the Israelites to call together a volunteer army, ready to overthrow the despot's authority at the first sign of weakness. The reforms of Hezekiah (II Chr. 29–31) and of Josiah (*see above*) were probably supported by this kind of volunteer army.

Deut. 12 prescribes that all Israelite worship is to be centralized in one place, at which place God will cause his name to dwell. In the reform of Josiah, this place is clearly understood to be Jerusalem. It is not certain, however, that this was the earlier understanding of the Israelites. From the period of the Conquest and the time of the judges, Israel had maintained a central gathering place for the twelve tribes. Under David, Jerusalem was intended to represent this central gathering place. It continued to have its rivals, however, as is indicated by the revolt of Jeroboam and the establishment of Bethel and Dan as the central places of worship for N Israel (I Kings 12). Already in the Covenant Code, specification was made that certain cases were to be settled "before God" (Exod. 21:6; 22:8-9—H 22:7-8; 23:15-17, 19).

With the development of the Jerusalem cultus, especially after the fall of the Northern Kingdom in 722-721 B.C., the place in which God had caused his name to dwell came to be understood as the Holy of holies of the Jerusalem temple. This concern with the "name" of Yahweh is characteristic of the Deuteronomic legislation and the recasting of the historical traditions in Joshua–II Kings by the Deuteronomic historian.

D. ***THE EXILE AND ITS SIGNIFICANCE FOR LAW.*** **1. The destruction of the temple.** The high hopes attached to the reform of Josiah very quickly were crushed. Josiah died in battle in 609/608 at Megiddo, vainly seeking to prevent the Egyptians from going to the aid of the embattled Assyrians in NW Mesopotamia. It is probable that Jeremiah had already sought to make clear to the Judeans that they should not pin too great hopes upon this reform and upon its talisman, the Jerusalem temple (Jer. 7; 8:8; 26). With the destruction of the city of Jerusalem and its temple by Nebuchadrezzar in 587 B.C., this safeguard to Israelite law and religion was swept away. A poet whose words were probably written just after the event has summed the matter up: "The law is no more" (Lam. 2:9).

One of the most remarkable features of Israelite life and faith is, however, that the destruction of the temple and the Babylonian exile did not destroy Israelite law or Israelite faith. On the contrary, it was during the Exile that the great bodies of priestly legislation were gathered together and elaborated.

2. Law and the priests. In the period before the Exile, the PRIESTS had been the primary interpreters of the law. The term "Torah" (תורה) is closely associated with the acts of oracle giving and the determination of the will of God on specific occasions. The priests were the custodians of the sacred traditions, and particularly of those associated with the acts of worship, the festivals, and the sacrificial rites. The role of the Levitical priests and teachers has already been noted in reference to the Deuteronomic legislation. The Jerusalem priesthood, however, was of even more decisive significance in the preservation and elaboration of the priestly legislation. During and following upon the Babylonian exile, the priestly laws took the shape which they now have in the OT, particularly in the books of Exodus, Leviticus, and Numbers.

3. The Holiness Code. One of the more ancient collections of priestly law is found in Lev. 17–26, which has been designated as the Holiness Code. The collection in its present form dates from the period following the fall of Jerusalem in 587 B.C., although the legal materials contained in it belong, no doubt, to a much earlier period and had been handed down within the priestly community in Jerusalem from generation to generation.

The laws are concerned primarily with the maintenance of Israelite HOLINESS and purity. Sacrifices are to be offered only before the tabernacle; this stipulation is to be understood to refer to the centralization of sacrifice in Jerusalem (17:1-7). Family purity is to be maintained through strict observance of the restrictions against marriage with near relatives (18:6-18). In the strongest terms the laws prohibit religious and social practices like those of the foreign peoples.

Ch. 19 contains a collection of laws similar in content and form to earlier laws, in particular the Ten Commandments and the Covenant Code. Other laws also have their connections with earlier legislation. These are treated, however, from the priestly point of view.

This point of view is clearly expressed over and over again: "You shall be holy to me; for I Yahweh am holy, and have separated you from the peoples, that you should be mine" (Lev. 20:26). A regular refrain concludes the particular prescriptions: "I am Yahweh." The priestly community has sought to draw the consequences of God's election of Israel from among all the nations to be his "own possession" (Exod. 19:5). God's people must be discernibly different from the other peoples. Nowhere in the OT legislation is this judgment expressed with such force and repetitiveness as in the Holiness Code.

4. Other priestly legal materials. Certain legal features are discernible in the framework within which the entire Pentateuch has been set by the priestly community during and following the Exile. God appears as lawgiver in the creation story itself. He speaks, and heaven and earth are provided, step by step, with their divinely ordained structure. The blessing upon man includes a specific command: "Be fruitful and multiply, and fill the earth and subdue it" (Gen. 1:28). This command is repeated in connection with the law against the taking of human life (Gen. 9:5-7). These laws apply to all men, although presumably they were understood to have particular force for the people of God.

With the law on CIRCUMCISION (Gen. 17:9-14) the priests introduce into their treatment of the early narratives the first commandment concerned specifically with Israel. Priestly legal concerns appear next in the Passover legislation, in connection with the last of the plagues (Exod. 12:1-13, 43-49). The major collections of priestly law are found, however, in the context of the events at Mount Sinai and in the wilderness.

The first large body of priestly law deals with the building and equipping of the TABERNACLE. Exod. 25–31 contains the prescriptions for this undertaking and for the consecration of the tabernacle to the worship of Yahweh. In Exod. 35–40, the execution of these commands is recorded.

The book of Leviticus consists entirely of priestly legislation. The book contains regulations on sacrifices (chs. 1–7), the consecration of priests (chs. 8–10), and clean and unclean animals (ch. 11); laws on impurity (chs. 12–15); and the ritual for the Day of Atonement (ch. 16). Following the Code of Holiness (chs. 17–26) is a concluding chapter (27) dealing with the making and fulfilment of vows to Yahweh.

The book of Numbers consists primarily of priestly materials, only a part of which are of a specifically legal character. The following are the major legal stipulations: on the service of the Levites in the tent of meeting (chs. 4; 18); on adultery and jealousy (ch. 5); on the making and fulfilment of vows (chs. 6; 30); on dedication of the Levites (ch. 8); on sacrifices (ch. 15); on uncleanness (ch. 19); on inheritance (ch. 27); on festivals and festival sacrifices (chs. 28–29); on the holy war (ch. 31); and on the Levitical and refuge cities (ch. 35).

In this legislation it is once again clear that the priests are employing older legal materials but that these are set in the context of that priestly understanding of the law referred to above. Israel is to be a holy people, consecrated to Yahweh. Her entire life is to be ordered by the understanding that Yahweh has set her apart to his service. It is remarkable that the priests, who have been closely associated with the kingship in Jerusalem, have not set forth their legal understandings as having been transmitted by the kings. All the priestly legislation is assigned to Moses, apart from those requirements which were understood to have been given by God at the Creation, or following the Flood, or directly to Abraham.

During the Exile, therefore, the priestly community has devoted itself to the study and elaboration of the divine law with almost single-minded purpose. The aim is the preservation of the holy community within an alien environment. Yet the priests, as well as other Israelite men of faith, have looked forward to a day when Israel should return from exile and be reconstituted as God's people in the holy land. The Israelite view of the "latter days" (Isa. 2:2), when God would bring his work among men to fulfilment, was of profound influence upon the development and understanding of law.

5. Law and eschatology. The Israelite conception of Yahweh as a God actively involved in the course of world history is of decisive importance for an understanding of OT faith. In reflection upon the meaning of Yahweh's redemption of Israel from Egyptian slavery, the OT theologians were led to develop a view of God as creator of heaven and earth. Through the same reflection, they were led to ponder the purpose of God's action among men, the end toward which it pointed. In the successive stages of Israel's history, the purpose of God could not be seen to have been fulfilled. Israel's repeated acts of apostasy, of failure to be God's people, were understood to have delayed the fulfilment of God's promise that through Israel all the families of the earth were to receive blessing (Gen. 12:3). In the century preceding the Exile, and particularly during the exilic period, prophets and poets of Israel arose to sketch in broad outline the features of the "latter days," when God's purpose would come to its culmination. These pictures of the day of fulfilment at the "end" of history are referred to by the term "eschatology," the doctrine of the last days or the last things. *See* ESCHATOLOGY OF THE OT.

In these "latter days," the law occupies a prominent place. First of all, the Last Day, the Day of Yahweh (*see* DAY OF THE LORD; cf. Isa. 2:12–3:15; Amos 5:18-20; Zeph. 1:7, 14-18) is a day of divine wrath upon those who have not been faithful to the covenant or obedient to God's law. God will appear in wrath against a faithless people. But this is not the major aspect of OT eschatology. Of greater prominence is the hope that in the "latter days" God will himself see to his promise. Israel will be restored to fidelity and obedience, and from Jerusalem, God's law will be taught to all the nations (Isa. 2:2-4; 42:1-4; Mic. 4:1-4; etc.). The various depictions of this Last Day do not constitute a unified eschatology, nor do all of them give the same prominence to the law. Three features of the Israelite view of the relation between law and eschatology should be noted, however:

a. Law and the New Covenant. One way of describing the action of God at the Last Day, by which his purpose for Israel and for mankind is brought to fulfilment, is provided by the prophet Jeremiah (31:31-34; cf. Isa. 49:8-13; Ezek. 11:17-20; 36:24-27; 37:26-28; Hos. 2:18-20). The day is to come in which Yahweh will make a new covenant with Israel and Judah, not like the covenant made with their forefathers, which they broke. God will put his law within them, write it upon their hearts, so that the teaching of the law will no longer be necessary. All will know it and will keep it. The sin and iniquity of Israel will be swept away, to be remembered no more.

It should be noted that, while a new COVENANT is promised, no new law is to be given. A new relationship between God and man is to be established, a relationship in which the law of the Old Covenant finds expression in the very being of the people of the New Covenant. It will no longer be a reality external to the people, to which they respond in obedience or faithlessness. The law will be within them, constitutive of their very life, so that simply to live will be to live in communion with God and in obedience to his law.

b. Law and the restored community. While the prophet Ezekiel seems to have shared this view of the Last Day with Jeremiah (Ezek. 11:17-20; 36:24-27; 37:26-28), he (or one of his disciples) has also provided a sketch of the restored commonwealth of Israel (Ezek. 40–48). These chapters certainly come from the period of the Exile, whether written by Ezekiel or by a later writer. The prophet reports a vision received in the twenty-fifth year of exile (40:1). He is transported to the temple area of Jerusalem, where he is shown a fully restored temple, the measurements of which are provided him. The glory of God then enters the temple (43:1-5), and the prophet is told that never again will Israel defile God's holy name (43:7). The prophet is given further details of the temple worship and service and is provided with the new boundaries of the twelve tribes.

This vision does not constitute a part of Israelite law, although it does contain a number of legal matters, some of which are not in agreement with the laws of the Pentateuch. But as a visionary description of the restored commonwealth of Israel it is significant for the way in which a prophet has related law and eschatology. Israel is to be reconstituted upon the Land of Promise. She is to be a holy people, charged not to let God's holy name come again into disrepute. All God's laws and statutes are to be strictly obeyed (44:23-24). In a new Jerusalem, a new temple, and a newly distributed land, Israel is to be God's people, recognizable by all as his people. The mission to the nations seems to consist in this fact alone: that they shall be able to see a faithful people of God, bent upon his service, maintaining their identity in the world as God's people.

c. Law and worship. Already in the early period of Israelite history, the worship of Israel (*see* WORSHIP IN THE OT) and the law of God are seen to be intimately related. The ceremony of covenant renewal included a reaffirmation of obedience to the covenant stipulations (*see* § C4 *above* and note in particular

Josh. 24). Priestly custodianship of the legal traditions guaranteed that in the acts of worship the people should be presented with the significance of God's law and of its background and implication in the totality of their life. In the Psalms, further evidence of the connection between law and worship is to be found.

Ps. 19 consists of two parts, perhaps originally independent of each other. The first (vss. 1-6—H 2-7) is a hymn in praise of the God of nature. The second (vss. 7-14—H 8-15) is in praise of God's law (תורה). In this psalm, as in several others (Pss. 1; 94; 119), the Israelite worshiper expresses his delight in God's law. He counts it as the greatest of gifts that God has taught him how to walk before God in faithfulness and obedience. Moreover, in meditation upon God's law (Ps. 1:2) the worshiper participates in that end time, in which the purpose and promise of God find their fulfilment. Israelite worship as anticipation of the final victory of God, and in which the law of God has an important place, provides another connection between law and eschatology. In the act of worship the entire sweep of God's dealings with man, from the Creation to the new creation, is gathered up into an experience by which man is judged, forgiven, is enabled to discern, if only for a time, the glory of God as judge, lawgiver, and redeemer.

E. *LAW IN THE POSTEXILIC PERIOD.* It is possible that during the Exile the site of the ruined temple had not been entirely abandoned by those who remained in the land. It was not, however, until a number of exiles had returned to Judah that the temple was rebuilt (Haggai; Zech. 6:9-15). Upon the resumption of Israelite worship in the temple, provision was made for many of the legal practices of the earlier periods, elaborated during the Exile, to be put into effect. Within a period of about one hundred years the final edition of the laws of Israel was completed. The "book of the law of Moses" referred to in Neh. 8:1 probably represents the Pentateuch in its present form.

The conditions of life in the Exile had led not only to elaboration and development of the laws of the earlier periods. In the process of such development, the law had been studied assiduously and its observance strictly impressed upon the community. Observance of the sabbath and of circumcision were of particular significance in the maintenance of Israel as a separate and distinct community. Gatherings of Israelites for the study of the law were probably a regular feature of the exile period (Ezek. 33:30-33). Thus the way was prepared for the emergence of the SYNAGOGUE as an institution of primary importance within Judaism following the Exile.

A further development occurred in connection with the law. Israel had to exist in exile without king or temple, and without the possibility of maintaining the tribal organization in anything more than an idealized form. Thus the sacral structure within which the law had developed had disappeared. In the period following the Exile, the consequences of this event emerged. The law came to be regarded as an independent reality, loosed from its moorings in the tribal system, in the acts of worship at the temple, and no longer the criterion by which kingship and other functions of an organized state could be judged. It may be that only by this means was the community of Israel preserved in the Exile. It is certain, however, that the consequences of the law's having been loosed from its institutional and structural moorings within Israel were serious indeed.

1. Law as the dominant reality within Judaism. Chief among these consequences was the appearance of an understanding of the law of Israel as containing within itself the totality of God's will for man. Israel had failed to keep the law; consequently, God's judgment had befallen them—just as the prophets had warned. Now that the community had returned to the Land of Promise, it was imperative that the law be strictly observed. Worship in the temple had to be carried out in rigid accord with the legal specifications; in fact, worship tended to be understood itself as the fulfilment of the law. The freedom with which earlier generations had dealt with the law was now exercised less in the development of that law than in its interpretation. Torah had become the basic reality for the life of the Jews.

It should be remembered, however, that Torah meant more than the legal requirements. It included the whole sweep of God's dealings with mankind from the beginning up to the death of Moses. Furthermore, the Torah was still understood to be the gift of God. The saving deeds of God still constituted the basis for Torah (Neh. 9). Israel had been chosen by God and then had been given the Torah; God's choice was not based upon obedience to Torah.

Even so, it cannot be denied that in postexilic Judaism the law and obedience to the law outweighed all other religious realities and obligations. The influence of the historical interpretations provided by the recasting of the old traditions by the Deuteronomic school (as seen in Joshua–II Kings) and by the Chronicler (I–II Chronicles; Ezra; Nehemiah) became of decisive importance. Obedience to the law would guarantee God's blessing; disobedience meant disaster (Mal. 3:6-12). The way was thus prepared for a doctrine of merits. Those who kept the law were the pious ones, whom God would surely reward for their piety. Those who spurned the law were evildoers, with whom the pious should have no dealings. The motivation for obedience to the law came to be understood less as gratitude to God for his gracious acts of redemption (Amos 2:9-12) and more as a means to secure God's favor.

2. Law and wisdom. The WISDOM tradition in Israel is as old as the people of Israel. Solomon was the legendary wise man in Israel and the collector and creator of a great store of wisdom (I Kings 4:29-34). The wise men of Israel were a distinct group alongside priests and prophets (Jer. 18:18). They were concerned primarily with practical matters: with the right relations between different groups in society; with protocol in business and politics; and in general with the maintenance of decency and order. In the postexilic period, however, as the law came to occupy such a central place in the life of the Jewish community, the law and the wisdom tradition became much more closely related to each other. The beginning of wisdom is the fear of Yahweh (Prov. 9:10). Wisdom was God's own gift, his creation at the beginning of his work, the first of his acts (Prov. 8:22). The teachers of wisdom in postexilic Judaism developed as a group devoted to the law, giving practical reinforcement to the legal requirements.

The next step, which was taken in the intertestamental period, was the virtual identification of the law and wisdom (Ecclus. 24; Wisd. Sol. 6-10). This is a further stage in the development of the notion of the law as a divine reality, an intermediary between God and man.

In the books of Job and Ecclesiastes, however, strong attacks are leveled against the more popular understanding of the wisdom school. The author of Job (*see* JOB, BOOK OF) presents the friends of Job as the protagonists of pragmatic wisdom and has no difficulty in showing up the untenability of their superficial judgments. The author of ECCLESIASTES attacks the bourgeois morality of the wisdom tradition point by point, insisting that the sum of all human actions is nothing but vanity.

3. Obedience to the law and the hope of Israel. It has been noted that in Israelite eschatology the law occupies a very significant place. This is equally true of that form of eschatology which is called APOCALYPTICISM. Foreign influences, notably from Persia, led to the development within Judaism of a picture of the "latter days" significantly different from that represented in earlier texts. The most prominent features of this apocalyptic eschatology are the following: The present age is viewed as being under the domination of evil powers, engaged in conflict with the forces of goodness, and more often than not prevailing over them. The struggle between good and evil is a cosmic struggle; it also has its counterpart in the heart of every man. At the last day, however, a pitched battle will ensue between good and evil. God will vanquish the evil forces and reconstitute the cosmos in accordance with his purpose at Creation.

The OT contains only a few documents which reflect this apocalyptic eschatology, among them Isa. 24-27; Ezek. 38-39; Daniel. The hero of the book of DANIEL is depicted as a scrupulous observer of the law of Israel. This document, which has arisen in its present form from the time of the persecution of Judah by Antiochus IV (*ca.* 165 B.C.), reveals the author's sympathy to be with the pious of Israel who hold fast to the law even in the face of persecution and death. The Maccabean brothers are looked upon as no more than a "little help" (11:34). The hope of Israel is seen to rest in unswerving obedience to the law. In the evil age in which men now live, the law is the one sure hope of mankind. Those who are righteous will pass through the great cataclysm of the last day and will arise to new life (Dan. 12:2; Isa. 25:8; 26:19).

In later Judaism, obedience to the law was considered the prerequisite to the coming of the Messiah. Should Israel keep the law perfectly for but a single day, then the Messiah would appear (*see* LAW IN FIRST CENTURY JUDAISM). Various movements within Judaism in the NT period, and shortly before, arose out of the dual conviction that the last day was close at hand and that at least a remnant within Israel should devote itself to the law with uncompromising rigor. One such movement is that of the Essenes, with whom the community of Qumran was probably closely related, if not identical.

In the OT, then, law is understood to rest upon the initiative of God, who has redeemed a particular people, entered into covenant with them, and provided the basic stipulations of this covenant relationship in the form of the covenant law. The love and grace of God constitute the setting for the giving of the law. Responsive love, gratitude, and faith provide the motivation for obedience to the law, although the OT does not too frequently express the matter in this way (but cf. Deut. 6:5; Ps. 18:1—H 18:2; Jer. 2:2). In the postexilic period the law tends to be viewed as an independent reality, less integrally related to the saving action of God, obeyed less from gratitude to God and more as an ordinance decreed at the creation. But the promise of a new covenant is not forgotten; and Torah is one day to come to the coastlands, to all the nations (Isa. 2:2-4; 42:4).

Bibliography. A. Jirku, *Das weltliche Recht im AT* (1927). G. von Rad, *Das Gottesvolk im Deuteronomium* (1929). F. Horst, *Das Privilegrecht Jahwes* (1930). A. Alt, *Die Ursprünge des israelitischen Rechts* (1934)—a study of fundamental importance. M. Noth, *Die Gesetze im Pentateuch; ihre Voraussetzungen und ihr Sinn* (1940). G. Östborn, *Tōrā in the OT; a Semantic Study* (1945). G. von Rad, *Der Heilige Krieg im alten Israel* (1951); *Studies in Deuteronomy* (1953). G. Mendenhall, *Law and Covenant in Israel and the Ancient Near East* (1955). J. B. Pritchard, ed., *ANET* (2nd ed., 1955), pp. 159-98. H. H. Schrey, H. H. Walz, and W. A. Whitehouse, *The Biblical Doctrine of Justice and Law* (1955). F. Horst, "Recht und Religion im Bereich des AT," *Evangelische Theologie*, 16 (1956), 49-75. *See also* bibliography under TEN COMMANDMENTS. W. J. HARRELSON

LAW IN FIRST-CENTURY JUDAISM [תורה; Aram. אוריתא, אורייפא; νόμος]. The term *torah* in Judaism, usually (under the influence of the LXX translation of it as νόμος, "law") rendered by "law," ranges in meaning from teaching or instruction to the totality of the divine revelation, written and oral. It is with this last that we are here concerned.

The nature and content of this revelation in first-century Judaism cannot be determined with exact certainty for three reasons: (*a*) the period was one of fluidity: the Jewish tradition had not been stabilized in the Mishna (redacted *ca.* A.D. 200-220; *see* TALMUD), but was still in lively process; (*b*) the law was so variously interpreted by different groups—e.g., the Pharisees, the Sadducees, and the Essenes—that no integrated description of it can be given, and a too systematic presentation of the material must be suspect; (*c*) the rabbinic sources directly dealing with the law (the Mishna, the Midrashim, etc.) are later than the first century, and, by and large, represent only one current in the Judaism of that time, and only the dominant element within this one current (the Pharisaism of Rabbi Johanan ben Zakkai and his collaborators at Jamnia), so that they can be used only with extreme caution. However, by very careful sifting of these sources, which contain traditional material going back to the first century and earlier, and by the critical use of the Apoc. and the Pseudep., Philo, Josephus, and the Dead Sea Scrolls, certain positions can safely be suggested, as characterizing first-century Judaism.

1. The written law
2. The oral law
    - *a.* Its rise
    - *b.* Its authority

c. Codification
d. Exegesis
3. Law as agent of salvation
4. Law as agent of creation
5. The law in the future
Bibliography

1. The written law. Judaism in the first century, as always, postulated that God exists and that he has revealed his nature, character, and purpose, and his will as to what man should be and do. And, as is the case in other revealed religions, Judaism claimed that, in the very act of revelation, there had been given a law, which was, therefore, of divine origin and authority, to govern man in all the details of his life. This law, it was believed, was partly enshrined in the documents now called the OT. The notion of inspired scriptures probably arose in connection with prophecy. While first-century Judaism continued to believe in the OT convictions that God could reveal himself, through angels, messengers, visions, dreams, and voices, the act of prophecy, through which God declared his will, had come to be particularly associated with the activity of the Holy Spirit; all the prophets spoke by the Holy Spirit, and with the last of the prophets the Holy Spirit had ceased from Israel (T.B. Yom. 9*b;* T.B. Sot. 48*b;* T.B. Sanh. 11*a;* etc.). The law of the prophet Moses, the books of the prophets themselves, and, by a natural evolution, all the other books now contained in the OT, came to be conceived as written by persons moved by the Holy Spirit. This connection with prophecy, and thereby with the Holy Spirit, gave to them an inspired character. Although much inspired material had not found a way into the writings of the OT, everything within them was inspired.

The names given to the OT varied. For long there was no generic title in use. The books of the OT were referred to as "the law and the prophets" (II Macc. 15:9; IV Macc. 18:10; Matt. 5:17; 11:13; Luke 16:16); then there was used the phrase "the law, the prophets, and the writings" (T.B. Sanh. 90*b*). Possibly the first term used to designate the whole of the Law was "the book," "the books," "the holy books" (βιβλίον, βιβλία=ספר, etc. [I Macc. 12:9; II Macc. 8:23]; ἡ ἱερά βίβλος; βιβλίον; βίβλος ἱερά, etc. [see an index to Philo]). In the NT we find "the scripture," ἡ γραφή (הכתוב); Philo has γράμματα, γραφή (Josephus has τὰ ἱερὰ γράμματα). The precise contents of "the scripture" we can deduce. After A.D. 70 there was still discussion in Judaism on the authority of certain books. The inspiration of Ezekiel can hardly have ever been seriously doubted, but the wisdom of placing it in the hands of all was questioned, because it contained contradictions of the Pentateuch; these were subsequently resolved (T.B. Shab. 13*b*, etc.). But the following books were in dispute: (*a*) Ecclesiastes, because it contradicted itself, and was more the product of Solomon's own wisdom than of the Holy Spirit; according to Jerome's Commentary on Eccl. 12:13, the closing words of the book alone eventually secured its place in the canon. (The dispute over this book was lively in the days of Hillel and Shammai [M. Eduyoth 5.3; M. Yadaim 3.5], and continued till the third century [Tosef. Yadaim 2.14].) (*b*) The Song of Songs, Proverbs, and Ecclesiastes were regarded by some as too profane (ARN 1.5); Proverbs contradicted itself (26:4-5). (*c*) Esther was in conflict with the fundamental principle that the law was complete (Lev. 27:34) and that no new institution was to be introduced by any prophet after Moses—Esther and Mordecai were concerned to introduce a new festival, the Day of Purim.

Eventually, at the school at Jamnia, Ecclesiastes and the Song of Songs were accepted as scripture. At the same time, other documents were excluded from the canon. Tosef. Yadaim 2.13 reads: "The Gospel [הגליונים] and the books of the heretics [ספרי המינים] are not sacred Scripture. The books of Ben Sira, and whatever books have been written since his time, are not sacred Scripture." The exact connotation of "the Gospel" and "books of the heretics" cannot here be discussed (*see bibliography*), but since Ecclesiasticus was rejected, because its author lived in comparatively recent times, when the Holy Spirit had departed from Israel, the same would apply to documents similarly dated, including the gospels and other Christian books (though it is surely incredible that the canonicity of these would ever have been even considered by Judaism).

By the end of the first century, we can be sure that the OT, as we know it, was regarded as canonical, although discussion of certain of its books continued to a later date. The phrase used to denote the canonical character of a book was that it "defiled the hands." M. Eduyoth 5.3 illustrates the usage: "According to the School of Shammai the book of Ecclesiastes does not render the hands unclean. And the School of Hillel say: It renders the hands unclean" (קהלת אינו מטמא את הידים כדברי ב . . . ש ובו . . . ה אומרים מטמא אתהידים). Is this to be taken to mean that the distinction between what defiles the hands and does not, as applied to the Scriptures, was opposed by Shammaites? In M. Yadaim 4.6 the Sadducees ascribe the distinction to the Pharisees. Thus "the Sadducees say, We cry out against you, O ye Pharisees, for ye say, 'The Holy Scriptures render the hands unclean,' [and] 'The writings of Harmiram [either the books of the heretics or those of Homer] do not render the hands unclean.' " The latter passage reveals that it was out of love for the Scriptures that the Pharisees declared them "to defile the hands," and both passages make it clear that they participate in the quality of things consecrated to God. As a consequence, the rolls on which the OT was written were treated with extraordinary respect. Rules concerning their form and the mode of their composition were multiplied: they could not be introduced into an impure place; the honor of the law was jealously guarded (Jos. War II.xii.2). The question was discussed as to the languages into which the law could be translated: according to Rabban Simeon Gamaliel, it could only be written in Greek, and, although targums were permissible in other languages (M. Meg. I.8; T.B. Meg. 3*a*), these were not to be used as lectionaries (cf. T.B. Shab. 115*a*). The law had become the consolation of Israel (I Macc. 12:9), for which many were prepared to die (I Macc. 1:56-60; T.B. 'A.Z. 17*b*); already in the first century it had become an important part of the liturgy of the synagogue and the chief object of study (M. Ab. 5.22). Josephus' words are apt: "But for our people, if anybody do but ask any one of them about our laws, he will more readily tell them all than he will tell his own name, and this in consequence of our having learned them immediately as soon as ever we became sensible of anything, and of our having them, as it were, engraven on our souls" (Jos. Apion II.xix). Exaggerated this may be, but nonetheless indicative. *See* CANON OF THE OT.

This last quotation refers us to the laws as such. Were there distinctions made between the different parts of the OT? So far, we have referred to the whole of the OT as Torah; and, while the translation of this term as "Law" is not strictly correct, because it merely covers the meaning of Torah as "commandment" (מצוה), nevertheless, the use of "Law" for the whole Torah is significant. Because the fundamental section of the OT was the Mosaic law contained in the OT, the Decalogue as such was given prominence (Mek. on 15:26; 20:1; Song of Songs Rabba 5.14-15; Philo *On the Decalogue*); but it was not to be regarded in any exclusive sense as *the* Torah. The withdrawal of its recitation from the synagogue service, when it was used by Christians as if it were the whole Torah, points to this (T.B. Ber. 12*a;* J. Ber. 3*c*). It is, however, difficult not to think of the Pentateuch, as a whole, as constituting the Mosaic law: it was called Torah, even in its nonlegal aspects (e.g., Gal. 4:21 ff).

The authority of the Mosaic law—i.e., the Pentateuch—was indicated variously. Its derivation directly from God (T.B. Sanh. 99*a;* on the relation of the Jewish law to God, see especially Jos. Antiq. Preface 3; Apion II.xviii ff), or by the mediation of angels from God (Jub. 1:27-28; 2:1 ff; 6:22; etc.) emphasized this (the notion that such mediation implied inferiority is a Christian development; Gal. 3:19; Heb. 2:2). On the other hand, this distinguished it from the Prophets, and the other writings of the OT, which, though produced under the inspiration of the Holy Spirit, only derived their authority from the Law—i.e., their agreement with the Pentateuch (T.B. Sanh. 30*b*); Moses was the first and greatest prophet; all that was communicated to prophets, who followed him, he had already received. No prophet could contradict him or change or add to what he had proclaimed (Lev. 27:34; Deut. 4:2; 13:1 ff; T.B. Shab. 104*a*). The prophets were guardians of the torah of Moses (II Macc. 2:1 ff). The writings outside the Pentateuch are designated "tradition," קבלה, and derive their authority from their "exposition" of the Mosaic law—i.e., from their Sinaitic character (T.B. Ned. 22*b*). While there was no doubt expressed as to the authority of the Law and the Prophets, the authority of certain documents among the Writings, we saw, was questioned. The Writings were not read in public worship, in the synagogue, as were the Law and the Prophets. Thus all writings in the OT outside the Pentateuch were of second rank, although inspired: that proof texts were often quoted in three verses, from the Law, the Prophets, and the Writings, did not mean that these were all on the same level of importance, but that the last two confirmed or reiterated what was in the Law (T.B. Meg. 31*a*).

Before we leave the written law, it is necessary to point to revelations of God's law made before that on Sinai. The basic laws essential to man, it was claimed, had been given to Adam (Mek. on 19:10; T.B. Sanh. 56*b;* Deuteronomy Rabba 2.17; Jub. 3:10-14, 30-31). In addition, Noah had been given, according to some, seven laws (Mek. on 20:2; Tosef. 'A.Z. 8.4). T.B. Sanh. 56*ab;* Jub. 7:20-21 speak of more general laws, and others refer to thirty commandments given to him (Genesis Rabba 98.9; J. 'A.Z. 2.1.40*c*). These Noachian commandments were placed on all mankind, and may roughly be taken to correspond to the Stoic "law of nature." Some scholars consider them to signalize the recognition on the part of Judaism of the extreme improbability that all nations would ever come to obey the whole law; it resigned itself to this fact by insisting only on a minimum of decency for Gentiles. It should also be noted that, after the exodus from Egypt, Israel had received some laws before the revelation on Sinai (Exod. 15:25), and that the patriarchs, especially Abraham, were thought to have practiced all the laws, either because they had discovered them for themselves or because they had received a revelation of them. In Philo, both Moses and Abraham are not only examples of lives after the law (νόμιμος βίος) but in themselves incarnations of the Law (Moses is νόμος ἔμψυχός, and Abraham νόμος αὔτος ὢν καὶ θεσμὸς ἄγραφος).

2. The oral law. ***a. Its rise.*** The term "torah" had reference not only to scriptures, but also to an unwritten tradition, partly interpreting and partly supplementing the written one, and usually referred to as the oral law. The phrase "oral law" (תורה שבעל פה) probably goes back to Hillel (T.B. Shab. 31*a*), or at least to Gamaliel II (Sifre Deuteronomy XXXIII.10). But, in the first century, it was little used, the term "tradition," קבלה, being preferred (so in the NT; Josephus uses παραδόσεις, "traditions"; *see* LAW [IN THE NT]; in Philo, νόμος ἄγραφος [see an index to Philo] refers to the natural law; again, in the Rabbis, as we saw, "tradition," קבלה, also refers to the non-Pentateuchal books—e.g., M. Ab. 3.13).

The development of such an oral law was natural on several grounds. No written law can be so exhaustive as to cover all the contingencies of life, and so the ritual and ceremonial, as well as the civil and criminal, law of the Pentateuch implies, or presupposes, a great deal of custom or usage, which was law, although it was not written. Thus Deut. 16:18 directs the appointment of judges, but gives no details as to the procedures they are to follow. Presumably such procedures were orally transmitted. Similarly "custom" was followed in matters such as divorce, the payment of taxes to priests, the observance of the sabbath. As to this last, e.g., the OT gives no definition of work that was prohibited, but custom gradually established certain patterns of rest. It is likely also that during the Exile written codes or collections of laws were lost which were never later replaced but whose contents were orally preserved, at least in substance.

More specifically, it may be said that while the Scriptures themselves recognize the need for the interpretation and adaptation of the law (e.g., Deut. 17:8–26:19) by the hands of priests and judges, the biggest impetus to this arose probably at three periods:

a) At the time of Ezra, when the returned exiles

had to resettle in Israel, and made the law the ground of their life. In this connection the description of Ezra in 7:6 ff is significant. *See* EZRA.

b) During the time when Persian rule gave place to Greek rule in Palestine. Under the Persians the scribes (*see* SCRIBE) had ruled Israel; they constituted an authoritative body of teachers, versed in "the Book" (hence their name, Soferim, from the Hebrew ספר), and up to the Greek period they faced conditions of continuity that were manageable in terms of the Book and their interpretation of it. The change to Greek rule interrupted the activity of the Soferim, as an authoritative body, and, at the same time, faced the nation with bewilderingly new conditions. New ideas and customs had to be met for which the Soferim and the law, which they had interpreted, were unprepared. Hence there had to be an expansion of interpretation and a new adaptability, and this meant the growth of oral tradition—i.e., a tradition alongside the written tradition. This condition of change received some regulation with the establishment of the SANHEDRIN in 190 B.C. This, an authoritative body of priests and laymen, taught and interpreted the law and sought to regulate the life of the people. But again under Antiochus IV Epiphanes (175-163 B.C.) books were burned, and there had to be a greater reliance on tradition as such, and this gave an impetus to the development of the oral law.

c) There can be little doubt that in the Roman period and in the first century, perhaps especially, economic tensions within the nation contributed to the same development. The needs of the expanding artisan and commercial elements in the nation have been claimed to dictate the concern of the Pharisees with the expansion of the oral law, and the interests of the patrician Sadducees, in maintaining the economic *status quo,* to govern their conservatism on the law (*see* PHARISEES; SADDUCEES). E.g., according to Deut. 15:2, all loans were remitted in the seventh year. The uncertainty which this introduced into commercial transactions is evident: it could lead to fraud and oppression (Deut. 15:9), and the advent of the seventh year would tend to paralyze the economy. Hillel accordingly enacted the rule of the Prosbol. This was a declaration, made before a court of law by a creditor, and signed by witnesses, to the effect that the loan in question would not be remitted under the terms of the seventh-year law (M. Sheb. 10.3 ff). (Was Hillel introducing Babylonian usage?)

b. Its authority. Various factors, then, inevitably produced a rich tradition alongside the written law, and the question arose as to the authority of this tradition. Ultimately, the oral tradition was rooted in long-established custom. At first, its authority was directly connected with the written law. By the use of midrashic methods of interpretation, each tradition was grounded in the Scriptures. There are illustrations of this in the Mishna at M. Soṭ. 8.1-6; Neg. 12.5-7; Sh. 5.10-13, where we have a running commentary on the scriptural text, as the basis of certain commandments. Attempts to prove that the oral law was first formulated without reference to the Scriptures, and later related to them, have failed. That view is most likely which finds the midrashic presentation of the oral tradition—i.e., its presentation in connection with the text of scripture—giving place, under the pressures, particularly of Hellenism, in the Greek period, when there was a rapid growth in oral laws, to the Mishnaic method—i.e., the presentation of the traditions independently of the sacred text, as in most of the Mishna. Not that the Mishnaic method of transmitting the oral law ousted the midrashic, but that the former came to coexist with the latter: both methods continued in use, the one culminating in the redaction of the Mishna, the other in the production of the great Midrashim.

c. Codification. What is clear, however, is that, although the oral law came to be presented in isolation from the text of scripture, nevertheless, it was regarded as of equal obligation as the written law, and was deemed to have been included in the revelation given at Sinai, just as was the latter. It was the attempt to connect the oral law with the Mosaic law that led to the development of rabbinic exegesis. Laws which could not be so connected were, probably at Jamnia, designated "Mosaic halakah from Sinai" (הלכה למשה מסיני); eventually the grammatical and exegetical rule and methods of rabbinic Judaism were traced back to Sinai. To what extent the statements concerning the equal derivation of the oral and written law from Moses are playful hyperbole is difficult to assess, although only of a few oral laws is it explicitly stated that they were revealed to Moses.

The first century was alive with the questions here referred to. On the one hand, the Mishnaic method had become so customary that that century saw collections of oral law made. There may have been collections of important laws dealing with the temple and its ritual, as early as the period of the Soferim, but these were probably never written down. The earliest code mentioned in postbiblical times is the Sadducean criminal code in force down to the time of Queen Alexandra (78 B.C.); the *Megillat Taanith,* the "Scroll of Fasts," a record of days which it is not lawful to keep as fasts, probably dated in part before A.D. 70, can be regarded as the earliest rabbinical code. This is an anti-Pharisaic work, but it is probable that in the time of Jesus, although the Pharisees for various reasons were seeking to hinder the writing of codes for the public (there was, in fact, no interdict against this), many scholars had secret books of *halachah,* which they considered important, in codified form (*see bibliography*). In that period the house of Hillel and the house of Shammai were submitting the oral law to intense discussion. They differed so much that there was a danger that Israel should be faced with two laws rather than one (Tosef. Soṭ. 14:9). The discussions between them could not but have produced grave religious uncertainty. Toward the end of the first century at Jamnia, under the influence probably of Gamaliel II, attempts were made to bring an end to this uncertainty. The decisions of the school of Hillel were adopted as standard, although in practice authority was often given to the school of Shammai (J. Ber. 3*b;* T.B. 'Er. 13*b*). But the work at Jamnia did not dispel the uncertainty, and it was Akiba's work in collecting *halachoth* that laid the fundamental outlines for the Mishna. Immediately before and after A.D.

70, the need for codification among scholars was probably "in the air." Immediately after 70, the pupils of Rabbi Johanan ben Zakkai, and his younger contemporaries, collected the treatises Yoma, Tamid, and Middot. It is certain that material from this period, as from before 70, which had already been codified, was later included in the Mishna.

d. Exegesis. On the other hand, along with the activity of a Mishnaic or codifying kind went another, which, however, is not to be regarded as inconsistent with this—namely, the development of "exegesis" to connect the oral law with the written law. Many have held that the rules of rabbinic exegesis, or hermeneutics, were derived from classical Greek, Aristotelian models, as employed in the schools of Alexandria (*see bibliography*). Others regard them as more popular, and less rationalized, than this view demands. What is clear is that, in the time of Jesus, rules of exegesis had been developed, though it must be understood that the aim of this exegesis was not so much the elucidation of the text, as the convincing imposition of particular laws upon it. The rabbinic tradition preserves certain catalogues of rules. It ascribes the first to Hillel. His catalogue contained seven rules, while that of Rabbi Ishmael (who flourished A.D. 120-35) had thirteen such. Possibly the rules of Hillel are older than he, consisting of the direct methods of earlier scribes. But that the first century saw developments in this field is clear (for Hillel's rules, see: Tosef. Sanh. 7.11, p. 427; ARN 37.10; for those of Ishmael, Siphra on Leviticus [preface]; there is an allusion to them in Mek. on Exod. 13:2). *See bibliography.*

If we now analyze the oral law, as it was in process in the first century, the following components of it emerge: (*a*) It contained long-established custom. (*b*) It incorporated regulations or decrees of a prohibitive kind (גזרות) and enactments of a positive kind (תקנות) issued by individuals or bodies, who at different times had authority to do this—e.g., the Prosbol of Hillel. Later than the first century this procedure was justified on scriptural grounds; for our period two things are noteworthy: many oral laws could not be connected with the written law—to such laws the appellation "Mosaic rules from Sinai" was given (*see* § 2 *above*); and much in the oral law was in direct contradiction to the written law. Authorities, when necessary, did not hesitate to modify and even to suspend the written law, on their own initiative, without any attempt at elaborate casuistry to justify their procedure. The Prosbol of Hillel is the classic example of this; for other instances, see M. Soṭ. 9.9. (*c*) The oral law grew from the very study of the written law; new laws were found to be implicit in the latter, which did not belong to the former, but which were then naturally proclaimed as demands which had fallen into desuetude. Along with this went the discovery of principles in the written law to meet the new conditions that were continually being faced.

It was over the validity of this growing oral law that the Pharisees and Sadducees were divided. Josephus has expressed the matter thus: "What I would now explain is this, that the Pharisees have delivered to the people a great many observances by succession from their fathers, which are not written in the law of Moses; and for that reason it is that the Sadducees reject them, and say that we are to esteem those observances to be obligatory which are in the written word, but are not to observe what are derived from the tradition of our forefathers; and concerning these things it is that great disputes and differences have arisen among them" (Antiq. XIII. x.6). It was in their attitude toward the law that other sects also differed (*see* ESSENES; SADDUCEES; PHARISEES). And it is over against a background of intense discussion on the relative claims of the written law and the oral, and of the meaning of the latter, that the ministry of Jesus is to be placed (*see* LAW [IN THE NT]). One caveat is to be issued. Under the impact of Josephus, who emphasized the importance of the Pharisees in the first-century scene, and of the NT, where they play a prominent role, the influence of the law in that century has been probably overestimated. While Pharisees, Sadducees, Essenes, and other groups would have been occupied with the law, they constituted only a small portion of the total population; the vast majority were not so interested, being what were technically called "people of the land" (*see* 'AM HA'AREZ), ignorant of the law and indifferent to rules of cleanness and uncleanness.

3. The law as the agent of salvation. So far, the content, written and oral, of the Torah, has been indicated. Clearly its scope was exceptionally wide, including what we should call canon, civil, criminal, and even international law, all in one, and embracing the whole range of human activity (*see* TALMUD). A third-century rabbi computed that there were 613 commandments placed upon Israel (T.B. Mak. 23*b*). Doubtless many of these had emerged after the first century, while the majority of them dealt with matters which did not impinge directly on the ordinary life or, as, e.g., in the case of laws on the priesthood and divorce, concerned only a few within the community. Nevertheless, the importance of the law in first-century Judaism is too obvious to need emphasis.

Because the law was regarded as the gracious gift of God to man, the yoke of the law was readily accepted by the pious, and there was joy in submission to it. No profound theological justification of obedience was offered or necessary; the stark statement that the law was commanded by God and was, therefore, to be obeyed, sufficed. (This did not prevent much discussion on the "grounds" or "reasons" for certain laws—the טעמי תורה: the *Doreshe Reshumoth* [דורשי רשמות] were concerned with these and other difficulties in the law. In one sense the development of rabbinic exegesis itself is an attempt at the rationalization of the oral law, this under Hellenistic influences.) The classic example of this acceptance is the statement of Rabbi Johanan ben Zakkai, who, on being questioned as to the meaning of the seemingly pointless rite dealing with the red heifer, simply asserted: "The Holy One, blessed be He, merely says: 'I have laid down a statute, I have issued a decree. You are not allowed to transgress my decree'; as it is written, 'This is the statute of the Law'" (Numbers Rabba XIX.8).

It was obedience to the law that secured merit (זכות) before God. This merit could, moreover, be assessed with some exactitude according to deeds committed, just as guilt (חובה) could be measured by the transgression of the law (עבירה). Every Israelite thus had to give a reckoning (חשבון) before God, and his destiny was determined according to his deeds. As Akiba "used to say: All is given against a pledge, and the net is cast over all living; the shop stands open and the shopkeeper gives credit and the account book lies open, and the hand writes and everyone that wishes to borrow let him come and borrow; but the collectors go their round continually every day and exact payment of men with their consent or without their consent" (M. Ab. 3.17). *See bibliography.*

At first sight such a view implied that man can fulfil the law, and that salvation is his own achievement. Moreover, when reward was so closely connected with observance, the temptation to a mechanical obedience unrelated to religious sincerity was a real one. But Judaism was aware of the dangers and difficulties of its attitude toward the Torah. On the ability of man to achieve his own destiny there were differences among Pharisee and Sadducee and others, but it is no accident that among the things enumerated as pre-existing creation was repentance (*see bibliography*). The rabbis recognized that the nature of man is so constituted that he cannot escape sin, so that repentance is a condition of his existence. Hence its premundane creation (*see* REPENT). Moreover, the law itself ordained the sacrificial system as a means of atonement for sin, though sacrifice without confession of, and compensation for, the wrong done—i.e., without true repentance—did not avail. So, too, Judaism recognized the danger of a merely formal obedience to the law by insisting on the necessity for a pure intention (כונה) behind all obedience (M. Ber. 2.1; M.R.H. 3.7), by distinguishing between moral and ceremonial demands, as even in Numbers Rabba XIX.8, by demanding a piety from the heart and not a merely "legal" piety (*see bibliography*). It is over against these considerations that criticisms of Pharisaism in the gospels must be assessed. The potency of repentance is such that a single day of it would bring in Israel's redemption (Pesiḳta 163*b*, dated A.D. 300; earlier are T.B. Yom. 86*b* [A.D. 110] and T.B. Sanh. 97*b* [A.D. 90]).

4. The law as the agent of creation. We have been concerned with the law mainly as the demand of God, by obedience to which salvation was to be achieved. But, so profound was the devotion of Judaism to the law, that it was not content merely to regard it as God's agent for human redemption.

The law was given a kind of personal existence. Despite the multiplicity of its demands, the law was conceived of as an entity, which could teach and speak ("The Scripture says, . . . speaks, . . . teaches, etc."; cf. Paul's personification of the law). The personalized unity given to the law is illustrated by the fact that the plural form, "laws" (תורות), occurs usually when it is necessary to deny the existence of more than one law (T.B. Sanh. 80*b*). The law was a living, unified reality (T.B. Shab. 31*a;* Tosef. Soṭ. 14.9).

It was given, not only a redemptive, but also a cosmic, significance. We have seen that the oral law was traced back to Sinai, but the whole law, conceived as revelation, was given still greater antiquity—in fact, a precosmic existence. The way was prepared for this, long before the first century, through the identification of wisdom with the law. WISDOM in the OT, especially in Prov. 8, is the agent both of redemption and of creation, its precosmic role being clearly defined. And, as early as Deut. 4:6, the law was associated with wisdom, and in Ecclus. 24:23 the identification of the two was made explicit, so that, by the first century, the precosmic existence of the law and its agency in creation were well established (Bar. 3:14–4:1; IV Macc. 1:17; *et passim*), and, although some of the testimonia adduced below are later than the first century, there can be little doubt that the motifs go back to that period. The following emphases are noteworthy:

a) The law, like wisdom in Prov. 8, was regarded as older than the world. Sifre on Deut. 11:10 takes Prov. 8:22 to mean that the law was created before everything. In Genesis Rabba 1, it is made clear that the law not only existed in the mind of God before creation, but that it had actually been created then.

b) The law was connected with the very act of creation. Rabbi Akiba (A.D. 120-35) said: "Beloved are Israel to whom was given a precious instrument wherewith the world was created. It was greater love that it was made known to them that there was given to them a precious instrument whereby the world was created, as it is said, Prov. 4:2" (M. Ab. 3.15; cf. Philo *On the Creation of the World*).

c) The Torah was thus one of the pillars of the universe (M. Ab. 1.2 in a saying ascribed to Simon the Just [either 280 or 200 B.C.]); later passages speak of the world as having been created for the law (e.g., Genesis Rabba 12.2).

d) It followed that in a real sense God himself was bound by and to the law: He had studied it and fulfilled it (T.B. 'A.Z. 3*b*).

e) It was corollary to this that the law was perfect and eternal (I Enoch 99:2; Bar. 4:1; Jos. Apion II; Philo *Life of Moses* 2.3.14), although later passages have been taken to suggest a distinction between the Pentateuch, at this point, and the rest of scripture, the former alone being eternal (J. Meg. 1.70). But see context.

How seriously are we to take these emphases? Are they merely the play of fancy? It may be argued, in the light of the ease with which Judaism ascribed pre-existence to other things than the law—repentance, Paradise, Gehenna, the throne of glory, the sanctuary, the name of the Messiah (Pes. 54*a;* Genesis Rabba 1.4, etc.)—that the category of pre-existence in itself was not highly significant. But it was otherwise with the idea of the law as the instrument of creation. This concept gives expression to one of the most fundamental convictions of Judaism: that the universe conforms to the law, that nature itself is after the pattern of it. To claim that the law was the instrument of creation was to declare that nature and revelation belonged together; in theological terms, that there was no discontinuity between nature and grace. It was to give cosmic significance to morality, and to cosmic speculation a sobriety it might otherwise have lacked. Nor is the close relation of God himself to the law to be lightly treated; for Judaism this meant that religion, revealed in law, was no secondary afterthought but primeval to God himself. Again these emphases raise the possibility that within Judaism there may have been conceptions not far removed from the Platonic doctrine of ideas, albeit expressed far more naïvely than in Plato. Thus the law had a kind of celestial existence before it came into being on Sinai, and we are reminded of Philo's doctrine of the Word conceived and residing in the mind (λόγος ἐνδιάθετος), the Word expressed (λόγος προφορικός; *see* PHILO JUDEUS). In any case, the law was regarded as existing in two places: first, in what Plato would have called the realm of ideas, and, secondly, in time. But this is part of the problem of the relation between symbolism and imagery in Judaism (especially apocalyptic) and Hellenism. It is, however, well to be on our guard against too sharp a distinction between what is Platonic or Hellenistic and what is Hebraic.

This is the best place to ask whether in Hellenistic-Jewish writers such as Josephus and Philo the understanding of the law was modified under Hellenistic influences. Josephus remained a Jew in his attitude toward the law, but in three ways he reveals a Hellenistic coloring. His praise of Moses, as a pious, wise man, probably stems from his desire to commend him to the Hellenistic world, as does his interest in supplying reasonable grounds for the law—he had intended to write a book on this theme; Hellenistic in its appeal is also his understanding of the law in terms of virtue. Hellenistic motifs are still more marked in Philo, although he remained a practicing Jew. He identified the law of Judaism with the law of nature, or the order of the world, because for him God is both creator and revealer. The fathers (Abraham, etc.) were able to live according to the law, before the law had actually been given, because reason and revelation are one. This attempt to equate revelation and nature, philosophy and law, led Philo to the use of the allegorical method, but his allegorism never led him to neglect the observance of the law. Along with his use of allegory went his attempt to find rational grounds for the law in order to avoid offense to the Hellenistic world.

5. The law in the future. Finally, we have to ask what role the law was expected to play in the messianic age or in the age to come. We have seen that it was regarded as perfect and eternal: it was impossible that it should ever be forgotten, no prophet could ever arise who would change it, and no new Moses should ever appear to introduce another law to replace it. Matt. 5:18 adequately expresses the dominant first-century doctrine. Note, however, the following:

a) There are a few passages which suggest the cessation in the messianic age of certain enactments concerning sacrifices and the festivals (Leviticus Rabba 9.7; Yalqut on Prov. 9:2); others suggest changes in the laws concerning things clean and unclean (Midrash Tehillim on 146.7; Leviticus Rabba 13.3); others often claimed to imply changes in the law are of doubtful weight (e.g., Sifre on Deut. 17:18).

b) Difficulties or incomprehensibilities in the law will finally be adequately explained. God himself would teach his people in the messianic age (Numbers Rabba 19.6). The passages which speak of a new law in the messianic age are of a late date, but they may be cogent enough to permit us to assert that the expectation of a new, messianic law was not incompatible with first-century Judaism (see Targ. on Isa. 12:3); it is possible that anti-Christian polemic may have caused the suppression of early evidence for this. In the age to come, beyond the messianic age, commandments were to cease (T.B. Ned. 61*b*). On the whole, however, the picture that emerges is that of a future, when God himself or his Messiah would study the laws, reveal their "grounds," return backsliders, and give the law to the Gentiles. Judaism could no more think of the future than of the past and present other than in terms of the eternal law.

Bibliography. In addition to standard works on Judaism, Josephus, and Philo, see the following: W. Bacher, *Die exegetische Terminologie* (1899-1905), pp. 90 ff. S. Schechter, *Some Aspects of Rabbinic Theology* (1909). R. Marcus, *Law in the Apoc.* (1929). G. F. Moore, *Judaism in the First Five Centuries of the Christian Era* (1927-30), I, 235-80; on Philo's use of γράμματα, γραφή, III, 64. H. L. Strack, *Introduction to the Talmud and Midrash* (1931), pp. 12 ff, on secret books of *halachah* in the first century A.D. H. L. Strack and P. Billerbeck, *Kommentar zum NT aus Talmud und Midrasch* (1922-28), I, 3-6, on the relationship of deeds and destiny; I, 13-15, on the distinction between true piety and "legal" piety. C. H. Dodd, *The Bible and the Greeks* (1935). J. Bonsirven, *Le Judaïsme Palestinien* (1934-35), I, 247 ff; *Exégèse Rabbinique et Exégèse Paulinienne* (1939), on the development of rabbinic exegesis in the first century. On the derivation of the rules of rabbinic exegesis from Aristotelian models, see D. Daube, *HUCA*, XXII (1945), 239 ff. W. D. Davies, *Torah in the Messianic Age and/or the Age to Come* (1952). T. Z. Lauterbach, *Rabbinic Essays* (1957), pp. 23-298.

W. D. DAVIES

LAW IN THE NT [νόμος; תורה]. By "law," or "the law," the NT usually means the law of God revealed in the OT. Except, by implication, in Matt. 17:24-27; Mark 12:13-17; Rom. 13:1 ff; I Pet. 2:13 ff, the civil and criminal laws of states are not dealt with. Even in I Tim. 1:8 the reference is probably to the Mosaic law, and in Rom. 2:12-16 the law written on the heart (*see* CONSCIENCE) is also probably to be understood as "what the [Mosaic] law requires" (vs. 15). Our main concern, therefore, will be with the law of the OT in the NT.

1. The law in the Synoptic gospels
   a. Criticism of the law
   b. Affirmation of the law
   c. Explanations of Jesus' dual attitude
2. The earliest Christians and the law
   a. Radicalism: Stephen
   b. Compromise
3. Paul and the law
   a. Terminology
   b. Life under law and "in Christ"
   c. Role in history
   d. Christ the end of the law
4. The Letter to the Hebrews
5. The Letter of James
6. The Fourth Gospel
7. Conclusion

Bibliography

1. The law in the Synoptic gospels. The term "law" (νόμος) does not occur in Mark at all; in Matthew and Luke it occurs eight and ten times respectively, always with the article, except in Luke 2:23, where also the reference is to the law of the OT.

Usually the term denotes the Pentateuch (e.g., Matt. 5:18-19). Probably the phrase "the law and the prophets" is used for the whole of the OT (Matt. 5:17; 7:12; 11:13; 22:40; Luke 16:16; 24:44 [here the psalms are distinguished]), as are also "the scripture" (ἡ γραφή; e.g., Mark 15:28) and "the scriptures" (αἱ γραφαί; e.g., Mark 14:49). The "oral law" (תורה שבעל פה) is not described as "law" (νόμος), but as the "tradition of the elders" (παράδοσις τῶν πρεσβυτέρων; Mark 7:5) or the "tradition of men" (παράδοσις τῶν ἀνθρώπων; Mark 7:8).

The meager incidence of the term itself is no measure of the deep significance of the problem of "the law" in the Synoptics. But at the outset it must be said that it is beyond dispute—however much it may have been exaggerated by some scholars—that in the course of their transmission, the words and works of Jesus have been colored by the experience and needs of the churches that preserved them. To distinguish the attitude of Jesus himself toward the law from that of the early church, therefore, is exceedingly difficult. Here the Synoptic evidence is presented without any attempt to establish how far it accurately represents the position of Jesus himself.

a. Criticism of the law. According to the Synoptics, the ministry of Jesus implied, and possibly explicitly recognized, that the law, as understood by Judaism, no longer regulated the ways of God with men, and that Jesus himself had taken over the place previously held by the law. "The law and the prophets were until John; since then the good news of the kingdom of God is preached" (Luke 16:16; cf. Matt. 11:11-13). The coming of Jesus has inaugurated a new order in which, in some sense, the law is superseded; the new wine of this new order cannot be put in old wineskins (Mark 2:22). This is most marked, not only in the parables, which illumine a crisis in which the KINGDOM OF GOD is now in the process of realizing itself, but also in the relationship of Jesus with publicans and sinners, the "people of the land." A "friend of sinners," he ignored limitations placed on social intercourse by the law, and by implication he broke down barriers essential to the maintenance of the distinction between "clean and unclean" (Mark 2:13-17; Matt. 11:19). An examination of his attitude toward the sabbath (Mark 2:23–3:6), toward things clean and unclean (Mark 7:1-24), and toward divorce (Mark 10:2 ff), reveals that: (*a*) Jesus rejected the oral tradition (in this sense he was, from one point of view, near the Sadducees); (*b*) he set one passage of scripture over against another, not to harmonize them, but to invalidate the one by means of the other (Mark 2:23-28; 10:5-9); and (*c*) he elevated moral above ceremonial commandments (cf. Mark 12:28-33).

Moreover, Jesus appealed to men to judge of themselves that which was good (Luke 12:57), and himself claimed the right to reinterpret the will of God (Matt. 5:17-48). Nurtured as he was in the Law and the Prophets, Jesus passed beyond his nurture to an intuitive awareness of the will of God. We cannot doubt that he followed the immediate deliverances of his own conscience, and the view is probable (though many would contest this) that his attitude toward the law implies his messianic awareness or consciousness. This may be implicit in his use of the messianic "I" in Matt. 5:21 ff (in the phrase "but I say to you," though some take this to be merely a rabbinic formula of no such significance) and even more so in his appeal to creation. The messianic age was to inaugurate a new creation comparable to the first. It is in the light of this that we are to understand the teaching of Jesus on divorce in Mark 10:2 ff, where he appeals to the order of creation as supplying a truer clue to the intention of God than the law, and much in the parables and other passages (Matt. 5:45 ff; 6:25-33). It is not surprising, therefore, that Mark sets Jesus in opposition to the scribes and Pharisees from the beginning (2:1–3:6), while Matthew places the ethical demands of Jesus in antithesis to those of the law (5:17 ff) and ascribes to Jesus a bitter attack on Pharisaic casuistry and hypocrisy (ch. 23), even while accepting the validity of the teaching of the Pharisees (23:1-2). Henceforth, it is man's relationship to Jesus, not to the law, that is decisive (Matt. 10:32-40; Mark 8:38). The inadequacy of even a strict adherence to the law, rather than humble readiness to receive God's grace, is clear in Luke 18:10-14.

b. Affirmation of the law. On the other hand, the Synoptics recognize that Jesus was not concerned (or, at least, not primarily) to annul the law. While some of the alleged evidence for this may be due to Jesus' desire to comply with necessary civil laws (Mark 1:44), his personal conservatism in the observance of the law is noteworthy. He goes to the synagogue on the sabbath (Mark 1:21; Luke 4:16; 13:10); he appears in Jerusalem at the festivals (Luke 2:41 ff; Mark 11:1 ff); he teaches in the synagogues and in the temple (Mark 1:29 ff; 14:49); he celebrates the Passover (Mark 14:12 ff; Luke 22:15-16); he does not speak disapprovingly of religious usages as such—fasting, almsgiving, prayer (Matt. 5:23-24; 6:1-18); he wears the prescribed fringes on his garments (Mark 6:56; Luke 8:44). Even where he, or his disciples, do break the law, this is justified, not in any spirit of iconoclasm or unprincipled "liberalism." Either this breaking of the law happens in the interests of the emerging messianic community (as in Mark 2:23-28, where the "Son of man" may connote the "people of the saints of the Most High"—i.e., Jesus and his disciples—and where no impatience with sabbatarianism is shown, but, rather, a desire to enlighten his opponents), or Jesus reacts to certain situations in immediate response to the will of God, thereby recognizing the supreme claims of that will without considering the effect of his action on the law (so Mark 3:1 ff, where no mere antisabbatarianism governed Jesus' action). Similarly, Jesus' inability, even against himself, to resist the priority of human need, or the claims of the rule of God, governs his action in Luke 13:10-13 rather than frivolous antisabbatarianism. What the latter called forth from him we see in the Western text (D) at Luke 6:5.

Unless Mark 7:15 be so interpreted, there is no explicit assertion of the annulling of the law by Jesus, and many interpret Mark 7:15, not as a rejection of the distinction between things clean and unclean, but as an assertion of the priority of the moral over the ritual. The moral demand of Jesus is expressed, in part at least, in terms of the Law and the Prophets (Matt. 22:34-40; Mark 12:28-34; Luke 10:25-28), and, in Matt. 5:17 ff, Jesus probably, as a second Moses (parallel to, and not only antithetic to, the first one), is sent, not to annul the law, but to fulfil it.

c. Explanations of Jesus' dual attitude. As the Synoptics present him, then, Jesus had a twofold attitude toward the law: he seemed to annul it, at least by implication, and at the same time to affirm it. This contradiction has been variously explained:

a) Possibly the attitude of Jesus toward the law changed during his ministry. As they now stand, our sources set Jesus in opposition to the Jewish religious leaders from the start, but there are indications that, at some stage in his ministry, Jesus attempted to be friendly with Pharisees. He well understood how natural it was for them to suspect his position, and sought to conciliate them (Matt. 23:23; Mark 12:28-29; Luke 5:39; 13:31; 17:20). Nevertheless, although there may have been development in the mind of Jesus, the chronology of the ministry is so confused that it would be hazardous to trace this too confidently.

b) The conservatism of Jesus on the law, it has been claimed, is the result of Jewish Christian influences on the tradition, which have "Judaized" Jesus. Thus Matt. 5:17-18 has been declared unthinkable on the lips of the historical Jesus; and Matt. 23, by making him attack merely scribal, and Pharisaic, hypocritical misuse of it, rather than the law itself, has falsified the position of Jesus. But the passage upholding the law in every iota and dot occurs, not only in the Jewish Christian source M, but in Q, which is often connected with the Gentile church at Antioch. There is nothing in Matt. 5:17-19 which cannot be connected with Jesus' ministry, with his encounter with the "people of the land," with discussions between Hillel and Shammai and others on knowing and doing the law and on heavy and light commandments. Since friend and foe could find sufficient cause, in both the practice and the teaching of Jesus, to stimulate the suspicion of iconoclasm, Matt. 5:17 ff could have been called forth by conditions, during the ministry itself, in which Jesus disclaimed any intention to annul the law.

c) The contradiction under discussion may be due to the fact that Jesus attacked, not the law itself, but the oral tradition. In his treatment of the sabbath and divorce, Jesus always criticizes the law from within the law (Mark 2:23-26; 3:1-6; 10:2-3). At two points, however, the attempt to relate Jesus' conflict with the law exclusively to the "fence" around it—i.e., the oral tradition—has been claimed to fail. In Mark 7:15, Jesus seems to annul the law itself (although even here he may still be attacking the ceremonial laws merely in order to emphasize the ethical), and in Matt. 5:31, 38, the law itself is cited, and particular provisions abrogated (although here too Jesus may merely be offering a new interpretation of the law; as we saw, scholars are divided as to the exact force of the phrase: "But I say to you"—some regard it as messianic in significance; others treat it as a customary rabbinic formula to denote that Jesus is merely presenting his understanding of the law).

d) Another possible explanation of Jesus' twofold attitude toward the law is that there was a distinction in Jesus' mind between the period before his death, which is the final culmination of the old order, and that which comes to birth through his death. In the former, the law is not annulled by him, although "signs" that it is passing are given. Only after his death has sealed the new covenant, and fully inaugurated the new order, does the law cease to govern relations between God and man. This may be the meaning of Matt. 5:18, the phrase "until all is accomplished" (ἕως ἂν πάντα γένηται) possibly referring to the death of Christ. This view has been little discussed, and is highly tentative; but it might explain why Paul connects the death of Christ so closely with the end of the law (Gal. 2:19-21; 3:13; 5:11; Eph. 2:13-14; Col. 2:14), and why Jesus, who looked to a future incursion of Gentiles into the kingdom (Matt. 8:10-11), nevertheless confined his ministry to the Jews.

e) The reference to the death of Jesus may supply us with a clue that we need. Jesus went to his death in obedience to the will of God (Mark 14:36), and thus fulfilled the law, as the demand of God, as he understood it (Luke 24:25-27). It may be impossible for us to disentangle the precise attitude of Jesus toward the ceremonial laws (he himself perhaps would not have made the rigid distinctions that we make at this point), but we can be sure that the moral demand of the law, as the expression of the will of God, Jesus never annulled. His very call to repentance implies this (Mark 1:15; Matt. 4:17); the prodigal son is to return to obedience to his father (Luke 15:19); to know and to keep the two great commandments of love to God and neighbor is to be near the kingdom (Mark 12:28-34); Jesus has his own yoke to impose (Matt. 11:25-30). The concept of "law" as the demand of God would not have repelled Jesus. Nevertheless, it was not in terms of the law of Judaism that he issued his call to repentance, but in terms of the kingdom of God (Mark 1:15). By setting the call to repentance in the context of the givenness and immediacy of the kingdom, Jesus freed it from mere moralism and utterly radicalized it. Thus, too, he came to understand the law in terms of the will of God, not the will of God in terms of the law. And the will of God for him was one of absolute love, so that God's demand was one for such love (Matt. 5:17-48). And to know the demand of God as such—i.e., as one of absolute love—is to recognize that one cannot "obey" it fully, nor set up any claim to merit before God, that the "broken and the contrite heart" alone is possible for us. This was at the root of the criticism that Jesus made of the scribal and Pharisaic tradition: that it assumed the "achievability" of a right relation to God on grounds of obedience, whereas to stand under the will of God as love, as Jesus understood it, was to know that, when we have done all that is commanded, we are unworthy servants (Luke 17:10). But Jesus does not deliver us from all commandments. He gives us a commandment, that of love, and we must ask whether this means that he introduced a new law. *See* ETHICS IN NT.

f) Matt. 5 possibly makes of Jesus a new Moses proclaiming new, radical commandments to be applied. It is, moreover, not unlikely that Jesus set himself in conscious parallelism to Moses. But we can only speak of the words of Jesus, as a new law, with extreme caution. The total obedience to the will of God, which is one of love, could not be reduced to a written code in a prescriptive sense. This obedience has to discover its own means of expression in any given situation, even though it be informed by the law, tradition, or even the words of Jesus himself. Precisely because the law could, and often did, hide the immediate demands of love, in any particular situation, and could, and often did, lead to external observance without the true intent, and to a concern for merit and reward, and hence to hypocrisy, Jesus opposed scribes and Pharisees. And he himself spoke, not, primarily at least, as a lawgiver, though he commanded, but as one sent of God in the last hour to reveal the absolute will of God. His hyperbolical statements of the demand of God, though to be taken with the utmost seriousness, are, therefore, to be interpreted, not as a "new law," but as pointers to the true nature of God's demand of love.

2. The earliest Christians and the law. ***a. Radicalism: Stephen.*** The ambiguity which marked the attitude of Jesus toward the law, according to the Synoptics, reappears in the attitude of the earliest Christians—i.e., the claims of the law are recognized and, at the same time, rejected. In the very earliest days, to judge from Acts, Christians continued to "practice Judaism," and were occupied more with asserting that Jesus of Nazareth was the Messiah than with what their attitude should be toward the law (Acts 2–3). This is true, probably, despite the work of the firebrand Stephen, who was accused of talking against the temple and the law (Acts 6:13 ff). Although in fact there is no attack on the law as such in Stephen, but only on the temple and on the history of the Jews, nevertheless, his attitude implies a detachment from the tradition of Judaism, which could lead to a rejection of the law on which the service of the temple was based. (Though Stephen was a Hellenist, it is not justifiable on this ground to ascribe his radicalism to liberal, Hellenistic influences, because Acts 6:9 ff makes it clear that the Hellenists opposed him; his attitude arose either from an antilegalistic and anticultic tradition in Judaism itself or under the influence of Jesus' example.) Stephen's wholesale dismissal of the temple, and, by implication, of the law, and his condemnation of the people of Israel, were not embraced by the church, which found his attitude too radical, and the problem of the relation between law and gospel too complex, to be thus summarily solved. This problem emerged fully only later, when numbers of Gentile converts entered the church.

b. Compromise. To judge from Gal. 2; Acts 15, there was common agreement among the leaders of the church that salvation was by faith in Jesus Christ and not by works of the law. Difficulties arose when the actualities of a community including Jews and Gentiles had to be faced. Did the acceptance of the gospel imply that Jews should now forswear the observance of the law in order to make it possible for them to enjoy table fellowship, and, especially, the Eucharist, with Gentile Christians; or, conversely, for the sake of Jewish sensibilities, should Gentile Christians be circumcised and submit to the observance of the law? No problems arose as long as communities were exclusively Gentile or exclusively Jewish; and the church tactfully recognized a division in its missionary task. In Jewish Christian churches, while justification was proclaimed on the basis of faith, it was acknowledged that Jewish Christians might obey the law—the mission to the circumcision was assigned to Peter. In Gentile churches obedience to the law was not observed—the uncircumcision was the field of Paul (Gal. 2:7-8). This approach to the law was virtually ratified in the Council of Jerusalem, and, either at this council or slightly after, the conditions on which there could be actual intermingling of Gentile and Jewish Christians were laid down (Acts 15:1-30). The exact significance of these conditions has been variously assessed, either as a minimal ethic to be observed by all (but the nature of the conditions, and the Jewish attitude toward the law as a unity, are against this), or as a safeguard against Gnostic influences (a vague phrase which does not take us very far), or as the Noachian commandments which Judaism laid upon all men—this is the most probable interpretation. The church virtually followed Judaism at this point, because the presence of Gentiles in many synagogues had long involved the mother faith in the same problem, and it had dealt with it in terms of the Noachian commandments. Here the actualities of the situation which confronted the church have to be grasped:

a) While most Christians were aware that salvation was only in the name of Jesus, they also had to recognize that, if there was to be any effective approach to Jewry, the law had to be honored. A movement that sat loose to the law would be self-condemned among Jews from the outset. Not only would it be difficult for Jews brought up in obedience to the law to reject it (even though they no longer placed their hope of salvation upon it), but Romans shows how naturally they feared moral laxity should the law be abandoned and justification by faith alone offered (Rom. 6). There were understandable reasons why the church was cautious on the question of law and took a *via media.*

b) In Galatians, however, Paul ascribes to certain champions of the law more dishonorable motives. They favored the law from fear of persecution, in order to make a good showing in the flesh (Gal. 6:12-13). It was these, who are usually referred to as the Judaizers, who, centered in Jerusalem, invaded the Pauline churches to undo the work of Paul. While it is possible to overemphasize the significance of the Judaizing movement, and to give to James, the brother of the Lord, and to Peter, a Judaizing role which they never played (they were not Judaizers), it is even more erroneous so to minimize the gulf between Paul and the primitive community as to deny the differences of emphasis between him and Peter and James, and, in particular, the reality of the Judaizing opposition which he faced. Two extreme positions are to be, therefore, avoided—the one which tends to equate the Christianity of the primitive church with that of later Jewish Christianity, so as to make it legalistic, and the other that would obliterate any real distinction between the primitive church and Paul. The Judaizing elements eventually led to Jewish Christianity, which demanded the observance of the law from all Christians, and to the Nazoreans, who held fast to the law for Jewish Christians only. Attempts to ascribe to Jewish Christianity a major role in the struggle of the church against Marcion and incipient Gnosticism have not always been convincing. *See bibliography.*

3. Paul and the law. ***a. Terminology.*** By the term "law" (νόμος) Paul usually means the law of God as contained in the OT, whether he uses "the law" or "law" without the article. This is so even when the law is not defined as the law of Moses (I Cor. 9:9) or the law of God (Rom. 7:22, 25; 8:7). Occasionally, perhaps, it refers to the Decalogue, as such (Rom. 2:20 ff; 7:7; 13:8-10), but there is no essential difference in Paul between the Decalogue and the rest of the law. Though he uses "the law and the prophets" for the whole of the OT (Rom. 3:21), and although "law" may refer to the Pentateuch in isolation, this is not to be pressed, because in I Cor. 14:21; Rom. 3:19, the single term "law" stands for all the OT. The term is also used without reference to the OT. In Rom. 3: 27 it seems to mean "dispensation" or "order," the order of faith over against the order of works (διὰ ποίου νόμου; τῶν ἔργων; οὐχί, ἀλλὰ διὰ νόμου πίστεως). In Rom. 7:21 "law" is a kind of inexorable necessity. Followed by a genitive, it refers to what we may call a governing principle, either internal (Rom. 7:21-25) or "external" (Rom. 8:2; Gal. 6:2), though this distinction is not to be pressed. In Rom. 7:1-3, "law" refers simply to a legal enactment; in Rom. 5: 13 to a "commandment"; in Rom. 2:14-15 to an interior law, written on the heart, but not to be identified with CONSCIENCE; in Rom. 13:8 "the law" is summed up in the commandment to love the neighbor.

Paul never uses the plural "laws," probably because he regards all "law," in and outside Judaism, as a unified whole. In Judaism this takes the form of the law of the OT, and among Gentiles of a "law written on the heart" (Rom. 2:15). In both cases "the law" is a living demand of God. This enables Paul almost to personify the law (Rom. 3:19; 4:15; 7:1; I Cor. 9:8); but this personification is found in Judaism also. *See* LAW (IN FIRST-CENTURY JUDAISM).

b. Life under the law and "in Christ." As a Pharisee, Paul would have regarded the law as the perfect expression of God's will. But his conversion (*see* PAUL) compelled him to reassess Judaism and, particularly, the law. Historical factors lay back of his concentration on the relation of the law to the gospel, rather than on other aspects of the relation between Judaism and Chrisianity—its cruciality in his previous life as a Jew, and the practical pressure of problems in the church on the relation between Jewish and Gentile Christians. But not only so. It was Paul's very zeal for the law of God that had blinded him to the Son of God and led him to persecute his church (Gal. 1:13-14; 3:13; Phil. 3:5-6)—the law had proved a veil to hide Christ (II Cor. 3:14-15). This fact governed his re-examination of the law. Its staggering character was reinforced by the difference which Paul found between his life under the law and "in Christ," which his antitheses set forth. The law was powerless; Christ was the power of God (Rom. 3:20-21, 27-28; 4:14; 8:3-4; 9:31-32; Gal. 2:16, 21; 3:2, 5, 11, 19; 5:4; Phil. 3:9). The law condemned; Christ saved from the wrath and curse and death (Rom. 3:21-25; 4:15; 5:1-11, 20-21; 6:22; 7:7-13; 8:1-14; I Cor. 1:30; 3:7; 15: 25-27; II Cor. 5:17-19; Gal. 1:3-4; 3:10, 13, 21-22). The yoke of the law was bondage (Gal. 3:23; 4:1-7, 21-23; 5:1-3); the service of Christ was freedom (Rom. 6:18-22; 8:2, 21). It is in the light of these antitheses, which arose out of his conversion—there being no evidence that before this Paul had found the law weak, condemnatory and tyrannical (Phil. 3:6)—that his understanding of the law is to be comprehended. What, then, was Paul's analysis and interpretation of the function of the law?

To begin with, it expresses the will of God, and is holy, just, good, and spiritual (Rom. 3:2; 7:12, 14); to be outside the law is to be at enmity with God (Rom. 7:12; 8:7). That the law cannot give life, does not mean that its demands are evil, but that no one can keep them; it is at the point of obedience, not of demand, that the law is to be judged; and it is an empirical fact that all have sinned, and, therefore, cannot be justified under the law (Rom. 3:20, 23). Why?

First, the law usually confronts us as prohibition, expressing the negative aspect of God's will (Rom. 7:7). And, while the prohibition makes man responsible, by revealing sin to him, it leaves him powerless in his responsibility.

The law actually incites to sin. This is not merely because prohibition promotes desire, but because, by confronting man with God's demand, it excites what lies behind all sin—namely, the rejection of God's rightful claims, the refusal to recognize dependence on him. And the rebellious desire thus created by the prohibition becomes the base from which sin attacks man. Thus, the law, intrinsically good, subserves the ends of sin, which is intrinsically evil, but which is, apart from the opportunity provided by law, impotent. What is good in itself, the law, thus becomes a power for evil. While sin is in man before he encounters the law, it is the latter that brings it to life by presenting the possibility for transgression (Rom. 4: 15; 5:20; 7:13; Gal. 3:19). The law even aims at transgression (Rom. 5:20; Gal. 3:19)..

Nevertheless, the law condemns sin (Rom. 2:12; 3: 19; 8:1), works wrath (Rom. 4:15; *see* WRATH OF GOD) and death (I Cor. 15:56; Rom. 7:9-10), and, if never to be identified with sin, by Paul comes to be closely connected with it (I Cor. 15:56; Rom. 3:20; 4:15; 6:14; 8:3).

But how is it that what was intrinsically good has been thus diverted to the service of sin? Paul would seem to give two answers:

a) The powerlessness of the law is due to its relation to the flesh (Rom. 8:3; *see* FLESH IN THE NT); and part of the meaning of II Cor. 3:6 ff is that this is due to the external character of the law, which works, not from within, but approaches man from without.

b) More important, Paul regards the law as related to the "elemental spirits of the universe" (τὰ στοιχεῖα τοῦ κόσμου; Gal. 4:3, 9; Col. 2:8, 20). Whether Paul thought of the law as itself one of the demonic principalities and powers, whose might was canceled on the cross (Col. 2:13-14), or as an instrument used by demonic, angelic powers (Gal. 3:19; 4:1-11; II Cor. 4:4), which had not only gained control of the law in Judaism, but, in the Gentile world, reigned under the form of pagan gods, is difficult to determine. Under the influence of these powers, we are best to understand, the law had itself come to serve an evil purpose, so that its functions would seem (it has been claimed) to correspond to those of Satan (as prosecutor, executioner, and tempter; Rom. 2:12; 3:19; 7:7-8; II Cor. 3:6 ff). *See* SATAN.

*c. **Role of the law in history.*** But if so, has the law any positive role in history? Yes; but only in a relative and transitory sense. Its role is relative because it came into being, not of God's primordial purpose, but as a result of his reaction to human sinfulness. God's dealing with man reveals two stages: (*a*) a covenant based on a gracious promise to Abraham (Gal. 3:1 ff; Rom. 4:20); (*b*) a covenant, which followed this, based on the law (Gal. 3:19, 22-25; Rom. 5:20). Thus, the law slipped in between the promise and its fulfilment in Christ, which means that now its writ is at an end. It was allowed to slip in to increase trespass (Rom. 3:20; 5:20; 7:7)—i.e., to reveal sin as sin—because sin is only seen as sin when it becomes transgression and thus engenders guilt. And the recognition of sin as sin, through the advent of the law, was an advance preparing the way for Christ. In this way the law was a custodian (παιδαγωγός) unto Christ (Gal. 3:24); it had quickened the recognition of the need for deliverance by deepening the sense of sin. The merely relative value of the law is apparent also to Paul in its ordination through angels (Gal. 3:19)—i.e., it was mediated from God indirectly, not directly, as was the promise to Abraham. From its very promulgation it was a phenomenon not capable of lasting (II Cor. 3:13).

*d. **Christ the end of the law.*** Paul's criticism of the law culminates in the claim that with the coming of Christ the law's dispensation is at an end (Rom. 6:14; Gal. 3:13, 25; 4:5; 5:1). But it has ceased only for those who have died and risen with Christ (Gal. 2:19; Rom. 7:4, 6; Col. 2:20)—this experience is symbolized in baptism (Gal. 2:21; Rom. 6). But that Christ is the end of the law (Rom. 10:4) signifies, not that the law has come to an end, but that it has reached its final purpose in him: Christ was the goal to which the law was directed (cf. Rom. 3:21); he has achieved its destiny. The cessation of the law was associated with the Cross (Gal. 2:19, 21; 3:13; 5:11; Eph. 2:13-14; Col. 2:14). But the Cross is also the most complete obedience to God, which is precisely the demand of the law (Rom. 8:34 ff). To share "in Christ" is to fulfil the law (Rom. 3:31). The demand of the law, in its essence, is not violated by the Christian, because it can be gathered up in love (Gal. 5:14; 6:2; Rom. 8:4; 13:8, 10). Paul is thus no antinomian. And he reveals the same ambiguity on the law as do Jesus and the early church (Rom. 3:31; 10:4).

This ambiguity is due not merely to fluidity in the use of the term "law," because it pervades Paul's personal conduct and missionary policy. Thus he allowed Jewish Christians to observe the law (Acts 21:21-26), and himself did so, certainly when necessary, possibly always (I Cor. 7:18; Acts 16:3, 21; 23:6). Certain practical considerations would incline Paul to this; any deviation from orthodoxy would inevitably close the doors of Judaism against him; and an increasingly ironic attitude toward the law emerges in his letters (cf. Gal. 4:25; 5:1; Rom. 7:12, 14; 8:3; II Cor. 3:14-18).

It became clear to Paul early in his ministry that obedience to the law of Christ sometimes demanded obedience to the old law (I Cor. 9:19-20; *see bibliography*). In giving rules to churches Paul even drew upon the law (I Cor. 9:8, 13). Nevertheless, he did so parenthetically, and he finally appeals to a commandment of the Lord (I Cor. 9:14). Here, as elsewhere, the law is understood in the light of Christ.

This is why scholars have, on the whole, been loath to admit that Paul understood Christ in terms of the law, but, only and always, the law in terms of Christ. But the possibility is not to be ruled out that much in Paul's understanding of his Lord, as the pre-existent agent of creation, e.g. (Col. 1:15 ff), may be due to his ascription to Christ of attributes ascribed by Judaism to the law. Certain it is that Christ, in his person and words, has taken the place of the law in Paul's life and thought, and, in this sense, has become for him a new Torah. The influence of the Reformation, because of its emphasis on the gospel as justification by faith, makes it difficult for us to do justice to this aspect of Paul's thought. His criticisms of the law belong chiefly to his polemic letters, Galatians and Romans; nor must they be minimized. Paul did come to believe that to accept life under the law as the means to salvation was to enter upon an impossible road marked either by despair at failure or by overweening, insensitive pride (ὕβρις, καύχημα) at achievement, but this was so only because the light of Christ had revealed the more excellent way to him. His criticism of the law is a consequence of his faith in Christ, but not its center. Polemic, and the historic circumstances attending the emergence of Christianity, have somewhat hidden the fact, but the center of Paulinism lies, not in the relation of gospel and law, but in Paul's awareness that with the coming of Christ the age to come was becoming present fact, the proof of which was the advent of the Spirit: it lies in those conceptions of standing under the judgment and mercy of a new Torah, Christ, of dying and rising with this same Christ, of undergoing a new Exodus in him, and of so being incorporated into a new Israel, the community of the Spirit.

4. The Letter to the Hebrews. The term "law" refers here again to the law of the OT, even in Heb. 7:16, where it may mean "order." The plural "laws" occurs only in quotations from the OT in 8:10; 10:16. Unlike Paul, who was concerned with the law as a system of prohibitions and commandments designed to make man righteous, and with the moral problem thus created for a Pharisee, Hebrews was concerned with the problem of worship, of access to the presence of the Holy God, which the priesthood and sacrifices were designed to achieve. Hence the law is significant for Hebrews as it is related to the priesthood and sacrificial system (the reference to foods in 13:9 is secondary). This relation is twofold. The law was, on the one hand, the foundation on which the priesthood and sacrifices were built, because it had ordained them (although 7:11 makes the law almost dependent on the priesthood, this must not be taken to mean that God was not the source of the law). On the other hand, because the law was broken, the media for expiation, the priesthood and sacrifices, became necessary for continued life under the law (7:5, 11-12; 8:4; 10:8). How then does Hebrews regard the law?

First, like the rest of the OT, the law was the word of God. Although mediated by angels—this mediation implied its inferiority (as in Gal. 3:19)—it was valid. There is nothing in Hebrews comparable to the radical dismissal of the temple and, by implication, the law, in Stephen (Acts 7:47-50); no suggestion that, in the past, the law should not have been obeyed. Moreover, the ordinances of the law had a positive value. They pointed upward to what was already eternally existent in the mind of God, and forward to a real fulfilment of that after which they grope in the future. The temple, the priesthood, the sacrifices, the covenant, all are copies of the real (8:5) and foreshadowings of better things to come (10:1). Thus the old covenant, including the law, was not false but imperfect, premonitory rather than satisfying. The force of this can be gauged only by reading the whole of Hebrews, but especially 7:1–11:1. For the merging of Platonic and eschatological concepts implied, *see* HEBREWS, LETTER TO THE.

Nevertheless, the critical attitude of Hebrews toward the law is noteworthy. The dispensation of the law had been ineffective. Priest and sacrifice had failed in their aim of bringing men near to God by the cleansing of their consciences (7:15; 9:14; 10:4). This was so because: (*a*) the OT ordinances were only outward arrangements, which could not effectively deal with sin and guilt (9:9-10); (*b*) the priests, the human agents of reconciliation, were themselves mortal and sinful and could not, therefore, really be effective (5:3; 7:27); and (*c*) the very repetitive nature of the sacrificial system showed its inefficacy (10:1 ff). Moreover, that the OT itself looked forward to better things to come (Jer. 31) *ipso facto* implied and recognized its incompleteness (Heb. 8:8-12).

Thus, though Paul and Hebrews are not concerned with the same aspects of the law, they agree in much of their understanding of it. The difference between them is clear. In Hebrews the law is especially connected with the priesthood (7:11). A change in priesthood meant a change in the law (7:12). Christ is a new kind of priest, after the order of Melchizedek. This priesthood was announced to Abraham before the Levitical priesthood existed, and the latter has not abrogated it. Had the Levitical priesthood procured access to God, the rise of a priest after the order of Melchizedek, as was predicted in Ps. 110:4, would have been unnecessary. But the antiquating of the cultus through the high priesthood of Christ carries with it the supersession of the law. The argument is very similar to that applied directly to the law by Paul in Gal. 3:17-18, except that for Paul it is the abrogation of the law in Christ that implies the supersession of the cultus. For both Paul and Hebrews, moreover, the Christian dispensation is a higher order than that of Judaism; but the element of discontinuity between them may be more marked in Paul, because he found in Christ what Judaism could not give, whereas Hebrews found in Judaism what pointed forward to Christ (but see Rom. 3:21).

5. The Letter of James. This letter is concerned with the relation of faith and works (not faith and law, as is Paul; 2:14 ff), and the term "law," which occurs ten times, refers not primarily to the OT law as such. In 1:25 the "law," with which James is occupied, is defined as the "perfect law . . . of liberty," and the context makes it clear that this is a summary description of the Christian message—i.e., the "Word" referred to in 1:21-23, the gospel itself. Does this mean that James understands the gospel in terms of law? This possibility, which is enforced by the explicit injunctions in 2:1 ff; 3:1 ff; etc., is offset by the emphasis on liberty or freedom in the phrase "perfect law of liberty." The "Word" demands obedience, but "in freedom."

The law of freedom is further defined in 2:8 ff as the "royal law," which in the light of 2:9 consists of the Golden Rule. This rule is to be obeyed in all its demands, but this demand is not expressed in specific directions for conduct. This is the implication of 4:11 ff. This passage echoes Rom. 14:4, which asserts that each man stands or falls before his own master —i.e., he is not subject to any fixed law, which can be discerned by outsiders, and which prescribes a set course of action. He is free himself to decide what he should do, under the constraint of love or of Christ; to judge another's action is to presume to know the meaning of that constraint for him, to judge the law of love itself, and this very judgment is itself a transgression of that law.

Thus James too, despite his sane earthiness, takes seriously the principle of freedom from specific enactments and in this is like Paul, as he is also like Paul in his ethical seriousness (1:22 ff; 2:14 ff *et passim*). Pauline controversies over the Jewish law, as such, are outside the purview of James, although the possibility is a real one that, especially in 2:14-26, he may be attacking certain misunderstandings of Paul which were current in his circles. The method of argument suggests this. *See* JAMES, LETTER OF.

6. The Fourth Gospel. Here "law" (νόμος) is used in three ways: (*a*) of a specific commandment (7:19, 23); (*b*) of the system governing the administration of justice among Jews, though this was for them part of the law of God (7:51; 8:17; 18:31; 19:7); (*c*) of the Pentateuch (1:45), the law of Moses (7:23), or the law given by Moses (7:19), or the law given by God through Moses (1:17), which was the authoritative basis for Jewish life; (*d*) of the whole of the OT (10:34; 12:34; 15:25; and probably 7:49).

Though an intimate knowledge of rabbinic interpretation of the law appears, the evangelist looks at the law from the outside also. E.g., 8:17, where he uses a phrase ("In your law it is written") used by Gentiles in discussions with Jews; 1:17, where grace and truth, particularly associated with the law in the OT (Pss. 25:10; 85:11; 89:15), are claimed to be in Christ, not in the law; and 5:39, where the true quest for eternal life in Christ is contrasted with the misguided quest for him in the law, point to a major theme of the gospel—namely, the superiority of the revelation of God given in Christ over that given in the law.

It is this point of view that largely governs the symbolic forms under which Christ is presented. In 2:6-10 the water of the dispensation of the law or again its inferior wine (2:10) is contrasted with the wine that Christ brings. Water, a symbol of the law in Judaism, is applied to Christ in 4:12-14; he is the living water; the evanescent manna, which probably here (through its association with bread, a regular symbol for it) stands for the law, is contrasted with the true bread, which Christ brings (ch. 6); similarly, Christ becomes the Light (8:12; 9:5; 12:35), the Way, the Truth, and the Life (14:6). Christ is source of the true light (1:9), the true bread (6:32), the true judgment (8:16), the true vine (15:1)—i.e., Christ introduces us to the world of realities. The law, it is implied, dealt only with shadows. Here the Fourth

Gospel and Hebrews show an affinity. But most noteworthy is the ascription to Christ, as "the Word," of attributes Judaism had reserved for the law. Pre-existence (1:1-2), association with God (1:1), sonship (1:14), light and life (1:4), creative activity in the beginning (1:3)—all these are ascribed to Christ as the Word, just as they are ascribed to wisdom in the OT and Judaism (*see* LAW IN FIRST-CENTURY JUDAISM) and to the law. The Prologue, no less than the rest of the gospel, thus proclaims the reality of the revelation in Christ as superseding that given in the law.

We have seen the parallelism between John and Hebrews. The concept of the law as a shadow is not explicit in John, however, although it is implicit. Does John ascribe a further positive value to the law? In 1:45 this would seem to be the case: the law has borne witness to Christ. To deny Christ is to deny the Scriptures (5:39 ff); and the law is fulfilled in his ministry (8:17; 10:34; 12:34; 15:25). But this fulfilment, while it lends partial validity to the law, also spells its end. For the Fourth Gospel, as for Paul, even though it is not concerned as was he with the law as a rule for life, as commandment, loyalty to Christ has replaced obedience to the law as the demand of God (5:19 ff; 7:17), and this means sharing in his love (13:34; 15:12-15).

7. Conclusion. The NT documents, throughout, reveal the same ambiguity in the evaluation of the law that we found in Jesus. Just as they reveal a parallelism between Moses and Christ, which is sometimes antithetic (John and Hebrews) and sometimes synthetic (Matthew and Paul, broadly speaking), so they find in the law both the passing shadow of the gospel to come and that which is completed or fulfilled "in Christ." They all affirm that the law, insofar as it is the expression of the holy will of God, remains valid, radicalized, and at the same time relativized, by the absolute claim of love.

Bibliography. B. H. Branscomb, *Jesus and the Law of Moses* (1930). W. G. Kümmel, "Jesus und der jüdische Traditionsgedanke," *ZNW,* 33 (1934), 105-30. Concerning the role played by Jewish Christianity in the church's struggle against Marcion and incipient Gnosticism, see H. J. Schoeps, *Theologie und Geschichte des Judenchristentums* (1949); see also his "Jesus und das jüdische Gesetz" in *Aus frühchristlicher Zeit* (1950), pp. 212-20. C. H. Dodd, *Gospel and Law* (1951). E. Schweizer, on Matt. 5:17-20, in "Anmerkungen zum Gesetzesverständnis des Matthäus," *TLZ,* 77 (1952), 479-84. On the necessity of Paul's obedience to the old law in his ministry, see C. H. Dodd, "Εννομος χριστοῦ," *Studia Paulina in Honorem Johannes de Zwaan* (1953), pp. 96 ff. There are excellent studies by A. Descamps and P. Demann in *Moïse l'Homme de l'Alliance, Cahiers Sioniens,* nos. 2-4 (1954), pp. 171-244. W. D. Davies, on Matt. 5:17-18, in *Mélanges Biblique Rédiges en l'honneur d'André Robert* (1957).

See the bibliographies in R. Schnackenburg, *Die Sittliche Botschaft des Neuen Testaments* (1954).

W. D. DAVIES

LAWLESS ONE [ἄνομος] (II Thess. 2:8-9); KJV WICKED. *See* ANTICHRIST.

LAWYER [νομικός, *from* νόμος, law]. One learned in the law, specifically in the law of Moses.

The Greek term occurs six times in Luke, twice in Titus, once in Matthew, but nowhere else in the NT (cf. IV Macc. 5:4). At Tit. 3:9 it is an adjective, describing those preoccupied in legalistic discussions (*see* TEACHER). In vs. 13 it refers to Zenas, who is otherwise unknown. It is evident from the context that he was on some urgent mission, but there is no way of telling whether the law in which he was engaged was Hebrew, Greek, or Roman.

At Matt. 22:35; Mark 12:28, the term is equivalent to "scribes" (*see* SCRIBE). Luke may have preferred "lawyer" to "scribe" as being more familiar to Gentile readers. Interestingly enough, however, he never has νομικός in passages drawn from Mark or Q.

Except at Luke 10:25 (which may be Luke's substitute for Mark 12:28 ff), the word always has a bad sense in the Third Gospel. Lawyers are among those who oppose Jesus' sabbath healings (Luke 14:3). They have rejected John the Baptist and, in so doing, rejected the purpose of God (7:30). They neglect justice, place unbearable burdens on their fellow men, and then refuse to help them (11:45-46). They refuse sound knowledge and hinder those who seek it (11:52). Most of these accusations are on Jesus' own lips, and in one case (11:45) a lawyer complains that Jesus is insulting them (ὑβρίζεις). Rarely elsewhere does Luke wax so polemical as this—though he often blames Jews, rather than Romans, for the sufferings of Jesus and his followers.

PIERSON PARKER

LAYING ON OF HANDS. *See* HANDS, LAYING ON OF.

LAZARUS AND DIVES lăz′ə rəs, dī′vēz [Λάζαρος=אלעזר, one whom God helps, *shortened form* לעזר *presupposed by the* Gr.; Vulg. *dives, see below*]. The beggar and the rich man in the parable told by Jesus (Luke 16:19-31). The Vulg. translates the adjective "rich" by *dives,* which has often incorrectly been taken to be the name of the rich man (*see* DIVES). Lazarus was a common Jewish name, as shown by many ossuary inscriptions. The poor man is distinguished by the only proper name reported in Jesus' parables, while the rich man remains nameless. Since biblical names have significance, Lazarus' name was well chosen: "God's help of a needy beggar."

Lazarus of the parable and LAZARUS OF BETHANY (John 11:1-44) are two different persons. Scholarly opinion is divided about whether or not there is any relationship between the parable of Lazarus and the narrative in John. The decision depends upon the unsettled question as to whether or not either of the gospel authors knew the other. Jesus may have created the story or adapted it from a somewhat similar tale about a rich and a poor man.

The parable has two parts: (*a*) an earthly scene; (*b*) a scene in the afterworld. Poor ulcerated Lazarus was laid at the large gate of the palace of a rich man who lived in the luxury of the finest clothing and food. Lazarus longed to eat, not "crumbs" (KJV), but whatever fell from the rich man's table, where bread was used for wiping the fingers. Even the street dogs, unclean animals, nosed the helpless beggar. Death called both men and reversed their situations. Lazarus was carried by angels to a place of honor nearest Abraham (*see* ABRAHAM'S BOSOM; cf. John 13:23) at a heavenly banquet. The rich man found himself tormented in flames in the underworld.

In Jewish belief such good and evil people could see one another, but their places were separated by a great chasm. Lazarus nowhere speaks in the parable, but the rich man called to Father Abraham to send Lazarus with water to cool his tongue. Abraham acknowledged his kinship ("son") but rejected the request, because justice required the reversed roles and because the chasm could not be crossed. The rich man wanted Lazarus sent to his five brethren to warn them lest they should come to the place of torment. Again Abraham denied his request, because the brothers had ample teaching from Moses and the prophets, and because not even one from the dead would make them repentant when they ignored God's revelation in the Scriptures.

This parable emphasizes three points: (*a*) warnings to the selfish rich; (*b*) an eventual evening-up of fate for rich and poor; (*c*) that a miracle like resurrection will not bring repentance if the teachings of God are not heeded.

Bibliography. H. Gressmann, "Vom reichen Mann und armen Lazarus," *Abhandlungen der preussischen Akademie der Wissenschaft* (1918), no. 7; B. D. T. Smith, *The Parables of the Synoptic Gospels* (1937), pp. 64-65, 134-41; S. MacL. Gilmour, Exegesis of Luke, *IB,* VIII (1953), 288-93; J. Jeremias, *The Parables of Jesus* (1954; trans. S. H. Hooke, from *Die Gleichnisse Jesu* [3rd ed., 1954]), pp. 128-30. D. M. BECK

LAZARUS OF BETHANY [לעזר, *abbreviation of* אלעזר, God has helped: Λάζαρος]. A friend of Jesus, living at BETHANY; brother of MARTHA and Mary (*see* MARY 3). He was raised from the dead by Jesus, and was present at the supper in their house six days before the Passover, at which his sister Mary anointed Jesus, according to John 11:1-44; 12:1-11.

Apart from those who deny on general principles the possibility of any miracles, there are many scholars who hold that the raising of Lazarus involves such formidable difficulties as to make it impossible to accept it as historical.

He had been dead for four days, whereas the other recorded raisings had been of persons only recently dead—Jairus' daughter (Mark 5:22-43) and the son of the widow at Nain (Luke 7:11-17). Both these, it can be argued, were not really dead, but only deeply unconscious—indeed, Jesus says in the former case: "The child is not dead but sleeping" (Mark 5:39).

A more serious objection is the silence of the other evangelists on what must have been the most astounding of Jesus' miracles, particularly in the case of Luke, who knew of the sisters Martha and Mary but not of Lazarus (Luke 10:38-42).

Moreover, while John attributes the decision of the high priests and Pharisees to kill Jesus to the consternation caused them by this miracle (John 11:47-53), the other evangelists, probably following Mark 11:18, attribute it to their anger at Jesus' action in cleansing the temple of the merchants and money-changers. Mark records the anointing at Bethany (14:3-9), but he mentions neither Lazarus nor Mary, and he places the anointing in the house of Simon the leper.

Accordingly, some scholars, seeking an explanation of the origin of the story, find it in the parable of Luke 16:19-31. It is argued that it originated as an illustration or reinforcement of the lesson of the parable: "If they do not hear Moses and the prophets, neither will they be convinced if some one should rise from the dead" (vs. 31). Jesus had indeed raised a Lazarus from the dead, and, so far from believing him, the authorities had planned his death.

This explanation does not, however, account for the association of Martha and Mary with Lazarus, for which no theological motive can be discerned.

Furthermore, while the raising of Lazarus is admittedly the most spectacular of Jesus' miracles, it is not absolutely unique. The naming of a character in a parable is, however, unique, and it may be argued accordingly that, since it is the unique that most demands explanation, the relationship of miracle and parable is the other way round. Jesus had indeed raised Lazarus, with the result known, and had named the poor man in his parable Lazarus with deliberate irony.

There are other examples of correspondences between John and Luke (*see* JOHN, GOSPEL OF, § C1), where it can be argued that Luke is dependent on the tradition found in John. This would account for Luke's knowing of Martha and Mary, and would also make it unlikely that in one instance only John is secondary to Luke.

The silence of the other evangelists on the raising of Lazarus remains to be explained. It could be due either to ignorance on the part of Mark's principal informant, or to deliberate suppression on the part of Palestinian tradition during the lifetime of Lazarus, in view of the determination of Jesus' enemies to kill Lazarus also (John 12:10). The confusion in the Synoptic accounts of Jesus' anointing is as readily explained on the assumption that John gives the best account as on any other view.

The remark of the evangelist: "Jesus loved [ἠγάπα] Martha and her sister and Lazarus" (John 11:5), may be a clue to the identity of the disciple whom Jesus loved (*see* BELOVED DISCIPLE; also John 13:23; 19:26; 21:7, 20, in all of which the verb ἠγάπα is found—in John 20:2 the verb is ἐφίλει, and the disciple here may be a different person; *see* JOHN, GOSPEL OF, § F). If Lazarus was this disciple, it would explain how Jesus' saying: "If it is my will that he remain until I come, what is that to you?" (John 21:22) came to be taken as meaning that he was not to die—he had already died once.

Bibliography. R. Eisler, *The Enigma of the Fourth Gospel* (1938), pp. 187-95; J. N. Sanders, *Those whom Jesus loved,* NTS, I (1954), 29-41; W. Bauer, Λάζαρος, *Griechisch-Deutsches Wörterbuch zu den Schriften des NTs* (5th ed., 1957), p. 914. "Lazarus," in F. L. Cross, ed., *The Oxford Dictionary of the Christian Church* (1957), p. 793, gives a brief account of later legends about Lazarus.

For commentaries on the Gospel of John, *see* bibliography under JOHN, GOSPEL OF. J. N. SANDERS

LEAD [עופרת]. A blue-gray metallic element (Pb), heavy, pliable, readily tarnishing to dull gray; in antiquity often confused with metals of similar physical properties, as tin.

Lead was regarded as the heaviest metal (Ecclus. 47:18). In lists of metals (gold, silver, bronze, iron, tin, lead) it is mentioned last (Num. 31:22; Ezek. 22:18, 20), and in Ecclus. 22:14 it is named "Fool." Yet it was an important metal. One significant use was

20. Lead figures: (1) figure of Hathor, found in a Hyksos tomb at Gaza; (2) either a votive offering of a bound soldier, or a victim of incantation, found at Tell Sandahannan in the debris above the floor level of the Seleucidan "barracks"

in the reduction of silver; the lead was placed in the crucible with the silver, and the heated lead oxidized and carried off the alloy, leaving pure silver (Jer. 6:27-30). It was used in weights (illustrated archaeologically), for fish-net sinkers (cf. Exod. 15:10), for sounding lines, plummets (*see* PLUMBLINE), and for heavy covers (Zech. 5:7-8). Figurines made of lead have been found in Egyptian and Palestinian excavations.* In Job 19:24 there is a reference to lead poured into letter forms cut in stone (as in part of the inscription of Darius I at Behistun), or to a lead tablet inscribed with an iron pen. Another Hebrew word, translated "plumbline" in Amos 7:7-8 (אנך; Akkadian *anâku,* "lead"), may also designate lead. Fig. LEA 20.

Tyre was an area distributing point for lead (Ezek. 27:12). Abundant galena (lead sulphide) ore is to be found in Asia Minor; Mesopotamian merchants trading for pure lead were settled there *ca.* 2000 B.C. Galena was used as eye paint in earliest Egypt, before 3400 B.C.

Bibliography. C. Watzinger, *Denkmäler Palestinas,* II (1935), 106-7, plate 33, figures 76-79; C. Singer *et al.,* eds., *A History of Technology,* I (1954), 582-85. P. L. GARBER

LEAH lē'ə [לֵאָה, wild cow *or* gazelle]. The elder daughter of Laban; Jacob's first wife, who bore him six sons and a daughter.

It was only by a ruse that the Aramean Laban tricked Jacob into marrying Leah, his weak-eyed and less attractive elder daughter, in addition to the younger and more beautiful Rachel (Gen. 29:15-30). The children born to the less favored (vs. 30; cf. 33:1-3) Leah were Reuben, Simeon, Levi, Judah (29:31-35), and later Issachar, Zebulun, and Dinah (30:14-24). Her handmaid, Zilpah, bore to Jacob Gad and Asher (30:9-13). Leah and her children went to Palestine with Jacob (ch. 31), and presumably she died there, since the Priestly Code (49:31) says she was buried in the cave at Machpelah.

The OT view of corporate personality (cf. Ruth 4:11) would suggest that the Leah traditions reflect tribal relations and history, although conclusions in this regard must be tentative.

It is possible that there was originally a Leah tribe or clan of cattle breeders, the totem of which was the wild cow. It is almost certain that the six Leah tribes belonged to the twelve-tribe amphictyony in which Israel was organized during the period of the judges and which is reflected in the grouping of Jacob-Israel's family. Some think there was a six-tribe Leah amphictyony before the twelve-tribe organization. JUDAH, the fourth of Leah's sons, became the dominant tribe in the S in Israel's later history.

Bibliography. M. Noth, *Das System der zwölf Stämme Israels* (1930); *Geschichte Israels* (1950); J. Bright, *Early Israel in Recent History Writing* (1956). M. NEWMAN

LEANNOTH lē ăn'ŏth. *See* MUSIC.

LEATHER, LEATHERN [עוֹר, skin; תחש (Ezek. 16:10; SHEEPSKIN *in* Num. 4:25; KJV BADGERS' SKIN *in* Ezek. 16:10); עור תחש (Num. 4:6, 8, 10, etc.) = GOATSKIN (KJV BADGERS' SKINS); δερμάτινος (Matt. 3:4; Mark 1:6), *from* δέρμα, skin, hide]. Animal skin tanned and prepared for human use. *See also* SKIN; TANNER.

We know that leather was widely used in the ancient Near East, and it is evident that it was equally common in biblical Palestine. There are references to the use of hides, probably tanned, as garments, girdles, and footwear (Gen. 3:21; Lev. 13:48; II Kings 1:8; Ezek. 16:10; Matt. 3:4; Mark 1:6; Heb. 11:37). It is possible that the "leprous disease" found in certain skin garments (Lev. 13:47-59) was due to the improper tanning of the leather. The skin coverings for the tabernacle (Exod. 26:14) and for its various furnishings (Num. 4:6, etc.) were undoubtedly tanned. Numerous secular objects were made of leather (Lev. 13:48; Num. 31:20), as probably was David's pouch (I Sam. 17:40). Complete hides of small animals, with the holes duly sewn, were widely used as water, milk, and wine containers (Gen. 21:14; Judg. 4:19; I Sam. 1:24; Job 38:37; Matt. 9:17; *see* WATERSKINS; WINE § 2*a*). Leather was also used for writing material, though Jeremiah's scroll (Jer. 36), which was readily combustible, may have been of papyrus. The Isaiah MS of the DSS, which comes from *ca.* 150 B.C., is written on a scroll made up of seventeen sheets of leather prepared from rather coarse skins sewn together, with the writing on the hair side. *See* WRITING AND WRITING MATERIALS.

Bibliography. On leather for writing purposes in the ancient Near East, see G. R. Driver, *Aramaic Documents of the Fifth Century B.C.* (1954), pp. 1-2. For references to leather articles in Mishnaic times, see M. Kel. 2.1; 15.1; 16.4; 24.12; 26.1-9; 28.3, 5. W. S. MCCULLOUGH

LEAVEN [שְׂאֹר, a piece of fermented dough; חָמֵץ, leaven, leavened, leavened dough; ζύμη]. Any substance which is added to dough or liquids to produce fermentation; a portion of fermenting dough reserved from a previous batch to be used for this purpose; figuratively, an element or admixture which tempers, moderates, debases and corrupts, or otherwise changes the whole by a progressive inward operation.

1. In biblical times. In biblical times leaven generally consisted of a portion of dough reserved from a previous batch. No other leaven than this sour dough is mentioned in the OT or the NT (for a list of leavens used in NT times, see Pliny Nat. Hist. 18.26; for directions as to the proper use of leaven by Jews in Mishnaic times, see Men. 5.1-2). This piece of fermented dough was named שאר in the MT, ζύμη in the LXX and the NT. Leavened dough, whether it had risen under the action of leaven or by spontaneous fermentation, was known as חמץ, "leavened," and when baked into bread as לחם חמץ, "leavened bread." The term חמץ is generally used as a substantive, sometimes meaning "leaven" (Lev. 2: 11), sometimes "that which is leavened" (Exod. 13: 3); nonetheless, the words שאר and חמץ are not entirely synonymous in the OT, for the former word is never used as the subject of the verb "to eat."

2. Leaven and sacrifices. Leaven was absolutely prohibited in connection with any sacrifices to the Lord (Exod. 23:18; 34:25), and in meal offerings (Lev. 2:11; 6:17; cf. Men. 5.2). It would seem likely that all offerings of bread to the Deity were unleavened throughout the Israelitic tradition; the injunction seems to be an ancient one and is so represented in later Israelitic tradition (Exod. 23:18). Leaven could, however, be used in offerings which were to be eaten by the priests or others (the peace offering in Lev. 7:13; the offering of the wave loaves in 23:17). The loaves of the bread of the Presence were unleavened, according to Josephus (Antiq. III.vi.6; x.7).

The Israelite was forbidden to eat leavened bread or to have leaven in his possession or household during the Passover season. Unleavened bread (מצה, or, more frequently in the OT, the plural form מצות) had been used during the Exodus because of the haste in which the Hebrews had left Egypt (Exod. 12:34-39); later practice continued this and other customs popularly associated with the first Passover. The eating of the unleavened bread during the days of the Passover celebration not only served to remind the devout Jew of the circumstances of the Exodus but also symbolized for him the manner of life which service to God requires (Exod. 12:39; Deut. 16:3).

3. Symbolic significance in the OT and the NT. The rationale for this prohibition was simply that fermentation was emblematic of a process of corruption; the leaven was capable of debasing and corrupting the mass of dough. That such an idea was suggested by association may be inferred from numerous OT passages and is explicitly shown in the NT, in which "leaven" is used for the unsound teaching of the Pharisees and the Sadducees (Matt. 16:11), and for the moral laxity of the Corinthians (I Cor. 5:6-8; cf. "yeast" in Gal. 5:9). The association of these ideas was also known in other traditions; among the Greeks it was made by Plutarch (*Quaest. Rom.* 109); the Roman satirist Persius used the word *fermentum,* "leaven," with reference to moral corruption (1.24).

"Leaven" is used in a good sense in the parable of the leaven (Matt. 13:33; Luke 13:20-21), in which Jesus likens the silent, unrelenting growth of the kingdom of God among men to the pervasive, assimilating action of the yeast. More generally, however, the NT uses of the symbol are based upon the traditional association of "fermentation" with political and moral corruption (Matt. 16:6, 11-12; Mark 8:15; Luke 12:1). Paul was fearful of the consequences of moral corruption and disobedience to Christ among the members of the Corinthian church, and he warned them with the reminder "that a little leaven leavens the whole lump"; he therefore admonished them to cleanse out the old leaven—i.e., the traces of the unregenerate condition—and to live the Christian life "with the unleavened bread of sincerity and truth" (I Cor. 5:6-8).

In rabbinical literature "leaven" symbolizes evil desires. The figure is also commonly used in Jewish theology to represent the inherited corruption of human nature.

See also SACRIFICE AND OFFERINGS; UNLEAVENED BREAD; WORSHIP IN THE OT. H. F. BECK

LEBANA lĭ bā'nə [לבנה, white] (Neh. 7:48); LEBANAH (Ezra 2:45; I Esd. 5:29); KJV Apoc. LABANA. Head of a family listed among the exiles who returned from Babylon.

LEBANON lĕb'ə nən [לבנון, *or with the definite article,* הלבנון, the white (mountain); Akkad. *Labnānu;* Egyp. *Ramanan;* Λίβανος; Arab. *Jebel Lubnān*]. The mountain range in Syria following the coast of the Mediterranean from Nahr el-Kebir in the N to Nahr el-Kasimiye (the lower part of Nahr el-Litany) in the S.

1. Landscape. The mountains of Lebanon and Anti-lebanon (*see* ANTI-LEBANON) are a part of the line of mountains which extends from the Amanus in the N to the Peninsula of Sinai in the S. The range of Lebanon is the mountain barrier between Nahr el-Kebir ("the great river"; the ancient name was Eleutherus), and Nahr el-Kasimiye (the lower part of Nahr el-Litany, Leontes). The latter river flows southward in the valley which divides Lebanon from Anti-lebanon. The name of the valley is Biqa'.

From *Atlas of the Bible* (Thomas Nelson & Sons Limited)

21. The Lebanons as seen from Baalbek

Another river, Orontes, flows northward in the valley. Their watershed is in the vicinity of Baalbek* at a height of *ca.* 3,770 feet above sea level. The Biqa' varies in breadth from *ca.* 6-10 miles. It is part of the great depression which was called Coele-Syria in antiquity. In Josh. 11:17 it is called the "valley of Lebanon." Fig. LEB 21.

The name of Lebanon, "the white," could be taken as an indication of the snow covering the mountain. In the winter much snow falls, and only during that season the higher parts are covered with snow. The mountain ridge is *ca.* 6,230 feet high, but there are summits of a height of more than 11,000 feet: the

Courtesy of Alfred Haldar

22. The hinterland near modern Beirut in Lebanon

highest peak is el-Qurnat el-Sauda' (11,024 feet). Other high summits are Dahr el-Qadib, Jebel Makmal, and Timarun. Jebel Sannin, overlooking Beirut and St. George Bay, is also of a majestic height (10,800 feet).* Particularly the S part of Anti-lebanon, HERMON, is often covered with snow, and the white crown of Hermon offers a majestic and impressive view. The mountain chains are divided into a N and a S part of the defile of Lebanon. The mountains are the result of a series of faults. This being so, there are a number of high peaks and summits, and between the higher parts of the range there are valleys and ravines. The communication between one part of the country and the other is often very difficult. Among the more important valleys may be mentioned the Holy Valley, which collects the water from the Mountain of the Cedars. This is the region where the Maronites found a refuge in the beginning of their history, and this cradle of the Maronite community has remained a holy place through the ages, from where the Maronite sect spread over a considerable part of Lebanon. The Valley of Adonis is another famous name. Through the valley flows the River of Adonis. To the Valley of Adonis, the pilgrimage of Adonis took place, at the end of the spring, when the verdure was in its greatest beauty. The ruins of a temple from Roman times still give a remembrance of the ancient Venus-Adonis cult, particularly the funerary reliefs sculptured on a high rock associated with Venus bewailing the death of Adonis. The Valley of Nahr el-Kelb is another name famous through historical reminiscences.* Two inscriptions, one Egyptian and one Assyrian, side by side on the same rock, record historical events showing the military importance of this route. Marcus Aurelius tells us about his work to open the coastal route. *See* PHOENICIANS. Figs. LEB 22-23.

Courtesy of the Oriental Institute, the University of Chicago

23. To the left is a probable relief of Shalmaneser III (858-824 B.C.); the upper part of the relief shows Ramses II (1301-1234 B.C.) before a god; at Nahr el-Kelb

2. Geological formation. Lebanon, as well as Anti-lebanon, has originated through faults. Both mainly consist of limestone from the Jurassic, Cretaceous, and Eocene periods, but also sandstone from the early Cretaceous period. Before the glacial age, the whole region of Syria and the neighboring countries was covered by water, and on the bottom of the sea stratifications accumulated, through which the limestone rocks originated which now constitute the main part of the W mountain range of Syria. During the following period, the Tertiary, earth movements took place, through which the bottom was lifted, and in this way the mountains originated. Thanks to animal remains, some of which are fossilized, in the sedimentations it is possible to determine the date. There are two limestone layers, the lower one covered by sandstone. This in its turn is covered by the upper limestone layer, which forms the mountain summits. It may vary in thickness from some hundred to five thousand feet. The upper layer of limestone has given Lebanon its scenery, which has its color from the grayish limestone. It has created the soil for the agriculture; its stones have been desired as building material. The thickness of the sandstone layer below the upper limestone may vary from a few hundred to a thousand feet. The sandstone is from the early Cretaceous period. It contains in some places lignite, which has been used as fuel in modern times.

3. Plants and animals. The valley between Lebanon and Anti-lebanon (el-Biqa') has favorable soil for agriculture. There is also good pasturage. On the mountains vegetation is perhaps not so rich as it was in ancient times (cf. Ps. 72:16; Isa. 35:2; 60:13). Particularly famous were its wine (Hos. 14:7—H 14:8), its cedars (I Kings 5:14; Ps. 29:5; Isa. 2:13; Ezek. 17:3; etc.), its cypresses (I Kings 5:8; II Kings 19:23; Isa. 14:8; etc.). In I Kings 7:2 ff the palace of Solomon is called the "House of the Forest of Lebanon." In Song of S. 4:11; Hos. 14:7, the fragrance of the trees is alluded to. The wild animals of Lebanon are mentioned in II Kings 14:9; Isa. 40:16; Hab. 2:17. Accordingly, Lebanon was famous also for its game. Today there is not much left of the cedar woods;* almost all of them are gone. The olive tree also played an important part in ancient times, and it is still cultivated, as well as the wine. Olive oil was used for various purposes: as food, for ointment and perfume, and as fuel in the lamps. The pasturage of the mountains is scanty, but sheep and goats are able to find enough food there. Pl. IX*a*.

Bibliography. H. Lammens, *Notes de géographie syrienne,* II-III, Mélanges de la faculté orientale, Université Saint-Joseph, Beyrouth, vol. I (1906); P. K. Hitti, *History of Syria* (1951); M. Dunand, *De l'Amanus au Sinaï: Sites et monuments* (1953).

A. HALDAR

LEBAOTH. *See* BETH-LEBAOTH.

LEBBAEUS lĕ bē'əs [Λεββαῖος=לבי(?), beloved child(?), courageous one(?)]. An alternative (Western) reading for "Thaddaeus" in Matt. 10:3 (so KJV); Mark 3:18; possibly a descriptive designation for "Judas the son of James" (Luke 6:16; Acts 1:13). *See* JUDAS 8.

Bibliography. J. Hastings, ed., *A Dictionary of Christ and the Gospels,* II (1908), 22-23; R. Harris, *The Twelve Apostles* (1927), pp. 28-36; V. Taylor, *The Gospel According to St. Mark* (1952), pp. 233-34.

E. P. BLAIR

LEBONAH lĭ bō'nə [לבונה] (Judg. 21:19). A town of sufficient importance to be mentioned in the

Courtesy of Herbert G. May

24. The Plain of Lebonah (Lubban) in the hill country of Ephraim, with the modern village of Lubban (biblical Lebonah) right of center at the foot of the hill (arrow)

identification of the location of Shiloh. The ancient name is preserved in the modern Lubban, *ca.* three miles NW of Shiloh (Seilun). Fig. LEB 24; Pl. XXV*b*.

W. L. REED

LEB-QAMAI. A cryptogram for "Chaldeans" (Jer. 51:1). *See* ATHBASH.

LECAH lē'kə [לכה] (I Chr. 4:21). Apparently a village in Judah; the location is unknown.

LECTIONARY. A book of scripture readings for worship services; specifically, one of the numerous Greek MSS of this type which have become increasingly valuable in textual studies. *See* TEXT, NT, § B5.

LEDGE. The translation of כרכב (Exod. 27:5; 38:4; KJV COMPASS) and עזרה (Ezek. 43:14, 17, 20; 45:19; KJV SETTLE), both of which refer to a projection on an altar. The altar of the tabernacle had a ledge halfway between the base and the hearth on top, possibly resembling the raised stone band on incense altars excavated at Megiddo (Fig. INC 5). The altar of Ezekiel's ideal temple possessed two steplike ledges between the base and the hearth. Fig. ALT 19.

See also ALTAR; TEMPLE, JERUSALEM.

L. E. TOOMBS

LEECH [עלוקה; *cf.* Arab. *'aliqa,* to hang, cling; *'alaq,* leech] (Prov. 30:15); KJV HORSELEACH. A wormlike, blood-sucking animal of the class *Hirudinea.*

It is certain—and this is confirmed by the ancient versions—that עלוקה (*'alûqâ*) is a leech, though there is no reason for taking it to be specifically the horseleech (*Haemopis* or *Aulostoma gulo*). On the several varieties of leech recorded by Tristram in Palestine, see, *NHB*, pp. 299-300.

See also FAUNA § G2*a*. W. S. MCCULLOUGH

LEEK [חציר, *ḥāṣîr*]. A bulbous herb of the lily family, *Allium porrum* L., which looks like an elongated onion. Leeks were an important part of the diet of the ancient Near East. During the wilderness period

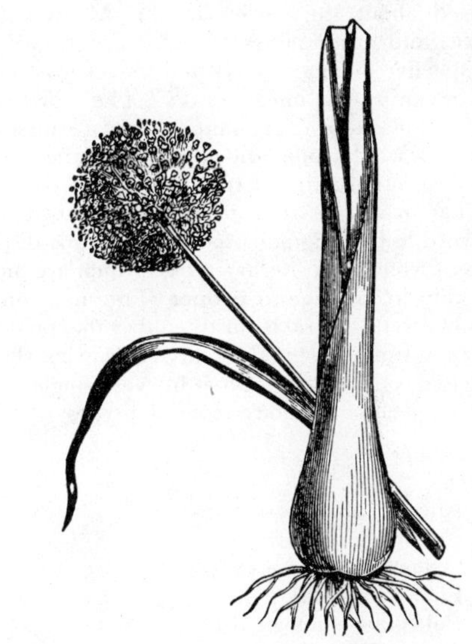

25. Leek

the Hebrews longed for them and for other foods of Egypt (Num. 11:5). *Ḥāṣîr* usually denotes GRASS (nineteen of twenty-one occurrences), and this leads some scholars to question the translation "leek," which goes back to the LXX (πράσα). Another green, cloverlike herb, *Tragonella foenumgraecum* L., popular in Egypt, is claimed, therefore, as the meaning here. The grasslike leaves of the leek and the association with ONIONS and GARLIC in Num. 11:5 provide stronger arguments for retaining the traditional meaning.

Fig. LEE 25.

See also AGRICULTURE; FLORA § A3*c;* FOOD.

Bibliography. I. Löw, *Die Flora der Juden,* II (1924), 131-38; H. N. and A. L. Moldenke, *Plants of the Bible* (1952), pp. 34-35.

J. C. TREVER

LEES [שמר]. The dregs remaining in a skin of WINE. In biblical times it was customary to allow wine to remain on the lees in order to gain strength and flavor; after it was strained, it was preferable to the newly fermented product. Thus in the age to come, Yahweh will prepare a feast (*see* BANQUET) of "wine on the lees well refined" (Isa. 25:6). The term is used as a simile for undisturbed peoples: (*a*) those "thickening upon their lees," who say that Yahweh will do nothing (Zeph. 1:12); and (*b*) the Moabites, who have "not been emptied from vessel to vessel" and have thus "settled on [their] lees" (Jer. 48:11). In the latter passage the author refers to the fact that Moab has never gone into exile. J. F. ROSS

LEFT HAND. *See* RIGHT HAND.

LEGEND. This word has in English a much wider use than, e.g., in German or Nordic scholarly terminology, and often includes both myth and fairy tale and all kinds of "folk tales." Legend in this wide sense is not restricted to "primitive" folk tales; there are learned or consciously artistic (poetic) legends as well.

Legenda was, at least since the twelfth century A.D., used about the stories of the Martyrs (*see* MARTYR) and other saints, which were "read" at their respective memorial days and thence gradually got the meaning of "miracle tale." The word was finally used often for every fanciful tale about some hero, even a secular one, and mostly with the implication of an invented, not true, story. In scholarly terminology it will be appropriate to restrict the use of the word to the original *religious* area, thus distinguishing it from other literary types, which are more or less akin to the legend proper. The mention of these other types here is justified by the popular usage of the word, by the difficulty of drawing sharp limits between the different types in every single case, and by the genetic relation among the types.

1. The fairy tale
2. *Sagn*
   a. Ancestor *sagn*
   b. Culture-hero tales
   c. Cosmological or cosmogonical *sagn*
   d. Etiological tales
   e. Cult-place etiological tales
   f. Hero tales
3. Historical narrative
4. The legend proper
5. Myth

Bibliography

1. The fairy tale. The fairy tale, or "chimeric" (German *Märchen*), is the oldest type of oral "literature," found everywhere and in all ages. It sprang from man's original and innate "lust of fabling," sometimes called "fabulating urge," and the thrill he experiences in the flight of his fancy. It plays beyond time and place—fairies, elves, trolls and other nature spirits, demons, animals, plants, and things are the acting persons, besides the hero, often the youngest son, despised by his brothers. After many dangers, trials, and marvelous adventures, he "gets the princess and half the kingdom" (a common finale in Norwegian folk tales).

In the OT we find the fairy tale only as poetical metaphor: the man who borrows the wings of the morning (Ps. 139:9); the Nessus shirt (109:18); or as motifs in legends and "short stories" with or without historical kernel: the speaking serpent (Gen. 3); Balaam's speaking ass; the sea monster that devours JONAH and spews him out again.

Here we have to do with international motifs, wandering from land to land. Of this type is also the story of the birth and childhood of Moses—the same story is told of the old Babylonian king Sargon, of Cyrus, Perseus, and Romulus and Remus (in the last-mentioned case combined with the motif of the hostile brethren). Sometimes the whole story is built upon such a motif, as in Solomon's judgment (I Kings 3:16-28), to which a close parallel is known from India. To Joseph and Potiphar's wife we have a parallel from an Egyptian *Märchen.* The Joseph narrative partly plays over the well-known motif—the hostile brethren—as does also the story of Jacob and Esau; the motif of the story of TOBIT, "the grateful dead," is found partly in older recensions, in many folk stories, as in Hans Christian Andersen's "Traveler's Companion" and a Norwegian *Märchen.* To this type of short stories or "historical novels" belong the stories of JONAH; ESTHER; JUDITH; and RUTH.

A didactic offshoot of the animal and plant *Märchen* is the FABLE.

2. *Sagn.* This Norwegian word (German *sage,* lit. "what is said") means a more or less fanciful story, which may be of the type described in § 1 *above,* but which is connected with some factual person or thing, an event, a locality, a sociological or cultural relation, and thus includes a kernel of fact. The living TRADITION always tends to glorify heroes and events by attaching to them all sorts of fairy-tale motifs and poetical decoration.

***a. Ancestor* sagn.** An important role among the Hebrews and other Semites is played by ancestor stories. The ancestor may be a mere *heros eponymos,* a fictitious person originating from the name of the tribe or clan; but he is nevertheless a personification of the ideals of the tribe, he lives on in the "sons," and events and customs from the history and life of the tribe have been connected with him—it is now mostly impossible to disentangle them (see the work of Bräunlich). Biblical instances of such stories, where the tribe characterizes itself, are: Cain and Lamech (Gen. 4); Tamar and Judah (Gen. 38); and others. The Lamech story shows that these characterizations often have taken poetical form (*see* LITERATURE § 5*a*). The ancestor is a sociological reality, sometimes with historical individual traits. This also holds good for the PATRIARCHS; it is more important to discern the sociological entities for which they stand ("Hebrew" tribes migrating to Canaan from NW Mesopotamia some three hundred to four hundred years before the migration of the Israelites from the S) than to speculate over individual persons—Abraham, Jacob, etc.

b. Culture-hero tales. Ancestors, among them also totem ancestors (*see* TOTEMISM), are often seen as the inventors and founders of the different kinds of human culture, even rituals and cults and secret "wisdom." They then are mostly considered as haveing lived in primeval times, and often as supernatural beings, as well—of the type of the Australian "originators" (see the work of Söderblom). In the OT we are told of Enoch, the first founder of a town; Jabal, the father of the tent dweller and cattle breeder; Jubal, the inventor of musical instruments and music and ancestor of the musicians; Tubal-Cain, the first smith; Noah, the husbandman who made the first wine; and Enosh, who "began to call upon the name of Yahweh" (Gen. 4:26). From here there is a short step to speculations and fancies about the first man —Adam, Enosh—and the origins of mankind.

***c. Cosmological or cosmogonical* sagn.** These are stories about the CREATION of the world and of the living beings, tales about the original happiness of man (*see* EDEN, GARDEN OF; PARADISE), and the present tragedy of man's life, etc. To a similar type of literature belong the fanciful speculations on the "primeval man" (*der Urmensch,* to be distinguished from the first created man)—an idea which later Judaism has taken over from Persia. The tales of the creation of man's world often reflect what is regularly created anew by the cult; they often have the character of a myth (*see* § 5 *below*). On the contrary, a myth may be "historified" into a *sagn* about later times; thus the creation out of the original water is reflected in the Babylonian and biblical stories of the FLOOD.

d. Etiological tales. The above-mentioned types often include an element of etiology. The tale will explain the reason (αἴτιον) for which things now are as they are: a striking locality, such as the "salt pillar" (explained as the petrified wife of LOT); or the tower of BABEL; the origin of a custom, a rite, a sociological or political state; the name of a person or of a tribe—which things then are the factual kernel of the *sagn* in question. Other instances: How came the holy well of Qadesh into existence? Why do the springs of Upper and Lower Gullot belong to the OTHNIEL clan and not to CALEB? What about the big tell of AI? Most of what the book of JOSHUA tells about the Conquest (*see* ISRAEL) is based upon such local etiologies.

e. Cult-place etiological tales. A special type of etiological tale is the story about the foundation of a holy place—in the OT commonly ascribed to one of the patriarchs. As the cultic place, in the opinion of the ancients, had its own sanctity, the story often tells how the hero discovered it, as Jacob did at BETHEL. A theological explanation is regularly given in the OT: the place has been sanctified and appointed by a revelation of the God. Such a "cult *sagn*" was told at the feast of the sanctuary, to the glorification both of the place and of the saint, and thus may be called a cult legend (cf. § 4 *below*).

f. Hero tales. These are connected with real historical persons, and the events related often include a greater or smaller historical kernel, although often overgrown by poetical embellishments, etiological and fairy-tale motifs, etc. To this type belong the tales of the so-called "great JUDGES," and even many of the stories about SAUL and DAVID, overgrown by legend.

3. Historical narrative. No sharp boundaries divide the hero tale from the historical narrative, to which the Norse word "saga," derived from the same root as *sagn,* should be restricted, according to its Old Norse use. Even here—e.g., in the stories from the deeds and life of David and his family—we have to reckon with the free poetical art of the storyteller and with his modeling of the events after the customs and rites of his own time (e.g., II Sam. 6). Even apparent historical events such as the two decisive battles through which Joshua conquered the land (Josh. 10–11) may be due to the constructive work of a later "sagaman" (cf. § 2*d above*).

4. The legend proper. This type has drawn upon all the above types of tales and motifs. It may be defined as a *sagn* with edifying, devotional tendency, a story from the life and works of some religious hero, a saint, a prophet, an ancestor and culture hero of the type in § 2*b above*. The wonders and the activity of the deity play an important role. To the tendency also belong the glorification of the saint, appealing to admiration, awe, and to imitation of his religious and moral virtues. As the cult aition, the legend is told at the festivals of the sanctuary with which the saint is connected. By definition even the legend may include a historical nucleus, as in the MOSES and Exodus (*see* EXODUS, BOOK OF) stories in their present form.

Here the "salvatory deeds," not of Moses, but of the Lord, are retold and re-experienced, and we may therefore call them the myth (*see* § 5 *below*) of the cultic feast.

Most of the legends in the OT are concerned with prophets and their miraculous predictions and wonders, often built up upon some fairy-tale motif (*see* § 1 *above*). Masterpieces of epic art are the Elijah legends (*see* ELIJAH THE PROPHET § 1), while the ELISHA legends contain more of the popular conceptions of the "holy man." Devotional tendency and legendary motifs are also in the ISAIAH tales (chs. 36–39). The spiritual situation of the DISPERSION is reflected in the DANIEL legend.

The postcanonical literature—such as the Ascension of Moses (*see* MOSES, ASSUMPTION OF); the book of JUBILEES; the "Genesis Apocryphon" from the Qumran caves (*see* DEAD SEA SCROLLS); the TESTAMENTS OF THE TWELVE PATRIARCHS; the Great Synagogue (*see* SYNAGOGUE, THE GREAT); etc.—swarms with legends and legendary motifs, partly more or less international fairy-tale motifs (*see* § 1 *above*), partly spun out of Bible passages by means of MIDRASH. A good instance of this sort is the legend of Balaam in Josephus and the Talmud. Late Judaism also offers examples of the martyr legend, as in II Maccabees (*see* MACCABEES, BOOKS OF) or the Martyrdom of Isaiah (*see* ASCENSION OF ISAIAH).

5. Myth. In principle the legend must be distinguished from the genuine MYTH, the epic account of the saving facts and deeds (*Heilstatsachen*) rehappening and re-experienced in the cult. But even here the border line is not sharp (*see* § 4 *above* on the Exodus legend, and § 2*c above*). Even the cult myth may under the hands of the poets lose its direct connection with the cult and become "epic poetry" of the *sagn* type (§ 2 *above*), with its own "place in life," the god becoming a semidivine hero, as the Sumerian Gilgamesh, or a (super)human dynasty founder, such as the Ugaritic Keret (*see* UGARIT).

Bibliography. W. Baumgarten, "Märchen" I-II, *RGG²*, III, col. 1824 ff, with references. H. Gunkel, *Elias, Jahve und Baal* (1906); *Esther* (1916). N. Söderblom, *Das Werden des Gottesglaubens* (1916), ch. 4. H. Gunkel, *Das Märchen im AT* (1917); *Genesis³⁻⁴* (1917), pp. 7-56. W. Bräunlich, "Beiträge zur Gesellschaftsordnung der arabischen Beduinen-Stämme," *Islamica* (1933), pp. 1-2. S. Mowinckel, *Religion und Kultus* (1953), pp. 94 ff.

See also bibliography under LITERATURE.

S. MOWINCKEL

LEGION [λεγιών, λεγεών; *loan word from* Lat. *legio*] (Matt. 26:53; Mark 5:9, 15; Luke 8:30). The principal unit of the Roman army. The composition of the legion varied as Rome was successively confronted with the tasks of conquering Italy and the world, of assimilating its conquests, and of maintaining peace and order throughout its vast extent and holding its frontiers. Originally made up of property-holding citizens, the legions were always regarded as the best and most trustworthy Roman soldiers and were carefully distinguished from the "allies," first the *socii* and then the *auxilia,* and other second-class troops. If, throughout its history, the quality and prestige of the legion were related to its emphasis on citizenship and consequent capacity for rigid discipline and arduous training, its effectiveness in warfare was due to its concentration on heavy infantry.

A legion in the republican army—the army which for nearly three centuries after 350 B.C. was engaged in conquering Italy and the world—was generally composed of 4,500 men—1,200 *hastati* (spearmen), 1,200 *principes* (mature and experienced men), 1,200 *velites* (light-armed troops or skirmishers), 600 *triarii* or *pilarii* (veteran reserves), and 300 *equites* (cavalry). Sometimes there might be as many as 6,000 men.

Toward the end of the Republic (509-27 B.C.), as a result of the reforms of Marius (157[?]-86 B.C.), the private-property qualifications for service in the legions were abolished. The legionaries became proletarian and professional. The legion also was reorganized as a body of 6,000 men divided into 10 cohorts (*see* COHORT) and 60 centuries. The unit of tactical action thus became 600. Marius also modified the legion by abolishing its cavalry. About this time the Roman franchise was extended to all Italians. This meant the conversion of allies (*socii*) and subjects into citizens, thus providing the increase of soldiery required by the growth of empire, although it threatened to weaken the distinction in status between the legions and the auxiliaries.

When Augustus (27 B.C.-A.D. 14) reorganized the imperial army of defense, he set up two grades of troops: first, the legions, made up of Roman citizens, whether in Italy or in the provinces; second, the *auxilia,* made up of subjects (not citizens) of the Empire in the provinces. To the Marian legion of 6,000 heavy infantry in 10 cohorts, Augustus added 120 cavalry. During the first century A.D., Italy provided the bulk of the recruits. After A.D. 70 the soldiers were drawn almost entirely from the Romanized towns of the provinces. The effort continued to be made to maintain the citizenship qualification for admission to the legion, although in times of stress this could sometimes be done only by granting citizenship on enlistment. Nevertheless, the legionary soldier continued to be thought of as the typical "Roman" soldier, even after Augustus had greatly extended the republican practice of using *socii* as auxiliary armies by creating a new order of *auxilia,* regiments (cohorts) of infantry and squadrons (*alae*) of cavalry, 500 to 1,000 strong, and composed of apparently voluntary recruits from the noncitizen populations of the provinces. Ultimately the numbers of the auxiliaries greatly exceeded those of the legions. These *auxilia* seem to have provided all the archers and most of the cavalry, and were originally important for the diversity of their fighting methods. Since military service was often professional and might last twenty years or more, the noncitizen on discharge was given a bounty, sometimes of both land and money, and Roman franchise for himself, his wife, and his children. And in turn the auxiliaries must generally have become Romanized.

Although at least three and sometimes more legions were quartered in Syria during the whole of the first century, the troops in Palestine at this time were normally auxiliaries. In times of special crisis legionary soldiers might be brought in. There may, indeed, have been some legionaries in the garrison at Jerusalem. However, in the main, the legions were stationed in the frontier provinces, and they do not appear prominently in Judea until A.D. 66.

The word "legion" never occurs in the NT in its proper military sense, nor does it occur at all in the LXX. In Josephus it is rare, if at all. In War II.v.44; III.viii.97, τάγμα ("corps, division") stands for "legion." In the NT, "legion" is used only for the hosts of demons (Mark 5:9=Luke 8:30; Mark 5:15) or the hosts of angels (Matt. 26:53). No greater tribute to the prestige of the legion in the Empire could be paid than this NT use of the word to refer to the armies of demons and angels.

Bibliography. M. P. Nilsson, *Imperial Rome* (1926), pp. 281-316; T. R. S. Broughton, "The Roman Army," note XXXII, in F. J. Foakes-Jackson and K. Lake, *The Beginnings of Christianity,* pt. I, vol. V (1933), pp. 427-45; F. J. Haverfield, "Roman Army," *Encyclopaedia Britannica,* XIX (1955), 395-99.

F. D. GEALY

LEHABIM lĭ hā'bĭm [להבים] (Gen. 10:13; I Chr. 1:11). A group named as offspring of Egypt, together with the Ludim, Anamim, Naphtuhim, Pathrusim, Casluhim, and the Caphtorim. They are completely unknown unless, as some scholars suggest, the name is to be emended to לובים, "Lubim." *See* LIBYA.

T. O. LAMBDIN

LEHEM lē'hĕm [לחם] (I Chr. 4:22). An unknown place in Judah, if it ever existed, to which, according to the RSV, Joash and Saraph returned after ruling in Moab. The KJV reads the corrupt text (וישבי לחם) as a personal name, ". . . and JASHUBI-LEHEM." But against the Commentaries, the correct reading is perhaps וישבו לחם (cf. LXX καὶ ἀπέστρεψεν αὐτούς). This requires the least textual emendation, the full phrase then reading: ". . . Joash and Saraph, who ruled in Moab, *but returned*" (lit., returned *to themselves;* Hebrew *lahem*). The same idiomatic form is found, e.g., in Num. 22:34; Deut. 5:30; I Sam. 26:12.

B. T. DAHLBERG

LEHI lē'hī [לחי, jawbone]. A place in Judah. Possibly some geological formation had a shape reminiscent of a jawbone and so gave the place its name, or the name may reflect the scene of the incident of Judg. 15:9 ff. It was probably in the region of Beth-shemesh, between Zorah and Timnah.

After Samson had burned some of the Philistines' crops, they retaliated with a raid against Lehi (Judg. 15:9). To placate the Philistines, the men of Judah attempted to put Samson into Philistine hands at Lehi, but he seized the jawbone (*leḥî*) of an ass and crushed the skulls of a sizable number of Philistines (vss. 14 ff). The place of the Philistine rout was called Ramath-lehi ("hill of the jawbone").

V. R. GOLD

LEMUEL lĕm'yo͞o əl [למואל, devoted to God, *or* belonging to God, God's (=לאל)] (Prov. 31:1, 4). A king to whom are ascribed words "which his mother taught him." Vss. 2-9 are presented as if spoken by the mother. Whether the words "Lemuel" and "king" refer to a historical individual or have some other significance is unknown.

Bibliography. C. H. Toy, *Proverbs,* ICC (1916), pp. 538-41. M. Noth, *Die israelitischen Personennamen* (1928), p. 249, no. 814; cf. pp. 32, 153.

B. T. DAHLBERG

LEND. *See* DEBT.

LENTILS [עדשים, *ʿadhāšîm* (*plural only*); Arab. *ʿadas;* LXX φακός (*singular*)]. The fruit of a leguminous plant of the pea family, *Lens esculenta* Moench (also called *Ervum lens* L.). Fig. LEN 26.

Jacob's pottage made from lentils (Gen. 25:34) was probably similar to the modern Arab dish called *mujedderah,* made from lentils, onions, and rice stewed in olive oil. The reddish-brown color of lentil stew seems to be connected with the name Edom (="red"; Gen. 25:30).

Lentils were included with other foods supplied to David and his men, when he was forced to flee to Mahanaim (II Sam. 17:28). Shammah, one of David's "Mighty Men" (*see* SHAMMAH 4) had a single-handed victory over the Philistines near LEHI in a "plot of ground full of lentils" (II Sam. 23:11). Lentils were included in the mixture of grains used by Ezekiel to make a bread symbolic of famine (Ezek. 4:9). Lentil bread (with a little barley added) is still an important part of the diet of the poor people of the Near East, especially in S Egypt.

26. Lentils

See also AGRICULTURE; FLORA § A1*f;* FOOD; POTTAGE; VEGETABLES.

Bibliography. I. Löw, *Die Flora der Juden,* II (1924), 442-52; H. N. and A. L. Moldenke, *Plants of the Bible* (1952), pp. 128-29.

J. C. TREVER

LENTULUS, EPISTLE OF lĕn'chə ləs. A medieval writing of uncertain date (thirteen-fifteenth century) describing the physical appearance of Christ (*see* APOCRYPHA, NT). Although in the oldest form the document purports to be from the "annal books of the Romans," it is commonly in the form of a short letter to the Roman Senate by Lentulus, a Roman official in Judea. The delineation gives medieval ideas of Christ's appearance and may well be a written description of one of the many traditional portraits. The theme was a popular one from the earliest days. Eusebius (Hist. VII.18.4) says that he had seen "the likenesses of both his apostles Peter and Paul and of Christ himself, preserved in pictures painted in colors." The tradition that Luke painted many such is very ancient.

M. S. ENSLIN

LEOPARD [נמר, Aram. נמר (Dan. 7:6), *cf.* Arab. *namir,* Akkad. *nemru;* πάρδαλις]. A formidable and ferocious carnivorous mammal, *felis pardus,* of the family Felidae, surviving in Palestine as late as the twentieth century. The cheetah, a variety of leopard that can be tamed and trained to hunt, and known for its speed, was also familiar in the biblical world and may be referred to in Hab. 1:8.

In the OT, apart from the references to the leopard's spots (Jer. 13:23), to the leopard's lying down with the kid in the future age of peace (Isa. 11:6), and to Lebanon and Hermon as being the home of leopards (Song of S. 4:8), the leopard serves either as a figure of speech or as an apocalyptic animal. In Hos. 13:7 Yahweh, who is about to punish Israel, is likened to a leopard, whereas in Jer. 5:6 the figure is applied to Israel's waiting enemy, presumably Babylon. In Hab. 1:8 Chaldean horses are paid the compliment of being swifter than leopards (or cheetahs). In Dan. 7:6 the third beast, likened to a winged four-headed leopard, appears to represent Achaemenid Persia; in Rev. 13:2 the composite beast, typifying the Roman Empire, is said to be like a leopard—a simile that many first-century Christians must have fully endorsed.

W. S. MCCULLOUGH

LEPROSY [צרעת; נגע צרעת; LXX *and* NT λέπρα]. One of the more serious genera of skin diseases which was particularly associated with the idea of uncleanness. The Hebrew term צרעת is generic, and is derived from a root which contains the idea of being struck or afflicted with an eruptive skin disease. The Greek rendering λέπρα originally signified an ailment which was characterized by the appearance of rough, scaly patches on the skin. This meaning is found in Hippocrates, Polybius, and other writers, and appears to correspond with psoriasis, a skin disease which assumes several different forms.

Another Greek medical term, ἐλεφαντίασις (ἐλέφας), or "elephantiasis Graecorum," describes a much more serious chronic disease, whose symptoms correspond largely to those associated with the leprosy of modern times. Quite probably the term λέπρα was indefinite and general in nature, with the result that the Greek translators of the Hebrew Bible employed it to include psoriasis, leucodermia, ringworm, and the like, as well as true leprosy. The usage of λέπρα in the NT, however, appears to be restricted to specific dermatological conditions exclusive of true leprosy. In medieval European medical writings, the Vulg. rendering *lepra* was employed as a designation of elephantiasis Graecorum, so that the symptoms of this much-feared affliction were associated descriptively with what was recorded about צרעת and λέπρα in the Scriptures. From this confusion arose the belief that the chronic, hopeless, medieval European leprosy was being described by the biblical references.

In antiquity leprosy was a familiar disease in Mesopotamia and the Orient, being described as far back as the third millennium B.C. Only one instance of true leprosy has been discovered on Egyptian mummies, and this leaves room for the contention that the individual concerned may have been an immigrant from Syria or Mesopotamia. In view of these observations it is curious that some classical writers associated leprosy almost exclusively with Egypt. Josephus (Apion I.xxvi) recorded that three Egyptian historians, Manetho, Cheremon, and Lysimachus, preserved the legend that the Hebrews under Moses (Osarsiph) were expelled from Egypt at the time of the Exodus because they were "leprous and scabby, and subject to certain other kinds of distempers," an allegation which Josephus indignantly repudiated.

While Herodotus did not mention that leprosy was endemic in Egypt, he recorded the incidence of a certain skin disease (λεύκη) among the Persians, which was such as to compel the sufferers to live outside towns and villages. Hippocrates also included this disease in a group of dermatological conditions which he described, and which may be suggestive of leprosy.

During the medieval period the term "leprosy" signified almost any cutaneous disease which erupted in rough, scaly patches over a period of time. In the eighteenth century it became apparent that the areas of skin affected by one particular disease became completely devoid of sensation. The true causative organism was discovered in 1871 by Hansen, who showed that leprosy was the result of infection by a minute schizomycetous fungus, Mycobacterium leprae (Hansen's Bacillus). The onset of this chronic endemic disease is often insidious, and the first indications are of lassitude, febrile interludes, and pains in limbs and joints. An eruptive stage follows, in which the cutaneous blotches may appear and disappear by turns, and when this activity has concluded, the disease assumes its particular form. There are three commonly described varieties of clinical leprosy, or Hansen's Disease, as it is often called today.

The nodular type results in the formation of lumps in the skin of the face, and the general thickening of the tissues produces a characteristic lionlike appearance. Degenerative changes also take place in the mucous membranes of the nose and throat. The anesthetic variety is less severe, and involves the cutaneous nerves. Depigmented areas of skin, in which there is no feeling, result from the thickening of the nerves, and after a time blisters form on these anesthetic patches. Perforating ulcers may also be present on the feet, while portions of the extremities frequently necrose and fall off, leaving a healed stump (*lepra mutilans*). This form of leprosy is chronic in nature, and may last up to thirty years. A third or mixed variety has a combination of all the above symptoms in varying degrees. Diagnosis of Hansen's Disease is established by the detection of the presence of the Bacillus leprae in the nodules or blisters.

A detailed description of the disease rendered in the English versions by "leprosy" is given in Lev. 13. The Hebrew is technical and obscure to the modern student, and the situation is further complicated by the obsolete English terminology employed to translate the Hebrew. These include "scall" (RSV "itch") and "tetter," the latter being virtually meaningless but still surviving, unfortunately, in the RSV (Lev. 13:39).

To the priesthood was committed the responsibility of pronouncing a man leprous, or of entertaining a differential diagnosis, and a number of symptoms are described carefully. The affliction might occur spontaneously (vss. 2-17); it might follow a furuncle (vss. 18-23) or a burn on the skin (vss. 24-28), or it might develop on the head or beard (vss. 29-44). The first symptoms were those of a swelling (שאת; LXX οὐλή) or subcutaneous nodule, a cuticular crust (ספחת; LXX σημασία), and a whitish-red spot (בהרת; LXX τηλαύγημα).

Taken together, these symptoms presented a picture of subcuticular penetration resulting in a whitening of the small hairs present in that portion of the skin under examination. If such was the case, the patient was tentatively pronounced unclean. But if only one of these symptoms was present, the priest imposed a seven-day quarantine. At the end of this period the patient was examined again, and isolated for another week if no further degeneration was apparent; after this time he could be declared clean.

A chronic form of the disease was indicated by the presence of white hairs and red granular or ulcerated tissue in a raised area of depigmented skin. When these symptoms occurred, the sufferer was pronounced unclean by the priest. But if the patient presented evidence of a white cutaneous disorder covering his whole body, he was considered clean (Lev. 13:13). In such instances he would probably be suffering from acquired leucodermia (vitiligo), characterized by an absence of pigment in the skin without other abnormalities. Less probable would be a diagnosis of psoriasis, a chronic cutaneous condition marked by a covering of white scales on reddened patches of skin, and found generally on the extensor surfaces of the scalp, knees, and elbows. This common affliction is neither infectious nor dangerous.

If, however, on subsequent examination by the priest, the sufferer was found to be ulcerated, he was to be declared unclean (Lev. 13:14). In the event that this ulceration merely constituted the mild pustulation common to most cutaneous diseases, the priest was empowered to declare the patient clean. Great importance was attached to the early recognition of leprosy, having regard to the various possibilities of differential diagnosis. The crux of the matter lay in the degree of cutaneous penetration which the disease had achieved. If it affected the epidermis or outermost layer of skin and did not produce pathological changes in the hairs, the affliction was not regarded as especially serious. As such it might consist of eczema, leucodermia, psoriasis, or some allied cutaneous disease. But if the affliction had infiltrated the dermis (corium) and had caused the hairs to split or break off and lose their color, then leprosy was to be suspected. The word "dim" (KJV "somewhat dark") indicates a fading spot or rash.

Another cutaneous affliction of importance in the larger diagnosis of leprosy was that which emerged as a white or inflamed spot on the site of an old boil or burn (Lev. 13:18-28). If the dermis had not been penetrated, a seven-day quarantine period was imposed, after which the priest re-examined the patient. If the pustule or swelling remained localized, the diagnosis of leprosy was excluded. The actual condition involved is obscure, and may have been a keloid, a connective-tissue growth of the skin which normally arises in the scar of some previous injury or disease. Less probable is the diagnosis of diffuse symmetrical scleroderma (*sclerema adultorum*), in which symmetrical patches of the skin become hardened and thickened.

The diagnostic principles mentioned above were applied to the incidence of disease affecting the scalp (Lev. 13:29-37), where the affliction was spoken of as נתק; (LXX θραῦσμα; RSV "itch"; KJV "dry scall"). If no black hairs were present, the patient was to be quarantined for one week. After this time he was required to shave off all the hair in the vicinity of the affliction without actually touching the affected portions of the skin. If after another week of quarantine it was apparent that the disease was spreading, the priest was empowered to declare the patient unclean, whether yellowish hairs were actually present in the skin or not.

But if there was evidence that the progress of the disease had been checked, and on examination there were seen to be black hairs growing on the affected area, the patient was to be pronounced clean. The general symptoms contemplated are those of favus (ringworm), a contagious cutaneous disease which frequently occurs in childhood. Caused by a fungus, *Achorion schönleinii*, it is marked by the formation of yellow, saucer-shaped favose scabs around the hair follicles.

The presence of dull white spots on the body indicated the outbreak of a disease which, however, did not render the patient unclean. This eruption (בהק; LXX ἀλφός) is apparently acquired leucodermia (vitiligo), the λέπρα of the Greek medical writers. It is a cutaneous condition marked by white patches in which there is an absence of pigment (*see* TETTER). Alopecia (baldness) was a clean condition (Lev. 13:40-41) unless complicated by the characteristic leprous eruptions. Where the chronic condition was diagnosed, the afflicted person was banished from society, and was ordered to dress distinctively and to announce his uncleanness. Appropriate ritual ceremonies were prescribed for those occasions on which spontaneous healing took place and the leper was declared clean (Lev. 14:1-32).

The deteriorated condition of garments (Lev. 13:47-59) probably resulted from the incursion of dampness, mold, or fungus. Its incidence was taken seriously, and the material was burned if the deterioration showed signs of spreading; otherwise washing would render the article clean. If discoloration of the walls of a house occurred (Lev. 14:34-47), the usual principles of quarantine applied. Affected stonework or woodwork had to be removed and replaced by new material. These regulations appear to have been directed at halting the spread of dry rot in the woodwork, and discouraging the growth of lichens, fungi, and mineral precipitates on the masonry of houses.

While the leper was regarded as ceremonially unclean, the Bible never refers to leprosy as a type of sin. Its incidence was regarded as an act of God, and in consequence the healing of the leper was invariably interpreted as a miracle of divine grace. The nature of the affliction which beset Moses (Exod. 4:7) is obscure, while the leprosy of Miriam, his sister (Num. 12:10-15), was of a transient nature, perhaps psoriasis. Naaman (II Kings 5) was permitted to mingle freely with his own people, indicating that he was not suffering from Hansen's Disease, but from some other complaint, possibly vitiligo. Since there are reasons for believing that emotional stresses frequently underlie the incidence of most cutaneous disorders, the injunction to wash in the Jordan may have constituted an important suggestive element in a regime of psychotherapy. The four lepers outside besieged Samaria (II Kings 7:3-10) seem typical of those victims of Hansen's Disease who had been banished from human society. Uzziah (II Chr. 26:19-21), who lived in a separate (KJV "several") house, also appears to have suffered from true leprosy. Job's ailment, in spite of popular opinion, was not leprosy (*see* BOIL).

In his ministry Jesus healed many described in the NT as λεπροί, and, according to Matt. 10:8, the cleansing of such people was one of the tasks allotted to the Twelve during their mission. In Mark 1:40-45 (=Matt. 8:2-4; Luke 5:12-15) Jesus healed a man from a skin disease by means of his touch and a pronouncement. Perhaps this condition was vitiligo rather than true leprosy.

The ten men whom Jesus healed on his way to Jerusalem (Luke 17:11-19) were instructed to satisfy the requirements of Levitical ceremonial law before returning to their homes. They, too, probably suffered from vitiligo, which, if psychogenic in nature, would respond to that suggestion which appears to have been undertaken as part of the treatment (Luke 17:19). The term εἱλκωμένος ("ulcerated") was used of the parabolic Lazarus of Luke 16:20 alone in the NT, and there is no reason for assuming that the brother of Martha and Mary was similarly afflicted.

R. K. HARRISON

LESHEM lē'shəm [לשם] (Josh. 19:47). Alternate name of LAISH; DAN 2.

***LETTER.** A written message sent as a means of communication between persons separated by distance. While historical books of the Bible, both in the OT and in the NT (Acts), occasionally incorporate examples of such correspondence at appropriate points in the narratives, the NT is especially rich in letters. In the older terminology, these were called "epistles," but in modern usage a technical distinction is often made between the terms "letter" and "epistle."

1. Biblical terminology
   a. In the OT
   b. In the NT
2. Ancient letter forms
3. Dispatch of letters
4. Distinction between letters and epistles
   a. Letters in the NT
   b. Epistles in the NT

Bibliography

1. Biblical terminology. ***a. In the OT.*** Both the KJV and the RSV regularly use "letter" in the sense of "missive" to translate four different Hebrew or Aramaic terms, the commonest being the Hebrew ספר, signifying a writing, more frequently translated "book." The other terms, all probably of Persian origin, are אגרא or אגרת, indicating a message dispatched by courier; נשתון, meaning a writing; and פתגם, a word. The term "epistle" is not used in an English version of the OT.

b. In the NT. The KJV uses "letter" in the sense of a missive, as well as "epistle," to translate the Greek ἐπιστολή. The RSV has abandoned the term "epistle" entirely. However, both versions also employ the term "letter" in a different sense—viz., for a character of the alphabet, thus translating the Greek γράμμα, in Luke 23:38 (RSV mg.; cf. KJV John 7:15; Rom. 2:27, 29; 7:6; II Cor. 3:6). Since the plural of this Greek term (γράμματα) clearly refers to a written message in Acts 28:21, the KJV interprets the dative plural (γράμμασιν) in the same sense in Gal. 6:11, where the RSV has more accurately "with what large letters"—i.e., the written characters. Thus, with the exception of Acts 28:21, the Greek term for "written correspondence" in the NT is always ἐπιστολή. In the LXX, likewise, ἐπιστολή is far more usual than γράμματα to designate a missive.

2. Ancient letter forms. About the precise forms in which letters were composed in antiquity, more information is available from Greek and Roman than from Hebrew sources. Scantiness of evidence in the latter case is due largely to the tendency in historical records in the Bible to abbreviate all such documents by eliminating everything not essential to the message. If Hebrew letters, in II Sam. 11:14-15; I Kings 21:8-9, appear curtly peremptory by any standard of polite address, this might be because they represent royal orders issued to subordinates. Since the same consideration cannot explain an equally terse message from one king requesting a favor from another, in II Kings 5:6, the assumption is that the narrator omitted the customary amenities for the sake of brevity. Evidence of such curtailment survives, in Ezra 4:11, where names of addressees and senders are followed by an Aramaic equivalent of *et cetera.* A hint of the normal greeting remains in Ezra 4:17: "peace, etc." (RSV "greeting"), while the salutation "all peace" occurs in Ezra 5:7. A Hebrew letter from Bar Cocheba, leader of the Second Jewish Revolt (A.D. 132-35), was discovered in a cave in the Wadi Murabba'at, in 1952; it is addressed "From Simeon ben Kosiba to Jeshua ben Galgola, peace."

Most letters included in the Apoc. use the characteristic Greek "greeting" (χαίρειν; lit., "to rejoice"), but II Macc. 1:1-2 combines this with the typically Semitic "good peace."

In the NT, Paul, who never opens a letter with χαίρειν, couples the Hebraic "peace" with "grace" (χάρις). Abundant evidence for the form of Greek letters came to light with discoveries of Egyptian papyri, which not only illustrate the external appearance of such correspondence, but also demonstrate that the various formulas of address and closing greetings found in NT letters are exactly those in common use. They include, in addition to χαίρειν (Acts 15:23; 23:26; Jas. 1:1; cf. II John 10-11), prayers for the reader's health (εὔχομαί σε . . . ὑγιαίνειν; III John 2); "making mention" of him before the Deity (μνείαν σου ποιούμενος; Philem. 4); thanksgivings (εὐχαριστῶ; Rom. 1:8; I Cor. 1:4; etc.; *see* THANKSGIVING). Urgent pleas begin: "I appeal to you" (παρακαλῶ ὑμᾶς; Rom. 12:1; I Cor. 1:10). At the close come greetings from the writer and those with him to the reader and others mentioned by name (ἀσπάξομαι in its various forms; Rom. 16:3 ff; III John 15), and "farewell" (ἔρρωσθε; Acts 15:29). Thus, in this, as in other respects, NT Greek reflects current Hellenistic usage.

Historical study of the NT would have been greatly facilitated, had not the various letters included in the canon been stripped of all indications of date. The commonest method of dating, at the end of a letter, was by reference to the year of the emperor (cf. Luke 3:1). However, published collections of ancient letters frequently omit date lines, though occasionally both date and place of writing are preserved. It is generally recognized that subscriptions appended to Paul's letters in some MSS are scribal conjectures affording no reliable data. E.g., Athens, Laodicea, and Rome, all unlikely, vie with one another as the place of writing of II Thessalonians, while Philippi rivals Ephesus (the probability) for I Corinthians.

3. Dispatch of letters. After writing, the sheet of papyrus was folded or rolled, tied, and often sealed to ensure privacy. Sealing is mentioned in I Kings 21:8; Esth. 3:12; 8:8, where it serves the double motive of secrecy and royal authority. Dispatch of letters by foot runners, or by mounted couriers, is described in Esth. 3:13; 8:10, but about the sending and delivery of NT letters little information appears in the sources. Since the official postal service of the Roman Empire (*cursus publicus*) did not carry private correspondence, wealthy families had their own slaves for this purpose, and large commercial enterprises likewise employed their own letter carriers, called *tabellarii* (from the wooden tablets, *tabella,* used for briefer communications). Hence, it is natural that, according to Acts 15:22, the bearers of the letter which follows were men chosen from the congregation for that purpose. II Cor. 8:16 suggests that Titus may have been entrusted with the message which mentions his approaching departure for Corinth; just as Phil. 2:25 may indicate Epaphroditus; Col. 4:7-8, Tychicus, as the respective carriers of those letters.

4. Distinction between letters and epistles. Since the English term "epistle" is derived from the Greek ἐπιστολή, Latin *epistula,* which in ancient usage designated precisely the kind of written missive now ordinarily called a "letter" (cf. Latin *litterae*), the technical distinction made by modern scholars in the application of these two terms requires brief explanation. The papyri preserve private correspondence of people in humbler walks of life, who never dreamed that the personal greetings and intimate bits of news they exchanged with relatives and friends would ever be read by other eyes. Collected letters of Greeks and Romans prominent in civic affairs, however, often include documents which, although composed in epistolary form, might more accurately be classified as public orations, philosophical treatises, political tracts, or moral exhortations. By mentioning in their opening address the name of some well-known individual, literary compositions of this kind were given the semblance of personal correspondence, even though intended for a much wider circle of readers. But unlike true letters characterized by some measure of confidential privacy, such *epistulae* have all the marks of having been written for general publication. It is to distinguish a work of this type from a genuinely personal "letter" that the term "epistle" is now frequently used.

a. Letters in the NT. The question arises how far this distinction may be applicable to documents in the NT canon. Does it contain any real letters? Limiting this term strictly to private correspondence between two individuals, the answer would be negative, with the exception of III John, for even PHILEMON is addressed to the "church in your house." Yet the message which follows is intensely personal, even if—as is likely—this is the letter which Colossian Christians were directed to obtain from Laodicea and read in their congregation (Col. 4:16). However, such directions for an exchange of letters addressed to two different churches, unique in Paul's correspondence, in no way indicates that the eventual collection and publication of his letters was ever part of the apostle's own intention. On the contrary, his frank discussion of scandalous conditions in certain local congregations, particularly at Corinth, suggests that wider publicity was far from his mind. Had a copy of the letter Paul received from the Corinthian church (I Cor. 7:1) likewise been preserved, the task of interpreting parts of his message would be less difficult, since certain obscurities stem from the fact that we possess only half this written "conversation." Such is the nature of a true letter, which is usually intelligible enough to its original recipient.

Because of its more formal rhetorical style, Romans is sometimes regarded as marking a transition from "letter" to "epistle." Nevertheless, ch. 15, especially vss. 22-29, must have served the purposes of genuine correspondence, even if at some time copies were circulated omitting the local address of 1:7; 15 (personal greetings in ch. 16 constitute a separate problem). *See* ROMANS, LETTER TO THE.

b. Epistles in the NT. Questions of pseudepigraphy are not our concern here. However, whether by Paul or not, "Ephesians" should be considered an encyclical. The earliest extant MS (P^{46}) preserves a text without reference to Ephesus in 1:1. The anonymous work called "Hebrews" lacks all suggestion of epistolary form until the closing lines (13:22-25), where it is described as a "message of exhortation." Despite their form as letters, the three Pastorals have more in common with a category of writings known as Church Orders.

Eusebius reports that early in the fourth century seven documents now in the NT were classified as "catholic"—i.e., general—epistles (Hist. II.xxiii.25). This description is not altogether inappropriate for James, I and II Peter, and Jude, although James after its opening lines is really a moral homily akin to the OT wisdom literature. I John, too, appears as a homily from an absent teacher. Finally, the letters to seven churches, or more accurately to their "angels," in Rev. 2:1–3:21, are simply literary introductions to a book which is itself cast in an epistolary framework (1:4; 22:21).

Bibliography. A. Deissmann, *Bible Studies* (1901), pp. 1-59; *Light From the Ancient East* (1911), ch. 3, especially pp. 217-38; for criticism of Deissmann's distinction between letters and epistles, see also W. M. Ramsay, *The Letters to the Seven Churches* (1905), pp. 23 ff. J. Moffatt, *Introduction to the Literature of the NT* (1911), pp. 47-55. M. Dibelius, *A Fresh Approach to the NT and Early Christian Literature* (1936), pp. 137-213. E. J. Goodspeed, *A History of Early Christian Literature* (1942), pp. 10 ff. H. L. Ginsberg, "Notes on the Two Published Letters to Jeshua ben Galgolah," *BASOR,* 131 (Oct., 1953), 25-27.

O. J. F. SEITZ

LETTUS. KJV Apoc. form of HATTUSH.

LETUSHIM lĭ to͞o'shəm [לטושים] (Gen. 25:3). A people mentioned as one of those descended from Dedan, the others being the Ashurim (Ashurites; *see* ASHUR) and the Leummim. The meanings of the names Letushim and Leummim are dubious, and their location uncertain; it may possibly have been the Sinai Peninsula.

S. COHEN

LEUCIUS lo͞o'shəs [Λεύκιος]. The reputed author of the Acts of John (*see* JOHN, ACTS OF); and subsequently considered the author not only of all five of those apocryphal Acts which the Manicheans are said to have substituted for the canonical Acts of the Apostles, but also of many other apocryphal writings.

M. S. ENSLIN

LEUMMIM lē ŭm'ĭm [לאמים, people, hordes(?)] (Gen. 25:3). A people reported to be descended from Dedan. *See* LETUSHIM.

S. COHEN

LEVI lē'vī [לוי, *possibly gentilic of* לאה (LEAH), wild cow; *or from lāwīyū,* person pledged for a debt or vow; *see bibliography*]. **1.** Either the eponymous ancestor or a personification—which one is unknown—of the tribe of Levi. In the sagas of the Hebrew patriarchs he is the third son of Jacob and Leah (Gen. 29:34; cf. 35:23; Exod. 1:2; I Chr. 2:1; etc.). The most ancient reputation ascribed to him, which means to the tribe bearing his name, is that of a predatory and merciless adversary. With his brother Simeon he cruelly avenges his sister DINAH on Shechem for having assaulted her (Gen. 34:25-31), and Jacob's "blessing" describes Simeon and Levi in phrases of abhorrence for their wanton anger against their enemies (49:5-7). It is the sons of Levi who at

Moses' behest slaughter three thousand of the apostate Hebrews in the wilderness and thus, according to one account, ordain themselves for the service of Yahweh (Exod. 32:25-29; cf. Deut. 33:8-11). Traditionally the three original sons of Levi were GERSHON (or Gershom); KOHATH; and MERARI (Gen. 46:11; Exod. 6:16; and many other references), ancestors of the three main divisions of the Levites. Num. 26:59 speaks of Moses' mother, Jochebed, as having been "born to Levi," but clearly this must mean the tribe and not the original ancestor.

For the role of this tribe in Israel's history and on the "Levites," "sons of Levi," "house of Levi," etc., *see* PRIESTS AND LEVITES. On Levi in the apocryphal and pseudepigraphical literature, *see bibliography*.

2. An ancestor of Jesus Christ (Luke 3:24); son of Melchi, and father of Matthat.

3. An ancestor of Jesus Christ (Luke 3:29); son of Symeon, and father of Matthat.

4. A local tax collector in Capernaum who became a follower of Jesus (Mark 2:14). According to the Lukan account, Jesus was also a guest in his home (Luke 5:27-32). In Mark he is called the "son of Alphaeus," but is otherwise unknown. Some of the Markan MSS read "James" for this name in 2:14, while the parallel account in Matthew reads "Matthew" instead of "Levi" (Matt. 9:9), whom it then identifies with Matthew one of the twelve apostles (10:3). The name Levi appears in none of the lists of apostles and cannot with any certainty be identified with the Matthew who is among the Twelve.

Bibliography. On the many proposed etymologies of the name Levi, see, besides the lexicons: J. Pedersen, *Israel*, III-IV (1940), 680; W. F. Albright, *Archaeology and the Religion of Israel* (1942), pp. 109, 204-5; T. J. Meek, *Hebrew Origins* (rev. ed., 1950), pp. 123-24; C. A. Simpson, Exegesis of Genesis, *IB*, I (1952), 703. For a complete index of the abundant references to Levi in the Apoc. and the Pseudep., see R. H. Charles, ed., *The Apoc. and Pseudep. of the OT* (2 vols.; 1913), II, 587. B. T. DAHLBERG

LEVIATHAN lĭ vī'ə thən [לויתן, coiled one, *from* לוה; Arab. *l-w-y*, coil, wind]. One of the names of the primeval dragon subdued by Yahweh at the dawn of creation (Ps. 74:14; Isa. 27:1). In apocalyptic literature (II Esd. 6:52; II Bar. 29:3-8), Leviathan is represented as destined to break loose from his bonds at the end of the present era, only to suffer a second and final defeat. A prototype of the cosmogonic myth appears in the Canaanite texts from Ras Shamra-Ugarit (fourteenth century B.C.), where Baal defeats the draconic *L-t-n;* while the apocalyptic version is probably influenced by parallel Iranian beliefs concerning the dragon Aži Dahaka (cf. Yasht 13.62). *See* COSMOGONY § D2*b*. Fig. LEV 27.

Courtesy of the American Schools of Oriental Research

27. Two deities are destroying a seven-headed serpent-dragon (cf. the Leviathan); an impression of a cylinder seal found at Tell Asmar in Mesopotamia; Akkadian period (*ca.* 2360-2180 B.C.)

In Job 41:1; Ps. 104:26, the term "Leviathan" is used by extension to denote a sea monster in general, without mythological implication. T. H. GASTER

LEVIRATE LAW. The legal provision that if brothers live together and one of them dies leaving no son, the other brother shall marry the widow. The first son of this union shall take the name of the brother who died (Deut. 25:5-10). *See* MARRIAGE § 1*g*.

LEVIS lē'vĭs. KJV Apoc. form of LEVI.

LEVITES. *See* PRIESTS AND LEVITES.

LEVITICAL CITIES. According to Josh. 21:1-42= I Chr. 6:54-81, forty-eight cities, with their surrounding pastures as grazing lands for their cattle, are to be set apart in Palestine as the dwelling places of the tribe of Levi (Num. 35:1-2). The sons of Aaron are to receive thirteen of these cities for their exclusive use. These cities, with houses and pastures, are the inalienable rights of the priests and Levites, and any which have been sold may be redeemed at any time, but must be released in any case to the Levites in the Year of Jubilee (Lev. 25:32-34). The six cities of refuge—i.e., for homicides, etc.—named in Num. 35:9-34; Deut. 4:41-43; Josh. 20:1-9, are included in the Levitical cities (Num. 35:1-8). An average of four cities per tribe is thus envisaged (Joseph =Ephraim and Manasseh).

But other passages presuppose a different situation. According to Num. 18:20; 26:62; Deut. 10:9, the priests are to have no inheritance or portion in the Promised Land. Accordingly the priests are classed with other needy members of Israel as deserving of charity (e.g., Deut. 14:28-29). What thus appears to be a contradiction in the laws has led many scholars to reject the regulations concerning the Levitical cities as unhistorical. They have felt themselves confirmed in this view by the differences between the lists in Josh. 21; I Chr. 6, by the fact that many of the Levitical cities did not become Israelite until later times, that the pastures surrounding some cities would have overlapped the pastures of other cities (e.g., Hebron and Holon, Anathoth and Almon), and that the whole scheme was patently impossible in postexilic days, to which period the Levitical legislation was thought to belong. The Levitical cities of Josh. 21 are thus best explained, according to these writers, as the adoption of the ancient holy cities of Canaan into Israel's religious system.

There has been an increasing tendency, however, to recognize that the priestly editors, though they were postexilic, were yet editors of material of varying dates. Accordingly, various scholars not only attributed the institution of cities of refuge to the time of David, but ascribed to his day the Levitical cities also. Comparative study of the lists has greatly lessened the differences between Josh. 21 and I Chr. 6, and has shown that many of the cities did not belong to Israel until the time of David, and that some of the cities were lost to Israel after the division of the monarchy. Albright, following Löhr and Stein, has further shown that other considerations point to the reign of David rather than that of Solomon as the time of origin. David's plan may only have existed on paper, but the laws prohibiting Levitical inheritance cited above suggest that a beginning was made with the plan, but that the possession of Levitical property was abused, and so gave rise to the prohibitions.

The Davidic origin of the plan is preferable to the postexilic date. On either view an idealizing element is largely present. It is also important to recall the theological basis of the conception. By this the Levitical cities are seen as part of the doctrine that all property belongs to God.

Bibliography. W. F. Albright, *Archaeology and the Religion of Israel* (1942), pp. 121-24; W. F. Albright, "The List of Levitic Cities," *Louis Ginzberg Jubilee Volume* (1945), pp. 49-73.

See also bibliography under PRIESTS AND LEVITES; CITIES OF REFUGE.

G. HENTON DAVIES

*__LEVITICUS__ lĭ vĭt'ə kəs. The third book of the Bible. The same word appears as the title of the book in the Vulg. This in turn is derived from the LXX to Λευεῖτικόν—i.e., the Levitical book, the book which deals mainly with the Levitical priests and their duties (cf. Heb. 7:11). The Hebrew title of the book is its first Hebrew word, ויקרא, "And he called." It is the third book of Moses, and a comparison of Exod. 40:1, 17, with Num. 1:1 shows that it belongs to the first month of the second year of the Exodus. There are but four legislative narratives in the book: Aaron's priesthood (chs. 8-9); the punishment of Nadab and Abihu (10:1-7); the ritual error of Eleazar and Ithamar (10:16-20); and the stoning of a blasphemer (24:10-14, 23). The remainder of the book contains legislation.

1. Sources
2. Contents
3. Character of the book
   a. Worship and sacrifice
   b. The priesthood
   c. The laws of purification
   d. The Day of Atonement
   e. The Code of Holiness
4. Leviticus and the Scriptures
Bibliography

1. Sources. Perhaps the least difficult of all the tasks of Pentateuchal criticism (*see* PENTATEUCH) has been the identification and isolation of the material now commonly ascribed to the P document. This is true of narrative material and even more true of legal material. Law (*see* LAW IN THE OT) is the domain of the priest (Jer. 18:18); and without denying that priestly activity and personality are behind other narrative and legal portions in the Pentateuch, nevertheless the priestly origin and character of parts of Exodus and Numbers and of all Leviticus are clearly recognized. It may be said then that Leviticus belongs to P. This is not to say, of course, that Leviticus is a unity, for there are various indications which show the contrary. The book, in fact, contains a number of smaller units of law dealing mainly with cultic matters. These smaller units of law may be detected by means of their introductory formulas or superscriptions, which may be an editorial framework, as in Lev. 1:1-2, or may be an exact title of the law which follows: e.g., "This is the law of the burnt offering" (6:9—H 6:2; cf. 6:9-13, 14, 25—H 6:2-6, 7, 18; 7:18). There are other superscriptions in Lev. 7:1, 11; 14:2. In addition, the end of such groups of laws or individual laws is also indicated by a closing formula, a subscription (Lev. 7:37—H 7:38; 11:46-47; 12:7; 13:59; 14:32, 54-57; 15:32-33). Both introductory and closing formulas are the work of an editor or compiler who was classifying and ordering his material, but they clearly enshrine the older, separate units. Eissfeldt points out that 14:54-57 serves not merely to round off a law or group of laws, but contains also in the words "to show when it is unclean and when it is clean" a rubric for its use. These corpora are styled "Agendas" by Eissfeldt and are really groups of professional directives for the priests in their ministry to the people. But it is also clear that besides these groups of laws intended for the priests for use in their ministry to the people, there were other laws and groups of laws which were intended directly as manuals or "agendas" for the laity. These will be found, e.g., in the directions concerning the calendars of feasts (23:9, 21, 39-43); in the regulations covering forbidden degrees of relationship for the purpose of marriage (18:6-18), and in the lists of those animals which may or may not be eaten (11:1-23, 41-47). It has also been suggested that the sacrificial tariffs known to us from Marseilles and Carthage would point to official announcements which would have lain behind such summary passages as 7:28-36 (cf. Deut. 18:1-5).

The next stage in the development of law was clearly the combination of laws of like character or similar theme into larger units or collections of laws. Such collections would be a stage on the way to the fully developed codes of law such as the Book of the Covenant (*see* COVENANT, BOOK OF THE); DEUTERONOMY; and the HOLINESS CODE. It is the recovery of these intermediate collections of laws which offers the greatest opportunity for subjective criteria of analysis. Indeed, one scholar has described these intermediary stages of law by the term "balks," and these are arrived at and isolated by the detection of duplicates, parallels, and variant traditions. The study of commentaries on Leviticus will show at once the criteria which enable various commentators to arrive at the intermediary groups of law. Thus, by way of example, it is claimed that 6:8-7:38 is parallel to and supplements 1:1-6:7. Then within these it is claimed that chs. 1; 3 belong together, but that ch. 2 has a different origin because of the different introductory formula (2:1). Though chs. 1; 3 and ch. 2 are thus said to be separate, both may be very old, whereas ch. 4 belongs to the late strand of P. Again, 5:1-6 belongs to a different source from that of ch. 4. So the division continues, and the whole book is divided into a considerable number of intermediary sections. But the arguments which prompt such divisions may be countered by other considerations, and this suggests that the precise analysis of these laws into intermediary sections is unwise. It is questionable, too, whether such documentary analysis, which is often so helpful to the study of Pentateuchal narrative, is really appropriate to the laws. In these circumstances it is best to regard these intermediary sections, if ever they existed, as the missing links in the growth of the major codes of law as they now exist in the OT. The analysis of case and categorical laws (*see* LAW IN THE OT) and the recognition of introductory and concluding formulas in individual laws or brief units of law is one thing. But beyond this until the greater corpora of law emerge, all is really uncertain, though, as will be seen below, there are exceptions. Adhering to this principle, the analysis of the contents of Leviticus will show the presence of several sizable corpora of law, including, of course, that separate code which is commonly styled the Law of Holiness (chs. 17–26). It should be noted that von Rad finds both his P^{A} and his P^{B} sources in Lev. 8:9; 10; 16.

Similarly, the dating of such laws is very difficult. There is, however, a growing recognition that many of the laws, both as to form and as to content, go back to old and very old times. There was thus a stream of law categorical in character which came from the Mosaic side of Israel's life, and there was another stream mainly of case law which Israel canalized from Canaanite sources. Of course, in their present codified form these laws belong to the latest pre-exilic days or later. A suggestion may be hazarded from the parallel of the book of Isaiah. The writings of Isaiah of Jerusalem come first in the book of Isaiah, though chs. 1–39 contain material from a later date. Isa. 40–55 is exilic and chs. 56–66 exilic and later. It is possible then that, with exceptions, the blocks of law in P in Exodus and Leviticus may reflect either a historical order or a priestly tradition of the chronological order of the laws. If there is any sort of validity in this conception, then the exilic dating of Lev. 17–26 might be a *terminus ad quem* from which the material could be dated into earlier periods. Then, too, the law of the Day of Atonement in Lev. 16 would stand largely at the end of P's laws, where, of course, it historically belongs. The principle, of course, may only be broadly applied.

2. Contents. The contents of the book may be analyzed and summarized as follows:

a) 1:1–6:7 is a code of laws concerning sacrificial worship addressed to Israelite worshipers through Moses. It contains the following laws:

Ch. 1. The law of the burnt offering (vss. 2*b*-9, of the herd; vss. 10-13, of the flock; vss. 14-17, of fowls).

Ch. 2. The law of the meal or cereal offering (vss. 1-3, of fine flour; vss. 4-13, cooked, baked, or fried; vss. 14-17, of first fruits).

Ch. 3. The law of the peace offering (vss. 1-5, of the herd; vss. 6-11, of the flock: sheep; vss. 12-16, of the flock: goats; vs. 17, perpetual statute concerning blood and suet).

4:1–6:7. The law of the sin offering (4:1-12, for an anointed priest; 4:13-21, for the whole congregation; 4:22-26, for a ruler; 4:27-31, for any person [a goat]; 4:32-35, a lamb; 5:1-6, for any person [lamb or goat]; 5:7-10, for poorer people [fowls]; 5:11-13, for the poorest [meal or cereal]; 5:14-16, guilt offering for deceit in holy things; 5:17-19, for unknown sins; 6:1-7, for crimes against a neighbor).

b) 6:8–7:38—H 6–7 is a code of similar laws addressed mainly to the priests through Moses (6:8). Note the recurring formula: "This is the law of . . . ." There are the following subdivisions:

6:8-13. The law of the burnt offering.

6:14-18. The law of the cereal offering.

6:19-23. The offering of the priest.

6:24-30. The law of the sin offering.

7:1-10. The law of the trespass offering, with priestly perquisites (vss. 8-10).

7:11-21. The law of the peace offering.

7:22-27. Exposition of 3:17; prohibition to eat fat or blood.

7:28-34. Selected portions; wave breast and heave thigh for the priests.

7:35-36. Further portion for the priests.

7:37-38. Conclusion.

It should be noted that the regulations in 1–7 correspond to the directions in Exod. 29. But the other requirement of Exod. 29—namely, the command to consecrate Aaron—is not fulfilled until Lev. 8. Thus Lev. 1–7 interrupts the connection between Exod. 29 and Lev. 8, and these interrupting chapters are themselves paralleled in Exod. 29. But further, Exod. 25–29 suggests that a complete law of the tabernacle and its contents is being presented, and 29:43-46 is the final religious formula which closes this section. But in Exod. 30:1-10 a law for the construction of the altar of incense is given, and thus it supplements the laws of chs. 25–29. In turn this altar is required for the special cases of the sin offering in Lev. 4. The author of Exod. 25–29 knows of no altar of incense or of its ritual. Thus one group of passages (Exod. 27:1-8; 29:38; Lev. 1–3; 5–6; 8–9; 16; Num. 16:46) refers to "the altar"—i.e., they know but one altar. This is the narrative of P proper. Other passages, however (Exod. 30:28; 31:9; 35:16; 38:1; 40:6, 10, 29), speak of the "altar of burnt offering." This second group of passages, then, which either mention the incense altar or point, by a distinguishing title such as "altar of burnt offering," to a second altar no doubt belongs to a different and later stratum of P. There is thus evidence of a long tradition of growth.

Of the two manuals in Lev. 1–7 it may be said that the first deals with the method and materials of sacrifices, whereas the second also deals with a great variety of more incidental detail. Certain differences in the order of sacrifices in the treatment of the fire (cf. 1:7; 6:12-13), not to mention the formula of 6:9, 14, 25; 7:1, 11, 37, suggest that the codes are by different hands. 7:37-38 is a colophon which suggests a concluding summary.

c) In chs. 8–9 the ordination of Aaron and his sons is according to the instructions given in Exod. 29:

8:1-5. The scene.

8:6-13. Washing, vesting, and anointing of Aaron and his sons.

8:14-30. The sacrifices (vss. 14-17, the bull of the sin offering; vss. 18-21, the ram of the burnt offering; vss. 22-30, the ram of ordination; vss. 31-36, the days of ordination).

Ch. 9. The initial sacrificial activity of Aaron (vss. 7-14, the atoning offering for himself; vss. 15-21, the atoning offering for the people; vss. 22-24, the blessing of Israel and the advent of God's glory).

d) Two legislative narratives are found in ch. 10:

Vss. 1-7. Punishment of Nadab and Abihu without priestly mourning.

Vss. 8-11. Prohibition of intoxicants for priests.

Vss. 12-15. Law concerning edible holy things.

Vss. 16-20. The ritual error of Eleazar and Ithamar.

Lev. 8 appears to be based on Exod. 29 as an expanded version of a more original and shorter narrative detailing the fulfilment of Exod. 29. Lev. 9 doubtless belongs to the main strand of P and continues the story of Exod. 29.

e) Chs. 11–15 contain the laws of purification:

Ch. 11. The law of food and clean and unclean animals (vss. 1-8, land animals; vss. 9-12, water animals; vss. 13-19, birds; vss. 20-23, winged creeping things; vss. 24-28, land animals; vss. 29-31, creeping things on earth; vss. 32-38, things unclean by contact; vss. 39-40, dead clean beasts; vss. 41-43, creeping things on earth; vss. 44-47, concluding summaries).

Ch. 12. Purification following childbirth.

Chs. 13–14. Diagnosis and treatment of leprosy (ch. 13, detection on various parts of the body; 14:1-8, the rites for leprosy; 14:9-32, the sacrifices for leprosy and for the poor; 14:33-57, leprosy in houses).

Ch. 15. Ritual for bodily excretions and discharges.

The analysis of chs. 11–15 shows that Lev. 11:2-23, 41-45, forms a continuous law on diet and animals marked by the Hebrew word שקץ, "abomination," or better, "detestation" while vss. 24-40 are a separate and probably interpolated section dealing with uncleanness from contact; 12:2*b* appears to refer to 15:19, so that chs. 12; 15, in view of their subject matter, may have belonged together; the laws of leprosy, though they represent various aspects of one theme, probably represent a long development in legal practice, and the material is from different dates and sources. The repetitions of ch. 15 on secretions similarly suggest a late date (cf. also the references to the sin offering).

f) Ch. 16 is concerned with the Day of Atonement:

Vss. 1-2. The occasion.

Vss. 3-10. The entry of Aaron into the holy place.

Vss. 11-28. The ceremonial in detail.

Vss. 29-34. Annual repetition of the DAY OF ATONEMENT.

To Lev. 16 belongs a long investigation of its unity, sources, and place in the P code. Various scholars have made critical analyses of different themes such as the cleansing of holy place, tent, and altar, and the atonement for persons, and have chosen various portions as the original or early form of the ritual. There is, however, no agreement. The different topics within the chapter must be accepted as evidence of a long development, but there are no agreed criteria for the analysis of the development, even though different ideas are present. The atomizing process in such detail is not suited to legal material, and the form history of legal material does not favor it.

g) Chs. 17–26 contain the Law of Holiness (H):

Ch. 17. Sacrifice (vss. 1-9, the place of sacrifice; vss. 10-14, eating meat with blood prohibited; vss. 15-16, eating of carcasses also forbidden).

Ch. 18. Sexual laws; various prohibitions and exhortatory conclusion.

Ch. 19. Moral and ceremonial laws.

Ch. 20. Miscellaneous laws (vss. 1-8, Molech-worship; vs. 9, respect for parents; vss. 10-21, sexual laws; vss. 24-26, exhortatory directions).

Chs. 21–22. Priesthood and sacrifice (21:1-9, priests; 21:10-15, high priests; 21:16-24, disqualifying blemishes; 22:1-6, clean and unclean food; 22:17-25, blemished sacrificial animals; 22:26-33, further directions and exhortatory conclusion).

Ch. 23. A sacred calendar (vss. 1-3, sabbath; vss. 4-8, Passover and Unleavened Bread; vss. 9-14, First Fruits; vss. 15-22, Feast of Weeks; vss. 23-25, New Year Festival; vss. 26-32, Day of Atonement; vss. 33-44, Feast of Tabernacles).

Ch. 24. Miscellaneous laws (vss. 1-4, lamps; vss. 5-9, the bread of the Presence; vss. 10-16, 23, the blasphemer; vss. 17-22, injuries; vs. 23, conclusion).

Ch. 25. The sabbatical year and the Year of Jubilee (vss. 1-7, the sabbatical year; vss. 8-23, Year of Jubilee; vss. 24-34, redemption of land; vss. 35-38, usury; vss. 39-55, slavery).

h) Ch. 26 contains a concluding exhortation and colophon to the code.

Chs. 17–26 are marked by their beginning (17:1-2) and by their ending (26:46) as a separate law code, which Klostermann entitled the "Law of Holiness" in reference to its recurring holiness formula (19:2; 20:7-8, 26; 21:6, 8, 15, 23; 22:9, 16, 32). Various writers have given lists of words and phrases that are peculiar to the code, and which show that the author is nearer to Ezekiel than to any other book in the OT.

Some passages in H, such as parts of ch. 23 and 24:1-9, are paralleled elsewhere in P; but when these are subtracted, what remains is unlike P. There are doublets (e.g., 17:12=19:26*a;* 19:27-28=21:5; 19:30=26:2; 19:31=20:6; 19:34=24:22; 19:30=26:2*a*), and these show that little groups of laws have been incorporated into H and the duplications allowed to remain. On the other hand, to detect such smaller codes as H^1 or H^2 and H^3 is difficult. Elements from P have been combined with parts of another destructive code of laws to provide H.

The analysis reveals that the code contains much exhortatory material and so is more closely akin to Deuteronomy. Von Rad has shown how sermonic utterances have been combined with various laws to form liturgical wholes. Thus Lev. 18 begins with exhortation in vss. 2-5; then follow the laws in vss. 6-23 and a concluding exhortation in vss. 24-30. Von Rad analyzes the material formally and thus reveals various runs of laws (e.g., 19:9*a*, 9*b*, 10*a*, 10*b;* or another series in vss. 11-12, 13*a*-18*a*). He finds a cultic series in 19:19*b*, 26-28. Again, 20:7-21 furnished a collection of various commandments with similar beginnings and endings, with a concluding exhortation in vss. 22-24. These illustrations show that von Rad is justified in his claim that H contains sermonic instruction for the community which is based on series of older laws and ordinances. In 26:3-45 is the last and longest of these sermonic exhortations, and it doubtless is also intended to mark the end of the code.

The demonstrable connections of H with Ezekiel, which have led some scholars to claim Ezekiel as the author of H, show that H and Ezekiel are roughly contemporary and possibly that H originated among the exiles in Babylon rather than in Jerusalem. It cannot be shown with certainty that H preceded Ezekiel or vice versa. Neh. 8:14-18 refers to Lev. 23:33-43, and this suggests that by Ezra's day H was a part of P and, indeed, of the Pentateuch.

i) Ch. 27. Vows and tithes (vss. 1-29, vows and their redemption; vss. 30-33, appendix on tithes and their redemption; vs. 34, conclusion).

3. Character of the book. The study of the book of Exodus and the four gospels has familiarized many people with the idea of *Heilsgeschichte*, "sacred and saving story." *Heilsgeschichte* both records the story of salvation and seeks to confer salvation. One scholar has coined a similar expression to describe the character and function of Hebrew law: Hebrew law is *Heilsgesetz*, "sacred and saving law." *Heilsgesetz* in the OT not only records and is the revelation of a divine order of society but also seeks to establish such a society in the commonwealth of Israel. The character and function of Leviticus then is summed up in this idea of *Heilsgesetz*. The themes of this Levitical saving law, as shown by the analysis of the book, are worship and sacrifice (chs. 1-7); the ministry of the priesthood (chs. 8-10); the purifying of Israel's life (chs. 11-15); the annual atonement (ch. 16); the holiness of God and Israel (H chs. 17-22; 24); the dedication of time, life, and property (H chs. 23; 25); and preaching (H chs. 26-27).

a. Worship and sacrifice. There are excellent summary tables of the differentia of sacrifices (*see* SACRIFICE AND OFFERINGS) provided in commentaries on Leviticus. As revelation is the approach of God to his people, so worship and sacrifice are the approach of Israel to God. Sacrifice is one of the bonds of Israel and God. Whether by gifts without ritual and without presentation at the altar—e.g., half-shekel temple taxes paid to the priests; by offerings such as first fruits presented at the altar but then given to the priest; by slain offerings, partly burned on the altar and partly consumed by the priests and by the offerers, such as peace offerings; by most of the sin offerings and guilt offerings, partly burned on the altar and with the rest consumed by the priests; or, lastly, by the burnt offerings in which the altar retained everything, the Israelites according to their need and condition came near to their God. Yet their approach is not of their making, for they come to fulfil divinely revealed requirements. In this fulfilment there lies hidden the grace of humility and obedience. There are, however, two major principles which throw further light on the meaning of this sacrificial system. The altar is essentially the place of slaughter, and there the blood of slain sacrifices is made over to God. The blood is the life, and sacrifice is surrendered life, and so involves surrendered time, surrendered property, and surrendered self (laying on of hands). Thus it is laid down that in the blood is the life of the flesh (17:11), but this important and oft-quoted maxim should not hide the reference to the still more important and by no means often-quoted principle stated in this same context—namely, that God gives this shed blood upon the altar to make ATONEMENT. The divine evaluation of the devoted blood is the key to the understanding of Israel's approach to God through sacrificial worship. God chooses to provide and to regard such blood as the means and the method of Israel's atonement. The thought of 17:11 is paralleled in the law of the meal offering (6:14-18), and it is noteworthy that in both passages there is a sudden emergence of the divine first person—no doubt, by way of urgent emphasis. *See further* WORSHIP IN THE OT.

b. The priesthood. Israel's saving law provided for the ministry of a permanent and hereditary priesthood. Again there is no need to recapitulate the ceremonies of washing, vesting, anointing, of ordination sacrifices which Lev. 8-10 describes in such detail. The priest is the permanent religious official in ancient Israel and fulfils both teaching and sacrificial functions. In Leviticus the teaching role is apparently much diminished, but it is still manifest in such features as the URIM AND THUMMIM, in the diagnosis of leprosy, in the directions concerning the clean and the unclean, in the moral and ethical portions of the book, and in the longer sermonic portions already noted. The priest is a revelatory organ, but he tended to neglect his teaching functions and to concentrate more on his sacrificial duties and function, and it is these which are more obvious in Leviticus. There are various points in the sacred law which are worthy of note. It has been pointed out that the priests offered a threefold sacrifice upon ordination. There was first the sin offering, which was a sign of the forgiveness of sins; then the whole burnt offering declared the totality of his consecration, and the ram of ordination, an elaborated peace offering, expressed the fellowship of God and Israel in the mediating priesthood. It is the blood of this ram which is put on the tip of Aaron's right ear, upon his right thumb, and upon the great toe of his right foot, and likewise upon Aaron's sons. Thus was consecrated their obedience, their office and possessions, and their way of life. "To fill the hand" is the Hebrew way of saying "to appoint to the priesthood," and the blood upon the hand must be thus interpreted.

It is remarkable that following upon Aaron's consecration and his first ministry for his people, there is in the legislative narrative of ch. 10 the story of the first priestly transgression and the punishment that accrued. It is not clear wherein lay the fault of Nadab and Abihu, the sons of Aaron, and commentators seek to relate the story to various parts of the ordination or to the regulation concerning intoxicants which appears in the same context (10:8-9). The detailed connection of the story may not be certain, though it is, of course, in some way connected with priestly access to God; but the *Heilsgesetz* implication of the story is clear. The priestly fault so soon after the ordination must be seen in the light of similar stories. There is the Garden, but then the sin in the Garden; there is the release of Noah and all his family from the ark and the accompanying sacrifice, and then comes the story of his drunkenness. Similarly, at Sinai there is first the theophany and the covenant, but then the golden calf. So priestly trespass emerges immediately upon priestly ordination. Even priests can go wrong, and they can go wrong in the very aftermath of ordination. The story, then, is designed to warn and thus to save the ministry in Israel, and no doubt rests upon some historical reminiscence, even if from another context.

c. The laws of purification. These chapters are, of course, very unattractive and in part decidedly repulsive. They are mainly of interest to the anthropologist and sociologist. Beneath these laws may be hidden early hygiene, ancient superstitions, customs now meaningless, simple prejudices, or perhaps deliberate revulsion from what were once known as the practices of the peoples in the service of their gods. However meaningless and irrelevant, these laws meant for the Israelite the fulfilment of a divinely appointed way of life. By the observance of these laws of purification Israel felt that it was dedicating its life to God. The laws of purification are, then, the dedication of Israel's national life. This is their redemptive purpose within the revelation.

d. The Day of Atonement. In Lev. 16 is the order of service for the annual service of atonement. Attempts at analysis have been abundant, but they cannot be said to have been successful. Attempts have been made to distinguish between old and newer rituals, between ritual for the place as distinct from that for the atonement of Israel. No doubt, various ideas are enshrined in different parts of the ritual, and they may have been drawn from different sources; but the ceremony is now presented as a whole, even if supplementary observations may be detected in places. The history of the development of the ritual is probably, for the time being, not possible.

First, there are various minor ideas which must be noted. Aaron, here representative of all succeeding high priests, must wash and be attired in his linen garments, coat, breeches, girdle, turban. At the conclusion of the ceremonies, he must doff these humble linen garments, wash, and resume his clothing—the beautiful and holy garments of his office: breastpiece, ephod, robe, checker coat, turban, and girdle (Exod. 28), robes which by their colors, decorations, and ornaments, including diadem, suggest royal status and function. Again, in the matter of the sacrifices of the Day, a comparison of Lev. 16:11-24 with the part played by Ezekiel's prince in the provision of sacrifices (cf. Ezek. 45:17-18, 21-22) will show a great similarity in the sacrifices and their purposes. Since both are really the ritual of New Year's Day, the comparison is instructive, for it bears again on the royal role of the high priest.

The ideas, then, which the Day represents are those of affliction (cf. Lev. 16:29, 31, and linen garments), purity, propitiation, substitution and transference of guilt, and death as the due reward for sin. But the all-embracing idea is that of performed intercession. It is the redeeming, sanctifying, of sanctuary with its system of sacrifice, of the priesthood of Aaron and of the people of Israel, that is the concern of the Day. The Day seeks to achieve the spiritual health and wholeness, the blessedness of all the community in all its parts for the succeeding year. It is the equivalent, if not indeed the same thing, as the שוב שבות restoration of fortunes of the pre-exilic psalms (Pss. 14:7; 53:6; 85:1; cf. Hos. 6:11; Amos 9:14). The intercession is in words (Lev. 16:21), and in the deeds of sacrifices and other activities of the Day.

The Day of Atonement became the supreme Jewish festival. Yet apparently there is no evidence for its observance in pre-exilic days, or, indeed, in Ezekiel or in Nehemiah. This has led to such conceptions as the idea of the growth of sin in exilic days and so on. Yet it is hardly possible that such a ritual burst newborn on Judaism like Jordan does at its source. There must be a prehistory to the Day. The obvious solution is, of course, that the Day was in some way connected with a possible New Year Festival or its Israelite equivalent in pre-exilic days, and that its ritual conceals in some ways pre-exilic royal ritual. Certainly references to mercy seat and testimony (Lev. 16:13) presuppose the holy of holies of the first, and not the second, temple. Similarly the ritual of AZAZEL must be very ancient.

e. The Code of Holiness. In the Code of Holiness (chs. 17–26) there are all the usual features of a ceremonial and moral law code and the theological ideas appropriate thereto. But the perusal of these chapters soon reveals a more sermonic style and the appearance in 17:10 of the divine first person. Apart from such blocks of laws as 18:7-23 (cf. 19:19*b*-25*a;* 20:9-21; 22:17-30; 23:12-21), the appearance of the divine first person, at the beginning, or at the end, or interspersed through the laws, is constant from Lev. 17:10 onward and is very prominent in the final exhortation in ch. 26. The final chapter of Leviticus, 27, which does not belong to H, shows no occurrence of this divine first person. These first-person sentences testify to the theocentric art of the Levitical preacher, and are reminiscent of Ezekiel and of Isa. 40–55. There are the expressions: "I am Yahweh," "I am Yahweh your (their) God" (cf. 18:2, 4, 30; 19:3, 10, 25, 31, 34; etc.), with the occasional addition of "who brought you out of the land of Egypt" (19:36; 25:38; 26:13) or some other clause of praise (cf. 20:8, 24; 21:8, 15, 23; 22:9, 16, 32). This divine utterance in the first person is an important form of revelation in both Testaments. God describes himself with a number of varying predicates. The utterance may thus be described as the self-predication of God. Especially in the phrase: "I, Yahweh, your God, am holy" (19:2; 20:26) is the self-predication almost "tautological," for holiness here has a theistic, rather than an exclusively moral, connotation. Holiness expresses thus the "godness" or deity of God, so that the sense is virtually: "I, Yahweh, your God, am God." Perhaps the best description of this quintessence of the theocentric art is W. Vischer's phrase by which he describes these divine-first-person sentences as *Autokerygma*—God's heralding of himself. In such sentences it is not really a question of *Heilsgeschichte* or *Heilsgesetz,* but *Heilspredigt,* "sacred and saving preaching," which, as ch. 19 shows, touches all departments of Israel's life. Here is the hallmark of revelation, and in the simple sentence: "I am Yahweh your God," the final, most complete, and sovereign sentence of all scripture, without exception. It is, in fact, the apotheosis of *Heilsgeschichte* and of scripture.

The Code of Holiness, however, does not close without bearing witness to that most characteristic feature of Israel's faith (cf. Exod. 33:16), which is given at Lev. 26:11-12: "I will make my abode among you . . . . And I will walk among you, and will be your God, and you shall be my people." Here the tabernacling presence and the guiding presence and the covenant faith are combined in an exceptionally rich autokerygmatic context.

4. Leviticus and the Scriptures. Wheeler Robinson's dictum that Leviticus and the Psalter should be studied side by side has long been a commonplace. He thought of them side by side in the post-exilic period, but equally it is true that many of the psalms and much of the ritual were side by side in the pre-exilic period also. It is studying Leviticus and Psalms that corrects the impression of silence that is gained from Leviticus. It is true that the book is a series of speeches, and there is much sermonic material, but the performance of the ritual appears to be silent. Thus the movement, vitality, and sound of the Psalter, not to mention such a passage as Ecclus. 50:5-21, provide the corrective. By such means Leviticus takes its place not merely among the codes of law but also among the manuals of worship in the OT.

Leviticus describes the performance of much ritual action, and the exposition that accompanies the ritual is missing. Deut. 26 offers an interesting illustration of the faith and the ritual. Similarly the promise made to Abraham (Gen. 15:18) is embodied and guaranteed in a series of ritual actions (vss. 9-19). Ritual is thus expressive of religion, just as morality often is the fruit of religion. Revelation and all the divine side of religion find an expressive outlet in ritual, and gospel is declared through sacrament. On the other hand, too, ritual aims at hallowing life through sacred ceremony. Ritual is thus the accompaniment of the revealed word and, as informed by a moral and numinous purpose, has its due place in the religious life; and this is the justification for Leviticus in the OT, even though the ritual dominates in the book.

It is also necessary to read Leviticus side by side with certain passages from the NT, notably the Letter to the Hebrews (*see* HEBREWS, LETTER TO THE). Jesus found in Lev. 19:18 the source for the second part of his summary of the law: "You shall love your neighbor as yourself" (Matt. 5:43; 19:19; 22:39; Mark 12:31; Luke 10:27; Rom. 13:9; Gal. 5:14). There are also the leprosy passages (Matt. 8:2-4; cf. Lev. 14).

The tabernacle is the shadow of the templehood of Christ and of the Christian believer (cf. II Cor. 6:16); the sacrificial system the pointer to the one atoning sacrifice of Jesus Christ; the Day of Atonement the parallel to Christ's cross; and the high priest the type of the apostle and high priest of the Christian profession (Heb. 3:1; 8–9 in general). There are other allusions too, such as Matt. 5:18; 19:17; 27:51; Rev. 4:5, which presuppose Leviticus.

On the face of it, the case against considering Leviticus as part of scripture is very strong. But in favor of it there is a case even stronger. There is first the testimony of the book to Jesus Christ; then there is its autokerygmatic emphasis. Finally, by his choice of Lev. 19:18 Jesus canonized Leviticus once for all.

Bibliography. A. R. S. Kennedy, *Leviticus and Numbers* (n.d.); A. T. Chapman and A. W. Streane, *The Book of Leviticus* (1914); R. Dussaud, *Les origines cananéenes du sacrifice israélite* (1921); G. B. Gray, *Sacrifice in the OT* (1925); A. Wendel, *Das Opfer in der altisraelitischen Religion* (1927); E. Kalt, *Genesis, Exodus und Leviticus* (1948), pp. 399-489; G. Contenau, *La civilisation phénicienne* (2nd ed., 1949); H. Cazelles, "Le Lévitique," *La Sainte Bible*, vol. I (1951); W. Kornfeld, *Studien zum Heiligkeitsgesetz* (1952), includes an extensive and up-to-date Bibliography; H. Schneider, *Leviticus* (1952); N. Micklem, Introduction, Exegesis, and Exposition of Leviticus, *IB*, II (1953), 3-134; G. von Rad, "Form-Criticism of the Holiness Code," *Studies in Deuteronomy* (1953), pp. 25-36.

G. HENTON DAVIES

LIA lī'ə. Douay Version form of LEAH.

LIBATION. *See* SACRIFICE AND OFFERINGS §§ A2b*i-ii*.

LIBER DE INFANTIA lē'bər dā ĭn făn'tĭ ə. Alternate name of the Gospel of Pseudo-Matthew. *See* PSEUDO-MATTHEW, GOSPEL OF.

LIBERTINES. *See* FREEDMEN.

LIBERTY [דרור, חפשה; ἐλευθερία; Lat. *libertas*]. Primarily, the state of those who are not slaves; and secondarily, though more fundamentally, the quality of personal and social life, here and hereafter, which is the given possession of those whom Christ has set free from human bondage.

1. In the OT. Liberty in the OT is almost exclusively the condition of those free from slavery, or of those exempt from forced labor, etc. It is significant that the more humane treatment of slaves by the Hebrews was a direct consequence of their religion, and that in Isa. 61:1 "liberty" is a metaphor of what God was about to effect in history in releasing his people from Babylon. Jesus took the metaphor to its final stage when, preaching at Nazareth, he used it to indicate the deliverance wrought by his own coming (Luke 4:16-21).

2. In the NT. In contrast to the Stoic idea of liberty of self-sufficiency (the free man is always "master of himself," never the "slave of circumstance"), the NT conceived of liberty as man's relationship to God.

a. Negative conditions. Man, a fallen creature in a fallen world, is in bondage to sin. The bondage is universal ("All have sinned and fall short of the glory of God"; Rom. 3:23) and absolute ("I know that nothing good dwells within me, that is, in my flesh. I can will what is right, but I cannot do it"; 7:18). Man is in bondage to the law, whether he knows it as divine revelation, as the work of conscience, or as positive human law; for while law was intended to enable man to achieve a righteousness acceptable as a basis of community between man and God, it proves incapable—human nature being what it is—to free men from sin (7:7-20). This leaves man in bondage to death, for, apart from sharing in the eternal life of God, man, with the whole creation, is in "bondage to decay" (8:21).

b. The Liberator. What the law could not achieve because of human nature, God has done in a human nature. God's Son became man, assumed flesh, took the form of a slave, yet, in remaining sinless, "condemned sin in the flesh" (Rom. 8:3), and brought human nature to its divine destiny. For "God raised him up, having loosed the pangs of death, because it was not possible for him to be held by it" (Acts 2:24).

c. The liberated. Such an achievement is the proclamation of liberty to those captives of sin, law, and death who believe and trust in Christ. They are free from the bondage of sin—now because adequate grace is available for them (II Cor. 12:9), and in the end because they no longer need to justify themselves to God, since Christ is their justification (Rom. 3:20-22). They are free from bondage to law because their life is no longer a vain attempt to keep perfect obedience to ordinances, but an acceptance of the given guidance of the Spirit (Gal. 5:5, 18), of the life of Christ himself in the believer (2:20). They are freed from bondage to death, for "the wages of sin is death, but the free gift of God is eternal life in Christ Jesus the Lord" (Rom. 6:23).

But Christian liberty is not simply freedom *from,* not license to "do as you like"; rather, it is so complete a surrender to God as to be called "slavery" to God, to righteousness (Rom. 6:18, 22). Liberty begets its own pattern of gracious living: "You were called to freedom, brethren; only do not use your freedom as an opportunity for the flesh, but through love be servants of one another. For the whole law is fulfilled in one word, 'You shall love your neighbor as yourself' " (Gal. 5:13-14). Love may be called the "perfect law of liberty."

Transition to the life of liberty is made at baptism, where the believer is crucified with Christ and raised to new life in him (Rom. 6:3-4). He is no longer a slave to the flesh, no longer alien from God, no longer exempt from God's service; he has become a son, whose meat it is to do the Father's will, and who, as a son, will abide in the Father's house forever. The transition is made in time, but the end is in eternity, and what the full liberty of the sons of God is like passes our poor imagination. "Beloved, we are God's children now; it does not yet appear what we shall be." (I John 3:2.) J. Marsh

LIBNAH lĭb'nə [לבנה, white]. **1.** A camp of the Israelites in the wilderness (Num. 33:20-21). The site is unknown; perhaps the same as Laban (Deut. 1:1).

* **2.** An important town in the SHEPHELAH (Josh. 15:42), probably on the border between Judah and Philistia (cf. II Kings 8:22, where Libnah's revolt against Judah implies that the town was located on the edge of Judahite territory).

Eusebius equated Libnah with a town "Lob(a)na" in the district of Eleutheropolis. The only important tell which can be said to lie within this district and which at the same time is located near the Judeo-Philistine border is Tell es-Safi, on the W end of the Valley of Elah (*see* ELAH, VALLEY OF); it was the site of the Crusader fortress of Blanche-garde. The white cliffs of the region doubtless gave the tell both its Hebrew and its French name.

Excavations at Tell es-Safi have uncovered pottery, the dates of which range from pre-Israelite times to the period of the Seleucids; several of the jar handles were imprinted with Hebrew royal stamps. Sections of the city wall were also discovered; it is similar in style to the wall at Ashur, which was built during the reign of Sennacherib. Five fragments of an Assyrian stele provide another indication of Assyrian occupation at this period (cf. II Kings 19:8). The absence of significant signs of the Greek and Roman settlement of Lobna may be due to the fact that only a small portion of the tell was available for excavation.

The chief objection to the identification of Libnah with Tell es-Safi is that it places this town farther N than any of the others in the same province and requires that a provincial boundary be drawn through the middle of the Valley of Elah. Hence some have sought the location of Libnah in the more southerly Wadi Zeita. Here the favored site is Tell Bornat.

Libnah first appears in the OT as one of the Palestinian cities captured by Joshua (Josh. 10:29-39; 12:15). However, these passages are of doubtful historical value; there is no indication in the Amarna Letters that Libnah was a Canaanite royal city.

Libnah seems to have served the S kingdom as a fortified border station, and appears to have been under Judah's control during most of its history. We do read of a revolt against Jehoram, when this king was trying unsuccessfully to subdue the rebellious Edomites (II Kings 8:22); but by the time of Hezekiah, Judah seems to have regained control. Libnah was one of the two major forts on Judah's W border to which Sennacherib laid siege (19:8). The mother of Jehoahaz was an inhabitant of this city (II Kings 23:31; Jer. 52:1).

The name Libnah is found in the Judahite province list (Josh. 15:42), which may come from either the ninth or the seventh century B.C., as well as in the list of LEVITICAL CITIES (21:13). Perhaps the *Rbwn* which appears in the list of towns which the Egyptian Sheshonk I (biblical Shishak; I Kings 14:25-26) claimed to have taken is to be interpreted as Libnah.

Bibliography. F. J. Bliss and R. A. S. Macalister, *Excavations in Palestine, 1898-1900* (1902), pp. 28-43. W. F. Albright, "Historical Geography of Palestine," *AASOR,* II-III (1921-22), 12-17; but contrast his "Researches of the School in Western Judaea," *BASOR,* 15 (Oct., 1924), 9. C. Watzinger, *Denkmäler Palästinas,* II (1935), 3. F. M. Cross, Jr., and G. E. Wright, "The Boundary and Province Lists of Judah," *JBL,* LXXV (1956), 217-18. R. W. Corney

LIBNI lĭb'nī [לבני, belonging to Libna(?), *or* white(?)]; **LIBNITES** —nīts. **1.** A family of Levite priests of the town LIBNA; one of four or five families of Levite priests located around HEBRON sometime between Deborah and David (Num. 26:58*a,* an ancient genealogy, possibly redacted by addition of "Mahlites" and rearrangement); possibly to be connected with 2 *below.*

2. In P and Chronicles, the eldest son of Gershon, and eponym of the Libnites, one of the two divisions of Levites descended from Gershon (Exod. 6:17; Num. 3:18, 21; I Chr. 6:17, 20).

3. A name in a list of Levites descended from Merari (I Chr. 6:29).

Bibliography. K. Möhlenbrink, "Die levitischen Überlieferungen des ATs," *ZAW,* LII (1934), 191-97.

T. M. Mauch

LIBYA lĭb'ĭ ə, lĭb'yə; **LIBYANS** lĭb'ĭ ənz. A large territory in North Africa, bordered by Egypt and the Sudan on the E, by Tunisia and Algeria on the W, and by French Equatorial and West Africa on the S. The name had a wider and less specific application throughout most of biblical and classical antiquity.

1. The name. Three distinct Hebrew words are rendered by "Libya" or "Libyans" in the versions. The following equations illustrate the existing variety:

a) כוב, "Libya" (Ezek. 30:5; KJV "Chub"; RSV mg. "Cub")=LXX Λιβυες(?).

b) לובים (*lûbhîm*), "Libyans" (II Chr. 12:3; 16:8; Dan. 11:43; Nah. 3:9; KJV alternately "Lubims")= LXX Λιβυες.

c) KJV פוט (*pût*), "Libya," "Libyans" (RSV "PUT"; KJV alternately "Put"; "Phut")=LXX φουτ, φουδ, or Λιβυες.

d) Λιβύη, "Libya" (Acts 2:10).

Further, it is possible that להבים (*see* LEHABIM) is also a variant of the ethnic term לובים, or at least refers to the same or a neighboring area and its inhabitants. Hebrew *lûbhîm* and Greek Λιβυες are both adaptations of the native name found in Egyptian sources as *Rbw* (*Lbw*).

2. Early history. For our knowledge of Libyan history before the classical period we are dependent almost entirely on Egyptian sources. The most ancient inhabitants of Libya about whom we know anything are the Tehenu, mentioned in texts of the Old Kingdom (third millennium B.C.). It is now thought that the Tehenu were not Libyans in an ethnic sense but rather an isolated group of people originally closely related to the Egyptians themselves. From the end of the Old Kingdom there is evidence of a steady invasion of Egypt from the SW by a light-skinned, blond, blue-eyed people identified by the Egyptians as the Temehu. During the first half of the second millennium the name Temehu became synonymous with the Libyans in general; and it is not until the New Kingdom that two groups, the Meshwesh and the Lebu, stand out in their conflicts with Egypt, notably under the reigns of Thut-mose III, Sethi I, and Ramses III. That Egypt was not able to subdue completely these tribes, which constantly threatened her W border, is evidenced by the fact that *ca.* 950 B.C. the Libyan prince Shishak (Shoshenq) mounted the royal throne of Egypt as pharaoh and ushered in the Twenty-second, or Libyan, Dynasty.

3. The Libyan Dynasty. Shishak, the founder of the Libyan Dynasty, is best known from OT sources as a supporter of Jeroboam I. His rise to power in Egypt marked the end of the weak, quasi-priestly rule of his predecessor, Psusennes II, last of the Tanite House (Twenty-first Dynasty). He adopted instead a policy of aggression, which resulted in his invasion of Palestine in an attempt to restore Egyptian dominion over this area. A brief account of this campaign is contained in I Kings 14:25-26, during the fifth year of Rehoboam. From the biblical narrative and from Egyptian sources, such as the list at Karnak of towns and cities taken by Shishak in this campaign, it is clear that the Egyptian ruler did not stay his forces at the confines of Judah but pushed well on into Israel. This effort, though successful, brought Egypt little more than plunder, for she was not able to establish any kind of permanent hold over the ravaged area. The dynasty ruled from the Delta city of Bubastis (*see* PIBESETH) for approximately two hundred years (until *ca.* 730 B.C.) and included the rules of Shishak I-IV, Osorkon I-II, Takelot I-II, and Pemou. The reconstruction of events which brought an end to this long dynasty is very complicated, but it appears that it was followed immediately in Bubastis by the Twenty-third Dynasty, which in turn was contemporary with the ascendant Tefnakht, precursor of the Twenty-fourth Dynasty at Saïs. This, too, was short-lived, falling, after the brief reign of Bocchoris, to the triumphant Ethiopic (Twenty-fifth) Dynasty under Shabaka *ca.* 715 B.C. *See* CUSH.

Bibliography. J. H. Breasted, *Ancient Records of Egypt,* IV (1906), 339-444; W. Hölscher, *Libyer und Ägypter,* Ägyptologische Forschungen, no. 4 (1955). T. O. LAMBDIN

LICE. For etymology and occurrences, *see* GNAT; FAUNA § E1. For bibliography, *see* ANT.

LICENTIOUSNESS [ἀσέλγεια]. Debauchery; sensual or sexual excesses. Licentiousness characterizes Gentiles (Eph. 4:17-19) and heretics (Jude 4; II Pet. 2:2, 18). Sexual excess is especially referred to in Paul's use of the word (Rom. 13:13; II Cor. 12:21; Gal. 5:19). B. H. THROCKMORTON, JR.

LIDEBIR lĭd'ə bĭr [לדבר]. RSV mg. translation in Josh. 13:26, where the text has DEBIR (3). The ל may be a dittograph of final consonant of the preceding word, גבול. It may also correspond to LODEBAR, a place in Gilead. C. T. FRITSCH

LIE. *See* LYING.

LIEUTENANT. *See* SATRAP.

LIFE. Notwithstanding the great differences between the OT and NT views of life, the biblical religion represents a common concept of life which differs conspicuously from all nonbiblical views. Failure to notice this fact has often misled exegetes into reading wrong features into the biblical record.

Over against the naturalistic-monistic view, which interprets all the manifestations of man's life as rooted in physiology, but also over against the dualistic separation of physical and mental life, the Bible teaches the oneness of man's life yet differentiates its functions according to the goals served. This fact implies also that while life has a common origin in all human beings, the differentiation into nations, sexes, and individuals adds an essential feature to it. Nobody is simply a human being. The biblical view is therefore above and beyond both individualism and collectivism. While Israel, like other nations, is regarded as a collective agent, its true life depends on the spontaneous and responsible participation of its individual members.

The idealistic view, found both in ancient Greece and in our age, according to which the value of life depends on what an individual or a group makes of its faculties, is rejected in favor of the belief that life's meaning depends primarily on the purpose God has with it. There is no room left for a fatalistic interpretation, according to which man is the passive organ of Life, or the slave of deities, so that at the best he can try to adjust himself to his destiny. Rather, the Bible emphasizes that he is free to make of his life what he pleases.

1. The OT view
2. The intertestamental literature
3. The NT view in general
4. John's view

5. Paul's view
Bibliography

1. The OT view. "Life" in the OT designates the sum total of spontaneous activities and experiences of an individual or group capable of preserving its identity in the flux of changing conditions. This power of identity, the *nephesh* (wrongly translated "soul"), is lost in death, and what remains of the organism disintegrates. The living organism is designated as *basar* ("flesh"); this term, however, does not indicate a material which is being animated, but rather the individual being in its earthly condition (e.g., Deut. 5:26; Ps. 56:4; Isa. 31:3). The spontaneity of life is described as "ghost" or "spirit" (*ruaḥ*), and the latter is said to be "given up" in death (e.g., Gen. 25:8, 17; 35:29; 49:33; Job 3:11; 10:18; 11:20; etc.; cf. Matt. 27:50; John 19:30). In other places, it is the *nephesh* which is breathed out (Job 11:20; Jer. 15:9), or poured out (Isa. 53:12). In other words, "life" designates the concrete existence of a being; it is not an energy operating in, or upon, a body. *Nephesh* indicates that each life is an articulate individual urge, not just the individuation of a species.

However, individual existence is not self-contained. Life is described throughout the OT as co-existence with other individuals of the same kind. This co-existence implies co-operation and mutual dependence, yet not equality. Superior power and authority, on the one hand, and subjection, on the other, are essential features of human life. By co-ordinating the origin of life with the creation story, the OT reminds the reader of the fact that life would not be possible if we were not living in a universe which is so arranged that each individual finds food and shelter (Gen. 1:28-30; Pss. 104:27-28; 145;15; 147:8-9; cf. Luke 12:24).

Life is experienced as something that essentially transcends purely material existence and that therefore represents something "numinous" for the ancient Hebrews. This fact is most frequently described by differentiating between the Word of God, by means of which the things of this world were brought into existence, on the one hand, and the Spirit of God as the giver of life, on the other (e.g., Gen. 2:7; 6:17; 7:15, 22; Ps. 104:29). God is the "God of life" (Num. 14:28; Deut. 32:40; Judg. 8:19; Ruth 3:13; I Sam. 14:39; 19:6; Jer. 5:2; etc.) or the "living God" (e.g., Deut. 5:26; Josh. 3:10; I Sam. 17:26; II Kings 19:4; cf. Matt. 26:63; Acts 14:15; Rom. 9:26; Rev. 7:2). His very nature is life, and thus he is able to impart it to the creatures. For this reason, life is basically the same in all that moves on earth (e.g., Job 12:10; Ps. 104:30; Isa. 42:5; cf. Eccl. 3:19; Ezek. 37:8-10; Acts 17:25). This does not mean, however, that with the gift of life creatures partake of the divine nature (Deut. 5:20; Ps. 56:4; Isa. 31:3; Jer. 25:31; etc.), but rather that by God's grace they are enabled to communicate with their Creator. Life is not regarded as an immanent creative principle in all that is, as in modern vitalism. Though man has no control or power over it, life is entirely, both in its origin and in its manifestations, in God's hands (e.g., I Sam. 2:6; Ps. 49:7, 9). Thus when God withholds his "breath" or "spirit," the creatures die (e.g., Job 4:9; 34:14; Ps. 104:29; cf. Deut. 5:23; Josh. 3:10; II Kings 19:4; Ps. 76:11-12; Isa. 37:17).

Accordingly, idols, with whom God has nothing in common, are "dead" (Pss. 113; 134; Isa. 44:9-20; Jer. 10:8-10, 14). In turn, the very fact that we are alive is to be considered a divine gift (e.g., Pss. 36:10; 42:8; 66:9; 139:13), which must be upheld by God (e.g., Job 33:4; Ps. 119:116; Isa. 38:16; Wisd. Sol. 3:1; 16:12). A similar idea is expressed by the images of the "tree of life" in paradise, over which God alone has control (Gen. 2:17; Prov. 3:18; 11:30; 13:12; cf. Rev. 2:7; 22:2, 14), and the "fountain of life" (Prov. 10:11; 13:14; 14:27), which has probably its parallels in the river which flows from the throne of God and the Lamb (Rev. 22:2) and the waters of life in paradise (Rev. 7:17; 21:6; 22:17). God was under no obligation to impart life to any creature. For the same reason the procreative ability is not to be regarded as a matter of course; rather, it is a divine blessing (e.g., Gen. 1:22, 28). Consequently, individual features and special abilities do not originate in heredity or physiological particularities, but rather are rooted in the divine Spirit's creativity (e.g., II Chr. 15:1; 20:14; Ezek. 2:2; 3:24; 11:5).

The individual's life is God's property. Hence the individual has no right to destroy his own life or wantonly to kill other life (Exod. 20:13; Deut. 5:17; cf. Gen. 4:10, 20-24). Human sacrifices are not demanded by God (Gen. 22). The death penalty, which has been fixed by God for certain crimes—e.g., adultery (Lev. 20:10; Deut. 22:22)—is therefore an indication of the degree to which God abhors them, and the wholesale destruction of sinful mankind by the Flood (Gen. 7:21-23) was a sign of its complete corruption. Since life is God's property, blood, as the "vehicle" of life, must be abstained from (Gen. 9:4; Lev. 3:17; 17:10; Deut. 12:23; etc.). The value of life can be seen in God's care for the preservation of the animal realm—e.g., when he commanded Noah to take a pair of each species into the ark (Gen. 7:2-3), or in his provision of food for all (e.g., Ps. 145:15). It is not surprising, therefore, that in the OT life is valued as the supreme earthly good, surpassed only by God's grace or mercy (e.g., Ps. 63:3).

This does not mean, however, that life is a gift to be enjoyed only. The seat of life is the heart (לב, לבב), and thus life is of a volitional and appetitive character (e.g., Exod. 34:21; Ps. 51:12), which manifests itself in the affections and emotions rather than in reflection. Life consists in willing and doing things (e.g., Ps. 90:10), or hating and fighting off dangers and evils. Having received his life from God, however, man is not free in the choice of his goals and actions. Life is always desire for something not yet appropriated; yet this self-transcendence, rightly understood, points ultimately to the fact that man is destined to live for God (e.g., Isa. 38:10-20). The legislation on Mount Sinai was not interpreted as a tyrannical act of Yahweh, but rather as a means by which God made the Israelites aware of their final destination as human beings. The true nurture of life consists in doing God's will (e.g., Lev. 18:5; Prov. 15:27) or feeding on God's word (e.g., Deut. 32:47; Ezek. 3:18; 14:13 ff; 18:1 ff; 33:1 ff; cf. Deut. 8:3). Apart from it, no good life may be expected (e.g., Ps. 16:11; cf. Prov. 2:19; 5:6; Ecclus. 4:12). Thus the divine gift of life and human responsibility are correlative terms in the OT.

The outright positive evaluation of life in the OT

seems at first sight strange, since the ancient Hebrews not only took a very sober and realistic view of life but also considered the hardships and dangers of it, as well as pain and mortality, the result of God's curse pronounced over a sinful mankind (Gen. 3:14-19). The shortness and frailty of human life are often bewailed (e.g., Pss. 89:47; 103:15-16; cf. 90:10). Life is like a grain of sand (Ecclus. 18:10), a dream (Job 20:8), a shadow (I Chr. 29:15; Job 8:9; 14:2; Pss. 39:6; 102:11; 109:23; 144:4; Eccl. 6:12; 8:13; Wisd. Sol. 2:5), a cloud (Job 7:9), a fleeting breath (Job 7:7), a mist (Job 7:16; cf. Jas. 4:14), a grass (Pss. 102:11; 103:15; Isa. 40:6-7; Ecclus. 14:18; cf. I Pet. 1:24), or a flower (Job 14:2; Ps. 103:15; Isa. 40:6; cf. Job 9:25-26; Jas. 1:10). Taken from the dust (Gen. 2:7), man must return to it (Gen. 3:19; Ps. 103:14). Thus an early death is believed to be a special penalty of sin (Job 8:13; 15:32; 22:16; Pss. 9:18; 31:18; 37:35-36; 55:23; Prov. 10:27; 22:23; Ecclus. 19:3; 40:8-10; Jer. 2:19; etc.). Some scholars deny that in Gen. 3 death is interpreted in this way. The truth is that man, like all the other earthly creatures, is described as having his life from God. Thus he possesses no natural, innate immortality. But being able to do the will of God, he had the opportunity to acquire unending life. However, with the transgression of God's commandment this possibility was destroyed, and death became the inescapable fate of man.

But the curse has not deprived life completely of its value. To those who keep God's commandments, long life and happiness are promised (Gen. 15:15; Exod. 20:12; Lev. 18:5; Deut. 5:15-16; 16:20; 30:19; Judg. 8:32; Ps. 91:16; cf. Gen. 25:7 ff; 35:28 ff; Ps. 34:12; etc.) so that "life" and "happiness" have become synonymous. Even under the curse, life is blessing (e.g., Deut. 30:16-18). While man is tripped all the time by life (Job 18:10; Jer. 5:26), God is man's refuge from danger (e.g., Deut. 33:27; Pss. 14:6; 46:1). No wonder that people wish to live until life is exhausted (e.g., Gen. 25:8; 35:29; Job 42:17). A good old age is the supreme good (Prov. 3:16), and thus people wish one another to live (e.g., Dan. 2:4; 3:9; etc.)—i.e., to enjoy a long and happy life. Man is willing to sacrifice everything for his life (Job 2:4). In turn, death, which is the result of old age, is accepted without sentimentality as the end willed by God (e.g., II Sam. 14:14; Ps. 89:48).

The idea of an afterlife was originally unknown in ancient Israel. People were interested only in the continuation of the nation (Isa. 56:3, 5) and/or the family (Ps. 37:27-28; note especially vs. 28). The later acceptance of the idea of Sheol, in which the individual *nephesh* survives (e.g., Job 3:12-19), was not intended to increase the value of life, as did the Orphic concept of afterlife; on the contrary. Originally it is often emphasized that the dead are cut off from the cultic community (Pss. 88:11-12; 115:17; cf. Pss. 6:5; 30:9; Isa. 38:10-11, 18; Ecclus. 17:27). The only passage in which resurrection is clearly stated in the OT is in Dan. 12:2. Other passages, such as Job 14:13; 19:25-27; Pss. 16:10; 49:15, which have been interpreted as speaking of individual resurrection, probably use "Sheol" as a metaphor for the affliction in which the individual finds himself, and the return from Sheol means deliverance from the present ills. Isa. 25:6-8; Ezek. 37 do not speak of individuals, but rather of the recovery of Israel as a nation (see also Isa. 26:19).

When in the sixth century B.C. the idea of man's responsibility and of the divine curse were coupled with that of personal life, the outcome was a differentiation between true life and actual life. Only life in obedience to God's law deserves to be called life (see particularly Ezek. 3:18; 14:13 ff; 18:1 ff; 20:1 ff, 11; 33:1 ff; cf. Deut. 30:15; Ecclus. 15:17). Such life will be rewarded by God. He will be with the righteous ones and defend them against all evils (e.g., Ps. 73:23; Jer. 21:5). Thus the life of obedience carries with it full satisfaction (Deut. 30:15, 20; Ps. 119:144; cf. Ps. 39:12; Ezek. 33:18-19; Amos 5:4), and sinners are admonished to repent in order to "live" (Ezek. 33:11; cf. Jer. 38:20; Ezek. 3:18; 18:4, 21; 20:11; Hab. 2:4), whereas the wicked ones will experience misery and death (e.g., Ps. 49:10).

2. Intertestamental literature. This literature, in particular the wisdom literature, shows signs, however, of recognition that this view in which the experiences of the collective life of the chosen people had been transferred to the individual did not square with the facts. While earthly life is still highly evaluated (e.g., Ecclus. 31:20; Tob. 8:17; 12:9-10; Bar. 3:14), the success of the wicked is an undeniable fact (Ps. 73:4-5; cf. Job 21:7; Pss. 10:13; 17:14-15; etc.). But wisdom is the light (Wisd. Sol. 7:25) by which the individual learns to combine obedience to God's law with a maximum of happiness. Thus wisdom (Prov. 4:10; 8:35; 9:6) or the successive experience of life (Eccl. 11:7-8), rather than Yahweh, is considered the source of true life and of happiness (Job 5:26; Ps. 91:16; Prov. 3:2, 16, 22; 4:10, 22; 8:35; 9:11; 10:27; etc.). Though the misery of life (Job 7:1; Ecclus. 40:1-4) and its futility (Eccl. 1:2, 17; 2:11; etc.) are strongly emphasized, life is sweet (Eccl. 9:4-6; 11:7), because the good man has the key to felicity.

In the apocalyptic literature, it is particularly by means of the idea of the resurrection and the Final Judgment that the success of the wicked and the misery of the righteous are shown to be provisional only. Thereby the life of the righteous one is rendered meaningful and the desire for a moral order is satisfied. The righteous ones will eventually be compensated for their present sufferings, whereas the evildoers will then receive their due (e.g., Dan. 12:2). But this apocalypticism lacked convincing power. Measured by the actual conditions, it looked like wishful thinking. Large sections of Judaism, and particularly the Sadducees, refused to hold such beliefs.

3. The NT view in general. The term "life" is found frequently in Paul's letters and the Johannine literature, including Revelation, but only occasionally in the other NT books. In the English Bible the picture is affected by the fact that not only ζωή and βίος, but also ψυχή, which corresponds to the Hebrew *nephesh,* has been rendered "life." Basically the NT view of life agrees with that of the OT. God is the living God (Matt. 16:16; 26:63; John 6:68-69; Acts 14:15; Rom. 9:26; etc.), who has life in himself (John 5:26; cf. Rev. 4:9-10; 10:6; 15:7) or immortality (I Tim. 6:16). God is Lord of life and death (e.g., Luke 12:20; II Cor. 1:9; Jas. 4:15; cf. Matt. 10:28 and parallels). Since human life is the life of flesh and blood—i.e., of the individual in its totality and concreteness (e.g., Matt. 16:17; I Cor. 15:50; Eph. 6:12)—βίος and ζωή are not to be differentiated as physical and spiritual life, but rather βίος designates the conduct of life (e.g., Luke 8:14; II Tim. 2:4; I John 2:16) and ζωή the human existence. In Mark 5:23; John 4:50, e.g., ζωή connotes "health."

However, the NT differs from the OT in the fact that Jesus has brought the true life to light (II Tim. 1:10). The terms "life" and "to live," used without further qualification, designate frequently the true life rather than the actual one (e.g., Matt. 7:14; 18:8-9; Mark 9:43, 45; Luke 10:28; Rom. 1:17; 8:13; I Thess. 5:10; Heb. 12:9; I Pet. 3:7, 10; II Pet. 1:3; etc.). This usage indicates that the "natural" life is no longer considered as being merely less perfect than the true life, as is the case in the OT, but rather as the perversion of the divine gift. The responsibility for this condition rests, in the first place, with the individual, who is free to seek his own life (e.g., Matt. 10:39); but, like Judaism (e.g., Wisd. Sol. 1:13; 2:24), the NT points out also that the possibility of sin was caused by the ancestor of the race (Rom. 5:12). It is on account of the Fall and our sins that death reigns in the world (Rom. 5:12-21). Thus unlike the Hellenistic mystery religion, the NT does not consider mortality the worst of evils, but rather sin. Also in contrast to Hellenistic individualism and Judaism, both of which believe in the good man's ability to render his life meaningful, the NT proclaims that only by a divine act of redemption embracing the whole human race can true life in the individual be set free. This is done by Jesus, who gave his life for the forgiveness of mankind's sin (e.g., Matt. 20:28; Mark 10:45; Rom. 5:6-7; Gal. 3:13; Eph. 5:2; Phil. 2:8; I Pet. 2:24; etc.). Thereby he brought to light a new feature of life. Life is not only mutual dependence and co-existence, but is also destined to be lived for mutual help. In living this life of love to the very limit by giving himself unto death, Jesus did not simply comply with a moral commandment given to him. Since he had this life in himself (John 5:20)—i.e., since it was his very nature—he was thereby able effectively to transform the life of mankind.

Through Jesus' redemptive life, the perverted life of people can be renewed and regenerated (e.g., John 3:3-8; I Pet. 1:3). This change is not merely one of conduct but of status. While the unregenerate man is "dead" (Luke 15:24, 32; Rev. 3:1; cf. Matt. 8:22), a follower of Christ has passed from death into life (John 5:24; cf. Eph. 2:1; Col. 2:13; I John 3:14). Thus the new life is not, as in Judaism, merely a condition to be hoped for, but rather a present experience (Matt. 18:20; 28:20; John 5:24; Rom. 6:4, 11; 8:6; Col. 3:3; I John 3:14; etc.). It is not acquired by adding a new quality or energy to our natural life. Rather, by the work of Christ man is freed from the inhibitions which had made it impossible for him unrestrictedly to practice love. Thus the true life is still man's concrete daily life, but he is no longer restlessly seeking to find his satisfaction therein, but rather he rests in God or Christ (e.g., Matt. 11:29), or "dwells in his Father's house" (e.g., Luke 15:31; John 14:1-15). That is to say, it is his privilege to use all God's resources and opportunities for the implementation of his new birth.

Just as with the "natural" life, this new or true life is not the result of man's efforts, but altogether God's gracious gift (John 6:63; Acts 17:25; Rom. 4:17; 6:23; I Cor. 15:45; I Pet. 3:7; Jude 21; cf. I John 5:12). It can therefore also be called the inheritance of God's children (e.g., Matt. 19:20; Mark 10:17; Luke 10:25; Tit. 3:7; I Pet. 3:7) or the kingdom—i.e., the domain into which the elect enter (e.g., Matt. 18:8-9; 19:17; Mark 9:43 ff; cf. John 3:5). In Christ this gift of true life is offered to the whole of mankind, but it is not distributed mechanically or indiscriminately. In order to receive it, people must be worthy of it (e.g., Matt. 25:46; Mark 10:17 and parallels; 10:30 and parallels; John 5:29; 12:25; Rom. 2:7; 6:22-23; Gal. 6:8; cf. Matt. 7:13-14; Luke 10:28). A person is worthy when he believes in Jesus—i.e., when he no longer considers his own activities as the source of true life, but rather hopes to receive the latter as a result of God's grace. A believer does not only look at Jesus' life as the highest type of life, but also is eager to follow him in order to be transformed into the likeness of his life (e.g., Matt. 10:25; John 5:39-40; I Tim. 1:16). Practically, this means both losing oneself—i.e., renouncing those goals of life which enhance only our individual or collective position in this world (e.g., Matt. 10:39; Luke 10:29; Rom. 6:2; II Cor. 5:15)—and positively serving God in love (Mark 10:17 ff; Luke 10:25 ff; cf. Matt. 25:46; Rom. 2:7; 14:7-8; II Cor. 5:15; Gal. 2:19; cf. Gal. 3:7; II Tim. 3:12; Tit. 2:12; I Pet. 2:24).

The new life is still lived in this body and thus requires food and care (e.g., Matt. 4:4 and parallels; Luke 12:15; I Cor. 9:14). But the sustenance of the body does not suffice to keep the new life alive. Rather, it is the service of God, based in a receptive way upon God's love and the means he provides, especially his "living words" (e.g., Acts 7:38; Heb. 4:12; I Pet. 1:23), which furnishes the food that sustains and strengthens the new life (Matt. 4:4 and parallels; Luke 12:15; John 4:8; 6:27, 32-58). Hence a person who feeds on it can be sure that God will take care of his physical life, too (e.g., Matt. 6:25). For, as the miracles of Jesus indicate, he is a God who wants to preserve and restore life (Matt. 9:18; Mark 5:23; John 3:15-16; 4:47 ff; 10:10; cf. Rom. 8:31-39). Life thus understood is therefore quite the opposite of modern subjectivism and existentialism. Rather than being "simple openness to God," it is a voluntary subjection of one's existence to God's plans. It is therefore not confined to a special psychological sphere of "spiritual life" but rather manifests itself as a special quality or outlook which informs a person's whole life (e.g., Matt. 7:21; Luke 6:46). Yet far from being mere passivity, such commitment implies spontaneity; otherwise it could not reach its climax in love. However, its spontaneity is one in which one's egotism is subordinated to God's will (e.g., Matt. 19:19; 22:39 and parallels).

Thus the new life, as the NT sees it, is the individual's personal life, or the life of his "spirit" (e.g., Matt. 26:41; Mark 14:38; Rom. 1:9; 7:6; 8:16; I Pet. 4:1-2; etc.), and its newness is due to his willingness to accept the love Christ shows for him. This offer of Christ's love is in the NT coupled with the Holy Spirit. Those willing to be redeemed by Christ will feel in themselves the stimulus of God's Spirit. This is the same Spirit who according to the OT conveys life; but by the death and resurrection of Jesus, life has reached a new level. Through him, it has been hallowed, and thus the Spirit has become the vehicle of hallowed life (e.g., John 3:5; 6:63; 7:39). Just as by our receptivity Christ's life is enabled to engender the new life in us, so in turn our new life is capable of bearing fruit—i.e., not only capable of acting in accordance with his life, but also of bringing about such life in others (Matt. 3:8-10; 7:16-20; 12:33; Mark 4:7-8, 29; 11:14 and parallels; John 4:36; 12: 24; 15:1-16; Rom. 1:13; 15:28; Eph. 5:9; Col. 1:10; Heb. 12:11; etc.).

While the NT writers refer frequently to the growth of the new life, they are not thinking of it in Hellenistic terms—viz., as a gradual perfection of one's moral or religious life—but rather as a growing awareness of the value and significance of the gift of Christ, and accordingly of the responsibility implied therein (*see* KNOWLEDGE). This explains the paradoxical fact that the new life is compatible with sins (e.g., Rom. 7:15-20; I John 1:8-10; 2:1-2) and spiritual weakness (e.g., Matt. 17:20; 26:30-35 and parallels; Rom. 8:16, 26; cf. Heb. 5:11-14). But these conditions are caused by the infirmity of our flesh (e.g., Matt. 26:41; Mark 14:38; Rom. 7:18)—i.e., the fact that even in the new life we are still subject to the conditions of this world. The sins of the believer differ essentially, nevertheless, from the unbeliever's sinfulness. Whereas the latter is a deliberate refusal to live for God's sake, the former show merely a temporal failure to actualize the new life. This difference accounts for the fact that despite their sins the disciples of Jesus continue to co-operate with him in his work of transforming this world, whereas apart from Christ man's works are dead (e.g., John 5:24; I John 3:14). No matter how great the outward changes may be which they bring about, such actions do not alter the nature of this universe, in which good and evil keep themselves in a permanent equilibrium (John 15:5).

The new life is an indestructible one. The believers are "living stones" (I Pet. 2:4-5) of which God's temple is built here on earth (e.g., Rev. 21:12, 14). In their service they offer themselves as "living sacrifices" (Rom. 12:1; cf. 6:13, 19). However, this life is constantly threatened by three enemies—viz., the devil, the law, and death. While no earthly power is capable of annihilating the new life, the latter is not preserved automatically. The devil is anxious to destroy it (Matt. 10:28; Luke 12:4-5; I John 3:10, 14-15), and only in the power of Christ can he be overcome (Rom. 8:37-39; Eph. 6:10-18). Furthermore, the new life is endangered by the law. The very fact that we are called into the service of God can be interpreted, as indeed the Pharisees interpreted it, as meaning that by his own moral efforts man provides life for himself. Yet believing so, man denies the givenness of the new life (e.g., Rom. 7:10, 13; II Cor. 3:4-6; cf. Jas. 1:15), and thus fails to receive or preserve it. Finally, physical death seems to terminate the individual's existence, as is implied in such expressions as "giving up one's spirit" (e.g., Luke 23:46; John 19:30; Acts 7:59) or "one's *psyche*" (e.g., John 10:11, 15, 17; 13:37; 19:30; I John 3:16). Yet those who have tasted the new life realize that it must be unending, if it is to be more than an imagination (e.g., Matt. 19:16 and parallels; 19:29; 25:46; John 3:15-16; 4:14; 6:27; Acts 13:46, 48; Rom. 2:7; 5:21; 6:22-23; Gal. 6:8; I Tim. 1:16; 6:12; Tit. 1:2; 3:7; Jude 21). The modern longing for death is the very opposite of the NT view of life.

The answer to man's quest for life everlasting is the NT belief in a personal resurrection. Its basis is the resurrection of Jesus, which was understood as a bodily one. Hence the Christian resurrection is not, as in Judaism, a compensation for the miseries of life, but rather the continuation of that true life which the disciples of Jesus enjoy already in their earthly existence (I Cor. 15:19). This belief explains the seeming paradox that the new life is sometimes spoken of as a present possession (e.g., Matt. 10:39; 16:25 and parallels; Luke 17:33) and sometimes as a future good (Matt. 7:14; 18:8-9; 19:16; Mark 9:43, 45; 10:30; Luke 18:30; Jas. 1:12; I Pet. 3:7, 10; II Pet. 1:3; Rev. 2:10; 3:1; 11:11; etc.). There is no contradiction between the two views. Rather, physical death is the death of the body (Matt. 10:28 and parallels; Rom. 7:24; Jas. 2:26; cf. Rom. 6:6; 8:23); yet in death the believer's self is raised, and will eventually receive a new spiritual body in the resurrection (I Cor. 15:44, 53). As a result, all the obstacles which presently beset the manifestation of the true life will then be removed. This new risen condition is called the "crown of life" (Jas. 1:12; Rev. 2:10). Since life is activity, the future life is not imagined in an Orphic-Platonic sense as taking place in an absolute vacuum, but rather in a "new world" (Rev. 21:1-4). The resurrection is coupled with the Final Judgment, in which it will appear whether or not those who held that they possessed the new life had actually apprehended it. Those who did not are destined for the "second death" (Rev. 20:14-15; cf. Matt. 25:44-46).

4. John's view. To this general view of life, both John and Paul add a few specific features. John's message is rooted in the OT idea that God is life. The evangelist emphasizes that in Jesus the eternal "word of life" (I John 1:2; cf. John 1:1-4; 5:26; 6:57; I John 5:11-20) had become man (John 1:14), so that the people who by faith had identified themselves with him would share in his life (e.g., John 3:16; 6:63; 10:10; 20:31; cf. I John 4:9). John is particularly anxious to stress the presence of the new life (e.g., John 3:36; 5:24; 6:47, 54) and thus our ability to do God's commandment (I John 2:29). Through Jesus alone, to whom it was given to have life in himself (John 5:26; cf. 11:25; 14:6), can people have life (e.g., John 4:14; 5:21; 6:33, 58; 10:10, 28; Rom. 6: 11, 23; Col. 3:4; II Tim. 1:1, 10), and in this life which is God's life (John 5:20-21; 17:2), they become children of God (John 1:12; 12:36; 14:11, 13, 26; 17:3; I John 3:1; cf. John 8:44).

Jesus' existence is an everlasting one because it is not lived in self-chosen freedom but rather in God's service (John 12:50; cf. 4:34; 5:19-20). However, unlike Buddhism, Jesus does not teach the equality of all life; on the contrary. It is only in his own life that God's purpose in imparting life to his creatures is fully disclosed (John 11:25; 14:6). The nature of God's life is thereby to be made known to the world (John 15:8; 21:19). Ultimately, life consists in the knowledge of God (John 17:3)—i.e., in conscious love of the Creator and the fellow creatures. In its freedom (John 8:32, 36; cf. Rom. 6:18; I Pet. 2:24) life bears witness to the God who gave it, and thus refutes fatalism. Though the new life appears only occasionally in the believer, it is a seed which will grow into a full plant (I John 3:9). Having this power of the Son in themselves, believers are therefore capable of influencing the course of this world (John 15:4), especially through prayer (John 15:7). In line with this, their resurrection is not thought of as an extraneous act but rather as the full manifestation of the resurrection power in the believers (John 11:23-25; cf. 5:28-29). However, the resurrection is definitely regarded as a future event by John (John 5:28-29; 6:39-40, 44, 51-56; 12:48; I John 2:28-29; 3:2; 4:17; cf. John 17:24). It is not feasible, without doing violence to the text of the Johannine writings, to eliminate all these passages in order to ascribe a non-futuristic eschatology to their author.

The undeserved divine gift of Christ's coming shows that the new life is not destined to be a privilege for a few people only, as in the mystery religions, but rather a blessing for the whole of mankind (John 3:15; 10:10; 14:9; cf. 1:4, 7, 12). Furthermore, "the life was the light of men" (John 1:4; cf. 8:12); i.e., knowledge of the true life does not so much depend on written information as on belief in Jesus (e.g., John 3:15, 36; 5:24, 40; 6:40, 47, 58; 8:51; 11:25; 14:6; 20:31; cf. 10:10; I John 3:15)—i.e., on contact with his saving life (John 6:51, 57) as it goes on through the ages (John 8:12; 15:1-8; 17:3; I John 4:9). Against this background John states very powerfully that what is commonly called life is but frustration and, in the last analysis, death (John 5:24; I John 3:14), because it is unwillingness to do God's will (John 7:17; cf. 3:19-21; 12:25). The true life is not an innate quality (John 4:14; 5:24; 6:33; 11:25) but a divine gift (John 3:15-16). However, John also emphasizes the faithfulness of Christ, who will keep his followers alive (John 6:40; 10:28; 15:4) and will eventually render them like himself (I John 3:2). Through his love he makes them willing to keep God's commandment (e.g., John 5:29; I John 3:14).

5. Paul's view. Paul's teaching on life resembles in many respects that of John, yet is couched in a different language, which shows both rabbinical and Hellenistic influences. Paul starts from the assurance (Hab. 2:4) that the prerequisite of true life is righteousness—i.e., the whole person's agreement with God's will (Rom. 1:17; cf. Gal. 3:11; Tit. 1:1-2). This true life which on account of man's sinfulness had never been a reality (Rom. 3:23), has by the grace of God become a historical fact in Jesus (Rom. 3:25; 5:15, 17; I Tim. 1:10). Other people, too, may share in it by believing in that gracious act of God (Rom. 3:24; 6:8 ff; I Tim. 1:16; cf. Acts 11:18; 13:46; 15:7-9). Basic for Paul is the contrast between the common life of man, which is "fleshly" (κατὰ σάρκα; e.g., Rom. 8:12), and the life in Christ, which is spiritual (κατὰ πνεῦμα). The former is worthless and futile (e.g., Eph. 2:12), because it leads inevitably to death (e.g., Rom. 5:14; 6:21; 7:5), whereas the latter is a priceless good (Phil. 3:7), since it has the promise of the life everlasting (e.g., Rom. 5:10, 21; I Cor. 15:19; Col. 3:4). The fleshly life is not understood in a Hellenistic sense by Paul as designating the passions and desires of the body, but rather it is man's life as adjusted to the demands which the earthly conditions make upon him. True life, on the other hand, is lived in Christ—i.e., it is one in which the individual believer has become a member of the body of the risen Lord (e.g., Eph. 4:13-16; cf. Rom. 6:11-13). Whereas according to John the true life is that which God works through the incarnation of the Word, Paul holds that it is the heavenly life of the risen Christ which vivifies the believer (e.g., Rom. 8:29; Eph. 2:5; Col. 1:18; 2:13). This change implies closest personal contact of the disciples of Jesus with their risen head (e.g., Phil. 1:21; I Thess. 3:8), but it guarantees also that the new life is experienced as a power, which reigns over the faithful (e.g., Rom. 5:21). Significantly, "Lord" is the principal title given by Paul to Jesus. Baptism is the specific act in which the incipient believer dies to sin and to his past (e.g., Rom. 6:1-11; cf. Gal. 2:19-20; 6:14) and enters completely into the Lord's life (e.g., Rom. 6:4; 8:10; II Cor. 4:8-10; 6:4-10; Gal. 2:19-20). He is thus under obligation to live in the historical movement initiated by Jesus and to serve it (e.g., II Cor. 2:16; 4:12) and thereby to engender such life in others, too (e.g., Rom. 6:22-23; Gal. 6:8; Phil. 3:8-14). Missionary activity is therefore incumbent on all Christians. The gospel—i.e., the proclamation of the Christ—is in turn life (II Tim. 1:10).

Since the life of the risen Lord is interpreted eschatologically as the conquest of the universe for God, the new life of the believer has both present (e.g., Rom. 5:12-21; 6:11; 8:2, 10, 20; Gal. 2:20; II Tim. 1:1) and also futuristic features (e.g., Rom. 1:17; 2:7; I Cor. 15:20-22, 44-49; II Cor. 5:1-10; Gal. 6:8). The power of Christ's life, manifested in his resurrection, has already overcome sin (Rom. 5:10) and brought to light his indestructible life (II Tim. 1:10). The believers are destined eventually to share in the glory of Christ (e.g., I Cor. 15:43; II Tim. 2:10; cf. I Pet. 5:1, 4, 10; Rev. 2:10), but that glorious life is still "hid with Christ" (Col. 3:3-4; cf. Rom. 8:35), because throughout this earthly life we must first participate in the suffering of Christ (e.g., Phil. 1:20; cf. II Cor. 4:7-12; 6:9). On account of the saving activity of the risen Christ, Paul notices how the believer's body of sin is gradually made subservient to the Lord's redemptive goal (e.g., Rom. 6:12-13; 8:11; 12:1). Nevertheless, only through the gift of a new spiritual body in the final resurrection (I Cor. 15:44, 51; II Cor. 5:1-5; Phil. 3:21; I Thess. 4:13-18) will the individual be able fully to actualize his new life.

Paul usually describes the manifestation of the life of the risen Lord as the work of the Holy Spirit. However, when he says that "the Lord is the Spirit" (II Cor. 3:17), he does not identify the two, but rather states that the life-giving work of the Spirit (e.g., I Cor. 15:45; II Cor. 3:6) has reached its goal in the risen Lord. Whereas the Spirit's power manifests itself in general in the lives of all the mortal creatures, in Christ it is realized in a way which is in accordance with the Spirit's own unlimited duration—i.e., as a never-ending life (Rom. 6:9). In the Lord's resurrection the work of the Creator was completed. Over against mortal Adam (Rom. 5:12; I Cor. 15:22, 45-49) the "man in Christ" is a new creation (II Cor. 5:17; cf. Rom. 6:4), which bears fruits of new life

(Gal. 5:19-22; cf. I Cor. 15:58; Gal. 6:8; Eph. 5:5, 9); i.e., he acts in the power of the risen Lord and performs spontaneously the will of God (Eph. 6:6; cf. Rom. 8:12; I Cor. 14:1; Gal. 5:22-25). His life is therefore one of living for Christ (Rom. 6:11, 13; II Cor. 5:15; Gal. 2:19-20; Phil. 1:20-22). Thereby he is enabled to know God (I Cor. 13:12) and to realize that earthly goods yield no real satisfaction (I Cor. 7:29-31). This effective operation of the Spirit is in turn taken by Paul as a guarantee that the believer has been made new (Rom. 8:23; II Cor. 5:5), and that he will therefore be raised from the dead (II Cor. 5:5; Phil. 1:6; II Tim. 1:10). For the work of the Spirit is a sign that Christ's love surrounds and protects us (Rom. 5:5; 8:35).

Bibliography. F. Delitzsch, *A System of Biblical Psychology* (English trans.; 2nd ed., 1869); J. Macpherson, "The NT View of Life," *Exp.*, 1st Series, V (1877), 72-80; J. Massie, "Two NT Words Denoting Life," *Exp.*, 2nd Series, IV (1882), 380-97; E. von Schrenk, *Die johanneische Anschauung vom Leben* (1898); S. D. F. Salmond, *Christian Doctrine of Immortality* (4th ed., 1901); E. Sokolovski, *Die Begriffe Geist und Leben bei Paulus* (1903); J. Laidlaw, *Bible Doctrine of Man* (rev. ed., 1905); R. Law, *Tests of Life, a Study of the First Epistle of St. John* (1905); F. C. Burkitt, "Life, Zoe, Hayyim," *ZNW*, 12 (1911), 228-30; G. Robinson, *The Christian Doctrine of Man* (1911); J. Lindblom, *Das ewige Leben: Eine Studie über die Entstehung der religiösen Lebensidee im NT* (1914); W. Baudissin, "Alttestamentliches 'hajjim Leben' in der Bedeutung von 'Glück,'" *Festschrift Eduard Sachau* (1915), pp. 43-61; A. Schulz, *Der Sinn des Todes im AT* (1919); J. B. Frey, "Le concepte de 'Vie' dans l'évangile de saint Jean," *Bibl.*, I (1920), 37-58, 211-39; G. Quell, *Die Auffassung des Todes in Israel* (1925); L. Dürr, *Die Wertung des Lebens im AT und im antiken Orient* (1926); N. B. Harrison, *The Gospel of Life, Love and Light; the Gospel of John and the First Epistle of John* (1929); J. McConnachie, *The Gospel of Life: Studies in the Gospel According to St. John* (1930); H. Pribnow, *Die johanneische Anschauung vom Leben* (1934); P. H. Loyd, *The Life According to St. John* (1936); W. E. Hocking, *Thoughts on Death and Life* (1937); J. A. Findlay, *The Way, the Truth, and the Life* (1940); E. K. Lee, *The Religious Thought of St. John* (1943), pp. 191-237; W. Eichrodt, *Man in the OT* (1951); F. Muszner, *Zoe: Die Anschauung vom "Leben" im vierten Evangelium unter Berücksichtigung der Johannesbriefe*, Münch. Theologische Studien, I, no. 5 (1952); C. H. Dodd, "Eternal Life," *The Interpretation of the Fourth Gospel* (1953), pp. 144-50; E. Schmitt, *Leben in den Weisheitsbüchern, Job, Sprüche und Jesus Sirach*, Freiburg Theologische Studien, LXVI (1954); W. Matthias, "Der alte und der neue Mensch in der Anthropologie des Paulus," *Evangelische Theologie* (1957), 385-97; R. L. Shinn, *Life, Death and Destiny* (1957).

See also works on the theology of the NT and of the various biblical books.

O. A. Piper

LIFE, BOOK OF [Τὸ βιβλίον τῆς ζωῆς; ὁ βίβλος ζωῆς]. A heavenly book in which the names of the righteous, as predetermined by God, are inscribed (cf. Ps. 139:16; I Enoch 104:1; Luke 10:20; Phil. 4:3; Heb. 12:23; Rev. 13:8; 17:8; 21:27; I Clem. 45:8). There is a corresponding book of destruction for the wicked (I Enoch 81:4; Jub. 30:22; Test. Levi 5:4). In the main the concept was predestinarian; however, through apostasy, e.g., a name might be removed; or possibly, through repentance, it might be added (cf. Ps. 69:28; Jub. 30:22; Rev. 3:5; Herm. Vis. I.3). Related to these books of life or of destruction are books of destiny, which predicted—if, indeed, they did not predetermine—future events. Notable examples are the book of seven seals in Rev. 5:1 ff and the heavenly tablets which Enoch (81:1-3) saw in heaven (cf. also Ezek. 2:9-10; Rev. 10:8 ff; Herm. Vis. II). These deterministic heavenly books remind one of the Babylonian concept that the zodiac with its constellations was a heavenly tablet controlling the destinies of mankind.

Heavenly books in which the deeds of men, good or evil, are recorded after they have occurred, not predicted or detemined beforehand, are obviously somewhat different (cf. Dan. 7:10; 12:1; II Esd. 6:20; I Enoch 47:1; II Bar. 24:1; Rev. 20:12, 15; Herm. Sim. II.9; Ascension of Isaiah 9:22). Some of these are to be opened at the Last Judgment.

See also Apocalypticism; Eschatology.

M. Rist

LIGHT, LIGHT AND DARKNESS [Light: *usually* אור; φῶς; Darkness: חשך, אפל, ערפל; σκότος, σκοτία]. **1. "Light" in the OT.** For the ancient Hebrews, light is one of the primal phenomena of this world (e.g., Job 38:19). Created prior to and independent of the heavenly luminaries (Gen. 1:3-5), light is the most general and most adequate manifestation of divine operation in a world which apart from it is darkness and chaos. The ancient Hebrews did not differentiate between natural and supranatural light. The phenomenon of dawn prior to sunrise was to them an evidence that God pursued a special goal in creating this world. The dawn indicates that darkness will not last and reign forever (e.g., Ps. 130:6; Hos. 6:3, 5). Light is therefore the essence of all the gifts through which God blesses his creatures.

This view implies that light is a substance or an energy which brings about certain effects in this world, and that it is primarily for man's benefit that the light shines. It is only in exilic times that we have clear evidence that light and the sun are seen in a causal connection (e.g., Isa. 60:19); and this fact, in turn, is clear proof that the high regard in which light was held in the Hebrew religion was at no time connected with the worship of the sun. The metaphorical use of "light" is rooted in the creation story.

The constant rhythm of night and day prevents a strictly dualistic view of the universe. Though light and darkness are opposites, the latter is as real as the former. Darkness is not merely the absence of light. The religious interest the Bible takes in light concerns the benefits which it imparts, rather than its nature. Hence it is practically impossible to differentiate between the natural and the metaphorical usage of the term. God is the creator of light and darkness (Isa. 45:6-7), he has made his covenant with day and night (Jer. 33:25; cf. Ps. 148:3-6; Jer. 31:35-36) —i.e., he watches over their orderly succession (e.g., Ps. 104:20; Amos 4:13). All things were originally in the darkness, which is, as it were, the womb in which everything exists. But through light God uncovers them (Job 12:22; cf. Dan. 2:22). Thus it is God's will that light and darkness shall coexist in this world. However, light curbs darkness (Pss. 91:5; 139:11-12); and since both are energies, this activity entails conflict. In this conflict, light by its limiting power proves its superior value (Eccl. 2:13).

Many are the effects of light. It is, above all, the source of life (e.g., Eccl. 11:7). "Seeing the light" is frequently used as a synonym for "being alive" (e.g., Job 3:20; Ps. 49:19) or "being born" (e.g., Job 3:16); cf. the "light of life" (Job 33:30; Ps. 56:13—H 56:14). Since life is not only truly life unless it can be enjoyed, "light" often designates the pleasures of life (e.g., Job 10:22; 30:26; Ps. 97:11; Isa. 45:7; 60: 19-20; Amos 5:18, 20). The phrase "Light dawns for the righteous" (Ps. 97:11; cf. Job 18:5; 38:15; Ps. 112:4) means that he sees good days. "In thy light do we see light" (Ps. 36:9) has originally nothing to do with knowledge, as Augustine interpreted it, but rather it states that man is happy when God's light shines upon him. In a more general way, light in the OT designates "salvation" or "rescue from danger," because salvation implies good days or happiness. The two concepts can hardly be separated in the OT, because all good fortunes are God's blessings—e.g., "When I sit in darkness, the Lord will be a light to me" (Mic. 7:8-9; cf. II Sam. 22:29; Pss. 18:28; 27:1-2; Isa. 9:2; 10:17).

In addition to life, light brings order to this world. This idea starts probably from the fact that the dawn appears with great regularity, so that the coming of light is the prototype of all order. At the same time, through the light the things in this world are shown in their relation to one another, and thus light becomes the source of knowledge. With the practical outlook of the OT, the two aspects are closely related. Order must manifest itself as underlying the whole of Creation if people are to walk accordingly. Light and truth are thus coupled in Ps. 43:3, and light symbolizes God's law in Ps. 19, where the regularity of the revolutions of the heavenly luminaries (vss. 1-6) points to God's law (vss. 7-13; see also Ps. 119:105; Prov. 6:23; Isa. 51:4). According to the dynamic realism of the OT, the light of truth and law operate upon man both by imparting knowledge (e.g., Pss. 19:8—H 19:9; 139:11-12) and by guiding him (e.g., Deut. 28:29; Job 12:24-25; 22:28; 43:3; 78:14; 119:105; Prov. 4:18; 6:23; Isa. 42:16; cf. Job 29:3; Ps. 43:3; Isa. 2:5; Mic. 7:8).

As a result of the reciprocal relationship between light and man, the recipient of light becomes a light himself. He shines both outwardly (Ps. 34:5; Eccl. 8:1) and inwardly, having been made wise by God's light (e.g., Prov. 4:18; 20:27; Eccl. 2:13-14; Dan. 5:11). Thus faithful Israel is to become a light for the Gentiles (Isa. 49:6; 60:3, 5; 62:1).

Similar views are found in other religions. The peculiar character of the OT view, however, lies in the fact that the wholesome effects of light are contingent on righteousness (Job 22:21, 28); that the rhythm of darkness and light is dependent exclusively on God's behest (Isa. 50:3; Jer. 4:23 ff; Amos 5:20), who can change it at will (e.g., Josh. 10:12-13; cf. Matt. 27:45); and that the light carries judgment with it (Ps. 37:6; Isa. 10:17; 51:4; Hos. 6:5; cf. Ps. 90:8). All this results from the fact that the manifestations of light are God's own work (Pss. 44:3; 89:15—H 89:16; 119:130), who dwells in light (Exod. 13:21; Ps. 104:2; Dan. 2:22; cf. Job 37:21; I Tim. 6:16).

The "light of God's face" shines upon his people (e.g., Num. 6:25; Pss. 4:6—H 4:7; 31:16—H 31:17; 44:3—H 44:4; 80:7; 90:8). This personalization of the work of light explains the eschatological hope that eventually the rhythm of darkness and light will give way to an eternal day, when God will be his people's light (e.g., Isa. 30:26; 60:19-22; Hos. 6:3; Zech. 14:7; cf. Eccl. 12:2; Isa. 2:1; 42:6; Rev. 21:23; 22:5).

2. "Darkness" in the OT. Strictly parallel with the view of "light" runs that of "darkness" or "night." In the beginning of Creation, darkness brooded passively over the primeval ocean (Gen. 1:2), and this darkness represents the original condition of the world. That this is not a "mere possibility rejected by God in the act of Creation" (K. Barth) can be seen in the power darkness has over the creatures (e.g., Job 12:24-25; Isa. 59:10; Jer. 13:16; 23:12; cf. Luke 22:53). Being originally related to chaos, darkness manifests itself as bad luck, evil fate or affliction (e.g., Job 17:12; 21:17; 29:3; Pss. 18:28—H 18:29; 23:4; Isa. 5:30; 8:22-9:1—H 8:22-23; Zeph. 1:15), and particularly death. There is no light in Sheol (e.g., Job 10:21-22; 38:17; Pss. 49:18—H 49:20; 88:11-13; Eccl. 6:4; Isa. 45:19).

Since light is the manifestation of God's nature, darkness also designates ignorance of God's saving and demanding will, and thus it is the sphere, or rather the source, of sin and iniquity (e.g., Job 18:5-6; 24:13-17; Pss. 10:8, 11; 74:20; Isa. 21:11-12; 29: 15; 59:9; cf. Rom. 13:12; Eph. 5:8-12). By its superior power, light, which manifests God's own purpose, is enabled to disclose the true nature of darkness (e.g., Job 34:21-22; Ps. 139:11-12), thereby passing judgment on it (e.g., Isa. 5:30; 13:10; Jer. 4:23-24; Joel 2:1-2, 31; 3:14-15) and delivering people from its sway (e.g., II Sam. 22:29; Job 29:3; Pss. 23:4; 139:11-12; Isa. 50:10; Mic. 7:8-9; cf. Luke 1:79).

3. "Light" in the NT. NT usage follows, on the whole, that of the OT. Unlike Hellenistic mysticism, in which light is identified with God, the NT emphasizes that light is a divine gift. While God dwells in the light (I Tim. 6:16), this brightness or GLORY of God is not itself imparted to man. Accordingly, there is no divine spark residing in human nature. Whatever light a person has has been received from God. This continuation of the OT view explains the absence of cosmological speculations about light and darkness in the NT. All the NT references to light are dealing with the function it has in the execution of God's saving purpose.

As the "Father of lights," God is the fountain of all good gifts (Jas. 1:17). Several of the OT passages referring to the light of salvation are quoted in the NT (e.g., Matt. 4:16; Luke 2:32; Acts 13:47; cf. also John 1:4; 8:12; 11:9; Acts 2:20; I Pet. 2:9; Rev. 18: 1), and the evaluation of the OT as a lamp or light is taken over (e.g., II Pet. 1:19). The term "light" is particularly used to designate the fact that it is through a divine revelation (e.g., Acts 9:3; 22:6, 9; Eph. 5:13; II Tim. 1:10; cf. Eph. 3:9) that men have been made aware of Christ's redemptive work. Revelation speaks of candlesticks that are placed in front of the heavenly Christ (Rev. 1:12-13, 20), and says that he has given one to each congregation (Rev. 2:5), symbolizing his revealing light. Conversion is described as illumination (e.g., Heb. 6:4; 10:32; cf. II Cor. 4:4-6), and this gift is a sign of election (e.g., Eph. 5:13; I Pet. 2:9). Thus for practical guidance the life of faith relies on the heavenly light (e.g., Rom. 13:12; Eph. 1:18). For by its coming from God the light makes visible what is and what is not in agreement with the Lord's will (e.g., Rom. 13:12; I Cor. 4:5; Eph. 1:18; 5:13; Heb. 10:32; cf. John 3:21; Eph. 5:11) and thereby divides mankind forever. This is the judgment (John 3:17-21; 8:15; 12:47).

More frequently than the OT, yet following a tendency already found there and intensified in the intertestamental Judaism, the NT emphasizes that the believers, or the whole people of God (Acts 26: 23; Col. 1:12; I Pet. 2:9), are "sons of light" (Luke 16:8; John 12:36; I Thess. 5:5; cf. Eph. 5:8). They have been so cleansed and transformed by the power of the heavenly light that they are the "light of the world" (Matt. 5:14; cf. Mark 4:21-22; Luke 2:32; Acts 13:47; Phil. 2:15). Whereas the OT, when speaking of the light, lays the emphasis upon the value it has for people, the NT stresses the believers' responsibility to act according to the light imparted to them (Matt. 6:22-23; Luke 11:34-36; John 9:4; 12:46-47; II Cor. 6:14; I Thess. 5:4-8; I John 2:10), because as a result of inactivity or indifference the gift may be lost (e.g., John 5:35; 12:35; I Thess. 5: 5-6). Consequently they must use that heavenly light as their armor or weapon (Rom. 13:12; Eph. 6:12; I Thess. 5:8; cf. Matt. 6:23) in their fight against the powers of darkness. By doing so they will not only bear fruits of the light—i.e., act in accordance with God's will (Eph. 5:9)—but also make that light shine forth for the rest of mankind (Matt. 5:16; 10:27; Luke 8:16; 11:33; 12:3; Acts 13:47; cf. Rom. 2:19).

Some entirely new features in the NT usage of "light" are called forth by the change in the eschatological situation brought about by Jesus. Instead of the intermittent manifestations of the heavenly light characteristic of the old aeon (*see* TIME), in which light and darkness alternate, as in the natural order, the light is now permanently present in Jesus Christ (Matt. 4:16; John 1:7-9; 8:12; 9:5; 12:46; Eph. 5:14; Heb. 1:3; cf. Matt. 17:5) and in the GOSPEL (e.g., Acts 26:23; II Cor. 4:4), through which the operation of his light is continued. Christ's coming announced the dawn of the New Age, which will never be followed by a night (Rev. 21:23; 22:5). The children of light are therefore the rulers of the world forever (Rev. 22:5; cf. I Pet. 2:9; Rev. 1:6). Though they are still surrounded by darkness (e.g., John 1:5; 8:12; 12:35, 46; Acts 26:18; II Cor. 6:14; Eph. 6:12; I Thess. 5:4; cf. John 3:19; I John 3:9, 11), the night is nearly spent (Rom. 13:12), and Christ is shining as the morning star (Rev. 2:28; 22:16). The darkness will be dispelled as a result of their splendor (Col. 1:12; I John 2:8; cf. Jas. 1:17) and of Christ's Parousia (Rev. 21:23-24).

As a result of this Christocentric and personalized view of light, darkness appears in two different ways. It may be the natural condition of man who has not yet been "enlightened" (John 1:4-5; 12:35, 46; Eph. 5:14), or it may be the result of one's turning away from the light (John 3:19-20). The former condition, though a deficiency, can nevertheless be remedied, because God's light shines to all men (John 1:9; 11: 10; Eph. 5:14; I Thess. 5:5-7); whereas of the latter condition men should be ashamed (Eph. 5:12; cf. John 3:20), for it is the devil's work in them (II Cor. 6:15; 11:14; Col. 1:13; I Thess. 5:4-5). By their self-inflicted darkness people are rendered spiritually blind (Acts 26:18; I John 2:9-11; cf. John 9:39-40), and if persisting in it bring upon themselves everlasting doom (Col. 1:13; II Pet. 2:17; Jude 13). The designation "outer" and "extreme" darkness (e.g., Matt. 8:12; 22:13; 25:30), used for the eschatological state of the doomed, indicates that darkness, though it is not destined ever to vanish from this world, yet will be permanently curbed.

John, who has a rather elaborate theology of light, thereby probably reflects his Jewish-Hellenistic background. However, over against the idealistic and naturalistic tendencies of the Hellenistic theology of light, John stands close to the Qumran "Hymns of Praise." He emphasizes that God "is light" (I John 1:5); this form of speech characterizes him as the source or creator of light (cf. John 4:24; I John 4:16), rather than as a substantial light; and by stating that Jesus is the light of the world (John 8:12) the Fourth Gospel points out that God's full blessing to mankind (John 9:5) is tied up with a definite historical event. Though the operation of the eternal Logos implies the shedding of light (John 1:9), full salvation can be found only where he is present as the incarnate One or in his proclamation (John 12: 35-36; cf. 9:4). In turn, since the coming of the light manifests God's love, true life in the light consists in keeping Jesus' commandments, especially in loving one's brother (I John 1:7; 2:8). He who hates his brother is therefore in the darkness (I John 2:11).

Bibliography. W. Bousset, *Kyrios Christos* (1913), pp. 208-14. G. P. Wetter, *Phos* (1915). F. J. Dölger, *Sol Salutis* (1920). E. Gulin, *Das Antlitz Jahwes im AT* (1923). F. Nötscher, *"Das Antlitz Gottes schauen" nach biblischer und bablyonischer Auffassung* (1924). V. Aptowitzer, "Zur Kosmologie der Agada. Licht als Urstoff," *Monatsschrift für die Geschichte und Wissenschaft des Judentums,* 72 (1928), 363 ff. E. R. Goodenough, *By Light Light: The Mystic Gospel of Hellenistic Judaism* (1935). H. G. May, "The Creation of Light in Gen. 1:3-5," *JBL,* vol. 58 (1939). A. M. Gierlich, *Der Lichtgedanke in den Psalmen* (1940). S. Aalen, *Die Begriffe "Licht" und "Finsternis" im AT, im Spätjudentum und im Rabbinismus* (1951). E. P. Dickie, *God Is Light: Studies in Revaluation and Personal Conviction* (1953). C. H. Dodd, *The Bible and the Greeks* (1953); *The Interpretation of the Fourth Gospel* (1953), pp. 201-12. O. A. PIPER

LIGHTNING. *See* THUNDER AND LIGHTNING.

LIGNALOES lĭn ăl'ōz [Vulg. *lignum aloes,* wood of aloes]. KJV translation of אהלים (RSV ALOES) in Num. 24:6.

LIGURE lĭg'yŏŏr. KJV translation of לשם (RSV JACINTH) in Exod. 28:19; 39:12.

LIKHI lĭk'hī [לקחי] (I Chr. 7:19). A Manassite. The name may be the result of an error for Helek (חלק, "portion"), which stands in the related lists of Num. 26:30; Josh. 17:2.

LILIES. *See* MUSIC.

LILITH lĭl'ĭth (RSV NIGHT HAG) [לילית, *lîlîth;* Akkad. *lilītu;* LXX ὀνοκένταυρος; Vulg. *Lamia*] (Isa. 34:14); KJV SCREECH OWL. A female demon who was believed to haunt desolate places. She is identified in a Canaanite charm of the eighth century B.C., and likewise in postbiblical Jewish literature, with the child-stealing witch Lilith of world-wide folklore. The name derives from Sumerian *lil,* "wind" (i.e., "spirit"), and has nothing to do with Hebrew *lāyil,* "night," as was formerly supposed.

See fully DEMON, § A4*a*. T. H. GASTER

LILY [שׁושׁן, *šûšan, šôšān* (*masculine*); שׁושׁנה, *šôšannâ* (*feminine*), *from* Egyp. *sššn;* κρίνον]. A flower of the *Liliaceae* family, or perhaps any showy flower with the general appearance of the lily. There is little agreement concerning the original meaning of the above Hebrew words. The Egyptian *sššn* was the sacred lotus water lily, *Nymphaea lotus* L., common along the edges of the Nile; it was the inspiration of the earliest pillar capitals in Egypt (cf. I Kings 7:19, 22), as well as prominent on reliefs and paintings.

Although the LOTUS may have once grown along the Jordan River, there is no evidence of it in the Holy Land today, and it seems unlikely that the Hebrew word ever referred directly to it. It may have come into the language meaning "lotuslike," and may have been applied to a certain Palestinian flower or to several. צאלים, *ṣe'ᵉlîm,* in Job 40:21-22 may possibly be a biblical reference to the Egyptian LOTUS, but it is not so considered by most scholars.

From *Plants of the Bible* (London: Crosby Lockwood & Son, Ltd.)

28. Lily (*Lilium candidum* L.)

The form of the capitals of the pillars of JACHIN AND BOAZ ("lily-work"; I Kings 7:19, 22) and the rim of the "molten sea" (I Kings 7:26 = II Chr. 4:5) in Solomon's temple may have been inspired by the lotus through Egyptian architectural influence (Fig. TEM 28). It could already have carried the meaning "flower," implying a stylized lilylike form (*see* TEMPLE, JERUSALEM). The prominence of the lotus on Canaanite Astarte plaques and Syrian god representations (*ANEP* 469-70, 472-75, 566; cf. 314-16) would suggest a wider Egyptian influence of this flower than previously thought, and may indicate an original meaning "lotus" for *šûšan.* The only lily in Palestine which could possibly have been intended, *Lilium candidum* L.,* does not fit any of the passages where these words appear in the Bible. *See* FLORA § A10. Fig. LIL 28.

The "lily of the valleys" in Song of S. 2:1 (cf. 6:11) is not the flower to which this expression normally applies today, *Convallaria majalis* L. (not found in Palestine), but would indicate a general reference to the many springtime flowers, or perhaps some predominant flower. The next verse refers to a "lily among brambles." Several times the idea of animals' feeding among "lilies" appears in these love songs: 2:14; 4:5; 6:3 (cf. 6:2). These passages bring to mind the springtime flower-studded open fields with their grazing flocks. "His lips are lilies" (5:13) could be a poetic allusion to shape rather than color, and therefore may not require a red flower. Although the evidence points to a relatively late date for the writing of the Song of Songs, the secular nature of these "wedding songs" raises the possibility of a connection between their use of *šûšan* and the Canaanite Astarte figurines holding the lotus flower, despite the evidence of the contexts to the contrary.

In a figure of the restoration of Israel (Hos. 14:5), "He shall blossom as the lily" implies both beauty and abundance, again bringing forth the vision of the colorful hillsides and valleys of springtime.

"Consider the lilies of the field" (Matt. 6:28 = Luke 12:27) is the most widely discussed allusion to the lily. The Greek κρίνον is more specific, usually referring to the *Lilium candidum* L., the white Madonna lily, even though the nature of the growth of this woodland lily clearly argues against its use in this context. The white lily has nevertheless played an important part in Christian symbolism through the centuries. Although many scholars think that Jesus intended specific flowers in his figure, the tendency today is to consider it a reference to the many prominent flowers so well known to Jesus' listeners. In the Holy Land one may be impressed with the progression of the brilliant scarlet anemones (*Anemone coronaria* L.), ranunculi (*Ranunculus asiaticus* L.), and poppies (*Papaver rhoeas* L. and *P. syriacum* Boiss. et Bl.), which appear in this order from late January to early May. Their similarity, abundance, delicate structure, and brilliance, appearing over such a long period of each year, would argue in favor of their having been in the mind of Jesus as he spoke. The distinctions between these flowers are not clearly apparent. Either the above predominant flowers or flowers in general would seem to be the best interpretation of the passage. Although yellow flowers seem to dominate the Galilean hillsides today, the scarlet flowers among them make a vivid impression. Jesus thought the array of the flowers of the field exceeded that of Solomon in all his glory.

Ecclus. 39:14; 50:8 may refer specifically to the *Lilium candidum,* or even the lotus, but could also be taken in the general sense of any flower.

SUSA (Shushan; Neh. 1:1, etc.), the winter residence of Persian kings, received its name from the lily, probably the *Fritillaria imperialis* L., which is still abundant in Persia.

For the references in the titles of some of the Psalms, *see* SHOSHANNIM. *See also* FLOWERS; SUSANNA.

Bibliography. I. Löw, *Die Flora der Juden,* II (1924), 160-84; G. E. Post, *Flora of Syria, Palestine and Sinai,* II (1933), 583-630; H. N. and A. L. Moldenke, *Plants of the Bible* (1952), pp. 41-46, 114-18, 129, 154-55. J. C. TREVER

LILY-WORK [מעשה שושן] (I Kings 7:19, 22). Decoration on the bowl-shaped capitals (I Kings 7:41) of the free-standing columns, JACHIN AND BOAZ, at the vestibule of Solomon's temple; and the part of the column immediately below the capital probably bore a similar decoration (*see* PILLAR). The lily motif was most likely suggested by the resemblance of the bowl-like capitals to the open calyx of a flower, a resemblance specifically noted in the case of the "molten sea" (I Kings 7:26).* Two incense altars from Megiddo illustrate the probable nature of lily-work. The first, a pottery altar, has stylized petals or leaves around the rim of the bowl with a second row a little farther down on the stand (Fig. INC 4). The other Megiddo altar, a more elaborate object, has the bowl decorated with lotus buds and open flowers

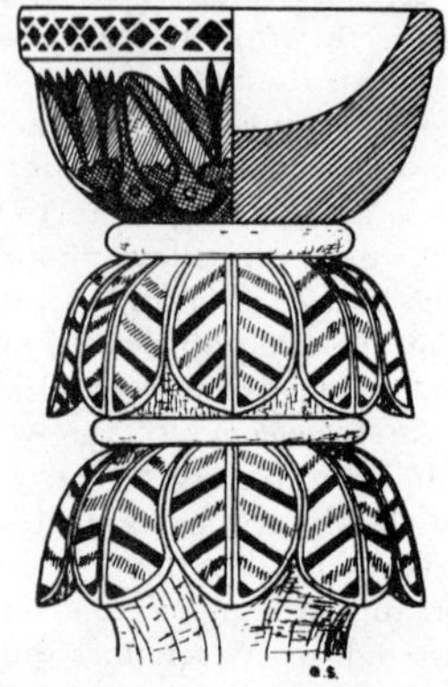

Courtesy of the Oriental Institute, the University of Chicago

29. Drawing of an incense stand, from Megiddo (*ca.* 1000 B.C.)

with two registers of downward-folding leaves below (Fig. LIL 29). Since this limestone incense stand resembles a pillar, it provides the closest analogy to the lily-work mentioned in I Kings. Fig. LAM 11.

Bibliography. H. G. May and R. M. Engberg, *Material Remains of the Megiddo Cult* (1935), pp. 20-23, plate XX; H. G. May, "The Two Pillars Before the Temple of Solomon," *BASOR,* 88 (1942), 19-27. L. E. TOOMBS

LIME [שיד, *cf. denominative verb* שיד (Deut. 27:2, 4), to whitewash; LXX κονία, a potash or alkali powder used as soap; Vulg. *cinis,* ashes]. A caustic, highly fusible solid, white when pure, obtained by calcining limestone, shells, etc.

Palestine limestone is a carbonate of lime, which, when heated, becomes quicklime, a chief ingredient of mortar. In Isa. 33:12 "lime" appears in connection with burning in a figure of ignominious destruction; the text could mean "burned to lime" (RSV) or a "burning of lime"—i.e., by lime. The former is more in keeping with Amos 2:1, which says that Moab will be visited because he burned the bones of the king of Edom to lime. Since the lime of these two

Courtesy of Herbert G. May

30. A Palestinian limekiln

passages is the result of the burning of bones, it must have been a phosphate of lime. In Deut. 27:2, 4, the word is translated "plaster."

Lime was produced for use as plaster of walls, floors, cisterns, etc., or for other purposes by burning crushed limestone in kilns (Fig. LIM 30). Slaked lime was used in setting the dye in preparing woolen cloth.

W. E. STAPLES

LINEN. The growing of flax (פשת) was not limited to Egypt, though that country was doubtless the most productive area for it in the ancient world. Specific biblical references indicate that it was raised also in Palestine—e.g., at Jericho (Josh. 2:6); cf. also the notice of the month for the plucking of flax in the Gezer Calendar (*see* INSCRIPTIONS § 3; CALENDAR § 3*b*). In Talmudic times it was grown around Beth-shan and Arbela. Egyptian linen was celebrated in antiquity, and extant pieces of royal linen are so finely woven that they cannot be distinguished from silk without the use of a magnifying glass. Even ordinary linen was of excellent quality.

Flax culture requires fertile soil for abundant production and good quality. When the stalks were ripe, they were pulled up by the roots, tied in bundles, and shocked to dry or spread upon a flat roof. When dried, the seed pods were removed and the stalks placed in a steeping pond, where they were weighted down with stones. They were allowed to remain there until they had softened to the point where the fibers could easily be separated. Then they were wrung out, dried in an oven, bleached, and cleaned. Finally they were pounded to loosen the fibers, then twisted into strands and combed to separate them from tow when it was ready for delivery to the spinners.

The spinners spooled the threads on the distaff; after this they were ready for the weaver (*ANEP* 42, fig. 143). *See* CLOTH § 5.

While there is no indication of colored linen in the Bible, we do know that there was such in Egypt (tomb of King Tut-Ankh-Amen). Blue linen threads were used in some of the textile materials found with the Qumran Scrolls (*see* CLOTH § 2*c*). Ordinarily garments were of bleached linen, though those of the wealthy were often interspersed with colored threads as bands or otherwise decorated. According to I Chr. 4:21, there was a family or guild of linen workers at

Beth-ashbea, and linen designers were present among the Israelites in the time of Moses (Exod. 35:35; 38:23).

Linen was commonly used for all kinds of clothing, for the swathing of the dead, bed sheets, curtains, and in the varied colored patterns of weaving. It was especially desirable for summer wear because of coolness. Imported linen was an item of luxury. The Egyptian mummies were bandaged exclusively with linen. The priestly garments and vestments were all made of this product of flax—undergarments, head-gear, tunics, etc. It was also used for sails for ships and as wrappers for scrolls.

There are a number of words translated "linen":

a) בד (LXX λίνον, βύσσινος), a word used in connection with the linen garments of the high priest (Lev. 16:23, 32), in which he carried out the ritual of atonement. The regular garment proper for conducting the burnt offering (Lev. 6:10—H 6:31) was linen. The linen garments of the priest consisted of the holy coat (Lev. 16:4), the breeches (Exod. 28:42; 39:28; Lev. 6:10—H 6:31; 16:4), the girdle (Lev. 16:4), and the turban (Lev. 16:4). The ephod was also made of linen (I Sam. 2:18; 22:18; II Sam. 6:14; I Chr. 15:27). The scribe with the six men in Ezekiel's vision was clothed in linen (9:2-3, 11; 10:2, 6-7), as was the man in Daniel's vision on the banks of the Tigris (10:5; 12:6-7).

b) שש (LXX βύσσος, βύσσινος), "fine linen," limited by tradition to Egyptian linen. When Joseph was made minister by the Pharaoh, he was arrayed in שש (Gen. 41:42). The offerings collected from the people for the tabernacle and its furnishings were also of this kind of linen (Exod. 25:4; 28:5; 35:6, 23, 25). The same is true of the tabernacle curtains (Exod. 26:1; 36:8), the veil (Exod. 26:31; 36:35), the screen for the tent door (Exod. 26:36; 36:37), the hangings for the tabernacle (Exod. 27:9; 38:9, 16), and the screen for the entrance of the court (Exod. 27:16, 18; 38:18). The priestly vestments—the ephod and its band (Exod. 28:6, 8; 39:2-3, 5), the breast-piece of judgment (Exod. 28:15; 39:8), the checker-work coat (Exod. 28:39; 39:27), the breeches (Exod. 28:42; 39:28), the girdle (Exod. 39:29), the turbans and caps (Exod. 39:28), and the pomegranate designs on the skirt of the robe of the ephod (Exod. 39:24)—all were of fine Egyptian linen.

c) בוץ (LXX βύσσος, βύσσινος), a fine white linen. This term replaced שש and does not occur before Ezekiel. The term is used in association with the Israelite family of linen workers noted above. Huramabi of Tyre was skilled in linen working (II Chr. 2:14). This linen was a valuable article of trade with Edom (Ezek. 27:16). David and the Levitical singers were clothed in linen garments when the ark was brought to Jerusalem (I Chr. 15:27), as were the members of the musical guild of the Solomonic temple (II Chr. 5:12). Mordecai wore a linen garment in the presence of the Persian king (Esth. 8:15). The veil of the temple was made of linen (II Chr. 3:14), and the hangings in the palace garden at Susa were held up with linen cords (Esth. 1:6).

d) פשתה (LXX λίνον, στιππύινος), "flax"—i.e., linen—apparently a more general term, as may be seen from the reference to leprous garments of flax and wool (Lev. 13:47-48, 52, 59) and the prohibition against the wearing of mixed clothes of flax and wool (Deut. 22:11). In a more specific sense the term is used of Jeremiah's waistcloth and the garments of the priests in Ezekiel's new order (44:17-18).

e) אטון (Egyptian *idmy;* Prov. 7:16), prized linen from Egypt.

f) Βύσσος, soft, fine linen. The rich man (Luke 16:19) wore clothes of such linen, and it was a valued article of trade brought to Rome (Rev. 18:12) by oriental merchants.

g) Βύσσινος ("material of βύσσος"), a linen garment. The term is used figuratively in Revelation to describe the luxury of the harlot city (18:16), the worthy raiment of the bride of the lamb (19:8) and the armies of heaven (19:14).

h) Σινδών, fine, costly linen (cloth). The young man who broke away on the night of Jesus' arrest had only such a linen cloth about him (Mark 14:51-52). The body of Jesus was wrapped in a linen shroud in preparation for burial (Matt. 27:59; Mark 15:46; Luke 23:53).

i) Ὀθόνη, a linen sheet or cloth. This term is used for the sheet let down from heaven, which Peter saw in a trance (Acts 10:11; 11:5).

j) Ὀθόνιον, a strip of linen used for swathing the dead (Luke 24:12; John 19:40; 20:5-7).

k) Λίνον, flax; linen as clothing, wick of lamp. This term is used of the apparel of the seven angels (Rev. 15:6) and the smoking wick (Matt. 12:20=Isa. 42:3; cf. Isa. 43:17).

In addition to these, the KJV uses "linen" in several other passages. On מקוה (KJV "linen yarn"; I Kings 10:28; II Chr. 1:16), *see* KUE. On סדין (KJV "fine linen"; Prov. 31:24; Isa. 3:23), *see* LINEN GARMENT. On שעטנז (KJV "a garment mingled of linen and woolen"; Lev. 19:19), *see* STUFF; CLOTH § 6.

Bibliography. S. Krauss, *Talmudische Archäologie,* I (1910), 138 ff; L. M. Wilson, *Ancient Textiles from Egypt* (1933); G. Dalman, *Arbeit und Sitte in Palästina,* V (1937), 23-30; L. Bellinger, "Report upon a Fragment of Cloth from Dead Sea Scroll Cave," *BASOR,* 118 (1950), 9-11; G. M. Crowfoot, "Linen Textiles from the Cave of Ain Feshkha in the Jordan Valley," *PEQ* (1951), pp. 5-31. J. M. MYERS

LINEN GARMENT [סדין; Akkad. *saddinu*]; KJV SHEET; FINE LINEN. A large rectangular sheet of linen, serviceable as a garment or as a cover. Because of its size and nature, it was quite valuable and highly prized. The term is used of the thirty sheets wagered by Samson on his riddle (Judg. 14:12-13), of one of the products of the industrious housewife (Prov. 31:24), and of one of the luxuries of the women of Jerusalem (Isa. 3:23). In later Jewish literature the word refers to the light summer garment. It was used for sails, curtains, bedspreads, and runners to protect carpets or rugs from being soiled.

For other occurrences of "linen garments" as a literal translation, *see* LINEN; DRESS AND ORNAMENTS.

J. M. MYERS

LINTEL [איל, משקוף; KJV כפתור (RSV CAPITAL)]. A wooden beam above the door. In I Kings 6:31, which is obscure, the meaning may be that the lintel in this case, instead of a horizontal beam, was two beams meeting at an angle, suggestive of the tent which originally contained the ark. In the Passover the lintel and the doorposts were sprinkled with blood (Exod. 12:22-23).

See also ARCHITECTURE; DOOR; HOUSE.

O. R. SELLERS

LINUS lī'nəs [Λίνος] (II Tim. 4:21). A Christian man who sent greetings to Timothy. An untrustworthy tradition in the Apostolic Constitutions 7.46 makes him the son of Claudia, who is found in the same verse. Linus in rescued from the obscurity surrounding so many others who are briefly mentioned in the NT letters by the tradition, first found in Irenaeus (Her. III.3.3) that the apostles Peter and Paul, after they had founded the church in Rome and set it in order, made Linus bishop of that church; at the same time he identifies him with the Linus of II Timothy. Many later church fathers repeat this tradition of Irenaeus, though Tertullian (Presc. Her. 32) implies that Clement was the first subapostolic bishop of Rome.

Many questions, difficult or impossible of solution, have been raised concerning Linus. First, is the identification of the Roman bishop with the Linus of II Timothy correct? Did Linus assume office before the death of Peter, and what was the nature of his power? Was he bishop jointly with Clement, or did each of them rule over part of the Roman church?

Eusebius (Hist. III.13) says Linus was bishop twelve years; a likely dating would be *ca.* A.D. 64-76. The Roman Breviary says he was born in Volterra in Etruria and martyred by the consul Saturninus; the latter statement seems unlikely, since there were no outstanding martyrdoms between Nero and Domitian. The Western church honors him September 23.

F. W. GINGRICH

LION [ארי, אריה (*so also* Aram.; Dan. 7:4, *etc.*), *cf.* Akkad. *arū;* כפיר, *possibly* covered one (*i.e., with mane*) *or* concealed one (*i.e., a tricky prowler*), *cf.* Arab. *kapara,* to cover, conceal; לביא, *lābhî'* (לבי *in* Ps. 57:4—H 57:5; Nah. 2:13; לביא, *lebhîyā', in* Ezek. 19:2), *cf.* Ugar. *lb', lbit;* Arab. *labā'a, etc.;* ליש (Job 4:11; Prov. 30:30; Isa. 30:6), *cf.* Arab. *laish;* Akkad. *nēšu;* שחל, *perhaps* noisy one, *cf.* Arab. *saḥala,* to bray (*of an ass, mule*); λέων; Lat. *leo*]; KJV LION'S WHELPS [בני שחץ, sons of pride] (Job 28:8; RSV PROUD BEASTS; cf. 41:34—H 41:26). A large carnivorous quadruped (*Panthera leo* or *Felis leo*) of a tawny color, and with a tufted tail, the male usually with a mane.

The lion of Palestine belonged to the Asiatic or Persian lion, *Panthera leo persica* Mey. Contrary to earlier assumptions, this subspecies contained maned lions, as well as the almost maneless, blackish-maned to pale-maned individuals. The mane stopped at the shoulders but covered most of the belly. Lions were common in Palestine in biblical times. They decreased until shortly after A.D. 1300. The last two reported lions were killed near Beisan (Beth-shan) and near Megiddo. In Mesopotamia lions died out only toward the end of the nineteenth century. Usamah ibn Munqidh gave us as late as the twelfth century very vivid descriptions of lion hunts in the Orontes Valley.

אריה (*'aryê*) is the most general word for "lion"; the others are all poetic names of strong lions in their full power. כפיר (*kephîr*) is often translated "young lion," but there is little justification for dintinguishing it in this way from the other general designations. In poetic parallelism it may be only a synonym for the different word for "lion" in the preceding line, as in Ps. 91:13; Ezek. 19:6; Hos. 5:14; etc.

The Assyrian sources indicate that lion-hunting was the sport of kings* (*see bibliography;* on the Syrian lion, see Aristotle *History of Animals* VI.31 [579*b*]). From the time of the judges (Judg. 14:5-9) through the age of Job (Job 4:10-11), and as late as the Mishna (B.K. 1.4; B.M. 7.9; Sanh. 1.4), Israel's literature has numerous references to these animals, including lionesses and cubs. While Samson (Judg. 14:6), David (I Sam. 17:34-36), and Benaiah (II Sam. 23:20) are credited with killing lions, others fared less well in such encounters (I Kings 13:24; 20:36; II Kings 17:25; M. Sanh. 1.4; on one method of capturing and killing lions, cf. Ezek. 19:4, 8; on lions in captivity, cf. Dan. 6). Generally speaking, the lion appears in the Bible as a bold, destructive creature, the bane of the flock (Amos 3:12), whose roaring inspires fear; Prov. 30:30 recognizes it as the mightiest of all the beasts. Although the lion, like all God's creatures, is sustained by divine providence (Job 38:39; Ps. 104:21), it is represented in forecasts of the future age of blessedness as being altogether absent (Isa. 35:9) or as domesticated (Isa. 11:6-7; 65:25). Fig. ASS 102.

The lion serves as a common metaphor or simile in the Bible. Thus "Judah is a lion's whelp" (Gen. 49:9); the wicked "lurks in secret like a lion in his covert" (Ps. 10:9); "a king's wrath is like the growling of a lion" (Prov. 19:12); Judas Maccabeus is "like a lion in his deeds" (I Macc. 3:4); etc. Even the Lord is likened to a lion (Job 10:16; Hos. 13:7), as is the devil (I Pet. 5:8). In Rev. 5:5 the Messiah is termed the "Lion of the tribe of Judah" (cf. 22:16)—a concept presumably resting on (*a*) the reference to Judah as a lion's whelp in Gen. 49:9, and (*b*) the view that the Messiah was a descendant of the house of David (cf. II Esd. 12:31-32).

The lion played a limited role in the religious symbolism of the ancient Near East. In Egypt it was associated with Horus and Re, while a number of goddesses manifested themselves as a lioness (e.g., Tefnut, Sekhmet).* Although in Babylonia, Ishtar and a lion are often grouped together, E. D. Van Buren (*see bibliography*) suggests that in early Mesopotamia "the lion was not the emblem of one particular god, but indicated that warlike strain which was latent in the character of most divinities." Later, when the natural lion was felt, despite its strength, to be inadequate to cope with evil spirits, its own powers were augmented by wings, etc., and it became a semidivine cherub, the *lamassu.* In the late Assyrian period the lion was seemingly regarded as a royal beast; thus weights, of the king's standard, were cast in the shape of a lion couchant. In Palestine the lion motif in the fine arts was established before the coming of the Hebrews, as we learn from the orthostat of a lion excavated in 1955 from a thirteenth-century Canaanite sanctuary at Hazor;* cf. the lions in the temple-palace at Tell Halaf and at Mari. It was Phoenician craftsmen who were responsible for the lions which graced Solomon's temple (I Kings 7:29,

Courtesy of the Museum of Fine Arts, Boston

31. A glazed brick lion, from the Processional Way, Babylon (sixth century B.C.)

Courtesy of the Palestine Archaeological Museum, Jerusalem, Jordan

32. Lions from the Samarian ivories (ninth century B.C.)

36) and palace (10:19-20); cf. the lion faces of the cherubim carved on the paneling of Ezekiel's temple (Ezek. 41:15-19). A seal depicting a lion, and belonging to Shema the servant of Jeroboam, was found at Megiddo (*see bibliography*); whether at this time the lion was a Hebrew symbol of royalty is uncertain. The ivories found at Samaria supply other examples of the use of the lion motif.* For illustrations, *see bibliography*. Figs. LIO 31; ART 86; LIO 32.

In view of the above evidence, the employment of the lion as a symbol of power and ferocity by biblical writers, especially by the apocalyptists, is quite intelligible. Ezekiel's cherubim have as one of their four faces that of a lion (Ezek. 1:10; 10:14); the first of the great beasts to come out of the sea in Dan. 7:1-4 was a winged lion; the first of the four living creatures around the throne of God in Rev. 4:7 is described as "like a lion"; and in Rev. 13:2 the seven-headed beast rising out of the sea is said to have a mouth "like a lion's" (cf. 9:8, 17).

Bibliography. For illustrations of lions, see: *Syria*, XIX (1938), plate 10 (lions at Mari); J. W. and G. M. Crowfoot, *Early Ivories from Samaria* (1938), plates IX-X; E. D. Van Buren, *The Fauna of Ancient Mesopotamia as Represented in Art* (1939), p. 4; A. Reifenberg, *Ancient Hebrew Seals* (1950), fig. 1 (a seal from Megiddo); M. Von Oppenheim, *Tell Halaf*, vol. III (1955), nos. 105-7; *BA* (Feb., 1956), p. 10 (orthostat excavated at Hazor).

On lion-hunting, see G. Contenau, *Everyday Life in Babylon and Assyria* (1954), pp. 134-35.

W. S. McCullough and F. S. Bodenheimer

***LISTS, ETHICAL.** Two main types of ethical lists occur in the NT letters: (*a*) catalogues enumerating moral obligations of individuals in specified relationships within a household or community; (*b*) catalogues with more general ethical content.

1. Terminology
2. Cultural background of household codes
   - *a*. Jewish
   - *b*. Greek and Roman
3. Development of household rules in the NT
4. NT rules for life in community
5. The other ethical lists

Bibliography

1. Terminology. In Luther's German translation of the Bible, two lists in particular, Eph. 5:21–6:9; Col. 3:18–4:1, are headed by the word *Haustafel* (lit., "household table"), now a technical term designating such a catalogue of domestic duties, much as "table" is employed in the OT for the Hebrew לוח (LXX πλάξ; Vulg. *tabula*)—e.g., in Deut. 5:22—for the actual stone tablets containing the Decalogue (cf. II Cor. 3:3; Heb. 9:4). Another term, *Gemeindetafel* (lit., "community table"), designates a more inclusive code of rules governing conduct of members within the church, or toward those outside (e.g., I Tim. 2:1-15; 5:1-21; 6:1-2; I Pet. 2:13–3:7). More general ethical lists usually take the form of catalogues enumerating certain sins, or vices, to be "put off," or virtues to be "put on" (Col. 3:5-14; cf. Gal. 5:19-23). The background and origin of all such lists has been widely debated.

2. Cultural background of household codes. ***a. Jewish.*** In the OT the Decalogue provided a nucleus for domestic regulations in the Fifth Commandment (Exod. 20:12; Deut. 5:16), quoted in Eph. 6:2-3 (cf. Mark 7:10, followed by a list of sins in vss. 21-22). Respect for parents likewise occupies a prominent place in the Holiness Code (Lev. 19:3), as well as in imprecations appended to the Deuteronomic Code (Deut. 27:16; cf. Exod. 21:15, 17). Honor due to God is deduced from that accorded a father by his son and a master by his slave, in Mal. 1:6. Similarly, rabbinic teaching coupled Exod. 20:12 with Prov. 3:9, and Lev. 19:3 with Deut 6:13 (Ḳid. 30*b*). Philo frequently connects filial piety with duty to God, as do Tob. 4:3-5; Ecclus. 3:1-16, in the Apoc. A Hebrew household (בית; LXX οἶκος; Vulg. *domus*) frequently included not only husband, wife, sons, and daughters, but also daughters-in-law (Gen. 7:1, 7), or mother-in-law (cf. Mark 1:29 ff), as well as slaves with their children (Gen. 15:3; 17:23; 24:2). The Mishna lists together wife, children, and slaves, as exempt from certain religious duties required of the man (Ber. III.3; Suk. II.8). A woman was subject to her father's authority until transferred to that of her husband (Keth. IV.3), while a man's responsibility for certain actions of his wife, slave, son, or daughter is discussed in B.M. I.5. A Jewish household code, more inclusive than any in the NT, occurs in Ecclus. 7:18-36, embracing obligations to friends, wife, slaves, domestic animals, children (especially marriageable daughters), parents, the Lord and his priests, together with the poor, the dead, mourners, and the sick. Lists given by Philo include many of the same items, the chief addition being duty to one's country and its rulers. Among the Dead Sea Scrolls, the Manual of Discipline provides rules for a community, but none for households.

b. Greek and Roman. Among familial obligations stressed by Greek and Latin moralists, respect for parents is often joined with reverence for the deities. Pythagoras is credited by Diogenes Laertius with teaching that, next to gods and heroes, parents should receive highest honor (*Lives of Eminent Philosophers* VIII.2). Similar connections are made by

Epictetus (II.xvii), Marcus Aurelius (V.31), and in a work on the *Education of Children* attributed to Plutarch. Greek and Roman households included not only those related by kinship and marriage but also domestic servants. On the one hand, the Latin *familia* designated, first of all, the retinue of *famuli* or household slaves; on the other hand, the adjective *familiaris* applied to friends, even acquaintances. By rule of *patria potestas* a father had absolute authority over his children, and a wife, given *in manu,* was transferred from parental authority to that of her husband. Since domestic relations were conducted in accord with unwritten custom, problems arose on which Stoic moralists gave advice of rather general nature. Seneca (*Epistle* 94) refers to that part of philosophy which counsels a husband how to treat his wife, a father how to bring up his children, a master how to govern his slaves. Marcus Aurelius (V.31) asks: "How have you dealt with the gods, with parents, brothers, wife, children, teachers, guardians, friends, relatives, domestic servants?" Epictetus (II.xiv) speaks quite as broadly regarding duties of son, father, brother, citizen, husband, wife, neighbor, companion, ruler, and ruled. Plutarch, if he wrote the work mentioned above, says: "One must reverence deities, honor parents, respect elders, obey laws, submit to rulers, love friends, be discreet with women, affectionate toward children and not mistreat slaves."

3. Development of household rules in the NT. The fervid eschatological expectations of the primitive church had the effect of weakening family ties, as concerns of an age soon to pass away (Mark 10:29-30; 13:12; cf. Matt. 8:21-22; 10:35 ff; Luke 12:52-53; 14:26). On such grounds, Paul could counsel everyone to remain in the state in which he was called; contracting marriage was held inadvisable, slavery a matter of indifference (I Cor. 7:17-35). Given this outlook, it is unlikely that, in I Thess. 4:4, the obscure phrase "to possess his vessel" (KJV) really means "to take a wife" (RSV), nor is the passage in which it occurs an incipient *Haustafel.* Although I Cor. 7:3-6 outlines mutual obligations of husband and wife, where both are believers, while vss. 12 ff treat special problems raised where one is an unbeliever, probably the earliest attempt to draw up a more comprehensive table of domestic relations is that in Col. 3:18–4:1. Here rules governing relations between slaves and masters, especially, probably bear upon the Letter to Philemon, where the Christian master of Onesimus is urged to accept him "no longer as a slave but more than a slave, as a beloved brother, . . . in the Lord" (vs. 16). That a domestic servant should be treated as a brother is taught in Ecclus. 33:31. Duties of wives and husbands, children and parents, are more briefly sketched in this list than in Eph. 5:22–6:4.

Some scholars believe that these and other such catalogues reflect current catechetical instruction given in preparation of converts for baptism (*see* EDUCATION, NT); they indicate that antecedents are to be sought in Judaism. Other investigators, pointing to similarities in content between these lists and those of Stoic moralists (*see* STOICS), maintain that the latter were taken over and adapted by early Christian teachers with only slight modifications; some suggest that in Colossians the table may be an interpolation, interrupting an original sequence from 3:17 to 4:2. Perhaps these two views are not mutually exclusive, for while some of the Greek terminology of the NT *Haustafeln* coincides with that of Stoic teachers, certain phrases used in them are characteristically Jewish. Examples in Col. 3:22 ff include "singleness of heart," "fearing the Lord," and "respect of persons" (partiality). Eph. 5:31 ff contains not only quotations from Gen. 2:24; Exod. 20:12, but other reflections of OT thought and language. The same is true of I Pet. 2:17 ff; 3:6; 5:5. On the other hand, requirements of a bishop, in I Tim. 3:2-7; Tit. 1:7-9, include qualifications from Hellenistic lists for a king, a general, and even a midwife.

4. NT rules for life in community. The Pastoral letters illustrate how tables of purely domestic duties could be adapted to the needs of church order. This is especially evident in I Tim. 3:4, 15, where a bishop must manage his own household well, in order to know how to take care of the congregation, which is God's household, as in Num. 12:7. Within this larger family, older men and women are to receive the respect due to father and mother; younger men and women are to be treated as brothers and sisters (I Tim. 5:1-2; cf. Matt. 23:8*b;* Mark 3:35). Yet ties of kinship are not broken, and filial responsibilities should not be shifted to the church (I Tim. 5:3-8). By the same token, Christian slaves whose masters are also believers must not take advantage of their brotherhood by failing to give them proper respect and service (6:2). That Christian masters should treat their slaves fairly (Eph. 6:9; Col. 4:1) is not repeated in the Pastorals.

Such community rules also urge the maintenance of good relations between church members and outsiders. Christian slaves of unbelieving masters should strive to give satisfaction, guarding the name of God and church doctrine from disrepute (I Tim. 6:1; Tit. 2:9-10; I Pet. 2:18 ff). On similar grounds, Christians are not only to pray for pagan rulers, but to submit to their lawful authority (I Tim. 2:1 ff; Tit. 3:1 ff; I Pet. 2:13 ff). If, in spite of good conduct, believers suffer unjust treatment, they should endure it patiently, following Christ's example; only they must never commit criminal acts justly punishable by the state (I Pet. 3:13 ff; 4:13 ff). Thus governmental authority might even be invoked to reinforce the moral code of the community.

5. The other ethical lists. Catalogues of pagan vices to be avoided sometimes accompany lists of household or community duties (Eph. 5:3-8; Col. 3:5-9; I Tim. 1:9-10; Tit. 3:3; I Pet. 4:3). Such lists also occur quite independently of *Haustafeln* (Rom. 1:29 ff; I Cor. 5:10-11; 6:9-10; Gal. 5:19 ff; II Tim. 3:2 ff). In at least two instances they are placed in direct contrast to lists of virtues (Gal. 5:22-23; Col. 3:12 ff; cf. Eph. 4:25 ff; 5:2; Tit. 3:2). Some scholars hold that all such lists go back to the teaching of Stoic moralists; they point out that parallels are rare in the OT, or in rabbinic teaching, although represented in Hellenistic Judaism, in Wisd. Sol. 14:25-26, and the work of Philo on the *Sacrifices of Cain and Abel* (V.32). The list in Rom. 1:28 ff is headed by a Greek phrase (τὰ μὴ καθήκοντα, "improper conduct"), derived from the Stoic term for "duty," while in the catalogue of II Tim. 3:2-4 nearly half the words do not occur in the LXX. Starting from such premises, it is suggested that the sins in Mark 7:21-22 are another example of the list-making activity of Hellenized Christianity, rather than a deposit from Palestinian tradition. Nevertheless, here every term occurs in the LXX, each (with the exception of ἀσέλγεια, "licentiousness") representing a Hebrew term. Moreover, the belief that evil thoughts and actions originate in the heart is typically Hebraic (cf. Gen. 6:5; Matt. 5:28).

A rabbinic catalogue of the heart's activities includes several sins listed in Mark 7:21-22 (Eccl. Rabbah I.16). Among the Dead Sea Scrolls, the Manual of Discipline lists certain counsels attributed to two spirits which contend within man's heart; counsels of the spirit of error include terms listed in Mark; several counsels of the spirit of truth coincide with virtues found in other NT lists (1QS IV.2 ff, 9 ff). While the scroll writer might have come under Hellenistic influence, evidence of this is lacking from his catalogues, which employ no terms borrowed from the Greek, but a purely biblical Hebrew vocabulary. If a community of Palestinian Jews residing near the Dead Sea drew up lists of this kind for its members, Jewish Christians may have done likewise. Even the reliability of the tradition attributing such a list to Jesus can scarcely be disproved by any objective criterion, although the esoteric device in Mark 7:17, as elsewhere, appears rather artificial.

In substance, the teaching of Mark 7:21-22 harmonizes with another saying of Jesus which likewise emphasizes the internal root of character, the human heart (Luke 6:45). It is further underscored by Paul's recognition of all virtue as the "fruit of the Spirit" (Gal. 5:22-23). The net result of the catalogue method, with its tendency to externalize both vice and virtue, the latter as something to be "put on," was a reintroduction of legalism. This limitation of formal ethical lists, whatever their actual content, may help explain their scarcity in the gospels.

Bibliography. K. Weidinger, *Die Haustafeln* (1928); W. K. L. Clarke, *NT Problems* (1929), pp. 157-60; K. E. Kirk, *The Vision of God* (1931), pp. 111-30; B. S. Easton, "NT Ethical Lists," *JBL* (1932), pp. 1-12; P. Carrington, *The Primitive Christian Catechism* (1940); B. S. Easton, *The Pastoral Epistles* (1947), pp. 197-202; E. G. Selwyn, *The First Epistle of St. Peter* (1947), pp. 363-466; W. D. Davies, *Paul and Rabbinic Judaism* (1948), ch. 6; D. Daube, *The NT and Rabbinic Judaism* (1956), pp. 90-140; W. D. Davies, "Paul and the DSS: Flesh and Spirit," *The Scrolls and the NT* (1957), pp. 169-72.

O. J. F. SEITZ

***LITERATURE.** In the broadest sense literature includes all that is written. WRITING was originally used for merely practical purposes. In the OT many sorts of such "literature" are mentioned: commercial documents and accounts (cf. the Samaria OSTRACA, letters (*see* LETTER; LACHISH), lists of state officials (I Kings 4), tax lists, population lists (Ezra 2), and other administrative documents. Even curses (*see* BLESSINGS AND CURSINGS) may early have been written with the magical letters to increase their power (Zech. 5:1 ff; cf. Ezek. 2:9 ff).

In the more restricted sense, however, literature designates artistic compositions, in poetry or in prose, which are related to the life and thought of a particular community. Biblical literature includes various genres or types which are similar in many respects to the literary pieces produced by Near Eastern and Greco-Roman antiquities.

1. Origins
2. Wisdom literature
3. Laws
4. Historiography
5. Poetic literature
   a. Popular poetry
   b. Epic poetry
   c. Sacral poetry
   d. Written texts
   e. Postcanonical religious poetry
6. Prophetic literature
   a. Prophetic sayings and poems
   b. Books
   c. Apocalyptic
7. Metrical forms

Bibliography

1. Origins. Behind practically all literary types and styles in the OT lies the oral stage transmitted by TRADITION. In the times of the tribal amphictyony neither administration nor cult needed written texts. A written literature came into existence with the kingdom. For his political relations with the neighboring powers the king needed scribes (*see* SCRIBE), educated in the knowledge of international affairs and in forms of expression necessary for their work. The historical kernel which may be found in the idea of Solomon as the patron of the "wisdom" of the scribes, is in all probability that he organized a school for scribes in connection with palace and temple. Both the study of foreign languages and the education in the beautiful art of writing and in the proper conduct of a king's scribe made models and texts necessary. Thus Israel simply stepped into an interoriental literary tradition with fixed types and styles, each of them according to its own "place in life"—with Canaan as intermediary. In fact, most of the Israelite literature has close parallels in the much older oriental literature, both as to types (*Gattungen*) and to style and phraseology, partly also as to religious and moral ideas.

2. Wisdom literature. WISDOM was the international word that also included the art of the scribes. In Egypt and Babylonia they long had laid down the self-consciousness and the ideals of their class as to education, morals, life style, and literary forms, in "wisdom books," with their specific didactic style and metrical form. Nothing was more natural than that such books were the first books with which the school and the scribes of Solomon were acquainted. Among the minor collections which are assembled in the book of PROVERBS is also one that drew directly on the Egyptian "Wisdom of Amen-em-ope." There can be little doubt that the oldest *written* literature in Israel was translations and imitations of foreign wisdom, gradually developing into an Israelite wisdom showing something of the spirit of Yahwism. Compared with that of the foreign models, the influence of the popular proverb was unimportant.

The older wisdom is of a merely practical and utilitarian kind. The presence of many advices for the career shows that this wisdom originates within the circle of the royal officials (cf. also the heading in Prov. 25:1). The younger collection, Prov. 1-9, reveals influence from foreign speculations on the metaphysical nature of wisdom. That also the fundamental problems of religion and philosophy of life in the course of time have been felt and taken up by the wise men, is seen from JOB, which shows a mixture of wisdom and psalm style, also found in the latest psalm poetry (*see* § 6 *below*), and the pessimistic ECCLESIASTES, while the book of ECCLESIASTICUS in this respect walks on the traditional path. Influence from Greek popular philosophy betrays the WISDOM OF SOLOMON, where the old metrical form mostly is given up.

3. Laws. The scribes of the palace had to deal with the affairs of the royal chapel, the temple, as well (cf. II Kings 22:3 ff; Jer. 36:10-12). This must have given strong impulses to written fixations of sacral traditions. The scribes, in a way, became the "traditionists" of a sacral literature. Already in pre-exilic times there may have existed written collections of psalms, as in Deut. 26:1-6, and of priestly TORAH, etc. Written laws (*see* LAW IN THE OT) very often have been among the first demands of a nation. The origin of the Israelite law is a double one: the orally transmitted separate decisions and "instructions" (*tôrôth*) and ordeals of the priest in the name of Yahweh, and the more "civil" right, expressed in casuistic "judgments" (*mishpāṭîm*), both stylistically and materially dependent on interoriental jurisprudence and certainly taken over from the Canaanites. Soon, they too came to be considered as the laws of Yahweh. The common man, of course, was first and foremost interested in the latter, and even the scribes might wish to have written the norms according to which they had to deal in public affairs or as judges at court. There is therefore good reason to think that one of the first written collections was the *"Mishpāṭîm"* (Exod. 21:1-22:27). The priestly, apodictic *tôrâ* style of the additions at the end (22:17-27) proves that they were transmitted within circles closely related to the temple, and adapted to Yahwistic ideas.

There are also laws of such nature and purpose that it was early felt necessary to inscribe them on tables and set them up publicly. Thence the word חק (חקה), from חקק, "cut in," "engrave," "inscribe." Such laws are the specific *leges sacrae* of a sanctuary, setting the conditions for entering the place and taking part in its blessings. An example of such old sacral law is reflected in the etiological anecdote (*see* LEGEND § 2*d*) in II Sam. 5:6-8: "The blind and the lame shall not come into the house"—i.e., the temple (cf. Lev. 21:18). In Jerusalem the idea of such conditions of entrance was connected with the idea of the fundamental commandments of the COVENANT, preferably in decalogue form, and thus got its place in the liturgies both as "conditions of entrance" (Pss. 15; 24:3-4) and at the annual renewal of the covenant (Pss. 81; 95). Various forms of decalogues may early have been written—the background of the legend in Exod. 32 and the "charter" (ספר הברית) in Exod. 24:7.

The greater law books have gradually been built up of such smaller, oral and written, collections. The "Book of the Law" found in the temple in Josiah's time probably was one of the sources of DEUTERONOMY; D itself (=Deut. 4:45-27:9; ch. 28) is best explained as the "constitution" of the consolidated Jewish congregation after the "restoration" (*ca.* 520 B.C.). Somewhat younger are probably the codification of the "Law of Holiness" (Lev. 17-26), the temple order proposed in Ezek. 40-48 and the last redaction of the laws now included in "P" (*see* § 4 *below*).

4. Historiography. This is the first of the two points where Israel's literature distinguishes itself from the rest of the ancient Near East. From the beginning the royal annals (ספר דברי הימים) belonged to the duties of the scribes. They knew the stories told at court, of the deeds of David and the splendor of Solomon. And their close connection with the temple also made them acquainted with the traditions and legends told at the festivals—the Exodus legends, the concentrated form of which was the "historical credo" (von Rad): "Yahweh thy God who led thee up from Egypt." The historical foundation of Israel's existence as Yahweh's elected people gave to its religion a feeling of history, unknown to the ancient Near East—Yahweh the Lord of history.

The beginning was the living tradition of the court and its oral connection with greater pragmatic complexes, as the Saul-Samuel and Saul-David traditions, the record of David's last years and the ascension of Solomon, where the vivid oral style and epic skill are easily recognizable. How early they were written, one cannot tell. Some of them may have been incorporated in the "book of the acts of Solomon" (I Kings 11:41). The "book of chronicles of the kings of Judah," or of "Israel," often referred to in Kings, was scarcely the original annals, rather a more epic and "popular" recension of these, that even may have included many prophet legends (*see* LEGEND).

The *opus magnum* of OT historiography is the national saga of J. Using all existing myths and *sagas* about the primeval times, the patriarchs, the Exodus, etc., J wrote the history of the Davidic "Great Israel" from the Creation to the conquest of Canaan, from a religious point of view—the election and the fulfilling of the promises to the fathers. In spite of his respect for the fixed tradition, J is no mere collector; he is a real author who has stamped his book with his own spirit. On the later expansion of his book *see* TRADITION § 5.

On all these sources the Deuteronomistic saga has drawn, dealing with the history from the last days of Moses to the fall of Jerusalem (587 B.C.) and the release of Jehoiachin twenty-seven years later. Of the events from the Exodus to Jordan it gives only a short résumé, in the form of a speech of Moses, dependent on the expanded J. Then follows the Law=D, the source of the author's theology and religious pragmatism—the fate of the people is determined by its right or wrong relation to the Law. The book was written after the consolidation of the Jewish congregation, that it might learn from history to walk on the path of life. The often accepted theory about a pre-exilic origin and a later redaction is very improbable (for another view, *see* DEUTERONOMY; PENTATEUCH).

The "memorial" (not "memoirs"!) of Nehemiah follows the literary line of the oriental royal inscriptions, with their "I" style and enumeration of the deeds of the king. This record of the governor's pious works is written to be laid down "before the face of God" in the temple, that he may "remember him them for good." *See* EZRA AND NEHEMIAH, BOOKS OF.

A later author, P, representing priestly traditions and interests, rewrote the history from the CREATION to the Conquest (*see* ISRAEL) as seen from a "church-historical" point of view—the origin and old history of the people of the covenant and of its sacral institutions. The greatest place is taken up by the inserted ritual laws; the history itself is only a short scheme, with some new, quite legendary elements. Later on, P was braided together with the expanded J, and this compound work and the Deuteronomistic saga were telescoped into each other, with the final result that the first part of this work, Genesis–Deuteronomy, has the character of a law book—"the Law"—and is considered as a book of its own. *See* PENTATEUCH; TORAH.

The CHRONICLES drew the consequences of the predecessor's philosophy of history. "Israel" is here Judah only, the history of which is told from David to EZRA; the older times are only given in the form of tribal genealogies (*see* GENEALOGY), partly old traditions, partly learned constructions. The legendary development of the TRADITION (*see* §§ 4-5) makes it easy to demonstrate the ideological pragmatism of the author. The original Chronicles had no room for Nehemiah, whose place was given to the more edifying Ezra narrative, representing a tradition (or a written source) of its own, partly imitating Nehemiah.

Later Jewish "historical" literature (*see* DANIEL; ESTHER; JUDITH; TOBIT) becomes more and more LEGEND, lacking real historical feeling. This, however, had a short revival at the time of national freedom (*see* MACCABEES, BOOKS OF).

5. Poetic literature. Also the POETRY originally lived in oral form. This means that in spite of the relative fixity of tradition, poems often may have been linguistically and ideologically "modernized," unconsciously and consciously—let alone other possible errors—and that even the written "Ur text" may have existed in different forms (see the double recensions of Pss. 14 and 53; Ps. 18 and II Sam. 22). *See* TRADITION § 5.

It follows from the old Israelite conception of life that no sharp distinction can be drawn between profane and sacral poetry. It is, however, possible to speak of a more "popular" poetry besides the strictly sacral one.

a. Popular poetry. One of the oldest types is the power-filled rhythmical word of blessing—used both at solemn occasions of private life, as betrothal (Gen. 24:60) or the last words of the dying father (Gen. 27), and at the cultic assemblies (Num. 6:22-27)—and of curse—used, e.g., together with cultic rites before the battle to break the force of the enemy (Num. 22–24). *See* BLESSINGS AND CURSINGS.

This type has often been combined with the tribal anthem (*cf.* LEGEND § 2*a*), characterizations of the tribe's nature and fate (e.g., Gen. 4:23; 27:27-29, 39-40), which then have been formed as effective words and mostly put in the mouth of the dying ancestor. The fate and actual situation of the tribe are explained as the result of a blessing or a curse of the ancestor. Collections of such *vaticinia ex eventu* we have in Gen. 49 and the younger Deut. 33, imitations in the Balaam oracles and the so-called "last words of David" (II Sam. 23:1-7—a typical mixture of prophetic and wisdom style).

Among folk songs may be mentioned the short workers' songs (also known from Egypt), both at vintage and harvest and at *corvée* (Neh. 4:4). It may also have the character of an effective incantation—e.g., at the digging of a well "with the [power-filled] scepters of the chiefs" (Num. 21:17-18). Further examples are the mocking songs, often hinted at; the harlot's song (Isa. 23:16); the drinking song (Isa. 22:13); the watchman's song (cf. Isa. 5:1 ff).

At the burials were heard the conventional funeral songs of the professional "mourning women" (II Sam. 3:33-34; Jer. 9:16; 22:18), with the characteristic beginning, אכה and the sad cry, "Oh, our brother!" They gave impetus to passionate personal poems such as II Sam. 1:19-27; and the style was often used both in earnest and ironically, in poems on the fall of a city or of a people ("political dirges"; *see* LAMENTATIONS, BOOK OF), and often was imitated by the prophets (Amos 5:2), sometimes combined with the tone of the triumphant mocking song (Isa. 47).

At weddings, but also at other assemblies, the love poetry had its place (*see* SONG OF SONGS) among the poems, of which also may be found echoes from the drama of the old fertility cult, "secularized" into popular game and song.

From the short war songs, improvisations on the battlefield or at the return of the victorious warriors (cf. Judg. 11:34; I Sam. 18:7), sprang a higher poetry—e.g., the so-called Song of Deborah (Judg. 5; *see* DEBORAH 2), which was already influenced by the style of the hymn of praise (*see* § 5*c below*). The so-called Song of Miriam (Exod. 15; *see* MIRIAM 1) is no popular poem, but a regular cultic festival hymn, commemorating Yahweh's salvatory deeds of old, thus belonging to the strictly sacral poetry (*see* § 5*c below*).

b. Epic poetry. There also seems to have existed an epic poetry. There is reason to believe that the Book of Jashar (*see* JASHAR, BOOK OF) and the Book of the Wars of the Lord (*see* WARS OF THE LORD, BOOK OF) are identical, and that it was a sort of national epos, dealing poetically with the traditions about the Conquest and the first kings. It may, as usual, have originated from the independent, separate songs of the "rhapsodes" (מושלים). The age may be that between the original J and its later expansions (*see* § 4 *above*), which draw upon it.

c. Sacral poetry. The strictly sacral poetry includes, above all, the cultic poetry of PSALMS, with their different types, each having its specific function in connection with the different cultic and liturgical acts and situations: general hymns of praise; hymns to the definite feasts, among them the group of the hymns at Yahweh's throne ascension; national (congregational) psalms of lamentation on the days of penitence and prayer in public disaster and danger, often put in the mouth of the king; general prayer psalms; national thanksgiving psalms at the feast after experienced deliverance, even these partly with the king as the speaking Ego; individual psalms of lamentation for the use of "Everyman" who had fallen in illness or any other disaster and had to offer his "sin offering"; individual psalms of thanksgiving; festal liturgies, reflecting the different acts of the ritual—e.g., the coming of the festal procession, its entrance through the temple gates, etc. (Pss. 24; 68; 118; 132 and possibly others).

To the sacral poetry must also be added the oracles of the cult prophets—e.g., at the anointment of the king (Pss. 2; 110; 72), or in connection with the recitation of a psalm of lamentation; likewise, the priest's formulas of blessing and curse (*see* § 5*a above*) as regular or casual part of the liturgy—sometimes, like the oracles, included in the transmitted psalm text. Even the king's promise, his "charter" (Ps. 101), may be mentioned.

Even some of the prophetic "books," such as HABAKKUK and JOEL, may have come into existence as cultic liturgies for a definite occasion.

Religious in its outlook and motivation is also the wisdom poetry (*see* § 2 *above*) from the beginning, and it tends more and more in this direction. "The fear of the Lord is the beginning of wisdom."

d. Written texts. The fixation in script gradually took place (*see* § 3 *above*). The "Wars of the Lord" is quoted as a "book" both by the expanded J (*see* § 4 *above*) and by the sources of the Deuteronomistic saga. Most of the postexilic poetry seems to have been written at once—an indication is the use of the alphabetic acrostic, a decoration more for the eye than for the ear, found in Lamentations and late psalms.

e. Postcanonical religious poetry. The same must be said of the postcanonical psalmody. It is partly found as poems made *ad hoc* and put into the mouths of the heroes of the legendary literature (Daniel and his friends, Tobit, Judith, etc.) or in the books of the "wise," such as ECCLESIASTICUS, and partly in separate collections, such as PSALMS OF SOLOMON; DEAD SEA SCROLLS. It tries to walk on the traditional paths, but demonstrates, however, a typical mixture of psalm and wisdom style and ideas. Characteristics of the Qumran Hodayoth are the overwhelming biblical reminiscences, the disintegration of the style of the classical thanksgiving psalm, the allusions to the external and the mystical experiences of the poet, and the religious reflections.

6. Prophetic literature. This represents the second point that demonstrates the originality of Israelite literature. In spite of pretended Egyptian and Babylonian models—which at best are remote formal analogies—it has nothing to be compared with in the ancient East. Phenomenologically and psychologically the prophets of Israel have close analogies almost everywhere in the ancient Near East. What these other נביאים said, however, was ephemeral only and is "gone with the wind." In Israel only the words of the נביאים gave rise to a literature of world importance. This fact is due to the spiritual originality of the prophets (*see* PROPHET) and the uniqueness of the religion of Israel, or, in other words, their experience and idea of God. The religion of the Psalms is the spiritual background of the prophets, who always stood in close connection with the temple and the cult.

a. Prophetic sayings and poems. The originally oral sayings of the prophets, sprung from the more or less ecstatic inspiration of the moment, were independent short units, giving Yahweh's "oracle" of fortune or misfortune, or his "instruction" for the definite historical situation (cf. II Sam. 5:19, 23-24). Genetically and formally they are connected both with the exclamations of the religious ecstatics and with the visions of the old seers (cf. Num. 24:17) and their power-filled words of blessing or curse, which in themselves had the virtue to influence the things to come (*cf.* § 5*a above*). The visuality, the impressionism, the vivid picturing of the events to come, the emotions called forth by the picture in the mind of the prophet, the changing scenes, the hinting-at instead of a description, the metaphors—all these point to the connection with the ecstatics and the vision. This is true even in later times, as the normal form of the oracle—under the influence of the idea of inspiration by the Spirit of Yahweh—became the "message," introduced by the messenger's (and letter's) formula: "Thus saith Yahweh: Go and say unto So and So." In this latter type, the auditory element, which is not lacking in the vision, becomes more prominent.

The form of blessing and curse has lived on in the prophetic words, giving occasion to a more or less detailed description of the fortune or destruction to come.

The classic prophetic style was fully developed before Amos. What distinguishes it from the older one is, above all, that the prophet now is not content only with telling *what* Yahweh will do; he must also say *why* Yahweh acts as he does. The scheme is as follows: "Because So and So has done [said] such and such, therefore I now shall do this and this"; or vice versa: "I shall do such or such, for So and So has done . . . ." These may be called "expanded, or motivated, oracles." Materially we may distinguish between oracles of doom (threats) and oracles of fortune and "salvation" (promises). In the former the scolding and the reproach, the enumeration of the sins of the people, often using the style of the lamentation in the psalms, and the threat, akin to the curse, become prominent elements. In the promises, which were in exilic and postexilic times the predominant form of prophecy, Yahweh's remembering of the covenant, his "trustiness" and "lovingkindness" (*ḥêsedh*), more and more became the usual motivation.

The oldest sayings were very short, as can be seen both in the prophetic legends (*see* § 4 *above*) and even in Amos, where the original units easily can be distinguished from one another through the use of standing introductory and finishing formulas; they often comprise only two or three up to eight or even ten biblical verses. The "expanded oracle," of course, tends to become longer, but even the Deutero-Isaiah collection includes forty-six originally independent sayings, while the prophecies from his circle of disciples, the so-called Trito-Isaiah, are longer and often have imitated the form of the cultic "compound liturgies"—these eleven chapters include fourteen separate prophecies. But even the longer compositions—e.g., Jer. 2—reveal the original independence of the smaller units; even here the logical and formal connection is very loose.

During the ages the prophets have used the styles and forms of practically all the given poetic types, to make their sayings the more impressive. The prophetic oracle was in itself a poem, often a perfect one, in the usual metrical forms (*see* § 7 *below*). Especially the prophecies of JEREMIAH can be viewed as an anthology of the prophetic variations of the most different literary types. The influence of the psalm style is very prominent, both in Jeremiah (especially the psalm of lamentation) and in Deutero-Isaiah (ideas and forms from the hymns of praise, especially from the throne-ascension hymns).

Probably under the influence of the "wise scribes" as the tutors of the laws (*see* §§ 2-3 *above*) there came up prophetic "sermons" in prose, clearly akin to the Deuteronomistic admonitions and warnings, mostly secondary and literary, as in the books of Jeremiah and Ezekiel. In this "evolution" also the oral transmission of prophetic sayings played a role (on this subject and on the occasional use of script, *see* TRADITION § 5).

b. Books. The prophetic books are gradually composed of smaller collections of orally transmitted sayings, arranged after the following pattern: prophecies of doom followed by prophecies of salvation and reestablishment, often with catchwords as the principle of collection. Sometimes also biographical stories, as in Baruch's Jeremiah book (*see* BARUCH), or in Amos 7:10 ff, and legends have been attached. Some introductory and final formulas have been preserved, but often the single oracles have been attached to one another, without any connecting link, sometimes, however, connected by short redactional remarks, often only a כי ("for") or על־כן ("therefore"). A useful means of distinguishing is the study of the stylistic forms and types.

In the partly oral, partly literary process of collection and redaction especially the "school" of disciples such as that of ISAIAH seems to have played an important role—a fact to which, e.g., the combination of the Isaian and Deutero-Isaian "books" may be due. Both collection and redaction sprang from the religious needs of the congregation, aiming at the edification and at the fortifying of the hope for the "restoration of the kingdom for Israel."

c. Apocalyptic. The last offshoot of the prophetic literature is APOCALYPTICISM and the apocalyptic books (*see* PSEUDEPIGRAPHA), the beginnings of which we have already in the OT: Isa. 24–27; JOEL in its present form; Zech. 9–14; part of EZEKIEL; and DANIEL, here and oftener combined with the legendary "history."

Apocalyptic is learned, not popular, literature, but imbued with the author's consciousness of inspiration—the "wise men" considered themselves the heirs of the prophets—and often expressing personal mystical experiences; the right understanding of the older prophecies has "come to them" from above.

7. Metrical forms. On the metrical forms of Hebrew POETRY—which, no doubt, are dependent upon older Near East tradition—opinions still disagree. The normal form is no doubt the double line, or stich (bicolon), the two parallel hemistichs (cola) of which make a "thought-rhyme"; sometimes also tripartite stichs (tricola) occur—certainly a later evolution, although already found in Ugaritic poetry. The thought-rhyme (*parallelismus membrorum*) is no metrical phenomenon, but a stylistic; it became, however, fundamental in Hebrew poetry. Even in verses where we find neither a synonymous nor an antithetical parallelism, the verse is logically, grammatically, and metrically divided in two halves through a caesura (by Lowth called "synthetical parallelism"). Even the hemistich (colon) very often is dipodic, but also monopodic verses occur. Very often also 2+2 stichs (bicola) are parallel, making the basic strophe, but even more artificial stanzas (3, 4, 5, 7 stichs) are found. According to the still generally accepted system of Sievers, the ordinary stich (bicolon) has 3+3 (often even 3+4, or 4+3, or 4+4) metrical beats. Others here find a 4+4 meter, exclusively used in the wisdom poetry and thence called "mashal meter." A brachycatalectic descendant of the mashal is the kinah meter, with 4+3 (according to Sievers 3+2) beats, especially used in funeral songs, but also by psalmists and by prophets.

Bibliography. E. Sievers, Metrische Studien, vols. I-III (1904-5). H. Gunkel, "Die israelitische Literaturgeschichte," *Die orientalischen Literaturen* (=P. Hinneberg, *Die Kultur der Gegenwart* [1906], I, 7). H. Gressmann, "Die literarische Analyse Deuterojesajas," *ZATW*, 34 (1914), 254 ff. S. Mowinckel, *Zur Komposition des Buches Jeremia* (1914); *Statholderen Nehemia* (1916); *Ezra den skriftlaerde* (1916). G. Hölscher, "Komposition und Ursprung des Deuteronomium," *ZATW*, vol. 40 (1922). H. Gunkel, "Die Propheten als Schriftsteller und Dichter," *Die Schriften des AT in Auswahl,* II (2nd ed., 1923), 34 ff. S. Mowinckel, Psalmenstudien, III: *Kultprophetie und prophetische Psalmen* (1923); V: *Segen und Fluch in Israels Kult und Psalmdichtung* (1924). H. Gressmann, "Die neugefundene Lehre des Amenemope und die vorexilische Spruchdichtung Israels," *ZATW*, 42 (1924), 272 ff. L. Rost, *Die Ueberlieferung von der Thronnachfolge Davids* (1926). S. Mowinckel, "Motiver og stilformer i profeten Jeremias diktning," *Edda*, 26 (1926), 233 ff; *Le Décalogue* (1927). J. Hempel, *Die althebräische Literatur* (1930). S. Mowinckel, "Die Komposition des deuterojesajanischen Buches," *ZATW*, 44 (1931), 87 ff, 242 ff. A. Alt, *Die Ursprünge des israelitische Rechts* (1934). S. Mowinckel, "Hat es ein israelitisches Nationalepos gegeben?" *ZATW*, 53 (1935), 103 ff. G. Hylmö, *Gamla testamentets litteraturhistoria* (1938). G. von Rad, *Das formgeschichtliche Problem des Hexateuchs* (1938). R. Pfeiffer, *Introduction to the OT* (1941), pp. 11 ff. M. Noth, *Traditionsgeschichtliche Studien,* vol. I (1941). S. Mowinckel, "Oppkomsten av profetlitteraturen," *Norsk Teologisk Tidsskrift*, 43 (1942), 65 ff; *Det Gamle Testament,* III (1944), 33 ff. J. H. Patton, *Canaanite Parallels in the Book of Psalms* (1944). A. Kapelrud, *The Question of Authorship in the Ezra Narrative* (1944). A. Lods, *Histoire de la littérature hébraïque et juive des origines à la ruine de l'État juif* (1950). S. Mowinckel, *Offersang og sangoffer* (1951), pp. 418 ff, 436 ff. A. Bentzen, *Introduction to the OT,* I (2nd ed., 1952), 108 ff (with references). G. Hölscher, *Geschichtsschreibung in Israel* (1952). S. Mowinckel, "Psalms and Wisdom," *Wisdom in Israel and in the Ancient Near East: Supplements to Vetus Testamentum,* III (1955), 205 ff; "Marginalien zur hebräischen Metrik" (with references), *ZATW*, 68 (1956), 97 ff.

See also bibliographies under LEGEND; TRADITION.

S. MOWINCKEL

LITTER [מטה, *miṭṭâ* (Song of S. 3:7), *from* נטה, recline; צב, *ṣābh* (Isa. 66:20), *from* Akkad. *ṣumbu,* wagon]. A curtained couch borne on men's shoulders.

The meaning of *miṭṭâ* in Song of S. 3:7 appears to be related to *'appiryôn* in 3:9 (*see* PALANQUIN). Elsewhere usually BED or COUCH is used.

The context of *ṣabbîm* (plural of *ṣābh*) in Isa. 66:20 suggests that the Akkadian meaning, "wagons," is more appropriate than the RSV "litters" (cf. "covered wagons" of Num. 7:3, and *see* CART, WAGON).

W. S. MCCULLOUGH

LIVER [כבד]. The liver is rarely mentioned in the Bible, and then usually in its literal, physiological sense. The Hebrew word is derived from the root "to be heavy," perhaps with the implication that, in view of its density, the liver is to be regarded as the preeminently heavy organ of the body.

In the offering of ordinary sacrifice the CAUL (RSV "appendage") of the liver, along with the KIDNEYS and some other specified portions of the viscera, is set apart to be burned upon the altar as a special gift to Yahweh (Lev. 3:4, 10, 15).

In the ancient Orient the markings on the liver were studied for the purpose of DIVINATION ("hepatoscopy").* There is no direct evidence that the Hebrews themselves engaged in this practice, but the OT records an example of it in the case of the king of Babylon (Ezek. 21:21). The book of Tobit (6:4-7; 8:2) relates an instance of the use of a fish's liver to drive away demons. *See* MAGIC. Figs. DIV 31-33.

The liver was undoubtedly regarded as a seat of the psychic life, especially in its emotional aspects, although only one passage in the present Hebrew Bible actually uses the word with this implication (Lam. 2:11 KJV; RSV "heart"). It is probable, however, that certain other passages which now speak—rather unintelligibly—of the "glory" of an individual originally spoke of his "liver." The word for "glory" or "honor" (כבוד) in consonantal Hebrew script, when written defectively (as in Gen. 49:6), is identical with the word for "liver." It seems likely that in such passages as Gen. 49:6; Pss. 16:9; 57:8 the more delicate sensibilities of a later age have caused the alteration of the crude word "liver" (*kābhēdh*), in the sense of "innermost person" (cf. RSV "spirit" or "soul"), into the poetic-sounding "glory" (*kābhōdh*), by a simple change of the vowel points.

R. C. DENTAN

LIVING CREATURE [חיות, *from* חיה, to be alive]. In his inaugural vision Ezekiel beheld four living creatures (cf. Ezek. 1:5, 13-15, 19-20, 22) which looked like men in form but each of which had four faces. The faces were of man, lion, ox, and eagle. The same unusual appearance was witnessed by Ezekiel in 3:13 and in the second vision of God, which is recorded in ch. 10.

The exact meaning of this mysterious vision would not be easily unraveled, since it probably is more or less a refraction of symbols whose real meaning has been lost. However, the rabbinic interpretation would seem to be on the right track—namely, that the four faces represent God's dominion over man, who was created to rule the earth; over the lion, which is king of the forest; over the ox, which is most powerful of domesticated animals; and over the eagle, which rules the air. In other words, this somewhat bizarre vision contains a profound truth: that God is universal ruler over all life, whose source he is.

Life itself is bound up in the presence of God and is so symbolized by the creatures who are in proximity to the Almighty. In Rev. 4:7-8 the living creatures are mentioned, but instead of an oxen face there is the face of a calf, and instead of four wings each possesses six. Always the living God is represented as being surrounded by living creatures; this would suggest that he is not only ruler over all life but its source also.

C. G. HOWIE

LIZARD [לטאה (Lev. 11:30), *possibly* clinger; *cf.* Arab. *laṭa'a,* to cleave (to the ground); שממית (Prov. 30:28; KJV SPIDER) *probably* poisonous one, *cf.* Arab. *samm,* poison; *sāmm,* gecko; Syr. *sam,* medicine, poison; *samomīthā,* poisonous lizard; Jewish Aram. סממיתא, spotted lizard, spider]. Any of a suborder (*Lacertilia*) of reptiles, mostly small, having a scaly body and generally four legs and a long tail; there are *ca.* 1,700 species, commonly arranged into 20 distinct families. Tristram, who noted the abundance of lizards in Palestine, collected 22 species, belonging to 18 genera.

The ancient versions and the context in Lev. 11 point to לטאה (*leṭā'â*) as being a lizard, but more precise identification is impossible. If, as Bodenheimer holds (*see* FAUNA § D), this is a "general name for lizards," it is rather odd that it appears in the middle of a list of words with more restricted meanings.

The ancient versions agree that שממית (*śemāmîth*) is a lizard, though the word in the Targ. can also mean "spider" (so Luther; KJV). If the term means "poisonous one," it reflects a popular superstition when applied to lizards in the Near East, for the only poisonous lizards (*Helodermatidae*) are found in the Western Hemisphere. Koehler takes the animal to be a gecko.

See also CHAMELEON; GECKO; GREAT LIZARD; SAND LIZARD.

W. S. MCCULLOUGH

LOAF. *See* BREAD, particularly § 1*d*.

LO-AMMI lō ăm'ī. KJV translation of לא־עמי, a symbolic name given by the prophet Hosea to his third child, to indicate God's decisive repudiation of Israel (Hos. 1:9; RSV lit. "Not my people").

LOAN [משא, משאה]. *See* DEBT.

LOCK. 1. Four Hebrew words refer to "lock of hair": ציצית (Ezek. 8:3); מחלפות (Judg. 16:13, 19); פרע (Num. 6:5; Ezek. 44:20); קוצות (Song of S. 5:2, 11). Another word, צמה, is translated "lock" in the KJV (Song of S. 4:1, 3; 6:7; Isa. 47:2; RSV "veil").

2. נעל. To fasten a door (Judg. 3:23-24). *See* BOLT; KEY.

3. KJV translation of מנעול (RSV BOLT) in Song of S. 5:5; Neh. 3:3, 6, 13, 15.

O. R. SELLERS

LOCUST. An insect species of the order *Orthoptera,* family *Acrididae,* which is capable at times—more or less periodically—of multiplying in appalling masses, of wandering into distant lands, and of causing frightful destruction of cultivated vegetation. Grasshoppers are also various members of *Acrididae,* but are distinctive in that they lack the locusts' capacity of swarming and mass migration.

The locust plague was the eighth of the ten Egyptian plagues (Exod. 10:3-20). Fig. ASS 05.

1. Locust terminology in the Bible
   a. In OT Hebrew
   b. In LXX Greek
   c. In NT Greek
   d. In the RSV and the KJV
2. The locust in the ancient world
3. The locust as a food
4. Definition and distribution
5. Biology of the locust
   a. Origin and mass outbreaks
   b. Development and behavior
   c. Wandering instinct
6. The locust as a destroyer
7. Modern control organization

Bibliography

1. Locust terminology in the Bible. ***a. In OT Hebrew.*** Twelve words are used in the Hebrew OT for "locust," or are rendered so in the translations and by exegetes:

a) ארבה (Akkadian *arbu, aribu, aribi, erebu;* Ugaritic *irby*). Occurring twenty-four times, this is the commonest word meaning "locust." It is generally used collectively, but is also used in the singular to refer to the individual members of the species—i.e., as a *nomen unitatis*—as in Exod. 10:19. This noun means the adult and winged insect adapted to fly (Exod. 10:13, 19).

b) חגב. This word occurs five times, used once (Eccl. 12:5) metaphorically. In the Talmud this word means any species of the short-horned grasshoppers, and it is said there (Hull. 63*b*) exaggeratively that there are eight hundred kinds of grasshoppers (חגבים). However, once (II Chr. 7:13) חגב is used in the sense of "locust" (cf. I Kings 8:37). *See* GRASSHOPPER.

c) גובי ,גבי (Amos 7:1; Nah. 3:17). This is a synonym of ארבה. In Aramaic it is גובא (Targ.) and גובאי or גוביי (Talmud). In Hull. 65*a* it is specifically identified with ארבה (Arabic *jāb, jābī*). The doubling גוב גובי (Nah. 3:17) may indicate many locusts ("clouds of locusts").

d) גבים (Isa. 33:4). This word is to be understood in the same meaning as *c,* for it is paralleled with חסיל (*see i-k below*).

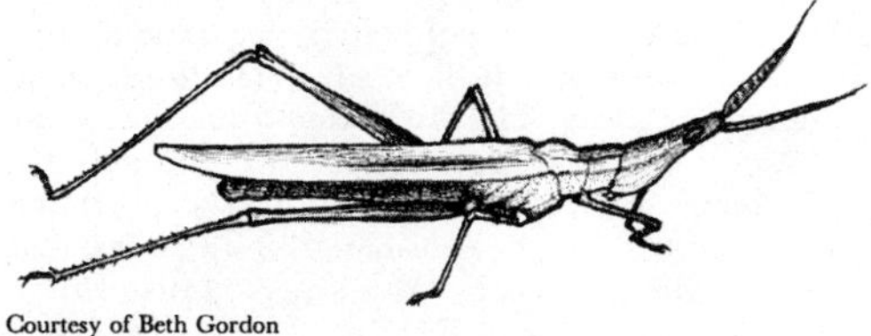

Courtesy of Beth Gordon

33. A female locust

e) סלעם (Lev. 11:22). From the morphological symptoms given for this grasshopper in the Talmud (Hull. 65*b*-66*a;* Yom. 77*b*), there is no doubt that this word means the very similar grasshopper genera *Truxalis* L. or *Acrida* F. (Fig. LOC 33) of the subfamily *Tryxalinae,* or slant-faced locusts.

f) חרגל (Lev. 11:22). From the discussion in the Talmud (Hull. 65*b*) we may with certainty conclude that this word means any species of the family *Tettigoniidae,* vernacularly named katydids or long-horned grasshoppers.

g) חנמל (Ps. 78:47; RSV "frost"). Targ., Symm., Midrashim, Rashi, and the Karaite Ḥassan render this word too as a kind of locust. But this meaning is not acceptable, since the sycamore of this verse is just one of those few trees which are not damageable by the locust (*see* § 6 *below*).

h) צלצל (Deut. 28:42). Most interpreters render this word as "grasshopper" or "cricket." The LXX translates ἐρυσίβη (after A: ἐρισύβη) and the Vulg. *rubigo* (or also four times for חסיל); both generally meant "rust," a fungus disease of plants. But Levy, Kohut, Jastrow, and Krauss in their lexicons identify ἐρμσίβη with the Talmudic ערצוביא (Hull. 65*a*) as a locust species. It may also be identified as *Gryllotalpa,* the mole cricket, which has a decided rusty color.

i-k) ילק (nine times), חסיל (six times), and גזם (three times). These three words doubtless signify the successive stages of the immature locust.

From the succession of ילק, חסיל, and גזם twice in Joel (1:4; 2:25), which differs with respect to the commencement of the series but is constant in consecution, it can be concluded that ילק means the first instar, חסיל the middle instars, and גזם the last ones of the immature locust. According to this opinion, ילק פשט ויעף (Nah. 3:16) may be rendered: "nymph [of the first locust instar] sheds [its skin] and flits."

l) הצפוני, "the northerner" (Joel 2:20). This expression is to be understood as a rhetorical epithet for the locust, on the one hand symbolizing the violent N intruding peoples who keep the Orient in awe (Jer. 1:14; Ezek. 38:15-16), and on the other the locusts themselves being symbolized by the N peoples.

b. In LXX Greek. The translation of the LXX for the twelve words pertaining to "locust" is not fully consistent. For ארבה it usually has ἀκρίς, which means "locust." 'Ακρίς is also the translation of חגב, גבי, and גבים; in one case (Lev. 11:22) ὀφίομαχην is written for חגב, and ἀκρίδα takes the place of חרגל, but this seems to be only a displacement, and is already corrected by the Vulg. 'Οφίομαχην = *ophiomachus,* the literal sense of which is "snake-combatant," may be suited as hyperbole for the giant preying katydid genus *Saga.* סלעם is translated αττακην, transliterated by the Vulg. *attacus,* the meaning of which is unknown. גזם is rendered by κάμπη, "caterpillar" or "nymph." ילק is usually rendered βροῦχος, "unwinged locust"; this word is once (II Chr. 6:28) used for חסיל, and the Vulg. has *bruchus* for חסיל also in Isa. 33:4; κάμπη and βροῦχος may fit the nymphal stages of the locust. Four times חסיל is translated ἐρυσίβη, a word used also for צלצל (*see* § 1*a above*). חנמל is rendered πάχνη = *pruina,* "rime." הצפוני is translated βορρᾶ = *Aquilone,* corresponding to "the northerner" of the RSV (*see* § 1*a above*).

c. In NT Greek. 'Ακρίδες, which corresponds to Vulg. *locustae,* is used in the four references to locusts in the NT (Matt. 3:4; Mark 1:6; Rev. 9:3, 7).

d. In the RSV and the KJV. The rendering of the Hebrew names for "locust" is not always consistent or certain in either the RSV or the KJV. "Locust" is given equally for ארבה (KJV "grasshopper" in Judg. 6:5; 7:12; Job 39:20; Jer. 46:23); חגב (only II Chr. 7:13; otherwise "grasshopper" [Lev. 11:22; Num. 13:33; Eccl. 12:5; Isa. 40:22]); גבי (Amos 7:1 RSV;

otherwise "grasshopper"); גבים; צלצל ("locust"); and, with corresponding adjectives, also for חסיל, ילק, and גזם. חרגל is translated "cricket" (Lev. 11:22 RSV), the root of which is "crick," an imitative of chirping sounds, and which commonly means insects of the unclean *Gryllidae* family, but "cricket" is also variously used as the name of different katydids (*Tettigoniidae*); the KJV "beetle" must be rejected. סלעם (Lev. 11:22) is rendered "bald locust," which quite fits the meaning of a slant-faced grasshopper (*see* § 1*a above*), recognized by a "high" face or front baldness (גבחת in Talmud: Hull. 65*b*). The rendering "hopping locust" or "hopper" for ילק, "destroying locust" or "destroyer" for חסיל, and "cutting locust" or "cutter" for גזם is only a verbal conception; but once (Ps. 105:34) we find for ילק a well-fitted equivalent: "young locusts"; "cankerworm," "caterpiller," and "palmerworm" of KJV are to be rejected, being the young stages of butterflies or moths only. חנמל (Ps. 78:47) is translated "frost," which is in accordance with LXX, Vulg., Syr., Sa'adia, and Ibn Janaḥ.

2. The locust in the ancient world. The locust plague, one of the severest evils of mankind, left many indelible impressions in the Bible and in other documents of the ancient world. It serves as a threat (Deut. 28:38) and as a harbinger of the day of the Lord (Joel 2:1, 11). Special days of praying, fasting, and trumpet-blowing were proclaimed to remove this plague (I Kings 8:37=II Chr. 6:28; Joel 2:12-17).

According to Talmudic regulations, the locust plague was, as in cases of drought (Palestinian Ta'an. 1.7), blight, mildew, invasions of wild beasts or despoiling armies, counteracted by general trumpet-blowing, and not only at the place where it broke out, because it was considered as a "walking plague" (Babylonian Ta'an. 3.5).

The Magi produced special amulets and sorcery stones presumed to protect against the locust plague (Pliny Nat. Hist. XXXVII.40). Here (VIII.43) it is also said, according to Marcus Varro, that a tribe in Africa was put to flight by locusts.

In the Bible the locust symbolizes powerful and large enemy armies completely destroying the earnings of man's toil (Judg. 6:5; Isa. 33:4; Jer. 46:23; 51:27; Joel 2:20; Nah. 3:15). Similar metaphors are frequent in the other oriental literatures (e.g., Ugaritic Legend of KRT, I K: 104-5, 192-94).

3. The locust as a food. Locusts were eaten, and they were esteemed as a dainty to adorn the king's table (Bereshith Raba 67.2; Pliny Nat. Hist. VI.35; VII.2).* In Lev. 11:21-22 the kinds permitted for food are designated; in the Talmud this matter is discussed in detail, and there are given precise specifications for clean locusts, to distinguish them from the unclean ones (Mishna, Hull. 3.7; Gemara, Hull. 65-66 *et passim*). Nowadays the Bedouins eat locusts raw, roasted, and cooked. They are preserved by drying and threading; they are also crushed and ground, and the grists are put into dishes or eaten with bread, sometimes mixed with honey or dates. Hasselquist (1746) states that in Arabia the locusts "never occasion a plague to the country, as they do in other places." Also the Jews of Yemen and North Africa prepare in many ways the allowed kinds of locusts for food. Fig. LOC 34.

34. Assyrian attendants carrying locusts and pomegranates on skewers

According to the analysis of Guggenheim in Jerusalem, the desert locust consists of 75 per cent proteins, 3.4 per cent fats, and 7.5 per cent carbohydrates; as to vitamins, he found 1.75 milligrams riboflavin and 7.5 milligrams nicotinic acid in each 100 grams. According to E. B. Uvarov (1931), this species is also rich in many minerals, especially in iron, calcium, and sulphur.

4. Definition and distribution. Only three of the hundreds of Acridids common in Bible lands are capable of increasing from time to time to immense multitudes, then to wander in frightful swarms and invade wide and distant areas, causing a total devastation of natural and cultivated vegetation. This alone is, according to B. P. Uvarov (1928), the true definition of "locust," in distinction from "grasshopper." Only one of these three species, namely the desert locust (*Schistocerca gregaria* Forsk. =*Acridium peregrinum* Oliv.) can be considered as the widespread plague in all Bible lands, and stray bands of them may penetrate as far as Transcaucasia and Transcaspia in the N, Burma in the E, the S parts of the Iberian Peninsula in the W, and the Cape Province in the S.

5. Biology of the locust. The following biological sketch is concerned mainly with the desert locust.

a. Origin and mass outbreaks. The native region of the desert locust is the spacious Sudan. The correct explanation for the swarming and wandering periodicity of locusts was at first proposed by B. P. Uvarov (1921) in his phase theory, affirming the principle of morphobiological phases as a base for this phenomenon.

Each locust species appears in two distinct phases: (*a*) *phasis solitaria* and (*b*) *phasis gregaria;* and there may also be distinguished an intermediate third phase, *phasis transiens*. The differences between the phases are manifest both in the immature and in the adult stages by external (color, form, and proportion differences) and physiological (metabolism, mobility, and general behavior differences) symptoms. A full reciprocity between the two series of symptoms was already proved both by natural observations and by laboratory experiments. The periodicity is bound up with the transition from the calm solitary phase to the extremely active and destroying gregarious phase. This transition occurs in the native area of the locust in years in which the quantity and temporal distribution of rains particularly afford adequate conditions for reproduction, because the locusts deposit their eggs and these develop only in moisty soil. One or two such years may bring into the world huge locust swarms in their gregarious phase.

In this phase the wandering instinct is the most peculiar trait of the locust's habit and is a result of its gregarious behavior. Because of the climatic conditions in the area invaded by him, the locust does not reach sexual maturity, and so it tarries here as a plunderous stranger only, and in the years between invasions "not a single locust [is] left in all the country" invaded (Exod. 10:19).

b. Development and behavior. After copulation, lasting from fifty minutes to a few hours, the female deposits eggs in a hole previously excavated in the ground by means of her ovipositor, for which purpose the abdomen can elongate twofold or more (Fig. LOC 35). A female is able to deposit 1-6 egg pods containing 28-146 eggs each. The egg is .3-.4 inch in length and yellow-grayish in color. During the oviposition a glutinous fluid is discharged which makes the eggs adhere to one another and also forms a foamlike bung to the egg burrow from above.

Courtesy of Dr. H. Bytinski-Salz

35. A female locust depositing eggs in a hole by means of her ovipositor

The larvae emerge from the eggs fifteen to forty-three days after oviposition, depending on the season and weather. The newborn larvae have a vermiform appearance and are covered with a rosy-whitish envelope, which they shed immediately after emergence, and they are already able to move by leaps, for which the locust larvae deserve their name: hoppers. Besides this intermediate molt, there are five regular molts in the larval stage of the locust. From molt to molt the larva increases about a fourth part in length and doubles in weight, and in the last instar even more. The hoppers of instars 4 and 5 already possess well-decided wing rudiments enveloped in flat sheaths. After the fifth molt appears a winged insect. This is the perfect, but not sexually mature, locust. The maturing period can continue some weeks, according to season, being longer in winter than in summer. In its gregarious phase the desert locust has at first a pink or reddish main coloration, and turns glossy lemon-yellow, bearing a brown network on forewings when it is mature. The female is larger than the male, and during maturation until oviposition it doubles in weight.

The adult locust, as its larvae, possesses six legs, as all other insects. The hind pair of legs is longer than the four other and is provided with very large and ample thighs, in which strong muscles enabling good jumping are placed. The ancients considered the hind legs of locusts as limbs by themselves; they do not include them in the number of legs and consequently give them a separate term: כרעים in the Bible and קרצולים in the Talmud. This view is also alluded to by Aristotle, who states: "All these creatures [leaping insects] have six feet, inclusive of the parts used for leaping" (*Parts of Animals* IV.6).

c. Wandering instinct. In the gregarious phase, from the second instar and afterward, the locust is overwhelmed by a strong wandering instinct, causing a random procession of overflowing masses which ignores any obstruction. The hopper swarms climb and pass unhindered over hills, rocks, and walls; trenches and pits are filled out by the bodies of the vanguard, and the afterguard marches over its brethren as on a plain; water dikes and rivers are crossed by swimming, and Ballard (1932) states that a swarm of hoppers even rushed across the Suez Canal. The prophet Joel (2:4-9) describes this phenomenon in an expressive style, with strong coloring.

There is only one firm regulator for the movement and power of action of the locust—temperature. Bodenheimer (1930) concludes from laboratory experiments that a temperature of 4-5 degrees centigrade conduces the hoppers to cold torpor; at 20-26 degrees they behave normally; 43-44 degrees causes maximal excitation; 49-50 degrees leads to heat paralysis; at 51 degrees centigrade appears heat death. These experimentally found facts are also observed in the behavior of the locust in nature and in the daily order of its activities, and are also used figuratively by the prophet Nahum (3:17).

Shortly after winging, the locusts set out from their larval home and fly in prodigious bands straight ahead, not altering the direction during the whole journey, extending sometimes three days without interruption. The desert locust is the most diligent and most skilful flyer among the locusts, and it is capable of moving up to 1,240 miles from its native place. The factors inciting and directing the wandering rage seem to be chiefly physiological ones, internally connected with the process of genital incretions. Similar stimuli are also observed in other animals during their sexual maturation period. An auxiliary journey-directing factor is the direction of the winds. This fact, which is already emphasized in the Bible (Exod. 10:13, 19) and also by Pliny (Nat. Hist. XI.35), is repeatedly verified by recent scientific observations.

6. The locust as a destroyer. Consuming almost every plant, the locust can cause an absolute devastation of the fresh vegetation in the areas invaded by it. Factually, indeed, the desert locust does not eat the carob, sycamore, and castor trees and the oleander bush. Also the olive and date trees do not seem to suit its taste, since it eats their foliage only in emergency cases. Among the alien plants, Melia Azedarach (bead tree), eucalyptus, and prickly pear are spared by the desert locust.

7. Modern control organization. Many natural enemies, parasites as well as predators, assail the mature locusts, the hoppers, and the eggs; but notwithstanding all their importance, they have not sufficient power "to remove this death" (Exod. 10:17) from mankind. However, the great desert locust outbreak in 1927-30 caused the United Kingdom government to establish a special Anti-Locust Research Centre, and brought also the other interested governments to international and interterritorial cooperation, resulting in the International Anti-Locust Conferences, the first of which took place at Rome in September, 1931. Since then much investigation work, both pure and applied, has been made—and now it may be hoped that step by step man approaches the final control of the agelong locust plague.

Bibliography. Tristram, *NHB,* pp. 306-18. S. Bochartus, *Hierozoicon* (1675), I, 69; II, 442-87. F. Hasselquist, *Voyages and Travels in the Levant* (1766), pp. 230-33. I. Aharoni, *Ha'arbê* (1920). L. Köhler, "Die Bezeichnungen der Heuschrecke im AT," *ZDPV,* XLIX (1926), 328-33. B. P. Uvarov, *Locusts and Grasshoppers* (1928). F. S. Bodenheimer, *Studien zur Epidemologie, Oekologie und Physiologie der afrikanischen Wanderheuschrecke* (1930). E. Ballard, *The Desert Locust in Egypt* (1932). F. S. Bodenheimer, *Insects as Human Food* (1951), *passim.* B. P. Uvarov, *Locust Research and Control* (1951). N. S. Shcherbinovsky, *Pustynnaia sarancha Schistocerca* (1952). L. W. Clausen, *Insect Fact and Folklore* (1956), pp. 55-59, 171-73.

Y. Palmoni

LOD lŏd [לֹד]; LYDDA lĭd'ə [Λύδδα]. A town of Benjamin near the S border of the Plain of Sharon and *ca.* eleven miles SE of Joppa. It was built by the sons of Elpaal, descendants of Benjamin (I Chr. 8:12), and, along with Hadid and Ono, was the ancestral homeland of more than 720 exiles who returned from the Babylonian exile (Ezra 2:33; Neh. 7:37; 11:35). With these sites, also, it constituted the westernmost district of the restored community.

Its strategic location, at the intersection of the great trunk road between Egypt and Babylon and the main highway from Joppa to Jerusalem, made it often-contested territory. Under the name Lydda, it was head of one of the districts of Samaria which Demetrius Nicator ceded to Judea in 145 B.C. at the request of Jonathan Maccabeus (I Macc. 10:30, 38; 11:28, 34, 57; Jos. Antiq. XIII.iv.9). Jewish rights in the site were removed by the Roman general Pompey, but Caesar promptly restored them. *Ca.* 45 B.C. the site was captured by Cassius and its inhabitants sold into slavery (Jos. Antiq. XIV.xi.2). Release was soon gained, however, by decree of Marcus Antonius (Jos. Antiq. XIV.xii.2-5). In A.D. 66, Cestius Gallus burned the vacated city while the inhabitants were celebrating the Feast of Tabernacles in Jerusalem (Jos. War II.xix.1), and, again, in 68 the site was occupied and resettled by Vespasian during the progress of his campaign in Judea (Jos. War IV.viii.1).

Lydda was the residence of an early Christian community (Acts 9:32), which was substantially increased as a result of the visit of Peter and the healing of Aeneas, a paralytic (vss. 33-35). News of these events soon reached the Christians of nearby Joppa, who straightway sought the ministry of the Apostle in the case of Tabitha (vs. 38).

Sometime in the second or third century Judaism was virtually eradicated from the site, and it was renamed Diospolis. Christianity, however, survived and flourished to the extent that the site was the seat of a bishop in the fourth century and the scene of the trial of Pelagius at the Synod of 415.

36. Air view of Lydda, the old town in the upper center

During the Crusader period the town bore the name of Saint George, who suffered martyrdom in 303, and over whose reputed tomb on the site the Crusaders built a church. The ruins of this church may still be seen, but the name of the site long ago reverted to its original form and is preserved in the Arabic Ludd.

Fig. LOD 36.

Bibliography. G. A. Smith, *The Historical Geography of the Holy Land* (1931), pp. 159-62; D. Baly, *The Geography of the Bible* (1957), pp. 135-36.

W. H. Morton

LO-DEBAR. Alternate form of DEBIR 3.

LODGE [מלונה (*alternately* HUT); מלון (*alternately* LODGING PLACE; PLACE WHERE ONE LODGES; RETREAT)]; LODGING [*see above;* ξενία (*alternately* GUEST ROOM)]. Usually a temporary resting place or campground (Josh. 4:3, 8; Isa. 10:29; Philem. 22). Paul's "lodging" in Rome (Acts 28:23) seems to have been more permanent, and Jeremiah may have wished for a permanent dwelling away from his sinful people (Jer. 9:2). The "lodge in a cucumber field" (Isa. 1:8) probably refers to a lean-to, used by the workers in the field (the same word is translated "hut" in Isa. 24:20). It is a symbol of desolation. *See* BOOTH. E. M. GOOD

LOFT. KJV translation of עליה (RSV "upper chamber") in I Kings 17:19. *See* ARCHITECTURE; CHAMBER; HOUSE; UPPER ROOM.

LOG. 1. A Hebrew liquid measure (Lev. 14:10). *See* WEIGHTS AND MEASURES § C4*b*.

2. A section of a tree trunk. "Log(s)" in this sense is the translation of the following words:

a) עצים (Eccl. 10:9; Ezek. 24:10; KJV "wood," which is perhaps better in the latter verse).

b) עצמים (Ezek. 24:5; KJV "bones," which is the meaning of the MT; the RSV "logs" is based on an emendation to עצים; cf. vs. 10).

c) קורה (II Kings 6:2, 5; KJV "beam").

d) Δοκός (Matt. 7:3-5; Luke 6:41-42; KJV "beam," which is precise, since δοκός is a long, shaped piece of lumber).

Hiram king of Tyre sent cedar, cypress, and algum wood, presumably in the form of logs tied together as rafts, by sea to Solomon for the building of the temple (I Kings 5:8-9—H 5:22-23; II Chr. 2:8, 16—H 2:7, 15).

The vivid saying of Jesus in Matt. 7:3-5; Luke 6:41-42 has a close parallel in the Babylonian Talmud: "Rabbi Tarfon [*ca.* A.D. 120] said: 'I wonder whether there is any one in this generation who would accept reproof. If one said, Take the mote from between your eyes, he would answer, Take the beam from between your eyes' " ('Arak. 16*b;* cf. B.B. 15*b*).

See also SPECK.

Bibliography. G. B. King, "The Mote and the Beam," *HTR,* XVII (1924), 393-404; P. L. Hedley, " 'The Mote and the Beam' and 'The Gates of Hades,' " *ET,* XXXIX (1928), 427-28; G. B. King, "A Further Note on the Mote and the Beam," *HTR,* XXVI (1933), 73-76. J. A. THOMPSON

LOGIA lō'jĭ ə. A term applied especially to collections of sayings employed by the gospel writers. The word is a transliteration of the plural of λόγιον (diminutive of λόγος; *see* AGRAPHA), which is used frequently in the LXX and several times in the NT ("oracles," "first principles").

This term is of special interest because of its use in a remark of Papias in the early second century, quoted by Eusebius, to the effect that Matthew was responsible for the arrangement or the writing down of the logia of Jesus in the Hebrew (Aramaic) language. Some have thought that Papias was referring to the Gospel of Matthew or to a lost Aramaic gospel such as the Gospel of the Hebrews. In support of this hypothesis may be cited some patristic tradition and the use of "logia" by Philo and others to mean "scripture," in a sense inclusive of both historical incidents and discourse. Against it, at least so far as Matthew is concerned, is the evidence that the First Gospel was composed in Greek from Greek sources.

The most popular hypothesis is that the logia of Papias are to be identified with a sayings source (*see* Q), used by both the First Gospel and the Third, its use by the First accounting for the connection of Matthew's name with that gospel. Alternative views, such as that the logia were a collection of messianic proof texts or that Papias was misinformed, have not commended themselves widely.

Ground for identifying Q and the logia exists in the restricted meaning the word usually has in the LXX, the NT, Clement of Rome, Polycarp, and Justin Martyr. Such an understanding of the logia also fits well with the practice in the early church of bringing together sayings of Jesus, considered as oracles, for didactic purposes, just as Judaism treasured the sayings of the rabbis. In this view the emphasis falls upon the sacred and oracular nature of a brief utterance of universal significance (cf. Matt. 5–7), as distinguished from both a saying of purely local significance, usually embedded in a narrative framework (Mark 2:23-28; Matt. 8:5-13=Luke 7:1-10), and a lengthy or reasoned discourse such as those in the Gospel of John.

D. T. ROWLINGSON

LOGOS lŏg'ŏs [λόγος]. *See* WORD, THE.

LOINS. The Hebrew and Greek words translated "loins" refer specifically to the hips or lower part of the back.

The normal Hebrew word מתנים (dual) is often used in a purely physical sense as indicating the middle of the body (Exod. 28:42; Ezek. 1:27; 47:4), as the place where a belt is fastened (II Kings 1:8; Isa. 11:5; Jer. 13:1), a warrior's sword is hung (II Sam. 20:8), or sackcloth is placed (Gen. 37:34; I King 20:32), and as the thickest part of the body (I Kings 12:10). There are a number of references to the practice of tying the long lower garments about the middle of the body ("the loins") in preparation for running (I Kings 18:46) or traveling speedily (Exod. 12:11; II Kings 9:1). The word is also frequently used in a figurative sense as representing the seat of man's physical strength (Nah. 2:1). In this sense "to loose the loins" (Isa. 45:1) or "make them shake" (Ps. 69:23) means simply to make a person weak. Also, in this sense, the loins can be thought of as the place where disease or misfortune most obviously manifests its presence (Ps. 66:11; Isa. 21:3; Nah. 2:10).

The word חלצים (dual) has approximately the same sense in Hebrew and covers much the same range of meanings, except that it is also taken as a symbol of the generative organs or powers and can therefore be used in the rhetorical description of a man's descendants as "those who come out of his loins" (cf. Gen. 35:11; I Kings 8:19). In this last sense the word ירך (properly "side") sometimes occurs as a synonym for חלצים (Gen. 46:26; Exod. 1:5).

The word כסל (lit., "flank") is also used to designate the loins, but (except for Ps. 38:7) only in the literal sense.

In the NT, the word ὀσφὺς covers the various meanings of the Hebrew words mentioned above: the middle of the body (Matt. 3:4; waist); the source of progeny (cf. Acts 2:30; Heb. 7:5, 10); and the place where garments are tied, in the metaphor "girding the loins" meaning "be prepared for activity" (Luke 12:35; Eph. 6:14; I Pet. 1:13; references are to the KJV; the RSV in many instances renders more freely). R. C. DENTAN

LOIS lō'ĭs [Λωίς, more desirable, better(?)] (II Tim. 1:5). The mother of Eunice, and grandmother of Timothy. Lois is commended for her Christian faith. "Paul" reminds Timothy that he has been nurtured in a family of believers and so exhorts him to "rekindle the gift of God." B. H. THROCKMORTON, JR.

LONGSUFFERING.

1. In the OT. This word occurs four times in the KJV of the OT—three times as an adjective (Exod. 34:6; Num. 14:18; Ps. 86:15) and once as a noun (Jer. 15:15)—as a translation of ארך אפים (lit., "length of wrath"). Elsewhere this same Hebrew expression is translated "slow to anger" in the KJV; the RSV uses this translation for the adjective and "forbearance" for the noun. The term characterizes one of the two aspects of God's dealing with Israel—its rebelliousness demands punishment, but he delays in order to give opportunity for repentance and amendment. The LXX translates the Hebrew expression by μακρόθυμος and μακροθυμία, an almost literal rendering.

2. In the NT. Although the Greek adjective does not appear in the NT, the noun is used fourteen times and the corresponding verb once. For them the KJV uses "longsuffering" thirteen times, "patience" twice (Heb. 6:12; Jas. 5:10). The RSV uses either "forbearance" or "patience." When the word is used of God (Rom. 2:4; 9:22; I Pet. 3:20), it has the same connotation as in the OT—i.e., "delay in inflicting a deserved punishment on sin, in the hope that repentance may take place" (cf. especially Rom. 2:4: "Do you presume upon the riches of his kindness and forbearance and patience? Do you not know that God's kindness is meant to lead you to repentance?" II Pet. 3:9: "The Lord is not slow about his promise as some count slowness, but is forbearing toward you, not wishing that any should perish, but that all should reach repentance"). In I Tim. 1:16; II Pet. 3:15 the word is used of Christ in much the same way.

When it is applied to men, it is generally one of a list of Christian virtues, "fruit of the Spirit"—"love, joy, peace, patience, kindness, goodness" (Gal. 5:22), which are necessary in preserving unity within the Christian fellowship (Eph. 4:2). In the light of the preceding, therefore, the meaning would seem to be that the child of God is to reflect God's attitude of forbearance toward wrongdoers, not condoning evil but hoping that PATIENCE will lead him to a better mind.

Bibliography. E. D. Burton, *Commentary on Galatians,* ICC (1920), p. 315; A. Richardson, "Long-suffering," *Theological Word Book of the Bible* (1950). E. J. COOK

LOOKING GLASS. *See* MIRROR.

LOOM [ארג (Judg. 16:14; KJV BEAM; WEAVER'S SHUTTLE *in* Job 7:6), weaver's bobbin; דלה (Isa. 38:12; KJV PINING SICKNESS; FLOWING LOCKS *in* Song of S. 7:5—H 7:6; *cf.* RSV mg.; KJV HAIR), thrum]. Apparatus for weaving. *See* CLOTH.

LOOPS [ללאת] (Exod. 26:4-5, 10-11; 36:11-12, 17). The cloth fastenings by which the two halves of the TABERNACLE were joined. The inner linen lining of the tabernacle consisted of two separate sections which were fastened together along one edge by running gold clasps through fifty matching loops on each half. The single flat piece thus formed was draped over the frame of the structure. The goatskin outer covering was made in the same way, except that the clasps were bronze, and the loops probably goats' hair. L. E. TOOMBS

LORD. The English rendering of various words that appear in biblical Hebrew, Aramaic, and Greek to express the idea of a person who commands respect or exercises authority. In many cases "Lord" is a title of honor and majesty used in addressing God, or a substitute for the special name Yahweh (KJV-RSV "the LORD").

a) אדון, "Adon," is the basic Hebrew word. It is a title of courtesy and respect used in addressing superiors—e.g., in the case of a slave speaking to his master or a subject to the king. God is called the "Lord of all the earth" (e.g., Ps. 97:5). Usually, however, when the title refers to God, it is vocalized *Adonai* as a plural of "majesty" (lit., "my Lords"). When the special name Yahweh was withdrawn from common usage, for fear of profaning it, Adonai was adopted as a substitute in public worship; this practice is reflected in the Masoretic vocalization of the Tetragrammaton (YHWH) with the vowels of the name Adonai. *See* JEHOVAH; GOD, NAMES OF, §§ B, C6.

b) בעל, "Baal" ("owner, lord"), is sometimes used of human leaders (Num. 21:28; Isa. 16:8) or the "master" of cattle (Isa. 1:3). Because of the associations of the name with the Canaanite nature god Baal, however, it was never finally approved as a name for Israel's God (cf. Hos. 2:16—H 2:18). *See* GOD, NAMES OF, § C5.

c) Less important words are גביר, meaning "master, commander" (Gen. 27:29, 37); סרן, the title of the Philistine rulers (e.g., Judg. 16:5). In the Aramaic portion of Daniel are found רב, רברבן, in the sense of "lord, noble" (Dan. 4:36—A 4:33; 5:1) and מרא in the sense of "exalted one, lord" (2:47; 4:19, 24—A 4:16, 21; 5:23). The latter is important for religious usage, for the Christians applied it to Jesus in the Aramaic prayer Maranatha, "Our Lord, come" (I Cor. 16:22; cf. Rev. 22:20).

d) The LXX uses κύριος to translate "Adon" and also to translate "Baal" when it has a nonreligious sense (e.g., Isa. 1:3). In the great majority of cases, however, it is a substitute for "Yahweh," although occasionally δεσπότης is used in compound titles like "the Lord God." The LXX usage carries over into the NT, though with the new development that κύριος is a confessional title applied to Jesus Christ (Rom. 10:9; Phil. 2:11). B. W. ANDERSON

***LORD (CHRIST)** [יהוה, אדוני; Aram. אדון, מר; ὁ κύριος]. The Hebrew word is used in the English versions of the OT to translate the divine names Yahweh and Adonai; the Greek Bible, both LXX and NT, employs ὁ κύριος for the same purpose. The Greek word has, however, a very wide reference, being used of the God of the OT (e.g., Acts 2: 34, quoting Ps. 110:1), of Jesus (e.g., Luke 10:1), of human masters (Acts 16:19), in address to an angel (Acts 10:4), or with the force of "Rabbi" or "Sir" (e.g., Matt. 8:6).

When characters in the gospels use the word in addressing Jesus, it often means no more than "Sir," but at other times it expresses full Christian faith, as in Thomas' ejaculation: "My Lord and my God!" (John 20:28). "The Lord" as a simple designation for Jesus is mostly confined to the narratives of Luke-Acts (e.g., Luke 17:5-6; Acts 9:10-11, 15, 17). Acts also frequently uses the phrase "the Lord Jesus" (e.g., 4:33), and speaks of faith in the Lord Jesus (16: 31) and baptism in the name of the Lord Jesus (8:16; 19:5). Evidently "Jesus is Lord" was one of the early formulas of faith, and in Acts 2:36 Peter is quoted as saying that God has made Jesus both Lord and Messiah.

Paul often uses the fuller phrase "the Lord Jesus Christ" in conjunction with the mention of God the Father (e.g., I Thess. 1:1; cf. II Cor. 13:14, where the Holy Spirit is also named). He also uses the simpler formulas "the Lord Jesus" (II Thess. 1:7) and "our Lord Jesus" (I Thess. 3:13). In contrast to the many so-called gods and lords, there is for Christians but one God, the Father, and one Lord, Jesus Christ (I Cor. 8:5-6). It has often been noted that the statement of I Cor. 10:21: "You cannot partake of the table of the Lord and the table of demons," is paralleled by the famous papyrus letter: "Chaeremon invites you to dinner at the table of the Lord Sarapis" (Oxyrhynchus Papyrus CX). Paul, like the author of Acts, knows of the formula "Jesus is Lord," and says that no one can say κύριος 'Ιησοῦς except by the Holy Spirit (I Cor. 12:3). In the important christological passage, Phil. 2:5-11, the "name which is above every name," which Jesus received at his exaltation, is probably κύριος (cf. Acts 2:36). The word is used in connection with the hope of his parousia (Phil. 3:20; 4:5; I Thess. 3:13), and at the conclusion of I Corinthians, Paul utters the Aramaic prayer: Μαράνα θά, "Our Lord, come!" (16:22; cf. Rev. 22:20: "Amen. Come, Lord Jesus!").

To an early Christian accustomed to reading the OT, the word "Lord," when used of Jesus, would suggest his identification with the God of the OT. It expressed Christ's divinity without explicitly asserting his deity, which was an idea startling to non-Christian Jews. A Christian of pagan background would find the word reminiscent of the god of a cult, like Sarapis. That even the Aramaic *mar* could have this meaning is shown by the fact that a god was worshiped at Gaza under this title, and his sanctuary was known as the Marneum. This does not, however, lead to the conclusion that Christians borrowed the title "Lord" from paganism. The evidence of Acts, taken together with I Cor. 16:22 and the very Jewish book of Revelation, shows that it belongs to the very earliest stratum of Christianity. Phil. 2:5-11 may, indeed, be representative of a pre-Pauline hymn or creed.

In the book of Revelation the title "Lord" has still another connotation. The Emperor Domitian liked to be called "our Lord," and one of his decrees began: "Our Lord and God commands that this be done" (Suetonius *Domitian* 13). To the author of Revelation, such lords and gods were blasphemous and demonic beasts (e.g., Rev. 13:1-6). His book implies that Christ, as King of kings and Lord of lords, is the only emperor whom Christians can recognize (19:16). The author of I Peter, who is much more friendly to the Empire, exhorts his readers to honor the emperor but to fear God (2:17) and to sanctify Christ as Lord in their hearts (3:15). *See* CHRIST.

Bibliography. E. Lohmeyer, *Kyrios Christos: eine Untersuchung zu Phil. 2:5-11* (1928); W. Bousset, *Kyrios Christos* (4th ed., 1935).

S. E. JOHNSON

LORD OF HOSTS *Yahweh S^{e}bhā'ôth* [יהוה צבאות; LXX κύριος τῶν δυνάμεων, κύριος σαβαώθ, κύριος παντοκράτωρ]. A special epithet for the God of Israel which was originally associated with the central sanctuary of the tribal confederacy at Shiloh (I Sam. 1: 3, 11). This form, which occurs most frequently in the OT (267 times), is often assumed to be an abbreviation of the allegedly older form "Yahweh, God of [the] hosts" (יהוה אלהי [ה]צבאות), which occurs 18 times (with the article: Hos. 12:5—H 12:6; Amos 3: 13; 6:14; 9:5; without the article: II Sam. 5:10; I Kings 19:10, 14; Jer. 5:14; Amos 4:13; 5:14-16; etc.). Since these passages do not necessarily represent an older tradition than those which associate the epithet with Shiloh, the ark (I Sam. 4:4; II Sam. 6:2, 18; cf. Isa. 37:16=II Kings 19:31), holy war (I Sam. 15:2; 17:45), the sacred oath (I Kings 18:15; II Kings 3: 14), or the cultus of Jerusalem (II Sam. 7:8, 26; Ps. 24:10, the likelihood is that יהוה צבאות is the original form and יהוה אלהי הצבאות an interpretive expansion. Other expansions are "Yahweh, the God of hosts, the God of Israel" (Isa. 21:10; Jer. 35:17; 38:17; 44:7; cf. Ps. 59:5—H 59:6); "Yahweh of hosts, the God of Israel" (II Sam. 7:27; Jer. 7:3, 21; Zeph. 2:9); "the Lord, Yahweh of hosts" (Isa. 1:24 [האדון]; 3:15 [אדני]).

It is possible grammatically to regard the two words, יהוה צבאות, as standing in apposition, in which case צבאות would be a second divine name rather than a genitive which determines the *nomen regens,* Yahweh (in the construct state). Nevertheless, the expanded forms of the divine epithet are probably correct in expressing the grammatical dependence of צבאות upon the proper name of Israel's God. The hosts over which Yahweh is sovereign are variously taken to mean the armies of Israel or the heavenly host—i.e., the celestial bodies or the angels. *See* HOST OF HEAVEN. B. W. ANDERSON

***LORD'S DAY** [ἡ κυριακὴ ἡμέρα]. The first day of the week, celebrated by the early Christians with joyful worship as the day of Jesus' resurrection, and sharply contrasted with Saturday, the Jewish SABBATH.

1. The NT phrase
2. Sunday and sabbath
3. Dating by the week
4. How the Lord's Day was observed
5. Sunday as a day of rest
Bibliography

1. The NT phrase. The actual phrase occurs only once in the NT, at Rev. 1:10, and although some scholars have suggested its meaning there as the eschatological "Day of the Lord" and not Sunday, this is highly doubtful. The Day of the Lord is always ἡ ἡμέρα τοῦ Κυρίου, never ἡ κυριακὴ ἡμέρα. Moreover, our phrase (though with the word ἡμέρα suppressed and understood) unquestionably refers to the Christian observance of Sunday in early Christian literature—e.g., Did. 14; Ign. Magn. 9.1; Gospel of Peter 9.35; 12.50. The phrase itself is similar to Σεβαστή ("Imperial"), by which the first day of the month was known in Egypt and Asia Minor, in honor of the emperor. The Christian day is the day of the Christian Lord or Emperor, Jesus.

That the first day of the week was given special prominence in the Christian calendar is clear from Acts 20:7, where a service of preaching and the Lord's Supper is referred to; from I Cor. 16:2, where Paul probably intends that weekly collections for the Jerusalem church be taken up at the time of the Lord's Supper; from John 20:19, 26, where the passages may reflect a paschal octave as well as the observance of Sunday; and from Luke 24:30 ff, where the Emmaus story is intended as a prototype of the weekly Eucharist at which the Lord is present.

That the day, moreover, was chosen to celebrate the resurrection of Jesus is clear from the emphasis of the evangelists on his having risen on the first day of the week (Matt. 28:1, etc.).

2. Sunday and sabbath. The Lord's Day stands in marked contrast to the Jewish sabbath, which up to the eleventh century never meant Sunday, but always Saturday. Since the NT gives no evidence that sabbath observance was a cause of strife in the primitive Jewish Christian church, as was circumcision, we may assume that the two days were at first celebrated together. Paul, e.g., frequently attended synagogue worship and preached there on his missionary journeys (Acts 13:14, 45; 16:13; 17:2; etc.). As Christianity spread in Gentile circles, however, the sabbath observance was soon dropped and never made binding on Gentile Christians. In Col. 2:16, Paul criticizes sabbath scrupulosity in reference to Gentile converts. Indeed, the observance of the sabbath soon distinguished Jewish Christian groups in contrast to the Gentile church, and its celebration was regarded as a feature of "Judaizing." For Ignatius, the Christian no longer "sabbatizes," but lives according to the Lord's day (Magn. 9.1). Similarly the peculiar turn of phrase in Did. 14: κατὰ τὴν κυριακὴν δὲ κυρίου συναχθέντες ("according to the Lord's [Day] of the Lord gathering together [for worship]"), seems to mean "meeting for worship on the Lord's Day—*his special day*," in contrast to the sabbath. It was not until the fourth century that Saturday (and then only in the East) became a liturgical day. Even there, its observance bore no reference to the Mosaic legislation on the sabbath. Indeed, the early Christian attitude toward the Fourth Commandment was the precise opposite of the later Roman Catholic and Puritan Sabbatarianism, which applied its restrictions to Sunday. Early Christianity viewed the Fourth Commandment as a ceremonial part of the law now abrogated. It was regarded as symbolic, not of Sunday, but either of a perpetual turning from sin (Just. Trypho 12) or of the future rest of the eschatological kingdom (Barn. 15.8; Iren. Her. 4.16.1).

3. Dating by the week. That Gentile Christians took over the observance of the Lord's Day from the Jewish Christian church implies also that they appropriated from Judaism the seven-day WEEK. Such a division of time is Babylonian in origin and based on astrology. Via the Canaanites, it was adopted by the Israelites, who developed their unique sabbatarianism from the seventh Babylonian day, which was a *dies non*—a day of prohibition on which it was unlucky to do important things.

The Roman calendar was entirely different, revolving around the calends, nones, and ides of the month. It was the cumbersome and unsatisfactory nature of the Roman reckoning, together with the spread of oriental and Jewish customs, especially through syncretic cults, that was responsible for the diverse ways of calculating the week in the early Empire (see Jos. Apion II.xl; Tert. Apol. 16; Nat. 13). In Mithra, e.g., the first day of the week was observed as the day of the sun, though the day of Saturn (Saturday) was more generally celebrated with rest and banqueting. Constantine's motives in finally legislating the public holiday of the "venerable day of the sun" in A.D. 321, while primarily determined by his Christian conversion, doubtless owed something to his desire to straighten out the Roman calendar, as well as to the influence of cults like Mithra and to the general importance of the sun-god in the Empire. Indeed, this god was the titulary divinity of Constantine's family, and from the fourth century there is an increasing assimilation of Christ to the sun-god (as Sun of Righteousness), the *Christos Helios* (cf. Euseb. *Life of Constantine* 1.4.18; and the notable mosaic of *Christos Helios* recently uncovered in the tomb of the Julii under the Vatican). However, this does not belong to the earlier period. The symbolism of Sunday is not that of relating Christ to the sun-god but of suggesting the correspondence in time between the original creation and the new creation in the risen Christ, both of which occurred on the first day of the week (Just. Apol. 67).

4. How the Lord's Day was observed. It is altogether impossible to tell exactly how the primitive Christians kept the Lord's Day. One thing only is certain—viz., that they held their distinctive service of worship on that day. But precisely what this included, how it was related to the preceding sabbath, and at what time it came, are dark questions indeed. When the church emerges into clear light in the second century, we know that around dawn there was a celebration of the liturgy which included scripture, prayers, sermon, and Eucharist on Sunday morning (Just. Apol. 67; *see* LORD'S SUPPER; WORSHIP IN NT TIMES, CHRISTIAN). For the Gentile church there was no sabbath observance, though some pious Christians in the West may occasionally have prolonged their Friday fast through Saturday, as early as the second century, but this had nothing to do with the Fourth Commandment.

What was the situation in the first century? The only NT passage we have to guide us is Acts 20:7-11; and the only other aids we have in reconstructing events are the unclear references in Pliny's letter (Epis. 10.96) and in Did. 9–10; 14. It is possible that the author of Acts wishes us to understand his story as a typical example of early Christian practice. On the first day of the week the disciples came together to "break bread" (a technical term for observing the Lord's Supper, which then was a regular evening meal). Paul first preached an inordinately long sermon, causing the near tragedy of Eutychus, and then, when the young man was restored, those present held their meal and talked on till daybreak. The Lord's Supper was thus an evening meal preceded by a sermon. But it is unclear whether the author wishes us to understand that the events occurred on what we should call Sunday evening or on Saturday evening. The difficulty arises from the fact that Jews dated their days from sundown, while the Romans (like us), from midnight. Which dating is here intended? On the whole, one is inclined to imagine it is Sunday evening, and that Paul leaves "on the morrow," in accord with his intention—that is, on Monday morning (vss. 7, 11). The dating would then be Roman, and the Eucharist story would fit the gospel patterns to which we have already referred, and according to which Sunday evening is viewed as the occasion of Jesus' revealing himself in Christian worship.

This, too, would correspond with Pliny's account. By his time the actual supper had been separated from the distinctively Christian service—or rather was in process of being separated. There is a service "before dawn," which consists of hymnody (probably the antiphonal reciting of the messianic psalms), the Decalogue (derived from synagogue worship), and doubtless prayers and lections which Pliny does not mention. But in the evening of the same day (Sunday) there is a supper, which is finally abandoned because of Trajan's edict forbidding evening dinners of unlicensed clubs. We can also read the Didache along the same lines. The simple eucharistic supper of chs. 9–10 would come on Sunday evening (ch. 14) and include, or be preceded by, a confession of sins. But of all this we cannot be absolutely sure, and it is possible to read the evidence (but not Pliny's evidence) to refer to events on Saturday evening. A late meal on Saturday evening (such as the Passover meal whose traditions have so vitally affected the Lord's Supper) would occur for a Jew on Sunday, since his day would begin with sundown.

In any case, the observance comes in the evening with a eucharistic meal. The origins of a service around dawn, which eventually absorbed the sacramental part of the meal (leaving only an *agape* or church supper in the evening, deprived of its original significance), are to be found in the needs and circumstances of the Gentile church. Trajan's edict outlawing dinners of unlicensed clubs naturally forced a change in the Christian mode of worship. Evenings, furthermore, were not a time when slaves, who formed so large a part of an early Christian congregation, would be free to attend a service. The increasing need, moreover, that a persecuted group act secretly led to the transfer of worship to the very early hours of the morning. Finally, the fact that Christ had risen around dawn doubtless lent an appropriateness to the solution. The Lord's Day was celebrated at the moment of the Resurrection.

5. Sunday as a day of rest. For the early Christian, Sunday was a regular day of work, just as any other day. The special liturgical observance could not alter the cultural context in which he lived. There was, moreover, no question of applying the Jewish sabbatarian rules to the Christian day. The two days were distinct; and the Fourth Commandment was viewed by the Gentile church as part of the ceremonial law which had been abrogated in Christ. It is not until the third century that we learn from Tertullian (*On Prayer* 23) that some stricter Christians even deferred their business in order the better to celebrate the joy of the Lord's Day. But while this practice is in line with Tertullian's somewhat rigorous tendencies, there is no hint that he has in mind the Fourth Commandment. The point is merely that the festive character of the day can be best celebrated in that way, just as the common custom of standing, rather than kneeling, for prayer on Sundays reflects the joyful mood of the Christian on the day of the Resurrection. Indeed, Tertullian's reference is absolutely unique, until the advent of Constantine's edict in 321, making the "venerable day of the sun" a public holiday (*Codex Justinianus* 3.12.3). The motives behind his action have already been suggested. It was to be a day of rest; workshops and law courts were to be closed, but rural labor was permitted so that "the bounty of heaven might not be neglected." It is from the required rest of the imperial edict that the tendency toward sabbatarianism arose in the fourth and fifth centuries. In Ambrose (in Ps. 47) and Chrysostom (Homily 10 on Genesis) we have the first theologians to defend the Sunday relaxation from work on the basis of the Fourth Commandment. Pseudo Athanasius (*De Semente* 1) says in his homily: "God transferred the day of the sabbath to the Lord's day."

The ecclesiastical legislation which reflects this growing sabbatarianism, however, is far from demanding a complete cessation of work. Most of the canons (e.g., Apostolic Constitutions 7.23; 8.33; Council of Agde in 506, Canon 47) are primarily concerned with church attendance, and with emphasizing that Sunday, and not Saturday, is the Christian day. For instance, the Council of Laodicea, Canon 29 (later fourth century), insists "Christians must not Judaize by resting on the sabbath"; it then goes on to stress the honor due to the Lord's Day, on which, "if they can," Christians should rest. The injunction to rest is thus far from absolute. Not until the sixth-century Synod of Orleans (Canon 28) is manual labor forbidden.

The severest restrictions on work on Sunday belong to later medieval Catholicism and to English Puritanism. In the former case, however, the actual observance of Sunday was far removed from the church's ideal. It is noteworthy, furthermore, that the early reformers refused to admit a literal reference of the Fourth Commandment to the Lord's Day. Typical is the position of John Frith, the Cambridge reformer, who after stressing Sunday worship goes on to observe: "That done, they may return into their houses and do their business as well as any other day." The work which, more than any other, influenced the stern Puritan attitude was Nicholas Bownd's *True Doctrine of the Sabbath* (1595), to which King James I in 1618 made his notable reply in *The Book of Sports.*

Bibliography. The best brief accounts are J. S. Clemens, in J. Hastings, ed., *Dictionary of the Apostolic Church* (1919), II, 707-10; M. G. Glazebbrook, in J. Hastings, ed., *Encyclopedia of Religion and Ethics* (1922), XII, 103-11. The best exhaustive study is by H. Dumaine in *Dictionnaire d'Archéologie chrétienne et de Liturgie,* vol. IV (1921), cols. 858-994. See also: P. Heylin, *History of the Sabbath* (1636); J. A. Hessey, *Sunday, Its Origin, History and Present Obligation* (1860)—a mine of information; T. Zahn, *Skizzen aus dem Leben der alten Kirche* (2nd ed., 1898), no. 5; L. Eisenhofer, *Handbuch der katholischen Liturgik* (1932), pp. 475-82; P. Cotton, *From Sabbath to Sunday* (1933); C. Callewaert, "La synaxe eucharistique à Jerusalem, berceau du dimanche," *Sacris erudiri* (1940), pp. 263-304. There is some interesting material in M. M. Knappen, *Tudor Puritanism* (1939), pp. 442-50. C. C. RICHARDSON

LORD'S PRAYER. The brief set of petitions ascribed to Jesus in Matthew and Luke, nowhere in the NT referred to under this title but possibly by the double term "Abba! Father!" (ἀββά ὁ πατήρ).

1. The texts of the prayer
2. Origin and context of the double tradition
3. Purpose and plan of the prayer
   a. The address
   b. The first petition
   c. The second petition
   d. The third petition
   e. The fourth petition
   f. The fifth petition
   g. The sixth petition
   h. The doxology
4. Eschatology and existence
5. An epitome of Jesus' teaching
6. Liturgical and personal use
Bibliography

1. The texts of the prayer. The two accounts, in Matthew and Luke, literally translated, may be compared as in the following column.

	Matt. 6		Luke 11
9*a*	Pray then like this:	2*a*	when you pray, say:
b	Our Father	*b*	Father,
c	who art in heaven,		
d	may thy name be hallowed;	*c*	may thy name be hallowed;
10*a*	May thy kindom come;	*d*	May thy kingdom come;
b	May thy will come to pass		
c	as in heaven so also on earth;		
11*a*	Our bread for the morrow	3*a*	Our bread for the morrow
b	give us today;	*b*	give us day by day;
12	And forgive us our debts, as we also have forgiven our debtors;	4*a*	And forgive us our sins, for we ourselves also forgive all who are indebted to us;
13*a*	And do not lead us into temptation,	*b*	And do not lead us into temptation.
b	but deliver us from evil (or, the evil one).		
c	Some MSS of Matthew (W, H, 13, bg etc., Byz., Sy^{c}, Sa, Did.) contain an added doxology: "because thine is the kingdom and the power and the glory for ever."		

Important variations are found in Luke. E.g., vs. 2*b* is found as above in important witnesses (א, B, 1, 118, etc., sy^{s}, Marcion, Origen), but the Matthean expansion is found in others (A, C, D, W, θ, 13, 69, etc., Byz., it, sy^{c}, sy^{pc}, sa, bo). Likewise vs. 2*d* is found as above (B, 1, 118, etc., sy^{c}, sy^{s}), but the Matthew form is found in many MSS (א, A, C, D, W, θ, 13, 69, etc., Byz., it, vg, sy^{pc}, bo). The variants are probably assimilations to Matthew. For Luke alone the shorter text is more original. A further important variant of Luke 11:2 is referred to in § 3*c below.* Other minor signs of assimilation in both gospels are found.

2. Origin and context of the double tradition. The Q hypothesis is of little help, or the suggestion that Jesus delivered two forms of the prayer on two separate occasions. It is more likely that the two forms reach us from independent sources, each evangelist recording the form familiar in the church services of his region (*see* MATTHEW, GOSPEL OF; LUKE, GOSPEL OF). All the essentials are found in the shorter form. A liturgical origin for the two versions is indicated in several ways. The appearance of the doxology in some MSS shows that liturgical development was still in progress before the text of Matthew became settled. The variations are better explained by liturgical tradition than otherwise, in particular the form of Luke 11:2*c* found in Marcion and Gregory of Nyssa (*see* § 3*c below*). Luke's form of the fourth petition, compared with Matthew's, shows adaptation to a liturgical situation. The use of "Abba! Father!" in Rom. 8:15 (cf. I Pet. 1:17); Gal. 4:6 suggests a liturgical usage intelligible to the reader, and the combination of Aramaic and Greek terms testifies to a liturgical situation where both languages were used, which would have been true of many places besides Jerusalem. Jewish parallels and the lack of anything more than editorial contexts in the gospels point in the same direction.

Matthew has intruded the prayer into the Sermon on the Mount at a point where it interrupts the parallel construction of a section on religious practices (see Matt. 6:1-4, 5-6, 16-18). Luke has also attached it to a section on prayer (11:5-13), with an editorial transition, which, however, is less artificial than Matthew's. Luke's immediate introduction referring to a custom of John the Baptist's (cf. 5:33) also applies to the rabbis. It was not unusual to provide a brief summary prayer, and if Jesus did so, its liturgical history would inevitably begin with the earliest Christian gatherings.

We cannot, therefore, point with confidence to a brief original testified to by Luke which might have stood in Q. A considerable history stands behind the forms which finally entered the gospels. The diverse liturgical origins also make problematical the reconstruction of an Aramaic original. So far as this is possible, the results for each gospel indicate that, like much of Jesus' teaching, the prayer was cast in a rhythmic form, reminiscent of poetry, with stresses, assonances, and a strophic structure which would make for ease in memorizing. While this consideration must be applied with caution in determining the form of words, the Eastern ability to retain and pass on oral tradition makes such structure probable.

3. Purpose and plan of the prayer. The claim of the two passages both to be a guide to prayer and to provide a specific set piece to be said corporately or individually is about equal. Certainly, to take it as a liturgical piece only would be to misconstrue the intent of the evangelists and, no doubt, of Jesus himself. It clearly served this purpose when the gospels were compiled and has continued to occupy a climactic place in Christian liturgies. The value of the Lord's Prayer as a plan upon which to base all prayer is indicated by each evangelist. Matthew, in offering it as a substitute for the wrong kind of prayer, establishes in it the priority of attention upon God and his kingdom. Luke, likewise, presents it in answer to a plea to be taught how to pray rather than to be taught a prayer. The similarity between the prayer and Jewish forms suggests the same thought. It forms a summary of the matter of prayer, and the Jewish rabbis provided such synopses. Tractate Berakoth (29*a*) reads: "What is the abstract of the eighteen? Rab said, 'An abstract of each benediction.' Samuel said, 'Give us understanding, O Lord our God, to know thy ways.' " There follows a brief prayer which summarizes the Eighteen Benedictions (cf. the *Habinenu* in the Jewish Prayer Book). This is later than Jesus, but there is no reason to think that the custom was not older than the Talmud. Jesus' prayer is in many respects a summary of the Shemoneh Esreh (Eighteen Benedictions) and doubtless was designed to cover in brief both an outline and order for the matter of prayer and a form which might be used as a short comprehensive prayer in itself.

The Lord's Prayer in the Didache is attributed to our Lord's command and presented as a substitute for "praying as the hypocrites" (revealing a knowledge of both the Matthean setting and the text). It is to be used three times a day (Did. VIII.2.3).

***a. The address* (*Matt. 6:9*b-c; *Luke 11:2*b).** It is not unknown for Jewish prayers to be addressed to God as Father. More frequent in the synagogue service, however, is: "Our Father, Our King" (*'abînû malkhênû*). "Our Father" occurs in connection with the Fifth Benediction (*'abînû*)—though there immediately appears in parallel: "O our King" (*malkhênû*)—and elsewhere occasionally alone. "My Father" is occasionally found among the rabbis (e.g., Sifra Lev. 20: 26; Mek. 68*b;* etc.). The OT thinks of God as Father (Creator; Deut. 32:6; cf. Mal. 2:10) and addresses him as such (Isa. 63:16; 64:8; Jer. 3:4, 19—passages which the Targums translate with some circumspection). The later literature tends to treat God as Father of a more limited group within Israel (Wisd. Sol. 2: 16, 18; Jub. 1:24-25; Pss. Sol. 13:8; 17:30; 18:4).

The Lord's Prayer tells us nothing of Jesus' mode of addressing God, but the gospels record two cases of Jesus' use of "Father" (Matt. 11:25-26 [cf. Luke 10:21]; Mark 14:36 [cf. Matt. 26:39: "My Father"]; Luke 22:42). Mark 14:36 has ἀββὰ, ὁ πατήρ, and since Mark does not interpolate his usual translation, this may reflect a liturgical familiarity (the Passion in Mark is arranged as if for liturgical use) rather than a reminiscence. "Abba" is an Aramaic word which may represent the form with a personal suffix or be translated, as in Luke, simply "Father." This seems to have been Jesus' mode of address. It would be more usual in prayer to find the noun with the pronominal suffix (Hebrew *'abînû;* Aramaic *'abûnā* or *'abûnan*), "our Father." The loss of the pronoun in Luke may be explained by its Gentile Christian provenance.

Jewish piety would tend to add: "who art in heaven," as in Matt. 6:9*c* (ὁ πατὴρ ὑμῶν ὁ οὐράνιος, "your heavenly Father," occurs, e.g., in Matt. 5:48; 6:14, 26; etc.; and ὁ ἐν τοῖς οὐρανοῖς, "who is in heaven," e.g., Matt. 5:16, 45; 7:21; etc.). Its absence from Luke is not a sign of more primitive, but of non-Jewish, usage. Many MSS bring Luke into conformity with Matthew at this point. The Didache varies Matthew with πάτερ ὑμῶν ὁ ἐν τῷ οὐρανῷ, an indication that in use the text was still being adapted. Origen refers to a "boldness of speech" on the part of Jesus in addressing God as Father which goes beyond Jewish practice. It has become the characteristic use of the Christian church, which knows God through Christ the Son.

***b. The first petition* (*Matt. 6:9*d; *Luke 11:2*c).** The first three petitions (two in Luke) have ultimately a similar meaning. To hallow God's name, to pray for the kingdom and for the doing of God's will, all suggest the affirmation of God's sovereignty in an eschatological hope. It is the prayer of a community living in an eschatological atmosphere, and this is properly what the church is when it prays this prayer.

The three petitions have in common the passive verb forms. Luke's verbs differ from Matthew's in the later petitions but not here. The passive imperatives are the language of prayer. Use of the passive was an act of reverence and may be widely illustrated in statements about God, as well as in prayers (e.g., Matt. 5:5, 7, 9; 7:1; Luke 14:14*b*). In the later petitions, where the subject is no longer God and the object no longer the divine situation, the active voice is used.

There is evidence in the Fathers that the variant petition for the Holy Spirit (*see* § 3*c below*) was sometimes found in place of this petition and the added ἐφ' ὑμᾶς, "upon us," found in D, may be a reflection of it (cf. Isa. 43:1; 63:19).

The name of God implied his nature and power. The danger petitioned against is represented in Rom. 2:24 (cf. Ps. 74:10, 18; Isa. 29:23; Ezek. 36:22-23). Ber. 40*b* asserts: "A benediction which contains no mention of the Divine Name is no benediction." The synagogue service in the *Atta hu ad* has the petitions: "Sanctify thy name upon them that sanctify it, yea, sanctify thy name throughout the world. . . . Blessed art thou, O Lord, who sanctifiest thy name among the many." The Kaddish begins: "Magnified and sanctified be his great name." To hallow God's name means to recognize and accept his nature and its demands, and the full answer to this petition presupposes the eschatological consummation. In the interim it is in every sense a "missionary" prayer, for it implies the spread of the knowledge of God's name until all men hold it sacred (cf. Rom. 10:13-15).

***c. The second petition* (*Matt. 6:10*a; *Luke 11:2*d).** This is also a completely Jewish prayer, though on Christian lips it is informed with Jesus' distinctive teaching and his own relation to the kingdom. "King" is a favorite designation for God. The synagogue Kaddish reads: "May he establish his kingdom during your life and during your days, and during the life of all the house of Israel." In Johanan's reply to the statement about the divine name, Berakoth states: "A benediction which contains no reference to the Divine Kingship is no benediction."

A few witnesses testify to the substitution for this petition in Luke the words ἐλθάτω τὸ ἅγιον πνεῦμα σου ἐφ' ἡμᾶς καὶ καθαρισάτω ἡμᾶς, "May thy Holy Spirit come upon us and cleanse us" (162, 700, Gregory of Nyssa, Maximus). It seems to be a Christian variant rather than an original reading, although it fits Luke's emphasis on the Holy Spirit. It may possibly have been a form connected with Christian initiation. Tertullian knew of it in Marcion as a substitute for the first petition.

This is also an eschatological prayer. The tension in Jesus' teaching about the kingdom as impending and yet operative is more obvious in the third petition in Matthew.

***d. The third petition* (*Matt. 6:10*b-c).** That God's will may be accomplished is an interpretation of the coming of the kingdom, since when God's will is completely fulfilled to the exclusion of all other wills, the sovereignty of God in his kingdom will be evident to all. As such this petition is a proper expansion of the last.

Pirke Aboth contains the saying of Jehuda ben Tema: "Be strong as a leopard, and swift as an eagle, and fleet as a hart, and courageous as a lion, to do the will of thy Father which is in heaven." Also the words attributed to Gamaliel: "Do his will as thy will, that he may do thy will as his will. Annihilate thy will before his will, that he may annihilate the will of others before thy will." This may be compared with Jesus' prayer in Mark 14:36, which provides support for the inclusion of this petition.

The second part (vs. 10*c*) suggests that the doing of God's will is intended in the absolute sense that the situation which obtains in heaven may also obtain on earth (but cf. Col. 1:20). For the Christian the fulfilment is found in Christ's complete response to the Father, as developed in the Fourth Gospel, so that the prayer for the coming kingdom is in a real sense a prayer for the coming of Christ, *Maranatha*.

Origen and many since have speculated whether this clause might not be applied to the preceding petitions (for Origen, all three). The usual punctuation attaches it to the prayer for God's will, but the petitions for hallowing God's name and for his kingdom are susceptible of the same application. It is probably a liturgical adaptation in which the present answer becomes an anticipation of the final reality.

***e. The fourth petition* (*Matt. 6:11; Luke 11:3*).** In the remaining petitions the verbs cease to be passive and become active. Matt. 6:11*a* and Luke 11:3*a* are identical, including the unusual word ἐπιούσιον. Origen thought the term, "invented by the evangelists," to have been derived from οὐσία, "substance," meaning "essential"—i.e., necessary for real life. So the Peshitta and Arabic are understood, and Jerome translates *panis supersubstantialem*. This suggests the OT "food that is needful" (לחם חקי) of Prov. 30:8. The combination of ἐπί and οὐσία is, however, grammatically unlikely, and οὐσία has usually another meaning.

The word is found only in the Lord's Prayer and in discussions of it, with the possible exceptions of a doubtful reading on an inscription now lost and a fifth-century A.D. papyrus (Sammelbuch 5224.20), where, if the incomplete form is correctly reconstructed, it seems to read: "for the day's (rations? expenses?)." In this case the term might be a form of ἐπιοῦσα construed with ἡμέρα (expressed or understood) to mean the coming day or the next day (cf. Acts 7:26; 16:11; 20:15; 21:18). This might justify Jerome's claim to have found *maḥar* in the Gospel of the Hebrews version, and he translates *crastinum, id est futurum*. The meaning then would be "of the morrow"—i.e., the day's ration for the next day. This could be given the weight of "daily," as is suggested by the Curetonian Syr., "continual bread" (Aramaic *lāḥman 'amînâ,* for Hebrew לחם התמיד); cf. Num. 4:7: "the bread of continuity" (LXX οἱ ἄρτοι οἱ διὰ παντός). There is possibly behind this nothing more than the simple Aramaic "our bread of the day" (*laḥman deyômâ*), but an original reference to the future seems more likely.

It is difficult to understand why so curious a word was used if it were not original, as its later introduction would be even more difficult to understand. It is best taken as a term fixed in the tradition and retained by liturgical conservatism and sanctity. The remaining and varying parts of the petition in Matthew and Luke then are not glosses (redundant if ἐπιούσιον meant "today's") but liturgical adaptations which apply the meaning to the circumstances of use and plead for the eschatological benefit to be applied to the present. The phrase is clearly a temporal one. The example of the manna in the OT suggests that the bread for the coming day would be sufficient for that day only. The term is best read as having no simply limited meaning. It is unlikely that it had a metaphysical one. The prevailing eschatological tone on the whole prayer shows that "bread of the coming day" could also suggest a share in the messianic banquet, of which the present, material bread, received thankfully, was a foretaste—an idea not remote from that of the "breaking of bread" or the Eucharist.

The remaining clause of the petition then becomes, in each case, easy to explain. Matthew's "give us today" (cf. Did. 8:2) interprets the petition to apply to bread needed for the day and would form a morning petition or, on Jewish reckoning, an evening one. The aorist, δὸς, fits the σήμερον. The Lukan present, δίδου, suggests a constant situation in keeping with the idiomatic τὸ καθ' ἡμέραν ("day by day"), a petition which might be used at any hour, better fitting a Hellenistic situation. (The Aramaic verbs give no guidance as to temporal sense.) If these clauses are taken to be liturgical adaptations of τὸν ἐπιούσιον, this *hapax legomenon* does not have to fit either to the exclusion of the other and shows that it had come to be understood most probably as "that portion designed for the day at hand." Most attempts to translate it (though "daily" is colorless) represent a possible meaning in its actual use but are not a sure guide to the original. The two versions are best explained as modes by which an eschatological term was adapted to the existential situation. An eschatological tension between future and present is not peculiar to the Lord's Prayer.

***f. The fifth petition* (*Matt. 6:12; Luke 11:4*a).** In the first clause the difference is Luke's substitution of τὰς ἁμαρτίας ("sins") for Matthew's τὰ ὀφειλήματα ("debts"). This is hardly significant, since Luke in the parallel clause follows Matthew (except grammatically). Luke uses synonyms wherever possible. The Didache has the variation τὴν ὀφειλὴν ἡμῶν (cf. Matt. 18:32). The commercial word represents the Aramaic *ḥôbhā* (Hebrew חוב), sin conceived as a debt, and "sins" would be a better translation in each case. (The term "trespasses," familiar to some liturgical uses, comes from neither version but is borrowed from Matt. 6:14-15: τὰ παραπτώματα.)

The fifth and sixth benedictions of the Shemoneh Esreh bless God, who delights in repentance, is gracious, and abundantly forgives, but there is no real parallel in Jewish prayers. The conditioning of God's forgiveness on man's, as in Matthew (reinforced by vss. 14-15), seems strange to Jewish ears. Matthew's aorist (ἀφήκαμεν, RSV "have forgiven") seems to imply a limit based on man's action. In Luke the present (ἀφίομεν) is used, suggesting concurrent practice. The tense may represent, however, an indeterminate Aramaic verb and be read as present or future. The NT present is sometimes used in a future sense. It is possible to read Luke's version, not as accomplished fact, but as intention: "Forgive our sins, for we ourselves will forgive." Matthew's insertion of vss. 14-15, choosing, as it does in its present context, one petition of the Lord's Prayer for comment, seems out of place (but cf. Matt. 18:23-34, with its added moral in vs. 35). The future sense is supported by Syr. versions for both gospels.

The difficulty, if it exists, may also be a sign of a reduced eschatological reference, the forgiveness referred to in each case being a final reckoning here made operative in current relationships (cf. Polyc. Phil. VI.2, where Rom. 14:10, 12, is quoted). Otherwise, it must be understood to mean that God's abundant grace, offered to all, must turn to judgment for those who will not themselves forgive. There is a self-commitment implied in the other petitions, especially in Matthew's parallelisms, but nowhere as emphatically as here. There seems no ground for limiting the application within the Christian community.

***g. The sixth petition* (*Matt. 6:13*a-b; *Luke 11:4*b).** In view of Jas. 1:13, this request has seemed strange, and in some of the versions and ancient liturgies it reads: "Do not let us succumb to temptation." Attempts have been made to reveal an underlying Aramaic idiom which could be translated: "Do not let us go under in temptation." The causative verb may have a permissive sense, but since the Hebrew little distinguished cause and result and all that happened came under God's control, this is not important. In Ber. 60*b* a prayer for retiring says: "Bring me not into the power of sin, iniquity, temptation or contempt; and let the good impulse have dominion over me but not the evil impulse." Similar words occur in the Jewish Prayer Book: "Lead us [*tᵉbhê'ênû*] not into sin or . . . temptation . . . ; let not the evil inclination [*yêṣer hāra'*] have sway over us." In Mark 14:38, Jesus counsels such prayer, and here the word πειρασμός refers to immediate dangers which will prove to be a test.

Πειρασμός means primarily a testing, and not enticement to sin. In the LXX it translates the verb and place name *Massah* (where God was put to the test; Exod. 17:7; Deut. 6:16; etc.; cf. Ps. 95:8), and the verb *anah*, "to be afflicted." Its peculiarly biblical use is for putting men to the proof (e.g., Gen. 22:1; Exod. 20:20; Judg. 2:22; Dan. 1:14; Heb. 11:17; etc.). Such testing is to be expected (Ecclus. 2:1-2), even for Jesus (Luke 22:28), and prayer for deliverance seems, in view of I Cor. 10:13, to provide a difficulty (yet cf. Mark 14:35-36). It may be met by the very probable solution that the petition referred primarily to the final time of trial, the messianic woes (cf. Matt. 24:21, 29; Mark 13:24; I Pet. 4:12; etc.). In this case the word usually is θλίψις, though πειρασμός occurs at Rev. 3:10. There is only one case of parallel use, when Luke 8:13 substitutes ἐν καιρῷ πειρασμοῦ for the θλίψεως ἢ διωγμοῦ of Mark 4:17. Probably an eschatological reference is here modified for use in a prayer which seeks deliverance from, but comes to imply deliverance within, testing. To limit the petition to enticement to sin is to narrow its meaning to the point of distortion.

Eschatologically, the addition in Matthew must be read: "Deliver us from the evil one"—namely, the Devil, Antichrist, etc. The words τοῦ πονηροῦ may be masculine or neuter, "evil one" or "evil," and both are found in the NT. The Didache text is the same, but in 10:5 it is applied in the neuter to the church (ἀπὸ παντὸς πονηροῦ), "from all evil." In the Jewish prayer *above*, evil is found in the *yêṣer hāra'* or "evil impulse." Neither possibility can be absolutely excluded. Whether evil comes from other men, inner impulse, circumstances, or the enemy finally disclosed, prayer for deliverance is appropriate, and we may be asked to be spared the final, overwhelming test.

***h. The doxology* (*Matt. 6:13*c *in some MSS*).** This is clearly a later addition and liturgical development, as the Didache shows. In 8:2 it is added to the prayer in the short form: "Thine is the power and the glory." It is clearly said by the people as a response and may have been so said after the Lord's Prayer. In Did. 9–10 it is repeated in a threefold pattern. The first two responses in each case are: "Thine is the glory for ever" (9:2-3; 10:2, 4), and the third: "for thine is the glory and the power through Jesus Christ for ever" (9:4) or "power and the glory" (10:5). These are responses to blessings and prayers over the wine and bread (9) and thanksgiving for the same and prayer for the church (10).

The addition of the doxology makes the Lord's Prayer a more complete act of worship. As a response it can also enlighten the meaning of each petition and give substance to the hope expressed. While fulfilment must await the last day, the kingdom, power, and glory are already in God's hands. We may pray for God's kingdom because the kingdom is his; for the hallowing of his name, because the glory is his;

for the doing of his will, because the power is his. We may share in the provision of bread, forgiveness, and deliverance also, because these are gifts that come with his kingdom; they express his power and manifest his glory.

4. Eschatology and existence. The doxology speaks of an existing state, promised but not realized, basic to the faith by which the prayer is prayed. In each petition it can be seen that there is a primary reference to an eschatological reality and hope. It most likely explains the difficulties involved in the present texts. In the first three petitions we are aware that the answer must be an ultimate reality, for they deal with what God must accomplish in the end, yet are brought into touch with our situation by the words: "as in heaven so also on earth." The last petitions deal with our relation to this final gift of the kingdom and in the text are already modified under the stress of applying the realizable fruits of the "coming near" of the kingdom to our present state. In every case we can pray for the final provision, forgiveness, and deliverance, but also for some anticipation of it in present experience. Thus the prayer of a community eschatologically conditioned becomes "existential" in use. What we pray for is an ἀρραβῶν, a "down payment."

5. An epitome of Jesus' teaching. In manifesting this tension the Lord's Prayer reflects that present in Jesus' teaching (and experience) between the kingdom near at hand and the kingdom yet to come. It also reflects clearly the priorities which he emphasized and applies them to the practice of prayer. Our first concern must be for God's concerns, as they were Christ's, and then our needs fall into perspective. The Lord's Prayer acts upon the injunction: "Seek first his kingdom and his righteousness, and all these things shall be yours as well" (Matt. 6:33). In affirming where our true treasure is, the petitions determine the proper nature of our interest (Matt. 6:9-21).

6. Liturgical and personal use. The developing forms revealed by the texts and by the doxology in particular indicate the propriety of both personal and corporate (liturgical) use. In each case the Lord's Prayer provides a plan upon which to base private practice and the priorities which ought to operate in public worship or liturgical order. The unvarying use of the prayer in every act of worship serves to bring that worship to a climax and at the same time to remind each worshiper to "pray like this."

Bibliography. The treatment of the several petitions, even words, is voluminous. The following will lead to the key materials: M. Margoliouth, *The Lord's Prayer No Adaptation of Existing Jewish Petitions* (1876). F. H. Chase, *The Lord's Prayer in the Early Church,* Texts and Studies, vol. I, no. 3 (1891). I. Abrahams, *Studies in Pharisaism and the Gospels,* 2nd Series (1924). C. F. Burney, *The Poetry of Our Lord* (1925). P. Fiebig, *Das Vaterunser* (1927). G. Dalman, *Die Worte Jesu* (1930). C. G. Montefiore, *Rabbinic Literature and Gospel Teachings* (1930). C. C. Torrey, *The Four Gospels* (1933); *Our Translated Gospels* (1946). M. Black, *An Aramaic Approach to the Gospels and Acts* (1946). E. Lohmeyer, *Das Vater-unser* (1946). E. F. Scott, *The Lord's Prayer* (1951). E. G. Jay, Origen *Treatise on Prayer* (1954). J. Lowe, *The Interpretation of the Lord's Prayer* (Hale Memorial Sermon; 1955). B. M. Metzger, "How Many Times Does *'epiousios'* Occur Outside the Lord's Prayer?" *ET,* vol. LXIX, no. 2 (Nov., 1957). J. Jeremias, "The Lord's Prayer in Modern Research," *ET,* vol. LXXI, no. 5 (Feb., 1960).

C. W. F. SMITH

LORD'S SUPPER [κυριακόν δεῖπνον]. The title given by Paul (I Cor. 11:20) to the common, sacred meals of the church, in continuation of the table fellowship of Jesus with his disciples, which was formally instituted by Jesus at the LAST SUPPER as a perpetual memorial of himself until his Second Coming.

1. Names of the rite
2. Times of observance
3. Form of the rite
   a. As a common meal
   b. Problems of the meal
   c. Separation from the meal
4. Ministers of the rite
5. Doctrine
   a. As a sacrament
   b. As a sacrifice

Bibliography

1. Names of the rite. The term "Lord's Supper" is not used by any other writers of the NT than Paul, but the phrase "marriage supper of the Lamb" in Rev. 19:9 is probably related to it. The word "supper" (δεῖπνον) is common in Greek writers, and in the papyri and inscriptions for cult meals of communion between gods and men. This circumstance may explain why the early church fathers seldom employed the term. Both Clement of Alexandria (*The Instructor* II.2.33) and Hippolytus (*Apostolic Tradition* XXVI.5) use it of the AGAPE, the informal suppers of the church for purposes of fellowship and charity that were not considered a sacramental rite.

The author of Luke-Acts favored the phrase "breaking of bread" (Acts 2:42, 46; 20:11; cf. Luke 24:35) to denote the common meals of the church, without clearly distinguishing between its sacramental and social characteristics. With "the prayers," the act is a peculiarity of the fellowship or "communion" of the church with the apostles. Paul also in one place uses the word "communion" with specific reference to the sacramental body and blood of Christ (I Cor. 10:16); otherwise, he employs "communion" in wider contexts of the fellowship of Christians with Christ and the Holy Spirit, with one another, and more particularly, of sharing in the spread of the gospel and in charity to the poor. *See* COMMUNION.

Christian writers from the second century on (e.g., the Didache, Ignatius, Justin, Irenaeus) preferred the title "Eucharist," derived from the thanksgiving over the bread and wine, the principal ritual act of the Lord's Supper. The absolute use of the noun "Eucharist" in this technical sense is not found in the NT, however, with the possible exception of I Cor. 14:16. Some commentators have found an allusion to the sacrament in the "sacrifice of praise" (Heb. 13:15), but the context suggests that it is a description of Christian life and worship in general, comparable to the summary of Col. 3:16-17; Eph. 5:19-20.

2. Times of observance. The primary form and meaning of the Lord's Supper were given to the church by Jesus in his words and actions at the LAST SUPPER with his disciples before his passion. It should not be overlooked that a primitive and recurrent aspect in the tradition of the Resurrection is the association of the appearances of the risen Lord to his disciples with the occasion of their table fellowship and common meals (Luke 24:30-43; John 20:19; 21: 9-14; Acts 10:41; and the appearance to James, recorded in the Gospel According to the Hebrews, as reported by Jerome *On Illustrious Men* 2). This intimate association of the resurrection faith with the "breaking of bread" explains the festive quality and character of the celebration of the Lord's Supper from the very beginning of the church's existence, as it is admirably summarized in Acts 2:46-47: "And day by day, attending the temple together and breaking bread in their homes, they partook of food with glad and generous hearts, praising God and having favor with all the people."

This passage from Acts suggests that the supper-fellowship of the earliest Jewish Christians was a daily observance. This may well have been the case, in view of their vivid expectation of the imminent return of Jesus from heaven in the Second Coming. The sayings of Jesus at the Last Supper had pointed to an impending fulfilment of God's promise of the revelation of his kingdom. The church, in these earliest days, was living in a continual Passover experience of redemption, reinforced by the sense of participation in the "last times" by the manifest outpouring of the Holy Spirit. The delay of Jesus' return, however, and the spread of the church outside the limited boundaries of the Jerusalem community, made so constant a resort to common meetings less urgent and practical. Though we cannot trace the development with any detail, it is no less clear that before the end of the apostolic period, the regular time of meeting of Christians was the "first day of the week," Sunday—or, as Christians called it, the LORD'S DAY (cf. Acts 20:7; I Cor. 16:2; Rev. 1:10; Did. 14:1; Barn. 15:9; Ign. Magn. 9:1).

We can only surmise the process whereby Sunday became the peculiar day for the corporate worship of the church. So long as the church's membership was predominantly Jewish, and the tension between Jewish and Christian beliefs about Jesus had not provoked an open breach of fellowship, we may suppose that Jewish Christians continued to worship on the sabbath in temple and synagogue. But at sundown on the sabbath, which marked for the Jews the close of the seventh and the beginning of the first day of the week, the Christian disciples would gather for their own peculiar observances, including the "breaking of bread." As the church became more and more Gentile in membership, and Jewish Christians were themselves separated from participation in the communal assemblies of Jewry, the meetings on Saturday evening, often lasting into the early hours of the morning (cf. Acts 20:7-11), would remain as the primary occasion of Christian worship. Whether the selection of the first day of the week for the church's worship was a fortuitous or a deliberate choice in the mind of Christians, it was soon understood as a providential guidance, and significant of the entire orientation of Christian faith around the resurrection of Jesus. Throughout the early centuries of the history of the church, Sunday was universally observed by the celebration of the Lord's Supper. This unanimous association of Sunday with the Eucharistic rites testifies, as does no other single fact, to the early Christian way of understanding the Lord's Supper, not only as a memorial of the Lord's death, but also of his resurrection, the earnest of eternal life in the age to come.

3. Form of the rite. The most debated question concerning the Lord's Supper in the apostolic age concerns the form of its observance. It is unanimously agreed that the celebration as a whole involved, as did the Last Supper, a full supper or meal. But critics disagree as to whether the earliest Christians distinguished the blessed elements of bread and wine, received in conscious memory of the Lord's special institution, as more sacred and sacramental in character than the rest of the meal and accompanying devotions. In other words, did the early church maintain a clear distinction between the Eucharist and the AGAPE?

a. As a common meal. The two types of observance, Eucharist and Agape, were certainly distinguished, not to say separated, from each other by the time of Justin Martyr (A.D. 150). By that time the Eucharist was a ceremonial meal, involving only the offering, blessing, and sharing of the elements of bread and wine, and carefully differentiated by its sacramental character from the fellowship and charitable suppers of the Agape and the funerary, memorial banquets for departed Christians. The passing references in writers of the subapostolic age are not detailed enough to afford a clue to the problem at an earlier phase of development. This includes the mention in Acts, as already noted, of the "breaking of bread." The fuller directives of the DIDACHE 9–10, 14, are themselves involved in this critical controversy, and are in any case an uncertain guide because of other problems of this document with respect to its date, location, and significance. We are thus dependent almost entirely upon the notice of Paul in I Cor. 11:17-34.

Among the Jews, even the most ordinary meals were sanctified by the benedictions—i.e., thanksgivings—offered to God by the head of the family, both at the beginning and at the end of the repast. The former of these benedictions was pronounced at the breaking of bread. At occasions of a more formal, religious nature, the thanksgiving after meals was said over a "cup of blessing" of wine mixed with water, which was then passed about the table for each member of the company to partake. The special grace thus shared in common was associated more especially with participation in the one blessing rather than with consecrated elements of food. The food and drink, however, were hallowed by the recognition that they were gifts of God's providence; and the special thanksgiving over the cup linked the remembrance of God's providence with the recalling of his past acts of redemption and his promise of the coming kingdom. In a setting such as this, the earliest Christian missionaries imparted to their converts the tradition of the Last Supper, translating the older Jewish table benedictions into terms recalling the redemptive act of Christ, the fulfilling of his church with the Spirit, and the sure hope and expectation of his imminent return to establish his kingdom.

Gentile converts to the faith were also familiar with cult meals in their pagan background. We know too little of the details of sacramental meals in the mystery religions, other than that they existed, since the more solemn ceremonies of these cults were kept with extraordinary secrecy. In addition, there were the feasts following upon religious sacrifices; and many guilds of tradesmen and funerary associations held common meals under the patronage, and in devotion to, particular tutelary deities. Such meals would be formally opened by libations offered to the gods; and in many cases special offerings of food would be set aside for the patron deity, as one present in the company of devotees. All too often, however, pagan cult meals degenerated into gluttonous feasting and drinking, and exceeded the limits of decent decorum.

b. Problems of the meal. The church in Corinth, founded by Paul, may not have been typical of Christian congregations; but the problems raised by their behavior at the Lord's Supper were no doubt symptomatic of the difficulty of preserving the decorous and sacred atmosphere of the Jewish tradition of religious meals among converts of heathen background. The particular abuses at Corinth to which Paul addresses his strenuous remonstrances had to do with three things: (*a*) the open divisions of the Corinthians in their celebration of the Supper; (*b*) the disregard of certain members, perhaps the wealthier and more leisured, for others by the way they began the observance of the Supper before all the church members had arrived; and (*c*) the excesses of certain members in eating and drinking. The divisions of the Corinthian church were not only social and economic, but ethnic and religious, for in the same letter Paul deals with the problem of Jewish-Gentile tension over eating meat that had been offered in pagan sacrifice, and with the partisan strife that centered in conflicting loyalties to several missionaries. *See* CORINTHIANS, FIRST LETTER TO THE.

By reminding them once more of the tradition as to how the Lord had celebrated the Last Supper, Paul roundly condemned the Corinthians' observance as a travesty upon it. He insisted that they should all begin the Supper together and share it together, with full regard for Christian charity to impoverished Christians who could not provide much in the way of food and drink for the meal. He recalled them to the religious solemnity of the occasion, as predominant over its social character. And he directed that any temptation to immoderate feasting be removed by reminding those who were hungry to eat at home.

There is no suggestion in Paul's directives that the Supper was to be reduced to a purely ceremonial meal upon the bread and wine. It is generally accepted by all commentators that Paul allowed for a continuation of a common meal, as at the Last Supper, between the blessing of the bread at the beginning and the blessing of the cup after supper. His one concern is that this meal be done by all together, with sobriety and devout remembrance of the Lord. It is certainly possible to distinguish, as many critics do, the two actions of blessing and sharing of the bread and the cup, respectively, from the rest of the meal, and to denote these actions only as sacramental and cultic. Support for this view can be found in I Cor. 10:16: "The cup of blessing which we bless, is it not a communion in the blood of Christ? The bread which we break, is it not a communion in the body of Christ?" Certainly the blessed bread and cup of wine had a greater significance than any other part of the meal, by virtue of the Lord's words about them at the Last Supper. There can be no denying this. But it is not clear, by any means, in the recital of I Cor. 11:20, that the title "Lord's Supper" refers only to the words and actions associated with the bread and the cup, and not to the entire observance of the meal.

c. Separation from the meal. There is no record of the time and place when and where the meal was detached from the memorial of the Last Supper and a clear separation made between the sacramental Eucharist and the fellowship meal of the Agape. A theory has been propounded that, in view of the universal and uniform development of this differentiation throughout the church by the middle of the second century at the latest, if not at a considerably earlier time, the arrangement was made by authority of the apostles. This is possible, but it is incapable of proof. We may surmise, however, the principal reasons for its taking place. One was undoubtedly the need of preserving the most sacred cult act of the church from the kind of abuses that happened at Corinth, and that was likely to be repeated as the membership of the church was drawn more and more from Gentiles of heathen background.

A practical consideration may well have been the limitations of space. As congregations grew in size, it would have been impossible to accommodate them at a regular meal, all at one time, even in the more commodious houses of well-to-do members, where in most places Christians would be enabled to meet. Unfortunately, no house-church of a primitive age has come to light. The oldest one as yet identified—that at Dura, dated 242—had probably ceased to be a private residence by the time it was taken over for use by the local church. It exhibits modifications in the interior arrangements, through the combination of several rooms to form one large meeting room, precisely to provide enough space for the gathering of the church at the Eucharist.

The separation of the Eucharist from the common meal led to an important modification in the ritual and manner of its celebration. With the dropping out of the meal, the older, separate thanksgivings over the bread and the cup were combined into a single prayer of thanksgiving over both elements together. Henceforth the bread and the wine were offered together and blessed together, with communion in both species following immediately. On Sundays, at least, this ceremonial meal was preceded by a synaxis, or corporate devotion of lessons, sermon, prayers, and kiss of peace, which presents analogies with the service of the Jewish synagogue, from which it may have been derived and developed. The lessons and sermon were open to any person, whether a member of the church or not—though, for security reasons, unbaptized persons must have been allowed to attend only upon invitation. Before the prayers, however, all non-Christians and unbaptized catechumens were required to leave, and the rest of the rite was observed by the faithful alone behind guarded doors to avoid profanation of the sacred mystery. In this respect, the sacramental rite of the church provided certain analogies to the cults of the mystery religions. The oldest, detailed account of such a celebration that we have is provided in Justin Martyr's first Apology, 65-67.

4. Ministers of the rite. From the time of Ignatius (*ca.* 110), it was a universal custom that only the bishop presided over the celebration and offered the consecratory prayer of thanksgiving over the bread and wine. In his absence, he could deputize this office to an elder (presbyter). The deacons assisted the celebrant in receiving the offerings of the people and in administering communion both to those present at the assembly and to the absent (the sick and prisoners). Whether or not this arrangement goes back to apostolic times cannot be exactly determined, since neither Paul nor the book of Acts gives us any precise information on this point. Doubtless an apostle, when present, took precedence over all other ministers in presiding over the celebration. Did. 10:7 allows a prophet to offer the thanksgiving "howsoever he wishes," but it is disputed by commentators whether this passage refers to the Eucharistic consecration or to the table blessings of the Agape. However, in ch. 15, after a precise mention of the Eucharist, the Didachist prescribes the appointment of bishops and deacons who "also minister the liturgy of prophets and teachers." It may be that this directive is a commentary upon Acts 13:1-3, where prophets and teachers at Antioch are described as "liturgizing" for the church there. In I Clem. 44.4, the bishop is especially described among those "who have offered the gifts"—i.e., the Eucharistic elements. Many scholars believe that the original and primary function of the office of bishop was that of "overseer" of the Eucharistic rite. *See* BISHOP; MINISTRY, CHRISTIAN, § 8.

5. Doctrine. The theological meaning of the Lord's Supper is obviously based upon the intention of Jesus in his words and actions at the LAST SUPPER (*see* § 3), though undoubtedly the understanding of them by the early Christians was colored by their own comprehension and beliefs respecting the nature of his person and atonement, and the character of his relation to his church. For Jesus, the Supper was the sign of the New Covenant, sealed in his death and resurrection, that constitutes the new Israel of God as the heir of the impending kingdom. It is a pledge that his disciples partake of the benefits of his redeeming work and hence have an earnest of the heavenly messianic banquet that they will share with him. The Supper is the means whereby those who belong to Jesus join with him in that entire, sacrificial self-offering to the Father's will that alone is the way to eternal life.

a. As a sacrament. Later NT teaching is basically faithful to this perspective of Jesus, both in its sacrificial and in its eschatological aspects. Paul developed and stressed especially the realistic communion that the Christian has with Christ and his fellow believers in the elements of the Supper. It is "supernatural food," typified in the OT by the manna and water from the rock enjoyed by the Hebrews in their wilderness wandering to the Promised Land (I Cor. 10:1 ff). This communion with Christ has two principal corollaries: (*a*) it is of such holiness and power that profanation of it by association with the communions of either Jewish or pagan sacrifices provokes the Lord to "jealousy" (I Cor. 10:16-22); and (*b*) it is such a bond of unity in the church that want of charity among the members of the one body, who share the one bread, brings judgment of damnation. More than that, unworthy participation in the consecrated bread and cup results in dire consequences, by not "discerning the body," not only in the spiritual, but also in the material, sphere of life (I Cor. 11:27-34). Thus, in Paul's thought, the sacrament seals the intimate union of Christ with his church, and of the several members of the church one with another.

The Fourth Evangelist also employs the typology of the manna to stress the supernatural receiving of Christ, "the bread . . . which comes down from heaven," in the eating of his flesh and the drinking of his blood. The sacrament is both the nourishment of the Christian in eternal life now during his life on earth, and a pledge of his being raised up "at the last day." The evangelist meets the scandal aroused by his intensely realistic language by the reminder that Christ offers us not his material, natural flesh and blood, but his risen and ascended life in Spirit, and that the gift of this life is received and appropriated in faith (John 6:25 ff).

Many modern critics see in the Pauline and Johannine sacramental realism the influence of pagan mystery cults, or, at least, a radical transformation of the historical and eschatological context of Jesus' words of interpretation into the nontemporal and metaphysical outlook of Hellenism with its concern for the redemption of matter by spirit. To some extent this is true, and perhaps inevitable in the process of translating the gospel into the terms of a Greek-speaking, Greek-thinking culture. The trend in this direction very early reached a term in the definition of the Eucharist by Ignatius (Eph. 20.2) as the "medicine of immortality, the antidote that we should not die but live for ever in Jesus Christ." On the other hand, it is not fair to include either Paul or "John" with those who conceived of sacraments as quasi-magical operations, infusing "immortality" in their mortal recipients. They guard the efficacy of the Eucharist by their insistence upon the conditions of faith and charity in the participants. Nor do they ignore the tension of future judgment which the sacrament places upon all who partake of it. Their teaching is loyal to the "realized eschatology" of the NT outlook as a whole. *See* ESCHATOLOGY OF THE NT.

b. As a sacrifice. The sacrificial character of the Lord's Supper is necessarily related to Jesus' own association of the bread and wine with the offering of his body and blood on the cross. It has been argued by some scholars that his very command, "Do this," implies that the performance of the rite itself is a sacrifice. Even if this be admitted, it does not help us to define the precise character of the Eucharistic sacrifice, especially in view of the varied kinds of sacrifice current in the ancient world among both Jews and Gentiles. *See* SACRIFICE AND OFFERINGS.

No writer of the NT uses the word "sacrifice" to denote the Eucharist. We have seen, however, that Paul draws an analogy between the Christians' communion in the sacramental elements and the meals of the sacrificial offerings of Jewish and pagan cult. Yet Paul does not suggest that the Eucharistic bread and wine are in and of themselves offered to God as a sacrifice. Insofar as Christians offer sacrifice at all, in Paul's view, they offer the totality of their lives in Christian service: "a living sacrifice, . . . your spiritual worship" (Rom. 12:1). The same thought underlies the statement of I Pet. 2:5, that Christians "offer spiritual sacrifices," and of Heb. 13:15-16: "Through him [i.e., Christ] then let us continually offer up the sacrifice of praise to God, that is, the fruit of lips that acknowledge his name. Do not neglect to do good and to share . . . , for such sacrifices are pleasing to God."

There is no need to exclude from these passages the Lord's Supper, since it was part and parcel of the Christian life of fellowship and sharing. But they contain no specific doctrine of a Eucharistic sacrifice apart from the obvious truth that the sacrament is a means, among others, whereby the faithful in Christ, being one with him, are participants by grace in the demands, as in the effects, of his one offering of himself once for all on the cross. It is therefore quite in accord with NT thought to speak of the Lord's Supper as a "memorial sacrifice" or as a "sacrifice of praise and thanksgiving." (The Christian sacrament, in this respect, shares many of the motifs of the Jewish Passover.) It is a thankful and joyous memorial of redemption, not in the way of mere mental recollection of a past event, but, more than that, a here-and-now experience of the mighty deliverance of God, with his promise—made sure for the Christian by Christ's victory—of salvation in the world to come.

The first Christian document to call the Eucharist a "sacrifice" as such was the Didache (14:2-3), by considering it a fulfilment of Mal. 1:11. The Eucharist is the "pure offering" magnifying God's name among all peoples throughout the world. This notion may not be very faithful to the original meaning of the prophet, but the idea was to have a rich development in second-century Christian theology. It fit into the trend of late Jewish and pagan philosophical thought, with its depreciation of material offerings—particularly "bloody" ones—and its emphasis upon true sacrifice as an inner oblation of the heart and mind of those who are in moral character fit for communion with God. The Christian development of the theme took one of its cues from Paul's concept of spiritual sacrifice in Rom. 12:1. Possibly Paul himself borrowed the phrase from current philosophical discussion. To trace the application of it to the Eucharist would take us, however, far beyond the boundaries of NT theology. *See* WORSHIP IN NT TIMES, CHRISTIAN.

Bibliography. *See* the bibliographies under AGAPE; LAST SUPPER; and for doctrine, *see* the Commentaries listed under JOHN, GOSPEL OF; CORINTHIANS, FIRST LETTER TO THE.

Other works: M. Goguel, *L'Eucharistie des origines à Justin Martyr* (1910). H. Lietzmann, *Messe und Herrenmahl* (1926). G. H. C. Macgregor, *Eucharistic Origins* (1928). W. Goossens, *Les origines de l'Eucharistie, Sacrement et Sacrifice* (1931). O. Cullmann, "La signification de la Sainte-Cène dans le Christianisme primitif," *RHPR,* XVI (1936), 1-22. E. Lohmeyer, "Vom urchristlichen Abendmahl," *Theol. Rundschau* IX (1937), 168-227, 273-312; X (1938), 81-99. F. L. Cirlot, *The Early Eucharist* (1939). G. Dix, *The Shape of the Liturgy* (1944), pp. 36-155, 238-67. A. J. B. Higgins, *The Lord's Supper in the NT* (1952). N. Clark, *An Approach to the Theology of the Sacraments* (1956).

M. H. SHEPHERD, JR.

LO-RUHAMAH lō'ro͞o hā'mə. KJV translation of לא־רחמה, a symbolic name given by the prophet Hosea to his second child, to indicate God's anger against Israel (Hos. 1:6; RSV lit. "Not pitied").

LOT lŏt [לוט; LXX *and* NT Λωτ]. Son of Haran, and nephew of Abraham (Gen. 11:27).

The Lot stories are now found intertwined with the more dominant Abraham narrative (Gen. 11:27-32; 12:4*a,* 5*a;* 13:1-13; 14:12, 16; 19). Viewed separately, however, they contrast Lot with his uncle, his neighbors the Sodomites, his wife, and his daughters.

1. Lot and Abraham
2. Lot and Sodom
3. Lot and his wife
4. Lot and his daughters

Bibliography

1. Lot and Abraham. Like Noah, Terah had three sons: Abram (the form Abraham is not used until 17:5; *see* ABRAHAM § A), Nahor, and Haran. Haran was the father of Lot and presumably also of Milcah and Iscah. He died before his father "in the land of his birth, in Ur of the Chaldeans" (11:26-29). Taking Abram, Lot, and Sarai (*see* SARAH), Terah left the ancient Sumerian city of Ur for the land of Canaan. But when he reached Haran, a flourishing city on the Upper Balih River, he settled there and died (vss. 31-32).

When Abram was called by Yahweh to leave Haran, he took with him Lot and all the members of their families (12:4-5*a*). Entering Palestine, Abram and Lot camped first at Shechem and then near Bethel, each time building an altar for the worship of Yahweh. Yet they "journeyed on, still going toward the Negeb" (the S—originally "dry"—country; vss. 6-9).

This movement of Hebrew patriarchs from Haran down to the S border of Palestine would indicate that Israelites shared in the general migration of Arameans into the W and SW sections of the ancient Near East during the Middle Bronze Age (2000-1500 B.C.).

Although the narrative in 12:10-20 does not explicitly state that Lot accompanied Abram and Sarai to Egypt, the three are named together upon their return to Palestine (13:1). Moreover, the Dead Sea Genesis Apocryphon (*see* DEAD SEA SCROLLS § 5*e*) has Lot not only accompanying Abram into Egypt (XX.11, 33-34) but also functioning as spokesman to Pharaoh's agent (lines 22, 24), acquiring great possessions, and obtaining a wife (line 34).

After their sojourn in Egypt, Abram and Lot went through the Negeb up into the Benjaminite hill country, seeking adequate pasturage for their flocks and herds, which had greatly increased in Egypt (12:16; 13:2). When they reached their former camp between Bethel and Ai, they parted. The earlier J source gives the reason as personal strife between their herdsmen (13:7*a*); the later P writer adds that "the land could not support both of them dwelling together" (vs. 6). The note that the Canaanites and Perizzites were then dwelling in the land (vs. 7*b*) serves two functions. First, it emphasizes the dimension of faith; for the land was not yet in the possession of the Hebrew patriarchs, to whom it had been promised (12:7; 13:14-17). Then it points up the acuteness of the economic situation; for not only must Abram and Lot find enough land to support their large flocks, but they must further reckon with the prior claims undoubtedly being urged by the native inhabitants.

Eschewing discord, especially between "men who are brothers," Abram gave his nephew first choice of the best of the land (13:8-9). Lot, having surveyed the scene, chose the whole Jordan basin (lit., the "circle of the Jordan," a technical term; *see* JORDAN § 4), whose fertile richness the editor compares with the garden of Yahweh and with Egypt. He journeyed through it and settled at Sodom (vss. 10-12). This story offers an intentional contrast between Abram's magnanimity and Lot's self-interest; and its closing words form both a judgment upon Lot and a connecting link with ch. 19, the second unit in the Lot tradition: "Now the men of Sodom were wicked, great sinners against Yahweh" (13:13).

Lot appears in ch. 14 as one of the captives taken by CHEDORLAOMER and his E confederates when they quelled the revolt of five Canaanite kings from the region of Sodom and Gomorrah (vss. 1-12). Lot was then rescued by Abram, whose valorous action brought him honor (vss. 13-24; *see* ABRAHAM § C3). Within this unique chapter the figure of Lot serves to link together two originally separate units (vss. 1-12, 13-24). Also, his capture brings Abram out into the international scene, dramatizing him as a military hero and a savior of his people.

2. Lot and Sodom. Other comparisons are found in the next section. Dwelling in one of the "cities of the plain," Lot himself forms a clear contrast with the perverted Sodomites, just as his hospitality to the angelic visitors is contrasted with the wickedness of the citizens (19:1-9). However, the story implies also a comparison with Abraham's hospitality (18:1-8) which is not favorable to Lot, who let the claims of courtesy transcend the moral obligations of fatherhood (19:6-8).

3. Lot and his wife. Again Lot is rescued (19:12-29; cf. ch. 14), this time by divine intervention which takes into consideration his relative righteousness (Wisd. Sol. 10:6-8; Luke 17:28-29; II Pet. 2:7-8) and accommodates itself to his weakness (Gen. 19:16-21; but cf. vs. 29[P]). Here Lot is favorably contrasted with the members of his own family. "His sons-in-law, who were to marry his daughters," given the chance to share in Lot's salvation, condemned themselves by their frivolous disbelief. Even his wife, though specifically warned (vs. 17), brought her own condemnation by refusing to give herself totally to the flight. Looking back because of reluctance or curiosity, "she became a pillar of salt" and so has served as a warning in later Jewish (Wisd. Sol. 10:7) and Christian (Luke 17:32) teaching. Fig. LOT 37.

From *Atlas of the Bible* (Thomas Nelson & Sons Limited)

37. One of the columns of rock-salt traditionally associated with the story of Lot's wife

4. Lot and his daughters. As the "cities of the valley" were being destroyed (*see* SODOM; GOMORRAH; DEAD SEA § 2*d*), Lot and his two daughters fled from ZOAR, where they had taken refuge (Gen. 19:17-22), up into the hills of Moab (vs. 30; cf. 14:10). Dwelling with their father in a cave, through incestuous relations Lot's older daughter becomes the mother of the Moabites; his younger, of the Ammonites (vss. 30-38; cf. Deut. 2:9, 19). Although these popular ethnic etymologies are historically and linguistically unsatisfactory, they preserve a memory of intermarriage between ancestors of the Israelites and inhabitants of S Transjordan (cf. also Gen. 36 [especially vss. 20-30]; I Sam. 22:3-4; Ruth; *see* MOAB; AMMON). The present form of the stories leaves no doubt as to Israel's feeling of superiority (cf. Isa. 15–16; Jer. 48; Amos 2:1-3; Zeph. 2:8-9).

The Lot narrative ends with the same theological motifs which characterize the whole J epic: God's election of Israel and his providential guidance of the patriarchs, his judgment of sin, his accommodation to man's weakness, and his saving grace.

Bibliography. S. R. Driver, *The Book of Genesis* (rev. ed., 1911), pp. 151-55, 197-205. G. von Rad, *Das erste Buch Mose*, Kap. 12/10—25/18 (1952), pp. 142-46, 184-92.

L. HICKS

LOTAN lō'tăn [לוטן, *probably connected with* LOT; *note frequent nunation in* Edomitic (Gen. 38) *and* N Arabian (Gen. 25:1-3) *personal names*]. The first son of Seir (Gen. 36:20; I Chr. 1:38); clan chief of the native Horite inhabitants of Edom (Gen. 36:22, 29 [אלוף לוטן]; I Chr. 1:39). L. HICKS

LOTHASUBUS. Apoc. alternate name of HASHUM.

LOTS.

1. In the OT. The employment of the lot (גורל), either in the form of casting it on the ground or of drawing it from a receptacle, was much in vogue in the ancient world (cf. Esth. 3:7, where the Akkadian *pûru* is equated with the Hebrew גורל; Joel 3:3—H 4:3; Jonah 1:7; Nah. 3:10). In the OT the use of the lot is reported on many occasions: to apportion the newly conquered land among the tribes (Num. 26:55; Josh. 14:2; etc.), to detect a guilty person who has broken a taboo (Josh. 7:14; I Sam. 14:42), to determine which of the two goats in the ritual of the Day of Atonement shall be sacrificed as a sin offering and which shall be sent away into the wilderness to Azazel (Lev. 16:7-10), etc. The same method was sometimes employed to solve exceptional political and labor problems. The first king of Israel was chosen by lot (I Sam. 10:20-21). The courses of the priests, singers, and gatekeepers in the temple were assigned by the same means (I Chr. 24:5; 25:8; 26:13). In times of emergency certain tasks, such as the provision of wood for the temple and the resettling of Jerusalem, were also accomplished by the casting of the lot (Neh. 10:34—H 10:35; 11:1). According to Prov. 18:18, the lot was used in settling disputes between powerful contenders.

The use of the lot was not considered a practice bordering on magic (cf. Josh. 18:6, 8, where the lot is cast "before the LORD our God"). Deut. 18:10-12, which condemns all forms of witchcraft, does not mention the lot; and Prov. 16:33 contends that though the lot is thrown, "the decision is wholly from the LORD."

The term "lot," as first used in Joshua as a method to apportion land, acquired later the meaning of hereditary land property (cf. Josh. 17:14; Ps. 16:5-6; etc.), and finally, in a metaphorical sense, that of "destiny" (cf. Isa. 17:14; Jer. 13:25; Dan. 12:13). The character and form of the lot in ancient Israel are not known.

See also URIM AND THUMMIM. I. MENDELSOHN

2. In the NT. Casting lots (βάλλειν κλῆρον) was a method of ascertaining the divine will, widely employed in pagan, Jewish, and to some extent in Christian antiquity. In our literature the practice rests upon the belief that a man's lot, his κλῆρος, is his inheritance, his κληρονομία, and that what he has has been assigned to him by God. To know God's will for oneself is, therefore, to know what God has assigned to one, to know what one's appointed "lot" is. This might be a tangible possession, such as a field; it might be a function, task, or office; it might be even a share in the final salvation. In any case, the emphasis is on the idea that it is something given by God, not earned or obtained. In order to magnify God's initiative, the NT will either minimize man's part in decision or overlook it entirely.

The method of casting lots—i.e., of putting stones, perhaps of various colors or with symbols marked upon them, into a vessel to be shaken until one jumped out—seemed to remove the human element, so that God might make the choice. This is the intent of Acts 1:26. Luke does not mean to say that the Eleven voted Matthias in, but that the Lord Jesus chose Matthias, as he had previously chosen the Twelve. As Judas had "turned aside" from his inheritance, so the Lord Jesus appointed a successor to this "lot." And Acts says, suggestively, that this was done in the casting of "lots." The number of the Twelve, the New Israel, could be made full only by the Lord Jesus himself.

That Acts does not hereafter note the practice again, may be due to the fact that after Pentecost, Luke regularly sets forth the divine activity in terms of the Holy Spirit or the Spirit of Jesus.

That the soldiers cast lots for the garments of Jesus (Mark 15:24=Matt. 27:35=Luke 23:34=John 19:24), will indicate the utter humiliation of Jesus before man. Here man dares to usurp God's prerogative, by seeking to dispose by "lot" of him who alone determines "lots."

Bibliography. F. J. Foakes-Jackson and K. Lake, *The Beginnings of Christianity,* pt. I, vol. IV (1933), p. 15; L. S. Thornton, "The Choice of Matthias," *JTS* (1945), pp. 51-59.

F. D. GEALY

LOTS, FEAST OF. *See* PURIM.

LOTUS [צאלים, *ṣe'ᵉlîm*] (Job 40:21-22); KJV SHADY TREES. A name which has been used as a popular name for many plants. In this case the identification is with the *Zizyphus lotus* (L.) Lam., a thorny shrub or low tree with small, oval leaves. It is found in dry places. This identification fails to fit the watery context of Job 40, in which the mythical

Courtesy of the Trustees of the British Museum

38. An ivory from Nimrud (eighth century B.C.), with man holding a lotus and saluting

beast Behemoth is described. The sacred water LILY of Egypt, *Nymphaea lotus* L., would fit the biblical context better, but not the linguistic evidence.

Figs. LOT 38; PER 29.

Bibliography. I. Löw, *Die Flora der Juden,* III (1924), 134-36; H. N. and A. L. Moldenke, *Plants of the Bible* (1952), p. 247.

J. C. TREVER

LOVE IN THE OT. Love in the OT is the basic character of the relationship between persons, a relationship with the qualities of devotion, loyalty, intimate knowledge, and responsibility. It is not simply an emotion but is the total quality of relationship. In its personal character, love is closely related to the sexual realm, even when the subject is God's love. And the "person" may be collective, as is the case in God's love for Israel as a whole. In all cases, love is the force which both initiates and maintains relationships, be it among persons or between God and man. The OT idea of the love of God is decisive for the NT ideas of love and GRACE. It includes the relationships of friendship, sex, covenant, loyalty, kindness, and sometimes mercy or pity.

1. The vocabulary of love
2. Human love
   - *a.* Sexual love
   - *b.* Familial love
   - *c.* Friendship and human society

3. Divine love
   a. The love of election
   b. The love of covenant
   c. Love and eschatology
4. Man's love of God
   a. Love and covenant
   b. Love and worship
   c. Love and ethics

Bibliography

1. The vocabulary of love. A large number of words are used to express the various aspects of love. The most important of these is perhaps אהב, a word which denotes both human and divine love, sometimes with a sexual connotation (Gen. 24:67; cf. Hos. 3:1). The verb is pointed by the Masoretes as stative (except in Gen. 37:3-4; Deut. 4:37; I Kings 11:1). Its primary connection with sexual love is suggested, but not proved, by the nominal derivatives *'ăhabh,* "carnal love" (Hos. 8:9; but cf. Prov. 5:19 in a good sense), and *'ôhabh,* used only in Hos. 9:10 of "idolatrous love." The noun אהבה corresponds in meaning to the range of meanings of the verb (see II Sam. 13:15; Song of S. 2:4; Isa. 63:9; Jer. 2:2; 31:3). אהב can also denote a perverted devotion, as where the object of love is evil (Ps. 52:3—H 52:5), food (Gen. 27:4), sleep (Prov. 20:13), etc. The other word which is most often used is the noun חסד, which has the principal connotation of "loyal love," the love which characterizes covenant (cf. Deut. 7:12; I Sam. 20:8). The RSV almost always translates חסד as "steadfast love," sometimes as "kindness" or "loyalty," while the KJV and the ASV usually have "mercy" or "lovingkindness" (cf. LXX ἔλεος, Vulg. *misericordia*). The verb חסד appears in the *Hithpa'el* in II Sam. 22:26=Ps. 18:26. One other term is found in all the main meanings of "love," the verb חשק (of human love: Gen. 34:8; Deut. 21:11; of divine love: Deut. 7:7; Isa. 38:17; of man's love of God: Ps. 91:14), which may be derived from a root meaning "to bind or press together."

Other words are narrower in sense. רעה generally means "to be friendly" (cf. Prov. 22:24), and its derivative, רע, is often "friend," though this becomes "lover" in the sexual sense (Song of S. 5:16; Jer. 3:1, 20). רעיה is to be found only in the Song of Songs (1:9, 15; 2:2; etc.; but cf. *Kᵉthîbh* of Judg. 11:37), where it refers to the bride (translated "love" in the nominal meaning). The corresponding masculine term in the Song of Solomon is דוד (1:13; 2:3; 5:2; etc.), which is also used for "uncle" (cf. Lev. 10:4, etc.) and for sexual love in general (Prov. 7:18; Ezek. 16:8; etc.). The probable cognate ידיד, "beloved," usually refers to Yahweh's love for men (see Deut. 33:12; Isa. 5:1; Ps. 60:5—H 60:7; but cf. the title to Ps. 45, where a secular love song may be meant), as does ידדות (Jer. 12:7; but cf. Ps. 84:1—H 84:2). עגב expresses sensual love carried to the inordinate extreme of desire (Jer. 4:30; Ezek. 23 *passim*), and its nominal derivatives עגב (Ezek. 33:32) and עגבה (Ezek. 23:11) refer to the same lust. Once רחם, normally "mercy" or "pity," refers to man's love for Yahweh (Ps. 18:1). The *hapax legomenon* חבב (Deut. 33:3) may be an Aramaic loan word (cf. חב, "bosom" [Job 31:33]), which, as the MT stands, denotes Yahweh's intense love for "the peoples" (עמים), though the RSV emends to "his people" (עמו), narrowing the scope of the expression. In Dan. 9:23; 10:11, 19; 11:37, Daniel is called "greatly beloved" (חמודה, a word which denotes something highly desirable and precious) by the angel.

2. Human love. Love is a pervasive quality in human relationships for the OT. It takes many forms: the sexual, quite possibly the romantic, the love within families and within the bonds of kinship, the love of friendship and of human covenant. From the highest pitch of sexual communion to the calmest and most detached kindness, the rightly ordered human relationship is one of mutuality in love.

a. Sexual love. On its most elemental level, love is sexual relationship. The OT has no trace of prudery with regard to sexuality. On the contrary, the primacy of the sexual relationship in the nature of man is evident in both P and J creation stories (*see* CREATION; MAN, NATURE OF, OT; SEX AND SEXUAL BEHAVIOR). In Gen. 1:28, the implication even seems to be that man is in the image of God in his nature as male and female, and this is further suggested by the importance of the term KNOWLEDGE as a symbol both of man's relationship to God and of the sexual relationship of man and woman (cf. Gen. 4:1, etc.). Though this element of man's love may be purely sexual (cf. Prov. 7:18, where the plural אהבים denotes sexual acts), on the whole it requires a deeper aspect to be a true love. There is present in several OT stories a love which is best described as "romantic," the love of first sight (Gen. 29:18, 20, 32) or of long intimacy (Deut. 21:15-16; I Sam. 1:5; Eccl. 9:9). This love includes the sexual dimension but is not comprised of it. It is rather the intimate devotion and loyalty of life together, which, at least in the early OT narratives, is not incompatible with polygamy (*see* MARRIAGE). The OT understands the danger of concentration on the sexual to the exclusion of the other aspects of human love, such as loyalty (cf. Gen. 20:13; Judg. 14:16; 16:4-5; Ezek. 16:8; 23:17; Hos. 3:1), mutuality (cf. Gen. 24:67), and responsibility (cf. II Sam. 13:1, 4, 15). The SONG OF SONGS is probably a collection of marriage poems, all praising the wonder of sexual love but with emphasis on the mutuality and devotion on which it is founded (cf. Song of S. 2:16; 3:1-8; 7:10; 8:6-7).

b. Familial love. Tribal and familial bonds were very strong in Israel. It is not surprising, therefore, to find love a significant element in the relationship of kinsmen. It is related to sexual love in Ruth 3:10, where the "kindness" (חסד) involves both the initiative of sexual love and the loyalty to next of kin. Elsewhere we meet this love usually within the FAMILY unit, most frequently of father and son (Gen. 22:2; 37:3; 44:20; 47:29; Prov. 13:24) or of parents and all the children (Prov. 15:17[?]; Hos. 9:16); in Ruth 4:15 it is of mother-in-law and daughter-in-law. Yet when familial love is too selective, serious difficulties arise. Isaac loved Esau, but Rebekah loved Jacob (Gen. 25:28), and this led to the hatred between Jacob and Esau. Jacob's overbearing love for Joseph (Gen. 37:3) made the other sons of Jacob hate Joseph (vs. 4). The very exclusiveness of love may be a point where hatred can enter, for love must be responsible as well as devoted. *See* JEALOUSY.

c. Friendship and human society. The social life of man is for the OT an important—perhaps the most important—area of human relationships. Here too we find the love of man for man a primary aspect. Just as the basic social units of family and tribe are maintained by love, the quality of life most desirable in a man is that of חסד, "kindness, loyalty" (Prov. 19:22; cf. 3:3). Though the word has primary religious connotations, they are extended into his responsibility in the whole of society. The specific relationships of human life are designated at various points as love: the respect of man for man (I Kings 5:1—H 5:15; Prov. 16:13); the consistent loyalty of friend for friend (Prov. 10:12; 17:9, 17); the joyful hero-worship of people for leader (I Sam. 18:16, 22, 28); the devotion of slave to master (Exod. 21:5; Deut. 15:16); the love of the neighbor (Lev. 19:18); the love of the individual and of society for the stranger (גר; Lev. 19:34; Deut. 10:19); the kindness (חסד) shown to the poor and unfortunate (Prov. 14:21, 31; 19:17; 28:8). When the love of human friendship is present, rebuke and reproof are accepted in the spirit of man's oneness (Ps. 141:5 [but read perhaps חסיד יוכיחני, "the loyal man may reprove me"]; Prov. 27:5): "Reprove a wise man, and he will love you" (Prov. 9:8). But when these loyalties of love break down, when the wicked show no kindness to the poor (Ps. 109:12, 16), when the friend shuns and despises his friend (Job 6:14; 19:19; Pss. 88:18—H 88:19; 109:4-5), when love is lavished on those who hate (II Sam. 19:6), then society is in danger.

In the OT, human society is principally a covenantal society, not only a society which lives under the divine covenant (*see* § 4 *below*) but also a society structured within itself by a multiplicity of covenants, each of which demands the same responsibility from the participants as does the national covenant with Yahweh. Indeed, the covenant between two men can be referred to as producing the חסד יהוה, the loyalty of Yahweh (I Sam. 20:14). The covenant between David and Jonathan is an excellent example. Jonathan loves David "as his own soul" (I Sam. 18:1, 3; 20:17), and their relationship is one of "sacred covenant" (20:8), the decisive quality of which is חסד, the loyalty of devoted love. David can even say that his covenantal love with Jonathan was a finer thing than the love of women (II Sam. 1:26). Jonathan gives David help in escaping from his father, and David reciprocates after Jonathan's death with unfailing kindness to the family of Jonathan (II Sam. 9:1, 3, 7). Human covenants are always reciprocal, and love is the characteristic of the relationship. Thus "to show kindness" (עשה חסד) is almost always to reciprocate in covenantal terms, in return for a favor (Gen. 40:14; Josh. 2:12, 14; Judg. 1:24; 8:35) or in response to previous loyal dealing (cf. I Sam. 15:6). Love in the covenantal context is therefore a consistent loyalty which the covenanting parties may expect (Gen. 21:23; II Sam. 10:2; I Kings 2:7; I Chr. 19:2), the breaking of which is regarded as evidence of total irresponsibility (cf. II Sam. 3:8; 16:17; II Chr. 24:22). Such a false covenant is the antithesis of true love, as when Jehoshaphat is accused of loving those who hate Yahweh (II Chr. 19:2).

The whole range of human relationships is therefore viewed in the OT as directed and determined by love. This love is, however, no abstract emotion, but the concrete acts of love and loyalty which go to the maintenance of human society.

3. Divine love. Consonant with the personal and active character of human love is the view of divine love in the OT. God's love is not the emotional or intellectual imposition of a favorable viewpoint upon an object of love, but is his redeeming activity in human history. To call it love is to recognize that this activity produces the relationship of persons between man and God. There is no doubt that the sexual magic of indigenous Canaanite fertility worship had its effect on the OT terminology and imagery, but considering the number of times where love is mentioned as an active characteristic of God, the rarity of the husband image is remarkable. The love of God manifests itself most strongly in Israel's history.

a. The love of election. Perhaps the prime focus of Israel's self-awareness is the notion that she is the chosen people (*see* ELECTION). The act of choice on God's part is analogous to a man's choice of a wife, as in Hos. 3:1: "Go again, love a woman who is beloved of a paramour and is an adulteress; even as Yahweh loves [אהב] the people of Israel" (cf. Jer. 2:2; Hos. 2:14-20—H 2:16-22). Hosea also uses the image of the father-child relationship (11:1), where Yahweh's calling Israel out of Egypt is the act of his love. The event of the Exodus, as the original act of election, is frequently referred to as an act of love (cf. Exod. 15:13 [חסד]; Deut. 4:37 [אהב]; 33:3 [חבב]; Neh. 9:17 [חסד]; Ps. 106:7 [חסד]; Hos. 11:4 [אהבה]). The election of the patriarchs, however, is seldom known as an election of love (cf. Ps. 47:4—H 47:5; Mal. 1:2, of Jacob; Deut. 33:12 [ידיד], of Benjamin). On the other hand, the love of Yahweh which elects can also be applied to persons chosen for a particular purpose (cf. II Sam. 12:24; Neh. 13:26, of Solomon; Ezra 7:28, of Ezra; Dan. 9:23; 10:11, 19, of Daniel). This electing love is always to a degree inexplicable. The efforts of the Deuteronomists to explain it come to the conclusion that Israel is God's chosen because "Yahweh loves you" (Deut. 7:8), though they move the step one generation back by referring to Yahweh's oath to the fathers (cf. 4:37). Considering the magnitude of the whole earth, which belongs to Yahweh, Israel can only marvel at God's special love for her (Deut. 10:15). But it is Yahweh's character to love and choose as he pleases, so that even the love for the sojourner in Israel is rationalized by Yahweh's love for the sojourner (Deut. 10:18-19). To this redeeming and elective love Israel responds, for it is the goodness which Yahweh lavishes on his people (Isa. 63:7, 9), the human curse which is turned to blessing (Deut. 23:5—H 23:6), the saving help and faithfulness for his own (Ps. 40:10—H 40:11), the revivification of a weary people (Ezra 9:9), the casting down of his people's foe (Isa. 48:14). This may also be applied to the individual, where deliverance from death is seen as an act of love intended to set the individual on the right way (Pss. 86:13; 103:4). Yahweh's redemption of Israel is the love which upholds the precious thing he has created (Isa. 48:14).

b. The love of covenant. The distinction between the love of election and that of covenant is a narrow one. It is not simply a matter of terminology (Snaith [*see bibliography*] treats אהב as election love and חסד as covenant love; but cf., e.g., Deut. 7:13). The two are closely related, since the act of Yahweh's choice of Israel and the covenant between Yahweh and Israel are two aspects of the same relationship. We may, however, make a distinction for analytic purposes between that love of God which manifests itself in the original choice of Israel and in the election of individuals and that love which presupposes the relationship of covenant and operates within it. Covenant love is therefore the love which maintains a relationship already established. It is to "keep covenant and steadfast love" (cf. Exod. 20:6; Deut. 5:10; 7:9, 12; I Kings 8:23; Neh. 1:5; 9:32; Ps. 89:28—H 89:29; Dan. 9:4). In many places חסד occurs either in the phrase ברית וחסד or in parallel with ברית (*see* COVENANT). חסד is therefore primarily covenant love, a love which presupposes the mutuality of relationship (cf. II Sam. 22:26: "With the *ḥāsîdh* thou dost practice *ḥésedh*" [עם חסיד תתחסד]). The covenant raises the possibility of Yahweh's love:

> He remembered for their sake his covenant,
> and relented according to the abundance of his steadfast love (Ps. 106:45).

The finality of the covenant also assures the continuance of Yahweh's love (cf. Isa. 54:10; 55:3). Yahweh will "keep" (שמר, "guard") his steadfast love for Israel (Exod. 34:7; I Kings 3:6); he will "continue" it to those who know him (Ps. 36:10—H 36:11). He will not remove it from Israel (II Sam. 7:15; I Chr. 17:13; Pss. 66:20; 89:33—H 89:34; Isa. 54:10; Lam. 3:22; cf. Ruth 2:20).

The covenant love of Yahweh is therefore a faithful love, a steadfast, unshakable maintenance of the covenantal relationship. This is most clearly shown by the associations between חסד and the root אמן, particularly the nouns אמת ("truth," "faithfulness") and אמונה ("faith," "faithfulness"; *see* FAITH). When חסד is paired with אמת or אמונה, the latter are usually translated "faithfulness" or "loyalty" by the RSV. Such love is shown in Yahweh's continuing acts of love to those in the covenant relationship: to Abraham (Gen. 24:27), to Jacob (Gen. 32:10—H 32:11), to the men of Jabesh-gilead in return for their loyalty (חסד) to Saul (II Sam. 2:6), to Ittai in return for his loyalty to David (II Sam. 15:20 LXX), to the king (Pss. 61:7—H 61:8; 89:24—H 89:25), to the individual (Ps. 40:10—H 40:11; cf. Ruth 1:8). In each case, the continuance of covenant love is a reward for faithfulness to a covenant on the part of the individual. Covenant love is also maintained for Israel (cf. Ps. 98:3), and for this love and faithfulness Israel gives thanks (Ps. 138:2) and glory to Yahweh (Ps. 115:1).

c. Love and eschatology. Because Israel knows the steadfastness of covenantal love, she looks forward to its continuance. The accompaniment of a recital of the events of the Exodus by the formula כי לעולם חסדו, "For his steadfast love endures for ever" (Ps. 136), is an expression of the faith that the covenant will continue, and that Yahweh's promises will be effective "for ever," as long as Israel can imagine (*see* TIME § 2*c*). The חסד of Yahweh is often referred to as being in force "for ever" (לעולם [I Chr. 16:34, 41; II Chr. 5:13; 7:3, 6; 20:21; Ezra 3:11; Pss. 100:5; 103:17; 106:1; 107:1; 117:2; 118:1-4, 29; 138:8; Jer. 33:11]; עולם ועד, "for ever and ever" [Ps. 52:8—H 52:10]). Therefore Israel can hope in Yahweh's love (Ps. 147:11), and so in Yahweh because he is a God of love (Ps. 130:7). For Yahweh watches over those who hope in his love (Ps. 33:18, 22). In the love of covenant there is great forgiveness (Hos. 14:4—H 14:5), and this forgiveness will come to Israel as it did in "days of old" (Mic. 7:18-20). Therefore, the psalmist may trust in the love of God as over against those who trust in earthly riches (Ps. 52:8—H 52:10; cf. vs. 7—H 9). To expect Yahweh's love and the fulfilment of his promises is to expect the same thing (119:41; cf. 77:8—H 77:9). For love is the character of God's judgment and is the mode in which he exercises his power (62:11-12—H 62:12-13). Therefore the description of the final restoration of Israel shows a time when "steadfast love and faithfulness [אמת] will meet" (85:10—H 85:11). And the expectation of ultimate salvation is the hope in Yahweh's covenantal love. He will save because of his love (ישע למען חסד [6:4—H 6:5]; פדה למען חסד [44:26—H 44:27; cf. 31:16—H 31:17]). His eschatological victory will be a renewal of Israel in love (Zeph. 3:17; read יחדש באהבתו with the LXX and the RSV for MT יחריש). Indeed, Yahweh's salvation and his love can be spoken of as synonymous (note the parallelism of Pss. 85:7—H 85:8; 119:41 [ישע]; 130:7 [פדות]). Salvation is to be found in the consummation of the covenant at an "acceptable time" (Ps. 69:13—H 69:14). And the psalmist, presuming that covenant love is possible only in life, asks in complaint: "Is thy steadfast love declared in the grave?" (88:11—H 88:12), unaware that the saving love of God would be found in death and a grave, an eschatological consummation which was unthinkable for the OT. *See* SALVATION.

4. Man's love of God. The covenantal love of God is primary in the divine-human relationship. Man is to love God, but his love is derived from God's primal establishment of covenantal relationship. It is because Yahweh loves that the "faithful" (חסידים; RSV "saints") are exhorted to "love Yahweh" (Ps. 31:23—H 31:24). Yahweh's faithfulness in attendance upon his people's prayer is cause for their love for him (116:1), and his gracious might exerted on their behalf motivates their love (רחם; 18:1—H 18:2). The great commandment: "You shall love Yahweh your God with all your heart, and with all your soul, and with all your might" (Deut. 6:5; cf. 13:3—H 13:4; 30:6), sets forth the most profound response to Yahweh's oneness, his uniqueness, and his sole claim to man's devotion ("Hear, O Israel; Yahweh our God is one Yahweh"). *See* DEUTERONOMY; SHEMA.

a. Love and covenant. It is not surprising, therefore, that in the Deuteronomic circle of writings, Israel is commanded to love Yahweh (Deut. 11:13, 22; 19:9; 30:16; Josh. 22:5; cf. 23:11). The love which Yahweh has shown is a love which initiates and sustains the COVENANT, and Israel's life in the covenant can properly be only a life of love to Yahweh. Therefore, the commandment of love is not the contradiction in terms which it might seem. It is a description of covenantal life, as well as an exhortation to responsibility in the covenant. To love Yahweh is life itself (Deut.

30:20: כי הוא חייך וארך ימיך, "for that means life to you and length of days"; cf. 13:3—H 13:4; 30:6). Those who love Yahweh are the objects of his "keeping covenant and steadfast love" (Exod. 20:6; Deut. 5:10; 7:9; Neh. 1:5; Dan. 9:4; cf. Ps. 145:20; *see* § 3*b above*). Yahweh delivers those who love him (חשק; Ps. 91:14). His custom (משפט, "justice," "regular practice"; *see* JUSTICE) is to have mercy on them (Ps. 119:132). And the faithful love not only Yahweh but also his promise (vs. 140). Israel's covenantal love, therefore, is the response to the love Yahweh has first shown by his establishment of the covenant. At a time of great apostasy and stress, Yahweh speaks through Jeremiah of his remembrance of Israel's youthful loyalty (חסד) and her "love as a bride" (אהבה; Jer. 2:2). But this covenantal devotion has been short-lived (cf. Jer. 2:5-37), and Israel's חסד is a "morning cloud, like the dew that goes early away" (Hos. 6:4). *See* RIGHTEOUSNESS.

b. Love and worship. Israel's worship (*see* WORSHIP IN THE OT) is thus undertaken in love to Yahweh. The combination of the two ideas is not often found, but worship is sometimes an expression of the love of the chosen people. Those who "love the name" of Yahweh will dwell in the restored Zion (Ps. 69:36—H 69:37), and the impression is that their dwelling in Zion is a continual ritual worship. The pious love Yahweh because he answers prayer (116:1). Those who love his name participate in ritual exultation in him (5:11—H 5:12; the text of the first part of the verse is in some disrepair). By extension, those who love Yahweh love also the temple in which he lives, "the place where [his] glory dwells" (26:8; cf. also 84:1—84:2 [ידידות]). Even foreigners may enter into the joyful worship of the people of the covenant if they

> join themselves to Yahweh,
> to minister to him, to love the name of Yahweh,
> and to be his servants (Isa. 56:6-7).

There is, of course, that false worship which is false love. Israel has "loved strangers" (Jer. 2:25), which seem in the context to be alien gods (cf. 8:2). Hosea twice specifies these "lovers" as the Baals (2:13—H 2:15; 9:10). And the indignant outcries of Hosea, Jeremiah, Ezekiel, and the author of Lamentations against Israel's seeking "lovers" among the nations carry the connotation of a departure from the exclusive and loving devotion to the worship of Yahweh, since political alliance in ancient times involved recognition of foreign deities (cf. Jer. 2:33; 3:1 [רעים]; 4:30 [עגבים]; 22:20, 22; 30:14; Lam. 1:2, 19; Ezek. 16:33, 36-37; 23:5, 9, 22; Hos. 2:12—H 2:14; 8:9).

c. Love and ethics. Just as love for man is a touchstone of the OT ethical outlook (cf., e.g., Lev. 19:18), so love for Yahweh provides the most profound impulse to responsible life. It is the חסד of the moral life which Yahweh desires, rather than the multiplication of external rituals (Hos. 6:6; Mic. 6:8). The time has come for Israel to sow the seed of righteousness (צדקה) and reap the fruit of covenant love (Hos. 10:12; read לפרי חסד with the LXX and the RSV for MT לפי חסד). Repentance involves the keeping of steadfast love and justice in human relations (Hos. 12:6—H 12:7). It is perhaps notable that for most of the OT, חסד is the love Yahweh shows for men, and אהבה is that of men for Yahweh. In Hosea, the terms are reversed: the love of Yahweh is אהבה, and man's reciprocal love is חסד. But though the terminology may be different, the fundamental idea is not changed. The ethical life takes place within the covenant. It is a life of love to Yahweh. To love Yahweh is to walk in his ways (Deut. 10:12; 11:22; 19:9; 30:16). Those who love Yahweh are those who keep his commandments (Exod. 20:6; Deut. 5:10; 7:9; 11:1; Neh. 1:5; Dan. 9:4; etc.). There is in the OT, therefore, no antithesis between love and law. The love of God is primary, and man loves both God and man in response to God's love. But the life of love is a life lived out in the relationship of the covenant. The law is the gift of God's love in order that man may have a framework in which he orders his devoted obedience (*see* LAW [IN THE OT]). Hence the psalmist can reiterate untiringly his love of Yahweh's law (Ps. 119:97, 113, 163-64), of his commandments (vss. 47-48, 127), of his testimonies (vss. 119, 167), of his precepts (vs. 159). To love Yahweh is to know his primary love and to live in responsible devotion to man and God. It is to "hear the voice of Yahweh and to cleave to him" (Deut. 30:20).

Bibliography. J. Köberle, *Sünde und Gnade im religiösen Leben des Volkes Israel* (1905); N. Glueck, *Das Wort Häsäd,* BZAW (1927); B. J. Bamberger, "Fear and Love of God in the OT," *HUCA,* VI (1929), 39-53; J. Ziegler, *Die Liebe Gottes bei dem Propheten,* Alttestamentliche Abhandlung, vol. XI, no. 3 (1930); G. Nagel, "Crainte et amour de Dieu dans l'AT," *RTP,* XXXII (1944), 175-86; N. H. Snaith, *The Distinctive Ideas of the OT* (1944), pp. 94-142; H. J. Stoebe, "Die Bedeutung des Wortes ḥäsäd im AT," *Vetus Testamentum,* II (1952), 244-54; A. R. Johnson, "HESEḎ and HĀSÎḎ," *Interpretationes ad VT pertinentes Sigmundo Mowinckel septuagenario missae* (1955), pp. 100-112; C. R. Smith, *The Bible Doctrine of Grace and Related Doctrines* (1956); C. Wiéner, *Recherches sur l'amour pour Dieu dans l'AT: Étude d'une racine* (1957).

E. M. GOOD

*LOVE IN THE NT [ἀγάπη].

1. Terminology
2. The Synoptic teaching of Jesus
3. Paul
   a. Divine love as manifested to man
   b. Man's answering love for God
   c. Man's love for neighbors and brethren
4. Acts; the sub-Paulines; the Catholic letters; Revelation
5. John
   a. The letters
   b. The Fourth Gospel

Bibliography

1. Terminology. Love language is much less common in the NT than one would expect (Acts has one example, Titus none). The verb is more frequent than the noun, of which there are no occurrences at all in Mark, Acts, Titus, James, or I and II Peter. Distribution among the users of the term is approximately as follows: Jesus, ten per cent; Paul, twenty-eight per cent; John (gospel and three letters), thirty-three per cent; sub-Paulines (Ephesians and the Pastorals), thirteen per cent; and the remainder, sixteen per cent. It is thus significant that John, who accounts for one tenth of the NT, provides one third of the references to love.

The great NT word for "love" is ἀγάπη; the adjective is ἀγαπητός (*see* BELOVED). Φιλία occurs once only, in Jas. 4:4 ("friendship with the world"; cf. Rom. 8:7; I John 2:15). The usual verb is ἀγαπάω; less common is φιλέω. It is doubtful if any distinction should be made between these verbs (cf. Matt. 23:6 and Luke 11:43; John 3:35 and 5:20; 11: 3, 5; 19:26 and 20:2; 21:15-17). Originally ἀγάπη seems to have meant "satisfaction," "sympathy," or "a hospitable spirit"; whereas the commoner φιλία denoted the affection of friend or of kinsman; each denotes passionless love. Contrasted with both is ἔρως, which denotes sexual desire, passionate aspiration, sensual longing. Despite the use of ἔρως in philosophical discussion for "upward longing to the eternal and divine," NT writers avoid the word.

'Αγάπη (the noun) is almost never found in pre-Christian Greek (one example in the Berlin Papyrus 9869), but it occurs some twenty times in the LXX for the Hebrew *'ăhăvâh.*

2. The Synoptic teaching of Jesus. In this body of material Jesus never says that God loves, and it may be that John preserves valuable traditions. For the general impression of what Jesus had to teach about God must surely be that of an infinite love, invincible in resources, altogether perfect in its good purposes. The two great commandments ("Love the Lord your God. . . . Love your neighbor as yourself" [Mark 12:30-31; Matt. 19:19]) depend on the prior assumption that God is, in fact, lovable and loving. Here Jesus served himself heir of the OT teaching reviewed *above* (*see* LOVE IN THE OT), and he reminded Jewish religious leaders that God preferred loving kindness (חסד) to a sacrificial cult (Matt. 9: 13; 12:7). But, as the Galileans soon recognized, there was in his message a new note (Mark 1:27; 2:22), which may be summed up as the doctrine of God as Father (Matt. 5:16; 6:9; 11:25-27; 16:17; 23:9; Mark 8:38; 11:25; 13:32; 14:36; Luke 6:36; 12:32; 22:29; 23:46 [and 34?]). The intimate tone of *Abba* ("Father") implies a deep fellowship of understanding and affection as well as obedience. Hence the idea of God's kingdom, imminent in his mission and already effective for the work of salvation, was transformed. For the Jews were summoned, not by the judgment blasts of John the Baptist or the warrior psalms of Qumran, but by the gentle, teasing words of the prophet from Nazareth. He proclaimed their fathers' God (cf. Mark 12:26), the high and holy One, the creator of heaven and earth; and yet the way of life demanded by the Father's incoming reign of righteousness was far different from the holiness of the priests or the Essenes, or the legalism of the Pharisees or the Zadokites of Qumran. God, said Jesus, cares for his creatures and for mankind: he clothes the grass and feeds the ravens (Luke 12:22 ff); he makes his sun rise on the evil and the good, and sends rain on the just and the unjust (Matt. 5:45); the cheapest sparrow does not die without God's remembrance, and the very hairs of our heads are all numbered (Luke 12:6-7). This is not quaint, poetic hyperbole so much as a tender declaration of the universal and intimate character of the divine love as Jesus knew it. Man is dependent; God is independent, the self-existent, without beginning and end, and yet God cares!

Three words may describe briefly what this love is: it is patient, merciful, and generous. The parable of the fig tree teaches the divine goodness that allows another chance, and at the same time the awful judgment if the opportunity is rejected; for God is God, and he is to be scorned and hated at our peril (Luke 13:6-9; cf. Matt. 18:35; Luke 12:5; *see* FEAR). The parables of Luke 15 (lost coin, lost sheep, lost boy) demonstrate the wonder of that gracious mercy from which forgiveness springs (cf. Mark 2:3 ff; Luke 7: 36 ff; 18:13: the penitent publican). Grace elicits love in return; this is the lesson of the incident in Luke 7:36 ff ("for she loved much"). But we must not press Luke 7:42-43 as if Jesus implied that love is in proportion to the sins forgiven! God's generosity is illustrated in the story of the laborers in the vineyard, which is not intended to apply to industrial wage disputes (Matt. 20:1-16; cf. 7:11; Luke 11:13; 12:32).

This divine love is an active benevolence that will go to any length to do good to the beloved object and to secure its well-being. Jesus, however, does not analyze the nature of love; his mind was concrete rather than speculative. Nevertheless, it would be true to his teaching to affirm that the divine love is sovereign, unmotivated save by the necessity to be itself, spontaneous, and redemptive.

Jesus revealed the meaning of love by his life, and the church proclaimed that this was because he is the unique Son of the Father. Not only so, but Jesus himself seems to have claimed this status. Hence in the gospels he is recognized from heaven as the "beloved Son" (Mark 1:11; 9:7), and he invites men to perceive the revelation of God in him and to follow him as Master (Matt. 11:25-30; Luke 10:21-22). Sonship may be implied too in the parables of the wicked husbandmen (Mark 12:1-11) and the marriage feast (Matt. 22:1-14; on this *see* SON OF GOD; CHRIST). But the most significant fact about the role of Jesus is that his mission was thought of in terms derived from the image of the Servant of the Lord; that he had come to seek and to save the lost; to heal the spiritually sick, and to do wonders among men as one in whom and through whom the Spirit of God was at work (Mark 1:10, 23 ff; 2:17; 10:45; Luke 7:22; 19:10).

Jesus therefore speaks the word of forgiveness (Mark 2:5), and demands the utmost in sacrifice for love's sake (Mark 9:34-37; 10:21; Luke 9:57-62). The divine compassion is overheard in his words to sufferers, "child" or "daughter," and seen in the pity he felt for the infirm and troubled (Matt. 9:36; Mark 1:41; 2:5; 5:34; 6:34). Cf. also the anguish of his cry over Jerusalem (Luke 13:34) and the patience of his dealings with the lunatic of Gerasa (Mark 5:1-13). It was offensive to the so-called godly that Jesus ate with tax collectors and public sinners (Mark 2:15-17; Luke 15:2), and that he often preferred to break the sabbath law if he could save or comfort a human life (Matt. 12:12; Luke 14:1-6). For his part, Jesus was justly angered by Pharisaic legalism and hypocrisy (Matt. 15:1 ff; Mark 3:5; 7:9 ff). This stern attitude, no less than his compassion, reflected love which is the holy, righteous love of God. Again, Jesus welcomed mothers with their children, rebuking the surly disciples for their fussy guardianship (Mark 10:13-16). His love understood, even when it could not approve (e.g., Mark 10:21 ff); it exhausted itself in the work of mercy for the sake of the kingdom; and at last his love embraced the Cross with all its agony and dereliction. In that full and perfect life of gracious concern and care for others, men have seen the revelation of God himself, and the name of that God is Love. The Son has given the exposition of the Father (John 1:18).

The consequent duty of man as the child of such a God is to love God with all his heart, soul, mind, and strength (Mark 12:30), and never to let Mammon (money or materialism) or self-interest usurp God's place (cf. Matt. 6:24; Mark 9:43-47; Luke 16:14). As the love of Jesus did not freeze in the crisis, neither should that of his disciples; but it does (Matt. 24:12). Even religion may get in the way of the spirit of genuine love, and this was the worst condemnation of the Pharisees and other opponents of Jesus (Luke 11:42: "You tithe mint and rue and every herb, and neglect justice and the love of God," where the last phrase must mean "love for God"; Matt. 23:23, with an echo there of Mic. 6:8). Nothing but a single-minded devotion to the cause of the kingdom can enable love to flourish in the disciple (Matt. 5:8; Luke 10:42). It is true that love is not mentioned in the Lord's Prayer, but it is surely implied in the opening word: "*Abba,* Father" (Luke 11:2). Secret prayer is a means to real fellowship with God, who is to be loved for himself alone (Matt. 6:1-6, 16-18).

Whatever the reason, these examples comprise all that Jesus, in the Synoptics, had to say about man's love for God. His primary emphasis was that his disciples should live as the "sons of God"; and full treatment of his meaning would demand an adequate discussion of Matt. 5:43-48. Because God is what he is, men are to be sincere, patient, kind, merciful, humble, and generous. Quite clearly, the Father's love is the exemplar, so that Nygren (*see bibliography*) properly asserts that the Christian ethic derives from the relation of fellowship with God: "It is the Christian conception of fellowship with God that gives the idea of Agape its meaning." Hence Jesus said that the second chief commandment was "like the first," for neighborly love is the will of God for his children. All through the NT it will be seen that the love of God may virtually be equated with love for the neighbor (e.g., Heb. 6:10; I Pet. 2:17; I John *passim*). E. Stauffer, however, writes that Jesus, "like a good Jew, . . . takes a sober view of the matter, and simply[!] tells us to love our neighbors as ourselves." In this way Jesus avoided a vague universalism and an impracticable idealism. Did Jesus merely love sinners "as himself"? Is this the meaning of the Cross? Or does this not rule out self-love altogether? Love gives to the uttermost; if it counts the cost (Luke 14:28-33), it is only that, in full self-consistency, it may recklessly "renounce all" to become a follower of the Christ of God.

Jesus never advised that reasonable self-love be the yardstick for a neighborly love that would not shame even the heavenly Father! He did not advocate love as a policy which ultimately promotes only the ends of the self—e.g., to be humble so that exaltation may follow, or to serve others in order to attain greatness (Mark 10:43-44; Luke 14:7 ff). Such motives and conduct would represent a complete misunderstanding of the mind and spirit of Jesus. A man's heart must be made clean (Mark 7:21), so that he may be sincere (Matt. 6:1; 7:3-5; cf. Mark 12:38-40). He must treat others positively as he would like to be treated (Luke 6:31; the negative form of the Golden Rule is found outside Christianity—e.g., Hillel, T.B. Shab. 31*a*). He is to be merciful (Matt. 5:7), forgiving seventy times seven (Matt. 18:21-22; cf. Gen. 4:24 on the vengeance of Lamech). He is to be tolerant of nonconformists (Mark 9:40) and to be generous (Luke 14:13). The whole point is that the disciple acts, not out of prudence, but from obedience to the Father, because his true destiny is to be a son of the Most High. He is committed, therefore, to an uncalculating loving kindness, for even the blow of insult is to be tolerated without reprisal. "Love your enemies," said Jesus (Matt. 5:44). James Moffatt (*see bibliography*) asserts: "To 'love' them does not mean that we are pleased with them in their present position, or that we are to be amiable to them; it means a new moral relationship, for which 'love' was a new term."

Thus there was always an ethical "plus" in the teaching of Jesus, corresponding to the gracious dealings of God the heavenly Father with men and women. Jesus demanded a righteousness that exceeded that of the scribes and Pharisees. Accordingly, disciples were not to pass by when they encountered the "outsider" in trouble, for any "outsider" is the neighbor to be loved (Luke 10:30-37; the choice of a Samaritan for this story was deliberate, since Jews hated Samaritans [John 4:9]). Love was not merely a matter of the emotions; on the contrary, it was much more of the mind and the will. Disciples must be obedient, and deeds count, as well as words (Matt. 7:21 ff; 10:42; 12:36-37). Love gives, expecting no return (Luke 6:35); love stoops to serve, like the master who waited on his laborers (Luke 12:37; cf. 17:7-8).

Love is rewarded. This does not involve any diminution of the quality of love, for the supreme compensation is membership in the new family of the kingdom (Matt. 23:8-9; Mark 3:34-35; 10:30). The self may be "lost," yet paradoxically it is "found" (Matt. 10:39 ff). Disciples enjoy the vision of God and life eternal (Matt. 5:8; 19:16, 29; 25:34-36). These are personal gifts, and "love" is the only word that does justice to the meaning of life as a system of personal relationships, created by God for his children.

Jesus stands alone in his proclamation that Love made the universe and watches over the creation; that sacrificial love is the pattern of the good life here for those who would serve God, so long as any evil and sin remain, and that mutual love is the eternal mark of life in God's kingdom; that ritual observance is therefore less important than active benevolence, and so men and women are called to display the neighborliness of a meek and loving heart that ignores the conventions of race and sex and culture. The good of the other must be a man's care. The favor of the heavenly Father, said Jesus—that shall be his reward.

3. Paul. The first considerable use of the noun ἀγάπη occurs in the letters of Paul, who so fills it with content and makes it so central that it virtually becomes a technical term.

Contrary to expectation, there is very little dependence on OT teaching. Hos. 2:23 (the beloved people) is cited in Rom. 9:25-26; Mal. 1:2-3 ("I have loved [i.e., preferred] Jacob") in Rom. 9:13; and there may be a reminiscence of Deut. 33:12 ("beloved of the LORD") in II Thess. 2:13. Paul's primary source was history rather than scripture. There was the private history of his own experience, though he hesitated to make much use of it in his correspondence (II Cor. 11:16 ff). It was the traditional kerygma of what God had done in Jesus Christ that formed the articles of first importance (I Cor. 15:3). In the fulness of time God had sent the Christ, his own Son and Image, to be the Redeemer. God reconciled sinners to himself graciously through the death of this same Christ; for it was God who had set him forth in his death as the personal means of propitiation (or expiation). All is of God, cried the astonished apostle (Rom. 3:21 ff; II Cor. 4:4-6; 5:14, 18 ff; Gal. 4:4-5). This divine act had brought to an end the religion based on law, replacing it with the religion of grace and faith. And the restoration of personal relations between God and man produced also a new society, a people consecrated in Christ Jesus, the church of God (*see* CHURCH, IDEA OF). Like any Magdalene or Zacchaeus, Paul the Pharisee had found in the brotherhood of the church "his place and his peace" (a phrase of Mrs. Elton Trueblood's). It was out of his life and service in the Christian fellowship, with all its joys and tribulations, that Paul's teaching on love emerged.

It is customary and, indeed, essential to discuss this teaching in terms of (*a*) the divine love as manifested to man; (*b*) man's answering love for God; (*c*) man's love for his neighbors and his brethren.

a. Divine love as manifested to man. Love is revealed at the Cross, and in the character of Jesus Christ. "God shows his love for us in that while we were yet sinners Christ died for us" (Rom. 5:8). This declaration is set in the context of the divine wrath against sin and sinners (Rom. 1:18; 2:5; cf. 9:22; 12:19; Col. 3:6; I Thess. 1:10; in I Thess. 2:16 Paul says that the divine wrath has already overtaken the Jews, who crucified Jesus and now hinder the preaching of the gospel). God, who is holy, requires moral integrity and obedience from men, both Jew and Gentile, and he rewards them according to their deeds (Rom. 2:6-11). Yet the Christ had been made a sin offering (II Cor. 5:21), and through the crucified Lord, God himself had provided a way of escape from the ultimate consequences of the wrath. "Christ died for us" means that Jesus chose to die and did this to redeem us; that somehow in him were concentrated the horror, the anguish and pain, of human guilt. Paul does not quite say that Christ bore our guilt; the atonement springs from the love of God and Christ's own love, so that there is an unfathomable mystery in the sin-bearing. The other side of this doctrine is that of baptism, for in its sacramental waters the man who believes in Jesus as the risen Christ and trusts in him is united with the Lord who died. The confession of guilt and the renunciation of sin, which one assumes as antecedents to the sacrament, involve a kind of spiritual death, a con-crucifixion (Gal. 2:20); and on rising out of these waters of death the believer is renewed in spirit by the divine Spirit; he is clothed upon with Christ and becomes a man in Christ, a new creation, a limb of his spiritual body, the church. Now he is a son of God, who should be led by the Spirit and live in the same love that Christ exhibits (Rom. 6:3 ff; 8:2-16; 13:14; I Cor. 12:12 ff; II Cor. 5:17; Gal. 5:16 ff; Col. 1:18, 22; 2:11 ff; I Thess. 3:12).

The wonder of the Cross, then, was the great new word it announced concerning the holy God whose wrath men feared. God was responsible for it in the last analysis, and he had made the enmity of men his tool. He had done what the law could not do in Judaism, nor any system of Gentile men outside the law. He had renewed Adam.

Paul's view rests on the Semitic notion of solidarity by which Adam is humanity and the king incorporates the nation, and on the actual moral transformations seen within the Christian community. He did not intend to evict moral responsibility from the redeemed life (e.g., "continue in sin that grace may abound" [Rom. 6:1]), nor did he conceive of Jesus Christ as a mere scapegoat. Rather, he had discovered that sin is primarily a rebellion against divine love and that atonement results from the sacrificial ministry of this love personally present in the human life of God's Son, and evoking in return the gratitude and loyalty of those who perceive the glory of God in the face of Jesus Christ. It is not surprising that, with such a grasp of what Christ is as love incarnate, Paul spoke seldom about repentance and never of penance; and that he called men and women to have "faith"—a loving, trustful attitude that involves the total personality in the acceptance of a free gift of grace (Rom. 4:16-25; 5:6-21).

Because the Cross stands for victory over sin and evil (princes and powers of evil, the apostle would have said), love is almighty. Divine providence means that God's care is constantly exercised for the good of mankind. This was a truth that Christians needed over and over again, because love also involved them in suffering. By tribulations are the sons of God to enter the kingdom (II Cor. 11:23–12:10; I Thess. 2:14; 3:3-4; II Thess. 1:5). Whatever threats there might be from the cosmic powers in the stars, from natural disaster, from the onset of the devil, or from any other source, believers could take courage from the assurance that love reigns and that God will never desert them; for God's love is precisely the same as Christ's love (Rom. 8:28-39).

Within the church also, God is immanent as a loving Power in the Holy Spirit, who knits the faithful into a communion (koinonia, partnership [II Cor. 13:14]; perhaps corresponding to יחד, the technical term for the Qumran brotherhood [1QS 1.12, 24; 9.2]). "We rejoice in our sufferings, . . . and hope does not disappoint us, because God's love has been poured into our hearts through the Holy Spirit which has been given to us" (Rom. 5:3, 5). Love is inspired in disciples by the Spirit (Gal. 5:22; Rom. 15:30: "by the love of the Spirit"), so that they should pray for one another. Paul can assume that such love emerges within a newly founded congregation, whoever the evangelist (cf. Col. 1:3-8; Epaphras was the missionary to Colossae). The reason for this is that, just as God is the Father of the Lord Jesus Christ, so the Holy Spirit must now be identified as the "Spirit of Jesus Christ" (Phil. 1:19; cf. Rom. 8:2, 9 ff; *see* SPIRIT; HOLY SPIRIT). The church is the family of God, through faith in his Son and the presence of his Son's Spirit (Rom. 8:14 ff, 29; Gal. 3:26, 29; 4:5-7).

Its members are "beloved by the Lord," elect, "holy and beloved" (Rom. 1:7; Col. 3:12; II Thess. 2:13). One is not surprised, therefore, to find grace, love, and fellowship combined in a Pauline benediction (II Cor. 13:14). Each word denotes what is virtually the identical spiritual reality; for grace is loving, and only love can effect a genuine communion among men and women of diverse race, color, culture, and wisdom. God is the "God of love and peace" (II Cor. 13:11), whose benefits are enjoyed by those who are obedient to Paul's teaching; and Paul claimed to have the "mind of Christ" (I Cor. 2:16; 7:40, in some readings).

This note of love is remarkable in one who had been a Pharisee. It was held together in his thought with others—e.g., judgment, righteousness, forgiveness, ministry—and was never alone. In this, of course, Paul stands in the central NT tradition (cf. Matt. 25:31 ff; Luke 12:4-12; John 3:16-21; 16:7-11; Heb. 2:14-18; 9:27-28; Jas. 4:12; I Pet. 1:13; 3:12; 5:10; II Pet. 2:4-10; I John 4:10, 17-18; Rev. 2–3). Like these other writers, Paul believed in God as the chief fact of his life, and had a prophetic conception of the divine work in history, electing and rejecting. The Eternal had to be thought of as personal will, so that Paul uses the terms "foreknowing," "predestining," "calling," and "justifying." The Ephesian continuator (*see* EPHESIANS, LETTER TO THE) rightly set all this in the context of a love that was active before the foundation of the world (Eph. 1:4-5). Love created, love saved, love sanctifies; and love will crown its work for the faithful when they are "with Christ" and have attained the "prize of the upward call of God in Christ Jesus" (Phil. 1:23; 3: 14). Paul is not far from that saying of I John which sums up the Christian revelation in three words: "God is love" (4:8).

In spite of the prominence given to our theme, the expression "God's love" does not occur in I Thessalonians, I Corinthians, Philippians, and Philemon. Its place is taken by such words as "grace" and "peace." In Philem. 9 "for love's sake" means: for the sake of that love of God which we have both known in Jesus Christ the Lord.

b. Man's answering love for God. If the references to the divine love for men are comparatively few, what is one to say of those to man's answering love for God? Excluding absolute uses and Eph. 6:24, there are at most five places where love toward God or Christ is mentioned:

a) II Thess. 3:5: "May the Lord direct your hearts to the love of God and to the steadfastness of Christ." Moffatt understands love here as God's "loyal care for the interests of His people in a time of strain," and the steadfastness is what God inspires and requires. The genitives are ambiguous, and the second phrase might mean "a steadfastness like that shown by Christ" or, more simply, "Christian endurance." As to the first, why should the Lord guide the Thessalonians toward God's care for them, when they have just been assured that God chose them, called them, and loves them (2:13 ff)? Paul wants them to prove their obedience to his instructions by deeds ("every good work and word" [vs. 17; 3:4]). Presumably he had taught them the first commandment of the Mosaic ten and the first of the two "great commandments"—to love God with everything one has—for those who had but lately abandoned the Greek pantheon for the God of Abraham, Moses, and Jesus needed this kind of teaching (cf. I Thess. 3:6: "the good news of your faith and love"; God is the natural object of both faith and love). It is interesting to note that Irenaeus read "the love of God" instead of "the love of the truth" in II Thess. 2:10, for the apostle had to warn the young church against the wiles of the devil (vs. 9; 3:3). Stand fast, he tells them; follow the example of Christ. At I Thess. 5:8 "faith and love" are substituted for "righteousness" (Isa. 59:17; cf. Eph. 6:14), probably under the influence of a favorite triad (I Cor. 13:13; Col. 1:4-5; I Thess. 1:3).

b) I Cor. 2:9: "What God has prepared for those who love him." If Paul is using Isa. 64:4, he has altered "those who wait for him" into "those who love him." There are exact parallels at Jas. 1:12; 2:5 (cf. *Epistle to Diognetus* 10.2; Luke 11:42). Paul is reminding the quarrelsome, conceited gnostics of Corinth that, in the eschatological crisis of that time (I Cor. 7:29-31), their duty is to learn "love's sweet lesson to obey," instead of preening themselves on the more glamorous gifts of spiritual ecstasy.

c) I Cor. 16:22: "If any one has no love for the Lord [the verb is φιλεῖ], let him be accursed." Paul's Christ was lovable. Had he not, though he was rich, yet become poor? (II Cor. 8:9; cf. Phil. 2:7-8.) Who but the Lord Jesus sat for the portrait of I Cor. 13:4-7? "Love is patient and kind." The apostle, therefore, set Christ before himself and his converts as an example (I Cor. 11:1; cf. Eph. 5:1). The force of this example is much heightened by the bridal theme to which Paul alludes at several places. A believer becomes "one spirit" with the Lord, as in a marriage (I Cor. 6:17). A church is betrothed to Christ so that its apostle may present it as a pure bride to its one husband (II Cor. 11:2, the source of Eph. 5:25 ff).

Such a unity is at once covenantal and contractual, and Paul thinks of himself as bound by the law of Christ, a law how different from the Mosaic! (I Cor. 9:21; cf. Rom. 6:16, where "obedience" is substituted for Christ; 7:6; 8:2.) Love too imposes a service; love is not antinomian or licentious. The proper way to progress in the knowledge of God's truth is to obey his will; and growth is to be desired (Phil. 1:9: "that your love may abound more and more, with knowledge and all discernment, so that you may distinguish [RSV 'approve'] what is excellent"; cf. John 7:17; 8:32, 42 ff).

d) I Cor. 8:3: "If one loves God, one is known by him" (the correct reading in spite of the omission of "God" by the important Papyrus 46). In this chapter, as in ch. 13, love is contrasted with knowledge (gnosis): love builds up; knowledge is arrogant. The issue for Paul was not so much whether the heathen gods exist, as that some of his converts were lamentably ignorant of the right relations which should obtain in the church as the body of Christ (8:10-13). The "know-alls" at Corinth did not understand the profound spiritual reality of the body, with its consequent sense of mutual involvement in joy and sorrow (Rom. 12:10-15; 14:7, 10; I Cor. 12:25-26). Only through love does one enter into the relation that might be expressed as the knowledge of God. Paul, however, inverts the phrase: "One is known by him," as in Gal. 4:9. Partly from reverence, partly perhaps because of the arrogant claims of Greek mystery cults, Paul avoids the direct statement, "One knows God" (but see Rom. 1:21). He was, in any case, inclined to emphasize the divine initiative both in revelation and in salvation (cf. I Cor. 12:3). It may be that with respect to I Cor. 8:3 the Hebrew sense of knowledge of persons as a love relationship would clarify the meaning. To "know" a woman is to love her sexually; and so to know anyone, including God, is to be bound up in the fellowship of love. If, then, we love God, it is only because God has loved us in Christ; how dare we take pride in our knowledge? Love is expressed by wonder, praise, adoration, and brotherly affection to others for whom the Son of God died.

e) Rom. 8:28: "We know that in everything God works for good with those who love him, who are called according to his purpose." This is part of Paul's exposition of the providential care of God. Christians, as the sons of God who hope for inheritance in his kingdom, are expected to love God. This is in direct continuity with the teaching of Jesus (cf. also I Cor. 14:1: "Make love your aim," where love to God and man is in view; Eph. 6:24: "Grace be with all who love our Lord Jesus Christ with love undying").

Why did Paul speak so rarely about love to God or Christ? From some sense of his own unfitness as a former persecutor? "Beloved," so common on his lips with reference to brother Christians, is never used of the Christ (Col. 1:13 is not an exception; but cf. Eph. 1:6). Paul is his Master's slave rather than his lover. Did he then abhor false emotionalism, or any love concepts, because of his environment? Hardly, in the light of the marriage imagery he employs. Perhaps he was influenced by local conditions in Corinth, for most of the passages that speak about loving God are associated with that city of Aphrodite Pandemos, goddess of love (*eros*). Paul the Jew, like Jesus himself, preferred the language of reverence and service (Rom. 11:20; II Cor. 5:11; 7:1; Col. 3:22; cf. Phil. 2:12).

Nygren's explanation is that "love," *agape,* is not proper to man's response to God, because *agape* is unmotivated. Man's devotion must therefore be called "faith." If we ask why Paul can use *agape* for brotherly or neighborly affection, the reply is that through the invasion of the Holy Spirit, God's free, dynamic love flows from the believer toward the neighbor. It is not really the believer's at all! This is to evacuate Christian love of any value, and it is to be rejected for the same reasons that one must reject the notion that faith is a moment of passivity. Nygren insists that Christians are to love the neighbor, not "God in the neighbor." Surely then it is the Christian who is to love, not simply "God in the believer." True, Paul stresses the predestining power of God, both in electing and in "hardening" (Rom. 9:16, 18; 11:7, 25; cf. 1QS 3.17-4.1, 15-26). He would therefore agree that it is God who "enables" the Christian to love. Yet the method of the Cross, the long-suffering goodness of God, ceases to impress us if it is in fact a form of irresistible grace. Paul safeguards himself to some extent by his use of love for man's attitude toward God. When he has occasion, he takes it.

c. Man's love for neighbors and brethren. Because it is grounded in a binding obligation to God in Christ, the new life could not be left at the whim of fluctuating emotion. God remained the holy One, and men were set free to be his servants (Rom. 6:22; I Cor. 6:20; cf. I Cor. 7:22; Gal. 6:17; Phil. 3:12; Col. 4:1). A God who is holy expects his people to be holy, as those dedicated to him, "saints" (II Cor. 6:14–7:1; I Thess. 4:3). This holiness must be defined in terms of the divine graces of love: patience, tenderness, fatherly affection, loyalty to promises, and humility (Rom. 2:4; II Cor. 1:18 ff; Phil. 1:8; 2:5 ff; Col. 1:12-13; I Thess. 3:11-13; II Thess. 2:16). Or the new life might be described as growth into the likeness of Jesus Christ the Lord, the head of the body (Rom. 14:7-9; Col. 2:6-7). Such a life, no longer "according to the flesh"—man's weak, creaturely, and sinful nature (the "old Adam")—was to be lived "according to the Spirit"—i.e., in the church of the "last Adam, the life-giver" (Rom. 8:5; I Cor. 15:45; cf. II Cor. 3:3; I Thess. 4:8). For only so could one become worthy of the inheritance that awaited at the end of the age (eschatological hope spans the entire range of Paul's ministry: Phil. 1:10; II Thess. 1:5). The motive to love one another did not, however, arise from thoughts of the Judgment so much as from gratitude for divine grace.

The sum of duty is given in Rom. 13:8: "Owe no one anything, except to love one another." A similar care for members of their community is found among the Zadokites of Qumran (1QS 1.8-10; 8.12-16; 1QM 10.9; 1QH 6.9-11; 11.11; CD 6.20, quoting Lev. 19:18; *see* DEAD SEA SCROLLS).

In the first instance such love was applied by Paul to fellow members of the church, the beloved brethren; but he went far beyond this, following the spirit of Jesus, and insisted that love should determine one's attitude toward outsiders and enemies: "Bless those who persecute you; bless and do not curse" (Rom. 12:14-21). At Qumran, on the other hand, the brotherhood were trained for a holy war and were commanded to hate (1QS 2.25; 3.1-5; 1QH 2.30-31; 4.6 ff). Of course, even Paul fell below the standard of love in his relationships with the churches, and his apostolic authority could appear overbearing; but he was conscious of his faults and emerges from controversy with the highest reputation (see I–II Corinthians *passim*). The most bracing challenge to love came from the sense that one must be worthy of the Lord or of God or of the gospel (Phil. 1:27; Col. 1:10; I Thess. 2:12).

For those who entered the church, ancient barriers of nationality, culture, and sex were broken down (Gal. 3:28). Master and slave became brothers beloved (Philemon); parents learned that children are to be loved, and this was sometimes a quite new thought in that age (Col. 3:21; cf. I Cor. 7:14); marriage too is consecrated, and divorce is forbidden (but the Christian spouse may separate from a pagan partner under definite circumstances: I Cor. 7; Col. 3:18-19). It followed that every form of sexual perversion must be abhorred (Rom. 1:24 ff; I Cor. 5; 6:15 ff; Gal. 5:19 ff; Col. 3:5 ff). Paul's principle in guiding his converts was that love sets bounds to individual liberty without destroying individual responsibility (Rom. 14:1–15:6; I Cor. 10:23-30; Gal. 6:1 ff). He makes no attempt to erect a Christian casuistry or to make brotherly love a legal enactment. Love, because it answers to the very nature of God in redemptive action, is the crown of every virtue: patience, gentleness, self-control, fidelity, kindness, are all so many expressions of love itself; and this love is the first fruit of the Holy Spirit (Gal. 5:22). Here is the source of the later doctrine that the Spirit is, in fact, Love. "Above all these put on love, which binds everything together in perfect harmony" (Col. 3:14). The Pythagoreans are said to have called *philia* the bond of all virtues. Moule suggests that Paul's meaning may be that *agape* gives coherence to conduct, in much the same way as Christ gives coherence to the universe; and Christ is the embodiment of *agape*.

It should be observed that Paul refused to translate the duty of neighborly love into a policy of revolution, not only because of the adventist hope (I Cor. 7:17 ff), but perhaps because he did not see to what lengths this new ethic must lead in the end. Wives, e.g., were not told to love their husbands, nor were children enjoined to love their parents. Yet the commandment: "Love your neighbor as yourself," must be relevant to family life. Paul seems to have been held by the Jewish idea that slaves, children, and wives belonged to the inferior classes, so that "submission," "obedience," and "reverence" were the appropriate words to be addressed to them about their duty. It was, nonetheless, a tremendous gain that the superiors were encouraged to love their inferiors, to treat them justly, to show kindness and long-suffering (*see* COLOSSIANS; PHILEMON; SLAVERY; MARRIAGE; FAMILY). At this point the NT ethic should be critically appreciated, especially in its bearing on modern social issues like the status and service of women in church and society.

Paul's sensitive awareness of the dignity and glory of genuine love came to its magnificent climax in the hymn of I Cor. 13. Despite the doubts of a few critics, who think the poem has been inserted between 12:31 and 14:1, its authenticity is beyond question. For Paul's rhetorical and poetic gifts were considerable, as we see from Phil. 2:5-11; Col. 1:15-20. "Love" is used absolutely in the poem, and this has led to divergent definitions of what is strictly in mind. Is it love to God (the Latin Fathers; Lütgert; Allo; Reitzenstein)? Is it love for the neighbor (the Greek Fathers; Harnack; recently C. Spicq most emphatically)? Are God and man both its objects (Cornely; Corssen; Huby; Schlier)? Nygren declares that it is just simply *agape,* God's free love that shines in its own light "regardless of any significance it might acquire from its object."

The context (I Cor. 12:27 ff) would suggest that Paul is concerned with human relationships, primarily behavior within the church. "This is the way in which love acts when it is genuine *agape,*" is the apostle's meaning (cf. 12:31, but "way" and "love" are not simply to be equated).

The first strophe (vss. 1-3) indicates what is false in the Christian life: *glossolalia* (speaking with tongues) without love; wisdom and faith without love; self-sacrifice without love. All these SPIRITUAL GIFTS (for they are gifts of the Spirit) are unprofitable and good for nothing if love is missing; for love alone edifies, and the Spirit distributes his gifts "for the common good" (I Cor. 8:1; 12:7).

The second strophe, noted already, delineates the positive character of love (vss. 4-7). "Love is patient and generous; love is not jealous or pretentious; love is not arrogant or dishonorable; love does not insist on its own advantage, is not irritable, does not reckon up a wrong. Love does not rejoice at injustice, but applauds the truth. Love bears all things, believes with unquenchable faith, ever hopes, endures to the uttermost. Love is for always." (This translation is partly indebted to Father Spicq.) "Love is not love which alters when it alteration finds."

The third strophe (vss. 8-13) contrasts love with prophecy and gnosis, then with faith and hope. All these belong to the imperfect, to life here and now, the life of struggle, defeat, and growth; and their time will run out. Love too is for now, but love is for the beatitude of heaven, where God is who loves us with an everlasting love. That is why love is the greatest thing in the world.

What is this love? Of course, it is love for God the Father, the Father of the Lord Jesus Christ! Of course, it is also love for friend and love for foe (so long as there are opponents and enemies). It is love, absolutely. It is genuine good will that puts first the needs and interests of the other; it is the secret of personal unity, and as such is forever relevant. Paul would gladly have signed the great sentence of Baron von Hügel: "Christianity taught us to care. Caring is the greatest thing, caring matters most."

4. Acts; the sub-Paulines; the Catholic letters; Revelation. The only example in Acts of a derivative from "love" is in 15:25, where Barnabas and Paul are described as "our beloved" in the letter from Jerusalem to the Gentile Christians of Syria and Cilicia. This agrees with Lukan usage, for, outside the teaching of Jesus and the heavenly voice at the Baptism and the Transfiguration, only the verb ἀγαπάω occurs (Luke 7:5; cf. Mark 10:21 for Mark). As distinct from the words, one finds the substance of Christian love in the early community of goods (2:44-47); Stephen's final cry (7:60), and the prayer meeting for Peter (12:5); the constant use of "brethren" (e.g., 1:16; 6:3; 9:17; *see* BROTHERHOOD); the affectionate embraces of Paul and the Ephesians at Miletus (20:36-38); and the protesting question of the apostle at Caesarea: "What are you doing, weeping and breaking my heart?" (21:13). Kindness is not confined to Christians, however (27:3; 28:2), and there is plenty to mar the idyllic unity of the first years (5:1 ff; 6:1; 11:2; 15:36-39; 20:29-30). The Golden Rule in its negative form is quoted in 15:29 in the Western text; and a lovely word of Jesus occurs in Paul's speech to the Ephesians (20:35): "It is more blessed to give than to receive."

EPHESIANS, thoroughly Pauline in tone and theology, emphasizes the love of God in predestination (1:5; but perhaps "in love" belongs with the preceding phrase). This is of special interest, because it rightly links the doctrines of creation and salvation (2:4-7; for Christ's love cf. 3:19; 5:2, adapted from Gal. 2:20; and 5:25). "The Beloved" (1:6) may be a messianic title. Love is associated with peace in the Pauline manner, in the closing prayer for divine blessing (6:23).

The love of Christians for one another is stressed in 4:2; 5:2, 25, 28, 33 (cf. 1:15, in spite of Codex Vaticanus and Papyrus 46). The absolute uses at 3:17; 4:15-16 look to brotherly love, probably, rather than love for God or Christ. Eph. 4:1-16 is important for the themes of church unity and growth, and it seems to envisage the development of a redeemed humanity in which Jesus Christ will find his completion. 4:15 should perhaps be translated: "Rather, practicing the truth, we are to grow up in love."

In ch. 5 the expansion of the section on husbands and wives is notable (cf. Col. 3:18-19). Christ's union with his church is put in terms of the marriage relationship in true OT and Pauline style; they constitute "one flesh" (5:29). Paul would have said "one Spirit." Christ is the Head, with full authority, and in consequence the advice to wives remains as in I Corinthians and Colossians. Husbands should love and cherish their wives; and wives should revere (or fear) their husbands, being duly subject as to the Lord (5:22, 33). The mutual submission of 5:21 does not imply that husbands are to be subject to their wives, for we still have to do with a hierarchy (cf. I Cor. 11:3). Tit. 2:4 remains the one place in the NT where wives are exhorted to love their husbands!

The inclusion of love in the lists of virtues in the Pastorals seems somewhat formal (I Tim. 1:5; 4:12; II Tim. 2:22; Tit. 2:2). The example of Paul, the great martyr-apostle, includes his love (II Tim. 3:10; cf. I Tim. 6:11). Women must pay the price of Eve's sin, and may win salvation by childbearing and perseverance in "faith and love and holiness" (I Tim. 2:14-15). A large number of nouns and adjectives compounded with *phil-*, "lover of," suggests the development of a new Christian vocabulary, but too much should not be made of this. They are: lover of children, of husbands, of strangers, of God, of the good; and, by contrast, lover of money, of pleasure, and of oneself (I Tim. 3:2; 6:10; II Tim. 3:2, 4; Tit. 1:8; 2:4; 3:4). Demas, "in love with this present world," is a deserter (II Tim. 4:10; cf. I John 2:15; note the object of the verb ἀγαπάω, and *see* § 5*a below* on I John). The genuine believers await the epiphany of Christ at the Day of Judgment (II Tim. 4:8): they "have loved his appearing." "Beloved" is still the appropriate adjective for fellow Christians—e.g., masters are beloved brethren of their slaves (I Tim. 6:2).

On the whole, the tone is colder than in Paul, yet grace and love belong together (I Tim. 1:14; cf. the "philanthropy" of God in Tit. 3:4; and the "God-lover" of II Tim. 3:4). God grants a "spirit of power and love and self-control" rather than timidity or fear (II Tim. 1:7; *see* FEAR), but this is not adequately related to the work of the Holy Spirit (in spite of II Tim. 1:14). It is difficult to evaluate the evidence of the Pastoral letters, and the tendency to underrate them must be resisted. Nevertheless, the final impression is that the author does not fully understand the meaning of love as a dynamic power, the effect of God's Spirit.

The Catholic letters and Revelation come from dark days of persecution and long days of disappointed hope, because Christ had not returned. Hence their God, though merciful and kind, is the God of discipline and judgment (Heb. 12:6-7; Jas. 5:9; I Pet. 4:17; Rev. 14:6–17:6). One may venture to respect him with awful reverence (Heb. 10:31; 12:9; Rev. 11:17-18); but also to love him (Jas. 1:12; 2:5; Jude 21; cf. I Pet. 1:8, of Christ: "Without having seen him you love him"). God's love is mentioned in Jude (1-2), and one doxology (Rev. 1:5-6) makes much of it: "To him who loves us and has freed us . . . and made us a kingdom, . . . to him be glory and dominion for ever and ever. Amen." Nothing else is said about the divine love explicitly, yet there is real nobility in I Peter, which is full of tender touches (e.g., 2:3, 25; 3:8, 15; 4:10-11). Hebrews too, with its concept of the high priest who understands us men from within, has a profound sense of what God has done for sinners in the work of salvation. We must not judge the writers merely by statistics.

Christians, as always, are beloved brethren in all these documents. Jas. 2:8 repeats the second great commandment (the royal law) to love one's neighbor, although the emphasis is on justification by works (vss. 14 ff). The profession of love without doing works of love is fatally easy for Christians, so that James must have rendered valuable service. His panegyric on wisdom (3:17) is somewhat reminiscent of the praises of love in I Cor. 13. Stress on the good works of love appears also at Heb. 6:10; 10:24, 34; 13:1-2; I Pet. 2:12 ff; Rev. 2:4-5, 19. It is indeed odd that II Pet. 1:7 requires the addition of love to brotherliness, though a pastor knows how formal piety may pay lip service to brotherly status, and even the word "brother," used of fellows in the same order or society, may be uttered in the oily tones of sheer hypocrisy. Christians who lived in the middle of the second century had to learn such lessons, and needed to be told their duty to "grow in the grace and knowledge of our Lord and Savior Jesus Christ" (II Pet. 3:18), since enemies and heretics would readily seduce them to another "knowledge" (cf. I Tim. 6: 20-21). In the sub-apostolic age apostasy was not unknown, rich members despised the poor, and even the presbyters had to be warned not to domineer or serve for petty gain (Heb. 10:29; Jas. 2:1-7; I Pet. 5:2; Rev. 2–3). So the line between church and world had to be clearly drawn (Revelation does this and inspires martyrs; I Peter is more cautious, but inspires equal loyalty).

The use of Prov. 10:12 ("Love covers all offenses") is found in Jas. 5:20; I Pet. 4:8; and also I Clem. 49. Apparently it was thought that love shown to the erring (James) or to the church (Peter) qualified one for the pardon of one's own sins; and if so, love has become a work of merit rather than the fruit of the Holy Spirit in the life of the redeemed (*see bibliography*). This would mark a very serious declension from the highest NT teaching on the divine love as grace, and the resulting birth of true love in those whom Christ has restored to the Father.

5. John. ***a. The letters.*** These documents, which are to be dated close to A.D. 100, reflect a situation when the church was gravely threatened by forms of Docetic and Gnostic heresy. John's opponents seem to have claimed that they had no need for redemption from sin (I John 1:8, 10; cf. 3:6). They could go beyond mere faith to actual vision of God (I John 2:4; 4:12), for they were the enlightened (I John 2:9; perhaps a reference to mystic initiation). In spite of their unlovely temper, and possibly immoral conduct, they said that they loved God (I John 4:20) and perhaps too that they had "passed from death into the life eternal" (I John 3:14; initiates into certain of the mystery cults claimed to have been "reborn into eternity"). And the sum of it all was their assertion that they enjoyed "communion with God" (I John 1:6; 2:6). Reading between the lines, one can see that John was distressed by the dreadful gap between the profession and the practice of those teachers who were seeking to corrupt the faithful Christians. Over and over again, therefore, he states the elementary truth that he who is "of God," who has been born anew, is one who acts righteously, and especially that he loves his brethren (e.g., I John 3:10). To live is to love, because it means "having the Son of the Father" and "having the Father" (I John 2:23; 5:11-12, 20; to have is to enjoy personal fellowship with). Hence John can speak about loving God (I John 2:5, 15; 3:17). This is not simply a counterassertion to heretical claims; John makes love a primary term in everything he has to say of religion and duty. For this reason many commentators have been impressed with the warmth of the letters.

John's "outstanding contribution to Christian theology" (Dodd) is the sublime sentence in the First Letter, "God is love" (4:8). It is assumed that God is, and that he is holy, faithful, and righteous, as the whole Judeo-Christian tradition taught (cf. I John 1:9). Again, God is invisible (I John 4:12, 20; but cf. III John 11; in the OT cf. Exod. 33:20). Nevertheless, the Christian knows that God is "light"—i.e., he reveals himself and is knowable. The proof is found, not so much in the history of Israel as in the historic life of Jesus, the Christ, the Son of the Father: in that incarnation denied or obscured by the heretics (I John 1:2-3; 4:2; 5:6; II John 7), and in the atoning death of the Son, who came to defeat the devil and be the Savior of the world (I John 1:7; 2:2; 3:5, 8, 16; 4:10, 14). The faithful, who may commit acts of sin in spite of the fact that God's children properly ought to be incapable of sinning, can rely on the exalted Son to be their Advocate (Paraclete; I John 2:2) and are blessed with the gift of the Spirit (I John 3:24; 4:13). But the Spirit is not so definitely linked to the moral life as one would expect; it stands here for the theological confession of the Incarnation, and for the witness to Jesus Christ as the Son in certain events of his life and in the sacraments (I John 4:2; 5:6-8). On the other hand, belief and love go together, as in Paul (I John 3:23; 5:1; II John 1: "whom I love in the truth"; III John 1). The truth is the final reality of God, disclosed in a human life and expressed in the doctrine of God's Son; hence to believe the truth is, in fact, to love the Son of God, Jesus Christ. For believers, Christ is always the norm; and as he defines the Godhead, so he defines the nature of the true life: the faithful are therefore the "children of God," and at the end they will be like Christ, for they shall see him as he is (I John 3:1-2). Love must issue in vision. At the same time love provides assurance and hope. Those who know that the Day of Judgment is still to come can await it without terror, if they love God and are in communion with the Father and the Son through the Spirit (I John 1:3-4; 4:17-18). Love brings the joy of fellowship (I John 1:4; II John 4, 12; III John 3-4).

"God is love" is no palindrome like "sin is lawlessness" (I John 3:4). John offered no Aphrodite substitute, "Love is God," for he meant that God is so perfectly loving that one can understand what love is only by knowing who God is and what he has done for men. John can say, however, that "love is of God," who is its fountainhead, who enables his children to be loving. "We love, because he first loved us" (I John 4:19). Or again: "If God so loved us, we also ought to love one another" (I John 4:11); and: "By this we know love, that he [here it is Christ] laid down his life for us; and we ought to lay down our lives for the brethren" (I John 3:16). Divine love elicits love from the redeemed, but this involves obedience to the divine will; and God's will is "that you follow love," the new commandment "that we love one another" (I John 2:3-5, 7 ff; 3:11, 18, 22-24; 4:21; 5:1-2; II John 5-6; cf. John 13:34-35). Hate, disobedience, mere profession in words without deeds, pride in one's "experience," all point to a fundamental hypocrisy. Notice that John's call for readiness to be a martyr states the royal law of neighborly love so effectively as to exclude any casuistic idea of loving the other only after we have taken care of loving ourselves. The test of sincerity is to walk in the steps of Christ, who gave up his life (I John 2:6). To live otherwise is to dwell in darkness (I John 1:6-7).

It may be thought that the "we love" of I John 4:19 is absolute and includes all possible objects (cf. vs. 14: Savior of the "world"). But, in fact, John seems to limit love to brotherly love (cf. 1QS 1.10; 5.4; 8.2; 10.26). He does not advise love for heretics (see II John 10-11), and denies that it is any use praying for one who has committed mortal sin, probably apostasy (I John 5:16). The "children of the devil" recalls the "sons of Belial" in 1QS. John believed that he was at war with those who put the whole cause of apostolic Christianity in jeopardy. Believers, then, must not love the world, the system of organized paganism (I John 2:15-17; 5:19; cf. 1QS 1.3-4; 2.7-8; 5.11; 9.17-18). Here as in II Tim. 4:10 ἀγαπάω has an object, and from this Nygren deduces that Christian *agape* was in danger of becoming a mere aspiration like *eros*. The fact is that NT evidence will not always fit into such a thesis. People do love the world, with a passion that should be reserved for devotion to God.

How much warmth is there in the brotherly love of the letters? Love "in the true faith" (II John 1-3) smacks of a theological virtue. There is greater warmth in III John (e.g., 15: "The friends send greetings. Give my greetings to my friends, each by name"; the RSV is misleading). The primary contribution of the letters is their rigorous insistence that love is not a matter of the lip but of the heart, that the love of God is meaningless if it is not expressed in love for one's fellow Christians, that Christ is the supreme example of love in a human life, and that such love touches the very heart of the ultimate reality with which we have to do.

b. The Fourth Gospel. Here too there is stress on the duty of obedience, and this book shares with I John an ambivalent attitude toward the world.

Disciple and Master share the same fate, because they are under the same obligation: "He who loves [φιλῶν] his life loses it, and he who hates his life in this world will keep it for eternal life" (12:25; cf. Mark 8:35; Luke 14:26; 17:33); note above all the sublime story in John 13 (vs. 15: "I have given you an example"). Cowardly disciples are mentioned in 12:43: "They loved the praise of men [ἀγαπάω, again with an object] more than the praise of God." Obedient disciples "bear fruit," and this involves "going," presumably to become witnesses (15:2, 8, 16, 27). They must give their testimony in a world that hates them (15:18 ff; 16:33; 17:14), so that their vocation may eventuate in martyrdom (15:13). But the Son has set them free to be spiritually responsible, and they are promised the guidance and help of the Holy Spirit, the Paraclete, as well as the joy of communion with the Father and the Son (8:31-32, 36; 14:16-17, 26; 15:26; 14:23). Nothing else is said to give body to the implications of obedience. In the Appendix, however, this theme recurs in the story of Peter's restoration and commission. Thrice Peter affirms his love (the verb is φιλέω); Jesus uses ἀγαπάω twice, and the third time φιλέω. "Are you really my friend?" might be the distinction from the first two questions: "Do you love me?" But it is perhaps oversubtle to press the difference in the language. Peter was not the disciple whom Jesus loved (19:26, etc. Was he a fiction?). In this scene, however, Peter becomes the disciple who truly loved Jesus, and here he receives authority to be a shepherd in the church (21:15-18; cf. 10:3 ff). The relationship of this dramatic and moving story to Peter's primacy in the church catholic is obscure. 21:22 ("What is that to you? Follow me!") reminds us that an apostle and even a bishop should attend to his own calling and get on with his immediate duty.

The duty of obedience may be summarily stated in terms of what Archbishop Ussher called the "eleventh commandment": "A new commandment I give to you, that you love one another; even as I have loved you, that you also love one another" (13:34). This is the peculiarly Christian limitation of the second great commandment of the Law (Lev. 19:18). If, then, it is new, the reason must be found in the clause: "even as I have loved you." It is the quality of Christ's graciously condescending, sacrificial love that is to be the model for that of his disciples in their relations with each other. We note that Jesus is represented as delivering this to the disciples as a commandment, and it may be asked, both of this saying and of the two great commandments of the OT, how love can be made a matter of law. The reason is that God is the one who has the right to make such demands of men, and that Jesus speaks in the name of God as the Word incarnate. Moreover, Jesus is the Master and Lord, with authority to lay down the conditions for discipleship. What is commanded, of course, is not merely the emotion of brotherly affection; it is rather a steady, disciplined will to seek the good of others. The moral imperative for the redeemed is that they should walk in the way of the Lord Christ, who is the Truth and the Life, following him who embodied in his own person and death the goodness that pleases the heavenly Father.

The world is the creation of God through his Word, and the Word became flesh in that Jesus Christ who, as the Lamb of God, ascended the cross in order to save the "world" (1:3, 29; 3:16; 12:19, 32). Yet the sacrifice of Jesus was in order to gather into one the "children of God who are scattered abroad" (11:52), and none may be saved unless the Father draw him and give him to Jesus (1:12; 6:44; cf. 8:47; 17:6). John seems to mean that spiritual realities demand spiritual insight for their apprehension (cf. I Cor. 2:13) and that believing in Jesus as the Word and Savior (he avoids the noun "faith") is the work of God within a man (cf. I Cor. 12:3). Unbelievers, like those who compassed the death of Jesus, belong to the devil, and on them rests the divine wrath (John 3:19-21; 5:29; 8:24, 44 ff).

Because of the situation in which he wrote (*see* § 5*a above*), John emphasized the care of God for the disciples (10:29; 16:27; 17:23; cf. 5:23; 12:26) and the love of Christ for his disciples (11:3: "he whom you love"; 13:1 ff; 15:15-16: "I have called you friends"; 19:26, his kindness to his mother at the Cross; and 20:17: "Go to my brethren"). There is a peculiarly Johannine tenderness in the language employed.

Almost nothing is said about love to God (5:42?) and little about love to Christ (8:42; 14:15, 21 ff). Love ideas lurk behind the theme of the Bridegroom (3:29). John seems to make more of the rewards and duties of love: freedom, joy, life (5:24; 6:40; 8:34 ff; 10:28; 12:50; 15:11). The church of disciples enjoys communion with the Son as he does with the Father, and through the Son's revelation and the work of the Holy Spirit their life in God is fulfilled. It is along this line that John develops what Paul understood by life in the body of Christ (cf. 14:17, 20; 15:1 ff: the "vine of God" is the Christ and is also his Israel and church; 17:20-26: "I in them and thou in me, that they may become perfectly one, so that the world may know that thou hast sent me and hast loved them even as thou hast loved me").

Two other elements are distinctive to the Fourth Gospel: the mutual love of the Father and the Son; and the paradox of the Son's obedience as the authentic mark of his divine glory. For the first, see 14:31 ("that the world may know that I love the Father"); 3:35; 5:20 (the Father loves the Son and has delivered all things into his hands); 10:17-18 (the sacrifice of the Son and his rising again fulfils the will of the Father: "For this reason the Father loves me"). Gnostic heresies that God was not in the crucified Christ are thus denied, just as Docetic error is refuted by 19:34. So the glory of Christ is a glory he had with the Father before the world began (17:5); and yet for the believer his supreme glory is that he should have died to redeem the sinful, and that he desires for them the love with which his Father loved him (17:26).

Following Martin Dibelius, Nygren would define this love of the Father as the "self-communication of God to the Son," and he finds in John the concept of a love that is motivated by the inherent worth of the Son. This at once denies his own definition of *agape* as a love freely outflowing and unmotivated. By what W. F. Howard called the method of "explicative emphasis," John is simply showing the deepest meaning of Jesus' recognition by the heavenly voice as "my beloved Son." The doctrine of the incarnation of the eternal Word or Logos is John's contribution to Christology, but he failed to proceed to the concept of the eternal Trinity of Father, Son, and Paraclete. He does provide material, however, on which the systematic theologian may build who would explore further the meaning of the Christian faith that "God is love." *See* CHRIST.

The obedience of the Son appears throughout the book: 4:34; 5:19, 30; 6:38; 8:28-29; 12:50; 14:31; 17:4, 6 ff. Is this not also the extension of the Synoptic theme of the Son of man, who came to minister (Mark 10:45)?

The sum of the matter is that the relations of the Father to the Spirit and the Spirit to the Son (14:16, 26; 15:26: "whom I shall send . . . , who proceeds from the Father") are all to be subsumed under the concept of love. With the First Letter one must say that God is love in all his being, works, and purposes. Consequently God is the Redeemer as well as the Creator of the world, and God stoops to win his children, patiently, graciously (1:17). God's will for those who turn to him through the Son and the Spirit is that they should live in love, forbearing one another, caring for the weak, seeking the truth, finding in simplicity and meekness of heart the way and the life. This is the entire secret of the NT gospel. In Jesus of Nazareth (1:45; 6:42) love had taken a human face and spoken by a human voice, for the sake of the scattered children of the Father. Love had offered the sufficient sin sacrifice and so had won fresh glory. Love had reached down from God to man, that man might rise up to enjoy life in God forever.

Bibliography. H. Drummond, *The Greatest Thing in the World* (1894). J. Moffatt, *Love in the NT* (1929). H. Preisker, *Die urchristliche Botschaft der Liebe Gottes* (1930). J. Burnaby, *Amor Dei* (1938). M. C. D'Arcy, *The Mind and Heart of Love* (1945). C. H. Dodd, *The Interpretation of the Fourth Gospel* (1953). A. Nygren, *Agape and Eros* (rev. English trans. by P. S. Watson; 1953)—on the distinction between love as a work of merit and as the fruit of the Holy Spirit, see especially pp. 248-49. C. Spicq, *L'Agapè de I Cor. XIII* (Analecta Lovaniensia Biblica et Orientalia; 1954); *Théologie Néo-Testamentaire de l'Agapè*, vol. I: *Analyse des Textes* (1957—).

G. JOHNSTON

LOVE FEASTS. *See* AGAPE, THE.

LOVINGKINDNESS. Occasional KJV and frequent ASV translation of חסד, which in the RSV is regularly rendered "steadfast love." *See* LOVE IN THE OT.

LOW COUNTRY, LOWLAND. Same as SHEPHELAH.

LOWER BETH-HORON. *See* BETH-HORON.

LOZON lō'zŏn [Λοζών]. Apoc. alternate name of DARKON.

LUBIM lōō'bĭm [לובים]. Plural of the gentilic לובי (*lûbhî*), "Libyan." *See* LIBYA.

LUCAS. KJV alternate form of LUKE.

LUCIFER. KJV translation of הילל (RSV DAY STAR).

LUCIUS lōō'shəs [Λεύκιος, Λούκιος]. **1.** A Roman consul who sent a letter (I Macc. 15:16-21) to Ptolemy VII of Egypt and to other Near Eastern rulers, stating the Roman Senate's backing for the Jewish state of SIMON (1) in his struggle with the Seleucids.

Identification of Lucius is difficult, since his full name is not given, and since the letter may be wrongly placed; even the genuineness of the letter has been questioned (*see* MACCABEES, BOOKS OF). The following identifications are most frequently suggested:

a) Lucius Caecilius Metellus, consul in 142 B.C. If he is intended, the letter would seem to belong in I Macc. 14 rather than in its present place in ch. 15, which puts it in 139 B.C.

b) Cnaeus or Lucius Calpurnius Piso, consul in 139 B.C. His consulship fits the date of the letter as it appears in I Maccabees, but his name most probably was Cnaeus, not Lucius (the sources differ on this point).

c) Jos. Antiq. XIV.145-48 inserts a letter which bears striking similarities to that in I Macc. 15:16-21. Josephus dates this letter in the time of Hyrcanus II (47 B.C.). Probably he has edited and inserted a letter from an earlier time, but scholars differ as to the proper date of Josephus' letter. He mentions a praetor, not consul, named Lucius Valerius, whom some have identified with the consul Lucius of I Maccabees. But identification of Josephus' Lucius Valerius with any other known Lucius is very precarious.

Bibliography. J. C. Dancy, *A Commentary on I Maccabees* (1954), pp. 189-90.

W. A. BEARDSLEE

2. Lucius of Cyrene, one of the prophets and teachers of the Christian church at Antioch (Acts 13:1).

3. An otherwise unknown Christian, probably a Jew by birth ("kinsman" = "fellow countryman"), who sent greetings from Corinth in Rom. 16:21.

The undoubted fact that LUKE (Λουκᾶς) is an alternate form of Lucius or Lucanus has led to an identification of this Lucius with the author of the Third Gospel and Acts, from Origen to Deissmann (*see below*). The great likelihood that Luke was a Gentile and Lucius a Jew tells heavily against this identification. There was also a tendency, shown in some variant readings, to identify Luke with 2 *above* (*see* the works of Cadbury in the *bibliography*). Finally, it is possible that Lucius 2 and Lucius 3 were the same man.

Bibliography. A. Deissmann, *Light from the Ancient East* (1927), pp. 435 ff. H. J. Cadbury, *Beginnings of Christianity*, vol. I, pt. 5 (1933), pp. 489-95; *The Book of Acts in History* (1955), pp. 155-56.

F. W. GINGRICH

LUD, LUDIM lŭd, lōō'dĭm [לוד, לודים, לודיים]. A people in Asia Minor, presumably. The name of Lud/Ludim can only be identified, to our present knowledge, with that of the Lydians, *Luddu* of Ashurbanipal's inscriptions (Rassam Cylinder II.95). Since the Lydians are an ancient population established in Asia Minor (*see* LYDIA), the biblical genealogies are somewhat difficult to reconcile with the historical situation. It seems, however, that at the basis of all the references there are some elements of historical reality.

In Gen. 10:22; I Chr. 1:17 Lud appears among the sons of Shem. In Gen. 10:13; I Chr. 1:11 Ludim is a son of Mizraim (i.e., Egypt), second son of Ham. The Lydians of Asia Minor were neither Semites nor Hamites, but the contradictory nature of the two classifications of Lud and Ludim would seem to emphasize that the people in question were only incidentally known to the Near East. This would be explained if the original habitat of the Lud/Ludim were remote, although they at times must have entered the horizon of Egypt and Babylonia.

Historically, the Lydians came into contact with Assyria and Egypt in the early seventh century B.C., when their king Gyges sent an embassy to Ashurbanipal in 668 or 660. The Assyrians then did not know the language of the Lydian envoys, but diplomatic contact was established, and from Gyges' rule on, the name of the Lydians was known in the Near East, although few people from oriental countries would have had personal experience of Lydia in a geographical sense. Better information about Lydia became available after the Persian army under Cyrus had conquered Lydia in 546 B.C. and had incorporated it in the Persian Empire.

The listing of Lud among the nations in Isa. 66:19, with Tubal, Javan, and the coastlands afar off, is perfectly consistent with the situation of Lydia in Asia Minor near the Ionian coast. This passage supports the identification of Lud as Lydia. The other references seem to know of Lydians employed as mercenaries in foreign armies. In Jer. 46:9 they are fighting with the Egyptians in the Battle of Carchemish (605 B.C.); in Ezek. 30:5 they are again listed among the helpers of Egypt.

The presence of Lydian mercenaries in Egypt goes back to the days of Gyges, who sent military aid to his ally Psammetichus of Egypt (663-609) against the Assyrian armies (Ashurbanipal, Rassam Cylinder II.114-15). This contingent would certainly have included Lydians, who were known as good soldiers in pre-Persian times (Herodotus I.79), and it would have been known under the collective name of Lydians. The Greeks report that mercenaries from Asia Minor ("bronze men from the sea") supported the Saite dynasty; according to Herodotus (II.152), they were of Carian and Ionian derivation. These mercenaries have left many graffiti in Egypt, one of which is in Lydian (Friedrich no. 49).

It does not seem probable that Lydians were important among the mercenaries in other foreign armies—e.g., in Tyre (Ezek. 27:10)—although after the Persian conquest the Lydians furnished a contingent to the Persian army. M. J. MELLINK

LUHITH lo͞o'hĭth [הלוחית, הלחית] (Isa. 15:5; Jer. 48:5). A city of Moab, associated with Horonaim. It was apparently at the top of an ascent, probably near the S end of the Dead Sea, since it seems to be a stage in the flight of Moabites to Zoar. Eusebius and Jerome identify it with Loueitha, a city between Areopolis (*see* AR) and Zoar. It is probably identical with לחיתו of a Nabatean inscription from Medeba. E. D. GROHMAN

LUKE (EVANGELIST) lo͝ok [Λουκᾶς, *an affectionate form of* Λούκιος (Lat. *Lucius*) *or* Λουκανός (Lat. *Lucanus*)]. A companion of Paul; a physician; and the probable author of our Third Gospel and the book of Acts. *See* LUKE, GOSPEL OF; ACTS OF THE APOSTLES.

Λουκᾶς ("Luke") occurs three times in the text of the NT (Col. 4:14; II Tim. 4:11; Philem. 24). Λούκιος ("Lucius") appears twice (Acts 13:1; Rom. 16:21).

From the first three references we learn that Luke was a physician beloved by Paul; Paul's fellow worker (συνεργός; Philem. 24) during Paul's imprisonment, probably in Rome; and a Gentile by birth (note the division of Paul's companions into "men of the circumcision" and those not so, in Col. 4:10-14).

It is possible, though not probable, that "Lucius of Cyrene" at Antioch (Acts 13:1) and "Lucius . . . my kinsman" (συγγενής; Rom. 16:21) are references to Luke. The appearance of "we" in the Western text of Acts 11:28, if not original, is at least witness to an early belief that the author was present at Antioch at the time of Agabus' prophecy. This would lead naturally to the view (as it did for Ephrem Syrus of the fourth century) that the author was the Lucius of Cyrene of Acts 13:1. Acts 20:3-6 may imply that Luke was with Paul at Corinth, the city from which the readers of Rom. 16:21 are greeted by "Lucius." Would there have been two men with the same name among Paul's companions? Against both identifications it has been argued that the Lucius of Rom. 16:21 was a Jew ("my kinsman"), while Luke was a Gentile; that Lucius was a very common Roman first name in this period and may well have been carried by several early Christians; and that the author, who seems studiously to avoid direct reference to himself, would hardly have flatly named himself in Acts 13:1. Certainty concerning the suggested identifications is impossible.

Luke's native country is likewise uncertain. The Western text of Acts 11:28, the possible identification of Luke with the Lucius of Acts 13:1, and persisting church tradition (in the so-called Anti-Marcionite Prologue to Luke, Eusebius, Jerome) favor Antioch in Syria as his place of residence. On the other hand, certain other data in Acts point toward Philippi. The "we" passages, beginning in 16:10, may indicate that the author of the book was himself the "man of Macedonia" and that he joined Paul and his associates at Troas for the journey to and evangelization of his native land. He seems to have remained in Philippi while Paul and his party journeyed into Achaia and rejoined them some years later when the missionaries again came through Philippi (Acts 20:5-6). His pride in the importance of Philippi (Acts 16:12) has been cited as supporting evidence. Antioch in Pisidia also has been suggested.

It is possible that Luke and Titus were brothers (II Cor. 8:18; 12:18)—a suggestion made by Origen and Jerome. This might account for the nonmention of Titus in Acts, surely a strange phenomenon in view of Titus' importance in the Pauline letters.

Luke's medical training may have been taken at Tarsus, which, along with Alexandria and Athens, was a famous center of learning. Until recent times it was believed that the vocabulary of Luke-Acts was saturated with medical terminology, final proof that the author of this two-volume work was a physician. But it has been shown conclusively that the writer of Luke-Acts used no language beyond the competence of the average, educated, nonmedical Greek of the period. *See* LUKE, GOSPEL OF.

If Luke the "beloved physician" and companion of Paul was the author of Luke-Acts, it is possible to derive from this work characteristics of the author's mind and spirit. He was broad in his sympathies, compassionate toward the poor and the outcasts of society, genuinely pious, self-effacing, radiantly joyful, charmingly urbane, and deeply loyal. He remained with Paul to the end, doubtlessly serving him in medical and other ways, and earned the great apostle's gratitude and admiration (Col. 4:14; II Tim. 4:11; Philem. 24).

The Anti-Marcionite Prologue to Luke says that he never married and that he died at the age of seventy-four in Bithynia (in some MSS "Boeotia"), "full of the Holy Ghost." Traditions are abundant and various concerning his later fields of activity and place and manner of death.

Bibliography. A. Harnack, *Luke the Physician* (1907). A. T. Robertson, *Luke the Historian in the Light of Research* (1920), pp. 16-29. H. J. Cadbury, *The Style and Literary Method of Luke* (1919-20); *The Making of Luke-Acts* (1927). A. Deissmann, *Light from the Ancient East* (1927), pp. 435-38. F. J. Foakes-Jackson and K. Lake, eds., *The Beginnings of Christianity,* II (1922), 207-64; V (1933), 489-95. A. M. Ramsay, *The Bearing of Recent Discovery on the Trustworthiness of the NT* (reprinted 1953). A. H. N. Green-Armytage, *A Portrait of St. Luke* (1955).

E. P. BLAIR

***LUKE, GOSPEL OF** [κατὰ λουκᾶν, *see* LUKE (EVANGELIST)]. The third book of the NT canon. This gospel is dedicated by the author to an unknown patron, the "most excellent Theophilus," but was intended for general circulation in a Gentile community. As the Preface (1:1-4) shows, the evangelist was capable of writing excellent Greek, but he adapts his style to that of his several sources.

He intended the gospel to be the first part of a larger work, for the book of ACTS is clearly a sequel to it. In Acts 1:1 he explains that "in the first book" (i.e., the gospel) he has dealt with "all that Jesus began to do and teach, until the day when he was taken up"—i.e., until his ASCENSION into heaven. Even apart from the fact that the word used here for "first" usually designates the former of two, there is no good reason to think that the author proposed to write a third book. In Luke 1:4 he describes the purpose which he has in view in the words: "that you may know the truth concerning the things of which you have been informed," thus referring to earlier instruction.

The fidelity with which he follows the language and style of his sources and his marked religious interests make his book of inestimable value as one of the basic documents of historical Christianity.

See map "Palestine: Matthew, Mark and Luke," under MARK, GOSPEL OF.

1. Authorship
2. Purpose
3. Contents
   a. The Preface
   b. The birth and infancy narratives
   c. The Galilean ministry
   d. The journey to Jerusalem through Samaria
   e. The Jerusalem ministry
   f. The passion and resurrection narrative
4. Distinctive characteristics
   a. Universalism
   b. An interest in social relationships
   c. A deep concern for outcasts, sinners, and Samaritans
   d. An interest in stories about women
   e. An emphasis on joy, prayer, and the Holy Spirit
   f. An emphasis on the graciousness and severity of the demands of Jesus
   g. The stress on the lordship of Christ
   h. The interest taken in the Passion
5. Sources
   a. Mark
   b. Q
   c. L
   d. The birth and infancy narrative
6. Proto-Luke
7. Date
8. Place of writing
9. Canonicity
10. Text
11. The value of Luke

Bibliography

1. Authorship. According to tradition the gospel was written by "Luke the beloved physician" (Col. 4:14). "Luke," writes Irenaeus (A.D. 185), "the follower of Paul recorded in a book the gospel that was preached by him." The Muratorian Canon (*see* CANON OF THE NT § 3*e*), which reflects the opinion of the church of Rome (A.D. 170-90), says: "The third book of the Gospel, according to Luke, Luke that physician, who after the ascension of Christ, when Paul had taken him with him as companion of his journey, composed in his own name on the basis of report." In view of the tendency to ascribe NT writings to apostolic authorship, this tradition has much weight, and is accepted by very many, although not by all, modern scholars. It is confirmed by the probability that Luke is the author of the "we sections"—i.e., the parts of the Acts which are written in the first person plural (16:10-17; 20:5-15; 21:1-18; 27:1–28:16). In these sections the writer is manifestly a companion of Paul, since he writes accurately and with considerable detail, and may well be Luke, since in them Luke himself is never mentioned. The retention of the first person ("we," etc.) is best explained by the view that the writer of these sections is also the author of the Acts as a whole; and strong linguistic arguments have been advanced to show that he is also the author of the gospel.

Lukan authorship is also supported, although by no means demonstrated, by the linguistic evidence which suggests that the author of Luke-Acts was a physician. Much less stress is laid on this "medical argument" today, in consequence of evidence which shows that many of the words formerly cited as "medical words" are used by contemporary and later writers who were not physicians. Other scholars think that this counterargument has been pressed too far and that, while the vocabulary and the style do not prove that the author was a physician, they tend to confirm the ancient tradition. In favor of this view they cite 4:38: "Now Simon's mother-in-law was ill with a high fever" (cf. Mark 1:30); 5:12: "There came a man full of leprosy" (cf. Mark 1:40); and 8:43, where Luke replaces Mark's description of the woman with the issue of blood ("who had suffered much under many physicians, and had spent all that she had, and was no better but rather grew worse"; Mark 5:26) by the statement that she "could not be healed by any one."

The objections to Lukan authorship turn mainly upon the historical problems which meet us in the Acts, especially the difficulty of reconciling the account of the Apostolic Council in Acts 15 with Paul's personal narrative in Gal. 2:1-10 and the problems raised by the decree in Acts 15:23-29 (*see* COUNCIL OF JERUSALEM). These problems belong mainly to the study of the ACTS and all that can be said here is that the difficulties have been exaggerated, especially if it is remembered that the aims and circumstances of Luke and Paul were different. Some scholars, it may be added, prefer (but on doubtful grounds) to identify Gal. 2:1-10 with Acts 11:27-30; 12:25. *See also* GALATIANS.

On the question of authorship we may, with some confidence, conclude that the Third Gospel was written by Luke the beloved physician. Much force belongs to B. H. Streeter's words: "The burden of proof is on those who would assert the traditional authorship of Matthew and John and on those who would deny it in the case of Mark and Luke."

2. Purpose. In considering this question we have the advantage of the author's personal explanation in his Preface (1:1-4). He writes to confirm in the minds of his readers the truth of what they have been already taught, presumably in the primitive Christian community. With this end in view he selects from his sources, and from oral tradition, material by which to present an outline of the life, ministry, and death and resurrection of Jesus Christ. Basically his interests are historical. This fact, it must be said, is one of his virtues, in spite of the tendency of many scholars to describe him in a depreciatory sense as a "historicizer" of the tradition. He does not write as a modern historian would write or within the limitations of his knowledge. His intention is to record what Jesus had said and done in the light of certain definite interests of his own. He is not primarily a theologian, and certainly not a "Paulinist." Irenaeus, we have seen, says that he recorded the gospel preached by Paul; but this statement is quite general and cannot be pressed. Like Paul, Luke speaks expressly of sin (5:8; 7:47), of forgiveness and reconciliation (15:11-32), and records teaching which reminds us of Paul (17:10; 18:14; 19:9-10); but in these respects he simply hands down primitive Christian teaching in which both writers shared. How little Luke had entered into Paul's deepest thoughts is shown by the quite general reference to justification in the apostle's sermon at Antioch of Pisidia: "Let it be known to you therefore, brethren, that through this man forgiveness of sins is proclaimed to you, and by him every one that believes is freed from everything from which you could not be freed by the law of Moses" (Acts 13:38-39). This statement is only a pale, and not very accurate, reflection of the kind of teaching we find in Paul's letters—e.g., in Rom. 3:27-31; Gal. 5:1, 13-15. Luke's purposes are not doctrinal, but practical in the best sense of the word.

It is a fascinating, and by no means improbable, suggestion that one of the reasons which shaped the writing of Luke-Acts was the desire to commend Christianity to members of the Roman court circle. T. Flavius Clemens, joint consul in A.D. 95, whose wife Domitilla was an adherent, if not a baptized member, of the church at Rome, was probably favorably disposed to the new faith, and excavations suggest that other members of leading families were also interested in it. The contents of Luke-Acts lend support to this suggestion. The gospel is related to world history in 3:1-2, and Tiberius is mentioned in 3:1 and Augustus in 2:1. Three times Pilate declares Jesus innocent (Luke 23:4, 14, 22), and although he passes sentence upon him, the guilt of the chief priests and rulers of the people is emphasized in the words: "And their voices prevailed," and the statement that he delivered up his prisoner "to their will" (23:24-25). In the Acts, Roman officials are not unfriendly, as the references to Sergius Paulus (13:4-12), to the magistrates at Philippi (16:35-40), to Gallio (18:12-17), and to the Asiarchs at Ephesus (19:31) show. To Festus, Paul says: "I am standing before Caesar's tribunal, where I ought to be tried; to the Jews I have done no wrong, as you know very well . . . . I appeal to Caesar" (25:10-11); and later Agrippa says to Festus: "This man could have been set free if he had not appealed to Caesar" (26:32). The climax of Luke-Acts describes Paul's preaching and teaching in Rome as being carried on "quite openly and unhindered" (28:30-31). Luke may well have wished to suggest that Christianity was not politically dangerous. This, of course, is not his main purpose, as Luke 1:1-4 makes clear, but it appears to have influenced his use of his material.

3. Contents. The gospel may be summarily outlined as follows:

I. The Preface, 1:1-4
II. The birth and infancy narratives, 1:5–2:52
III. The Galilean ministry, 3:1–9:50
IV. The journey to Jerusalem through Samaria, 9:51–19:48
V. The Jerusalem ministry, chs. 20–21
VI. The passion and resurrection narrative, chs. 22–24

a. The Preface. There are several important statements in this passage, the only one of its kind in the Synoptic gospels. Luke speaks of many predecessors. Many, he tells us, had undertaken to compile a narrative of the "things which have been accomplished among us," and they had done this "just as they were delivered to us by those who from the beginning were eyewitnesses and ministers of the word" (1:1-2). Mark is certainly one of these early evangelists, but whether the other narratives amounted to gospels is uncertain. Who the others were we do not know, and it is idle to guess. Luke may be referring to those, including perhaps himself, who had already strung together groups of narratives and sayings illustrative of various aspects of the ministry of Jesus. He modestly says that it seemed good to him to write an orderly account inasmuch as he had followed the course of all things closely (or "accurately") from the first.

b. The birth and infancy narratives. The change from the excellent Greek of the Preface to the Hebraistic Greek of 1:5–2:52 is noted by all commentators. Semitic idioms and the biblical style of the narratives suggest that the evangelist either is using a Hebrew or Aramaic document or is deliberately adapting his language to that of the Greek OT. A series of narratives which announce the birth of John the Baptist, the son of Zechariah and Elizabeth, his conception, birth, and circumcision, is balanced at every point by a second series concerning Jesus which ends with the story of his visit to Jerusalem and the temple at the age of twelve. It has been conjectured that the basic cycle is that concerning John and that the evangelist has shaped the narratives about the birth and infancy of Jesus in accordance with it. A reference to the Virgin Birth appears in 1:34-35: "And Mary said to the angel, 'How can this be, since I have no husband?' And the angel said to her,

> 'The Holy Spirit will come upon you,
> and the power of the Most High will overshadow you;
> therefore the child to be born will be called holy,
> the Son of God.' "

Some think that this passage may have been added at the time of the composition of the gospel, or less probably later, since it is difficult to harmonize it with the terms of the messianic prophecy in 1:30-33, but most commentators conclude that it is an original element in the cycle. The beauty and restraint of the whole section, its marked Jewish-Christian character, as seen in the great hymns which have come to be known as the Benedictus, the Magnificat, the Gloria in Excelsis, and the Nunc Dimittis, and the deep religious spirit which prevails throughout—these are some of the characteristics of these matchless chapters.

c. The Galilean ministry. As in Mark and Matthew, the early ministry is introduced with an account of the preaching of John and the baptism of Jesus. Distinctive of the gospel is the elaborate, sixfold date in 3:1-2. After a summary reference to the imprisonment of John and a brief account of the baptism of Jesus, a genealogy is introduced which traces his descent from Adam, "the son of God" (3:23-38). "Full of the Holy Spirit," Jesus is led into the wilderness and "tempted by the devil"; and returning "in the power of the Spirit," he begins a teaching and healing ministry in Galilee, "being glorified by all" (4:1-15).

With intention Luke sets at the beginning of the ministry an independent account of the preaching of Jesus in the synagogue at Nazareth (4:16-30), a story which sounds the note of universalism characteristic of his special interests. From this point he is dependent mainly on his principal sources, but he introduces material peculiar to his gospel in the narratives of the call of the first disciples (5:1-11), the raising of the widow's son at Nain (7:11-17), the woman of the city (7:36-50), and the ministering women from Galilee (8:1-3). In 6:20-49 he introduces the Great Sermon. The form is more compact than Matthew's SERMON ON THE MOUNT (Matt. 5–7). This is followed by other material from the same sayings source.

The rest of the section consists of portions of Mark. Thus Luke retells the stories of the storm on the lake (8:22-25), the Gerasene demoniac (8:26-39), the raising of Jairus' daughter (8:40-56), the mission of the Twelve (9:10-17), the confession of Peter (9:18-22), the Transfiguration (9:28-36), the epileptic lad (9:37-43), the second prophecy of the Passion (9:43*b*-45), the child in the midst (9:46-48), and the man casting out devils who was not a disciple (9:49-50). This Markan material consists of extracts (Mark 1:21-39; 1:40–3:19; 3:31-35; 4:1-25; 4:35–6:44; 8:27–9:40), some of them long, as will be seen. In these sections Mark's order is meticulously followed, with transpositions only in 3:7-19, 31-35. Clearly for this part of his gospel Luke had little special information of his own apart from isolated traditions noted above.

d. The journey to Jerusalem through Samaria. It would be tedious, and it is not necessary, to list all the narratives and sayings in this long section of some ten chapters. In 9:51–18:14 Mark is not used at all, except possibly in a few phrases.

The section opens with a summary statement: "When the days drew near for him to be received up, he set his face to go to Jerusalem" (9:51). Its amorphous contents are linked loosely together by such passages as 13:22: "He went on his way through towns and villages, teaching, and journeying toward Jerusalem"; 17:11: "On the way to Jerusalem he was passing along between Samaria and Galilee"; and by briefer captions introducing single narratives and groups of sayings and parables. Manifestly, Luke had no detailed chronological knowledge of the course of events in this journey.

Various reasons have been suggested for this want of continuity. It has been conjectured that accounts of three separate journeys have been loosely compiled. It has even been suggested that the evangelist has selected and arranged his material so as to present a sequence corresponding to the book of Deuteronomy. A better suggestion is that he is making use of existing groups of tradition compiled for the guidance of individual missionaries on such topics as the charge of Jesus to his disciples, prayer, miracles, wealth, forgiveness, and mammon. More is to be said for the view that Luke has followed the order of Q (*see* § 5*b below*), and has introduced his special tradition at appropriate points. This view would not rule out the probability that Q was preceded by groups of allied materials.

More important than the origins of this long section is the distinctively Lukan material which it contains. It is this section more than any other which gives to the gospel its peculiar stamp. Outstanding among the contents are the parables of the good Samaritan, the friend at midnight, the rich fool, the tower builder, the rash king, the lost sheep, the lost coin, the lost son, the unjust steward, the rich man and Lazarus, the farmer and his servant, the unjust judge, the Pharisee and the tax collector, and the pounds; and such stories as Martha and Mary, the woman who cried: "Blessed is the womb that bore you," Herod's threat, Zacchaeus, and the weeping over Jerusalem. The religious value of this material cannot be estimated.

e. The Jerusalem ministry. In this section Luke is again largely dependent on Mark for his account of the controversies in Jerusalem and at least part of the eschatological discourse on the Mount of Olives. The discourse is of special importance because in 21:20-36 he appears to be using a special tradition. Several American and British scholars have more or less independently maintained that the evangelist has inserted short Markan extracts (vss. 21*a*, 23*a*, 26*b*-27,

29-33) into a section which otherwise is non-Markan. The importance of this contention is that, if this view is accepted, it disposes of the common objection that Luke would probably not deliberately have interpolated verses from Mark into another source. The apparent fact that he does this very thing in 21:20-36 bears closely upon the vital question of the origins of his passion and resurrection narrative.

As for the discourse itself, in spite of much that has been said to the contrary, one can be far from certain that it reflects a knowledge of the siege of Jerusalem in A.D. 68-70, as indeed we should have to conclude if Luke 21:20-24 is only an editorial expansion of Mark 13:14-20.

A feature of the Lukan discourse is that it emphasizes the political more than the eschatological aspects of the teaching of Jesus. In 21:37 Luke adds the summary statement: "Every day he was teaching in the temple, but at night he went out and lodged on the mount called Olivet. And early in the morning all the people came to him in the temple to hear him." This passage appears to be more than a mere editorial expansion of Mark 11:19.

f. The passion and resurrection narrative. The nature of chs. 22–24 presents the greatest difficulties to the commentator, and, at the same time, is a matter of great importance for the general reader. If, as is commonly held, this section is a re-edited version of Mark's account, with certain Lukan additions, its historical value will be appreciably less than the estimate we may put upon it if, in fact, it contains an independent Lukan account of the Passion with Markan supplements. Some of the facts connected with the problem are undoubted. Luke 22:1-13 is certainly a re-edited version of Mark 14:1-2, 10-16; and Luke 24:13-53 (the journey to Emmaus, the appearance to the Eleven, and the Ascension) is a part of Luke's special tradition. In the intervening section, Luke 22:14–24:11 (24:12 is no part of the original text: *see* § 10 *below*), there are also several passages which have indubitably been drawn from Mark. These include Luke 22:19*a*, 22, 34, 46*b*(?), 50*b*, 52-53*a*, 54*b*-61; 23:3, 26, 34*b*(?), 38, 44-45, 50-54; 24:10(?); and perhaps other passages in 22:39-46, 47-53; 23:18-25.

The beauty, pathos, and religious value of the distinctively Lukan elements in chs. 22–24 are recognized by all. This applies especially to the narratives of the Agony (22:39-46), the women of Jerusalem (23:27-31), and the Emmaus story (24:13-35). On the other hand, the appearance to the Eleven (24:36-43) contains legendary elements in the references to "flesh and bones" and the eating of "broiled fish." The passion narrative, and the gospel as a whole, find an impressive climax in the words: "Then he led them out as far as Bethany, and lifting up his hands he blessed them. While he blessed them, he parted from them. And they returned to Jerusalem with great joy, and were continually in the temple blessing God."

4. Distinctive characteristics. ***a. Universalism.*** This quality has already been noted in the account of the sermon at Nazareth, in the references to the widow at Zarephath and Naaman the Syrian (4:25-27). It runs throughout the gospel—in the birth stories, where the promised salvation is described as a "light for revelation to the Gentiles" (2:32); in the parable of the great supper, in which the servant is bidden to "go out to the highways and hedges, and compel people to come in" (14:23); and in the story of the appearance to the Eleven according to which the disciples are to preach repentance and the forgiveness of sins "to all nations, beginning from Jerusalem" (24:47).

b. An interest in social relationships. This concern appears in the beatitudes addressed to the poor and woes addressed to the rich (6:20-26). Illustrations from finance are frequent—e.g., in many of the parables, such as the two debtors, the rich fool, the tower builder, the rich man and Lazarus, and the pounds. There are also several references to almsgiving (11:41; 12:33), and frequent allusions to lodging and entertainment (2:7; 9:12; 21:37; also 7:36 ff; 10:38 ff; 13:26; etc.).

c. A deep concern for outcasts, sinners, and Samaritans. See 5:1-11; 7:36 ff; 9:51-55; 10:29-37; 17:11-19; 18:9-14; 19:1-10; 23:39-43. The remark of Harnack has often been quoted: "He has a boundless—indeed a paradoxical—love for sinners, together with the most confident hope of their forgiveness and amendment."

d. An interest in stories about women. This interest is illustrated in portraiture of the Virgin, Elizabeth, Anna, the widow at Nain, the penitent harlot, the ministering women from Galilee, Martha and Mary, the bent woman, and the women mentioned in the parables of the lost coin and the unjust judge. The same interest, it will be recalled, is manifest in the Acts in the stories about Tabitha, Lydia, Priscilla, and the four daughters of Philip the evangelist.

e. An emphasis on joy, prayer, and the Holy Spirit. The angelic message to the shepherds speaks of "good news of a great joy which will come to all the people" (2:10). Prayer is mentioned in 5:16; 6:12; 11:1; 22:32, 41-42. On the cross Jesus prays: "Father, forgive them; for they know not what they do," and commends himself to the Father in the words: "Father, into thy hands I commit my spirit" (23:46). The Holy Spirit is mentioned in 4:1, 14, and again at 10:21, and the gift of the Spirit to the disciples is promised in the words: "Behold, I send the promise of my Father upon you; but stay in the city, until you are clothed with power from on high" (24:49). These same interests are abundantly illustrated in the Acts.

f. An emphasis on the graciousness and severity of the demands of Jesus. The graciousness of the Lukan Jesus is universally recognized. At Nazareth "all spoke well of him, and wondered at the gracious words which proceeded out of his mouth" (4:22). Tenderness and compassion shine in the narratives of the woman of the city, Zacchaeus, and the penitent bandit. It is not always immediately recognized, however, that along with this graciousness there is an imperious note in the sayings of Jesus. Without counseling hatred, he demands undivided loyalty to himself in the saying: "If any one comes to me and does not hate his own father and mother and wife and children and brothers and sisters, yes, and even his own life, he cannot be my disciple" (14:26); this saying appears in a more challenging form than in the parallel in Matt. 10:37. Complete renunciation is required in the words which follow the parable of the rash king: "So therefore, whoever of you does not renounce all that he has cannot be my disciple" (14:

33). The saying on salt (14:34-35; cf. Matt. 5:13; Mark 9:50), which closes this group, appears in a form more searching and more absolute than in the parallel versions: "Salt is good; but if salt has lost its taste, how shall its saltness be restored? It is fit neither for the land nor for the dunghill; men throw it away. He who has ears to hear, let him hear."

g. The stress on the lordship of Christ. The sonship of Christ, while fully recognized in Luke (cf. 1:35; 3:22; 4:3, 9; 10:22), is not emphasized to the degree illustrated in the Pauline letters and the Johannine writings. The stress lies, as indeed it does in the case of Paul, upon the lordship of Christ. This is true also of the Acts. In fact, we may say that the Christology of Luke-Acts is that of primitive Christianity. The evangelist uses the title "the Lord" at least eighteen times, and in various combinations nearly fifty times in the Acts. There can be little doubt that it expresses an attitude of marked religious veneration.

h. The interest taken in the Passion. In this respect the gospel resembles Mark, but there is perhaps a greater interest in its tragic aspects. In 9:51 Jesus sets his face to go to Jerusalem. In 12:50, in a saying found only in Luke, Jesus says: "I have a baptism to be baptized with; and how I am constrained until it is accomplished!" (cf. Mark 10:39). In reply to the threats of Herod Antipas, he says: "Behold, I cast out demons and perform cures today and tomorrow, and the third day I finish my course" (13:32); and, at the Last Supper, he quotes Isa. 53:12 in the words: "I tell you that this scripture must be fulfilled in me, 'And he was reckoned with transgressors'; for what is written about me has its fulfilment' " (22:37). The last clause in this passage has even greater point if, with a number of scholars, it is rendered: "For my life draws to its end." In Luke, Christ is the divine Son and Lord who in filial obedience fulfils a ministry of grace which culminates in suffering, death, and resurrection.

5. Sources. Already, in discussing the ideas characteristic of this gospel, it has been found difficult to avoid references to its sources. They are Mark, Q, L, and the birth and infancy narrative.

a. Mark. The evangelist's use of Mark is beyond question. It is one of his principal sources, and is generally held to provide the framework of his gospel. In 3:1–4:30 the phrases "preaching a baptism of repentance for the forgiveness of sins" (3:3) and "the thong of whose sandals I am not worthy to untie" (3:16) appear to have been drawn from Mark. In 22:14–24:11 a greater use of Mark is made. In both these sections, however, the question of sources is very complicated and is still open to argument.

A most copious use of Mark is obvious in the long intervening section 4:31–22:13, and it is here more than anywhere else that we can best assess Luke's dependence upon this source. Here the Markan sections are: Luke 4:31-44; 5:12–6:11 (19); 8:4–9:50; 18:15-43; 19:29-36, 45-46; 20:1–21:11, 16-17; 22:1-13. In these passages the proportion of words shared with Mark ranges from 52 to 68 per cent, in spite of changes of vocabulary and style. (Only in 4:40-44; 5:36-38; 6:6-19; 9:28-45; 19:47-48, does the agreement fall below 45 per cent.) Percentages may be thought a mechanical means of deciding dependence, but they draw attention to, and confirm, conclusions suggested by a close linguistic comparison, and the upshot is to show that Luke uses Mark with a high degree of fidelity to his source, despite additions and changes. They justify hesitation when elsewhere in the gospel commentators find it necessary to describe Luke's narratives as "editorial" or as a "radical revision of Mark."

It is important to observe that, while Luke uses Mark, he omits nearly half the material in his source, and that the verses which he takes over do not amount to a third of his own gospel (300-350 verses out of 1,149). Luke is indebted to Q, L, and oral tradition to a far greater extent than he is to Mark.

b. Q. This is the sayings source used independently by Matthew and Luke. The material Luke derives from Q amounts to some 220-30 verses. It includes the following passages: Luke 3:7-9, 16-17, 21-22; 4:1-13; 6:20-23, 27-49; 7:1-10, 18-28, 31-35; 9:57-60; 10:2-16, 21-24; 11:2-4, 9-26, 29-35, 49-51; 12:2-12, 22-31, 33*b*-34, 39-46, 51-53, 57-59; 13:18-29, 34-35; 14:11, 15-24, 26-27; 16:13, 16-18; 17:1-6, 23-24, 26-27, 33-35, 37; 22:30*b*. Probably also it contained a few passages not found in Matthew, including 6:24-26; 9:61-62; 12:35-38, 47-48, 54-56. Q may have been preceded by short groups of sayings and parables, but there can be little doubt that it was in the form of a document at the time when Matthew and Luke wrote. This inference is suggesed by two facts: (*a*) that many sequences of passages can be traced between Luke and the five groups Matt. 5–7; 10; 13; 18; 23–25; and a sixth group consisting of the rest of Matthew; and (*b*) that the sayings not in sequences are those which the First Evangelist has conflated with material derived from other sources (Mark and M). There are good grounds for believing that Luke reproduces Q in its original order, and that he adheres closely to its text. After decades of further research the probability remains that, whether Luke recorded the words of Jesus from Mark or found them in Q, he seldom made any changes for the sake of giving them wider scope or application.

An important fact bearing upon the composition of the gospel is that material from Mark is not introduced into Q contexts and that Q sayings are not inserted in Markan contexts. The contents of the two sources are segregated. In contrast, material peculiar to Luke, usually designated by the symbol L, is commonly and freely connected with the Q passages listed above.

c. L. The evangelist owes more of his material to L than to any other source. Some 400-450 verses belong to this source apart from the 132 verses in Luke 1–2. It has been maintained that L was a document, but it may be doubted that this view can be sustained, if the birth stories belong to a separate source. It is best to regard L as a body of oral tradition which Luke first reduced to writing at Caesarea.

It is the L material which gives much of its distinctive character to the Third Gospel. To it belong the parables and narratives peculiar to Luke which already have been enumerated (*see* §§ 3*c-f above*). Besides these parables and narratives Luke has derived groups of sayings from this cycle: on dividing the inheritance (12:13-15); on being invited to a banquet and on issuing invitations (14:7-14); on mammon (16:9-12); on wealth (16:14-15); on true greatness (22:24-

30); together with the non-Markan parts of 21:12-36.

A reasonable conjecture is that this L material was collected by Luke *ca.* A.D. 60, when, as he tells us in Acts 21:8-9, he remained with his companions "many days" in the house of Philip the evangelist at Caesarea. Philip, he tells us, had four unmarried daughters. In view of the special interest in women which marks the L tradition, it may well be that these women were the evangelist's intermediaries. The probability that his information reached him in an oral form is supported by the fact that his distinctive style is especially marked in the narratives and parables derived from this source—in 5:1-11; 7:36-50; 10:29-37; 17:11-19; 19:41-44; 23:5-12, 14-15, 39-43; 24:13-35, 36-53.

d. The birth and infancy narrative. The biblical style and the Semitic idioms of Luke 1–2 have already been mentioned. The question arises how far these linguistic features are due to Luke himself and how far they are distinctive features of a source. Upon this issue critical opinion is divided. It may be that Luke is dependent on oral tradition and that he deliberately used the idioms of the LXX as being peculiarly appropriate to these stories. The alternative is to suppose that he drew upon Hebrew or Aramaic sources, possibly already translated into Greek, and that he embellished them by the artistry of his style. These stylistic features are more strongly marked in the annunciation to Mary (1:26-38) and the visit of Mary to Elizabeth (1:39-45, 56), and again in the narratives of Luke 2, than they are in the Baptist stories (1:5-23, 57-80); and to this extent the hypothesis that the Baptist cycle is basic is supported. The intermediaries are probably women, perhaps those who handed down the L tradition. It has often been conjectured that the ultimate authority for the birth stories is Mary the Virgin, and support for this view is afforded by the delicacy of the narratives and by 2:19: "Mary kept all these things, pondering them in her heart," and 2:51: "He went down with them and came to Nazareth, and was obedient to them; and his mother kept all these things in her heart." This suggestion must remain conjectural, since it depends for its force upon the view taken of the historical value of the birth and infancy tradition. The date when this tradition first became a matter of general knowledge in the church is the period A.D. 60-80. How much older it is, we do not know.

How Luke has used the four sources described above is a question upon which opinion is divided. The generally accepted view is that Mark forms the framework of the gospel, into which, mainly at two points, Luke introduced the matter he drew from Q and L, prefacing the whole with the birth and infancy section and inserting his special tradition in the passion and resurrection narrative. The two sections in the body of the gospel in which non-Markan material has been introduced are 6:20–8:3; 9:51–18:14, the so-called "lesser" and "greater interpolations." How far this construction is sound depends on the view taken of the Proto-Luke hypothesis, of which some account must now be given. *See* SYNOPTIC PROBLEM.

6. Proto-Luke. Although the existence of Proto-Luke is disputed, a summary statement of the hypothesis must be supplied, in view of its wide acceptance and the probability that, in some form or other, it represents a stage in the composition of the Third Gospel. Proto-Luke is not a lost gospel, but a first draft on which, it is presumed, Luke drew when composing his gospel. According to the hypothesis, he began with Q and expanded it with material from L and an account of the Passion and the Resurrection. Later he enlarged it with many longer or shorter extracts from Mark, with the birth stories, and with the Preface to the gospel. The hypothesis is represented by the formula: (Q + L) + Mark + the birth stories + the Preface = Luke.

For a detailed account of this hypothesis, reference must be made to the textbooks. Here only a brief summary of the main points can be offered.

As already observed, the Q passages in the gospel are constantly combined with material from L, but Q and the Markan passages stand apart. The presumption is that Q + L represents a stage antecedent to the composition of the gospel. This part of the hypothesis would be widely conceded.

The Markan sections in Luke, which consist of larger or shorter extracts, do not form a whole, but appear to be inserted in non-Markan contexts (Q + L). The same structure is present in the eschatological discourse (Luke 21) and in the passion narrative (Luke 22–24). If this is so, Proto-Luke is an original entity. This view would not necessarily be inconsistent with the widespread opinion that Mark supplies the ground plan of the gospel.

The non-Markan parts of Luke form a readable whole with a continuity of their own.

If Luke expanded Proto-Luke, we see why he omitted so much of Mark. He passed by material to which he already had parallel or similar versions.

The sixfold date in 3:1-2 and the position of the genealogy in 3:23-38 are intelligible if they stood at the beginning of Proto-Luke, and the statement in the Preface, that the evangelist has "followed all things closely for some time past" (or better, "from the beginning"), is in harmony with the hypothesis.

The passages which, it is suggested, belonged to Proto-Luke include: 3:1–4:30; 5:1-11; 6:20–8:3; 9:51–18:14; 19:1-28, 37-44, 47-48; 22:14–24:53 (minus the Markan insertions). (*See* § 3*f above.*) The obvious difficulties of the hypothesis are the gaps between 8:3 and 9:51 and before 22:14. Whether 21:20-38 formed part of Proto-Luke cannot be demonstrated, and the same is true of the original introduction to the passion narrative, which, apparently, the Markan passage, Luke 22:1-13, has replaced. In general, one must say that the hypothesis has suffered from attempts to determine too precisely the contents of Proto-Luke, especially in the passion narrative; but that Q + L had been compiled before the gospel was written has much probability. If this is so, the importance of Proto-Luke, as a source slightly earlier than Mark and comparable with it, is great; and we have a broader basis for the gospel tradition and a better insight into Luke's methods as an evangelist.

7. Date. The date is not easy to determine, but most is to be said for a date *ca.* A.D. 80. The main competing views are as follows:

a) A date *ca.* A.D. 60 was suggested by A. Harnack as a consequence of his submission that Acts was compiled shortly after Paul's imprisonment for two years in his "hired house" (RSV "at his own expense") in Rome (Acts 28:30-31). The difficulty in accepting this date is that it compels us to assign Luke-Acts to a period earlier than the contents of these writings would naturally suggest, and to date Mark as early as 50-60. Mark 13:14 suggests that the investment of Jerusalem by the Romans was imminent, and this circumstance makes it impossible to date Mark earlier than *ca.* 65-67. If this opinion is accepted, the composition of Luke must be later.

b) Many scholars have held that Luke is indebted to Josephus, who wrote his *Jewish War* before the death of Vespasian in 79 and his *Antiquities* in 93. If this is so, the gospel must be dated *ca.* 100. Luke's language, it is held, reflects the vocabulary and style of Josephus. In particular, it is argued, he was misled by what Josephus wrote about LYSANIAS (Luke 3:1) and THEUDAS (Acts 5:36-37). As regards the former, to whom Luke refers in the phrase "Lysanias tetrarch of Abilene," we now know from an inscription that there was a younger Lysanias, and Luke's statement is thus correct. The difficulty in the allusion to Theudas is less easily met, but even if Luke is guilty of an anachronism, it is far from probable that he was misled by what he read in Jos. Antiq. XX.v.1, where Josephus speaks of a revolt under Theudas when Fadus was procurator of Judea (A.D. 44-46). The linguistic argument for dependence upon the works of Josephus is held by very many scholars to be "not proven" or "not quite conclusive." It does not seem necessary, therefore, to date the gospel at the end of the first century.

c) The commonly accepted view, that in consequence of his use of Mark, Luke's Gospel belongs to the period 70-80, must be held to stand. It is often argued that Luke 21:20: "When you see Jerusalem surrounded by armies, then know that its desolation has come near," is a conscious modification of Mark 13:14: "When you see the desolating sacrilege set up where it ought not to be (let the reader understand), then let those who are in Judea flee to the mountains." If this plea is accepted, the date must be subsequent to 68-70. It does not seem necessary to take this view of Luke 21:20 in the light of other references to the fate of the city (Luke 13:34-35; 19:41-44); but, in any case, a date after the fall of Jerusalem seems probable, and toward the end of the decade 70-80 rather than earlier. The use of the name "the Lord" for Jesus and the development of the tradition as it appears in the Acts, in the account of the Apostolic Council (Acts 15) and in other narratives, support this view. It should be remembered, however, that while the actual composition of the gospel is comparatively late, it draws upon much earlier sources, which, we have maintained, were used with fidelity.

8. Place of writing. Where the gospel was written we do not know. The Anti-Marcionite Prologue mentions Achaea. This tradition is attested by Gregory of Nazianzus (*Oratio* 23.11) and is reflected by Jerome (Preface to Matthew), but there are no strong arguments in its favor. The further tradition, that Luke was buried at Thebes in Boeotia, throws no light upon the place of composition. The probability that Luke first read the Gospel of Mark at Rome, and the possibility that one of the reasons Luke-Acts was written was to present the case for Christianity (*see* § 2 *above*) support the Roman origin of the Third Gospel. It is also consistent with this suggestion that Acts describes the expansion of Christianity from Jerusalem to Rome, reaching its climax in the reference to Paul's preaching and teaching in Rome "quite openly and unhindered" (28:30-31). These arguments do not amount to demonstration, and no more can be said than that of all suggestions regarding the place of writing the view that the Gospel of Luke was written at Rome is the most probable.

9. Canonicity. The gospel has been included among the books recognized as authoritative in the church from the time when the NT writings first began to be collected and regarded as scripture (*see* CANON OF THE NT). As is true of all the gospels, its history in the first half of the second century is obscure. Some scholars think that it is quoted in the letter of Clement of Rome to the church at Corinth written *ca.* 95, but the echoes of gospel tradition in this writing are uncertain; and the same is true of alleged quotations in Ignatius, Polycarp, Barnabas, and the Didache in the opening decades of the second century. It is more widely agreed that Marcion (*ca.* 140) abbreviated Luke's Gospel in forming his canon, although some scholars prefer to think that he used an earlier form of the gospel on which also Luke depends. With Justin Martyr (*ca.* 150) the situation becomes clearer, for by general consent he drew upon all the Synoptic gospels in writing his *Apologies*. The Anti-Marcionite Prologue (A.D. 170) alludes to the composition of the gospel by Luke and says: "Afterwards the same Luke wrote the Acts of the Apostles." The same testimony is given by the Muratorian Canon (A.D. 170-200), as we have seen (§ 1 *above*), while Tatian, the pupil of Justin Martyr, used all four gospels in forming his gospel harmony known as the *Diatessaron* (A.D. 170). Irenaeus (*ca.* 185) not only speaks of the composition of the gospel by Luke, but attests the existence of the fourfold gospel canon by curious arguments from the four quarters of the world, the four universal winds, and the fourfold shape of the cherubim. Among other things he says: "The Gospel according to Luke, as having a sacerdotal character, begins with Zacharias the priest offering incense to God" (Her. III.11.8). At the end of the second century the gospel occupied an undisputed place among the books recognized as scripture by all parts of the Christian church.

It is not necessary to proceed further than the period covered by the testimonies of Irenaeus, Tertullian, and Clement of Alexandria. When councils spoke, the gospel had already established itself in the usage of the church, and it is universally accepted by every part of the church today.

10. Text. Several interesting questions arise, some of which are of historical importance, especially in the additions, and still more in the omissions, of Codex Bezae (D), the chief authority for the text current in many quarters, both in the East and in the West, in the second century A.D.

The additions consist of the following:

a) After 6:4, D reads: "On the same day beholding a certain man working on the sabbath day he said to him, 'Man, if you know what you are doing, blessed are you; but if you do not know, you are accursed and a transgressor of the law.'" This passage may well be authentic tradition, but it is not part of the original text of the gospel.

b) In 9:55, supported by other MSS and versions, D adds: "And he said, 'You do not know of what spirit you are.' " In this case there is a greater possibility that the passage is original. The same may also be true of the addition in vs. 54: "as Elijah did" (A C D etc.).

c) In 11:2-4 (the Lord's Prayer), besides smaller additions ("Our Father who art in heaven" instead of the vocative "Father"), D reads: "Let thy kingdom come upon us." Two other MSS (700 and 162) read: "Let thy Holy Spirit come upon us." Some scholars think that this reading is original and that it has support in D. The reference to the Holy Spirit, whose activity is a characteristic interest of Luke, may be held to support this view, but on the whole it is more likely to be a liturgical expansion of the text.

d) In 23:38, with the support of Codex Sinaiticus, Codex Alexandrinus, and many early versions, D adds the phrase: "in letters of Greek and Latin and Hebrew," but this reading is probably an assimilation to the text of John 19:20.

e) In 23:53 a picturesque, but probably not original, addition is made by D in the words: "And when he laid him there, he had a stone placed before the tomb that twenty men could scarcely roll."

The omissions of Codex Bezae are of more importance than the additions, since the tendency of this MS is to add rather than to omit. Among the principal omissions are the following:

a) 5:39: "And no one after drinking old wine desires new; for he says, 'The old is better.' "

b) 7:7*a:* "Therefore I did not presume to come to you."

c) 10:42: "Few things are needful, or only one."

d) 11:35-36: "Therefore be careful lest the light in you be darkness. If then your whole body is full of light, having no part dark, it will be wholly bright, as when a lamp with its rays gives you light."

e) 12:19: "laid up for many years; take your ease, eat, drink."

f) 19:25: "And they said to him, 'Lord, he has ten pounds!' "

g) 22:19*b*-20: " 'which is given for you. Do this in remembrance of me.' And likewise the cup after supper, saying, 'This cup which is poured out for you is the new covenant in my blood.' "

h) 24:6: "He is not here, but has risen."

i) 24:12: "But Peter rose and ran to the tomb; stooping and looking in, he saw the linen cloths by themselves; and he went home wondering at what had happened."

j) 24:36: "And said to them, 'Peace to you!' "

k) 24:40: "And when he had said this, he showed them his hands and his feet."

l) 24:51: "and was carried up into heaven."

m) 24:52: "worshiped him, and."

In most of these omissions Codex Bezae is supported by important OL MSS and often by the Old Syr. version, Marcion, and Tatian. The tendency of textual critics and commentators is to reject these passages. Those in ch. 24, along with 22:19*b*-20, are assigned to the margin by the RSV. Westcott and Hort enclose them in double square brackets and describe them as "Western non-interpolations." A better name would be "Alexandrian" or "Neutral insertions." Recently a more favorable estimate has been formed of some of these passages, notably 22:19*b*-20; 24:51. The former, which belongs to the longer text of the narrative of the institution of the Lord's Supper, is accepted as original by a number of scholars, but is still rejected as based on Mark 14:24; I Cor. 11:24-25, by very many others. 24:51: "and was carried up into heaven," the only allusion to the Ascension in the Synoptic gospels, is also accepted by many who suggest that it may have been canceled because it does not harmonize with the forty days' interval mentioned in Acts 1:3.

Two other passages must be mentioned because they are omitted by a number of MSS: 22:43-44, which describes the agony and bloody sweat, and 23:34: "And Jesus said, 'Father, forgive them; for they know not what they do.' " The former is omitted by Codex Vaticanus (B) and the Washington Codex (W), and by many other authorities, but its Lukan characteristics suggest that it is original, its omission being due to the feeling that it was derogatory to the full divinity of Christ. The latter, which is omitted by many of the same MSS, is recognized as containing genuine tradition by many who reject its authenticity. It should probably be read, since it may well have been omitted because in the second century some found it difficult to believe that God could, or ought to, forgive the Jews. Both passages are read by the RSV with notes in the margin.

It will be seen that the textual problems of the Third Gospel are as interesting as they are difficult. The difficulties are enhanced by the fact that Marcion often agrees with Codex Bezae in the omissions listed above, and it is hard to determine how far Marcion is a witness to the original text and how far his omissions are deliberate cancellations. Where it is not possible to show that the omissions represent his known doctrinal views, he should be regarded as an early and valuable witness to the original text of Luke. *See* TEXT, NT.

11. The value of Luke. An outstanding feature of the gospel is the variety and extent of its points of value. The close bearing of its use of sources upon historical problems is one of these. When both Mark and Luke record the same incident, we naturally turn to Mark as our primary authority; but Luke's version is always of interest because he is the earliest commentator on that gospel, and because we can trace the influence of his special interests upon all that he writes. Luke's Gospel, along with that of Matthew, is the starting point for any useful study of Q, and it is also a mirror in which we can faintly see stages behind the compilation of that source.

His special tradition, however, is the theme of greatest interest on the critical side, for the artistry of his writing should not be allowed to conceal from us the wealth of the early tradition he records. There is doubtless a kind of film overshadowing his narratives, so that the rugged character of the earliest tradition is hidden from us. One notices a certain tendency for details from one narrative to pass over to another. Thus, in his account of the Great Commandment (10:25-28) he introduces the question: "Teacher, what shall I do to inherit eternal life?" and there are correspondences between the story of the woman of the city (7:36-50) and that of the anointing at Bethany in Mark (14:3-9) and John (12:1-8). The stories have been shortened and rounded in the course of transmission and developed by Luke's art, so that in them there is a combination of simplicity and directness with a certain vagueness of outline.

The textual value of Luke has been sufficiently indicated. Luke-Acts is the gateway to many textual studies.

The charm and literary value of the gospel will always be highly esteemed, and it is not surprising that later tradition speaks of the evangelist as an artist. Perhaps the greatest service of the gospel is its value to the preacher, in its broad humanity, the beauty of its parables, and its portraiture of Jesus. How much we owe to the statement that "Jesus increased in wisdom and in stature, and in favor with God and man" (2:52)! Each of the gospels has its special dignity and worth. Luke's Gospel will always stand out as that of a "scribe of the gentleness of Christ" (Dante *De Monarchia* 1.16[18]).

Bibliography. Commentaries: A. Plummer, ICC (4th ed., 1908), still of very great value. M.-J. Lagrange (2nd ed., 1921). B. S. Easton (1926). E. Klostermann, *Handbuch zum NT* (2nd ed., 1929). J. Weiss, *Die Schriften des NT* (4th ed., 1929). J. M. Creed (1930). W. Manson, Moffatt NT Commentary (1930). H. K. Luce, Cambridge Greek Testament (1933). S. MacLean Gilmour, *IB*, vol. VIII (1952). See also introductions to literature of the NT by Goodspeed, Moffatt, Jülicher, McNeile, A. S. Peake, F. B. Clogg, E. F. Scott, etc.

Special studies: A. Harnack, *Luke the Physician* (1911); *The Date of Acts and of the Synoptic Gospels* (1911). C. S. Patton, *Sources of the Synoptic Gospels* (1915). J. C. Hawkins, *Horae Synopticae* (1909). H. J. Cadbury, *The Style and Literary Method of Luke* (1919). V. H. Stanton, *The Gospels as Historical Documents,* vols. I-III (1909-20). A. M. Perry, *The Sources of Luke's Passion Narrative* (1920). B. H. Streeter, *The Four Gospels* (1924). E. Meyer, *Ursprung und Anfänge des Christentums,* vol. I (1924). V. Taylor, *Behind the Third Gospel* (1926); *The Gospels* (1930). W. Bussmann, *Synoptische Studien* (1925-31). F. J. Foakes-Jackson and K. Lake, *The Beginnings of Christianity,* vols. I-V (1920-33). J. H. Ropes, *The Synoptic Gospels* (1934). V. Taylor, *The Formation of the Gospel Tradition* (2nd ed., 1935). J. Knox, *Marcion and the NT* (1942). C. S. C. Williams, *Alterations to the Text of the Synoptic Gospels and Acts* (1951). V. Taylor, "The Order of Q," *JTS,* N.S., IV (1953), 27-31. J. Huby, *L'Évangile et les Évangiles* (new ed. by Xavier Léon-Dufour; 1954). L. Vaganay, *Le problème synoptique* (1954). A. Farrer, "On Dispensing with Q," in D. E. Nineham, ed., *Studies in the Gospels* (1955), pp. 55-88. J. Jeremias, *The Eucharistic Words of Jesus* (1955). P. Benoit, "L'Enfance de Jean-Baptiste selon Luc I," *NTS,* III (1957), 169-94. W. L. Knox, *The Sources of the Synoptic Gospels,* vol. II (1957). H. C. Kee and F. W. Young, *Understanding the NT* (1957). V. Taylor, "The Original Order of Q," *NT Essays in Memory of T. W. Manson* (1959), pp. 246-69.
V. TAYLOR

LUMBER. *See* WOOD.

LUNATICK. Once a popular term for "epileptic" (so RSV; *see* EPILEPSY); used by the KJV to translate σεληνιάζεται, σεληνιαζομένους (Mark 4:24; 17:15). The verb from which the Greek word is derived means "to be affected by, or under the influence of, the moon [σελήνη]." In the same way, "lunatick" is derived from Latin *lūna,* "moon."

In 4:24 Matthew uses σεληνιαζομένους in a series with δαιμονιζομένους, as if a distinction from demon-possession was being indicated; but in 17:15 the epilepsy is cured when the demon is expelled. So the use in series in 4:24 is popular and inexact, and does not exclude possession. Probably the popular belief was that the influence of the moon had caused a DEMON to enter.

Matt. 17:15 should be compared with the earlier account in Mark 9:17, which says that the boy has a "dumb spirit." Luke 9:39 attributes the ailment to a spirit which seizes the child.

The popular conception among the Greeks is described by Hippocrates *The Sacred Disease* I; Lucian of Samosata *Lover of Lies* 16.

Bibliography. S. V. McCasland, *By the Finger of God* (1951), pp. 32-38.
S. V. MCCASLAND

LUST [נפש, soul as the seat of appetites; תאוה, delight; עגבה, erotic pleasure; ἐπιθυμία, ὄρεξις, *etc.,* desire; θυμός, πάθος, passion]. The biblical terms that are usually translated by this word carry the meaning of "passionate desire," especially "sexual desire," or "desire for worldly pleasures."

In the OT the root עגב, "to have inordinate sensuous love," is related largely to the entire community of Israel or to other nations, in the context of religious PROSTITUTION and sexual corruption. Other figures are also used to convey the idea of "lust." Babylon is said to be "wanton as a heifer at grass" and to "neigh like stallions" in heat (Jer. 50:11). Although such usage represents the personification of the nations concerned, it undoubtedly reflects the experience of personal lust also.

The NT has words for "lusts," "passion," "burn with sexual desire," and the like (θυμός, πυρόω). A man must not look lustfully at a woman (Matt. 5:28); wicked men dishonor their bodies among themselves in the lusts of their hearts (Rom. 1:24). Passion and evil desire are to be put to death (Col. 3:5); and the believer should take a wife in holiness and honor, not in a heathenish passion of lust (I Thess. 4:4-5). Timothy is advised to shun youthful passions (II Tim. 2:22), for desire produces sin and sin death (Jas. 1:14-15). Believers are urged to set an example by abstaining from passions of the flesh (I Pet. 2:11-12); they are to live no longer by human passions but by the will of God (4:2). Lust and defiling passion produce corruption and evil in the world (II Pet. 1:4; 2:10; cf. 2:13-14, 18, 20-22).

See also SEX; HOMOSEXUALITY. O. J. BAAB

LUSTRATION. The cultic act of purification as by propitiatory sacrifice or ritual washing. *See* CLEAN AND UNCLEAN; SACRIFICE AND OFFERINGS.

LUTE. *See* MUSICAL INSTRUMENTS.

LUZ lŭz [לוז]. **1.** The early name of the Canaanite city renamed BETHEL by Jacob (Gen. 28:19; 35:6). Jacob later recalled to Joseph the appearance of El Shaddai to him at Luz. In the definition of the boundary of Benjamin, Luz is mentioned and identified as Bethel (Josh. 18:13; see also Judg. 1:23). A later commentary on Jacob's experience makes the same identification (Jub. 27:19, 26).

Josh. 16:2 merits special consideration because it contains the expression "from Bethel to Luz" (מבית אל לוזה), as if two different cities existed at the same time on the N border of Joseph. More probably the two names in this passage refer to a single city, which we might designate as Bethel-Luz (cf. a LXX variant reading εἰς βαιθηλ Λουζα).

With a theory that Luz and Bethel were originally distinct towns, Luz has been located by some scholars at et-Tell, near Bethel. A city by the name of *Rwś* (for *Lwś*) appears in the list of places conquered by Thut-mose III. It has been proposed that this may be Luz, although it may rather be LAISH of Judg. 18:27.

2. A city in the land of the Hittites built by a man from Bethel (Luz) who was spared when the Israelites conquered Bethel (Judg. 1:26). The location of the city might be any place in Syria or Lebanon, which were at one time within the great Hittite Empire. W. L. REED

LXX. Abbreviation for SEPTUAGINT.

LYCAONIA lĭk'ĭ ō'nĭ ə, lī'kĭ— [Λυκαονία]; LYCAONIAN —ən. A region in S central Asia Minor. Its borders varied and often do not appear clearly defined, but in general Lycaonia was bounded on the N by GALATIA proper, where the Gauls who invaded Asia Minor had settled; on the E by Cappadocia; on the S by Cilicia (Strabo and others included Isauria in Lycaonia); and on the W by Pisidia and Phrygia. The region was, for the most part, a high, treeless plateau, not well watered and with a more than average salt content in the soil. Strabo says that water was scarce and wells were deep in Lycaonia (*Geography* XII.6.1). The vegetation, however, proved suitable for sheep-raising; and when Amyntas was king, he had three hundred flocks in this region.

The origin of the Lycaonians is uncertain. These wild and warlike people were able to keep free of Persian domination, but from Alexander the Great's time they were under outside control. The Seleucids ruled the region until Antiochus the Great was defeated by the Romans at Magnesia (190 B.C.). The Romans gave Lycaonia to the king of Pergamum, but actually continued to exercise ultimate control over the area. The N portion came to be united with Galatia, the E part with Cappadocia, and the S part with Cilicia. This last part was given to Polemon in 39 B.C. and soon after, in 36 B.C., was given to Amyntas, king of Pisidia, who was then made king of Galatia. On his death in 25 B.C. the Romans took over his kingdom and made it the province of Galatia. Thus Lycaonia, except for an E section which had been given to Antiochus of Commagene and was thereafter called Lycaonia Antiochiana, was during the apostolic age a part of Galatia. Later, Galatia and Cappadocia were combined for a time; and in the second century A.D., Lycaonia, Isauria, and Cilicia were united in one province.

Lystra and Derbe were leading cities of Lycaonia. Iconium was in earlier times considered Phrygian, and in the apostolic age was sometimes reckoned as part of Phrygia. This usage seems implied in Acts 14:5-6, where Paul fled from Iconium to Lystra and Derbe, and only these two latter cities are called "cities of Lycaonia."

Under the Seleucid rulers the Hellenization of Lycaonia, especially in the main cities, made some progress. The Lycaonian language did not die out, however; for when Paul healed the crippled man at Lystra, the crowd, either because most of them normally spoke Lycaonian or because in their excitement they fell back into the use of their native tongue, cried out in Lycaonian that "the gods have come down to us in the likeness of men" (Acts 14:8-11). Little is known of the Lycaonian language. The fact that Paul could preach in Greek and be understood shows that Greek was common in Lycaonian cities.

The book of Acts clearly reports the presence of

aggressive Jews at Pisidian Antioch and Iconium, but gives little evidence of a Jewish community at Lystra and Derbe. The one event reported on Paul's first visit to Lystra (Acts 14:8-18) reflects the continued vitality of pagan religion there; nothing is told of the religious situation Paul found at Derbe, except that he made many disciples there. However, since Timothy came from Lystra and his mother was a Jewess (16:1-3), it seems clear that there were Jews in Lystra; moreover, the influence of Jews of Antioch and Iconium on people at Lystra must have had a point of contact through Jews of Lystra (14:19). Such a conclusion would go well with the fact that there were large numbers of Jews in Asia Minor, and that Paul's regular practice was to preach to Jews first.

Paul visited cities in Lycaonia at least three times. In Acts 13-14 he and Barnabas came from Pisidian Antioch and Iconium to Lystra and Derbe, and then retraced their route to Pisidian Antioch and returned through Pamphylia to Syrian Antioch. In 16:1-5, Paul and Silas, after leaving Tarsus in Cilicia and passing through the Cilician Gates to reach the high tablelands of central Asia Minor, strengthened the churches of Derbe and Lystra and took Timothy, who probably had been converted on the earlier visit, as a helper on their further missionary journeys. In 18:23 the route of Paul when he left Syrian Antioch is not clearly indicated. Probably he again went up the road through the Cilician Gates and passed through Lycaonia, revisiting the churches there. This is certain if the reference to Galatia, as seems probable, means the Roman province of Galatia and has in view the S Galatian churches of Antioch, Iconium, Lystra, and Derbe.

Christian inscriptions show that the church had made great headway in Lycaonia by the third century.

Bibliography. W. M. Ramsay, *A Historical Commentary on St. Paul's Epistle to the Galatians* (1900); A. H. M. Jones, *Cities of the Eastern Roman Provinces* (1937), ch. 5. F. V. Filson

LYCIA lĭsh′ĭ ə [Λυκία]. A rugged, mountainous district in SW Asia Minor. It is bounded on the NW by Caria; on the N by Phrygia and Pisidia; on the NE by Pamphylia; and on the E, S, and W by the Lycian Sea, which is a N portion of the Mediterranean.

The fertile valleys of the Xanthus and other streams supported a highly civilized and politically capable group of cities, whose federation continued strong through centuries and to a great extent preserved freedom even under foreign rulers. Lycia was ruled by the Persians, Alexander the Great, and the Seleucid and Ptolemaic dynasties before the power of Rome began to be felt. Then, after a period of indirect and loose control, the Emperor Claudius in A.D. 43 made Lycia a Roman province. This arrangement lasted but a short time, and Lycia was perhaps free again for a few years. Later, in 74, Vespasian united it with Pamphylia in a more clearly defined provincial organization. Throughout its pre-Roman history, however, the Lycians, even when subject to foreign powers, retained their unity as a federation of cities, and this local vigor continued under the Romans.

Among the important ports of Lycia were Myra (Acts 27:5) and Patara (21:1; some MSS include here a stop at Myra also). These references call attention to two features of first-century sea travel: (*a*) These Lycian ports were natural stopover points for ships carrying Jews from ports in the W Mediterranean or from the Aegean Sea to Jerusalem for Jewish feasts. (*b*) Alexandrian grain ships, when the prevailing winds were from the W, worked N past Palestine and Syria, often going E of Cyprus, and used shore winds to work westward along the S coast of Asia Minor; this would make the ports of Lycia natural ports of call.

The letter the Romans sent to the confederation of Lycian cities *ca.* 139 B.C. to urge good treatment of the Jews (I Macc. 15:23) shows that there were Jews in at least the important cities of Lycia. The book of Acts gives no hint of Christian churches in Lycia, and I Pet. 1:1 likewise offers no suggestion of the early spread of Christianity there. A petition against the Christians was directed by Lycians to the Emperor Maximin in A.D. 312. This act suggests that Christianity was then known in Lycia but was actively opposed.

Bibliography. Strabo *Geography* XIV.3.2-10; *Cambridge Ancient History*, XI (1936), 590-97; A. H. M. Jones, *The Cities of the Eastern Roman Provinces* (1937), ch. 3; D. Magie, *Roman Rule in Asia Minor* (1950), pp. 516-39. F. V. Filson

LYDDA. *See* Lod.

LYDIA lĭd′ĭ ə [Λυδία, *see below*]. A woman from Thyatira in Asia Minor whom Paul met at Philippi. Perhaps her name had originally been an adjective—"a woman of Lydia"—for Thyatira was a Lydian city. Her name occurs only in a narrative in Acts 16:11-40; Paul does not refer to her. Possibly, though not probably, she was a Jewess: the conclusion depends on whether the words "a worshiper of God" (Acts 16:14) are here a technical expression designating a non-Jew worshiping in the synagogue.

Lydia sold purple-dyed goods which she had brought to Philippi from Thyatira—a city which, like all the land of Lydia, was famous for its dyeing. Its guild of dyers is known from inscriptions. She was apparently well-to-do, for a considerable amount of capital was needed to trade in such articles.

Lydia heard and conversed with Paul; and eventually (Acts does not say when) she and her household were baptized. At her urging Paul and his companions stayed in her house. Her hospitality thus relieved the apostle of the necessity of earning his living in Philippi, as he was required to do elsewhere. Not only was Paul taken care of when he was in Philippi, but we know from his letters that he accepted gifts from the Philippian church when he was at other churches (cf. II Cor. 11:8; Phil. 4:16). He thus permitted the church there to support him as he did not allow any other church to do (Phil. 4:15).

Paul's Letter to the Philippians reveals his special love for their church (cf. 1:3-8; 2:12, 15-16; 4:1, 15-16, 18); and Lydia's help must have been a chief cause of this unique relationship.

Bibliography. W. W. Ramsay, *St. Paul the Traveller* (1896), pp. 214-15. F. W. Foakes-Jackson and K. Lake, *Beginnings of Christianity* (1933), IV; V, pp. 86-87.
B. H. Throckmorton, Jr.

LYDIA (PLACE) [Λυδία]. A country in SW Asia Minor which received its name from an old component in the population of the peninsula, the Lydians. Its territory lies mostly in river valleys. To the N it extends beyond the Hermus (modern Gediz); it includes the Cayster Valley (modern Küçük Menderes) and is bordered on the S by the Meander (modern Büyük Menderes). Its W border varies with the development of Greek colonization along the coasts of Asia Minor. The Lydians never seem to have been interested in naval expansion. They quarreled with the Greek cities on the coast, but their own strength lay inland, as is demonstrated by the location of their capital, SARDIS, deep in the Hermus Valley. The borders to the E were disputed with the Phrygians.

1. History
   a. Prehistory
   b. Hittite period
   c. Lydian kingdom
   d. Persian period
   e. Hellenistic and Roman times
2. Language
3. Art and industries
4. Religion
Bibliography

1. History. ***a. Prehistory.*** In prehistoric times the region belonged to a culture which, though part of a larger Anatolian complex, developed local traits typical of W Asia Minor. Little excavation has taken place so far for the preclassical periods. Indications point to a contrast between a conservative inland element and a more active coastal region where commerce and warfare had more scope.

b. Hittite period. In the records of the Hittite Empire no specific references to the Lydian region can be identified, although there is some probability in a theory which localizes Ashshuwa (later Asia) in Lydia. Rock-cut monuments of the Hittite period exist in two Lydian sites: the "Niobe," an image of a seated goddess near Magnesia ad Sipylum; and the reliefs of a warrior (god?) near Karabel which Herodotus mentions (II.106). Both reliefs are inscribed in Hittite hieroglyphs. They show that the Lydian area was exposed to Hittite cultural penetration, although we have to distinguish regional variants in this period as much as in the third millennium.

c. Lydian kingdom. Our direct historical information begins after the fall of the Bronze Age empires and the subsequent dark ages. Lydia then appears in Assyrian, Persian, and Greek texts. The most extensive account is found in Herodotus (I.6-86); but more reliable chronological inferences can be drawn from Assyrian sources. Herodotus mentions a Heraclid Dynasty whose last king, Candaules-Myrsilos, was ousted by the historical figure of Gyges, founder of the Mermnad Dynasty.

Gyges ruled *ca.* 685-652 B.C. Under him, Lydia gathered considerable strength as an independent country. Gyges attacked Greek cities on the coast and maintained friendly relations with Delphi. To the E, his country was threatened by the raids of the Cimmerians (*see* GOMER) in Asia Minor. In this emergency Gyges entered into contact with Ashurbanipal (*ca.* 668 B.C.), in whose Annals the Lydian king is referred to as Guggu of Luddu (Rassam Cylinder II.95; *see* GOG). The Lydian ambassador caused embarrassment in Nineveh, where nobody understood his language. Previous contact of the Assyrians with Asia Minor had been via the Mushki-Phrygians (*see* MESHECH), whose power had been destroyed by the Cimmerians. The Assyrians may have aided Gyges indirectly. The Lydian king succeeded in defeating the Cimmerians and sent two prisoners with presents to Ashurbanipal. Soon he felt no longer obliged to continue his respects and sought an alliance with Psammetichus I of Egypt, whom he sent troops to help liberate Egypt from Assyria (*ca.* 654 B.C.). *See* LUD.

The Cimmerians ransacked Lydia after this, and Gyges died in these raids. His son Ardys (*ca.* 652-615 B.C.) restored good relations with Assyria. The Cimmerians were still active during his rule and that of his successor Sadyattes (*ca.* 615-605); but Alyattes (605-560) finally expelled them from Lydia. In the meantime the Indo-European migrations had brought the Scythians and Medes into action in Asia Minor. The Medes under Cyaxares rose to power as a major adversary of Alyattes. After several battles (during one of which an eclipse was observed—May 28, 585 B.C.) peace was established, whereby the Halys River became the border between the Lydian and the Median empires. The power of Lydia had extended far beyond its original limits, to include what used to belong to Phrygia. Lydia entered an international phase: the peace with Cyaxares was mediated by the kings of Cilicia and Babylonia; and a daughter of Alyattes was married to Astyages, son of Cyaxares.

The most famous of Lydian kings, Croesus (560-546 B.C.), appeared to Greek historians as the prototype of a wealthy oriental monarch. His intensive contacts with the Greeks in Asia Minor led to their vassalage and his Hellenization. His gifts to Delphi were spectacular; and his support to Greek culture in Asia Minor is exemplified in his subsidy to the building of the archaic temple of Artemis at Ephesus, on which his name is preserved.

d. Persian period. The Persians, successors to the Median Empire, proved too strong for the Lydian kingdom. After an undecided battle between Cyrus and Croesus, E of the Halys, Cyrus pursued the unsuspecting Lydians W and captured Sardis in 546 B.C. This meant the end of political independence for Lydia, which until 334 B.C. figured as a satrapy of the Persian Empire, with the satrap's residence established at Sardis. The Persians again separated the important satrapy of Lydia from the coastal strip, which was the satrapy of Ionia. The Hellenization of Lydia continued under Persian rule; but as a considerable number of Persians resided in the capital, Achaemenian culture was blended with the old Greek elements.

e. Hellenistic and Roman times. After the Battle of the Granicus in 334 B.C., Lydia fell to Alexander the Great, who restored some of its cultural autonomy. In the Hellenistic period Lydia at first belonged to the Seleucids, but as a result of the defeat of Antiochus III at Magnesia in 190 B.C., it was given to the Pergamene Dynasty. This battle and its conse-

Courtesy of Machteld J. Mellink

39. Mountain pass in the territory of ancient Lydia, showing a Hittite relief of Karabel

quences for Lydia are reported on in I Macc. 8:8. In 133 B.C. Lydia was bequeathed to Rome by the testament of Attalus III.

Under the Roman emperors Lydia was prosperous as a part of the province of Asia, to which Mysia, Phrygia, and Caria also belonged. Lydia did not become a separate entity again until the reign of Diocletian, who made Lydia a district of the dioecesis Asiana, with Sardis as its capital (after A.D. 297).

2. Language. The Lydian language is insufficiently known, although a good number of inscriptions were found at Sardis. It may well be an old Indo-European idiom. From the royal names of Myrsilos, Sadyattes, and Alyattes one may gather that the period of the Lydian kingdom had linguistic ties with the second millennium, when Murshilis was a Hittite royal name and names in *-attes* (e.g., Maduwattash) appeared in W Asia Minor. The Lydians thus seem to represent part of the Bronze Age heritage in the peninsula, rather than an intrusive element.

Fig. LYD 39.

3. Art and industries. Lydian art, so far as known especially from the excavations at Sardis, is strongly influenced by E Greek and Persian styles. In architecture and metallurgy one notices excellent craftsmanship and a taste for the luxurious. The wealth of Croesus was proverbial; ancient stories told about gold washed down by the Pactolus River; the amount of gold found in Sardis is not inconsiderable, and the dedications by Gyges and Croesus in Delphi were lavish. Lydia established a reputation also for its textile and carpet industries. In Roman times guilds of woolworkers and dyers are known. Lydian perfumes were sold in containers of an elegant shape known as Lydion.

4. Religion. The old cults of Lydia were tenaciously preserved into Roman times. Worship of the Anatolian mother-goddess and a youthful male god is attested under various names, often with Phrygian intrusions into the Lydian stratum. The later rulers of the country introduced various other cults. There was a Jewish element in Lydia, since Antiochus III (223-187 B.C.) probably settled two thousand Jewish families from Babylonia in Lydia and Phrygia (Jos. Antiq. XII.iii.4). Sardis and Thyatira both had Jewish communities in Roman times. The rise of Christianity in Lydia can be measured by the presence of three of the seven churches of Revelation in this country: Thyatira, Sardis, and Philadelphia, called churches of Asia (rather than Lydia) in accordance with the Roman provincial classification.

Bibliography. L. Burchner, J. Keil, and G. Deeters, "Lydia," in Pauly-Wissowa, *Reallexikon der Altertumswissenschaft,* vol. XIII (1927), cols. 2122-2202; J. Friedrich, *Kleinasiatische Sprachdenkmäler* (1932), pp. 108-23; P. Naster, *L'Asie Mineure et l'Assyrie aux VIIIe et VIIe siècles avant Jésus-Christ* (1938), pp. 91-98; H. T. Bossert, *Altanatolien* (1942), figs. 141-98, 557-62; D. Magie, *Roman Rule in Asia Minor* (1950), pp. 45-50; A. Goetze, *Kleinasien,* Kulturgeschichte des alten Orients, vol. III, no. 1 (1957), pp. 206-9. M. J. MELLINK

LYE [בר (Job 9:30; Isa. 1:25; *cf.* KJV); נתר (Jer. 2:22; KJV NITRE)]. A substance used for cleansing purposes. נתר is, no doubt, Greek νίτρον or Latin *natrum,* in which case it may have been sodium carbonate. This occurs naturally and is referred to by ancient writers as appearing in Egypt and Armenia. However, it may also have referred to potassium carbonate, a strongly alkaline solution made from wood ashes or other vegetable matter. In Palestine it was probably the latter, since we have no knowledge of natural deposits of sodium carbonate in this part of the world.

Both potassium carbonate and sodium carbonate possess excellent detergent qualities and would have been suitable for washing purposes.

The putting of vinegar on such an alkali (Prov. 25:20) would render it useless; hence the RSV is probably correct in rejecting the Hebrew and following the Greek text at this point ("wound").

H. N. RICHARDSON

LYING. The sin of speaking or acting falsely, deceitfully, or treacherously. It may occur with or without deliberate intent.

There are a number of terms which suggest "lying": in the Hebrew, כזב ("falsehood"), שקר ("deception"), שוא ("vanity"), כחש ("disappointment"), בגד ("treachery"), and derivatives of רמה ("beguile"); in the Greek, ψεῦδος ("falsehood"), δόλος ("craftiness"), πλάνη ("error"), and ideas associated with the verbs δολιόω ("deceive"), ἀπατάω ("beguile"), and παραλογίζομαι ("cheat").

In Hebrew thought, lying appears as a spiritual distortion which does violence to a man's true being, to his communal relations, and to his standing with God. Although in the NT it is construed more in intellectual terms, it retains its religious character as opposition to God's saving TRUTH. Since God (Num. 23:19; I Sam. 15:29; Rom. 3:4) and Christ (John 1:17; 14:6) are absolutely true and bring the truth, and since "no lie is of the truth" (I John 2:21), it follows that falsehood is ultimately attributed to the devil (John 8:44).

As truthfulness is admonished in God's people, lying and all deceit are forbidden (cf. Zech. 8:16-17; Col. 3:9). A heinous sin is the bearing of false witness (Exod. 20:16; Deut. 19:18; etc.; cf. ψευδομαρτυρία in Mark 14:56-57, etc.).

Diviners and prophets who bring false oracles are frequently condemned (e.g., Isa. 9:15—H 9:14; Jer. 14:14; 23:25-26; 28:15; Ezek. 13:6-7; 21:29—H 21:34; 22:28; Mic. 2:11; Zech. 10:2; 13:3). Because they are vain and deceitful, idols are spoken of as "lies"

(Ps. 40:4 KJV—H 40:5; Isa. 44:9 ff, especially vs. 20; Jer. 10:14; Amos 2:4; Hab. 2:18; Rom. 1:25).
S. J. De Vries

LYRE. *See* Musical Instruments.

LYSANIAS lī sā'nī əs [Λυσανίας]. The Tetrarch of Abilene. When Luke (3:1-2) introduces John the Baptist, he fixes the date by mentioning the fifteenth year of the Roman emperor Tiberius, the procuratorship of Pilate, the tetrarchies of Herod (Antipas) and of Philip, the tetrarchy of Lysanias, and the high priesthood of Annas and Caiaphas.

No other reference to any Lysanias in this period (perhaps A.D. 28 or 29) has survived. However, a Lysanias is known from Josephus, though the time factors obstruct identifying these two as the same person; this Lysanias succeeded his father, Ptolemaeus, to the throne of Chalcis and was executed by Mark Antony in 36 B.C. (Antiq. XV.iv.1; Euseb. Chron. I.170, reading Λυσανίου for Λυσιμάχου). On the assumption that there was only this one Lysanias, many responsible scholars have concluded that Luke committed a rather striking error in chronology.

While no other Lysanias is directly mentioned in the sources, there are some scattered data which are used to acquit Luke of error. Thus, Josephus (Antiq. XV.x.1; War I.xx.4) relates that "a certain Zenodorus purchased (leased) the house of Lysanias." Again, an inscription, regrettably partially indistinct, seems to identify this Zenodorus as the son of a Lysanias who lived later than the Lysanias executed by Mark Antony.

Moreover, Abilene, the history of which is obscure, was added to the kingdom of Agrippa II in the time of Claudius (*ca.* A.D. 53). Josephus relates that Claudius bestowed "Abila of Lysanius" upon Agrippa and that Abila ('Αέλλα) had been the "tetrarchy of Lysanias" (Antiq. XIX.v.1; XX.vii.1; see also War II.xi.5). The question can be asked, Is the Lysanias in these latter passages the one who reigned some ninety years earlier? And did his name still attach to the territories, despite a short and undistinguished reign? Or do these passages refer to a second Lysanias? The inscription cited above names both a Lysanias and Zenodorus, the son of Lysanias, though the latter is a partly restored reading. A second inscription increases the probability that there was this second Lysanias; on the inscriptions, *see bibliography.*

If it appears established that there was actually a second Lysanias, then conceivably in the ninety-three years between 40 B.C. and A.D. 53 there could have been even more men who bore this name, and quite conceivably some Lysanias could have been the tetrarch of Abila/Abilene *ca.* A.D. 28-29, and therefore Luke need not be charged with error.

Yet to vindicate Luke, respecting Lysanias, does not in itself eliminate other acute chronological problems in Luke, such as the date of the census of Quirinius or the high priesthood of Annas and Caiaphas. Nor does it answer the enigma which has puzzled many scholars—namely, why should unimportant Abilene have been selected from the various areas near Judea for Luke's chronological purposes? The standard commentaries on Luke supply conjectures which need not be repeated here; the matter remains an enigma.

Bibliography. *Corpus Inscriptionum Graecarum,* no. 4521 (also in Dittenberger, *Orientis Graeci Inscriptiones Selectae,* no. 606), no. 4523. R. Savignac, "Texte complet de l'inscription d'Abila relative a' Lysanias," *RB,* N.S. IX (1912), 533-40. J. M. Creed, "Lysanias, Tetrarch of Abilene," *The Gospel According to St. Luke* (1930), pp. 307-9. The inscriptions are reproduced in E. Schürer, *A History of the Jewish People in the Time of Jesus Christ* (English trans.; 1891), div. 2, vol. II, pp. 335-39. On the possibility of an error in Luke derived from an imprecise use of Josephus, see M. Krenkel, *Josephus und Lucas,* pp. 95-98.
S. Sandmel

LYSIAS (SYRIAN) lĭs'ĭ əs [Λυσίας]. The regent appointed by Antiochus Epiphanes to rule Syria in 166-165 B.C., while he was fighting the Parthians (I Macc. 3:31-37; *see* Antiochus 4). In this capacity Lysias sent Ptolemy, Nicanor, and Gorgias with a large army against Judas Maccabeus. They miserably failed, and the next year Lysias came to attack Judas himself. The accounts in I and II Maccabees conflict with each other, but what probably happened is as follows: Lysias encamped at Beth-zur, S of Jerusalem, and either Judas was successful (I Macc. 4:34-35) in a skirmish with Lysias or it was inconclusive; a peace treaty was signed between them, approved by Antiochus Epiphanes (II Macc. 11), which took away the restrictions on the worship of Judaism. It was a glorious thing for the faithful Jews and led immediately to the cleansing of the temple by Judas from the pollution of the worship of Zeus, and to the inauguration of the Hanukkah Feast. *See* Dedication, Feast of; Hanukkah.

The next year, 164, on the death of Antiochus Epiphanes, Lysias invaded Judea once again, taking with him the boy-king Eupator (*see* Antiochus 5), on whose behalf he was claiming to act as regent. He defeated Judas Maccabeus at Bethzacharia, near Beth-zur, and laid siege to Jerusalem. But just then he heard that a rival for power, a general named Philip, had set himself up in Antioch, and Lysias was compelled to make terms with the Jews and retire. He finally subdued Philip, but he was unable to resist another claimant, Demetrius, and met his own death when Demetrius came to the throne in 162.
N. Turner

LYSIAS, CLAUDIUS klô'dĭ əs [Κλαύδιος Λυσίας] (Acts 23:26). Commander of a cohort (detachment of a thousand) of Roman troops in Jerusalem at the time of Paul's arrest, and apparently military commander there.

He was not a Latin, as his Greek name, Lysias, and his purchase (perhaps by emancipation from slavery) of Roman citizenship (Acts 22:28) indicate. His garrison was quartered in the tower Antonia, NW of the temple area and connected to it by a staircase (Acts 21:35, 40; Jos. War V.v.8).

He rescued Paul from the crowd (Acts 21:31-36; 22:24); discovered his Roman citizenship (22:24-29); had him examined by the Sanhedrin (22:30); and sent him to Caesarea (23:23-33). The wording of his letter to Felix (vss. 26-30) was probably formulated by the author of Acts (note vs. 25: "to this effect").

Bibliography. H. J. Cadbury, *The Book of Acts in History* (1955), pp. 66-68.
W. A. Beardslee

LYSIMACHUS lī sĭm'ə kəs [Λυσίμαχος]. **1.** Son of Ptolemy. He is reported (Add. Esth. 11:1) to have translated the book of Esther into Greek.

2. Brother of the Menelaus who supplanted Jason as high priest. The name had once been borne by a Thessalian general who became one of the successors of Alexander the Great. Menelaus, described as "having the hot temper of a cruel tyrant and the rage of a savage wild beast" (II Macc. 4:25), named "his own brother Lysimachus as deputy in the high priesthood" (vs. 29). With the connivance of Menelaus, Lysimachus personally appropriated some of the temple wealth and committed other acts of sacrilege. When the people became "aroused and filled with anger," Lysimachus sent against them troops to the number of three thousand. He had scarcely reckoned upon the resistance he encountered; "some picked up stones, some blocks of wood, and others took handfuls of the ashes that were lying about, and threw them in wild confusion at Lysimachus and his men. As a result, they wounded many of them, and killed some, and put them all to flight; and the temple-robber himself they killed close by the treasury" (vss. 41-42). J. C. Swaim

LYSTRA lĭs'trə [ἡ Λύστρα, τὰ Λύστρα] (Acts 14:6, 8, 21; 16:1-2; II Tim. 3:11). A town in the central part of S Asia Minor.

Lystra is an ancient site in the district of Lycaonia, the plateau SW of the Salt Lake in central Anatolia. Its nearest important neighbor is Iconium, some twenty miles to the NE; but Iconium, inhabited by Phrygians, was politically rather separate from the region to the S and the SE, where Lystra and Derbe were the most prominent Lycaonian centers.

The Lycaonians were a small Anatolian tribe speaking their own idiom, presumably one of the many surviving Bronze Age languages spoken along the fringe of the Anatolian Plateau. The story of the healing of the crippled man in Lystra (Acts 14:8-11) refers to the popular usage of the Lycaonian language in the days when Greek had become the cosmopolitan idiom. Lycaonian was still spoken in the sixth century A.D.

The site of Lystra has been known with certainty since 1885, when the finding of an inscription confirmed a guess made by Leake as early as 1820 that Lystra was to be sought in a ruined mound slightly

Courtesy of William Sanford La Sor

40. The mound of ancient Lystra

N of Hatunsaray. The mound, variously referred to as Zoldera or Zordula hüyük, is a prehistoric tell with accumulations dating back to the third and second millenniums B.C., but actively inhabited in classical times.* On and around it the city of Lystra must have been located; but no excavations have been made, and some scattered blocks are all that is left of the ancient buildings on the surface. Fig. LYS 40.

The name of Lystra presumably goes back to prehistoric times and can be attributed to the Lycaonian language. The uncertainty of its gender in Greek emphasizes the non-Greek character of the name.

The plain around Lystra is fertile. Two small streams flow N and S of Hatunsaray, and the N one skirts the W side of the mound. The choice of this well-watered site for an early settlement is a logical one, although the location was barely of commercial or strategic advantage. In early history Lystra therefore plays no role. It existed as a rural settlement into Hellenistic and Roman times, much on the lines of many other early villages marked by mounds in the neighborhood. Its vicissitudes under Persian and Hellenistic rule can be inferred from general references to the Lycaonian district, which was subject to the Seleucids (280-189 B.C.) first, then to the Attalids (189-133), and finally to the Romans. For a short time in the first century B.C., Lystra was under control of a local potentate Antipater who ruled from Derbe, but it passed to Amyntas of Galatia until 25 B.C.

Augustus decided to make use of the old but inconspicuous settlement of Lystra to found one of his military colonies as a Roman stronghold against the mountaineers to the S. Lystra thus received some Roman settlers, mostly veterans, and was partly Romanized *ca.* 6 B.C. Its name became Julia Felix Gemina Lustra, as attested on coins and in the inscription which allowed the definite identification of the site (CIL III.6786). Local coinage began under Augustus. This status of a Roman colony allowed Lystra later on to send a statue of Concord to its "sister" colony of Antioch in Pisidia.

The Romanization of the mountainous districts of N Pisidia was also furthered by the construction of roads under Augustus' rule. A branch of the Via Sebaste, which led to Iconium, continued to Lystra. From there a road led to Derbe and the Cilician Gates.

The later history of Lystra is similar to that of Derbe. The two towns were ruled by the client-king Antiochus IV of Commagene (A.D. 38-72), but returned to Roman provincial administration in 72. Antoninus Pius made them part of Cilicia.

The somewhat rustic character of Lystra, in spite of the Roman colonization, is reflected in Acts 14: 6-21. Paul and Barnabas fled the hostility of the Jews at Iconium to Lystra and Derbe. The reaction of the Lycaonian natives of Lystra to the healing of the crippled man must be typical of the local beliefs in epiphanies of the old gods. The reference to the "priest of Zeus, whose temple was in front of the city" (Acts 14:13), is a topographical indication of remains awaiting excavation at the foot of the Zordula mound. At this first visit of Paul the local people of Lystra were friendly until Jews from Antioch and Iconium created disturbances. Timothy of Lystra presumably had been converted before then (II Tim. 3:10-11). Paul and Barnabas left for Derbe, which is *ca.* sixty miles to the SE of Lystra. They probably followed the Roman road from Lystra to Derbe, a road which Paul traveled in the opposite direction, coming from the Cilician Gates, for his second visit to Derbe and Lystra (Acts 16:1).

The coins of Lystra continue into the rule of Marcus Aurelius (161-80). The later history of the site is obscure. There are some listings of bishops, and on the E side of the mound at Lystra there are foundations of a small Byzantine church.

Bibliography. H. S. Cronin, "First Report of a Journey in Pisidia, etc.," *JHS,* XXIV (1904), 121-24; W. M. Ramsay, *The Cities of St. Paul* (1908), pp. 407-18; D. Magie, *Roman Rule in Asia Minor* (1950), pp. 463, 1324.

M. J. MELLINK

M. A symbol used to designate one of the alleged sources of the Gospel of Matthew. *See* SYNOPTIC PROBLEM.

MAACAH mā′ə kə [מעכה, *perhaps* dull, stupid; *see bibliography*]; KJV usually MAACHAH; MAACATHITE mā ăk′ə thīt′; KJV MAACHATHITE; KJV MAACHATHI —thī′ in Deut. 3:14. Alternately: MAACATH mā′ə kăth [מעכת] (Josh. 13:13); ARAM-MAACAH âr′əm— [ארם מעכה, *see* ARAM] (I Chr. 19:6); KJV SYRIA-MAACHAH sĭr′ĭ ə—. **1.** Eponymous ancestor, or a personification, of 10 *below;* a son of Nahor, Abraham's brother (Gen. 22:24).

2. Evidently the wife of Machir (I Chr. 7:16), although called his sister in vs. 15 (the text is corrupt); generally interpreted as a personification of 10 *below* (*see bibliography; also* JABESH-GILEAD § 2).

Bibliography. E. L. Curtis and A. A. Madsen, *Chronicles,* ICC (1910), pp. 151-52.

3. A concubine of Caleb, ancestor of the Calebites (I Chr. 2:48).

4. The wife of Jeiel of Gibeon, an ancestor of Saul (I Chr. 8:29; 9:35).

5. One of King David's wives, and the mother of Absalom (II Sam. 3:3; I Chr. 3:2).

6. The father or an ancestor (if not the town of this name) of Hanan, one of David's Mighty Men (I Chr. 11:43).

7. The father or ancestor of Shephatiah, the chief officer of the tribe of Simeon in David's reign (I Chr. 27:16).

8. The father or ancestor of Achish king of Gath, a contemporary of Solomon (I Kings 2:39).

9. According to I Kings 15:2, the mother of King Abijam of Judah. In vss. 10, 13, she is called the "mother" of Abijam's son King Asa, but the latter reference probably signifies "queen mother," which she had remained after her son's death (cf. vs. 13). She was, moreover, probably the granddaughter, rather than the daughter, of Absalom (Abishalom; cf. I Kings 15:2 with II Chr. 11:20-22; *see bibliography*). MICAIAH (1) in II Chr. 13:2 is probably an error for Maacah, since the latter name occurs in connection with this person several times.

Bibliography. M. Noth, *Die israelitischen Personennamen* (1928), p. 250. N. H. Snaith, Exegesis of I Kings, *IB,* III (1954), 133-34. B. T. DAHLBERG

10. An Aramean kingdom forming, together with Geshur, the W border of Bashan, in which was situated Argob, the territory of Jair son of Manasseh (Deut. 3:14; Josh. 12:5; 13:11, 13). The kingdom of Bashan was situated S of Mount Hermon. Accordingly Maacah may have been situated SW of the mountain. In Josh. 13:13 we are told that the invading Israelites did not oust the Maacathites and the Geshurites, but they lived among them. According to II Sam. 10:6-8; I Chr. 19:6-9, Maacah, together with Zobah and Beth-rehob, was allied to the Ammonites in their war with King David.

A. HALDAR

MAADAI ma′ə dı [מעדי] (Ezra 10:34). One of those compelled by Ezra to give up their foreign wives. In I Esd. 9:34 the name is Momdius (Μομδιος).

MAADIAH mā′ə dī′ə [מעדיה, *perhaps from* יעד, Yahu assembles, *or from* מעד, Yahu promises (*the latter as in* Old S Arab.)] (Neh. 12:5). One of the priests who returned from Exile with Zerubbabel, perhaps identical with the Moadiah of Neh. 12:17, or the Maaziah of Neh. 10:8 (this latter variant is also in the LXX of 12:5). J. M. WARD

MAAI mā′ī [מעי] (Neh. 12:36). A musician in the procession at the dedication of the wall of Jerusalem after it was rebuilt.

MAALEH-ACRABBIM. *See* AKRABBIM.

MAANI. KJV Apoc. form of BANI.

MAARATH mā′ə răth [מערת, barren field] (Josh. 15:59). A village in Judah's hill-country district of Beth-zur; possibly identical with Maroth (Mic. 1:12). Maarath may be Khirbet Qufin, just NE of Beit Ummar, *ca.* two miles N of Beth-zur. V. R. GOLD

MAASAI mā′ə sī [מעשי, *perhaps shortened from* מעשיהו, work of Yahu; *see* MAASEIAH] (I Chr. 9:12); KJV MAASIAI mā ăs′ĭ ī. One of the priests who returned from the Babylonian exile. "Amashsai" (Neh. 11:13) apparently stands for this name and may be a corrupted form of it. Again, both names may be forms of "Amasai" (עמשי). B. T. DAHLBERG

MAASEIAH mā′ə sē′yə [מעשיה, מעשיהו, work of Yahu; *cf.* BAASEIAH; MAASAI; Apoc. Μαθήλας (A; I Esd. 9:19), Μάνης (BA; I Esd. 9:21), Μασσίας (A; I Esd. 9:22)]; KJV Apoc. MATTHELAS măth′ə ləs (I Esd. 9:19); EANES ē′ə nēz′ (I Esd. 9:21); MASSIAS mə sī′əs (I Esd. 9:22). Alternately; MASSEIAH [Μαιάννας] (I Esd. 9:48; KJV MAIANEAS mā ăn′ĭ əs); MOOSSIAS mō′ə sī′əs [Μοοσσίας] (I Esd. 9:31; KJV MOOSIAS). **1.** A Levite musician of the second order among those appointed to accompany worship before the ark in the tabernacle during David's reign (I Chr. 15:18, 20).

2. A military officer who took part in the rebellion led by the priest Jehoiada against Queen Athaliah to put Joash (*ca.* 837-800 B.C.) on the throne (II Chr. 23:1).

3. An officer in Judah during the reign of King Uzziah (*ca.* 783-742 B.C.) who helped prepare the military lists mentioned in II Chr. 26:11.

4. A son or brother of King Ahaz of Judah (*ca.* 735-715 B.C.) who was slain in the war with the N kingdom, Israel (II Chr. 28:7).

5. Governor of Jerusalem during the reign of King Josiah (*ca.* 640-609 B.C.; II Chr. 34:8).

6. The father of the prophet Zedekiah, whom Jeremiah the prophet charged with "prophesying a lie" (Jer. 29:21).

7. The father of Zephaniah the priest, a contemporary of Jeremiah the prophet (Jer. 21:1; 29:25; 37:3).

8. KJV form of MAHSEIAH.

9. A doorkeeper in the temple at Jerusalem, and a contemporary of the prophet Jeremiah (Jer. 35:4). Presumably he was a Levite (cf. I Chr. 26:1, where Meshelemiah may be the same individual as Shallum here).

10. A man of Judah among the residents of post-exilic Jerusalem (Neh. 11:5). In I Chr. 9:5 the name has been rendered "Asaiah" (עשיה).

11. A Benjaminite ancestor of a resident of post-exilic Jerusalem (Neh. 11:7; lacking in I Chr. 9:7-8).

12. A priest among those contemporaries of Ezra who had married foreign wives. He was of the family of Jeshua the high priest (Ezra 10:18; I Esd. 9:19).

13. Another priest, of the family of Harim, who had married a foreign wife in the time of Ezra (Ezra 10:21; I Esd. 9:21).

14. A third priest such as 12-13 *above*, of the family of Pashhur (Ezra 10:22; I Esd. 9:22).

15. A layman who had married a foreign wife in the time of Ezra (Ezra 10:30; cf. I Esd. 9:31).

16. The father or ancestor of the Azariah who helped repair the wall of Jerusalem for Nehemiah (Neh. 3:23).

17. One of the "chiefs of the people" signatory to the covenant of Ezra (Neh. 10:25); possibly the same as 15 *above* and 18 *below*.

18. One of those who stood beside Ezra at the public reading of the law (Neh. 8:4). They were probably laymen; possibly the same as 15 or 17 *above*, or both. In I Esd. 9:43 the name is Baalsamus.

19. One of those Levites who assisted as interpreters of the law when Ezra read from it to the people (Neh. 8:7; cf. I Esd. 9:48).

20. A priest among those taking part in the ceremonies dedicating the rebuilt walls of Jerusalem in the time of Nehemiah (Neh. 12:41). *See* 21 *below*.

21. Another priest among those noted in 20 *above* (Neh. 12:42). Either person may be the same as 12, 13, or 14 *above*. The distinctions, if any, between some of the foregoing individuals are obscure.

B. T. DAHLBERG

MAASIAI. KJV form of MAASAI.

MAASIAS. KJV Apoc. form of MAASEIAH.

MAASMAS mā ăs'məs [Μαασμᾶν (BA), Σεμεια (Luc.)] (I Esd. 8:43); KJV MASMAN măs'mən. One of the leading men who returned with Ezra from the Exile. The corresponding name is Shemaiah in Ezra 8:16.

C. T. FRITSCH

MAATH mā'ăth [Μάαθ] (Luke 3:26). An ancestor of Jesus.

MAAZ mā'ăz [מעץ, angry(?)] (I Chr. 2:27). A Jerahmeelite.

Bibliography. M. Noth, *Die israelitischen Personennamen* (1928), p. 250; cf. p. 235, no. 97.

MAAZIAH mā'ə zī'ə [מעזיהו (I Chr. 24:18), מעזיה (Neh. 10:8—H 10:9), Yahu is a refuge]. Eponym of a division of priests listed as contemporaries of King David (I Chr. 24:18), and perhaps represented by the priest of this name who signed the covenant of Ezra (Neh. 10:8—H 10:9).

Bibliography. M. Noth, *Die israelitischen Personennamen* (1928), p. 250; cf. p. 157.

B. T. DAHLBERG

MABDAI măb'dī. KJV form of Mamdai. *See* BENAIAH 9.

MACALON măk'ə lŏn. KJV form of MICHMASH.

MACCABEES, MACCABEAN REVOLT. The Maccabees (or Hasmoneans; *see* HASMONEAN) were the leaders of Judea during the last two centuries B.C., especially in the earlier stages (second third of the second century), during the epic struggle of the Jewish people against Hellenistic culture and imperialism.

Judas (i.e., Judah), son of Mattathias, was nicknamed "Maccabee" (I Macc. 2:4; Ἰουδας ὁ καλούμενος Μακκαβαῖος; cf. 2:66; 3:1), probably meaning "the Mallet-headed" (Aramaic מקבא, *maqqābâ*). Judas' brothers all had nicknames, also probably reflecting physical characteristics. Several popular etymologies were later derived from, and then attributed to, the name "Maccabee"—e.g., Judas the "Hammerer" (or "Quencher"; from the root כבה, *kābâ*) of the enemy; or מכבי, representing the initial letters of the four well-known words: מי כמוך באלים יהוה, "Who is like Thee, O LORD, among the mighty [RSV 'gods']?" (Exod. 15:11).

The name "Maccabees" never occurs in the rabbinic literature; it is the term "HASMONEAN" that is there employed. The title "(Books of the) Maccabees," deriving from Judas' nickname, originated in the church, apparently so designated for the first time in the second century by Clement of Alexandria; in the third century it is so referred to by Hippolytus, Tertullian, and Origen, among others.

Ancient Israel's career was invariably one of involvement; it could not be otherwise, since Israel's land constituted a bridge between Western Asia and Africa. This involvement, however, reached its peak in antiquity in the Greco-Roman period, thanks to the revolutionary conquests under Alexander the Great. Never before in history had so many countries and peoples and religions come simultaneously under the influence of a single, dominant culture and way of life as did those of Asia and Africa in relation to Hellenism. Judea, Judaism, and the Jewish people, partly because of geography but chiefly because of unique religious beliefs and practices, became more involved—and more dramatically—than any other ethnic-religious-political group. Indeed, not only do we have a more complete literary record of Judaism's experience in that hectic period, but Judaism turned out to be the sole survivor among the cultures with which Hellenism came in contact.

Alexander himself was favorably disposed toward the Jews. Most of the Jews at the end of the fourth century B.C. lived outside Judea, along the Mediterranean coast of Asia and in Babylonia and Persia. It was sensible policy, therefore, for Greek strategy to curry favor with the Jews in the attempt to overcome the Persian Empire of Darius. Thus Alexander supported Jerusalem as the site of the temple against the Samaritans' Mount Gerizim, and he added to Judean territory several important cities of Samaria. Legend added that Alexander, on the way from Tyre to Egypt, turned off to Jerusalem and offered sacrifices in the temple to Israel's God (Jos. Antiq. XI.viii.4-6; Talmud Yom. 69*a*).

After Alexander's death in 323, General Seleucus acquired Babylonia and General Ptolemy obtained Egypt. But three years later Ptolemy invaded Judea—on a sabbath, when their law prevented the Jews from fighting—only to retreat in the face of another of Alexander's generals, Antigonus. Subsequently, Seleucus and Ptolemy joined forces against the too-powerful Antigonus, and in 312 they overcame his fleet at Gaza. Seleucus then emerged as the strongest ruler in Western Asia, and the year 312—the "year of the Greeks," it came to be called—became year 1 of the Seleucid era.

Alexander's empire suffered a second major division after the Battle of Ipsus, in 301. Judea, as part of Syria, fell to Seleucus; but Ptolemy rushed in and occupied the little, but very strategic, country. And for over a century thereafter, Judea became a pawn and sometimes also a battlefield for Syria and Egypt.

Generally, the Jews supported the Seleucids in this struggle. Ever since the Persian restoration of Judah in the sixth century B.C., the Jews had been living in Western Asia under a single rule. This was true also under Alexander, and would be true under the Seleucids. And there were other factors. E.g., the vernacular of Babylonian Jewry, Aramaic, resembled that of Judea, whereas the Jews of Egypt had acquired that country's vernacular, Greek. Again, the temple in Jerusalem received considerable support from Babylonian and Persian Jewry, and the priesthood preferred the centralized rule of the Seleucids throughout Western Asia. And so, *ca.* 250, the high priest Onias II sided with Seleucid II, against Ptolemy III; and when the latter was defeated by the former in 242, Onias refused to pay him even the token tribute of twenty talents. But another faction of Jews, led by Joseph (a nephew of Onias) and his father, Tobiah (husband of Onias' sister), opposed Onias because it had business dealings with Egypt, and counseled payment of the tribute, in the interest of increased Mediterranean trade. As a consequence of this clash of interests, Joseph—who was not of male priestly descent—became secular head of Judea, while Onias retained the priestly authority. And Judea remained loyal to the Ptolemies.

Joseph then intrigued for additional power, to Judea's hurt. He borrowed money from some Samaritan friends, went to Ptolemy's court in Alexandria as Judea's ambassador of good will, and with the money he bribed enough important officials to secure the lucrative post of tax collector of Coele-Syria. Jerusalem, as the seat of the chief tax collector, became an even more important city, and civil authority became the property of Joseph's descendants—the "sons of Tobias," as they came to be known.

Judean Jewry henceforth became essentially a divided people. Under the influence of the Tobiads, and because of the greatly increased Jewish population in Egypt, the cultural influence of Hellenized Egypt upon the commercial aristocracy of Judea became ever more prominent. Greek became increasingly their vernacular, and Hellenism in various social and cultural forms became more apparent. After Joseph's death, his son Hyrcanus continued his father's pro-Egyptian policy, whereas his half-brothers—Joshua, Onias, and Simon—deprived of authority, sided with Syria.

But for several decades neither Syria nor Egypt could long remain the superior power, and tiny Judea often suffered the consequences. In 219 Antiochus III* the Great conquered Coele-Syria and Transjordan; and two years later Ptolemy IV Philopator reconquered this territory. Again, in 201, after a special meeting of Judea's council of elders (ἡ γερουσία) had been convoked and had decided in favor of Syria over Egypt, an Egyptian army reconquered several Judean cities and punished many pro-Seleucid Jews; and a garrison was stationed in Jerusalem. Finally, two years later, Antiochus invaded Coele-Syria and destroyed the Egyptian army. Judea was now lost to the Ptolemies forever. Fig. ANT 33.

In 192 Antiochus and Ptolemy signed a treaty in which, *inter alia,* the problem of Coele-Syria seemed settled; but each party soon claimed that the other had misunderstood the clause in question, and each laid a claim to that area. Nevertheless, international conditions appeared bright for Judea. In several concrete ways Antiochus demonstrated his appreciation of its efforts in his behalf: he canceled its taxes for three years; he promised compensation for the cities destroyed by the wars; he exempted priests, scribes, temple singers, and the like from the poll and crown taxes; he provided duty-free timber for the reconstruction of Jerusalem's walls and the temple's cloisters; he made moneys available for sacrifices; Jewish captives were restored to freedom.

But the storm broke loose over Judea's head after 175, in large part as a result of Rome's entering upon the Near Eastern scene of history. In that year Seleucus IV was assassinated, and his brother, Antiochus IV Epiphanes,* after bringing about the murder of the designated successor, Seleucus' infant son, occupied the throne. Antiochus had spent some time as a hostage in Rome (after his father's defeat at the Battle of Magnesia in 190) and had lived in Athens. Antiochus realized that Rome would surely seek control of all Western Asia. Accordingly, he sought to prevent this imperialistic expansion by conquering Egypt and uniting it with Syria. An important step in this direction was the Hellenization of the heterogeneous populations of these areas. It was this leveling process of Hellenization that was the immediate cause of the Judean revolt led by the Maccabees. Fig. ANT 34.

Within Judean Jewry there were opposing forces at work. It is true that one part of the ruling class was pro-Syrian, the other pro-Egyptian; after all, it was simply not possible for this class to remain independent in the face of the greatly superior economic, political, and military forces around it. But in one major respect the ruling class was united—namely, in the desire to imitate and assimilate the current Hellenistic culture of these same superior forces. Increasingly these Jews spoke Greek instead of Hebrew, and adopted Hellenic and Hellenized forms of names. Many laws of Judaism became irksome for them. Their economic interests impelled them, through the medium of Jason (*né* Joshua), who had supplanted his brother Onias as high priest, to request Antiochus Epiphanes for "permission . . . to establish . . . a gymnasium and a body of youth [ephebeum] . . . , and to enrol the men of Jerusalem as citizens of Antioch" (II Macc. 4:9)—in other words, to turn the Holy City into a Hellenistic city with the right to strike its own coinage. Indeed, Jason did build a gymnasium in Jerusalem, where the youth, even priests, took part in games, with their bodies exposed.

The Tobiads, however, wanted all power in their own hands. In 175 Jason had occasion to send one of the Tobiads, Menelaus Onias, to Antiochus, "to carry the money to the king and to complete the records of essential business" (4:23 ff). Menelaus, however, flattered the king with such unction that he secured the high priesthood for himself, "outbidding Jason by three hundred talents of silver." But Jason and his supporters fought back, and Menelaus might well have failed in his purpose had not Antiochus sent a military force to his aid in Jerusalem.

International and domestic strife now came simultaneously to a head. Antiochus began an all-out campaign to annex Egypt. In 171 Syria and Egypt went to war for control of Coele-Syria, and a year later Egypt capitulated. On his return to Syria, Antiochus turned off to Jerusalem, entered the temple, and robbed much of its gold treasure. "He committed deeds of murder," the account in I Maccabees continues (1:20-28; cf. II Macc. 5:11-26),

> and spoke with great arrogance.
> Israel mourned deeply in every community,
>
> . . . .
>
> and all the house of Jacob was clothed with shame.

But Antiochus was not destined to annex Egypt. Rome had by now become powerful and interested enough to thwart this obstacle to her own imperialistic program. Rome ordered Antiochus to leave Egypt at once; and he did. He retreated along the coast of Judea, determined at least to retain that little state as a buffer against Egypt and as an outlet to the sea.

Rumor spread that Antiochus had died. Jason then organized a Jewish force and attacked Jerusalem, forcing Menelaus to seek refuge in the citadel. Consequently Antiochus took sweeping revenge, determined to stamp out all opposition to his regime. He gave orders for "the Jews to depart from the laws of their fathers, to cease living by the laws of God, and to pollute the Temple. . . . This onset of evil came to be harsh and odious for everyone" (II Macc. 6; cf. I Macc. 1:29-64). On the site of the temple hill a fortress, called Acra, was built, and a permanent garrison was placed there.

While the Judean upper class did not oppose the Hellenization of their religion and way of life, the common people, most of them farmers, craftsmen, menial workers, petty merchants, and the like, having little or nothing to gain from collaboration with either Syria or Egypt, did not favor it. Why should they give up the Judaism of their fathers for alien paganism? Some of these Jews actively opposed the foreign and brutally enforced attempt to alter their religious and social beliefs and practices.

Most prominent among these activists was the priestly family of Mattathias, which had moved from Jerusalem to Modein; he and his five sons "rent their clothes, put on sackcloth, and mourned greatly" (I Macc. 2:14). When the king's officers came to Modein to enforce improper sacrifice, Mattathias slew both the king's official and the first Jew who stepped forward to oblige the aliens. He then tore down the altar and proclaimed throughout the town: "Let every one who is zealous for the law and supports the covenant come out with me!" (I Macc. 2: 15-27). Mattathias and his sons and followers fled to the mountains, and the spark of revolt was lit.

Mattathias was soon joined by many other Jews, among them the Hasidim, who realized that in order to gain religious freedom they would have to battle also militarily and politically; indeed, they agreed with Mattathias to set aside the law of the sabbath, if it became necessary for them to defend themselves on that day (2:28 ff). Mattathias' forces proceeded to wage war against the Jews who had complied meekly with Antiochus' orders. They tore down altars, circumcised Jewish children that had been left uncircumcised, and exhorted Jews everywhere to join in the revolt. "They rescued the law out of the hands of the Gentiles and kings, and they never let the sinner gain the upper hand" (vss. 45-48).

Mattathias knew he was dying. He called together his sons and told them, somewhat in the manner of Jacob the biblical patriarch: "Behold, I know that Simeon your brother is wise in counsel; always listen to him; he shall be your father. Judas Maccabeus has been a mighty warrior from his youth; he shall command the army for you and fight the battle against the peoples" (2:49-68; 168-167 B.C.).

Under Judas the revolt continued to spread. When Apollonius, governor of Samaria, mustered a large force to stop him, Judas routed them and killed the governor. A Syrian army under General Seron shortly afterward suffered the same fate at Beth-horon. Antiochus realized for the first time that the Judean revolt was a very serious matter.

But Antiochus was now beset also by other troubles. His treasury was low, and he was forced to lead an expedition to Persia, there to acquire additional revenues. He designated Lysias, a "prominent man of royal lineage," next in command, assigning to him half his forces and ordering him to liquidate the Judean menace: "to wipe out and destroy the strength of Israel and the remnant of Jerusalem; . . . to banish the memory of them from the place, settle aliens in all their territory, and distribute their land" (3:35-36).

Forty thousand infantry and seven thousand cavalry marched into Judea, pitching camp near Emmaus; there they were joined by additional forces. Judas and his followers realized their crucial position. They could scarcely hope to achieve victory; but, they said, "it is better for us to die in battle than to see the misfortunes of our nation and of the sanctuary. But as his will in heaven may be, so he will do" (3:59-60).

General Gorgias took five thousand infantry and a thousand horsemen and marched out by night, planning to catch Judas' forces by surprise. But Judas learned of it. He broke camp at once and marched out to attack the enemy at Emmaus. With his small force of three thousand, Judas routed the much more numerous enemy: "They pursued them to Gazara, and to the plains of Judea [RSV 'Idumea'], and to Ashdod [RSV 'Azotus'] and Jamnia" (4:1-15). This done, Judas turned on the forces under Gorgias and routed them also. Much booty fell into their hands. And "Israel had a great deliverance that day."

The following year Lysias sent another powerful army against the Judean rebels. Once again, however, Judas' force, numbering some ten thousand, discomfited the Syrian army of some sixty thousand picked men and five thousand horsemen, for, as Lysias himself had noted, they were ready "either to live or to die nobly" (4:35).

With the first phase of the war of liberation accomplished, Judas set about to achieve the second. He selected "blameless priests devoted to the law," and they proceeded to cleanse the temple. They tore down and removed every vestige of uncleanness and reproach. In 165, on the twenty-fifth day of the ninth month (Chislev), proper sacrifices to the Lord were offered up in the temple, amid prayers of thanksgiving and rejoicing. For eight days the dedication (חנכה, *Ḥ^a^nukkâ*) was observed, "and all the assembly of Israel determined that every year at that season the days of the dedication of the altar should be observed with gladness and joy for eight days" (4:59).

But Judas did not forget that he was beset by enemies in his midst and around him. He "made war on the sons of Esau in Idumea, at Akrabattene [near Shechem], because they kept lying in wait for Israel. . . . He also remembered the wickedness of the sons of Baean. . . . He crossed over to attack the Ammonites. . . . He also took Jazer and its villages" (5: 1-8). When the Jews in Galilee and in Gilead urgently asked for help, a great assembly (ἐκκλσία μεγάλη) was convoked, and it was decided that, meager as Judea's forces were, the Jews in the N and in the E could not be abandoned. Judas left a small force to guard Judea, and to his brother Simon he said: "Choose your men and go and rescue your brethren in Galilee; I and Jonathan my brother will go to Gilead" (5:14-19). The subsequent campaigns, with but few exceptions, were eminently successful.

Far off in Persia, Antiochus had heard of Lysias' defeat, and "he was astounded and badly shaken" (6:8). The one great fortress still under his control was the citadel in Jerusalem, Acra. He gathered a force of "a hundred thousand foot soldiers, twenty thousand horsemen, and thirty-two elephants accustomed to war" (6:30 ff), to rescue the garrison and annihilate all Judean opposition to his rule.

But death (October, 165) cut Antiochus short, and a certain Philip was appointed to take charge for his successor, Antiochus V Eupator.

Judas did not know that the hated Antiochus IV was no more when the temple was dedicated (December; II Macc. 9:1 ff). But Lysias heard the report. Having decided to return to Antioch, to forestall his demotion and perhaps even his death, Lysias persuaded Antiochus V to grant the Jews religious freedom: "Let us come to terms with these men, . . . and agree to let them live by their own laws as they did before; for it was on account of their laws which we abolished that they became angry and did all these things" (I Macc. 6:58-59; cf. II Macc. 11:22-33).

Civil war once again broke out in Syria. In 163-162 Demetrius, nephew of Antiochus IV and a hostage in Rome, made his escape with the aid of Polybius the historian. In Tripoli he established himself as king. He and his followers made their way to Antioch, where the army had arrested Antiochus V and Lysias. The latter were killed, and Demetrius became king of Syria (I Macc. 7:1-4).

The repercussions were felt soon enough also in Judea. "Then there came to him [Demetrius] all the lawless and ungodly men of Israel; they were led by Alcimus, who wanted to be high priest. And they brought to the king this accusation against the [Jewish] people: 'Judas and his brothers have destroyed all your friends' " (7:5-7).

A Syrian army, under Bacchides, with Alcimus as the new high priest, was soon dispatched to punish Judas and Judea. A group of Jewish scholars ("scribes"), including Hasidim, sought peace with the Syrians. They were content with religious freedom, and were not sympathetic with Judas' desire for political independence also. They were happy to receive a sworn promise of religious liberty from Alcimus and Bacchides—until sixty of them were arrested and slain in one day (7:12-18). Judas' group, however, had not been deceived by these glib promises (vss. 10-11).

Unable to halt the activities of Judas, Alcimus returned to Antioch, "and the king sent Nicanor, one of his famous officers, who hated and despised Israel, and ordered him to get rid of the people" (7:26). After several skirmishes, the two forces met in battle. Nicanor's army was shattered (161 B.C.), "and the land of Judah was quiet for a little while" (7:50).

Judas now went beyond the purely military range of leadership. He initiated a pact of friendship with Rome, having heard "that they pledged friendship to those who came to them." The Roman Senate accepted the proposal of Judas (8:1 ff).

But Demetrius persisted. He sent a fresh army, under Bacchides and Alcimus, to subdue Judea. Judas now found himself with but 800 men—after some 2,200 had fled—against about 20,000 of the enemy. In the losing battle that ensued, Judas was killed, and he was replaced as leader by his brother Jonathan, aided by his brother Simon (9:1 ff).

The prospects for Judea appeared black indeed. "The lawless emerged in all parts of Israel . . . . In those days a very great famine occurred" (9:23-24).

Jonathan and Simon and all their men had to flee, seeking refuge in the wilderness of Tekoa. To all intents and purposes Syria was in control of Judea. Yet opposition was not really dead. On several occasions Bacchides and his Hellenized Jewish supporters had a falling out. Several Bedouin groups joined with Jonathan against Syrian attempts to dominate them. Alcimus himself became paralyzed from a stroke and died in great agony. Bacchides was constantly being harassed. Consequently, Jonathan considered the circumstances ripe for a proposal of peace. Bacchides "agreed, and did as he said . . . . He turned and departed to his own land, and came no more into their territory . . . . And Jonathan dwelt in Michmash. And Jonathan began to judge the people, and he destroyed the ungodly out of Israel" (9:55-73).

Judea was now further helped by internal struggles for power in Syria, Alexander Epiphanes (Balas) of Smyrna laid claim to the throne of Antiochus V; but so did the latter's son, Demetrius. The two claimants vied with each other for Judea's support. Demetrius abandoned all the fortified posts—except Beth-zur—that Bacchides had established in Judea, and authorized Jonathan to gather an army as his ally. Alexander, in turn, designated Jonathan high priest and "friend of the king." Demetrius then relieved Jerusalem, as a holy city, and the Jews of many taxes, attached to Jerusalem three toparchies previously belonging to Samaria, and recognized the high priest as the highest authority over the Jews. Fortunately, Jonathan sided with Alexander Balas, for the latter disposed of Demetrius in battle and then—by marriage—acquired the Egyptian royal house as ally (ch. 10).

Subsequently, war between Egypt and Syria, as well as within Syria itself, furthered the interests of Judea. Alexander Balas (151-146) had to flee Syria and lost his life. Demetrius II Nicator (146-139) and Antiochus VI Epiphanes (146/5-143/2)*—the latter supported by Alexander Balas' adjutant, Trypho—like their predecessors, vied with each other for Judea's support. Jonathan sided with Antiochus, and a Judean force defeated part of Demetrius' army marching on Galilee (ch. 11). Fig. ANT 35.

Jonathan then turned again to the diplomatic field of battle. He sent an embassy to Rome to renew the bond of friendship between them, and sought one for the first time with the Spartans. However, in the midst of his high-water mark of leadership, Jonathan was killed. Trypho cleverly arranged the arrest of both Antiochus and Jonathan, obtained from Simon as ransom a hundred talents of silver as well as two of his sons as hostages, and then killed his two rival rulers. Trypho became ruler of Syria, and Simon remained in control of Judea (chs. 12-13).

Simon rebuilt the fortresses of the land and stored food in them, and then offered his support to Demetrius II in a common struggle against Trypho, "for the sole activities of Trypho were to plunder." Demetrius agreed to the pact, and renounced forever all Syrian claims to Judea: "King Demetrius to Simon, the high priest and friend of kings, and to the elders and nation of the Jews, greeting. We have received the golden crown and the palm branch which you sent, and we are ready to make a general peace with you and to write to our officials to grant you release from tribute. All the grants that we have made to you remain valid, and let the strongholds that you have built be your possession. We pardon any errors and offenses committed to this day, and cancel the crown tax which you owe; and whatever other tax has been collected in Jerusalem shall be collected no longer [= *de facto* and *de jure* recognition of Judea as a sovereign state]. And if any of you are qualified to be enrolled in our bodyguard, let them be enrolled, and let there be peace between us." And so, "in the one hundred and seventieth year [144-143 B.C.] the yoke of the Gentiles was removed from Israel, and the people began to write in their documents and contracts, 'In the first year of Simon the great high priest and commander and leader of the Jews'" (13:36-42). Subsequently, the citadel itself was also captured, and the day of its purification observed as a festival (vss. 49 ff).

With this incident the original Book of the Hasmoneans ended. The author began with the account of the capture and pollution of Jerusalem by Antiochus IV Epiphanes, followed this with the story of the Hasmonean revolts against the alien and pagan elements in control of the country, and concluded with the grand deliverance of the land under Simon. The philosophy of our historian is clear and consistent: While God was with the Hasmoneans in their righteous struggle against paganism, it was largely the heroic deeds of the Hasmoneans and their followers, together with their alert exploitation of the struggles between and within Syria and Egypt, that achieved independence for Judea. Even Rome now recognized this little country.

For Simon's reign and the succeeding Hasmonean rulers, *see* HASMONEANS.

Bibliography. E. Kautzsch and A. Kamphausen, I and II Maccabees respectively in E. Kautzsch, ed., *Die Apokryphen und Pseudepigraphen des AT,* vol. I (1900). W. O. E. Oesterley and J. Moffatt, I and II Maccabees respectively in R. H. Charles, ed., *The Apoc. and Pseudep. of the OT,* vol. I (1913). E. Schürer, *Geschichte des jüdischen Volkes in Zeitalter Jesu Christi,* vol. I (5th ed., 1920); vol. III (4th ed., 1909). E. R. Bevan, "Syria and the Jews," *Cambridge Ancient History,* VIII (1930), 495-533, with references to Bevan's important works *The House of Seleucus* (1902); *A History of Egypt Under the Ptolemaic Dynasty* (1927). G. H. Box, *Judaism in the Greek Period* (1932). E. Bickermann, *Der Gott der Makkabäer* (1937); *Die Makkabäer* (1935; English trans., 1947). F.-M. Abel, *Les Livres des Maccabées* (*Études bibliques;* 1949). R. H. Pfeiffer, *History of NT Times with an Introduction to the Apoc.* (1949). The best statement on the Maccabean period is in S. Zeitlin and S. Tedesche, *The First Book of Maccabees* (Dropsie College ed.: *Jewish Apocryphal Literature;* 1950), Introduction, Critical Notes, and Appendices (with references to Zeitlin's numerous publications *passim*); the English translation of I Maccabees employed here is either from this edition or from the RSV. S. Zeitlin and S. Tedesche, *The Second Book of Maccabees* (1954), Introduction, Critical Notes, and Appendices. V. Tcherikover, "Introduction" and "Prolegomena" in V. A. Tcherikover and A. Fuks, *Corpus Papyrorum Judaicarum,* vol. I (1957); *Hellenistic Civilization and the Jews* (1959).

H. M. ORLINSKY

MACCABEES, BOOKS OF [Μακκαβαίων; Lat. *Machabaeorum; see* JUDAS 10; MACCABEES]. A group of historical and quasi-historical books concerned with the struggle of Judaism for survival under the pressure of forcible Hellenization, particularly during the persecution of Antiochus IV Epiphanes (*see*

Antiochus 4). I and II Maccabees belong to the Apocrypha, and, together with III and IV Maccabees, were cherished by the early church for their inspiration to faith and loyalty during persecution.

- A. The book titles
- B. I Maccabees
  1. Original title
  2. Contents
  3. Message
  4. Chronology
  5. Literary sources
     - *a.* Letters and official documents
     - *b.* A Seleucid chronicle
     - *c.* A biography of Judas
     - *d.* The Mattathias tradition
     - *e.* Annals of the high priests
     - *f.* Poetic source
  6. Integrity
  7. Original language
  8. Authorship and date
  9. Importance for the NT
- C. II Maccabees
  1. Original title
  2. Contents
  3. Message
  4. Chronology
  5. Literary sources
     - *a.* Jason's history
     - *b.* Letters
  6. Sources of Jason's history
     - *a.* The biography of Judas
     - *b.* A Seleucid chronicle
     - *c.* The temple archives
  7. Integrity, problem of disarrangements
  8. Original language
  9. Authorship and date
     - *a.* Hasidic affinities
     - *b.* Relationship to Daniel
     - *c.* Affinities with the War Scroll
     - *d.* Anti-Hasmonean and pre-Roman
     - *e.* Egyptian provenance
  10. Importance for the NT
- D. III Maccabees
  1. Original title
  2. Contents
  3. Message
  4. Historical sources
     - *a.* An anti-Ptolemaic history
     - *b.* Jewish traditions
  5. Literary affinities
     - *a.* Comparison with Esther
     - *b.* Comparison with II Maccabees
  6. Authorship and date
  7. Importance for the NT
- E. IV Maccabees
  1. Original title
  2. Contents
  3. Message
  4. Literary classification
  5. Literary source
  6. Integrity
  7. Occasion
  8. Authorship and date
  9. Importance for the NT
- F. Canonicity
- Bibliography

A. ***THE BOOK TITLES.*** Τὰ Μακκαβαϊκα ("The Things Maccabean") was employed as a designation of both I and II Maccabees as early as the late second century A.D.; but it was probably used originally only for II Maccabees, since the surname Maccabeus belongs properly to Judas, who alone features prominently in this book, whereas I Maccabees tells also the history of his brothers and successors, who had other distinguishing epithets (I Macc. 2:2-5). *See* Maccabees.

Clement of Alexandria (*ca.* A.D. 195) distinguishes between these books by designating I Maccabees as

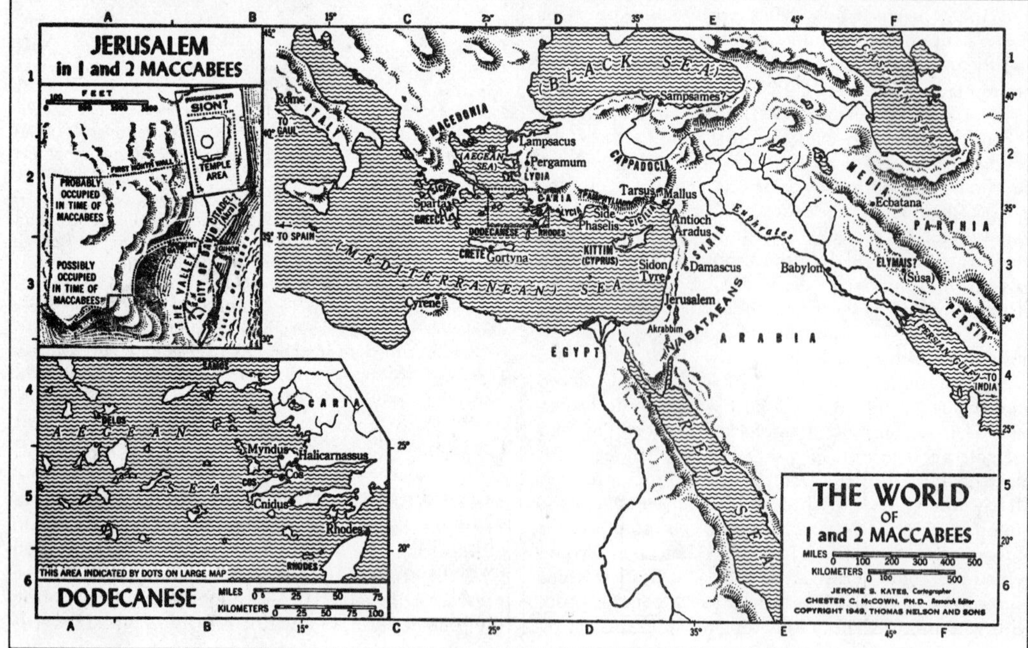

τὸ [Βιβλίον] τῶν Μακκαβαϊκῶν and II Maccabees as ἡ τῶν Μακκαβαϊκῶν ἐπιτομή—"The [Book] of Things Maccabean" and "The Epitome of Things Maccabean," respectively. Cyprian (*ca.* 250) uses the Latin title *Machabaei* for citing either I or II Maccabees. Eusebius sometimes employs indiscriminately ἡ γραφή τῶν καλουμένων Μακκαβαίων ("The Scripture of the Things Called Maccabean"); yet with precision he mentions also ἡ πρώτη καλουμένη τῶν Μακκαβαίων Βίβλος ("The First Book Called Maccabees"). Most Greek MSS distinguish them as Μακκαβαίων Α' and Μακκαβαίων Β'.

The titles III and IV Maccabees (Μακκαβαίων Γ' and Μακκαβαίων Δ') are commonly employed to designate two other books, through an extension of the name Maccabee to refer to any Jewish martyr in the struggle against Hellenism, whether those who suffered for their faith during the reign of Antiochus Epiphanes in Syria Palestine (as in IV Maccabees), or even in the supposedly earlier persecution in Egypt under Ptolemy Philopator (as in III Maccabees). For further discussion of the titles, *see* §§ B-E *below.*

B. *I MACCABEES.* 1. Original title. As seen above, the designation "Maccabees" cannot be original. More appropriate would be "The Book of the Hasmonean House"; for (according to Jos. Antiq. XII.vi.1) Mattathias, the father of Judas and his brethren, was descended from one who bore the name Hashmoneus, and the concern of the book is with the adventures of all the sons of Mattathias, and not merely with those of Judas Maccabeus.

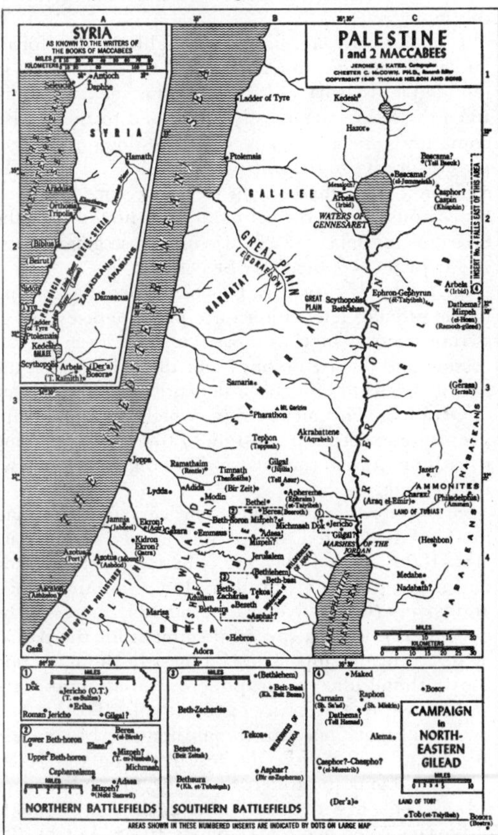

Early Hebrew and Aramaic writings do not know the term "Maccabee," but employ the term "Hasmonean." The Hebrew *Josippon* (a free translation of Josephus' *Jewish Wars*), written perhaps as early as the fourth century A.D., concludes its account of the wars of Judas by declaring: "The rest is written in the *Book of the House of the Hasmoneans.*" Rabbi Saadia seems to know a book entitled either *Megillath Bēth Ḥashmōnā'î* ("The Scroll of the Hasmonean House") or *Kitabh Benê Ḥashmōnā'î* ("The Writing of the Sons of Hashmoneus").

Several scholars have sought to recover from a transcription of Eusebius a similar Semitic title. Upon the authority of Origen, Eusebius cites the name σαρβηθ σαρβαναιελ (Euseb. Hist. VI.25.2). This is perhaps a corruption of σφαρ βηθ σαραχαι ελ, transliterating Aramaic *sephār bēth sārekhê ēl* ("The Book of the House of the Princes of God"). This Aramaic title would be equivalent to the Hebrew *sēpher bēth ḥashmōnā'îm,* provided *ḥashmōnā'î* is only an honorific title meaning "prince." Cf. πρέσβεις ("dignitaries") as a translation of *ḥashmanîm* (KJV=ASV "princes"; Ps. 68:31—H 68:32—G 67:32) in Origen's Hexapla. For other etymologies, *see* HASMONEANS.

2. Contents. After a brief account of the origin of Greek rule in the East (1:1-9), the book sketches briefly the background of the Maccabean revolt against the Seleucid king Antiochus Epiphanes (1:10-64) and its inception under the leadership of Mattathias and his sons (ch. 2) and then portrays at length the military and political careers of Mattathias' sons Judas (3:1–9:22), Jonathan (9:23–12:53), and Simon (13:1–16:17). The book concludes with a brief summary of the rule of Simon's son John. For fuller treatment of this history, *see* MACCABEES; HASMONEAN.

3. Message. I Maccabees teaches the continuing providence of God over his people Israel during the Greek era. It was probably intended as a sequel to the OT Hebrew book of Ezra-Nehemiah; for as the latter depicts the Jewish history of the Persian period against the background of the conquests of Cyrus, so I Maccabees portrays Jewish history against the backdrop of the conquests of Alexander the Great. In its citation of official correspondence, it is also reminiscent of Ezra-Nehemiah. Frequent allusions to God's saving acts of the past, as encouragement for the present, underscore the belief that the history of salvation begun in the OT continues into Maccabean times. Victory over implacable enemies depends more upon loyalty and faith in God than upon the size of the armies. *See* WAR, IDEAS OF.

The Maccabees were agents of God's salvation from pagan oppressors. Mattathias, burning with zeal for the law, like the ancient Phinehas (2:26; cf. Num. 25:10-15), sparked the Maccabean Revolt; and like the patriarch Jacob (Gen. 48–49), his final testament (I Macc. 2:65-68) determined the course of Hebrew history. Judas was the "savior of Israel" (9:21), as truly as the judges and kings of old (Judg. 3:9; II Kings 13:5). Jonathan *judged* the people at Michmash (I Macc. 9:73; cf. I Sam. 14). Thus the Maccabees fulfilled the hope of future "saviors" who would govern the nation (Obad. 21).

Although prophecy has ceased, one still awaits the coming of the "prophet" foretold in Deut. 18:15, 18, to determine what should be done with desecrated altar stones (I Macc. 4:46) or who should be priest or ruler after the interim appointment of Simon and his heirs (14:41). Messianism per se does not appear, but the revival of Israel as a state seems to presage the messianic age. Hence Simon is extolled in language borrowed from messianic prophecy (14:4-15; cf. Mic. 4:4; Zech. 8:4-6, 12).

The Maccabees may be blamed for not being content with the achievement of religious liberty, for launching their own new aggressions against Gentile neighbors; but they argued that it was their destiny to re-establish the borders of ancient Israel (15:33). Had not the prophets foretold the repossession of Edom, Philistia, Ammon, and Moab (Isa. 11:14; Obad. 21)? Significantly I Maccabees uses these archaic names in referring to Jewish conquests of these areas.

4. Chronology. Dates in I Maccabees are regularly according to the "year of the kingdom of the Greeks" (1:10). Therefore, for the period concerned, the book provides the backbone for any Jewish chronology in relation to world history. The era, as Josephus explains (Antiq. XIII.vi.7), is that of the "Syrian Kingdom, reckoned from the time when Seleucus, surnamed Nicator, occupied Syria."

The decisive event which initiated this epoch was the Battle of Gaza, of the summer of 312 B.C. The official Seleucid calendar followed the Syrian custom of beginning the year in the autumn, as also the pre-exilic Hebrew calendar, so that the Seleucid era began officially in the autumn of 312. Postexilic Jewish practice, however, followed the Babylonian custom of calculating the year from the spring, in the month Nisan, but anomalously retained the tradition of an autumnal New Year's celebration dated to the seventh month, Tishri. (For spring as the beginning of the Jewish Year, see Jos. Antiq. III.x.5; *see also* CALENDAR.) This complicates the problem of dates in I and II Maccabees.

Did the Jews antedate the beginning of the Seleucid era to Nisan, 312 B.C., or even more radically to Tishri, 313? Or did the Palestinian Jews wait until Nisan of 311 for beginning the Seleucid era? Competent scholars have espoused each one of these positions, or have argued for more than one method of calculation among the divergent sources of I and II Maccabees. The enumeration of the months in I Maccabees supports the reckoning of the year from the spring; but which spring? The footnotes explaining the dates in the RSV are all calculated from the year 311, which may be seen by subtracting a number one less than the ordinal number given from 311. Thus the reign of Antiochus Epiphanes, which began in the 137th year of the Seleucid era, is dated to 175 B.C. (311 minus 136). This rough calculation cannot always be correct, even assuming a Nisan, 311, era; for the year overlaps the Julian calendar. On the other hand, some of the year dates may be accurate, even if one begins the era in the spring or autumn of 312, for these years would be completed in the spring or autumn of 311.

Recent research has led to the analysis of the dates into official Syrian and popular Jewish datings. The former are all of the most general character, not giving the number or name of the month, whereas the latter are mostly very precise, recording not only the month, but often even the day. The former are especially related to general events of Syrian history (as the accession year of a king), whereas the latter are concerned with internal Jewish affairs or with Syrian history as it impinged directly upon Judea. These differently calculated dates stem from the sources utilized by the author, and they seem to find their best resolution if one calculates the year's beginning in each case from the year 312. *See* § C4 *below. See also* CHRONOLOGY OF THE OT.

5. Literary sources. So rich is I Maccabees in accurate, detailed, and circumstantial historical information that it is scarcely conceivable that it could have been written, even by an eyewitness, without some aid from written sources. The following source analysis may be examined:

a. Letters and official documents. Numerous documents are quoted, whose genuineness has often been called in question; but there is a growing conviction that most, if not all, are genuine. Characteristically they interrupt the flow of the narrative; but this does not prove them to be later interpolations. Thus ch. 8, which contains a letter from Rome, breaks the continuity of chs. 7; 9; but it is clearly presupposed by the narrator at 12:1. Similarly, 6:1 resumes the narrative concerning Epiphanes, which had been abandoned at 3:37, but this may be readily explained by the introduction of a different literary source on the part of the original author, as also by the exigency of keeping two interrelated stories going at the same time.

I Maccabees mentions a probable source for its quoted documents, the archives of the chief priest in the temple treasury (14:23, 49). This seems natural, since the letters are mostly addressed to the Jewish community, or are copies of foreign documents prepared for the high priest (8:22; 11:37; 15:24). In such an archive there might well have appeared even a previously forged document like the letter of the Spartans to Onias (12:20-23)—of whose genuineness one is justly skeptical. *See* SPARTA.

b. A Seleucid chronicle. The events dated according to the official Seleucid era are prominent events of Syrian history, such as those which concern the accession and demise of kings. For this information the author seems to have been dependent upon a Greek or Aramaic chronicle, from which he made appropriate excerpts from time to time, interweaving it with his Jewish sources, and often giving it a Jewish coloring.

c. A biography of Judas. The very fact that half the book is devoted to a period of only seven years (166-160 B.C.) in Judas' life, whereas the remaining half is devoted to his brothers Jonathan and Simon and covers twenty-five years (160-135), suggests the dependence upon a special document for the period of Judas' leadership. The vividness of the narration shows that Judas' biographer was a contemporary and eyewitness of many of the events. To this biographical work perhaps the author of I Maccabees alludes at 9:22: "Now the rest of the acts of Judas . . . have not been recorded, for they were very many." This negative reversal of a familiar OT mode of literary reference (cf. II Kings 10:34; II Chr. 25:

26) seems to allude, not merely to the inexhaustible unwritten traditions concerning Judas, but also to the author's sole dependence upon written material which has been substantially embodied. *See* § B5*d, below.*

d. The Mattathias tradition. The stories of Mattathias in ch. 2 give structure and coherence to the entire book, for here we meet his sons who figure prominently in the subsequent narrative. Judas, Jonathan, and Simon each in turn took up the cause of Israel bequeathed to them by their father.

The present account of Mattathias contains within it a section which originally belonged to the biography of Judas; for 2:29-48 is clearly distinguished from the rest of the chapter by style and content. Most notably, it is "Mattathias and his friends" who figure here, whereas in the material preceding and following it is Mattathias and his sons. Since this material alone really advances the course of events in ch. 1, it appears probable that this piece originally referred to "Judas and his friends" (cf. 9:26, 28). A comparison with II Maccabees confirms this conjecture, where the same sequence for the acts of Judas is followed: the wilderness withdrawal (I Macc. 2:29-30; II Macc. 5:27), refusal to fight on the sabbath (I Macc. 2:31-41; II Macc. 6:11), Judas' recruitments (I Macc. 2:42 ff; II Macc. 8:1), Judas' early exploits (I Macc. 2:44-48; II Macc. 8:5-7). Further, II Macc. 5:27 makes explicit the origin of the circle of friends which appears already formed in I Macc. 2:39. The defection of the Hasideans from Judas, as recorded in I Macc. 7:13-14, implies their previous alliance with him as related in 2:42 (cf. II Macc. 14:6).

The legends of Mattathias, then, were only two: his heroic action in withdrawing to Modein, where he resisted pagan sacrifice (2:1-28), and his final testament to his sons (vss. 49-70). These are obvious interpolations into the Judas source, for they break the original sequence of 1:62-64; 2:29-48; 3:10 ff. The author of I Maccabees made brilliant use of the Mattathias legends by way of tying together his entire narrative of the Maccabean movement. He filled the hiatus between the legends of Mattathias by transforming a section of the Judas biography into stories about Mattathias. Thus Mattathias usurped the role of Judas as the dynamic initiator of the Maccabean Revolt—appearing now as the patriarchal head of a family of heroes. Judas was then made the first successor to his noble father (3:1-9). *See* MATTATHIAS 1.

e. The annals of the high priests. Judas' brothers Jonathan and Simon became high priests. In this capacity they doubtless followed the ancient custom of keeping official chronicles of the outstanding events of each year. Of Simon's son John it is written: "The rest of the acts of John . . . are written in the chronicles of his high priesthood" (16:23-24). The assumption that such annals had been kept since the time of Jonathan would explain satisfactorily the accurate and carefully dated history of the deeds of Jonathan and Simon. However, the reader is not referred to them in connection with these men, since the author believed he had made adequate use of their material in piecing together this history. In the case of John, one is directed to the annals, since the author chose to conclude his story with John's accession and only a brief digest of his rule.

These chronicles were probably kept in the temple treasury along with other official documents (*cf.* § B5*a above*). Naturally, they followed the Jewish system of dating; but they were interwoven in the narration with material gleaned from the Seleucid chronicle employing the official calendar. *Cf.* § B4 *above.*

f. Poetic source. Interspersed through the book are a number of poetic sections: laments upon Antiochus' ravaging of Jerusalem (1:24*b*-28), the desolation of the sanctuary (1:36-40), the ruin of Zion (2:7-12; 3:45, 50*b*-53), and the death of Judas (9:21); an imprecatory prayer against Nicanor (7:37-38); and eulogies of Judas (3:3-9) and Simon (14:4-15). There is also a free quotation of Ps. 79:2-3, lamenting the slaughter of the Hasideans (I Macc. 7:17). This last shows that the author was capable of quoting and adapting poetic material to the needs of the historical content of his work. He may have composed some of these poems himself. Yet some or all may have been borrowed from a body of Maccabean psalms. Like the hymnody of the ancient Essenes, which is probably contemporary with our author, this poetry is saturated with phraseology borrowed from the OT. *See* DEAD SEA SCROLLS.

6. Integrity. The genuineness of the final chapters has been contested by many scholars because Josephus discontinued his use of I Maccabees as his historical source for *Jewish Antiquities* after the selection of Simon as high priest (Jos. Antiq. XIII. vi.7). There are several views as to the original termination of the book: 13:42; 13:53; 14:13; 14:15. Though small inner contradictions of ch. 14 have reinforced the opinion of an originally shorter work, these occur mostly between the poetic eulogy of Simon (vss. 4-15) and the following prose narrative, as also between the inscription on the bronze tablets honoring Simon (vss. 27*b*-45) and the sequence of events elsewhere. None of these disagreements is serious, but all are well explained as discrepancies between the author and the documents he cites.

Josephus' abandonment of I Maccabees at this point is easily explained as a falling back upon an earlier work of his, *Jewish Wars,* in which he had drawn heavily upon Nicholas of Damascus, in apparent ignorance of I Maccabees. Even so, some scholars allege that the account of *Jewish Antiquities* is not devoid of coloring from I Maccabees for the latter part of Simon's rule. There is insufficient justification, therefore, for denying the genuineness of the final chapters. On Josephus' writings, *see* JOSEPHUS.

7. Original language. I Maccabees was originally composed in the Hebrew language, according to the explicit testimony of Jerome in his *Prologus Galeatus.* The extant Greek text, from which the later versions were made, is full of Hebrew idioms. Often this text may be corrected upon the assumption of an error in the reading or copying of the original Hebrew—which, unfortunately, is no longer extant.

8. Authorship and date. The author of I Maccabees, writing *ca.* 110 B.C., perhaps at the prompting of Simon's son John, undertook an official history of the Hasmonean house, beginning with the patriarchal leadership of Mattathias and reaching its climax in the hereditary rule of Simon. The accession of John Hyrcanus I (*see* HASMONEANS) is presented, with a brief summary of his rule, by way of showing the establishment and durability of Simon's line. The descendants of Mattathias are presented as an elect family without whose hegemony victory is impossible (5:55-62).

Though the final verses seem to indicate that John's rule was well advanced, there is nothing to indicate that the annals of his priesthood had been completed. The author's dynastic concern may indicate that he wrote against the background of the growing discontent of all Hasidic elements (including PHARISEES and ESSENES) with the Hasmonean leadership. John's reign closed with an open rupture between him and the Pharisees and his espousal of the Sadducean cause (Jos. Antiq. XIII.x.6). The authorization of Simon's line had been qualified "until a trustworthy prophet should arise" (14:41)—with adverse allusion to such prophetic figures as the Qumran Teacher of Righteousness (*see* DEAD SEA SCROLLS) and Judas the Essene, who by implication were not "trustworthy."

The history of I Maccabees appears to be nonpartisan, espousing the views of neither Sadducee nor Pharisee. It was therefore written before the open break of the Pharisees with Hyrcanus. With deference to the Sadducean point of view, it avoids doctrines which would offend them; but at the same time it represents all the sons of Mattathias as zealous champions of the law and opponents of paganism, at one in their aims with the Hasideans. It is therefore not anti-Pharisaic. It does record, however, the misguided gullibility of the Hasideans who had welcomed Alcimus as chief priest, despite the suspicions of Judas and his brothers (7:8-18). This partial defection of the Hasideans, with all its tragic consequences, is reported as a caution against disaffection in the author's own day.

9. Importance for the NT. The book illustrates the contrast between Jewish national aspirations and the universal KINGDOM OF GOD envisaged by Jesus; for I Maccabees belongs to the dispensation of the Old Covenant, which was to terminate with the coming of the Prophet (4:46; 14:41), whom early Christians were to identify with Jesus. *See* JESUS CHRIST.

Other religious parallels are few. I Maccabees 2:52 combines Abraham's offering up of Isaac (Gen. 22) with his justification by God (Gen. 15:6) in precisely the same way as Jas. 2:21-23. Similarly the Scriptures are regarded as the true source of encouragement (παράκλησις), in I Macc. 12:9; Rom. 15:4.

Alcimus' destruction of the wall of the inner court of the TEMPLE, separating Jews from Gentiles (9:54), finds an interesting parallel and contrast in Eph. 2:14. The former is the work of a sacrilegious priest, imperiling the existence of Judaism; but the latter is the redemptive act of the Messiah, extending the moral power of Judaism to the whole world. *See* EPHESIANS, LETTER TO THE.

C. *II MACCABEES.* 1. Original title. The book may well have been qualified by the adjective "Maccabean" (*cf.* § A *above*) from the beginning, since it is primarily concerned with the history of Judas Maccabeus. Clement of Alexandria called it appropriately ἡ τῶν Μακκαβαϊκων ἐπιτομή, since it claims to be a condensation of a five-volume work of Jason of Cyrene (2:23). Even more apt is the title of the colophon at the end of the book in MS V: "An Epitome of the Deeds of Judas Maccabeus."

2. Contents. II Maccabees is introduced by two epistles from the Jews of Judea to their brethren in Egypt (1:1-9; 1:10–2:18). Both letters are concerned with the observance of the Feast of Dedication (*see* DEDICATION, FEAST OF) in commemoration of the reconsecration of the sanctuary after its profanation by Antiochus IV Epiphanes (*see* ANTIOCHUS 4). *See also* § C5*b*.

After a prologue describing the author's condensation and embellishment of the history written by Jason of Cyrene (2:19-32), we reach the epitome proper. Any adequate outline of II Maccabees must be theological, not merely chronological. The following principal heads may be given:

I. God's blessing of Jerusalem and protection of the temple from desecration by Heliodorus, during the devout administration of the high priest Onias, under Seleucus IV, ch. 3
II. God's punishment of Jerusalem—Antiochus IV's profanation of the temple and proscription of Judaism—resulting from the evil intrigues of Simon and the Hellenizing priests Jason and Menelaus, chs. 4-7
III. God's merciful deliverance of the Jews and the reconsecration of the temple, resulting from the devout and heroic action of Judas and his men, as also from the timely death of Antiochus IV, 8:1–10:9
IV. God's loyal support of Judas and his men in their numerous victories, during the reign of Antiochus V, 10:10–13:26
V. God's self-manifestation in his defense of Jerusalem and the temple through Judas' defeat of Nicanor, during the reign of Demetrius I, 14:1–15:36
VI. Epilogue, 15:37-39

3. Message. The sanctity of the temple is the unifying theme of the entire narrative, as may be seen from the foregoing outline. One will note the perfect balancing of the headings I and V, and the neat reversal of II in III. Headings III and V are also in strict parallelism, since the former led to the establishment of the Feast of Dedication (10:5-8) and the latter to the institution of Nicanor's Day (15:36; *see* NICANOR 1). The Jerusalem temple is the greatest, most famous, and holiest of the entire earth (2:19, 22; 5:15; 14:31; 15:18), for through it God dwells among his people (14:35-36).

Judas' role is deliverer of people and sanctuary. In the second introductory letter (*see above*), he is also preserver of the Scriptures, but primary attention is given to his purification of the altar of burnt sacrifice. In both respects he labored as a second Nehemiah; but as a kindler of the holy fire upon the altar, he stands in the tradition of Moses, Solomon, and Jeremiah.

Theodicy dominates the book; for everywhere the perfect justice of God is maintained. The persecution of the Jews by Antiochus Epiphanes was occasioned by national apostasy under the leadership of the Hellenized priests. To be sure, this involved the suffering of the righteous; but it was a kindly discipline intended to bring the people to repentance. God is quick to scourge his own in order to deter them from further sin; but he is forbearing with the heathen until their sins are ripe for an annihilating judgment (6:13-16; 7:33; 10:4). God's wrath toward Israel was turned to mercy through the prayers and obedience of Judas and his party (8:1-5, 27). Their observance of the law guaranteed their success in battle (8:34-36). There are numerous examples of the principle of exact retribution, or punishment in the same place or manner as the crime committed (4:16, 38; 5:9-10; 7:17; 8:33; 9:5-6; 13:8).

Monotheism and the absolute sovereignty of God are stressed, not only by the narrative, but also by the appellations given him. Seldom is he simply "God" or "Lord," but rather "the Almighty God [or Lord]" (3:22; 8:18), "God [or Lord], the righteous Judge" (12:6, 41), "great Sovereign of the world" (12:15, 28), "him who sees all things" (12:22), etc. Always the appellation is that which best suits the historical context. The strongest assertion of divine sovereignty is Judas' ascription to "Almighty God" the ability "with a single nod to strike down those who are coming against us and even the whole world" (8:18). So great is God's power, he created the world from nothing (7:28). Here is the first explicit expression of the doctrine of creation *ex nihilo*.

The battles in which the Jews engage are supermundane, for angels participate in the struggle. Here is perpetuated the OT concept of the "Lord of hosts," or "Sovereign of spirits" (3:24), who commands heavenly as well as earthly legions. The angelic warriors appear regularly as horsemen mounted upon glorious steeds (3:25; 10:29-31; 11:8), but sometimes simply as resplendent young men (3:26, 33). The coming of a good angel renders the Hebrew armies invincible (11:6, 8; 15:23); but the forty-day apparition of contending cavalries charging over the sky of Jerusalem (ch. 5) was an evil omen, as similar apparitions reported by Josephus (War VI.v.3) and Tacitus (Hist. V.13) which presaged the destruction of Herod's temple. Contrast the good omen of II Sam. 5:23-24 (I Chr. 14:14-15). For angelic horsemen and charioteers in the OT, cf. II Kings 2:11; 6:17; 13:14; Zech. 1:8; 6:1-8. *See* ANGEL.

The martyred saints are also profoundly concerned with the human struggle; for in Judas' vision the priest Onias and the prophet JEREMIAH appeared as the people's intercessors (II Macc. 15:11-14). Jeremiah handed Judas a golden sword with which to strike down his adversaries (vss. 15-16).

The doctrine of the RESURRECTION is presented as a stimulus for heroic dying for the sake of religious conviction. The descriptions of the dauntless deaths of Eleazar (6:18-31), of the mother and her seven sons (ch. 7), and of Razis (14:37-46) are the earliest known martyrologies. *See* MARTYR.

The resurrection of the dead is described in such strongly physical terms as to suggest a resuscitation to participate in the earthly blessings of the messianic age. Apparently only the righteous are to be raised (7:14). On one occasion, Judas made atonement for his men who fell in battle, by sending money to provide a sin offering on their behalf at the temple. The purpose was to guarantee the resurrection of those whose religion was compromised by their wearing pagan amulets (12:39-45).

4. Chronology. II Maccabees follows the official system of calculating the beginning of the Seleucid era from the autumn of 312 B.C. (*cf.* § B4 *above*). This method, of course, is used in the official correspondence of ch. 11, where within the same year is found the sequence: Dioscorinthius (11:21) and Xanthicus (11:33)—the former being the autumn month Dios and the latter corresponding with the Jewish month of Nisan (roughly, April), which for the Jews began the new year. "Dios" was qualified by "Corinthius" in Lysias' letter, apparently out of his admiration for things Greek.

The same CALENDAR is followed in the narrative of the book, for where I Macc. 7:1 reports a Syrian dating, II Macc. 14:4 agrees. On the other hand, where I Macc. 6:20 reports a Jewish dating for the summer of 163 B.C., it reckons it as the 150th year, whereas II Macc. 13:1 locates the same event in the 149th year. Year 150 according to the Jewish calculation began the spring preceding, but according to the official Seleucid calendar it would not begin until the following autumn. The availability of mulberry juice at the time (I Macc. 6:34) points to the summer. The fact that the Jews were hindered in their defense of BETH-ZUR by food shortages (I Macc. 6:49, 53) occasioned by the SABBATICAL YEAR also reinforces the dating, for this holy year was calculated from the autumn (Tishri, 164), so that food shortages would have been felt by the following summer.

5. Literary sources. ***a. Jason's history.*** The author of II Maccabees, commonly called the "epitomist," names the principal source of his historical narrative as the five-volume work of Jason of Cyrene (*see* JASON 3). He describes his process as one of omitting tedious and uninteresting matters and of embellishing the material appropriated in order to improve its literary style (2:23-31). Some incidents, particularly the martyrdoms, are dealt with at such length and with such striving for emotion-stirring effect that they can hardly be regarded as in any sense an epitome, but more probably an elaboration of a simpler narrative in Jason's work. Yet other materials are so highly condensed that they appear to be a hasty summary of events told more fully in the original source (13:22-26).

The epitomist also omitted whole episodes. Thus in ch. 14 he omits an account of Bacchides' expedition to install Alcimus as high priest (I Macc. 7:5-7, 25; II Macc. 14:4-10) and records only the later dispatch of Nicanor to reinstall Alcimus (II Macc. 14:11-27), which parallels I Macc. 7:26-32. The author makes it clear that he knew that Alcimus had been made high priest earlier (II Macc. 14:3), and the same is indicated indirectly by his knowledge of the date of Alcimus' initial visit (II Macc. 14:4; I Macc. 7:1).

The book divides into five clear-cut divisions, corresponding to the outline given above (*see* § C2). Each of these ends with a summary statement marking the formal close (3:40; 7:42; 10:9; 13:26*b;* 15:37*a*). Many scholars believe that these correspond with the fivefold division of Jason's work.

b. Letters. To the epitome are prefixed epistles

from the Palestinian Jews to those of Egypt, urging the observance of Hanukkah—the festival commemorating the purification of the temple after its desecration by Antiochus IV (*see* DEDICATION, FEAST OF). The letters are generally explained as two in number: (*a*) 1:1-9, written in the 188th year (124 B.C.), but citing an earlier letter (vss. 7-8) written in the 169th year (143); and (*b*) 1:10–2:18. The latter, however, appears to be composite; for 2:16 resumes the epistolary thread of 1:18, so that the intervening legendary matter may not have been an original part of this letter. It bears no date, but the situation implied would assign it to 165, prior to the first celebration of the Feast of Dedication. Since, however, its account of the death of Antiochus does not accord with the accounts found elsewhere, it is probably spurious (*see* ANTIOCHUS 4). These letters were prefixed to the historical work either by the epitomist himself or by a later editor. *See* § C7 *below*.

6. Sources of Jason's history. ***a. The biography of Judas.*** Since Judas' career is presented in close agreement with the life of Judas employed by I Maccabees (*cf.* §§ B5*c-d above*), it appears probable that Jason knew and ultilized this same biography. Jason, apparently, enriched his written material with the oral legends which the author of I Maccabees disdained to use (cf. I Macc. 9:22).

b. A Seleucid chronicle. For his knowledge of profane history, Jason may have consulted a Seleucid chronicle, employing the official Seleucid system of dating; but it was not necessarily the same document as that employed by the author of I Maccabees (*cf.* § B5*b above*); for in such matters as the number of soldiers employed in a battle, I and II Maccabees are not in agreement.

c. The temple archives. Jason must have had access to the archives of the temple, if we are to believe in the genuineness of the documents cited by the epitomist (II Macc. 9:19-27; 11:16-38). In these same archives may have been found the annals of the pre-Hasmonean priests containing some of the information concerning Onias, Jason, and Menelaus. Yet much of this material may have been transmitted by tradition which was embellished by supernatural occurrences. To have obtained so rich, extensive, and often accurate material, Jason must have visited the Holy Land. *See* JASON 3.

7. Integrity, problem of disarrangements. The origin of the introductory letters and of the disarrangements in the proper historical sequence of the book must be explained. The most obvious chronological error is the placing of the death of Antiochus IV prior to the rededication of the temple by Judas, both in the prefixed correspondence (1:11-18) and in the historical narrative (9:1–10:9). In the case of the latter, there is an obvious literary dislocation; for 10:9 ("Such then was the end of Antiochus") should stand immediately after 9:29 as the conclusion of the account of Antiochus' death. Yet it also belongs immediately before 10:10, as affording the proper antecedent for "that ungodly man." The reconsecration of the temple (10:1-8) is therefore an intrusion in its present context and should doubtless be placed prior to Antiochus' death, as in I Macc. 4–6.

There are other errors in sequence. II Macc. 8:30-33 intrudes an account of battles with Timothy and Bacchides between vs. 29 and vs. 34, breaking the original continuity of the account of the defeat of Nicanor (vss. 23-29, 34-36). At the same time vss. 30-33 presuppose the Maccabean recovery of Jerusalem, which has not yet been recorded, but which is correctly presented as the result of Judas' first defeat of Lysias in I Macc. 4; but the parallel account of II Maccabees is 11:1–12:1*a*, erroneously placed under the reign of Antiochus V, rather than Antiochus IV. The proper sequence would therefore be: (*a*) Lysias' campaign and defeat (11:1–12:1*a*); (*b*) the rededication of the temple (10:1-8); (*c*) the defeat of Timothy and Bacchides (8:30-33); (*d*) the death of Epiphanes (ch. 9; 10:9). The wars with neighboring peoples in 12:3-45 might also be properly placed before the death of Epiphanes, as in I Macc. 5; but it is highly probable that some of these battles occurred later, during the rule of Eupator.

These passages cannot be merely reshuffled, however, to restore the text to its original form; for they are clearly integrated in their present context. Thus the result of assigning the events of the Seleucid year 148 to the reign of Eupator in ch. 11 is to assign the death of Epiphanes to the year 147 and to shorten the period of the temple's desecration from three years (I Macc. 1:54, 59; 4:52) to two years (II Macc. 10:3). Moreover, in 11:1 Lysias is not the guardian of the king's son, as in I Macc. 3:33, but of the king himself. Hence Eupator has already become king, with the implication that Antiochus Epiphanes has died. Similarly the letter of II Macc. 11:22-26 (of doubtful genuineness) alludes to the death of Epiphanes, signifying that Lysias' campaign (11:1–12:1*a*) really occurred after Eupator became king. Finally, the dating of the reconsecration of the temple after the death of Epiphanes not only accords with the variant account of 1:10-18; it also makes for an over-all parallelism in the book, whereby the first half concludes with the institution of the Feast of Dedication (10:5-8), while the second half concludes with the establishment of Nicanor's Day (15:36).

Are these dislocations to be assigned to the epitomist or to a later editor? On the side of the first alternative, it may be claimed that the complete integration of the materials and the literary balance of the present book point to its composition in the form known to us. On the side of the second alternative, one may note the great discrepancy between the accounts of the death of Antiochus Epiphanes in chs. 1; 9 and question whether the epitomist, with his high regard for Jason's work, would have incorporated such a contradictory account as 1:13-16 (with Epiphanes actually killed in the Persian temple which he tried to rob, rather than suffering the later affliction described in ch. 9) and then have proceeded to rearrange the events of Jason's history to fit the implied historical sequence. Whoever wrought this confusion was doubtless influenced by the account of 1:13-16, for he surely would not have himself composed such a variant story. The epitomist may have been as likely content with a simple chronological adjustment of the text as a later editor; for he does not appear to be a man with acumen for historical research (2:28). It appears unnecessary, therefore, to attribute either the introductory epistles or the disarrangements to an editor; for the prologue to the epitome (2:19-32), as also its epilogue (15:37-39), discloses an author who had more concern for literary effectiveness than for historical accuracy. As the painter of a landscape does not hesitate to move, or even remove, any tree which obscures an aesthetically attractive view, so the epitomist felt free to rearrange or omit as suited his intention.

8. Original language. The epitomist was a skilled rhetorician who wrote good literary Greek, though his love of bombast and pathos too often descends to bathos to appeal to modern literary tastes. The original language was certainly Greek, unless it be for the introductory letters, which disclose sufficient Semitisms as to suggest the possibility that they may have been composed in Hebrew or Aramaic.

9. Authorship and date. ***a. Hasidic affinities.*** Judas Maccabeus, the chief hero of the book, is presented as the leader of the Hasideans (14:6). No reference is made to their defection from him, as in I Macc. 7:12-16. Their refusal to fight on the sabbath day, even in self-defense, is presented with approval (6: 11). The compromise of fighting in self-defense (I Macc. 2:39-42) is not recorded. Judas' leaving off pursuit of Nicanor is explained by the approach of the sabbath in II Macc. 8:25-26, whereas a military explanation is employed in I Macc. 4:16-18. II Macc. 15:1-5 discloses how sabbath-keeping Jews thwarted Nicanor's attempt to attack Judas in the region of Samaria. In all his prayers and speeches, Judas is a true Hasid. *See* HASIDIM; HASIDEANS.

b. Relationship to Daniel. It has often been pointed out that a knowledge of II Maccabees (as well as of I Maccabees) is necessary for an understanding of the historical allusions of Daniel, not only those which relate to the arrogance and cruelty of Antiochus Epiphanes, but also those which pertain to the details of his reign (especially in Dan. 11:21-39). Allusions to Heliodorus (Dan. 11:20; cf. II Macc. 3), to the martyrdom of Onias (Dan. 9:26; cf. II Macc. 4:30-36), and to Judas Maccabeus (Dan. 11: 34) have been alleged (*see* DANIEL). It is likewise important to note the influence exercised by Daniel upon II Maccabees and his forebear Jason of Cyrene —since the two cannot be clearly distinguished.

The martyrs of II Maccabees (6:10–7:42; 14:37-46) act with the courage and piety of Daniel and his three companions in refusing to compromise with paganism. Their trust in the resurrection of the dead reflects the popularity of the book of Daniel (11:35; 12:2). There is a similar prominence given to angels. Judas, if alluded to in Daniel, is only a "little help" (11:34); for direct intervention of God is necessary for salvation: sending a fatal plague upon Epiphanes and dispatching the archangel Michael (11:45–12:1). II Maccabees, however, represents Judas' victories as miracles achieved through the help of angels, though, of course, the human struggle is very real. In both books pagan rulers are compelled to recognize the might and divinity of the Lord (Dan. 2:47; 3:28; 4:34-37; 6:25-27; II Macc. 3:35-39; 8:36; 9:17). Since the book of Daniel was written by a Hasidean, these affinities strengthen the Hasidic character of II Maccabees.

c. Affinities with the War Scroll. There is also a close conceptual relationship with the ancient military manual known as the War of the Sons of Light and the Sons of Darkness (*see* DEAD SEA SCROLLS). The battle slogans of Judas—"God's Help" (II Macc. 8:23; cf. 12:11; 13:13, 17; 15:7-8, 35) and "God's victory" (13:15)—are similar to those inscribed on the banners of the Sons of Light. Both works give a prominent place to the restoration of the temple and its cult. In both fighting is avoided during the sabbatical years. The military manual forbids it, and the epitomist does not represent the fighting in 11: 1-12 as occurring during the sabbatical year, as indicated by I Macc. 6:49, 53. In the War Scroll there is the same supermundane character of the conflict as in II Maccabees; for the Sons of Light are supported by good angels in their war with the Sons of Darkness, who also for their part are supported by evil angels (*see* § B3 *above*). Since the ESSENES, who possessed the scroll, evolved from the Hasideans, once more the affinities reinforce the Hasidic character of II Maccabees. The author cannot be identified with either Pharisee or Essene; the most we can assert is that his outlook was Hasidean.

d. Anti-Hasmonean and pre-Roman. It is only in the second introductory letter that there is any direct allusion to the Hasmonean dynasty established by Simon (2:17). The fact that Simon appears in the narrative only in a somewhat unfavorable light (10: 18-22; 14:17-19) probably indicates that the epitomist was anti-Hasmonean. In any case, his Hasidic affinities would place him in the company of those who opposed that dynasty, including both PHARISEES and ESSENES. The first introductory letter, dating from *ca.* 124 B.C. (1:9), was written during the rule of Simon's son John Hyrcanus. Though Hasidic discontent with the Hasmonean dynasty arose earlier (*cf.* § B8 *above*), Hyrcanus' open break with the Pharisees occurred near the end of his rule (*ca.* 106). It is doubtful that II Maccabees should be assigned a date much before 100. Since Jerusalem is still in the possession of the Jews (15:37), the book must be pre-Roman, prior to 63.

The work of Jason, upon which the epitomist depended, would be earlier, but probably not prior to the early part of Hyrcanus' rule—which lasted from 135 to 105; for time has to be allowed for the developed state of the traditions he recorded, as also for the composition of Judas' biography which was used by him (*see* § C6*a above*). Jason and the author of I Maccabees appear to have labored independently, for all the striking agreements between them are easily accounted for by their use of common sources, especially the biography of Judas. Jason probably wrote earlier than I Maccabees, but outside the Holy Land, so that his work was unknown to the author of I Maccabees.

e. Egyptian provenance. The fluent Greek of the epitome would seem to point to its composition by a Jew of the DISPERSION. Also, only outside Palestine would confessing oneself to be a Ιουδαῖον (6:6) mean to "confess himself to be a Jew," rather than a "Judean." Though it has been suggested that Antioch may have been the place of composition, upon the assumption that some of the martyrdoms occurred there (7:3; cf. 6:8), the prefixing of letters addressed to the Egyptian Jews supports the prevalent view that the book was written in Egypt, perhaps at Alexandria. The stress upon the unique sanctity of the Jerusalem temple may have been directed against the rival Jewish temple at HELIOPOLIS. Similarly, the impressing upon them of the observance of the Feast of Dedication was intended to promote the unity of Egyptian and Palestinian Jews.

10. Importance for the NT. The Letter to the Hebrews refers to the martyrdoms of II Macc. 6:10–7:42, when at Heb. 11:35 it declares: "Some were tortured, refusing to accept release, that they might rise again to a better life." The allusion of Heb. 11:38 is especially to II Maccabees (5:27; 6:11; 10:6; cf. I Macc. 2:30-31), when again it describes the martyrs as "wandering over deserts and mountains, and in dens and caves of the earth."

The influence of II Macc. 8:13 appears in the language of Rev. 21:8—"those who were cowardly and distrustful [οἱ δειλανδροῦντες καὶ ἀπιστεῦντες] of God's justice ran off and got away" being echoed by "the cowardly, the faithless [τοῖς δειλοῖς καὶ ἀπίστοις]," in the latter. The former reference makes clear that ἀπίστοις should be understood, not simply as "faithless" in the sense of disloyal, but also as "unbelieving" (KJV). Faith is the wellspring of the martyr's faithfulness.

For the interpretation of the coming of the Christ, II Maccabees affords important antitheses. In the NT, the Christ replaces the temple as God's abiding presence among his people (John 2:19-21; Rev. 21:22); and the glory of God, which was expected to return to the temple (II Macc. 2:8), has been manifested in him (John 1:14). Similarly, one may contrast the spurious divinity of Epiphanes, who "had just been thinking that he could command the waves of the sea, in his superhuman arrogance" (II Macc. 9:8), with God's unique Son, whom winds and sea obeyed (Luke 8:25).

Christ's expiatory suffering is adumbrated by the suffering of the martyrs, who thought of an atoning value in suffering (II Macc. 7:37; 8:3), though their vengeful attitude toward their enemies was not emulated by him. The necessity of an atonement with validity for the next world (in contrast with the OT sacrifices for this world only) underlies the crudity of prayer and sacrifice for the dead in 12:42-45. In fulfilment of this need is the "once for all . . . eternal redemption" of Christ (Heb. 9:12, 25-26). *See* ATONEMENT.

The supermundane character of the struggle of God's people is stressed in the NT, as also in II Maccabees. Jesus, in his wilderness trial, was tempted by Satan and ministered to by holy angels (Mark 1:13). In the agony of Gethsemane he was strengthened by an angel (Luke 22:43); but, unlike Maccabeus (II Macc. 11:6; 15:23), he accepted suffering rather than appeal for heavenly legions (Matt. 26:53-54). His death and resurrection are represented as the undoing of Satan (John 12:31; 14:30; 16:11; Col. 2:15; Heb. 2:14; Rev. 12:7-9). For Paul, the struggle of the saints is with the "spiritual hosts of wickedness in the heavenly places" (Eph. 6:12). *See* § C3 *above*.

In the area of custom one may note that the practice of mixing water with wine (II Macc. 15:39) prevents Jesus' command of drawing water for wine jars from appearing strange (John 2:7)—the novelty appears only in their having been filled with water alone. Perhaps against this background we are to understand I Tim. 5:23: "No longer drink only water, but use a *little* wine" (*see* WINE AND STRONG DRINK). John the Baptist's diet of locusts and wild honey (Mark 1:6) is well explained by the practice of the Hasideans, who in their wilderness retreat sought to avoid defilement by subsisting "on what grew wild" (II Macc. 5:27). *See* JOHN THE BAPTIST.

There are Greek words in the NT whose meanings are illumined by II Maccabees. Thus God's redemptive "appearance" (ἐπιφάνεια) occurs repeatedly in II Maccabees, not merely through the apparitions of angels (2:21; 3:24-25, 33; 12:22), but also through the military might of Maccabeus (15:27). God's epiphany in the NT is in the incarnation of his Son (Luke 1:79; II Tim. 1:10) and in his expected return in glory (II Thess. 2:8; I Tim. 6:14; II Tim. 4:1, 8; Tit. 2:13). Likewise, the persecutor in II Macc. 7:19 is one who dares "to fight against God" (θεόμαχειν); the same verb is employed as in Acts 5:39 for the persecutors of the church.

D. *III MACCABEES*. 1. Original title. The present name is a misnomer (*cf.* § A *above*). Consequently, where the listing of the *Synopsis Athanasii* mentions Μακκαβαϊκὰ βιβλία δ′, Πτολεμαϊκά ("four Maccabean books, Ptolemaica"), it is supposed that we should emend δ′ to καί, so as to read "the Maccabean books and Ptolemaica"—the latter being III Maccabees. Its proximity to I and II Maccabees in MSS of the SEPTUAGINT probably gave rise to its present name. This association was not without reason; for its affinities with II Maccabees (*see* § D5 *below*), together with the fact that its history precedes that of II Maccabees, makes the book an excellent prolegomenon to II Maccabees.

2. Contents. The book presents three stories of conflict between Ptolemy Philopator and Judaism—each being the outgrowth of the preceding. The first (1:1–2:24) is his attempt to enter the sanctuary of the Jerusalem TEMPLE, following his victory over Antiochus III in the Battle of Raphia. After popular protest and the eloquent prayer of the high priest Simon (*see* SIMON 1), Philopator swooned. Gradually recovering his wits, he withdrew with bitter threats to Alexandria.

The second story (2:25-33) is his spiteful effort to exclude the Jews from Alexandrian citizenship, by requiring all citizens to sacrifice at the royal temples. All who refused were to be enrolled as serfs and branded with the ivy leaf, the emblem of the god Dionysus. Only a few Jews acquiesced; the rest resorted to bribery in order to avoid the enrollment, and even ostracized their apostate brethren.

In the third story (chs. 3–7) the king brought with great cruelty all the Jews of the Egyptian interior to the hippodrome near Alexandria, where they were to be enrolled for execution; but this was hindered by a failure in the supply of papyrus and pens, so that after a period of forty days the census was still incomplete. Impatiently, the decree was given that they should be trampled by drunken elephants; but this was delayed on two successive days, first by the king's oversleeping, and then by his complete forgetfulness—events presented as miracles, but placed in the setting of the king's carousals. When the event was in readiness, the Jews gave themselves to prayer, being led by an aged priest, Eleazar. Two angels descended; this panicked the elephants and turned them back upon Philopator's own soldiers.

Moved to penitence, the king released the Jews, feasted them for a week, and then dismissed them with a letter which indicated their loyalty. He also gave them permission to kill their weaker brethren who had apostatized. En route home, they celebrated a second week of festivity after reaching Ptolemaïs (apparently "Ptolemaïs of the harbor," twelve miles SW of Cairo). Then they completed their homeward journey in safety. After each of the foregoing weeks of feasting, the Jews ordained to commemorate the occasion by instituting an annual festival.

3. Message. III Maccabees is an apologetical work intended to make the Jews more steadfast in their faith and practice and designed also as a warning to all would-be persecutors; for the Jews are a unique people, the sanctity of whose temple cannot be safely violated (1:8–2:24) and the purity of whose religion cannot be contaminated even under duress (2:25–7:23). They are loyal citizens, who have always been devoted to the Egyptian government, having manned her fortresses from of old (3:21; 6:25; 7:7; *see* ARISTEAS; ELEPHANTINE PAPYRI). Though they reside in the lands of their enemies, they are protected by the special providence of God (6:15), who is the "eternal saviour of Israel" (7:16).

4. Historical sources. ***a. An anti-Ptolemaic history.*** The book is so replete with obvious exaggerations and needless resort to miracles that a cursory reading suggests a historical romance. Yet the author is so well informed that he must have been dependent upon a written history of the period. His account of the Battle of Raphia is remarkably close to that of Polybius of the second century B.C. (*Histories* V.80-86). Philopator's visit to nearby cities and their enthusiastic welcome of him is duly recorded by Polybius, as also by III Macc. 1:6-8. In this setting, it is most reasonable that he should have visited Jerusalem. The ancient monuments attest his lavish expenditures upon temples, in full accord with his gifts to Syrian shrines and his sacrifices at Jerusalem (1:7-10). He enacted two censuses: one in 220-219 B.C., the other in 206-205. The second, which alone follows the Battle of Raphia (217), is too far removed to have been a vengeful act occasioned by his rebuff in Jerusalem; but it is late enough for the king to refer to his children (7:2)—his legitimate son having been born in 208. His life of dissipation and misgovernment is attested by Polybius (*Histories* V.34), as also by Plutarch (*Lives of Agis and Cleomenes* XXXIII-XXXIV), who depicts him as "absorbed with women and Dionysiac routs and revels."

Though such characterizations may not be wholly fair, it is obvious that the author had access to some good historical information. Unexplained differences in detail prevent us from identifying his source with the *Histories* of Polybius—though his *memoriter* usage of it is possible. Since a certain Ptolemy of Megalopolis, who served as governor of Cyprus under Philopator, wrote an uncomplimentary biography of his overlord, it is suggested that his work was the primary source of both Polybius (who was also of Megalopolis) and III Maccabees for the history of this period. His writing is believed to have been characterized by extravagances adaptable to the use of III Maccabees. Unfortunately, only fragments of his work survive.

b. Jewish traditions. The political rights of the Jews in ALEXANDRIA were ambiguous and often contested, so that an attempt to curb them may well have occurred upon the occasion of a census—knowledge of which was transmitted by tradition.

The elephant story was an independent legend, unrelated to the census; for Josephus (Apion II.v) presents us with a variant account which locates the event under Ptolemy IX Physcon (146-117 B.C.), as an act of political reprisal against the Alexandrian Jews for supporting the rival claims of Queen Cleopatra. This setting is intrinsically more probable. Yet the identity of the Ptolemy may have been indefinite in popular lore, enabling the author of III Maccabees to fuse the story with other traditions and history.

The sharp distinction drawn between the Jews of Alexandria and those of the interior, as also between the two festivals inaugurated—one at Alexandria, the other at Ptolemaïs—points to the fusion of variant traditions into one dramatic story.

5. Literary affinities. ***a. Comparison with Esther.*** The work combines the elements of religious oppression characteristic of Daniel with the purely ethnical oppression of the canonical ESTHER. The conspiracy of Theodotus (1:2) recalls that of the chamberlains of Esth. 2:21-23; and Dositheus saves the king's life (III Macc. 1:3), as does Mordecai (Esth. 6:2). Similar charges of disloyalty are brought against the Jews (III Macc. 3:19; Esth. 3:8). In each case an attempted pogrom was abortive and recoiled upon the perpetrators, ending with the institution of a commemorative festival. In both books the delivered Jews are given license to kill. In Esther (ch. 9) this is a mostly vengeful slaying of hostile Gentiles, but in III Maccabees (7:10-15) it is a heartless slaying of their weaker brethren. The tone of Esther is almost secular, whereas that of III Maccabees is profoundly religious; but this difference is remedied by the apocryphal additions of the Greek Esther. *See* ESTHER, APOCRYPHAL.

b. Comparison with II Maccabees. In III Maccabees (2:27-30), as also in II Maccabees (4:9; 6:1-9), an effort was made to impose an alien citizenship upon the Jews involving compromise with Hellenism. In both books remarkable deliverances are commemorated by festivals. The abortive effort of Philopator to penetrate into the sanctuary at Jerusalem (III Macc. 1:9–2:24) recalls the similar incident of Heliodorus (II Macc. 3). Heliodorus' vision of scourging angels (vs. 25) is paralleled by those which terrify the Egyptians and their elephants in III Macc. 6:18-21. Prayers for the protection of the sanctuary figure in both works (II Macc. 3:15-23; 14:34-36; III Macc. 2:1-20).

6. Authorship and date. Since Alexandria is the focal point of the story, there is no room to doubt that the author was an Alexandrian Jew. He was a true Hasidean who believed in loyalty unto death to the law of Moses. In the spirit of the Bible, his defense of Judaism was based upon history alone, not upon philosophical argument—in this respect being quite unlike ARISTEAS, PHILO JUDEUS, and the author of IV Maccabees (*cf. below*). His faith in miracles parallels that of Daniel, whose stories are recalled in Simon's prayer (III Macc. 6:6-7). No mention is made of Esther, for in the story there is no room for hero or heroine, but only for the "mighty works" of God (6:13). The focus upon deliverance is sufficient to explain the absence of any reference to the resurrection, precisely as in the stories of Dan. 1–6, despite that faith which finds expression later in the same book (Dan. 11:35; 12:2). The author believed in "glorified angels of terrifying aspect" (III Macc. 6:18); but naturally he allowed them to be seen by the Egyptians only, mercifully shielding the Jews from any further terror. Though he wrote in Greek for Greek-speaking Jews, his religion is scarcely influenced by his Hellenistic environment.

The book could not have been written prior to the first century B.C., as may be inferred from the influence of II Maccabees. The author probably knew Esther and Daniel only in the enlarged Greek recension. His description of three youths in the fiery furnace (6:6; cf. Dan. 3:20-25) reflects the language of the Greek Daniel (Song Thr. Ch. 26-27). Linguistic similarities with the Greek Epistle of Aristeas (*see* ARISTEAS) also suggest a date not earlier than the first century B.C. Epistolary formulas indicate the same period. The Ptolemies did not use personal epithets like "Philopator" (III Macc. 3:12; 7:1) in official correspondence before *ca.* 100 B.C.

The author's intention was to prepare a religious scroll to meet the inspirational and instructional needs of the distinctive festivals of Egyptian Jewry. This alone may be sufficient occasion for his writing, without there being any especially severe persecution in his own day. There is no reference to emperor-worship or to the erection of images in synagogues expected in a work written in the time of Caligula (cf. the persecution of A.D. 38-39, described in Philo's work *On Flaccus*). Though it has been claimed that the word for "census," λαογραφία (2:28), is distinctively Roman, the evidence is ambiguous; for though in Roman usage it applied to noncitizens only as in 2:28-30, it was concerned with a poll tax, of which nothing is said in III Maccabees. Hence the word may be used in a nontechnical pre-Roman sense of an enrollment for general purposes of administration and taxation. Allowing for the ambiguity, the book may be safely dated to the first century B.C., either before or after Roman rule, which began in 30 B.C.

7. Importance for the NT. The book affords additional examples of God's "manifestation" (ἐπιφάνεια) in history (2:9; 5:8, 51). God "manifests" his mercy (2:19), his might (5:13), and his presence (6:18) in order to protect his temple and his people. He is, indeed, through the deliverances of this book "the manifest God" (5:35)—but how much more through the redemption of Christ! *Cf.* § C10 *above.*

E. *IV MACCABEES.* 1. Original title. The common name of this book in Greek MSS is IV Maccabees (*cf.* § A *above*). But through a false attribution to JOSEPHUS, it appears also among his works, entitled *On the Supremacy of Reason* (Περὶ αὐτοκράτορος λογισμοῦ), and is thus cited by Eusebius (Hist. III. x.6) and Jerome (*On Illustrious Men* 13). Variant forms of the title appear in some MSS of Josephus. Whatever the original name, *On the Supremacy of Reason* is most apt.

2. Contents. The book contains a philosophic discourse on the supremacy of religious reason over all passions of body and soul. After a statement of the theme (1:1-12) and a careful definition of the philosophical terms (1:13-30*a*), the author illustrates his oft-reiterated thesis by OT examples (1:30*b*–3:17). The greatest demonstration of his proposition, however, is to be found in the heroism of those who died for their religion during the persecution of Antiochus Epiphanes: Eleazar, the seven brothers, and their mother. To them he refers at the outset (1:8-12), and to them he devotes the major part of his book (5:1–18:24).

3. Message. The book is dedicated to the proposition that the law is the most authentic expression of true philosophy, as seen by the following propositions: "Reason, then, is the intellect choosing with correct judgment the life of wisdom; wisdom is knowledge of things human and divine and their cause. Such wisdom is education in the Law, through which we learn things divine reverently and things human advantageously" (1:16-17, translated by Hadas; *see* WISDOM). Reason is frequently denominated "religious wisdom," ὁ εὐσεβὴς λογισμός (1:1; 7:16; 13:1; 15:23; 16:1; 18:2), or the "reason whose source and essence is piety," ὁ λογισμός τῆς εὐσεβείας (7:4, 23; 16:4). By claiming that God designed Jewish food laws in accordance with that which was fit for the soul (or physical life?), the author equates the law of Moses with natural law, as in Stoicism (5:25-26; *see* STOICS; CLEAN AND UNCLEAN). There is also an echo of universal brotherhood, grounded in the common nature of man (12:13).

The human passions are capable of an Aristotelian division into pleasure (ἡδονή) and pain (πόνος); but associated with these are desire (ἐπιθυμία) and joy (χαρά), fear (φόβος) and grief (λύπη)—a fourfold classification of emotions similar to that of Stoicism (1:20-23; *cf.* STOICS). Anger (θυμὸς) is common to both pleasure and pain, and the inclination to EVIL (ἡ κακοήθης διάθεσις) is a form of pleasure including many emotions of body and soul (1:24-28). This last is derived from rabbinic Judaism, wherein the evil inclination (*yeṣer ha-ra'*) stands opposed to the good inclination (*yeṣer ha-tobh*). Accordingly it is elucidated so as to include the appetite for forbidden foods (vs. 27). Equally Jewish is the author's repudiation of the Stoic notion that the sage achieves freedom from passion (ἀπάθεια); for virtue is achieved, not by eradication of God-given emotions, but by their subjection to religious reason (2:21-23). *See* GREEK RELIGION AND PHILOSOPHY.

Judaism may boast of her philosophers, of whom the aged priest Eleazar and even the seven youths are outstanding examples (5:4; 7:7-9; 8:1). Like Socrates in Plato's *Gorgias,* they believe that it is better to suffer evil than to do evil, also that the evildoer is more miserable than the man wronged (9:30). On the other hand, Antiochus, like the opponents of Socrates, advocates hedonism and opportunism (5:6-12; 8:5-10; 12:3-4). By choosing death in preference to apostasy, the noble "Maccabees" reveal (1:6, 18; 3:1) that they possess the qualities of: prudence (φρόνησις), justice (δικαιοσύνη), courage (ἀνδρεία), and self-control (σωφροσύνη)—virtues acclaimed by the Stoics, but Platonic in origin. The amazing endurance (ὑπομονή) of these martyrs, whereby they demonstrated their Stoic strength, proves (9:18) that "the Hebrews alone are invincible in virtue's cause."

As with Socrates and Plato, the ultimate moral sanctions are rooted in the doctrine of immortality: eternal life with God for the righteous (7:3; 9:22; 14: 5-6; 16:13; 17:12; 18:23), but eternal punishment for the wicked (9:9, 31; 10:15, 21; 12:12, 18; 13:15; 15: 27; 18:5, 22). Immortality, as in Greek thought, seems to be wholly spiritual—nothing is made of a physical resurrection, but some of the language is suggestive of a spiritual resurrection. *See* § E9 *below; see also* RESURRECTION.

The author sometimes uses philosophic titles for God: Providence, πρόνοια (9:24; 13:19; 17:22); Justice, δίκη (4:21; 8:14, 22; 9:9; 11:3; 12:12; 18:22); and Power, δύναμις (5:13). These attributes are never hypostatized, however, as in PHILO JUDEUS. We have rather the traditional angelology (4:10; 7:11). *See* ANGEL.

The most astonishing doctrine is the expiatory power of the blood of the martyrs. It dissolves the power of tyranny (a punishment for the nation's sin), cleanses the fatherland, and renews the observance of the law (1:11; 17:21; 18:4). Atonement is explained in strongly substitutionary terms (6:28-29; 17:21)—life for life (a ψυχή becomes an ἀντίψυχος)! Like the blood of Abel (Gen. 4:10-11), it calls down the wrath of God upon the wrongdoer (IV Macc. 11: 22; 12:17-18). The expiatory death of the SERVANT OF THE LORD in Isa. 53 partially anticipates this doctrine; but the closest parallels are in the Essene Manual of Discipline, where the Council of the Community must "expiate iniquity through practicing justice and through the anguish of the refining furnace" (VIII.3-4), and as "the chosen of divine acceptance must atone for the land and render to the wicked their desert" (VIII.6-7; cf. 9-10). *See* DEAD SEA SCROLLS; *cf.* § C10 *above.*

4. Literary classification. The book has been variously assessed, as: (*a*) a sermon, (*b*) a diatribe (or lecture), and (*c*) a panegyric on Maccabean martyrs. Its religious tone, including the use of doxologies (1: 12; 18:24), suggests its delivery in the context of worship; but the fact that it develops a philosophical dogma rather than a biblical text favors its classification as a diatribe, rather than a sermon. Still the element of eulogy and frequent apostrophizing favors even more a panegyric. In any case, the book was written for oral delivery and is a splendid piece of Hellenistic oratory. It is quite declamatory and employs many rhetorical devices to create the moods of pathos, horror, admiration, and conviction.

5. Literary source. The historical material of the book seems to be dependent upon II Maccabees. The background of the Seleucid persecution of the Jews (IV Macc. 3:19–4:26) summarizes II Macc. 2–6:11. The martyrologies (IV Macc. 5:1–18:24) expand and elaborate II Macc. 6:18–7:42. Reference is also made to the cruel fate of Antiochus Epiphanes (IV Macc. 18:5), with allusion to II Macc. 9. The only alternative to the use of II Maccabees is a possible dependence upon Jason of Cyrene, whose work II Maccabees professes to condense. (*cf.* § C5*a above*). In support of this dependence are notable differences in the narrative and the considerably fuller account of the martyrdoms; but these are easily explicable as the author's own free deviations—especially since in the story of King David's thirst (IV Macc. 3:6-16), he embellishes and alters the biblical account (II Sam. 23:13-17; I Chr. 11:15-19).

6. Integrity. The genuineness of three sections has been questioned. IV Macc. 17:23-24; 18:6-19 interrupt the context and do not accord in language or tenor with the rest of the book. The latter passage gives a speech of the martyr mother concerning the domestic teaching of the now deceased father, in order to attribute the endurance of the sons to their paternal instruction. Its citations of Deut. 30:20; 32: 39; Ezek. 37:3 (at IV Macc. 18:17-18) allude to a doctrine of physical resurrection at odds with the rest of the work (*cf.* § D3 *above*). Despite claims to the contrary, 18:5*b* is defensible as genuine and in its proper place as an explanation of how Antiochus met his end (vs. 5*a*), and no mere gloss accounting for Jewish military successes (vs. 4). It accords also with the author's method of simplifying the more complex historical situations of II Maccabees—leaving Antiochus in the vicinity of Jerusalem (4:22–5:3) until the martyrdoms were over and he himself was ready to march to his death in Persia.

7. Occasion. Since IV Maccabees was composed to commemorate those "who at this season died" (1: 10; cf. 3:19), one is led to inquire as to the identity of the "season." As early as the fourth and fifth centuries A.D., the Greek and Syriac churches observed an anniversary of the martyrdoms on August 1. The tomb (or tombs) was (or were) believed to be near a synagogue in the Kerateion Quarter of Antioch (*see* ANTIOCH [SYRIAN]). However, 18:5*b*-6*a* (*cf.* § D6 *above*) would contradict this location of the tomb; and there is late Arabic attestation to a synagogue built over the remains of these martyrs—the first constructed after the destruction of the second temple (*see* TEMPLE, JERUSALEM) and therefore supposedly at Jerusalem. Consequently, even though the book was written as a memorial, since its composition was probably outside the Holy Land (*cf.* § D8 *below*), it could not have been intended for delivery at (or near) the place of burial—the only allusion to the tomb (17:8-10) being wholly rhetorical.

The stories are highly embellished legends which record the execution of Eleazar as taking place at a common trial with the seven youths and their mother. These were separate incidents in II Macc. 6:18-31; 7:1-41, with the king present only for the latter, which can be presumed to be historical only in the sense that it is a legend growing out of real persecution and martyrdom. Therefore, no death date could have been known, and any memorial address must have been assimilated to some other occasion.

Since the Christian commemoration of August 1 approximates the Jewish Ninth of Ab lamentations of the destruction of the first and second temples, it may have been borrowed from the Kerateion Synagogue of Antioch, where it was recited on that occasion. However, this observance did not come into vogue until after 70, whereas IV Maccabees bemoans the suppression of the temple cult by Antiochus as a great tragedy (4:20) from which the faithful suffering of the martyrs has brought relief. Consequently, the temple is presumed still to stand, and the book was composed prior to 70, and therefore for some other festival.

The book's constant emphasis upon atonement wrought by the martyrdoms would make it suitable for reading on the annual Day of Atonement. Analogously, a rabbinic legend of the execution by Hadrian of ten teachers of the law is included in the synagogue liturgy for that day.

The Feast of Dedication (*see* DEDICATION, FEAST OF) would be most apt of all for commemoration of Maccabean martyrs, though no reference is made to the festival in this book. Yet it reiterates the theme of the purified fatherland (1:11; 17:21) through the suffering of the martyrs for the people (6:29), in harmony with II Maccabees' representation of the festival as one of purification (II Macc. 1:18; 2:16, 19; 10:3, 5). The doctrine of the inviolability of the temple while the law is faithfully observed is borrowed from II Maccabees, as also the explanation of Antiochus IV's profanation as due to the sins of the Jews. Since the deaths of the "Maccabees" under torture have undone the desecration of the tyrant, the book would be appropriate for the Feast of Dedication, with its commemoration of the renewed altar and purified temple. In harmony with this, there is some evidence for the Jewish recitation of a rabbinic variant of the story of the seven brethren and their mother (though assigned to the persecution of Hadrian) at this feast. To be sure, one might expect some allusion to the noble Hasmonean house, to whom much credit was due from recovery of the temple; but in pious circles the HASMONEANS fell more and more into ill repute, and our author represents the deliverance as achieved through martyrdom rather than by military prowess (17:22; 18:4).

8. Authorship and date. The book was written in a semiclassical style of Greek (making frequent use of the archaic optative) by a writer versed in Greek philosophy, who addressed a Jewish audience expected to follow and appreciate his learned reasoning. This suggests that he was a Jew of the Diaspora. It is commonly claimed that he was ignorant of the topography of Jerusalem, since he locates a gymnasium *upon* the citadel of the city (4:20) instead of *under* it as in II Macc. 4:12. However, he employs ἐπ(ί) with the dative, which in both classical and koine Greek often means "near," or "at," rather than "upon." Even so, the sense of detachment from the place, indicated by the change of preposition, does imply composition outside the Holy Land. The assimilation of Greek philosophy by Judaism is well attested for ALEXANDRIA. Therefore, the author of IV Maccabees has often been assigned to this city. If, however, the Greek of IV Maccabees is Asiatic (as good authorities claim), composition at the great cultural center of Antioch (*see* ANTIOCH [SYRIAN]) seems more probable. In that case, pious "invention" had not yet located the Maccabean tomb in that city, or the author would not have represented the martyrdoms as taking place at Jerusalem.

As already seen (§ E7 *above*), the book was written while the temple was still standing. The most precise criterion for dating is the alteration of the title of Apollonius from "governor of Coelesyria and Phoenicia" (II Macc. 4:4) to "governor of Syria and Phoenicia and Cilicia" (IV Macc. 4:2); for CILICIA was connected administratively with Syria and Phoenicia only for the brief span of A.D. 18-55. The persecution by Caligula occurred in the middle of this period (38-39); but this time, as also the years following, is excluded, since the auditors of the panegyric find it difficult to believe their ears concerning the cruelty of Antiochus (14:9). So, then, IV Maccabees was written between 18 and 37.

9. Importance for the NT. As a writing roughly contemporary with Jesus and the apostles, IV Maccabees is very important for establishing the thought of the Diaspora Judaism at that time. However, one must not draw too rigid a distinction between the religion of the Jews inside and outside the Holy Land; for the Greco-Roman world was largely one.

Jesus' admonition not to fear him who can kill the body alone, but rather him who can kill both body and soul (Matt. 10:28; Luke 12:4-5), is paralleled by IV Macc. 10:4; 15:8; II Macc. 6:30—from which it is apparent that Jesus referred to God as the one to be feared (*see* FEAR). Reception of the righteous dead into the fellowship of the patriarchs was a current view (IV Macc. 7:19; 16:25) appearing at Luke 16:23, an idea combined also with the phrase "live to God" (Luke 20:37-38). The sympathetic suffering of the mother with each of her sons (IV Macc. 15: 12, 16, 22) is applied to Mary the mother of Jesus in a parenthetical remark of Luke 2:35*a*. The association of sweat with blood (IV Macc. 7:8) appears likewise at Luke 22:44. If the last two Lukan references are genuine to Luke, and not glosses, Luke may have been influenced by IV Maccabees.

Paul had not necessarily read IV Maccabees shortly before writing I Corinthians; but when he wrote (13:3*b*): "If I deliver my body to be burned, but have not love, I gain nothing," it was a poignant criticism of IV Maccabees and similar stories. Paul's great moral trilogy of faith, hope, and love—of which the greatest is love (vs. 13)—strikingly suggests an antithesis to the four Hellenistic virtues, prudence, justice, courage, and self-control—of which the greatest is prudence (IV Macc. 1:18-19). Most significantly, in this letter Paul developed fully his doctrine of the spiritual body (I Cor. 15:35-57), which may have been suggested in part by IV Macc. 9:22: "As though he were being transformed into incorruption [μετασχηματιζόμενος εἰς ἀφθαρσίαν] by the fire, he nobly endured the torments" (cf. I Cor. 15: 52-54; Phil. 3:21). The "as though" (ὥσπερ) of IV Maccabees seems to indicate a mere figure of speech, yet the author also speaks of receiving pure and deathless souls at physical death (18:23)—an idea somewhat suggestive of Paul's "spiritual body" (cf. II Cor. 5:1-4). *See* PAUL; RESURRECTION.

The "history of religion" (ἡ τῆς εὐσεβείας ἱστορία) for IV Maccabees (17:7; cf. 3:19) is not the usual *Heilsgeschichte* (salvation story) of the Bible, but a record of human endurance under trial. So also in the Letter to the Hebrews, where likewise FAITH is a heroic principle of doing and suffering for righteousness' sake (Heb. 11; cf. IV Macc. 15:24; 16:22; 17:2). Heb. 11:34-35 suggests IV Maccabees as background, but it may rather be accounted for by II Maccabees (*cf.* § C10 *above*). The common figure of the spectators in the stadium (Heb. 12:1; IV Macc. 17:11-16), observing the gladiators, would cause no pause, if "looking to Jesus" (Heb. 12:2) were not reminiscent of "looking unto God" (IV Macc. 17:10) —in each case the Greek ἀφορῶντες εἰς. Sanctification by the expiatory blood of the martyrs in IV Macc. 1:11; 6:29; 17:21-22 is paralleled by the sanctifying death of Christ in Heb. 1:3; 2:11; 10:10, 14, 29; 13:12—the former, however, being limited to the Jews and the Holy Land, whereas Christ's expiation is universal. Neither has Christ's blood the vengeful effect ascribed to that of the Maccabean martyrs (*cf.* § E3 *above;* Rev. 6:9-10), but it "speaks more graciously than the blood of Abel."

In IV Maccabees "to conquer" (νικᾶν) continually means to endure martyrdom without apostasy (6:10; 7:4, 10-11; 8:1; 9:6; 11:20), thereby defeating tyranny (1:11; 9:30; 16:14) and proving the power of religious reason over the passions (3:17; 6:33; 13:2, 7; 17:15). Similar meanings are common for the word in Johannine literature (John 16:33; I John 2:13-14; 4:4; 5:4-5; Rev. 2:7, 11, 17, 26; 3:5, 12, 21; 11:7; 12:11; 13:7; 17:14; 21:7). In both IV Macc. 17:18; Rev. 7:15, the martyred dead stand before the throne of God.

The Gospel According to John traces the ministry of Jesus through a sequence of Jewish feasts, including the Feast of Dedication (10:22). If stories of Maccabean martyrs were told on such an occasion (*cf.* § E7 *above*), a comparison with John is most instructive; for here Jesus is threatened with martyrdom (vss. 31-39) and like a good shepherd will lay down his life for others (vs. 15). The raising of Lazarus signifies that Christ has the power of renewal (note ἐγκαίνια as a name for the festival). This Lazarus (whose name is a form of Eleazar) was himself in danger of being martyred (12:10-11); but it was Jesus who was destined to be the vicarious sacrifice (11: 49-53). *See* ATONEMENT.

F. *CANONICITY.* The books of Maccabees, along with other APOCRYPHA and PSEUDEPIGRAPHA, owe their preservation solely to the church, which cherished them as historical works of God's people Israel and as examples of heroic defense of the truth. Although I and II Maccabees are cited by some church fathers as scripture, the more scholarly of them who could read Hebrew, or who were acquainted with the Jewish Bible, did not include these among the canonical writings. I and II Maccabees had no place in the original Vulg. of Jerome, although they were in the OL Version and from there gained later admission into the Vulg. III Maccabees was well received only in the Eastern churches (Greek, Syriac, and Armenian), where it was received along with I and II Maccabees. IV Maccabees was widely influential in the writing of martyrologies and for celebrating the heroism of the Maccabean martyrs; and it appears in some MSS of the LXX. However, it has rarely received recognition as canonical. As late as the time of Luther, prominent Roman Catholic scholars rejected all the Apoc. It was in opposition to the Reformers that the Roman church at the Council of Trent in 1546 decreed the canonization of the Apoc., including I and II Maccabees. *See* CANON OF THE OT.

As regards historical and religious value, I Maccabees compares favorably with Kings, II Maccabees with Chronicles, and III Maccabees with Esther. IV Maccabees, either as a philosophical treatise or as a panegyric, is without any counterpart in the Bible. For biblical scholarship, the concept of canon is an irrelevance; for all literature is welcome material of study for the light it can shed upon the OT (as these books upon Daniel) or the NT. The Maccabean books are also appreciated for themselves as the religious literature of God's chosen people, wherein great truths often find apt expression.

Bibliography. Commentaries: R. L. Bensly, *The Fourth Book of Maccabees and Kindred Documents in Syr., with an Introduction and Translations* (1895), shows Christian interest in this book. See the following commentaries in R. H. Charles, *The Apoc. and Pseudep. of the OT* (1913): W. O. E. Oesterley, "The First Book of Maccabees," II, 59-124; J. Moffatt, "The Second Book of Maccabees," I, 125-54; C. W. Emmet, "The Third Book of Maccabees," I, 155-73; R. B. Townshend, "The Fourth Book of Maccabees," II, 653-85. C. W. Emmet, *The 3rd and 4th Books of Maccabees* (translations of early documents; 1918): of popular character. A. Dupont-Sommer, *Le quatrième livre des Machabées,* Librairie Ancienne Honoré Champion (1939): very valuable. F.-M. Abel, *Les livres des Maccabées,* EB (1949): valuable for the first two books, with critical Greek text. M. Hadas, *The Third and Fourth Books of Maccabees,* Jewish Apocryphal Literature (1953): valuable, with critical Greek text. J. C. Dancy, *A Commentary on I Maccabees* (1954): semipopular, with notes on II Maccabees also. S. Tedesche (trans.) and S. Zeitlin (commentator), *The First Book of Maccabees,* Jewish Apocryphal Literature (1950); *The Second Book of Maccabees,* Jewish Apocryphal Literature (1954): both important studies with critical Greek texts. See also Introductions to the Apoc. by E. J. Goodspeed, B. M. Metzger, W. O. E. Oesterley, R. H. Pfeiffer, C. C. Torrey, etc.

Special studies: J. P. Mahaffy, *The Empire of the Ptolemies* (1895), pp. 243-88: on Ptolemy IV and III Maccabees. I. Abrahams, "The Third Book of the Maccabees," *JQR,* IX (1896-97), 39-58: defends the historicity of the book. R. de Tindaro, "Martyre et sépulture des Machabées," *Revue de l'Art Chrétien,* XLII (1899), 290-305, 457-65: on the tradition of the Maccabean tomb at Antioch and later removals of the relics. B. P. Grenfel, A. S. Hunt, and J. G. Smyly, *The Tebtunis Papyri,* I (1902), 447-48: on pre-Roman use of λαογραφία in Egypt. B. W. Bacon, "The Festival of Lives Given for the Nation in Jewish and Christian Faith," *The Hibbert Journal,* XV (1916-17), 256-78, contains discussion of the Feast of Dedication in relation to IV Maccabees and John. A. Deissmann, *Paulus* (2nd ed., 1925), p. 76: for Paul's knowledge of IV Maccabees. E. Bickermann, on the first three "Makkabäerbücher," in *Paulys Real-Enzyklopädie,* vol. XIV, no. 1 (1928), cols. 779-800. I. Heinemann, on IV Maccabees and its use for the Feast of Dedication, in *Paulys Real-Enzyklopädie,* vol. XIV, no. 1 (1928), cols. 800-805. J. Obermann, "The Sepulchre of the Maccabean Martyrs," *JBL,* LI (1931), 250-65: on the tomb at Jerusalem. E. Bickermann, *Der Gott der Makkabäer* (1937). M. G. Dagut, "II Maccabees and the Death of Antiochus IV Epiphanes," *JBL,* LXXII (1953), 149-57. K.-D. Schunck, *Die Quellen des I und II Makkabäerbuches* (1954): important for chronology as a guide to source analysis.

W. H. BROWNLEE

MACCABEUS măk'ə bē'əs [Μακκαβαῖος]. Surname of Judas, son of Mattathias, who gave the name to his family and to their celebrated revolt against the Syrian king. The meaning is often said to be "hammerer"; but it has been pointed out that, if this is so, the word from which it is derived does not mean a heavy hammer, as might be expected, but a small workman's tool.

See also MACCABEES.

N. TURNER

***MACEDONIA** măs′ə dō′nĭ ə [ἡ Μακεδονία]; MACEDONIAN —ən. The region N of ACHAIA in what is now the Balkan Peninsula.

Macedonia is predominantly mountainous but also has many fertile plains. Stretching from the Adriatic Sea to the Aegean, its most important cities were on the Aegean coast. Analysis of the ancient population indicates a pre-Indo-Germanic stratum overlaid by Thracian, Illyrian, and Macedonian tribes, with later Greek and Latin colonization and additional immigration from the N and the E.

According to Herodotus (VIII.139), the founder of the Macedonian kingdom was Perdikkas I, who must have reigned in the first half of the seventh century B.C. He was succeeded in turn by six descendants named by Herodotus, among them Philip I, Amyntas I, and Alexander I. Amyntas I may be placed in the second half of the sixth century, Alexander I *ca.* 480-450 B.C. The next kings were Perdikkas II (*ca.* 450–*ca.* 413 B.C.) and Archelaus (*ca.* 413–*ca.* 399). Of the latter, Thucydides (II.100) says that he did more than all his eight predecessors together to build up the roads and the military forces of Macedonia. In the following decades a number of different rulers struggled for and held the power; then in 359 B.C., Philip II, son of Amyntas III, came to the throne. It was the work of Philip II, by war and diplomacy, to weld together the Macedonian kingdom as never before, and then, with victory at the Battle of Chaeroneia in 338 B.C. (Diodorus XVI.85-86), to establish the supremacy of Macedonia over most of the Greek states. Thereafter he proposed war against Persia and in 336 sent an advance force across the Hellespont; but before he himself could follow, he was assassinated by a Macedonian noble. Alexander III, son of Philip II and Olympias, at thirteen a student of Aristotle, at eighteen a commander in the Battle of Chaeroneia, and now but twenty, acted swiftly to claim the kingdom. In the meteoric career which followed, Alexander, known to history as the Great, accomplished such amazing conquests

1. A Macedonian coin, bearing the Greek inscription

that by the time of his death in Babylon in 323 B.C. the Macedonian name belonged to an empire which extended from his native highlands to the Nile and the Indus (Plutarch *Alexander*). Fig. MAC 1.

The regent of Macedonia during Alexander's expedition to the East was Antipater, formerly an ambassador of Philip II to Athens. Before his death in 319 B.C., Antipater handed power to Polyperchon, former phalanx leader under Alexander, passing over his own son Cassander. Cassander took up the struggle and by 316 was master of Macedonia (Diodorus XIX.52). When Antigonus Cyclops, former general of Alexander and claimant to all his empire, fell at the Battle of Ipsus (301 B.C.), Cassander was recognized as king of Macedonia. Alexander, son of Cassander, followed the latter in 297 B.C. but was soon slain by Demetrius Poliorcetes, son of Antigonus Cyclops, who reigned from 294 to 287 (Plutarch *Demetrius*). After that there were years of confused struggles and also of invasion by migrating Gauls; then in 276 B.C., Antigonus II Gonatas, son of Demetrius, consolidated his position as king of the land (Polybius II.45; IX.29). Henceforward, till the coming of the Romans, Macedonia was the realm of the Antigonids.

In 168 B.C., Perseus, king of Macedonia and last of the Antigonids, was defeated at the Battle of Pydna by the Roman consul L. Aemilius Paullus (Polybius XXIX.xvii-xxi; Plutarch *Aemilius Paullus* XVI-XXII). In the settlement made the next year, Macedonia was declared free but divided into four districts (μερίδες) and placed under annual officials (Livy XLV.xvii-xviii, xxix-xxx). The first district extended from the River Nestos to the Strymon; the second from the Strymon to the Axios; the third from the Axios to the Peneios; the fourth from W of Mount Bora to the borders of Illyria and Epirus. The capitals were Amphipolis, Thessalonica, Pella, and Pelagonia (probably Heraclea Lyncestis) respectively. In 149 B.C. the Roman army under Q. Caecilius Metellus crushed the revolt of a certain Andriscus, who claimed to be the son of King Perseus and attempted to re-establish the monarchy. After that, Macedonia was made a Roman province; and the date of its foundation as a province, 148 B.C., was taken as the beginning of an official era. From A.D. 15 to 44, Macedonia was combined with Achaia and Moesia in a large imperial province under the legate of Moesia; but from 44 on, it was again a senatorial province. The Roman governor was a proconsul of praetorian rank, and the seat of administration was the free city of Thessalonica.

Macedonia provided the major land route between

MACEDONIA AND GREECE

Jack Finegan

Asia and the West; and soon after it became a province, the Romans constructed the famous Via Egnatia, which is mentioned already by Polybius (XXXIV.12), who died *ca.* 125 B.C. From a double point of departure on the Adriatic at either Dyrrhachium or Apollonia this route ran across the mountains to reach the sea at Thessalonica and then went

Courtesy of Harriet-Louise H. Patterson

2. Plain in Macedonia, where Philippi was situated

on through another Apollonia to Amphipolis, Philippi,* Neapolis, and beyond. Strabo (VII.322) says that it was marked by pillars from Apollonia on the W coast to Kypsela beyond the Hebros River in Thrace and that the distance was 535 Roman miles or, at 8 stadia to the mile, 4,280 stadia. The apostle Paul must have traveled on this road from Neapolis to Philippi, Amphipolis, Apollonia, and Thessalonica (Acts 16:11-12; 17:1). Fig. MAC 2.

Bibliography. Geyer and Hoffmann, "Makedonia," *Pauly-Wissowa,* vol. XIV, pt. i (1928), cols. 638-771. *Cambridge Ancient History,* VI (1927), 200-71, 352-504; VII (1928), 75-108, 197-223; VIII (1930), 241-78; IX (1932), 441-42; X (1934), 341, 681; XI (1936), 566-70. J. A. O. Larsen, "Roman Greece," in T. Frank, ed., *An Economic Survey of Ancient Rome,* IV (1938), 259-498.

J. FINEGAN

MACHABEES măk'ə bēz. Douay Version form of MACCABEES.

MACHAERUS mə kĭr'əs [Μαχαιροῦς]. The strongest Jewish castle, after Jerusalem. It was situated to

From *Atlas of the Bible* (Thomas Nelson & Sons Limited)

3. Remains of the fortress of Machaerus, where tradition says John the Baptist was imprisoned and suffered death

the E of the Dead Sea (the modern Mkaur). The place had originally been fortified by Alexander Janneus (*see* JANNEUS, ALEXANDER; HASMONEANS § 3*d*), according to Josephus, but was later demolished. Herod the Great refortified it and used it as one of his chief residences, and at his death it passed to Herod Antipas. After the Nabatean wife of Antipas had been divorced, she was imprisoned here; and, according to Josephus, this was where John the Baptist also was sent as a prisoner and perished.* The gospels do not identify the place; indeed, Mark's reference to the notables of Galilee suggests a place much farther N. The fortress became a stronghold of the Jews in the war against the Romans (A.D. 66-70). Fig. MAC 3. N. TURNER

MACHBANNAI măk băn'ī [מכבני] (I Chr. 12:13—H 12:14); KJV MACHBANAI măk'bə nī. One of the famed warriors from the tribe of Gad who joined the outlaw band of David at Ziklag; subsequently appointed as an officer in David's army.

MACHBENAH măk bē'nə [מכבנה] (I Chr. 2:49). A town in Judah; possibly the same as Meconah. The location is unknown.

MACHI mā'kī [מכי, reduced(?), *or* bought(?)] (Num. 13:15). The father of Geuel, who was sent from the tribe of Gad to spy out the land of Canaan.

Bibliography. M. Noth, *Die israelitischen Personennamen* (1928), pp. 39, 232.

MACHIR mā'kĭr [מכיר, bought (*as an orphan or waif*)]; MACHIRITES mā'kə rīts. **1.** Son of Manasseh. Little is known of him as an individual. The ancient list in Josh. 17:1-2 calls him Manasseh's first-born. The Chronicler names Asriel as his brother (I Chr. 7:14) and Maacah as his wife, who bore him Peresh and Sheresh (vs. 16*a*). An unnamed daughter is mentioned in 2:21; but further information from 7:15-18 is questionable.

Of Machir as a clan (Num. 26:29) two aspects are notable:

a) Anciently Machir was named among the tribes settled W of the Jordan, presumably as a constituent part of the Israelite federation (Judg. 5:14). But other references locate Machir in Transjordan, occupying specifically the territory from Mahanaim, N of the Jabbok, to the Yarmuk River (Deut. 3:15; Josh. 13:29-31; 17:1). Probably the warlike Machirites helped conquer part of central Palestine, then moved back E, dispossessing the Amorites from Gilead in Transjordan (Num. 32:39-40). This tribal movement was represented stylistically by calling Gilead Machir's son (Num. 27:1; 36:1; Josh. 17:3). *See* GILEAD 1.

b) Whatever its original position among the Israelite tribes—and some admixture with Arameans is indicated (*see* JAIR 1; Deut. 3:14; I Chr. 2:21)—Machir emerges as the dominant Manassite family. Gen. 50:23 is an ethnic etiology, explaining Machir's adoption into the "house of Joseph." *See* MANASSEH 2.

Bibliography. M. Noth, *Die israelitischen Personennamen* (1928), p. 232; *The History of Israel* (1958), pp. 61-62, 72, 89-90. L. HICKS

2. Son of Ammiel of Lo-debar, presumably near Mahanaim. As a loyal supporter of the house of Saul, Machir afforded a gracious sanctuary to Meribbaal (Mephibosheth) during the anxious days that followed the regicide of his uncle Ishbaal (Ishbosheth), until David accorded the lame son of Jonathan a princely status at his court (II Sam. 9). Converted, no doubt, by this kindly act of the king, Machir became a loyal adherent of David and subsequently joined two other wealthy Transjordanian patricians, Shobi the Ammonite prince and Barzillai the Gileadite, in supplying David and his men with ample supplies of food and equipment when they had established their quarters at Mahanaim during their flight from the usurper Absalom (II Sam. 17:27-29). E. R. DALGLISH

MACHMAS. KJV Apoc. form of MICHMASH.

MACHNADEBAI măk năd'ə bī [מכנדבי, *possibly a corruption of* מכרנבו, possession of Nebo, *or more probably, as* I Esd. 9:34 *suggests, a corruption of* ומבני זכי, and from the sons of Zaccai (*cf.* Ezra 2:9)] (Ezra 10:40; I Esd. 9:34). One of those compelled by Ezra to give up their foreign wives. M. NEWMAN

MACHPELAH măk pē'lə [המכפלה, the double (cave)].

1. Location. A place in the center of modern el-Khalil (Hebron) in which there is a cave purchased by Abraham for use as a family sepulchre. In it were buried Sarah (Gen. 23:19) and Abraham (25:9), Isaac (35:29) and Rebekah, Jacob and Leah (49:31; 50:13), and perhaps others. The biblical datum locates it "east of Mamre." The traditional identification with the area now covered by the Haram el-Khalil ("sacred precinct of the friend of the merciful one, God") is almost certainly correct. Ancient Hebron was built on a hill, er-Rumeideh, W of the present site. During the Middle Ages the earlier site was abandoned, and the city began to grow around the sanctuary below it.

2. Biblical history. The only reference outside Genesis to the patriarchal sepulchre is obliquely in the sermon of Stephen (Acts 7:15-16). Here Stephen says that Jacob was returned from Egypt and buried in the tomb Abraham had bought from the sons of Hamor in Shechem. According to Gen. 50:13, Jacob was buried in Machpelah; it was Joseph who was buried at Shechem (Josh. 24:32). In the pseudepigraphic Testament of the Twelve Patriarchs, Joseph is said to have been buried at Hebron (Test. Joseph 20:6). Where the other tribal ancestors were buried is not mentioned in the Bible, but Josephus (Antiq.

II.viii.2), the Testament of the Twelve Patriarchs, and the book of Jubilees (46:9-10) say they were buried in Hebron. On the other hand, Jerome (*Epistles* 47.10; 108.13) says that their tombs were also pointed out at Shechem. This double location may reflect the hostility between the Jews and the Samaritans. The traditions had been confused, and Stephen's words reflect the confusion.

The "field of Machpelah" in which the cave lay belonged to one Ephron, a Hittite, and was legally purchased by the Amorite chieftain Abraham. The account in Gen. 23, usually assigned to P, has customarily been interpreted as a typical example of the lengthy negotiations characteristic of the East, with Ephron getting a large price under the guise of pretended generosity. It has been pointed out, however, that this is rather a typical example of land purchase under Hittite law. Abraham's first request is countered with an offer to use or lease but not buy (vs. 6). He insists on buying the cave at the edge of the field belonging to Ephron, who first offers both the cave and the field as a gift. Abraham refuses and insists on paying for it. Ephron's price of four hundred shekels is accepted by Abraham and weighed out in the presence of witnesses. The point of the protracted negotiation and Ephron's insistence on the sale of the field is that under Hittite law the purchaser of property also became liable to the feudal service required of the landowner. Thus Ephron was trying to rid himself of this obligation—whatever it was—by selling the whole tract to Abraham. Also typical is the mention of the trees in the account, for in Hittite business documents it was customary to list all the trees when a plot of land was purchased. Thus the story reflects a situation in which Hittite legal practice was observed.

From the patriarchal days to the Roman period, nothing is known of the tombs of the patriarchs except that the tradition seems to have remained current throughout this long period. In the Hellenistic period we meet the traditions already cited in which the patriarchs, their wives, and Jacob's sons (including Joseph) were buried at Hebron (Jubilees, Testament of the Twelve Patriarchs). The book of Jubilees also mentions frequently a tower or house of Abraham (29:17-19; 31:5; 33:21; 36:20), and this tower played a role in the conflict between Esau and Jacob (chs. 37-38). These accounts not only reflect in legendary form the conflicts between the Jews and the Idumeans, but also preserve a memory of some kind of monument at the site of the tomb of the patriarchs, of which there is no longer any trace.

3. Postbiblical history. Our first archaeological evidence is from the time of Herod, who erected a splendid enclosure around the site, *ca.* 197 feet long and 111 feet wide, with walls *ca.* 8 feet thick, oriented in a NW-SE direction. The original entrance, located to lead to the opening of the cave, was probably where the present "Tomb of Joseph" is. In 1917, from the cenotaph of Abraham, an English army officer entered a chamber which may have been the vestibule of Herod's day before one entered the cave consisting of two chambers cut in the rock. On the upper level Herod built monuments or cenotaphs to mark the tombs. It would be these to which Josephus refers as "of really fine marble and of exquisite workmanship" (War IV.ix.7). The Pilgrim of Bordeaux (333) mentions the quadrangle and the marble tombs. A century or so later, Peter the Deacon speaks of the church without a roof and the house of Jacob to be found at Abramiri (ʼΑβραὰμ μεσίς, "field of Abraham").

At the time of Eudocia (mid-fifth century) or Justinian (early sixth century), a basilica was built in the E part of the enclosure. *Ca.* 570 another traveler noted the church which one could see there, as well as the patriarchal tombs, including the tomb of Joseph—Joseph had been finally "annexed" to Hebron by a tradition competing with that of Shechem, it would seem. After the Arab invasion, the church became a mosque.

In 670, Arculf, after a visit to the shrine, does not speak of the church but of three large cenotaphs for Abraham, Isaac, and Jacob and three smaller ones for Sarah, Rebekah, and Leah. The six probably came from the Byzantine period and are not the ones seen today. Of interest is the mention of a monument to Adam, which reflects a Jewish tradition, also accepted by Jerome, that Adam was buried at Hebron. Indeed, the ancient name of Hebron, Kiriath-arba, was said to refer to the four tombs of Adam, Abraham, Isaac, and Jacob.

The description of Muqaddasi (985) indicates that the cenotaphs were then placed as they are today. The monuments to Isaac and Rebekah were built by the Mamluks, those to Abraham and Sarah by the Abbasids or Omayyads. The Persian traveler Naṣir-i-Khosrau (1047) speaks in glowing terms of the beauty of the mosque and notes that Caliph Mahdi (in 918) made a new entrance, probably because the old one was obstructed by the "tomb of Joseph."

With the coming of the Crusaders, the shrine again became the property of the Christians. The mosque was reconverted to a church, and in 1168 it became the seat of a bishopric.

In June, 1119, according to two Arab writers and a Latin account, the bones of the patriarchs were found. Some of the paving stones were removed from the floor of the church. A small vestibule was found from which a corridor led westward to a small, circular hall, then to a chamber cut in the rock, and finally, at the end of this, to a second chamber. The remains in the first chamber were attributed to Jacob, those in the second to Isaac, while the body of Abraham was apparently sealed in a sarcophagus. In addition, there were fifteen clay jars filled with bones. The twelfth-century investigators had entered from the SE corner of the church, which entrance is now sealed (though its location can be seen), and reached the chamber into which one may peer from the twelve-inch hole in the floor of the present mosque, near the NW wall *ca.* ten feet SW of the main entrance. This is the same chamber visited by the English officer in 1917 by an opening which had been hidden since the time of the Crusades, the first of the two burial chambers. The Crusader clergy placed some bones in the main altar of the church and returned the rest to the graves. A Jewish traveler, Benjamin of Tudela, was allowed to visit the sepulchre in 1170. He tells of six sarcophagi on which "the Gentiles" had inscribed the names of the patriarchs and their wives. In his short visit, the

English officer caught a quick glimpse of one of the medieval tombs. The Crusaders rebuilt the church on its Byzantine plan but embellished it with vaults supported by massive pillars built around the earlier columns, and added an entrance porch.

After the fall of the Frankish Kingdom, the shrine again became Muslim. For a time visits by pilgrims were permitted, but after the fourteenth century all Christians and Jews were forbidden entrance to the cave and the enclosure above it. The church became a mosque, with few alterations. The marble veneer and the present cenotaphs date from Malik en-Naṣer, son of Qalaûn (1332). The description of the shrine by Mudjir ed-Dîn in 1496 fits the present establishment, including the Tomb and Mosque of Joseph (from the time of Barquq, 1395).

See also HEBRON.

Bibliography. M. Lehmann, "Abraham's Purchase of Machpelah and Hittite Law," *BASOR,* 129 (1953), 15-18; R. de Vaux, "Machpelah," *Dictionnaire de la Bible, Supplément,* vol. V (1953), cols. 618-27, and bibliography cited there.

V. R. GOLD

MACRON mā'krŏn [Μάκρων, *perhaps* long-headed]. A name of the Ptolemy who, according to II Macc. 10:12, was governor of Cyprus at the time of Ptolemy Philometor. He was regarded as a gifted governor (Polybius 1.27.13; 5.61). He deserted Philometor VI in favor of Antiochus Epiphanes IV. Because of his pro-Jewish policies, taking "the lead in showing justice to the Jews because of the wrong that had been done to them" (II Macc. 10:12), he was accused before Antiochus Eupator by the king's friends, presumably Lysias. Since he could not maintain the honor of his position, he took poison and thus ended his life.

Some identify him with son of Dorymenes (I Macc. 3:38). Such identification is not well founded, because of the different attitudes taken toward the Judeans. Ptolemy son of Dorymenes was the one who induced the king to change his mind favorably, to clear Menelaus of the accusations by the Jews that he allowed his brother Lysimachus to steal golden vessels from the temple. He also was the one who issued the order to the Jews to conform with Greek manners and sacrifice (II Macc. 6:8).

Bibliography. S. Tedesche and S. Zeitlin, *II Maccabees* (1954), pp. 142, 191.

S. B. HOENIG

MADAI mā'dī [מדי, Mede(s)] (Gen. 10:2; I Chr. 1:5). An eponym; one of the "sons" of Japheth. *See* MAN, DIVISIONS OF, § A1*a;* MEDIA.

MADIABUN. KJV form of EMADABUN.

***MADMANNAH** măd măn'ə [מדמנה]. A city in S Judah, mentioned next to Ziklag (Josh. 15:31). In the parallel list of cities of Simeon (Josh. 19:5) it is replaced by BETH-MARCABOTH, but the two are probably the same city. According to I Chr. 2:49, it was founded by Shaaph the son of Caleb (i.e., Shaaph was the "father" of Madmannah); hence Madmannah was probably the older name, which was altered when Solomon selected the place as a good location for the manufacture and storage of chariots (cf. II Chr. 9:25).

S. COHEN

MADMEN măd'mĕn [מדמן, dung pit] (Jer. 48:2). A town mentioned in Jeremiah's dirge upon the destruction of Moab; possibly identical with DIMON. It may be located at Khirbet Dimneh, 2½ miles NW of Rabbah.

MADMENAH măd mē'nə [מדמנה, dunghill] (Isa. 10:31). One of the places on the N invasion route to Jerusalem. The location is unknown, though it was certainly N of Jerusalem, perhaps at Shu'fat.

The invasion may be that of Sennacherib in 701, though the route itself may well have been used earlier, so that this would be a sort of "traditional" description (for a similar description from the S, see Mic. 1:10-15).

V. R. GOLD

MADNESS [שגעון, מתהלל; μανία, παραφρονία, ἄνοια]; MADMAN. Mental disease of a chronic nature was not uncommon in the ancient Near East, although there are comparatively few instances of insanity recorded in the Scriptures. The Hebrew root שגע, akin to an Akkadian verb meaning "to be furious," appears to include violent rage as one manifestation of madness, while the verb הלל may originally have been used of those thought to be "moonstruck." In the OT, however, the latter verb is used of one who makes a fool of another, or who behaves like a madman. The Greek words of the LXX and the NT envisage mental disorders in general.

In antiquity the madman was held in universal dread, since it was believed that his insanity was the result of special contact with a deity, generally through demon possession. In consequence no one dared to interfere with the mentally infirm in any way, and in practice all contact with them was sedulously avoided. Even at the present day there is very little interest anywhere in the Near East in the plight of the insane.

In the Pentateuch, madness was regarded as a divine punishment to be meted out to those who disobeyed the laws of God (Deut. 28:28), while elsewhere its incidence was attributed to a spirit sent by the Lord (I Sam. 16:14; cf. I Kings 22:19-23).

The picture of psychological deterioration presented by Saul has often been interpreted in terms of typical manic-depressive insanity. But in actual fact he seems to have been suffering from the more malignant psychotic reaction of paranoid schizophrenia. This disease is frequently characterized by delusions of grandeur and of persecution, which may be complicated by fluctuations of the general mental condition. The patient is usually moody and suspicious, and his attempts to compensate for personality weaknesses not infrequently result in hallucinations and delusions. As the disease progresses, a violent act may be committed, particularly against someone who is suspected of being an actual or even potential enemy. The condition frequently terminates in complete intellectual and emotional deterioration (cf. I Sam. 18:11; 20:30-34; 28:20; 31:5; *see* SAUL). The attitude characterizing the thinking of the day was reflected in the behavior of Achish, king of Gath, toward David (I Sam. 21:12-15), which contributed materially to the success of the stratagem employed by the desperate fugitive.

The madness attributed to Nebuchadnezzar (Dan.

4) has every appearance of being historical, despite the understandable reluctance of contemporary historians to record or discuss it. He suffered from a psychotic condition (monomania), the symptoms of which were related to a specific paranoid delusional concept, and which assumed the rare form of *boanthropy*, where the sufferer believed himself to be an animal and acted as such. A damaged Babylonian inscription recovered by Sir Henry Rawlinson may perhaps provide independent confirmation of this situation. *See* DISEASE.

NT demoniacs were believed to be possessed by evil spirits (*see* DEMON; DISEASE), for which exorcism was the only reliable therapy. Jesus healed many such persons afflicted with neurotic and psychotic conditions (cf. Luke 8:2, 30; 11:14; etc.) and commanded his disciples to do likewise (Matt. 10:1; Mark 16:17).

R. K. HARRISON

MADON mā'dŏn [מדון] (Josh. 11:1; 12:19). A Canaanite town in Galilee, whose king joined Jabin's unsuccessful confederacy against Israel. It is identified with the LB–Iron I (*ca.* 1550-900 B.C.) site on the summit of Qarn Hattin, NW of Tiberias.

Bibliography. W. F. Albright, "Among the Canaanite Mounds of Eastern Galilee," *BASOR,* 29 (1928), 5-6.

G. W. VAN BEEK

MAELUS mā ē'ləs. KJV Apoc. form of MIJAMIN 2.

MAGADAN măg'ə dăn [Μαγαδάν]. A place of uncertain location on the Sea of Galilee, according to Matt. 15:39 in the best MSS. Some MSS and the RSV mg. read "Magadan" also in Mark 8:10, where the best MSS read "DALMANUTHA." *See also* MAGDALA.

D. C. PELLETT

MAGBISH măg'bĭsh [מגביש, thick(?)] (Ezra 2:30). A town of Judah to which the descendants of former residents returned after the Exile; possibly to be identified with Khirbet el-Mahbiyeh, *ca.* three miles SW of Adullam.

MAGDALA măg'də lə. KJV translation of Μαγδαλά (Μαγαδάν in the best MSS; Aramaic מגדלא, "tower") in Matt. 15:39 (RSV MAGADAN); and RSV mg. alternate translation in Mark 8:10 (DALMANUTHA in the text). The city called Magdala was on the W shore of the Sea of Galilee. The adjective "Magdalene" occurs in the gospels as the identification of a particular Mary probably identifying her as from Magdala. In NT times the Greek name for Magdala was probably Tarichea, which was well known as a flourishing city and center of the fishing industry (Jos. War II.xxi.8; III.ix.7–x.5).

The modern Mejdel almost certainly preserves both the name of the ancient city and the correct identification of the site. Mejdel is in a strategic location at a junction of the road along the lake from Tiberias and the road coming down from the hills into the plain through the Valley of Robbers. Apparently the city was named because it served as a guard tower or fort. The Talmud identifies Magdala as a short distance from Tiberias and in terms not inconsistent with the fact that Mejdel is *ca.* three miles N-NW of Tiberias (J.T. 'Er. V.1 [IV.3]; T.B.

4. Magdala, on the shore of the Sea of Galilee, with the Plain of Gennesaret in the foreground

Pes. 46*a*). Medieval travelers spoke of Mejdel and identified it with Magdala. Fig. MAG 4.

Bibliography. G. Dalman, *Orte und Wege Jesu* (1919), pp. 123-26; W. F. Albright, "Contributions to the Historical Geography of Palestine," *AASOR,* II-III (1923), 29-46.

D. C. PELLETT

MAGDALENE măg'də lēn [Μαγδαληνή; Aram. מגדליתא, the one from Magdala]. The standard term in the gospels for designating one of Jesus' most prominent Galilean female followers (Matt. 27:56, 61; 28:1; Mark 15:40, 47; 16:1; Luke 8:2; 24:10; John 19:25; 20:1, 18; lit., "Mary, the one [the woman] from Magdala").

Magdala is not mentioned in the gospels or in Josephus ("Magdala" in Matt. 15:39 KJV should read "Magadan," as in אBD; so RSV). In the Talmud, Magdala is located near Tiberias and is called "Migdal Nunya" ("fish tower"; Pes. 46*a*). It lay at the S end of the fertile Plain of Gennesaret (Ginnesar).

See also MARY 2.

E. P. BLAIR

MAGDIEL măg'dĭ əl [מגדיאל, choice gift from God(?)] (Gen. 36:43; I Chr. 1:54). An Edomite clan chief (but perhaps "clan chief of Magdiel").

MAGED. KJV Apoc. alternate form of MAKED.

MAGGOT [רמה] (Job 25:6; Isa. 14:11); KJV WORM. Alternately: WORM.

***MAGI** mā'jī [*singular:* μάγος; Lat. *magus;* Old Pers. *magu*]. The wise men in the nativity story. According to Matt. 2:1-12, after Jesus was born in Bethlehem, while Herod was king, "wise men from the East" arrived in Jerusalem with gifts for the newborn Messiah, saying that they had seen his star in the East. Led by the star to the very house in which the child was, they presented their gifts of gold, frankincense, and myrrh, and worshiped him. But warned in a dream of threats of Herod, they departed; and the strange visitors, whose identity and homeland are uncertain, are heard of no more. The episode is not mentioned elsewhere in the Bible. Who were they? Why are they unknown to other biblical writers? What does the story mean?

1. Translations
2. Identity of the Magi
   a. Shaman caste of ancient Medes
   b. Zoroastrian priests

c. Scholarly profession in Mediterranean world
d. Adepts in magic of various types
e. The term finally adopted by some Christians
3. Identity of the Magi of the gospel story
4. Interpretation of the story
Bibliography

1. Translations. The Greek expression in Matt. 2:1 is μάγοι ἀπὸ ἀνατολῶν. The RSV translates this as "wise men from the East" (KJV "wise men from the east"; ASV "Wise-men from the east"; Moffatt "magicians from the East"; Goodspeed "astrologers from the east").

2. Identity of the Magi. ***a. Shaman caste of ancient Medes.*** Most of our information about the Magi in the ancient period is based on statements of Herodotus. He mentions them in I.101, 107, 120, 132; III.65, 73, 79; VII.19. He states in I.101 that the Magi are a γενεά of the Medes, listing them along with five other groups. It is probable that he uses γενεά here in the sense of "caste." The Magi then would probably be a priestly caste, similar to medicine men and shaman groups of various early peoples, and somewhat parallel to the Brahmans of India in their earlier period. In I.107, 120; VII.19, Herodotus indicates that the Magi specialized in interpreting dreams.

b. Zoroastrian priests. On the other hand, Herodotus indicates that in his time the Magi were priests of Persia. As the religion of Persia was Zoroastrianism at that time, the Magi, therefore, were Zoroastrian priests. It has been suggested that when this aboriginal group of shamans was conquered by the invading Aryans, they succeeded in adopting the religion of their conquerors, but they also transformed it to the extent that they became its priests. In their adopted religion they eventually came into a position of great power. In the fourth century A.D. the Magi were in such a dominant position that they were able to instigate a deadly persecution of both Christians and Jews in Persia.

c. Scholarly profession in Mediterranean world. But Magi ranged far beyond the bounds of Persia. Such writers as Strabo (XV.727, 733) and Plutarch (*On Isis and Osiris* 46) are familiar with them in the Mediterranean area. As we have seen, they appear in Matt. 2:1-12. Acts 8:9-24 tells of SIMON MAGUS at Samaria. Acts 13:6-11 gives an account of ELYMAS, a magus at the city of Paphos on the Island of Cyprus associated with Sergius Paulus the proconsul. Josephus also in Antiq. XX.vii.2 tells of a magus of Cyprus named Atomos, who was attached to the court of Governor Felix at Caesarea. Magi were common in the Mediterranean world and were well known to early Christians. The three just named were Jews. This makes it clear that the Magi were by no means limited to persons of Persian nationality. The term had come to indicate a profession rather than any particular citizenship or culture. They were no longer necessarily associated with Persia in the popular mind.

Except for the Magi who came bearing gifts for the Christ child, the NT gives an unfavorable impression of these men. Simon Magus and Elymas Magus are presented as vile men without either true understanding or moral principles. That Magi were attached to the courts of such highly placed Roman officials as the proconsul and the governor indicates that some of them, at any rate, possessed qualities which made them welcome guests in the cultured social life of the age. This view is strongly supported by Philo of Alexandria, who in *Every Good Man Is Free* 74 and *On the Special Laws* 100 highly commends the Magi for their research into the facts of nature. This type of knowledge he calls the "true magic." A similar appreciation of the Magi is also implied by Cicero in his *On Divination* I.91, where he says that no Persian is able to become king who has not first mastered the scientific discipline of the Magi—a fact which is also mentioned by Philo. It is clear that some Magi in the Mediterranean area had established a sound reputation for both character and learning.

d. Adepts in magic of various types. But it is evident also that *magus* indicates adepts in MAGIC of various kinds. In his *Special Laws* III.101, Philo refers to them in this broader sense. He says that this type of practice is a counterfeit and perversion of art; that it is pursued by charlatan mendicants and parasites, but especially by low-grade women and slaves, who use charms, incantations, etc. Philo compares them to vipers, scorpions, and other venomous creatures.

Somewhat similar evidence may be derived from the Greek translations of the OT, which are relevant here because on account of their dates they neatly span the period of the writing of the NT. The LXX of Dan. 2:2, 10, uses *magus* to translate אשף, which the Hebrew lexicon defines as "conjurer" or "necromancer." This translation must have been made *ca.* 100 B.C. Theodotion, who translated Daniel in the second century, renders אשף by *magus* in Dan. 1:20; 2:2, 10, 27; 4:7; 5:7, 11, 15. Fragments of Aquila, also of the second century, use *magus* to render *'ob* in Deut. 18:11; I Sam. 28:3, 7-9; II Kings 21:6; 23:24; Isa. 29:4. אוב means either a necromancer or the spirit which he possesses in order to perform his art. Symmachus, another second-century translator, renders חרטמים as *magi* in Gen. 41:8, 24. This word means "magicians" or "interpreters of dreams." In all these cases *magus* is used to designate magicians of foreign cultures, such as Egyptian, Persian, and Babylonian, or outlawed practitioners among the Hebrews.

Yet the Bible presents some heroes of its own, such as Joseph and Daniel, who specialize in oneiromancy (interpretation of dreams). Several instances of this are presented also in the NT. Note Matt. 1:20, 24; 2:12-13, 19, 22; 27:19; Acts 2:17.

When Aquila translates אוב as *magus* in I Sam. 28:3, 7-9, in vss. 3, 8, and 9 it means the medium, but in vs. 7 it is the spirit which the medium possesses. The necromancer visited by the desperate King Saul at night possesses a *magus*. This same point of view is reflected in Mark 3:22-30, where the scribes accuse Jesus of possessing Be-elzebub and by this means casting out demons. The accusation is renewed in John 7:20, where the people say he has a demon or devil. The words thus used in parallel are אוב, "Be-elzebub," *daimonion*, and *magos* or *magus*. In other words, the scribes accuse Jesus of being a *magus*. The same charge could have been brought against the apostles and other early (and later) Christians who followed the practice of casting out demons.

In spite of the view of such a writer as Ignatius in Eph. 19.3 that by the birth of Christ all magic had been overthrown, it is evident that magic was variously used. When Philo idealizes it and Ignatius scorns it, they use the word in different senses. Although Jews and Christians ordinarily applied the word only to phenomena in other religions, they themselves nevertheless habitually practiced many of the same things but called them by different names.

e. The term finally adopted by some Christians. The cycle appears to have become complete when in the third century Cyprian, bishop of Carthage, in *Confessio Sancti Cypriani* 7, refers to himself as *magos philosophos* and in his *Homologia* as *Cyprian the Magus* busied with magic and possessing magical scriptures.

3. Identity of the Magi of the gospel story. Matthew makes no effort to identify the Magi. He only says that they are from the East, which could mean Arabia, Mesopotamia, or regions beyond. But they know the stars and understand their meaning; this knowledge was a science which was deeply rooted in various peoples of the ancient Orient. In his story of the Magi, Matthew recognizes that the science in this case was right. But he is not the only biblical writer who holds that stars and other heavenly bodies may serve as signs, portents, and wonders revealing God's will. Note Gen. 37:9; Joel 2:28-32; Mark 13: 24-27; Acts 2:17-21; Rev. 6:12-17.

4. Interpretation of the story. While Matthew does not identify the Magi (nor can we), it appears that they have come from far away. They are not Hebrews; their questions indicate this. They are pagans. The wonder, mystery, and reverence of the Magi are tribute to the Messiah from unnamed peoples; and the world's oldest learning pays homage. The Scriptures provide the background for this. In view of Matthew's fondness for the fulfilment of scripture, it is remarkable that he did not mention Num. 24:17, which says that a star will arise from Jacob, or Isa. 60:3:

> Nations shall come to your light,
> and kings to the brightness of your rising.

Other relevant passages are Pss. 68:29; 72:10, which tell of kings bearing gifts. These poetic statements are probably the origin of the later belief that the Magi were kings. All these and possibly other similar passages have prepared the way for, even if they have not outrightly inspired, Matthew's beautiful story. A half-century after Matthew wrote of the Magi a violent Jewish messianic movement named its leader, Simon, *Bar Cocheba,* "Son of the Star," a name suggested by Num. 24:17.

While geography, ethnology, and Eastern religions shed a dim light on the Magi, they become fully luminous only to eyes of faith in the Christmas season.

Bibliography. E. Hatch and H. A. Redpath, *Concordance to the LXX* (1897). S. V. McCasland, "Portents in Josephus and in the Gospels," *JBL,* vol. LI, no. iv (1932), pp. 323-335. F. J. Foakes-Jackson, K. Lake, and H. J. Cadbury, *Beginnings of Christianity,* vol. V (1933): R. P. Casey, "Simon Magus," pp. 151-63; A. D. Nock, "Paul and the Magician," pp. 164-88. M. S. Enslin, "The Christian Stories of the Nativity," *JBL,* vol. LIX, no. iii (1940), pp. 317-38. S. E. Johnson and G. A. Buttrick, *IB,* VII (1951), 256-59. S. V. McCasland, "Signs and Wonders," *JBL,* vol. LXXVI, no. ii (1957), pp. 149-52.

S. V. McCasland

MAGIC, MAGICIAN. In any polytheistic system the gods, by virtue of their multiplicity and limitation of power, are incapable of securing for themselves, for nature, and for mankind the stability and security essential for the continuation of things as they are. This deficiency forced both gods and men to make use of magic—an inactive power independent of gods and men, but which could be activized by the aid of incantations and rituals in order to accomplish supernatural deeds. The employment of magic by gods as a means to achieve definite purposes is well attested in the Sumero-Akkadian and Canaanite religious literatures. The Babylonian Creation Epic (Enuma Eliš) tells us that in the struggle against the primeval pair Tiamat and Apsu, the hero of the young generation of gods, Ea-Enki, killed Apsu with the aid of a spell which he recited (Tablet I, 60-70). It was because of his knowledge of effective spells and rituals that Ea-Enki had the epithet "Lord of Incantation," and was considered as the god of magic par excellence. The gods sought his advice to combat the malevolent deeds of evil spirits, and when the great Marduk once betook himself to his father for such help, Ea-Enki told him:

> O my son, what dost thou not know,
> What more can I give thee?
> How can I add unto thy knowledge?
> What I know thou knowest also.

In his fight against the monsters created by Tiamat to destroy her rebellious offspring, Marduk the champion of the gods used, among other weapons, a "red paste" which he held between his lips (The Babylonian Creation Epic, Tablet IV, 61; red was the magic color for warding off evil influences). Tiamat, on her part, did not rely solely on her armies either; in the midst of the battle she "recited a charm and cast a spell." Marduk, however, emerged victorious from the encounter, because he proved himself to be a better magician than the primeval Mother Tiamat. Furthermore, it would seem that the very vitality of the gods depended on a talisman which the chief deity carried on his body. In the Myth of Zu (*ANET* 111-13) we are told that when the bird-god Zu stole the tablets of Destinies from Enlil, all the norms of life were suspended and the gods themselves wasted away until the Tablets of Destinies were recovered and returned to Enlil. The gods wear amulets to protect themselves and to ensure victory in their undertakings. The goddess Ishtar wore charms when she descended to the nether world (Descent of Ishtar to the Nether World, *ANET* 106-9; cf. *bibliography*). A classic example of the use of magic is related in the Babylonian Creation Epic. Before proclaiming Marduk as their chief the gods in assembly put him to the test in order to find out whether he possessed the magical know-how, without which no god could rule supreme. They placed a piece of cloth before him and said:

> "Lord, truly thy decree is first among the gods.
> Say but to wreck or create; it shall be.

Open thy mouth: the cloth will vanish!
Speak again, and the cloth shall be whole!"
At the word of his mouth the cloth vanished.
He spoke again, and the cloth was restored.
When the gods, his fathers, saw the fruit of his word,
Joyfully they did homage: "Marduk is king!"
(Tablet IV, 21-29).

In comparison with the wealth of material available relating to the part played by magic in the Sumero-Akkadian religion, the sources from Canaan (Syria and pre-Israelite Palestine) are very meager. However, the references in the OT to magic practiced by the Canaanite inhabitants of Palestine and the data supplied in the myths and legends from Ugarit give us a clear insight into the role of sorcery in the Canaanite religion of the second millennium B.C. When Keret, king of Ugarit, fell ill, the supreme deity of the Ugaritic pantheon, El, addressed himself to the assembly of the gods, saying: "Who among the gods can remove the sickness, driving out the malady?" After having repeated the same question seven times without any of the gods' volunteering for the task, El decided to act himself. He declared: "I will work magic [*'iḫtrš,* Gt form of the root *ḥrš* "magic"; cf. חרשים (Isa. 3:3)], and will surely compass the removal of illness, driving out the malady." The next few lines of the text are partially broken off, but from what follows it is clear that El fashioned a creature (from clay?) called Sha'taqat, who brought about the complete recovery of the king. Her method consisted of washing his body clean of sweat and restoring his appetite for food, with the result that "death on the one hand, is broken; Sha'taqat, on the other, has prevailed" (The Legend of King Keret; cf. *ANET* 148*b*). A graphic description of the restoration of fertility by sympathetic magic is preserved in the Baal Epic. After Baal, the god of fertility, was killed by Mot, the god of sterility, the goddess Anath avenged the death of her brother in the following manner:

She seizes the Godly Mot—
With sword she doth cleave him.
With fan she doth winnow him—
With fire she doth burn him.
With hand-mill she grinds him—
In the field she doth sow him
(*ANET* 140*b*).[1]

By the process of dissecting Mot's body and planting it in the ground, fertility returns to the land. In a vision El perceived that "the heavens rain with fat, the wadies flow with honey" (Poems About Baal and Anath; cf. *ANET* 140*b*). This is a sure sign that Baal is alive again and that nature is responding with abundance once more.

Some human beings are endowed with magical power and can foretell future events or reveal hidden things by observing and interpreting omens. Of Paghat, the daughter of the legendary Daniel, it is said, she

who observes the water,
Who studies the dew from the drip,
Who knows the course of the stars
(The Tale of Aqhat, *ANET* 153*b*).[1]

[1] J. B. Pritchard, ed., *Ancient Near Eastern Texts* (Princeton University Press; rev. ed., 1955).

Paghat is also credited with the ability "of using magic against the dwellers in the tents" (Gordon, *Ugaritic Handbook,* I Aqhat, 221-22).

That the Hebrews engaged in magic practices is amply attested in the OT. The repeated prohibition of the use of magic by law, as well as the zealous and fervent struggle waged against it by the prophets, proves how deep-rooted was the belief in the efficacy of this art. Saul, who is reported to have banished the "mediums and the wizards" from the land, sought their help in a critical situation (I Sam. 28:3, 7). When Joram, king of Israel, asked Jehu whether he came in peace, the latter answered: "What peace can there be, so long as the harlotries and the sorceries [כשפיה] of your mother Jezebel are so many?" (II Kings 9:22). When Isaiah (3:2-3) placed the "diviner" [קסם], the "skilful magician" [חכם חרשים], and the "expert in charms" [נבון לחש] on the same plane as the "mighty man and the soldier, the judge and the prophet," he merely stated a known fact—namely, the importance attached to these practitioners in the life of the people and of the state. And it was in keeping with this high regard for magicians that King Manasseh made public use of their services (II Chr. 33:6). But it was not the kings only who sought help from magicians and sorcerers. The people, of course, did likewise. Jeremiah (27:9) appeals directly to the people not to put trust in "your [false] prophets, your diviners [קסמיכם], . . . your soothsayers [עננכם], or your sorcerers [כשפיכם]." Ezekiel (13:18-20) reports of women "who sew magic bands [כסתות] upon all wrists, and make veils for the heads of persons of every stature, in the hunt for souls" (i.e., witches who subjugate the mind of the victims to their power).

Not all the forms of magic, as known to have been in vogue in the ancient Near East, are mentioned in the OT. The reason for the omissions might be either that the Palestinian practices were less elaborate and did not attain the high level of specialization as in Egypt and Babylonia, or that our texts simply failed to record all the aspects of the art prevalent in the country. The difficulty in assessing the range of magical practices in biblical Palestine is further complicated by the uncertainty of the primary meanings of the technical terms used in the OT to describe these activities. The law of Deut. 18:10-11, which prohibits all magic art, lists its most important features in the following order: קסם קסמים, "one who practices divination"; מעונן, "a soothsayer"; מנחש, "an augur"; מכשף, "a sorcerer"; חבר חבר, "a charmer"; אוב, "a medium"; ידעני, "a wizard"; and דרש אל המתים, "a necromancer." The professions omitted in this passage are לחש or מלחשים, "charms, charmers"; and חרשים, "magic, magicians." (The הברי שמים and החזים בככבים, "astrologers"; חרטמים, "magicians"; אשפים, "enchanters"; and אטים, "shades of a dead person," referred to elsewhere in the OT, are not mentioned in this law, since they all represent Egyptian and Babylonian practitioners.) All terms, with the exception of חרשים and מכשף, are discussed respectively under ASTROLOGER; DIVINATION; ENCHANTER; FAMILIAR SPIRIT; INCANTATIONS; SHADES.

Figs. AMU 23-24.

The term חרש, whatever its etymology be, has long been known from Aramaic and Syriac (*ḥaršā*), and it has been found now also in Ugaritic (*ḥrš; see above*), with the general meaning of "magic, sorcery." It is mentioned only once in the OT (Isa. 3:3), in the form חכם חרשים ("skilful magician"), but its use in Ugaritic proves that it is an old West Semitic word. The abstract noun כשפים, "sorceries" (participial forms מכשף, מכשפה, plural כשפים and מכשפים), has its cognate in Akkadian *kišpu* and *kaššāpūtu,* "sorcery, magic." We may assume that, while the other terms, mentioned above, designate specific magical practices, חרשים and כשפים denote the generic name for "magic" in all its aspects (for the all-inclusive meaning of כשפים, see in particular Exod. 22:18; II Kings 9:22; and the reference to Assyria in Nah. 3:4 as בעלת כשפים, "mistress of magic arts" [RSV "deadly charms"; KJV "mistress of witchcrafts"]).

Magic in any form is forbidden by law, and its practitioners are to be put to death (Exod. 22:18—H 22:17; Lev. 19:26, 31; 20:6, 27; cf. the Code of Hammurabi, paragraph 2, and the Middle Assyrian Laws, paragraph 47). The sorcerers are an antisocial group, and they are considered as enemies of the people. Their practices are equated with that of the offering of human sacrifices (Deut. 18:10-11; cf. II Kings 17:17; II Chr. 33:6). They are liars and deceivers (cf. Isa. 44:25; Jer. 27:9-10; Ezek. 22:28; Zech. 10:2; etc.). Isaiah (57:3) calls the guild of the sorcerers (בני עננה; lit., "sons of the sorceress") the "offspring of the adulterer and the harlot"; and Malachi (3:5) puts them in the same category with those who oppress the widow and the orphan. Micah cherishes the hope that in the near future the Lord will

> cut off sorceries from your hand,
> and you shall have no more soothsayers
> (5:12—H 5:11).

The apostolic writers held substantially the same view of magic. Paul called the magician Bar-Jesus (=Elymas) "you enemy of all righteousness, full of all deceit and villainy" (Acts 13:10); he compares sorcery to immorality, licentiousness, and idolatry (Gal. 5:19-21; and see II Tim. 3:8). John places the sorcerer on the same plane as liars and murderers (Rev. 9:21; 18:23; 21:8; 22:15).

Bibliography. Babylonia and Egypt: L. W. King, *Babylonian Magic and Sorcery* (1896). E. A. W. Budge, *Egyptian Magic* (1899). R. C. Thompson, *The Reports of the Magicians and Astrologers of Nineveh and Babylon in the British Museum* (2 vols.; 1900); *The Devils and Evil Spirits of Babylonia* (2 vols.; 1903-4); *Semitic Magic: Its Origin and Development* (1908). F. Lexa, *La magie dans l'Egypte antique . . .* (3 vols.; 1925). E. D. Van Buren, "Amulets in Ancient Babylonia," *Orientalia,* XIV (1945), 21 ff. G. Contenau, *La magie chez les Assyriens et les Babyloniens* (1947).

OT: T. W. Davies, *Magic, Divination, and Demonology Among the Hebrews and Their Neighbours* (1898). H. Kaupel, *Die Dämonen im AT* (1930). A. Guillaume, *Prophecy and Divination* (1938).

Postbiblical Jewish magic: L. Blau, *Das altjüdische Zauberwesen* (1898). J. Trachtenberg, *Jewish Magic and Superstition: A Study in Folk Religion* (1939). I. MENDELSOHN

MAGISTRATE [στρατηγός (Acts 16:20, 22, 35-36, 38)]. Alternately: CAPTAIN, CAPTAIN OF THE TEMPLE (Luke 22:4, 52; Acts 4:1; 5:24, 26). A word used in Acts 16 five times, always in the plural, to designate, we may suppose, the highest officials of the Roman colony of Philippi. The Greek word στρατηγός itself had an extensive usage. It could mean a leader of an army or general, or a governor of a city-state; it was the title of the ten officers annually elected in Athens to command the army and the navy; it was used to designate the chief magistrates of the cities of Asia Minor and of other Greek states; in Ptolemaic and Roman Egypt, it could mean the military and civil governor of a nome; it could refer to a consul or proconsul, to the *praetor urbanus,* or to the *praetor;* and it was also used for the *duumviri* or chief magistrates of Roman colonies. An informed person reading Acts would be at least somewhat aware of the varied and important official connotations of the term.

In the cities under Roman rule the στρατηγοί would ordinarily be the governing officials. There could have been three, four, more commonly five, but sometimes even ten or twelve of such making up the magisterial board, which had in charge the administration of civic affairs. Since the terms ἄρχοντες (Acts 16:19) and στρατηγοί are both frequently used in letters addressed to communities by emperors or Roman officials, it may be regarded as probable that the former term was merely the general designation for the governing board. Most probably Luke does not intend his readers to understand him as meaning that "rulers" (vs. 19) and "magistrates" are two different groups.

The functions of the board of στρατηγοί involved the administration of the community. They would include the management of public finances, the enforcement of the enactments of the Council and People. They could have to do with trying those accused of violating laws, and with their punishment if found guilty. Sometimes their names and titles appeared on the bronze coins issued by a city. They are frequently attested as having responsibility for maintenance of order. It is known that Smyrna had a "στρατηγός in charge of arms," whose duty may have been to furnish weapons for suppressing riots.

It is clear enough what Luke intends his readers to understand by στρατηγός. However, the question is raised whether Luke, in using the word, accurately reflects the historical situation. The usual Latin word for στρατηγός, it is affirmed, is *praetor;* the governing officials in a Roman colony, however, were *duumviri,* a title carrying somewhat lesser prestige than *praetor.* We may say either that Luke—and this is possible for well-understood reasons—designates the magistrates at Philippi by the most impressive term available; or—and this is probable—that the Latin *praetor,* like the Greek στρατηγός, was broadly and somewhat imprecisely used and could refer to *duumviri.* In any case, Luke was writing for Greek, not Latin, readers, and what other term than στρατηγός could he have used?

Since Luke does not give the number of the magistrates, he may think of them as two or more.

Bibliography. The most important new material on the word is to be found in D. Magie, *Roman Rule in Asia Minor* (1950), pp. 643-44, 844-46, 1,006-7, 1,508-9. F. D. GEALY

MAGNIFICAT măg nĭf'ə kăt [Lat. *magnifico,* magnify]. The Song of Mary, the first of three psalms contained in the infancy narrative of the Gospel of Luke (1:46-55). *See also* BENEDICTUS; NUNC DIMITTIS.

The song is modeled, in structure and expression, upon the Song of Hannah in I Sam. 2:1-10, with numerous reminiscences of the Psalms and other OT poetry. The Magnificat is a beautiful summary of the OT hope of God's redemption of his people, as it is brought to concrete realization in the Incarnation, in the womb of God's handmaiden of "low estate." Characteristic of Hebrew poetic and prophetic utterance in exalted moments of the spirit is its celebration of the saving acts of God, which are expected in the future, in tenses that speak of them as already accomplished. His mighty deeds of old are a surety of the fulfilment of his promises for the coming days.

Several Old Latin MSS and a few Western fathers, such as Irenaeus and Nicetas of Remesiana, ascribe the song to Elizabeth rather than to Mary. A number of modern critics, noting the greater similarity between Elizabeth's circumstances and those of Hannah, have adopted this view. But the greater weight of all the Greek MSS and most of the versions in the attribution to Mary cannot be easily set aside. Nor is it necessary to suppose, with some critics, that the song is in reality a Jewish psalm adapted for the church by the interpolation of vs. 48, or that it emanated originally from the circle of disciples of John the Baptist. The piety of early Palestinian Christians, nurtured as it was almost solely upon the OT, was certainly capable of producing a piece of this kind. Nor is there any cogent reason for denying the possibility of its having been composed by Mary herself. In particular, the song reflects the humble situation of early Christian believers, such as is outlined in the BEATITUDES.

In the Eastern liturgies the Magnificat is sung at the morning office of Lauds. Benedict of Nursia, possibly following Roman custom, appointed it in his monastic rule as the climax of Vespers, with which office it has been associated ever since, in the daily prayers of the Western church.

Bibliography. Commentaries on Luke, especially that of J. M. Creed (1930), pp. 13-16, 22-24, 303-307. For liturgical use, J. Mearns, *The Canticles of the Christian Church Eastern and Western in Early and Medieval Times* (1914).

M. H. SHEPHERD, JR.

MAGOG mā'gŏg [מגוג; Μαγωγ] (Gen. 10:2; I Chr. 1:5; Ezek. 38:2; 39:6; Rev. 20:8). The land from which GOG came, whose attack on Israel is described in Ezek. 38–39; it constitutes his kingdom and territory. Some have thought that this name resulted from a גוג מגוג play on "darkness from darkness," but the presence of the name in the Genesis table of nations makes this very unlikely. It is possible that Magog might be identified with the Scythian hordes who wrought such havoc in the sixth century B.C.

Again, though there may be some identifiable place called Magog, Ezekiel did not know of such a locality and so chose the name to symbolize that great kingdom of men who would challenge the rule of God. There is no land of Magog except as every land is such.

The usage in Revelation illustrates how the passage of time allows a place to become a person (Rev. 20:8); but even so, the original concept of evil in array against the Almighty is carried over from prophecy to apocalypse. Magog is the focal point in human history where men join together in a desperate effort against God and are defeated. After defeat, God's people become secure, and God's kingdom is established.

C. G. HOWIE

MAGOR-MISSABIB mā'gôr mĭs'ə bĭb. KJV translation of מגור מסביב (RSV lit., TERROR ON EVERY SIDE), the name given by Jeremiah to the priest Pashhur son of Immer, who had put him in the stocks for prophesying the destruction of Jerusalem by the Chaldeans (Jer. 20:3). The same phrase appears elsewhere, though not as a name (Ps. 31:13; Jer. 6:25; 20:10; 46:5; 49:29; Lam. 2:22). The absence of the words "on every side" from the LXX, which renders "Magor" by Μέτοικος ("exile"), and from the interpretation in Jer. 20:4, suggests that they may be a later addition, conforming to the complete phrase in 6:25; 20:10.

J. MUILENBURG

MAGPIASH măg'pĭ ăsh [מגפיעש] (Neh. 10:20). One of the chiefs of the people, signatory to the covenant of Ezra.

MAHALAB mā'ə lăb [מחבל; Akkad. maḫālīb] (Josh. 19:29). A town in the territory allotted to Asher; identical with AHLAB. The different order of the last two consonants in the Hebrew form probably results from metathesis (cf. LXX). It is listed among the towns captured by Sennacherib in his third campaign (*ca.* 701 B.C.).

G. W. VAN BEEK

MAHALALEL mə hăl'ə lĕl [מהללאל, God shines forth, *from* הלל (*Hiph'il*), flash forth light; *cf.* יהללאל; LXX *and* NT Μαλελεηλ]; KJV MAHALALEEL —lēl. Alternately: MAHALALEEL (Luke 3:37); KJV MALELEEL mā'lə lēl. **1.** Son of Kenan; father of Jared (Gen. 5:12-17; I Chr. 1:2; Luke 3:37).

2. A postexilic Judahite (Neh. 11:4).

Bibliography. M. Noth, *Die israelitischen Personennamen* (1928), pp. 168, 205.

L. HICKS

MAHALATH mā'ə lăth. *See* MUSIC.

MAHALATH LEANNOTH mā'ə lăth lē ăn'ŏth. *See* MUSIC.

MAHALI mā'ə lī. KJV alternate form of MAHLI 1.

MAHANAIM mā'ə nā'əm [מחנים, double camp]. A city of some importance, located in Gilead in the territory of the tribe of Gad, close to the territory of Manasseh (Josh. 13:26, 30; 21:38). The name is twice explained: as due to the fact that Jacob saw an encampment of angels beside his own (Gen. 32: 1-2—H 32:2-3), or that his family had grown large enough to become two companies (vs. 10—H vs. 11). Egyptian records give the name in the form *Ma-han-ma;* so it is possible that the original Hebrew form was "Mahaneh" ("encampment"), lengthened by mimation to "Mahanem," which in turn became "Mahanaim" (cf. *yᵉrûshālēm* and *yᵉrûshālayim* for "Jerusalem").

Mahanaim must have been a place of considerable strength, as it twice served as a place of refuge. After the defeat of Saul at Mount Gilboa, the shattered remnants of his army fled to Mahanaim, where Ishbosheth, his son, set up a kingdom, and eventually recovered control of the greater part of Palestine (II Sam. 2:8-9). It was in this city that the king was murdered by Rechab and Baanah (4:5-7), and thus David became ruler over the entire country. David, in turn, while fleeing from Jerusalem after the sudden coup of Absalom, halted his retreat at Mahanaim, where his troops received refreshment and allies arrived (17:24-27). He waited at the gate of Mahanaim as his troops went forth to battle with those of Absalom in the forest of Ephraim, and it was there that David uttered his poignant lament: "O my son Absalom . . . ! Would I had died instead of you" (ch. 18).

During the reign of Solomon, Mahanaim was the capital of his seventh district, which comprised a part of Gilead. *Ca.* 925 B.C. the city was sacked by Shishak of Egypt in his raid on Palestine. There are no later references to the city, but it is possible that the "dance before two armies" mentioned in Song of S. 6:13 may be the "dance of Mahanaim," as the Hebrew word has both meanings.

The site of Mahanaim has not been identified. The identification with Tulul edh-Dhahab has been proved false by investigation, and this site is rather PENUEL. There is a Khirbet Mahneh N of the Jabbok and not far from the village of Ajlun which seems to have preserved the name, but this needs further confirmation. The biblical data are so vague that Mahanaim could have been almost anywhere in the hill country of Gilead, in the neighborhood of Ajlun to the N or es-Salt in the S, the two present-day centers of the Gilead area. S. COHEN

MAHANEH-DAN mā'ə nə dăn' [מחנה דן, camp of Dan] (Judg. 13:25; 18:12). A place W of Kiriath-jearim where the Danites camped en route from Zorah and Eshtaol to the hill country of Ephraim.

MAHARAI mā'ə rī [מהרי]. One of the members of the Mighty Men of David known as the "Thirty" (II Sam. 23:28; I Chr. 11:30). He came from the city of Netophah in Judah and was of the clan of the Zerahites. He was also in command of the Davidic militia that served for the tenth month (I Chr. 27:13). E. R. DALGLISH

MAHATH mā'hăth [מחת, tough(?)]. **1.** A Kohathite Levite (I Chr. 6:35—H 6:20).

2. One of the Levites assisting in the reforms of King Hezekiah (II Chr. 29:12) and appointed to be one of the overseers of the offerings brought into the temple (31:13).

Bibliography. M. Noth, *Die israelitischen Personennamen* (1928), p. 225. B. T. DAHLBERG

MAHAVITE, THE mā'ə vīt [המחוים] (I Chr. 11:46). A gentilic name used to describe Eliel, who was a member of the company of the Davidic Mighty Men known as the "Thirty." The reading is unintelligible and may be emended to read המחנימי or המחני, "the Mahanaimite." E. R. DALGLISH

MAHAZIOTH mə hā'zĭ ŏth [מחזיאות]. According to I Chr. 25:4, 30, one of the sons of Heman appointed to prophesy in the sanctuary with music. But these names appear to form a liturgical prayer and may not refer to real persons. *See* GIDDALTI.

MAHER-SHALAL-HASHBAZ mā'ər shăl'əl-hăsh'băz [מהר שלל חש בז]. The symbolic name of the second son of Isaiah (Isa. 8:1, 3; cf. vs. 18). Its meaning is: "The spoil speeds, the prey hastes" (RSV mg.), and its import is that the doom of Syria and Ephraim is irrevocable. This doom is doubly attested, first by the writing of the words on a tablet in the presence of witnesses and in letters that all might read, and a year later by the birth of the child bearing the name.

See also SHEAR-JASHUB; IMMANUEL § 1.

C. R. NORTH

MAHLAH mä'lə [מחלה, weak one(?)]. **1.** One of the five daughters of Zelophehad who through Moses received the family territorial inheritance in W Manasseh after the death of their father (Num. 26:33; 27:1; 36:11; Josh. 17:3). The names of the five daughters seem originally to have been the names of Canaanite towns, but the location of Mahlah is unknown.

2. A descendant of Manasseh, presumably male (I Chr. 7:18). M. NEWMAN

MAHLI mä'lī [מחלי, *possibly* shrewd, cunning; *cf.* Arab. *mihālun;* Apoc. Μοολί]; KJV MAHALI mā'ə lī in Exod. 6:19; KJV Apoc. MOLI mō'lī; MAHLITES mä'līts. **1.** A Levite; son of Merari; brother of Mushi; eponym of a priestly house (Exod. 6:19 [cf. Test. Levi 12:3]; Num. 3:20, 33; 26:58; I Chr. 6:19, 29—H 6:4, 14; 23:21; 24:26, 28; Ezra 8:18; I Esd. 8:47).

2. A Levite; son of Mushi, and grandson of Merari (I Chr. 6:47—H 6:32; 23:23; 24:30).

Bibliography. M. Noth, *Die israelitischen Personennamen* (1928), p. 249. B. T. DAHLBERG

MAHLON mä'lən [מחלון] (Ruth 1:2, 5; 4:9-10). One of the two sons of Elimelech and Naomi. He migrated with his family to Moab, where he married the Moabitess Ruth and later died.

MAHOL mā'hŏl [מחול, place of dancing, dancing (*cf.* Ps. 30:11—H 30:12; Jer. 31:13), *from* חול, to circle, dance] (I Kings 4:31—H 5:11). The putative father of Ethan, Heman, Calcol, and Darda, wise men who are said to have been surpassed in wisdom by Solomon. However, the phrase "the sons of Mahol" is more correctly taken to mean "members of an orchestral guild." Since wisdom and music were closely associated in the Hebrew mind, it is not surprising that wise men were included among the members of the ancient Israelite musical guild (cf. I Chr. 25:2 ff; II Chr. 29:30).

Bibliography. W. F. Albright, *Archaeology and the Religion of Israel* (3rd ed., 1953), pp. 127, 210. "Canaanite-Phoenician Sources of Hebrew Wisdom," *Wisdom in Israel and in the Ancient Near East: Supplements to Vetus Testamentum,* III (1955), 13. E. R. DALGLISH

MAHSEIAH mä sē'yə [מחסיה, Yahu is a refuge; Apoc. Μαασαίας] (Jer. 32:12; 51:59; Bar. 1:1); KJV

MAASEIAH mā'ə—; KJV Apoc. MAASEAS mā'ə sē'əs. Grandfather of Baruch the scribe of Jeremiah.

MAIANEAS. KJV Apoc. form of MAASEIAH 19.

MAID, MAIDEN [אמה, בתולה, נערה, עלמה, שפחה; κοράσιον, παιδίσκη; KJV παῖς (Luke 8:51, 54; RSV "child")]. A young unmarried woman, usually of the servant class.

1. In the OT. With SLAVERY an accepted institution, female slaves were used in many households. The term אמה emphasizes this aspect, and its alternative translations ("female slave," "bondwoman," "bondmaid," "maidservant"; KJV "handmaiden") follow out this understanding. These maidens were to be well cared for, according to the law (Lev. 25:6; Deut. 15:12 ff; cf. Job 31:13). They participate in God's blessing and receive his protection (Deut. 5:14; 12:12; Ezra 2:65). They sometimes became concubines and substitute wives when the first wife was sterile (Gen. 30:3; 31:33). As a term of humility אמה is used by Abigail before David (I Sam. 25:24 ff; cf. II Sam. 14:15); so, too, by Ruth (3:9) and Bathsheba (I Kings 1:13, 17). The devout and pious woman may call herself אמה of God (I Sam. 1:11 [cf. Luke 1:38, 48]; Pss. 86:16; 116:16).

Closely paralleled to this word is שפחה (alternately "female slave," "maidservant," "handmaid"), which is characteristic of the patriarchal narratives for slaves (Gen. 24:35; 30:43; etc.) and for the concubines who were originally maids of the free wife (cf. Hagar, Zilpah, and Bilhah). As a token of humility the woman of Endor speaks of herself as a "handmaid" before Saul (I Sam. 28:21), and the word is also used in a different narrative by a woman before David (II Sam. 14:6).

The Hebrew בתולה refers to a young woman of marriageable age. She is often a "virgin" (Exod. 22:16; Deut. 22:17). עלמה is simply a "girl" (Exod. 2:8) or "young woman" (Isa. 7:14), presumably a virgin (Prov. 30:19; the LXX uses παρθένος, with the meaning "virgin," in Isa. 7:14). Similarly, נערה is used for unmarried girls (II Kings 5:2), but also for female servants (Ruth 2:8; Esth. 2:4).

2. In the NT. The κοράσιον is simply a child or young "girl" (Matt. 9:24-25; the parallel in Luke 8:51, 54, uses παῖς, "child"). The παιδίσκη is a servant girl, not necessarily indentured (Matt. 26:69; Mark 14:66; John 18:16).

The pious formulation of Mary reflects the OT use of "servant," and so she uses δούλη, "handmaid" (Luke 1:38, 48). The same Greek word is used for the slave in the Pentecost quotation from Joel's prophecy (Acts 2:18; "maidservant").

C. U. WOLF

MAIL, COAT OF. *See* COAT OF MAIL; WEAPONS AND IMPLEMENTS OF WAR § 4*b*.

MAINSAIL. KJV translation in Acts 27:40 of what is evidently a FORESAIL.

MAKAZ mā'kăz [מקץ, a cutting off, end] (I Kings 4:9). A city in Solomon's second administrative district; possibly Khirbet el-Mukheizin, S of Ekron.

MAKED mā'kĕd [Μακέδ] (I Macc. 5:26, 36); KJV MAGED —gĕd in I Macc. 5:36. A city in Gilead from which Judas Maccabeus rescued the Jews who were threatened by their Greek neighbors. The site is unknown.

S. COHEN

MAKHELOTH măk hē'lŏth [מקהלת, קהל, to assemble] (Num. 33:25-26). A stopping place of the Israelites in the wilderness. There is a strong similarity to KEHELATHAH, mentioned in Num. 33:22-23. The location is unknown.

MAKKEDAH mə kē'də [מקדה, place of shepherds]. A Canaanite royal city near which was a cave in which the five kings of a S Canaanite alliance against Gibeon, an "ally" of the invading Israelites, took refuge after their rout at the hands of Joshua's forces. Joshua ordered the cave sealed and put under guard, set up headquarters at Makkedah, and directed the "mopping up" of the remnants of the Canaanite forces.

After the second phase of the battle was completed, the five kings were brought out of the cave, executed, and their bodies hung on trees until sundown, when they were returned to the cave for final burial. The populace of Makkedah was put to the sword, as were other cities southward (Josh. 10:16-39).

Later on, Makkedah was included in the Shephelah district of Judah, of which Lachish was the district capital (Josh. 15:41).

The location of Makkedah is uncertain. Eusebius placed it eight (Roman) miles E of Eleutheropolis (Beit Jibrin), but most scholars feel it would make better sense to place it N of this city. At present, Tell es-Safi, S of Hulda, appears to be the most likely identification.

V. R. GOLD

MAKTESH măk'tĕsh. KJV translation of מכתש (RSV MORTAR, THE).

MALACHI măl'ə kī [מלאכי, the messenger or angel of Yahweh; LXX Μαλαχίας]. The last of the short books which constitute the collection of the Twelve Prophets; the last book of the OT prophetic canon. Together with the books of Haggai and Zechariah, it forms a block of postexilic prophecy, and, like them, affords valuable evidence of religious and social conditions in this scantily documented period.

Superficially its closest connection is with the concluding chapters (9–14) of the book of ZECHARIAH, in that it would appear to be the third section of a collection of prophecies (Zech. 9:1–Mal. 4:6) which at some point have been added to the Book of the Twelve, two of the sections (Zech. 9–11; 12–14) having been added to the work of the sixth-century prophet Zechariah, and the third section having been given a separate identity under the name of Malachi.

This association is suggested by the fact that each of the three sections has a similar and distinctive superscription: "An oracle of the word of the LORD" (cf. Zech. 9:1; 12:1; Mal. 1:1). The detachment of the third section from the book of Zechariah has been explained as an editorial device to complete the sacred number of twelve prophets, but clearly the basic justification for the separate existence of this book is that both the theological content and the historical background are entirely different from those of Zech. 9–14. Apart from the sole resemblance to Zech. 9–14 lying in the fact that these prophecies are in all probability anonymous, they bear the distinctive mark of a single author and can be dated with considerable certainty.

The author, who may have been a cult prophet, was active in Jerusalem in the period of Persian rule *ca.* 450, shortly before the appearance of Nehemiah. His chief concern is with the correct conduct of the worship of the temple and with the danger of mixed marriages. He depicts a state of affairs where religious duties were taken lightly and ethical standards were loosely observed. It is obvious that a more rigorous policy, even with its dangers, was at this stage urgently required, and in paving the way for the work of Nehemiah and Ezra (*see* EZRA AND NEHEMIAH, BOOKS OF), who introduced such a policy, the author made an important contribution to the development of Judaism.

From the point of view of NT studies, however, the most significant feature of the prophecies is the reference to the messianic herald (3:1) which is applied by the Synoptists to JOHN THE BAPTIST (Mark 1:2, etc.), who is likewise regarded by Jesus as the fulfilment of the prediction concerning Elijah (*see* ELIJAH 1) in Mal. 4:5 (Mark 9:11-13).

See map "Palestine: Haggai, Zechariah and Malachi," under ZECHARIAH, BOOK OF.

1. The author
2. Date
3. Jerusalem *ca.* 450 B.C.
4. The prophecies
   a. The first oracle
   b. The second oracle
   c. The third oracle
   d. The fourth oracle
   e. The fifth oracle
   f. The sixth oracle
   g. Conclusion of the book
5. The significance of Malachi
Bibliography

1. The author. The evidence for attributing this book to a prophet who bore the name of Malachi is the superscription of 1:1. This, however, is clearly an editorial preface to the prophecies which begin in 1:2 (cf. Zech. 9:1; 12:1). It is possible, but unlikely, that Malachi is a personal name. The suggestion has been made that it is an abbreviation for "Malachiah." This, however, would tend to mean "Yahweh is a messenger or angel," an impossible concept, rather than "the messenger or angel of Yahweh," which is the usual translation of "Malachiah."

A stronger argument against the view that Malachi was the name of the prophet is that it appears to have its origin in the Hebrew word for "my messenger" in 3:1 (מלאכי, *mal'ākhî*). But since the LXX reads "his messenger" in 1:1 (מלאכו, *mal'ākhô*) and both the Talmud and the Targum of Jonathan identify "my messenger" in 1:1 as Ezra the Scribe, an explanation which was accepted by Jerome, it is unlikely that the author bore the name of Malachi at all.

The tradition in favor of Ezra as the author is no more valuable than similar traditions in favor of Nehemiah and Zerubbabel. Both the themes and the historical allusions of the book would suggest any one of these names as possible authors, and it would seem most probable that the writer is unknown, an editor of the Book of the Twelve having bestowed the name of Malachi upon the author of this anonymous collection of prophecies on the basis of the phrase in 3:1. For convenience, however, he is generally referred to as Malachi.

2. Date. Although we know nothing of the author, he gives us sufficient indication of the conditions of his time to enable us to date his prophecies with a reasonable degree of accuracy. Since the land is ruled by a Persian governor (*Pechah;* 1:8; cf. Neh. 5:14; Hag. 1:1), the time must be after the return from exile. There is, however, no reference to a derelict temple or to the need for its rebuilding, as in Haggai and Zechariah. On the contrary, the cultus is in full operation (1:10; 3:1, 10), and this points to a date later than 516—indeed, a good many years later, since the prophet's complaint is that the priests have grown weary of the ritual (1:13).

He inveighs against mixed marriages (2:10-16), but there is no suggestion that there is any official legislation against them. This would point to a date before 444, when Nehemiah appeared in Jerusalem and proceeded, among other things, to deal with this problem (Neh. 13:23-27). It was, in fact, during Nehemiah's second term of office that he took action on this matter, and for this reason some scholars regard these prophecies as dating from the period between Nehemiah's first and second administrations. This is, however, more than evidence warrants. For it is clear that the prophet's strictures on the inadequacy of the temple cultus (e.g., 1:8) are based on the Deuteronomic Code of 621 and not on the Priestly Code of *ca.* 450-400. The fact that the reference to tithe law in 3:10 is based on P (Num. 18:21), rather than on D (Deut. 14:22-29), does not necessarily point to a date later than the promulgation of the Priestly Code, since any codification may include some legislation which is already established practice.

Further, the author's conception of the priesthood (2:4-9) makes no distinction between priests and Levites, thus agreeing with the Deuteronomic view (cf. Deut. 17:9), whereas the Priestly Code distinguished between the Aaronic priesthood (Lev. 1:5) and the Levitical assistants (Num. 18:1-4). For these reasons most support is given to a date somewhere *ca.* 460-450. If it were possible to date the Nabatean invasion of Edom (1:2-5), an even closer approximation might be reached.

3. Jerusalem *ca.* 450 B.C. If the date of these prophecies may be reckoned to be approximately the middle of the fifth century B.C., the picture which Malachi gives of the state of society at that time is indeed somber. The land is under the domination of Persia, and, even if there is no evidence of oppression or abuse of power, the lot of a subject state and its people is never a happy one. Under the most liberal regime vassals must bear the cost of occupation, and levies for Persian military exploits in the region must have been a drain on the limited man power of the small community. Nature herself had added her quota of afflictions in the form of drought, blighted vineyards, and plagues of locusts (3:10-11).

The return from exile almost a century before was

a fading memory, and disillusion had followed the glowing promises of Second Isaiah (e.g., Isa. 49; 54). The exiles had returned to a troubled heritage and not to the joyous and blissful era which they had been led to expect. Roused to fresh heights of endeavor by HAGGAI and Zechariah, they had set to work to rebuild the shattered temple and had completed it with laudable speed. But once more the prophetic promises had not come true. Haggai's pledges of prosperity once the house of the Lord was restored had come to nought (Hag. 2:6-9). Zechariah's plea for deeper commitment to Yahweh had been mocked by the apparent failure of Yahweh to safeguard even the primary needs of his people (Zech. 8:4-13).

Men had therefore lost heart and, worse still, lost faith. The more devout section of the community, the precursors of the HASIDIM, wept bitter tears by the altar (2:13) and mourned before the Lord of hosts (3:14). But skepticism and indifference were more common, and the cleavage which became more obvious in the Hellenistic period between the pious minority and the lax "progressive" majority was beginning to make its appearance. Many had come to doubt whether Yahweh still cared for his people at all (1:2) and whether their obedience meant anything to him (2:17; 3:15). The less scrupulous had already gone beyond questioning and were treating organized religion with contempt (1:14; 3:7-12). Adultery, perjury, and victimization of the underprivileged were rife (3:5). Intermarriage with pagan women (2:10-12), with its attendant infiltration of heathen religious practices into the homes of the people, was but an outward sign that the covenant relationship had ceased to matter.

The spiritual leaders were little better than the laity. Priests were perfunctory in their offices. They were bored with religion (1:13). They paid so little heed to the ordinances of the sacred law that they reckoned any kind of offering to be good enough for Yahweh (1:7-8). All in all, it is a dismal scene which the prophet surveys and which he now seeks to restore to something more worthy of the people of Yahweh. *See* ISRAEL, HISTORY OF.

4. The prophecies. ***a. The first oracle.*** Mal. 1:2-5 is a reaffirmation of Hosea's proclamation of Yahweh's love for Israel (e.g., Hos. 11). Malachi is faced with a body of skeptical opinion among the people of Jerusalem, which questions whether Yahweh still cares for his people. Subjection to a foreign overlord (1:8), plagues of locusts, and lack of the rainfall which was vital to their economy (3:11) were a sorry caricature of what might be expected by the people of Yahweh's choice. Where was the fulfilment of the rosy prospect of peace and plenty which Second Isaiah, Haggai, and Zechariah had spread before them?

The prophet's reply is in the spirit of the man in the proverb who complained that his shoes pinched until he met a man who had no feet. He points to the even sorrier plight of Edom. Traditionally, Jacob, the father of the tribes of Israel, and Esau, the progenitor of the tribes of Edom (Gen. 36:1), were twin brothers (Gen. 25:21-27). Yet Jacob and his descendants had been singled out for Yahweh's blessing, while Esau and his line had been visited with divine displeasure.

The Jews had many reasons for perpetuating bitter feud with the Edomites (*see* EDOM; OBADIAH, BOOK OF). They had exulted over Jerusalem's downfall (cf. Ps. 137:7) and by their hostility had incurred the condemnation of more than one prophet (e.g., Jer. 49:7-22; Ezek. 35; Amos 1:11-12). But now apparently some major disaster had overtaken them, which Malachi cites as evidence that in comparison with Yahweh's wrath against Edom his love for Israel is abundantly plain.

The disaster referred to was doubtless the invasion of Edomite territory by Nabatean Arabs, who drove the population out of their lands S of the Dead Sea, forcing them eventually to settle in the S part of Judah, which was later known as Idumea. The prophet's message is that Edom will never recover its ancestral home, whereas Israel, whatever its present afflictions, has at least seen the fulfilment of the promise that it should once more, after the discipline of the Exile, inhabit Mount Zion. Ironically, it was a descendant of the ancient Edomites, Herod, who later became king of the Jews. Paul quotes Mal. 1:2*b*-3*a* in Rom. 9:13 in connection with his doctrine of election.

b. The second oracle. 1:6–2:9 is a denunciation of the priesthood for their failure to give the moral and religious leadership that Yahweh demands of his ministers, implying their responsibility for the hardships which the people are suffering, and for their lack of spiritual resources to meet them. Yahweh asks his priests where are the reverence and honor that even a human father would expect from his children. Instead of receiving these, he has been treated with contempt (1:6).

The law (Lev. 22:20-22; Deut. 15:21; 17:1) ordained that nothing but the best should be regarded as a fitting offering to the Lord—the sacrificial animals must be without blemish. Yet the priests had become so casual in their office that they were prepared to accept from the people and offer to Yahweh maimed animals, which they would not even dream of offering to their Persian governor (1:7-8). How could priests like these intercede for the people before Yahweh (1:9)? Far better were it that they should close the temple doors and quench the altar fires forever (1:10).

Even among the Gentiles there was more reverence, and purer worship was offered to Yahweh by them than by his own priests (1:11), who were so bored with their religious office that they no longer cared how they performed it (1:13). The curse of Yahweh would fall upon the man who dared to bring to the temple an offering which he knew to be a makeshift and a second best (1:14), and a like curse would fall upon the unworthy priests who encouraged him (2:1-2). Their authority would be taken from them, and they would be thrown aside like the ordure of the animals they sacrificed (2:3).

Yahweh had founded the priesthood on Levi (Deut. 18:1-8; 33:8-11), who was the pattern of what every priest should be (Mal. 2:4). In return for the knowledge of the meaning of life and the inward peace divinely given, which came by virtue of his sacred office, the true priest must stand in awe before the Lord and reverence his holy name (2:5). His words must be words of truth; integrity must inspire his actions. Men must know that from him they would learn the will of Yahweh (cf. Deut. 17:8-12), and his life must be dedicated to turning men from their sins to the service of the living God. For the true priest is nothing less than the "messenger of the LORD of hosts" (Mal. 2:6-7).

But the priests of Israel have failed woefully to fulfil their vocation. They have prevented their people from offering proper worship. They have corrupted the true relationship between Yahweh and his people (2:8). Now they stand exposed as false and unworthy pastors, currying favor with the well-to-do, so that even their own flock despise them (2:9). *See* PRIESTS AND LEVITES.

c. The third oracle. 2:10-16 is concerned with mixed marriages and divorce. It is addressed to the laity. They too have broken covenant with Yahweh and with one another. Disregarding their common Father and the fact that they are a community of brothers, some of them have gone outside the family of Israel to find wives, who bring with them religious beliefs and practices which are contrary to the law (2:10-11). They cannot expect such actions to go unpunished (2:12). When they pour out their lamentations to Yahweh because of their present plight, let them remember that they have only themselves to blame (2:13). They cannot imagine that Yahweh will bless with prosperity men who for the sake of some young and pretty foreign face divorce the wives who have borne their children. Marriage is a lifelong companionship (cf. Gen. 2:24), not just a biological necessity (Mal. 2:14-15). Ill-treatment of a faithful wife is abhorrent to Yahweh. DIVORCE is anathema to him (2:16). *See* MARRIAGE.

d. The fourth oracle. 2:17–3:5 is a prophecy of the coming of Yahweh in judgment. He has grown weary of the constant complaints of the people that there is no justice in the world, that the wicked prosper, and that Yahweh merely strengthens their hand (2:17). But suddenly the Day of Yahweh will be upon them, and the Lord himself will come in judgment (*see* DAY OF THE LORD), heralded by his messenger (3:1-2). The priesthood will be the first to be subjected to the sifting of the faithful from the faithless (cf. 1:6–2:9) so that the worship of the temple may become once more acceptable to Yahweh (3:3-4). Next the laity (cf. 1:14; 2:10-16) will be purified, and punishment will be meted out to all who have been guilty of offenses against the Lord—and, in this, religious and moral crimes will be condemned alike (3:5).

e. The fifth oracle. 3:6-12 traces the divine disfavor, of which the people complain, to their failure to give Yahweh his dues. His attitude toward his people does not suddenly change without cause. It changes because they have failed to keep his laws. If they will return to their proper service of obedience, Yahweh will restore their prosperity (3:6-7). Their particular offense lies in their failure to pay the correct amount of tithe (Num. 18:21). Once this obligation is fulfilled, the curse of Yahweh will be lifted: the rains will come and the fields will burgeon. Locusts will no longer devour their crops, and rich harvests will gladden their hearts and impress their neighbors (Mal. 3:8-12).

f. The sixth oracle. 3:13–4:3 returns to the problem of the moral order of the universe (cf. 2:17). The devout and faithful section of the community wonder what profit lies in obedience to Yahweh. They perform their religious obligations, but, despite this, the arrogant and highhanded unbeliever seems to fare better and to suffer no penalty for his sins (3:13-15). The prophet's reply is that a record is kept in heaven of the deeds of the righteous. When the terrible Day of the Lord comes, Yahweh will remember their good works. The world will see then that the service of Yahweh is one that brings rich reward (3:16-18). For when the great Day dawns, the wicked will be destroyed, whereas the faithful servants of Yahweh will know blessedness and joy (4:1-3).

g. Conclusion of the book. The concluding verses (4:4-6) are probably editorial additions. The compiler of the Book of the Twelve may have added vs. 4 as a summary of what he considered to be the essence of the message of Malachi, or he may have meant to suggest that prophecy had now come to an end and that the words once spoken by Yahweh to Moses, and now contained in the written law, should take the place of the words more recently spoken by Yahweh through his prophets. The reference to Elijah in vs. 5 is presumably intended to clarify the allusion to the "messenger" in 3:1.

5. The significance of Malachi. Malachi cannot be reckoned among the great prophets. He does not share the profound and original insights into the nature and purpose of God which were given to men like Amos, Jeremiah, and Second Isaiah. He lived at a time when prophetic utterances were no longer accepted without question as direct communications from Yahweh. Although prophecy had not yet sunk to the depths described in Zech. 13, it is clear from the dialectic character of Malachi's oracles (1:2-3, 6-7; 2:13-14, 17; 3:7-8, 13-14) that a prophet's words were no longer taken at their face value. He had to argue his case in a way that his predecessors in the heyday of classical prophecy had never been obliged to do. *See* PROPHET.

Men were dissatisfied with the old and sometimes oversimplified answers that had been given by the great prophets to the problems of good and evil, rewards and punishments, and they now were beginning to question the providential government of life, both in the narrower community and in the world at large. Malachi obviously enters into their difficulties insofar as he sees that it is not enough merely to enunciate high doctrine and moral principles, but seeks to enshrine them in a practical code of behavior and points toward a final solution of the world's disorder in the Day of Yahweh.

He shares the genuine prophetic insight which knows that true obedience to God must come from personal commitment, but he also recognizes that for ordinary mortals this must be expressed in sundry small acts of discipline and religious observance.

Thus, on one side, Malachi, with his insistence on the correct fulfilment of the worshiper's obligation to the priesthood (3:8-10), his stress on the importance of offering unblemished sacrifices (1:7-8), his fear of the infiltration of foreign religious practices through mixed marriages (2:10-11), points through Ezra and Nehemiah to the hardening of the spiritual arteries of the prophetic faith, which reached its apex in Pharisaism. *See* PHARISEES.

On the other hand, there are many echoes of the older voice of true prophecy to be found in these oracles. There is not only the recognition of the holiness and righteousness of God but also the conviction that his true service includes moral obedience. Correct ritual is obligatory, but so also are honesty, justice, and mercy (1:14; 3:5). Here too is the recognition that fundamentally the first step toward the right relationship with God is repentance (3:7), that reverence and awe are the foundations of true religion (3:16), and that iniquity will not forever go unpunished (4:1).

The limitations of Malachi's thought are obvious (e.g., 1:2-5; 3:10; 4:3), but these were common to the prophetic outlook as a whole. More significant, however, is the equally obvious fact that in the early stage of Judaism which he reflects, the basis of the desire for correct ritual is that nothing but the best is good enough for Yahweh (1:7-8), and that a casual attitude toward the ordinances of religion betrays a fundamentally casual attitude toward God (1:12-13).

We may be grateful to this unknown author for his impressive and moving conception of the vocation of the holy ministry (2:5-7) and for his daring and, for these times, astounding recognition that worship offered in sincerity and truth under the auspices of any religion whatever is in effect offered to the one true God (1:11; cf. Acts 10:35). In his high doctrine of the institution of marriage and his condemnation of easy divorce, he is more akin to the spirit of the NT than the OT (cf. Deut. 24:1-4 with Mark 10:2-12).

His eschatology is partly conventional and partly original. The Day of the Lord in these oracles is largely of the normal prophetic pattern (cf. Amos 5:18-20; Zeph. 1:7-18), but a new note is introduced with the conception of the book of remembrance in which are recorded the names of the righteous (Mal. 3:16) and which points toward later developments in the belief in a future life.

Significant too is the conception of a forerunner to "prepare the way" for the coming of Yahweh at the great Day (3:1). It is not clear whether the author had in mind two separate figures, the "messenger" and the "messenger of the covenant," or whether the latter is an editorial emendation. Nor is it clear whether the "messenger" is a prophetic figure who will proclaim a last chance of repentance before the judgment, and who, as we have seen, one of the editors of the oracles believed to be the author himself (1:1), or whether the concept is rather that of a supernatural "angel of Yahweh," almost a manifestation of Yahweh himself.

On the basis of the editorial note in 4:5, which identifies the messenger with Elijah redivivus (cf. II Kings 2:11), the idea of a herald of the messianic age came to play a large part in later apocalyptic. Our Lord clearly regarded the prophecy as foreshadowing the mission of John the Baptist (Mark 9:11-13), and the early church without hesitation saw in the relationship of the work of the Baptist to the messianic kingdom inaugurated by Jesus, the perfect fulfilment of this oracle (Mark 1:2; Luke 1:17).

Bibliography. Commentaries: S. R. Driver, Century Bible (1906); J. M. P. Smith, ICC (1912); W. E. Barnes, *Cambridge Bible* (1917); G. A. Smith, *EB* (1928); E. Sellin, *KAT* (1929); F. Horst, *HAT* (1954); R. C. Dentan, *IB* (1956).

Special studies: A. von Bulmerincq, *Der Prophet Maleachi* (2 vols.; 1926-32); O. Holzmann, *Der Prophet Maleachi und der Ursprung des Pharisäertums,* ARW, XXIX (1931), 1-21.

W. NEIL

MALACHIAS măl′ə kī′əs. Douay Version form of MALACHI.

MALACHY. KJV Apoc. form of MALACHI.

MALCAM măl′kăm [מלכם, *perhaps shortened from* Akkad. *Abdi-milḫi,* servant of the king (deity)] (I Chr. 8:9); KJV MALCHAM. A Benjaminite.

Bibliography. M. Noth, *Die israelitischen Personennamen* (1928), p. 118.

MALCHIAH. Alternate form of MALCHIJAH.

MALCHIEL măl′kĭ əl [מלכיאל, Malki is God]; MALCHIELITES —ə līts. A descendant of Asher (Gen. 46:17; Num. 26:45; I Chr. 7:31).

Bibliography. M. Noth, *Die israelitischen Personennamen* (1928), pp. 36, 118, 140.

MALCHIJAH măl kī′jə [מלכיה, מלכיהו, Yahu is king; Apoc. Μελχίας]. Alternately: MALCHIAH —ə; Apoc. MELCHIAS mĕl kī′əs; KJV MELCHIAH —ə (Jer. 21:1). **1.** A Gershonite Levite, ancestor of Asaph the temple musician (I Chr. 6:40 —H 6:25).

2. A priest or priestly family listed as contemporary with King David (I Chr. 24:9). Pashhur, a subdivision of this family, is listed among the residents of postexilic Jerusalem (I Chr. 9:12; cf. Ezra 2:38; Neh. 11:12).

3. A royal prince who owned the cistern in which the prophet Jeremiah was imprisoned (Jer. 38:6). He may also have been the same Malchiah who was the father of the Pashhur mentioned in Jer. 21:1; 38:1 (and to be distinguished from 2 *above*).

4. One of those Jews contemporary with Ezra who are listed as having married foreign wives (Ezra 10:25*a;* I Esd. 9:26).

5. Son of Harim; one of those who helped build the Jerusalem wall with Nehemiah (Neh. 3:11). He may have been the same person who is listed in Ezra 10:31 as having a foreign wife (cf. I Esd. 9:32).

6. Son of Rechab; one of those who helped build Nehemiah's wall (Neh. 3:14).

7. A goldsmith who worked on the wall of Jerusalem in Nehemiah's time (Neh. 3:31).

8. One of the priests taking part in the ceremony dedicating the rebuilt Jerusalem wall in the days of Nehemiah the governor (Neh. 12:42).

9. One of those standing beside Ezra during the public reading of the law (Neh. 8:4). Probably they were laymen.

10. A priest signatory to the covenant of Ezra, or the priestly house represented among the signers (Neh. 10:3). If the latter, perhaps the same as 2 *above.*

11. KJV translation in Ezra 10:25*b.* The LXX and I Esd. 9:26 show this Malchijah to be an error for HASHABIAH (8), and the RSV omits the name.

B. T. DAHLBERG

MALCHIRAM măl kī′rəm [מלכירם, my king is exalted] (I Chr. 3:18). Son of Jeconiah (Jehoiachin).

MALCHISHUA măl'kə shōō'ə [מַלְכִּי־שׁוּעַ]; KJV MALCHI-SHUA —kī— in I Chr. 8:33; 9:39; MELCHISHUA mĕl'— in I Sam. 14:49; 31:2. The youngest of the three sons of Saul by his wife Ahinoam. The Philistines slew Malchishua in the battle on Mount Gilboa (I Sam. 14:49; 31:2; I Chr. 10:2).
E. R. DALGLISH

MALCHUS măl'kəs [Μάλχος = מלך, king] (John 18:10). The high priest's slave whose ear was cut off by Peter.

The name is found in Josephus and in Palmyrene and Nabatean inscriptions, usually of kings (Malchus I and II of Nabatea) or of chieftains. The slave may have been a Syrian or a Nabatean, attached to the high priest's (Caiaphas'; John 18:13) household, in his personal service, or even captain of the temple police.

Whether he was an onlooker or a key figure at the arrest of Jesus is unclear. Peter's attack on him and Jesus' immediate rectification of the damage (Luke 22:51) suggest that the injury occurred directly before Jesus and not at the fringe of the motley band. If he was Caiphas' personal representative in the arrest, according to ancient Hebrew conceptions he was entitled to the same respect as the high priest himself. That Peter's offense was heinous, Jesus saw immediately.

Only the Fourth Gospel offers the names of the attacker and the attacked—possibly evidence of a special tradition behind this gospel.

Bibliography. H. L. Strack and P. Billerbeck, *Kommentar zum NT aus Talmud und Midrasch,* II (1924), 568; M. Rostovtzeff, Οὖς δεξιὸν ἀποτέμνειν, *ZNW,* 33 (1934), 196-99; V. Taylor, *The Gospel According to St. Mark* (1952), pp. 559-60.
E. P. BLAIR

MALELEEL. KJV NT form of MAHALALEL 1.

MALLET [הַלְמוּת] (Judg. 5:26); KJV HAMMER. The workman's tool with which Jael killed Sisera. It may have been the instrument with which the tent pegs were driven (cf. Judg. 4:21, where מַקֶּבֶת, "hammer," is mentioned as the tool used for that purpose). *See* HAMMER.
H. F. BECK

MALLOS. KJV form of MALLUS.

MALLOTHI măl'ə thī [מַלּוֹתִי] (I Chr. 25:4, 26). One of the sons of Heman among the priests appointed to prophesy in the sanctuary with music. But the names in this verse appear to constitute a liturgical prayer and may not refer to real persons. *See* GIDDALTI.
B. T. DAHLBERG

MALLOW [מַלּוּחַ, *mallûaḥ*]. Any plant of the genus *Malva.* The translation "mallow" in Job 30:4 seems to have come from the similarity to the Greek word for the true mallow (μαλάχη). The association of the Hebrew word with *melaḥ,* "salt," the LXX ἅλιμον, and the context of Job 30:4 have led most scholars to identify it with the *Atriplex halimus* L., the "shrubby orache," or other similar shrubs common to the salt marshes of the Holy Land. In the Job passage the "disreputable brood" of men is reduced to a state of eating these salty shrubs (cf. Zeph. 2:9).

In Job 24:24 the RSV reads after the LXX "like the mallow," instead of "like all." The context fits the *Malva* better than the *Atriplex.* The pink flowers of the *Malva sylvestris* L. are very prominent around Jerusalem in the late spring.

See also FLORA § A9*k;* SALT.

Bibliography. I. Löw, *Die Flora der Juden,* I (1926), 345-46; II (1924), 231-32. H. N. and A. L. Moldenke, *Plants of the Bible* (1952), pp. 53-54.
J. C. TREVER

MALLUCH măl'ək [מַלּוּךְ; Apoc. Μαλούχ]; KJV Apoc. MAMUCHUS mə mū'kəs. **1.** Ancestor of a Levitical singer in Solomon's temple (I Chr. 6:44—H 6:29).

2. A priest who accompanied Zerubbabel in the return from the Exile (Neh. 12:2).

3. Son of Bani, and one of the laymen whom Ezra required to put away their foreign wives (Ezra 10:29).

4. Son of Harim in the same list as 3 *above* (Ezra 10:32).

5. A priest who witnessed the covenant renewal under Ezra (Neh. 10:4); perhaps identical with 2 *above.*

6. A chief of the people in the same list as 5 *above* (Neh. 10:27); perhaps identical with 4 *above.*
J. M. WARD

MALLUCHI măl'ōō kī [מַלּוּכִי]; KJV MELICU mĕl'ĭ kū (Neh. 12:14). A family of priests in the time of Joiakim; headed by Jonathan. The name should probably be read "Malluch," as in Neh. 12:2.

MALLUS măl'əs [Μαλλώτης] (II Macc. 4:30); KJV MALLOS. A Cilician city of considerable size situated in the SE part of the region on the River Pyramus at the head of the river's delta. In the Seleucid period the city contained a small Greek element in addition to the native Cilician and oriental people. The city joined with Tarsus in a revolt against the proposal of Antiochus Epiphanes to present the two cities as gifts to his concubines—a common practice of Persian and Seleucid rulers (cf. Thucydides I.138.5; Cicero *Against Verres* II.3.33; I Macc. 10:89).

Bibliography. F.-M. Abel, *Les Livres des Maccabées* (1949), p. 340.
E. W. SAUNDERS

MALTA môl'tə [ἡ Μελίτη] (Acts 28:1); KJV MELITA mĕl'ĭ tə. An island S of Sicily.

As described in the first century B.C. by Diodorus of Sicily (V.12), there are three islands which lie out to sea off Sicily, each of which possessed a city and harbors capable of offering safety to ships in stress of weather. These are Malta, Gaulus (modern Gozo), and Kerkina. Malta is ninety miles (eight hundred stadia, according to Diodorus) from Syracuse, sixty miles from the nearest tip of Sicily.

The position of Malta made it significant for Mediterranean travel both from E to W and also from the N to Africa. Presumably it was the last relationship which led Ptolemy (*Geography* IV.3) to list Malta among islands along the coast of Africa. According to Diodorus, the island was colonized by the Phoenicians, who in the course of extending their trade to the W ocean found it a safe retreat, since it was well supplied with harbors and lay out in the

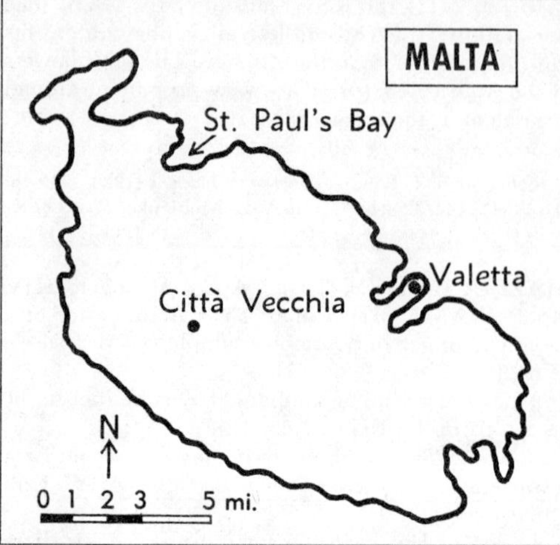

Jack Finegan

open sea. For the same reason, he says, the inhabitants of the island received much assistance from the sea merchants and accordingly advanced rapidly in manner of living and in renown.

Malta is approximately eighteen miles long and eight miles wide. The highest point is 845 feet above sea level. On the SW side the cliffs descend abruptly to the sea, but on the NE coast there are many inlets and bays. The largest harbor is the site of the present city of Valetta; the bay to which the name of Paul is given, as the traditional place of the shipwreck of the apostle, is *ca.* eight miles farther NW, toward the upper tip of the island.

On the voyage on which he was shipwrecked on Malta, Paul left Fair Havens, Crete, after the fast (Acts 27:9). This was the Day of Atonement, which came on the tenth day of the seventh month, Tishri (Lev. 16:29), and in A.D. 57 fell on September 27. The ship drifted for over thirteen days (Acts 27:27); therefore the wreck on Malta must have been not far from the middle of October. At that time it was cold and raining (28:2). According to one set of observations in Valetta, October temperatures ranged from a maximum of 73 to a minimum of 59 degrees, and there was rain on from five to twelve days of the month.

Archaeological investigation has found extensive remains of a Neolithic culture on Malta, characterized particularly by megalithic structures in double-oval form, which were probably cult places. Later, objects of the Bronze Age are found, doubtless indicating the arrival of a new population. The first landings of the Phoenicians were probably made in the course of their voyages to Spain soon after the beginning of the first millennium B.C., and it may have been in the eighth or seventh century B.C. that they built the city of Malta on the site of the present Città Vecchia, near which Phoenician graves are found. Stephen of Byzantium (sixth century A.D.) states (*De Urbibus*) that the city of Acholla in Libya was a colony of Malta, and, since such colonization in North Africa would hardly have been possible after the rise of Carthage to dominance in the sixth century B.C., the power of Phoenician Melita prior to that time is shown.

With the rise of Carthage, it was natural that Malta should come under its dominance; and the first historical reference to Malta, a notice in the middle of the fourth century B.C. in the *Periplus* attributed to Scylax, states that the island, with its city and harbor, was under the Carthaginians. During the wars between Carthage and Rome, Malta passed back and forth between the two powers and was finally surrendered to Rome at the beginning of the Second Punic War in 218 B.C., when the Roman consul Titus Sempronius Longus landed on the island (Livy XXI.li.1-2). Under the Romans the administration of Malta was placed in the hands of the governor of Sicily. This governorship was held by Gaius Verres for three years just preceding 70 B.C., when Cicero, himself quaestor at Lilybaeum, Sicily, in 75 B.C., prosecuted him for misgovernment and extortion. In his speeches Cicero told how Verres plundered an ancient temple of Juno which stood on a headland not far from the town of Malta, and also referred to the hordes of pirates who infested neighboring waters in those days and spent their winters on Malta (*Against Verres* II.4.103-4). When he himself went into exile in 58 B.C., Cicero would have liked to go to Malta (*To Atticus* III.4). With the reorganization of the Empire under Augustus, the Maltese islands appear to have been placed directly under a procurator, and an inscription from Malta mentions a "procurator of the islands of Malta and Gaulus." On Malta itself the leading local official seems to have borne the simple title "chief," or "first" (ὁ πρῶτος or *primus*), as shown by inscriptions in both Greek and Latin. This is the title of Publius in Acts 28:7 (ὁ πρῶτος τῆς νήσου).

There are many Jewish and Christian catacombs on Malta. The Christian tombs are usually considered, although without sufficient evidence for a positive decision, to date from the fourth century. *See bibliography.*

Bibliography. A. Mayr, *Die Insel Malta im Altertum* (1909); J. Weiss, "Melite," *Pauly-Wissowa,* vol. XV, pt. i (1931), cols. 543-47.

On the catacombs, see: E. Becker, *Malta Sotterranea* (1913); H. Leclercq, "Malte," *Dictionnaire d'archéologie chrétienne et de liturgie,* vol. X, pt. i (1931), cols. 1332-39. J. FINEGAN

MAMAIAS. KJV alternate form of SHEMAIAH.

MAMDAI măm'dī. Alternate name of BENAIAH 9.

MAMMON măm'ən [μαμωνᾶς=Aram. ממון, ממונא]. A word of uncertain Semitic origin meaning "wealth," "money," "property," or "profit." The term appears in the NT only in the words of Jesus (Matt. 6:24; Luke 16:9, 11, 13), but it was known well enough to need no explanation (S-B, I, 434-35). It is found in Ecclus. 31:8 (H); Enoch 63:10; M. Ab. 2.12; and in the Targums repeatedly. Jesus' use of the word displays two aspects:

a) In Matt. 6:24; Luke 16:13, service to God forbids service to mammon. No one (οὐδεὶς; Matthew), no slave (οὐδεὶς οἰκέτης; Luke), can serve two masters. Not the possession of money, but the unshared service of it as a slave serves his owner, makes impossible an undivided obligation to God. Ultimate loyalty belongs to God alone.

b) In Luke 16:9, 11 (cf. Ecclus. 5:8), mammon, like the steward, is described as unrighteous (ἀδικία). Its acquisition often involves injustice and wickedness, "tainted money," but it is to be used to make friends to win eternal security with God. Faithfulness to earthly possessions prepares one to be entrusted with true mammon (riches).

Bibliography. J. T. Marshall, in J. Hastings, *Encyclopedia of Religion and Ethics* (1916), VIII, 374-75; A. M. Honeyman, "The Etymology of Mammon," *Archivum Linguisticum*, vol. IV, fasc. 1 (1952), pp. 60-65; J. Jeremias, *The Parables of Jesus* (1954); trans. S. H. Hooke, from *Die Gleichnisse Jesu* (3rd ed., 1954), pp. 31-36. D. M. Beck

MAMRE măm'rĭ [ממרא]. **1.** An Amorite, brother of Aner and Eshcol. All three are pictured as allies of Abram in the routing of Chedorlaomer (Gen. 14:13, 24). *See 2 below.*

2. A place, Ramet el-Khalil ("height of the friend [of the merciful one, God]"), *ca.* 1⅔ miles N of the later site of Hebron.

It seems to have been the focal point of the general area in which Abraham lived. According to the biblical tradition, it was named after an Amorite, Mamre, who, with his brothers, joined Abraham in the pursuit and defeat of Chedorlaomer and his allies (Gen. 14:13 ff). Abraham erected an altar here, "by the oaks of Mamre" (13:18), and later pleaded for the sparing of Sodom and Gomorrah here (18:1 ff). The cave in the field of MACHPELAH, E of Mamre, was purchased by Abraham for use as a tomb in which he, Sarah, and the other patriarchs and their wives were buried (23:17 ff; 25:9; 35:27; 49:30; 50:13).

Because of its patriarchal associations, the precinct became sacred to the Jews. A pavement from the ninth-eighth centuries B.C., found in the course of excavation, is a tangible witness to this long-standing tradition. A break in the pavement just NE of the "well of Abraham" may mark the location of an earlier "oak of Abraham."

In Josephus' day an oak, said to have been there since Creation, was pointed out as the Oak of Abraham (War IV.ix.7; Antiq. I.x.4). Josephus' distance from Hebron (⅔ mile N) is *ca.* a mile short of the oak described by fourth-century travelers and may be an error.

The enclosure built by Herod bears striking similarities to that of the Haram around the site of the Cave of Machpelah in Hebron and the temple enclosure in Jerusalem. Destroyed in 70, it was rebuilt by Hadrian and in A.D. 135 was the scene of the sale of Jewish prisoners captured in the course of putting down the Second Revolt, led by Bar Cocheba, in the course of the famed "Fair of Terebinthos" (i.e., Oak of Abraham).

The mixed population of S Palestine used the precinct, its altar, and its well for assorted rites, largely superstitious, which the construction of the Constantinian basilica and the destruction of the altar in the fourth century failed to halt. The pagan practices apparently continued until the Arab invasion. The basilica was destroyed by the Persians in 614 and partially rebuilt.

Today the walls of the enclosure, rebuilt during the centuries, still rise to a height of eighteen feet in one place. The Herodian masonry still rests upon some courses of pre-Herodian stonework. Chalcolithic and Early Bronze remains reveal that this site was a gathering place for people for perhaps nearly two millenniums before the new city of Hebron eclipsed it; even then its religious significance prevented its being forgotten "to this day."

Bibliography. R. de Vaux, "Mambré," *Dictionnaire de la Bible, Supplément*, vol. V (1953), cols. 754-58, and the bibliography cited there. A. E. Mader, *Mambrie. Die Ergebnisse der Ausgrabungen im heiligen Bezirk Râmet el-Ḫalîl in Südpalästina* (2 vols.; 1957). V. R. Gold

MAMUCHUS. KJV Apoc. form of MALLUCH.

MAN, ETHNIC DIVISIONS OF. The OT deals often with relations between Israel and her neighbors; it also has an interest in the interrelations of the various subdivisions of mankind. In both these areas the OT offers ethnographic information that adds up to a substantial amount. The whole reflects stated principles of classification and broad geographic horizons; but it suffers inevitably from the scientific limitations of that age. The material, moreover, is uneven in regard to sources, date, and emphasis. Consequently, the detail often proves confusing, and at times self-contradictory. Many of the difficulties can be clarified by co-ordinating the biblical evidence with the mass of pertinent information to be found in extrabiblical sources.

- A. The ethno-geographic evidence of the OT
  - 1. The Table of Nations
    - *a.* Japhethites
    - *b.* Hamites
    - *c.* S(h)emites
  - 2. Lists of pre-Israelite nations
  - 3. Descriptive contexts
- B. The modern ethno-linguistic picture of Bible lands
  - 1. The Semito-Hamitic group
    - *a.* Akkadians
    - *b.* Amorites
    - *c.* Canaanites
    - *d.* Arameans
    - *e.* The Arabic group
    - *f.* Egyptians and Cushites
  - 2. The Indo-European family
    - *a.* Hittites
    - *b.* Indo-Aryans
    - *c.* Philistines
    - *d.* Others
  - 3. Unassigned groups
    - *a.* Sumerians
    - *b.* Elamites
    - *c.* Kassites
    - *d.* Hurrians
    - *e.* Anatolians
    - *f.* Others
- C. Biblical and extrabiblical data compared
  - 1. Canaanites and Amorites
  - 2. Hittites
  - 3. Hurrians
- Bibliography

A. *THE ETHNO-GEOGRAPHIC EVIDENCE OF THE OT.* Biblical terminology uses "people" (עם)

primarily for a genetically related group, and "nation" (גוי) largely for a political entity centered in a given locality. These terms may be interchanged, yet the underlying distinction is still apparent for the most part. For purposes of national classification, therefore, it is thus גוי that is the more suitable term; hence the Table of Nations employs it repeatedly (Gen. 10:5, 20, 31-32), but dispenses with עם altogether. According to the same source, the subdivision of a nation is the "clan, family" (משפחה), but the main criteria are "language" (לשון) and "land" (ארץ; vss. 5, 20, 31). Nor is the genealogical factor left out of account, since "direct descent" (תולדות) is explicitly recognized (vs. 32). Historically, of course, some nations are known to have been superseded by others: "The Horites . . . lived in Seir formerly, but the sons of Esau dispossessed them" (Deut. 2:12; cf. vss. 10, 20, 22-23).

Yet not all these theoretical criteria have uniform validity in practice. Although language is duly stressed, and peoples can be distinguished by their vocabulary (e.g., Deut. 3:9)—indeed, the proper pronunciation may sometimes be a matter of life or death (Judg. 12:6)—it is recognized that a mastery of more than one language was possible (II Kings 18:26= Isa. 36:11). On the other hand, there are some otherwise prominent distinctions that the Table of Nations ignores. Circumcision was not practiced by the Philistines (e.g., I Sam. 18:25, 27) or, at least originally, by the Hivites (Gen. 34:13-14), but was customary with many other peoples (Jer. 9:24-25) aside from the Israelites. The formal lists are silent on this point. The same holds true, significantly enough, of pigmentation, even though the color of skin could loom large in other contexts (Jer. 13:23). It thus follows that race in the anthropological sense was viewed as incidental. In short, the principal criteria for classifying the subdivisions of mankind were nation and country. The basis was thus essentially ethno-geographic.

1. The Table of Nations. This name has long been applied to Gen. 10, a chapter devoted in its entirety to ethnographic matters. In it the peoples of the world are subdivided according to stated principles of classification. This is an ambitious undertaking, the first of its kind known from anywhere. Naturally, the achievement has to be viewed in terms of the knowledge and the methods of its particular age. As such, it operates with a very large canvas, extending from Transcaucasia to Ethiopia and from Iran to the Aegean; but the coverage is concentric and fades out on the peripheries. The Table, moreover, is by no means self-consistent—a fault that derives in part from the composite character of the work. Portions of it come from the J document, notably vss. 8-19, 25-30. The remainder stems from P, except where the ultimate compiler left some additions and dislocations. In any case, even the later entries cannot be put after the seventh century, since their substance was known to both Jeremiah and Ezekiel.

a. Japhethites. The Table traces the nations of the world to the three sons of Noah, thereby accounting for the progressive repopulation after the Flood, and providing a starting point for subsequent scientific terminology. In the original use, however, geography took precedence over linguistics. The Japhethite branch (vss. 2-4) includes Cimmerians (Gomer), Medes, Ionians (Javan), Scythians (Ashkenaz), and Cypriotes (Elisha and Kittim), among others. Its settlements thus skirt the Fertile Crescent from the N and penetrate the maritime regions in the W. The fact is worth stressing that no Japhethite list has come down from J, evidently because that particular horizon was as yet closed to the J source.

b. Hamites. The main subdivisions of this branch (vss. 6-20) are the peoples of the S shores of the Red Sea (Cush), Egypt (Mizraim), Canaan, and the as-yet-ambiguous Put (probably Cyrene rather than Somaliland).

The case of Cush was complicated by the fact that there were originally two independent bearers of this name, which led to their becoming telescoped in the OT (*see* § B3 *below*). This is why the Nimrod passage (vss. 8-12), at one time an extension of the Mesopotamian Cush, is now inserted with Ethiopia under the Hamites. No such accident, however, can be held responsible for the inclusion of both the Philistines and the Cretans (Caphtorim) under Egypt (vss. 13-14). The author (J) was surely aware that no ethnic or linguistic bonds linked the Egyptians and the Philistines; the main reason, then, for such a connection had to be geographic, with Crete drawn in as the Philistines' previous home. The mention of Ludim in the same company remains enigmatic, if the name stands for Lydians, unless this is an echo of the invasion of Egypt by the so-called Sea Peoples, an event in which the Philistines participated; another, and no less puzzling, Lud is listed with the Semites (vs. 22).

Most difficult of all, however, is the placing of Canaan within this branch (vs. 6), in view especially of Canaan's further subdivisions. The main one is Sidon (Phoenicia), which is appropriate enough, since the Phoenicians themselves called their country Canaan; but Sidon's brothers became the eponyms of the Hittites (Heth), along with Jebusites, Amorites, Hivites, and others (vss. 15-18). Now the authors (both J and P) could not but know that Phoenician was very close to Hebrew, but quite different from Egyptian, not to mention the other dialects in question. To be sure, the lists of Canaanite nations (*see* § A2 *below*) had something to do with this situation, and the tradition behind the curse of Canaan (Gen. 9:25-26) must also have been a factor. Yet such socio-political arguments cannot very well be stretched to Phoenicia or Egypt. It would thus seem to follow that the basic principle of classification was once again neither ethnic nor linguistic alone, but ethno-geographic. By this token, the biblical Hamites extended from Phoenicia down through W Palestine, and from there into Africa. Only the Amorites (vs. 16) are partly out of focus in this picture; but vss. 16-17 are now commonly ascribed to the final compiler ("R").

c. S(h)emites. This branch is given special prominence because it comprised, among other groups, "all the children of Eber" (vs. 21)—i.e., the Hebrews in the broader sense. Under it were subsumed, naturally enough, the related groups of Assyrians and Arameans, as well as numerous tribes of Arabia. What is less transparent is the inclusion of the Elamites (vs. 22), whose center was in SW Persia. Here again, however, geographic considerations must have played a part. Elam was the nearest E neighbor of Mesopotamia; for this reason, therefore, it could properly be cited together with Asshur. On the other hand, Arpachshad still defies explanation as the ancestor of Eber and the Hebrews (vs. 24); the name itself appears to be non-Semitic.

No less puzzling, at least at first glance, is the omission of Israel from this list, together with Israel's E neighbors and relatives, such as the Edomites, the Moabites, and the Ammonites. All these peoples should have been listed under Peleg, but no descendant of this first-born son of Eber is here recorded. His detailed genealogy, however, is given in Gen. 11:18-27. It is likely, therefore, that the J document had originally dealt with Peleg at greater length, but the details were later left out in favor of P's separate statement. Another notable omission is that of Babylon. Quite probably, this name had figured at one time under descendants of a Mesopotamian Cush (cf. vs. 10), as part of the Semitic branch, only to be shunted aside in the technical merger with the Hamitic Cushites.

All in all, the Table of Nations, for all its reshuffling and dislocations, remains an achievement remarkable for its wide scope and analytical approach. As such, it stands out as a pioneering effort among the ethnographic inquiries of the ancient world.

2. Lists of pre-Israelite nations. These are incidental and stereotyped groupings of the occupants of Palestine prior to the Israelite settlement. There are twenty-two such lists, ranging in number from two (Canaanites and Perizzites; Gen. 13:7; 34:30; cf. Judg. 1:4-5) to ten (Gen. 15:19-20). More commonly, however, the enumerations center on the following intermediate group: Amorites, Canaanites, Hittites, Perizzites, Hivites, Jebusites, and Girgashites—in this approximate order of prominence. All seven are given in Deut. 7:1; Josh. 3:10; 24:11. As a rule, however, the number is six (eleven instances), the Girgashites being usually the ones left out; but the LXX tends to restore the higher figure. The sources range all the way from the J document to the Chronicler (II Chr. 8:7), thus suggesting a common underlying tradition.

Of the seven nations just cited, the first five—and more particularly the first three—may be used inclusively as general terms for larger ethnic blocks. Moreover, either the Canaanites (e.g., Gen. 12:6) or the Amorites (e.g., Gen. 15:16) may stand, in descriptive contexts, for the entire population of Palestine. The choice in such cases is not automatically a matter of source pure and simple. It is true that the J document favors the Canaanites as a comprehensive ethnic designation, whereas the E document has a similar partiality for the Amorites; yet E does not hesitate to employ the term "Canaan" as a land name (e.g., Gen. 42:13, 29, 32; 45:17, 25), and there is no geographic term "Amor" as such. One may, therefore, posit as a general hypothesis that "Canaan" actually started out as a geographic name, but took on extra duty for ethnic and even linguistic (Isa. 19:18) purposes, whereas "Amorite(s)" was never extended beyond its original ethnic use. Both terms would thus be basically independent, their diverse employment in the OT pointing to a mixed population in early biblical times.

This conclusion is supported by the evidence of the extrabiblical sources (*see* § B *below*) as well as that of sundry narrative passages in the Bible (*see* § A3 *below*). It is borne out, furthermore, by the lists themselves. Mention has already been made of "the Canaanites and the Perizzites." On another occasion, moreover, we hear of "the Hivites, the Canaanites, and the Hittites" (Exod. 23:28). It follows that behind the broader distinction between Canaanites and Amorites—insofar as these terms were not regarded as interchangeable—there was usually the concept of other ethnic groups. These in turn could be subsumed either under the Perizzites or under the Hivites and Hittites.

3. Descriptive contexts. As opposed to the bare lists, there are in the OT various scattered passages in which ethnic elements in Palestine and vicinity are linked to particular localities or events. Thus Amorites are located in Hebron (Gen. 14:13), and especially in Transjordan (Deut. 1:4; 2:24; 3:2, 8; etc.). According to Num. 23:29, "the Amalekites dwell in the land of Negeb; the Hittites, the Jebusites, and the Amorites dwell in the hill country; and the Canaanites dwell by the sea, and along the Jordan." Another significant passage,. as preserved in the LXX, is Isa. 17:9, in that it brackets together "the Hivites and the Amorites"; in the case of the former, the MT points to Horites instead (*see* HORITES § 2). There is, lastly, Ezekiel's reference to Jerusalem as the offspring of an Amorite father and a Hittite mother (16:3, 45). All such combinations, stemming as they do from various authors and periods, serve to emphasize the fact that Israel thought of the earlier population of the country as composed, not just of Canaanites and Amorites alone, but of other elements as well.

Biblical literature abounds, of course, in descriptive and poetic references to nations near and far with which Israel had direct contact at one time or another. These include comments about Israel's close relatives in Edom, Moab, and Ammon, as well as other ethnic groups in Egypt, Syria, Mesopotamia, and the like. There are also occasional antiquarian references to such older elements as the Emim (Deut. 2:10), the Horites (vs. 12), the Rephaim or Zamzummim (vs. 20), and the Avvim (vs. 23); cf. also Gen. 14:5-6.

B. *THE MODERN ETHNO-LINGUISTIC PICTURE OF BIBLE LANDS.* Whereas the OT refers only to such nations or tribes as were part of its own historical experience, modern scholarship reconstructs the ethnic picture of the biblical age from many different sources. Skeletal remains provide certain anthropometric data. Ancient paintings and sculptures show how the given human types were portrayed by artists. Innumerable written documents, in a profusion of languages and from many areas of the ancient Near East, furnish a vast amount of information on the history, culture, and location of a truly bewildering array of peoples. And finally, there is the internal linguistic evidence of the documents that have come down to us: the structure of each particular language, and its family relations, if any.

Of all these and other similar sources, it is the linguistic material alone that is fully dependable and capable of scientific control. To arrive at a satisfactory ethnic classification, therefore, it is necessary to match, if at all possible, a given people with the language which that group commonly employed. Accordingly, herein such terms as "Akkadians" or "Amorites" will be understood to refer primarily to native speakers of "Akkadian" or "Amorite." On this basis, the "Canaanites" in an ethno-linguistic sense correspond only in part with the ethno-geographic Canaanites of the OT. And by the same token, the Elamites can no longer be classified as Semitic, the Hittites as Canaanite, or the Philistines as Egyptian. Nevertheless, it will be seen that the differences between the biblical and the modern groupings are less drastic than one might expect, for there remains a substantial area of agreement.

1. The Semito-Hamitic family. Modern research leaves no doubt that the Semitic languages, Egyptian, and the Hamitic languages had a common ancestry. The original home of this family would seem to suggest a location in North Africa, though this is by no means certain. In any case, after separating from the parent stock, the Semites are found in Asia, where they can be eventually distinguished by a number of separate languages.

a. Akkadians. The principal historic speakers of the language called "Akkadian" (after the city of Akkad; Gen. 10:10) by the ancient users and modern students alike were the Babylonians and Assyrians. The language itself is the oldest and easternmost branch of Semitic. Its main difference from all its sister languages consists in a distinctive verbal system. The OT contains various Akkadian personal names and some special terms (e.g., טפסר, Akkadian *ṭupšarru*, "scribe" [Jer. 51:27; RSV "marshal"; Nah. 3:17]; מִסְכֵּן, "pitiable," Akkadian *muškênu* [Eccl. 4:13; 9:15-16]). The Table of Nations gives Asshur a prominent place under the descendants of Shem (Gen. 10:22), but lists Babylon (Babel) only as a city (vs. 10). *See* § A1*c above.*

b. Amorites. Akkadian texts often mention a land Amurru, and this name is known to interchange with the written Sumerian form *MAR.TU.* Whether these two forms referred originally to separate lands is as yet uncertain; but both occur in the same sense in the Alalakh texts from the Old Babylonian stratum. The gentilic term in Akkadian was *Amurrû*, and the corresponding Hurrian term was *Amur(r)uḫḫi* (in Alalakh). Because Amorites were the nearest historic neighbors to the W of Akkadian Mesopotamia, the Akkadian term for "west" came to be *amurru.*

Bearers of distinctive W Semitic personal names appear in Mesopotamia toward the end of the third millennium, and their numbers increase appreciably by the beginning of the second millennium. These intrusive elements have generally been traced back to the Amorites. They proceeded to establish a number of new dynasties, notably at Larsa, Babylon, Mari, and Asshur. The First Dynasty of Babylon, whose best-known ruler was the celebrated Hammurabi (or rather, Hammurapi), is frequently referred to for this very reason as the Dynasty of Amurru. That all these newcomers were soon thoroughly assimilated is proof of the cultural superiority of Babylonia, but not of a want of Amorite enterprise.

Later in the second millennium, the Amarna Letters cite the Amorites repeatedly as invading or threatening various places in Phoenicia and vicinity. The Hittite archives have yielded several treaties with rulers of Amurru. Nor are references to the land lacking in later Assyrian records. Nevertheless, the exact location of Amurru is difficult to establish, possibly because its boundaries were fluid and its people widely scattered outside their own homeland. The general region, however, is not seriously in doubt. Amurru lay to the S of Aleppo and Alalakh, and E of the Phoenician strip. When political conditions favored their expansion, Amorite holdings might impinge on the old states of the Mesopotamian area in the E, and spread to the Jordan watershed in the S. It should be noted that some of the Asiatic names in the Egyptian execration texts of the patriarchal age appear to be Amorite in origin.

c. Canaanites. Whereas the Amorites are cited early and all the way E in Lower Mesopotamia, both as an ethnic group and by country, the Canaanites are not alluded to before the middle of the second millennium, to judge from the sources available thus far; except, moreover, for a rare lexical reference, the name is reflected in the Mesopotamian area only at Nuzi; its concentration was in the W, and its older use is primarily geographic. Thus the Alalakh texts of the Mitannian period speak of the "land of" *Ki-in-a-nim* (with the so-called "broken" spelling reflecting a medial ʿ-sound) and *Ki-na-a-ni.* Amarna texts record eleven occurrences of a land name *Kinaḫḫi, Kinaḫ/na,* as against a single gentilic *Ki-na-ḫa-ay-u.* A geographic connotation underlies also the Nuzi adjective *Kinaḫḫu,* which describes a type of purple wool imported from the W. Egyptian *p' Knʿn* and Phoenician כנען likewise refer to a land, the latter to Phoenicia itself. The corresponding gentilics (including Ugaritic *knʿny*) are met with less frequently, outside the OT. There is thus good reason for assuming that the primary connotation was geographic, the areas being Phoenicia and Palestine.

Thus both usage and distribution impose a sharp distinction between Canaanites and Amorites. Linguistic evidence points to a similar conclusion. Although there is little early material on the subject—mostly personal names—it indicates nevertheless certain dialectal differences, both in the treatment of the sibilants and in the morphology of the verb. E.g., the personal name "X has listened" appears as *(Y)išma(ʿ)-X* in Canaanite, but *Yasmaʿ-X* in Amorite; the corresponding Akkadian form is *Išme-X.*

On geographical grounds, Ugaritic should be classed with Canaanite, and there is considerable linguistic evidence to confirm this expectation. There is, however, also some contrary evidence. The problem may prove to be largely one of chronology, inasmuch as Ugaritic is older than the extant Canaanite material.

If Canaan was originally the geographical name for Phoenicia and the adjoining districts of Palestine, then anyone settled in those areas could have been described as a Canaanite, regardless of his native language; and such, indeed, is the bearing of many biblical occurrences of the term. If one starts, however, with the language of the historical Phoenicians and calls it, quite properly, "Canaanite," then the related dialects of the Israelites and the Moabites should likewise be classed as Canaanite. The latter usage is found already in Isa. 19:18; and it is reflected in modern linguistic terminology, which groups together under "Canaanite" (or "Hebrew") the same group of dialects—or, in other words, the speech of the Pelegite branch of Eber as well as that of the Phoenicians. The term has thus a dual application, one geographical (OT) and the other linguistic.

d. Arameans. This group poses no problems in the present context, in that OT and modern terminology are this time in complete agreement. The eponymous Aram was a descendant of Shem (Gen. 10:22), and the speech of that people is a long-recognized member of the Semitic family. The ARAMEANS superseded the Amorites as menacing neighbors of Mesopotamia along its W borders. They harassed Assyria for centuries, and were an even more serious threat to Israel.

Courtesy of the Cairo Museum; photo courtesy of the Metropolitan Museum of Art

5. Libyans, Syrians, and Negroes represented as prisoners, on the interior of a state chariot of Tut-ankh-Amon

And the Aramaic language was to show unprecedented vitality long after the political decline of the Arameans, spreading over the whole of the ancient Near East, and becoming the main speech of Palestine and Syria. The extensive Aramaic portions of the OT, glosses in the NT, the Targums, and much of the Talmud are among the many witnesses to the pervasive force of that language.

Fig. MAN 5.

e. The Arabic groups. Current terminology employs "Arabian" for geographical, "Arab" for ethnic, and "Arabic" for linguistic purposes. The first two usages speak for themselves, but the last lends itself to misunderstanding in that it is applied to two independent branches of Semitic: North Arabic, or the group of dialects now included under Arabic proper; and South Arabic, which is so named on account of its relation to the Arabian Peninsula rather than to Arabic. The logical designation for the latter is Southeast Semitic. This is a sizable subdivision of Semitic, comprising, in the main, ancient Sabaean, Minaean, and Ethiopic (in the strict linguistic sense), as well as numerous modern descendants. On internal linguistic grounds, Southeast Semitic proves to be a very old member of the family. It displays certain intimate links with Akkadian. The Table of Nations, moreover, hints at similar ties with "Hebrew" by tracing such elements as Sheba and Hazarmaveth (modern Hadramaut) to Joktan, who was the second son of Eber (Gen. 10:25-27). But it also names Seba, Sheba, and Dedan under Cush, brother of Canaan (vss. 6-7). This vacillation is readily explained, however, inasmuch as the Cushitic listing goes back to the P document, and the Hebrew connection to J. In any case, contacts with actual North Arabians are rare, and they are signified both in the cuneiform sources and in the OT by explicit use of the term "Arab."

f. Egyptians and Cushites. Within the larger Semito-Hamitic family, both Egyptian and Cushitic depart markedly from Semitic proper. For cogent methodological reasons, Egyptian is classified as a separate branch, whereas Cushitic has long been grouped under Hamitic proper. Egyptian is represented in the OT by certain proper names and a small number of loan words. Cushitic—in the linguistic sense, and hence distinct from Ethiopic, which is a Southeast Semitic language, and from Kassite—happens to show a striking, yet unmistakable, tie with certain pronominal forms of Akkadian. Together with pertinent details of phonology and verbal structure, this is a highly significant, though isolated, reminder of linguistic conditions in the oldest stratum of the common Hamito-Semitic stock.

2. The Indo-European family. Indo-European elements are reflected in Bible lands and in the OT in various periods and circumstances. Midway through the second millennium the Near East was host to speakers of the two distinctive branches of this family: the *centum* group (which includes Greek, Italo-Celtic, and Germanic, among others) is represented by Hittites; and the *satem* group (which lists Indo-Aryan and Balto-Slavic among its members) is attested by an early wave of Indo-Aryans. By the end of the second millennium a coastal strip of Palestine was occupied by the Philistines, whose meager linguistic traces hint at an Indo-European background. In the following millennium other groups of Indo-Europeans made their appearance in increasing numbers, notably Iranians, Scythians, Celts, and Greeks.

a. Hittites. This name carries several conflicting connotations, which derive in part from local Anatolian usage, in part from the terminology of the Table of Nations, and in still another part from the nature of the subject itself. There is thus the ancient Anatolian land name *Ḫatti*, whose "Hattic" people spoke "Hattic" and had their capital at *Ḫattus* (modern Boghazköy). This is evidently the source of the biblical Heth, listed in the Table of Nations as the brother of Sidon (Gen. 10:15); hence our term "Hittite." The Hattic language was neither Semitic nor Indo-European. Now when Hatti was overrun by a foreign people, the conquerors retained the old geographic names for the country and its capital, but imposed on the territory their own language. This

Courtesy of the Oriental Institute, the University of Chicago

6. Prisoners from the foreign conquests of Ramses III, showing (left to right) Libyan, Syrian, Hittite, Philistine (sea people), Syrian; from the Temple of Ramses III, Medinet Habu

language has proved to be Indo-European—or Indo-Hittite, in a highly technical sense. Its modern decipherers can hardly be blamed for calling it "Hittite," even though it turned out eventually to have nothing in common with Hattic. This Indo-European Hittite is now known to have had several relatives in the area, among them Luwian and so-called Hieroglyphic Hittite, so that "Hittite" today can be used for this whole interrelated group. In this broader linguistic sense Hittite is attested in Anatolia and parts of N Syria through most of the second millennium. Fig. MAN 6.

Against this complex background the biblical occurrences of the term pose a difficult problem of their own: do they reflect the ancient Anatolian Hattians, the intrusive Hittites, or at times the former and other times the latter? *See* HITTITES; *and cf.* § C2 *below.*

b. Indo-Aryans. Toward the middle of the second millennium much of the Near East was devastated by invaders under the leadership of E Indo-Europeans, or Indo-Aryans. In the wake of this irruption, Vedic deities entered the Hittite pantheon, Aryan kings ruled the new state of Mitanni, and Aryan princes were found in various cities of Syria and Palestine—as shown in particular by the Amarna correspondence. The success of the invaders was facilitated apparently by their large-scale employment of horses; small wonder, therefore, that cuneiform records of that age contain Aryan technical terms for chariot racing and for breeds and colors of horses. Before long, however, the newcomers were absorbed by the local elements, and the *status quo* was restored. Thus the whole fateful, though relatively brief, episode appears to have left no tangible mark in the OT.

c. Philistines. As here considered, the PHILISTINES are an offshoot of the Sea Peoples deposited in Palestine shortly after 1200 B.C.; this dating is supported by archaeological remains and historical references. Accordingly, the appearance of this ethnic term in earlier OT contexts would seem to indicate an extension of the name to prior, and perhaps related, settlers. In any case, the historical Philistines came, according to the Table of Nations, either from or by way of Caphtor (Gen. 10:14, where the last two words have been accidentally misplaced). What little information can be gathered from the few original personal names and a handful of possible Philistine loan words in Hebrew is not inconsistent with the assumption that the language was a dialect of Indo-European, perhaps related to Illyrian.

d. Others. By the seventh century, when the latest entries in the Table of Nations had been recorded, Mesopotamia and Syria had long been in contact with many other groups of Indo-Europeans. Visitors from Ionia (OT Javan) were not uncommon, Cimmerians (Gomer) and Scythians (Ashkenaz) were thorns in the side of Assyria, and the Medes (Madai) were soon to leave Nineveh in ruins. A few decades later, the Persians extended their empire over the entire Near East, only to give way in time to Greeks and Macedonians. It is natural, therefore, that the later books of the OT should show increasing evidence of Indo-European connections, chiefly in the form of Iranian personal names and loan words. There is even an ascertained Greek loan word, the term פסנטרין, פסנתרין (Greek ψαλ Τήριον; the name of a musical instrument; Dan 3:5, 7, 10, 15). By then, however, the West was well established throughout the Near East.

3. Unassigned groups. The Semitic-Hamitic and Indo-European families were not the only stocks in the ancient Near East any more than they are today. The modern population includes Turks, who are relatively recent arrivals, and also—in the northernmost districts—various ethno-linguistic elements of the large Caucasic family. The past knew likewise, especially in the Fertile Crescent and Anatolia, a number of such separate groups. Some of these proved to be exceptionally important cultural and historical factors. Aside from the Sumerians, moreover, these scattered elements appear to represent the earliest population of the area.

a. Sumerians. Immensely important though they were culturally and historically, the Sumerians (*see* SUMER) remain linguistically isolated, and hence ethnically, too, a group apart. The weight of the evidence would seem to point to their arrival in Lower Mesopotamia late in the prehistoric period, probably from a considerable distance. The OT calls their land Shinar (actually *Šin'ar,* Akkadian *Šumer,* from Sumerian *Kiengir;* cf., e.g., Gen. 10:10; 11:2; 14:1, 9). And it is a measure of the far-reaching influence of that people that Sumerian loan words found their way into the OT: e.g., *'ēdh,* "underground swell" (Gen. 2:4), and—in all probability—the name Eden. The common Semitic terms for "chair" and "carpenter" also go back to Sumerian. These borrowings, however, reflect the stratified character of the cultural and ethnic picture of the ancient Near East; for both these words had been taken over, in turn, from the pre-Sumerian inhabitants of the land.

b. Elamites. A people settled in SW Iran since early prehistoric times, the Elamites continued as a significant local factor down to the Persian period. The Elamite language, known from records that span many centuries, has no demonstrable relatives. There is not enough material to decide whether such neighboring groups of the Lullu and the Guti were linguistically affiliated with Elamites; conceivably, all three might be ancestral to some of the languages of modern Caucasic. The Table of Nations lists Elam with the Shemites (Gen. 10:22), apparently for geographical reasons. Some of the later notices in the OT could well allude to Persians.

c. Kassites. A people originally from W Iran, the Kassites (Akkadian *Kaššû,* Nuzi Akkadian *Kuššu-;* cf. Κοσσαῖοι) made themselves masters of Babylonia following the fall of the First Dynasty, and held this position for several centuries. In the Middle Babylonian period "Kassite land" was synonymous with Babylonia. The people had a distinctive language of their own, which remains isolated thus far. The corresponding biblical term is "Cush" (Gen. 2:13; 10:8), wholly distinct from the more common and better known Cush in the region of the Upper Nile, but inevitably confused with its Nilotic namesake.

d. Hurrians. A people widely diffused throughout the Near East, the HURRIANS had intimate relations with Mesopotamia, Anatolia, Syria, and various districts of Palestine. The OT appears to have known them locally as HIVITES; JEBUSITES (*see* JEBUS); and perhaps Perizzites (*see* PERIZZITE), whereas the pertinent term "HORITES" is used in this connection only in the LXX. Linguistic witnesses of the diffusion of Hurrians are now known from many areas of the Near East. The language itself may have been an early representative of the Caucasic group. Its only known relative is Urartean, the speech of pre-Indo-European Armenia; the cognate biblical term is ARARAT.

e. Anatolians. Of the various ethnic groups that were settled in Anatolia before the Indo-European invasion, the most important is that of the Hattians. It is they who gave their name to the land of the later Hittites, and to the biblical eponym Heth (Gen. 10:15; *cf.* § B2*a above*). The Hattic language is once again an isolated medium.

f. Others. The above survey does not fully delimit the ethnic horizons of the ancient Near East as reflected in extrabiblical sources. It is known, e.g., that contacts were maintained with Cyprus (cuneiform *Alašiya;* OT Elishah) and with Crete (cuneiform *Kaptara;* OT Caphtor). But until the original languages of these islands have been deciphered, we shall remain in ignorance of their linguistic connections. Similarly, the source or sources of certain cultural terms that are common to Semitic and Indo-European—such as those for "wine," or "iron" (Hebrew *barzel;* Latin **ferzom*>*ferrum*), and the like—must remain undetermined. Large areas have been illuminated. But there are still many dark corners.

C. *BIBLICAL AND EXTRABIBLICAL DATA COMPARED.* A comparison of the two sets of data that have been outlined above bears out the initial assumption that they differ not so much in content as in methodology; as has already been stressed repeatedly, the biblical criterion was primarily ethnogeographic, whereas ours is ethno-linguistic. The Shemites and Hamites of the OT are now subsumed for the most part under the joint Semito-Hamitic label. That Philistines and Hurrians and Elamites were included with these categories in the past, but must now be excluded from them, is accounted for by former political and geographical considerations. Just so, the largely maritime nations which the OT combines under Japhethites must now be classified on other terms; some of the entries prove to be Indo-European, while others emerge as unrelated.

The main problems that are still to be reviewed stem from the scattered notices of pre-Israelite nations rather than the comprehensive ethnic image of the Table of Nations. The over-all results may be summarized as follows:

1. Canaanites and Amorites. It was shown above that these two terms had separate and independent meanings in nonbiblical sources. The former goes back to a geographic concept applied, in the main, to the Phoenician coast and the neighboring districts of Palestine. The latter is met with in earlier times and over a much larger area. Its use is more pronouncedly ethnic than geographical; and insofar as location is involved, Amurru paralleled Canaan to the E. Furthermore, Canaanite and Amorite were separate and distinctive dialects, if not fully differentiated languages. Significantly enough, this dialectal division is actually attested in the OT. For we learn from Deut. 3:9 that "the Sidonians [i.e., Phoenicians, or, in other words, Canaanites] call Hermon Sirion, while the Amorites call it Senir."

During the Amarna age and immediately thereafter, there would thus be a predominance of Canaanites in Palestine, and of Amorites in Transjordan. But we also know from local cuneiform sources that Palestine was inhabited at that time by other groups in addition to Semites; Hurrians and Aryans have been positively identified. It is self-evident, moreover, that a contemporary user of a local Semitic dialect could readily tell the difference between a fellow Semite and a non-Semite, on the basis of speech, personal names, or the like. And such distinctions were bound to be reflected in local traditions.

How would such traditions be recorded in the OT? As a geographic designation, the established name for Palestine was Canaan; and on this basis, anyone living in Canaan would be a "Canaanite," no matter what his native speech. But if one wished to particularize the various ethnic elements, he would specify Canaanites, Amorites, Hittites, Hivites, and others, precisely as is done in some of the lists of pre-Israelite nations. On the other hand, if a more comprehensive ethnic summary were attempted, we would speak today of Semites and non-Semites. The OT offers instead "Canaanites and Perizzites" or, in reverse ethnic order, "Hivites and Amorites" (LXX; *cf.* §§ A2-3 *above*), with Canaanites or Amorites being equivalent to Semites, and Perizzites or Hivites to non-Semites. The Table of Nations does much the same thing in subdividing Canaan into Sidon and Heth (Gen. 10:15). As a transition to the detailed lists, Exod. 23:28 gives us "Hivites, Canaanites, and Hittites."

Thus both "Canaanites" and "Amorites" could designate the entire Semitic population of the area, depending on the particular vantage point, period, and author. In addition, however, each term had its own specialized and more precise meaning.

2. Hittites. In its early biblical application, this term should refer to the pre-Indo-European Hattians of Anatolia, and by extension to Anatolians in general. That some elements from this region may have been settled in Phoenicia and Palestine is inherently probable, but conclusive evidence is lacking. On the other hand, Indo-European Hittites could not be expected in that region prior to the Amarna age, at least not in substantial numbers. In any event, the biblical term has to be regarded as ambiguous. In Ezek. 16:3, 45, moreover, this *ethnicon* harks back to "Jebusite" and is thus descriptive of a Hurrian rather than an Anatolian element. Yet elsewhere we find Hurrians distinguished from "Hittites" (e.g., Exod. 23:28). All in all, therefore, the usage was flexible. The term could express (*a*) Hattians; (*b*) Indo-European Hittites; (*c*) Anatolians in general, as distinct from Hurrians; (*d*) non-Semites as opposed to Semites, under the geographical concept of Canaan (Gen. 10:15).

3. Hurrians. There is ample extrabiblical evidence that Hurrians were settled in Palestine in the latter half of the second millennium. Yet the MT fails to record them by name, the Horites being confined there to the area of Edom. It follows, therefore, that Hebrew tradition had come to refer to Hurrians under some other name or names; the LXX still locates them in Palestine in several significant instances. On various grounds, both the Hivites and the Jebusites may safely be linked with Hurrians. It is immaterial how these local designations may have come into vogue; the fact that accidental similarity in sound led to confusion with the Semitic Horites of Edom could well have worked against retention of the ethnic term for the Palestinian and non-Semitic Hurrians.

The term "Perizzites" cannot be ignored in this connection. Its vocalization would seem to suggest non-Semitic origin, and its use can be comprehensive enough to express the concept of "non-Semites," as in the phrase "Canaanites and Perizzites" (Gen. 13:7; 34:30; Judg. 1:4-5). The suffix *-izzi* is independently attested in Hurrian. There is thus the inherent possibility that the Perizzites were originally yet another local group of Hurrians, alongside the Hivites and the Jebusites. No confident conclusion, however, can be founded on such meager evidence.

There is, finally, one other question that remains to be posed. Among the intrusive ethnic groups that are witnessed in Palestine during the Amarna age, Indo-Aryans have been identified just as positively as Hurrians. Their numbers, however, were smaller, and there is nothing to indicate that they played a part in the cultural life of the country. In these circumstances, would some ethnic reference to these Indo-Aryans have found a place in later traditions? It is highly improbable that the term "Perizzites" is the answer to this question. At best, one might reserve for the purpose the as-yet-unplaced name Girgashites, which occurs only in the routine biblical lists, aside from some Phoenician inscriptions. It is much more likely, however, that the local Indo-Aryans did not keep their ethnic identity long enough to find a permanent place in biblical tradition.

Bibliography. General: E. Meyer, *Die Israeliten und ihre Nachbarstämme* (1906); F. Böhl, *Kananäer und Hebräer* (1911)—still a very useful survey; E. A. Speiser, *Mesopotamian Origins* (1930); A. Götze, *Hethiter, Churriter und Assyrer* (1936); I. J. Gelb, *Hurrians and Subarians* (1944); R. T. O'Callaghan, *Aram Naharaim* (1948); J. R. Kupper, *Les nomades en Mésopotamie au temps des rois de Mari* (1957).

Special studies: E. A. Speiser, "The Name *Phoinikes*," *Language*, XII (1936), 121-26; W. F. Albright, "The Rôle of the Canaanites in the History of Civilization," *W. G. Leland Volume* (1942), pp. 11-50; B. Maisler, "Canaan and Canaanites," *BASOR*, CII (1946), 7-12; B. Landsberger, *Journal of Cuneiform Studies*, VIII (1954), 56-61; J. Simons, "The Table of Nations," *Oudtestamentische Studien*, X (1954), 155-84; E. A. Speiser, "In Search of Nimrod," *Eretz-Israel*, V (1958), 32-36; A. van Selms, "The Canaanites in Genesis," *Oudtestamentische Studien*, XII (1958), 182-213.

E. A. Speiser

MAN, NATURE OF, IN THE OT. The OT knows nothing about autonomous man. Man's nature is determined entirely by his relation to God, a relation which preserves the distance between God and man, between the Creator and the creature. The belief that man was created in the divine image defines his relation both to God and to the rest of nature. He cannot claim divine descent, but he is called to a unique fellowship with God, which involves obedience to the will of God.

Since God is transcendent to nature, man's duty cannot be defined in terms of any kind of mystical identification of himself with nature so as to achieve harmony with it. The OT thinks of man as a psychophysical organism which is related to God as a whole. There is in man no immortal part which can survive death on its own account.

Man has worth, though not in his own right. On account of his creatureliness and in the absence of faith, man is in a state of anxiety. Man is sinful—though this is not to be included in the definition of man—and this reveals itself especially in self-assertion and arrogance.

The OT has a conception of humanity as a whole. The special privilege and responsibility of Israel is due to God's choice and not to any racial superiority. Israel was called to be representative man, and, as such, experienced to the full the responsibility of being involved in historical existence.

History has an end as well as a beginning, but man's destiny was not fully understood within the OT period.

1. Terminology of man in the OT
   a. In biblical Hebrew
   b. In LXX Greek
2. Creation of man
3. Constitution of man
4. Characteristics of man
   a. Worth
   b. Frailty
   c. Sinfulness
5. Humanity
6. Man's responsibility
7. Man's destiny
Bibliography

1. Terminology of man in the OT. ***a. In biblical Hebrew.*** There are five words translatable by "man." Certain other words rendered occasionally in English versions by "man" are not significant for our purpose.

a) אדם, "mankind" (=*homo*), is sometimes used of individual man, but the more precise expression is בן־אדם (etymology doubtful). Jos. Antiq. I.xxxiv connects אדם and אדמה ("earth") with the root אדם, "red." This view is now generally abandoned. אדם is now usually connected with Arabic *'adām,* collective for "creatures, mankind" (cf. Akkadian *amêlu*).

b) For איש, "man (=*vir*), husband, individual," two derivations have been suggested: (*a*) the root איש or אוש, "to be strong" (cf. Akkadian *ûšu,* "power"); (*b*) the root of Hebrew אנוש and Arabic *'insān.* The former is more probable. No etymological connection between איש and אשה ("woman") has been established in spite of Gen. 2:23.

c) For אנוש, "man, mortal," two derivations have been suggested: (*a*) the root אנש, "to be weak" (cf. Akkadian *anâšu* and Arabic *'anutha*), which would suggest the meaning "frail man" or "mortal"; (*b*) Arabic *'anisa,* "to be friendly, social" (cf. Ugaritic *'anš,* "to be friendly," and Arabic *'insān*).

d) גבר, man as strong in distinction from women, children, etc., is related to Arabic *gabara,* "compel" (cf. Akkadian *gapru,* "strong").

e) מת, only found in the plural, מתים, "males, men, people," is related to Akkadian *mutū,* "husband."

These words are often used synonymously, especially in poetry. They may reflect in some measure the differing aspects of human nature as conceived by the Hebrews.

b. In LXX Greek. As might be expected, no consistent system of equivalences is followed. The following are among the terms used: ἄνθρωπος, ἀνήρ, βροτός, θνητός, ψυχή, ἄρσην, ἀνδρεῖος, δυνατός, γηγενής.

2. Creation of man. There are two distinct accounts in Genesis of the creation of man. The first (1:26-30) is attributed to the P source, and may represent the fruit of centuries of priestly reflection. Man is represented as the climax of creation. The word אדם is not the proper name Adam. Neither is it collective, so as to lay the emphasis on men as a group. Rather is the word generic ("man"). The words "Male and female he created them" (vs. 27) imply at least two individuals, but not necessarily only two. What interests the author is primarily man's nature when summoned into being by God.

The creation of man is signalized by an introductory reference to the divine deliberation: "Let us make man." This is usually now regarded as referring to the divine court, beings subordinate to God but superhuman and along with God forming the category אלהים. Perhaps, however, we have merely the equivalent of an impersonal construction. God deliberates: "Let us make man in our image [צלם], after our likeness [דמות]" (*see* IMAGE OF GOD). The usage in the OT of צלם suggests a concrete meaning here, as does the appearance of the same two words in Gen. 5:3 with reference to the resemblance between Adam and his son Seth. Yet perhaps the use of two words in Gen. 1:26; 5:3 (though not in 1:27; 9:6) suggests the effort to express a difficult idea or to guard against misunderstanding. Moreover, Hebrew thought did not distinguish sharply between physical and spiritual. Yet, even though "image" has a concrete meaning, this need not exclude a reference to the dignity of man as in a certain respect like God. Man is a being who can be given authority and responsibility. While the reference to two sexes does not prove that the word "image" cannot be meant physically, there is no suggestion here of the deification of sex. The reference to two sexes merely points forward to the command to human beings to reproduce themselves. God's intention from the beginning was, according to this narrative, that the human race should go on. Moreover, man is given the charter of civilization. He is to have authority over the lower creatures and use the world to satisfy his legitimate needs. Cf. also Ps. 8, which speaks of man's dignity and responsibility.

The second account of the creation of man (Gen. 2:7-8, 18-23) is attributed to the J source. We are told that God created man as the center of creation. Man is referred to generically in vs. 7, but immediately, in the naïve manner found also in fables (e.g., Aesop's fables), the generic passes into the individual use, until finally (3:20-21; 4:1) the first pair are named ADAM and EVE. In this account God does not "make" or "create" man; he forms him—the word used is that which describes the activity of the potter. Cf. the vivid descriptions in Job 10:8-11; Ps. 139:13-16, which reveal, not only a knowledge of natural procreation, but an understanding of the truth that man's origin is hidden in the thought and intention of God.

The creation of the woman as partner of the man is preceded by the creation of the animals and birds. The man names them, thus asserting his authority (cf. 1:28), but none of the lower creatures meets man's need of a Thou. The primitive idea that the woman was fashioned from a rib taken from the man's side, while he lay in a magic sleep which preserved the mystery of creation, may have etiological significance, but this is not the chief interest of the story for the author.

3. Constitution of man. The second account of Creation not only tells how God formed man, but makes a classic statement on the constitution of man which is basic to the Hebrew view of man's nature. We read (Gen. 2:7): "Then the LORD God formed man of dust from the ground, and breathed into his nostrils the breath of life; and man became a living being." The expression "living being" (נפש חיה), signifying a living individual, is here unique. (Contrast the usage in Gen. 1:20, 21, 24.) Actually נפש alone would have meant the same thing (*see* SOUL). Man's uniqueness is also implied by God's direct action in communicating the breath of life (נשמת חיים). By Yahweh's communication of the vitalizing breath to the earthen man he had fashioned, we are not to conclude that man is compounded of two separate entities, body and soul—the view characteristic of Orphism and Platonism. To use the now classic phrase, the Hebrew conceived of man as an animated body, not as an incarnated soul. The material of which man is made is called "flesh" (בשר) as soon as he is a living being (*see* FLESH [OT]). But neither נפש nor נשמה is the soul conceived of as able to exist in separation from the flesh. נפש is both the vital principle which gives form to the flesh and the living being itself (*see* SOUL). It is not pre-existent, and it cannot survive the body. Man is a psychophysical organism made up of many parts forming a unity or totality.

Curiously enough, Hebrew has no word meaning "BODY" apart from several words which properly signify "corpse" (גופה, נבלה, פגר, גויה, the last named occasionally denoting the living body). Yet there is a clear awareness that all the different members cohere in a unity. Hebrew makes do with the word "flesh," while NT Greek has both σάρξ and σῶμα. The Hebrew did not think of the soul as having a body but as being a body which was alive, and this he called נפש with the emphasis on its "livingness." The word נפש, however, while it can mean "self," "person," does not clearly mark off one self from another. It can be used collectively (e.g., II Kings 9:15) in accordance with the principle of "corporate personality." Man is constituted as an individual, not by the boundary of his physical being, but by the responsibility to which he is summoned by God.

OT thought had at its disposal a rich vocabulary to describe the functions of the self. It is a natural extension of the meaning of the word נפש to make it the subject of the sentient and emotional life in all its different shades and expressions. Incidentally, one gets the impression from the OT that the Hebrew was characterized by a certain emotional instability which expressed itself in a tendency to swing from one extreme to another. The words for "flesh" and "bone" are also sometimes made the subjects of emotion.

It was noticed, however, that some men exhibited from time to time an exceptional access of life and power, and a special word was used to express this, "spirit" (רוח). This power was thought of as invasive and normally as coming from God (*see* SPIRIT; HOLY SPIRIT). Unusual skill or strength or insight or power of leadership was supposed to originate in this way. Men were lifted above themselves. The OT does not speak of human genius; it prefers to think of endowments of the spirit. Spirit, however, is not always invasive, but, like soul, can be used to describe the ebb and flow of vitality. Spirit is essentially power (cf. Isa. 31:3, where it means "strength" in contrast to "flesh," which means "weakness"). Spirit, too, can express aspects of human character which are conceived of as energies of the self, and, when thus used, it signifies the human, not the divine, spirit. As such it has no separate existence any more than soul has. In Ps. 51 we have the interesting attempt to relate the human and divine spirits.

Hebrew can express a remarkable number of psychological shades of meaning by the use of this or that term denoting a part of the body. These terms can represent the self by synecdoche. The suggestion that the Hebrews believed in a diffusion of personality throughout the body is to be rejected. It is not surprising that, related as they are to the totality, the terms tend to overlap in meaning.

The Hebrews had no knowledge of the nervous or muscular or respiratory systems or of the circulation of the blood. The significance of the brain as the center of the nervous system was completely overlooked by them. The word "HEART" (לבב לב), however, plays a very large part in descriptions of man's inner life, often in association with the words already referred to. Occasionally used with reference to the emotions, it more often occurs where we would speak of the mind or will or conscience, knowledge and action (following upon volition) being closely associated in Hebrew thought. To express emotion, the word "bowels" (מעים) is employed and to a much lesser extent the word "liver" (כבד). The kidneys or reins (כליות) too are regarded as the seat of the emotions and affections, and, in conjunction with the heart (in Psalms and Jeremiah), describe the inmost character exposed to the testing scrutiny of God. רחמים, the plural of רחם ("womb"), is used to signify "compassion." Further, the head and certain of its parts (face, eye, ear, nostrils, mouth, tongue, etc.), the limbs and their parts (especially the hand), serve to express a great variety of psychological shades of meaning. This, however, in no way implies diffusion of personality.

4. Characteristics of man. ***a. Worth.*** The OT does not credit man with any worth in his own right, though he is tempted to arrogate such worth to himself. Yet, as the crown or center of creation and as made in the image and likeness of God for fellowship with God, man has worth as God's gift. In a number of places the self is designated by the word כבוד ("honor, glory"), and it should probably not be emended to כבד ("liver"). The most notable expression of the worth of man in God's sight is in Ps. 8, which tells how God condescends to man and grants him royal honors (כבוד והדר) and a status little less than divine. In spite of Gen. 3:17-19, man shares with God the dignity of work (Gen. 1:28; 2:15; Ps. 104:23).

b. Frailty. In himself man is frail. The classic statement of this is Ps. 103:13-16:

> He [God] knows our frame;
> he remembers that we are dust.

The psalmist goes on to compare man to the grass, which withers. The same comparison is found in Isa. 40:6-8, where the prophet declares: "All flesh is grass." This is one of a limited number of passages where "flesh" is used with the connotation of weakness (e.g., II Chr. 32:8; Ps. 78:39; Isa. 31:3; Jer. 17:5). Man is also described as "dust and ashes" (Gen. 18:27).

Man's frailty shows itself in his liability to disease, in the fact that such strength as he possesses diminishes with age (except in rare cases [Deut. 34:7]), and in his mortality (*see* DEATH). Man is a being who knows that he must die. As a result of his frailty, vulnerability, and mortality, man experiences anxiety and fear, one of the commonest emotions referred to in the OT. *See* FEAR § 2*a*.

c. Sinfulness. Though the OT does not theorize about sin and certainly knows nothing of the loss of man's likeness to God (*see* IMAGE OF GOD), it tells much of man's sinfulness (*see* SIN, SINNERS). Sinfulness, however, is not part of the definition of man. The most remarkable analysis of the human situation is in Gen. 3–11, which may be regarded in intention as the story of Everyman. Man sins because he wishes vainly to assert his autonomy over against God. Adam and Eve, Cain, Lamech, the builders of the Tower of Babel, all exemplify this (J). The priestly writer, too, knows that man is a sinner and even approaches stating a doctrine of total depravity, though such a view is not characteristic of the OT as a whole. Both before and after the Flood, P asserts that the thoughts of the human heart are corrupt. Cf. Ps. 143:2 with Ps. 51:5, which represents the psalmist as acknowledging his sinfulness from birth.

It was, above all, the prophets who brought home the fact of sin to the conscience of Israel, and in whose words is found that searching analysis of the nature of sin as estrangement from God and rebellion against God which corresponded to their conviction that God was holy, loving, and righteous. Man's creaturely weakness, though not itself the cause of sin, might tempt him to lack of faith in God and to self-assertion and arrogance. The sin of Adam and Eve was the attempt to be "like God, knowing good and evil." The builders of the Tower of Babel wished to make a name for themselves, and there was no limit to their ambition. A prophecy is directed against the king of Babylon (Isa. 14:13-14):

> You said in your heart,
> "I will ascend to heaven;
> . . . .
> I will make myself like the Most High."

The prince of Tyre (Ezek. 28:2) is condemned because in his pride he said: "I am a god, I sit in the seat of the gods." It is characteristic of Isaiah, who had a vision of the Lord high and lifted up, that he denounces in God's name all human pride (see especially 2:12-19) and condemns the glaring example of such pride shown by the king of Assyria, who attributed his victories to his own strong hand. Isaiah also appears in the lists to oppose Ahaz and urges him to find security in faith. Elijah opposes the pretensions of Ahab.

5. Humanity. In spite of Israel's belief in its election by God, which it often arrogantly interpreted as election to special privilege instead of to special service, the OT is clear that humanity is one. Paul was in accord with Hebrew thought when he declared at Athens that God had "made from one every nation of men to live on all the face of the earth" (Acts 17:26). In the table of the nations in Gen. 10 the Hebrew people takes its place among all the others (*see* MAN, ETHNIC DIVISIONS OF), and when Abraham is summoned to his special destiny, it is with the promise to him that by him "all the families of the earth will bless themselves."

It may well have been in the spacious days of the United Monarchy that Israel reached this broad, human outlook on the world. When later they lost it, a Hebrew voice was uplifted to remind them that all men are equal before God. God is concerned with Ethiopians, Philistines, and Syrians as with Israel itself (Amos 9:7). A prophet said: "Blessed be Egypt my people, and Assyria the work of my hands, and Israel my heritage" (Isa. 19:25). The international outlook finds its finest expression in the picture of the Servant of the Lord in Second Isaiah (Isa. 42:6), who is to be a "light to the nations"; in the vision of a unified mankind with its religious center in Jerusalem (Isa. 2:2-4; Mic. 4:1-3); and in the books of Jonah and Ruth. In the P source in Genesis, God makes a covenant with all mankind (Gen. 9:8-17).

Israel was unaware of the kind of distinction which for the Greeks divided mankind into Greeks and barbarians. If Israel was chosen from the other nations, this was not because of any particular merit (Deut. 7:6-8; 9:4-5), but because of the mysterious will of God. In Job 31:13-15 even the distinction between master and slave is denied. Alongside its intolerance, Deuteronomy is also marked by a fine sympathy for the unprivileged classes in society, including the sojourner (גֵּר).

One of the merits of the OT is that it depicts for us Hebrew man as representative man, Everyman. This was possible because the Hebrew in the circle of the chosen people found himself confronted and challenged by God, and in this relationship learned what it is essential that man should know about himself, and what God ultimately demands of all men.

6. Man's responsibility. It is characteristic of the OT that man is represented as a being responsible to God, who has made his will known and expects it to be obeyed. This is made clear in both the creation narratives. The call to obedience is the burden of Law and Prophets alike, a call which is grounded in God's grace (see Exod. 20:2; Deut. 5:6; Isa. 1:2; Mic. 6:4). Deuteronomy links obedience and life (30:15-16; 32:46-47). Hence the importance of man's heart, which is the organ of will. Cf. Prov. 4:23:

> Keep your heart with all vigilance;
> for from it flow the springs of life.

While individualism is no late phenomenon in history, it is true that the Hebrew had a strong sense of the importance of the institution, and exemplified throughout the centuries the primitive sense of corporate personality. Yet this did not prevent his leaders from impressing upon him his individual responsibility for the institutions of family (Gen. 2:18) and state, and characteristically the OT ignores the distinction between secular and religious law. Man is summoned by God, both to the worship of God and to the practice of righteousness toward his fellows (cf. Mic. 6:8, addressed to man!). In all the relationships of life man is responsible to God for his conduct, and God has made his mind known (*see* MAN AND SOCIETY). Man is to understand himself, not just as a part of nature, but as having his place in history as responsible to the Lord of history, whose will for man is not a static law revealed once for all, but a law which is made known in the crises of history, when man must make the decisions on which his life depends.

7. Man's destiny. As history had its beginning, so it will have its end. There were times when Israel was little conscious of the end toward which history was moving, but, by and large, the OT has an eschatological accent upon it. Yet when Hebrew seers looked forward, what they saw on the horizon of time was the consummation of God's rule upon earth in a people or in humanity obedient to his will (*see* ESCHATOLOGY OF THE OT). That individual man had a destiny on the other side of DEATH, either through resurrection on this earth or in some other world, was, if ever entertained, little more than a wild surmise, with two exceptions (see Isa. 25:8; 26:19; Dan. 12:2-3). What the OT does teach, however, is the possibility of a faith in God's care and forgiveness and of a fellowship with him, without which in the fulness of time a more positive view of man's destiny would scarcely have been possible.

Bibliography. OT Theologies of Eichrodt, Imschoot, Jacob, Köhler, Von Rad, and Vriezen. H. W. Robinson, *The Christian Doctrine of Man* (1911), ch. 1, pp. 4-67; *The People and the Book* (ed. A. S. Peake; 1925), ch. 11. J. Pedersen, *Israel,* I-II (1926). H. W. Robinson, "Hebrew Psychology," *Inspiration and Revelation in the OT* (1946), pt. II, pp. 353-82; "God and Man," pp. 49-105. A. R. Johnson, *The Vitality of the Individual in the Thought of Ancient Israel* (1949). W. Zimmerli, "Das Menschenbild des AT," *Theologische Existenz Heute,* N.F. 14 (1949). W. Eichrodt, *Man in the OT* (1951), p. 84. C. Ryder

Smith, *The Bible Doctrine of Man* (1951), p. 274. J. A. T. Robinson, *The Body* (1952), ch. 1, pp. 11-16. G. Pidoux, *L'homme dans L'AT* (1953). L. Köhler, *Hebrew Man* (1956). H. H. Rowley, *The Faith of Israel* (1956).

N. W. Porteous

***MAN, NATURE OF, IN THE NT** [ὁ ἄνθρωπος]. Man has intelligence, emotions, free will, moral responsibility, and a possibility of eternal life.

A. Jesus
  1. Psychological terms
  2. Spirit possession
  3. His words and stories
B. Paul
  1. Natural religion
  2. The self
    a. Desire
    b. Reason
    c. Will
  3. Will of God versus will of man
  4. Salvation
    a. Redemption
    b. Sanctification
    c. Immortality
C. Other NT writers
Bibliography

A. *JESUS.* The views of Jesus about the nature of man are derived mainly from the Synoptic gospels, on the assumption that the reports which they give are the most authentic record of his teachings. The Gospel of John, by contrast, appears to be a somewhat later, entirely new exposition of the gospel of Jesus along the lines of its author's own, individualistic thinking.

1. Psychological terms. The most general impression derived from a survey of passages in the Synoptic gospels which might indicate the ideas of Jesus about the nature of man is that, on the whole, his views are essentially those of the OT. First of all is the concept of the physical body, which is expressed by either σῶμα, "body," or σάρξ, "flesh." In Mark 5:29: "She felt in her body that she was healed," the word is σῶμα. This word appears also in 14:8: "She has anointed my body beforehand"; and in 15:43: "Joseph . . . asked for the body of Jesus." On the other hand, in 14:22: "This is my body," σῶμα obviously means "flesh." Mark 10:8 uses σάρξ, "flesh," to mean the sexual function, which simply preserves the meaning of *bāsār*, "flesh," in Gen. 2:24. In a popular way Mark 14:38: "The spirit indeed is willing, but the flesh is weak," seems to indicate a dualistic view, but this is not actually the case. It is characteristic of Jesus, as it was also of the OT, to think of personality as a unity.

In Mark 13:20: "No human being would be saved," the word for "human being" is σάρξ, "flesh": no flesh would be saved. "Flesh" in this sense is a metonym for man, a usage which is frequent in the OT (cf. Isa. 40:5). "Body," on the other hand, as in Matt. 5:29: "that your whole body be thrown into hell," is a metonym for "person" or "personality," a figure which appears also in Matt. 6:22: "The eye is the lamp of the body." Of course, in this passage "eye" is a metaphor for "mind." There is nothing in these uses of σῶμα and σάρξ which was not often expressed by *bāsār* in the OT.

In Mark 3:4: "to save life or to kill," the word for "life" is ψυχή, which is our word "psyche." It is used in this sense also in 10:45: "to give his life as a ransom for many." In 8:35, however: "Whoever would save his life will lose it," a pun is involved. For here "psyche" means not only "life," but also "soul," in the sense of "eternal life." Jesus means that in the effort to save your temporal life you may lose it eternally. This idea that man possesses an eternal soul had developed toward the end of the OT, but was not evident in the earlier writings.

Mark 14:34: "My soul is very sorrowful, even to death," shows that "psyche" or "soul" is used in the sense of the first-person pronoun "I." The idea expressed is, "I am sorrowful." This again is a common idiom in the OT (cf. Pss. 6:3; 7:2; etc.).

The translation of Deut. 6:5, which occurs in Mark 12:30; Matt. 22:37; Luke 10:27, introduces the Greek word διάνοια, "mind," into the Hebrew quotation. But this is only an effort of Jesus himself, or the translator whom he is quoting, to show that the Hebrew word *nephesh,* "soul," in the passage includes an intellectual element. It introduces no new idea. Psyche in the words of Jesus could, almost without exception, be turned back into the Hebrew *nephesh.*

2. Spirit possession. *Pneuma,* "spirit," is used of the Holy Spirit, as in Mark 1:8, 12; 3:29; 12:36; 13:11; or it can refer to the spirit of an individual person, as in 2:8; 8:12. Both these uses are common enough in the OT. The use of *pneuma* with reference to "unclean, evil spirits" or "demons" goes beyond the OT. It occurs with great frequency in the Synoptic gospels. In the OT we are limited to such passages as I Sam. 16:14: "An evil spirit from the Lord tormented him"; or I Kings 22:23: "The Lord has put a lying spirit in the mouth of all these your prophets." The appearance of evil spirits is far more frequent in the gospels, and also the theology is different. In the OT the evil spirits are under God's control, while in the gospels they are subject to Satan. In both cases, however, the references throw important light on the view of man's nature. Like his OT predecessors, Jesus assumes that a spirit has an objective existence of its own; that it may succeed in gaining entrance into the personality of a human being, where it can either expel or dominate the human spirit, and take up residence in the body; and also that such a spirit may be overcome and driven out by an exorcist who understands how to do it. This phenomenon of possession and exorcism was an ancient way of diagnosing and treating what we call mental illness, with its neuroses and psychoses (*see bibliography*). A similar view of personality is shown also in the belief that the Holy Spirit objectively entered into persons. In Mark 1:10, "the Spirit descending upon him" is actually in the Greek ". . . into him" (εἰς αὐτόν).

3. His words and stories. The most basic element in Jesus' view of the nature of man is his assumption throughout that man has intelligence, free will, and emotions which require discipline. Man's intelligence enables him to understand God's will; his freedom makes it possible for him to choose the will of God; and his autonomy permits him to do it.

These qualities of intelligence, freedom, and responsibility are indicated in such a saying as Matt.

15:19: "Out of the heart come evil thoughts, murder, adultery, fornication, theft, false witness, slander." The same insight into personality is shown in Matt. 5:28: "I say to you that every one who looks at a woman lustfully has already committed adultery with her in his heart." In such passages Jesus assumes that all acts of the moral life spring from the autonomy of the self. "Heart" in these sayings is similar to "flesh" in Paul's vocabulary, as illustrated in Gal. 5:19, where he gives a catalogue of sins which are the "works of the flesh." The insight of Jesus here is certainly no less profound than that of Paul. However, "heart" means much more for Jesus than "flesh" does for Paul in such contexts. It includes in its range what Paul lists in Gal. 5:22-23 as "fruits of the Spirit." Jesus knows that the inner self of man is capable of good things as well as bad; and so he is able to say in Matt. 5:8: "Blessed are the pure in heart, for they shall see God." Such purity is within reach of the devout man who responds to the grace of God by keeping his commandments.

In the eyes of Jesus, sin is a deliberate, wilful, evil deed. He says in Mark 9:42: "Whoever causes one of these little ones who believe in me to sin, it would be better for him if a great millstone were hung round his neck and he were thrown into the sea." This saying is based on the responsibility of a man for his evil deeds. The same principle is implied in Mark 10:21, where Jesus says to the young man: "You lack one thing; go, sell what you have, and give to the poor, and you will have treasure in heaven; and come, follow me." This shows that the truly moral and spiritual life is based squarely on the individual autonomy of decision, which belongs to the genius of man's nature by virtue of the fact that he is created in the image of God.

The same view of personality is reflected in the parables. In the story of the sower in Mark 4:3-20, Jesus says the seed fell in four different kinds of soil: in the uncultivated footpath, where obviously nothing could grow; in rocky soil, where there was no depth; in thorns, where young plants were quickly crowded out; and in good soil, which produced abundantly. The parable illustrates four types of persons. But even here Jesus does not mean that a man's character is determined by heredity. He assumes as a matter of course that a man is responsible for the sort of soil he is.

The story of the wayward son in Luke 15:11-32 shows the same principle. The father, who represents God, allows his son complete freedom in arriving at the decision to leave home. Moreover, the son returns only after he has freely made up his mind that it is best for him to go back.

The story of the rich man and Lazarus in Luke 16:19-31 lets the rich man suffer for the course he has deliberately chosen to pursue. The ten maidens of Matt. 25:1-13, who are going to a wedding, are allowed to decide freely whether to keep their lamps trimmed and burning; and in the Last Judgment of Matt. 25:31-46 the Son of man pronounces his blessing on those who have freely shown compassion on needy persons.

While Jesus was not attempting to set up a system of psychology or ethics, the moral and spiritual structure of personality and the principles which are at the basis of man's nature are transparent in all his words and stories. Although his principles are those of the OT, no prophet before him had seen so clearly what it means to be created in the image of God.

The idea of life after death has little place in the OT, although it would seem to have been implicit in the concept that man was created like God (Gen. 1:27). But for long centuries Hebrews believed that the religious drama came to its end in death. Nothing but a dreary Sheol was to follow. But this view was finally replaced by such writers as that of Dan. 12:1-3; and at the very end of that era Wisd. Sol. 2:23 was to say:

> God created man for incorruption,
> and made him in the image of his own eternity.

Jesus was the heir of this faith. For him it was fundamental. There is hardly a word in his teaching which does not presuppose that the possibility of eternal life belongs to the nature of man (see Matt. 6:19-21; 13: 37-43, 47-50; 22:30-32; 25:10, 34, 41, 46; Luke 16: 19-31; 18:18, 29-30; John 5:25; 6:27, 40, 44, 47, 51, 54, 58; 11:25-26).

B. *PAUL*. 1. Natural religion. Although the general exposition of salvation in Paul's letters is stated in terms of the supernatural, his understanding of faith, nevertheless, is based on a solid foundation of natural religion. In Rom. 1:19-20 he writes: "What can be known about God is plain to them, because God has shown it to them. Ever since the creation of the world his invisible nature, namely, his eternal power and deity, has been clearly perceived in the things that have been made. So they are without excuse." The idea in this passage is that God is revealed to the intelligence of man by his works of creation. This is natural revelation, and it is apprehended by the natural reason of man. It is possible for man, entirely apart from historical revelation—such, e.g., as that given through Moses and the prophets—from a study of the natural world itself to arrive at belief in the existence of God, and in a conception of divine law, which he ought to obey. Paul goes on to say that man has not lived up to his opportunity and obligation in this respect, but it is not because of lack of natural ability to know God and comprehend his law. Man's failure is due rather to some innate perversity of his own nature, which causes him to sin.

Paul carries his statement about natural religion further and makes it more explicit in Rom. 2:14-15: "When Gentiles who have not the law do by nature what the law requires, they are a law to themselves, even though they do not have the law. They show that what the law requires is written on their hearts, while their conscience also bears witness and their conflicting thoughts accuse or perhaps excuse them." In these words Paul recognizes that among Gentiles who have never heard the law of Moses there are good people who obey God; and the reason they are able to do this, although they have never heard of Moses, is that God has written his law on their hearts. Their consciences are therefore divinely equipped to direct them in the moral life.

This sympathetic view of the Gentile world is an extension to all mankind of what Jeremiah had said long before about Israel. In 31:33 this prophet spoke of a time when God would write his law upon Hebrew hearts, so that they would have a natural knowledge of the divine will. Paul takes this insight and makes it universal, although he is quick to point out that Gentiles have usually fallen short of their opportunity and obligation.

Paul's views of the religious capacity with which human beings are endowed are in line with the OT idea that man is created in the image of God (Gen. 1:27). The prophets and psalmists (cf. Pss. 8; 19; Isa. 40:26; Amos 5:8-9) make the original religious endowment of man a basic assumption. Paul is mainly preoccupied with man's tendency to sin, but at times the optimistic humanism of his Hebrew heritage comes to expression. His mood usually calls for somber colors as he paints human nature. Nevertheless, he has brighter hues at his disposal into which he sometimes dips his brush.

2. The self. The failure of Gentiles to live by natural revelation, like that of Jews to keep the law of Moses, led Paul into a searching analysis of human nature in an effort to isolate the element of perversity which causes man to be a sinner. He succeeded in penetrating deep recesses of personality. Picturesquely, but also profoundly, and quite unintentionally, he was the first great introspective psychologist. The school of depth psychology has been powerfully influenced by his insights.

But Paul was neither a psychologist nor a philosopher in a technical sense. His language is closer to that of a poet. The first step that one must take in understanding what he writes is to recognize the figurative nature of his vocabulary. If he knows scientific forms of thought, he does not use them. He likes to play with words. There rushes from his pen a torrent of colorful metaphors, metonyms, and puns. In the course of a few sentences he will use the same word in so many different meanings that the reader may find himself lost in a maze. There is an element of the fox in Paul as he baffles his pursuers. Yet in spite of the poetic subtleties with which he expounds the Christian faith, and the difficulty of defining his terms with complete certainty, the broad outlines of his thought are fairly clear.

Among the important words which Paul uses in his analysis of personality are "soul" (ψυχή), "spirit" (πνεῦμα), "body" (σῶμα), "flesh" (σάρξ), "sin" (ἁμαρτία), "reason" (νοῦς), "death" (θάνατος), "law" (νόμος), "heart" (καρδία), and the adjectival forms derived from them.

a. Desire. Paul does not limit himself to one word to express desire. Indeed, it seems doubtful that he actually had an abstract concept of desire. His thought in this respect is Hebrew rather than Greek. Yet, whether he was conscious of it or not, desire was the most determinative idea in his vocabulary of personality. This is such a decisive concept for Paul that one could say that it was his prepossession, not to say obsession. In this respect he moved far away from his classical Hebrew heritage and speaks more like a man of the Far East. He reminds us of Gautama Buddha, whose most basic affirmation was that the tragic human predicament results from desire—a view which he held in common with Jains and various ascetic elements of Hinduism. While not a Gnostic in the sense of regarding the flesh as totally evil, or a Manichaean in the sense of going in for extreme asceticism, especially with reference to sex, yet Paul must inevitably be placed in the ancestry of these later cults.

Paul associates desire very closely with the flesh. In Gal. 5:16-21 he says: "Walk by the Spirit, and do not gratify the desires of the flesh. For the desires of the flesh are against the Spirit, and the desires of the Spirit are against the flesh; for these are opposed to each other, to prevent you from doing what you would. But if you are led by the Spirit you are not under the law. Now the works of the flesh are plain: immorality, impurity, licentiousness, idolatry, sorcery, enmity, strife, jealousy, anger, selfishness, dissension, party spirit, envy, drunkenness, carousing, and the like." And in vs. 24: "Those who belong to Christ Jesus have crucified the flesh with its passions and desires."

In such passages one must distinguish between individual passions and desires and the "flesh," which is the seat of them all. In the latter sense "flesh" is a metonym for "desire." Some desires, such as hunger and sex, have such specific and obvious location in the flesh of the body that "flesh" becomes a metonym for all desire. So in the passages quoted above, flesh is referred to as if it were a person. Flesh as a sort of foreign, alien person seems to reside in the body.

Paul also uses "body" in the same sense. In Rom. 6:6 he says: "We know that our old self [Greek 'our old man'] was crucified with him so that the sinful body might be destroyed, and we might no longer be enslaved to sin." Again in 6:12: "Let not sin therefore reign in your mortal bodies, to make you obey their passions." Here "body" has the meaning of "flesh" in the passages quoted from Galatians, and "sin" is introduced in the same sense. Paul can use "flesh," "body," and "sin" interchangeably in these contexts, and they mean essentially the same thing.

In Rom. 8:13 he says: "If you live according to the flesh you will die, but if by the Spirit you put to death the deeds of the body you will live," where "flesh" is equated with "body." If we bear in mind that "flesh," "body," and "sin" are metonyms for the same thing—i.e., for "desire"—an important step has been taken toward understanding Paul. His statement in Rom. 7:20: "It is no longer I that do it, but sin which dwells within me," is intelligible as soon as we are aware that "sin" is a metonym for "desire." In this case, as sin so often results from desire, it is substituted for desire itself.

b. Reason. In line with his tendency to avoid abstract terms, Paul rarely mentions reason or mind. Yet his respect for natural religion, as we have seen, implies that rationality is an important element in personality as he sees it. But the word "reason" itself appears in certain key passages. A notable example of this occurs in I Cor. 14, where Paul draws his famous contrast between inspired ecstatic phenomena and Christian rational behavior, showing that he has high respect for the latter. In 14:14-16 he writes: "If I pray in a tongue, my spirit prays but my mind [νοῦς] is unfruitful. What am I to do? I will pray with the spirit and I will pray with the mind [νοῦς] also; I will sing with the spirit and I will sing with the mind [νοῦς] also." In vs. 19 he continues: "I would rather speak five words with my mind [νοῦς], in order to instruct others, than ten thousand words in a tongue."

But Paul's most relevant use of "reason" for our

purpose occurs in Rom. 7:22-23: "I delight in the law of God, in my inmost self [*see* INNER, INWARD MAN], but I see in my members another law at war with the law of my mind [νοῦς] and making me captive to the law of sin which dwells in my members." The context shows that in this case Paul equates "reason" with "inmost self," which makes it of basic importance in his analysis of personality. The passage occurs at a crucial point in his great discussion of the nature of man (Rom. 5–8).

c. Will. Nor do we find will dealt with by Paul in abstract, technical terms. Yet some of the obscure statements in his exposition of human nature are clarified only if we realize that here is a description of will struggling with alien forces which have overcome it and hold it in bondage. The demonic monsters which overpower the will are called variously: "body," "flesh," "law," "sin," "death." In I Cor. 15:56 death is conceived as a dragon which bears sin embedded as a mortal sting in its tail.

The predicament of man, as Paul sees it, appears in Rom. 7. Here the human self is constructed with three levels at the same time. Above is reason, which apprehends the law of God and knows well what man's duty is. At bottom is the flesh, whose overriding desire blocks the performance of duty. But in between, on another level, is the conscious "I," which is aware of both the upward challenge of God's law and the downward pull of carnal desire. The "I" has will at its disposal, but finds it constantly thwarted and made impotent by desire. Such is man's condition. Yet at the same time, the "I" cannot stand aside as a mere spectator and observe the struggle between reason and desire. Paul knows well that this trinity of the self is also a unity; that reason, desire, and the conscious will are together components of the one self, the one nature of man. Although figuratively there are three selves, the "I" can, and does, in this passage from verse to verse speak from the point of view of first one of these selves and then the other. Yet it knows that in a true sense it absorbs and includes them all. Thus Paul concludes in vs. 25: "So then, I of myself serve the law of God with my mind, but with my flesh I serve the law of sin." In this statement Paul summarizes his triangle of the self.

3. Will of God versus will of man. There is also an element of determinism in Paul's understanding of man. Human destiny is shaped by decrees of the divine will. This idea is formulated in Rom. 8:29-30: "Those whom he foreknew he also predestined to be conformed to the image of his Son, in order that he might be the first-born among many brethren. And those whom he predestined he also called; and those whom he called he also justified; and those whom he justified he also glorified." Paul knows that no man holds his own destiny entirely in his own hands. But this is an election of love. There is no predestination of punishment in Paul's mind. Nor does he say that God ever invades man's autonomy or coerces his will. God's sovereignty and man's freedom both find their place in Paul's thought. But man finds true freedom only when he brings his will into harmony with the will of God. Paul himself enjoys being a slave of Christ.

4. Salvation. Paul's study of human nature shows that without aid from beyond or above himself, man is lost. He does not say that help has not been available. God has constantly sought to come to man's rescue. From the beginning of time he has been revealing himself in nature (Rom. 1:19-20). Then he sent Moses and the prophets. Man has good inclinations; he apprehends the truth; but desire has paralyzed his will, and holds him in bondage. Salvation is impossible unless someone sets him free (Rom. 7:17-25).

a. Redemption. Freedom from slavery can be achieved only by running away or through redemption (*see* REDEEM). The former is impossible because man can never escape from himself. Nor can he redeem himself, as he is bankrupt (7:24-25). The only possibility is redemption by another, which is freely offered by Christ to those who have faith. Faith is necessary because God does not override man's will (Rom. 1:16-17). But Christ is ready to deliver man from law, flesh, body, sin, and death, the monsters which hold him in bondage. This is Paul's gospel (Gal. 2:19-21).

b. Sanctification. Salvation is thus a mutual experience in which both God and man inevitably participate. The only way in which redemption can occur without violating the nature and dignity of man is through his full response to God in mind, heart, and will, which is faith. As the commitment involves the entire personality, it means that all of man's faculties must be transformed into the likeness of Christ. This is SANCTIFICATION. The real Christian is changed into the divine image (II Cor. 3:12-18); this is a process both moral and spiritual which continues throughout life, but reaches culmination only in the hereafter (I Cor. 13:12). But sanctification is not a humanistic achievement. Its source is God through Christ (I Cor. 1:30; I Thess. 4:3).

c. Immortality. *Pneuma* in the Pauline sense inherits from classical Greek *pneuma,* on the one hand, and from Hebrew *nephesh,* on the other, the idea of shadowy survival in Hades or Sheol as a natural quality; but IMMORTALITY, which is the hope of the Christian, is for Paul, not the heritage of the first Adam, but the hope of the second Adam (I Cor. 15:45-50). The first man is of the dust; the second is from heaven. "Just as we have borne the image of the man of dust, we shall also bear the image of the man of heaven." This is the final possibility of man.

Just as Paul sees the forces of sin which hold man in bondage as cosmic powers, he assumes that the inanimate creation has also been "subjected to futility" and "groaning in travail together until now." But he appears to contemplate that in the final consummation, when the sons of God are revealed, all nature will participate in some marvelous way in the "glorious liberty of the children of God" (Rom. 8:18-25).

C. *OTHER NT WRITERS.* Nowhere else among NT writers do we find such deep concern about man's nature. The Gospel of John (1:6-9) sees the drama of redemption in cosmic terms. It is a struggle between light and darkness. Man cannot enter the kingdom of God unless he is born again (1:13; 3:3-7). This writer assumes the depravity of man, but he does not stop to analyze it. The same is to be said of I Peter (1:23). Both these authors appear to stand in Paul's debt. II Peter, Jude, and Revelation share Paul's view that the natural world is to be renewed, but this idea they, as well as Paul, have drawn from Jewish apocalyptic writers in general. They make no contribution to a study of man. The author of Hebrews breaks new ground with his original interpretation of Jesus as the incomparable high priest; but insofar as man is concerned, he is a son of the OT. This is true also of James, whose letter shows more similarity to the words of Jesus than any other document in the NT. The letters of John are concerned with Christian ethics in a simple, unspeculative way.

Bibliography. E. D. Burton, *Spirit, Soul and Flesh* (1918); *Commentary on Galatians* (1921). F. C. Grant, *Introduction to NT Thought* (1950), pp. 160-86. S. V. McCasland, "The Image of God in Paul," *JBL*, vol. LXIX, pt. ii (1950), pp. 85-100; *By the Finger of God* (1951)—on ancient methods of diagnosing and treating mental illness. R. Bultmann, *Theology of the NT*, vol. I (1951). J. Knox, "Romans," *IB*, IX (1954), 355-668.

S. V. McCASLAND

MAN, SON OF. *See* SON OF MAN.

MAN AND SOCIETY. The word "society" does not appear in the English versions of the Bible. The term is of somewhat indeterminate nature, applicable to many human groups and relationships. These may involve families, tribes, nations, religious communities, or even world-wide humanity. All these appear in the Bible; hence the social nature of man is assumed therein at every turn. Man is man only as a member of a social group. Monotheism in Israel, once attained, had as its corollary the sovereignty of God over all peoples. But the societies at the focus of attention in the OT and the NT, being religiously grounded, felt both their differences from and their responsibilities toward other societies in the world.

1. Terminology employed in the Bible
   a. In biblical Hebrew
   b. In NT Greek
2. Man and society in the OT
   a. The social nature of man in the OT
   b. The place of the law in OT society
3. Man and society in the NT
   a. In the gospels
   b. In Acts and Paul's letters
   c. In other NT writings

Bibliography

1. Terminology employed in the Bible. Although there is no word in the Bible corresponding to our word "society," there are many words which refer to what we may call the constituent elements of the social order.

a. In biblical Hebrew. The basic unit of society is designated either by משפחה ("FAMILY"; LXX πατριά; I Sam. 9:21) or by בית אב ("father's house," "household"; LXX οἶκος τοῦ πατρός; Gen. 24:7, 38). These terms are sometimes used interchangeably (Exod. 12:3, 21). The family seems to have been a social unit between the "father's house" and the tribe (Num. 2:34; Josh. 7:14; "tribe" is מטה and שבט, both terms deriving from words meaning the staff of the ruler). Two terms ordinarily employed for stated meetings for worship are קהל ("assembly"; LXX ἐκκλησία) and עדה ("congregation"; LXX συναγωγή), but these words could also designate the permanent community of all Israel (Deut. 23:2-3; Mic. 2:5). The term רע ("NEIGHBOR") usually meant "fellow Israelite" (Deut. 15:2; Jer. 31:34; cf. Lev. 19:18). The SOJOURNER was given legal protection by the Book of the Covenant (*see* COVENANT, BOOK OF THE; Exod. 22:21-22; cf. Deut. 5:14).

b. In NT Greek. The NT uses some of the same words as the LXX; e.g., πατριά for "family" (Luke 2:4; Eph. 3:15) and οἶκος for "household" (Luke 19:9; Acts 10:2). Another word, κόσμος, peculiar to the LXX—the OT Hebrew has no comparable word—is used in the NT for the created world, especially the sphere of human relations or the world of men (Matt. 18:7; John 1:29). The words used for the Christian community and its members are many. Members are called "Christians" thrice (Acts 11:26; 26:28; I Pet. 4:16); "disciples" (μαθητής; Acts 6:1; 15:10); "brethren" (ἀδελφός; Rom. 7:4; cf. I Pet. 2:17); "saints" (ἅγιος; Acts 26:10; Col. 1:4, 26). The Christian community was called a "fellowship" (κοινωνία; Acts 2:42; I Cor. 1:9; cf. I John 1:3, 7); a "household of faith" or "of God" (οἶκος; Gal. 6:10; Eph. 2:19); "God's elect" or "chosen" (ἐκλεκτός; Rom. 8:33; Tit. 1:1); the "body of Christ" (σῶμα χριστοῦ; I Cor. 12:27; cf. Eph. 4:12; Col. 1:18*a*); the "Israel of God" (Gal. 6:16). The "church" (ἐκκλησία) is the term most commonly used for the Christian community, either for separate churches or for the church as a whole (Acts 9:31; I Cor. 12:28; Eph. 3:21). The "church of God" is also found (I Cor. 10:32; Gal. 1:13; cf. II Thess. 1:4).

2. Man and society in the OT. In both testaments it is assumed that no man by himself can live a complete life; he needs a society to fulfil his true nature, and he gains stature to the extent that he carries out his responsibilities to God as well as to society.

a. The social nature of man in the OT. In the early nomadic period especially, the solidarity of family, clan, and tribe was of necessity such that the individual could scarcely hope to survive outside his kinship group. A man's life was merged into the collective or corporate personality (Num. 16:1-35; Josh. 7:10-26; cf. II Sam. 24:10-15). This concept of corporate personality is often exaggerated to the degree that individualism is thought to have been entirely absent from Israel until the time of Jeremiah and Ezekiel. It is true that these prophets voiced the first definitive statement of individualism (Jer. 31:29-30; Ezek. 18:4, 20; cf. Deut. 24:16), yet it is equally true that individual leadership and responsibility, as well as personal religious experience, were recognized long before this. It is true also that the thought of Israel remained distinctly social throughout OT times. The prophets were conspicuous for their urging man's responsibility for his neighbors' welfare and insisting that mercy and justice be accorded the least and humblest of them (Isa. 3:13-15; Amos 8:4-6). The same note of social responsibility is often struck in the Psalms and the wisdom books (Job 31; Ps. 15).

Beyond this, the prophets discerned within the community of Israel a faithful group which should be a means of salvation, even though disaster might overtake others. Isaiah made this a characteristic of prophetic faith (*see* REMNANT; Isa. 10:20-22). In the hands of Second Isaiah this religiously faithful portion of Israel, perhaps, was to spread the Yahweh faith among other peoples (Isa. 42:1-4; 49:5-6).

b. The place of the law in OT society. The law was also on the side of social justice and responsibility (*see*

LAW IN THE OT). The Book of the Covenant calls for the individual's obedience to the divine will as expressed in the law and as the basis of moral and social conduct. The Decalogue (*see* TEN COMMANDMENTS) demands that every man respect his neighbor's rights (Exod. 20:12-17). Even the rights of Hebrew slaves were recognized (Exod. 21:1-6; cf. Deut. 15:12-18). The book of DEUTERONOMY, owing perhaps to prophetic influence, is especially important for its high quality of social legislation. One writer has called Deut. 17:14-20 the "Magna Charta of Israel," because it puts limitations upon the monarchy to protect the dignity and personal value of the common man. There are suggestions in both the legal and the prophetic books that the ideal society would be one in which all men were equal in the sight of God and deserving of equal rights to consideration and justice from others.

3. Man and society in the NT. Many of the concepts in this category in the NT are rooted in the OT, yet with significant differences and extensions. For one thing, just as in the OT Israel felt itself to be a unique creation of God, different in nature from all other peoples, so in the NT the "new Israel" was felt to be a separate and radically different kind of society —a "new creation" (Gal. 6:15-16)—different in a qualitative, not a racial or social, sense.

a. In the gospels. Jesus can hardly be called a social reformer, nor was he interested primarily in ethical teaching per se (*see* ETHICS IN THE NT). He did, however, as the prophets before him, enunciate many ethical and social principles, as a means to the end that men might gain true fellowship with God and thus truer fellowship with one another. He regarded himself as a teacher in the prophetic tradition (Mark 6:4; Luke 13:33). He did not nullify the law which had governed the OT community for centuries; rather, he fulfilled it (Matt. 5:17; cf. 22:36-40). In his teaching on the moral duty of the individual man, Jesus gave greater weight to the inward motive than to the external command or the overt act (Matt. 5:19-22, 27-28, 38-48).

The KINGDOM OF GOD, the main theme in the Synoptic gospels, was in one sense the envisioning of a new kind of society, for which men were urged to prepare and in which all would acknowledge God's sovereignty. But in a larger sense it was an eschatological expectation which had already begun to manifest itself (Matt. 12:28; cf. Luke 17:20-21), and which was to come in its fulness in the coming age (Matt. 13:36-43; cf. Mark 10:29-30).

b. In Acts and Paul's letters. The apostles' preaching in Acts proclaims the risen Jesus as the coming Messiah (Acts 3:20-21; cf. 1:11; 10:39-42). There was as yet no thought of Jesus' followers' breaking with Judaism to form an independent society. They constituted an eschatological community within Judaism, expecting the new age to appear soon and their Messiah to return at any moment. This was the bond which held them together and distinguished them from their fellow Jews.

But it was not long before the movement reached out beyond Judaism (Acts 8:5-8, 14-17; 10:9-16, 34-35, 44-48). The Christian movement was now on its way to becoming a separate community. And with Paul's mission to the Gentiles, the separation became more fully marked (Acts 13:43-46). The new society was now a "people" (Acts 15:14), made up of men of various nations and classes. When men entered this society, they ceased to be Jews or Gentiles, slaves or freemen. They were "one body in Christ" (Gal. 3:28-29; Col. 3:11-15; cf. Rom. 12:5, 9-10).

The separateness of the new community may be seen in the various names applied to it (*see* § 1*b above*). The very term "church" (ἐκκλησία) means "called out," as does the term "elect" or "chosen" (ἐκλεκτός). "People of God," "Israel of God," "household of faith," connoted a community intimately bound together. The "body of Christ" implied also a single vital organism, somewhat like the OT concept of corporate personality (*see* § 2*a above*) or better, a "remnant" (cf. Rom. 11:5).

Yet despite its sense of separateness from the world, the Christian community did not remain aloof from the world. It could not do so if it would, for it felt a responsibility for the world and sought to win as many as possible from the world before the end time should come (I Cor. 9:19-23; cf. 7:29*a*, 31). The Christian society, the church as the eschatological community, may thus be called a new type of society, the prototype of the still more inclusive and perfect world society which is to be (Eph. 2:19-22).

c. In other NT writings. In later books of the NT the Christians are shown more fully aware than ever of their differences from all other societies. They are to be distinguished from Jews in that they are the community of the "new covenant" (Heb. 9:15; 12:24; cf. II Cor. 3:6), and as "God's own people" (I Pet. 2:9-10; cf. Tit. 2:14). They are advised to keep themselves "unstained from the world" (Jas. 1:27), and they are warned that "friendship with the world is enmity with God" (Jas. 4:4; cf. I John 2:15-17). It is said also that the Christian society is "of God" and others are "of the world" (I John 4:4-6). "The Lord knows those who are his" (II Tim. 2:19).

The Christians must expect persecution from evil men (II Tim. 3:12-13; I Pet. 4:12-19). But they must not allow this to deter them from living exemplary lives among themselves (Heb. 13:3-7; I Pet. 1:22; 3:8-9) or from exercising the ethic of love toward those outside their fellowship (I Tim. 2:1-4; I Pet. 2:12-16; 3:15-17).

The Christian community was still the eschatological community and the end time was imminent (I Tim. 6:14-15; I Pet. 4:7, 17; I John 2:28). Yet, though it awaits consummation, it has already begun, for the church represents the household of faith, the pattern of the future kingdom of God (Jas. 2:5; cf. Eph. 2:19-22; Heb. 12:28). The church is, indeed, the "first fruits of his creatures" (Jas. 1:18; cf. Rev. 14:4*c*), a society which is in the world but not of it (cf. I Cor. 2:12), yet a society responsible to the world —to human society—for the salvation of all men (I Tim. 2:3-6; cf. 4:10).

Bibliography. J. Pedersen, *Israel, Its Life and Culture*, vols. I–II (1926). W. A. Irwin in H. and H. A. Frankfort, *The Intellectual Adventure of Ancient Man* (1946), chs. 10-11. E. F. Scott, *Man and Society in the NT* (1947). W. Eichrodt, *Man in the OT* (Studies in Biblical Theology No. 4; trans. K. and R. G. Smith; 1951), pp. 9-20, 35-39. G. E. Wright, *The Biblical Doctrine of Man in Society* (Ecumenical Biblical Studies No. 2; 1954). R. Bultmann, *Theology of the NT* (trans. K. Grobel;

1951, 1955), I, 33-62, 92-108, 254-69; II, 15-17, 95-100. R. P. Shedd, *Man in Community* (1958). J. W. FLIGHT

MAN OF LAWLESSNESS [ἄνθρωπος τῆς ἀνομίας] (II Thess. 2:3). A mythical satanic character who is to be the personal adversary of Jesus Christ at the time of his second advent. *See* ANTICHRIST.

MANAEN măn′ĭ ən [Μαναήν = מנחם (Menahem), comforter] (Acts 13:1). Listed along with Barnabas, Symeon called Niger, Lucius the Cyrenian, and Saul as one of the "prophets and teachers" in the church at Antioch.

He is called a σύντροφος of Herod the tetrarch—i.e., Herod Antipas, who in 4 B.C. succeeded his father, Herod the Great, as ruler over a part of his domain (4 B.C.–A.D. 37). The word σύντροφος occurs only here in the NT (cf. the LXX of III Kings 12:24; also I Macc. 1:6; II Macc. 9:29). It should be translated either as "member of the court" (so RSV) or "courtier," or as "intimate friend"; and it probably does not mean in this passage "foster brother." Manaen had apparently been a close friend of Herod, perhaps since childhood.

Bibliography. A. Deissmann, *Bible Studies* (1901), pp. 310-12; J. Moulton and J. Milligan, *Vocabulary of the Greek NT* (1914-19), p. 615. B. H. THROCKMORTON, JR.

MANAHATH măn′ə hăth [מנחת, *apparently* resting place, settlement; *cf. place name* מנחת *and personal names* נחת, מנוח]. **1.** The second son of clan chief Shobal; ancestor of a Horite subclan in Edom (Gen. 36:23; I Chr. 1:40). L. HICKS

2. A site, probably in Judah, to which were exiled certain Benjaminite inhabitants of Geba (I Chr. 8:6); generally identified with Manocho, a city appearing in the list of towns in the hill country of Judah, which the LXX adds to the Hebrew text of Josh. 15:59. The ancient site is probably represented by modern Malha, a village three miles SW of Jerusalem in the vicinity of Bittir. W. H. MORTON

MANAHATHITES măn′ə hăth′īts [מנחתי]; KJV MANAHETHITES —hĕth′—. A clan mentioned only in I Chr. 2:54, where they are said to belong to the genealogy of Judah. It is therefore assumed that the town of MANAHATH was reckoned to the tribe of Judah. *Cf.* MENUHOTH. E. R. ACHTEMEIER

MANASSEH mə năs′ə [מנשה, one who causes to forget—*e.g., some misfortune (thus correctly in* Gen. 41:51); *originally the name of a person*]; MANASSITE —īt [מנשי]; Apoc. MANASSEAS —ĭ əs (I Esd. 9:31); KJV Apoc. and NT MANASSES —ēz. **1.** The first-born son of Joseph, and the eponymous ancestor of one of the twelve tribes. Born of Asenath, the daughter of the Egyptian priest (Gen. 41:51; 46:20), he was adopted, along with his brother Ephraim, by Jacob (48:5). Although Manasseh is regularly specified in the tribal lists, the name is never found in the lists of the sons of Jacob, where only Joseph is mentioned. Manasseh also appears elsewhere occasionally as an individual (e.g., Gen. 50:23), but for the most part his function as *heros eponymos* of the tribe of Manasseh can be discerned.

The tradition that Ephraim and Manasseh were adopted by Jacob (Gen. 48) already contains clear etiological statements concerning history. It has to explain not only the equal status of the younger tribes alongside the older tribes, but, above all, the reversal of political importance which occurred in the course of time in the younger group itself. The old assumption is still to be preferred—that only the Joseph or Rachel group (at least in part) was in Egypt in the course of the "Israelite" occupation of the land, and then only later joined the movement toward Canaan as a second, large wave, after the Leah group, which was already settled there. The common point of departure was probably the region of Kadesh-barnea. From here the Leah group had penetrated into Palestine directly from the S and had gradually spread through the whole wooded hill country which had been but slightly developed by Canaanite cities, until in the central area the tribes of Simeon and Levi were suddenly smitten by the catastrophe which forced them to retreat to the S edge of the cultivated land (Simeon), and even to the point of departure in Kadesh (Levi). From here, too, the Joseph or Rachel group, having returned from Egypt, began its new advance, respecting, however, the land taken by its kindred—i.e., the territory of Judah (and, not least of all, the crossbar of Canaanite cities from Jerusalem to Gezer) no less than that of the Edomites, the Moabites, and the Ammonites. They advanced on a new route which led them to their goal from the E, into the country in which Simeon and Levi had once tried in vain to gain a foothold (Gen. 34:30; 49:5-7). While Benjamin crossed the Jordan near Jericho and apparently had to suffer severe casualties, the Joseph group either crossed at the same spot (but not until later) and/or at fords farther N. In any case, they were able to preserve their large number and gradually capture the whole area from Bethel to the Plain of Jezreel.

To these people also belonged the group later called Manasseh. That they had to restrict themselves to the hill country and were unable for a long time to penetrate the coastal plain or the Plain of Jezreel and its E continuation, the Plain of Beisan, is stated expressly in the document preserved in Judg. 1:27 ff and is shown, likewise, by the old anecdote in Josh. 17:14 ff. The particulars as to the composition of the group and how it coalesced are, naturally, beyond our cognizance. Presumably it absorbed parts of the older wave which were scattered throughout the country. From a later, but still pre-statehood, period, a document has been preserved for us in connection with the border descriptions in the book of Joshua, a document which permits a glimpse into the further development of the tribe of Manasseh—i.e., Josh. 17:2 and (without the genealogy) perhaps also vs. 3. Canaanite cities such as Helek, Shechem, and Hepher had already been incorporated, also Hoglah and Tirzah; alongside them were communities like Abiezer and Azriel, which can be recognized as purely Israelite by their names. The document is only a fragment, but it is instructive insofar as it shows that the Manassites have already captured cities and settled in them, and surely not everywhere by destroying the native population. At first, to be sure, they, like all the Israelites, avoided the Canaanite cities and established themselves in the open country in new settlements by clans. A clear-cut example of this is furnished again by Josh. 17:8, an old notice interspersed in the boundary description of Manasseh itself. According to this, Manasseh settled at first only the area belonging to Tappuah (Tell Sheikh Abu Zarad). The town itself, located on the S border, was occupied only at a later stage, and then by the Ephraimites. By the time the boundary which divided the city from its territory was fixed, in the period before statehood, the people of Joseph had already developed separately. This development may have been based in part on blood differences. Certainly the physical and political contrasts of the regions in the N and the S also played a role. The S part of the country, more reminiscent of Judah, was furrowed by deep valleys in which it was also easier to maintain one's own character because of the absence of Canaanite cities. Because this area sealed itself off, the N was left alone and more and more had its own destiny, which was determined, not so much by the struggle against the forest (Josh. 17:15) as by the conflict with the Canaanite city-states (vss. 2-3). Being larger in extent and with a more friendly terrain, not so closed up, and with many smaller plains scattered in it, it attracted the greater number of settlers. This accounted for its initial pre-eminence. The fact that the N lost its pre-eminence to the S is connected with political development. Not by chance did Ephraim produce such important men as Joshua, Samuel, and Jeroboam I.

The name Manasseh probably did not come into constant use as a general designation for the N until relatively late. Before that it was in competition with the name Machir, if the latter is not really the older. In any case, the Song of Deborah mentions the same name, Machir (Judg. 5:14), and connects it with Issachar and Zebulun, but clearly separates it from Ephraim, with which Benjamin appears and which is named first. The Blessing of Moses also knows both parts and gives Ephraim precedence, but designates the brother tribe as Manasseh (Deut. 33:17) and combines both as Joseph and praises them for the wild-ox strength with which they struck down nations. The Joseph saying in the Blessing of Jacob (Gen. 49:22-26) mentions neither Manasseh nor Machir, and reveals that a true center of political power lies with Joseph, the "consecrated one" (for the holy war), the champion "among his brothers." When the fertility of the land is emphasized, Manasseh is thought of primarily.

Machir was probably, like Manasseh, originally the name of an important leader, and his clan was in the N section of the territory of Joseph. The clan in part emigrated again in the period before the kings, and drew others along with it and after it. From this comes the idea of Machir as the "son of Manasseh" (Gen. 50:23; Num. 26:29; 32:39-40; Josh. 13:31) and the "father of Gilead"—i.e., of the country lying across from Manasseh N of the Jabbok (Josh. 17:1; I Chr. 2:21, 23; 7:14; also Num. 26:29; 27:1; 36:1; Josh. 17:3). Thus originated the tradition of the "half-tribe of Manasseh" as possessor of the N land E of the Jordan, alongside Reuben and Gad to the S (Num. 32:33; 34:14; Deut. 3:13 [cf. 4:43]; Josh. 1:12; 4:12; 12:6; 18:7 [cf. 20:8]; 21:6, 27; 22:1 ff [cf. II Kings 10:33]; I Chr. 5:18, 23, 26; 6:47, 56; 12:38; 26:32; 27:21). This was an instance of colonization rather than a seizing or occupation of the land (*Landnahme*). At first it involved only the ascents to the hills out of the Jordan Valley. Even the boundary description in Josh. 13 restricts the Israelite territory N of the Jabbok to a narrow strip which runs to the Sea of Chinnereth (vs. 27). With the strength they gained in the period of the kings, the Israelites naturally attempted to extend their territory; there is talk more than once of battles, evidently border battles, against the Arameans at Ramoth, some sixty miles E of the Jordan (I Kings 22; II Kings 8-9). Already in the time of Solomon a N Israelite district official resided here (I Kings 4:13). Obviously no uniform tribal relationship existed in this colonial territory, nor was it settled exclusively by Israelites. One can hardly be wrong if he conceives of the first stage of colonization in the pre-statehood period in all the land E of the Jordan as not too grand and especially not too vast in area. Indeed, limits were set every place there for the advance of the Israelites beyond the belt of forest by the states of the Moabites and the Ammonites in the S and of the Arameans of Rehob and Maacah in the N. The latter, in turn, probably exploited the great forest area of "Gilead" from the E for their purposes. Coexistence with Arameans is also confirmed by the tradition, fixed at a late date, that Machir married Maacah (I Chr. 7:15-16), although this tradition may refer to the situation at the time of the kings. The fact that different tribes participated in the colonization of Gilead is illustrated by Judg. 12:4, where the Gileadites take revenge on the Ephraimites because the latter have reproached them with being "fugitives of Ephraim" ("Gileadites in the midst of Ephraim and Manasseh"). On the other hand, the colonists of Manasseh also did not hesitate at settling in Gadite territory; for Nobah, which is included in Manasseh in Num. 32:42, probably lay in the region of Jogbehah (Judg. 8:11) in Gadite territory (Num. 32:35)—in any case, S of the Jabbok line (Judg. 8:4-9), S of Sukkoth and Penuel, the first of which is likewise designated as Gadite in Josh. 13:27. The so-called tent villages of the Manassite Jair, on the other hand (Num. 32:41; Deut. 3:14; Josh. 13:30; I Kings 4:13), are to be sought in Gilead N of the Jabbok. Jair was buried in Kamon, perhaps modern Qamm (Judg. 10:3-5). That the Manassite groups on the other side of the Jordan did not withdraw from the obligation to Israel as a whole, is shown by the fact that Gideon of the Manassite clan of Abiezer (Judg. 6:15) was able, with the levy of the amphictyony (6:35; 7:23), to pursue the Midianites from the Plain of Jezreel far across the Jordan, where he attacked their camp once more E of Nobah and Jogbehah. This presupposes undoubtedly the manifold assistance of the Manassites who lived there. In a similar fashion Jephthah was able to count on them (Judg. 11:29).

In the period of the kings Isaiah mentions Manasseh (Isa. 9:1—M 9:20). Ps. 60:7—H 60:9 = 108:8—H 108:9 names Gilead and Manasseh before Ephraim; Ps. 80:2—H 80:3, Ephraim (and Benjamin?) before Manasseh. The later literature presents the name of Manasseh frequently in statistical contexts: thus P in Num. 1:10, 34-35; 2:20; 7:54; 10:

23; 13:11 always has Manasseh after Ephraim; this order is reversed only in Num. 26:28-34; 34:23. In the list of the Levite cities the W "half-tribe of Manasseh" ranks after Ephraim, separated from it by Dan, which is inserted for geographical reasons (Josh. 21:5, 25=I Chr. 6:61, 70—H 6:46, 55). The E half-tribe is once placed before Reuben and Gad—but taken along with the Galilean group—and has, therefore, displaced Zebulun as last of the E Jordan group (Josh. 21:6=I Chr. 6:62—H 6:47). Another time it is put at the beginning of the Galilean group, so that it follows immediately after the W half-tribe (Josh. 21:27=I Chr. 6:71—H 6:56). In Ezek. 48:4, Manasseh is ranked, because of geography, ahead of Ephraim. The lists of Chronicles show in I Chr. 12 the W half-tribe of Manasseh after Ephraim (vs. 31); the E, after Reuben and Gad at the end (vs. 37); and in I Chr. 27:20-21, both together after Ephraim. In the arrangement of I Chr. 1-9 the E part appears as the "half-tribe of Manasseh" after Reuben and Gad (5:23-26), with a note about the abduction by Tiglath-pileser; the W, as "Manasseh" before Ephraim (7:14-19). Elsewhere the Chronicler has all kinds of unverifiable things to report about Manasseh—i.e., Manassites who live in Jerusalem (I Chr. 9:3), Manassites who go over to David (12:20-21), wards protected by the laws of the land under Asa (II Chr. 15:9), participants in the Passover at Jerusalem under Hezekiah (30:1, 10-11, 18), those who broke down the pillars and the Asherim (31:1), the purge of the cult in the Manassite territory under Josiah (probably the single historical fact), and the payment of the temple taxes (34:6, 9). In the NT, Manasseh appears in Rev. 7:6, strangely enough, alongside Joseph, who represents here Ephraim—if Manasseh is not conceived of as meaning only the portion E of the Jordan.

For Manasseh in Judg. 18:30 MT-KJV *see* JONATHAN 1. For the territory of Manasseh *see* TRIBES, TERRITORIES OF, § 3*b*. For bibliography *see under* ASHER.

K. ELLIGER

2. King of Judah *ca.* 687-642 B.C.; son and successor of Hezekiah. Manasseh came to the throne at the age of twelve and is said to have reigned for fifty-five years (II Kings 21:1*a;* II Chr. 33:1). His mother was Hephzibah (II Kings 21:1*b*). If we assume that Hezekiah died *ca.* 687, and that the recorded years of the reigns of Amon and Josiah are correct, the length of Manasseh's reign must be shortened to *ca.* forty-five years. It is probable that during his reign under Assyrian influence the system of postdating, instead of antedating, became the accepted custom in Judah.

Practically the whole account of Manasseh's reign (II Kings 21:1-18) is devoted to a description of his attempt to establish polytheistic worship in the land. The Chronicler paints the same picture for the earlier part of his reign (II Chr. 33:1-9). But he tells also of an invasion of Judah by the Assyrians, of Manasseh's being carried to Babylon as a captive, of his repentance and return to Jerusalem, and finally of his restoration of Yahweh-worship (vss. 11-17). Of these things the Deuteronomist makes no mention.

After the death of Hezekiah a reaction followed under Manasseh. This is not surprising. Hezekiah's reformation was only partly successful. Presumably it met with considerable opposition. Perhaps many people even attributed the misfortunes which Judah suffered as a result of Sennacherib's invasion to Hezekiah's rejection of the old ways. Manasseh succeeded to the throne at the age of twelve, and apparently came under the influence of the pro-Assyrian party. His apostasy consisted in restoring the high places—i.e., the local Yahweh shrines—which Hezekiah had abolished. With the erection of an altar to the Baal and the making of an Asherah, Baalism once again came to be officially recognized. Not only Baalism, but astral worship as well, flourished in Judah. It was a feature of Assyrian policy to impose the worship of the Assyrian gods on conquered peoples. The OT contains various references to the worship of the host of heaven (cf. Jer. 7:18; Amos 5:26; Zeph. 1:5; etc.). That such a practice was abhorrent is clear from the injunctions against it (cf. Deut. 4:19; 17:3; etc.). Popular worship of this type had a profoundly demoralizing effect upon the people. In addition, human sacrifice was reintroduced, and a revival of necromancy took place, with consultation of the spirits of the dead (II Kings 21:6). On the evidence of cuneiform records the use of magic and divination was widespread during this period. No small subject nation of the time could successfully resist such encroachments. Syncretistic worship was the order of the day.

In addition to these specific acts of apostasy Kings records that "Manasseh shed very much innocent blood, till he had filled Jerusalem from one end to another" (II Kings 21:16). Traditionally this has been interpreted as a reference to the slaughter of the prophets and their followers, and Isaiah was reported to have been sawn asunder during Manasseh's reign (cf. the Ascension of Isaiah; cf. also Heb. 11:37). The king was repeatedly warned by prophetic voices that inevitable punishment would follow the course of action he was pursuing (II Kings 21:10). It is true that during this period the voice of prophecy was apparently silenced. At least no record has survived. But such an interpretation is questionable. For the most part, the person of a prophet was regarded as sacrosanct (cf., however, Jer. 26:20-23). It is to be doubted that Manasseh would have gone to such lengths. This datum stands by itself, unconnected with his idolatrous acts. It seems much more probable that it is a general reference to injustices and even acts of violence for which the king was responsible. It must also be remembered that his countermeasures to Hezekiah's reformation must have met with bitter opposition from those who remained loyal to Yahweh.

The problem of Manasseh's reign centers round the historicity of the events recorded by the Chronicler in II Chr. 33:11-17. Punishment came upon the king in the form of an Assyrian invasion of the land. Manasseh was treated with humiliation and carried off in bonds to Babylon. There he repented and in his need called upon Yahweh, who brought him back to Judah. He spent his remaining years in furthering the restoration of the Yahweh cult.

The Chronicler gives no historical reason for the appearance in Judah of the Assyrian army commanders. No mention is made of any act of disloyalty on Manasseh's part against the king of Assyria. Two opportunities, however, presented themselves. From the Assyrian inscriptions of Esarhaddon (*ca.* 681-669) and his son Ashurbanipal (*ca.* 669-630) we know that Egypt was conquered and brought into subjection to Assyria (cf. Nah. 3:8). It is possible that Manasseh came under suspicion in connection with these events. It is to be noted, however, that in his first campaign against Egypt, Ashurbanipal lists among his vassals twenty-two kings, of whom one was Manasseh. In 652 a serious rebellion broke out against Assyria, led by Babylon. The commander of the rebel forces was Shamashshumukin, brother of Ashurbanipal. This civil war lasted until *ca.* 648, and ended with the capture of Babylon. If Manasseh was actually guilty of rebellion, this would seem to have been the most opportune time. Perhaps at this time, too, the Arab tribes of the Syrian Desert began to press into the territory of Transjordan. Ashurbanipal fought them there. He mentions specifically Ammon, Edom, and Moab. This may have been the occasion for the lament over the fall of Moab preserved in Isa. 15–16; Jer. 48. Perhaps the Babylonian revolt was the signal for a more widespread rebellion, of which details are lacking. Manasseh may have been summoned to Babylon, where the Assyrian king resided frequently after 648, along with the heads of all the subject states, to renew their loyalty to Assyria. But this does not explain the Chronicler's statement of the presence of an Assyrian army in Judah. Consequently, it seems better to assume that Manasseh actually joined in the rebellion against Assyria and was carried to Babylon at the close of the campaign directed chiefly against the Arabs. It is most surprising that no mention of Manasseh's action appears in the Assyrian inscriptions. That Manasseh was taken to Babylon and then restored to Jerusalem constitutes no difficulty. Neco I of Egypt was also among the royal captives at Ashurbanipal's court, and was later restored.

On his return Manasseh is said to have built an outer wall to the city of David (II Chr. 33:14), presumably in order to strengthen its defenses. He also put army commanders in all the fortified cities of Judah. But all the fortified cities had been captured by Sennacherib (II Kings 18:13). They must, therefore, have been recovered by Judah. Vs. 14 interrupts the connection between vs. 13 and vss. 15 ff, but it gives the impression of furnishing reliable data. Who was the enemy against whom Judah strengthened her defenses? It could not have been the Assyrians, for they had allowed Manasseh to return. It must then have been Egypt, which in the meantime had succeeded in regaining her independence, *ca.* 652. Assyria's purpose was clearly to safeguard this outpost of the Empire against a possible Egyptian attack.

That Manasseh had an actual change of heart in Babylon is possible; but, if so, it was temporary. The reform measures which the Chronicler attributes to him are unhistorical. They stand in sharp contradiction to such passages as II Kings 23:4-6, 26; 24:3; Jeh. 15:4, even if one makes allowance for Amon's evil reign.

From the Chronicler's viewpoint there must have been some reason why such an evil king reigned such a long time—the longest reign of any king of the S kingdom. To explain this, he assumed that a complete change must have taken place in the king's life —a change necessarily accompanied by religious reforms in accordance with his change of heart.

Are there two separate sources mentioned in II Chr. 33:18-19—the "Chronicles of the Kings of Israel" and the "Chronicles of the Seers"—or is the latter a part of the former? It seems preferable to adopt the second viewpoint. From this passage the "Prayer of Manasseh" (*see next entry*) took its title.

Bibliography. R. H. Charles, *The Apoc. and Pseudep.* (1913), I, 612-24; II, 155-62. M. Noth, *Die israelitischen Personennamen* (1928), p. 222. W. O. E. Oesterley and T. H. Robinson, *A History of Israel,* I (2nd ed., 1934), 400 ff. W. F. Albright, "The Chronology of the Divided Monarchy of Israel," *BASOR,* 100 (1945), 16-22, especially p. 22, note 29. A. Bentzen, *Introduction to the OT,* II (1948), 212. J. Simons, *Jerusalem in the OT* (1952), pp. 207, 328 ff. J. B. Pritchard, ed., *ANET* (2nd ed., 1955), pp. 291, 294. W. F. Albright, *Archaeology and the Religion of Israel* (4th ed., 1956), p. 203, note 31.

H. B. MacLean

3, 4. Two Israelites who put away their foreign wives (Ezra 10:30, 33; I Esd. 9:31, 33).

MANASSEH, PRAYER OF. A short penitential psalm of fifteen verses (thirty-seven *stichoi*) ascribed to King Manasseh (*see* Manasseh 2) on the basis of the account in II Chr. 33:11-13. Here, in contrast to the narrative in II Kings 21–24, he is represented as being taken prisoner to Babylon and there repenting of his sins and uttering this prayer for forgiveness. Our document, while of much later origin, came to circulate with the Apoc. in some MSS and editions (*see below*), doubtless in part because of its intrinsic worth. It is then generally found among the Odes or Canticles which were often appended to the Psalter in Greek MSS, as well as in Syriac, Armenian, and such other versions as were made from the Greek. But in some of the versions it stands after II Chronicles.

The prayer opens with a long apostrophe in which God is addressed as God of the fathers and of the righteous, creator and orderer of all things, punisher of sin, and dispenser of mercy. He has appointed repentance, not for the righteous, but for sinners. Among these is Manasseh, who acknowledges that his sins are as the sands of the sea in number and who prays fervently for forgiveness. He promises that if God in his mercy will forgive him, he will continually praise him as long as he lives. Manasseh's iron fetters are mentioned in vs. 10, and the various references to the heavens and to the "host of heaven" are thought to reflect aspects of the idolatrous worship which, according to the biblical accounts, he encouraged.

The prayer is typical of Judaism of the postexilic period. Ideas generally regarded as evidence of this are the mixture of universal and particularistic elements, the designation of God as God of the righteous, and the notion of the sinless patriarchs. The afterlife, however, is spoken of in terms of Sheol. Comparison is often made with such documents as Ps. 51 and the Prayer of Azariah in the Greek of Daniel. While the Prayer of Manasseh may be somewhat inferior to these, it breathes a spirit of genuine piety and devotion.

The exact origin of our document is an unsolved problem. Its contents, form, diction, and history all point to a relatively late date—i.e., probably in the first century A.D. or B.C. But it has been variously dated from the second century B.C. to the third A.D. One theory derives it from the Didascalia (*see below*); another supposes that it was part of the original LXX of Chronicles, displaced by the version of Theod. Both of these are questionable. There is no evidence that it was originally part of the LXX; nor is it found in any list of Jewish canonical or extra-canonical books. However, its form and content and the Jewish legends about Manasseh (*see below*) point to Jewish authorship, perhaps in Alexandria, the composer's purpose being doubtless to supply the prayer which is referred to in Chronicles and also described there as found in the "acts of the Kings of Israel" and in the "acts of the seers" (cf. II Bar. 64:8).

The repentance of Manasseh was subject to much legendary embellishment and speculation. The underlying motivation, beginning with the Chronicler or his sources, was doubtless to explain how the king could have enjoyed so long a reign. In Chronicles he returns to Jerusalem and carries out the reforms which in the Kings account are ascribed to Josiah. The narrative in II Kings had blamed the Babylonian captivity, along with the destruction of Jerusalem and the temple, upon the wickedness of Manasseh (II Kings 21:13-14; 23:26-27; 24:3-4), in spite of the reforms of the good King Josiah. The Chronicler, however, appears to make King Zedekiah responsible for these calamities (II Chr. 36:14-21). Later sources, such as II Bar. 64, the Jewish Targums, and various rabbinic writings (*see bibliography*), spell out in detail the experience of Manasseh in Babylon and speculate upon the acceptance of his repentance and the possibility of his having a share in the world to come. Rabbinic sources are generally negative on the latter point, although admitting that God must have forgiven his sins, as he would those of any truly repentant sinner.

The original language of the prayer is also in doubt. The admittedly Semitic structure and Semiticisms naturally suggest Hebrew or Aramaic; but these are not such as to preclude composition in Greek. There are also reflections of LXX phraseology. Most scholars have therefore favored the Greek, although the brevity of the document makes judgment difficult, and composition in a Semitic language in Palestine or elsewhere is not positively excluded.

The earliest extant text is actually in the Syr. Didascalia (II:21), a church manual of the first half of the third century A.D. The Greek is found in Codex Alexandrinus of the fifth century (Ode 8, following Isa. 38:9-20) and later codices. It was unknown to Jerome, but appears in medieval Latin MSS, on the basis of which it is included in printed editions of the Vulg., beginning with R. Stephanus (1540). Before the Council of Trent it was placed at the end of II Chronicles; afterward, in an appendix following the NT. The Council did not include it in its endorsement of the Apoc., but it appeared in such important editions as the Complutensian Polyglot (1514-17) and the Clementine Vulg. (1592). The Bibles of Luther (1534) and the French Protestant Olivétan included it, but it was omitted in the Zwingli Bible (1527-29) and the Zurich Latin edition (1543). It is often omitted in editions of the LXX.

In English the prayer first appears in the Wyclif Bible, reflecting the Vulg. tradition. Its initial printing was in the "Matthews" revision of the Coverdale Bible (1537). It is then continued in the "authorized" editions: the Great Bible (1539), the Bishops' Bible (1568), and the KJV (1611). It is part of the Apoc. of the ERV-ASV and the RSV. Early editions of the Reims-Douay Bible (1609-10) and the Geneva (1560) include it, the latter after II Chronicles. *See also* APOCRYPHA.

Bibliography. H. Wace, ed., *Apocrypha,* vol. II (1888). E. Schürer, *Geschichte des jüdischen Volkes,* III (3rd ed., 1909), 458-60. P. de Lagarde, *Didascalia apostolorum Syriace* (reprint, 1911): a critical edition of the Syr. text; English trans. by R. H. Connolly, *Didascalia Apostolorum* (1929). H. E. Ryle in R. H. Charles, *The Apoc. and Pseudep. of the OT,* I (1913), 612-24: for the Greek and versional MSS and editions, and a critical discussion. O. Bardenhewer, *Geschichte der altkirchlichen Literatur,* II (2nd ed., 1914), 304-12. A Rahlfs, *Psalmi cum Odis* (1931), is the best critical Greek text; cf. H. B. Swete, *The OT in Greek,* vol. III (1894); A. Rahlfs, *Septuaginta* (1935). L. Ginzberg, *The Legends of the Jews* (7 vols.; 1910-37), *passim* —for rabbinic sources and special articles, see IV, 106-8. R. H. Pfeiffer, *History of NT Times with an Introduction to the Apoc.* (1949).

A. WIKGREN

MANASSES mə năs'ēz. KJV Apoc. and NT and Douay Version form of MANASSEH.

MANDRAKE [דודאים, *dûdhā'îm*]. A stemless perennial herb with large, deep-green rosetted leaves and a divided fleshy root, *Mandragora officinarum* L., common in uncultivated fields throughout the E Mediterranean region. The major biblical reference to it (Gen. 30:14-16) parallels the legends which have persisted regarding the herb throughout the centuries. Its small, plumlike berry and fleshy root were reputed to induce human fertility. (It is commonly called the "love apple.") Apparently the original Genesis story purported to relate how RACHEL, to relieve the embarrassment of her own barrenness, bargained for the mandrakes which Reuben, the son of LEAH, had found in a field. Later editors, however, wove a religious motif into the story to cover the primitive elements (vss. 17-24). The Arabic

Courtesy of the Société Botanique de Genève

7. Mandrake

name, *bayḍ ul-jinn* ("eggs of the jinn-spirits"), has perpetuated the superstition. The fruit ripens to a bright yellow in May, about the time of the wheat harvest (Gen. 30:14). Although considered edible by the natives, the somewhat poisonous fruit produces a purgative effect. It is closely related to the deadly poisonous nightshade, *Atropa belladonna* L.

In Song of S. 7:13 the fragrance of the plant is emphasized. This has occasioned much discussion about identification, since the odor of *Mandragora officinarum* is considered fetid by Westerners. Oriental tastes, however, are known to differ radically from those of the West. Post calls the fruit "fragrant."

In the ancient legend of 'Anat in Ugaritic three occurrences of *ddym* ('nt III:12; IV:53, 73) have been thought by some to refer to mandrakes.

See also FLORA § A16*c*.

Fig. MAN 7.

Bibliography. H. N. and A. L. Moldenke, *Plants of the Bible* (1952), pp. 137-39. J. C. TREVER

MANES. Same as MANI 2.

MANGER [φάτνη] (Luke 2:7, 12, 16; 13:15); KJV STALL in Luke 13:15. A trough or box for feeding cattle. The main OT equivalent is CRIB (אבוס). The context in which this word is used in Job 39:9; Isa. 1:3 would suit "manger" as well as "stall." In Prov. 14:4 the RSV follows most commentators in emending the text, though a footnote gives "manger" as the translation of this word itself.

The exact reference of the Greek φάτνη is not so clear. It is used, e.g., in the LXX of II Chr. 32:28 ("stalls [ארוֹת] for all kinds of cattle, and sheepfolds") and of Hab. 3:17:

> the flock be cut off from the fold
> and there be no herd in the stalls [רפתים],

where the parallelism in both cases favors "stall" rather than "manger." The general evidence, however, of both biblical and classical usage favors "manger" as the normal meaning.

The evidence of archaeology and of modern Arabic custom suggests two possibilities as to the location of the stable and its manger: (*a*) Most poorer Palestinian homes consisted simply of one large room divided into a lower and a higher section. The lower section was at ground level and nearer the entrance. This was naturally where the animals would find shelter and be fed, especially in colder weather. The other section was separated, not by a partition, but by being raised eighteen inches or more above the level of the lower. Here the family slept and ate their meals. In such homes the manger would be a stone box set against a wall of the lower section, or carved in a natural outcropping of rock, or constructed of masonry. Stone mangers were found *in situ* in the stables at Megiddo (*see* MEGIDDO; STALL). They were cut out of single pieces of limestone rock and were *ca.* three feet long, eighteen inches wide, and two feet deep. Cut into the corners of the pillars beside them, just above the tops of the mangers, were holes for the tie ropes of the horses (Fig. MAN 8). Mangers constructed of masonry were found in a cave stable at Lachish, dated from *ca.* 1200 B.C., and also, though less relevant to biblical times, in some Crusaders' stables near Acre in N Palestine, dated

Courtesy of the Oriental Institute, the University of Chicago

8. Manger from the Megiddo stables (period of Solomon?)

from *ca.* A.D. 1200. (*b*) The other possibility for the location of the stable and manger is in a natural cave near the house, or beneath the house in the limestone foundation. At Lachish, from early Israelite times, such a cave found beneath the remains of a house bore marks of having been used as a stable and still contained the masonry manger mentioned above. Another, larger cave, originally a quarry, also bore marks of use as a stable, or as a dwelling, or both. W. M. Thomson (*The Land and the Book*) mentions seeing inns, or *khans,* built thus over caves in which were mangers for cattle. In such cases the mangers are usually carved out of the limestone walls of the cave, though they may be stone boxes like those at Megiddo.

The tradition that it was in a cave stable that Jesus was born was current at least as early as Justin (*ca.* A.D. 150) and is reflected in some of the apocryphal gospels of the early centuries. In the fourth century Constantine enclosed the traditional cave of the Nativity with a basilica, which has become the Church of the Nativity in Bethlehem, with its many later chapels around it. However, the evidence of Luke's Gospel would point as easily to a simple shelter in or near a house. S. V. FAWCETT

MANI. **1.** mā'nī. KJV Apoc. alternate form of BANI 6.

2. mä'nē; also MANES mā'nēz (Μάνης) or MANICHEUS măn'ə kē'əs (Μανιχαῖος). Founder of the religion MANICHEISM. Born in Babylonia of Iranian origin, Mani lived A.D. 216-77(?), during the reigns of the first rulers of the Sassanian Dynasty (*see* PERSIA § D6). He traveled extensively, and as a result Manichean communities were established in Persia and India. He is the author of religious scriptures and letters addressed to his followers, who, at one time, were located in an area stretching from North Africa to China. Until a few years before the end of his life Mani enjoyed the official favor of the Sassanian ruler Shapur I (239/41-270/73), but he suffered violent death at the instigation of the Zoroastrian priesthood under the accusation of heresy.

Bibliography. For Mani's biography with detailed bibliographical references, see: H.-C. Puech, *Le Manichéisme, son fondateur, sa doctrine* (1949), pp. 15-57. On his personality, see: A. V. Williams Jackson, "The Personality of Mânî, the Founder of Manichaeism," *JAOS*, LVIII (1938), 235-40. For conventionalized portraits, see: A. von Le Coq, *Die buddhistische Spätantike in Mittelasien,* vol. II: *Die manichäischen*

Miniaturen (1923), plate Ia; J.-P. de Menasce and A. Guillou, "Un cachet de la Bibliothèque Nationale, *RHR,* CXXXI (1946), 81-84 (with photographs). For a description of Mani's appearance, see: Hegemonius *Acta Archelai* XIV.3 (ed. C. H. Beeson, *Die griechischen christlichen Schriftsteller der ersten drei Jahrhunderte,* vol. XVI). The most recent discussion of the years of Mani's life is to be found in "The Dates of Mani's Life by S. H. Taqizadeh, Translated from the Persian, Introduced, and Concluded by W. B. Henning," *Asia Major,* New Series, VI (1957), 106-21. M. J. DRESDEN

MANICHEISM măn'ĭ kē ĭzm'. The religious movement initiated by MANI (Manicheus) in the third century A.D.

1. Sources
2. Mani's works
3. Mani's doctrine
   - *a.* Religious background
   - *b.* Basic characteristics
   - *c.* Cosmogony
   - *d.* Salvation
   - *e.* Expansion and survival

Bibliography

1. Sources. The sources of documentation for the Manichean faith are of a great variety. Until recently they consisted of the indirect, apologetic, and often untrustworthy testimonies of the Greek and Roman church fathers, Christian Syriac chroniclers, and Persian and Arabic Muslim authors (*see bibliography*). This documentation was supplemented by the discovery of original Manichean texts in such distant areas as Chinese Turkistan in the E and the Egyptian Fayum in the W, which testify to the extension of Manicheism at one time. The documents unearthed in Central Asia in the beginning of the twentieth century were written in three Iranian languages (Middle Persian, Middle Parthian, and Sogdian; *see* PERSIA § C2), in Chinese, and in Uigur (Old Turkish). In 1931 the Egyptian Fayum yielded a library of Coptic translations of Manichean texts (*see bibliography*). It is easy to see that these original materials gave new impulses to the study of Manicheism and will continue to do so as their publication progresses.

2. Mani's works. The Manichean canon seems to have consisted of the following scriptures, which, presumably, were originally written in Aramaic: (*a*) the "(Great Living) Gospel," (*b*) the "Treasure of Life," (*c*) the "Pragmateia" or "(Historical) Treatise," (*d*) the "(Book of) Secrets," (*e*) the "Book of the Giants," (*f*) the "Epistles," (*g*) the "Psalms" and "Prayers." Another popular work was the "(Book of the) Two (Great) Principles," which originally may have been composed in Middle Persian. Besides, references are made to the "(Great) Drawing," apparently a picture book illustrating Mani's teachings, and to the "Tradition."

3. Mani's doctrine. ***a. Religious background.*** In the beginning of the third century A.D., W Iran was the meeting place of a prodigious manifoldness of either indigenous or imported creeds and beliefs (*see* PERSIA § D6*b*). These included ancient local pagan faiths, Zoroastrianism, Hellenistic philosophy and science, and Judaism. Christianity, introduced in Persia by Arameans belonging to the church of Syria, sectarianism of various coloration (called *Mughtasila* by the Arabic and *Mnaqdē* by the Syriac authors), and gnostic philosophies, all had their followers in that area. It seems even likely that Brahmins and Buddhist monks exercised some influence, although the main center of their activities lay, naturally, in E Iran. For the understanding of Manicheism the possible attribution of its constituent components to any one of these potential sources is a necessity. Labeling such Manichean doctrinal elements as the belief in metempsychosis, the duality of Light and Darkness, and the important role assigned to the Paraclete and Jesus, as simple borrowings from Buddhism, Zoroastrianism, and Christianity respectively, is not much more, however, than a truism. Closer scrutiny is required before these parallels can be evaluated. Similar caution is recommended when it comes to a classification of Mani's system of thought. Such commonly used terms as "syncretistic," "dualistic," and "gnostic" are to be taken only as general indicators of its character.

b. Basic characteristics. Manicheism claims to be a universal religion: "The previous religions existed (only) in one land and in one language. My religion, however, is such that it will become manifest in every country and will be taught in the remote(st) lands." Mani, the "seal of the prophets" such as the patriarchs, Buddha, Zoroaster, and Jesus, considered himself the supreme and final revelator.

It is a missionary religion, and each servant of the church, after the example set by Mani himself by his frequent trips, has the obligation to "wander forever in the world while preaching the doctrine and guiding men in truth."

It is a religion of the book. Since, according to Mani, previous religions failed partly because their founders neglected to put their teachings down, Mani took great pains to commit his words to writing and to have them canonized during his lifetime.

c. Cosmogony. In order to explain to man his condition in this world and make him understand from where he comes, why he has fallen down, what he is, and where he is going, Mani conceived a grandiose cosmological myth. In it it is said that in the beginning two antagonistic substances existed, the one Good and the other Evil, or Light and Darkness, or God and Matter. The acceptance of the duality of the "two principles" is one of the two fundamental dogmas of the Manichean credo, the other being the belief in the three "periods" or "moments." By means of an attack executed by the forces of darkness, the unmixed state of separation between the two principles is followed by a state of mixture in which part of the luminous particles of light is imprisoned in and made subservient to the dark substance of matter. The operation of delivering the light particles and transferring them back to their place of origin lasts for the duration of the world. The visible world is organized by God through a series of complicated processes, which all aim at the restoration of the original situation. This move is counteracted by Matter, which creates the first couple of human beings: Adam and Eve. Adam's eyes were opened by a savior known, among other names, as *yyšw' zyw',* "Jesus-splendor," to the divine origin of his soul; but Adam's offspring continues to procreate in accordance with the design of Matter. This is the state mankind is in at present. The third moment of the Manichean myth is to be inaugurated by a series of apocalyptic upheavals. After a Last Judgment the world will burn for a period of 1,486 years. The last light particles will be reunited with the light world, the material world will come to an end, and darkness will be restricted to its own original domain. The absolute and eternal separation of the two principles brings about the closure of the cycle.

d. Salvation. From this bare outline of the cosmogonic myth, which in the Manichean scriptures is expounded in complex detail and in ornate language which in some of its verse parts reaches great suggestive power, it will appear that understanding of the dual nature of whatever exists and of man himself opens the road to man's salvation. Since in the "mixed" world in which man lives most things, plants, animals, and others contain light particles, violence against them constitutes an act of sin. Manichean ethics, therefore, prescribe not to have sexual intercourse, not to kill, not to eat meat or to drink wine, not to possess, not to sow or harvest, etc. Rigorous observation of these rules is required only of the elite, however, and the rules are somewhat relaxed for other members of the community. The latter—in theory, at least—cannot escape from subsequent reincarnation, while the former at the time of their death shall return to the Paradise of Light.

e. Expansion and survival. There is no way to give a fair estimate of the number of followers of the Manichean faith for the almost twelve centuries it was active or provoked repercussions in areas as far apart as North Africa and China. In the eighth and ninth centuries it was the official state religion in the Uigur state on the River Orkhon in Outer Mongolia, and in spite of severe prosecution Manichean communities managed to survive in the province of Fukien in SW China.

The vicissitudes of the "religion of light" in the Western world, from its successes in North Africa —the future Saint Augustine was among its members —to its decline under the pressure of state and church in the Roman Empire, cannot be related in full.

The relationship between Manicheism and such medieval sects as the Paulicians, Bogomils, Cathares, and Albigenses still offers many unsolved puzzles.

Bibliography. General: I. de Beausobre, *Histoire critique de Manichée et du Manichéisme,* vols. I-II (1734-39). G. Flügel, *Mani, seine Lehre und seine Schriften* (1862). K. Kessler, *Mani, Forschungen über die manichäische Religion,* vol. I: *Voruntersuchungen und Quellen* (1889). P. Alfaric, *Les écritures manichéennes,* vols. I-II (1918-19). F. C. Burkitt, *The Religion of the Manichees* (1925). H. H. Schaeder, *Urform und Fortbildungen des manichäischen Systems* (1927). F. C. Baur, *Das manichäische Religionssystem* (1831; rev. ed., 1928). H. J. Polotsky, "Manichäismus," *Real-Enzyklopädie der klassischen Altertumswissenschaften,* Supplement vol. VI (1935), pp. 240-71. E. Rose, *Die Christologie des Manichäismus* (1941). G. Widengren, *Mesopotamian Elements in Manichaeism, Studies in Manichaean, Mandaean and Gnostic Religion* (1946). H.-C. Puech, *Le manichéisme, son fondateur, sa doctrine* (1949). A. Adam, *Texte zum Manichäismus* (1954).

Sources in Arabic: For al-Bīrūnī: C. E. Sachau, trans. and ed., *Chronology of Ancient Nations* (with Notes and Index; 1879); *India, an Account of the Religion, Philosophy, Literature, Chronology, Astronomy, Customs, Laws and Astrology About A.D. 1030,* vols. I-II (with Notes and Indexes; 1910). For al-Ya'qūbī, al-Mas'ūdī, and aš-Šahrastānī: K. Kessler (*see above*). For an-Nadīm's account: G. Flügel (*see above*).

Sources in Coptic: H. J. Polotsky, *Manichäische Homilien,* Manichäische Handschriften der Sammlung A. Chester Beatty, vol. I (1934). C. R. C. Allberry, ed., *A Manichaean Psalm-Book,* pt. II, Manichaean Manuscripts in the Chester-Beatty Collection, vol. II (1938). H. J. Polotsky and A. Böhlig, *Kephalaia,* I, Hälfte, Manichäische Handschriften der Staatlichen Museen Berlins, vol. I (1940).

Sources in Chinese: E. Waldschmidt and W. Lentz, "Die Stellung Jesu im Manichäismus," *APAW* (1926); "Manichäische Dogmatik aus chinesischen und iranischen Quellen," *SPAW* (1933). G. Haloun and W. B. Henning, "The Compendium of the Doctrine and Styles of the Teaching of Mani, the Buddha of Light," *Asia Major,* New Series, III (1952), 184-212.

Sources in Greek: A. Adam (*see above*), pp. vi-vii.

Sources in Iranian (Middle Persian, Middle Parthian, and Sogdian; *see* PERSIA § C2): F. C. Andreas and W. Henning, "Mitteliranische Manichaica aus Chinesisch Turkestan," *SPAW,* vols. I-III (1932-34). W. B. Henning, "Ein manichäisches Bet- und Beichtbuch," *APAW* (1936). M. Boyce, *The Manichaean Hymn-Cycles in Parthian* (1954).

Sources in Latin: Augustine's writings in *CSEL* 25 and Migne, *SL* 32, 37, 42. A. Adam (*see above*), pp. vii-viii.

Sources in Syriac: A. Adam (*see above*), pp. viii-ix.

Sources in Uigur: For a bibliography, see A. von Gabain, *Alttürkische Grammatik* (2nd ed., 1950). A. von Gabain and W. Winter, "Türkische Turfantexte IX, Ein Hymnus an den Vater Mani auf 'Tocharisch' B mit alttürkischer Übersetzung," *Abhandlungen der Deutschen Akademie der Wissenschaften zu Berlin, Klasse für Sprachen, Literatur und Kunst* (1956), p. 43.

On the survival of Manichaeism: S. Runciman, *The Medieval Manichee* (1947); D. Obolensky, *The Bogomils* (1948); A. Borst, *Die Katharer* (1953). The recent literature on Bogomils, Catharism, and related medieval movements is discussed by H.-C. Puech, "Catharisme médiéval et Bogomilisme," *Accademia Nazionale dei Lincei, Convegno di Scienze Morali, Storiche e Filologiche* (1957), pp. 56-84. M. J. DRESDEN

MANIFESTATION [ἀνάδειξις (Luke 1:80; KJV SHOWING), φανέρωσις (I Cor. 12:7; II Cor. 4:2 KJV [RSV OPEN STATEMENT]); KJV ἀποκάλυψις (Rom. 8:19; RSV REVEALING)]. In Luke 1:80 reference is to John the Baptist's "manifestation to Israel," when God publicly appointed him as the forerunner of the Messiah. In I Cor. 12:7, Paul refers either to what is given by the Spirit or to the Spirit's own appearing. The English word appears also in the RSV at I Cor. 14:12 in a rendering of πνευμάτων.

See also REVELATION. B. H. THROCKMORTON, JR.

MANIUS, TITUS tĭ'təs mā'nĭ əs [Τίτος Μάνιος] (II Macc. 11:34); KJV TITUS MANLIUS măn'lĭ əs [Μάνλιος]. One of the ambassadors of the Romans to the nation of the Jews bringing greetings in 165 B.C. Polybius (XXXI.9.6) records a Manius Sergius as one of the envoys to Antiochus Epiphanes in 163. Livy (XLIII.11) notes a Titus Manlius Torquatus on a mission to Egypt in 164. However, attempts at identification have been unsuccessful.

Bibliography. R. H. Charles, *Apoc. and Pseudep. of the OT* (1913), I, 148. S. B. HOENIG

MANNA măn'ə [מָן; μάννα]. An edible substance on which the Israelites subsisted for part of their food during their forty years of wilderness wandering. Its name was connected in popular etymology with מָן הוּא (*mān hû'*), "What is it?" the question the Israelites are reported to have asked one another when they first found it on the ground in the morning (Exod. 16:15). It is described as a "fine, flake-like thing, fine as hoarfrost . . . . It was like coriander seed, white, and the taste of it was like wafers made with honey . . . [or] cakes baked with oil" (Exod. 16: 14, 31; Num. 11:8). It could be ground in mills or beaten in mortars, boiled in pots, and made into cakes (Num. 11:7-8).

It was first given after Israel arrived in the Wilderness of Sin (*see* SIN, WILDERNESS OF). In response to the murmuring of the hungry Israelites against Moses and Aaron, the Lord promised to Moses that he would rain bread from heaven, and the people should go out and gather a day's portion every day, but on the sixth day they would be permitted to gather an additional portion for the sabbath. The daily ration could not be kept overnight, lest it become wormy and spoiled—the only exception to this was the portion for the sabbath (Exod. 16:1-30). The supply did not cease until the Israelites arrived at the border of Canaan, according to one tradition (vs. 35); and according to another, until they came to Gilgal and "ate of the fruit of the land of Canaan" (Josh. 5:12).

In order that future generations might see the bread with which God had fed their forefathers in the wilderness, Aaron was commanded by Moses to "take a jar, and put an omer of manna in it, and place it before the LORD, to be kept throughout your generations" (Exod. 16:33).

Manna is also mentioned in Deut. 8:3, 16; Neh. 9:20; Ps. 78:24, where it is called "grain of heaven" (דגן שמים); and in Ps. 105:40 it is alluded to as "bread from heaven" (לחם שמים).

Christ spoke of manna as the "bread from heaven," and referred to himself as the "living bread which came down from heaven," and added that if anyone ate of this bread, he would live forever (John 6:31-65). Paul called manna the "supernatural [Greek 'spiritual'; RSV mg.] food" (I Cor. 10:3). In Rev. 2:17 "some of the hidden manna" is promised as a reward "to him who conquers."

From time to time investigations have been made in the Sinai region to discover a substance that would accord with the description of manna in the OT references.

Josephus claimed that manna was still coming down in his day. "Even now, in all that place, this manna comes down in rain" (Antiq. III.i.7). On the other hand, the Greek monks who lived in Sinai in the early Christian centuries associated the biblical manna with the manna produced by the tamarisk thickets. The tamarisk bush produces in June a granular type of sweet manna from pinhead to a pea size. It appears on the tender twigs of tamarisk bushes for a period of three to six weeks. The quantity of manna depends upon the winter rainfall.

Certain wadies such as Wadi Nasib and the Wadi esh-Sheikh are famous for their manna production. At the peak of season a steady worker may collect over half a pound (kilogram) per day. This, however, is hardly enough to have supplied the daily food for the wandering Israelites. It must have been its sweetness which justified its inclusion into the reports of the wilderness wandering.

Until recently this manna was regarded as a secretion of the tamarisk. However, a study of the tamarisk production of manna in the valleys of Central Sinai led to the conclusion that manna is produced by excretions of two closely related species of scale insects.* One of these, *Trabutina mannipara* Ehrenberg, produces it in the mountain regions; and the other, *Najacoccus serpentinus* Green, produces it in the lowlands. Fig. FAU 10.

A chemical analysis of these excretions revealed that they contain a mixture of three basic sugars with pectin. The plant saps on which these insects feed are rich in carbohydrates but extremely poor in nitrogen content. In order to acquire a minimum amount of nitrogen for their metabolism, they must consume great quantities of sap. The excess passes from them in honeydew excretions which in the dry air of the desert quickly change into drops of sticky solids. These manna pieces later turn a whitish, yellowish, or brownish color.

On the basis of these findings, manna production is a biological phenomenon of the dry deserts and steppes. The liquid honeydew excretions of a number of Cicadas, plant lice, and scale insects speedily solidify by rapid evaporation. From remote time the resulting sticky and often granular masses have been collected and called manna.

See also FAUNA § E3.

Bibliography. F. S. Bodenheimer, *Ergebnisse Der Sinai-Expedition 1927* (1929), pp. 45 ff; *BA*, vol. X, no. 1 (1947), pp. 2 ff.

J. L. MIHELIC

MANOAH mə nō'ə [מנוח, rest]. A Danite of Zorah; the father of SAMSON. The narrative in Judg. 13 relates that the barren wife of Manoah was instructed in a vision that she was to become the mother of a son, who would be a lifelong Nazirite and who would begin to deliver Israel from the oppression of the Philistines. When the man of God reappeared in answer to the petition of Manoah, the latter requested additional instructions concerning the nurture of the child. The former directions,which stipulated that the mother should abstain from unclean food and intoxicating drink, were simply reiterated. Manoah then invited the man of God to partake of a meal, but was bidden to offer the food as a burnt offering instead. When the flame ascended from the altar, the man of God went up in the flame, disclosing his identity as none other than the angel of Yahweh. Terrified at this discovery, Manoah was seized with the fear of death because as a mortal he had seen God; but his wife persuaded him that the gracious promise and acceptance of the offering by the angel contradicted his fears.

The tomb of Manoah was located between Zorah and Eshtaol, where the remains of Samson were also interred (Judg. 16:31). E. R. DALGLISH

MANSION. The KJV translation of μονή in John 14:2. The Greek word comes from μένω, "to remain," and means "an abiding place." The RSV more accurately renders it "room": "In my Father's house are many rooms." S. A. CARTLEDGE

MANSLAYER. *See* CRIMES AND PUNISHMENTS § C2*b*.

MAN-STEALING. *See* CRIMES AND PUNISHMENTS § C6*a*.

MANTELET [סכך] (Nah. 2:5); KJV DEFENSE. A movable structure used to shield besiegers while attacking a city.

The word occurs in a description of an attack on Nineveh, and its exact meaning is uncertain. The Hebrew root means "to weave together," as well as "to screen, protect." Both the LXX (προφυλακή) and the Vulg. (*umbraculum*) understood the word as a protection of some sort; hence the rendering "mantelet" seems likely to be approximately correct.

J. W. WEVERS

MANTLE. The translation of a number of words:

a) אדרת (alternately: "robe"), a cape or loose coat. In Josh. 7:21, 24, the term is used of a mantle (KJV "garment") of Shinar (Babylon). Elijah had such a mantle (I Kings 19:13, 19), which fell from him when he was taken from Elisha (II Kings 2:8, 13-14). A mantle made of hair (a hairy mantle) was evidently worn by the prophets (Zech. 13:4; KJV "rough mantle"). Esau was as hairy as such a mantle (Gen. 25:25; KJV "hairy garment"). In Jonah 3:6 the word refers to a garment of state.

b) מעיל (alternately: "robe"), a sleeveless coat. Ezra possessed one (Ezra 9:3, 5), as did Samuel (I Sam. 15:27; 28:14) and Job and his friends (Job 1:20; 2:12). The word is used figuratively in Ps. 109:29 with shame and in Isa. 59:17 with fury as the mantle of the Lord.

c) מעטה, a wrap; used figuratively in Isa. 61:3 as a mantle of praise.

d) מעטפה, an over-tunic. In Isa. 3:22 it is one of the luxuries of the women of Jerusalem.

e) שמלה, a wrap, robe. It was an article possessed by the Israelites at the time of the Exodus (Exod. 12:34 [KJV "clothes"]; 22:27—H 22:26 [KJV "raiment"]). It was a sign of respectability (Isa. 3:6-7; KJV "clothing").

f) KJV translation of שמיכה (RSV RUG) in Judg. 4:18.

g) מטפחת (Ruth 3:15 [KJV "vail"]; Isa. 3:22), a cloak.

h) תכריך (Esth. 8:15; KJV "garment"), a robe.

i) רדיד, the veil-like garment worn by the women of Jerusalem (Isa. 3:23; "veil") and the maiden in Song of S. 5:7. The LXX understood it as being a thin summer garment (θέριστρον), probably something like the stoles worn by women today.

j) Aramaic סרבל (Dan. 3:21, 27; KJV "coat"; alternately: "tunic"), garment, trousers.

k) KJV שמיכה (Judg. 4:18; RSV RUG).

l) Ἱμάτιον, an outer garment. *See* DRESS AND ORNAMENTS § A1.

m) Χιτών, an undergarment. *See* DRESS AND ORNAMENTS § A2.

n) Περιβόλαιον, an outer garment. *See* DRESS AND ORNAMENTS § A1.

J. M. MYERS

MANURE [κοπρία] (Luke 13:8; cf. KJV). The droppings of animals or birds, used as fertilizer. Sometimes the animals are pastured in those fields which have to be fertilized. Road scrapings are also spread on fields or made into compost heaps. Varro reports on various types of fertilizers in Roman times. In more primitive society DUNG was more important as a fuel than as fertilizer.

C. U. WOLF

MANUSCRIPTS. Any hand-written documents; particularly the copies of the Bible known on papyrus, vellum, parchment, and leather. They date from shortly before the beginning of the Christian era to the sixteenth century.

See also DEAD SEA SCROLLS; VERSIONS, ANCIENT; TEXT, NT and OT.

Pls. I-VIII.

M. M. PARVIS

MAOCH mā'ŏk [מעוך] (I Sam. 27:2). The father of Achish, king of Gath, where David and his men took refuge from the relentless pursuit of Saul. While Maoch has sometimes been identified with MAACAH (8), the father of Achish (I Kings 2:39), it is more likely, in view of the elapsed time, that Maacah may have been the son of Achish I and the grandson of Maoch. *See bibliography*.

Bibliography. A. Šanda, *Die Bücher der Könige*, I (1911), 46.

E. R. DALGLISH

MAON mā'ŏn [מעון, dwelling]; **MAONITES** —ə nīts. **1.** A descendant of Caleb; son of Shammai, and the father of Bethzur (I Chr. 2:45). As elsewhere in this section, this is probably a collective referring to the village or city and implying some sort of relationship between the inhabitants. The location is the same as 2 *below*.

2. The chief town of a hill-country district of Judah (Josh. 15:55); identified with modern Tell Ma'in, 1½ miles S of Carmel of Judah (Kirmil) and 8½ miles S of Hebron. It is situated on a high, isolated hilltop. Scattered along the hillside are a few fragments of Early Iron (Iron I) pottery indicating occupation at the time of David. There are no remains of a wall from this period on the rocky crest. Traces of a wall, possibly that of a watchtower guarding the approach to the Roman fortress at Chermula (Carmel, Kirmil), can be seen. Maon may have served to protect the fields in the small plains around it (cf. I Sam. 25:2 ff).

David took refuge from Saul in the "wilderness of Maon," E of Maon. Only an urgent message concerning a Philistine raid prevented Saul from capturing David and his men (I Sam. 23:24-25).

Nabal, a property holder in Maon, refused hospitality to David, who had seen to it that his men did not disturb the crops and flocks of NABAL (I Sam. 25:2 ff).

The next reference to Maon appears in the Talmud, which calls it "Maon of Judah" to distinguish it from Beth Ma'on near Tiberias.

V. R. GOLD

MARA mâr'ə [מרא, bitter] (Ruth 1:20). The name chosen by NAOMI after God had "dealt bitterly" with her.

MARAH mâr'ə [מרה, bitter, bitterness]. The first source of water which the Israelites found after three days' journey in the Wilderness of Shur (Exod. 15:23), which is also called the Wilderness Etham (Num. 33:8). Bitter and otherwise unpalatable water pools and wells are found frequently in desert areas.

This is an etiological story, explaining how this place received its name. The Israelites, after wandering for three days in a waterless waste, came upon water which was undrinkable because of its bitterness. Hence the place was called "bitterness." The account continues in a typical form. The people were helpless without a leader. They murmured against Moses, and he prayed to the Lord, who showed him a tree, which he threw into the water and the water became sweet.

The site cannot be definitely located. It may perhaps be 'Ain Hawarah, which is *ca.* two hours before Wadi Gharandel (Elim?). *See* EXODUS, ROUTE OF.

Bibliography. E. Robinson, *Researches in Palestine*, I (1856), 67. J. L. MIHELIC

MARALAH. KJV form of MAREAL.

MARANATHA mărʹə năthʹə [μαραναθά; Aram. מרן אתא, Our Lord has come, *or* Our Lord, come!]. An Aramaic expression used by Paul as a part of his closing salutation in I Cor. 16:22, and probably to be taken imperatively as a transliteration either of מרנא תא or of מרך אתא, "Our Lord, come!" One may compare the equivalent Greek (with the addition of the name Jesus) in Rev. 22:20: ἔρχου Κύριε 'Ιησοῦ ("Come, Lord Jesus!"). Editors of Greek texts have differed in dividing the words in accordance with the supposed Aramaic. Tischendorf, Hort, von Soden, Merk, and Vogels read μαρὰν ἀθά; Nestle and Bover read μαράνα θά. The MS evidence in general would show no division, and this was followed by B. Weiss.

Treatments of the phrase in some Christian sources and by early editors and translators had erroneously connected it with the preceding word, "ANATHEMA," and made it part of the curse in the Corinthian passage. The nondivision of words in the MSS and ignorance of Aramaic most likely account for this. It so appears in several English Bibles, down to and including early printings of the KJV. Another explanation would find in the expression a possible equivalent of *shamathâ* (Aramaic שמתא), meaning a "curse" or "ban" (lit., "The name [i.e., God] comes"). A number of reputable scholars have suggested that the phrase be taken to mean "Our Lord is the sign," reading the underlying Aramaic as מרן אתא; or as "Our Lord is the *aleph* and *tau*"—i.e., the Aramaic or Hebrew equivalent of the familiar Greek "*alpha* and *omega*" (e.g., Rev. 1:8).

The fact that these occurrences are both part of a more or less formal salutation and that Paul is using Aramaic in addressing a Gentile group would indicate that the phrase had become a familiar watchword of hope and encouragement among the early Christians at a time when the return of Jesus was a lively element in their faith. It is used in the Didache (X.6), of the early second century, in the context of a Eucharistic prayer with strong eschatological overtones. Cf. Phil. 4:5: "The Lord is at hand."

See also PAROUSIA.

Bibliography. G. Dalman, *Die Worte Jesu*, I (1930), 269-70, treats *māran* and *māranâ* and their Greek equivalents; K. J. Kuhn in R. Kittel, *TWNT*, IV (1942), 470-75 (excellent discussion and additional bibliography); E. J. Goodspeed, *Translation Problems in the NT* (1945), pp. 166-68, gives the data from early English Bibles; W. F. Arndt and F. W. Gingrich, *A Greek-English Lexicon of the NT* (English trans. by W. Bauer; 5th ed., 1957). C. F. D. Moule, "A Reconsideration of the Context of Maranatha," *NTS*, 6 (1960), 307-10, endorses the possible connection with *anathema* and gives further data and bibliography. A. WIKGREN

MARBLE [שיש, שש, *šeš*, *cf.* Akkad. *šaššu*, white marble *or* alabaster] (I Chr. 29:2; Esth. 1:6; Song of S. 5:15 KJV). Marble differs from common limestone in being more or less crystallized by metamorphism. It can take a good polish. The color of marble varies from white to black.

In I Chr. 29:2 the LXX reads πάριον (cf. Vulg. *marmor Parium*); Paros is the source of the finest marble for the classical world. It is doubtful, however, that David obtained his building stone for the temple from Paros. It seems more likely that he used the limestone of the country from the hill Bezetha, N of the temple area. This classical allusion to Paros as a source of fine marble is repeated in Esth. 1:6, in the LXX and Vulg. translations in which שש is used for pillars and pavement stones in the garden court at Susa. The Persians obtained marble locally for the buildings at Persepolis. Ashurbanipal also boasted of having carried off marble statues from Elam. It should be noted also that Sennacherib obtained marble from Mount Amnana. In the Song of S. 5:15 "ALABASTER columns" (KJV "pillars of marble") describe the legs of the lover. Egyptian alabaster, a crystalline form of calcium carbonate, was certainly known to the author, even if only in the guise of jars for ointment mentioned in Matt. 27:7, etc. W. E. STAPLES

MARCHESHVAN mär kĕshʹvăn [מרחשון; μαρσουάνης]. The Hebrew form of the Akkadian-Babylonian name *Arahsamna*, meaning "eighth month," corresponding to the Macedonian *Dios* (October-November). It occurs first in Aramaic papyri of the Jews in Egypt in the fifth century B.C. Modern Hebrew regards the name as properly Heshvan. *See* CALENDAR. E. W. SAUNDERS

MARCION, GOSPEL OF märʹshən [Μαρκίων]. A gospel used by Marcion, a highly influential second-century reformer and ardent Pauline Christian, easily (but mistakenly) dismissed as "another Gnostic" and archheretic.

This gospel, together with his version of ten Pauline letters and his own *Antitheses*, formed for him and his many followers a canon of scripture in place of the OT, which latter he rejected *in toto*. This gospel, which Marcion adopted and to which he added no further designation, is commonly regarded a version of the canonical Gospel of Luke, purged of what Marcion believed to be accretions and Jewish interpolations, notably the birth story, and thus restored to its primitive form. In the "primitive" form it began: "In the fifteenth year of Tiberius Jesus Christ [or God?] came down to Capernaum, a city of Galilee, and taught in the synagogue." To what extent Marcion's text differed from the one he had inherited is not easily said. It would appear to have been substantially an abridgment, with very little actual interpolation by Marcion himself. Nor is it to be overlooked that in both this gospel and the

Apostolicon (the Pauline letters) many of the variations, formerly ascribed to his pen, must now be regarded as primitive (pre-Marcionite) readings, which were subsequently altered in what may be styled the "ecclesiastical texts," as we know them.

Frequent guesses as to why Marcion selected Luke as the one best embodying what he believed to be the primitive gospel have been made. Obviously Matthew would have been quite unacceptable; John, which Marcion presumably knew, would have contained some highly congenial material—"All who came before me are thieves and robbers" (John 10:8)—but such material as the Prologue, the high appraisal of John the Baptist, the incident at Cana, would have been quite impossible. On the other hand, he must have *one* gospel, for one gospel, like the Pauline letters, must have been genuine although (unfortunately) adulterated by Jews and Jewish Christians, against whom, he argued, Paul had so valiantly contended. Only Mark and Luke would thus seem to have been prominent enough to come into choice. Perhaps the scanty amount of discourse material in Mark tended to weight the balance in favor of Luke. Nor is it impossible that in Pontus the Gospel of Luke had been the one in common use and thus the one to which Marcion had been accustomed in the days before he broke away from orthodoxy. It is not without interest that the Gospel of Basilides (*see* BASILIDES, GOSPEL OF) may with some plausibility also be regarded as a revision of the canonical Luke.

Occasional voices have been raised at this identification of Marcion's gospel. John Knox would see Marcion making use of an "early Luke" or "proto-Luke" (but not the proto-Luke of Streeter). Sometime after Marcion this early Luke was revised and combined with other materials to form our Luke-Acts. Knox's arguments are not lightly to be dismissed and merit more attention than they have apparently received.

Bibliography. The fullest and most adequate treatment of Marcion and his writings is to be found in A. von Harnack, *Marcion: das Evangelium vom fremden Gott* (2nd ed., 1924). See also J. Knox, *Marcion and the NT* (1942). M. S. ENSLIN

MARCUS. KJV alternate form of MARK. *See* MARK, JOHN.

MARDOCHAI mär′də kī. Douay Version form of MORDECAI.

MARDUK mär′do͝ok. The state god of Babylon, BEL, to whom in the time of Hammurabi (*ca.* 1700 B.C.) were transferred the functions and exploits of the storm-god and creator En-lil. The name is Hebraized as Merodach. In the myth and ritual of the Babylonian New Year Festival each spring his victory as champion of the gods over the chaotic waters and his creation of nature and man were celebrated, and he was acclaimed as king. This ideology was expressed in the myth and cult of Baal in Syria, and influenced Hebrew thought regarding the kingship of Yahweh.

See also BAAL; ASSYRIA AND BABYLONIA.

Fig. MAR 9.

Bibliography. M. Jastrow, *The Religion of Babylonia and Assyria* (1898), pp. 52-55, 96, 132-42; E. Dhorme, *Les Religions de Babylonie et d'Assyrie* (1945), pp. 139-50; J. Bottéro, *La religion babylonienne* (1952), pp. 40-41; *Larousse Encyclopedia of Mythology* (1959), pp. 54-56. J. GRAY

9. The Babylonian god Marduk and horned demon; lapis lazuli (ninth century)

MAREAL mâr′ĭ əl [מרעלה] (Josh. 19:11); KJV MARALAH mär′ə lə. A border town in Zebulun. Tell Ghalta, located in the Valley of Jezreel, N of Megiddo, has been suggested as a possible site, but this is uncertain.

Bibliography. F.-M. Abel, *Géographie de la Palestine,* II (1938), 379. G. W. VAN BEEK

MARESHAH mə rē′shə [מרשה, head place(?); LXX Μαρισα]; KJV MESHA mē′shə [מישע]. **1.** The first-born son of Caleb, and the father of Ziph and Hebron (I Chr. 2:42). The text is confused, indicating some accident in transmission. In the Hebrew text Caleb's son is first named Mesha and then, apparently, Mareshah. The RSV's consistent use of Mareshah follows the LXX.

2. A Judahite, son of Laadah (I Chr. 4:21).

R. F. JOHNSON

* **3.** Modern Tell Sandahannah, one mile SE of Beit Jibrin (Eleutheropolis). Mareshah was a Canaanite city (Amarna *Muḫrashti*) which became chief city of a Shephelah district of Judah (Josh. 15:44).

Rehoboam (*ca.* 922-915 B.C.) fortified it (II Chr. 11:8), and Asa (*ca.* 913-873) apparently strengthened the fortifications. Zerah, an Ethiopian commander of a garrison in Gerar, presumably established by Shishak after his invasion in *ca.* 918, marched against Judah. Asa met and defeated him near the fortress city of Mareshah and chased the Ethiopians back to Gerar, thirty miles SW of Mareshah (II Chr. 14:9-

14). Mareshah was the home of Eliezer, son of Dodavahu, who correctly predicted that the joint merchant-marine program of Ahaziah of Israel (*ca.* 850-849) and Jehoshaphat (*ca.* 873-849) would come to naught (II Chr. 20:37). In a section of Micah's prophecy noted for its play on words, Mareshah is one of the cities which will be destroyed (Mic. 1:15).

During the Exile the Idumeans (Edomites) infiltrated S Judah, and Marisa (Μαρισ[σ]α=Mareshah) became one of their capitals. In 312 it changed hands twice (Seleucids–Ptolemies–Seleucids), and for the next 150 years the exchange continued, with the city being under Egyptian control longer than under Seleucid. *Ca.* 250 a Sidonian colony under Apollophanes settled in Marisa. In the course of the archaeological investigation of the site, one of the most unusual discoveries was that of the painted tombs, the earliest one bearing the name of Apollophanes.

Though under Egyptian rule, the process of Hellenization in this part of the Near East was so rapid at this time that the Sidonians began to use Greek names after a couple of generations rather than Phoenician. Excavation revealed a city built according to Hellenistic practice, with streets running at right angles whenever possible and houses arranged in regular blocks.

Marisa was a center for the Idumean slave trade as a record of Zeno from 259 B.C. indicates. The tombs near Mareshah not only provide us with Phoenician and Greek names but also Idumean, many of them including the name of the Idumean god Qos.

During the Maccabean period Marisa remained important. First, Georgias, governor of Idumea, used it for a refuge in 164 (II Macc. 12:35; cf. I Macc. 5:66). Possibly *ca.* 110 it was captured by John Hyrcanus (134-104), who granted the Idumeans permission to remain if they submitted to circumcision (Jos. Antiq. XIII.ix.1). In 63, Pompey restored Marisa to the Idumeans, and *ca.* 57, Gabinius, the Roman governor of Syria, ordered the rebuilding of Marisa's fortifications, perhaps destroyed by John Hyrcanus. By order of Caesar, Idumea was again annexed to Judea in 47, when he appointed Hyrcanus high priest and Antipater, the Idumean, procurator of Judea (Jos. Antiq. XIV.viii.5; x.6). Later, Herod, Antipater's son, fled to Marisa to escape Antigonus and his Parthian allies (Jos. Antiq. XIV. xiii.9). In 40 B.C., Marisa was captured and destroyed by the Parthians. It was never rebuilt. Its place in the region was taken by Eleutheropolis (Beit Jibrin). Fig. CIT 33.

Bibliography. J. P. Peters and H. Thiersch, *Painted Tombs in the Necropolis of Marissa (Mareshah)* (1905). F.-M. Abel, *Histoire de la Palestine,* I (1933), *passim.* W. F. Albright, "Egypt and the Early History of the Negeb," *JPOS,* 4 (1924), 146-47; *Archaeology of Palestine* (1932), pp. 152-53; *Archaeology and the Religion of Israel* (1942), pp. 144 ff. B. Kanael, "The Partition of Judea by Gabinius," *IEJ,* 7 (1957), 98-106.

V. R. GOLD

***MARI** mä′rē [Akkad. *Ma-ri*[KI]; Sumer. MA-ER]. An ancient city of MESOPOTAMIA, on the right bank of the EUPHRATES.

1. Location
2. Excavations
3. The royal archives
4. History
5. Relations to the Bible

Bibliography

1. Location. The site of Mari, known today as Tell Hariri, is situated 6.8 miles N-NW of Abu-Kemal, a townlet on the Syrian side of the Syro-Iraqi frontier. Mari owed its importance to its location at the intersection of two caravan roads: one, crossing the Syrian Desert, linked the city with Syria and the Mediterranean coast; the other, descending from N Mesopotamia through the valleys of the rivers Habor and Euphrates, was one of the main highways leading from Assyria to Babylonia. *See* ASSYRIA AND BABYLONIA.

Fig. MAR 11.

Courtesy of Editions des Musées Nationaux, Paris

10. Statue of Ebih-il, steward to Ishtar, in which he sits on a stool of basketwork; from the temple of Ishtar at Mari (middle third millennium B.C.)

2. Excavations. In 1933, Bedouins searching for stones near the summit of Tell Hariri unearthed a headless stone statue. Excavations were started soon afterward under the auspices of the Louvre Museum and under the direction of A. Parrot. When the outbreak of the Second World War interrupted the excavations in 1939, six highly successful campaigns had taken place. The work was resumed in 1951 but, after four further campaigns, was broken off again in 1956 as a consequence of the Suez incident. The most important buildings uncovered were: (*a*) a temple of the goddess ISHTAR,* located near the perimeter of the city and consisting of four superposed buildings from various periods, the latest belonging in the time of the First Dynasty of Babylon; (*b*) a *ziqqurrat,* or

From *Atlas of the Bible* (Thomas Nelson & Sons Limited)
11. Air view of Mari, showing the palace

temple-tower, with an adjoining sanctuary dedicated to the "Divine King of the Land" (*[d]Šarru-ma-tim*); (*c*) a sprawling palace, contemporary of the First Dynasty of Babylon, occupying the center of the mound and containing almost three hundred rooms. The throne room furnished some of the rare specimens of well-preserved wall paintings.* (*d*) In the postwar campaigns, the excavators investigated mainly the older strata, reaching buildings from the time of the Dynasty of Akkad and the pre-Sargonic period. Figs. MAR 10, 12-13.

Courtesy of James B. Pritchard
12. Lamgi-Mari, king of Mari

3. The royal archives. In the palace area were found some twenty thousand cuneiform tablets the bulk of which dates from the time of kings Iasmaḫ-Adad, under whose reign the construction of the palace was begun, and Zimri-Lim, under whom it was completed. With the exception of a few texts of a religious character written in Hurrian and some bilingual Sumero-Akkadian inscriptions, the documents are written in Akkadian, even though the personal names and some peculiarities of the vocabulary indicate that the ruling class of Mari was of West Semitic origin. Several rooms contained particularly economic, administrative, and juridical texts relating to everyday life in the palace, and others furnished the royal correspondences. King Iasmaḫ-Adad corresponded in particular with his father, the powerful empire-builder, King Shamshi-Adad I of Assyria, and with his brother, King Ishme-Dagan I of Assyria, as well as with his representatives in the provinces of his realm. King Zimri-Lim's correspondence comprises letters exchanged with King Ḥammu-rapi (*see* HAMMURABI) of Babylon, King Iarîm-Lim of Aleppo, and other royal personages, as well as with several vassal kings. Two letters sent from Aleppo to Zimri-Lim concerned prophetic utterances pronounced in the name of the god Adad (*see* HADAD) of Aleppo, the subject and tenor of which are reminiscent of biblical prophecies.

Courtesy of James B. Pritchard
13. Ishtup-ilum, of Mari

4. History. The earliest reference to Mari is found in an inscription of King Eannatum of Lagash (middle of the third pre-Christian millennium), who prides himself on having conquered Mari. The next conqueror of Mari was King Sargon of Akkad (*see* SARGON 1). At the time of the Third Dynasty of Ur, Mari was ruled by governors (*šakkanakku*) of the kings of Ur. Eventually, however, a prince of Mari, Ishbi-Irra, who had brought the city-state of Isin

Courtesy of the Musées d'Archéologie d'Istanbul

14. Puzar-Ishtar, governor of Mari, Ur III period (*ca.* 2060-1955 B.C.)

under his domination (*ca.* 2021 B.C.), was instrumental in bringing about the downfall of the Dynasty of Ur.* Iaḫdun-Lim, a king of Khana, expanded his realm by conquering several adjoining kingdoms including Mari. He was defeated by King Shamshi-Adad I of Assyria (1818-1786 B.C.) and lost his life in a palace revolution (*ca.* 1793 B.C.). Four years later, Shamshi-Adad placed his younger son, Iasmaḫ-Adad, on the throne of Mari. Iaḫdun-Lim's son, Zimri-Lim, taking advantage of Shamshi-Adad's death, assembled a coalition against this king's sons, Ishme-Dagan I of Assyria and Iasmaḫ-Adad of Mari. Under the protection of the army of Eshnunna and of the powerful king of Aleppo, he ascended his father's throne in 1780 B.C. He lost his independence when Ḫammu-rapi of Babylon conquered Mari in 1765 B.C., but continued to rule until *ca.* 1746 B.C., when the Kassites conquered and destroyed Mari. Figs. MAR 14, 13.

5. Relations to the Bible. The texts from the royal archives frequently mention a tribe named TUR^{MEŠ}-*ia-mi-na.* Whereas it is not established yet whether the first element of this name must be read *mârê*^{MEŠ} (with the Akkadian term for "sons") or *binû*^{MES} (with its West Semitic equivalent), the meaning "sons of the South" is beyond doubt. The tribe so named was renowned for its military prowess. It had, at least to a large extent, given up nomadic life and was settled in towns and villages along the rivers Habor, Euphrates, and Balikh, S of the city of Harran. The names of the tribesmen are West Semitic, with a high percentage of theophorous names alluding to the moon-god (Eraḫ or Sîn), the grain-god Dagan (*see* DAGON), and others. One letter mentions an alliance between the "sons of the South" and another tribe concluded in the temple of Sîn at Harran. Whereas other peoples and tribes were ruled by kings, they were headed by "chieftains" (*suqâqû*) and "elders" (*šibûtum*). When not engaged in warfare, they tilled the soil. The relation of this tribe to the Israelite tribe of BENJAMIN (1) is obvious; it remains to be investigated whether they migrated from Mesopotamia to Palestine, taking with them from their former habitat near Harran the traditions centering around this famous holy city, as reflected in the patriarchal stories.

Bibliography. On excavations: A. Parrot, *Syria,* XVI (1935), 1-28, 117-40; XVII (1936), 1-31; XVIII (1937), 54-84, 325-54; XIX (1938), 1-29; XX (1939), 1-22; XXI (1940), 1-29; *Archiv für Orientforschung,* XVI (1953), 366; XVII, no. 1 (1954-55), 197; XVII, no. 2 (1956), 424; *Le Palais* (*Mission Archéologique de Mari,* II; 1958).

On royal archives: F. Thureau-Dangin, *Revue d'Assyriologie,* XXXVI (1939), 1-28; *Archives Royales de Mari, Musée du Louvre, Département des Antiquités Orientales,* vols. I-VIII (1946-58).

On history: F. Thureau-Dangin, *Revue d'Assyriologie,* XXXI (1934), 137-43; *Revue d'Assyriologie,* XXXIII (1936), 49-54. G. Dossin, *Syria,* XXI (1940), 152-69. H. Lewy, *Annuaire de l'Institut de Philologie et d'Histoire Orientales et Slaves,* XIII (1953), 241-53. G. Dossin, *Syria,* XXXII (1955), 1-28. H. E. Werdner, *Archiv für Orientforschung,* XVII, no. 2 (1956), 424.

On relations to the Bible: G. Dossin, *Mélanges syriens offerts à M. René Dussaud* (1940), pp. 981-96. A. Lods, *Une tablette inédite de Mari, intéressante pour l'histoire ancienne du prophétisme sémitique* (*Studies in OT Prophecy Presented to Th. H. Robinson;* 1950), pp. 103-10. M. Noth, *Mari und Israel* (1953).

H. LEWY

MARIMOTH. KJV form of MERAIOTH 1 in II Esd. 1:2.

MARINER. *See* SHIPS AND SAILING.

MARISA mărʹə sə [Μαρισ(σ)α] (I Macc. 5:66; II Macc. 12:35). Greek form of the name MARESHAH.

MARK, GOAL, SIGN [אות, מפת, תו, נס, משאת; σημεῖον, σκοπός, στίγμα, χάραγμα, παράσημος].

1. In the OT. Cain's "mark" (אות) may have been a facial tattoo later characteristic of Kenites (Gen. 4:15). A similar purpose was served by the "mark" (תו, a cross, the archaic form of the letter *tau*) of Ezek. 9:4, 6. The marks prohibited in Lev. 19:28 were probably Canaanite cultic signs. The heavenly luminaries are "signs" (אתת) marking time divisions (Gen. 1:14). Moses' miracles were "signs" of the genuineness of his commission (Exod. 4:8-9); in this sense אות overlaps with מפת ("portent"), translated "sign" in I Kings 13:3, 5; II Chr. 32:24 (corresponding to אות in II Kings 20:8-9=Isa. 38:7, 22); Ezek. 12:6, 11; 24:24, 27 (of the prophet as a "sign " to his audience; cf. אות and מפת together in Isa. 8:18 of Isaiah and his children). In Ps. 74:4, אות is used of standards; cf. נס in Exod. 17:15 ("The LORD is my banner") and in the sense of "warning" in Num. 26:10. The "signal" of Jer. 6:1 is a fire beacon (משאת).

2. In the NT. The commonest word for "sign" in the NT is σημεῖον. As Jonah was a "sign" of impending judgment to the Ninevites unless they repented, so was the Son of man to his contemporaries (Luke 11:30). In apostolic times prophecy and glossolalia were "signs" for believers and unbelievers respectively (I Cor. 14:22). The most distinctive use of the word in the NT denotes Jesus' mighty works as "signs" of the kingdom of God, or (in John) of the incarnate Word (*see* SIGNS AND WONDERS; SIGNS IN THE NT). The "mark" of Phil. 3:14 KJV (σκοπός) is Paul's "goal" (RSV) in his apostolic service. The "marks [στίγματα] of Jesus" (Gal. 6:17) are the scars left by Paul's beatings, stoning, etc.—brand marks which he bears as Christ's slave, contrasted with the mark of circumcision. The "mark" (χάραγμα) of the beast (Rev. 13:16-17) is Antichrist's name or cryptogram tattooed on his devotees. The "sign" (παράσημος) of the ship in Acts 28:11 was its figurehead.

F. F. BRUCE

*__MARK, GOSPEL OF__ [Μᾶρκος, *see* MARK, JOHN]. The second book in the NT canon. This gospel was written, probably in Rome, by Mark, who was able to draw on the personal reminiscences of Peter, with whom he had been associated. After an initial period of extensive influence it was for many centuries thought to be merely an abridgment of Matthew and so tended to be the least valued and least read of the gospels. It is now widely recognized as the earliest gospel and our primary source of information concerning the ministry of Jesus. Within the fourfold testimony it has its own characteristic and outstanding merits, besides being fundamental to the study of the other gospels.

1. Early tradition
2. Authorship
3. Date
4. Place of writing
5. The earliest gospel
6. Contents and sources
7. Arrangement and purpose
8. Historical reliability
   a. Of Mark's sources
   b. Of Mark himself
   c. Some special questions
9. Theology
   a. The Lord who "was rich"
   b. The Lord who "became poor"
   c. The Lord who is exalted
   d. The Lord who is coming
10. Problem of the ending
11. Style
12. Canonicity
13. Text

Bibliography

1. Early tradition. The earliest extant statement about the gospel comes from a lost exposition of the Lord's sayings written by Papias, bishop of Hierapolis, *ca.* A.D. 140. It is quoted by Eusebius in his *Ecclesiastical History* (III.39) and may be translated as follows: "This also the Elder said: Mark, who became Peter's interpreter, wrote accurately, though not in order, all that he remembered of the things said and done by the Lord. For he had neither heard the Lord nor been one of his followers, but afterward, as I said, he had followed Peter, who used to compose his discourses with a view to the needs [of his hearers], but

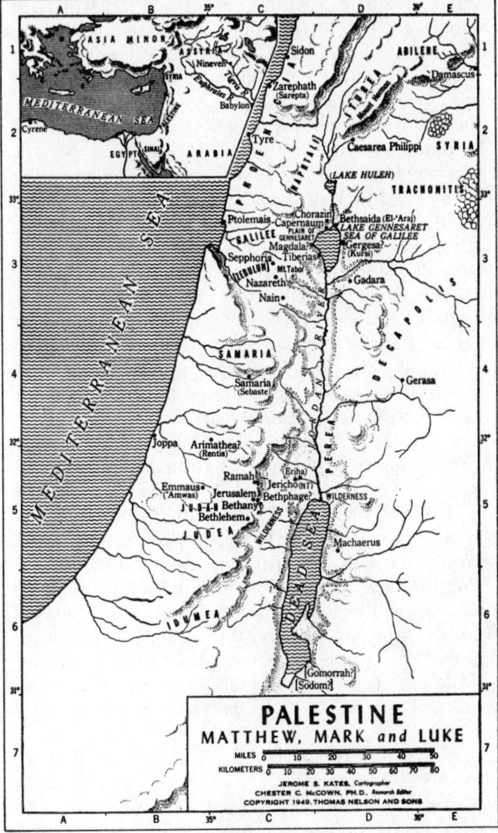

not as if he were composing a systematic account of the Lord's sayings. So Mark did nothing blameworthy in thus writing some things just as he remembered them; for he was careful of this one thing, to omit none of the things he had heard and to state no untruth therein." The first sentence, at any rate—and this is the vital one—is a quotation within a quotation and gives us the testimony of an older contemporary of Papias (probably to be identified with the elder John who is mentioned by Papias in another passage which Eusebius has just quoted). It is thus evidence of what was believed in the province of Asia at the beginning of the second century. It affirms a close connection between Mark and Peter (the significance of "interpreter" is perhaps that Mark translated Peter's Aramaic into Greek or perhaps that he committed Peter's reminiscences to writing and so acted as his spokesman) and testifies to Mark's accuracy, while at the same time indicating that his gospel was criticized for a certain deficiency of order (whether the complaint related to chronological order or to systematic arrangement and comprehensiveness is not certain). The second and third sentences, though probably not part of the Elder's words, probably do correctly interpret them. They explain the deficiency of order as due to the fact that Mark was not himself a firsthand witness but derived his information from Peter's discourses, and they underline the Elder's testimony to Mark's carefulness.

Only a little later than the Papias passage is Justin Martyr's reference (Dial. 106) to Peter's "memoirs" (Πέτρον . . . ἐν τοῖς ἀπομνημονεύμασιν αὐτοῦ). If

Mark is meant, as seems likely, since the words to which Justin is referring occur in Mark and in no other gospel, then this is another testimony to the close connection between this gospel and the apostle Peter.

The Anti-Marcionite Prologue to Mark is perhaps to be dated as early as 160-80 (though some would date it much later). The first part is lost. The rest is as follows: "Mark declared, who is called 'Stump-fingered' because he had small fingers in comparison with the size of the rest of his body. He was Peter's interpreter. After the death of Peter himself he wrote down this same gospel in the parts of Italy." This adds two details of importance to the information given by Papias: that the gospel was written after the death of Peter; that it was written in Italy. (The former of these is perhaps implied by the references to remembering in the Papias passage.)

The witness of Irenaeus (*ca.* 180) agrees with the Anti-Marcionite Prologue in dating Mark after the death of Peter. In Her. III.1.2 he says: "And after their [i.e., Peter's and Paul's] deaths Mark, the disciple and interpreter of Peter, himself also handed down to us in writing the things preached by Peter."

The first line of the Muratorian Canon (*ca.* 200; *see* CANON, NT) refers to Mark (what follows makes this clear), but it is only the end of a sentence. It reads: ". . . at which he was present, and so wrote them down." It seems reasonable to suppose that the lost antecedent of "which" referred to Peter's discourses.

Later writers repeat the tradition of the Petrine connection. The tendency was to heighten it, as is seen in the references of Clement of Alexandria to the subject. According to him the gospel was written during the lifetime of Peter, and, while in one place he says that Peter "neither actively hindered nor encouraged the undertaking" (quoted in Euseb. Hist. VI.14), in another place he actually affirms that the apostle "ratified the writing for reading in the churches" (Euseb. Hist. II.15).

The testimony of early tradition to Mark's authorship and to the connection of the gospel with Peter is thus clear and constant from the beginning of the second century onward. There is early and reliable support for dating the gospel after Peter's death. Irenaeus had been in Rome, and his dating may well reflect the local Roman tradition. That the place of writing was Rome would seem to be the implication of the early testimonies. Chrysostom's statement that Mark wrote it in Egypt is doubtless a mistake due to the tradition that he was the first bishop of Alexandria.

2. Authorship. The gospel itself is anonymous; but it contains nothing which forbids us to accept the universal tradition that its author was Mark, the associate of Peter, and much which points to a close connection with PETER (*see* § 6 *below*). The fact that, in spite of the strong tendency to claim direct apostolic authorship for the gospels, tradition persistently named one who was not an apostle as the author of this gospel, itself goes a long way toward guaranteeing the truth of the tradition. That the author was Mark is not open to serious doubt.

But is this Mark (cf. I Pet. 5:13) to be identified with the Mark of Acts 12:12, 25; 13:13; 15:37-39; Col. 4:10; II Tim. 4:11; Philem. 24? The objections which have been urged against this identification by some scholars are hardly convincing. The apparent tentativeness with which Jerome identifies the Mark of Philem. 24 with the author of the gospel: "Mark, . . . whom I take to be the author of the gospel," is certainly a little strange, but probably only reflects the scholar's cautiousness. The failure of earlier writers to make this identification explicitly may well be due to the fact that it never occurred to them that anyone would think otherwise. The objection that the gospel contains blunders with regard to Palestinian matters such as one who had been a resident in Jerusalem would not have been likely to make is not very weighty; for some, at least, of the alleged blunders are probably not blunders at all (the most notable example is Mark's dating of the Last Supper and the Crucifixion in relation to the Passover). We may take it as virtually certain that the Mark who wrote the gospel and who is referred to in I Pet. 5:13 and the Mark of Acts and the Pauline letters are one and the same person. For further information about Mark, *see* MARK, JOHN.

3. Date. That the gospel was written after the death of Peter is explicitly stated by the Anti-Marcionite Prologue and by Irenaeus, is probably implied by Papias, and is borne out by the internal evidence. The striking frankness with which details to the discredit of Peter are related is best accounted for on the assumption that he had already died a martyr's death, so that the unsparing recital of his past failures would not offend the church for which the gospel was written but would rather be welcomed as an encouragement to weak Christians. That Peter was martyred in the Neronian persecution (A.D. 64-65) seems certain. So we have 65 for our *terminus a quo.* The use of Mark by the later Synoptists makes a date later than 70 unlikely, and the fact that ch. 13 is in no way colored by awareness of the actual events of the tragic Jewish War of 66-70 (contrast Luke 21:20-24) suggests that the gospel was written before the later stages of that war. We may date the gospel, then, between 65 and 70, and probably within the narrower period 65-67.

4. Place of writing. The fact that Mark explains Jewish customs (7:3-4; 15:42) and gives a translation of Aramaic expressions (3:17; 5:41; 7:11, 34; 15:22) suggests that he was writing for Gentiles. The Anti-Marcionite Prologue states that he wrote the gospel "in the parts of Italy." Clement of Alexandria implies that it was in Rome. The testimony of I Pet. 5:13 to Mark's presence with Peter shortly before Peter's martyrdom is in favor of Rome. The mention of the sons of Simon of Cyrene in 15:21, which suggests that they were known to the church for which the evangelist was writing, may possibly be another pointer to Rome—if the Rufus whom Mark names is the same as the Rufus mentioned in Rom. 16:13 and if Rom. 16 was really addressed to Rome (*see* RUFUS; ROMANS, LETTER TO THE). Other points in favor of Rome as the place of writing are the special interest shown in the subject of persecution and martyrdom (e.g., 8:34-38; 13:9-13), which fits in well with the gospel's having been written there soon after the Neronian persecution; and the fact of the gospel's rapid and wide dissemination (attested by the use made of it by the other Synoptists and probably also by the Fourth Evangelist), which suggests that it had behind it the authority of no less important a church than that of Rome. The presence of a number of Latin loan words and of some possible Latinisms of idiom is scarcely evidence of an Italian origin, for the influence of Latin must have been strong throughout the Empire; but the special frequency of these in Mark possibly points to a Western origin. The arguments which have led a few scholars to suggest Antioch as the place of writing are weak in comparison with those which support Rome.

5. The earliest gospel. It is now very widely agreed that Mark is the earliest of the Synoptic gospels (that it is earlier than John is universally admitted). The arguments on which this conclusion is based may be indicated here briefly (for fuller discussion, *see* SYNOPTIC PROBLEM): (*a*) The substance of over ninety per cent of Mark's verses is contained in Matthew, the substance of over fifty per cent in Luke. (*b*) Where the same matter is contained in all three Synoptic gospels, usually more than half Mark's actual words are to be found either in both Matthew and Luke or in one of them; and, while there is often agreement in sentence structure and collocation of words between both Matthew and Luke and Mark or between one of them and Mark, it hardly ever happens that Matthew and Luke agree against Mark, except in some instances covered by *d* below. (*c*) The order in which the material is arranged in Mark is usually followed by both Matthew and Luke; where either of them differs from Mark, the other usually agrees with him. (*d*) Often where Matthew and/or Luke and Mark differ in language, the language of Matthew and/or Luke is either grammatically or stylistically smoother and more correct than that of Mark. (*e*) On other occasions something in Mark which could perplex or offend is either absent from, or appears in a less sharp form in, Matthew and/or Luke (cf., e.g., Mark 4:38*b* with Matt. 8:25; Luke 8:24; and Mark 6:5 with Matt. 13:58; and Mark 10:17-18 with Matt. 19:16-17). (*f*) In Mark the disciples' pre-Resurrection mode of addressing Jesus (as "Teacher," "Rabbi") is faithfully reflected, whereas Matthew and Luke often represent him as addressed by the title "Lord," thus reflecting the post-Resurrection usage of the church.

Against the hypothesis that Matthew was written first and was used by Mark (the suggestion that Luke in the form in which we have it was the original gospel is not made) the following points may be made, in addition to those indicated above: (*a*) Matthew is much more succinct than Mark, and, while Matthew's omission of Mark's unnecessary words and phrases in order to make room for additional matter is easily understood, the contrary process of omitting valuable material in order to make room for verbosity is hard to imagine. (*b*) Where Matthew's order differs from Mark's, it is often clearly secondary (e.g., the series of stories in Mark 2:1-3:6 appears in part in Matt. 9 and in part in Matt. 12; and cf. Mark 6:6*b*-33 with Matt. 9:35; 10:1, 9-11, 14; 14:1-13).

If Mark, then, is the earliest of the gospels, its special importance as our primary source of information about the ministry of Jesus is obvious.

6. Contents and sources. The material contained in the gospel is not all of the same kind.

There are narratives which by their vividness and wealth of detail give the impression of being derived directly from the reminiscence of an eyewitness. Some of these are narratives in which Peter figures prominently or which must have had a special interest for him (e.g., 1:16-20; 1:29-31; 1:35-38; 14:27-31, 54, 66-72; 14:32-42); others relate incidents at which only a few, but including Peter, were present (e.g., 5:21-24, 35-43). In 9:14-27 it is noticeable that the story is told from the point of view of the three disciples who return with Jesus. It is reasonable to suppose that as far as these narratives which have a special Petrine interest, and also most of the other narratives which are distinguished by special vividness and wealth of detail, are concerned, the tradition of Mark's dependence on the reminiscences of Peter is correct.

But there are other narratives (e.g., 2:18-20; 2:23-26; 3:31-35) which show signs of having passed through the processes of oral tradition, in the course of which details have been lost and the stories molded by frequent repetition into a rounded form. Often these narratives are pronouncement stories—i.e., stories in which the interest is concentrated on a saying of Jesus to which the story leads. For a discussion of the various "forms" according to which the form critics have sought to classify the gospel material, *see* FORM CRITICISM.

In addition to narratives which are probably derived directly from Peter (or occasionally perhaps from some other eyewitness) and narratives which are units of oral tradition which had been in circulation in the primitive Christian communities, two other kinds of narrative material may be distinguished: narratives which seem to have been constructed by Mark on the basis of tradition (e.g., 3:13-19; 6:6*b*-13; 6:14-16; 6:30-33; 6:53-56) and brief statements which indicate in summary form what was happening over a period of time (e.g., 1:14-15; 3:7-12; 4:33-34). Narratives of the former sort, while they rest on tradition, seem to be Mark's own composition and not actual units of tradition. They lack vivid details and tend to be somewhat vague. On the question how far passages of the latter sort reflect a traditional outline of the ministry of Jesus, *see* § 8*c below*.

The gospel also contains a considerable amount of sayings material. While sometimes tradition preserved the memory of the circumstances which had called forth a particular saying (hence the pronouncement stories mentioned above), more often the circumstances were forgotten and the sayings preserved as independent units of tradition. So it comes about that the same saying can appear in different contexts in the different gospels (cf., e.g., Mark 4:22 with Matt. 10:26; Luke 12:2). Collections of sayings would seem to have been made in the various churches and used for catechetical purposes (*see* Q). It is likely that Mark drew upon a collection in use in the church of Rome. Traces of the groupings of sayings in his source (or sources) according to catchwords and according to topics are to be seen from time to time in the gospel. A particularly interesting example is 9:37-50. It looks as if 42 may first have been joined to 37 because of the presence of "one such child" in 37 and "one of these little ones" in 42; and afterward 38-40 may have been inserted after 37 because of another catchword, "in my name" in 37 and "in your name" and "in my name" in 38-40; and 41 similarly inserted after 38-40 because it contained "because you bear the name of Christ" (ἐν ὀνόματι, ὅτι Χριστοῦ ἐστε—which should probably rather be translated "on the ground that you belong to Christ," though it contains the Greek word for "name"). The connection between 42 and 43-48 is the verb "cause to sin," the expression "it would be [is] better," and the verb "throw." Again, the connection between 48 and 49 is the word "fire," and between 49 and 50 the verb "to salt" and the noun "salt." Such a grouping made it easier to memorize the sayings.

It is probable that the narrative material also was to some extent collected into groups of units before the compilation of the gospel. In the case of the passion story, it is almost certain that some kind of summary continuous narrative was traditional. It seems likely that the Markan passion narrative represents such a traditional narrative filled out with additional material derived from the reminiscences of an eyewitness or eyewitnesses. In other parts of the gospel there are narrative "complexes"—i.e., groups of narrative units—of which some, at least, appear to have been brought together at an earlier stage than the compilation of the gospel. One such group that has often been noticed is the series of conflict stories, 2:1–3:6. It is noticeable that in some of these groups there are no connecting links between the units other than a simple "and"; the stories are merely placed one after another. In these groups the bond between the different narratives is topical. In other groups the separate stories are joined together by temporal or geographical links, and the connection would seem to be historical. Examples of this sort of group are to be seen in 1:21-38; 4:35–5:43; 8:27–9:29. While complexes of this latter sort probably go back to the memory of an eyewitness, the topical complexes would seem to have originated in the catechetical requirements of the primitive church.

To what extent, if any, the sources mentioned were written, it is difficult, perhaps impossible, to decide.

A further question with regard to the sources of Mark arises at this point: Was there perhaps an intermediate stage (or stages) between the sources of the sort we have been discussing and the actual composition of the gospel as we know it? Various hypotheses about extensive written sources have been put forward. Some have posited a first edition of Mark (*Ur-Markus*) earlier than the gospel we possess and lacking the passages which both Matthew and Luke lack; according to this theory Matthew and Luke used, not our Mark, but Ur-Markus (*see* SYNOPTIC PROBLEM). Others have suggested that the evangelist combined a "disciple source" and a "Twelve source"; or that he used three sources—a Palestinian gospel written in Aramaic, a gospel of the Dispersion written by Mark himself, and a Gentile gospel written for the Pauline mission; or, again, that the gospel arrived at its present form by three stages—first an original form used by Luke, then that form expanded by a Galilean redactor, which was the gospel as used by Matthew, and finally this expanded form edited by a Roman editor, which is our Gospel According to Mark. But none of these hypotheses has met with anything like general acceptance.

7. Arrangement and purpose. The central turning point of the gospel, which marks its rough division into two halves, is the narrative of Peter's confession of Jesus as the Messiah and of the first prediction of the Passion (8:27-33). The second half of the gospel falls easily into four main divisions: 8:27–10:52; 11–13; 14–15; 16. It is not so easy to see exactly what are the main divisions of the first half. That 1:1-13 is the introduction or prologue to the gospel is clear enough. But commentators divide 1:14–8:26 differently. On the whole, it seems best to divide it into 1:14–3:6; 3:7–6:13; 6:14–8:26. We thus get the scheme:

I. Introduction, 1:1-13
II. Beginnings of the Galilean ministry, 1:14–3:6
III. Later stages of the Galilean ministry, 3:7–6:13
IV. Jesus goes outside Galilee, 6:14–8:26
V. The way to Jerusalem, 8:27–10:52
VI. Ministry in Jerusalem, chs. 11–13
VII. The Passion, chs. 14–15
VIII. The Resurrection, ch. 16

The whole of the latter half of the gospel is dominated by the Passion (see, e.g., in the earlier part of the latter half, 8:31; 9:9-13, 31; 10:32-34, 38-39, 45). In the former half, too, there are many features which point forward to it: e.g., the reference to the arrest (the verb παραδίδωμι is used; cf. 9:31; 10:33; 14:10, 41; 15:1, 10, 15) of John the Baptist (the Forerunner) in 1:14; the crescendo of opposition indicated in 2:1–3:6, culminating in the plot against Jesus' life (3:6); the scribes' accusation in 3:22; the rejection at Nazareth (6:1-6); and the account of Herod's fears ("John, whom I beheaded, has been raised"), followed by the story of John's end (6:14-29). The movement of the gospel is the march of Jesus toward the Cross and the Resurrection.

Mark's emphasis on the Passion is an indication of his purpose to set forth the good news of the Deed of God for the world's salvation. It is not, however, intended to suggest that what preceded the actual Passion was unimportant, but rather to illumine the significance of the whole. To describe the gospel as a passion narrative with a rather full introduction might mislead; for God's Deed included more than the cross, resurrection, and exaltation of Jesus. His miracles, his mixing with sinners, his choice of the Twelve, his teaching both the crowds and the disciples—these and other things were also part of that Deed,,and so accounts of them find their place in the gospel. But these things are rightly understood only when they are seen in the light of what followed them.

Mark's general purpose in compiling the gospel may be summed up in the language of John 20:31. He wrote in order that those who should read or hear his words might believe that Jesus is the Messiah, the Son of God, and that believing, they might have life in his name. Within the framework of this general purpose, which he shared with all three later evangelists, it is possible to discern his special motives. He had in mind primarily, it seems, the church in Rome and the Gentile mission. The gospel was intended to supply a catechetical and liturgical need and a need of the church's missionary preaching, to nourish and sustain the faith of Christians in Nero's Rome, and to strengthen and guide their obedience.

8. Historical reliability. We have seen that the gospel was written from faith to faith. Its purpose was not simply to pass on some historical information, but to support faith. Its contents are not the coldly objective depositions of neutral observers, but the testimony of people who believed in Jesus of Nazareth as the Son of God. We have seen too that, while some of the material in the gospel probably derives from the reminiscence of Peter, much of it bears the marks of having undergone the processes of oral tradition over a considerable period. In view of these facts, what can we say about the historical reliability of the gospel?

Here we must distinguish two questions: that of the general reliability of the sources Mark used and that of Mark's own reliability.

a. Of Mark's sources. According to the more skeptical of the form critics, much of the narrative material which Mark received was legend and ideal construction, and many of the sayings ascribed to Jesus were similarly the creation of the primitive community. The tradition, according to them, is evidence of the faith and the interests of the early church (it is, indeed, indirectly evidence of the historical ministry of Jesus, since it would not have arisen had there not been some sufficient cause to give rise to it; but it is only indirect evidence), and tells us what Jesus had become for Christian faith, not what he actually had been in his historical life. Some have even gone so far as to assert that of the historical Jesus we can now know next to nothing. But there are many considerations to be set over against this radical skepticism, considerations which have led other scholars to believe that there was preserved through the oral-tradition period a substantially reliable picture of the historical Jesus.

We may mention some of them: (*a*) The survival of eyewitnesses, hostile as well as believing, throughout the oral-tradition period must have limited severely the church's freedom to invent and even to embellish. (*b*) The prominence in the NT of the words μάρτυς, μαρτυρέω, μαρτυρία, μαρτύριον ("witness," "bear witness," etc.) implies that the primitive community was conscious of its obligation to tell the truth (the word μάρτυς means primarily a witness in court). I Cor. 7, in which Paul distinguishes carefully more than once between that for which he has the authority of a definite word of the Lord Jesus and that which he is saying on his own account as a Christian, illustrates its sense of responsibility in the matter. The fact that the primitive community believed that it was speaking about God's Deed made its sense of responsibility all the stronger (cf. I Cor. 15:15). (*c*) The main outline of events, especially the story of the Passion, must have been constantly repeated in preaching and liturgy, and so kept clear in the memory. (*d*) The fact that the church grew up within the Jewish community, a community with a long-established and highly revered oral tradition of its own, must not be forgotten. Among the rabbis the most meticulous care was taken to preserve the oral tradition of their teachers unaltered. (*e*) The form of much of the teaching of Jesus (poetry, epigram, parable) made it particularly easy to remember accurately. (*f*) The respect paid by the later evangelists to Mark is something we should not expect if the early church had really felt as free to invent and embellish as some would have us believe. (*g*) The presence of Semitisms in many of the sayings of Jesus and also in many of the narratives of the gospel, while it does not, of course, guarantee the historical accuracy of the material, tells strongly against any theory which sees in it corruptions of the tradition due to Hellenistic influences. (*h*) The fact that material which was discreditable to Peter and the other apostles, and, still more, such sayings of Jesus as his admission of ignorance of the date of the Parousia (13:32) and his cry of dereliction on the cross (15:34), which we know puzzled and embarrassed the early church, have been preserved, goes a long way toward guaranteeing the general reliability of the tradition.

b. Of Mark himself. Can we make out anything of the way in which Mark used his sources? Did he treat them with respect, recognizing an obligation to pass them on as he received them, or did he feel free to embellish them or to smooth away difficulties? Was he a creative writer?

Here several things must be said: First, there is the fact, to which reference has already been made (*see* § 5 *above*), that some statements in Mark that could offend or perplex are either omitted or softened down in Matthew and/or Luke. To the examples already given, others may be added: e.g., the request ascribed in Mark 10:37 to James and John is in Matt. 20:21 ascribed to their mother; the statement that Jesus "began to be greatly distressed and troubled" (Mark 14:33) is softened in Matt. 26:37 (λυπεῖσθαι is much weaker than ἐκθαμβεῖσθαι) and omitted altogether in Luke; the picture of the three disciples' failure to watch with Jesus in Gethsemane is considerably softened by the addition of the words "for sorrow" in Luke 22:45; in Mark 14:71 (cf. Matt. 26:74) Peter is said to have begun "to invoke a curse on himself and to swear, 'I do not know this man . . . ,' " but Luke has the much less offensive "Man, I do not know what you are saying" (Luke 22:60); and the cry of dereliction (Mark 15:34; Matt. 27:46) is omitted in Luke. There is also the fact (mentioned in § 5 *above*) of Mark's retention of the pre-Resurrection mode of address, which contrasts with the frequent use of "Lord" in Matthew and Luke. These two features not only point to the priority of Mark; they also suggest that Mark was strikingly frank.

It is very noticeable, also, that the Markan constructions (i.e., those passages which Mark, in the absence of an actual unit of tradition to incorporate at a particular point, has himself composed on the basis of a general knowledge of what had happened —e.g., 3:13-19; 6:6*b*-13; 6:14-16; 6:30-34; 6:53-56) are singularly lacking in vivid details, in striking contrast with such passages as 5:1-20; 9:14-29; 10:17-22. The most natural explanation would seem to be that, where Mark did not find vivid details in the material which he had received, he refrained from creating them. The evidence does not point to Mark's having been a born storyteller, the sort of person who just cannot tell a story badly, as has sometimes been suggested; rather it suggests that the vividness characteristic of so much of the gospel must be attributed, not to Mark, but to his sources. The gospel Mark has left us gives us no solid grounds for acclaiming him as an artist and a creative writer. On the contrary, the evidence points to his having been something which on the surface seems very dull in comparison but which in actual fact is from our point of view of infinitely greater worth—a careful and conscientious compiler. Since we need not suppose that he could not have made his own constructions more interesting had he wished, we may attribute their lack of vividness to a deliberate choice on his part. His peculiar merit as an evangelist would seem to have been that of self-restraint—the virtue of a witness. It reflects a real reverence for the sacredness of historical events which he believed to have been the very Deed of God.

Mark has shown this same self-restraint in the matter of connecting links between his sections. When he has received a unit of tradition in isolation and has no reliable information about its historical context, he does not supply from his imagination suitable temporal and geographical details to link it with the context in which he sets it, but prefers to introduce it with a simple "and." By contrast, Matthew and Luke sometimes introduce connecting links where Mark has none: e.g., Luke connects the question about fasting with the supper in Levi's house (οἱ δὲ εἶπαν in 5:33; contrast Mark 2:18); and Matthew connects Jesus' withdrawal in 14:13 with the execution of the Baptist by the phrase "Now when Jesus heard this" (contrast Mark 6:30-31). The same restraint is apparent in the way Mark leaves intact groups of units which he has received as such, even where the grouping is clearly topical, not historical (e.g., 2:1–3:6).

The conclusion to be drawn from this evidence is surely that we may have very great confidence in Mark's own reliability.

c. Some special questions. There are several special problems which should at least be mentioned here, even though it is impossible to discuss them at all adequately.

There is first the problem of the Markan framework or outline, about which opinions differ widely. On the one extreme there are those who, placing great weight on the order in which the various incidents are related, are confident that they can trace in considerable detail the successive stages of the ministry of Jesus and even of his inner psychological development. On the other extreme there are those who regard the Markan order as purely artificial, apart from chs. 14–16 and perhaps one or two complexes like 1:21-38. A middle position was taken up by C. H. Dodd (*see bibliography*), and his view has been widely supported. According to him, while "it is hazardous to argue from the precise sequence of the narrative in detail . . . , there is good reason to believe that in broad lines the Marcan order does represent a genuine succession of events, within which movement and development can be traced." While some of his arguments are perhaps less conclusive than they seemed at first, he was probably right in thinking that Mark received, in addition to a number of independent units of tradition and a number of complexes (some of which were continuous narratives in which the connection between the parts was historical, while others were merely topical), an outline of the ministry of Jesus. Dodd seems to think of this outline as something that was a familiar part of the general oral tradition of the church; but, while it is certainly likely that a simple and summary outline of the ministry was traditional in this sense, it seems rather unlikely that such a long and detailed outline as he seems to envisage ever was. It seems more reasonable to suppose that the summary statements (*see* § 6 *above*), which form to a large extent the framework of the gospel, were composed by Mark on the basis of a knowledge of the course of the ministry which he possessed as a result of his association with Peter (and perhaps other eyewitnesses) rather than that they are fragments of an outline that was a familiar part of the general oral tradition. If we allow, as we surely must, that Peter is likely to have retained a fairly accurate memory, not only of particular incidents but also of the general course of the ministry, we need not accept the view that the Markan framework is purely artificial; on the other hand, we must make due allowance for the fact that much of Mark's material seems to have come to him as isolated units carrying no indications of their proper historical contexts, while some was already grouped, not historically, but topically. We must examine on its merits the relation of each separate unit of tradition to the outline.

Other special questions concern the accounts of miracles, the references to angels, Satan, demons, and the suggestion of Bultmann that the NT contains a mythological element which it is proper to attempt to "demythologize." That all these matters would have to be considered in any full discussion of the historical reliability of Mark's gospel is obvious; but, as they are problems not just of Mark but of the NT as a whole, and as any worth-while treatment of them would require considerable space, it suffices here to make, in addition to some suggestions in the bibliography, this one observation—that, in view of what we have seen in §§ 8*a-b above*, we shall be wise to listen attentively to, and to take very seriously, what Mark has to say, and to beware of rejecting anything simply because it cannot easily be reconciled with our twentieth-century presuppositions.

With regard to the question whether the material contained in Mark has been affected by the influence of Paulinism, it is perhaps enough here to register the now widely held opinion that, while there are many contacts between the teaching of the gospel and the teaching of Paul, there is very little, if anything, that can justifiably be claimed as distinctively Pauline.

On two other questions—that of the alleged distortion of some of the teaching of Jesus as a result of the preoccupation of Mark and the church of his time with apocalyptic hopes, and that of the alleged coloring of the material by a doctrine of a "messianic secret"—some light will, it is hoped, be shed by § 9 *below*.

9. Theology. Christology is by no means the whole of Christian theology, but it is the heart of it. We shall get as clear and adequate a picture of the theology of this gospel as belongs in a summary article if we concentrate on its Christology.

The whole gospel presupposes the early church's faith that Jesus is Lord (cf. Rom. 10:9; I Cor. 12:3; II Cor. 4:5; etc.)—it would never have been written if Mark had not shared this faith. But, because he had a sense of responsibility about historical truth, he avoided representing Jesus as being called "Lord" during his ministry. Only once in the gospel does the vocative κύριε occur as a form of address to Jesus (it is read in 1:40 and 10:51 in some MSS, but is rightly omitted by the RSV); this is in 7:28, where, on the lips of the Syrophoenician woman, it only means "Sir." In the body of the gospel Jesus is never referred to as "the Lord" (unless in 11:3; but here it is probable that ὁ κύριος should be translated, not "the Lord" as in the RSV, but "its [i.e., the colt's] owner"). But there is one place in the Prologue to the gospel where "the Lord" may well refer to Jesus. In 1:3 Mark quotes Isa. 40:3, but by substituting "his" for "of our God" (LXX; RSV has "for our God") he makes it possible, though not necessary, to identify the preceding "the Lord" with Jesus. It seems probable that Mark intends κυρίου in the quotation to be understood of Jesus (though it is often taken to refer to God), and that here in the Prologue he is pointing to the truth (which he will not be able to express in so many words in the course of the gospel) that the One whose ministry he is about to record is the One whom the church acknowledges as "the Lord." But whether or not this is correct of 1:3, there is no doubt that the gospel was written from the faith that Jesus is Lord.

The Christology of the gospel may be considered conveniently under four heads:

a. The Lord who "was rich." If we were right about 1:3, then that verse is an eloquent pointer to the Lord who—in Paul's language (II Cor. 8:9)—"was rich"; for it would be an example of something which is common elsewhere in the NT—the application of an OT passage, in which κύριος stands for "Yahweh," to Jesus. And this usage points to belief in the pre-existence of him who in his earthly life was known as Jesus of Nazareth; for "Lord" in this sense is something which no Jew worthy of the name could think of a man's becoming. Only he who had from all eternity been Lord could at a particular moment become or be designated or made Lord in this sense.

A claim to pre-existence is probably implied by Jesus' self-designation SON OF MAN (*see also bibliography*); for in Enoch 46:1-3; 48:2-7; 62:7 a heavenly pre-existence of the Son of man seems to be assumed (though this has been disputed). It is also perhaps implied by the sayings which begin "I came" or "the Son of man came" (Mark 2:17; 10:45; possibly also 1:38).

Specially important here is the title SON OF GOD (*see also bibliography*), which is a prominent theme of the gospel—1:1 (*see* § 13 *below*); 1:11; 3:11; 8:38; 9:7; 12:6; 13:32; 14:36, 61; 15:39. It is not to be explained as merely a messianic title (though some would so explain it); for the evidence of its use as a messianic title in pre-Christian Palestinian Judaism is scanty and doubtful. Its use is rather to be explained as having its origin in the filial consciousness of Jesus. The absolute use of "the Son" in 13:32 is specially interesting; for this saying is one of which the genuineness cannot reasonably be doubted (an assertion of Jesus' ignorance is not likely to have been created by the early church). It is evidence of Jesus' having thought of himself as the unique Son of God.

While it is true that the Gospel According to Mark contains no explicit statement such as is found in the Prologue of John—that the Word, which from the beginning was with God and was God, became flesh (i.e., assumed human nature) in Jesus—the Christology of Mark, though less directly stated, is every bit as high as that of the Fourth Gospel.

b. The Lord who "became poor." While the whole gospel presupposes the heavenly riches of this Lord's pre-existence (and also his exaltation and the hope of his coming again), it is the history of his poverty that it is throughout the first fifteen chapters concerned to record.

Mark begins at the point where Jesus, the first quiet stages of his course completed, makes his mature self-dedication to the fulfilment of his life's mission of complete self-identification with sinners by submitting to John's baptism of repentance. This was the first decisive step on the road of the Servant, which led down into the very lowest depths of human anguish and shame. The poverty he had to endure included not merely death but death under the curse of God. In Mark, of all the gospels, the horror of this stands out most starkly. The temptation to depict Jesus as the supreme Christian martyr is not yielded to. Here we see, not the calm courage of the martyr, but the inexpressible fear and horror (14:33-34) of one who knows that for him death must mean drinking the cup of God's wrath to the dregs (14:36; cf. Isa. 51:17-23; Jer. 25:15-28; 49:12; 51:7, etc.). The cry of dereliction (15:34), which is not to be explained away, bears witness to a real abandonment by God his Father, endured by him on our behalf and in our place. That is what it meant "to give his life as a ransom for many" (10:45); and the fact that in some way beyond our comprehension the unity of the Blessed Trinity was even then unbroken does not permit us to gloss over the awful reality of that abandonment.

The history Mark records is the history of the hidden Lord, the Lord who, having laid aside every outwardly compelling evidence of his divine glory, had become one whose claim to authority could only appear to the world paradoxical and problematic. This hiddenness was an essential part of the cost of redeeming the "many"; for, while his presence placed men in a situation of crisis, the hiddenness was necessary in order that they might be allowed sufficient room in which to make a personal decision. Everything in the ministry of Jesus has to be seen in the light of this hiddenness of the divine Lord. Here is the clue to the understanding of his refusal to give a sign (8:11-12), his silencing of the demoniacs (1:25, 34; 3:12), his efforts to limit the publicity of his miracles (1:44; 5:43; 7:36; 8:26), his teaching the multitudes by means of parables, indirectly, and confining his more direct teaching about himself and the kingdom of God to his disciples (4:33-34), his enjoining secrecy on the disciples (8:30; 9:9), and also the slowness of the disciples to understand (4:13, 40; 6:52; 8:17-21). These features, most of which Wrede (*see* SECRET, MESSIANIC) supposed were the invention of the primitive church read back into the story in order to get over a dogmatic difficulty (the alleged fact that Jesus neither claimed to be Messiah during his life nor was recognized as such by the disciples), are an integral part of the history, connected with this hiddenness, that was necessary for the fulfilment of Jesus' mission.

In the last hours of the ministry the hiddenness deepens. Forsaken by his disciples (14:50; note the hammerlike blows with which the original Greek drives home his loneliness), rejected and condemned by the religious leaders of Israel (14:63-64), denied by Peter (14:66-72), sentenced to death by Pilate (15:15), scourged (15:15), mocked by the soldiers (15:16-20), physically exhausted (15:21), he is brought to the place of execution, and there, powerless in the hands of his enemies, the defenseless object of men's gibes (15:29-32), he dies, abandoned by God (15:34), the death that the law declares accursed (Deut. 21:23), to all outward appearance the absolute antithesis of kingly and divine dignity and power. In those last hours the truth about him is expressed only indirectly and unconsciously—the truth of his messiahship (15:9, 12, 18, 26, 32), his saviorhood (15:31), and his divine sonship (15:39).

But the hidden Lord was really Lord, and the history of his poverty is the history of God's mighty Deed. In him the KINGDOM OF GOD, God's kingly rule, God's sovereign and effective claim upon men, had come near to men (1:15) and was confronting them in mercy and judgment, in command and promise. The "secret of the kingdom of God" (4:11), which had been revealed to the disciples, was the secret of its presence in him. His miracles, though they were not compelling proofs or signs of the sort demanded by the Pharisees (8:11) and though, as far as unbelievers were concerned, the amazement they caused was counterbalanced by the apparent weakness and unimpressiveness of him who wrought them, were indeed the power of God in action and the expression of God's own compassion (5:19). For the eye of faith they were an effective manifestation of his divine glory. His exorcisms were a spoiling of Satan's house (3:27), the evidence that Satan had suffered a decisive defeat, though he still remained strong. In his teaching too the kingdom of God was present and active. And finally, his death in all its horror and loneliness was the fulfilment of the divine purpose, to which the Scriptures bore witness (9:12; 14:21); the redemption of "many" (10:45); the etablishment of God's new covenant with men (14:24); and the opening of the way for sinners into the presence of God (15:38).

c. The Lord who is exalted. The whole gospel is written from the point of view of faith in the living and exalted Lord. There can be no doubt that the faith which the writer of the longer ending (*see* § 10 *below*) expressed so magnificently—"So then the Lord Jesus, after he had spoken to them, was taken up into heaven, and sat down at the right hand of God" (16:19)—was shared by Mark. The very fact of his having put pen to paper to write an altogether new and special sort of book, which was not a mere memoir or biography or history but a "gospel," points to such a faith.

Direct references to the "Lord who is exalted" are naturally not to be expected in any number in the gospel, since it is concerned with the historical life of Jesus, though there are such passages as the account of the angel's message at the empty tomb (16:1-8), the reference to the Son of man's "sitting at the right hand of Power" (14:62), and—more direct, if they are, as seems probable, Mark's own comments made from his viewpoint—the words: "But that you may know that the Son of man has authority on earth to forgive sins" (2:10) and the statement: "So the Son of man is lord even of the sabbath" (2:28). But it is not necessary to search for special references. The whole gospel implies the existence of a church living by faith in a risen and exalted Lord, whose presence it joyfully greeted in its celebrations of his Supper and whose power to save it experienced daily in the midst of trials and persecutions.

d. The Lord who is coming. The Lord to whom the gospel bears witness is also the Lord who is to come. From beginning to end it breathes the hope of his coming. The sayings of Jesus contrast the present hiddenness and apparent weakness of the kingdom of God with its future manifestation. God's kingly rule had indeed come near to men in his person and works and words; but it was veiled, something which could be recognized only by faith, a μυστήριον (4:11). Now in its apparent weakness and insignificance it was like the mustard seed, "which, when sown upon the ground, is the smallest of all the seeds on earth" (4:31); but, as the tiny mustard seed, proverbial among the Jews for its smallness (Matt. 17:20), becomes a great shrub "and puts forth large branches" (4:32), so the kingdom of God will one day be made manifest in its real splendor. The parable of the lamp (4:21) has a similar point. One does not carry a lighted lamp into a house merely in order to conceal it. If one brings it in, it is because one intends to put it on the lampstand. And God has not sent his Son into the world merely in order to hide him. For a while he is indeed hidden (cf. 4:22), but God's ultimate intention is that he should be manifest to all. The point of the parable contained in 4:26-29 is similar. It is another parable of contrast. As sowing is followed in due course by the joy of harvest, so the present obscurity of the kingdom of God will be followed by the glorious unveiling.

To attempt to explain this contrast between the kingdom's present veiledness and future manifestation by reference to the small beginnings of the church in the lifetime of Jesus, on the one hand, and, on the other hand, its later world-wide expansion, would be to ignore not only the ambiguousness and questionableness which mark the church's life in history but also the evidence of other material in the gospel. The contrast intended is rather between the veiledness of the kingdom in the ministry of Jesus (and in the witness of his church throughout history), on the one hand, and the glorious manifestation of the kingdom at the PAROUSIA, on the other.

The subject of NT eschatology is beset with difficulties. So it will be well, before indicating briefly the witness of Mark's gospel to the coming Lord, to say something about these difficulties and about the various solutions which have been suggested. The main problem is that which is posed by the NT insistence on the nearness of the Parousia and the fact that many centuries have passed and the Parousia has not yet occurred.

One suggested solution of this problem, which has had considerable popularity, is that the early church misunderstood the teaching of Jesus at this point.

Jesus never envisaged a second coming at all. Insofar as sayings of an apocalyptic nature with a future reference are allowed to be authentic, they are explained as symbolic: the future tenses are "an accommodation of language" and signify, not a future event, but "the timeless fact." But the teaching of Jesus has, according to this view, been subjected to reinterpretation along the lines of the apocalyptic interests of the early church. Such is the solution of thoroughgoing "realized eschatology" (*see* ESCHATOLOGY OF THE NT). It has the effect of transferring from Jesus to the early church the responsibility both for an unfulfilled prediction and for the idea of a second coming so uncongenial to those who are consciously or unconsciously under the influence of Platonism.

A less extreme form of this "mistake of the early church" solution is that which allows that Jesus did envisage a future coming of the Son of man but ascribes to the early church the emphasis on its imminence and the apocalyptic color with which it is depicted.

Another suggested solution, which is also widely supported, is that Jesus himself was mistaken. He expected the final manifestation of the kingdom of God to take place in the immediate future, and his expectation was not fulfilled.

Before indicating the other possible solution, which seems the most probable, it is necessary to refer to the special difficulties connected with ch. 13. Since the publication of T. Colani's *Jésus-Christ et les Croyances Messianiques de son Temps* in 1864 the theory that ch. 13 contains a Jewish Christian apocalypse (the "Little Apocalypse" theory) has been very widely held—though there has been much disagreement as to what exactly the alleged apocalypse contained. This theory has suffered damaging criticism from different directions; but even the scholars who reject or drastically modify the theory tend to agree with its supporters in thinking that the chapter as it stands gives a false picture of the eschatological teaching of Jesus. Apart from a general dislike of anything savoring of apocalyptic, three main objections have been brought against the authenticity of 13:5-37: (*a*) it is asserted that the passage is not self-consistent, that the idea of a sudden Parousia cannot be reconciled with that of a Parousia heralded by signs; (*b*) it is asserted that the passage is inconsistent with the teaching of Jesus given elsewhere in the gospels, the idea of a Parousia heralded by signs being incompatible with such a passage as Luke 17:22-37; (*c*) it is asserted that 13:5-37 is incongruous with its immediate context, since it makes Jesus reply to a question about the date of the destruction of the temple by talking about the end of the world.

But these objections are not so conclusive as at first sight they seem. To *a* and *b* it may be replied that, while vss. 5-31 make use of the language of apocalyptic, they differ widely from typical apocalyptic in form. Whereas it is characteristic of Jewish apocalyptic that the seer either is himself addressed or else relates in the first person what he has seen and heard, this discourse is characterized by the use of the second person plural imperative. It is therefore not to be taken for granted that the purpose of the signs is to enable the disciples (or the reader) to predict the date of the Parousia (as one would expect if this passage were typical apocalyptic); and, if this is not their purpose, then the listing of them is not necessarily incompatible with the idea of a sudden and unexpected Parousia (*see further below* on the signs). In answer to *c* it may be pointed out that the idea of the replacement of the old temple by a new was already an element of Jewish eschatological expectation (e.g., Enoch 90:28-29). So it would be natural for the disciples to connect Jesus' prediction in 13:2 with the end of the world, and Matt. 24:3 may well be a correct gloss of Mark 13:4.

While it is likely that the discourse (13:5-37) is composite (i.e., that it was not all spoken as a continuous discourse, but that sayings on the same theme have been brought together in what seemed a suitable context), there seems to be no sufficient reason for maintaining that it misrepresents the eschatological teaching of Jesus.

It is now possible to indicate briefly what seems the most likely solution to the problem of the NT insistence on the nearness of the Parousia, and at the same time to sum up what seems to be the significance of Mark's witness to the coming Lord. Jesus apparently did assert the imminence of his parousia, but probably neither he nor the NT writers meant by this that it must necessarily occur within a few years or months (passages such as Matt. 10:23; Mark 9:1; 13:30; I Cor. 15:51; I Thess. 4:15-17, which at first sight seem to imply this, are patient of other interpretations), though it was only natural that some elements in the early church should have misunderstood what was meant in this way (see, e.g., II Pet. 3:3-9). In one sense the interval between the Ascension and the Parousia might be long or short; but there was a more important sense in which it could only be described as short; for this whole period is the "last days"—the epilogue, so to speak, of history—since it comes after the decisive event of the life, death, resurrection, and ascension of Christ. Indeed, the Incarnation-Crucifixion-Resurrection-Ascension, on the one hand, and the Parousia, on the other, are essentially but one event, one saving act of God; and the interval between them is the time of God's patience, during which the final manifestation of the kingdom of God is held back in order to give men opportunity for repentance and faith. So Mark witnesses to the nearness of the Lord's coming (13:29). It will be sudden and unexpected (13:33, 35); not even the Son of God himself in his earthly life knows when it will be (13:32). Because they do not know when their Lord will come, the disciples must be always prepared for him, always engaged in those tasks with which he has charged them (13:33-37). But his coming, though it will be unexpected, is nevertheless heralded by signs (13:5-23). Faith is to see in the events of history reminders and pledges of his coming and of its nearness. The signs are listed in 13:5-23, not in order that disciples may be able to predict the date of the Parousia, but in order that, recognizing the signs as they occur, they may have their attention, which is so easily distracted, directed back again and again to its proper object, their coming Lord.

10. Problem of the ending. Mark 16:9-20, though found in the majority of Greek MSS, is omitted by ℵ B k sy [s] and by some MSS of the Georgian, Ethiopic, and Armenian versions. Both Eusebius and

Jerome regarded these verses as unauthentic in view of their absence from almost all the Greek MSS known to them. The OL MS k gives in their place a shorter ending, while L and a few other Greek MSS and also some Coptic and Ethiopic MSS give both this shorter ending and 16:9-20 as alternatives. One tenth-century Armenian MS, which has 16:9-20, attributes it to "the presbyter Ariston" (probably meaning the Aristion whom Papias mentions). There is a possible echo of 16:20 in Just. Apol. I.45, but the earliest definite testimony to these verses as a part of Mark is Iren. Her. III.10.6. Probably they were added sometime before the middle of the second century, in order to fill what was an obvious gap. The clumsiness of the connection, however, shows that they were not written for the purpose. Apparently they were originally compiled as a catechetical summary and may have been in existence for a considerable period before being attached to Mark. The lengthy gloss (often referred to as the "Freer Logion"), which is read by W at the end of vs. 14, was apparently known to Jerome, since he quotes the first part of it as found in some MSS; it was probably added at the end of the second or the beginning of the third century, apparently in order to soften the rebuke of the apostles in that verse.

To the question why the gospel as written by Mark ends with 16:8, there seem to be four possible answers: (*a*) that it was never finished, because Mark was prevented in one way or another from finishing it; (*b*) that the conclusion was lost or destroyed by some mischance; (*c*) that the conclusion was deliberately suppressed; (*d*) that 16:8 was intended to be the end of the gospel. Of these *c* is unlikely; and *b* is not very likely, since it involves assuming both that Mark was unavailable to rewrite the conclusion and also that the gospel had not been in use long enough for someone else to be able to restore the conclusion from memory. Since the fact of resurrection appearances was clearly an element of the primitive preaching (cf. I Cor. 15:5-7; and also Acts 1:22; 2:32; 3:15; 10:41; 13:31), *d*, though it has received a good deal of support, should surely be rejected. It is extremely improbable that Mark intended to conclude his gospel without recording at least one resurrection appearance. The most probable answer to the question is *a*.

11. Style. The style of the gospel is unpretentious and close to the everyday speech of the time. While it lacks the refinements of literary Greek, it has the merits of simplicity and directness. The Semitic flavor is unmistakable. But the Greek of the gospel, though it reflects strongly the influence of Aramaic and though it is certainly rough and colloquial, is not incompetent; that Mark had a reasonable grasp of the language is indicated by his careful use of the tenses.

The vividness and dramatic power which are so characteristic of the gospel should probably be attributed to Mark's sources rather than to Mark himself. *See* § 8*b above*.

12. Canonicity. Mark is contained in all the ancient versions of the NT and is mentioned in all the early lists of the canon. No evidence is extant of any doubt about its authority having been expressed in the early church.

13. Text. From the point of view of textual criticism Mark is specially interesting, because as a result of the comparative neglect which it suffered in the early church it quite often happens that a MS has a more primitive type of text in Mark than it has in the other gospels (so, for instance, the Codex Washingtonianus I [W], the Codex Sangallensis [Δ], and the Codex Koridethianus [Θ]).

The following are examples of the more interesting textual problems in this gospel:

1:1: Should υἱοῦ θεοῦ be read or omitted? Probably it should be read, for the attestation is very strong. Furthermore, the phrase could easily have been omitted by homoeoteleuton. "Son of God" is a theme of the gospel (*see* § 9*a above*), and it is intrinsically likely that it would be found in the first verse; at a time when the divine sonship of Jesus was taken for granted, the phrase could have been omitted on stylistic grounds in order to diminish the ugly series of genitives. The patristic evidence for omission is not very significant, as a Father's omission of words that are not relevant to the point he is making does not prove that they were not in the text which he knew.

1:41: Here the reading ὀργισθείς should probably be accepted in place of σπλαγχνισθείς; for, while an original ὀργισθείς would be likely to be changed to the easier σπλαγχνισθείς, it is difficult to account for the substitution of ὀργισθείς for an original σπλαγχνισθείς; and it is noticeable that neither Matthew nor Luke has reproduced σπλαγχνισθείς here, which would be surprising if it was in Mark as known to them.

6:3: Here the question which has to be decided is whether it is easier to account for an original ὁ τέκτων, ὁ υἱὸς τῆς Μαρίας (let us refer to it as reading A) in Mark being changed by Matthew to ὁ τοῦ τέκτονος υἱός; οὐχ ἡ μήτηρ αὐτοῦ λέγεται Μαριάμ, by Luke to υἱὸς Ἰωσήφ, and by a copyist of Mark to ὁ τοῦ τέκτονος υἱὸς καὶ (τῆς) Μαρίας, or for an original ὁ τοῦ τέκτονος υἱὸς καὶ (τῆς) Μαρίας (reading B) in Mark being reproduced by Matthew as ὁ τοῦ τέκτονος υἱός; οὐχ ἡ μήτηρ αὐτοῦ λέγεται Μαριάμ changed by Luke to υἱὸς . . . Ἰωσήφ, and by a copyist of Mark to ὁ τέκτων, ὁ υἱὸς τῆς Μαρίας. If reading A was original, then the alterations in Matthew and Luke may be explained as due to a feeling that the idea of Jesus' being a carpenter would offend Gentile readers and/or a feeling that ὁ υἱὸς τῆς Μαρίας was derogatory—tantamount to a charge of illegitimacy; and the other reading in Mark can be explained as assimilation to Matthew. On the other hand, if reading B was original in Mark, while the Matthew and Luke texts give no difficulty, it is not easy to explain the alteration in Mark. The suggestion that it was made in the interests of the doctrine of the Virgin Birth is unsatisfactory; for both Matthew and Luke are content that the people of Nazareth should call Jesus the son of the carpenter (of Joseph), though it is in their gospels that the doctrine is clearly expressed. Moreover, Jesus would in any case be the legal son of Joseph (cf. Luke 3:23—ὡς ἐνομίζετο), so that for the people to refer to Jesus as the son of the carpenter Joseph would not be in any way incompatible with the truth of the Virgin Birth. The conclusion to be drawn would seem to be that the reading A is original, and that Origen's denial (in reply to Celsus) that Jesus is anywhere described in the gospels current in the churches as an artisan was due either to a lapse of memory, or, more probably, to his knowing a Markan text already assimilated to Matthew.

8:38: Here W k* sah Tert(?) omit λόγους, and this reading has been preferred by a number of scholars. The meaning of τοὺς ἐμούς would be "my disciples." The fact that D it (some MSS) sy[c] Orig omit λόγους in the Luke parallel supports the omission in Mark. The support for omitting λόγους is small in quantity but impressive in quality, and warrants the recognition that there is a real possibility that λόγους is not original; but in view of the ease with which it could have been omitted accidentally by homoeoteleuton, we should hardly be justified in omitting it, supported as it is by the overwhelming majority of authorities.

14:62: Θ fam.13 *pc* geo arm Orig attest σὺ εἶπας ὅτι ἐγώ εἰμι. This reading would account for Matt. 26:64; Luke 22:70, while it is not near enough to them to be easily explicable as assimilation. It is, moreover, intrinsically quite probable, being consistent with the attitude of Jesus to the messianic title (cf. his immediate substitution of "Son of man" in this same verse); for according to this reading his reply, though affirmative, is more reserved than the direct ἐγώ εἰμι of the majority of MSS. It indicates that while Jesus knows himself to be the Messiah, he has different ideas from those of the high priest about the meaning of messiahship. If, on the other hand, the direct ἐγώ εἰμι is read, we have a clear affirmative reply, the explanation of which would presumably be that now at last, when he is in the power of his enemies and the claim can only seem altogether paradoxical, it is consistent with his mission to declare openly what previously it was necessary to veil. Here the balance of probability would seem to be in favor of the reading of Θ, etc.

Bibliography. Commentaries: J. Calvin, *Commentary on a Harmony of the Evangelists, Matthew, Mark and Luke* (1555; English trans. reprinted 1949)—still of immense value. H. B. Swete, Macmillan NT Commentary (3rd ed., 1909). A. E. J. Rawlinson, WC (1925). M.-J. Lagrange (4th rev. ed., 1929). J. Schniewind, *NT Deutsch* (1934). A. Schlatter, *Der Evangelist Markus* (1935). E. Lohmeyer, *Kritisch-exegetischer Kommentar über das NT* (1937). V. Taylor, Macmillan NT Commentary (1952)—the fullest English Commentary and indispensable for the serious student. J. Schmid, *Regensburger NT* (4th rev. ed., 1958). C. E. B. Cranfield, Cambridge Greek Testament Commentary (1959).

General studies of Mark: R. H. Lightfoot, *The Gospel Message of St. Mark* (1950). W. L. Knox, *The Sources of the Synoptic Gospels*, vol. I: *St. Mark* (1953). J. M. Robinson, *The Problem of History in Mark* (1957). See also: *Interpretation*, IX (1955), 131-256, which was a special Mark number. F. C. Grant, *The Earliest Gospel* (1943).

On the historical reliability of Mark's sources: V. Taylor, *The Formation of the Gospel Tradition* (1935). W. Manson, *Jesus the Messiah* (1943). C. H. Dodd, *About the Gospels* (1950).

On the Markan framework: K. L. Schmidt, *Der Rahmen der Geschichte Jesu* (1919). C. H. Dodd, "The Framework of the Gospel Narrative," *ET*, XLIII (1932), 396 ff. D. E. Nineham, "The Order of Events in St. Mark's Gospel," *Studies in the Gospels* (1955), pp. 223-39.

On miracles: A. Richardson, *The Miracle Stories of the Gospels* (1941). W. Manson, *Jesus the Messiah* (1943), pp. 33-50. W. A. Whitehouse, *Christian Faith and the Scientific Attitude* (1952), pp. 73-77.

On angels: K. Barth, *Kirchliche Dogmatik*, III/3 (1950), 426-608. C. E. B. Cranfield in *Scottish Journal of Theology*, V, 284-88.

On Satan and the demons: K. Barth, *Kirchliche Dogmatik*, III/3 (1950), 327-425, 608-23.

On "demythologizing": H. W. Bartsch, ed., *Kerygma and Mythos* (English trans., 1953). K. Barth, *Rudolf Bultmann: Ein Versuch, ihn zu verstehen* (1952).

On Jesus' self-designation "Son of man": T. Preiss, *Le Fils de l'Homme* (1951), is especially valuable.

On "Son of God": W. Manson, *Jesus the Messiah* (1943), pp. 103-9. J. Bieneck, *Sohn Gottes als Christusbezeichnung der Synoptiker* (1951).

On the hiddenness of the Messiah: C. E. B. Cranfield in *Scottish Journal of Theology*, V, 61-64.

On Mark 13: G. R. Beasley-Murray, *Jesus and the Future* (1954); *A Commentary on Mark Thirteen* (1957). C. E. B. Cranfield, "St. Mark 13," *Scottish Journal of Theology*, VI, 189-96, 287-303; VII, 284-303.

For a full discussion of the vocabulary, syntax, style, and Semitic background, reference should be made to V. Taylor, Macmillan NT Commentary (1952), pp. 44-66; and on the text see pp. 33-43, and the literature cited there.

C. E. B. CRANFIELD

MARK, JOHN jŏn märk [Μᾶρκος; Lat. *Marcus*, a large hammer; Ἰωάν[ν]ης, *from* יוחנן, יהוחנן, Y is gracious]. Son of Mary of Jerusalem (Acts 12:12); a companion of early Christian missionaries; and the probable author of our Second Gospel.

Around Peter and Paul were many secondary figures whose names appear now and then in the fragmentary literary records of the early days of Christianity. One such was called John or Mark—John was his Jewish and Mark his Roman name (Acts 12:12, 25; 15:37)—in keeping with the custom of Hellenistic Jews of this time (cf. Saul-Paul; Joseph-Justus [Acts 1:23]).

When we first meet John Mark, he is living in Jerusalem, apparently in the home of his mother, Mary (Acts 12:12, 25; *see* MARY 6). She appears to have been a widow of some means, inasmuch as she is described in Acts as the owner of a house spacious enough to accommodate a large Christian gathering and as having the services of a maid (Acts 12:12 ff). It has been suggested that the Last Supper was held in her home and that John as a boy may have witnessed some of the final events of Jesus' life. It is further conjectured that the young man who fled away naked in the Garden of Gethsemane (Mark 14:51-52) was John, that he was serving as caretaker of the family garden, and that at the time of the arrest of Jesus he had been sleeping there in the watchtower. This would explain the young man's state of dishabille.

Such conjectures are attractive but unprovable. Against them are the facts that the Upper Room is said to have belonged to a male "householder" (Mark 14:14-15), that John Mark (if he was the evangelist) seems to have possessed little detailed personal knowledge of the closing events of Jesus' life, and that Papias cites a tradition to the effect that Mark "had neither heard the Lord nor been his personal follower" (Euseb. Hist. III.39.15).

John comes clearly before us in Acts 12–15, where he is said to have journeyed to Antioch with Barnabas, his cousin (Col. 4:10), and Saul (Paul). He was taken by these men on the so-called first missionary journey as an assistant (ὑπηρέτης; Acts 13:5). The nature of his duties has been much debated. Was he to make travel arrangements, care for food and lodging, handle requests for interviews with Paul and Barnabas, assist with baptisms, and the like? Or was he a catechist, whose responsibilities were primarily instructional? "Assistant" (ὑπηρέτης) in Luke 4:20

(RSV "attendant") means the *hazzan,* the caretaker and instructor in the synagogue school, and in Luke 1:2 it signifies persons who handed down the gospel tradition. In the papyri the word frequently means a person who handles documents and delivers their contents to others. It is likely that John was a teacher as well as a travel secretary.

For some unknown reason John forsook Paul and Barnabas at Perga in Pamphylia (Acts 13:13) and returned to Jerusalem. Perhaps he was irritated at Paul's wresting of leadership in the missionary venture from his cousin Barnabas. Whatever the cause, it was sufficiently serious in Paul's eyes to lead to his refusal to take John on the second journey and to warrant a break with Barnabas (Acts 15:36-40). The cousins went back to Cyprus, and Paul took Silas into Cilicia and Galatia.

Nothing more is heard of Mark until near the end of Paul's ministry. In Col. 4:10; Philem. 24, Paul refers to him in such a way as to indicate that a reconciliation has taken place. Mark is with him (in Rome or in Ephesus) as a fellow worker (συνεργός), and apparently Mark plans to visit the Colossians soon. In II Tim. 4:11, Paul is represented as instructing Timothy to bring Mark (from Asia Minor?), "for he is very useful in serving me." Whether Mark returned to Paul is not said. The evidence is clear that the young man finally had made good in the eyes of the venerable missionary.

In I Pet. 5:13, Mark is referred to as Peter's "son," who joins the church in Rome ("Babylon" here is a sobriquet for Rome) in sending greetings to the readers. Whether I Peter in some sense was written by Peter or is a pseudepigraph, the phrase "my son" offers evidence of close attachment between Peter and Mark (such as may be assumed from Acts 12:12-17), and makes probable the alleged association of the two in Rome (probably after the death of Paul). That Mark during this period could be associated with both Paul and Peter indicates the extent to which old chasms had been bridged.

Papias of Hierapolis, according to Eusebius (Hist. III.39.15), quotes a tradition to the effect that Mark was Peter's "interpreter" and that he wrote down what he remembered from Peter's preaching concerning the "things said or done by the Lord." That the record referred to is our Gospel of Mark can scarcely be doubted, though it is not absolutely certain that the Mark mentioned is John of Jerusalem. Furthermore, our gospel is certainly not derived simply from Peter's preaching. *See* MARK, GOSPEL OF.

Many traditions connect Mark with the founding of Alexandrian Christianity. According to Hippolytus (*Refutation of All Heresies* VII.30), he was "stump-fingered." The Paschal Chronicle claims that he suffered a martyr's death.

Bibliography. H. B. Swete, *The Gospel According to St. Mark* (1898), pp. ix-xxiii; E. D. Jones, "Was Mark the Gardener of Gethsemane?" *ET,* XXXIII (1921-22), 403-4; B. T. Holmes, "Luke's Description of John Mark," *JBL,* LIV (1935), 63-72; F. C. Grant, *The Earliest Gospel* (1943), pp. 34-57; V. Taylor, *The Gospel According to St. Mark* (1952), pp. 27-31; H. Rolston, *Personalities Around Paul* (1954), pp. 43-47. E. P. BLAIR

MARKET PLACE [רחב (Ps. 55:11; KJV STREETS); ἀγορά]. The usage in Ps. 55:11 is metaphorical. In the NT we must distinguish between the market places referred to in the gospels and those mentioned in Acts. The market places in the gospels were all Jewish-Palestinian—i.e., they were streets of shops something like the "bazaars" of modern oriental towns. Here children sat and called to their playmates (Matt. 11:16; Luke 7:32); here the sick were laid and Jesus healed them (Mark 6:56), and men stood idle (Matt. 20:3), and scribes in long robes were saluted (Mark 12:38 and parallels). The Pharises also loved salutations in the market places (Luke 11:43); and, having left a market place, they "purified themselves" before they ate (Mark 7:4).

In Acts, however, the two market places mentioned are in Greek cities—Philippi (16:19) and Athens (17:17).* These were the centers of public life, being open places full of statues and colonnades, and surrounded by numerous temples and other public buildings. It was to the "market place" (Lake-Cadbury "courthouse") in Philippi that Paul and Silas were dragged to appear before magistrates. And in the market place of Athens, Paul disputed with "those who chanced to be there." Fig. ATH 114.

B. H. THROCKMORTON, JR.

MARMOTH mär'mŏth. KJV form of MEREMOTH.

MAROTH mâr'ŏth [מרות, bitterness, bitter fountains] (Mic. 1:12). A town in Judah; possibly identical with MAARATH.

*__MARRIAGE.__ The institution of marriage in the Bible reflects a long history of sociological and cultural development, as to some stages of which there can be no absolute certainty. However, the main characteristics of this institution are clear.

The status of the bride (wife) and her personal relations to her husband show the influence of Greco-Roman and Christian conceptions in the later biblical literature. In the background of biblical teaching about marriage is the idea of the marriage of the gods, which is adapted to the faith of Israel. For the literary expression of their views the biblical writers made considerable use of the figure of marriage and its relationships. Marriage was understood to signify also the fulfilment of God's purpose in creation by the spiritual and sexual union of a man and his wife.

1. Forms of marriage
   a. Matriarchal marriage
   b. Patriarchal marriage
   c. Polygamy
   d. Monogamy
   e. Exogamy
   f. Endogamy
   g. Levirate marriage
2. The marriage transaction
   a. The initiation of the marriage transaction
   b. Marriage by capture
   c. Marriage by purchase
   d. Marriage by covenant
   e. The betrothal
   f. Circumcision
   g. The marriage ceremony
3. The figurative use of marriage
4. The theological use of marriage

5. The function and purpose of marriage
Bibliography

1. Forms of marriage. Scholars have identified many patterns or forms of marriage in the Bible. Assuming as an essential hypothesis the continuity of Israel's social culture with that of the ancient Near Eastern world, they have found verification of this assumption in the biblical documents. The pertinent passages from the Bible are readily compiled. Their bearing upon specific forms of marriage must be determined with caution. For full presentation of the various arguments, *see bibliography*.

a. Matriarchal marriage. This type of marriage assumes the authority of the mother but is also used to identify the way relationship is determined. So-called "sadiqa" marriage is of two types, the "beena" and the "mota." The term "beena" marriage is sometimes used when the children remain under the mother's control and the husband settles in his wife's home more or less permanently. In "mota" marriage the visits are periodic. "Matrilinear" signifies that descent is reckoned from the mother, and "metronymic" suggests that the wife remains with her own kin and is visited there by her husband from time to time. For examples of "beena" marriage the cases of Jacob and Moses are used. Both lived in the homes of their wives (Gen. 29:1-30; Exod. 2:21-22) for a considerable length of time. To illustrate "mota" marriage, Samson's visits to his wife at Timnah have been noted (Judg. 15:1). When Abimelech went to "his mother's kinsmen" (9:1) and visited the "whole clan of his mother's family," they listened to his plea because they realized that he was their brother (vs. 3). The literal meaning of "metronymic," "named after the mother," is evident here.

In further support of the matriarchal idea, references to the wife's possession of her own quarters have been gathered. When Abraham's servant arrived at the city of Nahor, he encountered Rebekah, who "ran and told her mother's household" about the meeting (Gen. 24:28). Leah had her own tent, as did Rachel (31:33). When Sisera fled from the victorious Hebrew troops, he entered the tent of Jael, the wife of Heber the Kenite (Judg. 4:17-18). Naomi urged her two daughters-in-law to return "each of you to her mother's house" (Ruth 1:8). The "mother's house" recurs in Song of S. 3:4. Some or all of these passages may, of course, simply signify that the wife or mother occupied a separate part of the family tent or had her own tent which was a part of a group of family tents concentrated in one place.

Another kind of evidence thought by some to point to matriarchal marriage is the appearance of maternal groups in opposition to one another in the same family. These are composed of children who have the same father but who are divided because they have different mothers. Listed in this category of mother-centered groups in tension is the account of the vengeance taken by the brothers Joab and Abishai upon Abner because he had killed their brother Asahel (II Sam. 3:30). In II Sam. 13:27-29 appears the record of Absalom's anger at his half brother Amnon for the violation of his sister Tamar. We may observe a similar incident in Gen. 34:13. These are hardly proof of survivals of matriarchal marriage, however. They may be referred more properly to blood feuds and the desire for revenge against any who bring injury or dishonor. Again, certain restrictions against marriage have been observed in the Pentateuch. These bar marriage with kin on the mother's side but not on the father's (cf. Gen. 20:12; Num. 26:59). On the other hand, marriage with the sister of the father or of the mother is forbidden (Lev. 18:12-13; 20:19).

The role of the wife in some parts of the Bible may lead to the conclusion that this reflects a survival of matriarchal authority. A wife has the right to give her maid to her husband as his second wife, e.g. (Gen. 16:3; 30:9). Even a secondary wife (Hagar) takes a wife for her son, evidently on her own initiative, without any challenge to her authority to do this (Gen. 21:21). The prevailing form of marriage in the Bible, the patriarchal, was perhaps not so suppressive of woman's rights as is commonly supposed.

In evaluating the various positions held by biblical scholars as to the presence of material which presupposes the matriarchal type of marriage, the student should realize how these positions have been influenced by research outside the biblical field, especially in the fields of anthropology and sociology. Drawn largely from primitive societies, data have been interpreted to fit into a concept of development from a stage of promiscuity, through subsequent stages of group marriage, matriarchy, etc., to monogamy. When this principle is applied to the culture of the Bible, the results are interesting, but unimpressive, partly because of the meagerness and inconclusiveness of the pertinent facts and partly because the Bible is preoccupied with the presentation of theological-religious rather than sociological phenomena. When we reject the necessity of confirming any hypothesis as to the history of marriage in the Bible, the facts at hand as to some kind of matriarchy are far from conclusive.

b. Patriarchal marriage. This relates to the authority of the father and the effect of this authority upon the entire marriage pattern. Descent is reckoned from the father. One notes the impressive proof of this in the genealogical and census lists (Gen. 5 [even though there are references to "other sons and daughters," no daughter is named]; 10; 36:9-42 [wives are named only to distinguish between the sons of the father]; Num. 1:1–3:39; 26:5-62; Ruth 4:18-22; I Chr. 1–9; Ezra 2:3-61; 10:18-43; etc.). The emphasis upon the authority of the father is perhaps suggested in the custom of the father's naming his child. In Hebrew thought the name was the essence of the self. This essence was transmitted by the father to his son. Through his son he could project his very being into the future after he had died and gone to his fathers. So the act of naming was of great importance. While the mother does this in a number of instances (Gen. 4:25; 29:32), we may observe some of the references in which the father assumes this significant function: Gen. 4:26; 5:3, 29; 16:15; 29:34(?); 38:3; Exod. 2:22. Related to this act is the deep and sometimes despairing desire for sons which the Bible describes (*see* FAMILY). This passionate longing for sons rather than daughters reveals the influence of the father concept upon the normal desire for children. For the theological effect of this concept, *see* FATHER; GOD, OT; GOD, NT.

The power a husband may exercise over his wife is also an indication of patriarchal marriage. She has rights and freedom only within the context of this authority, although there are apparent exceptions to this, or developments beyond it, in the later books of the Bible. The husband may even revoke a vow that his wife has made to God, if he sees fit (Num. 30:10-14). Wives are classified with chattel property: both fields and wives, Jeremiah announces, will be seized by the enemy (Jer. 6:12). Paul speaks plainly of the husband's authority: "The head of a woman is her husband" (I Cor. 11:3); and this view is repeated by other writers (Eph. 5:22; cf. Col. 3:18; I Pet. 3:1-2). משל, "rule," "have dominion," is used of man's relation to his wife; evidently her subjection to her husband is regarded as punishment for disobedience in the garden (Gen. 3:16). Other proofs of the subordination of the wife to the husband which characterize a patriarchal society support this concept of authority. Such terms as נתן לאשה, "give to wife" (Gen. 29:28; 34:8, 12; Josh. 15:16-17; Judg. 1:12-13; etc.), and לקח לאשה, "take to wife" (Gen. 4:19; 6:2; 11:29; 12:19; 20:2-3; etc.), show the woman is an object acted upon, rather than the initiator of action. Her father or her husband determines her marriage and her fate.

Again, the meaning of the term בעל, "baal," is both "owner of property" and "husband." The verb may mean "to possess" or "to marry." As a divine name it means "Lord." The meaning "husband" in the context of ownership and control is significant (Gen. 20:3; Exod. 21:22; Deut. 22:22; 24:4; II Sam. 11:26; Esth. 1:17, 20; Prov. 12:4; 31:11, 23, 28; Joel 1:8). The use of forms of the verb supports the idea of male authority in marriage (Gen. 20:3; Deut. 21:13; 22:22; 24:1; Isa. 54:1, 5; 62:4-5; Mal. 2:11). This term signifying father-control has been applied by some authorities to the form of marriage it connotes —i.e., "baal" marriage—over against "beena" marriage (*see* § 1*a above*). In Hebrew marriage, as will be seen below (§ 2*c*), a distinction was made between ownership and control, however. The power of the husband-father must be understood within the total framework of the patriarchal idea as set forth in the Bible.

Within the over-all structure of the patriarchal form of marriage specific elements have been identified. The children are identified with the father, particularly sons; they descend from him. Sociologists call this patrilinear descent. Related to this practice is the custom of naming the child after the father, a custom that is called patronymic. These terms, together with so-called "baal" marriage, serve to single out the principal aspects of patriarchal marriage recorded in the Bible.

c. Polygamy. The term "polygamy" literally means "many marriages." In actual use, it simply signifies more than one marriage alliance existing concurrently in the same family or family group. The term may be applied to either of the two major types of marriage, the matriarchal or the patriarchal. Polygamy was widespread in ancient Israel. It assumed the form of polygyny (marriage with more than one woman) rather than polyandry (marriage with more than one man). The latter has been found as the background of levirate marriage (*see* § 1*g below*). Polygamy is also largely bigamous; social position and economic status usually determine the possession of more than two wives. Social change and the breakdown of the seminomadic way of life, as well as the effect of other cultures, reduced the practice of polygyny (polygamy) and encouraged the more general practice of monogyny.

The practice of polygamy in biblical times was due to several values derived therefrom. Biblical examples will show what these values were. Sarai, Abram's wife, bore him no children. So she gave him Hagar, her Egyptian maid, as a second wife (Gen. 16:3). Jacob worked seven years in order to secure Rachel as his wife, because he loved her (29:18), and he worked seven more years when her sister Leah was foisted upon him (vss. 25, 30). Another barren wife gave her maid to her husband that she might have children by him (30:1-5). Other allusions to polygamous marriage recite the names of sons born to David of the wives and concubines he took from Jerusalem (II Sam. 5:13-16); the alliances of Solomon with foreign princesses ("He had seven hundred wives, princesses, and three hundred concubines"; I Kings 11:1, 3); the size of Rehoboam's household (II Chr. 11:21); and, with considerable embellishment, the passion of David for Bathsheba, which resulted in murder and matrimony (II Sam. 11:15, 27). In Deut. 21:15 the existence of polygamy is assumed. The harems of a Persian ruler are noted in the book of Esther (2:3, 14). The reasons for polygamy, therefore, are love and lust, the desire for children, and diplomacy on the part of the nation's rulers. Undoubtedly the need and the desire for sons was the most prominent factor. In the seminomadic and agricultural periods of Israel's history the possession of several wives made a large working force available to tend the flocks and the fields. The maintenance of the nation's manpower could also have been a consideration in the perpetuation of polygamy.

The desire for sons was paramount in marriage. A wife was regarded as a means of securing this result. If she failed, either polygamy or divorce was demanded. The powerful craving of a man for a son of his own conception made the alternative of ADOPTION unthinkable. The practice of levirate marriage promoted polygamy, for the levir might himself already possess a wife before marrying his deceased brother's widow.

In polygamous marriage, and perhaps in a special way when there are only two wives, the appearance of conflict and dissension is apparent. One wife might be the husband's favorite, and bitter rivalry could ensue, especially if the husband showed a preference for the son of such a wife (II Chr. 11:21-22). The Deuteronomic Code deals with such a situation when it requires the father, in the event his first-born is the son of a "disliked" wife, to acknowledge his first-born "by giving him a double portion of all that he has" (Deut. 21:15-17). It is significant that the common Semitic name for "second wife" is צרה, the root meaning of which is "show hostility toward," "vex" (Ecclus. 26:6; 37:11; I Sam. 1:6).

d. Monogamy. In opposition to the earlier view of the history of human marriage which saw it in an evolutionary pattern ranging from primitive promiscuity to monogamy, many now believe that early man probably had a form of temporary monogamy (*see bibliography*). However this may be, the general practice of monogamy in the biblical records cannot be denied. It is frequently evident in the OT, and it is regularly presupposed in the NT. The creation account in Genesis writes of the first marriage in clearly monogamous terms: "A man . . . cleaves to his wife" (2:24). Many of the Hebrew laws strongly imply this form of marriage (Exod. 20:17; 21:5; Lev. 18:8, 16, 20; 20:10; 21:13; Num. 5:12; Deut. 5:21; 22:22; 24:5; etc.). In its various admonitions regarding the good life, the book of Proverbs is silent on polygamous life (cf. Prov. 12:4; 18:22; 19:13). The skeptic writes that a man should "enjoy life with the wife whom [he] love[s]" (Eccl. 9:9). The extravagant expression of the goodness of life under the God of Israel includes a description of the fruitful wife in the home of the faithful (Ps. 128), while the love poetry of the Song of Songs reports the passionate longing of two lovers for marriage to each other. Faithlessness to the wife of one's youth is condemned in a revealing championship of fidelity in marriage to one woman (Mal. 2:14).

e. Exogamy. Interacting with each other, and sometimes in conflict with each other, are the tendencies toward exogamy and toward endogamy in Hebrew marriage. A marriage can be at one and the same time exogamous and endogamous. It may be exogamous in its demand that marriage take place outside a defined kinship circle; it may also be endogamous in its rejection of marriage with those who are too far outside, such as members of another ethnic group. With respect to exogamous marriage we must ascertain the limits of this kind of marriage. Who may be included and who must be excluded? We discover that Esau married Canaanite women (Gen. 36:2), while Joseph (41:45) and Moses (Exod. 2:21) also married foreign women. An Israelite woman's son, we are told, had a father who was an Egyptian (Lev. 24:10); and the daughter of Sheshan, who had no sons, married an Egyptian slave whose name was Jarha (I Chr. 2:34-35). An understandable development of exogamous marriage attended the occupation of Canaan, as the documents reveal. Gideon married a Canaanite woman (Judg. 8:31), and the Hebrew sons of Elimelech married Moabite girls (Ruth 1:4). And Samson asked his parents to obtain a certain Philistine girl for his wife (Judg. 14:2).

In the postexilic period marriages with foreign women, Canaanite, Hittite, and Ammonite, had taken place (Ezra 9:1-2). These indications of marriage by members of the biblical community with persons outside it reflect in some instances a response to exceptional circumstances, such as residence among foreigners. Other examples of so-called exogamy may be accounted for on the ground of the interpenetration of cultures and peoples during the long process conventionally called the conquest of Canaan. The encounter between the Hebrews and the mixed people living in or near Canaan inevitably resulted in intermarriage. But these examples do not constitute a pattern which was defended and promulgated by the Israelite group. It is evident that to use the term "exogamy" at all in connection with Hebrew marriage, it must be used in a restricted sense, as a means of identifying the outer limits of permissible endogamous marriages. This conclusion is supported by passages already cited. The references to marriages with Hittites and Ammonites, e.g., in Ezra are made in connection with a statement of the drastic action which was taken to annul these marriages.

f. Endogamy. Marriage in biblical society was restricted to members of the group both by custom and by conscious support of custom. Thus it was endogamous in that it excluded marital relations with communities outside Israel. Marriage between members of different clans was not forbidden, however. This means there was exogamy with respect to relations between Israelite clans and endogamy with respect to non-Israelite people. We may therefore say that the Israelite community as a whole was endogamous. This endogamy was supported by both sociological and theological considerations, which biblical writers sometimes enunciate with great vigor. The power of the community was mobilized in its defense. We observe the concern of Abraham to secure a wife for his son from his kindred from whose land he had moved (Gen. 24:4, 10). Similarly, Jacob was commanded not to marry a Canaanite, but to take one of the daughters of Laban his uncle (28:1-2). When their son besought them to arrange a marriage with a Philistine girl for him, the parents of Samson urged him to take an Israelite girl (Judg. 14:3). Tobit married Anna of his own kin group (Tob. 1:9; cf. 4:12; 6:12).

When David took Bathsheba the wife of Uriah the Hittite, he encountered strong opposition (II Sam. 11:3; 12:14). Kings are rebuked for their "expedient" exogamy, which was nonetheless in defiance of the Lord's command (I Kings 11:1-2; 16:31). The books of the Law take up this theme of denunciation and attack marriages outside the community and ardently defend intragroup alliances. Israel is to take heed lest she take the daughters of the Canaanites and related peoples for her sons, thereby creating idolatry (Exod. 34:16). And, as already noted, marriages with the "peoples of the lands" in the postexilic community were abrogated by mass action by the men of Israel. They took an oath to put away their foreign wives and their children (Ezra 10:5; cf. Neh. 10:28-30; 13:23-27). In Neh. 13 the reason for the wholesale purge of foreign wives is pointedly stated—because such marriages were a great evil and treachery against the God of Israel.

Apart from the threat of social and cultural breakdown through intimate association with foreign peoples, the real danger, religious leaders realized, was the deadly threat to Israel's faith. Through intermarriage with these people the integrity of Israel's faith could be undermined and ultimately destroyed. This was the supreme biblical argument for endogamy and against exogamy. In a modified form, because the people of the covenant had become the community of Christ, this is the NT case for in-group marriage and marital relations. Paul prohibits marriage with unbelievers (II Cor. 6:14-15). Of course, if a wife already has an unbeliever as a husband (which must have been the situation in many of the early Christian homes), she is to exhibit patience, reverence, and chastity, in order to win her spouse to her Christian faith (I Pet. 3:1-2).

The terms "endogamy" and "exogamy" are complementary rather than contradictory to each other, as already suggested. The former determines that marriage must occur within the group. As far as the OT is concerned, this group is Israel. When endogamy is applied in a more limited sense—to a clan or family, e.g.—how close can be the relationship of the partners to a marriage? An opposing, exogamous force becomes operative in determining this question. For purposes of marriage a man must go outside a specified series of kinship classifications. Women who fall within these classifications may not be taken in marriage. On the precise nature of these prohibitions, *see* INCEST.

g. Levirate marriage. The term "levirate" comes from the word "levir" meaning "a husband's brother." This term is applied to that form of marriage which is defined in the book of Deuteronomy (25:5-10). It may also be applied to marriages which involve a deceased husband's brother and his widow, without necessarily conforming at every point to the Deuteronomic legislation (*see* LEVIRATE LAW). The purpose of the law is clear—to prevent marriage of the Israelite girl to an outsider and to continue the name of the dead husband in Israel. This purpose underscores the value of endogamous marriage (*see* § 1*f above*) and the importance of sons. One example of the levirate form of marriage is contained in the story of Judah and Tamar (Gen. 38). Judah took a wife for his first-born son, Er. Upon the latter's untimely death, Judah instructed a brother of Er, Onan, to "perform the duty of a brother-in-law to her, and raise up offspring" for Er (vs. 8). When Onan understood that the children of his union with Tamar would not be his, but his dead brother's, he avoided making her pregnant (vs. 9). When still another brother was not given to her in marriage (vs. 14), she by subterfuge caused her father-in-law to have intercourse with her. The effort of both Judah and Tamar to raise up offspring for her late husband reveals a strong interest in the levirate principle, even though it is hardly a typical instance of this kind of marriage.

The book of Ruth is another notable illustration of this form of marriage. Although at certain points it differs from the form envisioned in Deut. 25, it recites in some detail the efforts of a Hebrew woman to secure a second husband for her widowed daughter-in-law. It will be noted that the appearance in this story of the matter of INHERITANCE (4:10) is one point of differentiation from the law in Deuteronomy. It differs also in that the two men who are confronted by the opportunity to marry Ruth and to redeem Elimelech's property are clearly not brothers of Ruth's deceased husband. Thus the term "levirate" in the strict sense of the word does not apply. The act of Boaz in the book of Ruth extends the levirate custom to other male relatives of the deceased in the event no brothers survive. Such an adjustment of the custom may also be seen in ancient Hittite law.

In Ruth the Hebrew word translated "do the part of next of kin" is from the root גאל, from which comes the word *goel,* "redeemer." In Gen. 38:8; Deut. 25:5, 7, the word is from the root יבם. Derivatives from this root have the meaning "husband's brother" in the first instance and "sister-in-law" in the second. In Matt. 22:24 the Greek text has the word ἀνίστημι, "to raise up, cause to be born." Here it is used in connection with the argument about marriage in the resurrection. One after the other, each of seven brothers married the same woman, none having any sons.

These allusions to levirate marriage raise several questions: Was the levirate widely practiced? Does the legislation in Deuteronomy indicate that it was endorsed by law? Does the levirate mean that both the widow and her husband's property became the possession of her brother-in-law—i.e., that it deals primarily with inheritance rather than with marriage? How can the differences noted above be explained? As to the first question, there is evidence that levirate marriage extended beyond the borders of Israel. It was certainly known to the Assyrians and the Hittites, and to the Canaanites as well. The extent to which it was in effect in Israel is uncertain, but the so-called levirate law in Deut. 25 indicates its practice and possibly its partial abandonment, the law being published in order to reaffirm it. Conceivably, the custom needed to be urged in this way because of the change in social patterns brought about by the increasing urbanization and commercialization of Israel's life. This affected marriage customs as well as other social institutions that had been based upon a patriarchal organization of life. A late priestly document indicates strong opposition to, or complete unawareness of, the levirate concept. Sexual relations (marriage) with one's brother's wife are forbidden (Lev. 18:16; 20:21). These prohibitions may, of course, be interpreted to mean that they are in effect only while the brother is alive. Yet the language is emphatic and unqualified.

It is unlikely that the Hebrew view of marriage would permit the levirate to develop as a simple matter of inheritance in the event of the death of a childless brother whose widow survived him. If a distinction may be made between casuistic and apodictic laws in the OT, as has been proposed, then it is conceivable that the passage in Deut. 25 has a Canaanite origin and content. This is based on the hypothesis that casuistic laws were taken over from the Canaanites, whereas the apodictic are Israelite in origin. If the Canaanite origin of the levirate law in Deuteronomy is upheld, it was obviously adapted to Israelite life and thought. In Hebrew law levirate marriage became entirely different from a provision for the inheritance of property. The emphasis in the book of Ruth upon redemption of the brother's estate is, by this reasoning, closer to the Canaanite practice than to the Hebrew.

While it may have been originally an inheritance law, its adaptation by the Israelites to their own customs and outlook cannot be doubted. The law in Deuteronomy includes the significant statement, introducing the legislation (or description of custom): "If brothers dwell together," etc. Here the reference is to a definitely Israelite practice and the preservation of a closely knit family. The purpose of this law is to preserve the homogeneity of the family group and the name of its male members in the ongoing life of Israel. Josephus, Jewish historian at the beginning of the Christian era, writes that the purpose of levirate marriage was threefold—to preserve the family name and the family estate and to provide for the welfare of the widow. In biblical thought the first of these is by far the most important (but *see* WIDOW). It assumed a special importance because among the Hebrews it was equivalent to the practice of ADOPTION among other peoples. Some authorities believe that levirate marriage may be traced to polyandrous marriage of the fraternal type, while still others assert that it grew out of ancestor-worship, where the need to provide sons to carry on the requirements of the cult was great. *See bibliography.*

2. The marriage transaction. The arrangement of a marriage, the means of selecting or securing a bride, the character of the marriage contract or agreement, and the marriage ceremony itself leading to the consummation of the union, although debatable at certain points, are rather clearly reflected in the biblical writings. Here again may be detected the continuity of biblical social customs with those of the ancient Near Eastern world. Archaeological research continues to support this generalization.

a. The initiation of the marriage transaction. The father as head of the household usually instituted the plans for marriage on behalf of his son. This included the selection of the bride. On her part, she was a more or less passive participant in the transaction, since her father gave her to be the wife of the man involved. Abraham directed his servant to take a wife for his son from his kindred (Gen. 24:4); Laban gave his daughters to Jacob (29:23, 28); and Hamor negotiated with Jacob to arrange a marriage between his son Shechem and the latter's daughter Dinah (34:8). Caleb promised to give his daughter as wife to the conqueror of Debir (Josh. 15:16; see also Gen. 29:19; 38:14; Exod. 2:21; Judg. 1:12; etc.). The mother took the initiative in arranging a marriage for her son Ishmael (Gen. 21:21). This role of the mother is exceptional, however. The place of the father in arranging marriage is consistent with the concept of the family in the Bible. It does not rule out some activity at this stage on the part of the potential bridegroom and bride. There is some indication of romance. We are told, e.g., that Michal loved David (I Sam. 18:20). At harvest festivals and at the village well the sexes met and mingled freely (Gen. 24:15-20; 29:2-11; Exod. 2:15-19).

b. Marriage by capture. Some anthropologists have used the idea of marriage by capture to account for the transition from matriarchal to patriarchal marriage. In this view, in primitive society daughters were a liability, and female infanticide was general. When this disturbed the balance between the sexes and girls became too scarce to meet the demand for wives, tribes raided one another. Thus the name for "wife" became synonymous with terms meaning a person with a subject or inferior status. Does the Bible contain support for marriage by capture? Supposed survivals of this type of marriage are found by some in the book of Judges (5:30; 14:11; 21:21) and in the Pentateuch (Lev. 18:17; Deut. 21:10-14). But none of these so-called survivals is convincing, and we must agree with the majority of scholars that there is no real evidence for marriage by capture in our sources.

c. Marriage by purchase. מכר, "to sell," in Gen. 31:15, used in connection with Jacob's marriage with Leah and Rachel, evidently refers to marriage by purchase. The two wives say of their father's action in giving them to Jacob: "He has sold us, and he has been using up the money given for us." Another word is used as a substantive in Gen. 34:12; Exod. 22:17—H 22:16; I Sam. 18:25, and as a verb in Ps. 16:4 (where the Hebrew text is uncertain) and in Exod. 22:16—H 22:15. It is translated in the Bible "marriage present," or "give the marriage present" in the case of the verb. The Assyrian equivalent is *m'aru,* "to send," whence *tamirtu,* "gift." However, this root has also been translated "to acquire by paying the purchase price, or bride price." An examination of the context in which this word is used in the passages listed above may be helpful. In the verse from Genesis, Shechem pleads with the father and brothers of Dinah to let him have her as his wife. He wants their favor and is willing to give whatever they say in the form of a marriage present and gift. Evidently to secure their favorable action he will allow them to set the amount of the gift or purchase price. This gift(?) is to be given to the father (and brothers?), but not to the bride. In I Sam. 18:25 the *mohar* ("marriage present") takes the form of the foreskins of one hundred Philistines, to be paid to Saul. This ghastly form of the *mohar* is evidently in lieu of the usual gift, which was waived because David was a poor man (vs. 23). In Exod. 22:16-17 provision is made that a man who seduces an unbetrothed virgin must give the *mohar* for her and make her his wife. Here the *mohar* also goes to the father, not in the payment of damages for seduction, but as a bride gift in the marriage transaction. If the father is unwilling to make this settlement of marriage, the offender must pay a sum of money to him equivalent in amount to the "marriage present for virgins."

The inconclusive results we have obtained from noting the use of the term *mohar* in the Bible require that we go beyond this term to actual or alleged instances of marriage by purchase in the Bible. Seemingly, a poor bridegroom might, instead of paying *mohar,* serve the family of his intended wife. This seems to have been the situation when Jacob served Laban (Gen. 29:20, 28) and possibly when Moses went to live with the priest of Midian (Exod. 2:21). The substitute for *mohar* might also take the form of some special act for the benefit of the bride's father. So a city is taken (Josh. 15:16-17; cf. Judg. 1:12); a giant is slain (I Sam. 17:25); one hundred of the enemy are killed and mutilated (I Sam. 18:25-27; cf. II Sam. 3:14). In return for such deeds as these the hero received a wife without, presumably, the payment of *mohar* as such. In Deut. 22:29 = Exod. 22:16-17, there occurs the specific amount of the *mohar* which is to be paid—fifty shekels of silver. In Ruth 4:5, *mohar* as purchase price may be indirectly alluded to: "You are . . . buying Ruth."

An ancient mythological poem from the Ras Shamra Tablets contains several words relating to the marriage contract (*see bibliography*). One of these is *mohar*. As there used, the word denotes some kind of payment by the bridegroom to the girl's father before marriage: "And thou wilt *mhr* her from her father for a thousand (shekels) of silver, and ten thousand of gold." This poem also uses *tlh*, which is equivalent to the Hebrew word שלוחים and is translated "parting gift" (of/to the bride). The Hebrew term occurs in Exod. 18:2; I Kings 9:16 (it is used figuratively in Mic. 1:14 also). In the first case, it refers simply to the departure of Zipporah, but in I Kings the reference is to a king's parting gift—i.e., dowry—to his daughter. The problem of the meaning of the "parting gift" or the *mhr* is complicated by the fact that gifts not described by either of these terms are also given. Abraham's servant took "all sorts of choice gifts" (Gen. 24:10), including a gold ring and two bracelets (vs. 22), which he put on the bride-to-be (vs. 47), and other jewelry and clothing, some of which was given to Rebekah's mother and brother (vs. 53). Achsah asked and received from her father, evidently as a marriage gift, choice land sites containing springs of water (Judg. 1:15). Again, these occurrences of gifts in relation to marriage pose the question of their use either as payment for value received or as noncommercial gifts. It is evident that gifts may have no connection with purchase and can be simply indications of friendship or good will. Or they may subtly suggest that the bridegroom is able to keep a wife.

Too many difficulties stand in the way of the idea of purchase marriage to justify its unqualified acceptance. It is impossible to identify any out-and-out commercial transaction where something of value is given and something of value is received. The bride is more than a commodity to be bartered. The penetrating insight of the author of Gen. 24 and the delicacy of his portrayal of human relations in the oriental community, as he recites the negotiation of a marriage transaction, supports this. Certainly Rebekah is not chattel to be bought in the market. The conception of the status of a wife found in Prov. 31 further supports the view that marriage by purchase is an untenable interpretation.

d. Marriage by covenant. In the Bible marriage is regarded as a covenant entered into by two families who thereby form an alliance through their representatives, the bridegroom and the bride. So marriage is both personal and communal. Our justification for using the word "covenant" derives in part from the use by biblical writers of the figure of marriage to describe the covenant relation between Yahweh and Israel (*see* § 5*c below*). and in part from the place of the covenant in social contracts of the biblical community. In the context of the covenant idea the special terms that have been presented above may be understood in their proper perspective. Two biblical books use the word "covenant" in relation to marriage (Prov. 2:17; Mal. 2:14). The establishment of a covenant between two parties, and in relations between members of Near Eastern communities generally, was not a simple process. The use of gifts was an important element. The gift was an object of value which was tendered for a number of reasons. One of these was to establish the prestige and social standing of the giver. This was doubtless one purpose of the bride gift or bride price, the *mhr* (cf. מתן; Gen. 34:12; Num. 18:11). Another was the expectation of a return which would reflect in some manner the value of that which was given. A third purpose—and this is peculiar to the biblical idea of possessions—was the transfer to the recipient of a part of the life of the giver. An object which a biblical man possessed was not detached from his self and his life; it was a genuine part of the self. It may have been, and often was, symbolized by a covenant of blood (*see* BLOOD; COVENANT), in which some kind of exchange and compensation are involved. The gift of *mhr* seals the covenant between two families, establishes the prestige of the husband and his family, and gives him authority, although not absolute control, over his wife. In this sense of compensation and ratification of a covenant, a kind of purchase may be understood. But we have in this view of the marriage transaction something more than a *quid pro quo*—what is added is drawn from the purpose of the gift and the personal and social nature of the covenant of marriage.

e. The betrothal. The word translated "betroth," ארש, in cognate languages, such as Arabic, has the root meaning "a fine," "pay the price," and so gain the right of possession, or "tribute" in Assyrian. We may note first its appearance in Exodus (22:16—H 22:15). In Deut. 20:7 a distinction is made between betrothing a wife and taking her. Another use of the word "betroth" appears in Deut. 22:23-24, where a man who performs the sexual act with a betrothed virgin is stoned to death because "he violated his neighbor's wife." In the same chapter (vs. 28) intercourse with a virgin who is not betrothed involves, not death, but marriage to the girl and payment of a fine to her father. Betrothing a wife appears to be equivalent to marrying her (Deut. 28:30; II Sam. 3:14). In Hos. 2:19-20—H 2:21-22 the word is used figuratively to affirm the meaning of the true covenant relation between God and his people Israel. The emphasis is upon faithfulness and permanence. Matt. 1:18; Luke 1:27; 2:5 contain the Greek term μνηστεύω, "woo and win," "betroth."

In at least one of these citations betrothal legally constitutes an actual marital relationship, as already noted. The account of the encounter between Lot and the men of Sodom (Gen. 19:14) assumes that the men who were to marry his daughters were already his sons-in-law. Samson's betrothed is also called his wife (Judg. 14:15; 15:1). The language of Matt. 1:18, 20, 24-25, shows that in being betrothed to Joseph, Mary was actually his wife, even though he did not know her sexually until after the birth of Jesus. This equivalence of betrothal and marriage is in harmony with the OT teaching on the subject. *See* VIRGIN BIRTH.

f. Circumcision. While the timing of the several elements of the marriage arrangements is not clear, the betrothal was probably sealed after the payment of the *mohar* and the exchange of other gifts. This did not complete the transaction, however, for the preparation included other factors, one of which was the performance of circumcision upon the bridegroom in anticipation of his sexual use of his wife. Of special interest is the Hebrew word for "bridegroom," חתן, which may also be translated "daughter's husband." From the same root the word for "wife's father" is derived: "one who circumcises." In the "Hymn to Nikkal, etc.," ancient Canaanite poem, the same word appears, in the sense of "son-in-law," and is used in relation to the rite of circumcision at marriage, showing that this practice existed in Palestine-Syria as early as 1500 B.C. *See* CIRCUMCISION.

g. The marriage ceremony. The completion of plans for the wedding was not climaxed by the execution of a written contract prior to the actual marriage ceremony itself, as far as available evidence from the Bible is concerned. In Aramaic papyri from the fifth century, however, there is a record of such a contract between Hebrews and the Egyptians whom they married (*see bibliography*). Further, in the apocryphal book of Tobit (7:14) we read of an "instrument of cohabitation" (RSV "contract") which a father wrote for his daughter and her groom, evidently as a private document. In any case, a covenant agreement, whether written or not, is presupposed as the basis for the actual ceremonies which culminated in a man's physical possession of his wife. For the wedding special attire was worn (Song of Songs; Isa. 61:10; Ezek. 16), and the bridal pair were bedecked with ornaments, including garlands and jewelry (*see* DRESS AND ORNAMENTS). A veil was evidently worn by the bride (Gen. 24:65). In the account of Laban's deception in giving Leah instead of Rachel to Jacob on his wedding night, the use of a veil by the bride may be inferred (29:23, 25). The bridegroom had his party of friends or attendants (Judg. 14:11). Jesus speaks of them by using the strange words "sons of the bridechamber" (RSV "wedding guests"; Matt. 9:15; Mark 2:19; Luke 5:34). Possibly one of these acted as best man and may be identified in the phrase "friend of the bridegroom" of John 3:29. The words "best man" actually occur in Judg. 14:20. The bride also had attendants (Ps. 45:14; Song of S. 3: 11; etc.).

A procession of some sort was a part of the wedding ceremonies. The two bridal parties left their places of assembly separately and met at a predetermined location (I Macc. 9:39). The processions were accompanied by music (Jer. 7:34); the combined parties moved to the house, usually the bridegroom's, where the wedding feast was to be held (but see Gen. 29:22, where the feast is held in the home of the father-in-law). One such feast lasted for seven days (Judg. 14:12), but in Tobit this period is doubled (Tob. 8:20). Music during the procession and perhaps during the feast itself is noted in Ps. 78:63; Song of Songs; Isa. 5:1; Ezek. 33:32.

The ceremony proper may have included a skirt-spreading ceremony, symbolizing that a woman is taken as a wife. In the book of Ruth, the widowed young woman approaches Boaz, uncovers his feet (genitals?), and lies down (Ruth 3:7). When Boaz awakens, she identifies herself and requests him to spread his skirt over her, because he is next of kin. This certainly signifies an effort on Ruth's part to secure Boaz as a husband. A modern observer has noted an Arab practice of throwing over the bride a cloak belonging to a man with the words, "None shall cover thee but such a one," naming the bridegroom (*see bibliography*). For the completion of the marriage ceremony a special tent or room is prepared as a bridal chamber.

The final ritual before the consummation of the marriage may have been formal proof of the bride's virginity. This practice is perhaps reflected in the provision of Deut. 22:13-21, to the effect that if a man marries a girl and fails to find in her the "tokens of virginity," then her parents shall submit the "tokens of her virginity" to the elders as proof of the falsity of his accusation. It further provides that the garment shall be spread before the elders for their inspection. In this connection, of interest is the action of Joseph, who, when he discovered that Mary was pregnant before he had taken her, refused to make this evidence that she was not a virgin a public matter and "resolved to divorce her quietly" (Matt. 1:19). It is conceivable, if a display of tokens of virginity was a customary part of the marriage ritual, that the so-called "friends of the bridechamber" mentioned in the gospels (RSV "wedding guests") functioned as witnesses to check on the bride's virginity in the bridal chamber (Mark 2:19).

3. The figurative use of marriage. With singular clarity and concreteness the biblical writers drew upon the common experiences of their day to communicate their message. The experience of marriage illustrates this point. The prophet expresses the compassion of Israel's God when he writes:

> Your Maker is your husband.
>
> . . . .
>
> For the LORD has called you
> like a wife forsaken and grieved in spirit,
> like a wife of youth when she is cast off
> (Isa. 54:5-6).

In the same book the persistent, purposeful love of God holds out the promise that his desolate people will receive a new name, Beulah, Hebrew for "married"; and her God will rejoice over her as the bridegroom rejoices over the bride (62:4-5). The book of Jeremiah stresses the awful desolation of the land which was imminent for Judah and Jerusalem by contrasting it with the joy and merriment of the wedding feast—the "voice of mirth and the voice of gladness, the voice of the bridegroom and the voice of the bride" shall cease (Jer. 7:34; 16:9; 25:10; cf. Bar. 2:23). In another context a poet describes the "garments of salvation" as bridal attire (Isa. 61:10). A dramatic and impressive lesson on the nature of the kingdom of heaven is driven home in Jesus' parable of the marriage feast (Matt. 22:1-14). Equally vivid and effective in using his audience' experience of marriage ceremonies is the story of the wise and foolish maidens in the same gospel (25:1-12). Again, language learned by familiarity with wedding festivities was utilized to explain why the disciples of Jesus did not fast (Mark 2:18-20). John the Baptist compares his own deep joy with that of the friend of the bridegroom, who rejoices at the happiness of the latter in his possession of the bride (John 3:29). *See* FAMILY; FATHER; PROSTITUTION.

4. The theological use of marriage. Since marriage was indeed a covenant (*see* § 2*d above*), its relationships served a theological purpose, that of defining the meaning of Israel's God and of her obligation to him. Beyond this, since Israel's faith was fashioned in the fires of religious and cultural tensions, the prominence of the concept of sacred marriage in the Canaanite culture made an Israelite adaptation of this concept a most effective weapon for defending the faith. In the Canaanite world the cycle of the seasons was believed to be intimately associated with sexual relations between gods and goddesses. These relations were momentous for the welfare of an agricultural community. *See bibliography; see also* PROSTITUTION.

Biblical writers wrote polemics against this widespread concept of marriage while at the same time adopting some of its terminology and adapting it to the biblical concept of marriage and of God. The use of the figure of marriage to express the relation between Yahweh and Israel has been suggested above, by its value in articulating the divine love. Yahweh speaks to Israel through his prophet:

> I remember the devotion of your youth,
> your love as a bride,
> how you followed me in the wilderness
> (Jer. 2:2).

Here the past is idealized by the prophet and Israel is depicted as the devoted, faithful bride of her Lord and Redeemer. This concretely affirms the personal dimension of the covenant relation between God and his people. This use of the husband concept to emphasize the relational theology of the covenant is brought out clearly in the book of Hosea. Here it is written that Yahweh the husband has repudiated his conjugal relation with his wife, Israel (Hos. 2:2), but that he will again betroth her to himself when she abandons her faithless practices (vss. 19-20). Then she will "know the Lord" in a deeply personal and ethical way comparable to the knowledge which a man has of his wife (*see* SEX; KNOWLEDGE). In the NT use of marriage for theological definition of the gospel, Paul's words are significant: "I betrothed you to Christ to present you as a pure bride to her one husband" (II Cor. 11:2). In admonishing his readers as to the proper relations between a husband and his wife, the writer of the Letter to the Ephesians states that "the husband is the head of the wife as Christ is the head of the church, his body" (Eph. 5:23). This affirms more than mere control, as vs. 25 shows—husbands are to love their wives, as Christ loved the church, and tenderly nourish and cherish them. With this background of the biblical use of marriage, the seer who has visions of the end time is able to announce that the marriage of the Lamb and his bride is about to be consummated; Christ and the faithful are to be united in marriage (Rev. 19:7-9). This union marks the appearance of the church triumphant, for the description of which the writer turns to the experience of marriage.

5. The function and purpose of marriage. Because of its importance in providing progeny and thus preserving the family name, marriage was practically universal in biblical society. There were widows, but no spinsters, in biblical times. Celibacy was limited to those who through injury were unable to function sexually (Deut. 23:1), and to those who through a congenital condition or through violence or choice had become eunuchs (Matt. 19:12; *see* EUNUCH). In the Dead Sea Scrolls the Manual of Discipline contains the words "bear seed," thereby showing that the particular Essene sect represented here were not celibates and thus did not resemble the Covenanters of Damascus. Josephus the ancient Jewish historian mentions the marrying sect of ESSENES. The power of the desire for sons and the value of the family made marriage a prominent institution in the life of biblical people.

Beyond this reproductive and social function of marriage a personal one may also be noted, although it is not conspicuous in most of the biblical books. Paul concedes the presence of sexual passion and grants that it had better be satisfied within marriage rather than in illicit relations (I Cor. 7:9). He recommends that husband and wife grant each other sexual pleasure on a reciprocal basis (vss. 3-4). The delights of marriage, largely on this level, are fully and beautifully set forth in the Song of Songs. Here deeply satisfying personal relations are described. At its best, the biblical account of the function of sex in marriage is presented in a setting of personal, spiritual, and social values, as an essential part of a partnership between persons who are creatures of God. Love in marriage is urged—a husband is to be "infatuated always" with his wife's love (Prov. 5:19). The heartbreak of the prophet Hosea over the tragedy of his marriage is second only to the truth it enabled him to enunciate—the persistent, forgiving love of God. And Malachi movingly states the personal meaning of marriage in describing one's wife as "companion" and "wife by covenant" (Mal. 2:14; cf. Ecclus. 7:19; 25:1, 8; 41:23).

At its deepest level, marriage is a personal-sexual-spiritual companionship ordained and instituted by God. This interpretation rests upon the biblical experience of marriage in the light of the biblical faith in the God who is both Creator and Redeemer. This faith is affirmed, as far as marriage is concerned, in clear terms: "A man leaves his father and his mother and cleaves to his wife, and they become one flesh" (Gen. 2:24). Jesus reads the Pharisees a lesson on divorce by using the same passage as a text when he says: "God made them male and female. For this reason a man shall leave his father and mother and be joined to his wife, and the two shall become one" (Mark 10:6*b*-8). By using the common terms for "man" and "woman"—איש; אשה—the writer of Gen. 2:23 stresses the close relation between man and woman. The words are pronounced similarly: *'îsh* and *'ishshâ*, the latter mistakenly taken by the biblical writer to contain as its last syllable a feminine ending of the former (in fact, איש probably derives from a root meaning "to lead," and אשה may come from אנש, "to be delicate"). *See* SEX.

Such an understanding of marriage may be more

clearly seen in the later rather than in the earlier documents of the Bible, although its appearance in the earlier period within the framework of the polygamous pattern must not be ignored. Doubtless the effect upon social institutions of the loss of nationality, the disintegration of the Exile, and the fuller exposure of the Israelites to foreign cultures may be detected in the developing personal emphasis upon marriage. Notably the impact of Greco-Roman thought and custom and of Christian teachings was considerable in the late OT and in the NT periods. *See bibliography.*

Bibliography. J. L. Burckhardt, *Notes on the Bedouins* (1830): data on skirt-spreading ceremony. J. F. McLennan, "The Levirate and Polyandry," *Fortnightly Review* (1877). L. Dargun, *Mutterrecht und Vaterrecht* (1892). J. Wellhausen, *Die Ehe bei den Arabern* (1893). S. A. Cook, *The Laws of Moses and the Code of Hammurabi* (1903). W. R. Smith, *Kinship and Marriage in Early Arabia* (1903). T. Engert, *Ehe und Familienrecht der Hebräer* (1905). A. Eberharter, *Das Ehe- und Familienrecht der Hebräer . . .* (1914). T. J. Meek, "Canticles and the Tammuz Cult," *AJSL,* 39 (1922), 1-14. A. E. Cowley, *Aramaic Papyri of the Fifth Century B.C.* (1923): a marriage document mentioned. G. A. Barton, *Archaeology and the Bible* (1925), pp. 326-28, 465. J. T. Pedersen, *Israel,* vols. I-II (1926): generally useful. R. Briffault, *The Mothers* (1927). J. M. P. Smith, *Origin and History of Hebrew Law* (1931). R. H. Kennett, *Ancient Hebrew Life and Social Custom* (1933). A. Alt, *Die Ursprünge des israelitischen Rechts* (1934): distinction between apodictic and casuistic law in connection with levirate marriage. G. A. Barton, *Semitic and Hamitic Origins* (1934). G. R. Driver and J. C. Miles, *The Assyrian Laws* (1935). C. H. Gordon, "Fratriarchy in the OT," *JBL,* 54 (1935), 223-31; "A Marriage of the Gods in Canaanite Mythology," *AASOR,* 65 (1937), 29-33. M. Burrows, *The Basis of Israelite Marriage* (1938). T. H. Gaster, "On a Proto-Hebrew Poem from Ras Shamra," *JBL,* 47 (1938), 81-87. A. Goetze, "The Nikkal Poem from Ras Shamra," *JBL,* 60 (1941), 353-74. L. M. Epstein, *Marriage Laws in the Bible and the Talmud* (1942). E. Neufeld, *Ancient Hebrew Marriage Laws* (1944), pp. 23-55: treatment of levirate marriage. A. van Praag, *Droit matrimonial assyrobabylonian* (1945). T. J. Meek, *Hebrew Origins* (2nd ed., 1950), pp. 62-65. D. R. Mace, *Hebrew Marriage* (1953). A. van Selms, *Marriage and Family Life in Ugaritic Literature* (1954). J. B. Pritchard, ed., *ANET* (2nd ed., 1955). L. Kohler, *Hebrew Man* (trans. P. R. Ackroyd; 1956), pp. 75 ff. G. A. Barton, A Liturgy for the Celebration of the Spring Festival at Jerusalem, *JBL,* 53 (1934), 61-78. R. de Langhe, "L'organisation familiale," *Les Textes de Ras Shamra-Ugarit II* (1946), pp. 355-77. E. Westermarck, *History of Human Marriage,* vols. I-III (5th ed., 1922).

O. J. BAAB

MARSENA mär sē'nə [מרסנא] (Esth. 1:14). One of the "seven princes of Persia and Media" ranking next after King Ahasuerus in authority within the kingdom.

Bibliography. L. B. Paton, *Esther,* ICC (1908), pp. 68-69, 152-53.

B. T. DAHLBERG

MARSH [בצה, *probably* soft place; גבא, cistern pool]. Except along the flat shore line of the Dead Sea (Ezek. 47:11), marshes are almost unknown in dry Palestine. The references in Job 8:11; 40:21 are probably to Egyptian marshes, where the papyrus grows and Behemoth is to be found.

L. E. TOOMBS

MARSHAL [טפסר] (Jer. 51:27); KJV CAPTAIN. A military officer in charge of the census of the troops. Cf. ספר, "SCRIBE" (KJV "writer"), in Judg. 5:14 (as well as γραμματεῦς in I Macc. 5:42), which in the military context of the Song of Deborah must denote an officer who mustered the troops. Cf. also II Kings 25:19, where "secretary" should probably be changed to "marshal."

J. W. WEVERS

MARS' HILL märz. KJV translation of Ἄρειος πάγος (Acts 17:22; RSV AREOPAGUS).

MARTHA mär'thə [Μάρθα; Aram. מרתא, lady, mistress]. Sister of Mary and Lazarus of Bethany (Luke 10:38-42; John 11:1–12:2).

That Martha had a sister named Mary (*see* MARY 3) is clearly indicated in the gospel tradition. That these sisters lived at Bethany and had a brother Lazarus is affirmed only in the Fourth Gospel. From Luke alone one would conclude that the sisters lived somewhere in S Galilee (see Luke 9:51; 10:38-42; 17:11). Luke's central section (9:51–19:27), however, is clearly a collection of materials from various periods of Jesus' ministry, with little regard for chronological and geographical order. The details concerning the sisters and their brother in John supplement the fragmentary information offered in Luke and serve to explain some obscure points in the Synoptic narrative (e.g., Mark 11:1-12; Luke 21:37). Many recent scholars look upon specific data of the Fourth Gospel not present in the Synoptics (personal names, place names, time notations, and the like) as evidence of a trustworthy special tradition, not as fanciful expansions of Synoptic material.

The character portrayal of the sisters in Luke and John is strikingly similar. Martha was the practical type: the mistress of the house (Luke 10:38; John 12:2); concerned that adequate provision for Jesus' physical needs be made (Luke 10:40; John 12:2); impatient over her sister's contemplative bent (Luke 10:40); collected enough in her bereavement to meet Jesus on his approach to Bethany and to explain the situation to him, while her sister sat at home in black despair (John 11:20); mindful of the unpleasantness of a body four days dead (John 11:39).

Jesus loved both sisters. The Fourth Evangelist even writes: "Now Jesus loved Martha and her sister and Lazarus" (11:5). Jesus undoubtedly accepted Martha's ministrations gratefully. He took note when customary courtesies were not extended to him (Luke 7:44-46). But he was distressed at Martha's petulant bondage to secondary concerns. Whatever the exact original wording of his rebuke of Martha (the text of Luke 10:41 has come down in several forms), his general meaning is clear: The kingdom of God is a value transcending all other values. Mary has set her heart on this. You, Martha, should seek first the kingdom of God and let other things take their proper place.

In John 12:1-8 we read of a dinner at Bethany at which Martha served Jesus, his disciples, and Lazarus, and Mary anointed Jesus' feet. In Mark 14:3-9 a meal at Bethany in the house of Simon the leper is described, during which Jesus' head was anointed by an unnamed woman. These are obviously variant reports of the same incident, however the similarities and differences are to be explained (*see* MARY 3). It is possible that Simon was a leper who had been cured by Jesus and that he was the father or the husband of Martha; or he may have been deceased and the house still known by his name.

Bibliography. P. Ketter, *Christ and Womankind* (English trans., 1937), pp. 278-93; H. D. A. Major, T. W. Manson, and C. J. Wright, *The Mission and Message of Jesus* (1938), pp. 280, 555-56, 836 ff; J. N. Sanders, "Those Whom Jesus Loved," *NTS,* I (1954-55), 29-41. E. P. BLAIR

MARTYR. A believer who has borne witness to Christ by shedding his blood for him.

1. The terms "witness" and "martyr." Both terms are translations of the Greek μάρτυς. WITNESS is the more primitive rendering. In the NT it is primarily applied to the apostles who bear witness to the risen Christ. They are prepared to suffer gladly "for the name" (Acts 5:41; 9:16), yet it is by their life and missionary work that they bear witness to Christ.

"Martyr" is a literal transcription from the Greek in order to give expression to a new meaning. In the second century and at a time of persecution the term "martyr" is commonly used to designate Christ's confessors who suffered martyrdom rather than deny their Lord. A witness bears testimony by his actual preaching. A martyr has borne testimony even by his death, which gives him his title and rank as a martyr (cf. Mart. Polyc. 14:2; 16:2; 17:3).

2. The martyrs in the NT. According to some scholars this new meaning is already apparent in the NT. We read in Acts (cf. 22:20) that the blood of Stephen the "μάρτυς of the Lord" has been shed. Versions translate either "witness" (ASV, RSV) or "martyr" (KJV, Moffatt). The translation "witness" might be recommended by the fact that Stephen had a preaching activity (Acts 6–7). Yet Stephen does not see the Lord at the beginning of his career and does not receive express command from him, as the other "witnesses" in Acts, the first disciples (cf. 1:8, etc.), and Paul (cf. 22:15; 26:16) do. He sees him only at the hour of his martyrdom. Thus it may be admitted that this use of the term μάρτυς is at least a step in the direction of the meaning of "martyr."

The same may be said about two passages in the book of Revelation. A Christian Antipas, "who was killed" (Rev. 2:13), is called a "witness" (ASV, RSV) or a "martyr" (KJV). Later (cf. 17:6) the "blood of the martyrs of Jesus" is spoken of. Elsewhere in the same book persecuted Christians who remained faithful unto death are not called "martyrs" (Rev. 6:9-11; 13:15; 18:20; 20:4), although they bore testimony to Christ (Rev. 6:9; 20:4). It may be concluded that in NT times the term μάρτυς began to receive the new connotation of "martyr," but that this new meaning was not yet in general use.

3. Discipleship and martyrdom. The first-century church had not yet undergone general persecution. Yet the believers had before their eyes the example of Christ, who died on a cross. They had been warned by their Master that God's messengers in the Old Covenant were persecuted (Matt. 23:34-35), and they had been themselves commanded to take up their cross and follow him (Mark 8:34-38; cf. 13: 9-13; John 15:20; 16:1-3). In all times true discipleship means readiness to suffer all kinds of ill-treatment for Christ's sake (cf. Phil. 1:29-30; I Thess. 2:14-15; I Pet. 3:14). During an age of persecution the faithful witness becomes the martyr of Christ.

Bibliography. D. W. Riddle, *The Martyrs: A Study in Social Control* (1931); R. P. Casey, "Μάρτυς," in F. J. Foakes-Jackson and K. Lake, *The Beginnings of Christianity,* V (1933), 30-37; E. Günther, "Zeuge und Märtyrer," *ZNW,* XLVII (1956), 145-61. P. H. MENOUD

MARTYRDOM OF MATTHEW. *See* MATTHEW, MARTYRDOM OF.

MARTYRDOM OF POLYCARP. *See* POLYCARP, MARTYRDOM OF.

MARVEL. *See* SIGNS AND WONDERS.

MARY mâr'ĭ [Μαριάμ (*e.g.,* Matt. 13:55; 27:61; 28: 1; Luke 1:27; 10:39; John 11:2; 20:16; Acts 1:14), *from* מרים, *perhaps from* מרא, the corpulent one; *also* Μαρία (*e.g.,* Matt. 1:16; 2:11; 27:56; 28:1; Mark 6:3; Luke 1:41; 2:19; John 11:1; 19:25; Acts 12:12; Rom. 16:6), *Grecized form of* מרים]. The name of the mother of Jesus and several other women of the NT; first made famous by Moses' sister (Miriam; Exod. 15:20; Num. 26:59). It appears in Josephus (Antiq. III.ii.4) as Mariamme (Μαριάμμη).

1. *See* MARY MOTHER OF JESUS.

2. Mary of Magdala (*see* MAGDALENE), one of the most prominent of the Galilean women who followed Jesus.

Magdala (probably also called by the Greek name Tarichaea), at the S end of the Plain of Gennesaret (Ginnesar), was an important agricultural, fishing, fish-curing, shipbuilding, and trading center, a city of considerable wealth. The population was predominantly Gentile, as evidenced by the presence of a hippodrome (Jos. War II.xxi.3). Rabbis later attributed the fall of the city to licentiousness (Midrash on Lamentations II.2), so bad was its reputation.

We do not know when or where Jesus met Mary of Magdala. It is not said that he visited the city, though its environs are mentioned (Mark 6:53; Matt. 14:34).

Neither do we understand Mary's condition when she first met Jesus. It is said that seven demons had gone out of her (Luke 8:2; cf. Mark 16:9). Since demon possession was at that time associated with both physical and moral-spiritual sickness, Luke's statement does not offer us much help. The reference to "seven demons" probably emphasizes either the seriousness of her condition (Luke 8:30) or the recurrent nature of it (Luke 11:26).

There is no solid reason for assuming that Mary had been a harlot and therefore is to be identified with the sinful woman of Luke 7:36-50. Luke surely did not intend this identification, as he introduces Mary Magdalene in a formal way in 8:2, with no suggestion that she has been presented in 7:36-50. It is, furthermore, doubtful whether Joanna, the wife of Herod's steward, would have traveled around Galilee (Luke 8:1-3) with a notorious courtesan.

Neither is Mary Magdalene to be identified with Mary of Bethany (John 11:1–12:8; Luke 10:38-42). The former was a Galilean (Mark 15:40-41; cf. Luke 8:1-3); the latter, with Martha and Lazarus, lived in Judea, in the village of Bethany, just E of Jerusalem (John 11:1 ff; on Luke's location of their residence, *see* 3 *below*). There is no suggestion in the narratives about Mary of Bethany that she had been delivered from a serious physical or moral illness. The aggressive role of Mary Magdalene in the distaff side of the gospel story (*see below*) contrasts sharply with the contemplative bent of Mary of Bethany (John 11; Luke 10:38-42).

The identification of Mary Magdalene, the sinner of Luke 7:36-50, and Mary of Bethany, widely accepted in the Western church from about the sixth century (but rejected in the Eastern), probably arose because of the similarities in the stories of the anointing of Jesus by women contained in Luke 7:36-50; John 12:1-8, and the unfounded supposition that Mary Magdalene's "seven demons" were demons of unchastity. The unsavory reputation of Magdala may have helped to blacken her character.

Mary Magdalene's devotion to Jesus and his cause is clearly underscored by her practical service. She participated in his itinerating mission in Galilee and contributed financially to the venture (Luke 8:1-3; Mark 15:40-41). She went with him and his followers to Jerusalem for his final appeal to the nation in its capital city (Mark 15:41). She was present at the Crucifixion (Mark 15:40; John 19:25), came to the tomb to anoint Jesus' body (Mark 16:1; Luke 23:55–24:1), reported the fact of the empty tomb and the message of the angels to the Eleven (Luke 24:1-11), and was the recipient of a personal appearance by Jesus after the resurrection (John 20:11-18).

Bibliography. P. Ketter, *Die Magdalenenfrage* (1929). F. C. Burkitt, "Mary Magdalene and Mary, Sister of Martha," *ET*, 42 (1930/31), 157-59. G. Dalman, *Sacred Sites and Ways* (English trans., 1935), pp. 125-28.

3. Mary of Bethany. As was pointed out in 2 *above,* she is probably not to be identified with Mary Magdalene or the sinful woman of Luke 7:36-50. Information about Mary of Bethany comes from Luke 10:38-42; John 11:1–12:8. That these two passages are concerned with the same Mary is hardly subject to doubt: in both she has a sister Martha; in both the same qualities of personality of the sisters appear; in both the same loving relationship to Jesus is pictured. Luke's location of the home of the sisters in S Galilee (Luke 10:38; 13:22; 17:11), rather than in Bethany near Jerusalem, is no argument against the identification, since Luke's whole central section is loosely arranged chronologically (*see* LUKE, GOSPEL OF). These two passages supplement and illuminate each other most strikingly.

The Lukan narrative represents Mary as the contemplative type, somewhat indifferent to mundane matters, single-mindedly absorbed in the truth about the kingdom of God and its inaugurator. The Johannine stories picture her as grieving inconsolably over her brother's death (John 11:20, 31), as deeply devoted to Jesus and cognizant of his power (vs. 32), and as effusively thankful for the superlatively wonderful restoration of her brother from the dead (12:1-3).

The stories of the anointing of Jesus by Mary in Mark 14:3-9 (without mention of her name) and in John 12:1-8 pose numerous problems: whether she anointed his head (Mark) or his feet (John); what her precise motive in the anointing was; the circumstances of the act (time, place, persons present); the literary relationship of these stories to the anointing recorded in Luke 7:36-50; and the like. It is widely believed that Mark is correct in asserting that Jesus' head was anointed by Mary, probably as her grateful ascription to him of royal dignity. Jesus reinterpreted the act in the light of his premonition of coming disaster and declared it an anointing of his body "beforehand for burying" (Mark 14:8). Whether there was an earlier anointing, as recorded in Luke 7:36-50, or simply one anointing, with variant reports of it, has not yet been settled. In any case Mary of Bethany figured in one—to her eternal credit (Mark 14:9)!

Bibliography. F. C. Burkitt, "Mary Magdalene and Mary, Sister of Martha," *ET*, 42 (1930/31), 157-59. D. Daube, "The Anointing at Bethany and Jesus' Burial," *ATR*, 32 (1950), 186-99. J. N. Sanders, "Those Whom Jesus Loved," *NTS*, I (1954-55), 29-41.

4. The mother of James the Younger and Joses; a Galilean follower and financial supporter (Mark 15:40; Luke 8:3) of Jesus. She is said to have accompanied him to Jerusalem (Mark 15:41; Matt. 27:55), stood by at the Crucifixion (Mark 15:40; Matt. 27:55-56; Luke 23:49), witnessed the entombment (Mark 15:47; Matt. 27:61; Luke 23:55), joined in the securing of spices for anointing Jesus' body (Mark 16:1; Luke 23:56), seen the empty tomb and heard the angelic announcement of Jesus' resurrection (Mark 16:2-7; Matt. 28:1-7; Luke 24:1-7), reported to the apostles what she had seen and heard (Matt. 28:8; Luke 24:9-11), and even to have seen the resurrected Jesus (Matt. 28:9-10).

It is possible that this Mary is to be identified with Mary the wife of Clopas (*see* 5 *below; see bibliography* under 5).

5. The wife of Clopas; one of the women standing near the cross (John 19:25). She almost certainly is not to be identified with the sister of Mary mentioned in this passage, since two sisters would not have possessed the same name.

CLOPAS may be identical with the ALPHAEUS of Mark 2:14; 3:18, but probably not with Cleopas of Luke 24:18. The latter is a pure Greek name (abbreviated from Κλεόπατρος), not a Greek rendition of a Semitic name.

Hegesippus mentions a Clopas who is said to have been a brother of Jesus' father, Joseph (Euseb. Hist. III.11; IV.22). If there is any truth in this tradition, Mary of Clopas was Mary the Virgin's sister-in-law. We may conjecture then that her husband was Clopas (Alphaeus) and that her children were James (one of the Twelve; Mark 3:18), Joses (Mark 15:40), and Levi (Mark 2:14).

"Mary of Clopas," as the text of John 19:25 reads literally, may mean "daughter of Clopas," in which case the neat solution suggested above is upset.

Bibliography. J. R. Harris, *The Twelve Apostles* (1927), pp. 64-76. J. R. Mackay, "The Other Mary," *ET*, 40 (1928/29), 319-21. E. F. F. Bishop, "Mary Clopas—Joh. xix.25," *ET*, 65 (1953/54), 382-83.

6. The mother of John Mark; the owner of a house in Jerusalem in which the early church met (Acts 12:12) and mother of the John who became a companion and helper of Paul and Barnabas and who was probably author of the Second Gospel (*see* MARK, JOHN).

7. A diligent worker in a Pauline church (Rome or Ephesus; *see* ROMANS, LETTER TO THE), who is saluted by Paul for her achievement (Rom. 16:6). She was probably of Jewish descent. E. P. BLAIR

MARY, BIRTH (OR DESCENT) OF. A Gnostic writing known only from a reference in Epiphanius (*Heresies* XXVI.12.1-9), and which, if fairly reported, would seem to have been a viciously anti-Jewish writing: the reason Zacharias had first been struck dumb and subsequently murdered was that he had seen, while offering the incense, the God of the Jews in the form of an ass; the reason the high priest was commanded by Moses always to wear bells on his garment was to warn this divinity to hide lest his form be seen. *See* APOCRYPHA, NT. M. S. ENSLIN

MARY, GOSPEL OF THE BIRTH OF. A Latin infancy gospel (*see* APOCRYPHA, NT) which repeats substantially that part of the Gospel of Pseudo-Matthew (*see* PSEUDO-MATTHEW, GOSPEL OF) which tells of the birth and life of the Virgin Mary until the birth of Jesus. Its alterations are severely editorial and pedestrian.

Mary was born at Nazareth, of the stock and family of David. The name Mary was given the child by command of the angel. The three-year-old Virgin, when brought by her parents to the temple, went up *all* the altar steps "in such a way that you would think she had attained full age." Joseph was the only one of "all those of the house and family of David that were unmarried and fit for marriage" who at first deliberately "withheld his rod."

After the annunciation to Mary the author quits his source with the word: "It will be long, and perhaps to some even tedious, if we insert in this little work everything which we read of as having preceded or followed the Lord's nativity; wherefore, omitting those things which have been more fully written in the gospel, let us come to those which are held to be less worthy of being narrated." These "less worthy" details are the return of Joseph to Mary after a three-month absence, "intending to marry the virgin." He found her pregnant, suspected fornication, was corrected by an angel of the Lord in a dream, took her as his wife, and kept her in chastity. Then her days were fulfilled, "and she brought forth her firstborn son, as the holy evangelists have shown."

The traditional ascription of this writing to Jerome is utterly without foundation. Its only source of information, except the canonical gospels, is Pseudo-Matthew, of which it is a distinctly inferior copy in artificially elegant Latin. Its influence upon medieval art is quite out of proportion to its own merits, for it was incorporated bodily into his *Golden Legend* by Jacobus de Voragine in the thirteenth century.

This is a totally different work from the Gnostic BIRTH OF MARY.

Bibliography. An English translation is available in the *Ante-Nicene Christian Library*, vol. XVI. A brief résumé of its contents is printed by M. R. James, *The Apocryphal NT* (1924), pp. 79-84. M. S. ENSLIN

MARY MOTHER OF JESUS. It is impossible to write a historical sketch of Mary's life, so inadequate are the data in the gospels and so unreliable are the traditions of the church. Such data as we have are contained in stories whose purpose is not historical narration but theological affirmation: they declare that God has come to men in a child born of a virgin, that he may redeem them from sin and death and lead them into his blessed kingdom. Mary is depicted as the instrument of God's gracious purpose (the "handmaid of the Lord" [Luke 1:38]).

1. Family background
2. Virginal conception
3. Marital relationship to Joseph
4. Place of Jesus" birth
5. Relationship to the child Jesus
6. Relationship to the adult Jesus
7. Relationship to other children in the family
8. Character
9. Christian tradition
Bibliography

1. Family background. We know very little concerning Mary's background. She was a devout Jewess, apparently living in Nazareth at the time when she conceived. Since both genealogies (Matt. 1:2-16; Luke 3:23-28) are Joseph's, we do not know whether she belonged to the Davidic line, though the angel's words in Luke 1:32 would at least imply that the early church believed that she was so descended. Davidic lineage is affirmed for Jesus outside the nativity stories (Acts 13:23; Rom. 1:3; II Tim. 2:8; Rev. 5:5; 22:16), but on what ground is not indicated. Elizabeth, "of the daughters of Aaron" (Luke 1:5), is called Mary's "kinswoman (σμγγενίς; Luke 1:36). If the kinship was of blood and not from marriage, Mary would seem to be of Levitic descent. It is not, of course, impossible that both lines lay behind her. Priests were not absolutely required to marry within their tribe, although it was held desirable that they should do so. The second-century Protevangelium of James identifies her parents as Joachim and Anna—possibly a reliable tradition.

2. Virginal conception. At the time when she conceived, she was betrothed to Joseph, who is said to have been "of the house of David" (Luke 1:27 and the genealogies). He is described in Matthew (1:18-25) as a God-fearing, law-abiding man, of considerate nature. Since betrothal in Judaism was tantamount to marriage, except for residence in the bridegroom's home (*see* JOSEPH HUSBAND OF MARY), Mary's pregnancy was at first a shock to Joseph. How could this condition have occurred except by an adulterous act? The stories in both Matthew and Luke explain the pregnancy as due to the Holy Spirit (Matt. 1:18, 20; Luke 1:35), the purpose of God being to raise up for his people a divine Savior ("Emmanuel" [Matt. 1:23]; "the Son of the Most High" [Luke 1:32]), who "will reign over the house of Jacob for ever" (Luke 1:33). Joseph's fears were allayed by the assurances of an angel, and he is said to have proceeded with his plans with respect to Mary.

How early belief in the Virgin Birth arose in the church it is impossible to say. Peter in the sermons of Acts and Paul in his letters never mention it, if they knew of it. In fact, in Gal. 4:4 Paul writes that Jesus was born of a "woman" (γυνή), when he might easily have used the more particular word "virgin" (παρθένος). Mark and John do not refer to the Virgin Birth (though some have read it into Mark 6:3; John 1:13). Outside Matthew and Luke it appears nowhere in the NT.

It has been argued that earlier forms of the birth stories now contained in Matthew and Luke lacked the virgin-birth explanation. Matt. 1:16 exists in three text forms, one of which reads: "Joseph, to whom Mary the virgin was betrothed, begat Jesus called the Christ" (syr^{s}). It has been contended that Luke 1:34-35 is an addition to the original text by some early Christian scribe or, more probably, that it is Luke's own addition to his source. It must seem queer to any perceptive reader that Luke, after telling the story of the Virgin Birth, should offer the comments contained in 2:33, 48-51. Is this an indication that he was utilizing sources which did not know of the Virgin Birth?

If the miraculous birth rests solely, as far as the NT is concerned, on the testimony of the writers of Matthew and Luke (both of whom clearly believed it, regardless of what their sources contained), the doctrine is, of course, not overthrown. It is indeed possible that Jesus was virgin born, even though only two writers of the NT record it. It is congruous with the pattern set by the Incarnation and the Resurrection. Jesus was unique, and it is not wholly incredible that he should have been uniquely born. However, it clearly is not an indispensable doctrine, or Peter, Paul, and other Christian preachers would have included it.

3. Marital relationship to Joseph. Roman Catholics have made much of Mary's response to the angelic announcement, as recorded in Luke 1:34: "How can this be, since I have no husband [lit. 'I am not knowing (γινώσκω) a man']?" They point out that the present tense expresses durative action and therefore means that Mary was then under a vow of perpetual virginity. The marriage of Mary and Joseph was thus never sexually consummated, and the so-called brothers and sisters of Jesus were really his cousins (*see* § 7 *below*). In response to the objection that the ideal of perpetual virginity was unknown in Judaism, they point to the Essenes, one group of whom eschewed marriage (Jos. War II.viii.2; Pliny Nat. Hist. V.15). In addition they cite Paul's advocacy of celibacy for some people (I Cor. 7).

It is doubtful whether Luke 1:34 can bear the heavy dogmatic weight heaped upon it. Why did Mary become betrothed to Joseph at all, if she already had vowed perpetual virginity? It will hardly do to answer, as some Roman Catholic scholars have, that she was obliged by the Mosaic Law (Num. 27:1-11; 36) and custom to enter this relationship because she was an heiress. The passages cited do not *require* marriage of heiresses, and that Mary belonged in this category is a gratuitous assumption. Neither does it help to cite the unreliable tradition in apocryphal literature (e.g., in the Protevangelium of James) that Joseph was an old man at the time of his betrothal (and therefore willing to forego the full marital relation). Lacking solid evidence to the contrary, one can only assume that the betrothal was the customary first stage in a relationship meant to be consummated. Matt. 1:24-25 says: "He took his wife, but knew her not until she had borne a son"; and in Luke 2:7 Jesus is called Mary's "first-born son"—these passages would hardly have been written in this way by persons who believed in Mary's perpetual virginity.

4. Place of Jesus' birth. According to Matthew and Luke, Jesus was born in Bethlehem. Luke, who holds that Joseph and Mary resided in Nazareth, explains their presence in Bethlehem as due to the necessity of enrollment in their ancestral city (2:1 ff). While there, Mary gave birth to her son in a stable, "because there was no place for them in the inn" (vs. 7).

The birth in Bethlehem has been challenged on various grounds: during the reign of Herod the Great a Roman census in Palestine is inherently unlikely; Quirinius, under whom Luke says it was held, was not then governor of Syria. C. J. Cadoux writes: "No government in its senses would have required a village-carpenter to undertake a journey of seventy miles simply in order to fill up the census-paper at the place where his *ancestors* had lived centuries before." And it is not likely that Joseph would have taken his wife in an advanced stage of pregnancy on such a trip. The story of the Bethlehem birth probably arose out of the church's reading of OT prophecy (Mic. 5:2).

Answers of varying value have been given to these objections. Evidence from Egyptian papyri indicates that a census was taken in the Roman world every fourteen years. One of these must have fallen *ca.* 8 B.C. and may have been somewhat delayed in Palestine. Quirinius, though not then properly governor of Syria, was in the East as commander in the Homanadensian War (10-7 B.C.) and may have supervised the census in Syria and Palestine. Further evidence from Egyptian papyri shows that in Egypt in A.D. 104 people were required to return to their own town for enrollment along with their kinsmen. It is likely that the same procedure was in effect in Syria-Palestine at the time of Jesus' birth. It is not impossible that Mary made the journey with Joseph, whether out of official or personal reasons. Finally, only extremely skeptical criticism assumes the unhistoricity of a NT statement because there is an OT prophecy corresponding to it. Though questions still remain (e.g., concerning Quirinius), it cannot be said that the NT affirmation of Jesus' birth at Bethlehem has been refuted.

5. Relationship to the child Jesus. Events following the birth are narrated by Luke and Matthew. Luke reports a visit of shepherds to the stable, the circumcision and naming of the child on the eighth day, and the purification ceremony for Mary forty days after the birth (Lev. 12), followed by the presentation of the child at the temple. The fact that Mary's sacrificial offering at the termination of her period of uncleanness consisted of a "pair of turtle doves, or two young pigeons," indicates the humble circumstances of the new parents (Lev. 12:6-8). The presentation ceremony recognized God's claim on the first-born, which, if not actually surrendered to him, had to be redeemed by an offering (Exod. 13: 2, 11-16; Num. 18:15-16). Luke makes no mention of this offering. He seems to interpret the presentation of Jesus by his parents in the light of the story about Hannah's grateful presentation of Samuel for the Lord's service (I Sam. 1:24-28). The prophetic declaration of Simeon is said to have caused Joseph and Mary to marvel at what was said about the child's future (Luke 2:33).

Matthew tells other infancy stories involving Mary. The Wise Men are said to have found her and the child in a house (Matt. 2:11), presumably in Bethlehem. A journey into Egypt by the holy family in order to escape Herod, and their subsequent return and settlement in Nazareth (vss. 13-23), are recorded.

Luke narrates one incident from the period of Jesus' youth in which Mary figures. When she and Joseph, after much searching, found him in the temple among the rabbis, they were "astonished" (2:48). She reproached her son for such treatment of his father and mother and was told that she should have expected him to be in his Father's house. This remark they did not understand (vs. 50), and Mary added this also to her store of matters for reflection (vs. 51). The story implies that Jesus knew who he was and something about his mission, but that the parents were still somewhat in the dark.

6. Relationship to the adult Jesus. Mary's perplexity and joy over Jesus appear to have continued during the period of his ministry. Joseph apparently was dead by this time, and Mary seems to have been living with Jesus' brothers and sisters at Nazareth (Mark 6:3). She is not represented as accompanying Jesus on his preaching missions in Galilee, as did Mary Magdalene, Joanna, Susanna, and "many others" (Luke 8:3). The picture of her offered in the Johannine story of the wedding at Cana (John 2:1-11) implies that she had faith in her son's ability to meet the emergency, but Jesus' mild rebuke of her shows that she had not entered very far into his understanding of the nature and conditions of his ministry. Similarly, when Jesus' mother and brethren sought him out—obviously to lodge some formal family appeal with him—his attitude reveals a marked independence of them. Instead of warmly welcoming them, he remarks to his hearers that his true relatives are those who join him in obedience to the will of God, that fleshly ties have no ultimate significance (Mark 3:31-35). The priority of the spiritual over the physical relationship to him is similarly emphasized in his response to the woman of the crowd who eulogized his mother: "Blessed rather are those who hear the word of God and keep it!" (Luke 11:27-28). When all allowance is made for the dramatic element in his teaching technique, it still must be said that his family according to the flesh, and even to a degree his mother, seem somewhat removed from him (cf. John 7:1-9).

Mary last appears in the gospels at the foot of the cross (John 19:25-27). Only deep mother love could have emboldened her to stand near a son who was being crucified as an enemy of the state. It is significant that Jesus' brothers are not mentioned as being present. During those last moments Jesus committed his mother to the Beloved Disciple, who thereupon took her to his own home (vs. 27). (Some interpreters view Mary at Cana and at the Cross as representative of Judaism.)

Mary is mentioned only once more in the NT: in Acts 1:14, where she and Jesus' brothers, together with the apostles, are pictured as participating in a prayer meeting following the Resurrection and Ascension. The brothers, like the scattered and confused disciples, had been reached by the testimonies concerning Jesus' resurrection, and James, at least, by a personal encounter with him (I Cor. 15:7). Mary is there, her hopes for her son transmuted and now gloriously realized.

7. Relationship to the other children in the family. Was Mary the mother of children besides Jesus? As noted in § 3 *above,* Roman Catholics affirm her perpetual virginity. The matter has been debated since early Christian centuries. Views fall into three categories: the Helvidian (advocated by Helvidius, *ca.* A.D. 380), which holds that these children (Mark 6:3; Matt. 13:55-56) were Jesus' blood brothers and sisters; the Epiphanian (from Epiphanius, *ca.* A.D. 382), that they were children of Joseph by a former wife; and the Hieronymian (Jerome, *ca.* A.D. 383), that they were the children of Mary, the wife of Alphaeus, the Virgin Mary's sister, and thus Jesus' cousins. Each view has had considerable support in both antiquity and modern times, the last now being favored by Roman Catholics.

Jerome's answer was shaped to meet the views of Helvidius. Jerome held that the word "brother" (ἀδελφός) is used in the Bible in a wide sense—to cover not only actual brotherhood, but also wider kinship, common nationality, and friendship. He argued that three women, not four, are mentioned in John 19:25 as standing at the foot of the cross, the second named being Mary's sister, identified here as "Mary the wife of Clopas," and that this Mary is said in Mark 15:40 to be the mother of James the Younger (i.e., James the Lord's brother [Gal. 1:19]). He believed this James to be the same as "James the son of Alphaeus" of the lists of the apostles (Mark 3:16-19; Matt. 10:2-4; Luke 6:14-16; Acts 1:13). Thus James the Lord's brother was really his cousin.

Later writers affirmed on linguistic grounds the identity of the names Alphaeus and Clopas and found the Judas and Simon mentioned in Mark 6:3 in Judas of James (Luke 6:16) and Simon the Zealot (Luke 6:15). Thus several of Jesus' cousins were held to belong to the Twelve.

Jerome's view, though superficially attractive, is undoubtedly erroneous. Though "brother" (ἀδελφός) is unquestionably sometimes used in the LXX and probably in the papyri in a wide sense, and therefore could have been used by the evangelists in the sense of "relative," its usual meaning is "brother" (blood brother). If they had meant "cousin," why did they not use the customary word (ἀνεψιός; Col. 4:10) for this relationship? Furthermore, to suppose that several of Jesus' cousins were members of the apostolic circle is to fly in the face of the flat statement in John 7:5 that his brothers did not believe in him (cf. Mark 3:21, 31-35). What is more, they are never associated with Mary of Clopas (the assumed wife of Alphaeus) in the gospels, but only with Joseph and Mary—exceeding strange if Mary of Clopas were their mother. And, finally, it is unlikely that John 19:25 means to make Mary of Clopas Jesus' mother's sister. Two sisters in the same home would hardly have borne the same name, Mary. Four women, rather than three, are undoubtedly meant in this passage. Jerome's hypothesis was devised to support his doctrine of the perpetual virginity of Mary.

The view of Epiphanius is less objectionable on NT grounds. It is possible that Joseph had children by a former wife. But the correlative hypothesis, that Joseph's marriage to Mary was never sexually consummated, seems not to have been believed by the evangelists. Would not the evangelists have avoided such statements as appear in Luke 2:7 ("her first-born son"); Matt. 1:25 ("Joseph . . . knew her not until she had borne a son") if they had believed in Mary's perpetual virginity?

The Helvidian view, that Jesus' "brothers" were also born of Mary, is supported by other ancients (notably Tertullian) and by many modern scholars. Jesus' committing his mother to the Beloved Disciple at the Cross, said to be unlikely if she had other sons, is no real argument against this, as it overlooks the fact that these sons were at this time hostile to Jesus. They were not at the Cross. And it is possible to argue that if Jesus had actual blood brothers and sisters, he entered more deeply into our humanity than the other views assume.

8. Character. The Mary of the NT represents all that was finest in Jewish womanhood and motherhood. Her deep spiritual sensitivity; her purity, faith, and obedience to the divine will; her scrupulous attention to the training of her son in the religious traditions of his people; her loyalty to him, as evidenced by her presence at the Cross, even when she did not fully understand him—all mark her as a person of remarkable qualities.

That she was mystified by much that her son did is not strange. Jesus did not fit the traditional messianic pattern. His most sensitive disciples were confused. In the light of the Resurrection both they and she began to see through the veil of mystery and to discern the divine purpose in Jesus' strangely wonderful life, death, and resurrection. For her as well as for them, he became "Lord and Christ" (Acts 2:36).

9. Christian tradition. There is no veneration of Mary in the NT. In fact, Jesus expressly warned against such (Luke 11:27-28). Mary takes her place in the NT as one of the servants of God through whom his redemptive purposes toward man were advanced.

However, Christian imagination soon set to work to embellish and expand the NT picture of Mary. In the second-century Protevangelium of James, Mary is said to have been born to rich but childless Joachim and Anna as a result of fervent prayer and to have been dedicated by her grateful parents to a life of service in the temple. There, from three years of age, she lived "like a dove that is nurtured." She was fed by an angel. At twelve she was taken from the temple by Joseph, a widower, as a result of a sign marking Joseph as her divinely ordained protector. Later she was appointed among seven virgins to the task of weaving a new curtain for the temple. During this work the angel of the Annunciation appeared to her. When she at length was found to be pregnant, both she and Joseph were forced to undergo the water test for adultery (Num. 5:16 ff), which they successfully passed. Near the end of the journey to Bethlehem, Joseph searched for a midwife while Mary rested in a cave. A cloud overshadowed the cave, a great light appeared, and the child was born and began to nurse. The midwife was astonished at the miraculous signs accrediting the Virgin Birth. The narrative proceeds to describe the visit of the Magi, the slaughter of the children at Bethlehem, and other happenings.

Legends concerning Mary's death and assumption began to appear. The earliest is contained in the Assumption of the Virgin (*Liber Transitus*), falsely attributed to Melito of Sardis; various recensions of it circulated in the fifth century. This book holds that Mary died in Jerusalem (another tradition says in Ephesus), attended by the apostles, who had been miraculously assembled. A Jewish priest, who during the funeral procession laid his hands in wrath on the bier to overturn it, found that he could not free his hands until he had confessed faith in Mary's divine Son. The body of Mary was placed in a new sepulchre and then raised by the command of Jesus, who appeared before the tomb with a band of angels. Angels straightway bore her into paradise.

Since the fifth century the bodily assumption of Mary has been widely believed in the Roman Catholic Church. A bull issued November 1, 1950, by Pope Pius XII declared that it is a "revealed dogma" that "the Virgin Mary, the Immaculate Mother of God, when the course of her life was finished, was taken up, body and soul, into the glory of heaven." Roman Catholic theology has increasingly ascribed to Mary many of the miraculous features associated with the birth, life, resurrection, and ascension of Jesus in the NT.

Bibliography. W. M. Ramsay, *Was Christ Born at Bethlehem?* (1898). V. Taylor, *The Historical Evidence for the Virgin Birth* (1920). M. R. James, *The Apocryphal NT* (1924), pp. 38-49, 194-227. J. G. Machen, *The Virgin Birth of Christ* (1930). M. Dibelius, *Jungfrauensohn und Krippenkind* (1932). J. J. Collins, "The Brethren of the Lord and Two Recently Published Papyri," *Theological Studies,* V (1944), 484-94. J. J. Lilly, "Jesus and His Mother During the Public Life," CBQ, 8 (1946), 52-57, 197-200, 315-19. P. S. Minear, *The Interpreter and the Birth Narratives* (1950). V. Taylor, *The Gospel According to St. Mark* (1952), pp. 247-49. J. B. Carol, ed., *Mariology,* I (1955), 51-108, 156-84; II (1957), 100-116, 228-96, 461-92.

E. P. Blair

***MASADA** mə sä'də [מצדה, mountain stronghold; Μασάδα]. Modern es-Sebbe; an impregnable rock fortress on the W shore of the Dead Sea *ca.* ten miles S of En-gedi, which was the scene of the last stand of the Jewish insurgents in the revolt which began in A.D. 66. It was taken by the Romans after a herculean effort in 73.

Although it plays no direct role in the NT narrative, Masada has been immortalized by the lengthy account of Josephus (War VII.viii.1-ix.2). Its history is brief and violent. According to Josephus it was first fortified by the high priest Jonathan, brother and successor of Judas Maccabeus (161-142 B.C.), but it came to prominence only in the time of Herod the Great. In 42 B.C., during the reign of Hyrcanus II, a certain Helix, an opponent of the brothers Herod and Phasael, came into temporary possession of the stronghold while Herod was away in Syria (Jos. War I.xii.1; Antiq. XIV.xi.7). Knowing its value full well, Herod soon recovered the citadel (Jos. War I.xii.2) and made it a haven for his family while he was away in Rome claiming his kingdom (40-39 B.C.; Jos. War I.xiii.7-8; xv.1; Antiq. XIV.xiii.8-9; xiv.6); one of Herod's first moves after his return was to force Antigonus to lift his siege of Masada, thus freeing Herod's relatives (Jos. War I.xv.3-4; xvi.1; Antiq. XIV.xv.1-2). Once in firm possession of his realm, Herod began serious work on the fortress and made it a monument to his genius as a builder and military strategist.

The Romans occupied the stronghold during the period of provincial governors in Judea (A.D. 6-66; cf. Jos. War II.xvii.2). In the summer of 66, however, a band of fanatical revolutionaries, known as the sicarii, took it from the Romans by ruse, and it became the focal point of sicarius activity throughout the war (Jos. War II.xvii.2, 8-9; xxii.2; IV.ix.3, 5). By 68 Vespasian had reduced the whole of Palestine save Jerusalem and the three wilderness fortresses of HERODIUM; MACHAERUS; and Masada. It was not until five years later that Flavius Silva, as commander of the Tenth Legion, raised an enormous earthwork and succeeded in breaching the walls. The 960 occupants, except for 7 women and children, formed and executed a suicide pact, which left the Romans masters of their bodies and the smoldering ruins of the palace (Jos. War VII.viii.1-ix.2).

Courtesy of the Orient Press Photo Company, Tel Aviv

15. Masada

The site of Masada is a mesa, the flat top of which comprises *ca.* twenty acres, much of which is still covered with soil; Josephus' statement that the land inside the fortress was cultivated is therefore not improbable. The sheer rock faces of the mountain rise *ca.* 820 feet on the E and 600 feet on the W above the surrounding valleys. The summit was approached by a "snake" path on the E and a less precipitous route on the W, the latter being guarded by a tower (Jos. War VII.viii.3). Fig. MAS 15.

Most of the extant ruins are to be attributed to Herod the Great. The whole plateau, except for a triple terrace on the N point, was encompassed by a formidable casemate wall with thirty-seven towers. Numerous cisterns were cut into the top of the mountain and into its face, particularly on the W, to ensure an abundant water supply (Jos. War VII.viii.3). A number of buildings are sufficiently well preserved to make evident their plan and function. Within the enclosure wall at the N end is a huge complex of buildings consisting of long, narrow rooms which served as arsenal and for stores (cf. Jos. War VII. viii.4); quarters for part of the garrison were also included in this structure. It is in this complex that the remains of an earlier tower—presumably belonging to Jonathan—are to be found. Adjoining the outer wall on the W is a large palace consisting of rooms grouped around three courtyards with store rooms attached; this residence was probably designed for Herod's entourage. Between the palace and the storehouse-arsenal lies another building, which probably served as the barracks for the Roman garrison during the period 6-66.

The plateau comes to a point on the N in a narrow finger which extends beyond the limits of the fortress proper and drops in two terrace-steps more than one hundred feet below the summit. It was this point which Herod, following his Hasmonean predecessors, selected for his personal palace. The upper palace, which was probably originated by Jonathan and rebuilt by Herod, consists of nine rooms and a semicircular terrace; on the second level sixty-five feet below is a circular structure the function of which is unknown. On the lower terrace, the small area of which abuts the precipitous cliffs, Herod erected a peristyle building with lavish appointments. The three levels of the palace are connected by stairways cut into the rock to hide them from view (Jos. War VII.viii.3).

The remains of two later buildings are found within the fortress: an apsidal church—probably Byzantine—and a monastic complex which may have gone with the church.

While the figures and description of Josephus are at points exaggerated or confused, he has accurately represented the formidableness and beauty of the Herodian stronghold.

Bibliography. E. Schürer, *A History of the Jewish People* (English trans., 1891), div. I, vol. II, pp. 251-53. A. Schulten, "Masada, die Burg des Herodes und die römischen Lager," *ZDPV*, 56 (1933), 1-185. M. Avi-Yonah *et al.*, *Masada* (1957); cf. *IEJ*, 7 (1957), 1.

R. W. FUNK

MASALOTH. KJV form of MESALOTH.

MASCHIL. KJV form of MASKIL.

MASH măsh [מש; Samar. משא; LXX Μοσοχ; *cf.* משך *in* I Chr. 1:17] (Gen. 10:23). A son of Aram. Mash is sometimes considered to be a mountain (mons Masius?), or, if identical with Akkadian *Māshu*, Lebanon–Anti-lebanon.

See also MISHAL.

A. HALDAR

MASHAL. Alternate form of MISHAL.

MASIAH mə sī′ə [Μεισαίας (B), Μασίας (A)] (I Esd. 5:34); KJV MASIAS —əs. Head of a family of "sons of Solomon's servants" who returned with

Zerubbabel. The name is omitted in the parallels Ezra 2:57; Neh. 7:59. C. T. FRITSCH

MASKIL măs′kĭl [מַשְׂכִּיל]; KJV MASCHIL. A word in the title of Ps. 32 and twelve other psalms. In Ps. 47:7—H 47:8 it is translated "a psalm" (KJV "with understanding"). The term is to be derived either from השכיל, "to have understanding" (e.g., Ps. 2:10; Isa. 44:18; cf. LXX συνέσεως in Ps. 32:1—H 31 title; συνετῶς in Ps. 47:7—H 47:8; εἰς σύνεσιν in Ps. 42:1—H 41 title) or from the musical term השכיל (II Chr. 30:22; cf. the parallelism מהללים ["praising"] in vs. 21 and משכילים in vs. 22). The term may signify a psalm accompanied by some special kind of music, or sung at a special (annual) festival.

Bibliography. S. Mowinckel, *Psalmenstudien,* IV (1922), 5-7; G. von Rad, *Das Geschichtsbild des Chronistischen Werkes* (1930), p. 103; W. O. Oesterley and T. H. Robinson, *An Introduction to the Books of the OT* (1934), pp. 183-84; G. W. Ahlström, *Psalm 89* (1959), pp. 21-26; H. D. Preuss, "Miktam in the Syrian Bible," *ZAW,* 71 (1959), 46; H. J. Kraus, *Psalmen* (1960), pp. xxii ff. J. HEMPEL

MASMAN. KJV Apoc. form of MAASMAS; SHEMAIAH.

MASON [גדר, *from verb* build a wall; חצב (*alternately* STONECUTTER), splitter, cutter; חרש קיר, cutter of a wall; חרש אבן קיר, cutter of a stone wall]. Though the ordinary man built his house, cutting his own stone, skilled masons, particularly Phoenicians or those trained by Phoenicians, played a considerable part in the life of Israel.* Solomonic structures show a high class of work in the cutting and laying of stones, including the use of mason's setting-out marks and identification marks (Fig. TEM 33). The tunnel which Hezekiah had made (II Kings 20:20; II Chr. 32:30) shows skill of the cutters in working from both ends toward the middle (Fig. HEZ 18). The palaces of Omri and Ahab at Samaria, together with the later additions there, are an example of excellent work with stone.* Remains of Herod's buildings are impressive in their masonry. Figs. WAL 1-2; SAM 10-11, 14-15, 20; TEM 11.

Much of the native stone in Palestine is soft and not difficult to cut, but becomes hard after exposure to air. A good mason could cut the stone so accurately that no mortar was needed in the laying of his wall. The mason who worked in brick would need mortar.

See also ARCHITECTURE. O. R. SELLERS

MASORA mə sôr′ə [מסורה, tradition]; MASORETES măs′ə rēts. Notes entered on the top, bottom, and side margins of MT MSS to safeguard the traditional transmission. They were subsequently assembled into independent collections; and during the later transmission and especially in printed Bibles, they were erroneously regarded as uniform. The Masoretes were the scribal preservers of the Masora.

See also TEXT, OT.

Bibliography. S. Frensdorff, *Ochlah we Ochlah* (1864). S. Baer and H. L. Strack, *Diqduqē ha-te'amim* (1879). C. D. Ginsburg, *The Massorah* (4 vols.; 1880-97); *Introduction to the Massoretico-Critical Edition of the Hebrew Bible* (1897). P. Kahle in H. Bauer and P. Leander, *Historische Grammatik der hebräischen Sprache* (1922). B. J. ROBERTS

MASORETIC ACCENTS măs′ə rĕt′ĭk.

1. Function. The MT of the OT contains accents of punctuation and other signs endowed with phonetic and musical meanings. Their significance for the proper reading of the text has been differently evaluated, from total neglect by the Lagarde school to high esteem by Delitzsch and Berliner. Two systems of accents are known: that of the twenty-one prosaic books and the system of the three so-called "poetic" books of Psalms, Job, and Proverbs.

The function of the Masoretic accents is at least twofold, in many cases threefold:

a) They constitute a most exact and intricate system of rhetoric punctuation of the MT. Problems of proper punctuation have frequently influenced the tradition of biblical exegesis, as, e.g., in Isa. 40:3. The Masoretic accents determine the punctuation thus:

> A voice cries:
> "In the wilderness prepare the way of the LORD,"

not:

> A voice cries in the wilderness:
> "Prepare the way of the LORD."

b) Many civilizations and ethnic groups of the fading ancient world used diacritical signs in their MSS in order to indicate to the reader the rise and fall of his voice. These primitive marks developed into the general ecphonetic notation, of which the Masoretic accents are one of many special cases. (The Byzantine, Armenian, Syrian, Nestorian, and Latin churches all developed ecphonetic systems of their own.) Aside from fixing the proper punctuation of a sacred text, the Masoretic accents became also the signs of a primitive notation, upon which the cantillation of scripture was based.

c) In many cases the Masoretic accents are also used to indicate, by their position, the stressed syllable of the respective word of the MT. This third function was imposed upon the Masoretic accent well after the first millennium.

2. The three systems. The external shape of the Masoretic accents has undergone several changes, as has their nomenclature. In correspondence with the three schools of MASORA, one distinguishes three sets of Masoretic accentuation. The oldest one is the so-called Palestinian system; it originated late in the fifth or early in the sixth century A.D. It marks only the strongest disjunctive accents, called in Hebrew מפסקים (full stop, half stop, semicolon, colon, comma, dash) by various arrangements of dots or small strokes. The second was the Babylonian, more complex and also more extensive than the earlier system. The last and definite system was established in Tiberias *ca.* A.D. 900 by Ben Asher and Ben Naphtali. It has been generally accepted by all Jewish groups and was "canonized" by the rabbinic authorities.

3. Age and provenance. The history of the Masoretic accents belongs to the most difficult aspects of textual criticism (*see* TEXT, OT). Its origin is still obscure, in spite of the efforts of Praetorius, Kahle, Grimme, and other scholars to discover the

Table 1			
8th–9th century			
EARLY MEDI-EVAL GREEK	ECPHONETIC NAME	LATIN NEUMES	HEBREW NEGINOT IN THE ('א׳מ׳ת׳-BOOKS)
	ὀξεῖα	Acutus (Virga)	Ṭiphḥâ
	βαρεῖα	Gravis	Legharmeh
	ὑπόκρισις	Quilisma descendens	Dargâ or Shalshéleth
	καθίστη	Circumflexa	Zarqâ
	κρημαστὴ ἀπ' ἔξω	Flexa	'Athnaḥ
	συρματική = περισπωμένη	Circumflexa	Zarqâ-sillûq
Later development 11th–12th centuries			
EARLY MEDI-EVAL GREEK	BYZANTINE	LATIN NEUMES	HEBREW NEGINOT ('א׳מ׳ת׳)
	ὀξεῖα	Virga	Tiphḥâ or Yethibh
	ὀλίγον (ἴσον)	Virga iacens	
	κρημαστή ἀπ' ἔξω	Flexa or clivis	'Atnaḥ
	κρημαστή ἀπ' ἔζω	Podatus	Shôphār or Babylonian Tiphḥâ
+	τέλεια	Punctus	Sôph Pasûq

Exod. 12:2 in Three Renditions (*see* p. 298)

starting point and origin of all ecphonetic notation, and in particular that of scriptural accentuation. Today many, but by no means all, scholars accept Kahle's suggestion that the accents of the Palestinian Masora originated in or near Nisibis (in E Syria) in the fifth century A.D.: the external resemblance of those accents with the oldest Syriac ones seems to sustain this hypothesis.

Whether the Masoretes borrowed their accents from Byzantine lectionaries, as Praetorius claimed, or whether they established their system in collaboration with a Nestorian school of catechetes, as Kahle proposes, or whether the method of Alexandrian grammarians played an essential part in the early Masora (Fleischer's assumption), remains problematic. However, there can be no doubt about the resemblance of Byzantine ecphonetic and Hebrew Masoretic accents (*see* Table 1). The ecphonetic accents became, in the course of many centuries, the forerunners of our Western musical notation.

4. Cantillation of the Hebrew Text. Masoretic accents have preserved the traditional features of ancient cantillation, a practice which was used long before the destruction of the temple (A.D. 70) and probably went back to Ezra himself in the fourth century B.C. Cantillation of scripture was governed by grammatical rules, syntactic analysis, and the interpretation of the text. The study of the Masoretic accents and of their significance for the cantillation of the text is therefore of extreme importance for the exegesis of the MT.

The practice of chanting biblical texts antedates by many centuries the establishment of the Masoretic accents, as we know from early tannaitic literature, since a rabbinic discussion in the Talmud (Meg. 32*a*) takes cantillation for granted and even closes with the categorical dictum: "Whoever reads Scripture without melody and the Mishna without chant, to him applies the biblical verse: 'I gave them laws which were not beautiful'" (from Ezek. 20:25). Rabbi Aqiba also championed the practice of cantillation (Tosef. Par. 4(3), 7, ed. Mandelkern). There is, however, no evidence that the chant of these early centuries was in any way regulated. We must assume that cantillation crystallized but slowly into a standardized pattern during the thousand years that preceded its regulation by Masoretic accents. But this new unity was lost again, when the subsequent migrations of the Jews broke up the once-effected general pattern. Thus, today, we make a distinction between three basic traditions of cantillation, typical of the Ashkenazic, Sephardic, and Yemenite Jews, respectively. Nonetheless, the same set of Masoretic accents has been accepted by all three groups as the basis of their scriptural chant. The latter is called *trôp* in Hebrew (from τρόπος), and must well be distinguished from the *ta'amê migrâ'*, as the Masoretic accents are called in Hebrew.

Of the three oral traditions of cantillation, the Yemenite one is doubtless the oldest. Three significant facts confirm this assumption: (*a*) The Yemenite Jews use the same group of motifs for both the Torah and the prophetic lesson; (*b*) the musical range of their cantillation is narrow and hardly exceeds a fourth; (*c*) there are resemblances and even identities between Yemenite cantillation and ancient

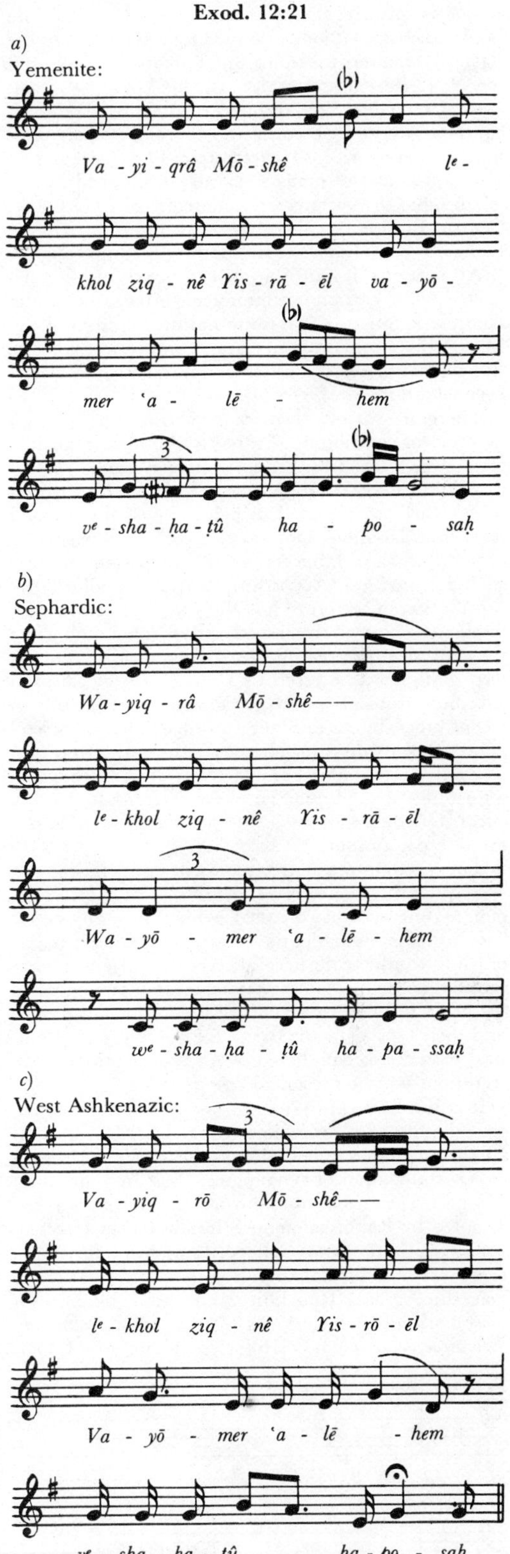

After A. Z. Idelsohn, *Jewish Music in Its Historical Development;* copyright, 1929, by Holt, Rinehart and Winston, Inc.; copyright renewed in 1956

elements of Gregorian chant (*see below*). The Sephardic cantillation is divided into two types of the Eastern Mediterranean group (Balkan, Turkey, and the Near East in general) and the Western group (Low Countries, England, France). However, their common origin is obvious, and there are many similarities between the two groups. The Ashkenazic tradition knows of many variants, influenced by the folk song of the various environments (SW Germany, Central Europe, Poland, Latvia, Lithuania, Russia, Hungary, etc.), but its basic identity is unmistakable.

All systems of cantillation are very closely connected with certain grammatical principles of the Hebrew language. The punctuating function of the Masoretic accents, upon which cantillation rests, is still evident in every chanted scriptural verse of whatever tradition.

There are various theories concerning the original function of cantillation. Probably the most plausible ones were offered by Franz Delitzsch and E. Hommel. Both scholars emphasize the gradual transition from clearly accentuated speech to musically intoned recitation. Hommel, moreover, gives many examples of peddlers' and laborers' cries which demonstrate such a transition. According to these scholars, the cantillation of scripture has the function of drawing public attention to the lesson and of solemnizing the ritual of scripture reading. A somewhat different interpretation was offered by the *Tossafists* (Talmud commentators of the High Middle Ages) and, in recent times, by A. Berliner and especially A. Ackermann. According to their view all cantillation had originally a mnemotechnical purpose, and they list a number of medieval Hebrew statements to this effect. Of course, the two theories mentioned do not exclude each other.

The various musical systems of cantillation are clearly distinguished by the motifs for the strong, punctuating accents (מפסקים), which, in many cases, have a distinctly cadential character. Since it is impossible to illustrate here all traditional systems of cantillation, let us confine ourselves to a comparative list of six disjunctive accents of the various traditions and their typical motifs (*see* p. 296). Finally, one biblical sentence as cantillated by each of the three main traditions will be presented (*see* p. 297).

It is but natural that these melodic patterns, repeated and heard three times every week, for at least a millennium, have exerted a powerful influence upon the crystallization of synagogue chant in general.

The first musical notation of cantillation was attempted by Rabbi Salomon Mintz in North Italy, *ca.* 1483 (MS in the Jews College, London). This, however, was an effort lacking in system and method. It was the great Reuchlin and his collaborator Böschenstein, who in his *De Accentibus Linguae Hebraicae* (Haguenau, 1518) gave the first exact notation of Pentateuch cantillation of the Ashkenazim. Many others followed Reuchlin's example—e.g., Sebastian Münster, A. Guarin, Bartolocci. Reuchlin's (or Böschenstein's) sources are somewhat obscure, although their notation reflects a cantillation which hardly deviates from today's Ashkenazic rendition.

Modern scholars have noticed in this version of cantillation a conspicuously pentatonic element, which does not occur in either the Sephardic or the Yemenite tradition. It has been pointed out that the German version of Gregorian chant during the Middle Ages exhibits very similar pentatonic motifs. The profound research of Peter Wagner let it seem probable that the preference for pentatonic formulas in the High Middle Ages was a result of the recent intrusion of secular Teutonic folk song. This theory might also account for the pentatonic elements in the Jewish tradition of Central Europe. However, there can be no doubt that the original tradition was not pentatonic, but based upon a tetrachordal structure of melodic invention, which is generally characteristic of all ancient strata of Jewish music.

This fact is demonstrated by the frequent resemblances between Yemenite cantillation and ancient elements of Gregorian chant (*see below*).

We observe that a syntactically ordered Hebrew sentence (according to Masoretic principles) and its melody have lost their original punctuating structure in the Latin version. Only the melodic flow was retained, including the characteristic cadence.

Bibliography. J. Reuchlin, *De accentibus linguae hebraicae* (1518). S. Dérenbourg, *Manuel du lecteur* (1871). W. Wickes, *Poetical Accentuation of the OT* (1881); *Accentuation of the So-called Prose Books of the OT* (1887). A. Ackermann, *Das hermeneutische Element der biblischen Akzentzeichen* (1893); "Der synagogale Gesang in seiner historischen Entwicklung," in Winter and Wuensche, *Die jüdische Literatur* (1897), III, 477-525. F. Praetorius, *Über die Herkunft der hebräischen Akzente* (1901), M. L. Margolis, "Accents in Hebrew," *Jewish Encyclopedia,* I (1902), 149-58. F. L. Cohen, "Cantillation," *Jewish Encyclopedia,* III (1902), 537-49. P. Wagner, *Einführung in die Gregorianischen Melodien,* III (1921), 111 ff. A. Z. Idelsohn, "Reste althebräischer Musik," *Ost und West* (1912-13), vol. XII, col. 1041; vol. XIII, col. 225; *Thesaurus of Hebrew Oriental Melodies,* vols. II, IV (1922-28). P. Kahle, *Masoreten des Ostens* (1913); in H. Bauer and P. Leander, *Historische Grammatik der hebräische Sprache* (1922); *Masoreten des Westens* (1927). H. Löwenstein, "Eine pentatonische Bibelweise in der deutschen Synagoge," *Zeitschrift für Musikwissenschaft,* XII (1930), 513-26. A. Gastoué, "Chant Juif et Chant Grégorien," *Revue du Chant Grégorien,* fasc. 6 ff (1930-31). C. Hoeg, *La notation ecphonétique* (1935). L. Kornitzer, "Die Pentatonik bei der Vorlesung der Thora," *Der Jüdische Kantor,* no. 3 (1936). J. Yasser, "Medieval Quartal Harmony," *Musical Quarterly,* XXIII (1937), 170, 333; (1938), 351 ff. R. Lachmann, *Jewish Cantillation in the Island of Djerbe* (1940). G. Reese, *Music in the Middle Ages* (1940), pp. 160 ff. E. Werner, "Preliminary Notes on Jewish and Catholic Musical Punctuation," *HUCA* (1940), pp. 335-66; "Two Obscure Sources in Reuchlin's De

accentibus linguae hebraicae," *Historia Judaica,* XVI (1954), 39-54; "Postbiblical Music," *New Oxford History of Music,* I (1957), 313-35 (and notes). S. Rosowsky, *The Cantillation of the Bible* (1957; use with great caution). E. WERNER

MASPHA măs'fə. KJV Apoc. form of MIZPAH (I Macc. 3:46 [*see* MIZPAH § 5]; I Macc. 5:35 [but read ALEMA; so RSV]).

MASREKAH măs'rə kə [משרקה, vineyard(?)] (Gen. 36:36; I Chr. 1:47). The home of Samlah, a king of Edom. The name may be preserved in Jebel el-Mushraq, near the Nabatean site of Khirbet et-Telajeh, twenty miles S-SW of Ma'an, near the Hismeh Valley. Eusebius puts it in the Gebalene, the N part of Edom. V. R. GOLD

MASSA măs'ə [משא]. The seventh son of Ishmael, and the eponymous ancestor of a N Arabian tribe (Gen. 25:14; I Chr. 1:30). A people of Mas'a (Mas'ai) are also mentioned by Tiglath-pileser III, along with the inhabitants of Tema (Gen. 25:15), Saba', Haiappa (? = Ephah; Gen. 25:4), Badana, Hatti, and Idiba'ileans (= Adbeel; Gen. 25:13), who submitted to his rule and paid tribute (*ANET* 283).

The name occurs also in Prov. 30:1; 31:1, where it is a part of the title. In Prov. 30:1 it appears with a definite article, המשא, and hence can be rendered as "the burden" or "the oracle." The term משא is frequently used of prophetic oracles or utterances (Isa. 13:1; Nah. 1:1; Hab. 1:1; etc.). However, as has been shown, משא has acquired in prophetic usage an ominous sense, suggesting the idea of an impending doom or the judgment of God. Such an idea, however, is not present in Prov. 30, and hence המשא cannot mean "the burden" or "the oracle" here. Perhaps the term was originally a gentilic, המשאי (="the Massait")—e.g., an inhabitant of Massa or a member of the tribe or the nation of Massa. On the other hand, in Prov. 31:1 the word is without a definite article, and it may be read "king of Massa." Thus, in Prov. 30:1; 31:1, "Massa" may refer, as in Gen. 25:14; I Chr. 1:30, to the N Arabian tribe of Massa.

The names of these two persons occur also in some form in certain Minaean and other ancient S Arabian inscriptions. In Bar. 3:23 there is a reference to the "sons of Hagar [Ishmaelites or N Arabians], who seek for understanding on the earth."

Bibliography. P. K. Hitti, *The History of the Arabs* (1953), p. 43; W. F. Albright, "The Biblical Tribe of Massa and Some Congeners," *Studi orientalistici in onore di Giorgio Levi della Vida* (1956), pp. 1-14. J. L. MIHELIC

MASSADA mă sā'də. Alternate form of MASADA.

MASSAH AND MERIBAH măs'ə, mĕr'ə bə [מסה, ומריבה, מסה, *from* נסה, to test, try; מריבה, *from* ריב, to strive, contend, find fault]. The names of a station of the Israelites in the wilderness.

The combination of these two words occurs three times: Exod. 17:7; Deut. 33:8; Ps. 95:8. The first refers to the locality where the lack of water caused the Israelites to grumble and to challenge Moses' position of leadership; and, as Moses implied in Exod. 16:7-8, this contention amounted to testing Yahweh's presence among them: "Is the LORD among us or not?"

In both the second and the third occurrence of this combination, the allusion is to the above experience in the wilderness, but with the following difference. In Deut. 33:8, Yahweh is said to have tested the tribe of Levi at Massah and contended with it at the waters of Meribah. This suggests an experience different from that contained in Exod. 17:7 or in the parallel account in Num. 20:13, of which otherwise there is no record. On the other hand, it is possible that the episode of Exod. 17:7; Num. 20:1-13 was interpreted by the writer of the Blessing of Moses (Deut. 33) as God's testing of Moses, who was of the tribe of Levi (Exod. 6:17-27). Deut. 33:8-10, however, breaks completely the style, meter, and content of the rest of the poem. The passage is regarded by some scholars as a late addition. On the other hand, in Ps. 95:8-9 the allusion is clear and corresponds with the actions presented in Exod. 17:1-7; Num. 20:1-13. Whether Deut. 33:8 is a reference to a now forgotten historical experience, in which Levi's faithfulness was subjected to a test, or whether it is a later, interpretative addition, as some scholars claim, or both, we do not know.

For the question of location and other allusions to Meribah, *see* MERIBAH.

Bibliography. F. M. Cross and D. M. Freedman, "The Blessing of Moses," *JBL,* LXVII (1948), 191-210; E. Arden, "How Moses Failed God," *JBL,* LXXVI (1957), 50-52; A. S. Kapelrud, "How Tradition Failed Moses," *JBL,* LXXVI (1957), 242. J. L. MIHELIC

MASSEBAH măs'ə bə. Transcription of the Hebrew מצבה (*massēbhâ*), used by archaeologists as a technical term for "sacred pillar." *See* PILLAR. Fig. PIL 55.

MASSEIAH; MASSIAS. Apoc. forms of MAASEIAH.

MASSORAH, MASSORETES. *See* MASORA.

MAST [תרן (Isa. 33:23; Ezek. 27:5); חבל (Prov. 23:34), *possibly* what is roped, *cf.* חבל, rope]. A long pole rising from the keel of a vessel through the deck to support the sail.

Of the three biblical references (Prov. 23:34; Isa. 33:23; Ezek. 27:5), only Ezek. 27:5 refers to the mast of a specific vessel, the mast (of cedar of Lebanon) of a Tyrian ship propelled by oar and sail.

The earliest masts on Egyptian river boats were bipod to give greater stability to the reed craft. Later a single-pole mast was used, and when it was not required for navigation, it was commonly unstepped and placed on deck. On seagoing Mediterranean vessels permanent masts, supported by shrouds, came to be standard equipment, but even these larger ships sometimes had masts that could be dismantled.

Bibliography. A. Neuburger, *The Technical Arts and Sciences of the Ancients* (trans. H. L. Brose; 1930), pp. 491-92.
W. S. McCULLOUGH

MASTEMAH măs'tə mə. *See* DEMON § B.

MASTER (AS TITLE OF JESUS). 1. A KJV translation of διδάσκαλος. *See* TEACHER.

2. A translation of ἐπιστάτης (from ἐφίστημι, "stand over"), a term meaning "manager" or "chief" and applied to various kinds of officials in the LXX and in Greek literature (e.g., to overseers of work, military officers, etc.). Only Luke uses it in the NT, each time in the vocative, ἐπιστάτα, as addressed to Jesus. At corresponding points Matthew and Mark use διδάσκαλε (cf. Luke 8:24; 9:49), or κύριε or ῥαββί (cf. Luke 9:33), or nothing at all (cf. Luke 5:5; 8:45; 17:13). Luke evidently regarded all these terms as roughly equivalent, using ἐπιστάτα chiefly for reasons of style. PIERSON PARKER

MASTIC [σχῖνον]; KJV MASTICK. A shrub or small tree whose sap provides a gumlike resin used for chewing and medicine in the Near East. The tree

16. Mastic

is referred to (in the garden of Joakim in Babylon) in Sus. 54. The shrubby tree, *Pistacia lentiscus* L., is common throughout the Mediterranean world, though the island of Chios is famed for high quality mastic.

See also BALM; BALSAM; FLORA § A7*b*.

Fig. MAS 16. J. C. TREVER

MATHANIAS. KJV Apoc. form of BESCASPASMYS.

MATHUSALA. KJV NT form of METHUSELAH.

MATRED mā'trĭd [מטרד, spear, *from* Arab. *mitrad*(?)] (Gen. 36:39; I Chr. 1:50). A parent of Mehetabel, the wife of Hadar (Hadad), a king of Edom. The MT makes Matred the daughter of Mezehab, but in Genesis the LXX and the Syr. more credibly make Matred the son of Mezahab. M. NEWMAN

MATRITES mă'trīts [מטרי] (I Sam. 10:21; RSV rightly includes the LXX addition); KJV MATRI —trī. A family of the tribe of Benjamin. In the selection of the king the lot fell upon them; and one of their members, Saul of Gibeah, was crowned the first king of Israel. E. R. DALGLISH

MATTAN măt'ən [מתן, gift (of God)]. **1.** A priest of Baal slain before his altar by the revolutionaries who killed Queen Athaliah and placed Joash on the throne of Judah (II Kings 11:18; cf. II Chr. 23:17).

2. The father of Shephatiah, a prince under King Zedekiah in the days of Jeremiah the prophet (Jer. 38:1).

Bibliography. M. Noth, *Die israelitischen Personennamen* (1928), pp. 37, 170. B. T. DAHLBERG

MATTANAH măt'ə nə [מתנה, gift] (Num. 21:18-19). A stopping place of the Israelites on their route from the Arnon into the territory of Sihon king of the Amorites. Khirbet el-Medeiyineh, on the left bank of the Wadi eth-Themed in the upper reaches of the Wadi el-Wala, has been suggested as the most probable location. Its distance SE of Madeba would agree with the figure of twelve miles given by Eusebius in his Onomasticon. A dry ditch or moat encircled the mound about halfway down the slope. Exploration disclosed also traces of a wall surrounding the top of the mound. The pottery sherds indicate occupation from perhaps shortly before 1200 to *ca.* 800 B.C., most of it belonging to the Early Iron I period (1200-900).

Bibliography. B. Baensch, *Exodus-Leviticus-Numeri* (1903), p. 580; N. Glueck, "Explorations in Eastern Palestine," *AASOR*, XIV (1934), 13-27. J. L. MIHELIC

MATTANIAH măt'ə nī'ə [מתניה, מתניהו; Apoc. Ματθανίας]; KJV Apoc. MATTHANIAS măth'ə-nī'əs. **1.** The original name of King Zedekiah of Judah (II Kings 24:17). The name was changed by the Babylonian conqueror Nebuchadnezzar.

2. The son of Mica, a Levite and Asaphite, and one of the first to return to Jerusalem after the Exile, according to the Chronicler (I Chr. 9:15).

3. A son of Heman, and a member of the temple musicians, who "prophesied" with lyres, harps, and cymbals (I Chr. 25:4).

4. A Levite and Asaphite (*see* ASAPH; II Chr. 20:14).

5. A son of Asaph, a Levite who took part in the sanctifying of the temple in the religious reform under King Hezekiah of Judah (II Chr. 29:13).

6. A Levitic leader of the temple choir in the time of Zerubbabel (Neh. 11:17, 22; 12:8).

7. A Levitic gatekeeper who guarded the storehouses of the gates in Jerusalem (Neh. 12:25).

8. A Levite, the father of Shemaiah (Neh. 12:35).

9. Grandfather of Hanan, a treasurer in the storehouse; and the father of Zaccur (Neh. 13:13).

10. Four of the returned exiles who had married foreign wives and were therefore thought to have broken the covenant (Ezra 10:26, 27, 30, 37; I Esd. 9:27, 31).

Some of the above may be identical, but it is now impossible to tell. E. R. ACHTEMEIER

MATTATHA măt'ə thə [Ματταθά] (Luke 3:31). One of the ancestors of Jesus. His father was Nathan, a son of King David.

MATTATHIAS măt'ə thī'əs [Ματταθίας = מתתיה, מתתיהו(?)]. **1.** Mattathias I, the father of the Hasmoneans. He was a native of Jerusalem but settled in Modin. A member of the priestly family of Jehoiarib (cf. I Chr. 24:7), his genealogy is listed in I Macc. 2:1 and in Jos. Antiq. XII.vi.3.

Mattathias defied King Antiochus' decree of violation of the law by declaring: "I and my sons and my brothers will live by the covenant of our fathers. Far be it from us to desert the law." He refused to sacrifice to heathens and slayed an offender. He commanded that the Jews fight on the sabbath rather than be cut down, and he conducted underground guerrilla warfare against the enemy, circumcised children, and thereby rescued the law (I Macc. 2 ff). His motto was: "Let every one who is zealous for the law . . . come out with me!"

He led for one year and died in 168/167 B.C. at the age of 146. His burial place was in the ancestral tomb in Modin.

His last will and testament to his sons was: "Obey the ordinance of the law." Therein, as portrayed by Josephus, he stressed the idea of immortality, "for though our bodies are mortal and subject to death, they can, through the meaning of our deeds, attain heights of immortality" (Antiq. XII.vi.3).

The rabbis spoke of Mattathias in glowing terms (Meg. 11*a*). As progenitor of the Hasmoneans, he is remembered in special Hanukkah prayers as the spearhead of the battle for religious freedom.

It has been suggested that Taxo in the Assumption of Moses is to be identified with Mattathias.

Bibliography. S. Zeitlin, "The Assumption of Moses," *JQR*, vol. 38 (1947); R. H. Pfeiffer, *History of NT Times* (1949), pp. 14, 80; S. Tedesche and S. Zeitlin, *The First Book of Maccabees* (1950), p. 32.

2. Mattathias II, third son of Simon the Hasmonean. He was murdered by Ptolemy, a brother-in-law, when the latter killed Simon and his sons at Jericho (I Macc. 16:14; Jos. Antiq. XIII.viii.1; War I.ii.3).

3. Son of Absalom; one of Jonathan's (the Hasmonean's) captains who escaped ambush. When the Syrians under Demetrius attacked the Hasmonean army, they fled at Hazor, but Jonathan then came to rout the Syrians (I Macc. 11:70).

Bibliography. R. H. Pfeiffer, *History of NT Times* (1949), p. 19.

4. Son of Ananos; appointed by Agrippa I as high priest (A.D. 42-43; Jos. Antiq. XIX.vi.4).

5. Mattathias ben Margalit, a scribe who, with Judas ben Sariphaeus, insurrected against Herod. Josephus (Antiq. XVII.vi.2) calls him a "celebrated interpreter of Jewish law." Mattathias and Judas incited young men to pull down the large golden eagle which Herod had erected over the gate of the temple. For this insurrection Mattathias was burned. Josephus remarks that on the night there was an eclipse of the moon (War I.xxxiii).

6. The father of Josephus; descendant of a distinguished priestly family; there are also two ancestors of the same name. One of the forefathers called Mattathias had married a daughter of Alexander Janneus (Jos. Life I; Antiq. XVI.vii.1).

7. Mattathias ben Theophilus, a native of Jerusalem who succeeded Simon ben Boethus as high priest appointed by Herod (5-4 B.C.). He became ritually unclean on the Day of Atonement and could not perform the services; he was then assisted by one Joseph ben Ellemus. Herod later deprived Mattathias of the high priesthood (Jos. Antiq. XVII.vi.4). In the Talmud his name is not mentioned in the narrative (Tos. Yom. 1.4; Yom. 12*b;* J. Yom. 38*d*).

8. Son of Theophilus; appointed high priest in A.D. 65 by Agrippa II. He succeeded Jesus ben Gamaliel, but was deposed before the siege. Because he was of the aristocratic peace party, he was put to death by Simon ben Giora, whom he had invited to Jerusalem (Jos. Antiq. XX.ix.7).

Bibliography. H. Graetz, *Monatsschrift* (1881), pp. 62-64.

9. Son of Boethus; high priest (Jos. War VI.xxii; IV.ix.11; V.xiii.1. S. B. Hoenig

MATTATTAH măt'ə tə [מתתה, gift (of God); Apoc. Ματταθίας] (Ezra 10:33; I Esd. 9:33); KJV MATTATHAH —thə; KJV Apoc. MATTHIAS mă-thī'əs. One of the laymen persuaded by Ezra to divorce their foreign wives.

Bibliography. M. Noth, *Die israelitischen Personennamen* (1928), p. 170.

MATTENAI măt'ə nī [מתני, gift (of God); Apoc. 'Αλταννaῖος (Codex A), Μαλταννaῖος (Codex B)]; KJV Apoc. ALTANEUS ăl'tə nē'əs. **1.** A priest in the days of Joiakim the high priest (Neh. 12:19).

2. A layman among those persuaded by Ezra to divorce their foreign wives (Ezra 10:33; I Esd. 9:33).

3. Another layman in the same group as 2 *above* (Ezra 10:37; the name is not recognizable in the parallel I Esd. 9:34).

Bibliography. M. Noth, *Die israelitischen Personennamen* (1928), pp. 38, 170. B. T. Dahlberg

MATTHAN măth'ăn [Ματθάν=מתן (II Chr. 23:17; Jer. 38:1)] (Matt. 1:15; Luke 3:23 ff in MS D). An ancestor of Jesus. F. W. Gingrich

MATTHANIAS. KJV Apoc. form of Mattaniah.

MATTHAT măth'ăt [Ματθάτ, Μαθθαθ, Μαθθατ, Ματταθ=מתת] (Luke 3:24, 29). The name of two ancestors of Jesus.

MATTHELAS. KJV Apoc. form of Maaseiah 12.

MATTHEW măth'ū [Μαθθαῖος, Ματθαῖος; Heb. *or* Aram. מתי *or* מתאי, *shortened from* מתתיה *or* מתניה, gift of Y]. One of the twelve apostles of Jesus, according to the four NT lists (Mark 3:18; Matt. 10:3; Luke 6:15; Acts 1:13).

Matt. 9:9; 10:3 assert that he was a tax collector before he became a follower of Jesus. In Mark 2:14 this man is called "Levi the son of Alphaeus" (D, Θ, and other MSS read "James the son of Alphaeus" here, obviously in an attempt to bring the name into line with the list in Mark 3:16-18). Luke calls him simply Levi (5:27, 29). *See* Levi 4; James 4.

In Mark and Luke, Levi and Matthew seem not to be regarded as the same person. Only in Matthew is this equivalence made. Is it historically correct?

It is argued that Jews frequently bore two names, that the name Matthew may have been given him after he became a disciple of Jesus (cf. Simon Peter), that the tradition lying behind the identification in Matthew is very early, and that there would be no good reason for the equivalence if it were not historical. Conversely, it is held that Mark and Luke know nothing of it, that it is not proved that Jews carried two Jewish names ("Peter" is an epithet, not a true name), that "the tax collector" of Matt. 10:3 is an early gloss intended originally to refer to James the son of Alphaeus (who in some texts of Mark 2:14 is said to have been the tax collector), and that Origen and others denied the identity of Levi and Matthew (*see below*).

It seems obvious from the many problems in coordinating the four NT lists and doing justice to other data about the apostles in the gospels that the exact membership of the first group was soon forgotten. The early tradition of the identity of Levi and Matthew may or may not be sound.

If Matthew was Levi, he was in the service of Herod Antipas near or at Capernaum. It was his duty to levy on merchandise carried over the Damascus-Acre road and perhaps to tax the fishing and other industries of the area. Jesus' ministry around Capernaum provided many opportunities for contacts between the two prior to the occasion of the call (Mark 2:14).

Luke says that Levi entertained Jesus and a large company of tax collectors at a banquet in his home (5:29; the location is unclear in Mark 2:15). Was this Levi's way of celebrating his break with the old life, his method of introducing others to Jesus, or simply a gesture of gratitude to one who looked on tax collectors and other despised persons, not as horrible sinners, but as potential members of the kingdom of God?

The early church believed that Matthew wrote our first gospel (*see* MATTHEW, GOSPEL OF). Heracleon (Clement *Stromata* IV.ix), Origen (*Contra Celsum* I.lxii), and others distinguished between Levi and Matthew. Eusebius said that Matthew first evangelized among Hebrews and then among other peoples (Euseb. Hist. III.24.6). Clement of Alexandria made Matthew a vegetarian (*Instructor* II.i). Heracleon (Clement *Stromata* IV.ix) held that he died a natural death, but late legend dramatized his death by fire or the sword. It tended to confuse Matthew and Matthias. The tradition in the Babylonian Talmud (Sanh. 43*a*) concerning the trial and execution of "Matthai" is probably of no historical value.

Bibliography. T. Zahn, *Introduction to the NT*, II (1909), 506-9, 522-24. M. R. James, *The Apocryphal NT* (1924), pp. 204, 460-62, 466-67. B. W. Bacon, *Studies in Matthew* (1930), pp. 39-41. V. Taylor, *The Gospel According to St. Mark* (1952), pp. 202-3. E. J. Goodspeed, *The Twelve* (1957), pp. 25-28, 41-43; *Matthew, Apostle and Evangelist* (1959). E. P. BLAIR

***MATTHEW, GOSPEL OF.** The first, in order, of the gospels, and the opening book of the NT.

See map "Palestine: Matthew, Mark and Luke," under MARK, GOSPEL OF.

1. The order of the gospels
2. The traditional theory
3. The structure of Matthew
4. Main sources: Mark and Q
5. Special source or sources
6. OT quotations in Matthew
7. Material peculiar to Matthew
8. The "ecclesiastical" gospel
9. Background, place, and date
10. Later influence
Bibliography

1. The order of the gospels. Matthew is the first of the gospels, in the traditional order. But this is not necessarily the chronological order, and there is good reason for thinking that Matthew was one of the later gospels, rather than the first. Tradition has maintained its early date, and the location of Matthew as the first book of the NT has in turn supported the tradition, at least has maintained its wide acceptance in popular thought. But, in the first place, it is quite certain that Matthew is later than Mark, upon which, like Luke, it is based (*see* GOSPELS); further, as we shall see, its formulation of the gospel tradition, the problems with which it deals, especially those of the Palestinian or Syrian church, the carefully arranged order and articulation of its contents—all these probably point to a later date than Luke. Nevertheless, the fact that Luke and Matthew reflect no influence of one upon the other—save as the MS text of Matthew has influenced Luke, as it has influenced the other gospels—makes it impossible for us to claim that either of these two gospels must be later than the other. And anyway, their dates must be somewhere within the same generation, approximately between A.D. 90 or 95 and A.D. 115. So far as internal evidence goes, it is only a general probability that the order of the gospels was Mark, Luke, Matthew, John.

But this literary probability is confirmed archaeologically:

a) Since the time of Irenaeus (A.D. 180), and even before, the four beasts named in Rev. 4:7 have been identified, in Christian exegesis and art, with the four evangelists—the fourfold gospel canon had been formed presumably thirty years before Irenaeus wrote his work *Against Heresies* (see III.11.8). The lion was Mark, the ox was Luke, the "living creature with the face of a man" was Matthew, the flying eagle John. But there is nothing in these gospels, either covert reference or literary or theological character, to suggest the identifications.

Why should Mark be symbolized by a lion, Luke by an ox, Matthew by a man? The description is based on Ezek. 1:10, but the symbolism is modified—in Ezekiel each figure had "the face of a man in front, . . . the face of a lion on the right side, . . . the face of an ox on the left side, . . . the face of an eagle at the back." The author of Revelation has made this over into four separate creatures, not alike in form or features. The ultimate origin of the symbol may have been ancient Assyrian mythology, or rather the later Assyrian astral lore, in which Nergal was a winged lion, Marduk a winged bull, Nebo a human being, Ninib an eagle. These four astral gods were identified with the four cardinal directions—a view reflected in Irenaeus' insistence that there must be four gospels—and can be only four—as there are four cardinal directions, east, west, north, south, and four winds, four quarters of the earth, etc. Four was also Plato's "perfect" number, as later expositors pointed out. But the strange and unaccountable thing is Irenaeus' assumption that his readers will recognize, as something already known, that the lion symbolized Mark, etc; and that, in other words, the order of the evangelists is the order of the four living creatures: Mark,

Luke, Matthew, John. This is unaccountable—unless it was the order in which, as some early Christians recalled (contrary to Papias, *ca.* A.D. 135, and others), the gospels had been written.

b) Further evidence for this tradition, as contrasted with the views of Papias and, later, Augustine, may be seen in the old Roman mosaics in the mausoleum of Galla Placidia, outside the Church of San Vitale at Ravenna. Here on a low, antique bookcase with sloping shelves the four gospels are pictured in the following order:

MARCVS	LVCAS
MATTEVS	IOANN ES

The date of the mosaic is *ca.* 440. Galla Placidia was the sister of Honorius, the Emperor of the West, and her adventurous and really heroic life ended at Ravenna soon after she had ordered her mausoleum to be built. The date of the mosaics, 440, is scarcely more than a century after the Council of Nicea (325), and only nine years after the Council of Ephesus (431). It was evidently early enough to antedate the popular acceptance of Augustine's conjecture, based on Papias, according to which Matthew came first, then Mark, "walking in Matthew's footsteps and abridging him," then Luke and John (Augustine *On the Agreement of the Evangelists* I.2.4).

It cannot be said that a specific tradition underlies this order at Ravenna, though it is not improbable. Some explanation there must be. Possibly some artist or scholar, uninfluenced by the Papian-Augustinian view, preserved what once had been the traditional order, the same as that presupposed by Irenaeus. For these mosaics are not Byzantine but Roman—i.e., old Italian. The same order is found elsewhere: e.g., in the nearby Accademia at Venice, where the medallion reliefs in the ceiling of the Sala della Presentazione preserve the same order. And there are other instances: e.g., a Spanish copper-gilt set of plaques of the four evangelists in the Metropolitan Museum, New York (M 167), probably from the twelfth century; or a modern Russian brass binding, in relief, of an Evangelisterion by Ovchinnikov, where the order is reversed—the binding is modern, but its motif is ancient.

Luke	Mark
John	Matthew

Of course, such evidence is not conclusive, but it supports the probability advanced on the basis of the literary data, and—to say the least—demands an explanation, the simplest being the one already suggested by the internal evidence of the gospels themselves. On the other hand, there is no similar archaeological or literary evidence, so far as we know, of a similar early date of origin, supporting the Papian-Augustinian order.

Other orders are found in various MSS, but they are more easily explained: e.g., the placing of the apostles' names first, as in the Clermont list (from Egypt, *ca.* 300), Matthew, John, Mark, Luke; or the Cheltenham list, discovered by Mommsen in 1885 and sometimes called the Mommsen list (from North Africa, *ca.* 360), Matthew, Mark, John, Luke—where the apostles are kept together but Mark, as the "abridgment" of Matthew, follows next to it; or in Codex Bezae, probably from the fifth century, which has Matthew, John, Luke, Mark, and reflects the low estimate of Mark held commonly after the fourth century. (It is surprising that the copyists of D did not bring Luke-Acts into sequence.) *See bibliography.*

c) Moreover, the simplest explanation of the present order, found in our NT today, is that when the Papian-Augustinian hypothesis came to prevail, and was accepted as genuine tradition, the order of the gospels was altered only to the extent of shifting Matthew to first place, leaving Mark, Luke, and John where they had always been.

2. The traditional theory. The view that Matthew was the earliest gospel rests mainly upon the statement of Papias quoted by Eusebius in his *Church History* (III.39.16): "Matthew compiled [and arranged: the Greek verb, συνετάξατο, means both] the *logia* [oracles] in the Hebrew language [lit., dialect], and each one interpreted them [i.e., either translated or expounded them, or both] as best he could." The modern view that by *logia* Papias meant a life of Christ, or a gospel, or the sayings of Jesus, or Q, is most improbable. For hundreds of years, *logion* had been the technical term, in Greek, for a divine oracle, an inspired utterance—e.g., the oracles of Apollo delivered at Delphi. In time the usage spread to the OT, viewed as a collection of such divinely inspired utterances (cf. the "living oracles" delivered at Mount Sinai [Acts 7:38] and the "oracles of God" in Rom. 3:2; Heb. 5:12; I Pet. 4:11). In time, also, but not before the second century, the utterances of Christ were described as oracles. That Papias (unlike some modern writers) did not confuse *logia* with *logoi* ("words") is clear from the same chapter in Eusebius, § 14, where also Papias is quoted. In view of the character of Matthew's materials, and the large number of his quotations from the OT, viewed as "prophecies" which Christ "fulfilled" (*see* § 6 *below*), it is most probable that Papias meant exactly what he said: "Matthew compiled the prophetic oracles [of the OT] in the Hebrew dialect, and each one [each teacher in the early church] interpreted them as best he was able."

The later church fathers assumed without question that Matthew, being a disciple and the collector of the logia, must have been the first evangelist to write. They overlooked the fact that Papias himself—as quoted by Eusebius—discusses Mark before Matthew. So Irenaeus assumed (Her. III.1.1; Euseb. Hist. V.8.2-6; the old Anti-Marcionite gospel Prologues, from the period between Papias and Irenaeus, unfortunately lack the Prologue to Matthew; and the Muratorian Canon, *ca.* 180-200, is likewise fragmentary, though Luke is described as the "third" gospel—the order presupposed is probably the one we now have). So Clement of Alexandria assumed (Euseb. Hist. VI.14. 5-7), who found it natural for the gospels to begin with Matthew's genealogy; so did Eusebius himself (Hist. III.24.5-8), and Jerome (*Proem to the Commentary on Matthew,* §§ 5-7), as well as Augustine. It cannot be proved that the order favored by the later church fathers rests upon early tradition. It looks more like the rationalization of a *fait accompli,* as fateful for the historical interpretation of the gospels as was the assignment of the Pentateuch to Moses, or the Psalms to David, the author of Daniel to the days of Belshazzar, or the writing of Hebrews to the apostle Paul.

But the theory that Matthew was the earliest gospel, and that Mark abridged it—a view in flagrant opposition to Papias' view of Mark as based on Peter's teaching (Euseb. Hist. III.39.15)—or, in its modern form, that Matthew was first written in Hebrew (or Aramaic, as some writers who hold this view maintain), and then translated into Greek after Mark was written, is impossible. If Mark is an abridgment, it must abridge both Matthew and Luke, as its relations are as close to one as to the other; but no one could abridge two works and show equal reliance upon both, keeping them in perfect balance, but betraying none of the peculiar literary qualities or theological views of either. By far the simplest and most natural view of the Synoptic gospels is the one which looks upon Matthew and Luke as two entirely independent gospels—both, however, being based upon Mark as one of their two primary sources, the other being Q (*see* Q; GOSPELS). Luke cannot have used Matthew, nor Matthew Luke, for similar cogent reasons: neither is influenced by the other's distinctive "ideas," language, or theological convictions, and neither is affected by the peculiar sources of the other (L or M). Their sole bond of connection is Mark, which both use almost *in toto.* (This is not to deny the later influence of the text of Matthew upon that of Luke, perhaps in the second century; but that was after the finished gospels had been in circulation for some time.) Further, the view that Matthew, or any other of our four gospels, was originally written in Aramaic, though warmly advocated by several modern scholars, has been almost universally repudiated. The gospel traditions undoubtedly once circulated in oral Aramaic; but the written gospels are Greek books, and the basic source for Matthew and Luke was unquestionably a Greek work, the Gospel According to Mark. Even the advocates of Aramaic gospels have to assume that the translators of Matthew and Luke kept their eyes on both the Aramaic original and the already-existing Greek translation of Mark—a complicated hypothesis for which there is no evidence in the gospels themselves.

3. The structure of Matthew. When we examine the structure of the Gospel of Matthew, it is evident that the work, whatever its sources, has been very carefully and artistically arranged. Like many ancient Jewish works, it is in five "books" or main divisions—cf. the five books of the Pentateuch, and the Psalms, the five Megilloth, the five chapters (now six) of Pirke Aboth read on sabbath afternoons following Passover. These five divisions are alike in structure: each contains a narrative section (i.e., Jesus' ministry), followed by a didactic section (i.e., Jesus' teaching). In outline the gospel is as follows:

I. The infancy narrative, chs. 1–2
II. Discipleship, chs. 3–7
  A. Narrative, the beginning of Jesus' ministry, chs. 3–4
  B. Discourse, the Sermon on the Mount, chs. 5–7
III. Apostleship, chs. 8–10
  A. Narrative, Jesus' ministry of healing and teaching, 8:1–9:34
  B. Discourse, the mission of the disciples, 9:35–10:42
IV. The hidden revelation, 11:1–13:52
  A. Narrative, growing opposition to Jesus, chs. 11–12
  B. Discourse, the hidden teaching of the parables, 13:1-52
V. The church, 13:53–18:35
  A. Narrative, messiahship and suffering, 13:53–17:23
  B. Discourse, church administration, 17:24–18:35
VI. The Judgment, chs. 19–25
  A. Narrative, controversies in Jerusalem, chs. 19–22
  B. Discourse, criticism of the scribes and Pharisees, ch. 23; the doctrine of the Parousia, chs. 24–25
VII. The passion narrative, chs. 26–27
VIII. The Resurrection, ch. 28

Comparing Matthew with Mark, one finds it most striking that Matthew has kept Mark's order, for the most part, as well as preserving almost the entire contents of Mark (Luke, on the contrary, has long omissions); and Matthew has done this while impressing upon his finished work the subject arrangement just described. The gospel is clearly the work of a first-rate literary artist and teacher, who has reflected long and deeply upon the substance of the Christian gospel—both Jesus' life and his teaching—and has combined the teaching material with the biographical (or anecdotal) narratives in a most appropriate way. That the evangelist has behind him a "school" of Christian teachers and interpreters is not improbable; this is the way teaching was usually transmitted in the ancient world, especially in Semitic areas. Although many persons still hold that the author was Matthew the tax collector (cf. 9:9), who would have been a man accustomed to writing, to keeping accounts and making records, the gospel itself points to a later author—or authors. As is true of most ancient books based upon tradition, partly oral, partly written, many persons (cf. Luke 1:1) had a share in handing on the stories and sayings upon which it was based, and even in its literary formation. The gospels do not rest upon the literary production of four men, or their own personal recollection, but upon the widespread social memory of the larger group, the whole Christian church, from its beginning, in the particular area where each gospel was finally produced. If the Gospel of Matthew was produced in Syria—i.e., either in Antioch or somewhere in its hinterland (as Bacon held)—this would still be within the area of bilingual Hellenized Semitic culture; this hypothesis well accounts, not only for the language of the gospel, its Jewish as well as its Greek background, its thought, the institutional development of the church which it takes for granted, but also for the same phenomena in the cognate writing, the Didache (or "Teaching of the Twelve Apostles," now found among the APOSTOLIC FATHERS). As Paul Wernle said (*see bibliography*), the author of Matthew was "a Hellenist."

4. Main sources: Mark and Q. In addition to his use of Mark as his basic source, the author also uses the collection, oral or written, of Jesus' sayings which modern scholars call "Q," from German *Quelle,* "source" (i.e., as Bernhard Weiss and others used the term, the "apostolic" source; *see also* SYNOPTIC PROBLEM). This was no doubt originally an Aramaic collection (and therefore not the logia collected by Matthew "in the Hebrew dialect," according to Papias, *see* § 2 *above*); but it had already been translated into Greek, and was used by both Luke and Matthew in its Greek form—though clearly with occasional reference—certainly in Matthew's use—to the underlying Aramaic. Since Matthew has arranged this sayings material to meet the requirements of his didactic organization of the gospel (i.e., by main subjects, in five "books"), it seems probable that the original order of Q is better preserved by Luke, whose aim is not so much subject arrangement as historical continuity, and who makes no effort to rearrange Q by any topical order of his own. In fact, when we examine this Q material, in its Lukan order, we find that it already had an order of its own, quite different from both Matthew's topical arrangement and the order of Luke's material. Obviously it begins with John the Baptist and the beginning of Jesus' ministry; obviously it had to end with Jesus' teaching about the coming Parousia of the Son of man and the Last Judgment. But the main, central section of Q is on the subject of discipleship, as if this were veritably an ancient "Master's Guide for His Disciples," which Matthew made over into a manual for church doctrine, order, discipline, and worship.

As identified by most modern NT scholars, the contents of Q were as in Table 1 (in the order of Luke). No special theory of origin, or of some possibly ampler form of which this is an abridgment, or of authorship, is presupposed by the following list. Q is simply the material, common to Luke and Matthew, not derived from Mark: its extraction and isolation is almost a mathematical or physical process. Obviously, some explanation of its origin ought to be possible. At the moment, the only fact to be emphasized is the high value placed on this source by both the later Synoptists, Luke and Matthew. In Table 1, probable passages, whose inclusion is all but self-evident, are cited within brackets.

Table 1
The Contents of Q

John the Baptizer:
- 3:[2*b*], 3*a*, 7*b*-9, John's preaching of repentance (cf. Matt. 3:1-10)
- 3:16-17, John's prediction of the coming Judge (cf. Matt. 3:11-12)

The ordeal of the Messiah:
- 4:1*b*-12, the Temptation (cf. Matt. 4:1-11)

Jesus' public teaching:
- 6:20-49, the Sermon on the Plain (or Mountain; cf. Matt. 5:3-12, 39-48; 7:12, 1-5, 16-27; 10:24-25; 12:33-35; 15:14)

The response to Jesus' teaching:
- 7:1-2, 6*b*-10, the centurion's faith (cf. Matt. 8:5-13)
- 7:18*b*, 19, 22-28, 31-35, John's emissaries; Jesus' words about John (cf. Matt. 11:2-6, 7-19)
- 9:57*b*-62, various followers (cf. Matt. 8:19-22)

The mission of the Twelve:
- 10:2-16, the mission of the disciples (cf. Matt. 9:37-38; 10:7-16, 40; 11:21-23)
- [10:17*b*-20, the return of the Twelve]
- 10:21*b*-24, the rejoicing of Jesus (cf. Matt. 11:25-27; 13:16-17)

Jesus' teaching about prayer:
- 11:2-4, the Lord's Prayer (cf. Matt. 6:9-13)
- [11:5-8, the parable of the friend at midnight]
- 11:9-13, constancy in prayer (cf. Matt. 7:7-11)

Controversy with the scribes and Pharisees:
- 11:14-23, the charge of collusion with Beelzebul (cf. Matt. 12:22-30)
- 11:24-26, the story of the unclean spirit (cf. Matt. 12:43-45)
- 11:29*b*-32, the warning contained in the "sign of Jonah" (cf. Matt. 12:38-42)
- 11:33-36, Jesus' sayings about light (cf. Matt. 5:15; 6:22-23)
- 11:39*b*, 42-43, [44], 46-52, the controversy with the scribes and Pharisees (cf. Matt. 23:4-36)

Jesus' teaching about discipleship (especially the duties of disciples when persecuted):
- 12:2-12, the testimony of disciples amid adversaries (cf. Matt. 10:26-33; 12:32; 10:19-20)
- 12:22-31, on freedom from care (cf. Matt. 6:25-33)
- 12:33*b*-34, on treasure (cf. Matt. 6:19-21)
- 12:39-40, 42-46, three parables on watchfulness (cf. Matt. 24:43-51*a*)
- 12:49-53, messianic divisions (cf. Matt. 10:34-36)
- [12:54-56, signs of the times (cf. Matt. 16:2-3)]
- 12:57-59, the duty of speedy reconciliation (cf. Matt. 5:25-26)
- 13:18-21, the parables of the mustard seed and the leaven: the steady growth of the kingdom despite opposition (cf. Matt. 13:31-33)
- 13:24-29, the narrow way (cf. Matt. 7:13-14; 7:22-23; 8:11-12)
- 13:34-35, the fate of Jerusalem (cf. Matt. 23:37-39)
- 14:11 = 18:14, on self-exaltation (cf. Matt. 18:4; 23:12)
- 14:16-23, the parable of the great supper (cf. Matt. 22:1-10)
- 14:26-27, on hating one's next of kin, and on bearing the cross (cf. Matt. 10:37-38)
- 14:34-35, the saying on salt (cf. Matt. 5:13)
- 15:4-7, the parable of the lost sheep (cf. Matt. 18:12-14)
- [15:8-10, the parable of the lost coin]
- 16:13, on serving two masters (cf. Matt. 6:24)
- [16:16-18, the Law and the Prophets were until John; on divorce (cf. Matt. 11:12-13; 5:18, 32)]
- 17:1-2, on offenses (cf. Matt. 18:6-7)
- 17:3-4, on forgiveness (cf. Matt. 18:15, 21-22)
- 17:6, on faith (cf. Matt. 17:20*b*)

The coming Parousia:
- 17:23-24, 26-30, 34-35, 37*b*, the Parousia (cf. Matt. 24:26-28, 37-39; 10:39; 24:40-41, 28)
- 19:12-13, 15*b*-26, the parable of the entrusted talents (cf. Matt. 25:14-30)
- [22:28-30, the apostles' thrones (cf. Matt. 19:28)]

A study of this table, especially of the section on discipleship, and even more a study of the passages in a "harmony" like *Gospel Parallels* (in English) by B. H. Throckmorton or the latest edition of A. Huck's

Synopsis of the First Three Gospels (in Greek, but with English headings, edited by H. Lietzmann and F. L. Cross) will make clear Matthew's method of using Q and rearranging it to fit the Markan outline, which he has already taken over, abridged, and reorganized.

5. Special source or sources. Not only has Matthew rearranged Q to suit his arrangement by subject; he has also added considerable material which is peculiarly his own, not shared with any other NT writer. Many scholars (e.g., B. H. Streeter) designate this material, or large parts of it, with the letter "M"—just as they designate Luke's peculiar material by the letter "L." Peculiar to Matthew is the genealogy of Jesus (1:1-17), which cannot be identified with that of Luke (3:23-38) save for thirteen names between Abraham and David—where the agreement probably rests upon a common use of I Chr. 2:1-15 or Ruth 4:18-22, but not I Chr. 3:10-19, except for the two names Shealtiel (Salathiel) and Zerubbabel (from I Chr. 3:17-19), and, of course, Joseph, who was known to Christian tradition as the father of Jesus. (Matthew and Luke do not agree on the name of Joseph's father, nor any other ancestors between Zerubbabel and Joseph, a period of *ca.* 460 years, to which Matthew assigns twelve generations, Luke nineteen.) But Matthew's genealogy is artistic, schematic, arranged (presumably) in three groups of fourteen generations (1:17), from Abraham to Jesus (actually there are fourteen plus fourteen plus twelve generations). The great point of the two genealogies is evidently Jesus' royal descent, from David and from Abraham, in Matthew; and his universal human ancestry, his descent from Adam, who was figuratively or typically the "Son of God," in Luke (3:38).

Peculiar to Matthew are also the account of the birth of Jesus and the story of his infancy, the Wise Men ("magi," or astrologers) from the East, the flight into Egypt, and the return to Palestine and settlement in Nazareth after Herod's death (1:18–2:23). All this special material, which has only the faintest parallels in Luke's infancy narrative (chs. 1–2) and is really incompatible with Luke's narrative as a whole, is an example of Jewish Christian "midrash"—i.e., the imaginative elaboration, in story form, of a striking text or series of texts, combined with a certain element drawn from historical tradition somewhat as a modern historical writer describes an event for which information is very scanty, but uses inference and imagination, and (above all) endeavors to write "in character"—i.e., appropriately—to the person or persons involved. Much of the "historical" writing in the OT is of this nature—not annalistic data drawn from written records, but imaginative, poetic, descriptive. Much of the ancient historical literature of the East, in general, had this character. And even the more "scientific" historical writing of the Greeks and Romans often allowed for such an element, especially in writers who dealt, not with a narrowly limited and fairly recent or contemporary period like Thucydides or Tacitus, but with the more distant past, as did Herodotus and Livy. Where annalistic or factually recorded history did not exist, we can either have its imaginative reconstruction, using whatever data are available (in this case chiefly OT texts), or go without—and the Christian church decidedly preferred an appropriate story. Thus Matthew's narrative begins: "Now the birth [or origin, *genesis*] of the Messiah was like this"—translating literally from what many scholars believe to be the best Greek text (1:18). Here the central text, in which the story centers, is Isa. 7:14 as read in the LXX, not the Hebrew:

> Behold, a virgin shall conceive and bear a son,
> and his name shall be called Emmanuel.

The doctrine of the Virgin Birth, found only here in Matthew and in Luke 1:34-35 (though Luke's present text may be due to textual conformation; *see below*), and nowhere else in the NT, is clearly an inference from the LXX translation of Isaiah; and in the first or second century such an inference would be perfectly natural and unquestioned. If many great and famous men were believed to be the sons of virgin mothers, or supernaturally born—and there was then no "scientific" objection to the belief—why should not Matthew conclude that the LXX verse referred to the birth of the Messiah, and had been "fulfilled" at Jesus' conception and birth? *See* JESUS CHRIST.

So also the story of the search for his birthplace, and its location in Bethlehem on the basis of ancient prophecy (2:1-6); and the terrible tale of Herod's murder of the children at Bethlehem, and of the flight into Egypt—a mingling of prophecy, interpretation, fancy, and fact, all "in character": for Herod was a grisly murderer, as we know from Josephus, and Rachel's "children" were slain (though Ramah was not Bethlehem), and Egypt was often a refuge for Jews driven out of their homeland (though *Nazōraios*, in 2:23, does not mean "Nazarene," and it is impossible to find this text in the OT). This "midrashic" type of narrative, immediately recognizable to anyone familiar with ancient Jewish literature, is not only found here and there in the main body of the gospel, which is based on Mark, but reappears in quantity again at the end. The story of Peter's walking on the water and his loss of faith (14:28-31), the blessing of Peter and the promise of the keys (16:17-19)—these are attached to Markan pericopes, and are few in number. Far more ample are the amplifications of the passion and resurrection narratives: the designation of Judas as the betrayer (26:25); the rebuke of Peter's resistance to and Jesus' acceptance of suffering as in accordance with the Scriptures (26:52-54); the death of Judas (27:3-10, also in accordance with scripture—three passages woven together—though the story contradicts the one in Acts 1:18-19); Pilate's wife's dream (27:19), and Pilate's dramatic washing his hands of responsibility and the impossible self-imprecation of "the people" (27:24-25); the earthquake following the death of Jesus on the cross (27:51*b*-53); the guard at the tomb (27:62-66); the second earthquake, at the Resurrection (28:2-4, again with a verse of scripture as the key [Eccl. 12:3 LXX]); the meeting of Jesus with the two Marys (28:9-10, a far better conclusion than Mark 16:8 provides); the bribing of the soldiers (28:11-15); and the resurrection appearance in Galilee (28:16-20) leading to the Great Commission—the sublime climax and conclusion to the whole gospel. All this special material is midrashic, and anyone familiar with the Jewish midrashim will recognize it as both typical and extraordinary. If one can rid his mind of the narrowly modern view of religious literature, which must be strictly factual to be "true," and can recognize in imaginative writing like this, in poetry and midrash, the presentation of something more than bare annals—viz., what the worshipers of Jesus came, in later Jewish Christian circles, to believe of him—the material will gain added meaning and value. It is like some of the material in the apocryphal gospels (*see* GOSPELS, APOCRYPHAL) or even in some of the imaginative "lives of Christ" of today; but it is older, more Jewish, more appropriate, and explicitly "in character." Fortunately, the question of "historicity" need not be raised—as in another example, the coin in the fish's mouth (17:24-27), or the two animals at the Triumphal Entry (21:1-7); for, as modern theologians now recognize, the Christian message of salvation is not dependent upon, or even proclaimed by means of, these elaborations of the gospel story. They must be viewed as fancies—pious fancies, no doubt, but still only the poetic or imaginative embellishment of the central narrative and message of the NT.

Another type of material, cognate to this, but more explicit, is found in the OT quotations which Matthew cites, predominantly—but not always—from the LXX.

6. OT quotations in Matthew. These are over sixty in number, as follows, not counting innumerable echoes of single words and phrases which give Matthew's style its marked "biblical"—i.e., OT—coloring.

1) Matt. 1:23 (Isa. 7:14 LXX):

> " 'Behold, a virgin shall conceive and bear a son,
> and his name shall be called Emmanuel'

(which means, God with us)."

The Hebrew reads "a young woman" and "she shall call." Matthew uses the LXX.

2) Matt. 2:6 (Mic. 5:2):

> And you, O Bethlehem, in the land of Judah,
> are by no means least among the rulers of Judah;
> for from you shall come a ruler
> who will govern my people Israel.

This follows approximately the MT. Matthew's unconcern for the doctrine of Christ's pre-existence is reflected in his omission of the last two lines of Mic. 5:2.

3) Matt. 2:15 (Hos. 11:1): "Out of Egypt have I called my son."

Hosea's reference was to God's redemption of Israel from slavery in Egypt; Matthew reinterprets.

4) Matt. 2:18 (Jer. 31:15):

> A voice was heard in Ramah,
> wailing and loud lamentation,
> Rachel weeping for her children;
> she refused to be consoled,
> because they were no more.

Again Matthew sees this "fulfilled," not in the history of Israel, but in the events surrounding the birth of Christ. Here is an example of early Christian midrash, or imaginative interpretation of the OT.

5) Matt. 2:23: "He shall be called a Nazarene [or Nazorean]."

This strange text, introduced by the same formula as other messianic prophecies in Matthew, is not from the OT, and may come from some lost apocryphal book. Just possibly it may be a covert "mystical" reference to Isa. 11:1 or 53:2.

6) Matt. 3:3 (Isa. 40:3 LXX):

> The voice of one crying in the wilderness:
> Prepare the way of the Lord,
> make his paths straight.

As in Mark 1:3, Matthew's text follows the LXX. The Hebrew had read: "In the wilderness prepare . . ."; but early Christian exegesis saw this verse "fulfilled" in John's preaching "in the wilderness."

7) Matt. 4:4 (Deut. 8:3 LXX):

> Man shall not live by bread alone,
> but by every word that proceeds from the mouth of God.

Matthew, following the Greek translation, renders as poetry what Deuteronomy had set forth in prose. The same is true of Jesus' quotations from Deuteronomy in vss. 7, 10—the temptation narrative is almost a mosaic of Deuteronomic verses applied to the career of Jesus as Israel's true Messiah, one of the profoundest themes in the Gospel of Matthew.

8) Matt. 4:6 (Ps. 91:11-12):

> He will give his angels charge of you.
> . . . .
> On their hands they will bear you up,
> lest you strike your foot against a stone.

These two verses, indeed the whole of Ps. 91—so violently in contrast with Ps. 22, the passion psalm—must have given rise to much painful questioning in the early church. Why should Jesus die? Above all, why had God permitted his chosen Messiah to die on a cross? The whole temptation narrative is a midrashic or exegetical answer to this question.

9) Matt. 4:7 (Deut. 6:16): "You shall not tempt the Lord your God."

Again Israel's experience—and the divine oracle addressed to the nation—is interpreted as referring to the individual and specifically to Christ: "You shall not put the LORD your God to the test, as you tested him at Massah." As generally in the Bible, "temptation" means "testing," "making trial of," "putting to the test" (see Ecclus. 2:1 ff).

10) Matt. 4:10 (Deut. 5:9; 6:13):

> You shall worship the Lord your God
> and him only shall you serve.

The whole OT forbids idolatry and polytheism—above all, the worship of evil spirits; positively, it commands the worship of God alone, the one and only God, as specifically in the Shema (Deut. 6:4-5) and in Isa. 43:11; 44:6, 8; 45:6, 21; 46:9; etc.

11) Matt. 4:15-16 (Isa. 9:1-2):

> The land of Zebulun and the land of Naphtali,
> toward the sea, across the Jordan,
> Galilee of the Gentiles—
> the people who sat in darkness
> have seen a great light,
> and for those who sat in the region and shadow of death
> light has dawned.

I.e., "Galilee of [or surrounded by] the Gentiles" will see the dawn of the new day in Jesus' proclamation of the gospel. This is another good example of messianic reinterpretation of the OT.

12) Matt. 5:5 (Ps. 37:11): "Blessed are the meek."

This is taken directly from the Psalter: "The meek shall possess the land," in order to complete the number (nine) of the Beatitudes in Matthew's recension.

13) Matt. 5:21 (Exod. 20:13; 21:12): "You shall not kill."

This and the other OT verses quoted in Matt. 5 belong to the reinterpreted halachah of the gospel, which widens and deepens the range of the law's demands by including, more explicitly than in the Pentateuch, the inner attitudes and motives of men. The law is not rejected or abrogated (5:17-20), but made more authoritative than ever, as contrasted with any purely external legal casuistry, dealing only with overt actions.

14) Matt. 5:27 (Exod. 20:14): "You shall not commit adultery."

15) Matt. 5:31 (Deut. 24:1): on divorce.

In the Pentateuch, the privilege of divorce is taken for granted, and the text in Deuteronomy rules out the possibility of collusion or blackmail through remarriage. But Jesus attacked the whole practice of divorce and remarriage (Mark 10:2-12; cf. Mal. 2:13-16).

16) Matt. 5:33 (Deut. 23:22): on oaths.

17) Matt. 5:38 (Deut. 19:21): the *lex talionis*.

18) Matt. 5:43 (cf. Lev. 19:18): "You shall love your neighbor and hate your enemy."

The second half of this command cannot be found in the OT, though it is presupposed in some passages (e.g., the command to exterminate the Canaanites, and the psalmist's "Do I not hate them that hate thee, O LORD?" [Ps. 139:21]). But Jesus' teaching included all men within the range of perfect love—which must be like the love of God.

19) Matt. 5:48 (Deut. 18:13; Lev. 19:2): "You, therefore, must be perfect, as your heavenly Father is perfect."

This is more than an echo of the OT; it reinterprets and applies the command to be upright in God's sight: one must be *like* God.

20) Matt. 8:17 (Isa. 53:4): "He took our infirmities and bore our diseases."

Like 12:18-21, this is an example of the evangelist's recognition of the character of Jesus as anticipated and described by Isaiah. The "fulfilment" was more than a series of external events; it involved deep insight into the divine purpose of God's revelation. To Matthew, the aspects of Jesus' messiahship which meant most were not power and glory—though he emphasizes these more than any other evangelist—but gentleness, tenderness, divine compassion.

21) Matt. 9:13 (Hos. 6:6; cf. I Sam. 15:22): "I desire mercy, and not sacrifice."

This is another instance of Matthew's religious interpretation of the OT.

22) Matt. 10:35 (Mic. 7:6): family divisions in the last time—a common feature in apocalyptic descriptions of the "messianic woes," the social and political chaos which was to precede the end of the present age.

23) Matt. 11:5 (Isa. 29:18-19; 35:5-6; 61:1; cf. Luke 4:18-19): the supernatural gifts of the Messiah —i.e., of the divinely appointed and anointed King of Israel in the age to come.

These were often emphasized: he should be a powerful ruler, as in Isa. 9; Ps. 110; but also, as in Ps. 72, he should be the friend of the poor and suffering, and should bring them relief and release.

24) Matt. 11:10 (Exod. 23:20; Mal. 3:1):

> Behold, I send my messenger before thy face,
> who shall prepare thy way before thee.

The words of Malachi have been transformed (as in the LXX, and in Mark 1:2) under the influence of Exod. 23:20, and then reinterpreted as a reference to the coming of John the Baptist, who is Jesus' predecessor and the preparer of his "way." Matt. 11:10 may be the source of the expanded text in Mark (1:2*b* is not in "Isaiah").

25) Matt. 12:7 (Hos. 6:6; cf. I Sam. 15:22; Matt. 9:13): identical with 21 *above*.

26) Matt. 12:8-21 (Isa. 42:1-4; cf. 41:9):

> Behold, my servant whom I have chosen,
> my beloved with whom my soul is well pleased.
> I will put my Spirit upon him,
> and he shall proclaim justice to the Gentiles.
> He will not wrangle or cry aloud,
> nor will any one hear his voice in the streets;
> he will not break a bruised reed
> or quench a smoldering wick,
> till he brings justice to victory;
> and in his name will the Gentiles hope.

This long quotation is approximately identical in wording with Isa. 42:1-4, but has been influenced by ch. 41. *See* 20 *above*.

27) Matt. 12:40 (Jonah 2:1): "As Jonah was three days and three nights in the belly of the whale, so will the Son of man be three days and three nights in the heart of the earth."

This gives Matthew's literalizing interpretation (cf. the literalism in 21:1-9) of the saying and its OT reference: the forms found in Mark 8:12; Luke 11:30; and here in Matthew represent a series of interpretations.

28) Matt. 13:14-15 (Isa. 6:9-10):

> You shall indeed hear but never understand,
> and you shall indeed see but never perceive.
> For this people's heart has grown dull,
> and their ears are heavy of hearing,
> and their eyes they have closed,
> lest they should perceive with their eyes,
> and hear with their ears,
> and understand with their heart,
> and turn for me to heal them.

Matthew gives in full the passage which the saying in Mark 4:12 gives briefly and which Luke 8:10 echoes. Matthew is surely right in explaining Jesus' use of parables "because seeing they do not see"—as against Mark's and Luke's "so that," as if Jesus intended to withhold the truth from his hearers. Their interpretation of Isa. 6:9-10 seems to be justified by the OT language, where the final result is ascribed to the divine purpose; but Matthew assumes that the judgment of blindness has already overtaken his hearers, and therefore Jesus had to use simple figurative language to help them understand.

29) Matt. 13:35 (Ps. 78:2):

> I will open my mouth in parables,
> I will utter what has been hidden since the
> foundation of the world.

This is a further scriptural support for the straightforward, natural understanding of Jesus' purpose in using parables. The psalmist is referred to as a "prophet"—for Matthew the whole of the OT was "prophetic" of the Latter Days and especially of Christ.

30) Matt. 15:4 (Exod. 20:12; Deut. 5:16; Exod. 21:17; Lev. 20:9): "Honor your father and your mother. . . . He who speaks evil of father or mother, let him surely die."

Both the positive commandment and the negative threat of penalty—a draconic survival of primitive custom—are given by Mark and Matthew. Together they set the background for Jesus' criticism of scribal laxity in interpretation of the halachah. This, of course, reflects Matthew's viewpoint also.

31) Matt. 15:8-9 (Isa. 29:13 LXX):

> This people honors me with their lips,
> but their heart is far from me;
> in vain do they worship me,
> teaching as doctrines the precepts of men.

The passage (given in the same form in Mark 7:6-7) differs somewhat from the MT (for which see RSV), and is doubtless in the form in which it circulated in the early Gentile churches, where it expressed the church's rejection of Jewish traditions.

32) Matt. 18:16 (Deut. 19:15): "Take one or two others along with you, that every word may be confirmed by the evidence of two or three witnesses."

This just and salutary provision in the Jewish law (see Num. 35:30; Deut. 19:15-21; 17:6) is taken over by Matthew into the Christian halachah, the subject of the present context. That it should be required among Christians is clear from I Cor. 6 and later history.

33) Matt. 19:4-5 (Gen. 1:27; 2:24): "Have you not read that he who made them from the beginning made them male and female, and said, 'For this reason a man shall leave his father and mother and be joined to his wife, and the two shall become one'?"

This passage is quoted as in Mark 10:6-8, approximately as in the Hebrew. So also is vs. 7 (Deut. 24:1).

34) Matt. 19:18-19 (Exod. 20:12-16; Deut. 5:16-20; Lev. 19:18): The commandments necessary for life, as in Mark 10:19; Luke 18:20; but in a different order from Exodus, and with the addition of Lev. 19:18 (which some ancient authorities omit; *see* 43-44 *below*).

35) Matt. 21:5 (Isa. 62:11; Zech. 9:9):

> Tell the daughter of Zion,
> Behold, your king is coming to you,
> humble, and mounted on an ass,
> and on a colt, the foal of an ass.

This is also quoted, in abridged form, in John 12: 15. In both passages there is a significant variation from the OT—the omission of line 4 of Zech. 9:9: "Triumphant and victorious is he," perhaps as inappropriate to the present occasion.

36) Matt. 21:9 (Ps. 118:25-26; cf. II Sam. 14:4): "Hosanna to the Son of David! Blessed be he who comes in the name of the Lord! Hosanna in the highest!"

All four gospels give this verse, but in different forms (cf. Mark 11:9-10; Luke 19:38; John 12:13). Matthew alone omits mention of "the king" or "the kingdom of David"—though the title "Son of David" implies it. *Cf.* 35 *above*.

37) Matt. 21:13 (Isa. 56:7; Jer. 7:11): "My house shall be called a house of prayer."

As in Mark 11:17; Luke 19:46, two OT quotations are combined: the description of the temple is from Isaiah; the criticism of the priesthood echoes that of Jeremiah, who accused them of murder and oppression, not merely of extortion as in some modern expositions of the gospels. The temple was no "den" of petty "thieves," but a "cave of armed bandits," robbers of the whole nation, including the poor.

38) Matt. 21:16 (Ps. 8:2):

> Out of the mouth of babes and sucklings
> thou hast brought perfect praise.

This is found only in Matthew. The text varies from the MT, but paraphrases it.

39) Matt. 21:33 (cf. Isa. 5:1-2; 27:2): "There was a householder who planted a vineyard, and set a hedge around it, and dug a wine press in it, and built a tower, and let it out to tenants, and went into another country."

The language echoes that of Isaiah, but this was only natural in the telling of the story. It is not cited as a quotation.

40) Matt. 21:42 (Ps. 118:22-23):

> The very stone which the builders rejected
> has become the head of the corner;
> this was the Lord's doing,
> and it is marvelous in our eyes.

As in Mark 12:10-11, abridged in Luke 20:17, this is understood as an explicit reference to Jesus, and a rebuke to his critics.

41) Matt. 22:24 (Deut. 25:5-6; Gen. 38:8): "Teacher, Moses said, 'If a man dies, having no children, his brother must marry the widow, and raise up children for his brother.' "

This is a typical "school problem," cited in Mark 12:19; Luke 20:28, and one which doubtless still caused trouble for early Christian believers in the resurrection—who usually (unlike Paul in I Cor. 15; II Cor. 5; etc.) viewed it as material and physical.

42) Matt. 22:32 (Exod. 3:6): ". . .'I am the God of Abraham, and the God of Isaac, and the God of Jacob.' He is not God of the dead, but of the living."

As in Mark 12:26; Luke 20:37, this is a fine example of early church exegesis which doubtless went back to Jesus' own expositions of the Scriptures, in the synagogues and elsewhere publicly.

43) Matt. 22:37 (Deut. 6:5): "You shall love the Lord your God with all your heart, and with all your soul, and with all your mind."

This commandment appears also in Mark 12:30; Luke 10:27. It was a part of the Shema, recited by every observant Jew twice or even thrice a day. But the unique thing about the teaching of Jesus was his combination of the "second commandment" with it, as follows:

44) Matt. 22:39 (Lev. 19:18): "You shall love your neighbor as yourself."

This is also in Mark 12:31; Luke 10:27. Rabbi Hillel had set forth the "Golden Rule" (Matt. 7:12), in its negative form ("Do not to another what you would not have him do to you"), as a "summary of the law." Jesus' characteristic emphasis added love to one's neighbor as like—or equal—to the first.

45) Matt. 22:44 (Ps. 110:1; cf. Mark 12:36; Luke 20:42-43):

The Lord said to my Lord,
Sit at my right hand,
till I put thy enemies under thy feet.

Clearly this was one of the favorite "messianic" texts used in the early church (see Acts 2:34-35; I Cor. 15:25; Heb. 1:13; 10:13). Indeed, it was a text which exercised considerable influence upon the formulation of early Christian doctrine and theology.

46) Matt. 23:39 (Ps. 118:26): "Blessed be he who comes in the name of the Lord."

This is found also in Luke 13:35. The verse from the "Psalm of Ascents" might have been thought to be fulfilled at the entry into Jerusalem (*see* 36 *above*), but both Luke and Matthew (i.e., Q) give it a further significance: its final fulfilment will come to pass at the Parousia—which, as in much Jewish and early Christian thought, was somehow related to the fate of Jerusalem.

47) Matt. 24:7 (Isa. 19:2): "Nation will rise against nation, and kingdom against kingdom, and there will be famines and earthquakes in various places."

This is from Mark 13:8; cf. Luke 21:10. The language is typical (cf. II Chr. 15:6), but the oracle against Egypt (Isa. 19:2) is still awaiting its complete fulfilment, on a universal scale.

48) Matt. 24:15 (Dan. 9:27; 11:31; 12:11): the "desolating sacrilege spoken of by the prophet Daniel."

As in Mark 13:14 (but reinterpreted in Luke 21:20 as the siege of Jerusalem), this famous oracle was taken to refer, not to the desecration of the temple in 168 B.C., or to Caligula's proposed statue in A.D. 40, but to Antichrist standing in the holy place at the end of the age. Apocalyptic was constantly reinterpreted, in generation after generation.

49) Matt. 24:21 (Dan. 12:1): the "great tribulation."

This is as in Mark 13:19; again Luke reinterprets.

50) Matt. 24:29-31 (Isa. 13:10; 34:4; Zech. 12:10 ff; Dan. 7:13; Isa. 27:13; Zech. 12:10-14; Deut. 30:4): a mosaic of apocalyptic detail.

Some of this is already combined in Mark 13:24-27. Luke considerably abridges and tones down. Matthew, as usual, expands and emphasizes apocalyptic details.

51) Matt. 26:15 (Zech. 11:12): the payment of Judas.

Matthew makes explicit the "thirty pieces of silver," which in Mark 14:11; Luke 22:5 is only "money." Thus he prepares for the "fulfilment" of the oracle of Zechariah in 27:3-10 (*see* 55 *below*).

52) Matt. 26:31 (Zech. 13:7): "I will strike the shepherd, and the sheep of the flock will be scattered."

This is in Mark 14:27. It is again one of the more obvious passages of the OT to be interpreted of Jesus and his disciples (cf. John 16:32). Another interpretation is found in Matt. 9:36.

53) Matt. 26:38 (Pss. 42:6, 11; 43:5): "My soul is very sorrowful, even to death."

A most appropriate quotation, from one of the Passion Psalms, this is as in Mark 14:34; it is omitted by Luke (though see 12:49 ff). It was deeply rooted in the early Christian tradition (see John 12:27; Heb. 5:7).

54) Matt. 26:64 (Ps. 110:1; Dan. 7:13; cf. Mark 14:62; Luke 22:69): "Hereafter you will see the Son of man seated at the right hand of Power, and coming on the clouds of heaven."

This is the cardinal passage for the apocalyptic interpretation of Jesus' second coming as Son of man in glory (see Mark 9:1; Luke 9:27; Matt. 16:28; Mark 13:26; Luke 21:27; Matt. 24:30; Acts 7:56; Rev. 1:7; etc.). It had already been interpreted as a reference to the heavenly Messiah, *the* Son of man, in the "parables" of the book of Enoch (and see Matt. 25:31).

55) Matt. 27:9 (Zech. 11:12-13; Jer. 18:2-12; 19; 32:6-9; Exod. 9:12 LXX): the prophecy concerning the pieces of silver.

The prophecy is basically that found in Zechariah, but conflated with material from other OT passages. Jerome says he found the same text in an "apocryphal book of Jeremiah" (*Commentary on Matthew* VII.1. 228*a;* but see his *Epistle* 57.7). A totally different account of the death of Judas is given in Acts 1:18-19, with other supporting OT quotations.

56) Matt. 27:34 (Ps. 69:21): the wine mingled with gall.

Cf. Mark 15:23; Luke omits. This and the many following details of the Passion were identified in the OT by the early Christian evangelists and teachers—i.e., interpreters of scripture. See also John 19:28-29, 36-37.

57) Matt. 27:35 (Ps. 22:18): the casting of lots for Jesus' garments.

Cf. Mark 15:24; Luke 23:34; John 19:24. The division of the spolia by the crucifixion squad was customary. John adds a unique and highly symbolic detail.

58) Matt. 27:39 (Pss. 22:7; 109:25): "Those who passed by derided him, wagging their heads."

Cf. Mark 15:29; Luke 23:35. This is a further "fulfilment" of the oracle in the greatest of the Passion Psalms.

59) Matt. 27:43 (Ps. 22:8; cf. Wisd. Sol. 2:13, 18-20): "He trusts in God; let God deliver him now, if he desires him; for he said, 'I am the Son of God.' "

This taunt is peculiar to Matthew. But the cry, and the scandal of such apparently misplaced trust in God, rings throughout the Psalms, the book of Job, Isa. 53, and many other parts of the OT.

60) Matt. 27:46 (Ps. 22:1): "My God, my God, why hast thou forsaken me?"

This is in Mark 15:43; Luke omits it, and substitutes Ps. 31:5 (Luke 23:46; cf. what he does in 23:34 and what John does in 19:30). The "cry of desolation"—or "cry of dereliction," as it is often called—was directly quoted from Ps. 22, either by Jesus himself, or by the early Christian evangelists, who took the cry to be the words of Jesus' last "great shout" (Mark 15:37).

61) Matt. 27:48 (Ps. 69:21): the sponge filled with vinegar.

As in Mark 15:36, even the tiny detail of the vinegar is added. Luke 23:36 takes it to be an act of mockery by the soldiers—not a very probable interpretation.

It is obvious that Matthew's "collection and arrangement of the OT oracles" (the logia), of which the sixty-one most obvious examples are listed here, is much fuller than that of any other evangelist—or any other writer in the NT, including Paul and the authors of Hebrews and Revelation. Not limited to a dozen or fifteen well-known "proof texts," it is by far the fullest and most complete collection of passages bearing on the theme "Christ in the OT"—chiefly in the book of Isaiah, the "evangelical prophet," and in the Psalms, but also representative of the OT as a whole: the Law, the Prophets, and the Psalms (Luke 24:27, 44). An early Christian writer like Papias, whose five books of exegesis on the "Oracles of the Lord" may have dealt with the same material, and who, like all other early Christians, greatly prized the testimonia found in the ancient Jewish scriptures, would naturally be strongly impressed by this feature in Matthew's work—the use of these same OT oracles—and therefore emphasized it in his account of the origin of Matthew's Gospel (Euseb. Hist. III.39.16; *see* § 2 *above*).

7. Material peculiar to Matthew. The "peculiar" material of Matthew clearly includes, not only the Christian midrashic "haggadah" just described, and the Christian "messianic" texts from the OT—i.e., texts messianically interpreted from the Christian point of view—but also examples of Christian exegesis and homiletics, and even of reinterpretation of the church's own tradition, such as we find in 3:14-15; 12:5-7; 13:36-43. It also includes formulations of Christian duty approaching those of a code—as in the Didache, the early Church Orders, and the early canons: the process of formulation is at least moving in that direction (see 10:41; 18:18; 19:10-12; 23:2-3, 8-10). Even early liturgical material is present, as in 11:25-30, the rejoicing of Jesus and the Evangelic Invitation, which some scholars view as a baptismal hymn, and the Great Commission in 28:18-20, which includes the baptismal formula. The Matthean version of the Lord's Prayer, in 6:7-13, which differs markedly from the parallel in Luke 11:2-4, must have been taken, as many scholars now believe, from the current worship of the church; and so is the oft-quoted promise: "Where two or three are gathered in my name, there am I in the midst of them" (18:20). The Sinaitic Syr. MS even reads, in vs. 19: "If two of you agree on earth about anything concerning which they shall be asked [this could be a literal Syr. rendering of the Aramaic impersonal plural, 'which they'—i.e., people—'shall ask'] it will be binding in heaven." Here we have the early Christian assembly united, not only in worship, but also judicially (as in I Cor. 5:4*b*-5) or legislatively; indeed, it is not even the whole assembly, but a Christian local Sanhedrin, assembled for the purpose of rendering a decision upon some matter of duty, practice, or observance. The Jewish Christian outlook of the passage is obvious.

One of Matthew's chief characteristics is its emphasis on apocalyptic eschatology, which is heightened and underscored repeatedly (see 13:24-30; 20:1-16; 22:1-14; 25, *passim*). Most of Matthew's parables are given this strongly apocalyptic-eschatological emphasis, and the climax is the great panorama of the Last Judgment in 25:31-46, where the ethics of the gospel—love and compassion for the poor and helpless—is woven in with every silken fiber of this majestic tapestry: "As you did it to one of the least of these my brethren, you did it to me"—i.e., to the heavenly Son of man, throned in glory, judging all nations on the Last Day.

8. The "ecclesiastical" gospel. Matthew is sometimes described as the "ecclesiastical" gospel, and appropriately, for its interests are far more thoroughly centered in the church than are those of any other gospel—or any other writing of the NT. Here the church is not an ideal, as it is in Ephesians or in John, but the actual living body of worshipers and devotees of Christ and his teaching—a sect which originated within Judaism, but which is now more or less completely separated and living a life of its own. It is still in contact with Jews and with Jewish beliefs and practices. Much of the SERMON ON THE MOUNT (ch. 5) deals with the Christian interpretation—i.e., Jesus' interpretation—of the great commandments in the Law, which he came, not to destroy, but to "fulfil" (5:17-20), to deepen, widen, apply more consistently, and interpret in the light of the divine intention behind the command. The practices of piety (discussed in ch. 6) are those of the Pharisees and increasingly of all Jews in the first century—but with notable omissions (tithing, the food laws, and sabbath observance). These were part of a rule of life—prayer, fasting, almsgiving—which was rooted deeply in the older Judaism reflected in the Apoc., especially in Tobit, Judith, and Ecclesiasticus. The admonitions contained in the rest of the Matthean Sermon—i.e., those in 6:19-34, which reinforce the requirement of sincerity and simplicity and the absence of ostentation and pride in the observance of the three rules of life, and in ch. 7, where censoriousness is forbidden and complete self-dedication to the will of God is commanded—conclude with the magnificent and unforgettable parable of the two housebuilders (7:24-27), the point of which is clearly the indispensable requirement of not only hearing but also doing the "words" of Jesus. The Christian disciple must not only say, "Lord, Lord," but actually practice the Lord's teaching (vss. 21-23).

Moreover, the Jewish ties of Matthew and his circle (teachers, presumably, in the early Palestinian or Syrian church) are implied in ch. 23, where "the scribes sit on Moses' seat." (The addition, "and the Pharisees," is perhaps an early gloss; the scribes were the official teachers, while the Pharisees were only a society of pious, devoted laymen who undertook to carry out the full requirements of the law as expounded by its scribal interpreters. Of course, the two groups were closely related.) As the authoritative "teachers of righteousness"—i.e., of the Jewish religion—they are to be obeyed: "So practice and observe whatever they tell you, but not what they do; for they preach, but do not practice." Here their authority is recognized, though their personal character is sharply criticized (23:1-12). Seven tremendous woes are pronounced against them in 23:13-33, each following a standard literary pattern; to this is added the threat of the impending Judgment (vss. 34-36), followed by the lament over Jerusalem (vss. 37-39)—a powerful introduction to the apocalyptic discourse in chs. 24-25. The evils of the present—religious insincerity and hypocrisy, greed, false teaching, a human tradition which obscured the divine commands and substituted the minutiae of petty legal rulings for the basic requirements of "justice, mercy, and faith"—these features in the religion of Jesus' day, and equally in that of the evangelist, are leading directly to the Day of Judgment. No OT prophet, no Jewish apocalyptist, no Qumran or Essene sectary, no Stoic or Cynic street preacher, ever castigated the evils of his time in more searching, more inescapable invective.

9. Background, place, and date. Hence the background of Matthew must be sought in some area where Judaism and early Christianity still overlapped, were in close contact—and in conflict. The area which best suits these requirements is probably N Palestine or Syria, perhaps Antioch; and the date, some time after the fall of Jerusalem in 70—probably a considerable time after this date, when apocalyptic eschatology has had a long enough period to decline and revive again—as in IV Ezra and II Baruch. A. H. McNeile and others have dated the book between 70 and 115, when Ignatius of Antioch apparently quotes the gospel, or at least is familiar with traditions which Matthew also uses. E.g., his Letter to the Ephesians, ch. 19, seems to show acquaintance with Matthew's birth narrative, though with a difference—including midrashic elements very like those in Matthew. "The virginity of Mary and her giving birth were hid from the Prince of this world, and so also was the death of the Lord. [There were] three mysteries of a cry [or, of shouting] which took place in the silence of God. How then was he manifested to the ages [or, aeons]? A star shone out in heaven, brighter than all other stars, and its light was indescribable and its newness [sudden appearance?] was most strange, and all the rest of the stars together with the sun and moon formed a chorus about it, but its light far outshone them all; and there was perplexity as to whence this novelty [astronomers would say, *nova*] came, so unlike them. In consequence, all magic was dissolved and every bond of wickedness disappeared; ignorance was taken away, the old kingdom [of evil] was wholly destroyed, God being manifested humanly for the renewal of eternal life, and what had been prepared by God had its beginning. Hence all things were moved, because the destruction of death was being set in motion."

Such a passage does not prove the dependence of Ignatius upon Matthew, but suggests it; and it also illustrates the midrashic type of exegesis and the quasi-Gnostic speculation which were current in the Syrian milieu of Ignatius and also—most probably—of Matthew. It was in such an atmosphere that early Syrian Gnosticism arose; and it was also the atmosphere of the surrounding Greco-Roman-Jewish syncretism in which Matthew lived and taught. The anchorage of the Christian tradition in actual history, rather than in theosophical fancy or speculation, and the valiant defense of Jesus' firm ethical and religious teaching, his proclamation of the coming kingdom of God, his actual death and resurrection, stand out ever more clearly against this background. The echoes of current debate which we catch between the lines of Matthew's gospel—as in 5:3: "poor in spirit" (contrast Luke 6:20); or 5:19, the threat of antinomianism; or 5:32; 19:9, the exception clause in the prohibition of divorce; or 19:12, the answer to the Encratites, who forbade marriage; or 18:22, the problem of the "unforgivable" sin; or 18:15 ff, the problem of scandal in the church; or 17:24-27, the problem of the temple tax (now, presumably, paid to Rome—i.e., the *Judaicus fiscus*)—all these and many more references to current issues help to fix upon a probable milieu and approximate date for Matthew—viz., Syria around the end of the first century.

The Judaism presupposed by Matthew is that of the postbellum period when the Jews were still crushed and defeated after the catastrophe of A.D. 70, when Jerusalem fell and the temple was destroyed. It was a time of recession and retreat, when renewed study of the sacred scriptures and deeper devotion to prayer and synagogue worship took the place of the ancient sacrificial system with its attendant liturgical forms. The Jews were determined to survive, despite the loss of their freedom, their temple, and their ancient ritual. The hierarchical party of the Sadducees disappeared, and the popular lay leaders, the Pharisees, with their scribal teachers, completely took over the religious leadership of what was left of the nation. Rabbi Johanan ben Zakkai, a saintly scholar who survived the fall of Jerusalem, obtained permission from the Romans to establish a school at Jamnia, which became a center of fresh religious learning and activity. Sectarian errors were weeded out. The malediction against the *minim* and the apostates (not necessarily limited to Christians) was added to the daily prayer, the Eighteen Benedictions. The canon of the OT was settled. The more recent and as yet unrecognized works which circulated in Greek at Alexandria (approximately our APOCRYPHA), and also the clandestine or "hidden" writings now called PSEUDEPIGRAPHA were firmly rejected. Only the books already in use in the synagogue—i.e., the Hebrew scriptures (our OT)—were recognized, pronounced canonical and inspired, and authorized for use in worship and study. The Greek translation of the OT, the SEPTUAGINT, was repudiated—one rabbi said that Israel should observe as a fast day the day on which it was completed—or begun! The world mission of Judaism was suspended, and writers like Philo of Alexandria, who had endeavored to synthesize Judaism and Greek culture or philosophy, were discouraged. (The Christians, not the Jews, preserved Philo's writings for posterity.) This was the rallying time of resurgent Judaism, and the beginning of what George F. Moore called the "rise of normative Judaism"—i.e., the movement which eventually resulted, in the fourth and fifth centuries, in the achievement of the classical, or normal, Judaism which has been known to history ever since.

Along with this revival of Judaism went a renewed emphasis upon and cultivation of apocalyptic thought, a movement which Matthew both reflects and shares. (Matthew's apocalyptic passages, when compared with those in Mark or Luke, fully illustrate this; cf. 24:4-36 with Mark 13:5-37; Luke 21:8-36; to this chapter Matthew appends ch. 25, which is wholly apocalyptic-eschatological in doctrine and emphasis.) The revived apocalypticism in contemporary Jewish religious thought is represented, as we have seen, by II Baruch and IV Ezra.

Another tie with contemporary history is the renewed emphasis on refusal to seize weapons and join the proposed revolt against Rome (e.g., 26:52). Sufficient time had elapsed for a revived Zealotism to emerge, promising a quick victory against the oppressor. This must have been long after 70, and may even reflect conditions under Trajan, when, apparently, the Jewish uprising in North Africa and in Cyprus and Syria was shared to some extent in Palestine—though the records are incomplete: this is one more lacuna in early imperial history. Certainly we know that just before and during the revolt under Hadrian (132-35) the Christians were urged and even compelled to join the forces of Akiba and Bar Cocheba in the great rebellion. Bar Cocheba may be one of the pseudo messiahs referred to in 24:5. The story of Hegesippus which describes the arrest and examination of Jude's grandsons (Euseb. Hist. III.20) in the time of Domitian also reflects the conditions of the time, and the Christian abstention from armed resistance or insurrection. Finally, 24:12 also reflects the growing tension: "Because wickedness [i.e., lawlessness, *anomia*] is multiplied, most men's love will grow cold."

10. Later influence. Throughout the centuries since this gospel was written, it has exercised a great and dominant influence. Not only have its MSS influenced the text of the other gospels (especially, e.g., in the Old Syr. version); not only have its pericopes been the favored ones in the church's liturgies, outnumbering those chosen from the other gospels; not only have its formulations of favorite passages (e.g., the Beatitudes, the Lord's Prayer, the passion narrative, as in Bach's setting) prevailed over the parallels in the other gospels; but its theology has been a dominant influence, comparable only with that of John.

Matthew's theology is a Christianized Jewish set of doctrines, with a far from normal Jewish or even later Christian emphasis upon apocalyptic eschatology. Yet it does not go all the way with modern "thoroughgoing" apocalyptic: Matthew has room for the world church and its world mission. His conception of the person of Christ is thoroughly apocalyptic; and yet the deeply religious and ethical characteristics of his Christology are unmistakable, and rarely matched (as in the "parables" of I Enoch), and not at all equaled in I Thess. 4; II Thess. 1; Jude; or Revelation.

Above all, the ecclesiastical influence of such a passage as Matt. 16:17-19 has been incalculable, and is fitly symbolized by the great inscription about the dome of St. Peter's in Rome: *Tu es Petrus et super hanc petram aedificabo ecclesiam meam.* There is no parallel to this in any other gospel, and its underlying assumption of Peter's primacy is rejected or ignored everywhere else in the NT. Modern scholars believe that this piece of midrash reflects the later position of Peter, either in Jerusalem, before his departure for "another place" (Acts 12:17), or in Antioch, where for a time he was looked upon as the "prince of the apostles," superior to James, John, James the Lord's brother, Andrew, and the rest of the Twelve—and certainly superior to Paul, whose "freedom from the law" seemed to the conservatives to go altogether too far. The commission to Peter, in Matt. 16:19, giving him the right to "bind and loose" (i.e., by decisions as to the interpretation and application of the law or of Jesus' own commands), is apparently shared by others in 18:18. Yet if Peter is only *primus inter pares,* he remains *primus.* The authority is centered in him, according to this passage. It is already within the range of the "monarchical episcopate" claimed by Ignatius of Antioch, and not far removed from the papal claims which date at least from the second century.

Bibliography. Commentaries: W. C. Allen, ICC (1907); A. Plummer (1909); A. H. McNeile (1915); P. A. Micklem, WC (1917); H. L. Strack and P. Billerbeck, *Kommentar zum Neuen Testament aus Talmud und Midrasch,* vol. I (1922; Index to the 4 vols., 1956); E. Klostermann, *Handbuch zum Neuen Testament* (1927); C. G. Montefiore, *The Synoptic Gospels* (2 vols.; 2nd ed., 1927); B. T. D. Smith, Cambridge Greek Testament (1927; also in Cambridge Bible); T. H. Robinson, *The Moffatt Commentary* (1928); F. W. Green, Clarendon Bible (1945); S. E. Johnson, *IB* (1951); F. C. Grant, *Harper's Annotated Bible* (1955).

For the order of the gospels in various MSS, see the lists in E. J. Goodspeed, *The Making of the NT* (1926), Appendix.

On the question of the text followed by Matthew, which at times agrees with the LXX, at others with the MT, at still others with neither, see McNeile's Commentary (1915) or S. Johnson, "The Biblical Quotations in Matthew," *HTR,* XXXVI (1943), 135-53.

Other works: P. Wernle, *Die Synoptische Frage* (1899); G. F. Moore, *Judaism* (3 vols.; 1927-30); B. W. Bacon, *Studies in Matthew* (1930); W. Bauer, *Rechtgläubigkeit und Ketzerei im ältesten Christentum* (1934); P. Volz, *Die Eschatologie der jüdischen Gemeinde im Neutestamentlichen Zeitalter* (1934); A. Barr, *A Diagram of Synoptic Relationships* (1938); G. D. Kilpatrick, *The Origins of the Gospel According to St. Matthew* (1946); M. Black, *An Aramaic Approach to the Gospels and Acts* (2nd ed., 1954).

For further bibliography, see F. C. Grant, *The Gospels: Their Origin and Their Growth* (1957), pp. 203-7. F. C. GRANT

MATTHEW, MARTYRDOM OF. A late, long-winded, and very confused account of the martyrdom of Matthew at the hands of the king of the Anthropophagi (cannibals), to whose city he had been ordered to return by Christ. The account is clearly dependent upon the Acts of Andrew and Matthias (*see* ANDREW AND MATTHIAS, ACTS OF), but is in no sense a consistent sequel.

Matthew, "a publican but now called an apostle by the Lord crucified by the Jews," has replaced Matthias in the older story. A church is in the land, with Plato as its bishop, but there is little other evidence of the earlier successful labors. The account is a loosely strung-together tale of Matthew's arrival at the city, his planting of a rod given him for this purpose by Christ, its speedy growth into a tree with resultant marvels; the exorcism of the demon Asmodeus from the wife and family of the king; Matthew's martyrdom by fire, in the course of which the fire had been as dew to him but had consumed the metal idols and had chased the king to his palace, whence he had returned as a momentary suppliant begging for aid; the burial of Matthew in an iron coffin, sealed with lead and sunk secretly at night in the sea by the once-more hostile king; the reappearance of Matthew on the sea, with two men in shining apparel and led by Christ in the form of a child; the emergence from the sea of the cross and at its end the iron casket; the long-delayed conversion of the king and his ordination, under the new name Matthew, to become the bishop of the city.

This is an example of the low ebb reached by many of these later apocryphal Acts. There is no apparent interest in either religion or dogma, orthodox or otherwise. It is simply a farrago of wonder tales appropriated from earlier sources, each one garishly exaggerated, and strung together with no attempt at consistency. The work is extant in Greek and Latin, with many differences in the several accounts.

See also APOCRYPHA, NT.

Bibliography. The full text is to be found in R. A. Lipsius and M. Bonnet, *Acta Apostolorum Apocrypha,* vol. II, no. 1 (1898). An epitome of its contents is provided by M. R. James, *The Apocryphal NT* (1924), pp. 460-62. M. S. ENSLIN

MATTHEW, PSEUDO-, GOSPEL OF. *See* PSEUDO-MATTHEW, GOSPEL OF.

MATTHEW BIBLE. A revision of Tyndale's Version of the English Bible by John Rogers, 1537. *See* VERSIONS, ENGLISH, § 3*b*. J. R. BRANTON

MATTHIAS mă thī'əs [Μαθθίας, Ματθίας, *shortened form of* Ματταθίας; מתתיה, gift of Yahweh]. The apostle selected to fill the place among the Twelve left by Judas Iscariot.

Peter preached to the "brethren"—"about a hundred and twenty" people (Acts 1:15)—that the scripture which prophesied Judas' betrayal of the Lord (Ps. 69:25) also prophesied that the place Judas left would be filled by another: "His office let another take" (Acts 1:20). Therefore, another must be enrolled with the Eleven.

The qualifications mentioned as needed for apostleship are that the candidate must have "accompanied" Jesus and the apostles from the days when John baptized to the time of Jesus' ascension, and that he be able to witness to Jesus' resurrection. The story assumes that apostleship was not possible apart from a close association with Jesus during his life and ministry and a witnessing of Jesus' ascension. Whether Acts 1:2 assumes that anyone other than the eleven apostles witnessed the Ascension is at least questionable, if not doubtful; but the account of the selection of Matthias may come from a different tradition.

Two men who fulfilled the necessary requirements were put forward as candidates—Joseph called Barsabbas, who was surnamed Justus, and Matthias. In the Western text D, the verb is in the singular: "He put forward," presumably referring to Peter. (In Greek the only change involved is a change in one letter, with an accompanying slight difference in pronunciation.) Augustine also read the singular verb, believing that Peter had the authority to select the two men, one of whom was to be made an apostle.

The choice was made by the casting of lots. But before lots were cast, the disciples prayed together to "the Lord" (probably Christ is meant) that he would guide them in their selection. This is the first corporate oral prayer recorded in the NT (cf. Acts 4:24). It was probably led by Peter. Then "they cast lots" (lit., they "gave" lots). The Hebrews had commonly decided issues by casting lots (cf. Lev. 16:8; Prov. 16:33). It was usually done by putting stones with the names written on them into a vessel. The vessel was then shaken until one stone fell out. But the verb ordinarily used to describe this practice would be a word for "casting," not "giving." Perhaps the meaning in the Acts passage is that they "gave votes." Or the use of "gave" may be a Hebraism, a literal rendering of נתן.

It is to be noted that in this early passage there is no mention either of the laying on of hands or of the Holy Spirit; but Irenaeus refers to Matthias as "ordained" (*ordinatus est*) in the place of Judas (Iren. Her. II-XX.2, 5).

According to Eusebius and Epiphanius, Matthias was one of the seventy disciples (Euseb. Hist. I.12.3; Epiphanius I.20). There is also a tradition that he preached in Judea and was stoned to death by the Jews. An early apocryphal gospel bore his name (cf. Euseb. Hist. III.25.6; Clem. Misc. II.163; VII.318); and he was later believed to have suffered martyrdom (cf. *Menologium Graece* III.198).

B. H. THROCKMORTON, JR.

MATTHIAS, ACTS OF ANDREW AND. *See* ANDREW AND MATTHIAS, ACTS OF.

MATTHIAS, GOSPEL OF. *See* MATTHIAS, TRADITIONS OF.

MATTHIAS, TRADITIONS OF. A work known only from Clement of Alexandria, who quotes from it three times and remarks that the Gnostics cited it in support of an ascetic abuse of the flesh. Origen, whose statements are repeated by Ambrose and Jerome, mentions a schismatic Gospel According to Matthias. A book by this title was condemned in the Gelasian Decree. Occasionally the Traditions and the Gospel have been considered the same writing, but our knowledge is too limited to make this certain or even to suggest the nature of either work. *See* APOCRYPHA, NT. M. S. ENSLIN

MATTITHIAH măt'ə thī'ə [מתתיה, מתתיהו, gift of Yahu; Apoc. Μαζιτίας (I Esd. 9:35)]; KJV Apoc. MAZITIAS măz'ə tī'əs. Alternately: MATTATHIAH [Ματταθίας] (I Esd. 9:43); KJV MATTATHIAS măt'ə thī'əs. **1.** A Levite, son of Jeduthun (I Chr. 25:3), and one of the musicians appointed to minister before the ark in the sanctuary (15:18, 21; 16:5; 25:21).

2. A Korahite Levite in charge of the baking of liturgical cakes for the sanctuary (I Chr. 9:31).

3. One of the laymen persuaded by Ezra to divorce their foreign wives (Ezra 10:43; I Esd. 9:35).

4. One of those attending Ezra at the public reading of the law (Neh. 8:4; cf. I Esd. 9:43).

Bibliography. M. Noth, *Die israelitischen Personennamen* (1928), p. 170. B. T. DAHLBERG

MATTOCK [מחרשה, *from* חרש, cut in, plow (I Sam. 13:20-21); KJV חרב (II Chr. 34:6; RSV "ruin"), מעדר (Isa. 7:25; RSV "hoe")]. A metal tool used for grubbing or breaking up the soil, having a blade at one end and usually a pick or narrow blade at the other. Constant use required that it be sharpened periodically.

Fig. MAT 17. H. N. RICHARDSON

MAUL. KJV translation of מפיץ (Prov. 25:18; RSV "war club"). *See* CLUB.

MAW. KJV translation of קבה (RSV "stomach"), the rennet-bag, the bag-shaped appendage of the stomach, in Deut. 18:3. It was one of the parts of the sacrificial animal given to the priests.

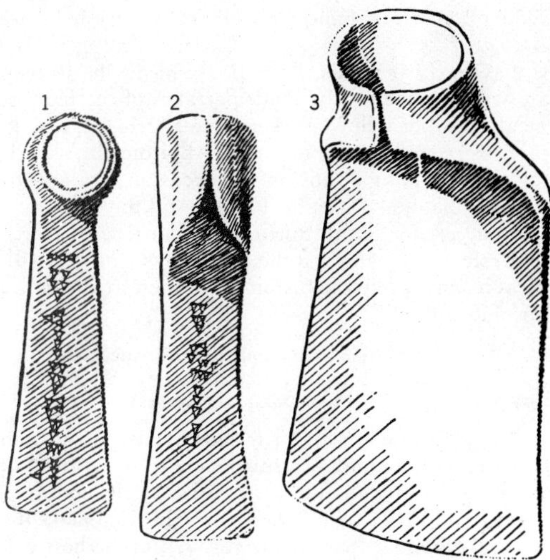

1-2) Courtesy of the Librairie Orientaliste Paul Geuthner, Paris; (3) from Petrie, *Gerar;* by permission of the Department of Egyptology, University College, London

17. 1-2) Bronze adzes or mattocks from Ugarit, with inscription *"Hrsn* [or 'adze of'] the chief priests," and "chief priests," respectively; (3) bronze mattock from Gerar

MAZITIAS. KJV Apoc. form of MATTITHIAH 3.

MAZZAROTH măz'ə rŏth [מזרות] (Job 38:32). A constellation mentioned in association with 'Ayish (עיש)—i.e., Arcturus or Aldebaran. Identification is disputed. The LXX omits the word; Symm. renders τὰ σκορπίσθεντα, "the scattered ones" (from the root זרה); and the Vulg., *Lucifer.* The Targ. equates with מזלות, "constellations," of II Kings 23:5 (where the LXX, indeed, has μαζουρωθ), and the Syr. translates *'agaltâ,* "Wain," a name of the Great Bear (cf. Talmudic עגלה ['Er. 56*a*]; Sumerian *MARGIDDA,* "Large Chariot"; English "Charles' Wain," etc., in the same sense). Some translations venture "the twelve signs" (i.e., of the Zodiac), an interpretation anticipated by Olympiodorus (in Migne, *PL,* XCIII, 408*d*) and Suidas (μαζουρωθ); while others, including the KJV and the RSV, content themselves with mere transliteration.

According to Michaelis and Dhorme, the name derives from נזר, "crown," and denotes the Corona Borealis. According to G. Hoffmann, it is from זרה, "sprinkle," and denotes the Hyades (cf. ὕειν). According to G. R. Driver, it should be vocalized *Mazzôreth* and derived from אזר, "engird," in the sense of the circle of the Zodiac.

It has been suggested also that *Mazzaroth* is simply a feminine variant of *Mᵉzārîm* (מזרים), mentioned in Job 37:9 as the place whence "cold" is sent forth. This reading, however, is itself suspect and should probably be emended to מזודים or מזוים, "storehouses," in accordance with the parallel: "From its chamber comes the whirlwind," and with the well-attested belief that snow and hail were conserved within celestial promptuaries (cf. Job 38:22; Enoch 69:23).

Bibliography. G. Hoffmann, *ZAW,* III (1883), 108, 279; G. R. Driver, *JTS,* VII (1956), 5-7. T. H. GASTER

MEAH, TOWER OF mē'ə. KJV translation of מגדל המאה (RSV TOWER OF THE HUNDRED). *See* HUNDRED, TOWER OF THE.

MEAL [קמח (*alternately* FLOUR; *see below*), סלת, עריסה (*see below*); ἄλευρον]. Meal is to be distinguished from FLOUR in that meal was ground from the whole kernels and the bran, whereas flour (usually termed "fine flour") was prepared from the inner kernels only. Normally meal was made from wheat, but the exception "barley meal" is to be found in Num. 5:15 (cf. II Kings 7:1). Possibly barley was used more extensively in the early history of Israel and was gradually replaced by wheat. However this may be, meal was much more commonly used than flour (I Kings 4:22—H 5:2); it was taken to soldiers at their camps (II Sam. 17:28; I Chr. 12:40) and was one of the last foods possessed by the widow of Zarephath in a time of drought (I Kings 17:12). Accordingly it is a sign of God's judgment when the grain has no heads and thus yields no meal (Hos. 8:7). Meal was rarely used in sacrifices, however; it appears only in Gideon's present to the angel (Judg. 6:19; קמח; KJV-RSV "flour"), in Hannah's offering at Shiloh (I Sam. 1:24; קמח; KJV-RSV "flour"), and in the offering required of a woman suspected of adultery (Num. 5:15). The "coarse meal" (עריסה; KJV "dough") mentioned in the offerings of first fruits (Num. 15:20-21; Neh. 10:37—H 10:38; Ezek. 44:30) was probably a barley paste.

The grinding of meal was done at dawn (cf. Prov. 31:15), usually by women (Exod. 11:5; Isa. 47:2; Matt. 24:41; Luke 17:35). Indeed, it was ignoble for a man to grind; as a result of the destruction of Jerusalem "young men are compelled to grind at the mill" (Lam. 5:13; cf. Judg. 16:21). Only enough meal was prepared to last the day; this was apparently three measures (*ca.* four pecks; Gen. 18:6; Matt. 13:33; Luke 13:21). The work was, of course, very difficult and noisy, particularly before the introduction of the rotary mill in Hellenistic times; the cessation of the sound of grinding is a mark of the destruction of a city (Jer. 25:10; Rev. 18:22).

For details on grinding and the construction of mills, *see* MILL. *See also* BARLEY; CEREALS; THRESHING; WHEAT.

Bibliography. G. Dalman, "Die Mehlarten im AT," *BWAT,* XIII (1913), 61-69; G. B. Gray, *Numbers,* ICC (1903), on Num. 5:15. J. F. ROSS

MEAL OFFERING. *See* SACRIFICE AND OFFERINGS §§ A2*b*i-ii.

MEALS. In the Near East, both ancient and modern, meals are not merely occasions for consuming food and drink; rather, they are also expressions of fellowship between man and man and between man and God. In addition, they provide the context for most of the entertainment enjoyed by all classes; although Koheleth is convinced that "money answereth all things," he also avers that "a feast is made for laughter, and wine maketh merry" (Eccl. 10:19 KJV).

1. Time of meals
   a. Everyday meals
   b. Banquets and feasts

2. Guests at meals
3. Customs at meals
   a. Seating arrangements
   b. Serving of food
   c. Entertainment
4. Meals in biblical imagery
   a. Meals in OT imagery
   b. Meals in NT imagery

Bibliography

1. Time of meals. ***a. Everyday meals.*** Ordinarily the day began without any meal; however, the laborer might fortify himself with a bit of bread and cheese and a few dates or olives. A meal corresponding to the modern breakfast is mentioned only in connection with one of the resurrection appearances: Jesus asks the disciples to "come and have breakfast" (John 21: 12). Elsewhere, eating a meal early in the day is condemned as childish (Eccl. 10:16; cf. Isa. 5:11; Acts 2:15, where Peter points out that the disciples cannot be drunk, "since it is only the third hour of the day"). Thus the first proper meal came late in the morning. According to the rabbis (Shab. 10*a*), the fourth hour (*ca.* 10:00 A.M.) was the mealtime for ordinary people, the fifth for laborers in the fields, and the sixth for scholars. Thus Peter becomes hungry "about the sixth hour" (Acts 10:9-10). There is no special name for this meal in the OT, although it is mentioned in connection with the harvest (Ruth 2:14). In the NT, however, it is specifically termed the ἄριστον (Matt. 22:4; Luke 11:38; 14:12; in all three passages both the RSV and the KJV have "dinner"). Contrary to Egyptian usage, where an elaborate meal was served at noon (Gen. 43:16, Joseph's meal for his brethren), this meal was not extensive in Palestine. It was as much a time for rest from one's labors as a time for eating. Only bread dipped in VINEGAR (RSV "wine") and PARCHED CORN are mentioned in the harvest meal eaten by Ruth (2:14) and Boaz.

The chief meal was therefore held in the evening, when there was not enough light for work (Judg. 19: 16, 21; Luke 17:7-8; cf. Ruth 3:2, 7). Accordingly, the ravens bring Elijah food both in the morning and in the evening (I Kings 17:6). The custom of eating two meals a day is traced back to the wilderness period; Yahweh tells Moses to command the people: "At twilight you shall eat flesh, and in the morning you shall be filled with bread" (Exod. 16:12). The same passage shows that the evening meal was the more substantial of the two; only then is meat appropriate. Again, there is no specific name for this meal in the OT; the NT, however, calls it δεῖπνον (John 12:2; 13:2; 21:20; I Cor. 11:20; etc.; both RSV and KJV "supper" in these passages, although elsewhere RSV renders "banquet" [e.g., Luke 14:17]).

b. Banquets and feasts. As in modern times, it was customary to hold banquets and feasts in the evening. The two angels come to Sodom "in the evening," and Lot prepares a feast for them (Gen. 19:1-3). There are exceptions, however. Jesus tells the ruler of the Pharisees not to invite only his friends to "a dinner or a banquet" (ἄριστον and δεῖπνον respectively; Luke 14:12). Abraham entertains the three men "in the heat of the day" (Gen. 18:1-8), and the family banquets of Job and his sons seem to have been held during the working day (Job 1:13-14). For the occasions upon which banquets and feasts were held, *see* BANQUET.

2. Guests at meals. At ordinary meals the women ate with the men; thus Ruth partakes of the harvest meal with her fellow workers (Ruth 2:14). But only men were invited to banquets. Absalom thus sends for only the king's sons on the occasion of a sheep-shearing banquet (II Sam. 13:23). And the three men have to ask for Sarah during their meal with Abraham; she was listening at the tent door (Gen. 18:9-10). Sirach makes the exclusion of women at meals an absolute rule:

> Never dine with another man's wife,
> nor revel with her at wine
> (Ecclus. 9:9).

Naturally one invited his friends, relatives, and rich neighbors to a banquet; thus he could be assured of receiving an invitation in turn. Jesus, on the contrary, urges that one invite "the poor, the maimed, the lame, the blind"; they cannot repay, and the host will be repaid at the resurrection (Luke 14:12-14). In any case, the official invitation to a banquet was in two parts: First, the host sent out servants announcing the forthcoming festivities. Then on the actual day of the banquet the servants were again dispatched, this time to inform the guests that all was in readiness (Matt. 22:3-4; Luke 14:16-17; cf. Esth. 5:8; 6:14).

When the guests arrived, they were dressed in a special garment (a "mantle of praise"; Isa. 61:3; cf. Matt. 22:11-12). Apparently this was to be of white material (Eccl. 9:8); furthermore, the head was adorned with flowers (Isa. 61:3; Wisd. Sol. 2:7-8). The latter custom is apparently referred to by Isaiah in his denunciation of the "proud crown of the drunkards of Ephraim" and the "fading flower of its glorious beauty" (Isa. 28:1). Thus arrayed, the guests were received by their host with a kiss (Jesus rebukes Simon the Pharisee for omitting this [Luke 7:45]), and their feet were washed (Gen. 18:4; 24:32; 43:24; Judg. 19:21; I Sam. 25:41; Luke 7:44). Finally the head and feet of the guest were anointed (*see* ANOINT); ordinarily this was done with oil (*see* OIL § 2*b*), but Mary used a "pound of costly ointment of pure nard" to anoint Jesus (John 12:3; cf. Matt. 26:7; Mark 14:3; Luke 7:38; for other references to anointing at banquets, cf. Ps. 23:5; Eccl. 9:8; Amos 6:6). The guests and their host then proceeded to the dining hall ("house of feasting"; Jer. 16:8).

3. Customs at meals. Seating arrangements at meals and proper etiquette in the consumption of food were of the greatest importance in biblical times, as in the modern Near East.

a. Seating arrangements. In the earliest times the Hebrews merely sat on the ground for their meals. This may be assumed from the description of Abraham's meal for the three strangers, at which the host stands under a nearby tree (Gen. 18:8). Similarly Gideon brings a kid, unleavened bread, meat, and broth and presents them to the angel "under the tree" (Judg. 6:19). Following Canaanite customs, however, the Hebrews later sat on chairs or stools, and the dishes were placed on small leather stands. Thus David says that he must not fail to "sit at table with the king," and Saul's "seat by the wall" is mentioned (I Sam. 20:5, 25). Lying on couches was probably a

Babylonian custom imported into Palestine. It is denounced as a mark of irresponsible luxury by Amos:

> Woe to those who lie upon beds of ivory,
> and stretch themselves upon their couches
> (Amos 6:4).

Elsewhere in the OT and the Apoc., however, such reclining is taken for granted. Couches are mentioned in connection with the feasts described in Esther (1:6; 7:8), and Judith's maid lays out "soft fleeces" upon which her mistress reclines (Jth. 12:15).

In NT times the guests still reclined, but the arrangements, ultimately derived from Greco-Roman usage, were much more elaborate. A square table was set up in the center of the dining hall (cf. Mark 7:28, where the Syrophoenician woman refers to the "dogs under the table"), and wide couches were arranged around three of the sides, the fourth side by the door being left free for the servants. Each of the couches could accommodate three persons (cf. Latin *triclinium*), and the usual practice was to lie at a right angle to the table, supporting oneself on the left elbow and leaving the right hand free for eating. On the basis of modern Arabic parallels it may be assumed that eating with the right hand was the universal practice; to eat with the left hand is an insult to the host.

At a banquet the guest of honor was given a place at the head of the table, opposite the entrance to the room (cf. I Sam. 20:25). Thus Samuel gives Saul and his servant a "place at the head of those who had been invited" (I Sam. 9:22). Similarly James and John ask Jesus: "Grant us to sit, one at your right hand and one at your left, in your glory" (Mark 10:37). Jesus advises his banquet companions to take the lowest place as a sign of humility, so that the host can later ask them to "go up higher" (Luke 14:7-11). Those other than the honored guests were seated according to age or importance; Joseph seats his brethren "the first-born according to his birthright and the youngest according to his youth" (Gen. 43:33).

After all the guests were in their places, servants circulated among them with ewers and basins (*see* VESSELS) in which the hands were washed. This was not only a matter of cleanliness, but also a ceremony of sanctification. Mark reports that "the Pharisees, and all the Jews, do not eat unless they wash their hands, observing the tradition of the elders" (Mark 7:3); therefore, the Pharisees criticize Jesus' disciples for eating "with hands defiled" (Matt. 15:1-2; Mark 7:2).

Finally the host offered thanks for the forthcoming food. Such a blessing, coupled with praise of the host, is spoken by Eleazar, the oldest of the priests invited to a banquet by Ptolemy Philadelphus (Aristeas 184-85). At the feeding of the multitude Jesus gives thanks for the loaves and fish (Matt. 15:36; cf. Mark 8:6-7, where Jesus gives thanks for the loaves but blesses the fish; cf. also Matt. 14:19; Mark 6:41; Luke 9:16). And at the Last Supper (*see* LORD'S SUPPER) Jesus gives thanks for both the bread and the cup (Matt. 26:26-27; Mark 14:22-23; Luke 22:17, 19; I Cor. 11:24; cf. Acts 27:35). Indeed, the name of the Christian sacrament, EUCHARIST, is derived from the Greek word meaning "to give thanks," εὐχαριστεῖν.

b. Serving of food. Meals were usually served by the women of the family; Peter's mother-in-law serves Jesus and some of his disciples after she has been cured of a fever (Matt. 8:14-15; Mark 1:30-31; Luke 4:38-39). But in the wealthier households male servants were employed. The queen of Sheba is astonished at the number of Solomon's servants (עבדיו [masculine]) and cupbearers (I Kings 10:5; II Chr. 9:4). The meal or banquet itself was divided into two main parts. In the first, food alone was served; in the second, wine was provided. Thus at Jesus' last supper with his disciples the bread is given before the wine. Similarly Jacob brings Isaac game, and he eats; only then is the wine served (Gen. 27:25; cf. Gen. 26:30).

In biblical times no eating utensils were used, and the only dishes were those on which the food itself was served. Consequently the guests ate out of the common bowl with their fingers:

> The sluggard buries his hand in the dish;
> it wears him out to bring it back to his mouth
> (Prov. 26:15).

Similarly Jesus identifies his betrayer as "one who is dipping bread in the same dish with me" (Mark 14:20; cf. Matt. 26:23; Luke 22:21). This also refers to the use of a piece of bread to sop up broths, sauces, and gravies (cf. John 13:26; Ruth 2:14; *see* BREAD § 2*a*). Of course, cups and goblets (*see* VESSELS) were provided for wine; we are told that all of Solomon's drinking vessels were made of gold (I Kings 10:21; II Chr. 9:20).

Naturally the best portions of food were given to the guest of honor. Joseph shows that Benjamin is his favorite by giving him a portion "five times as much as any of [his brothers]" (Gen. 43:34). And Samuel has his cook put aside a special piece of meat for Saul (I Sam. 9:23-24). Especially enjoyed were the fat pieces. Thus, in the days to come, Yahweh will prepare a feast for all peoples, "a feast of fat things, a feast of wine on the lees, of fat things full of marrow" (Isa. 25:6). But the guest is not to be greedy; he must not marvel at the quantity and quality of the food, or reach out for everything in sight. Rather, he is to eat "like a human being," and is to be the first to stop (Ecclus. 31:12-18).

c. Entertainment. The chief form of entertainment at a banquet was music and song. Amos condemns those who "sing idle songs to the sound of the harp" (Amos 6:5), and Isaiah is no less scathing in his sarcasm (Isa. 5:12; cf. 24:9). But in later times musical accompaniment to banquets was generally accepted. Sirach exclaims:

> A ruby seal in a setting of gold
> is a concert of music at a banquet of wine.
> A seal of emerald in a rich setting of gold
> is the melody of music with good wine
> (Ecclus. 32:5-6).

Furthermore, at the return of the prodigal son his father holds a feast with "music and dancing" (Luke 15:25). Naturally, drinking songs were sung at such celebrations; one is preserved in Wisd. Sol. 2:6-9.

Dancing (*see* DANCE; cf. the parable of the prodigal son) was also a feature of important banquets. On Herod's birthday his stepdaughter danced before the assembled multitude; the king was so pleased that he offered to grant her any wish (Mark 6:21-22; Matt. 14:6-7).

Finally, it was not uncommon for the guests to be entertained by riddles at a festive occasion. At his wedding banquet Samson puts a riddle to his thirty guests and challenges them to answer it within the seven days of the feast; having found out the answer, the guests propose a counterriddle (Judg. 14:12-18). A large part of the Letter of Aristeas (*see* Aristeas) is taken up with hard questions put by Ptolemy to his guests, the Jewish elders who had been commissioned to translate the Torah into Greek (Aristeas 187-294).

Naturally the rich food and wine and lavish entertainment at banquets could lead to excess, and this is often condemned in both the OT and the NT. The views of Amos and Isaiah have already been noted, but they are not alone. Paul urges the Romans not to engage in "reveling and drunkenness" (Rom. 13:13), and cites "drunkenness, carousing, and the like" as "works of the flesh" (Gal. 5:19, 21). Similarly the author of I Peter says that the time is past for "drunkenness, revels, [and] carousing" (4:3). Even Koheleth warns that princes should hold their feasts at the proper time and eat and drink "for strength, and not for drunkenness!" (Eccl. 10:17). *See* Drunkenness; Wine § 4.

4. Meals in biblical imagery. Since biblical imagery generally makes use of the things and events of everyday life, it is natural that meals and eating customs should be used metaphorically.

a. Meals in OT imagery. Since laughter and joy are naturally associated with banquets, it can be said that "a cheerful heart has a continual feast" (Prov. 15:15). More frequent, however, is the metaphor of a feast prepared by Yahweh. Such a feast can be an expression of blessing, as in Isaiah's "feast of fat things" for all people (25:6; cf. 61:3), but it can also be a threat of judgment. Thus Jeremiah says of the Babylonians:

> While they are inflamed I will prepare them a feast
> and make them drunk, till they swoon away
> and sleep a perpetual sleep
> and not wake, says Yahweh (51:39).

b. Meals in NT imagery. Reference has already been made to the use of banquets in Jesus' parables (Matt. 22:1-10; Luke 14:16-24; etc.). In addition, however, the coming kingdom of God is often connected with a feast. This usage is derived from Isa. 25:6 (*see* § 4*a above*) and the concept of the messianic banquet found in the Pseudep. (Enoch 62:14; Syr. Apocal. Bar. 29:5-8; for the parallel from the Qumran sect, *see bibliography*). At the Last Supper, Jesus says that he will not drink wine again "until . . . I drink it new with you in my Father's kingdom" (Matt. 26:29; cf. Mark 14:25; Luke 22:18). The universality of the gospel is likewise expressed in terms of a banquet in the kingdom of heaven, at which there will be "many . . . from east and west" along with Abraham, Isaac, and Jacob (Matt. 8:11; cf. Luke 13:29). Finally, the twelve are to "eat and drink at [Jesus'] table in [his] kingdom, and sit on thrones judging the twelve tribes of Israel" (Luke 22:30; cf. Luke 14:15; Rev. 19:9).

See also Food; Wine.

Bibliography. V. Zapletal, *Der Wein in der Bibel,* Bibl. Stud., XX.1 (1920), pp. 44-46; J. Döller, "Der Wein in Bibel und Talmud," *Bibl.* IV (1923), 269-76; A. C. Bouquet, *Everyday Life in NT Times* (1954), pp. 69-74; E. W. Heaton, *Everyday Life in OT Times* (1956); L. Köhler, *Hebrew Man* (1956), pp. 86-87; M. Burrows, *More Light on the Dead Sea Scrolls* (1958), p. 395 (on the messianic banquet at Qumran).

J. F. Ross

MEANI mē ā'nī. KJV Apoc. form of Meunim.

MEARAH mē âr'ə [מערה] (Josh. 13:4). Probably identical with the caves called Mughar Jezzin, E of Sidon; mentioned among the places remaining to be conquered after Joshua's conquests.

MEASURES. A term used to translate many Hebrew and Greek words indicating units of uncertain value. *See* Weights and Measures.

MEAT. *See* Food.

MEAT OFFERING. *See* Sacrifice and Offerings §§ A2*b*i-ii.

MEBUNNAI mĭ bŭn'ī [מבני]. An apparently corrupt form appearing in II Sam. 23:27 as the name of one of the Davidic "Thirty." It should, no doubt, be Sibbecai, as it appears in the parallel passages (I Chr. 11:29; 27:11).

MECHERATHITE mĭ kĕr'ə thīt [מכרתי] (I Chr. 11:36). The title given to Hepher, one of David's army. It probably should be "Maacathite" (*see* Maacah 1), following II Sam. 23:34.

MECONAH mĭ kō'nə [מכנה, foundation] (Neh. 11:28); KJV MEKONAH. A town in S Judah, between Ziklag and Ain-rimmon. The site is unknown.

MEDABA. KJV Apoc. form of Medeba.

MEDAD mē'dăd [מידד, beloved(?); LXX Μωδαδ] (Num. 11:26-27). An Israelite who prophesied in the wilderness camp. After seventy elders had been equipped by the spirit of Yahweh to assist Moses, Medad and Eldad were similarly equipped by exceptional divine action.

Bibliography. M. Noth, *Die israelitischen Personennamen* (1928), p. 223.

R. F. Johnson

MEDAN mē'dăn [מדן] (Gen. 25:2; I Chr. 1:32). The third son of Abraham and Keturah, and hence the name of an Arabian group. It is mentioned just before Midian and is possibly a corrupt dittograph of the latter. However, there was an Arabian god named Madan, known from the famous family name Abd-al-Madan, and this may have been the original vocalization. There was also a place called Badan, which was conquered by Tiglath-pileser III of Assyria in 732 B.C. and which was located to the S of Tema; this may be Medan, as the consonants "b" and "m" are often interchanged in Arabic.

S. Cohen

MEDEBA mĕd'ə bə [מידבא; Apoc. Μήδαβα]; KJV Apoc. MEDABA. A city in Transjordan, *ca.* fifteen miles SE of the entrance of the Jordan into the Dead Sea.

Medeba was a Moabite town taken by the

Amorite king Sihon from Moab just before the Israelite conquest, and in turn taken by the Israelites in their victory over Sihon (Num. 21:30). The territory allotted by Moses to the tribe of Reuben included all the tableland of Medeba (Josh. 13:9, 16). In David's time it seems to have been in Ammonite hands, for the Syrian allies of the Ammonites encamped there before their defeat by Joab (I Chr. 19:7). According to the Moabite Stone, the Israelite king Omri had retaken Medeba (מהדבה), probably from Moab, and Israel dwelt there in his time and in half of his son's time, forty years. Mesha recaptured and rebuilt it, along with other cities of the area. Jeroboam II "restored the border of Israel from the entrance of Hamath as far as the Sea of the Arabah" (II Kings 14:25), probably pushing Moab S of the Arnon and taking once again the area including Medeba. Israelite possession was probably short-lived, and Medeba was included in Isaiah's oracle against Moab (Isa. 15:2), although not in Jer. 48, where we would also expect to find it mentioned.

In Maccabean times (*see* MACCABEES) John, the oldest son of Mattathias, was ambushed just outside Medeba (I Macc. 9:36) by the children of Ambri (Josephus: Amarios). Jonathan and Simon, John's brothers, avenged themselves by lying in wait outside Medeba and killing a wedding party of their enemies (I Macc. 9:35-42; Jos. Antiq. XIII.i.2, 4). Later John Hyrcanus, Simon's son, captured Medeba after a six-month siege (Jos. Antiq. XIII.ix.1).

Medeba was an early Christian center. In the sixth century A.D. an artist constructed an illustrated mosaic map of Palestine on the floor of a church in Medeba. In 1890, unfortunately, most of the map was destroyed when a new church was being built.

Medeba is still occupied today, being called Madeba. It is in the midst of rich farm lands, and it would seem that most pre-Nabatean remains have been wiped out by the heavy subsequent occupation and cultivation. Madeba is on the main N-S highway through Transjordan, which has followed practically the same route since the Early Bronze Age, over four thousand years ago. *See* KING'S HIGHWAY.

Bibliography. F.-M. Abel, *Géographie de la Palestine,* II (1938), 381-82.
E. D. GROHMAN

MEDIA mē'dĭ ə [Heb.-Aram. מדי; Aram. *determinative* מדיא *Kethibh,* מדאה *Qere;* Akkad. *ma-da-a-a;* Elam. *ma-da;* Old Pers. *māda*]; MEDES mēdz [מדי; Μῆδοι]. An ancient area in NW Iran, situated between the Elburz Mountain range, the Salt Desert, Fārs (Persia), and Mesopotamia; the capital was ECBATANA. Later a distinction was made between Southern, or Greater, and Northern Media or Atropatene (Azerbaijan).

Both the Medes and the Persians (Esth. 1:19; Dan. 5:28; 6:8, 12, 15; cf. Media and Persia in Esth. 1:3, 14, 18; 10:2; *see* PERSIA) are among several groups whose idioms show features characteristic of the (Indo-)Iranian branch of the Indo-European language group, and who entered the Iranian and adjacent territories in the course of several centuries between approximately 1400 and 1000 B.C. in subsequent waves. In the Table of the Nations in Gen. 10, Madai (מדי, Media) is a "son" of Japheth, along with Gomer, Magog, Javan, Tubal, Meshech, and Tiras (Gen. 10:2; I Chr. 1:5; *see* MAN, ETHNIC DIVISIONS OF, § A1*a*). Fig. MED 18.

Some of the most important information on the ancient Medes is contained in Assyrian sources. They are first mentioned in a passage in which the Assyrian king Shalmanezer III (858-824), in a campaign to the N, invaded the territory of the *Parsua* and then, turning to the SW, entered the land of the Medes. Other references from documents of Shamshi-Adad V (823-810), Tiglath-pileser III (745-727), Sargon II (721-705), and Sennacherib (705-681) show the continuous relations between Assyria and Media over a period of almost two centuries. The name *Dayaukku* of a prisoner of Sargon captured in 715 calls to mind the Deioces mentioned by Herodotus (*see below*). From Sargon until *ca.* the middle of the seventh century Media seems to have been in the position of a subject to the Assyrian kings.

Courtesy of the Oriental Institute, the University of Chicago

18. Head of a Mede, with his high rounded hat, beard and mustache; from the stairway of the Apadana, Persepolis (521-465 B.C.)

Among the places to which Sargon exiled the Israelites were the "cities of the Medes" (II Kings 17:6; 18:11). Fig. MED 19.

In a well-known passage Herodotus (I.96-98) reports that Deioces (Δηιόκης) succeeded in uniting the Medes and persuaded them to build the city of Ecbatana (see Ezra 6:2; Tob. 3:7). The list of other Median rulers—Phraortes (φραόρτης; Old Persian *fravarti*), Cyaxares (κυαξάρης; Old Persian [*h*]*uvaxštra*), Astyages ('Αστυάγης)—given by the same authority and the longer lists of Ctesias (Diodorus 2.32.6) and other, later historians show an effort to harmonize conflicting data. The details are still under debate. The succession of the rulers over a period of more than a century seems to have been: (*a*) Deioces, (*b*) Phraortes (675?-653?), the same, perhaps, as the *Kaštarita* (Old Persian *xšaθrita*[?]) mentioned in As-

Courtesy of the Oriental Institute, the University of Chicago

19. The stairs of the Apadana at Persepolis (521-465 B.C.), showing the relief of Median nobles

syrian sources, (*c*) Cyaxares (625?-585?), and (*d*) Astyages (585?-550?).

In the first half of the seventh century Cimmerians (*Gimirrai; see* GOMER) and SCYTHIANS (*Išguza*) were in frequent contact with the Medes. At one time they made common cause with them against the Assyrians.

Cyaxares' role in the formation of the short-lived Median Empire was large. He succeeded in pushing back the Scythian hordes, became Nabopolassar's ally in the campaigns (620-605) which led to the final downfall of the Assyrian power, and was successful in campaigns against Lydia. The possibility of a Median attack upon Babylon, envisaged in Isa. 13:17-18; Jer. 51:11, 28, never materialized (see also Jer. 25:25).

His successor, Astyages, was defeated *ca.* the middle of the sixth century by Cyrus the Great. Media became part of the vast Persian Empire, and its importance was similar to any other of its many provinces. In Sassanian times the name Media was still used and appears on a list of provinces (*Ammianus Marcellinus* XXIII.6.14). The Muslim authors use the name *Jibāl* for the area approximately corresponding to ancient Media.

No written documents in the Median language have so far come to light. A number of Old Persian words show phonological features which can be explained by assuming that they were borrowed from Median. Herodotus' note (I.110) contains the expected initial group *sp-* in the Median word σπάκα, "dog," which afterward is incorporated in the Greek lexicons (Hesychius σπάδακες· κύνες). Among the Jews at Jerusalem at Pentecost were Parthians, Medes, Elamites, and others (Acts 2:9).

See also DARIUS THE MEDE (Dan. 5:30; 6:1 ff; 9:1; 11:1).

Bibliography. E. Herzfeld, *Archäologische Mitteilungen aus Iran,* vol. I (1929); F. W. König, *Älteste Geschichte der Meder und Perser* (1934); G. G. Cameron, *History of Early Iran* (1936); I. M. D'yakonov, *History of Media from the Earliest Times Until the End of the Fourth Century A.D.* (1956; Russian). On the Median loan words in Old Persian, see R. G. Kent, *Old Persian* (1950), pp. 8-9. M. J. DRESDEN

MEDIATOR, MEDIATION. Religious thinking necessarily implies a distinction between natural and supernatural, the human and the divine; and at the same time it affirms the possibility of relationship between the two. Mediation means the establishing and maintaining of this relationship, and every religion makes available "means of grace"—i.e., religious rites by which deity and worshipers are brought into communion with one another. However wide and deep may be the gulf envisaged between man and God, religion depends on the assumption that it is bridgeable. God may be estranged by the evil in human conduct, and may be imagined as at enmity with man; and certain aspects of human experience, e.g., suffering, may be interpreted as evidence of this enmity. But something in man's heart encourages the hope that this enmity can be put away; there is some atonement which transforms estrangement into reconciliation.

Apart from the consideration of human sinfulness, the problem is posed by the very differentiation between man and God, particularly when divine transcendence is emphasized. If God is exalted above his creatures, what communion between him and them is possible? How can the high and lofty one who inhabits eternity have any habitation among mortal beings? This line of consideration will be concerned with the more philosophic aspect of the problem, with knowledge and revelation, faith and reason, time and eternity. Where the approach is determined, as in the Bible, by the thought of human sin and divine holiness, the discussion will be more concerned with ATONEMENT and RECONCILIATION.

All offers of redemption imply some idea of mediation. If the deity is conceived as personal, "reconciliation" is the more appropriate term. The basic problem for man is how he shall be brought into a right relationship with his environment, that environment being understood as including supernatural factors which, together with natural, condition human life and determine human destiny.

This subject has wider scope than is suggested by the relatively few occurrences of the Hebrew and Greek terms translated "mediator," etc.

A. Linguistic introduction
B. Mediation in the OT
   1. Sin and the covenant
   2. Moses
   3. The law
   4. The prophets
   5. The priests
   6. The king
   7. Sacrifice
   8. Hypostatic mediation
      a. Wisdom
      b. Word (Logos)
      c. Spirit
   9. Servant of the Lord
   10. Messiah
C. Mediation in the NT
   1. Christian beginnings
   2. Jesus' own conception of his work
      a. Fulfilment
      b. The kingdom
      c. Messiah
      d. Son of God
      e. Son of man
      f. Self-sacrifice
   3. Paul
      a. The lordship of Christ
      b. The divine sonship of Christ

c. Christ as liberator
d. Christ as reconciler
e. Christ as second Adam
f. Cosmic Christology
4. John
a. Christ as revealer (Logos)
b. Christ as Son of God and Son of man
c. Christ as Lamb of God
d. Discipleship: the divine society
5. Hebrews
a. The finality of Christ's work
b. The perfect sacrifice
c. The perfect priest
6. I Peter
7. Revelation
D. Summary
Bibliography

A. *LINGUISTIC INTRODUCTION.* The word "mediation" does not occur in the English Bible, but "mediator" (μεσίτης) is found six times in the NT, and the cognate verb (ἐμεσίτευσε) once, with God as subject, in the sense of "interpose," "give a guarantee" (Heb. 6:17). The noun μεσίτης (Gal. 3:19-20; I Tim. 2:5; Heb. 8:6; 9:15; 12:24; also once only in the LXX, Job 9:33) has the sense of one who intervenes between two parties to inaugurate a contract. It may be translated "negotiator," "intermediary." The sense of reconciling differences is not to the fore in these NT passages. The reference in Gal. 3 is to Moses; he was commonly so regarded in Judaism (cf. Philo's *Life of Moses* II.166 [Loeb] and *On Dreams* I.143; cf. also Asmp. Moses 1:14; 3:12). The other four references are to Christ: his efficacy for man's salvation, or (in Hebrews) his inauguration of the new covenant —i.e., right relationship between man and God.

B. *MEDIATION IN THE OT.* 1. Sin and the covenant. The status of mankind is illustrated in the third chapter of Genesis in terms of man's disobedience. This unflattering affirmation is reinforced by the use made of the story of the Flood (Gen. 6–8), where full attention should be given to the theological introduction which Hebrew authors have provided before their adaptation of this old Babylonian saga (Gen. 6:5-12; cf. also for the same implication 4:1-16; 11:1-9; 13:13; 15:16). There are insights here which are basic for the whole of the OT. Man is capable of conforming to the divine will, which is his highest good (Gen. 1:26-27, which ascribes to man alone of all created beings the image and likeness of God, is always presupposed), but in fact he does not do so. No generation of men can make such a boast, not even the favored recipients of revelation (Israel, the posterity of Abraham; Gen. 12:1-3). Just as Noah's generation "corrupted their way," so does Israel continually.

Similar is the teaching of the prophets. God's rebuke is sounded by the earlier prophets against Baal worship and its accompanying social evils, and against the syncretism and moral degeneration of the later pre-exilic period by Jeremiah and Ezekiel (Jer. 2:26-28; 5:1-9, 23-31; 13:23; Ezek. 8; 22–23). For the period after the Exile we may refer to Isa. 56–66 and Malachi. Not only is man's actual behavior antisocial, but his affection is alienated from God and his fellow man: "Their hearts are far from me" (Isa. 29:13).

> The heart is deceitful above all things,
> and desperately corrupt (Jer. 17:9;
> cf. Gen. 8:21; Ps. 51; Ezek. 36:26).

The deliverance from Egypt was interpreted (if not by Moses at the time, at least by later tradition) as Yahweh's intervention on Israel's behalf. This is an aspect of divine election—Yahweh *chose* a people to be in this special relationship with him. They need him more than he needs them, and his ministration to their need is his invitation to them to be in covenant with him. He has rescued them at a major crisis, and promises prosperity in the future. Their response should be to live as he directs, to "keep the statutes and the ordinances." The book of Deuteronomy sets out the fundamentals of the covenant idea (7:6-13; 26:16-19; 30:15-20). The Ten Commandments (Exod. 20:1-17) and the "ordinances" (Exod. 21:1–23:22) are to be understood as representing the human obligations under the covenant.

But in ancient Israel the covenant involved much more than a contract in which each side received advantage and accepted obligations. The distinctive feature of the OT is the perception that when man (Israel) fails in his obligations—in other words, breaks the commandments—God does not look upon the covenant as null and void. In ordinary contracts, if one partner defaults, the contract is at an end and the other party is free of obligation. This kind of legality is not applicable to OT religion, for Yahweh's justice far transcends it. In strict logic the prophets of Israel should have argued that because the nation had repeatedly sinned, their God would punish them with sickness, bad harvests, and defeat in battle, and even cast them off utterly. They do in fact say this. But they have an intuition that there is something more to be said; they discern that Yahweh will never utterly cast off his covenant people. Israel may not keep the statutes and the ordinances, but he can be relied on to keep the covenant and to show mercy (Deut. 4:31; 7:9). His justice is more than the justice of law court or moralist upon earth. *See* COVENANT; cf. Ps. 103:7-18; Isa. 54:1-10; 55:3-9; Jer. 31:28-34; Hos. 11.

2. Moses. As mediator of the law and inaugurator of the covenant of Sinai, Moses claims a unique place among agents of the biblical revelation. See Exod. 20:19; Deut. 5:2-5; and the quaint narrative of Exod. 33:18-23, according to which he was permitted to see more of the divine presence than was vouchsafed to any other mortal. By comparison with this the later priests and prophets were subordinates, officers of lower commission. His intercession on behalf of the calf-worshipers (Exod. 32:11-14, 30-34) shows a more personal aspect of his mediation. Abraham's pleading for Sodom (Gen. 18:22-33) is similar, as also perhaps the experience of Jeremiah (Jer. 1:4-10; 8:18-22; 15:15-21; 20:7-18).

3. The law. The law itself was regarded as a mediating factor. It was not a hard task to be performed so much as a privilege to be enjoyed (Ps. 19:7-11). It was an imperative which assured those who endeavored to fulfil it that they were in communion with one whose providence was an inspiration. The author of this imperative was not taskmaster but deliverer (Deut. 7:6-8). Later speculation equated Torah with wisdom as mediator (Ecclus. 24:23-29).

4. The prophets. The prophet had a new word to deliver, directed to contemporary circumstances, a true understanding of which had been revealed to him directly by Yahweh. He did not conceive himself to be declaring his own views, in the manner of a newspaper columnist; he was certain that thoughts had been communicated to him by God. And this was doubtless admitted by the audience who heard him preface his utterance with: "Yahweh's word came unto me." Doubts might arise for the hearers if the utterance was contrary to their private wish or traditional customs. But it was generally accepted that a man might appropriately dare to speak thus in the name of Yahweh, and to mediate between Yahweh and his worshipers in this way. *See* PROPHET; INSPIRATION AND REVELATION.

5. The priests. Priests were the custodians of the old revelation rather than the bearers of new revelation. They interpreted and applied the written word of law. It was not their privilege, as it was that of the prophet, to announce a spoken word that had been heard in the counsel of Yahweh. It is the priests, rather than the prophets, who are to be regarded—if the comparison be allowed—as the regular clergy of Israel. They were attached to the various centers of worship and pre-eminently to the great temple in Jerusalem (the only center of worship in the postexilic period). One thinks of them more particularly as the administrators of the system of sacrifice, which was designed as the means by which even the sinner could approach God. The priest then was the mediator by whose agency worshipers could become acceptable to God and feel that the barriers created by their sins were removed.

The priest was in attendance at the temple to advise people what their duty was, what sort of offering they should make in view of their wrongdoing or as a thank offering for benefits received. He carried out the ritual observances, and also interpreted the laws, of Hebrew religion. This included some duties of the modern physician—e.g., certification of freedom from infectious disease (see Lev. 13–14; Mark 1:44). Where the existing body of statutes was not explicit, the priests might be asked to give a judgment in a disputed case, as in Hag. 2:11-13. Thus, in addition to the more technical tasks of their profession, priests were looked up to as the appointed guides of the nation in morals and religion (Leviticus; Ezek. 40–48; cf. Deut. 33:8-10; Hos. 4:1-9; 6:6-9; Mal. 2:4-7). The priest's responsibility involved in some sense his bearing of the iniquity of the whole people (Ezek. 4:4). The vestments of the high priest symbolized the representative character of his functions (Exod. 28, especially vs. 29).

In the light of this we can look on the priests and prophets as colleagues rather than as rivals. It is not inappropriate to conceive the mediation of the prophet as, so to speak, a downward movement, and that of the priest as an upward movement, provided they are seen as complementary, not contrasted. There were occasions when a happy complementing of functions did not obtain, but we are outlining what the respective functions of priest and prophet were in principle. The priest was essentially the man who maintained the traditional religion, in its ritual and also its moral aspect. The prophet was not concerned so much for custom and outward form as for inner principle and for new revelations from Yahweh. But the prophet could reassert the "old" traditional religion if it seemed to him that current practice had departed from it (cf. Jer. 7:22-28); in this case the prophet is a reformer, not an innovator. He judges the present and actual in the light of an ideal—namely, God's will—whether as revealed at Sinai to Moses in the classic past, or as freshly revealed to the prophet of a later day.

6. The king. As Yahweh's anointed, the king is the representative of Yahweh to the people. He may even have been regarded as superhuman. He is Yahweh's son (Pss. 2:7; 89:26-27). In II Sam. 14:17, 20; Ps. 110; Jer. 22:18, he is lord. In I Sam. 16:13; II Sam. 23:1-5; Isa. 11:2; 61:1, the king has the divine spirit. But he is also the people's representative before Yahweh. He is their "shield" (Pss. 84:9; 89:18). The people is in some sense embodied in him, and he is the expression of their ideals. Their conduct, whether good or bad, is, as it were, focused in him. Like people, like king; a wicked king is both cause and consequence of a wicked people (cf. II Kings 16 [Ahaz]; 21:1-16 [Manasseh]); similarly in the case of good kings like Hezekiah (II Kings 18–20) and David. Generally, on the king as inseparable from the kingdom, see II Sam. 3:28; 21:1-14; I Kings 18:18.

The king's function included the performance of cult acts which were later the exclusive prerogative of the priests (I Kings 8). In the view of some scholars he did even more: he performed a ritual act which fell to no priest of a later day, not even to the postexilic high priest. At the New Year festival, which was a re-enactment of Creation, he was annually enthroned, and this was viewed as an impersonation of Yahweh (just as in the Babylonian cult the king impersonated Marduk); Yahweh was triumphing over the winter-death of vegetation, as he did over primeval chaos, and this triumph guaranteed the fruitfulness of earth and man for another year, victory over enemies, and general prosperity. An additional element in this cultic drama in Israel was the conception of the renewal of the covenant. The OT evidence supporting this theory is not as definite as could be desired. It is mainly derived from the Psalms (especially 93–99; 132–35). Not all scholars are willing to allow that the Babylonian rites must have had their parallel in Israel. For discussion of Babylonian religion, *see* ASSYRIA AND BABYLONIA.

A distinctive feature of Yahwism was the limitation of the king's autocracy by the assumption of his responsibility for upholding the covenant. Only insofar as he accepts this responsibility is he a king "after Yahweh's own heart" (Deut. 17:14-20; Ps. 72). The ideal of kingship was not always realized (cf. I Sam. 8; Jer. 22:13-17; and the summaries in I–II Kings).

7. Sacrifice. The sacrificial system among the Hebrews figures largely in their experience of mediation. There is need here only to mention in general terms what was implied in the ritual. (*See also* SACRIFICES AND OFFERINGS.) No rationale of ancient sacrifice can be given, because our ancient sources give us no information about the intention of worshipers. The theories that sacrifice was essentially man's offering a gift to his deity, or seeking communion, or making available the magic potency of blood, or annulling sin and thereby restoring a right relationship with an offended deity—all have some truth in them and might all in varying degrees be in the minds of those who stood around an altar.

We note the part played by priests as mediators, and by the high priest in particular, in the ritual of the Day of Atonement (Lev. 16). But apart from the priestly agency, the system in itself meant that God was willing to be on good terms with his people, whether there were normal relations, so to speak, and the people came conscious simply of their humanity vis-à-vis their god (as in the kind of sacrifice known as peace offering [Lev. 3], which was followed by the jollity of a feast); or whether good relations had been violated and the people approached with a deep consciousness of sin (as with the postexilic sin, or guilt, offering, which was not accompanied by feasting). However little the average Israelite may have understood the details of the ritual of the later period, and however little he may have reflected on the significance of it, he must have accepted it as the means provided by God himself by which man could be freed from the sense of alienation from God. God was willing to be approached in this way; reconciliation was effected by this means.

The sacrificial system of Israel dealt with sins of ritual uncleanness rather than of moral transgression (Lev. 5:17-19; Num. 15:22-29; Ps. 19:12). For deliberate sins, "with a high hand" (Num. 15:30-31), presumptuous sins (Ps. 19:13), no sacrifice availed—e.g., for the disobedience of Adam in Gen. 3, or for the moral failure described in Rom. 1–2; 7. In the older legislation there had to be restitution where possible (Lev. 5:16; 24:17-21) and penalties, including extermination (Exod. 32:30-35; Lev. 20:2-27; Num. 15:30-36). In the Prophets it is realized that the real need is at a deeper level: what God requires most is repentance (Ps. 51; Ezek. 18). If the sinner has come to a penitent attitude, the grace of God forgives and restores, even though the consequences of his sin still have to be faced. This is beautifully clear in the account of David's sin with Bathsheba and the prophetic rebuke of it (II Sam. 12:13). Doubtless the performance of the sacrifices presupposed penitence on the part of the offerer and were not believed to be efficacious *ex opere operato.* "If one sacrifices from what has been wrongfully obtained, the offering is blemished," says Ben Sirach (Ecclus. 34:18-26), though he recognizes the necessity of sacrifice (35:1-11; 50:1-21). This may be taken as typical of how the system was regarded in the later period (second century B.C.). Jews of the Dispersion could not attend the temple, and had to concentrate on observances other than sacrifice—e.g., prayer, almsgiving, fasting. This was an unwitting preparation for the time when the temple cult was forcibly terminated (A.D. 70). It meant a certain spiritualizing and individualizing of religion, though it also laid stress on human effort in the endeavor for acceptance with God.

8. Hypostatic mediation. The postexilic period saw an increasing emphasis on the divine transcendence, and this led to the conception of mediating agencies other than the definitely human ones we have already considered (prophet, priest, king). The thought is now rather of the wisdom or word or spirit of Yahweh visualized as in some sense distinguishable from him but representing his dealing with man. The three terms mentioned are certainly used as more than mere attributes of Yahweh, and wisdom in particular is almost personified. Some scholars would place the Isaianic figure of the Servant in this category. A more popular type of thinking which is increasingly in evidence is the conception of angelic mediation. *See* ANGEL.

The word "hypostasis" (ὑπόστασις) means literally "solid basis," "essential nature," as in Heb. 1:2; 11:1. It is a more philosophic term than "angel," but like "angel" signifies something between a person and a pure abstraction, related to and dependent on God Most High, though distinct from the supreme majesty of the Godhead.

a. Wisdom. WISDOM appears in the OT as practical knowledge, but it rises to theological significance when understood as the principle of order in the universe. The relevant passages for this are Job 28:23-27; Ps. 104:24; Prov. 1:20-33; 3:13-19; and, above all, Prov. 8:22-31. In this last passage wisdom is not only the enlightener of mankind, but also the agent of God in the creation of the universe. The modern mind naturally assumes that this implies pre-existence—an independent existence of wisdom, apart from God though proceeding from him, seems to be implied. Some scholars, however, hesitate to attribute such precision to the author of Proverbs, and prefer to speak of poetic personification.

Two later passages in the Apoc. leave no doubt as to the substantive independence of wisdom (Ecclus. 24:3-6; Wisd. Sol. 7:22–8:4). The latter passage is the most important of all, and its agreement with Prov. 8 is plain, although the influence of Greek thought on the author of the Wisdom of Solomon is clear. The extra feature found in Ecclus. 24 is the conception of the embodiment of wisdom in the Torah or law of Israel. This is developed from the idea of wisdom's heavenly origin and immanence in the universe, with which the chapter opens. But the main thought is of the special relationship of wisdom to Israel (vs. 8: "Make your dwelling in Jacob"). This chapter stands by itself, and it is not possible to say that this identification of wisdom with law underlies all the references to wisdom in Ecclesiasticus (4:11-19; 6:18-22; 14:20-27; 51:23-26). But it is significant that the identification was made. With it may be connected the rabbinic idea that at the Creation Yahweh consulted the law, as an architect looks at his plans. The law, like wisdom, was in existence before the world. The significance of Ps. 119 must not be forgotten in this connection.

b. Word (Logos). For the word of God in the OT we have to distinguish three main usages: (*a*) The natural world is thought of as deriving its existence from the divine word or command (Gen. 1; Ps. 33:6-9; Isa. 40:26). (*b*) There is the legal word, divine commands for the moral guidance of society. (*c*) There is also the prophetic word, fresh revelation for the guidance of the people transmitted by the medium of the prophet. These three senses are combined in the conception of the word as the sovereign power and purpose of Yahweh. This conception dominates Deuteronomy and is reflected in some postexilic passages (Deut. 4:4-8; 8:3-4; Pss. 147:15-20; 148:8; Isa. 44:24-28; 45:18-23).

The prophets, both before and after the Exile, emphasize the objectivity of the word; it comes to them from God, and is not confused with their own thinking (Isa. 55:10-11; Jer. 20:9; 23:29). We may compare also the crystallization of this thought in Ps. 147:15-19; Wisd. Sol. 16:12; 18:15. This prepares for the definite hypostatization of the word, and its visualization as a distinct entity. This stage was not definitely reached, however, until after Greek philosophy had begun to influence Judaism.

The particular theme in Greek philosophy which is here meant was the teaching about the LOGOS which may be translated "Word" but always signifies thought, reason, rational principle, as well as its utterance—a twofold signification which other languages cannot reproduce. For Plato the Logos mediated between this imperfect world and the higher world of perfect archetypes, between the world of sense perception and the real or "intelligible" (νοητός) world. It might be called all-pervasive mind, but it is not personified. Later Platonists were more inclined to regard it as divine. In Stoicism, which was pantheistic and did not make the Platonist distinction of the two worlds, Logos was reason immanent in the world. It could be thought of as natural law, as the power that sustains the world, and as the mental power of individual men. As such it was divine, and might be identified with certain of the traditional gods.

The differentiation of Logos from the supreme God —i.e., its hypostatization in the strict sense—is seen first in Philo the Jew of Alexandria (*ca.* 20 B.C.–A.D. 49). Philo makes Logos one of the divine "powers" or agencies of the will of God. It is the instrument by which the world was created, the mediator of the law, the image (εἰκών) of God, the messenger (ἄγγελος), and the son (υἱός) of God. But it is neither personal nor pre-existent. Our present consideration is of the Logos figure as a cosmological principle, and—a more distinctively religious concept—as the medium both of God's providential control of the world and of man's knowledge of God. Full personification of the Logos had to wait for John's Gospel and Christian theology.

In later thought, represented in the Hermetic writings (A.D. 200-300), Logos became identified with Hermes, the messenger of the gods, who was variously thought of as the mediator of creation and the mediator generally between gods and men, as revealer of truth and savior, son of the supreme God, second god (δεύτερος θεός). In the Gnostic systems of the second century A.D., Logos tends to appear as one of the divine aeons or emanations who mediate between the supreme God and the world.

c. Spirit. The third main example of hypostatic conceptions is the developed doctrine of the SPIRIT. The thought of the OT is no more systematic here than in other connections, but we may define the functioning of the Spirit as meaning God's creative activity, whether in nature (Gen. 1:4; Job 33:4; Ps. 104:29-30) or in history and human experience (Neh. 9:20; Isa. 4:4; 61:1; Ezek. 37:1-14; 36:27; Zech. 4:6). The eschatological sense, of God's new creation at the end of history, is the climax of this. This is not much ascribed to the Spirit in the OT, but there is the well-known passage Joel 2:28-32, which seemed so significant to the first Christians (Acts 2:17-21). The idea that this creative divine energy is imparted to individuals is very common—e.g., in the case of Bezalel, with reference to artistic skill (Exod. 31:1-5), or with reference to extraordinary feats, as in the case of Samson (Judg. 14:16) and Saul (I Sam. 10:6-11; 11:6-15). This applies particularly to prophets (cf. Num. 11:25; 24:2; Neh. 9:30; Hos. 9:7; Zech. 7:12). The great prophets seem to show a certain caution in claiming God's spirit behind their utterances, and to prefer to speak of Yahweh's hand being upon them (Isa. 8:11; Jer. 15:17; Ezek. 1:3; 8:1).

The phrase "*holy* Spirit" occurs three times (Ps. 51:11; Isa. 63:10-11), and some have felt a suggestion here that the Spirit is distinct from Yahweh. Passages like Ps. 139:7 ("Whither shall I go from thy Spirit?"); Isa. 40:13; 48:16; Hag. 2:5 might be taken as lending support to this view. Caution is advisable here. The basic OT thought about the Spirit is as Yahweh personally in operation, making his will known to men, increasing their moral and religious potentialities, granting special quickening to certain people as agents of his purpose. This is not a conception of a divine hypostasis, but of God himself as *dynamis* (δύναμις) energy; in more Hebraic terms, the OT does not say so much that God has spirit (רוח), as that he is spirit (cf. John 4:24).

The later Judaism continued to think of the Spirit as power and heightened vitality, with special emphasis on its place in the temple cultus and in the person of the high priest. The living voice of a prophet was no longer heard, but the prophets of old were believed to have been prompted by the Spirit, as was scripture generally. We read much of the Spirit as source of morality and wisdom in the Testaments of the Twelve Patriarchs (Test. Simeon 4:4; Test. Levi 18:7, 11; Test. Judah 20:1; 24:2-3). Here we note the connection of the Spirit with wisdom, which is also found in Dan. 5:11-14; Wisd. Sol. 9:17; and frequently in Philo. The idea of the Spirit as a cosmic potency is found—doubtless under Stoic influence—in Wisdom of Solomon and Philo (cf. Wisd. Sol. 1:7; 7:23–8:1; 12:1). It is this line of development which leads to the hypostatization of the Spirit (if it is indeed justifiable to differentiate Spirit from its divine author)—namely, the notion of divine immanence in creation. The parallelism with wisdom no doubt contributed. Much of what is said about the activity of wisdom in Wisd. Sol. 7–8 might equally well be said of the Spirit (cf. Wisd. Sol. 1:4-7; 9:17).

9. Servant of the Lord. The mediatorial role of the much-debated figure of the Servant of Yahweh (Isa. 53) must not be overlooked. Recent discussion has introduced the suggestion that it is a king of Israel whom the prophet has in mind, and this, of course, brings the conception into closer relation with the concept of Messiah. Other interpretations keep to the thought of a prophetic figure, who displays, not in preaching but in bitter experience, the value for sin's atonement of obedience unto death. *See* SERVANT OF THE LORD.

10. Messiah. The significance of the Messiah similarly must not be overlooked. Even if Messiah was not strictly a mediating figure, he was the representative of Yahweh, whether his function was conceived as political (i.e., Messiah as ideal king of the future) or spiritual. The conception must be evaluated in the light of the king ideology referred to above. Some scholars bring it into relation with the figure of the Servant, and it is then suggested that Judaism had the doctrine of a suffering Messiah.

Judaism certainly had a brief in the atoning potency of the suffering of righteous men. This is presented in its most sublimated form in Isa. 53, and the trials of good men in later times (e.g., during the Maccabean Revolt) were seen as exemplifications of it. It may be that the concept of the Messiah tended to be interpreted in the light of this. But the real fusion of these ideals had to wait for the creative experience of Jesus. *See* MESSIAH, JEWISH.

C. ***MEDIATION IN THE NT.*** **1. Christian beginnings.** The most primitive Christian proclamation declared that in the life of Christ the power of God was at work; even his death was part of God's purpose; his resurrection meant, not only his vindication against adversaries and doubters, but also his exaltation to the presence of God, as Messiah and Lord (Acts 2:23-24, 32-36; 10:36-42; Rom. 1:4).

Through this Messiah, who had not been king in Jerusalem, and was not of priestly stock, but a humbly born Galilean carpenter, God was acting redemptively as never before. For this divine activity was that of the "end time" to which Israel's prophets had pointed (Acts 2:16-24; 10:43; I Cor. 15:3-4; I Pet. 1: 10-12). Through this Lord a new deliverance is available for Israel; that is the significance of the fresh outpouring of divine empowering Spirit (Acts 2:1-11; 3:16; 4:31-35; 5:32; 11:15-18). A new opportunity to attain moral triumph over sin is being offered (Acts 2:38-40; 3:26; 11:18). Christ is God's Righteous One, the Author (or Pioneer) of life (Acts 3:14-15). He is also the final arbiter of human destiny (Acts 10:42).

2. Jesus' own conception of his work. ***a. Fulfilment.*** The interpretation of Jesus' work as fulfilment was the original deposit of faith after the first Christians' eyes had been opened to the significance of their Master by the event of his resurrection and the experience of Pentecost. The basis of it was the Master's own understanding of his person and task. This may be reconstructed, in barest outline, from the Synoptic gospels as follows:

Whereas prophets spoke the word of God, Jesus incorporated it in himself. He knew himself to be greater than the prophets (Mark 8:27-38); greater than Jonah (Matt. 12:41); greater than John the Baptist (Matt. 11:2-11). Whereas the priests of Israel put men in touch with imperfect means of bridging the gulf caused by sin, Christ effected the perfect means of atonement, and inaugurated the new covenant (Mark 10:45; 14:24). Something greater than the temple was there during his ministry to Israel (Matt. 12:6). Christ made a higher claim on men's allegiance. He was the true king of Israel; he embodied the divine sovereignty. "Something greater than Solomon is here" (Matt. 12:42). Even the mediator Moses has now to acknowledge that a greater than he has come to the service of men (Mark 9:7).

b. The kingdom. Recent study has interpreted Christ's teaching and work as centering round the idea of the KINGDOM OF GOD. This is illuminating, provided the idea of God's fatherhood is not minimized. From this point of view his mediatorial achievement consisted in enabling his followers to take seriously the loving sovereignty and redemptive reality of God. In this sense the kingdom of God drew near to men (Mark 1:15); it could even be said to have come (Matt. 12:28).

The ethical teaching of Jesus is best understood as the laws of the kingdom. As men gathered round Jesus and heard him teaching, they stood under the kingdom's authority and felt the urge to obey. This was the authority with which he spoke, and the obedience of faith which his words inspired (Mark 1:22-27; 4:37-41). Negatively, he attacked the evil influences that plagued men. This is the inner significance of the healings and exorcisms; the kingdom of Satan was being overthrown that the kingdom of God might be inaugurated (Matt. 12:15-29). The advent of Jesus on the human scene made Satan recognize the limitations of his power. He had been strong in his tyranny over mankind, but he is now bound and his evil works are being undone by one stronger than he.

Such is the testimony of the gospels to the inner significance of Jesus' acts of healing and compassion, and critical scholarship cannot deny that this represents also the self-consciousness of Jesus himself (Mark 9:1; Luke 4:1-21; 10:1-24; 11:14-32; 13:10-17; 16:16 [cf. Matt. 11:11-12]; 17:20-21). He created conditions in which people could realize God's fatherly nearness, and could be reconciled to him and submit to his sovereignty with humble joy. This is clear not only from passages which explicitly mention the sovereignty, but also in incidents like those described in Luke 7:36-50; 19:1-10; and in the parables of Luke 15; 18:11-14. Christ's ministry was the supreme event in the long series of God's mighty acts on man's behalf. By it the divine love was brought down to man's level, and man was placed within its reach. Christ, as no other, enables the prodigal son to come to himself and return to the welcoming Father. So man's deepest need is satisfied, and mediation and reconciliation effected.

c. Messiah. The christological titles of the gospels are intended to express this concept (*see* CHRIST and related articles).

Such titles as "prophet" or "rabbi" (Matt. 16:13-20) were inadequate to express the fact that the divine sovereignty was making itself real among men through him. He could be no less than Messiah, in Jewish terminology. But this involved him in embarrassment, because of its prevailingly political connotation at that period. In the highest sense of the term he was Messiah, the peacemaking Messiah of Zech. 9:9-10, as hinted in the drama of the Entry into Jerusalem (Mark 11:1-10). But to have allowed this fact to be broadcast earlier in his ministry would have exposed him to the charge of being a Zealot nationalist. Hence the remarkable reticence of the Jesus of the Synoptic gospels about his messiahship.

"Lord" is fairly frequent in Luke as a title of Jesus, but elsewhere it is rare, and the proper inference from our Synoptic gospels is that deliberate thinking about Jesus as Lord (κύριος; Aramaic מר) was the usage of the early church rather than of the first disciples and Jesus himself.

d. Son of God. Jesus certainly thought of himself as the Son of God. Even if with extreme critical caution we set aside as unhistorical the acclamation of him as Son of God by disciples, by the centurion at the Cross, by demons, and also in the narratives of birth, baptism, temptation, and transfiguration, there are still three basic passages in which his own conviction, if not his public teaching, about himself, as in a unique filial relationship to God, is clear: Matt. 11:25-27; Mark 12:1-12; 13:32. Proper reverence must be preserved about our ability to reconstruct the inner life of Jesus, but it is reasonable to assume that this filial consciousness was the basis of all Jesus' thinking about himself and his duty. The significance of it is that Jesus was appropriating to himself as a title what the OT used as a description of Israel's relation to her God (Hos. 11:1, etc.). It could be applied to an individual—e.g., the king (II Sam. 7:14; Ps. 2:7)—but seems not to have been a normal designation of the Messiah. The gospels, however, take it as synonymous with "Messiah," and probably this was a Christian innovation.

e. Son of man. The self-designation most favored by Jesus appears to have been the enigmatic title "Son of man." The primary meaning of this phrase, whether in the classical Hebrew (as in Ps. 8:4; Ezek. 2:1; etc.) or in the Aramaic of Jesus' time, was "man," "human being," "anybody." By using this term of himself, therefore, Jesus was indicating his sense of kinship with ordinary humanity. But this can hardly have been the whole of his intention. Modern sentiment tends to assume that Jesus thought of himself as the ideal man, but this ignores the categories that were available to him as a Jew of the first century. It is clear, however, that whereas the title "Son of God" expresses his relationship with his Father, "Son of man" expresses his relationship with his human brethren, the words "son of" in each case being a Hebraism for "likeness to" or "affinity with."

The uncertainty about the term "son of man" arises from its symbolic use, as in Dan. 7:13-27, where a human figure, in contrast with animal figures, is made to represent the "saints of the Most High." There is a further uncertainty whether the later use of the term in apocalyptic writing (I Enoch) was familiar to Jesus or not. There is less tendency among scholars now than a generation ago to assume this. Mark 14:62 is more likely to reflect the beliefs of the first Christians than to be an actual statement of Jesus. But the eschatological Son of man is firmly embedded in Mark and Q, and there can be no doubt that Jesus spoke in these terms (Matt. 19:28; 24:27, 37, 44; Mark 8:38; 13:26; 14:62). Whether Jesus fully identified himself with this conception of the vicegerent of God intervening at the end of history, and whether it expresses his distinctive thought, is more doubtful. It is certainly wrong to regard his earthly career as only a prelude to final intervention.

The view has been advocated that, as in Dan. 7, so in the thought of Jesus, the "Son of man" stands for a messianic community rather than an individual Messiah. This links back with Hebrew ideas of corporate personality, and points forward to the church as the new Israel, the new society "in Christ." On this view Jesus, in gathering disciples round him, was constituting the nucleus of the new covenant, the redeemed society, the kingdom of God on earth. This foreshadows the Pauline doctrine of Christ as the second Adam.

f. Self-sacrifice. The very ambiguity of the term "Son of man" may have made it welcome to Jesus, in the sense that it was more susceptible than the term "Messiah" of fresh meaning which he was waiting to pour into it. This new connotation is the element of self-sacrifice. For in the Markan presentation the Son of man is one destined not only to come on the clouds in a glorious denouement, but first to be humiliated and crucified (Mark 8:31; 9:12, 31; 10:33, 45; 14:21, 41). Some scholars have regarded this as unhistorical, but there is growing recognition that it was the characteristic thought of Jesus to accept death as the climax of his obedience to God and his service to his fellow men, and not to reject it as incompatible with messiahship. The full interpretation of these passages seems also to require the assumption that Jesus conceived his destiny in terms of Isa. 53. If Jesus thought of himself as that Servant of God who voluntarily made himself an offering for sin and poured out his soul to death, this expresses not only his relation to God (as Son of God) and his relation to men (as Son of man), but also the extent of his devotedness to his fellow men.

Summing up, we discern in Jesus' sense of mission a unique fusion of complete self-sacrifice with assurance of triumph as God's representative. He was convinced that, in the divine overruling, to lose his life was to save it; that God was undertaking for him and would make his suffering potent for the establishment of the divine society and the liberation of men from their sins.

3. Paul. The problem to which mediation is the answer is seen by PAUL in terms of man's sin and need of deliverance from it. No other NT writer takes it so seriously in these terms except the author of Hebrews.

There is a characteristic Pauline doctrine of the inability of man's idealism and moral consciousness (in biblical terminology, knowledge of law), with all the moral endeavor that may be prompted by it, to solve the basic problem of man's existence (Rom. 2:17-29; 3:9-20; 7; 8:3-4; 10:4; Gal. 2:16-21; 3:21; Phil. 3:9).

Christ's fitness to effect mediation is expressed in the titles "Lord" and "Son of God," which Paul ascribes to him as part of his inheritance from the primitive Christology. The marks of his own reflection on that Christology, and of his attempts to bring out its significance, particularly for non-Jewish Christians, are to be seen in the conception of Christ as emancipator of the human race, as reconciler, as second Adam, and as wisdom.

a. The lordship of Christ. Christ as Lord is presupposed everywhere, and it is superfluous to quote references (*see* CHRIST). The most illuminating passages are probably Rom. 10:9; 14:8-9; I Cor. 8:6; II Cor. 3:16-18; Phil. 2:6-11. We note in the two Romans passages the connection with the Resurrection; this was in the most primitive preaching the signal proof of Christ's lordship, as we may infer from Acts 2:36. There is an individual apprehension of this in Phil. 3:8-10. The general idea needs little elucidation: it is that of Christ's complete control, directly in the church, indirectly in the whole universe, and ultimately (Phil. 2:11) over all existing beings, natural and supernatural. The references to Christ's final appearance at the end of history may be considered in this connection (I Cor. 1:8; 16:22; Phil. 1:6, 10; 2:16; 3:20; I Thess. 1:10; 3:13; 4:13-17; 5:2, 23; II Thess. 1:7-10; 2:1-8). Similarly, the references to Christ as "head" (κεφαλή) may be treated as one aspect of his lordship. These teach a general or cosmic primacy, as in Col. 2:10, and are also particularized in the church, as in Col. 1:18; 2:19; the two conceptions not being in contrast, but mutually interpenetrating. There is a similar interpenetration of thought about Christ's headship in the whole universe and in the church in Eph. 1:22-23; 4:15-16; 5:23. The envisaging of the goal of the divine purpose as the creation of a unified community of supernatural and natural beings under Christ's primacy also belongs to this line of development. The parallel with the lordship of Christ in Phil. 2:11 is close.

The precise meaning of "head" in these passages is not to be confined to the meaning "primacy in a series," which it derives from the use of κεφαλή to render the Hebrew ראש; by the time of the NT it was a commonplace in the sense of "head of state," and this meant the absolute ruler.

b. The divine sonship of Christ. It might be said that Christ's lordship was not so much an inherent capacity to effect mediation as an achievement resulting from his life, suffering, and resurrection. Having made mediation possible, he is properly addressed as Lord. The term "Son of God" more unambiguously asserts his antecedent right, and relates him primarily to God rather than to men. But its significance is not ontological, as in John. Paul uses the term with reference, not to incarnation or pre-existence, but to resurrection and redemption (Rom. 1:4; Gal. 4:4-5). The divine love motivates the Son and flows through him until a new society or kingdom (Col. 1:13) is created where men are freed from the bondage of sin. This is seen as the sacrifice of love on God's part (Rom. 8:31-39), as also on Christ's part (Gal. 2:20); and the new society which results is said to be raised to the level of sonship (Gal. 4:5). This sonship is connected with the work of the Spirit (Rom. 8:14-17; II Cor. 1:19-22; Gal. 4:6-7; Eph. 1:13-14). Perfect humanity, which is the goal of the process, comes from knowledge of the Son of God (Eph. 4:13).

c. Christ as liberator. Christ liberates men from their sins. Paul's own sensitiveness to the power of sin caused him to reflect searchingly on this aspect of the significance of Christ. We note three distinctive features in it:

a) The fact of sin is understood—in distinction to specific acts—as a sinister power, semipersonified, which has control over all men. It is more objectively conceived, and more comprehensive, than guilt, which is man's consciousness of sin; but in Paul's sense a man is sinful even before he can feel guilt. We are sinners by the simple fact of being born; guilt arises only with the development of moral sense (Rom. 5:13; 7:7-11).

b) Paul has his own peculiar understanding of the moral law or categorical imperative as exerting a thralldom over us (Rom. 7:7-23; Gal. 2:15-21; 3:18-25). Law merely defines sins; it gives no power to avoid them (Rom. 3:20). To a moral intensity and spiritual sensitiveness such as Paul's this only aggravated the moral demand.

c) Connected with sin, as punishment or inevitable consequence, is death (Rom. 5:12-14, 21; 6:16-23; cf. Jas. 1:15). Christ's deliverance from sin includes deliverance from death. To the modern mind this may seem illogical, but it must be remembered that in the Bible death is not simply a biological fact; it means separation from God. *See* DEATH.

But Christ brings deliverance, in view of all these aspects of the problem. He broke the power, loosed the strangle hold, of sin. This was a fact of experience for Paul before it was taken up into his theology (Rom. 7:24–8:4). That experience was one of release, of a new freedom which arises from being in a right relationship with God, and which may without arrogance be called divine sonship (Rom. 8:12-17; II Cor. 3:17; Gal. 1:4; 2:15-20; 3:23–4:7; 4:21–5:1). This freedom includes freedom from death (Rom. 5:17-21; 6:20–7:6; 8:11). Christ's resurrection was evidence of this (Rom. 6:4-11; I Cor. 15:12-26). Paul makes the point that Christ, having actually faced death, now offers the same immunity from it to his worshipers. A later Paulinist says Christ abolished death (II Tim. 1:10; cf. Acts 2:24; Heb. 2:9-14).

The notion of Christ's overcoming Satan is firmly embedded in NT Christology, and is prominent among NT suggestions as to how he effected mediation. It appears in the Synoptic gospels in the accounts of exorcisms. In Paul it is seen in Rom. 8:37-39; I Cor. 2:8; 15:24; Gal. 4:8-9; Col. 2:14-15. This mythological language expresses the conviction that the malign forces which affect human life were drawn to issue by Christ and deprived of their power to frustrate the divine purpose.

Explanation of how Christ secured his benefits for mankind followed other lines too. In Rom. 3:21-25 the thought is of the expiatory power of his death, on the analogy of OT sacrifice which was believed to restore the relationship broken by sin.

But for Paul the significance of Christ's death did not depend only on comparison with sacrificial animals. It demonstrated how unreservedly he entered into the consequences of human sin, as indicated in the bold hyperbole of II Cor. 5:21: God "made him to be sin who knew no sin." Christ identified himself with sinful humanity to the extent of sharing the curse which the Mosaic law pronounces upon its transgressors (Gal. 3:10-13). The meaning here apparently is that Christ took the sinful entail upon himself and, as it were, absorbed it, thus exhausting the "curse." Again, the Cross shows the length to which Christ went in conforming to the will of God —i.e., in moral obedience such as man could never render to God (Phil. 2:7-8). And this is not simply his own achievement, for which he is exalted (vss. 10-11), but it inspires the same quality of life in his worshipers while still on earth (vss. 1-5). These worshipers will ultimately follow their Redeemer in his upward path to the heavenly regions where he belongs and is exalted as Lord, and where they belong too (Phil. 3:20).

d. Christ as reconciler. The new status of freedom and sonship is reconciliation with God (II Cor. 5:18-21; Eph. 2:12-18; Col. 1:13-14). Paul's reflection on human sinfulness, in the light of the biblical teaching about the divine righteousness and holiness, necessarily implied that there is a state of alienation (ἔχθρα, "hostility, enmity") between man and God (Rom. 5:1-11). But Christ's self-offering unto death (Rom. 5:6; Phil. 2:7-8) meant divine initiative toward overcoming that situation. It imparted righteousness to men ("justified by his blood" [Rom. 5:9], a phrase that needs Rom. 3:21-26 for its elucidation). It is positively a righteous act (Rom. 5:18), and a signal example of divine grace (Rom. 5:20-21).

e. Christ as second Adam. Further, Christ is the second Adam, the new representative man. This is clearly implied in Rom. 5:12-21; I Cor. 15:22, 45-49; supporting passages are Rom. 8:1-2, 10-11, 29; 12:4-5. Ancient ideals of primeval man and modern ideas of ideal man offer only partial parallels, for Paul's thought is strongly Hebraic and corporate. Modern individualistic thinking has to make special efforts to recognize the inclusive and representative nature of this conception. The parallelism between Christ and Adam is not that of two individuals, but each is a typical and representative figure. Adam stands for actual, sinful, mortal humanity; and Christ stands for humanity re-created (II Cor. 5:17), united in veneration for him (what Paul calls faith), capable of fulfilling the moral law, destined for perfection and eternal life. A Paulinist developed this thought into the conception of Christ controlling the moral evolution of mankind (or at least the church) toward a final unity with all other spiritual beings, a unity unattainable in conditions of ordinary human life (Adam), but of which Christ is architect and "head" (Eph. 1:10, 19-23; 4:13-16). A middle term in this development of thought is Paul's own application of headship to Christ in Col. 1:15-20; 2:9-15; 3:11.

f. Cosmic Christology. This cosmic Christology of Col. 1:15-17 owes something to the hypostatic speculation about wisdom referred to *above* (§ B8*a;* cf. I Cor. 1:24, 30). The meaning is that man depends, not on any other spiritual authority or principality (cf. 2:20), not even on what the Jews called wisdom, but on Christ alone, both for his physical existence and for his proper development as a spiritual being. Christ is the supreme agent, or mediator, of God in creation and redemption.

The use of the wisdom or Logos concept makes it possible to deal with mediation in the sense of the relation of a transcendent God to the material world. In the NT, although the major attention is directed to Christ's significance in relation to human sin, his relation to the whole cosmos is also recognized—in other words, his cosmological as well as his soteriological significance (for this, in addition to Col. 1:15-17, see Rom. 8:18-25; I Cor. 8:6; and also, outside Paul, John 1:1-5; Heb. 1:2). To isolate soteriology from cosmology, as Marcion was to do a century later, in reaction to the cosmological speculations of Gnosticism, was to make it meaningless. But the NT is proof against this, for it conceives the redemptive activity of Christ as extending to the natural world as well as to man. And this is not merely a daring speculation of Paul's in his argument against Colossian Gnosticism. It is the implicit logic of the Christian belief in God as creator and redeemer. The divine concern is for the totality of the universe, and mediation can have no lesser scope.

4. John. ***a. Christ as revealer (Logos).*** In the Johannine presentation Jesus mediates between man and God by bringing the true revelation. It is a more intellectualist conception than that of Paul or I Peter or the early church generally. The superiority of Christ is strongly emphasized, as compared with other mediators or revealers of divine truth—e.g., Moses (1:17; 5:45-47; 6:31-58; 9:28-33); Abraham (8:56-58); John the Baptist (1:6-8, 15, 30; 3:30; 5:36). The stress on the uniqueness of Christ is carried sometimes to the point of denying progressive revelation (1:18; 6:46; 10:7-10; 14:6; 18:37). This dogmatic intransigency is not altogether peculiar to John, for we find similar affirmations elsewhere in the NT—e.g., Acts 4:12; Col. 2:9-10.

The Johannine Prologue introduces the thought of mediation in terms of the Logos, whose characteristic function it is. Its essential being is the thought of God, but its outreach is to the world and to mankind. It brought the world and human life into existence, and in this setting its crowning work is performed—namely, the illumination of life, the transformation of mere existence into true life, life of grace and truth, which has affinity with the life of God. In order to achieve this the Logos concentrated itself in a particular human life. Then at last it was possible for those who are in the flesh to behold the glory of God, to receive grace and truth, to "know" God. God, through his Logos, in Christ, had made this possible; mediation was complete.

The decisive point in this divinely controlled process is the Incarnation, rather than the Passion or Resurrection. This is a particular feature of the Johannine theology; but it keeps in conformity with NT theology as a whole by its doctrine of the Passion as the special "hour" when the glory of the Father and of Christ is to be revealed (7:30; 12:33; 13:1; 17:1). Moreover, the Good Shepherd has come, not simply to gather his flock, but to lay down his life for them (10:15-18; cf. 11:50-53).

b. Christ as Son of God and Son of man. At the end of the Prologue, when the thought becomes more concrete and personal, "Logos" gives way to "Son," and it is mainly as Son of God that Christ appears in the pages of this gospel. The Prologue reminds us that the author understands sonship in terms of Logos. The traditional terms "Messiah" and "Son of man" are also used, as roughly equivalent to "Son of God" and as requiring no further explanation. For "Messiah," cf. 1:41-49; 4:25; 7:31; 10:1-30 (in the light of Ezek. 34); 11:27; 12:12-15; 18:33-37 ("King," as 1:49; 19:19-22); 20:31. For "Son of man," cf. 5:27; 6:27, where the idea is the conventional apocalyptic one. But in 1:51; 3:13-14; 6:62; 8:23, 28; 12:34 the title has a different connotation, and expresses the Hellenistic idea of an archetypal man who belongs to the divine realm but descends into this world conveying revelation; his return makes it possible for recipients of the revelation to ascend also, leaving the earthly sphere of evil and attaining new life in the supernatural realm. There is thus a parallel in John to the conception of the "Son of man" as a corporate entity of the saints, and to the Pauline thought of Christ as the Adam who re-creates humanity. "Son of man" in this sense is the perfect mediator between heaven and earth.

For "Son of God," cf. 3:16-18, 35-36; 5:17-27; 10:30-38; 14:10-13, 28; 17:1-3. John has kept the Synop tic title, but stresses the relationship with the Father in its ontological aspect as well as in its aspect of obedience to the Father's will. This goes beyond the Hebraic sense of "Son of God" as meaning "people of God," or "special representative of God." It makes clear Christ's right to effect mediation between man and God, and defines his relationship with God more precisely than was done in the earlier Christian tradition.

c. Christ as Lamb of God. In 1:29 Jesus is called the "Lamb of God, who takes away the sin of the world." The term "sin" does not figure prominently in the Gospel of John. The First Letter is somewhat closer to the rest of the NT when it declares Christ to be the expiation for sins, as in Rom. 3:25 (cf. I John 1:8–2:2; 4:10). It even affirms the possibility of sinlessness for those who abide in Christ. But in the gospel there is the theme of a parallel development of faith and unbelief, and sin must be defined in reference to it. The fundamental sin is refusal to believe in Christ (16:9).

d. Discipleship: the divine society. The benefits arising from the Incarnation are mainly described throughout this gospel in terms of life or eternal life (3:15-16; 5:21-26; 6:35-40; 10:28; etc.). The contrast between this higher life and ordinary existence or physical needs is made clear in 4:10-14, 31-34. It is the nourishment of man's spirit (6:32-35, 47-58); it is the reception of Christ's teaching (6:68); it is communion with God in true worship and petitionary prayer (4:21-24; 14:14; 15:7, 16; 16:23-24); it is knowing God (17:3); and, of course, it endures beyond death (14:1-6; 17:24). Its chief mark in outward conduct is love (13:34-35; 15:12-14); this is dealt with in more detail in I John (see especially 4:7-21).

Those who receive these benefits have come out of darkness into light, and belong no more to the world —i.e., the mass of mankind apart from Christ (10:26-27; 17:16). They can appreciate the wonder of the Shepherd's concern for them which impelled him to lay down his life for them (10:1-18). Their status is that of children of God (1:12-13), for their response to Christ is a kind of rebirth. Their relationship is not only with one another and with Christ, but also with the Father. For knowledge of him is the highest life, and Christ's mission was to make this knowledge possible (17:3). The ultimate goal is his presence, and the purpose of Christ's death is to pioneer the way thither (14:1-7). He alone mediates knowledge of God and communion with God (15:9-16; 17:6-19; 20:17). After his withdrawal from the earthly scene his presence with his disciples is still available, for the Spirit of truth will be their counselor (14:16-17, 26; 15:26-27). This he has arranged with the Father on their behalf as the continuing manifestation of himself and as a bond with the Father which neither death nor all the hatred of the world can break. Thus the ultimate goal is this ideal community in God, secure beyond time and evil; and it was made possible through the incarnation of the eternal Logos in Jesus of Nazareth.

5. Hebrews. ***a. The finality of Christ's work.*** The Letter to the Hebrews opens with the statement that God's self-communication in Christ is more complete than in previous revelations. By nature Christ was better equipped to do this, being the agent of creation and superior to angels. The terminology shows that the author is influenced by Hellenistic-Jewish speculation about the agency of wisdom and the Logos. Christ's work is described summarily as "purification of sins." Elsewhere it is "eternal redemption" (9:12; cf. 5:9)—i.e., of eternal effectiveness, as contrasted with the rites of OT sacrifice, which needed to be repeated. What Christ achieved was "once for all," complete and final (cf. 7:25; 10:11-14). There is an element of Platonism in this use of the adjective "eternal" (cf. 9:15; 13:20); it implies that Christ belongs to the realm of perfect archetypes, where all have this eternal or ideal quality.

b. The perfect sacrifice. The significance of Christ's saving work is brought out by reference to the Hebrew sacrificial system and priesthood. It is argued that this system was imperfect, a mere adumbration (8:5) of how man's moral need is to be met. This need is not for outward purification, but for purification of the conscience (9:13-14). It is then claimed that Christ's ministry is effectual just here. He is the "surety" (ἔγγυος, "guarantor"; 7:22) and "mediator" (μεσίτης; 8:6) of a superior covenant. Israel's refractoriness had annulled the old covenant, and the most discerning prophets had visualized a new covenant—i.e., a relationship between man and God founded on a more perfect understanding of God's ways. This new covenant is now in being, as a result of Christ's life and death. His blood was the sacrificial blood necessary, according to Jewish ideas, for the inauguration of a covenant (9:22). His willingness to pour out his lifeblood is the perfect obedience which divine justice requires of men but had received neither from the first Adam nor from any of his posterity (5:8; 10: 5-10; 12:2).

The logic here is not simply that Christ's death is declared to have the efficacy which the slaying of animals was reputed to have in the sacrificial rituals of the ancient world. It rises above this analogy in the confidence that there is no limit to what God can do with a life of perfect obedience culminating in death voluntarily accepted. At one point in history this offering was made, and the Christian conviction is that God, who accepted the offering, makes it fruitful for all who attach themselves to Christ by faith.

c. The perfect priest. Interwoven with this argument is the conception of Christ as high priest. The Jewish high priest entered the inner sanctuary of the temple, the holy of holies, once a year on the Day of Atonement (Lev. 16:2, 17). That holy place signified the presence of God, and it was realized that man, as man—i.e., as sinner—was not fit to approach God. The seriousness with which this was recognized is a mark of the superiority of Hebrew to pagan religion: the Hebrews felt that only the holiest of men, their high priest, might venture to enter the divine presence, and he only once in the year. The affirmation of our letter is that Christ has entered God's presence in heaven itself on behalf of men (9:24; 10:20; the temple veil seems to be compared alternatively to the sky and to Christ's body, rent open as he hung bleeding on the cross). In entering heaven he has returned to his rightful dignity, but he has done so representatively for us, after his human experience, which, as it were, earned him a family of brethren (2:11-12), whom he now presents to his heavenly Father. In a different metaphor, he has pioneered man's approach to God. He is our forerunner (6:20) or pioneer (2:10; 10:19-20). He has secured this both by his personal qualities and by his actual achievement in his earthly life (2:9-18; 7:25-27). Men need no longer feel that their sin unfits them for fellowship with God. By his continued agency and intercession they may draw near to God (7:25), with confidence (4:16).

Subordinate ideas to be noted are: (*a*) that of Christ as example, arising out of his self-identification with man (2:9-18; 5:8-9; 12:2); (*b*) that of victory over death and the devil (2:14-15).

6. I Peter. In I Peter, Christ's achievement as Savior is illuminated in three passages: (*a*) 1:19 compares the Cross for its efficacy with the lamb of sacrifice, as in Rom. 3:25; Hebrews. No material means can raise human life from futility (1:18), but only sacrificial suffering, and this was his destiny from eternity (1:20). (*b*) Christ's innocence and exemplary quality are stressed, and also the vicarious nature of his sacrifice, in 2:21-24. (*c*) 3:19-20 enlarges the vicariousness of his death to include former generations. The "spirits in prison" are probably to be taken as referring to departed souls in Hades (Sheol). The thought, then, is that in the interval between his death and resurrection Christ visited Sheol and proclaimed his victory over sin and death. This is mythological in form, but expresses the conviction that the salvation Christ offers is available not only for the generation contemporary with his earthly life, and all subsequent generations to whom the gospel may be preached, but to past generations as well. This conception of the scope of salvation is impressive. Christ's work has significance for the whole of mankind, from Adam to the end of history.

7. Revelation. Revelation presupposes as general background a world situation degenerating not simply from bad to worse but from corruption to chaos. The fall of Rome is imminent and will be the prelude to a final outburst of evil when good will be in conflict with the worst that evil can perpetrate; not merely with the beast—i.e., Rome—symbolizing human tyranny, but with the dragon—i.e., demonic evil (19:11–20:10). Revelation therefore offers no doctrine of mediation but the assurance that in spite of appearances God is in control, evil will be done away with, and ideal conditions will be ultimately created (21:1-4).

There are many references to Christ, most of which are rooted in the primitive Christian kerygma, but they are isolated. E.g., Christ is "the first-born of the dead, and the ruler of kings on earth" (1:5); he has authority over Death and Hades (1:18) and over the churches on earth (chs. 2–3); he is victor (3:21; 12:10).

He is referred to twenty-nine times as the "Lamb who was slain" (5:6-13, etc.). He is Son of God (2:18; 3:5) and Word of God (19:13). His second coming is mentioned (1:7; 3:3; 19:11-16). Most impressive of all, his loving self-sacrifice, which freed men from their sins and created a new kingdom or priesthood, is recorded (1:5-6; 5:9-10). But although these elements of the faith are retained, they are not integrated into the general pattern, and the characteristic logic of this book is that the decisive act for man's salvation is still future, and God rather than Christ will be the actor, Christ's function being to preside over a millennial reign with the martyrs (20:4-6), after he has inflicted the divine wrath on the sinful of all nations (19:11-21).

D. *SUMMARY.* The NT has a compact answer to questions concerning mediation, and its neatest formulation comes from a writer who gives us no sustained argument but has a rare facility for pregnant phrase: "There is one God, and there is one mediator between God and men, the man Christ Jesus, who gave himself as a ransom for all" (I Tim. 2:5-6). This sounds more like the quotation of a primitive creed than theological reflection, but it expresses the heart of the matter.

The lines of development in thought upon this problem converge upon Christ. By this is meant no mechanical fulfilment of OT conceptions, but the affirmation, repeated with varying emphasis throughout the NT, that the ideals of prophet, priest, and king were realized in Christ, and that he was the living embodiment of what the OT knew as the word of God and the wisdom of God; the Spirit of God descended upon him, guided his ministry, and was the means of his continued presence among men after his physical presence was withdrawn. As the one who in the daily experience of his disciples had made God a Father real and near, he could not but be proclaimed as Messiah and Son of God; for had not the kingly rule of God come upon them through his teaching and acts? The enigma of a Messiah crucified (I Cor. 1:23) had passed from inexplicable tragedy to the glorious conviction that his death was that vicarious suffering of God's truest servant which Isaiah had discerned as destined to forward the divine purpose and cause many to be accounted righteous (Isa. 53:10-11).

This was no peculiar theologoumenon of Paul; it was the common testimony. As the Johannine author testifies: "He is the expiation for our sins, and not for ours only but also for the sins of the whole world" (I John 2:2), and: "No one has ever seen God; the only Son, who is in the bosom of the Father, he has made him known" (John 1:18).

The lesser minds also in their own idiom affirm the uniqueness of Christ as mediator and revealer over against all other religious leaders. Consider Acts 4:12, from a writer who made no claim to be a theologian, quoting from an early source: "There is salvation in no one else, for there is no other name under heaven given among men by which we must be saved."

Bibliography. In addition to Commentaries and works on biblical theology, see, for the OT and Judaism: W. Bousset and H. Gressmann, *Die Religion des Judentums* (3rd ed., 1926); G. F. Moore, *Judaism* (1927); C. H. Dodd, *The Bible and the Greeks* (1935); J. Pedersen, *Israel: Its Life and Culture* (1926-40); H. A. Wolfson, *Philo* (1947); A. R. Johnson, *Sacral Kingship* (1955); R. Bultmann, *Primitive Christianity in Its Contemporary Setting* (trans. R. H. Fuller; 1956); S. Mowinckel, *He That Cometh* (trans. G. W. Anderson; 1956); H. H. Rowley, *The Faith of Israel* (1956).

For the NT: V. Taylor, *Jesus and His Sacrifice* (1937); W. L. Knox, *St. Paul and the Church of the Gentiles* (1939); V. Taylor, *The Atonement in NT Teaching* (1940); W. Manson, *Jesus the Messiah* (1943); W. D. Davies, *Paul and Rabbinic Judaism* (1948); G. S. Duncan, *Jesus Son of Man* (1948); T. W. Manson, *The Teaching of Jesus* (2nd ed., 1948); C. H.

Dodd, *The Interpretation of the Fourth Gospel* (1953); G. B. Caird, *Principalities and Powers* (1956). E. C. BLACKMAN

MEDICINE. While comparatively little appears in the earlier biblical writings on the care of the sick, it must be remembered that the Hebrews shared with other peoples of the ancient Near East the tradition of a priesthood trained and equipped to cope with a wide variety of ailments. In the Pentateuch the priest and the midwife were held responsible for communal health, and it was not until the period of the monarchy that physicians as separate individuals put in an appearance, which contrasts markedly with what is known of earlier civilizations.

1. The priest-physician in antiquity
   a. Mesopotamia
   b. Egypt
   c. Israel
2. Medical functions of priests and prophets
3. Medical treatments in the NT
4. Surgery
5. Surgical disease and accident
6. Obstetrics
7. Medical folklore in the Bible

Bibliography

1. The priest-physician in antiquity. ***a. Mesopotamia.*** In ancient Mesopotamia two distinct classes of exorcist priests were responsible for the prevention or control of disease. The intensely superstitious Mesopotamians regarded illness as the result of attack by malignant demons, and therefore the services of competent exorcists were always in demand. As in all ancient civilizations, the priesthood monopolized education, and the study of medicine was no exception.

Courtesy of the Wellcome Historical Medical Museum, London

20. Seal of a Sumerian physician, Ur-Lugal-edinna

Patients were often treated in the precincts of temples or shrines by a variety of means, which invariably included an incantation. Herbs such as caper, garlic, rue, and the mandrake had magical qualities assigned to them, while others like castor oil were used empirically in Babylonian medicine.* The Code of Hammurabi gave proper professional status to the doctor and laid down the conditions under which he could pursue his vocation. A variety of extant cuneiform tablets have to do with therapeutics, and testify to the remarkable development of empirical medicine in Mesopotamia. Fig. MED 20.

b. Egypt. The ancient Egyptian priesthood had its medical branch from an early period, one of the most celebrated pioneers of empirical therapy being Imhotep. The medical traditions of Egypt have been preserved in part in a number of medical and surgical papyri which have survived. These documents show that in Egypt, as in Mesopotamia, magico-religious considerations occupied a dominant place in any estimate of diseased conditions. Illness was held to result from the activity of evil spirits, which could only be counteracted most effectively by magic. In consequence the Egyptian priest-physicians employed magical rites for diseases of the eyes, gynecological disorders, burns, injuries, and many other pathological conditions. Herbs and animal substances were used empirically, but generally needed the assistance of an incantation to be most effective. Only one surgical papyrus is free from obvious magical influences, and even this has a number of incantations written on the verso. The "physicians" of Gen. 50:2 were the embalmers, whose work constituted an important specialty, and whose rituals and techniques have been preserved, notably by Herodotus (II.86). Like other medical specialists in ancient Egypt, they formed one branch of the priesthood. Fig. MED 21.

21. Hes-Re, the chief of dentists and physicians, an Egyptian medical specialist (*ca.* 3000 B.C.)

c. Israel. The medical principles of the early Hebrews, as enshrined in the Pentateuch, represented a notable advance upon contemporary theories of disease in that they repudiated magic completely, and sought to consider disease either from an empirical standpoint or else in terms of the personal spiritual relationship existing between the sufferer and his God. The principles of personal and social hygiene contained in the medical sections of Leviticus are unique in antiquity as rational assessments of pathology. The responsibility for propagating and enforcing these enactments rested with the priests, to whom guidance was given on the question of how certain diseases were to be treated, notably LEPROSY.

The first reference to physicians outside the Pentateuchal writings is in II Chr. 16:12, which speaks rather disparagingly of those to whom Asa resorted at the end of his life (*see* DISEASE). The Hebrew רפה originally meant "one who repairs," "one who sews together," and seems to have been used of the tending of wounds and injuries. Since God was the acknowledged Supreme Healer (Exod. 15:26), the physicians of the Monarchy can have been little more than practicing apothecaries or herbalists. The reference in Jer. 8:22 which associates physicians with therapeutic substances (*see* BALM) indicates that this state of affairs continued in Israel. The presence of a physician gave some hope of relief from sickness, while his medicaments included the aromatic antiseptic resins and gums popular at that time.

The prestige of the physician appears to have increased considerably by the time Ecclesiasticus was written (second century B.C.), for he is described in quite different terms. While God is still the Healer, he has committed gifts of healing to men and has provided medicines for the cure of sicknesses. But the person who sins against the Lord must also be expected to behave arrogantly in the presence of a physician (Ecclus. 38:1-15).

Jesus mentioned physicians occasionally in his teaching, quoting popular proverbs about them (Matt. 9:12; Luke 4:23), and indicating that they were generally fairly competent. Periodically, however, they were confronted with a situation with which they were unable to cope (Mark 5:26), when they resorted to a succession of therapeutic expedients without avail. Luke is spoken of as the "beloved physician" (Col. 4:14), and his writings are notable for the accurate recording of the healing ministry of Jesus. His special use of medical terms which occur occasionally in the writings of nonmedical authors shows beyond reasonable doubt that he was trained in the Greek medical tradition.

2. Medical functions of priests and prophets. The medical responsibilities of the early Hebrew priests were closely connected with their religious duties. The book of Leviticus contains seven forms of purification, in which medical, as well as religious, considerations are involved. They are: puerperal (ch. 12), leprous (ch. 13), venereal (15:2-15), spermatorrheal (15:16-18), concubital (15:18), menstrual (15:19-30), and cadaveric (21:1-3). The "jealousy ordeal" (Num. 5:11-31) included the administration of a special potion mixed by the priest. The dramatic ritual and suggestibility of the whole procedure are reminiscent of the forms of treatment undertaken by the Babylonian priest-physicians in the second millennium B.C. This account is the only biblical one which mentions the oral administration of potions or medicines.

The art of the perfumer (Exod. 30:35) was employed for purposes other than the purely medicinal, although the substances used, such as myrrh, frankincense, balm, aloes, cassia, cinnamon, and other aromatic vegetable products, were widely used in folk medicine (*see* PERFUME). The OT contains no reference to the use of the well-known oriental narcotics, though they may have been imported along with other commodities.

Part of the prophetic office included prognostication of sickness, as with Nathan (II Sam. 12:14), Elijah (I Kings 17:17; II Kings 1:4), Ahijah (I Kings 14:4), and Elisha (II Kings 5:3; 8:7). Elisha exhibited unusual medical abilities in neutralizing the poisonous herbs (II Kings 4:41) and in purifying the waters of Jericho (II Kings 2:20-21), as well as participating in the cure of Naaman (II Kings 5:3-14) and the son of the Shunammite (II Kings 4:18-37). An important instance of prophetic prognosis and treatment relates to the BOIL of Hezekiah (II Kings 20:1-7), which constitutes the only prescription proper in the OT. Wounds and putrefying sores were treated with a variety of medicaments including balm and oil (Isa. 1:6). Most of the resinous gums were antiseptic and astringent in nature, making them suitable for emollient dressings. While there are grounds for believing that fractures were commonly left untreated at an early period (cf. Lev. 21:19), the reference in Ezek. 30:21 indicates that subsequently attempts were made to reduce fractures. Ezekiel makes no mention of splints such as were common in Egypt, though the use of the bandage (KJV "roller") would probably imply some such procedure.

In the apocryphal period, the place of medicines in the treatment of sicknesses was dignified in proportion to the increased stature of the physician. Medicines were regarded as natural products, and therefore beneficial to mankind. The prudent would submit themselves to the skill of the apothecary, according to Ben Sirach (Ecclus. 38:1-15), and derive advantage from the medical gifts of the physician. But it appears from the Talmud that contemporary practitioners advised patients to wear amulets, indulge in magical exercises of various kinds, and resort to therapeutic procedures of extremely questionable value. Something of this sort may have befallen the woman with an issue of blood (Mark 5:25).

3. Medical treatments in the NT. The NT has very little indeed to say about medical treatment, and such references as occur appear in an incidental manner. The Good Samaritan rendered effective first aid (Luke 10:34) by applying antiseptic and soothing dressings to the unfortunate victim of an assault. The anointing of Luke 7:37-38 was more of a cosmetic technique than a specifically therapeutic one. This practice was one of several connected with the preparation of a corpse for burial (Luke 23:56). The anointing with spittle (John 9:6) was of a symbolic nature, and as employed by Jesus was not strictly a therapeutic procedure.

The administration of sour wine mixed with gall and myrrh to those being crucified (Mark 15:23) was an act of charity intended to lessen the sufferings of the victims. But unless the potion contained some such narcotic as opium, its effect on the crucified persons would be negligible, since myrrh is only slightly sedative.

The kindly counsel of Paul to Timothy (I Tim. 5:

23) is typical of folk medicine in all ages. Probably Timothy was suffering from flatulent dyspepsia, the discomfort of which would be relieved temporarily by alcohol. However, there seem to be good reasons for believing that the gastric condition was only a part of a larger pathological pattern ("frequent ailments"), which was probably psychosomatic in nature. The anointing with oil in the name of God was symbolic rather than therapeutic, and intimately associated with the "prayer of faith."

4. Surgery. The only surgical operation mentioned in the Bible is CIRCUMCISION.* While this procedure was known among other peoples, notably the Egyptians, who regarded it as the hallmark of a civilized upbringing, it never claimed the quasi-religious nature that it had among the Jews. While Abraham was the first to submit to it according to OT records, the rite is almost certainly far older than the Hebrew patriarchs. The Semites of the Bronze and Iron Ages still used the obsolete flint knives for the operation, which would indicate something of the antiquity of the rite itself. Resection of the prepuce was performed on all male Israelite children on the eighth day after birth (Lev. 12:3), and also upon household slaves (Gen. 17:11). Among the Hebrews its religious significance was paramount, and it was never regarded primarily as a hygienic or prophylactic measure. Fig. CIR 29.

What might be classed as a minor surgical procedure was the boring of the servant's ear by means of an awl (Exod. 21:6) used in the stitching of hides and skins. This rite established the relationship between master and servant by which the latter covenanted to serve the former for life; and it was of a religio-social, rather than a medical, character.

5. Surgical disease and accident. There are comparatively few references in the Bible to surgical disease as such (*see* DISEASE). In Exod. 21:18-19 the person who injures or maims another in a quarrel is to be held responsible for the complete restoration to health of the injured man, and for compensating him for the loss of his working time. To what extent such injuries were treated by the priests is unknown, but attempts may have been made in later times to reduce and bandage fractures (Ezek. 30:21).

The hunchback and the dwarf were *ipso facto* disqualified from the priesthood. These two categories probably covered all forms of physical assymetry, but whereas the dwarf might not necessarily have been deformed (physiological dwarf), the hunchback was invariably the victim of caries and destruction of the spinal vertebrae. Spinal kyphosis appears to have been fairly common in ancient Egypt.

The woman who had had a "spirit of infirmity" for eighteen years (*see* DISEASE) and who could attend the synagogue although she could not straighten herself fully (Luke 13:11) was probably suffering from spondylitis deformans. This is an arthritic condition of the spine which results in a rigid kyphosis and allows little free spinal movement.

A further instance of surgical accident may be seen in the case of Malchus, whose right ear was cut off (John 18:10). No doubt, Peter aimed the sword at the head of the high priest's servant with the intention of doing more serious damage, but in the event only the pinna was severed. If complete separation from the adjacent tissues took place, the healing which ensued was strictly miraculous (cf. Luke 22:51), since neither ancient nor modern surgery would avail under such circumstances.

6. Obstetrics. Some of the most primitive references to biblical medicine are to obstetrics. In fact, the midwife was the first public-health worker to be mentioned in scripture, and she occupied an important position in the community. This is of significance when it is remembered that oriental women as a whole were discouraged from engaging in public duties. The midwives seem to have formed a regular professional guild or class, and the names of the two head midwives in Egypt (Exod. 1:15) have been preserved for posterity; this fact further attests to the importance of their status in the community.

The decree of Pharaoh (Exod. 1:16) appears to have been an obvious violation of their professional ethics, as well as constituting a grossly inhuman act. The reason which they subsequently adduced for disregarding this injunction was that precipitate labor had invariably taken place before the midwife arrived to supervise the confinement. It would appear that the Hebrew midwives gave professional care to the Egyptian women also, since they were able to compare their relative performances during parturition. The confinements seem to have been conducted with the mother supported on the low seat or birthstool, a device which is still in use among Egyptian fellahin.

In two confinements the mother died after giving a symbolic name to her offspring. Rachel suffered a fatal dystocia (Gen. 35:16-19), which may have been due to some obstruction in the birth canal or to uterine anergia (maternal dystocia). Some idea of the hardship which a woman could experience in childbirth may be seen in the name "son of my sorrow," which Rachel gave her son just before her death. The wife of Phinehas (I Sam. 4:19-22) was about to undergo confinement when tragic news reached her. The resultant shock precipitated labor, and after the child was delivered, she became comatose and died.

Two instances of the birth of twins are recorded in Genesis. Rebekah (Gen. 25:21-26) experienced considerable fetal agitation during her pregnancy. When Esau was born, he was still covered with the lanugo, a downy growth which appears on the fetus from the fourth month of gestation, but which has normally disappeared by full term. The birth of Jacob followed almost immediately after the delivery of Esau.

An unusual and difficult condition existed in the case of Tamar (Gen. 38:27-30), who was with child by her father-in-law. The twins were apparently locked, and one of them was presenting transversely. A prolapsed arm was suitably marked by the midwife, who seems to have performed some sort of turning operation, with the result that the other twin was born first. Then his brother was delivered, apparently by spontaneous evolution. A perineal laceration appears to have been indicated by the symbolic name given to one of the twins, Perez ("breach"). This difficult obstetrical situation was seemingly handled with great competence by the attending midwife, who was evidently a woman of considerable skill and resource.

Elderly primiparas, or women who are pregnant for the first time at a later period in life, include Sarah

(Gen. 21:2), the wife of Manoah (Judg. 13:24), Hannah (I Sam. 1:20), and Elizabeth (Luke 1:36).

The postnatal procedures mentioned in scripture (cf. Ezek. 16:4-5) include dividing of the umbilical cord, washing of the infant, and the removal of the uterine sebacious material (*vernix caseosa*) by means of salt. The newborn infant was then "swaddled" by being placed diagonally on a square of cloth, the ends of which were then folded over the body and the feet and held in position by strips of material (swaddling bands) passed around the outside of the bundle. A dusting powder of myrtle leaves was used to prevent chafing, and the baby was frequently rubbed with oil. "Swaddling" was continued until the baby was at least six months old.

7. Medical folklore in the Bible. Some examples of popular medical folklore as found in the Bible may receive brief notice. When Jacob desired to increase his own share of Laban's flocks (Gen. 30:31), he resorted to a device based on the age-old concept of maternal impressions. Although Laban had promised him the black and speckled offspring in the flocks, he had removed the male speckled animals so as to render the increase of that variety impossible. But Jacob took boughs of trees, peeled away sections of the bark at random to produce a dappled effect, and placed them near the feeding troughs where the ewes could see them at impregnation and when eating. By this means he hoped that the speckled appearance of the branches would impress itself upon the pregnant ewes and influence the physical appearance of the fetus. Even to the present, some persons attribute harelip in a baby to a prenatal encounter by the mother with a rabbit or hare. In actual fact, such deficiencies are congenital, and governed by the genes rather than by visual impressions retained by the unconscious mind.

The use of mandrakes by Leah (Gen. 30:14-16), who was anxious to resume bearing children after a period of sterility, points to popular superstition concerning the plant *Mandragora officinarum*. In antiquity it had wide repute as a magical charm to offset sterility and promote venery and fertility, hence the desire of both Rachel and Leah to make use of the root which Reuben had found. Whatever general effect it may have had probably resulted from psychological suggestion, with consequent alteration of endocrinal secretions, rather than the aphrodisiac qualities of the plant itself. *See* MANDRAKE.

In extreme old age David (I Kings 1:1-4) was provided with a maiden, in the belief that by his drawing heat from her body and breathing her breath, his own life would be prolonged. It is also possible that the king's potency was being tested in accordance with the magico-ritual understanding of the royal function. *See* KING.

The opinion, widespread in all ages, that the moon could exert an injurious influence on the minds of people, is also reflected in scripture. One of the psalms (121:6) assures that the moon will not harm by night, thus precluding the incidence of insanity by this particular means. The words "lunatic" and "moon-struck," along with the Greek σεληνιαζόμενος (Matt. 4:24) and σεληνιάζεται (Matt. 17:15), have perpetuated the tradition that people can be affected mentally by lunar phases.

An interpolation in the KJV of John 5 (vs. 4, omitted in the RSV text) preserves a popular explanation of the troubling of the waters in the pool of Beth-zatha. This comment, which is not found in the earliest Greek MSS, is an explanatory gloss which ascribed the healing virtues of the pool to specifically supernatural agencies. Holy wells and springs of this kind can be found in a great many countries, and invariably their alleged healing powers can be explained satisfactorily along rational lines. The agitation of the water in the pool of Beth-zatha may have been caused by the liberation of underground pockets of natural gas. The tradition of healing by immersion in the waters may have been perpetuated by the periodic cure of certain varieties of psychosomatic pathology.

Bibliography. C. R. Smith, *A Physician Examines the Bible* (1950); R. K. Harrison, "Medicine of the Bible," *Canadian Association of Medical Students and Internes Journal*, vol. X, no. 1 (1951), pp. 17-20; R. Labat, *Traité akkadien de diagnostics et pronostics médicaux* (2 vols.; 1951); A. R. Short, *The Bible and Modern Medicine* (1953); R. K. Harrison, "The Mandrake and the Ancient World," *Evangelical Quarterly*, vol. XXVIII, no. 2 (1956), pp. 87-92; L. Köhler, *Hebrew Man* (1956), pp. 48-60; F. Jonckheere, *Les médecins de l'Egypte pharaonique* (1958).

R. K. HARRISON

MEDITERRANEAN mĕd'ə tə rā'nĭ ən. *See* GREAT SEA; WESTERN SEA; SEA.

MEDIUMS. *See* DIVINATION.

MEEDA. KJV Apoc. form of MEHIDA.

MEEKNESS. A translation of πραύτης, and a KJV translation of ענוה (Ps. 45:4; Zeph. 2:3 [RSV "humility"]).

The adjective "meek" is found a number of times as a translation of ענו, the primary meaning of which is "poor," "needy" (Deut. 15:11; *see* POOR). From this there is developed the idea of "weak," "oppressed by the rich and powerful" (cf. Amos 2:7); Israel oppressed by wicked nations (Isa. 14:32); or the pious in Israel oppressed by their wicked compatriots (Ps. 10:17). Thus it came about that the word was used to express the attitude of the truly religious person, as opposed to the rich and arrogant, who, relying upon themselves or upon secular alliances, were defiant toward God and oppressive toward those weaker than themselves. "Meekness" is the opposite of pride, which in turn is basically an attempted reliance upon the self, and the root of sin. The variety of connotations of the word is shown by the different translations of it in the RSV—"oppressed" (Ps. 76:9), "downtrodden" (Ps. 147:6).. "Meekness," therefore, in the OT is used to describe primarily the proper attitude of complete dependence upon God, and secondarily the attitude shown toward others by one who is "meek toward God."

The ordinary translation of ענו in the LXX is πραύς, which is found four times in the NT, translated always in the KJV by "meek" and in the RSV by "meek" (Matt. 5:5), "humble" (Matt. 21:5), "gentle" (Matt. 11:29; I Pet. 3:4). Matt. 5:5 shows most clearly the connection with its OT background; "Blessed are the meek, for they shall inherit the earth," comes directly from Ps. 37:11. In contrast to those who rebel against God and are insolent to man, and whom the Lord will destroy, are the meek, who take a proper view of themselves in relation to God and hence to man; these are they who shall possess the kingdom of God. Matt. 21:5 is a quotation from Zech. 9:9; and in Matt. 11:29 πραΰς is paired with ταπεινός, which also has a long history of use in the OT (*cf.* HUMILITY). In I Pet. 3:4 it is used with "quiet" to describe what should be the attitude of a Christian woman, a "gentle and quiet spirit" in contrast to mere "outward adorning."

There are eleven occurrences of the cognate noun, πραΰτης, all of them outside the Gospels. In II Cor. 10:1 it is used of Christ: "I entreat you, by the meekness and gentleness of Christ" (cf. Matt. 11:29 above; also Phil. 2:8: "humbled himself"). In all other examples it is a virtue enjoined upon Christians. Jas. 1:21; 3:13 may have something of the flavor of the OT usage; but in the other cases, although the word has been used by pagan writers in an ethical sense, it has acquired distinctly Christian overtones. Aristotle had said that "meekness" was the mean between "irascibility" (ὀργιλότης) and "sluggishness" (ἀοργησία), "and he finds it worthy of praise, more because by it a man retains his own equanimity and composure than for any nobler reason" (Trench, *Synonyms of the NT*). The RSV translates πραΰτης by "meekness" when it is a question of one's inner attitude, and by "gentleness" when it is a matter of dealing with others; and in Tit. 3:2 "perfect courtesy" well brings out the meaning.

Rich though the word has become through the long history of its use in both Jewish and pagan connections, its full meaning in the Christian tradition comes out only as seen in its portrayal of a quality in Christ (Matt. 11:29; II Cor. 10:1) which Christians are to emulate and share (Phil. 2:5).

Bibliography. R. C. Trench, *Synonyms of the NT* (1880), pp. 148-57; O. J. Baab, *Theology of the OT* (1949), p. 119; A. Richardson, ed., "Pride," *Theological Word Book of the Bible* (1950).

E. J. COOK

*__MEGIDDO__ mə gĭd'ō [מגדו]; KJV MEGIDDON mə gĭd'ən [מגדון] in Zech. 12:11 (*see also* ARMAGEDDON). An important Canaanite, and later Israelite, city overlooking the Valley of Jezreel or the Plain of Esdraelon.

1. Location
2. Excavation
3. History
   a. From the first settlement through the Early Bronze Age
   b. The Middle Bronze Age
   c. The Late Bronze Age
   d. The Iron Age
Bibliography

1. Location. Analyses of literary sources and of the results of excavations have shown that Megiddo is to be identified with Tell el-Mutesellim (the "mound of the commander").* The site, which has a surface area of *ca.* thirteen acres, occupies a spur of

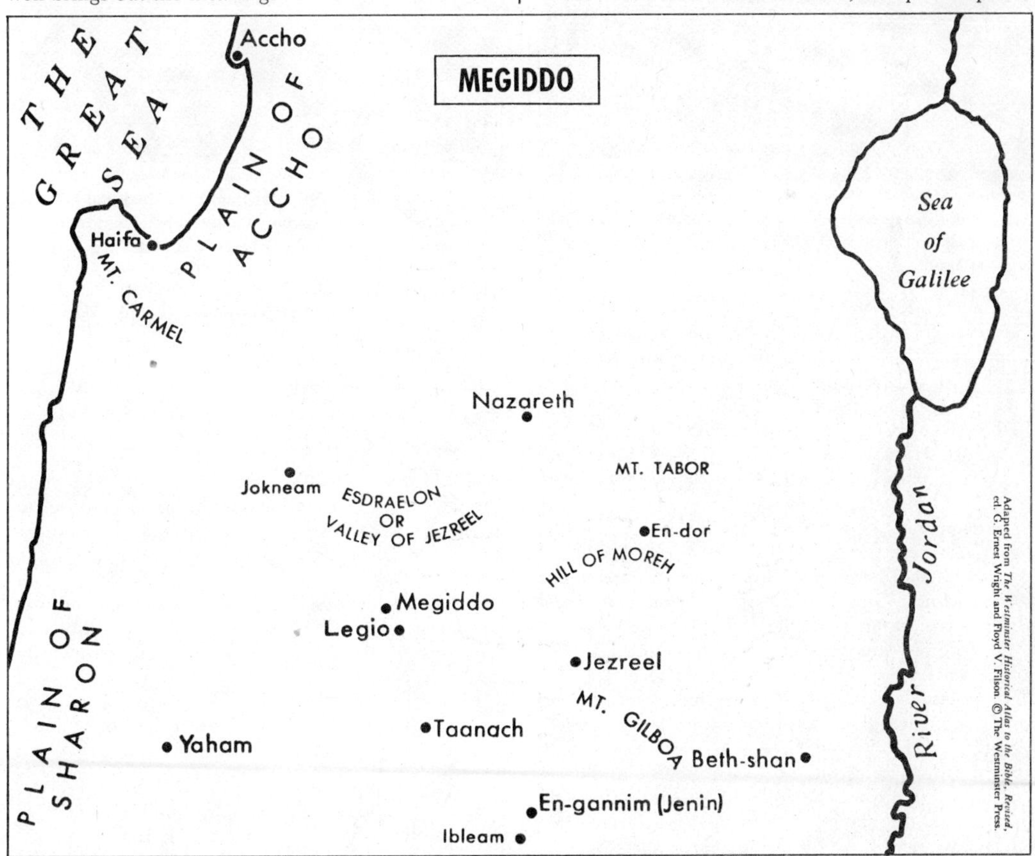

Adapted from *The Westminster Historical Atlas to the Bible, Revised*, ed. G. Ernest Wright and Floyd V. Filson. © The Westminster Press.

Courtesy of Herbert G. May

22. Site of Megiddo (Tell el-Mutesellim), with field house of expedition staff on the terrace

Courtesy of the Oriental Institute, the University of Chicago

23. The Palestine mound at Megiddo viewed from the E

Courtesy of the Oriental Institute, the University of Chicago

24. The Plain of Esdraelon with the mound of Megiddo at the left center, and below it the Arab village of el-Lejjun

the Carmel Range that projects into the Plain of Esdraelon from the SW. It is located approximately twenty miles S-SE of Haifa and eleven miles N-NW of Jenin; less than one mile to the S is the village el-Lejjun (derived from Latin *Legio*, "Legion"), the site of a Roman encampment. Figs. MEG 22-23, 24.

A more strategic site than Megiddo is difficult to find. From its summit can be seen the entire breadth of the Plain of Esdraelon to the hills of Galilee on the N, and much of its length along Mount Carmel on the W to where the W extension of the Galilee hills hides the Mediterranean from view, and eastward toward Mount Gilboa and Little Hermon, between which is the watershed where the plain drops away to the Jordan Valley, with the Transjordan hills beyond. Across the plain and to the right of Little Hermon rises Mount Tabor. Two important ancient routes intersected just E of the mound: one linked Egypt with the Fertile Crescent; the other linked central and E Palestine with the Phoenician coast. The former followed the coast of Palestine through Philistia and the Plain of Sharon, passed through the Carmel Range by way of Wadi 'Arah, which runs along the E side of Megiddo, and then crossed the Plain of Esdraelon to Syria and Mesopotamia. Since the Wadi 'Arah is the best pass through the Carmel chain, and since Megiddo guarded its N entrance, possession of the site permitted absolute control of this route. During Roman times, when Megiddo was no longer occupied, the Romans exercised similar control over this pass by stationing troops at Legio. The second route followed the central N-S ridge of Palestine to Jenin, led along the N side of the Carmel Range by Taanach and Megiddo to the Plain of Acre, and northward to Phoenicia. Since this route also skirted Megiddo, it too was subject to control from the site. Because of its strategic location, Megiddo was the scene of many battles; the prize to the victor was domination of the city itself, and of the routes which it controlled.

2. Excavation. The first excavations at Megiddo (1903-5) were conducted by G. Schumacher for the Deutschen Orient-Gesellschaft. A large N-S trench across the middle of the mound, an extensive area on the E side, and a number of soundings and probe trenches were dug during these campaigns. Schumacher's excavations on the mound revealed eight

Courtesy of the Oriental Institute, the University of Chicago

25. Air view of the Oriental Institute expedition house and mound at Megiddo. The deep trenches are from the earlier Schumacher excavations.

strata, ranging in date from MB II (from the nineteenth century) to the Persian period. Fig. MEG 25.

Nothing more was done at Megiddo until 1925, when the Oriental Institute of the University of Chicago organized the Megiddo Expedition, the largest ever to work in Palestine. The excavations, which continued until 1939, were successively directed by C. S. Fisher (1925-27), P. L. O. Guy (1927-29), and Gordon Loud (1935-39). Excavation was begun on the lower E slope of the mound to provide an area for dumping debris, and a number of tombs were brought to light in this area. On the mound itself, the top five strata in the SE section (area C) were cleared. In 1929 the entire mound was purchased, with a view to excavating it completely from top to bottom. The five strata previously cleared in area C were then systematically removed in all other areas of the summit. Later the plan to excavate the whole mound had to be abandoned, and work was concentrated in several areas (A and B on the S side, E on the SW side, and D on the N side). When the complete excavation of these areas proved impossible, it was decided to dig several smaller areas in different parts of the site to bedrock

Courtesy of the Oriental Institute, the University of Chicago

26. Completed excavations in one of the areas at Megiddo

(areas AA and DD on the N side, BB on the E side,* and CC on the S side), in order to recover a complete cultural history of the site. Only in area BB did the excavators reach bedrock; here a total of twenty strata—several with more than one phase—were distinguished, covering more than 3,500 years, from early Chalcolithic (i.e., the early fourth millennium) to the Persian period, with only a few occupational gaps. Fig. MEG 26.

More recently (1960), a sounding was conducted by Y. Yadin on the NE side of the mound to investigate problems of stratigraphy of the Solomonic period.

3. History. The primary source for the history of the site is the information gleaned from archaeological excavation. Supplementing this source are a number of literary documents in which Megiddo is mentioned, including Egyptian and Assyrian texts, the Tell el-Amarna Tablets, and the Bible.

a. From the first settlement through the Early Bronze Age. The earliest occupation of the site, stratum XX, was founded on bedrock. Only a small area of this stratum has been exposed, and no over-all view of the occupation can be given. Architectural remains consist of a few circular walls and a series of holes cut in bedrock.* Prominent among the objects are flint implements, including sickle blades, scrapers, and javelin heads. The pottery is mixed: some of it belongs to the Early Chalcolithic period, proving that Megiddo came into being in the early fourth millennium B.C.; the remainder belongs to the following Chalcolithic phases, terminating *ca.* 3200 B.C. Stratum XIX, dated *ca.* the thirty-second or thirty-first century B.C., by examples of band-slip and gray burnished pottery, is also represented by fragmentary remains and includes at least two phases. The most noteworthy structure is a rectangular shrine with an altar against the back wall opposite the entrance.* The following occupation, stratum XVIII, belongs to EB II (*ca.* 2900-2600) and features the largest city wall yet found at the site; it is nearly twenty-six feet thick—including a buttressing wall—and is preserved to a height of more than thirteen feet. Strata XVII and XVI—dated early in EB III (*ca.* 2600-2300)—contain better-preserved buildings than earlier strata. Of special interest is an enormous round altar, the finest yet discovered in Palestine (Figs. ALT 20; MEG 27). In the debris surrounding its base were found a great quantity of animal bones, which indicate animal sacrifice. With the end of stratum XVI, the site was unoccupied for at least two centuries. Figs. WAL 2; TEM 41.

Courtesy of the Oriental Institute, the University of Chicago

27. Burnt-offering altar at Megiddo, as rebuilt in Stratum XVI

Little is known about the inhabitants of Megiddo during this period. Skeletal remains from Chalcolithic and EB tombs found on the E slope of the mound indicate that the inhabitants were of medium stature with long, narrow heads (dolichocephalic), characteristically Mediterranean in type. Animal bones discovered in the tombs and on the mound prove that the ass, large and small ox, roe deer, pig, dog or jackal, and several species of sheep and goats were known in Chalcolithic and EB times; gazelle, lion, and bear were also known in Chalcolithic times.

b. The Middle Bronze Age. This period is fully represented at Megiddo by five strata, XV to X, several of which include more than one phase. The first of these, stratum XV, belongs to MB I and IIA, covering the twenty-first to the early nineteenth centuries. The great altar of strata XVII and XVI continued to be used during this occupation, but was now associated with three shrines or temples, each consisting of an altar room, porch, and side chamber (*see* TEMPLES § 2*a*).* To this stratum probably belongs the statuette of Thut-hotep—a high official at Hermapolis under Sesostris III—which was found reused in a stratum VII wall. Whether it indicates Egyptian control of or simply friendly relations with Megiddo is unknown, although the former is probable. Fig. ARC 51.

Stratum XIV includes two phases, which belong to the nineteenth and eighteenth centuries. One of the three temples of stratum XV survived, but was radically modified. Carved reliefs in ivory, and bronze figurines, axes, and adzes first appear in this stratum. The following occupation, stratum XIII, also consists of two phases, which belong to the eighteenth century. This city was protected by a mud-brick wall nearly five feet thick, and an exceptionally strong L-shaped gateway built of mud brick on the N side of the mound (area AA). Noteworthy among the finds were the first HYKSOS scarabs, presaging Hyksos ascendancy in Palestine. These scarabs are exceedingly common in strata XII-X, indicating that these strata were contemporary with the major period of Hyksos dominance.

During stratum XII (*ca.* eighteenth-early seventeenth centuries), the earlier (stratum XIII*) city wall continued in use, but a buttressing wall was added to its outer face. Within the city several well-preserved large houses were discovered, each consisting of a central court enclosed on two or three sides by single rows of rooms. In this and the following two strata (XI and X), a number of stone-built tombs containing multiple burials were found inside the city—an unusual custom in Palestine. Equipment in the tombs included a quantity of bone inlays used to decorate small wooden funerary boxes, in addition to the usual deposits of pottery, jewelry, and implements. In the next occupation, stratum XI (seventeenth century), a group of even larger houses was built over the remains of the strata XIII-XII city wall. A new city wall, slightly more than three feet thick, was built with small buttresses on the inner face and a sloping glacis against its outer face; the latter is a characteristic feature of the Hyksos period. In stratum X (late seventeenth–early sixteenth centuries) many of the earlier stratum XI buildings continued in use, but with repairs and additions. Most of the objects are similar to those of strata XIII-XI, but a number of new pottery forms—which become common in LB—appear for the first time, proving that the Middle Bronze period at Megiddo was drawing to a close. Fig. ARC 55.

Courtesy of the Oriental Institute, the University of Chicago

28. Skeleton of a child, along with jugs, found in a burial jar at Megiddo (Middle Bronze II)

During this period Megiddo was a prosperous city, as shown both by the architectural remains and by the fine objects recovered. But it enjoyed little peace; the number of strata and phases of strata in this period point to repeated destruction. The tombs of the early part of the period (MB I) were predominantly of the shaft type; during MB II some of these were reused, and other types—e.g., jar burials* and stone-built tombs (*see above*)—became common (Fig. MEG 28). From skeletal remains, it appears that the population was changing; the inhabitants were still of medium stature, but were sturdier and had broader skulls, approaching the Alpine type; this type predominates throughout later occupations. Fig. TOM 67.

c. The Late Bronze Age. With the expulsion of the Hyksos from Egypt, *ca.* 1550 B.C., and the Egyptian conquest of Palestine that followed, Megiddo once again came under Egyptian domination; it remained a city-state in the Asiatic empire of Egypt throughout the Late Bronze Age. Three strata belong to this period: IX, VIII, and VII. The plans and arrangements of the buildings of these strata generally follow those of stratum X, though with minor modifications. A good example is the palace just inside the city gate in area AA; its basic plan and orientation are the same through strata X-VII, with only minor alterations of plan, and construction of new floors during these occupations. Stratum IX (*ca.* 1550-1468) is particularly noted for its excellent examples of bichrome pottery. This fabric belongs exclusively to LB I, and examples of it have been found in Palestine, Syria, Egypt, and Cyprus (Pl. XX). This occupation was destroyed by the great Egyptian king Thut-mose III (*ca.* 1490-1436), after defeating a coalition of Syro-Palestinian princes, led by the king of Kadesh, at Megiddo. The account of this battle is vividly told by Thut-mose' scribes on the Armant Stele and in the Annals of Karnak. After this disaster Megiddo probably lay in ruins for several decades.

The next occupation, stratum VIII (fourteenth century), features a number of important structures.

Courtesy of the Oriental Institute, the University of Chicago

29. Excavations at Megiddo, showing the temple of Stratum VIII

The gateway of the city (area AA), which may have earlier phases in stratum IX or X, consisted of a narrow passage flanked by three pairs of piers, access to which was gained by means of a paved road on the NE slope of the mound.* During this or the following period (VIIB), a new temple (Figs. MEG 29; TEM 45) was built over the remains of the earlier altar and shrines; this area seems to have been considered sacred during all Canaanite occupations. The temple was rectangular in plan and contained one large room. Its entrance on the N was guarded by two large towers (*see* TEMPLES § 2*a*). Beneath the floor of one of the palace rooms a treasure hoard of gold and ivory objects was found, including an ivory wand decorated with incised animal and human figures on one side and an Egyptian text on the other. These attest to the wealth of Megiddo at this time. This occupation is contemporary with the Amarna Age in Egypt, during which Egyptian control over its Asiatic empire was weak and ineffective (*see* TELL EL-AMARNA). Among the letters from the city-states of Palestine to the Egyptian capital are a number from Prince Biridiya of Megiddo (spelled "Magidda" or "Makida"). In these letters Biridiya describes his loyalty to the Egyptian throne and accuses the princes of other city-states of treachery and failure to assume their obligations. Altogether these letters vividly portray the chaotic political conditions of this period. To about this time perhaps belongs a fragment of a clay tablet containing part of the Gilgamesh Epic, which

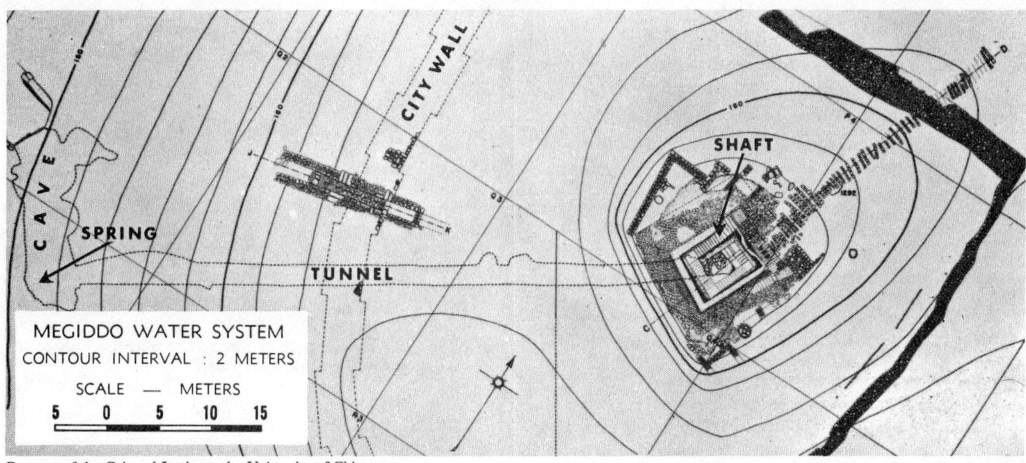

Courtesy of the Oriental Institute, the University of Chicago

30. Plans of the Megiddo water system

was found at the site by a shepherd in 1955. Fig. ARC 55.

Stratum VII, covering the thirteenth century and the first three quarters of the twelfth, consists of two phases, the first of which was violently destroyed. The second phase properly belongs to the beginning of the Iron Age, but for purposes of stratigraphic continuity, it is included in the Late Bronze period. The city represented by this phase was rebuilt immediately along the lines of VIIB and VIII, with only minor modifications. The city gate remains the same except for the laying of new pavement. The temple was rebuilt—probably during this phase—with walls of ashlar and a lime plaster floor; otherwise it was virtually identical with the earlier structure. The palace was also slightly altered in plan, especially by the addition of a three-room treasury below ground level. It contained a great quantity of beautiful ivory objects carved in relief or incised, including especially a model pen case inscribed with the name of Ramses III and a small box decorated with lions and sphinxes,* together with many other valuable objects such as gold jewelry, semiprecious stones, and alabaster jars (Figs. ART 70; BAN 18-19; IVO 18-19, 21; *see also* IVORY). It was probably in this period that the great water system was dug in area E, in order to assure a water supply inside the city during siege. It consisted of a deep vertical shaft cut through earlier occupational debris and bedrock, and a long, horizontal, rock-hewn tunnel

Courtesy of the Oriental Institute, the University of Chicago

31. Bronze statue base of Ramses VI, discovered at Megiddo

leading from the shaft to a spring in a cave at the foot of the mound; water flowed from the cave through the tunnel to the bottom of the shaft. This water system continued in use for centuries, with periodic cleaning and minor alterations (Figs. MEG 30; WAT 7; *see also* WATER WORKS § 3). The discovery of a bronze statue base of Ramses VI under a VIIB wall proves that this occupation was under Egyptian control.* Megiddo is also mentioned among other Syro-Palestinian towns in the Papyrus Anastasi, a letter written by an Egyptian official in the late thirteenth century B.C. Fig. MEG 31.

During this occupation the Israelites invaded Palestine. Megiddo lay in the territory allotted to the tribe of Manasseh (Josh. 17:11; I Chr. 7:29). In spite of the historical summary in Josh. 12:21—according to which Joshua and the children of Israel defeated the king of this city—the Israelites were unable to occupy Megiddo at this time (Judg. 1:27), because the Canaanite inhabitants were equipped with superior weapons such as iron chariots (see Josh. 17:16).

d. The Iron Age. Stratum VII was followed by a period during which Megiddo was unoccupied. It was during this occupational gap that the battle between Barak and the Canaanite Sisera took place at Taanach, by the waters of Megiddo, as told by Deborah (Judg. 5:19). The next occupation, stratum VI, covers the first half of the eleventh century and consists of two phases. The building tradition that persisted throughout LB is now broken, and the structures of this occupation bear no resemblance to those of earlier periods. During the first phase the town was probably unprotected, having neither a wall nor a city gate. But in the second phase (VIA) a new gateway was constructed, of which only the approach remains; the fortress gate itself was destroyed by the builders of the VA-IVB gateway (*see below*). Just W of the city gate, new houses were built on totally different lines from the earlier palaces. To this period also belongs the third and last phase of the Canaanite temple—as shown by its pottery—suggesting that the inhabitants were still Canaanites. Noteworthy objects are a bronze statuette of a seated man (or deity) overlaid with gold,* a fragment of a rectangular shrine of clay, a hoard of silver jewelry in cloth bags, and a fragment of an ivory cup carved with scenes in relief. This stratum was largely destroyed by a great fire that baked many of the mudbrick walls of the buildings. Fig. ART 64.

Courtesy of the Oriental Institute, the University of Chicago

32. Cult objects from the Solomonic stratum at Megiddo, including two horned incense altars and three cylindrical incense stands

After a decade or two, the site was again occupied, probably by Israelites during the reign of Saul (*ca.* 1020-1000 B.C.). The remains of the buildings of this stratum (VB) are fragmentary—having been largely destroyed by the builders of VA-IVB—but enough is preserved to show that in both plan and orientation they differed from those of preceding occupations. An exception is the VIA gateway, which probably continued in use, though with minor additions. Of interest among the objects found are a number of pieces of Cypriote pottery, proving that trade with Cyprus—which had been going on throughout LB and Iron I—continued during this period; a bronze statuette; and a small proto-Ionic CAPITAL—the earliest example known in the ancient Near East. *See* ARCHITECTURE. Fig. MEG 32.

This stratum, which came to an end in the second quarter of the tenth century, covered the reigns of Saul (*ca.* 1020-1000) and David (*ca.* 1000-961). Since it is inconceivable that David would have left any Palestinian stronghold or fortress in Canaanite hands while pursuing his program of conquest, it can be assumed that Megiddo was an Israelite city at this time. A number of lines of evidence indicate that this occupation gradually gave way to stratum VA-IVB during the early years of the reign of Solomon (*ca.* 961-923) and possibly during the last years of David. In the transition, the VB inhabitants were evicted, and their homes were torn down as each new VA-IVB structure was built.

The next stratum is called VA-IVB, because the buildings that were assigned by the excavators to separate phases VA and IVB actually belong to one occupation. During this occupation Solomon transformed Megiddo from an urban center into a royal chariot city (I Kings 9:15, 19). Although it has been generally believed that all the stable complexes at Megiddo were built by Solomon, Yadin's excavation proved that at least the N stables belong to stratum IVA (*see below*). The S stable, however, exhibits a slightly different plan and finer workmanship than the N stable, and was almost certainly constructed by Solomon. It contained several units, each consisting of a paved central aisle flanked by two rows of paved stalls, which were equipped with tie posts and mangers. Outside was an enclosed exercise yard with a water trough in the center.* Two large residences,

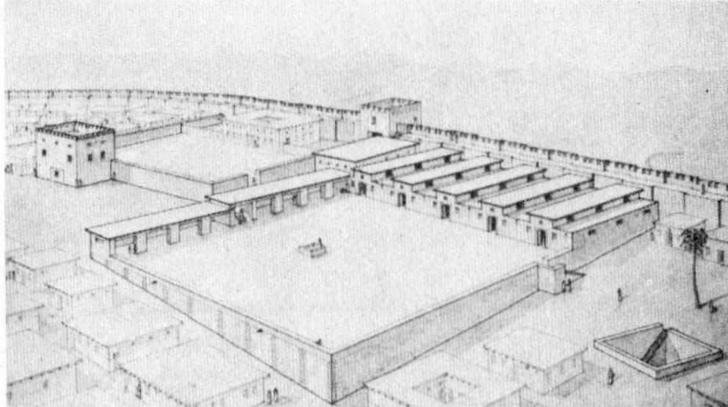

Courtesy of the Oriental Institute, the University of Chicago

33. Reconstruction of S stables at Megiddo (Stratum IVA), with entrance to water system at the right and "palace" compound to the left

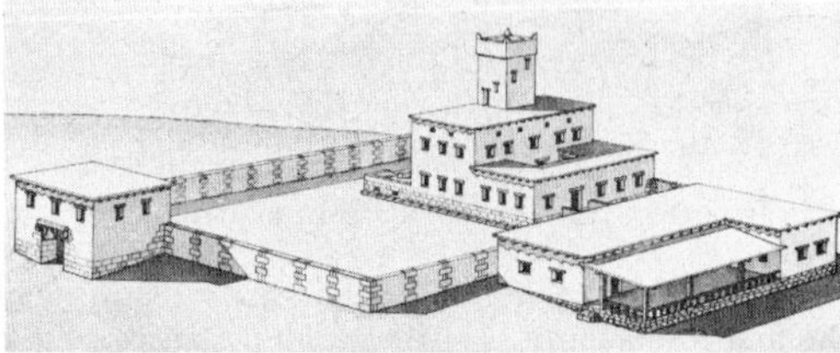

Courtesy of the Oriental Institute, the University of Chicago

34. Reconstruction of residence (Stratum IVB) beside S stable compound at Megiddo

Courtesy of the Oriental Institute, the University of Chicago

35. One of two large residences from Stratum IV at Megiddo, near which several proto-Ionic pilaster capitals were discovered

one in the S* and one in the N, were also found. One of these probably served as the residence of Baana, one of the twelve district officers appointed by Solomon (I Kings 4:12). Near these buildings several proto-Ionic pilaster capitals were discovered (Figs. CAP 8; MEG 35). Just W of the city gate was a series of smaller buildings, presumably houses, which contained, in addition to a quantity of pottery, a number of cult objects such as altars and incense burners. The city was protected by a casemate wall, traces of which are preserved along the NE edge of the mound, and a new fortress gate, consisting of a paved passage flanked by four pairs of piers. A paved road approached the gate at a sharp angle from the E and was protected by a second gateway consisting of two piers. Figs. MEG 33, 34, 36-37; ARC 53.

After Solomon's death Megiddo became part of the newly formed N state of Israel under Jeroboam

Courtesy of the Oriental Institute, the University of Chicago

36. Reconstruction showing the walls, gate, and towers at Megiddo, Stratum VA-IVB (Solomonic)

Courtesy of the Oriental Institute, the University of Chicago

37. Excavations viewed from the N, showing the Stratum VA-IVB gateway

I. This occupation was brought to an end by Shishak of Egypt, in the course of his Palestinian campaign *ca.* 918. Although the Bible describes only his attack on Judah (I Kings 14:25-26; II Chr. 12:2-9), the discovery of a stele at Megiddo bearing Shishak's name (Fig. SHI 53), and the appearance of Megiddo in Shishak's list of conquered Syro-Palestinian towns on the Bubastite Portal at Karnak, prove that Megiddo fell at this time. Only a few buildings and the casemate fortifications were destroyed in this attack. Three stables (Figs. STA 78-80) were built in the NE area of the site, probably by Ahab, who is reported, in the annals of Shalmaneser III, to have had two thousand chariots. These stables were separated from one another by paved streets which led to another exercise yard with two large bins, probably for the storage of fodder. Together with the S stable, which seems to have survived the Shishak raid and to have been repaired and remodeled in this period, they provided accommodation for approximately 450 horses. A new city wall, solidly built with offsets and slightly more than nine feet thick, and a new gateway, consisting of a central passage flanked by three pairs of piers, were also constructed. It was during this period that Ahaziah king of Judah died in Megiddo (II Kings 9:27) from wounds inflicted by Jehu at the beginning of Jehu's revolution in Israel (*ca.* 842). Although the destruction of this occupation is not specifically mentioned in any source, probably it can be attributed to Hazael king of Syria, who devastated Israel *ca.* 815 (II Kings 13:3-7).

Whether stratum III began immediately after the destruction of IVA or during the reign of Jeroboam II (*ca.* 786-746), after a lapse of several decades, cannot be determined. In this period Megiddo once again became a city of houses and shops, and no longer served as a royal chariot city. It was well planned throughout; buildings were similarly oriented and laid out in blocks bounded by parallel streets. The VA-IVB city wall and gate approach still protected the city, but a new fortress gate was built, reusing in part the foundations of the earlier gate. Unlike its predecessor, this gate was designed with only two pairs of piers flanking the passageway. A noteworthy feature of this stratum was a circular grain storage pit more than twenty-one feet deep, thirty-five feet in diameter at the top tapering to *ca.* twenty-one feet in diameter at the bottom, with an estimated capacity of *ca.* 12,800 bushels (Fig. GRA 37). One of the most interesting finds was a seal, inscribed with two lines of Hebrew: "(belonging) to Shema, servant of Jeroboam" (Fig. SEA 35, no. 20); it probably belonged to an officer of King Jeroboam II. This occupation was destroyed in 733 by the Assyrians under Tiglath-pileser III, only a few years before the collapse of the N kingdom of Israel.

The city was soon rebuilt and became the capital of an Assyrian province under an Assyrian governor. One of the governors was a certain Ishtu-Adadaninu, who ruled Megiddo (spelled "Magidu[nu]" in Assyrian) in the year 679. During this occupation, stratum II, the city was without an encircling wall. The general layout of the town remained the same as in stratum III, though it was more highly developed. A large building with walls 6½-8 feet thick, and with rooms on three or possibly four sides of a central court, probably served as the fortified residence of the governor. This occupation was destroyed by Neco of Egypt in 609, after he defeated and killed Josiah of Judah at the Battle of Megiddo (II Kings 23:29-30; II Chr. 35:20-24).

Soon after this battle the site was reoccupied. Like stratum II, this occupation (stratum I) was largely residential and lacked a protective city wall. The last biblical reference to Megiddo (Zech. 12:11) probably belongs to this period or slightly later. Here mourning in Jerusalem is compared to mourning in the plain of Megiddo. This may refer specifically to mourning for Josiah, or in a more general sense to mourning for all who had lost their lives in the historic battles that were fought near the city. With the end of stratum I, probably in the early fourth century, occupation of Megiddo ceased.

Courtesy of the Oriental Institute, the University of Chicago

38. Roman-period tomb at Megiddo, with cover slabs removed

Among the remains of stratum I and in the cemetery area on the SE slope of the mound, a number of graves of the Roman period were discovered.* At the time, there was a large Roman community S of the mound in the vicinity of the modern village el-Lejjun, and it was probably the inhabitants of this settlement who used the site as a burial ground. Fig. MEG 38.

Bibliography. General: O. Schroeder, *Keilschrifttexte aus Assur verschiedenen Inhalts* (1920), pp. 27, 113. G. A. Smith, *The Historical Geography of the Holy Land* (25th ed., 1932), pp. 411-12. J. Simon, *Handbook for the Study of Egyptian Topographical Lists Relating to Western Asia* (1937), pp. 178-81. F.-M. Abel, *Géographie de la Palestine,* II (1938), 21-22, 59, 80, 87, 219. J. B. Pritchard, ed., *ANET* (2nd ed., 1955), pp. 228, 234-38, 263-64, 475-77, 485 (for reliable translations of most of the texts referring to Megiddo). W. F. Albright, *The Archaeology of Palestine* (1956), pp. 66-142 *passim.*

Excavation publications: G. Schumacher, *Tell el-Mutesellim I* (1908). C. Watzinger, *Tell el-Mutesellim II* (1929). R. S. Lamon, *The Megiddo Water System* (1935). H. G. May, *Material Remains of the Megiddo Cult* (1935). P. L. O. Guy and R. M. Engberg, *Megiddo Tombs* (1938). R. S. Lamon and G. M. Shipton, *Megiddo I* (1939). G. Loud, *The Megiddo Ivories* (1939); *Megiddo II* (1948). Y. Yadin, "New Light on Solomon's Megiddo," *BA,* 23 (1960), 62-68.

Reviews: W. F. Albright, review of Megiddo I, *AJA,* 44 (1940), 546-50. J. W. Crowfoot, "Megiddo . . . A Review," *PEQ* (1940), pp. 132-47. W. F. Albright, review of Megiddo II, *AJA,* 53 (1949), 213-15 (especially important for strata XX-XVI). G. E. Wright, review of Megiddo II, *JAOS,* 70 (1950), 56-60. G. W. VAN BEEK

MEGIDDO, PLAIN OF [בקעת מגדון] (Zech. 12:11); KJV VALLEY OF MEGIDDON mə gĭd'ən. That portion of the Valley of Jezreel in the vicinity of MEGIDDO; a place of great mourning. The reference in Zechariah may allude to the death of Josiah (see II Chr. 35:22), or to all who died on this historic battlefield. G. W. VAN BEEK

MEGIDDO, WATERS OF [מי מגדו]. A perennial stream near MEGIDDO; probably Wadi el-Lejjun, the scene of the battle of Sisera and Barak (Judg. 5:19).

MEGILLOTH mĭ gĭl'ŏth. The plural form of *megillah* (מגלה), meaning "scroll [of papyrus]" (Jer. 36:28-29; Ezek. 3:1-3; etc.). "The five *megilloth*" were each read on an annual festival: Song of Songs (Passover), Ruth (Pentecost), Lamentations (the ninth of Ab), Ecclesiastes (Tabernacles), and Esther (Purim). R. H. PFEIFFER

MEHETABEL mĭ hĕt'ə bĕl [מהיטבאל, God does good]. **1.** The wife of Hadar (Hadad), a king of Edom (Gen. 36:39; I Chr. 1:50).

2. An ancestor of Shemaiah, a false prophet, who was hired by Tobiah and Sanballat to intimidate Nehemiah (Neh. 6:10). M. NEWMAN

MEHIDA mĭ hī'də [מחידא, *possibly for* מחירא, bought (as slave); Μαουδά (Ezra 2:52), Μεειδά (Neh. 7:54)]; KJV Apoc. MEEDA mē ē'də. Eponym of a family of Nethinim, or temple servants (Ezra 2:52; Neh. 7:54; I Esd. 5:32).

Bibliography. W. Rudolph, *Esra und Nehemia* (1949), p. 12. B. T. DAHLBERG

MEHIR mē'hər [מחיר] (I Chr. 4:11). A descendant of Judah.

MEHOLATHITE mĭ hō'lə thīt [מחלתי]. Descriptive adjective of Adriel, who was the husband of Merab daughter of Saul (I Sam. 18:19; II Sam. 21:8); he was the son of Barzillai. The name denotes an inhabitant of ABEL-MEHOLAH and may indicate that Saul contracted this alliance with a chief of this important Gileadite city in order to strengthen his rule. S. COHEN

MEHUJAEL mĭ hū'jĭ əl [מחויאל, מחייאל; LXX Μαιηλ] (Gen. 4:18). Son of Irad; J counterpart to P's "Mahalalel."

MEHUMAN mĭ hū'mən [מהומן] (Esth. 1:10). One of the seven eunuchs who served King Ahasuerus as chamberlain.

Bibliography. L. B. Paton, *Esther,* ICC (1908), pp. 67, 148.

MEHUNIM, MEHUNIMS. KJV forms of MEUNIM, MEUNITES.

ME-JARKON mē jär'kŏn [מי הירקון, waters of the Jarkon (pale green, *perhaps the color of the water*)] (Josh. 19:46). Part of the territory of Dan; the name probably does not refer to a place but rather to a watercourse, very possibly the Nahr el-'Auja, which flows into the Mediterranean 3¾ miles N of Joppa (modern Tell Aviv). The Nahr el-'Auja rises at Ras el-'Ain, some ten miles inland, and is one of five perennially flowing streams draining the Plain of Sharon and the Judeo-Samaritan highland beyond. It flows to the sea first through swampy land and then through a deep channel.

The Mishnaic term *Mê-Pîga* ("the Jarkon") reflects the Hellenistic city of Pegae at Ras el-'Ain, the Aphek of an earlier day. After Herod's founding of Antipatris in 9 B.C., the Jarkon became the "River of Antipatris," which the Arabs after the Muslim conquest adopted as the Nahr Abi Futrus. In the Middle Ages, Arab historians and geographers began using the modern name, Nahr el-'Auja ("the winding river").

Bibliography. W. F. Albright, "The Site of Aphek in Sharon," *JPOS,* 3 (1923), 50-53; F.-M. Abel, *Géographie de la Palestine,* I (1933), 160, 472-73. V. R. GOLD

MEKONAH. KJV form of MECONAH.

MELATIAH mĕl'ə tī'ə [מלטיה, Yahu has set free] (Neh. 3:7). A man of Gibeon who helped rebuild the wall of Jerusalem in the time of Nehemiah.

MELCHI mĕl'kī [Μελχί=מלכי] (Luke 3:24, 28). The name of two ancestors of Jesus.

MELCHIAH. KJV form of MALCHIJAH.

MELCHIAS. KJV Apoc. form of MALCHIJAH.

MELCHIEL mĕl'kĭ əl [Μελχιήλ; *cf.* מלכיאל] (Jth. 6:15). The father of Charmis, one of the magistrates of Bethulia to whom Judith made her appeal for aid. J. C. SWAIM

MELCHIOR. *See* MELKON.

MELCHISEDEC. KJV NT form of MELCHIZEDEK.

MELCHI-SHUA. KJV alternate form of MALCHI-SHUA.

***MELCHIZEDEK** mĕl kĭz'ə dĕk' [מלכי־צדק, *see* § 1 *below;* LXX *and* NT Μελχισεδεκ]. An OT figure, appearing also in the Letter to the Hebrews.

1. Name
2. In the OT
   a. Gen. 14
   b. Ps. 110
3. In the NT

Bibliography

1. Name. Traditionally interpreted "king of righteousness" (Heb. 7:2), this name actually represents a good, ancient Canaanite formation, parallel to OT ADONI-ZEDEK and ABIMELECH; Akkadian *Milki-ilu* (*cf.* OT MALCHIEL) and *Ili-milku* (*cf.* OT ELIMELECH); and Ugaritic *mlkn'm* (*cf.* OT ABINOAM), *'ilmlk,* and *ṣdq'il* (*cf.* OT ZEDEKIAH). The proper translation is uncertain but is usually given as (*a*) "The (my) king is Zedek" (a deity), or (*b*) "Milki [a deity] is righteous" or "The (my) king is righteous(ness)."

2. In the OT. Historically Melchizedek was probably a Canaanite king of pre-Israelite Jerusalem (*see below*), as was ADONI-ZEDEK. He is mentioned in two OT passages. In Gen. 14:18-20 Melchizedek prepares a (cultic) meal for Abram (Abraham), blesses him in the name of God Most High, and receives his tithe. In Ps. 110:4 he is the representative priest in whose succession the Davidic king is ordained.

a. Gen. 14. Literarily the Melchizedek pericope (vss. 18-20) now lies embedded in two larger units, of which, however, it furnishes the high point. The larger includes the entire present chapter, which brings Abram into conflict with a league of powerful Eastern kings (*see* AMRAPHEL; ARIOCH); the smaller (vss. 17-24) leads the king of Sodom out to meet the victorious Abram (*see* ABRAHAM). What the setting and function of the ancient Melchizedek tradition may have been, is, accordingly, difficult to determine. Certainly it is odd to find the Canaanite cultus presented in so favorable a position vis-à-vis the religion of Israel. But Melchizedek's position gives the key; for the chapter, in its present form being late, is best seen against the background of the Israelite monarchy.

First, Melchizedek is recognized as "king of Salem" (*shālēm*), which was identified with Jerusalem (as Ps. 76:2—H 76:3 and Targ. and Dead Sea Genesis Apocryphon on Gen. 14:18 indicate; *see* SALEM; JERUSALEM § 1). Second, he is "priest of God Most High" (אל עליון); this is quite probably an appellation of the high god worshiped by the Canaanites in pre-Israelite Jerusalem (*see* GOD, OT). Clearly he is presented as the sacral king, exercising both royal and priestly authority in the city later to become Israel's holy capital. By virtue of his unique office Melchizedek towers over all the other important people in this crowded chapter. To him only, Abram submits himself (vs. 20*b*).

b. Ps. 110. The figure of Melchizedek as sacral king is here associated with the Davidic messiah. Now Melchizedek appears as a prototype of the Davidic king, who is also Yahweh's adopted son (Ps. 2:7) and anointed prince (Pss. 18:50—H 18:51; 132:17). As ideal king, the "son of David" establishes righteousness (צדק [same as "*-zedek*"]) and peace (שלום [cognate with SALEM]; Pss. 72:1-7; 99:4). As ideal priest, he heads Israel's worship (II Sam. 6; I Chr. 13; 15–16) and mediates between his people and God (I Kings 8; Ps. 132:9-10). Since this priesthood is eternal (Ps. 110:4*a*), it transcends the Aaronic (Levitical) order. *See* MESSIAH (JEWISH); PRIESTS AND LEVITES §§ D2*a-b*.

3. In the NT. Melchizedek is mentioned only in Hebrews (5:6, 10; 6:20; 7:1, 10-11, 15, 17). A major theme of this letter is the superiority of Christ above all creatures and the pre-eminence of his mediatorial office over all earthly ministries (*see* HEBREWS, LETTER TO THE, § 4*b*); and the OT Melchizedek tradition is offered as part of its scriptural proof. Christ is designated "high priest after the order of Melchizedek" (5:5-10; 6:20; cf. 7:21; Ps. 110:4). Being both king of righteousness and peace and a unique (without parents or kin) and eternal (without beginning or end) priest (though never "high priest"), Melchizedek resembles the Son of God (7:1-3). Since Melchizedek himself was greater than the patriarch Abraham (vss. 4-10) and the priest Aaron (vss. 11-17), he is the "type" of Christ, whose royal, holy high priesthood transcends all human orders (vss. 23-28; 8:1–10:18).

Bibliography. M. Noth, *Die israelitischen Personennamen* (1928), pp. 161-62; G. von Rad, *Das erste Buch Mose, Genesis Kapitel 12,10–25,18* (1952), pp. 150-52; A. R. Johnson, *Sacral Kingship in Ancient Israel* (1955), pp. 31-46, 120-22.

L. HICKS

MELEA mē'lĭ ə [Μελεά] (Luke 3:31). An ancestor of Jesus.

MELECH mē'lĕk [מלך, king] (I Chr. 8:35; 9:41). A Benjaminite, and the grandson of Meribbaal. *See also* MOLECH.

MELICU. KJV form of MALLUCHI.

MELITA. KJV form of MALTA.

MELITO, PSEUDO-, NARRATIVE OF mĕl'ĭ tō. A Latin narrative of the ASSUMPTION OF THE VIRGIN.

MELKON mĕl'kŏn. Alternately: **MELCHIOR** mĕl'kĭ ôr. In late tradition, one of the Magi (Matt. 2:1-12). Many curious and purely imaginative traditions arose to amplify the terse canonical account. In the increasingly common form of the tradition which limited the number of the Magi to three (on the basis of the three gifts mentioned in Matthew), Melkon is regularly pictured as the king of Persia, and occasionally as the brother of his two associates: Gaspar, a king of India, and Balthasar, a king of Arabia. In the very prolix account in the Armenian Gospel of the Infancy (*see* APOCRYPHA, NT) Melkon delivers to the infant Jesus, along with the traditional gifts, a letter to Adam, written and sealed by God, and long stored in the archives of the kings of Persia. In the West he is commemorated as a saint, most commonly together with Gaspar and Balthasar, on

January 6; in the East, on December 25. Among others of the utterly irresponsible legends which have attached themselves to the three is that identifying them with Shem, Ham, and Japheth. Less grotesque fancy sees them receiving baptism at the hands of Thomas and acting as missionaries in Persia. They are often styled the Three Kings of Cologne, from one form of the medieval legend, which recounts that their bodies were brought by the Empress Helena (mother of Constantine) to Constantinople, and thence were transferred by Eustorgius to Milan, and subsequently by the Emperor Henry to Cologne.

Bibliography. S. Baring-Gould, *The Lives of the Saints* (1872).

M. S. ENSLIN

MELONS [אבטחים, *'abhaṭṭiḥîm;* Arab. *baṭîḫ*]. A fruit, common in Egypt, for which the Israelites longed when in the wilderness (Num. 11:5). The word is probably generic, referring to several kinds of melons, *Cucumis melo* L. (muskmelon; *cf.* FLORA § A3*e*) and *Citrullus vulgaris* Schrad. (watermelon), common in N Egypt.

See also CUCUMBER; FLORA § A3*d*.

Bibliography. H. N. and A. L. Moldenke, *Plants of the Bible* (1952), pp. 80-81.

J. C. TREVER

MELZAR mĕl'zär. KJV translation of מלצר (Dan. 1:11, 16; RSV correctly "the steward"). The word occurs each time with the definite article (המלצר) and is not a proper name.

MEM mĕm (Heb. mām) [מ, *m* (*Mēm*)]. The thirteenth letter of the Hebrew ALPHABET as it is placed in the KJV at the head of the thirteenth section of the acrostic psalm, Ps. 119, where each verse of this section of the psalm begins with this letter.

MEMBERS. A term of importance only in the NT (μέλη), where it is used, not only of the organs of the body, and inclusively of the body as a whole (e.g., Matt. 5:29; Rom. 6:13; 7:23; 12:4; I Cor. 12:12; Jas. 3:6; 4:1), but also of the members of the church (e.g., Rom. 12:5; I Cor. 12:27; Eph. 4:25; 5:30)—two uses not so divergent as they may appear, since the church might be looked upon as the body of Christ. For a striking instance of the association of the two ideas, see I Cor. 6:15, where our "bodies" are described as "members" of Christ. Although the idea of "members" is present in I Cor. 6:5; Eph. 2:19; 3:6 (see RSV), the Greek word is not found.

See also CHURCH, IDEA OF; BODY OF CHRIST.

J. KNOX

MEMMIUS, QUINTUS kwĭn'təs mĕm'ĭ əs [Κοίντος Μέμμιος] (II Macc. 11:34). A Roman envoy who, with Titus Manius, is reported to have brought a letter to the Jewish people; these *legati Romanorum* (Vulg.) are otherwise unknown to history, and some infer that the incident of the letter is a fabrication.

J. C. SWAIM

MEMORIAL, MEMORY [זכר, to remember, *and nominal forms;* μιμνήσκομαι]. In addition to the words translated thus, "memorial" or "memory" is implied by (*a*) such phrases as "record," "be mindful," "come to mind" (lit., "rise up"; e.g., Jer. 3:16; Ezek. 14:3; etc.), "remind" (i.e., "cause to remember"), and "reminder"; (*b*) certain examples of the use of the verb "to visit" (e.g., I Sam. 15:2; Pss. 80:14; 106:4; Hos. 8:13 = 9:9 = Jer. 14:10, where "visit" either parallels or approaches "remember" in meaning); (*c*) the words for "forgetting" (e.g., Isa. 17:10) and their synonyms.

Some of the older Bible dictionaries did not include a study of "memory," but the act of memory plays a significant role in the Bible and in all life. Recent writers have tended to emphasize that the biblical memory is not merely theoretical—i.e., the recalling of an objective memory image—but that it recalls conditions and determines the behavior of him who remembers. But to a certain extent this is true also of the most intimate, personal, and religious memories of modern man. It is as well to know that for the Hebrew the recollection of the past means that what is recalled becomes a present reality, which in turn controls the will. Various shades of meaning may also be discovered in the Hebrew usage. Besides (*a*) "remember, call to mind" (cf. Isa. 65:17; Jer. 3:16), used basically of the recollection of past events, there is (*b*) "remember" almost in the sense of "know" (Gen. 31:50; Judg. 9:2). In Isa. 47:7 "remember their end" could also be translated by "know" or even "anticipate." And there are: (*c*) Jer. 17:2, where "remember" is almost "delight in"; Acts 10:31, where remembered alms are parallel to prayers that are heard; and lastly, (*d*) "remember" appears to mean "commemorate" in Esth. 9:28, "commemorated" or "addressed" in Exod. 3:15, and "affirm" in Ps. 78:35.

1. God as subject of the verb. God remembers such people as Noah, Abraham, Rachel, Hannah. Then he also remembers or will remember "my covenant" (Gen. 9:15; Exod. 2:24; 6:5; Lev. 26:52; Ezek. 16:60); or he is ever mindful of his covenant (I Chr. 16:15; Pss. 105:8; 111:5); his steadfast love (Ps. 98:3); his holy promise (105:42). He does not remember (Isa. 43:25; Jer. 31:34) or does remember (Jer. 14:10) sins, evil works (Hos. 7:2), iniquity (Hos. 8:13; 9:9; Rev. 16:19; 18:5). He remembers that Israel is dust (Ps. 78:39), or he remembers Israel's low estate (136:23). He is mindful of man (Ps. 8:4) and of Israel (115:12), but he remembers the dead no more (88:5). He causes his name to be remembered at sanctuaries (Exod. 20:24), and likewise his works (Ps. 111:4). In John 14:26 the Holy Spirit is to create remembrance of Jesus Christ and his words in the disciples.

2. Israel and Israelites as the subject of the verb. God, like Moses, David, Nehemiah, seeks to stir up Israel to remember. God bids Israel remember the sabbath day (Exod. 20:8; Mal. 4:4); or to remember to keep the commandments (Num. 15:39; cf. Ps. 103:18); or to remember (Isa. 46:8-9) or not to remember (Isa. 43:18) the former things. Israel's remembrance figures prominently in Deuteronomy and Psalms, and probably a cultic explanation is essential to both. In Deuteronomy, Moses bids Israel remember (*a*) God (8:18; also Ps. 42:6; Eccl. 12:1; Isa. 57:11; 64:5; Jer. 51:50; Ezek. 6:9; Zech. 10:9; cf. Judg. 8:34; Neh. 4:14); (*b*) the deeds of God (Deut. 7:18; cf. I Chr. 16:12; Pss. 77:5, 11; 105:5; 106:7; 119:55 [name]), including the Exodus (Deut. 11:3; cf. Exod. 14:31); (*c*) the desert journey (Deut. 8:2; cf. 24:9);

(*d*) the days of old (Deut. 32:7; cf. Pss. 77:5; 143:5; Ezek. 16:43); (*e*) that they were once slaves in Egypt (Deut. 15:15; 16:12; 24:18, 22), for such memories will instruct them how to regard and treat resident aliens in their own midst; (*f*) Amalek (Deut. 25:17, 19; cf. Exod. 17:14). Consideration of the "memory" passages in Deuteronomy suggests that the mode of the remembrance was preaching or sacred recital in the sanctuaries, and it is so prominent as to amount to a Deuteronomic presentation of remembrance.

It may also be said that Moses bids Israel remember their fare in Egypt (Num. 11:5); Joshua (1:13) reminds certain tribes of Moses' word. Nehemiah reproaches Israel that they were not mindful of God's mercies (Neh. 9:17). Individuals use the formula "remember" in pleas of various kinds—e.g., Abigail to David (I Sam. 25:31); Shimei to David (II Sam. 19: 19); Jehu to Bidkar (II Kings 9:25); etc. A remembrancer or recorder appears among David's officials (II Sam. 8:16; 20:24; cf. II Kings 18:18, etc.).

3. In prayer and intercession. The appeal to God to remember is, of course, a frequent formula of prayers, as these references show: Samson (Judg. 16: 28); Hannah (I Sam. 1:11); Solomon (II Chr. 6:42); Hezekiah (II Kings 20:3); Nehemiah (Neh. 1:8 and frequently); Habakkuk (3:2); Job (Job 7:7, etc.). Jeremiah petitions God to remember his covenant (Jer. 14:21) and poignantly: "Remember me and visit me" (15:15; cf. 18:20). Similarly Israel prays to God in these terms (Lam. 3:19; 5:1). Such passages prepare us for the place of remembrance in the prayers of the psalmists. They ask God to remember not the sins of youth but rather to remember his people (Ps. 25:7; cf. 79:8; 106:4), or to be mindful of his mercy and of his steadfast love (Ps. 25:6). They pray that God will remember the scoffers (74:18, 22), or will remember his word (119:49). The formula of remembrance is also characteristic of the language of intercession. Thus Moses intercedes for Israel by asking God to remember Israel's three patriarchs (Exod. 32: 13; Deut. 9:27). The psalmists pray that God will remember (*a*) their king (Pss. 20:3; 89:47, 50; 132:1); (*b*) Israel (Ps. 74:2); (*c*) Mount Zion (74:2); (*d*) the day of Jerusalem against Edom (137:7). The intercessors are, of course, priests, and perhaps the high priest himself.

The role of remembrance in the Psalms points to an important principle of the religious life. The psalmist says:

> My soul is cast down within me,
> therefore I remember thee (Ps. 42:6; cf. Jonah 2:7; II Pet. 1:12-15; 3:1).

Remembrance is revival for the downcast. It is the means whereby spiritual vitality and joy in God are re-created. Earlier in Ps. 42 the psalmist, as he pours out his soul, remembers his place in the festal procession. Indeed, he was the marshal of the procession, and he recalls the noise, the people, and the festival. Memory revives faith. In turn, in the cultic ceremonies themselves Israel remembers her ancient story, the works of God, his marvelous deeds in times past. Thus cult is sacred memory becoming sacred reality and life for the participants. The bearing of all this on the role of remembrance in the words for the institution of the Lord's Supper (Luke 22:19; I Cor. 11:24-25) is clear. Through the elements Christians are to remember Jesus Christ, but it follows from this meal that the presence of Christ is not merely remembered, but becomes a real presence through the remembrance. Their remembrances thus are the medium for the holy reality of Jesus Christ, and in this holy reality the life of the spirit is quickened and revived. Remembrance in religion always means revival. Thus in II Tim. 1:6 spiritual gifts are revived through the laying on of hands.

A different aspect of the matter is seen in those passages where God is invited to remember, or things are done to serve as a reminder to God. In Second Isaiah, God bids Israel remind him of any case she may have (Isa. 43:26). Similarly trumpets are to be sounded at the time of battle, that God may remember Israel and that victory may be ensured (Num. 10:9). The same principle is extended to various types of sacrifices over which trumpets are to be blown so that the sacrifices shall serve Israel for a remembrance before God (Num. 10:10). In this latter passage the Hebrew word for "remembrance" means a memorial or reminder to God, and it is attached to various objects. In Num. 10:10 it refers to trumpets; in Exod. 17:14 to a book (cf. Esth. 6:1; Mal. 3:16); in Exod. 28:12 to stories of remembrance (cf. 28:29; 39:7); in 30:16 to atonement money. All these objects are memorials—they are the things in which the memory or the name or the meaning is enshrined; and when presented to God, they serve to remind God of the people concerned. In other references the memorial is a reminder to Israel (Exod. 12:14; Num. 16:40—H 17:5; Josh. 4:7; Zech. 6:14; etc.). Similarly the אזכרה, "memorial offering," is P's word for that portion of various sacrifices and incenses burned before the Lord. The memorial portion thus bears the offerer into the presence of God. Through the memorial offering the worshiper is presented to God. In Isa. 62:6 Jerusalem's watchmen fulfil this role. They are not to cease putting the Lord in remembrance until he restores Jerusalem.

In the NT, apart from the memorial features connected with the Last Supper, there is little to mention. There is the recollection of OT events (Luke 17:32) or OT passages (Heb. 8:12). There is remembrance of fellow Christians (Col. 4:18), especially in prayers (Eph. 1:16; II Tim. 1:3; Philem. 1:4), and of Jesus Christ (II Tim. 2:8). The recollection of the words and events of Jesus (Matt. 16:9; Luke 24:6; John 15:20; Acts 20:35; Rev. 3:3; cf. Matt. 26:75, etc.) obviously represent the early stages in the formation and transmission of the gospel tradition. No doubt, short creedal statements like "Jesus is Lord" and I Tim. 3:16 were memorized and sung by the early Christians. "Tomb" (Mark 15:46; Luke 23: 53; cf. Acts 7:16; Rev. 11:9) in Greek is the sign or place of remembrance.

In Acts 10:4 prayers and alms are a memorial before God. This verse thus suggests a sacrificial nuance, but it is highly improbable that there is any sacrificial intention with a godward reference in "Do this in memory of me" in the Last Supper.

Bibliography. F. Schwally, "Miscellen," *ZAW*, 11 (1891), 169-83 (especially 176-80); J. P. Peters, "Critical Notes," *JBL*, 12 (1893), 47-60 (especially 57-59); B. Jacob, "Beiträge zu einer Einleitung in die Psalmen," *ZAW,* 17 (1897), 48-80; I. J. Peritz, "Women in the Ancient Hebrew Cult," *JBL,* 17 (1898), 111-48; J. Pedersen, *Israel,* I-II (1926), 245-59; J. Begrich, "Sofer und Mazkir," *ZAW,* 58 (1941), 1-29; N. Dahl, "Anamnesis," *Studia Theologica,* I (1947), 69-94; W. D. Davies, *Paul and Rabbinic Judaism* (1948), pp. 250-51; H. Lietzmann, "An die Korinther I-II," *Handbuch zum NT* (4th ed., 1949), pp. 49-57; W. Vollborn, *Studien zum Zeitverständnis des AT* (1951), pp. 191-97; D. Jones, "'Ανάμνησις in the LXX and the Interpretation of I Cor. xi.25," *JTS,* vol. 6, pt. 2 (Oct., 1955), pp. 183-91.

G. HENTON DAVIES

MEMPHIS mĕm'fĭs [נֹף, *Nōph;* מֹף, *Mōph* (Hos. 9:6); LXX Μέμφις]. A city located *ca.* thirteen miles S of modern Cairo on the W side of the Nile; the chief city of Lower (N) Egypt during most of that country's early history.

1. Name
2. History
3. Archaeological significance
4. Religious significance

Bibliography

1. Name. According to native tradition, the city was founded by Menes, the first ruler of a united Egypt in the First Dynasty (*ca.* 2800 B.C.). The Egyptian name of the city, *Mn-nfr,* which appears in Hebrew as *Mōph* and (by a dissimilation of the initial labial) *Nōph,* dates from the Sixth Dynasty and is originally the name of the pyramid of Pepi I, which was constructed in the city's environs at that time (*ca.* 2300 B.C.). While there is some dispute over the meaning of the name, it most probably should be translated "The goodness [of Pepi I] endures" or similarly. Another, less widely accepted interpretation is "the good port (or station)," as suggested by

From *Atlas of the Bible* (Thomas Nelson & Sons Limited)

39. Palm trees at Memphis where once stood the palaces of the Pharaohs of the Old Empire

Plutarch (*De Iside et Osiride* 20). Extrabiblical attestations of the name include Assyrian *Mempi, Mimpi* from the Annals of Ashurbanipal, and the Coptic forms *Membi, Memfi,* etc. It is interesting to note that the sacred name of Memphis, Egyptian *Ḥ(w)t-kꜣ-Ptḥ,* "the house of the Ka of Ptah," written in the cuneiform of Tell el-Amarna as *Ḫi-ku-up-taḫ,* is the forerunner of Greek Αἴγυπτος and thence of the modern designation Egypt.

Fig. MEM 39.

2. History. One of Egypt's oldest cities, Memphis rose gradually in political importance during the Thinite Period (First and Second Dynasties), and, following a shift of power during the latter part of the Second Dynasty, became the capital of Egypt at the beginning of the Third Dynasty, the most significant ruler of which was Djoser. The city apparently enjoyed unrivaled political supremacy until the close of the Fifth Dynasty, at which time the ruling power at Memphis became feeble and was eclipsed by various minor local dynasties during the first intermediate period (*ca.* 2190-2052). When Egypt was again unified by the pharaohs of the Eleventh Dynasty, THEBES replaced Memphis as the capital, and from this time on, Memphis never again achieved its former political importance. For a short time, however, during the second intermediate period (*ca.* 1750-1570) Memphis was the capital of the HYKSOS ruler Salatis, but was replaced shortly thereafter by Avaris-Tanis in the Delta. Memphis figures prominently in the accounts of Piankhi, a Nubian king who *ca.* 720 B.C. marched victoriously through Egypt to the Delta but after a short reign retired to his Nubian capital, Napata. His account of the capture of Memphis is a high point of the narrative and demonstrates the important position still held by that city. Memphis was captured by Esarhaddon during the retreat of Taharka (Twenty-fifth Dynasty, *ca.* 715-663) before the invading Assyrian forces, but is mentioned again as being recaptured by Tanutamun. The latter's victory was brief, however, for he was driven southward again by reinforced Assyrian troops. Memphis remained in Assyrian hands until Psamtik, the first king of the Saite Dynasty (663-525), shook off the restraint of Asian rule and Egypt entered the period known as the Saite restoration.

What remains of Memphis today gives little indication of the glorious past the city enjoyed. Its fall was gradual, however, and due first to the founding of Alexandria shortly after the conquest of Egypt by Alexander the Great in 332 B.C. Strabo (17.1.32) mentions explicitly that Memphis was second to Alexandria in population. Much later, in A.D. 638, Old Cairo was founded by the Arab conquerors, and the ruins of Memphis, which until that time had been quite extensive, were exploited for building materials to the extent that even the temple of Ptah, which seems to have been one of the few stable elements of the city, whose position shifted repeatedly because of different concentrations of building activity, was dilapidated beyond recognition. Nothing survives to indicate the splendor of this its principal architectural monument, enlarged and elaborated by successive dynasties of pharaohs.

3. Archaeological significance. The prominent position held by Memphis during Egyptian history is perhaps most forcibly attested by the major pyramid fields in its immediate vicinity on the west bank of the Nile. Among the most important of these are (*a*) Abusir, the location of the Fifth Dynasty pyramids of Sahure and his successors; (*b*) Dahshur, where the famous "bent" pyramid of Sneferu (Third Dynasty), as well as the less imposing tombs of several Twelfth Dynasty kings, were built; (*c*) Gizeh, the site of the world-famous trio of pyramids constructed by the Fourth Dynasty rulers Cheops, Chefren, and Mycerinus; and (*d*) Sakkarah, where were built the once magnificent step pyramid of Djoser (Third Dynasty); the Fifth and Sixth Dynasty pyramids of Userkaf, Teti, Pepi I, Pepi II, and Merenre, whose burial chambers have yielded to modern scholars the invaluable Pyramid Texts; and numerous great tombs of the First Dynasty, the recent excavations of which have added immensely to our knowledge of the earliest phases of dynastic history and material culture. It is possible that Hosea was mindful of these splendid monuments of Egypt's buried glory when, in speaking of the fate of Israel's unfaithful, he declared (9:6):

Behold, they are going to Assyria;
 Egypt shall gather them,
 Memphis shall bury them.

4. Religious significance. Memphis rivaled HELIOPOLIS as a center of religious activity. The local theology is well known to us through the famous document commonly called the *Denkmal memphitischer Theologie,* which is preserved in an inscribed copy on black granite, the execution of which was ordered by Shabaka, founder of the Twenty-fifth Dynasty. The Memphite system reckons Ptah as the oldest of the gods and creator of mankind. His dominant position in the local pantheon is reflected also in the sacred name of the city, as cited above. Ptah was identified by the Greeks with Hephaestus and is so mentioned by Herodotus (II.99), who states that Menes constructed in Memphis the great and most noteworthy temple to that god. Ptah was also worshiped in the form of APIS and like the latter was closely associated with OSIRIS as the god of the dead. Worship of numerous other deities was centered at Memphis; among the most important of these were native gods such as Sokaris (whose name survives in the place name Sakkarah), Osiris, Suchos, as well as foreign gods like Baal, Kadesh, and especially Astarte.

Bibliography. A. Erman, *Ein Denkmal memphitischer Theologie* (1911); B. Porter and R. L. B. Moss, *Topographical Bibliography of Ancient Egyptian Hieroglyphic Texts, Reliefs, and Paintings,* III: *Memphis* (1931); H. Junker, *Die Götterlehre von Memphis, Abhandlungen der preussischen Akademie der Wissenschaften* (1940); I. E. S. Edwards, *The Pyramids of Egypt* (1949), *passim;* A. Scharff and A. Moortgat, *Ägypten und Vorderasien im Altertum* (1950), *passim.* T. O. LAMBDIN

MEMPHITIC VERSION mĕm fĭt'ĭk. An obsolete designation of the Bohairic (Coptic) Version of the Bible. *See* VERSIONS, ANCIENT, § 5.

MEMUCAN mĭ mōō'kən [ממוכן] (Esth. 1:14, 16, 21). One of the seven princes of Persia and Media at the court of King Ahasuerus, who were consulted for their legal knowledge. Their names are Persian.

MENAHEM mĕn'ə hĕm [מנחם, comforter]. King of Israel *ca.* 745-738 B.C.; son of Gadi. He succeeded to the throne through the assassination of Shallum.

The root of the name is נחם, here found in the *pi'el* participle. It is used of one who comforts over the death of a relative, or it is perhaps the name given to a child who takes the place of another child who has died. In Assyrian inscriptions it appears as *Me-ni-ḫi-im-me; Mi-in-ḫi-im-mu* (cf. also Μανεεμος).

After the death of the powerful Jeroboam II (*ca.* 746) chaotic conditions prevailed in the N kingdom. Jeroboam's son Zechariah followed him on the throne but was murdered by Shallum the son of Jabesh, after a brief reign lasting six months (II Kings 15:8-10). Shallum in his turn was assassinated by Menahem after reigning only one month (vss. 13-14; Hos. 7:7*b;* 8:4*a*).

Menahem belonged to Tirzah, the former capital city. It seems clear that at the time of the murder of Zechariah there was more than one aspirant to the throne. Shallum was the leader of one party, Menahem of another. This may serve to throw some light on the very difficult verse (II Kings 15:16): "At that time Menahem sacked Tappuah and all who were in it and its territory from Tirzah on; because they did not open it to him, therefore he sacked it, and he ripped up all the women in it who were with child." For "Tappuah" the MT reads here "Tiphsah." Earlier exegetes identified Tiphsah with the well-known Tiphshah-Thapsacus on the Euphrates (cf. I Kings 4:24—H 5:4); but such an identification is not possible. The view now commonly accepted is that, instead of "Tiphsah," "Tappuah" should be read—the reading of the Lucian MS of the LXX. Tappuah has been identified with the modern Sheikh Abu Zarad, a few miles S of Shechem. This identification, however, cannot be accepted as certain, and the alteration is perhaps unnecessary. The reference may be to Tiphsah, located some six miles SW of Shechem. The most reasonable explanation of Menahem's atrocities against this city, after he had captured it, is that it had supported Shallum and refused to surrender to his murderer.

Menahem is said to have reigned for ten years (II Kings 15:17), but the date of his death is uncertain. He seems to have been still alive in 738, when he paid tribute to Tiglath-pileser III. Thereafter no further mention is made of him. Because of this uncertainty it seems best to assume that he died very soon afterward. The chronology of this period is very complicated, but recent investigation of the events which occurred in the first years of Tiglath-pileser's reign, based on Assyrian records, has thrown considerable light on this question.

If the Azriau Ia-ú-da-a-a- named in the Assyrian Annals is correctly identified with Azariah (Uzziah) of Judah—an identification which is quite convincing—a synchronism has been established for Tiglath-pileser and Azariah. The two reigns must have overlapped, at least in part. Tiglath-pileser also claims to have received heavy tribute from Me-ni-ḫi-im-me-al Sa-me-ri-na-a—i.e., Menahem of Samaria. This helps to establish a further point of reference. The dates of Tiglath-pileser's reign have been established from Assyrian sources, *ca.* 745-727.

The older view considered 738 as the year of Tiglath-pileser's expedition mentioned in the Assyrian inscriptions, and consequently the year when Menahem of Samaria paid tribute to him. This date speaks against the equation of Azriau with Azariah. It has now, however, been shown that Tiglath-pileser led an expedition against Syria, *ca.* 743-742. The campaign that followed lasted six years and was the beginning of his conquest of the whole Syro-Palestinian territory. This date enables us to identify Azriau and Azariah of Judah, and to give at least an approximate date for Azariah's death. It is not necessary, however, also to assume that at this time Menahem paid tribute to Tiglath-pileser, and that he died soon thereafter. Menahem may very well have paid tribute both in 743-742 and in 738. The datum mentioned in II Kings 15:19 must have occurred at the latter date, in view of the clear statement of vs. 20*b:* "So the king of Assyria turned back, and did not stay there in the land." This seems to be confirmed by the evidence of the inscriptions which indicate that Tiglath-pileser did not return to the west until his tenth year—i.e., 736—and did not appear in Israel until his twelfth year—i.e., 734.

The outstanding event of Menahem's reign was the supremacy of Assyrian power in the West. This is confirmed in detail from Assyrian sources. The writer of Kings records that "Pul the king of Assyria came against the land; and Menahem gave Pul a thousand talents of silver, that he might help him to confirm his hold of the royal power" (II Kings 15:19). The picture becomes clearer if the reading of the LXX is adopted, which transfers "all his days" (vs. 18) to the beginning of vs. 19 and reads "in his days." This verse contains two points of special importance:

a) The first is the reference to Pul as the name of the king of Assyria. On the basis of I Chr. 5:26 it was quite naturally assumed by older commentators that Pul and Tiglath-pileser were two distinct and separate kings of Assyria, both of whom conquered Israel. It is now clear, however, that Pul and Tiglath-pileser are two names for one and the same Assyrian ruler. When Tiglath-pileser III of Assyria took the throne of Babylon in 729, he assumed the name Pūlu. This is the form of the name given in the Babylonian King List. Other forms of the name are given as Πωρου in the Ptolemaic Canon and Φουλος in Eusebius. Thus the identification of the two names is certain.

An alternative explanation of the names has been advanced—that Pul was his personal name, Tiglath-pileser his throne name. The suggestion is interesting in the light of the similar practice found in the case of certain of the kings of Judah.

b) The second point is the words: "that he might help him to confirm his hold of the royal power." The implication is that Menahem sat uneasily on the throne of Israel, and that his position was far from secure. It is even possible that Menahem had obtained the throne by buying Assyrian support (cf. Hos. 5:13).

In his annals Tiglath-pileser records the receiving of tribute from various nations of the West—Menahem of Samaria, Rezin of Damascus, Hiram of Tyre, Sibittibi'li of Byblos, etc. A fragmentary text adds further details about Menahem. He was overwhelmed like a snowstorm and fled like a bird, alone, and bowed to the feet of his conqueror, who returned him to his place and imposed tribute upon him. Tiglath-pileser also claims that all the inhabitants of Israel "and their possessions I led to Assyria." No confirmation of this is found in the biblical sources. Kings records the amount of tribute as a "thousand talents of silver." Menahem secured this sum by levying a poll tax of fifty shekels on every wealthy Israelite (II Kings 15:20). It has been calculated that this represents a figure of *ca.* sixty thousand men who were in a position to pay. This is an interesting commentary on the financial position existing in the land and sheds light on the violent denunciations of the contemporary prophets, Amos and Hosea, against the excesses of the wealthy.

It is noteworthy that alone of the last six kings of Israel is it recorded that Menahem died a peaceful death and slept with his fathers (II Kings 15:22).

Bibliography. M. Noth, *Die israelitischen Personennamen* (1928), p. 222; K. Galling, *Biblisches Reallexikon* (1937), p. 186; F.-M. Abel, *Géographie de la Palestine,* II (1938), 475-76, 485-86; E. R. Thiele, *The Mysterious Numbers of the Hebrew Kings* (1951), pp. 75-98; J. B. Pritchard, ed., *ANET* (2nd ed., 1955), pp. 272, 283-84; M. Noth, *Geschichte Israels* (3rd ed., 1956), pp. 233 ff.

H. B. MacLean

MENAN. KJV form of Menna.

MENE, MENE, TEKEL, AND PARSIN mē'nĭ, tē'kəl, tĕk'əl, pär'sĭn; KJV MENE, MENE, TEKEL, UPHARSIN ū fär'sĭn. The enigmatic inscription recorded in Dan. 5:25.

1. Text. MT מנא מנא תקל ופרסין, m^{e}nê m^{e}nê t^{e}qēl ûphārsîn; LXX (5:1 chapter summary) Μανη φαρες θεκελ; Theod. 5:25 Μανη, θεκελ, φαρες; Jos. Antiq. X.xi.3; and Vulg. *mane, thecel, phares,* agree with Theod. Some scholars think the three-word text of the versions is original and omit the second *m^{e}nê* as dittography. Similarly, *upharsin* is often corrected to *p^{e}rēs*. But Eissfeldt retains the MT on the grounds that in this kind of explication we have to recognize not *Auslegung* (exegesis) but *Einlegung* (eisegesis). He substantiates this by reference to the explication of the dream in ch. 2 and by parallels from the Habakkuk Pesher from Qumran. In *Einlegung* the explanation often slightly adapts the text to the desired meaning, and the words actually commented upon are not identical with the text as given. In this view, the versions, wishing to make the wording fit more closely the explanation given in 5:27-28, have altered the text, which the MT gives more faithfully. As we shall see below, there are good grounds for accepting Eissfeldt's contention.

2. Interpretation. The debate turns on the question whether the author of Daniel has coined his own phrase or whether he has employed an already popular proverbial saying. (For discussion of the author's dependence on traditional materials, *see* Daniel.) If the saying was already current, then Eissfeldt's contention noted above is greatly strengthened, and we must reckon with two elements: the original saying and its meaning, and the fresh meaning given to it in Daniel's exposition.

The inscription appeared upon the wall, written by a detached hand. Whether we are to understand that the characters of the inscription baffled the "Chaldeans" or whether it employed a normal script is not clear. Probably we are to think of an (unvocalized) Aramaic script, and the puzzle was so to vocalize it (by pronunciation) that the words could be construed into a meaningful sentence or phrase. If the saying were proverbial, the reading should have baffled none, but this kind of realism is not to be expected in Daniel. Presuming that it was currently a proverb and that we must retain the MT text, we may proceed as follows: the three words of the inscription refer to weights and their equivalent monetary values. "Mene" (Aramaic מנא = Hebrew מנה) is the mina; "Tekel" (Aramaic תקל = Hebrew שקל) is the shekel; and "Upharsin," of which the "u" is simply the copulative "and," is *p^{e}rēs* in the plural, meaning "halves." The word has been found on half-mina weights and occurs in the Talmud in the sense of a half mina, but Eissfeldt successfully contends that it simply means "half" and gets its meaning as half mina simply from the context. Here then it is to be taken as half shekel, and there is no need to rearrange the order, as the LXX does. Thus we get "mina, shekel, and half shekels." The use of these WEIGHTS not only to designate monetary values but also to express estimates of character (cf. Hebrew כבוד, GLORY, in the sense of "soul, person," and Latin *gravis* used of a man) is found in the Talmud. To what then did this proverbial saying, "A mina, a mina, a shekel, half shekels," refer? Presumably to any situation of family degeneration (cf. the Lancashire proverb "From clogs to boots and boots to clogs"—i.e., family wealth is gained and lost again in four generations). Probably the Jews applied it to the occupants of the Neo-Babylonian throne: Nebuchadnezzar is the mina, Evil-merodach is the shekel, and Nabonidus and Belshazzar are the half shekels. Why is *mn'* repeated? Either because the saying was adapted to some succession of four kings, including Nabonidus and his crown-prince, Belshazzar, as one, or because it was made to conform to the four-kingdom pattern also featured in Dan. 2; 7 (*see* DANIEL § 2*e*). Or, again, perhaps the first *mn'* was to be differently pointed (*m^enâ'* instead of *m^enê'*) and read: "He has weighed: a mina, a shekel, and half shekels." In any case, it was probably used to suggest the answer to the question: "What is the worth of the kings of Babylon?" The answer is that God has weighed them and found them to be steadily losing weight. There is, however, another way of accounting for the plural *ûphārsîn,* which suggests that when the Neo-Babylonian kingdom fell, the old riddle was pressed into further use by using the assonance between *pārăs* (Persia) and *p^erēs* to imply that while Nebuchadnezzar was worth a mina, the Persians were worth only half shekels; and if the double nature of the Medo-Persian kingdom were in mind, we may take the term as dual and say that the riddle maintained that the Medes and Persians together were worth only one sixtieth of the great Chaldean. What is past often seems so much preferable to what is present.

So much for the ancient riddle. The use to which Daniel put it is in little doubt. By punning on the three terms used, he brings out of the riddle an oracle of doom. He changes *mn'* to the *lamedh-he* root and vocalizes it as *m^enâh* ("he numbered")—God has checked over the number of the days of your kingdom and has found that the allotted figure has been reached; *tql* he vocalizes as *t^eqal* ("he weighed")—God has weighed Belshazzar and has found him to be underweight and has therefore condemned him on this account; *prs* he vocalizes as *p^eras* ("he divided")—God has already divided up your kingdom and given it to the Medes and the Persians. We might try something of the same wordplay in English if the phrase "Stones, pounds, quarters," were current among us as a proverb indicating that great men have lesser sons and even lesser grandsons. Then a modern Daniel could have explained it as: "Stone—you are to be stoned to death; pound—your power will be pounded to pieces; quarter—your kingdom has been quartered and distributed among others." That Daniel's exposition alters the form of the words somewhat is in full accord with Jewish exegetical practice as illustrated by Eissfeldt in the article mentioned above.

Since we can thus fully account for the form of words given in Dan. 5:25 MT, there is no need to emend them to the form given in the versions; to adopt their reading would be only to follow them in correcting an error which never existed.

Bibliography. J. A. Montgomery, *Daniel,* ICC (1927); R. H. Charles, *Commentary on Daniel* (1929); E. G. Kraeling, "The Handwriting on the Wall," *JBL,* 63 (1944), 11; O. Eissfeldt, "Die Mene-Tekel Inschrift," *ZAW,* 63 (1951), 105; A. Bentzen, *Daniel,* HAT (2nd ed., 1952). S. B. FROST

MENELAUS mĕn'ə lā'əs [Μενέλαος = Heb. MENAHEM]. An unscrupulous and usurping high priest, in the reign of Antiochus Epiphanes. He was probably the leader of the Tobiads, the Jerusalem supporters of the Seleucids. The high priest Jason sent him to Antioch in 171 B.C. to take the tribute which Jason had promised, but Menelaus himself offered Antiochus a heavier tribute, and was therefore allowed to supplant Jason (II Macc. 4:23 ff). Jason had to flee, but Menelaus did not pay the tribute he had promised and was summoned before Antiochus. The king was away from Antioch when Menelaus arrived, and the latter thereupon took advantage of the occasion for a little more bribery. According to II Maccabees, the veracity of which is not above reproach, he had stolen some vessels from the temple; and by presenting these to Andronicus, who was acting as deputy for Antiochus, Menelaus completely gained his sympathy. He persuaded Andronicus to assassinate the pious ex-high priest Onias III (*see* ONIAS 3), who was tricked out of his place of refuge at Daphne, because Onias was doing his best to make the sacrilege of Menelaus public. Greeks and Jews alike were appalled by this murder, and reported the matter to Antiochus. Andronicus paid for this with his life, but Menelaus emerged unscathed. Back in Jerusalem the brother and deputy of Menelaus, Lysimachus, had caused a riot by his sacrilege in the temple and been killed by the mob. A deputation complaining of Menelaus was sent by the Jews to Antiochus at Tyre. But meanwhile Menelaus had not neglected his gift; and by bribing an influential courtier, Ptolemy Dorymenes, to put in a word to the king, Menelaus obtained both his own acquittal and the execution of the hostile witnesses. At this point the usurped Jason appeared once more, probably at the head of the Oniads, attacking Jerusalem while Antiochus was absent in Egypt. He caused Menelaus to flee for refuge, but Antiochus took a serious view of the attack and massacred the inhabitants of Jerusalem, plundering the temple with the help of the scoundrel Menelaus. He and the Tobiads were thus restored to power for a time, but he was not high priest when the temple was cleansed (165-164). He reappears in 162 in the reign of Eupator, whom he did not succeed in winning over so easily. The king was warned by the Syrian chancellor LYSIAS of the true nature of the man, and he brought about his execution by having him thrown into a tower of ashes, according to one account (II Macc. 13:3-8).

Bibliography. F.-M. Abel, *Les Livres des Maccabées* (1949), pp. 337-38; R. H. Pfeiffer, *History of NT Times* (1949), p. 11.
N. TURNER

MENESTHEUS mĭ nĕs′thĭ əs [Μενεσθεύς] (II Macc. 4:4). The father of Apollonius, the governor of Coele-Syria and Phoenicia.

Bibliography. S. Tedesche and S. Zeitlin, *I Maccabees* (1950), p. 73; *II Maccabees* (1954), p. 151.

MENI mə nē′ [מְנִי, *from* מנה, to count, apportion]. With Gad, a deity or genius of good luck worshiped by Jewish apostates probably in the postexilic period (Isa. 65:11). Manat is known from the Quran (Surah 53.20) as a deity worshiped in Arabia before Islam. The name is found, possibly in a plural form, in Nabatean inscriptions from the Hejaz. The Arab association is interesting in view of Edomite or Arab penetration of Palestine in the postexilic period, to which Isa. 65:11 probably refers (*see* DESTINY 1).

Bibliography. G. A. Cooke, *A Textbook of North Semitic Inscriptions* (1903), pp. 217-23.
J. GRAY

MENNA mĕn′ə [Μεννά] (Luke 3:31); KJV MENAN mē′nən [Μαϊνάν]. An ancestor of Jesus.

*__MENORAH__ mə nôr′ə [מְנוֹרָה, *from* נוּר, light]. The Hebrew *mᵉnōrâ* might refer to any lampstand; but as it is used in the OT, it is a technical term for the seven-branched LAMPSTAND (KJV "candlestick") of the tabernacle and the temple, and the lampstand in Zechariah's vision (Zech. 4:2, 11).
L. E. TOOMBS

MENSTRUATION. *See* CLEAN AND UNCLEAN.

MENUHOTH mə no͞o′hŏth [מְנֻחוֹת, resting places] (I Chr. 2:52); KJV MANAHETHITES măn′ə-hĕth′īts. An unknown family, unless "Manahathites" (הַמָּנַחְתִּי) be read, in which case they would be the other half of the MANAHATHITES of vs. 54, who are of the clan of Salma, living S of Jerusalem, around Bethlehem, while those of vs. 52 are of the clan of Shobal, living NW of Jerusalem, toward Kiriath-jearim.

Bibliography. W. Rudolph, *Chronikbücher* (1955), pp. 23 ff.
V. R. GOLD

MEONENIM, PLAIN OF mē ŏn′ə nĭm. KJV translation of אלון מעוננים (RSV DIVINERS' OAK).

MEONOTHAI mē ŏn′ə thī [מְעוֹנֹתַי] (I Chr. 4:13-14). Son of Othniel, a Judahite, and the father of Ophrah.

MEPHAATH mĕf′ĭ ăth [מֵיפַעַת, מֵפַעַת, מוֹפַעַת]. A town given to the tribe of Reuben (Josh. 13:18), assigned to the MERARITES (Josh. 21:37; I Chr. 6:79—H 6:64; *see* LEVITICAL CITIES). In Jeremiah's time it was possessed by Moab (Jer. 48:21). It is perhaps modern Jawah, *ca.* six miles S of Amman. This place name is common in S Arabia.
E. D. GROHMAN

MEPHIBOSHETH mĭ fĭb′ə shĕth [מְפִיבֹשֶׁת, he who scatters shame, *or* from the mouth of shame]. **1.** Jonathan's son, to whom David granted generous concessions out of respect for his father's friendship. The original name of this scion of the house of Saul may be presumed to have been MERIBBAAL (I Chr. 8:34).

Mephibosheth was five years old when the fateful news of his father's death in Mount Gilboa reached the household of Saul. Fleeing in panic lest the prince share a similar fate, the nurse of Mephibosheth let the child fall from her arms and permanently crippled his two feet (II Sam. 4:4).

When his uncle Ishbaal was assassinated, the youthful Mephibosheth was, no doubt, the presumptive heir to the throne of Saul, but he never pressed his claim, contenting himself in those troublous days with the relative security he found in the home of his benefactor, Machir the son of Ammiel, a powerful Transjordanian noble. When Mephibosheth was finally summoned to the royal court, David gave evidence of his good will by granting to him all the property of the house of Saul, committing it to the custody of Ziba, the steward of Saul, while Mephibosheth himself he invested as a permanent member of the king's board (II Sam. 9).

All went well with Mephibosheth until the rebellion of Absalom, when his unavoidable detention in Jerusalem, which was maliciously caused by Ziba, was slanderously misrepresented by the latter to be an endeavor to secure the throne for himself. This studied duplicity was perpetrated when Ziba brought generous supplies to David, as he fled from Jerusalem. Moved by this evident token of solicitous concern and beguiled by the deceit of Ziba, David ordered that all the possessions of Mephibosheth be transferred to Ziba (II Sam. 16:1-4).

When David had crushed the rebellion of Absalom, Mephibosheth went down to meet the returning king at the Jordan and betrayed visibly, with untrimmed beard and unwashed clothes, his deep grief at the misfortune David had suffered. Sternly accosted by the king as to the reason why he abode in Jerusalem, Mephibosheth exposed the ruse of Ziba and presented movingly his firm loyalty and profound gratitude for David's singular kindness. No doubt persuaded of Mephibosheth's integrity but thankful for the timely supplies he had received of Ziba, David decided that Mephibosheth should share equally with Ziba in the lands of Saul. With an altruism reminiscent of his father, Mephibosheth replied, "Oh, let him take it all, since my lord the king has come safely home" (II Sam. 19:30; cf. vss. 24-29).

Because of the oath Jonathan and David had sworn together (II Sam. 21:7; I Sam. 20:12-17), Mephibosheth was spared the tragic death which befell seven of the sons of Saul at the hands of the Gibeonites.

Mephibosheth had a son named Mica (II Sam. 9:12), from whom a well-known family in Israel was descended (I Chr. 8:35; 9:41).

2. A son of Saul by his concubine Rizpah, daughter of Aiah. With his brother, Armoni, and the five sons of Merab, daughter of Saul, Mephibosheth was delivered by David to the Gibeonites to be hanged before Yahweh in order to expiate the guilt incurred when Saul violated an ancient oath by slaughtering the Gibeonites (Josh. 9:15 ff; II Sam. 21:1-9)—which guilt was oracularly interpreted to be the cause of the existing famine. The mother of Mephibosheth stationed herself by the seven corpses, guarding them from molestation until the rain fell, which was believed to indicate the passing of the divine wrath. Their remains were then gathered and interred by the order of David, presumably in the tomb of their grandfather Kish in Zela (II Sam. 21:10-14).

E. R. Dalglish

MERAB mĭr'ăb [מרב, *probably from* רבב, become many, much]. The elder daughter of Saul (I Sam. 14: 49). Saul promised her to David, to spur him on to reckless valor in the wars with the Philistines, so that he would be killed. Merab was actually given, however, to Adriel the Meholathite, and her younger sister, Michal, became the wife of David (I Sam. 18: 17-27). When David later had seven of the sons of Saul put to death in order to appease the Gibeonites, the five sons of Merab were probably among them (II Sam. 21:8; two Hebrew MSS, one LXX, and the Syr. are probably correct in reading "Merab" at this point; other Hebrew MSS read "Michal").

D. Harvey

MERAIAH mĭ rā'yə [מריה, *probably from* אמריה, Yahu has promised; *see* Amariah] (Neh. 12:12). Head of a priestly family, the sons of Seraiah, in the time of the high priest Joiakim.

MERAIOTH mĭ rā'yŏth [מריות, *hypocoristic for* obstinate, rebellious; Apoc. Μαραιώθ, Μαρερώθ]; KJV Apoc. MEREMOTH mĕr'ə mŏth (I Esd. 8:2; RSV omits the name with Codex B); MARIMOTH măr'ĭ mŏth (II Esd. 1:2—G 7:3). **1.** A priest descended from Aaron (I Chr. 6:6-7, 52—H 5:32-33; 6:37). The same individual is probably referred to in I Chr. 9:11; Neh. 11:11, in spite of divergences between the two genealogies. The Chronicler represents him as an ancestor of Ezra the scribe (Ezra 7:3; I Esd. 8:2 KJV; II Esd. 1:2—G 7:3).

2. A priestly house in the postexilic period (Neh. 12:15); perhaps descended from the foregoing, unless the name here is an error for "Meremoth," which occupies the corresponding position in the list of Neh. 12:3.

B. T. Dahlberg

MERAN mĭr'ăn. KJV form of Merran.

MERARI mĭ râr'ĭ [מררי, *probably* bitterness, gall, *from* מרר, be bitter; *cf.* Arab. *mirratun;* LXX Μεραρι]. **1.** Third son of Levi, and younger brother of Gershon and Kohath (Gen. 46:11; Exod. 6:16; Num. 3:17; I Chr. 6:1—H 5:27; 6:16—H 6:1; 23:6). Through his sons, Mahli and Mushi (Exod. 6:19; Num. 3:20; I Chr. 6:19—H 6:4; 23:21; 24:26), were descended the Merarites.

2. The father of Judith (Jth. 8:1; 16:7—G 16:6).

L. Hicks

MERARITES mĭ râr'īts [בני מררי (*usually*), *twice* משפחות מררי, *once* המררי]. A significant Levitical family, descended from Merari 1. All information about the person and the family comes through either the Priestly writer (*see* Pentateuch § A5) or the Chronicler (*see* Chronicles, I and II, § 4) and falls into the periods of the Exodus and Conquest, the Monarchy, and the Restoration.

1. During the Exodus and Conquest. When the Tabernacle was constructed in the wilderness, the three chief Levitical families—the Gershonites, the Kohathites, and the Merarites—were stationed around it and charged with its care and transit. The Merarites, divided into the families of the Mahlites and the Mushites, numbered 6,200 males from one month upward (Num. 3:33-34), and 3,200 from thirty years old up to fifty (4:42-45). Their station was on the N side of the tabernacle; and their "appointed charge" was the care of the less important items: the frames, bars, pillars, bases of the tabernacle, and their accessories; also the pillars of the court with their bases, pegs, and cords (3:35*b*-37; cf. 4:29-33). For transporting this equipment they received four wagons and eight oxen (7:8; cf. 10:17).

At the occupation of Palestine the Merarite families were allotted twelve cities from the tribes of Reuben, Gad, and Zebulun, including a "city of refuge" (Josh. 21:7, 34-40; cf. I Chr. 6:63, 77-81—H 6:48, 62-66).

2. During the Monarchy. When David "prepared a place for the ark of God, and pitched a tent for it," he gathered 220 Merarites, under Asaiah as chief (I Chr. 15:6), to bring the ark up into Jerusalem. Then Ethan was appointed to represent them in the cultic music (vss. 17, 19; *see* Musical Instruments § B1*b*). Moreover, certain Merarites served as doorkeepers (26:10, 19). *See* Doorkeeper; Temple, Jerusalem, § A1.

In 725 B.C., when Hezekiah called upon the Levites to purify Judah's cultic practices, Kish and Azariah represented the Merarites (II Chr. 29:12). Similarly, when Josiah undertook to repair the temple in 621, the Merarites Jahath and Obadiah were among the supervising Levites (34:12).

3. After the Exile. In the postexilic period Sherebiah, of the Mahlite family, and other Merarites assisted Ezra as temple ministers (Ezra 8:18-19; cf. I Esd. 8:47-48—G 8:46-47). *See* Ezra and Nehemiah, Books of, § 3*d*.

L. Hicks

MERATHAIM mĕr'ə thā'əm [מרתים] (Jer. 50:21). A region in S Babylonia, near the mouth of the Tigris and Euphrates, perhaps the *nār mārratu* of the inscriptions. Here it is used as a play on the word "to be rebellious" (מרה), in a dual form to accentuate the meaning. Thus Babylon's name is "twofold rebel."

J. Muilenburg

MERCHANT [כנעני, סחר, רכל; ἔμπορος]. The Babylonians, Arameans, Canaanites, Phoenicians, and Greeks were all great merchants. The Israelites were not a great merchant nation in biblical times. The word "Canaanite" (כנען, כנעני) became a popular term for "merchant" or "trader" (Prov. 31:24; Hos. 12:7; etc.). The merchants thus designated were perhaps originally traders only of purple dye and purple dyed wool.

The merchant sometimes went from house to house like a peddler (Neh. 13:16). He visited farmers and made purchases of homespun (Prov. 31:24). The merchants' traveling about is reflected in the Hebrew roots (סחר, רכל, תור), all meaning "go about" or "turn." The Greek ἔμπορος was a traveling merchant (Matt. 13:45), as distinct from a purely local peddler (κάπηλος). The merchant brought his goods to the bazaar and set up shop (Neh. 3:31; 13:19 ff; cf. I Kings 20:34). Markets were very noisy (Matt. 11:16). There were some women merchants.

Merchants traveled far to pick up their merchandise: ivory and gold from Africa, silk and amber from Asia, incense and spices from Arabia and India, lumber from Syria, etc. Khans or caravansaries were established for the merchants on the overland routes. Storehouses are known in the Bible (Gen. 41:49; I Kings 10:28). Jacob's sons traded in Egypt (Gen. 43:11). The greatest expansion of Israel was under Solomon (I Kings 9:26-27; 10:28). During the Exile many Jews became wealthy merchants. They returned rich (Neh. 5:1-13). Merchant princes are mentioned in Isa. 23:8. Merchant guilds helped Nehemiah rebuild the walls of Jerusalem (Neh. 3:8, 31-32).

Many business documents have been found by archaeologists at Mari and Nuzi which illustrate some of the customs of the ancient Semitic merchants. Mosaic law and the Hammurabi Code regulated weights and measures (Deut. 25:14). Seals were often used to ratify deeds. Receipts were often written on ostraca. Ben Sirach warns against cheating (Ecclus. 26:28; 37:12; 42:5). Philo reports on regulations in the Alexandrine markets. After the fall of Jerusalem to the Romans in A.D. 70 some rabbis still supported themselves by merchant activities.

See also TRADE AND COMMERCE; CHAPMAN.

C. U. WOLF

MERCURIUS mər kyŏŏr'ĭ əs. KJV translation of Ἑρμῆς (RSV HERMES 1) in Acts 14:12. Mercurius, in English more frequently called Mercury, was the Latin name (from *merces*, "commerce") for the Olympian god Hermes.

F. W. BEARE

MERCY, MERCIFUL; COMPASSION; PITY. The meaning of "mercy" in the Bible is extremely varied. When applied to God or to Jesus Christ, it can denote an inner feeling of sympathy or love which is expressed outwardly in helping action; it can mean an affection or yearning similar to that of a parent for his child; it can signify simply forgiveness. Generally, however, it denotes the divine love, manifested in saving acts of grace, which God holds for his covenant people. Human mercy, on the other hand, is usually a consideration, manifested in outward works, for the condition and needs of one's fellow men. However, the demands of such consideration are often defined by a communal relationship.

1. Terminology
2. In the OT
   a. God's mercy
   b. Man's mercy
3. In the NT
   a. The mercy of Jesus Christ
   b. God's mercy
   c. Man's mercy

1. Terminology. The vocabulary of mercy in the Bible is rich, and no one word in the original languages can be said to have only one possibility of translation. The most frequently employed verb in the Hebrew is רחם, "to have compassion"; רחמים forms the noun "compassion," and רחום the adjective "compassionate." However, חנן, "to show favor," "to be gracious"; חמל, "to spare," "to have compassion"; and חוס, "to pity," "to look upon with compassion," are often used. חמלה is twice nominally employed, both times of the mercy of Yahweh (Gen. 19:16; Isa. 63:9). The KJV frequently translates חסד "mercy." However, the RSV consistently renders חסד "steadfast love" (*see* LOVE for the meaning of this important biblical term).

In the NT, ἐλεέω, "to have mercy on," is the usual verb; ἔλεος forms the noun "mercy," and ἐλεήμων the adjective "merciful." However, οἰκτείρω, "to pity," "to have compassion on," with its noun, οἰκτιρμός, and the adjective, οἰκτίρμων, are also used, as are σπλαγχνίζομαι, "to be moved with compassion," with its noun, σπλάγχνον, and συμπαθέω, "to sympathize with."

2. In the OT. ***a. God's mercy.*** It has often been pointed out that one Hebrew word for "mercy" or "compassion," רחמים, derives from the stem רחם, meaning "womb," and that its original meaning was brotherly or motherly feeling—i.e., the feeling of those born from the same womb or the love of a mother for her child. Thus Yahweh's mercy has been defined in terms of such familial love, and some OT passages support this reasoning: in Ps. 103:13; Isa. 63:15-16; Jer. 31:20, Yahweh is a father to Israel (cf. Hos. 11); in Isa. 49:15 a mother; in Isa. 54:4-8 a husband (cf. Hos. 1–3). As such, the Lord welcomes his sinful child or wife back to him with overflowing yearning and love and forgiveness.

It is a mistake, however, to define Yahweh's mercy only in terms of such familial affection, more of one to view it solely as an inward feeling. God's mercy in the OT, like his faithfulness, his steadfast love, his righteousness, his judgments (cf. Hos. 2:19), represents his continual regard for the covenant which he has established with his chosen people, Israel (cf. Exod. 33:19; Isa. 63:9). Not once is God's mercy granted to those outside the covenant relationship. Further, although mercy signifies, more than the other terms listed above, an affection or love within the divine person (cf. II Chr. 36:15), it is never described in the OT apart from its concrete manifestation in some outward act by Yahweh within history. It is, in general, a loving act of Yahweh by which he faithfully maintains his covenant relationship with his chosen people.

Thus God's mercy could be manifested in many different ways: in forgiveness, whereby individual or nation was restored to relationship with him (Deut. 13:17; II Sam. 24:14; II Kings 13:23; Pss. 25:6; 40:11; 51:1; 79:8; 103:4; Isa. 54:8; 55:7; Lam. 3:32; Dan. 9:9, 18; Hos. 1:6-7; Joel 2:18; Mic. 7:19; Hab. 3:2; Zech. 1:12, 16); in his deliverance of his chosen ones from their enemies (Neh. 9:27-28; Pss. 25:6; 40:11; 69:16; 79:8; Isa. 30:18; Jer. 42:12); in the fulfilment of his promise (Deut. 13:17; Jer. 33:26); in his gathering of his exiled people and the restoration of them to their land (Deut. 30:3; Isa. 14:1; 49:13; Jer. 12:15; Ezek. 39:25); in his provision for them in the wilderness (Neh. 9:19; Isa. 49:10); in his restoration of them to communion with himself (II Kings 13:23; Hos. 2:19, 23). Whatever the specific act, it was outward proof of the fact that Yahweh, who had chosen Israel and covenanted with her, continued to love her, to provide for her, and to protect her from harm (cf. Exod. 33:19; Isa. 54:10). Yahweh's mercy was his fulfilment of his covenant obligations, not out of duty but out of love.

Israel therefore could appeal to Yahweh's mercy for help in any situation (Pss. 51:1; 57:1; 79:8; 86:16; 123:2; Isa. 33:2; Dan. 9:18), not because she was righteous and not because she herself had any right to do so (cf. Dan. 9:18), but because she had been given the guarantee of God's faithfulness to her in his gift of the covenant. Israel's claim to Yahweh's mercy was wholly dependent on his primary, covenantal initiative. Unless God had first chosen Israel, Israel had no reason to expect anything from God. But because he had so chosen, Israel raised her voice to the Lord, whom she knew in faith to be "merciful and gracious, slow to anger, and abounding in steadfast love" (Exod. 34:6; Neh. 9:17; Pss. 86:15; 103:8; 145:8; Joel 2:13; Jonah 4:2). Indeed, Israel knew that among the good things of the End, when history reached its climax and finish, there would be found the mercy of God (Isa. 14:1; 49:13; 54:7; Jer. 12:15; 33:26; Ezek. 39:25; Zech. 1:16). Mercy became part of the eschatological hope.

There are some passages in the OT in which God's mercy seems to consist merely in a consideration for the conditions and needs of man. These are those in which the Hebrew employs the verb חמל (Job 27:22; Lam. 2:17, 21; 3:43; Zech. 11:6) or חוס (Jer. 13:14; Ezek. 7:4; 5:11; 7:9; 8:18; 9:10; 24:14) in connection with the judgment of Yahweh upon his sinful people. In such cases the Lord is said to have no more pity for his chosen ones, destroying them mercilessly. However, the full meaning of such passages can, again, only be seen in the context of the covenant relationship.

b. Man's mercy. The mercy of man in the OT consists often in a consideration for the condition and needs of his fellow man, although it is usually the absence of such mercy which is noted. Thus the conqueror in warfare rarely shows consideration for the helplessness of the defeated or captive enemy (Deut. 7:2, 16; Jer. 6:23; 21:7), though sometimes the Lord intervenes to inspire mercy for the loser (I Kings 8: 50; II Chr. 30:9; Ps. 106:46; Jer. 42:12). There is, too, no judicial pity wasted on the idolater (Deut. 13: 8), the murderer (Deut. 19:13), or the false witness (Deut. 19:21). However, some such as Nehemiah (1:11), Daniel (1:9), and Saul (I Sam. 23:21) find unexpected consideration from those upon whom they are dependent for life or prosperity.

Beyond such manifestations of humanity, or lack of them, there is a structure of communal relationship within the OT which governs the limits and demands of mercy. The closest ties which the Hebrew knew were those of the family. Within the family circle, mercy—help, love, consideration of need—was not only expected; it was a duty. Where a family was, there was mercy. Where mercy was lacking, the familial ties were gone. Thus mercy was to be rendered to the brother (Amos 1:11; Zech. 7:9). Next in importance was the tribe or the community. The neighbor and the friend were deserving of help and consideration (Job 19:21; Prov. 21:10). And finally there were those who were dependent on the community—the children, the aged, the poor, the fatherless, the widows. These had special claim to mercy, because without communal concern and aid they were helpless and destitute (Ps. 72:13; Ezek. 16:5; cf. Zech. 7:9-10; Exod. 2:6). Thus one of the worst characteristics of the armed conqueror was his lack of consideration for these poor and needy (II Chr. 36: 17; Isa. 13:18; 47:6). Man's mercy in the OT, like God's, is understood in the context of a relationship. And the human relationship then becomes part of the relationship to God. To truly love God, one must also love one's neighbor. Mercy given to man was homage rendered to the Lord.

3. In the NT. *a. The mercy of Jesus Christ.* In the gospels, those who are sick or suffering repeatedly appeal to Jesus for mercy (Matt. 9:27; 15:22; 17:15; 20:30-34; Mark 5:19; 9:22; 10:47; Luke 17:13; 18:38), and such appeals are naturally understood as cries for succor or healing. Thus Jesus' mercy is understood first in this sense. To have mercy—and here the verb ἐλεέω is used—means to render aid.

When describing Jesus' reaction to such need, however, the NT uses the verb σπλαγχνίζομαι, literally "to be moved in one's bowels." The Greek poets from Aeschylus down regarded the bowels as the seat of violent passions such as anger and love, but the Hebrews regarded them as the center of the tenderer affections, especially of kindness, benevolence, and pity. The bowels were for them equivalent to our heart as the seat of compassion. When Jesus was confronted with human need, the NT therefore says he was moved in his bowels—i.e., he had pity and compassion (Matt. 9:36; 14:14; 20:34; 15:32= Mark 8:2; Mark 1:41; 6:34; Luke 7:13). In this sense mercy is an inner feeling. Nevertheless, it is worthy of note that such feeling in Jesus always gave rise to an outward act of succor. His pity led him to heal the blind (Matt. 20:34), to cleanse the leper (Mark 1:41), to teach the ignorant (Mark 6:34), to raise the dead (Luke 7:13), to feed the hungry (Matt. 15:32; Mark 8:2). Jesus willed man, as man, with all his sins and shortcomings, to be whole. His compassion led him to grant man such wholeness.

In the Letter to the Hebrews the mercy of Jesus Christ is thought of as his forgiveness (2:17; 4:6), while twice in the NT it is defined in eschatological terms (II Tim. 1:16, 18; Jude 21). In the latter passages, Christ's mercy consists of the gift of eternal life to true Christians at the time of his return to judgment (cf. I Pet. 1:3).

b. God's mercy. The OT understanding of God's mercy is very often carried over, without alteration, into the NT. Thus God's loving faithfulness to his covenant people is specifically emphasized in the opening chapter of Luke (vss. 50, 54, 72, 78) and in passages such as I Pet. 2:10, which recalls to mind Hos. 2:23. Again, Paul's great argument of Rom. 9 reflects the same Hebraic background, and certainly the OT understanding of mercy is to be seen in the benedictions of Gal. 6:16; I Tim. 1:2; II John 3; Jude 2. Indeed, the NT's use of the term "mercy" is fully comprehended only in the light of the OT (cf. Rom. 15:9), and such verses as Matt. 5:7; Rom. 12:1; Eph.

2:4; Jas. 5:11; I Pet. 1:3, take on new meaning in such light. God's chosen people Israel had become the church, but God's loving faithfulness to them remained the same.

As in the OT, God's mercy could be manifested in many different ways. To the barren Elizabeth it came in the gift of a child in her old age (Luke 1:58), to the ailing Epaphroditus in healing (Phil. 2:27), to the persecutor Saul in forgiveness and a new life (I Tim. 1:13; cf. I Cor. 7:25) and the rigors of the Christian ministry (II Cor. 4:1). Primarily, however, God's mercy was made manifest in his gift of salvation through Jesus Christ (Rom. 9:23; 11:30-32; 12:1; Eph. 2:4). In Christ, God's covenant with his own was given its final, loving, and perfect confirmation, a seal unbreakable by any power (Rom. 8:38-39), a deed and a promise for all eternity. And in this light, too, mercy in the NT must always be understood.

c. Man's mercy. Again the OT understanding of mercy is to be found. The term is used generally to designate a consideration for one's fellow men, manifested in acts of aid and relief (Matt. 18:27; Luke 10:37; 16:24; Rom. 12:8; Phil. 2:1; Col. 3:12; Heb. 10:34; Jas. 3:17; I John 3:17). But there is, especially in the Gospel of Matthew, perhaps the most Hebraic of the gospels, also the thought of the compassion and mercy which one member of the covenant community owes to another (Matt. 9:13; 12:7; 23:23; cf. 5:7). Members of a community, no matter who they be—scribes, Pharisees, tax collectors, sinners—are to give love and aid and comfort to one another. This is their communal obligation. Indeed, this is part and parcel of their faith. As God loves them, they are to love one another. They are to be merciful as God is merciful (Luke 6:36; cf. Matt. 5:7). E. R. ACHTEMEIER

MERCY SEAT [כפרת, *from* כפר, cover; LXX *usually* ἱλαστήριον; Vulg. *propitiatorium; properly,* propitiating thing *or* means of propitiation] (only in P: sixteen times in Exod. 25–31; 35–40; Lev. 16:2, 13-15; Num. 7:89; I Chr. 28:11). A slab of specially refined gold on top of P's ark of the testimony (*see* TABERNACLE), 2½ by 1½ cubits (approximately half yards). It was not a lid or covering to the ark, but the support (thickness unknown) of the two cherubim, which formed one piece with it and the base above, which was the tabernacling PRESENCE (cf. "footstool" in I Chr. 28:2; Pss. 99:5; 132:7). It was sprinkled with blood on the Day of Atonement. The noun is derived from the *Piel,* one of the active tenses in Hebrew, and so the feminine noun is active, "she who wipes out." Hence, like the cognate Arabic *kafarat,* the words mean "propitiation, instrument of propitiation." The Greek is best taken in this sense in Rom. 3:25 (RSV "expiation"). G. HENTON DAVIES

MERED mĭr'ĕd [מרד, rebel] (I Chr. 4:17-18). A Judahite with two wives, one the daughter of "Pharaoh," one a Jewess. Whether "Pharaoh" indicates marriage into Egyptian royalty is uncertain. However, only the Egyptian wife is named.

E. R. ACHTEMEIER

MEREMOTH mĕr'ə mŏth [מרמות; Apoc. Μαρεμώθ]. **1.** A priest who returned with Zerubbabel from the Exile (Neh. 12:3).

2. A priest of the time of Ezra and Nehemiah. His family was at first unable to prove its priestly lineage (Ezra 2:61; as sons of Hakkoz, cf. Neh. 3:4), but was later recognized and allowed to participate in the receipt of the temple vessels (Ezra 8:33), the rebuilding of the wall of Jerusalem (a double assignment; Neh. 3:4, 21), and the covenant renewal (10:5). "Meremoth" should also be read in place of "MERAIOTH" (as the Greek and Syr. versions show) in Neh. 12:15.

3. Son of Bani; a layman in the list of those whom Ezra required to give up their foreign wives (Ezra 10:36). J. M. WARD

MERENPTAH mĕr'ən ptä'. Variant spelling of MER-NE-PTAH.

MERES mĭr'ēz [מרס] (Esth. 1:14). One of the "seven princes of Persia and Media" who ranked next after King Ahasuerus in authority within the kingdom.

Bibliography. L. B. Paton, *Esther,* ICC (1908), pp. 68, 152-53.

MERIBAH mĕr'ə bə [מריבה, *from* ריב, to strive, contend]. The name of two different stations of the Israelites in the wilderness. The word occurs by itself in Exod. 17:7; Ps. 95:8, mentioned with Massah (*see* MASSAH AND MERIBAH). In Num. 20:13; Deut. 33:8 (mentioned with Massah); Pss. 81:7—H 81:8; 106:32 there occurs the expression "waters of Meribah" (מי מריבה; in Ps. 106:32 KJV "waters of strife"). In two of these occurrences (Num. 20:13; Ps. 106:32) the expression refers to the rebellious attitude of the people toward Yahweh. In Deut. 32:51; Ezek. 47:19; 48:28 the phrase used is "the waters of Meribath-Kadesh." According to Deut. 33:8, the faithfulness of the tribe of Levi was tested by Yahweh at Massah-Meribah; and in Ps. 81:7—H 81:8, Yahweh tested the people at the waters of Meribah. In all these cases the reference is to the waters which came from the rock when it was struck by Moses (Exod. 17:1-7; Num. 20:10-13).

The problem of the exact locality in the above two narratives is difficult to resolve. In the former the Israelites are said to be at REPHIDIM, and the rock is at HOREB; while in the latter account, they are in the Wilderness of Zin (*see* ZIN, WILDERNESS OF) in KADESH. The references to the latter locality (Num. 27:12-14; Deut. 32:51; Ezek. 47:19; 48:28) are clear, while the others allude to the experience at Meribah without localizing it more precisely; and still others (Deut. 8:15; Pss. 78:15, 20; 105:41; 114:8; Isa. 48:21) make only an allusion to the waters flowing from the rock. J. L. MIHELIC

MERIBATH-KADESH mĕr'ə băth kā'dĭsh [מריבת קדש]; KJV MERIBAH-KADESH —bə—. Alternate name of KADESH-BARNEA. *See also* MERIBAH.

MERIBBAAL mĕr'ə bāl [מריבעל]. The original name of MEPHIBOSHETH 1. The original form of this name was "Meribaal." Names compounded with "Baal" were not uncommon in the early monarchical period, but after the struggle with the Baal cult in the ninth century B.C., it would seem that "Meribaal" ("man/hero of Baal," or "loved by Baal") was changed into "Meribbaal" ("opponent of Baal" [so Rudolph; cf. Judg. 6:31]), which was subsequently disguised as "Mephibosheth" ("he who scatters shame," or "from the mouth of shame"). Similar mutations are seen in "Jerubbosheth" from "Jerubbaal," in "Ishbosheth" from "Ishbaal," and in "Eliada" from "Baaliada" (MT "Beeliada").

E. R. DALGLISH

MER-NE-PTAH mĕr′nĕp tä′ [Egyp. *mr-n-ptḥ,* the beloved of (the god of Memphis) Ptah]. A pharaoh of the Nineteenth Dynasty (*ca.* 1224-1214 B.C.).

Mer-ne-Ptah is often taken to be the Pharaoh of the Exodus, because his father, Ramses II, is the traditional Pharaoh of the Oppression. There is no specific Egyptian evidence in support of the tradition. Indeed, a poetical composition of Mer-ne-Ptah's fifth year, the "Israel Stele," associates the people Israel with the inhabitants of Canaan, allowing no time for a forty-years' wandering. Fig. MER 40.

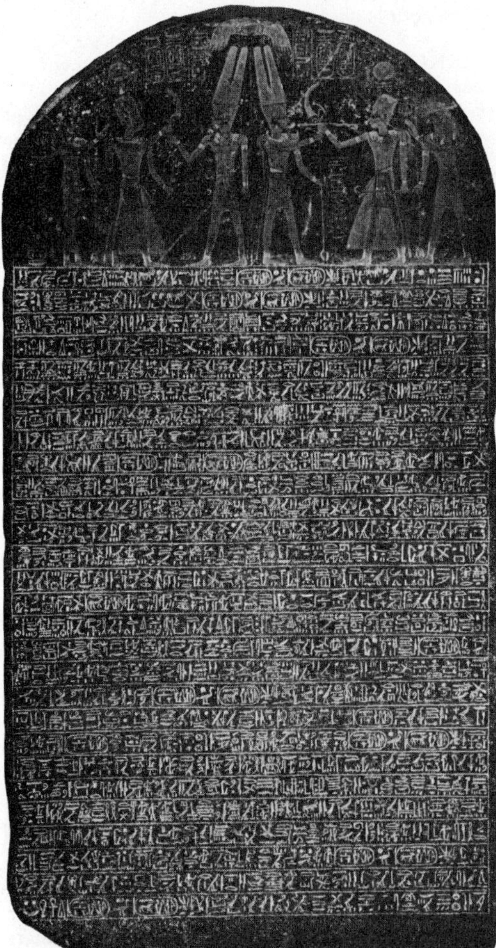

From *Atlas of the Bible* (Thomas Nelson & Sons Limited)

40. The "Israel" stele of Mer-ne-Ptah (1224-1214 B.C.), showing Mut on the extreme left, Horus on the extreme right, and the double figure of Amon giving a sickle-shaped sword to the king; while above Amon's helmet is the sun disk

Mer-ne-Ptah had to defend his NW frontier against an invasion of Libyans, Achaeans, and others. His name may be retained in a Canaanite place name NEPHTOAH.

Bibliography. H. E. Winlock, "The Pharaoh of the Exodus," *Bulletin of the Metropolitan Museum of Art,* XII (1922), 225-34; J. H. Breasted, *Cambridge Ancient History,* II (1924), 164-70.

J. A. WILSON

MERODACH mĕr′ə dăk, mĭ rō′— [מרודך, Heb. *version of* MARDUK]. The name of the god of Babylon, cited in apposition to his title BEL in Jer. 50:2, and used in the theophoric names Merodach-baladan (II Kings 20:12; Isa. 39:1) and Evil-merodach (II Kings 25:27; Jer. 52:31).

MERODACH-BALADAN mĕr′ə dăk băl′ə dən, mĭ-rō′— [מרדך בלאדן (Isa. 39:1), בלאדין (Isa. A 39:1); Akkad. *Marduk-apal-iddin,* Marduk has given a son]; KJV BERODACH-BALADAN bĕr′ə—, bĭ-rō′— [בראדך בלאדן] in II Kings 20:12. Ruler of the Chaldean tribe Bīt-Yakin, and twice king of Babylon (721-710 and 704 B.C.).

Merodach-baladan, who claimed to be of royal descent and mentioned King Erība-Marduk (782-762) of the Eighth Dynasty of Babylon as a forefather, appears first in the inscriptions of Tiglath-pileser III as king of the Sea Country. At that time he, together with the rulers of the other Chaldean tribes, paid homage to the Assyrian king. Under the rule of Sargon II, Merodach-baladan succeeded in making himself king of Babylon, after having obtained powerful military aid from Elam. When Sargon met the Elamite army at Dēr, Merodach-baladan conveniently came too late for the battle, but he enjoyed the consequences of its indecisive outcome. Since Sargon was not able to mount another attack until 710, Merodach-baladan could rule in peace in Babylon. Even when the Assyrian king succeeded in taking Babylon and making himself king there, he was unable to oust Merodach-baladan from his tribal realm in Bīt-Yakin. Merodach-baladan was even reinstated by Sargon. He appears again under Sennacherib, when he ousted Marduk-zākir-šumi, whom the inhabitants of Babylon had made their king in 703. Through his new allies, the Arabs, he tried to incite the Assyrian vassals in the W to rebellion. He sent a letter to this effect to Hezekiah of Judah (II Kings 20:12 ff). Of course, he had—as did all the rebels in Babylonia—to rely on Elam for armed support, although he must have known how unstable and unreliable the royal rule was in that country. This time Merodach-baladan's reign in Babylonia was very short, because Sennacherib reacted immediately and took Babylon, from which Merodach-baladan retreated into his homeland. Relentlessly pursued by the Assyrians, Merodach-baladan had to look for asylum in Elam, which was, of course, granted to him. After a short return to Bīt-Yakin, he had to take refuge in Elam once more, and his throne in Babylon was occupied by Sennacherib's son Ashurnadinshumi. When the intrigues kept up by the Chaldean refugees along the Elamite coast of the Persian Gulf continued to foment rebellions in

S Babylonia, Sennacherib attacked these coastal cities in a sea-borne invasion and destroyed them, without, however, mentioning Merodach-baladan, who must have died before 692; but his son Nabushumishkun was taken prisoner by Sennacherib in the Battle of Halulê.

The tenacious struggle of this tribal chieftain against Assyrian influence in Babylonia, his clever use of Elamite ambitions, and the scope of his political planning must inspire admiration. In spite of his misfortunes, which made him fail where Nabopolassar succeeded because of the collapse of Assyria, he kept returning from exile to fight not only the Assyrian kings but also the large cities of Babylonia, which had no sympathy for the proud tribal lords, who hampered trade and communications and constantly had to be bribed. A. L. Oppenheim

MEROM, WATERS OF mĭr'əm [מי מרום]. A wadi in Upper Galilee, where Joshua defeated a coalition of Canaanites. Several locations for the Waters of Merom have been proposed. From the Middle Ages to recent times, the Waters of Merom were generally identified with Lake Huleh, but the marshy terrain of this area does not satisfy the topography implicit in the military action described in Josh. 11:1-9. Another suggested site is the wadi N of Jebel Marun, located *ca.* ten miles N-NW of Safed. The similarity of the modern name to the LXX Μαρών for Merom and the suitable topography of this district make this identification attractive, but no ancient remains have been reported in this area. The most probable site of Merom is the village of Meiron, situated on the lower slopes of Jebel Jermaq, approximately four miles W-NW of Safed. This site is located on the main E-W route through Upper Galilee; while this route was not so important as the routes in the Valley of Jezreel, it was of considerable local significance, because it made this region accessible. Surface explorations have shown that Meiron was occupied in the LB, Iron I, Hellenistic-Roman, Byzantine, and Islamic periods. Since the Conquest took place at the end of LB, this site admirably fits the archaeological requirements of the Joshua narrative. On the E slopes of the mountain are the remains of a synagogue of the late second or early third century A.D., and in the vicinity of the village are many rock-cut tombs, where according to tradition a number of well-known rabbis, including Hillel, Shammai, and Simeon ben Johai of the first and second centuries A.D., are buried.

Below Meiron and along the S foot of the mountain is a valley known as Wadi Meiron, which carries water from a large perennial spring nearby. This wadi runs eastward and then turns southward, where it becomes known as Wadi el-Tawahin. In its southward course it is joined by another wadi running southward from near Safed, and in this area it is called Wadi 'Amud. Changing course to the SE, the wadi emerges from the mountains, crosses the plain S of Chinnereth, and empties into the Sea of Galilee. It is with the upper reaches of this wadi, in the vicinity of the village of Meiron, that the Waters of Merom are probably to be identified. This area, with its rugged hills and wadies, was well suited to the form of combat which the Israelites used successfully.

Merom first appears in historical records in the Karnak list of towns captured by Thut-mose III in the fifteenth century B.C.; it is number twelve in this list and is spelled *mrm* in Egyptian. Merom is also included among the towns Ramses II claimed to have destroyed in the thirteenth century B.C. In the latter part of that century it was at the Waters of Merom that a confederation of Canaanites, under the leadership of Jabin, king of Hazor, assembled to do battle with Israel, and was put to rout when the Israelites, led by Joshua, attacked suddenly.

Bibliography. C. R. Conder and H. H. Kitchener, *Survey of Western Palestine,* I (1881), 251 ff; W. F. Albright, "New Israelite and Pre-Israelite Sites: The Spring Trip of 1929," *BASOR,* 35 (1929), 8; F.-M. Abel, *Géographie de la Palestine,* I (1933), 492-93; J. B. Pritchard, ed., *ANET* (2nd ed., 1955), pp. 243, 256; D. Baly, *The Geography of the Bible* (1957), pp. 111-14, 191. G. W. Van Beek

MERONOTHITE mĭ rŏn'ə thīt [מרנתי] (I Chr. 27:30; Neh. 3:7). A title given to Jehdeiah and Jadon from Meronoth, near Gibeah. The exact location of Meronoth is unknown.

MEROZ mĭr'ŏz [מרוז] (Judg. 5:23). A town condemned in the Song of Deborah, because of the failure of its inhabitants to participate in the battle against Sisera. The exact location of the town is unknown, although numerous sites have been proposed. One suggested site is Khirbet Marus, situated approximately three miles NW of Hazor, but there is nothing in the poem which can be construed to support a location so far from the scene of battle. Nor is it likely that "Meroz" is a mistake for "Madon" (Josh. 12:19) or "Merom" (11:5). On the other hand, it is possible that "Meroz" is a corrupt reading of "Meron," one element of the double name Shimron-meron (12:20). The latter is perhaps to be identified with Semuniyeh, a mound on the edge of the Valley of Jezreel, N of Megiddo. In any case, Meroz was probably located in or near the Valley of Jezreel.

Bibliography. W. F. Albright, "Earliest Forms of Hebrew Verse," *JPOS,* 2 (1922), 79, 284-85; F.-M. Abel, *Géographie de la Palestine,* II (1938), 385; A. Alt, "Meros," *ZAW,* 58 (1940-41), 244-47. G. W. Van Beek

MERRAN mĕr'ən [Μέρραν] (Bar. 3:23); KJV MERAN. A place name, derived by an error in transliteration from Midian.

MERUTH. KJV Apoc. form of Immer.

MESALOTH mĕs'ə lŏth [Μαισαλωθ, Μεσσαλωθ] (I Macc. 9:2); KJV MASALOTH măs'—. A place in Arbela taken by Bacchides and Alcimus in their march on Judah. Its location is unknown.

MESECH. KJV form of Meshech 1 in Ps. 120:5.

MESHA mē'shə [מישא (*in* 1-2 *below*), משא (*in* 3 *below*)]. **1.** A Benjaminite in Moab (I Chr. 8:9).

2. KJV form of Mareshah in I Chr. 2:42.

E. R. Achtemeier

3. One of the limits of the territory of the Joktanites (Gen. 10:30). It is apparently the same as the Massa of the Ishmaelite group (Gen. 25:14;

Prov. 31:1). The Assyrian records mention a district called Mash, in the region of Jebel Shamar in the N part of Arabia; this is probably the same as the Maciya of the Naqs-i-Rustam inscription of Darius I of Persia. Hence "Mesha" should be vocalized as "Massa" and is to be located on the line between the head of the Gulf of Aqaba and the Persian Gulf.

See also MESHA KING OF MOAB. S. COHEN

MESHA KING OF MOAB mō'ăb [מֵישַׁע (MT), משע (Moabite Stone), salvation *or* succor; *an abbreviation of* Chemosh is salvation(?)]. Ninth-century-B.C. ruler of the Moabites who rebelled against Israel. In II Kings 3:4 he is called a נֹקֵד, or owner of a breed of sheep called in Arabic *naqad*—a breed noted for the quality of its wool (cf. Amos 1:1). In Ugaritic the phrase "chief of the *nqdm*" appears as an honorific title.

During the reign of Omri, MOAB was under Israelite control, and apparently paid an enormous annual tribute to the Israelite king (II Kings 3:4; the MT lacks "annually," though the iterative sense of the Hebrew verb suggests it; cf. Isa. 6:1). According to II Kings 3:5, Mesha rebelled against the overlordship of Israel after the death of Omri's son and successor, Ahab. However, the MOABITE STONE, which Mesha himself erected to commemorate the rebellion, claims that the revolt took place in the middle of the reign of Omri's "son," forty years after Omri had begun his oppression of Moab. The two dates may be reconciled if we take "son" to mean "grandson" (cf. 8:26, where the daughter of Ahab [vs. 18] is called "daughter of Omri"). A date toward the end of the rule of the Omrides is also indicated by the reference to forty years, since the house of Omri retained control of the N kingdom for only thirty-five years.

Mesha began his revolt by seizing the towns of Ataroth, Nebo (Khirbet el-Mekhaiyet), and Jahaz, which was the base of Israel's operations against the Moabites. He then appears to have protected his N frontier by the erection of the fortress towns of Medeba, Beth-diblathen, and Baal-meon. Joram, king of Israel, determined to reconquer the lost territory, sought the aid of Jehoshaphat, king of Judah. The allies, together with Judah's tributary kingdom Edom, invaded Moab from the S, thereby avoiding the strongly fortified N frontier and the danger of an attack in the rear by the Arameans. A counterattack by the Moabites was beaten off, and the allies advanced to Kir-hareseth, which they besieged. After an abortive attempt on the part of Mesha to escape to the king of Aram (II Kings 3:26, reading "Aram" for "Edom"), the Moabite king sacrificed his eldest son to CHEMOSH. The Israelites, frightened of the consequences to themselves of Mesha's act, raised the siege (vss. 6-27; into the account of the invasion has been woven a miracle story from the Elisha cycle).

Mesha also describes himself as a constructor of cities and the builder of a highway, which would seem to indicate that Moab enjoyed a fair amount of prosperity during his reign. However, archaeological exploration indicates that during this period Moabite culture suffered a decline. Probably Moab was unable to recover from the material destruction wrought by the allied invasion.

Bibliography. M. Noth, *Die israelitischen Personennamen* (1928), p. 155. N. Glueck, *Explorations in Eastern Palestine,* I, in *AASOR,* XIV (1933-34), 82; "The Boundaries of Edom," *HUCA,* XI (1936), 150. C. H. Gordon, *Ugaritic Handbook* (1947), p. 67. A. Lods, *Israel* (1953), p. 285. A. D. Tushingham, *Excavations at Dibon in Moab, 1952-1953,* in *BASOR,* no. 133 (Feb., 1954), p. 25. R. W. CORNEY

MESHACH. *See* SHADRACH, MESHACH, ABEDNEGO.

MESHECH mē'shĕk [מֶשֶׁךְ]; KJV MESECH mē'sĕk in Ps. 120:5. **1.** A people and country in Asia Minor; the name occurs among the sons of Japheth (Gen. 10:2; I Chr. 1:5) with Gomer, Javan, Tubal, and others. Merchants from Javan, Tubal, and Meshech trade in copper vessels (Ezek. 27:13). The association with Tubal is most frequent (Ezek. 32:26; 38:2-3; 39:1). The combined evidence fits the identification of Meshech as the Mushki (*Muški*) of Assyrian sources and the Μόσχοι of the Greek tradition, both equally involved with TUBAL (Tabal); GOMER (Cimmerians); and JAVAN (Ionians). Fig. MES 41.

Courtesy of Machteld J. Mellink

41. Sangarios River in the foreground, with two city mounds of Gordion in the distance, and a Phrygian tumulus (burial mound) at the right

The Mushki first appear *ca.* 1100 B.C. in Assyrian texts of Tiglath-pileser I, who defeated five of their kings with twenty thousand men in the land of Kutmuhi E of the Euphrates. This conflict seems the result of migrations by tribes which had been active in the destruction of the Hittite Empire.

The most extensive historical references to Mushki belong to the time of Sargon (722-705). One of his major adversaries in Asia Minor is King Mita of Mushki. The chronology of the various conflicts is as follows: In 717 Pisiris, king of Carchemish, was punished in spite of his alliance with Mita. In 715 Sargon took three cities which Mita had conquered in Que (Cilicia). In 713 Ambaris of Tabal, who had shifted his allegiance from Sargon to Mita, was stripped of his power. The Assyrians then consolidated their border against Mushki by the building of three fortresses, Usi, Usian, and Uargin, sites possibly to be identified S of the Halys River. In 709 the Assyrian governor of Que made a successful raid against Mita and the land of Mushki. He captured two of Mita's fortresses and forced Mita into submission in the form of an offer of services and tribute (Annals 72 ff, 119 ff, 194 ff, 445 ff).

The relations of Mita to King Rusa of Urartu (Ararat) were mostly friendly. Both kings were allies of Ambaris of Tabal against Sargon (Annals 199-200).

The name Mita occurs in a Hittite text of the late thirteenth century as that of a disloyal vassal in the Armenian highlands (KUB XXIII, 72); and Mita, as well as Mushki, may stand for an oriental component in the population of Asia Minor. On the other hand, the eighth-century Mita of Mushki is undoubtedly to be identified with Midas of the Greek tradition. In the Greek tradition Midas is the king of Phrygia who ruled earlier than Gyges of Lydia. He dedicated a throne at Delphi (Herodotus I.14) and died in 696/5 B.C. in the destruction of his empire by the Cimmerians (Eusebius). His name occurs as Mida(s) on the Phrygian rock façade at Yazilikaya (Friedrich 1).

The discrepancy in nomenclature (Mushki, Phrygians) seems to be due to the mixed nature of the population under Midas' rule. The Greeks knew the immigrant Thracian element best, which was Western and near them (Herodotus VII.73). The Assyrians were familiar with the Mushki who were geographically and perhaps originally oriental (these Mushki to the Greeks are a minor tribe, Μόσχοι, associated with Τιβαρηνοί—Tabaleans; Herodotus III. 94; VII.78). Both ethnic elements, Phrygians and Mushki, must have been strongly represented in the kingdom of Mita. Mita's capital was situated in the W at Gordion, well out of reach of the Assyrian troops, but it was destroyed violently by the Cimmerians. Archaeological evidence gathered from royal burials at Gordion confirms the connections with Urartu and Assyria and proves the excellence of Phrygian metallurgy (cf. Ezek. 27:13).

Bibliography. P. Naster, *L'Asie Mineure el l'Assyrie aux VIIIe et VIIe siècles avec Jésus-Christ* (1938), pp. 36 ff, 50 ff; K. Bittel, *Kleinasiatische Studien* (1942), pp. 66-116; O. R. Gurney, "Mita of Pahhuwa," *AAA,* 28 (1948), 32-47; A. Goetze, *Kleinasien* (Kulturgeschichte des alten Orients III.1 (1957), pp. 201-6.

2. An otherwise unknown Aramean tribe (I Chr. 1:17; MASH in the parallel passage, Gen. 10:23).

M. J. MELLINK

MESHELEMIAH mĭ shĕl'ə mī'ə [משלמיה (I Chr. 9:21), משלמיהו (I Chr. 26:1-2, 9), Yahu is recompense]. A Levite, son of Kore; gatekeeper in the sanctuary. In I Chr. 26:14 he is called Shelemiah, which is a shortened form of this name; and the name SHALLUM, another form, may refer to the same individual in I Chr. 9:17, 19, 31; Ezra 2:42.

Bibliography. M. Noth, *Die israelitischen Personennamen* (1928), pp. 31, 145.

B. T. DAHLBERG

MESHEZABEL mĭ shĕz'ə bĕl [משיזבאל, God delivers; *cf.* Aram. שיזב]; KJV MESHEZABEEL —bēl. **1.** Ancestor of one of those who helped repair the wall of Jerusalem under Nehemiah (Neh. 3:4).

2. One of the "chiefs of the people" signatory to the covenant of Ezra (Neh. 10:21).

3. A man of Judah; father of a certain Pethahiah (Neh. 11:24).

B. T. DAHLBERG

MESHILLEMOTH mĭ shĭl'ə mŏth [משלמות]. Alternately: MESHILLEMITH —mĭth (I Chr. 9:12). **1.** A priest, son of Immer (Neh. 11:13). The identification is made on the basis of the genealogies and MS evidence.

2. An Ephraimite who apparently was from a leading family of the tribe (II Chr. 28:12).

E. R. ACHTEMEIER

MESHOBAB mĭ shō'băb [משובב] (I Chr. 4:34). A Simeonite, a prince, who with his tribal compatriots found prosperity in a now uncertain region of Judah.

MESHULLAM mĭ shōōl'əm [משלם; Apoc. Μεσολλαμ]; KJV Apoc.: MOSOLLAM mō sŏl'əm; MOSOLLAMON mō sŏl'ə mən; OLAMUS ŏl'ə məs. **1.** Grandfather of Shaphan (II Kings 22:3).

2. One of the sons of Zerubbabel (I Chr. 3:19).

3. A Gadite who dwelt in Bashan (I Chr. 5:13).

4. Son of Elpaal (I Chr. 8:17).

5. The father of Sallu (I Chr. 9:7).

6. Son of Shephatiah (I Chr. 9:8).

7. A member of an important family of priests; son of Zadok, and the father of Hilkiah (I Chr. 9:11). For the history of this family and its connection with the religious life of Israel, *see* ZADOK THE PRIEST.

8. Another priest of the Zadokite family (I Chr. 9:12).

9. A Kohathite, one of the overseers of the temple repairs made during the reign of King Josiah (II Chr. 34:12). For the history of the religious reform in which such repairs resulted, *see* JOSIAH.

10. In Ezra 8:16, the name given to one of the "leading men" whom Ezra sent to procure a Levite to join the company of exiles returning to Jerusalem. He is also mentioned in I Esd. 8:44; 9:14. Assuming that the same individual is meant, it is reported in Ezra 10:15 that he opposed the course of action laid out by Ezra and the company of returned exiles regarding mixed marriages. The reason for such opposition would be clear if we could assume that Meshullam, the son of Bani, mentioned in Ezra 10: 29; I Esd. 9:30, is the same individual mentioned in Ezra 8:16; 10:15: he himself had married a foreign wife and was loath to give her up.

11. Son of Berechiah, and one of those who helped repair the wall of Jerusalem (Neh. 3:4, 30). The marriage of his daughter to Jehohanan is mentioned in Neh. 6:18.

12. Son of Besodeiah, and one of those who helped repair the Old Gate of Jerusalem after the return from exile (Neh. 3:6).

13. One of those who stood at Ezra's left hand during the ceremony of the reading of the Law before the people in the seventh month of the year (Neh. 8:4). The position taken by Meshullam here is reminiscent of the place of honor afforded leading men in the ceremony of the third- and second-century-B.C. synagogues.

14. A priest who set his seal to the covenant made between the people and God after the return from the Exile (Neh. 10:7).

15. A chief of the people, signatory to the covenant made between the people and God after the return from the Exile (Neh. 10:20).

16. Head of a priestly house in the time of the high priest Joiakim (Neh. 12:13).

17. Head of another priestly house in the time of the high priest Joiakim (Neh. 12:16).

18. A gatekeeper who guarded the storehouses of the gates in the days of Joiakim (Neh. 12:25; *see also* MESHELEMIAH).

19. One of those who participated in the procession which was held during the dedication of the rebuilt wall of Jerusalem (Neh. 12:33). According to the text he was a prince in Judah.

E. R. ACHTEMEIER

MESHULLEMETH mĭ shōōl'ə mĕth [משלמת, *from* שלם, restitution (for child lost through death)] (II Kings 21:19). The wife of Manasseh, king of Judah; the mother of Amon.

MESOBAITE. KJV form of MEZOBAITE.

MESOPOTAMIA mĕs'ə pə tā'mĭ ə [ארם נהרים, Aram-naharaim (*see superscription of* Ps. 60—H 60:2); Μεσοποταμία]. Strictly speaking, the land between the Tigris and Euphrates rivers. Politically and culturally, the borders of Mesopotamia varied in the long course of the land's history. At various times, expansion to the E into Elam and Media, and N into what is now Turkish territory, and from the NW into Canaan and Egypt, made of Mesopotamia the most influential common source of both Hebrew and Greek civilizations. The cultural pioneers of Mesopotamia were the Sumerians, who established the foundations of their literate civilization *ca.* 3000 B.C. They and their Semitic successors (the Akkadians) fostered a well-regulated economy with written records under law. Sumer (as S Babylonia is called) lacked mineral resources, and yet Sumerian civilization excelled, from the start, in the arts of metallurgy and stonework. Accordingly, foreign trade was fostered at quite distant points to secure raw materials and to exchange processed goods. Mesopotamian merchants, under royal sponsorship and protection, spread their native traditions of economy, law, and literature. The Mesopotamian contribution was a major part of the legacy that the Hebrews inherited upon settling in Canaan. While the Hebrews transcended this heritage in many ways (notably in religion, literature, and historiography), they fell below its standards in others (notably in economics and law). In Canaan, where the Mesopotamian merchants were the creditors exacting interest from the native debtors, the Hebrews reacted by outlawing interest collected by Hebrews from Hebrews.

The Hebrews were linked repeatedly with Mesopotamia throughout their history. The patriarchs hailed from the HARAN sector of PADDAN-ARAM in the far N (see Gen. 11:31–12:4; 24:10; 28:6 ff). In the time of the judges a Mesopotamian king subjugated Israel (Judg. 3:8). The Ammonites hired Mesopotamian chariots and horsemen in their war against David (I Chr. 19:6; cf. superscription of Ps. 60). During the Divided Monarchy the Assyrians deported many of the Israelites and Judeans to various parts of Mesopotamia; and Nebuchadnezzar of Babylon continued the process. The Exile shifted the center of gravity in Jewish life to Babylonia, where a large part of the OT was written, and where postbiblical Judaism was destined to produce its greatest rabbinic monument: the Babylonian Talmud. There were residents of Mesopotamia at Jerusalem on the day of Pentecost (Acts 2:9). Stephen referred to Abraham's living in Mesopotamia before he lived in Haran (Acts 7:2).

Courtesy of the Oriental Institute, the University of Chicago

42. Gypsum statuette man from Tell Asmar with clean-shaven head and face; Early Dynastic II (early third millennium)

Fig. MES 42.

Bibliography. C. H. Gordon, "Homer and the Bible," *HUCA,* XXVI (1955), 43-108; H. Schmökel, *Keilschriftforschung und alte Geschichte Vorderasiens* (Handbuch der Orientalistik II, 3; 1957).

C. H. GORDON

MESSENGER [מלאך, *from* לאך, send (LXX ἄγγελος); NT ἄγγελος, ἀπόστολος; Apoc. ἄγγελος, πρεσβύτης]. Alternately: ENVOY; ANGEL; KJV AMBASSADOR. One who is sent with a message. He may carry messages of private (Gen. 32:3, 6; Num. 24:12; I Kings 19:2; etc.) or public (Num. 20:14; Deut. 2:26; Judg. 6:35; I Sam. 16:19; II Sam. 2:5; II Kings 16:7; etc.) interest. He may be part of the royal messenger service of ancient kingdoms and so a COURIER. He may proclaim the triumphal entry of a conqueror or some other public decree as a HERALD.

The Hebrew word may be used for a PROPHET sent by God with a message to his people (II Chr. 36:15-16; Isa. 42:19; 44:26; Hag. 1:13). It may refer to the priest (Eccl. 5:6; Mal. 2:7; *see* PRIESTS AND

LEVITES). Such a one will announce the advent of the DAY OF THE LORD (Mal. 3:1). The anger of a king is said to be a messenger of death (Prov. 16:14). The messenger may bring evil news or cause destruction (Ps. 78:49 ["angel"]; Prov. 13:17). In the majority of OT passages this word is used for "ANGEL," the heavenly messenger from God to man.

So in the NT, ἄγγελος is the messenger—i.e., angel—of God. In pagan literature this word is used for the messenger of the gods. But he may be an envoy sent by man to prepare the way (Gen. 32:4 LXX; Jth. 1:11; I Macc. 1:44; Luke 7:24; 9:52). Thus the forerunner of the Messiah is designated a messenger (Matt. 11:10; Mark 1:2; Luke 7:27; cf. Mal. 3:1). Joshua's scouts are so designated (Jas. 2:25).

Also in the NT ἀπόστολος is the delegate, envoy, or AMBASSADOR, and the word is so used of the prophets and the apostles (John 13:16 ["he who is sent"]; II Cor. 8:23; Phil. 2:25; etc.). *See* APOSTLE.

C. U. WOLF

***MESSIAH, JEWISH** mə sī'ə [Μεσσίας, *from* Aram. משיחא = Heb. משיח]. In the biblical final expectation, the designation of the God-appointed king of the end of time; literally, the "anointed one."

In the OT the ruling king of Israel was generally called the "anointed of Yahweh" (*see* KING), as investigation of the terminology (§ 1 *below*) shows. If the name has been transferred to the ideal king of the future (*see* ESCHATOLOGY OF THE OT), then it is to be expected, as a matter of course, that this eschatological hope will exhibit connections with the OT (and ancient Near Eastern) conception of a king, even if not all of its individual features can be traced back to it (*see* § 2 *below*). In the history of the OT expectation of the future (*see* § 3 *below*), as also in the late Jewish eschatology (*see* § 4 *below*), the messianic hope by no means plays a dominant role everywhere, even in those areas where it is verified at all. One is, therefore, not justified in using the concept "messianic" synonymously with the more general concept "eschatological," although for the Christian theology of fulfilment in Christ the messianic expectation naturally dominates all other eschatological expectations. On the other hand, however, in spite of the connections between the messianic expectation and the OT or ancient Near Eastern ideology of a king, one should not as yet apply the concepts "messianic" and "messianism" to the blessings which are expected from the present king, but should reserve them for the expectations of a king which are truly of an eschatological character (i.e., directed toward a new, different kind of future).

1. Terminology
   a. The "anointed one" in the OT
   b. The "anointed one" in the NT and in the late Jewish literature
2. Origin and nature of the Messiah expectation
   a. King and Messiah
   b. Original man and the Messiah
   c. Yahweh and Messiah
3. The messianic expectation in the OT
   a. Gen. 49:10-12; Num. 24:17
   b. Isaiah
   c. Micah
   d. Jeremiah
   e. Ezekiel
   f. Deutero-Isaiah
   g. Haggai and Zechariah
   h. Deutero-Zechariah
4. The messianic expectation in late Judaism
   a. Sources
   b. Person and work of the Messiah

Bibliography

1. Terminology. The expression "the anointed one" was by no means applied only to the figure of the king of the last days. On the contrary, we often find a messianic expectation even when the title of Messiah is lacking or is replaced by another name (e.g., BRANCH; SON OF MAN).

a. The "anointed one" in the OT. The word משיח, "anointed," derived from the verb משח, "to anoint," occurs thirty-nine times in the OT. It designates primarily and in most cases the king of Israel or of Judah who ruled at that time (twenty-nine times; in II Sam. 1:21 the text should be emended); once it is applied to CYRUS of Persia (Isa. 45:1). In postexilic writings it is sometimes applied to the high priest, who has inherited certain functions of the king (Lev. 4:3, 5, 16; 6:22—H 6:15; Dan. 9:25-26; *see* PRIESTS AND LEVITES), and finally, once probably to the patriarchs who were regarded as prophets (Ps. 105: 15=I Chr. 16:22). The basic form of the title "the LORD's anointed" (of Saul: I Sam. 24:6, 10—H 24: 7, 11; 26:9, 11, 16, 23; II Sam. 1:14, 16; of David: II Sam. 19:21—H 19:22; of Zedekiah, the last king of Judah: Lam. 4:20), appears in varied ways, according to the context, as "mine anointed" (of the Davidic king: I Sam. 2:35; Ps. 132:17), "thine anointed" (of the Davidic king: Pss. 84:9—H 84:10; 89:38, 51—H 89:39, 52; 132:10; Hab. 3:13; of Solomon: II Chr. 6:42), "his anointed" (of Saul: I Sam. 12:3, 5; of the king to be designated by Samuel: I Sam. 16:6; of David: II Sam. 22:51=Ps. 18:50—H 18:51; of a king or descendant of David who is not more precisely designated: I Sam. 2:10; Ps. 2:2; 20: 6—H 20:7; 28:8), once also as the "anointed of the God of Jacob" (of David: II Sam. 23:1). These expressions point to the intimate connection between Yahweh and the king. Such a connection is guaranteed by the anointing and finds expression in the inviolability of the king (I Sam. 24; 26; II Sam. 1:14, 16; 19:21—H 19:22) and his endowment with the spirit of Yahweh (I Sam. 16:13). *See* ANOINT.

Although in Lam. 4:20 the anointed one, probably in imitation of the custom of foreign courts, is once extravagantly called the "breath of our nostrils"—i.e., the one who transmits the life-giving power of God—nevertheless, one cannot discern in any of the passages mentioned a specifically messianic meaning of the title. This is also true of Isa. 45:1, where Yahweh addresses Cyrus as "his anointed." While some scholars already see here the *terminus technicus* for the ultimate king of the world—a title which was first commonly used in late Judaism—transferred to the king of the Persians, others correctly regard the expression as a special title of honor, fashioned to express the lofty position of God's chosen instrument.

b. The "anointed one" in the NT and in the late Jewish literature. Only in NT times is there evidence of the "anointed one" (משיח; Aram. משיחא; χριστός) as one of the various designations for the eschatological king. In the NT the Grecized Aramaic form Μεσσίας is found only in John 1:41; 4:25, in both instances followed by the Greek translation; elsewhere the translation is always used (*see* CHRIST). The title is not found in the Apoc. nor in the Mishna (except for Soṭ. 9.15). On the other hand, it is found in the Qumran literature (1QS IX.11; 1QSa II.11 ff; CDC XII.23; XIV.19; XIX.10; XX.1; 4Q Patriarchal Blessings I.3), in individual works of the Pseudep. (Pss. Sol. 17:32; 18:5, 7; Enoch 48:10; 52:4; II Esd. 7:28-29; 12:32; II Bar. 39:7; 40:1; 70:9; 72:2), as well as in old Jewish prayers or in the literature of the Targums and the Talmud.

2. Origin and nature of the Messiah expectation. As a single and subordinate line within the OT eschatology (*see* ESCHATOLOGY OF THE OT) the OT Messiah, like OT eschatology, has no real counterpart in the ancient Near Eastern milieu. Its source must, therefore, be sought within the OT faith. To be sure, many of the concepts which are a part of the picture of the Messiah are also to be found in the intellectual world of the Babylonians, the Egyptians, and other cultures of the Near East. But in these cases they lack the specifically Israelitic projection toward the final goal of history.

The Messiah expectation is, in the first place, linked with the well-developed world of ideas which surrounded the historic Davidic kingship. In addition, however, mythological ideas of an original man as king of paradise also seem to play a part in it. The development of this Messiah expectation is not left to free fancy but is always directly related to the expected full revelation of Yahweh.

a. King and Messiah. The Israelitic kingship (*see* KING) did not attain central significance for religion, as was the case in many ancient Near Eastern nations, because it was established only at a comparatively late date and for entirely secular and political reasons. However, kept under constant criticism by the belief in Yahweh, this institution, thanks to the exceptional rule of DAVID, also won a place for itself in religion and became the foundation for the Messiah expectation. Two points of departure should be observed here: (*a*) The kingdom of David obtained its religious legitimation by the so-called Nathan prophecy (II Sam. 7; cf. 23:1-7). In it the dynasty of David was promised eternal existence (II Sam. 7:16, 29; 23:5; cf. Pss. 89:3-4, 29-37—H 89:4-5, 30-38; 132:11-12), and the son-father relationship with all its blessings (II Sam. 7:14; Ps. 2:7) was promised between any particular king of the house of David and Yahweh. Taking the place of the mythological legitimation found in Egypt or Mesopotamia, is the view of the Davidic kingdom as a new pledge of redemption by Yahweh, within the already-existing Yahweh-Israel COVENANT (II Sam. 7:10-11: "my people Israel"; 23:3*a:* "God of Israel," "Rock of Israel"). As the covenant with Abraham, according to the Yahwist, aims at the goal of redemption (Gen. 12:1-3), so the covenant with David, especially when the great promise had no outlook for adequate fulfilment in the present, was gradually adjusted to an eschatological fulfilment. (*b*) Various forms and phrases of the so-called court style, which served to glorify the king, were taken over from the world surrounding Israel, with its various forms of sacred kingship, perhaps also from the pre-Davidic kingship of Jerusalem (Gen. 14:18; Ps. 110:4; *see* MELCHIZEDEK)—however, in such a way that the actual deification of the king was eliminated by the belief in Yahweh. Especially in the royal PSALMS (Pss. 2; 18; 20; 21; 45; 72; 101; 110; 132) extravagant statements are heaped upon the king. He is Yahweh's adopted son (2:7). He provides for law and justice in the land (72:1-4, 12-14) and secures for his people the blessings of God (72:6-7, 16). He defeats all enemies (21:8-12—H 21:9-13) and will rule forever (21:4—H 21:5; 72:5) over the whole world (2:8; 72:8-11). This kingly ideology in the royal psalms, with its prototypes and parallels in the ancient Orient, must by no means be interpreted yet as messianic eschatological, although, naturally, the fact that the ideal (which was, after all, largely unfulfilled in the present) was transferred again and again, from one king to another, presupposes a certain eschatologically adjusted attitude. However, as soon as the expectations which were cherished in relation to the empirical king were transferred to an eschatological king, it was from this complex of ideas concerning the ideal king that the belief in a Messiah was formally nurtured. Hence it is not surprising that the royal psalms came to be interpreted in later times as thoroughly messianic (Ps. 2 in Acts 4:25 ff; 13:33; Heb. 1:5; 5:5).

b. Original man and the Messiah. In the Messiah expectation of Isaiah and Micah occur features which cannot be traced back directly to the kingly ideal—e.g., the origin of the Messiah in primitive times (Mic. 5:2—H 5:1); his mysterious birth (Isa. 7:14; Mic. 5:3—H 5:2); milk and honey, known elsewhere as food for the gods (Isa. 7:15); the peace of paradise (Isa. 11:6-8). Also Jacob's blessing of Judah, which probably dates from the time of David (Gen. 49:8-12), with its difficult-to-interpret promise of a ruler from Judah (vs. 10; *see* SHILOH; *see also* § 3*a below*), seems to promise the restoration of the conditions of paradise. The unifying element among these scattered traces has been presumed to be the mystical figure of original man or the king of paradise. Motifs based on this figure can also be found elsewhere in the OT (Job 15:7-8; Ezek. 28:12 ff; cf. Ps. 8:5-8—H 8:6-9; *see* PARADISE). It is, therefore, not easy to decide whether we may infer from this the existence of an expectation of a savior, which would be anterior to, and independent of, the Davidic kingship. In any case, the idea of the original man and king of paradise, which in itself does not show any eschatological features, may well have enriched the expectations of a Davidic Messiah by all kinds of features. More evident in late Jewish eschatology are the influences of the oriental-Hellenistic idea of the original man (Anthropos) on the expectation of a SON OF MAN, who must be distinguished from the Messiah.

c. Yahweh and Messiah. In the eschatology of the OT the coming of Yahweh to complete his dominion through judgment and salvation is the central content (*see* ESCHATOLOGY OF THE OT § 1). What is the relation of this to the coming of the Messiah ("comes" in Gen. 49:10; Zech. 9:9; "come forth" in

Isa. 11:1; Mic. 5:2—H 5:1; "be born" in Isa. 7:14; 9:6—H 9:5; "raise up" in Jer. 23:5; "set up" in Ezek. 34:23), who, as a sort of double of Yahweh, will perform all the functions of a ruler (unlimited authority over the nations in Gen. 49:10; Isa. 9:7—H 9:6; Mic. 5:4—H 5:3; Zech. 9:10; judgeship in Isa. 11:3-5; Jer. 23:5; bringer of peace and prosperity in Gen. 49:11-12; Isa. 11:6-9; Jer. 23:6; Mic. 5:4—H 5:3; Zech. 9:10)? What is said of Yahweh in Zech. 2:10 ff—H 2:14 ff is applied to the Messiah-king in Zech. 9:9-10; and very similar phraseology is used here. At first sight the waiting for the special figure of an ultimate king seems to have no proper place alongside the hope for the unlimited dominion of Yahweh. There are also prophetic passages which seem to exclude the reign of any king but Yahweh (Isa. 24:23; Obad. 21; Zeph. 3:15; Zech. 14:9). However, we must understand clearly that in OT expectations of the future the Messiah always plays only a subordinate role. Whenever he is mentioned at all, he is more of a symbol (Gen. 49:11-12; Isa. 7:14 ["God with us"]) and a gift (Isa. 9:6—H 9:5) of the time of salvation ushered in by Yahweh himself (Isa. 9:3-5—H 9:2-4; Jer. 23:1-4; Ezek. 34:20-23; Zech. 9:8). In the OT—different, e.g., from the late Jewish eschatology—the effecting of the change is not really the task of the Messiah. He is the representative and instrument of Yahweh (Jer. 23:5-6; Ezek. 34:23; Mic. 5:4—H 5:3: "in the strength of the LORD, in the majesty of the name of the LORD his God"), bearer of the spirit of Yahweh (Isa. 11:2). As in the figure of the ANGEL of Yahweh (e.g., Gen. 16), which at one time is Yahweh's messenger, at another his double, so we may probably also recognize in the figure of the Messiah the dynamic will of the OT God to reveal himself and to be personally present with his own, without, however, losing his supernatural character or destroying man by his unveiled presence (Exod. 33:20). The problems of NT Christology announce themselves here already.

3. The messianic expectation in the OT. In connection with several passages there is controversy as to whether the text has a messianic significance or not. Frequently, e.g., the re-establishment of the monarchy or a change on the throne is promised although no mention of a real messianic king is made (Jer. 30:21; Ezek. 17:22-24; 21:32; Amos 9:11). In the following, only the unambiguous and the more important texts are to be discussed.

a. Gen. 49:10-12; Num. 24:17. In Jacob's blessing of Judah (Gen. 49:8-12) the supremacy of the tribe of Judah, which was actually historically achieved by the kingship of David, seems to be taken for granted (vss. 8, 10*a*). The promise: "until שילה comes . . . , and to him shall be the obedience of the peoples," clearly goes beyond the condition attained under David ("until . . . comes") and must refer to a new messianic ruler in a new era of paradisaical fruitfulness. Unfortunately, however, the decisive word cannot be interpreted with certainty (*see* SHILOH), so that this ancient messianic promise, which probably still dates from the tenth century, remains quite unclear.

Probably also from the time of David is the second Yahwist prophecy of BALAAM in Num. 24:15-19, with its promise of a warlike king:

> I see him, but not now;
> I behold him, but not nigh:
> a star shall come forth out of Jacob,
> and a scepter [or comet] shall rise out of Israel;
> it shall crush the forehead of Moab,
> and break down all the sons of Sheth.

Since this is probably not a genuine prophecy, but an imitation oracle in honor of David, and since only warlike successes, but no creation of essentially new conditions, are foretold, the passage is not to be regarded as messianic. The question is, however, whether such a *vaticinium ex eventu* existing in a clearly marked form does not permit us to infer older prototypes of genuinely messianic oracles.

b. Isaiah. For a discussion of the difficult Immanuel prophecy in Isa. 7:10-17, *see* IMMANUEL. If the messianic interpretation of the Immanuel symbol is correct, Isaiah, in the political crisis of the so-called Syrian-Ephraimitic War (734/733) predicts for the faithless King Ahaz the impending birth of the Messiah—as a sign of punishment upon Ahaz and Judah, but also as a symbol of salvation for the faithful remnant. In Isa. 9:1-7—H 8:23–9:6; 11:1-9 the messianic expectation is fully developed. The so-called Christmas promise dates from the time between 732 and 722, when the territories mentioned in 9:1—H 8:23 had already become an Assyrian province. Vss. 2-5—H 1-4 laud the impending liberation of these regions, which according to vss. 6-7—H 5-6 would coincide with the crowning of a new (messianic) king of the house of David. The birth or begetting in vs. 6—H 5 is, according to Ps. 2:7, to be regarded as the adoption of the king by Yahweh as he began his reign; then follow the investiture and the conferring of the coronation titles

> Wonderful Counselor, Mighty God,
> Everlasting Father, Prince of Peace,

in which the foundation and program of the eternal messianic reign in justice and peace are defined. The title of king is appropriately avoided, because of the opposition between the Messiah and the empiric kingship. The prophecy in Isa. 11:1-9 begins with the metaphor of the Messiah shoot, which will come forth from the stump of Jesse (vs. 1), the present ruling house of David which is to be destroyed. The Messiah is related to the house of David as the REMNANT (*see also* ESCHATOLOGY OF THE OT § 2*d*) is related to the nation. The new type of messianic ruler (vss. 2-5) is distinguished by the fact that the spirit of Yahweh will abide in him as a permanent force. The relationship of the messianic king to Yahweh is determined by the spirit of acknowledgment (being concerned about the will of God; *see* KNOWLEDGE) and the fear of Yahweh (reverential fear and loving obedience; *see* FEAR § 2*e*); for his subjects he is the just judge, who helps the poor and humble obtain justice and destroys the godless. The description of the ruler is followed by that of his realm (vss. 6-9); it is a paradiselike realm of peace in which animals get along well with one another and men commit no evil.

c. Micah. The expectation of a Messiah in Micah presents strong affinities with that of Isaiah (Mic. 5:2-5*a*—H 5:1-4*a*). The origin and birth of the Messiah are mentioned with mysterious intimations. On the one hand, he is a descendant of David; he does not, however, come from Jerusalem, but constitutes a new beginning from David's kinsmen the Ephrathites (I Sam. 17:12; *see* EPHRATHAH), as whose dwelling place Bethlehem was added. On the other hand, the one "who is to be the ruler in Israel" is also one

> whose origin is from old,
> from ancient days.

Does this refer to the distant old days of Jesse and David, or did ideas of the coming again of the original man have influence here after all? With his mysterious birth the present distress will come to an end:

> Then the rest of his brethren shall return
> to the people of Israel (vs. 3—H 2).

This need not refer to the return of the exiled to their home, so that Micah's prophecy would have to be denied, but may just as well refer to the restoration of the kingdom of David, which had been split up since the death of Solomon and especially since the Assyrian annexations. Vs. 4—H 3 pictures the reign of the Messiah as a representative of Yahweh in his universal kingdom:

> And he shall stand and feed his flock in the strength of the LORD,
> in the majesty of the name of the LORD his God.
> And they shall dwell secure, for now he shall be great
> to the ends of the earth.

Probably vs. 5*a*—H 4*a* in the translation "And he will be LORD of peace" also belongs to it.

d. Jeremiah. In Jeremiah's picture of the future the Messiah expectation is not prominent. The new representative from the line of David in Jer. 23:5-6 is contrasted by the designation "righteous Branch" (probably tying in with Isa. 11:1; later *terminus technicus* for the Messiah; cf. Zech. 3:8; 6:12; *see* BRANCH) and also by the title of honor "Yahweh is our justice" with the present king, Zedekiah, whose name likewise contains the element "justice" (*see* ZEDEKIAH 4). All supernatural wondrous features are lacking in the kingly ideal. As a wise and just king, appointed by Yahweh (the title of king is not avoided here), he provides for the welfare and safety of Israel. The national political hopes have become very modest.

e. Ezekiel. As in Jeremiah, the Messiah image in Ezekiel is rather faint. Passages 17:22-24; 21:25-27 —H 21:30-32 are not productive and can also be applied to a nonmessianic ruler. On the other hand, 34:23-24; 37:22, 24-25, promise that Yahweh, after he himself has brought about the change and has brought the reunited people back to Palestine, will appoint his shepherd, his servant David, over them: "I will set up over them one shepherd, my servant David, and he shall feed them: he shall feed them and be their shepherd. And I, the LORD, will be their God, and my servant David shall be prince [נשיא] among them; I, the LORD, have spoken" (34:23-24). Only a little is said about the blessings derived from the reign of the Messiah. His reign does not extend beyond Israel, aside from the fact that the peoples "shall know that I, the LORD their God, am with them, and that they, the house of Israel, are my people" (34:30; cf. 37:28). It is clear that the Messiah is only *one* gift of the time of salvation, among others; as "servant"—i.e., minister—he is overshadowed completely by Yahweh. In 34:23-24 the title "king" is avoided. Ezekiel uses only the term "prince," which, according to the testimony of the LXX, should probably be used in 37:22, 24, instead of "king." Also to be noted is the eschatological statement in 37:25: "David my servant shall be their prince *for ever,*" which should not be rationalistically turned about by a collective interpretation of "David my servant" to mean an uninterrupted dynasty.

f. Deutero-Isaiah. As in Amos, Zephaniah, and other prophets, we find in Deutero-Isaiah (Isa. 40–55) no expectation of a Messiah. Yahweh himself is the king at the time of salvation (52:7). On the other hand, the prophet has cognizance of various instruments which God uses to achieve his plan of salvation. As in the case of Jeremiah's "Nebuchadnezzar, the king of Babylon, my servant" (Jer. 27:6), so in Deutero-Isaiah the historic person of CYRUS has become the executor of an eschatological mission:

> who says of Cyrus, "He is my shepherd,
> and he shall fulfil all my purpose"
> (44:28).

In 45:1 Yahweh even addresses him as "his anointed." Nevertheless, he is not a messianic king of the end of days (*see* § 1*a above*), since in the case of the earlier prophets Yahweh himself brings about the change before the Messiah begins his reign, while here Cyrus appears merely as the politico-military forerunner of salvation in the service of Yahweh. Even the Suffering Servant of God, with his prophetic and soteriological mission, cannot be regarded as a messianic king, even if he has probably acquired certain kingly features (*see* SERVANT OF THE LORD). He, like the figure of the SON OF MAN, was brought into synthesis with the figure of the Messiah only in NT times or in the person of Jesus.

g. Haggai and Zechariah. Toward the end of the year 520 B.C., Haggai announced to the governor of the community of Jerusalem, who was appointed by the Persians, that Yahweh would bring about a great revolution in the immediate future (Hag. 2:21). The nation's instruments of military power would disappear (vs. 22). "On that day, says the LORD of hosts, I will take you, O Zerubbabel my servant, the son of Shealtiel, says the LORD, and make you like a signet ring; for I have chosen you, says the LORD of hosts" (vs. 23). As "servant" and as "signet ring" —i.e., as God's governor (cf. Jer. 22:24; *see* SIGNET) —the descendant of David, Zerubbabel, will be the messianic ruler of the last days. Here, then, the coming of the Messiah is no longer awaited, but only his enthronement. A similar imminent messianic hope is found with a contemporary of Haggai, the prophet Zechariah. In the passage Zech. 6:9-14 the prophet, according to the presumedly original text, was (in a symbolic act) to crown as the coming Messiah, not the high priest Joshua, but Zerubbabel. The title "BRANCH" (cf. Jer. 23:5) has here already become a messianic name of honor. When the fulfilment of the promise did not materialize, the wording was changed secondarily so that the high priest Joshua was to receive the crown as a sign that the Messiah would come (in the future). The unfulfilled imminent expectation of the Messiah thus became here again the expectation of a future Messiah.

h. Deutero-Zechariah. A last direct evidence of the messianic expectation in the OT is found in the supplement to the book of Zechariah, in the passage which is difficult to date but is probably rather late, Zech. 9:9-10. After the cry of the herald:

> Rejoice greatly, O daughter of Zion!
> Shout aloud, O daughter of Jerusalem!
> Lo, your king comes to you,

the Messiah is pictured as a humble king of peace:

> Triumphant and victorious is he,
> humble and riding on an ass,
> on a colt the foal of an ass.

The ass, originally the royal mount (Gen. 49:11), is now, in contrast to the horse, the symbol for the king's love of peace:

> He [LXX; Hebrew "I"] will cut off the chariot from Ephraim
> and the war horse from Jerusalem;
> and the battle bow shall be cut off,
> and he shall command peace to the nations.

His world-wide dominion is expressed in the traditional formula of Ps. 72:8. The most varied elements of earlier prophetic expectations are here once more combined into an impressive Messiah image.

4. The messianic expectation in late Judaism. From the confusing abundance of views on the coming of an ultimate ruler in the late Jewish period of the first century B.C., we can pick out only a few of the more important points. The penetration of the apocalyptic dualism, with its separation between this life and the life beyond, the present and the coming aeon (*see* APOCALYPTICISM; ESCHATOLOGY OF THE APOCRYPHA AND THE PSEUDEPIGRAPHA), also had a far-reaching influence on the messianic hope. The figure of the "SON OF MAN" (Dan. 7; Enoch 37–71; II Esdras; II Baruch) was, moreover, in accord with the otherworldly, universal tendencies, as that of a pre-existent, heavenly angelic being who, at the end of time, will appear at the side of God as judge of the world. In contrast to this, the Messiah born on earth from the line of David, who in the time of salvation will lead the people of Israel to power and rule them brilliantly, always remained a more mundane nationalistic expectation. But the two conceptions have influenced each other in many ways. In addition to these, however, there also emerge a number of other figures of the final days; mention is made of a Levitic Messiah (Test. Levi 18), a Messiah ben Joseph, a Messiah ben Ephraim. Only the older, more worldly nationalistic expectation of a Davidic Messiah, through the late Jewish literature, will be traced here.

a. Sources. In some works the messianic expectation is lacking completely, as, e.g., in Daniel, in the Apoc. (I and II Maccabees; Tobit; Judith; Baruch; Ecclesiasticus; Wisdom of Solomon), in some of the Pseudep. (Jubilees; Assumption of Moses; Ethiopian Enoch 1–36; Slavonic Enoch), in the Mishna, and in Philo. In other works the idea of the Son of man or a combination of the Messiah and the Son of man is dominant (Enoch 37–71; II Esdras; II Baruch). The most detailed picture of the Davidic king is drawn in Pss. Sol. 17:21 ff; 18:6-9), with considerable use of OT passages. Information on the Messiah doctrine(s) of the Qumran sect (*see* DEAD SEA SCROLLS; ESSENES) is given in some rather obscure passages such as 1QS IX.10-11; 1QSa II.11 ff; CDC XII.23; XIV.19; XIX.10-11; XX.1; cf. also CDC VII.18 ff; 1QSb V.20-29; 1QM V.1; also fragments from 4Q. The Messiah is often mentioned in late Jewish prayers—e.g.: "The Shoot of David do Thou cause to shoot forth speedily" (Eighteen Benedictions). The Targums and Talmudic literature are another main source. Not only the actual messianic prophecies but also other passages are given messianic interpretation—e.g., Gen. 3:15; the bridegroom in the Song of Solomon; in a peculiar reinterpretation, also the servant of God of Isa. 53. Also of some significance for the messianic faith of the masses, finally, were the "false messiahs" about whose rebellions Flavius Josephus tells (cf. Acts 5:36-37). Simon bar Cocheba ("Son of a Star") regarded himself in the Jewish uprising of 132-35 as the "star of Jacob" proclaimed in Num. 24:17, and he was greeted as Messiah by Rabbi Akiba.

b. Person and work of the Messiah. A systematic theory of the Messiah cannot be ascertained from the various sources, with their frequently divergent teachings. A picture which is not yet very far removed from the OT expectations is given in the PSALMS OF SOLOMON. The king and son of David has the task of purging Jerusalem of the heathen and destroying the godless (17:21-25). Then he will establish the realm of holy people; strangers are not admitted (vss. 26-29). The subjugated heathen come from afar to Jerusalem to see her glory and bring back the scattered members of the nation (vss. 30-31). The just, wise, strong, and sinless king depends on God alone; he introduces a blessed era (vss. 32 ff; 18:6-9). Here as also elsewhere (II Esd. 12:31-34; II Bar. 40:1-2) it is clear that the Messiah plays a considerably more active role in the deliverance of Israel and the subjugation of the enemies than in the OT.

Concerning the time of the coming of the Messiah, the most divergent opinions were current. The apocalyptic writers attempted to calculate the duration of the world era; according to others, no one but God knows the day and hour. He will come when the wickedness of the world has reached its peak, when the "messianic woes" (war, pestilence, famine, dissolution of all order) have come. According to certain rabbis, penitence and obedience to the law will hasten his coming, while sin and impenitence delay it; but other authorities deny that the coming of the Messiah depends upon the penitence of Israel. The concept of a forerunner of the Messiah (Elijah, Moses, Enoch, the "prophet") plays an important role. Most widespread was the belief that Elijah would return to prepare Israel for the coming of the Messiah (Mal. 4:5-6—H 3:23-24; Ecclus. 48:10; Luke 4:25; etc.; *see* ELIJAH 1). It was also taught that the Messiah was already present unrecognized, but concealed still because of the sins of Israel.

When the Messiah comes, he will destroy the hostile world power (under the name of Gog and Magog, Rome, Babylon, Edom) and establish on Zion his glorious kingdom, which is essentially limited to Israel. The struggle against the Antimessiah or Antichrist, the resurrection of the dead, and the general last judgment over the good and the wicked do not belong in his sphere of duty. These ideas belong to the more recent, more transcendental and cosmic, universalistically directed line of apocalyptic thought, in which the decisive deeds at the beginning of the new aeon are reserved for God himself or the otherworldly Son of man. Between this new, transcendental expectation and the old, more worldly and nationalistic hope for a messianic kingdom, there exists a real conflict of feeling. A partial adjustment between the two was finally arrived at by thinking of the messianic kingdom as the end of the present aeon. It was to endure for a limited time (forty, four hundred, one thousand, two thousand years are mentioned) and then be followed by the new aeon. At the end of this interval (*see* MILLENNIUM) the Messiah was to die and be resurrected with his own in the new aeon. II Esd. 7:28-29 reads: "My son the Messiah shall be revealed with those who are with him, and those who remain shall rejoice four hundred years. And after these years my son the Messiah shall die, and all who draw human breath" (cf. also II Bar. 30:1; 40:3; 74:2). The rabbis make a distinction between the "days of the Messiah," which belong to the present aeon, and the world of the future.

As a result of extensive messianic interpretation of OT passages in late Judaism, the messianic king could also, from time to time, acquire all kinds of prophetic traits. A Messiah who suffers and dies as a substitute for all men in the NT sense was unknown in Judaism. To be sure, there is evidence for suffering *or* for death of the Messiah, but not for a Messiah who suffers *and* dies. In addition to the already-mentioned view of the dying of the Messiah at the end of the passing world age, it should also be mentioned that—e.g., on the basis of passages such as Zech. 12:10—one could also speak of a dying Messiah ben Joseph. The suffering of the Messiah is connected with his effort in establishing the messianic kingdom; or with the fact that all the just must suffer; or, finally, with the fact that before he reveals himself and is publicly recognized, he must lead a hidden and despised existence. The ideas of Isa. 53 did not affect the Messiah image, although the Servant of God has now and then been considered messianic. In the Targ. of Isa. 53 the text is transformed: "Then shall the glory of all the kingdoms be despised and come to an end; they shall be infirm and sick even as a man of sorrows and as one destined for sicknesses, and as when the presence of the Shekinah was withdrawn from us, they shall be despised and of no account. Then he shall pray on behalf of our transgressions and our iniquities shall be pardoned for his sake, though we were accounted smitten, stricken from before the Lord, and afflicted. But he shall build the sanctuary that was polluted because of our transgressions and given up because of our iniquities; and by his teaching shall his peace be multiplied upon us, and by our devotion to his words our transgressions shall be forgiven us . . . . He was praying, and he was answered, and before he opened his mouth he was accepted; the mighty ones of the peoples shall he deliver up like a lamb to the slaughter, and as a ewe that before her shearers is dumb, and there shall be none before him opening his mouth or speaking a word . . . . And he shall deliver the wicked unto Gehinnam, and those that are rich in possessions which they have obtained by violence unto the death of destruction, that those who commit sin may not be established, nor speak deceits with their mouth." (Vss. 3-5, 7, 9.)[1]

Bibliography. F. Delitzsch, *Messianische Weissagungen in geschichtlicher Folge* (1890). E. Hühn, *Die messianischen Weissagungen des Volkes Israel* (1899). K. Begrich, "Das Messiasbild des Ezechiel," *Zeitschrift für wissenschaftliche Theologie,* XLVII (1904), 433-61. M.-J. Lagrange, *Le messianisme chez les juifs* (1909). E. Sellin, *Die israelitisch-jüdische Heilandserwartung* (1909); "Der Heiland," *Der alttestamentliche Prophetismus* (1912), pp. 167-83. W. Eichrodt, *Die Hoffnung des ewigen Friedens* (1920). E. König, *Die messianischen Weissagungen des AT* (1923). L. Dürr, *Ursprung und Ausbau der israelitisch-jüdischen Heilandserwartung* (1925). G. Hölscher, *Die Ursprünge der jüdischen Eschatologie* (1925). H. Schmidt, *Der Mythus vom wiederkehrenden König im AT* (1925). W. Bousset, "Die Religion des Judentums im spät-hellenistischen Zeitalter," *Handbuch zum NT,* vol. XXI (3rd ed., ed. H. Gressmann; 1926). A. von Gall, βασιλεία τοῦ θεοῦ (1926). H. L. Strack and P. Billerbeck, *Kommentar zum NT aus Talmud und Midrasch,* vols. I-IV (1922-28). H. Gressmann, "Der Messias," *FRLANT,* vol. XLIII (1929). W. Gronkowski, *Le messiasnisme d'Ezéchiel* (1930). G. F. Moore, *Judaism in the First Centuries of the Christian Era to the Age of the Tannaim,* vols. I-III (1927-30). G. von Rad and K. G. Kuhn, βασιλεύς, in G. Kittel, *TWNT,* I (1933), 563-73. P. Volz, *Die Eschatologie der jüdischen Gemeinde im neutestamentlichen Zeitalter* (2nd ed., 1934). E. Sellin, "Der Messias," *Theologie des AT,* II (1936), 128-35. H. W. Wolff, "Herrschaft Jahwes und Messiasgestalt im AT," *ZAW,* LIV (1936), 168-202. W. Staerk, *Soter: Die biblische Erlösererwartung als religionsgeschichtliches Problem,* vols. I-II (1933-38). G. von Rad, "Erwägungen zu den Königspsalmen," *ZAW,* LVIII (1940-41), 216-22. A. H. Edelkoort, *De Christus-verwachting in het Oude Testament* (1941). M. J. Gruenthaner, "The Messianic Concepts of Ezekiel," *Theological Studies,* II (1941), 1-18. G. von Rad, "Das judäische Königsritual," *TLZ,* LXXII (1947), 211-16 (on Isa. 9). H. H. Rowley, *The Relevance of Apocalyptic* (1947). O. Procksch, "Die messianische Hoffnung," *Theologie des AT* (1950), pp. 582-600. C. Steuernagel, "Strukturlinien der Entwicklung der jüdischen Eschatologie," *Festschrift für A. Bertholet* (1950), pp. 479-87. H. Ringgren, "König und Messias," *ZAW,* LXIV (1952), 120-47. H. H. Rowley, "The Suffering Servant and the Davidic Messiah," *The Servant of the Lord and Other Essays on the OT* (1952), pp. 59-88. A. Alt, "Jesaja 8,23–9,6; Befreiungsnacht und Krönungstag," *Kleine Schriften zur Geschichte des Volkes Israel,* II (1953), 206-25. A. Bentzen, *King and Messiah* (1954). L. Cerfaux *et al., L'attente du Messie* (ed. B. Rigaux; 1954). E. Jacob, "Le royaume messianique," *Théologie de l'AT* (1955), pp. 263-75. E. L. Ehrlich, "Ein Beitrag zur Messiaslehre der Qumransekte," *ZAW,* LXVIII (1956), 234-43. S. Mowinckel, *He That Cometh* (trans. G. W. Anderson; 1956), with detailed bibliography. J. Klausner, *The Messianic Idea in Israel* (1956). H. Ringgren, *The Messiah in the OT* (1956). W. Eichrodt, "Die Vollendung des Bundes," *Theologie des AT,* I (5th ed., 1957), 320-41. G. Fohrer, *Messiasfrage und Bibelverständnis* (1957). T. C. Vriezen, "Das Königreich Gottes in der Zukunftserwartung," *Theologie des AT in Grundzügen* (1957), pp. 302-22. A. S. van der Woude, *Die messianischen Vorstellungen der Gemeinde von Qumran* (1957).

E. JENNI

MESSIAH (TITLE FOR JESUS). *See* CHRIST.

MESSOS, APOCALYPSE OF mĕs'əs. A Gnostic work in Coptic, discovered at Chenoboskion in 1946 (*see* APOCRYPHA, NT). It is thought to be one of the five apocalypses which Plotinus is reported by Porphyry to have combatted. This document suggests

[1] J. F. Stenning, ed. and trans., *The Targum of Isaiah* (Oxford: The Clarendon Press, 1949).

that Messos, long an uncertain figure, was neither Moses nor some mystic mediator nor a holy place, but a Gnostic seer or prophet. M. S. Enslin

*METALLURGY. The metals known and used in ancient Palestine were gold, silver, copper, lead, tin, and iron. The art of working gold and copper goes back into remote antiquity and was probably discovered in more than one place independently. Although the earliest metal objects so far discovered are of copper (or of meteoric iron), there are reasons for believing that gold was the first metal to be utilized by man. It occurs in the form of glittering yellow particles which attract attention; unlike copper, it does not require to be smelted from ore, and it is soft enough so that it can be easily worked. Hence it was early used for the making of simple ornaments.

1. The origin of copperworking
2. Tubal-cain
3. Smelting sites in the Arabah
4. Smelting methods
5. The great smelter at Tell el-Kheleifeh
6. Metallurgical centers in Palestine
7. Prophetic references to smelting

Bibliography

1. The origin of copperworking. The discovery that metallic copper can be produced by the simple process of heating malachite ore in a wood or charcoal fire was probably made accidentally when someone built a fire on or against rocks containing malachite. The use of copper does not appear suddenly in Egypt; on the contrary, it is possible to trace a gradual evolution from the simple to the complex in the forms of the copper objects produced. This fact indicates that the art of working copper was an indigenous development in that country and not an importation from outside, although the theory of an Asiatic, more specifically an Anatolian, origin has its advocates (*see bibliography*). However, the presence of ancient copper mines and slag heaps in Anatolia, the Caucasus, and N Iran shows that the metallurgical art was known and practiced in these areas also in ancient times.

The inhabitants of the E side of the Wadi Arabah (*see* Arabah) probably learned the arts of mining and metalworking from the Egyptians. A natural route of transmission is formed by the existence of Egyptian copper mines in Sinai (*see bibliography*). The Hebrews, in turn, seem to have learned these arts from the Transjordanians (*see bibliography*).

2. Tubal-cain. Hebrew tradition associates the beginnings of metallurgy with a figure called Tubal-cain (Gen. 4:22). The unusual compound name and the fact that its bearer is made to be the first worker in two different metals, copper and iron, which, as we know, were introduced at widely different periods of time (*see* Copper; Iron), suggest that we are faced with a telescoping of two different traditions, one of which traced the invention of copperworking (and perhaps ironworking as well) to Cain, and another which traced the introduction of ironworking to Tubal. The Cain of the tradition is almost certainly to be regarded as a personification of the Kenite tribe, or as the eponym of this tribe. Since "Cain" (*qayin*) in Arabic means "smith," it is highly likely that the Kenites were engaged in the exploitation of the copper and iron deposits of the Arabah (*see* Mining) and that they derived their name from their occupation. Associated with the Kenites were the Kenizzites (*see* Kenaz), who, according to I Chr. 4:13-14, lived in the Valley of Smiths (Ge-harashim). It was not until after the Israelites came into contact with the Kenites and Moses had taken a second wife in the person of the daughter of Hobab the Kenite (as is implied by the references to Hobab as Moses' father-in-law in Num. 10:29; Judg. 4:11) that Moses "made a bronze [or rather, copper] serpent, and set it on a pole" (Num. 21:9). The position of the story of this incident in the narrative supports the view that the Israelites learned the art of metalworking from the Kenites.

3. Smelting sites in the Arabah. It is very probable that a metal industry flourished at Feinan (Punon) as early as 2000 b.c. (*see* Mining). But the period of most intense activity was the Iron I Age (1200-900), as is attested by the presence, along the edge of the Arabah, of a considerable number of mining and smelting camps littered with sherds of the Iron I-II periods. Heaps of slag and small smelting furnaces leave no doubt as to the character of the remains. The largest center was at Mene'iyyeh, on the W side of the Arabah and *ca.* twenty-one miles from the head of the Gulf. Khirbet en-Nahas, *ca.* fifty-two miles farther N, on the E side of the wadi, was the center of another important mining and smelting area, which included Khirbet el-Gheweibeh and Khirbet el-Jariyeh.

4. Smelting methods. The ore was probably first broken into small pieces, then placed in the smelting furnace on top of a bed of charcoal. A few of the smelting furnaces are still standing. One at Khirbet el-Jariyeh is roughly circular in form and measures from 8½ to 9½ feet in diameter. Another, of square pattern, measures nearly 9 feet to the side. A furnace at Khirbet en-Nahas exhibits two compartments, one above the other. The fuel employed was charcoal, obtained from the neighboring wooded hills of Mount Seir. There is no evidence of the use of bellows to supply a forced draft. The melted copper would collect in a mass at the bottom of the furnace, from which it would be removed and broken up into chunks for further treatment. The use of such primitive means meant that a good deal of metal was not extracted from the ore, as examination of the slag shows. Furthermore, the copper produced in this way would be rather spongy and would require considerable hammering in order to consolidate it and free it from impurities.

5. The great smelter at Tell el-Kheleifeh. Glueck's excavation, in 1938-40, of Tell el-Kheleifeh at the S end of the Wadi Arabah (*see* Ezion-geber) uncovered the largest copper smelter to be found in the whole of the Arabah or, for that matter, in the whole of the ancient Near East. The archaeological evidence shows that it was built in the tenth century b.c.; hence it seems reasonable to attribute it to Solomon, who, as we know, showed considerable interest in the head of the Gulf of Aqabah (cf. I Kings 9:26-28; 10:22). The smelter, in its earliest form, com-

Courtesy of Nelson Glueck

43. Smelter at Ezion-geber with a double row of flues

prised three large rooms and three smaller ones. The brick walls, which had been *ca.* thirteen feet high, were pierced by two rows of flues. Glueck believes that the lower flues, located *ca.* four feet above the hearth bottom, were designed to permit gases forming in one chamber to pass into the next and preheat its contents. The upper flues, which connected with a system of air channels inside the walls, were intended to supply a draft. The smelter was oriented so that the strong wind which blows almost constantly down the Arabah from the N would enter the upper row of flues, thus making the use of bellows unnecessary. Fig. MET 43.

The smelter stood in the middle of a fortified rectangle against whose inner face was a line of rooms, possibly workshops where copper articles were manufactured. Copper objects found on the site included fishhooks, arrowheads, spear points, fibulae, and fragments of utensils and tools. The presence of some iron objects has suggested that the smelter may have been used occasionally for treating iron ore.

In the course of time the flues and air channels became choked with sand, and some other means of supplying a draft must have been devised. The archaeological evidence indicates that the smelter continued to function, at least intermittently, down to the fifth century B.C. (*see bibliography*). The fact that as late as A.D. 1800 world production of copper amounted to only ten thousand tons is a warning, however, against envisaging a miniature Pittsburgh at the head of the Gulf in biblical times. The exact relationship of the Tell el-Kheleifeh smelter to the smaller, contemporary smelters at Mene'iyyeh and Khirbet en-Nahas is not certain, but it seems probable that at the large smelter the copper was subjected to further heating and refining. The presence of a number of pottery crucibles, each with a capacity of *ca.* fourteen cubic feet, suggests that this was the case. W. F. Albright has suggested that the Phoenician word for such a smelter or refinery was *tarshîsh.*

6. Metallurgical centers. In Palestine itself a number of small smelting furnaces have been discovered in the course of excavation, some of which were used for the treatment of copper and some for the treatment of iron. At Tell Jemmeh, Petrie found four such furnaces (*Gerar* [1928], pp. 14-18); E. Grant found two at Ain Shems (*Rumeileh* [1934], pp. 20, 42, Pl. XII*a*). Others have been discovered at Ai (cf. *RB*, XXXVIII [1929], 96; XLVI [1937], 254) and at Tell Qasile near Tell Aviv (*IEJ*, I [1950], 74-75).

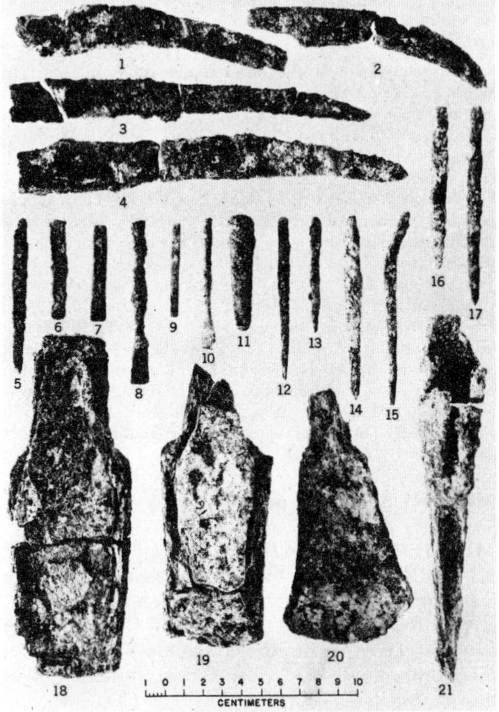

Courtesy of the Oriental Institute, the University of Chicago

44. Metal implements, from Megiddo: (1-4) iron knife blades (sickles?); (5-15) bronze chisels; (16-19) iron chisels; (20) iron axe; (21) bronze goad(?)

All these furnaces date from the Early Iron Age. One of the furnaces at Tell Jemmeh had flues on both sides, which were so aligned as to take advantage of the prevailing westerly wind. Others, no doubt, relied on bellows (Hebrew *mappûaḥ;* cf. Jer. 6:29) or blowpipes. A portable bellows appears in the early-nineteenth-century-B.C. wall painting in the tomb of Khnum-hotep III at Beni-hasan in Upper Egypt, showing a group of Asiatics (Fig. JOS 29). Blowpipes, and open stone molds which could be used for making a variety of tools and weapons at the same time, are well illustrated. Fig. MET 44.

7. Prophetic references to smelting. The spectacle of smiths at work suggested various ideas to the minds of the prophets. Ezekiel sees in the hot smelting furnaces, operated by bellows or blowpipes, the kind of treatment which God will accord wicked Israel: "I will put you in [the furnace] . . . and blow upon you with the fire of my wrath, and you shall be melted in the midst of it" (22:20-21). Isaiah uses the smelting process as a figure of speech for the manner in which God will remove from Zion her base elements:

> [I] will smelt away your dross as with lye
> and remove all your alloy (1:25).

Jeremiah, on the other hand, conceives of God's attempt to purge Israel of dross as futile:

> The bellows blow fiercely,
> the lead is consumed by the fire;
> in vain the refining goes on,
> for the wicked are not removed.

Refuse silver they are called,
for the LORD has rejected them
(6:29-30).

Bibliography. On the Egyptian copper mines in Sinai, see W. M. F. Petrie, *Researches in Sinai* (1906). For the foot-operated bellows used in both ancient Egypt and the modern Sudan, see T. C. Crawhall, "Iron Working in the Sudan," *Man,* XXXIII (1933), 41-43. On the theory of an Anatolian origin for copperworking, see, e.g., A. G. Barrois, *Manuel d'Archéologie Biblique,* I (1939), 365. N. Glueck, "The Excavations of Solomon's Seaport: Ezion-geber" (Report of the Smithsonian Institution; 1941), pp. 453-78. For a reconstruction of the smelter at Tell el-Kheleifeh, see N. Glueck, *The River Jordan* (1946), fig. 75, p. 142. H. Maryon, "Metal Working in the Ancient World," *AJA,* LIII (1949), 93-125. R. J. Forbes, *Metallurgy in Antiquity* (1950). J. Kelso, "Ancient Copper Refining," *BASOR,* 122 (1951), 26-28. J. B. Pritchard, *ANEP* (1954), pp. 40-41. On the Transjordanians' transmission of the art of metalworking, see J. Perrot, "The Excavations at Tell Abu Matar, Near Beer-sheba," *IEJ,* V (1955), 185-89. F. C. Thompson, "The Early Metallurgy of Copper and Bronze," *Man,* LVIII (1958), 1-7. F. V. WINNETT

METERUS. KJV form of BAITERUS.

METHEGH-AMMAH mē'thĕg ăm'ə [מתג האמה]; KJV METHEG-AMMAH. A phrase of uncertain meaning in II Sam. 8:1. The KJV and the RSV interpret it as the name of a place of the Philistines taken by David. The ASV translates "the bridle of the mother city"; the Amer. Trans. "the control of the metropolis." The parallel in I Chr. 18:1 has "Gath and its villages." It is not certain whether I Chronicles has the right reading or only incorporates a later guess. W. F. STINESPRING

METHUSAEL. KJV form of METHUSHAEL.

METHUSELAH mĭ thōō'zə lə [מתושלח, *often* man of the javelin, *but perhaps* man (worshiper) of (the deity) Šelaḥ; *cf.* Old Akkad. *Sumu-Ea,* Old Babylonian *Šumu-Sīn,* Amarna *mutu-ba'al,* Ugar. *mtb'l,* Heb. פנואל, בתואל; Μαθουσάλα]; KJV NT MATHUSALA mə—. Sethite patriarch (Gen. 5:21-22, 25-27; I Chr. 1:3; Luke 3:37); P counterpart to Cainite Methushael.

Bibliography. M. Tsevat, "The Canaanite God Šälaḥ," *Vetus Testamentum,* IV (1954), 41-49. L. HICKS

METHUSHAEL mĭ thōō'shĭ əl [מתושאל, *often* man of God, *as if* Akkad. **mutu-ša-ili, but highly questionable;* LXX Μαθουσαλα] (Gen. 4:18); KJV METHUSAEL —sĭ əl. Cainite patriarch; J counterpart to Methuselah.

MEUNIM mĭ ū'nĭm [מעונים, *plural of the gentilic of* Maon (*Ma'ân*)]; KJV HABITATIONS in I Chr. 4:41; MEHUNIM —hū'— in Ezra 2:50. Alternately: MEUNITES —nīts; KJV AMMONITES ăm'ə-nīts in II Chr. 20:1; MEHUNIM in II Chr. 26:7. An Arab tribe centered about the town of Ma'an, twelve miles SE of Petra. Some of them, with the Ammonites and the Moabites, launched a raid into Judah which got as far as En-gedi before Jehoshaphat (*ca.* 873-849) heard of it. He raised a force to counterattack in the wilderness E of Tekoa at the ascent of ZIZ. The forces of the coalition were routed (II Chr. 20:1-23). The reference to Mount Seir (vss. 22-23) is to the direction from which they came, not to the Edomites, who were not involved in this raid. The homeland of the Meunim lay to the E of the line of Edomite border fortresses protecting the E frontier of Edom from invasion from the desert.

That the Meunim continued to be troublesome is suggested by the note that Uzziah (*ca.* 783-742) had to subdue them (II Chr. 26:7). The implication of the context is that they now lived in S Judah. In the list of returnees from the Exile, Meunim are listed among the Nethinim, the temple servants (Ezra 2:50; Neh. 7:52). During the century or so after Uzziah, it appears that the Meunim, or at least some of them, were assimilated into the Judahite community; possibly, at the outset, they were prisoners of war.

The Meunim are probably not the same as the Mineans (cf. LXX).

"Meunim" in I Chr. 4:41 is probably a scribal error and should be read "their dwellings." In II Chr. 20:1 the RSV reads "Meunites" for Hebrew "Ammonites," in the light of 26:7.

Bibliography. W. F. Albright, "Egypt and the Early History of the Negeb," *JPOS,* 4 (1924), 147-48; W. Rudolf, *Chronikbücher,* HAT, 21 (1955). V. R. GOLD

MEZAHAB mĕz'ə hăb [מי זהב, waters of gold] (Gen. 36:39; I Chr. 1:50). The father of Matred, and the grandfather of Mehetabel, who was the wife of Hadar (Hadad), a king of Edom. Since the name sounds more like a place than a person, it has been plausibly proposed to read מן די זהב for בת מי זהב, making Matred a male resident of the Dizahab mentioned in Deut. 1:1. M. NEWMAN

MEZOBAITE mĭ zō'bĭ īt [מצביה] (I Chr. 11:47); KJV MESOBAITE. The title given to Jaasiel of David's army. The text is dubious and perhaps should read "Mizzobah" (מצבה).

MEZUZAH mə zōō'zə [מזוזה]. The Hebrew word usually translated "doorpost" or "post." It is virtually suppressed in the translation "doors" in Prov. 8:34, and in I Kings 7:5 is usually replaced by the word for "windows" (so LXX, RSV).

The word is used of doorposts of a local sanctuary (Exod. 12:7, 22-23; Deut. 6:9; 11:20), though these references are sometimes taken to mean a dwelling house. A dwelling house is presupposed in Prov. 8:34; Ezek. 43:8. Likewise in Judg. 16:3 the reference is to the city gates. Otherwise the gates of the temple are meant: e.g., Shiloh (I Sam. 1:9), Solomon's temple (I Kings 6:33), Ezekiel's temple (Ezek. 41:21; 43:8; 45:19).

Like the threshold, the doorposts were sacred and were used for blood sprinkling (Exod. 12:7, 22-23, etc.) and for the attachment of passages of scripture (Deut. 6:9; 11:20). The figurative interpretation of these latter passages is doubtful. Probably at first doorposts shared the holiness of the threshold; later the custom grew up of attaching scriptures to the doorposts. Lastly, *Mezuzah* came to mean the container of such scriptures attached to the doorposts.

See also THRESHOLD; PHYLACTERIES.

G. HENTON DAVIES

MIAMIN. KJV form of MIJAMIN.

MIBHAR mĭb'här [מבחר] (I Chr. 11:38). Son of Hagri (KJV Haggeri); included by the Chronicler among the Mighty Men of David known as the "Thirty." However, in the parallel catalogue the words "Mibhar the son of Hagri" are read "of Zobah, Bani the Gadite" (II Sam. 23:36), which, though not free from difficulties, appears to be the original reading. E. R. DALGLISH

MIBSAM mĭb'săm [מבשם]. **1.** A son of Ishmael, and hence the name of an Arabian group (Gen. 25:13; I Chr. 1:29). Its location is unknown.

2. A descendant of Simeon (I Chr. 4:25), the father of Mishma. S. COHEN

MIBZAR mĭb'zär [מבצר, fortification] (Gen. 36:42; I Chr. 1:53). An Edomite clan chief. Eusebius identifies the name with Μαβσαρά in N Edom; others suggest Bozrah (cf. Gen. 36:33; Amos 1:12: בצרה).

MICA mī'kə [מיכא, who is like E(l)] (II Sam. 9:12; I Chr. 9:15; Neh. 10:11—H 10:12; 11:22); KJV MICAH, MICAIAH, MICHA. Alternately: MICAH [מילה] (I Chr. 8:34-35; 9:40-41; 11:17); MICAIAH mĭ kā'yə, mī— [מיליה, who is like Yahu] (Neh. 12: 35). **1.** A son of Mephibosheth, and grandson of Jonathan son of Saul. Mica no doubt shared the fortunes of his father as a recipient of the generosity of David for the sake of Jonathan, as well as the subsequent penalization by David because of the duplicity of Ziba (II Sam. 9:12; cf. 19:24-29). He appears to have become the progenitor of a well-known family in Israel and the father of four sons (I Chr. 8: 34-35; 9:40-41).

2. An Asaphite, son of Zichri (I Chr. 9:15; Zaccur in Neh. 12:35; Zabdi in 11:17); the father of Mattaniah, who was in charge of the songs of thanksgiving in the postexilic worship (Neh. 11:17; 12:8). Mica's descendants include Uzzi, who was the later overseer of the Levites in Jerusalem (11:22), and Zechariah, who was a trumpeter in the thanksgiving processional at the rededication of the walls of Jerusalem in the days of Nehemiah (12:35).

3. One of the Levites who set their seals to the covenant made in the time of Nehemiah (Neh. 10: 11—H 10:12). E. R. DALGLISH

MICAH mī'kə [מיכה, מיכא, *abbreviated forms of* מיכיהו, who is like Yahu?]. **1.** The Ephraimite in the ancient Yahwistic narrative of Judg. 17–18, a postexilic addition to the Deuteronomic edition of the book of Judges. According to the story, Micah's mother has made for him from two hundred pieces of silver a graven image and a molten image, to be set up as a shrine, along with ephod and teraphim, in his house. The priest of the shrine is one of Micah's sons. A better priest is soon found, however, in the person of a young Levite from Bethlehem in Judah, who, after the offer of wages, clothing, board, and room, is installed in Micah's house as a permanent spiritual "father." But five Danites seeking a territory for their tribe learn of the Levite's presence, and upon returning to Ephraim with six hundred armed men, they persuade the Levite to accompany them to Laish, where they ultimately establish their home. With them they take also Micah's ephod and teraphim and graven image. Micah protests this action, but is helpless in the face of superior strength and returns home empty-handed. His graven image becomes a shrine in the city of Dan.

2. A descendant of Reuben (I Chr. 5:5).

3. The son of Meribbaal (*see* MEPHIBOSHETH; I Chr. 8:34-35; 9:40-41). He is called Mica (KJV "Micha") in II Sam. 9:12.

4. A Levite who lived during the last days of David (I Chr. 23:20; 24:24-25).

5. The father of Abdon (II Chr. 34:20). The same person is called Micaiah in the parallel passage, II Kings 22:12. E. R. ACHTEMEIER

*__MICAH THE PROPHET__ [מיכה, *abbreviated form of* מיכיה, Who is like Yah? (Jer. 26:18); LXX Μειχαίας]. A Judean prophet, contemporary of Isaiah (end of eighth century B.C.). The book of Micah is the sixth in the collection of the Twelve.

See map "Palestine: Micah, Nahum, Habakkuk, Zephaniah," under ZEPHANIAH, BOOK OF.

A. Home and date
B. Ministry
  1. The doom of Samaria
  2. Warnings to Judah
  3. The Judean rulers
  4. The prophet's inspiration
  5. The doom of Jerusalem
C. The book
  1. Oracles of messianic hope
  2. Prophetic threats and promises
    a. Yahweh's controversy
    b. Warnings against Samaria
    c. A lament on a corrupt people
    d. A psalm of hope
Bibliography

A. ***HOME AND DATE.*** According to the superscription, the prophet came from a town named Moresheth, or Mareshah (1:1, 14-15; cf. Jer. 26:18), probably MORESHETH-GATH, near the old Philistine town of Gath (LXX κληρονομίας Γεθ; 1:14). It has been identified with Tell el-Menshiyeh, near 'Araq el-Menshiyeh, *ca.* 6½ miles W of Beit Jibrin and 7½ miles SW of Tell ej-Judeideh. The prophet lived, therefore, in a small village of the Shephelah or the low foothills of SW Palestine halfway between Jerusalem and Gaza, near the Judean stronghold of Lachish and close to the Philistine cities. The nature of the prophet's home and its location may help to explain two of the prominent features of his message: (*a*) Micah loved poor farmers and shepherds and felt that these humble country people were the backbone of the nation (3:2-4); (*b*) he observed international affairs in a way which was not exceptional for a dweller of a village placed on the route of foreigner invasions.

A chronological note (1:1) indicates that Micah received the "word of Yahweh" during the reign of Jotham (*ca.* 750-735), Ahaz (*ca.* 735-715), and Hezekiah (*ca.* 715-687). If the editor of the book is right, Micah's activities began a long time before the fall of Samaria (721) and continued for many years, running simultaneously with that of Isaiah in Jerusalem.

Tekoa, where Amos had been reared, lay only

17½ miles E of Moresheth, and the influence of Amos' thoughts upon Micah as he grew into young manhood was probably great (cf. Mic. 2:6 with Amos 2:12; 5:11; 7:10-11). It is almost certain that Micah of the countryside was familiar with the cry for justice that was characteristic of Amos. It is also likely that he had often been in Jerusalem in the days when Isaiah was preaching there. According to Jer. 26, Micah had preached in Jerusalem so forcibly that he, like Isaiah, had influenced Hezekiah and had led him to inaugurate a reform which later inspired the Deuteronomic reform of Josiah (Jer. 26:16-19).

B. *MINISTRY*. 1. The doom of Samaria. It was to Samaria, the capital of the kingdom of Israel, that Micah turned early in his prophetic ministry. All eyes were on Samaria. Thus far it had withstood the shock of the Assyrian invasion of Israel, but Assyria was ruthless and strong, and Israel's future was most uncertain. The prophet was well aware that Samaria could not long hold out against Assyrian attack. Micah sought to awaken the capital to the fact of its imminent destruction:

I will make Samaria a heap [of ruins] in the open country,
 a place for planting vineyards;
and I will pour down her stones into the valley,
 and uncover her foundations (1:6).

The capital city was besieged and captured by Sargon (721 B.C.). The majority of its population (close to thirty thousand people) was taken captive, and in its place were brought in captives from other regions which the Assyrians had mastered (II Kings 17:24-34).

2. Warnings to Judah. Micah took the occasion to appeal to his fellow Judeans, that they might take a lesson from Samaria's collapse. He resorted to symbolic prophecy to awaken his people to the degenerating influences of the fertility rites. Naked and barefoot like a slave, he went at an impulse from Yahweh and lamented—as do the people in their wailings—over the sins of the N and their corrupting influence pouring into Judah:

For this I will lament and wail;
 I will go stripped and naked;
. . . .
For her wound is incurable;
 and it has come to Judah,
 it has reached to the gate of my people
 (1:8-9).

When at length the Assyrians withdrew from invading the SHEPHELAH without having invaded the hill country of Judah, and indeed without having aroused any of the Judean people to serious thought or earnest repentance, Yahweh spoke a message of lament, for his people would soon know the galling experience of a foreign yoke (2:3-5, 11).

Suddenly, however, into the situation came an eschatological vision: Yahweh's people and their king passing on before them in dignity and triumph, and Yahweh at their head (2:12-13).

3. The Judean rulers. The prophet then turned to the aristocracy of Judah. Are they worthy to lead? Have they really any right to be called "rulers of the house of Israel," when they constantly hate what is good and love what is evil (3:1-2*a*)? Are they sensitive to the responsibility of a leadership that truly serves?

With the official prophets of his time Micah dealt sharply, for they gauged the quality of their revelation by what the people paid them. He said to them:

Therefore it shall be night to you, without vision,
 and darkness to you, without divination.
The sun shall go down upon the prophets,
 and the day shall be black over them (3:6).

Tragic indeed is the time when the seer does not see and when he whose calling it is to declare: "Thus saith the LORD," has to cover his lips in embarrassed chagrin, "for there is no answer from God." The channels of divine disclosure are clogged.

4. The prophet's inspiration. Micah has been criticizing those who belong to the same high calling as that to which he belonged. What he saw of the prophets, taken as a whole, was to him a cause of heart-searching as to his own inner spirit. He did not find the task of prophesying easy, and it touched him to the quick to see among his high calling of spokesmanship for God and for human duty, as illumined by the divine spirit, men who were in it for what they could get out of it. The word of God so lived in his own person and made upon him such a powerful demand of utterance that he could not stand to see about him in the office of prophet superficial time-servers. It is in this mood—not in that of self-congratulation—that he gives us now, in contrast, a glimpse of his own soul. He was aware that Yahweh had laid his hand upon him.

As for me, I am filled with power,
 with the Spirit of the LORD,
 and with justice and might,
to declare to Jacob his transgression
 and to Israel his sin (3:8).

Micah was constantly learning as he worked at the searching calling of prophecy. He now was at the point of leaving the quiet countryside of Moresheth-gath to go to Jerusalem, Judah's capital city and spiritual center.

5. The doom of Jerusalem. Did Micah see Isaiah in Jerusalem? Did he hear him speak? Or did Isaiah, brilliant and dedicated Jerusalem spokesman for God, hear his colleague from the countryside of Moresheth-gath? It was clear to Micah that the capital city of Jerusalem was in reality the chief source of licentious and corrupt living. And it was plain to him that as Jerusalem went, so went the nation.

What is the sin of the house of Judah?
 Is it not Jerusalem? (1:5.)

It was most likely his first direct contact with the political and spiritual leaders. The civil officials were criminal profiteers. The judges' hands were itchy for bribes. The priests so manipulated the priestly oracle as to enrich themselves. The prophets had become infected with a materialistic motivation of their sacred calling as the Lord's spokesmen. It is reasonable to believe that 3:9-11*a* was Micah's first utterance in Jerusalem and most likely at the temple.

Micah's country background made all the more clear to him the sense of responsibility that should characterize these heads and rulers, these spiritual guides. Boldly, the prophet predicted the destruction of the capital and even the downfall of the temple (3:12).

C. *THE BOOK.* Like the Isaianic collection, the book which bears the name of Micah appears to be composite. Chs. 1–3 (with the exception of 2:12-13) contain exclusively threats of doom; chs. 4–5 contain promises; 6:1–7:6 contains threats of doom, and 7:7-20 promises. It would seem that the final editor, whose task it was to bring the various oracles of the prophet before a reading public, balanced the two phases of prophecy, oracles of doom and gracious promises.

Contemporary scholars believe that the genuine oracles of Micah are to be found chiefly in the first three chapters of his book, while chs. 4–7 contain two later anthologies (chs. 4–5; 6–7) which may include one or two oracles of the eighth-century prophet.

1. Oracles of messianic hope (chs. 4–5). This booklet of comfort opens with the poem on universal peace (4:1-4) which is found also in Isaiah (2:2-4). It contains the apostrophe to Bethlehem as the birthplace of the Messiah to come (5:2-4). There is no apparent thread connecting the various pieces of this anthology, and many hypotheses have been proposed in attempts to remove the contradictions. The date of one part of the collection is at least later than the Battle of Carchemish (605), since it presents Babylon as the place of exile (4:10). The poems which follow (4:11-13; 5:7-9) suggest the nationalistic eschatology of the Ezekiel school (chs. 38–39).

2. Prophetic threats and promises (chs. 6–7). The last section is constituted by the juxtaposition of four independent poems:

a. Yahweh's controversy (6:1-8). This dramatic dialogue, of high literary quality, raises a central question in the religious life, whether of nations or of individuals; shows the alternative answers that Judah has made to it historically; and then in climactic fashion gives a prophetic answer in one of the noblest utterances of holy scripture. It has been suggestively called the Magna Charta of prophetic religion.

The picturesque setting of the piece is that of a lawsuit between Yahweh, party of the first part, and Judah, party of the second part. The poet chose a time for this utterance when the Judean leaders in great numbers were present in the temple. The opening utterance (6:1*a*) presents the debate as "the word" which Yahweh is speaking to Israel. The debate grew out of the questioning on the part of Israel of Yahweh's real leadership and concern for his people. The prophet, in Yahweh's name, calls Israel to attention. Israel is to plead its case before the Lord (6:1-2).

Yahweh opens the debate, recalling how he has brought Israel out of Egypt, from bondage into freedom, sending before them great leaders—Moses, Aaron, and Miriam, three significant leaders, all from one dedicated family (6:3-4). He recalls that when Israel was actually entering Canaan, the Moabite king Balak commanded Balaam, the Moabite seer, to curse the Israelites as they were in the process of invading Canaan, for he was overcome with fear of them. But Balaam the seer refused to curse them. Said he:

> How can I curse whom God has not cursed?
> How can I denounce whom the LORD has not denounced?
> (Num. 23:8).

The prophet then (Mic. 6:4-5) recalls to Israel, as among the saving acts of the Lord, his redemption of them from Egyptian bondage, his sending before them great leaders—Moses, Aaron, and Miriam—and the refusal of the Moabite seer to curse the invading Israelites. Shittim (vs. 5) was the last camp of the Israelites on the march toward Canaan before they crossed the Jordan River, and Gilgal was the place of their first encampment after they had crossed. "From Shittim to Gilgal" represents the sustaining help of God which made this epochal crossing possible.

The prophet asks at last: When I come before Yahweh to bow myself before God on high, *what shall I bring?* The prophet himself provides an answer:

> He has showed you, O man, what is good;
> and what does Yahweh require of you
> but to do justice, and to love kindness,
> and to walk humbly with your God?
> (vs. 8).

The pathetic accent of the divine questioning (vs. 3) contrasts sharply with the tone which prevails in the rest of the book, and it shows marked affinity with the styles of Hosea, Deuteronomy, and Jeremiah. A deep anxiety prompts the people's cultic uncertainty (vss. 6-7). Reference to human sacrifices (vs. 7*b*) may point to the time of Manasseh (687-642; II Kings 21:1-18), although the reign of Ahaz (735-715 B.C.) should not be excluded (II Kings 16:3). Critical opinion concerning the date and authorship of this poem is divided, and several scholars ascribe it to Micah. The prophetic answer which it offers (vs. 8*b*) summarizes the preaching of Amos (righteousness), Hosea (steadfast love), and Isaiah (humility and faith).

b. Warnings against Samaria (6:9-16). This poem may originate from Micah, since it is directed against the leaders of a corrupt city (vs. 9) and allusions are found in it to Omri and Ahab (vs. 16). Its language, however, points to a later age.

c. A lament on a corrupt people (7:1-6). This dirge may come from Micah. It is written in the first person, and it deplores the absence of a single godly man in the land of Judah.

d. A psalm of hope (7:7-20). The last piece of the book is a song of trust in which the poet experiences his hope in the God of his salvation (vs. 7*b*). Affinities with Habakkuk; Ps. 137; Isa. 40–66 indicate an exilic date.

Bibliography. Commentaries: R. F. Horton, *The Minor Prophets,* The Century Bible (n.d.); J. M. P. Smith *et al., A Critical and Exegetical Commentary on Micah, Zephaniah, Nahum, Habakkuk, Obadiah, and Joel,* ICC (1911); W. Nowack, *Die kleinen Propheten* (1922); E. Sellin, *Das Zwölfprophetenbuch* (1922); G. L. Robinson, *The Twelve Minor Prophets* (1926); G. A. Smith, *The Book of the Twelve Prophets* (1929), vol. I; H. Junker, *Die zwölf kleinen Propheten* (1939); A. Weiser, *Das Buch der zwölf kleinen Propheten,* vol. I (1949); J. Coppens, *Les douze Petits Prophètes: bréviaire du prophétisme* (1950); M. Schumpp, *Das Buch der zwölf Propheten* (1950); A. George, *Michée, Sophonie, Nahum* (1952); J. Marsh, *Amos and Micah* (1954); T. H. Robinson, *Die zwölf kleinen Propheten* (rev. ed., 1954); N. H. Snaith, *Amos, Hosea and Micah* (1956); R. E.

Wolfe, Introduction and Exegesis of Micah, *IB*, VI (1956), 897-949; J. Fichtner, *Obadja, Jona, Micha* (1957); R. F. von Ungern-Sternberg, *Der Rechsstreit Gottes mit seiner Gemeinde: Der Prophet Micha*, Die Botschaft des AT (1958).

Special studies: A. F. Kirkpatrick, *The Doctrine of the Prophets* (1912); J. A. Tait, *The Prophecy of Micah* (1917); K. Budde, "Micah 2 und 3," *ZAW*, XXXVIII (1919), 2-22; J. Jeremias, "Moreseth Gath, die Heimat des Propheten Micah," *PJ* (1923), pp. 42-53; J. Lindblom, *Micah Literarisch untersucht* (1929); W. C. Graham, "Some Suggestions Toward the Interpretation of Micah," *AJSL*, XLVII (1931), 237-58; R. E. Wolfe, "The Editing of the Book of the Twelve," *ZAW*, vol. LIII (1935); E. A. Leslie, *The Prophets Tell Their Own Story* (1939); H. M. Weil, "Le Chapitre II de Michée," *RHR*, CXXI (1940), 146-67; G. W. Anderson, "A Study of Micah 6:1-8," *Scottish Journal of Theology*, IV (1951), 191-97; M. B. Crook, "The Promise in Micah 5," *JBL*, LXX (1951), 313-20; J. P. Hyatt, "On the Meaning and Origin of Micah 6:8," *ATR*, XXXIV (1952), 232-39; J. T. Milik, "Fragments d'un midrash de Michée dans les manuscrits de Qumran," *RB*, LIX (1952), 412-18; L. P. Smith, "The Book of Micah," *Interpretation*, VI (1952), 210-17; A. Alt, "Micha 2:1-5," *Norsk Teologisk Tidsschift*, LVI (1955), 13-23; W. Beyerlin, *Die Kulttraditionen Israels in der Verkündigung des Propheten Micha* (1956); T. Rüsch, *Gnade im Gericht: Die Botschaft des Propheten Micha ausgelegt* (1956); E. Balla, *Die Botschaft der Propheten* (1958).

E. A. LESLIE

MICAIAH mĭ kāy'yə, mī— [מיכיהו, מיכיה, מיכה, who is like Yahu?]; KJV MICHAIAH for all except 3 *below*. Alternately: MICAH mī'kə (II Chr. 34:20); MICA (Neh. 11:17, 22); KJV MICHA in Neh. 11:17, 22. **1.** The mother of Abijah king of Judah; daughter of Uriel of Gibeah (II Chr. 13:2). The name Micaiah appears to be a corruption of MAACAH (10).

2. A prince under the reign of Jehoshaphat of Judah (II Chr. 17:7). He was sent by the king, together with other princes, into the cities of Judah to teach the law of the Lord.

3. Son of Imlah; a prophet during the reign of Ahab of Israel (I Kings 22:8-28; II Chr. 18:7-27).

Ahab, in an attempt to recapture Ramoth-gilead, planned a military attack on the Syrians of Damascus. In consultation of the divine will, Ahab summoned four hundred prophets who prophesied favorably in regard to the king's undertaking. One prophet, Micaiah the son of Imlah, was not called upon, for he was *persona non grata* with Ahab because his prophecies were never favorable to the king. But at the request of Jehoshaphat the king of Judah, who was an ally of Ahab, a messenger was dispatched for Micaiah. The messenger tempted Micaiah to conformism and suggested that he give a favorable answer to the king's inquiry. Micaiah, imitating the four hundred prophets, repeated their favorable oracle, but the king was suspicious of the veracity of the oracle and adjured him to speak the truth. Then the prophet gave a prophecy of doom and announced that he saw the defeated army of Israel as sheep without a shepherd. In support of his minority voice, Micaiah then reported his vision of the court of the Lord. He said he saw the Lord sitting upon his heavenly throne with all the hosts of heaven standing before him. The Lord asked the heavenly host who would volunteer to entice Ahab to attack Ramoth-gilead. One of the spirits then offered himself to be a lying spirit in the mouth of all the prophets of Ahab. Hearing this discreditation of the favorable oracle of the four hundred prophets, Zedekiah, one of the prophets, denounced Micaiah and smote him on the cheek. Finally, Micaiah was put in prison at the command of the king, to await the king's return; but when he was led away to prison, he still prophesied doom to Ahab, who actually died in the battle of Ramoth-gilead.

This short episode, preserved from the life of this ninth-century prophet, is significant in three aspects: One of these is the fact that, in the ninth century B.C., the Lord was pictured as a heavenly king in the midst of his court, surrounded with ministering spirits. This concept is indicative of the monotheistic implications of primitive Yahwism.

The second aspect that is apparent is that the strict monistic outlook of the primitive Yahwism regarded the Lord as the source of all happenings, including the evil ones. The destruction of Ahab is decreed by the Lord and completed by the instrumental role of a spirit of the heavenly court. This "lying spirit" had not yet the distinguished role of the adversary (*see* SATAN), but he is represented as merely one of the spirits.

The third aspect is that the supernatural origin of prophecy in general is maintained, and there is a clear distinction between the inspiration by the "lying spirit" and by the "Spirit of the LORD." This distinction leads to the problem of true and false prophets, which is one of the most difficult questions of the whole OT.

4. The father of Achbor (II Kings 22:12; II Chr. 34:20).

5. A contemporary of Jeremiah, son of Gemariah and grandson of Shaphan. After hearing the words of Jeremiah read by Baruch in the temple on a fast day in the fifth year of Jehoiakim, he reported them to the princes (Jer. 36:11-13).

6. Great-great-grandfather of Zechariah, a priest in the time of Nehemiah (Neh. 11:17, 22; 12:35).

7. One of the priests in the time of Nehemiah (Neh. 12:41). He was in the group of priests who blew the trumpet in the festal procession which dedicated the rebuilt walls of Jerusalem.

Bibliography. J. Pedersen, *Israel, Its Life and Culture*, I-II (1926), 141-45; H. W. Robinson, "The Council of Yahweh," *JTS*, XLV (1944), 151-53.

S. SZIKSZAI

MICE. *See* MOUSE.

MICHA. KJV form of MICAH 3 in II Sam. 9:12 and of Mica (*see* MICAIAH 6) in Neh. 11:17, 22.

MICHAEL mī'kəl [מיכאל, who is like God? Μιχάηλ]. An Asherite, father of one of the men sent by Moses to spy out the promised land (Num. 13:13).

2. A Gadite otherwise unknown to us (I Chr. 5:13).

3. Another Gadite (I Chr. 5:14).

4. One of the forebears of Asaph; a Levitical singer (I Chr. 6:40).

5. One of the sons of Izrahiah of the tribe of Issachar (I Chr. 7:3).

6. A Benjaminite (I Chr. 8:16).

7. One of the men of the tribe of Manasseh who deserted to David at Ziklag (I Chr. 12:20). He had been a "chief of thousands" in Manasseh and was made a commander in David's army.

8. The father of Omri of Issachar (I Chr. 27:18).

9. One of the sons of King Jehoshaphat of Judah (II Chr. 21:2). He was slain by his brother Jehoram upon the latter's ascension to the throne.

10. The father of Zebadiah, one of those who went up from Babylonia with Ezra in the reign of King Artaxerxes (Ezra 8:8). E. R. ACHTEMEIER

11. A celestial prince, or archangel.

A product of the elaborate angelology that developed during the Hellenistic period of Jewish history, Michael is mentioned but three times in the OT and only twice in the NT. References to him are, however, not infrequent in the deuterocanonical scriptures and in later Jewish and Christian writings.

Michael is portrayed as the patron angel of Israel (Dan. 12:1; Jub. 1:29; 2:1; Enoch 20:5; Test. Levi 5:6). He champions God's people against the rival angel of the Persians (Dan. 10:13, 20) and will lead the celestial hosts in the final battle against the forces of evil (12:1), variously represented as Belial, Gog and Magog, or—perhaps under the influence of the Iranian legend of Aži Dahak—the primordial Dragon (Rev. 12:7). In later rabbinic literature, he is depicted analogously as the vindicator of Israel against Edom—i.e., Rome (Exodus Rabbah 18.5). In this capacity, Michael is styled "general" or "chief captain" (II Enoch 22:6; 33:10), and his name is emblazoned on the escutcheon of one of the four divisions ("towers"; cf. Latin *turris*) of the troops of God (1QM IX.14-16). In medieval Christian art he is often furnished with the heraldic device of a banner hung from a cross.

Michael's championship of Israel is, however, not always so bellicose. He appears also as the people's intercessor before God (Test. Dan 6:2; Ascension of Isa. 9:23 [Latin]; cf. also Apocalypse of Paul 42; Pesîqtâ Rabbathî 44), characterized by his charity and forbearance (Enoch 40:9).

In Dan. 12:1 it is said of Michael that when he ultimately rises against the wicked, "your people shall be delivered, every one whose name shall be found written in the book." This bred the notion that he was also a recording angel (Ascension of Isa. 9: 22-23 [Latin]). As the heavenly "librarian," however, he was likewise the custodian of other wondrous scriptures. Thus, he served as the intermediary between God and Moses at the giving of the law on Mount Sinai (Greek Apocalypse of Moses; Jub. 1:27; 2:1; Ascension of Isa. 11:21; Herm. Sim. VIII.3.3; Palestinian Targum, Exod. 24:1; cf. Acts 7:38; Deuteronomy Rabbah 11.10); and he is also the guardian of the magical formulas by which heaven and earth are established (cf. Enoch 60:12). Fragments of an Aramaic work beginning: "Words of the book which Michael rehearsed unto the angels," have been recovered among the Dead Sea scriptures; and a later Hebrew composition, entitled the Book of Elijah, purports to record apocalyptic secrets revealed to the prophet by this angel.

In Jude 9 allusion is made to a dispute between Michael and the devil about the body of Moses. According to Origen and other ancient authorities, this was related in the pseudepigraphic Assumption of Moses, but it is not to be found in the incomplete Latin text of that work that has come down to us. There are, however, sundry indications of such a story in later rabbinic literature (e.g., Deuteronomy Rabbah 10.11; Midrash Peṭîrath Môšeh, in Jellinek, *Bêth Ha-Midrash,* VI, 75; cf. L. Ginzberg, *Legends of the Jews* [1938], VI, 159). Michael similarly acts as a psychopompos in the Testament of Abraham (ch. 19). He opens the paradisal gate to the righteous (Ethiopian Apocalypse of Bar. 9:5; so too in a Sephardic funeral chant, *see bibliography*); and in a Syriac History of the Blessed Virgin, he reveals Mary's body in the clouds. *See bibliography.*

Michael is one of the specially privileged "angels of the presence" who stand beside the throne of God (Enoch 9:1; 40:2; 90:22; Sibylline Oracles 2:15; Palestinian Targum, Deut. 34:6; Targ. Job 25:2). The number of these is variously given, but Michael is usually associated with Gabriel and Raphael. Indeed, it is to be noted that he sometimes discharges functions elsewhere attributed to the former. Thus, in later Arabic tradition, it is Gabriel, not Michael, who reveals the heavenly scripture (i.e., the nuclear Koran) to God's prophet; and, whereas it is usually Gabriel who sounds the Last Trump, in a medieval Jewish midrash (*Ôthôth Ha-Mašîaḥ,* "Signs of the Messiah," in Jellinek, *Bêth Ha-Midrash,* II, 61-62), this role is assigned to Michael.

Bibliography. For the Syriac History of the Blessed Virgin, see W. Wright, *Contributions to the Apocryphal Literature of the NT* (1865), p. 42. For the Sephardic Jewish funeral chant, see T. H. Gaster, trans., *The Holy and the Profane* (1955), p. 146. T. H. GASTER

MICHAH. KJV form of MICAH in I Chr. 23:20; 24:24-25.

MICHAIAH. KJV alternate form of MICAIAH.

MICHAL mī'kəl [מִיכַל, *probably shortened form of* מִיכָאֵל, *from* מִי, כְּ and אֵל, who is like God? *cf.* MICAIAH]. The younger daughter of Saul (I Sam. 14: 49). Saul learned that she loved David and offered her to David, making the bride price a hundred dead Philistines, and hoping in this way to entice David to his death (18:20-25). David, however, was successful in the ordeal, won great popularity, married Michal, and aroused Saul's jealousy still more. Finally, when Saul sent messengers to kill David, Michal contrived his escape (19:11-17). Saul then gave Michal to Paltiel son of Laish (I Sam. 25:44; II Sam. 3:15). Later, when David made his treaty with Abner, one of the terms of the agreement was that Michal should be returned to him. This was done, much to the grief of Paltiel (II Sam. 3:13-16). When David brought the ark to Jerusalem, and performed the wild dancing associated with the Canaanite cult as part of the ceremony, Michal rebuked him. David apparently retaliated by giving her "no child to the day of her death" (6:16-23).

The reference to Michal in most MSS of II Sam. 21:8 is probably an error for Merab (so RSV), Michal's older sister and wife of Adriel.

Bibliography. M. Noth, *Die israelitischen Personennamen* (1928), p. 144. D. HARVEY

MICHEAS mī'kĭ əs. KJV Apoc. form of MICAH.

MICHMASH mĭk'măsh [מִכְמָשׂ, *mikhmāś, mikhmash* (I Sam. 13:2 ff; 14:5, 31; Neh. 11:31; Isa. 10:28); Μαχμάς (I Macc. 9:73), KJV MACHMAS măk'măs]; MICHMAS mĭk'măs [מִכְמָס, *mikhmās,* hidden(?) (Ezra 2:27; Neh. 7:31)]. A city of Benjamin in the mountains *ca.* seven miles NE of Jerusalem.

1. Location. The ancient name is preserved in Mukhmas, a village located *ca.* seven miles NE of Jerusalem on a hill *ca.* two thousand feet above sea

From *Atlas of the Bible* (Thomas Nelson & Sons Limited)

45. In the background lies the desert of Judah, while in the foreground Michmash (1) lies to the left and Geba (2) to the right of the pass between them (3).

level, N of the rugged Wadi es-Suwenit, the narrow pass leading from the Jordan Valley to the hills of Ephraim.* According to I Sam. 14:4, two rocky crags named BOZEZ and SENEH were in the vicinity of Michmash. Fig. MIC 45.

2. History. Michmash first appears in biblical history in connection with the description of the military struggles against the Philistines on the part of Saul and Jonathan (I Sam. 13–14). This description is based, for the most part, on an intimate knowledge of the geographical features of the Michmash area, and the terrain was an important factor in the military strategy. The distribution of three thousand men between Michmash, where Saul was in charge, and GEBA under Jonathan (I Sam. 13:2-3; most commentators read "Geba" in both verses), placed the Israelites in a mountain area where the superiority of Philistine numbers and equipment would be at a disadvantage. Control of Michmash and the pass would keep open lines of communication between Saul's forces in the Jordan Valley and those in the hills of Ephraim.

The record of the conflict which follows seems to be based upon a conflation of early and late sources, thus explaining the occupation of Michmash by the Philistines without a clear statement of Saul's withdrawal from the place, although it may be implied in vs. 4. Philistine strength in Michmash is probably greatly exaggerated in vs. 5, which is usually taken to be from a late source. The figure of three thousand chariots (see LXX, Syr.) in vs. 5 seems large in view of the fact that in more favorable terrain the Egyptians operated with six hundred chariots (Exod. 14:7) and the Canaanites with nine hundred (Judg. 4:3). The complete rout of the Philistines came when Jonathan, with his armor-bearer, succeeded in scaling a mountain at Michmash and killing the sentries, and Saul's forces were quick to take advantage of the panic which ensued in the Philistine camp (I Sam. 14:5, 31).

Isaiah, in a poem which envisages an attack on Jerusalem, pictures the enemy storing his baggage at Michmash (Isa. 10:28). The attacker is most likely Assyria or a Syro-Ephraimite army. Isaiah's authorship of the poem is doubted by some on the basis of stylistic considerations. The usual interpretation is that heavy equipment would be left at Michmash to make the force mobile enough to ascend the mountains to Jerusalem. Some scholars have doubted that any force would make an attack on Jerusalem from this direction. Michmash appears in a list of Israelites returning from Babylonia. In Ezra 2:27; Neh. 7:31 the men of Michmash (Michmas) are numbered as 122. The occupation of the city by returning exiles is further attested in Neh. 11:31-36 by a reference to it, along with Aija, Bethel, Anathoth, and other nearby places, in the territory of Benjamin at the time of Nehemiah.

In the Maccabean period Michmash was the place of Jonathan's residence following the withdrawal of Bacchides to Antioch (I Macc. 9:73). The statement that he began to judge the people there has been taken as indicating that Jonathan set up in Michmash a government in opposition to that in Jerusalem, which had come under the influence of the Hellenistic forces from Syria. See also Jos. Antiq. XIII.i.6.

Bibliography. W. F. Albright, "The Assyrian March on Jerusalem," *AASOR,* IV (1922-23), 134-40. W. L. REED

MICHMETHATH mĭk'mə thăth [מִכְמְתָת] (Josh. 16:6; 17:7); KJV MICHMETHAH —thə. A place said to be near Shechem and on the border of Ephraim and Manasseh. A problem exists by reason of the statements in Josh. 16:6 that Michmethath is on the N boundary of Ephraim; and in 17:7 that Michmethath is E of Shechem and on a border of Manasseh, which, if E of Shechem, would not be contiguous with the N boundary of Ephraim. It is probable that the text has been disturbed and that the editors were uncertain as to the location of the place. Two possible sites for Michmethath have been proposed: Khirbet Makhneh el-Foqa, located on a hill *ca.* five miles SE of Shechem and W of the road from Jerusalem; and Khirbet Juleijil, E of Shechem.

Bibliography. W. F. Albright, "The Northern Boundary of Benjamin," *AASOR,* IV (1922-23), 150-55. W. L. REED

MICHRI mĭk'rī [מִכְרִי] (I Chr. 9:8). A descendant of Benjamin; otherwise unknown to us.

MICHTAM. KJV form of MIKTAM.

MIDDIN mĭd'ən [מִדִּין] (Josh. 15:61). A village of Judah in the "wilderness" district. The LXX reading, Μαδών (Madon), is probably correct. It is identified with modern Khirbet Abu Tabaq in el-Buqe'ah (the Valley of Achor).

Bibliography. F. M. Cross, Jr., and J. T. Milik, "Explorations in the Judaean Buqê'ah," *BASOR,* 142 (1956), 5-17; F. M. Cross, Jr., "A Footnote to Biblical History," *BA,* 19 (1956), 12-17. V. R. GOLD

MIDIAN mĭd′ĭ ən [מדין]; **MIDIANITE(S)** mĭd′ĭ ə nīts [מדינים (Gen. 37:28; Num. 25:17; 31:2); מדיני (Num. 10:29)].

1. Origin and territory
2. The "land of Midian"
3. Earliest history
4. Theory of a Midianite Sinai-Horeb
5. War with Midian in the Plains of Moab
6. The Midianite invasion
7. Later history of Midian

Bibliography

1. Origin and territory. According to biblical tradition, Midian was one of the sons of KETURAH, Abraham's third wife (Gen. 25:2; I Chr. 1:32). Through their eponymous ancestor, the Midianites are thus acknowledged to have traced their origin from the father of the Hebrews, thereby tacitly implying kinship with the Hebrews themselves. Geographically, however, the territories assigned to Midian and Israel were clearly separate, for while Abraham was still living, he is said to have sent away the "sons of his concubines," among whom Midian was reckoned, "eastward to the east country" (Gen. 25:6); and at the beginning of the eleventh century B.C. we find the Midianites still associated with the People of the East (*see* EAST, PEOPLE OF THE; Judg. 6:3, 33; 7:12)—i.e., in the Syro-Arabian Desert. The territory over which the nomadic Midianites wandered, however, never seems to have had clearly demarked boundaries. Moreover, its limits appear to have fluctuated considerably at different periods.

2. The "land of Midian." The "land of Midian" appears in the early thirteenth century B.C. as a definite geographical entity (Exod. 2:15). Most scholars are agreed in defining this as a tract of land in NW Arabia on the E shore of the Gulf of 'Aqabah. In this same region Ptolemy (*Geography* VI.7, 27) cites a city which he calls Μοδίανα, located directly on the coast, and another Μαδίανα, situated farther inland, approximately twenty-six miles from the Gulf (modern el-Bed'). The latter would seem to correspond with the Μαδιάμ of Eusebius (*Onomastica* 136.31, ed. Lagarde) and the Μαδιάν of Josephus (Antiq. II.xi.1), as well as with the Madyan of the Arab writers. The nomadism of the Midianites, however, is clearly attested in the OT, where we find them radiating from 'Aqabah to penetrate W into Sinai (Num. 10:29), N into Moab (Gen. 36:35; I Chr. 1:46) and the reaches of the Syrian Desert E of Moab and Ammon (Judg. 7:25; 8:18-19), and finally into the E Jordan Valley (Num. 25:6-7; 31:2-3; Josh. 13:21) and Canaan (Judg. 6:1-6, 33; 7:1).

3. Earliest history. Before the thirteenth century B.C., little is known of the Midianites. They first emerge in the biblical story of Joseph, where they are characterized as "traders" (סחרים), who sold Joseph to the Ishmaelites "for twenty shekels of silver" (Gen. 37:28). The interpretation of the narrative at this point is difficult, and many scholars consider the account to be conflate, representing the skilful fusing of two traditions, one which told of the selling of Joseph to a caravan of ISHMAELITES and another which related the "kidnaping" of Joseph by Midianites. It is not impossible that in the original tradition the Ishmaelites and Midianites were identified through the stylistic device of parallelism (cf. Judg. 8:24), a literary phenomenon well attested in written sources from the second millennium B.C. (*see* JOSEPH SON OF JACOB § 2*d*). It must be remembered, however, that the Midianites and Ishmaelites are usually distinguished in the OT, in respect to both genealogical relationships and sphere of operation.

Moses, prior to the Exodus, had fled to the "land of Midian" (Exod. 2:15), where he was befriended by Jethro, priest of Midian. According to a persistent Israelite tradition, Moses' father-in-law was a Kenite (Judg. 1:16; 4:11). This has led many scholars to maintain that the metalworking KENITES were actually a clan of Midianites, or at least closely associated with them. Archaeological investigation has shown that in the Early Iron Age, Midian was much richer in copper ores than either Sinai or Edom. It is not unexpected that the Midianites would take advantage of this source of economic prosperity. Midian at this time was occupied by seminomadic tribes linked by ties of commerce and industry with Egypt and Canaan. The Midianites (or Kenites) among whom Moses lived are also described as a pastoral people, tending their flocks, and thus were at least partly nomadic in character. In addition, they were well acquainted with the trade routes leading from the S to the N (cf. Exod. 18:5; Num. 10:29-31). All this forms a striking contrast to the picture of camel nomads, as the Midianites are portrayed at the beginning of the eleventh century. *See* § 6 *below.*

4. Theory of a Midianite Sinai-Horeb. While Moses was still living in the land of Midian, he made a journey "to the west side of the wilderness [אחר המדבר], and came to Horeb, the mountain of God," where he experienced a divine theophany (Exod. 3:1-2). It is not specified that Mount Horeb was located in the land of Midian, but a number of scholars have so interpreted it, pointing out that some of the most ancient biblical traditions referring to the desert regions in which the Hebrews wandered (cf. Deut. 33:2; Judg. 5:4-5; Hab. 3:3) call for a site which more appropriately fits the land of Midian than the more traditional Sinai Peninsula (*see* SINAI, MOUNT). However, a careful study of the relevant biblical passages points to an area, not in the land of Midian proper, but farther N in the Arabah W of Edom (but cf. Hab. 3:7).

5. War with Midian in the Plains of Moab. The "elders of Midian" near the end of the Exodus period became associated with the Moabites in a venture to expel the Israelites from the Plains of Moab, the territory E of the Jordan opposite Jericho (Num. 22:4, 7). The precise relationship between Moab and Midian at this time is not known, but apparently some Midianite clans had been permitted to live peacefully in the land of Moab. Following the Israelite conquest of the Amorites, the Midianites and Israelites seem to have had conflicting interests (Num. 22:4). Thus the king of Moab secured Midian's co-operation in hiring the N Syrian diviner BALAAM, whose effort to impair the Israelites by magical means eventually came to naught. While the Israelites paused for a time in the Plains of Moab, one of the Israelites married a Midianite woman (Num. 25:6-7; *see* COZBI). The story seems to be composed of various fragmentary elements, the details of which are not always clear, but the conclusion drawn in vs. 17 would seem to imply that the association of the Midianites and the Israelites had given rise to some hostility between the two peoples, not only because there had been an Israelite-Midianite intermarriage, but also because the Israelites had been seduced into Midianite pagan worship (if this is, indeed, what vs. 18 means). The idolatry was blamed on the treacherous counsel of Balaam (31:16)—a tradition which persisted into NT times (cf. Rev. 2:14). These episodes led to a war of vindication, which God commanded Moses to carry out against Midian (Num. 31:1-12; Josh. 13:21). The Midianites were defeated, including the so-called five "kings" of Midian, whose personal names are curiously preserved in the biblical record. The Midianite cities and encampments were burned and pillaged, and the women and children taken captive. Moses was angry because the Israelites had kept alive the women who had led them to practice idolatry. Thus all Midianite women except virgins were slain, along with all their male children.

6. The Midianite invasion. *Ca.* 1100 B.C. the first known camel nomads irrupted into Palestine in the form of a Midianite razzia. As far as we now know, the Midianites were among the first to make effective use of the recently domesticated CAMEL, thereby increasing considerably their nomadic mobility and swift striking power. Surging forth from the Wadi Sirhan to the Hauran, the initial impact of the Midianite invasion caused consternation in W Palestine, forcing the Israelites to seek refuge in the hill country, while the ruthless invaders, abetted by the Amalekites and the People of the East, penetrated as far as Gaza, pillaging both crops and cattle for a period of seven years (Judg. 6:1-6). These devastating raids were finally repulsed by Gideon, with the help of men of Ephraim who captured two of the Midianite princes, Oreb and Zeeb (Judg. 7:24-25). Gideon pursued a remnant of the fleeing nomads across the Jordan as far as their original habitat at Karkor in the Wadi Sirhan (8:10), where he captured the two kings of Midian, Zebah and Zalmunna, and dispersed their armies (vs. 12). The war with Midian in the days of Hadad king of Edom, who is said to have defeated Midian in the country of Moab (Gen. 36:35; I Chr. 1:46), should be reckoned as a part of this movement. In any event, the Midianites were thoroughly routed, never again to threaten the peace and stability of Palestine (Judg. 8:28). Gideon's decisive victory was to be long remembered both by the prophets and by the psalmist (Ps. 83:9, 11—H 83:10, 12; Isa. 9:4; 10:26; 60:6; Hab. 3:7).

7. Later history of Midian. Although the Bible records nothing further after the eleventh century B.C. about Midianite history, two of the descendants of Midian may appear in the Assyrian texts. In the Annals of Tiglath-pileser III (*ca.* 732) a tribe known as the Haiappu is mentioned as bearing tribute of gold, silver, camels, and all kinds of spices as a sign of submission to the Assyrian monarch. The Haiappu are identified with biblical EPHAH, the first-named son of Midian listed in Gen. 25:4, which has the same basic consonants. In the following Assyrian record the name Haiappu comes immediately after that of the Sabeans. In Isa. 60:6, where the "camels of Midian" are mentioned, both Ephah and Sheba appear in conjunction. The name Haiappu may survive at Ghuwafa, SW of Tebuk in NW Arabia. Finally, in a report of Sargon's campaign in 715 B.C., the Haiappu again appear.

Bibliography. A. Musil, *The Northern Heğâz* (1926), pp. 278-98. D. Luckenbill, *Ancient Records of Assyria* (1927), vol. I, sections 778, 799, 818; vol. II, sections 17, 118. F.-M. Abel, *Géographie de la Palestine* (1933), I, 285-87, 392-93. J. Montgomery, *Arabia and the Bible* (1934), pp. 9-10, 43-44, 47, 52, 186. W. F. Albright, *From the Stone Age to Christianity* (1940), pp. 120, 194-96, 200, 219; *Archaeology and the Religion of Israel* (3rd ed., 1953), pp. 60, 100, 132, 206. R. Walz, "Zum Problem des Zeitpunkts der Domestikation der altweltlichen Cameliden," *ZDMG,* 101 (1951), 29-51; "Neue Untersuchungen zum Domestikationsproblem der altweltlichen Cameliden," *ZDMG,* 104 (1954), 45-87. G. M. LANDES

***MIDRASH** mĭd′răsh [מדרש, *from root* to search, to investigate, *hence* to expound]. The name given to that exegesis of the Bible which emanated from the rabbinic schools in ancient Palestine. Its aim was to elucidate the meaning of the text of the Holy Writ, to penetrate into its inner significance, to deduce from it new laws and principles, and to establish by reference to it authentic religious and ethical doctrines. There are two types of midrash: HALACHAH, which deals with the legal parts of the Bible; and HAGGADAH (הגדה, "narration"), which deals with the nonlegal parts, and is hence homiletical. In the domain of Haggadah Midrash left its deep impress on the Bible itself. Thus we find passages in Chronicles which are midrashic glosses, supplementing in many details the narratives in the book of Kings. There is also a Midrash to the book of Kings mentioned in II Chr. 24:27, while reference to the Midrash of Iddo the prophet is made in 13:22. Midrash was also employed by Ezra in his public reading of the Law at the memorable convocation in the year 444 B.C., and by successive generations of teachers who followed him. *See* TALMUD.

This mass of accumulated midrashic material, with numerous adaptations and expansions, was arranged in separate collections which constitute the extensive midrashic literature, of varying age, provenance, and character, presented in the form of commentaries on different books of the Bible. The earliest of these collections are the Halachic Midrashim compiled *ca.* the middle of the second Christian century: the Mekilta of Exodus, the Sifra on Leviticus, and the Sifre on Numbers and Deuteronomy. Of the Haggadic Midrashim the earliest is the Midrash on Genesis, going back in its larger part to the third century. Of a later date are the Midrashim on the other books of the Pentateuch, and on the Song of Songs, Lamentations, Ecclesiastes, Ruth, and Esther, which together with the Midrash on Genesis make up the Midrash Rabbah, the most popular of midrashic works. Other Midrashim of a later date include the Yalkut Shimeoni, a kind of midrashic thesaurus on the whole of the OT (compiled probably in the first half of the thirteenth century); the Pesiḳtha Rabbathi (probably compiled in the eighth century), containing special discourses for special sabbaths and festivals; and the ethical midrash Tanna debe Eliyyahu (probably compiled in the second half of the tenth century), the universal humanism of which is reflected in its utterance: "I call heaven and earth to witness that whether a person be a Jew or non-Jew, bondman or bondwoman, according to the deed he performs the Holy Spirit rests on him."

Bibliography. M. Mielziner, *Introduction to the Talmud* (1925); M. Waxman, *A History of Jewish Literature,* vol. I (1930); H. L. Strack, *Introduction to the Talmud and Midrash* (1931); I. Epstein, *Judaism* (1939; rev. ed., 1945).

I. Epstein

MIDWIFE [מילדת, one who brings to birth, *from* ילד, to bear, bring forth]. A woman who assists the delivery of a child. The most extensive reference to women serving in this capacity is found in the first chapter of Exodus. Here two Hebrew midwives named Shiphrah and Puah serve the Hebrew women with the help of a Birthstool. They are ordered to destroy all the male infants that are born to Hebrew women. Because of their refusal to do this, they are rewarded by the God of Israel with families. There may be a suggestion here that barren women with no families acted as midwives.

Although not specifically named as midwives, on two occasions women who probably assisted at a birth are mentioned. When Ruth's child was born, women from the community were present to congratulate the grandmother and to name the child (Ruth 4:14, 17). They may well have helped deliver the infant. When the wife of Phinehas was about to give birth, she had pains suddenly and was on the point of death, when the women who were attending her consoled her by saying: "Fear not, for you have borne a son" (I Sam. 4:20). Helping with a delivery, they ascertained the sex of the child as quickly as possible.

O. J. Baab

MIGDAL-EL mĭg′dəl ĕl′ [מגדל אל, fortress tower of El] (Josh. 19:38). A fortified town in the territory allotted to Naphtali. The site is unknown, but according to context, it must have been located in Upper Galilee, in the vicinity of Iron.

MIGDAL-GAD mĭg′dəl găd′ [מגדל־גד, tower of Gad] (Josh. 15:37). A village of Judah in the Shephelah district of Lachish; probably to be identified with Khirbet el-Mejdeleh, five miles S of Beit Jibrin (Eleutheropolis), near ed-Dawa'imeh.

MIGDOL mĭg′dŏl [מגדל, מגדול *in* Jer. 46:14; LXX Μάγδωλον]. A town or city in Lower Egypt mentioned in the OT in three different contexts: (*a*) as a place on the route of the Exodus near Pi-hahiroth, Baal-zephon, and the sea; (*b*) by Jeremiah (44:1; 46:14) as a residence of the Jews in Egypt, along with Memphis and Tahpanhes; and (*c*) by Ezekiel (29:10; 30:6) as a place in N Egypt contrasted with Syene in the extreme S. It is not certain that these three places are to be identified with one another, but there is no direct evidence to the contrary. The name Migdol is Semitic and means "tower" or "fortress." The word appears in Egyptian as a borrowing, both as a common noun meaning "fortress" and as the proper name of various military stations on the NE frontier. A similarly named Egyptian city, *Ma-ag-da-lí,* is mentioned in Tell el-Amarna Letter 234:29, but the context does not specify its location.

The exact identification of the exodus sites in Egypt is difficult because neither the biblical narrative nor contemporary Egyptian sources provide sufficient information. The Migdol of the Exodus may be located with certainty in the E Delta. Papyrus Anastasi V.19 mentions a Migdol of Seti I in the vicinity of Tjeku, and if the identification of the latter place with Succoth (modern Tell el-Maskhutah) is accepted, the equation of this Migdol with that of the Exodus is possible. An alternative identification of Migdol in general is with the Magdolo of the Antonine Itinerary, roughly midway between Pelusium and Sele and equated tentatively with modern Tell el-Her. The latter location suits the Migdol of Jeremiah and Ezekiel better than that of the Exodus account, but the choice rests with the total picture of the route outlined in Exodus rather than with any single detail.

Bibliography. A. H. Gardiner, "The Ancient Military Road Between Egypt and Palestine," *JEA,* 6 (1920), 107-10.

T. O. Lambdin

MIGHTY MEN [גבורים]. The designation accorded to proud, bold, and strong heroes. It is applied to legendary heroes of the dim, mythical past (Gen. 6:4) and also to heroic contemporaries (II Sam. 17:10). It refers to foreigners (Josh. 10:2) as well as to Israelites (II Sam. 17:8), but it is also a technical term for the mercenaries and warriors of David. This host of mercenaries included the Cherethites and the Pelethites (I Kings 1:38) and the Gittites (II Sam. 15:18), and were led by Joab (II Sam. 10:7) and Benaiah (I Kings 1:10). The heroic exploits of the "three mighty men" of David and those of "the thirty" were preserved in biblical records (II Sam. 23:8-39).

S. Szikszai

MIGHTY WORKS. *See* Signs and Wonders; Miracle.

MIGRON mĭg′rŏn [מגרון]. A town of Benjamin, at some distance from Gibeah, where Saul sat under a pomegranate tree to observe the movements of the invading Philistines (I Sam. 14:2). It is also mentioned in Isaiah's account of the march of the Assyrian army upon Jerusalem as the place where its baggage train halted (Isa. 10:28). In the first passage Migron is obviously S of the pass of Michmash, while in the latter it is located N of it. Albright, reconstructing the passage in Isaiah, has therefore proposed to transfer the positions of Michmash and Migron, so as to bring the latter next to Geba, which would agree with the passage in I Samuel; Geba would then be the lodging place of the Assyrian army after its first day's march, while the baggage train would be encamped at Migron. The site has not been identified.

Bibliography. W. F. Albright, *AASOR,* IV (1924), 37, 135-38.

S. Cohen

MIJAMIN mĭj'ə mĭn [מִיָּמִן, מִיָּמִין, *contraction of* מִנְיָמִן, Miniamin; Apoc. Μεαμίμ, Μειαμείν, Μειμίν]; KJV MIAMIN mī'ə mĭn in Ezra 10:25; Neh. 12:5. A name that has been found in Neo-Babylonian and Persian business documents and is therefore probably not to be equated with בִּנְיָמִין (Benjamin), in spite of the fact that the Syr. of Ezra 10:25 reads the latter in place of Mijamin.

1. A priest of David's time (I Chr. 24:9), the supposed ancestor of a postexilic priestly family.

2. A layman, son of Parosh, who was among those required by Ezra to put away their foreign wives (Ezra 10:25).

3. A priest who "set his seal" to the covenant under Ezra (Neh. 10:7).

4. A priest who accompanied Zerubbabel in the return from the Exile (Neh. 12:5). J. M. Ward

MIKLOTH mĭk'lŏth [מִקְלוֹת]. **1.** One of the descendants of the Benjaminite Jeiel, who resided at Gibeon, and the father of Shimeah (I Chr. 8:32; cf. 9:37-38). In I Chr. 8:31 the words "and Mikloth" should doubtless be restored, in conformity with I Chr. 9:37.

2. The chief officer who served under Dodai, the officer in charge of the Davidic militia for the second month (I Chr. 27:4 RSV mg.). However, the text is undoubtedly corrupt, and the words "and his division and Mikloth the chief officer" are best omitted.

E. R. Dalglish

MIKNEIAH mĭk nē'yə [מִקְנֵיָהוּ, Yahu acquires, *or* Yahu creates] (I Chr. 15:18, 21). A Levite of the second rank; one of the leaders with lyres appointed by David. The omission of his name from the similar list in I Chr. 16:5 may indicate that it is secondary here.

Bibliography. P. Humbert, "*Qana* en hébreu biblique," *Festschrift Alfred Bertholet* (1950), pp. 259-66.

R. W. Corney

MIKTAM mĭk'təm [מִכְתָּם, *see below*]; KJV MICHTAM. The heading of Pss. 16; 56–60; and probably of the hymn in Isa. 38:9. The etymology of the word is uncertain (LXX στηλογραφία). Luther (*Güldenes Kleinod*) combined it with כֶּתֶם, "gold"; Mowinckel (and others) with Akkadian *katâmu*, "to cover" (cf. *naktamu*, "covering"), "to expiate." "Miktam" would then be a "psalm of covering the sin, of expiation."

See also Music.

Bibliography. S. Mowinckel, *Psalmenstudien*, IV (1922), 4-5.

J. Hempel

MILALAI mĭl'ə lī [מִלֲלַי] (Neh. 12:36). One of the musicians taking part in the dedication of Nehemiah's wall. The name is lacking in the Greek and may be an error due to dittography (cf. the following name, Gilalai).

MILCAH mĭl'kə [מִלְכָּה, queen; *cf.* Akkad. *malkatu*, princess, *a title of the Babylonian goddess Ishtar*]. **1.** A daughter of Haran, Abram's brother, who became the wife of Nahor, also Abram's brother (Gen. 11:29 J), and bore him eight sons (22:20-23 J). Through her son Bethuel she was the grandmother of Rebekah (24:15, 24, 47, J).

2. One of the five daughters of Zelophehad who through Moses received the family inheritance in W Manasseh after the death of their father (Num. 26:33; 27:1; 36:11; Josh. 17:3). The names of the daughters seem originally to have been the names of Canaanite towns, but the location of Milcah is unknown. M. Newman

MILCOM mĭl'kəm [מִלְכּוֹם]. Hebrew distortion of the name of the national god of Ammon. *See* Molech.

MILDEW [יֵרָקוֹן, yellow, pale]. It is uncertain if a plant blight is intended by this word. It is always associated with שִׁדָּפוֹן, "withering" of crops (RSV "blight"; KJV "blasting"; I Kings 8:37; Amos 4:9; cf. Gen. 41:6) as divine punishment, and apparently is connected with the blowing of hot, dry wind of sirocco (Deut. 28:22-24). *See* East Wind; Palestine, Climate of. R. B. Y. Scott

MILE [μίλιον] (Matt. 5:41). The Roman mile, which was a little shorter than the American mile. *See* Weights and Measures § D4*e*.

***MILETUS** mī lē'təs [Μίλητος] (Acts 20:15,17; II Tim. 4:20). A prominent Greek harbor city on the W coast of Asia Minor.

Miletus, a city with a pre-Greek name, was presumably founded in prehistoric times to serve as a safe station for coastal shipping. It was located on a promontory projecting from the S shore of the Latmian Gulf, which served as the estuary of the Maeander River. Miletus had four harbors, a location sheltered but favorable to commerce, and enough local supplies to support a sizable population.

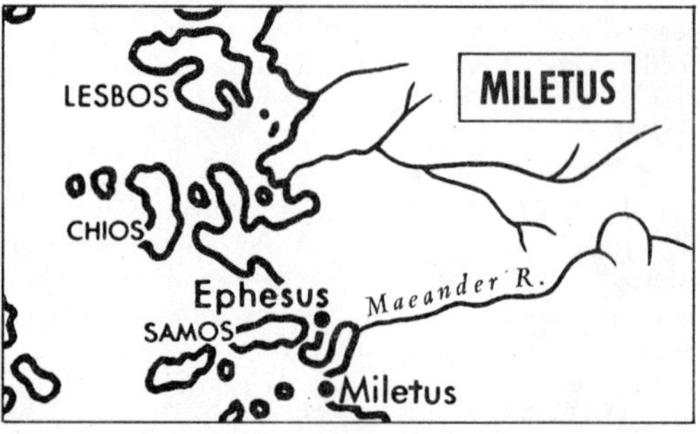

The geological situation in the Latmian Gulf was subject to constant change because of the accumulation of silt by the Maeander. Whereas anciently the gulf cut deep into the coast with the island of Lade sheltering the W side of Miletus, the modern coastline has been closed in front of an inland lake. The harbors are filled in, the course of the river has shifted, and the ruins of Miletus are now five miles from the coast. This change began to be detrimental to shipping in late Roman times; but in the days of Paul's visit the port was still active and prominent.

Miletus was first colonized by Cretans of the period of Minoan expansion, later to be taken over by Mycenean Greeks and made into a fortified outpost in the fourteenth century B.C. It may well be identical with Millawanda, referred to in Hittite texts as a coastal town in W Anatolia. Although destroyed in disturbances *ca.* 1200 B.C., Miletus was perhaps never abandoned by the Greeks but reinforced by Ionian immigrants. It emerged as the leading center of Ionian naval enterprise in the seventh century B.C. Its ships carried colonists to the far shores of the Black Sea and Egypt, accumulating new resources for the prosperous mother city. Some rivalry with the Lydian kingdom arose, without affecting the sea power of Miletus. The city came to a favorable understanding with the Persians after 546 B.C.

The commercial expansion of early Miletus was matched by her artistic and intellectual importance. Famous philosophers (Thales, Anaximander, Anaximenes) were Milesians. The city was among the first to mint coins. Its best sculpture and architecture were produced for the oracle temple of Apollo at Didyma, some ten miles S of Miletus. The sacred road connecting town and sanctuary was partly lined with statues.

The Ionian revolt against the Persians put an end to this phase of prosperity. Miletus was involved in its beginning (499 B.C.) and fell a victim to its unfortunate ending in 494. The city was captured by the Persians, its inhabitants killed or deported as slaves, the temple in Didyma plundered and burned.

After the Persian defeat at Mykala (479 B.C.), Miletus was liberated and rebuilt along modern lines by the town-planner Hippodamus, a Milesian, who laid out the regular pattern preserved in the later city. Miletus joined the Delian League, fell to Persia after the intrigues against Athens at the end of the fifth century, and was for some time under control of such Carian dynasts as Maussollos (377-353).

Alexander captured Miletus in 334 B.C. The city became free again but had to cope with the interest in its naval base by various competing Hellenistic rulers. This period marks the revival of grandiose city architecture in Miletus, and several of the Hellenistic monarchs sponsored monumental building projects.

Courtesy of Ahmet Dönmez

46. The Roman remains of the ancient city of Miletus

The period of the Roman Empire meant increased prosperity and trade for Miletus. The emperors were benevolent recipients of honors and dedicators of buildings; and private citizens added their gifts. The late first and second centuries A.D. saw great architectural activities.* The threat of decline came from the silting-up of the harbor rather than from a lack of local enterprise. The size of the city shrank, and the Byzantine town was no more than a small citadel. Fig. MIL 46.

When Paul visited Miletus, it was the natural stopping place en route from Lesbos, Chios, Samos to the S, and near enough to Ephesus for the elders of the church to be called in for consultation (Acts 20:15-17). The message to Ephesus would have been sent across the gulf to Priene and from there by road to Ephesus.

The reference in II Tim. 4:20 seems to mention another visit to Miletus.

From *Atlas of the Bible* (Thomas Nelson & Sons Limited)

47. Miletus: the theater in the foreground and the harbor in the background

In the first century A.D., Miletus had not yet reached the climax of its architectural embellishment. Even in this period, however, the city was remarkable for the elaborate but regular layout of its public buildings. It had two market places built of colonnades combined at right angles, creating vast open spaces as well as magazines and shops. A council house stood between the two markets, not a simple covered theater but a building with a lavish exterior and colonnaded court. This complex was essentially Hellenistic, as was the large theater overlooking one of the harbors.* In Roman times such display pieces as the triple gateway to the S market were added. Fig. MIL 47.

At Didyma the temple of Apollo was being rebuilt during Hellenistic and Roman times. Never finished, it yet became one of the largest and most magnificent Ionic shrines, unique in design because of the peculiar nature of its oracle cult.

Miletus was excavated by a German expedition 1899-1914, again in 1938 and 1955.

Bibliography. T. Wiegand *et al.*, *Miletus Ergebnisse der Ausgrabungen und Untersuchungen* (1906—); D. Magie, *Roman Rule in Asia Minor* (1950), pp. 73-74. M. J. MELLINK

MILK. Milk products were among the staples of the diet in biblical times (Ecclus. 39:26), but fresh milk was not commonly drunk.* Rather, it was made into CHEESE and CURDS; thus "in that day" there will be a sufficiency of curds because of the abundance of milk (Isa. 7:22; cf. Prov. 30:33). Goat's milk (Prov. 27:27) was the most widely used; however, we also read of "milk from the flock" (Deut. 32:14; I Cor. 9:7) and human milk (Isa. 28:9). Milk was kept in skins (Judg. 4:19) and offered to a guest (Gen. 18:8; Judg. 5:25). Figs. COW 51; MIL 48-49.

The most common use of the term "milk" is figurative: (*a*) for abundance (Deut. 32:14), including that of the eschatological age (Isa. 55:1; Joel 3:18—

Courtesy of James B. Pritchard

48. Cylinder seal showing a man milking a goat from behind; from Early Dynastic III (*ca.* 2700 B.C.)

Courtesy of the University Museum of the University of Pennsylvania

49. Mesopotamian cattle scenes from a First Dynasty temple at al-'Ubaid (*ca.* 2700 B.C.)

H 4:18); (*b*) for whiteness of teeth (Gen. 49:12) or skin (Lam. 4:7); (*c*) for Israel's vindication (Isa. 60: 16; she will drink the milk of the nations); (*d*) for the excellencies of a loved one (Song of S. 4:11; 5:12); (*e*) for the rudiments of teaching (I Cor. 3:2; Heb. 5:12-13); and (*f*) for unfalsified Christian doctrine (I Pet. 2:2).

The common phrase "a land flowing with milk and honey" (Exod. 3:8; Num. 13:27; Deut. 6:3; Jer. 11:5; Ecclus. 46:8; Bar. 1:20; etc., descriptive of Canaan; Num. 16:13, of Goshen) may have a mythological origin, but more probably it refers to the fertility of the land as seen from the viewpoint of those wandering in the wilderness. The prohibition against boiling a kid in its mother's milk (Exod. 23:19; 34: 26; Deut. 14:21) is most probably directed against Canaanite sacrificial practices; a reference to such a custom is found in Text 52:14 from Ras Shamra. *See* UGARIT.

Bibliography. C. H. Gordon, *Ugaritic Literature* (1949), p. 59.

J. F. Ross

MILL, MILLSTONE. A machine consisting of two stones used for grinding grain into flour. רחים, a dual form, is the more common, generic term for the hand mill, which is of two types. One consists of one stone more or less rectangular in shape and usually slightly concave, with one end a little thicker than the other. A good example found at Megiddo measured *ca.* thirty inches in length. The archaeologist refers to this stone as a saddle quern. The upper or grinding stone is flat on one side and elliptical on the other and is much smaller, usually the length being about equal to the width of the lower stone and the width of it just enough to be easily grasped by the hands. The grinding was done by pushing the upper, smaller stone back and forth on the larger stone, upon which the grain was placed. Probably not much grain could be ground at one time in such a mill as this, but this mill was the only one in use down to Hellenistic times. Fig. MIL 50.

The second type of hand mill consists of two round stones. The lower stone is convex on the top, while the upper stone is concave so as to fit snugly over the lower stone. Some examples of this type have a hole in the center of the top stone, through which the grain was poured. This type of mill became common in the Hellenistic period and onward, and variations of it are frequently seen today. The stones of both types of hand mills were commonly of black basalt, which is hard and porous, thus providing a constantly rough surface of many cutting edges.

Both these types of mills were used in the home and were operated by the women of the household; this was their daily chore, for which they arose early in the morning. In a household where there were maidservants or slaves, the task of grinding would undoubtedly fall to them (Exod. 11:5; Isa. 47:2).

Courtesy of the Museum of Fine Arts, Boston

50. Statuette of a woman grinding grain with a millstone, from Gizeh; Fifth Dynasty, Old Kingdom (*ca.* 2500-2350 B.C.)

Likewise captives often found themselves burdened with the task of operating the mill (Judg. 16:21; Jer. 52:11 LXX).

פלח רכב is the term used for the upper millstone (Judg. 9:53; II Sam. 11:21), while פלח תחתית is used for the lower millstone (Job 41:24—H 41:16).

Large community mills in which a heavy stone shaped like a wheel was rolled around on a large, heavy, round lower stone by an animal also existed in ancient times. טחון may be the term used for this type of mill (Lam. 5:13). The large animal- or water-operated mill is today called in Arabic *ṭaḥûbun.* In Greek this type of mill is known by the term μύλος ὀνικός (Matt. 18:6; Mark 9:42).

Since the hand mill was absolutely necessary, the law prohibited the taking of either the mill as a whole or the upper millstone in pledge for a debt, since this would deprive the family of the equipment necessary for making flour, out of which bread, the basic item in the daily diet, was made.

The upper millstone was an effective weapon, as in the case of the death of Abimelech (Judg. 9:53). No doubt, the sound of the grinding in the early morning was a very familiar one in the cities and villages of Palestine. When it was no longer heard, this was a sign of complete desolation (Jer. 25:10; Rev. 18:22).

Bibliography. A. G. Barrois, *Manuel d'archéologie biblique,* I (1939), 317 ff; R. S. Lamon and G. M. Shipton, *Megiddo I* (1939), pl. 114:11; C. C. McCown, *Tell en-Nasbeh* (1947), p. 250, pl. 91:4; G. Loud, *Megiddo II* (1948), pl. 264:11.

H. N. RICHARDSON

MILLENNIUM [Lat. *mille,* thousand, *plus annus,* year]. Strictly speaking, the thousand-year reign of Jesus Christ with certain resurrected martyrs, and with them alone, which is to occur following his second advent as an interregnum between this present, evil, temporal age under Satan and the future, righteous eternal age under God, as described all too briefly in Rev. 20:4-6. This passage, brief though it is, has had a great deal of influence upon Christian thinking. Furthermore, it has been misinterpreted as a rule, for few have taken it literally in its historic context. First of all, coming out of the persecution by the Romans, the passage limits the enjoyment of the millennium to a special group, those who had died as martyrs because they had refused to worship the Roman emperor-gods (the beast), and to them alone. They, and no one else, are restored to life in the first resurrection for this reward. Secondly, the author was convinced that the millennium would be established very soon after his prediction, 3½ years, in all probability. Consequently, if the prediction had been fulfilled, the millennium would have begun *ca.* A.D. 100 and would have ended *ca.* 1100. Failure to take the author literally has caused the millennium to be a subject for almost endless speculation.

1. Jewish sources. The messianic interval as presented in Revelation is apparently traceable to earlier Jewish thinking in which the prophetic ideal of a messianic kingdom was combined with the apocalyptic hope. Certainly, a messianic interim is not an essential element of apocalypticism; as evidence for this, there is no messianic reign in such typical apocalypses as Isa. 24–27; Daniel; the Assumption of Moses; and the Apocalypse of Abraham. In fact, there is no mention of a messiah in the first three.

An interim period without a messiah is presented in the source of I Enoch 91:12-17; 93, known as the Apocalypse of Weeks. Past history is divided into seven uneven "weeks" of time, beginning with the birth of Enoch and ending with the degenerate time of the author of this apocalyptic fragment, possibly before the Maccabean period. These seven weeks will be followed by three more: the eighth a period of righteousness, the ninth a time in which the world will be marked for destruction, and the tenth a week in which the angels will be judged. This will all be followed by an eternity of weeks in a new heaven. There is no messiah in this scheme, hence no messianic interim; however, the inclusion of a messiah within this pattern could be made rather readily.

A somewhat similar eschatological chronology, and likewise without a messiah, is provided in II Enoch 32:3–33:1. This present world age is to consist of seven days of a thousand years each. The seventh, a millennial day of rest, will be followed by an eternal eighth day. The seventh day is not a messianic reign, for no messiah is mentioned. However, it would be easy to adapt this scheme to the messianic millennium, as was done in early Christian sources.

In II Bar. 39–40 a messianic kingdom, which is to follow the destruction of four world kingdoms (the last one is Rome), is to endure until this world of corruption is ended. However, this may not be a good parallel, since the passage in which it is found is not unquestionably apocalyptic.

The closest parallel in a Jewish work no later in date than Revelation is in II Esd. 5:2–7:4. First, this evil and degenerate age is to be brought to an end by God himself. Next, the messiah, who apparently had no other function, will appear and reign for four hundred years with those who have gone to heaven without tasting death (Enoch, Elijah, possibly others as well) and with the righteous on earth who have survived the woes of the last times. After the four-hundred-year interim of rejoicing, the messiah, his work finished, will die, together with all who have human breath. This will be followed by a general resurrection and judgment, and the new age under God. That this pattern of belief was current in later Judaism, at least, is noted by Hippolytus (first half of the third century), who states that the Jews believe that following a battle with the nations a warrior-messiah will gather the Jews into Jerusalem and reign over them. Another war, in which the messiah will be killed, will ensue, to be followed by the termination of this universe, the establishment of a new age, a general resurrection, and a judgment, with recompense to all according to their deeds. Also, certain Christian opponents of millennialism stigmatized it as Jewish.

The closest Jewish parallel to the eschatology of Revelation is in the Neo-Hebraic Apocalypse of Elijah, written *ca.* 261 but based on earlier sources. An antimessiah, it predicts, is to wage a series of devastating wars, but in time the messiah will appear with angels of destruction to destroy the nations. With this present evil age ended, the messiah will rule in Jerusalem with the righteous Jews for forty years, which will be a period of great plenty. At its close God (*sic*) will raise Gog and Magog against the holy city, but they and their armies will be destroyed. A resurrection and judgment follow; the wicked will be sent to a fiery pit, but the righteous will dwell in the new age with God in a new Garden of Eden and in a heavenly Jerusalem come down to earth.

This work is thoroughly Jewish throughout, showing no dependence upon Revelation despite close similarities. Quite likely the authors of both (as well as Lactantius in his *Divine Institutes* VII) have followed a common apocalyptic tradition. The basic pattern is the same; the differences (such as the forty-year duration of the kingdom) are minor.

2. Christian sources. Turning to the Christian sources, strangely enough we can find no allusion, even, in the NT to a messianic interregnum outside of Revelation, except in I Cor. 15:23-28 (cf. Col. 1:

13), not even in adventist passages like Mark 13 (and parallels); I Thess. 4:13-18; II Thess. 2:1-12: II Pet. 3:1-12. Paul in the Corinthians reference states briefly that with Christ's second coming there will be a resurrection, and that he will rule until all the cosmic enemies, including death, are abolished. Then he will turn all things over to God (cf. Col. 1: 13: "the kingdom of his beloved Son"). The Ascension of Isaiah in its present form is a Christian work from about the time of Revelation. In 4.1-18 it is promised that Christ in his return from heaven with his angelic armies will defeat the antichrist Beliar and will drag him and his armies to Gehenna. Then he will give rest or refreshment (for an unspecified period of time) to the still living godly, who have execrated Beliar, along with the saints in heaven who will descend. After this messianic interim all will leave their bodies and ascend to heaven.

Bar. 15 (first part of the second century) is more specific concerning the time. As in II Enoch, there are seven days of a thousand years each. Everything will be completed in six days; then the Son will return, destroying the time of the wicked one and judging the godless. After changing the sun, moon, and stars, he will rest on the seventh day. This implies a messianic interim reign of a thousand years.

The millennial hope became quite popular in the next few centuries, with the term "chiliasm" used to denote a belief in a materialistic concept of the millennium with sensuous delights and pleasures. Among the second-century believers in the millennial reign, some more chiliastic than others, were Cerinthus, Papias, Justin Martyr, Irenaeus, Tertullian, and Montanus, with Hippolytus and Lactantius in the following century.

Justin Martyr said that many Christians accepted the doctrine, which he supported by OT prophecy and Rev. 20:4-5 (written by John the apostle). However, he frankly admitted that many pious Christians rejected it. Cerinthus is said to have depicted the future kingdom of Christ as providing sensual pleasures: eating, drinking, and marriage festivities. Papias ascribed to Jesus a prophecy of a marvelously productive earth, in terms similar to a messianic promise in II Bar. 29 (Iren. Her. V.33).

Lactantius is even more detailed. The heavenly bodies will give more light during the interim reign of Christ; the earth will produce food of its own accord; the mountains will drip with honey; there will be streams of wine and milk; all animals and birds will live in peace (*Divine Institutes* VII.24).

As Justin remarked, there were many Christians who rejected millennialism; their rejection was in some measure due to crass materialistic expectations of other Christians; some, for no evident reason, ignored the doctrine. E.g., the Didache, an early Christian manual, concludes with an apocalyptic passage predicting the reign of the antichrist and the second coming of the Lord on the clouds, but without any mention of the messianic reign.

Origen allegorized the millennium: Christ will not establish a physical kingdom; instead, he has a spiritual one in which he instructs all those capable of receiving him, reigning in them until he has subjected them to the Father (*On First Things* II.1; III.6). The Eastern church tended, in fact, to reject Revelation, along with a materialistic millennial hope.

Augustine also allegorized Revelation. There is to be no actual second advent of Christ before the final judgment, for his coming occurs continually in the church and its members. The first resurrection is figurative, symbolizing the change in the status of people as they die to sin and rise to a new life. The thousand-year reign of Christ on earth actually began with Jesus himself, for it is the Christian church wherein the saints reign (*City of God* XX.6-7).

The millennial hope, however, never died out in the Western church; indeed, from time to time it became quite prominent in one form or another. It was emphasized in the Reformation period by reformers and by some Anabaptists. The scholarly Bengel in his commentary in 1740 fixed the beginning of the millennium at 1836. Irvingites, Mormons, Millerites (Seventh Day Adventists), and Russellites (Jehovah's Witnesses) are among the more modern popular movements that stress, not only adventism, but some form of millennialism as well. Not only is it a basic tenet of a number of the more fundamentalistic denominations and sects, but it is also accepted in one way or another by an untold number of members of other denominations as well. Some Christians are premillennialists, believing that Christ will come before the millennium; others are postmillennialists, placing the Advent after the interim; still others, like Origen and Augustine, allegorize or spiritualize the concept. Consequently, understanding of its original meaning for the author of Revelation, the probable background for his views, and the early history of the doctrine are of great importance. *See also* APOCALYPTICISM.

Bibliography. J. A. MacCulloch, "Eschatology," in J. Hastings, *Encyclopedia of Religion and Ethics* (1912), V, 373 ff; R. H. Charles, *A Critical History of the Doctrine of a Future Life* (2nd ed., 1913); S. J. Case, *The Millennial Hope* (1917).

M. RIST

MILLET [דחן, *dōḥan;* Akkad. *duḫnu;* Arab. *dukhn;* κέγχρος]. The smallest of grass seeds cultivated for food. A poor quality of bread is made from its flour, though it is more commonly mixed with other grains.

דחן is included with other grains mixed together to make a symbolic bread for Ezekiel's dramatization of the siege of Jerusalem (Ezek. 4:9). The Syr. of Ezek. 27:17 uses "millet" for the puzzling PANNAG, but *see* FIG. The Douay Version, following the LXX and the Vulg., mistakenly uses "millet" for *nismān* in Isa. 28:25 (RSV "proper place").

Post and Löw favor the identification of *dōḥan* with sorghum (*Sorghum vulgare* Pers.), the *durra* of the Arabs, but most others prefer the equally common *Panicum miliacum* L., millet. The Hebrew may refer to several similar seeds.

See also GRAIN; FLORA § A1*d*.

Bibliography. I. Löw, *Die Flora der Juden,* I*b* (1928), 738-46; H. N. and A. L. Moldenke, *Plants of the Bible* (1952), pp. 166-67.

J. C. TREVER

MILLO mĭl'ō [מלוא, *from* מלא, to fill; *cf.* Assyrian *mulû,* terrasse]. **1.** The name of an element of fortification of the city of David (*see* DAVID, CITY OF). It is mentioned in connection with the constructions which David undertook after the conquest of Jerusalem (II Sam. 5:9; I Chr. 11:8). The construction of the Millo is formally attributed to Solomon in I Kings 9:15, 24; 11:27. It is referred to as the "house of Millo" (בית מלא) in the account of the death of Joash (II Kings 12:20—H 12:21). The location of the Millo to the NW of the city of David, while plausible, remains unproved. The etymology suggests a structure built on an artificial platform of stamped earth. *See* JERUSALEM § 5*b*.

Bibliography. H. Vincent, *Jérusalem Antique* (1912), pp. 171-82; J. Simons, *Jerusalem in the OT* (1952), pp. 131-37.

2. The proper name of a quarter in the city of SHECHEM (Judg. 9:6, 20), in the expression בית מלוא, "Beth-millo" (RSV), "house of Millo" (KJV).

G. A. BARROIS

MILLSTONE. One of two stones which together made up the hand mill used in the home for grinding grain into flour. *See* MILL.

MINCING [טפף, to go like a little child (טף) —*i.e.*, to trip along]. An affectedly nice or elegant manner of walking, acting, or speaking. The word is used in Isa. 3:16 of the haughty daughters of Zion. Perhaps the phrase in which it is used should be read "tripping along as they go."

H. G. MAY

MIND. A word used in the English Bible to translate a considerable number of Hebrew and Greek words of various meanings, none of which has precisely the same connotations as the English word, although all of them certainly include the idea of the human capacity for rational thinking. The translator's chief difficulty is that the Bible is the product of the Hebraic mind, which had no real interest in psychological analysis and no conception of the division of the human personality into separate organs or faculties, each governing some particular phase of man's psychic activity. Feeling, thinking, planning, and willing were all conceived to be functions of the entire personality, so that the conception of "the mind" as the special seat or organ of reflective thinking as distinguished, e.g., from the heart as the seat of the emotions would have been, for the Hebrews, almost unintelligible.

While the vocabulary of the NT, at first glance, seems more precise than that of the OT, and includes a number of words which had already acquired a technical psychological sense in the works of the Greek philosophers and, in some instances, an equally technical but different sense in pagan religious thinkers of mystical tendencies, it seems clear that these words are used quite loosely by the NT writers, who were under the influence of LXX usage and whose thinking was largely set in Hebraic categories, so that the meaning of the words must be determined rather by context than by history or etymology.

One word commonly translated "mind" in the English OT is לב or לבב, properly HEART, which does not refer, as in English usage, to the center of man's emotional life, but rather to the inmost center of his entire personality, the hidden part of his being, in which take place all those activities—affective, volitional, and intellectual—which finally determine the direction of his external acts. The word is translated "mind" in passages where the emphasis seems to be especially on the heart as the seat of recollection (Isa. 65:17; Jer. 3:16) or purpose (Num. 16:28 KJV; Jer. 19:5). The translators of the LXX appear already to have caught this nuance of the word, since in a number of places they have preferred to translate לב or לבב by νοῦς ("mind") rather than by the more usual καρδία, although their practice in this respect follows no obvious pattern of logic or consistency. Since the words נפש ("soul") and רוח ("spirit") can similarly be used to designate the deepest part of man, though in a dynamic rather than merely local sense, they also are occasionally translated "mind" in the English versions, as in Gen. 23:8 KJV; I Sam. 2:35; II Kings 9:15 (נפש); and in Gen. 26:35 KJV; Ezek. 11:5 (רוח). In one familiar passage, Isa. 26:3, the underlying Hebrew word is יצר, more commonly translated IMAGINATION. In all these passages where the English word "mind" appears and the idea of thinking obviously occupies an important place, it is primarily thinking related to action, either recalled from the past or planned for the future. The idea of pure, disinterested thinking for its own sake is alien to the Hebrew mentality.

The Greek word νοῦς, which in the NT occurs almost exclusively in the writings of Paul and in the Pastoral letters (the only exceptions being Luke 24:45; Rev. 13:18; 17:9), is the exact equivalent of "mind" in Greek philosophical usage, but is used by Paul in a less technical sense which is closer to that of ancient popular Greek. Plato's view of the human person as divided into three parts, of which the νοῦς is the highest, e.g., is largely irrelevant for understanding the Pauline use of the term.

For Paul the "mind" is the thinking, reasoning, reflective, and purposing aspect of man's consciousness. It is a purely human element, part of man's nature as such, which makes it possible for him to comprehend the revelation of God and to act accordingly. It is, therefore, *potentially* a designation for his higher nature as opposed to the FLESH; which is frequently a name for the lower nature; but it is also capable of being corrupted (Rom. 1:28; Col. 2:18; I Tim. 6:5) and so diverted from its true end (Rom. 1:28). Fortunately it is also capable of recovery and renewal (Rom. 12:2). Although the mind in Pauline thought is the means whereby men apprehend God's truth, it is never confused with SPIRIT in the theological sense, the divinely infused instrument or agent by which man is brought into direct relationship to God. Indeed, in I Cor. 14:15 "the mind" is set in sharp, and not at all unfavorable, contrast to "the spirit." The only passage in which the two concepts might possibly seem to be confused is I Cor. 2:16 ("We have the mind of Christ"), where the context shows that "mind" means "spirit"; but Paul's unusual usage here is entirely determined by his quotation from the LXX (Isa. 40:13) in which the Greek translators, contrary to their normal rule, inexplicably rendered the Hebrew רוח by νοῦς. According to Bultmann's elaborate and subtle analysis, "the mind" in Pauline thought means the whole of the self conceived as the subject of its thinking, feeling, and judging, whereas the BODY is the same self regarded as the object of these activities. It is true, in any event, that for Paul, as for the rest of the Bible, "mind" in some sense includes the whole man and can, in fact, often be taken as practically equivalent to "character" (Rom. 1:28; 11:34; II Tim. 3:8).

Three other words, etymologically related to νοῦς, are also sometimes translated "mind." Διάνοια, which often has in classical Greek the sense of "thinking" or "reflecting" and is, therefore, more specifically an intellectual concept than νοῦς, is the word which underlies the familiar "You shall love the Lord your God . . . with all your mind" in Matt. 22:37 and its parallels. Twice the word νόημα, which properly means "thought," is rendered "mind" by metonymy (II Cor. 3:14; 4:4). The KJV, in the same way, uses "mind" as a translation of ἔννοια in I Pet. 4:1, although the RSV more accurately translates "thought." The English versions also use "mind" to translate φρόνημα (in Rom. 8:7, 27) and, rarely, ψυχή ("soul"; Acts 14:2; 15:24; Phil. 1:27; Heb. 12:3 KJV); πνεῦμα ("spirit") in occasional idiomatic use (II Cor. 2:13; 7:13); καρδία ("heart"; Rom. 1:21); and νεφρὸς (KIDNEY; Rev. 2:23). In addition to those passages where "mind" translates an original noun, there are several where it is used to render a verb or verb phrase. Most notable of these is Phil. 2:5: "Let this mind be in you which was also" (KJV), where the Greek τοῦτο φρονεῖτε ἐν ὑμῖν ὃ καὶ can hardly be translated literally into grammatical English. The verb in this passage, φρονέω, is ordinarily translated by some such phrase as "to set the mind on" (Rom. 8:5) or "be minded" (Phil. 3:15). In similar fashion σωφρονέω, which in Tit. 2:6 is translated "control oneself," appears in Mark 5:15; Luke 8:35 as "to be in one's right mind."

Bibliography. R. Bultmann, *Theology of the NT* (trans. K. Grobel; 1954), I, 211-16. R. C. DENTAN

MINEANS mĭ nē′ənz. A Semitic people of S Arabia; possibly to be identified with the MEUNIM. The Minean kingdom, known as Ma'in, was centered in the Jof, a region in the NE corner of modern Yemen, approximately fifty miles NW of Marib. In antiquity, intensive cultivation of the soil and control of the major caravan route (*see* SABEANS) supported a number of cities in this area. The ancient capital of Ma'in was Qarnaw, modern Ma'in.

Recent discoveries have discredited the old "high" chronology which placed the Mineans in the second millennium B.C. (*see also* SABEANS), and have shown that Ma'in was founded by the kings of Hadhramaut (*see* HAZARMAVETH) *ca.* 400 B.C. Ma'in expanded rapidly, and by the second century B.C. its territory reached far to the N to include DEDAN. During this period it overshadowed its neighbor Saba. *Ca.* the middle of the first century B.C., Ma'in lost its independence through conquest by Qataban. There have been no archaeological excavations in this area.

Bibliography. J. A. Montgomery, *Arabia and the Bible* (1934), pp. 133-36, 182-83. H. von Wissmann and M. Höfner, *Beiträge zur historischen Geographie des vorislamischen Südarabien* (1952), pp. 9-17. W. F. Albright, "The Chronology of the Minaean Kings of Arabia," *BASOR,* 129 (1953), 20-24; "Dedan," *Geschichte und Altes Testament* (1953), pp. 1-12.
G. W. VAN BEEK

MINIAMIN mĭn′yə mĭn [מִנְיָמִין, מִנְיָמִן, luck (*lit.*, from the right hand); *see also* MIJAMIN]. **1.** One of those who assisted Kore the Levite in supervising the gathering of the freewill offerings in the reign of King Hezekiah (II Chr. 31:15).

2. A priestly house in the time of Joiakim the high priest (Neh. 12:17).

3. One of the trumpet players participating in the dedication of Nehemiah's wall (Neh. 12:41).

Bibliography. M. Noth, *Die israelitischen Personennamen* (1928), pp. 60n, 224. B. T. DAHLBERG

MINING. The absence of any special word for "mine" or "mining" in biblical Hebrew indicates that mining was not an occupation with which the Hebrews were very familiar. In Job 28:1 the word מוֹצָא, "mine" (KJV "vein"), occurs as a designation of the place from which silver may be obtained, but the word means simply "source." In the Siloam Inscription (*see* SILOAM) the word used for tunneling operations is נקבה (used in the OT of "boring" a hole; cf. II Kings 12:9, etc.), miners are called חצבם (the root of which is used in the OT for "hewing out" cisterns; cf. Deut. 6:11; Jer. 2:13), and a miner's pick is called a גרזן. However, the author of Job is familiar with mining operations to the extent that he knows that they are carried on in out-of-the-way places: "They open shafts in a valley away from where men live" (28:4). They "search out . . . the ore in gloom and deep darkness" (vs. 3).

1. Copper mines. Copper ore, principally malachite, occurs on both sides of the Wadi Arabah (*see* ARABAH), and especially in the tributary wadis entering it from the E. Some veins in the sandstone are quite rich, containing up to forty per cent of metal.

Courtesy of Nelson Glueck

51. The entrance to Umm el-'Amad, looking N

The deposits seem to be connected geologically with similar deposits in the Peninsula of Sinai. The Sinai mines were among the main sources from which Egypt obtained her supply of copper in early times and were worked intermittently from predynastic times down to the Twentieth Dynasty. The exploitation of the deposits in the Arabah began later, since the earliest sedentary occupation in the Arabah, at PUNON, dates only from *ca.* 2200-1800 B.C. Doubtless it was the interest shown by the Egyptians in the Sinai deposits which awakened the interest of the inhabitants of Mount Seir in the copper deposits along their own W border. The mine which was worked by the inhabitants of Punon seems to have been the one now called Umm el-'Amad, located *ca.* 5½ miles to the SE. The mine owes its name, meaning "Mother of Pillars," to the rock pillars left by the ancient miners to support the roof. Fig. MIN 51.

During the Iron I-II Age (1200-600 B.C.) there was an intensive exploitation of the copper deposits of the Arabah, as is attested by the remains of mining and smelting camps, littered with Iron I-II sherds. It is highly likely that this exploitation was carried on, in the first instance, by the Kenites, who, according to Num. 24:21, had their center at Sela (modern Sil'?), not far from the copper mines. (For the tradition which associates the beginnings of metallurgy with Tubal-cain, *see* METALLURGY.) It was doubtless from the Kenites that the Hebrews learned the arts of mining and smelting. The establishment of a Hebrew monarchy led to rivalry with the Edomite kings for the control of the mineral resources of the Arabah; and this, together with the desire to secure access to the Gulf of Aqabah, was probably the chief cause of the wars between Judah and Edom from the time of David to that of Jehoshaphat, and from Amaziah to Ahaz. See EDOM.

The most important mining center in the N part of the Arabah was at Khirbet en-Nahas ("Copper Ruin"), approximately 16½ miles S of the Dead Sea and near the extensive ore deposits of the wadis Gheweibeh and Jariyeh. Its identification with Ir-nahash ("Copper City") of I Chr. 4:12 has been suggested. In the S Arabah the largest mining center was at Mene'iyyeh, which lies on the W side of the Arabah, *ca.* 22 miles from the head of the Gulf. Glueck reports the presence here of huge deposits of copper ore. The intense summer heat in the Arabah, combined with the scarcity of water (except at Feinan), makes it highly likely that the mining operations were carried on only during the rainy season. That slave labor was employed is suggested by the presence of large, walled enclosures at the two main camps mentioned above. These enclosures must date from the period of the Hebrew monarchy, for it is very improbable that the Kenites possessed sufficient political power to employ slaves on the scale suggested by the size of the enclosures.

2. Iron mines. The presence of a certain amount of iron slag at the mining and smelting camps along the Arabah is evidence that iron ore, as well as copper, was discovered and mined there during the Iron Age. The exact site of the iron mines is, however, uncertain. A considerable deposit of iron ore is known to exist in the Wadi es-Sabrah, *ca.* 4⅓ miles SE of Petra, but it does not seem to have been worked until the Nabatean period.

Smelting furnaces discovered near 'Ajlun in N Transjordan (Gilead) are believed to be of medieval date, but the iron mine not far away at Magharat Warda, between the Nahr Zerqa (Jabbok) and the Wadi Rajib, may have been worked in ancient times. The tradition (Deut. 3:11) that Og, king of Bashan, possessed a "bed" (ערש) of iron points to the working of this mine, or some other in N Transjordan, as early as the time of Moses, or earlier. (Among the Transjordanians the word ערש may well have had the meaning "throne," as does Arabic *'arš,* in which case we are reminded of the iron throne which was presented to one of the pre-Hittite kings of Asia Minor, Anittas [*cf.* the work of O. R. Gurney in the *bibliography; see* BEDSTEAD].) By the time Deut. 3:11 was composed, Og's ערש was identified with some megalithic monument at Rabbah (modern er-Rabbah) in S Transjordan. The fact that a Gileadite of the time of David bore the name BARZILLAI ("Iron-Man") also suggests an early connection of Gilead with ironworking. The assertion of the author of Deuteronomy (put into the mouth of Moses) that the Promised Land was one "whose stones are iron, and out of whose hills you can dig copper" (8:9), points to a belief that the working of iron, as well as of copper, went back to the Mosaic period.

Bibliography. F.-M. Abel, *Géographie de la Palestine,* vol. I (1933), ch. 7: "Mineralogie"; N. Glueck, *Explorations in Eastern Palestine, II-IV, AASOR,* vol. XVII (1938); vols. XVIII/XIX (1939); vols. XXV-XXVIII (1951); *The Other Side of the Jordan* (1940), ch. 3: "King Solomon's Copper Mines." O. R. Gurney, *The Hittites* (2nd ed., 1954), pp. 20, 83.

F. V. WINNETT

MINISTER IN THE OT. "Minister" translates משרת, the *Pi'el* participle of שרת, "to minister, serve," a verb that is used to describe service that is not menial. For menial service the root עבד, "to work, serve," is used; though this word is also used of service in worship which is not menial. In the LXX the verb שרת appears almost exclusively as λειτουργεῖν. Other words are the verb λατρέυειν (Num. 16:9; Ezek. 20:32, of priestly function) and the noun θεράπων (lit., "devoted caretaker"), which is used of Joshua in Exod. 33:11. The Aramaic verb פלח, "pay reverence to, serve God," occurs in Dan. 3:12, 14, 17-18, etc., in participial form and in Ezra 7:24 of the servants of the house of God.

Joshua is Moses' minister and deputy and as such serves Moses as his personal attendant and as his deputy in religious duty (cf. Exod. 24:13; 33:11 [E]; Num. 11:28 [J]; Josh. 1:1 [D]), just as Elisha personally attended Elijah (I Kings 19:21). Solomon's domestic attendants were among the features of his court that so astonished the Queen of Sheba (cf. I Kings 10:5, 11; II Chr. 9:4). The verb is also used of higher domestic service, as in the case of Joseph (Gen. 39:4; 40:4); of Elisha's chief servant (II Kings 4:43); and of royal domestics (Esth. 2:2; 6:3; cf. Abishag in I Kings 1:4, 15). These examples show the personal and intimate character of the service. In Ps. 103:21 the hosts of the Lord—i.e., the heavenly company of the angels, God's personal attendants—are named his ministers, and in 104:4 flames of fire are also his ministers (but see the Commentaries for this verse). Isa. 61:6 shows an interesting parallelism between "priests" and "ministers," but both terms are used of Israelites in general in the messianic age. There is an approach in this prophecy, which has been identified by some scholars as a fifth Servant Song, to the idea of the universal priesthood and ministry—i.e., to the ministry of each of God's children, as distinct from the ministry of all believers in a corporate body. As such they will share in the riches and favors of the Gentiles (cf. 56:6; 60:10).

This prophetic parallelism of "priest" and "minister" is grounded in the fact that "minister" often occurs of specifically religious duties and in connection with the priests. Thus Jer. 33:21 (and cf. the strange phrase in the Hebrew of 33:22) identifies the Levites, the priests, as "my ministers." Ezekiel, too, permits Levites to be ministers in Yahweh's sanctuary (44:11; 45:5), but the real ministers are the priests, the ministers of the sanctuary, who come near to minister to Yahweh—i.e., the Zadokite priests (44: 11). In Joel priests are described as the ministers of the altar, and ministers of God, and as such they weep and make intercession between the porch and the altar (Joel 1:9, 13; 2:17). Similarly the verb is used (*a*) of religious duties in the sanctuary (cf. Exod. 28:43); (*b*) of Levites with various accusatives, including Aaronic priests (Num. 3:6; 8:26), the Lord (I Chr. 15:2; II Chr. 29:11), etc.; (*c*) of Zadokite priests in Ezekiel (42:14, etc.); (*d*) of Aaronic priests (Exod. 28:35, etc. [P]). Ezekiel also uses the verb once (20:32) of the idolatrous worship of wood and stone.

A comparison of the participle and the ordinary verb in their general and cultic usages shows that the ministry described is both personal and devoted. The emphasis on personal attendance in the general usage of the word must be carried over to the understanding of the close personal attendance of the priests on Yahweh. Similarly the emphasis on religious devotion in the priestly usage of the word must figure in the understanding of the devoted ministry of attendants in the general sense.

See also PRIESTS AND LEVITES.

Bibliography. H. Lietzmann, "Zur altchristlichen Verfassungsgeschichte," *Zeitschrift für wissenschaftliche Theologie,* LV (1914), 97-153. W. Brandt, *Dienst und Dienen im NT* (1931). A. C. Headlam and F. Gerke, "The Origin of the Christian Ministry," in R. Dunkerley, ed., *The Ministry and the Sacraments* (1937), pp. 326-67. K. L. Schmidt, "Le ministère et les ministères dans l'église du NT," *RHPR,* XVII (1937), 314-36; "Amt und Ämter im NT," *Theologische Zeitschrift,* I (1945), 309-11. A. M. Farrer, "The Ministry in the NT," in K. E. Kirk, ed., *The Apostolic Ministry* (1946), pp. 113-82. T. W. Manson, *The Church's Ministry* (1948). P. H. Menoud, *L'Eglise et les ministères selon le NT* (1949), pp. 35-55 (especially 50-55). H. J. Carpenter, "Minister," in A. Richardson, ed., *A Theological Word Book of the Bible* (1950), pp. 146-52.

G. HENTON DAVIES

MINISTRY, CHRISTIAN. Few subjects in the history of the church have received such disputed interpretations as the origin and development of the ministry. The differences of interpreters stem in part from the meager, and apparently contradictory, notices on the subject in the NT and early patristic sources. To a greater degree, however, they are the result of conflicting theological views respecting the nature of the church, and the necessity or expediency of certain forms of ministry for the essential constitution of the church, both in its inner organic unity and in its outer historic structure. Involved in these disputes have been questions concerning the several sources of ministerial authority, the manner of selection and ordination of ministers, and the transmission of ministerial authority to succeeding generations of the church's ongoing life and mission.

These issues are not entirely modern in origin. Many are reflected in the apostolic and postapostolic writings. E.g., Paul was often engaged in defense of his own apostolic commission and authority. At an early date the primitive church found itself faced with the necessity of providing criteria for judging between true and false prophets and teachers. The letters of Clement and Ignatius reveal serious divisions among the Christians of the postapostolic generation regarding the position and prerogatives of the episcopate.

1. Jesus and the ministry
2. The Twelve and the Seven
3. James and the apostles
4. Origin of elders
5. Prophets and teachers
6. Other charismatic ministries
7. Bishops, elders, and deacons
   a. Jewish prototypes
   b. Gentile prototypes
   c. In Paul and Acts
   d. The postapostolic age
8. The monarchical episcopate
9. Apostolic succession

Bibliography

1. Jesus and the ministry. Any consideration of the origin of the Christian ministry must of necessity begin with the intention and action of Jesus, since all ministries of the Christian churches claim to be ministries of Christ. Two characteristics of Jesus' teaching about ministry are noteworthy, with regard both to himself and to his disciples. One is represented by the word "to send" (ἀποστέλλειν), the other by the word "to serve" (διακονεῖν). In many passages of the gospels, Jesus describes himself as "sent" upon his mission by the Father (Matt. 15:24; Mark 9:37; Luke 9: 48; John 3:17; 5:36; 6:29, 57; 7:29; 8:42; 11:42; 17: 3, 8, 18, 21, 23, 25; 20:21). The same theme occurs in several of the parables, notably that of the wicked husbandmen (Mark 12:1 ff and parallels).

Similarly, in turn, Jesus "sent" forth the Twelve (Matt. 10:5, 10; Mark 3:14; 6:7; Luke 9:2; John 4: 38) and the Seventy (Luke 10:1), with the pronouncement that whoever received them also received him who "sent" them (Matt. 10:40), in the same manner that those who received Christ received the Father who "sent" him (Mark 9:37; cf. Luke 10:16; John 17:8, 25). Underlying all these sayings is the meaning that those who are thus sent are especially chosen by the divine will for their mission, and they bear the authority of him who sent them forth.

Jesus also emphasized the quality of "serving" as a fundamental characteristic of such a ministry. Again, he pointed to himself as the model and example. "I am among you as one who serves" (Luke 22:27; cf. John 13:13-15). Greatness in the ministry is accounted, not in outward rank, but in proportion to service (Matt. 20:25-28; Mark 10:42-45; Luke 22: 24-27). And only for service is there promise of great reward. "If any one serves me, he must follow me; and where I am, there shall my servant be also; if any one serves me, the Father will honor him" (John 12:26).

A more difficult problem concerns the question whether Jesus' outlook was purely eschatological, in his expectation of the imminent coming of the kingdom of God as the climax of his own mission, or whether he foresaw an interim period, of whatever span of time, between his ascension and his second advent and hence provided some kind of organization for his disciples during the interval. There is no indication in the gospels that Jesus formally repudiated—despite his trenchant criticism of their leadership and character—the hierarchies of Judaism established in Sanhedrin, temple, and synagogue. He was himself subject to their ministrations, and counseled his followers to be likewise (cf. Matt. 23:3).

2. The Twelve and the Seven. It is true that Jesus selected from his followers, upon his own authority and for the purpose of fulfilling his divinely predestined ministry, the TWELVE. The number was symbolic of the twelve tribes that constituted the Israel of God (cf. Rev. 21:14). To them he gave particular training and a definite commission to assist and extend his work of preaching and healing among the people (Mark 3:13 ff and parallels; cf. John 6:70). And to the Twelve he gave a promise that they should sit enthroned with him in the coming judgment upon Israel (Matt. 19:28; Luke 22:30).

If these passages stood alone in the gospel narratives, the case would be clear that the Twelve were chosen by Jesus solely for a ministry during his earthly career and at the eschatological judgment. But the resurrection narratives contain a definite commission by the risen Lord to the eleven witnesses (Judas having defected) to carry the gospel to the whole world (Luke 24:46-48; Acts 1:8), with authority to baptize (Matt. 28:19) and to remit sins (John 20:23). Such a commission implies, at the least, the formation and governance of a specific historical community of Christian disciples.

The resurrection commission, it is true, was not exclusively granted to the Twelve, but to a wider number of "apostles" (*see* § 3 *below*); and it is probable that the narratives of the Resurrection reflect in some degree the ex-post-facto experience of the early church. But the intention of Jesus for a ministry of the Twelve to the community of his disciples after the close of his earthly life finds support in the promise to Peter of a peculiar position of leadership (Matt. 16:18; cf. Luke 22:32), and in the command to repeat the Supper of the Lord (Luke 22:19; I Cor. 11:24-25; *see* LAST SUPPER). The critic who rules out the historical authenticity of all these passages lays himself open to the charge of manipulating the evidence in the interest of preconceived theories.

In any event, the evidence of Acts 1–6 presents the Twelve (with Matthias in the place of Judas), under the leadership of Peter, in charge of both the missionary propaganda of the church and the liturgical, teaching, and disciplinary activities of its corporate life.

At an early stage in the church's growth, it became advisable for the Twelve to delegate a pastoral responsibility for the Hellenist widows to a group of seven disciples. These men were chosen by the entire community of believers on the basis of their character, wisdom, and evident endowment with the Holy Spirit. The Twelve ordained them with prayer and the laying on of hands. The author of Acts possibly viewed this ordination of the SEVEN as the institution of the ministerial order of DEACON. Yet he does not use the noun "deacon" to designate them, though he employs the verb διακονεῖν ("to serve") to describe their function of ministering charity from the "tables" of the church. In his brief accounts of their ministry, however, he portrays them as preachers, similar to the Twelve; and in a later passage (21:8) he denotes one of them, Philip, as an EVANGELIST. The selection and ordination of the Seven may well have been a singular act in the life of the early church, called forth by a particular need at a given time. But it may well have served as a model of later differentiations of ordained ministries in the church. For the qualifications of office, and the means of selection and conferral of ministerial authority, in the case of the Seven, were adopted for other and similar ordinations.

3. James and the apostles. Following upon the narrative of the Seven, the author of Acts abandons the use of the term "Twelve" to describe the leaders of the church in Jerusalem, and thenceforward employs the word "APOSTLE." With ch. 15, the governing group are named "apostles and elders," over whom there presides, not Peter, but James the Lord's brother. This transition in leadership is in no place explained by the author of Acts, nor do we find any clues to the change in the letters of Paul. The latter mentions the Twelve once (I Cor. 15:5), in connection with the resurrection appearances. Otherwise Paul speaks only of "apostles" at Jerusalem, including James (Gal. 1:17, 19; cf. 2:9, where James, Cephas, and John are called "pillars"). In general, Luke-Acts employs the terms "Twelve" and "apostles" synonymously—the chief exceptions being Acts 14:4, 14. It is obvious from Paul's own vigorous defense of his claim to be an apostle, and his use of the term for others besides the Twelve, that the word "apostle" denoted a wider circle of leaders than the Twelve (cf. Rom. 16:7; I Cor. 15:7; Gal. 1:19). By Paul's definition, an apostle was a witness of the Resurrection who had received a commission to preach the gospel directly from the risen Lord (cf. I Cor. 9:1 ff), and the same view is implied in Acts (1:21-22).

The ministry of James, apostles, and elders in the mother church of Jerusalem was unique of its kind, and presented a Christian counterpart to the Jewish SANHEDRIN under the leadership of the high priest, with much the same dignity and, doubtless, with claims to much of the same prerogatives among Christian believers. Besides immediate oversight of the spiritual and material needs of the local congregation in Jerusalem, this group exercised a general supervision over the churches of Judea, and certain of its more orthodox Jewish members conceived of it as a final authority for the whole church. It was this council that determined, in consultation with Paul and Barnabas, the conditions of Christian communion between Jewish and Gentile Christians (Acts 15; Gal. 2), thus exercising a supreme judicial and disciplinary prerogative. Some of its emissaries attempted to control the behavior of Jewish Christians in churches far afield (cf. Gal. 2:12), but any such interference in mission churches outside Judea was stoutly resisted by Paul, though Paul himself was not unsubmissive to its directives when he was a visitor in Jerusalem (cf. Acts 21:18 ff).

The leadership of James (*see* JAMES 5) over the Jerusalem church was due not merely to his apostolic dignity and the reputation of his character and piety, but in large measure to a dynastic principle. As the nearest male relative of the Messiah, he was his personal representative on earth until Christ's return. Streeter described the situation as a "caliphate." After James's death, the headship of the church in Jerusalem continued to be held by members of Jesus' family until, apparently, the line died out with Simeon in the early years of the second century. To describe James, in the usage of later generations, as the first "bishop" of Jerusalem is anachronistic; nor can his rule be termed as absolutely monarchical, since he appears in all fundamental decisions to have acted only in counsel with the other apostles and elders. It is possible, however, that the ordering of the church in Jerusalem in the earliest days may have served in some way as a model for the later emergence throughout the church of the monarchical episcopate.

The apostles, by virtue of their singular commission to evangelize, were traveling missionaries and founders of churches. Jerusalem was not of necessity a base of operation for all of them. There may be some significance in the fact that at the time of Paul's last visit to Jerusalem he found no apostles (Acts 21:18). We know very little of the labors of most of the apostles, other than Paul. Their authority in the churches that they founded, if we may judge from Paul's claims, was absolute, they being final arbiters in all questions of worship, discipline, and doctrine. Obviously, the force of this authority was tempered by the personal abilities and the powers of persuasion of the individual apostle himself. In larger communities, where several apostles carried on missionary activity, there were bound to be conflicts of loyalty and party divisions. We do not know, however, how such churches as those of Ephesus, Corinth, or Rome—to name but a few of the more distinguished that claimed more than one apostolic founder—achieved organic unity about a commonly accepted ministry.

4. Origin of elders. The NT does not record the original institution of elders (or presbyters) in the church; but it is obvious that the office was modeled upon the Jewish eldership, both of the Jerusalem Sanhedrin and of the local presbyteries found in all organized Jewish communities. Acts 14:23 informs us that Paul and Barnabas ordained elders in the churches they founded on their missionary journey in Asia Minor. One may infer from this that it was a customary procedure of the apostles to provide their churches with responsible leaders who would have oversight of the churches during their absence and advise them of any difficult or special problems.

The elders would be chosen from the wiser and more experienced members of the community, usually but not necessarily "old" men. Vacancies, when no longer supplied by the apostles, would be filled by coöptation, with ordination to office by prayer and the laying on of hands of the apostle (if present) and the entire presbyterial group (cf. I Tim. 4:14). So much may be assumed by analogy with the Jewish prototype, but the NT evidence is very scant.

It is even more difficult to determine the exact ministerial duties of the elders in apostolic times. The office is not once mentioned in the genuine letters of Paul, and the evidence of the later NT writings of the postapostolic age must be used with caution in view of the more developed concept of the office. The word "elder" has been taken by some critics to be more of a description of status and dignity than of a specific ministerial order. But if the analogy of Jewish elders may be used, the Christian elders must have had at least some responsibilities of a judicial nature, both in the interpretation of permissible doctrine and usage and in the discipline of offenders against the church's faith and ethic. Such responsibility would imply some kind of pastoral ministry (cf. Jas. 5:14), and at least, in the absence of other qualified persons, a capacity to lead the church's worship. *See* ELDER IN THE NT.

5. Prophets and teachers. Highly regarded in the life of the primitive church were the ministries of prophets and teachers. There is no hint that these were in any way ordained men. Their ministry rested upon recognition in the church of their immediately inspired character. Their model was Christ himself. Jesus was taken by many of the people to be a prophet (Mark 8:28 and parallels; Luke 7:16; 24:19; John 4:19; 6:14; 7:40; 9:17), and he accepted the role of prophet (Matt. 23:37; Mark 6:4 and parallels; Luke 13:33-34; John 4:44). He was commonly addressed, even by his enemies, as "rabbi" or "teacher" (Matt. 26:25, 49; Mark 9:5; 10:51; 11:21; 14:45; John 1:49; 3:2; 4:31; 6:25; 9:2; 11:8; etc.). Both prophets and teachers were well known in Judaism, though prophecy had become virtually extinct until suddenly revived by John the Baptist and Jesus.

The prominence of prophets and prophesying in the early church stemmed in large degree from the fervor of religious experience and in particular from the possession by the church of the Holy Spirit, whose outpouring on the believers was a sign of the dawn of the age to come (cf. Acts 2:17 ff). Paul's ranking of prophets and teachers immediately after apostles, in the order of spiritual gifts (I Cor. 12:28; cf. Rom. 12:6; Eph. 4:11), was probably not a singular opinion of his own.

Prophets and teachers were not permanently attached to one community, but wandered from place to place as prompted by the Spirit. In Acts we meet a few of them by name: Agabus, a Judean, prophesying at Antioch (11:28) and Caesarea (21:10); Judas and Silas, who accompanied Paul and Barnabas from Jerusalem to Antioch (15:32)—the latter of whom (Silas) was later associated with Paul in missionary labors in Asia Minor and Greece. Prophetic inspiration—as in Judaism—was not confined to men. The four unmarried daughters of Philip were prophetesses (Acts 21:9). After some time spent with their father in Caesarea, they later moved with him to Asia Minor, where they settled in Hierapolis (Euseb. Hist. III.31.3-4; V.24.2).

In Acts 13:1-3 a primitive tradition informs us that for a time the church in Antioch was actually led by a group of prophets and teachers who presided over the worship and directed, through inspiration by the Spirit, its missionary ventures. How typical this situation may have been in Gentile mission churches, we cannot say. But the custom appears to have continued in many places in Syria into the second century, if we may trust the Didache (11-15), which portrays Christian congregations without a settled ministry and dependent upon wandering prophets and teachers. Even as late as the latter part of the second century, the challenge to episcopal authority presented by the new prophecy of Montanism reveals the strength of prophetic leadership in the primitive tradition of the church.

6. Other charismatic ministries. The earliest Christians highly esteemed "spiritual gifts" quite apart from any ecclesiastical rank or office held by those who possessed them. In all his extant correspondence Paul has little to say about official ministries, other than that of an apostle, though he is not unmindful of the obedience and love owed to those who labor and lead and admonish his congregations "in the Lord" (I Cor. 16:15-16; I Thess. 5:12). Unruly elements were not lacking in his churches, and Paul was enough of an authoritarian himself to appreciate a strong hand of discipline and a sound voice of instruction. But to Paul, ministry in the church was primarily a function or a grace, not an office. It was an exercise by each and every member of the church of his own charism of the Spirit to the edification of all (Rom. 12:6-8; I Cor. 7:7; 12:4-11, 28-31; cf. I Pet. 4:11; I Clem. 38:1; Did. 1:5). Even apostleship was to Paul a "spiritual gift"; and it is as charism that he describes to the Roman Christians his projected apostolic visitation (Rom. 1:11). These gifts were not severally exclusive; a Christian might possess one or many. Nor were they of equal value. Paul certainly thought prophesying of more worth than speaking in tongues. And he would have placed the gifts of grace—faith, hope, charity—above all others. His famous "hymn to charity" as the "more excellent way" follows immediately upon his discussion of the greater charisms (I Cor. 12:31). *See* SPIRITUAL GIFTS.

The difficulties inherent in reliance upon charismatic ministries were always apparent. They had to be tested, both as to their genuineness and as to their edifying effect. Yet such tests, if not purely subjective, ran the risk of "quenching the Spirit" (cf. I Cor. 12:3, 14; I Thess. 5:19-21). Jesus had warned his disciples of the coming of false prophets (Matt. 24:24; Mark 13:22), and the warning, as repeated in the traditions peculiar to Matthew (7:15; 24:11), reflects a real problem in the time the first gospel was written. To his chagrin, Paul acknowledged that the uninhibited exercise of charisms, as at Corinth, was more conducive to disorder than to edification. In the literature of the postapostolic age, references to false prophets and teachers become cumulative (e.g., I Tim. 4:1; 6:3-5; II Tim. 4:3; II Pet. 2:1; I John 4:1; Polyc. Phil. 7:2). The directions given in the Didache for testing them, though they strike the modern reader with mild amusement, were no less a real attempt to give objective criteria of judgment.

On the other hand, the esteem of charisms had a lasting effect upon the church's concept of an ordained ministry. For whatever the office to which a man was called and commissioned by the laying on of hands, it was demanded that evidence be forthcoming that he had received a charism appropriate to his particular ministerial order. So I Clem. 42:4 affirms that the apostles "appointed their firstfruits, after testing them by the Spirit, as bishops and deacons." In the Pastorals, Timothy is reminded of the charisma "which was given you by prophetic utterance when the elders laid their hands upon you" (I Tim. 4:14; cf. II Tim. 1:6). The oldest ordination prayers extant, those in Hippolytus' *Apostolic Tradition*, pray God to "pour forth the power that is from Thee of the princely Spirit" and to "grant the spirit of grace."

7. Bishops, elders, and deacons. The most difficult problem in the history of the development of the Christian ministry has to do with the transition from the varied ministries of the apostolic age to the threefold orders of bishops, elders (or presbyters), and deacons that were universally established and recognized in the church by the time of Ignatius and Polycarp (*ca.* A.D. 120). The principal questions debated are: (*a*) the relation of bishops and elders—whether they were originally the same, and, if not, how they were distinguished one from the other; (*b*) the emergence of a single, monarchical bishop as the head of each Christian community; and (*c*) the means of selection and ordination of these orders. For more detailed discussion of these problems, *see* BISHOP; DEACON; ELDER IN THE NT.

a. Jewish prototypes. There is no question about the derivation of the order of elders from the Jewish presbyterate (*see* § 4 *above*). But the terms for "bishop" (ἐπίσκοπος, "overseer") and "deacon" (διάκονος, "servant") are not found in Jewish sources to denote cultic or governmental offices of any kind. In view of the close association of bishops and deacons with the church's worship, it has frequently been suggested that Jewish prototypes of these ministries existed in the two officials of the synagogue who exercised somewhat analogous functions. The ruler of a synagogue (ἀρχισυνάγωγος; cf. Mark 5:22 ff; Luke 8:49; 13:14; Acts 13:15; 18:8, 17; *see* SYNAGOGUE), normally elected for life, presided in the synagogue worship and served as general arbiter of synagogue affairs in much the same way that the Christian bishop acted in the corporate religious life of the churches. The ruler had a helper, the hazzan (ὑπερέτης; cf. Luke 4:20), who performed lesser duties, ranging from that of caretaker of the synagogue building to that of schoolteacher for the children.

Since the earliest Christian churches were initially gathered from synagogue congregations, it is reasonable to suppose that an organization developed in the church comparable to that found in Jewish congregations. The principal objection to such a theory—apart from its failure to explain the origin of the terms "bishop" and "deacon"—is the fact that bishops and deacons were sacramental ministers, and were also engaged in a greater degree of pastoral and charitable duties than is indicated by the sources with regard to the synagogue officials.

The finds of the DEAD SEA SCROLLS have brought to the fore some discussion of the possible influence of the Qumran and similar "Essene" communities upon the organization and ministry of the early church. The Manual of Discipline, e.g., divides the community into ranks of priests, elders, and people. A council of fifteen—three priests and twelve laymen—has special charge of expounding the law and administering discipline. (One is inevitably reminded here of the Twelve and the three "pillars" of the Jerusalem church; cf. Gal. 2:9). There is also an overseer (מבקר) who supervises the new members and looks after the finances of the community. Scholarly research on these new materials has not advanced sufficiently to date, however, to justify any positive conclusions respecting the relation of these groups to primitive Christianity; but the parallels of organization should not be ignored by students of Christian origins.

b. Gentile prototypes. The terms "bishop" and "deacon," denoting officers of pagan cults and associations, are frequently found in Greek inscriptions from all parts of the Mediterranean world. But it is difficult to determine their precise meaning in these contexts. In central Syria, especially, the title *episkopos* occurs in both sacral and civil lists, always with something of its primary meaning of "overseer"; but it describes not only directors, curators, and cashiers, but also supervisors of provisions and buildings. The word "deacon" is much less frequent; often it denotes waiters in some cult association. The total evidence is not weighty enough to demand a secular or pagan derivation for Christian use of these titles. It only shows that the terms were known and flexible enough to admit of varying connotations depending upon the specific community that employed them.

c. In Paul and Acts. In no place does Paul mention elders; but in the address of Phil. 1:1 he singles out "bishops and deacons" for particular greeting. Both the KJV and the RSV translate the terms thus, though it has been disputed whether the words here have so technical a sense. But Philippians is a letter of thanks for charitable assistance sent the apostle during his imprisonment. It would be natural, therefore, for Paul to mention those who were especially charged with its supervision and service.

Paul also uses the word translated "deacon" in other letters in a more general sense of "servant" or "helper" in the work of evangelism. Thus he uses the term of Christ (Rom. 15:8; Gal. 2:17); of himself and other missionaries (I Cor. 3:5; II Cor. 3:6; 6:4; 11:15, 23; Col. 1:23, 25; cf. Eph. 3:7); of helpers such as Timothy (I Thess. 3:2), Tychicus (Col. 4:7; cf. Eph. 6:21), and Epaphras (Col. 1:7); and also of civil magistrates as "God's servants" (Rom. 13:4). In one place (Rom. 16:1), Paul may have used the term technically of a deaconess.

With the reference of Phil. 1:1 is often associated the speech of Paul to the Ephesian elders related in Acts 20:17 ff, in the course of which Paul addresses them as *episkopoi* (vs. 28; RSV "guardians"; KJV "overseers"). The speeches of Acts are probably compositions of the author, and therefore represent the outlook of his own generation. The interpretation of this passage is particularly problematic, however; for some have taken it to mean an original identity of bishops and elders, while others claim that in this instance the elders addressed were but a select group of men with specifically episcopal responsibilities. Still others (as the translators of the KJV and the RSV) maintain that *episkopoi* has in this context only a general, not a technical, sense.

d. The postapostolic age. Similar ambiguities surround other scattered notices in the later NT books. In I Pet. 5:1 ff, the author, reputedly an apostle, but describing himself also as an elder, exhorts his fellow elders to "exercise oversight" (ἐπισκοποῦντες) in their care of God's flock. But the context shows that elders are here distinguished from younger members, and may therefore mean no more than "older" men, upon whom leadership and responsibility in the church must fall. The same writer also uses ἐπίσκοπος of Christ (2:25; RSV "Guardian"; KJV "Bishop").

Little can be established from the single reference to elders in Jas. 5:14, or from the much-disputed figure who styles himself "the elder" in the addresses of II and III John. Whether the latter was the apostle John, or another John—a disciple of apostolic dignity, a monarchical bishop, or an elder of repute, or merely an old man of experience and authority—cannot be determined from the ambiguous traditions that have developed about his personage.

The evidence of the PASTORAL LETTERS would be more helpful if these letters could be dated and placed with greater security; for they provide the clearest testimony in the NT to the developed norm of a threefold hierarchy. Qualifications for all three orders are listed in Tit. 1:5-9; I Tim. 3:1-13, but with the curious circumstance that deacons are not mentioned in the former passage, nor elders in the latter. Moreover, the abrupt transition in Tit. 1:7 from the discussion of elders to that of bishops is awkward, and has suggested to some critics possible interpolation. I Tim. 4:14 contains, too, a reference to ordination by the laying on of hands of the elders; but it is uncertain whether Timothy himself is the ordinand, or whether his name merely stands for some bishop or elder to whom the letter was actually addressed. Thus, while the Pastorals provide reference to the three ministerial orders, in an apparently distinguishable form, they do not clarify with precision their respective relationship or means of transmission.

The DIDACHE is likewise a document of disputed date. Concerned with the uncertain quality of charismatic ministries, the author advises the churches to appoint "bishops and deacons worthy of the Lord, meek men and not lovers of money, truthful and tested, for they also minister to you the 'liturgy' of prophets and teachers" (15:1). No mention is made of elders. The context shows that bishops and deacons are especially responsible for worship, and also, presumably, for the offerings of the people. The qualifications for these offices are much the same as those enumerated in the Pastoral letters. Nothing is said, however, as to how these ministries are to be appointed and ordained.

The letter of the Roman church to the church in Corinth, *ca.* A.D. 95, known as the First Epistle of Clement (*see* CLEMENT, EPISTLE OF), is concerned particularly with the deposition by the Corinthians of their bishops and deacons and the factional disputes caused thereby. The writer believes (see especially 42-44) these ministries were not only divinely ordered and prophesied in the OT, but were also established by specific regulation of the apostles and continued through other "approved" and "eminent" men who succeeded to the ministry of the apostles. He condemns, therefore, the removal from office of those who have "blamelessly and holily offered the sacrifices" (i.e., the Eucharist). And, says he, "blessed are the elders who have finished their course before now . . . for they have no fear lest anyone shall remove them from their appointed office."

It is by no means clear whether the author of I Clement employs "elders" in this passage in a technical sense, as synonymous with "bishops" and "deacons," or whether he is thinking merely of men of a past and older generation. The passage is also patient of an interpretation which distinguishes elders in general from elders that have an appointed office—namely, the bishops and deacons who offer the Eucharistic gifts.

Thus none of the surviving documents of the postapostolic age provides sufficient material to explain the emergence of the threefold, clearly distinguishable orders of bishop, elders, and deacons that stand out so clearly from the letters of IGNATIUS, the martyr-bishop of Antioch, which were written before A.D. 117 (*see also* BISHOP). Not only does Ignatius make the elders, no less than the deacons, subordinate to the bishop; but he is the first clear witness to the "monarchical" episcopate—i.e., the custom of a single bishop's presiding as authoritative leader over the entire Christian community in any one city or place. Ignatius does not speak in any passage, however, of ordination or ministerial succession.

8. The monarchical episcopate. Two theories, each with variations of detail, generally claim the allegiance of scholars in explaining the significance of the data outlined in the previous section. One is the classic hypothesis of Lightfoot, that originally "bishops" and "elders" were synonymous terms, but that the episcopate arose out of the presbyterate by "elevation" into a distinct and higher order. Harnack, who held this view, stressed the distinction between the universal ministries of apostle, prophet, and teacher, and the local ministries of bishops-elders and deacons. Streeter saw in some instances evidence of a mediate stage of a collegiate episcopate before the monarchical system was firmly established.

The other theory maintains an original distinction of the two orders of bishop and elder, without denying that bishops may also have been numbered among the presbyterate. But not all elders were bishops. The bishops were "appointed elders," specifically ordained for liturgical, pastoral, and economic functions, in which the deacons assisted them. There may have been one or more bishops in the earliest communities, depending upon their size and number of congregations. But in any event, the office of bishop was always distinct, and its origin goes back to apostolic appointment of those who, being tested by the Spirit, manifested the appropriate charism for the office. The elders enjoyed a position of honor, not of ministerial office. But with the rise of the monarchical episcopate, elders had delegated to them by the bishops certain ministerial functions of a liturgical and pastoral nature. This theory, developed by Sohm and Lowrie, is thus the opposite of the other: the episcopate did not arise by elevation out of the presbyterate; but the presbyterate as an order of ministry and not merely a title of honor came into being by delegation from the episcopate.

Neither of these theories solves, however, the obscure problem of ordination and succession. The sources are too scanty to allow positive statements. The apostles may very well have ordained the first bishops and elders; or they may have been ordained by prophets and teachers, or any other "eminent" leaders. It is even possible that some of the early bishops were placed in their office by popular acclamation. Similarly, the succession of ministers from one generation to the other might have been maintained by bishops or by elders, or by both together, with or without the assistance of prophets and other charismatics. It is only at the turn of the third century, in the work of Hippolytus, that the first clear notice survives of what was then viewed as "apostolic tradition" in the matter of ordination—namely, bishops were ordained by other bishops; elders were ordained by a bishop with the assistance of other elders; deacons were ordained by a bishop alone.

9. Apostolic succession. The concept of regular succession to office and ministry was not unknown to Judaism, being associated both with the eldership and with the rabbinate, and, in a different way, with the idea of a succession of prophets raised up by God for his people. But the Jews did not make a doctrine out of succession, or stress the need of an uninterrupted series of ordinations by the laying on of hands. The early Christians of apostolic times could hardly have had much interest in the matter, however, in view of their eschatological hope of the early return of the Lord from heaven. It was the tension of threatened schism and the rise of heretical teaching in the postapostolic age that brought to the fore concern for an identifiable succession of leaders who could claim authority to speak for the faith and order imparted to the church by its original founders and the disciples of the Lord.

The first explicit description of a ministerial succession from the apostles occurs in the Letter of Clement, cited above. But the same idea is implicit in the Pastoral letters, with their emphasis upon a regular appointment of ministers who will teach sound doctrine and manifest exemplary character. Crystallization of the doctrine of apostolic succession, borne by the church's episcopate, came into clear focus only in the latter half of the second century. It was a reaction to the claim of Gnostic heretics to possess an esoteric teaching handed down to them in secret succession from the apostles. Orthodox leaders, notably Irenaeus (Her. III.3-4), countered this claim by an appeal to the open teaching of the true, apostolic faith maintained by the bishops who had succeeded the apostles in the government of the chief churches. Not only Irenaeus, but others also drew up lists of names of bishops who had thus succeeded one another uninterruptedly. The interest of these orthodox fathers was not as yet involved in the question of ordination. They were concerned solely with identifying a series of ministers who had guarded the apostolic doctrine. Similarly, with the outbreak of the Montanist schism, church leaders and theologians such as Hippolytus drew up lists of orthodox prophets from apostolic times to counter the claims of the new prophets of Montanist inspiration. Only in later times, when the bishops themselves, who were the supposed guardians of the apostolic faith, were in disagreement as to that faith, did the doctrine of apostolic succession necessarily undergo a change of emphasis, and a greater concern develop with respect to the agents and the manner of ordination.

Bibliography. J. B. Lightfoot, "The Christian Ministry," *Saint Paul's Epistle to the Philippians* (rev. ed., 1890), pp. 181-269; E. Hatch, *The Organization of the Early Christian Churches* (1892); R. Sohm, *Kirchenrecht,* vol. I (1892); W. Lowrie, *The Church and Its Organization in Primitive and Catholic Times* (1904); A. Harnack, *The Constitution and Law of the Church in the First Two Centuries* (1910); T. M. Lindsay, *The Church and the Ministry in the Early Centuries* (4th ed., 1910); H. Lietzmann, "Zur altchristlichen Verfassungsgeschichte," *Zeitschrift für wissenschaftliche Theologie,* LV (1913), 97-153; H. B. Swete, ed., *Essays on the Early History of the Church and the Ministry* (1921); B. H. Streeter, *The Primitive Church* (1929); O. Linton,

Das Problem der Urkirche in der neueren Forschung (1932); R. Dunkerley, ed., *The Ministry and the Sacraments* (1937); M. H. Shepherd, Jr., "The Development of the Early Ministry," *ATR,* XXVI (1944), 135-50; K. E. Kirk, ed., *The Apostolic Ministry* (1946), pp. 113-303; T. W. Manson, *The Church's Ministry* (1948); G. W. H. Lampe, *Some Aspects of the NT Ministry* (1949); A. Ehrhardt, *The Apostolic Succession in the First Two Centuries of the Church* (1953); H. F. von Campenhausen, *Kirchliches Amt und geistliche Vollmacht in den ersten drei Jahrhunderten* (1953); E. Molland, "Le développement de l'idée de succession apostolique," *RHPR,* XXXIV (1954), 1-29; F. W. Beare, "The Ministry in the NT Church: Practice and Theory," *ATR,* XXXVII (1955), 3-18; J. Knox, *The Early Church and the Coming Great Church* (1955), pp. 101-29. *See also* the bibliographies under APOSTLE; BISHOP.

M. H. SHEPHERD, JR.

MINNI mĭn'ī [מִנִּי] (Jer. 51:27). A people and a state, to be located in the area directly S of Lake Urmia.

In the only place where it is mentioned in the OT, the kingdom of Minni, together with the kingdoms of Ararat and Ashkenaz, is summoned by Yahweh to destroy the wicked Babylon. As Ararat is the same as Urarṭu of the Assyrian cuneiform sources, the name of a region to be located S of Lake Van; and as Ashkenaz corresponds to Ašguzaya, Iškuzaya (applied to the people later known as Scythians) in the Assyrian sources, which often refer to the people thus designated in connection with the Urarteans; it seems logical to locate the Minni of the OT in the same general area and to connect them with the Manneans, who are regularly mentioned along with the Urarteans in the historical inscriptions of the late Assyrian kings. The cuneiform *Mannaya* (or *Mannay*), a gentilic formation from *Man* or *Manna,* corresponds to the OT *Minnī,* in view of the phonetic change *a>i,* well known in Hebrew (as in the case of the form attested in cuneiform as *Ḫatti,* which changes to *Ḥittīm* in Hebrew). The attested history of the Manneans begins with the reign of the Assyrian king Shalmaneser III (858-824 B.C.) and continues until the end of the Assyrian Empire. A connection between the Manneans-Minni and "Minyas in Armenia" mentioned in Jos. Antiq. I.iii.6 must be rejected, because these names cannot be associated in accordance with phonetic principles. For an article concerning the exact area occupied by the Manneans in Assyrian times, *see bibliography.*

Bibliography. M. Streck, "Die Mannäer-Gebiete," *ZA,* XIV (1899), 134-48. I. J. GELB

MINNITH mĭn'ĭth [מִנִּית] (Judg. 11:33). One of the "twenty cities" involved in Jephthah's military conquest of the Ammonites (Judg. 11:29-33). The precise location is unknown, although it must have been situated in the general area W and S of Rabbah-ammon (modern Amman) in E Palestine. In Eusebius *Onomastica* (140.3; ed. Lagarde), it is identified with a village some four Roman miles NE of Heshbon which still bore the name Μαανιθ. Several contemporary antiquity sites have been suggested, among them Khirbet Hanizeh (or Khirbet umm el-Hanafish), halfway between Heshbon and el-Yadudeh.

Bibliography. A. Alt, "Die Ausflüge und Reise (Strassen um Philadelphia)," *PJB,* 29 (1933), 27-28. G. M. LANDES

MINSTRELSY. *See* MUSIC.

MINT [ἡδύοσμον, *lit.,* sweet odor]. A sweet-smelling herb, the leaves and stems of which contain an aromatic oil which is used in medicine and food-seasoning. Mint is referred to in Matt. 23:23 (=Luke 11:42) in connection with Jesus' criticism of the Pharisees, who required the tithing even of mint, DILL, and CUMMIN (cf. Luke 11:42: mint, RUE, and every herb; cf. also Deut. 14:22-23), but had "neglected the weightier matters of the law, justice and mercy and faith" (cf. Mic. 6:8).

Several species of mint (*Mentha*) are found growing wild in the Holy Land, in moist places, especially along banks of streams. *Mentha longifolia* L. (commonly called "horse mint") is the more common variety today.

52. Mint

Mint apparently was included with those herbs used as BITTER HERBS (Exod. 12:8; Num. 9:11) with the Pascal lamb, according to the Jewish Talmud (Pes. 2.6).

Fig. MIN 52.

Bibliography. I. Löw, *Die Flora der Juden,* II (1924), 67-68, 75-78; G. E. Post, *Flora of Syria, Palestine and Sinai,* II (1933), 329-32; H. N. and A. L. Moldenke, *Plants of the Bible* (1952), pp. 139-40. J. C. TREVER

MINUSCULE mĭ nŭs'kyəl. The small (hence the name) cursive writing developed out of the earlier, UNCIAL style (large, separated letters) and characteristic of virtually all Greek and Latin MSS of the Bible after the ninth century; also, a MS written in this style. *See* TEXT, NT, § B4. J. KNOX

MIPHKAD, GATE. KJV translation of שער המפקד (RSV MUSTER GATE).

***MIRACLE.** An event, whether natural or supernatural, in which one sees an act or revelation of God.

Did the miracles of the Bible occur? If so, how are

we to interpret them? Do all the miracles of the Bible have the same degree of authenticity? What do history, science, philosophy, literature, and theology have to say about miracles? What are we to believe about miracles in other cultures and religions? Did miracles cease at the end of the biblical period? What was the attitude of the prophets and Jesus toward miracles? Are miracles an essential element of Christian faith? Is our universe controlled by laws to which there are no exceptions? What should be one's attitude toward the possibility of miracles in the world today?

1. Terminology
   a. In translation
   b. In the OT
   c. In the NT
2. Definitions
   a. Presuppositions
   b. Spinoza
   c. Hume
   d. The unknown
   e. The absurd
   f. Not contrary to nature
   g. Outside the order of nature
   h. Essential miracles
   i. Providence
   j. Mutation, atomic nucleus, and free will
3. The Bible and the laws of nature
   a. The biblical view
   b. Philosophy and science
   c. Revelation
   d. The laws of nature
4. Miracles of nature
5. Miracles in human life
6. Miracles in national history
7. Miracles of healing
8. Miracles and literary forms
   a. Saga
   b. Short story
   c. Apocalypse
   d. Myth
   e. Legend
   f. Poetry
   g. Portents
   h. Parables
   i. Cult stories
9. Miracles versus prodigies
10. Miracles and faith

Bibliography

1. Terminology. ***a. In translation.*** Translators of the Bible have had no little difficulty in rendering the various words which carry the idea of "miracle." The KJV uses the word "miracle" no fewer than thirty-seven times. Five of these are in the OT, and thirty-two in the NT. The ASV has apparently eliminated the word from the OT, but uses it eight times in the NT. The RSV has reinstated it at least six times in the OT, but uses it only seven times in the NT. Goodspeed's NT has apparently not used the word "miracle" at all.

Other words frequently used in English versions are "sign," "wonder," "work," and "mighty work." Translators tend to avoid "portent" and "prodigy," but the RSV has used "portent" seven times. Goodspeed introduces this term in Acts 2:22; Heb. 2:4. Among the words used in Jerome's Latin Vulg. are *signum, virtus, ostentum, mirabilium, portentum, prodigium,* and *miraculum* (Isa. 29:14). Another English word which frequently occurs in the context of "miracle" is "judgment," as an act of God (I Chr. 16:12; Ps. 105:5). This catalogue is by no means an exhaustive list of words used by the translators, but it shows something of the variety of words which have been employed. Behind this variety of words lie the different ideas in the original languages, but also the uncertainties of translators as to the nature of miracle.

This tendency to avoid the word "miracle" has been unfortunate. Most of the other terms used are in themselves neutral. They acquire the connotation of the supernatural only from the context. The words "sign" and "wonder" are used so frequently in our ordinary language that they do not in themselves carry any definite overtone of the supernatural. The only word in our idiom which is unequivocal on this point is "miracle." It ought to be used more often in translations. In this particular, the KJV is superior to all its successors. Other related terms which could be used to good advantage are "portent" and "prodigy." They fit well in many contexts of the Bible and at the same time immediately relate the biblical material to similar phenomena in other literatures.

b. In the OT. The two Hebrew words most commonly used for "miracle" occur in Deut. 13:1, as translated by the RSV: "If a prophet arises among you, or a dreamer of dreams, and gives you a sign or a wonder. . . ." The word for "sign" here is את, and for "wonder," מופת. The LXX reproduces את as σημεῖον, "sign," and מופת as τέρας, "wonder." The Vulg. uses *signum* and *portentum.* את is derived from a verb which means to make a sign or mark on an object to identify it. The noun is used with the meaning of "sign," "pledge," or "token" in such passages as Gen. 1:14, where the sun and moon are signs of day, night, and seasons; Exod. 12:13, where blood is a sign of the Passover; Josh. 4:6, where memorial stones are signs; Gen. 17:10, where circumcision is a sign of the covenant; Num. 2:2, where the word means a military standard. But in such contexts as those in which we are interested, it means an omen, portent, prodigy, or miracle, which is an expression of divine intention and power. It is a sign of the supernatural, an event or act which, to those who behold it, reveals something about God.

The derivation of מופת is uncertain, but it means "wonder," "sign," "portent," or "miracle." It is a special display of God's power, as in the case of Moses and Aaron in Egypt, or by a false prophet (Deut. 13:1-3). Along with את, it is applied to the effects of a curse in Deut. 28:46. Also it can be a sign or token of a future event; or it may designate a person who serves as a symbol or sign. The Greek word τέρας, used by the LXX to translate it, is the ultimate source of our word "terror."

Another Hebrew word for "miracle" is פלא, which means something beyond one's power to do or to understand. It appears in Exod. 15:11 referring to wonders of the Exodus; but in Ps. 89:5-6, it means wonders of the natural world. A closely related word is נפלאות. It also means the wonderful acts of

God. In Exod. 3:20; Judg. 6:13, it refers to events of the Exodus. But in Job 5:9 it includes rainfall, which God sends upon earth and fields. These two words are frequently rendered in the LXX by θαυμάσια, "marvels"; and in the Vulg. by *mirabilia*, "marvels." They occur often in poetry and mean portents and prodigies, providential control of history, or wonders of God in natural phenomena. אות and מופת, "sign" and "wonder," are so closely related to each other that we should not attempt to differentiate them sharply. In Exod. 4:8, where God has shown Moses how to perform certain wonders, he uses the word אות to designate the wonders. Yet in 4:21, with reference to the same wonders, he says מופת. This shows that the words can be used as synonyms with approximately the same meaning. They were bound together so closely that they entered into a standard idiom, אתות ומופתים, "signs and wonders." In this form the idiom occurs in Deuteronomy alone some nine times (4:34; 6:22; 7:19; 13:1; 26:8; 28:46; 29:3; 34:11). It is used also in Exod. 7:3; Neh. 9:10; Ps. 105:27; Isa. 8:18; Jer. 32:20; and in the Aramaic of Dan. 3:32-33; 6:27. This shows how closely the two words were related to each other and how they were used together to express the idea of miracle. The LXX in turn uses a standard Greek idiom to reproduce this Hebrew expression. It says σημεῖα καὶ τέρατα, "signs and wonders." We know also that the LXX is not merely reproducing Hebrew idiom, because this Greek idiom is used by Hellenistic writers. It occurs in Wisd. Sol. 8:8; 10:16; Jos. Antiq. XX.viii.6; War *Pref.* 11; Philo *Moses* I.95; Plutarch *Alexander* 75; Polybius III.112; Aelian *Variae Historiae* XII.17. *See* SIGNS AND WONDERS.

c. In the NT. This widespread usage interests us especially when we observe that the idiom σημεῖα καὶ τέρατα, "signs and wonders," is often used in the NT in precisely the same sense. One encounters it in Matt. 24:24; Mark 13:22; John 4:48; Acts 2:43; 4:30; 5:12; 6:8; 7:36; 8:13; 14:3; 15:12; Rom. 15:19; II Cor. 12:12; II Thess. 2:9; Heb. 2:4. These passages demonstrate that σημεῖα καὶ τέρατα was a common idiom for NT writers, one which they had taken over from the Greek of the Hellenistic period, on the one hand, but from the LXX, on the other, which had used the idiom to translate the Hebrew אתות ומופתים. The idiom shows a common interest in portents and prodigies among the Hebrews, early Christians, and the Greek world generally.

Along with σημεῖον and τέρας, "sign" and "wonder," the NT often uses δύναμις, "power." This means the power of God, of the Holy Spirit, or of Jesus. But by metonymy, in Mark 14:62 it is used as a name for God. In a similar way, metonymy makes it possible also to designate with this word the act performed. Mark 5:30 relates that when Jesus performed a healing he felt power go out from him. But in Mark 6:5, where it is said that Jesus was unable to perform any miracle because of unbelief, δύναμις means the miracle itself. It also has this meaning in 9:39. Mark 6:2 speaks of the δυμάμεις performed by the hands of Jesus. Paul mentions his power to work δυνάμεις in Gal. 3:5. In Rom. 15:19; II Thess. 2:9; Heb. 2:4, δύναμις appears to have entered into an idiom with σημεῖα and τέρατα as a general expression for "miracles." Yet a writer like John could limit himself almost exclusively to one word for "miracle." He preferred σημεῖον, "sign." This occurs in John 2:11, 18, 23; 3:2; 4:54; 6:2, 14, 26, 30; 7:31; 9:16; 10:41; 11:47; 12:18, 37; 20:30. On the other hand, to show that he was familiar with the standard idiom for miracles, in 4:48 he used σημεῖα καὶ τέρατα, "signs and wonders." *See* JOHN, GOSPEL OF.

A similar preference for σημεῖον is evident also in Revelation, where it occurs in 12:1, 3; 13:13, 14; 15:1; 16:4; 19:20. Here the σημεῖα ("signs") are performed by the red dragon, the beast, the seven angels, demons, the false prophet, etc. *See* REVELATION, BOOK OF.

But ἔργον, "work," is also used with the specialized meaning of "miracle." Matt. 11:2 states that when John, who was in prison, heard of τὰ ἔργα, "the works" (RSV "deeds"), of Jesus, he sent his disciples to ask him whether he was the one to come. But it is the Gospel of John again which shows the greatest preference for this term. It occurs in 5:20, 36; 7:3; 10:38; 14:11, 12; 15:24.

Thus the NT writers had at their disposal σημεῖον, "sign"; τέρας, "wonder"; δύναμις, "power"; and ἔργον, "work," when they wished to say "miracle." Each of these words has an element of uniqueness in its meaning. Σημεῖον points to something beyond itself; τέρας indicates the reaction of awe or terror; δύναμις refers to the power which performs the act; ἔργον refers to the act itself. Both δύναμις and ἔργον are metonyms. In the former, the act is designated on the basis of the power which causes it; in the latter it is designated on the basis of the action which produces it; or it is the work which is worked. It is clear, however, that these distinctions were not always maintained, and that in a general sense the four words were used as synonyms. While they can be translated as "sign," "wonder," "power," and "work"—and such renderings are useful in some contexts—all these English terms are predominantly neutral. They lack the strength necessary to carry the full meaning of the supernatural which is involved. The only word adequate for this is "miracle." *See* SIGNS IN THE NT.

2. Definitions. ***a. Presuppositions.*** A clear and useful definition of miracle can be formulated only from a consciously limited point of view. One who gives a definition, in order to make intelligible what he means, must state the principles on the basis of which his definition is formulated. A definition is only as valid as its presuppositions. If one starts with an assumption that miracles are impossible, he has already excluded the basis on which a definition could be worked out. It is just as necessary to state the presupposition with which one operates as it is to put down a foundation before building a house. Nor should one ever forget, or be allowed to forget, the assumption which is inevitably implicit in his definition. The issue is joined only in the presupposition, and must be decided there.

The argument over the possibility of miracles and the effort to define miracle have consumed much time and energy, yet these are secondary questions. The primary question, and in a sense the only real question, in religion, is God. If one believes in God, that God creates the universe, sustains it, and controls it, most of the difficulties of miracle have thereby been dealt with. One who believes in God will believe in the possibility of miracles. On the other hand, he will admit that his belief in miracles results from his belief in God and in God's continuing control of the world. This faith is assumed herein.

On the other hand, one's view of miracle is related to his concept of what we call the natural world. It is not unusual to encounter the belief that the world is controlled by universal laws which are unalterable, that there are no exceptions whatever to the workings of these laws. Such laws are regarded as mathematical descriptions of chains of causality which are expressed in all the processes of nature. Whatever occurs is said to be in harmony with some natural law. Every event is the result of a cause or a group of causes. These causes operate in a mechanistic and inexorable fashion. Now, if miracle were defined as a violation of natural law taken in this sense, one would be forced to conclude that no miracle has happened or could happen.

b. Spinoza. This is the view which was held by Benedict Spinoza, who in a sense has voiced the doubt of miracles felt by the modern world. Most of the skeptical views have been mere variations of the position of Spinoza. His view that a miracle is a violation of natural law is the concept most frequently encountered in our time. In the course of his argument in the pamphlet entitled *A Theological-Political Treatise,* he first states this inclusive mechanistic concept of the world, and then proceeds to show that the miracles of the Bible were events which happened according to natural law. Of course, Spinoza believed in God, but one might almost say that he worshiped the universe. Although he formally denied the possibility of miracles, since he believed that natural laws are inexorable, the universe itself with all its wonderful processes was essentially a miracle for him. Spinoza never ceased to wonder at the marvelous things of the natural world. So his reverence for the processes revealed by chemistry, physics, biology, and the other sciences took the place of awe with respect to miracles in traditional religion; and one must recognize that Spinoza expressed the feeling of a large segment of mankind. Indeed, there is something of Spinoza in all of us. His view shows how it is possible for one to retain a feeling of deep reverence although he doubts the occurrence of some of the miraculous events related in the Bible. We must not forget to do justice to his contribution to our understanding of religion. He has shown many persons how to retain faith in spite of mechanistic views. Naturalism in theology is deeply indebted to Spinoza.

c. Hume. David Hume is no less well known than Spinoza for his skepticism as regards miracles. This view pervades his philosophical writings in general, but he gave it most pointed expression in his "Essay on Miracles." He also assumes that "miracle is a violation of the laws of nature," and reasons that "as a firm and unalterable experience has established these laws, the proof against a miracle, from the very nature of the fact, is as entire as any argument from experience can possibly be imagined." But in this same essay, in his effort to demonstrate that faith cannot be based on reason, he shows that rational investigation of evidence as to whether an event has occurred can at best lead to no more than probability. This is a sound conclusion. But this line of reasoning shows that the laws of nature on which he depends for his rejection of miracles can be no more than matters of statistical probability. So his argument against miracles as a possibility is inadequate. Yet Hume's logic, with its negative conclusion, has a valuable result for theology. Its demonstration of the limitations of reason shows that faith must not depend too much on reason for its validity. This is an insight which was well known to biblical writers. In his negative way, Hume assists theology to get back on a biblical basis. So we are indebted to him for reminding us that religion lives by faith. He succeeds in showing that miracles cannot be validated by historical research and that Christian theology cannot be based solely on reason. What Hume did was to demonstrate the bankruptcy of a theology which attempts to equate faith with historical information, scientific facts, or philosophical speculation. This was a contribution of great value.

d. The unknown. Another approach, followed by numerous writers, retains the concept of a natural order but holds that a miracle is simply a phenomenon produced by the operation of a natural law which we do not know, or which, if we did know, we could not employ. Thus a miracle is a purely natural event. Only from our point of view, it might be regarded as a supernatural event, since we are ignorant of its natural cause. This approach limits miracle to phenomena occurring in those areas of the natural order which science has not yet investigated. In other words, miracles occur only in those aspects of the universe which we do not yet understand. It is assumed that when science has finally mastered those areas of existence, as presumably it will, all miracles will become just as intelligible as other events which we have understood all along. This approach is theoretically possible, but it should be kept in mind that it eliminates the supernatural from miracles, so that in the end miracles tend to become just like all other natural events, with no more significance for religion.

On the other hand, that there is probably much truth in this position does not need to be denied. It is entirely possible that some of the episodes related as miracles in the Scriptures were so regarded only because the people of that time did not understand the natural processes of their world. There has been a tendency on the part of man to associate things which he could not understand with the supernatural. But this type of reasoning tends to eliminate God from the world. Such a definition of miracle is based on a naturalistic approach which would have been acceptable to either Spinoza or Hume. While it may seem to lend a hand in dealing with certain miracle stories, in the end it leaves faith with an unanswered question. *See* SCIENCE.

e. The absurd. Not many persons would state the definition of miracle in terms of the famous epigrams of Tertullian: "It is to be believed absolutely, because it is absurd; . . . it is certain, because it is impossible" (*On the Body of Christ* 5). Yet one must understand Tertullian's statement in its context. For one thing, an epigram, in order to achieve picturesqueness, usually states a half-truth, which can be misleading. But Tertullian was thinking of the birth, death, and resurrection of God's Son, which appear incomprehensible to reason. He assumes the fact of revelation, and his words should be interpreted on the basis of this assumption. As a scientific or philosophical statement, they are unsound. But they have the virtue of recognizing that there are elements in truth which are beyond discursive reason. While Tertullian does not make this explicit, he realizes that rational thought is based on presuppositions which in themselves are not achieved by reason. In this sense his statement is profoundly true, and worth keeping in mind when one attempts to define miracle.

f. Not contrary to nature. Replying to those who doubted miracles of scripture in his time, Augustine was concerned especially with the concept of nature. In *The City of God* XXI.8 he considers the charge of skeptics that biblical miracles are contrary to nature. On the one hand, he says that miracles are not contrary to nature, for nature is nothing but the will of God with reference to any particular object. It is an error to say that a portent is contrary to nature when it occurs according to the will of God, who causes it. Nature, therefore, according to Augustine, must include, not merely the observed order of things about us, but also whatever God does in the universe. The natural is identified with the will of God. If one assumes the existence of God as creator and ruler of the world, there is no necessary problem connected with miracles. On the other hand, Augustine questions the rigid and inexorable character of the order and laws of nature. By pointing to numerous phenomena known in his time which, he thought, did not conform to the order of nature, his approach to the question anticipated the modern view. Scientists are not so confident today of the absoluteness of nature's laws. They readily admit that the laws to a considerable extent are an imposition of abstract principles upon phenomena which in themselves are not necessarily as orderly as logical inference from the laws might appear to indicate.

g. Outside the order of nature. Thomas Aquinas bases his discussion of miracles on Augustine, but his conception of nature appears to be more rigid. He deals with the question in his *Summa Theologica* I.cx.4; I.cxiv.4; II.ii.178.1-2. Unlike Augustine, he says that a miracle is something that occurs outside the order of nature (*aliqua fiunt praeter ordinem totius naturae creatae*). A miracle is therefore not a violation of nature.

But since we do not know all of the order of created nature, in our ignorance we may call something a miracle which really is not. As only God can operate outside the order of nature, only God can perform a miracle. Thomas' concern in this connection is to deny that angels, demons, magicians, etc., can work miracles—a possibility which Augustine seems to allow. His reasoning is that since all these beings are themselves creatures, they are within the order of nature, and so cannot operate outside it. Therefore they cannot work miracles.

h. Essential miracles. René Descartes showed something of the modern attitude toward the definition of miracle when he said: "The Lord performed three miracles: creation, freedom of will and the Incarnation." In these words he deals with the definition of miracle in its essential terms. What he is saying is that the essence of miracle is God, and that there are three real manifestations of God in our universe. The first is creation itself; the second is the freedom of man's will; and the third is the manifestation of God in Christ. These are essential items of Christian faith. Once they are accepted, one is in a position to use discrimination in his evaluation of events reported as miracles.

i. Providence. It is an error, however, to think of miracles only in terms of violations of the order of nature or as happenings outside the order of nature. It may well be that miracles could and do in some cases fit into one or the other of these categories. One has no right to say that God could not operate contrary to the usual processes of nature, or outside them. But to limit miracles to such cases is to overlook the mysterious character of the natural processes. The doctrine of creation involves miracles not only in the sense that God created the universe with all its forms at some time in the past. It means also that he is continuously in the process of creation.

God is like a dynamo which generates electricity that keeps a current going to all the motors, machines, and light globes throughout all the system supplied by the power plant. But we must not be misled by this simple analogy to think of God merely in terms of the physical energy of the world. The analogy must apply also to life in all its forms, to mind, and to all aspects of truth, goodness, and beauty. Paul must have had this in mind when he said in Acts 17:28: "In him we live and move and have our being." In other words, the doctrine of creation involves also the concept of providence. The two are inseparable. Providence must not be thought of merely as something outside, or contrary to, processes of nature. It applies to these processes themselves. Spinoza was right in emphasizing this aspect of the manifestation of God in the world.

j. Mutation, atomic nucleus, and free will. In our time we are in a better position to implement the insight of Descartes. We not only have before us the facts of creation as he knew them. The advance of biological science has revealed the phenomenon of mutation, which is one of the genuine marvels of our universe. The biologist can tell us something of the chromosomes and genes in the cell, but he cannot explain the origin of the new form of life which he calls a mutant, which becomes the first in a new series called a species. Here, it seems, one can see the actual process of creation at work. It may be that in time science will be able to give a complete description of mutation, but such a description is not an explanation.

Another great achievement is the exploration of the atom and the release of atomic energy. We are amazed by the discovery, however, that the electrical particles which constitute the nucleus of the atom do not conform to any known pattern of order and regularity. One might say, therefore, that in the mutant and in the nucleus of the atom we encounter phenomena of discontinuity which transcend what has been considered the order of nature. Yet it would probably be accurate to say that, in some way which we do not understand, both the mutation of biological forms and the strange operation within the atom, each in its own mysterious way, somehow are included in the order of nature. In a profound sense, therefore, nature itself is a miracle.

Not the least of miracles is the freedom of man's will. This is illustrated in his use of the materials and forces of nature. Man's intelligence enables him to analyze both his own needs and desires and the things of nature. Then he is able to create things for his own use which do not exist in nature. A man who cannot cross the seas by his own natural strength builds a ship; one who cannot fly builds an airplane; and so man constructs automobiles, radios, and all the instruments and machines with which we are familiar. These things are examples of the freedom of man's will, by means of which he goes outside the order of nature to make things for his use and enjoyment.

This same freedom of will is also evident in man's recognition of good and evil, and in the moral choices which he is continually making. Descartes was right in recognizing the freedom of man's will as one of the truly great miracles. It is something outside the mechanistic order of nature. Yet it is not outside nature if we think of nature as all of that which comes from God. It is God who gives man intelligence and freedom of will. In this way God makes it possible for man to have a moral character. This is what the Bible means when it says that man is made in the image of God.

3. The Bible and the laws of nature. As is clear from § 2 *above,* the main difficulty that modern persons feel as they consider the question of miracle arises from the way in which miracle is defined. That is to say, the problem of miracles faced in our time is faced with respect to a particular definition of miracle. The definition that is almost universally held is that a miracle is a violation of the laws of nature. It is against miracle so defined that many persons feel they must rebel. We have seen that the laws of nature are not so absolute as they were once thought to be, so that even in the framework of these laws there is still theoretically a place for miracle. At the same time, after we have stated this possibility of error, we must acknowledge that there is a generally observed order of nature and that the usual phenomena of the world occur according to this order. So it is difficult for a person who is familiar with this orderly aspect of the world to accept any event which is reported to be in violation of it. This is a problem the theologian must face with both sympathy and realism.

a. The biblical view. We can find help in dealing with this problem by going back to the Bible itself. Here we discover that the people of the Bible never faced a problem of miracle. The reason for this is that the problem as we know it has been formulated in terms of a philosophy that has arisen since biblical times. It is a problem for persons who have been trained in philosophy and science. In other words, it is a philosophical problem. The people of the Bible, however, were not familiar with science in our sense of the word, or with philosophy. The Bible has some very great writers, but one will not find there a Plato, an Aristotle, a Newton, or an Einstein.

b. Philosophy and science. The essential element of philosophy and science is their humanistic character. They are achievements of the unaided human mind. Philosophy and science are what the human mind by means of its own powers can achieve by way of understanding our world. They are secular enterprises, proceeding on the assumption that man himself discovers the truth. As man learns about his world, he interprets and generalizes his finds in terms of principles or laws which are universal; and so he arrives at the concept of the laws of nature. This is a process which—in our culture, at any rate—began with the ancient Greeks. It has continued down to the present time and flowered into the achievements of the sciences. The entire enterprise is centered in man. *See* SCIENCE.

c. Revelation. Biblical thought, on the other hand, proceeds on the assumption that knowledge comes from God. Instead of reason, it uses the concept of revelation. Biblical people regard the world as God's creation and under his control. True wisdom is conceived in terms of life in fellowship with God, who makes himself known to man and enables man to live a good life by giving him commandments to keep. The great enterprise of biblical people, therefore, is religion. The meaning and purpose of life are found in God. The wise men of the Bible are priests, prophets, and sages. (The sage comes nearer to the philosophic ideal than either of the others.) Toward the end of the OT period they began to produce what we know as the wisdom literature. This includes such books as Job, Proverbs, Ecclesiastes, and the Wisdom of Solomon. In some places these writings deal realistically and profoundly with the problems of life, but never in merely secular, philosophical terms. They retain the general background of faith and revelation. *See* REVELATION.

d. The laws of nature. Biblical culture never developed the concept of universal laws of nature. In the OT proper there is no word for "nature." One comes upon it first in the apocryphal writings, in which affinities with Greek culture begin to appear. In Wisd. Sol. 7:20 there is a reference to the natures of animals. In IV Macc. 5:7 Antiochus pleads with an old Jew to save his life by eating the "delicious meat of a pig which is a gift of nature." There are numerous casual references to nature in the NT. In Rom. 1:26 Paul refers to certain sexual acts as being against nature. According to Rom. 11:24, the grafting of the wild olive into the tame is against nature. In 2:14-15 Gentiles may know the works of the moral law by nature. Paul argues in I Cor. 11:14 that nature teaches men and women how to wear their hair. Paul's statements no doubt show the incipient stages of theological development among early Christians. From his Stoic contemporaries he had absorbed the idea of living in harmony with nature.

Yet in none of these passages in the Bible do we encounter the concept of nature on the grand scale. Certainly it is never thought of in the rationalistic, secular sense of philosophy and science. Nowhere would one find the idea of universal laws of nature which are autonomous and inexorable. The Stoic idea that all men are by nature children of God appears in Luke 3:38; Acts 17:28, whereas the usual idea in the Bible is that men are sons of God only by faith. The Stoic concept of the rational Logos which pervades all the universe is clearly reflected in Heb. 4:12-13. But these stray affinities with Greek thought do not represent general philosophical thinking in the biblical writers. They are only intimations of what is to come later as Christian theology comes to its maturity.

It is clear, therefore, that even the most powerful minds among biblical people never faced the problem of miracle as it has been stated in our philosophical tradition. They could not have understood Spinoza and Hume. The reason for this is not that they lacked the intellectual power, but that their thought moved on the basis of a different presupposition. As was stated above, a definition can be understood only in terms of its presupposition. This applies also to questions and problems. Our scientific tradition first arrived at a concept of the world which is secular in nature. It ignored the biblical presupposition, which is that the ground of all being is God. Once modern thought, however, had formulated its secular, essentially atheistic philosophy of the world, it then stated its criticism of miracles on this basis. If one has first accepted the secular philosophy, obviously he faces a problem of miracle which may be insoluble. Philosophers have made the problem more difficult than it actually is. They have made an unbiblical approach to a biblical question; and the problem becomes less difficult if we state it in terms of the stories found in biblical records and on the basis of presuppositions of biblical faith.

4. Miracles of nature. Instead, then, of looking for what are labeled as signs, wonders, portents, prodigies, or miracles, let us examine the miraculous quality of existence itself.

First of all is the creation of the world. What Hebrews believed about the origin of the world is picturesquely summarized by the P writer of Gen. 1:1–2:3 (*see* PENTATEUCH). The story is told again in a somewhat different way by the J writer of Gen. 2:4–3:24. In order to appreciate these stories properly, we should try to think ourselves back to a time when no connected ideas of creation had been achieved by the Hebrew people. But they lived in a world basically not so different from our own—earth, sea, sky, people, and animals. The ancestors of the Hebrews looked out upon that world with amazement and wonder; they felt a sense of awe and reverence; in and through all the bewildering phenomena about them they sensed the existence of the Reality which is the source and ground of all being. They were conscious of something in their hearts which they believed was the revelation of God. Through those objects of the external world God was speaking to them. This sense of revelation is the primordial fact of religion. Those early people saw the world about them as a continuing miracle.

In Ps. 8:3 a poet sings:

> When I look at thy heavens, the work of thy fingers,
> the moon and the stars which thou hast established . . . .

Another, in the Nineteenth Psalm, hears the heavens telling the glory of God and the firmament proclaiming his handiwork. The prophet Amos in 4:13 speaks of the One

> who forms the mountains, and creates the wind,
> and declares to man what is his thought;
> who makes the morning darkness,
> and treads on the heights of the earth.

The author of Isa. 40:26, as he attempts to revive hope in discouraged exiles, points to the stars of the night sky and says:

> Lift up your eyes on high and see:
> who created these?
> He who brings out their host by number,
> calling them all by name;
> by the greatness of his might,
> and because he is strong in power
> not one is missing.

No more beautiful poem of nature has ever been written than Ps. 65:6-13, where God establishes the mountains, stills the roaring seas, controls day and night, waters the earth with rain, and causes the crops of fields and pastures to come to maturity.

Special acts of God are seen in eclipses (Joel 2:30-31; Matt. 27:45), storms (Exod. 14:21; 15:10), earthquakes (Judg. 5:4-5; Matt. 27:51), volcanic activity (Exod. 19:16-18), growth of agriculture (Hos. 2:8), and the lilies of the field (Matt. 6:28-29).

This concept of nature runs all through the Bible. It is one of the most profound expressions of the revelation of God. The world of nature to biblical people never loses its miraculous character. The importance of this insight is recognized by Paul in Rom. 1:19-20. He says that because of this universal revelation no man can plead ignorance of God as an excuse for immoral conduct. This element of biblical thought shows that a miracle is not necessarily an event outside nature or in violation of its laws, but is any occurrence whatever which arouses a feeling of awe, amazement, terror, or wonder, and causes the one who beholds it to see, not merely the phenomenon of nature, but God, whose being it expresses. The secular thought of the modern period tends to deprive man of this source of his faith.

5. Miracles in human life. Biblical faith also presents human life in terms of miracle. In Gen. 2:4-24, J tells how God shaped man's body out of the earth and then breathed into his nostrils the breath of life. As man was unhappy in the vast solitude, the Lord made the animals one by one in an effort to overcome man's loneliness. When they proved inadequate, the Lord put man to sleep, took out one of his ribs, and made it into a woman to be his companion. In this way J explains why it is that a man leaves his own parents and enters into a lifelong companionship with his wife. P, on the other hand, in Gen. 1:27, in his more sophisticated way, says that God created man in his own image. At the same time he made man both male and female, or husband and wife. Marriage, therefore, belongs to human life by the divine fact of creation. Biblical writers never cease to be amazed at the wonder of marriage. Prov. 18:22 says that a wife is a favor of the Lord; 30:18-19 expresses the incomprehensible mystery of love; 31:10-31 marvels at the energy and wisdom of a good wife; Song of S. 8:6-7 knows the deadly jealousy which lurks in love and also its priceless quality; Eph. 5:21-33 uses the wonder of marriage to express the deepest miracle of the Christian life.

No less marvelous is the moral life. While P explains this by saying that man is created in the image of God, J resorts to allegory. Man eats of the tree of knowledge of good and evil, and so his conscience is born. The way to understand this allegory is to realize that every man who ever lived is Adam and every woman is Eve. Each of us recapitulates the story. Prov. 20:27 recognizes the wonder of conscience as the lamp of the Lord. Jer. 31:31-34 tells of a new covenant when God's law will be written in the conscience of every man. Paul in Rom. 2:15 refers to the moral law which is stamped in the heart. This insight of biblical writers arises from their recognition that there is something about the knowledge of good and evil and the freedom of the will which transcends determinism and mechanism and finds its explanation only in God.

Miracle was seen also in the conception of a child. Eve received Seth from the Lord (Gen. 4:25); the Lord gave Isaac to Abraham and Sarah in their great old age (Gen. 17:15-21), twins to Rebekah (Gen. 25:21), a son to the barren Rachel (Gen. 30: 22), a son to Ruth and Boaz (Ruth 4:13), Samuel to his desolate mother, Hannah (I Sam. 1:19), John to the barren and elderly Elizabeth and Zechariah (Luke 1:7-13), and Jesus to Mary and Joseph (Matt. 1:20; Luke 1:26-31).

The Lord's providence for those who are faithful to him continues throughout life. This belief in God's constant care stands out as a dominant theme in all the stories of the patriarchs in Genesis, but it appears also throughout both OT and NT. The religion of the Bible would be incomprehensible without it. How impoverished would be the faith of the Bible without the Twenty-third Psalm, or the Ninety-first, or the words of Jesus about anxiety in Matt. 6:25-34, or the confidence of Paul in Rom. 8!

The specifically religious experiences of life are all thought of in the sense of miracle. There is, of course, no real differentiation between the religious qualities of different areas of experience according to the Bible. Yet there are certain experiences which stand out. The prophets' are typical. These men believed that their messages came directly from God. According to Amos 1:1, the prophet delivers a message he has seen. To "see" in this sense means to have a religious vision, in which, by insight, or intuition, or faith, one comes to an understanding of what God wants him to say or do. Amos says in 7: 15 that the Lord took him from behind the flock. Exod. 3:2 ff relates how Moses had his first prophetic vision in the presence of a shrub which burned without being consumed. He was in the wild solitude of a mountain. Isa. 6, on the other hand, describes a vision which came to Isaiah in the temple. Ezek. 1: 4-28 tells a story of the prophet's vision as he heard the roar of wind and watched lightning flashes and swiftly changing forms of a rain cloud on a summer day.

In the Bible prayer always has a miraculous character. There are numberless passages in which prayer is presented as an interview between a man and God, where all the dialogue that took place between them is recorded. This reflects the realism of their experience of prayer and the genuine possibility of communion with God. Such a concept is the basis of worship wherever it is presented, either in the OT or in the NT. The Christian idea is the worship of a resurrected and living Christ, not of one who belongs only to antiquity, but of one who is eternally alive and present wherever his disciples gather to worship, or wherever an individual turns to him in faith.

The concepts of vision, revelation, and inspiration are characteristic of biblical religion. They always have a miraculous nature. The miracle is not one which one reads about in a book, but one which is experienced in the heart. In this way one discovers the constant miracle of the religious life.

6. Miracles in national history. According to Gen. 12:1-6, the miraculous hand of God appears first in Hebrew history when the Lord tells Abram to leave Haran and migrate to Canaan. The divine control of Hebrew history is continuous from that date. The exodus from Egypt and the conquest of Canaan are presented in the Bible as notable examples of the miraculous control of history. So are the first struggles toward national unity in Judges; the rise of the nation under Saul and David; the division of the kingdom at the death of Solomon (I Kings 11: 11); the destruction of Israel by Assyria in 721 B.C. (II Kings 17:18), of Judah by Babylon in 586 B.C. (II Kings 24:2-4); the victory of the Maccabeans in 165 B.C. (Dan. 7:13-14; I Macc. 3:18-19; 4:10, 24, 55; 16:3); and the destruction of Jerusalem by the Romans in A.D. 70. Josephus (War VI.v) gives a list of seven portents and prodigies which had foretold this catastrophe.

The divine control of history was stated clearly by Amos *ca.* 760 B.C. It applies not only to the Hebrews. His book begins with a cycle of seven oracles about Damascus, Gaza, Tyre, Edom, Ammon, Moab, and Judah. Then he concentrates his attention on Israel, about whom he is mainly concerned. Moreover, according to Amos 9:7, God's call of Israel is not unique. He has also called the Ethiopians, Philistines, and Syrians. This faith of Amos was shared by all his great successors among the prophets. It is stated in Dan. 4:31-32 by a voice from heaven to Nebuchadnezzar, who has been given the mind of a beast because of his sins. The voice says to the king that his affliction will continue "until you have learned that the Most High rules the kingdom of men and gives it to whom he will"—a view shared by Paul in Rom. 13:1.

If one is to avoid intellectual confusion, however, it must be noted that this view of history is an intuition of faith. It is not a fact of history in the sense that historical research can either prove it or disprove it.

7. Miracles of healing. The cure of illness was often considered miraculous in both the OT and the NT. Records of this type cluster about Elijah, Elisha, Jesus, his first disciples, and the apostles Peter and Paul. They are attested for the patristic period by Justin (Dial. LXXXV; II Apol. VI, VIII), Minucius Felix (Octavius XXVII), Origen (Against Celsus II. 33), and Augustine (City of God XXII.8); and miracles of healing continue to be reported in both Roman Catholic, Eastern Orthodox, and Protestant circles down to our own time.

These reports ought to be set in the context of records of miraculous cures in other cultures of both ancient and modern times. Religious healing was well known in the Hellenistic world. The Greek god Asclepius (Roman "Aesculapius") was devoted to the cure of disease. His temples were the hospitals of the ancient Greek world. Both Pausanias (II.xxvii.3) and Strabo (VIII.374) mention testimonials inscribed on the walls of the shrine at Epidaurus recording cures. Archaeologists have recovered some of these inscriptions (P. Cavvadias, *Fouilles D'Epidaure* [1893], I, 24 ff.), and also some from the temple of Aesculapius at Rome (*Corpus Inscriptionum Graecarum*, vol. III, p. 804, no. 5980). Cures are mentioned in *The Lover of Lies* by Lucian of Samosata, and also in *The Life of Apollonius of Tyana* by Philostratus. Such reports of divine healing from many parts of the world make it probable that in some cases, at least, cures were effected in the names of divine beings. It goes without saying, however, that in this area one must be on guard against legends.

Our primary concern is with the biblical records, which report miraculous cures of various diseases, and there are a few instances of raising the dead. From a theological point of view, it is possible that God could perform all these miracles if he chose to do it. From the point of view of history, however, which does not make the theological assumption, one can feel certain only of healings which can be confirmed by medical science of our time. It is probable that many of the reported cures of the Bible fall into this category, and that they occurred essentially as they are recorded. The most certain of these are the cases of driving out demons. Verification of this type of healing is possible when we recognize that what biblical writers call demon possession is called mental illness today. Psychiatrists are now able to recognize with reasonable certainty the following types of mental illness in the biblical records: (*a*) the manic-depressive psychosis, illustrated by King Saul (I Sam. 16:14 ff) and by the man of Gerasa (Mark 5:1-20); (*b*) epilepsy (Mark 9:17-27); (*c*) hysteria (Mark 1:23-26; Acts 16:16-18). It appears probable that various other psychoses were encountered in cases of mental illness referred to in the Bible, but they are not described fully enough to allow identification. On the basis of purely historical criteria, we may accept the cures of mental illness essentially as they are reported. But we have no way of knowing whether the cures were permanent, as no further records of them have survived.

That some other diseases were healed by faith is also probable. It is well known that real faith contributes to good health and the healing of disease. Faith is an aid even in organic disease, but medical science would say that it has limits in this respect. So far as we know, faith cannot restore missing eyeballs or amputated limbs. On the other hand, in the area of diseases which are psychogenic in origin the healing value of faith can scarcely be overemphasized. This is the area in which many of the psychoses occur. That Jesus and other persons of the Bible performed cures of other types must be allowed as a possibility, but we are not able to verify them at the present time.

8. Miracles and literary forms. One of the main reasons for the problem of miracles is the monolithic view of the Scriptures which has characterized traditional interpretation. This view fails to recognize that the Bible is a literature composed of various types of writing. The first obligation of the interpreter is to recognize the type or form of writing with which he is dealing in any particular case. The Bible was first of all the literature of an ancient people. It was produced in the course of no less than a thousand years. It covers the life of the Hebrews from the time when they lived as nomads to the rise of their nation, the period of the monarchy, the division of the kingdom, the fall of both kingdoms, the Exile, the struggles to return and rebuild the nation, domination by foreign powers, and final destruction in A.D. 70 by the Romans. The NT continues the story with the life of Jesus, the origin of Christianity, and its spread throughout the Mediterranean world. The Bible comprises the literary masterpieces of that long period. It is somewhat parallel to an anthology of English literature from Caedmon and Chaucer to the present time. It contains early ballads, historical records, law codes, prophets, psalms, wisdom literature, short stories, parables, letters, apocalypses, myths, legends, and possibly other types of writing.

a. Saga. The story of Samson in Judges is a saga. Samson is parallel to the Greek Hercules. His deeds should be interpreted in this light. The truth of the saga is that it presents the agelong struggle between Hebrews and Philistines, a conflict which was never resolved. It brought only tragedy to both peoples. Samson represents the Hebrews who waste the power which God has given them.

b. Short story. Jonah is a short story which has been misunderstood because of the fish episode. It is a satire on Hebrew nationalism and sets forth God's love for all nations. The incident of the fish is irrelevant to the main point. It was used by the writer as a convention to get his story read. He drew the motif from folklore. There are parallel stories in various cultures of a man's being swallowed by a beast of some kind and finally surviving.

c. Apocalypse. The book of Daniel is a collection of stories in the form of an apocalypse (*see* APOCALYPTICISM). These stories are fiction, although they deal in most cases with a historical person, Daniel. They are best understood as allegorical expressions of faith in the providence of God for his people. They urge the Jews to be faithful to their religion in opposition to the Syrians, who are attempting to destroy it *ca.* 165 B.C. (*see* DANIEL). The Revelation to John is similar to Daniel. It also is a work of religious fiction. Its purpose is to encourage loyalty in early Christians as they face Roman persecution. *See* REVELATION, BOOK OF.

d. Myth. The Garden of Eden is a myth. It gives a picture of human nature. Adam and Eve are everyman and everywoman, and the serpent is the voice of temptation which each of us knows in his heart. The story is a profound study of the moral life. Gen. 9:8-17 gives the myth of the rainbow, and 11:1-9 presents the myth of languages. *See* MYTH.

e. Legend. The plagues in Egypt and other wonders which accompanied the Exodus and the conquest of Canaan are thinly veiled natural phenomena which Hebrews saw as acts of God. *See* LEGEND.

f. Poetry. Some miracle stories have a poetic origin. The episode about the sun's standing still in

Josh. 10:12-14 is of this type. What the author writes down in prose is a misconstruction of the poem he has just quoted (*see* POETRY). It is possible that this approach applies also to the VIRGIN BIRTH, which occurs in Matt. 1:18-25; Luke 1:26-38, and is based on Isa. 7:14 in Greek. The withering of a fig tree in Mark 11:12-14, which is out of character for Jesus, appears to be a misinterpretation of one of his poetic sayings.

g. Portents. The list of portents which Mark 15: 33-38 says occurred while Jesus was on the cross mentions only an eclipse of the sun and the rending of the veil of the temple, but Matt. 27:51-53 inserts an earthquake, rending of rocks, rising of saints, and their appearance in the city. These portents are parallel to prodigies which Josephus lists in his War VI.v in connection with the destruction of the temple in A.D. 70 and to similar events reported by numerous Greek and Roman writers. They are dependent partly on OT passages, such as Joel 2:30-31, which announces portents to precede the day of the Lord. *See* SIGNS AND WONDERS.

h. Parables. In some cases miracles are used as parables. This is true especially in the Gospel of John. *See* JOHN, GOSPEL OF; *see also* § 9 *below.*

i. Cult stories. Belief in the resurrection of Jesus is based on statements of those who testified that he appeared to them alive. The oldest record is I Cor. 15:1-8. The Christian story has literary parallels in cult narratives of Osiris, Attis, Adonis, and Persephone, who symbolize the death and resurrection of vegetation in autumn and spring. Important differences, however, are that Jesus was a historical person and that belief in his resurrection is based on testimony of eyewitnesses. *See* RESURRECTION IN THE NT.

9. Miracles versus prodigies. As we have seen, the word "miracle" is a flexible term which may include phenomena of many kinds, such as acts of God in creation, processes of nature, spiritual elements and experiences of human personality, or spectacular phenomena believed to be either outside the processes of nature or in violation of them. This last type is usually designated as a sign (*see* SIGNS AND WONDERS), portent, or prodigy. It is evident, therefore, that a prodigy must be a miracle, but a miracle is not necessarily a prodigy.

The religion of the Bible is based on the concept of miracle throughout, but it is not always based on prodigies. The truly great persons of the Bible almost never make use of a prodigy. Prodigies are most frequent in those sections of the Bible which have a popular character. Of this type are the records of the Exodus, of the conquest of Canaan, of the prophets Elijah and Elisha, and some of the gospel material —e.g., the infancy stories and the lists of portents which occurred when Jesus died. The first part of Acts is also of this popular character.

Great prophets like Amos, Hosea, and Isaiah, who have left autographic records, did not rely on portents and prodigies. They depended on miracles of the other type. The same is true of Paul. While he makes numerous references to miracles in his letters, he does not exploit them as portents. He depends on miracles of other kinds as the basis of Christian faith.

Opposition to the use of portents and prodigies is evident also in Jesus. In the temptation story of Matt. 4:1-11, where Satan challenges Jesus to turn stones into bread or to leap from a pinnacle of the temple, Jesus declines. He refuses to base his claims on prodigies. When the Pharisees, according to Mark 8:11-12, ask Jesus to give them a sign from heaven, he sighs deeply and then says that no sign will be given. This is the first stage of this particular tradition. The second stage comes from the Q document, as preserved in Matt. 16:4; Luke 11:29. Here Jesus says that no sign will be given except the sign of Jonah, and it is clear from what follows in Luke that the sign of Jonah was his preaching to Nineveh. But this tradition continues its development and appears in its third stage in Matt. 12:39-40, where Matthew has inserted into the Q tradition the three days and nights of Jonah in the belly of the whale. So, he has Jesus say, the Son of man will be three days and nights in the heart of the earth. The third stage of the tradition is in conflict with what Jesus himself had said about a sign from heaven. It shows what happened to this tradition as it was carried along in popular circles.

One notes also Jesus' refusal to allow his miracles of healing to be treated as prodigies. It was his custom to charge those whom he healed not to say anything about what had happened. This is shown in Mark 1:25, 34, 44; 3:12; 5:43; 8:26. While he performed numerous miracles, they were done out of compassion for persons in need. He healed their diseases because he loved them, but he was unwilling to have his deeds exploited as prodigies.

It is true, however, that other persons, including the disciples, soon began to regard the miracles of Jesus as portents and prodigies. In places the gospels exhibit this interest characteristic of popular circles of both the ancient and the modern world. The Gospel of John appears at first reading to be a notable example of this interest. It presents a series of seven spectacular miracles of Jesus. Each of them is usually called a sign, and the author comes to his culmination in 20:30 by saying that Jesus did many other signs which are not written in his book, but that those which he has recorded are for the purpose of producing faith in Jesus as God's son. However, a careful study of the Fourth Gospel shows that even this author is not primarily interested in prodigies in the popular sense. One discovers that these seven prodigies are in fact used as allegories of Christian truth. They replace parables which are so prominent in the Synoptic gospels but are lacking here. *See* JOHN, GOSPEL OF.

10. Miracles and faith. Christianity is a historical religion. It has its setting in a context of real events. Historical research can establish that many of these events occurred. Yet because of its naturalistic presupposition, research can never demonstrate that an event is an act of God. It assumes that any event with which it deals has a naturalistic explanation. This is not to say that historians are necessarily unbelievers, but the method with which they deal is limited to the natural order. Only faith is able to apprehend the hand of God in an event. Revelation is a fact of faith but not a fact of historical information. A fact of faith is not the kind of fact with which historical research can deal. It can neither be proved nor be disproved by it. As God and faith are beyond the naturalistic order, research is unable to give us information about them. An ordinary event as apprehended by faith may be a miracle. Historical research assumes that the same event is neutral, colorless, naturalistic, secular. Faith must challenge this assumption with its deeper intuition. At the same time, the believer as a natural man does not forget the question which reason asks. Faith has to accept the doubt which it transcends.

One should keep in mind that a miracle is any event, whether natural or supernatural, in which one sees a revelation of God. Whether a miracle is outside the laws of nature or a violation of them is essentially irrelevant for faith. It is evident in many ways that religious faith is grounded in the sense and possibility of miracle. Faith is man's response to his apprehension of God's revelation. But faith must not be equated with historical, scientific, or philosophical information. It is not an achievement of the intellect alone. Hume demonstrated that whoever attempts to base faith solely on reason will land in skepticism. There is something of the skeptic in every man. Reason always challenges faith with the threat of unbelief.

How faith comes is a mystery. Some find it by reading the Scriptures; others, in a sermon, or the liturgy, or the sacraments; or it may come from the contemplation of nature, or the wonders in human life. Faith is contagious; it passes in strange ways from one person to another; but whenever it comes, one knows it; one feels the miracle within oneself. The outcome of the debate over whether certain miracles of the Scriptures occurred can never provide the real answer to man's religious question. While such miracle stories are not unimportant as expressions of ancient faith, they are subordinate to the miracle which occurs in one's own life when he is born of the Spirit of God.

Blaise Pascal was right when he said the heart has reasons which the mind does not understand. This is the meaning of Paul's words in I Cor. 1:22-25, where he condemns Jews who seek after prodigies and Greeks who are in search of wisdom, and then affirms that the gospel, while it appears to be foolishness, is in fact the redeeming power of God. Paul himself never ceases to wonder about the nature of faith, but the nearest that he is able to come to its secret is to say in Eph. 2:8 that it is a gift of God.

Bibliography. B. F. Westcott, *Characteristics of the Gospel Miracles* (1859). M. E. Canney, *Encyclopaedia Biblica,* vol. IV (1903), cols. 5350-53. J. A. MacCulloch, *Encyclopaedia of Religion and Ethics,* VIII (1916), 676-90. S. J. Case, *Experience with the Supernatural in Early Christian Times* (1929). E. Lewis, *Abingdon Bible Commentary* (1929), pp. 921-30. S. V. McCasland, *The Resurrection of Jesus* (1932); *By the Finger of God* (1951), which interprets demon possession as mental illness. P. Tillich, *Systematic Theology,* I (1951); *Biblical Religion and the Search for Ultimate Reality* (1955); S. V. McCasland, "Signs and Wonders," *JBL,* LXXVI (1957), 149-52.

S. V. McCasland

MIRIAM mĭr'ĭ əm [מרים, *see* 1 *below*]. **1.** The daughter of Jochebed, and the sister of Moses and Aaron. Although not mentioned by name, she is presented in the E document as watching after the basket into which the infant Moses had been put and fetching his mother as a nurse (Exod. 2:4, 7-8). She is also remembered as a "prophetess" in connection with her song of victory on the occasion of the crossing of the Sea of Reeds (15:20-21); the song is one of the earliest fragments of Hebrew poetry (*see* Poetry, Hebrew, § G6). But she was also involved in, if not the leader of, the rebellion against Moses when he married a Cushite woman. Along with Aaron, she claimed to be an oracle of Yahweh. But Yahweh heard their boasts and rebuked them; Miriam was struck with leprosy, but Moses interceded for her, and she was healed after a quarantine period of seven days (Num. 12). She is not mentioned again until the occasion of her death and burial at Kadesh (20:1). In later times she was remembered both as a leader sent by Yahweh (Mic. 6:4) and as an example to Israel in cases of leprosy (Deut. 24:9). Later Jewish legends present her as the eldest of the three children, as a wife of Caleb, and as a prophetess who foretold the birth of Moses as a savior. Jerome says that her tomb was exhibited close to Petra. *See* Sela 1.

The name Miriam has been variously interpreted. The rabbis understood it to mean "bitterness," while Jerome proposed "star of the sea." Modern interpretations are: (*a*) "plump one," from the root מרא III; (*b*) "the wished-for child," from Arabic *marām;* (*c*) "one who loves or is loved by Yahweh," from Egyptian *mer,* "love"; and (*d*) simply "the beloved," from the same Egyptian word. The LXX has Μαριάμ, which is NT Greek for Mary. The name was common in NT times; Josephus mentions six women with the name Mariamne, among them the second and third wives of Herod.

2. A relative of Shammai and Ishbah (I Chr. 4:17). The KJV follows the MT and does not give either the mother or the father; the RSV inserts a sentence from vs. 18 and makes Miriam a son or daughter of Mered and Bithiah. The text of the LXX is also corrupt.

Bibliography. O. Bardenhewer, *Der Name Maria,* Biblische Studien, vol. I, no. 1 (1895); F. Zorell, "Was bedeutet der Name Maria?" *Zeitschrift für katholische Theologie,* XXX (1906), 356-60; H. Bauer, "Die Gottheiten von Ras Schamra," *ZAW,* LI (1933), 87; A. H. Gardiner, "The Egyptian Origin of Some English Personal Names," *JAOS,* LVI (1936), 194-95; I. Hösl, "Zur orientalischen Namenkunde: Maria—Moses—Aaron," in H. J. Kissling and A. Schmaus, eds., *Serta Monacensia F. Babinger . . . dargebracht* (1952). J. F. Ross

MIRMAH mûr'mə [מרמה] (I Chr. 8:10). A Benjaminite, one of the seven sons of Shaharaim by his wife Hodesh.

MIRROR [מראה, ראי, *from* ראה, to see; ἔσοπτρον]. Ancient mirrors were made of polished metal, as is suggested by Exod. 38:8; the laver of the tabernacle was made by melting the bronze mirrors of the women who "ministered at the door of the tent of meeting." Job 37:18 compares the sky to a "molten mirror," obviously of metal. Glass mirrors were not available until late Roman times. Hence the rendering of the Hebrew and Greek words for mirror by "looking glass" (KJV) is an archaeological anachronism, and the "molten looking glass" of Job 37:18 KJV is doubly erroneous. For the same reasons, the translation of the Hebrew גלינים by "glasses" (Isa. 3:

Courtesy of the Palestine Archaeological Museum, Jerusalem, Jordan

53. Palestinian bronze mirror from 'Athlit (fifth century B.C.)

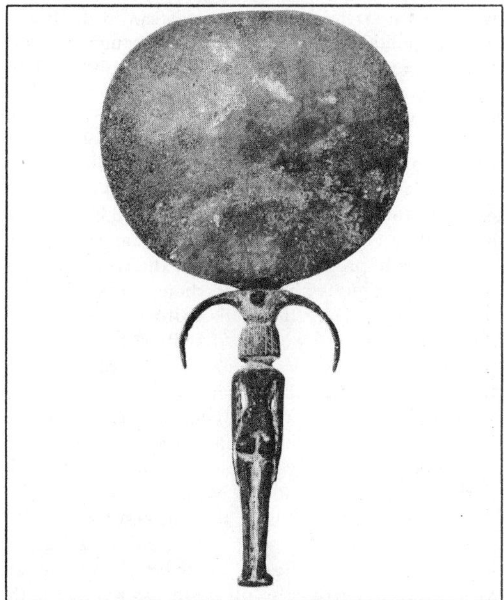

Courtesy of the University Museum of the University of Pennsylvania

54. Bronze mirror with bone handle; from Abydos, Egypt

23 KJV) is also to be rejected. These objects, which according to context are articles of women's apparel, might indeed be mirrors, but then they are not of glass; and if they are made of glass, then they are not mirrors, but glass beads and trinkets. The RSV rendering, "garments of gauze," is highly hypothetical. The etymology suggests something shiny or transparent, but does not lead to more precise conclusions.

Mirrors were considered at first as highly valuable objects. They are mentioned often among the presents which kings and princes made to one another. Thus the documents of TELL EL-AMARNA refer to a gift of thirty-two mirrors of polished bronze from Egypt by Amenophis IV to Burraburiash and of a silver mirror by the Hittite king. Figs. COS 47, 49; MIR 53-54.

One may not necessarily infer from Exod. 38:8 that the women bearing mirrors, who stood watch at the entrance of the tabernacle, were fulfilling recognized functions in the official worship. A text of I Sam. 2:22 refers to similar persons as actually engaged in prostitution at the gates of the temple at Shiloh. At any rate, there is no reason why the mirrors of Exod. 38:8 should be classified among utensils designated for the worship of Yahweh.

By reason of the relative luxury brought in by the all-pervading Hellenistic culture, the use of mirrors became widespread, and ceased to be the privilege of court ladies or of high-rank prostitutes.

Specimens of bronze mirrors have been found in Palestine in the course of excavations, most of the time together with miscellaneous jewelry and articles of women's apparel. They are circular in shape, sometimes of one piece, but more frequently with a handle of wood or ivory, or without a handle at all. A bronze mirror from Tell el-'Ajjul near Gaza, the handle of which is shaped like a lotus flower, is probably an Egyptian import from the Eighteenth Dynasty. The greater number of mirrors found in Palestine and Syria range from the postexilic period to the Roman times. The ornamentation of their handles, showing engraved dots and circles, volutes, etc., belongs to the composite art of the Mediterranean seaboard, characterized by the fusion of Egyptian, Mesopotamian, Aegean, and Anatolian traditions. The unpolished face of the mirrors was usually bare. One Hellenistic specimen from Gezer, however, had its back side adorned with a cluster of grapes in relief.

Pl. XVIII.

Bibliography. K. Galling, *Biblisches Reallexikon* (1937), cols. 493-94; G. A. Barrois, *Manuel d'Archéologie Biblique,* I (1939), 393-94.

G. A. BARROIS

MISACH mĭs'ăk. Douay Version form of MESHACH.

MISAEL. KJV Apoc. form of MISHAEL.

MISCARRIAGE. *See* UNTIMELY BIRTH.

MISGAB mĭs'găb. KJV translation of המשגב (lit., "the height"), as a Moabite place name, in Jer. 48:1. The RSV treats the word as a common noun and translates "the fortress."

MISHAEL mĭsh'ĭ əl [מישאל, *possibly* who is what God is?; Apoc. Μισαήλ]; KJV Apoc. MISAEL mĭs'—. **1.** A Levite, son of Uzziel and cousin of Aaron (Exod. 6:22), who with his brother Elzaphan was obliged by Moses to dispose of the bodies of Nadab and Abihu, who had desecrated the altar of the Lord (Lev. 10:4; cf. vss. 1-3).

2. One of those who stood beside Ezra during the public reading of the law (Neh. 8:4; I Esd. 9:44).

3. One of Daniel's three friends (Dan. 1:6-7, 11, 19; 2:17; Song Thr. Ch. 66; I Macc. 2:59; IV Macc. 16:3, 21; 18:12); surnamed by the Babylonians Meshach (Dan. 1:7; *see* SHADRACH, MESHACH, ABEDNEGO).

Bibliography. M. Noth, *Die israelitischen Personennamen* (1928), p. 249. B. T. DAHLBERG

MISHAL mī'shəl [משׁאל] (Josh. 19:26; 21:30); KJV MISHEAL mĭsh'ĭ əl. Alternately: MASHAL mā'shəl [משׁל] (I Chr. 6:74—H 6:59). A Levitical town on the border of Asher. Mishal is no. 39 (Egyptian *msh'r*) in the list of towns conquered by Thut-mose III. Its exact location is unknown. G. W. VAN BEEK

MISHAM mī'shăm [משׁעם] (I Chr. 8:12). A Benjaminite; one of those who built Ono and Lod.

MISHEAL. KJV form of MISHAL.

MISHMA mĭsh'mə [משׁמע]. **1.** A son of Ishmael, and hence the name of an Arabian people (Gen. 25:14; I Chr. 1:30). A Jebel Mishma is given on some maps, between Teima and Jebel Shamar, but the reading is uncertain.

2. A descendant of Simeon, and son of Mibsam (I Chr. 4:25). The presence of the two names Mibsam and Mishma here, as well as in the Ishmaelite genealogy, may indicate that the two were Arabian tribes that had become affiliated with Simeon in the course of the latter's expansion southward (vss. 38-43).
S. COHEN

MISHMANNAH mĭsh măn'ə [משׁמנה] (I Chr. 12:10—H 12:11). One of the famed Gadite warriors who joined the proscribed followers of David at Ziklag; he subsequently became an officer in David's army.

MISHNA mĭsh'nə [משׁנה, *from* שׁנה, *shānâ*, repeat]. A term used generally to denote the body of Jewish law transmitted orally, as distinct from *mikrâ* (מקרא), denoting the law transmitted by written documents (scripture) and learned by reading. More specifically, the term "Mishna" denotes the collection of oral laws compiled by Rabbi Judah the Prince (born in the year 135 of the Christian era). The Mishna is divided into six orders (סדרים, *Sedharîm*), which in turn are grouped into sixty-three treatises, or tractates (מסכתות, *Massekhtôth*), embracing the whole of the Jewish religio-legal system as taught in the schools of Palestine up to the time of its compiler.

See also TALMUD.

Bibliography. M. Waxman, *A History of Jewish Literature*, vol. I (1930); H. Danby, *The Mishnah* (1933).
I. EPSTEIN

MISHRAITES mĭsh'rĭ īts [משׁרעי] (I Chr. 2:53). One of the families of Kiriath-jearim, from whom came the Zorathites and the Eshtaolites.

MISPAR mĭs'pär [מספר; Apoc. 'Ασφαράσος] (Ezra 2:2; I Esd. 5:8); KJV MIZPAR mĭz'—; KJV Apoc. ASPHARASUS ăs făr'ə səs. Alternately: MISPERETH mĭs'pə rĕth [מספרת (*feminine*)] (Neh. 7:7). One of those who returned with Zerubbabel from the Exile.

MISREPHOTH-MAIM mĭz'rə fŏth mā'əm [משׂרפות מים, *see below*] (Josh. 11:8; 13:6). A place in the neighborhood of Sidon; now called 'Ain Mesherfi, where there are warm springs. Some scholars think the place is identical with Khirbet el-Musheirefeh, where ruins have been found, but 'Ain Mesherfi seems more likely.

The name may mean "lime-burning at the water." Joshua pursued the Canaanites, defeated at the waters of Merom, as far as Misrephoth-maim, on the boundary of the Sidonians. A. S. KAPELRUD

MISSIONS. The sending of representatives of a deity for the purpose of conveying a message or carrying out a task. In a larger sense, activities of a religious community dedicated to the propagation of its faith in other communities.

From time immemorial, messengers have traveled back and forth between peoples, bearing messages and performing acts as empowered representatives of their senders. Though such messengers are most frequently attested as representatives of kings, we hear in the Mari Letters also of a message delivered by a functionary of a god of Aleppo (indirectly) to the king of Mari, in a neighboring state. So far as is known, there was little deliberate attempt in antiquity (before the Hellenistic period) to convert people from one religion to another except in the framework of political and military action, though the Mari letter mentioned above was intended to impose religious (cultic) obligations upon the king of Mari. Assyrian imperialism certainly had close ties with religion, and resulted in certain religious obligations being imposed upon their vassals (II Kings 16:10-16). The attempt of the "heretic king" Akh-en-Aton of Egypt to impose a new religion upon his land was also closely connected with political concerns.

There is impressive evidence for the wide diffusion of certain religious cults, even though it is frequently unknown precisely how this diffusion took place. Egyptian gods were worshiped at Byblos in Phoenicia perhaps before the First Dynasty of Egypt. Deities of the Third Dynasty of Ur were worshiped at Haran in N Syria, and at Qatna in central Syria, long after Ur fell. Canaanite deities had temples and considerable popularity in Egypt during the New Empire, and in the same period the Mitannian king perhaps deserves credit for devising the simplest form of missionary activity: he sent the goddess Ishtar of Nineveh herself to Egypt in order to receive the honor due her from the pharaoh; and we hear the same thing had taken place in the preceding generation. The Philistines seem to have taken over a god (Dagon) who is first attested a thousand years earlier in E Syria, and the Canaanite Baal in many cases was the storm-god Hadad, who also seems to have originated in the same region. The diffusion of worship of certain gods and goddesses thus is well known long before there is any direct evidence of missionary activities in the modern (i.e., since Alexander the Great) sense of the term. This kind of transplanting of religions is closely tied up with diffusion of other cultural features, and may very well have been a direct result of migrations of peoples as well. It is probable that certain temples enjoyed a sort of international prestige in particular types of activities such as law, omenology, healing, and the like, on account of highly specialized priestly traditions.

It is not, therefore, surprising that examples of such religious diffusion are to be found in the Bible. According to the historical narratives, Canaanite deities were received in Israelite cities from the time of the judges on. Ahab and Athaliah evidently established the cult of the Tyrian Baal (Melqart) as the (or an) official state religion (I Kings 16:31-32; II Kings 11:18) of Israel and Judah respectively. The king of Moab sent to N Syria for the diviner Balaam (Num. 22), just as the king of Cyprus sent to Egypt for a specialist in divining by the flight of birds (if this is the correct interpretation of Amarna Letter No. 35:26, Knudtzon). The king of Damascus sent an officer, Naaman, to the king of Israel to be healed of leprosy (II Kings 5). The prophet Elijah received a commission to anoint Hazael king of Damascus (I Kings 19:15).

In addition to this type of propagation of particular religious traditions and techniques carried, so to speak, by political, economic, and personal concerns, there is some reason to believe that the OT faith was at the beginning an active missionary religion. Josh. 24 seems to present a narrative of a message to those outside the religious community urging them to transfer their religious loyalty to Yahweh, God of Israel. Though the problem of the identification of Yahweh with the "god of the fathers" is difficult, it may well have been that Moses' mission to the Hebrews (=people without a political status) in Egypt was essentially a transference of religious loyalty. Finally, the historical difficulty, if not impossibility, of accounting for the large population of the twelve tribes even before the monarchy (possibly a quarter of a million), makes it necessary to assume that a considerable part of the population of Palestine was converted to Yahwism during the Conquest, since it is biologically impossible that they all should have been lineal descendants of the group who emerged from Egyptian slave-labor camps under the leadership of Moses.

After the initial formation of the twelve-tribe federation, there seems to have been little further expansion. Whether the empire of David resulted in any diffusion of Yahwistic traditions in foreign lands is completely unknown; it is also not at all certain that obligations to Yahweh were imposed upon non-Israelite peoples. (Does Ps. 2 possibly reflect some such pattern of thought?)

Though the prophets occasionally addressed oracles of Yahweh to foreign NATIONS from Amos on, the first direct statements of conversion of foreign peoples comes, surprisingly enough, from the time of the Exile. Isa. 56:3 presupposes that foreigners had been converted, and the same prophet contemplates future wholesale acknowledgment of the God of Jacob by pagan lands (45:14; 49:6; 55:5; 60:6, 10-14). Political and economic implications are present even here, but, interestingly enough, they are the result, not the cause, of religious attachment to Yahweh. The book of Jonah also presupposes a missionary activity to a foreign people, and it is hard not to take this as based upon some sort of known activity on the part of the religious community of exilic or postexilic times.

The missionary activities of Judaism also are well attested, and evidently had considerable success in the Hellenistic period. Jesus refers to them in Matt. 23:15, and proselytes (*see* PROSELYTE) are mentioned in Acts 2:11; 6:5; 13:43. The Qumran community, on the other hand, may not have sought out converts, though it is difficult to believe that they exercised no initiative in this direction during the two centuries of their existence.

The extent to which early Christianity followed previous Jewish customs and patterns in its mission to non-Jews cannot be determined with certainty. Though the term "APOSTLE" corresponds linguistically to late Hebrew שליח, the differences historically are too great to regard these plentipotentiaries of rabbinic Judaism as the historical model for the Christian apostles. Rather, the prophets of the OT seem to correspond much more closely to the early Christian conception of their function. Jesus himself, in the gospel narratives, is "sent" with a message (Matt. 15:24; Luke 4:18), as is John the Baptist (Matt. 11:10). Jesus, in turn, sends out the Twelve with power (Matt. 10), and the Seventy (Luke 10: 1-20).

Regardless of the historical problem of the antecedents of the apostolic function, there can be no doubt that the Christian community from the very beginnings regarded the proclamation of the message of the GOSPEL to all peoples as a most important aspect of its religious obligation. That mission was soon separated (if not from the very beginnings) from the process of diffusing particularistic Jewish cultural and religious features, but, on the other hand, early Christianity could not entirely identify itself with Hellenistic-Roman culture (Gal. 3:28). The church had to depend upon religious motivations, for it was not a high-prestige group (I Cor. 1:26-30; 2:1-5; 4:9-13).

Though the book of Acts gives much information about missionary journeys of those scattered after the death of Stephen (8:4), of Peter (ch. 10), of Barnabas (11:22), and of others (11:19-20), little is known in detail about the beginnings of the churches in Damascus, Lydda, Antioch, and Rome. There can be little doubt that the persecution following the martyrdom of Stephen directly resulted in more widespread missionary activities, and very soon these activities were directed to non-Jewish peoples as well as Jews (Acts 10:28-29; 11:19-20). Paul's mission to the GENTILES is thus the continuation on a wider scale of that which had begun at the time of his conversion.

Bibliography. B. Sundkler, "Jésus et les païens," *RHPR*, XVI (1936), 462-99; reprinted in *Arbeiten und Mitteilungen aus dem neutestamentlichen Seminar zu Uppsala*, VI (1937), 1-38. H. H. Rowley, *The Missionary Message of the OT* (1945). F. M. T. de Liagre-Böhl, "Missions- und Erwählungsgedanke im Alt-Israel," *Festschrift Alfred Bertholet* (1950), pp. 77-96. E. Lohmeyer, " 'Mir ist gegeben alle Gewalt!' Eine Exegese von Matt. 28:16-20," *In Memoriam Ernst Lohmeyer* (1951), pp. 22-49. J. Hempel, "Die Wurzeln des Missionswillens im Glauben des AT," *ZAW*, LXVI (1954), 244-72. T. C. Vriezen, "De Zending in het Oude Testament," *De*

Heerbaan, VII (1954), 98-110. T. W. Manson, *Jesus and the Non-Jews* (1955). E. Jacob, "The Mission," *Theology of the OT* (1958), pp. 217-23. J. Jeremias, *Jesus' Promise to the Nations* (trans. S. H. Hooke; 1958), includes an excellent bibliography of literature on the whole subject. G. E. MENDENHALL

MIST [אד (Gen. 2:6; Job 36:27; KJV VAPOR), *probably* a subterranean stream of water, flood; *cf.* Akkad. *edû,* flood, waves, swell, *a loan word from* Sumer.; נשאים (Jer. 10:13; 51:16; KJV VAPORS), fog *or* clouds, *from verb* to lift up; ענן (Isa. 44:22; Hos. 13:3, KJV CLOUD); ἀτμίς (Jas. 4:14; KJV VAPOR); ἀχλύς (Acts 13:11), mistiness which darkens the vision of the blind]. In Gen. 2:6 אד refers to the water which was essential to God's creation of organic life. The creation story beginning in Gen. 2:4*a* reflects a background in the flood-valley culture of Mesopotamia; this is suggested in part by the origin of אד (*'êdh*) in the Akkadian *edû,* which indicates an underground source of fresh water. In a Sumerian-Akkadian vocabulary it is associated with *butuqtum,* meaning "break-through" of the subterranean water, and *mēlu,* "flood" or "ground flow." Job 36:27 suggests a Palestinian adaptation of this idea, in that here God distils rain from the mist which rises from the earth. God's creative power is attested by the waters in the heavens, the wind in his storehouses, and the "mist" which he causes to come up "from the ends of the earth" (cf. Jer. 10:13; 51:16). The other occurrences of "mist" noted above are figurative.

Bibliography. W. F. Albright, *The Archaeology of Palestine and the Bible* (1935), pp. 139 ff; *JBL,* 58 (1939), 102-3. E. A. Speiser, " *'Ed* in the Story of Creation," *BASOR,* 140 (1955), 9-10. G. B. COOKE

***MITANNI** mĭ tăn'nē. An important kingdom in N Mesopotamia during the Amarna Age (fifteenth-fourteenth centuries B.C.). While the main stratum of its population was Hurrian (*see* HORITES), and its monarchs occasionally used Hurrian as a language for royal correspondence, the Mitannian aristocracy were Indo-Iranian warlords in control of horse-drawn chariotry. At the height of Egyptian power under Thut-mose III (*ca.* 1502-1448 B.C.), the Euphrates River was the border between Mitanni and the Egyptian Empire. Thereafter, Mitanni princesses entered the royal Egyptian harems and achieved great influence in Pharaonic circles.

The importance of Mitanni in the Bible world is not so much political as cultural. The Hurrians (who were a major ethnic element throughout the Near East during the second millennium B.C.) exerted considerable influence outside the Mitannian borders, and the ruler of Jebusite Jerusalem bears the Hurrian title האורנה (the *iwirne*), "the chief, ruler," in II Sam. 24:16. *See* ARAUNAH.

Bibliography. H. Schmökel, *Geschichte des alten Vorderasien,* Handbuch der Orientalistik, vol. II, no. 3 (1957), pp. 145-70. C. H. GORDON

MITE. *See* MONEY, COINS, § 3*c.*

MITHKAH mĭth'kə [מתקה] (Num. 33:28-29); KJV MITHCAH. One of the wilderness stations of the Israelites after Hazeroth. The location is unknown.

MITHNITE mĭth'nīt [מתני] (I Chr. 11:43). A title applied to Joshaphat, one of David's army. The text is questioned.

MITHREDATH mĭth'rə dăth [מתרדת, *from Pers.,* gift of Mithra (the deity)]; Apoc. MITHRIDATES mĭth'rə dā'tēz [Μιθραδάτης, Μιθριδάτης]. **1.** The treasurer under Cyrus king of Persia who delivered the temple vessels to Sheshbazzar to be returned to Jerusalem (Ezra 1:8; I Esd. 2:11). I Esd. 4:57 attributes the return of the vessels to Darius.

2. A Syrian officer in the reign of Artaxerxes II who was among those opposing the rebuilding of Jerusalem (Ezra 4:7; I Esd. 2:16).

Bibliography. R. A. Bowman, Exegesis of Ezra, *IB,* III (1954), 599. B. T. DAHLBERG

MITRE. KJV word for certain types of headdress. *See* TURBAN.

MITYLENE mĭt'ə lē'nĭ [Μιτυλήνη] (Acts 20:14). The chief city of the Aegean island of Lesbos off the SE coast of Asia Minor, on the route of Paul's third journey.

Liberated in 479 B.C. by the Greeks from the domination of Persia, the city joined the Delian Confederacy, but was brought to the verge of destruction as a result of two secessions from the league. For a time it was a vassal city of Lysander the Spartan, but in the fourth century B.C. an alliance with the Attic League and Athens was renewed. Freed by Alexander, it passed under successive rules of the Ptolemies and the Seleucids. It became a popular holiday resort for Roman leaders and suffered severe punishment for the support given by its citizens to the revolt of the Pontic king Mithridates. The city's acropolis and walls were stormed and destroyed in 80 B.C. by the Romans in reprisal for a revolt over taxation; but freedom was restored by Pompey, who found asylum here from Julius Caesar. The city continued to be a favorite residence for influential Romans, regaining its freedom after losing it for a time under Vespasian. It was devastated by an earthquake in A.D. 151-52. During the Middle Ages the name of the city was applied to the island as a whole.

In the return to Syria from Achaia (Acts 20:2; presumably Corinth), Paul and his companions sailed from the W coast port of Assos to Mitylene, departing the following day toward Chios and Samos, and stopping overnight at each until Miletus was reached. Fig. MIT 55.

Courtesy of Ernest W. Saunders

55. The harbor at Mitylene

Bibliography. Pauly-Wissowa, *Real-Enzyklopädie,* vol. XVI (1935), cols. 1411-27; M. Rostovzeff, *The Social and Economic History of the Hellenistic World* (3 vols.; 1941), *passim.*

E. W. SAUNDERS

MIXED MULTITUDE [ערב רב; *cf.* אספסף, rabble; LXX ἐπίμικτος *for both words*] (Exod. 12:38). A heterogeneous group of camp followers who joined the Hebrews in the exodus from Egypt. The Hebrew term is used elsewhere to designate "those of foreign descent" attached to Judah (Neh. 13:3), Egypt (Jer. 25:20; "foreign folk"), and Babylon (50:37; "foreign troops"), and in Jer. 25:24 the "mixed tribes" of the desert.

See also NATIONS; FOREIGNERS. E. J. HAMLIN

MIZAR mī'zär [מצער, littleness] (Ps. 42:6—H 42:7). A mountain mentioned in connection with the region of the Jordan and Hermon. Since this whole psalm contains allusions to the sources of the Jordan near Dan, Mizar is apparently some locality in the neighborhood. On the other hand, the word may be merely an adjective, used to contrast the majestic Hermon with the "smallest" mountain. The site is unidentified. S. COHEN

MIZPAH, MIZPEH mĭz'pə [מצפה]. The name of several towns in Palestine and neighboring lands; usually spelled "Mizpah," but also "Mizpeh." The former spelling always appears with the definite article except in Hos. 5:1; the latter spelling has the article (Josh. 15:38; 18:26), but more often is in construct relation, as in "Mizpeh of Moab" (I Sam. 22:3) or "Mizpeh of Gilead (Judg. 11:29). The word is derived from צפה, "to look out," "to spy," or "to watch"; hence the meaning "watchtower" or "outlook point" (II Chr. 20:24; Isa. 21:8). In several instances the LXX translates the name as a common noun, as in Judg. 10:17; 11:29 (ἡ σκοπία). It is not surprising that the name should be applied to many places or that the verbal root should be reflected in other names like Zephath (Judg. 1:17), Ramathaim-zophim (I Sam. 1:1), or Zophim (Num. 23:14). The Greek text gives a number of forms for the word: Μασσηφά (Judg. 11:11, 34); Μασφέ (Neh. 3:19); Μασφά (II Chr. 16:6); Μασσώχ (Josh. 11:8); Μασσηφάθ (II Kings 25:23; but Μασσηφα in vs. 25, A). In the familiar context of Jacob's covenant with Laban it has ἡ ὅρασις.

1. Mizpeh of Gilead (מצפה גלעד; Gen. 31:49; Judg. 10:17; 11:11, 29, 34; Hos. 5:1[?]). While the topographical clues are meager in the Genesis context and rather obscure in Judges, it is clear in the former that Jacob is moving S toward the "mountain of Gilead" (Gen. 31:21, 25; הר הגלעד; RSV "hill country") and only later crosses the Jabbok. Many proposals have been made for the identification of the site: Ramoth-gilead; Suf, a locality near Jerash (Conder); and especially Jebel Jel'ad (De Vaux, Kraeling). Glueck is doubtless correct, however, in insisting upon a region in N Gilead, both for the scene of the covenant in Genesis and for Jephthah's home and base of operations.

After a bitter quarrel concerning Jacob's flight from Paddan-aram, Laban proposed a covenant between them (Gen. 31:43-55). The event was solemnized by the erection of a pillar (*maççēbâ*) and by a heap of stones. The word *maççēbâ* has fallen out of the text in vs. 49, because of its similarity with "Mizpah," and is correctly supplied by the RSV (for מצפה the Samar. reads מצבה). The two covenant makers called the cairn the "heap of witness," Laban in his native Aramaic, Jacob in Hebrew (גל עד). But the pillar was named Mizpah (i.e., "Watchpost"), in memory of Jacob's words: "Yahweh watch between you and me, when we are absent one from the other." The story is plainly etiological, and the words probably become the *hieros logos* of a sanctuary.

At the time of Jephthah the Ammonites mobilized their forces in order to drive out the Israelites from Gilead (Judg. 11). The Israelites pleaded with Jephthah to be their leader against the foe. The Israelites were encamped at Mizpah, and there they entered into a bond with Jephthah, sealed significantly with the words: "Yahweh will be witness between us" (בינותינו; lit., "hearer between us"; Judg. 11:10; cf. Gen. 31:44, 48, 52). The cultic language is clear, notably in vs. 11: "Jephthah spoke all his words before Yahweh at Mizpah." The Spirit of Yahweh fell on him, and under its power he passed through Gilead and Manasseh and on to Mizpah. When he returned to his home at Mizpah, he was greeted by his daughter and was compelled to fulfil his terrible vow by sacrificing her. Hos. 5:1 may well refer to this Mizpah of Gilead.

2. The land of Mizpah (ארץ המצפה; Josh. 11:3); the valley of Mizpeh (בקעת מצפה; vs. 8). A region to the N of Palestine. After defeating Jabin king of Hazor and his allies by the waters of Merom (*see* MEROM, WATERS OF), the Israelites under Joshua chased them as far as Great Sidon and Misrephoth-maim and eastward as far as the valley of Mizpeh.

In the list of northern peoples the Hivites are described as living "under Hermon in the land of Mizpah." This land cannot be far from the "waters of Merom," probably Wadi Marun N-NW of the Lake of Galilee, E of "Great Sidon" and Misrephoth-maim (Josh. 11:8). It may be the plain along the lower Wadi et-Tem or in the region of modern Banias.

3. Mizpeh of Judah (המצפה; Josh. 15:38). One of the cities assigned to the tribe of Judah in the settlement of the land; located in the Shephelah, and often identified with Tell es-Safieh. Eusebius and Jerome refer to a place by that name in this region (Euseb. Onom. Μασφα).

4. Mizpeh of Moab (מצפה מואב; I Sam. 22:3). The location of the site is unknown. It has sometimes been identified with Kir-Moab (Kerak; *see* KIR 1). Musil (*Moab,* pp. 270 ff) assigns it to a conspicuous height, Ruzm el-Mesrife, to the W-SW of Madeba. It was at Mizpeh of Moab that David delivered his parents into the custody of the Moabite king when Saul was pursuing him.

5. Mizpah of Benjamin (המצפה; Josh. 18:26; I Sam. 7:5-7, 11-12, 16; 10:17; I Kings 15:22=II Chr. 16:6; II Kings 25:23, 25; Neh. 3:7, 15, 19; Jer. 40:6, 8, 10, 12-13, 15; 41:1, 3, 6, 10, 14, 16; I Macc. 3:46). A city of Benjamin on the border between Judah and Israel. This is the most important of all the OT references to Mizpah.

The site of Mizpah of Benjamin is one of the most

controversial of Palestinian topography. It has been most frequently identified with Nebi Samwil the lofty and impressive height some five miles to the N of Jerusalem. Its association with the prophet Samuel has naturally been a strong argument in its favor (cf. I Sam. 7; 10:17), and the tradition obviously reaches deep into the past. It has received the support of Edward Robinson (*Biblical Researches* [1856], I, 575), F. Buhl, Rudolf Kittel, G. A. Smith originally, and W. F. Albright. The chief competitor to Nebi Samwil has been the ancient mound of Tell en-Nasbeh, *ca.* eight miles to the N of Jerusalem, on the highway to Samaria, the "great road" often referred to in the OT. To the S are Gibeah (Tell el-Ful) and Ramah (er-Ram); to the W, Gibeon (el-Jib); to the N-NE, Beeroth and Bethel. It is situated on top of a large, rounded limestone hill with sharp declivities on all sides, although the N decline is less precipitate. It, too, has been identified with Mizpah by many scholars, notably Raboisson, Dalman, Alt originally, Vincent, and W. F. Badè. The excavation of the tell by W. F. Badè from 1926 to 1935 has strengthened the case for Tell en-Nasbeh, although the arguments in its favor cannot be said to be coercive (*see* CITY § B2*a-f*). W. F. Albright believes it to be the site of ATAROTH-ADDAR.

The archaeological remains uncovered at Tell en-Nasbeh fit the history of Mizpah recounted in the OT very closely, its termini being from the beginning of the Iron Age, *ca.* 1200 B.C., into the Persian Age or even Hellenistic times. The area within the walls was *ca.* seven acres. The walls were the most impressive of any Palestinian mound exposed up to that time, with a probable height of some thirty-five to forty feet and a breadth of fifteen to twenty feet. The great gate facing the N contained a large court, and in it were benches upon which the elders doubtless sat to adjudicate disputes. All this suggests that it was a place of some importance, in all likelihood the boundary fortress between Judah and Israel. If so, it comports well with the biblical representation of Mizpah. Nebi Samwil has never been thoroughly excavated, but such remains as have been recovered nearly all come from a much later period. Nevertheless, it must be considered as a possibility for Mizpah of Benjamin.

A critical scrutiny of the relevant texts in which Mizpah of Benjamin is mentioned reveals the striking fact that in one set of passages it is the place of prayer and worship for all Israel (Judg. 20–21; I Sam. 7; 10:17-27), while in another (I Kings 15:22= II Chr. 16:6; II Kings 25:23, 25) its importance is chiefly military and political. Logically there is no reason why Mizpah should not have been both, as Jerusalem was from the time of David. But it has long been recognized that the passages which refer to Mizpah as a center for worship bear many signs of lateness and have little claim to historicity, not only because of their language and style but also because of the way they contradict contiguous passages which are indisputably reliable. But whence then does this representation of Mizpah as a place of worship come? There can be little doubt that the period following the fall of Judah in 597 B.C., after the city and the temple were destroyed, provides us with precisely the proper temporal and social milieu. The increasing stress upon prayer which we find in the prophecies of Jeremiah and the cultic interests of Ezekiel found expression in the exilic community; and Mizpah, which became the capital of the Babylonian province, also became the center of worship. Mizpah took the place of Jerusalem as both a political and a religious center. The tragic associations of the fall of state and temple now clustered about the community which sought to perpetuate their ancient traditions, the venerable cult, and the teachings of the prophets.

Mizpah appears for the first time in the list of cities assigned to the tribe of Benjamin after the Conquest (Josh. 18:21-28). The list is doubtless early, though not so early as the period of settlement. The first historical reference of great importance comes in the context of the boundary wars between Judah and Israel in the years following the disruption of the United Monarchy (I Kings 15:16-22). Baasha king of Israel, of the tribe of Issachar, eager to secure his S border against invasion from Judah, undertook to block the N approach to Jerusalem by building a fortress at Ramah. Asa king of Judah retaliated by making an alliance with Ben-hadad, king of Aram, who forthwith invaded Israel's N provinces, with the result that Baasha was compelled to give up his fortification of Ramah. Asa, in turn, countered Baasha's aggressive acts by fortifying Geba and Mizpah with the stones and timber from Ramah. Baasha's penetration of Judah violated the natural frontiers between the two lands, while Asa's counterthrust succeeded in placing fortresses at two strategic locations.

Mizpah again emerges as an important center after the fall of Jerusalem, when it became the capital of the Babylonian province. Gedaliah, the grandson of Shaphan, who had figured so largely in the reformation of 621, was appointed governor. Here he gathered his weak band of followers and sought to inspire them with hope and courage. The prophet Jeremiah, released from prison, joined his countrymen. But the times were chaotic and harsh. Through Ammonite intrigue, Ishmael fell upon Gedaliah and murdered him, and later "all the Jews who were with Gedaliah at Mizpah, and the Chaldean soldiers who happened to be there" (Jer. 41:3). The next day a procession of eighty men from Shechem, Shiloh, and Samaria, on their way to bring offerings to the house of Yahweh in Jerusalem, were waylaid by Ishmael, and most of them were slain and cast into a cistern. The signal of revolt had been raised, and Ishmael was forced to flee to the land of Ammon, with Johanan ben Kareah and his followers in hot pursuit. They were overtaken "by the great waters that are at Gibeon," and Ishmael and most of his companions were killed. What happened to Mizpah in the succeeding months and years we do not know; the period is one of the most obscure in Jewish history. There are those who believe that it continued on even into the Persian age. If so, we may understand how it came to achieve the reputation as a great center for prayer and worship, reflected in I Macc. 3:44-46.

Bibliography. The literature on Mizpah is extensive, but is best represented in the following journals: *PJB, JPOS, ZDPV,*

BASOR, and *RB.* The succinct summaries in Grollenberg's Atlas and especially in F.-M. Abel, *Géographie de la Palestine* (1933), are valuable. The following are among the most important discussions in the history of the subject: Raboisson, *Les Maspeh* (1897). E. Baumann, "Die Lage von Mizpa in Benjamin," *ZDPV,* 34 (1911), 119-37. A. Alt, "Mizpa in Benjamin," *PJB,* 6 (1910), 46; 21 (1925), 129-30. G. Dalman, Annual reports in *PJB,* 7 (1911); 21 (1925). W. F. Albright, "Mizpah and Beeroth," *AASOR,* vol. IV (1922/23), Appendix I, pp. 90-112. H. L. Vincent, *RB* (1924), pp. 637-38. A. Jirku, "Wo lag Gib'on?" *JPOS,* 8 (1928), 187-90. W. F. Badè, "The Seal of Jaazaniah," *ZAW,* 12 N.F. (1933), 50 ff. J. Muilenburg in C. C. McCown, *Tell en-Naṣbeh* (2 vols.; 1947); "Mizpah of Benjamin," *Studia Theologica,* vol. VIII (1955).

J. Muilenburg

MIZPAR. KJV form of Mispar.

MIZPEH. Alternative form of Mizpah.

MIZRAIM mĭz'rĭ əm [מצרים, Ugar. *mṣr;* Akkad. *Muṣur, Muṣru, Miṣir*]. Mentioned as one of the sons of Ham in Gen. 10:6, 13 KJV (RSV Egypt). This is the regular Hebrew word for Egypt, more technically transliterated *miṣrayim,* which occurs in many passages (Gen. 12:10; 13:10; 25:18; 47:20; etc.). It is possible that in a few instances (I Kings 10:28; II Kings 7:6; II Chr. 1:16-17) it refers, not to Egypt, but to the land Musri, mentioned in nonbiblical records—e.g., in the annals of Shalmaneser III (858-824 B.C.). He reports that he got "camels whose backs were doubled" as tribute from Musri. This reference to the Bactrian camel indicates that Musri was located in Asia. Also Tiglath-pileser III (744-727) and Sargon II (721-705) mentioned a Musru. So did also Sennacherib (704-681) and Esarhaddon (680-669), but both they and Sargon speak about Musru and Musri in a way which indicates that they mean Egypt. The name could probably be used with different meanings, because the basic meaning of it is "march," and it could thus be used about several kinds of "border country," whether they were found in Asia Minor or in Egypt.

In I Kings 10:28 the Hebrew word *miṣrayim,* is mentioned together with Kue (RSV) as a place which exported horses to Solomon. Kue, or Que, or Qewe, is an ancient name of Cilicia, and there is reason to suppose that Mizraim here means a land in Asia Minor.

A. S. Kapelrud

MIZZAH mĭz'ə [מזה; LXX Μοζέ, Μοχέ] (Gen. 36:13, 17; I Chr. 1:37). An Edomite clan chief (אלוף מזה, perhaps "clan chief of Mizzah"); the last of the four sons of Reuel 1.

MNASON nā'sən [Μνάσων] (Acts 21:16). A Christian with whom Paul lodged on his final visit to Jerusalem. This is a common Greek name, occurring among Romans as Nason, and among Jews as Jason. The Greek text of Acts makes it difficult to determine whether Mnason lived in Jerusalem (implied by the oldest MSS) or in a village between Caesarea and Jerusalem (implied by the Western text). Both types of text agree in affirming (*a*) that he was from Cyprus and (*b*) that he was an early disciple. Some commentators interpret the word "early" to mean that Mnason was one of the original disciples, although not one of the Twelve. More plausibly, he was an early convert.

Bibliography. R. J. Knowling, *Expositor's Greek Testament,* II (4th ed., 1910), 447, includes a full discussion of the textual problem. For further conjectures about Mnason, see F. J. Foakes-Jackson and K. Lake, *Beginnings of Christianity,* pt. I, vol. IV (1933), p. 270.

H. C. Kee

*__MOAB__ mō'ăb [מואב, מאב; LXX Μωαβ; Akkad. *Ma'aba, Ma'ab, Mu'aba;* Egyp. *M-'-b; for the popular etymology, see* § 1 *below*]; MOABITE —ə bīt' [מואבי, מאבי, בני מואב], Moabitess. A state in Transjordan, E of the Dead Sea and of the S few miles of the Jordan River. Moab was of frequent concern to Israel from the time of the Exodus to the fall of Jerusalem.

1. Name and origin
2. Geography
3. History
   a. Prebiblical
   b. Early Bronze Age IV–Middle Bronze Age I (twenty-third through twentieth centuries B.C.)
   c. The rise of the Iron Age civilization
   d. The period of the Exodus (thirteenth century B.C.)
   e. The period of the Israelite judges
   f. The period of the United Monarchy (*ca.* 1020–*ca.* 922)
   g. The period from Israelite division to the beginning of Moab's Assyrian vassalship (*ca.* 922–*ca.* 735)
   h. The period from Assyrian vassalship to Moab's end as a state (*ca.* 735–*ca.* 600)
   i. Later events
4. Religion

Bibliography

1. Name and origin. According to Gen. 19:30-38, the ancestor of the Moabites was Moab, son of Lot and of the older of his two daughters, born in the hills above Zoar, apparently in S Moab. No etymology of "Moab" is given in MT. However, after "[she] called his name Moab," the LXX adds: "saying, from my father," as if the MT had originally included לאמר מאבי. Possibly the LXX reflects the original text, since an etymology for "Moab" would correspond to the name Ben-ammi in vs. 38. No other mention is made of this ancestor of the Moabites, and elsewhere in the Bible, "Moab" indicates either the land or the people.

2. Geography. Essentially, Moab consisted of the high, gently rolling plateau immediately E of the Dead Sea, *ca.* 3,000 feet above sea level, and therefore *ca.* 4,300 feet above the Dead Sea itself. The extreme N-S extent of Moab was *ca.* sixty miles, but in times of weakness the N section was lost, and the remaining distance was *ca.* thirty-five miles. The E-W extent was *ca.* twenty-five miles—of course, not all cultivable land, since this distance includes the steep descent to the Dead Sea on the W, and since the land becomes increasingly dry to the E. The rather narrow N-S strip is well watered and produces fine crops of grain. In periods of heavy occupation, cultivation was undertaken in every square foot of land possible, even to the extent of

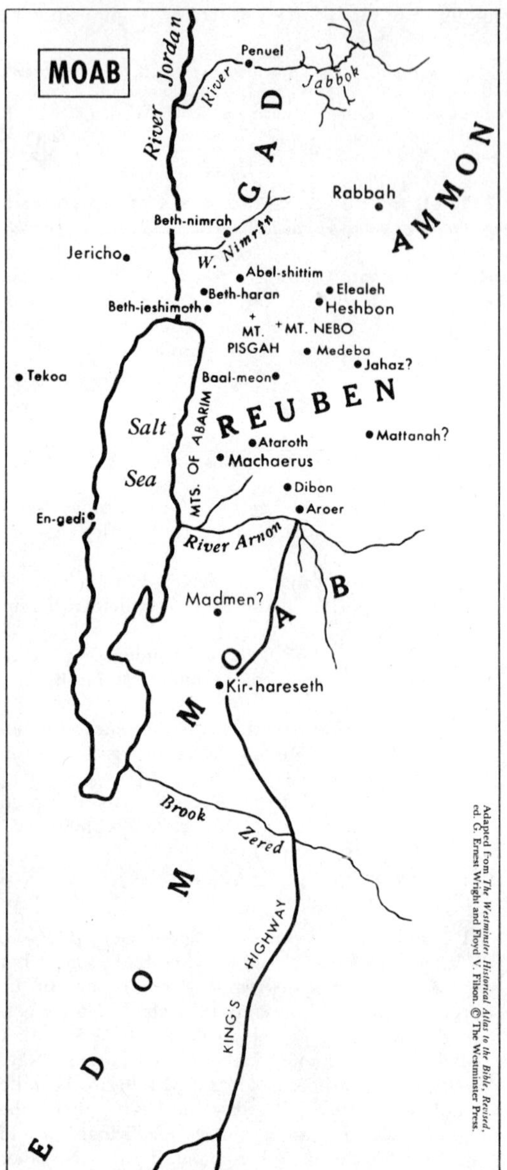

Adapted from *The Westminster Historical Atlas to the Bible, Revised*, ed. G. Ernest Wright and Floyd V. Filson. © The Westminster Press.

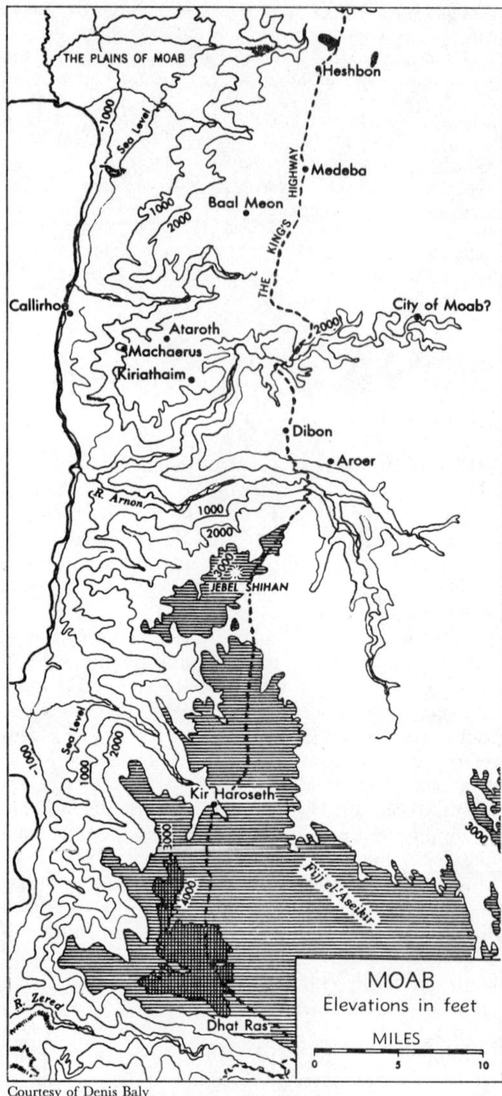

Courtesy of Denis Baly

terracing steep hillsides, as, e.g., the S slope leading down to the Wadi Hesa. Everywhere there are sheep, as there were when Mesha was royal sheepmaster to the king of Israel (*see* § 3*g below*). The flocks move E into the Syrian Desert during the rich season of spring and return W in the drought of summer.

On the W the descent from the plateau to the Dead Sea is very steep, and there is no continuous route of travel along the shore, since tall cliffs frequently rise directly from the sea. At intervals the mountains are cut by narrow gorges, through which flow the streams from the plateau. The largest of these is the River Arnon (now called the Wadi Mojib), entering the Dead Sea just N of its mid-point. *Ca.* two thirds of the way S along the shore, a broad peninsula, called the Lisan ("tongue"), extends into the sea. It reaches to within three miles of the W shore, and it was formerly possible to ford the strait. The Lisan itself is unproductive, but the small plain lying at the foot of the plateau is watered by the Wadi Kerak and other streams, and is agriculturally useful. There are also several small watered deltas.

The Wadi Hesa (probably the biblical Brook Zered; *see* ZERED, BROOK) forms a very definite S boundary for Moab. Its N bank was well fortified by Moab, and its S bank by Edom (*see* § 3*c below*). Except on rare occasions (*see* § 3*g below*), the border was not transgressed by Moab or Edom. Through most of its course the Wadi Hesa flows through a great canyon with very high and steep banks, which contributed to the strength of the boundary. E.g., the SW corner of the plateau is more than 2,500 feet above the stream in the chasm below; at the ford of the King's Highway at Aineh, *ca.* seventeen miles upstream from the outlet of the wadi, there is still a steep climb of over 1,500 feet up to the plateau. Farther E, of course, the valley becomes more shallow and more easily crossed.

The E boundary of Moab was less definitely

marked. The land gradually becomes too dry for practical occupation, but there is no precise point where this stage is reached. It depends on small variations of climate, pressure of population, efficiency in the use of water, and other factors. Many of the E border fortresses were located in areas beyond the limit of cultivation. *See* § 3*c below.*

The N border of Moab fluctuated greatly with Moab's changing fortunes. What may be called the original border, or the ideal border, may be identified approximately with a line including the Wadi Hesban, and Qasr el-Al and Khirbet er-Rufaiseh E of the wadi, a line which would be *ca.* four or five miles N of the Dead Sea. However (*see* § 3 *below*), Moab's border varied at different times between this line and that of the tremendous chasm of the River Arnon, *ca.* twenty-five miles farther S.

A rather individual area was the "Plains of Moab," a rich and comparatively well-watered district along the River Jordan, stretching from the Dead Sea N to the Wadi Nimrin, a distance of *ca.* eight miles. Several perennial streams flow through the area from the E hills, including the wadis Nimrin, Kefrein, and Rameh. Several important cities were also located here (*see* SHITTIM 1; BETH-HARAM;

Courtesy of Denis Baly

56. The mountains of Moab from the E shore of the Dead Sea

BETH-JESHIMOTH; BETH-NIMRAH). The area figures often in Israelite history, especially in the period of the Exodus. Presumably Moab possessed this area early in its political history, since it was already called the "Plains of Moab" when the Amorite king Sihon dispossessed Moab S to the Arnon.

Of course, an estimate of the population of Moab can be made only with the greatest caution. Judging from the intensity of cultivation, Nelson Glueck has suggested a possible figure of 450,000 for all of Transjordan in Iron Age I-II, which might allow an estimate of about 100,000-150,000 for Moab. However, this is merely a rough estimate. Fig. MOA 56.

3. History. ***a. Prebiblical.*** The most conspicuous prebiblical remains are the numerous fields of dolmens and menhirs scattered here and there in Moab and throughout Transjordan. A dolmen is a structure of massive stone slabs which form the walls and roof of a chamber or series of chambers, often buried under a tumulus of earth or stones. The dolmens are probably imitations of the houses in which people lived. A menhir is a great standing stone; often several are set up in a row or circle. In Moab these monuments stem from the Neolithic Age, dating *ca.* 6000-4500 B.C. Individual stones often weigh several tons.

E.g., Khirbet Iskander is a site *ca.* 13½ miles E of the Dead Sea, on the N bank of the Wadi Wala.

Courtesy of Nelson Glueck

57. Menhir at Ader

Courtesy of Nelson Glueck

58. Menhir at Khirbet Iskander

The E section of the site is dotted with menhir circles and large standing or fallen menhirs.* The circles range from 5 to 18 feet in diameter, with individual menhirs averaging 5½ by 1½ by 1 feet, excluding the portion sunk in the soil. One large fallen menhir is 13 feet long, 4¼ feet wide at its base, and tapers to 2 1/10 feet at its top. Figs. MOA 57-58.

An unusually extensive dolmen field exists along the S slope of the valley of Wadi Jideid, *ca.* two miles S of Mount Nebo. In an area of *ca.* two square miles, 162 dolmens have been examined. Of one of many in good condition, the capstone measured 8½ by 8 feet; the S side stone was 8½ by 3½ by 1¾ feet; two N side stones were 3 by 5 and 5 by 7 feet, each 2 feet thick. *See* DOLMENS.

b. Early Bronze Age IV–Middle Bronze Age I (twenty-third through twentieth centuries B.C.). At the end of the Early Bronze Age there was an intensive sedentary occupation in Moab, as in all of Transjordan. Large, firmly established farming communities represent a highly advanced civilization. Most of the sites are strongly walled, and usually are built on an eminence easy to defend. In many instances large fields of from three to ten acres or more were walled in and cultivated, although intensive cultivation was carried on outside the walls as well. There seems to have been political disunity, the fortifications being directed as much against neighbors as against foreign enemies. The sites were generally near a spring or perennial stream to provide water. The inhabitants used much excellent, although rather coarse, handmade pottery, showing no substantial differences from contemporary pottery in W Palestine.

Careful use was made of water and land. E.g., there are three EB IV–MB I sites on the S slope leading down from the Moabite Plateau to the Wadi Hesa: el-Aineh, Khirbet Umm Sedeirah, and Khirbet Serareh. Agricultural communities could survive here only under the pressure of dire necessity, when every available bit of land was being used.

Khirbet Iskander (*see* § 3*a above*) is a typical EB IV–MB I site. It is a large, low, completely destroyed mound, with its S side reaching to the very edge of the N bank of the Wadi Wala. The W section of the site, located on a rise, is enclosed by the remnants of a strong wall, measuring *ca.* 500 feet square, with traces of large square towers at each corner and near the middle of each wall. The best preserved wall measures *ca.* 5.6 feet thick. Clear foundation remains of houses are against the inside faces of the walls.

At this time, there was a well-defined N-S trade route through central Transjordan—practically the same route that has been used in all subsequent ages up to the present. When an army led by Chedorlaomer moved down this route as far as El-paran in Edom (Gen. 14:5-7), it was able to conquer the fortified sites one by one. Apparently no united defensive attempt was made. This defeat may have contributed to the disappearance of the EMIM, a group of the REPHAIM said to have lived in Moab before the Moabites (Deut. 2:10-11).

This sedentary civilization in Moab and S Transjordan generally ended *ca.* the twentieth century B.C. From the River Jabbok S there is a gap from before 1900 to after 1300, during which the area was peopled almost exclusively by nomads, who left no pottery trace of their sojourn. The reason for the break lies, not in climatic change, but rather in political and economic factors. The Amorite movement (*see* AMORITES) in Mesopotamia seems to have been of great influence. There was increasing pressure by Amorite nomads in the Fertile Crescent between 2200 and 2000, when it also penetrated into Egypt. The effective settlement of the Amorite nomads in Mesopotamia did not begin until after the fall of the third dynasty of Ur, *ca.* 1950. However, in Moab, the inhabitants continued a nomadic life until the thirteenth century. This Amorite nomadism was not as mobile as was later Arab nomadism, since effective domestication of the camel did not come until the latter part of the second millennium B.C. The Amorites were dependent on pasturage for their herds of cattle, sheep, goats, and asses. Many of the details of the situation in Moab from *ca.* 1900 remain obscure, but the general picture of nomadic occupation is clear.

c. The rise of the Iron Age civilization. The long period without sedentary occupation in S Transjordan closed at the very end of the Late Bronze Age in the thirteenth century B.C. The nomads who had held the land since *ca.* 1900 settled down, and the kingdom of Moab arose, as well as the kingdoms of Edom and Ammon, and those of the "Amorite" kings Sihon and Og. From the topographical lists of Rameses II (1290-1224) at Luxor comes the first mention of Moab in extrabiblical sources (*ANET* 343). In Num. 24:17, Moab occurs parallel to the expression "the sons of Sheth" (בני שת). Sheth (שת) is an archaic tribal name. The Egyptian texts from the nineteenth century mention a nomadic people of the same name, the Shutu (*Šwtw*), somewhere in Palestine (*ANET* 329). Upper and Lower Shutu both have princes, and may roughly correspond to later Ammon and Moab. At any rate, nomads such as these began to settle down in the thirteenth century, presumably passing through a seminomadic stage before becoming fully sedentary. At the time that the Israelites passed through Transjordan, the Moabites probably exhibited a mixture of seminomadic and sendentary culture, feeling strong attachment to their territory and bitter resentment toward any encroachment upon it.

The Iron Age kingdom of Moab was defended by a very strong system of fortresses. Several guarded the S border, where the plateau descends to the Wadi Hesa. The KING'S HIGHWAY crossed the Wadi Hesa *ca.* seventeen miles E of its outlet into the Dead Sea. This pass was important for communication and trade, and the springs of Aineh watered a fertile area nearby. To guard the area was the fortress el-Medeiyineh, situated on an almost impregnable, high hill. The walls of the fortress form an irregular rectangle, measuring *ca.* 128 by 200 by 206 by 206 feet, with an additional enclosed section on the E. When the King's Highway reached the top of the slope, it had perforce to go around a long rock outspur. On the spur was a second fortress, el-Akuzeh. The entire spur, *ca.* 750 by 45 feet, was walled, and it was cut off from the rest of the ridge by a deep and wide moat. There were towers at each end and in the middle.

Guarding the SW corner of Moab was a strong walled fortress, Dhubab, *ca.* 550 yards below the SW corner of the plateau. Not far N and lower on the slope was Khaneq en-Nasara. And on a completely isolated hill on the plateau proper was Medinet er-Ras, where a great wall 6½ feet thick enclosed an area *ca.* 475 by 55 feet. At the S end of the site was a very strong fortress. Medinet er-Ras completed the S fortifications and began those guarding the descent to the Dead Sea on the W edge of Moab.

To guard against invasion from the desert, the E border of Moab was guarded even more strongly than the S border. The southernmost and key fortress on the E border was Mahaiy, on the fairly flat top of a high steep hill, *ca.* 1600 feet long and 400-800 feet wide. A great outer wall surrounded the hilltop, and there was a strong watchtower on a small rise within the fortress. Mahaiy commanded a clear view of the desert areas to the E and the NE, and also dominated the slope down to the Wadi Hesa. No large group could invade Moab from the SE without coming into range of Mahaiy.

N of Mahaiy was a carefully worked-out and well-integrated system of fortresses, many within sight of one another. There were large fortresses similar to those described above and also smaller blockhouses to supplement them. E.g., almost four miles N-NW of Mahaiy is the large fortress of Medeibi. *Ca.* two miles N-NW of Medeibi is the blockhouse of el-Mahri.* It is well built, measuring 52 by 66 feet, with walls 4½ feet thick. At one corner the wall is still fourteen courses high, totaling 16 feet. On almost every rise in the entire district are the remains of a

Courtesy of Nelson Glueck

59. Border fortress at el-Mahri

Courtesy of Nelson Glueck

60. Wall of a Moabite border fortress, at Qasr Abu el-Kharaq

large or small watchtower or police post, many from the Iron Age. The line of fortification continues N along the entire E border of Moab. In the important area of the Arnon there are several strong fortresses located in inhospitable areas near which there was probably never any habitation or cultivation. Their garrisons must have been provisioned from outside and their water drawn from their own cisterns. Figs. MOA 59-60.

Since the N boundary of Moab fluctuated more than the E and the S, the border defenses are not so clear. Furthermore, the interior of Moab did not rely for protection solely on the border fortresses. Practically every site throughout the land consisted of a great fortress or a strong blockhouse. Sometimes it consisted of a strong central structure about which the dwellings of the inhabitants clustered, all within a great fortification wall. The land was cultivated outside the strongholds, and the inhabitants returned every night. As in EB, all available land was cultivated to supply the needs of a dense population.

An important difference between the Iron Age culure and that of EB involved water. In EB, sites were generally located near springs or perennial streams. However, by the Iron Age the technique of constructing water-tight cisterns by the use of plaster made with slaked lime had been developed. This allowed settlement in areas away from natural water sources, dependent on the storing of rain for their water supply. Often cisterns were located on the top or sides of the hill on which a settlement was built; sometimes they were inside or around the buildings themselves. Many were hewn directly from the natural rock. In the Moabite Stone, Mesha stated (*ca.* 830 B.C.) that there was no cistern inside the town at Qarhoh. Therefore, he commanded all the people that each should make for himself a cistern in his house. From the contents of the Moabite Stone, Qarhoh seems to be identical with DIBON, Mesha's capital. Possibly Qarhoh may be a common noun, meaning "its citadel." In the topographical lists of Ramses II at Karnak and of Ramses III at Medinet Habu, the same word, *q-r-h,* is mentioned. Additional evidence for the identification of Qarhoh with Dibon is provided by the fact that no fewer than sixty-seven cisterns have been catalogued on the N mound of modern Dhiban, and thirty more on the sides of the surrounding wadi.

Courtesy of the Palestine Archaeological Museum, Jerusalem, Jordan

61. Stele from Balu'ah in Moab

In 1930 a stele was discovered at Baluʿah, *ca.* fifteen miles N of Kir-hareseth. Its inscription is too worn to be read, but it seems to date in the latter part of the Early Bronze Age. However, the relief on the stele seems to be secondary, dating to *ca.* the twelfth or eleventh century B.C. The figure on the left is a god, wearing the crown of Upper and Lower Egypt; that on the right is a goddess. The central figure is a suppliant, standing with upraised hands before the god. Fig. MOA 61.

Whereas there was no distinguishable difference between the EB pottery of E and W Palestine, there are enough peculiarities in the early Iron Age to put the Transjordan pottery in a class of its own. Part of the distinctiveness of this pottery, particularly in Moab and Edom, may be attributed to influences coming S from Syria along the King's Highway. In this period the orientation of Transjordan was to the N and the S—i.e., to Syria and Arabia—rather than to W Palestine. The pottery attests a high civilization, with potters skilled in ceramic craft and having high artistic sense.

We find, therefore, that the Iron Age civilization in Moab, as elsewhere in Transjordan, was no less developed than that in W Palestine. Judged by houses, fortresses, cisterns, agriculture, pottery, commercial activities, density of population, political organization, Moab was a highly advanced kingdom.

d. The period of the Exodus (thirteenth century B.C.). After the episode discussed in 1, Moab came on the biblical scene next at the time of the Exodus. It was the first stage of the Iron Age kingdom that we have just discussed which the Israelites encountered in Moab. Shortly before the Israelite arrival in Transjordan, Sihon, a king of the Amorites, had defeated the previous king of Moab (Num. 21:26) and appropriated the N section of Moabite territory as far S as the Arnon. We do not know the precise extent of Moab before Sihon's conquest, but it must have reached far enough N to include the Plains of Moab, NE of the Dead Sea, since this area had already received its name. At any rate, after his victory over Moab, Sihon ruled the territory from the Jabbok to the Arnon, and was commonly known as king of Heshbon. The song in Num. 21:27-30 seems to refer to this Amorite conquest of Moab.

It is difficult to trace the precise course of events as the Israelites moved through Transjordan on their way to the Promised Land. The chief passages from which we derive our information about Israel's dealings with Moab are the accounts in Num. 21–33, Moses' words in Deut. 2:8-37, and Jephthah's message to the king of the Ammonites in Judg. 11:12-28. In Num. 21:10, the Israelites have detoured around Edom and encamped at Oboth. Then they encamped at Iye-abarim, "in the wilderness which is opposite Moab, toward the sunrise," and next in the Valley of Zered. They crossed the Arnon, and after a further series of encampments (cf. Num. 21:10-20; 33:41-49) the Israelites arrived at the "valley lying in the region of Moab by the top of Pisgah which looks down upon the desert" (Num. 21:20), which may correspond to the encampment "in the mountains of Abarim, before Nebo" (Num. 33:47).

Next, Num. 21 relates the Israelite victories over the two Amorite kings Sihon and Og. We would have expected these conflicts to have taken place before the Israelites moved W from the wilderness toward Canaan, not after they had reached their encampment by Nebo. According to Jephthah's message in Judg. 11:17, the kings of Edom and Moab refused to let the Israelites pass through their lands, although we are told that the Moabites who live in Ar later sold the Israelites provisions (Deut. 2:29). After the refusal, Israel journeyed around Edom and Moab, and used the victories over Sihon and Og to gain access to Canaan.

According to Deut. 2:9, the Israelites had been forbidden to contend with Moab in battle, because God had "given Ar to the sons of Lot for a possession." In Deut. 23:3-6, no Moabite (or Ammonite) may "enter the assembly of the LORD; even to the tenth generation . . . ," because they did not meet Israel with bread and water on the way, and because they hired Balaam to curse Israel. Yet exclusion to the tenth generation is not permanent separation. This provision and the order to refrain from battle with Moab illustrate the fact that Moab and Israel are always felt to be related peoples, as understood in the light of common ancestry. However, according to Josh. 24:9, Balak the king of Moab "arose and fought against Israel"; of such a conflict we know nothing more.

The Israelites then proceeded down to their encampment in the Plains of Moab, across the Jordan from Jericho (Num. 22:1 ff). Moab was in great fear of Israel because of the defeat of the Amorites. The king of Moab, Balak, the son of Zippor, sent messengers to Balaam, son of Beor, at Pethor by the Euphrates, asking him to come and curse Israel (Num. 22–24). After some complications, Balaam acquiesced, but the result was a blessing upon Israel instead of a curse.

While Israel was encamped at Shittim in the Plains of Moab, the people entered into illicit relations with Moabite women. The latter invited the Israelites to the sacrifices of their gods, and Israel "yoked himself to Baal of Peor" (Num. 25:3). Also involved in the situation were the Midianites. God's anger was kindled; the offenders were slain, and a plague came upon Israel in punishment.

The tribes of Reuben and Gad were attracted by the territory in Transjordan, including the N section of Moab which the Israelites had taken from Sihon (Num. 32). They possessed many cattle and saw that it would be good grazing land, so they asked for their territorial assignment there, rather than W of the Jordan. After arranging that their men of war should assist the rest of Israel W of the Jordan, the assignment was made. Many former Moabite cities were rebuilt by the tribes of Gad and Reuben (Num. 32:34-38).

At the close of the Israelite stay in the Plains of Moab, Joshua was commissioned as Moses' successor, and Moses ascended Mount Nebo to view the land and then to die (Num. 27:12-23; Deut. 32:48-52; 34:1-8). Moses was buried "in the valley in the land of Moab opposite Beth-peor," and the Israelites mourned for him thirty days. Joshua sent the two spies to Jericho and received their report (Josh. 1–2). The Israelites moved from Shittim to the Jordan, encamped three days, and then passed on to their conquest of Canaan (Josh. 3:1 ff).

e. The period of the Israelite judges. At least for a time in the period of the Israelite judges, Moab must have regained most, if not all, of its N territory. In Judg. 3:12-30 we have the account of the "judge" Ehud. Eglon, king of Moab, allied himself with the

Ammonites and the Amalekites, and they took the "city of palms" (i.e., Jericho). The Moabites must first have pushed N from the River Arnon the approximately twenty-five miles to the N end of the Dead Sea, and probably several miles farther. This corresponds well with the general picture of Israelite weakness and disunity in the time of the judges. For eighteen years the Israelites are said to have served Eglon. Perhaps this was the occasion for Samuel's reminder that God had sold Israel into the hand of the king of Moab (I Sam. 12:9). Then there arose a deliverer, Ehud, a Benjaminite, who assassinated Eglon. Moabite territorial control seemed to end at the "sculptured stones near Gilgal" (Judg. 3:19, 26), although we do not know what they were. At the fords of the Jordan, which the Moabites were compelled to cross in retreat, the Israelites killed "about ten thousand of the Moabites" (vs. 29), so Moab was subdued and the land of Israel had rest for eighty years (vs. 30). However, there was no Israelite invasion E of the Jordan into Moab proper. The defeat was simply of Moab's occupying forces.

The events in the book of Ruth are said to have taken place "in the days when the judges ruled" (Ruth 1:1). Unfortunately, no precise geographical data are given as to where in Moab Elimelech's family settled, although certainly the N section would be reached first. After ten years, Naomi returned to Bethlehem, accompanied by her daughter-in-law Ruth, who became the wife of Boaz and the great-grandmother of King David. This story, with its easy travel between Moab and Israel, and the lack of hostility in either land toward foreigners from the other, illustrates the friendly relations that must have existed from time to time between the two peoples.

In a time of Ammonite oppression of Israel, Jephthah, a Gileadite, arose to deliver Israel (Judg. 10:17–12:7). In his message to the Ammonites, Jephthah denied that Israel had taken away the land of the Ammonites or of the Moabites at the time of the Exodus. He recounted Israel's journey around Edom and Moab, and the defeat of the Amorite king Sihon. He argued that Israel had been left in peace for "three hundred years" in the area of Heshbon, and of Aroer, and along the banks of the Arnon, so the Ammonites should not be making war against Israel now on this account. Jephthah's words to the contrary, much of this N area of Moab had been regained by the Moabites, allied at least for a time with the Ammonites and the Amalekites, at the time of Ehud (*see above*). At any rate, Jephthah's arguments were unsuccessful, and the Ammonites were subdued by force.

Some inferences can be drawn from incidental information in Judges. Judg. 10:6 tells of the Israelites' serving many foreign gods of surrounding nations, including "the gods of Sidon, the gods of Moab, the gods of the Ammonites," and others. In Judg. 6–8, the Midianites, the Amalekites, and the people of the East are said to have oppressed Israel. They raided in great numbers, using the recently domesticated camel. In 6:33 they are said to have crossed the Jordan and encamped in the Valley of Jezreel, before Gideon's great victory. Whether or not this particular raid had struck Moab before crossing the Jordan, it seems likely that Moab suffered from similar invasions from time to time, giving us a clearer understanding of the occasion for the strong border defenses described in § 3*c above*.

***f. The period of the United Monarchy* (ca. *1020*–ca. *922*).** The time of the United Monarchy in Israel, beginning just before the end of the eleventh century, was a time of Israelite strength and domination in Transjordan, and in Moab in particular. The first major event of Saul's kingship was the victory over Nahash the Ammonite, who was besieging Jabesh-gilead, a little more than thirty miles N of N Moab. Saul's successes covered Transjordan, including victories over Moab, the Ammonites, Edom, and even the kings of Zobah in the NE (I Sam. 14:47). We do not know whether this was an extension of his victory over Nahash or whether it was a separate campaign, fitted in between encounters with the Philistines.

While David was a fugitive from Saul, he is said to have gone to Mizpeh of Moab and entrusted his parents to the king of Moab (I Sam. 22:3-5). The Moabite king would probably sympathize with David's flight from Saul, and possibly would be favorably inclined toward David because of his Moabite great-grandmother, Ruth. Perhaps Ithmah the Moabite, who is listed as one of David's mighty men (I Chr. 11:46), became attached to him at this time.

At the beginning of David's reign there was civil war between David's followers in the S and those of a surviving son of Saul, Ish-bosheth, in the N and the E (II Sam. 2–4). Ish-bosheth's headquarters were at Mahanaim, in Transjordan, which was also later to serve as refuge for David in his conflict with Absalom (II Sam. 17:24, 27). Most likely Moab took advantage of the temporary Israelite weakness to reassert its independence. It may be as a result of some such action that David defeated Moab (II Sam. 8:2; I Chr. 18:2). We are told that he measured them with a line, putting two lines to death and sparing one line, presumably of the men captured in battle. The gold and silver spoil from Moab, with that from other nations, was dedicated to the Lord (II Chr. 18:11). Most likely it was the fact that Moab was already under Israelite domination that caused the Ammonites to look to the Syrians for help against Israel (II Sam. 10:6 ff), rather than to Moab or farther S to Edom. Also during David's reign, Benaiah the son of Jehoiada smote two warriors of Moab (II Sam. 23:20; I Chr. 11:22; RSV "ariels"; KJV "lionlike men"; the meaning of "ariel" is known from Egyptian transcriptions).

In Solomon's time Israel presumably maintained its domination over Moab. The seventh of Solomon's twelve administrative districts (I Kings 4:13-14) was administered from Mahanaim, and it probably extended S along the Dead Sea to include at least part of N Moab. Solomon provided places of worship for the gods of the nations of his many wives, including the building of a "high place for Chemosh the abomination of Moab" (I Kings 11:7); apparently Solomon himself engaged in the worship of the foreign gods (vs. 33).

***g. The period from Israelite division to the beginning of Moab's Assyrian vassalship* (ca. *922*–ca. *735*).** This is the most important period in the history of Moab. After the division of the United Monarchy in 922,

Moab probably continued for a time under the domination of the N kingdom. As Jeroboam is said to have "built Penuel" (I Kings 12:25) on the Jabbok, Israel seems to have maintained its strength for a time in Transjordan. The administrative districts set up by Solomon seem to have been preserved, since II Kings 20:14-15, 17, 19, speaks of their governors, and the ostraca of Samaria (*ca.* 778-770) reflect the same structure (*see* INSCRIPTIONS § 3). N Moab, then, probably continued to be included in the district of Mahanaim.

Probably early in the ninth century, Moab attempted to assert its independence of Israel and regain its territory N of the River Arnon. Success was short-lived, for soon after Omri ascended the Israelite throne (*ca.* 876), he "occupied the land of Medeba," and Israel remained there in his time and half the time of his son, forty years (Moabite Stone). Omri's "son" is apparently his grandson, Joram, so Israel maintained its control over Moab through most of the Omride dynasty. At the Battle of Karkar (Karkara) in 853, the Assyrian Shalmaneser III was faced by a coalition including Aram, Israel, and Ammon (*ANET* 278-79). However, neither Moab nor Edom was mentioned, and this confirms the fact that they were not independent.

Shortly thereafter, war broke out between Aram and Israel. In an attempt, with the help of Jehoshaphat of Judah, to recover Ramoth-gilead in Transjordan, Ahab was killed (I Kings 22:1-40; II Chr. 18). Meanwhile, the Moabites, the Ammonites, and some Meunites invaded Judah from the S (II Chr. 20:1 ff). Very possibly the Aramean Ben-hadad instigated the attack, hoping to relieve the pressure of Israel against the Aramean penetration. Furthermore, Jehoshaphat was attempting to reopen sea trade with South Arabia (I Kings 22:48-49; II Chr. 20:35-37), which would mean serious competition for the overland caravan route along the King's Highway through Transjordan. At any rate, before Jehoshaphat realized the danger, the allies had penetrated as far as En-gedi on the W shore of the Dead Sea, possibly crossing the Dead Sea from Moab at the ford between the Lisan and the W shore. As a result of Jehoshaphat's prayer (II Chr. 20:6-12), the Lord "set an ambush" against the allies as they came up the ascent of Ziz, near Tekoa, and they were routed. The allies turned against each other, and the invasion came to a disastrous end.

Nevertheless, successful rebellion by Moab was shortly to come. For some time before the death of Ahab, the "king" of Moab had been Mesha, a sheep raiser. "He had to deliver annually to the king of Israel a hundred thousand lambs, and the wool of a hundred thousand rams" (II Kings 3:4). There exists an Ugaritic parallel to the term "sheep raiser" (נקד), in which an individual is known as "chief priest, chief shepherd" (*rb khnm rb nḳdm*). Thus, Mesha occupied the official position under Ahab of Israel of royal sheepmaster, like "chief butler," "chief baker," in Gen. 40:2.

After the death of King Ahab of Israel, Mesha rebelled (II Kings 3:5 ff). Joram of Israel, Jehoshaphat of Judah, and the king of Edom marched against Moab "by the way of the wilderness of Edom" (II Kings 3:8), apparently in 849 B.C., since only for this year did Joram and Jehoshaphat rule simultaneously. They made a circuitous march of seven days, through waterless country (II Kings 3:9). As was seen in § 3*c above,* the strong defense system along Moab's S border and the deep chasm of the Wadi Hesa were good reasons for their going out of their way to attack Moab from the E. Yet here also there were strong defenses, including the powerful fortress of Mahaiy (*see* § 3*c above*). The night before the battle, the dry stream bed separating the forces was filled with water, coming from the E. Early in the morning the Moabites saw the sun reflected in the water, thought the allies must have fallen out and slaughtered one another, rushed headlong to the attack, and were slaughtered by the Israelites. Moab fled, pursued by the Israelites, who destroyed the cities, threw stones on the good land, stopped the springs, felled the trees, and shut up Mesha in Kir-hareseth. Mesha with seven hundred swordsmen tried to break through opposite the king of Edom, but could not. Then as a last resort, Mesha took his eldest son and offered him as a burnt offering upon the wall, apparently raising such superstitious fear in the hearts of the besiegers that they raised the siege and gave up the invasion (II Kings 3:27). According to Mesha, the house of Omri was defeated, and "Israel perished forever!"

In his inscription, Mesha described his further victories. He regained the land of Medeba, which Omri had taken. He took the land of Ataroth from the men of Gad. (The tribe of Reuben is not mentioned on the Moabite Stone.) Nebo was taken in a battle continuing from the break of dawn until noon; seven thousand Israelites were reportedly slain. Thus the Moabites gained their complete independence from Israel and regained much of their old N territory. After his victories, Mesha engaged in fortifying various cities, providing water supplies, and executing other public works, in part at least by the use of Israelite captives (line 25). The Ammonites had already regained their independence, and Edom also successfully rebelled against Judah (II Kings 8:20-22), so that by the death of Joram of Judah in 842, all three Transjordan states were independent.

Throughout most of the remaining ninth century, Israel was very weak, and Aram was the dominant power in Syria-Palestine. The Arameans under Hazael overran Transjordan as far S as the Arnon (II Kings 10:33). Possibly Moab welcomed Aram as an ally against Israel, freeing the King's Highway from Israelite domination. Moab may have become an autonomous vassal of Aram, although we have no direct evidence of this.

However, *ca.* 806, Hazael died. The Assyrians, under Adad-nirari III, moved W, subdued Aram, and imposed a heavy tribute. Also mentioned as paying tribute are Tyre, Sidon, Philistia, Israel, and Edom, but it does not seem that Assyria actually invaded Palestine or tried to conquer all the former Aramean territory (*ANET* 281-82). Moab probably kept intact the territory it had regained under Mesha. Shortly after Joash became king of Israel (*ca.* 801), we are told that "bands of Moabites used to invade the land in the spring of the year" (II

Kings 13:20). This seems to imply that the territory to the N end of the Dead Sea was under Moabite control, so that the marauding bands would have access to Israel.

Yet, from about the beginning of the eighth century, Moab began to decline. In Moab there is a scarcity of pottery remains from the latter half of the Iron II period. In spite of Mesha's success in the N, perhaps Moab never fully recovered from the destruction wrought by Joram and Jehoshaphat in the S. Many of the cities they destroyed were probably never rebuilt. Contributing to Moab's decline was the successful campaign of Amaziah of Judah against Edom (II Kings 14:7), giving Judah control of the South Arabian commercial trade, diverting it from the King's Highway in Transjordan. Israel took leadership from Judah with Joash's defeat of Amaziah (II Kings 14:11-14; II Chr. 25:21-24), but Moab was not further affected until the reign of Uzziah (*ca.* 783-742).

Uzziah strengthened Judah's hold on the N-S trade by rebuilding the port of Elath (II Kings 14:22). He imposed tribute on Ammon (II Chr. 26:8), probably after the death of Jeroboam II (*ca.* 746), since Jeroboam II had restored at least part of Transjordan to Israelite sovereignty (II Kings 14:25). When Uzziah exacted tribute from Ammon, he must also have subjected Moab, thereby giving Judah control of Ammon, Moab, and Edom. Ammon (but not Moab) rebelled soon after Uzziah's death (*ca.* 742), but Jotham subdued Ammon and imposed a large tribute (II Chr. 27:5). From time to time, after *ca.* 750, parts of S Gilead and N Moab seem often to have been in Ammonite hands. Since Uzziah and Jotham imposed tribute on Ammon, we infer that Ammon had grown W and SW so as to be within reach of Judah. However, the Palestine scene was now to be changed very greatly by the return of the Assyrians. Whereas up to this point the most common direction from which danger had come to Moab was the W, now in the closing days danger was to come from the NE.

h. The period from Assyrian vassalship to Moab's end as a state **(ca. *735*–ca. *600*).** The period of Assyrian weakness that began with the death of Adad-nirari III (*ca.* 783) continued until the accession of Tiglath-pileser III (*ca.* 745). After success elsewhere, by 738 Tiglath-pileser was in Palestine-Syria, and received tribute from Menahem of Israel (II Kings 15:19-20; also mentioned in Tiglath-pileser's annals) and other kings of the area. When Ahaz took the throne of Judah (*ca.* 735), he found himself under attack from Aram and Israel in the N, Edom in the S, and the Philistines in the W. Ahaz sent tribute and asked Tiglath-pileser for aid. In 733, Tiglath-pileser's army swept over N Israel, Philistia, and Transjordan. He took captive the Reubenites, Gadites, and half-Manasseh (I Chr. 5:26); created the new Assyrian province of Gal'azu (Gilead); and received tribute from various kings, including Salamanu of Moab, Jehoahaz of Judah, and those of Edom and Ammon. Direct Assyrian control may have extended S to the Arnon, and the Transjordan states became vassals of Assyria (*ANET* 282-84).

Presumably, as time went on, Moab continued to pay tribute to Assyria. Israel fell to Sargon II in 722/1. Azuru, king of Ashdod, tried to muster a coalition of Philistia, Judah, Edom, and Moab, with the support of Pir'u (Pharaoh Bocchoris) of Egypt. In 711, Sargon defeated Ashdod and made it an Assyrian province, but the allies seem to have withdrawn in time, since Sargon mentions having subjugated only Ashdod (*ANET* 286-87).

After Sargon's death, Sennacherib took the Assyrian throne (*ca.* 704). In 701, Sennacherib moved W to put down a general rebellion. He conquered Judah, blockaded Jerusalem, and received tribute from Hezekiah. Ammon, Moab (whose king was Kammusunadbi), and Edom also paid tribute, whether or not they were involved in the rebellion (*ANET* 287-88).

From a letter, apparently written to king Esarhaddon (681-669), we learn that Moab paid him a tribute of one mina of gold (=1/60 of a talent). Moab's weakness is seen in this small tribute, only half that of Ammon (two minas) and about equal to that of Judah (ten minas of silver). Also in Esarhaddon's time, Musuri king of Moab is mentioned in a list of twenty-two kings (including those of Judah, Edom, and Ammon) who were compelled to provide building materials for the royal palace at Nineveh (*ANET* 291).

Under Ashurbanipal (669–*ca.* 630), Assyria reached its climax of prestige and wealth. However, during the civil war between Ashurbanipal and his brother Shamash-shum-ukin (652-648), the Arabs flooded E Syria and Palestine, including Moab. One of the Arab chiefs, Ammuladi, king of Kedar, was captured by Kamashallay(?) of Moab, whose name seems also to be recorded on a cylinder seal. Kamashallay, acting as a vassal of Ashurbanipal, sent Ammuladi in bonds to Nineveh (*ANET* 298). However, this catastrophe of the Arab invasion spelled the end of Moab as a strong autonomous state. It continued to exist for a generation or two, but in a greatly weakened condition.

The dirge on the fate of Moab contained in Isa. 15–16; Jer. 48 probably refers to the events of this catastrophe, *ca.* 650 B.C. The Arabs seem to have swept over Moab from the N, attacking Heshbon and Elealeh first and then pushing S. Fugitives seem to have fled from them in a southerly direction (cf. Isa. 15:5, 7; 16:1 ff; Jer. 48:4-6, 28, 34, 45). The desert raiders may have come in from the E between Ammon and Moab; been repelled by the strong line of fortresses protecting the Ammonite capital, Rabbah; and then swung S through Moab, finding the Moabite strongholds more vulnerable (Jer. 48:1, 18, 41).

During the reign of Josiah (*ca.* 640-609), Zephaniah's oracle (2:8-11) was pronounced against Moab and the Ammonites in reaction to their taunts of the Israelites. Ammon at this time was relatively strong, but Moab definitely of little importance. Jehoiakim (609-598) became a vassal of Nebuchadnezzar the Babylonian, who had also made raids against the Arabs in Transjordan. When Jehoiakim rebelled against Nebuchadnezzar, bands of Chaldeans, Syrians, Moabites, and Ammonites raided Judah in punishment (II Kings 24:2). As late as 598 we hear of a king reigning in Moab (Jer. 27:3). At the time of the destruction of Jerusalem, many fled to Moab,

Ammon, and Edom, some returning when Gedaliah was appointed governor (Jer. 40:11-12).

Archaeological exploration has shown that Moab was largely depopulated from *ca.* the beginning of the sixth century, and in many sites from *ca.* the eighth century. From the sixth century on, nomads wandered through the land until political and economic factors made sedentary life possible again in the last centuries B.C.

i. Later events. After several centuries without sedentary occupation, almost all of what had been Moab (as far N as the N end of the Dead Sea) was settled by the NABATEANS. Heavy as the settlement had been in earlier periods, the Nabatean population at its height was perhaps twice as intensive. Even more efficient use was made of water; even more difficult land was put under cultivation. Practically all the defense posts and fortresses were reused or strengthened, and others were built. The Nabateans flourished from the first century B.C. through the first century A.D., almost all of the Nabatean kingdom being incorporated into a Roman province by Trajan in A.D. 106. Occupation continued to be heavy in the Roman and Byzantine periods.

During the twelfth century, the Crusaders built a magnificent castle at Kerak (*see* KIR-HARESETH), where Mesha sacrificed his son to drive off the Israelite invaders.

4. Religion. The Moabite Stone says much about the attitude of the Moabites toward their national deity, CHEMOSH. Mesha speaks of his father's having "made this high place for Chemosh in Qarhoh" (Dibon; *see* § 3*c above*). It is because Chemosh was angry at his land that Omri was able to humble Moab. That Chemosh dwelt in Medeba in Mesha's time signifies Moab's recapture of that city (lines 8-9; some scholars read "restored"). All the people of Ataroth were slain as a sacrifice for Chemosh. At the command of Chemosh, Nebo was taken from

Courtesy of Nelson Glueck

62. Head of a Semitic king or deity

Israel, and its population was slain for the god Ashtar-Chemosh. The king of Israel was driven out of Jahaz before Mesha by Chemosh. Fig. MOA 62.

"Chemosh" was a common element in Moabite names. We have mentioned Kammusunadbi (Chemosh-nadab) and Kamashallay (Chemosh-

Courtesy of Nelson Glueck

63. Two figurines from el-Meshhed

Courtesy of Nelson Glueck

64. Female figurine, from near Kerak

hallay). According to the Moabite Stone, Mesha's father's name, although damaged, was a compound with "Chemosh." From seals we find the names כמשיחי (Chemosh-yeḥi) and כמשצדק (Chemosh-ṣedeq).

However, Chemosh should not be pictured in purely Moabite terms. Once in the Moabite Stone he is mentioned as Ashtar-Chemosh (עשתר כמש), being identified with Ashtar, the Canaanite god of the morning star. The winged sun disk occurs several times as a motif on seals in connection with names formed with "Chemosh." Also, in the Babylonian vocabularies of the second millennium, Chemosh (Kammush) appears as a name of Nergal, the lord of the City of the Underworld. So Chemosh must be considered in the light of the general Semitic pantheon.

Small pottery figurines found at various places in Moab contribute to our knowledge. As was also true of the Canaanites, the gods and goddesses of fertility were prominent in Moab (*see* FERTILITY CULTS).* Near Mount Nebo and near Kerak have been found figurines of fertility goddesses holding loaves of bread or some other sacred object.* Heads of similar figurines were found at el-Medeiyineh and Balu'ah, one with the prong for attaching it to the body still intact.* Figurines of animals or of animals with riders have also been found. An additional find at el-Medeiyineh

Courtesy of Nelson Glueck

65. Heads from el-Medeiyineh (right) and Balu'ah (left) in Transjordan

was an interesting figurine head of a Semitic king or deity. The features are quite clear, including headdress, braided hair, and pointed beard. Figs. MOA 63, 64, 65.

Bibliography. N. Glueck, *Explorations in Eastern Palestine:* vol. I in AASOR, vol. XIV (1933-34); vol. II in AASOR, vol. XV (1934-35); vol. III in AASOR, vols. XVIII-XIX (1937-39); vol. IV in AASOR, vols. XXV-XXVIII (1945-48). These are an invaluable series of archaeological surveys, including hundreds of sites in Transjordan. The first deals particularly with Moab, but the others also contribute very greatly. Other works by Glueck are: *The Other Side of the Jordan* (1940), a popular summary of the first three annuals mentioned above; *The River Jordan* (1946). See also: D. D. Luckenbill, *Ancient Records of Assyria and Babylonia* (2 vols.; 1926-27). F.-M. Abel, *Géographie de la Palestine,* vol. I (1933); vol. II (1938). W. F. Albright, "The Biblical Period," reprinted from L. Finkelstein, ed., *The Jews: Their History, Culture and Religion* (1949). H. L. Ginsberg, "Judah and the Transjordan States from 734 to 582 B.C.," *Alexander Marx Jubilee Volume* (1950), pp. 347-68. F. V. Winnett, "Excavations at Dibon in Moab, 1950-51," *BASOR,* no. 125 (1952), pp. 7-20. A. D. Tushingham, "Excavations at Dibon in Moab, 1952-53," *BASOR,* no. 133 (1954), pp. 6-26. J. B. Pritchard, ed., *ANET* (2nd ed., 1955). W. F. Albright, *The Archaeology of Palestine* (1956). D. Baly, *The Geography of the Bible* (1957).

For further study, consult the general biblical Commentaries for the passages relating to Moab, the general histories of Israel for the events involving Moab and Israel, and the general Bible atlases for the geography of the area.

E. D. GROHMAN

MOABITE STONE. A stela of black basalt measuring forty-four by twenty-eight by fourteen inches, found at Dhiban (OT DIBON) in Transjordan and containing an inscription of MESHA, king of Moab, in which he recounts his victory over Israel.

1. Discovery
2. Language
3. Historical significance
4. Translation

Bibliography

1. Discovery. Although the stela was first shown in 1868 to F. A. Klein, a Prussian missionary, the French orientalist Clermont-Ganneau had already been apprised of its existence and was able subsequently to obtain a copy of some lines and a squeeze of the inscription. Shortly after this the natives, suspecting the value of the antiquity, smashed it into several fragments, hoping thereby to dispose of each piece separately and thus command a higher

From *Atlas of the Bible* (Thomas Nelson & Sons Limited)

66. The Moabite Stone, stele of Mesha king of Moab

price. Most of the fragments were eventually acquired by the Louvre, where, with the aid of Clermont-Ganneau's squeeze, they were reassembled, so that the stone as at present exhibited is a combination of original pieces and plaster restorations of the remainder. Fig. MOA 66.

2. Language. This stela is the only major inscription in Moabite, a language or dialect very closely related to Hebrew. Epigraphically, the forms of the letters are of importance in illustrating the development of Canaanite writing in the latter half of the ninth century B.C. The language shares with Hebrew such characteristic features as the "*waw* consecutive," the relative particle אשר, and the accusative particle את. It differs from Hebrew, however, in contracting all diphthongs *ay* and *aw* to *ê* and *ô* respectively, in exhibiting a masculine plural and dual termination in *n* rather than *m,* in preserving the *iphte'al* theme of the verb, and in employing a feminine ending *-t* in place of *-at,* as in *št* (=*šatt*) for OT *šānâ* (<*šanatu*), "year."

3. Historical significance. The inscription is dedicated to the god CHEMOSH in thankfulness for a Moabite victory over the Israelites. The account opens (line 5) with Chemosh' anger against his people and the resultant punishment of Moab by Israelite domination under Omri. This supplements the OT account in I Kings 16 by supplying the information that Omri was responsible for the conquest of N Moab. Lines 6-7 then describe how, on the accession of Omri's son to the throne of Israel, the latter determined to continue the subjection of Moab, but that Mesha succeeded in breaking the Israelite yoke so that Israel "completely perished for ever."

According to II Kings 1:1; 3:5, Moab took advantage of the confusion following the death of Ahab to revolt. Mesha's account states (lines 7-8) that Omri had gained control of the territory about Medeba and that Israel held it for a period of forty years during his reign and half that of his son. Since Omri reigned twelve years (I Kings 16:23) and Ahab twenty-two (vs. 29), the combined reign and half reign would be only twenty-three years. If, however, the בנה of line 8 refers to Omri's grandson (for "son" meaning "grandson" cf. Gen. 29:5) Jehoram, who reigned for twelve years (II Kings 3:1) after the short one-year reign of his brother Ahaziah, then the combined years of Omri, Ahab, and Ahaziah and one half the years of Jehoram's reign would total forty-one.

According to II Kings 3:4-27 it was Jehoram who set out to crush the rebellious Moabites, allied with Jehoshaphat of Judah and the Edomite king, and encouraged by the prophet Elisha. Although they carried all before them, they were finally forced to retire when Mesha, in the utmost extremity, offered his eldest son as a sacrifice to Chemosh. There is no reference to this in the Moabite Stone. On the other hand, there is no reference in the OT to the Moabite victory which forms the theme of the stela. Mesha's gloating allusion to the complete destruction of Israel may refer, not only to his military success, but also to the overthrow of the Omrid dynasty by Jehu in 841 B.C.

Certain facts of interest for the religion of the period also emerge. The OT custom of the חרם or BAN was likewise observed in Moab (line 17). Just as Israel's victory was due to Yahweh (II Kings 3:18), so Moab owed hers to Chemosh (line 4; cf. Judg. 11:24). Lines 14-18 mention a Yahweh sanctuary in the city of Nebo, although the OT gives no indication of this.

4. Translation. (1) It was I, Mesha son of Chemosh-[. . .], king of Moab, the (2) Dibonite, who, when my father had ruled over Moab for thirty years, ruled (3) after my father and made this high place for Chemosh in Qericho as a h[igh place(?) of] (4) victory, because he delivered me from all the kings[? or vicissitudes?], and because he let me triumph over all my foes. Omri, (5) king of Israel, oppressed Moab for a long time, because Chemosh was angry at his land. (6) His son succeeded him, and he too said, "I will oppress Moab!" It was in my time that he said [this], (7) but I triumphed over him and his dynasty, Israel having completely perished for ever. When Omri took possession of all [the re]gion (8) of Medeba [cf. Josh. 13:9], he inhabited it during his time and half the time of his son [or grandson]—forty years. (9) Chemosh restored it in my time, so that I built Baal-meon [cf. Num. 32:38], made the reservoir in it and built (10) Kiriathaim [cf. Josh. 13:19]. Now the men of Gad had always lived in the region of Ataroth [cf. Num. 32:34], so the king of (11) Israel built Ataroth for them. I fought against the city, captured it and slew all the people of (12) the city as satisfaction for Chemosh and Moab. Bringing Ariel [cf. II Sam. 23:20; or the altar hearth of (cf. Ezek. 43:15-16)] its DWD back from there, I (13) dragged him [or it] before Chemosh in Kerioth [cf. Jer. 48:24]. In it I settled men of Sharon and men of (14) Maharith. Then Chemosh said to me, "Go, capture Nebo [cf. Num. 32:38] from Israel!" (15) So I went by night and fought against it from break of dawn till noon. I (16) captured it, slaying all of [it]—seven thousand men, boys, women, [girls], (17) and female slaves, for I had put it under the ban for Ashtar-Chemosh. Taking from there the (18) accoutrements of Yahweh, I dragged them before Chemosh. Now the king of Israel had built (19) Jahaz [cf. Josh. 13:18] where he stayed when he fought against me, but Chemosh drove him out before me. (20) From Moab I took two hundred men, its very best, brought them against Jahaz and captured it, (21) in order to add it to Dibon. It was I who built Qericho, the wall of the two honeycombs [i.e., the two mounds honeycombed with cisterns (suggestion of F. V. Winnett); or forests?] and the wall of (22) the citadel; I who built its gates; I who built its towers; I (23) who built a palace; I who made the retaining walls of the reservoir [for the wa]ter[? or spring?] inside (24) the city. Since there was no cistern inside the city at Qericho, I said to all the people, "Each of you (25) make himself a cistern in his house!" It was I who cut the beams[?] for Qericho, using (26) Israelite captives; I who rebuilt Aroer [cf. Josh. 13:16]; I who made the highway in the Arnon [valley; cf. Num. 21:13]; (27) I who built Beth-bamoth [cf. Josh. 13:17?], because it was razed; I who rebuilt Bezer [cf. Josh. 20:8], because it was in ruins, (28) using fifty men of Dibon, since all Dibon is obedient to me. It was I who reigned (29) . . . in the cities which I added to the land; I who rebuilt (30) . . . [Mede]ba and Beth-diblathaim [cf. Jer. 48:22]. As for Beth-baal-meon [cf. Josh. 13:17], I brought there the fin[est (31) of the oxen and the best of] the sheep of the land. As for Horonaim [cf. Isa. 15:5], there settled in it . . . (32) . . . Chemosh said to me, "Go down, fight against Horonaim!" So I went down, [fought (33) against the city and captured it.] Chemosh [resto]red it in my time . . . (34) . . . .

Bibliography. G. A. Cooke, *A Text-Book of North-Semitic Inscriptions* (1903), pp. 1-14; R. Dussaud, *Les monuments palestiniens et judaïques* (1912), pp. 4-22. For the interpretation of line 12, cf. W. F. Albright, *BASOR*, no. 89 (1943), p. 16, note 55.

R. J. WILLIAMS

MOADIAH mō'ə dī'ə [מועדיה, Yahu promises] (Neh. 12:17). A priestly family of the time of Joiakim. *See* MAADIAH.

MOAT [חרוץ; Akkad. *ḫariṣu*] (Dan. 9:25); KJV WALL. A ditch or trench surrounding the walls of a fortress or city for purposes of protection; a detail of the rebuilt city of Jerusalem.

MOCHMUR mŏk'mər [Μοχμούρ] (Jth. 7:18). A brook SE of DOTHAIM. Possibly it is identical with Wadi Makhfuriyeh, S of Nablus. The OL reads *Machur;* the Vulg. omits the name. P. WINTER

MOCK. *See* SCOFFER.

MODEIN mō'dēn [Μωδεΐν=מודיעין, declarers]; KJV MODIN mō'dĭn. The home and burial place of the early Maccabean leaders (*see* HASMONEANS). In both late Jewish and early Christian sources, Modein is variously indicated as a village or a city. Certain rabbinic writings, and also Jerome's Vulg. throughout, name the place Mount Modein (*in monte Modin*). It is most probable that this nomenclature has local physiographic significance.

1. Location
2. History
3. The Hasmonean mausoleum
4. The man from Modein

Bibliography

1. Location. Modern Ras Medieh undoubtedly marks the site of the Hasmonean Modein. All available evidence—and there is a great deal of it—so demonstrates. Included are intertestamental descriptions of Modein-based battles, rabbinic and Talmudic specifications of distance from Jerusalem, nearness to Lydda emphasized in major Palestinian Onomastica, and the placement of Modein on the Medaba Map.

These miscellaneous data are doubly paralleled and confirmed by two sequences of evidence, linguistic and archaeological, in the form of place names and artifacts here localized and demonstrating habitation on the site. Such synchronized data are available for main periods from Hellenistic times on.

67. Area around Modein

Ras Medieh is a typical Palestinian tell in the midst of the Shephelah, standing some seven hundred feet high. It is located above the ancient Jerusalem-Jaffa road, almost equidistant between Lower Beth-horon and Lydda. The modern village of Medieh nestles at its base.

Fig. MOD 67.

2. History. Modein is most famed because here in 167 B.C. the aged priest Mattathias, a descendant of Hasmon, dramatically incited his fellow townsmen and his sons to revolt against the attempt of Antiochus IV Epiphanes to force religious and cultural Hellenization onto Jewish life in Palestine. The story of that revolt, narrated earlier in I Macc. 2:1-28, and retold by Josephus in Antiq. XII.vi.2, continues to be one of the great religio-national classics of Jewish literature. The immediate result, won in fairly brief time, was the firm establishment of Jewish liberty, religious and civil, achieved under Hasmonean leadership, and maintained within the framework of the "Second Jewish Commonwealth."

In this struggle Modein itself was repeatedly the field base for well-directed actions against invading armies (I Macc. 16:4-10; II Macc. 13:14-17). It served excellently for this purpose; for it was handily defensible, and it overlooked one of the main invasion routes into the Judean uplands.

In view of Jewish family customs, it was most natural for Modein to get lasting repute as the burial place of the heroic group of early Hasmonean leaders. Three times over, I Maccabees narrates—and Josephus reiterates—accounts of local burial and national mourning for Mattathias himself, and for one and another of his valiant sons (I Macc. 2:70; 9:18-21; 13:25-26; Jos. Antiq. XII.vi.4; XII.xi.2; XIII.vi.6).

3. The Hasmonean mausoleum. Simon "the Guide," who outlived his four brothers, erected a monumental family sepulchre at Modein, which was a pre-eminent memorial of that period. The descriptions of it in I Maccabees (13:27-30) and the Antiquities (XIII.211-12) are so vivid and detailed as to enable its reconstruction with considerable confidence. It was characterized by seven pyramids, memorializing the parents and their five sons. Colonnades with panoplies and ships' prows in the intercolumniations were also featured. Elements indigenous and Egyptian and Hellenistic were thus strikingly synthesized. It was a prototype for the sturdy Herodian memorials known from Jerusalem and elsewhere. *See* TOMB.

Apparently it was an astonishingly permanent structure. The Onomastica of Eusebius and of Jerome recorded familiarity with it in the fourth and the fifth centuries respectively. The current consensus is that it was constructed on the very summit of the Ras itself.

4. The man from Modein. It is all but forgotten that Modein made distinctive and personal contribution to the elaboration and summarization of normative Judaism. Rabbi Eleazar was the teacher, native to Modein, who did this. He was known simply as the Modiite (*ha-Modii*); and he was quoted with evident esteem in Aboth and Mishna and the Talmuds. The beginning and the ending of his teaching career were his association with Rabbi Gamaliel II, the Nasi at Jamnia, and his execution on the order of Bar Cocheba himself in 135, on a false suspicion of treason. His dictum quoted in Ab. 3.12 is accepted as a typical analysis of religious heresy from the viewpoint of rabbinic Judaism, of which he was a loyal and a skilful exponent.

Bibliography. I. Abrahams, "Modin," *Encyclopedia Biblica,* vol. III (1902), cols. 3180-82; C. Watzinger, Denkmäler Palästinas, II (1933), 22-23; F.-M. Abel, *Géographie,* III (1938), 391; S. Tedesche, *The First Book of Maccabees* (1950); I. Press, מודיעים, *Topographical-Historical Encyclopedia of Palestine,* III (1952), 557.

H. R. WILLOUGHBY

MOETH. Apoc. name of NOADIAH 1.

MOLADAH mŏl'ə də [מולדה, generation]. A city of Simeon in the S of Judah, not far from Beer-sheba

(Josh. 15:26; 19:2). The name indicates that it was a shrine whither women came to pray for children. Since one of the descendants of Jerahmeel bore the name Molid (I Chr. 2:29), it has been suggested that Moladah was a part of the Jerahmeelite settlement, which is known to have been in the S of Judah (I Sam. 27:10). In the postexilic period Moladah was one of the towns resettled by the returning Jews (Neh. 11:26). Later on, the Edomites occupied the region, and so it is probably the same as the fortified town of Malatha, where Herod Agrippa I, in retirement at the time of his disgrace, was dissuaded from suicide by his wife, Cypros (Jos. Antiq. XVIII.6.2). The site is unknown. S. COHEN

MOLDING [זר, wreath, border]; KJV CROWN. The decorative ledge of gold around the ark of the covenant (Exod. 25:11; 37:2), the table (25:24-25; 37:11-12), and the incense altar (30:3-4; 37:26-27). In form it was likely either a rope molding or a projecting flat surface with simple floral decoration. Judging by ridges on known stone altars from antiquity, its position was part way up on the side of the structure, although it may have been at or near the upper edge.

See ALTAR; ARK OF THE COVENANT; TABERNACLE.

L. E. TOOMBS

MOLDY; KJV MOULDY. The translation of נקדים in Josh. 9:5, 12 (only the plural form is used in the OT; CAKES in I Kings 14:3 [KJV CRACKNELS]).

MOLE [חפרפרה (Isa. 2:20, *emended text*), *possibly* digger, *from* חפר, to dig; KJV תנשמת (Lev. 11:30; RSV CHAMELEON)]. Any of several small insect-eating mammals of the family Talpidae, the true mole being of the genus Talpa. Both Tristram and Bodenheimer agree that the mole, like the shrew (Soricidae), has never been found in Palestine.

It is surmised that חפרפרה designates the great mole rat (*Spalax typhlus*). This animal, of molelike appearance, six to nine inches long, is a member of a small family of Old World rodents adapted to a purely subterranean life, whose little earth hills testify to its assiduous tunneling in search of bulbs and roots (cf. the postbiblical Hebrew אשות). With respect to Isa. 2:20 it must be observed that the mole-rat and the bat do not have the same habitat, though each moves in a world of darkness.

See also FAUNA § A2*hi*. W. S. MCCULLOUGH

MOLECH, MOLOCH mō'lĕk, —lŏk [*the deliberate misvocalization of the name of a pagan god, the consonants,* מלך, king, *being retained and the vowels of* בשת, shame, *used; cf.* ASHTORETH]. A deity to whom human sacrifice was made, particularly in the Valley of Hinnom, which bounds Jerusalem on the SW (II Kings 23:10; Jer. 32:35), at a site known as Topheth, which probably means "firepit" as in Syriac. The deity is associated with Ammon in I Kings 11:7, and is here identical with MILCOM, the national god of Ammon. This is not the proper name of the deity, but a title—"the king"—as is suggested probably in the oracles against Ammon in Amos 1:15; Jer. 49:1, 3, which read "their king," rendered "Milcom" by the LXX. Jer. 49:3 mentions "his priests and his princes" in parallelism with "their king" (RSV "Milcom"), so that it is beyond doubt that "king" here is the title of the god. The LXX generally bears this view out in Lev. 18:21; 20:2-5 (*see below*); Jer. 32:35. The form "Moloch," used by the LXX here and in II Kings 23:10, is interesting in view of the discovery by G. Dossin of a god Muluk in the tablets from Mari on the mid-Euphrates (date *ca.* 1700 B.C.). This is an abstract form, a verbal noun, and may be rendered "kingship." In spite of the LXX "Moloch," however, which is actually used only twice, it seems more likely that the god of the Ammonites was named by his title "the king"—Malik with the final afformative *m,* which is used with the force of a definite article.

Eissfeldt thinks that in the phrase "to sacrifice, or pass a child through the fire למלך," the last word means, not "to Molech," but "as a votive offering." This view is based on the significance of the phrase in Punic inscriptions *ca.* 400-150 B.C., the vocalization of מלך being known from the Latin of bilingual inscriptions as *molc,* denoting a sacrifice made to confirm or acquit a vow. In view of this evidence the significance of למלך in the stereotyped phrase cited *above,* as in Lev. 18:21; 20:3-5; II Kings 23:10; Jer. 32:35, must remain an open question. In I Kings 11:7, however, "Molech" is visualized definitely as the national god of Ammon.

From Jephthah's reply to the Ammonites (Judg. 11:24) it is apparent that the national god of Ammon was identical with CHEMOSH, the national god of Moab. From the compound divine name Athtar-Chemosh, by which the national god of Moab is named in the inscription of Mesha, it appears that the proper name of the god was Athtar—both Chemosh and Milcom being his local titles. Athtar is well known in Arabian mythology as the Venus Star. From the Ras Shamra texts we see that the morning and evening star might be thought of as twins, SHAHAR and SHALEM. From the name of the city we may reasonably infer that the cult of Shalem, and conceivably also of his twin Shahar, was practiced at Jerusalem in pre-Israelite times, so that when Solomon built high places for Chemosh of Moab and Molech of Ammon, probably on the Mount of Olives, he was establishing local varieties of a cult already practiced at Jerusalem.

Apart from general references to Molech in Jer. 49:1, 3, and perhaps Amos 1:15, or to his cult in I Kings 11:7, 33; Zeph. 1:5, the rest of the references to Molech are associated with human sacrifice (Lev. 20:2-5), specifically by making one's children pass through the fire (Lev. 18:21; II Kings 23:10; Jer. 32:35). There Molech is not associated with Ammon, and the view of Eissfeldt (*see above*) is feasible.

Human sacrifice in Israel is first explicitly attested under Ahaz in Judah (II Kings 16:3) and in Israel under Hoshea (II Kings 17:17); and, though Molech is not named, the parallel passage in II Chr. 28:3 adds that the scene of this abomination was the Valley of the Son of Hinnom, specifically Tophet, which is associated with Molech in Jer. 32:35. Apart from the sacrifice of the son of Mesha of Moab (II Kings 3:27), which would naturally be made to Chemosh, the national god of Moab, whom we have identified with Molech, human sacrifice was made by the Assyrian military colonists in Samaria after 722 B.C. Here the gods so honored are given as Adrammelech and Anammelech. The first of these may have been Molech, actually Malik—Adrammelech means "the lordship of the King"—and Anammelech may be a case of the syncretism of the local god Molech and Anu, the supreme sky-god of Mesopotamian religion.

In spite of the reformation of Hezekiah, which does not mention the cult of Molech, this cult survived until the time of Josiah, when Zephaniah condemned it (Zeph. 1:5). This passage, associating the worship of Milcom ("their king") with the cult of the host of heaven, supports our contention that Molech was primarily an astral deity. In the account of Josiah's reformation the scene of human sacrifices, Tophet in the Valley of Hinnom, was desecrated (II Kings 23:10), and the sanctuaries of Milcom and Chemosh (the Ammonite and Moabite manifestations of the god Athtar), which had survived from the time of Solomon, were destroyed.

Bibliography. O. Eissfeldt, *Molk als Opferbegriff im Punischen und Hebräischen und das Ende des Gottes Moloch* (1935); J. Gray, "The Desert God Aṯtr in the Literature and Religion of Canaan," *JNES*, VIII (1949), 72-83; W. F. Albright, *Archaeology and the Religion of Israel* (1953), pp. 162-64.

J. GRAY

MOLI. KJV Apoc. form of MAHLI.

MOLID mō'lĭd [מוליד] (I Chr. 2:29). A descendant of Judah; the son of Abishur and his wife Abihail.

MOLOCH. *See* MOLECH.

MOLTEN IMAGE [מסכה, נסיך, נסך, *all from* נסך, to cast, to pour]. The appearance of these words in the OT reflects the common practice among ancient peoples of making representations of deity for use in worship (*see* IDOL; GRAVEN IMAGE). Molten images were made by pouring molten gold, silver, iron, or bronze over a prepared form or into a mold (Lev. 19:4; Deut. 27:15; Isa. 40:18-20). The prohibition of IDOLATRY in the Ten Commandments implies that Israelites were exposed to this practice. Small bronze images of Baal or Resheph or other deities have been found in the excavations, on occasion overlaid with gold. Silver and gold figurines are also known, as well as cast bronze animal figurines. Although no representations of Yahweh have been found, instances of the use of molten and other types of images or cult objects in Israel are attested by the stories of the golden calf (Exod. 32; *see* CALF, GOLDEN) and Micah's idols (Judg. 17–18), and by prophetic denunciations (e.g., Isa. 30:22; 40:19; Hos. 13:2). It is also possible that some Israelites made use of Canaanite images in their worship of Yahweh.

Bibliography. H. G. May, *Material Remains of the Megiddo Cult* (1935), pp. 33-34, plate XXXIV; A. G. Barrois, *Manuel d'Archéologie Biblique,* II (1953), 389-98; G. E. Wright, *Biblical Archaeology* (1957), pp. 115-18.

G. B. COOKE

MOLTEN SEA. *See* SEA, MOLTEN.

MOMDIS mŏm'dĭs. KJV Apoc. form of MAADAI.

MOMENT. *See* TIME § 1*a*.

MONEY BOX [γλωσσόκομον] (John 12:6; 13:29); KJV BAG. A small receptacle. The term is used in reference to the apostles' receptacle for their funds.

MONEY, COINS. Movable objects which are generally accepted as means of barter or evalution. The modern conception of money developed:

a) from barter—i.e., exchange of superfluous objects for desirable ones or delivering of objects of daily use or products for duties, taxes, or tributes;

b) from exchange of metal (gold, silver, copper, iron) for desirable objects or payment of duties;

c) from the use of minted metal of fixed weight and purity as means of exchange or payment.

Although this development took place chronologically, the several phases existed also simultaneously, so that, e.g., we find pure barter at periods when minted money was long in use.

The accounts of the Bible on money transactions are best understood if we keep in mind these three phases of development, as in the following discussion.

1. Barter
2. Exchange of metal for objects or duties
3. Use of minted metal
   a. In the OT period
   b. In the intertestamental period
   c. In the NT period
4. Jewish numismatics
5. Illustrations

Bibliography

1. Barter. The primitive economy sufficed on its own products, but a steady growth of the community soon multiplied its demands. The peculiarities of the geographical situation and the specialization of the handicraft eventually made a mutual exchange of products necessary. Barter was therefore generally practiced. The most important movable possession of the primitive man—his cattle—became the accepted means of evaluation. This is proved by the Latin word for "money," *pecuna* (*pecus*="cattle"), and the Hebrew מקנה (*miqnê*), which stands for "cattle" (Gen. 13:2; 31:18; etc.) or "purchase" (17:12-13; 23:18). Smaller objects suitable for barter were sheep, asses, goats, but also corn, oil, and wine. The religious practice of the period, which made cattle the most important offering to the gods, also weighed heavily in favor of making animals the most common currency of barter. The great herds which thus accumulated at the holy places could not be consumed by the priests but were traded for other goods. Thus the temples became the oldest places of commerce, the celebration of offerings the first fairs.

The Bible gives us many examples of barter at this period. King Solomon paid Hiram with wheat and olive oil for his help with the erection of the temple (I Kings 5:11). The tribute of King Mesha of Moab consisted of lambs and rams (II Kings 3:4). The Israelites were taxed for the court of the king with grain, wine (I Sam. 8:15), wheat, barley, oil, sheep (Ezek. 45:13-16).

2. Exchange of metal for objects or duties. Exchanging objects (cattle, wheat, etc.) proved unsatisfactory because of their fluctuating value and because of their inconvenient size. As civilization grew to be more and more based on metals, metals became dominant as fixed and easily transportable means of evaluation. Everybody needed copper, the most important material for the manufacturing of weapons and of agricultural implements which were much more durable and therefore more economical than stone implements. A man who had copper had no difficulty whatsoever in trading it for whatever he wanted. Silver and gold were used for larger transactions. Abimelech gave to Abraham "a thousand (pieces of) silver" (Gen. 20:16). The Midianites paid for Joseph "twenty (shekels of) silver" (37:28). Micah gave to his mother "eleven hundred (pieces of) silver" (Judg. 17:2). Here the translator has added "pieces" or "shekels." The original has only כסף (*keseph*), "silver." This must have meant pieces of silver of now unknown weight.

The estimation of the value by eye was likely to be uncertain. Therefore, uniformly shaped pieces of metal were molded in the form of ingots, bars, tongues, heads of animals, or bracelets. The bracelets could be worn as ornaments. So the spoil of the Midianites (Num. 31:50) consisted of "articles of gold, armlets and bracelets, signet rings, earrings, and beads," objects which were not only of ornamental use but also convenient articles of barter. This practice persists today among primitives who use strings of coins as adornment or wear their property in the form of gold bracelets and other valuable and tradable finery. The forms of these pieces of metal were probably normed and represented an accepted value (or weight), so that buying and selling could be accomplished with their help. Achan reported to Joshua that among the spoil of Jericho was a "bar of gold" (Hebrew "tongue of gold"; Josh. 7:21). The servant of Abraham gave Rebekah "a gold ring weighing a half shekel, and two bracelets for her arms weighing ten gold shekels" (Gen. 24:22). The children of Jacob purchased corn in Egypt with annular currency. Their money is described as "bundles of money"—i.e., it could be gathered together and bound with strings (42:35; *see* Weights and Measures § B1). We read in Deut. 14:25 of the money which was intended for the sanctuary: "Bind up the money in your hand, and go to the place." This tying up is understandable only if this currency had the form of rings. Each of the brethren and sisters of Job gave him a "ring of gold." These rings represented money, since otherwise not everyone would have given him the same present (Job 42:11). At Gezer two pieces of gold in the forms of a circle and a tongue were excavated, the only examples yet found (*see* No. 1 in § 5 *below*). This scarcity is explainable because gold and silver were rare in these periods, and because the gold was subject to continuous remelting into more contemporary forms till it was at last struck into coins.

But even these shaped and perhaps normed pieces of metal were no reliable means of evaluation. They could be assured only after ascertaining their exact weight. The weighing system of the Bible was taken over from the Sumero-Babylonian method (*see* Weights and Measures § B2). It is based on the shekel, which at first meant the object to be weighed, but later was used in the sense of "balance" or "weight." The weight of the shekel was *ca.* 11.5 grams silver (*ca.* .4 ounce). Silver was much more common than gold, and became therefore the real medium of evaluation. Thus the Hebrew word for "silver" (כסף, *keseph*) later meant plainly "money" (as *argentum* in Latin and *argent* in French). The necessary amount of silver was weighed in front of the dealer. Therefore, it is said of the purchase of the Machpelah cave by Abraham: "Abraham weighed out for Ephron the silver . . . , four hundred shekels of silver, according to the weights current among the merchants" (Gen. 23:16). Jeremiah bought in Anathoth the field of his uncle's son and "weighed out the money to him, seventeen shekels of silver" (Jer. 32:9).

The value of the shekel cannot be calculated simply by summing up the amount of silver and comparing it with modern silver prices. Such a calculation would give an entirely misleading picture, because we would equal the purchasing power of today with that of biblical times, which was quite different. Our only reliable help is the biblical account itself. It was possible then to buy a ram for 2 shekels (*ca.* 23 grams of silver; Lev. 5:15), a homer of barley (*ca.* 370 liters or 11 bushels; or, by the reckoning suggested in Weights and Measures § C4*a*, 134 liters or 3.8 bushels) for 50 shekels (Lev. 27:16), or a measure (סאה, *seah; ca.* 12:5 liters or *ca.* 1.5 pecks; *see* Weights and Measures § C4*f*) of fine meal for a shekel, or two measures of barley (*ca.* 25 liters or 3 pecks) for a shekel (II Kings 7:16). Though the weight of the shekel differed during various periods, it is possible to guess approximately which quantities of silver passed from hand to hand in the described transactions. We will not be far wrong if we assume that a shekel had 11.5 grams of silver, a mina (50 shekels) 575 grams, and a talent (60 minas) 3,450 grams. *See* Weights and Measures §§ B2, 4*g*.

The continual weighing and examination of the purity of the metal took up much time and naturally enticed cheating. The weights consisted mostly of pieces of bronze or iron or dressed stones which never had been gauged. So the Bible warns: "You shall not have in your bag two kinds of weights [Hebrew 'a stone and a stone'], a large and a small . . . . A full and just weight [Hebrew 'stone'] you shall have" (Deut. 25:13, 15).

> A false balance is an abomination to the Lord,
> but a just weight [Hebrew "stone"] is his delight
> (Prov. 11:1; cf. 20:10).

Also, Amos (8:5) mentions tricks used in weighing.

In order to find a remedy, the authorities (kings) gauged and stamped the weights, which were then declared sacred:

> A just balance and scales are the Lord's;
> all the weights in the bag are his work
> (Prov. 16:11).

The next logical step was to stamp directly on the tongues, bars, or bracelets to be bargained with, in order to guarantee their right value, as stamps or seals are used on documents to guarantee their genuineness.

3. Use of minted metal. The further development was a piece of metal whose weight and purity were ascertained by a stamp—i.e., a coin. This was a tremendous success. Now it was no longer necessary to examine the purity of the metal and the accuracy of the weight, although fraud was still possible. We know of great numbers of antique coins which were forged, struck from inferior metal, and were coated with silver. Frequently antique coins display a deep cut by a sharp instrument which shows that somebody wanted to investigate if the metal was real silver. Furthermore, the edges of the coins were not marked in antiquity—this is an invention of the eighteenth century A.D.—so that it was easy to cut off parts. As protection against this practice, one had to weigh the coins again in order to get full value.

a. In the OT period. The ingenious invention of coins, which has not been superseded—either in the shape or in the character of the coins—does not go back farther than the seventh century B.C. It is assumed that it took place simultaneously in Aegina in Greece and in Lydia in Asia Minor. We know, therefore, that the Israelites could not have become acquainted with the first coins before the Babylonian exile. When the Bible refers to money in an earlier period, it must be understood as bars, ingots, bracelets, etc., stamped or unstamped, from one of the phases of the preliminary development.

In the Bible the first money is mentioned in Ezra 2:69. When returning from the Exile, the Jews donated for the erection of the temple "sixty-one thousand darics of gold, five thousand mines of silver." Today the explanation is generally accepted that "darics" (דרכמונים, *dark^e^mônîm*) meant the Persian gold coin *dareikos*. This name is derived from King Darius I (521-486 B.C.). These coins are of pure gold (8.424 grams) and illustrate a very early phase of coinage. They are oval and have only a deep incuse of varying form on the reverse (*see* No. 2 in § 5 *below*). Nevertheless, the account of Ezra makes clear that the greatest part of the offerings was uncoined silver and gold. This shows that at this period (sixth century B.C.) still not enough coins were current, and the demand was covered only partially. Likewise we read that Ezra carried with him for the temple "twenty bowls of gold worth a thousand darics" (Ezra 8:27). Darics are similarly mentioned in Neh. 7:70-72. The fact that these gold coins were already called darics at the time of King Cyrus (550-530 B.C.)—i.e., well before the reign of King Darius, who presumably gave them this name, leads to the assumption that this term is probably of a much earlier date. We find an explanation in an older Assyrian denomination (*see* DARIC), but most probably the term "daric" is best accounted for when we assume that the author of the book Ezra, who lived in the fifth century B.C., habitually called every current gold coin "daric," and therefore also used this name for the coins which Ezra brought with him. The same interpretation is indicated for the mentioning of darics at the time of King David (I Chr. 29:7).

It is probable that the mint for these darics was at first in Sardis and was taken over by the Persians after the conquest, because only at that time were the experience and skilled craftsmen available.

On the other hand, it seems that, at least in the W part of the Persian Empire, the Greek silver coinage was most current. The oldest Greek coin was found in an excavation in Shechem in 1956, dated from the sixth century B.C. and originating from N Greece. More current were the tetradrachmas of Athens in the fifth century B.C. The intensive trade connection between Greece and Asia Minor and the Phoenician towns in the N of Palestine made these coins an international currency. This also explains their frequent discovery at excavations in Palestine (*see* No. 3 in § 5 *below*). The Athenian tetradrachma was far more developed, having both obverse and reverse dies, while the darics have only obverse dies.

Courtesy of the Trustees of the British Museum

68. Coin with inscription YHD (*Yehud,* Judah) in the British Museum (from Gaza? fourth century B.C.)

It is proved that there was a local mint already in the Persian province יהד (*Y^e^hûdh*)—i.e., Jehud—in the fourth century B.C. From Ezra 5:1, 8; 7:14; Dan. 2:25; 5:13 it is ascertained that *Y^e^hûdh* was the official name for Judea (*see* Nos. 4-5 in § 5 *below*). It is clearly to be observed that these coins are conceived in pure Greek style, and that No. 4 is an imitation of the tetradrachma of Athens. All show the inscription "יהד." As they are of silver, they must have been issued with permission of the Persian commanding officer or satrap. Only a few specimens are known to exist, which indicates that they were struck in small numbers or during a short period. Fig. MON 68.

After Alexander's conquest of the Persian Empire the unified coinage of the new empire was valid for Palestine. The current coins were the gold stater and the silver tetradrachma (*see* No. 6 in § 5 *below*). The nearest mints were Acre and Sidon. But the great traffic in the unified world, together with the many movements of troops, brought tetradrachmas from various mints into the country. The Bible does not provide any clues for this period; consequently these coins are not mentioned. But it is proved by excavations and finds in Palestine that the above currency and the following coins of the Ptolemies were circulating abundantly.

The Ptolemies, the heirs of Alexander, added more mints (Gaza, Jaffa, Tyre), but the style of the coin type did not change much. *See* No. 7 in § 5 *below.*

b. In the intertestamental period. The control of the Ptolemies over Judea expired in 198 B.C., when they were overrun by the Seleucids (*see* No. 8 in § 5 *below*).* The books of the Maccabees describe how the latter tried to suppress the ancient religion of the Jews in the attempt to force Hellenism upon them. In 167 B.C. the Maccabees led their people in the revolt against this suppression. After much trouble, victories, and defeats they forced the Seleucids into granting them some sort of independence. In 139 B.C., when Antiochus VII (Euergetes) started to fight against the usurper Trypho for the supremacy of the Seleucid Empire, he tried to win over Simon the Maccabee as an ally, and wrote him a letter offering him his friendship and guaranteeing him the independence of his country. He bestowed on him the right of coinage: "I permit you to mint your own coinage as money for your country" (I Macc. 15:6). But after the consolidation of his reign, following the successful war against his rival, he rejected the Jewish auxiliary troops which were sent to him (138 B.C.), canceled all former promises, and forced Simon to pay tribute. This quick change from an independent state to one subject to tribute did not allow for sufficient time to start issuing coins. When in 135 B.C. John Hyrcanus followed his father as ruler, Antiochus brought the rest of the autonomy to an end. He conquered Jerusalem and forced him into complete subjugation (134 B.C.). In 132/31 Antiochus struck his own coins in Jerusalem which bore his name and confirmed his rule. *See* No. 9 in § 5 *below*. Fig. SEL 37.

The fight of the descendants of Antiochus after his death in 129 B.C. weakened the power of the Seleucids to such a degree that John Hyrcanus declared his independence simultaneously with others. As a sign of his sovereignty he started to mint his own coins with the inscription: "Johanan the high priest and the community [*ḥebher*] of the Jews" (*ca.* 111/10 B.C.). These are the first real Jewish coins, and all assumptions of a probable previous coinage ascribed to Simon the Maccabee must be disregarded.

John Hyrcanus I accomplished what Simon could not do. He had sufficient time on his hands, and he certainly needed it, because neither a mint nor skilled craftsmen were available. It is even unlikely that there existed skilled Jewish diesinkers in other Gentile mints. The Second Commandment: "You shall not make yourself a graven image" (Exod. 20:4), did not allow a Jew to engrave the head of the king or the emperor, which was an indispensable part of the obverse of ancient coins. Thus, on account of lack of experience, the first Jewish coins could only be extremely modest, quite unlike the coins of the contemporary Eastern world, which, guided by experienced Greek artists, could look back on hundreds of years of tradition. The obverse of these first Jewish coins displayed inside a wreath the inscription mentioned above. For the lettering the ancient Jewish script was chosen. The Dead Sea Scrolls indicate more use of this Paleo-Hebrew script than has been formerly supposed. To the Jews it probably seemed the best suitable script for coins, in part because it was well known to them from the Sidonian and Tyrian currency. From now on it remained traditionally in use on all later Jewish issues, with the exception of the coins of the Herodian rulers. The title of high priest for John Hyrcanus I does not seem strange if we consider that the Jewish state in the postexilic period was a hierarchy with the high priest as its leader. The Maccabees as princes had also the hereditary title of high priest. For the reverse of the coins a double "horn of abundance" (cornucopia) and a poppy head were chosen, both symbols of plenty and fertility, originating in Greek myths and frequently employed on Seleucid coins. Here it should signify the prosperity of the reign of John Hyrcanus I. It shows that the concept of the first Jewish coinage leaned heavily on the contemporary currency, although the design was deviating intentionally from all known types. *See* No. 10 in § 5.

The denomination of this and the following coins is to be understood as the second smallest unit (פרוטה, *p*e*rûṭâ;* διλεπτον). In the meantime the Seleucids continued to mint silver coinage, which was struck by the Phoenician cities at their order. This money was the recognized currency in Palestine. To issue silver coins was the acknowledged and sole privilege of full autonomy. If the Maccabees had started to strike silver of their own, it might have been interpreted as an open revolt, which could have led to an unnecessary complication of the involved situation.

John Hyrcanus I started striking his own coins only in 111/110 B.C. The coins of his son and successor Judas Aristobulus (106/105 B.C.) are few, consonant with his short-lived rule. The coin type remains the same. The inscription reads: "Jehuda, the high priest and the community [*ḥebher*] of the Jews." After his untimely death his brother Alexander Janneus (105-78 B.C.) took over the reign and the office as a high priest. This pugnacious and active Maccabee enlarged the boundaries of the country in the course of victories and defeats, and used for the first time the title "king" on his coinage. There are essentially three types of coins. No. 10 (§ 5 *below*), which has "Jonathan" in the place of "Johanan," continues the tradition of the very first coin type. No. 11 is certainly an imitation of the coin of Antiochus VII (*cf.* No. 9) minted in Jerusalem. There exists an old controversy whether the design on the obverse of No. 12 should be interpreted as a star or a wheel (sun-wheel), but recently it has been assumed that it should be understood as a star. None of the contemporary coins displays a star of this peculiar form, so that it remains guesswork where this symbol comes from and what allegorical significance it has. It is believed that the anchor was chosen by Alexander Janneus as his special symbol because he added several harbors (Raphia, Jaffa, Dora) to his kingdom. The Greek inscription on his anchor coins indicates that it was intended to circulate among his non-Jewish subjects and his neighbors. His successor, John Hyrcanus II (67 and 63-40 B.C.), was a weak man, who continually fought with his brother for the rulership. He was forced by his brother Aristobulus II to abdicate, and was restored again by Pompeius, but only as a high priest. The sons of Aristobulus contended with him for this office, too, till he lost his importance entirely when Julius Caesar in 47 B.C. appointed Herod as procurator of Judea. There is a dispute as to which coins were issued by John Hyrcanus I and which by John Hyrcanus II, as both have struck coins identical in type and in legend as well. The last of the Maccabees, Antigonus (Mattathias; 40-37 B.C.), fought desperately for his throne. Immediately after he conquered Jerusalem with the help of the Parthians, he demonstrated his new power with his own coinage. As a consequence of this hurry, all these coins are carelessly minted; the alloy contains much lead, and they are therefore badly preserved. His most remarkable coin is the one showing the seven-branched lampstand. This is the very first representation of the sacred lampstand from the temple, which is known to us from its classical depiction on the arch of Titus in Rome (*see* No. 13 in § 5 *below*). Most of his other coins are repetitions of the issues of his predecessors (wreath with inscription and cornucopias). *See* No. 14 in § 5 *below*.

All these coins, except No. 12*a*, are to be regarded as dileptons (in the NT, κοδράντης; in Hebrew, פרוטה, *perûṭâ*).

c. In the NT period. Herod I (36-4 B.C.) was appointed king in Judea by the Romans. With him we enter the period of the NT. His whole nature was Hellenistic. He founded towns in Greek style, sponsored the building of Gentile temples and prize fights in the Roman manner. But this did not prevent him from considering the feeling of his Jewish subjects when minting coins. These either showed the old symbols (anchor, cornucopias) or, in case of new designs, did at least not offend the population. His rebuilding of the temple in Jerusalem is largely regarded as an attempt to acquire the sympathy of the Jews. But each impulse of good will thus created was forfeited again by his unsurpassed cruelty, which did not stop at his own family. His coins are the first Jewish coins bearing dates (*see* Nos. 15-17 in § 5 *below*). The inscription is Greek only. The symbols of Nos. 15-16 are intentionally derived from Greek models. On No. 17 the symbols are the same as on coins of John Hyrcanus, Alexander Janneus, and Aristobulus.

Archelaus (4 B.C.-A.D. 6), son of Herod I, was confirmed by Augustus as ethnarch for Judea, Samaria, and Idumea only. The title "king," therefore, does not appear on his coins. He, too, considered the feelings of his Jewish subjects when he issued new coins, and kept to neutral symbols (*see* Nos. 18-19 in § 5 *below*). He competed in cruelty with his father. When Joseph "heard that Archelaus reigned over Judea in place of his father Herod, he was afraid" (Matt. 2: 22). Augustus exiled him after ten years of cruel reign, on account of the general discontent. The government of the land was then taken over by Roman procurators.

His brother Herod Antipas (4 B.C.-A.D. 39) became tetrarch of Galilee and Perea. In atrocity, despotism, and treachery he equaled his father. Jesus compared him to a fox (Luke 13:32). He put to death John the Baptist (Matt. 14:3-12; Mark 6:17-29; Luke 9:9). Jesus was sent to him by Pilate for examination. In A.D. 18 Herod Antipas founded Tiberias in honor of the Emperor Tiberius, made it his capital, and chose it as his mint (*see* No. 20 in § 5 *below*). Caligula finally sent him into exile.

Philip (4 B.C.-A.D. 34) was the last son of Herod and tetrarch of Trachonitis, Paneas, etc., an essentially non-Jewish region. He was the first ruler who dared to set aside the commandment: "You shall not make yourself a graven image," which had been strictly adhered to till then, and he endeavored to put the head of the Roman emperor on his coins (*see* No. 21 in § 5 *below*). As all of them probably were minted in Paneas, we may assume that the building on the reverse is the temple his father had built there in honor of Augustus (Luke 3:1).

Herod Agrippa I (37-44), with the help of the Emperor Caius Caligula, unified the small districts which were ruled by his predecessors, so that he could call himself on his coins "great king, friend of Caesar." He was the first to put his own portrait on his coins. An unsolved numismatic problem remains (*see* No. 22 in § 5 *below*). Till recently the object on the obverse had been explained as an umbrella, a mark of distinction of an oriental ruler. But numismatic scholars did not accept this interpretation wholeheartedly. No other coin with an umbrella design was elsewhere known. Other theories and interpretations were developed, none of which gave a satisfactory explanation. The three ears of corn on the reverse of the coin signify plenty and wealth. The Bible reports about Herod Agrippa that "he killed James the brother of John with the sword" (Acts 12:1-4). He also put Peter in prison. One of his coins (No. 23 in § 5 *below*) was minted in Caesarea in connection with the great prize fights during which he suddenly fell ill and died (vss. 21-23).

Herod Agrippa II (50-100) was the last ruling descendant of the house of Herod. The greatest part of his provinces consisted of non-Jewish districts. Neither his regency nor his coins show any connection with the Bible.

During the reign of the Idumean princes part after part of the real power was taken over by Rome. The first procurator who ruled from Caesarea was sent by Augustus in the year 6, right after Archelaus was exiled. These procurators were continually changed by the emperors. According to imperial orders they minted copper coins, which remained the small currency of the country till 58/59. Their issue was interrupted only during the reign of Agrippa I. These coins are found in abundance in Palestine. All the procurators conformed with the tradition introduced by the Maccabees and refrained from issuing designs or coin types which might have offended Jewish feelings—i.e., portraits or figures of gods. So their issues differed completely from the customary Roman coinage. They show symbols of the country (palms, vine leaves), or products of the country in the form of containers of wine or oil or cornucopias, which stand for plenty and wealth. They were inscribed with the name or the title of Caesar and with the year of his reign. The denomination equaled the Roman quadrans or the Greek dilepton, forming the small currency during the time of the NT. *See* Nos. 24-26 in § 5 *below*.

Two coins which were struck by Pontius Pilate differ from the other issues. The first shows a simplum (ladle) and the second a lituus (curved staff or wand). Both these objects were well-known emblems of Roman priests. Pontius Pilate had been an augur himself before he took over the reign of Judea, and Tiberius was a great disciple of the augurian trend. It was thought that Pilate chose these symbols in honor of Tiberius, as well as for a sign of his own dignity; but this interpretation, which was accepted until now, seems to be no longer valid. Recent coin finds show a date which points unmistakably to the predecessor of Pontius Pilate, Valerius Gratus, which proves that Pontius Pilate did not create this coin type himself, but only took it over. *See* Nos. 27-28 in § 5 *below*.

In the NT we find many different coin names. It would be interesting to establish which sort of money went through the hands of Jesus and his disciples. This seems not too difficult a task, considering that the coins of this period are all well known to us, but nevertheless there arise some difficulties:

a) In the first century A.D. various coins were current in the country. In addition to the procurators, the cities of Caesarea and Ascalon minted bronze, and the coins of the Phoenician cities (mostly Tyre and Sidon) were brought through the trade routes. Additionally, Roman copper and silver coins flooded the country through troop movements and commerce; and further, there was the imperial coinage of this region, which was minted in Antiochia. Accordingly, we meet with bronze coins from various parts of the Empire and silver coins from Rome, Antiochia, Tyre, Alexandria, and Caesarea in Cappadocia.

b) We do not know the denomination of the bronze coins because it is indicated on none of them, and we must be careful in drawing conclusions from their size and weight, as these were not constant.

c) The translator of the Greek text (especially of the KJV) rendered the problem still more difficult, inasmuch as he used the same word for different Greek designations. Further, in order to make comparisons possible for the reader, he tried to substitute modern specifications ("penny," "farthing," "mite") for the ancient coin names, so that we are forced to go back to the original.

Notwithstanding these difficulties, we know in many of the cases to which coin the Bible is referring. The most frequently mentioned coin is the denarius (δηνάριον), which is translated "penny" in the KJV. It was the most current silver coin in the first century and was mainly minted in Rome under the supervision of the emperor. In the East the right of coinage was given only to Antiochia and Caesarea in Cappadocia. The denarius was used to pay the troops and quickly superseded all Greek silver coins of the same value. One denarius was the daily wage of a laborer (Matt. 20:9-10, 13), and it was used to pay tribute to the emperor. When it was suggested that Jesus had enticed the people to withhold these taxes, he asked for the money which was used to pay tribute. They brought him a denar, and he pointed out the portrait and the name of the emperor and retorted: "Render therefore to Caesar the things that are Caesar's" (Matt. 22:21), and explained that money that belongs to the emperor should be given to him (*see* No. 29 in § 5 *below*). This "civil tribute" (Matt. 22:19: τὸ νόμισμα τοῦ κῆνσου, "money for the tax," KJV "tribute money"; Mark 12:14: κῆνσος, "taxes," KJV "tribute"; Luke 20:22; 23:2: φόρος, "tribute") was the duty the Jews had to deliver to Rome after Judea lost its independence (after A.D. 70). Subsequent to the destruction of the temple by Vespasian, all Jews under Roman rule had to pay two drachmas per head to the temple of Jupiter Capitolinus. This tribute was abolished by Nerva but reinstalled by Hadrian after the suppression of the War of Bar Cocheba. This tax consisted purposely of the same sum each Jew had formerly been bound to pay as annual sacred tribute (Matt. 17:24: τὰ δίδραχμα, "half-shekel," KJV "tribute money") to his own temple. This duty had been—according to Exod. 30:13, 16; 38:26—half a shekel or two drachmas, which are approximately two denars. In the Roman period the shekel or didrachma was no longer current, so that the payment was in denars.

Matt. 26:15 refers to another sort of silver coin, where it is said that the high priest paid to Judas Iscariot thirty pieces of silver (ἀργύρια) for the betrayal of the Lord. According to Exod. 21:32, thirty shekels were the compensation which had to be paid for a servant who was accidentally slain (cf. Matt. 27:6: "blood money," KJV "price of blood"). This parallel leads to the assumption that the coins paid to Judas were thirty shekels which were coined in Tyre, or their equivalent—thirty tetradrachmas of Antiochia. Nos. 30-31 in § 5 *below* show specimens of the coins which must have been in Judas' hands.

In Matt. 28:12 we meet with the expression "a sum of money" (KJV "large money"), with which the guards of the holy sepulchre were bribed. Small money was the regular denar. With "large money" they must have had in mind shekels or tetradrachmas, the only large silver coins in circulation.

In Mark 12:42 a small coin is mentioned which is called in the KJV "mite." The poor widow cast in the treasury "two mites, which make a farthing" (RSV "two copper coins, which make a penny"). For better understanding the translator used here the names of small contemporary copper coins. The original reads: λέπτον and κοδράντης. The λέπτον corresponds to the smallest Greek copper coin, whereas κοδράντης is the Greek name for the smallest Roman copper coin: quadrans (=two leptons or a dilepton). We have therefore to regard the regular copper coins depicted in Nos. 10-12, 17-19, 22, 24-28 (§ 5 *below*), as dilepton (Hebrew *perûṭâ*) with a weight of *ca.* 1.5-3.0 grams. Different from them in weight and size and sometimes also in careless execution was the lepton (the mite), which was the smallest denomination (a half quadrans, a half *perûṭâ;* No. 12*a*), weight *ca.* 0.5-1.0 gram. Such a lepton was the gift of the widow. The smallness of this donation was especially pointed out by Jesus.

4. Jewish numismatics. For the treasury of the temple only Jewish coins were fit to be donated—i.e., coins with symbols which did not offend the religious feelings of the Jews. This means that only coins of Hyrcanus, Alexander, Janneus, Herod, and the procurators, as mentioned before, could be used, all of them of copper. It can be assumed that this currency was still circulating at that period or could at least be obtained from the money-changers in the temple. But we must conclude from the presence of coined silver in the temple treasury that it must have been necessary to depart from the rules of the law, because there was no current money which fulfilled its strict conditions. We know that Tyrian shekels were preferably accepted (*see* No. 31 in § 5 *below*), not because the image of the god Heracles-Melqart was less offensive to the law than the portraits of other gods or rulers, but because experience had shown that these coins had the best content of silver.

It was the praxis of the Roman emperors to shift the procurators in Palestine after some years, so that they could not enrich themselves excessively during their government. But with each new official came a new extortioner. The last of them was Gessius Florus (64-66), who was offendingly unscrupulous in his ways of extracting money from the unhappy population. If extortion did not work, he used robbery. He stirred the controversy between Greeks and Jews in order to get more bribes. But when his officials were impudent enough to demand a great sum out of the temple treasury, even the quietest citizen could not be restrained any more, and an open revolt broke out. After some preliminary victories over the few Roman troops, the latter retreated and the greatest part of the country was liberated from its tormentors. Now the Jews believed that the hour of freedom of Zion had finally come, and they set up their own government. As one of the manifestations of independence they issued their own money, and this time they struck silver. In the Roman Empire this was the exclusive privilege of the emperor, and to infringe upon it was a challenge to the entire Roman authority. The minting of silver shekels in the first war of independence has therefore to be regarded, from the Roman point of view, as a very grave revolutionary act. It was a remarkable innovation; they were the first Jewish silver coins ever to have been minted. The whole workshop of a mint (die-cutting, metal-casting, etc.) had to be created anew, because a hundred years had passed since the last issuing of Jewish coins. As for the designs—this new and consciously national coinage must have rejected each sort of strange prototype influenced from the Gentile world. We must therefore assume that the devices used were generally known and accepted Jewish symbols. The main object must have been to stress the liberation of Zion, and we must therefore take it that the symbols used were connected with the most important Jewish institution—the religion and the temple service in Jerusalem. Accordingly, we must regard the cup on the obverse of the silver shekel (*see* No. 32 in § 5 *below*) as a prominent and familiar temple implement. The symbols represented on the other coins are connected with feasts of pilgrimage, which assembled the whole Jewish people in Jerusalem for the service. So we may assume that this cup belongs to the paraphernalia of those celebrations too. This leads to the conjecture that we have here the golden "omer" vessel into which an offering of barley, the first fruit of the land, was measured for the temple on the second day of Passover. The swinging of this cup during the temple service was seen by everybody and must have been a significant and impressive ceremony. The reverse of the shekel shows a bunch of pomegranates with three buds, which must have been a popular symbol too, the more so as it is one of the seven celebrated fruits of the country (Deut. 8:8). It was used as an ornament on the JACHIN AND BOAZ columns of the temple (I Kings 7:18, 20), and was depicted on the vestment of the high priest (Exod. 39:24-26). Its numerous seeds made the fruit a symbol of fertility.

The shekel had the same weight (14 grams) as the Tyrian shekel or the tetradrachma of Antioch, and was given a similar value in order to supplant the foreign currency. The necessary silver probably came out of the temple treasury. The writing is in the ancient Hebrew script. We have shekels and half shekels from the first to the fifth year (66-70).

In the second and third years of the war of independence bronze coins were added which displayed an amphora on one side (wine or oil container) and a vine leaf with tendril on the other side (*see* No. 33 in § 5 *below*). Vine belongs to the distinguished fruits of the country (Deut. 8:8). The source of the cultivation is traced back to Noah (Gen. 9:20), and it was a drink offering in the temple (Lev. 23:13; Num. 15: 5, 7). Isaiah compares Israel to a vineyard (Isa. 5: 1 ff; Jer. 2:21; Ezek. 19:10: Hos. 10:1), and vine is a symbol for blessing and fecundity (Ps. 128:3; Hos. 14:7). The custom of blessing wine and bread became a ceremony at each Jewish feast, and was taken over by the Christians at the Holy Communion.

From the fourth year of the war of independence we have half-, quarter-, and eighth-shekels, all of bronze. Perhaps it had become necessary to close the gap between the silver shekels and the small currency. It is also possible that the decision to mint tokens of bronze was due to the exhaustion of the silver treasury of the temple in the fourth year of minting. The bronze coins (*see* No. 34 in § 5 *below*) show on the obverse two lulabs (a palm branch, myrtle, and willow tied together) and between them the ethrog (citron), all symbols of the Feast of Tabernacles (see Lev. 23:40). During the celebration the lulab was to be held in the right hand and the ethrog in the left. The reverse of the coin shows two baskets filled with fruits under a palm tree (see Deut. 26:2). The baskets on these coins indicate the offerings to the temple at the "feast of first fruits" (Pentecost). The palm tree as a coin motif is already familiar to us from coins of Herod Antipas and the procurators. Walls, doors, and columns of the temple were adorned with palm motifs (I Kings 6:29, 32; 7:36; Ezek. 40:16-17; 41:18-19). It became the symbol of Judea because it was said to grow there more abundantly than in all other sections of Palestine.

We have seen now how the tendency of all coins of the first war of independence points unmistakably to the temple service, offerings, and celebrations which all Jews were bound to attend in yearly pilgrimages. The devices depicted were familiar to them in connection with their visits in Jerusalem. They were chosen to point out their all-uniting bond, the service to the God of Israel.

Rome razed Jerusalem to the ground; an imperium stood against the smallest nation. Notwithstanding this inequality in power, the victor immortalized his success with an arch of triumph in Rome and with the issue of new coins, bearing the inscription *Judaea capta*. This coin—so far removed from Jewish religion—seems to illustrate the words of Isaiah:

> Your men shall fall by the sword
> and your mighty men in battle.
> And her gates shall lament and mourn;
> ravaged, she shall sit upon the ground
> (Isa. 3:25-26).

It seems that the victor could not escape the impression of the Judean landscape. Again the palm is used on this coin in a central position. *See* No. 35 in § 5 *below*.

The flame of revolution never died in Judea. It was kindled by the expectation of the Messiah, who would rebuild the Holy City and the destroyed temple and expel the hated oppressors. It was stirred by the intention of Hadrian to re-create the city as a Roman colony, "Aelia Capitolina," and excited by his plan to erect a temple dedicated to Jupiter on the place of the Holy of Holies. In 132-35 Judea was aroused to the second war of independence. Simultaneously with the expulsion of their enemies, they again started minting silver and bronze coins as a sign of their regained sovereignty. But this time they lacked the raw material which had been supplied by the temple treasury in the first war. This supply had been plundered thoroughly by the Romans after the conquest of Titus. The Jews had no choice now but to use the current coinage and stamp their own symbols on the foreign devices. We can well imagine their feelings of satisfaction when the hated portraits of their oppressors vanished under the die and their own symbols were re-created. All circulating Tyrian and Syrian tetradrachmas, Roman denars, and bronze coins were thus overstruck. This was sometimes hurriedly done, so that traces of the former coinage remained visible. This proved a great help for the numismatic scholars, who only thus could date these coins with certainty. The aim of the second war of independence was to rebuild the Holy City and revive the temple service. In this light we have to interpret the symbols on the coins. First of all, the coin designs of the first war of independence were repeated: palm, grape, vine, and vine leaf. We read the name of Eleazar, the priest who seemed to have been associated in rule with Simon (Bar Cocheba), who was the military commander of the war and whose name is constantly found on the coins of this period. Dated coins exist only from the first and second years. It must be assumed that the coins with the inscription "Redemption of Jerusalem" were struck in the last year of the war, when Jerusalem seems to have already been lost to the Romans, and instead of the manifestation of freedom the hope for freedom is expressed.

The tetradrachma (*see* No. 36 in § 5 *below*) has on the obverse a temple with four columns and within a shrine with shelves and two scrolls of the Law, or—in another opinion—only a door. Most scholars see in this design a representation of the Holy of Holies. The reason is that on Gentile coins the statue of a god takes the central place inside a temple, so it is plausible that the most holy object in Jewish ritual—namely, the scrolls of the Law—should here be depicted. We must not take the design of the temple as an actual reminiscence of what it had looked like. More than sixty years had passed since its destruction, so we cannot expect either that the memory of its construction still lingered on or that laymen had more than a very vague conception of the Holy of the Holies. The reverses show lulab and ethrog, which we have met already on the bronze coins of the first war. On the denars (*see* Nos. 37-41 in § 5 *below*) we find lyres, trumpets, amphorae, grapes, and palm branches. The trumpets correspond to a description of Flavius Josephus (Antiq. II.xii.6). A representation in relief is to be seen on the arch of triumph of Titus in Rome, where they are carried beside the seven-branched lampstand as remarkable pieces of the spoil. Flavius Josephus traces these trumpets back to Moses. In ancient times they were sounded for assembling the people or as a signal of departure, at the celebration of feasts and at similar occasions. During the period of the temple they were used at the Feast of Tabernacles when praying for rain, and during the water libation, as we learn from the Talmud. The lyre is represented in two manners, either chelys-shaped or in the form of a cithara with three strings. These are the lyres and harps which are many times mentioned in the Bible (II Sam. 6:5; I Chr. 13:8; 15:28; Ps. 150:3). They were the priestly instruments of praise and rejoicing (I Chr. 25:1-7; cf. II Chr. 5:13). The palm branch had already been used on coins of the procurators. The continuous repetition of this motif points to a general knowledge of its significance and use. It was an important part of the lulab which was used in the ritual of the Feast of Tabernacles; it signified peace (I Macc. 13:37) and symbolized dignity, honor (II Macc. 14:4), and prosperity (Ps. 92:12-13). Grapes are always depicted in clusters. Not only was wine an important product of the country; it also belonged to the temple ceremonial (cf. vine leaf on coins of the first war of independence). The one-handled jug with a narrow neck was used at the Feast of Tabernacles for water libation, with the purpose of inducing rain. In a solemn procession water was drawn in a golden vessel at the fountain of Siloah, and was then brought to the temple and poured on the altar. The palm branch, which is depicted on the side of the amphora, was used on each festive occasion. On these coins Bar Cocheba wanted to symbolize that the re-erection of the temple and the restoration of the water libation would result in well-timed rainfall. Belated rainfall, deplored by the population, was said to have been the rule since the destruction of the temple. On the bronze coins (*see* Nos. 42-43 in § 5 *below*) most of the motifs of the silver coins are repeated, with the addition of a two-handled amphora. Wine and water for libation were not the only liquids used in the ritual. Much oil was necessary for the meal offerings, breads, and foremost for the menorah, for which purest oil was demanded (Exod. 27:20). We must conclude that the amphora on these coins was also a part of the temple service, and it is most probable that it was an oil container for the menorah, or lampstand.

The Bar Cocheba war brought the last and most handsome flowers of Jewish numismatics. Its symbols have a close contact with the former worship in the temple, and are standing, therefore, still under the full influence of the Bible.

5. Illustrations.

1. Tongue and circle of gold from Gezer

(R. A. S. Macalister, *Gezer II*, p. 259, fig. 405; used by permission of the Palestine Exploration Fund)

2. Persian daric, gold, 8.424 grams

Obv. King kneeling, in left hand a bow, in right a spear.

Rev. Irregular incuse square.

3. Athenian tetradrachma, silver, 17.5 grams maximum

Obv. Head of Athena, helmeted.

Rev. Incuse square, owl within it, behind it olive spray and small decrescent moon; inscription: ΑΘΕ (Athens).

4. Silver

Obv. Bearded male head, with turbanlike headdress.

Rev. Owl, a fleur-de-lis-shaped flower to the left; in field: יהד (Judea).

5. Silver

Rev. Male divinity seated on a winged wheel; on his extended left hand, a hawk; above, inscription: יהד (Judea); to the right, a bald-headed mask.

6. Silver, 14.5 grams

Obv. Head of young Herakles, wearing lion skin.

Rev. Zeus seated on throne, his left hand grasping top of scepter, on his extended right hand an eagle; inscription: ΒΑΣΙΛΕΩΣ ΑΛΕΞΑΝΔΡΟΥ (King Alexander).

7. Silver, 13-14 grams

Obv. Head of Ptolemy I, diademed.

Rev. Eagle standing on thunderbolt; left, in field; club and monogram; inscription: ΠΤΟΛΕΜΑΙΟΥ ΒΑΣΙΛΕΩΣ (King Ptolemy).

8. Silver, 16-17 grams

Obv. Head of Antiochus IV.

Rev. Zeus seated on throne, left hand resting on scepter, Nike on extended right hand; inscription: ΒΑΣΙΛΕΩΣ ΑΝΤΙΟΧΟΥ ΘΕΟΥ ΕΠΙΦΑΝΟΥΣ (King Antiochus, magnificent god, or god who manifests himself).

9. Bronze

Obv. Lily.

Rev. Anchor; inscription: ΒΑΣΙΛΕΩΣ ΑΝΤΙΟΧΟΥ ΕΥΕΡΓΕΤΟΥ (King Antiochus, benefactor); date: ΑΠΡ=132/31 B.C.

10. Bronze

Obv. Inscription: יהוחנן הכהן הגדל וחבר היהדים (Johanan the high priest and the community of the Jews).

Rev. Double cornucopia, a poppy head within.

11. Bronze

Obv. Half-opened flower; inscription: יהונתן המלך (Jonathan, the king).

Rev. Anchor within a circle; inscription: ΒΑΣΙΛΕΩΣ ΑΛΕΞΑΝΔΡΟΥ (King Alexander).

12*a.* Dilepton (Hebrew *p^e^rûṭâ*), bronze, 1.5–3.0 grams

Obv. Within the intermediate spaces of rays of a star, an inscription: יהונתן המלך (Jonathan, the king).

Rev. Anchor; inscription: ΒΑΣΙΛΕΩΣ ΑΛΕΞΑΝΔΡΟΥ (King Alexander).

12*b.* Lepton, bronze, 0.5–1.0 gram

Obv. Same as 12*a*, without inscription.

Rev. Same as 12*a*, without inscription.

13. Bronze

Obv. Uncertain object.

Rev. The seven-branched candlestick; inscription: ΒΑCΙΛ ΑΝΤΙΓ (King Antigonus).

14. Bronze

Obv. Wreath of ivy; inscription: [ΒΑCΙΛ]ΕΩC ΑΝΤΙΓ[ΟΝΟΥ] (King Antigonus).

Rev. Double cornucopia; inscription: מתתיה הכהן הגדל וחבר היהודים (Mattathias the high priest and the community of the Jews).

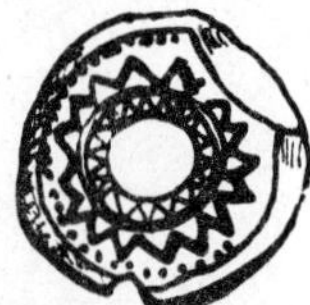

15. Bronze

Obv. Helmet with crest and cheek piece; inscription: ΒΑΣΙΛΕΩΣ ΗΡΩΔΟΥ (King Herod); date and monogram as in No. 15.

Rev. Circular shield, surrounded by a wavy line.

16. Bronze

Obv. Tripod with bowl; in field right, monogram: ⳨ ; left, date: LΓ (year 3); inscription: ΒΑΣΙΛΕΩΣ ΗΡΩΔΟΥ (King Herod).

Rev. Thymiaterium (incense burner) between two palm branches.

17. Bronze

Obv. Anchor; inscription: ΒΑCΙ ΗΡWΔ (King Herod).

Rev. Double cornucopia with caduceus between horns.

18. Bronze

Obv. Anchor; inscription: ΗΡW[ΔΟV] (Herod).

Rev. Within wreath, an inscription: ΕΘΝΑ (Ethnarch).

19. Bronze

Obv. Bunch of grapes with leaf; inscription: ΗΡWΔΟΥ (Herod).

Rev. Helmet with cheek pieces and double crest; left, small caduceus; below, inscription: ΕΘΝΑΡΧΟΥ (Ethnarch).

20. Bronze

Obv. Palm branch; in field, date: LΛΓ (33=A.D. 29/30); inscription: ΗΡWΔΟΥ ΤΕΤΡΑΡΧΟΥ (Herod, Tetrarch).

Rev. Within wreath, an inscription: ΤΙΒΕ ΡΙΑC (Tiberias).

21. Bronze

Obv. Head of Tiberius; inscription: [CEB]ACTW [KA]ICAPI (Caesar Augustus).
Rev. Tetrastyle temple; inscription: ΦΙΛΙΠΠΟΥ TET[PAPXOY] (Philip, Tetrarch); date: LIB (12=A.D. 8/9).

22. Bronze

Obv. Umbrella with fringe (?); inscription: BACI-ΛEWC AΓΡΙΠΑ (King Agrippa).
Rev. Three ears of corn; date: LS (6=A.D. 42/43).

23. Bronze

Obv. Head of Agrippa I; inscription: BACIΛEVC ΜΕΓΑC ΑΓΡΙΠΠΑC ΦΙΛΟΚΑΙCAP (Great King Agrippa, friend of Caesar).
Rev. Female figure holding rudder and palm branch; inscription: KAICAPIA H ΠΡOC [CEBACTΩ ΛΙΜΕΝΙ] (Caesarea at the harbor Sebastos).

24. Bronze

Obv. Ear of corn; inscription: KAICAPOC (Caesar).
Rev. Palm tree with two bunches of fruit; date: L ΛΓ (33=A.D. 5/6).

25. Bronze

Obv. Vine leaf; inscription: TIBEP (Tiberius).
Rev. Cantharus (wine jug); date: L Δ (4=A.D. 17/18); inscription: KAICAP (Caesar).

26. Bronze

Obv. Palm branch; date: L E (5=A.D. 58/59); inscription: KAICAPOC (Caesar).
Rev. Within a wreath, an inscription: NEPWNOC (Nero).

27. Bronze

Obv. Simplum (ladle); inscription: TIBEPIOY KAICAPOC (Tiberius Caesar); date: L IS (16=A.D. 29/30).
Rev. Three ears bound together; inscription: ΙΟΥΛΙΑ KAICAPOC (Julia Caesar).

28. Bronze

Obv. Lituus; inscription: TIBEPIOY KAICAPOC (Tiberius Caesar).
Rev. Within a wreath, the date: L IZ (17=A.D. 30/31).

29. Roman denar, silver; tribute money

Obv. Head of Tiberius; inscription: TI CAESAR DIVI AUG F AUGUSTUS (Tiberius Caesar, son of the divine Augustus, Augustus).
Rev. Pax seated, holding branch; inscription: PONTIF MAXIM (High priest).

30. Syrian tetradrachma, silver

Obv. Head of Augustus; inscription: ΚΑΙΣΑΡΟΣ ΣΕΒΑΣΤΟΣ (Caesar, Augustus).
Rev. Tyche of Antiochia; at his feet, the river-god Orontes; inscription: ΑΝΤΙΟΧΕΩΝ ΜΗΤΡΟ-ΠΟΛΕΩΣ (Capital of the Antiochian); date: ΔΝ (54; after Pharsalus), Ϛ Λ (36 after Actium=A.D. 5).

31. Silver Tyrian shekel

Obv. Head of Melqart-Herakles.
Rev. Eagle, palm branch over right shoulder; in

field, date: PNB (152=A.D. 26/27); inscription: ΤΥΡΟΥ ΙΕΡ[ΑΣ ΚΑΙ ΑΣΥ]ΛΟΥ (Tyre, sanctuary and asylum).

32. Silver

Obv. Cup, above date: א (1 year); inscription: שקל ישראל (Shekel of Israel).
Rev. Bunch of pomegranate with three buds; inscription: ירושלם קדשה (Jerusalem the Holy).

33. Bronze

Obv. Amphora; inscription: שנת שתים (Year 2).
Rev. Vine branch with leaf and tendril; inscription: חרות ציון (Deliverance of Zion).

34. Bronze

Obv. Ethrog between two lulabs; inscription: שנת ארבע חצי (Year 4½).
Rev. Palm tree between two baskets filled with fruits; inscription: לגאלת ציון (For the redemption of Zion).

35. Bronze

Obv. Head of Vespasian; inscription: IMPerator CAESar VESPASIAN AUGustus Pontifex Maximus TRibunicia Potestas Pater Patriae COnSul III.
Rev. Palm tree; on the left, a Jew standing, his hands tied behind his back, behind him a shield; on the right, a Jewess seated on a cuirass, weeping; inscription: JUDAEA CAPTA, in exergue: S. C. *(Senatus consulto:* With permission of the Senate).

36. Tetradrachma of the Bar Cocheba War, silver, 14 grams

Obv. Temple with four columns, within a shrine with shelves and two scrolls of the Law; inscription: ירושלם (Jerusalem).
Rev. Lulab and ethrob; inscription: שב לחר[ות] ישראל (Second year of the freedom of Israel).

37. Denar, silver

Obv. Within wreath, an inscription: שמעון (Simon).
Rev. Two trumpets; inscription: לחרות ירושלם (For the freedom of Jerusalem).

38. Denar, silver

Obv. Bunch of grapes; inscription: שמעון (Simon).
Rev. Palm branch; inscription: שב לחר[ות] יש[ר]אל (Second year of the freedom of Israel).

39. Denar, silver

Rev. Lyre (chelys-shaped) with three strings; inscription: שב לחר[ות] ישאל (Second year of the freedom of Israel).

40. Denar, silver

Rev. Lyre (cithara); inscription: לחר[ות] [י]רשלם (For the freedom of Jerusalem).

41. Denar, silver

Rev. Jug with palm branch to the right; inscription same as in No. 40.

42. Bronze

Obv. Palm tree with two branches of fruit; inscription: שמעון (Simon).

Rev. Vine leaf; inscription: לחרות ירושלם (For the freedom of Jerusalem).

43. Bronze

Obv. Within a wreath, an inscription: שמעון (Simon).

Rev. Two-handled amphora; inscription: שב לחר[ות] ישראל (Second year of the freedom of Israel).

Bibliography. F. W. Madden, *Coins of the Jews* (1881); E. Rogers, *A Handy Guide to Jewish Coins* (1914); A. Reifenberg, *Ancient Jewish Coins* (1940); P. Romanoff, *Jewish Symbols on Ancient Jewish Coins* (1944); F. Banks, *Coins of Bible Days* (1955).

H. HAMBURGER

MONEY-CHANGER [κολλυβιστής, κερματιστής; שולחני, one who sits at a table, *like* Greek τραπεζίτης]. The term applied to those who in ancient times served many of the functions of the modern banker. Among their services was the exchange of the currency of one country or province for that of another, and of small coins for those of larger denomination. For such services they collected a small fee, called in Greek κόλλυβος; this term was also adopted in Hebrew and Aramaic.

The half-shekel offering imposed by scripture (Exod. 30:11 ff) on every adult male had to be paid, according to the ruling current in NT times, in Tyrian silver coins. The assistance of the money-changers was essential if the people were to discharge properly this universally recognized obligation. Accordingly the Mishna (Sheḳ. 1.3) reports that the tables of the money-changers were set up in the provinces on the fifteenth day of Adar (a month before the Passover) to facilitate regional collections. Ten days later, when pilgrims would be arriving in growing numbers from foreign countries, the money-changers transferred their operation to the temple courts.

The first activity of Jesus after his triumphal entry into Jerusalem is reported to have been the "cleansing of the temple" (Matt. 21:12 ff; Mark 11:15 ff; Luke 19:45 ff—the briefest version; John 2:13 ff). On this occasion he drove out of the temple those who traded in animals or birds for sacrifice, overthrew the tables of the money-changers, and according to Mark forbade anyone to carry a vessel through the temple areas. And alluding to Jer. 7:11, he accused the objects of his wrath of turning the temple into a den of robbers.

Although the "money-changers in the temple" have become a familiar symbol of the sordid, especially of the profaning of religion by commercialism, the real meaning of this episode is by no means certain. Jesus paid the half-shekel tax for himself and Peter (Matt. 17:24 ff) and enjoined the healed leper to bring the prescribed offering (Matt. 8:4; Mark 1:44; Luke 5:14). Evidently he was not opposed to the maintenance of the temple and its sacrificial system. His objection to carrying a vessel through the temple (Mark 11:16) is further proof of his regard for the sanctity of the place, and is in full accord with the Pharisaic injunction against using the temple area as a short cut (M. Ber. 9.5). Why then did he object to an arrangement which enabled worshipers more easily to make their contribution to the support of the temple?

The most plausible explanation is that he regarded the charge made by the money-changers as excessive. Contemporary Jewish sources, it is true, do not confirm this suggestion directly; according to the tradition of the majority, the charge was a twenty-fourth of a shekel. (In fact, only one of the scholars whose views are reported held that the money-changers retained this profit for themselves. The others state that the entire transaction was under temple auspices, and that the income was devoted to the public welfare: see M. Sheḳ. 1.7; Tosef. Sheḳ. 1.8.)

But we do have accounts of profiteering in the sale of sacrificial doves. On one occasion, the Mishna reports, the price of doves rose to an outrageous figure. Thereupon Simeon the son of Gamaliel, who had succeeded his father as leader of the Pharisees, modified the law so as to reduce the number of mandatory sacrifices—and the price of doves soon dropped sharply (Ker. 1.7).

This episode reflects the bitter hostility of the people and their Pharisaic representatives toward the venal priesthood who, in the last days of the Second Temple, obtained or retained the higher positions only by bribing or otherwise conciliating the Roman rulers.

It seems probable that the ire of Jesus against the money-changers derived from some incident, not directly reported, in which the temple authorities had tried to increase their gains by excessive charges —or at least from a widespread belief among the plain folk of the province that such exploitation was going on.

Bibliography. S. Krauss, *Talmudische Archäologie* (1911), II, 411; I. Abrahams, *Studies in Pharisaism and the Gospels,* First Series (1917), pp. 82-89. B. J. BAMBERGER

***MONOTHEISM** mŏn'ə thē ĭz'em. *See* GOD, OT VIEW OF, § D6.

MONSTER [תנין] (Jer. 51:34); KJV DRAGON. *See* SEA MONSTER.

MONTH. *See* CALENDAR § 3.

MONUMENT. The tombstone or grave marker (ציון) of the man of God which Josiah permitted to stand when other tombs at Bethel were being defiled (II Kings 23:17; KJV "title"). The word also designated a signpost or temporary marker for a grave (Ezek. 39:15; "sign") and a road marker on a highway (Jer. 31:21; "waymark"). The word יד (lit., "hand") is translated "monument" in I Sam. 15:12; II Sam. 18:18; I Chr. 18:3; Isa. 56:5 (cf. Matt. 23:29), where the contexts suggest memorial standing stones or pillars. The KJV renders נצורים as "monuments" (RSV "secret places") where the term seems to refer to places or structures associated with tombs (Isa. 65:4).

See also MASSEBAH; PILLAR. W. L. REED

MOON. The moon is mentioned thirty-four times in the OT and nine times in the NT, as well as in several passages of the Apoc. and the Pseudep. References to it occur especially in cosmogonic and eschatological contexts, but there are also divers allusions to the heathen worship of it and to popular legends and customs associated with it. Occasionally, too, it is introduced as a symbol of permanence.

1. Terminology
2. The moon in cosmogony and eschatology
3. Cult and worship of the moon
4. The moon in the calendar
5. The moon in biblical folklore
6. The moon in idiomatic expressions
Bibliography

1. Terminology. The usual Hebrew term for "moon" is ירח, a word common to all the Semitic languages and seemingly connected with the verb ארח, "journey, travel," in reference to the progress of the luminary across the sky. An alternative, but purely poetic, designation is לבנה, "White Lady" (Song of S. 6:10; Isa. 24:23; 30:26), used always as a parallel to חמה, "hot one," a fanciful term for the sun.

The new moon is called חדש, "renewal"; and the full moon, כסא (Job 26:9; Ps. 81:3—H 81:4; Prov. 7:20). The latter corresponds to the Akkadian *kuse'u,* "headgear, crown," and bears reference to the idea, well attested in Mesopotamian literature, that at the plenilune the moon wears a hat or crown.

In Enoch 78:2 the names of the moon are given as: Asônjâ, Eblâ, Benâsê, and Erâe. The complex *Labenaserraë* clearly conceals לבנה, כסא, ירח; but what underlies *asonyaeb* (patently corrupt) is obscure.

2. The moon in cosmogony and eschatology. The moon was fashioned and placed in the firmament on the fourth day of creation, to illumine the night and regulate the seasons. Its light is represented as independent of the sun, and its movement as controlled entirely by the external will of God (Gen. 1:14-19; Pss. 104:19; 136:9; Ecclus. 43:6-8). At the end of the present era, when all things revert to primordial chaos, the moon will be darkened (Isa. 13:10; Joel 2:10; Matt. 24:29; Mark 13:24), or turn to blood (Joel 2:31—H 3:4; Rev. 6:12), or shine abnormally by day (II Esd. 5:4 [where read, perhaps, *in die jugiter* for *in die ter* of the MSS]). Eventually, however, on God's day of triumph, it will shine again and thenceforth never wane (Isa. 60:20).

A fanciful, astronomical description of the moon and its movements is given in Enoch 78.

3. Cult and worship of the moon. As among all the Semitic peoples, the worship of the moon figured prominently in the early pagan cults of Palestine and Syria, where it was regarded as a male deity, most commonly known as Yaraḫ. Sacrifices to him are prescribed in the temple tariffs from Ras Shamra–Ugarit (1.14; 5.11, 14), where reference is also made to a special offering "on the day of the new moon" (3.48; *bym ḥdṯ*); while the popularity of his cult among the W Semites in general is attested by the occurrence of such personal names as Abdu-Eraḫ, "servant of the Moon-god"; Zimri-Eraḫ, "the Moon-god is a protection"; and Yantin-Eraḫ, "the Moon-god gives," in documents from Mari and other sites. Under the name of Śahar (cf. Aramaic *sahᵃrâ;* S Arabic name of goddess Ś-h-r, "moon"), his worship is attested also at Hamath and Nerab, in Syria, in the seventh century B.C. (*ANET* 502*a*).

Nor was it only among the Semites of Canaan and Amurru that the moon was adored. The corresponding deity, Kusuḫ, is likewise mentioned in Hurrian (Horite) texts from Ugarit (4.16); and the extent to which the Semites were subjected to such foreign influence may be gauged from the fact that an adaptation (or direct translation?) of a Hurrian myth dealing with the marriage of the moon-god figures among the poetical texts from that site. *See bibliography.*

The city of Jericho (יריחו) was named for the ancient moon-god. On the other hand, the oft-repeated statement that Sinai and the Wilderness of Sin derive their names from that of the Mesopotamian moon-god Sin must now be discounted, for there is no evidence that that particular name was ever used in Canaan or by the Semitic nomads of Palestine.

The worship of the moon, as of other heavenly bodies, was forbidden in the religion of Yahweh, as impugning the uniqueness of that deity (Deut. 4:19; 17:3); and there is no sound reason for supposing that this prohibition was but a late innovation, however late may be the literary redaction of the code in which it is now found embodied. The ancient pagan cult was, however, adopted officially in Judah by the apostatic king Manasseh (687-641 B.C.; II Kings 21:3, 5), and was maintained by other rulers and by the populace in general (Jer. 8:2), though it was formally proscribed in 621 B.C. by Josiah (II Kings 23:5). A feature of this cult was the worship of the moon on roof tops (Jer. 19:13; Zeph. 1:5); and it seems also to have been a popular custom to salute it reverently as it "sailed in beauty" (cf. Job 31:26-27).

4. The moon in the calendar. The standard calendar in Israel was lunar, and the major seasonal festivals of spring and fall—viz., Pesaḫ ("Passover") and 'Āsîph ("Ingathering")—commenced at full moon. At new moon, trumpets were blown (Num. 10:10; Ps. 81:3—H 81:4)—originally, no doubt, as a means of scaring demons believed to be especially rampant in the "dark o' the moon." Special offerings were also prescribed for this occasion (Num. 28:11-15). At full moon, persons traveling on business returned home, if possible (Prov. 7:20). This probably reflects the widespread notion that the waning moon, and especially the night when it begins to wane, is unpropitious for the conduct of affairs.

On the theory that the sabbath was originally the full moon, *see* SABBATH.

5. The moon in biblical folklore. Two items of popular lore relating to the moon are mentioned in the OT:

a) When Yahweh took to the warpath, the moon, like the sun, could be halted in its course (Hab. 3:11); and this was believed actually to have happened in the days of Joshua, when the Israelites engaged their enemies at Gibeon (Josh. 10:12). *See* SUN.

b) The moon could exert a baleful influence and "strike" a man (Ps. 121:6), rendering him "lunatic." This fairly universal superstition appears also in the NT (Matt. 4:24; 17:15).

6. The moon in idiomatic expressions. Like the sun, the moon was regarded as a symbol of permanence (Pss. 72:5; 89:37—H 89:38—an idea well attested also in Akkadian literature).

Quite obscure is the meaning of the expression "output of the moons" (גרש ירחים; RSV "rich yield of the months") in Deut. 33:14, where it stands parallel to "choicest fruits of the sun." According to some (e.g., LXX, Targ. Onqelos, Palestinian Targ.), the plural form of the word indicates that it really means "lunar months," in which case the reference will be to seasonal crops and fruits (so RSV). According to others, the allusion is to dew, which was often regarded in antiquity as an efflux of the moon.

Bibliography. J. M. Lagrange, *Études sur les religions sémitiques* (1905), pp. 450 ff; A. Jirku, "Der Kult des Mondgottes im altorientalischen Palästina-Syrien," *ZDMG*, C (1930), 202-4.

On the Hurrian myth of the marriage of the moon-god, see: H. L. Ginsberg, *Orientalia,* VIII (1939), 317-27; A. Goetze, *JBL,* LX (1940), 353-74.

On the moon as a symbol of permanence, see: K. Tallquist, *Hakedem,* I (1906), 3-5. T. H. GASTER

MOOSSIAS; KJV **MOOSIAS.** Apoc. forms of MAASEIAH 15.

MORASTHITE môr'əs thīt. KJV translation of מורשתי (RSV "of Moresheth") in Jer. 26:18; Mic. 1:1. *See* MORESHETH.

MORDECAI môr'də kī [מרדכי = Akkad. *Marduk, name of the chief Babylonian deity*]; KJV Apoc. MARDOCHEUS mär'də kē'əs [Μαρδοχαῖος]. **1.** One of those whose names head the list of Jewish exiles returned from Babylon to Jerusalem with Zerubbabel (Ezra 2:2; cf. Neh. 7:7; I Esd. 5:8).

2. The Jewish hero of the book of Esther. He and Esther, his cousin and ward, who became queen to the Persian king Ahasuerus, triumphed over the evil plotting of Haman, vizier of the king. Haman would have destroyed not only Mordecai but all Jews in the Persian Empire (Esth. 2:5–10:3).

Scholars consider the story of Esther to be fictitious and the persons within it scarcely historical (*see bibliography and* ESTHER, BOOK OF), although it is the author's purpose to write as if he were narrating history. Thus Ahasuerus is believed to represent the Persian king Xerxes I (*ca.* 486-465 B.C.), and Mordecai is probably meant to be identified with the Mordecai of Ezra 2:2 (*see* 1 *above*). But Esth. 2:6 declares that Mordecai had been taken into Babylonian exile with King Jeconiah (JEHOIACHIN)—i.e., in the first deportation *ca.* 597 B.C. This raises serious historical problems, since for Mordecai then to be flourishing in the reign of Xerxes I, he would have to be well over a hundred years old. The writer clearly telescopes history. Of more interest as an indication of the writer's point of view is the genealogy of Mordecai, on the one hand, which makes him a descendant of Kish, ancestor of King Saul (Esth. 2:5), and the ancestry of Mordecai's enemy Haman, on the other hand, which makes the latter a descendant of Agag, king of the Amalekites (3:1)—recalling the victory of Saul over Agag (*ca.* 1020 B.C.; cf. I Sam. 15:1-9, 17-33), and in general the lasting enmity between the Amalekites and Israel. In the Jewish synagogue today the Torah reading for Purim, the feast which celebrates the tradition of Esther and Mordecai, is Exod. 17:8-16, which concludes with the words: "The LORD will have war with Amalek from generation to generation" (vs. 16). It would seem that in the ancient writer's view the contest between the Jewish Diaspora and Haman was part of a continuing struggle.

On the other hand, that Mordecai's name is the equivalent of Marduk, the name of the Babylonian deity, and that Esther's name is the equivalent of Ishtar the goddess, has led interpreters of the story to find in the book of Esther a thinly veiled Babylonian or other pagan myth describing a cosmic conflict having to do originally with the cycle of the seasons. That the story of Esther takes its plot and motifs to a certain extent from some pagan festival with which the Jews of the Dispersion were acquainted is not improbable (*see bibliography*), but it has been here historicized and made subservient to Jewish interpretations of history.

In this regard, reference must be made to a single undated cuneiform document from the Persian period, found at Borsippa (*see bibliography*), which refers to a certain Marduka who was a finance officer of some sort in the Persian court at Susa during the reign of Xerxes I. While a connection between such an individual and the Mordecai of the book of Esther is in no sense established, the possibility of such a historical event as is related in Esther actually forming a factual nucleus to the book cannot be dismissed out of hand.

It remains finally to mention that II Macc. 15:36, concluding an account of the defeat of the Syrian armies of Nicanor by Judas Maccabeus, declares that "Nicanor's day" is to be celebrated on the day before "Mordecai's day"—i.e., the first day of the two-day feast of Purim. From this passage it has been conjectured that the Purim festival and the story of Mordecai and Esther were devised in the beginning to celebrate and commemorate the victory of Judas Maccabeus over the Syrians (*ca.* 161 B.C.; *see bibliog-*

raphy). This explanation is not impossible, although it has not received general acceptance among biblical scholars.

Jewish tradition, beginning with the apocryphal Additions to the Book of Esther (*see* ESTHER, APOCRYPHAL) and continuing in the rabbinical literature, has built a wealth of legend, supported by fanciful biblical exegesis, about the already largely legendary figure of Mordecai found in the canonical book. *See bibliography*.

See also ESTHER; PURIM.

Bibliography. L. B. Paton, *Esther,* ICC (1908), pp. 75, 77-79, 85, 88-91, 166-72. R. H. Pfeiffer, *Introduction to the OT* (rev. ed., 1948), p. 746. B. W. Anderson, Introduction and Exegesis of Esther, *IB,* III (1954), 826, 840-41. On theories of mythological origins, see, besides the foregoing works: T. H. Gaster, *Festivals of the Jewish Year* (1953), pp. 215-21, 230-31. On the Mordecai inscription from Susa, see: A. Ungnad, "Keilinschriftliche Beiträge zum Buch Esra und Ester," *ZAW,* XVII (1940-41), 243-44; XVIII (1942-43), 219. On Mordecai in the rabbinical literature, see: the survey by M. Seligsohn, "Mordecai," *JE,* IX (1905), 7-9.

B. T. DAHLBERG

MOREH môr'ə [מורה, מרה, place of instruction or divination(?), *or* teacher(?)]. **1.** The site of the "oak of Moreh" (אלון מורה; KJV "plain of Moreh" is incorrect), a sacred tree in the vicinity of Shechem. Here Abraham encamped and built an altar to Yahweh, who had appeared to him (Gen. 12:6-8). It is evident that this was an old Canaanite place of worship. The fact that Abraham is not reported as having planted the oak of Moreh (see Gen. 21:33, where he is said to have planted a tamarisk tree in Beer-sheba) suggests that the place of theophany at Shechem was Canaanite prior to its visitation by the patriarchs. Jacob hid the foreign gods (teraphim) under the oak which was near Shechem (Gen. 35:4). In Deut. 11:30 the oak of Moreh is mentioned in designating the location of nearby Mount Ebal and Mount Gerizim and the land of the Canaanites, which the Israelites would possess. At Shechem, Joshua took a great stone "and set it up there under the oak in the sanctuary of the LORD" (Josh. 24:26).

The Diviners' Oak at Shechem in Judg. 9:37 (cf. the "oak of the pillar" at Shechem in vs. 6) is probably to be identified with the oak of Moreh. A connection between Moreh and MORIAH is improbable.

2. A hill near which the Midianites encamped in the valley (Judg. 7:1). This was the Valley of Jezreel, and the hill of Moreh may be identified with the hill now called Jebel Dahi across the valley from Mount Gilboa. It was probably called the hill of Moreh because a sanctuary where divination was practiced was located on it.

Some scholars have held that the hill of Moreh was located in the vicinity of Shechem; but if the camps of the Hebrews and the Midians had been established near Shechem, it is more probable that Mount Gerizim or Mount Ebal, rather than the hill of Moreh, would have been mentioned to identify their locations.

W. L. REED

MORESHETH môr'ə shěth [מורשת גת, possession of Gath]. The home of the prophet Micah (Jer. 26:18; Mic. 1:1), and one of the cities mentioned in the wordplay section of Micah's prophecy (Mic. 1:14).

The ancient site of Moresheth is identified with modern Tell ej-Judeideh, a site occupying a strategic location *ca.* 1⅔ miles N of Beit Jibrin (Eleutheropolis). Pseudo-Epiphanius says that Micah was buried in his home near the cemetery of the Anakites, in the vicinity of Eleutheropolis. Eusebius and Jerome locate Moresheth (N)E of Eleutheropolis. The Map of Madeba shows a vignette NE of Eleutheropolis with the note: "Morasthi, from which the prophet Micah came," and nearby a small church, possibly dedicated to Micah, though the note is broken here. The Byzantine name of the place, Birathsatia ("castle of Satia") or Chariasati ("village of Satia"), appears in the references by Sozomen (fifth century A.D.) and Peter the Deacon.

Tell ej-Judeideh was abandoned at the end of the Bronze Age and not reoccupied until during the closing centuries of the monarchy (*ca.* 750). A half mile S, Khirbet Es'id, first successor to the old Moresheth and settled in Iron I (1200-900), retains a name reminiscent of Chariasati. An ancient necropolis, just to the S, apparently dates from Seleucid times. Khirbet el-Basal, a short distance to the N of Khirbet Es'id, is the later successor to Moresheth after its second abandonment. Here, in the Byzantine village, are the foundations of a church, possibly the one pictured on the Madeba Map.

Bibliography. F.-M. Abel, *Géographie de la Palestine*, vol. II (1938); J. Jeremias, "Moresheth-Gath, die Heimat des Propheten Micha," *PJB,* 29 (1933), 42-53; K. Elliger, "Die Heimat des Propheten Micha," *ZDPV,* 57 (1934), 119 ff.

V. R. GOLD

MORIAH mō rī'ə [המריה *with the article*]. **1.** The "land of Moriah" (ארץ המריה) is mentioned in Gen. 22:2 as a mountainous district, at a three-days' journey from Beer-sheba. The location is otherwise unspecified. Abraham was directed by God to offer Isaac in sacrifice on one of the mountains of that region, but was prevented from consummating the sacrifice by a direct intervention of the angel of the Lord. The narrator concludes the episode by recording popular etymologies of the name, allegedly derived from the radical ראה, "to see" or "to provide," and explained as follows (Gen. 22:14): "The LORD will provide" (KJV "Jehovah-jireh," meaning "Jehovah shall see"), or "On the mount of the LORD it shall be provided" (KJV ". . . seen"). The Vulg. has interpreted "land of Moriah" as "land of the vision" (*in terram visionis*), in general conformity with the Hebrew tradition. The expression "land of Moriah" is replaced in the LXX by "the hill country" (εἰς τὴν γῆν τὴν ὑψηλήν) and in the Syr. by "the land of the Amorite." The reading of the Samar. המוראה suggests a possible relation of Moriah to the oak of MOREH (*see* MOREH 1), as if seeking to locate the sacrifice of Isaac in the vicinity of SHECHEM and Mount Gerizim (*see* GERIZIM, MOUNT).

2. Mount Moriah (הר המריה) is the rocky hilltop of Jerusalem N of the city of David, where Solomon built the temple (II Chr. 3:1). The same text specifies that this was the place which David had chosen, and purchased from Ornan the Jebusite (*see* ARAUNAH). Since the name Moriah appears nowhere else in the texts relative to the topography of Jerusalem, there is good reason to suspect that the author of Chronicles intended to ascribe an early origin to the royal

69. Air view of Mount Moriah, which became the site for Solomon's temple, and where today the Muslim "Dome of the Rock" is located

sanctuary, by identifying the unnamed hilltop formerly used as a threshing floor with the mountain in the land of Moriah, where Abraham had made ready to sacrifice his son. This identification is explicit in Josephus (Antiq. I.xiii.224, 226; VII.xiii.333) as well as in the Book of the Jubilees (18:13), and in rabbinical literature. It was accepted without discussion by Jerome (*Hebrew Questions on Gen.* 22.2; *on Jer.* 26.4), and it has influenced the Muslim folklore of the Dome of the Rock, in which the *maqam el-Khalil,* "Abraham's place," is shown to the pilgrims.

Fig. MOR 69.

Bibliography. G. A. Smith, *Jerusalem,* I (1907), 267-68; G. Dalman, *Jerusalem und sein Gelände* (1930), p. 125; F.-M. Abel, *Géographie de la Palestine,* I (1933), 374-75; J. Simons, *Jerusalem in the OT* (1952), p. 383; E. Nielsen, *Shechem* (1953), pp. 333-34.

G. A. Barrois

MORNING STAR [φωσφόρος] (II Pet. 1:19); KJV DAY-STAR. The Venus-star, heralding the Dawn.

MORTAL SIN [ἁμαρτία πρὸς θάνατον]. Literally, sin or sinning (which leads) to death. The expression occurs in the NT only in I John 5:16-17 (four times). John distinguishes between sin which is mortal and sin which is not mortal, both kinds being committed only by those who are not "born of God" (5:18). By "mortal sin" John may have meant sin which by its nature excluded the sinner from the church—as, e.g., hating a Christian brother (3:15); or he may have meant denying that Jesus is of God (4:3). Intercession for these is not exhorted. (Cf. Heb. 6:4-6; 10:26-31; 12:15-17.) *See* Sin, Sinners.

B. H. Throckmorton, Jr.

MORTAR. 1. מכתש מדכה. A vessel in which substances are crushed with a pestle. The most common use of the mortar and pestle was in the preparation of grain, either in husking or in grinding into flour, but it was also employed in crushing herbs (medicinal mortars); in the preparation of Cosmetics and dye pigments; and in other processes in which materials such as spices had to be reduced to fine grains or powder. In some cases a channel cut through the rim of the vessel functions as a drain and indicates that the mortar and pestle were also used in the preparation of small quantities of certain liquids—e.g., oil.

Manna was pounded in a mortar (מדכה) and also ground by millstones. "Mortar" (מכתש) and "pestle" (עלי) are used figuratively in Prov. 27:22. מכתש, *makhtēsh,* is used descriptively of a "hollow place" (the shape of a mortar) in Judg. 15:19 and as a place name in Zeph. 1:11 (KJV "Maktesh"; *see* Mortar, The).

Mortars are most often made of basalt (lava) because of its roughness and hardness, although limestone is also used, especially in the case of cosmetic mortars or palettes. The shape of the mortar varies from the simple cylindrical block with a concave depression on top to elaborate footed and decorated types; they are sometimes made in imitation of ceramic forms. In form the footed mortar is not easily distinguished from the Brazier.

The pestle was normally an elongated cylindrical or conical (occasionally oval) tool made to be grasped in the hand; the head was shaped to correspond to the curvature of the mortar with which it was used.

Courtesy of the Oriental Institute, the University of Chicago

70. Mortars and pestles, from Megiddo

Pestles are frequently made of basalt, but examples in granite and limestone are common.

See also MILLSTONE.

Fig. MOR 70.

Bibliography. See archaeological reports, such as: R. S. Lamon and G. M. Shipton, *Megiddo I* (1939), pls. 112-14. W. F. Albright, "Tell Beit Mirsim III," *AASOR*, vols. XXI-XXII (1941-43), pp. 83-84 and pls. 30:6-7 (64:12, 57:1, 3), 29:16 (63:32), 64:13 (simple and footed types); pp. 80-81 and pls. 27, 30, 57 (cosmetic palettes). C. C. McCown, *Tell en-Nasbeh I* (1947), pp. 249-50; p. 266 and pls. 92:1-4, 106; p. 68 and pl. 12:5-6 (in imitation of a ceramic form); pl. 97:5.

R. W. FUNK

2. חמר. A building material. Generally mortar was of clay, for which the same Hebrew word is used. Its basic meaning is "red." The binding mortar was of the same material as bricks, generally mixed with straw and applied while damp and soft. The Israelites in Egypt were compelled to work in both mortar and brick (Exod. 1:14). The foe from the N is to "trample on rulers as on mortar, as the potter treads the clay" (Isa. 41:25). In Nah. 3:14 there is a reference to treading mortar in connection with the brick mold. The builders of the tower of Babel had brick for stone and bitumen (KJV "slime") for mortar (Gen. 11:3).

Another word, עפר, which means "dust," is translated "mortar" in the KJV (RSV better PLASTER; Lev. 14:42, 45).

In the proverbial "untempered mortar" (Ezek. 13:10-11, 14) the translation "mortar" for תפל is conjectural and italicized in the KJV; the word means something weak or insipid (RSV WHITEWASH). Evidently the reference is to covering the wall with something that would not harden sufficiently to resist a shower. Mortar was not always used in building a wall. Excavations have uncovered many walls with stones so accurately cut that they hold together without other binding.

See also ARCHITECTURE; BRICK; MASON.

O. R. SELLERS

MORTAR, THE [מכתש, *makhtēsh*] (Zeph. 1:11); KJV MAKTESH măk′tĕsh. The quarter of Jerusalem in which the silver traders and the silversmiths conducted their business under the reign of Josiah. It is mentioned in connection with the Mishneh, or SECOND QUARTER, and with the FISH GATE. It has been tentatively identified with the upper course of the Valley of the Tyropoeon (*see* JERUSALEM § 6*d*); this is a plausible, yet unproven, localization.

Bibliography. J. Simons, *Jerusalem in the OT* (1952), p. 52, note 2.

G. A. BARROIS

MORTGAGE [ערב, take on pledge, give in pledge, exchange] (Neh. 5:3; cf. Gen. 43:9; 44:32; Ezra 9:2; Ps. 106:35; Prov. 6:1; 11:15; 14:10; 17:18; 20:16; 24:21; 27:13; Isa. 36:8 [cf. II Kings 18:23]; 38:14; Jer. 30:21; etc.).

The word "mortgage" is used only once in the Bible, as a verb in a passage depicting the internal economic conditions in Judah in the time of Nehemiah and Ezra (see Neh. 5:1-13). Several charges were made by the poor against their wealthy Jewish brethren; among these is the complaint that it was necessary for the poor to mortgage their fields and houses during the famine in order to buy food. They were also obliged to borrow money in order to pay taxes (vs. 4).

H. F. BECK

MOSAIC PAVEMENT [רצפה]. While the Hebrew word, from רצף, "fit together," may mean simply "pavement" (so KJV), the context in Esth. 1:6 clearly shows that it refers to the mosaic pavement at SUSA.

MOSERAH mō′ zə rə [מוסרה] (Deut. 10:6); KJV MOSERA. Alternately: MOSEROTH —rōth [מסרות] (Num. 33:30-31). A stopping place of the Israelites in the wilderness after they left Beeroth Bene-jaakan. According to this account, Aaron died at Moserah and was buried there, and his son Eleazar became a priest in his stead. This is a variant tradition of the death and burial of Aaron. According to Num. 33:38, he died at Mount Hor. Moreover, in vs. 30 we have a different order of itinerary: the Israelites came to Bene-jaakan after they had left Moseroth.

The locality is unknown.

J. L. MIHELIC

*__MOSES__ mō′zĭz, —zəs [משה, *see below*]. Leader of the Hebrew tribes in their exodus from Egypt and during their consolidation prior to the invasion of Canaan.

The exodus from Egypt is the creative center of the OT. In countless ways the literature of Israel reveals the magnetic power of this event for generations far removed from it in time.

When Israel went forth from Egypt,
the house of Jacob from a people of strange language,
Judah became his sanctuary,
Israel his dominion. (Ps. 114:1-2.)

The Exodus is the hour of Israel's birth as a people. It is this moment which remains decisive even when the family tree is traced back through the ancestors, Abraham, Isaac, and Jacob, whose lives God orders in anticipation of the deliverance from Egypt. The Exodus also maintains its creative priority over the circumstances of Israel's life in Canaan. The OT does not consistently attempt to conceal the significant changes Israel undergoes on account of its situation in Canaan. The defining marks of Israel's identity, the delineation of common responsibility and destiny, the ethnic complexion of the Israelite folk, and the forms for ordering its varied life, all change with time and circumstance. Yet, throughout the centuries of Israelite life which the OT mirrors, the Exodus remains the symbol by which subsequent events are interpreted. It persists as the judge and corrective of this newness. Witness to this can be found in the OT in narrative, poetry, legal formulation, cultic rubric, prophetic oracle, and eschatological rhapsody.

1. Historicity
   a. Biblical evidence
   b. Analysis of Pentateuchal traditions
   c. Appraisal
2. Background
   a. Nativity story
   b. Levite ancestry
   c. Egyptian influence
   d. Midianite influence
3. Mission
   a. Commissioning
   b. Task in Egypt
   c. Passover
   d. Crossing the sea
   e. Life in the wilderness
   f. Revelation at Mount Sinai
4. OT summary
5. Moses in postbiblical Judaism
   a. Hellenistic Judaism
   b. Palestinian Judaism
6. Moses in the NT
Bibliography

1. Historicity. The link between Moses and Israel's emergence from Egypt is such an intimate one in the biblical narrative that it seems almost impossible to question its authenticity. However, when the connection between Moses and the birth of Israel is examined more closely, two seemingly contradictory things appear. These call for investigation.

a. Biblical evidence. Moses appears, first of all, to dominate the exodus traditions. The magnetic power of the man attracts attention from every strand of biblical material, early or late, which sets its story in the exodus period. The great variety of roles which this same material ascribes to Moses is an equally impressive phenomenon. He performs almost every function attached to the offices and callings that were subsequently known in Israel (important exceptions were kingship and priesthood). He represents in germinal form the whole future life of Israel. Condensed into this one man are the figures of prophet, priest, judge (a foreshadowing of the king), lawgiver, intercessor, victor, exile, fugitive, shepherd, guide, healer, miracle-worker, man of God, and rebel. Moses does not merely assist at the birth of Israel; in him Israel is born. So in closest parallelism it can be affirmed that God

> made known his ways to Moses,
> his acts to the people of Israel
> (Ps. 103:7).

And yet a second observation must be made about Moses. In the oldest reference to the exodus event now contained in the OT, Moses is not mentioned. It is only Yahweh's triumph that is to be celebrated after Israel has escaped from the Egyptians:

> Sing to Yahweh, for he has triumphed gloriously;
> the horse and his rider he has thrown into the sea
> (Exod. 15:21).

Similarly, Israel's ancient creedal recital of the mighty deeds of God makes no mention of Moses in connection with the deliverance from Egypt (Deut. 26:5-9). In the biblical material outside the Hexateuch, the attention paid to Moses is almost equally slim. Among the pre-exilic prophets only Jeremiah (15:1) and possibly Micah (6:4) give his name, although Hosea alludes to him (12:13—H 12:14). Later prophetic material sees no significant increase. Moses' name does occur somewhat more frequently in Kings, Chronicles, and Psalms—a development probably due to the influence of the Deuteronomic picture of Moses as the lawgiver.

Since such large blocks of the OT pass over Moses in silence, suspicion is raised about the historicity of this mighty figure. He looms large in the Pentateuch, but perhaps his dominant position there results from the piety of later generations of Israelites. If they have not actually created the figure of the nation's founder, perhaps they have magnified his importance and pictured him in such a way as to derive sanction for their own practices and values.

Yet the infrequent mention of Moses outside the Pentateuch may be due to forces of a very different sort. The cult of heroic personalities is unable to gain a foothold in Israel's faith. Since Yahweh is the primary actor in every event, it is to him, and not to his human agent, that faith is attached once the event has occurred. Human agency is not insignificant in the OT understanding of God's ways, but no historical or human pattern can dictate the future.

Hosea may allude to Moses long after the latter's day, but he calls him a prophet, because the authentic prophet is the one who points away from himself to the divine word and deed. "By a prophet Yahweh brought Israel up from Egypt" (Hos. 12:13—H 12:14). Consequently, the failure of the oldest literary fragments in the Pentateuch to mention Moses is not strong evidence of his nonhistoricity. If Moses is not named in the old creedal statement of Deut. 26:5-9, neither is anyone else.

The resurgence of interest in Moses, apparent in the D and P literature, indicates an attempt to recover Israel's earlier dynamic in the face of the impending collapse of the Judean state. In some sense, it is as if the mission of Moses had not been fulfilled and hence demands a recasting of his work and witness in fresh garb. This development is akin to the OT's attitude about prophets. The name of a prophet is rarely mentioned after the period of his active ministry. If a prophet's word is fulfilled, his role is concluded. It was only because his word about Jerusalem had remained unfulfilled, that Micah was mentioned a hundred years after his time in defense of Jeremiah (Jer. 26:18). In the OT, frequency of citation is not by itself an indication either of historicity or of significance.

b. Analysis of Pentateuchal traditions. Another method for investigating the historicity of Moses employs analysis of the history of the traditions in which he figures. The exodus and wilderness traditions, in which Moses is now a principal character, appear to consist of four large themes: the exodus from Egypt, the revelation at Sinai, the wandering in the wilderness, and the entrance into the Promised Land. The biblical story of Moses proceeds through these themes, and the ability to reconstruct his career obviously depends upon the interlocking movement of events from theme to theme. It has been long recognized, however, that the theme "the revelation at Sinai" shows evidence of only a very loose connection with the other themes. It appears as an excursus, interrupting the narrative at the end of Exod. 18 and allowing it to resume in Num. 10:29.

Recently a more radical thesis has been advanced about the history of the Pentateuchal themes. It has been argued that originally there was no integral connection between any of them. Their present form, in which Moses is the great unifying figure found in them all, is held to be secondary. Moses has become the link binding these once-unrelated thematic episodes into a narrative sequence. This obviously means that the framework of Moses' career, moving from Egypt to the mountains of Transjordan, cannot be considered historical. The historicity of Moses as a person—in a minimal sense—has not been denied, but it has been held that the only reliable datum about his life is the tradition of his death and burial at a Transjordanian site (Deut. 34:6). Beginning with this meager information, the Israelite tradition has clothed Moses with a substantial history and, in creating him, has created the present Pentateuchal narrative sequence. *See* PENTATEUCH.

c. Appraisal. One of the fundamental supports for the hypothesis just described is the conclusion that the Pentateuchal themes were, in fact, originally separate cycles of tradition, complete in themselves. This analysis is far from established, however. The theme "the revelation at Sinai" is, indeed, absent from Deut. 26:5-9, the creedal recitation of Yahweh's mighty deeds. But the other themes—exodus, wandering, land—are already united there. Furthermore, the omission of Sinai from this recitation is probably explained by the suggestion that the creedal formula was recited in a ceremony of covenant renewal—i.e., in a setting where the Sinai theme was presented liturgically rather than narratively. Figs. SIN 63-64.

The most serious objection to any nihilistic view of the work of Moses is the difficulty it creates for understanding early Israelite history in Palestine. The Song of Deborah (*ca.* 1125 B.C.) indicates that common action was undertaken by several Israelite tribes approximately a century after the invasion of Canaan (Judg. 5). This concerted action is motivated by common allegiance to Yahweh, in whose cause the tribes are bound together as the "people of Yahweh." Without the prior activity of Moses it becomes quite difficult to give an effective explanation of this Israelite tribal "confederacy." If analysis of the Pentateuchal themes leaves the traditions of pre-Palestinian Israel dismembered, then they describe only disjointed episodes involving unconnected groups of people coming together in the land of Canaan. What brought them together with such swiftness and distinctiveness as the Song of Deborah reveals is then hard to discover.

Moreover, if credence is to be denied the general biblical framework of Moses' career, the task of explaining why and how later generations created such a person becomes a formidable one. Moses is a central figure in both the J and the E narratives and, presumably, also in the earlier, common tradition upon which both narratives apparently drew. A common tradition of this sort must have been in existence by the beginning of the Israelite monarchy (*ca.* 1020 B.C.), if not earlier. This means that one must explain the entrance within a span of not more than two hundred years of "Israelitish" elements into Canaan, the emergence of Israel as a self-conscious and effective entity, and the expansion of Moses into the unquestioned position of founder and leader of all Israel. No one can prove, of course, that such a development could not have occurred without the Moses whom the Pentateuch pictures. But it is easily possible to consider the biblical account of Mosaic leadership a more credible explanation of Israel's early period in Palestine than any other available thesis.

2. Background. The only source of information for the life and work of Moses is the Bible. Archaeological evidence may confirm the essential credibility of biblical events to which Moses is related, such as the enslavement of Hebrews in Egypt and the assault upon Canaan. But it affords no specific confirmation of either the existence or the work of Moses. Within the Bible some retrospective deductions about Moses' influence may be drawn from the faith and practices of post-Mosaic Israel, but hope of reconstructing any coherent career of Moses depends mainly upon the oldest versions of Israel's traditions related by the Yahwist and Elohist historians. Although Deuteronomic and Priestly accounts add details to the picture, they are of more significance in indicating the impact of Mosaic religion upon their respective circumstances.

a. Nativity story. The story of Moses' birth employs folklore to introduce the future deliverer (Exod. 2). Folkloristic themes suggest dimensions of meaning and mystery for which the reader should be alert. Appropriate portents, e.g., announce a man of extraordinary powers and suggest an ominous future. In spite of its own edict, the Egyptian throne gives shelter to the powerless infant who will one day humiliate it and face it with death. Such themes do not need to be originally Israelite. The story of the baby set afloat in a basket of bulrushes, e.g., resembles the birth story of Sargon of Agade (*see* SARGON 1), who was rescued from the Euphrates and became, in his adulthood, the founder of the great Babylonian city-state of Akkad. Moses is thus introduced in imagery common to ancient Near Eastern expectations of extraordinary achievement and deliverance.

b. Levite ancestry. The connection of Moses' ancestry with the house of Levi (Exod. 2:1) may reflect tendencies of another sort. The contradiction between Exod. 2:1-2, where Moses appears as the first-born of his parents, and references implying that Miriam and Aaron are older than he (cf. Exod. 2:7; 6:20; 7:7; Num. 26:59), suggests the possibility that Moses' Levite connection is not original. If not, it would have originated with interests eager to attach Moses to a priestly family. Although Moses performs sacerdotal functions, he is not pictured in the bulk of the traditions primarily or exclusively as a priest. Priestly actions are undertaken by others—by Aaron and the Levites (Exod. 32:5, 29), and by young men, apparently laymen, who offer the sacrifices at the ratification of the covenant (24:5).

c. Egyptian influence. The tradition of Moses' connection with Egyptian circles seems authentic, however. His name is apparently the old perfective of the Egyptian verb "to be born," which is frequently combined with divine titles to form personal names, as in Ra-meses. The derivation attributed to Pharaoh's daughter: "She named him Moses, . . . 'Because I drew him out of the water' " (Exod. 2:10), represents popular etymology based upon assonance. The use of names of Egyptian derivation like Phinehas, Hophni, and Merari (probably also Aaron and Miriam) for several generations in Levitical genealogies (Exod. 6:16, 25; I Sam. 1:3) is additional evidence of Egyptian connection, although not certain proof that either Moses or the Levites have an Egyptian background. Apart from the birth story, there is no indication of Moses' connection with the Egyptian court. No reference is made to it in Moses' negotiations with Pharaoh, although the absence of a language barrier between the two might have been understood against this feature of the narrative. Attempts to connect Moses with the learning of Egypt and the religious reform of the so-called monotheistic pharaoh, AKH-EN-ATON, have not been noticeably successful (cf. Acts 7:22). Egyptian influences of many sorts may have touched Moses, but the evidence is not available to establish or refute such connection. What is certain is that Moses' awesome energy and power stem from another source.

d. Midianite influence. Moses' connection with MIDIAN is well attested. Tradition is not likely to have invented such involvement in view of the later hostility between Israelites and Midianites (cf. Judg. 6:2; Isa. 9:4—H 9:3). Tradition pictures Moses as finding refuge in Midian after fleeing from Egypt. Here he also finds employment as a shepherd, and Zipporah, daughter of Jethro, becomes his wife (Exod. 2:15-3:1). Zipporah is perhaps to be identified with the "Cushite woman," whom Moses marries according to another narrative (Num. 12:1).

Whether Moses and Mosaic Yahwism are more deeply indebted to Jethro, the "priest of Midian," for cultic and cultural instruction and forms is a question long debated. One aspect of the question involves the possible origin of the divine name Yahweh among the Kenite clan to which Jethro belonged (*see* GOD, NAMES OF; JETHRO). Apart from this highly specialized problem, it is likely that in its earliest days, as all through its history, Israel borrowed both cultic and cultural forms from its environment in order to express its life as the community of Yahweh.

3. Mission. The account which Israel preserves of its founder's call reveals a perspective about itself and its own vocation (Exod. 3–4). Moses is called to bring a people to Yahweh, and this mission which thus constitutes him Yahweh's servant also constitutes the people whom he serves. In this regard, the limited character of the task assigned to Moses appears to be a crucial feature in his call. He is called to engage himself at the outset of Israel's life only, not to make himself the enduring center of that life. No timeless significance is to be attached to his person. No words of his are to be transmitted as the sacred lore about God. Moses is to bring the sons of Israel out of Egypt under a sign that points them to the future; the guarantee of God's presence is simply that "when you have brought forth the people out of Egypt, you shall serve God upon this mountain" (Exod. 3:12). The religion with which Moses is to be involved will be able to survive without him (although it may also rediscover him), just as the entrance into the Promised Land will occur without his presence or direction (Deut. 34:4). Israel is thus free to meet the future instructed, but not shackled, by the past.

a. Commissioning. Moses does not volunteer to be the liberator of Israel. Although he appears in the vicinity of Mount Sinai as a sequel to his concern for the oppressed Hebrews in Egypt (Exod. 2:11-15), little else suggests him to be a firebrand in the cause of liberty. Nor is Moses a man of unusual piety. He does not come to the "mountain of God" (Exod. 3:1) as a religious exercise. He stumbles unsuspectingly upon what proves to be a holy place, and he does this in the course of his duties as a shepherd. Perhaps the mountain was already a shrine of the Kenites. This seems unlikely, however, in view of Moses' failure to mention his experience there when he requests leave from Jethro to return to Egypt (Exod. 4:18). In short, Moses is drafted for his job.

Moses is certainly no *tabula rasa* prior to the encounter with Yahweh at the burning bush. What turns him into a man of destiny, however, is the convergence of a concrete, historical task and the new knowledge of God which grasps him. This galvanizes the extraordinary and diverse powers of the man in an endeavor which will henceforth dominate him utterly. He is a man set apart under God's election and endowment, charismatically empowered, for a particular task in a moment of time. He can misconstrue his calling as though it were a summons to eloquence, which he lacks (Exod. 4:10). But in fact his calling is to obey Him in whose purposes Moses' inability will prove adequate: "Now therefore go, and I will be with your mouth and teach you what you shall speak" (vs. 12).

Yahweh's disclosure of himself to Moses is portrayed through the magnificent symbols of the burning bush, the holy ground, and the divine name. In revealing himself, what Yahweh discloses is that he is involved in the plight of the Hebrews in Egypt and that he intends to act in this setting. This is tantamount, in the biblical idiom, to communicating one's name or character, and explicit disclosure of the divine name climaxes Yahweh's meeting with Moses (*see* NAME). Both the E and the P historians indicate that the proper divine name Yahweh was not known prior to its disclosure to Moses, although, in effect, it was Yahweh whom the patriarchs knew under another name (Exod. 3:13-15; 6:2-3). J makes this latter identification explicit by employing the name Yahweh from earliest times (Gen. 4:26). The significance of the divine name for the story of Moses, however, is not to be judged in terms of its novelty. The name does not conceal esoteric religious information but proclaims a God who has openly declared his intention to act in the affairs of Egypt. What Moses has to convey to his kinsmen in Egypt, therefore, is not secret learning about divine mysteries, but the character of the times in which they live. Since God is the primary actor in human events, to read the times aright will be to disclose him.

Whatever the previous history of the name Yahweh may have been, its derivation from the verb הוה in Exod. 3:14 (*see* GOD, NAMES OF) underscores the intensive and enduring nature of Yahweh's presence in the events of every age. "But I will be with you" (vs. 12), is the dynamic explication of Yahweh's name and also the promise which fashions Israel's destiny from beginning to end (cf. the elaboration of this theme in Isa. 43:1-13).

The Priestly account of the call of Moses is placed after Moses' return to Egypt (Exod. 6:2–7:13). It serves as divine reassurance after Moses' initial audience with the Pharaoh has failed. The theme of God's action in the historical situation is still present, although the Exodus is now viewed as a less epochal divine disclosure. For P it is the covenant God made with the patriarchs which warrants his present action in Egypt (Exod. 2:24). For P the role of the priest at the founding of the nation is also of great interest. Hence, Aaron stands alongside Moses and executes the word which the latter has received from God (7:2). But as genealogy testifies, it is now Aaron's descendants, not Moses', who constitute the living continuation of the Levite line and the current extension of the work of Moses (6:25).

b. Task in Egypt. Moses is sent from Sinai to Egypt. He is to interpret what occurred to him at Sinai in its impact upon those who are in Egypt, Egyptian as well as Hebrew. He is the mediator who bears what has happened to himself to the people for whom it has happened. He is singled out in such extraordinary fashion that no one else is like him. But all this occurs so that Yahweh may create a community of his own from a motley group, bearing almost no marks of communal identity.

Thus, Moses' task is defined by the scope of Yahweh's intention. It involves more than religious instruction, for ideas alone do not create a community. It involves leading a group into and through a common experience that will be new and perilous. This experience will then have to be given enduring form in the social, economic, legal, and cultic structures necessary for communal living in the world. And although these structures may be formally patterned upon those of Israel's neighbors, they must also be able to bear the meaning appropriate to a community created by a unique historical experience.

The initial task of Moses is to win the allegiance of the "mixed multitude" (Exod. 12:38) in Egypt and to devise a strategy for their departure. The biblical account of Moses' efforts is cast in highly dramatic form, for the ultimate protagonists are Yahweh and Pharaoh. Behind Pharaoh is arrayed the entire power of the Egyptian state, marshaled in its magicians and armies as well as in its embodiment of divinity, the crown. Although the gods of Egypt are mentioned only once as Yahweh's opponents (vs. 12), their power is at stake in the contest. It underlies the occult arts of the magicians of Egypt, as well as the presumptuous arrogance of the Pharaoh, who means to show that there is none like himself in all the earth (5:2; 9:16-17).

Moses is equipped with extraordinary powers which are intended to validate him before his people and win Pharaoh's compliance with the divine order: "Let my people go, that they may hold a feast to me in the wilderness" (Exod. 4:30–5:1). The essentially dramatic and symbolic character of the Mosaic signs and plagues is indicated by their failure to carry conviction (*see* PLAGUES OF EGYPT). They are schematized in the seesaw battle between faith and doubt, obedience and defiance; and their ability to persuade can give way before Israel's doubts or Pharaoh's obstinacy (8:15—H 8:11; 14:11-12).

From these stories it is impossible, then, to reconstruct the methods by which Moses rallied his people and accomplished their departure from Egypt. The Israelites are pictured as murmuring frequently against his leadership (Exod. 14:11-12; 16:3; Num. 11:4-5), but against this view must be set prophetic traditions which picture the exodus period as the time of Israel's fidelity (Jer. 2:1-3; Hos. 9:10*a-b*). The account of tension between Moses and his people may have been colored by the tension between prophet and people characteristic of a later time. This may also be true of the P representation that the people initially did not trust Moses (Exod. 6:9), a view contrary to that in the older J source (3:18; 4:31).

Tendencies to explain Moses' power by categorizing him as an exhibitionist wonder-worker, adept in the secrets of magic, do not succeed. The power wielded by Moses in the plague stories or in the war against Amalek (Exod. 17) or in the erection of the brazen serpent (Num. 21:9) is not glorified as fundamental to his mission. The strength of the man—not to mention his weakness—is too diversified to allow such a development. He cannot be explained as a wizard. He is unable to alter circumstances at will. His followers can disbelieve him and even struggle with him for power (Num. 12; 16). He dies without setting foot on the land which is the goal of his labors. And quite appropriately, his grave is unknown and cannot be made into a cultic site (Deut. 34:6). Thus, although the account of how Moses rallies his people may be illuminated by features of magic provenance, it cannot be explained by them.

The negotiations between Moses and the Pharaoh must be judged in similar fashion. Since Yahweh claims obedience from every aspect of his world, the throne of Egypt, as well as men and nature, must bow before him. In order to accomplish his purposes, he will do as he wills with what he has made, "that you may know that the earth is the LORD's" (Exod. 9:29). As long as Pharaoh's consent to the demands of Moses is given with reservations or may be revoked, the issue between him and Moses can never be concluded. Yahweh demands total surrender from the world, as he will from his covenant people (20:3), and the scenes at Pharaoh's court are described accordingly.

Consequently, there is little in the biblical narrative upon which to reconstruct Moses' strategy in Egypt. In itself the tradition that the Pharaoh granted audiences to the Israelite leader is not implausible. If the Exodus (*see* EXODUS, ROUTE OF) is to be dated in the early thirteenth century B.C., as much evidence now suggests, the Egyptian dynasty involved would be that of the Ramessides (Nineteenth Dynasty, *ca.* 1308-1216), who are known to have permitted appeals to the royal court from their slaves. In the same period the Egyptian capital was relocated in the Delta area at Avaris, the vicinity of the Hebrew settlement (Gen. 46:28-34; Exod. 2:5-10; *see* GOSHEN; EGYPT). Hence such features of the biblical story as Moses' movements between the palace and the Hebrew enclave or the labor of the Hebrew slaves on the Ramesside building projects in the Delta (Exod. 1:11) would be possible.

c. Passover. Israel's departure from Egypt is preceded, in the biblical account, by rites of cultic character (Exod. 12:1–13:16). The roots of later Israelite observances—PASSOVER AND FEAST OF UNLEAVENED BREAD, and dedication of the FIRST-BORN—are here planted in the soil of the exodus deliverance. From the complex cluster of ideas and rites connecting these observances with the Exodus, it is apparent that they are adaptations of heterogeneous, pre-Israelite practices. Borrowed from a sharply different interpretation of man's existence, in which they once commemorated the recurrent features of nature, they have been reinterpreted to celebrate a uniquely revealing and redeeming moment of history. Now they assert that Yahweh has taken possession of his people. Whether Moses is to be connected with such reinterpretation may be an open question, but scarcely more can be said than that it would be appropriate to his work as interpreter of his people's experience in word and form. Interpretation of these observances is not unalterably fixed in any period of the OT, although the essential testimony to Israel's origin in the divine deliverance from Egypt remains unchanged. The impact of Moses upon Israel's self-understanding did not lead to canonization of the earliest forms of the exodus traditions.

d. Crossing the sea. Historical and literary analysis pinpoints the Israelites' crossing of the Sea of Reeds (*yam sûph*) as the catalytic moment in the experience of deliverance (Exod. 14:15-22). Just as the immediate reaction is to interpret the event as Yahweh's triumphant action (15:21), so considered reflection will necessitate interpreting all existence in its light (cf. Ps. 114; Isa. 51:9-11). In giving life to his people, Yahweh has asserted the subordination of nature and history to his ultimate purposes. Israel's future interpreters must view the life of man, situated at the juncture of nature and history, from this controlling perspective.

This critical moment is one in which the undisputed lordship of God can be shared with no one, not even Moses. The watchword which Moses proclaims asserts this: "Fear not, stand firm, and see the salvation of the LORD, which he will work for you today" (Exod. 14:13). Subsequent embellishments of what appears to be the earliest prose form of the story (vss. 15, 19*a*, 21*a*β-*b*α, 22*a*) seek to heighten the significance of Moses as well as the scope of the wonder (cf. vss. 16, 22, 26). Yet Moses' chief responsibility seems to be to maneuver the Israelites into a position between the Egyptians and the sea from which only Yahweh's aid can extricate them (vss. 1-4). The crossing of the sea does not glorify Mosaic strategy, therefore, but divine sufficiency. Yahweh alone is adequate to deliver his people. *See* RED SEA.

e. Life in the wilderness. A similar perspective colors the narrative of Israel's years in the wilderness (Exod. 15:22–18:27; Num. 10:29–31:54). Details of geography, logistics, and history are subordinate to the dominant concern with Yahweh's possession and nurture of his people. Framing the great core of dramatic and legal material now centered upon Israel's stay at Mount Sinai (Exod. 19:1–Num. 10:28) is a series of episodes recounting Israel's experiences in the wilderness. The narrative describes the struggle to survive—efforts to find water and food, to discover the way, to hold an oasis, to preserve unity and order within the ranks, to escape annihilation by foes. Clearly, Yahweh's deliverance of Israel at the Sea of Reeds has not transformed the harsh conditions of life in the Sinaitic Peninsula. But Yahweh is represented as involved in his people's struggle, preserving their life while at the same time testing their resolve to live as the people whom he has borne "on eagles' wings and brought" to himself (Exod. 19:4).

From whatever subsequent period they date, the biblical narratives of the Mosaic era are primarily concerned with the ultimate issue of Yahweh's mastery of men and events for his own purposes. Yet this does not lead to a caricature of either men or events. God chooses to give meaning to history, not to abrogate it. So the biblical account of Mosaic leadership during the wilderness years affords glimpses of Moses' character and tactics while also depicting the chief protagonist in the drama, Yahweh. Indeed, a rich and varied picture of Mosaic leadership is drawn.

On the one hand, Moses appears in radical self-denial as intercessor for his people (Exod. 32:30-33); on the other, in quick-tempered chafing under the burden of their care (Num. 11:10-15). "Turn from thy fierce wrath, and repent of this evil against thy people," as Moses implores Yahweh (Exod. 32:12), is a request very different in substance, although not in boldness, from: "Did I conceive all this people? Did I bring them forth, that thou shouldst say to me, 'Carry them in your bosom, as a nurse carries the sucking child . . . ?' " (Num. 11:12).

Again, while Moses appears to be only incidental to the provision of quail and manna (Exod. 16:12 P) and at most only an executor of Yahweh's directions in obtaining water (15:22-25 J; 17:5-6 E), he acts independently on other occasions. He himself makes the decision to accept his father-in-law's proposal for accelerating judicial processes (18:13-27). The strategy in the battle against Amalek is devised without divine instruction: "Moses said to Joshua, 'Choose for us men, and go out, fight with Amalek;

tomorrow I will stand on the top of the hill with the rod of God in my hand' " (17:9). However, the posture assumed by Moses, the outstretched hands, and the rod of God are intended as evidence of the present power of God, apparent only to faith.

Many of the wilderness episodes appear to have occurred in or near Kadesh-barnea (Num. 13:26; *see* KADESH), an oasis somewhere SW of the Dead Sea. The battle with the Amalekites may well have been a struggle for possession of this oasis (Exod. 17:8-16). The persistent enmity between Israelites and Amalekites (cf. I Sam. 15) may stem in part from this critical struggle for survival. It is also probable that Moses sought to consolidate his leadership of the people during a long stay at Kadesh. Apart from the recurring theme that hardship causes Israel to disbelieve the promises of God and to revolt against Moses' authority, several pointed attacks upon his authority appear to have been launched at Kadesh. Miriam and Aaron seek to undermine the position of their brother, ostensibly because of his marriage, but actually because of their claim to prophetic office: "Has Yahweh indeed spoken only through Moses? Has he not spoken through us also?" (Num. 12:2). DATHAN and Abiram allege that Moses' failure to gain the promised "land flowing with milk and honey" has been compounded by his own pretensions as to princely authority (16: 12-15 JE). The ill-fated revolt of KORAH, now interwoven in the narrative of Dathan and Abiram's agitation, is motivated by a charge of more priestly cast —namely, that Moses and Aaron have claimed superior sacerdotal status and denied that "all the congregation are holy" (16:1*a*, 3-11, P).

Separatist tensions and power struggles within the emerging wilderness community certainly seem credible. The task at hand was an enormous one. A community had been created almost out of nothing by a radically reorienting event. The endeavor to articulate its implications and to subject inherited and traditional forms of life to these implications was as demanding as the job was boundless. Little wonder that many chafed under a redemption that made slave rations in Egypt seem preferable to the desert fare of freemen. Little wonder that there were rival interpretations and definitions of what Israel was. Indeed, the fundamental problems in this early period were those that would engage the OT community throughout its entire life.

That all was not strife and contention in the wilderness, however, is suggested by the consecration of the seventy-two elders to aid Moses in bearing the burden of the people (Num. 11:16-30). They receive a share in the same energizing spirit which rests upon Moses in an incomparable manner. Just how far Moses is from wanting to assert totalitarian claims to authority is indicated by his exclamation: "Would that all Yahweh's people were prophets, that Yahweh would put his spirit upon them!" (vs. 29). Many scholars, however, believe that this story reflects a later situation (cf. Gen. 46; Num. 26).

It has been suggested that the formative role of Kadesh in the early life of Israel is considerably more extensive than is now indicated by the biblical narratives. One thesis would recognize in Kadesh a pre-Mosaic cult and legal center, under the direction of Aaron and Miriam. Marah, where Yahweh made a "statute and an ordinance" for Israel (Exod. 15:25), is perhaps to be equated with Kadesh (cf. Exod. 15: 22-27 with 17:1-7; Num. 20:1-3, 13). This would then identify Kadesh as a center for proclaiming and administering law. If Aaron and Miriam are Kadesh figures, their quarrel with Moses about his marriage (Num. 12) may conceal a deeper struggle in which they were dispossessed and supplanted by Moses as proprietor and priest of the center.

Undoubtedly, Israel's stay at Kadesh provided more than a respite from the rigors of the Sinaitic Peninsula. If Jethro's visit with his son-in-law is to be located at Kadesh (Exod. 18), it would be here that Israel adopted certain judicial forms proposed by Jethro (vss. 13-27). What is apparently implied is that Midianite-Kenite judicial institutions were imitated by Moses, thus introducing into Israel a lay judiciary and a distinctive method, perhaps the sacred lot, for obtaining instruction directly from God. Since Jethro is acknowledged as the "priest of Midian," his competence would extend also to cultic as well as legal matters, and it would be natural to assume Israelite indebtedness at this point to Midianite-Kenite forms. Jethro appears to act as priest on this occasion, which the biblical account now depicts as a kind of family reunion, although some obscurity is created by the statement that Jethro "took" (not "offered," as in the RSV) "a burnt offering and sacrifices to God" (Exod. 18:12). Whether or not the ensuing notice: "Aaron came with all the elders of Israel to eat bread with Moses' father-in-law before God" (vs. 12), implies that Jethro was inducting them into the cult of Yahweh depends upon the conclusion drawn about Jethro's connection with the origin of Yahwism in Israel. *See* JETHRO.

Two other features of Israel's wilderness encampment connected with Moses deserve attention: the tent and the ARK OF THE COVENANT. The tent, pitched outside the camp, is a tent of meeting between Yahweh and Moses, and in this proper sense it is a cult object that pertains to Moses alone (Exod. 33:7-11 E). The divine presence is manifested at the tent, not because the Deity maintains uninterrupted residence there, but because he graciously wills to approach Moses there. The descending PILLAR OF CLOUD AND FIRE announces the advent of the God who wills to let himself be consulted, but who, in effect, must also be sought while he may be found (cf. Num. 11:24-25; 12:5-8). As a cult symbol of the presence of the holy God of Sinai, who does not abandon his people when they depart from that mountain, the tent is appropriate to Mosaic Yahwism.

The suitability of the ark to the wilderness period has been more contested. Admittedly, it figures extensively in Israel's settlement in Canaan until David removes it to Jerusalem (cf. II Sam. 4–6). It appears to have been a symbol especially adapted to affirming God's presence with his people in times of military conflict and struggle for survival. As such it need not have been out of place as a wilderness shrine. One of the oldest OT fragments connects it with such a setting: "Whenever the ark set out, Moses said, 'Arise, O Yahweh, and let thy enemies be scattered; and let them that hate thee flee before thee.' And when it rested, he said, 'Return, O Yahweh, to the ten thousand thousands of Israel' " (Num. 10:35-36). If the ark originally represented a portable throne upon which Yahweh was conceived as invisibly enthroned, its power as a symbol in both the wilderness and conquest periods is understandable.

The wilderness shrine of the P historians, the tabernacle (Exod. 25), incorporates elements from both tent and ark traditions. Features borrowed from the Davidic tabernacle (II Sam. 6:17) and the Solomonic temple have also been used to describe this imaginary construction, but its theological significance for P lies in the combination of emphases from the two ancient wilderness traditions. The tent, ancient symbol of God's gracious descent into the midst of his people, now houses the ark, ancient symbol of God's continuing presence with his people. The ark, set within P's tabernacle and provided with the "mercy seat on the top" (Exod. 25:21), is now made to witness to man's dependence on the redemptive mercy of God, mediated in Israel's cultic establishment. Thus, the original witness of the tent of meeting to God's transcendent majesty finds an echo in the priestly theology. *See* TABERNACLE.

f. Revelation at Mount Sinai. Since Moses has been pre-eminently the man of the law in Jewish and Christian tradition, it appears incongruous at first that uncertainty should exist about the exact scope and character of legal material attributable to him. It is, however, highly significant that the actual role of Moses in Israel's emergent years did not stultify future legal, cultic, or social developments. From the fundamental beginning made through his agency, further wrestling with the will and guidance of the living God could be expected. Variations in the transmission of the law, adaptations of it to new circumstances, and existence of multiple forms of the Decalogue testify that this did happen. Declaration and interpretation of the divine will remained alive in Israel's legal and prophetic movements.

The vitality of Israel's legal heritage makes a chronological reconstruction of its manifestations difficult. Amendments, additions, rearrangements, and codifications took place without regard to the niceties associated with modern jurisprudence. The cluster of material now attached to the revelation at Mount Sinai is diverse in date, structure, and content. Its literary connections are largely with the Priestly Pentateuchal material, including Exod. 25–31; 35–40; Leviticus; Num. 1–10:28, speaking generally. JE material is found in Exod. 19–24; 32–34. Since Deuteronomic legal formulation is cast as an exhortation to those about to enter Canaan, its locale is not Sinai but Transjordan.

The form in which OT legal matter is now found reflects conditions of an agricultural society, settled in Canaan (e.g., Exod. 22:5-6—H 22:4-5). This does not imply that such a code as the "Covenant Code" (Exod. 20:23–23:19 E) originated entirely in post-Mosaic Israel. Legal traditions are long-lived and, in the case of Israel's legal formulations, reach back into the exodus period, as well as into the common legal heritage of the Semitic world (*see* LAW IN THE OT). The age of a tradition, legal or otherwise, is not established by the date when it was reduced to writing.

Efforts to isolate legal material of Mosaic origin are closely related to attempted reconstructions of Mosaic Yahwism, in which the Sinaitic covenant is central. The way in which the covenant relationship is conceived determines the kind of legal material which can be credited to Moses. However, questions about the connection of the Sinai theme with the other themes of the exodus and wilderness traditions have been indicated above (*see* § 1*b*). If the story of Israel at Sinai originally existed as a separate tradition, unconnected with its present context, serious question would be raised about the part Moses plays in the story. It might be supposed that he was imported into the Sinai narrative from an original connection with the Exodus. Or, on the other hand, the apparent disjunction between the Sinai theme and the other Pentateuchal themes may be due to the history of the respective traditions rather than to the events which underlie them. That is to say, the attachment of Moses to both groups of events would be original, but the traditions would have developed in their several, separate ways as determined by later cultic and cultural forces. It should be noted, however, that the exodus and Sinai themes are already linked in the Decalogue. The initial words spoken by the divine lawgiver are: "I am the LORD your God, who brought you out of the land of Egypt" (Exod. 20:2). *See* § 1*c above.*

Thus, the revelation at Mount Sinai confirms and climaxes the deliverance from Egypt. The dynamic exodus event is given enduring significance in the dynamic covenant relationship—a mutual, albeit unequal, commitment between Yahweh and Israel. "You have seen what I did to the Egyptians," says Yahweh, "and how I bore you on eagles' wings and brought you to myself. Now therefore, if you will obey my voice and keep my covenant, you shall be my own possession among all peoples; for all the earth is mine, and you shall be to me a kingdom of priests and a holy nation" (Exod. 19:4-6*a* J or E). The earth-shattering implications of dependence upon a deliverer who is holy are now dramatically portrayed. Even Mount Sinai trembles when "the LORD descends upon it in fire" in order to meet his people. The appropriate response which God seeks from his people, however, is not cowering fright, but free and vigorous obedience. As Moses interprets God's engagement with his people, "God has come to prove you, and that the fear of him may be before your eyes, that you may not sin" (20:20). In the present ordering of the biblical material the solemn ceremony of sealing the covenant (ch. 24) takes place only after God's will has been proclaimed in the law (chs. 20–23). Having promised obedience to this will, the people as a whole are bound to their covenant Lord in the power of sacrificial blood (24:6-8). Since the covenant is made with all Israel and not with individuals or groups, the nation's existence is thus grounded in him and governed by him. *See* COVENANT.

In the Sinai narrative the characteristic mark of Mosaic Yahwism is apparent: the intensely personal, dynamic will of the holy God, who claims exclusive allegiance from all areas of life. His will is formulated in two general types of law found in the Pentateuch (*see* LAW IN THE OT). The type which occurs more frequently formulates requirements conditionally, describing specific penalties for specific actions (cf.

Exod. 21:26-27). The casuistic formula employed is part of the common Semitic legal heritage. The other type of law states the divine requirement unconditionally: "You shall not utter a false report" (23:1). The Decalogue is of this latter type, and probably in its original form contained only pithy, unconditional commands, such as: "You shall have no other gods before me" (20:3).

The origin of unconditional law must lie in Israel's unique encounter with the divine lawgiver as holy, personal will. Moses, the interpreter of this encounter, may be responsible for the creation of this kind of legal formulation. The DECALOGUE of Exod. 20 in its original, brief form could thus come from Moses himself, although there are significant difficulties for this view.

The tables of the law with which Moses is provided in the context of the golden-calf story do not come into consideration at this point. Presumably they would include more than a compact decalogue, being inscribed on both sides and thus necessitating Moses' unexpectedly long stay on the mountain (Exod. 32:1, 15). The so-called "ritual decalogue" of Exod. 34:14-26 is not a likely repository of Mosaic legislation either. It reflects conditions of an agricultural society and is, in fact, a probable fragment of the J "Covenant Code" rather than a decalogue.

What stands out clearly, however, in all the Sinai narratives is that it is Moses who proclaims Yahweh as the God of uncontainable energy and passion, a "jealous God" (Exod. 34:14), who wills in grace and in judgment to be Lord. Without expressing itself in abstract terms about the existence or nonexistence of other gods, Mosaic Yahwism knows a God from whose demands no power in heaven or earth can provide an escape (*see* MONOTHEISM). It was this witness which the prophets recovered in later centuries, and with which they laid open their society before the claims of the living God. The power with which Moses stamped such witness upon biblical faith is the incomparable work he accomplished in the history of Yahweh's people.

4. OT summary. The biblical material itself acknowledges the incomparable position of Moses in very interesting ways. He is unique not only among his contemporaries but also among his successors. Post-Mosaic developments can be referred to him and set under the prestige of his name as in Deuteronomic and Priestly circles (*see* PENTATEUCH). But no imitator or rival appears in the history of Israel. Perhaps King David comes closest to being such—a fact that suggests the fateful character of the Davidic monarchy for OT faith.

The failure of Israel to create a "Mosaic type" of man or office is all the more striking when set against the Pentateuchal picture of Moses' incomparability. This is depicted in terms of intimacy and immediacy of relation to God. It is Moses who as a servant is entrusted by God with all his house. This servantship is one, not of servility, but of confidence and freest exchange between lord and servant. "With him I speak mouth to mouth, clearly, and not in dark speech; and he beholds the form of Yahweh" (Num. 12:7-8; cf. Isa. 50:4-5). The conversation is "face to face," the kind of stance in which "a man speaks to his friend" and does not dissimulate or conceal anything (Exod. 33:11). And even if Moses' request to be shown Yahweh's glory must be denied, the divine name is proclaimed to him. He is thereby set in relation to the deepest mystery of the Deity, who declares his name to mean: "I will be gracious to whom I will be gracious, and will show mercy on whom I will show mercy" (vs. 19). But the intimacy of relation to God which sets Moses apart is not a human or religious capacity, capable of imitation. "There has not arisen a prophet since in Israel like Moses, whom the LORD knew face to face" (Deut. 34:10). "Moses did not know that the skin of his face shone because he had been talking with God" (Exod. 34:29).

The absence of imitators of Moses is probably due to the same forces which prevent any characterization of him as a demigod. Moses must finally stand together with all the personages of the OT under a common judgment: there is no perfectly obedient man in Israel. Moses can be exalted in the story of the golden calf to the position of mediator between God and people. The renewal of the covenant with faithless Israel takes place in him, and he offers to set his life in place of those whose disobedience has made their life forfeit (Exod. 32:32; 34:9). Yet, just as his position as mediator confirms the distance between God and man, so his own career finally sets him on the side of men (cf. 32:33). The "epitaph" which concludes that career underscores the "not yet" of every human attainment when compared with the promises of God: "And the LORD said to him, 'This is the land of which I swore. . . . I have let you see it with your eyes, but you shall not go over there" (Deut. 34:4). Fig. NEB 10.

5. Moses in postbiblical Judaism. Those tendencies to glorify Moses which the OT appears to have resisted make themselves felt in the Judaism of the late pre-Christian and early post-Christian centuries. Because of the centrality of Torah (law) in late Judaism, Moses is easily the most significant figure in the history of the Jews, and he is exalted in both Hellenistic and Palestinian Judaism.

a. Hellenistic Judaism. Moses is praised as the greatest of men, the benefactor of mankind in his role as the father of learning and skills. Truth in Egyptian religion and in Greek philosophy has come from the Mosaic fountainhead. For Philo the Alexandrian Jew of the first century A.D., Moses is the epitome of ideal humanity, reconciler and mediator between God and man, and revealer of the changeless law which existed with God before the creation of the world. Hellenistic Judaism views Moses in terms of its own ideals as a superhuman figure, a divine man (θεῖος ἀνήρ).

b. Palestinian Judaism. A more restrained extension of the significance of Moses takes place in Palestinian Judaism. More characteristically biblical patterns are employed, portraying Moses as mediator of the divine word, servant of God set apart by marks of patience and humility, and the recipient of the complete and final revelation of God. All scripture is but reiteration of this revelation, and the prophets can be subordinated to Moses to the extent of asserting that he spoke their words in addition to his own. The body of unwritten law, cultivated so diligently by the Pharisees, is also derived from Moses. The twofold law, written and unwritten, is revealed to him in its entirety, and some of the unwritten law is called "Mosaic rule of law from Sinai." Through ordination the spirit of Moses is transmitted to the scribes in unbroken succession. Moses thus becomes Israel's teacher in a supreme sense. *See* LAW IN FIRST-CENTURY JUDAISM.

Several pseudepigraphical works are ascribed to Moses in Palestinian Judaism (*see* PSEUDEPIGRAPHA). Generally, they represent Moses as the recipient of revelation that unveils the future. To him God discloses all events and the final hour. Concern is also shown with the biblical tradition of Moses' death. The dominant interpretation of the tradition is that Moses died but that his corpse did not decay. There is, however, another view, that Moses was bodily translated into heaven. In the former view it is considered necessary that Moses should have died and been buried in the wilderness. Only through the atoning efficacy of his death and burial would the wilderness generation rise from the dead and be allowed entrance into the Promised Land.

The biblical tradition that God would raise up for his people a prophet like Moses (Deut. 18:15-18) is variously interpreted in Judaism. Although the passage is applied in rabbinic literature to the post-Mosaic succession of prophets, it may also have received a messianic interpretation in Judaism, as it did among the Samaritans. In the literature of the Qumran sect the "prophet to come" appears as one of the eschatological figures of the messianic age, along with the priestly and the royal messiahs. Apart from the Deuteronomic reference, there is a general tendency in both rabbinic and Qumran literature to relate Moses and the messianic age: "As the first redeemer [Moses], so the last redeemer [the Messiah]." Indeed, the Qumran community retreated to the wilderness in preparation for the new, eschatological exodus and renewal of God's elect community. In many features, then, the messianic age is conceived after the pattern of the age of Moses.

6. Moses in the NT. In the NT the most frequently mentioned OT figure is Moses. The NT picture of Moses corresponds more closely to the restrained characterization of the OT than to the later developments of Judaism, although some new features are added to the Pentateuchal tradition. Instead of the stammering and reluctant figure of Exod. 4, Moses is pictured as "mighty in his words and deeds" and versed in "all the wisdom of the Egyptians" (Acts 7:22), and now he receives the law through the mediation of angels (vs. 38).

Moses appears in the NT in many of his OT roles, but he is dominantly the lawgiver (Matt. 8:4; Mark 7:10; John 1:17). The designation "Moses" may by itself refer to the law of Moses (Mark 7:10; Luke 16:29; II Cor. 3:15). Although the ultimate fulfilment of every iota and dot of the law may be asserted (Matt. 5:18), Jesus appeals beyond the Mosaic law on divorce to the absolute criterion of God's will and action (Mark 10:2-9).

As a prophet, Moses speaks of the coming of the Messiah and his suffering (Luke 24:25-27; Acts 3:22). The appearance of Moses together with Elijah at the transfiguration of Jesus suggests the witness of the Law and the Prophets that the Messiah must suffer (Matt. 17:1-8; Mark 9:2-8; Luke 9:28-36). The location of the transfiguration story between the first two predictions of the Passion indicates that this is at least a significant function of the story (cf. Luke 9:31).

It is not only as lawgiver and prophet, however, that Moses concerns the NT. Quite apart from any single aspect of his work, his entire career and the history in which he is involved are taken to be patterns of life under the new covenant. The nativity story of Jesus reveals the Mosaic theme of the infant deliverer snatched from the evil designs of an earthly tyrant (Matt. 2:13-18). The appearance of John the Baptist in the wilderness, in fulfilment of the prophecy of Isa. 40:3, anticipates a final deliverance patterned after the Mosaic one (Matt. 3:1-4). The proclamation of the new law from the mountain (Matt. 5:1) presents Jesus as the living voice from Sinai, the authoritative interpreter of the will of God (cf. Mark 10:2-9), as he is also mediator of the new covenant (Mark 14:24).

The Mosaic era may also offer a kind of obverse pattern for the new. The old "dispensation of condemnation" is far exceeded in splendor by the new "dispensation of righteousness." The distinguishing mark of the latter is the presence of the Spirit in the community, creating a ministry in the Spirit. In contrast to the veil of Moses, the new community beholds the glory of the Lord with unveiled face and is "being changed into his likeness from one degree of glory to another; for this comes from the Lord who is the Spirit" (II Cor. 3). The counterbalancing of Moses and Christ is especially pronounced in Hebrews. Moses was a faithful servant in God's house; Christ is a son (Heb. 3:5-6). Moses was able to seal the covenant only with the blood of calves and goats; Christ is the mediator of a new covenant sealed in his own blood (Heb. 9:11-22). The contrast between Moses and Christ is also underscored in John's Gospel. The distinction that "the law was given through Moses; grace and truth came through Jesus Christ" (John 1:17), is perhaps meant in a supplementary, not antithetical, sense. Although no claim is made that the manna in the wilderness was given by Moses, a sharp contrast is implied between Moses, who did not give bread from heaven, and Jesus, who is the "bread of life" (John 6:30-35).

In another sense the NT has described the first Moses from the perspective of the second Moses. The pre-eminence of the Cross has led to emphasis upon Moses as a suffering figure. He prefers abuse for Christ to the treasures of Egypt, and ill-treatment shared with God's people to the "fleeting pleasures of sin" (Heb. 11:23-28). He knows the anguish of rejection by those very people for whose sake he has been sent (Acts 7:25, 39).

In the NT, Christ and Moses, church and Israel, are inseparably linked to one another, declaring the unity and the distinction within the one story of God's mighty deeds of salvation.

Bibliography. H. Gressmann, *Mose und seine Zeit* (1913); P. Volz, *Mose und sein Werk* (2nd ed., 1932); W. Eichrodt, "Der Religionsstifter," *Theologie des ATs,* I (1933), 142-45; M. Buber, *Moses* (1946); J. Bright, *Early Israel in Recent History Writing* (1956); C. A. Keller, "Von Stand und Aufgabe der Moseforschung," *Theologische Zeitschrift,* XIII (1957), 430-41;

A. Néher, *Moses and the Vocation of the Jewish People* (1959); R. Smend, *Das Mosebild von Heinrich Ewald bis Martin Noth* (1959). R. F. JOHNSON

MOSES, ASSUMPTION OF. A Jewish pseudepigraph, extant in a Latin version from a defective sixth-century MS and probably representing the combination of two earlier works, the Testament of Moses and the Assumption of Moses. The combined work might better be entitled the Testament of Moses, for it does not contain any reference to the assumption of Moses (save for an obvious interpolation in 10:12). In fact, it is stated repeatedly that Moses was to die in a normal manner (1:15; 10:12-14; 11:8) and be buried.

That a (real) Assumption (Ascension) of Moses once existed is attested by Origen, who writes that Jude 9, which refers to a dispute between Michael and the devil for Moses' body, was taken from a little treatise entitled the Ascension of Moses (*On the Principles* III.2.1; cf. *Homily on Joshua* II.1). Somewhat earlier Clement of Alexandria in his *Comments on the Epistle of Jude* relates Jude 9 to the assumption of Moses (cf. *Stromata* VI.5: "Moses is with the angels," and I.23: "He had a third name in heaven, after his ascension"). The appearance of Moses with Elijah on the Mount of Transfiguration (Mark 9:4 and parallels) and the probable identification of the two heavenly witnesses of Rev. 11:3 ff as Moses and Elijah testify to the early currency of the legend among Christians, if not to the existence of the book itself. The circulation of the tradition, at least among the Jews, is indicated by the rabbinic denial that neither Moses nor Elijah had ascended to heaven (*Dukkah* 5*a*).

Both a Testament of Moses and an Assumption of Moses are included in lists of apocryphal books. The section 3:10-13 of our text, which may be assigned to the Testament, was possibly a source for II Bar. 84:2-5, written *ca.* A.D. 100.

It is conjectured that the two works were combined at an early date. Jude (125-50) not only reflects use of the Assumption in vs. 9, but vs. 16 may be a conflation of 7:7, 9; 5:5, which is in the Testament. When the two works were combined, they may have been given the title of one, the Assumption of Moses. The otherwise puzzling interpolation in 10:12 of the word "assumption" ("For there shall be my death and assumption"; orig. tr.) may indicate that the missing conclusion of our text contained an account of Moses' assumption.

1. Contents
2. Special problems
   a. Text
   b. Date
   c. Author
   d. Taxo
   e. Moses
   f. Eschatology
Bibliography

1. Contents. Moses, as death approaches, is represented as giving a charge to Joshua (similar to one of the Testaments of the Twelve Patriarchs) in which he briefly predicts the future of Israel to the consummation at the end of days, which will be marked by a time of repentance. First, the people will possess the land (Canaan) which had been promised them, and will be ruled over by their chiefs (judges) and kings. The kingdom will be divided, and then they will be taken captive by a king from the East (Nebuchadnezzar) and live in exile seventy-seven years. One of their number (Daniel) will offer up a prayer for God's mercy. A compassionate king (Cyrus) will send them back to their own land. Some will return, but the ten tribes will stay with the Gentiles. Then will come a day of reckoning under evil kings (the Seleucids); certain of the priests will turn to strange gods (the Hellenizing high priests, Jason and Menelaus). Strangely enough, there is no mention here of the Maccabees; but their successors, evil priest-kings (the Hasmoneans), are predicted, along with their successor, an arrogant king who is not a priest (Herod). His reign of thirty-four years will be longer than that of any of his sons. Next, a mighty king from the West will conquer them, burn part of the temple, and crucify some (Varus, governor of Syria, who quelled a revolt in 4 B.C.).

From here on, the identification of persons and events is quite uncertain; apparently the writer has begun to predict (in Moses' name) events beyond his own time. Thus, unidentified impious rulers who claim to be righteous will reign. Then great vengeance and wrath such as have not been on the land before will come upon the Jews (cf. Dan. 12:1), and a king of the kings of the earth will persecute and torture them. A Levite, with the curious name Taxo, will refuse to transgress the laws of God, but will fast with his seven sons, and then will go into a cave to await death. By doing this they may expect to be avenged in the sight of the Lord.

This period of persecution is followed by the only apocalyptic section in the book, a poem of ten stanzas of three lines each. The devil, it is predicted, who is the ruler of this world, will be brought to his end by an angel (Michael), and sorrow will be no more. By implication, he is the cause of the persecution. God himself will intervene directly to avenge his children. There will be great earthquakes; the sun will be darkened; the moon will turn into blood; the courses of the stars will be disturbed; and water will disappear from the sea and the rivers. God will also destroy the idols of the Gentiles. Israel will then mount upon the wings and neck of the eagle (i.e., Rome). Next, God will exalt Israel to the heaven where he himself dwells, and Israel will look down on her adversaries on earth (Gehenna?) and rejoice.

All this, Joshua is told, will be consummated 1,750 years (250 weeks of years) after Moses' death (*ca.* A.D. 75-107). Joshua is grieved upon hearing these predictions, but Moses assures him that all will be worked out according to God's providence. (The text breaks off in the middle of a sentence.)

2. Special problems. *a. Text.* The Latin text is both incomplete and corrupt; the translators have depended upon a number of emendations. The conclusion, as we have seen, is missing. The Latin is from a Greek text, which in turn is probably based upon a Hebrew (or Aramaic) original. No text, except fragments, of the Ascension mentioned by Origen has survived.

b. ***Date.*** If the work was a source for II Baruch, then its date is no later than the end of the first century A.D. This is supported by the calculation that the consummation would occur 1,750 years after the death of Moses, or *ca.* 75-107. However, earlier limits than this may be set. It was predicted that Herod's reign of 34 years would be longer than that of any of his sons. This is actually in error; Archelaus, it is true, had a short rule, being deposed in A.D. 6; but Philip reigned 37 years and Antipas 43. Apparently the work was composed before the reigns of his sons exceeded that of Herod's, or before A.D. 30. If so, it was written during Jesus' lifetime.

c. ***Author.*** The author was quite likely a Palestinian Jew, loyal to God, to Israel, to the temple, to the law (written rather than oral), and to the memory of Moses, his great hero. There is no evidence that he was a Sadducee; unlike the Zealots, although he hated Roman rule, he did not advocate revolt; his interest in the temple is enough to preclude his having been an Essene. He has been termed a "quietistic" Pharisee, but his apocalypticism seems to indicate that he was not a Pharisee. In other words, he was an apocalyptic Jew who may have had no affiliation with any formal group.

d. ***Taxo.*** The mysteriously unique name Taxo has been considered by some to be a cipher. It has been resolved to Eleazar, a martyr of the Maccabean period; and to Mattathias, the father of the Maccabees and progenitor of the Hasmoneans. According to one suggestion, Taxo was some contemporary of the author's who cannot be identified. Could it be, however, that Taxo is symbolic, that he and his sons typify the faithful, loyal Jews who will endure with patience the persecutions that are to precede the coming of the end of this age? If this is so, then Charles's theory that the Taxo section (chs. 8–9) reflects the Maccabean period and should be placed just before the mention of the Hasmoneans in ch. 6 is unnecessary.

e. ***Moses.*** Moses was ordained from the foundation of the world to be the mediator of the covenant for Israel, God's chosen people, for whom the world was created. As a prophet he knows the future without having it revealed to him by an angel or through a trip to heaven. No place will be suitable for his burial; all the world will be his sepulchre.

f. ***Eschatology.*** The apocalyptic hope is evidently based on Dan. 12:1 ff. There will be a time of vengeance such as the world has never seen. There is no Messiah; instead, an angel (Michael) will overthrow the devil (possibly identified with Antiochus in 8:1?), and God will punish the Gentiles. As in Daniel, the righteous will enjoy an astral immortality (their future home is not to be on earth), and the wicked persecutors will dwell in Gehenna.

Bibliography. R. H. Charles, *The Assumption of Moses* (trans. from the sixth-century Latin MS, the unemended text of which is published herewith, together with the text in its restored and critically emended form; 1897); G. Beer, "Die Himmelfahrt Moses," in Kautzsch, *Die Apokryphen und Pseudepigraphen des Alten Testaments* (1900), II, 311-31; R. H. Charles, "The Assumption of Moses," *Apoc. and Pseudep. of the OT* (1913), II, 407-24; W. J. Ferrar, *The Assumption of Moses* (1917); H. H. Rowley, "The Figure of 'Taxo' in the Assumption of Moses," *JBL*, LXIV (1945), 141-45.

M. RIST

MOSOLLAM, MOSOLLAMON. KJV Apoc. forms of MESHULLAM.

MOST HIGH. The usual translation of the Hebrew name Elyon (עֶלְיוֹן, "the Exalted One"), an ancient West Semitic name for El (God), the heavenly father of the gods. The name was appropriated by Israel and redefined according to the Yahweh faith (Pss. 21:7—H 21:8; 46:4—H 46:5; 47:2—H 47:3; 91:1; etc.). It appears in Greek in the NT as ὕψιστος (e.g., Acts 7:48). *See* GOD, NAMES OF, § C2*b*. B. W. ANDERSON

MOST HOLY PLACE [קֹדֶשׁ קָדָשִׁים, קֹדֶשׁ הַקֳּדָשִׁים, holy of holies]. A phrase designating, first, the innermost room of the tabernacle (Exod. 26:34). It was partitioned from the rest of the tabernacle by a veil, bearing the figures of cherubim. Inside was the ark of testimony (*see* ARK OF THE COVENANT), on which was the MERCY SEAT. According to priestly law, in this room the high priest made yearly atonement for the people (Lev. 16). *See* ATONEMENT; ATONEMENT, DAY OF; TABERNACLE.

The phrase "most holy place" is applied also to the innermost room of the Jerusalem temple, sometimes called "Debir." The room was a cube of twenty cubits (*ca.* thirty feet) in each dimension (I Kings 6:16), and it contained two olivewood cherubim whose wings reached from wall to wall. At the dedication of the temple the ark of the covenant was brought into the most holy place (I Kings 8:6; II Chr. 5:7) through doors of olivewood, later apparently replaced by curtains (*see* VEIL OF THE TEMPLE). In Hebrews, the inner shrine, sometimes called the "Holy Place," is a symbol of the redemption wrought by Christ (cf. Heb. 9:11-28; 10:19-20).

The place where Aaronic priests were to eat the offerings reserved from the fire was also called a most holy place (Num. 18:10), as was the portion of land to be allotted for residence to the Zadokite priests (Ezek. 48:12). The "most holy place" in Dan. 9:24 is ambiguous; the reference to an "anointed one" in vs. 25 may mean that קֹדֶשׁ קָדָשִׁים should be read "most holy one" (KJV "Most Holy"). E. M. GOOD

MOTE. KJV translation of κάρφος (RSV SPECK) in Matt. 7:3-5; Luke 6:41-42. "Mote," which formerly had the meaning "straw," appeared in Wyclif's Version, based on the Vulg. *festuca,* "straw" or "twig."

MOTH [עָשׁ, consumer, waster; Akkad. *ašašu,* fish moth, *uššu,* grief; Arab. *'uth,* to be thin, weak; Syr. *'ša';* Ethio. *'eṣē;* σής]. The clothes moth, an insect (order Lepidoptera), whose Palestinian representative is *Tineola biselliella.* Eggs are laid in wool or furs, upon which the larvae then feed, often causing irreparable damage. This destructive quality is referred to in Ps. 39:11—H 39:12; Isa. 50:9; 51:8; Hos. 5:12; Matt. 6:19-20; Luke 12:33. Job 4:19; 27:18 (RSV "spider's web," with LXX, Syr.) compare the moth or his house to the inadequacy or frailty of man. Job 13:28 compares ungodly man, and Jas. 5:2 (σητόβρωτος) compares riches, to worthless, "motheaten" garments.

See also FAUNA § F5. *See* bibliography under ANT.

W. W. FRERICHS

MOTHER. *See* FAMILY; WOMAN.

MOTHER-IN-LAW. *See* FAMILY.

MOTHER-OF-PEARL [דר; Arab. *dur*]; KJV WHITE. Part of the material in the mosaic pavement at Susa (Esth. 1:6).

MOUND, SIEGE [סללה; χάραξ]. A temporary structure built outside the wall or rampart of a city or fortress in order to lay siege to it. The siege mound (סללה) is mentioned with דיק ("siege wall" in Ezek. 4:2; 17:17; "siege tower" in 21:22), but the difference between them is not clear (*see* WAR, METHODS OF, § 8). Upon the siege mound a siege tower would be erected, or a siege engine would be driven from which to hurl arrows and stones and attack the ramparts or scale the wall.

Joab used siege mounds to beleaguer the little town of Abel of Beth-maacah, in which Sheba the son of Bichri, who had rebelled against David, had taken refuge (II Sam. 20:15). It is said that Sennacherib had to withdraw from Jerusalem before he had built a siege mound against it (II Kings 19:32; Isa. 37:33).

Both Jeremiah (6:6) and Ezekiel (4:2; 17:17; 21:22—H 21:27) speak threateningly of the siege mounds with which the Babylonians will besiege Jerusalem (cf. Isa. 29:3). Jesus, too, prophetically warns Jerusalem of the siege mound ("bank"; KJV "trench") which will be cast up against her by invading armies (Luke 19:43). J. A. SANDERS

***MOUNT, MOUNTAIN.** The translation of several words used in the Bible. *See also* HILL, HILL COUNTRY; MOUND (SIEGE) § 2.

The usual words translated "mountain" are הר (Gen. 12:8; 14:10; Exod. 19:3; Josh. 15:8; Judg. 5:5; Isa. 2:2) and ὄρος (Matt. 4:8; Mark 5:5; I Cor. 13:2). Where context and geographical data make such translations appropriate, the RSV renders הר as "Mount" (Lev. 7:38; Deut. 27:4); rarely, "mount" (II Kings 23:16; Isa. 16:1), "mountain" (I Sam. 17:3; I Kings 11:7), "hill" (Judg. 16:3; II Kings 1:9), and "hill country" (I Kings 12:25; II Chr. 19:4). The KJV usually renders הר as "mount" or "mountain," but occasionally "hill" (Judg. 16:3; I Kings 11:7).

Other words for "mount" or "mountain" are: הרר, usually plural (Gen. 14:6; Num. 23:7; Deut. 33:15); מצב (Isa. 29:3; KJV "mount"; RSV correctly "towers"); סללה (Jer. 6:6 [KJV "mount"; RSV correctly "siege mound"]; Ezek. 4:2 [KJV "mount"; RSV "mound"]); Aramaic טור, טורא (Dan. 2:35, 45).

The mountains or hills of Bible lands include two "ridges," one W of the Jordan Rift, composing the elevated terrain in Galilee, Samaria, and Judah; the other E of the Jordan, extending from Mount Hermon through Gilead, Ammon, Moab, and Edom. In comparison with mountains in Europe and America, these are not high, although their proximity to the Mediterranean Sea and the Dead Sea (*ca.* 1,300 feet below sea level) adds to their impressive appearance. The following figures in feet indicate elevations of famous mounts: EBAL, 3,084; GERIZIM, 2,890; GILBOA, 1,630; HERMON, 9,230; NEBO, 2,630; TABOR, 1,930; SINAI (Jebel Musa), 7,500. Other biblical mountains include the mountains of ABARIM, the mountains of ARARAT, and the following mounts: CARMEL; EPHRON; HALAK; HOR; JEARIM; MORIAH; OLIVES; Perazim (*see* BAAL-PERAZIM); SEIR; SHEPHER; ZALMON; ZEMARAIM; ZION. The highest peak in Cisjordan is Jebel Jermaq (3,973 feet). For the geologic formation of the mountains in Palestine, *see* PALESTINE, GEOLOGY OF. For topographical aspects, *see* PALESTINE, GEOGRAPHY OF.

Mountains are mentioned as places of worship (Exod. 19:20; Deut. 12:2); part of God's creation (Ps. 104:8); features of geographical boundaries (Josh. 15:8); places of ambush (Judg. 9:25); scenes of military combat (I Sam. 23:26); the habitat of goats (Ps. 104:18) and birds (I Sam. 26:20; Ps. 11:1—H 11:2); places of refuge (Judg. 6:2) and spiritual retreat (I Kings 19:8). Mountains are often mentioned figuratively in referring to stability (Ps. 30:7—H 30:8), obstacles (Zech. 4:7; Matt. 17:20), and God's power over nature (Ps. 97:5). W. L. REED

MOUNT OF ASSEMBLY [הר מועד]; KJV MOUNT OF THE CONGREGATION. In a mythological description (Isa. 14:12-15) Babylon is likened to the ill-fated DAY STAR (הילל), son of DAWN (שחר), who attempted to scale the heights of heaven and "sit on the mount of assembly [of the gods] in the far north" (cf. Ps. 82; Ezek. 28:11-19).

See also SHAHAR; MYTH. C. R. NORTH

MOUNT OF CONGREGATION. *See* MOUNT OF ASSEMBLY.

MOUNT OF OLIVES. *See* OLIVES, MOUNT OF.

MOUNTAIN-SHEEP [זמר] (Deut. 14:5); KJV CHAMOIS. The זמר (*zemer*) cannot be identified (cf. LXX καμηλοπάρδαλις, "giraffe"). It can only be described as a reasonable supposition that the animal is a species of wild sheep. Wild sheep are still known in the Mediterranean area (*Ovis musimon* of Corsica and Sardinia; *Ovis orientalis* of Armenia and Persia; *Ammotragus lervia* of North Africa), and it is probable that they were found in or near biblical Palestine. *See* CHAMOIS. W. S. MCCULLOUGH

MOURNING. Lamentation and other funerary rites were as imperative a duty as burial, and their absence was considered a grave misfortune (I Kings 14:13; Job 27:15; Jer. 16:4, 6; 22:18; 25:33; 34:5). All who were affected by mourning participated in the lamenting (I Sam. 25:1; 28:3; II Sam. 1:12; 3:31; I Kings 13:29-30; Jer. 16:5; 22:18), first of all the members of the family (Gen. 23:2; 50:10; II Sam. 11:26; Ezek. 24:16). The Hebrew term for this act is ספד, whose original meaning, kept in Syriac, evokes the gesture of striking oneself. The substantive מספד means a shrill cry or wail, as is apparent from the association of ספד with הילל (Jer. 4:8; 49:3; Joel 1:13; Mic. 1:8). To this cry were added exclamations of grief: הו or הוי (Amos 5:16); more commonly, הוי אחי, הוי אחות—i.e., "Ah! my brother," "Ah! my sister" (cf. I Kings 13:30; Jer. 22:18); הוי אדון, when the lamenting was for a king (Jer. 22:18; 34:5). These laments were not left to the inspiration of grief, but were determined by ritual. In describing a מספד for a god who dies and comes to life again, the prophet

Zechariah insists on the orderliness which must govern ceremonies of this kind (12:11-14). Likewise tears were to be shed ritually and only at the proper moment (Mal. 2:13; Matt. 11:17; Luke 7:32). Lamentation began immediately following death (Gen. 23:2), in the very presence of the corpse, as the NT still shows (Matt. 9:23; Mark 5:38). It was continued on the way to the tomb and around the tomb itself, but did not end with burial. In general, mourning lasted seven days (Gen. 50:10; I Sam. 31:13; I Chr. 10:12; Jth. 16:24; Ecclus. 22:12). For Moses and Aaron it lasted thirty days (Num. 20:29; Deut. 34:8), and for Jacob seventy days, according to the Egyptian custom (Gen. 50:3). On account of the stability of funeral customs, it is possible to supplement biblical information by studying the funeral lament as it is practiced in the Orient today. Dalman, Kahle, Littmann, Musil, Wetzstein, Jahnow, and Cramer have collected important documentation which may be consulted with profit (*see bibliography*).

Courtesy of Gaddis Photo Stores, Luxor, Egypt

71. Women and girls mourning for the deceased; from a tomb at Thebes (fourteenth century B.C.)

Courtesy of James B. Pritchard

72. Four women mourners on the sarcophagus of King Ahiram of Byblos (tenth century B.C.)

The predominance of the ritual aspect over the psychological led to giving a very important place to professional mourners (II Chr. 35:25; Eccl. 12:5; Jer. 9:17 ff—H 9:16 ff; Ezek. 27:32; Amos 5:16). Women had the chief role. They are called שרות, "singing women" (II Chr. 35:25); מקוננות, "mourning women" (Jer. 9:17—H 9:16); and also חכמות, "cunning women" (Jer. 9:17 KJV—H 9:16). This suggests that not only was a certain technique expected of them, but also more or less magical knowledge and gifts, the secrets of which were handed down from generation to generation (Jer. 9:20—H 9:19). The predominance of women may be explained by their greater emotivity and sensitivity. Professional mourners were paid, and frequently showed themselves very jealous of their prerogatives (cf. Matt. 9:24). Figs. MOU 71-72.

These mourners not only uttered cries, but also composed poems, whose length was proportionate to the importance of the dead person. The OT has preserved several funeral elegies, sung for the dead or for persons or groups considered as such. Among the former may be cited the elegies of David for Saul and Jonathan (II Sam. 1:18-27) and for Abner (II Sam. 3:33-34). The lamentations of Jeremiah and the satirical laments for Babylon, Tyre, and Egypt may be mentioned as examples of the latter type (Isa. 14:4-21; Ezek. 27:2 ff; 32:2-16). Except for the great part of irony in the prophetic elegies for foreign peoples, all these compositions follow a similar scheme in both content and form. Taking as an example the elegy of David for Saul and Jonathan (the depth and expressiveness of which could hardly have been equaled in ordinary compositions), we may distinguish three essential themes in the lament:

a) The main theme is the eulogy of the dead. This eulogy generally exceeds historical truth: the dead person is always handsome, strong, and good; his family origins are stressed (Ezek. 19:2, 10), as is his valor in war (II Sam. 1:27; Ezek. 32:27); and his human value is unique and incomparable (II Sam. 1:19; Isa. 14:10; Ezek. 27:32). It is important that the name of the dead be uttered (II Sam. 1:26; 3:33—H 3:34; Ezek. 19:2 ff; 26:17 ff; 27:3 ff; 28:12 ff; 32:2 ff).

b) The second theme is the lament, generally introduced by the words איך or איכה—"how?" or "what?"—suitable for bringing into relief the tragic aspect of the demise. The lament is particularly passionate in cases of violent death, and it is often transformed into a demand for vengeance or a curse upon the enemy (II Sam. 1:21—H 1:22). The rejoicing that the particular death may have caused is stigmatized (II Sam. 1:20—H 1:29; Lam. 1:3, 7, 21; 2:15 ff). Past splendor and prosperity are contrasted with present misery, e.g., in Lam. 1 and in the images of the fallen star (Isa. 14:12), the captive lion (Ezek. 19:8), and the felled cedar (Ezek. 31:10). The dreariness of existence in Sheol is frequently contrasted with life on earth.

c) The third theme is consolation. The good memory left by the dead person, the posterity that will perpetuate his name, and the fact that the funeral duties have been correctly performed attenuate the sorrow of those who remain behind.

The lament for Judas Maccabee, in re-employing the terms of the lamentation for Saul and Jonathan, furnishes proof of the stability of the form (I Macc. 9:21).

The elegy—in Hebrew, קינה, a word which probably means an artful composition—employs a verse whose second part is always shorter than the first. This limping rhythm is not restricted to the elegy (e.g., Ps. 136; Isa. 1:10 ff; 40:9 ff; Jonah 2:3 ff; and even the Song of Songs), but if it is not exclusively used for the funeral lament, it nonetheless expresses better than other rhythms the feelings of sadness and despair. It is interesting to note the occurrence of the same rhythm in Ugaritic in a passage where the god El laments the death of Baal:

Dead is Alyin Baal,
Perished is the Prince, Lord of Earth
(Gordon, p. 42; *ANET* 140).

Certain indications seem to point to a dialogue form of the lament. The recurrent refrain is taken up by the choir—e.g.: "How are the mighty fallen!" (II Sam. 1:19, 25, 27); "Go down, and be laid with the uncircumcised" (Ezek. 32:19 ff); "Alas! alas! thou great city" (Rev. 18:10 ff). One may also recall the words of Jesus: "We wailed, and you did not mourn" (Matt. 11:17).

The lament was accompanied by musical instruments. The flute was the preferred instrument of mourning because of the succession of high and deep tones (Jer. 48:36). It is true that the same instrument is also used in happy circumstances (I Kings 1:40; Isa. 5:12; 30:29). Josephus speaks of the flute players at a time of mourning (War III.ix.5), and the Mishna specifies that even for the poorest burial there must be at least two flutes and a wailing woman (Keth. IV.4), which seems to conform to the usage described in the NT (Matt. 9:23).

Both the מספד and the קינה were entirely profane; God's name was never pronounced, not even at a time when a relationship between death and the cult of Yahweh was acknowledged (cf. II Sam. 1:14 ff with II Sam. 1:19 ff; and II Sam. 3:28, 39, with II Sam. 3:33 ff). It must not be concluded from this that the dead man was deified. The lamentation for the gods, which was an important element of the fertility cults (cf. Judg. 11:30-40), bears only a formal analogy with the rites of mourning. The dead person was only a human being whose life had value purely in terms of the way it had been lived and not in terms of what it was destined to become. The advent of more positive beliefs in an afterlife was to give a new orientation to the lament, diminishing its importance considerably.

See also DEATH; IMMORTALITY.

Bibliography. J. G. Wetzstein, "Die syrische Dreschtafel," *Zeitschrift für Ethnologie,* 5 (1873), 270 ff; K. Budde, "Das hebräische Klagelied," *ZAW* (1882), pp. 1 ff; E. Littmann, *Neuarabische Volkspoesie* (1902); A. Musil, *Arabia Petraea,* vol. III (1908); H. Jahnow, "Das hebräische Leichenlied im Rahmen der Völkerdichtung," *BZAW,* vol. 36 (1923); P. Kahle, "Die Totenklage im heutigen Ägypten," *Eucharisterion,* FRLANT, 19/1 (1923), pp. 346 ff; P. Heinisch, "Die Totenklage im AT," *BZF,* H.9/10 (1931), pp. 13-14; M. Cramer, *Die Totenklage bei den Kopten* (1941); C. H. Gordon, *Ugaritic Handbook II—Texts in Transliteration* (1947), p. 149.

E. JACOB

MOUSE [עכבר; *cf.* Jewish Aram. עכברא; Syr. *'ûqbrâ*]. Any one of a large number of rodents of the family Muridae. The true mice and rats belong to the genus Mus, the mice being the smaller.

In Lev. 11:29 the mouse is stated to be unclean, עכבר probably being a general term to cover all varieties of rats, mice, and related animals; Tristram identified no fewer than twenty-three members of this group in nineteenth-century Palestine (*NHB* 122).

Isa. 66:17 seemingly refers to a non-Yahwistic cultic practice in which mice were eaten. The rodent in question may have been the jerboa, the common hamster, the dormouse, or the large sand rat, the flesh of all of which is edible (cf. *NHB* 122). Maimonides preserves the tradition that the Harranians sacrificed field mice.

The reference in I Sam. 6:5 to "mice that ravage the land" (cf. vss. 4, 11, 18) may point to a local variety of vole (*microtus*), a rodent which when numerous can cause great havoc to agriculture. Whether, as is sometimes assumed, the vole in this case was also the carrier of an epidemic disease (I Sam. 5:6, 9, 11-12; 6:3-4) is problematical.

See also FAUNA § A2*h*ii. W. S. MCCULLOUGH

MOUTH [פה; Assyrian *pû;* Aram. פם; חך *in* Job 20:13; Prov. 8:7; *etc.;* στόμα]. The word is used extensively and with the following principal connotations in the OT and the NT:

a) The organ of eating and drinking (Judg. 7:6; I Sam. 14:26-27). Figuratively, that which finds things sweet (Job 20:12; Ps. 119:103); the mouth of the earth, which swallows up (Gen. 4:11; Num. 16:30, 32); and Sheol (Isa. 5:14; cf. Ps. 69:15—H 69:16).

b) An external organ (II Kings 4:34; Prov. 30:20), used for kissing (I Kings 19:18; Job 31:27; Song of S. 1:2) and for mocking (Job 16:10; Ps. 35:21; Isa. 57:4).

c) Much more often, the organ of speech (Gen. 45:12; Deut. 32:1; II Sam. 1:16; Matt. 5:2; 12:34; 13:35) and of laughter (Job 8:21; Ps. 126:2), as the mouth of God, which proclaims (Isa. 1:20; 40:5; Jer. 9:12—H 9:11; Matt. 4:4); the mouth of animals which speak (Gen. 8:11; Num. 22:28; Isa. 10:14; Rev. 12:16; 13:2); and with reference to human foes under the figures of ravenous beasts (Ps. 22:21—H 22:22; Ezek. 34:10).

d) The mouth of God, from which fire comes forth (II Sam. 22:9=Ps. 18:8—H 18:9).

e) The opening or orifice of a well (Gen. 29:2-3, 8, 10), of a cave (Josh. 10:18, 22, 27), of an abyss (Jer. 48:28), of Sheol (Ps. 141:7), of a sack (Gen. 42:27-28; 44:1-2, 8).

פה is used in combination with various prepositions: אל פי, "according to the measure of," "in accordance with" (Josh. 15:13; 17:4); כפי, "according to the command, or mouth, of," "in proportion to" (Lev. 25:52; Num. 6:21; also as a conjunction in Zech. 2:4; Mal. 2:9); לפי, "according to" or "as" (Gen. 47:12; Exod. 12:4); על פי, "according to the command, or mouth, of," "in accordance with" (Gen. 45:21; Exod. 17:1; Lev. 27:8). H. F. BECK

MOWING [גזז, to shear or cut; גז *usually means* fleece] (Amos 7:1). The reference to the "king's mowings" (גזי המלך) in Amos 7:1 is to the first growth cut as taxes to support the ruler. Cf. the reference to "mown grass" left lying on the ground in Ps. 72:6.

H. N. Richardson

MOZA mō'zə [מוצא]. **1.** A descendant of Judah, born of the concubine of Caleb (I Chr. 2:46).

2. A descendant of Saul; son of Zimri; father of Binea (I Chr. 8:36-37; 9:42-43).

MOZAH mō'zə [המצה] (Josh. 18:26). A city in Benjamin, mentioned after Chephirah. Its name is stamped on the handles of vessels excavated at Jericho and Tell en-Nasbeh, showing that it was a royal pottery. After the Great War Against Rome (A.D. 66-73), Vespasian settled eight hundred soldiers there, giving it the name Colonia Emmaus. This is confirmed by the Jerusalem Talmud (Suk. IV.5), which states that Mozah was the place where willows were gathered for the Feast of Sukkoth and that it was the same as Koloniya. The site is at or near the Arab village of Qaluniya, four miles NW of Jerusalem on the road to Tel Aviv.

S. Cohen

MUFFLER. KJV translation of רעלה (RSV Scarf).

MUGHARAH, WADI EL- wä'dĭ ĕl mo͝o gär'ə [Arab., valley of the caves]. A valley in which caves containing important prehistoric remains have been found. Fig. MUG 73.

The Wadi el-Mugharah is located on the lower

Courtesy of Herbert G. May

73. Wadi el-Mugharah

Courtesy of the Palestine Archaeological Museum, Jerusalem, Jordan

74. View of the three caves at Wadi el-Mugharah, at the close of the excavations in 1934

Courtesy of Herbert G. May

75. Photographing skeletons at Mugharet es-Skhul, Wadi el-Mugharah

W slope of Mount Carmel, approximately eleven miles S of the N promontory of the mountain, and two miles from the Mediterranean Sea. Flanking the mouth of the valley are two limestone bluffs; in the S one are four caves, Mugharet el-Wad ("cave of the valley"), Mugharet ej-Jamal ("cave of the camel"), et-Tabun ("the oven"), and Mugharet es-Skhul ("cave of the kids"; Fig. MUG 74). From 1929-34, these caves were excavated by Dorothy A. E. Garrod and Theodore D. McCown for the British School of Archaeology in Jerusalem and the American School of Prehistoric Research. With the exception of Mugharet ej-Jamal, which was practically empty, each cave contained the stratified remains of several Stone Age cultures. Fig. MUG 75.

These excavations firmly established the Stone Age chronology of Palestine through the discovery of a long and apparently continuous series of flint industries* from Tayacian (Early Paleolithic) to Natufian (Mesolithic). With this sequence of cultures, it was possible to relate the previously known isolated Stone Age deposits of Palestine, and to make detailed comparisons between the Stone Age cultures of Palestine and those of Europe and Africa. Important light was also shed on the development of early man. In Mugharet es-Skhul—in an early Levalloiso-Mousterian deposit—a number of skeletons were found which show characteristics of both paleanthropic man (*Homo neanderthalensis*) and neanthropic man (*Homo sapiens*), suggesting that a mixture of these races took place in Palestine (Fig. MUG 76). In addition, much was learned about the characteristic fauna of the different periods from the bones found in the cave deposits. The study of the

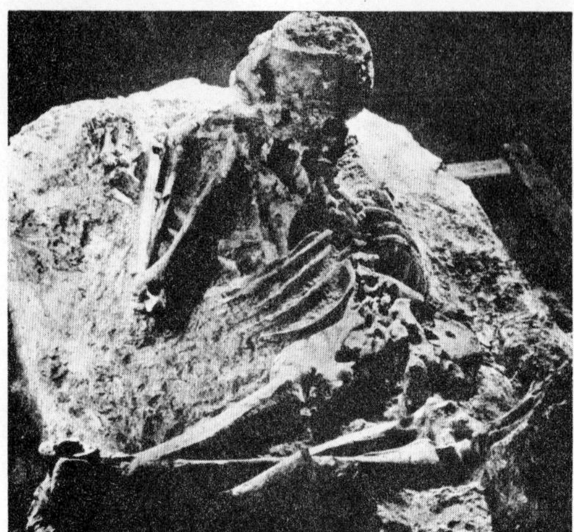

From Garrod and Bate, *The Stone Age of Mount Carmel* (Oxford: Clarendon Press)

76. Early Paleolithic Levalloiso-Mousterian skeleton removed in block of marl from cave at Wadi el-Mugharah

fauna, in turn, has thrown light on changes of climate in Palestine during the Stone Age. Fig. FLI 17.

Bibliography. D. A. E. Garrod and D. M. A. Bate, *The Stone Age of Mount Carmel,* vol. I (1937). G. W. Van Beek

MULBERRY TREES. The KJV translates בכא (*bākhâ*) "mulberry" in II Sam. 5:23-24; I Chr. 14:14-15 (RSV Balsam). Reference to the fruit of the mulberry (*Morus nigra* L.) is found in I Macc. 6:34 (μόρον), where the blood-red juice was used to incite the elephants of Antiochus' army during the battles against the Maccabees. In Luke 17:6, Jesus refers to this tree, here called συκάμινος (*see* Sycamine), in a parable concerning faith.

The black (or red) mulberry, *Morus nigra* L., is common in Palestine, and its juicy fruit is highly prized. The white mulberry (*Morus alba* L.), so necessary for the silkworm industry of the Orient, was apparently not introduced into Palestine until postbiblical times.

See also Flora § A2*e;* Rephaim, Valley of; Silk. Fig. MUL 77.

Bibliography. H. N. and A. L. Moldenke, *Plants of the Bible* (1952), pp. 140-41. J. C. Trever

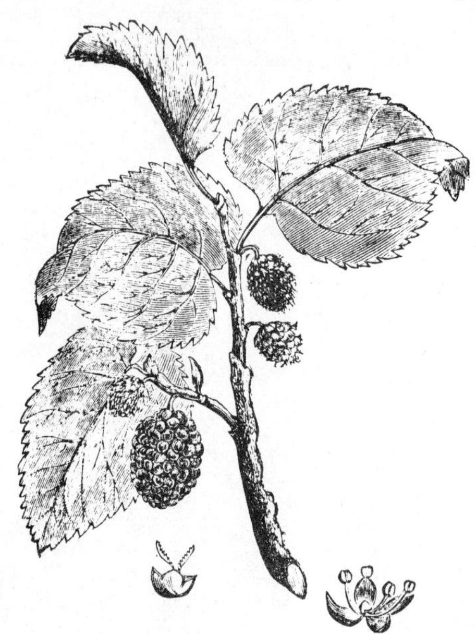

77. Mulberry

MULE [פרד, פרדה, *possibly* separated one; KJV רכש (Esth. 8:10, 14; RSV "swift horse"), ימם (Gen. 36:24; RSV "hot springs"; "adder" *in* L. Koehler, *Lexicon*)]. A quadruped, the hybrid offspring of an ass and a horse, properly of a male ass and a mare; the product of a she-ass and a stallion is a hinny.

Mules first appear in the OT only in the time of David (II Sam. 13:29), the reason doubtless being the comparative rarity of the horse among the Hebrews and their neighbors prior to 1000 B.C. Since the law against the crossbreeding of animals (Lev. 19:19) was generally observed, any mules the Hebrews possessed must have been obtained from Gentiles. Tyre imported horses and mules from Beth-togarmah (possibly in Armenia or N Syria), and Phoenicia may therefore have been one of the sources of the mules used in Israel (Ezek. 27:14). On later Jewish conventions regarding mules, see M. Kil. 1.6; 8.4-5.

78. Mules used in threshing grain, from Saqqarah tomb, Old Kingdom (3200-2475 B.C.)

Mules, controlled by bit and bridle (Ps. 32:9), are first mentioned as riding animals, but all the references indicate that they were used as such principally by the court and the aristocracy (II Sam. 13:29; 18:9; I Kings 10:25; 18:5). They were also employed as burden-bearers (II Kings 5:17; I Chr. 12:40; cf. Jos. Life XXVI.26 [127]). In the animal resources of the post-exilic Judean community, recorded in Ezra 2:66-67, the number of mules is given as 245; the horses, camels, and asses were much more numerous.

See also Fauna § A1*a*.

Fig. MUL 78. W. S. McCullough

MUPPIM mŭp'ĭm [מפים; LXX Μαμφιν] (Gen. 46:21). Son of Benjamin. Elsewhere the name exhibits different forms. *See* Shephupham.

MURATORIAN FRAGMENT myŏŏr'ə tôr'ĭ ən. A fragment of a corrupt Latin MS, named for its discoverer, L. A. Muratori (in 1740), and comprising the greater part of a list of the Christian writings accepted as canonical by someone probably at Rome near the end of the second century. The document has great importance in the history of the NT canon. *See* Canon of the NT. J. Knox

MURDER. *See* CRIMES AND PUNISHMENTS § C2*a*.

MURMUR [רגן, לון לין; γογγύζω (GRUMBLE *in* Matt. 20:11; I Cor. 10:10), διαγογγύζω]; MURMURING [תלנות; γογγυσμός]. To express dissatisfaction or anger by subdued, often inarticulate, and always resentful complaint.

MURRAIN mûr′ĭn. KJV translation of דבר (Exod. 9:3; LXX θάνατος; RSV PLAGUE), referring to an infectious disease affecting animals.

MUSHI mo͞o′shī [משי, מושי]; MUSHITES —shīts. One of four or five families of Levite priests located around Hebron sometime between Deborah and David (Num. 26:58*a*, an ancient genealogy, possibly redacted by the addition of "Mahlites" and rearrangement). In P and Chronicles, Mushi was the second son of Merari and the eponym of one of the two divisions of Levites descended from Merari (Exod. 6:19; Num. 3:20, 33; I Chr. 6:19, 47; 23:21, 23; 24:26, 30).

Bibliography. K. Möhlenbrink, "Die levitischen Überlieferungen des ATs," *ZAW*, LII (1934), 191-97.

T. M. MAUCH

***MUSIC.** The concept of art as a de luxe commodity of life, a concept of our time, was utterly alien to the ancient world. Then music was an organic part of daily life, linked with a thousand bonds to all human concerns, from birth to death. All the biblical references to music must be understood from this perspective. Moreover, as the narrative portions of the OT cover a long span of history, it is but natural that music, its forms, and its functions have undergone significant changes in the course of these many centuries.

A. The evidence
 1. General usage and function of music
 2. Music in worship
 3. Extrabiblical sources
B. Interpretation of musical references
 1. Terminology
 2. Forms and structures
 3. Practice and performance
  a. Popular songs
  b. Professional liturgical music
 4. Character of biblical music
  a. Continuity and unity of Jewish musical tradition
  b. Remnants of ancient Hebrew songs in plain chant of church and synagogue
  c. Development of research in ancient Jewish chant
C. Music in the NT and in the rabbinic era
 1. Organized versus spontaneous praying and singing
 2. Scriptural versus extrascriptural poems
 3. Fusion with Hellenistic music
 4. Vocal versus instrumental music
 5. Rise of monasticism and its influence upon ecclesiastical chant
Bibliography

A. *THE EVIDENCE.* 1. General usage and function of music. As in most cultures, the first biblical reference links music with a mythical personage, "Jubal, who was the father of all those who play the lyre and pipe" (Gen. 4:21). The name is related to the Hebrew word for "ram" (*yôbhēl*). Jubal's brother was Jabal, the first cattle-breeder; his half brother Tubal-cain, the first smith; his half sister Na'amah, whose name signifies beauty. The parallel with Aphrodite, Hephaestos, and Dionysos, has been recognized early.

The main functions of music in the early times of biblical history were social merrymaking, martial noisemaking, magic incantation, and worship. Merrymaking in particular was the main function of music during the age of patriarchs and judges (e.g., Gen. 31:27; Exod. 32:17-18; Judg. 11:34-35), sometimes even licentiously practiced (e.g., Isa. 23:16).

Often the music barely exceeded the level of organized noisemaking, especially when the purpose was to terrorize the enemy, as in Exod. 32:17-18; Judg. 7:18-20. Other manifestations of functional music are the mocking song (Job 30:9) and the "working songs" of harvesters (Isa. 16:10; Jer. 48:33) or of well-diggers (Num. 21:17). All this, however, alludes to distinctly popular, nonartistic singing and playing; no professionals are as yet mentioned. When Amos (6:5) caustically chastised the *nouveaux riches* and their "artistic" extravagances, he stressed for the first time the age-old feud between the professional and the dilettante (orig. tr.):

> They chant idle songs to the sound of the harp
> And fancy to play their instruments like David.

Indeed, not before David's time do professional musicians appear in the Bible. From where did they come? Considering the apparent connection of professional musicians with the institution of monarchy, we must bear in mind that in the neighboring countries, Egypt and Assyria, the professional musician was an old and familiar figure. It seems that the midrash alludes to an ancient tradition when it relates that King Solomon's Egyptian wife, daughter of the Pharaoh, carried in her dowry a thousand foreign instruments. Yet an instrument is of no use without a musician able to play it. Hence, we may assume that the systematic import and subsequent training of professional musicians took place in the era of David and Solomon.

Before the establishment of the kingdom under Saul, it was the women who, as in every young civilization, played a major part in the performance of music. Such figures as Miriam, Deborah, Jephthah's daughter, and the women hailing the young hero David (I Sam. 18:6-7) have become almost archetypes of female musicians. Characteristic of all these cases is the familiar picture of a female chorus, dancing and singing, accompanied by frenzied drum-beating. This is a scene known to the entire Near East, and not even the severe rule of Islam could wholly suppress this age-old practice. Remnants of these choruses of dancing women are still extant in isolated Jewish communities, such as Yemen on the island of Djerba, of whose chants we possess a penetrating study by Robert Lachmann (*see bibliography*): "The women's songs have preserved, to some extent, the qualities of uninfluenced chant: they belong to the group of tunes directed by motoric impulse (as in dance or occupational songs). . . . In the isolated Jewish communities of the Near East the women accompany their songs on frame-drums or cymbals which they beat with their hands." These observations read as if they expounded the women's songs of biblical times. But no, they refer to present-day conditions in North Africa and Arabia.

With the emergence of professional musicians, active in the temple and the royal courts, the women's songs dwindled to insignificance. Henceforth, trained singers and instrumentalists were considered functionaries of high rank. This development is certainly connected with the religious and secular centralization of Israel in Jerusalem in the years 950-850 B.C. The tabulation in Table 1 will illustrate this.

Table 1

Function	Scriptural Passage
Family parties	Gen. 31:27 (farewell party for Jacob) Luke 15:25 (home-coming party for prodigal son)
Acclamation of heroes	Judg. 11:34 (welcome of Jephthah) I Sam. 18:6 (triumph of David)
King's enthronement and martial music	Judg. 7:18-20 I Kings 1:39-40 II Kings 11:14 II Chr. 13:14 II Chr. 20:28
Harem and court music	II Sam. 19:35 (Barzillai's refusal of David's invitation: "Can I still listen to the voice of singing men and singing women?" Josephus adds here "which delights those who live with kings" [Antiq. VII.xi.4]) Eccl. 2:8 (as if said by Solomon: "I got singers, both men and women, and many concubines, man's delight")
Banquet and feast	Isa. 5:12 Isa. 24:8-9
Occupational songs	Num. 21:17 Judg. 9:27 Isa. 16:10 Jer. 31:4-5, 7; 48:33
Dirges and laments	II Sam. 1:17-18 II Chr. 35:25 Matt. 9:23 The customary wailing women
Magic-apotropaic incantations, etc.	Exod. 28:35 Josh. 6:4-20 I Sam. 16:6 ff II Kings 3:15

2. Music in worship. There is but one step from a musical incantation to religious music. In the Bible, apotropaic practices are perfectly compatible with monotheistic worship. Thus, cultic music appears on three or four levels in the OT: in the frenzied songs of the professional prophets (I Sam. 10:5-6); in the early numinous ordinances of the P Code in Leviticus and Numbers, and, eventually, in the organized songs, chants, and psalms of the temple and of the professional Levitic musicians. The OT retains vestiges of the magic use of music, which antedates most of the biblical narratives by many centuries. The collapse of Jericho's wall, after the ritual sounding of the ram's horns, is mythologically akin to the Greek legend of Amphion of Thebes, whose lyre-playing moved the stones to rebuild the broken wall (cf. Homer *Odyssey* XI.260 ff). Basically apotropaic functions accounted for the bells on the robe of the high priest (Exod. 28:34-35), and also for the *shôphār* and trumpet blowing at the time of the New Moon and similar occasions. To the same concept belongs the story of David's soothing Saul with music (I Sam. 16:16-23). This anecdote and that of Elisha's prophetic inspiration restored by minstrelsy (II Kings

3:15) reveal the importance of the "ethos doctrine" of music, a conception common to all nations of the ancient world, even though its systematic formulation was achieved by the Pythagoreans.

It is difficult to ascertain when liturgical music became a regular institution in Israel; for the report of II Chr. 7, which credits King David with the organization of temple music, was written many centuries after David. The earlier historical accounts, especially in II Samuel, do not mention organized temple music. There, David appears as a talented singer, player, and composer. The famous passages II Sam. 6:14-15, where "David danced before the LORD with all his might," bear little resemblance to the stately ceremony reported at the same occasion in I Chr. 15.

It is important to bear in mind that all music of the temple, regardless of the period, was nothing but an accessory to its sacrificial ritual. Without sacrifice the music loses its *raison d'être*. What was the inherent connection between the sacrifice and its accompanying music? This is still an unsolved puzzle. It is possible to compare a banquet for honored guests, whereby quantities of burned meat, incense, and music were offered, to a sacred meal for a still anthropomorphically conceived deity, whose prestige demanded sacrifice, incense, praise, as well as musical entertainment. Whatever the original function of sacrificial music, it was forbidden immediately after the destruction of the temple in A.D. 70. Nor do we know all the details of the temple's musical practice. This lack of continuous information is not a simple consequence of Jerusalem's destruction by the Roman legions, for the Jewish tradition has in most other points survived that disaster intact. There is ample reason to believe that the Levites refused to divulge their "trade secrets" and took them to their graves.

3. Extrabiblical sources. The music of the temple has been a subject of fascination to many authors, to whom it became almost a romantic image. It was considered an unattainable aim to create music that could match it in grandeur. The Jews consider themselves a particularly musical people, as we learn from their literature. Indeed, there is external evidence to affirm this strange belief. An Assyrian bas-relief's inscription praises the victory of King Sennacherib over King Hezekiah and relates the latter's ransom and tribute. It consisted, aside from precious metals, of Judean musicians, male and female. In Ps. 137 we read that the Babylonians demanded from their Hebrew prisoners "songs of Zion." To ask for musicians as tribute and to show interest in the folk music of a vanquished enemy was unusual indeed. During the Hellenistic era, the geographer Strabo praises the singing girls from Palestine as the most musical in the world. Obviously the apocryphal Acts of Thomas speaks of such a maiden: The apostle had just landed in India and was somewhat homesick; "then a piper stood over him and played at his head for a long time: now this piper girl was by race a Hebrew." The testimonies to the temple's musical glories, whether they come from the nostalgic pen of a Josephus or from the poisonously anti-Jewish one of John Chrysostom, say essentially the same as the Wisdom of Solomon (18:9): "Our fathers already led the sacred songs of praise" (orig. tr.).

B. *INTERPRETATION OF MUSICAL REFERENCES.* 1. Terminology. For instruments and their names, *see* MUSICAL INSTRUMENTS.

The enigmatic musical superscriptions which occur mainly at the opening of psalms constitute a real musical terminology, which, however, is almost unintelligible to us. Many of these headings must have been obscure at the time when the LXX was written—i.e., during the existence of the temple. This fact admits two possibilities: either the original meaning of these musical terms was then generally forgotten, or, on account of the continuous tradition of the temple, it was still understood, but as a secret closely guarded by the priestly caste. Naturally, the rabbinical translators of the LXX were not privy to these priestly arcana. As an analogous obscurity prevails in the realm of sacrificial procedure, the second possibility seems more likely.

Close examination of the Hebrew texts reveals three categories of psalm headings:

a) Titles, such as "A Psalm [מזמור, *Mizmôr*] of the Sons of Korah. A Song [שיר]" (Ps. 87), or "A *Maskîl* [משכיל] of Asaph" (Ps. 78). To this group belong the terms *Mizmôr* (from *zimmer,* "to play, sing"); *Maskîl* (from *haskēl,* "to reason, meditate," perhaps "A Meditation"); *Mikhtām* (מכתם; etymology unknown; LXX στηλογραφία, "inscription, engraving"; Pss. 16; 56-60); Song of Ascent or Degrees (שיר המעלות; LXX ᾠδή τῶν ἀναβαθμῶν; Vulg. *Cantus graduum; see below*).

b) Remarks concerning a type or kind of performance. To this category belong a group of nouns, usually with a preposition such as "with," "upon," etc. They seem to refer to accompanying instruments, as in Ps. 5: "for the flutes" (נחילות), *'ᵃlāmôth* (עלמות), perhaps "flutingly" (cf. ἔλυμος, "small flute or pipe"); others interpret it "in the style of maiden"—e.g., in high tones (cf. עלמה, *'almâ,* "young woman"). The following two terms suggest a musical mode or melodic pattern: *Shᵉmînîth* (שמינית; Pss. 6; 12), which indicates the eighth mode. The older interpretation which connected it with the octave (שמונה, "eight") is untenable, as the division of the octave into eight tones was unknown to the ancient Hebrews. The RSV translation of *nᵉghinôth* (נגינות), "stringed instruments," does not fully cover the significance of the term (Pss. 4; 6; 54-55; 61; 67; 76). This is obvious in Ps. 69:12—H 69:13, where *nᵉghînôth* stands for a song, and a drunkard's song at that! The interpretation "melodic pattern" has been widely accepted. In this sense it is used as a marginal gloss, which later became part of the text, in Hab. 3:19. *'Al maḥᵃlath* (etymology obscure, perhaps related to מחלה, "dance, roundel") seems to indicate a choreographic direction in Ps. 88, where it is coupled with *lᵉ'annôth,* indicating a responsorial or antiphonal performance by two groups. *Shiggāyôn,* plural *shighyōnôth* (שגיון, from שגה, "to go astray, err"), is used in Ps. 7; Hab. 3:1. Perhaps the interpretation "tumultuous dithyramb" approximates the true meaning; it certainly would suit the form and content of Hab. 3. This chapter indicates also the intimate connection between prophecy, temple service, and music. *Higgayôn* (הגיון, from הגה, "to murmur, meditate, whisper") seems to occur in a twofold meaning: as "meditation, thoughtful reflection," in Ps. 19:14, and in a strictly musical sense as in Pss. 9:16—H 9:17; 92:3. There, it seems to indicate the murmuring glissando of the low strings as a kind of accompaniment.

c) Cue words. The majority of psalm headings consist of "cue words," which suggest the *incipits* of songs popular at the times of the psalmists. This practice of setting new words to an old tune (contrafacts) is common to the hymnology of every age.

Thus occur *'al-'ayyéleth hash-sháḥar* ("Hind of the Dawn"; Ps. 22); *'al-tashḥēth* ("Do Not Destroy"; Pss. 57–59; 75); *'al-yônath 'élem reḥōqîm* ("Dove on Far-off Terebinths"; Ps. 56); *'al-mûth-labbēn*, which should probably read *'al-'alāmôth labbēn* ("Upon Maiden," "To the Son"; Ps. 9); *'al-shōshannîm* ("Upon the Lilies"; Ps. 45); *'al-shûshan 'ēdhûth* ("The Lily of the Testimony"[?]; Ps. 60). All these songs are long forgotten, and their melodies lost forever. Special mention should be made of the "Destroy Not" incipit of Pss. 57–59; 75. It has sometimes been construed as an allusion to the new wine or to a vintage song (on account of Isa. 65:8). Of the four psalms that bear this heading, only one uses wine in its imagery. The content of these psalms, however, suggests that their heading did not at all refer to music, but to a common idea—viz., the curse of the wicked and the plea for salvation. *'Al-hag-gittîth* ("In the Fashion of Gath"[?]; Pss. 8; 81; 84) has no clear meaning, and its etymology is controversial. Some scholars derive it from a word for "wine press" and attribute to these psalms the gay spirit of the wine harvest.

The famous heading *Shîr ham-ma'alôth* ("Song of Ascent"; LXX ᾠδή τῶν ἀναβαθμῶν; Vulg. *cantus graduum;* Pss. 120–34) admits several interpretations. According to the rabbinic (and patristic) explanation, these fifteen psalms were sung by the Levites standing on the fifteen steps between the court of the women and that of the Israelites. The more recent interpretation, "Pilgrimage Song," which alludes to the pilgrims' ascending the high city of Jerusalem at the occasion of the three "pilgrimage festivals," has now been generally accepted. It is interesting to note that the musical term "gradual" stems directly from the rabbinic-patristic translation "Song of Steps," *cantus graduum.*

d) *Selāh* (סלה; LXX διάψαλμα; "interlude"). This is probably a direction for the conductor that now a signal of the cymbals should interrupt the even flow of chant. Probably *Selah* was originally a marginal gloss, which in the course of centuries has crept into the text. It occurs seventy-one times in thirty-nine psalms and in Hab. 3:3, 9, 13. Most expressive is the combination *Higgāyôn Selāh* in Ps. 9:16, indicating the end of the main thought by a soft whispering of strings, followed by a clash of cymbals.

e) *Lam-menaṣṣēah*, "To the choirmaster" (למנצח >√נצח, "to excel, to lead, to conquer," LXX εἰς τὸ τέλος [?]; Aq. τῷ νικοποιῷ; Symm. ἐπινίκιος; Vulg. *victori*). It occurs fifty-five times in Psalms and in Hab. 3:19. It seems to suggest a person's title or office, because in Ps. 39:1 Jeduthun is mentioned as "leader." Yet, the translation "choirmaster" is alien to ancient tradition. The fact that the Thrice-Holy (Isa. 6:3) is called ὕμνος ἐπινίκιος ("triumphal hymn"), following Aq. and Symm., even in the earliest Christian liturgies, seems to suggest either the title "head of musicians" or "master of ceremonies" or else the character of psalms with this heading, which perhaps implies "to the triumphator" or "triumph-maker."

2. Forms and structures. In the surprisingly large Hebrew vocabulary of music, the terms for vocal music outnumber by far the purely instrumental ones. The various forms or types of songs all have designations of their own; thus, the formal structure of chant in biblical times is not as enigmatic to us as some of the psalm headings or references to instrumental performance. All chant was inseparably bound to the word, and the word has remained with us.

A certain distinction is made in the OT between a spontaneous hymn, inspired by a specific occasion, a more or less popular song, and a liturgical composition or chant. The songs of Deborah or of Moses are clearly designated as inspired hymns (שיר). Rabbinic as well as patristic authors have numbered and collected these canticles, and were well aware of their special status. The same holds true of the Psalms (תהלים), which held a preferred position in the liturgy of the temple. Imitations of psalms were widespread and popular, from the apocryphal Odes of Solomon to the Hymns of Thanksgiving in the Dead Sea Scrolls. In comparison with these highly developed and artistic forms, only a few of the popular ditties have come down to us, as profane sprinklings in an otherwise theocratic text (e.g., Lamech's song [Gen. 4:23-24], or the well song [Num. 21:14-18], or the chants of the harvesters).

Of all the songs, it is the Psalms which display most clearly their musical structure. There is ample evidence, both in scriptural and in rabbinical sources, that the art of singing was diligently cultivated, especially in the temple. I Chr. 25 not only relates the initial organization of the temple singers, but uses in its terminology the words "trained in song" (מלמדי־שיר) and "skilful" (מבין). The Talmud even hints that lack of correct singing annulled the value of the sacrifice (B. 'Arak. 11*a*). The musical training of a Levitical singer took at least five years of intensive preparation (B. Hullin 24*a*).

Under such circumstances, all exegetes of scripture, beginning with the church fathers and rabbis, felt obligated to expound and explain every biblical statement, however obscure, which refers to the musical part of the temple's liturgy. As all chant depended upon the relation between word and tone, the textual structure of the Psalms is of eminent importance for all investigations of ancient Hebrew chant.

It may not be amiss to remind the student that the musical structure today called psalmody was certainly not the original practice of psalm-rendering. For it presupposes a strictly systematized rendition, whereby each verse is sung, or recited, according to a rigid formula. Yet the very diversified headings of the psalms seem to preclude a uniform psalmody and with it the assumption that the chant of primitive Christianity was a direct heritage of the temple.

Nonetheless, there are indications or "stage directions" in the text of psalms, which reflect their practice of performance in the Second Temple. Some of these directions are heeded even today. They are:

a) The formal doxologies at the end of each of the five books of the Psalter, with their responsorial acclamations (41:13—H 41:14; 72:19; 89:52—H 89:53; 106:48; Ps. 150 as a whole).

b) The strophic structure of some psalms—e.g., Ps. 29, where the expression "voice of the LORD" occurs seven times, or Ps. 119 with its eightfold alphabetic stanzas.

c) The frequent appearance of refrains, as in Pss. 118:1-4, 29; 136; also the recurrent acclamations "Blessed" (אשרי) or "Hallelujah."

By far the most unifying feature of the Psalter is its poetic parallelism, which expresses every verse in two "rhymes of thought," be they analogous or antithetical (*see* POETRY, HEBREW). This well-known poetic device suggests a corresponding musical rendition—in fact, a musical dichotomy. This dichotomy may be implemented by responsorial performance or by antiphonal musical parallelism.

Four forms of music, born of the genius of the psalmists, have become the outstanding patterns of synagogal and ecclesiastical chant: (*a*) plain psalmody (e.g., Ps. 46:1); (*b*) response (e.g., Ps. 67:1-2); (*c*) antiphony (e.g., Ps. 103:20-22) rendered as antiphonal song:

> Bless Yahweh, O you his angels,
> you mighty ones who do his word,
> hearkening to the voice of his word!
> *Bless Yahweh, all his hosts,*
> his ministers that do his will!
> *Bless Yahweh, all his works,*
> in all places of his dominion.
> *Bless Yahweh, O my soul!*

(*d*) litany with refrain (e.g., Ps. 80:2-3, 6-7, 18-19):

> Stir up thy might,
> and come to save us!
> Restore us, O God;
> *let thy face shine, that we may be saved!*
> . . . .
> Thou dost make us the scorn of our neighbors;
> and our enemies laugh among themselves.
> Restore us, O God of hosts;
> *let thy face shine, that we may be saved!*
> . . . .
> Give us life, and we will call on thy name!
> Restore us, O Yahweh, God of hosts!
> *let thy face shine, that we may be saved!*

These closely knit poetic structures were intended for solemn and well-organized musical representation. Both synagogue and church have made full use of these music-inviting forms. The Hymns of Thanksgiving of the Dead Sea Scrolls elaborate on these archetypes, and much of Eastern Christian liturgies consists of paraphrases of such structures.

3. Practice and performance. This is perhaps the most obscure of all the problems which concern the music of the Bible. The concept of nonfunctional art, which the West has taken for granted for the last two hundred years, is alien to the ancient Orient. Even the loftiest psalm, a truly spiritual creation of music or literature, served a more or less definable purpose. The functions of music were: merrymaking, dance, minstrelsy, lament, accompaniment of exalted prophetic utterances, mnemonics, magic, theurgy, working songs, military signals and calls, and, of course, the liturgical chant of the temple and synagogue. Naturally, the musical practices were as different as were the respective functions.

The Bible itself provides us with but scant technical details, and they pertain almost exclusively to religious music. All the other functions, mentioned above, are also to be found in the Bible, but mostly in the form of laws, narratives, or anecdotal incidents (e.g., the concept of the apotropaic power of music in Exod. 28:33; 39:25-26; I Sam. 16:14-23; 19:9). Postbiblical Jewish sources, such as Josephus and the tannaitic descriptions, must be read with caution; they were written after the destruction of the temple, mostly by laymen (not Levites), and naturally glorify the temple music. Apocryphal writings tell us little about the subject of music; and the Hellenistic authors take interest in it only toward the end of the second century A.D., when the relation between Judaism and Christianity intrigued their curiosity. In view of the dearth of documents, the student of ancient music must consider these late sources no less than those of the old Mesopotamian, especially Aramean and Akkadian, cultures.

In the following examination a distinction is made between folk music and that of professional musicians. The former designation refers chiefly to mass-singing, ditties, acclamations, etc.; professional musicians emerged in Israel about the time of David and Solomon. From then on, we have abundant historical evidence of the role which the professional musicians played in the organization of the temple ritual.

a. Popular songs. The biblical literature describes these songs almost invariably as spontaneous outbursts of excited or exalted masses. Granted that the editors of our final text may have smoothed the language and its rhythm, there is no reason to doubt the original spontaneity of such musical transports. Here, the testimonies of neighboring civilizations are of little value, as they concern chiefly the music of courts or temples, which in Sumer, Babylon, and Canaan was then in the hands of professional priest-musicians. We have only a few remarks of Herodotus about Egyptian practices, which were similar to those of ancient Hebrew popular singing. He refers to the "lament for Linos," also to women's chants in processions of the cult of Osiris and the Diana of Bubastis (Hist. II.60;79; also Plutarch *De Iside* 17). In Phoenicia and Syria almost all popular music reflected the worship of Ishtar, the goddess of fertility. Thus, popular song was usually a prelude to sexual orgies in honor of the goddess, led and organized by her thousands of hierodules.

Israel's early popular singing resembled those practices closely in performance but differed radically in its intent. The two lost books "The Wars of the Lord" (ספר מלחמת ה; cf. Num. 21:14) and "The Book of *Yashar*" (ספר הישר; cf. II Sam. 1:18, perhaps even a mistake for ספר השיר) seem to have contained a collection of texts of popular songs. Expressly to the latter book belonged the famous lament of David for Saul and Jonathan. The crucial passage here demands that "it should be taught to the people of Judah" (II Sam. 1:18). The quotation of the "Wars of the Lord" might give us a faint inkling of the kind of singing then in vogue.

There is no doubt that some of the Hebrew texts approximate the metric principle of isosyllabism (equal number of syllables per *stichos*). Accordingly, this system could be imitated in English as follows (Num. 21:14-18 orig. tr.):

Line	Syllables
Wahab which is in Suphah	7
And valleys of Arnon.	6
And descents of its brooks	6
That turn to the seat of Ar	7
And leans on Moab's border.	7
And thence to the well;	5
[This is the well where the Lord said to Moses]	
"Gather the people	5
I'll give them water."	5
Then did Israel sing	6
This song did it sing:	5
Spring up, well, sing to it!	6
Well, which the princes dug,	6
Which nobles of the people delved,	7
With their scepters and staves.	6

Such short lines of five to seven syllables are usually sung upon one and the same melodic phrase; this kind of rendition is even today an archetype of Near Eastern chant. If such phrases are accompanied by tambourines or light percussion instruments, the result may have resembled an antiphony of Yemenite Jewish women (Example 1):

Example 1

From E. Gerson-Kiwi, "Musique dans la Bible," *Dictionnaire de la Bible* (ed. Pirot; Supplément, 1955); by permission of Letouzey et Ané, Paris

Other typical folk songs are laments or acclamations, as they appear, e.g., in I Sam. 17:7; I Kings 12:16 (in mocking fashion); Jer. 9:19-20. In the same way ditties were chanted, almost like our nursery rhymes; they also display the characteristic sequence of accents: 3/2 or 4/3. According to Budde, this rhythmic arrangement is typical of the *Qinah* (dirge), but this is a somewhat disputed theory. Be that as it may, this arrangement was probably reflected in their melodies. It is possible that regular accentual patterns like 3/2 or 4/3 had stereotype melodies, so-called contrafacts, which could be adjusted to any text that fitted the number of beats. Example 2 illustrates this practice.

Example 2

Yemenite Mode of Penitence and Lamentations

(Idelsohn)

Gregorian Mode of Lamentation

(after O. Fleischer and P. Wagner)

By permission of Breitkopf & Härtel, Leipzig

Other expressions of popular singing are the working songs, of which the early rabbinic literature speaks with contempt. Furthermore, there are riddles, as in Judg. 14:14, with the accentual pattern 3/3, somewhat like

> From the eáter came sómething to éat.
> From the stróng came sómething swéet.

Here, words and tune must have formed a close unity. Military calls or signals, such as Num. 10:35, must be imagined sung to a strictly rhythmical tune in keeping with the beats of the text (in Hebrew). The stressed words rhyme:

Qu-mā̧ Ya-ha-wę́, wə-ya-phų́-ṣu *ǫ-yə-vę́-kha*, vəyanų́-su *məsa-nę́-kha mipanę́kha*.

To a related category belong the remnants of bardic songs, such as the well-known "Song of Lamech" (Gen. 4:23-24). Here, the rhythmic scheme approximates metrical poetry.

b. Professional liturgical music. Widespread is the naïve notion which assumes for the temple in Jerusalem a never-changing, inflexible musical tradition. There is a lack of technical information in our sources; its cause is the deliberate silence of the priests, which is, however slightly, lifted but once, by Josephus, himself a priest. Only in one passage he discloses one of the internal "stage secrets" of the priest's performance: "The King, with the suffrages of those that came into the synhedrion, granted the singers (Levites) this privilege, that they may lay aside their former garments, and wear such a linen as they desired; and as a part of this tribe (of the Levites) ministered in the Temple, he also permitted them to learn those hymns as they had besought him for. Now all this was contrary to the laws of our country. Whenever these laws were transgressed, we have never been able to avoid the punishment of such transgressions" (Antiq. XX.ix.6).

Whether or not one pays attention to Josephus' gloomy *vaticinium ex eventu,* the fact emerges that the Levites studied—i.e., memorized—text and music of "new hymns." What these new hymns were, we do not know; but that a change in the musical repertoire was nothing unheard of, is proved by the repeated exhortation: "Sing to the Lord a new song!"

The rendition of longer canticles or psalms must have been strophic, as without any such repetition (and, of course, without notation) it was not possible to keep together the vocal and instrumental ensemble. The instrumental accompaniment was probably heterophonic—i.e., it reproduced the vocal line in an instrumental unison with slight melismatic deviations. The instruments were used independently only for signaling purposes (cymbal strokes, trumpet calls, etc.).

According to the Talmud, during the existence of the temple there was a distinction made between certain archetypes of Levitical songs. This statement must be treated with great caution, as the Talmud idealizes a priori everything pertaining to the temple. At the same time, we know from the Talmud itself that hardly 150 years after the temple's destruction the great rabbis could not, and did not, agree on the performance of the most popular group of Psalms, the Hallel (Soṭ. 30*b*). With this reservation, the passages concerning the archetypes of song are here briefly extracted (Giṭ. 7*a*).

The solemn, straightforward type of the *shîrâ* (שירה) applies to poetic texts on festive occasions.

The exuberant, probably melismatic chant of praise, *hālîlâ* (הלילא), is suitable for high festivals.

The syllabic psalmody *zimra* (זמרא) is appropriate for the study of the Mishna or the plain reading of the Psalms. Perhaps it denoted also a primitive type of scriptural cantillation.

Every melody (נעימה) has its own prosody (טעם) and pitch (הגבה קול), which must be observed (Midrash *Canticum Rabba* 8.12).

These archetypes of performance constituted the usual temple ritual. Yet, there was one annual event which served as pretext for all kinds of extravagances in music and dance. Again, we must, to a certain extent, rely upon the Talmudic description, which, however, in this case is confirmed by passages of early rabbinic literature and extensive descriptions by Josephus. This, the merriest of all the festivals, was the "Feast of Drawing Water" (שמחת בית השואבה). It was the most joyous and the most musical of the temple's festivities. Its description in the Mishna text opens with the significant words: "Whosoever has not seen the joy of the House of Water-Drawing has never seen real joy in his life" (M. Suk. 5.1). After the preparations, which occupied the entire afternoon of the first day of Tabernacles, the "men of good deeds" began to dance before the people in the temple court with burning torches. The Levites, having stationed themselves upon the fifteen steps leading from the women's court to the Inner Court, took up their harps, lyres, cymbals, trumpets, pipes, flutes, clarinets, etc., all instruments greatly augmented in number, and intoned the fifteen "Songs of Ascent." Thus, the night passed in dancing, singing, and general merrymaking. At the sound of the first cockcrow, the priests intoned the triple blast תקיעה, תרועה, תקיעה upon their ritual trumpets. These signals ended the general frolicking, and the crowd ranged itself into an orderly procession to the well of Siloah.

Today, this music and dance festival is understood as the one remnant of old Canaanite fertility rituals, which, in the monotheistic pseudomorphosis of the temple ceremonies, was to ensure an abundant crop of plants, animals, and even human beings.

This was perhaps the only occasion where popular music-making was allowed to mix with the otherwise sternly guarded prerogative of Levitical music. Consequently, secular, superstitious, even popular licentious elements were here introduced in the pure performance of the temple's liturgical music.

4. Character of biblical music. Considering the rather fantastic notions which have been proposed in the past, the following examination distinguishes between documentary evidence, working hypotheses, and personal opinions.

We have no technical evidence concerning the details of popular and secular song in Israel; but with regard to temple music, there are certain historical facts which lend themselves at least to musicological interpretation. They concern (*a*) the problem of continuity and unity of the Jewish musical tradition, (*b*) certain remnants of ancient Jewish music in the plain chant of Judaism and Christianity, and (*c*) the melodic archetypes of ancient Jewish chant.

a. Continuity and unity of Jewish musical tradition. Among modern musicologists, we encounter rather different attitudes toward this problem. L. Saminsky denies any continuity of musical tradition since the destruction of the second temple. He does not, however, support his thesis with any factual evidence. He is inclined to ascribe all resemblances of Jewish and Christian chant to Jewish borrowings. The crucial case of the Yemenite Jews, whose music shows conspicuous identities with the oldest strata of Gregorian chant, yet who never came in contact with any of the churches, is ignored. An opposite view is held by J. Yasser, who, in his various publications, assumes a rigid and strict adherence to ancient tradition. But, being a cautious scholar, he is aware of the fact that the farther back we are able to trace a melody, the more the number of its notes diminishes.

A moderate line is held by Curt Sachs, who has adduced historic documents to prove the continuity of musical tradition in Judaism. The most important agency for the preservation of musical tradition was the institution of the *maʿ*[a]*mādhôth* (מעמדות), the "bystanders" in the temple, lay delegations from all parts of Palestine. During the last century of the temple's existence, the Pharisees (rabbis) succeeded in establishing a synagogue in the very area of the temple. This synagogue, a democratic institution within the hierarchical confines of the temple, was the renowned "Hall of Stones" or "Solomon's Hall" of the NT. There, the bystanders were instructed in the chants of the sanctuary by outstanding Levites. We know the names of two of these Levitical instructors for the laymen: Rabbi Joshua ben Ḥananya and Rabbi Eliezer ben Hyrcanus ('Arak. 11*b*). Rabbi Joshua, a disciple of Rabbi Johanan ben Zakkai, assisted his master in preserving as much as possible of the temple's ritual customs for the academy of Jabne (Suk. 53*a*). He and his contemporaries formed a strong link in the chain of tradition at a most critical time.

Aside from these historical circumstances, the manifold and conspicuous resemblances of melodic archetypes in ancient Hebrew tradition with old strata of Christian plain chant, impel us to assume a common source for such similarities. Whether this source was the temple or the contemporary synagogue remains problematical.

b. Remnants of ancient Hebrew songs in plain chant of church and synagogue. Already some of the church fathers have insisted that the church be considered the *heres de facto* and *de jure* of temple and ancient synagogue. Ambrose and some of his contemporaries went so far as to claim for the church a direct Jewish legacy in ritual and chant. On the Jewish side, Manuello of Rome, a contemporary of Dante, wrote the caustic distich:

> What has the science of music to say to the Christians?
> "Stolen, yea stolen was I" from the Hebrews' own land!

(The second *stichos* is, in the original Hebrew, a sardonic quotation of Gen. 40:15.)

The first serious examination of the interrelation between Christian and Hebrew chant was made by Padre Martini, young Mozart's benevolent teacher, in his *Storia della Musica*. Martini arrives at the cautious conclusion that there are undeniable resemblances, but because of the dearth of primary Jewish and Christian sources it is in most cases impossible to state who lent and who borrowed.

A hundred years after Martini, the Jewish composer and writer Samuel Naumbourg (1815-80) published his *Recueil de chants religieux des Israélites* (1874), which opens with an intuitive study on the sources of Hebrew musical tradition. He compares some characteristic archetypes of Gregorian chant with their Hebrew counterparts and comes to the conclusion that both are based upon a common source. He refrains, however, from speculating further and concludes by emphasizing the main differences of Gregorian and Hebrew plain chant.

It was the French musicologist Amédée Gastoué who, through historical, paleographical, and musical methods, gave the first conclusive proof of the ancient relationship of Jewish and Christian chant. Shortly thereafter, A. Z. Idelsohn, the foremost Jewish musicologist of his generation, demonstrated the close connection of certain melodic archetypes of the Yemenite tradition with the oldest strata of Gregorian chant. This was a significant discovery, as the Yemenites had left Palestine at the time of incipient Christianity and had never been in contact with any of the churches. The outstanding scholar Peter Wagner took up the cue in his Gregorian research and discovered important Jewish roots in the chant of the early church. With the works of these three scholars a solid foundation was laid; and yet, the methodology of their comparisons leaves much to be desired in cogent reasoning, on account of a principal uncertainty concerning the "case histories" of most synagogal or Gregorian tunes.

Egon Wellesz, the protagonist of Byzantine chant, added new evidence to the problem of Jewish-Christian musical interrelation, specializing in the liturgical chant of the Eastern churches.

By abandoning the method of comparing individual tunes with one another, and by replacing the single melody by archetypes or structural prototypes, one is able to base his research upon the methods of comparative liturgy and comparative musicology.

c. Development of research in ancient Jewish chant. The judicious scholars of Renaissance and Reformation broke with the medieval tradition of a mystic temple. Parallel with the increasingly critical interpretation of scripture went a growing understanding of music as it occurs in the Bible. Johannes Reuchlin's evaluation and notation of Jewish scriptural cantillation heralded a new attitude toward the music of the ancient Near East. The two subsequent centuries produced such scholars as the Jesuit Athanasius Kircher, the theologians Père Mersenne, G. Bartolocci, A. Pfeiffer, the renowned Abbot Gerbert, all of whom occupied themselves with Hebrew music in general and that of the temple in particular. They limited themselves, however, to the study of texts and documents and overlooked the possibility that the Near East of their own times might have preserved traces of ancient Semitic music. *See* MASORETIC ACCENTS.

This idea was championed, in word and deed, by G. A. Villoteau (1759-1839), who participated in Napoleon's expedition to Egypt and the Near East. There he investigated at first hand, and with incredible industry but inadequate equipment, the music of Syria and Egypt. He devoted a special chapter to the musical traditions of the Jews in Egypt and Palestine. His learned disquisitions are contained in the monumental volumes of the government-commissioned *Description de l'Égypte*. Though many of his findings and conclusions have been superseded during the subsequent years, some of his fundamental statements and the basic principles of his approach remain landmarks of comparative musicology. He pointed out what he considered the indigenous elements of all Semitic and Egyptian music and analyzed them in detail.

Modern research utilized the newly excavated treasures of cuneiform libraries. The triad of linguistics, history of culture, and comparative musicology has produced some startling new discoveries. Many ancient musical instruments from Ur, Kara-Tepe, from ancient Mesopotamia, and Egypt were brought to light, and most recently the soil of Israel has yielded a few of its musical relics. Entire or fragmentary liturgies of Sumer, Akkad, Egypt, Ugarit, have been reconstructed and published. Finally, concerted efforts have been made to compare the most ancient melodic elements of the Near East and to establish criteria for their age and provenance.

Thanks to the efforts of many scholars, we may, with a certain amount of certainty, set down the following characteristics of ancient Hebrew music:

a) The general nature of its melos is diatonic and tetrachordal.

b) Hebrew music inclines to crystallizing stereotyped melodic patterns, which were established in a set of fairly defined modes.

c) Each of these musical modes was believed to possess an ethos of its own, which corresponded to the four elements, the four humors of the human body, and the four seasons of the year.

d) Clement of Alexandria has left to us a general description of the psalmody of Egyptian Jewry, which, according to Philo, was shaped in conformity with the chant of Palestinian Jewry. Plutarch gives an exact analysis of the mode mentioned by Clement, the so-called *Tropos Spondeiakos*. In accordance with these sources, the mode may be reconstructed as in Example 3:

Example 3

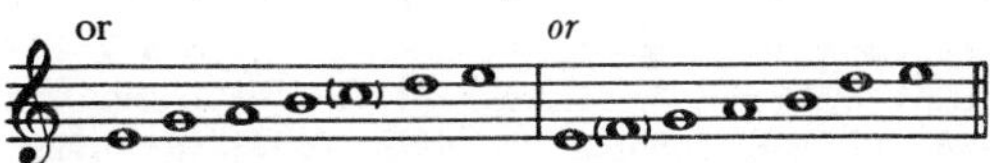

(According to Clement of Alexandria *The Pedagogue*, II.4; Plutarch *De musica*)

Indeed, melodies based upon this mode can be found in Gregorian, Armenian, Byzantine, and Hebrew chant. *See* Example 4.

Example 4

Yemenite *Sh*[e] *ma*'

Gregorian

By permission of Breitkopf & Härtel, Leipzig

e) Certain psalmodic formulas and cadences occur in Yemenite as well as in the oldest strata of Gregorian chant. Their common source must be Palestinian, as the Yemenites, after their emigration from Judea, did not come into contact again with organized Christianity. *See* Example 5.

Example 5

Yemenite psalmody

The Eighth Gregorian Psalm Tone

Example 6

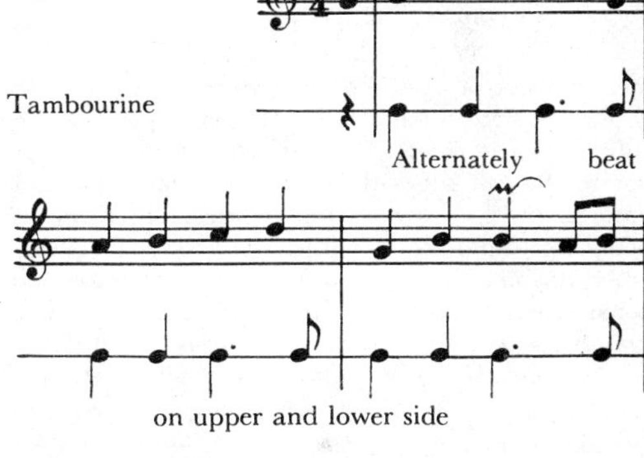

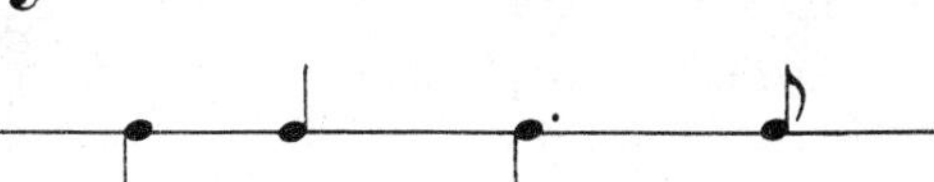

From E. Gerson-Kiwi, "Musique dans la Bible," *Dictionnaire de la Bible* (ed. Pirot; Supplément, 1955); by permission of Letouzey et Ané, Paris

f) Ancient Hebrew music did not make the distinction between composer and performer; every singer composed, or rather improvised, his songs upon the motifs which belonged to the treasury of common folk songs and were familiar to all his listeners. He was more a compounder of well-known motifs than an original composer. The idea of "originality" is unknown to Semitic musicians even up to this day.

g) The chant of ancient Hebrews was rhythmical, but probably free of fixed meter. Perhaps the only exceptions were the dancing songs of women, usually accompanied by percussion instruments. *See* Example 6 *above*.

C. *MUSIC IN THE NT AND IN THE RABBINIC ERA.* The books of the NT, clearly destined for the practical activities of the incipient church, are, from a historical point of view, limited to a short period. They encompass the span of seventy years before the destruction of the temple; geographically, they address themselves to the world of Hellenism. Moreover, neither the gospels nor the epistolary literature display any particular interest in the ritual and the liturgy of the temple. It might even be said that the apostles considered the institution of the temple as a panel for religious disputation at best, as a seat of corruption at worst. They all came from the synagogue and were at home there. They had no use for hierarchical traditions and were, in this respect at least, in accord with the Pharisees, opposed to the ruling class of the Sadducees, who dominated the temple. Indeed, all evidence points to the chant and music of the primitive church as practically identical with the customs and traditions of the synagogue.

Aside from the customary music of temple and synagogue, the books of the NT speak of music mainly as an integral part of the daily life of Palestine and the Hellenistic communities. This statement admits of one important exception: the book of Revelation, whose eschatological visions contain a great deal of exalted musical imagery (*see below*). As far as the references to musical activity in the other books of the NT are concerned, they may be easily listed. *See* Table 2.

Table 2

Religious or liturgical chant	Obsequies	Prophetic passages	Merrymaking	Metaphorical usage of musical terms
Matt. 26:30 Mark 14:26 Acts 16:25 I Cor. 14:15 I Cor. 14:26 Eph. 5:19 Col. 3:16 Heb. 2:12 Jas. 5:13	Matt. 9:23	Matt. 24:31 I Cor. 15:52 I Thess. 4:16 Heb. 12:19	Luke 15:25	Matt. 6:2 Matt. 11:17 Luke 7:32 I Cor. 13:1 I Cor. 14:7-8

This tabulation of relatively few passages contains a rather disproportionate number of metaphorical sentences, where music or its instruments are not to be understood literally, but are used as similes or rhetorical figures. The most celebrated of these poetical passages is Paul's glorification of love in I Cor. 13. He opens this dithyrambic praise of *agape* with a startling metaphor: "If I speak in the tongues of men and of angels, but have not love, I am a noisy gong or a clanging cymbal." This passage cannot be fully understood without some knowledge of the attitude toward music taken by Pharisaic Jewry. Explicitly stated here is the primacy of vocal performance over any instrumental music. Implicit is the contempt of all instrumental music, and the emphatic disparagement of "gong" (χαλκός) and cymbals, two of the temple's percussion instruments. This sentiment was vastly different from the Gentile attitude, which favored these instruments. Paul, however, denounced their usage on account of their role in the mystery cults, and thus reflected the views of the orthodox Pharisees as well as some ideas of Philo's philosophy.

Paul, himself a "Pharisee of the Pharisees," shared fully these views; in all his exhortations, he speaks only of "psalms and hymns and spiritual songs" (Eph. 5:19; Col. 3:16). The terminology of this phrase is still somewhat controversial, especially with regard to the term "spiritual songs" (ᾠδαὶ πνευματικαὶ). Whether he understood by this expression the musical form of glossolalia, a kind of wordless hymn, then much in vogue in Judaism, is at least problematical. Occasionally Paul even speaks of an instrument, but like the DSS, he uses it only for metaphorical or rhetoric purposes (as the "bugle," σαλπίγξ, in I Cor. 14:8). In general, however, he considers all musical instruments "lifeless" or "soulless" (ἄψυχα; vs. 7). His attitude toward women in the ecclesia is exactly that of an orthodox Pharisee. The dictum "The women should keep silence in the churches" (vs. 34) has its parallel in the rabbinic principle "The voice of a woman leads to licentiousness" (T.B. Ber. 24*a*).

Music, both vocal and instrumental, plays an exceptional, highly exalted role in some of the apocalyptic writings, especially in Revelation, the Mithra liturgies, Jewish apocalypses, and even in the Judeo-Christian Pseudo-Clementine liturgy (Apostolic Constitutions). To these and similar compilations there must now be added the Dead Sea Scroll of the War of the Children of Light and the Children of Darkness. In some of these visions the actual experience or the idealized image of the temple seems to have set the pattern, from which the author's imagination took its cue—e.g., the harps and trumpets with the Hallelujah singing of the angels (Revelation). In other cases, as in the Hymns of Thanksgiving (*Hôdhayôth* in the Dead Sea Scrolls), we are confronted with a number of references to music which are, as in some Paulinic passages, mere rhetorical devices—e.g.:

> They roared abuse of me
> To the play of the lyre
> And in mocking-songs uttered their sneers
> (ch. V, orig. tr.).
>
> But suddenly I saw
> That there was no distress
> To tear me with pain.
> I played then my harp
> With sounds of redemption,
> My lyre to joyful strains,
> Yea, I blew the pipe and the flute
> In ceaseless praise
> (ch. XI, orig. tr.).

Such allegorizing passages contain the nucleuses of the later substance, and perhaps the presage of the future trends of Christian music. The first three centuries of the church witnessed many controversies; some of them concerned themselves directly with music. The most important of these issues were: (*a*) organized versus spontaneous praying and singing; (*b*) scriptural versus extrascriptural poems; (*c*) fusion with Hellenistic music; (*d*) vocal versus instrumental music; (*e*) the rise of monasticism and its influence upon ecclesiastical chant.

1. Organized versus spontaneous praying and singing. The best examples of this long-lasting controversy, whose results affected all church music, are offered by the various doxologies of the first three Christian centuries. If we define a doxology as a praise of God in the third person with emphasis upon his infinity, the church had, during its first centuries, developed a great number of spontaneous and highly individualized doxologies. Such passages are, e.g.: Rom. 11:36; II Cor. 11:31; Phil. 4:20; I Tim. 1:17, all patterned after the Hebrew models in the Psalter. When the pressure of Arian heresy threatened the unity of the church, the "standardized" lesser doxology *Gloria Patri*, etc., was introduced (cf. Cassian *De Instit. Coenob.* II.8, in *Patrologia Latina*, vol. 49, col. 94), and finally ratified at the second synod of Vaison in 529. *See* Doxology.

The musical consequences of this process of standardization are obvious: organized prayer and chant gain a decided victory over spontaneous worship. Besides, Western chant tends more and more toward codification and systematization, certainly to a larger degree than that reached by the liturgical chant of the Eastern churches. In spite of all these divergences the oldest strata of Gregorian and synagogue plain chant have retained certain common elements in ancient doxological chants. *See* Example 7.

2. Scriptural versus extrascriptural poems. Already at the end of the second century the Byzantine, Syrian, and later the Armenian church showed a marked preference for new, nonscriptural hymns, despite all warnings by the catholic authorities. Even Canon 59 of the Council of Laodicea (360-81), which expressly prohibited nonscriptural texts, was constantly circumvented and openly violated, as the

Example 7

Yemenite

Gregorian

enormous hymn literature of the Eastern churches demonstrates. The fact that, e.g., the Maronite or Uniate Armenian churches came under Roman jurisdiction did in no way diminish the quantity of free hymns in their liturgies. Such inclinations are obviously remnants of ethnic, possibly pagan, predilections, which no doctrine, however strict, could eliminate. Musically speaking, this results in the relatively larger number of metrical tunes in the Eastern tradition in comparison with the Latin ritual. The West remained conservative, faithful to scripture, and admitted rather late (seventh to eighth century) metrical Latin hymns to its official liturgy.

3. Fusion with Hellenistic music. Another important factor in the formation and expansion of early Christian music was its Gentile wing, which brought the Palestinian-Syrian tradition into close contact with the Hellenized world. According to some scholars, the passage Phil. 2:6-12 might perhaps be understood as a free poetic outburst. If their view is correct, we must consider it the first perceptible deviation from spirit and structure of Hebrew poetry. There is no parallelism, not even a trace of lines similar to each other in length or in the number of accentuated syllables. If such a piece was ever sung, which is doubtful, it could not have been performed in the manner of traditional Jewish psalmody or like a canticle.

An instructive example of the synthesis of Hellenistic and Jewish chant is presented by the melos of the Oxyrhynchus Hymn, the oldest notated Christian hymn. This composition seems to be typical of Christian chant outside Palestine, in the second and third centuries A.D. In Example 8 (*see below*) its best transcription (by R. Wagner) is given, together with a translation (original). The scriptural influence upon this composition is undeniable. The allusion to Pss. 93:3-4; 148:4 (the waters praising God); Ps. 19:1-2 (the heavens and stars) and to similar biblical passages seems obvious. The closing doxology is added in strictly orthodox fashion. Hellenistic chant, as we know from its remnants, limited itself to a strictly syllabic relation of word and tone. Thus, one syllable corresponded to one and only one tone, a principle which naturally excludes any melismatic, nonsyllablic motifs. The Oxyrhynchus Hymn breaks with this principle, especially in the four Amens, which are placed at the end of verses. Thus, the Semitic element of so-called "punctuating melismata"

Example 8

Transcription after O. Ursprung, *Bulletin de la Société "Union Musicologique"* (1923), vol. III; by permission of Martinus Nijhoff, The Hague

Translation

". . . all splendid creations of God . . . must not keep silent, nor shall the light-bearing stars remain behind. . . . All waves of thundering streams shall praise our Father and Son, and Holy Ghost, all powers shall join in: Amen, Amen! Rule and Praise (and Glory) to the sole Giver of all Good. Amen, Amen."

has entered into a basically Hellenistic structure. A Hebrew heritage, the melismatic formulas, is recognizable in a hymn of the Gentile church; yet we must not overlook the most important type of Hebrew chant—i.e., psalmody, which directly influenced the ecclesiastical music. According to available patristic writings, the introduction of psalmody into the ancient Greek and Roman world came like a revolutionary event. Writers unfamiliar with psalmody found it strange—e.g., Pliny the Younger, Clement of Alexandria, Socrates, and Diodor of Tarsus. All these writers were either pagans or Gentile Christians. No such wonderment can be found in the writings of the apostles or fathers with Hebrew-Aramaic background. Paul refers to psalmody as to something quite familiar to him.

4. Vocal versus instrumental music. The superiority of vocal over instrumental music was a general tenet of Christian aesthetics, although the degree of hostility to instrumental performances varied in different places, at different times. This attitude seems to run parallel to the rabbinic prohibition of instrumental music, but the underlying reasons were by no means identical. For the short span of Israel's prosperity under the first Hasmoneans, instrumental music was particularly popular at banquets. However the Pharisees might have felt about the temple orchestra, which was exclusively in Sadducean hands, banquet music was welcome in their houses. Maxims of etiquette and deportment refer to secular music—e.g., the adhortations of Ben Sirach (Ecclus. 32:3-6 orig. tr.):

> Do not disturb the musicians!
> Where there is music,
> Do not pour out speech
> And do not be importunate in showing thy wisdom.
> Like a ruby shines in its golden setting,
> So is the musician's ensemble at a banquet of wine.
> As the precious emerald in a golden frame
> So adorn melodies of musicians a feast of wine.
> (Listen in silence
> And thy modesty will be rewarded by good will.)

This urbane attitude vanished under the unceasing pressure of Pharisaic puritanism, especially in the realm of liturgical music. While Paul's contempt of musical instruments was based upon the Pharisaic view (*see* § C *above*), the later Christian authorities had much more cogent reasons for their antagonism against all instrumental music. The pagan theater and circus, with their licentious female musicians, attracted vast masses of Gentile Christians, who were accustomed to these spectacles. The wild vigils of martyr's anniversaries; the various, only slightly camouflaged, popular festivals, disguised as memorial days of saints, were the occasions when instrumental music was taken for granted. The church needed three centuries of severe legislation to eradicate at least the worst of these orgiastic customs.

5. Rise of monasticism and its influence upon ecclesiastical chant. The most decisive steps in the development of Christian chant were taken under the aegis and championship of early monasticism. Through the Dead Sea Scrolls we know today that both concept and practice of monastic life grew directly out of dissident Jewish sects during the last two centuries of the Second Jewish Commonwealth. From the very beginning, even during its Jewish phase, monasticism cultivated choral singing as an integral part of its observance (cf. Manual of Discipline and Hymns of Thanksgiving). A later historiographer of the church, Eusebius, was aware of the musical predilections of the old ascetic sects in Judaism. In fact, he excerpted Philo's description of the ritual of the Alexandrinian Therapeutes, which he likened to the Christian practice of his own time (four centuries later): "The men and the women rise, each group forming a choir, and sing thanksgiving hymns to God the Redeemer" (Hist. II.17).

The majority of Christian monks in Egypt and Palestine championed organized choral chant, often in the face of a sternly opposed authority. When all historical circumstances are taken into account, there can be no doubt that the tremendous expansion and refinement of Christian chant before Pope Gregory was due to the intensive and continuous musical activities of the monks. The musical endeavors of the monastic orders came to fruition in the West, however, and deteriorated in the Near East. This paradoxical fact is probably due to the specific musical traditions and predilections of the various, recently Christianized nations of the East. Perhaps Augustine may be considered the pivotal figure in this development. By birth and inclination a Semite, he was won over to Western culture and views in the field of music (cf. his *De Musica*). He was the last exponent of a uniform musical tradition within the church. Soon after his death, the regional-ethnic forces of Gentile Christianity caused the split in the liturgico-musical development of the Eastern and Western churches. While the former remained essentially stagnant in liturgical chant, the latter became the main agent in the gigantic development of Western music.

Bibliography. Bibliographical reference works: *Bibliography of Asiastic Musics* (Library of Congress), third instalment: "The Jews, Ancient and Modern"; fourth instalment: "Hebrews, Jews and Early Christians"; fifth instalment: "Christians"; in "Notes," vol. V, no. 3 (1948), pp. 354-62; vol. V, no. 4 (1948), pp. 549-62; vol. VI, no. 1 (1949), pp. 122-36. A. Sendrey, *Bibliography of Jewish Music* (1951).

General: A. Ackermann, "Der Synagogale Gesang," *Winter und Wünsche, Geschichte der Literatur der Juden* (1897), F. Leitner, *Der gottesdienstliche Volksgesang im jüdischen und christlichen Altertum* (1906). S. Krauss, *Talmudische Archäologie* (1912). A. Z. Idelsohn, *Thesaurus of Hebrew Oriental Melodies* (1914-31). C. Sachs, *Musik der Antike* (1924). D. D. Luckenbill, *Ancient Records of Assyria and Babylonia* (1926-27). G. Dalman, *Arbeit und Sitte in Palästina* (1928-42). A. Z. Idelsohn, *Jewish Music in Its Historical Development* (1929). R. Lachmann, *Jewish Cantillation and Song in the Island of Djerba* (1940). C. Sachs, *History of Musical Instruments* (1940); *The Rise of Music in the Ancient World* (1943). L. R. Wiley, *Bible Music* (1945). E. Werner, "Jewish Music," in G. Grove, *Dictionary of Music* (5th ed., 1952-54); "The Origin of Psalmody," *HUCA*, vol. XXV (1954). E. Gerson-Kiwi, "Musique dans la Bible," *Dictionnaire de la Bible*, Supplement (1956).

On music in the OT: J. Reuchlin, *De accentibus linguae hebraicae* (1518). P. G. Martini, *Storia della Musica* (1757-81). G. A. Villoteau, *Description de l'Egypte*, I (1809), 833-43, 1,011 ff. S. Naumbourg, *Recueil de chants religieux des Israélites* (1874). A. Buechler, "Jur Geschichte der Tempelmusik und der Tempelpsalmen," *ZAW*, XIX (1899), 96-133, 329-44; XX (1900), 97-135. A. Buechler, "Zur Geschichte des Tempelcultus in Jerusalem," *Chwolson-Festschrift* (1899). K. Budde, *Geschichte der althebr. Literatur* (1906). A. Gastoué, *Les origines du chant romain* (1907). P. Wagner, *Einführung in die Gregorianischen Melodien* (1911-22). S. Krauss, *Synagogale Altertuemer* (1922). A. Gastoué, "Chant juif et chant grégorien," *Revue du Chant Grégorien* (1931), pp. 11 ff. L. Saminsky, *Music of the Bible and of the Ghetto* (1937). E. Werner, "The Doxology in Synagogue and Church," *HUCA*, vol. XIX (1945/46). E. Kolari, *Musikinstrumente und ihre Verwendung im AT* (1947). R. Patai, *Man and Temple* (1947). E. Wellesz, *Eastern Elements in Western Chant* (1947). E. Werner, "The Conflict Between Hellenism and Judaism in the Music of the Early Church," *HUCA*, XX (1947). H. Schneider, "Die biblischen Oden im christlichen Altertum," *Bibl.*, XXX (1949), 28-65. E. Werner, "The Common Ground in the Chant of Church and Synagogue," *Acts of First International Congress of Catholic Music* (1951). J. Yasser, "The Traditional Roots of Jewish Harmony," *Proceedings of the Cantors' Assembly* (1951). M. Burrows, *The Dead Sea Scrolls* (1955). E. Werner, "Musical Aspects of the Dead Sea Scrolls," *Musical Quarterly*, XLIII (1957), 21-37. M. Wallenstein, "Hymns of Thanksgiving," *Bulletin of the John Rylands Library*, vol. 38 (1955-56).

On music in the NT: Diodore of Tarsus, in *Texte und Untersuchungen zur Geschichte der altchristlichen Literatur* (ed. Harnack), N.F. VI (1901). Eusebius on Philo in Hist. II.17 (ed. Schwartz). Plutarch *De Iside*, etc. (ed. Parthey; 1850); *De Musica* (ed. R. Volkmann; 1856). F. X. Funk, ed., *Constitutiones Apostolorum* (1905). *Patrologia Latina* (ed. Migne; 1907); *Patrologia Graeca* (ed. Migne; 1907); *Patrologia Orientalis* (eds. Griffin and Nau; 1907 ff). Pliny the Younger *Letters* (ed. W. Melmoth; 1915). B. P. Grenfell and A. S. Hunt, *The Oxyrhynchos Papyri*, vol. XV (1922). R. Wagner, *Philologus*, vol. 79 (1923). L. Saminsky, *Music of the Ghetto and of the Bible* (1934). Clement of Alexandria *The Pedagogue* (ed. Stählin), in *Die griechischen christlichen Schriftsteller*, vol. 12 (1936). Augustine *De musica*, in *Patrologia Latina*, vol. 32 (trans. C. R. Taliaferro; 1939). E. Werner, "The Attitude of the Early Church Fathers Towards Hebrew Psalmody," *Review of Religion*, vol. VII (May, 1943); "The Origin of the Eight Modes of Music," *HUCA*, vol. XXI (1948); *The Sacred Bridge* (1957/58). C. H. Kraeling, "The Music of the Bible," *New Oxford History of Music*, vol. I (1957). E. Werner

MUSICAL INSTRUMENTS. Many books of the OT and some of the NT refer in detail to musical instruments. From the time of the earliest exegetes—i.e., rabbis and church fathers—the instruments of the temple and, later, quite generally all musical instruments mentioned in scripture became a subject of curiosity, research, and often of unfounded hypotheses and illusions.

A. Sources
B. Classification

1. Idiophones
   a. Bells
   b. Cymbals
   c. Rattler-sistrum
   d. Gong
2. Aerophones
   a. Flute, pipe
   b. Clarinet
   c. Horn
   d. Trumpet
   e. *Shôphār*
3. Membranophones
4. Chordophones
   a. Lyre
   b. Trigon
   c. Lute
   d. Harp
5. Spurious terms
   a. "Bagpipe"
   b. "Sackbut," "viol," and "cornet"
6. Collective terms
   a. "Stringed instruments"
   b. "Instruments of music"

Bibliography

A. *SOURCES.* Our sources belong to two main categories: (*a*) written or printed documents and (*b*) archaeological findings.

The first category consists of three components: the Bible and its translations; rabbinic and patristic literature; and descriptions transmitted by Roman or Greek authors. While the Bible is reliable, its substance is meager and its terminology unclear and apparently extremely sparse in its few explanations. Rabbinic and patristic literature should be used only with great caution; while the texts deal mainly with the music of the temple—in an idealizing fashion—they were written at least 150 years after the temple's destruction. Many, if not all, of them rely upon hearsay. Roman and Greek descriptions also demand prudent evaluation, though for different reasons. To Josephus, who had been born into the priestly class, everything connected with the temple was *ipso facto* admirable. To the early church fathers, much of the temple's ritual was either holy or suspect, especially to Epiphanius and John Chrysostom. Of Gentile Hellenistic authors we have only some rather fantastic remarks on Jewish civilization (cf. Diogenes Laertius, Plutarch).

The archaeological evidence consists of pictorial representations of temple instruments or discoveries of musical instruments in Palestine and the neighboring countries. To the first category belong the famous relief on the Arch of Titus in Rome and the coins, issued by Hasmonean kings and Bar Cocheba, on which lyre and trumpet are depicted. Richer are the findings of archaeological excavations. Of Palestinian instruments the following were discovered: the mouthpiece of a חליל (by N. Glueck; *see* § B2*b below*), several bone flutes (by E. Garstang), and a trumpet made of a large sea shell (by Y. Yadin). Many instruments were discovered in or near Ur, at Lake Mari, etc., and there is abundant pictorial representation in reliefs, sculptures, and pictures of Sumerian, Babylonian, Hittite, Mittani, and Egyptian musical instruments.

B. *CLASSIFICATION.* In accordance with C. Sachs's generally recognized method we distinguish idiophones, aerophones, membranophones, and chordophones. To the idiophones (the instrument's own material produces the tone) belong: bells, castanets, rattler-sistrum, triangle (tabret), cymbals, and certain chimes. Aerophones (air is directly vibrated) are: flute, horn, trumpet, oboe, clarinet, pipe, ram's horn (*shôphār*), bugle, bagpipe, and the puzzling, erroneously named sackbut. Membranophones (the tone is produced by vibrating membranes) are: tambourine, timbrel, and drum. Chordophones (strings produce the tone) are: harp, lute, lyre, sambuke, cittern, dulcimer, psaltery, and viol.

1. Idiophones. *a. Bells.* There are two types of bells mentioned. פעמנים (from פעם, "to strike, push") were used as apotropaic protective instruments fastened to the hem of the high priest's robe (Exod. 28:33; 39:25-26). These bells, presumably without clapper, alternated with pomegranates; both were made of pure gold. By striking against one another at every movement of the priest, they produced a jingling sound, which had the function of chasing away the evil spirits from under the threshold of the holy of holies when the high priest entered it. Their apotropaic value was still understood by the early rabbis, and there are many analogous phenomena known in anthropology.

מצלת (from צלל, "to rattle, jingle"; properly "jingle bells") are mentioned only in Zech. 14:20, as ornaments or amulets of horses. These bells were shaped like little metal disks and fastened to the bridles or breast straps of the horses (cf. Targ.; M. Par. 12.8).

b. Cymbals. Cymbals (מצלתים, צלצלים; κύμβαλα) occur in three slightly different forms of the same archetype: (*a*) The word מצלתים clearly represents a pair of cymbals, as indicated by the dual form of the Hebrew. They were used only by men, perhaps even only by priests. All thirteen references to them accentuate their ritual or ecstatic function. Their main usage seems to have been priestly; they accompany mostly instruments such as the trumpets (Ezra 3:10), the sacerdotal lyre (I Chr. 25:1; Neh. 12:27), and the "instruments for sacred song" (I Chr. 16:42). (*b*) The second type are the צלצלים, which have been interpreted as either cymbals or even castanets (I Chr. 16:5). "Castanets" can hardly be accepted, inasmuch as the LXX uses here the term κυμβάλοις ἀναφωνῶν, perhaps "cymbals of shouting" (or proclamation). This rendering corresponds to the account of the Talmud (M. Tam. 7, 3; b'Arak. 11*b*), where the cymbal (צלצל) is understood as a purely signaling instrument, in contradistinction to the מצלתים, which team up with lyres and trumpets. Castanets could never have functioned as signal instruments in so spacious and public a location as the temple. (*c*) The צלצלים are qualified in Ps. 150:5 as צלצלי שמע and צלצלי תרוע. According to C. Sachs, the distinction refers both to the shape of the instruments and to the way they were held, horizontally* or vertically.* As the psalm passage cannot be applied to the temple ritual, the "sounding and loud clashing cymbals" had a truly musical function and were not just signaling instruments. Sachs's hypothesis therefore becomes plausible. Figs. MUS 79, 80.

From *Atlas of the Bible* (Thomas Nelson & Sons Limited)

79. Army musicians playing lyres, drum, and horizontal cymbals at military celebration; horses walking to music; from Nineveh (Quyunjiq), period of Ashurbanipal (668-631 B.C.)

Courtesy of the American Schools of Oriental Research

80. Vertical cymbals (Assyria)

c. Rattler-sistrum. The מנענעים (from נוע, "to quiver, to be shaken"; RSV "castanet," KJV "cornet") is mentioned only once (II Sam. 6:5). The LXX has κύμβαλα, the Vulg. correctly *sistra*. This interpretation is demanded both by the etymology of the name and by the instrument's use, as a noise-maker for joyous and sad occasions. The Mishna knows it (M. Kel. 16.7) as one of the wailing women's instruments. It served, exactly as in Egypt, the emotional extremes of jubilation and deep mourning. The oldest sistrums were found in Ur, Kish, and in Sumerian excavations; the instrument has come from Mesopotamia via Palestine to Egypt. Fig. MUS 81.

Paul may have reference to cymbals in I Cor. 13:

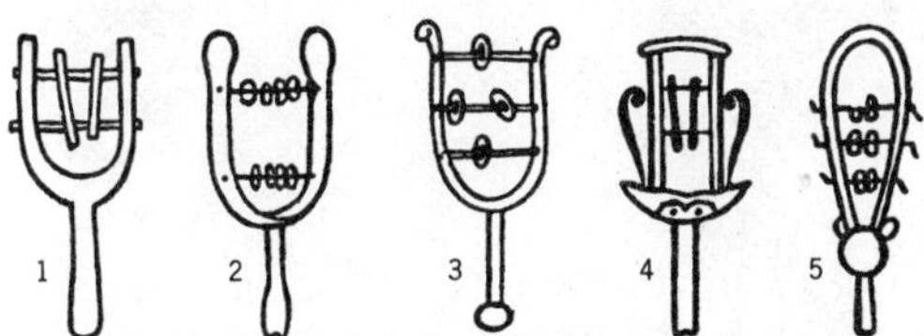

From F. W. Galpin, *Music of the Sumerians* (Cambridge University Press)

81. Sistrums or noisemakers: (1) "spur shaped" from Egypt (twenty-second century B.C.); (2) Georgian (Transcaucasian); (3) Abyssinian; (4) "temple shaped" (Ancient Egypt); (5) "stirrup shaped" (Ancient Egypt)

1 (χαλκός, "copper"; KJV "brass," RSV "gong").

d. Gong. The χαλκός (I Cor. 13:1; KJV BRASS) is known in the rabbinic literature as אירוס (Aramaic), a bronce-gong, which was a characteristic instrument for weddings and similar joyous occasions; in its smaller form it appeared as a kind of hand bell (M. Soṭ. 9, 14). In the famous passage in I Corinthians, Paul seems to allude to *erus* and *ṣilṣelim*.

82. Painting from an Eighteenth Dynasty (*ca.* 1570-1310 B.C.) tomb in Egypt, showing girls playing the harp and lute

2. Aerophones. ***a. Flute, pipe.*** "Flute" and "pipe" are used to translate several words. All pipes and flutes belong to the category of orgiastic-dionysiac instruments which served wild joy as well as ecstatic lament.

The RSV uses "pipe" for עוגב (from עגב, "to love passionately"; KJV "organ"), which occurs four times in the OT and is always translated in the Targumim as אבובא (*aboba*), "shrill pipe or flute." The עוגב was apparently a secular instrument and is never listed in the temple orchestra; only in Ps. 150:4 is it mentioned in a religious (but not ritual) function. Its ethos was not blameless at all, as we see from Genesis Rabbah 50: "The angels said to Lot: 'There are players of the עוגב in the country,

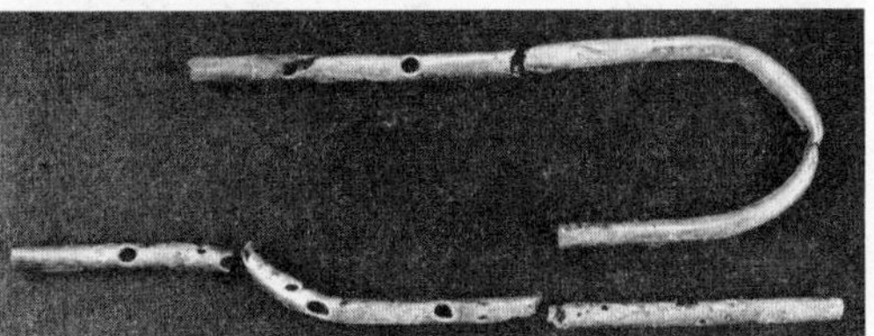

Courtesy of the University Museum of the University of Pennsylvania

83. A silver flute from Ur

hence it ought to be destroyed.'" Its rabbinical identification with the *aboba*, the flute of the notorious Syrian *bayaderes* (cf. Horace *Satires* I.2), emphasizes the erotic element which already the Hebrew name suggests. As both the LXX and the Vulg. translate עוגב with ὄργανον=*organum* in Ps. 150:4, "organ" has become a popular, though erroneous, interpretation. Fig. MUS 83.

משרקיתא (from שרק, "to whistle"; LXX συρισμός; "pipe"; KJV "flute") occurs four times in the Aramaic portions of Daniel; a similar expression (שרקות in Judg. 5:16) indicates the shepherd's piping for his flock. The instrument, made of reeds, wood, or bones, was as primitive as its tone was coarse. As in Theod., this pipe was generally identified with the *syrinx* (cf. the root שרק), or "Pan's pipe." It was not considered fit for liturgical purposes.

b. Clarinet. חליל (KJV "pipe") is translated "flute" in I Sam. 10:5; Isa. 5:12; 30:29; Jer. 48:36. The proper translation of חליל (from חלל, "to pierce"; LXX αὐλός; Akkadian *ḫalḫallatu,* "double pipes"), often erroneously called "flute" or "oboe," is "clarinet." Αὐλός (I Cor. 14:7), "flute" in the RSV, is "pipe" in the KJV. This was the most popular of woodwinds in the Near East. Its Greek counterpart is noted in Matt. 9:23; 11:17; Luke 7:32; I Cor. 14:7; Rev. 18:22. The instrument was no flute or oboe, but a primitive clarinet. Since Nelson Glueck's happy discovery of the mouthpiece of a חליל near Aqaba, we know that it was practically identical with the αῦλος. The proper translation of the Hebrew term would be *shawm* (cf. French *chalumet* and Latin *calamus*), which Raši has already used. The ambiguity of the term חליל was already known to the rabbis. States Rabbi Obadya: "Many kinds of musical instruments were there, but because the sound of the חליל was more audible than the rest, all of them are called by its name" (M. Suk. 5.1).

Long before Israel's existence, we find in Akkadian tablets the word *ḫalḫallatu* for "double clarinet," and we have many ancient representations of this instrument.* As the עוגב, so served also the חליל to express extreme joy as well as deep mourning. Its liturgical function is dubious, to say the least. According to rabbinic literature, the days were limited

Courtesy of the Trustees of the British Museum

84. King's private band of clarinets and harps at Susa, paying homage to King Ashurbanipal of Assyria

to twelve, or maximally eighteen, when the חליל was to be played before the altar (M. 'Arak. 2.3). Fig. MUS 84.

Extremely popular for secular purposes, the חליל was played at weddings, banquets, and funerals. At funerals it served as accompaniment to the customary wailing women; this is the meaning of Matt. 9:23. The chief characteristics of the חליל were: popularity, juxtaposition with hand drum and lyre, expression of extreme emotionalism, and symbolic meaning of fertility and resurrection.

c. Horn. The "horn" (קרן; κέρας; Latin *cornu;* Aramaic קרנא) was a wind instrument made of horn, wood, or metal. In the Hebrew form it is mentioned but twice (Josh. 6:5; I Chr. 25:5 [see KJV]), but as Aramaic קרנא it occurs in Dan. 3:5, 7, 10, 15 (KJV "cornet"). It seems to stand for any kind of horn and/or tuba. Apparently the horn in its primitive form was popular in Canaan before the time of Joshua, as it is mentioned in the Tell el-Amarna correspondence. Tusratta, king of Mitanni, sent (1380 B.C.) to the Pharaoh Amenophis III, his prospective son-in-law, a list of his daughter's dowry, wherein horns are mentioned.

d. Trumpet. A number of words are translated "trumpet." יובל (from יובל, "ram, ram's horn"; LXX σαλπίγξ), which occurs by itself only in Exod. 19:13, is coupled with שופר (*shôphār;* frequently translated "trumpet"; *see* § B2*e below*) in vs. 16. The יובל, as the *shôphār*, was strictly a signaling instrument. The other meaning of יובל, that of "jubilee," originated from the—possibly totemistic—use of the instrument (Lev. 25:9 ff). Its function in the Dead Sea Scrolls (War Scroll) is clearly patterned after Josh. 6.

חצוצרה is translated "trumpet" in Hos. 5:8, as is תקע in Ezek. 7:14. The חצוצרה (perhaps onomatopoetic, "to shatter"; LXX σαλπίγξ; Vulg. *tuba*) was the instrument of the priests par excellence. Its function is similar to, but not quite identical with, that of the שופר (*shôphār; see* § B2*e below*). Trumpets were used in pairs from the very beginning (Num. 10:1-10); their number increased from 2 to 120 at special occasions; sometimes even more were employed, especially at the Feast of Drawing Water. *See* MUSIC.

These instruments were made of metal (bronze, copper, silver, gold), bones, and shell. The tone of the trumpet must have been high and shrill, as the sounding air column was not quite two feet in length. To facilitate the blowing, mouthpieces were added, as we see in the trumpets depicted on the Hasmonean coins or on the famous Arch of Titus.* As the instruments were straight, they could produce some natural overtones. The question whether or not the pitch of the trumpet could be regulated accurately was long controversial (in spite of II Chr. 5:12, where 120 trumpets sounded in unison). This question was settled when the Dead Sea Scroll of the War of the Sons of Light and the Sons of Darkness was discov-

From *Atlas of the Bible* (Thomas Nelson & Sons Limited)

85. Sacred trumpets, from the Arch of Titus

Courtesy of Smithsonian Institute, Washington, D.C.

(*a*) ***Precious stones of the Bible:*** **(1) amethyst, (2) carnelian, (3) sardonyx, (4) turquoise, (5) jasper, (6) agate, (7) coral, (8) zircon, (9) beryl, (10) amber, (11) lapis lazuli, (12) topaz, (13) coral**

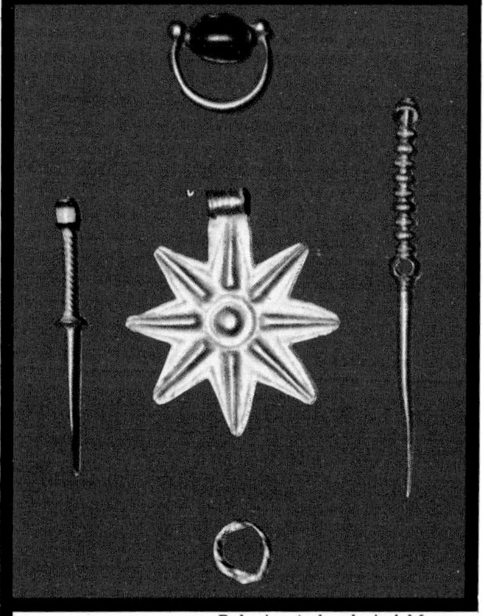

Palestine Archaeological Museum

(*b*) *Star pendant, two gold toggle pins, gold finger ring* with a scarab of amethyst, and *twisted gold earring;* Late Bronze Age, *ca.* 1550-1200 B.C.

Palestine Archaeological Museum

(*c*) *Necklace* mostly of agate stones, *flying hawk ornament* of gold, *gold earring, head of giraffe;* Late Bronze Age, *ca.* 1550-1200 B.C.

Royal Ontario Museum

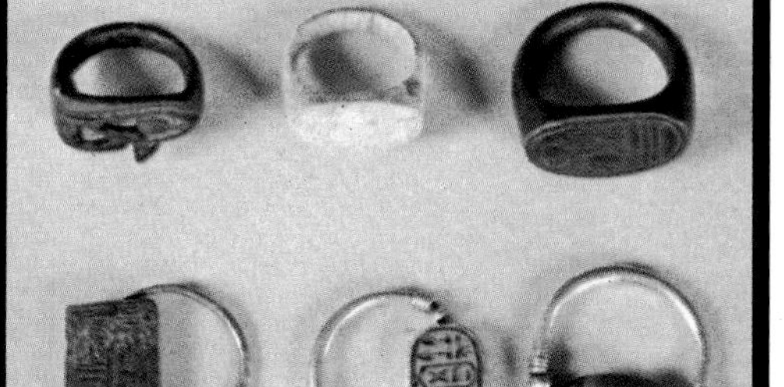

(*d*) Group of *Egyptian rings*

PLATE XVII

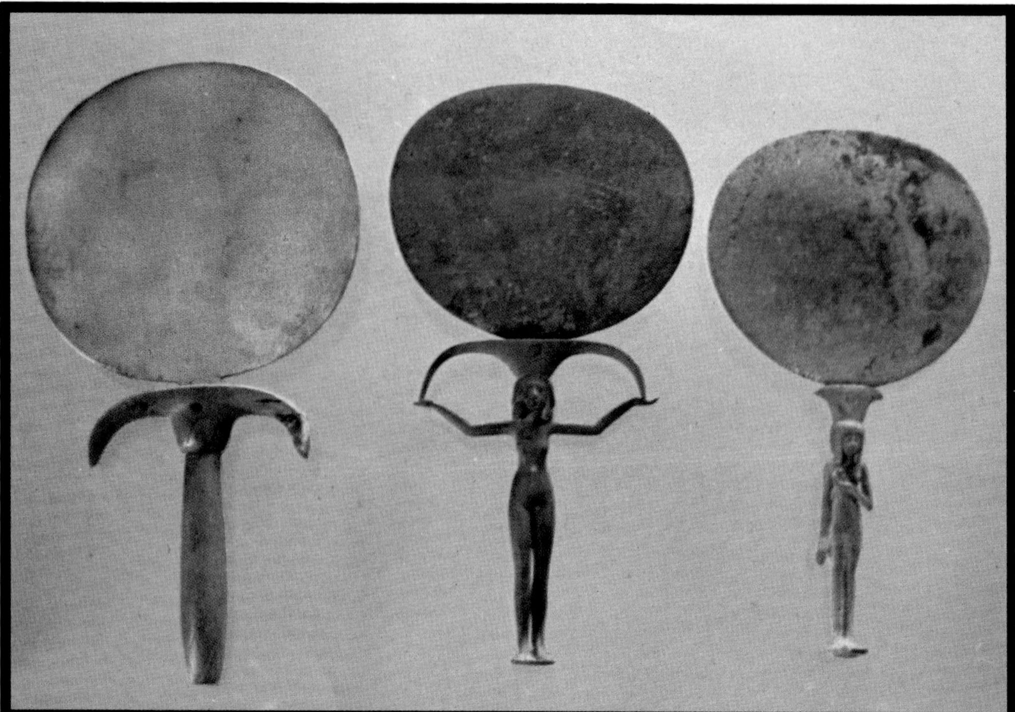

Royal Ontario Museum

(*a*) ***Three Egyptian bronze mirrors,*** **New Kingdom, sixteenth to thirteenth century B.C.**

Royal Ontario Museum

(*b*) ***Egyptian polychrome glass cosmetic bottle,*** **Eighteenth Dynasty**

PLATE XVIII

(*a*) ***Representation of incense altar*** **with "bowl" capital and "lily work," from Megiddo, *ca.* tenth-ninth century B.C.**

Herbert G. May

G. Schumacher and C. Steuernagel, Tell el-Mutesellim *(frontispiece; Leipzig: J. C. Hinrichs, 1908)*

(*b*) ***Pottery incense altar*** **with "lily work" decoration, from Megiddo Stratum VI, period of the judges, *ca.* 1100 B.C.**

PLATE XIX

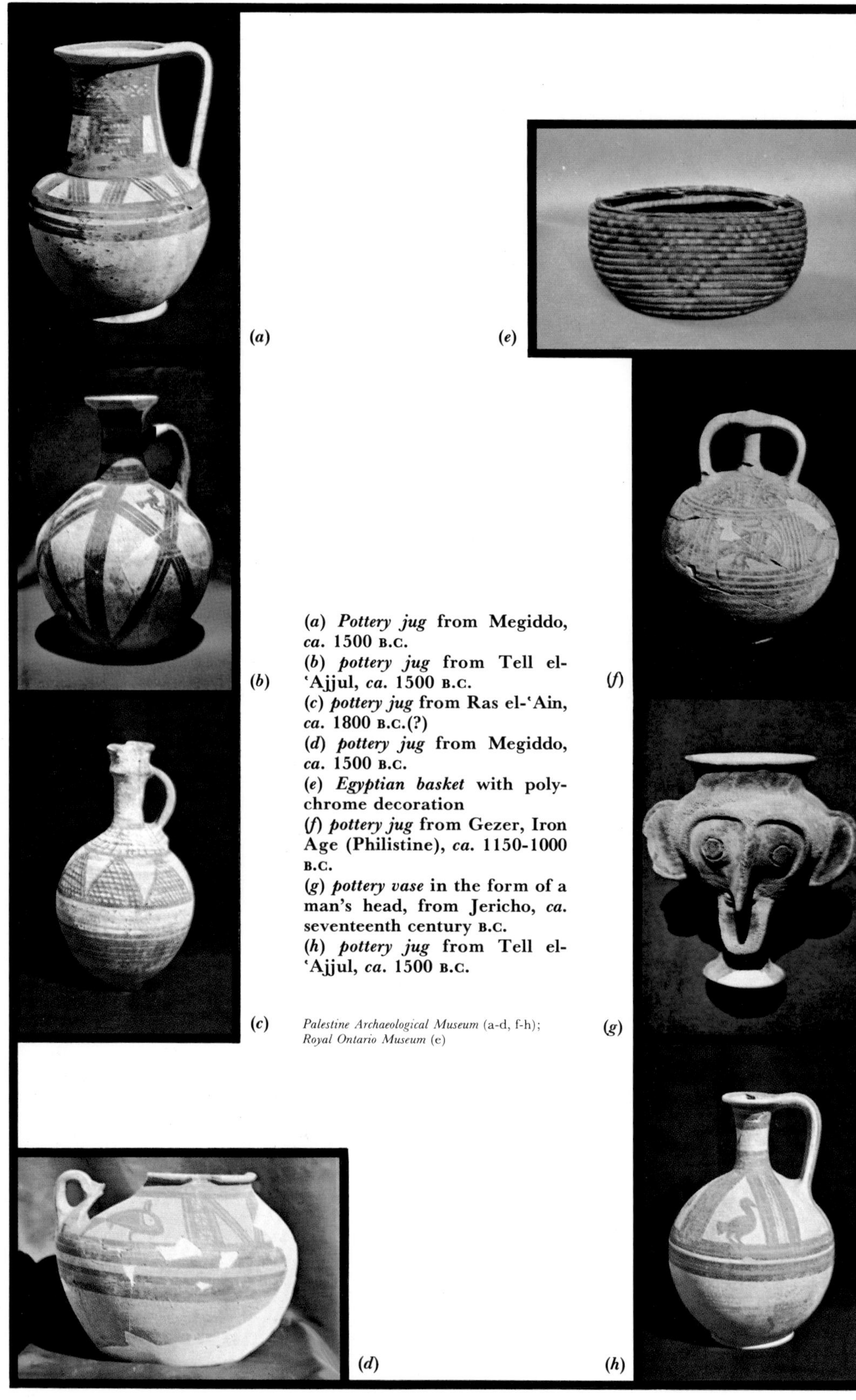

(*a*) *Pottery jug* from Megiddo, *ca.* 1500 B.C.
(*b*) *pottery jug* from Tell el-'Ajjul, *ca.* 1500 B.C.
(*c*) *pottery jug* from Ras el-'Ain, *ca.* 1800 B.C.(?)
(*d*) *pottery jug* from Megiddo, *ca.* 1500 B.C.
(*e*) *Egyptian basket* with polychrome decoration
(*f*) *pottery jug* from Gezer, Iron Age (Philistine), *ca.* 1150-1000 B.C.
(*g*) *pottery vase* in the form of a man's head, from Jericho, *ca.* seventeenth century B.C.
(*h*) *pottery jug* from Tell el-'Ajjul, *ca.* 1500 B.C.

Palestine Archaeological Museum (a-d, f-h); *Royal Ontario Museum* (e)

(*a*) (*b*) (*c*) (*d*) (*e*) (*f*) (*g*) (*h*)

PLATE XX

William L. Reed

(*a*) ***Pottery lamps*** **from Dibon (Dhiban), ninth century B.C.**

Palestine Archaeological Museum

(*b*) ***Basalt mill*** **for grinding grain; found in the excavations at Khirbet Qumran**

Palestine Archaeological Museum

(*c*) ***Pottery mold*** **for casting metal instruments, from Balatah, Middle Bronze Age, *ca.* 1600 B.C.(?)**

Royal Ontario Museum

(*d*) **From left to right: *Pottery juglet,* polished black ware, ninth-eighth century B.C. (Early Iron II), from Beth-shemesh; *pottery juglet,* polished red ware, with black painted decoration, Cypriote origin—a frequent import into Palestine, seventh-sixth century B.C.(?; Iron II); *alabaster* (gypsum) *juglet* from Jericho, *ca.* 2300-2000 B.C. (Intermediate Early Bronze-Middle Bronze Period); *faïence pot* from Jericho, *ca.* 2300-2000 B.C. (Intermediate Early Bronze Period).**

PLATE XXI

Above: (*a*) ***Three jars*** **found in Cave I, Khirbet Qumran**

Palestine Archaeological Museum; photo John C. Trever

Below: (*b*) *House-shaped ossuaries,* from Azor near Tel-Aviv, Chalcolithic Age, fourth millennium B.C.

Department of Antiquities, Israel; photo John C. Trever

Department of Antiquities, Israel; photo John C. Trever

(*c*) *Churn* from Beer-sheba, Chalcolithic Age, fourth millennium B.C.

Department of Antiquities, Israel; photo John C. Trever

(*d*) *"Khirbet Kerak" ware;* pottery vessel from Beth-Yerah (Khirbet Kerak), Early Bronze III, *ca.* 2600-2400 B.C.

PLATE XXII

Royal Ontario Museum

Pottery figurines from Palestine: (*a*) ***bird-face figurine*** **(left), site unknown, fifteenth to thirteenth century B.C. (Late Bronze Age), type frequently found also in Cyprus;** (*b*) ***"pillar type" figurine*** **(right) from Beth-shemesh, ninth-eighth century B.C. (Early Iron II)**

Royal Ontario Museum

(*c*) ***Lion relief*** **on glazed bricks, from palace of Nebuchadrezzar**

Royal Ontario Museum

(*e*) ***Mummy case of Djed-Maat-es-ankh,*** **the songstress of the god Amon, Twenty-sixth Dynasty (663-525 B.C.)**

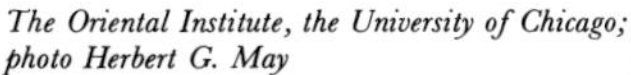

The Oriental Institute, the University of Chicago; photo Herbert G. May

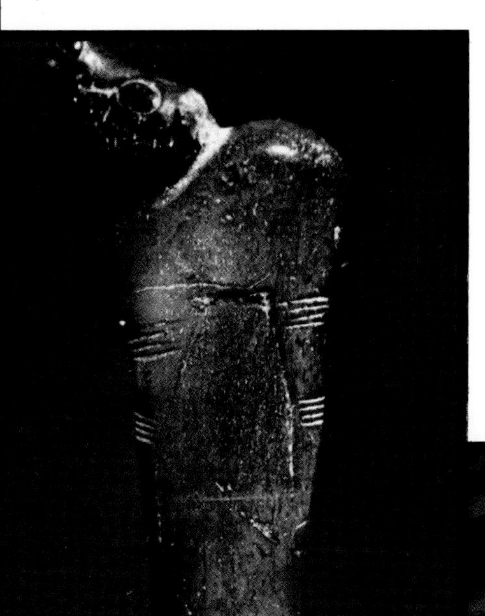

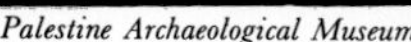

Palestine Archaeological Museum

(*d*) ***Carving of fawn*** **(?) on bone, perhaps a sickle haft, from Mugharet al-Wad, early Mesolithic (Middle Stone) Age**

(*f*) ***Upper part of red-quartzite colossal statue*** **of Tut-ankh-Amon (1362-1352 B.C.) in the Oriental Institute Museum**

PLATE XXIII

(*a*) *Ivory inlays* found at Samaria

Palestine Archaeological Museum; photo John C. Trever

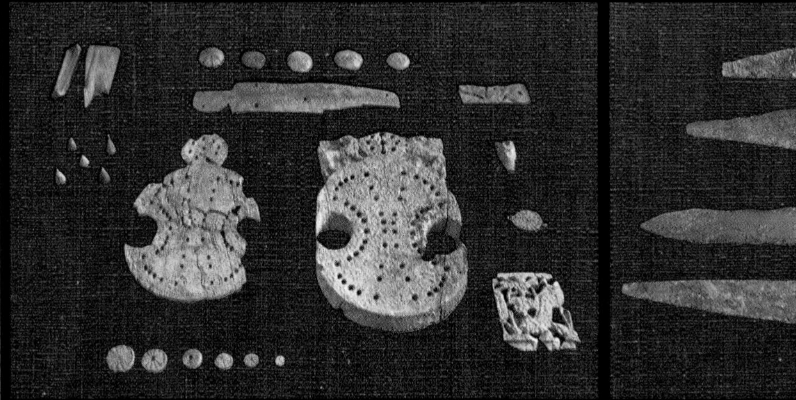

Palestine Archaeological Museum; photo John C. Trever

(*b*) *Ivories* from Stratum VII palace at Megiddo; two game boards (near center), game pieces, and other ivory carvings (early twelfth century B.C.)

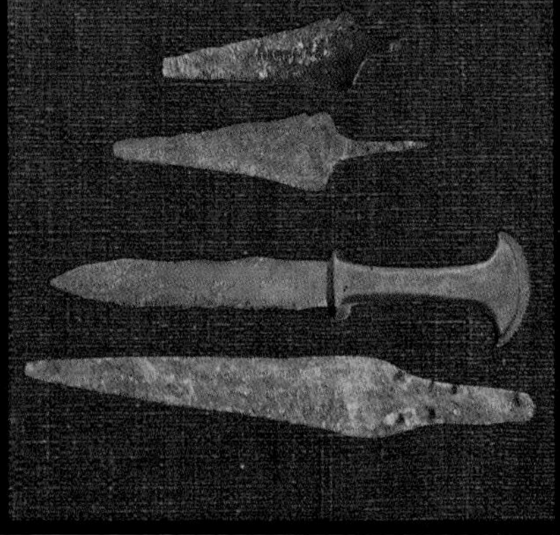

Palestine Archaeological Museum; photo John C. Trever

(*c*) *Bronze dagger* and *dagger blades,* Middle Bronze Age; the one on the left from Lachish, with early alphabetic inscription, dated *ca.* 1700-1600 B.C.

Royal Ontario Museum

(*d*) *Game board* from Egypt (Thebes?), late fourteenth-thirteenth century B.C. (Nineteenth Dynasty); thirty-square type for the game "senet," with squares of glazed steatite, five of which are inlaid with lapis lazuli; faïence game pieces

Palestine Archaeological Museum; photo John C. Trever

(*e*) *Copper bowl, iron hoe,* and *pottery vessel* from excavations at Khirbet Qumran

PLATE XXIV

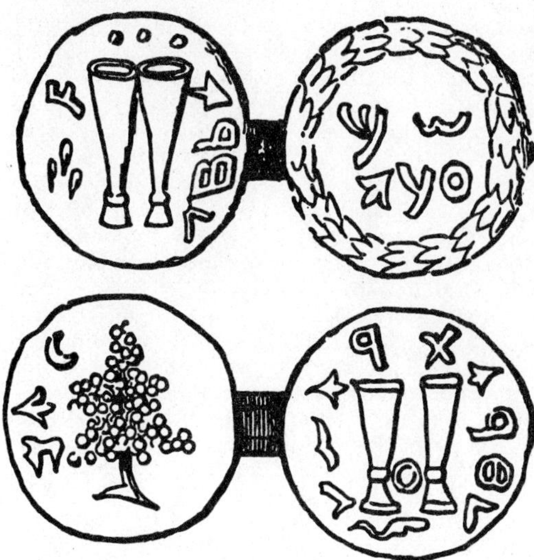

By permission of Novello and Company Ltd., London

86. Coins with trumpets surrounded by the motto, "The deliverance of Jerusalem"

From F. W. Galpin, *Music of the Sumerians* (Cambridge University Press)

87. Ancient trumpets: (1) Egyptian trumpet (*ca.* 1200 B.C.); (2) Hittite trumpet (*ca.* 1000 B.C.)

ered and examined. Therein, the trumpets were assigned a number of complicated signals, which implied their ability of blowing legato, staccato, and trills, and tonguing, all in unison, not "simultaneously," but "as with one mouth." Moreover, these apocalyptical trumpets bear different names: trumpets of assembly, of battle, of the slain, of ambush, etc. In general, they were used to terrorize the enemy into panic (cf. Gideon's use of trumpets in Judg. 7:19-20). Their function was, for all practical purposes, identical with that of the trumpets of Revelation. In the temple the signals of the trumpet introduced every ceremony and every sacrifice. Figs. MUS 85-86, 87.

***e.* Shôphār.** The שופר (from Akkadian *šapparu*, "wild ibex"; LXX σαλπίγξ or κερατίνη; Vulg. *buccina* or *cornu*) was the Jewish ritual instrument par excellence. The term is translated "ram's horn" or (erroneously) "trumpet," also "cornet" (KJV) and "horn" (I Chr. 15:28; II Chr. 15:14; Hos. 5:8).

The שופר is by far the most frequently named biblical instrument. It is called σάλπιγξ in the NT (usually "trumpet," but "bugle" in I Cor. 14:8; throughout the book of Revelation the seven apocalyptic trumpets appear to be שופרות).

Courtesy of the Trustees of the British Museum

88. A bas relief from Carchemish showing four military musicians playing a *shôphār* and drum (ninth-eighth century B.C.?)

According to Josh. 6:4, 6, 8, 13, the *shôphār* was a ram's horn, but in the second temple the horns of the ibex or the antelope were used.* The synagogue, however, uses the ram's horn exclusively as a memorial of the ram which replaced Isaac as sacrificial animal (Gen. 22, which is read on New Year's Day just before the *shôphār* ritual). How close to the surface lay still magic or totemistic conceptions may be seen in the prohibition of using a cow's horn instead of the *shôphār* for the temple's signals. The Talmud (R.H. 26*a*) indicates that a cow's horn or similar substitutes might seriously impair the spiritual affinity of the signal instrument with the sacrificial beast. (Cows were not sacrificed!) Fig. MUS 88.

All the various usages of the *shôphār* can be viewed under one category: that of a signaling instrument. It sounded all signals in war and peace; it announced the new moon, the beginning of the sabbath, the death of a notable; it warned of approaching danger; it heralded excommunication; it was instrumental in exorcisms and magic healing.

In its strictly ritual usage it carried the cries of the multitude to God. At special occasions he himself or his angels may sound the *shôphār* (Isa. 27:13; Zech. 9:14; Rev. 8:2, 6, 12; 9:1-13; cf. also the *Tuba mirum* of *Dies irae*). It is hardly possible to consider the *shôphār* a musical instrument. It can produce just the first two harmonic overtones, and these only approximately. Rarely does it appear together with other instruments, especially at solemn occasions of cultic significance, such as a transfer of the ark (II Sam. 6) or a procession with the entire staff of the temple (I Chr. 15:28; II Chr. 15:14). Only in Ps. 150:3 is it mentioned with most of the other really musical instruments. Hence, we must conclude that the function of the *shôphār* was to make noise—be it of earthly or of eschatological character—but not to make music. After the destruction of the temple and the general banishment of all instrumental music, the *shôphār* alone survived, just because it was *not* a musical instrument.

In the early rabbinic literature *shôphār* and "trumpet" (חצוצרה) were frequently confused. The nonchalance of this usage was an aspect of the studied indifference to all things artistic by the puritanical rabbis; it also reflects their efforts to attain in the world of the synagogue similarity with the institutions of the temple (B. Soṭ. 43*a;* Shab. 36*a*). Jerome, who equates the *shôphār* with the Roman *buccina,* is likewise mistaken, for the *buccina* was a trombone made of metal. Such confusions do not occur in the OT or the Dead Sea Scrolls. Both sets of documents state that only the trumpets, never the שופרות, should be blown "as with one voice"—i.e., "in unison" (cf. II Chr. 5:13; War Scroll). Passages such as Num. 10:2, 8; 31:6 accentuate the Aaronide's privilege of sounding the trumpet, whereas the *shôphār* was normally used by Levites.

Tradition has conveyed to us only three kinds of signals with their descriptions:

a) תקיעה ("to push, hit");

b) תרועה ("to make noise, alarm");

c) שברים ("to break," indicating a staccato or tremolo sound). In musical notation these signals would appear as in Example 1.

Example 1

Signals in Occidental Tradition (German Jews)
(After Abraham Baer)

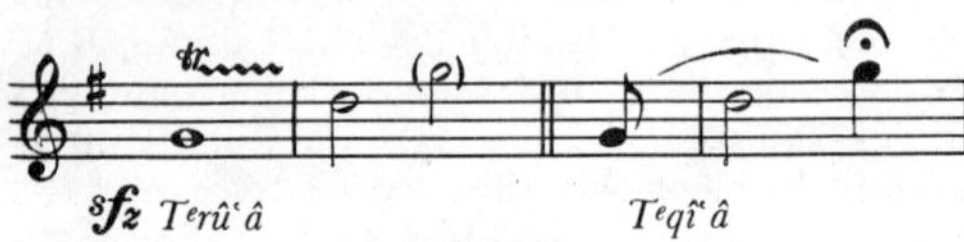

Oriental Jews:

Shebhārîm

From E. Gerson-Kiwi, "Musique dans la Bible," *Dictionnaire de la Bible* (ed. Pirot; Supplément, 1955); by permission of Letouzey et Ané, Paris

According to rabbinic interpretation, the first signal, תקיעה, was for gathering or assembly; the second and third were danger or alarm calls. From the Dead Sea Scrolls we learn, however, that these were by no means the only signals known to the Hebrews. *See* § B2*d above.*

3. Membranophones. The תֹּף (from onomatopoetic stem תפף; cf. τύμπανον; Arabic *duff*), translated "timbrel" and "tambourine" (KJV "timbrel" and "tabret"), was a typical women's instrument. It is mentioned seventeen times in the OT; thus it must have been very popular. Although it occurs in the Psalter and in religious hymns (Exod. 15; Jer. 31:4), it was not permitted in the temple. Its function in the Bible was restricted to secular or religious frolicking, cultic dances, or processions (e.g., II Sam. 6:5; I Chr. 13:8; Ps. 68:25—H 68:26). Its absence in the temple ritual was possibly due to the strong female symbolism, which always accompanied the tambourine, and which made its use so popular at all fertility rites. The תף was carried and beaten by hand; in archaic times it may have been a tambourine with two membranes, with pieces of bronze inserted in the rim and shaken by hand. Remnants of such instruments have been discovered in Mesopotamia.

4. Chordophones. ***a. Lyre.*** Two terms are translated "lyre" (KJV "harp"). The כנור (perhaps from Persian-Arabic *kunnâr,* "lute," or from the root meaning "lotus plant"; LXX κίθαρα [see I Cor. 14:7; Rev. 5:8; 14:2; 15:2], κινύρα [see I Macc. 4:54; KJV "harp"], ψαλτήριον; Vulg. *lyra, cithara, psalterium*) was the instrument of David and the Levites, considered the noblest instrument of all. It was used in a sacred milieu as well as in a secular one (cf. Isa. 23:16: in the hand of a harlot). In the temple never fewer than nine lyres were in use (M. Arakh. 2.5), but their number could be increased ad libitum.

The number of the strings of the כנור varies and is, according to most reports, dependent upon cosmological and other symbols; the minimum is three, the maximum twelve. Figurative representations of the lyre on Assyrian reliefs, Mesopotamian paintings, and Jewish coins show an enigmatic and curious re-

Courtesy of the Metropolitan Museum of Art

89. An oblique lyre, from Thebes, Eighteenth Dynasty (*ca.* 1570-1310 B.C.)

Courtesy of the Museo Archaologico di Firenze

90. A horizontal harp of ten strings, from an Egyptian tomb (*ca.* 1000 B.C.)

semblance to Cretan-Minoan instruments. In Mesopotamia and the E shore of the Mediterranean the lyre dates back to prehistoric times.

The כנור was played with the fingers or with a plectrum, as S. Krauss has shown. Being the instrument of the aristocracy, it often was made of silver or ivory, embellished by the craftsmanship of great artists, as, e.g., the golden lyre of Ur, only one of many such examples of precious artistry and material. Fig. UR 17.

The earliest Semitic representation of the כנור has been found in the famous tomb of the Beni-Hasan of the twentieth century B.C. Later forms tend to perfect the symmetry of the artistic framework of the lyre.

The Aramaic קיתרם (LXX κίθαρα; KJV "harp"), found only in Dan. 3:5, 7, 10, 15, was a strictly secular instrument for merrymaking, and it fits well into the picture of Nebuchadnezzar's banquet. It probably must be identified with one of the many Asiatic variants of the classic Greek κίθαρα.

Figs. MUS 89-90.

b. Trigon. Another type of lyre was the Aramaic שבכא (LXX σαμβυκή; Vulg. *sambŭca*), which appears only in Dan. 3:5, 7, 10, 15, and is translated "trigon" (KJV "sackbut"). We must rely upon the etymology of the name to determine its identification, as we have no representation from authentic sources. According to some linguists, its root may be שבע, "seven" (cf. Akkadian *sabītu,* "seven-stringed lyre"). As "sambuke" the instrument was well known, though of ill repute, as that of vulgar musicians and harlots (Macrobius *Satires* III.14.7), and Plato forbade it altogether (*Republic* III.399*d*). Athenaeus (*Deipnosophists* 634*a*) mentions the sambuke as resembling a ship and ladder joined together; an instrument exactly fitting this description has been excavated in Ur (*see* the work of V. Christian in the *bibliography*). It belonged, however, not to the instruments of Israel, but to the Babylonian orchestra.

c. Lute. The שלישים (from שלש, "three," referring to triangular form or to the three strings of the instrument; LXX κύμβαλα; Vulg. *sistra;* KJV-RSV "instrument of music"), which occurs in I Sam. 18:6, is interpreted as "lute" by some. Other suggestions are "triangle" and "hand drum" (Gressmann), "cymbals" (Sachs). Not being a temple instrument, it was, like the tambourine, usually played by women. Its name corresponds with the Akkadian *šalaštu,* which, according to Galpin, was a *"tambour* with a long neck like the lute." Fig. MUS 82.

d. Harp. The identification of the נבל (LXX ψαλτήριον, νάβλα, ὄργανον; Vulg. *psalterium, nablium, lyra, cithara, vas psalmi;* KJV alternately "psaltery," "viol") is not absolutely certain. It was a stringed instrument, for Josephus testifies to its twelve strings (Antiq. VII.xii.3). By way of elimination, the most probable interpretation seems to be "harp," although "cittern" and "lyre" (not "lute," as in Pss. 92:3; 150:3) cannot be excluded altogether. Fig. MUS 84.

The נבל occurs frequently in the OT; as the Greek equivalent of "lyre" and "harp," it plays a significant part in the image of the "heavenly Jerusalem" in Revelation (especially 14:2-3, where we encounter in the description the conspicuous Hebraism "κιθαρῳδῶν κιθαριξόντων ἐν ταῖς κιθάραις αὐτῶν"). The נבל is mainly an instrument of religious or liturgical character; only three passages mention it in a purely secular function (Isa. 5:12; 14:11; Amos 5:23).

Not unlike the lyre, the harp was an instrument of the aristocratic hierarchy, and therefore often made of precious woods and metals (e.g., I Kings 10:12; II Chr. 9:11). No pictorial representation of a נבל has come down to us, and we must depend upon the findings of instruments from neighboring countries.

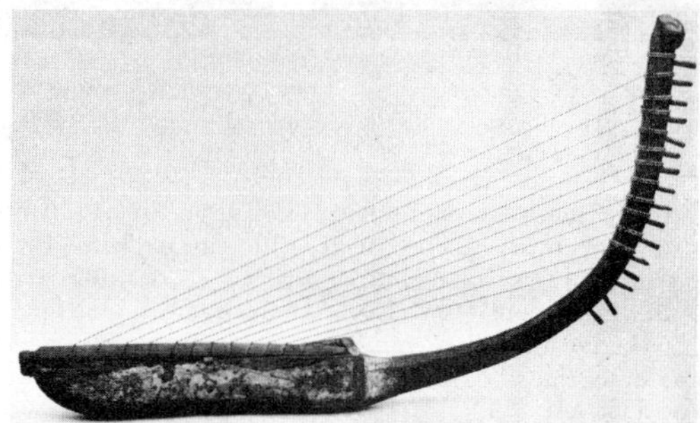

Courtesy of the Metropolitan Museum of Art

91. Egyptian wooden harp (restored), Eighteenth Dynasty (*ca.* 1550-1200 B.C.)

The harp was the favorite instrument of the Egyptians and generally well known in the ancient Near East. If we equate the Egyptian harp with the נבל, as some scholars suggest, it approximated a cithara-harp with ten to twenty strings, up to four yards high, and was mostly played without a plectrum.* In the temple there were never fewer than two harps, rarely more than six (M. Arakh. 2.3). The harp is a typical men's instrument; as such it belongs, with the lyre and the *shôphār,* to the Levitical orchestra. Fig. MUS 91.

The פסנטרין (LXX ψαλτήριον; KJV "psaltery"), also translated "harp," was the old dulcimer, the Persian-Arabic *santir.* The word occurs only in Dan. 3:5, 7, 10, 15. Although the name hints at the foreign provenance of the instrument, its occurrence is amply ascertained for the entire area of the E Mediterranean since the first millennium B.C. In Greece, the psaltery was a kind of cittern and is so understood in medieval Islamic culture. We find it first on Assyrian reliefs, where it consists of a two-foot-long, one-foot-wide resonator over which ten strings are drawn. The strings are struck with a little rod; consequently we behold a veritable dulcimer-Hackbrett.

The medieval Arabic *santir* was built on similar

From *Atlas of the Bible* (Thomas Nelson & Sons Limited)

92. The blind harper of Leiden, from a temple of Hatshepsut at Karnak; Amarna period (*ca.* 1400-1350 B.C.)

lines; this instrument was still played in the nineteenth century, according to Villoteau exclusively by Arabic Jews. The *santir* is probably identical with the instrument עשור (LXX ἐν δεκαχόρδῳ ψαλτηρίῳ; with Jerome, *Psalterium decachordum*), which is, of course, the so-called "ten-string."

Fig. MUS 92.

5. Spurious terms. ***a. "Bagpipe."*** This term (KJV "dulcimer") is an erroneous translation and misunderstanding of the Greek συμφωνία as it occurs in Dan. 3:5, 10, 15 (for סומפוניא). Both the error and the true meaning were known to Jerome. The misunderstanding originated in Spain through Isidor, who interpreted συμφωνία as either a drum or a bagpipe, in the Near East through Saadya Gaon.

Since Galpin's and Sachs's explanations, we are fairly sure that סומפוניא, always the last term on the list of the Babylonian orchestra, was not an instrument but referred to the ensemble playing of all the instruments mentioned individually before.

b. "Sackbut," "viol," and "cornet." These are fanciful mistranslations of the earlier English versions. The sackbut was some kind of trombone, which did not exist in biblical times (RSV uses "trigon"); the same holds true, *mutatis mutandis,* for the viol (RSV "harp") and the cornet (RSV "horn").

6. Collective terms. ***a. "Stringed instruments."*** The term מנים (LXX χόρδαι; Vulg. *chordae*) occurs twice (Pss. 45:8—H 45:9; 150:4), but only the reference in Ps. 150:4 ("strings") is clear. Here the stringed instruments are used together with secular instruments, such as תף and עוגב, whereas the preceding and parallel vs. 3 lists only the priestly instruments. The implication is that all the world, priest and layman alike, shall praise the Lord! This is the only time that all the priestly and most of the secular instruments are mentioned together in a religious but nonliturgical hymn.

b. "Instruments of music." The use of such terms as נגנה, כלי שיר, נבל, and זמרא (the last-named only in Dan. 3:5, 7, 10, 15) indicates emphatically the predominant place of stringed instruments in biblical music, for all the passages in which these terms appear refer to harps or lyres, in contrast to other priestly instruments such as trumpets or cymbals (e.g., I Chr. 16:42; II Chr. 5:13; cf. II Chr. 7:6; Amos 6:5).

Bibliography. For the older literature, see B. Ugolinus, *Antiquitates* (1744-68), vol. XXXII (in Latin).

Modern studies: F. Delitzsch, *Biblischer Kommentar ueber die Psalmen* (4th ed., 1883). H. Gressmann, *Musik und Musikinstrumente im AT* (1903). J. Garstang, *Land of the Hittites* (1910). S. H. Langdon, ed., *Sumerian Liturgies and Psalms* (1919). C. Sachs, "Altägyptische Musikinstrumente," *Reallexikon der Musikinstrumente, Der Alte Orient,* vol. XVII (1920). S. H. Langdon, "Babylonian and Hebrew Musical Terms," *JRAS* (1921). F. Thureau-Dangin, *Rituels accadiens* (1921). E. Chiera, *Sumerian Religious Texts* (1924). S. B. Finesinger, "Musical Instruments in the OT," *HUCA,* III (1926), 21-77. I. Benzinger, *Hebräische Archäologie* (3rd ed., 1927). J. Wellhausen, *Reste arabischen Heidentums* (2nd ed., 1927). C. Sachs, *Geist und Werden der Musikinstrumente* (1929): by far the most extensive and systematic work on the subject. M. Weir, *A Lexicon of Akkadian Prayers in the Rituals of Expiation* (1934). C. L. Woolley and H. R. Hall, *Ur Excavations,* vols. I-II (1927-36). F. W. Galpin, *The Music of the Sumerians* (1937). V. Christian, *Altertumskunde des Zweistromlandes* (1940): for the Ur instrument fitting the description of the sambuke, see vol. I, table 247. C. Sachs, *The History of Musical Instruments* (1940). E. Kolari, *Musikinstrumente und ihre Verwendung im AT* (1947). P. Gradenwitz, *The Music of Israel* (1949). E. Gerson-Kiwi, "Musique dans la Bible," *Dictionnaire de la Bible,* Supplément T.V. (1955). E. Werner, "Jewish Music," in G. Grove, *Dictionary of Music* (5th ed., 1955). Y. Yadin, *The Scrolls of the War of the Sons of Light Against the Sons of Darkness* (1955; in Hebrew). H. Hickman, *Musique et vie musicale sous les Pharaons,* vol. I (1956).

E. WERNER

MUSICAL MODES. *See* MUSIC.

MUSICIANS. *See* ASAPH; DAVID; ETHAN; HEMAN; JEDUTHUN; KORAH; MIRIAM. *See also* MUSIC.

MUSRI mo͞os′rĭ. A land in Asia Minor mentioned in cuneiform inscriptions and thought to be referred to in the OT. *See* MIZRAIM.

MUSTARD [σίναπι]. A sizable annual plant with very small seeds, probably *Brassica nigra* (L.) Koch (also called *Sinapis nigra* L.). The word appears only in the sayings of Jesus, in his parable of the mustard seed (Matt. 13:31; Mark 4:31; Luke 13:19) and in his simile concerning faith (Matt. 17:20; Luke 17:6 Q). In the parable the emphasis is upon the growth of the kingdom (or the spread of the gospel?) from small beginnings to the large, world-embracing events of the future, similar to the tiny mustard seed which grows so rapidly into a large plant. In the other saying the power of faith is likened to the commonly observed possibilities intrinsic within the tiny mustard seed.

Much debate has raged over the literal implications of the parable, which make the common mustard unsuitable for the illustration, even though the Greek clearly refers to it. We know now that the

93. Mustard

orchid seed, not the mustard seed, is the smallest. The mustard does not grow to tree size, for it is an annual plant. Though fast-growing, it could not be suitable for nesting birds in the early spring. In a parable, however, one expects some literary license to emphasize the point.

If the text must be rendered "make nests in its branches" (so RSV), the exaggeration would be immediately apparent to even the common man. Botanists avoid this problem by insisting that the verb translated "make nests" means only "settle upon" or "light upon" (cf. Amer. Trans. "roost"), referring only to small birds. The apparent allusion to Dan. 4:11-12, 20-21, seems to support the RSV translation, in which case the only solution is to take the expression as hyperbole (cf. Matt. 17:20).

See also FLORA § A6*f;* NETTLE; PARABLE.

Fig. MUS 93.

Bibliography. I. Löw, *Die Flora der Juden,* I (1928), 516-27; H. N. and A. L. Moldenke, *Plants of the Bible* (1952), pp. 59-62.

J. C. TREVER

MUSTER GATE [שער המפקד, gate of the lookout *or* of the inspection] (Neh. 3:31); KJV GATE MIPHKAD mĭf′kăd. A city gate in the NE section of Jerusalem, restored by Nehemiah. Perhaps this gate is the same as the Benjamin Gate. *See* BENJAMIN, GATE OF.

See map under NEHEMIAH. *See also* JERUSALEM §§ 6*e*, 7*b*.

G. A. BARROIS

MUTH LABBEN mŭth lăb′ən. *See* MUSIC.

MUTILATION. Physical mutilation of the bodies of man and beasts was not common in biblical times, because of a belief in the sacredness of life (*see* FAUNA; LIFE; MAN, NATURE OF, IN THE OT; MAN, NATURE OF, IN THE NT). Physical defects disqualified a priest from serving at the altar; among those named in the Holiness Code is a "mutilated face" (Lev. 21:18; KJV "flat nose"; חרם occurs only in this passage, where the context does not make clear whether the particular disfigurement was congenital, accidental, or the result of self-mutilation). It was forbidden to sacrifice animals that were "mutilated" (חרוץ; Lev. 22:22; KJV "maimed") or had suffered "mutilation" (משחתה; vs. 25; KJV "corruption"). *See* SACRIFICE AND OFFERINGS.

However, self-mutilation is reported concerning the prophets of Baal, who "cut themselves after their custom with swords and lances, until the blood gushed out upon them" (I Kings 18:28). The Hebrew prophets condemned the practice of self-mutilation (Jer. 47:5; Hos. 7:14; *see* GASH), and Jeremiah appears to have recognized it as a sign of mourning among the people of Shechem, Shiloh, and Samaria (41:5), and Moab (48:37). Mutilation of the bodies of enemies in time of war must have been common, as evidenced by the reports that Adoni-bezek cut off the thumbs and great toes of his enemies and suffered the same fate himself (Judg. 1:6-7); the Philistines gouged out Samson's eyes (16:21); the Ammonites threatened to gouge out the right eyes of all the men of Jabesh (I Sam. 11:2); the murderers of Ish-bosheth had their hands cut off, probably after death (II Sam. 4:12); Nebuchadnezzar threatened his servants that they would be torn limb from limb (Dan. 2:5). For a discussion of mutilation involved in the punishment of criminals, *see* CRIMES AND PUNISHMENTS.

Paul, in two curious passages, seems to have thought of CIRCUMCISION as mutilation. He warned against "those who mutilate the flesh" (τὴν κατατομήν; Phil. 3:2; KJV "the concision"), and expressed the wish that the troublemakers among the Galatians "would mutilate themselves" (ἀποκόψονται; Gal. 5:12; here the reference may be to the practice of emasculation, common in the Cybele-Attis cult, but by implication, to circumcision also).

W. L. REED

MUZZLE [חסם; φιμόω]. According to Deut. 25:4, it was illegal to put a muzzle on an ox while he was treading out grain on the threshing floor. The law is peculiar to Deuteronomy and is commonly regarded as a reflection of the humanity which is characteristic of that code. The prohibition was twice cited by Paul (I Cor. 9:9; I Tim. 5:18), who used it to illustrate the principle that "the laborer deserves his wages."

Jewish commentators, including Rashi, have suggested that the law applied to any animal doing work in connection with the production of foodstuffs. And yet it may be worth considering to what extent the ox received this treatment as a result of the fact that he was held in high regard in Israel, as in many surrounding cultures. He was a symbol of strength and fertility. However heretically in the minds of later generations, the golden calf had been at least emblematic of Yahwism in the kingdom under Jeroboam and his successors (I Kings 12:28 ff; II Kings 10:29; II Chr. 13:8), just as it had been to some of their ancestors in the wilderness (Exod. 32:1 ff). The fact that oxen were used extensively in sacrificial rites in Israel (Num. 7:87-88; II Sam. 24:22; II Chr. 5:6; 7:5; etc.) may also be of some significance in this regard. H. F. Beck

MYNDOS mĭn'dəs [Μύνδος]; KJV MYNDUS. A city on the coast of Caria in Asia, noted for silver mines; the modern Gumushli. A letter is alleged to have been sent here, and to other cities and islands, including SICYON; DELOS; and COS, from the Roman consul Lucius to the benefit of the Jews, in 139 B.C. (I Macc. 15:23). If this is so, Myndos had some independence, and it would also have possessed a Jewish colony—the Jews being attracted probably by the commercial prospects of the silver trade. Myndos never achieved great importance. N. Turner

MYRA mī'rə [τὰ Μύρα]. An important city of LYCIA; one of the six largest and most influential cities in the long-existing confederation of Lycian cities. Myra proper was situated on the River Andracus, *ca.* 2½ miles from the sea. Its port, with a good harbor, was Andriaca; but common usage included the port town in Myra. Under the Roman Empire, Myra was made the capital of the separate province of Lycia. The ruins at Dembre, the modern name of the site, include a large theater, many tombs, and inscriptions.

Acts 27:2-6 attests the importance of Myra for sea travel. At Caesarea in Palestine the centurion charged with taking Paul and other prisoners to Rome put them on a ship of ADRAMYTTIUM, a port of NW Asia Minor. The ship sailed N to Sidon, continued N past the E end of Cyprus and then W along the S coast of Asia Minor to Myra. Here the centurion took passage with his prisoners on an Alexandrian grain ship which had crossed from Egypt to Myra and planned to work its way W from there to Rome. In the E Mediterranean the prevailing winds were from the W, and grain ships regularly followed this route. Frequent sailing service between Lycia and Egypt, developed when the Ptolemies ruled Lycia, continued under Roman control.

In Acts 21:1, Codex D and some other authorities add the words "and Myra" after "Patara." Such a succession of stops was possible, but the limited evidence for the addition leaves doubt whether it is original. The Acts of Paul and Thecla have a legendary story of the preaching of Paul at Myra. In reality, nothing is known of the presence of Christianity in Myra in the first century. Nicholas, bishop of Myra under Constantine, became the patron saint of sailors, replacing a pagan deity at whose shrine sailors had earlier worshiped.

Bibliography. W. M. Ramsay, *St. Paul the Traveler and the Roman Citizen* (1896), pp. 297-300; A. H. M. Jones, *The Cities of the Eastern Roman Provinces* (1937), pp. 99-102, 107-8.
F. V. Filson

MYRIAD [μυριάς]. Literally, ten thousand. Sometimes it signifies more generally "countless" or "numberless." In the RSV the Greek word is transliterated as "myriads" in Jude 14; Rev. 5:11; but in Luke 12:1; Acts 19:19; 21:20; Heb. 12:22; Rev. 9:16 it is translated differently.
B. H. Throckmorton, Jr.

MYRRH mûr [לֹט, *lōṭ;* מֹר, מוֹר, *môr;* Ugar. *mr;* Akkad. *murru;* Arab. *murr;* נֵשֶׁק, *nēšeq* (KJV ARMOUR, HARNESS); σμύρνα]. Fragrant substances derived from the exudation of various shrubs and trees.

While most translations have "myrrh" in Gen. 37:25; 43:11, the word (לט) is identified by many scholars with the fragrant gum of a species of *Cistus* (commonly called "rockrose"), the ladanum (not "laudanum"!) of ancient trade (Akkadian *ladunu,* Arabic *ladan*). Zohary (*see* FLORA § A7*j*) takes it to be the resin of *Commiphora opobalsamum* (L.) Engl. (*see* SPICES). It was an item of trade carried from Gilead to Egypt by the Ishmaelites (Gen. 37:25); and was one of the "choice fruits of the land" which Jacob had his sons carry to Joseph in Egypt (43:11).

Myrrh (מוֹר, *môr;* σμύρνα) was the fragrant resin of *Commiphora myrrha* (Nees) Engl., found mostly in S Arabia. Apparently it was available in liquid (cf. Exod. 30:23; Song of S. 5:5, 13; "oil" in Esth. 2:12) as well as solid forms. That it was prized as early as the second millennium B.C. is clear from the Ras Shamra documents ("pitcher of oil of myrrh"; Ugar. 12:2, 8, 15; 120:15) and its apparent use in Egyptian embalming (cf. Herodotus II.86).

Myrrh was an important ingredient of the sacred anointing oil (Exod. 30:23). As an important ingredient of perfumes, it was used for beauty treatment (Esth. 2:12; cf. Song of S. 5:5) and for scenting clothing (Ps. 45:8; Prov. 7:17; Song of S. 1:13; 3:6), and appears in poetic symbolism (Song of S. 4:6, 14; 5:1, 13; Ecclus. 24:15). It was among the gifts given to the infant Jesus (Matt. 2:11). Jesus was offered "wine mingled with myrrh" (as an anodyne; Mark 15:23). Myrrh and aloes were brought by Nicodemus for Jesus' burial (John 19:39; cf. "spices" in Mark 16:1; Luke 24:1).

נשק (I Kings 10:25 = II Chr. 9:24; KJV "armour," "harness") normally means "armor"; but here the LXX has στακτή, on the basis of which the RSV

Courtesy of Winifred Walker

94. Myrrh (*Commiphora myrrha*)

uses "myrrh." The next word is ובשמים *ûbhᵉsāmîm* ("and spices"), which is a good co-ordinate to "myrrh." It was therefore probably among the gifts given to Solomon.

The RSV translates μύρον "myrrh" in Rev. 18:13, but "ointment" (KJV) or "perfume" (Amer. Trans.) would be more accurate.

See also FLORA § A7*j;* SPICES; STACTE.

Fig. MYR 94.

Bibliography. I. Löw, *Die Flora der Juden,* I (1926), 305-11, 362-63; H. N. and A. L. Moldenke, *Plants of the Bible* (1952), pp. 77, 82-84. J. C. TREVER

MYRTLE [הדס, *hᵃdhas*]. A leafy shrub, *Myrtus communis* L. Myrtle branches were included with other leafy branches for covering the booths at the Feast of Succoth (Neh. 8:15; cf. Lev. 23:40 and numerous references in the Talmud; *see* BOOTHS, FEAST OF). Myrtle growing in the wilderness and "instead of the brier" is part of the eschatological symbolism of Second Isaiah (Isa. 41:19; 55:13). An angel appeared to Zechariah in a vision of a man standing among myrtle bushes (not trees!) with horses (Zech. 1:8, 10-11).

The other name of Esther was HADASSAH (הדסה), the feminine form of the Hebrew word for "myrtle" (Esth. 2:7).

See also FLORA § A9*l.*

Bibliography. I. Löw, *Die Flora der Juden,* II (1924), 257-74; H. N. and A. L. Moldenke, *Plants of the Bible* (1952), pp. 143-45. J. C. TREVER

MYSIA mĭsh'ĭ ə [Μυσία]. The NW region of Asia Minor. Its extent varied considerably with different writers, but the boundaries generally set were the Aegean Sea on the W, the Hellespont and Propontis on the N, Bithynia and Phrygia on the E, and Lydia on the S. The E border was in the vicinity of Mount Olympus; the S border included Pergamum in Mysia. The region was not so fertile and prosperous as some other parts of Asia Minor. While the Mysians had a history reaching back to Homeric times—Troy was in the region later called Mysia—and enjoyed tribal freedom at times, the people of Mysia were never a definite or influential nation. In 133 B.C. the region was made a part of the Roman province of Asia. Mysian cities which appear in the NT are Alexandria, Troas, Assos, Adramyttium, and Pergamum.

Acts 16:6-11 tells of Paul's first visit to Mysia. He had revisited Derbe, Lystra, Iconium, and, no doubt, "Pisidian" Antioch, and had been turned aside from preaching in the province of Asia. He had gone northward until "opposite Mysia" (κατὰ τὴν Μυσίαν), on its E side. Here, perhaps at Dorylaeum, where the roads parted, Paul and his companions at first intended to go N into Bithynia, where Greek cities were located, especially on the coast of the Euxine Sea. In some way they were turned from this plan by the "Spirit of Jesus." "So, passing by Mysia," without making it a field of intensive missionary preaching, they came to the port of Troas, where Paul received a specific call to preach in Macedonia. While this leaves no room for extensive mission work in Troas, possibly he won a few converts on this first visit. Paul later found an open door there (II Cor. 2:12), and still later visited Christians there and perhaps also at Assos (Acts 20:5-14).

Bibliography. Strabo *Geography* XII.4.1-6; 8.1-4. A. H. M. Jones, *Cities of the Eastern Roman Provinces* (1937), ch. 2 (see Index). F. V. FILSON

MYSTERY. 1. Terminology. Μυστήριον (whether or not derived, as used to be said, from μυέω, "to close [the eyes]") seems to be in its earliest known occurrences a genuinely Greek religious term, denoting (generally in the plural) secret rites or the implements or teaching connected with them. Eventually it came, perhaps through metaphorical use, to mean more generally a secret of any sort, not necessarily religious.

Whether owing to chance or not, there was a similar Hebrew root, סתר, "to hide," yielding the noun מסתרים, "hidden things or secrets"; and inevitably, when the Greek word was transliterated into Semitic letters, the two were approximated. But the fact remains that the genuinely Hebrew word was not an exact equivalent of the Greek one, the Greek word having religious associations which the Hebrew did not so obviously possess; and it was perhaps not until biblical Greek adopted the word μυστήριον that the biblical vocabulary possessed a word meaning a "religious secret." Not that, even in the Bible, this word invariably has a religious connotation. In the wisdom literature it is sometimes used simply in connection with the sin of divulging secrets (e.g., Ecclus. 22:22; 27:16-17, 21). But, once it was in the Bible, it became especially a vehicle for conveying ideas peculiar to the biblical conception of revelation. In the Latin Bible, *sacramentum,* "an oath," which had associations with initiatory rites, is occasionally used for μυστήριον.

2. OT usage. In the Greek OT, μυστήριον occurs mostly in the books written in Greek or with lost or only fragmentary Hebrew originals—viz., Tob. 12:7, 11; Jth. 2:2; Wisd. Sol. 2:22; 6:22; 14:15, 23; Ecclus. 3:18 (some MSS only, derived from the [extant] Hebrew of vs. 20, סוד, "[secret] counsel"); 22:22; 27:16-17, 21; II Macc. 13:21. But in Dan. 2:18-19, 27-30, 47 (twice), it is used by the LXX for רז, which is said to be a Persian loan word meaning "a secret" (it occurs also in the Dead Sea Scrolls). The Aramaic participle מסתרתא, meaning "the hidden things," in Dan. 2:22 is rendered, not by μυστήριον, but by σκοτεινά (LXX), ἀπόκρυφα (Θ). Μυστήριον occurs in other Greek versions as follows:

a) Theod.: Dan. 2 (as above); 4:9—H 4:6, where the LXX is not extant (=רז, "again"); Job 15:8; Ps. 24:14—H 25:14; Prov. 20:19 (all=סוד, "[secret] counsel"); Isa. 24:16 (twice=רזי, *rāzî,* said to mean "leanness" or "wasting," and, if so, mistaken [possibly even by the Massoretes] for *rāz,* "secret").

b) Symm.: Isa. 24:16 (as above); Prov. 11:13 (=סוד).

c) Quinta: Ps. 24:14—H 25:14 (as above).

In these passages the LXX renders the Hebrew (or Aramaic) variously, if at all. Note that μυστήριον in Rev. 10:7 appears to represent סוד in Amos 3:7 (where the LXX has παιδεία, "instruction").

In several of the above occurrences, the word relates simply to ordinary "human" secrets. The RSV in the canonical books gives the following renderings: "mystery" in Dan. 2; 4; "council" in Job 15:8; "friendship" in Ps. 25:14; "secrets" in Prov. 11:13; 20:19; "I pine away" in Isa. 24:16 (רזי־לי). For the Pseudep. and the Dead Sea Scrolls, see R. E. Brown (*bibliography*).

3. NT usage. In the NT the word is used exclusively in religious senses, which may be broadly classified as follows:

a) That closely connected (by a strange paradox) with REVELATION—viz., a divine plan, concealed from all except the recipients of revelation, or concealed until God's good time; or, in other words, a divine secret indeed, but one designed by God to be revealed: an "open secret" in some sense. The word used thus is almost equivalent to the Christian gospel. The following passages may be classed here:

Mark 4:11 (=Matt. 13:11; Luke 8:10). Those who have come to Jesus to ask the meaning of the parables are told that, whereas for those who are outside, everything is done "in parables," they, by contrast, have been "given the secret of the kingdom of God" (Mark 4:11). Matthew and Luke have: "given to know the secrets." (For the difference [the latter perhaps an accommodation to ecclesiastical interests], see the commentaries.) In Mark the meaning would appear to be that the secret being revealed to this inner circle is that, in some sense, Jesus himself in his ministry is to be identified with the kingdom of God. A revelation is in process of being given: the μυστήριον is being divulged.

Rom. 11:25: "Lest you be wise in your own conceits, I want you to understand this mystery, brethren: a hardening has come upon part of Israel, until the full number of the Gentiles come in." Here the mystery is a special aspect of the divine evangelic plan, as Paul sees it—the partial eclipse of Israel until the Gentiles are won. (Possibly this passage should be included in *b below*.)

Rom. 16:25-26: "the mystery which was kept secret for long ages but is now disclosed and through the prophetic writings is made known to all nations." The Pauline authorship and the meaning of the "prophetic writings" are disputed; but in general, this is a perfect example of the sense of the word "mystery" now being illustrated.

I Cor. 2:1, a variant reading for μαρτύριον, "testimony" (see RSV mg.). If "mystery" is here read, it must mean simply the gospel, the subject of the apostle's proclamation. This, at any rate, is clear in 2:7: "We impart a secret and hidden wisdom of God [θεοῦ σοφίαν ἐν μυστηρίῳ], which God decreed before the ages for our glorification." So in 4:1, the apostles are "stewards of the mysteries of God."

In Ephesians the mystery is, in particular, that aspect of God's evangelic plan which consists of the unification of the universe, including Jew and Gentile: "the mystery of his will, according to his purpose which he set forth in Christ as a plan for the fulness of time, to unite all things in him, things in heaven and things on earth" (Eph. 1:9-10); "the mystery was made known to me by revelation, . . . the plan of the mystery hidden for ages in God who created all things; that through the church the manifold wisdom of God might now be made known to the principalities and powers in the heavenly places" (3:3 [cf. vs. 4], 9-10). In Eph. 6:19 (cf. Col. 4:3) it is again simply the gospel.

In Col. 1:26-27; 2:2, the divine secret, long hidden but now divulged, seems to be boldly identified with Christ himself. But in 1:26-27 the expression seems, in fact, to be very close to the Ephesians idea: the mystery is "Christ in you" (i.e., the Gentiles), the "hope of glory"; i.e., it is that Christ is among the Gentiles no less than the Jews.

Once again, in I Tim. 3:9, 16, the "mystery of the faith" or "of our religion" seems to be simply the gospel.

So, too, in Rev. 10:7, the "mystery of God, as he announced to his servants the prophets," is to be fulfilled. It is the divine plan which is ultimately to be completed.

Finally, perhaps it is right to include here also the "mystery of lawlessness" (II Thess. 2:7), if this means a kind of satanic parody of God's mystery, a sort of demonic gospel. This is Satan's "plan," which has to be worked out before it can be ultimately destroyed and dispatched by Jesus at his coming (vs. 8).

In most of these instances, it is noticeable that "mystery" is coupled with words of manifesting and divulging. *See* REVELATION.

b) Another sense seems to be closer to a more private, exclusive, less generally to-be-divulged "secret," although it is still a religious secret.

It is possible that Rom. 11:25 (*above*) should fall here, as a special revelation given to the apostle.

At any rate, in I Cor. 13:2 it is something special; for it is useless even to "understand all mysteries" (i.e., to have reached an exceptionally high degree of religious insight), unless one also has love.

In I Cor. 14:2 the man who utters unintelligible sounds under the stress of religious experience "utters mysteries in the Spirit."

And in I Cor. 15:51, "Lo! I tell you a mystery" introduces what seems to be a special revelation about the coming of the Lord.

c) In Eph. 5:32 the phrase "This is a great mystery, and I take it to mean Christ and the church" appears to apply to the exegesis of the passage from Gen. 2:24 cited in the preceding verse. Mystery may thus signify the "inner meaning" of a passage whose more obvious and literal sense is something other. If so, here is an anticipation of the long history of "mystical" exegesis. Near to the same sense, in that case, may be Rev. 1:20: "As for the mystery of the seven stars . . . , the seven stars are the angels," and 17:5: "On her forehead was written a name of mystery: 'Babylon the great.' "

4. Conclusions. Thus, from its early pagan religious use in allusion to the Greek mystery cults, the word "mystery" moved, in nonbiblical usage, to a general, secular usage in the sense merely of "secret" (though in later pagan usage it is found again in the cultic context); but it was taken up by the literature of revealed religion for a special meaning in connection with God's "open secret," his revelation; and Christianity in particular used it to epitomize the gospel—hidden for long ages, to be divulged in the Incarnation, and even then hidden from all except those who used their ears to hear and their eyes to see. And, in a secondary degree, Christianity used it for special secrets divulged by God to chosen vessels, or for the inner meaning behind a phrase or a symbol. The way is thus prepared for the postbiblical usage in application to the sacraments. The Vulg., which renders most of the occurrences in Dan. 2 and in the NT by *mysteria,* occasionally uses *sacramentum* —viz., in Dan. 2:18, 30, 47 (second occurrence); 4:6; Tob. 12:7; Wisd. Sol. 2:22; 6:24 (*sic*); Eph. 1:9; 3:3, 9; 5:32; Col. 1:27; I Tim. 3:16; Rev. 1:20. The word perhaps offered a bridge from the sense associated with the oath of initiation to the sacramental connotation.

Bibliography. J. A. Robinson, *Ephesians* (1903), excursus; D. Deden, *Le mystère paulinien* (1936); K. Prümm, " 'Mysterium' von Paulus bis Origenes," *Zeitschrift für katholische Theologie,* LXI (1937), 391 ff; W. L. Knox, *St. Paul and the Church of the Gentiles* (1939), pp. 227-28; L. Cerfaux, *La théologie de l'Eglise suivant S. Paul* (1942), pp. 239 ff; W. D. Davies, *Paul and Rabbinic Judaism* (1948), ch. 5; J. Dupont, *Gnosis* (1949), pp. 194 ff; C. L. Mitton, *Ephesians* (1951), pp. 86 ff; R. E. Brown, "The Semitic Background of the NT *Mysterion,*" *Biblica,* 39 (1958), 426-48; 40 (1959), 70-87; "The Pre-Christian Semitic Conception of 'Mystery,' " *Catholic Biblical Quarterly,* XX (1958), 417-43. C. F. D. MOULE

MYTH, MYTHOLOGY. In the narrower sense, a myth is a story about gods or other superhuman beings, or one told to account for a custom, institution, or natural phenomenon. In the broader sense, myth is that expression of the creative imagination which interprets the real in terms of the ideal, punctual events in terms of continuous situations. *See bibliography* § 1.

A. Ancient Near Eastern myth in the Bible
- 1. Direct parallels
  - *a.* The story of the Dragon
  - *b.* Creation and Paradise
  - *c.* The Deluge
- 2. Allusions
  - *a.* The revolt of the gods
  - *b.* Star myths
  - *c.* Hero myths
  - *d.* Myth in riddles?
  - *e.* The dying and reviving god
  - *f.* The wondrous child
- 3. Myth in figurative expressions
  - *a.* Thunder
  - *b.* Wind
  - *c.* Sun
  - *d.* The mountain of the north
  - *e.* The land flowing with milk and honey
  - *f.* The Book of Fate
  - *g.* Demons
  - *h.* Obscured allusions
- 4. Myth in history and apocalypse
- 5. Date of the mythological passages

B. Myth and ritual

C. Mythology in biblical exegesis

Bibliography

A. *ANCIENT NEAR EASTERN MYTH IN THE BIBLE.* Thanks to the rediscovery, in recent times, of considerable portions of Mesopotamian, Egyptian, Hittite, and Canaanite literature, it is now possible to recognize in the Bible several traces of ancient Near Eastern mythology. These appear in three main forms: (*a*) direct parallels; (*b*) allusions; and (*c*) survivals in figurative expressions. In all cases, they are accommodated to the religion of Israel by boldly transferring to Yahweh the heroic feats of the older, pagan gods. *See bibliography* § 2.

1. Direct parallels. Direct parallels to ancient Near Eastern myths are represented principally by (*a*) the fight of Yahweh against the Dragon; (*b*) the stories of Creation and Paradise; and (*c*) the tale of the Deluge.

a. The story of the Dragon. This story, pieced together from scattered passages in the prophetic and poetic books of the OT, tells how Yahweh primordially fought a monster variously termed LEVIATHAN—i.e., "Coiled One, Wriggly" (Job 3:8; Ps. 74:14; Isa. 27:1); RAHAB, "Arrogant" or "Rager" (Job 9:13; 26:12-13; Ps. 89:10; Isa. 30:7; 51:9-10); Tannîn—i.e., "Dragon" (Job 7:12; Ps. 74:13; Isa. 27:1; 51:9); Yam—i.e., "Sea" (Job 7:12; Ps. 74:13; Isa. 51:10; Hab. 3:8); or Nahar, "River, Stream" (Ps. 93; Hab. 3:8). The monster had several heads (Ps. 74:13-14); even the gods were alarmed by it (Job 41:25—H 41:17), but eventually Yahweh overcame it by hacking it to pieces (Isa. 51:9 [1QIs[a] "smiting" it, as in Job 26:12]), transpiercing it (Job 26:13; Ps. 89:10; Isa. 51:9), crushing it (Ps. 89:10), or bludgeoning its heads (Ps. 74:13-14), at the same time discomfiting its allies (Job 9:13). According to another version, however, he merely kept it under restraint (Job 7:12), and it is destined, at the end of the present world, to break loose and renew the fight, though abortively (Job 3:8; Isa. 27:1; cf. II Esd. 6:52; II Bar. 3:8; Palestinian Targ. Num. 9:21-27; Shab. 30*b;* Sanh. 97*b;* Keth. 111*b;* Mandean Ginza, pp. 298, 419, trans. Lidzbarski).

All this is simply the Hebrew version of the story told in the Ugaritic Myth of Baal concerning the victory of that god over the draconic Yam (alias Nahar), the genius of sea and rivers; and this in turn finds further parallels in: (*a*) the Mesopotamian tale (Enuma Eliš) of Marduk's combat with Tiamat; (*b*) the Hittite tale of the conflict between the storm-god and the dragon Illuyankas (*Keilschrifttexte aus Boghazköi* III.7; *Keilschrifturkunden aus Boghazköi* XII.66; XVII.5-6; cf. *ANET* 125-26); (*c*) the Sumerian myth of Ninurta's triumph over the monster Asag; (*d*) the Egyptian myth of Re's fight against 'Apep (Book of the Dead XXXIX); and (*e*) Horus of Beḥdet's against "the Caitiff"; and (*f*) the Phoenician story of the primordial battle between Zas (i.e., Baal) and Ophion (cf. ὄφις, "serpent"), to which allusion is made by Apollonius Rhodius (*Argonautica* I.503 ff), Maximus Tyrius (*Dissertationes* XXIX), and Celsus (Origen *Contra Celsum* VI.42, etc.; cf. also Milton, *Paradise Lost,* book X, lines 570-72). Moreover, the story is portrayed on rock sculptures at Malatiyeh and Karatepe and likewise on many Mesopotamian cylinder seals. It also possesses more remote analogues in the Iranian tale of the rout of Aži Dahaka (Yasht 19.38-44; Bundahish 29.9), the Vedic tale of the subjugation of Vṛtra by Indra (Rig Veda I.32), the Greek tale of Zeus's fight with Typhon (Hesiod *Theogony* 820 ff; Aeschylus *Prometheus Vinctus* 351 ff), and, of course, the familiar legend of Saint George and the Dragon (located near Laodicea, in Syria!).

The parallels cover not only broad theme but also specific details. Thus, in the Ugaritic myth, there is likewise mention of Leviathan (*Ltn;* I*AB, i.1) and Tannîn (*Tnn;* I AB, vi.13), as also of Yam and Nahar (AB, *passim*), and the monster is called by the very same epithets as are applied to it in Isa. 27:

1—viz., "evasive" (ברח) and "crooked" (עקלתון). There too it is said to possess several (lit., seven) heads (I*AB, i.2-3), while six-headed and seven-headed dragons are not unknown to Mesopotamian literature (cf. E. Ebeling, *Keilschrifttexte aux Assur religiösen Inhalts* no. 6) and art (seal from Tell Asmar in the Oriental Institute, Chicago). In the sister versions, the dragon likewise affrights the gods: Ninurta at first flees from Asag, Anu from Tiamat (Enuma Eliš II.81-82), Indra from Vṛtra (Satapatha Brahmaṇa, I Khaṇḍa, 6 Adh., 4 Br.), and the gods in general before Typhon (Apollodorus *Bibliotheca,* I.6.3). Furthermore, the fate of the monster is portrayed in the same way as in the Bible. In Egyptian sources, it is likewise said to have been "sword-pierced" (*m d ś*) or transfixed by a harpoon; while in the Ugaritic version it is smitten on the head (III AB, 24) or "between the eyes" (III AB, 21, 25). Lastly, the idea that it was merely held captive, but destined again to break loose, features prominently in the Iranian version and is also presupposed in the Greek myth of Typhon.

The myth was probably designed in the first place to symbolize the annual subjugation of the swollen rivers and winter floods; both the Mesopotamian and Hittite versions were in fact recited at seasonal festivals—viz., at the feasts of Akîtu and Puruli respectively.

b. Creation and Paradise. These stories likewise hew close to ancient Near Eastern myth.

The notion that man was formed out of dust or clay (Gen. 2:7; cf. Job 33:6) occurs already in the Babylonian myth of Atraḫasis (*ANET* 99-100) and in other Mesopotamian texts (*Die Keilinschriften und das Alte Testament,* 3rd ed., p. 506); while among the Egyptians, he was said to have been fashioned by the potter-god, Khnum. *See* COSMOGONY § B2.

Similarly, the idea that man was formed to tend the garden of God (Gen. 2:15) accords with the statement in an ancient Assyrian myth (*Keilschrifttexte aus Assur religiösen Inhalts,* I, no. 4) that he was created to "carry the basket and seed-bag, direct the course of the runnels, water the soil, cause plants and green things to grow."

The concept of the tree of life is likewise a mythological relic, to which the scriptural writer has given a new turn. Mesopotamian glyptic often portrays a scene in which a king draws life and strength by touching a sacred tree, while Egyptian sculptures likewise show the pharaoh beside a sacred tree in the company of divine beings who promise him countless years, etc. Similarly, too, in the Celtic paradise of Avalon, gods and men partook of the life-giving nuts of the hazel tree. *See bibliography* § 3*a*.

Lastly, the cherubs (griffins) posted at the entrance to Eden (Gen. 3:24) doubtless derive from the familiar mythological dragons who guard the magic tree or the hidden treasure. *See bibliography* § 3*b*.

c. The Deluge. That the biblical story of the Deluge is dependent on earlier Mesopotamian myth is apparent from its affinities with similar stories in the Epic of Gilgamesh (*ANET* 93-94) and the Legend of Atraḫasis (*ANET* 104-6). There, too, an ark is built (Gilgamesh XI.24, 28-31; Atraḫasis X.7-12) and sealed with bitumen (Gen. 6:14; Gilgamesh XI.54, 65-66); the hero's family and livestock are placed in it (Gen. 6:19-20; 7:2-3, 7-9; Gilgamesh XI.27, 84-86; Atraḫasis C.6-10); the Flood comes both from above and from below (Gen. 7:11; 8:2; Gilgamesh XI.98, 102; Atraḫasis II.29-30; III.44-46); birds are dispatched (Gen. 8:6-12; Gilgamesh XI. 145-55); the ark grounds on a remote mountain (Gen. 8:4; Gilgamesh XI.140), and egress from it is followed by a sacrifice which the deity savors (Gen. 8: 20-21; Gilgamesh XI.156-61).

To be sure, the OT writers sometimes manipulate time-honored myths to fit their own outlook. Thus, while they take over from the Mesopotamians the idea that man was molded out of clay, they represent his function as that of ruling creation (Gen. 1:27; Ps. 8:6-9), not, as did the Babylonians, of performing menial chores for the gods. Similarly, while they retain the conception of a divine bow hung in the sky, they identify it with the rainbow and not, as did the Babylonians, with a constellation; and they take it to be a sign of God's promise not to send another flood (Gen. 9:12-15), rather than, as in other cultures, his victorious weapon hung in the sky as a warning to future upstarts. In the same vein, too, the Canaanite plague-god Resheph is accommodated to Israelite monotheism by being made a mere attendant upon Yahweh (Hab. 3:5), and even then he is more of a poetic figure of speech than a full-fledged deity.

2. Allusions. ***a. The revolt of the gods.*** Familiar throughout the ancient Near East was the story of a primordial revolt in heaven. This forms the central theme, e.g., both of the Mesopotamian Epic of Creation (Enuma Eliš) and of the Hittite myth of Kumarpi (*ANET* 120); and it is probable that it was also one of the major elements in the Ugaritic Poem of Baal. Moreover, it has well-known classical analogues in the revolt of Zeus against Kronos, and of the giant Titans against Zeus. OT allusions to this myth may be recognized in (*a*) Ps. 82:6-7, which speaks of a sentence of mortality and discomfiture imposed by Yahweh on certain upstart minor gods, or celestial beings, and (*b*) Isa. 14:12-25, where the arrogant king of Tyre is likened to a certain celestial character named Hêlal (LXX ἑωσφόρος; Vulg. *Lucifer;* RSV "Day Star"), who was eventually thrust down to the nether world. Moreover, it may be suggested that there is a further reference to it in Judg. 5:13*b,* where the defeat of the Philistines is portrayed in words which may perhaps be rendered: "Then was Yahweh's army [עם] marching, [this time] for me, against the Giants [עם יהוה ירד לי בגבורים]!"

Another version of the tale, which depicts the offense of the heavenly beings as that of consorting with human women, is related briefly in Gen. 6:1-4 and not infrequently in later, pseudepigraphic literature (e.g., Enoch 6:6; Jub. 4:15; Zadokite Document, A II.18; Genesis Apocryphon 1).

b. Star myths. The Israelites seem also to have inherited a number of star myths, for in Job 38:31-32 allusion is made to (*a*) the chains (מענדות; so read for MT מעדנות, which the KJV renders "sweet influences"!) which bind together the cluster of the Pleiades (כימה; cf. Akkadian *kimtu,* "cluster, group, family"); (*b*) the cords of Orion, which are evidently his "belt"; and (*c*) the Great Bear and her "children," which recall the Latin Septentriones (i.e., "seven oxen") and the Egyptian "seven cows following the bull" as designations of the stars which accompany that constellation. Moreover, the Hebrew name of Orion—כסיל, "Fool"—seemingly implies a myth involving the widespread popular association of giants with dunderheads. *See fully* ARCTURUS; ORION; PLEIADES.

c. Hero myths. Traces of ancient Hebrew hero myths may be detected in the reference (Gen. 5:24) to Enoch, who "walked with God; and he was not, for God took him," and to Nimrod, the mighty (or giant) huntsman (10:8-9). Furthermore, the occasional use of the name David to denote the future messianic king (Jer. 30:9; Ezek. 34:23-24; 37:24; Hos. 3:5) probably reflects a version of the widespread myth that great national heroes (e.g., Arthur of Britain, Friedrich Barbarossa) do not die, but will return to their peoples in the hour of need. *See bibliography* § 3*c*.

The fact that Enoch is said to have lived 365 years (Gen. 5:23) has suggested to some scholars that elements of a sun myth may have been grafted upon the folk tale of that ancestral sage. Such mythological traits have been recognized also in the story of Samson (cf. שמש, "sun"). Here, however, caution is in order. It is quite unnecessary, e.g., to explain the shearing of Samson's locks as symbolizing the curtailment of the sun's rays at dusk, for the motif that a man's strength lies in his hair is, in fact, widespread in folk tale and is often associated with heroes who possess no solar traits whatsoever. Moreover, the equivalent of Hebrew Samson occurs as an ordinary proper name at Ugarit and elsewhere. *See bibliography* § 3*d*.

d. Myth in riddles? Further allusions to traditional myths are perhaps furnished by Prov. 30:4, where a number of riddles are propounded as examples of that "knowledge about divine beings" (דעת קדשים)—i.e., hagiology—of which the author professes himself ignorant. Thus, the question: "Who has ascended to heaven and come down?" may allude to Etana, who, in the familiar Mesopotamian story (*ANET* 114-18), aspired thither on the back of an eagle, only to fall into the sea. Similarly, the question: "Who has gathered the wind in his fists [LXX 'bosom']?" may refer to some ancient Near Eastern analogue of Aeolus (cf. *Odyssey* X.1-76); and "Who has established all the ends of the earth?" to some counterpart of Atlas, or of the Hittite-Hurrian Upelluri (*ANET* 112), who supported the world on his shoulders.

e. The dying and reviving god. Apart from these more or less overt allusions, attempts have been made to detect in the OT traces of the ancient Near Eastern myth of the dying and reviving god (i.e., Tammuz, Osiris, Adonis), who allegedly suffered an annual passion and resurrection, or slept in the nether world during the dry summer, to wake with the return of vegetation. It has been claimed that this figure underlies (*a*) the Suffering Servant of Isa. 53, and (*b*) the psalmists' several appeals to Yahweh to "wake" (Pss. 35:23; 44:23—H 44:24; 59:4—H 59:5); that the Song of Songs is an adapted version of ritual chants used in the cult of the divine lovers Ishtar and Tammuz, and that Hosea's imagery of Yahweh's marriage to Israel is inspired by the myth and ritual of the "sacred marriage" between a god and a goddess as a means of ensuring fertility.

All these theories, however, must be treated with caution. The Suffering Servant may be derived more plausibly from the misshapen man or condemned felon (e.g., the *bêl ḫiṭṭi* of the Babylonian Akîtu ceremonies [*Vorderasiatische Abteilung, Thontafelsammlung* 9555, rev. 10-11]) and the φαρμακός in Greece, who sometimes served as a human scapegoat at ancient seasonal festivals and the scourging of whom was believed to bring health and fertility to the community as a whole. Moreover, the similarities with the Tammuz texts are, at best, vague and superficial. Similarly, the invocations to Yahweh to "wake" are more probably connected with a common ancient practice of waking the god every morning. This has therefore nothing to do with an identification of the Hebrew god with Tammuz.

All love songs everywhere are bound to sound alike, and those of the Ishtar-Tammuz cult would necessarily imitate the type of thing familiar to their human worshipers. The similarity, therefore, proves nothing; and, as a matter of fact, even closer affinity exists with ancient Egyptian erotic poetry (*ANET* 467-68) and even with the chants of modern primitive peoples.

The marriage of Yahweh and Israel in Hosea symbolizes only a tie of affection and loyalty (חסד), and is not represented as a means of ensuring fecundity. It is simply another expression of the basic covenantal relationship (ברית), and finds its counterpart in the constant use of the term "go a-whoring" (זנה) in the sense of "commit apostasy" (e.g., Exod. 34:15-16; Isa. 57:3; RSV "play the harlot").

It should be observed also that the very existence of an ancient Near Eastern myth revolving around the theme of a god who annually dies and revives has recently been called into question, for it would now appear that the story of Tammuz really ran on somewhat different lines. *See bibliography* §§ 3*e-g*.

f. The wondrous child. A further vestige of ancient myth has been recognized in the famous prophecy of Isa. 7:14: "A virgin [עַלְמָה] shall conceive and bear a son," and in Isaiah's subsequent description (9:6-7) of an infant prodigy destined to wield sovereignty and bring eternal peace. This has been linked, with great probability, to the fairly widespread ancient myths—familiar especially from the Iranian lore of the Saoshyant (Savior) and from Vergil's Fourth Eclogue—of the virgin-born hero and of the Miraculous Child who is to usher in the New Age. *See bibliography* § 3*h*.

3. Myth in figurative expressions. Poetic imagery is everywhere a rich repository of traditional myth, and such reminiscences of more ancient popular lore are not wanting in the Bible. A few examples are:

a. Thunder. Thunder is the voice of God (II Sam. 22:14, etc.), as in the Ugaritic texts (II AB, v.8, vii. 29-35; I Aqhat, i.46), the Tell el-Amarna Letters (147.14-15), and frequently in Mesopotamian literature and elsewhere. *See bibliography* § 3*i*.

b. Wind. The wind is winged (II Sam. 22:11; Ps. 104:3; Hos. 4:19), as in the Mesopotamian myth of Adapa (*ANET* 101), the Sumerian wind-eagle (IM. DUGUD and IM.GIG), and as in the widespread belief that storms are caused by the flapping of the wings of a giant bird. *See bibliography* § 3*j*.

c. Sun. The sun, too, is said in Mal. 4:2—H 3:20 to be winged—a notion which harks back to the familiar Near Eastern "winged solar disk," so often portrayed in Egyptian and Mesopotamian art, as also among the Hittites and Hurrians, and on monuments from Susa. *See bibliography* § 3*k*.

d. The mountain of the north. In Isa. 14:13 the gods are said to hold assembly on a mountain in the north; and in Ps. 48:2, Zion is apostrophized as this mountain. So in the Ugaritic myths, the gods convene in the "recesses of the north" (*ṣrrt Ṣpn*)—a concept which recurs in Mesopotamian, Egyptian, Indic, and Iranian mythology and is mentioned also in the book of Enoch (24:3; 25:1). Often, indeed, the abode of the supreme god is celestially located, in pagan myths, near the North Star. *See bibliography* § 3*l*.

e. The land flowing with milk and honey. The familiar description of the Promised Land as one "flowing with milk and honey" portrays it, in mythological terms, as an earthly paradise, for honey is a medium of immortality, and rivers of milk and honey are a common feature of that blissful realm. Rivers of milk also characterize the future Golden Age (Joel 3:18). *See bibliography* § 3*m*.

f. The Book of Fate. In Ps. 139:15-16, mention is made of a book kept by God in which a man's days are prescribed before his birth. Somewhat similarly, the Hittites believed that certain goddesses called "the Inscribers [*Gulses*]"—analogous to the Schreiberinnen and Norns of Teutonic folklore, the Fata Scribunda mentioned by Tertullian (*De anima* C.39), and the Roman Parcae—inscribed the course of men's lives (*Keilschrifturkunden aus Boghazköi* XII 85, rev. 5 ff; XXXIII 118, 17-19; XXXIV 53, ii.14, etc.); while a Punic inscription of the third-second century B.C. appears to allude to the gods' recording a man's name and mark "from the beginning." *See bibliography* § 3*n*.

g. Demons. There are also in the OT sundry references to such demonic figures of ancient mythology as LILITH, the night hag (Isa. 34:14), and RESHEPH, the Canaanite god of pestilence. The latter is described as accompanying Yahweh on his warlike sorties (Hab. 3:5), and his "sons"—i.e., the plague demons—as hovering in the air (Job 5:7). *See* DEMON.

h. Obscured allusions. Lastly, it may be noted that our increasing knowledge of ancient Near Eastern mythology has enabled us to recover in the OT certain allusions previously concealed beneath popular distortions of language or the inevitable errors of scribes. Thus, in Ps. 68:4, where the God of Israel is described as רכב ערבות—i.e., "[he] who rides through the deserts"—it is now possible to recognize a distortion of the more ancient *Rkb ʿrpt*, "[he] who rides upon the clouds," a common designation of Baal in the Ugaritic myths. Similarly, from the unintelligible words of Hos. 8:6: "For *from Israel* [מישראל], and he—a workman made him, and he is no god," we can now restore, by mere regrouping of the letters, an effective gibe at the chief god of the Canaanites, called by his standard Ugaritic name—viz.: "For *who is El, the Bull* [מי שר אל]? He is one whom a workman made, and he is no god!"

4. Myth in history and apocalypse. Another type of mythological allusion is represented by the tendency of OT writers to portray historical events in language reminiscent of traditional myths, thereby envisaging them as the punctual realizations of ideal situations. Thus, in the song celebrating the crossing of the Red Sea (Exod. 15), the safe passage of Israel is depicted as Yahweh's leading his people to the mountain of his inheritance (i.e., estate), where, in a permanent abode (מכון) upreared by his own hands, he will reign forever (vss. 17-18). In this we may see an allusion to what is said of Baal in the Ugaritic myth of his victory over Yam; thereby he acquires eternal kingship (III AB, A 7-10), ensconcing himself in a palace on Mount Ṣapân, described as the mount of his inheritance (V AB, C 28-29). Similarly, in the Mesopotamian myth, Marduk is enthroned in the newly built shrine of Esagila, after routing Tiamat and her allies (Enuma Eliš, iv.14, 28; vi.50-72).

This tendency appears especially in apocalyptic passages where, in accordance with the developing notion that history is a cyclic rather than a linear process (*see* COSMOGONY), the future Golden Age is frequently portrayed as a repetition of primordial or primeval events recorded in traditional myth and saga. Thus, both in the Pseudep. and in Revelation, the eventual "renewal of the world" will involve a renewed combat against the Dragon and against the rebellious forces of Satan or Belial; while in Deutero-Isaiah, the restoration of Israel from exile is depicted as a duplication of its former redemption from Egypt and of its passage through the wilderness to the Promised Land.

5. Date of the mythological passages. Most of the mythological passages of the OT occur in books usually dated during or after the Babylonian exile. It was therefore held by nineteenth-century scholars that such material was picked up by the Jews in the course of their captivity. In the light of more recent discoveries, however, this view is untenable. Not only do the Ras Shamra Texts show clearly that much of it goes back to indigenous Canaanite sources, but there is also abundant evidence that as early as the second millennium B.C. the myths of the various ancient Near Eastern peoples circulated freely beyond their native borders. We have, e.g., both Hittite and Hurrian versions of the Mesopotamian Epic of Gilgamesh, and an Egyptian version of the Canaanite myth of Baal (*ANET* 17-18); while a fragment of the former has been found in the Palestinian city of Megiddo, and of the Mesopotamian myths of Adapa and of Nergal and Ereshkigal among the Tell el-Amarna Tablets.

As to why this mythological heritage is more evident in the later than in the earlier portions of the Hebrew scriptures, two explanations have been advanced. According to W. F. Albright (*see bibliography*), this was due to a general archaistic trend which swept the Near East in the seventh and sixth centuries B.C. and which is represented especially by the archaeological activities of Ashurbanipal (669-633) and Nabonidus (556-539) in Mesopotamia, and by the literary and architectural styles effected by the Saite kings (Twenty-sixth Dynasty, 660-625) in Egypt. In Israel, it found expression especially in the work of the Deuteronomists, and was doubtless continued through the desire of the Jews, both during the Exile and in the ensuing troubled period, to recapture the glories of the past. On the other hand, according to J. Morgenstern (*see bibliography*), the ancient pagan myths were adopted and adapted by the Jews of the Restoration in a deliberate effort to proselytize the "heathen" and to give the ancestral faith a more universal or cosmopolitan complexion. To these theories may be added the further consideration that mythological material is everywhere more naturally embodied in poetry than in other forms of literature; and OT poetry just happens to be mainly of this later date. *See bibliography* § 4.

B. *MYTH AND RITUAL.* Modern anthropological studies have shown that myths are commonly recited among primitive peoples at seasonal festivals, to explain and validate an accompanying ritual. This discovery has inspired the theory that several of the literary myths that have come down to us from antiquity may represent refined and sophisticated versions of such more primitive compositions, and that their successive incidents may reflect, basically, the sequence of elements in a seasonal rite. The theory has been applied, e.g., to the elucidation of Greek tragedy and comedy, to certain hymns of the Rig Veda, to the Elder Edda, and even to early Chinese festal chants. In the field of ancient Near Eastern literature, it has been proposed that the Ugaritic myth of Baal is basically the counterpart of a ritual pantomime (*sacer ludus*) enacting the seasonal conflicts between rain, subterranean waters, and aridity, and that it was originally designed for an autumnal festival inaugurating the wet season. A similar explanation would apply to the Mesopotamian Epic of Creation (Enuma Eliš) and to the Hittite myth of Illuyankas (*ANET* 124-25), both of which celebrate the victory of the primary god over a dragon and both of which were, in fact, recited at seasonal festivals.

Along the same lines, it has been suggested that some of the OT psalms may really be mythological chants designed for the New Year celebration. Those, e.g., which begin: "Yahweh has become king" (RSV "The Lord reigns") may have accompanied a ritual pantomime enacting the annual victory of that god over the floods and the powers of chaos, and his subsequent installation, like Baal or Marduk, as king of the earth. Some psalms (e.g., Pss. 29; 93) might even be blatant adaptations of earlier Canaanite hymns.

In appraising this hypothesis, however, it is important to draw a much sharper distinction between the ultimate origin of a literary genre and that of a particular composition. While it is plausible enough that certain types of literature were conditioned in the first place by the exigencies of rituals for which they were designed, these types may well have survived as fossilized literary conventions long after the rituals themselves had died out. Accordingly, it no more follows that an OT psalm celebrating Yahweh's defeat of the Dragon or his subsequent enthronement actually accompanied a ritual ceremony than that every performance of the children's game of blindman's buff actually involves the selection of a victim for human sacrifice—the rite to which folklorists have traced it! In other words, we must distinguish between myth which survives in poetry, and myth which survives in ritual.

A word should be said also concerning the fundamental relationship of myth and ritual. This has been variously formulated. According to some scholars, the myth is simply a later explanation of the rite; according to others, the opposite is the case and rites were essentially enactments of myths. The truth would seem to be, however, that neither is actually an offshoot of the other; rather are they the "longshot" and "close-up" views of the same thing. Ritual presents a situation in its immediate, myth in its ideal, terms. When, e.g., the king is ceremonially deposed and subsequently reinstated in primitive rituals, this represents and epitomizes the seasonal demise and revival of his actual community; but in the corresponding myth, it will be portrayed in ideal terms as the death and resurrection (or withdrawal and restoration) of a durative, preterpunctual god. Similarly, when the king takes a sacred bride as an immediate measure to promote fecundity, he merely punctualizes an ideal fertilizing "marriage in heaven."

C. *MYTHOLOGY IN BIBLICAL EXEGESIS.* It has been pointed out by Ernst Cassirer that myth issues from an activity of the human mind or psyche distinct from, and independent of, that which produces philosophy or speculative thought, and that its most natural medium is artistic fancy. Accordingly, we must expect to find in biblical poetry a constant undercurrent of mythopoeic imagery, suggestion, and association. Furthermore, the comparative study of folk literature has shown that traditional sagas tend likewise to be tinged with mythological coloration, historical persons (e.g., Arthur of Britain) and events being thus assimilated to ideal, mythic characters and situations.

A growing awareness of this fact has led several modern scholars (notably those of the so-called "Scandinavian school") to construe diverse utterances of the OT prophets in a mythic rather than a solely historical context—to see, e.g., in reference to the expulsion of enemies to the desert an allusion to the fate meted out to the rebels against God in some ancient myth. It may be objected, however, that this method of interpretation fails to distinguish properly between metaphor and literary borrowing. The figures and images used in poetry may indeed be the same as those which are more elaborately worked out in literary myths, but this does not mean that wherever they are employed, they are necessarily taken over from such myths. A poet might say, e.g., that a man's fortunes have been eclipsed, but this does not imply specific identification of him with the hero of a standard solar or lunar myth! Once again, the common mainspring of poetry and myth must be recognized; the former does not have to be derived from the latter.

Equally precarious is the older tendency to apply comprehensive theories of mythology to the stories of the OT—e.g., to construe them as the detritus of solar, lunar, astral, vegetation, or "world-cycle" myths, or to see in the patriarchal and monarchical narratives mere historicizations of standard mythic heroes like Gilgamesh or Heracles. In the first place, such theories all too often assume that the same astral figures were recognized everywhere—which is simply not true—and that, even when they were, the same myths were told about them. Secondly, these comprehensive systems are themselves little more than armchair constructions of ancient and primitive data, for there is often no assurance that the myths which are cited for comparative purposes actually bore to those who invented and recited them the interpretations imposed on them by nineteenth-century anthropologists. Lastly, many of the parallels adduced from primitive cultures turn out to be anything but primitive, being really mere distortions of Bible stories told by missionaries, or (conversely) native tales transmogrified by missionary rapporteurs!

It is well known that the NT stories of the Virgin Birth and of the death and resurrection of Jesus possess parallels in ancient religious mythologies—e.g., in what is told about the Saoshyant in Iranian lore and about so-called "dying and reviving gods" in classical sources. For liberal Christians this has posed a perplexing problem, commonly resolved along one of two main lines. Either (*a*) the unique historicity of the gospel narratives is held to be quite independent of mere mythological analogues; or (*b*) an attempt is made to strip the character and identity of Jesus of all "mythic" traits and to validate his mission solely by his human experience and the ethical qualities of his teachings.

In considering this problem, however, one should bear in mind that events of the past can, in general, be religiously significant and relevant in the present only insofar as they are lifted out of the specific contexts of their occurrence and taken as symbols of continuing, universal situations. And to effect such a translation from the punctual to the ideal is precisely the function of myth. Myth, therefore, is, in the last analysis, the supreme vehicle of the Word, as indeed of all religion—the element which gives them eternal life and pertinence. The exodus of the Israelites from Egypt, e.g., would be for the modern Jew no more than an antiquarian datum, were it not transfigured by myth into a symbol of his people's continuous experience, an evidence of God's continuous design and providence, and an exemplification of all men's continuous progress out of their Egypts, forward to their Sinais, and thence, through trial in the wilderness, to the entry of their children into their inheritance. By the same token, the story of Jesus becomes religiously significant to a Christian only when the man of Nazareth is regarded as incarnating and "punctualizing" an ideal, durative figure, variously represented, in terms of traditional mythology, as the Son of God, the Son of man, or the Christ (Messiah), and as symbolizing the constant role of God in man—traduced, yet triumphant. Such religious significance is in no way impaired because it is conveyed through antique symbols, born of other and less sophisticated times. For if the Bible is the Word of God, it is a word just as much as it is of God; it must speak perforce in the idiom of its day and age, and the Spirit must assume the calculated risk that it may at times be smothered by the mortal clay into which it is breathed. "In many and various ways God spoke of old to our fathers"; and in articulating his message, he has, indeed, often chosen "what is foolish in the world, to shame the wise." *See bibliography* § 5.

Bibliography. 1. On myth in general, see: B. Malinowski, *Myth in Primitive Psychology* (1926). E. Cassirer, *Language and Myth* (trans. S. Langer; 1946). R. Pettazzoni, *Studi e Materiali di Storia delle Religioni*, XXI (1947-48), 104-16. *Proceedings of the VIIth Congress for the History of Religions* (1951). A. E. Jensen, *Mythos und Kult bei Naturvölkern* (1951). T. H. Gaster, "Myth and Story," *Numen*, I (1954), 184-212.

2. The principal myths of the ancient Near East are translated in J. B. Pritchard, ed., *ANET* (2nd ed., 1955). For the Sumerian myth of Asag, see: S. N. Kramer, *Sumerian Mythology* (1944), pp. 80-82. T. Jacobsen, *JNES*, V (1946), 146-47. For the Egyptian myth of the fight between Horus of Beḥdet and "the Caitiff," see: A. Blackman and H. W. Fairman, *JEA*, XXI (1937), 26 ff; XXVIII (1942), 32 ff; XXIX (1943), 3 ff.

For general discussions of ancient Near Eastern myths, see: Y. Kaufmann, "The Bible and Mythological Polytheism," *JBL*, LXX (1951), 179-97. H. Frankfort *et al.*, *Before Philosophy* (1952). S. H. Hooke, ed., *Myth, Ritual and Kingship* (1958). E. O. James, *Myth and Ritual in the Ancient Near East* (1958). J. R. Clarke, *Myth and Symbol in Ancient Egypt* (1959). T. H. Gaster, *Thespis* (1950; rev. ed., 1961).

3. Special topics:

a) The Tree of Life (Mesopotamian): C. J. Gadd, *Ideas of Divine Rule in the Ancient East* (1948), pp. 90-92. Egyptian: J. Breasted, *The Development of Religion and Thought in Ancient Egypt* (1912), p. 134. General: H. Bergema, *De Boom des Levens* (1938).

b) Dragons (cherubs) as guardians of treasure: G. Elliot Smith, *The Evolution of the Dragon* (1919), pp. 161-65.

c) Rex redivivus: H. Schmidt, *Der Mythos vom wiederkehrenden König im AT* (1923).

d) The Samson cycle: P. Carus, *The Story of Samson* (1907). H. Gunkel, *Internationale Monatsschrift für Wissenschaft, Kunst und Technik* (1913), pp. 875-94.

e) The Song of Songs as an adaptation of Tammuz-Ishtar chants: T. J. Meek, *JBL*, XLII (1924), 245-52. W. Wittekindt, *Das Hohelied und seine Beziehungen zum Ishtarkult* (1926).

Traces of the fertility cult in Hosea: H. G. May, *AJSL*, XLVIII (1931), 73 ff.

f) The *pharmakos*, or human scapegoat: Frazer and Gaster, *The New Golden Bough* (1959), pp. 533-44, 555-56.

g) Ritual waking of the god in the morning: R. de Vaux, *Bulletin du Musée de Beyrouth*, V. 17 ff. A Moret, *Le rituel du culte journalier en Egypte* (1902), p. 121.

h) The wondrous child: E. Norden, *Das Geburt des Kindes* (1924). G. Gutknecht, *Das Motiv der Jungfrauengeburt in religionsgesch. Beleuchtung* (1953).

i) Thunder as the voice of God: F. Rück, *Hommel Festschrift* (1917), pp. 279-83.

j) The wind as winged: T. H. Gaster, *Thespis* (1950), p. 158.

k) The winged solar disk: G. Contenau, *Manuel d'archéologie orientale*, III (1931), 1445. B. Perring, *Archiv für Orientforschung*, VIII (1933), 281-96. V. Christian, *Archiv für Orientforschung*, IX (1934), 30. O. Eissfeldt, *Forschungen und Fortschritte*, XVIII (1942), 145-47.

l) On the Mountain of the North: T. H. Gaster, *Thespis* (1950), pp. 86, 170.

m) The "land flowing with milk and honey": H. Usener, *Rheinisches Museum*, LXII (1902), 177-92. I. Guidi, *Revue biblique*, XII (1903), 241 ff.

n) The Book of Fate: J. Friedrich, *JCS*, I (1947), 283-84 (Hittite). M. Lizbarski, *Ephemeris*, I (1902), 164 (Punic).

4. On the date of mythological passages in the OT, see: J. Morgenstern, *HUCA*, XIV (1939), 26 ff. W. F. Albright, *From the Stone Age to Christianity* (Anchor Books ed., 1957), pp. 315-19.

5. On myth in biblical exegesis, see : K. Grobel, "Bultmann's Problem of NT Mythology," *JBL*, LXX (1951), 99-

103. R. Josefson, "Die Entmythologisierung des Evangeliums," *Ny Kinklig Tidskrift* (1951). I. Henderson, *Myth in the NT* (1952). G. Henton Davies, "An Approach to Myth in the OT," *PEQ*, LXXXVIII (1956), 83-91. R. Bultmann, *Myth and Christianity* (1958). B. S. Childs, *Myth and Reality in the OT* (1960).
T. H. Gaster

*__MYTH IN THE NT__ [ὁ μῦθος]. An invented story, fable, tale, legend (I Tim. 1:4; 4:7; II Tim. 4:4; Tit. 1:14; II Pet. 1:16). The term carries with it the classical Greek significance (since Pindar and Herodotus)—i.e., the opposite of Logos or truth. The Vulg. translates the term with *fabula*. In the LXX it does not appear. The obvious NT understanding is that myth is to be rejected as a form of dangerous or foreign teaching, even a form of Heresy.

Modern historians of religion use the word as a technical term for that literary form which tells about otherworldly things in this-worldly concepts. Thus myth expresses truth in a hidden or indirect language, not in an open and direct way. Therefore, it cannot be objectified. It is agreed among NT scholars that earliest Christianity used myth and mythological patterns in its writings. Yet there is no consensus on how far one must, or is permitted to, go with this definition, and there is the open question concerning how to interpret myth in order to preserve the deeper truth in it.

1. The cosmological conception of the NT
2. The eschatological myth
3. The christological myth
4. Demythologizing
   a. Problem and program
   b. Critical evaluation

Bibliography

1. The cosmological conception of the NT. In general, this is carried over from the Jewish tradition. It reflects the concept of antiquity and presupposes the Cosmogony of the OT: a tripartite world consisting of heaven above, hell beneath, and earth between. In other words, the conception of the universe is not scientific but mythological. Such is pagan in its design, though transformed through Israel's introduction of monotheism (cf. Mark 9:48; Luke 16:23 ff). While Greek and Jewish mythology gave detailed descriptions of the world of Hades and of the place of death, the NT writers are restrained. The same is true for heaven and eternal life. As Satan and demons are at home in Hades or Gehenna, God is enthroned in heaven with the risen Christ and surrounded by angels (Mark 8:38; 10:37; 13:27; 14:62; Acts 7:55). Only Revelation (*see* Revelation, Book of), perhaps because it uses Jewish sources, gives a fanciful design of an otherworldly city (cf. Rev. 4; 21:1–22:5). In order to recognize the difference from later times, one may compare with the Shepherd of Hermas (*see* Hermas), Vis. III, Sim. IX.

The earth also is scarcely seen in the NT in mythological terms, and a nature mythology is lacking. The primary interest is in man, living between divine and demonic forces (*see* Demon), open to and threatened by the world above and beneath. This is the point where mythical patterns often are used. Angels are God's servants and proclaim coming events (Matt. 1:20; 2:13; Luke 1; 2) or act as God's hand (Matt. 28:2-3) or interpret the questions of the present (Matt. 28:5 ff). They punish the disobedient man (Acts 12:23) and protect the obedient believers in Christ (Matt. 12:7 ff). On the other side there are demons under the leadership of Satan, tempting man and often regarded as the cause of sickness. Thus the healing miracles of Christ are understood as his victory over Satan and demons and as proving his divine power. Sinners and unbelievers alike are in the bondage of Satan (I Cor. 5:5; 10:20-21; 11:10; etc.) and even Peter, after his confession, "You are the Christ" (Matt. 16:16), when he tried to hinder Jesus' way to Golgotha, must hear the words: "Get behind me, Satan!" (Matt. 16:23).

The question is how far this cosmic mythology expresses a cosmological dualism or is taken up only as the common picture-language of the age. The historical origin of cosmological dualism seems to be the Iranian myth, which enters Judaism not later than the second century B.C. How far it has been transformed into an ethical dualism or preserved its cosmological basis is still an open question and is connected with an adequate understanding of the Dead Sea Scrolls. In early Christian literature one feature is obvious in spite of all mythology: God is the creator and only designer of the universe and its history (cf. Matt. 7; Rom. 9–11; etc.). Nothing happens or will happen without his omnipotent will. Combined with this OT monotheism, which expresses itself in the pattern of prophecy and fulfilment and the acting of God in the election and rejection of men, is the Jewish belief that history leads to a goal designed and planned by God. Thus we must conclude that the cosmic mythology of the NT is used as a means of common language and does not demand a metaphysically dualistic conception of its meaning.

2. The eschatological myth. Here the problem becomes most crucial, because Iranian and Jewish traditions come together. When we read in Matt. 24:19 ff: "Immediately after the tribulation of those days the sun will be darkened, and the moon will not give its light, and the stars will fall from heaven, and the powers of the heavens will be shaken; . . . and they will see the Son of man coming on the clouds of heaven with power and great glory," we have a combination of Iranian astrology and Jewish mythology and a picture used since earliest Christian times (cf. I Thess. 4:16-17). No doubt, earliest Christianity believed in the actual and factual occurrences of this prophecy.

The problem of myth and mythology is whether or not the point of eschatology is inherently bound to its mythological setting. There can be no question as to whether Jesus proclaimed the kingdom of God as coming (cf. Matt. 6:10; Mark 1:15; etc.). Albert Schweitzer's thesis that this was an error of Jesus which must be eliminated has been answered by NT theologians in the following way: The point of the proclamation of the kingdom of God is not the mythological frame but the religious truth that God arrives out of the future and will establish his reign. "How" we describe this reign of God is of minor significance—the "that," and not the "how," is the kerygmatic truth. Whether there is a postponement of the eschatological event, whether Jesus erred or not, is without theological importance. The truth of God's coming action is decisive. Not only the Synoptic gospels, but also Paul, the letters of Peter, Hebrews, and—not the least—the book of Revelation, set forth the myth. A cosmic drama is expected. Since the change of aeons (*see* TIME) has already taken place, the Antichrist soon will come, and apocalyptic signs are present or just around the corner. The eternal reign is at hand. The human reckoning of its arrival as a result of this-worldly development, Jesus explicitly rejects (Luke 17:20-21). Yet there are pictures of its future appearance as when Jesus refers to a heavenly meal (Matt. 8:11; Luke 14:15; often taken up in the paintings of Roman catacombs), or when Paul speaks of the believers who will participate in the final act of judgment (I Cor. 6:2), or when he gives the sequence of eschatological occurrences in I Thess. 4. All mythological patterns include, of course, an idea of history and a specific idea of God.

3. The christological myth. This developed after the crucifixion and resurrection of Jesus. In order to explain the significance of this event, earliest Christianity took up a great variety of designs. The faith in Jesus as the Messiah and Son of God, as redeemer and coming judge of the world, led to the pictures of his supernatural birth (Matt. 1; Luke 2), to the empty-tomb stories, to the idea of a DESCENT INTO HADES (I Pet. 3:19). The main intention is to demonstrate Jesus' cosmic and universal role. NT Christology shows a plurality of interpretations, though it seems to be rather difficult to determine a clear historical development. On the one hand, Jesus appears as the adopted Son (at his baptism [Mark 1:9 ff]; after or together with his resurrection [Rom. 1:3 ff]). On the other hand, his pre-existence is affirmed (Phil. 2:6 ff), and he participated in God's creation of the world (Heb. 1:2). OT prophecies are projected into the life of Jesus, and oriental and Gnostic speculations are related to it. In Rev. 12 we have a complete mythical picture of the Christ event. Wonders are changed into miracles in order to prove the divinity of the historical Jesus.

The question has often been discussed whether Jesus of Nazareth is a historical person at all or simply a mythical figure. Today there is agreement that we have Christian and non-Christian sources enough to reject the doubts of Jesus' historicity. On the other hand, nonhistorical features were added to his life, so that an increasing tendency can be seen to emphasize the supernatural and miraculous aspects.

4. Demythologizing. The widespread mythology of the NT creates difficulties in teaching and preaching. Theological responsibility forbids the method of merely eliminating all those passages which we regard as bound to a prescientific concept of a tripartite world. Thus the German scholar Rudolf Bultmann in a very influential paper published in 1941 demanded "demythologizing" or, what means the same in positive terms, "existentialist interpretation."

a. Problem and program. The problem may be defined by the question: How can we preserve the theological essence of the Christian faith—i.e., that God acted with men in and through Christ Jesus—without demanding the acknowledgment of the mythological pattern of its biblical presentation? Can we retain the deeper truth of the resurrection of Jesus as Christ without taking the emptiness of the tomb as a historical fact; the truth of Jesus as Son of God without acknowledging the virgin birth; the truth of the coming kingdom of God without taking literally the apocalyptic panorama of the "Son of man" returning "on the clouds"? Should not we stress the stumbling-block character of the gospel where it belongs—i.e., in the proclamation of Christ Jesus as the crucified and risen Lord—yet not establish obstacles where a time-bound language is mythologically conditioned?

The program of demythologizing starts with the insight that all mythology expresses a truth, though in an obsolete way. It is impossible and meaningless to sanction the preaching or dogmatizing of the mythological elements of the Bible: impossible because the concept of the universe has radically changed since the first century, and no modern man can honestly believe in the world of spirits above and below; meaningless because most of the mythical elements of our NT are pagan in their origin and not an inherent part of the Christian message. In order to lay bare the deeper truth and to overcome the literal misunderstanding, a consistent method must be used. The task is a hermeneutical one. *See* INTERPRETATION.

The method of an "existentialist interpretation" presupposes that the mythologies do not have their very point in that which they tell in objective and anthropomorphic terms about God or otherworldliness, but in the specific self-understanding of man. It confesses itself in the form of time-bound clothes and must be rediscovered by interpretation. The leading question in dealing with myth must be: What is principally said about man's existence before God, of man's self-understanding in the midst of this world and history?

Three questions are often raised against this approach: (*a*) Do we not artificially modernize and thus falsify the NT message by interpreting myth? Answer: All interpretations throughout history are the result of a personal dialogue with the texts. The involved existence of an interpreter can never be excluded; he participates in the problem of his sources and tries to understand it for his own situation. Furthermore, the NT not only permits but demands the interpretation of myth and begins this task itself. The demand is obvious when we take seriously the often contradicting mythical designs. With the Synoptic writers and Revelation, e.g., we find an imminent eschatological expectation. Yet with Paul (e.g., II Cor. 6:2) and especially with John (e.g., John 5:24-25; 11:25-26; 12:31) there is a transformation of it which stresses the "now," the present "kairos." The futuristic, apocalyptic end drama is widely replaced by the conviction that every moment contains the possibility of being the eschatological one in our crisis before God. The same is the case with christological diversities in which only a consistent method of interpretation can overcome the plurality of pictures and overlapping titles that are rooted in different traditions.

b) Can we ever dismiss the mythical language and

symbolic pictures as a vehicle of religious thought? Is not myth a cipher, making transparent that which in its essence is transcendent? Answer: Demythologizing does not intend to eliminate the mythopoetical language, but to clarify the kerygmatic content of myth by a defined terminology and by a consistent method. Symbols are needed; yet they must be understood as symbols and not misunderstood as fundamental definitions.

c) Since myth is conceived as worldly speech about nonworldly things and as an objective presentation of a non-objectifiable transcendence, how can demythologizing preserve the proclamation that God acted with man in Christ Jesus? Is not the speaking of an action coming from God, concrete in Jesus, necessarily mythological? Answer: The speaking of God as acting with man is neither symbolic nor mythological, but means an objective fact, though perceived by faith only. Yet it involves analogy, thinking of the God-man relationship in terms analogous to the relation between a human "I" and "thou." We express by this way of speaking that God is a reality outside our own selves, outside any faith in his absolute being, although he reveals his being only in a personal revelation, encountered in faith.

b. Critical evaluation. Bultmann's approach and program of demythologizing is the result of an uncompromising biblical criticism. It takes up the heritage of a theological liberalism at the beginning of the twentieth century and the basic ideas of the "theology of crisis," but leads beyond the positions of both by avoiding their shortcomings. The primary intention is hermeneutical and combines with it a missionary aim—namely, to set forth the existential content of the NT Kerygma (*see* PREACHING) for modern man. While earlier attempts demythologized by allegorical or typological exegesis—thus forcing the texts—and others escaped the difficulties by means of elimination or arbitrary selection, here a consistent interpretation is used.

The critics of a more fundamentalistic background reject demythologizing by saying that the objectivity of sacred facts (virgin birth, miracles, empty tomb, and physical resurrection) is dissolved in subjectivity. They disregard the hermeneutical problem which is involved in all exegetical work. Critics of a strictly liberal or unitarian background say that the demythologizing approach is not radical enough, since the kerygma is never touched, and that consistent remythologizing should be demanded. They overlook that there must be a theological presupposition, given in the event of Christ Jesus as such, which is needed in order to preserve faith as "the one faith."

One may question the actual theological results of Bultmann's demythologizing in its details, which he presents in outline. Yet his statement of the problem and even his program provide a fruitful stimulation for exegesis as well as for a preaching of the Bible.

Bibliography. A. N. Wilder, "Mythology and the NT," *JBL,* LXX (1950), 99 ff. E. Dinkler, "Existentialist Interpretation of the NT," *JR,* XXXII (1952), 87 ff. H. W. Bartsch, ed., *Kerygma and Myth* (trans. R. H. Fuller; 1953). F. Gogarten, *Demythologizing and History* (1955). J. Macquarrie, *An Existentialist Theology* (1955). R. Bultmann, *History and Eschatology* (1957); *Jesus Christ and Mythology* (1958).

E. DINKLER

MYTILENE. Classical and modern form of NT MITYLENE.

NAAM nā'əm [נעם] (I Chr. 4:15). One of the descendants of Caleb, son of Jephunneh, of the tribe of Judah.

NAAMAH nā'ə mə [נעמה, pleasant, delightful, sweet]. **1.** Sister of Tubal-cain (Gen. 4:22). *See* LAMECH 1.

2. Ammonitess wife of Solomon; mother of Rehoboam (I Kings 14:21 [LXX A Νααμα; LXX B Μααχαμ], 31 [cf. LXX B]; II Chr. 12:13). *See* REHOBOAM. L. HICKS

3. A village of Judah in the Shephelah district of Lachish (Josh. 15:41). Though the name lingers on in 'Araq Na'aman, the modern location is probably at the nearby Khirbet Farad, between Timnah and Eltekeh. V. R. GOLD

NAAMAN nā'ə mən [נעמן, pleasantness]; NAAMITES —mīts. The name occurs in an Ugaritic genealogy, and the word *n'm* is a common term for "charm" or "loveliness" and an epithet of heroes in that language. The reference in Isa. 17:10 to the fertility-cult practice of planting PLEASANT PLANTS (נטעי נעמנים) suggests that the name may have been an epithet of ADONIS.

1. An obscure Benjaminite (Gen. 46:21; I Chr. 8:4, 7), the eponymous ancestor of the Naamites (Num. 26:40).

2. Commander of the army of the king of Aram (Syria) who was cured of leprosy by the prophet Elisha (II Kings 5). The kingdom was that of Damascus (vs. 12) and the king probably Ben-hadad II (*ca.* 850 B.C.; 8:7). The name of the Israelite king in the account (5:5-8) is unknown, and it is impossible to date the story precisely.

The exact nature of Naaman's leprosy is not known, since the biblical term covers several types of disease and even household mold or mildew (Lev. 13–14; *see* LEPROSY). It must not have been highly contagious, since neither he nor Gehazi, upon whom the blight subsequently fell (II Kings 5:27; 8:4), was isolated from society. There is a curious mixture of motifs surrounding the disease and its occasions in this story. Naaman was reported leprous without the disease being interpreted as a punishment for moral evil; while the transfer of the malady to Gehazi, under the power of Elisha, was the retribution for his designing greed. No moral responsibility was laid upon Naaman as the concomitant of his new-found health. He was led, however, to confess spontaneously his faith in the God of Israel, by whose power his cure was effected, as an exclusive loyalty, albeit qualified somewhat by the demand of court etiquette that he give lip service to his Syrian national god (5:18).

The interplay of motives and attitudes is rich and vivid throughout the account. The general's Israelite maidservant took compassion upon him in his distress, even though she was a war captive (5:2). She seemed interested only in his cure. Elisha, however, was concerned primarily to demonstrate his own power as a prophet of Yahweh (5:8). Once healed, Naaman seemed preoccupied simply with the grateful desire to acknowledge the sole godhead of Yahweh (vss. 15, 17). His unquestioning gratitude, of which Gehazi took advantage, is in marked contrast to the Israelite king's suspicion (vs. 7*b*). Gehazi surprises us in the sequel (8:5) by extolling the powers of the prophet who cursed him with leprosy.

A strange blend of the universal and the local characterizes Naaman's conception of God. On the one hand, he swore that he would worship only the Lord, who alone is God (5:15-17); but, on the other hand, he apparently believed that sacrifice to Yahweh could be offered only on Israelite soil. He therefore took the two mules' burden of earth back to Syria with him (vs. 17). The idea that Yahweh was God of the whole cosmos but administered some historical affairs through the agency of members of a heavenly court seems to have been current in the period of the Israelite monarchy (cf. Deut. 32:8-9 LXX; I Kings 22:19-22; Ps. 82). The gods of the nations were probably identified by many with these lesser heavenly beings.

The kind of international hospitality in medicine that is illustrated here was apparently common in the ancient world. Ramses II of Egypt offered medical aid to a Hittite princess, and a physician and exorcist were sent from Babylon to the Hittite king Hattushil (*ca.* 1275 B.C.), according to documents found in the modern era.

It has frequently been held that the reply of the Israelite king to Naaman's request: "Am I God, to kill and to make alive, that this man sends word to me to cure a man of his leprosy?" (II Kings 5:7), is evidence of a belief in the divinity of kings in ancient Israel, here modified by a later editor. Such an interpretation strains the text. The healing, or, indeed, life-giving (cf. 4:32-37), power of Elisha was not considered a mark of his divinity. Therefore, the king's exclamation was implicitly an oversimplification of the current belief. He might better have exclaimed: "Am I God, or a prophet of God . . . ?" Greater powers, of a superhuman sort, were attributed to prophets in Israel than to kings.

Parallels between the healing miracles of Jesus and those of Elijah and Elisha have often been drawn (*see* MIRACLE). Naaman's cure was alluded to by Jesus as an example of God's gracious concern for the non-Israelite (Luke 4:27).

Bibliography. J. A. Montgomery, *The Books of Kings,* ICC (1951), pp. 373-81. J. M. WARD

NAAMATHITE nā'ə mə thīt [נעמתי]. A resident of Na'ameh, perhaps Djebel-el-Na'ameh, in NW Arabia. The term is used in the OT only of Zophar (Job 2:11; 11:1; 20:1; 42:9), one of the friends of Job.

NAARAH nā'ə rə [נערה, girl]; KJV NAARATH —rāth in Josh. 16:7. Alternately: NAARAN —răn [נערן] (I Chr. 7:28). **1.** One of the two wives of Ashhur, a man of Judah (I Chr. 4:5-6).

B. T. DAHLBERG

2. A city on the E border of Ephraim, not far N of Jericho (Josh. 16:7), the first city of Benjamin. It lay in the fertile plain near the Jordan, one of the most densely populated regions of Canaan. It is the Naara of Josephus (Antiq. XVII.xiii.1). In Roman times it was called Noaran, and there is a reference in the Midrash to the proverbial hostility between its inhabitants and those of Jericho. Eusebius calls it Noarath and states that it was five Roman miles N of Jericho.

The site of Naarah has generally been considered to be at or near 'Ain Duq, at the foot of the mountains NE of Jericho. In 1918, during World War I, a shellburst opened up a buried synagogue, which was excavated by the École Biblique et Archéologique Française of Jerusalem in 1921. It was apparently built in the fourth or fifth century A.D. and has a fine mosaic floor with a zodiac, an ark of the Law, and other figures. N. Glueck (*see bibliography*), however, notes that no early remains have been found at this spot and suggests instead Khirbet el-'Ayash, near the Wadi el-'Auja, which is definitely as early as the Israelite period and more nearly five miles from Jericho than 'Ain Duq is.

Bibliography. N. Glueck, *AASOR,* vols. XXV-XXVIII, pt. 1 (1939), pp. 412-13.

S. COHEN

NAARAI nā'ə rī [נערי] (I Chr. 11:37). Son of Ezbai, and one of the members of the company of Davidic Mighty Men known as the "Thirty." In the parallel catalogue he is called Paarai the Arbite (II Sam. 23:35).

NAASHON. KJV alternate form of NAHSHON.

NAASSON. KJV NT form of NAHSHON.

NAATHUS nā'ə thəs [Λάθος (B), Νααθος (A)] (I Esd. 9:31). One of the sons of Addi who put away his foreign wife and children; possibly a variant form of ADNA in the parallel Ezra 10:30.

C. T. FRITSCH

NABAL nā'bəl [נבל, fool, churl]. A wealthy Calebite. His rude treatment of David's demand for provisions as a compensation for the protection his flocks had received would have spelled disaster had it not been for the astuteness of his wife, Abigail, who took it upon herself to propitiate David with generous supplies (I Sam. 25).

Nabal resided in Maon but pastured his large flocks of sheep and goats in Carmel (now el-Kurmul) on the edge of the wilderness of Judah. As he was celebrating the shearing of his sheep, David, whose band of followers appears to have protected the flocks of Nabal from the predatory raids of the Bedouins, sent ten of his men to collect "payment" for this service. Nabal not only categorically refused to give the messengers anything, but also grievously insulted David and his followers. Taking four hundred of his men with him to avenge this effrontery, David was met by Abigail, who by ample stores of food, as well as by graciousness of manner and personal charm, dissuaded David from his contemplated revenge. Her husband, she said, was incorrigibly insensible; indeed, Nabal ("churl") was his name, and churlishness (נבלה) was with him (i.e., his nature; I Sam. 25:25). When Nabal was informed of his wife's action on the morrow after his nocturnal debauch, he suffered a stroke and died within ten days. Shortly thereafter David took Abigail for his wife (I Sam. 27:3; 30:5; II Sam. 2:2; 3:3).

E. R. DALGLISH

NABARIAH năb'ə rī'ə [Ναβαρίας; Vulg. *Nabadias*] (I Esd. 9:44); KJV NABARIAS —əs. One of those standing upon Ezra's left hand as "he read aloud in the open square."

J. C. SWAIM

NABATEANS năb'ə tē'ənz [Ναβαταῖοι] (I Macc. 5:25; 9:35); KJV NABATHITES năb'ə thīts. An Arab people playing an important role in the history of Palestine and the neighboring countries in the last centuries B.C. and the first A.D. They are not mentioned by name in the OT or the NT, but Paul relates that he barely escaped arrest in Damascus on the orders of the governor of King Aretas IV (II Cor. 11:32; a somewhat different version of this event is in Acts 9:23-25); in another place (Gal. 1:17) he speaks of journeying into Arabia before returning to Damascus, by which is meant, not the Arabian Peninsula, but the territory of the Nabateans.

Up until modern times the only information about the Nabateans came from the works of such ancient writers as Diodorus Siculus, Strabo, and Pliny the Elder, which have proved to be inaccurate in many respects, and the notices of wars between them and the Jews given in the works of Josephus. It was not until 1812 that Burckhardt succeeded in reaching and describing the wonders of Petra, the Nabatean capital in the biblical Edom. In subsequent years considerable progress was made in the deciphering of the Nabatean inscriptions, which are mostly of a funerary or votive nature. It was not until the 1930's and after, however, that a thoroughgoing archaeological survey of the Nabatean territory yielded much more definite information as to the Nabatean civilization and the extent of their kingdom.

1. History. The early history of the Nabateans is comparatively unknown. Attempts to identify them with the Ishmaelitic group of NEBAIOTH have generally been rejected on the ground that this name is spelled with a *Tau* (ת) and that of the Nabateans with a *Ṭeth* (ט). The original home of the Nabateans was in NW Arabia, as can be seen by the fact that their remains are found as far as El-Heger (Medain Salih), *ca.* 250 miles SE of Petra. From there they came, perhaps as early as the sixth century B.C., to occupy the territory of the Edomites, who were pushed up into the S of Judah; it is not known whether this came about by armed conquest or as a result of steady infiltration. By the fourth century B.C., as is seen by archaeological evidence, they had settled all of Edom and Moab and had occupied the Wadi el-Arabah and the S part of the Negeb. They took over in these territories the fortress system of the original peoples and extended it to the S and the E, and in the succeeding centuries they built such strongholds as Abde, Kurnub, and Sbeita in the Negeb region. At first they were nominally subject to Persian rule, but they gradually attained an independent position, which they retained after the conquest of Alexander the Great (333 B.C.).

The first definite date in Nabatean history is 169 B.C., when Jason, one of the contenders for the office of Jewish high priest, vainly sought sanctuary with Aretas, the "tyrant" of the Nabateans (II Macc. 5:8). A second Aretas is mentioned as reigning in 96 and trying to intervene in the dynastic wars of Syria (Jos. Antiq. XIII.xiii.3). From that time on, the names of the Nabatean kings and the probable time of their reigns are known: Obodas I (95-87); Rabel I (*ca.* 87); Aretas III (87?-62); Obodas II (62-47); Malichus I (47-30); Obodas III (30-9); Aretas IV (9 B.C.–A.D. 40); Malichus II (40-70); Rabel II (70-106). During the greater part of this period there were wars between the Nabateans and the Jews; for though at first the former helped the latter in their struggle against the common Syrian enemy, later territorial and economic rivalry soon brought the two peoples into conflict. One war, indeed, was caused by Herod Antipas' divorce from the daughter of the Nabatean king in order to marry his niece and sister-in-law, Herodias (Jos. Antiq. XVIII.v.1). The fortunes of these wars swayed to and fro, but the general result was that the Nabateans established themselves in the N part of Transjordan, to the E of the Jewish Perea and the Greek Decapolis. In 85 B.C., Aretas III was summoned by the citizens of the free city of Damascus to rule over them, and the Nabateans may have remained in power until 65, when Pompey occupied the city. *Ca.* A.D. 37, Caligula again gave the city to the Nabateans, and they remained there till the beginning of the reign of Nero, *ca.* 54. Thus the Nabatean kingdom consisted of a N and a S part; the S part, limited on the N by a line drawn E to W through Medeba and on the E by Bayir Wells, was thickly settled by the Nabateans; the N part had merely Nabatean governors. The connection between the two was the Wadi Sirhan, in the desert E of Palestine, a trade route under Nabatean control.

After the death of Rabel II in 106, Trajan annexed all the Nabatean kingdom, probably to secure his S flank in his projected war against the Parthians. From that time on, the Nabateans ceased as an independent nation, though their prosperity continued for a while; it is even possible that Philip the Arab, Roman emperor from 244 to 249, was a Nabatean, as he was born in Bostra in the Hauran. In the course of time, however, the loss of independence and the disasters which befell the Roman Empire had their effect; the Nabateans lost their identity and disappeared among the other inhabitants of the country.

2. Civilization. Before their entrance into Palestine the Nabateans were a typically Arab group, living in tents, traveling about on camels, and getting their subsistence from dates and the flesh of animals. With their entrance into the territories of Edom and Moab, their life changed. They inherited the trade routes of the Edomites, and their caravans now traversed the country from Arabia to the SE, to Damascus to the N, and to Gaza and Alexandria to the W, whence they were transshipped as far as Asia Minor and Italy. The most important source of their prosperity, however, was their intense devotion to agriculture. They utilized every source of water supply, building dams and cisterns to store up the water in the wadis and from the rains; they were so successful that the population in the areas settled by them was the greatest at any time in history. They reached out into the stretches of the Negeb that before their time had been but thinly populated, and filled them with settlements; in fact, the roads which they made through that area were just as much to connect their cities as to facilitate trade. They continued to work the copper and iron mines of the Edomites, and formed port cities at Aila on the Gulf of Aqabah, and at Negra (Agra) and Leuké Komé (Hauara) on the Red Sea.

Their language must originally have been a form of Arabic, but the inscriptions, which come from the

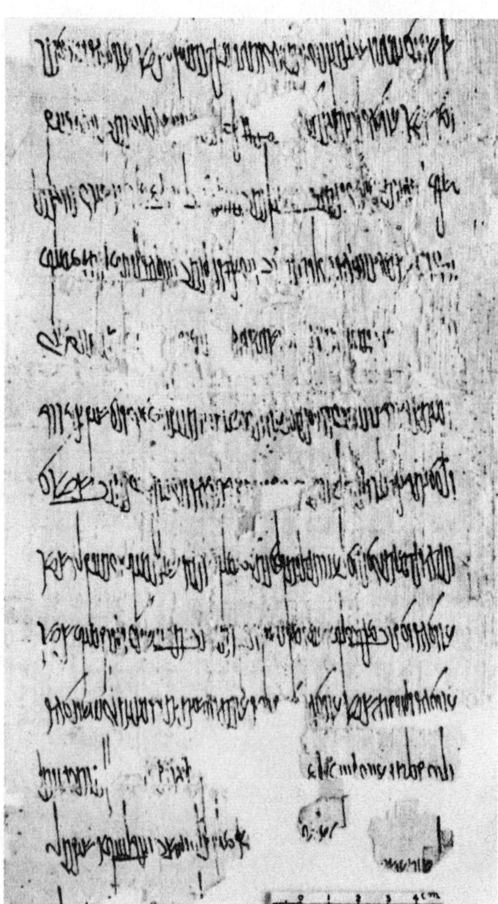

From Milik, *Ten Years of Discovery in the Wilderness of Judaea* (London: SCM Press, 1959; U.S.A.: Alec R. Allenson Inc.)

1. Earliest known Nabatean papyrus, a deed about property titles (*ca.* A.D. 100)

latter period of the kingdom, are written in Aramaic, which had become the universal tongue of Palestine, which shows that they learned to use it as their native language; while the fact that some of the inscriptions are partly in Aramaic and partly in Greek indicates that many were familiar with the Koiné that was widespread after the conquest of Alexander. The alphabet that they used in their Aramaic inscriptions is a distinctive one; it has letters similar to those of ancient Hebrew, but made almost rectangular and connected frequently by ligatures at their bottom lines; it is thus an intermediate stage between the uncial square Hebrew-Aramaic character and the cursive writing of the later Arabs. A number of Nabatean papyri of the first century A.D. have been found in the Qumran neighborhood, revealing for the first time the written form of their script. They appear to be contracts and indicate that at that time Nabateans and Jews were living closely together. Fig. NAB 1.

The religion of the Nabateans took the same course as that of the early Israelites in that it added to its own deities those of the countries they conquered. Their supreme god was always Dushara (דושרא); others were Allat, the Arabian mother-goddess, Ara, and several others. In the course of time they began also to worship Hadad, the storm-god; Atargatis, the fish-goddess;* and Gad, the god of luck. Later, in the syncretism of the times, they began to identify their gods with those of the Greeks: Dushara with Dionysius or Zeus, Hadad with Zeus, Gad with Tyche.* The kings, beginning with Obodas I, were regularly deified, like the Ptolemies; like the latter, they tended to marry their sisters, whose portraits are found frequently with theirs on coins. Figs. NAB 2, 3.

In addition to being clever traders and skilled agriculturists, the Nabateans were fine artists. Their pottery, remarkably thin and beautifully decorated, surpasses any in Palestine before their time. Their statuary, with its well-cut reliefs in plant designs, and especially their tombs cut out of the solid rock at PETRA and other places, bear witness to the skill of their sculptors.* Though they have left behind them no literature, the genius of the Nabateans is demonstrated by the engineering feats and the artistic remains that still attest to the high degree of their civilization. Figs. NAB 4, 5.

Courtesy of Nelson Glueck

2. Atargatis, the fish-goddess; from a relief at Khirbet Tannur

Courtesy of Nelson Glueck

3. Tyche, the guardian goddess of the city; from a relief found at Khirbet Tannur

Courtesy of the Palestine Archaeological Museum, Jerusalem, Jordan

4. Line of Royal Tombs at Petra

Courtesy of the Palestine Archaeological Museum, Jerusalem, Jordan

5. The large theater at Petra

Bibliography. There are no books that give the complete story of the Nabateans. J. Cantineau, *Le Nabatéen* (1930-32); A. Kemmerer, *Pétra et la Nabatène* (1929), supply the information known in their time. Later archaeological information is found in N. Glueck, *The Other Side of the Jordan* (1940), pp. 158-200; and throughout his "Explorations in Eastern Palestine," *AASOR,* vol. XIV (1934); vol. XV (1935); vols. XVIII-XIX (1939); vols. XXV-XXVIII (1951).

S. COHEN

NABONIDUS năb'ə nī'dəs [Lat. *form of* Ναβουνάϊδος, Λαβύνητος, *etc.;* Akkad. *Nabû-na'id,* Nabû is awe-inspiring]. The last king of Babylon (555-539 B.C.).

Although a variety of historical sources cover the reign of Nabonidus, very little more than the most salient facts is known, and the key to a real understanding of the unusual happenings of this final phase of Babylonian history is still lacking. Not only Herodotus but also Xenophon (*Cyropaedia*) and Josephus (*Antiquities*) discuss the events leading to the fall of Babylon to the Persians. There are also two passages from the lost work of the late Babylonian historian Berossus, who wrote in Greek on that subject—not to speak of the book of Daniel—which reflect this critical period in many ways. As to cuneiform sources, we have a number of quite unique documents which in themselves bespeak the extraordinary personality of Nabonidus. Apart from conventional foundation documents referring to the rebuilding of sanctuaries, etc., and from about sixty very broken lines in a chronicle, we have three texts that describe the background and activities of Nabonidus from widely differing viewpoints. These are, first, a basalt stela which contains his own report on his rise to kingship and which has been termed, not without reason, an apologia; then a memorial inscription coming from Harran in Upper Syria, in which his mother tells the story of her life; and, lastly, a damaged tablet that contains a political poem directed against Nabonidus and which is very revealing as to the political situation during the last days of Babylon before the conquest by Cyrus. It should be noted, furthermore, that a new stela has recently been found in the ruins of a mosque near Harran, in which were used stones taken from the temple of Sin erected by Nabonidus. Its text deepens, rather than solves, the mystery surrounding him. Under circumstances to which Nabonidus himself referred in his autobiographical inscription only cursorily and with obvious reluctance, when he was a military commander, in his sixties, he was made king of Babylon. We do not know what political forces brought Nabonidus to the throne, thus terminating the short reigns of the three successors of Nebuchadnezzar II: his son Evil-merodach (561-559), his son-in-law Neriglissar (559-555), and his grandson Labashi-Marduk (555).

Nabonidus was a native of Harran, where his father and mother seem to have been high Assyrian officials, and his sympathies in the crucial question of Assyrian policy toward Babylonia were clearly on the pro-Babylonian side, as references to Sennacherib as the destroyer of Babylon and to the conquest of the Assyrian Empire by the Medes, in the just-mentioned text, indicate. Nabonidus soon after his accession left his capital for the W; in fact, he was absent from the New Year's Festival for nearly ten years—a fact which the chronicle marks every year with resentful consistency. His sojourn in the W was taken up by minor military operations in Syria (Hamat); the rebuilding of the sanctuary of Sin in Harran, upon which his building inscriptions dwell with special care; a short stay in the Anti-Lebanon, where the king fell sick for some time; and the advance against and conquest of Adummu and the oasis city of Tema' in NW Arabia. For reasons still unknown, Nabonidus made the latter city the center of his activities in Arabia, and he stayed there for many years, visiting the larger towns, among them even Jatrib, later Medina (see Harran stela). Explanations of this long stay in Arabia, ranging from sentimental reasons to considerations of international policies, have been offered, but for none can any proof be found. The interest of all the rulers of the new Chaldean dynasty in the Phoenician cities and in overland trade, which became more evident of late, suggests an explanation in that direction. The fact that Nabonidus made his son Belshazzar ruler of Babylon and commander of the main part of the army when departing westward indicates that he was guided by careful planning rather than by spontaneous decisions. The length of the absence is perhaps even more startling than the travelings of a Babylonian king along the caravan roads of W Arabia.

Very little is known about the situation in Babylon. Some kind of understanding which seems to have existed between Nabonidus and Cyrus at the beginning of his reign must have come to an end when the latter defeated his most powerful enemy, Astyages the Median. With the subsequent defeat of Croesus and the fall of Sardis (546 B.C.), Cyrus became the most powerful king of the ancient Near East, and Babylon was in mortal danger. We know from the chronicle that Nabonidus did eventually return to Babylon, but the cuneiform sources are silent about the years between the fall of Sardis and the actual attack of Cyrus on Opis and Sippar (538); for this we have only Greek sources, which are not very reliable. In some desperate last move, Nabonidus seems to have attempted to bring all the images from the temples of Babylonia into the capital, but the chronicle stresses that the images of Borsippa, Cutha, and Sippar did not come. After the fall of Opis, Ugbaru, the governor of Gutium, with the Persian army entered Sippar and Babylon without a fight. While Nabonidus fled, Cyrus entered occupied Babylon to the jubilation of the population. It should be kept in mind that the chronicle itself, as well as the so-called Cylinder of Cyrus, not to speak of the poem against Nabonidus, is definitely pro-Persian and must be assumed to be a distorted report on the entire reign of Nabonidus. The reasons given for this strange attitude are somewhat too obviously religious to be fully acceptable. Nabonidus, whose religious sympathies seem clearly to have been favorable to the cult of Sin in its older and quite antiquated forms, is consistently represented as an impious innovator with sacrilegious intent, to be contrasted with Cyrus, who was praised for his piety and tolerance. Still, the large number of building inscriptions, inscribed bricks, etc., of Nabonidus demonstrate that he was as concerned with the traditional care of sacred sites as any other king of the last dynasty, and that such work went on in the sanctuaries of Babylonia in spite of the absence of the king. It is quite possible that Nabonidus was steeped in the tradition of the Assyrian concept of kingship and that this caused friction in Babylonia, where the king had traditionally no part in the religious activities of the great sanctuaries; or that his personal piety, which speaks out from many of his inscriptions, set him at odds with the formalized religion of his kingdom. The reinauguration of the office of an *entu* (high priestess) of Sin in Ur, for which he rebuilt a special sanctuary in the temple and in which he installed his own daughter, may represent only one example of his attitude toward established cults.

It should be finally mentioned that his unprecedented absence from his capital, as well as other still undetermined unconventional acts of Nabonidus, gave rise to the legend of a mad king of Babylonia, which is reflected in Dan. 4 (although transferred to Nebuchadnezzar) and in a Hebrew literary work of which some small fragments have been found in Qumran.

Bibliography. S. Smith, *Babylonian Historical Texts Relating to the Capture and Downfall of Babylon* (1924), pp. 27 ff, 98 ff; R. P. Dougherty, *Nabonidus and Belshazzar* (1929); J. Lewy, "The Late Assyro-Babylonian Cult of the Moon and Its Culmination at the Time of Nabonidus," *HUCA,* 19 (1946), 405-89; J. T. Milik, "Prière de Nabonide et autres écrits d'un cycle de Daniel," *RB,* 62 (1956), 407 ff.

A. L. OPPENHEIM

NABOPOLASSAR năb'ə pə lăs'ər [Akkad. *Nabû-apal-uṣur,* Nabû protect the son!]. King of Babylon (626-605 B.C.); first king of the Chaldean Dynasty; father of Nebuchadrezzar II. Of the twenty regnal years of Nabopolassar, all but the years 4-9 are mentioned in the several tablets containing the chronicle of the Neo-Babylonian period. Nabopolassar seems to have been a Babylonian general of the Assyrian king Sinsharishkun. He rebelled in the very year in which the latter succeeded his father, Ashurbanipal. After an unsuccessful siege of Nippur, which was held by its Assyrian garrison, Nabopolassar had to retreat toward Uruk; but he was soon able to enter Babylon, whose inhabitants had just defeated an Assyrian contingent marching against them. After Nabopolassar had become king of Babylon and another Assyrian attack had failed to reach even Sippar, he began to take the large cities one by one, Nippur in 622, Uruk in 623. In his tenth year we find Nabopolassar advancing along the Euphrates River, where Assyrian control was clearly on the wane. He still was rather wary of any encounter with Assyrian troops, but it can be gleaned even from the terse remarks of the chronicle that the military potential of Nabopolassar's army was increasing. An attack on Asshur, the old capital of Assyria, in 615 failed. In 614 Asshur fell to the Medes, but the army of Nabopolassar—intentionally or not—came too late for the battle. On that occasion he met the king of the Medes, Cyaxares, and established an alliance with him, which turned out to be of great political importance. The Medes apparently left the remnants of the Assyrian Empire to Nabopolassar, while they were to take the spoils of Nineveh. It is possible that a marriage between Nabopolassar's son Nebuchadrezzar and the daughter of the king of the Medes was to seal this alliance, which proved a boon to the new Babylonian Empire. Without fear of any attack from the mountain tribes, Nabopolassar could now compel all the former vassals of Assyria, as far as Palestine and Cilicia, to pay tribute to him. The next year (612) saw the fall of Nineveh, in which Nabopolassar fought side by side with his ally. In the annual campaigns of the next years Nabopolassar succeeded in dislodging the leftovers of the Assyrian army from Harran and in preventing their efforts and their Egyptian allies' efforts to regain that city. Then the Babylonian king directed his attention to the N, to keep the inhabitants of the foothills of the Zagros Range from moving into the fertile plain, now without Assyrian military protection. In 606 Nabopolassar again took up the Euphrates front, where the Egyptian hold on Carchemish posed a threat to the entire Western part of his newly won empire. There Babylonia met with success only when Nebuchadrezzar, the crown prince, acting for his ailing father, achieved the conquest of Carchemish and drove the Egyptian army back home in the year of the death of his father (605).

In his inscriptions Nabopolassar represents himself as a pious man who rose from low status to kingship, but he refers with pride to his victory over Assyria.

Bibliography. D. J. Wiseman, *Chronicles of the Chaldean Kings* (1956), pp. 5-21.

A. L. OPPENHEIM

NABOTH nā'bŏth [נבות, *perhaps from a stem cognate of* Arab. *nabata,* to sprout]. Owner of a vineyard in Jezreel adjacent to the country palace of king Ahab (I Kings 21). Ahab sought to extend his estate by purchasing the vineyard, but Naboth refused because of his obligation to maintain the land as a family inheritance. Jezebel, Ahab's queen, deplored the king's pouting meekness in this encounter and proceeded to secure the land for him by devious means. Naboth was stoned to death on a false conviction of blasphemy brought by a court under Jezebel's control (vss. 8-14). The prophet Elijah condemned Ahab for this crime (vss. 17-20*a*), prophesying that the king would die at the place of Naboth's death.

Jehu interpreted his killing of Joram, son of Ahab, as the fulfilment of Elijah's oracle (II Kings 9:21-26). This event took place outside Jezreel. Most commentators believe that I Kings 21:20*b*-29 is a late editorial addition to the account of Elijah's curse of Ahab, through which the initial malediction (vss. 17-19) and the ultimate facts of the fall of Ahab's house (II Kings 9-10) were made to correspond.

Some interpreters have held that Ahab had a collateral right of inheritance to Naboth's vineyard, which he could legally exercise after the owner's death. There is no evidence, however, to contravene the view that the land was appropriated for the crown by simple royal confiscation. Elijah was surely correct in denouncing a double crime (I Kings 21:19).

Bibliography. J. A. Montgomery, *The Books of Kings,* ICC (1951), pp. 330-45, 401-2.

J. M. WARD

NABUCHODONOSOR năb'ə kō dŏn'ə sôr. Douay Version form of NEBUCHADNEZZAR.

NACHON. KJV form of NACON.

NACHOR. KJV form of NAHOR in Josh. 24:2; Luke 3:34.

NACON nā'kŏn [נכון] (II Sam. 6:6); KJV NACHON. The owner of a threshing floor near which Uzzah was smitten of God, during the transfer of the ark of the covenant from Baale-judah (Kiriath-jearim) to Jerusalem. The parallel passage in I Chr. 13:9 reads "Chidon" instead of "Nacon." The place was called subsequently PEREZ-UZZAH.

G. A. BARROIS

NADAB nā'dăb [נָדָב, (Yahweh is) willing *or* liberal; *an abbreviation of* נדבאל *or* נדביה(ו); Apoc. Νασβᾶς]; KJV Apoc NASBAS năz'bəs in Tob. 11:19; AMAN ā'mən in Tob. 14:10. **1.** Eldest of the four sons of Aaron (Exod. 6:23; Num. 3:2; I Chr. 6:3—H 5:29); always associated with Abihu, Aaron's second son.

With Moses and Aaron, Abihu, and seventy of the elders of Israel, Nadab took part in the ceremony of the ratification of the covenant at Mount Sinai (Exod. 24:1, 9 ff). This account belongs to the J source.

Afterward he became a priest (Exod. 28:1). Later tradition repudiated both Nadab and Abihu because they "offered unholy fire before the LORD" (Lev. 10: 1; Num. 3:4). As a result they were consumed by fire (Lev. 10:1-7; Num. 26:61). The expression "offered unholy fire" occurs only in connection with this event, and probably means that Nadab and Abihu offered what was contrary to the express command of God. The nature of the actual offense, however, remains obscure. An old tradition explains the story on the ground that they offered unholy fire while under the influence of wine, but such an explanation is very unlikely. The source of this tradition is almost certainly the command in Lev. 10:9 forbidding Aaron and his sons to drink wine or strong drink when they went into the tent of meeting. Both brothers died without offspring (Num. 3:4; I Chr. 24:2).

2. A Judahite of the family of Hezron; descendant of Tamar, daughter-in-law of Judah (I Chr. 2:28, 30).

3. A Benjaminite, son of Jeiel and Maacah; brother of Kish, who was the father of King Saul (I Chr. 8:30; 9:36).

H. B. MACLEAN

4. King of Israel *ca.* 901-900 B.C.; son and successor of Jeroboam I; murdered by Baasha.

He is said to have reigned for two years (I Kings 15:25); but if he began to reign in Asa's second year (vs. 25), and Baasha succeeded him in Asa's third year (vs. 33), it is clear that he can have occupied the throne for only one year and part of a year.

The only noteworthy event recorded for his reign was the siege of GIBBETHON by the Israelites (I Kings 15:27). This was a Philistine city in the territory formerly occupied by the Danites (Josh. 19:40-46). It has not been identified with certainty but may be the modern Tell el-Melat, W of Gezer. No reason is given for Nadab's attack on this city, but from the Israelite point of view its capture must have been considered important, for it was again the object of attack in the reigns of Elah and Zimri (I Kings 16: 15). In the course of the siege a revolt broke out in the army, led by Baasha. This resulted in Nadab's death and the extermination of the house of Jeroboam (15:29). The prophecy of Ahijah the Shilonite had been fulfilled (14:10-11).

Nadab's murder after such a short reign indicated how unstable was the political situation in the N kingdom. The usual notice of burial is lacking in the case of Nadab, presumably because of his assassination. The reference to his capital is likewise omitted.

5. Nephew of Ahikar. When Tobias returned with Sarah, his bride, Nadab and his uncle came to the marriage ceremony, which "was celebrated for seven days with great festivity" (Tob. 11:18-19).

Though the texts contain many variations in the name (e.g., Ναβάς, Nabal, Laban), all of them difficult to account for, Nadab is now thought to be identical with the Nadab of Tob. 14:10-11. There Tobit, as part of his dying counsel, bids his son remember "what Nadab did to Ahikar who had reared him, how he brought him from light into darkness, and with what he repaid him. But Ahikar was saved, and the other received repayment as he himself went down into the darkness. Ahikar gave alms and escaped the deathtrap which Nadab had set for him; but Nadab fell into the trap and perished."

In each of the above instances, A and other MSS read "Aman" ('Αμάν), making it apparently a reference to Haman, the villain of Esther, and Mordecai.

Bibliography. J. R. Harris, *The Story of Ahikar* (1898), pp. xxix, xiv.

J. C. SWAIM

NADABATH năd'ə băth [Ναδαβαθ] (I Macc. 9: 37); KJV NADABATHA nə dăb'ə thə. Revenging the capture and execution of their brother John by the Jambrites, a Nabatean tribe, Jonathan and Simon Maccabeus ambushed a tribal wedding procession traveling from the bride's home at Nadabath to Medeba. This Transjordan city may be the Nabatha mentioned in Jos. Antiq. XIII.i.4, the ancient Nebo, NW of Medeba in the region still called en-Neba. It has also been identified with the modern Khirbet et-Teim, *ca.* 1.2 miles S of Medeba.

Bibliography. N. Glueck, *Explorations in Eastern Palestine*, I, *AASOR*, XIV (1933-34), 33.

E. W. SAUNDERS

NAGGAI năg'ī [Ναγγαί] (Luke 3:25); KJV NAGGE —ī. An ancestor of Jesus.

NAHALAL nā'ə lăl [נַהֲלָל]; KJV NAHALLAL nə hăl'əl in Josh. 19:15. Alternately: NAHALOL nā'ə lŏl (Judg. 1:30). A Levitical town in Zebulun (Josh. 19:15; 21:35), from which Zebulun was unable to expel the Canaanite inhabitants (Judg. 1:30). Although its exact location is unknown, it is perhaps to be identified with Tell en-Nahl, a small mound with evidence of occupation in the LB and Iron I periods, situated N of the Kishon River near the S end of the Plain of Acco.

Bibliography. W. F. Albright, "Contributions to the Historical Geography of Palestine," *AASOR*, 2-3 (1923), 26; "Bronze Age Mounds of Northern Palestine and the Hauran . . . ," *BASOR*, 19 (1925), 10.

G. W. VAN BEEK

NAHALIEL nə hā'lī əl [נַחֲלִיאֵל, torrent valley of God, *or perhaps* God is my inheritance] (Num. 21: 19). A stopping place of the Israelites in Transjordan between Mattanah and Bamoth. If it is a torrent valley, it might be the Wadi Zerqa Ma'in, which enters the Dead Sea between the Arnon and Mount Nebo. Another possibility is the Wadi Wala, an important N tributary of the Arnon. If Nahaliel is a particular town, its precise location is unknown.

E. D. GROHMAN

NAHALLAL; NAHALOL. *See* NAHALAL.

NAHAM nā'hăm [נחם] (I Chr. 4:19). The brother-in-law of Hodiah of Judah (MS evidence supports the RSV against the KJV, which takes Hodiah as the name of Naham's sister).

NAHAMANI nā'ə mā'nī [נחמני, *hypocoristic for* נחמיה, Yahu has comforted] (Neh. 7:7). One of those who returned from the Exile with Zerubbabel (cf. I Esd. 5:8, which reads "Bigvai"; KJV "Enenius" [Ενήνιος]; the name is lacking in Ezra 2:2).

Bibliography. M. Noth, *Die israelitischen Personennamen* (1928), pp. 39, 175. B. T. DAHLBERG

NAHARAI nā'ə rī [נחרי] (II Sam. 23:37; I Chr. 11:39); KJV NAHARI in II Sam. 23:37. One of the company of the Mighty Men of David known as the "Thirty"; the armor-bearer of Joab. He was from the city of Beeroth.

NAHASH nā'hăsh [נחש, serpent; *or* Akkad. *nuḫšu,* magnificence]. **1.** Ruler of the seminomadic Ammonites. His attack on Jabesh-gilead and subsequent defeat by the troops which Saul had collected to come to the aid of the besieged town was the occasion of Israel's accepting Saul as king (I Sam. 11:1-11). The attack by Nahash did not have as its primary purpose the extortion of tribute. Nahash coveted the honor which would accrue to him if he could inflict a shameful mutilation on his enemy. Hence he allowed the inhabitants of Jabesh-gilead to send for aid; for the more numerous the enemy, the greater the share of honor their defeat would bring. In this case Nahash miscalculated the size of the force Israel could send in response to the plea from the men of Jabesh-gilead, and the Ammonites suffered a stunning defeat. The fact that Saul was a mutual enemy may account for the friendship between Nahash and David (II Sam. 10:2).

Two of Nahash' sons, Hanun (II Sam. 10:1) and Shobi (17:27), appear to have ruled the Ammonites after him, the latter as David's viceroy.

2. II Sam. 17:25 mentions "Abigal the daughter of Nahash, sister of Zeruiah." It is not clear whether "sister of Zeruiah" refers to Abigal or to Nahash. If the latter, Nahash must be a woman's name. If the former, Nahash may be the Ammonite ruler. According to I Chr. 2:16, Abigail was David's sister, though David's father was not Nahash but Jesse. If I Chr. 2:16 is reliable, then the relationship between Abigail and David would be traced through their mother, as was the custom in the beena marriage, where children were considered to belong to the family of the mother and not the father. This relationship between Abigail and David might be another reason for the friendship between Nahash and David.

On the other hand, it is possible that "daughter of Nahash" is a textual corruption, with "Nahash" an insertion from the following verse, and that we should read "daughter of Jesse" (so LXX L).

Bibliography. M. Noth, *Die israelitischen Personennamen* (1928), p. 230; J. Morgenstern, "*Beena* Marriage (Matriarchate) in Ancient Israel and Its Historical Implications," *ZAW,* VI (1929), 91-110; J. Pedersen, *Israel,* I-II (1954), 221, 241. R. W. CORNEY

NAHATH nā'hăth [נחת, *usually* descent (נחת) *or* rest, quietness (נוח), *but possibly* pure, clear; *cf.* Arab. *naḥtun*]. **1.** An Edomite clan chief (אלוף נחת, perhaps "clan chief of Nahath"; Gen. 36:17 [LXX Νάχοθ, Νάχωρ]); first son of Reuel (Gen. 36:13 [LXX Νάχοθ, Νάχομ]; I Chr. 1:37 [Νάχεθ, Νάχες]).

2. A Levite, grandson of the Kohathite Elkanah (I Chr. 6:26—H 6:11 [LXX Νάαθ, Καῖναθ]); probably same as Toah (תוח) in 6:34—H 6:19 and Tohu (תחו) in I Sam. 1:1.

3. OVERSEER in the time of Hezekiah (II Chr. 31:13 [LXX Νάεθ, Μάεθ]). L. HICKS

NAHBI nä'bī [נחבי, hidden(?), *or* timid(?)] (Num. 13:14). A member of the tribe of Naphtali sent to spy out the land of Canaan; son of Vophsi.

Bibliography. M. Noth, *Die israelitischen Personennamen* (1928), p. 229.

NAHOR nā'hôr [נחור, *apparently from* Assyrian *place name Til-Naḫiri,* the mound of Naḫuru; *cf. Naḫaran, Niḫaru, Niḫaran, in* Old Assyrian *texts, and Nuḫuru in an inscription of Asshurbanipal;* Ναχωρ]; KJV NACHOR nā'kôr in Josh. 24:2; Luke 3:34. **1.** Son of Serug, of the line of Shem (Gen. 11:22-25; I Chr. 1:26; Luke 3:34); father of Terah, and grandfather of Abraham. After the birth of Terah in his twenty-ninth year, Nahor lived 119 years longer and had other children.

2. Son of Terah, and brother of Abraham and Haran (Gen. 11:26; Josh. 24:2). He married Milcah, daughter of Haran and sister of Iscah, and she bore him eight sons (Gen. 11:29; 22:20-22).

The relations of this Nahor serve to link the Hebrew patriarchs both vertically and horizontally with other peoples of the ancient Near East. The genealogy of Shem, like that of Seth (Gen. 5:6-32), to which it is related, comes to a climax with three brothers (11:27), whose appearance delineates a further rank of the human family leading more immediately to the Israelites themselves. This particular Semitic genealogy focuses attention upon the family of Abraham as the principal group. Nevertheless, the Israelites neither forgot nor denied their ancient relationship with other Semites; and the Nahorite genealogy in Gen. 22:20-24 embodies traditions concerning them. If the names there have the function of eponyms, this unit would present Abraham's brother Nahor as the progenitor of twelve kindred tribes, thus similar to Ishmael (25:13-16) and Jacob (35:22*b;* 49). The larger group, listing the sons of Nahor's wife, would relate the Israelites to the Aramean tribes who dwelt to the E and NE of Palestine; the smaller group, listing the sons of his concubine, to the Arameans who dwelt primarily in the region between Damascus and Kadesh. Being the offspring of the concubine, this latter group may represent hybrid or alien stock. *See* ARAMEANS.

In concluding the covenant at MIZPAH, Jacob swore by the "God of Abraham"—or more specifically, the "Fear [perhaps 'Kinsman'] of his father Isaac" (פחד אביו יצחק); and Laban, by the "God of Nahor," perhaps a patriarchal patron deity. Indications of the same type of worship of the family deity —the God with whom one's father had associated himself—are found in Old Assyrian cuneiform texts (Cappadocian correspondence) and the Mari Tablets, which are roughly contemporary with Israel's patriarchal age. *See* GOD, OT VIEW OF.

3. A city mentioned in Gen. 24:10. The reference may be either to a city called Nahor itself or to a city of the Hebrew (Aramean?) patriarch bearing this name (2 *above*). *Naḫur* occurs frequently in the Mari Texts (*see* MARI) as a city situated E of the upper Baliḫ River, and in Middle Assyrian documents. Although close by Haran (cf. Gen. 29:4-5), the city of Nahor is not identical with it but is probably to be located to the S or the E.

See also ARAM-NAHARAIM; HARAN 4.

Bibliography. A. Alt, "Der Gott der Väter," *BWANT,* vol. III, no. 12 (1929); H. G. May, "The Patriarchal Idea of God," *JBL,* vol. LX (1941); W. F. Albright, *From the Stone Age to Christianity* (2nd ed., 1946), pp. 179-89; J. P. Hyatt, "Yahweh as 'The God of My Father,' " *Vetus Testamentum,* vol. V (1955). L. HICKS

NAHSHON nä'shŏn [נחשון, little(?) serpent; Ναασσών]; KJV NAASHON nā ăsh'ən in Exod. 6:23; KJV NT NAASSON nā ăs'sən. Leader of Judah; son of Amminadab (Num. 1:7; 2:3; 7:12, 17; 10:14); one of twelve tribal chiefs (*see* PRINCE) or deputies who assisted Moses in taking a census of Israel and in other tasks in the wilderness. In Exod. 6:23, Nahshon is identified as a brother-in-law of Aaron, who married his sister Elisheba. His ancestry is traced to Perez, son of Judah and Tamar (I Chr. 2:4-10); while among his own descendants are named Boaz, his grandson, and King David (Ruth 4:20-22). Nahshon is included in the NT genealogies as an ancestor of Jesus Christ (Matt. 1:4; Luke 3:32).

Bibliography. M. Noth, *Die israelitischen Personennamen* (1928), pp. 229-30. R. F. JOHNSON

NAHUM nā'əm [נחום; Ναούμ]; KJV NT NAUM.
1. *See* NAHUM, BOOK OF.
2. An ancestor of Jesus (Luke 3:25).

NAHUM, BOOK OF. The seventh book of the collection of the Twelve Prophets. Nothing is known about the prophet except his name, which means "comfort," "compassion" (cf. Isa. 57:18), and the place of his birth—ELKOSH, a town in SW Judah, in the region where the tribe of Simeon had settled, close to the Philistine and Egyptian borders, between Beit Jibrin and Gaza. (G. Nestle in *PEQ* [1879], pp. 136-38, identifies it with Kessijeh, a little SW of Beit Jibrin. U. Cassuto, however, in *Giornale della Società Asiatica Italiana* [1914], pp. 291 ff, identifies it with Umm Lagish, halfway between Beit Jibrin and Gaza; cf. R. H. Pfeiffer, *HTR,* 27 [1932], 282. This latter locality fits the evidence from Epiphanius.)

See map "Palestine: Micah, Nahum, Habakkuk, Zephaniah," in ZEPHANIAH, BOOK OF.

1. Date
2. Nature of the book
3. The acrostic poem (1:2-10)
4. Promise and threat (1:11-15)
5. The destruction of Nineveh (chs. 2–3)
6. Literary and religious value

Bibliography

1. Date. The *terminus post quem* for the composition of the book of Nahum is the fall of Thebes to Assyria *ca.* 663 B.C. (Nah. 3:8). The fall of the Assyrian capital, NINEVEH, in 612 is the *terminus ante quem* in the view of those scholars who regard the book as looking forward to the destruction of this long-time center of oppression. Those who regard the book as composed after the event agree that the chief portion must be dated immediately thereafter. Some have suggested that most of the book was composed in anticipation and additions were made afterward.

In 625 the Chaldean NABOPOLASSAR founded the Neo-Babylonian state, which was destined to be the leading power in the Middle East for nearly three quarters of a century. He soon brought all Babylonia solidly under his control, then mobilized his forces against Assyria (see British Museum Tablet No. 21,901 in C. J. Gadd, *The Fall of Nineveh,* 1923). Marching up the Euphrates to Qablinu, he inflicted on the Assyrian army a decisive defeat. Meanwhile the Medes began attacking from the east. In 614 they took and sacked the major Assyrian city of Asshur, and Nabopolassar made an alliance with their king. Together the Medes and Chaldeans continued their attacks, until at length mighty Nineveh itself fell. The collapse of this imperial capital marked the end of an epoch, and its reverberations were felt throughout the then-known world.

2. Nature of the book. It is most likely that Nahum was himself a temple prophet. According to some scholars, he "historified" elements from the myth of Creation. He identified a historical enemy with the cosmic adversaries who had been conquered at the beginning of the world and whose fight was re-enacted in the New Year Festival. In any case, the book has the character of a prophetic curse pronounced against the enemy. It also expresses gratitude for the anticipated freedom from tyranny. To curse such an enemy, the very incarnation of Evil, is a way of professing loyalty to God.

3. The acrostic poem (1:2-10). After the superscription (1:1), there begins an alphabetic, acrostic hymn which describes a theophany. It extends at least through vs. 9. Each of the separate lines respectively begins with a different letter of the Hebrew alphabet, taken in order from א, the first letter, to נ, the fourteenth letter. Eissfeldt, by a slight transposition of lines, secures also a ס line in vs. 10, beginning with the word סבואים. There have been various attempts on the part of scholars to recover what many have thought was intended by the original author to be a complete acrostic poem, reaching as far as Nah. 2:3 or 2:4, but such attempts have produced no conclusive results. It is best to view the acrostic poem as ending with the ס strophe, which carries the acrostic through the first half (א to ס) of the Hebrew alphabet. Such procedure is also the case with the liturgical poetry of medieval Judaism.

4. Promise and threat (1:11-15). In 1:1-13; 2:1, 3, is contained a message of promise for Judah, but in 1:10-11(14?); 2:2 we have the beginning of a threat directed against Nineveh, which continues in 2:4-14.

The word of promise has to do with the destruction of the oppressing power and the consequent recovery of Israel (1:1-13; 2:1, 3). The oppressing power is clearly Nineveh.

Yahweh, "slow to anger and of great might," takes vengeance on his enemies (1:2-3). In whirlwind and storm he comes, drying up sea and rivers. Fertile pastureland, such as Bashan, dense forests that cover Mount Carmel, tree sprouts of Lebanon's majestic cedars, wither before him. Streams of lava from volcanic mountains pour down the mountainsides. All nature reacts as in terrified awe to its Creator.

The prophet is sensitive to the divine fury poured out like fire. Who can stand before it? Not even mighty Nineveh—such is his inference—can stand before God's righteous wrath (vs. 6*b*).

The prophet's thought suddenly turns, in vivid contrast, to the blessing on the part of this mighty Lord, of those who take refuge in him (vs. 7); to them he is a "stronghold in the day of trouble." But the enemies he will annihilate (vs. 9), just as fire consumes crackling thorns. Yahweh has used Assyria to discipline his people, but now his disciplinary use of Assyria is a thing of the past. He will break the Assyrian yoke (vs. 13) from upon Israel. The Lord of all the earth speaks his mighty threat in vss. 12-14 against and directly to Nineveh:

> No more shall your name be perpetuated;
> . . . .
> I will make your grave, for you are vile.

Then Nahum sings a song of triumph (vs. 15). It is a beautiful word lifted up centuries later in another context by the Deutero-Isaiah in Isa. 52:7:

> Behold, on the mountains the feet of him
> who brings good tidings,
> who proclaims peace! (Nah. 1:15).

And Nahum summons Judah, rejoicing in glad release, to observe her festivals and to fulfil her vows (vs. 15*b*). God is on the point of restoring the majesty of Israel (2:2).

5. The destruction of Nineveh (chs. 2-3). Diodorus and Xenophon tell how Nineveh was destroyed as the result of an exceptional rising of the Tigris. In Nah. 2:6, 8—H 2:7, 9, this is vividly pictured:

> The gates of the canals are opened,
> and the palace melts away [i.e., in dismay].
> . . . .
> Nineveh is like a pool of water,
> its waters in tumult (orig. tr.).

We read in 2:9-13 how the conquerors of Nineveh leap upon the fabulous spoil of that great city and carry it off in vast quantities. Nineveh used to be like a den of lions, but now it becomes a mass of corpses. The once great kingdom falls in ruin (3:7), sacked by her conquerors just as mighty Thebes (*No Amon*), chief city of Egypt and of the world, was sacked a half century before.

Nineveh's fortress capitulates to the rapacious Chaldeans and Medes, who devour it as first-ripe figs are devoured by hungry men. Her defenders are effeminate and traitorous. And her king perishes in the fire he himself kindled (Nah. 3:12-13; Diodorus II.27).

The destruction of Nineveh is the cause of well-nigh universal rejoicing. The city falls because it deserves to fall. Its "shepherds" are drowsy; its "nobles" are asleep. Moreover, its fall is irrevocable. There is no healing for Assyria's hurt (3:18-19).

The liturgy ends in the mood of irony. Let Nineveh try to recover, shaping many bricks for her destroyed walls and cementing them with mortar. Let it multiply warriors like locusts. It can never recover. Nineveh's rulers have been asleep, and severe are the consequences. And every neighboring nation which has felt Nineveh's brutal heel glories in its fall.

6. Literary and religious value. Nahum's poetic genius ranks with the highest in the Hebrew Bible. He sketches scenes of warfare with a vivid sense of the picturesque or horrible detail—e.g., the cavalry and chariotry charge (2:3-5), the panic of the queen's servants (vs. 7).

Many commentators have noted that Nahum is different from the other literary prophets of the OT, since he concerns himself not with national corruption but with the defeat of a hated oppressor. He is animated by an intense faith in Yahweh, the universal judge, whose jealousy and avenging wrath will not fail to destroy the guilty. The prophet shows also the importance of a dedicated leadership and the ultimate failure of injustice in a national policy.

Bibliography. Commentaries: S. R. Driver, ed., *The Minor Prophets*, New Century Bible (1906), vol. II. J. M. P. Smith *et al.*, *A Critical and Exegetical Commentary on Micah, Zephaniah, Nahum, Habakkuk, Obadiah and Joel*, ICC (1911). A. B. Davidson, *The Books of Nahum, Habakkuk and Zephaniah*, Cambridge Bible (1920). W. Nowack, *Die kleinen Propheten* (1922). E. Sellin, *Das Zwölfprophetenbuch* (1922). C. V. Pilcher, *Three Hebrew Prophets* (1928). G. A. Smith, *The Book of the Twelve Prophets* (1929), vol. II. G. G. Stonehouse, *Nahum*, WC (1929). J. Coppens, *Les douze Petits Prophètes: bréviaire du prophétisme* (1950). K. Elliger, *Das Buch der zwölf kleinen Propheten*, vol. II (1950). A. George, *Michée, Sophonie, Nahum* (1952). F. Horst, *Die zwölf kleinen Propheten* (1954), vol. II. C. L. Taylor, Introduction and Exegesis of Nahum, *IB*, VI (1956), 953-79.

Special studies: H. Gunkel, "Nahum I," *ZAW*, XIII (1893), 223-44. A. Billerbeck and A. Jeremias, "Der Untergang Nineveh's und die Weissagungschrift des Nahum von Elkosch," *Beitrage zur Assyriologie und semitischen Sprachwissenschaft*, III (1895), 86-188. W. R. Arnold, "The Composition of Nahum 1:2-2:3," *ZAW*, XXI (1901), 225-65. C. J. Gadd, *The Fall of Nineveh: The Newly Discovered Babylonian Chronicle* (1923). P. Humbert, "Essai d'analyse de Nahoum 1:2-2:3," *ZAW*, XLIV (1926), 266-82; "Le problème du livre de Nahoum," *RHPR*, XII (1932), 1-15. E. A. Leslie, *The Prophets Tell Their Own Story* (1939). A Haldar, *Studies in the Book of Nahum* (1947). J. L. Mihelic, "The Concept of God in the Book of Nahum," *Interpretation*, II (1948), 199-215. J. Leclercq, "Nahum," in P. Béguerie, *Études sur les Prophètes d'Israël* (1954), pp. 85-110. J. M. Allegro, "Further Light on the History of the Qumran Sect," *JBL*, LXXV (1956), 89-95. H. H. Rowley, "4Qp Nahum and the Teacher of Righteousness," *JBL*, LXXV (1956), 188-93. D. Leibel, "Some Remarks on the [4Q] Commentary on the Book of Nahum," *Tarbiz*, 27 (1957-58), 12-16.

E. A. Leslie

NAIDUS nā′ə dəs. *See* Benaiah 9.

NAIL. 1. צִפֹּרֶן, Aramaic טְפַר (Deut. 21:12; Dan. 4:33—H 4:30). Covering of a finger or toe (in Dan. 7:19 "claw" of a beast). A captive woman, brought to the home of a Hebrew, had to shave her head, pare her nails, and go through a month's mourning before she could be accepted as his wife.

2. מסמר; ἧλος. A carpenter's nail. Isa. 41:7; Jer. 10:4 speak of nails to hold household idols in place. I Chr. 22:3 tells how David stored quantities of iron for nails for the temple gates, and II Chr. 3:9 refers to gold nails used in the inner sanctuary.

Nails have been found in excavations at most biblical sites, though not in great numbers. The earliest nails are of bronze. Later the larger nails were mostly of iron, while smaller ones continued to be made of bronze. Nails found, many with wood still adhering to them, run pretty much the range of size and shape of modern nails, except for our smaller sizes. Some are long—iron spikes found at Samaria were 7-9 inches; some are short—1-1½ inches. Some have small, squared heads; others have broad, flat-domed heads. Most have squared shanks rather than round, and taper more gradually to a point than modern nails.

Two short, bronze nails from Tell Abu Hawam (near Acre), dated in the thirteenth century B.C., had broad, flat-domed heads, covered with gold foil. These, and similar, silver-sheeted nail heads from Nuzi, are surely ornamental nails and may suggest what the gold nails used in the temple were like.

John 20:25 ff refers to the prints of the nails used to fasten Jesus to the cross. Large iron spikes, 5-7 inches long, have been found in several excavations around Jerusalem in the Roman levels of *ca.* the first to the third centuries A.D.

3. Translation of the verb προσηλόω. Col. 2:14 states that God canceled the bond which stood against us, nailing it to the cross. Some have explained this reference by supposing a custom of nailing up a copy of a decree in a public place when it was declared null and void. There is no actual evidence of such a custom.

4. KJV alternate translation of יתד. *See* PEG.

S. V. FAWCETT

NAIN nān [Ναΐν, *perhaps from* נעים, pleasant, delightful] (Luke 7:11). A town of SW Galilee mentioned in the Bible only in connection with the raising of a widow's son.

1. Location. The place can hardly be the same as that of a city called Nain which Josephus mentions, for he speaks of it as along the border of Idumea (War IV.ix.4-5). The location of the Nain of the gospel is hardly in doubt, for the name survives in the modern Arab village of Nein, a site which fits the biblical evidence. This identification has the support of most scholars.

Nein lies on the lower slope of the NW side of Nebi Dahi, a hill between Gilboa and Tabor. In OT times it was known as the hill of Moreh (Judg. 7:1), and has also been called Little Hermon. The site is *ca.* two miles SW of Endor. Its position agrees approximately with the statement of Jerome, who places it two miles S of Tabor and near Endor (*De Situ et Nom. Loc. Hebr.* 255). The village is *ca.* five miles SE of Nazareth and *ca.* twenty-five miles or a day's journey from Capernaum (cf. Luke 7:11 RSV mg.).

2. Description. The town of Nein has a fine view of the Plain of Esdraelon, which may explain the origin of the name in its Hebrew form of Naim נעים; *see above*). Not only is the view pleasant, but a spring makes possible attractive groves of olives and figs. There is a midrash which explains that the description of the land of Issachar as the "land [that] was pleasant" (Gen. 49:15) is a reference to the village of Naim (Midrash Rabbah Ber. XCVIII.12).

The village of Nein now consists of a few houses and *ca.* two hundred inhabitants, but there are ruins which indicate that it was once a town of some importance. Outside and above the village to the SE are tombs and caves in the rock of the hillside. In the Middle Ages the intended grave of the young man and the home of his mother were shown to the faithful (Petri Diaconi, *ca.* A.D. 1137; Migne, *Patrologiae Latina*, CLXXIII, 1127). Today there is a small Franciscan church on the site of a medieval church. Nearby are the ruins of another shrine.

It was near the village of Nain that Jesus and his disciples met the funeral procession of the only son of a widow as it was coming out. The setting of the miracle of the raising of the son was near the gate of the village (Luke 7:11-16).

Bibliography. G. Dalman, *Orte und Wege Jesu* (1919), pp. 190-92; F.-M. Abel, *Géographie de la Palestine,* II (1933-38), 394-95.

D. C. PELLETT

NAIOTH nā'yŏth [נוית, dwellings(?)]. A name designating the common dwelling place (precinct or special structure) of a prophetic fraternity in Ramah under the leadership of Samuel (I Sam. 19:18-24). Here David fled for refuge from the jealous wrath of Saul (vss. 18-19); here Saul and his messengers sought him, but were seized with prophetic frenzy (vss. 20-24); and from here David fled for his rendezvous with Jonathan, soon thereafter to become captain of a refugee band (20:1; 22:1-2).

The etymological background of the name Naioth is quite obscure. Though it is possible that it may have denoted "dwelling," the derivation of such a meaning is quite precarious. The context, however, is rather suggestive, for, since Naioth is repeatedly described as being "in Ramah" (I Sam. 19:19, 22-23), a separate place name is apparently not intended. On the other hand, the reference to residence there (vs. 18), the prevalence of prophetic activity (vs. 20), and the protection of the supernatural (vss. 20-24) bespeak the presence of a sanctuary with appropriate accommodations—perhaps associated with the high place and hall where Saul had previously been the guest of Samuel (I Kings 9:19, 22-25). In this connection, the possibility of a settlement or coenobium of the prophets, patterned after the one under the supervision of Elisha near the Jordan, has been suggested (II Kings 6:1-7). In support of such a possibility, the Targ. renders for "Naioth": "house of instruction," suggesting the further possibility of a sort of prophetic school.

Bibliography. H. P. Smith, *Samuel,* ICC (1899), p. 181; S. R. Driver, *Notes on the Hebrew Text and the Topography of the Books of Samuel* (1913), pp. 158-59; E. G. Kraeling, *Bible Atlas* (1956), p. 184.

W. H. MORTON

*__NAME.__ In biblical thought a name is not a mere label of identification; it is an expression of the essential nature of its bearer. A man's name reveals his character. Adam was able to give names to beasts and birds (Gen. 2:20) because, as Milton says, he understood their nature (*Paradise Lost,* bk. VIII, ll. 352-53). This was a concept shared by the peoples of the ancient world. Hence to know the name of God is to know God as he has revealed himself (Ps. 9:10). The full disclosure of his nature and character is given in Jesus Christ, who has manifested his name (John 17:6, 26).

- A. Terminology
  - 1. In biblical Hebrew
  - 2. In LXX Greek
  - 3. In NT Greek
- B. Name in the OT
  - 1. Name and existence
  - 2. Name and personality
  - 3. Name and reputation
  - 4. Name and revelation
    - *a.* The being of God
    - *b.* The hidden God
    - *c.* "For his name's sake"
    - *d.* Revelation and response
    - *e.* Theological development
- C. Hebrew proper names
  - 1. Place names
    - *a.* Pre-Israelitish, Greek, and Latin
    - *b.* From local characteristics
    - *c.* From animals and plants
  - 2. Names of persons
    - *a.* From circumstances and characteristics
    - *b.* From animals and plants
    - *c.* Compound
    - *d.* Divine
- D. Name in the Apoc. and the Pseudep.
- E. Name in the NT
  - 1. Distinguishing term
  - 2. Name and personality
  - 3. Name and reputation
  - 4. The name of God
  - 5. The name of Christ
    - *a.* Belief in the name
    - *b.* Baptism in the name
    - *c.* Acting in the name
    - *d.* Persecution for the name
- Bibliography

A. *TERMINOLOGY.* The word "name" and associated words ("fame," "renown," "memory," "memorial," "remembrance") occur over 800 times in the English versions of the OT and some 180 times in those of the NT. For the most part they render into English two Hebrew words, one Aramaic word, and one Greek word.

1. In biblical Hebrew. The common Hebrew term for "name" is the noun שם (*shēm*). Its Aramaic equivalent, *shum,* occurs only in the books of Ezra and Daniel, in which it is found eleven times. The derivation of שם, which is an ancient term, is uncertain and obscure. It may be derived from the root שמה, "to be high," and hence have the primary meaning of "monument" or "memorial" (cf. Gen. 11:4; II Sam. 8:13; Isa. 55:13 ["memorial"]; 56:5 ["a monument and a name"]). This would imply the sense of "majesty" and "excellence" (Ps. 54:1). Another possible derivation is from the root ושם (Arabic *wshm*), "to brand or mark," in which case the original meaning would be "sign" or "token." שם is also translated "renown" in Gen. 6:4; Num. 16:2 KJV; "fame" in I Chr. 14:17; and "well-known" in Num. 16:2.

A lesser-used term is the noun זכר (*zēker;* lit., "remembrance" or "memorial"; *see* MEMORIAL)—derived from the verb *zākar,* "to remember." זכר is translated "name" in Pss. 30:4—H 30:5; 97:12; 102:12; Hos. 12:5—H 12:6. It is used as a parallel to שם in Exod. 3:15; Job 18:17; Ps. 135:13; Prov. 10:7; Isa. 26:8 (לשמך ולזכרך is rendered "thy memorial name"), and it has a closely related meaning in Ps. 145:7 ("fame"); Eccl. 9:5 ("memory"); Hos. 14:7—H 14:8 ("fragrance"; KJV "scent").

2. In LXX Greek. The LXX translators render the Hebrew שם and its Aramaic equivalent *shum* by the Greek ὄνομα, which is the common Greek term for "name." The other Hebrew word, זכר, when used in this sense, is rendered by μνήμη (Pss. 30:4—H 30:5; 97:12; 145:7; Prov. 10:7; Eccl. 9:5), μνημόσυνον (Exod. 3:15; Job 18:17; Pss. 102:12; 135:13; Hos. 12:5), and μνεία (Isa. 26:8).

3. In NT Greek. In the NT the noun ὄνομα, "name," in addition to being used as a distinguishing term, has meanings foreign to classical usage which can be traced to its use in the LXX as translating the Hebrew word שם. As a result of this Hebraistic influence, ὄνομα in the NT has acquired much of the content and associations of the Hebrew term. Thus it is used, e.g., for the rank associated with a prophet (Matt. 10:41), the authority or power of someone on whose behalf another acts (Matt. 21:9; Acts 3:6; 4:7), and the revealed character of God (John 17:6, 11). In Acts 1:15; Rev. 3:4; 11:13, the plural ὀνόματα has the meaning of "persons" (cf. שמות [Num. 1:2, 18, 20; 3:40, 43; 26:53]).

B. *NAME IN THE OT.* The uses of the word "name" in the OT are all related to the central conception of name as denoting essential being. This applies with regard to both man and God.

1. Name and existence. In Hebrew as in Babylonian thought, name is inextricably bound up with existence. Nothing exists unless it has a name. "Whatever has come to be has already been named" (Eccl. 6:10*a*). Its essence is concentrated in its name (cf. Gen. 27:36). Hence the act of creation is not complete until all creatures have received a name (Gen. 2:18-23). The Creator of the heavenly host, in bringing them into being, calls them all by name (Isa. 40:26). Personal existence is regarded as continuing posthumously in the name which is perpetuated by a man's descendants. To cut off a name, therefore, is to end the existence of its bearer (I Sam. 24:21; II Kings 14:27; Job 18:17; Ps. 83:4; Isa. 14:22; Zeph. 1:4). God's promise that his people's name shall remain is a pledge of their continuing existence (Isa. 56:5; 66:22).

2. Name and personality. The name in the OT is the essence of personality, the expression of innermost being. Esau says of his unscrupulous brother: "Is he not rightly named Jacob? For he has supplanted me these two times" (Gen. 27:36; *see* JACOB; *see also* § C2*a below*). As such, a name is regarded as possessing an inherent power which exercises a constraint upon its bearer: he must conform to his essential nature as expressed in his name. Thus Abigail makes excuse for her husband: "As his name is, so is he; Nabal [fool] is his name, and folly is with him"

(I Sam. 25:25; *see* NABAL). Hence a change of name accompanies a change in character. The changing of the patriarch's name from Jacob to Israel indicates a change in the personality of the man himself (Gen. 32:28). *See* JACOB.

To speak or act in someone's name is to act as the representative of that person and hence to participate in his authority (I Sam. 17:45; 25:5, 9; I Kings 21:8; Esth. 2:22; 3:12; 8:8, 10; Jer. 29:25). Similarly, to be called by a person's name (lit., "to call a name upon") implies ownership by the person. Whatever is so called comes under the authority and the protection of the one whose name is called upon it. Joab warns David that if he, and not David, completes the conquest of Rabbah, the city will be called by Joab's name—i.e., he will claim authority over it (II Sam. 12:28). Isaiah foresees that Jerusalem will be so depopulated that seven women will urge one man: "Only let us be called by your name," so that they may enjoy the protection of being owned by a husband (Isa. 4:1).

This is the secular application of a phrase which has frequently a religious significance. That which is called by Yahweh's name is his possession and therefore comes under both his authority and his protection (Deut. 28:10; II Chr. 7:14; Isa. 43:7; 63:19; 65:1; Dan. 9:18-19).

3. Name and reputation. When the character and achievements of a person become widely known, he gains a reputation. This is, as it were, an extension of his personality; it is his name writ large. Hence "name" comes also to mean "renown," "glory," "fame." E.g., the builders of the Tower of Babel seek a reputation through the magnitude of their work: "Let us make a name for ourselves" (Gen. 11:4). Abraham is promised renown if he obeys the divine command: "I will bless you, and make your name great" (Gen. 12:2). David wins a name for himself through his military exploits (I Sam. 18:30; II Sam. 8:13). Thus in Prov. 22:1; Eccl. 7:1 "name" by itself (the word is unqualified in the original) means a good reputation, which is of supreme worth. Conversely, men of bad reputation are said to be nameless (Job 30:8; בלי שם ["disreputable"; KJV "base"]).

4. Name and revelation. When used of God, "name" in the OT has a revelatory content. The name of God means primarily his revealed nature and character—the Savior God as he has manifested himself and desires to be known by man. For the Hebrew, God is both transcendent and immanent. He is the hidden God, dwelling in the high and lofty place in light unapproachable; nevertheless, he comes into saving relations with men. The gap between the Deity as ontologically remote and as dynamically near is bridged in OT thought by various related conceptions of the manifestation of God—his ANGEL; his FACE; his GLORY; his "name." Of these the name is the most comprehensive and significant. As expressing essential nature, it implies the most complete divine self-disclosure, while the identification of name and person safeguards the unity of God.

a. The being of God. The name of God is frequently used as a synonym for God himself, particularly in the postexilic period. As such it is the object of fear (Deut. 28:58; Ps. 61:5—H 61:6), of love (Pss. 5:11—H 5:12; 69:36—H 69:37; 119:132; Isa. 56:6), of blessing (Job 1:21; Pss. 96:2—H 96:3; 103:1), of thanks (I Chr. 16:35; Ps. 54:6), and especially of praise (II Sam. 22:50; Pss. 7:17; 9:2; 18:49—H 18:50). To know the name of God is to know God himself as he is revealed (Pss. 9:10—H 9:11; 91:14; Isa. 52:6; cf. 64:2; Jer. 48:17). In Lev. 24:11 "the Name" alone is used to denote God. This, however, is the only instance in the OT of a usage which became popular in the late Hellenistic period (*see* § D *below*) and may be due to a copyist rather than to the original writer. (In Lev. 24:16 read "name of the LORD" with LXX and Vulg.; but cf. Deut. 28:58.)

b. The hidden God. On two occasions in the OT the divine name is withheld. The mysterious being who wrestles with Jacob at Jabbok withholds his name (Gen. 32:29), as does also the "angel" who appears to Manoah and his wife (Judg. 13:18). It has been customary to explain this in terms of primitive ideas regarding the power which resides in the name—to know a person's name is to have power over the person; to disclose a name is to surrender that in which the power of the personality resides. But such explanations are inadequate and take no account of the theological significance of these stories. What we have here is an attempt to express the Hebrew awareness that the *deus revelatus* is also the *deus absconditus.* Common to both stories is the theme of perseverance. Jacob must persevere in his attempt to triumph over his weakness of character and win a spiritual blessing, without knowing whom he is encountering. Through his inward struggle, so powerfully dramatized in this story of his tenacious wrestling, he receives the divine blessing, becomes a new man, and is given a new name: "Perseverer with God" (*see* ISRAEL, NAME AND ASSOCIATIONS). But only when the encounter is ended does he realize that he has been face to face with God (Gen. 32:30).

In the same way, although to a lesser degree, Manoah and his wife must persevere in their attempt to know the divine will for their son whose birth has been foretold, without knowing the supernatural nature of the one with whom they are speaking. Only afterward are they constrained to say: "We have seen God" (Judg. 13:22).

In both cases the name is withheld—the divine self-manifestation is veiled until the recipient, by his resolve and importunity, has shown that he is fit to receive it. The encounter is a discipline and a test: "To him that hath shall be given." In the actual moment of visitation, God is hidden; only in retrospect does the *deus absconditus* become the *deus revelatus*.

c. "For his name's sake." God's name is great (Ps. 76:1—H 76:2; Jer. 10:6; 44:26), glorious (Deut. 28:58; cf. 32:3), and majestic (Ps. 8:1—H 8:2); it is also holy (Lev. 20:3; 22:32; I Chr. 16:10, 35; 29:16; Pss. 33:21; 103:1; 105:3; 106:47; 145:21; Isa. 57:15; Ezek. 20:39; 36:20-22; 39:7, 25; 43:7-8; Amos 2:7; *see* HOLINESS), and he is concerned for it (Ezek. 36:21) and jealous of it (20:9, 14, 22; 39:7, 25). When God acts for his name's sake, he is acting in accordance with his revealed character and to uphold the honor of his revelation, which has been staked upon his elect people, Israel. Since God has chosen to accomplish his redemptive purpose for mankind through the election of Israel, he will not allow the nation to be destroyed (I Sam. 12:22; Ps. 23:3; Isa. 48:9, 11; Ezek. 20:9, 14, 44; 36:22-23). This is the ground upon which appeal is frequently made to him (Pss. 25:11; 31:3—H 31:4; 143:11; Jer. 14:7, 21).

d. Revelation and response. When the people to whom this revelation has been given behave in a way which is contrary to the revealed character of God and as a result suffer dishonor, his name is profaned (Ezek. 36:20-21; Amos 2:7) or defiled (Ezek. 43:8) or reviled (Ps. 74:10, 18) or despised (Isa. 52:5).

On the other hand, the divine self-manifestation evokes from those who recognize it the response of worship. This is the meaning of the expression "call upon" (lit., "call with") the name of God (e.g., Gen. 4:26; 12:8; 13:4; 21:33; 26:25; II Kings 5:11; Pss. 75:1; 79:6 = Jer. 10:25; Isa. 65:1). To call upon the name of God is to invoke him on the basis of his revealed nature and character. The same phrase is used in a slightly different sense, and with reference to both Yahweh and the Tyrian Baal, in Elijah's contest with the prophets of Baal on Mount Carmel (I Kings 18:24-26; cf. vss. 36-37). Here it refers to a specific appeal to each of the deities to display his power.

The declaration of Zech. 14:9: "The LORD will be one and his name one," is also to be understood in terms of the principle of revelation and response. God's unity, which is already a reality, will ultimately be acknowledged by all men (cf. Isa. 56:6-7). And in Isa. 48:9, the parallel clause: "for the sake of my praise," suggests that "name" may be used here in the transferred sense of the worship called forth by the divine self-disclosure.

e. Theological development. In the early OT literature, "the name" is applied to temporary manifestations of Yahweh. The name of God said to be "in" the angel who leads and guards Israel in the wilderness signifies that during this limited period he acts as God's representative or plenipotentiary (Exod. 23:20-21; cf. 33:14). The implication is that when the wilderness wanderings are over, he will return to Yahweh. In Canaan altars are to be built and sacrifice offered wherever God causes his name to be remembered (Exod. 20:24 [KJV "records" his name]). From the way in which this law was observed, it is clear that such a place was the scene of a temporary self-disclosure of God. Altars were, in fact, built in places hallowed by some special indication of the divine presence—a theophany or a great deliverance (Gen. 12:7; 22:9; 26:24-25; Judg. 6:11-24; I Sam. 14:31-35). This is what is meant, therefore, by God's causing his name to be remembered. Indeed, the prophet Isaiah speaks of the name itself in terms of a theophany: it "comes from far, burning with his anger, and in thick rising smoke" (Isa. 30:27; cf. 59:19).

Deuteronomy, however, envisages a permanent manifestation of the divine presence at Jerusalem: there God causes his name to dwell (Deut. 12:5, 11). Thus in the writings of the Deuteronomic school the name becomes a symbol of faith in a *deus revelatus*. Jerusalem is the city where God has chosen to put his name (I Kings 11:36; cf. Isa. 18:7 [probably postexilic]). The temple is built as a habitation for the name of God (II Sam. 7:13; II Chr. 20:8), and in it his name dwells (I Kings 9:3; Ps. 74:7). Yahweh's own dwelling place is still in the heavens; but his presence is manifested on the earth through the quasi-independent entity of his name, which is nevertheless one with him (I Kings 8:27-30). In this way the antinomy between the transcendence of God and his abiding presence with his people is resolved by a virtual hypostatizing of his name. It is the instrument through which he comes to man's aid and prospers his way (Pss. 54:1—H 54:3; 89:24—H 89:25).

This theological development of the name of God is to some extent paralleled by the personification of his wisdom (Prov. 8) and of his creative word (Gen. 1:1-27; cf. John 1:1-14). With the latter it has a particular affinity, since in the OT a name is to a person as a word is to a thought. Its full significance is apparent only in the light of its consummation, when the name of God is manifested by him who is the Word made flesh (John 17:6-26).

C. *HEBREW PROPER NAMES.* Hebrew proper names may be classified in several different ways. They may be considered in two main groups according to whether their formation is simple or compound. Simple names consist of only one element, which is essentially an epithet—e.g., Jacob = "supplanter"; Nabal = "fool." Compound names have more than one element, and, while some are epithets (e.g., Obadiah = "servant of Yahweh"), most form a sentence (e.g., Elijah = "my God is Yahweh"; Nathaniel = "God has given"). Almost all compound names have a religious significance; simple names frequently have not.

Another classification is on the basis of origin. The name of a place, e.g., may reflect its physical features or some characteristic of its inhabitants; or it may be named after some animal or plant. A person's name may derive from circumstances attending his birth, or some physical characteristic, or some aspiration of his parents; or he also may bear the name of an animal or plant. On the other hand, he may be merely named after some kinsman or distinguished person of the past.

The most obvious division, however, is between the two main groups of place names and personal names, to which must be added a third category—the divine names.

1. Place names. Place names are, on the whole, more obscure and ambiguous than are the names of persons. For the most part, they are also more ancient. It seems, however, that the two are sometimes related—personal names, in some instances, are derived from names of places and place names, on other occasions, from names of persons.

a. Pre-Israelitish, Greek, and Latin. Many of the place names in Palestine are older than the Israelite conquest of the land. While, therefore, they may be for the most part Semitic, they originated with some branch of the Semites other than the Hebrew invaders. Most of them would seem to be of Canaanite origin, but there are isolated names, like Ziklag, which are clearly non-Semitic. Place names, therefore, do not necessarily offer evidence of Israelite beliefs and practices.

Direct evidence of the preconquest existence of over thirty OT place names is afforded by the lists of Thut-mose III, Seti I, and Ramses II (probably the Pharaoh of the Oppression) and by the Tell el-Amarna Tablets. The list of the conquests of Thut-mose III (1501-1448 B.C.) in his Karnak Inscription dated 1494 B.C. mentions twenty-one Palestinian towns including Gath, Gaza, Joppa, and Migdal. In the other Egyptian lists of Seti I (1314-1292 B.C.) and Ramses II (1292-1225 B.C.) are the names of Beth-anath, Luz, and Secu, and of two other towns which may possibly be Jabneh and Heres. A further ten names, including Aijalon, Jerusalem, Lachish, and Megiddo, occur in the Tell el-Amarna Tablets (fourteenth century B.C.).

Greek and Latin names are confined to the Apoc. (e.g., Σκυθῶν πόλις [Jth. 3:10; cf. Judg. 1:27 LXX]) and the NT (e.g., Antipatris [Acts 23:31]; Caesarea [Matt. 16:13]; Ptolemaïs [Acts 21:7]).

b. From local characteristics. Outstanding characteristics of the locality, whether permanent physical features or changing social and religious customs, account for many place names. Some names refer to physical features—e.g., Giba, Gibiah, Gibeon= "hill"; Shechem="shoulder of a hill," or a ridge; Ramah, Ramoth, Rumah="height"; Sela="the cliff"; Beth-emek="house of the valley"; Lebanon is derived from the root meaning "white" and probably refers to the white cliffs. Other names are derived from climate, water supply, and soil—e.g., Zion="waterless"; Horeb and Jabesh="dry"; Beer="well"; En="spring"; Abel="meadow"; Argob="rich soil"; Carmel="garden land."

Variable characteristics such as size, produce, occupation, give rise to yet other names—e.g., Rabbah="large"; Zoar="small"; Gath="wine press"; Bethlehem="house of bread"; En-mishpat="spring of judgment" (i.e., a place for the settling of disputes); Bezer, Bozrah="a fortified place." Such names, of course, only correspond with the local characteristics of the time in which the particular name was given.

This applies also to a number of compound names which express religious beliefs and customs—e.g., Beth-shemesh, "house or temple of the sun," and Beth-anath, "house or temple of Anath," indicate the worship there, at some indefinite past date, of these deities. Similarly, Sin and Sinai bear the name of the Babylonian moon-god Sin. Bethel means "house of God" and Penuel "face of God." Names which are compounded with Baal (="owner") are abbreviations. In their present form they are, strictly speaking, titles of deities rather than place names—e.g., Baal-tamar="owner of the palm-tree," and Baal-hazor="owner of the village." These, however, are abbreviations of Beth-baal-tamar, meaning "house [or temple] of the owner of the palm tree," and Beth-baal-hazor, meaning "house [or temple] of the owner of the village." Sometimes the "baal" instead of the "beth" is omitted in the abbreviation, thus giving rise to three variant forms of the name—e.g., Beth-baal-meon ("house of the owner of the town of Meon"; Josh. 13:17)=Baal-meon (Ezek. 25: 9)=Beth-meon (Jer. 48:23).

c. From animals and plants. Some thirty-three Palestinian towns bear the names of animals. Such names are not uniformly distributed but occur almost entirely in the S, only four being found N of Shechem. Their origin has been attributed to a totemistic stage either in early Hebrew society or among some of the S Canaanite peoples, but they do not necessarily demand such an interpretation, which assumes that they have been derived from the names of clans.

Some towns have the names of wild animals—e.g., Aijalon="stag"; Arad="wild ass"; Laish, Labaoth= "lion"; Ophra, Ephron="gazelle." Others are named after domestic animals—e.g., En-gedi="fountain of the kid"; Eglon="calf" (cf. En-eglaim="fountain of the calves"); Hazor-susah="village of the horse"; Parah="cow"; Telaim="lambs." The names of birds occur—e.g., Beth-hoglah="house [or place] of the partridge"; Etam="birds of prey." Reptile and insect names are also found—e.g., Ir-nahash="city of the serpent"; Humtah="lizard"; Akrabbim= "scorpions"; Zorah="cricket."

The names of trees and plants, or compound words containing them, occur frequently as place names. The apple tree (תפוח) gives its name to Tappuah, Beth-tappuah, and En-tappuah; the palm tree (תמר) to Tamar, Baal-tamar, and Hazazon-tamar. Dilan means "cucumber." Atad and Shamir bear the names of different kinds of thorn bushes. Grape clusters account for the name of the Valley of Eshcol and balsam trees for that of the Valley of Baca.

2. Names of persons. In early OT times a child was usually named by the mother—perhaps a relic of a primitive matriarchate (Gen. 4:1, 25; 16:11; 19: 37-38; 29:32-35; 30;6, 8, 11, 13, 18, 20-21, 24; 35: 18; 38:4-5; Judg. 13:24; I Sam. 1:20; I Chr. 4:9; 7:16). The name, however, could be altered by the father (Gen. 35:18) and was, indeed, frequently given also by him (Gen. 4:26; 5:3, 28-29; 16:15; 17:19; 21: 3; 41:51-52; Exod. 2:22; Judg. 8:31; I Chr. 7:23; Job 42:14; Hos. 1:4, 6, 9; cf. Isa. 7:3). In exceptional circumstances a child might receive his name from someone other than the parents (Exod. 2:10; Ruth 4:17; II Sam. 12:25). It seems that the name was given at birth or shortly after. Only in NT times do we find the giving of the name associated with CIRCUMCISION on the eighth day after birth (Luke 1:59; 2:21).

There is a marked difference in the way personal names were regarded before and after the Exile. In the early period a child was given a particular name because of its intrinsic significance. After the fifth century B.C., however, it became customary to name a child after some relative, especially the grandfather. Along with this practice went the revival of distinguished names of the past and the adoption of certain foreign names—Persian, Greek, and Roman. Early personal names are usually simple; later ones are compound.

a. From circumstances and characteristics. In the early period the name was vitally and indefeasibly related, in some way or other, to the personality of the child. It frequently signified some circumstance attending his birth. Thus at the birth of Rebekah's twins, the hand of the younger was holding the heel of the elder, as if trying to hold him back. The younger was therefore called Jacob—i.e., "one who takes by the heel," meaning "supplanter" (Gen. 25: 26). Rachel, dying in childbirth, gave to her son the name Ben-oni—i.e., "son of my sorrow" (Gen. 35: 18). The defeat of Israel by the Philistines, involving the capture of the ark and the death of Eli and Phinehas, prompted the dying wife of the latter to call her son Ichabod—i.e., "Inglorious," saying: "The glory has departed from Israel" (I Sam. 4:21).

Sometimes the name indicated some personal characteristic of the child. Esau, meaning "hairy," was so called because of his appearance at birth (Gen. 25:25). The head of a family of returning exiles must have been a very tiny baby, because he was named Hakkatan, meaning "the small one" (Ezra 8:12). The father of an Israelite captain at the time of the Exile was evidently lacking in hair when born, since his name was Kareah, meaning "bald" (II Kings 25:23).

Personal names frequently express the parents' gratitude to God for a child, or their aspirations concerning him. Thus Leah says at the birth of her fourth son: "This time I will praise the LORD," and calls the boy Judah, which means "praised." In this connection a name is often given for reasons of assonance rather than etymology—e.g., Hannah's child is called Samuel, which actually means "name of God," because the name Samuel recalls the sound of the Hebrew phrase meaning "asked of God" (I Sam. 1:20; cf. Gen. 5:29; 32:28; Judg. 6:32; I Chr. 4:9). A common name like Obadiah, meaning "worshiper, or servant, of Yahweh," obviously records the parents' wish concerning the child.

The children of a prophet are sometimes given symbolic names which epitomize his oracles. Isaiah's doctrine of the remnant finds expression in the name of his son Shear-jashub, which means "A remnant shall return" (Isa. 7:3). The formidable name of his other son, Maher-shalal-hashbaz, meaning "The spoil speeds, the prey hastens," signifies the speedy destruction of Rezin and Pekah by the Assyrian king (Isa. 8:3). Hosea's eldest son is called after the city of Jezreel as a token of the prophet's condemnation of the massacre of Ahab's family there (Hos. 1:4). The names of his daughter, Lo-ruhamah, meaning "Not pitied," and second son, Lo-ammi, meaning "Not my people," express Hosea's conviction that Israel had forfeited all claim to God's mercy and protection (1:6-8).

b. From animals and plants. Altogether a hundred names of animals are used as proper names in the OT. Most of these, however, occur as the names of places, clans, or foreign individuals. Only twenty-two are the names of Hebrew individuals, and all these are pre-exilic—e.g., Aiah = "vulture"; Caleb = "dog"; Deborah = "bee"; Jonah = "dove"; Rachel = "ewe"; Zibiah = "gazelle"; Zimri = "mountain sheep."

A strong argument for a totemistic origin of such names is their recrudescence in the time of Josiah, when the names which occur are those of unclean animals—Achbor = "mouse"; Huldah = "weasel"; Shaphan = "rock badger." The explanation offered is that superstitious practices derived from primitive totemism were revived in the religious syncretism of Manasseh's reign. Hence children were given the names of animals which were sacred according to these ancient beliefs although unclean in the Israelite code (cf. Isa. 66:17; Ezek. 8:10). As with animal place names, however, the derivation of these personal names is not necessarily totemistic. They may be accounted for in terms of natural poetry. People living in the open air would quite naturally name their children after beasts or birds—as do the Arabs—especially if such an animal name expressed qualities which the child seemed to possess, or which they desired it to have.

Personal names which are the names of trees or plants are less frequent—e.g., Elah, Elon = "oak" or "terebinth"; Tamar = "palm tree"; Hadassah = "myrtle"; Rimmon = "pomegranate"; Susanna (apocryphal Additions to Daniel and NT) = "lily."

c. Compound. Whereas in early times personal names are simple, there is an increasing tendency, especially in the seventh century B.C., to use compound names which state a fact or express a wish. Early compound names, although less numerous, are more varied and do not, for the most part, consist of sentences, as do the later ones. Some, which denote kinship, are compounds with Ab(i) = "father," Ah(i) = "brother," and Am(mi) = "kinsman"—e.g., Abigail, Ahihud, Ammiel. Each of these forms, however, occurs fewer than twenty-five times, and they all became obsolete before the Exile.

Less frequent are names denoting dominion which contain the words Melech = "king," Adoni = "lord," and Baal = "owner"—e.g., Abimelech, Adonijah, Merib-baal. Melech, Adoni, and Baal do not appear to have been used by the Hebrews as proper names, either of Yahweh or of some other deity, but as appellatives—i.e., they are descriptive titles of Yahweh. These forms would seem to have come into use after the settlement in Canaan, and they ceased to be used after the Exile.

The most numerous compounds are those containing the divine names El and Yah. Compounds with El are extremely ancient and, indeed, are common to all Semitic languages. Out of some 135 mentioned in the OT, 22 are the names of places or foreigners, and the remaining 113 are personal Hebrew names—e.g., Elijah, Elimelech, Ishmael, Nathaniel. Names compounded with Yah number over 150 and are almost entirely personal or family names—e.g., Jehoram, Jehoahaz, Adonijah, Obadiah. In the earliest period they are infrequent and are confined to certain circles and families. But they increase rapidly from the time of David onward, displacing almost all other compounds except those containing El. There is also a significant change in the positions of El and Yah in verbal compounds. In the early period they stand, for the most part, at the beginning of the names, but they come to stand increasingly at the end. This change of position in a verbal compound has the effect of moving the emphasis from the subject to the predicate. The earlier compounds are essentially assertions about El or Yah as opposed—implicitly, at least—to other deities. But as the ethical monotheism of prophetic teaching permeates the popular consciousness, it becomes unnecessary to emphasize the subject, since the one God is behind all actions. And so the emphasis falls on the divine activity expressed by the name.

d. Divine. A variety of names for God are found in the OT. They are all used here with reference to the one God of Israel, but some of them may have denoted separate and distinct deities at an earlier time. *See* GOD, NAMES OF.

D. *NAME IN THE APOC. AND THE PSEUDEP.* In the literature of the Apoc. and the Pseudep.

the term "name" has the same meaning and uses as in the OT. Personal existence continues in the name (Ecclus. 44:14; 46:12). It denotes reputation (Tob. 3:15; Ecclus. 40:19; 41:12-13). The name of God is frequently a synonym for God himself (Wisd. Sol. 10:20; Ecclus. 39:35; Song Thr. Ch. 3, 30; Enoch 39:13). God's protection is claimed for the people and temple over which his name has been called (Bar. 2:15, 26; I Macc. 7:37). In exile God's name is invoked (Bar. 3:7). We find also "the Name" used as a substitute for the divine name Yahweh (e.g., Ecclus. 23:10; cf. Wisd. Sol. 14:21).

E. *NAME IN THE NT.* Apart from having at times a more general sense, "name" is used in the NT in ways which are both parallel and complementary to its OT usage. With the name of God there is now linked the name of Jesus Christ, who declares it and so "fulfils" the OT revelation.

1. Distinguishing term. In the NT the term "name" is frequently used in the ordinary sense merely as a means of distinguishing one person or thing from another. The shepherd "calls his own sheep by name" (John 10:3). Gallio dismisses the accusation brought against Paul by the Jews of Corinth as a "matter of questions about words and names and your own law" (Acts 18:15). The writer of III John bids the recipient greet the friends "by name" (III John 14 KJV [κατ' ὄνομα]). The names of Christians are in the book of life (Phil. 4:3; cf. Rev. 3:5; 13:8; 17:8). In the book of Revelation the heavenly Jerusalem has inscribed on its gates the names of the twelve tribes of the sons of Israel (Rev. 21:12) and on the foundation of its walls the twelve names of the twelve apostles of the Lamb (vs. 14).

The term is used extensively in the same way to introduce personal proper names, such as those of the twelve apostles (Matt. 10:2), the parents of John the Baptist (Luke 1:5), the mother of Jesus and her betrothed husband (Luke 1:27), and the false prophet of Paphos (Acts 13:6; cf. Matt. 27:32; Mark 5:22; Luke 2:25; 24:18; John 1:6; 18:10; Acts 28:7; Rev. 9:11).

2. Name and personality. The characteristic NT usage of "name," however, links it very closely with personality, as in the OT. Hence the choosing of a child's name was a matter of great importance. This is evident in Luke's account of the naming of John the Baptist (Luke 1:13, 59-63). Joseph is charged by the angel to call the son whom Mary shall bear "Jesus"—the Greek form of the Hebrew name Joshua, meaning "Deliverer" or "Savior," "for he will save his people from their sins" (Matt. 1:21; cf. Luke 1:31). The author of Matthew's Gospel sees in this the fulfilment of Isaiah's prophecy concerning the birth of a child called Emmanuel, which means, as he points out, "God with us" (Matt. 1:22-23).

As in the OT, a change in character or status is accompanied by a change of name. After his great confession at Caesarea Philippi, Simon is renamed Peter, "rock man" (Matt. 16:17-18; cf. Mark 3:16; Luke 6:14). Sometimes such a change takes the form of the addition of another name to denote some characteristic of personality. Thus James and John, because of their fiery disposition, are surnamed BOANERGES, meaning, as Mark explains, "sons of thunder" (Mark 3:17; cf. Luke 9:51-56). When Saul of Tarsus enters upon his missionary vocation to the Gentile world, his name is appropriately changed from the Hebrew form, Saul, to the Roman, Paul (Acts 13:9).

Another example of the typically Hebraistic linking of name with personality may be seen in the question put by the Sanhedrin to Peter and John after the healing of the lame man: "By what power or by what name did you do this?" (Acts 4:7). The meaning of the last clause is: As whose representative? or, By whose authority? Similarly, to receive a prophet "in the name of a prophet" (Matt. 10:41 KJV) means "in his capacity as a prophet"—i.e., as Moffatt, Phillips, and the RSV translate it: "because he is a prophet."

3. Name and reputation. The use of "name" as denoting "renown" or "fame" is rare in the NT. Indeed, there are only four instances of it. King Herod heard of the reputation of Jesus: His "name had become known" (Mark 6:14; KJV "His name was spread abroad"). The disciples are warned that because of their association with Jesus, they will lose their reputation: men will cast out their name as evil (Luke 6:22). Because of his humility and obedience unto death, Christ has been given the highest glory and renown: "God has highly exalted him and bestowed on him the name which is above every name" (Phil. 2:9). The church in Sardis has a false reputation: "You have the name of being alive, and you are dead" (Rev. 3:1).

4. The name of God. This is mentioned some forty times in the NT. In fifteen places it occurs in a quotation from the OT (Matt. 12:21; 21:9; 23:39; Mark 11:9-10; Luke 13:35; 19:38; John 12:13; Acts 2:21; 15:17; Rom. 2:24; 9:17; 10:13; 15:9; Heb. 2:12), and at other times it is referred to in phraseology reminiscent of the OT (e.g., Matt. 6:9; John 17:6, 26). Everywhere it is used in the OT sense of the revealed nature and character of the Savior God.

As in the OT, the name of God is frequently used as a synonym for God himself. It is the object of worship (Heb. 13:15), of fear (Rev. 11:18), and of love (Heb. 6:10 KJV). It is holy (Luke 1:49), and the divine fatherhood manifested to men is to be hallowed (Matt. 6:9 = Luke 11:2). The name must not be defamed (I Tim. 6:1).

The prophets spoke in the name of the Lord—i.e., with divine authority (Jas. 5:10)—and, in accordance with OT prophecy, God has visited the Gentiles to take out of them a people for his name—i.e., for his own possession (Acts 15:14-18). Christ's claim to have come in his Father's name means as the Father's representative (John 5:43). His works done in that name bear witness to the Father's authority, which he shares (10:25). In him there has been given to men the complete revelation of the divine nature: he has manifested and declared the name of God (12:28; 17:6, 26).

5. The name of Christ. The distinctive feature of NT usage is the way in which the name of Jesus is either substituted for, or placed alongside, the name of God. Phrases which are used in the OT of the name of God are applied in the NT to the name of Jesus. Thus prophesying or speaking in the name of God becomes prophesying or speaking in the name of Jesus (e.g., Matt. 7:22; Acts 4:17-18; 5:40; 9:29;

cf. Deut. 18:22; I Chr. 21:19; Jer. 20:9; Dan. 9:6). The old Israel is called by the name of God (II Chr. 7:14), the new Israel by the name of Christ (Jas. 2:7; cf. Acts 11:26). Believing in the name of Jesus (John 1:12; I John 3:23) corresponds to trusting in the name of God (Ps. 33:21; Isa. 50:10). Calling on the name of God (Gen. 13:4; Ps. 105:1; etc.) is paralleled by calling on the name of Christ (Acts 9:14, 21; I Cor. 1:2; cf. Acts 2:21; I Pet. 1:17). That is to say, worship is offered to Christ as to God.

Just as in the OT the name of God is a synonym for God himself, so also in the NT the name of Jesus is a synonymous term for Jesus himself (John 1:12; 2:23; 3:18; I John 3:23; 5:13). It epitomizes his personality as known.

a. Belief in the name. The expression "to believe in the name of Jesus" is restricted to the Johannine writings, where it occurs five times (John 1:12; 2:23; 3:18; I John 3:23; 5:13). There is no foundation for the theory that in these and similar references to the name there is an assimilation of the use of the name of Jesus to ancient magic. This theory fails to take account of the influence of OT thought, with its immeasurably higher ideas, on Jesus and his disciples; it is obviously inapplicable to many passages in which the name occurs (e.g., Matt. 18:5); and it is incongruous with the general use which the NT writers make of this concept. In the foreground of the Fourth Gospel there is the idea of a mystical faith-union between the believer and Christ (*see* FAITH), and a significant feature of this gospel is the alternation of the phrases "to believe in the name of Jesus" and "to believe in Jesus" (e.g., John 3:18), which clearly mean the same thing. Belief in his name is linked with the discernment of the significance of his miracles as "signs" of the Messiah (John 2:23) and with salvation unto eternal life (3:16-18). It corresponds to "receiving" him (1:12) and, as an obligation associated with loving one another, is the command of God (I John 3:23). Believing in the name of Jesus, therefore, involves an acceptance of Jesus himself as Messiah and Savior, and of the obligation to show forth his love.

b. Baptism in the name. This is mentioned five times in the NT (Matt. 28:19; Acts 2:38; 8:16; 10:48; 19:5) along with the parallel phrase "baptized into Christ" (Rom. 6:3; Gal. 3:27). The use of three different Greek prepositions, however, gives shades of meaning which are absent from the English versions. In Acts 10:48 the preposition is ἐν, which has the force of the Hebrew ב and conveys the idea of acting on the authority of another. Peter commands Cornelius and his company to be baptized on the authority of Jesus Christ. The preposition ἐπι in Acts 2:38 gives the sense of resting upon, or being devoted to, the person of Christ. Here the appeal is to receive baptism on the ground of the hearers' faith: in being baptized they repose their trust in Christ. In the three remaining passages another preposition, εἰς, is used. This is equivalent to the Hebrew ל in the sense of "with regard to." The Christians at Samaria (Acts 8:16) and the disciples at Ephesus (19:5) receive baptism as the outward symbol of union with Christ. This would seem to be the meaning also of the commission of the risen Christ (Matt. 28:19). The trinitarian formula is generally seen as a later expansion.

c. Acting in the name. There is no reason to believe that in NT times the name of Jesus was used in any magical way as a "theurgic formula"—a view based largely on evidence from early Christian fathers which is to be attributed to the influence of Greek superstition. Some itinerant exorcists certainly attempted to use the name in this way, but with unhappy results (see Acts 19:13-16). When interpreting the NT, it is rather to the Hebraic ideas and influence of the OT that we must look.

In considering the various actions "in the name of Jesus" of which the NT writers speak—preaching, healing, exorcism, etc.—the force of the Greek prepositions, as influenced by their use in the LXX, must once again be taken into account. The same three prepositions, in addition to the simple dative case, are used. The most frequent is ἐν (ב), usually denoting participation in authority. It is used in this sense in passages relating to the casting out of demons (Mark 9:38 = Luke 9:49; Mark 16:17; Luke 10:17; Acts 16:18) and in the account of the healing of the lame man by Peter and John (Acts 3:6), of Paul's judgment concerning the case of incest in the Corinthian church (I Cor. 5:4), and of his command to the Thessalonians (II Thess. 3:6). In each case "in the name" of Christ means acting on his behalf, by his authority. The phrase is probably to be understood in this sense in Jas. 5:14—the elders of the church, as participating in the authority of Christ, are to anoint the sick. Here, however, "in the name" could also mean "by invoking the name"—i.e., while calling upon Christ. In Acts 9:27, 29, ἐν reflects a peculiar instrumental use of the Hebrew ב (cf. קרא בשם [Exod. 33:19; 34:5]), so that Paul's preaching boldly in the name of Jesus means his proclamation of Christ. A still different sense of ἐν is found in the Johannine sayings regarding prayer in the name of Jesus (John 14:14; 15:16; 16:23-24, 26). Here it is associated with the mystical faith-union concept of the Fourth Gospel, to which reference has been made, and has the meaning of being rooted in Christ. Hence prayer in his name is prayer that is prompted by the mind of Christ and in accordance with his character. In Mark 9:41 the giving of a cup of water ἐν ὀνόματι (KJV "in [my] name") is explained as meaning because the recipient belongs to Christ.

In another group of passages, confined to the Synoptic gospels and the Acts, the preposition ἐπι is used. This also represents ב but has the sense of relying upon. Thus to receive a child in the name of Christ (Matt. 18:5 = Mark 9:37 = Luke 9:48) is to receive him upon the ground of devotion to Christ—i.e., for Christ's sake. Those who shall come in Christ's name (Matt. 24:5 = Mark 13:6 = Luke 21:8) will come claiming the authority which properly belongs only to him—i.e., they will claim to be the Messiah. Preaching, teaching, and healing in the name of Christ (Luke 24:47; Acts 3:16; 4:17-18; 5:28, 40) are all carried out in reliance upon his messianic authority, to which appeal is made.

In only one instance is the preposition εἰς (ל) used in this connection (Matt. 18:20). To be gathered together in Christ's name means here that Christians are assembled with their minds directed toward him. He is the reason for their assembling, and it is his will that they seek to know. In such an assembly the name is made manifest: Christ himself is present with his people.

The use of the simple dative case in Matt. 7:22 conveys the idea of acting by the power of Christ's name—i.e., by invoking his authority.

d. Persecution for the name. In all except one of the references to Christ's followers' being hated or persecuted for his name's sake, "name" means Christ himself (Matt. 10:22; 24:9; Mark 13:13; Luke 21:12, 17; Acts 9:16; 21:13). The exception is Acts 5:41, where "the Name" (like "the Way" [*see* WAY]; Acts 9:2; 19:9) is a technical term for the Christian faith. Hence to suffer for the Name means to suffer as a Christian. The only other instance of this usage in the NT is in III John 7, where reference is made to brethren who have gone forth "for the sake of the Name" (ERV-ASV).

Bibliography. E. Nestle, *Die israelitischen Eigennamen nach ihrer religionsgeschichtlichen Bedeutung* (1876). B. Stade, *Geschichte des Volkes Israel,* II (1888), 247-48. H. Schultz, "Revelation and Names of God," *OT Theology,* II (English trans.; 1892), 122-25. M. von Grunwald, *Die Eigennamen des AT* (1895). G. B. Gray, *Studies in Hebrew Proper Names* (1896), is the most thorough and comprehensive work in English on the subject of Hebrew proper names. W. Heitmüller, *Im Namen Jesu* (1903). B. Jacob, *Im Namen Gottes* (1903). A. B. Davidson, "The Idea of the Divine Name," *The Theology of the OT* (1904), pp. 36-38. J. Pedersen, "Name," *Israel,* I-II (1926), 245-59, presents a clear and comprehensive summary. M. Noth, *Die israelitischen Personnamen* (1928). O. Grether, "Name und Wort Gottes," *BZAW,* vol. 64 (1934). G. von Rad, "Shem und Kabod," *Deuteronomiumstudien* (1948). E. Jacob, "The Name of God," *Theology of the OT* (English trans.; 1958), pp. 82-85.

R. ABBA

NANEA nə nē'ə [Ναναία]. A temple in Persia despoiled by Antiochus IV (I Macc. 6:2). It is called by Josephus (War LXVI; Antiq. XII.ix.1) and Polybius (31.4) the Temple Artemis. In it were the golden shields and arms of Alexander the Great. The inhabitants arose against Antiochus when he sought to plunder this temple, and he returned with great distress to Syria ("Babylon"). The Syrian goddess Nanea is Nana of the Babylonians and is identified by Appian (*Syrian Wars* 66) with Aphrodite of the Greeks and Venus of the Romans.

II Macc. 1:13-18 relates that when the king arrived in Persia with a strong army, he was defeated by the guile of the priests. On the pretext that he intended to marry the goddess, he came into the temple to claim its treasury as dowry. The priests had displayed the treasures but shut the temple gates after Antiochus had entered. From a secret opening in the ceiling they hurled stones at the king and struck him down, decapitated him, and threw his head out to those waiting outside.

Some scholars believe the incident refers to Antiochus III, who lost his life when he sought to plunder the temple of Bilus in the Elymean hills (Strabo 16.1.18). Others regard this as being Antiochus Sidetes VII, who was killed in his campaign against the Parthians in 129 B.C. (Appian *Syrian Wars* 68).

Bibliography. S. Tedesche and S. Zeitlin, *I and II Maccabees* (1954).

S. B. HOENIG

NANNAR năn'är [*originally Nar-nar,* lightgiver]. A title of the Sumerian moon-god Sin, under which he was worshiped at Ur, the chief center of the lunar cult in S Mesopotamia.

Bibliography. M. Jastrow, *The Religion of Babylonia and Assyria* (1898), pp. 74-79; E. Dhorme, *Les religions de Babylonie et d'Assyrie* (1945), pp. 54-60.

J. GRAY

NAOMI nā ō'mĭ [נעמי, my joy, my pleasant one; *cf.* Ugar. *n'm,* be pleasant, lovely; *probably a feminine form of Naaman*]. One of the leading characters in the book of Ruth. In a time of famine Elimelech of Bethlehem, his wife Naomi, and their two sons sought refuge in Moab. Here the sons married, and Elimelech and both sons later died. Naomi resolved to return to Bethlehem in Judah, and urged her two Moabite daughters-in-law to go back to their own families. One, Orpah, eventually yielded to her entreaty. The other, Ruth, declared her devotion to her mother-in-law (1:16-17), and accompanied her to Bethlehem. On their arrival, at the beginning of the barley harvest, Naomi contrasted the meaning of her name with the bitterness of her lot, and asked to be called Mara, "bitter" (1:20-21).

Ruth, going out to glean in the fields, happened to come to the field of Boaz, and attracted his favorable attention (2:5, 10-16). When Naomi learned this, she encouraged Ruth to remain with Boaz' maidens, since he was a kinsman of Elimelech. Later Naomi sent her daughter-in-law to find Boaz where he was spending the night at the threshing floor, and to ask his protection as next-of-kin. Boaz accepted the request, redeemed the property of Elimelech, and married Ruth. Their child was hailed as a "son . . . born to Naomi" (4:17). The line of Elimelech was thus preserved, and Naomi's heroic perseverance was splendidly rewarded.

See also RUTH, BOOK OF.

D. HARVEY

NAPHATH-DOR nā'făth dôr' [נפת דור (Josh. 12:23; KJV COAST OF DOR), נפת דאר (I Kings 4:11; KJV REGION OF DOR)]. Alternately: NAPHATH [נפת] (Josh. 17:11; KJV COUNTRIES); NAPHOTH-DOR nā'fŏth dôr' [נפות דור] (Josh. 11:2; KJV BORDERS OF DOR). A city or region identical with or adjacent to DOR. The term "Naphath" probably refers to the coastal plain in the vicinity of Dor.

W. L. REED

NAPHISH nā'fĭsh [נפיש]; KJV NEPHISH nē'— in I Chr. 5:19. The eleventh of Ishmael's twelve sons (Gen. 25:15; I Chr. 1:31), also designated "twelve princes [נשיאים] according to their tribes" (Gen. 25:16), perhaps indicating their position in a sacral institution (cf. Gen. 22:20-24; Num. 1:5-16; 13:4-15; 34:17-28); located in NW Arabia. The tribe was subdued by the Israelite Transjordan tribes (I Chr. 5:19 [LXX Ναφισαιων, Ναφεισαδαιων]).

Bibliography. M. Noth, *Geschichte Israels* (1950), section 8.

L. HICKS

NAPHISI. KJV Apoc. form of NEPHISIM.

NAPHOTH-DOR. Alternate form of NAPHATH-DOR.

NAPHTALI năf'tə lī [נפתלי, *presumably originally the name of a place or region; folk etymology derivation in* Gen. 30:8 *from* פתל, to wind, to twist]. The sixth son of Jacob, and the *heros eponymos* of the tribe of Naphtali. Jacob's second son by Rachel's maid Bilhah, and the full brother of Dan (Gen. 30:6-8), Naphtali is usually mentioned along with Dan in the lists of the sons (Gen. 35:25; 46:24; Exod. 1:4). In I Chr. 2:2 the two are probably separated by Joseph and Benjamin only inadvertently.

The special relationship of the tribe to Dan, which is expressed in the genealogy of the sons of Jacob, is easy to understand because of their geographical proximity in Galilee. The relationship of Dan to the Rachel group, which is also indicated there, is understandable in the light of Dan's original sojourn in the region SW of the Ephraimite territory, but it is not immediately in the case of Naphtali. Naphtali's territory, which according to the old description of the boundaries consisted of a broad strip parallel to the Jordan from Lake Huleh to the S end of the Lake of Gennesaret (Josh. 19:32-39), is separated from the Rachel group by the Leah tribes of Issachar and Zebulun. It could be conjectured that Naphtali, like Dan, migrated there northward after an initial settlement in central Palestine. The alternative assumption is just as valid—namely, that the Naphtali group had already separated from the main group of Rachel at the time of the crossing of the Jordan, which presumably took place at the more northerly fords. Coming into the upper valley of the Jordan and up the E slope of the Galilean Mountains, it came into the territory of the city of Hazor, whose king in the Amarna period, like Labaja of Shechem, had apparently been able to extend his rule beyond the compass of a normal city-state at the expense of the neighboring cities. In any case, the king of Hazor occupied a leading position among the Canaanites even at the time of the Israelites (Josh. 11:10; Judg. 4:2). It is quite conceivable that Naphtali had to make so many concessions to the Canaanites that the tribe was henceforth valued only as half-caste. The name of the tribe, which was taken from the region and probably is not of Semitic origin, may be proof of this. One may add to this the notation in the "negative inventory of possessions" that the Naphtalites "dwelt among the Canaanites, the inhabitants of the land" (Judg. 1:33). A Naphtalite tradition from the period of the occupation of land seems to be concealed in the description of the battle at the Waters of Merom, which has been expanded into a description of the conquest of the N half of Palestine (Josh. 10). Otherwise the earliest sources have not much to report concerning the tribe, which was unimportant as a result of its peripheral location. In the Blessing of Jacob, Naphtali as the last of the Galilean tribes gets a somewhat gloomy comment; it is compared to an unleashed hind, and this probably suggests the danger of its impulsive strength (Gen. 49:21). The Naphtali saying in the Blessing of Moses is essentially religious in content, but it speaks, too, of possession of the sea—i.e., the Sea of Chinnereth. The designation of the "Southland," which follows, scarcely takes its point of orientation from the sea. In that case it would refer to a part of the Jordan Valley S of the sea. But as this area belonged to Issachar, it more probably designates a pre-Israelite center of power N of the Sea of Chinnereth, probably Hazor. If this is the region actually meant by "Southland," then it would follow that the "Northland," still farther N, did not come into Naphtali's possession. As a matter of fact, the towns Abel-beth-maacah (Abil el-qamh) and Ijon (Tell Dibbin), which were later Israelite, seem not to have been included in the old system of border descriptions in the book of Joshua. They are mentioned for the first time at a late date: Abel, not until the time of David (II Sam. 20:14-15); Ijon, four generations later (I Kings 15:20). Both seem to have been settled relatively late by Israelites and then perhaps by others who immigrated from farther S, so that for a while a gap separated Naphtali and Dan. The Song of Deborah lauds Naphtali because of its death-defying action for the freedom of Israel (Judg. 5:18). The leader of the amphictyonic levy came from Naphtali (4:6, 10). Under Gideon, Naphtali proved its loyalty to the amphictyony by participation in the expulsion of the Midianites (Judg. 6:35; 7:23).

In the period of the kings Naphtali constituted a separate region in Solomon's arrangement of districts (I Kings 4:15). Solomon's brass-founder, Hiram, was Naphtalite on his mother's side (7:14). Under Baasha the territory of Naphtali suffered under the invasion of the Arameans allied with Asa (15:20; apparently Ijon and Abel-beth-maacah, even as Dan, are not reckoned to Naphtali, and only the fourth one in the list, "all Chinnereth," is included in "all the land of Naphtali"). Finally, Naphtali is found in a comment on an extract from the annals which described the route of Tiglath-pileser III, in the war which ended with the incorporation of Galilee and the land E of the Jordan into the Assyrian provincial system (II Kings 15:29; II Chr. 16:4). Isaiah alludes to the same event (Isa. 9:1—H 8:23), and his oracle has influenced Ps. 68:27—H 68:28.

The later literature mentions Naphtali almost exclusively in statistical contexts—primarily, of course, the P stratum of the Pentateuch. Here, except for the list of scouts (Num. 13:14), Naphtali always stands at the end (1:15, 42-43; 2:29; 7:78; 10:27; 26:48-50; 34:28). In the Deuteronomic historical work, Naphtali appears in the lists of the Levite cities (Josh. 21:6, 32; I Chr. 6:62—H 6:61) and the cities of refuge (Josh. 20:7), in Deut. 27:13 at the end of the group uttering the curse, and in 34:2 in a geographical survey which goes from N to S. In the apportionment of the land in Ezek. 48:3, Naphtali receives the third strip in the N, next to Dan and Asher, while Issachar and Zebulun are forced to emigrate to the S. In vs. 34 the last gate is given the name of Naphtali. Only in the lists of the Chronicler is Naphtali never ranked at the end (I Chr. 12:35; 27:19), not even in I Chr. 7:13. Otherwise "Naphtali" serves as a designation of the N in I Chr. 12:40; II Chr. 34:6.

In the NT, in addition to the quotation in Matt. 4:13, 15, Naphtali appears in the fifth position in the list of the sealed (Rev. 7:6).

For the territory of Naphtali, *see* TRIBES, TERRITORIES OF, § D5. *See* the bibliography under ASHER.

K. ELLIGER

NAPHTHA năf′thə [νάφθα] (Song of Thr. Ch. 23). An inflammable substance. This is referred to as "nephthar" (KJV "naphthar") in II Macc. 1:36. There the term is interpreted as meaning "purification" and is associated symbolically with the purification of the temple (cf. Num. 31:23). Strabo (16.1, 15) speaks of a liquid "which they call naphtha; if it is brought near fire it catches the fire." The etymology of the word is obscure.

NAPHTHAR. KJV form of NEPHTHAR.

NAPHTUHIM năf'tə hĭm [נפתחים; LXX Νεφθαλιιμ]. An unidentified ethnic group.

The Naphtuhim are mentioned only in the ethnographic lists of Gen. 10:13; I Chr. 1:11, where they are placed between the LEHABIM and the PATHRUSIM. Although we have no reason to believe that these lists are arranged according to an accurate geographical pattern, the identification of the Lehabim as Libyans and the Pathrusim as the inhabitants of Upper Egypt has led scholars to find in the term "Naphtuhim" a reference to the residents of the Egyptian Delta. None of the suggestions posed to date is without difficulties, but among the more likely correct is that of W. Spiegelberg (*see bibliography*)—namely, that "Naphtuhim" = Egyptian **na-patōḥ*+-*îm*, where the Egyptian word is a plausible, but conjectured, late form for "those of the Delta."

Bibliography. W. Spiegelberg, "נפתחים (Gen. X,13)," *OLZ*, 9 (1906), 276-79.

T. O. LAMBDIN

NAPKIN [σουδάριον, *from* Lat. *sudarium*, a cloth for wiping away perspiration, a handkerchief]. Alternately: CLOTH, HANDKERCHIEF. A small cloth. In Luke 19:20 it refers to the small cloth in which the one-talented man concealed his pound for safekeeping against the day of reckoning. In John 11:44 ("cloth") it is the cloth wrapped around the face of the dead. According to John 20:7, Jesus' face had been bound with a napkin which, after the Resurrection, was found in a place by itself. In Acts 19:12 ("handkerchief") the word doubtless refers to the small sweat-cloth handkerchiefs which had come into contact with Paul and were thus thought to possess some of the healing power of the apostle which could be transmitted through them to the sick.

J. M. MYERS

NARCISSUS när sĭs'əs [Νάρκισσος] (Rom. 16:11). The head of a household (including family and slaves), some of whom were Christians. The most famous bearer of this name was the freedman of the Emperor Claudius (A.D. 41-54), but it is quite unlikely that his household is meant here.

F. W. GINGRICH

NARD närd [נרד, *nērd, loan word from* Sanskrit *via* Pers.; νάρδος]. A costly fragrant ointment prepared from the roots and hairy stems of an aromatic Indian herb, *Nardostachys jatamansi* (Wall.) D. C. (also known as *Valeriana jatamansi* Wall.). In the OT it appears in the Song of Solomon as a perfume giving fragrance to the king's couch (1:12) and as one of several fragrant spices listed symbolically in praise of the bride (4:13-14). The expression translated "pure nard" in the RSV and "spikenard" in the KJV (νάρδος πιστική) in Mark 14:3; John 12:3 (cf.

6. Nard

Matt. 26:6-13; Luke 7:36-50) designates the costly ointment which the woman used to anoint Jesus when he visited Bethany. The obscure πιστική has been variously translated "pure," "genuine," "liquid," and traditionally "spike" (cf. Vulg. *spicatus*—i.e., the spikelike form of the root and lower stem of the young plant). *See also* FLORA § A7*k;* OINTMENT; SPICE.

Fig. NAR 6.

Bibliography. I. Löw, *Die Flora der Juden*, III (1924), 482-88; H. L. and A. L. Moldenke, *Plants of the Bible* (1952), pp. 148-49.

J. C. TREVER

NASBAS. KJV form of NADAB 5.

NASH PAPYRUS năsh pə pī'rəs. A pre-Christian papyrus containing the Decalogue (Exod. 20:2-17 or Deut. 5:6-21) and the Shema (Deut. 6:4-5).

The Nash Papyrus, first published in 1903 by S. A. Cooke, was purchased from a native Egyptian dealer by W. L. Nash, then secretary of the Society of Biblical Archaeology. The papyrus is of unknown provenance, although allegedly from the Faiyum, and consists of a single sheet, not from a scroll, apparently used for teaching or lectionary purposes. The text itself does not correspond exactly to the MT or to the LXX but stands closer to LXX A than to B. The writing may be assigned to somewhere in the Maccabean period, between 165 and 37 B.C., on the basis of the paleography, for which the Aramaic papyri from fifth-century Egypt provide a *terminus post quem* and the Herodian inscriptions a *terminus ante quem*.

Bibliography. F. C. Burkitt, "The Hebrew Papyrus of the Ten Commandments," *JQR*, 15 (1903), 392-408. S. A. Cooke, "A Pre-Massoretic Biblical Papyrus," *PSBA*, 25 (1903), 34-56. W. F. Albright, "A Biblical Fragment from the Maccabean Age: The Nash Papyrus," *JBL*, 56 (1937), 145-76; "On the Date of the Scrolls from 'Ain Feshka and the Nash Papyrus," *BASOR*, 115 (1949), 10-19.

T. O. LAMBDIN

NASITH. KJV Apoc. form of NEZIAH.

NASOR nā'sôr. KJV Apoc. form of HAZOR.

NATHAN nā'thən [נתן, gift; Ναθάν]. **1.** A son of David. He was David's third son born in Jerusalem (II Sam. 5:14; I Chr. 14:4). His mother's name was Bathshua, and thus he was an elder brother of Solomon (I Chr. 3:5). His descendants, as a subordinate branch of the Davidic family, appear, together with the latter, in the "Day of the LORD" apocalypse of the book of Zechariah (12:12). Jesus' genealogy is traced through this son of David in the Gospel According to Luke (3:31).

2. A prophet contemporary with David. He appears three times at the scene of the events of the Davidic court. The first time he was consulted by David (David had just finished the building of his palace) concerning the king's plans to erect a temple for the Lord. At first, Nathan approved the king's plans, but later he revealed to David the divine word which prohibited the building of a sanctuary but promised the establishment of the Davidic dynasty forever (II Sam. 7:1-17).

When David committed adultery with Bathsheba and murdered Uriah, her husband, Nathan presented a fictive legal case to David in which a rich man took away the only lamb of a poor man. When the enraged David announced that the rich man deserved to die, Nathan courageously confronted the royal murderer with his own crime (II Sam. 12:1-15).

In Solomon's succession to the throne of David, Nathan, together with Solomon's mother, Bathsheba, played an important role (cf. II Sam. 12:25). When Nathan was told that Adonijah, the elder brother of Solomon, had attempted to seize the royal throne, he sent Bathsheba to the senile David to ask him to fulfil his promise to make Solomon his successor; and later he, himself, went to the aged king to confirm her words. This plot of Bathsheba and Nathan was successful, for David ordered Nathan and Zadok the priest to anoint Solomon to be king over Israel on that very day (I Kings 1:5-48).

The Chronicler maintains that Nathan wrote chronicles on the acts of David (I Chr. 29:29) and of Solomon (II Chr. 9:29) and played a role in the development of temple music (29:25).

Apparently Nathan was a court prophet who had an intensive interest in the Davidic dynasty. This fact has prompted some scholars to deny the historicity of his denunciation of David. However, association with the court of David did not necessarily mean the servility of the prophet.

3. A man of Zobah; father of Igal, who was one of the thirty Mighty Men of David (II Sam. 23:36); and in the Chronicler's list of the heroes (I Chr. 11:38) he is the brother of Joel.

4. Father of two sons: Azariah, a chief officer of Solomon; and Zabud, a priest and the king's friend (I Kings 4:5). He is possibly identical with 1 or 2 *above*.

5. A descendant of the patriarch Judah, in the clan of Jerahmeel; son of Attai, and father of Zabad (I Chr. 2:36).

6. One of the leading men in the group of returnees, who was, along with a delegation, sent by Ezra to Iddo in Casiphia to ask for servants for the house of God (Ezra 8:16). He is probably identical with one of the returnees named Nathan who pledged that he would divorce his wife, since she was of foreign origin (10:39).

Bibliography. H. S. McKenzie, "The Dynastic Oracle: II Sam. 7," *Theological Studies,* VIII (1947), 187-218; S. Mowinckel, "Natanforjettelsen 2 Sam. Kap. 7," *Svensk Exegetisk Årsbok* (1948), pp. 204-13. S. SZIKSZAI

NATHANAEL nə thăn'ĭ əl [Ναθαναήλ=נתנאל, God has given; *see also* NETHANEL]. **1.** A priest required by Ezra to dismiss his foreign wife (I Esd. 9:22).

2. An ancestor of Judith (Jth. 8:1).

3. KJV Apoc. form of NETHANEL 7-8.

4. A guileless Israelite whom Jesus called to become a disciple and witness of his future glory (John 1:45-51).

Nathanael, from Cana in Galilee (John 21:2), was brought to Jesus by Philip, who had come to believe in Jesus' messiahship (1:45). Nathanael's initial skepticism concerning Jesus' right to this dignity (vs. 46) was overcome by a personal experience in which Jesus' knowledge of "what was in man" (2:25) deeply impressed him.

By describing Nathanael as a true, guileless Israelite (1:47), Jesus meant, not that he was sinless, but that he was utterly sincere, enlightened, and completely dedicated to God. Evidence for this judgment had come from Jesus' observing his actions under a fig tree (vs. 48). Fig and olive trees and grapevines offered rabbis suitable places for study and teaching of the law. Was Nathanael reading in the Scriptures, meditating, praying, and repenting when Jesus first saw him? Such activity would indicate clearly that he was an Israelite at heart, not merely in outward appearance.

Jesus' response to Nathanael's confession of faith contains an allusion to Jacob's experience at Bethel (Gen. 28:12). He says in effect, "If you follow me, you will become conscious that where I and my disciples are is the very presence of God, the veritable doorway to heaven."

Nathanael is not mentioned in the other gospels. The fact that his name occurs alongside those of important apostles (John 1:35-51; 21:2) has led many to equate him with persons appearing in the Synoptics (Bartholomew, Matthew, James the son of Alphaeus, John the son of Zebedee, Simon the Cananaean), the most favored identification being BARTHOLOMEW.

Whoever he was, Nathanael serves in the Fourth Gospel as a symbol of the pious, God-fearing Israelite who, good as he is, stands incomplete, and who must be willing to pass beyond his intellectual difficulties concerning Jesus into saving faith in him.

Bibliography. R. B. Y. Scott, "Who Was Nathanael?" *ET,* XXXVIII (1927), 93-94; J. Jeremias, "Die Berufung des Nathanael (Joh. 1, 45-51)," ΑΓΓΕΛΟΣ, III (1930), 2-5; W. Bauer, *Das Johannesevangelium* (3 *Aufl.;* 1933), pp. 41-43; U. Holzmeister, "Nathanael fuitne idem ac S. Bartholomaeus apostolus?" *Bibl.,* XXI (1940), 28-39. E. P. BLAIR

NATHANIAS. KJV form of NETHANIAH 5.

NATHAN-MELECH nā'thən mĕl'ĭk [נתן־מלך, the king has given, *or* Melech (a god) has given]. A

EUNUCH or chamberlain under King Josiah near whose quarters the sacrificial horses for sun-worship, which was purged by Josiah, were kept (II Kings 23:11). The title designated both high (25:19) and low (I Kings 22:9) officers and is identical with Assyrian and Babylonian usage (cf. II Kings 18:17: Rabsaris, "chief eunuch"). It is possible, though unlikely, that the name Nathan-melech is theophorous. *See* MOLECH.

J. M. WARD

NATIONALITY. The concept of nationality, in the sense in which the term will be employed here, with special reference to the ancient Near East, is the state or quality of a people living in a given territory and bound together by a more or less common language, common traditions, history, customs, government, and often a common religion, and possessing a greater sense of common interest and interrelation than exists between them and other peoples.

In the Bible, especially concerning Israel, the term usually has a religious connotation, distinguishing those who worshiped Yahweh from those who served other gods. It often has strong geographical as well as ethnological significance (Deut. 32:8-9; cf. Acts 17:26-27).

Nationality became symbolized, in the political sense, by monarchy. E.g., when Israel aspired to become a nation, the desire was for a king that they might be "like all the nations" (I Sam. 8:5). Nationality frequently took the form of nationalism, or even of exclusivism. Yet with the mingling of peoples there came at times an ephemeral sense of interdependence, as typified in what has been called the "first internationalism" in the ancient Near East from *ca.* the fifteenth to the thirteenth centuries B.C.

1. Nationality in the ancient Near East
   a. In Egypt
   b. In Mesopotamia
2. Terminology of nationality in the Bible
   a. In biblical Hebrew
   b. In LXX Greek
   c. In NT Greek
3. Nationality in the OT
   a. In Israel
   b. Israel an elect nation
   c. Future of Israel's nationality
4. Nationality in the Apoc. and the Pseudep.
5. Nationality in the NT
   a. Jesus' attitude toward nationality
   b. Paul's attitude toward nationality
   c. Other NT writers' attitudes toward nationality

Bibliography

1. Nationality in the ancient Near East. In the two largest areas of the ancient Near East, Egypt and Mesopotamia—excluding Palestine—the principal terms of our definition were met.

a. In Egypt. We cannot speak of actual nationality in EGYPT until the beginning of the dynastic period, although it may have been present in germ before that time. The Egyptians, being somewhat isolated from neighboring peoples, drew a distinction between themselves as "men" and other peoples as "humans"—to us a distinction without a difference, but to the Egyptians it meant that other peoples were in some manner inferior beings. When an alien, however, came to live permanently in Egypt, learned the language, followed the customs of the land, etc., he might ultimately be accepted as a member of the nation, whatever his race or color. E.g., Joseph, an alien, could even rise to a position of distinction (Gen. 41:40 ff).

b. In Mesopotamia. In the earliest historical periods Mesopotamia was made up of city-states, constantly warring and absorbing one another. To be sure, strong kings arose whose subjects gave these rulers their complete loyalty, which might presume some degree of nationality, but it was impermanent at best. The real beginnings of nationality belong, perhaps, to the periods of Sargon of Akkad in the twenty-fourth century B.C., and of the first dynasty of Babylon (Hammurabi's time) in the eighteenth century B.C. Thus a pattern was set for the two dominant nations, Assyria and Babylonia, each of which fostered a high degree of national feeling (*see* ASSYRIA AND BABYLONIA; SARGON 1; HAMMURABI). These two nations had much in common in their cultural heritage, so they could live in peaceful coexistence, but frequently tensions between them led to open warfare.

2. Terminology of nationality in the Bible. The word "nationality" does not appear in English versions, but there are several words, variously translated in these versions, which express the idea of nationality.

a. In biblical Hebrew. The most common Hebrew word for "nation" is עַם, denoting usually, not invariably, the nation Israel as the "people of God" (Judg. 20:2; II Sam. 14:13) or "people of Yahweh" (II Sam. 1:12; Ezek. 36:20). Other nations were designated usually by גּוֹי (Isa. 34:1*a*). Occasionally the word לְאֹם was employed to refer to other nations (Isa. 34:1*b*). A very common name for the nation—long familiar to readers of the KJV—was "children of Israel" (RSV usually "people of Israel"; Jer. 16:14).

b. In LXX Greek. The LXX translators usually rendered the common Hebrew word עַם by the Greek λαός (Isa. 10:22; Jer. 7:12). They employed the Greek ἔθνος for the Hebrew גּוֹי (Isa. 42:1; Jer. 16:19). For Hebrew לְאֹם they vacillated between ἔθνος (Hab. 2:13*c*) and ἄρχοντες, "rulers" (Isa. 41:1).

c. In NT Greek. The uses of λαός and ἔθνος follow much the same pattern as in the LXX: λαός used of the Jews (Luke 21:23; Heb. 11:25); of the Christians (Acts 18:10; I Pet. 2:10); ἔθνος of the Gentiles or other nations (Matt. 10:18; Rom. 15:9-10). In a few cases the latter term is used of the Jewish nation (Acts 10:22; 26:4).

3. Nationality in the OT. Most of the books of the OT have a strong interest in nationality, not so much in the political sense as in the social and religious sense. The first place we meet the idea of nationality is in the table of nations in Gen. 10, in which the Priestly writer (10:1-7, 20, 22-23) says all nations were descended from Noah's three sons. In Gen. 11:1-9, however, the J document attributes the division of mankind into separate language groups to the divine displeasure at their overweening pride in having built themselves a "city and a tower" to "make a name" for themselves "lest we be scattered"

(11:4). Thus, they felt, they would possess power for achievement which would make them self-sufficient. In the one case we have the origin of separate nationalities in natural kinship, divinely sanctioned; in the other, they came about in consequence of the arrogance of men.

a. In Israel. The first point at which Israel is named is Gen. 32:28—H 32:29, where Jacob's name is changed to Israel (*see* ISRAEL, HISTORY OF). But this is not the real beginning of nationality for the people Israel. We cannot truly speak of nationality as concerns ancient Israel until the establishment of the amphictyony (an association of tribes for protection of and worship at a particular shrine) at the common religious center of Shiloh (Judg. 18:31*b;* 21:19; I Sam. 1:3; 2:14*b;* 4:3*b*-4). Yet—and here interpreters differ—nationality may have been germinally present in the Mosaic age (*see* MOSES; COVENANT), was developed in the confederation of tribes during the conquest and settlement of Canaan, and was consummated at the time of the founding of the monarchy under Saul (I Sam. 11:15).

b. Israel an elect nation. The Israelite nation came to regard itself as the chosen people of Yahweh, its God (Deut. 7:6; I Kings 3:8; Jer. 13:11; *see* ELECTION).

The J writer had traced the idea of election as a central doctrine as far back as Abraham (Gen. 12:1-3: *see* ABRAHAM; PATRIARCHS), and continued the theme in the PENTATEUCH. This theme was carried through the subsequent history by succeeding writers. Israel was constantly reminded of its nationality as the "people of God"—a phrase often repeated, either directly (Judg. 20:2; II Sam. 5:2;) or indirectly as "my, thy, his people" (II Sam. 5:2; Pss. 14:7; 47:9).

The covenant at Sinai (Exod. 19:5-6) was usually looked upon as the seal of the divine choice, making Israel more than a political state; indeed, it was a religious community. The covenant was conditioned upon the nation's remaining faithful to her God. The prophets often denounced the nation and threatened calamity or destruction—loss of nationality—for breaking the covenant (Jer. 11:3-4, 8-11; Hos. 8:1-3; cf. Jer. 15:6-7; Ezek. 16:59-60). Yet always there was hope that the nation would repent and be restored.

c. Future of Israel's nationality. In view of the Israelite belief in the "everlasting" nature of the covenant (cf. Ezek. 16:60, etc.) it was inconceivable that her nationality should ever perish. The prophets nurtured this hope even in the darkest times. It was not a shallow optimism on their part, but based upon a trust in the mercy and forgiveness of the God of the covenant (Deut. 7:9) if the people remained faithful or repented when they had sinned against him. This hope of survival of nationality took several forms at various times in the history of Israel. Some passages predict that the whole nation will survive (Deut. 30:3-5; Hos. 2:14-15, 23; 14:1-7). Many postexilic interpolations express a similar idea (Isa. 11:12; Amos 9:14-15; Zeph. 3:20). Other apparently authentic passages, written at a time of impending or actual calamity, cling to the hope that a REMNANT will remain faithful or repent and survive (Isa. 1:9; 10:20-22; Amos 5:15). Certain late interpolated passages contemplate a messianic king (*see* MESSIAH), usually of Davidic lineage, who will in the future become ruler of the restored nation (Isa. 32:1-5; Jer. 33:14-17; Mic. 5:2-4). Still other late passages speak of the nations coming to acknowledge Israel's God (Isa. 2:2-4; 66:23; Zech. 14:16) or of the wealth of nations flowing to enrich Israel (Isa. 60:5, 11; cf. 45:14; Hag. 2:6-8). Additional late eschatological passages (*see* ESCHATOLOGY OF THE OT) look for a coming destruction of other nations or their harmlessness to Israel (Isa. 17:9; cf. 60:12; Jer. 30:10-11; Ezek. 28:24).

The most magnanimous hope for the enduring survival of Israel—and this would include other nations also—was that of Second Isaiah (Isa. 40–55), the prophet of the Exile, who hoped for a reconstitution of the nation in the homeland. This writer sounded a call for more than restoration of his own nation, for Israel, as the SERVANT OF THE LORD, is to "bring forth justice to the nations" (42:1) and to be a "light to the nations" (49:6). Israel, in short, is to bear responsibility for other peoples, far beyond her care for her own nationality and the harboring of her own national faith (cf. Ruth 1:22; 4:17-22; Jonah 4:11).

The actual history of succeeding periods did not bear out this burgeoning hope. Israel lost her political nationality under the subjection of the Babylonians, the Persians, and the Greeks. Yet through it all she maintained her status as a religious community, a holy nation, or people (Exod. 19:6; Deut. 26:19; cf. Lev. 20:26). In the time of Nehemiah and Ezra this meant a type of THEOCRACY with a strong sense of "peoplehood" and a stressing of purity of blood, prohibition of intermarriage with people of other nationalities, and strict obedience to the law. Following the Greek period came a century of religious, then political, freedom under the HASMONEAN kings. Then occurred the Roman conquest, marking once more for the Jews a cessation of political independence. But still for them nationality—of the religious kind—persisted.

4. Nationality in the Apoc. and the Pseudep. The OT book of Daniel attests the Jewish struggle for religious and political independence, as is true also of the apocryphal book of I Maccabees. The period was marked by a new sense of nationality, which is eloquently shown by I Macc. 3:59. The spirit of patriotism, marked by religious zeal, was kept alive by the book of Judith (11:10; 16:17-18). Again, the OT book of Esther, a secular work, introduced the feast of Purim and called for vengeance against the enemies of the Jews (4:14; 9:1-19). The Additions to Esther (apocryphal), supplying the religious element lacking in OT Esther, reveals also a high feeling for nationality (10:8-12; cf. 11:9). Even Ecclesiasticus (ch. 50), though a wisdom writing, carries a note, rare in such works, of nationalistic sentiment, urging that certain aspects of the national faith were beneficial in maintaining the separateness of the Jewish nation. Wisd. Sol. 6:1-5 states that the dominion of the kings of the nations derives from God (the God of Israel), and he shall punish them for not acknowledging this God (cf. Enoch 46:5). Jub. 22:12-20; 30:7-14 defend Jewish nationality by permitting no interrelations (intermarriage, interdining) with Gentiles. An opposing view is held by Test.

Benj. 1-6; 9:2; 10:5—showing a friendly attitude toward the Gentiles, for they too may be saved.

5. Nationality in the NT. The NT contains certain emphases on nationality similar to, and others differing from, those in the OT. The earliest followers of Jesus were Jews living under Roman rule, so they could not assert political nationality. But Jewish nationality in the religious sense remained strong. Many of the Jews who opposed Jesus, especially those of the official parties, did so on at least two grounds: either because in his teaching Jesus seemed to be thrusting aside many of the religious requirements of the national life, or because in proclaiming himself "King of the Jews" he was subverting Roman power (Mark 15:12, 26; cf. Luke 23:1-3). When the Christian movement actively reached out toward non-Jews, the problem changed, for here it came into conflict with imperial Roman claims which had their own implications of political (and religious?) nationality. But there is in the NT no hint of the organization of a Christian state, or any evidence of a sense of nationality on the part of the Christians, as there was in Judaism (*see* MAN AND SOCIETY).

a. Jesus' attitude toward nationality. Jesus himself was a Jew by nationality and never forswore it. In his teaching, while he minimized some of the legalistic aspects of the national religion, he centered his emphasis upon the spiritual core of the prophetic faith. What little Jesus may have said that had any bearing upon nationality would have had to do with the Roman state. He avoided political complications in his teaching, for he was concerned with man's relation to God and to his fellow men, and not to the Roman political order. Evidences of the nonpolitical character of his ministry are many (Luke 20:20-26; John 18:33-36; cf. Matt. 4:1-10). Yet, paradoxically, he was condemned to death as a revolutionist (Mark 15:26, 32*a*), owing in part to his accusers' distortion of the tribute saying (Luke 23:2). On the basis of this saying (Luke 20:21-25) it appears that Jesus accepted the state as belonging to the present world and as entitled to receive from its subjects the taxes necessary to its existence. Elsewhere we find that Jesus did not think of the state as the final form of society, in view of the end time (Mark 1:15; cf. Matt. 8:29; Greek *kairós*), which was to see the ushering in of the KINGDOM OF GOD. The kingdom of God was already being fulfilled (Matt. 12:28; Luke 17:20-21), and it is to come in its fulness in the future (Mark 14:25; Luke 13:29-30; *see* ESCHATOLOGY OF THE NT). Jesus appears definitely to have rejected the method of the ZEALOT to use force or the sword against the Roman state to re-establish Jewish political nationality (Matt. 26:52*b;* cf. 11:12).

b. Paul's attitude toward nationality. Paul enjoyed dual nationality, one political and one racial and spiritual, both of which he esteemed. He was a Roman citizen (Acts 22:25-28; 23:27; *see* PAUL), and he was of Jewish lineage and religion (Acts 21:39; 23:3; Phil. 3:3-6). This dual nationality sometimes proved advantageous to him during his missionary career.

The *locus classicus* for Paul's pronouncement on the Roman state is Rom. 13:1-2, often interpreted as calling for unconditional obedience of all subjects because the state is a divinely ordained institution. But if this passage is read in its context and considered with other verses in this chapter and in the light of at least one other passage (I Cor. 6:1-6), it may be seen that Paul took a position somewhat similar to that of Jesus. To Paul also the state is a necessary institution in this world (cf. I Cor. 6:3*b*), ordained of God (Rom. 13:1-2, 4), entitled to receive taxes (vss. 6-7; cf. Matt. 22:21); but in view of the end time (vs. 11), it is impermanent. Similar to Jesus' attitude but more explicit in this instance, is Paul's in viewing the state with critical judgment. His Roman nationality did not prevent him from being critical of Roman courts of law (I Cor. 6:1-6) and advising Christians to avoid civil lawsuits. Christians are changed men (vs. 11), and therefore they are not to bring their grievances to the courts to be judged by "unrighteous" (vs. 1) and "unbelievers" (vs. 6).

Paul shows in the final analysis that his gospel and the Christian movement transcend nationality (Rom. 1:16; 3:29; Gal. 3:26-28; Col. 3:11; cf. Rom. 11:11-15).

c. Other NT writers' attitudes toward nationality. In the book of the REVELATION the Roman Empire is called a "beast" (13:1-10). The term is not one that Paul would have used, but this book was written in a time of persecution of Christians by the Roman overlords, and this is the kind of imagery commonly employed by apocalypses to designate the persecuting power (cf. Dan. 7:3-6). Yet even while condemning the state, the book does not summon its Christian readers to revolt. Instead it advocates passive resistance, endurance, and faithfulness (13:10; cf. 2:10, 26), since the final victory and the destruction of the Roman state rests with God. At the same time the author sees a "new Jerusalem," by whose light the nations shall walk and the "kings of the earth shall bring their glory into it" (21:2, 24-26; cf. 7:9-10; 22:2). Allowing for the kind of imagery used here—partly borrowed from Isa. 60:11—it is uncertain whether these eschatological passages foresee the destruction or the survival of nationality.

Four other passages in the NT, most of them written probably to people facing or anticipating persecution, treat of Christian attitudes toward the Roman state. I Pet. 2:13-17; Tit. 3:1 offer much the same counsel to Christian readers as Paul did in Rom. 13:1-2. Heb. 10:32-39; I Pet. 3:13-17 (cf. 4:12-14) call for the Christians to manifest confidence, endurance, and faith in the presence of trials that have come or may come to them from the state. In any case, they know that everything will be resolved for them soon (Heb. 11:36-37; cf. I Pet. 1:6-7, 13).

One final passage, I Tim. 2:1-6 (cf. 4:10), advises Christians to pray "for all men, for kings and all who are in high positions," and states that God "desires all men to be saved and to come to the knowledge of the truth." This exhibits an attitude of magnanimity and universality similar to that which we observed in Paul and in the message of Second Isaiah. Nationality was thus transcended at certain points in both the OT and the NT.

See also CHURCH; MAN AND SOCIETY; NATIONS.

Bibliography. J. Pedersen, *Israel, Its Life and Culture,* vols. I-II (1926); W. F. Albright, *From the Stone Age to Christianity* (1940); M. Burrows, *An Outline of Biblical Theology* (1946); H. and H. A. Frankfort, *et al., The Intellectual Adventure of Ancient Man* (1946), chs. 3-4, 6, 11; W. Eichrodt, *Man in the*

OT, Studies in Biblical Theology (trans. K. and R. G. Smith; 1951); G. E. Wright, *The Biblical Doctrine of Man in Society*, Ecumenical Biblical Studies (1954); O. Cullmann, *The State in the NT* (1956).

J. W. Flight

NATIONS. In the biblical drama there are three dramatis personae: God, the nations, and Israel. The nations are the matrix of Israel's life, and the *raison d'être* of her whole history and calling. In the table of nations in Gen. 10 there are over seventy different ethnic groups mentioned, among which are the ancestors of the Hebrews. It includes the whole of mankind as known by the author, divided roughly into racial groups. It is unique in ancient literature. This interest in the nations accurately reflects the biblical emphasis on History as the vehicle of revelation and the nations as the object of God's redeeming purpose. Such preoccupation with history cannot be found in any other sacred literature of the world.

After the first period of world prehistory as presented in the Bible, which ends with the Flood, mankind makes a new start with Noah and differentiates into families, languages, lands, and nations (Gen. 10: 5, 20, 31). Each of these categories reveals the particularities of mankind from which arise the infinite varieties of social, political, cultural, and religious expressions which form the fabric of the life and history of mankind. From the very beginning the Bible takes these particularities seriously, and all through it they form the problem of Israel's life and the object of her mission, until, at the end, "a great multitude which no man could number, from every nation, from all tribes and peoples and tongues," stands before the throne of the Lamb (Rev. 7:9).

1. Terminology
   a. In the OT
   b. In the NT
2. The holy people among the nations
3. The nations in "patriarchal" theology
   a. Mission to the nations
   b. Goal of the nations' pilgrimage
   c. Rule over the nations
4. The nations in the "exodus" theology
   a. As enemies
   b. As temptations
   c. As observers
5. The nations in "exile" theology

Bibliography

1. Terminology. ***a. In the OT.*** There are three Hebrew words used more or less synonymously to refer to the nations; each of these may be used in the singular to refer to a particular nation, including the Hebrew nation.

עמים (cf. Ugaritic *'m*, "clan"; Vulg. *populi* or *nationes;* LXX ἔθνη or λαοί), "peoples." The original meaning of the word places stress on kinship as the basis of the group, though the limits may be a clan, a city, or a nation. In the singular it is the word most often used to refer to Israel as the עם of Yahweh. In this case the LXX translates λαός. The LXX uses ἔθνη for the plural in the Pentateuch, Joshua, and Judges; elsewhere both ἔθνη and λαοί are used.

גוים (Akkadian loan word from West Semitic, *ga'u*, "gang" or "group" [e.g., of workmen]; Vulg. *gentes;* LXX ἔθνη), "nations"; KJV alternately "heathen." This word stresses political and social rather than kinship bonds.

לאמים (cf. Akkadian *li'mmu*, "thousand"; Ugaritic *l'm*, "people"; Vulg. *populi;* LXX ἔθνη), "peoples"; KJV (incorrectly) "the people." According to I. Mendelsohn, this term originally meant a city which could produce a thousand soldiers in time of war. The word is often used in the prophetic books and the Psalms in parallel with גוים.

b. In the NT. The main term used in the NT is ἔθνη (Vulg. *gentes*), taken from LXX usage. It is translated "nations" thirty-seven times, "Gentiles" eighty-nine times, "heathen" three times, "pagans" twice.

"Gentiles" is used when the reference is interpreted to be to the non-Jewish nations in contrast to the Jews (Luke 21:24; Acts 9:15; I Cor. 1:23), or in contrast to followers of Christ (Matt. 6:7, 32; 10:5; 20:19; Eph. 2:11-12). "Nations" is used when the reference is interpreted as to all nations including the Jews (Matt. 24:9, 14; Mark 11:17; Rev. 7:9; etc.). Exceptions to be noted are Acts 13:19; 14:16; Gal. 3:8.

The NT uses λαοί, "peoples," in the plural only eight times, four of which are in parallel to ἔθνη, indicating Semitic style or LXX quotation (Luke 2:31; Acts 4:25, 27; Rom. 15:11), and four in Revelation in a formula with "nations, tongues, and tribes," reminiscent of Gen. 10; Dan. 3:4, 7; etc.

2. The holy people among the nations. Israel understood her origin to lie, not in her own soil or in a common ancestor, but among the nations, through the calling of and covenant with Yahweh. This is expressed in terms of generations in the early chapters of Genesis where the ancestry of Abraham is gradually differentiated from the sons of Noah, through the Semitic peoples of Mesopotamia and Arabia. In terms of ethnic origin, records show major sources among the Arameans (Deut. 26:5), Hittites, and Amorites (Ezek. 16:3), with elements being added in the early years from Egypt (Gen. 41:50; Lev. 24:10), the Kenites (Exod. 18:11; Num. 10:29 ff; Judg. 1:16; 4:11), Gibeonites (Josh. 9:3 ff), and others (*see* Proselyte for a list of Israelite aliens [גרים] who were gradually assimilated). The Mixed Multitude (Exod. 12:38) that went up from Egypt with the Hebrews also testifies to the heterogeneous nature of early Israel. To these we should add the Palestinian Habiru, who joined the Israelites at Shechem (Josh. 24), and the Canaanites (I Sam. 7:14).

We find the same understanding of origins in the NT. Jesus' common ancestry with all the nations of men is asserted in the Lukan genealogy (Luke 3:36-38); while in terms of geography, the new people of God is formed from all nations and peoples of the Roman Empire.

3. The nations in "patriarchal" theology. ***a. Mission to the nations.*** The Yahwist historian has so arranged his material that the scattering and mutual alienation of the nations of mankind (Gen. 11:1-9) is immediately followed by Yahweh's call of Abraham (12:1-3). Following the picture of the nations living under a curse, the new nation (גוי) is chosen to receive blessing and to be the means of the spread of this blessing to all nations: "By you all the families of the earth will bless themselves" (vs. 3). The reflexive form of the verb serves to underline the fact that in this motif, the nations will not merge their identity in a common humanity, but each will receive the particular blessing fitted to its character and destiny, like the particular blessings received by the sons (tribes) of Jacob (Gen. 49; Deut. 33; *see* BLESSINGS AND CURSINGS). The meaning of the covenant blessing is summarized in Deut. 28:1-14. It is this kind of blessing which is to spread to all the nations, according to this promise to Abraham. It implies universal peace, so that the well-being of one may not be at the expense of the others (cf. Mic. 4:1-4), and likewise the establishment of a covenant relationship between Yahweh and the nations as the normative ordering of their national lives in blessing.

The importance of this motif for the Yahwist is underscored by its fivefold repetition in Genesis (12:3; 18:18; 22:18; 26:4; 28:14; cf. the threefold repetition of the curse, Gen. 12:3; 27:29; Num. 24:9; cf. the Elohist version of the Joseph cycle, when "all the earth came to Joseph to buy grain"; 41:57).

The COVENANT word to Moses as the representative of Israel fits well into this motif (Exod. 19:3-6). Yahweh makes a nation (גוי) out of all the peoples to be a kingdom of priests for the whole earth. The association of the priest (*see* PRIESTS AND LEVITES) with the giving of torah and the cultic blessing gives the connection of the vocation of Israel with her mission to the nations as found in the J tradition of Abraham.

The motif comes to the surface again in the royal theology at the climax of a coronation hymn (Ps. 72:17):

> May men bless themselves by him [the king],
> all nations call him blessed!

The blessing received by God's nation would spread through her king to the nations of the earth, according to this hymn. We find the same idea in a harvest hymn (Ps. 67) where Yahweh's blessing of Israel involves the faith that this blessing must extend to the peoples at the end of the earth, though Israel's role in the process is not clear. The internationalism of Solomon's reign is seen in the prayer of Solomon that Yahweh will answer the petitions of the foreigner who prays toward the temple. This foreigner would then become by implication the bearer of Israel's blessing to his nation, so that, in time, "all the peoples of the earth" might know the name of Yahweh (I Kings 8:41-43).

The collapse of the royal theology as an interpretation of Israel's mission to the nations is seen in the use of the motif by Jeremiah, just before the end of the monarchy. If Israel will truly return to Yahweh, says Jeremiah,

> Then nations shall bless themselves in him
> [i.e., in Yahweh, not the king],
> and in him shall they glory (Jer. 4:2).

This conditional promise, however, comes at the penultimate climax of the poem (3:1–4:4), while the closing note is one of doom for the nation, including the kingship.

When Israel shares the curse of the nations (Gen. 11:1-9) by being herself scattered among them, a new interpretation of her vocation is given by Deutero-Isaiah. The picture is now held up of the humble servant going out to the nations with תורה and משפט, for which the nations eagerly wait (Isa. 42:1-4; cf. 51:4-5), as instruments of blessing. Light and covenant, opening of eyes for the blind, release for captives, are parts of the blessing which the servant brings (Isa. 42:7; 49:9; cf. 61:1). Thus Israel appears as the bearer of the great invitation to the peoples to turn to Yahweh for salvation (i.e., blessing; Isa. 45:22).

In the postexilic literature is found the prophecy that the blessing will one day be restored to Israel as at first (Zech. 8:13), and it will be so powerful that it will spread to her ancient enemies and oppressors, Assyria and Egypt (Isa. 19:24-25). The book of Jonah reveals a similar spirit in urging Israel to carry the word of God's judgment and mercy to Nineveh. Finally there is the recurrence of the royal theology in the prophecy of the messianic king who will command the blessing of peace upon the nations (Zech. 9:9-10).

Although this motif becomes fainter and fainter in the postexilic and postcanonical period, its persistence is seen in the review of Israel's history by Ben Sirach. Abraham's faith resulted in God's assurance "that the nations would be blessed through his posterity" (Ecclus. 44:21).

In the NT there appears a consciousness that the promise made to Abraham is now being fulfilled. The evangelists compile their narratives with this emphasis in mind. In the words of Simeon, Jesus is described as a "light for revelation to the nations" (RSV "Gentiles"; Luke 2:32). The early days of his life are placed, not in Israel, but among the nations —i.e., in Egypt (Matt. 2:15). He begins his ministry, not in Bethlehem or Jerusalem, but in "Galilee of the nations" (RSV "Gentiles"; Matt. 4:15). During his ministry there, many come from the neighboring peoples to him (Mark 3:8). Later he makes a journey into Tyre and Sidon, beyond the borders of the Jewish population. On this trip he exorcises the demon in a Phoenician girl whose mother recognizes him as the giver of the bread of life (Matt. 15:21-28; Mark 7:24-30), cures a deaf mute in the Decapolis (Mark 7:31-37; cf. Matt. 15:29-31) and feeds the four thousand in the wilderness (Matt. 15:32-39; Mark 8:1-10). Subsequently he heals the servant of a centurion, with commendatory words for the faith of this man from the nations (Matt. 8:5-13; Luke 7:1-10; cf. John 4:46-54, where this healing is taken as one of the great signs of Jesus' power), and a demoniac in Gerasa, whom he sends as a missionary of God's grace to his own people (Mark 5:19-20). The mission of the Seventy, recorded in Luke 10:1 ff, is intended to be to the nations. Jesus gives his disciples the mission of the servant as the light and salt of the world (Matt. 5:13-14; cf. Isa. 42:6; 49:6; and on the fact that salt may imply covenant, cf. Num. 18:19; II Chr. 13:5). His triumphal entry into Jerusalem revealed him as the messianic king who will bring the blessings of peace unto the nations (Matt. 21:5; cf. Zech. 9:9-10).

The early Christians knew that the risen Christ had sent them to the nations (Matt. 28:19-20; Mark 16:15; Luke 24:47; Acts 1:8) on a mission which is in a line with the eschatological signs of the earthly ministry of Jesus, the prophecies of Deutero-Isaiah, the royal (messianic) theology, the Sinai covenant, and the ancient promise to Abraham.

Paul found the purpose of the death of Christ to be that "in Christ Jesus the blessing of Abraham might come upon the nations" (RSV "Gentiles"; Gal. 3:14; cf. vs. 8). However, this fulfilment of the promise to Abraham in Christ brought Israel to a crisis, for it implied the end of her national aspirations. According to Jesus the nations themselves will judge Israel for her hardness of heart (Matt. 12:41-42). Peter quotes the promise to Abraham to encourage the Jews to take up their mission to the nations (Acts 3:25-26), and Paul quotes Isa. 49:6 as a judgment on the Jews for refusing to see their mission (Acts 13:47). Christ was meant to be a light to both the Jews and the nations; but since the Jews reject the light, the apostles turn to the nations (Acts 13:46; 18:6; 28:28). Paul finally concludes that it is in the providence of God that the very disobedience of Israel after the flesh should mean that the blessing would reach the nations through Christ (Rom. 11:11-12).

The last appearance of the mission of Israel to the nations is seen in Revelation, where in the midst of world catastrophe and the martyrdom of Christians there is an "angel flying in midheaven, with an eternal gospel to proclaim to those who dwell on earth, to every nation and tribe and tongue and people" (Rev. 14:6). It is the invitation of God in the style of Deutero-Isaiah: "Fear God and give him glory, for the hour of judgment has come" (vs. 7; cf. Isa. 45:22).

b. Goal of the nations' pilgrimage. If the J tradition of Genesis shows us the spread of the blessing of Yahweh to the nations through Israel's mission, the P tradition anticipates a reverse movement. In Gen. 17:3-8 the following promises are made to Abraham by El Shaddai: "I have made you the father of a multitude of nations. . . . I will establish my covenant between me and you and your descendants after you . . . , to be God to you . . . . I will give to you, and to your descendants after you, . . . all the land of Canaan." Here the "multitude of nations" (המון גוים) is parallel with the "descendants" of Abraham, who will inherit the covenant and the land of Canaan. Thus Canaan is seen as the gathering place for the nations and peoples as sons of Abraham and worshipers of El Shaddai.

The promise is repeated with variations twice to Jacob by Isaac (Gen. 28:3) and El Shaddai (35:11-12). Here the term קהל גוים is used, suggesting a religious assembly or CONGREGATION. Jacob passes on the same blessing to Joseph (48:4) with the words קהל עמים, and in the E tradition Jacob gives it to Ephraim (48:19), with the words מלא־הגוים.

The late date of the P narrative in written form should not be taken as an indication that this tradition is late. At the climax of an enthronement hymn of the monarchy stands the assertion:

> The princes of the peoples gather
> as the people of the God of Abraham
> (Ps. 47:9—H 47:10).

In Ps. 68, the procession of the tribes of Israel to the temple is suddenly joined by kings and people from Egypt and Ethiopia and the kingdoms of the earth, bearing gifts for the temple and singing praises to God. In both cases, cultic gatherings at the temple are seen as anticipations of the gathering of the nations and peoples of the earth to the shrine of Israel's God, who is over the nations.

In their hymns Israel called on "kings of the earth" to praise the name of Yahweh (Ps. 148:11-12; cf. 113; 117), while in their laments the deliverance of the sufferer prompts the worshiper to hope that one day

> All the nations thou hast made shall come
> and bow down before thee, O Lord
> (Ps. 86:9, quoted in Rev. 15:4;
> cf. Pss. 22:27-28—H 22:28-29;
> 102:18-22—H 102:19-23).

Although it does not occur elsewhere in the P tradition, the motif becomes most prominent in the exilic and postexilic eschatological prophecies. In Deutero-Isaiah we see the descendants of Israel returning from exile to Zion, in contexts which indicate that both the Diaspora Jews and the "survivors of the nations" are reckoned among these descendants (Isa. 44:1-5; 45:22-25; 49:12-20; 53:10). When, as a result of the suffering and mission of the Servant, the peoples at the ends of the earth are waiting for Yahweh's rule, then their survivors join themselves to Israel to converge on Jerusalem (55:5).

In later passages the motif appears in greater detail (*see* ESCHATOLOGY OF THE OT). Those from all the languages of the nations join the returning Jews (Zech. 8:21-23), and the alienation of Babel is removed when Yahweh gives them a pure speech so that they may call on his name (Zeph. 3:9). Kings lead their nations (Isa. 60:3, 11) in a great procession which extends "from sea to sea and from mountain to mountain" (Mic. 7:12), bringing the wealth of seas and nations on camels (Isa. 60:5-6), driving before them animals for sacrifice, and carrying the sons and daughters of Israel in their arms (vs. 4). They join themselves to Yahweh and become his people (Zech. 2:11) and go up every year to the Feast of Tabernacles in Jerusalem (14:16).

The object of the pilgrimage is the world sanctuary at Zion, which shall become a house of prayer for all nations (Isa. 56:7; cf. Mark 11:17). Zion is the navel of the earth (Ezek. 5:5; 38:12), the throne of Yahweh (Jer. 3:17), and the world mountain symbolizing the supremacy of Yahweh over all the nations and their gods (Ps. 99:9; Isa. 2:2-4 = Mic. 4:1-4; Isa. 66:20; Dan. 2:35): Then Zion will be called the birthplace of the nations (Ps. 87).

The eschatological pilgrimage will be climaxed by a great "festal banquet on Mount Zion," when Yahweh will invite "all peoples" and "remove the veil" that has alienated the nations from him, "destroy death," and "take away the reproach of his people" (Isa. 25:6-8). Thus do the nations become sons of Abraham and inherit Canaan as their land.

The Jewish mission to the nations in later postexilic times (*see* PROSELYTE) belongs properly to this motif. For the object of the mission was to make Jews of the people of the nations, to bring them to worship God at Jerusalem. It was also closely linked with Jewish nationalism and legalism. This was behind Jesus' severe condemnation of the proselyte movement (Matt. 23:15).

In the NT John the Baptist begins his preaching with a rebuke to the Jewish nationalists. Sons of Abraham are not confined to Israel according to the flesh (Matt. 3:9). Jesus spoke of a new temple (Mark 14:58) to be the universal sanctuary for the nations, and this lies behind his cleansing of the court of the Gentiles of the old temple (Mark 11:15-18). Jerusalem is the city on the hill, whose glory cannot be hidden, as the signal for the eschatological pilgrimage (Matt. 5:14; cf. Isa. 60:1-3). There will be a gathering of all nations before the throne of the King (Matt. 25:32), and the righteous among the nations (i.e., the sons of Abraham) will receive their inheritance in the kingdom of God.

In Acts, the joy of Jewish Christians at the response of the nations is a foretaste of the joy of the kingdom. The very purpose of Christ's becoming a servant to the Jews was that the nations might glorify God for his mercy (Rom. 15:7-13). It is possible that Paul saw the offering of the nations for the Jerusalem community as a kind of anticipation of the offering to be brought to Zion in the final age (Rom. 15:16, 25-27; cf. Isa. 60:5). Paul, indeed, sees the promise made to Abraham fulfilled in the justification of the nations by faith (Rom. 4:13-18).

The eschatological pilgrimage appears finally in Revelation. Those who have conquered the beast sing praises to the "King of the nations" (RSV mg.), with the prophecy that "all nations shall come and worship thee" (Rev. 15:1-4). After the seven bowls of wrath have been poured out and Satan finally destroyed, kings and nations come to the new Jerusalem with the "glory and the honor of the nations" to walk in the light of the glory of God, which is shed by the Lamb, who is the lamp, giving light to all that are in the house (Rev. 21:22-26).

*c. **Rule over the nations.*** Isaac blesses Jacob with the words:

> Let peoples serve you,
> and nations bow down to you
> (Gen. 27:29 J).

Jacob's blessing on Judah was that peoples would be obedient to a king from that tribe (49:10 J). In the oracle of Balaam, Israel is likened to a wild ox devouring the nations who are his adversaries (Num. 24:8 JE), while in Moses' blessing Joseph is seen as a bull pushing the peoples with his horns to the אפסים (Akkadian *'apsu,* "primordial abyss") surrounding the inhabited earth (i.e., the "ends of the earth"; Deut. 33:17 JE). According to Exod. 19:6, Israel is chosen for a vocation of kingship as well as priesthood, and the covenant blessing to obedient Israel in Deuteronomy is that "you shall rule over many nations, but they shall not rule over you" (Deut. 15:6).

As might be expected, this motif is prominent in the royal theology. Like the kings of other nations, the Israelite kings had to save their people from the enemies round about her (I Sam. 9:16; 10:1). The picture of success over enemies, cringing foreigners, slave peoples (Ps. 18:37-45—H 18:38-46), is not unique; nor is the claim to rule the whole earth different from that of the kings of Mesopotamia or Egypt. With the Israelites as with other peoples, the KING was adopted as "Son of God" at his coronation (Ps. 2:7). Thus as the regent of the God of the whole earth, and the champion of Israel his people, the king had the right to rule over the nations. In effect, this meant the ideal of an Israelite empire modeled after that of David, but stretching "from sea to sea, and from the River to the ends of the earth" (Ps. 72:8)—i.e., the whole inhabited world. This concept was like that of the great world powers, from whom it doubtless originally came.

But with Israel there was always the qualifying idea which arose at least as early as the monarchy itself, that the nations are not ultimately enemies to be crushed, but creatures of God meant for blessing. Israel, through her king, was thus meant to fulfil God's purpose among the nations of the world. Hence Ps. 72, which tells of the world rule of the Israelite king, ends with the Abrahamic blessing, while the meaning of "heritage" in Ps. 2:8 must be defined in terms of the family of Abraham's descendants (*see above*).

In the exilic period the motif of dominion over the nations is subordinated to that of the servant who suffers at the hands of the nations and is despised by rulers. However, in the eschatological time, kings and rulers will bow down to Israel and serve the servant (Isa. 14:1; 49:7, 22-23; 60:10-14; 61:5). Peoples come to rebuild Jerusalem as the servants of Israel, and bring the wealth of nations as tribute to her (Isa. 60:1-3, 10-18) because of the glory of God on Israel.

In the postexilic period the royal theology is applied to the Messiah, whose rule will extend "from sea to sea, and from the River to the ends of the earth" (Zech. 9:10). The dominion of Israel over the nations is most clearly expressed in Daniel. The stone "cut out by no human hands," which breaks the image into powder and then becomes a great mountain to fill the whole earth (Dan. 2:34-35), is God's kingdom, "which shall never be destroyed, nor shall its sovereignty be left to another people" (vs. 44). In another vision, the Son of man, who is identified with the "saints of the Most High," is given dominion, glory, and kingdom,

> that all peoples, nations, and languages
> should serve him;
> his dominion is an everlasting dominion,
> which shall not pass away
> (Dan. 7:14; cf. vss. 18, 26-27).

In the NT, Jesus assumes the role of the servant, and teaches his disciples not to try to "exercise authority" like the nations (Mark 10:42-45). Yet the Triumphal Entry is a kind of momentary unveiling of the future king of Zech. 9:9-10, who would rule the whole inhabited earth. The disciples ask seats at his side when he comes in glory (Mark 10:37). He appoints thrones for the Twelve to judge the tribes of Israel (i.e., the sons of Abraham; Luke 22:30). Paul reminds the Corinthian Christians that they (the saints) will rule the world (I Cor. 6:2).

Thus there is the anticipated fulfilment of the promises made to the patriarchs and to Israel, and repeated in Daniel. By his death, Christ

> ransom[ed] men for God
> from every tribe and tongue and people and nation,
> and hast made them a kingdom and priests to our God,
> and they shall reign on earth (Rev. 5:9-10).

In the midst of persecution comes the promise that to everyone who "conquers and who keeps [Christ's] works until the end," Christ will give "power over the nations, and he shall rule them with a rod of iron" (2:26-27).

At the PAROUSIA, Christ himself will come to take up his reign over the nations (Rom. 15:12), and the reign of his saints on earth with him will begin (Rev. 20:6; *see* MILLENNIUM). Although many features of Revelation agree with Jewish apocalyptic speculation of the time (*see* APOCALYPTICISM), the kingdom of the Lamb is established through suffering, and the reign of the saints as manifest on earth is expressed through self-sacrifice and service.

4. The nations in the "exodus" theology. ***a. As enemies.*** In the OT this motif is seen in three aspects corresponding to the historical periods of Israel's life.

a) The holy war. This aspect is uppermost in the period of the exodus from Egypt and the conquest of Canaan. The major facts are the defeat of the Egyptian power by Yahweh (Exod. 15:21) and the defeat of the inhabitants of Canaan (3:8). These events are retold throughout Israel's history (I Chr. 17:21; Pss. 44:2—H 44:3; 78:53-55; 80:8—H 80:9; 135:10; Acts 7:45; 13:19). In this period Israel was led by Yahweh into battle, and the holy war was just as much a part of their sacred obligation as cultic worship (*see* WAR, IDEAS OF). The outcome lay entirely with Yahweh, while the warrior's duty was simply to fight in his power against the enemy's superior numbers and armament.

b) The chastisement of Israel. The ideology of the holy war continues through David's reign; and, though after that it loses its sacral character, the role of the nations as enemies of Yahweh and his anointed is retained in the royal theology (Pss. 2; 18; 47; 110; 144; 147).

The prophets, however, gave a new dimension to Israel's understanding of the nations as her enemies. In the prophetic teachings, Israel's role in the holy war is reversed. Instead of following Yahweh into war, she becomes the victim of the attacks of her enemies by express appointment of Yahweh as his judgment on his people. She will suffer the fate of any conquered enemy in time of war—desolation, death, disease, and slavery.

Yet the picture is not completely consistent. For the nations themselves were under God's righteous judgment (Isa. 10:8-14; Amos 1–2). The "multitude of all the nations" who made up the Assyrian army gathered against Jerusalem in the days of Hezekiah would not succeed (Isa. 29:7-8), and Yahweh was about to "sift the nations with the sieve of destruction" (30:27-28).

It is in this category that many of the oracles against the foreign nations belong. They deal in general with God's judgment on the nations for their pride and violence, and are related to Amos 1:3–2:4. We may group them here for convenience, though they come from different periods. They include Egypt (Isa. 19:1-15; Jer. 46; Ezek. 29–32), Ethiopia (Isa. 18), Elam (Jer. 49:34-39), Babylon (Isa. 13; 14:3-23; 21:1-10; Jer. 50:1–51:58), Kedar (Jer. 49:28-33), Philistia (Isa. 14:28-32; Jer. 47; Ezek. 25:15-17), Edom (Isa. 34; Ezek. 25:12-14), Moab (Isa. 15–16; Jer. 48; Ezek. 25:8-11), Ammon (Jer. 49:1-6; Ezek. 25:1-7), Tyre (Ezek. 26:1–28:19), and Sidon (Ezek. 28:20-26).

In the later years of the monarchy, confidence in Yahweh's ultimate protection in spite of historical disaster was shaken. Habakkuk asked: "Is he [i.e, Babylon] to keep on . . . mercilessly slaying nations for ever?" (Hab. 1:17). Jeremiah saw the cruel and merciless people from the N country and asked Yahweh to destroy the "nations that know thee not" (Jer. 10:25). However, knowing the corruption within his own nation, Jeremiah could not ask for protection. He urged submission to the yoke of Nebuchadrezzar as the just judgment of Yahweh (27:12-15). But the nation was not ready for it. Judah was despoiled by Babylon. In the words of Lamentations:

> She dwells now among the nations,
> but finds no resting place
> (Lam. 1:3).

c) The vindication of Israel. After the fall of Jerusalem the nations appear mainly as oppressors and plunderers of Israel (Isa. 41:11-12; 42:23-25). The holy war against the nations has now become a holy suffering at the hands of and for the sake of the nations (50:4-6; 53:1-9). However, such humiliation is not to last forever. The tormentors of Israel will disappear before the victories of Cyrus (41:11-12). The despised slave will be exalted (49:7, 23; 52:13). Instead of being a vessel of no purpose (Hos. 8:8), the very purpose (חפץ, "will") of Yahweh will prosper in his hand (Isa. 53:10) after his intercession and sacrificial death for his enemies (vs. 12; cf. 52:15).

In the postexilic literature the holy-war motif appears again, but this time Israel no longer plays an active role. In the new exodus, Yahweh will overthrow the nations (Hag. 2:7), cast down those who have scattered Judah (Zech. 1:21), make the plunderers plunder for Israel (Zech. 2:8-9), and trample the people in anger (Isa. 63:6). Jerusalem herself will be a cup of reeling to all peoples (Obad. 16; Zech. 12:2).

In the early apocalyptic literature (Isa. 24–27; Ezek. 38–39; Joel 3—H 4; Zech. 9–14; *see* APOCALYPTICISM) the enmity of the nations toward Israel grows in intensity until the climactic struggle at Mount Zion, where Yahweh both summons them and punishes them for their violence on Israel. The author of Daniel sees this final struggle taking place in the persecution under Antiochus Epiphanes. This literature shows us the extreme enmity between the Jews and the nations, and the cry for revenge and vindication by direct intervention of God, born of intense suffering and faith in God. There is thus a complete polarization between Israel and the nations in contrast to the situation in earlier periods, so that the word גוים, ἔθνη ("nations" or "Gentiles"), becomes a technical term for the non-Jews as enemies and aliens. Yet the retention of the term is a significant link with the earlier tradition with its emphasis on the mission of Israel to the nations.

Yet there are, even in apocalyptic literature, hints that some among the nations will be saved in the final day, if they call on the name of Yahweh (Joel 3:12), and that there is a polarization within Israel as well as between Israel and the nations

(Zech. 14:14). The latter theme is developed fully in late apocalyptic literature where the punishment of the apostate Jews is described in vividly graphic terms.

In the NT, Israel is seen to exist among the nations as enemies. Now, however, the line is not between Jews and nations but between the Christian community and the nations. The Son of man will be handed over to the nations (Matt. 20:19; Mark 10:33; Luke 18:32), but also to "men" (Matt. 17:22; Mark 9:31; Luke 9:44), and rejected by the Jewish leaders (Matt. 16:21; Mark 8:31; Luke 9:22) and by "this generation" (Luke 17:25). Thus all nations, including the Jews, are at enmity with him, and his disciples will suffer a like fate (Matt. 24:9; cf. 10:7-18; John 15:18-20).

The alliance of Jew and Gentile against the followers of Jesus is a prominent theme of Acts (12:1-5; 14:2; 16:10-24; cf. II Cor. 11:26). The fulfilment of Ps. 2:1-2 is seen by the early church when "both Herod and Pontius Pilate, with the nations [RSV 'Gentiles'] and the peoples of Israel" gathered against God's Anointed (Acts 4:24-30). The promise of the risen Christ to Paul was to deliver him both from the people (Jews) and from the nations (Acts 26:17).

Suffering at the hands of the nations is a prominent theme in I Peter and Revelation, where the Roman persecutions are beginning to be felt. The nations play a large part in the apocalyptic drama in Revelation, as the enemies of God. They trample the Holy City for forty-two months (Rev. 11:2; cf. Luke 21:24). However, the time has come to destroy the destroyers (Rev. 11:18), so the mighty Babylon (Rome), who made the nations drunk (14:8; 18:3, 23; cf. Jer. 51:7), will be broken, and the nations will be defeated (16:19). Satan, deceiver of the nations, will be bound (20:3) during the reign of the saints, then released to deceive the nations at the four corners of the earth, so that the great apocalyptic battle takes place before the "camp of the saints" and the "beloved city" (20:7-9). In the end they are destroyed, Satan is cast into the lake of fire, and the dead are raised for judgment. This is the end of the nations as enemies of God and the prelude for the healing of the nations (*see above*).

b. As temptations. The first two commandments of the Decalogue define the nations, not as enemies, but as temptations for Israel. Her mission among the nations exposed her to these temptations, while her character as a holy nation demanded that she give her exclusive loyalty to Yahweh in cult and in social life. The ways of her neighbors were attractive to Israel—their fertility cult (cf. I Kings 14:24; II Kings 17:10; *see* FERTILITY CULTS), their occult arts (Deut. 18:9-14; Isa. 8:19), their sacral kingship (Deut. 17:14; I Kings 8:5;) and royal splendor (I Kings 4:22-26), their cultural achievements (I Kings 6–7), military power (Isa. 30:1-5; 31:1-3; Jer. 2:18; Hos. 8:9-10), and aristocracy (Amos 3:14–4:3; Mic. 2:1-2) all exercised a fascination on her. There was also the pressure of the overlord to adopt the imperial cult (II Kings 16:10-18).

The danger to which Israel was exposed in her life in Canaan is expressed repeatedly in Deuteronomy (6:14; 12:2, 30; 13:7; 18:9, 14; 29:16-18; cf. Josh. 23:7, 12; Judg. 2:12), and the fear of contamination lies behind the command to exterminate the peoples of the cities which she is to attack (Deut. 20:16).

The mystery of the great systems of idolatry in the presence of the God of the nations was not a subject of much speculation on the part of the Hebrews. However, in Deuteronomy they are seen as a kind of interim concession by Yahweh, who allotted the nations the sun, moon, and stars to worship (Deut. 4:19; cf. LXX of Deut. 32:8; Acts 14:16-17). Jeremiah even implies a certain praise of the loyalty of the nations to their gods, which is in contrast to Israel's faithlessness to her own God (Jer. 2:11), while in Mal. 1:11 it is said that Yahweh's name is great among the nations.

It is also important to note that cultural borrowing from the nations is not in every case condemned in itself. Hymns to Baal could be changed to Yahwist hymns while retaining literary form and style (e.g., Ps. 29). Myths from Mesopotamia could be so converted as to express the Hebrew understanding of God and man as sharply opposed to the Mesopotamian view. One stratum of early tradition makes no criticism of the kingship (I Sam. 9:1–10:16), which is fully accepted by Israel, and later, forms the basis for messianic prophecy. The agricultural festivals which were borrowed from Canaan are transformed by Israel, and the prophets' criticism is only of their corruption. Cultic practices in use in the temples of the nations could be adapted for Israelite priestly purposes as long as they did not threaten loyalty of the nation to Yahweh. The same is true of the LAW and WISDOM, where there was much in the way of borrowing. In all such borrowing, Israel's ideal response should be:

> For all the peoples walk
> each in the name of its god,
> but we will walk in the name of Yahweh our God
> for ever and ever (Mic. 4:5).

However, the prophetic and historical literature gives ample evidence that the strain imposed by such existence was too great. In the intense struggle in which prophets, nomadic idealists (*see* RECHABITES; NAZIRITES), and reforming kings all tried to recall her to faithfulness, Israel met defeat after defeat from inner corruption rather than outward attack, and the end result was her destruction as a nation. The Deuteronomist historians are careful to document the record (I Kings 11:2; 14:24; II Kings 16:3; 17:8, 11, 15; 21:2, 9; cf. I Chr. 5:25; 16:26; Ps. 106:34-37; Jer. 9:26; Hos. 7:8). The prophets denounce Israel as a faithless wife turned harlot (Jer. 5:7-8), and the reflection of a psalmist summarizes the whole of Israelite history to the Exile:

> They mingled with the nations
> and learned to do as they did
> (Ps. 106:35).

In the Exile, Israel reacts in two different manners to the temptation of the nations. First there is a revulsion from the ways of the nations among whom she had been cast. "What is in your mind shall never happen—the thought, 'Let us be like the nations, like the tribes of the countries, and worship wood and stone' " (Ezek. 20:32). The Exile was, according to Ezekiel, a shock to call Israel to repentance. Yahweh would then restore Israel as a holy people and thus vindicate his own holiness in the eyes of the nations (36:23).

According to Deutero-Isaiah, the temptation for Israel in exile is to renounce her faith in the purpose of the Lord of history, to give up to despair, or to adopt a historically irrelevant or simply nationalistic religion like that of the nations. Israel is not to manifest the holiness of God by withdrawing from the nations, but by going to them to proclaim his Lordship (Isa. 52:7); their gods are discredited. While she does this, she is to keep free from defilement (vs. 11) and in the face of suffering maintain her faith in her vindicator (50:8).

In the postexilic period, Israel's effort to maintain her cultural identity without political power led to her virtual separation from the peoples in order to exclude their "pollutions" and immoral practices (Lev. 18:24; Ezra 6:21; 9:1-2, 11, 14; 10:2; Neh. 10: 28, 30-31). Contact with the surrounding nations, and especially intermarriage with them, posed a threat to the very existence of the people of God. Her emphasis on law and holiness enabled her to maintain her separate existence and gave the Hasidim the will to resist forcible Hellenization under the Seleucids. "Be it known to you, O king, that we will not serve your gods or worship the golden image which you have set up." (Dan. 3:18.)

On the other side there was considerable borrowing from Iranian and Hellenistic cosmic speculation and philosophy, while a party favoring accommodation with Hellenism grew up under the leadership of the priestly group (I Macc. 1:1-15; II Macc. 4:10-14).

The temptations posed by the nations in the NT are seen in the descriptions of their way of life as over against that of the people of God. They salute their brethren only (Matt. 5:47), pray loudly in public places (6:7), and seek after material things (6:32; Luke 12:30). They are "darkened in their understanding, alienated from the life of God because of the ignorance that is in them, due to their hardness of heart" (Eph. 4:18; cf. Col. 1:21; I Thess. 4:5; I Pet. 4:3), led astray by speculation (Col. 2:8), given up to immorality (I Cor. 5:1, where "pagans" is the translation; cf. Rom. 1:26-32), idolaters (I Cor. 10: 20 ["pagans"]; 12:2 ["heathen"]; cf. Rom. 1:23). To "learn Christ" was to put off the old nature, that of the nations, and put on the new, that of Christ, which was "created after the likeness of God in true righteousness and holiness" (Eph. 4:20-24).

On the other hand, this separation from the nations was not a withdrawal from them. Jesus mixed freely with the irreligious people of his day, including harlots and tax collectors. The risen Christ sent his disciples (Matt. 28:19; Acts 1:8) and his church (Acts 10:1-43) out among the nations to mingle with them, to proclaim and serve in their midst. Paul became "all things to all men" (I Cor. 9:22), and Peter implied a conversation with the nations in counseling his readers to "be prepared to make a defense to any one who calls you to account for the hope that is in you" (I Pet. 3:15).

In Revelation, the community of saints is composed of those who have resisted the temptation under persecution to worship the emperor (Rev. 13: 4, 14-17; 14:9-12; 15:2), and who have not been deceived by the sorcery of Babylon (18:23). In the final destruction of Babylon and Satan, the temptation of the nations for Israel is removed, and all nations walk with Israel in the light of the Lamb (21:24).

*c. **As observers.*** When God brought Israel out of Egypt with mighty signs and wonders, the nations were looking on in fear (Exod. 15:14). In the biblical drama they are cast in the role of witnesses, for Israel is the primary locus of God's redeeming activity among the nations, and they will be able to behold his salvation in the saved people. They will hear God's word as Israel carries it to them, and they will understand God's way when they see suffering love in Israel and the true Israelite.

The nations are pictured as fearing Yahweh because of his power, displayed in Israel (Exod. 15:14; Josh. 4:24; Pss. 77:14—H 77:15; 98:2-3), or as fearing Israel because of Yahweh's power (Deut. 2:25; 28:10; I Chr. 14:17; Neh. 6:16).

On the other hand, they witness the wisdom and understanding of Israel (Deut. 4:6-7; 28:10) especially in the person of Solomon, Israel's great sage (I Kings 4:31, 34; 10:6-8; cf. also the wisdom psalm which Israel addresses to all peoples, Ps. 49:1—H 49:2; cf. Isa. 49:1).

Yahweh's motive for redeeming Israel is that the nations may know his power and name (I Kings 8: 60; Ps. 67). Moreover, his acts are motivated in part on the basis of what the nations will think. Moses appeals for mercy with the words: "Now if thou dost kill this people as one man, then the nations who have heard thy fame will say, 'Because the LORD was not able to bring this people into the land which he swore to give them . . .' " (Num. 14:15-16). In Ezekiel the chief motive for the restoration of Israel is that Yahweh's name might not be "profaned" among the nations (Ezek. 20:9, 14, 41; 36:23, 36; 37:28).

Therefore, the nations and peoples of the earth are exhorted to praise the God of Israel for his deliverance of his people and, by implication, his deliverance of all who turn to him (Deut. 32:43; Pss. 47:1—H 47:2; 66:4-12—H 66:5-11; 68:32—H 68:33; 96:7-9=I Chr. 16:27-28; Pss. 117:1; 148:11; Jer. 31:7), or it is said that they do now or will in the future praise Yahweh (Pss. 46:10—H 46:11; 97:6) and that they will behold his glory on Jerusalem (Isa. 60:2; Jer. 33:9) or his vindication of his people (Isa. 52:10; 61: 11; 62:2, 10-11; Mic. 7:16). For this reason Israel herself declares Yahweh's praise among the nations for them to hear and know him (Pss. 9:11—H 9:12; 18:49-50—H 18:50-51=II Sam. 22:50-51; Pss. 57: 9—H 57:10=108:3—H 108:4; 96:3, 10).

When Yahweh is about to judge his people for their unfaithfulness, he summons the peoples as witnesses and explains the reasons for his action (Mic. 1:2; cf. Jer. 6:18). In the midst of a controversy with his people, Yahweh suddenly says:

> Ask among the nations,
> who has heard the like of this?
> (Jer. 18:13; cf. 2:10).

The nations observe the fate of Israel as a result of her disloyalty to her God, and use her name for a curse word or a joke among themselves instead of the blessing she was meant to be (Deut. 28:37; I

Kings 9:7=II Chr. 7:20; Neh. 5:9; Ps. 44:13-14; Jer. 22:8; 26:6; 29:18; 44:8; Ezek. 5:14-15; 20:48; 22:4; Joel 2:17; Mic. 6:16).

In Deutero-Isaiah, Yahweh calls his servant to the attention of the nations twice with the dramatic word: "Behold!" The first time is at the close of the trial of the nations (Isa. 41:1–42:4), when the gods have been discredited and the nations fasten their gaze on the servant people. The second is in 52:13, where the nations fix their eyes on the exalted Servant, whom they had so misunderstood:

for that which has not been told them they shall see,
 and that which they have not heard they shall understand
 (vs. 15).

Their reaction is to shut their mouths in silent surprise and respect (Isa. 52:15; cf. Mic. 7:16), and then they give their testimony in Isa. 53:1-9:

But he was wounded for our transgressions,
 he was bruised for our iniquities;
upon him was the chastisement that made us whole,
 and with his stripes we are healed (vs. 5).

In the NT the salvation of God has been prepared "in the presence of all peoples" (Luke 2:31). The setting for Jesus' early ministry is "Galilee of the nations" (RSV "Gentiles"), in plain sight of those who "sat in darkness" (Matt. 4:15-16; cf. Isa. 9:1—H 8:23). In Phoenicia and Transjordan, as well as in Galilee, the peoples join the "lost sheep of the house of Israel" in gathering about him (Matt. 4:24; Mark 3:7; Luke 6:17). When he was dying on the Cross, Matthew reports the soldiers there watching him, one of them exclaiming at the end: "This was a son of God!" (Matt. 27:36, 54).

The early Christians were aware that they were living under the gaze of the nations. "Maintain good conduct," says Peter, "among the nations [RSV 'Gentiles'], so that in case they speak against you as wrongdoers, they may see your good deeds and glorify God on the day of visitation" (I Pet. 2:12; cf. Matt. 5:16). Their suffering at the end of history would be under the gaze of the "men from the peoples and tribes and tongues and nations," who gaze on the dead bodies of the two witnesses whom they have killed (Rev. 11:1-3, 7-9). Later, the witnesses are raised, and "in the sight of their foes" (vs. 12) they ascend to heaven.

5. The nations in "exile" theology. Israel is often pictured as God's flock (Ps. 100:3) under his care and that of his shepherds. Micaiah Ben Imlah saw the army of Israel in defeat as a flock scattered on the mountains, like sheep that have no shepherd (I Kings 22:17). The threat to scatter Israel for her disobedience originated in the wilderness, almost at the moment God had been gathering her from the slavery of Egypt (Ps. 106:27), although the covenant curse (Deut. 4:27-28; 28:36-37, 62-68; Jer. 9:16; Ezek. 4: 13; 12:15; cf. Pss. 44:11, 22; 106:41; Zech. 7:14) is not without a promise to gather a repentant remnant (Deut. 4:29-31; 30:1-4).

In Gen. 11:1-9, mankind is scattered abroad in division and alienation from one another, but Israel is gathered from among them in Abraham and at the Exodus. In the midst of the curse of scattering, there is the blessing of gathering. At the destruction of At the destruction of Samaria and Jerusalem, Israel receives the same curse as the nations and is scattered among them. However, there is a difference. For the scattered people is still the covenant people. The scattering is interpreted by the exilic prophets in two ways. The first is repentance: "They shall know that I am Yahweh, when I disperse them among the nations and scatter them through the countries" (Ezek. 12:15). The second is that of witness, seen negatively by Ezekiel: "that they may confess all their abominations among the nations" (vs. 16), and positively by Deutero-Isaiah. The silent suffering of the sheep led to slaughter among the nations, with no shepherd to save them (Isa. 53:7; cf. Ps. 44:11), is redemptive, and part of the purpose of God (Isa. 53: 10). The curse ("smitten by God" [vs. 4]) is changed into a blessing ("we are healed" [vs. 5]). The nations who like sheep are scattered ("gone astray" [vs. 6]) behold the silent suffering of the Lamb led to the slaughter as a bearing of their iniquities (vss. 6, 11). And so the scattering of judgment is reinterpreted as the scattering of mission.

Jesus saw the people as sheep without a shepherd (Matt. 9:36), and felt himself with a special mission to the scattered (lost) sheep of Israel (Matt. 10:6; 15: 24; cf. I Pet. 2:25, where the life of the nations is seen as that of scattered sheep, reminiscent of Gen. 11:1-9; Isa. 53:6). He scattered his disciples as sheep among wolves when he sent them out to proclaim the kingdom of God (Matt. 10:16). At the death of Jesus, the disciples will be scattered in tribulation (John 16:32-33), but this must be associated with the scattering of mission among the nations (Matt. 28: 19). Persecution in Jerusalem after the martyrdom of Stephen results in the scattering of the Christians in tribulation and mission throughout the region of Judea and Samaria (Acts 8:1).

The companion motif to scattering is gathering. Jeremiah sends out the word to all nations that "he who scattered Israel will gather him." He will keep Israel as a shepherd keeps his flock, with tenderness and love (Jer. 31:10; cf. Isa. 40:11; 54:7; Ezek. 11: 14-21; 20:34; 28:25; 34:11-16, 28-29; Zech. 10:8-12).

The postexilic community understood its own gathering as a foretaste of the final gathering (Neh. 5:8, 17), and the prayer for the gathering of the scattered flock of Israel has been a petition on the lips of the Jews ever since (Ps. 106:47).

In Matt. 25:32 ff, the picture of the gathering of the scattered flock is extended to the nations, for whose gathering Jesus dies (John 10:16; 11:51-52; cf. Heb. 13:20; I Pet. 2:25).

Thus, the purpose of God is fulfilled as Israel is scattered in tribulation and mission among the nations, then gathered symbolically in worship and praise from the nations, bringing with them the sons of the kingdom in anticipation of the final gathering of every nation before the throne of the Lamb (Rev. 7:9), to join the marriage supper of the Lamb (19:9) and partake of the fruit of the tree of life and its leaves, which are "for the healing of the nations" (22:2).

Bibliography. A. Bertholet, *Die Stellung der Israeliten und der Juden zu den Fremden* (1896). A. Causse, *Israël et la vision de l'humanité* (1924). H. Schmökel, *Yahweh und die Fremdvölker* (1934). B. Sundkler, "Jesus et les païens," *RHPR*, 16 (1936), 462 ff. W. Eichrodt, "Gottesvolk und die Völker," *Evangelische*

Missionsmagazin (1942). H. H. Rowley, *The Missionary Message of the OT* (1944); *The Biblical Doctrine of Election* (1950). S. Aalen, *Die Begriffe 'Licht' und 'Finsterniss' im AT, im Spätjudentum, und in Rabbinismus* (1951). T. W. Manson, *Jesus and the Non-Jews* (1955). E. Jacob, *Theology of the OT* (1958), pp. 217-23, 231-32, 317-44, contains good bibliographies. J. Jeremias, *Jesus' Promise to the Nations* (1958). E. J. HAMLIN

NATURAL HISTORY. *See* FAUNA; FLORA.

NATURE, NATURAL PHENOMENA. *See* WORLD.

NAUM. KJV form of NAHUM 2.

NAVE. 1. היכל (lit., "temple, palace," from Sumerian *E.GAL;* Akkadian *ekallu,* "great house"), the main room of the temple, between the vestibule and the inner room (I Kings 6 *passim;* 7:50 [KJV "temple"]; II Chr. 3:4-5, 13; 4:22 [KJV "house"]; Ezek. 41 *passim* [KJV "temple"]). *See* TEMPLE, JERUSALEM.

2. KJV translation of גב (I Kings 7:33), a block or center of a wheel through which the axle passes. This was a detail of the wheels of the stands of bronze in the temple. The reference is more probably to the rim (so RSV) of the wheels. E. M. GOOD

3. KJV Apoc. form of NUN.

NAVEL STRING [שר] (Ezek. 16:4; FLESH in Prov. 3:8; RSV mg.-KJV NAVEL). The mention of an uncut navel string was Ezekiel's dramatic way of reminding his people that their very survival was an act of mercy on the part of God (16:1-14). Israel, the foundling child, was heathen by parentage (vs. 3); she did not receive even the most elementary medical attention at her birth (vs. 4: "Your navel string was not cut"); and she was shortly discarded upon the open field, presumably to die of exposure (vs. 5; cf. 33:27; for the suggestion that female infants were sometimes buried alive among the ancient Arabs, see the Qur'an 81:8). God found and loved and cared for this abandoned child.

Vs. 4 suggests the simple duties of a midwife. Then, as among modern Arab peasants, these included the cutting of the navel cord (for indications of the importance of the navel and the belly muscles, see Job 40:16; Prov. 3:8 RSV mg); rubbing the child with salt, water, and oil; and wrapping him in swaddling cloths for seven days.

Bibliography. E. W. G. Masterman, "Hygiene and Disease in Palestine in Modern and in Biblical Times," *PEQ* (1918), p. 118. H. F. BECK

NAZARENE năz'ə rēn. A NT term used almost exclusively as an appellation of Jesus (as to Acts 24:5, *see below*). Two forms occur in the Greek text: Ναζαρηνός and Ναζωραῖος. Mark prefers the first; Matthew, John, and Luke, the second (Luke 4:34; 24:19 derive from older tradition). Yet there is no noticeable difference in meaning. In the view of the NT authors this appellation is connected with Jesus' origin from Nazareth (Matt. 2:23; the prophecy here alluded to can hardly be identified; see the Commentaries); consequently it is synonymous with the expression "the one from Nazareth" (ὁ ἀπὸ Ναζαρέθ; Matt. 21:11; Mark 1:9; John 1:45; Acts 10:38). Figs. NAZ 7-8.

Such a derivation, however, presents a problem with regard to the unusual spelling of the second form, Ναζωραῖος. To be sure, in Aramaic it is not philologically impossible, as many scholars assume, to relate the term to "Nazareth" (Aramaic נצרת): the difficult ω could stand for an unaccented, indistinct vowel. The transcription of צ with ζ is attested elsewhere; and besides, the spelling of Jesus' home town varies in the tradition (*see* NARAZETH), so that no fixed rules can be set up for building the adjectival derivative. The Syriac equivalent for both Greek forms is *nāṣ^e^rājā;* in this form the word was later carried over as a designation for the Christians into Arabic-Mohammedan, Armenian, and Persian usage. Notwithstanding these considerations, it remains unexplained how in Greek the unusual form Ναζωραῖος could maintain its position so consistently alongside the simpler form Ναζαρηνός, which was, after all, available. Furthermore, according to Acts 24:5, not only Jesus, but also the Christians were called Ναζωραῖοι; it would certainly be unusual if they were referred to as "people from Nazareth."

Now in Acts 24:5, and on the tongue of a Jew, reference is made to the *sect* of Nazarenes (ἡ τῶν Ναζωραίων αἵρεσις); and elsewhere the term appears outside the Christian community as a Jewish term of abuse for the Christians (נוצרים in the Talmud; Ta'an. 27*b,* or in the famous twelfth section of the Eighteen Benedictions according to the Palestinian Recension; see further Tert. Marcion IV.3; Jerome Commentary on Isa. 5:18 and *passim*). This makes it probable that originally, prior to the connection with the name of the locality Nazareth, the term was the name of a Jewish sect or heresy, derived from the root נצר, "observe," and meaning "observant," "devotee," a term later used of the Christians (see Celsus in Origen *Against Celsus* 7.8). M. Lidzbarski added support to this thesis especially by pointing to the self-designation of the Mandeans, a pre-Christian Gnostic sect which often called itself נצוראיא. It is, of course, possible that we have to do here simply with the self-designation of a Jewish Christian group united with the Mandeans; it was precisely heretical Jewish Christian groups which perpetuated the ancient designation of Christians as Ναζωραῖοι, according to patristic allusions (Epiphanius Panar. I, Haer. 29,6; Jerome Commentary on Isa. 11:1). However, Epiphanius lays particular emphasis upon a distinction between Jewish Christian Ναζωραῖοι and a pre-Christian Jewish sect of Νασαραῖοι (Panar. I, Haer. 18). If such a sect really did exist, then we have in its name "observants" the basic term which has been preserved as נוצרים for Jesus and the Christians, as Ναζωραῖοι (=Nazoraei) for the Jewish Christians, and as נצוראיא for the Mandeans.

Bibliography. In addition to the Commentaries on Matt. 2:23, see especially H. H. Schaeder, *TWNT,* IV (1942), 879-84. See further: F. C. Burkitt, "The Syriac Forms of the NT Proper Names," *Proceedings of the British Academy* (1911-12), pp. 391-400. G. F. Moore, "Nazarene and Nazareth," in F. J. Foakes-Jackson and K. Lake, eds., *The Beginnings of Christianity,* I (1920), 426-92. H. Zimmern, "Nazoräer (Nazarener)," *ZDMG,* 74 (1920), 429-38. M. Lidzbarski, *Man-*

däische Liturgien (1920), pp. xvi-xix; *Ginza: Das grosse Buch der Mandäer* (1925), pp. ix-x. H. Smith, *JTS,* 28 (1927), 60. W. F. Albright, *ZAW,* 44 (1926), 229-30; *JBL,* 65 (1946), 397-401. M. Black, *An Aramaic Approach to the Gospels and Acts* (1946), pp. 143-46. J. S. Kennard, *JBL,* 66 (1947), 79-81. H. J. Schoeps, *Theologie und Geschichte des Judenchristentums* (1949), pp. 9-10. B. Gärtner, *Die rätselhaften Termini Nazoräer und Iskariot* (1957). P. Winter, *NTS,* 3 (1957), 138, note 1.

O. CULLMANN

NAZARENES, GOSPEL OF THE [Ναζαρηνοί]. An Aramaic Targ. of the canonical Gospel of Matthew, current in the second century in Aramaic-speaking N Syria. Endless confusion has been caused by Jerome's utterly unwarranted claim to have translated this "Gospel According to the Hebrews . . . which Origen often uses," which has suggested that this Aramaic gospel was not only the original form of the canonical Matthew but to be identified with the actually very different Gospel According to the Hebrews (*see* HEBREWS, GOSPEL ACCORDING TO THE). Jerome seems to have first heard of this Aramaic Targ. from Apollinaris, who used it heavily in his own commentaries and appears to have believed it to be the original form of the gospel. Jerome's many citations from this "gospel which the Nazarenes use" are apparently largely from the commentaries of Apollinaris. At the time he was writing his *History* (*ca.* 325), Eusebius appears to have known this gospel only by hearsay (Hist. V.10.3-4); later, in the *Theophany,* he has come to know it at first hand, apparently in the eight-year interval having obtained a copy of it for the library at Caesarea. It was apparently this copy which Jerome subsequently saw for the first time and thereafter insisted that he had for the first time translated into Greek and Latin. In addition to taking material from Apollinaris, who had actually used this Aramaic Targ., Jerome also made free use of extracts from Origen, which passages the latter scholar had cited from the totally different Gospel According to the Hebrews. The researches of A. Schmidtke and B. W. Bacon have done much to untangle the confusion so largely caused by Jerome's unscrupulous claims and misstatements, and to suggest that most of the citations from Jerome, which are now conveniently collected by M. R. James (*see bibliography*), as stemming from the Gospel According to the Hebrews are more safely to be ascribed to this quite different Aramaic Gospel of the Nazarenes, which appears to have been quite as complete as the canonical Matthew, containing, as it did, the infancy chapters, and to have had frequent variant readings and embellishments—as, e.g., the man with the withered hand was a mason; it was not the veil but the lintel of the temple, of wondrous size, which fell at the time of the Crucifixion; Jesus' reply to his mother's suggestion that they go to John for baptism; the reply of the rich man, who scratched his head in perplexed displeasure at Jesus' word that he demonstrate his love for his poor neighbor. Many variants are now preserved as marginal readings, with the rubric τὸ 'Ιουδαϊκόν (i.e., "the Hebrew gospel") in the so-called Zion MSS, which were apparently made in Jerusalem in the late fourth or fifth century.

Bibliography. M. R. James, *The Apocryphal NT* (1924), pp. 3-6. For amplification of the identification sketched above, see A. Schmidtke, "Judenchristliche Evangelien," *Texte und Untersuchungen,* vol. 37 (1911); "Zum Hebräerevangelien," *ZNW,* vol. 35 (1936). B. W. Bacon, *Studies in Matthew* (1930), pp. 478-95. *See also* bibliography under APOCRYPHA, NT.

M. S. ENSLIN

NAZARETH năz'ə rĭth [Ναζαρέτ, Ναζαρέθ (*the best attested of the many variants*), *probably from* נצר, guard place, watchtower, *or* נצר, sprout, shoot (*so* Matt. 2:23), *in spite of the difficulty of the transliteration of* צ by ζ *which occurs elsewhere in* Gr. *and which here may be due to the false analogy of* Ναζιραῖος (Nazirite); *above etymology supported by* Syr. *Nâṣrat,* Arab. *Nâṣirah*]. A village of Lower Galilee; home of Joseph, Mary, and Jesus.

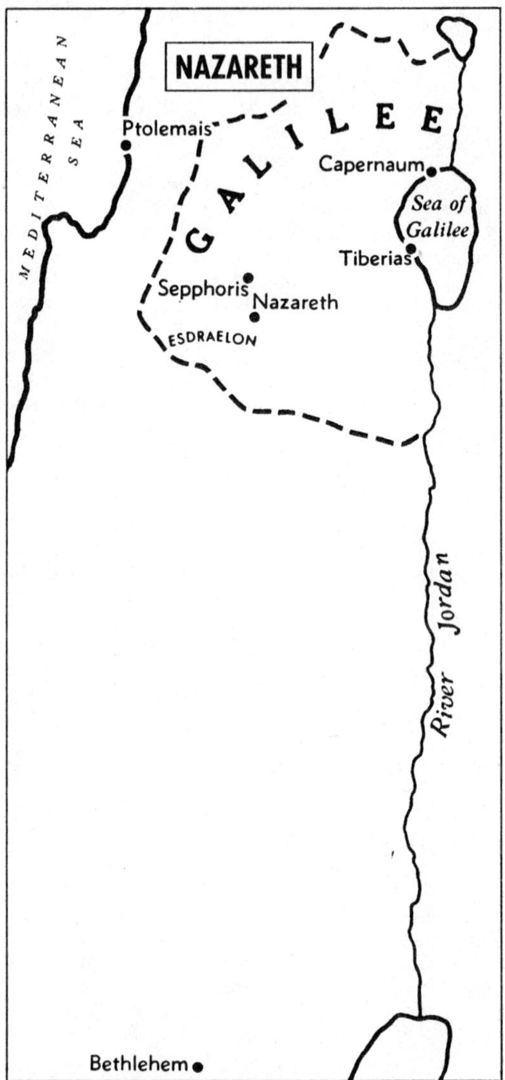

1. Location and description. The identification of the site of the ancient village with the modern Nazareth (*see above*) is generally accepted. Questions have arisen because there is no mention of Nazareth in the OT, the Talmud, the Midrash, or Josephus. This is understandable if it was an insignificant village (cf. John 1:46). Aside from the NT, the earliest evidence for Nazareth is from Julius Africanus (A.D. 170-240), as cited by Eusebius (Hist. I.7.6-12), but there is no suggestion that it had just been founded and was not in existence before the birth of Jesus. This location is confirmed by the *Onomasticon* (Jerome *De Situ et Nom. Loc. Hebr.* 255).

Nazareth lies to the N of the Plain of Esdraelon in a valley or basin open only to the S. The village is on the sides of a hill facing to the E and the SE. It is *ca.* fifteen miles from the Sea of Galilee and *ca.* twenty miles from the Mediterranean. The altitude is *ca.* 1,300 feet above sea level. The altitude and the protected position make for a moderate climate. The climate and the rainfall are favorable to vegetation, but the town has always been handicapped by possessing only one spring which must be supplemented by cisterns.

Courtesy of the Israel Office of Information, New York

7. Nazareth set within the hills of Galilee

From *Atlas of the Bible* (Thomas Nelson & Sons Limited)

8. A street in Nazareth

The ancient village seems to have extended farther up the hill, judging by the few remains to be seen (cf. Luke 4:29). In Jesus' day it was a small village, secluded, and not on any main highway, although it was near Sepphoris, an important city which was just S of the main road from Tiberias to Ptolemaïs.

Although various traditional holy places are shown as connected with the gospel accounts, the only one which may be authentic and go back to the time of Jesus is Mary's well. Other shrines are at the Church of the Annunciation, the House of Joseph, the Synagogue Church, the Mensa Christi (Table of Christ), the Church of Gabriel, and the Maronite Church of the Precipice.

Figs. NAZ 7-8.

2. In the NT. Nazareth is first mentioned as the home of Joseph and Mary at the time of the Annunciation (Luke 1:26). From there they set out for Bethlehem, and to it they returned after the birth of Jesus (Matt. 2:23; Luke 2:4). As a boy Jesus continued to live there with his parents (Luke 2:39, 51). He left Nazareth to go to be baptized by John (Mark 1:9). When Philip spoke to Nathanael and referred to Jesus as from Nazareth, Nathanael replied: "Can anything good come out of Nazareth?" (John 1:45-46). This implies that the village was insignificant, which is supported by the absence of references to it in ancient non-Christian sources. *See* § 1 *above*.

No reason is given as to why Jesus left Nazareth to dwell in Capernaum (Matt. 4:13). Only once is it specifically said that Jesus returned to Nazareth "where he had been brought up" (Luke 4:16; cf. Matt. 13:54; Mark 6:1). The only other occurrences of the noun form, and which speak of Jesus as from Nazareth, are in the account of the Triumphal Entry (Matt. 21:11) and in Peter's sermon before Cornelius (Acts 10:38).

There are many passages in which Jesus is identified as "the Nazarene" (RSV "of Nazareth"; e.g., Mark 1:24; 10:47; John 18:5, 7; Acts 2:22; 3:6). Only once are Jesus' followers referred to as "the Nazarenes" (Acts 24:5). Although there has been much discussion as to the significance of "NAZARENE," the most common and the most probable interpretation is that in the NT the word means "of Nazareth," as is specifically stated in Matt. 2:23.

3. Later history. Nazareth did not become an important Christian shrine until the reign of Constantine (A.D. 324-37). According to Epiphanius, before Constantine only Jews were permitted to live there (*Adv. Haer.* XXX.136). The first mention of a church built there is by Arculf (670). Nazareth suffered much persecution and destruction under the Muslim conquest (*ca.* 700). It regained its freedom and importance during the Crusades and was made the seat of a bishop (*ca.* 1108). Although it was captured by Saladin in 1187, it was retaken by Frederick II in 1229. During the Crusades its churches were rebuilt, but at the end Nazareth was captured and finally destroyed in 1291 by the Mamluke Beybars. Under the Turks it continued to be unimportant, but the modern resurgence of Nazareth as a Christian shrine and city began in 1620 when the Franciscans were granted permission to establish themselves there as the guardians of the holy places. Nazareth was captured by the British in 1918. Modern Nazareth has an estimated population of nearly twenty thousand. It is an important city in its district and is the largest Christian city in Israel.

Bibliography. G. Dalman, *Orte und Wege Jesu* (1919), pp. 46-74; F.-M. Abel, *Géographie de la Palestine,* II (1933), 203, 395; G. F. Moore, "Nazarene and Nazareth," in F. J. Foakes-Jackson and K. Lake, *The Beginnings of Christianity,* I (1942), 426-32; E. G. Kraeling, *Bible Atlas* (1956), pp. 358-59.

D. C. PELLETT

NAZIRITE năz′ə rīt [נזיר, one consecrated, devoted, separated, *from* נזר, to consecrate (*cf.* נדר, to vow); LXX ναζιρâιον, ναζιρ, ναζιρâιος, ναζιρâιοι, *words derived from* ἐύχομαι (to vow) *and* ἁγίζω (to consecrate)]. One who marks his status of special sanctity or his vow of self-dedication by letting his hair grow and abstaining from wine and strong drink.

Historically the Nazirite was a sacred person. In later times he acquired his special status by a vow he made himself, but in the beginning he was a charismatic by virtue of a mysterious divine endowment and/or the vow of his mother. In a Nazirite's status the motif of consecration predominated. He was a devotee who separated himself, or found himself "separate," *to* God (Num. 6:2, 6-8, 12; Judg. 13: 5, 7; 16:17). The consecration is not an ascetic separation but an expression of loyalty to God in which forms of abstinence are illustrative rather than constitutive.

References to Nazirites span all of OT history and extend into the early Christian period. At first the commitment was spontaneous and lifelong, expressing the charismatic gifts of the individual. Later the institution was standardized and regulated by law, so that any person who made a vow to observe a specified pattern of conduct could become a Nazirite for a temporary period. Thus the Nazirite was no longer primarily a sacred person because of a special endowment, but a person vowed to perform a sacred duty. The transformation was probably very gradual. It seems to have gained momentum in the era of the later monarchy; but, for want of adequate materials, it is not possible to document its progress in detail. Eventually, because of the transformation, the offering at the termination of the vow became the most important part of a Nazirite's dedication.

1. The Nazirite as a sacred person. In early Israel the holy man played a very large role. This was also true in the non-Israelite Near East (and elsewhere); what is unique in the OT is its theocentric way of understanding him. Holy men were under the power of the Spirit of the Lord. Holiness was manifest in psychic and physical forms rather than in ethical qualities. Invariably, spontaneity, expressed in ecstasy and enthusiasm, characterized these sacred persons. Early prophets and warriors were of this order. Saul and the prophets he joined (I Sam. 10: 9-13) played an involuntary, spontaneous role. Likewise, when he heard of the siege of Jabesh, Saul was brought to holy fury by the "spirit of God," so that he became a warrior (11:5-11). The early Nazirite seems to have been a holy person in this sense. He stood in a peculiar relation to God by virtue of the gifts at his disposal.

There are many affinities between the Nazirite and the warrior. Samson, who is called a Nazirite, was a holy warrior much like Saul. The "Spirit of the LORD" (Judg. 14:19, etc.) gave him special physical power. He was a charismatic figure with long hair. War in early Israel was a holy enterprise, and while on active duty the warrior was in a state of sanctity marked by a special pattern of conduct (Deut. 23:9-14; I Sam. 21:4-6; II Sam. 11:11-12). The Naziriteship of Joseph (Gen. 49:26; Deut. 33: 16) in relation to the other tribes may rest on the military prowess of that tribe in Israel's early history in Canaan. Princes may have been Nazirites (Lam. 4:7) in the sense that they were warrior chieftains.

Amos mentions the prophet and the Nazirite together as persons with a special vocation whose role has been frustrated (2:11-12). God had called both; beyond this we lack evidence to describe the relation between the two. Samuel was a prophet and a Nazirite, to be sure. But Samuel was also a priest and one for whom residence in a holy place had displaced the ecstatic sanctity of prophet and warrior. His hair was uncut (I Sam. 1:11), which may not have been true of priests later (Lev. 21:10); and the LXX adds that he abstained from wine (I Sam. 1:11). Like the early Nazirite, Samuel was a lifelong devotee. In many ways he was the figure who served as the bridge by means of which the transformation of the Nazirite from a spontaneous devotee with special gifts to a man under a voluntary vow completed by an offering was facilitated.

2. The law of the Nazirite. All the prescriptions in the Pentateuch concerning the Nazirite are found in Num. 6. This law indicates that the charismatic aspects were subsiding in favor of a standardized communal control. It assumes that a man or woman became a Nazirite by a voluntary vow for a specified term (vss. 2, 5). The Rechabites (Jer. 35), who exhibit many of the features of the Nazirite, combined the voluntary vow with a hereditary and lifelong commitment. But with the exception of their founder, they were not charismatics. Amos said God "raised up" (2:11-12) Nazirites. Samson was so designated by the angel, and Samuel lived under his mother's vow (I Sam. 9–11). The law makes no provision for such; we cannot even be certain that this type still continued. The reference in Amos makes improbable the suggestion of some that charismatics did not originally bear the title Nazirite but that it was applied to them by later writers.

In the law of his consecration the Nazirite was bound by three provisions that became marks of his sanctity: (*a*) he must avoid wine, strong drink, and all "that is produced by the grapevine" (Num. 6:4); (*b*) for the duration of his separation his hair might not be cut; and (*c*) he must avoid the presence of the dead, even of his parents. It seems doubtful that all these were observed by the older Nazirites. As noted, Samuel's abstinence from wine is mentioned only in the LXX. Samson's mother reportedly did abstain, but this may be a later interpretation; in any case it is unlikely that Samson did so (Judg. 13:4; 14:10). The practice of avoiding the presence of the dead is never mentioned in the older accounts. In its strictness it places the Nazirite in the same sphere of sanctity as the high priest (Lev. 21:11), ahead of the other priests (vss. 1-10). This provision may be evidence of an accommodation to the role of the priesthood in the law of the Nazirite.

The practice of not cutting the hair is present throughout. But it must be noted that, while in the earlier Nazirite the main thing is the lifelong growth of the hair, in the law of Num. 6 the focus is upon the cutting and offering of the hair at the completion of the vow (vs. 18). Like blood, hair symbolized the life of a person. Hair offerings as a form of self-dedication were common in the ancient Semitic cultus and elsewhere. Though crowded by the offerings of Israel's own cultus in Num. 6, the hair is still put on the fire; and the Mishna calls it an offering (Naz. 4.7). Further, it provides that in the case of one whose vow has miscarried (6.9-12), the hair must be buried rather than put on the altar fire (Ter. 7.4). In the case of a permanent Nazirite such as Samson, the hair is not a symbol of a person's life but of the charismatic divine power with which he is endowed. While this function of the hair also has pre-Israelite roots, the meaning is very different. We must conclude that the law prescribed for the Nazirite had drawn on and assimilated a wide range of antecedent forms. Likewise, abstinence from wine is often explained as nomadic reaction against the social patterns of agricultural Canaan. But in many cults, and also in Israel (Lev. 10:8-9), the priest performing his ministry avoided wine. The sources for the provisions in the law of the Nazirite were numerous and complex.

3. Later developments. The duration of a Nazirite's consecration was normally indicated at the time he made his vow. The Mishna says that it is to be for thirty days if such specification is lacking (Naz. 1.3). The brevity indicates that, increasingly, the offerings became more important than the status itself. In time it became a virtuous act for non-Nazirites to assume the expenses for the one who was and for whom the cost of release was burdensome (I Macc. 3:50; Jos. Antiq. XIX.vi.1; Acts 21:24). Aside from the fact that the days of his consecration had to be repeated in full, the real burden incurred by a Nazirite polluted by the dead (cf. Num. 6:9-12; 19:11 ff) was the cost of the additional sacrifices. Gentiles could not become Nazirites (Naz. 9.1), but women and slaves could, though under certain circumstances a father or husband could void a woman's vow, and this seems to have occurred mainly for economic reasons (cf. Num. 30).

There are many elements of similarity between the Nazirite's vow in its later stages and the vow of Ihrâm made by Muslim pilgrims. In both, the abstinences are preparatory to the fulfilment in the offering, which is to take place at a specified place and includes the cutting of the hair. In both, remnants of very ancient ritual forms, descriptive of a sacred state indicated by spontaneous charismatic gifts, have been recast to serve as rules governing the performance of a sacred duty.

Bibliography. J. Wellhausen, *Reste Arabischen Heidentums* (2nd ed., 1897), pp. 79-94. I. J. Peritz, "Woman in the Ancient Hebrew Cult," *JBL,* XVII (1898), 111-48. G. B. Gray, "The Nazirite," *JTS,* I (1899-1900); *Numbers,* ICC (1903). W. R. Smith, *Religion of the Semites* (rev. ed., 1907), pp. 323-35, 479-85. E. Binns, *Numbers,* WC (1927). H. Salmanowitsch, *Das Naziräat nach Bibel und Talmud* (1931). J. Pedersen, *Israel,* III-IV (1940), 264 ff. G. von Rad, *Der heilige Krieg im alten Israel* (1951). W. Eichrodt, *Theologie des AT,* I (5th ed., 1957), 200-202.

J. C. Rylaarsdam

NEAH nē'ə [נֵעָה] (Josh. 19:13). A border town in Zebulun. The site is unknown.

NEAPOLIS nē ăp'ə lĭs [ἡ Νέα πόλις *or* Νεάπολις] (Acts 16:11). The seaport of Philippi.

Neapolis is mentioned as a city in Thrace in an Athenian tribute list of the fifth century B.C. (*see bibliography*). In 188 B.C. it was visited by the army of the Roman consul Gnaeus Manlius Volso (Livy XXX.41). In 42 B.C., when Brutus and Cassius were camped at Philippi, they had their depot on the island of Thasos, a hundred stadia distant; and their triremes were anchored at Neapolis, at a distance of seventy stadia, as Appian (*Civil Wars* IV.106) narrates.

In Byzantine times Neapolis was called Christoupolis, and it is the modern Greek town of Kavalla. The distance from Kavalla to Philippi is ten miles, which corresponds to the seventy stadia indicated by Appian. Archaeological discoveries at Kavalla include vestiges of a Hellenic village, with a structure of the fourth or fifth century B.C. identified as the sanctuary of the goddess Parthenos, otherwise known as the chief deity of Neapolis. Latin inscriptions show

Courtesy of the Zion Research Library

9. Neapolis (modern Kavalla), the port of Philippi

that in the Roman period the port was dependent upon Philippi, and that some leading persons of the latter colony made their residence there.

See also MACEDONIA.

Fig. NEA 9.

Bibliography. B. D. Meritt and A. B. West, *The Athenian Assessment of 425 B.C.* (1934), p. 83, contains an Athenian tribute list mentioning Neapolis; V. Hiller, "Neapolis," *Pauly-Wissowa,* vol. XVI, pt. ii (1935), cols. 2110-12; G. Bakalakis, "Νεάπολις—Χριστούπολις—Καβάλα," 'Αρχαιολογικὴ 'Εφημερίς, Περιοδικὸν τῆς ἐν 'Αθήναις ἀρχαιολογικῆς 'Εταιρείας (1936), pp. 1-48; P. Collart, *Philippes, ville de Macédoine, depuis ses origines jusqu'à la fin de l'époque romaine,* École Française d'Athènes, Travaux et Mémoires, fasc. V (1937), pp. 102-32.

J. FINEGAN

NEARIAH nē'ə rī'ə [נעריה, *possibly* Yahu's young man, *or a corrupted gentilic from* נער—*i.e.,* a Nearite]. **1.** A remote descendant of David (I Chr. 3:22-23).

2. A Simeonite commander of Hezekiah's time who destroyed the remnant of the Amalekites (I Chr. 4:42).

J. M. WARD

NEBAI nē'bī [נובי (*Kethibh*), ניבי (*Qere*)]. One of the chiefs of the people signatory to the covenant of Ezra (Neh. 10:19—H 10:20).

NEBAIOTH nĭ bā'yŏth [נביות]; KJV NEBAJOTH —jŏth in Genesis. The eldest son of Ishmael, and brother of Kedar (Gen. 25:13; 28:9; 36:3; I Chr. 1:29); which means that there were clans of this name among the Ishmaelite Arabs. Both the Kedar and the Nebaioth Arabs were famous for sheep raising (Isa. 60:7). The Nebaioth Arabs are apparently identical with the *Nabaiati,* who are mentioned by Tiglath-pileser III in the eighth century B.C.; Ashurbanipal defeated and took booty from the *Nabaiati* and the *Qidri* (Kedar; *ANET* 298-300), and Pliny refers to the Nabatei and the Cedrei in his *Natural History.* Some scholars have sought to identify the Nebaioth with the NABATEANS of the sixth century B.C. and later; but the fact that the former is written with the Hebrew letter "tau" and the latter with a "teth" makes this equation very unlikely.

S. COHEN

NEBALLAT nĭ băl'ət [נבלט] (Neh. 11:34). A town in the hills overlooking the SE end of the Plain of Sharon and settled by Benjaminites following the restoration from exile; modern Beit Nebala, four miles E of Lod and nearly two miles N of Hadid. The name may preserve the memory of Nabu-uballit, presumably an Assyrian governor of Samaria in the seventh century B.C.

Bibliography. W. F. Albright, *AASOR,* vol. IV (1924), p. 106, note 15.

W. H. MORTON

NEBAT nē'băt [נבט] (I Kings 11:26, etc.). The father of King Jeroboam I. The name, common in S Arabic, is not identical with Naboth, as some suppose.

NEBO nē'bō [נבו, *transliteration of* Akkad. *nabu, from a verbal root meaning* to announce; *in* 2-3 *below,* a height, *or perhaps connected with the god* Nabu]. **1.** A Babylonian deity mentioned by Isaiah in his taunt song on the downfall of Babylon and her gods. He was specifically associated with Borsippa (modern Birs Nimrud) and was regarded as the son of MARDUK. His image and that of Marduk were together carried in the sacred procession in the spring New Year Festival at Babylon, hence the point in the association of the two in Isa. 46:1. Nebo was specifically associated with writing and speech; he was a Mesopotamian Mercury, though in his cult center his province included nature—he was originally a water deity. His cult was particularly popular during the Neo-Babylonian period (612-538 B.C.); his name appeared as an element in the names of three of the last six kings, Nabopolassar, Nebuchadrezzar, and Nabonidus.

Bibliography. W. Muss-Arnolt, *A Concise Dictionary of the Assyrian Language* (1905), pp. 632-34; E. Dhorme, *Les Religions de Babylonie et d'Assyrie* (1945), pp. 150-56.

J. GRAY

2. A city in Moab, requested by the tribes of Reuben and Gad as good grazing land (Num. 32:3) and rebuilt by the Reubenites (vs. 38), mentioned in connection with Bela among the descendants of Reuben (I Chr. 5:8). The MOABITE STONE, lines 14-18, records its capture by the Moabite king Mesha: "And Chemosh said to me, 'Go, take Nebo from Israel!' So I went by night and fought against it from the break of dawn until noon, taking it and slaying all, seven thousand men, boys, women, girls, and maid-servants, for I had devoted them to destruction for (the god) Ashtar-Chemosh. And I took from there the [. . .] of Yahweh, dragging them before Chemosh." Needless to say, Mesha's estimate of seven thousand killed is greatly exaggerated. Nebo is also mentioned in the oracles against Moab (Isa. 15:2; Jer. 48:1, 22).

Eusebius located Nebo eight Roman miles S of Heshbon. The most likely identification is Khirbet Mekhayyet, *ca.* five miles SW of Heshbon. Large quantities of Moabite Iron Age I-II (twelfth until beginning of sixth century B.C.) pottery were found. The fortress is built on an outspur and isolated by a moat. At one end are remains of a Byzantine church with a beautiful mosaic floor.

See also NEBO, MOUNT.

Bibliography. N. Glueck, *Explorations in Eastern Palestine,* II, AASOR, XV (1934-35), 110-11.

3. A town mentioned just after Bethel and Ai in the lists of repatriated Israelites (Ezra 2:29; Neh. 7:33). In Nehemiah it is called "the other Nebo" (נבו אחר), probably to distinguish it from 2 above. By some, this Nebo is identified with Nob (Neh. 11:32; Isa. 10:32). The site in question may be modern Nuba, NW of Beth-zur and *ca.* fifteen miles SW of Jerusalem.

E. D. GROHMAN

NEBO, MOUNT [הר נבו, mountain of the height, *or perhaps* mountain of (the god) Nabu]. A mountain of the Abarim range opposite Jericho, *ca.* twelve miles E of the mouth of the Jordan River. One of the Israelite stopping places was "in the mountains of Abarim, before Nebo" (Num. 33:47). After Moses' song in Deut. 32, he was commanded to "ascend this mountain to the Abarim, Mount Nebo, which is in the land of Moab, opposite Jericho" (vs. 49). There he was to view the land of Canaan and to die on the mountain. After Moses' final blessing of the people in Deut. 33, he "went up from the plains of Moab to Mount Nebo, to the top of Pisgah, which is opposite Jericho. And the LORD showed him all the land. Gilead as far as Dan, all Naphtali, the land of Ephraim and Manasseh, all the land of Judah as far as the Western Sea, the Negeb, and the Plain, that is, the valley of Jericho the city of palm trees, as far as Zoar" (34:1-3).

In OT times Mount Nebo changed hands several times. Shortly before the Israelite conquest, the Amorite king Sihon had taken the territory N of the River Arnon, including Mount Nebo, from Moab (Num. 21:26-30). In turn, the Israelites captured it from Sihon (vss. 23-32), and to this area Balak king of Moab brought Balaam to curse the Israelites (23:14, 28). The territory was assigned to the tribes of Reuben and Gad (ch. 32). In the time of the judges, Eglon king of Moab was in possession of Jericho, and so must also have possessed Mount Nebo (Judg. 3:12-30). King David subdued Moab (II Sam. 8:2, 12), so at least by his time Mount Nebo was again Israelite. King Mesha of Moab rebelled against Israel and reconquered territory that would include Mount Nebo (*see* MOABITE STONE; for the further vicissitudes of the area, *see* MOAB §§ 3*g-h*). Moab ceased its independent existence toward the end of the seventh century B.C.

Mount Nebo is probably modern Jebel en-Neba, its altitude being *ca.* 2,740 feet above the level of the Mediterranean, and so *ca.* 4,030 feet above the Dead Sea. Seen from the E, Mount Nebo is just a spur of the Moabite Plateau; however, it is a noteworthy mountain, seen from the Plains of Moab just W of its foot. The peak of Jebel en-Neba is separated by a saddle from Ras es-Siyaghah, a slightly lower summit just to the NW, which may well be the "top of Pisgah" from which Moses viewed the Promised Land. *See* PISGAH, MOUNT.

As indicated by Deut. 34:1-3, Mount Nebo, and especially Ras es-Siyaghah, commands a magnificent view to the N, W, and SW. To the N and the NE is the fertile plateau of Transjordan. Far to the N, under favorable conditions can be seen snow-capped Mount Hermon. As the eye moves S, there can be seen Tabor, Ebal, and Gerizim, the heights of Judah and Benjamin, the ridge stretching to the S on which lie Bethlehem and Hebron, the Dead Sea as far as Engedi. Directly below is the Valley of the Jordan. The Mediterranean cannot be seen because of the mountains intervening.

Near Mount Nebo a number of Iron Age I-II (twelfth to the beginning of the sixth centuries B.C.) and one Early Bronze IV–Middle Bronze I (twenty-third through twentieth centuries B.C.) sites have been found. Immediately below Ras es-Siyaghah to the NE are the strongly flowing waters of the 'Ayun Musa ("springs of Moses"). In the Moabite period the springs were well guarded by a strong fortress on top of a steep hill. It was once surrounded by a strong wall and cut off from the broken plateau by a dry moat. Large quantities of Iron Age I-II potsherds have been found. *Ca.* two miles SE of Ras es-Siyaghah is Khirbet Mekhayyet, probably the ancient town of Nebo (*see* NEBO 2). *Ca.* three miles below Mount Nebo to the W, on the plain stretching to the Dead Sea, is Rujm el-Heri, a small site sur-

10. Mount Nebo in the Abarim Range of Moab

rounded by a wall, where Iron Age I-II Moabite sherds were found. *Ca.* three miles NE of Ras es-Siyaghah is Khirbet Qurn el-Kibsh, a great wall having enclosed an area of *ca.* 935 by 310 feet. Large quantities of Early Bronze IV–Middle Bronze I sherds were found. Thus in the area of Mount Nebo, as in the rest of Moab, there was a sedentary occupation in Early Bronze IV–Middle Bronze I, followed by a nonsendentary period down to the thirteenth century, during which roaming Bedouins left no remains. Another sedentary period in Iron Age I-II, tapering off toward the end of Iron II (seventh century B.C.), was followed by a nonsedentary period down to the Nabatean period, beginning *ca.* the third century B.C.

Fig. NEB 10.

Bibliography. F.-M. Abel, *Géographie de la Palestine,* I (1933), 379-84; N. Glueck, *Explorations in Eastern Palestine,* II, *AASOR,* XV (1934-35), 109-11. E. D. GROHMAN

NEBUCHADREZZAR nĕb'ə kəd rĕz'ər, nĕb'yŏŏ— [נבוכדראצר; Akkad. *Nabû-kudurri-uṣur,* Nabu protect my boundary stone]. Alternately: NEBUCHADNEZZAR nĕb'ə kəd nĕz'ər, nĕb'yŏŏ— [נבוכדנאצר; LXX Ναβουχοδονοσόρ]; KJV Apoc. NABUCHODONOSAR năb'ə kə dŏn'ə sär; NABUCHODONOSOR —sôr. King of Babylonia 605-562 B.C.; son of NABOPOLASSAR, and father of EVIL-MERODACH.

The salient historical features of the rule of Nebuchadrezzar have been known for quite some time, but only the chronicles published by D. J. Wiseman (*see bibliography*) have allowed us a real insight into the political concepts that governed the activities of this king.* The new texts show Nebuchadrezzar, a Babylonian, acting in every respect as would an Assyrian king. He conducted annual campaigns to collect the tribute that would be forthcoming under the pressure of the presence of a well-equipped army. His planning was on a wide and international scale, and he punished the defeated enemy as cruelly as any Assyrian king would have done. Of the forty-three years of his reign, only the first ten are well known; for the balance we have but little evidence, and that of a kind which does not shed any light on the domestic situation. Two minor rebellions during his first ten years should be pointed out, if only to illustrate the existence of internal tensions which the historical sources of that period do not reflect. Even while he was still crown prince, Nebuchadrezzar had been in command of a Babylonian army; and when the health of his father began to fail after a campaign along the Euphrates against the Egyptians encamped at Carchemish, Nebuchadrezzar was sent out as commander-in-chief to the same front. His victory at Carchemish over the forces of Pharaoh Neco II (605) brought all of Syria and Palestine to its knees. He pursued the beaten Egyptians as far as the frontiers of their country, without entering the little kingdom of Judah (II Kings 24:7). Jehoiakim of Judah submitted to the victor. Nebuchadrezzar then had to leave in haste for Babylon, after having received news of the death of his father; but he soon returned as king and, with his army, collected tribute, which was rendered quickly enough because of the presence of the army and the impression made by the victory just won. In each of the following years, Nebuchadrezzar appeared with his army to conquer recalcitrant cities, such as Ashkelon, until, in 601, he fought a battle with Egyptian troops, from which he emerged just short of being defeated. The Egyptians, under Pharaoh Hophra, reconquered Gaza, and their influence was definitely increasing, especially in Jerusalem, in spite of the constant warnings of the prophet Jeremiah. According to Josephus, Jehoiakim still paid his tribute to Nebuchadrezzar, who appeared in 599 with newly strengthened troops, ready again to assert the supremacy of Babylonia over Egypt in that region. Nebuchadrezzar concerned himself on this occasion mainly with the Arabs to the E of Syria and Palestine, who lost not only their herds but also their images to Nebuchadrezzar. At the end of the year 598, Nebuchadrezzar started out from Babylon, this time quite clearly ready to attack the kingdom of Judah. He laid siege to what the Chronicler calls the "city of Judah," where in the meantime Jehoiachin had succeeded to his father's throne. On the fifteenth and sixteenth of March, 597, the city was captured and had to pay heavy tribute and to accept a new king of Nebuchadrezzar's choosing, Zedekiah. Jehoiachin lived in exile in Babylon, as we know from administrative texts dated from the tenth to the thirty-fifth year of Nebuchadrezzar. Of the next three years of Nebuchadrezzar we know that he continued his campaigns in Syria, with the exception of his ninth year, when he went to the region beyond the Tigris against Elam. Fig. JEH 10.

In the last thirty-three years of Nebuchadrezzar's reign fall the following events, which, however, cannot be clearly dated from cuneiform sources: the siege of Tyre, which, according to Josephus, lasted thirteen years; the second siege and destruction of Jerusalem in 586; his intervention in a border arrangement between the Medes and the Lydians at the Halys River in Asia Minor; and a campaign against Pharaoh Amasis, the successor of Hophra, in Nebuchadrezzar's thirty-seventh year—i.e., in 567.

Nebuchadrezzar had the great advantage over all Assyrian kings in having as ally the Medes—he was married to Amyitis, daughter of the king of the Medes—which secured the frontiers of his empire to the N and the NW. Much of the tribute collected on his campaigns went into the decoration of the temples he built in Babylon and other cities, into the immense fortification of the capital, and into his palace. The famous "hanging gardens" cannot be identified among the impressive ruins of Babylon. The reference in Dan. 4 to the madness of Nebuchadrezzar may refer to Nabonidus, whose unconventional acts as king provoked much opposition and may well have earned him the reputation of insanity.

Bibliography. D. J. Wiseman, *Chronicles of the Chaldaean Kings* (1956), pp. 20 ff. A. L. Oppenheim

NEBUSHAZBAN nĕb'ə shăz'băn [נבושזבן; Akkad. *Nabû-šūzibanni*, Nabû save me!] (Jer. 39:13). The chief eunuch of Nebuchadrezzar; mentioned among the "princes of the king of Babylon."

NEBUZARADAN nĕb'ə zə rā'dən [נבוזראדן; Akkad. *Nabû-zēr-iddin*, Nabû has given offspring] (II Kings 25:8, etc.). A high court official of Nebuchadrezzar. He destroyed the temple, the palace, and the houses of Jerusalem with fire and tore down the walls of the city. He reappeared four years later to deport more people (Jer. 52:30). His official title is given as "chief cook or butcher," but it should be noted that such a designation of a court official is unknown in Babylonia. A. L. Oppenheim

NECHO, NECHOH. KJV forms of Neco.

NECK, STIFF. *See* Stiff-necked.

NECKLACE [ענק; רביד, RSV *emendation in* II Chr. 3:16 *for* MT דביר, inner sanctuary]; KJV CHAIN. *See* Jewels and Precious Stones.

NECO nē'kō [נכו, נכה; Assyrian *Nikū;* Egyp. *Nk'w;* LXX Νεχαώ; Herodotus Νεκῶς]; KJV NECHO (II Chronicles); PHARAOH-NECHO (Jer. 46:2); PHARAOH-NECHOH (II Kings). A pharaoh (609-594 B.C.) of the Twenty-sixth Dynasty, who slew King Josiah and installed Jehoiakim in place of Jehoahaz (II Kings 23:29-35).

In 671 B.C. the Assyrian king Esarhaddon invaded Egypt and took Memphis, sending the Ethiopian pharaoh Tirhakah in flight to the S. Esarhaddon confirmed in rule a number of Delta princes, among them a certain Neco of Saïs and Memphis. Later a son of this Neco, Psammetichus I (663-609), claimed the rule of all Egypt and founded the Twenty-sixth Dynasty, with the capital at Saïs. The new dynasty was supported by Assyrian patronage and by the employment of Lydian and Ionian mercenaries.

A second Neco succeeded his father in 609, three years after the fall of Nineveh. The situation seemed ripe for the enlargement of Egyptian power, before the newly powerful Babylonian state had the opportunity to move into Syria and Palestine. Neco captured Gaza and Ashkelon, to establish entry bases into Palestine (Jer. 47:1, 5). He then moved N along the Philistine Plain and the Plain of Sharon, intending to make a juncture with the remnants of the Assyrian army near Carchemish on the Euphrates. At the Megiddo pass through the Carmel Range, Josiah of Judah attempted to withstand Neco's Greek mercenaries and was killed for his boldness (II Kings 23:29; II Chr. 35:20-24). When the people of Jerusalem chose another anti-Egyptian king, Jehoahaz, Neco brusquely haled the new ruler N to the Egyptian camp at Riblah, deposed him, and imposed a crushing fine upon the land of Judah. Jehoahaz was sent to Egypt, to end his years in captivity; and Neco appointed Eliakim king of Judah, changing his name to Jehoiakim (II Kings 23:33-35). Thus Egypt broke the independent power of Judah and gained a vassal at Jerusalem.

For a few years Neco enjoyed success in Asia. A fragment of a monument of his has been found at Sidon, and a letter written in Aramaic—probably from the ruler of Ashkelon and probably to Neco—shows another Palestinian vassal. With the remnants of the Assyrian army and with his own Anatolian and Aegean mercenaries, he was able to fortify Carchemish, cross the Euphrates, and threaten the rising power of Nabopolassar of Babylon. However, in 605 B.C., Nabopolassar sent his son Nebuchadrezzar N, and Neco suffered a crushing defeat at Carchemish (II Kings 24:7; Jer. 46:2). The pharaoh retreated hastily into Egypt. Nebuchadrezzar pursued him as far as the River of Egypt, but was called back home by his father's death. In 601-600, Nebuchadrezzar again fought at the Egyptian frontier, with heavy losses on both sides. Neco had learned a hard lesson and did not again venture out of Egypt. It was a dozen years before Egypt, under Hophra, again intervened actively in Asiatic politics.

For other events in Neco's reign our chief sources are classical, rather than Egyptian. However, since the first such source, Herodotus, visited Egypt only a few generations after Neco's reign, the tradition was relatively recent. At great cost of life, Neco tried to push a canal through the Wadi Tumilat from the Nile to the Red Sea. The project was not achieved, and was left to the Persian Darius to finish. The tradition that Neco sent out sailors to circumnavigate Africa is also insistent and accords with the mercantile curiosity of the day (Herodotus II.158; IV.42; Diodorus I.33).

Bibliography. *Cambridge Ancient History,* III (1925), 210-12, 297-300, 395-98; J. Bright, *BA,* XII (1949), 46-52; D. N. Freedman, *BA,* XIX (1956), 50-60; H. Tadmor, *JNES,* XV (1956), 226-30. The historical reality of Neco's canal is doubted by G. Posener, *Chronique d'Égypte,* no. 26 (1938), pp. 259-73.

J. A. WILSON

NECODAN. KJV Apoc. form of NEKODA 2.

NECROMANCY. Divination by means of communication with spirits of the dead. *See* FAMILIAR SPIRIT; DIVINATION.

NECTAR [נפת, *lit.,* dropping juice, flowing honey, comb; *in full,* נפת צופים (Ps. 19:10—H 19:11)] (Song of S. 4:11). Alternately: HONEY (Prov. 5:3); HONEYCOMB (Prov. 16:24). The sweet fluid secreted by the nectaries of plants; the principal source of the honey of bees, by which it is collected.

H. F. BECK

NEDABIAH nĕd'ə bī'ə [נדביה, Yahu has impelled] (I Chr. 3:18). A son of Jeconiah (Jehoiachin).

NEEDLE [ῥαφίς, βελόνη] (Matt. 19:24; Mark 10:25; Luke 18:25). An instrument for sewing with leather thong or thread. Needles have been found at most excavations in the Near East, from earliest to latest periods. Earliest examples, dating from the sixth millennium B.C., are of bone, usually flat strips tapering in width from base to tip and perforated at the wider end by boring from both sides. A number of bone needles, blunt at both ends, were found at Megiddo from the fourth millennium, and are identified as shuttle needles for weaving.

In the OT period bone needles were rarer and bronze needles more common. Most of these were made by flattening one end slightly and perforating it, the result being much like modern needles. Some, however, were made by looping the head end and bending it in tightly in such a way that it would not catch on the cloth. Sizes also approximate those of modern needles. At Tell en-Nasbeh they ranged from *ca.* 1½ to 5½ inches—i.e., from a small sewing needle to a large darning needle, in our terms. Fig. NEE 11.

In the NT period bronze needles continued to predominate, but bone needles are found and some very fine examples of ivory needles as well.

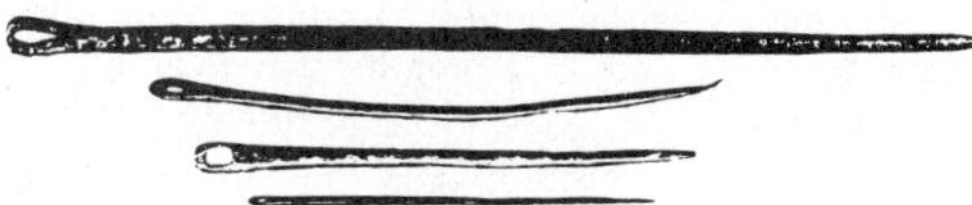

Courtesy of the American Schools of Oriental Research

11. Bronze needles from Mizpeh (Tell en-Nasbeh)

Jesus used the figure of the impossibility of a camel's going through the eye of a needle, to teach the difficulty of a rich man's entering the kingdom of God. Some late Greek MSS and other versions read κάμιλος ("cable, rope") for κάμηλος ("camel"), apparently to lessen the harshness of the saying. A much later interpretation made the saying refer to a postulated small gate called the "Needle's Eye," through which a camel would go with difficulty. Neither interpretation is justified.

S. V. FAWCETT

NEEDLEWORK. *See* EMBROIDERY.

NEEMIAS. KJV Apoc. alternate form of NEHEMIAH 3.

NEESINGS. Archaic term used as KJV translation of עטישה (RSV SNEEZINGS) in Job 41:18—H 41:10.

NEGEB, THE nĕg'ĕb [הנגב, the dry land]. One of the main regions of Canaan, comprised in an inverted triangle, with one side along the Wadi el-Arabah; another near the Sinai Peninsula, from the Gulf of Aqabah to the vicinity of Gaza; and its base a somewhat irregular line from the coast to the Dead Sea a little N of Beer-sheba. As it lay to the S of the hill country of W Palestine, the word has come to mean "south," and it is sometimes difficult to determine in biblical passages whether the district or the direction is denoted. Thus in Gen. 12:9; 13:1 the term is correctly rendered by "the Negeb" (so RSV), while the KJV incorrectly translated it as "the SOUTH."

Despite the fact that the name Negeb indicates a region which has considerably less rain than the rest of the country, the district was never a desert in prebiblical or biblical times. This may be partly due to the fact that in those times vegetation which helped hold the moisture in the soil was more abundant, and that this has been lost by the neglect of more modern times. Nelson Glueck, in his explorations in the region from 1952 on, found hundreds of sites of former settlements, indicating that the region was frequently well populated and an important area.

Evidences have been discovered of the presence of settlements as far back as Paleolithic times, and even more so in the Neolithic (seventh-fifth millenniums B.C.), Chalcolithic (fifth millennium to thirty-second century), and Early Bronze (thirty-second–twenty-first centuries) periods. A large number of these settlements were found along the main highways of the region: a N-S route continuing the water-parting route of the hills to the N through Beer-sheba and Kadesh-barnea ('Ain el-Qudeirat) down to the Sinai Peninsula and on to Egypt; and routes from Beer-sheba and Kadesh-barnea to Kurnub connecting with the Wadi el-Arabah route. There was a very extensive period of settlement in the Middle Bronze I age (twenty-first–nineteenth centuries), the latter part of which was the age of Abraham. When the latter journeyed in the Negeb on his way to and from Egypt (Gen. 12:9–13:1), he was thus able to find numerous cities and places of pasturage for his very large retinue of servants and animals.

This abundant settlement disappeared at the end of the period, possibly as a result of the invasion of Chedorlaomer and his allies, which swept across the "country of the Amalekites" as far as Kadesh-barnea (Gen. 14:7). Since this was a raid and not a conquest, it probably created an intentional desolation, tearing down the houses and filling up the wells. This may explain why Hagar, deprived of these familiar landmarks, lost her way below Beer-sheba (21:14); and why the patriarchs no longer journeyed into the further Negeb, but remained in the untouched areas, such as Gerar, Beer-sheba, and Hebron.

The Israelites appeared in the region after the Exodus and their fruitless attempt to storm the land of Canaan from Kadesh-barnea (Num. 14:44-45; Deut. 1:44); the route they followed was probably the old N-S route through the Negeb. It was not until many years later that the tribes of Judah and Simeon came down from the N and, after conquering the hill country, began to push into the Amalekite region of the Negeb. At that time the area was devoted to the raising of sheep and goats rather than to farming, though the Amalekites had at least one city, with Agag as king, which was destroyed by Saul (I Sam. 15). A little later, at the time when David settled in the region, there is mention (27:10; 30:14, 29) of separate districts of the Negeb: the Negeb of the Cherethites, near Ziklag; the Negeb of Judah, around Beer-sheba, occupied principally by the tribe of Simeon; the Negeb of the Calebites, near Hebron; the Negeb of the Jerahmeelites; and the Negeb of the Kenizzites (LXX; superior to the MT "Kenites"). All these were later incorporated by David into the kingdom of Judah.

In the times after David conquered Edom and got possession of the Arabah, and particularly after Solomon began his commercial and industrial expansion in that region, the settlement of the Negeb came into its own. Numerous fortresses and settlements all over the region during Iron Age II (900-600 B.C.) testify to the expansion of the Israelites to the S. The tribe of Simeon in particular enlarged its territory, spreading over the region near Gerar (I Chr. 4:39-40, where "Gerar" is to be read instead of "Gedor") and annihilating the last of the Amalekites and other aborigines of the area (vss. 41-43).

Courtesy of Denis Baly

12. The Negeb: interior of the "Great Cauldron," or Jebel Hathira

After the fall of the Judean state and the deportation of its people from 597 on, the N part of the Negeb was occupied by the Edomites and formed part of their kingdom of Idumea; the central and S parts were later occupied by the expanding population of the Nabateans. The latter not only settled in the previously occupied sites but also created new ones of their own; they built along the routes of the Negeb such large cities as Abde, Kurnub, Sbeita, Auja, and Elusa, which were prosperous for centuries. They practiced there their customary skill in water conservation; they built dams, dug cisterns, and created terraces to hold in every bit of moisture. As a result, under their rule the Negeb soil showed its underlying fertility, and the region became once more a place for farming as well as for animal raising, while caravans of camels crossed it in every direction. This was the state of the Negeb all through NT times, and it was only the devastations of war and neglect that, centuries later, caused it to be regarded as a desert. Fig. NEG 12.

Bibliography. N. Glueck, *BA*, XVIII (1955), 2-9; *BASOR*, 131 (1953), 6-15; 137 (1955), 10-22; 138 (1955), 7-29; 142 (1956), 17-35; 145 (1957), 11-25; 149 (1958), 8-16; 155 (1959), 2-13; *Rivers in the Desert* (1959). D. Baly, *Geography of the Bible* (1957), pp. 260-66. S. COHEN

NEGINAH, NEGINOTH nĕg'ĭ nə, —nŏth. *See* MUSIC.

NEHELAM nĭ hĕl'əm; KJV **NEHELAMITE** —ə mīt. A translation of הנחלמי ("of Nehelam"; KJV "the Nehelamite"; Jer. 29:24, 31-32). The name, referring to Shemaiah, one of the false prophets whom Jeremiah rebuked, may be that of an unknown locality, his home. The LXX B reads 'Αιλαμείτην. However, Nehelam might be a family name. On the other hand, some scholars regard it as a play on the word חלום, "dream," and so "dreamer" (cf. Jer 23:25, 32); but this is less probable.

J. MUILENBURG

NEHEMIAH nē′ə mī′ə [נחמיה, Yahu has comforted; Νεεμία]; KJV Apoc. NEHEMIAS —əs (I Esd. 5:8);

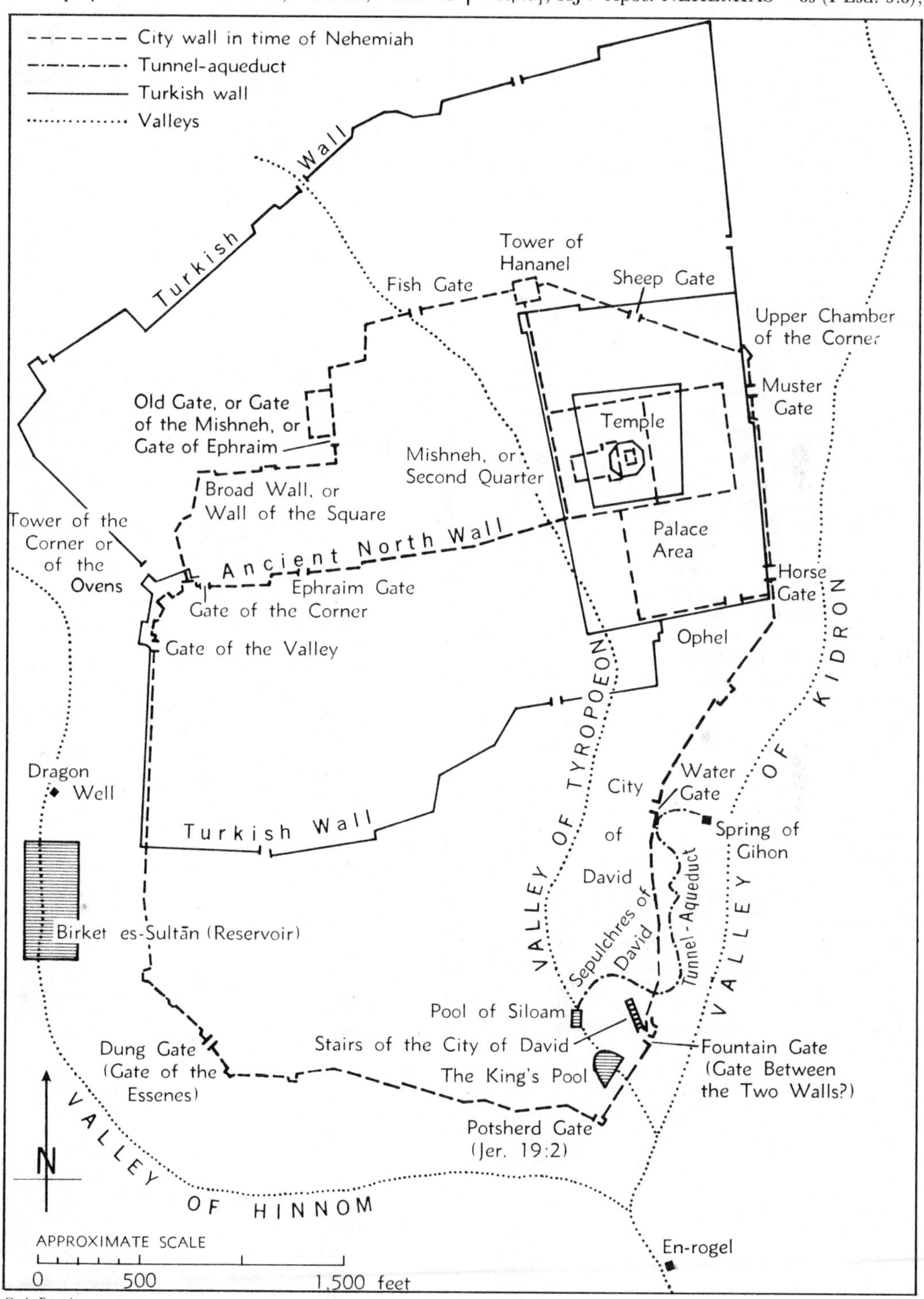

G. A. Barrois

13. Jerusalem in the time of Nehemiah

NEEMIAS (II Macc. 1:18-36; 2:13; Ecclus. 49:13).

1. One of those whose names head the list of exiles returned from Babylon with Sheshbazzar in 538 B.C. (Ezra 2:2; Neh. 7:7; I Esd. 5:8).

2. Son of Azbuk, and "ruler of half the district of Beth-zur"; one of those who aided Nehemiah governor of Judah in rebuilding the wall of Jerusalem in 444 B.C. (Neh. 3:16). B. T. DAHLBERG

3. Son of Hacaliah; cupbearer of Artaxerxes I king of Persia (465-424 B.C.). Upon receiving the news of the said plight of the Jews in Jerusalem from his kinsman Hanani in 444, Nehemiah became ill with grief and was allowed by his king to go to Jerusalem as governor (Neh. 1:1–2:8). Arrived at Jerusalem, he made a secret inspection of the ruined city walls (2: 9-16).* His decision to rebuild them provoked the scorn of Sanballat and Tobiah (2:17-20), but in spite of the opposition of the enemies the walls were rebuilt by devoted Jews (chs. 3–4). Serving unselfishly as governor, Nehemiah corrected some of the worst economic hardships (ch. 5). In spite of the plots of his enemies (6:1-14), Nehemiah completed the building of the walls (vss. 15-19) and set guards at the gates of Jerusalem (7:1-3). Alarmed by the smallness of Jerusalem's population (7:4-73*a*), Nehemiah ordered one out of ten Jews to live in the capital (11:1-2); the list of the inhabitants of Jerusalem is given in Neh. 11:3-19, and of other inhabitants of Judea in vss. 20-36. These lists may have been added by the Chronicler to the memoirs of Nehemiah, as well as the account of the dedication of the walls of Jerusalem (12:27-43) and of the list of the collectors of offerings due to the clergy (vss. 44-47). In 432 B.C., on his second visit to Jerusalem, Nehemiah drove Tobiah out from the temple (13:4-9), and enforced the payments due to the Levites (vss. 10-14) and the observance of the sabbath (vss. 15-22). In his effort to abolish mixed marriages (13:23-27), Nehemiah drove out a grandson of the high priest who had married a daughter of Sanballat (vss. 28-29). Nehemiah closes his memoirs begging God to remember his efforts to enforce the divine law (13:30-31). Fig. NEH 13. *See also* Map II under JERUSALEM.

Nehemiah, in contrast with Ezra, was a successful man of action. Through his energy, unselfishness, and cleverness he brought new life to the dying Jewish community in Jerusalem. He strengthened it physically through the new city walls, socially by helping the needy, and nationally by enforcing the law of Moses. Cf. also II Macc. 1:18-36; 2:13; Ecclus. 49:13.

Possibly Nehemiah is one of the "three of those sheep" signified in Enoch 89:72 who rebuilt Jerusalem and the temple (cf. Ezra 2:2). The Apoc. wrongly intrudes his name in I Esd. 5:40 for the "governor" of Ezra 2:63.

For bibliography, *see* EZRA AND NEHEMIAH, BOOKS OF. R. H. PFEIFFER

NEHEMIAH, BOOK OF. *See* EZRA AND NEHEMIAH, BOOKS OF.

NEHEMIAS. KJV Apoc. form of NEHEMIAH.

NEHILOTH nē'ə lŏth. *See* MUSIC.

NEHUM nē'hŭm [נחום] (Neh. 7:7). One of those whose names head the list of exiles returned from Babylon. The parallel list in Ezra 2:2 (cf. I Esd. 5:8) has REHUM (רחום); the latter is probably the correct form and the former a copyist's error.

NEHUSHTA nĭ hŏŏsh'tə [נחשתא, *probably* serpent (*cf. the name* Nahash), *or* bronze, strong as brass] (II Kings 24:8). The wife of Jehoiakim king of Judah, and the mother of Jehoiachin. She and Jehoiachin, together with other leading citizens, were taken into exile to Babylon by Nebuchadrezzar in the first deportation in 597 B.C. (II Kings 24:12, 15). D. HARVEY

NEHUSHTAN nĭ hŏŏsh'tən [נחשתן] (II Kings 18: 4). The bronze snake destroyed by King Hezekiah in his campaign to purify Hebrew worship. The record of this act is surprisingly brief for so important an act of reformation. It is apparent that the writer believed that the object destroyed by Hezekiah was the actual image fashioned by Moses in the wilderness (Num. 21:8-9). He notes also that its destruction was accompanied by the removal of the high places and symbols associated with the Baal religion and the hated symbol of ASHERAH.

It has been assumed by some scholars that the name Nehushtan was given to it by Hezekiah in contempt—"a thing of brass" (actually copper or bronze). The name is markedly close to the Hebrew נחושה, "bronze"; and there may have been a play upon words, a pattern delightful to Hebrew orators. It is more probable that the RSV is correct in rendering: "It was called Nehushtan," and that this had long been the name of the object.

It is probable that Nehushtan was the name of a deity, perhaps the snake-god, associated with a form of Baalism. This is supported by the fact that the mother of King Jehoiakim was named Nehushta (II Kings 24:8). She would scarcely have been named after a metal, but may have been named in honor of a nature deity.

Tensions between the prophetic party, protagonists for the Yahweh religion, and the adherents of Baalism are notable throughout much of biblical history. King Hezekiah gave his support to the cause of Yahwism. The snake was a hated symbol of Canaan's Baal religion. W. G. WILLIAMS

NEIEL nē ī'əl [נעיאל] (Josh. 19:27). A border town in Asher. It is probably to be identified with Khirbet Ya'nin, a site located on the E edge of the Plain of Acco, with LB and Iron I remains.

Bibliography. A. Saarisalo, "Topographical Researches in Galilee," *JPOS*, 9 (1929), 38. G. W. VAN BEEK

NEIGHBOR [רע, friend, companion, *from* רעה, to pasture (*cf.* רעה, shepherd); *in a weaker sense,* fellow citizen *or simply* another person with whom one stands in a reciprocal relationship; קרוב, near one; שכן, inhabitant, dweller; עמית, associate, relative, fellow; γείτων, fellow countryman, one who lives nearby; περίοικος, one dwelling nearby; ὁ πλησίον (*an adverb*, near, *used as a noun*), the one near or close to].

1. In the OT. "Neighbor" in the OT generally denotes a fellow member of the people of the covenant; it is therefore similar to "brother" (Lev. 25:25, probably 35-36, 39, 47; Deut. 15:2-3, 7, 9, 11-12; 17:15; 19:18-19; 22:1-4; 23:7, 19-20; Neh. 5:1 ff; Jer. 34:8, 17). This fellowship among the covenant people involved the assumption of moral obligations and the guarantee of certain rights for each member. Evidences of this sense of moral obligation toward one's neighbor are particularly clear in Exod. 20 (especially vss. 16-17 = Deut. 5:20-21; see also Exod. 22; Deut. 15; 19; 22:1-4; 27:17 ff); this obligation is categorically enjoined in Lev. 19:18: "You shall love your neighbor as yourself," an injunction which is quoted with hearty approval in the NT (Matt. 19:19; 22:39; Mark 12:31, 33; Luke 10:27; Rom. 13:9; Gal. 5:14; Jas. 2:8).

2. OT legislation concerning neighborly relations. In OT thought, relations among neighbors were subject to the law (Exod. 20:16-17), and care was urged so that these relationships should be properly maintained (22:5-15, 25-27; cf. Lev. 6:2 ff; 19:9-18; 25:13-17, 25-28, 35 ff). According to the law a man who has hurt his neighbor has done an evil thing, and "as he has done it shall be done to him" (Lev. 24:19-20, 22; Deut. 19:11-13; cf. Deut. 27:24; I Kings 8:31-32 = II Chr. 6:22); it is as though he had hurt his brother (Deut. 15:2; Jer. 34:9, 17; etc.). Cities of refuge were established in Israel so that if a man should unintentionally kill his neighbor, he might escape and so save his life (Deut. 4:41-43; 19:1-14; Josh. 20). This relationship of a man with his neighbor in Israel was subject to the law because the relationship had been established by God himself (Job 16:21). Conversely, moral disintegration and national catastrophe follow when men deny the rights of their neighbors and when neighbors disregard their reciprocal obligations. Men lie and slander their neighbors and so incur the divine wrath (Pss. 12:2; 101:5; cf. Prov. 11:9, 12; 14:21; 21:10; 25:18; 26:18-19). These circumstances will be widespread in the evil days which precede the day of the Lord's judgment (Isa. 3:5; Jer. 9:4-9; Mic. 7:5-6; cf. Jer. 19:9). The individual's treatment of his neighbor and his neighbor's wife is a prominent criterion in Ezekiel's distinction between the righteous and the sinful man (ch. 18; cf. ch. 22).

In the age of the New Covenant which Jeremiah envisaged, the law will be written upon men's hearts, and they will live together in peace (31:34); Zechariah envisaged an equally blissful state, when "every one . . . will invite his neighbor under his vine and under his fig tree" (3:10).

Throughout the OT one of the fears of the Israelite was that he should fall onto bad times and so become a subject of derision and scorn among his neighbors, whether Israelite or foreign (Job *passim;* Pss. 44:13; 79:4; 80:6; 89:41; etc.). The terrible pathos of the sorrows of captive Zion is underscored in Lamentations by the observation that the Lord has made Jacob's neighbors become his foes (1:17).

3. In the NT. In the NT, where the injunction from Lev. 19:18 is repeated with approval, the most important definition of the theological meaning of "neighbor" is presented in the parable of the Good Samaritan (Luke 10:25-37). Superficially the parable suggests that Jesus would have his followers recognize their neighbors as those in need of services, as individuals to whom assistance would be helpful and to whom it therefore should be offered. But actually Jesus did not use the parable in order to suggest that the man in need was the neighbor; rather, it was the man who had compassion who "proved neighbor to the man who fell among the robbers" (vs. 36). The ancient interpretation which viewed the Good Samaritan as a portrait of Christ himself properly proclaimed that he was the compassionate neighbor. For the Christian it follows that when the individual stops "desiring to justify himself" (vs. 29), and sees in Christ the compassionate neighbor, the individual then becomes the recipient of God's love; it then becomes possible for the individual to love God and his neighbors. In the same Christian terms it further becomes the obligation of the followers of Christ to serve as compassionate neighbors in the world, whence Jesus' directive to the lawyer (vs. 37). In this christological setting one's neighbors are those of his fellow beings who come forth in a variety of ways to do him good, whether by offering services to him or by confronting him with their own desperate need and so involving him with Christ in the fellowship of suffering humanity (cf. Matt. 25:31-46).

Jesus extends the term "neighbor" until it is essentially coextensive with "mankind." This wider interpretation belongs to the term in the rest of the NT. Both Paul (Rom. 13:9) and James (Jas. 2:8) regarded the commandment: "You shall love your neighbor as yourself," as the royal law and, in a sense, the summary of all law.

Bibliography. C. G. Montefiore, *The Synoptic Gospels* (2nd ed., 1927), II, 463-68; J. Moffatt, *Love in the NT* (1930); A. Nygren, *Agape and Eros* (trans. A. G. Hebert; 1941); A. C. Knudson, *The Principles of Christian Ethics* (1943), pp. 118-56; S. Kierkegaard, *Works of Love* (1946); K. Barth, *Kirchliche Dogmatik*, 1, 2 (4th ed., 1948), pp. 408-42, 457-74; G. A. Buttrick, *The Parables of Jesus* (1948), pp. 148-56; W. Eichrodt, *Theologie des Alten Testaments* (1948), I, 120-24; P. Ramsey, *Basic Christian Ethics* (1950), pp. 92-132, 234-48; P. E. Johnson, *Christian Love* (1951), pp. 23-48.

H. F. Beck

NEKEB nĕk'ĕb. KJV translation of הנקב ("tunnel, shaft, mine") in Josh. 19:33. If it is a town, it may be located at el-Bossa. However, it is almost certainly part of the place name Adami-nekeb (so RSV).

Bibliography. F.-M. Abel, *Géographie de la Palestine,* II (1938), 398.

G. W. Van Beek

NEKODA nĭ kō'də [נקודא]; KJV NECODAN —dən in I Esd. 5:37; NOEBA nō ē'bə in I Esd. 5:31. **1.** Eponym of some temple servants who returned to Jerusalem after the Exile (Ezra 2:48 = Neh. 7:50; I Esd. 5:31; II Esd. 17:50).

2. Eponym of some returned exiles who were unable to prove their Israelitic descent (Ezra 2:60 = Neh. 7:62; I Esd. 5:37).

E. R. Achtemeier

NEMUEL nĕm'yo͞o əl [נמואל]; NEMUELITES —ə līts. **1.** A Simeonite; head of the Nemuelites (Num. 26:12; I Chr. 4:24); called Jemuel in Gen. 46:10; Exod. 6:15.

2. A Reubenite; brother of Dathan and Abiram (Num. 26:9).

NEOLITHIC AGE nē'ə lĭth'ĭk. The second cultural stage, marked by the domestication of plants and animals, permitting settled communities, and by the technique of grinding as well as chipping stone implements. *See* PREHISTORY.

NEPHEG nē′fĕg [נֶפֶג]. **1.** A Levite; son of Izhar, and brother of Korah and Zichri (Exod. 6:21).

2. One of the sons of David who were born at Jerusalem (II Sam. 5:15; I Chr. 3:7; 14:6).

NEPHI nĕf′ī. KJV form of NAPHTHA.

NEPHILIM nĕf′ə lĭm [נפלים] (Gen. 6:4; Num. 13:33); KJV GIANTS. The exact meaning of the word is uncertain; it is therefore left untranslated. Although the word is rendered "giants" in the KJV, it should not be confused with the more widely used Hebrew words for "giant"—רפא, רפה, and רפאים.

In Gen. 6:1-4 we have a fragmentary narrative which purports to show that in the early history of the race the sons of God chose wives from among the daughters of men. From these unnatural unions a race of giants arose who represented a union of the divine spirit and human flesh. They were probably regarded as being intermediate between the divine and the human orders; and vs. 3 would seem to suggest, however obscurely, that they introduced an element of confusion into the world. Even though these Nephilim are referred to only once again in the OT (Num. 13:33), the tradition of such a race survived into historic times in Israel (Deut. 1:28; 2:10; and the various references to the REPHAIM cited above). We seem to have in this tradition the Hebraic version of a theme common in many ancient literatures, according to which men of great stature inhabited the earth in very early times, and in which marriages between supernatural beings and mortals were common. The myth in Gen. 6:1-4 therefore seems to serve an etiological purpose.

There is no clear basis for the long-standing interpretation that this passage is an introduction to the story of the Flood. That story does not allude to any such Nephilim, and the mere position of the fragment does not support the widespread inference. We are, as suggested, free to infer from vs. 3 that these Nephilim introduced some disorder into the world, and Jewish tradition commonly regards the Nephilim as the fallen or inferior ones. (Various other traditions have grown up in this connection. Adam, Eve, Seth, and Enoch are often designated as the sons of God whose children are the Nephilim. It is sometimes suggested that certain of the wives of Noah's sons were from this race and so bore giants after the Flood; or that certain giants escaped the Flood, thus accounting for the survival of these superhuman beings in later Hebraic tradition.) In the main, however, no sin is imputed to mankind for these marriages, and the blame is put, at least by inference, upon the Nephilim.

The reference to the Nephilim (of which J is the commonly accepted source) has been abridged so drastically that no real continuity holds the verses of the fragment together. Probably such an abridgment resulted from the writer's or a later editor's distaste for the mythological character of the narrative—he included these verses as an attempt to account for the origins of the Nephilim, about whom stories and beliefs continued to be popular. It is probable that the legend of the Nephilim was considerably more popular in the Hebrew tradition than the treatment of it by the editors of the Hexateuch would indicate. Vs. 4 clearly suggests that the existence of Nephilim was not restricted to the remote period mentioned in vs. 1. In Ezekiel's description of the nether world (ch. 32) we may have further allusions to these "fallen mighty men of old" (vs. 27).

See also ANAK; GIANT; SONS OF GOD.

Bibliography. K. Budde, *Die Biblische Urgeschichte* (1883), pp. 30 ff; J. Wellhausen, *Die Composition des Hexateuchs* (2nd ed., 1889), p. 14; H. G. Mitchell, *The World Before Abraham* (1901), pp. 190-94; S. R. Driver, *The Book of Genesis* (1904), pp. 82-84; J. Skinner, ICC (1910), pp. 145-47; O. Eissfeldt, *Hexateuch-Synopse* (1922), pp. 6-8, 225-26; C. A. Simpson, *The Early Traditions of Israel* (1948), pp. 61-62, 452, 499.

H. F. BECK

NEPHIS nē′fĭs. KJV Apoc. form of MAGBISH.

NEPHISH. KJV form of NAPHISH in I Chr. 5:19.

NEPHISIM nĭ fī′sĭm [נפיסים (*Kethibh*); Apoc. Ναφισί] (Ezra 2:50; I Esd. 5:31); KJV NEPHUSIM —fū′— [נפוסים (*Qere*)]; KJV Apoc. NAPHISI năf′ĭ sī. Alternately: NEPHUSHESIM nĭ fo͝osh′ə sĭm [נפושסים (*Kethibh*)] (Neh. 7:52); KJV NEPHISHESIM —fĭsh′— [נפישסים (*Qere*)].

Eponym of a family of Nethinim, or temple servants, listed among the exiles returned from Babylon; possibly related to the NAPHISH Ishmaelites (*see bibliography*). The form in Neh. 7:52 probably represents a superimposition of one variant spelling on another, the one with *sh,* the other with *s.*

Bibliography. L. W. Batten, *Ezra and Nehemiah,* ICC (1913), p. 89; R. A. Bowman, Exegesis of Ezra, *IB,* III (1954), 584.

B. T. DAHLBERG

NEPHTALI nĕf′tə lī. Douay Version form of NAPHTALI.

NEPHTHALI —thə lī. KJV Apoc. form of NAPHTALI; Kedesh Naphtali (*see* KEDESH 2).

NEPHTHALIM —lĭm. KJV NT form of NAPHTALI.

NEPHTHAR nĕf′thär [νεφθάρ] (II Macc. 1:36); KJV NAPHTHAR năf′—. A term of obscure etymology. *See* NAPHTHA.

NEPHTOAH nĕf tō′ə [נפתוח]. A place name, used only in the phrase "Waters of Nephtoah" (Josh. 15:9; 18:15). It is generally identified with modern Lifta with its spring, *ca.* three miles NW of Jerusalem. Other identifications have been proposed, particularly Atam, S of Bethlehem; but the nearness to KIRIATH-JEARIM fits Lifta.

Some scholars emend to read "waters of Merenptah" (מינפתח for נפתוח). *See* MER-NE-PTAH.

O. R. SELLERS

NEPHUSHESIM, NEPHUSIM. *See* NEPHISIM.

NER nûr [נר, light]. A Benjaminite whose son Abner was the commander of the army under Saul (I Sam.

26:5, 14, etc.). Although nothing is known of the life of Ner beyond the mere mention of his name, it is of importance to determine his relationship to the house of Saul. Some have considered Ner the uncle of Saul and the brother of Kish (e.g., Jos. Antiq. VI.vi.6). To arrive at this conclusion, it is necessary to interpret the antecedent of the words "Saul's uncle" in I Sam. 14:50 as Ner, to emend the following verse to read "sons of Abiel" instead of "son of Abiel," and to replace the first occurrence of Kish in I Chr. 8:33 (=I Chr. 9:39) with Abner. Support is sought for this interpretation in I Chr. 9:36, where a Kish is presented as a brother of Ner. However, the verses immediately following appear to demand two persons bearing the name Kish: one who is the brother of Ner, and one who is the son of Ner. Moreover, the change suggested in I Chr. 8:33 is simply foreign to the purpose of the Chronicler, which is to present the genealogy of the house of Saul.

On the other hand, if Ner is considered to be the grandfather of Saul and the father of Kish and Abner, no textual emendation is necessary except perhaps to insert "the son of Ner" immediately after the name Kish in I Sam. 9:1. The Benjaminite genealogy of the relationship of Ner to the house of Saul is then self-consistent (cf. also I Sam. 10:14-15).

E. R. DALGLISH

NERAIAH. Apoc. form of NERIAH.

NEREUS nĭr'o͞os, nĭr'ĭ əs [Νηρεύς]. A Christian who receives a greeting, together with his sister, who remains nameless, in Rom. 16:15. It has been conjectured that Philologus and Julia were the parents of Nereus, his sister, and Olympas, all mentioned in the same verse; the order of names supports this.

Nereus in Greek mythology was the wise old man of the sea, father of fifty daughters known as Nereids. It may seem strange that a Christian should bear and retain the name of a pagan divinity, but the same thing is true of Phoebe in vs. 1 and Hermes in vs. 14.

F. W. GINGRICH

NERGAL nûr'găl [*probably Ne-uru-gal,* the lord of the great city]. A Mesopotamian god whose name occurs in II Kings 17:30 and in a theophoric name Nergal-sharezer (Jer. 39:3, 13).

Nergal was a god worshiped by the military colonists settled by the Assyrians in the province of Samaria after the final collapse of Israel in 722 B.C., particularly by those of Cutha, of which he was the city god. Originally he was associated with fire and the heat of the sun, and then with war, hunting, and disasters which destroyed men en masse. The consort of Ereshkigal, mistress of Hell, he had as his cult animal the lion. One of his titles is "lord of weapons and the bow" (cf. "RESHEPH of the arrows" among the W Semites).

Bibliography. M. Jastrow, *The Religion of Babylonia and Assyria* (1898), pp. 65-68; W. Muss-Arnolt, *A Concise Dictionary of the Assyrian Language* (1905), pp. 726-27; E. Dhorme, *Les Religions de Babylonie et d'Assyrie* (1945), pp. 38-44.

J. GRAY

NERGAL-SHAREZER nûr'găl shə rē'zər [נרגל שר־אצר; Akkad. *Nergal-šar-uṣur,* Nergal protect the king!] (Jer. 39:3, 13). Rabmag, official of Nebuchadrezzar, mentioned among the "princes of the king of Babylon."

Possibly he is identical with King Neriglissar (559-556 B.C.), who was, according to Berosus, a son-in-law of Nebuchadrezzar, whose son Evil-merodach he killed in a rebellion. Of Neriglissar nothing is known besides a report on a campaign of his deep into Cilicia, which is described with unusual detail in a new fragment of the Babylonian Chronicle. It occurred in his third and last year. He was the son of a private citizen, and his name appears in legal texts, as do those of Nabonidus and Belshazzar.

Bibliography. D. J. Wiseman, *Chronicles of the Chaldaean Kings* (1956), pp. 37 ff.

A. L. OPPENHEIM

NERI nĭr'ī [Νηρί = נר, lamp] (Luke 3:27). An ancestor of Jesus.

NERIAH nĭ rī'ə [נריה, Yahu is light]. Alternately: NERAIAH nĭ rā'yə [Νηρίας] (Bar. 1:1); KJV NERIAS nĭ rī'əs. A Judean whose two sons served Jeremiah: Baruch as amanuensis (Jer. 32:12; 36:4; etc.), and Seraiah as bearer of the prophet's oracles against Babylon (51:59).

NERO nē'rō. Nero Claudius Caesar, successor of CLAUDIUS as Roman emperor (54-68). His mother, Agrippina, was the great-granddaughter of Augustus, sister of Caligula, and niece and later (49) wife of Claudius. To her and her previous husband, L. Domitius Ahenobarbus, the child Nero was born in 37. In 50 Agrippina persuaded Claudius to adopt Nero as guardian of his son and heir, Britannicus. Four years later Claudius died, probably poisoned by his wife, and Nero, hailed as emperor by the praetorian guard at her instigation, was confirmed by the Senate. In 55 Britannicus was murdered. Nero's empire was governed for him by his mother, by his tutor Seneca, and by Burrus, the praetorian prefect. In 59, weary of restraint and encouraged by his tutor and his mistress Poppea, Nero had his mother put to death. Three years later Burrus died, Seneca retired, and Nero divorced his wife in order to marry Poppea.

He was now free to turn to chariot races, shows of various kinds, and a promiscuous search for pleasure. He was genuinely enthusiastic about Greek poetry and music, but unfortunately he lacked talent. And his heavy expenses, including the costs of a successful war in Britain and a stalemate in Armenia,

Courtesy of the American Numismatic Society

14. Profile of Nero on Roman coin

led to the confiscation of estates (including those of the six largest landowners in Africa) and the depreciation of the currency. Both gold and silver coins were reduced in weight. Fig. NER 14.

On July 19, 64, a disastrous fire broke out in the city of Rome. It destroyed nearly a quarter of the city, and after the catastrophe public prayers were offered to the underworld deities, and propitiatory offerings were made to all the gods. A rumor persisted that Nero had ordered the fire started in order to provide space for his building operations, and he diverted attention from himself by finding scapegoats among "those whom, hated for their crimes, the mob called Chrestians" (Tac. Ann. XV.44). Tacitus does not specify these crimes except by referring to Christian superstition and inhumanity. The first to be arrested confessed either incendiarism or Christianity (it is not clear which accusation is involved), and then accused others, who were convicted "not so much for the crime of incendiarism as for hatred of the human race." They were afflicted with cruel and unusual punishments; some were clad in animal skins and attacked by dogs; others were crucified and burned in Nero's gardens, W of the Tiber. The emperor himself, with his usual dramatic flair, dressed as a charioteer and mingled with the crowds, sometimes mounting a chariot to drive through them. The result of his "savagery" was that doubts as to the Christians' guilt arose among the people. Seneca, who knew Nero well, had already warned him against this trait in his character, and was to refer to it again when he died as Nero's victim.

It is probable that the apostles Peter and Paul were put to death in this persecution, for the letter of Clement of Rome, written a generation later, indicates that both perished then. In this letter we read of the "noble examples of our own generation" —Peter and Paul, both presumably martyrs at Rome. "With these men was gathered a great multitude of the elect"; Tacitus also speaks of a "great multitude." "Women were persecuted as Danaids and Dircae"; here there are allusions to the mythological plays of which Nero was so fond. In Greek mythology the daughters of Danaus (Danaids) were given as prizes in a gymnastic contest, and Dirce was put to death by being tied to a wild bull. Clement is describing the persecution at Rome under Nero, and his account supplements that of Tacitus.

Two years later, the ex-consul Petus Thrasea was put to death for criticizing the emperor, while revolt broke out in Judea when the daily sacrifices for the emperor were suspended. On the other hand, Tiridates, king of Armenia and a Mithraic priest, came with his attendant Magi to reverence the emperor, addressing him as "master" and saying: "I have come to you my god, worshipping you as I worship Mithra" (Dio Cassius *History* LXIII.5). In return Nero confirmed Tiridates' rule over Armenia. This event may help explain oriental beliefs in Nero's survival of death.

The emperor then went on an extended tour of Greece (67-68); he won eighteen hundred crowns in various contests and proclaimed an imaginary "freedom for Greece" at Corinth, where he had the praetorian guards try to complete a canal through the Isthmus. The political situation, however, steadily grew worse. Nero demanded and received the suicides of a successful general and of two governors in Germany, but in the spring of 68 revolt broke out in Gaul, Spain, and Africa. The emperor returned to Rome but had to flee; he committed suicide on June 9. A year of anarchy followed. Galba, governor in Spain; Otho, friend of Nero and previous husband of Poppea; and Vitellius, a general in Spain, came to power in rapid succession. Stability was restored only when VESPASIAN became emperor.

Since the Senate had already declared Nero an enemy of the state, there was no question of his deification. His memory was detested by the aristocracy as well as by the Christians, who came to believe that he was responsible for all the imperial legislation against them. On the other hand, there were many who believed that he had not really died but would return, perhaps from the East. In the year 69 a pseudo-Nero arose in Asia and Achaea, anticipating Parthian aid, but he was soon caught and put to death. In 88 another pretender in Asia declared that he was Nero and that he had been in hiding; he was able to escape to the Parthians, but only temporarily. As late as the early second century, Dio Chrysostom (*Orations* XXI.10) says that "most men believe that Nero is still alive." The same belief was held by some Jewish-Christian apocalyptic writers (*Sibylline Oracles* IV.119; V.363; VIII.70). And the return of Nero may be symbolically mentioned in Rev. 13:3, 12 ("Its mortal wound was healed").

As far as Nero's relation to the Christian church is concerned, it is a fact that he persecuted Christians at Rome; it is also a fact that later Christian writers (e.g., Melito and Tertullian) believed that in the first century only he and Domitian persecuted the church. It is by no means so certain that an edict of Nero (*Institutum Neronianum,* as Tertullian calls it) actually served as the legal basis for later persecutions. Tertullian's evidence is ambiguous. In another connection he mentions no special law but speaks of Christians as condemned on grounds of sacrilege, enmity toward the state, and treason (*maiestas*). If there was such a law, passages from a few Christian writers suggest that it read: "It is not lawful for Christians to exist." But the very sporadic nature of later persecutions suggests that there was no such law. Furthermore, according to Tacitus the crime for which Christians were put to death was arson. He hints at other charges, but the penalty of being burned alive suggests that arson was the main point. We may also suspect the efforts of Christian writers to make the unpopular Nero and Domitian scapegoats for a policy of persecution which we know was followed by "good" emperors such as Trajan and Marcus Aurelius.

The reign of Nero, together with the subsequent fall of Jerusalem, strongly influenced the Christian church. In the first place, Nero deprived the church of some of its chief links with the earliest times and made necessary the preservation of apostolic memories in writing. It is likely that the Gospel of Mark is a product of Nero's reign. In the second place, it became evident that persecution and the fall of Jerusalem were not signs of the immediate end of the world, and a process of "rethinking apocalyptic" was intensified. Under these circumstances there was also an increased concern for the continuity of the church and of its ministry, as well as for the significance of martyrdom.

At the same time, there was now a relatively clear distinction between Judaism and Christianity. Before the Jewish Revolt began, the Christians of Jerusalem left the city for Pella, across the Jordan. And it has been suspected, though without evidence, that Nero chose Christians rather than Jews as his scapegoats because of the influence of Poppea, who, according to Josephus, was interested in Judaism. It was now hard to view Christianity as a Jewish sect.

Bibliography. B. W. Henderson, *The Life and Principate of the Emperor Nero* (1903); M. P. Charlesworth, *Documents Illustrating the Reigns of Claudius and Nero* (1939). On legislation against Christians, J. W. P. Borleffs, "Institutum Neronianum," *Vigiliae Christianae,* VI (1952), 129-45.

R. M. Grant

NEST. The word used to translate קֵן in certain OT passages. The verbal form from the same root, קִנֵּן, "to make a nest," is used also in several OT passages. Usually the reference is to birds and their nests, though at times it is to a temporary abiding place for a human being.

The word translated "nests" in the parallel passages Matt. 8:20; Luke 9:58, κατασκήνωσις, means literally "to put down a tent."

S. A. Cartledge

NET. A fabric of twine or cord, woven into meshes and used for catching fish, birds, and other animals.

1. Terminology
2. Cord nets
   - *a.* Antiquity, general use, and materials
   - *b.* Fishing
   - *c.* Fowling
   - *d.* Wild animals

Courtesy of the Editions des Musées Nationaux, Paris

15. Limestone stele from Telloh, showing the enemies of Eannatum, king of Lagash, snared in a net (middle third millennium)

3. Metal netting
4. Figurative use of "net"

1. Terminology. "Net" and similar terms are used to translate a number of Hebrew and Greek words. In the OT, מכמר (*makhmōr* in Ps. 141:10; *mikhmār* in Isa. 51:20) and מכמרת (*mikhmōreth* in Isa. 19:8; *mikhmereth* [SEINE; KJV DRAG] in Hab. 1:15-16) are probably from Akkadian *kamâru*, "press down, overpower" (noun *kamaru*, "net, snare"). מצודה (*m*e*ṣôdhâ* in Eccl. 9:12; *m*e*ṣûdhâ* [SNARE] in Ezek. 12:13; 17:20) and מצוד (Eccl. 7:26; SNARES) are from צוד, "to hunt." The KJV translates חרם "net" in Ezek. 32:3 (RSV DRAGNET; from חרם, "to slit"). Words similar to "net" are: רשת (מעשה רשת), "network" (Exod. 27:4; 38:4), from ירש, "subdue, take possession of"; שבכה, "network," "pitfall" (KJV variously "snare," "wreath," "wreathen work"; cf. Arabic *šabaka*, "be interwoven"). Words translated "net" in the NT are: αμφίβληστρον (Matt. 4:18), from ἀμφιβάλλω, "throw (or put) around"; δίκτυον, from δικεῖν, second aorist "throw, cast"; and σαγήνη (Matt. 13·47).

2. Cord nets. ***a. Antiquity, general use, and materials.*** Cord and rope making is one of the oldest human skills, and nets made from such cordage have been traced back to the Mesolithic period. The graphic and literary sources from both Egypt and Western Asia, as well as the biblical references, make it clear that all the commoner uses of the net were well known in the world of the biblical writers. The principal materials used for the cording were flax, hemp, palm fiber, and papyrus.

In the OT the precise difference between a net and a snare is not always clear, for some snares must in fact have been concealed nets.

b. Fishing. While the biblical data do not permit definitive conclusions, it seems probable that fishing nets were mostly of two kinds. One was a hand casting net, cone-shaped with leads around its wide mouth to pull it below the surface of the water (Matt. 4:18-21; Mark 1:16-19; etc.). The second was a seine or large draw net, its head supported by floats and its foot fitted with sinkers; it was often hauled ashore in a wide semicircle (Isa. 19:8; Ezek. 26:5, 14; 47:10; cf. 32:3 ["dragnet"]; Matt. 13:47). *See ANEP* 112-13. *See also* FISHING.

c. Fowling. Fowling nets are referred to in Prov. 1:17; Hos. 7:11-12, but we can only conjecture how they were operated. In the art of ancient Egypt a large clapnet for securing waterfowl in a pond or marsh is occasionally pictured. It was pulled shut by five men. *See* FOWLER. Fig. FOW 22.

d. Wild animals. Either a fleeing animal would be overtaken and a net thrown over it, or animals would be driven into an ambush in which nets were concealed (Isa. 51:20; Ezek. 19:8). *See* HUNTING.

3. Metal netting. According to Exod. 27:4-5; 38:4, a grille ("net" or "network") of bronze went around the altar of the temple. In Exod. 35:16; 38:5, 30; 39:39, this is called a "grating," מכבר, of bronze.

The OT informs us (I Kings 7:17-20, etc.; cf. Jos. Antiq. VIII.iii.4) that the two pillars, Jachin and Boaz, which stood at the entrance to the temple, had some bronze "network" as part of the decoration of their capitals. *See* JACHIN AND BOAZ.

4. Figurative use of "net." In the OT, but nowhere in the NT, the net serves frequently as a figure of speech. It is used to designate the Lord's chastisement of Israel (Ps. 66:11; Lam. 1:13; Hos. 7:12), of Zedekiah (Ezek. 12:13), of Job (Job 19:6), and of Egypt (Ezek. 32:3). It represents the plots or snares of Israel's leaders (Hos. 5:1) and of the enemies of the psalmists (Pss. 9:15—H 9:16; 31:4—H 31:5; 35:7-8; 57:6—H 57:7; 140:5—H 140:6; 141:10), man's exploitation of man (Ps. 10:9; Mic. 7:2; Hab. 1:15-17), and something akin to fate (Job 18:8; Ps. 25:15; Eccl. 9:12) or to an evil end (Job 18:8; "pitfall"). In Prov. 29:5 it typifies the wiles of the flatterer, and in Eccl. 7:26 the seductiveness of a woman. The meaning of Hab. 1:16 ("He sacrifices to his net") is obscure, as also of Prov. 12:12 KJV ("the net of evil men"). Fig. NET 15 represents enemies contained in a net. W. S. McCullough

NETAIM nĭ tā'əm [נטעים, plantings] (I Chr. 4:23). A place in Judah where some royal potters lived. The site is unknown.

NETHANEL nĭ thăn'əl [נתנאל, God gives; Apoc. Ναθαναήλ, Ναθανάηλος]; KJV NETHANEEL —ĭ əl; KJV Apoc. NATHANAEL nə thăn'ĭ əl. **1.** A leading chief of Issachar; son of Zuar (Num. 1:8); commander of 54,400 men (2:5; 10:15). He took part in the dedication of the altar of the tabernacle (7:18-23).

2. The fourth son of Jesse, and a brother of David (I Chr. 2:14).

3. A priest who was to blow the trumpets before the ark (I Chr. 15:24).

4. One of the princes of Judah sent out by King Jehoshaphat to instruct all the cities of Judah in the "book of the law of the LORD" (II Chr. 17:7-9).

5. A Levite; the father of Shemaiah (I Chr. 24:6).

6. A Levite; son of Obed-edom, a gatekeeper in the temple (I Chr. 26:4).

7. A Levite; brother of Conaniah, and one of those chief Levites who contributed to the Passover offering in the time of Josiah (II Chr. 35:9; I Esd. 1:9).

8. Son of Pashhur; one of the priests who had married a foreign wife while in exile (Ezra 10:22; I Esd. 9:22). He is perhaps identical with 10 *below*.

9. Head of the priestly house of Jedaiah in the days of the high priest Joiakim (Neh. 12:21).

10. A priest who took part in the dedication of the rebuilt wall of Jerusalem (Neh. 12:36). He is perhaps identical with 8 *above*. E. R. Achtemeier

NETHANIAH nĕth'ə nī'ə [נתניה, נתניהו, Y gives]; KJV Apoc. NATHANIAS năth'ə nī'əs. **1.** The father of Jehudi (Jer. 36:14).

2. The father of Ishmael, murderer of Gedaliah (II Kings 25:23, 25; Jer. 40:8, 14-15; 41).

3. A Levite sent by King Jehoshaphat to teach the law of the Lord throughout Judah (II Chr. 17:8).

4. A Levite, and one of the sons of Asaph whom David set apart to prophesy with lyres and harps and cymbals (I Chr. 25:2, 12). E. R. Achtemeier

5. A layman who divorced his foreign wife and children in Ezra's reform (I Esd. 9:34; equivalent to NATHAN [6] in Ezra 10:39).

NETHER WORLD. *See* DEAD, ABODE OF, § 3*d*.

NETHINIM nĕth′ə nĭm [נתינים, those given (*i.e., to the service of the sanctuary*), *from* נתן; *Kethibh* הנתונים *in* Ezra 8:17; LXX οἱ δεδομένοι; Josephus ἱερόδουλοι, sacred slaves]. The lists in Ezra-Nehemiah portray five clerical orders among the returned exiles: priests, Levites, singers, porters, and Nethinim (RSV "temple servants"; KJV "Nethinims")—i.e., persons appointed for the lowest menial tasks of the temple (cf. Ezra 2:36, 40-43; Neh. 10:28).

Very little is known of temple slaves in the pre-exilic period. Moses is said to have taken one of every fifty captive Midianites and beasts and given them to the Levites (Num. 31:30, 47). Josh. 9:27 relates how Joshua punished the wily Gibeonites for their ruse by making them hewers of wood and water carriers for the congregation and for Yahweh's altar. Ezra 8:20 mentions the temple servants or slaves whom David and his princes had given to the Levites. Ezra 2:58 likewise mentions Solomon's servants. It is the descendants of these earlier temple slaves who now appear in the lists of the returned exiles (Ezra 2:43-54; Neh. 7:46-56). 392 Nethinim and the descendants of Solomon's servants accompanied Zerubbabel to Jerusalem in 538 B.C. Later, either in 458 (Artaxerxes I) or in 398 (Artaxerxes II), Ezra came to Jerusalem, and 220 Nethinim were sent with him to swell his company. These and 38 Levites came from a Jewish colony at Casiphia (Ezra 8:16-20).

It is noteworthy that the lists show:

a) The Nethinim were organized under family heads. The Ezra list gives thirty-five families and ten families of Solomon's servants. The Nehemiah list gives thirty-two families; and in 11:21 it is stated that two chiefs, Ziha and Gishpa, were in charge of the whole company (cf. Ezra 2:43). These are all mentioned by name (Ezra 2:43 ff; for the phrase, cf. I Chr. 12:31; 16:41; etc.), and this suggests lists or even family registers.

b) The Nethinim were largely of foreign extraction. Thus the pre-exilic evidence above quoted, the evidence also concerning Solomon's servants, and the foreign names in the present lists tend to confirm the traditional view that the Nethinim were descended from prisoners of war—i.e., alien peoples. Hence arose the denunciation of Ezekiel (44:6-7) that Israel had delegated the care of the temple to uncircumcised foreigners.

c) Solomon's servants are mentioned next after the Nethinim. Their functions then were similar, even if they belonged to a slightly lower order. In Ezra 2:55 (=Neh. 7:57) the children of Solomon's servants (i.e., slaves) are distinguished from the Nethinim, and are separately classified in their families; but generally they are included as Nethinim.

1. Status. The Nethinim, though unmentioned in the Pentateuch, were the lowest class of temple servants and were "given" for service to the priests. Though they are carefully distinguished from Levites (e.g., lists above and I Chr. 9:2), they nevertheless were considered to belong to the congregation (Neh. 10:28). Like the other listed classes, they clung to the congregation and participated in the covenant and its accompanying curse to observe God's law in respect of mixed marriages, sabbathkeeping, etc. Likewise Ezra 7:24 shows that they shared in the privileges of the priests and Levites in tax exemption.

Later Jewish traditions in the Talmud (cf. Yeb. 2.4; Kid. 4.1) mention Nethinim with contempt and forbid the marriage of Jews and Nethinim. This latter prohibition is, of course, one of the articles of the covenant actually embraced by the Nethinim (Neh. 10:29 ff), so the Talmud tradition probably represents that view of the origin of the Nethinim which connected them with Gibeonites and other Canaanite captives. So far from the Talmud tradition's being true for the Persian period, it is likely that the lot and status of the Nethinim showed a progressive improvement. This would be inevitable if the Nethinim maintained their vows not to marry non-Jews. Thus Levites are described as Nethinim for Aaron, and this usage reveals a growing respectability for the term (cf. Num. 3:9; 18:6 [P]; I Chr. 6:48; I Esd. 1:3).

2. Residence. From Neh. 3:26 it seems clear that a good proportion, at least, of the Nethinim dwelt in *Ophel*—i.e., in their own quarter on the S extension of the temple hill. They were near the water gate, which led to the virgin's spring, and this location may well be significant for their duties. For from here they had easy access both to water and to the temple. Neh. 3:31 ascribes a residence to the Nethinim on the wall probably NE of the precincts of the temple, possibly a residence for more important Nethinim. Ezra 2:70 (=Neh. 7:73) indicates that Nethinim lived in other cities as well, and these were probably Levitical cities.

Bibliography. J. Pedersen, *Israel*, III-IV (1940), p. 183. *See also* the bibliographies under PRIESTS AND LEVITES; SOLOMON'S SERVANTS.

G. HENTON DAVIES

NETOPHAH nĭ tō′fə [נטפה, dropping; Νετέβας]; NETOPHATHITES —thīts. A town in the hill country of Judah, closely associated with Bethlehem (I Chr. 2:54; Ezra 2:21-22; Neh. 7:26). Two of David's Mighty Men, Maharai and Heleb, were natives of the site (II Sam. 23:28-29; I Chr. 11:30) and were commanders for the tenth and twelfth of the king's twelve monthly military divisions (I Chr. 27:13, 15).

A certain Netophathite, Seraiah the son of Tanhumeth, was among the captains of the scattered Judean forces which loyally gathered about Gedaliah, the puppet governor of Judea, subsequent to the fall of Jerusalem to the Babylonians in 587 B.C. (II Kings 25:23; Jer. 40:8-9).

Fifty-six men who counted Netophah their ancestral home were among those who returned with Zerubbabel from the Babylonian captivity (Ezra 2:22; Neh. 7:26; cf. I Esd. 5:18). Levites, also, who were returnees from the Captivity took up residence in the "villages of the Netophathites" (I Chr. 9:16), including certain "sons of the singers" among them who assembled in Jerusalem on the occasion of the dedication of the wall of the city (Neh. 12:27-28).

The ancient town of Netophah is probably represented by the ruin presently called Khirbet Bedd Faluh. The site occupies the spur of a ridge formed by the conjunction of two valleys *ca.* 3½ miles SE of Bethlehem and in the vicinity of Herodium. In the same general area is the spring called 'Ain en-Natuf, which preserves the ancient name of the district of Netophah with but slight change.

W. H. MORTON

NETTLE [חרול, *ḥārûl;* קמוש, *qimmôš*]. An annual wild plant of the genus *Urtica,* noted for its stinging toxic effect when touched. At least four species are common in Bible lands, particularly *Urtica pilulifera* L.

Many scholars conclude that the meaning of חרול is generic, referring to scrub brush that grows up over neglected fields (cf. Amer. Trans. use of "scrub" and "weeds"). The word is used in a description of men reduced to the lowest state of poverty (Job 30:7), the weeds which occupy the field of a lazy man (Prov. 24:31), a land "possessed by nettles and salt pits" (Zeph. 2:9). Many different weeds might fit these contexts. Royle's theory that חרול refers to the wild mustard, *Brassica nigra* (L.) Koch (or *Sinapis arvensis* L.), is worthy of consideration. The Mishnaic Hebrew חרדל and Arabic *khardal* for "mustard" might have derived from the OT word.

The second word above (קמוש) is more generally agreed to be the word for "nettle." It appears in Prov. 24:31 (RSV "thorns") parallel to חרול, which argues against translating both words "nettle." Describing a lazy man's field, the passage might refer to nettles and wild mustard, two weeds which are commonly seen even today in neglected fields. Nettles growing over deserted ruins dramatize the destruction and desolation (Isa. 34:13; Hos. 9:6).

See also FLORA §§ A12-13*a;* MUSTARD; THISTLES.

Bibliography. I. Löw, *Die Flora der Juden,* III (1924), 478-81; H. N. and A. L. Moldenke, *Plants of the Bible* (1952), pp. 220-21, 237.

J. C. TREVER

NETWORK. 1. רשת (Exod. 27:4-5; 38:4). A bronze grating on the altar of burnt offering before the tabernacle. *See* GRATE.

2. שבכה (I Kings 7:18, 20, 41-42; II Kings 25:17; II Chr. 4:12-13; Jer. 52:22-23; KJV NET). Bronze latticed work on the capitals of the two pillars, JACHIN AND BOAZ, in Solomon's temple. I Kings 7:17-18 describes the network as covering the capitals themselves (cf. II Kings 25:17). I Kings 7:41-42 describes the network as covering the bowls (גלת) of the capitals (cf. II Chr. 4:12-13). A "rounded projection" (בטן; KJV "belly") also figures in I Kings 7:20, being close beside the network. This may be the bowl of I Kings 7:41-42. The network may have been a grill of bronze covering the sides of huge lamp bowls on the pillars and serving as material upon which the pomegranates which adorned them were fastened. I Kings 7:20 indicates that the network had two hundred bronze pomegranates in two rows around it, though Jer. 52:23 knows of only one hundred pomegranates, four being placed at the cardinal points and the other ninety-six filling the remaining space in a row (and cf. II Chr. 3:16). The precise relationship of the network, the bowl, and the CAPITAL remains uncertain.

E. M. GOOD

NEW. The translation of חדש; καινός; νέος.

The common word for "new" in the NT is καινός, but occasionally νέος is used. It has generally been held that καινός means "new" in reference to character, whereas νέος means "new" in reference to time ("young, recent"). This distinction is sometimes apparent, but it cannot be pressed in every case. It is not supported by the evidence of the papyri, and in the NT it is difficult to see any distinction, e.g., between the "new man" or "new nature" in Eph. 2:15; 4:24 (καινός) and in Col. 3:10 (νέος). The NT also uses πρόσφατος ("newly manifested") of the "new" way to God opened up by Christ (Heb. 10:20; in the LXX this word appears, e.g., in Eccl. 1:9: "nothing new under the sun"); and ἄγναφος ("unlaundered, unshrunk") of "new" cloth (Mark 2:21 = Matt. 9:16 KJV).

The most significant OT occurrences of the concept of "newness" are connected (*a*) with the beginning of the month, year, etc. (*see* CALENDAR; FEASTS AND FASTS; NEW MOON; NEW YEAR); and (*b*) by analogy with these, with the new age to come, the day of the Lord, when he will perform a "new thing" (Isa. 43:19; cf. Jer. 31:22), make "a new covenant" with his people (Jer. 31:31 ff; cf. Ezek. 34:25; 37:26), implant a new heart and a new spirit within them (Ezek. 11:19; 18:31; 36:26), call them by a new name (Isa. 62:2), and create new heavens and a new earth (Isa. 65:17; cf. 66:22). This consummation is fittingly celebrated by a new song (Ps. 96:1; 98:1; cf. Isa. 42:10, where the return from exile heralds the new age).

In the NT these ideas are taken up and applied to the kingdom of God introduced by Christ. His hearers recognized in his ministry a "new teaching" (Mark 1:27); he himself compared his ministry to "new wine," which requires "fresh skins" (Mark 2:22). The new age which dawns with his ministry is the "regeneration" (Matt. 19:28 KJV; RSV "the new world"); those who are "created in Christ Jesus" (Eph. 2:10) constitute a "new creation" (II Cor. 5:17; cf. Gal. 6:15); for them "the old has passed away, behold, the new has come" (II Cor. 5:17). By the new birth which they receive through faith-union with Christ, they inherit the promise of a new heart and spirit foretold by Ezekiel; with them Jeremiah's "new covenant" is ratified (Heb. 8:8 ff)—a covenant sealed by their Lord's self-sacrifice (I Cor. 11:25)—and the "newness of life" (Rom. 6:4) which they henceforth enjoy is expressed sacramentally by baptism. In them the "new nature" or "new man" is formed, whether we think of their personal life (Eph. 4:24; Col. 3:10) or their communal life in Christ (Eph. 2:15). This new man is, by implication, Christ himself (cf. Gal. 4:19, and the references to the "second Adam"); Ignatius speaks explicitly of the "new man Jesus Christ" (Ign. Eph. 20:1). From Christ his people receive a "new name" (Rev. 2:17; 3:12), which is his own name (Rev. 22:4); and a "new commandment" (John 13:34), which is the old commandment of love (I John 2:7 ff), filled with a deeper and fresher meaning by its re-enactment and fulfilment by Jesus.

No wonder, then, that they celebrate his redemptive act by singing a new song, even as the people of Israel sang a new song to the Lord to celebrate the wonders of his delivering power and to hail his coming to judge the world in righteousness. The "new song" which saints and angels sing in heaven is the song sung by the church militant here on earth:

> Worthy art thou . . . ,
> for thou wast slain and by thy blood didst ransom
> men for God
> . . . .
> and hast made them a kingdom and priests to our God,
> and they shall reign on earth (Rev. 5:9-10; cf. 14:3).

Here and now the people of Christ have as their spiritual mother the "Jerusalem above" (Gal. 4:26); but the day will come when that heavenly city, "new Jerusalem" (Rev. 21:2), will come down to earth. An OT prophet had drawn the blueprint of a new Jerusalem for the new commonwealth which would take shape with Israel's return from exile (Ezek. 40:1 ff), and others had elaborated the details of his vision, as we now know from fragmentary documents found at Qumran; but in Rev. 21:2 ff this vision is taken up afresh and used to portray the day when "the dwelling of God is with men," when "the former things have passed away" and the declaration is made from the throne of God: "Behold, I make all things new" (an apocalyptic version of what is expressed as an inward experience in II Cor. 5:17). Thus a new meaning, in terms of NT fulfilment, is given to the words in which the prophet announced an earlier redemption:

> Behold, the former things have come to pass,
> and new things I now declare (Isa. 42:9);

and his picture of new heavens and a new earth (65:17) is realized in a completely new order, "in which righteousness dwells" (II Pet. 3:13; cf. Rev. 21:1). *See also* NEW EARTH; NEW JERUSALEM; REGENERATION.

Bibliography. R. A. Harrisville, "The Concept of Newness in the NT," *JBL,* LXXIV (1955), 69-79. F. F. BRUCE

NEW BIRTH. A concept which may be seen in a number of biblical expressions. "Born anew" occurs in I Pet. 1:3, 23, for ἀναγεννᾶν and in John 3:3, 7, for γεννᾶν ἄνωθεν to designate REGENERATION. In I Pet. 2:2 "newborn" translates ἀρτιγέννητος (lit., "recently born"). A term for "newness" (*see* NEW) is not actually present in these expressions for "rebirth." Yet "newness" of life, as an OT concept (Ps. 51:10; Ezek. 11:19; 18:31; 36:26) and an idea inherent in the NT eschatological outlook, does occur in some NT designations for regeneration:

a) "Renewal": ἀνακαίνωσις (Rom. 12:2; Tit. 3:5).

b) "Renew": ἀνακαινίζειν (Heb. 6:6; "restore" in vs. 4); ἀνανεοῦσθαι (Eph. 4:23); and, as a continuing process, ἀνακαινοῦσθαι (II Cor. 4:16; Col. 3:10).

c) "New creation" (KJV "new creature"): καινὴ κτίσις (II Cor. 5:17; Gal. 6:15).

d) "New nature" (KJV "new man"): νέος (ἄνθρωπος) (Col. 3:10); καινὸς ἄνθρωπος (Eph. 2:15 ["new man"]; 4:24). *See also* NEW MAN.

e) "Newness": καινότης (of life in Rom. 6:4; of spirit in 7:6).

Bibliography. A. von Harnack, "Die Terminologie der Wiedergeburt und verwandter Erlebnisse in der ältesten Kirche," *Texte und Untersuchungen,* vol. XLII, no. 3 (1918), especially pp. 101-3. J. M. ROBINSON

NEW EARTH, NEW HEAVEN [οὐρανὸν καινὸν καὶ γῆν καινήν]. The phrase used to impart the idea of a new creation, a part of John's theodicy in Rev. 21:1. This concept is a derivative from Isa. 65:17; 66:22 (cf. also I Enoch 45:4-5; II Esd. 7:75; II Bar. 32:6; II Pet. 3:13). Like Paul, the apocalyptist saw the former creation judged unworthy because of the "futility" which it shared with man in his sin (Rom. 8:19 ff; Rev. 20:11; cf. Gen. 3:17 ff; Eccl. 1:2).

Bibliography. In addition to the Commentaries listed in the bibliography under REVELATION, BOOK OF, see: E. Stauffer, *NT Theology* (trans. from 5th German ed. by John Marsh; 1955), ch. 58: "The New Created Order," pp. 225-28; cf. J. W. Bowman, *The Drama of the Book of Revelation* (1955), pp. 146-47. J. W. BOWMAN

NEW GATE (Jer. 26:10). A gate of the TEMPLE of Jerusalem. The Hebrew text, probably corrupted, reads שער יהוה החדש. A likely emendation would be שער בית יהוה החדש, "New Gate of the house of the LORD" (so RSV). The exact location is unknown. G. A. BARROIS

NEW JERUSALEM [τῆς καινῆς Ἰερουσαλὴμ (Rev. 3:12); τὴν πόλιν τὴν ἁγίαν Ἰερουσαλὴμ καινὴν (21:2; cf. vs. 10)]. The capital city of God's new creation (21:1). The conception is found in the OT and in later Jewish literature (cf. Isa. 54; 60; Ezek. 40; 48; II Esd. 10:27; II Bar. 4:3; Test. Dan 5:12), as also in the NT (Gal. 4:26-27; Phil. 3:20; Heb. 12:22). The description of this city in Rev. 21:2 as one like a "bride adorned for her husband" makes certain its identification with the church, the true people of God (cf. Isa. 61:10; Hos. 1–3; Eph. 5:25 ff; Heb. 11:10).

Bibliography. See the Commentaries listed in the bibliography under REVELATION, BOOK OF. J. W. BOWMAN

NEW MAN [νέος (ἄνθρωπος) Col. 3:10 KJV; RSV NEW NATURE); καινὸς ἄνθρωπος (Eph. 2:15; 4:24 KJV; RSV NEW NATURE)]. The exalted, cosmic Christ, the church his body, and thus man's true self. The christological title "the new man Jesus Christ" (Ign. Eph. 20:1) developed beyond the titles SON OF MAN, the "last Adam" (I Cor. 15:45), the "second man" (I Cor. 15:47; *see* SECOND ADAM), and the "perfect man" (Eph. 4:13 KJV; Ign. Smyr. 4:2), on the basis of the common concept of a "primal man": The cosmic reconciliation effected by Christ at his exaltation (Eph. 2:14; 4:8 ff; *see* ASCENSION) created "one new man" (2:15) or "one body" (vs. 16), which the church is equipped by the "one Spirit" (vs. 18; 4:3 ff) to realize ("build up"; Eph. 4:12 ff). Since the Christian imperative is thus rooted in the kerygmatic indicative, ethical exhortation takes the pattern: "Put on the new nature" (Eph. 4:24; Col. 3:10; cf. Epistle to Diognetus 2.1), just as, on a simpler christological level, one "put on Christ" (Rom. 13:14; Gal. 3:27). In this "new nature" man reaches his true destiny of the image of God (Eph. 4:24; Col. 3:10; cf. Rom. 8:29), so that the term is not only christological, but, like the term "Christ" itself (Rom. 8:10; Gal. 2:20; Phil. 1:21; Col. 3:3-4), also designates man's true self (cf. the "inner man" [II Cor. 4:16; Eph. 3:16-17]; and *see* REGENERATION), and points to the goal of Col. 1:28: "every man mature in Christ."

Bibliography. A. von Harnack, "Die Terminologie der Wiedergeburt und verwandter Erlebnisse in der ältesten Kirche," *TU,* vol. XLII, no. 3 (1918), especially pp. 135-38; H. Schlier, "Der himmlische Anthropos," *Christus und die Kirche im Epheserbrief* (1930), pp. 27-37. J. M. ROBINSON

NEW MOON [חדש(ה), (the) new one, month (*see* CALENDAR); ראש חדש, beginning (first) of the month (cf. Num. 10:10; 28:11); LXX νεομηνία *or* νουμηνία (Jth. 8:6)]. The festal religious observance of the first day of the month as indicated by the appearance of the new moon.

Israel's communal and religious life has centrally been based on a lunar calendar. In its notation on Exod. 12:2 the Mekilta states that "the nations" reckon by the sun, but Israel by the moon. The feasts of PASSOVER and BOOTHS were not set simply by the general lunar calculation, but on the basis of the appearance of the new moon of the month in which they occurred, PENTECOST depending on Passover in this respect. Easter and the Christian Pentecost still reflect this pattern. The earliest and only significant exception to this order of the religious year in Israel was the sabbath, which was separate from the lunar cycles and occurred every seventh day. Though it is impossible to document this fully, it seems probable that the sabbath was originally also part of this natural cycle of time, related to the phases of the moon, and that, following its separation, the Feast of the New Moon continued as a separate observance.

The observance of the New Moon was similar to sabbath observance in many ways. There was rest from work (Amos 8:5); the day was characterized by rejoicing (Hos. 2:11), and fasting and mourning were suspended (Jth. 8:6). In the worship of the temple special sacrifices were prescribed. These were even somewhat greater than those for the sabbath (cf. Num. 28:9-15), and the ceremonies were proclaimed with trumpets (Num. 10:10; Ps. 81:3). Formal festal eating seems to have formed part of the observance. It seems that the New Moon of especially significant months was particularly sacred (cf. I Sam. 20:6; Aq. Sym. on Ps. 81:3—H 81:4); the New Moon of the seventh month was especially important (Lev. 23:24; Neh. 8:2), probably because it once may have marked the beginning of the year. The New Moon seems to have been the appropriate time to consult a prophet (II Kings 4:23), and Ezekiel often records his visions as granted on the first day (26:1; 29:17; 31:1; 32:1; cf. Isa. 47:13; Hag. 1:1, of Babylonian seers).

In postexilic Judaism the importance of the New Moon feast apparently increased. Ezra read the law to the people at a New Moon (Neh. 8:2). In Isa. 66:22-23 the New Moon is coupled with sabbath in an eschatological pronouncement about the worship of "all flesh" in Jerusalem, and it is a significant fact that all historic Jewish rites for the announcement of the New Moon, made on the preceding sabbath, contain a prayer of eschatological content. The rationale for the observance was God's creation of the moon as a "sign" of the unbreakable covenant with Israel, the "times" of whose cultus it decreed (Ps. 104:19; Ecclus. 43:6-8). This eschatological meaning in the context of the covenant was linked with an emphasis upon God as Creator of time, illustrated in the formula of Blessing of the New Moon: "Praised art thou, LORD, that renewest the months" (Ber. 13*d*). Though the observance of New Moon was not continued in the Christian church, this was not for a want of awareness of the comprehensive significance attached to it in Judaism (Col. 2:16-17; cf. 1:16-17).

Before the dates of the New Moon were set by a fixed calendar, they were determined each month by actual observation. Following the destruction of the temple, it was a function of the supreme rabbinic council thus to designate the date. The special Torah reading for the day is Num. 28:1-15. Ps. 104 is also read, and the festal character of the observance is indicated by the chanting of the HALLEL. Since the sixteenth century the day preceding a New Moon has been a fast day, often called a little yom kippur.

Bibliography. I. Elbogen, *Der jüdische Gottesdienst* (2nd ed., 1924), pp. 122-26; G. Dalman, *Arbeit und Sitte in Palästina* (1927), pp. 3-19. J. C. RYLAARSDAM

NEW TESTAMENT [ἡ καινὴ διαθήκη] I Cor. 11:25; II Cor. 3:6; Heb. 8:8, 13; 9:15; cf. Jer. 31:31-34); RSV NEW COVENANT. In current usage, the twenty-seven books which form the second part of the Christian Bible, in continuation and distinction from the Old Testament (Covenant), or the Hebrew scriptures.

See also COVENANT; TESTAMENT. D. M. BECK

NT CANON. *See* CANON OF THE NT.

NT CHRONOLOGY. *See* CHRONOLOGY OF THE NT.

NT LANGUAGE. The language of the NT is, in general, the common nonliterary Greek of NT times. *See* GREEK LANGUAGE, THE, § 4*b*.

NT TEXT. *See* TEXT OF THE NT.

*__NEW YEAR__ [ראש השנה, *lit.* Head of the Year]. Naturally each of the several calendars employed by Israel during the biblical period of its history (*see* CALENDAR) had its own specific New Year's Day. The earliest, the pentecontad calendar (*see* SABBATH), was distinctly agricultural in character, directly associated with the successive stages of the annual crop. Its New Year's Day was, quite appropriately, the day of cutting the first sheaf of the new crop. This followed immediately upon and climaxed the seven-day *Maṣṣôth* Festival (*see* PASSOVER AND FEAST OF UNLEAVENED BREAD). During this festival, observed during the closing week of the old year, all that remained of the crop of that year, the embodiment of the god of vegetation for that year, had to be eaten, and what could not be eaten had to be destroyed completely, usually by burning. Under no condition might any of the old crop remain when the cutting of the new crop was begun. The god of vegetation of the old year must be dead and vanished before his successor, the god of the new year, could appear. Probably the cutting of the first sheaf of the new crop symbolized the birth, from the womb of Mother Earth, of the god of vegetation of the new year.

Of the ceremonial observance of this New Year's Day of the pentecontad calendar we know relatively little. This calendar itself, with all its various institutions and sacred days, was employed originally by the Canaanites and was borrowed from them by the Israelite newcomers in the land.

There is abundant evidence that the rebellion of Absalom (*see* ABSALOM 1) and his attempt to wrest the crown from DAVID were timed for the *Maṣṣôth* Festival and the ensuing New Year's Day, and this with good reason. On the first day of the festival the king of Jerusalem, in this instance David, led a solemn procession forth from the city, across the Kidron Brook, and up the Mount of Olives to the sanctuary at its summit (II Sam. 15:32). According to some scholars, the king was mourning in part (cf. vs. 30) for the dead god of vegetation. But in far larger measure the king was himself enacting the role of the god of the annual crop. In the folklore of Jerusalem the Mount of Olives was thought to cover the exit from, and therefore to be in the realm of the king of, the nether world. This was accordingly the deity who was worshiped on the summit of the Mount. There, nominally in the custody of the god of the nether world, the king, still playing the role of the dead vegetation god of the old year, would normally abide during the seven days of the *Maṣṣôth* Festival. Then upon the eighth day, the New Year's Day, just at sunrise, the very moment of the inauguration of the new year, the Mount of Olives was thought to split asunder, thus laying bare the exit from the nether world, and through this opening the god of vegetation, resurrected or born anew, would ascend into this world of life above and, still embodied in the person of the king, would return in solemn procession from the realm of death, back across the Kidron Brook to Jerusalem, the god to his sanctuary and the king to his palace. There, still early upon this New Year's Day morning, the שופר (*šôphār*), "ram's horn," would be blown. At its sound the king would solemnly ascend or reascend the throne (II Sam. 15:10; I Kings 1:34-35, 39; II Kings 9:13); and thus the new year would be formally inaugurated.

These two ceremonies, the blowing of the ram's horn and the formal ascension or reascension of the throne by the king, coupled with the promptly ensuing exodus of the people to their fields, there to cut ceremonially the first sheaf of the new crop, were the distinctive ritual acts of the New Year's Day of the pentecontad calendar. Also this New Year's Day was one of the three festal occasions in the year when the maidens of each community would go out to dance in the vineyards, there to be seized and taken as wives by the men of the community, waiting in hiding for this purpose (Gen. 34:1 ff; Exod. 15:20-21; Judg. 21:19-23; Jos. Antiq. V.ii.12; M. Ta'an. IV.8).

In response to evolving political, economic, and social conditions in Israel and the consequent need for a new calendar, one of wider range and more universal character, Solomon finally adopted the solar calendar of his Tyrian neighbors and allies as the official calendar for Israel (*see* YEAR). The year of this calendar was, of course, specifically solar. Solomon set its New Year's Day upon the day of the autumnal equinox, in the month of Etanim, the first month of the year of his calendar (cf. Targ. to I Kings 8:2), although the seventh month according to later reckoning. The exact incidence of this equinoctial day could be determined quite accurately, for on this day the first rays of the sun, rising over the Mount of Olives, shone on a straight line through the outer, E gate of the temple, tightly sealed throughout the remainder of the year, but opened on this one day for just this particular ceremony, then onward across the E temple court and over the great altar therein, then across the porch and through the doors of the temple, between the two brazen pillars which stood there on each side of the doorway, and on down the long axis of the temple into the *d^ebhîr*, the sacred recess, at its W end. This meaningful ceremony, in all its significant details, inaugurated the new year. Deviation of the first rays of the sun from this line to the extent that they no longer passed between the two brazen pillars and into the temple proper would indicate that a day must be added to the year, thus making it a leap year. The coming of the first rays of the rising, equinoctial sun, the *k^ebhôdh Yahweh*, the "radiance of Yahweh," as they were called, into the temple upon this day symbolized the entrance into his sanctuary of Yahweh, conceived of as the resurrected sun-god, entering upon his annual course through the heavens.

There in the temple, in fiery, radiant form, surrounded by his heavenly host, Yahweh held court and passed judgment and determined fates for nations and for men for the new year just commencing (I Kings 22:19-23; Job. 1:6-12; 2:1-7; Ps. 82; Isa. 6; Zech. 3:1-7). Moreover, there is considerable evidence that at the very commencement of the seven-day Festival of Ingathering (*see* BOOTHS, FEAST OF), which Solomon had appropriated from the earlier, pentecontad calendar, but the time of celebration of which he had shifted so that it would mark the final seven days of the solar year, and so immediately precede the New Year's Day, the sacred fire upon the altar was extinguished. Then seven days later, upon the solar New Year's Day, this sacred fire was rekindled from the rays of the rising, equinoctial sun, as they passed over the altar, or perhaps over the unkindled censer which the king, or eventually the high priest, held aloft at this decisive moment. Furthermore, several authorities maintain (*see bibliography*) that the king of Judah, clothed in radiant garb, enacted the role of the resurrected sun-god, rising from the nether world through the sundered Mount of Olives, which was split apart just at sunrise of this day, and returning in radiant glory to his sanctuary and his people (II Kings 15:5; 16:15; II Chr. 26:16-21; Zech. 14:4-5; cf. Jos. Antiq. IX.x.4; XIV.viii.2).

Closely linked with this vivid and meaningful ceremony upon this solar New Year's Day was the formal ascension or reascension of his throne by the king, and the heralding of this act and also the official inauguration of the new year by the ancient rite of blowing the *šôphār*. For this reason the years of the reigns of the kings of Judah were regularly reckoned from the first New Year's Day after actual succession to the kingship, the day of each king's first ceremonial throne-ascension.

In the course of the seventh century B.C. the Assyrian system of designating the months of this solar calendar by number, commencing with the month of the vernal equinox, rather than by their former Tyrian names, was introduced. Now the New Year's Day fell upon the tenth of the seventh month (Ezek. 40:1; cf. Lev. 16:29; 25:8-10). Upon this day, still as of old, the maidens would go out to dance in the vineyards. Upon this day too the dedication of Solomon's temple reached its culmination (I Kings 8: 10-11, 65), and also, according to one late tradition,

Aaron and his sons were consecrated as priests and the tabernacle-sanctuary was dedicated (Lev. 9:1–10:2). In the postexilic period, so long as the second temple stood (516-485 B.C.), the solar calendar continued in official use. The "anointed priest" (Lev. 4:3, 5, 16; 6:15), as his meaningful title indicates, replaced the king in the ancient, solar ritual of the New Year's Day (Zech. 3:1-7). A number of the Psalms, notably 47 (note vss. 6, 9); 81 (note vss. 4-5); 98 (note vss. 5-9), which are unmistakably the literary products of this period, reflect the persistent New Year's Day ceremonies of the rising, equinoctial sun, the coming of its first rays into the temple, the blowing of the *šôphār,* and with all this the throne-ascension of Yahweh, during this brief period regarded as Israel's true and only king.

In the mixed calendar current in Judah during the Exile (*see* YEAR) and again in the period following immediately upon the destruction of the second temple in 485 B.C., and apparently employed continuously thereafter by various Jewish sects for their own distinctive time-reckoning and religious practice, the New Year's Day seems to have been observed upon I/1 (cf. Exod. 12:2; 40:2 [both passages from P2]; Ezra 6:14-22).

Finally, in the last quarter of the fifth century B.C., after the erection of the third temple by Ezra and the religious and social reforms inaugurated by him and Nehemiah, in the lunar calendar then adopted, recorded in the Priestly Code (*see* YEAR), the New Year's Day was formally transferred from the tenth to the first day of the seventh month (Lev. 23: 24-25; Num. 29:1-6). With this went hand in hand the transfer of the heralding of the new year by the blowing of the *šôphār* and the traditional, but now merely symbolic, reascension of the divine throne by Yahweh in his role as the sole, universal King. Still today in the ritual of Judaism for the New Year's Day the blowing of the *šôphār* is the distinctive ceremony, while the throne-reascension of the Deity in his role as world-ruler is one of its major themes. Despite this transfer of dates, however, VII/10, the ancient New Year's Day, continued to be observed as a day of especial sanctity by the people at large, and this so generally that, probably as a concession to popular demand by the priestly authorities, it was reinstituted as a day of particular sanctity (Lev. 16; 23:27-32; Num. 29:7-11), as the Day of Atonement (*see* ATONEMENT, DAY OF). As such, and, in fact, even as it had been from remotest times, as the supremely sacred day of the religious year it has persisted in Jewish ceremonial practice to the present. A faint reminiscence of the original character of the day may be noted in the ceremony of *Ne'îlāh,* or "Closing [of the Gate—i.e., the E gate of the temple]," and of the blowing of the *šôphār* as the concluding ritual procedures, nominally performed just at sunset, of the day.

Bibliography. In addition to the references cited under YEAR, see the following: J. Morgenstern, "Two Ancient Israelite Agricultural Festivals," *JQR,* N.S., VIII (1917), 31-54; "The Origin of Maṣṣoth and the Maṣṣoth Festival," *AJT,* XXI (1917), 275-93; "The New Year for Kings," *Gaster Anniversary Volume* (1936), pp. 439-56; "The Mythological Background of Psalm 82," *HUCA,* XIV (1939), 29-126.

J. MORGENSTERN

NEZIAH nī zī'ə [נציח, faithful; *cf.* Arab. *naṣīḥun;* Apoc. Νασί]; KJV Apoc. NASITH nā'sĭth. Eponym of a family of Nethinim, or temple servants, listed among the exiles returned from Babylon (Ezra 2:54; Neh. 7:56; I Esd. 5:32).

Bibliography. M. Noth, *Die israelitischen Personennamen* (1928), p. 228.

B. T. DAHLBERG

NEZIB nē'zĭb [נציב, pillar, garrison] (Josh. 15:43). A village of Judah in the Shephelah district of Libnah-Mareshah; identified with modern Khirbet Beit Nesib, E of Lachish, *ca.* two miles from Khirbet Qila (KEILAH).

NIBHAZ nĭb'hăz [נבחז] (II Kings 17:31). A deity worshiped by Syrian colonists from Iwwa settled by the Assyrians in Samaria after 722 B.C. As in the case of TARTAK, no such Mesopotamian deity is known, and an Elamite origin has been conjectured. This is unlikely, since the worshipers are Syrian. More probably "Nibhaz" is a corruption in the early text, or possibly a wilful Jewish distortion of *mizbēaḥ* ("altar"), such as is known to have been deified and so the object of worship. An analogy to the deification of the altar is the deification of the house of God (*bēth 'ēl*), attested in the Aramaic papyri from Elephantine.

Bibliography. A. Cowley, *Aramaic Papyri of the Fifth Century B.C.* (1923), pp. 18-19; J. A. Montgomery, *Commentary on Kings,* ICC (ed. H. S. Gehman; 1951), pp. 474-75.

J. GRAY

NIBSHAN nĭb'shăn [נבשן] (Josh. 15:62). A village of Judah in the "wilderness" district; identified with Khirbet el-Maqari in el-Buqe'ah (the Valley of Achor), SW of Jericho.

Bibliography. F. M. Cross, Jr., and J. T. Milik, "Explorations in the Judaean Buqê'ah," *BASOR,* 142 (1956), 5-17; F. M. Cross, Jr., "A Footnote to Biblical History," *BA,* 19 (1956), 12-17.

V. R. GOLD

NICANOR nī kā'nər [Νικάνωρ, conqueror]. **1.** A general of Antiochus Epiphanes; son of Patroclus, according to II Macc. 8:9; a friend of the king, according to I Macc. 3:38. He was certainly an enemy to the Jews. He was one of the three generals who in 166 B.C. were sent by the regent Lysias to put down the revolt of Judas Maccabeus. Nicanor may have been in command of the two other generals, Gorgias and Ptolemy; he occupies the prominent place in the narrative of II Maccabees, but Gorgias does so in that of I Maccabees. In this campaign Judas Maccabeus was gloriously successful, and through his spectacular victory was able to convince the Syrian king, as well as his own people, that he was the man to seek terms which would lead to the cleansing of the temple in Jerusalem and of the Jewish religion in general, and to the restoration of the services.

The course of events seems to have been as follows: Nicanor and the invading forces took up positions at Emmaus, within a few miles of Jerusalem, but received such an onslaught at the hands of Judas that all was confusion, and the Syrian generals fled from Judea into Philistia. The writer of II Maccabees has added the embellishment that Nicanor fled to

Antioch in disguise (II Macc. 8:34-36), and it does appear that for a time the Syrians were powerless against Judas. Nicanor's fortunes revived, however, when after Lysias' death Demetrius made him governor of Judea and sent him there well equipped. Here II Maccabees does not agree with I Maccabees. According to the latter, by a trick which failed Nicanor tried to capture Judas, and the only result was a battle at Capharsalama in which Nicanor sustained great losses but may have inflicted still more on Judas. The Jewish champion did not trust the wily Syrian and kept out of the way when Nicanor sought peace. In the ensuing battle at Adasa and Beth-horon in March, 161 B.C., Nicanor had received reinforcements, but they did not save his army or himself. He himself was slain in the early stages, his body was retrieved from the field, and was badly mutilated and exposed in Jerusalem in 160.

This renowned victory over the Syrians was afterward celebrated annually, on the thirteenth of March (Adar), as "Nicanor's Day." On this triumphant note the author of II Maccabees closes his history.

N. TURNER

2. One of the SEVEN chosen to administer the daily distribution of food in the Jerusalem church (Acts 6:1-6).

NICODEMUS nĭk'ə dē'məs [Νικόδημος, conqueror of the people]. A Jewish leader who appears in the Fourth Gospel as a questioner of Jesus, and later as a secret follower.

The name Nicodemus was common among both Greeks and Jews in the NT period, but appears in the Bible only as the name of a member of the Jewish SANHEDRIN who came at night to talk with Jesus (John 3:1 ff). He was not only a "ruler of the Jews," but a teacher as well (vs. 2). In fact, the presence of the definite article in the Greek text of John's Gospel—"*the* teacher"—points to his pre-eminence as a teacher, and therefore as one who should have known the truth about God and his people. But the course of his conversation with Jesus shows that he did not understand the basic truths about the kingdom of God. Nicodemus was a Pharisee, and as such should have had interest in and knowledge about the coming of the kingdom, but Jesus' answers to his questions are more provocative than explanatory, and make him appear as a symbol of Israel's spiritual blindness. Some commentators have identified Nicodemus with a man of that name (also called Buni) mentioned in the rabbinic writings, who was living at the time of the destruction of Jerusalem in A.D. 70, but it seems unlikely that a man who was a ruler at the time of Jesus would still have been alive and active in 70.

In keeping with John's practice of using words with double meanings, the detail that Nicodemus came "by night" to see Jesus points both to the fact that Nicodemus and other Jewish leaders associated with Jesus only in secret (John 19:38), and to the darkness of understanding out of which Nicodemus asked his questions. In regard to his lack of understanding, John uses Nicodemus here as a symbol of the Jewish nation as a whole, who—according to John's estimate—are blind to the truth of God (John 1:11; 3:19; 9:39-41). Nicodemus, therefore, represents the Jewish inquirer who, though he does not yet believe fully, seeks fuller understanding of the meaning of Jesus.

Nicodemus' cautious sympathy with Jesus is attested in John 7:50-52, where the inclination on the part of Jewish officialdom to condemn Jesus is called into question, on the grounds that they have not heard at first hand what he teaches. The final mention of Nicodemus occurs in 19:39, where it is reported that he joined with JOSEPH OF ARIMATHEA in preparing the body of Jesus for burial. Nicodemus, who must have been a man of considerable wealth, provided a huge amount of spices—myrrh and aloes—to be placed between the folds of the linen cloth in which the body of Jesus was wrapped for burial. Even this act of devotion was carried out in secrecy, "for fear of the Jews" (vs. 38).

Bibliography. H. L. Strack and P. Billerbeck, *Kommentar zum NT,* II (1924), 412-20; J. Klausner, *Jesus of Nazareth* (English trans., 1925), pp. 28-30; C. K. Barrett, *Gospel According to St. John* (1955), pp. 169-82. H. C. KEE

NICODEMUS, GOSPEL OF. A title ascribed since the fourteenth century to the Acts of Pilate. *See* PILATE, ACTS OF.

NICOLAITANS nĭk'ə lā'ə tənz [Νικολαΐτης] (Rev. 2:6, 15). Followers of a Nicolaus. Their works and teaching in the churches of EPHESUS and of PERGAMUM are condemned by John. Since the same practice and teaching of immorality and of idolatry appear in the church of Thyatira, the Nicolaitans, though not named, were probably present also in this church (Rev. 2:20-25). Thus three out of the seven churches to whom John wrote were afflicted with this heretical sect. In Ephesus their deeds were hated by the church and by Christ; in Pergamum there were some who held their doctrine; in Thyatira the woman Jezebel, self-styled a prophetess, was tolerated and allowed to teach and to beguile Christ's servants. The name JEZEBEL, from the infamous Phoenician queen of Ahab, is chosen to typify this kind of leadership.

John conveys Christ's messages to the seven churches. The Ephesians are commended (Rev. 2:6). At Pergamum censure is due; unless the church there repents, it will face the coming of Christ, who with the sword of his mouth (2:16; cf. 1:16; 19:15) will war against the Nicolaitans. The Thyatirans, who refused the teaching of Jezebel, receive no other burden (cf. Acts 15:28), but must hold fast to what they have until Christ comes. Jezebel, who refused repentance, will be thrown into sickness; her followers will suffer great tribulation, while her children will be struck dead (Rev. 2:20-25).

Nothing is confidently known about the Nicolaitans beyond John's references to them. Their works are hated, but not described, in the letter to Ephesus. In Pergamum their teaching is held in like manner to those who held the teaching of BALAAM (Num. 25:1-2; 31:16; II Pet. 2:15; Jude 11). In early OT days Balaam had taught Balak, the Moabite king, to cause the Israelites to fall into fornication and idolatry. These same sins were taught and practiced by the Nicolaitans. Food sacrificed to idols (cf. I Cor. 8) referred not only to actual offerings but also to the remainder left on hand for home or market place, after the pagan gods had received their share. To eat this food might influence a Christian to return to idolatry. Pagan feasts thus might foster immorality, which is understood literally as licentiousness, or possibly in an allegorical way as unfaithfulness to God. Since the eighteenth century there has been some support for the attempt to identify Balaamites and Nicolaitans by a rough etymology (Νικᾶ-λαόν= בלע עם), but this claim is questioned or rejected by many. At Thyatira followers of Jezebel claim to know the deep things of Satan. Perhaps John quotes an actual claim or contrasts sarcastically the knowledge of Satan with the true depths of knowledge of God (cf. I Cor. 2:10). This claim to special knowledge of deep mysteries marks the incipient Gnosticism which flourished a century later (Iren. Her. II.2.2). The Nicolaitans may be taken to be a heretical sect, who retained pagan practices like idolatry and immorality contrary to the thought and the conduct required in Christian churches. The Christian could not avoid in daily life his contacts with heathen culture. But a deep cleft separated church and world, and at Thyatira the prophetess who taught indulgence was not to be tolerated.

Irenaeus asserts (Her. I.26.3; III.11.1) that the Nicolaitans were heretical followers of Nicolaus, the proselyte from Antioch, one of the Seven appointed by apostles in Jerusalem (Acts 6:5). This assumes that Nicolaus fell from the faith. Hippolytus supports Irenaeus and adds that Nicolaus departed from correct doctrine (*Philosophoumena* VII.36). There is much dispute whether this is fact or inference. Tertullian reports the lust and the luxury of the Nicolaitans, cites evidence from Revelation, and adds that there was another sort of Nicolaitans, a satanic sect, called the Gaian heresy (Tert. Marcion I.29; Presc. Her. 33; de Pudic. 19). Clement of Alexandria knows of followers of Nicolaus, "lascivious goats," who perverted his saying that it was necessary to abuse the flesh (*Stromata* II.20; III.24). Some orthodox Christians thus honored rigorous asceticism. Clement undertakes to show that Nicolaus was a true ascetic and that the later, immoral Nicolaitans were not his followers, though they claimed him as their teacher. In the fourth century Eusebius indirectly supports Clement by stating that the Nicolaitans arose for a brief time but soon became extinct (Euseb. Hist. III.29). Later their name flourished as a designation for heretics.

This division of opinion about whether the Nicolaitans of Revelation had any connection with Nicolaus of Antioch, and about whether they continued as a sect, remains to the present time. But the weight of recent scholarship supports the view (*a*) that we know little about Nicolaus, the proselyte, and nothing about his relationship to the Nicolaitans; (*b*) that we know only the information about the Nicolaitans in Revelation, with no certain connection between them and later sects of similar name.

Bibliography. L. Seesemann, "Die Nikolaiten," *Theologische Studien und Kritiken,* 66 (1893), 47-82; G. Wohlenberg, "Nikolaus von Antiochien und die Nikolaiten," *NKZ,* VI (1895), 923-61; W. M. Ramsay, *The Letters to the Seven Churches* (1904), pp. 298-302, 335-53; W. F. Cobb in J. Hastings *et al.*, eds., *Dictionary of the Apostolic Church* (1916), II, 90-91; R. W. Moss, in J. Hastings, ed., *Encyclopedia of Religion and Ethics* (1917), IX, 363-66; A. von Harnack, "The Sect of the Nicolaitans and Nicolaus the Deacon of Jerusalem," *JR,* III (1923), 413-22; E. B. Allo, *Saint John L'Apocalypse* (3rd ed., 1933), Excursus XII, pp. 57-59; M. Goguel, "Les Nicolaites," *RHR,* 115 (1936), 5-36.

D. M. Beck

NICOLAUS nĭk′ə lā′əs [Νικόλαος, conqueror of the people] (Acts 6:5); KJV NICOLAS nĭk′ə ləs. One of the Seven appointed by the church at Jerusalem to preside over the distribution of food and common goods. He is described as "a Proselyte of Antioch," which raises the question as to whether or not the others of the Seven—all of whom bear Greek names—were also proselytes. The fact that their names are Greek proves nothing, since Jews in Palestine, as well as in other regions of the Roman Empire, often gave Greek names to their children. Josephus reports that in Antioch there were large numbers of Greeks who attached themselves to the Jewish worship. Apparently it was among proselytes like Nicolaus that Christianity caught hold so rapidly in Antioch. Nicolaus was believed by some of the early church fathers to have apostatized from the true faith and become the founder of a heretical sect called the Nicolaitans (Rev. 2:6).

Bibliography. F. J. Foakes-Jackson and K. Lake, *The Beginnings of Christianity,* pt. I: "The Acts of the Apostles," vol. IV (1933), pp. 65-66. On the name see J. H. Moulton and G. Milligan, *The Vocabulary of the Greek Testament* (1924), p. 427.

H. C. Kee

NICOPOLIS nĭ kŏp′ə lĭs [ἡ Νικόπολις] (Tit. 3:12). Probably the city of this name in Epirus in NW Greece.

The name Nicopolis, meaning "city of victory," was bestowed upon many ancient towns. In order to determine the place probably indicated in Tit. 3:12, it is necessary to find a city of that name which was in the region of Paul's known travels, in existence in his lifetime, and likely to be thought of as a location in which it would be desirable to spend the winter. The Nicopolis built by Pompey in Lesser Armenia (Strabo XII.555) and that founded by Augustus near Alexandria, Egypt (Jos. War IV.xi.5), were too far distant to come into consideration. Nicopolis on the Nestos River on the border between Thrace and Macedonia (Ptolemy III.11) was founded by Trajan and thus, like several other cities of the same name, dated from a time after Paul. The Nicopolis in Bithynia (Pliny Nat. Hist. V.150) would hardly be chosen as a wintering place, nor would the one in NE Cilicia (Strabo XIV.676), to which either Tarsus or Antioch would seem preferable.

The most likely place, therefore, is that which is also otherwise the best known, Nicopolis in Epirus. This city was founded by Octavian to celebrate his decisive victory over Mark Antony in the naval battle of Actium (31 B.C.) and was located on the very site of his own camp, which was on the N side of the entrance to the Sinus Ambracicus or Gulf of Arta. Herod the Great interested himself in the city, and Josephus (Antiq. XVI.v.3) states that he built most of the public buildings there. Later Nicopolis was famed as the residence of the philosopher Epictetus, who moved there after being expelled from Rome by Domitian in A.D. 89 (Aulus Gellius *Attic Nights* XV.xi.5). While Tacitus (Ann. II.liii) calls Nicopolis an Achaian town, Epictetus (Arrian's *Discourses* of Epictetus III.iv.1) and Ptolemy (*Geography* III.13) refer to it as in Epirus.

In Codex Alexandrinus an added note at the end of the Letter to Titus states that the letter was "written from Nicopolis," but this is presumably nothing more than an inference from 3:12 and an incorrect one at that, for Nicopolis is spoken of "there."

Bibliography. T. Zahn, *Einleitung in das Neue Testament,* I (1897), 434-35; F. Schober, "Nikopolis," *Pauly-Wissowa,* vol. XVII, pt. i (1936), cols. 511-18. J. FINEGAN

NIGER nī′gər [Νίγερ, *from* Lat., black] (Acts 13:1). The surname of Symeon, one of the group of prophets and teachers in the church at ANTIOCH. It has been conjectured that he was the SIMON (8) of Cyrene mentioned in the gospels (Mark 15:21 and parallels). H. C. KEE

NIGHT [לילה, ליל, Aram. לילי; *inexactly* חשך (Job 26: 10 KJV); נשף (Isa. 5:11 KJV; 21:4 KJV; 59:10 KJV); ערב (Gen. 49:27 KJV; Lev. 6:20 KJV; Job 7:4; Ps. 30:5—H 30:6); νύξ]. Alternately: DARKNESS (Job 26:10); EVEN (Gen. 49:27); EVENING (Lev. 6:20; Isa. 5:11); TWILIGHT (Isa. 21:4; 59: 10). The dark period from sunset to sunrise.

For the Hebrews the night was contrasted to the day as darkness is to LIGHT; hence the expression "day and night" (יום ולילה; Gen. 8:22; cf. Ps. 1:2, etc.), and the mode of counting time by days and nights (Gen. 7:4, 12; Exod. 24:18; I Kings 19:8; etc.; *see* DAY 1). References to the night occur more than two hundred times in the OT. The beginning of the night was called "evening" (ערב), and its end "dawn" (שחר), while the "twilight" (נשף) was the time of semidarkness following the sunset and preceding the dawn. The Hebrews spoke of "midnight" (Exod. 11:4; 12:29; I Kings 3:20), and divided the night into watches (Ps. 90:4; Lam. 2:19; cf. Ps. 130: 6; Isa. 21:11-12), of which there were three in the later Jewish system and four according to the Greco-Roman reckoning.

A particular night might receive a special significance from a notable event of circumstance. Thus there were nights of feasting (Isa. 30:29), of suffering and sorrow (Job 7:3, etc.), of sudden assault (Isa. 15: 1), etc. The night is the symbol of blessing in Isa. 16:3, but the symbol of calamity in Mic. 3:6. Particularly for Job, the night is a time of dread and anxiety (cf. 4:12 ff; 24:14; 35:10; 36:20). DREAMS, so important a vehicle of divine revelation in both the OT and the NT, are associated with the night (cf. Dan. 7:2, etc.). There is little evidence in the OT of belief in the night as a time of demonic activity, as in later Judaism (however, *see* LILITH).

The NT employs νύξ in contrast to ἡμέρα ("day") in a manner similar to the OT usage (cf. Mark 5:5, etc.). By Jesus' time the night was divided into hours (*see* HOUR; Luke 12:39, etc.) and into watches. Mark 13:35 names the four night watches: the "evening" (ὀψέ), "midnight" (μεσονύκτιον), "cockcrowing" (ἀλεκτοροφωνίας), and "morning" (πρωΐ).

Night assumes an ominous symbolical importance in John 9:4 (cf. 11:10), where it becomes equivalent to death, the end of opportunity for work. In Rom. 13:12 night is the dark time of evil, which will soon disappear before the daybreak of salvation. The contrast between night and day, as opposite spiritual principles, is made especially sharp in I Thess. 5:5-7. All these passages evince a radical moral antithesis best illuminated by the strikingly similar views of the Qumran sect appearing in some of the Dead Sea Scrolls. According to certain late apocalyptic writings, night is to be done away with as the symbol of evil and sorrow (Zech. 14:7; Rev. 21:25; 22:5; II Enoch 65:9). S. J. DE VRIES

NIGHT HAG. A common, but incorrect, translation of Hebrew "LILITH" (לילית), the name of a female demon mentioned in Isa. 34:14. The rendering is based on the assumption that the name is connected with *lāyil,* "night." Actually, however, it derives (through Akkadian *lilîtu*) from the Sumerian *lil,* "air," and is a popular contraction of *kiskil-lil-la,* "air(-borne) maiden," a common designation of the *succuba,* a special type of female demon.

See fully DEMON § A4*a.* T. H. GASTER

NIGHTHAWK [תחמס, *perhaps* violent one; LXX γλαῦξ, little owl; Vulg. *noctua,* owl; Targ. (Onq.) ציצא, night hawk] (Lev. 11:16; Deut. 14:15). By "nighthawk" presumably the English translators mean the night jar (genus Caprimulgus of the order Caprimulgiformes), of which *ca.* ninety-five species are known. These rather small birds, whose food consists entirely of insects, fly about in the early evening, making a peculiar clapping noise seemingly with their wings. Tristram observed three species in Palestine in the nineteenth century.

The identity of the unclean bird תחמס is uncertain. It is improbable, however, that it is a night jar. The latter is not raptorial, nor in the biblical period is it likely to have been readily caught or to have been a probable article of food. Tristram, following the LXX and the Vulg., favors identifying the bird in question with the barn owl (*Tyto alba*); both Bodenheimer (*see* FAUNA § B2) and G. R. Driver (*see bibliography*) also prefer one of the owls.

Bibliography. G. R. Driver, *PEQ* (1955), p. 13.
W. S. MCCULLOUGH

NIGHT MONSTER. *See* DEMON §§ A4*a, f.*

NILE nīl [יאר, יאור]. The river which flows in an irregular course nearly 3,500 miles in length from the highland regions of East Central Africa to the Mediterranean. The watershed of the river is estimated to be over 1,000,000 square miles in area and includes a large territory with extremely heavy rainfall. At Khartum, just S of the sixth cataract, two branches known as the White Nile and the Blue Nile unite to form the Nile itself, which is then joined by only one other important tributary, the Atbara or Bahr el-Aswad, on its northerly course. The White Nile may be reckoned as originating at Lake Victoria in Uganda and Tanganyika but is augmented by a vast and complex system of tributaries before its confluence with the Blue Nile; the name of the river

Courtesy of the Arab Information Center, New York

16. The Nile River near Cairo

changes several times, however, as one journeys toward this remote source. The Blue Nile rises in the Gojam Highlands of Abyssinia in the region S of Lake Tsana. Between Khartum and Wadi Halfa to the N the Nile is roughly in the shape of an "s"; it is in this section of the river that the series of rapids known as the cataracts (sixth to second) are located. The first cataract, the most northerly, is at Assuan, ancient SYENE. At the apex of the Delta, just N of modern Cairo, the Nile divides into two main branches, the Rosetta and the Damietta, whereby it flows into the Mediterranean. Fig. NIL 16.

The steady flow of the river, so devoid of tributaries in its N half, is assured by the system of lakes and areas of repose in the vicinity of lakes Victoria, Albert, and Albert Edward in the S. Excessive seasonal rainfall at the headwaters of the E affluents, the Blue Nile and the Atbara, results in an annual inundation of the river valley in Egypt, the occurrence of which was the mainstay of ancient Egyptian agriculture, both for the water thus supplied and for the rich alluvium carried down by the river. At Assuan the Nile reaches its minimal level at the end of May, rises steadily during July and August, and attains its maximum at the beginning of September. The measurement of the height of the river was of the greatest importance in antiquity; the most important measure, or Nilometer, was located on the island of Elephantine at Assuan, with others at Philae, Edfu, and Esna.

In spite of the numerous suggestions which have been offered, the origin of the Greek word Νεῖλος remains obscure. The most ancient name of the river in Egypt itself was *ḥʿpy,* which also served as the designation of the Nile god. By the Middle Kingdom, however, the word *itrw,* at first meaning simply "river," had become the name of the river par excellence and continued as the ordinary appellation of the Nile down to the Greco-Roman period. This word, under a slightly modified form, was taken into Hebrew as a loan word and appears as יאר. Extra-biblical attestations of the name include the Assyrian transcription *ya-ru-'-ú* in the Annals of Ashurbanipal and Coptic *yero,* both of which reflect the compound form *itrw* ʿ3, "the great river," commonly used in the later periods. Hebrew יאר is employed in both the singular and the plural as the name of the Nile; it is generally assumed that the use of the plural refers to the several branches of the river which coursed through the Delta to the sea. In two instances, however (Job 28:10; Isa. 33:21), the plural יארים seems to mean, not the Nile, but streams or rivers in general.

The absolutely vital role which the Nile played in the agricultural life of the ancient Egyptian led very early to the personification of the river in the Nile-god Hapi. The annual inundation was greeted with both official and popular celebrations; we find lyrical references to the occasion as early as the Pyramid Texts, where we read: "The god's offerings descend, the face of men is bright, and the heart of the gods rejoices." The most famous of the hymns preserved for us is known as the "Adoration of the Nile" and survives in copies from the Nineteenth

Courtesy of the Oriental Institute, the University of Chicago

17. The Nile Valley seen from the cliffs by Medinet Habu; to the lower right can be seen within the enclosure the temple of Ramses III (1195-1164 B.C.) and other buildings.

Dynasty and later. Corresponding to his function as provider, Hapi is pictured as bringing offerings of food and drink to other deities, thus symbolizing the abundance provided by the river itself. This association is further represented by a portrayal of physical corpulence, especially in the breasts, which has led some scholars to interpret the figure as bisexual, thus emphasizing the self-generative fruitfulness of the Nile. Hapi never attained a strong position in the Egyptian pantheon; this was due partly to the gradual identification of Osiris, a much more important deity, as the lord of the inundation. The crocodile-god Sobek was also celebrated as the bringer of the annual flood. Fig. NIL 17.

The exact locations and names of the Delta branches of the Nile in antiquity remain a vexing issue, important not only for the geography of the Delta in general but also for the solution of certain problems in the topology of the Exodus. Because the courses of the Delta branches were constantly changing, we cannot assume that the information available from one period reflects the same geographical situation existing at another. In Ramesside times the three principal courses were known as (*a*) the Great River, corresponding in name to the Μέγας Ποταμός of Ptolemy, but more probably to be identified with the Sebennytic branch of classical times; (*b*) the Water of Prēʿ, the easternmost branch, possibly the same as the later Bubastic (also Pelusian) River; and (*c*) the Western River, which may be equated with the later

Canopic mouth. Other names are attested in both Egyptian and classical texts, but the precise equations to be made between these and the names mentioned here must await further evidence.

Fig. EGY 6; Pl. XV*a*.

Bibliography. O. Toussoun, *Mémoire sur l'histoire du Nil* (1925); A. H. Gardiner, *Ancient Egyptian Onomastica* (1947), II, 153*-170*. T. O. LAMBDIN

NIMRAH. Alternate form of BETH-NIMRAH.

NIMRIM, THE WATERS OF nĭm'rĭm [מי נמרים, *perhaps* waters of leopards]. Waters in Moab which are said to have become desolate, in oracles against Moab (Isa. 15:6; Jer. 48:34). Apparently they supported cultivation, since Isaiah continues:

> The grass is withered, the new growth fails,
> the verdure is no more.

Some would identify the Waters of Nimrim with the Wadi en-Numeirah, a small stream flowing into the E side of the Dead Sea, *ca.* 8½ miles from its S end. There are traces of former cultivation in the area. If this location is correct, the Waters of Nimrim would have been one of the streams watering the area of Sodom and its sister cities before their destruction.

Others would identify the Waters of Nimrim with the Wadi Nimrin, which flows into the Jordan from the E, *ca.* 8 miles N of the Dead Sea. The land in the area of the Wadi Nimrin is fertile and very productive when irrigated, as it has been from earliest historical times. The Plains of Moab, where the Israelites encamped before crossing the Jordan, stretch southward from the Wadi Nimrin to the NE end of the Dead Sea.

Bibliography. F.-M. Abel, *Géographie de la Palestine,* I (1933), 178; II (1938), 399. N. Glueck, *Explorations in E Palestine,* vol. II, *AASOR,* XV (1934-35), 7-8; vol. IV, *AASOR,* XXV-XXVIII (1945-48), 366-67. E. D. GROHMAN

NIMROD nĭm'rŏd [נמרוד, נמרד, *see* § 1 *below;* LXX Νεβρωδ].

1. Etymology and identification. The etymology of the name Nimrod is quite uncertain. If originally Hebrew, which is highly improbable, then it is apparently from מרד, "to rebel." Even as a foreign word, it could bring this meaning to the Hebrew reader's mind. However, it is probably Mesopotamian in origin. The name most frequently suggested as its source is Ninurta, though this is not without philological difficulty or opposition.

If the form "Ninurta" is accepted and assumed to refer strictly to a god, it would point to the Babylonian deity Ninurta, a war-god who is also called "the Arrow, the mighty hero," and whose cult assumed widespread importance in Mesopotamia during the late second millennium B.C. If it refers to a historical person, the Assyrian king Tukulti-Ninurta I (*ca.* 1246-1206 B.C.) is an attractive choice, for he was the first Assyrian monarch to rule over all Babylonia (cf. Gen. 10:10). According to Speiser, he served also as prototype for the composite Greek hero Ninus, associated with Nineveh. If, however, the Cushite origin of "Nimrod" (vss. 6, 8*a*) is maintained, the Egyptian monarch Amenophis III (1411-1375) would be suitable according to von Rad.

Regardless of origin, Nimrod must have become a figure of legendary proportions in the ancient Near East, whose story was extremely fluid. It was adopted by, and adapted to, many phases of ancient culture, lived on in medieval chronicles, and is still reflected in the *Nimrûd* of place names in Mesopotamia today.

2. In the OT. Nimrod appears only at Gen. 10:8-12; I Chr. 1:10; Mic. 5:6—H 5:5.

Nimrod son of Cush (I Chr. 1:10, perhaps here indicating the Kassites or Cosseans [Akkadian *Kaššu*], who conquered the Babylonians in the second millennium B.C.), was the first to become a mighty hero (גבור) on the earth. He was so renowned as a great hunter (גבור ציד, "mighty in the chase") that the expression "like Nimrod a mighty hunter before Yahweh" became proverbial (Gen. 10:8-9). "Before Yahweh" (לפני יהוה) may here be equivalent to "on the earth" or perhaps a conscious addition by the Yahwist to Hebraize this pagan tradition.

Nimrod was famed also for his kingdom in Mesopotamia. Its principal cities were Babel (Babylon), Erech, Accad, and CALNEH (so MT, LXX, Targ., Vulg., KJV; but cf. Samar., Pesh., and RSV) in the land of SHINAR (vs. 10). Further, he was closely associated with Asshur (for the word order of vs. 11*a,* cf. KJV with RSV) and Nineveh (vss. 11-12), so that Assyria is once called the "land of Nimrod" (Mic. 5:6—H 5:5). *See* ASSYRIA AND BABYLONIA § C3.

The appearance of a Nimrod story in the OT may be due not only to its immense popularity but also to the Yahwist's frequent use of ancient material for his cultural and ethnic etiologies. Here it helps him account for the origin of the great Assyro-Babylonian civilization.

Bibliography. E. A. Speiser, "In Search of Nimrod," *Eretz-Israel,* V (1958 [Mazar Volume]), 32-36, cites much of the pertinent literature. L. HICKS

NIMSHI nĭm'shī [נמשי]. Grandfather (according to II Kings 9:2, 14, which is probably original) or father (according to I Kings 19:16; II Kings 9:20; II Chr. 22:7) of King Jehu. The name has been found on an ostracon from Samaria.

NINEVEH nĭn'ə və [נינוה; LXX Νινευή] (Gen. 10:11-12; II Kings 19:36=Isa. 37:37; Jonah 1:2; 3:2, 3-7; 4:11; Nah. 1:1; 2:8; 3:7); MEN OF NINEVEH Νινευιται (Matt. 12:41; Luke 11:30, 32); KJV NINEVITES nĭn'ə vītz. One of the oldest and greatest cities of Mesopotamia, capital of Assyria at its height, but since its fall in 612 B.C. a symbol of Assyria's utter collapse.

1. Location. The city was situated on the E side of the Tigris, directly across the river from the site of modern Mosul. The ruins of Nineveh are marked primarily by two large mounds, Quyunjiq and Nebi Yunus, and are surrounded by an almost regular rectangle of walls nearly eight miles in circumference.* The area enclosed was thus exceptionally large, but it must have loomed ever so much larger in the hearsay accounts of outsiders; according to Jonah 3:3, it took "three days' journey" to cover it. Fig. NIN 18.

Nebi Yunus ("the prophet Jonah"), though much the more compact of the two mounds, is almost entirely out of reach of excavators because of its mod-

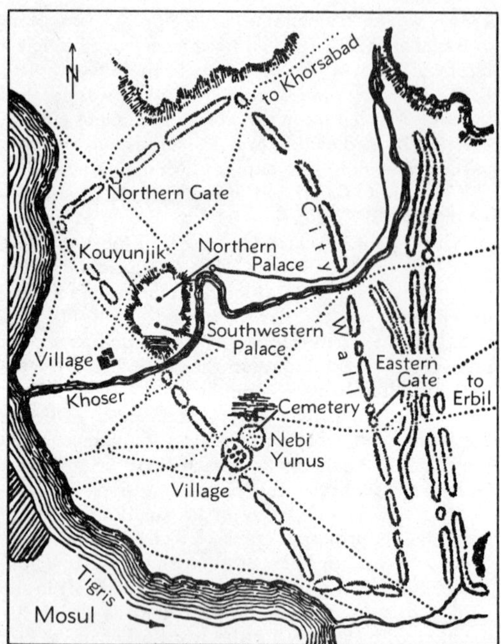

Courtesy of the Philosophical Library

18. Map of Nineveh today

Courtesy of the Philosophical Library

19. Views of Nineveh: Tell Nebi Yunus (above); Tell Quyunjiq (below)

ern village, its cemetery, its mosque, and its "Jonah's tomb." Quyunjiq, on the other hand, which is twice the size of Nebi Yunus, was an abandoned ruin already in the days of Xenophon, and was to attract little active interest until the age of modern archaeology. Excavations on this site were begun by the French in 1842, under P. E. Botta, and were continued intermittently by the British until 1932. Fig. NIN 19.

2. Name and history. The *Ninua* of cuneiform sources goes back to an earlier form, *Ninuwa,* which is still found at Mari and would seem to underlie the received biblical writing. The name itself appears to be of Hurrian origin. In addition to the syllabic spelling, the cuneiform texts also use a pseudo-logographic form, *Ninā,* a sign representing an enclosure with a fish inside. This particular variant must have given rise to considerable popular speculation, which in turn left its mark on more than one subsequent tradition. Another line of folk interpretation is found in Greek writers who call the city *Nînos,* after the legendary hero by that name whose eponymous role was influenced by accidental similarity in sound. Nevertheless, the very interest of outsiders in the background of Nineveh is indirect proof of the reputation and importance of the city itself.

The earliest occupation of Nineveh dates back to remote prehistoric times. Among the older historical witnesses, there is an inscription which was left in the city by the celebrated Naram-Sin of the Dynasty of Akkad; and the place is named in the Prologue of the Code of Hammurabi as the site of a famous temple of Ishtar. Statues of Ishtar of Nineveh were sent by Mitannian kings to Egyptian rulers as gifts worthy of exceptional attention. And extensive building activities in Nineveh are recorded repeatedly by kings of the Middle Assyrian period.

The city reached the height of its fame at the turn of the eighth century, when Sennacherib made Nineveh the capital of a steadily expanding Assyrian Empire. When Assyria held sway over Egypt, under Esarhaddon and Ashurbanipal, Nineveh had no rival anywhere in the world. Yet the end was only decades away. In 612 B.C. the city fell to the combined forces of the Babylonians and the Medes; its proud temples and palaces and engineering wonders soon crumbled and were forgotten. Only the great library that Ashurbanipal had assembled was to be reactivated, some twenty-five centuries later, thus furnishing the essential clue to the intellectual and spiritual treasures of the long-lived civilization of Mesopotamia.

3. Nineveh and the Bible. The earliest biblical mention of Nineveh is found in Gen. 10:11, where the place is listed together with other major Mesopotamian centers founded by Nimrod. The next verse speaks of "Resen between Nineveh and Calah; that is the great city." The same description is applied to Nineveh in Jonah (1:2; 3:3; 4:11). It is very doubtful, however, whether it was intended for that city in the present instance; the word order suggests Calah, which antedated Nineveh as the capital of Assyria. It is clear, nevertheless, that the fame of Nineveh had already spread to Israel in time to be reflected in the J document. A more tangible historical reference is given in the parallel passages II Kings 19:36; Isa. 37:37, which record Nineveh as the place that witnessed the assassination of Sennacherib by his sons.

The end of Nineveh is proclaimed by two contemporary biblical prophets, Zephaniah and Nahum. The former does so incidentally, but the entire record of the latter's prophecy is entitled "an oracle concerning Nineveh." Nahum's poem manages to evoke from a great distance, yet with all the impact of an eyewitness, and with unexcelled imagery and power, an event that was one of the major junctures in world history. The only comparable work in Assyrian literature is the Epic of Tukulti-Ninurta I, which deals with the struggle between Babylonia and Assyria in the late thirteenth century.

Another biblical work which centers on Nineveh is the book of Jonah. This time, however, historical facts are reshaped so as to serve the purposes of an unforgettable moral lesson. Such literary touches as the "king of Nineveh" (3:6) or the "three days'" circuit of the city's walls (3:3), among others, could scarcely ever have been mistaken for authentic data. Yet in his own way Jonah, too, tells of the glory that was once Nineveh. The Ninevites, the inhabitants of Nineveh, to whom Jonah preached, would arise at the Last Judgment to condemn the generation of Jesus, according to Matt. 12:41; Luke 11:30, 32.

Bibliography. R. C. Thompson and R. W. Hutchinson, *A Century of Exploration at Nineveh* (1929); A. Parrot, *Ninive et l'AT* (1955). E. A. Speiser

NINLIL nĭn′lĭl. An epithet of "the Mistress" (Belit), consort of En-lil, god of Nippur. *See* Sumer.

Bibliography. E. Dhorme, *Les religions de Babylonie et d'Assyrie* (1945), pp. 29-30.

NINURTA nĭ nŏŏr′tə. In Sumerian mythology the son of the storm-god En-lil; in the Gilgamesh Epic the name designates the herald of the gods. *See* Nimrod; Sumer.

Bibliography. E. Dhorme, *Les religions de Babylonie et d'Assyrie* (1945), pp. 102-5; *Larousse Encyclopedia of Mythology* (1959), pp. 58-59.

NIPHIS nī′fĭs. An Apoc. form of Magbish.

NIPPUR nĭ pŏŏr′. A city *ca.* 100 miles S of Baghdad. It was founded by the "Ubaid" people (*see* Sumer) *ca.* 4000 B.C. From the early third millennium B.C. to the days of Hammurabi, Nippur was Sumer's undisputed religious and cultural center. It wielded no political power and was never the seat of a Sumerian dynasty. But because of some still unknown momentous historical developments, the Sumerians came to adopt the credo that Nippur's tutelary deity, Enlil, was the chief of the Sumerian pantheon and the monarch of the entire universe. The rulers of Sumer, no matter where their capital, found it indispensable, therefore, to have Enlil "legitimize" their royal authority; and Enlil's temple at Nippur, the *Ekur,* "mountain house," became Sumer's leading shrine. According to a later tradition, it was Enmebaraggesi, the last ruler but one of the "Etana" dynasty of Kish, who first built Enlil's temple at Nippur. Following him, practically all the rulers of Sumer made sure that they either built or rebuilt parts of it. By the time of Hammurabi, Nippur had yielded to Babylon as a religious and cultural center, but it continued to be an important city down to Parthian times. Fig. NIP 20.

Nippur was the seat of Sumer's most important *edubba,* "academy" (see *Sumer*). In the myths and hymns composed and redacted in this *edubba,* Nippur and its leading deities, Enlil, his wife Ninlil, and his son Ninurta, played a large role. According to one literary document, Enlil sent the barbaric Guti to devastate Sumer because Naram-Sin had plundered Nippur and desecrated the *Ekur.* The destruction of Nippur itself is vividly described in a specially composed lamentation which also eulogizes its delivery and restoration by Ishme-Dagan (*ca.* 1900 B.C.).

Excavations conducted in Nippur by American expeditions in 1890, 1893-96, 1899-1900, 1948, and every other year from 1949 through 1958, laid bare parts of the *Ekur,* and its ziggurat; a small temple dedicated to an unknown deity; a large temple dedicated to the goddess Inanna; and the houses of the

Courtesy of the University Museum of the University of Pennsylvania

20. Clay-tablet map of Nippur, showing plan for temple, walls, canals, and gates

Courtesy of the University Museum of the University of Pennsylvania

21. A terra-cotta plaque from Nippur showing the worshiper being led by his "personal goddess"

Courtesy of the Oriental Institute, the University of Chicago

22. General view of Nippur, showing an Early Dynastic temple

scribal quarter of the city.* Among the most important finds are the votive inscriptions on vases, bowls, bricks, brick stamps, door sockets, and tablets—all invaluable for the political history of Sumer—as well as thirty to forty thousand tablets and fragments among which are close to four thousand inscribed with Sumerian literary works. Figs. NIP 21, 22.

Bibliography. H. V. Hilprecht, *The Excavations in Assyria and Babylonia* (1904), pp. 289-577. *Bulletin of the University Museum,* vol. 13, pt. 4 (1948); vol. 14, pt. 1 (1949); vol. 16, pt. 2 (1951). V. Crawford, *Archaeology,* vol. 12, no. 2 (1959), pp. 74-83. Publications of the Babylonian Section of the University Museum (a whole series of volumes devoted primarily to tablets). S. N. KRAMER

NISAN nī'zăn [ניסן; Νισαν]. The first month of the Hebrew CALENDAR, Akkadian *nisānu* (March-April). It was called ABIB before the Exile.

NISROCH nĭz'rŏk [נסרוך] (II Kings 19:37; Isa. 37:38). A deity worshiped by Sennacherib; in his temple Sennacherib was killed.

The name is quite unknown in our sources for Mesopotamian religion, and is probably a corruption by Hebrew scribes. If the corruption was unintentional and made while the records were still in the proto-Hebraic script, the original reading may have been either "Nusku" or "Marduk," the former being nearer the later script of the MT. The LXX readings Ἐσδρὰχ, Ἐσθρὰχ, and Ἀσρὰχ do not elucidate the matter, since they offer no alternative to the real difficulty, the last three consonants of the MT.

Regarding the identity of Nisroch with Marduk, the city-god of Babylon, it has been suggested, on inadequate evidence, that Sennacherib was assassinated there. Such information, however, as is extant suggests that the king was murdered at Nineveh, and evidence has been adduced that the cult of Marduk was transplanted there from Babylon.

Nusku, the fire-god, was the son of Sin, the moon-god, and his consort Ningal. Nusku was regarded as an intermediary between the great gods and men, and is so mentioned in Assyrian inscriptions. His cult, though native to S Mesopotamia, was practiced also in the N, especially at Harran and in its vicinity, and is attested in the period of Assyrian ascendancy to which II Kings 19 refers. Hence Nisroch should probably be identified with Nusku.

Bibliography. G. A. Cooke, *A Textbook of North Semitic Inscriptions* (1903), pp. 186-91; E. Dhorme, *Les religions de Babylonie et d'Assyrie* (1945), pp. 59, 111-12; J. A. Montgomery, *Commentary on Kings,* ICC (ed. H. S. Gehman; 1951), pp. 499-500, 506. J. GRAY

NITRE nī'tər. KJV translation of נתר in Prov. 25:20; Jer. 2:22. *See* LYE.

NO nō. KJV translation of נא, the Hebrew name, from Egyptian, of THEBES.

NOADIAH nō'ə dī'ə [נועדיה, Yahu has met by appointment—*i.e.,* has revealed himself]. Alternately: MOETH mō'ĭth [Μωέθ] (I Esd. 8:63—G 8:62). **1.** A Levite, son of Binnui; one of those given charge of the temple treasures brought by Ezra from Babylon (Ezra 8:33; I Esd. 8:63—G 8:62).

2. A prophetess referred to by Nehemiah as among those who had wanted to make him "afraid" (Neh. 6:14).

Bibliography. M. Noth, *Die israelitischen Personennamen* (1928), p. 184. B. T. DAHLBERG

NOAH nō'ə [נח, *Nōaḥ;* LXX *and* NT Νῶε; *see below*]. Alternately: NOE. Survivor, with his family, of the FLOOD; and discoverer of the art of making wine. He is considered everywhere in the Bible, apart from Gen. 9:20-29, only as the hero of the Flood (Isa. 54:9; Matt. 24:37-38; Luke 17:26-27), an exemplary righteous man (Ezek. 14:14, 20; I Pet. 3:20; II Pet. 2:5), who, with his family, was preserved from annihilation because of his faith in God and his obedience to the divine command (Heb. 11:7). It is possible, however, that the connection of Noah with the Deluge, as the Hebrew counterpart to the Babylonian Utnapishtim (*see* FLOOD § 3*c*), is not original but was made in Syria-Palestine for a figure who entered the area originally as a gardener. *See* § 2 *below.*

1. The biblical data. The son of LAMECH, ninth descendant of ADAM through SETH, Noah was born 126 years after the death of Adam. His birth was the first after Adam's death, and he thus becomes the second father of mankind after all other descendants of Adam have been destroyed. He has been called the "bringer of the new age, who rescued mankind from the return to chaos in the deluge, a messianic figure" (Jeremias 120).

The reason Lamech gives for naming his son Noah is that "out of the ground which Yahweh has cursed this one shall bring us relief from our work and from the toil of our hands" (Gen. 5:29*b*). Noah lived five hundred years before he "became the father of SHEM, HAM, and JAPHETH" (vs. 32). He himself was a "righteous man, blameless in his generation" (Gen. 6:9; cf. II Pet. 2:5) at a time when the world was "corrupt in God's sight" (Gen. 6:11). Therefore, when God determined to destroy "man and beast and creeping things and birds of the air" (vs. 7) from the earth, "Noah found favor in the eyes of the LORD" (vs. 8). God announced to him his determination "to make an end of all flesh," to "destroy them with the earth" (vs. 13), and ordered Noah to build an ARK of gopher wood—i.e., "some resinous wood" (Skinner), equipped with cells and covered "inside and out with pitch" (vs. 14); for the catastrophe was to be a world-wide deluge (vs. 17). Noah obeyed the command (6:22; 7:5) and, together with his family and the living creatures taken by him into the ark, was saved from annihilation. The Flood occurred "in the six hundredth year of Noah's life" (7:11); and one year later, "in the six hundredth and first year, in the first month, the first day of the month, the waters were dried from off the earth" (8:13). Noah, however, awaited God's command to disembark (vs. 15) and finally stepped onto dry ground seven weeks later (vs. 14), "in the second month, on the twenty-seventh day of the month."

After Noah had attended to the disembarkation of every creature in the ark, he "took of every clean animal and of every clean bird" and offered to God an enormous sacrifice of propitiation (vs. 20). God accepted the worship and determined that he would "never again curse the ground because of man" (vs. 21), for the evil of man cannot be cured by his wholesale destruction. Therefore, the alternation of the seasons would never again be disturbed by any catastrophe like the Flood. Then Noah, as the second father of mankind, received the same injunction which God had given to Adam: "Be fruitful and multiply, and fill the earth" (9:1*b*), and in addition the prohibition from eating blood (vs. 4) and from committing murder (vss. 5-6). As a sign of his promise not to destroy man again by a flood, God adopted the rainbow (vss. 8-17). Thus from Noah and his three sons (and Canaan) "the whole earth was peopled" (vs. 19).

Noah is also referred to (J) as the "first tiller of the soil" (9:20)—a strange contrast to 3:23. The best rendering of 9:20 is that of Skinner: "Noah the husbandman was the first who planted a vineyard"; but even this translation does not obviate the difficulty of referring to Noah as *the* husbandman, as though he were a gardener of some reputation, if not also the inventor of agriculture. The emphasis in the narrative, however, is on Noah's discovery of the culture of the vine and the consequences of "immoderate indulgence in its fruit." In his drunkenness he "uncovered himself in his tent" (vs. 21; RSV "lay uncovered" does not convey the force of the Hebrew) and was found in that state by his second(?) son, HAM, who told his brothers (vs. 22). Shem and Japheth then took a garment and entered the tent, walking backward in order not to see the shame of their father, and covered his nakedness (vs. 23). When Noah recovered and learned what had happened, he cursed CANAAN with slavery and blessed Shem and Japheth (vss. 24-27).

Noah lived after the Flood 350 years and died at the ripe old age of 950 years (9:28-29). The story of the generations of Noah (6:9) is concluded with a formula reminiscent of Gen. 5. *See* CHRONOLOGY OF THE OT.

2. Noah the gardener. The Noah of Gen. 9:20-27 almost certainly belongs to a tradition different from that of the blameless hero of the Flood. The two stories bear no intrinsic relation to each other and can be harmonized only with difficulty. Suspicion that a character other than the hero of the Flood is meant is aroused at vs. 20 by the reference to Noah as *the* man of the ground—i.e., *the* farmer—as though he were well known, not as the builder of the ark, but rather as the gardener par excellence. Further, Noah's sons are represented (vss. 22-24) as minors rather than as the married men of the flood story. In addition, the offender in vs. 24 is the youngest son of Noah, who is named in vs. 25 Canaan (not Ham) and whose brothers are Shem and Japheth. The attribution of the evil deed to "Ham, the father of Canaan" (vs. 22), along with the notice "Ham was the father of Canaan" (vs. 18*b*), is more than likely an attempt to harmonize the two accounts, to help bridge the hiatus between vs. 18 and vs. 20. Two chronologies apparently have been harmonized, one which gives Noah's sons as Shem, Ham, and Japheth, and one which lists them as Shem, Japheth, and Canaan. Moreover, the incident also breaks the connection between 9:19 and 10:1 and must therefore be an interpolation from another (older) source, which, if it knew the flood story, did not know Noah as its hero. Finally, the obvious allusion to 5:29 makes it probable that the story belongs somewhere within the J tradition, even though it did not form a part of the J narrative of the Flood. The incident may be part of a third source (J^1). *Cf.* FLOOD § 2*a*.

The story is clearly a culture myth describing the discovery of wine. It presupposes a state of transition from nomadic to agricultural life. Noah and his two sons Shem and Japheth are tent dwellers (vss. 21, 27); but Noah, no longer a nomad, has advanced beyond the simplest forms of agriculture to the more specialized, complicated art of vine cultivation. That the result of this occupation can be degrading is illustrated by the acts of Noah and Canaan. There appears in this story the same nomadic mistrust of and hostility toward settled agricultural life as that which exists in the story of Cain and Abel (4:1-16). Here Semitic contempt for the refinements of Canaanite civilization is summed up in Noah's curse of his youngest son (vs. 25).

3. The name Noah. The combination in Gen. 5:29 of the name Noah with the verb נחם (*pi'el*), "to comfort," "to cheer," is a late, fanciful interpretive derivation. The verse seems to have been misplaced from 9:20. Not only does ינחמנו make no sense in its present context with reference to Noah's role in the Deluge, but its meaning is also forced, when with obvious reference to wine Lamech remarks: "This one shall bring us relief from our work and from the toil of our hands" (5:29*b*). The *pi'el* נחם means "to comfort," "to dispel sorrow." Even Jer. 16:7, which refers to the "cup of consolation," does not refer so much to the properties of wine as to a mourning custom. Both Rabbi Johanan and Rabbi Simeon ben Lakish remarked that in Gen. 5:29*b* name and etymology do not correspond. "Either he named him *Nōaḥ* from *yənîḥēnû* or *Naḥmān* from *yənaḥəmēnû*" (Berakoth Rabba, Genesis, section 25, quoted by I. Goldziher, 208). Either an emendation of *yənaḥəmēnû* to *yənîḥēnû* (agrees with LXX διαναπαύσει),

"He will cause us to rest," is necessary, or the name Noah must be emended to Naham. The first alternative is preferable.

The LXX rendering indicates that the form *yənaḥəmēnû* did not enter the MT until the late Jewish period. It has been suggested that Gen. 5:29 preserves the "nucleus of a perhaps more extended birth-legend of Noah," which perhaps is found in the pseudepigraph Enoch 106. According to this theory, the infant Noah would be identified with the infant sun-god whose birth is associated with the winter solstice. The Canaanite or early Hebrew farmer would then "regard the solstice as ushering in his season of rest after the toil of spring, summer and autumn." The flood story, therefore, appears to have been a cult legend used in connection with a seasonal festival.

But even if the original biblical etymology connected the name Noah with the Hebrew root *nûaḥ*, little is won for the meaning and origin of the name. All etymologies of ancient names are, of course, uncertain, but some tentative theories must nevertheless be propounded in the light of the evidence. Originally the name was thought to derive from Assyrian *nâxu, inûx*, "to rest," but this derivation was given up when it was learned that Akkadian *x* and Hebrew *ḥ* do not represent the same consonant. Another suggested connection was with Old Babylonian *nuḫiya*, but this is an Akkadian diminutive of a name formed from the element *nūḫ*, which does not correspond vocalically with Noah. Two suggestions have received scholarly support: (*a*) that Noah is derived from a stem נחח, which in Arabic gives the word *naḥaḥe*, "liberality," "generosity"; and (*b*) that it is connected with the Akkadian element *nâḫ*. The discovery of the Akkadian names *Nāḫ-ilum* and *Muutnaḫa*, combinations with *Nâḫ*, make some connection of Noah with *Nâḫ* seem probable, for the change from Akkadian *Nâḫ* to Canaanite-Hebraic *Nōaḥ* is easily possible. *Nâḫ* is apparently a divine name. The name Noah, therefore, may be theophoric and the personage represented by the name pre-Israelite in origin.

If the Akkadian derivation for Noah be correct, a multitude of unanswerable questions are raised: Was *Nâḫ* in Mesopotamia originally a god or only a secondarily deified figure? Was he native to Mesopotamia, or was he brought there by invaders of the nineteenth-eighteenth centuries? Was he already known in connection with the flood story in the Mari region? In what role did he enter Syrian-Palestinian cultural tradition? Was he brought into Mesopotamia directly by the invaders of the nineteenth-eighteenth centuries, or was he mediated by them from Lower Mesopotamia? Did he come as a god or as a human figure? Did he already have some connection with the Flood at his first appearance in the Syrian-Palestinian area? These queries rightly focus scholarly attention on the problem of the Babylonian sources for most of the early stories of Genesis, which were mediated to the Hebrews through the Amorites and proto-Arameans of the Upper Euphrates region. The original Noah, therefore, may have had nothing to do with the flood tradition but was a gardener associated with the discovery of wine, as in Gen. 9:20-27. With this occupation the suggested biblical etymology of his name would agree; he is no longer a wanderer but is settled, at rest, an agriculturalist.

Bibliography. I. Goldziher, "Zur Geschichte der Etymologie des Names Nûḥ," *ZDMG*, 24 (1870), 207-11; P. Haupt, *Purim* (1906), p. 27; R. H. Charles, *The Book of Enoch* (2nd ed., (1912); E. G. Kraeling, "The Interpretation of the Name Noah in Gen. 5:29," *JBL*, 48 (1929), 138-43; A. Jeremias, *Das alte Testament im Lichte des alten Orients* (4 Aufl.; 1930); J. Skinner, *Genesis*, ICC (2nd ed., 1930); G. R. Berry, "The Hebrew Word Nûᵃḥ," *JBL*, 50 (1931), 207-10; S. Spiegel, "Noah, Danel, and Job," *Louis Ginzberg Jubilee Volume* (1945), pp. 305-55; M. Noth, "Noah, Daniel and Hiob in Ezekiel xiv," *Vetus Testamentum*, 1 (1951), 251-60. J. H. MARKS

NOAH (DAUGHTER OF ZELOPHEHAD) nō'ə [נֹעָה, *probably a place name*]. One of the five daughters of Zelophehad who asked for and received an inheritance, although their father was dead and they had no brothers (Num. 26:33; 27:1-11; 36:10-12; Josh. 17:3-6).

NOAH, APOCALYPSE OF. A pseudepigraphal writing mentioned by name in Jub. 10:13; 21:10; more properly, BOOK OF NOAH. Portions of it have been identified in Jub. 7:20-39; 10:1-17; Enoch 6–11; 39:1-2*a;* 54:7–55:2; 60; 65:1–69:25; 106; 107(?). Some fragments, corresponding to I Enoch 8:4–9:3; 106:1, have appeared among the DEAD SEA SCROLLS. The book is obviously earlier than JUBILEES, which may have been written *ca.* the middle of the second century B.C.

The extant fragments show a special interest in the legend of the fallen angels who introduced evil into the world when they had intercourse with the daughters of men (cf. Gen. 6:1 ff), and with the terrible punishments awaiting them. Through their demoralization of mankind they are held responsible for the Deluge. The fragments also contain a description of the marvelous events connected with the birth of Noah, a remarkable child, and also relate his death. In addition, a messianic kingdom is predicted.

On the basis of the fragmentary evidence the writing is not an apocalypse in the strict sense of the term (*see* APOCALYPTICISM). The title given in Jub. 10:13, the "Book of Noah," is preferable to the modern designation.

Bibliography. R. H. Charles, *The Apoc. and Pseudep. of the OT* (1913), vol. II; N. Schmidt, "The Apocalypse of Noah and the Parables of Enoch," *Oriental Studies for Paul Haupt* (1926), pp. 111-23. M. RIST

NO-AMON nō ăm'ən [נא אמון] (Nah. 3:8 RSV mg). A fuller form of No, the Hebrew name, from Egyptian, of THEBES.

NOB nŏb [נֹב]. A town in Benjamin.

1. History. Ahimelech the priest was in charge of the sanctuary which had been at Shiloh (I Sam. 14:3) and evidently was moved to Nob after the destruction of Shiloh (Jer. 7:14). Under Ahimelech was a large body of priests caring for sacred objects, including holy vessels, the "bread of the Presence," the ephod, and Goliath's sword. David on his flight from Saul came to Nob and, pretending to be on a secret mission from the king, persuaded Ahimelech to give him sacred bread and Goliath's sword (I Sam. 21:1-9). When this was reported to Saul by Doeg the Edomite, who had been present at David's visit to Nob, Saul in his anger summoned Ahimelech and all his father's house, the priests who were at Nob, and ordered them slain. The servants of the king refused to lay hands on the priests; so Saul told Doeg to carry out the order. Consequently Doeg killed eighty-five persons "who wore the linen ephod" and put to the sword the city of Nob—men, women, children, and animals. Only one son of Ahimelech, Abiathar, escaped, and he fled to David (I Sam. 22:9-23).

2. Location. That Nob was in Benjamin and near Anathoth is shown in the list of postexilic inhabited cities (Neh. 11:31-32). Another mention of Nob is in Isa. 10:27*b*-32, where the prophet tells of the imminent approach of the Assyrian. After discomfiting the cities of Benjamin, including Michmash, Geba, Gibeah, and Anathoth,

> This very day he will halt at Nob,
> he will shake his fist
> at the mount of the daughter of Zion,
> the hill of Jerusalem.

Thus it would seem that Nob is between Anathoth and Jerusalem and sufficiently high to command a view of the holy hill. Some have considered that this Nob is different from the Nob which contained the sanctuary, but the present prevailing view favors considering the two identical. A most likely location is Mount Scopus, the hill a little less than a mile NE of the ancient city. Titus camped there when he was approaching Jerusalem. Another possibility is Qu'meh, a low hill *ca.* a mile N of Scopus. It has the advantage of being nearer Gibeah, while Mount Scopus is a more likely location for one shaking his fist at Jerusalem. There is no satisfactory etymological explanation of the name Nob, nor is there as yet any archaeological evidence of its location.

O. R. SELLERS

NOBAH nō'bə [נבח]. **1.** Apparently a chieftain of the tribe of Manasseh; conqueror of KENATH during the Israelite conquest of Canaan (Num. 32:42). The account of the Manassite conquest of Gilead in Num. 32:39-42 appears to be a fragment, unrelated to its present context but similar to the account given in Judg. 1 of independent action by various Israelite tribes in the conquest of Canaan. Thus, Nobah's capture of Kenath and its villages forms part of the Manassite tribe's occupation of GILEAD. Num. 32:40 is an editorial attempt to reconcile the independent action of the Manassite clans with the preceding account of Moses' efforts to secure united Israelite action against Canaan. R. F. JOHNSON

2. A town in Gilead (Num. 32:42); formerly KENATH; named for its conqueror (*see* 1 *above*).

3. A town in the E of Gilead, near Jogbehah; Gideon made a circuit around the two towns in order to surprise the Midianites at Karkor (Judg. 8:10-11). The site is unknown. S. COHEN

NOBLE [אדיר, majestic (one); גדול, great; חורים; נגיד, leader, ruler, prince; נדיב, generous, princely, willing (one); נכבד, honored (one); פרתמים, *loan word from* Old Pers.; קר, cool of spirit, self-possessed; Aram. יקירא, honorable, difficult; εὐγενής, wellborn; εὐγενής ἄνθρωπος, a wellborn man, nobleman; καλός, beautiful, pleasing, honest, goodly; τιμή, (to, unto) honor]. A word descriptive of persons of illustrious deeds or otherwise distinguished for skill or genius; of persons of high birth, rank, title, or exalted position (Judg. 5:13; Ezra 4:10; Esth. 6:9; Prov. 17:26; I Cor. 1:26); of persons having high moral qualities and ideals who are recognized for their moral dignity and superiority (Ps. 16:3; Isa. 32:5, 8; Acts 17:11); of persons or things which are grand or stately in appearance, splendid in proportions, or very useful; generally, anything having qualities of a very high order (Ezek. 17:8, 23: a noble vine or tree, because productive; I Tim. 3:1: a noble task; Luke 21:5: noble stones and offerings).

The primitive meaning of חורים, the most common Hebrew noun for "nobleman," is "freed man" or "freeman," whence one of the connotations attaching to the idea of the nobility in the late period. The idea of the root (חרר), which is common to several Semitic languages, is "to become free, to set free" (in contrast to עבד, "to work, to serve"). *See* FREEDOM; FREEWILL OFFERING.

A nobleman freely supports and defends his community. He has a generous (נדיב) heart (Exod. 35:5, 22; II Chr. 29:31; cf. Num. 21:18; I Chr. 28:21). Thus, the repentant psalmist asks God to uphold him with a "free spirit" (רוח נדיבה; Ps. 51:12 KJV—H 51:14)—i.e., a "willing" (so RSV) or "noble" spirit.

H. F. BECK

NOD nŏd [נוד wandering]. A country E of Eden where Cain went and dwelt (Gen. 4:16). Possibly the name represents a play on words, a place of wandering for the condemned wanderer. Some have suggested that the words "east of Eden" are a gloss, added in order to attach the story to the Eden narrative of Gen. 3. D. M. C. ENGLERT

NODAB nō'dăb [נודב] (I Chr. 5:19). A Hagrite people mentioned in connection with Jetur and Napish as waging war against the Israelite tribes of Transjordan. Since Jetur, Napish, and Kedemah are mentioned together as the sons of Ishmael, the son of Hagar (Gen. 25:15; I Chr. 1:31), it is obvious that Kedemah and Nodab are different names for the same people, and it is even possible that one name may have arisen as a textual corruption of the other. The name Nodab is preserved in that of the village Nudebe in the Hauran. S. COHEN

NOE. KJV NT form of NOAH.

NOEBA. KJV Apoc. form of NEKODA.

NOEMI nō'ə mī. Douay Version form of NAOMI.

NOGAH nō'gə [נגה] (I Chr. 3:7; 14:6). One of the sons of David who were born at Jerusalem. Since the name is missing in the parallel list (II Sam. 5:15), some scholars are of the opinion that it is a dittographic corruption of the following name, NEPHEG (2), and consequently has erroneously been included in the lists of the Chronicler. E. R. DALGLISH

NOHAH nō'hə [נוחה]. The fourth born of Benjamin, according to I Chr. 8:2 (but cf. Gen. 46:21).

NOMADISM. A way of life in which a people have no permanent home or dwelling, but move from place to place seeking game or pasture. It is the repeated shifting of a people's habitat to find sustenance. It is not, therefore, unrestricted or aimless wandering but is focused around centers or in a certain directional pattern. Even in the wilderness of Judea the Ta'amira tribe has a generally defined territory. Climate, topography, and technological advance determine the type of nomadism. All types are found in all periods of history. The nomad is respected by more sedentary neighbors, despite his seeming POVERTY. His skill, strength, and stamina cause fear even among people with more advanced weapons.

1. Types of nomadism
   a. Hunting and collecting
   b. Pastoral
   c. Agricultural
2. Camel and ass nomadism
3. Nomadism in the ancient Near East
4. Nomadism in the Bible
   a. The patriarchal period
   b. After the Conquest
   c. Conflict with the sown and the settled
   d. The nomadic ideal

Bibliography

1. Types of nomadism. There are three significantly different types of nomadism found in all parts of the world and in all periods of history.

a. Hunting and collecting. The hunting and collecting nomads are made up of separate bands (*see* BAND), who rarely assembled together as tribes (*see* TRIBE) for some religious ceremonies. The size of the band depends on the changing food supply as well as the size of available territory. There is little surplus and no developed division of labor. Poverty is more prevalent than wealth, although all members of the band are relatively equal. Therefore, society is generally democratic, with all heads of families (*see* ELDER) vested with authority in the tribal council. Marriage is usually endogamous, although marriage by capture is not unknown. Individuals seldom join another tribe. The recognition of family hunting, fishing, and collecting rights is sometimes made within the larger tribal territory. Some of these bands may become pastoral nomads, but this is not a simple, direct evolutionary pattern, as commonly supposed.

b. Pastoral. The pastoral nomads follow a consistent pattern of grazing, regulated by the season and the type of herd or flock. The sheep and goat herders of modern Palestine and the ancient ass nomad traveled slowly, seeking pasture. The camel and horse nomad, the Bedouin in Arabia, can rapidly cover the length and breadth of the country. Wealth is in the herd. Territory is defined and is the property of specific families. Some families become wealthy, but all have a greater security than the hunting nomad. Milk and young animals are the major food supplies. Skin and hair are the source for clothing, tents, water bottles, etc. The same democratic practice prevails, but the voice of the wealthier elder is more likely to carry the day. The division of labor is on the sex basis, with men usually doing the herding and the women preparing hides and goatskins and erecting tents. Marriage is either exogamous or endogamous. Such tribes may settle down briefly for a season and raise a crop, but they do not build permanent structures. Eventually some may infiltrate or settle down on the edge of the territory and become agriculturists.

c. Agricultural. Agricultural nomads stay in one spot until the crop has exhausted the land. They then move on to new fertile territory, and the process is repeated. Perhaps these should not be considered real nomads.

2. Camel and ass nomadism. Most present-day Bedouins are camel nomads who also possess the horse. It is a fallacy of nineteenth-century scholarship to believe that the modern nomad is a pattern of the patriarch, and that his customs and religion can be projected back without any other supporting evidence into the pre-exodus period. The CAMEL is mentioned in several stories of the patriarchs (Gen. 24:64; 31:34), but, according to many authorities, these are anachronistic references, since the Midianites *ca.* the twelfth century B.C. are probably the first true camel nomads. It was apparently at this time that the camel was domesticated. This true camel nomadism is not reflected in the patriarchal stories. Nevertheless, despite the introduction of the camel and the horse, ass nomadism continues to the present day and does not necessarily fit into an evolutionary hypothesis. Similarly the excavations at Jericho and Ghassul show that well-developed cities go back far into Neolithic times, and a pattern of cultural development within the historical period of the Bible is not a simple line from nomad to agriculturist. Nomadism and strict moralism are by no means a first stage in the evolution of Israel. The patriarchs seem to be typical ass nomads, as depicted in Egypt under the descent of the Beni-hasan tribe. It is interesting to note the Beni Hamor ("sons of the ass") at Shechem (Gen. 34:2 ff). The ass was sacrificed by the Amorites in Mari, where many other patriarchal customs are paralleled. The ass was not necessarily a humble beast but was in that period ridden by kings and deities (Zech. 9:9). *See* UGARIT.

3. Nomadism in the ancient Near East. Nomads are erupting into the centers of civilization at the beginning of our records. By the end of the fourth millennium B.C., Semitic nomads are infiltrating Sumer. A large group of Akkadians settled down in the middle of the third millennium. Amorite nomads appear in the Fertile Crescent at the beginning of the second millennium. The pressure of nomads on settled communities is reflected in many of the documents from MARI. These documents also show how a group of nomads adapted themselves to a previously established culture. Some think the HYKSOS and the HABIRU also reflect Semitic nomadic movements. The Arameans came into the picture about the middle of the second millennium. At the time of the Conquest camel-riding Midianites appear in the E. At about this same time Edom and Moab settle down.

In addition to these Semitic nomads there are eruptions of others from the steppes to the N. The Hurrians, Hittites, and later the Medes and still later the Parthians perhaps reflect this same pattern of conquest and renewal in the ancient Near East. *See* ISRAEL, HISTORY OF.

4. Nomadism in the Bible. ***a. The patriarchal period.*** JABAL, a descendant of Cain, is the father of nomads, described as possessing cattle and dwelling in tents (Gen. 4:20), although Abel seems to represent this ideal over against Cain. The patriarchs are pictured as ass nomads. Abraham moved his tent from place to place (Gen. 13:3, 5, 18; 20:1; etc.; cf. Heb. 11:9). He possessed cattle (Gen. 12:16—the reference to camels may be anachronistic). He had grazing rights established with Lot (Gen. 13:8 ff). His tent may have been divided into two, with the wife behind the curtain in her quarter (Gen. 18:9-10).

The Ishmaelites are throughout the OT and even in modern times related genealogically to the Arab nomads (Gen. 37:25; Isa. 21:13). The prophecy of Ishmael's future suggests this nomadic life (Gen. 16:11; vs. 12 sees him as a "wild ass," and it is interesting that modern Syrians sometimes use a similar epithet to describe the Bedouins). The place names and encampments of the Ishmaelites support this identification with the Arabs (Gen. 25:13-18). It is significant that under David, an Ishmaelite is in charge of the camels (I Chr. 27:30). The Ishmaelites are linked with the Edomites among the enemies of Israel (Ps. 83:6).

The story of Isaac involves nothing that is not consonant with this seminomadic state. He settles down for a season and raises grain, then moves on (Gen. 26:12). The ass is important in this history (Gen. 22:3; 24:35; 30:43; 32:5). The fear of vengeance is strong, as in the contrast in the figures of the striving brothers, Jacob and Esau, the reputed ancestors of the Israelites and the Edomites.

Jacob's return from Laban is described almost like the movement of a small tribe of nomads with its several tents (Gen. 31:33). The descent of Jacob's family seeking provender from Joseph in Egypt is paralleled by many similar events in Egypt, such as that of the Beni-hasan (Gen. 42; cf. Gen. 46:34; 47:4). Joseph's dream indicates the seminomadic state of his family (Gen. 37:5 ff).

The Kenites and the Midianites seem to be tent-dwelling nomads (Judg. 5:24; 6:4-5). The eruption of camel-riding Midianites is verified in nonbiblical records, as is the settling of the Edomites in their territory. In Egypt the Israelites lived in the area frequented by nomads and seminomads (*see* GOSHEN, EGYPT). Moses takes refuge among a pastoral nomadic tribe (Exod. 2:15 ff), and tends sheep (Exod. 3:1 ff). The promise of a land flowing with milk and honey is calculated to appeal not only to slaves but also to such nomads whose traditions were on a mere sustenance level. In the wilderness wandering, Israel was again a seminomadic people moving with their cattle from oasis to oasis (Num. 33:1 ff; cf. Num. 10:31). The TABERNACLE can be appropriate only as a shrine for people with such a nomadic tradition. The tribal organization also suited tent dwellers more than city people (Num. 1:52, etc.).

b. After the Conquest. In the Conquest as described in Joshua and Judges there are elements of ass nomadism (Josh. 15:18 [cf. water in vs. 19]; Judg. 10:4; 12:14; etc.). Some of Israel remained in tents and were shepherds long after the settlement (Deut. 5:30; II Sam. 20:1; I Kings 12:16). Nabal's wealth is reckoned like that of a nomad, in terms of sheep and goats (I Sam. 25:2). The nomadic origin of Israel could not be forgotten. Imagery from the tent is in the poetic and prophetic books (Pss. 78:55; 104:2; Song of S. 1:5, 8; Isa. 33:20; 40:22; Jer. 10:20; etc.). The Rechabites (*see* RECHAB) only intensified this traditional nomadic ideal (Jer. 35:6 ff; *see below*). All the prophets championed this nomadic ideal against the seductiveness and idolatry of urban society. The memory is clearly confessed when it is declared: "A wandering Aramean was my father" (Deut. 26:5). Some even think the word HEBREW may mean "wanderer" (Gen. 14:13).

In the later books the nomads are located in the E (Jer. 49:29) and in the desert (Jer. 25:24). They are possibly already called Arabs (Isa. 13:20). They give tribute to Jehoshaphat of rams and goats (II Chr. 17:11). The story of Job has features from both the nomadic and a settled background (Job 1:3, 14, 17, 19; 6:18-19).

c. Conflict with the sown and the settled. Throughout history the conflict between the desert and the sown, between nomads and city dwellers, has continued. The clash is intensified whenever drought brings on a scarcity of game or pasture. The nomad raids the agricultural settlements for food. The boundary of desert and sown is fluid and fluctuates frequently. The nomad acquires foreign wives by capture and is perhaps influenced by his latest acquisition to abandon some of his nomadic traditions and ideals. For some reason the nomadic tribe which seeks to conquer an agricultural society usually prevails, as Israel did over Canaan, or the Amorites over Mari. Thus political leadership may go to the nomads, and there is an ethical stratification of society.

The Near East saw many raids, infiltrations, and conquests of settled communities by nomadic and seminomadic tribes. This conflict reaches back into the very first chapters of the Bible, when murder is committed by one whose posterity largely represents urbanized society (Gen. 4:8, 17). The tower of Babylon (Gen. 11) and Sodom and Gomorrah (Gen. 13:12-13; 18–19) indicate the same distrust of city life. Jacob and Esau renew the rivalry of Abel and Cain (Gen. 25:27 ff). The Israelites themselves raided, conquered, and opposed the remnants of Canaanite civilization, but were in turn harassed by Midianites, Moabites, Ammonites, etc. Not until the settlement did Israel practice much agriculture or viniculture. There was within Israel a conflict between those who became urbanized or Canaanized and those who lived as seminomads with flocks, holding strongly to their nomadic ideals. The God of the nomads is in conflict with the gods of the Canaanites.

d. The nomadic ideal. The prophets from Nathan to Elijah tried to keep the nomadic ideal alive. It reached its zenith in the Rechabites. Some scholars believe the tradition of JOHN THE BAPTIST and Qumran represents the same retreat from the temptations of urban society. For development of this idea, *see* the work of John Flight in the *bibliography*.

Since pastoral nomads do not practice viniculture, wine is considered an evil (Jer. 35:7, 9). The Rechabites (vss. 6, 8) and modern Muslims do not drink wine. Perhaps the stories of Noah (Gen. 9: 21 ff) and Lot (19:30 ff) reflect this aversion to strong drink (Lev. 10:9; Deut. 32:32; etc.). The NAZIRITE also abstains (I Sam. 1:15; Luke 1:15).

A certain type of moralism, strictly enforced, characterizes the nomad in all periods of history. The Rechabites urge that all symbols of pagan civilization be overthrown and that Israel return to living in tents as the only proper dwelling for God's people (Jer. 35:9-10).

The democratic ideal is most strong in Israel. It is reflected in the laws of the covenant and especially in the Deuteronomistic concept of history and its judgment on the kings. It reaches its epitome in the antimonarchic speech of Samuel (I Sam. 8:10 ff) and in his apologia (12:1 ff). But the action of Gideon (Judg. 8:23) and the parable of the trees (Judg. 9:8 ff) have the same attitude.

e. Miscellaneous customs. Outside the Bible, the Beni-hasan give a clear picture of the Semitic ass nomad. The tribe had about thirty-seven families. They wore woolen tunics, and sandals; and they used the composite bow, throw sticks, and javelins for weapons. It is obvious that these nomads used their herds for everything from dwelling place to bottle. Tents were made of goat hair; tunics, of wool; sandals, of leather; bottles, of goatskin (cf. Mark 2: 22 [KJV "bottles"; RSV "skins"]). The flat tent and the pole of the modern Arab nomad may perpetuate the tent of the early Israelite (Isa. 33:20). Grazing ground was arranged by custom and agreement.

Vengeance is characteristic of nomadic society and is perhaps reflected in the "eye for eye, tooth for tooth" (Exod. 21:24; Lev. 24:20; although this law sets a limitation for vengeance). Vengeance is not merely getting even with the enemy, but is a method of repairing the breach in one's own organization. Lamech's Song is a clear song of vengeance (Gen. 4:23-24).

In direct contrast, hospitality is also traditional in nomadic society (Heb. 13:2; cf. Gen. 18:1 ff; *see* SOJOURNER). This custom was horribly broken in Sisera's murder by Jael (Judg. 4:17 ff).

Bibliography. J. Flight, "The Nomadic Idea and Ideal in the OT," *JBL,* XLII (1923), 158 ff; G. E. Wright, "People of the Desert and People of the Sown," *BA,* vol. III, no. 3 (Sept., 1940), pp. 29 ff; S. Nyström, *Beduinentum und Jahwismus* (1946); A. Haldar, *The Notion of the Desert in the Sumero-Akkadian and West-Semitic Religions* (1950); E. Jucker, Nomaden, *Eigenbrötler und Schamanen* (1955); M. F. von Oppenheim, *Die Beduinen* (3 vols.; 1939-53); R. de Vaux, *Les Institutions de l'AT, I: Le Nomadisme et les survivances, institutions familiales, institutions civiles* (1958). C. U. WOLF

NON nŏn. KJV form of NUN in I Chr. 7:27.

NOPH nŏf. KJV translation of נֹף; a dissimilated form of Moph, the Hebrew name of MEMPHIS.

NOPHAH nō'fə [נֹפַח] (Num. 21:30 KJV; RSV mg.). A town of Moab, mentioned in the poem about the exploits of Sihon king of the Amorites. The text is doubtful; the RSV, comparing the LXX and the Samar., reads *nuppaḥ 'ēsh,* "fire spread," for *nōphaḥ 'asher,* "Nophah which," by omission of a single consonant. S. COHEN

NORTH. *See* ORIENTATION.

NORTH COUNTRY, THE [ארץ צפון, land of the north]. A name applied by the prophets to the country of any invader of Palestine that approached from the N. Since Palestine was a land bridge in the ancient world, with the Mediterranean Sea to its W and the Syro-Arabian Desert to the E, its principal international highways ran N and S. Egypt lay to the S, and all the other great powers (Assyria, Babylonia, Syrians, and the non-Semitic folk of Anatolia, the Caucasus region, Media, Persia, and Elam) had access to Palestine from the N. "North country" could thus refer also to E lands (Isa. 41:25).

For those Hebrews who accepted the Canaanite concept that the mountain of the gods lay far to the N (Ps. 48:2-3; Isa. 14:13-14), and who believed that manifestations of their own god, Yahweh, likewise came from the N (Job 37:22; Ezek. 1:4), a prophet's vague and nonspecific reference to a visitation by a foe from the N might well have been interpreted as an encounter with an army of God's own avengers. Usually such an enemy was directed against Judah, but Yahweh's agents from the N country were also sent against Egypt (Jer. 46:10, 20, 24) and Philistia (47:2).

When a dominant nation menaced the Hebrews, a veiled reference by the prophet to the foe from the N country would be readily identified by the people. Often, however, historical or geographical references in the context aid in identifying the N country. Sometimes it is Assyria, together with its W provinces in Mesopotamia, by the Euphrates (Jer. 46:10; Zeph. 2:13), the place to which men of Israel had been exiled (II Kings 17:6) and from which they were expected to return (Jer. 3:12, 18; 16:15; 23:8; 31:8). It is at other times the Chaldean kingdom in Babylonia (Ezek. 26:7; Zech. 2:6-7), the kingdom of Persia (Isa. 41:25; Jer. 50:3, 9, 41), or the Seleucid kingdom of Syria (Dan. 11:6 ff).

Sometimes non-Semitic northerners are mentioned (Ezek. 38:6), but it has been demonstrated that the earlier assumption that the N foe in the book of Jeremiah is to be identified with the Scythians mentioned by Herodotus (I.103-106; IV.11), is historically improbable. Where tribes or nations of the N are differentiated from the Babylonians (Jer. 1:14-15; 25:9; 50:9, 41), they appear to be but mercenary allies or dependents in the armies of the stronger nation.

Bibliography. F. Wilke, "Das Skythenproblem im Jeremiabuch," *Alttestamentliche Studien für Rudolf Kittel* (1913), pp. 222-54; A. C. Welch, *Jeremiah* (1928), pp. 97-131.

R. A. BOWMAN

NORTHEASTER, THE. The translation of Εὐροκλύδων, Εὐροκύλων (variant readings, the former two words meaning "east wind" and "wave" and the latter two words meaning "east wind" and "north wind"), the name of a northeasterly gale wind before which Paul's ship was driven (Acts 27:14). The KJV transliterates "Euroclydon"; ASV "Euraquilo." *See* EAST WIND; PALESTINE, CLIMATE OF. R. B. Y. SCOTT

NORTHERNER [הצפוני] (Joel 2:20). A term which apparently refers to the LOCUST swarms which, contrary to usual circumstances, came to Jerusalem from the N (as in 1915). Having promised to restore fertility to the land, God also promised removal of the locust plague and with it the shame and economic distress which the plague had caused (vs. 19). This was probably to be done by a great wind (cf. Exod. 10:19), which would drive the locusts to their death in the desert, the Dead Sea, and the Mediterranean (a phenomenon witnessed by Jerome).

Joel's choice of the term "northerner" for the locusts must have reminded many of the earlier prophecies concerning the enemy from the N (Jer. 1:14; 13:20; Ezek. 38:6, 15; 39:2). Moreover, the word was charged with many mythological associations. *See* NORTH COUNTRY.

Bibliography. J. D. Whiting, "Jerusalem's Locust Plague," *National Geographic Magazine,* XXVIII (1915), 513; A. S. Kapelrud, *Joel Studies* (1948), pp. 93-114. H. F. BECK

NOSE RING [נזמי האף, *plural, lit.,* rings of the nose] (Isa. 3:21); KJV NOSE JEWELS. The word "ring" (נזם) may designate a nose ring; cf. the gold ring presented by Abraham's servant to Rebekah at the well (Gen. 24:22, 30) and specifically said to have been placed on the nose (Gen. 24:47). Figurative reference is made to putting a ring on the nose, as a gift of the Lord to Israel, in Ezek. 16:12. *See also* RING. J. M. MYERS

NOT MY PEOPLE [לא עמי] (Hos. 1:9); KJV LO-AMMI lō ăm'ī. Symbolic name given by the prophet Hosea to his third child, a son, to indicate God's impending judgment upon Israel.

NOT PITIED [לא רחמה] (Hos. 1:6, 8); KJV LO-RUHAMAH lō'ro͞o hā'mə. Symbolic name given by the prophet Hosea to his second child, a daughter, to indicate God's impending judgment upon Israel.

NUMBER, NUMBERING, NUMBERS. The Hebrews do not appear to have taken any interest in theoretical mathematics, but were content to apply such arithmetical tools as they had to cope with various practical problems. That they were greatly indebted to the older and more advanced civilizations of Egypt and Mesopotamia in respect to mathematics, as well as to other aspects of culture, is abundantly clear.

1. Egyptian mathematics
2. Mesopotamian mathematics
3. Biblical mathematics
   a. Basic operations and terminology
   b. Representation of numbers
   c. Number and text criticism
4. Rhetorical uses of numbers
5. Cultic and symbolic uses of numbers

Bibliography

1. Egyptian mathematics. As early as the fourth millennium B.C. the Egyptians had developed a method of writing large numbers. On a royal mace of *ca.* 3500 B.C. there is a record of 120,000 prisoners, 400,000 oxen, and 1,422,000 goats. Egyptian mathematics was based on a rigid decimal system. The units were represented by single strokes, the tens by a symbol like an inverted "u," and there were symbols for 100, 1,000, 10,000, 100,000, and 1,000,000. The Egyptians never discovered that with a decimal system ten figures could serve for all possible numbers by being arranged in the order of units, tens, hundreds, etc. To write the number 985, e.g., required five units, eight tens, and nine hundreds—twenty-two symbols instead of the minimum of three. Addition and subtraction were no problem to the Egyptians, but they had some difficulty with multiplication and division. The problem of common fractions was too much for them to cope with, so they avoided them in computation, using unit fractions wherever possible. As early as 1700 B.C. the Egyptians arrived at a method of converting common fractions into a series of decreasing unit fractions—e.g., 3/4 could be written as the unit fractions 1/2 + 1/4, or 7/8 as 1/2 + 1/4 + 1/8. The fraction 2/3, however, did not yield to this treatment. Complementary fractions—i.e., those having a numerator one less than the denominator (2/3, 3/4, 4/5, 5/6, etc.) were frequently used, and there were special terms and symbols for them. A notable accomplishment of the Egyptian mathematics was the equation of the area of a circle with a square whose sides were 8/9 of the diameter—i.e., they came very close to the value of π as 3.1605. Egyptian mathematics reached its peak of development in the second millennium B.C., and most of our knowledge of it is derived from two documents: the Moscow Papyrus, dating *ca.* 1850 B.C., which deals with some twenty-five mathematical problems; and the Rhind Mathematical Papyrus, *ca.* 1650 B.C., with some eighty-five problems. Egyptian mathematics did not advance beyond the achievements reflected in these two papyri, and for a millennium afterward there was no significant development. Although Egyptian and Sumero-Akkadian mathematics were of about equal antiquity, the Egyptian remained the more primitive. Perhaps the reason for the lag of Egyptian mathematics behind the Sumero-Akkadian is to be seen in the characteristic modes of thought of the two cultures, the Egyptian being intuitive and the Mesopotamian abstract.

2. Mesopotamian mathematics. In Mesopotamia a remarkable level was achieved in mathematics and geometry. From earliest times the Sumerians and Akkadians knew both the decimal and the duodecimal or sexagesimal systems of numeration. The Sumero-Akkadian system was essentially sexagesimal, although there are influences of the decimal system. The decimal system was a Hamito-Semitic heritage, antedating the separation of Egyptian and Semitic, as indicated by the fact that the names of some of the numbers are obviously cognate. The sexagesimal system was the contribution of the non-Semitic Sumerians. The two systems blended without difficulty, preserving the advantages of each. The duodecimal base has the notable advantage of maximum divisibility, and its use continues in our divisions of time, the degrees of a circle, the dozen, and the gross. In the cuneiform system, as in the Egyptian, unity was represented by a vertical stroke or wedge and the other units to nine by combinations of such wedges. Ten was represented by a tailless wedge and the other numbers by tens and units. The symbol for unity was also used for sixty and as well as for any power of sixty; this occasions some difficulty for the modern interpreter of cuneiform mathematical texts. Another cause of uncertainty is that a blank space sometimes indicated zero. A special symbol for zero was not devised until the late sixth century B.C. The problem of common fractions was partially solved by converting them, wherever possible, to sexagesimal fractions—i.e., the common fraction $\frac{m}{n}$ was resolved into m x $\frac{1}{n}$, the unit fraction then converted to its corresponding sexagesimal fraction and multiplied by m; e.g., 3/4=3 x 1/4=3 x 15/60= 45/60.

The Sumerians and Akkadians made extensive application of practical mathematics in their complex business dealings, making use of bills, receipts, and notes in their accounting. Interest, varying from twenty to thirty per cent, was charged on loans. Besides the four basic arithmetical processes, the Mesopotamian mathematicians knew how to square and to extract the root of a number. They could compute the area of a triangle, quadrangle, and trapezium, and the volume of solid figures. They were acquainted with the Pythagorean theorem and the relation of the diameter and circumference of the circle. They were able to make practical application of their knowledge in metrology and in building. They prepared tables for convenience in reckoning. The rudiments of algebra were known to them. The progress achieved by the Sumerians and Akkadians in this field, as in other areas of culture, benefited the whole of the ancient Mediterranean world, and the Hebrews were heirs to some of this knowledge through the Canaanite civilization.

3. Biblical mathematics. The OT presents considerable data on the Hebrews' use of numbers, but most of it is simple enumeration.

a. Basic operations and terminology. The Hebrews were familiar with the four basic arithmetical operations, and they had at least an elementary control of fractions. The verbs ספר and מנה are the common words for the action of counting, and the derivatives מספר and מנין the common nouns for "number." The verb פקד, "attend to, visit, muster," is used of mustering and reviewing troops, of taking census of population, and of accounting and inventory of goods, and is thus equivalent to a verb of counting; its passive participle is used to designate the persons or things counted. The verb הוסיף, "add," is sometimes applied to specific numerals (Lev. 5:16; 6:5; 22:14; 27:13, 15, 19, 27, 31; II Kings 20:6=Isa. 38:5), but its opposite, גרע (cf. Deut. 4:2; 12:32—H 13:1) does not occur in connection with any specific numeral, nor does the term עדף, "remainder." The basic arithmetical operations are illustrated in a number of simple examples: addition, Num. 1; 26; subtraction, Gen. 18:28-33; multiplication, Lev. 25:8; Num. 7:84-86; division, Num. 31:27. More complicated operations are seen in Lev. 25:50 ff; 27:18, 23. The unit fractions, of course, presented no problem and were widely used. Since the Hebrew system was decimal, the tenths were much used, even the common fractions 2/10 and 3/10. The problem of converting mixed fractions to a common denominator was apparently avoided. In the Ugaritic epic of Keret there is a striking illustration of disregard for exactness in dealing with fractions of diverse denominators. A series of catastrophes wipe out the Keret's progeny in its entirety, but piecemeal in the proportions of 1/3, 1/4, 1/5, 1/6, and 1/7. The sum of these fractions amounts to 459/420=153/140=1 13/140. The poet may have been vaguely aware of the discrepancy but hardly exercised by it, since the best mathematicians of his time would not have been able to add these fractions.

The OT use of complementary fractions (*see above*) shows the influence of Egypt and Mesopotamia. The Hebrew idiom פי שנים (lit., "two mouths") originally meant "two parts out of three," or 2/3, exactly as the Akkadian *šenē pū* or *šenē pātu,* with which it is cognate. The expression still has this original sense in Zech. 13:8. The expression quite naturally developed the sense of "a double portion" or "twice as much" (II Kings 2:9; Ecclus. 12:5; 18:32; 48:12), and it always has this meaning in the Mishna and the Talmud. In Deut. 21:17 the sense is uncertain and may designate, in the original sense of the term, ⅔ of the entire estate rather than merely a double share among the brothers. The rabbis were aware of this archaic use of fractions and applied the terms "outside" (מלבר) and "inside" (מלגו) to distinguish the two concepts of ordinal and divisional fractions—e.g., the ordinal 1/5 of 20 considers 20 as 4/5 of a unit, with the missing 1/5 to be added, while the divisional or inside 1/5 of 20 considers the 20 as the whole. Thus an outside 1/5=an inside 1/4, and an outside 1/6=an inside 1/5, etc.

The Egyptians also used "mouth" in the sense of "proportion" in complementary fractions, thus the hieroglyph for "r" with two strokes attached designated 2/3 and with three strokes 3/4. Akkadian *śittā qātātu* and Hebrew שתי הידות, "two hands," meant "two parts (out of three)" or 2/3, and similarly "the four hands" of Gen. 47:24 means "four fifths" (so RSV). This form of the idiom, like "two mouths," also came to mean "twice as much," so that in Gen. 43:34 "five hands," originally "five parts (out of six)" or 5/6, means "five times as much" (so RSV), and similarly nine and ten "hands" (II Sam. 19:43; Neh. 11:1; Dan. 1:20) originally meant 9/10 and 10/11.

The measurements of the molten sea in the temple, ten cubits diameter and thirty cubits circumference (I Kings 7:23), show that the value of π was known only approximately. The Mishna ('Er. I.5) also gives the value of π as three. The earliest Hebrew treatise on geometry, *Mishnat ham-Middot,* composed *ca.* A.D. 150, gives the value of π as 3 1/7. This treatise also deals with the terminology and rules of plane and solid geometry from a practical rather than theoretical standpoint. This document was doubtless the basis of the forty-nine measurements quoted by Rashi, Ibn Ezra, and others. Unfortunately, we have little or no data outside the OT to illustrate the ancient Hebrews' dealing with numbers.

b. Representation of numbers. In the OT the numerals are always spelled out, and this is true also in the Moabite Stone and the Siloam tunnel inscription. The fact that we have no evidence for the early use of symbols for numbers among the Hebrews does not necessarily mean that they did not have and use some system of figures. At Ugarit the numerals in the literary texts are always spelled out, but in the administrative documents they are written ideographically with the Sumero-Akkadian symbols. The Old Aramaic inscriptions from Zenjirli, the Aramaic documents from Elephantine, and some Phoenician inscriptions spell out the numerals and also use figures. In the Eshmunazar Inscription the date is given both in words and in figures. On the Aramaic lion weights from Nineveh (eighth-seventh centuries B.C.) the numbers are doubly represented in words and figures. In South Arabic inscriptions also the numbers are sometimes written in full and sometimes represented by figures. In view of the fact that other peoples around them used symbols as well as the written names for the numerals, it seems altogether likely that the pre-exilic Israelites also used symbols, and most likely the same symbols and system as the Egyptians, Phoenicians, Arameans, and South Arabians.

The use of the letters of the alphabet for arithmetical figures is first found on Maccabean coins, and here also the numbers are spelled out as well. The Mishna (Sheḳ. III.2) states that the three chests used in the second temple were marked א, ב, ג; and this device may very well have been in use for some time before the second century B.C. Traces of this system are found in Origen, in the Cambridge MS of the Mishna, in the Jerusalem Talmud, and in a Hebrew inscription from Aden in the British Museum, and it came to be the standard system for numeration in postbiblical Hebrew writing. The units are denoted by א-ט, the tens by י-צ, the first four hundred by ק-ת, five hundred to nine hundred by ת plus the symbol for the other hundreds. The thousands are indicated by the units with two dots above. For the numbers fifteen and sixteen the combinations of nine plus six and nine plus seven are used to avoid the short forms of the divine name, יה and יו.

c. Number and text criticism. Some of the numbers given in the OT are manifestly absurd, discrepant, or otherwise suspect, and the question whether some system of symbols for numerals, and what system, if any, may lie behind these suspect numbers, is a concern that possibly belongs in the area of textual criticism. In the MT of II Sam. 24:13 the number of years of famine is given as seven, while the LXX and the parallel passage in I Chr. 21:12 give three. It has been suggested that behind this discrepancy lies the confusion between the letters ג and ז. Again in Judg. 8:10 the MT has "fifteen thousand," while Josephus (Antiq. V.vi.5) gives "eighteen thousand." The supposition that the confusion of יה and יח gave rise to this discrepancy is complicated by the question of the origin of the custom of substituting טו for יה to avert profane use of a form of the ineffable name. Apparently יה was used for some time to denote "fifteen," then later the order of the letters was inverted, and finally טו, nine plus six, was substituted. The discrepancy between the MT and Josephus may indicate that "fifteen" was represented by יה in Josephus' time. Recourse to the theory that suspect numbers of the OT are due to misreadings from the system of literal notation is defensible in very few cases, although it may conceivably be the correct explanation in these few cases. For the most part, such recourse is to no avail; and in the case of the Chronicler's startling figures, which are an integral part of his work, there is no remedy except the proverbial grain of salt.

4. Rhetorical uses of numbers. The rhetorical and symbolic use of numbers is a notable feature of biblical literature and of other ancient Near Eastern literatures as well. Many of the uses to be noted here have analogues and parallels in the older literatures of the Egyptians, Sumerians, Akkadians, Canaanites, and Hittites. The Ugaritic texts in particular share with the OT some striking rhetorical and symbolic uses of numbers. Perhaps the best way to deal with this topic is to treat the various numbers more or less in order. Because of their special importance in symbolic use, separate treatments are accorded SEVEN and TWELVE.

The various uses of the number "one" in the Bible present nothing especially remarkable. Hebrew has no indefinite article, but "one" is sometimes used as its virtual equivalent (Gen. 22:13) and often as the equivalent of an indefinite pronoun "someone, anyone," "a certain man." The ordinal, ראשון, "first," is frequently used in a series, as might be expected, but the cardinal, אחת, אחד, is also used for the ordinal, notably in the P creation story (Gen. 1:5) but also in Ruth 1:4; I Sam. 1:2; and in dates (Gen. 8:5, 13; Ezra 10:16; Dan. 9:1). The use of the cardinal for the first of a series is a striking literary device, perhaps a conscious archaism, and is found also in Akkadian, Hittite, Tocharian, Greek, Latin, Middle High German, and Slavic (cf. W. Winter's article in the *bibliography*).

The number "one" is basic to the doctrine of monotheism (Deut. 6:4; Mark 12:32; I Cor. 8:6), to the Christian assertion of the unity of Christ with God (John 10:30) and the unity of the church as the body of Christ (I Cor. 12:12-14), as well as to the Judeo-Christian doctrine of marriage (Gen. 2:24; Matt. 19:5; I Cor. 6:16; Eph. 5:31).

Hebrew usage prefers concrete rather than abstract forms of expression; thus a definite number is often used when only a guess or rough approximation is intended. The number "two" is used in the sense of "a few" (Num. 9:22; I Kings 17:12), or the next higher number may be added to emphasize that the figure is only approximate (II Kings 9:32; Job 33:29; Isa. 17:6; Amos 4:8; Matt. 18:20), like the Latin *bis terque*. Similar is the expression "yesterday and the day before," meaning "formerly, a short while ago" (Gen. 31:2, 5; Exod. 5:7, 14; 21:29, 36; Deut. 4:42; 19:4, 6; Josh. 3:4; 4:18; 20:5; Ruth 2:11; I Sam. 4:7; I Chr. 11:2). Emphasis is achieved by a twofold repetition of a word (I Kings 13:2; Isa. 43:25; 65:1; Matt. 7:21; 25:11; Luke 6:46).

"Three" is even more common than "two" as the designation of a small number (Gen. 30:36; 40:10, 12; 42:17; Exod. 2:2; 3:18; 5:3; 8:27; 10:22; 15:22; Lev. 19:23; Josh. 1:11; 2:16, 22; II Sam. 24:13; I Kings 12:5; II Kings 11:5; 13:18; 20:5; I Chr. 21:12; Esth. 4:16; Isa. 16:14; 20:3; Dan. 1:5; Jonah 1:17). It is, of course, not always possible to tell whether the number is intended to be exact or only approximate. The addition of the next higher number makes it certain that neither figure is to be taken as exact (Exod. 20:5; Deut. 5:9; Jer. 36:23; cf. *Odyssey* V.305: τρισμάκρες Δαναοὶ καὶ τετράκις, Latin *ter et quater*). Any number may be thus raised: "two or three berries . . . four or five" (Isa. 17:6); "five or six times" (II Kings 13:19). Such expressions are common in Akkadian (cf. Middle Assyrian Laws No. 24; Amarna letter 29.17, 20). Emphasis may be strengthened by triple repetition (Isa. 6:3; Jer. 7:4; 22:29; Ezek. 21:27).

The collocation of a numeral with its sequel within the same clause, either syndetically or asyndetically, is related to a similar rhetorical device in Northwest Semitic poetry in which the consecutive numbers stand in synonymous parallelism. This usage is common in Ugaritic and OT poetry and appears to be relatively rare elsewhere. The collocation of "one" and "two" is fairly common in the OT (Deut. 32:30; Job 33:14; 40:5; Jer. 3:14) but does not occur in the extant Ugaritic texts. "Two" and "three" are frequently used in this way in Ugaritic—e.g.:

Two feasts Baal hates,
three the Cloud Rider;

He smites him twice on the pate,
thrice on the ear;

Double I will give in silver,
treble in gold;

and in the OT (Hos. 6:2; Ecclus. 23:16; 26:28; 50: 25). "Three" and "four" are juxtaposed in Prov. 30: 15, 18, 29; Amos 1:3–2:6; Ecclus. 26:5, but this pair is missing in the Ugaritic texts. In Isa. 17:6 we have the combination of "two or three" paralleled by "four or five." "Five" and "six" do not occur in parallelism in the OT (II Kings 13:19 is not a case in point), nor in the Ugaritic poems. "Six" and "seven" are so used in the OT (Job 5:19; Prov. 6:16), but not in Ugaritic. "Seven" and "eight" are especially favored in the Ugaritic poems:

Seven years let Baal fail,
eight the Cloud Rider;

(Take) with you your seven lads,
your eight swine;

El answers in the seven chambers,
within the eight crypts;

and occur once in the OT (Mic. 5:5—H 5:4), or twice if we include Eccl. 11:2. The juxtaposition of "nine" and "ten" of Ecclus. 25:7 is not attested elsewhere in the OT or in Ugaritic. Once in the Ugaritic texts "eighty" and "ninety" are used, but this may be a scribal error for the characteristic Ugaritic use of ascending multiples of eleven:

Sixty-six cities he takes,
seventy-seven towns;

He lies with her seventy-seven times,
. . . eighty-eight

(cf. Gen. 4:24: "sevenfold" and "seventy-sevenfold"). Another striking numerical device of the Ugaritic myths and epics is the seven-day cycle with the enumeration of each day and its event and with the climax on the seventh day.

5. Cultic and symbolic uses of numbers. The frequency of certain numbers in connection with cultic concerns suggests that these numbers had special significance and importance of themselves, or as symbols of something deemed significant. The reasons for the special importance of some of the sacred numbers are rarely simple or obvious.

Next to the number SEVEN, the number most frequently used in connection with sacred matters is three. This number naturally suggests the idea of completeness—of beginning, middle, and end. The ancients conceived of the universe as consisting of three divisions, heaven, earth, and nether world. Gods often were grouped in triads, in relation to the three parts of the universe, or of the family—father, mother, child. Three played an important part in Egyptian cult practices, being the common number of times or periods which cult operations were repeated or continued. So it is also in the OT: certain sacrificial animals are to be three years old (Gen. 15:9); the fasts are three per year (Exod. 23:14); a three-year taboo was set on fruit (Lev. 19:23); ritual baths were required on the third and seventh days (Num. 19:12; 31:19); the times of daily prayer were three (Dan. 6:10). In many cases it is difficult to tell whether the number three has symbolic significance, or is used merely for a small round number or as a specific number with no symbolic significance. The division of a military force into three is purely a matter of strategy (Judg. 7:16; Job 1:17). In the dreams of Pharaoh's butler and baker (Gen. 40) the number three plays a special role. Periods of three days (Gen. 30:36; Exod. 3:18; 19:11), three months (Exod. 2:2), or three years (I Chr. 21:12) are common. The three times Elijah stretched himself on the widow's child (I Kings 17:21) must have had magical import. The number three was apparently important for the cities of refuge, for they were to be augmented by an additional three (Deut. 19:7, 9). Three daughters and seven sons is the ideal proportion of progeny (Job 1:2; 42:13). There are three heavenly witnesses (I John 5:8). Tripartite composition occurs in a number of striking cases without mention of the number. The formula "and God blessed" occurs three times in the P creation story (Gen. 1:22, 28; 2:3). The sanctuary had three divisions—court, holy place, and most holy place (Exod. 26:33; 27:9; I Kings 6:16-17). The blessing of Aaron (Num. 6:24-26) mentions the divine name three times and predicates three pairs of divine action. In Nah. 1:2 the divine name is repeated thrice. The Trisagion of Isa. 6:3 is only a species of superlative. The Qumran scroll here has the word "holy" only twice! The association of deity with "three" in the OT is no evidence of trinitarian doctrine; cf. the affirmations of unity and uniqueness of Deut. 6:4; Isa. 41:4; 44:6; 48:12. The "I AM" of Exod. 3:14 is expanded to cover the past, present, and future (Rev. 1:4; 4:8). The baptismal formula (Matt. 28:19) and the apostolic benediction (II Cor. 13:14) receive their threefold character from the doctrine of the Trinity. The three-day descent into Hades (Matt. 12:40) is an ancient mythological motif (cf. Ishtar's Descent into the Netherworld).

Multiples of three present nothing particularly noteworthy. There are the thirty-day month, thirty shekels (Exod. 21:32), three hundred shekels (Gen. 45:22). In I Maccabees three thousand is a frequent figure. The figures 3,600 and 30,000 are used occasionally (Josh. 8:3; II Chr. 2:2—H 2:1).

Four is a sacred number the world over, doubtless deriving its significance primarily from the four cardinal directions. Among the ancient Egyptians four played an important part, and so also among the Mesopotamians. In the OT four often occurs in relation to the universe: the rivers of paradise (Gen. 2:10); the corners of the earth (Isa. 11:12); the winds (Jer. 49:36; Dan. 7:2; Zech. 2:6; Rev. 7:1). Four is common in the measurements and components of sacred furniture (Exod. 25–27; I Kings 7:5, 19, 27, 30-32, 34, 38; Ezek. 41–43). Four-day periods are uncommon—e.g., the term of mourning for Jephthah's daughter (Judg. 11:40). The destroyers are of four kinds (Jer. 15:3); the sore acts of judgment are four (Ezek. 14:21); four horns scatter Judah (Zech. 1:18-21); the angels of destruction are four (Rev. 9:13-15). The guardians of the throne of God are four (Ezek. 1; 10; Rev. 4:6-7; 5:6, 8, 14; 6:1; 15:7; 19:4). The throne of God is transported (Ezek. 1; 10) and guarded (Rev. 4:6, 8; 5:6, 8, 14; 6:1; 15:7; 19:4) by four creatures. Four chariots patrol the earth (Zech. 6:1-8), and four horsemen bring calamity on the earth (Rev. 6:1-8).

Of the multiples of four, the most significant as a symbolic and sacred number is forty. It is used as a round number to designate a fairly long period of time in terms of human existence or endurance. Forty years is the approximate length of a generation. Isaac and Esau married at forty (Gen. 25:20; 26:34). A man was full grown at forty (Exod. 2:11; Acts 7:23; cf. Josh. 14:7; II Sam. 2:10). The Koran 46.14 says that this is the age at which man attains to his full strength. This was the age at which Mohammed received his call and at which Abu Baqr was converted. Thrice forty was the maximum span of life (Gen. 6:3; Deut. 34:7); and twice forty was ripe old age (II Sam. 19:34-35; Ps. 90:10). The forty-year period in the wilderness (Exod. 16:35; Deut. 2:7; 8:2; 29:5; Josh. 5:6; Neh. 9:21; Ps. 95:10; Amos 2:10; 5:25) was long enough for a whole generation to die off (Num. 14:33; 32:13). The 480 years from the Exodus to the building of the temple (I Kings 6:1) is counted as twelve generations in I Chr. 6:3-8—H 5:29-34. The forty-year rules of the tribal chieftains (Judg. 3:11; 8:28; 13:1; I Sam. 4:18) represent roughly a generation, and the eighty years of Judg. 3:30 amount to two generations. The forty-year reigns of David, Solomon, and Joash (II Sam. 5:4; I Kings 2:11; 11:42 [cf. I Chr. 29:27; II Chr. 9:30]; II Chr. 24:1) are proof of divine favor. Saul's reign of forty years (cf. Acts 13:21; Jos. Antiq. VI.xiv.9) was dropped from the MT (I Sam. 13:1), as incompatible with divine disfavor. The Mesha Stela sets Israel's oppression of Moab at forty years. Forty days or years was the common duration of critical situations, of punishment, fasting, repentance, vigil (Gen. 7:4, 12, 17; 8:6; Exod. 24:18; 34:28; Num. 13:25; Deut. 9:9, 11, 18, 25; 10:10; I Sam. 17:16; I Kings 19:8; Ezek. 4:6; 29:11-13; Jonah 3:4; Matt. 4:2 [cf. Mark 1:13; Luke 4:2]; Acts 1:3). The Egyptian process of embalming took forty days (Gen. 50:3). Forty lashes (Deut. 25:3), but not more (II Cor. 11:24), was the maximum flagellation.

Other miscellaneous examples of the application of forty are Judg. 12:14 (sons); II Kings 8:9 (loads of earth); Neh. 5:15 (shekels); Ezek. 41:2; 46:22 (measurements).

In Acts 23:13, 21, "more than forty" shows the figure to be a round number for a moderately large sum. Similar uses of "forty" are common with Greek and Roman writers. In Persian the figure is often used as the equivalent of "many." The terms for "centipede" (e.g., in Persian and Turkish) attribute to the creature "forty feet."

Other multiples of four and forty are four hundred (Gen. 15:13; Judg. 21:12) and four thousand (I Sam. 4:2; Matt. 15:38; Acts 21:38). The number forty thousand is common for a very large round number (Josh. 4:13; Judg. 5:8; II Sam. 10:18; I Kings 4:26; I Chr. 12:36; I Macc. 12:41; II Macc. 5:14), and four hundred thousand for a still larger number (Jos. Antiq. VII.xiii.1).

Five as half of the basic number ten is important in the Bible (I Kings 7:39, 49; Matt. 25:2) and is often used as a small round number (Lev. 26:8; I Sam. 17:40; 21:3; II Kings 7:13; Isa. 19:18; 30:17; Matt. 14:17, 21 [=Mark 6:38, 44; Luke 9:13; John 6:9]; I Cor. 14:19; II Esd. 14:24). Five is a common figure in penalties (Exod. 22:1; Num. 3:47; 18:16) or rewards (Gen. 43:34; 45:22), as is a fifth (Lev. 5:16; 22:14). Multiples of five are common in measures (Gen. 6:15; Ezek. 40:15), in compensation (Deut. 22:29), and in administrative divisions of civil or military personnel (Exod. 18:21; Deut. 1:15). The fifty days or years of the Feast of Weeks and the Jubilee (Lev. 23:16; 25:10-11) are comprised of seven squared plus one. The multiples up to 500,000 are fairly frequent (Gen. 5:32; 11:11; Exod. 30:23-24; Josh. 8:12; Judg. 20:45; II Sam. 24:9; I Chr. 29:7; II Chr. 13:17; Esth. 9:6, 12; Ezek. 42:16-20; 45:25; 48:15; Matt. 14:21 [=Mark 6:44; Luke 9:14]; I Cor. 15:6).

The number six seldom, if ever, has symbolic or sacred meaning. The six years of Exod. 21:2 correspond to the work days of the week (Exod. 20:9). The six steps of Solomon's throne are of less symbolic significance than the twelve lions (I Kings 10:19-20). The six-cubit measuring reed of Ezekiel's vision (Ezek. 40:5; 41:8) was standard. The sixth of an ephah of Ezek. 45:13 equals half a seah (*see* Weights and Measures). The six wings of the seraphim (Isa. 6:2) were functional, a pair each for purposes of reverence, modesty, and locomotion.

The numbers eight and nine have no apparent symbolic import. The eighth day for circumcision (Gen. 17:12), redemption of the first-born son (Exod. 22:29), defilement of a Nazirite (Num. 6:10), and the holy convocation (Lev. 23:36) is merely the day after the all-important period of Seven days. Nine is sometimes significant as one less than ten (Neh. 11:1; Luke 17:17), and ninety-nine as a hundred minus one (Matt. 18:12).

The convenience of ten as the basis of the decimal system derives obviously from the use of the fingers for simple calculations. In the Cabalistic Book of Creation (ספר יצירה) 1.13, the ten spheres are deduced from the fingers of the hand. The simplest use of ten is to denote a round or complete number, and it is frequently so used throughout the Bible (Gen. 24:10, 22; 31:7; Lev. 26:26; Num. 14:22; Josh.

22:14; Judg. 17:10; I Sam. 1:8; 17:17; II Sam. 18:11; I Kings 14:3; II Kings 5:5; 20:9-11; Neh. 5:18; Job 19:3; Eccl. 7:19; Isa. 6:13; Jer. 41:8; Zech. 8:23; II Esd. 5:46; Tob. 4:20; Matt. 25:1, 28; Luke 15:8; 19:25; Rev. 2:10). As a sacred number, ten may derive some of its significance from the fact that it is the sum of the two other especially sacred numbers, three and seven. The Ten Words (Exod. 34:1; Deut. 4:13; 10:4) may have been arranged as a mnemonic device, but the sanctity of the commandments lent itself to the number. The TITHE as a convenient fraction also became a sacred figure. Ten is much used in ritual connections. Many of the furnishings of the tabernacle and the temple were arranged or measured in tens (Exod. 26; I Kings 6–7; II Chr. 4; Ezek. 45). Ten is a prominent feature in apocalyptic symbolism (Dan. 7:7, 20, 24; Rev. 12:3; 13:1; 17:3, 7, 12, 16). In the creation story of Gen. 1 the clauses "and God said," "and God saw," "and God blessed," occur ten, seven, and three times, respectively, and it seems unlikely that this is pure accident. The LXX has "and God saw" once more (vs. 8*b*) than the MT, thus spoiling the pattern. If the LXX reading is original, the MT has altered it to conform to the sacred number. The antediluvian patriarchs are ten (Gen. 5), and the postdiluvian ten (Gen. 11:10-30). Ten times the Israelites in the wilderness put the Lord to the test (Num. 14:22), ten times Abraham was tempted (Jub. 19:8), and Augustine mentions ten persecutions (*City of God* XVIII.52).

Of multiples of ten, fifty is a common round number (Gen. 6:15; 7:24; 8:3; 18:24; Exod. 18:21; 26:5; Lev. 23:16; 25:10; 27:3; Num. 4:3; 16:2; Deut. 22:29; Josh. 7:21; II Sam. 24:24; I Kings 18:4; II Kings 1: 9-14; Ezra 8:6; Isa. 3:3; Jth. 1:2), and so also a hundred (Lev. 26:8; II Sam. 24:3; I Chr. 21:3; Prov. 17:10; Eccl. 6:3; 8:12; Matt. 19:29; Mark 10:30; Luke 8:8; Tob. 14:11; Jth. 10:17) and a thousand (Exod. 20:6; 34:7; Deut. 1:11; 7:9; 32:30; I Sam. 18:7; 21:11; 29:5; II Sam. 18:12; I Chr. 12:14; 16:15; Job 9:3; 33:23; Pss. 50:10; 84:10; 90:4; 91:7; 105:8; 119:72; Eccl. 6:6; 7:28; Isa. 30:17; 60:22 [clan]; Jer. 32:18; Amos 5:3; Mic. 6:7). The etymology of the word for "thousand" (אלף) connects it with the idea of "gregariousness," "crowd"; hence it is applied to cattle (herd) and to men (tribe, clan; Num. 1:16; Josh. 22:21, 30; Judg. 6:15; I Sam. 10:19; 23:23[?]; Isa. 60:22; Mic. 5:2—H 5:1; Zech. 12:5-6).

Multiples of a thousand are used for hyperbole: seven thousand (I Kings 19:18); ten thousand (Lev. 26:8; Deut. 32:30; I Sam. 18:7; 21:11; 29:5; Pss. 3:6; 68:17; 91:7; Song of S. 5:10; Hos. 8:12; Mic. 6:7; Wisd. Sol. 12:22); seventy thousand (II Sam. 24:15). A million (I Chr. 21:5; 22:14; II Chr. 14:9; Dan. 7:10), "thousands of ten thousands" (אלפי רבבה; Gen. 24:60), and "ten thousand times ten thousand" (רבו רבון; Dan. 7:10; cf. Enoch 40:1; Rev. 5:11) press the limits of numerical imagination. In the Ugaritic poems (Keret A 89-91) the highest number expressed is three hundred myriad (*tlt̠ mat rbt*)—i.e., three million—and beyond this the poet can adduce only the parallels "innumerable" and "beyond reckoning" (cf. Gen. 41:49; I Chr. 22:4; Job. 5:9; 9:10; 21:33; Pss. 40:12—H 40:13; 104:25; Heb. 11:12; 12:22).

Josephus in the preface to his *Antiquities* says that Moses expressed some things enigmatically, but Josephus apparently did not understand this to apply to numbers in particular. Aristobulus the philosopher (Euseb. Prep. Evang. XIII.12-13) interpreted the number seven mystically, and Philo followed suit, elaborating the hidden wonders of the number in considerable detail (*On the Creation of the World* XXX ff). The Talmudic, Midrashic, and Cabalistic literatures developed and used for the interpretation of the Scriptures a sort of numerology called Gematria (גמטריא), a Hebraized form of γεωμετρία, which sought to discover the hidden sense of the Hebrew text through the numerical values of the letters of the alphabet. This method was recognized as the twenty-ninth of the thirty-two hermeneutical rules of Rabbi Eliezer ben Jose. A famous example is the number 318 of Gen. 14:14, which is the numerical equivalent of Eliezer (אליעזר = 1 + 30 + 10 + 70 + 7 + 200), and so the Talmud interpreted it. Christians took over this mode of exegesis, and the Epistle of Barnabas interpreted the number to refer to the crucified Christ, the three hundred being T, the cross; and the eighteen, I H, the abbreviation of Ιησοῦς. In Gen. 49:10 the enigmatic יבא שילה has the numerical value of 358, which is also the value of the word "messiah" (משיח), hence the traditional messianic interpretation. Here this mode of interpretation has a bearing on textual criticism, since the normal spelling of Shiloh, שלה, as in the Samaritan Pentateuch, would not give the desired sum. This numerical interpretation may have influenced the copyists to spell the word with the vowel letter. In Num. 12:1 "the Cushite" has the numerical value of 735, or with variant spelling 736, which is the same as the value of "good looking" (יפת מראה), as in Gen. 12:11; hence Moses' wife was beautiful, and the Targ. Onkelos replaces the word "Cushite" by the Aramaic word for "beautiful," שפירתא. In Deut. 32 the initial letters of the first six verses are equal in numerical value to Moses' name; hence these verses are the epitome of Moses' lifework. This mode of interpretation has almost limitless possibilities and was carried to fantastic limits in the Cabalistic literature. Even in modern times such methods continue to have devotees who "discover" hidden meanings in numerical relationship all over the Bible.

The one authentic example of this sort of number game is the mysterious 666 (variant 616) of Rev. 13:18. Various interpretations have been suggested. Irenaeus took it to refer to the Roman Empire and derived the sum from Λατεῖνος (30 + 1 + 300 + 5 + 10 + 50 + 70 + 200). Other candidates are Nero and Trajan Hadrianus, both of whom can be made to add up to either 666 or 616 (נרון קסר; 50 + 200 + 6 + 50 + 100 + 60 + 200 = 666, or with omission of the final ן = 616), and טריון אנדרינוס = 666, or טריון אדרינוס = 616. Caligula as Γάϊος καῖσαρ comes to 616. Even the Hebrew for the "Primeval Abyss," תהום קדמוניה, which also adds up to 666, has been proposed. There can be no certainty, but Nero appears to be the most likely candidate.

Bibliography. K. Sethe, *Von Zahlen und Zahlworten bei den alten Ägyptern* (1916); E. von Dobschütz, "Zwei-und dreigliedrige Formeln; Ein Beitrag zur Vorgeschichte der Trinitätsformel," *JBL*, 50 (1931), 117-47; O. Neugebauer, *Vorgriechische Mathematik* (1934); H. L. Ginsberg, "The Development of the Graded Numerical Dictum," *Minhal David* (Jubilee Volume;

1935), pp. 76-82; A. Heller, *Biblische Zahlensymbolik* (1936); J. Bernardin, "A NT Triad," *JBL* (1938), pp. 273-79; A. Bea, "Der Zahlenspruch im Hebräischen und Ugaritischen," *Bibl.*, 21 (1940), 196-98; S. Gandz, "Complementary Fractions in Bible and Talmud," *Louis Ginsberg Jubilee Volume* (1945), pp. 143-57; O. Neugebauer, *The Exact Sciences in Antiquity* (1951); W. Winter, "Gruppe und Reihe; Beobachtungen zur Systematik indogermanischer Zählweise," *Zeitschrift für vergleichende Sprachforschung*, 71 (1953), 3-14; J. Finkel, "A Mathematical Conundrum in the Ugaritic Keret Poem," *HUCA*, 26 (1955), 109-49; O. Becker, *Das mathematische Denken der Antike* (1957).

M. H. Pope

***NUMBERS, BOOK OF.** The fourth book of the Pentateuch or traditional five books of Moses. It contains elements from all four of the principal Pentateuchal sources—J, E, D, and P—and its narrative is continuous with the books which precede and follow it. For a general discussion of the literary problems of these books, *see* PENTATEUCH.

See maps "Canaan: Numbers and Deuteronomy," under DEUTERONOMY, BOOK OF; "Egypt and Sinai: Exodus to Deuteronomy," under EXODUS, BOOK OF.

1. The name
2. Outline
   a. The narrative framework
   b. The legal and statistical contents
   c. Relation to other books
3. Sources
4. The narratives
5. The laws
6. Statistical material
7. Historical value
8. Religious value
Bibliography

1. The name. The name of the book in the English Bible is derived from the Latin Vulg. *Numeri*, which is in turn a translation of the title in the Greek LXX ('Αριθμοί). It is the only book of the Pentateuch which has had its title translated rather than merely transliterated from the Greek. Its name in the modern Hebrew Bible is במדבר, "in the wilderness," a phrase which occurs in the first verse and is perhaps a more accurate designation than the familiar English one. The name וידבר, "The Lord spoke," the opening phrase of ch. 1, was also used in antiquity and was known to Jerome and Epiphanius. The numbering of the tribes, to which the English name refers, occupies only the opening chapters (1:1-4:26) and ch. 26, and is by no means the most distinctive feature of the book.

2. Outline. Since the book has no real unity and was not composed in accordance with any logical, predetermined plan, whatever outline may be imposed upon it will have to be recognized as largely subjective and arbitrary. In general, one may say that it relates the adventures of the people of Israel from the final days at Sinai to the time when they encamped in the plains of Moab on the borders of the Promised Land. The broad sweep of the narrative, which provides the framework of the book, as of other parts of the Pentateuch, suggests a rough division into three major periods: (*a*) Israel's journey from Sinai to Canaan, culminating in an unsuccessful attempt to conquer the land from the S (chs. 1-14); (*b*) the traditional forty years of wandering "in the wilderness" (chs. 15-19?); (*c*) the final, triumphant march to the edge of the Jordan opposite Jericho (chs. 20?-36).

The geography of the book suggests a rather different and more accurate division: (*a*) events at Sinai (1:1-10:10; the beginning of this long episode having been related in Exod. 19:1); (*b*) events in the desert to the S of Palestine (10:11-20:13); and (*c*) events in Edom and Moab, E of the Dead Sea (20:14-36:13). The first of these divisions involves a period of twenty days (cf. 1:1 with 10:11); the second, a period of *ca.* thirty-eight years (cf. 10:11 with 33:38 [which dates the event recorded in 20:23-29]); the third, a period of somewhat over five months (cf. 33:38 with Deut. 1:3).

a. The narrative framework. The first section (1:1-10:10) can hardly be said to have any real narrative content, since it is entirely concerned with details of the census and other information of a purely legal or ecclesiastical character.

The second section (10:11-20:13) contains the stories of the complaints of the people about their diet and the choice of seventy elders to assist Moses in the government of the community (ch. 11); the vindication of Moses as Israel's leader in the face of Miriam and Aaron's opposition (ch. 12); the discouraging report of the spies (ch. 13); the people's unfortunate attempt to invade Canaan after their condemnation to forty years of wandering (ch. 14); the rebellion of Korah, Dathan, and Abiram—the one extended episode recorded for the "forty years" (ch. 16); and, finally, the summoning of water from the rock at Kadesh (20:1-13).

The third section (20:14-36:13) is in some ways the most important, containing as it does so many valuable fragments of ancient Hebrew poetry. The narrative begins with the refusal of the king of Edom to allow the Hebrews to pass through his realm (20:14-29); goes on to tell of the brazen serpent and Israel's defeat of Sihon the Amorite king and of Og the king of Bashan (ch. 21); and reaches its climax in the account of the triumph of Israel and her God over Balak of Moab and his seer, Balaam (chs. 22-24). Its concluding stories deal with the apostasy of the Israelites to Baal-peor (ch. 25); the second census (ch. 26); the appointment of Joshua (27:12-23); the slaughter of the Midianites (ch. 31); and the settlement of Reuben, Gad, and half of Manasseh E of the Jordan (ch. 32).

b. The legal and statistical contents. Strung out upon this thread of narrative and geography, and interspersed often without apparent logic among its episodes, are the laws and statistical summaries which are likely to be so wearisome to the ordinary reader and which, by their profusion, tend to obscure the course of the story. Thus the first section of the book records the size of the different tribes, the arrangement of the camp, and the numbers and duties of the Levites (chs. 1-4); together with laws governing the treatment of lepers and wives accused of adultery (ch. 5); the nature and fulfilment of a Nazirite vow (ch. 6); an enumeration of gifts to the sanctuary (ch. 7); directions for the ordination of Levites (ch. 8); and regulations with regard to the supplementary passover (ch. 9) and the use of the silver trumpets (10:1-10).

The second section adds to the basic narrative some laws with regard to sacrifice (ch. 15); the income of the priests and Levites (ch. 18); and purification after contact with the dead (ch. 19).

The third section contains the statistics of the second census, at the end of the forty years (ch. 26); regulations governing inheritance in the female line (27:1-11; ch. 36); a schedule of sacrifices to be offered during the course of the ecclesiastical year (chs. 28–29); casuistic decisions with regard to the validity of a woman's vows (ch. 30); a résumé of Israel's itinerary from Egypt to the plains of Moab (33:1-49); directions concerning the conquest and apportionment of the Promised Land (ch. 34); and provisions for the establishment in Canaan of Levitical cities and places of refuge for homicides (ch. 35).

c. Relation to other books. It will be evident from the above summary of contents that the material in the book is of the most heterogeneous character and that its arrangement, at least as respects the non-narrative elements, is largely fortuitous. Since any unity one may attribute to Numbers must be artificially imposed upon it, it is perhaps better not to think of it as a book so much as a more or less arbitrary division in the larger structure of the Pentateuch. Or, to express the same thought more accurately, one might say that it is the last division of the Tetrateuch (Genesis–Numbers), since its relation with the books which precede is organically much closer than with Deuteronomy, which follows.

3. Sources. The Deuteronomic element in Numbers is confined to a single small passage, 21:33-35 (=Deut. 3:1-3), whereas J, E, and P, the major sources of the Tetrateuch, are all generously represented. The principal source is P, which accounts for nearly three fourths of the book and nearly all the non-narrative portions. As in other parts of the Pentateuch, P is obviously not homogeneous, but consists of several layers of material. Gray (*Numbers*, ICC) distinguishes three in particular: P^g, the basic work embodying the history of Israel's sacred institutions; P^s, clearly later than P^g and itself coming from several hands; and P^x, matter not demonstrably later than P^g, but certainly not part of the original P document. In many cases P^x may be assumed to describe customs and institutions of great antiquity. JE in Numbers is readily distinguishable from P, but J and E cannot be so easily separated from each other, since some of the criteria available for earlier parts of the Pentateuch (in particular, that of the divine name) are only occasionally to be found. The continued existence of parallel narratives is evident, but it is usually difficult to determine which elements should be assigned to a particular source. One notable exception to this general statement is the Balaam story (chs. 22–24), in which 22:1-21, 35*b*-40, can with considerable confidence be derived from E, while 22:22-35*a* is plainly J, as is shown by the use of the name Yahweh instead of Elohim. In other sections various commentators show a wide divergence in their analysis of the JE document.

4. The narratives. While some of the legal and statistical material in the opening chapters is written in ostensibly narrative form, the true narrative of the book begins in 10:11-36, which tells of the breaking up of the camp at Sinai and the beginning of the march toward Canaan. Vss. 11-28 exhibit the typical features of the P document (the date, the concept of the cloud, the artificial disposition of the tribes, etc.), while vss. 29-36 (except for 34?) are equally characteristic of JE and pick up the thread of the JE story which was dropped at Exod. 34:28. At the end of the chapter (vss. 35-36) the JE editor has preserved two ancient battle cries associated with the movements of the ark.

Chs. 11–12 (entirely JE) have for their theme the problems which Moses faced as leader of a dissatisfied and rebellious people. The three opening verses of ch. 11 contain the fragmentary account of an incident in which Moses acted as intercessor when Israel's complaints had aroused God's anger against them. This sets the tone for the rest of the chapter, which tells the story of the people's protest against their meager diet and of the arrival of the death-bearing quails (vss. 31-34; an incident partly paralleled in Exod. 16, P); into this has been interwoven in a rather complicated way the story of the choice of seventy elders and their endowment with a portion of the spirit which rested on Moses (vss. 16-29, in the main). In ch. 12, God punishes Miriam with leprosy because she and Aaron had questioned the unique character of Moses' authority (the Cushite woman of vs. 1 seems irrelevant to the rest of the story).

The next two chapters (13–14) deal with the dispatch of spies into the Promised Land and the misadventures which followed their return. The narrative here is clearly composite and the P and JE strands can be separated without much difficulty (to P may be assigned 13:1-17*a*, 21, 25, 26*a*, 32*a;* 14:1*a*, 2, 5-7, 10, 26-39*a*). According to P, the spies went through the whole land and, with Caleb and Joshua dissenting, brought back a report that it was unproductive; in JE they go only through the Negeb as far as Hebron and report, Caleb dissenting, that the land, though productive, was populated by giants. In ch. 14, the people's petulant reaction to the spies' report is punished by their condemnation to forty years of wandering in the desert; when, in spite of this, they attempt to advance into Canaan from the S, they are defeated at Hormah.

The story of the rebellion of Korah, Dathan, and Abiram in ch. 16 is also clearly composite, as is shown by its frequent redundancies and inconsistencies. Here, actually, two quite different stories are interwoven: In the JE account Dathan and Abiram (and, in vs. 1, On), members of the tribe of Reuben, complain of Moses' arrogance in making himself the civil leader of the community, despite his failure to fulfil his promises (vss. 12-14); according to P, the revolt of Korah was in support of a doctrine of the "priesthood of all believers." It was his contention that Moses and Aaron's claims to ecclesiastical authority had no justification, since "all the congregation are holy" (vs. 3). It is generally agreed that there is now a third story (introduced by P^s), in which Korah is represented as a Levite and the dispute is said to have arisen over the claims of the Levites to equality with the priesthood. Each of the stories ends disastrously for the rebels: the party of Dathan and Abiram, with their families and possessions, is swallowed up by the earth (vss. 31-34, omitting "and all the men that belonged to Korah" in vs. 32), while the party of Korah is consumed by fire from heaven (vs. 35). The original P story is found in vss. 1*a*, 2*b*-11, 16-24, 27*a*, 32*b*, 35-50—H 16:35–17:15; the P^s supplement is contained in vss. 7*b*-11, 16-17, 36-40—H 17:1-5.

The theme of ch. 17 is closely related to that of the Korah story in its original form. The miraculous budding of Aaron's rod is a vindication of the exclusive claims of the tribe of Levi to serve in the tabernacle.

Ch. 20 tells of the transition from the period of wilderness wanderings (concerning which there are no traditions whatever, unless the story of ch. 16 is to be placed here) to that of renewed progress toward the Promised Land when the forty years were over. The first verse, which is composite (vs. 1*a* being P; 1*b*, JE), relates the death of Miriam at Kadesh. The next incident (vss. 2-13) explains, none too clearly, why neither Moses nor Aaron was permitted to enter Canaan with the tribes. Both were guilty, it is said, of some unspecified sin of disbelief in connection with the people's demand for water at Meribah (probably identical with Kadesh), but reverence for their memory has caused the omission of the specific charge against them. The story of Aaron's death is narrated in vss. 22-29. Vss. 14-21 tell of the resumption of Israel's march toward Canaan, this time through the lands E of the Dead Sea rather than from the S. Moses requests permission for his people to pass peacefully through the territory of Edom, but, when this is refused, he leads them by a different and more circuitous route (21:4), which first takes them S in the direction of the Gulf of Aqabah.

The opening verses of ch. 21 (1-3) seem to be misplaced, since the incident they relate can hardly belong to this period. In vss. 4-11, which, along with an itinerary, include the story of the bronze serpent, the course of Israel's journey is more naturally continued; and with vs. 12 they reach the S borders of Moab in their northward travels through Transjordan. Two quotations of ancient Hebrew poetry are included in this section, which briefly tells of their passage through Moab to Mount Pisgah (vss. 13-20); the first of these is a mere fragment from the Book of the Wars of the Lord (*see* WARS OF THE LORD, BOOK OF THE) and the second a little folk song, only fancifully connected with the context, which is addressed to the waters of a newly dug well (Hebrew *be'ēr*). The remainder of the chapter (vss. 21-35), which contains another and quite enigmatic fragment of an old poem (vss. 27-30), describes victory over the Amorite king Sihon, who is said at this period to have ruled all the region between the Arnon and the Jabbok from his capital, Heshbon, and over Og, king of Bashan, who was sovereign of N Transjordan. The whole chapter is from JE, with the exception of vss. 10-11 (P), 33-35 (D; cf. Deut. 3:1-3).

In many ways the most valuable and interesting part of Numbers is chs. 22–24, which not only tell of the defeat of the Moabite king Balak by Israel, but also contain the legend of Balaam the seer and a series of undoubtedly ancient oracles which are attributed to him. Here the redundancies and contradictions of the narrative make necessary some analysis into sources, although the whole of it (with the exception of 22:1, which is from P) is derived from JE. The analysis of ch. 22 must begin with the obvious peculiarities exhibited by vss. 2-21, 35*b*-41, when compared with vss. 22-35*a;* the former of which must be assigned to E, the latter to J. Further analysis of some kind seems to be called for in parts of vss. 1-21. The oracles of chs. 23–24, together with their narrative framework, are patently derived from more than one source, although there is no general agreement as to the details of the analysis. While the antiquity of the oracles as a whole (probably tenth century B.C.) can hardly be denied, serious questions have been raised about the concluding, and contextually irrelevant, prophecies of 24:18-24. The "star . . . out of Jacob" of 24:17 almost certainly refers, by a *vaticinium ex eventu*, to David.

Ch. 25, which tells of the apostasy of the people at Shittim, can be divided between JE (vss. 1-5) and P (vss. 6-18). 27:12-23, which describes Joshua's appointment as the successor of Moses, is to be assigned to P, as is ch. 31, a late addition to the priestly document which purports to describe the extermination of the Midianites, but is actually an unhistorical midrash intended to illustrate certain legal themes such as the purification of warriors (vss. 19-24) and the method of dividing the spoil of battle (vss. 25-54).

Ch. 32, the concluding narrative of Numbers and the last to exhibit traces of the JE document, tells of the settlement of Reuben and Gad (and half of Manasseh [vs. 33]) E of the Jordan. The story is obviously composite, but attempts at analysis have not as yet produced universally acceptable results. With this story (to which must be added the account of Moses' death, in Deut. 34), the narrative of the Tetrateuch concludes, and the way is prepared for the opening scene of Israel's conquest of Canaan, as related in the beginning chapters of Joshua. The long "farewell address" of Moses in the book of Deuteronomy, with the supplementary material which follows it, interrupts the flow of the story and is obviously from a different source.

5. The laws. As previously noted, the narrative of Numbers is in many places used simply as an artificial setting for the publication of certain laws, both civil and religious, often introduced without regard for suitability of context. Without exception, these belong to P, although they may be assigned to different strata within it, and many of them are undoubtedly of high antiquity. Ignoring here certain regulations concerning the Levites, which are embedded in the statistical material of chs. 1–4, the first important collection of laws is found in chs. 5–6, which deal with leprosy and related defilements (5:1-4), contributions to be made to the priesthood in case of "breaking faith" with God (5:5-10), the procedure to be followed in the case of a wife accused of unchastity (5:11-31), and the law of the Nazirite (6:1-21). It is evident that this material is not homogeneous and that no discernible principle governs its compilation or its insertion into the present context. The primitive character of the procedure imposed upon the accused woman is sufficient guarantee of the antiquity of the present law. It provides the classic instance of the use of the ordeal in the OT, the woman being required to drink holy water in which have been mixed dust from the sanctuary and the blotting of a curse imposed upon her by the priest. The inconsistent and repetitive account of the transaction shows that the present law has a long literary history behind it. The other important law in this section, that governing the Nazirite, deals with an ancient institution, but in its latest form, in which the vow is not taken for life, as in the case of Samson and Samuel, but only for a specified period of time.

The first three verses of ch. 8 give directions with regard to the lampstand of the tabernacle which are simply a summary repetition of material already contained in Exod. 25. The remainder of the chapter deals at length with the purification and dedication of the Levites, who are to serve the Lord in the tabernacle as surrogates for the first-born of all the people of Israel (vss. 16-18). The period of service assigned to the Levites in vss. 23-25 does not agree with the provision of 4:3; this disagreement is one of the numerous indications that the P document itself is of composite origin and has had a complex literary history.

9:1-14 provides that those who are unable to take part in the Passover because of ceremonial uncleanness may celebrate it a month later on the same date. The remainder of the chapter, which is not legal in character and is unrelated to what precedes and follows, describes the behavior of the cloud which accompanied the tabernacle during the travels of the Israelites.

10:1-10 gives directions for the blowing of the two silver trumpets, which are to be used for calling an assembly, sounding an alarm, and signaling the breakup of the camp.

The laws of ch. 15 have no relation either to the context in which they are now found or to one another. The first section (vss. 1-16) regulates the amount of meal, oil, and wine which is to accompany the animal sacrifices. The next (vss. 17-21) orders the gift to the Lord of the first part of the "coarse meal" (RSV; the precise meaning of the Hebrew word [עריסה] so translated is uncertain). Vss. 22-31 are of great importance for the clear distinction they make between unwitting offenses (vs. 24) and sins done "with a high hand" (vss. 30-31). Without a clear understanding of this distinction, the interpreter is likely to misinterpret the whole priestly system of atonement. For sins deliberately committed, no sacrifice or other atonement is possible; the sacrificial system is a gracious provision of Yahweh designed to protect those who fall into sin unwittingly. It is probable that the story of the man who gathered sticks on the sabbath (vss. 32-36) was introduced here to illustrate vividly the fate in store for those who sinned "with a high hand." The remaining verses (37-41) prescribe the wearing of tassels.

Ch. 18 is more closely related to the narrative than is ordinarily the case. It is appropriate that the stories of the rebellion of the Levites under Korah (ch. 16) and the vindication of the superiority of the Aaronic priesthood through the budding of Aaron's rod (ch. 17) should be followed by a chapter which deals with the proper functions of the Levites (18:1-7) and the income provided for the support of both priests and Levites.

Ch. 19 once again exhibits the phenomenon of complete irrelevance to context, dealing as it does with the subject of the purification of those who have become unclean through contact with a dead body. It can hardly have been a part of the original P document, although the primitive and magical character of the procedure enjoined (equaled elsewhere in Numbers only by the law of 5:11-31), involving the use of water in which have been mixed the ashes of a red heifer, perfect in form and unbroken to the yoke, is sufficient guarantee that it preserves a custom of considerable antiquity.

In distinction to the laws previously discussed, which have been of an ecclesiastical or ceremonial character, the law of 27:1-11 (which is supplemented by a further regulation in ch. 36) is of a civil nature, dealing with the inheritance of property. Ancient Hebrew law allowed only sons to inherit; the law of the levirate marriage (Deut. 25:5-10) provided an ingenious means of escape from the situation in which a man dies without male issue. The present law, which seems to be quite late, provides a more rational method of dealing with the same problem by allowing inheritance to descend in the female line. Since it was a basic principle of Hebrew jurisprudence to preserve property within the original social unit, ch. 36 provides that women who inherit property in this fashion shall, in order to prevent alienation of the property, marry only within the tribe.

Chs. 28–29 contain a schedule of the public offerings which are to be made in the tabernacle on the fixed holy days throughout the year. As a summary of the ecclesiastical calendar, it is comparable to Lev. 23. Sacrifices of a specific character are provided for the following occasions: daily (28:3-8); the sabbath (vss. 9-10); New Moon (vss. 11-15); Passover and the Feast of Unleavened Bread (vss. 16-25); Pentecost (vss. 26-31); first day of the seventh month—i.e., New Year's Day (29:1-6); Day of Atonement (29:7-11); the Feast of Tabernacles (29:12-38).

The whole of ch. 30 is occupied with a discussion of the conditions under which vows made by women are valid.

35:1-8 returns again to the subject of the Levites, so frequently treated in this book, and provides in an obviously Utopian manner for the assignment to them of forty-eight cities in the new land of Canaan. This legislation is clearly inconsistent with the principle stated in 18:24. The remainder of the chapter orders the establishment of cities of refuge to which homicides may flee until their guilt or innocence has been judicially determined. This represents a late effort to modify the unrestricted application of the *lex talionis.*

6. Statistical material. It is the large amount of purely statistical information incorporated in Numbers which makes much of it seem tedious to the modern reader. The question of the origin of this material is not easy to answer and can really be discussed only in connection with the individual examples. Some of it seems purely idealistic and unhistorical, while in other cases it seems evident that there must be some good historical information behind it. The geographical list in 34:1-15, e.g., from whatever period it may come, will hardly have been invented *ad hoc* and may well be based upon an ancient document; even the incredible figures assigned to the tribes in chs. 1–2 and 26 may be derived from misplaced census records of a much later time; but such a list as that of the princes' offerings in ch. 7 can scarcely have any other origin than the fertile imagination of a priestly scribe.

The opening chapters of the book (1–4), which are responsible for its familiar name, contain the results of the census supposedly made at Sinai toward the end of the sojourn at the holy mount: chs. 1–2 give the numbers of the warriors by tribes, the final total amounting to 603,550 (2:32), while chs. 3–4 give the names of the priests (3:1-4) and the numbers of the Levites by families, incidentally explaining their relation to Israel, their functions as a group (3:5-13, 40-51), and the particular task reserved on the march for each of the three major divisions—Gershonites, Kohathites, and Merarites. Ch. 7 lists in detail the offerings alleged to have been made by the chief men of the tribes on the day when the tabernacle was finished and its furnishings consecrated. In ch. 26 a second census of Israel and the Levites is recorded at the end of the forty years of wandering, when the previous generation had almost entirely died out (vss. 64-65). The total this time was 601,730 (vs. 51). Ch. 33 contains a late résumé (based upon JE and P and possibly some third source) of the journeys of Israel from the departure from Egypt until their arrival at the plains of Moab opposite Jericho. Finally, ch. 34 describes the ideal boundaries of the land of Canaan (vss. 1-15), which was soon to be allotted to the tribes, and lists the names of those who were to supervise the apportionment (vss. 16-29).

7. Historical value. The question of the historical value of Numbers really belongs to the larger question of the historical reliability of the Pentateuchal narrative as a whole. The following observations, however, may be in order: The P document in Numbers can be largely disregarded, so far as history is concerned, since most of its meager narrative elements are manifestly late and artificial. The JE material is very fragmentary (when compared with the unified tradition of the Exodus) and deals chiefly with two periods: the first approach to Canaan from the S (10:11–14:45) and the second approach, forty years later, from the E (20:1–25:5). It is thought by many scholars that these two sections preserve the memory of two different invasions, made at widely separated periods by different groups of tribes, and that the two events were fused by later tradition into the single, continuous movement of a unified people. It is probable that some genuine historical memories are preserved in the place names which frequently occur in the JE narrative, but less reliance can be placed upon the incidents connected with them, some of which are merely etiological legends (e.g., 11:1-3; 21:5-9), while others are only artificially related to their present context. The JE document in Numbers is good historical evidence for the traditions of the Hebrew people in the days of the early monarchy; the value of these traditions themselves, concerned as they are with events which occurred before the rise of written history in Israel, can be determined only after rigorous analysis and careful study, and even then the results will be largely hypothetical.

8. Religious value. Along with the rest of the Pentateuch, Numbers bears witness to some of the basic convictions of Israel: that God manifests himself in history, that he demands obedience to his righteous will, and that he is able (in spite of man's incurably rebellious spirit) to accomplish his good purposes toward his people and bring them out of bondage to the Promised Land.

Furthermore, the character of Moses in this book appears in a more attractive and religiously suggestive light than it does elsewhere. In Numbers we see him, not simply as a strong-willed hero, who leads Israel out of slavery, but as a deeply compassionate human being, who sympathizes with others even in their sins and is a constant intercessor for them (11:12; 12:13; 14:19). According to 12:3 he is the "meekest" of men, although the term here hardly has its common English meaning. Some elements from this traditional picture of Moses have undoubtedly entered into the portrait of the Servant of the Lord in Second Isaiah (see also Exod. 32:30-32).

Finally, one must admit that much of Numbers—the legal and statistical portions in particular—can hardly be regarded as having any direct religious significance for the modern reader. But even these parts are valuable as a reminder that the OT story is intended to be read as history and not as myth. The ancient Hebrew mind was not mythopoeic. The laws of Numbers, e.g., are set in (and sometimes derived from) concrete historical situations; and, extravagant and unreliable as the statistics usually are, they show us how earnestly the Hebrew writers strove to clothe the bare skeleton of the narrative tradition with precise historical information. If one would understand the religion of the OT, he must first of all grasp this history-centered mentality of the people who produced it.

Bibliography. B. Baentsch, *Exodus-Leviticus-Numeri* (1903); H. Holzinger, *Numeri* (1903); G. B. Gray, *A Critical and Exegetical Commentary on Numbers* (1903); A. H. McNeile, *The Book of Numbers* (1911); A. R. S. Kennedy, *Leviticus and Numbers* (n.d.); H. Gressmann, "Die Anfänge Israels," in *Die Schriften des Alten Testament in Auswahl* (1922); L. E. Binns, *The Book of Numbers* (1927); P. Heinisch, *Das Buch Numeri* (1936); W. F. Albright, "The Oracles of Balaam," *JBL,* LXIII (1944), 207-33; J. Marsh, Introduction and Exegesis of Numbers, *IB,* II (1952), 137-308; K. F. Krämer, *Numeri und Deuteronomium* (1955); G. E. Mendenhall, "The Census Lists of Numbers 1 and 26," *JBL,* LXXVII (1958), 52-66.

R. C. Dentan

NUMENIUS nōō mē'nĭ əs [Νουμήνιος] (I Macc. 15:15). Son of Antiochus, and one of Simon the Hasmonean's ambassadors to Rome. In 141 B.C., Simon sent an embassy led by Numenius with a gift of a gold shield weighing a thousand pounds. In 139, Numenius returned with copies of letters sent by Lucius the Roman consul to the neighboring states. In it there was a declaration of friendship of the Roman people for the Jews and for the embassy sent by the high priest Simon to Rome. The neighboring states were forbidden to injure the Jewish people, and extradition was demanded in the cases of any dissenters against Simon who had fled to their countries. Numenius also had been previously sent by Jonathan, along with Antipater son of Jason, to the Spartans to renew a pledge of brotherhood.

Some have questioned the authenticity of the document. It is recorded also by Josephus (Antiq. XIV. viii.5), who agrees in naming Lucius as Roman consul and Numenius as head of the Jewish embassy, but who dates the event in the reign of Hyrcanus II.

S. B. HOENIG

NUN (PERSON) nŭn [נוּן, fish; LXX Ναυή]. The father of Joshua (Exod. 33:11; Num. 11:28; 13:8, 16; Deut. 1:38; 32:44; Josh. 1:1; Judg. 2:8; I Kings 16:34; Neh. 8:17; etc.). Nothing is reported about Nun except that he was the father of Joshua and consequently a member of the tribe of Ephraim. Nun is named as the father of Hoshea (Num. 13:8, 16; Deut. 32:44 KJV) and of Jeshua (Neh. 8:17), variant forms of JOSHUA.

Bibliography. M. Noth, *Die israelitischen Personennamen* (1928), p. 230.

R. F. JOHNSON

NUN nŭn (Heb. nōōn) [נ, *n* (*Nûn*)]. The fourteenth letter of the Hebrew ALPHABET as it is placed in the KJV at the head of the fourteenth section of the acrostic psalm, Ps. 119, where each verse of this section of the psalm begins with this letter.

NUNC DIMITTIS nŭngk′ dĭ mĭt′ĭs [Lat., now lettest thou depart]. Traditional designation of the Song of Simeon (Luke 2:29-32), one of three psalms contained in the Lukan account of the nativity and infancy of Jesus (*see also* BENEDICTUS; MAGNIFICAT). The song emphasizes the universal implications of the Incarnation: it is both the "glory" of Israel and a "light" for the Gentiles (cf. Isa. 49:6; 52:10). It thus summarizes aptly the major theme of Luke's Gospel and Acts. Since the fourth century, the song has been associated with the evening Offices, with Vespers in the East, and with Compline in the West.

See also HYMNS. M. H. SHEPHERD, JR.

NURSE. A woman engaged to suckle or to take charge of an infant. Israelite women usually nursed their own children (Gen. 21:7; Exod. 2:7; I Sam. 1:23; I Kings 3:21; Song of S. 8:1; II Macc. 7:27). Children were nursed longer than today, perhaps up to three years of age (I Sam. 1:22-24). Weaning was a time of family jubilation (Gen. 21:8; I Sam. 1:23-24). At the fall of Jerusalem to Babylon, nursing was destroyed (Lam. 4:4; Joel 2:16).

A wet nurse (מינקת) was occasionally used. Such women had a firm place in the family circle, and honor was theirs (Gen. 24:59; II Kings 11:2). Moses' mother was hired as his wet nurse by the daughter of Pharaoh (Exod. 2:7-9). Deborah apparently remained in the family as a servant after the weaning of her charge (Gen. 35:8). In Jonathan's family the nurse (אמנת) cared for a five-year-old (II Sam. 4:4). Perhaps this is the status of Naomi, nurse to her own grandson (Ruth 4:16). In most instances the nurse seems to remain as servant (Isa. 49:23-24; cf. II Kings 11:2; II Chr. 22:11). It is probable that male tutors (perhaps eunuchs) were sometimes considered nurses (II Kings 10:1, 5). Thus it is not unnatural to call Moses "nurse" (אמן) of Israel (Num. 11:12). Paul considered himself "nurse" (τροφός) to the Thessalonians (I Thess. 2:7). In these two men the analogy may be to the early nurturing of the people of God, as well as to the gentleness of their care. *See* FAMILY.

C. U. WOLF

NUTS [אגוז, *'eghôz;* Arab. *jawz;* KJV בטנים, *boṭnîm* (RSV PISTACHIO NUTS); Akkad. *buṭnu;* Arab. *buṭm*]. The edible seeds of several species of fruit trees.

"I went down to the nut [אגוז] orchard" (Song of S. 6:11; KJV "garden of nuts") is part of a description of the springtime, perhaps with cultic significance. The generic meaning "nut" follows the LXX καρύα, which refers to various kinds of nuts, but also specifically to the walnut, *Juglans regia* L. (cf. Jos. War III.x.8, which tells of walnut trees by the Sea of Galilee). A native of Persia, the walnut tree and its Hebrew name apparently were introduced into Palestine from there. The Arabic supports this identification. *See* FLORA § A2*f*.

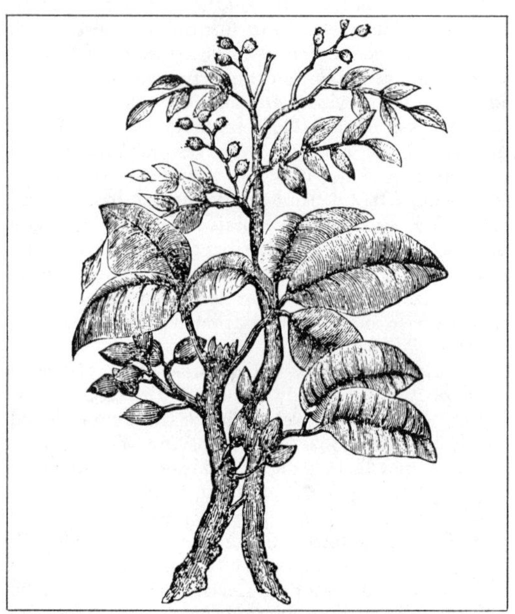

23. Nut

Some of the "choice fruits of the land" sent by Jacob down to Egypt included pistachio nuts (בטנים; KJV "nuts"). That pistachio nuts from the tree, *Pistacia vera* L., are intended seems quite certain. Indeed one of the "choice fruits of the land," the pistachio nut is considered a delicacy in all the Near East. Although the word may refer to nuts from other trees of the genus *Pistacia* (*see* FLORA § A2*f*), in Gen. 43:11 only the best quality would be sent by Jacob. Botanists disagree about the edible nature of the nuts from the other species. Coming mostly from Syria, the roasted nuts are readily available in the markets of Jordan. The city BETONIM (Josh. 13:26), E of the River Jordan, may have received its name from orchards of these trees there.

See also TEREBINTH; ALMOND. Fig. NUT 23.

Bibliography. I. Löw, *Die Flora der Juden*, I:1 (1926), 198-200; II (1924), 29-59. H. N. and A. L. Moldenke, *Plants of the Bible* (1952), pp. 118-20, 179-80. J. C. TREVER

***NUZI** nōō′zĭ [*cuneiform* (city of) *Nu-zi*, or *Nu-zu-e*, *always in the genitive*]. A city to the E of Ashhur and a short distance W of Arrapkha, which flourished in the middle centuries of the second millennium B.C. The Nuzi Texts throw much light on the social customs of the patriarchal age, and are also a primary source on the HABIRU. The records were written in Akkadian, but the vast majority of the people of that district were HURRIANS.

1. Local data. The present site of Nuzi is Yoghlan Tepe, a mound some 150 air miles N of Baghdad and near the foothills of S Kurdistan. It was excavated in 1925-31 by a joint expedition of the American School of Oriental Research in Baghdad and Harvard University. The name Nuzi was in use during the Hurrian occupation of the city. Although attested already in the Mari Tablets (period of Hammurabi), the name is best known to us from local documents which cover the fifteenth-fourteenth centuries, at which time the whole area was a province of the kingdom of Mitanni. Since all the occurrences of the place name are in the genitive case, the underlying nominative form of this non-Akkadian word has to be conjectured. Internal linguistic evidence would seem to favor *Nuzi*, but *Nuzu* has also been advocated. The city itself declined rapidly after its conquest by the Assyrians, in the late fourteenth or early thirteenth century.

Prior to the mass Hurrian settlement, the place was occupied by a different ("Subarian") ethnic group. In the Old Akkadian period the city bore the name of Gasur. The earliest occupation goes back to prehistoric times.

Courtesy of the American Schools of Oriental Research

24. Cuneiform tablet found at Nuzi

The cuneiform texts of the Nuzi period number several thousand. Most of them come from Nuzi itself and comprise private as well as public archives. There is, however, also a small but important collection from nearby Arrapkha (modern Kirkuk), some nine miles to the E. Together, these documents provide a vivid and many-sided commentary on the life and customs of the intrusive Hurrians, settled in an area that was peripheral to both Babylonia and Assyria. Fig. NUZ 24.

2. Bearing on the Bible. That so relatively obscure and remote a place should be of great interest to the modern student of the Bible is due mainly to chance and circumstance. Before their arrival in Palestine the patriarchs lived in the region of Haran, in the Middle Euphrates Valley, and they maintained contact with their original home for some time afterward. That region was thickly populated by Hurrians and was soon to be the focal center of Hurrian-dominated Mitanni. As social and political masters of the land, the Hurrians were bound to affect in many ways the life and habits of their Semitic neighbors, and among them the forefathers of the Hebrews. But little contemporary material has as yet come to light in that area. Nuzi, however, although far to the E, was likewise the seat of an authentic Hurrian community. Hence the results obtained at Nuzi are valid, by extension, for the W Hurrians as well. It is in this roundabout way that the Nuzi records have a significant bearing on the patriarchal narratives of the Bible. Fig. NUZ 25.

Courtesy of the American Schools of Oriental Research

25. Tablet found at Nuzi with seal impressions

The following are some of the many available instances of biblical concepts and practices that had long been puzzles, but can now be readily traced back to the Hurrians with the aid of the Nuzi records: Perhaps the most impressive single example is the appropriation by Rachel of the teraphim, or "house gods," of her father, Laban (Gen. 31:19, 30). Innumerable attempts were made to account for this strange behavior. But none could come close to the mark as long as the necessary data on the family law in Laban's land had been lacking. The texts from Arrapkha and Nuzi have at last supplied the details. In special circumstances, property could pass to a daughter's husband, but only if the father had handed over his house gods to his son-in-law as a formal token that the arrangement had proper sanction. A similar instance of legalizing the irregular—but this time duly explained as such—is to be found in Ruth 3:7; this usage, too, has significant antecedents at Nuzi. It is worth noting in this context that the common Nuzi clause "to go to the gods"—for purposes of a juridical ordeal—is echoed in Exod. 21:6, and more especially in 22:8; in the latter case the noun in question is still construed as plural.

In three passages (Gen. 12:10-20; 20:2-6; 26:1-11) the wife of a patriarch is introduced as his sister, for no apparent worthy reason. The Nuzi Texts, however, demonstrate that in Hurrian society the bonds of marriage were most solemn when the wife had legally, though not necessarily through ties of blood, the simultaneous status of sister; so much so that the terms for "sister" and "wife" could be interchanged in official use under the right circumstances. Thus, in falling back on the wife-sister equation, both Abraham and Isaac were availing themselves of the strongest safeguards that the law, as they knew it, could afford them.

Nuzi marriage contracts occasionally include the statement that a given slave girl is presented outright to the new bride, exactly as is the case with Leah (Gen. 29:24) and Rachel (vs. 29). Such was evidently the accepted practice in Hurrian circles, and hence also in culturally affiliated societies. Other marriage provisions in the Nuzi Documents specify that an upper-class wife who had borne her husband no sons was expected to furnish him with a slave girl as concubine; in that case, however, the wife was entitled to treat the concubine's offspring as her own. This last provision illuminates the otherwise cryptic statement in Gen. 16:2, with its punning: "I shall obtain children by her"="I shall be built up through her." The related law in the Code of Hammurabi (paragraph 144) offers no complete parallel; for there the wife is a priestess and is not entitled to claim the concubine's children for herself.

Lastly, in Hurrian society birthright was not so much a matter of chronological priority as of paternal decree. And such decrees were binding above all others when handed down in the form of a deathbed declaration, identified by the introductory formula: "Now that I have grown old." Against this stylized background, the ceremonial account in Gen. 27 acquires a new significance, with its opening clause (vs. 2), its solemn testatory pronouncements, and its arbitrary treatment of the birthright. Literary tradition may have obscured some of the content in the course of the intervening centuries. Indeed, the custom itself had to be outlawed (Deut. 21:16), manifestly because it was no longer suitable in the changed surroundings. But the underlying framework was preserved, enough so to be restored to its original meaning with the aid of pertinent cuneiform sources.

3. Nuzi and the Habiru. Aside from thus supplying an authentic background for various biblical passages relating to the patriarchal age, the Nuzi Tablets also help to clarify the complex problem of the HABIRU, or Hapiru. In the first place, these texts furnish a substantial number of personal names of the Habiru, and thus afford for the first time an insight into the ethnic composition of that group. The results show that a majority of the Habiru at Nuzi were of Akkadian origin; the rest bore Hurrian names, except for a few that cannot as yet be analyzed. Secondly, all the Habiru of these documents, including those with Hurrian names, were outsiders. What they have in common is not an ethnic or geographical classification but an inferior social status; their position throughout is that of underprivileged foreigners. To be sure, the Nuzi evidence is not necessarily valid for other lands and periods; the ethnic composition would certainly be subject to local variations. But the material before us bears out fully the conclusion that the term "Habiru" was largely, and perhaps from the very start, a designation for a particular class of people, and not a distinctive ethnic name.

All in all, the small city of Nuzi, although situated in an obscure peripheral area and gone from the stage of history before the time of Moses, left us resources that can still illuminate large stretches of the ancient Near East, including Palestine.

Bibliography. E. Chiera and E. A. Speiser, "A New Factor in the History of the Ancient Near East," *AASOR,* VI (1926), 75-90. R. F. Starr, *Nuzi* (1939). C. H. Gordon, "Biblical Customs and the Nuzu Tablets," *BA,* III (1940), 1-12. I. J. Gelb, P. M. Purves, and A. A. MacRae, *Nuzi Personal Names* (1943). E. A. Speiser, "Of Shoes and Shekels," *BASOR,* LXXVII (1940), 15-18; "I Know not the Day of my Death," *JBL,* LXXIV (1955), 252-56. M. Greenberg, *The Ḫab/piru* (1955), pp. 65-70. A. E. Draffkorn, "*Ilāni*/Elohim," *JBL,* LXXVI (1957), 216-24.

E. A. SPEISER

NYMPHA nĭm'fə [Νύμφα (*feminine*)]; KJV NYMPHAS —fəs [Νυμφᾶς (*masculine*). A Christian in whose house a church held its meetings, and to whom Paul sends greetings in Col. 4:15.

Since the name occurs only in the accusative, Νυμφαν, it could come from a masculine nominative Νυμφᾶς, a short form of Νυμφόδωρος, or from a feminine Νύμφα. Uncertainty in this matter dates back to a very early period, for the pronoun which follows the name is variously given in MSS as αὐτοῦ, "his" (KJV); αὐτῆς, "her" (RSV); αὐτῶν, "their" (ASV). It is impossible to decide which is right, though the feminine form has the disadvantage of being Doric for the more usual Attic Νύμφη.

Bibliography. C. F. D. Moule, *Colossians and Philemon* (1957), p. 28, note 1.

F. W. GINGRICH

OAK [אלון, *'allôn, and see below;* Akkad. *allânu;* δρῦς]. A tree noted for its great size and strength, probably *Quercus coccifera* L. ("kermes oak"), *Quercus aegilops* L. ("valonea oak"), and other species and subspecies about which there is much difference of opinion (*cf.* FLORA § A9*n*). אלון clearly means "oak" and is consistently so translated in Gen. 35:8; Isa. 2:13; 6:13; 44:14; Ezek. 27:6; Hos. 4:13; Amos 2:9; Zech. 11:2. Several other, similar Hebrew words have been translated "oak": אלון, *'ēlôn* (Gen. 12:6; 13:18; 14:13; 18:1; Deut. 11:30; Josh. 19:33; Judg. 4:11; 9:6, 37; I Sam. 10:3); אלה, *'ēlâ* (Gen. 35:4; Judg. 6:11, 19; II Sam. 18:9-10, 14; I Kings 13:14; I Chr. 10:12; Isa. 1:30; 6:13; Ezek. 6:13; Hos. 4:13); אלה, *'allâ* (Josh. 24:26); אילים, *'êlîm* (Isa. 1:29; 57:5; 61:3). The RSV mg. adds "terebinth" at Gen. 12:6; 13:18; 14:13; 18:1; Deut. 11:30. אילות is translated "oak" in Ps. 29:9 (RSV mg. and KJV "hinds").

That there was confusion even in Bible times concerning the meanings of these words is apparent from the use of *'ēlâ* in Gen. 35:4; *'allâ* in Josh. 24:26; and *'ēlôn* in Judg. 9:6—all for what was apparently the same sacred tree at Shechem! That *'êlâ* and *'allôn* refer to different trees, however, is clear from the occurrence of both words in Isa. 6:13; Hos. 4:13, where "terebinth" and "oak" are now recognized. Many scholars have come to feel that *'allôn* always meant "oak" and the other four words usually TEREBINTH. A notable exception is *'ēlâ* in II Sam. 18:9-10, 14, where the Forest of Ephraim, in which the death of Absalom occurred, seems to require an identification with *Quercus aegilops,* or some subspecies of the deciduous oaks common to the forests of Gilead.

The great oak shown SW of Hebron as Abraham's "oaks of Mamre" (Gen. 13:18; 14:13; 18:1) is a relatively recent tradition; but at Ramet el Khalil, N of Hebron, remains indicate the probable site.

The related Aramaic אילן, *'îlān,* of Dan. 4:10-26—Aram. 4:7-23 refers to an unusual "tree" of Nebuchadnezzar's dream, symbolic of the Babylonian Empire and perhaps of the mythological TREE OF LIFE (cf. Ezek. 31:3-14: "cedar"). A special (sacred?) oak outside Jerusalem is mentioned in II Bar. 6:1; 77:18; II Esd. 14:1.

See also ALLON 2; ALLON-BACUTH; ALOES; ELATH; ELM; EL-PARAN; HOLM; TEIL.

Bibliography. I. Löw, *Die Flora der Juden,* vol. I, no. 2 (1928), pp. 621-34; G. E. Post, *Flora of Syria, Palestine, and Sinai,* II (1933), 519-24; H. N. and A. L. Moldenke, *Plants of the Bible* (1952), pp. 193-99. J. C. TREVER

OAK, DIVINER'S. *See* DIVINER'S OAK.

OAK OF THE PILLAR [אלון מצב]; KJV PLAIN OF THE PILLAR. A sacred tree at a shrine at Shechem, beside which Abimelech was crowned (Judg. 9:6). Apparently this was the tree (אלה, "oak") under which Jacob hid the gods and jewelry of his wives (Gen. 35:4) and under which Joshua set up a "great stone" as a witness to the dedication of the people to the law of the Lord (Josh. 24:26).

See also OAK; FLORA § A9*n;* PILLAR.

J. M. MYERS

OAR [משוט, *miššôṭ* (Ezek. 27:6); משוט, *māšôṭ* (Ezek. 27:29); שיט, *shayiṭ, lit.* rowing (Isa. 33:21); *cf.* שׁוט, *shôṭ,* scourge, whip; Arab. *sâṭa,* to mix, whip]. A polelike wooden implement ending with a slightly curved blade, used to propel a boat.

The oar, which seems to have been a later refinement of the paddle, perhaps due to the appreciation of the value of a fulcrum for a steering paddle, appears in Egypt at an early date. Before 2000 B.C. the larger Nile River boats were rowed by men seated on stools on the deck; one such vessel was propelled by twenty-two oars. Fig. OAR 1.

Courtesy of the Oriental Institute, the University of Chicago

1. Limestone relief of boat with oars, carrying Syrian captives as they pay homage to the Egyptian king Sahu-Re; from mortuary temple of Sahu-Re, Fifth Dynasty (*ca.* 2500-2350 B.C.)

All the biblical references to oars and rowing relate to galleys (Isa. 33:21; Ezek. 27:6, 8, 26, 29). In Ezek. 27:6 the oars of Tyre are said to be of oak. Most galleys before the Christian era had only one tier or bank of oars. On the contentious question of the meaning of "bireme," "trireme," etc., *see* the bibliography under GALLEY. *See also* SHIPS AND SAILING. Figs. SHI 47, 50. W. S. MCCULLOUGH

OATHS. The security of a society demands that its members speak the truth in crucial situations and keep their promises in matters of serious import. The oath is an ancient and universal means of impressing this obligation on the responsible parties in an agreement or an investigation. The obligation is fortified by holy words and holy acts which create confidence and afford a sense of security that serves to hold the community together.

The oath was an important part of the cult life of the Hebrew community, as it was among other peoples. The legal procedure of which the oath was a part was closely associated with the shrines and the priesthood, because the oath as a holy act was properly pronounced in a sacred place or administered by a holy person, in contact or connection with holy objects. Perjury and the violation of an oath were serious matters, the profanation of the name of the Lord (Lev. 19:12), which could not go unpunished (Ezek. 17:13, 16, 18-19). An oath must be kept, though to one's hurt (Ps. 15:4), and even rash oaths (Lev. 5:1-4). The covenant between Isaac and Abimelech was backed by mutual oaths at the sacred well of oaths, Beer-sheba (Gen. 26:28-31). The oath for the suspected adulteress was administered with a drink of holy water containing dust from the tabernacle floor (Num. 5:17). Jephthah, when he became chief of the Gileadites, "spoke all his words before the LORD at Mizpah" (Judg. 11:11). These words were probably promises of exploits which he swore to carry out on behalf of the people, and it is likely that both parties sealed their agreement with oaths. The old sanctuaries at Gilgal and Beth-aven were places where oaths were administered and taken (Hos. 4:15). At the time of the composition of Solomon's prayer of dedication of the temple, oaths were administered before the temple altar (I Kings 8:31-32; II Chr. 6:22-23).

The oath is validated by the invocation of a deity, which for the Israelite should be none other than "the Lord, the God of heaven and earth." The Third Commandment (Exod. 20:7) forbids the invocation of the Lord's name for evil intent, which would include a false oath, black magic, or the like. The psalmist (Ps. 16:4) declares that he will not take the name of another god on his lips. Oaths by the god Ashimah of Samaria, and heathen gods at the shrines of Dan and Beer-sheba, are condemned by Amos (8:14). The Jews of Elephantine in Egypt took oaths by the deities Anathyahu, Harambethel, and the Egyptian goddess Sati. In later time one swore by heaven, earth, Jerusalem, the temple, or one's own head. The oath by one's head, common in Arabic, was also apparently frequent in Jesus' day (Matt. 5:36). In I Chr. 12:19 the Philistines swear by their heads.

The oath is accompanied by symbolic acts. The gesture of the oath was to raise the hand toward heaven (Gen. 14:22; Deut. 32:4; Dan. 12:7 [both hands]; Rev. 10:5-6 [the right hand]). To lift the hand, therefore, means to swear, and even God swears thus (Exod. 6:8; Ezek. 20:5). It is by his right hand that the Lord swears (Isa. 62:8; cf. the Arabic oath by the right hand of Allah and the meaning "oath" for the word *yamīn*, "right hand"). In Ps. 144:8, "whose right hand is a right hand of falsehood" refers to those who swear falsely.

The swearer may lay hold of some sacred and potent object, as the genitals of the patriarch (Gen. 24:2; 47:29). The rabbis understood the placing of the hand under the thigh as an oath by Abraham's circumcision (cf. Midrash Rabba, Palestinian Targum, and Rashi); but in view of the importance of the divine gift and attribute of fertility which the male organ symbolized, it seems unlikely that this form of oath had originally anything to do with circumcision. The later Jewish custom of taking hold of the Scriptures or phylacteries in a judicial oath furnished the model for the present-day procedure of swearing on the Bible.

Sacrifices accompanied the oath in connection with a covenant. The Hebrew idiom for making a covenant is "to cut a covenant with" someone. In Arabic the verb *qasama,* "cut," in the causative stem, *aqsama,* means "to swear," and the noun *qasam* means "oath." In the sacrifices of the covenant the animals were cut in two, and one or both parties passed between the pieces (Gen. 15:10, 17). In Jer. 34:18 those who break the covenant with the Lord are told that they will be made like the calf which they cut in two and passed between its parts. This suggests that the oath which bound the parties to a covenant may have stipulated in the conditional curse that the violator should be treated like the sacrificial animal. The Lord's covenant with Israel was conceived as having been sealed by mutual oaths, so that the promises of the covenant are referred to as things that the Lord swore to do (Gen. 24:7; 26:3; 50:24; Exod. 13:5, 11; 33:1; Num. 14:16, 30; 32:11; Deut. 1:8, 35; 6:10; etc.).

There are two varieties of oaths in the OT. The generic term שבועה designates the simpler form. The root of the word is the same as that of the number seven, and the verb "to swear" is the reciprocal verbal aspect (*Niph'al*) נשבע, which indicates that the swearer in some way enters into a relationship with the magical number seven. In the oath between Abraham and Abimelech at Beer-sheba (the well of seven, or well of the oath), Abraham set apart seven ewe lambs as a witness that he dug the well (Gen. 21:22-31). According to Herodotus (3.8), in Arab covenant oaths seven stones were smeared with blood. The second term, אלה, often translated "oath," properly means "curse." The two terms are used jointly (Num. 5:21; Neh. 10:29; Dan. 9:11). The oath for the suspected adulteress is termed the "oath of the curse," שבועת האלה (Num. 5:21). The curse is pronounced by the priest, and the woman accepts it by saying: "Amen, Amen." The terror of the curse is calculated to extract a confession from the guilty in advance of the administration of the oath, and was doubtless successful in many cases. When, e.g., Micah heard his mother's curse on the thief who had stolen her eleven hundred pieces of silver, he promptly confessed the theft (Judg. 17:2). For the suspected adulteress it was not sufficient simply to have her accept the curses by saying "Amen" to the priest's words; the curses were written down and the words washed off into the bitter water which the woman was made to drink; thus she took the poison of the curses into her body. If she were guilty, the curses would surely take effect; and if innocent, she would be immune. A fanciful example of a written curse with magical power is given in Zech. 5:1-4, where the prophet sees a vision of a large flying scroll inscribed with a comprehensive curse for every thief in the land; the scroll enters the house of the thief and the one who swears falsely by the Lord's name, and destroys the house. This vision was apparently called forth by the prophet's suspicion that there were many thieves in the land who had taken the oath of innocence falsely.

The full, unexpurgated oath includes a conditional curse intended to carry the conviction that the swearer is speaking the truth. The more serious the issue at stake, the more terrible would be the curses that are designed to enforce the oath. Because of the fear which the curse induces, the actual content of the curse is ordinarily suppressed, leaving only an eviscerated form of the oath. A common oath formula of the OT is: "May God the Lord do so to me and more also, if" I do, or do not, thus and so (Ruth 1:17; I Sam. 3:17; 14:44; II Sam. 3:35; I Kings 2:23). This formula may be varied and made more emphatic by the swearer's pronunciation of his own name (I Sam. 20:13; 25:22; II Sam. 3:9). When this formula is used by the pagan non-Israelites Jezebel (I Kings 19:2) and Ben-hadad (I Kings 20:10), it has a polytheistic turn, with the verb in the plural: "So may the gods do to me, and more also." As God is the guardian of the oath and fulfils or nullifies the curses in accordance with justice, one may make his asseveration an oath by calling God to witness (Gen. 31:50; I Sam. 12:5; 20:23 [reading *'ēdh* instead of *'adh*]; II Cor. 1:23; Gal. 1:20; Phil. 1:8) or to watch (Gen. 31:49) or to judge (Gen. 31:53). Since the validity of the oath depends ultimately on the deity who sanctions it, the most common asseveration is: "As the LORD lives" (Judg. 8:19; I Sam. 14:39, 45; 19:6; 20:3, 21; 25:26, 34; 26:10, 16; 28:10; 29:6; etc.), to which one may add a like asseveration by the life of the persons to whom he is speaking (I Sam. 20:3; II Sam. 11:11). The Lord swears by his own life (Ezek. 17:16; Zeph. 2:9) or by himself (Gen. 22:16).

The reluctance to pronounce the full oath replete with imprecations, for fear that, even though divine agency is assumed, the words themselves might inflict harm, led to the suppression of the conditional curse and the further reduction of the formula until only a vestige of the protasis remained: "if," and "if not." With the omission of the curse in the apodosis, the positive conditional protasis becomes a negative asseveration (if I do thus and so, may I be accursed —i.e., I surely will not do it), and the negative condition becomes a positive asseveration (if I do not thus and so, may I be accursed—i.e., I surely will do it).

In a few cases we have the full form of the oath with elaboration of the curses (Num. 5:19-28; Pss. 7:4-5; 137:5-6). These are exceptional cases, where the issue is grave and the emotion is very strong. The classic example is Job's apology for his life (ch. 31), which consists of a sort of negative confession in the form of a series of oaths complete with curses, which call down on himself such calamities as loss of property, alienation of his wife, the mutilation and maiming of his body, etc. In extremity of desperation and in his anxiety to impress both God and his hearers with his sincerity and innocence, Job breaks the taboo and calls down on himself the most terrible curses he can conceive. Here we see the oath in all its force as a kind of ordeal and spiritual combat. The swearer puts his whole soul and all that he has into the oath and exerts himself to the utmost to prove his integrity. The tension is extreme, but the just man will bear up under it, while the unjust man will break under the strain. In more ancient times it is probable that the families and households of the opposing parties stood behind the principals and gave their support and placed themselves in jeopardy. In Deut. 21:1-10 the elders of the city nearest the place where a slain man is found take responsibility for the whole city and affirm the city's innocence and ignorance of the killing before the Lord.

According to the NT, Jesus' attitude toward the prevalence of the oath in everyday Jewish life resembled that of the Essenes, who, as Josephus tells us (War II.viii.6), esteemed swearing on ordinary occasions as worse than perjury. Jesus urged that all oaths be omitted (Matt. 5:34; cf. Jas. 5:12). His own use of "Amen, Amen," however, while not strictly an oath, is a solemn asseveration akin to an oath and goes beyond the simple "Yes" and "No" which he recommended (Matt. 5:37). His strictures against oaths by the temple, the temple gold, the altar, or heaven (Matt. 23:16-22) are aimed at the casuistry which attempted to classify oaths, according to degrees of validity. Nevertheless, at the trial he deferred to custom in some measure: when the high priest asked simply if he had no answer to the testimony against him, he remained silent; only when the high priest adjured him by the living God to say whether he was the Christ, did he give answer (Matt. 26:63). This is in accordance with the Mishna (Shebu. 4.13), that if one adjures another by heaven and earth, it is not binding, but if one adjures another by one of the divine names, it is binding.

Peter's denial at the trial (Matt. 26:69-75) covers all three modes of Jewish asseveration. First, he simply denied, then he denied with an oath, and lastly he invoked a curse on himself and swore that he did not know the man.

Paul uses a form of oath attested in the OT when he calls God to witness his asseveration (II Cor. 1:23; Gal. 1:20; Phil. 1:8).

Oaths had an important place among the sectarians at Qumran. An oath of strict and complete allegiance to the law was required of every candidate for membership in the order. The text of the oath is not given, but it was certainly reinforced with curses, which are several times referred to in the Manual of Discipline as the "Curses of the Covenant" (אלות הברית), and similarly in the Damascus Document.

See BLESSINGS AND CURSINGS; COVENANT; VOWS.

Bibliography. J. Pedersen, *Der Eid bei den Semiten* (1914); J. Hempel, "Die israelitischen Anschauungen von Segen und Fluch im Lichte altorientalischen Parallelen," *ZDMG*, IV (1925), 20 ff; S. Blank, "The Curse, Blasphemy, the Spell and the Oath," *HUCA*, 23 (1950-51), 73-95; V. Rogers, "The Use of ראש in an Oath," *JBL*, 74 (1955), 272-73; M. Greenberg, "The Hebrew Oath Particle *Ḥay/Ḥē*," *JBL*, 76 (1957), 34-39.

M. H. POPE

OBADIAH ō'bə dī'ə [עֹבַדְיָהוּ, עֹבַדְיָה, servant of Y]. **1.** The chief of King Ahab's household, and a devout follower of Yahweh (I Kings 18:3-16).

2. A descendant of David (I Chr. 3:21).

3. A chief of the tribe of Issachar, and a son of Izrahiah (I Chr. 7:3).

4. A Benjaminite, son of Azel (I Chr. 8:38; 9:44).

5. A Levite who was among the first exiles to return to Jerusalem (I Chr. 9:16). He is called Abda in Neh. 11:17.

6. A Gadite chief who joined David's army and became an officer (I Chr. 12:9).

7. The father of Ishmaiah, one of the chiefs of Zebulun in the last days of David (I Chr. 27:19).

8. One of the princes whom King Jehoshaphat sent to teach the "book of law of the LORD" to the people in all the cities of Judah (II Chr. 17:7-9).

9. A Levite overseer of the temple repairs in the time of King Josiah of Judah (II Chr. 34:12). For the important religious reform which resulted from such repairs, *see* JOSIAH.

10. One of the priests who accompanied Ezra in his return to Jerusalem and who put his seal to the covenant between the people and God (Ezra 8:9; Neh. 10:5).

11. A gatekeeper who guarded the storehouses of the gates in the days of the high priest Joiakim (Neh. 12:25). E. R. ACHTEMEIER

OBADIAH, BOOK OF [עבדיה, *a common name* (cf. I Kings 18:3, 7, 16; I Chr. 27:19; II Chr. 34:12; etc.), servant of Yahweh]. A book of prophecy, the shortest in the OT and the fourth of the Book of the Twelve. It belongs to a literature of anti-Edomite polemic (Gen. 27:39-40; Ps. 137:7; Isa. 34:5 ff; 63:1-6; Ezek. 25:12-17; 35; Amos 1:11-12; Mal. 1:2-4; cf. Jer. 49: 7-22) and of Day-of-the-Lord prophecies (Isa. 2:6-22; Ezek. 7; Joel 1:15–2:11; Amos 5:18-20; Zeph. 1:7, 14-18), to which it bears numerous affinities in thought, style, and diction.

1. Historical setting and occasion
2. Contents
3. Composition and integrity
4. Date
5. Text

Bibliography

1. Historical setting and occasion. Israel's hatred of Edom was inveterate. The aetiological narratives

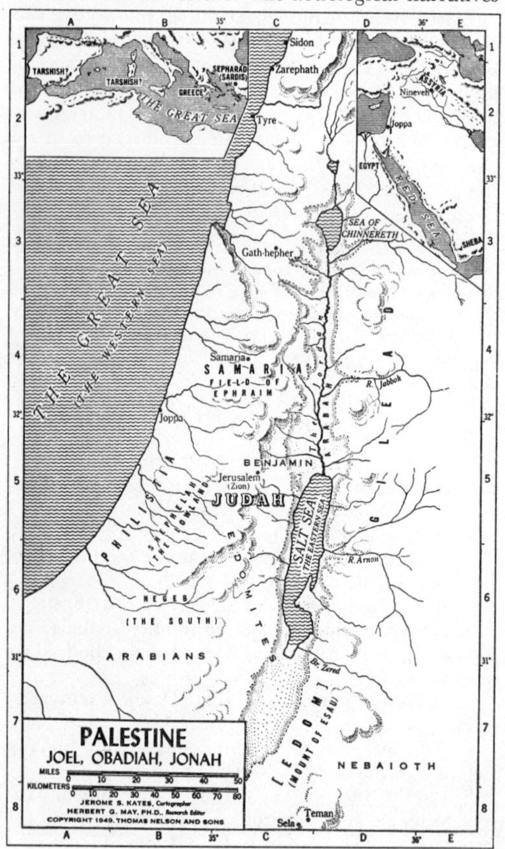

of Genesis record the tensions between Jacob-Israel and Esau-Edom (Gen. 25:23; 27:39-40). From the time of the United Monarchy the control of Edom was a fixed policy of the kings of Israel and Judah. The lucrative trade from Ezion-geber (modern Tell el-Kheleifeh), the port on the Gulf of Aqabah, passed through Edomite territory, and wars, as a consequence, were not infrequent (II Sam. 8:13-14, reading אדם for ארם; I Kings 11:14-17; II Kings 14: 22; 16:5-6; II Chr. 20; 21:8-10). When Jerusalem fell in 597, Edom exploited Judah's plight, rejoiced in its fate (Lam. 4:21), "acted revengefully" against her (Ezek. 25:12), joined with the Babylonians in her destruction, and occupied the Negeb (Ezek. 35: 10). The description of Edom's behavior in Obad. 11-14 is the most definite of all the anti-Edomite oracles, and is generally held to reflect conditions after 597. The only question is whether it should refer to contiguous verses in the book; on this matter there has been considerable diversity of opinion among scholars.

2. Contents. The superscription is brief: "The vision [חזון; cf. Isa. 1:1; Nah. 1:1] of Obadiah." The oracular formula, "Thus says Lord Yahweh," is awkward in the context of the following: "We have heard," and should probably be excised (so Eissfeldt). In an ecstatic audition the prophet has heard "tidings" (reading "I have heard" with the LXX, Jer. 49:14: שמועה שמעתי) from Yahweh, and a messenger has been sent among the nations to call them to battle. *Edom delenda est.* From her lofty dwelling "in the clefts of the rock" (probably Petra, and its fortress rock Umm el-Bayyarah) she is brought down, pillaged, and plundered. "On that day" (ביום ההוא) Yahweh will destroy her wise men and mighty warriors. Teman, modern Tawilan, is five miles E of Petra. The references are certainly to the future, not to the past. The grounds for this awful fate are given in vss. 11-14, 15*b:* as Edom has done to Judah, so it shall be done to her. Vss. 15*a*, 16-21, describe the imminent coming of the Day of the Lord. The classical motif of reversal, characteristic of many such oracles, is sounded here (cf. vs. 15*b*): the house of Jacob shall possess Edom's possessions. Mount Zion will rule Mount Esau, and the kingdom will belong to Yahweh.

3. Composition and integrity. The structure of the book may be delineated as follows:

- I. Superscription: vision of Obadiah concerning Edom, vs. 1*a*
- II. An ecstatic audition, 1*b*
- III. Edom's imminent destruction and its justification, 2-14
  - A. The divine judgment on Edom, 2-10
    1. Her pride brought low, 2-4
    2. Destruction, pillage, abandonment, 5-7
    3. The day of her shame, 8-10
  - B. The day of her treachery, 11-14, 15*b*
    1. Edom's aloofness when Jerusalem fell, 11
    2. Her evil gloating over Judah's distress, 12
    3. Her invasion of Jerusalem, 13
    4. Her support of the Babylonians, 14
    5. Judgment, 15*b*

IV. The Day of Yahweh, 15*a,* 16-21
   A. The reversal of fate, 15*a,* 16-18
   B. The lands repossessed, 19-21

Many views have been held regarding the composition of the book: (*a*) T. H. Robinson resolves it into a series of independent oracles from different times (vss. 1-5, 6-7, 8-11, 12-14, 15-16, 17-18, 19-21); (*b*) Sellin takes vss. 1-10 and vss. 11-14, 15*b,* as two separate pieces stemming from different periods; (*c*) Rudolph and Weiser support the essential integrity of the book, though with some reservation.

The issues involved in reaching a decision on the matter of composition are as follows:

a) The literary relation of Obad. 1-10 to Jer. 49: 7-22. That the two passages are parallel, there is no doubt, but the question of the priority of one over the other has been much controverted. It is now quite generally agreed that the passage in Jeremiah is secondary. While the text of the latter is admittedly superior, Obadiah is better ordered, more vigorous in style, and more closely knit.

b) The historical situation. While it is generally held that vss. 11-14 reflect conditions after 587, it is not clear that this is the background for the whole book. Many feel that vss. 15*a,* 16-21, reflect the thought of a later period. Thus the unity of Obadiah is quite generally called into question, and for the following reasons: (1) In the first major section (III) the nations are the divine instrument of judgment, in the second (IV) they are its objects; in the first section only Edom is punished, in the second the nations also, while Israel is the instrument. (2) The first section is addressed to Judah through the prophet's ecstatic audition; the second section is addressed to Edom.

But against these considerations others are to be weighed: (1) The motif of the Day persists throughout (8*a,* 11-15*a*), and the corresponding diction and imagery are present. (2) Throughout, Esau-Edom (cf. also Mount Esau [8, 9*b*]) is the central object of concern. (3) The motif of reversal is common to both (cf. 15*b,* 16-18). (4) So far as vss. 15*a,* 16-21, are concerned, the motif of possession is pervasive.

In view of all these considerations, it is hazardous to deny the possibility of an essential unity. The transition from the historical to the eschatological is by no means unparalleled; moreover, the appeal to difference in language carries little force. The books of Joel and Zephaniah are not greatly different.

4. Date. Wellhausen assigned the book to the fifth century, and many have followed him in this. He believed that the true background was to be discovered in the pressure of Arab tribes upon the Edomites and that the verbs in vss. 1-9 referred to past events. But there is no clear allusion to an Arab invasion, and the reference in the verbs is clearly to the future. While many other dates have been proposed, some of them in the pre-exilic period (Keil: 889 B.C.; Sellin: *ca.* 850 in the context of II Kings 8:20-22), others in the postexilic (Hitzig: 312), the unity of vss. 1-14, 15*b,* can be said to be established; the date would then be determined by vss. 11-14, the period shortly after 597. If the second major section, especially vss. 15*a,* 16-18, is from Obadiah, then the date is the same; if not, it is to be dated sometime later. If we hold to the essential integrity of the book, it comes from the time shortly after 587.

5. Text. The text of Obadiah has been well preserved. As a whole, the LXX is certainly inferior, but occasionally may be of help in restoring the original, as in vs. 1, where we should probably follow the LXX in reading שמעתי for the MT שמענו. In vs. 9 the final words, "by slaughter," are transferred to the beginning of vs. 10: "for the slaughter and violence." In vs. 16 the MT reads לעו (LXX ἀναβήσονται, adopted by some scholars). In vs. 21, where the MT has משעים, "saviors," the LXX and the Syr. read: "those who have been saved." This is also accepted by many scholars as original.

Bibliography. Commentaries: J. Bewer, ICC (1911); Sellin, *KAT* (1929-30); Weiser, *ATD* (2nd ed., 1956); N. F. Langford, *IB* (1956). See also the Introductions by Driver, Eissfeldt, and Weiser.

The following studies are of special importance: T. H. Robinson, "The Structure of the Book of Obadiah," *JTS* (1916), pp. 402-8; W. Rudolph, "Obadja," *ZAW* (1931), pp. 222-31; J. Starcky, "The Nabateans," *BA* (1955), pp. 84-106.

J. MUILENBURG

OBAL ō'bəl [עובל] (Gen. 10:28). Alternately: **EBAL** ē'bəl [עיבל] (I Chr. 1:22). A son of Joktan, and hence the name of an Arabian group. The location of the tribe cannot be established with certainty. Abil is a frequent geographic name in Yemen; there is also an Ubal located between Hadeida and Sanaa, the capital of Yemen. On the other hand, the group of tribes that immediately precedes Obal—viz., Hadoram, Uzal, and Diklah—is probably to be located farther to the N, in the neighborhood of Mecca; and hence Obal may have been in this region.

S. COHEN

OBDIA. KJV Apoc. form of HABAIAH.

OBED ō'bĭd [עובד, עבד, worshiper; 'Ιωβήδ]. **1.** The son of Boaz and Ruth; the father of Jesse; the grandfather of King David (Ruth 4:17, 21-22; I Chr. 2: 12). As a child, he was nursed by Naomi, and according to Matt. 1:5; Luke 3:32, he became an ancestor of Jesus Christ.

2. A Judahite (I Chr. 2:37-38).

3. One of David's Mighty Men (I Chr. 11:47).

4. A gatekeeper in Solomon's temple (I Chr. 26:7).

5. The father of Azariah, a commander in the days of Queen Athaliah of Judah (II Chr. 23:1).

E. R. ACHTEMEIER

OBED-EDOM ō'bĭd ē'dəm [עבד־אדם, עבד־אדום, servant of (the god) Edom(?); *cf.* Phoen. מלך־אדם; *or* servant of man(?), *reading 'ādhām for 'aedhōm*]. **1.** A Philistine from Gath residing between Kiriath-jearim and Jerusalem. It was at his house that David left the ark after the death of Uzzah. The good fortune which Obed-edom enjoyed during the three months the ark was in his house convinced David that he should bring the ark into Jerusalem, as he had originally intended (II Sam. 6:10-12; I Chr. 13:13-14; 15:25).

2. Keeper of the S gates of the temple and the storehouse (I Chr. 26:4-8, 15); probably a Korahite, since the Merarites are not mentioned until vs. 10, and vs. 19 limits the gatekeepers to these two families. The phrase "for God blessed him" (vs. 5) may indicate that he is to be identified with 1 *above* (cf. I Chr. 13:14).

3. A Levitical musician (I Chr. 16:5). In the list of singers in I Chr. 15:16-24 he appears as the "gatekeeper Obed-edom" (vs. 18); vs. 24 implies that he was both gatekeeper and musician. I Chr. 16:38 makes him the son of the musician Jeduthun, but gives his job as that of gatekeeper. It may be that the gatekeepers of the temple took the Philistine Obed-edom as their eponymous ancestor. Because of their involvement in the service of the temple, they would naturally be transformed into Levites (cf. II Kings 11; II Chr. 23; the foreign troops of the former passage become Levitical gatekeepers in the latter). Eventually the guild changed from gatekeepers into a guild of musicians, and this accounts for the association of Obed-edom with Jeduthun.

4. Guardian of the sacred vessels of the temple. He was taken as a hostage by Joash of Israel after his defeat of Amazaiah of Judah and the capture of Jerusalem (II Chr. 25:24; his name does not appear in the parallel account of II Kings 14:14).

Bibliography. S. R. Driver, *Notes on the Hebrew Text of the Books of Samuel* (1890), p. 206; R. H. Pfeiffer, *Introduction to the OT* (1948), p. 623.

R. W. CORNEY

OBEDIENCE. In the OT the common Hebrew word for "obedience" and its cognates is the root שמע, which literally means "hear." Translators are constantly faced with the problem of when to translate שמע by "hear" and when by "obey."

While the term is used in the OT to express such action in ordinary human relationships, it is the relationship between God and man—or more specifically God and Israel—which provides the proper context for understanding its full meaning. The basic presupposition is that God has revealed himself to Israel through his "word" or his "voice" (Gen. 27: 8; Exod. 19:5; Deut. 28:12; Jer. 7:23). When God speaks, he does so through his chosen representatives, a patriarch or judge (Judg. 2:17), prophet, priest (Deut. 17:12), king (II Kings 10:6), etc. His word not only reveals what he purposes to do, but also points to that action whereby he is already fulfilling or is about to fulfil his purpose. Indeed, the one through whom God declares his word is already made participant in his action. Abraham fully understands God's word that he should sacrifice his son when, in the act of sacrificing, God acts to provide the lamb (Gen. 22:1-19). Moses fully understands God's word to lead the Israelites out of Egypt (Exod. 5) when, in the act of leading, God brings the plagues on Egypt (chs. 8 ff) and separates the waters of the sea (ch. 14). Jeremiah understands God's word of judgment on Judah as he hears the snorting horses (Jer. 8:16) God brings from the N and the false cries of "Peace, peace," when there is no peace (Jer. 6:14; 8:11).

To "hear" God's word involves a single response that can be described from three different standpoints. First, it is a word which always involves the physical sense of hearing, since God fulfils his purposes in and through human beings. Second, to understand what one hears demands that the hearer respond in faith and trust in God's word and action. Third, such response involves the hearer in obedient action to fulfil God's intention for his part in the divine action. To understand the ambiguity of the word "hear" is necessary to grasping the full meaning of the word. To really hear God's word inevitably involves one in an obedient response in action prompted by faithfulness to and faith in the God who is revealing himself in and through particular historical events. Not to respond in obedient action is tantamount to unbelief—and so the prophet chastises his people for their blind eyes and deaf ears (Isa. 6: 9-10), which betray their faithlessness. The inevitable consequence of failing to hear is rebellion or disobedience. But rebellion is not just the wilful disobedience of one who has heard. Rebellion is the sign that one has not really heard, since to hear implies a faith-obedience response.

The history of Israel can be treated as the story of Israel's hearing or failure to hear God's word. In the early period of her history God speaks to Israel through appointed leaders, through whom God makes covenants—the climactic covenant being established through Moses in the giving of the law with its demands and promises. In the prophets God speaks anew to Israel, condemning her rebellion, calling her to faithful remembrance and obedient action in each new historical situation. Amos repeatedly says: "Hear this word" (3:1; 4:1; 5:1; 8:4). Jeremiah reminds his people: "But this command I gave them, 'Obey my voice, and I will be your God, and you shall be my people; and walk in all the way that I command you, that it may be well with you' " (Jer. 7:23). One of the major themes of postexilic Judaism is that Israel had failed to hear Moses and the prophets. When the returned exiles had been settled, one of the first acts of Ezra was to read the "book of the law of Moses" to all "who could hear *with understanding*" (Neh. 8:1-2). As late as the book of Daniel the relentless charge is made: "We . . . have not obeyed the voice of the LORD our God by following his laws, which he set before us by his servants the prophets" (Dan. 9:10). After the close of the prophetic period (*see* PROPHET) the Jews directed their attention increasingly to the law as the revealed word of God. There developed, then, a tendency to understand faith-obedience in moralistic and legalistic terms. *See* LAW (IN THE OT).

The NT presupposes the OT understanding of obedience. The usual term is ὑπακοή, but, again, "to hear" (ἀκούω) often means "to obey." In the characteristic word of Jesus: "He who has ears to hear, let him hear," the word "hear" bears the full meaning of שמע in the OT. He was not only asking people to hear his word in the physical sense, but that in faithful response they accept his word as a word from God and act in obedience to it. "Every one then who hears these words of mine and does them will be like a wise man who built his house upon the rock" (Matt. 7:24). As in the OT, to "hear" involved the hearer in the belief that Jesus was chosen of God to be the bearer of his word and that in his ministry God's action was already revealed. The sign that men had heard was repentance and belief in the good news of the kingdom (Mark 1:14-15). While Jesus called men to obedience to the good news of the kingdom, he did not see his message as contradicting the obedience called for in the Law (Mark 10:17 ff). Nevertheless, his own understanding of God's voice led him to an interpretation of the specific demands of the law which conflicted with the interpretation of others (Mark 2:23-28; 7:1-23; 10:1-12). This meant that his word was hard to "hear," not only because of Jesus' rigorous demands, but also because it implied an immediate awareness of a revelatory word of God in Jesus' words and ministry. Only those who had received the secret of the kingdom could understand (Mark 4:11-12); others did not *really* "hear." Obedience to his words presupposed believing and trusting him in his mission.

The earliest Christian community was confident that God had spoken anew through Jesus Christ. In Acts, Peter says: "Men of Israel, hear these words" (2:22). The crucial center of the message was the death and resurrection of Jesus, who was now fully manifest as Messiah. The sign of hearing was repentance in faith (6:7). Hearing or obedience was the faith-response to the gospel, now understood as a decisive word of God spoken through the death and resurrection of Jesus. Paul refers to the response to the gospel of the Galatian Christians as "hearing with faith" (Gal. 3:2; ἐξ ἀκοῆς πίστεως). The word translated "hearing" refers both to that which is heard and to the hearing itself. Paul's apostleship to the Gentiles is for the bringing about of the "obedience to the faith" (Rom. 1:5; ὑπακοὴν πίστεως). Hearing or obedience, then, is used in the closest relationship to faith, not as two distinct acts, but as one and the same response. "Faith comes from what is heard, and what is heard comes by the preaching of Christ" (Rom. 10:17). In the NT obedience is understood as faith-response to God's word in Jesus Christ, with special emphasis on Christ's own obedience (Phil. 2:8; Heb. 5:8). Whereas Adam and all men sin and are disobedient, Christ alone was truly obedient (Rom. 5:18-21). And it is through his obedience that believers receive righteousness and eternal life (Rom. 5; Heb. 5:9). Christians are "obedient children" (I Pet. 1:14), since through faith in Christ they share in the benefits of his obedience, and also in their lives of faith they act in obedience to him (Rom. 6:16; II Cor. 10:5-6; I Pet. 1:22). The life of obedience is not primarily the submission of the will to laws, either of the Old Covenant or of the New. It is life lived in obedience to the Spirit, which has made the "hearing with faith" a possibility (Gal. 3:2-5). Believers are "sanctified by the Spirit for obedience to Jesus Christ and for sprinkling with his blood" (I Pet. 1:2). Obedience understood from the standpoint of ethical conduct is first and foremost the "fruit of the Spirit" (Gal. 5:22), which is the "fruit of righteousness" that is through Jesus Christ (Phil. 1:11 ff). "My sheep hear my voice, and I know them, and they follow me," says the Gospel of John (10:27). But they do this as the Spirit speaks (John 14:25-26; 16:12-15). It is the obedience of the "heart" that leads to righteousness (Rom. 6:16-19). Obedience, as in the OT, is both a religious and an ethical term. This is also true of disobedience, which at one and the same time refers to faithlessness and to the immoral acts which are its outward signs (Acts 19:19; Rom. 11:31; Tit. 1:16; 3:3; I Pet. 4:17).

F. W. Young

OBEISANCE. In the OT, השתחוה (short form השתחו; cf. Ugaritic *tšthwy*, from *ḥwy*), "to do/make obeisance," "to do/make homage," "to bow down," means to prostrate oneself on the ground as a gesture of worship, homage, or submission.

In the NT, this Hebrew word is normally translated by προσκυνέω, "to worship." *See* Worship in NT Times, Christian. W. J. Harrelson

OBELISK ŏb'ə lĭsk [מצבה, pillar, standing stone] (Jer. 43:13); KJV IMAGE. Because of the context, the Hebrew word in this passage is interpreted as a reference to the obelisk, a type of sacred monument native to ancient Egypt. Figs. OBE 2; ELE 24.

Trans World Airlines Photo

2. Obelisk at a temple at Thebes, Egypt

In its normal form the obelisk is a tall, slender, four-sided stone pillar, gently tapering toward the top, which is mounted by a pyramidion. The obelisk originated in the Egyptian cult center of Heliopolis and seems at first to have been associated with the principal deity, Atum-Re, the sun-god. Earlier forms of the fetish are pictured which are shorter and broader. The exact reasons for the association of this type of monument with Atum-Re are not clear, but we do at least have mention of the god's both living in and resting on the obelisk. The Egyptians called the object the *ben* or *benben* and associated it with the rays of the rising sun, perhaps merely because of the similarity in sound to the verb *wbn*, "to rise, shine" (of the sun).

Through the constant extensions and syncretisms characteristic of Egyptian religion the obelisk assumed a variety of uses and significances beyond the original one. In the New Kingdom, e.g., the obelisk (usually in pairs) was erected with an appropriate inscription to commemorate the celebration of the king's Thirty-Year Festival. It is also found as a symbol of the moon, as well as being used for purely ornamental purposes.

Bibliography. H. Schafer, "Die Sonne auf dem Obelisk," *OLZ*, 32 (1929), 723-25; H. Bonnet, *Reallexikon der ägyptischen Religion* (1952), pp. 539-42. T. O. Lambdin

OBETH ō'bĕth. KJV Apoc. form of Obed.

OBIL ō'bĭl [אוביל, camel-driver; *cf.* Arab. *'abbal*] (I Chr. 27:30). An Ishmaelite who was one of the royal stewards of the property of King David and had charge of the royal camels.

OBLATION [מנחה] (I Kings 18:29, 36); KJV EVENING SACRIFICE. *See* Sacrifice and Offerings §§ A2*b*i-ii.

OBOE. *See* Musical Instruments.

OBOTH ō'bŏth [אבת, fathers] (Num. 21:10-11; 33:43-44). A station of the wilderness wanderings of the Israelites, between Punon and Iyye-abarim in Moab. It has been identified by some with 'Ain el-Weiba, not far from Feinan, the biblical Punon; but since the route of the Israelites between Punon and the borders of Moab is not known with certainty, this identification is not definite. S. Cohen

OBSOLETE TERMS. A major reason for revision of the KJV is afforded by changes in English usage.

1. Obsolete words
2. Words with obsolete meanings
   a. Words with changed meanings
   b. Words which have acquired worse or more violent meanings
   c. Words which have acquired less evil meanings or good connotations
3. Other archaic usage
4. A selected list of obsolete terms and their meanings

Bibliography

1. Obsolete words. The KJV contains some words, current in 1611, which have become archaic or obsolete. Examples are: "afore," "agone," "albeit," "all to brake," "astonied," "chapiter," "dure," "to ear," "emerods," "flowers," "folden," "to fray," "goodman," "gorget," "graff," "habergeon," "hoise," "knop," "leasing," "to list," "magnifical," "marish," "to mete," "neesing," "ouches," "ravin," "scrip," "sith," "taches," "trow," "wist," "wot." The meaning of these words may usually be inferred from the context, and they are not often misleading.

2. Words with obsolete meanings. More dangerous are the English words which are still in constant use but now convey a different meaning from that which they had in 1611 and in the KJV. These words were once accurate translations of the Hebrew and Greek scriptures; but they have so changed in meaning, or have acquired such additional meanings, that they have become ambiguous or misleading. They no longer say to the reader what the KJV translators meant them to say.

a. Words with changed meanings. "Prevent" is always used by the KJV in the obsolete sense of "be or go ahead of, precede." "I prevented the dawning of the morning" means "I rise before dawn" (Ps. 119:147). "Let" appears three times in the sense of "hinder" or "prevent" (Isa. 43:13; Rom. 1:13; II Thess. 2:6-7). "Suffer" is used sixty-nine times in the sense of "undergo" or "endure," and sixty times in the archaic sense of "let, allow, permit." "Allow" is always used in the sense of "praise, approve, accept."

By "conversation" the KJV always refers to conduct, behavior, or manner of life. Hence the injunction to "put off concerning the former conversation the old man" means "put off your old nature which belongs to your former manner of life" (Eph. 4:22), and "filthy conversation" means "licentiousness" (II Pet. 2:7). "Convenient" is applied to what is fitting and proper, rather than to what suits one's personal ease or comfort or lies near at hand (Eph. 5:4). The KJV uses "communicate" for "share" (Heb. 13:16), "evil communications" for "bad company" (I Cor. 15:33), "communed" for "discussed" (Luke 6:11), and "condescend" for "associate" (Rom. 12:16). "The darkness comprehended it not" means "The darkness has not overcome it" (John 1:5). In Rom. 8:19-23, 39, the word "creature" is employed in the sense of the "created universe"—the "whole creation," as the KJV itself translates the same Greek word in vs. 22. "Every creature of God" means "everything created by God" (I Tim. 4:4), and a "new creature" means a "new creation" (II Cor. 5:17; Gal. 6:15).

b. Words which have acquired worse or more violent meanings. Some words are used by the KJV in a good, or at least harmless, sense but now have acquired worse or more violent meanings. "Base" simply means "humble" (II Cor. 10:1), and "our vile body" means "our lowly body" (Phil. 3:21). "Demanded" means "asked" (Luke 3:14); "addicted themselves" is "devoted themselves" (I Cor. 16:15); and "unspeakable" means "inexpressible" (II Cor. 9:15). "Riot" and "rioting" refer to revelry and loose living rather than to turbulence and violence (Tit. 1:6; Rom. 13:13). The "feebleminded" are not mentally deficient, but simply "faint-hearted" (I Thess. 5:14). The word "covet" is used for earnest desire and zeal for the higher things of life, as well as for inordinate passion for its more material comforts (I Cor. 12:31). To "tempt" is sometimes used in the sense of "try" or "test," without the present implication of seeking to lead into evil (Mark 12:15).

c. Words which have acquired less evil meanings or good connotations. Some words that were used by the KJV in a bad sense have now acquired less evil meanings or even good connotations. "Debate" is listed among the characteristics of the reprobate mind (Rom. 1:29), and "emulation" among the works of the flesh (Gal. 5:20). "Delicacies" and "deliciously" are used for wanton licentiousness in Rev. 18:3, 7, 9.

To be "highminded" in 1611 was to be proud or haughty (Rom. 11:20; I Tim. 6:17; II Tim. 3:4); the term is now used for noble character and high principles, with no suggestion of unworthy pride. "Naughtiness" is really bad in the KJV; it means downright wickedness (Jas. 1:21).

Not only "anon," but also "by and by," "presently," and "out of hand" mean "immediately" in the KJV. "Discover" means to uncover, strip, lay bare. "Offend," as translation of the Greek verb σκανδαλίζω, means "cause to sin." In all but two cases, KJV uses "occupy" in the obsolete meanings of "use" and "trade with."

The "outlandish" women who led Solomon astray were simply "foreign" women (Neh. 13:26). A "peculiar people" means a people of God's own, both in Deut. 14:2; 26:18 and in Tit. 2:14; I Pet. 2:9. The word "virtue" means "power" in Luke 6:19; 8:46. A "virtuous woman" (Prov. 31:10) means a "good wife." The word "wealth" was used in the sixteenth century not only for "riches," but also in the sense of "weal, well-being, welfare." Unless this is remembered, Paul's counsel in I Cor. 10:24 looks like encouragement to theft: "Let no man seek his own, but every man another's wealth."

"Possess" in the KJV almost always has the archaic meaning "to take possession of, acquire, gain." "Tithes of all that I possess" (Luke 18:12) is properly "tithes of all that I get"—i.e., the tithe is based upon income. Paul's counsel that each should "know how to possess his vessel" means "know how to take a wife" (I Thess. 4:4).

"Take no thought" means "Do not be anxious" (Matt. 10:19). "Be careful for nothing" means "Have no anxiety about anything" (Phil. 4:6). The word "follow" once meant "imitate," but this meaning is now obsolete, and modern translations forsake "follow" in the eleven cases where the Greek calls for "imitate" or "imitators." A striking example is Heb. 13:7, where the KJV reads: "Remember them which have the rule over you, who have spoken unto you the word of God: whose faith follow, considering the end of their conversation." The RSV reads: "Remember your leaders, those who spoke to you the word of God; consider the outcome of their life, and imitate their faith."

3. Other archaic usage. More pervasive than the appearance of particular words in obsolete meanings, is the archaic usage of prepositions and indefinite pronouns, and the insertion of "manner" and "even."

The most versatile and ambiguous preposition in the KJV is "of." It is used where we would now say "by"—Jesus is said to be baptized *of* John and led *of* the Spirit into the wilderness to be tempted *of* the devil. "Which was spoken of the Lord by the prophet" (Matt. 2:15) seems to mean the prophet's word concerning the Lord; the clause is cleared of ambiguity by the ASV: "which was spoken by the Lord through the prophet," and by the RSV: "what the Lord had spoken by the prophet." "Which I have heard of God" means "which I heard from God" (John 8:40). "The zeal of thine house" is "zeal for thy house" (John 2:17). The expression "I am sick of love" (Song of S. 2:5) now implies surfeit and distaste; the Hebrew is better translated: "I am sick with love." Timothy is urged, not to "be . . . an example of the believers," but to "set the believers an example" (I Tim. 4:12). Other prepositions used in various archaic senses are "after," "against," "at," "by," "to," and "touching." In Matt. 20:31 the conjunction "because" is used in the obsolete sense of "in order that."

Indefinite pronouns, referring to any person, use the masculine form in the Greek, just as we in English often use the pronoun "he" in a general statement which includes both men and women. The KJV overdoes this masculine habit by its use of "no man" and "any man" where the meaning is "no one" or "any one." This practice limits many statements unduly, and results in occasional infelicities. In Matt. 11:27 it is said that "no man knoweth the Son, but the Father." The word "but" is ambiguous here, for it may mean that men do not know the Son but do know the Father. This is absurd. But if the meaning is that no man knows the Son except the Father, the text involves a worse absurdity by implying that the Father is a man. The Greek is perfectly clear, and the revised versions translate it clearly by using the expression "no one." The RSV translates: "No one knows the Son except the Father."

The word "manner" is used 234 times in the KJV, and in more than one third of the cases is unnecessary. There is, in these cases, no corresponding Hebrew or Greek word to call for its use, and the meaning of the text can be conveyed more directly and simply without it. "No manner of work shall be done" (Exod. 12:16) is simply "No work shall be done." "No manner of fat" is "no fat," "no manner of blood" is "no blood," and "any manner of blood" is "any blood" (Lev. 7:23, 26-27). In the gospels "all manner of disease" means "every disease" (Matt. 4:23; 10:1); "all manner of sin" is "every sin" (Matt. 12:31); "all manner of herbs" is "every herb" (Luke 11:42).

The adverb "even" is used 1,032 times in the KJV OT, and in 928 of these cases there is no corresponding word in the Hebrew text. This surprising fact is due in part to the disposition of the translators in 1611 to write "even so" for "so," "even as" for "as," and "even unto" where we should now say "to" or "up to" or "as far as." It is due chiefly, however, to their use of "even" to introduce an additional word or words intended to explain more clearly or fully some preceding word or words. The word "even" was for them a sign of equivalence or identity; it meant that the person or thing or subject referred to in what followed was the same person or thing or subject referred to in what preceded. "The men of the city, even the men of Sodom," means "the men of the city, the men of Sodom"—the same persons are meant by the two phrases (Gen. 19:4). So also "the man, even Lot," means "the man Lot" (19:9). "Jacob set up a pillar . . . , even a pillar of stone" (Gen. 35:14), has no "even" in the Hebrew. In such cases, the word "even" has a function similar to "namely" or "that is." The use of "even" in this colorless sense is now obsolete, and it has become a misleading feature of the KJV. "Even" is now used to indicate an extreme case or something not to be expected. So the reader of Gen. 10:21 is likely to wonder what was the matter with Shem to occasion the statement that "even to him were children born."

4. A selected list of obsolete terms and their meanings. A selected list of obsolete terms and meanings follows, with one reference for each term. Other occurrences can be located in a concordance. No attempt is here made to give a complete list of obsolete terms in the KJV. Their number is well over a thousand, and in a complete list account must be taken of a wide variety of contexts. The RSV replaces these terms with their equivalent in living English. It is not for the sake of novelty that the RSV replaces "alleging" with "proving" in Acts 17:3; it is to restore the meaning of the Greek, the meaning which the word "alleging" had when it was used by the KJV translators, but has now lost.

Term	Reference	Meaning
abhor	I Sam. 2:17	treat with contempt
abide	Acts 20:23	await
abroad	Deut. 24:11	outside
addicted	I Cor. 16:15	devoted
admiration	Rev. 17:6	astonishment
admire	II Thess. 1:10	marvel at
advertise	Ruth 4:4	tell
advise thyself	I Chr. 21:12	decide
affect	Gal. 4:17	make much of
affections	Gal. 5:24	passions
affinity	I Kings 3:1	marriage alliance
after	Ps. 28:4	according to
again	Gen. 24:5	back
allege	Acts 17:3	prove
allow	Rom. 14:22	approve
all to brake	Judg. 9:53	crushed
amazed	Mark 14:33	distressed
amazement	I Pet. 3:6	terror
amiable	Ps. 84:1	lovely
ancients	Isa. 3:14	old men, elders
and	Matt. 24:48	if
angle	Isa. 19:8	hook
anon	Matt. 13:20	immediately
any	Jas. 5:19	any one
any thing	Judg. 11:25	any
any thing at all	Acts 25:8	at all
any ways	Lev. 20:4	at all
apparently	Num. 12:8	clearly
appointed	Judg. 18:11	armed
apprehend	Phil. 3:12	make one's own
armholes	Jer. 38:12	armpits
artillery	I Sam. 20:40	weapons
ask at	Dan. 2:10	ask of
assay	Acts 9:26	attempt
assuaged	Gen. 8:1	subsided
attain to	Acts 27:12	reach
attendance	I Tim. 4:13	attend to
attire	Ezek. 23:15	headdress, turban
audience	I Sam. 25:24	hearing, ears
avoid	I Sam. 18:11	evade
away with	Isa. 1:13	endure
backside	Exod. 26:12	back
bands	Judg. 15:14	bonds
bank	II Sam. 20:15	mound
barbarian	I Cor. 14:11	foreigner
base	I Cor. 1:28	lowly, humble
because	Matt. 20:31	in order that
beside	Josh. 22:19	besides, other than
bestow	Luke 12:17	store
bewray	Matt. 26:73	reveal, betray
blow up	Ps. 81:3	blow
book	Job 31:35	indictment
botch	Deut. 28:27	boils
bottle	Matt. 9:17	wineskin
bowels	Phil. 1:8	affection
breaking up	Exod. 22:2	breaking in
broided	I Tim. 2:9	braided
broken up	Matt. 24:43	broken into
bruit	Jer. 10:22	rumor
bunch	Isa. 30:6	hump
bursting	Isa. 30:14	fragments
but	Amos 3:7	except, without
by	I Cor. 4:4	against
by and by	Matt. 13:21	immediately
by that	Exod. 22:26	before
by the space of	Acts 19:10	for
cabin	Jer. 37:16	cell
captivity	Judg. 5:12	captives
careful	Luke 10:41	anxious
carefully	Phil. 2:28	eagerly
carefulness	I Cor. 7:32	anxiety
careless	Judg. 18:7	free from care
carelessly	Isa. 47:8	securely
carriage	I Sam. 17:22	baggage
cast	Jer. 38:11	castoff
cast	Luke 1:29	consider
cast about	Jer. 41:14	turned about
castaway	I Cor. 9:27	disqualified
certify	Gal. 1:11	make known to
challenge	Exod. 22:9	say
chambering	Rom. 13:13	debauchery
chapman	II Chr. 9:14	trader
chargeable	II Sam. 13:25	burdensome
charged	I Tim. 5:16	burdened
charger	Matt. 14:8	platter
charges	I Cor. 9:7	expense
charity	I Cor. 13:13	love
check	Job 20:3	censure
churl	Isa. 32:5	knave
cieled	Ezek. 41:16	paneled
closet	Matt. 6:6	room
clothed upon	II Cor. 5:4	further clothed
clouted	Josh. 9:5	patched
clouts	Jer. 38:11	rags
coasts	Acts 19:1	country
come at	Luke 8:19	reach
comely	Eccl. 5:18	fitting
comfortably	Isa. 40:2	tenderly
comfortless	John 14:18	desolate
commune	Luke 6:11	discuss
communicate	Gal. 6:6	share
communications	I Cor. 15:33	company
compact	Ps. 122:3	bound firmly
compacted	Eph. 4:16	knit together
compass	Josh. 6:3	march around
compass, fetch a	Acts 28:13	make a circuit
compel	I Sam. 28:23	urge
comprehend	John 1:5	overcome
concupiscence	I Thess. 4:5	lust
condescend	Rom. 12:16	associate
confection	Exod. 30:35	incense blended

confectionaries	I Sam. 8:13	perfumers
confidences	Jer. 2:37	those in whom you trust
confound	I Cor. 1:27	shame
confusion	Ps. 44:15	disgrace
conscience	Heb. 10:2	consciousness
consist	Col. 1:17	hold together
consort with	Acts 17:4	join
constant	I Chr. 28:7	resolute
constantly	Acts 12:15	confidently
contain	I Cor. 7:9	exercise self-control
convenient	Prov. 30:8	needful
not convenient	Rom. 1:28	improper
were conversant	I Sam. 25:15	went
conversation	Heb. 13:7	life, behavior
convert	Isa. 6:10	turn
convince	John 8:46	convict
corn	Ps. 65:13	grain
corn of wheat	John 12:24	grain of wheat
corrupt	Luke 12:33	destroy
corruptible	I Cor. 9:25	perishable
cousin	Luke 1:36	kinswoman
covet	I Cor. 12:31	earnestly desire
creature	Rom. 8:19	creation
cumber	Luke 13:7	use up
cumbered	Luke 10:40	distracted
cumbrance	Deut. 1:12	weight
cunning	Gen. 25:27	skilful
cunning	I Kings 7:14	skill
curious	Acts 19:19	magical
curiously	Ps. 139:15	intricately
daily	Ps. 56:1	all day long
damnable	II Pet. 2:1	destructive
damnation	I Cor. 11:29	judgment
damned	Rom. 14:23	condemned
in danger of	Mark 3:29	guilty
darling	Ps. 22:20	life
daysman	Job 9:33	umpire
dayspring	Job 38:12	dawn
deal to	Isa. 58:7	share with
dearth	Acts 7:11	famine
debate	Rom. 1:29	strife
declare	Matt. 13:36	explain
decline	Ps. 44:18	depart
degree	I Tim. 3:13	standing
degrees	II Kings 20:9	steps
delectable	Isa. 44:9	that they delight in
delicacies	Rev. 18:3	wantonness
delicately	I Sam. 15:32	cheerfully
delicates	Jer. 51:34	delicacies
deliciously	Rev. 18:9	wantonly
demand	Luke 17:20	ask
denounce	Deut. 30:18	declare
descry	Judg. 1:23	spy out
desire	II Chr. 21:20	regret
despite	Ezek. 25:6	malice
despitefully use	Luke 6:28	abuse
do despite unto	Heb. 10:29	outrage
device	Jer. 51:11	purpose
devotions	Acts 17:23	objects of worship
diet	Jer. 52:34	allowance
dig up	Prov. 16:27	plot
disallow	I Pet. 2:4	reject

disannul	Isa. 14:27	annul
discomfit	Judg. 4:15	rout
discover	Mic. 1:6	uncover
disorderly	II Thess. 3:6	in idleness
dispensation	Eph. 3:2	stewardship
by disposition of	Acts 7:53	as delivered by
dispute	Mark 9:33	discuss
dissolve doubts	Dan. 5:12	solve problems
divers	Mark 1:34	various
doctor	Luke 2:46	teacher
doctrine	Matt. 7:28	teaching
done away	Num. 27:4	taken away
dote	Jer. 50:36	become fools
doubt	Acts 10:17	be perplexed
doubtful mind	Luke 12:29	anxious mind
doubting nothing	Acts 10:20	without hesitation
draught	Matt. 15:17	privy
draught house	II Kings 10:27	latrine
duke	Gen. 36:15	chief
dure	Matt. 13:21	endure
ear	I Sam. 8:12	plow
eared	Deut. 21:4	plowed
earing	Gen. 45:6	plowing
earnest	Eph. 1:14	guarantee
edification	I Cor. 14:3	upbuilding
edify	Eph. 4:16	upbuild
either	Lev. 10:1	each
either	Luke 6:42	or
eminent	Ezek. 16:24	lofty
emulation	Gal. 5:20	jealousy
enable	I Tim. 1:12	give strength
end	Jer. 31:17	future
enlargement	Esth. 4:14	relief
ensue	I Pet. 3:11	pursue
entreat	Matt. 22:6	treat
equal	Ezek. 18:25	just
equal	Lam. 2:13	liken
espoused	Matt. 1:18	betrothed
estate	Acts 22:5	council
estate	Col. 4:8	state, condition
every	II Sam. 21:20	each
evidence	Jer. 32:10	deed
evidently	Acts 10:3	clearly
example	Heb. 8:5	copy
exceed	Job 36:9	behave arrogantly
exchanger	Matt. 25:27	banker
exercise	I Tim. 4:7	train
exercise myself	Acts 24:16	take pains
expect	Heb. 10:13	wait
expectation	Ps. 62:5	hope
fable	I Tim. 1:4	myth
faint	II Cor. 4:16	lose heart
fair	Zech. 3:5	clean
fame	Gen. 45:16	report
familiars	Jer. 20:10	familiar friends
fan	Jer. 4:11	winnow
fan	Matt. 3:12	winnowing fork
fanners	Jer. 51:2	winnowers
fashion	II Kings 16:10	model
fast	Ruth 2:8	close
fat	Joel 2:24	vat
feebleminded	I Thess. 5:14	faint-hearted
fenced	Num. 32:17	fortified
fine	Job 28:1	refine
fining pot	Prov. 17:3	crucible

flagons	Song of S. 2:5	raisins
flood	Josh. 24:3	river
floor	Matt. 3:12	threshing floor
flux	Acts 28:8	dysentery
follow	Heb. 13:7	imitate
footmen	Jer. 12:5	men on foot
for all	John 21:11	although
for because	Gen. 22:16	because
forecast	Dan. 11:24	devise
forepart	Acts 27:41	bow
foreship	Acts 27:30	bow
foretell	II Cor. 13:2	warn
for that	I Tim. 1:12	because
for to	Luke 4:16	to
forward	Gal. 2:10	eager
forwardness	II Cor. 9:2	readiness
fowl	Gen. 1:20	birds
fray	Deut. 28:26	frighten
freely	Matt. 10:8	without pay
froward	Deut. 32:20	perverse
furniture	Gen. 31:34	saddle
gainsay	Luke 21:15	contradict
gender	Gal. 4:24	bear children
generation	Matt. 3:7	brood
glass	I Cor. 13:12	mirror
go about	John 7:19	seek
go aside	Num. 5:12	go astray
go beyond	I Thess. 4:6	transgress
go to	Gen. 11:3	come
governor	Jas. 3:4	pilot
grace	Ruth 2:2	favor
grief	Job 6:2	vexation
grieve	Gen. 49:23	attack
grudge	Jas. 5:9	grumble
be guilty of	Matt. 26:66	deserve
hale	Luke 12:58	drag
halt	Matt. 18:8	lame
halt	I Kings 18:21	go limping
hardly	Matt. 19:23	it is hard for
hardness	II Tim. 2:3	suffering
harness	I Kings 20:11	armor
headstone	Zech. 4:7	top stone
heady	II Tim. 3:4	reckless
on heaps	Ps. 79:1	in ruins
heavily	Ps. 35:14	in mourning
heaviness	Prov. 12:25	anxiety
heavy	I Kings 20:43	resentful
herb	Gen. 1:29	plant
high	Prov. 21:4	haughty
highminded	Rom. 11:20	proud
his	I Cor. 15:38	its
hitherto	Job 38:11	thus far
hold	I Sam. 22:4	stronghold
hold peace at	Num. 30:11	say nothing to
honest	Phil. 4:8	honorable
honestly	Rom. 13:13	becomingly
honourable	I Sam. 9:6	held in honor
hough	Josh. 11:6	hamstring
howbeit	II Sam. 12:14	nevertheless
how that	Matt. 16:12	that
husbandman	II Tim. 2:6	farmer
husbandry	I Cor. 3:9	field
if so be	Rom. 8:9	if
illuminated	Heb. 10:32	enlightened
imagination	Deut. 29:19	stubbornness
imagine	Gen. 11:6	propose

impart	Luke 3:11	share
implead	Acts 19:38	accuse
impotent	Acts 14:8	crippled
incontinent	II Tim. 3:3	profligate
inn	Gen. 42:27	lodging place
inquisition	Esth. 2:23	investigation
instant	Luke 23:23	urgent
instantly	Luke 7:4	earnestly
have intelligence with	Dan. 11:30	give heed to
be intreated	I Chr. 5:20	grant an entreaty
inward	Job 19:19	intimate
inwards	Exod. 29:13	entrails
jangling	I Tim. 1:6	vain discussion
judge	Luke 19:22	condemn
kerchief	Ezek. 13:18	veil
latchet	Mark 1:7	thong
laugh on	Job 29:24	smile on
lay at	Job 41:26	reach
lay away	Ezek. 26:16	remove
lay from	Jonah 3:6	remove
lay out	II Kings 12:11	pay out
leasing	Ps. 5:6	lies
left	Acts 21:32	stopped
let	Isa. 43:13	hinder
lewd	Acts 17:5	wicked
lewdness	Acts 18:14	crime
light	Judg. 9:4	reckless
light	I Kings 7:4	window
light bread	Num. 21:5	worthless food
lightly	Gen. 26:10	easily
lightness	Jer. 23:32	recklessness
liketh him	Deut. 23:16	pleases him
in good liking	Job 39:4	strong
worse liking	Dan. 1:10	in poorer condition
limit	Heb. 4:7	set
list	John 3:8	choose, will
lively	Acts 7:38	living
lover	Ps. 38:11	friend
lucre	I Tim. 3:3	gain
lunatick	Matt. 4:24	epileptic
lust after	Deut. 12:15	desire
mad	Eccl. 7:7	foolish
make	Judg. 18:3	do
make for	Ezek. 17:17	help
with the manner	Num. 5:13	in the act
man of war	Luke 23:11	soldier
mansion	John 14:2	room
mar	I Sam. 6:5	ravage
master	Matt. 10:24	teacher
maul	Prov. 25:18	war club
mean	Prov. 22:29	obscure
meat	Gen. 1:29	food
meat offering	Lev. 2:1	cereal offering
meet	Gen. 2:18	fit
memorial	Ps. 9:6	memory
merchantman	I Kings 10:15	trader
me thinketh	II Sam. 18:27	I think
minding	Acts 20:13	intending
minister	Luke 4:20	attendant
minister	II Cor. 9:10	to supply
mock	Jer. 38:19	abuse
moderation	Phil. 4:5	forbearance
the more part	Acts 27:12	the majority
mortify	Rom. 8:13	put to death

motions	Rom. 7:5	passions
munition	Isa. 29:7	stronghold
murrain	Exod. 9:3	plague
muse	Luke 3:15	question
naughtiness	Jas. 1:21	wickedness
naughty	Jer. 24:2	bad
neesing	Job 41:8	sneezing
nephew	Judg. 12:14	grandson
noisome	Ps. 91:3	deadly
set at nought	Prov. 1:25	ignore
nourish	Gen. 45:11	provide for
nursing father	Num. 11:12	nurse
nurture	Eph. 6:4	discipline
observe	Mark 6:20	keep safe
occupier	Ezek. 27:27	dealer
occupy	Judg. 16:11	use
occupy	Luke 19:13	trade
occurrent	I Kings 5:4	misfortune
odd	Num. 3:48	excess
offence	Gal. 5:11	stumbling block
offend	Matt. 18:8	cause to sin
often	I Tim. 5:23	frequent
once	Jer. 13:27	ever
open	Acts 17:3	explain
ordain	Ps. 8:3	establish
order	I Kings 20:14	begin
or ever	Prov. 8:23	before
outgoings	Josh. 17:18	farthest borders
outlandish	Neh. 13:26	foreign
out of hand	Num. 11:15	immediately
overcharged	Luke 21:34	weighed down
overlive	Josh. 24:31	outlive
overpass	Jer. 5:28	know no bounds
overrun	II Sam. 18:23	outrun
pap	Luke 11:27	breast
part	Acts 2:45	distribute
in particular	I Cor. 12:27	individually
particularly	Acts 21:19	one by one
passage	Judg. 12:6	ford
passengers	Prov. 9:15	those who pass by
pastor	Jer. 23:1	shepherd
pattern	Heb. 9:23	copy
a peculiar people	I Pet. 2:9	God's own people
peradventure	Gen. 24:5	perhaps
persecute	Ps. 71:11	pursue
persuade	I Kings 22:20	entice
persuaded	Rom. 8:38	sure
persuading	Acts 28:23	trying to convince
pillow	Ezek. 13:18	magic band
pitiful	Jas. 5:11	compassionate
plead	Judg. 6:31	contend
plagued	Ps. 73:5	stricken
plain	Gen. 25:27	quiet
possess	Deut. 1:8	take possession of
post	II Chr. 30:6	courier
power	II Chr. 32:9	forces
have power with	Gen. 32:28	have striven with
prefer	Esth. 2:9	advance
presently	Matt. 21:19	immediately
pressfat	Hag. 2:16	winevat
prevent	I Thess. 4:15	precede
prey	Josh. 8:2	booty
prick	Acts 26:14	goad
printed	Job 19:23	inscribed
privily	Acts 16:37	secretly
privy to	Acts 5:2	with knowledge of

profane	Ezek. 22:26	common, ordinary
profess	Matt. 7:23	declare
prolong	Ezek. 12:25	delay
proper	Heb. 11:23	beautiful
prove	I Thess. 5:21	test
provide	Heb. 11:40	foresee
provoke	II Cor. 9:2	stir up
publican	Mark 2:15	tax collector
publish	Deut. 32:3	proclaim
pulse	Dan. 1:12	vegetables
purchase	I Tim. 3:13	gain, obtain
purge	John 15:2	prune
purtenance	Exod. 12:9	inner parts
put down	II Chr. 36:3	depose
put to	Ezra 6:12	put forth
quarrel	Mark 6:19	grudge
question	Mark 9:16	discuss
quick	Num. 16:30	alive
quicken	Eph. 2:1	make alive
reap down	Jas. 5:4	mow
rear up	Exod. 26:30	erect
reason	Acts 6:2	right
reasoning	Luke 9:46	argument
record	Phil. 1:8	witness
recover	II Kings 5:7	cure
refrain	Job 7:11	restrain
refuse	Ps. 118:22	reject
rehearse	I Sam. 17:31	repeat
reins	Jer. 12:2	heart
remembrance	Job 13:12	maxim
remove	Ps. 46:2	change
repent himself	Ps. 135:14	have compassion
replenish	Gen. 1:28	fill
report	Acts 6:3	repute
reprobate	Jer. 6:30	refuse
require	Ezra 8:22	ask
resemble	Luke 13:18	compare
residue	Zech. 8:11	remnant
respect persons	Deut. 1:17	be partial
rid	Gen. 37:22	rescue
ringstraked	Gen. 30:35	striped
riot	I Pet. 4:4	profligacy
rioting	Rom. 13:13	reveling
riotous	Prov. 23:20	gluttonous
road	I Sam. 27:10	raid
room	Luke 14:7	place
safeguard	I Sam. 22:23	safekeeping
scall	Lev. 13:30	itch
scrip	Matt. 10:10	bag
search	Ezek. 34:11	search for
secure	Judg. 8:11	unsuspecting
seethe	Exod. 16:23	boil
sentence	Acts 15:19	judgment
set by	I Sam. 18:30	esteemed
settle	Ezek. 43:14	ledge
sever	Exod. 9:4	make a distinction
several	II Kings 15:5	separate
severally	I Cor. 12:11	individually
shambles	I Cor. 10:25	meat market
shamefacedness	I Tim. 2:9	modesty
simple	Rom. 16:19	guileless
simplicity	Rom. 12:8	liberality
sincere	I Pet. 2:2	pure
can skill	I Kings 5:6	know how
could skill of	II Chr. 34:12	were skilful with

sleight	Eph. 4:14	cunning
slime	Gen. 11:3	bitumen
so as	Rev. 8:12	so that
sober	I Tim. 3:2	sensible
sod	Gen. 25:29	boiled
sodden	Exod. 12:9	boiled
softly	Isa. 8:6	gently
some	Rom. 5:7	one
sometime	Col. 3:7	once
sometimes	Eph. 2:13	once
sop	John 13:26	morsel
sore	Gen. 19:9	hard
sore	Ps. 38:11	plague
sorer	Heb. 10:29	worse
so that	I Kings 8:25	if only
sottish	Jer. 4:22	stupid
space	Acts 5:34	while
spare	Job 30:10	hesitate
special	Acts 19:11	extraordinary
specially	Acts 25:26	especially
sped	Judg. 5:30	succeeded
speed	Gen. 24:12	success
spend up	Prov. 21:20	devour
spitefully	Matt. 22:6	shamefully
spoil	Gen. 34:27	plunder
spoil	Col. 2:8	make a prey of
stagger	Rom. 4:20	waver
stand to	Deut. 25:8	persist
stand to	II Kings 23:3	join in
stand upon	II Sam. 1:9	stand beside
stay	Job 37:4	restrain
still	Ps. 84:4	ever
stoutness	Isa. 9:9	arrogance
strain at	Matt. 23:24	strain out
strait	Job 36:16	distress
strait	Matt. 7:13	narrow
straitly	Gen. 43:7	carefully
straitness	Jer. 19:9	distress
strake	Gen. 30:37	streak
strength	Ezek. 30:15	stronghold
strike his hand	II Kings 5:11	wave his hand
strike hands	Prov. 22:26	give pledges
study	II Tim. 2:15	do your best
stuff	I Sam. 30:24	baggage
substance	Deut. 11:6	living thing
succour	II Sam. 8:5	help
succourer	Rom. 16:2	helper
such like	Mark 7:13	such
suddenly	I Tim. 5:22	hastily
suffer	Matt. 19:14	let
to supple	Ezek. 16:4	to cleanse
surely	Prov. 10:9	securely
surfeiting	Luke 21:34	dissipation
swellings	II Cor. 12:20	conceit
taber upon	Nah. 2:7	beat
table	Luke 1:63	tablet
tablet	Exod. 35:22	armlet
take thought	Matt. 6:25	be anxious
take wrong	I Cor. 6:7	suffer wrong
tale	I Sam. 18:27	number
target	I Sam. 17:6	javelin
tell	Gen. 15:5	number
temperance	Acts 24:25	self-control
tempered	Exod. 29:2	mixed
tempt	Gen. 22:1	test
temptation	Deut. 4:34	trial
thankworthy	I Pet. 2:19	approved
tire	II Kings 9:30	adorn
tire	Ezek. 24:17	turban
translate	II Sam. 3:10	transfer
translation	Heb. 11:5	was taken
true	Gen. 42:11	honest
turtle	Song of S. 2:12	turtledove
tutor	Gal. 4:2	guardian
twain	I Sam. 18:21	a second time
at unawares	Num. 35:11	without intent
uncomely	I Cor. 7:36	not properly
uncorruptness	Tit. 2:7	integrity
unction	I John 2:20	anointing
unjust	Luke 16:8	dishonest
unspeakable	II Cor. 9:15	inexpressible
unto	Gen. 3:21	for
unto	Num. 35:25	until
untoward	Acts 2:40	crooked
usury	Matt. 25:27	interest
vagabond	Gen. 4:12	wanderer
vain	Judg. 9:4	worthless
vanity	Rom. 8:20	futility
venison	Gen. 25:28	game
vex	Exod. 22:21	wrong
vile	Phil. 3:21	lowly
virtue	Mark 5:30	power
vocation	Eph. 4:1	calling
void place	I Kings 22:10	threshing floor
volume	Ps. 40:7	roll
wait upon	Ps. 123:2	look to
want	II Cor. 11:9	be in want
to the mercy seatward	Exod. 37:9	toward the mercy seat
to us-ward	Ps. 40:5	toward us
to thee-ward	I Sam. 19:4	to you
to you-ward	II Cor. 1:12	toward you
waster	Isa. 54:16	ravager
wasting	Isa. 59:7	desolation
wax	Luke 13:19	become
wealth	I Cor. 10:24	good
wealthy	Jer. 49:31	at ease
went for	I Sam. 17:12	was
when as	Matt. 1:18	when
whether	Matt. 21:31	which
which	Matt. 6:9	who
whiles	Matt. 5:25	while
wholesome	Prov. 15:4	gentle
willing	Heb. 13:18	desiring
win	Phil. 3:8	gain
winefat	Isa. 63:2	wine press
wink at	Acts 17:30	overlook
without	II Cor. 10:13	beyond
witty inventions	Prov. 8:12	discretion
woe worth	Ezek. 30:2	alas for
work	Rom. 5:3	produce
have worship	Luke 14:10	be honored
worthy	Rom. 1:32	deserve
would God	II Kings 5:3	would that
would to God	Josh. 7:7	would that
wrest	Deut. 16:19	pervert

Bibliography. T. L. O. Davies, *Bible English* (1875). W. A. Wright, *The Bible Word-Book* (2nd ed., 1884), deals with 2,316 archaic or obsolete terms in the KJV and the Book of Common Prayer, and contains a bibliography of six books on Bible words which were published from 1832 to 1864. L. A. Weigle, *Bible Words That Have Changed in Meaning* (1955), has a selected list of 857 terms, with references. L. A. Weigle, *The Living Word* (1956), was published in Edinburgh with the title *Bible Words in Living Language* (1957). R. Bridges and L. A. Weigle, *The Bible Word Book* (1960). The *Oxford English Dictionary* is an indispensable tool for the study of archaic and obsolete terms. L. A. WEIGLE

OCCUPATIONS. The word "occupation" is rare in the English versions. Joseph's brothers are coached to answer Pharaoh's inquiry about their occupation and so answer that they are "keepers of cattle" (Gen. 46:34) or "shepherds" (Gen. 47:3). The sailors ask Jonah a similar question, but he does not answer (Jonah 1:8). In Corinth, Paul stayed with those who had the same occupation (RSV "trades")—i.e., tentmakers (Acts 18:3). The guild in Ephesus consisted of those who had the same occupation—i.e., silversmiths (Acts 19:25).

Usually the English versions distinguish skilled craftsmen (*see* CRAFTS) from other workers, but, as in the NT examples above, this is not completely correct. If occupations are to be classified, the crafts engaged in by skilled craftsmen, usually freeborn laborers, should be noted first.

The occupations engaged in around the household were many and varied. Some of these were crafts, since the members of a household often produced their own necessities. Household occupations included: baking, cooking, dressmaking and all that goes with it, ropemaking, tentmaking, needlework, basketry, potterymaking, husbandry, winemaking, herding cattle, shepherding sheep, tending goats and swine, butchering, etc.

The occupations that render personal services were performed by both free and slave labor. These included: apothecary, barber, watchman, bath attendant, physician, midwife, innkeeper, nurse, money-changer, maid, servant, harlot.

The political organization and the institution of royalty afforded additional occupational opportunities, such as king, prince, ambassador, interpreter, steward, duke, butler, chamberlain, chancellor, counselor, cupbearer, deputy, eunuch, doorkeeper, elder, herald, wardrobe keeper, governor, procurator, centurion, overseer, tax collector, recorder, secretary, scribe, magistrate, judge, lawyer, minstrel, officer, quartermaster, soldier, archer, charioteer, armor-bearer, diviner, astrologer, exorcist, priest, executioner, etc. Among the religious professions were priest, prophet, sacred prostitute, diviner.

Other, miscellaneous occupations are as follows: brewer, musician, dancer, mourner, jeweler, sailor, schoolmaster, aqueduct builder, hydraulic engineer, merchant, trader, embalmer, well digger, painter, camel driver, beggar, criminal of any type, fowler, fisherman, farmer, laborer, quarryman, mason, miner, refiner.

Women engaged in many of the occupations listed above, such as basketmaking, weaving, potterymaking, and the domestic tasks. They were also bath attendants, midwives, nurses, harlots, maids, servants, judges, merchants, mourners, musicians, dancers.

As the word "job" is sometimes used in a derogatory sense when contrasted to "profession" or "vocation," so it is possible that "trade" is so used

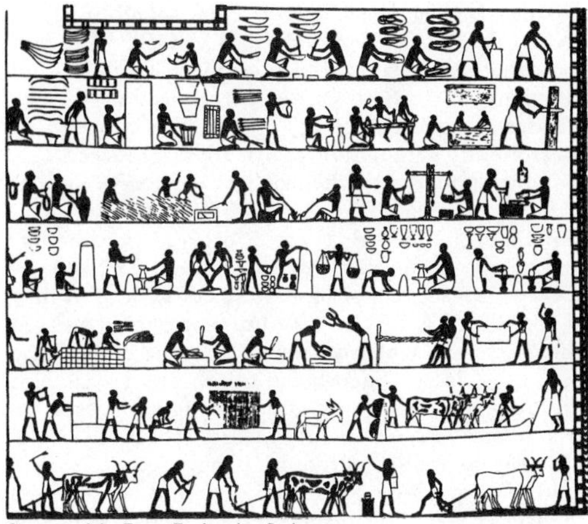

Courtesy of the Egypt Exploration Society

3. Scene from the Egyptian tomb of Amen-em-het at Beni-hasan, which describes the various trades, arts, and agricultural labors of the Middle Kingdom; Twelfth Dynasty, Sen-Usert I (1971-1928 B.C.)

when Jeremiah comments on prophets and priests who "ply their trade" (Jer. 14:18). In this sense the cleansing of the temple protects it from becoming a "house of trade" (John 2:16).

Fig. OCC 3. C. U. WOLF

OCHIEL. Alternate name of JEIEL.

OCHRAN ŏk′rən [עָכְרָן, trouble(?)]; KJV OCRAN. The father of Pagiel, who was the leader of Asher in the wilderness (Num. 1:13; 2:27; 7:72, 77; 10:26).

Bibliography. M. Noth, *Die israelitischen Personennamen* (1928), p. 253. R. F. JOHNSON

OCIDELUS ŏs′ə dē′ləs. KJV form of GEDALIAH 5.

OCINA ō sī′nə [Ὀκεινά] (Jth. 2:28). A coastal place S of Tyre. It has been variously identified—e.g., with Sandalium (Iskanderun)—with localities near the Phoenician-Palestinian border. Though no definite proposition appears justifiable, the name recalls ACCO, which would geographically fit the location. P. WINTER

OCRAN. KJV form of OCHRAN.

ODED ō′dĭd [עוֹדֵד, timekeeper(?) *or* restorer]. **1.** The father of Azariah, prophet of Asa's time (II Chr. 15:1).

2. A prophet who protested Pekah's enslavement of Judahites at the time of Ahaz (II Chr. 28:8-15).

ODOLLAM ō dŏl′əm. A form of ADULLAM.

ODOMERA ŏd′ə mĭr′ə [ὀδομηρά, ὀδοαρρής] (I Macc. 9:66); KJV ODONARKES ŏd′ə när′kēz. Chief of a Bedouin clan, struck down by Jonathan the Maccabee in a raid.

ODOR [רֵיחַ, scent, fragrance, *properly* breath, *usually in the construct state as part of the technical term* רֵיחַ נִיחֹחַ, soothing odor (to God), pleasing odor (of ascending sacrifices); ὀσμή, smell, savor]; RSV usually PLEASING ODOR; KJV SWEET SAVOR. The term "pleasing odor" is used frequently in Leviticus and Numbers and often stands in apposition to such phrases as "burnt offering" and "offering by fire"; it is essentially synonymous with these phrases in the OT. Burnt offerings, whether the sacrifices of animals (Gen. 8:21; Exod. 29:15-25; Lev. 1:3-9; etc.), of vegetables and cereals (Lev. 2; 6:19-23), of libations and drink offerings (Exod. 29:41; Lev. 23:13; Num. 15:1-10, 22-26; 29), or of mixtures of various of these (Exod. 29:22-25), were a prominent part of the sacrificial system, which was central in the cultic life of post-exilic Israel. Such burnt offerings were an integral part of the morning and evening services in the temple and of the appointed feasts (Num. 28–29; cf. Lev. 23), as well as of thanksgiving (Gen. 8:21), memorial (Lev. 2:1 ff), and ordination and consecration services (Exod. 29). Burnt offerings were specified as acceptable sin, guilt, and trespass offerings (Lev. 4–6; 7:1-10), and peace offerings (Lev. 3; 7:11-36).

The essentially synonymous liturgical meaning of the terms "burnt offerings," "offerings by fire," and "pleasant odors" is made clear in such verses as Num. 28:1-2: "The Lord said to Moses, 'Command the people of Israel, and say to them, "My offering, my food for my offerings by fire, my pleasing odor, you shall take heed to offer to me in its due season." ' " Such odors were popularly understood as sustenance for deity and as being pleasing to him. Such pleasing odors would seem often to have been influential in gaining forgiveness and favor for the worshiper who offered the sacrifices through the priestly mediator. A schedule of burnt offerings which were appropriate to the appointed feasts and to the circumstances of the individual worshiper was set forth as a part of the revelation to Moses (Lev. 1–7; 23; Num. 28–29). Generally, in the OT, Israel's loyalty to the covenantal relationship was thought to be manifested in her response to the obligation of offering sacrifices. In immediate pre-exilic times Ezekiel forewarned his people of their impending downfall; among their chief sins he noted the apostasy involved in a careless offering of "pleasing odor to all their idols" (6:13; cf. 16:19). In postexilic Judaism it was a commonplace observation that Israel's future security depended upon her compliance with these cultic injunctions (e.g., Neh. 10:28-39—H 10:20-40).

H. F. BECK

OFFERING. *See* SACRIFICE AND OFFERINGS.

***OFFERING FOR THE SAINTS.** An offering which Paul collected for the poor of the Jerusalem church and took to that city toward the end of his career. Such voluntary help to those in need, especially to widows and orphans, was strongly emphasized in the OT and in first-century Judaism. It was particularly needed by a large proportion of the Jerusalem Christians in the apostolic age; Jerusalem was never an independent economic unit, Palestine at that time was disturbed by unrest and revolutionary tendencies, the Jerusalem church had many Galilean Christians and dependent widows to support, and persecution and famine increased the severity of the problem. The surrender of possessions by individual Christians (Acts 4:37) gave only temporary help. The church at Antioch in Syria sent a gift to aid when famine struck (11:27-30). Later, at the COUNCIL OF JERUSALEM, Paul agreed—though Acts says nothing of this—to "remember the poor" at Jerusalem with gifts from the Gentile churches (Gal. 2:10). For Paul such aid was not only a work of mercy but also a means by which the Jewish and Gentile Christians could be brought closer in sympathy and friendship. It is clear from Rom. 15:25-31; I Cor. 16:1-4; II Cor. 8–9 that Paul did not feel free to turn to work in the West until he had gathered a liberal collection in his Gentile churches and had taken it to Jerusalem, even though he knew that in going there he was risking his life. The seven men named in Acts 20:4 went with him to deliver the collection; Luke does not mention this fact, and in Acts 24:17 seems to refer to the gifts as only personal contributions by Paul; but the letters of Paul show that Paul and his companions brought the gifts of the Gentile churches to relieve the economic need of the Jerusalem Christians.

F. V. FILSON

OFFICER. A servant or minister of the king, the army, or the temple. The Hebrew and Greek words translated by "officer" are not narrowly defined. It is difficult to assign specific functions for each term except perhaps the EUNUCH and the JUDGE. A SCRIBE or secretary may be an officer of the king. The leaders in synagogue and temple are officers. The military is controlled by its officers. Many subordinates to the king in palace, court, and harem are called officers—e.g., prince, steward, chamberlain, deputy, chancellor, overseer.

1. In the OT. The שטרים were subordinate officers in Israel. They may have originally been scribes or secretaries (Akkadian *šaṭâru,* "write"). They were taskmasters and overseers in Egypt (Exod. 5:6, 14). They were related to the elders in the judicial organization (Num. 11:16; Deut. 16:18; I Chr. 23:4; II Chr. 19:8; *cf.* Josephus in § 2 *below*). They conveyed orders and were adjutants in time of war (Deut. 20:5; Josh. 1:10; 3:2). They were very influential in the assembly of Israel (Deut. 29:10; 31:28; I Chr. 26:29; etc.). How they attained their position is unknown.

The שרים were most frequently princes. They were very close to the palace (Ezra 7:28). They served as leaders in the army (II Chr. 32:3; Neh. 2:9; etc.).

The שלשים were originally the leaders of a chariot group, perhaps the third man in the chariot (Exod. 14:7; 15:4). This later was broadened to include the officers of the guard (II Kings 10:25).

The concept of head man or chief is seen in both ראש and רב (Esth. 1:8; Jer. 41:1; Ezek. 23:15). In Esther it is collectively used for all the officials of the king.

The סרים was the eunuch. Originally a castrated harem attendant, he later became a confidant of the king. In some instances the term has no biological connotations (II Kings 24:12, 15).

The נצב was the appointed deputy. The officials in Edom are so called (I Kings 22:47). In Israel they seem to have been appointed by the king (I Kings 4:5; 5:16; 9:23). The term is also used collectively for all of Solomon's officers (II Chr. 8:10).

Forms of the root פקד refer to those appointed as overseers. Captains and military officers are noted in Num. 31:14; II Kings 11:15; 25:19; II Chr. 23:14; etc. In general civil government they were stationed in one area or province by the king to oversee all work (Judg. 9:28; Isa. 60:17). At times they may be deputized for special duty (Esth. 2:3). From among the priests and Levites temple officials (II Chr. 24: 11; 31:13; 35:8; Jer. 20:1; 29:26) were appointed. They were watchmen or guards in the temple (II Kings 11:18).

2. In the NT. Πράκτωρ occurs in Luke 12:58, while the parallel passage Matt. 5:25 uses the more common Greek word ὑπηρέτης, "guard of the prison." The original meaning, "under oarsman," has been lost except as a homiletic device. John uses the latter term to designate the deputies or bailiffs of the chief priests and Sanhedrin sent against Jesus (John 7:32, 45-46). They find Jesus in the garden of Gesthemane (John 18:3, 18, 22), but Jesus says that although he has such officers, they will not fight, since his kingdom is not of this world (vs. 36). They accuse Jesus in court (John 19:6). They are to be distinguished from the Roman soldiers (John 18:12). The apostles are also sought out by these representatives of the council (Acts 5:22, 26).

Paul considers himself steward or servant of God (I Cor. 4:1).

Josephus uses this Greek term for the judges appointed by Moses. A similar title was given to the clerks in Jewish courts (Jos. Antiq. IV.viii.14). In Mark 6:21, Herod includes his officers or captains (χιλίαρχος) as guests at his banquet. C. U. Wolf

OFFSET [מגרעה, *lit.,* diminished place]; KJV NARROWED REST. A ledge formed on a wall by a decrease in its width. The beams of the second and third stories of the side chambers in Solomon's temple rested on offsets, so that they would not penetrate the wall of the sacred structure (I Kings 6:6). According to the LXX, a similar arrangement pertained in Ezekiel's ideal temple, although the MT of the description is corrupt (Ezek. 41:6-7).

See also Temple, Jerusalem. L. E. Toombs

OG ŏg [עוג, עג]. Giant king of the land of Bashan, N of the River Jabbok, whose territory was occupied by the tribe of Manasseh (Num. 21:33; 32:33; Deut. 1:4; 3:1, 3-4, 10-11, 13; 4:47; 29:7—H 29:6; 31:4; Josh. 2:10; 9:10; 12:4; 13:12, 30-31; I Kings 4:19; Neh. 9:22; Pss. 135:11; 136:20).

Og is remembered in Israelite tradition as a legendary figure, a member of the race of giants, whose immense iron bedstead was on exhibition in Rabbath-ammon long after his death (Deut. 3:11). The bedstead was probably a dolmen of basalt blocks, a monument of the megalithic culture which gave rise to the traditions about giants in Canaan. Yet it is unlikely that information about the kingdom of Og contains no historical foundation, for it is accorded considerable attention in Deuteronomic material. The settled character of the region is stressed with its numerous fortified cities and Og's two capitals at Edrei and Ashtaroth (Josh. 12:4). During the fourteenth century B.C. city-states controlled this region, but it is possible that at some time in the next two centuries a King Og of Ashtaroth ruled the land of Bashan. The settlement of Manasseh in the region is said to follow upon a massive defeat of Og (Num. 21:35; 32:33 ff), but Israelite control of Bashan was always tenuous and disputed from time to time by the Aramean state of Damascus.

Bibliography. M. Noth, "Beiträge zur Geschichte des Ostjordanlandes," *Beiträge zur biblischen Landes- und Altertumskunde,* 68 (1951), 10-18. R. F. Johnson

OHAD ō'hăd [אהד; *cf.* אחוד] (Gen. 46:10; Exod. 6:15). Son of Simeon. The name is lacking in the parallel lists Num. 26:12-14; I Chr. 4:24-25.

OHEL ō'hĕl [אהל, tent, *possibly* family (of God), *or* (God is) shelter; *see bibliography*] (I Chr. 3:20). A descendant of King David; perhaps a son of Meshullam, son of Zerubbabel.

Bibliography. W. F. Albright, "The Date and Personality of the Chronicler," *JBL,* XL (1921), p. 110; M. Noth, *Die israelitischen Personennamen* (1928), pp. 158-59. B. T. Dahlberg

OHOLAH ō hō'lə [אהלה, she who has a tent]; KJV AHOLAH ə—. A name which refers to Samaria (Ezek. 23:4-5, 36, 44). Doubtless the expression has some tenuous connection with the history of the tabernacle, which was the tent of meeting in the early history of the Hebrew people.

Oholah and Oholibah are described as sisters of one mother, both of whom had scarlet careers in their dealings with neighboring lands. Oholah, who is identified with Samaria, was the elder sister (Ezek. 23:4), who played the harlot with the Assyrians, wantonly adopting both their habits and dress—a tendency which dated back to her youthful days in Egypt. As punishment Yahweh delivered this woman into the hands of the Assyrians, among whom she became a byword. This allegory was the way by which Ezekiel described the sordid history of Samaria and Jerusalem, both of whom lacked loyalty to God. The height of Assyrian syncretism was reached in the days of Manasseh after the death of Hezekiah, and it is to this era that allegorical reference is made. For such lewd conduct as idolatry and false worship Yahweh promised utter destruction. Through an allegorical figure of a scarlet woman Ezekiel drove home in yet another way the promise that God would judge. C. G. Howie

OHOLIAB ō hō'lĭ ăb [אהליאב, tent of the (divine) father(?)]; KJV AHOLIAB ə—. A Danite, son of Ahisamach, appointed with Bezalel to make the tabernacle and its equipment (Exod. 31:6; 35:34; 36:1-2; 38:23). The skills to be exercised by Bezalel and Oholiab in their crafts are traced to the Spirit of God.

Bibliography. M. Noth, *Die israelitischen Personennamen* (1928), p. 158. R. F. Johnson

OHOLIBAH ō hō'lĭ bə [אהליבה]; KJV AHOLIBAH ə—. *See* Oholah.

OHOLIBAMAH ō hō'lĭ băm'ə [אהליבמה, *usually* tent of the high place; *cf.* אהליאב (Exod. 31:6), אהליבה (Ezek. 23:4); Phoen. אהלבעל, אהלמלך; Sabean

אהלבאל]; KJV AHOLIBAMAH ə—. **1.** Wife of Esau (Gen. 36:2, 5, 14, 18, 25) and daughter of Anah. However, her name does not appear in other lists of Esau's wives (Gen. 26:34; 28:9).

2. An Edomite clan chief (Gen. 36:41; I Chr. 1:52).

Bibliography. M. Noth, *Die israelitischen Personennamen* (1928), pp. 158-59. L. HICKS

OHRMAZD ôr′məzd. Alternately: ORMAZD; ORMUZD. Middle Persian form of AHURA-MAZDA.

OIL. Oil was considered to be one of the necessities of life in biblical times. Thus, when the rest of her food had been exhausted in a time of drought, the widow of Zarephath still had "a handful of meal in a jar, and a little oil in a cruse" (I Kings 17:12; cf. II Kings 4:2). Furthermore, oil is specifically mentioned (along with grain [KJV "corn"] and wine) as a provision placed in the royal storehouses (II Chr. 32:28; cf. II Kings 20:13; II Chr. 11:11; Isa. 39:2).

Naturally it was considered to be a gift from Yahweh. Grain, oil, and wine are expressions of his goodness (Jer. 31:12; Joel 2:19); Israel sins when she does not know that Yahweh, not Baal, has given her these things (Hos. 2:8—H 2:10). Correspondingly, grain, oil, and wine will be taken away because of the nation's disobedience (Deut. 28:51; Joel 1:10; Hag. 1:11). Nor was oil less highly valued in NT times; it is mentioned as part of the cargo of Babylon alongside gold, silver, jewels, ivory, marble, spices, wine, fine flour, etc. (Rev. 18:12-13).

1. Preparation
2. Uses
   a. Food
   b. Anointing
   c. Sacrifice
   d. Lamps
   e. Medicinal
3. In figurative expressions

Bibliography

1. Preparation. Whereas sesame oil was widely used in Mesopotamia, Palestinian oil was prepared from olives (*see* OLIVE TREE). However, in Esth. 2:12 "oil of myrrh" is mentioned as an aid to beauty. It occurs several times in inventories from Ras Shamra (*see* UGARIT), but does not seem to have been widely used in Palestine. As for the olives used in making oil, certain varieties were preferred above others. The Mishna (Men. 8.3) states that those of Tekoa are the best, followed by those of Regeb. Still other varieties are listed in Tractate Peah 7.1. The olives were harvested in September and October, and those from a good tree could be expected to yield from ten to fifteen gallons of oil each year. *See* AGRICULTURE § 3*b*.

In OT times the olives were crushed in a mortar or in a rock-hewn press; occasionally wine vats (*see* WINE § 2*a*) may also have been used for the production of oil. The olives were picked before they were quite ripe, and the best fruit was either trodden out with the feet (cf. Mic. 6:15: "You shall tread olives, but not anoint yourselves with oil") or crushed with a large stone. In the first stage the pulp was transferred to wicker baskets and gently shaken to and fro. The baskets acted as strainers, and the oil was collected in jars. The top layer was skimmed off and was called "pure" or "beaten" oil (שמן כתית). It is prescribed for the lamp that is to burn continually in the sanctuary (Exod. 27:20; Lev. 24:2) and as a constituent of the continual burnt offering (Exod. 29:40; Num. 28:5). It also formed a part of Solomon's annual payment to Hiram (I Kings 5:11—H 5:25).

In the second stage the olive pulp was heated and again put into the vat. Pressure was applied by means of a large beam, one end of which was inserted into a niche in a wall and the other weighted with stones. The resulting oil was allowed to stand until the sediment had subsided; occasionally salt was used to clarify it. For this oil the simple Hebrew term שמן is used (Greek ἔλαιον). The term יצהר is also frequent, almost always in conjunction with דגן ("grain"; KJV "corn") and תירוש (one of the words for "wine"); this is, however, probably a traditional expression and does not denote a special kind of oil. *See* WINE § 1*a*.

2. Uses. Oil was used for many purposes in biblical times. The more important of these are mentioned below:

a. Food. Curiously enough, there are relatively few references to oil as a foodstuff in the Bible, although on the basis of modern parallels it may be assumed that many foods were cooked in oil. However, we do read that on her way to the camp of Holofernes, Judith took along a flask of oil in addition to other provisions (Jth. 10:5). Furthermore, the taste of manna is compared to that of cakes baked with oil (Num. 11:8). The use of oil in sacrifices (*see* § 2*c below*) may also be taken as an indication of its use in ordinary COOKING.

b. Anointing. Perhaps the most frequent use of oil mentioned in the Bible is that of anointing. Most familiar is the custom of anointing a king (I Sam. 10:1; 16:1, 13; II Kings 9:3, 6; 11:12), a priest (Lev. 8:30), or a prophet (Isa. 61:1). Since this anointing oil was called "oil of gladness" (Ps. 45:7—H 45:8; cf. Prov. 27:9; Isa. 61:3), it may be assumed that it was a joyous occasion. The shield of a warrior was also anointed (Isa. 21:5; cf. II Sam. 1:21), probably as a symbol of dedication to Yahweh.

But anointing was not confined to holy persons. Indeed, Koheleth says that one should always have oil upon the head (Eccl. 9:8). Such oil makes the face shine (Ps. 104:15); it is to be omitted only on the occasion of mourning (II Sam. 14:2). Even when a person is fasting, he should anoint his head and wash his face (Matt. 6:17); one is as important as the other (cf. Ezek. 16:9). Such anointing is especially necessary after bathing (II Sam. 12:20; Ruth 3:3), since at that time the skin is more vulnerable to the sun. And it is also a sign of honor when an individual anoints his neighbor; a guest should be anointed when he arrives for a BANQUET (Ps. 23:5; Amos 6:6; Luke 7:46). *See* ANOINT.

c. Sacrifice. The use of oil as a part of the continual burnt offering has already been noted. In addition, all cereal offerings were to be provided with oil; the oil was either mixed with the FLOUR or spread on the WAFERS (Lev. 2:4). This practice replaced the earlier custom of making a libation of oil, still mentioned in the patriarchal narratives (Gen. 28:18; 35:14). *See* SACRIFICE AND OFFERINGS.

d. Lamps. Of course, oil was also the chief fuel for lamps (*see* LAMP). Since the ordinary lamp was relatively small, the wise person provided himself with an adequate supply of oil (Matt. 25:3-8).

e. Medicinal. Finally, oil was widely used in healing. It had the effect of softening the wound (Isa. 1:6), but may also have been regarded as a symbol of God's protection. Thus the disciples healed by anointing (Mark 6:13), and elders are instructed to pray over the sick person and anoint him with oil (Jas. 5:14). The use of a mixture of oil and wine in healing a wound (Luke 10:34) is also attested in the Talmud (Shab. 134*a*). *See* MEDICINE.

In view of its various uses, it is natural that oil would occur in lists of exports from Palestine. Solomon's payment to Hiram has already been cited; similarly the Jews gave oil to the Sidonians and Tyrians in exchange for the cedar for the Second Temple (Ezra 3:7). The same trade may also be referred to in Ezek. 27:17, where oil is mentioned alongside wheat, olives, honey, and balm. Furthermore, oil was naturally a part of the internal commerce of the nation. Elisha advised the widow of one of the sons of the prophets to sell oil and pay her debts (II Kings 4:7), and the foolish virgins are told to replenish their supplies from a dealer (Matt. 25:9).

3. In figurative expressions. Since God provides oil for his people, its possession is a symbol of prosperity. Asher, who is to be the "favorite of his brothers," will "dip his foot in oil" (Deut. 33:24). Similarly Job longs for the day

> when my steps were washed with milk,
> and the rock poured out for me streams of oil!
> (Job 29:6).

Naturally the eschatological age will be a period of abundance:

> The threshing floors shall be full of grain,
> the vats shall overflow with wine and oil
> (Joel 2:24).

So also there are streams of honey, milk, oil, and wine in heaven (II Enoch 8:5).

Elsewhere the persuasive power of an enemy's words is compared to the softness of oil (Ps. 55:21—H 55:22); the psalmist also asks that his enemy's curses soak into his bones like oil (Ps. 109:18). The speech of a loose woman is said to be smoother than oil (Prov. 5:3).

Thus it is not surprising that the olive tree boasts that its fatness honors gods and men (Judg. 9:9). Nevertheless, "he who [inordinately] loves wine and oil will not be rich" (Prov. 21:17).

Bibliography. R. J. Forbes, *Studies in Ancient Technology,* III (1955), 101-4 (on the preparation of oil); G. E. Wright, *Biblical Archaeology* (1957), p. 180. J. F. ROSS

OIL TREE. KJV translation of עץ שמן, *'ēṣ šemen* (lit., "tree of OIL"), in Isa. 41:19 (RSV "olive"). The wood of this tree was used for the carved cherubim in the temple (I Kings 6:23, 31-33; "olivewood"), and its branches for the Feast of Booths (Neh. 8:15; cf. Lev. 23:40). It was included with other trees in a figure of the transformed desert (Isa. 41:19). It was mentioned poetically (in parallel with the olive) in praise of a high priest in Ecclus. 50:10 ("cypress"; cf. 24:13, where the same words were probably used in praise of wisdom).

עץ שמן is interpreted as the OLIVE TREE in the passages in Kings. In Neh. 8:15 the translation is "wild olive" (KJV "pine branches"). The variety of LXX translations alone is an indication of early confusion about the tree's identification, and the different contexts in which the references occur add to the present confusion. Strong claims have been made that it was the *zaqqûm* tree of the Arabs (*Balanites aegyptiaca* [L.] Del., found only near Jericho; *see* BALM), the WILD OLIVE (*Olea europaea,* var. *oleaster* DC.), the true oleaster (*Elaeagnus angustifolia* L.), and several species of pine (*see* FLORA § A9*m,* and so apparently the Mishna) or cypress (so LXX). It is reasonable to suppose that the Hebrew intended some tree related to the olive, either the wild olive or the oleaster or both (they are easily confused in appearance). An oil-producing conifer is also possible (*see* FLORA § A9*m*). Thus "oil tree" is probably the best translation for the present.

Bibliography. H. N. and A. L. Moldenke, *Plants of the Bible* (1952), pp. 97-98. J. C. TREVER

OINTMENT. Anointing oil. In the culture of the ancient Near East as reflected in the Bible, ointment had many uses.

1. Terminology
2. Contents of ointment
   a. Oil
   b. Perfumes
3. Manufacture
4. Value
5. Containers
6. Uses
   a. As a cosmetic
   b. In hospitality
   c. A sign of joy
   d. As medicine
   e. In mortuary processes
   f. On shields
   g. In consecration
7. Figurative references

Bibliography

1. Terminology. Hebrew words translated "ointment" are: (*a*) שמן (Eccl. 7:1; 10:1; RSV "oil" in Exod. 30:25; II Kings 20:13; Ps. 133:2; Prov. 27:9, 16; Amos 6:6); (*b*) derivatives of the root רקח, *rāqāḥ,* "to prepare perfume or ointment": רקח, *rōqaḥ* (Exod. 30:25 KJV; RSV does not translate); מרקחת, *mirqaḥath* (I Chr. 9:30 KJV; RSV "mixing"); מרקחה, *merqaḥah,* "pot of ointment" (Job 41:31—H 41:23); (*c*) תמרוק (lit., "rubbings" or "cleansings"; Esth. 2:3, 9 [KJV "things for purification"], 12 [KJV "things for the purifying"]).

The Greek word translated "ointment" is μύρον (Matt. 26:7, 9, 12; Mark 14:3-4; Luke 7:37-38, 46; John 11:2; 12:3, 5; RSV "myrrh" in Rev. 18:13).

2. Contents of ointment. *a. Oil.* In Israel olive oil (שמן) was the chief base of ointments, and was itself an ointment (Deut. 28:40; *see* OIL). The surrounding nations used other bases for ointment also: in Babylonia sesame oil and animal fats; in Egypt *balanos* oil, almond oil, and animal fats.

b. Perfumes. To the olive oil various perfumes were added (*see* PERFUME § 3*c*). Sometimes a descriptive adjective with "oil" or "ointment" indicates that it was perfumed—e.g., "precious" (II Kings 20:13; Eccl. 7:1), "fragrant" (Song of S. 1:3), or "finest" (Amos 6:6).

3. Manufacture. On ointment-mixers, *see* PERFUME § 3*c*. To make ointment, the raw material was crushed, boiled in oil, and stirred. The thrashing of a crocodile in water is compared to this process in the ointment pot (Job 41:31—H 41:23). This was the method of the Egyptians, the Jews (T.B. Ker. 5*a*), and of the Greeks and Romans (Pliny Nat. Hist. XIII.7).

4. Value. The great value placed on ointments is illustrated by the fact that they were included among the treasures of King Hezekiah (II Kings 20:13) and of the Pharaoh of Egypt in the New Kingdom. Robbers broke into the tomb of Tut-ankh-Amon of Egypt especially to steal the ointments, leaving objects of gold behind. The high cost of nard (imported from distant India), with which Mary anointed Jesus (John 12:3, 5), is confirmed by Pliny (Nat. Hist. XII.42-45).

5. Containers. The oil for anointing kings was carried in a VIAL for Saul (I Sam. 10:1), in a FLASK (same Hebrew word) for Jehu (II Kings 9:1), or in a "horn" for David (I Sam. 16:1) and Solomon (I Kings 1:39). According to Matt. 26:7, the ointment with which Jesus was anointed at Bethany was in an

Courtesy of Foto Marburg

4. Handle of a wooden ointment spoon, showing a Syrian porter carrying a jar, from the New Kingdom in Egypt (*ca.* 1550-1090 B.C.)

Courtesy of the Palestine Archaeological Museum, Jerusalem, Jordan

5. An ivory ointment flask hollowed from an elephant tusk; from Tell ed-Duweir (*ca.* 1400-1200 B.C.)

ALABASTER jar. Pliny (Nat. Hist. XIII.19) states that alabaster was the best material for ointment containers, and according to customs records in Palmyra, the best ointments were transported in such jars. Many ancient alabaster ointment jars have been found in Egypt and in Palestine. That the lids of these jars were sealed shut explains why Mary broke the vessel, probably the neck, to pour the ointment on Jesus' head. This is illustrated by the Mishna's reference (Kel. XXX.4) to a nard flask with a broken neck.

Figs. OIN 4-5.

6. Uses. ***a. As a cosmetic.*** In the dry climate of the Near East anointing is a common practice (Mic. 6:15) to prevent dessication of the skin. Ointment could be applied to the head (Matt. 6:17) or to the whole body after a bath (Ruth 3:3; II Sam. 12:20). Perfumed ointments were used by Judith before she met Holofernes (Jth. 10:13) and by Esther before approaching Ahasuerus (Esth. 2:12). Sweet ointments were also employed by men to attract the other sex (Song of S. 1:3). According to Josephus (War II.viii. 3), oil was not used as a cosmetic by the Essenes.

b. In hospitality. At a banquet it was a mark of honor to anoint the head of a guest with oil (Ps. 23:5). In Luke 7:46, Jesus contrasts his host, Simon the Pharisee, who had omitted anointing his head even with ordinary oil, with the sinful woman who had anointed his feet with perfumed ointment. The heads or rabbis were sometimes anointed at Jewish weddings (T.B. Keth. 17*b*). Ancient Egyptian banquet scenes show the guests being anointed with oil and with cones of melting ointment on their heads. The rabbinic commentary Siphre on Deut. 33:24 speaks of slaves' anointing people's feet with oil. Fig. OIN 6.

Courtesy of the Trustees of the British Museum

6. A wall painting from a tomb at Thebes, showing Syrian tribute-bearers bringing their offerings, among which is an ointment horn by the figure at the extreme right in the upper register; from the time of Thut-mose IV (1421-1413 B.C.)

c. A sign of joy. Anointing with the oil of gladness (Ps. 45:7—H 45:9; Isa. 61:3) was a sign of rejoicing. Conversely, in times of mourning or sorrow such anointing was usually omitted (II Sam. 12:20-21; 14:2; Dan. 10:3). The rabbis forbade anointing with oil in time of mourning (T.B. M.Ḳ. 15*b*), during special fasts in time of drought (M. Ta'an. I.6), and on the Day of Atonement (M. Yom. VIII.1). Jesus, on the other hand, urged that during fasts the head be anointed as usual, to avoid outward parade of religiosity (Matt. 6:17).

d. As medicine. Oil was used as a medical ointment for wounds (Isa. 1:6; Luke 10:34) and for diseases (Jer. 8:22; Mark 6:13; Jas. 5:14). The oil applied to the cleansed leper may have had a medicinal as well as a symbolic purpose (Lev. 14:15-18, 26-29). The church of Laodicea is asked to buy eye salve (for which the city was famous) for spiritual sight (Rev. 3:18).

e. In mortuary processes. In ancient Egypt several ointments (e.g., cedar oil, myrrh, resin) were used in the elaborate process of embalming and wrapping a body. This Egyptian process was applied to Jacob (Gen. 50:2-3) and to Joseph (vs. 26). Jesus received the ointment from Mary as anointing in advance for his burial (Mark 14:8). Women followers of Jesus prepared ointments to anoint his body (Mark 16:1; Luke 23:56). The Mishna (Shab. XXIV.5) mentions the practice of anointing bodies for burial.

f. On shields. Shields were anointed with oil, probably to preserve the leather and to make the surface slick to deflect weapons (II Sam. 1:21; Isa. 21:5).

g. In consecration. Jacob consecrated the stone at Bethel by pouring oil over it (Gen. 28:18). The sacred anointing oil was used to consecrate the tabernacle and its furniture (Exod. 30:26-29).

Aaron and his sons were consecrated as priests with the sacred oil, which was not to be used for "ordinary men" (Exod. 30:30-32). Kings were anointed in Israel (*see* § 5 *above*), as in ancient Egypt. That the sacred anointing oil of the priests was also used for the kings and that this oil made in Moses' time sufficed for all subsequent history till Josiah (so T.B. Hor. 11*b*, 12*a*) is not stated in the Bible. The anointing of one prophet, Elisha, is commanded (I Kings 19:16). In I Sam. 16:13 anointing with oil is associated with empowerment by the Spirit of the Lord. *See* ANOINT.

7. **Figurative references.** In Ps. 133:2 brotherly unity is said to be as pleasant as the sacred oil. That anointing oil was used for consecration in the OT makes it an apt symbol of the Holy Spirit in the NT (I John 2:20, 27).

Bibliography. S. Krauss, *Talmudische Archäologie,* I (1910), 233-37. B. Meissner, *Babylonien und Assyrien,* I (1920), 242-44, 353, 403, 411. A. Erman and H. Ranke, *Ägypten und ägyptisches Leben im Altertum* (1923), pp. 67, 141, 245, 259-61, 287, 412, 611. A. Schmidt, *Drogen und Drogenhandel im Altertum* (1924), pp. 25-36, 39-45. G. Dalman, *Arbeit und Sitte,* IV (1935), 259-68; V (1937), 266, 267, 274, 339. A. Lucas, *Ancient Egyptian Materials and Industries* (3rd ed., 1948), pp. 353, 355, 359-64.

J. A. THOMPSON

OLAMUS. KJV Apoc. form of MESHULLAM.

OLD GATE [שער הישנה] (Neh. 3:6; 12:39). A gate of Jerusalem, restored by Nehemiah; perhaps to be read "Gate of the SECOND QUARTER" (המשנה instead of הישנה). Then it might be identical with the EPHRAIM GATE in Neh. 12:39.

See map under NEHEMIAH. G. A. BARROIS

OLD LATIN VERSIONS. *See* VERSIONS, ANCIENT, § 3.

OLD TESTAMENT. In current usage, the Hebrew scriptures. The LXX, out of reverence for God, translated ברית, "[divine] covenant," with διαθήκη ("testament") instead of συνθήκη ("covenant"), which occurs only in Wisd. Sol. 12:21 in this sense. The change was made because in a covenant the two parties are of equal rank and discuss terms, while in a testament the testator is dead and decides all matters. The "old covenant" was made with Jews (II Cor. 3:14; Heb. 9:15); the "new covenant" was promised in Jer. 31:31—G 38:31 and made with Christians (I Cor. 11:25; II Cor. 3:6; Heb. 8:6-13; 10:16-17; cf. Luke 22:20; etc.). R. H. PFEIFFER

OT CANON. *See* CANON OF THE OT.

OT CHRONOLOGY. *See* CHRONOLOGY OF THE OT.

OT LANGUAGE. The language of the OT is Hebrew. Certain passages (Ezra 4:8–6:18; 7:12-26; Jer. 10:11; Dan. 2:4*b*–7:28) are in the related Aramaic language. Just as in English, however, we use such words as "piano," "contralto," "concerto," which have been borrowed from Italian, or "baptize," "deacon," "eucharist," "presbyter," which are Anglicized forms of Greek words, so in the OT are to be found Hebraized forms of words borrowed from other Near Eastern languages spoken in OT times. *See* HEBREW LANGUAGE; ARAMAIC LANGUAGE; LANGUAGES OF THE BIBLE; LANGUAGES OF THE ANCIENT NEAR EAST. A. JEFFERY

OT TEXT. *See* TEXT, OT.

OLIVE TREE [זית *zayith;* Ugar. *zt*(?); Aram. זיתא, *zêthâ;* Arab. *zaytûn;* ἐλαία]. An evergreen tree and its edible fruit, *Olea europaea* L. The importance of the olive tree to the whole Mediterranean area from very early times is witnessed by numerous references to it in ancient literature. Use of the tree and its fruit for food, fuel, light, carpentry, ointments, medicines, etc., touched almost every phase of daily life. Numerous references to the tree, its wood, fruit, and oil, in the Bible indicate in almost every case the prime importance of the olive tree (frequently associated with the vine; Exod. 23:11, etc.) to the life of ancient Israel. Fig. OLI 7.

Courtesy of Winifred Walker

7. Olive

Although new stock must be grafted from productive stock (cf. Rom. 11:17-24), and new trees mature very slowly, olive cultivation is simple, requiring only occasional loosening of the soil. It grows luxuriantly in the rocky soil of the Holy Land, requiring little water, and thus enduring the frequent droughts. The tree continues to produce heavily (usually every other year) for hundreds of years. Its chief enemy is the locust (Amos 4:9).

The tree may be seen everywhere in the Near East today, but is particularly prominent in the central highlands of Palestine around Hebron, Bethlehem, Jifna, and N of Nablus. Gnarled trees clinging to terraced, rocky hillsides are a common sight. In biblical times the OIL was essential for lamps (Lev. 24:2).

The production of olive oil was a major industry in biblical times, judging by the number of ancient stone olive presses still to be seen even where orchards no longer grow. A thick, vertical stone wheel, operated by a long, pivoted wooden bar, was rolled over the olives on another flat, circular stone, grooved to carry the oil to a basin at one side (Mic. 6:15). The familiar name GETHSEMANE in the gospels

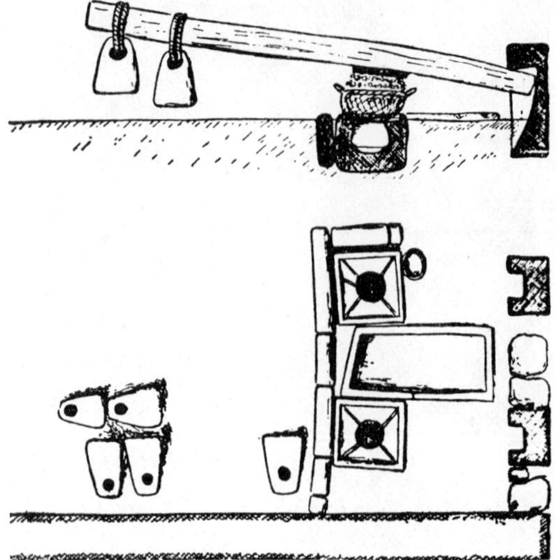

By permission of the Palestinian Exploration Fund

8. An ancient Palestinian olive press at work

(e.g., Mark 14:32) meant "oil press" in Aramaic. Fig. OLI 8.

In early Mesopotamian art the olive is occasionally depicted as the TREE OF LIFE, and in Gen. 8:11 the familiar story of the dove returning to Noah with an olive leaf suggests the symbolism of peace and friendship. The olive tree is depicted as a part of the glory of the Promised Land to the Hebrews poised to enter Canaan (Deut. 6:11; 8:8), but it is also included in Moses' curse upon the nation if it fails God (28:40). According to the law, some olives were to be left for the gleaners (Deut. 24:20; Isa. 17:6; cf. 24:13) during the late fall harvest.

Particularly frequent are the references to the tree in allegory, poetic imagery, and symbolism. In Jotham's fable, where the olive is the first choice for king of the trees, it answers: "Shall I leave my fatness, by which gods and men are honored . . . ?" (Judg. 9:8-9). Eliphaz eloquently describes the demise of an evil man as a shower of minute olive blossoms falling with the wind in the springtime (Job 15:33). A family blessed with many children is likened to olive shoots which spring from the roots of the old parent trees (Ps. 128:3). It is symbolic of Israel's past and future spiritual beauty (Jer. 11:16; Hos. 14:6). In Zechariah's vision (4:3, 11-12) Zerubbabel and Joshua are portrayed as olive trees (cf. Rev. 11:4) standing beside a seven-branched lampstand.

Paul's familiar allegory of the grafting of the olive trees, though revealing a lack of knowledge of horticulture, is a forceful presentation of his hope for Gentile Christianity (Rom. 11:17-24).

See also FLORA § A2*g;* OIL TREE; OINTMENT; WILD OLIVE; ZETHAN.

Bibliography. Pliny Nat. Hist. XV; G. Dalman, *Arbeit und Sitte in Palästina,* IV (1927), 153 ff; I. Löw, *Die Flora der Juden,* II (1924), 286-95; H. N. and A. L. Moldenke, *Plants of the Bible* (1952), pp. 157-60. J. C. TREVER

OLIVES, MOUNT OF [הר הזיתים, *also* מעלה הזיתים (II Sam. 15:30); τὸ ὄρος τῶν ἐλαιῶν (ASCENT OF THE MOUNT OF OLIVES [KJV MOUNT

OLIVET]); *also* τὸ ὄρος τὸ καλούμενον ἐλαιών]. Alternately: OLIVET, THE MOUNT CALLED (Luke 21:37; Acts 1:12); OLIVET, THE MOUNT THAT IS CALLED (Luke 19:29). A mountain E of Jerusalem, across the Valley of Kidron. *See* KIDRON, BROOK.

1. Description
2. In the OT and late Judaism
3. In the NT
4. Christian and Moslem sanctuaries

Bibliography

1. Description. The Mount of Olives is part of the main range of mountains which runs N-S through central and S Palestine. It has the shape of a ridge *ca.* 2½ miles in length, the three summits of which tower high over the barren hills that slope down E toward Jericho and the Jordan Valley. To the W, the Mount of Olives overlooks Jerusalem across the deep cut of the Kidron. The first summit, to the NE of the Old City, is the highest, with an altitude of 2,963 feet above Mediterranean Sea level, according to a recent survey. It is often called Mount Scopus, although this name, which occurs in Josephus (War II.xix.4, 7; V.iv.1), properly applies to the NW extremity of the entire range, the Ras el-Mesharif, which the Nablus Road negotiates 1½ miles from the Damascus Gate.

The second summit, right opposite the Haram esh-Sherif or temple area, which it overlooks, is separated from the Scopus by a very slight depression. It is called by the Arabs "Jebel et-Tur," and is partly occupied by the village known as Kafr et-Tur. These toponyms are derived from the Syriac *Ṭūrô Q^{e}dishô,* "the Holy Mountain," thus named for the miscellaneous Christian churches and memorials built in these parts. Figs. OLI 9-10.

Courtesy of Pan American World Airways

9. View of Gethsemane and the Mount of Olives, the Church of All Nations at lower left, and the Church of Magdalene right of center

The modern high road from Jerusalem to Jericho cuts the crest of the mountain between the Jebel et-Tur and the third summit, called in Arabic "Jebel Batn el-Hawa," at the foot of which the Kidron winds to the SE in the direction of the Dead Sea. This third summit, which is the lowest of the three, is located immediately above the village of Selwan, and overlooks the ancient site of Canaanite and Davidic Jerusalem, S of the temple area.

The entire mountain was named for extensive olive groves. It is called הר המשחה, "Mount of the Ointment," in the Talmud, and in modern Arabic usage Tur Zaita—i.e., Tur Olivet, an alternate to Jebel et-Tur. The olive groves today are only a fraction of what they must have been in antiquity, and the flanks of the mountain are bleak and partly occupied by modern Jewish cemeteries.

2. In the OT and late Judaism. The Mount of Olives is mentioned only twice in the OT. David, unable to stem the revolt of Absalom and forced to abandon his capital, took the path leading over the crest of the mountain, on his way to a temporary exile in Transjordan. The term used in II Sam. 15:30, מעלה, suggests a steep ascent, possibly with broad steps cut out of the rock. Toward the summit was a place of worship (II Sam. 15:32). It has been identified with the sanctuary of NOB, the location of which is most uncertain; remains of an ancient settlement discovered in 1907 while digging for the foundations of the German Hospice might be taken into consideration. Another point of David's itinerary is the village of BAHURIM (II Sam. 16:5) on the E slopes of the Mount of Olives, and tentatively identified with Ras et-Tmim, N of an ancient road leading to Jericho. Another road farther N crossed the crest of Mount Scopus in the direction of ANATHOTH.

The other reference of the OT to the Mount of Olives is found in the prophecy of Zechariah on the ruin of Jerusalem, when the mountain would split in two, prior to the day of the coming of the Lord (Zech. 14:4).

The S summit of the Mount of Olives, above the modern village of Selwan, is likely to be identical with the Mount of Corruption (*see* CORRUPTION, MOUNT OF), thus named by reference to the worship of idols introduced by the foreign wives of Solomon (II Kings 23:13). In this passage there is a probable play on the words משחית, *mash-ḥîth,* "corruption," and משחה, *mash-ḥâ,* "ointment," the latter referring to the oil from the olives grown on the mountain.

According to the Talmud, the rite of burning a red heifer to ashes for the preparation of lustral water (Num. 19:1-10) was performed on the Mount of Olives, opposite the E gate of the temple (Par. 3.6). A bridge and a path connected the temple with the mountain, on the summit of which fire signals were lighted to notify the apparition of the new moon for the computation of the months. These signals could be seen and were relayed from a second station, located on the Alexandrium, or Qarn Sartabeh, twenty-seven miles to the N-NE (R. H. 2.2).

3. In the NT. The Mount of Olives was the theater of some of the activities of Jesus during the last week of his earthly life, and is again mentioned in the book of Acts in connection with the last meeting of the disciples around their risen Lord prior to the Ascension. The name of the Mount of Olives occurs in a series of NT texts relative to the triumphal entry of Jesus into Jerusalem, six days before the Passover. It seems that Jesus and his disciples started from BETHANY, a village on the E side of the Mount of Olives, to be sought near el-'Azariyeh, presumably to the W of the modern village. They proceeded from there to BETHPHAGE, a hamlet the site of which is not known with absolute certainty. The

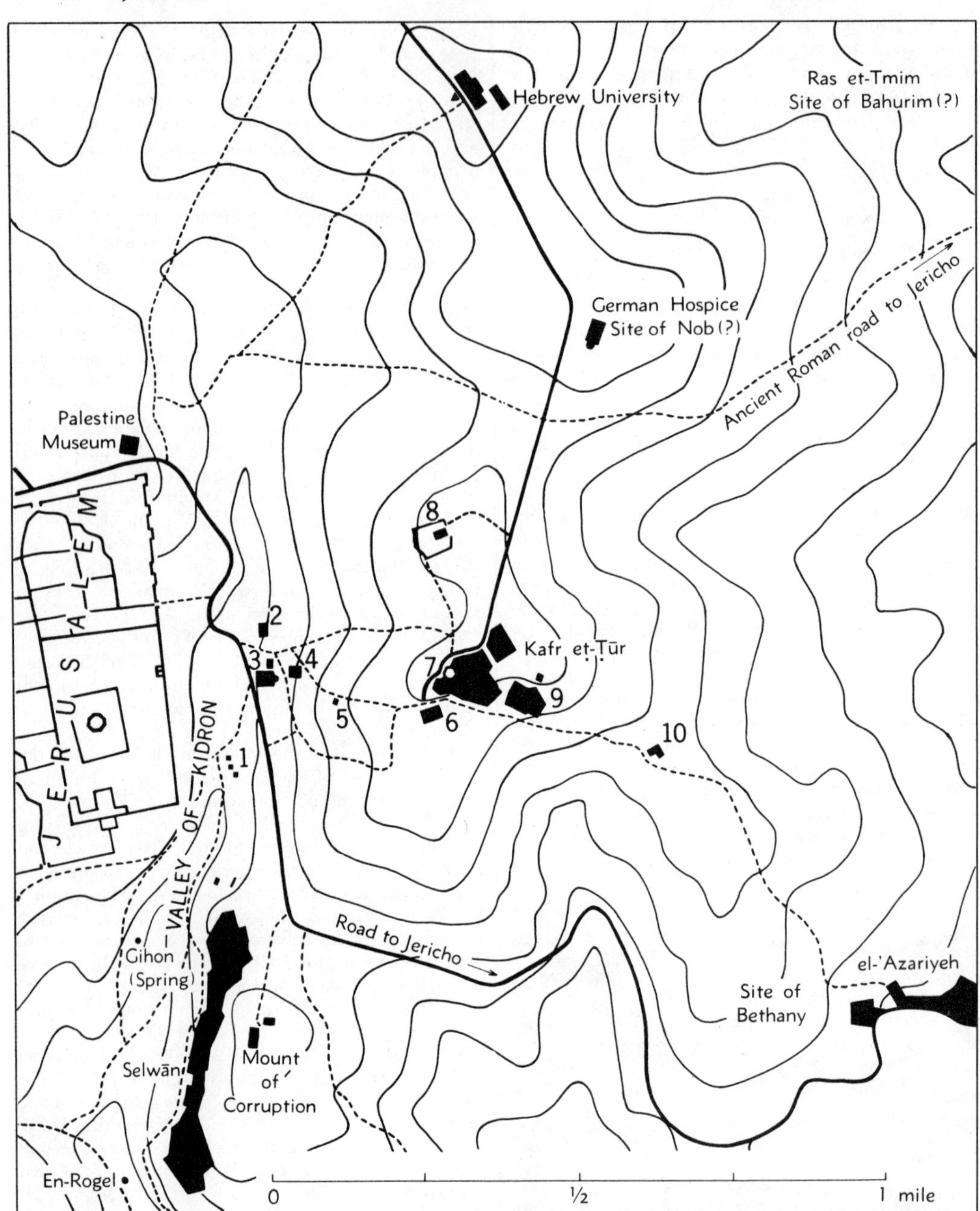

G. A. Barrois

10. Map of the Mount of Olives: (1) ancient Jewish tombs (two locations); (2) Tomb of Mary (church); (3) Garden and Church of Gethsemane; (4) Russian Church of St. Magdalene; (5) Chapel of the Tears of Jesus; (6) monastery of Carmelites (Eleona); (7) Ascension (mosque); (8) "Men of Galilee" (chapel); (9) Russian tower; (10) Bethphage (chapel)

Synoptic narratives imply the immediate proximity of the crest of the Mount, and Bethphage may accordingly be identified with, or localized in, the surrounds of Kefr et-Tur (Matt. 21:1; Mark 11:1). Luke adds that Jesus, coming in sight of Jerusalem, obviously from a point on the path affording a commanding view of the city, wept over it (Luke 19:41).

The prophecies of Jesus on the ruin of Jerusalem and the passing of this world were delivered on the Mount of Olives (Matt. 24:3; Mark 13:3-4; Luke 21:5 ff). They echo the words of Zech. 14:1-5, which contain a reference to the Mount itself. Matthew adds to the so-called Little Apocalypse a number of parables pointing to the duty of being watchful and ready to face the judgment (Matt. 24:32-51; ch. 25). There is no telling, however, whether they were actually pronounced on the Mount of Olives, even though contextual affinities make this not unlikely.

The Synoptics agree on the fact that, during the week preceding his arrest, Jesus, after visiting the temple by day, returned at night to the Mount of Olives. This may be inferred circumstantially from the Little Apocalypse and from the introduction to the pericope of the adulteress (which is misplaced in John 8:1-11 and should be taken rather as a tradition of the last week, perhaps originally a part of Luke); and it is formally stated by Luke 21:37. Where exactly Jesus did spend the nights, however, is not clear: either in Bethany, in the house of Simon the leper (cf. Matt. 26:6; Mark 14:3), or in the estate of GETHSEMANE, on the lower slopes of the Mount of Olives, where he "often met . . . with his disciples" (John 18:2), "as was his custom" (Luke 22:39).

The episode of the last meeting of Jesus with the disciples, after the Resurrection, when he parted from them and was lifted up, must be localized on, or in the vicinity of, the Mount of Olives, as may be inferred from Luke 24:50, which states that "he led them out as far as Bethany," and from Acts 1:12, where the disciples are depicted on their way back "from the mount called Olivet," immediately after the Ascension.

4. Christian sanctuaries. The first sanctuary in date is the basilica of the Eleona, the name of which results from the artificial addition of the Aramaic desinence *ā* to the Greek adjective ἐλαιών. It was built above a grotto in which Jesus was believed to have taught his disciples before the Crucifixion and to have met with them on the morning of the Ascension. The construction began in A.D. 325. It was destroyed in 614 by the Persians. Partial excavations conducted before the war of 1914-18 have unearthed part of the foundations and miscellaneous remains, near the monastery of the French Carmelites, on the S border of the village of Kefr et-Tur. The Eleona was replaced during the Middle Ages by a small chapel which was shown to the pilgrims as the place where Jesus allegedly taught the Lord's Prayer to his disciples. Still at a later date, the composition of the Apostles' Creed was localized nearby.

Toward 375, an octagonal church was built on the presumed site of the Ascension, on the summit of the Jebel et-Tur. It was restored by the Crusaders, but fell into the hands of the Moslems in the thirteenth century. Very little subsists today of the original construction, with the exception of the foundations of the octagon and the central shrine, which marks the exact spot where, according to popular tradition, Jesus was taken up to heaven. The shrine is adorned with medieval columns; the dome which covers it originates in a later restoration by the Muslims, who have built a minaret near the entrance, and a prayer niche (*miḥrab*) in the shrine.

The localization of Gethsemane on the lower slopes of the Mount, right opposite the so-called Golden Gate, is well founded in history and tradition. Excavations conducted before and during the war of 1914-18 have led to the discovery of two churches partly superposed. The lower, and more ancient, church, built toward the end of the fourth century, kept the memory of the prayer of Jesus in the garden. It was destroyed in 614, and its exact location had been forgotten when the Crusaders took Jerusalem and built a new church, the orientation of which differs from that of the early one. After the destruction of the medieval church in the fourteenth century, a nearby grotto was shown to the pilgrims as the place of the agony of Jesus, until a modern basilica, completed in 1924, was erected on the foundations of the fourth-century church, the mosaic pavements of which have been preserved in part in the new structure. Huge old olives are seen in the garden surrounding the basilica. Fig. GET 25.

To the N and at a lower level, a church had been built *ca.* 455 over what Jerusalem Christians regarded as the tomb of Mary, mother of Jesus. It was destroyed by the Persians. The underground church which one sees today is actually the crypt of the abbatial church of Saint Mary of Josaphat, which was built by the Crusaders and destroyed by Saladin in 1187. *See* JEHOSHAPHAT, VALLEY OF.

Since the fourteenth Christian century, the place where Jesus wept over the city is marked by a little chapel, S of the path which leads directly from Gethsemane to et-Tur. An olive grove to the NW of et-Tur has been identified in the local folklore as the place where the disciples were addressed as "men of Galilee" after the Ascension (Acts 1:11). Recent foundations, such as the Russian church of Saint Mary Magdalene, above the garden of Gethsemane, the Russian monastery on the Jebel et-Tur, and the German Hospice (Kaiserin Augusta Viktoria Stiftung) on the S end of the crest of the Scopus, have no connection with the gospel history.

Bibliography. H. Vincent and F.-M. Abel, *Jérusalem Nouvelle,* I–II (1914), 301-419; IV (1926), 808-10, 821-31, 1007-13. G. Dalman, *Jerusalem und sein Gelände* (1930), pp. 21-55. F.-M. Abel, *Géographie de la Palestine,* I (1933), 372-75.

G. A. BARROIS

OLYMPAS ō lĭm'pəs ['Ολυμπᾶς, *a short form of* Olympiodorus *or some other long name compounded with* Olymp-] (Rom. 16:15). A Christian man to whom a greeting is sent. He may have been a son of Philologus and Julia, and a brother of Nereus, all of whom are mentioned in the same verse.

F. W. GINGRICH

OLYMPIAN ZEUS, TEMPLE OF ō lĭm'pĭ ən zōōs [Διὸς 'Ολύμπιος] (II Macc. 6:2); KJV TEMPLE OF JUPITER OLYMPIUS jōō'pĭ tər ō lĭm'pĭ əs. The name given to the temple of Jerusalem when it was polluted by the Greeks. The Jews were compelled "to forsake the laws of their fathers and cease to live by the laws of God."

S. B. HOENIG

OMAERUS ō mĭr'əs. KJV Apoc. form of AMRAM.

OMAR ō'mär [אומר, *cf.* אמר, אמרי, אמריה] (Gen. 36:11, 15; I Chr. 1:36). An Edomite clan chief (אלוף אומר, perhaps "clan chief of Omar"); second son of Eliphaz.

OMEGA ō mĕg'ə, ō mē'gə [ὦ]. The last letter of the Greek alphabet; used symbolically to indicate the end, but it never appears thus apart from its opposite, ALPHA.

OMEN. Any circumstance, fact, or event which portends good or evil; any foreboding or augury of good or evil to come; a prophetic sign; a token significant of the nature of a future event. The word "omen" is not used in the KJV and is used only five times in the RSV: Num. 24:1 (נחשים, "omens"; KJV "enchantments"); I Kings 20:33 (ינחשו, "were watching for an omen," largely supplied in the KJV); Isa. 44:25 (אתות, "omens"; KJV "tokens"); Zech. 3:8 (אנשי מופת, "men of good omen"; KJV "men wondered at"); Phil. 1:28 (ἔνδειξις, "clear omen"; KJV "evident token"). In addition, however, את, "sign," "mark," or "token," often conveys the idea of "omen" in OT usage (Gen. 1:14; 9:12-13; 17:11; Exod. 3:12; 4:8-9, 17, 28, 30; 7:3; 8:23; 10:1-2; 12:13; 13:9, 16; 31:13, 17; etc.). Σημεῖον, "sign," "mark," "signal," or "portent," is the NT equivalent of נחש and את and almost invariably conveys the idea of "omen" (Matt. 12:38-39; 16:1, 3-4; 24:3, 24, 30; 26:48; Mark 8:11-12; 13:4, 22; 16:17, 20; Luke 2:12, 34; 11:16, 29-30; 21:7, 11, 25; John 2:18; 4:48; 6:30; 20:30; Acts 2:19, 22, 43; 4:30; 5:12; 7:36; 8:13; 14:3; Rom. 4:11; 15:19; I Cor. 1:22; 14:22; II Cor. 12:12; II Thess. 2:9; Heb. 2:4; Rev. 15:1).

The connotation of the word "omen" as a sign or portent is intended in I Kings 20:33 ("Now the men were watching for an omen"). The verb נחש means "to practice divination, to observe the omens" (Gen. 30:27; 44:5, 15). The related noun (Nöldeke and others maintain that the verb is a denominative) is used only in the story of Balaam (Num. 23:23; 24:1).

According to I Kings 20:26-34, the servants of Ben-hadad, the defeated king of Syria, now in hiding, came to Ahab of Israel in order to seek guarantees for the life of their king. Having placed their request before Ahab, they watched for an omen, possibly after the manner of diviners, but more probably as men who realize that their fate is related to that of their monarch. They await anxiously any signs of compassion from Ahab. His use of the word "brother" with reference to Ben-hadad (vs. 32) must have seemed a very good omen to them. Such searchings for omens or signs in a variety of situations, whether as the occupation of self-styled or popularly recognized diviners, of ordinary individuals, or as the preoccupation of whole generations, are frequently alluded to in both Testaments (Deut. 28:46; Josh. 2:12; 4:6; Ps. 86:17; Isa. 7:11, 14; 38:22; 55:13; Matt. 12:38-42; 16:4; 24:3; Luke 2:12; 11:14-23; John 6:14-15).

In what may be, in part, a late introduction to Balaam's third prophecy (Num. 24:1 ff), point is made of the fact that BALAAM, evidently contrary to his usual custom as a recognized curser and blesser, does not go "to meet with omens." On this occasion, having observed that the Lord means to bless Israel, and having seen that Israel is encamped before him, Balaam is taken up in a state of ecstasy; he "hears the words of God" and "sees the vision of the Almighty" (vs. 4), and becomes the spokesman for the Lord. There are now no such preparatory omens for the divine communication as he had experienced during his journey when the Lord came upon him in dreams (Num. 22:9-20) and sent an angel to waylay him and caused the ass to act strangely and then to speak (vss. 21-35). The mode of prophetic inspiration is more refined in Num. 24; nonetheless, throughout the story the foreign prophet, even though in the service of the Moabite king, refuses to speak or act except as he is directed by signs and omens from the God of Israel.

Reference is made in Isa. 44:25 to the "omens of liars," which the God of Israel is capable of frustrating. These are the omens of boasters or babblers (cf. Jer. 50:36). In the context both of the historical period and of the strophe (Isa. 44:24-28), the reference would seem to be to soothsayers, possibly the priestly ones of the Babylonian cults, who imagined that the signs of the times were revealed to them by their gods. Since the future is under the control of the God of Israel, who is the Lord of history, such devotees of foreign deities can only proclaim foolishness; they can neither know nor understand (cf. Isa. 47:1-15; Ezek. 21:21-22).

An undue concern for signs and omens seemed to Jesus of Nazareth to be prevalent in his time, and this concern may be regarded as a result of a keen interest in apocalyptic among his contemporaries.

Paul suggested to the Philippians (1:28) that if they would live so as to be worthy of the gospel of Christ, and would abide in the unity of the faith unswervingly, the very quality of their witness would be an omen to their antagonists. The implication is that such self-possession and faithfulness would be discouraging to the enemies of the Christian community. His friends at Philippi were to understand that a witness so borne is the mark of the Christian life and the sign of salvation.

See also ENCHANTER; SIGNS IN THE NT; SIGNS AND WONDERS.

Bibliography. J. Wellhausen, *Reste arabischen Heidentums* (1897), pp. 200-201. A. Guillaume, *Prophecy and Divination* (1938), especially pp. 133-41. J. Pedersen, *Israel, Its Life and Culture* (4 vols. in 2; 1926-40), I, 168-70; II, 15-18, 42, 112, 491, 499, 553. C. A. Keller, *Das Wort Oth als "Offenbarungszeichen Gottes"* (1946). G. E. Wright, *The OT Against Its Environment* (1950), pp. 78-93.

H. F. BECK

OMER ō'mər [עמר] (Exod. 16:13-36). A measure equal to a tenth of an ephah, a little more than two dry quarts. *See* WEIGHTS AND MEASURES § C4*h*.

OMRI ŏm'rī [עמרי]. **1.** A Benjaminite, a son of Becher (I Chr. 7:8).

2. One of the descendants of Judah; the son of Imri (I Chr. 9:4).

3. The son of Michael, and chief officer over the tribe of Issachar in the time of King David (I Chr. 27:18).

E. R. ACHTEMEIER

OMRI, KING [עמרי, worshiper of Yahweh; *cf.* Arab. *'Omar, 'Umar, from 'amara,* to live *or* to worship; *cuneiform* Ḫumri; LXX (Ζ)αμβρ(ε)ι]. King of Israel *ca.* 876-869 B.C.; successor of Zimri; founder of the Omride Dynasty.

The sources contain confusing and contradictory statements regarding the length of Omri's reign (I Kings 16:15, 21-22, 23, 29). If he began to reign in the thirty-first year of Asa king of Judah (vs. 23), and was succeeded by his son Ahab in the thirty-eighth year of Asa (vs. 29), it is clear that he reigned for eight years, not twelve years as stated (vs. 23). But Zimri, who reigned only seven days, came to the throne in the twenty-seventh year of Asa (vs. 15).

This would seem to indicate a period of twelve years, from Asa's twenty-seventh year to his thirty-eighth year, when Omri was in control. The confusion was due to the circumstances surrounding his becoming king.

A state of anarchy prevailed in the country following Elah's assassination by Zimri, one of his army commanders. The army in the field made Omri, the commander-in-chief, king. He moved at once to overthrow the usurper, who committed suicide in Tirzah when he saw that his cause was lost. But another aspirant to the throne appeared in the person of Tibni son of Ginath, of whom no details have been preserved. A period of civil war followed, with the people equally divided between Tibni and Omri (vs. 21). The struggle for power continued for four (five?) years and ended with Tibni's death. The Greek texts at this point add the words: "And his brother Joram (died) at the same time" (vs. 22). This addition almost certainly is historical. Only then was Omri formally acknowledged as king by the people, thereby confirming the army's choice (vs. 16). The figure of twelve years for Omri's reign was arrived at by adding the four years of civil war to the eight years of his sole rule. In reality the two periods overlapped in part.

It is to be noted that the name of Tibni's father is given, but no mention is made of Omri's father. The probable explanation is that Omri, like Zimri, was a foreigner, a non-Israelite, who had achieved his position through his own efforts and abilities. Tibni may have owed his position to the fact that he was a member of a known family in Israel.

Omri was a vigorous and capable ruler who demonstrated his ability both abroad and at home. He must be regarded as one of the greatest kings of Israel, despite the brief notice given him in Kings. The summary of his reign mentions the "might that he showed" (I Kings 16:27), but no actual details are given, apart from the civil war against Tibni. The writer of Kings was more interested in his religious policy than in his political achievements, but even here no details are given for the adverse judgment he passed on the king. He simply asserts that "Omri did what was evil in the sight of the LORD, and did more evil than all who were before him" (vs. 25).

Under Omri's strong leadership the latent power of Israel began to make itself felt. No mention is made of continuing war with Judah. It is clear that friendly relationships were established between them, cemented later by a marriage between the two royal houses. Omri succeeded in subjugating Moab and laying it under heavy tribute. The biblical narrative makes no specific reference to this conquest, but the amount of annual tribute paid to Israel and Moab's successful revolt under its King Mesha after the death of Ahab are recorded (II Kings 3:4). Fortunately, details have been preserved on the famous MOABITE STONE. These include Omri's name, and indicate that Moab endured afflictions for "many years." Moab had been independent since Solomon's time. As a result of Omri's victory much of the territory N of the River Arnon was occupied by the Israelites. Doubtless he hoped to use this newly won territory as a base of operations to recover the regions in NE Palestine which had been lost to Aram (I Kings 15:20). The sources are silent regarding any interference from Aram during this period. The probable explanation is that the relative strength of the two powers was approximately equal, so that neither was willing to attack the other. It is possible, however, that Omri achieved some success against Aram, which encouraged his son Ahab to continue the struggle for mastery.

Following in the footsteps of David and Solomon, Omri entered into an alliance with Phoenicia. This was sealed by the marriage of Ahab, Omri's eldest son, to Jezebel the daughter of Ethbaal (Ittobaal), the Sidonian king of Tyre (I Kings 16:31). This alliance was to have disastrous results for Israel, and was finally to bring about the downfall of the Omride Dynasty, but at the time it seemed to offer great advantages. It served as a check to the steadily growing power of Aram. Phoenicia was at the height of its power, and the alliance resulted in increased facilities for trade and the acquisition of considerable wealth by both countries. To this period belongs the rise of a new class in Israel—the merchant class. The wealth of these merchants stood in sharp contrast to the poverty of the majority of the people and profoundly affected the national life.

Closely allied to this change in the direction of Israel's policy came another strategic move which was to have far-reaching results for the whole future history of Israel. *Ca.* 870 Omri transferred his capital from Tirzah, where he had reigned for six years (vs. 23), to SAMARIA (the modern Sebastīyeh, *ca.* seven miles NW of Shechem). From the new capital the name Samaria came to be applied not only to the whole N kingdom but later to the Assyrian province as well. It was also the name often used by the prophet Hosea for his native country (Hos. 10:5, 7, etc.).

The reputation Omri won by his achievements is evidenced by the fact that for over a century after his death Samaria was called in the Assyrian records "House of Omri" (Ḫumri) and the land of Israel the "land of Omri." Even Jehu, who overthrew the Omride Dynasty in a blood bath, is called "son of Omri" in the black obelisk inscription of Shalmaneser III (*ca.* 842). The greatness of Omri is also exemplified by the reference in the prophet Micah (6:16) to the "statutes of Omri."

Bibliography. J. W. Crowfoot, K. Kenyon, and E. L. Sukenik, *Early Ivories from Samaria* (1938); *The Buildings at Samaria* (1942), pp. 5 ff. M. B. Rowton, "The Date of the Founding of Solomon's Temple," *BASOR,* 119 (1950), 20 ff. J. B. Pritchard, ed., *ANET* (2nd ed., 1955), pp. 320-31. G. E. Wright, *Biblical Archaeology* (1957), pp. 151-56.

H. B. MACLEAN

ON ŏn [און, vigor (*cf.* ONAM; ONAN); *in* 1 *below,* LXX B Αυν, LXX A Αυναν; *in* 2 *below,* LXX Ων]. **1.** A Reubenite who rebelled against Moses (Num. 16:1; but cf. Commentaries).

2. The Hebrew form of the Egyptian name of HELIOPOLIS; note also AVEN (1); City of the Sun; Ir-ha-heres.

ONAM ō'nəm [אונם, vigorous; LXX Ωμαν, Ωναν]. **1.** Ancestor of a Horite subclan in Edom (Gen. 36:23; I Chr. 1:40); fifth son of Shobal.

2. The father of a Jerahmeelite clan in Judah (I Chr. 2:26, 28); probably related to 1 *above.*

ONAN ō′nən [אונן=און, power, wealth, *plus ân; cf. personal name* אונם]. Second son of Judah and a Canaanitess (Gen. 38:4-10; 46:12; Num. 26:19; I Chr. 2:3). After the death of his older brother Er, Onan refused to accept the obligations of levirate marriage (*see* MARRIAGE § 1*g*) laid upon him both by social custom (cf. Deut. 25:5-10) and by explicit parental command (Gen. 38:8: יבם [RSV "perform the duty of a brother-in-law" preferable to KJV or LXX]). Instead, whenever he went in to her (the tenses are frequentative; G-K, §§ 112gg, 159o), he would spill his semen on the ground (so KJV and RSV; but ושחת ארצה="would spoil on the ground"—i.e., make it ineffective). For this refusal, rather than for the supposed sexual perversion bearing his name, Yahweh slew him. L. HICKS

ONESIMUS ō nĕs′ə məs [Ὀνήσιμος]. The slave in whose behalf Paul wrote his letter to Philemon. He is also mentioned in the Letter to the Colossians (4:9) as accompanying Tychicus, the bearer of the letter, and is spoken of there as "one of yourselves." His story, as gathered from the Letter to Philemon, is that he was the slave of either Philemon or Archippus, that he had not only run away but had also robbed his master to do so, had become acquainted with Paul, had been converted, and had become very dear to Paul. The relationship between him and Paul has become like that of father and child (Philem. 10). Paul says that in sending him back, he is sending his "very heart." Paul wishes that he might have kept Onesimus with him in his imprisonment, because his service has been so helpful and so faithful. Here Paul plays on the name Onesimus, which in Greek means "useful." Formerly, he says, the man was useless to his master, but now he has become useful to Paul (vss. 11-12). It is Paul's faith that the freed slave will be received as a beloved brother by his former owner, and that the latter will give him up to Paul. This, Paul implies, is the Christian obligation of the owner; but he refrains from commanding that it be so, lest the exercise of authority should make the act of freeing the slave a compulsion rather than Christian brotherhood.

The story of Onesimus may be carried further if two identifications are considered legitimate to make. Is he Onesimus the bishop, who is mentioned in laudatory terms in the second-century letter of Ignatius of Antioch to the church at Ephesus? If so, we have a glowing description of his leadership, a plea to his people to live worthily because they have so noble a bishop. The same pun on the name Onesimus as appears in the Letter to Philemon occurs here. Since it is a common name for slaves, and a less than common one for a free man, it is not too bold an assumption to say that the Bishop of Ephesus might have been a slave, and if a slave, most probably the slave whose freedom for Christian service Paul was asking in his letter to Philemon. The matter of his age at *ca.* A.D. 115 is a deterrent to some in making this identification; but if Onesimus were a young lad, as is quite possible when Paul wrote the Letter to Philemon, he would be in his seventies when Ignatius wrote—a not unsuitable age for a bishop who has proved himself by his commendable service.

The other identification in question is with the ONESIPHORUS mentioned in II Tim. 1:16-18. The case for this identification is more tenuous than for the identification with the bishop of Ephesus mentioned by Ignatius. The matter of Pauline authorship for this section of the Letter to Timothy would first need to be settled. Suffice it to say that the personal messages are the most likely parts of the Pastoral letters to hold for Paul. But the matter of the different form of the name is a greater problem to some. But P. N. Harrison (*see bibliography*) points out that we are willing to accept the identification of Silas with Silvanus, of Prisca with Priscilla, and perhaps Epaphras with EPAPHRODITUS; and so he asks, Why not Onesimus and Onesiphorus? If so, we have a warm commendation of him in Paul's words: "May the Lord grant mercy to the household of Onesiphorus, for he often refreshed me; he was not ashamed of my chains, but when he arrived in Rome he searched for me eagerly and found me—may the Lord grant him to find mercy from the Lord on that Day—and you well know all the service he rendered at Ephesus" (II Tim. 1:16-18). Again at the close of the letter he comes in for mention: "Greet Prisca and Aquila, and the household of Onesiphorus" (4:19). If this identification is not accepted, and the former one is, it would seem a real coincidence that two persons of similar names were not only ministering to Paul in prison but also giving excellent community service in Ephesus. To be sure, we have assumed that the prison service mentioned in the Letter to Philemon as given by Onesimus to Paul (*see* PHILEMON, LETTER TO) was in Ephesus rather than in Rome, and here Rome is explicitly mentioned. Those who accept this identification of Onesiphorus with Onesimus must either reject the Ephesian locale for this ministry or assume that the "far more imprisonments" of II Cor. 11:23 would allow for such ministration to take place in two different imprisonments. In any event, this identifying of Onesimus with Onesiphorus is somewhat more strained than is the case with the Bishop of Ephesus mentioned by Ignatius.

Onesimus traveled with Tychicus to carry both the letter to the Colossian church and the Letter to Philemon from the imprisoned Paul to the Christians at Colossae (Col. 4:7-9). The same friends of Paul send greetings in these two letters, and in the Colossian letter their names are linked with the promise that the two of them will tell the Christians in Colossae all the news of Paul. Both Tychicus and Onesimus are cited as "beloved brothers" and are described as faithful in work. If the view of John Knox (*see bibliography*) is accepted that Archippus, the slaveowner, is at Colossae, and that Philemon, the church leader of the Lycus Valley churches, is at Laodicea, then the letters were intended to go via Laodicea to their final destination at Colossae.

Bibliography. For Knox's views about Archippus and the identification of Onesimus with the Bishop of Ephesus, see *Philemon Among the Letters of Paul* (rev. ed., 1959). For the views of P. N. Harrison on Onesimus and Onesiphorus, see "Onesimus and Philemon," *ATR,* vol. XXXII (1950).

M. E. LYMAN

ONESIPHORUS ŏn'ə sĭf'ə rəs ['Ὀνησίφορος, profit-bearing]. A Christian from Ephesus who is praised for his loyalty and service to Paul and to the church (II Tim. 1:16-18). "Paul" prays that the Lord will grant mercy to the household of Onesiphorus (vs. 16), asks Timothy to greet the household of Onesiphorus (4:19), and recalls Onesiphorus' past devotion to him both in Ephesus and in Rome as a prisoner. Because of the references to the household of Onesiphorus, and not to Onesiphorus personally, one infers that at the time of the writing of II Timothy, Onesiphorus was either absent from home (so Dibelius) or no longer living. If he were dead, we would have in 1:18 the earliest prayer for the dead in Christian literature. Prayer for the dead had a Jewish precedent (cf. II Macc. 12:43-45) and became a common practice in the early church (cf. Tert. *On the Soldier's Chaplet* 3, *On Monogamy* 10; Cyprian *Epistles* 57, 66; Arnobius *Against the Heathen* IV; etc.; *see bibliography*).

When Onesiphorus went to Rome, he searched out Paul in prison, no doubt having difficulty finding him who was shortly to be condemned to death. He was "not ashamed" of Paul's imprisonment, and often "refreshed" Paul—no doubt, with his presence and with his gifts. Finally, a testimony is paid to Onesiphorus for all the services he had rendered not only in Rome but also in Ephesus—probably both to Paul and to the church there; and in the light of this tribute to Onesiphorus, Timothy, a "son," is bidden to be "strong in the grace that is in Christ Jesus" (II Tim. 2:1). *See also* ONESIMUS.

Bibliography. On prayer for the dead, see A. Plummer, *Expositor's Bible* (1888).

B. H. THROCKMORTON, JR.

ONIAS ō nī'əs [חוניו, חוני; 'Ονίας]. The name of several persons of priestly family in the Maccabean period.

1. Onias I, high priest in Judea (*ca.* 320-290 B.C.), the son of high priest Jaddua and father of high priest Simon I, who is called "the Just" by Josephus (Antiq. XI.viii.7; XII.iv.1). Onias I was a contemporary of the Spartan king Arius, who reigned 309-265, and he contracted an alliance with him to the effect that they were kinsmen (I Macc. 12:7 ff). The priestly family of Onias traced its lineage to Zadok, the high priest appointed by Solomon (I Kings 3:35).

Bibliography. E. Schürer, *A History of the Jewish People in the Time of Jesus Christ* (English trans.; 1891), vol. I, div. 1, p. 188.

2. Onias II, son of Simon I. His sacerdotal rule came only after that of his uncle Eleazar and the latter's uncle Manasseh, both of whom had succeeded Simon I before the son did; apparently Onias was still too young for the succession. Onias II, for politico-religious reasons, refused to pay the token tribute of twenty talents to King Ptolemy III, *ca.* 242 B.C. (Antiq. XII.iv.1). He was pro-Seleucidean and made an alliance with Seleucus II because of the economic needs of the temple. He believed that there was a greater kinship with Babylonian (Seleucid) Jewry than with the Ptolemaic Jewry. Ptolemy threatened to seize the country and parcel out the land, but Onias II persisted. His nephew Joseph (son of Tobias, the husband of Onias' sister), because of his business connections with the Egyptian court, handled the situation and thereby assumed civil leadership of the Jews, gaining temporal power over the high priesthood. Thus, by Onias II's action, the sacerdotal office was now divided; political control was relinquished, and the high priesthood henceforth retained only ecclesiastical power. This was the beginning of the high-priestly decline and the Tobiade domination in Judea. Onias II was succeeded by his son Simon II (who is also called "the Just"; Ecclus. 50).

Bibliography. S. Tedesche and S. Zeitlin, *The First Book of Maccabees* (1950), p. 5.

3. Onias III, son of Simon II and high priest in the time of Seleucus IV (*ca.* 180 B.C.). Unlike his father and his grandfather, he forsook the Seleucids and became an adherent of the Ptolemies. He felt that association with the Egyptians would be of greater advantage to Judea because of the large Jewish population in Alexandria and also because the disturbed roads to Syria prevented pilgrimages to Jerusalem. His cousins, the sons of Joseph ben Tobias, however, who had financial control of the state, sided with the Seleucids.

One of the Tobiade sons, Simon, the captain of the temple, informed King Seleucus that hidden in the temple were sums of money belonging to Hyrcanus, his half brother, who was a Ptolemaic agent. When Seleucus sent his minister Heliodorus to confiscate the money, Onias refused the latter admittance, insisting that the money belonged to widows and orphans. Heliodorus insisted but, upon entering the temple, was panic-stricken by an apparition of a rider, and he was flogged by youths. Onias prayed for Heliodorus' recovery, fearing that he would be punished as the instigator of the mischief (II Macc. 3:10 ff).

Simon, the temple captain, accused Onias, who thereupon went to Antioch to plead before King Seleucus. But the latter was assassinated by Heliodorus and was succeeded by his brother, Antiochus Epiphanes IV. Onias then fled to Egypt, where he built a rival temple in Heliopolis, called the temple of Onias (Jos. War VII.x.2; see also M. Men. 13.10). Onias' brother Joshua, called Jason, was subsequently established as high priest in Jerusalem. II Maccabees, however, depicts Onias as having been killed in Antioch when he left the asylum of Daphne (II Macc. 4:33 ff). Scholars disagree over the question whether the story of this murder is historical. It is to be assumed that the death of Onias III in Antioch was only a false rumor because of the death of the delegation protesting against Menelaus, who supported his cousin Jason. It was therefore thought that Onias, too, had been killed. Moreover, the passage in Jos. Antiq. XII.v.1, noting that this Onias was called Menelaus, is spurious.

Onias III is definitely to be regarded as the founder of the Onias temple. This temple in Heliopolis could have been built only in 169-168 B.C., when there was animosity between the Seleucids and Egyptians. It was Onias III who favored the Ptolemies and consequently received permission from Ptolemy V for the establishment of the sanctuary in Egypt. It could not be in the time of Onias IV (164-163 B.C.; *see below*), because already in 164 religious freedom had been established, and a rival temple in Egypt was not in demand. Josephus has many discrepancies about the Onias who built the Heliopolis temple (Jos. Antiq. XX.x.1; War VII.x.2).

Bibliography. S. Zeitlin, Prolegomena, *History of the Second Jewish Commonwealth* (1933), pp. 23, 26; R. H. Pfeiffer, *History of NT Times* (1949), p. 12; S. Tedesche and S. Zeitlin, *The Second Book of Maccabees* (1954), pp. 4-5; V. Tcherikover, *Hellenistic Civilization and the Jews* (1959).

4. Onias IV, son of Onias III. Josephus (Antiq. XII.ix.7; XIII.iii.1; XX.x.1) relates that when Antiochus V killed Menelaus, giving the priesthood to Alcimus, this Onias fled to Egypt and built a rival temple (*see* 3 *above*). A Jewish military colony in Leontopolis, near Memphis, was founded by Onias IV. His sons are recognized as prominent generals under Cleopatra III, dissuading her from warfare against the Judeans. *See* ALEXANDER JANNEUS.

Josephus also says that Onias V built the temple (Antiq. XIII.x.4).

Bibliography. S. A. Hirsch, "The Temple of Onias," *Jews' College Jubilee Volume* (1925), pp. 39-80; R. H. Pfeiffer, *History of NT Times* (1954), p. 179; V. A. Tcherikover and A. Fuks, *Corpus Papyrorum Judaicarum,* I (1957), 3, 44 ff; S. Baron, *A Social and Religious History of the Jews* (1952-58), 219 and bibliography on 394, note 11.

5. Onias, known as Menelaus, one of the sons of Joseph ben Tobias and cousin (*exadelphos*) of Onias III. He obtained the high priesthood through the military force of Antiochus IV after the deposition of Joshua-Jason, his cousin, by promising greater sums. Since he could not raise the money, he went to Antioch, placing his brother Lysimachus as acting high priest. Lysimachus committed sacrilege, robbing the temple in order to obtain the funds, but was lynched. Members of the Judean *gerousia* complained to the king about Onias-Menelaus, but they were executed summarily.

Bibliography. A. Büchler, *Die Tobiaden und die Oniaden* (1899), p. 80; S. Tedesche and S. Zeitlin, *The Second Book of Maccabees* (1954), p. 80. S. B. HOENIG

ONION [בצל, *bāṣāl* (*plural only*); Aram. בוצלא, *bûṣlâ;* Arab. *baṣal*]. A bulbous vegetable of the lily family, *Allium cepa* L. It was one of the foods of Egypt for which the Hebrews longed in the wilderness (Num. 11:5). It was popular as a food in Egypt as early as the third millennium B.C. (Herodotus II.125). Ancient writers extol the quality of Egyptian varieties.

See also AGRICULTURE; FLORA § A3*a;* FOOD.

Bibliography. H. N. and A. L. Moldenke, *Plants of the Bible* (1952), p. 33. J. C. TREVER

ONLY BEGOTTEN. A mistranslation in the KJV of the Greek μονογενής (RSV "only"; John 1:14, 18; 3:16, 18; Heb. 11:17; I John 4:9). Μονογενής is derived from μόνος, "single," and γένος, "kind," and means "one of a kind," "only," "unique," not "only begotten," which would be μονογέννητος. This is consistent with the LXX usage in Judg. 11:34; Pss. 22:20; 25:16; 35:17; Tob. 3:15; Wisd. Sol. 7:22; and with I Clem. XXV.2, where it is used of the phoenix. Jerome revised the translation in the Old Latin MSS from *unicus,* "only," to *unigenitus,* "only begotten," out of interest for theological dogma, not for the demands of linguistic study. In Luke 7:12; 8:42; 9:38, where no theological question is involved, the Latin *unicus* was left as the translation of μονογενής. Jerome was, no doubt, influenced by the theological orations of Gregory of Nazianzus, whom he had heard in Constantinople (379-81). Gregory's *Oration* XXIX, in discussing the eternal relation between the Father and the Son, spoke of the Father as γεννήτωρ, "begetter," and of the Son as γέννημα, "begotten."

William Tyndale (*see* VERSIONS, ENGLISH, § 3), the first to translate the NT from Greek into English, failed to correct Jerome in John 1:14, 18; Heb. 11:17; I John 4:9; but his editions of 1526 and 1534 corrected the error in John 3:16, 18, with the translation "only sonne." The KJV of 1611, under the influence of the Latin Vulg., returned to "only begotten" in John 3:16, 18.

The meaning of μονογενής in the Johannine writings has great significance for Christology. In I John the Son is declared the revealer of God (4:9) and the redeemer of men (4:10). The two ideas are elaborated in John's Gospel. The Son reveals God as the Logos (Word) becoming flesh with a "glory as of the only Son from the Father" (1:14). This relation is so important in historical revelation that John 1:18 does not hesitate to call the Son μονογενὴς θεὸς, "only God." The Son is proclaimed the redeemer of men, both in reference to his work as the sacrifice for sin (3:16) and in reference to his person, which is linked with believing on his name (3:18). The distinctive vocabulary of the Johannine writings reserves the term υἵος, "son," for the Son of God alone (John 1:34, 49; 3:18; 5:25; 10:36; 11:4, 27; 17:1; 19:7; 20:31; I John 1:3, 7; 3:8, 23; 4:9, 15; 5:5, 9-12, 20; II John 3), so that in a real sense Jesus is the only Son. Believers are called "children" (τέκνα; John 1:12; I John 3:1-2; 5:2). It would be awkward for John to speak of the Son as "begotten," since the word for "beget," γεννάω, is used to designate the relation between God and all his children (John 1:13; 3:3, 5-8; I John 2:29; 3:9; 4:7, 9; 5:1, 4, 18).

Bibliography. D. Moody, "God's Only Son," *JBL,* vol. LXXII, pt. IV (Dec., 1953), p. 72. D. MOODY

ONO ō′nō [אונו, אנו]; KJV Apoc. ONUS ō′nəs ['Ωνους, *genitive form*]. A town of Benjamin near the S border of the Plain of Sharon some seven miles SE of Joppa. With Lod (Lydda) and Hadid, it constituted the ancestral homeland of more than 720 exiles who returned from the Babylonian captivity (Ezra 2:33; Neh. 7:37; 11:35; I Esd. 5:22) and with them also represented the westernmost settlement of the restored community.

It appears in the Karnak list of Thutmose III (*'Unu*) and is described in the Mishna ('Arak. 9.6) as a walled city since the days of Joshua. Its construction by the sons of Elpaal, descendants of Benjamin, also testifies to its importance as an early fortified town (I Chr. 8:12).

The village of Kefr 'Ana in the Wadi Musrara preserves the name of the biblical site, and the broad wadi itself was the Plain of Ono—the setting for the intrigues of Sanballat and Geshem against Nehemiah (Neh. 6:2). W. H. MORTON

ONUS. KJV Apoc. form of ONO.

ONYCHA ŏn′ĭ kə [שְׁחֵלֶת, nail, claw, husk, flap, *or* that which hangs loose (down); LXX ὄνυξ] (Exod. 30:34). An ingredient (probably obtained from a marine animal, most probably from the closing flaps of certain mollusks) in the mixture to be burned on the altar of incense. A corresponding verbal root in Arabic is the basis for a noun denoting the husks of wheat and barley. A related postbiblical Hebrew word, שחלים, is used as the name for garden cress.

J. C. Rylaarsdam

ONYX. A chalcedony whose bands are milk-white alternating with black (*see also* Agate). "Onyx" is used to translate the following stone names:

a) שֹׁהַם, *šōham* (cf. Akkadian *sâmu*, "dark red"). The Vulg. renders this word "onyx" except in Job 28:16, where it reads "sardonyx." The LXX varies: in Gen. 2:12, λίθος ὁ πράσινος, "stone of leek green"; in Exod. 25:7; 35:9, λίθος σαρδίου, "carnelian" or "sardius"; in 28:9; 35:27, σμαράγδος, "emerald"; in 28:20, βηρύλλιον; in I Chr. 29:2, the transliteration σόομ. With gold and bdellium, onyx is a product of Havilah (Gen. 2:12). It is acceptable as an offering for the ephod and breastpiece (Exod. 25:7; 35:9, 27). It comprised the engraved shoulder pieces of Aaron's ephod (28:9; 39:6). It is a stone in the breastpiece of judgment (28:20; 39:13). It was building material assembled by David for the temple of Solomon (I Chr. 29:2). It was used in the evaluating of wisdom (Job 28:16).

b) יָשְׁפֵה, *yāšᵉphê*. In Ezek. 28:13, "beryl" is used for שהם (*above*) and "onyx" for ישפה. In Exod. 28:20, where the RSV translates "jasper," the LXX reads "onyx." It is one of the stones in the covering of the king of Tyre.

c) Σαρδόνυξ (Rev. 21:20; cf. Job 28:16 Vulg.; *see* Sardonyx), the fifth stone of the foundation of the wall of the New Jerusalem.

W. E. Staples

OPHEL ō′fĕl [עֹפֶל]. According to etymology, a swelling, a bulge; hence, a knoll, a mound. As a common appellative it occurs in the Hebrew text of Isa. 32:14 (RSV "the hill"; KJV "the forts") and of Mic. 4:8 (RSV "hill"; KJV "stronghold"). In several instances, the term "Ophel" applies to a specific mound and becomes a proper name. This may well be the case in II Kings 5:24 MT, which refers to the Ophel of Samaria, where the house of Elisha stood; the RSV, however, reads "the hill," and the KJV "the tower." Ophel is used undoubtedly as a proper name in the inscription of Mesha, line 22: "I built QRḤH (Kerak) . . . and the wall of the Ophel." *See* Moabite Stone.

The name Ophel was given to a quarter of ancient Jerusalem, to the fortification of which the late kings of Judah gave repeated attention (II Chr. 27:3; 33:14). After the Exile, the temple servants or Nethinim were quartered on the Ophel, and they repaired the ramparts that lay in ruins (Neh. 3:26-27; 11:21). The topographical details contained in all these texts point to a location on the NE portion of the triangular hill on which stood the City of David (*see* David, City of), S of the Haram esh-Sherif, in a commanding position above the slopes of the Kidron (*see* Kidron, Brook). Josephus calls the same quarter ʼΟφλᾶς, a Hellenized transcription of the Aramaic עפלא. He makes clear the proximity of Ophel to the temple, the S portico of which was contiguous with the city wall above the Kidron (War V.iv.2; vi.1), and he formally distinguishes ʼΟφλᾶς from ἄκρα, the citadel of the Syrians in the time of the Maccabees, which he localizes on the same hill, perhaps by confusion.

Various excavations conducted on the SE hill of Jerusalem have uncovered important elements of fortifications, particularly toward the angle of the Haram esh-Sherif overlooking the Kidron, and right above Gihon (*see* Gihon, Spring), ranging from the pre-Israelite period to the late Hellenistic. They can be regarded as the last remains of the system of ramparts and towers of the Ophel. Unfortunately, the chronological and architectural connections between structures excavated at long intervals of time and inadequately recorded remain often obscure. It should be noted that, in modern archaeological literature, the name of Ophel is sometimes given (abusively) to the entire hill, from the temple to Siloam.

See map under Jerusalem.

Bibliography. G. A. Smith, *Jerusalem*, I (1907), 152-54; H. Vincent, *Jérusalem Antique* (1912), pp. 187-90; G. Dalman, *Jerusalem und sein Gelände* (1930), pp. 123-25; J. Simons, *Jerusalem in the OT* (1952), pp. 64-67.

G. A. Barrois

OPHIR ō′fər [אוֹפִיר, אוֹפִר (Gen. 10:29), אֹפִיר (I Kings 10:11); LXX ουφιρ, οφερ, ωφιρ, σουφιρ, σουφειρ, σωφιρ, σωφειρ, σωφηρα]. **1.** A people descended from Shem through the lineage Arpachshad, Shelah, Eber, and Joktan (Gen. 10:29; I Chr. 1:23). On the location of their territory, *see* 2 *below*.

2. A region or territory chiefly known for its production of fine gold and Almug trees. Ophir first appears in historical narrative during the United Monarchy as the source of the 3,000 talents of fine gold left by David for the temple (I Chr. 29:4). It was also the place from which a fleet of ships, built by Solomon at Ezion-geber and manned by Phoenicians and Israelites, brought 420 talents of gold (II Chr. 8:18 reads 450 talents), silver, almug trees, precious stones, ivory, and two kinds of monkeys (*qôphîm* and *tukkîyîm; see* Fauna § A2*k*) to Israel (I Kings 9:28; 10:11 = II Chr. 8:18; 9:10). In the ninth century, Jehoshaphat attempted to duplicate Solomon's expeditions to Ophir, but his ships were broken up at Ezion-geber before setting sail (I Kings 22:48—H 22:49). Ophir is also mentioned in an inscription on a sherd found at Tell Qasileh, probably biblical Aphek. The inscription, which belongs to *ca.* the eighth century B.C., reads: "Gold of Ophir for [or belonging to] Beth-horon, 30 shekels." This is the first nonbiblical mention of Ophir discovered to date (Fig. OPH 11). The fame of Ophir's fine gold is also mentioned in poetic and prophetic passages as a symbol of greatest opulence (Job 22:24; 28:16; Ps. 45:9—H 45:10; Isa. 13:12).

The location of Ophir has been much disputed; it has been variously placed in India, Arabia, and Africa. Those who hold to an Indian location draw their support from the LXX reading "Sophir" with an initial "s" (*see above*); from Jerome, who once renders "Ophir" by "India" (Job 28:16); and from Josephus, who describes the destination of Solomon's

From *Journal of Near Eastern Studies*, published by the University of Chicago Press; copyright 1956 by the University of Chicago

11. Ostracon from Tell Qasile with inscription: "Gold of Ophir to Beth Horon . . . thirty shekels" (*ca.* 589/588 B.C.)

fleet as Sopher, which belongs to India (Antiq. VIII.vi.4). Basing themselves on this tradition, which goes back at least to LXX times, they identify Sophir with the city of Supara, located a few miles N of Bombay. This identification, however, is quite unlikely for several reasons. All available evidence suggests that before the first century B.C., trade between the Mediterranean lands and India was controlled by Arab and Indian merchantmen, and that Egyptian, Phoenician, and Greek fleets obtained Eastern products from middlemen in S Arabian and East African ports. Furthermore, there can be little doubt that the MT correctly preserves the name Ophir, the identification of which by Hellenistic times had been forgotten, and that the tradition identifying Ophir with Sophir = Supara was an attempt to locate this place.

Other scholars have sought to locate Ophir in the Arabian Peninsula, and virtually every coastal region from Yemen to the Persian Gulf and some inland areas have been suggested, including: Ma'afir, a territory in the extreme SW corner of Yemen; Dhofar, on the S coast; Nazwa, a site on the S slope of Jebel el-Akhdhar in Oman; Apir, a region on the Persian Gulf S of Elam; the wells at U'ayfirah, not far W of the S Tuwaiq range in central Arabia. All these proposed identifications, which are located E of the Aden Protectorates, are open to the same geographical objection that applies to the Indian identification (*see above*). The only possible part of Arabia in which Ophir might have been located is the SW corner of the peninsula, in view of the association of Ophir with Sheba (*see* SABEANS) and HAVILAH; but the one suggested identification in this area, Ma'afir, is linguistically impossible.

Two regions in Africa have been suggested as possible locations for Ophir: the ruins of Zimbabwe in Southern Rhodesia, and the East African coast in the general vicinity of Somaliland. The first of these is impossible, since the ruins of Zimbabwe date *ca.* the eighth century A.D. The second, the region of Somaliland, with a possible extension to the neighboring coast of S Arabia, is the most probable identification of Ophir as yet proposed. The products of Ophir (I Kings 9:28; 10:11) are the same as those of the Egyptian Punt, and included such characteristic African products as gold, silver, ivory, and two kinds of monkeys, the words for which in Egyptian, *qf* and *ky*, are the same as in Hebrew. It is therefore likely that Ophir and Punt were in the same general region and possibly the same place. It is certain that Punt was located in the vicinity of Somaliland, from Egyptian reliefs which portray an African culture and environment and list imported products such as myrrh trees, which in Africa grow only in this region. Thus it is quite probable that Ophir was located in this same region. The voyage to Ophir is said to have required three years, which probably meant one full year and parts of two others, according to Semitic reckoning. The fleet would leave Ezion-geber in the late autumn of one year, call at Ophir and possibly other ports en route as well during the second year, and return to Ezion-geber in the spring of the third year. Such voyages to a region no more distant than Ophir were quite possible, since we have numerous records of Egyptian voyages to Punt from the Fifth Dynasty through the period of the New Kingdom.

Bibliography. *The Periplus of the Erythraean Sea* (trans. and annotated by W. H. Schoff; 1912), p. 175; A. Grohmann, *Südarabien als Wirtschaftsgebiet* I in *Osten und Orient* (1922), p. 122; J. A. Montgomery, *Arabia and the Bible* (1934), pp. 38-39, 176-79; W. F. Albright, *Archaeology and the Religion of Israel* (1946), pp. 133-34; G. W. Van Beek, "Frankincense and Myrrh in Ancient South Arabia," *JAOS,* 78 (1958), 141-52; G. Ryckmans, "Ophir," *Supplément au Dictionnaire de la Bible* (1959), cols. 744-51: an excellent summary.

G. W. VAN BEEK

OPHNI ŏf'nī [עָפְנִי]. A town in the territory allotted to Benjamin (Josh. 18:24). Though the site remains unknown, its listing in company with Geba suggests the N central district of the tribal territory.

Modern Jifna, the Gophna of Josephus, is often suggested as a possible identification of the OT site. This town was located *ca.* three miles NW of Bethel and was strategically situated near the intersection of the Jerusalem-Shechem highway and the road leading up to Bethel from the Plain of Sharon. As head of one of the toparchies of Judea, Gophna was, in Josephus' day, second in importance only to Jerusalem (Jos. War III.iii.5). The suitability of this suggested location presupposes a slight northward bulge in the rather loosely delineated N boundary of Benjamin near Bethel.

Bibliography. G. A. Smith, *The Historical Geography of the Holy Land* (1904), p. 351.

W. H. MORTON

OPHRAH ŏf'rə [עָפְרָה, hind]. **1.** A son of Meonothai and descendant of Judah through Kenaz and Othniel (I Chr. 4:14).

2. One of the cities allotted to Benjamin (Josh. 18:23). Related cities in the list suggest a location in the hill country to the NE of Jerusalem. The site is also associated with one of three raiding parties dispatched from the Philistine camp at Michmash (I Sam. 13:17-18). With Saul's forces situated to the S at Geba, one Philistine party turned westward toward Beth-horon, another eastward toward the border overlooking the wilderness, and a third in the direction of Ophrah, which must, therefore, have lain northward from Michmash.

Ophrah is probably identical with Ephron of II Chr. 13:19; Ephraim of II Sam. 13:23; John 11:54; and Aphairema of I Macc. 11:34. If so, proximity to Bethel, Baal-hazor, and the wilderness becomes an additional factor in determining its location.

Jerome equates the ancient site with the town of Ephraim and locates it five Roman miles E of Bethel. Accordingly, it is probably correctly identified with modern et-Taiyibeh, five miles N of ancient Michmash and four miles NE of Beitin (Bethel).

3. A town in the Cis-Jordan territory of Manasseh, distinguished from others of like name as the one belonging to the clan of Abiezer (Judg. 6:11, 15, 24; 8:32; cf. Josh. 17:2; I Chr. 7:18). It was Gideon's home where he both experienced the oppression of the Midianites and received the divine commission to deliver Israel from it (Judg. 6:11, 14). Here, also, he built an altar to the Lord and destroyed the local idolatrous installations (vss. 24-27). From the spoil of his triumph over Midian he made a golden ephod for Ophrah, which became an apostatizing snare both to Israel and to his own family (8:27). Here Gideon died and was buried in the family sepulchre (vs. 32); and here Abimelech, ambitious to be king, slew seventy of his brothers as possible rivals to his claim —only Jotham managed to escape (9:5).

The geographical situation of Ophrah of Abiezer remains uncertain. The only available clues to its location are the rather general ones associating the Gideon episodes with the Valley of Jezreel, the hill of Moreh, the spring of Harod, and Tabor, plus the impression that the home of Gideon was not far removed from the scene of these activities (Judg. 6:11, 33-35; 7:1; 8:18-19). Several rather widely separated sites have been suggested for its location. Among them may be mentioned et-Taiyibeh, S of Tulkarem; et-Taiyibeh, NW of Beth-shan; Ferata, W of Shechem; Silet ed-Dahr, N of Shechem; and a site NW of Megiddo. No one of them, however, has sufficient evidence in its favor to encourage confidence in its identification with Ophrah.

Bibliography. F.-M. Abel, *Géographie de la Palestine,* II (1938), 95; E. G. Kraeling, *Bible Atlas* (1956), p. 154.

W. H. Morton

ORACLE [נאם (KJV SAY); משא (KJV BURDEN), *lit.*, speech, utterance, pronouncement]. An introductory formula to a divinely inspired message. These two Hebrew words are used in the prophetic literature (*see* Prophet). For the employment of oracles in early Israel, *cf.* Urim and Thummim.

I. Mendelsohn

ORACLES, SIBYLLINE. *See* Sibylline Oracles.

ORAL TRADITION. *See* Tradition.

ORATORY. *See* Rhetoric and Oratory.

ORCHARD [פרדס, *loan word from* Persian=Paradise (Song of S. 4:13; FOREST *in* Neh. 2:8; GARDEN *in* Eccl. 2:5); גנה, garden (Song of S. 6:11); זית, olive tree(s)]. Olive, pomegranate, or nut trees collectively; also, a park or Garden. "Fruit trees" in Neh. 9:25 suggests trees other than those mentioned above.

H. N. Richardson

ORDINANCE. A frequent translation of משפט ("judgment") and חק, חקה ("statute") in English versions (*see* Law in the OT).

משפט is one of the most significant OT words. It is derived from an ancient Semitic root meaning "to decide" and originally describes the decision of a local judge in cases of civil disputes. It is not unlikely that the plural, משפטים, was once a technical term for the casuistic Canaanite law, which made up a large part of Israel's legal corpus (cf. Exod. 21:1; 24:3). Derivatively, the word may mean "judgment," "justice," a "legal case," "claim," "that which is right, fitting" (hence "manner," "custom").

The words חק, חקה, are derived from a verb which means "inscribe" or "engrave," and thus "that which is fixed in writing," "decree," "statute." חק may then be used of anything which is prescribed, in the widest sense, including secular and divine law. חקה infers somewhat more narrowly "that which is due," "statute."

משפט is frequently translated "ordinance" for the KJV "judgment" when the particular law itself is intended, rather than "judgment" before the law, which the older term tends to convey to modern ears (similarly, "justice" for KJV "judgment" when the right of a person before the law is involved). חק, חקה, are normally translated "statute" when they appear parallel to other synonyms for the law.

Reminiscences of the ancient secular statutes and ordinances established for the social order are found in Gen. 47:26; I Sam. 30:25, where they are instituted by human authority (cf. I Kings 3:3; II Kings 17:8, 19; Dan. 6:7-8). Even within the cultic order, certain ordinances are instituted by men (cf. Judg. 11:39; II Chr. 8:14; 35:25).

In the theology of Deuteronomy a variety of etymologically distinct terms for "law" are used quite synonymously for the law of God: "statutes and ordinances" (Deut. 4:1, 5, 14; 5:1; 11:32); "statutes, commandments, ordinances, testimonies" (I Kings 2:3); "statutes, ordinances, . . . all this law" (Deut. 4:8; cf. 33:10; cf. also I Kings 8:58; 9:4; 11:33; II Kings 17:34, 37). The ordinances are grounded in the vital command of God (Deut. 4:5, 14; 5:31 ff; 6:1-2, 24-25) based upon his gracious activity (Deut. 4:32-40; 6:20; 7:6-8 [cf. 9:4-29]; 29:2-9), and therefore may not be understood in terms of mere legalism. For the Deuteronomist, all law can be summed up in the injunction to "love the Lord your God" with heart, soul, and might (Deut. 6:5; *see* Shema; cf. Deut. 4:29; 10:12, 16; 11:1; 30:10, 14). The purpose of obedience is clearly to keep Covenant with God, in order that his covenant promises may be fulfilled (Deut. 7:6-16; cf. 6:2-3; 11:8-25; 30:1-10). It is not necessary at this period to think of a fixed canon of sacred law, which eventually is implied in such passages as Ezra 7:6, 10; Neh. 1:7. Several of the Psalms employ the terms "ordinance" and "statute" in a typically Deuteronomic way (Pss. 18:22; 19:7-10; 89:30-31; 119; 147: 19-20; see also Ezek. 5:6-7; 20:11, 13, 16; 36:27; but cf. 20:25, which is distinctly non-Deuteronomic).

In the language of the cult, כמשפט, "according to the ordinance," becomes a technical term for fulfilling the priestly prescriptions. More than "custom" or "usage" is implied, and the RSV rightly translates "ordinance" for KJV "manner" (Lev. 5:10; 9:16; Num. 29). A typically priestly term is חקת עולם, "perpetual statute, ordinance" (Exod. 12:14, 17, 24; Lev. 16:29, 31, 34; 23:41; Num. 10:8; etc.).

Bibliography. W. Eichrodt, *Theologie des Alten Testaments,* I (1933), 26-41; A. Alt, *Die Ursprünge des israelitischen Rechts,* in *Kleine Schriften zur Geschichte des Volkes Israel,* I (1953), 278-332; G. E. Wright, *IB,* II (1953), 352; L. Koehler, *OT Theology* (English trans., 1957), pp. 201-9. J. A. WHARTON

ORDINATION, RAM OF. The animal (איל; *see* RAM) sacrificed in connection with the ordination (המלאים; lit., "that which fills" [τελειώσις], from מלא, "to be full," in some forms "fulfil," "institute," "ordain" [cf. Judg. 17:5; I Kings 13:33]; KJV CONSECRATION) of the Aaronic priesthood in Exod. 29:22 ff; Lev. 8:22 ff. *See* PRIESTS AND LEVITES; SACRIFICE AND OFFERINGS; MINISTRY.

J. A. WHARTON

ORE [אבן, *lit.,* stone]; KJV STONE. The rock from which metals are obtained. Job 28:2-3 refers to the deep mine shafts in remote valleys from which ore was obtained. *See* METALLURGY.

OREB AND ZEEB ôr'əb, zē'əb [עורב, raven; זאב, wolf]. Two Midianite princes who were captured and put to death by the Ephraimites after Gideon's surprise attack had routed their forces.

After seven years of subjugation to the devastating invasions of Arabian bands, whose recent domestication of the camel had greatly extended their predatory migrations, Gideon led his chosen followers in a successful attack against the Midianites and their allies as they encamped by the Hill of Moreh in the Valley of Jezreel (Judg. 6–7). The Ephraimites, who had been summoned by Gideon to cut off the retreat by commanding the waters to the E of the enemy, seized two Midianite princes, Oreb and Zeeb, and promptly executed them.

Each of these leaders appears to have bequeathed his name to the place where he was slain: Oreb to the rock of Oreb, and Zeeb to the wine press of Zeeb. However, it may be argued that the name of places gave rise to the names of the princes, who were perhaps not named in the original text.

The heads of these enemy leaders were presented to Gideon and constituted, in his words, such a rich war prize that the Ephraimites, who were angry because they had not been invited to participate earlier in the campaign, were completely pacified (Judg. 7:24–8:3). The execution of Oreb and Zeeb, as well as the defeat of Midian, became proverbial in the thought of Israel (Ps. 83:11—H 83:12; Isa. 9:4; 10:26). E. R. DALGLISH

OREN ôr'ən [אורן, fir tree] (I Chr. 2:25). A descendant of Judah, and one of the sons of Jerahmeel.

ORGAN. *See* MUSICAL INSTRUMENTS.

ORGIES [המון, tumult] (Jer. 3:23); KJV MULTITUDE. That "orgies on the mountains" refers to the fertility rites of the syncretistic West Semitic religions (*see* BAAL [DEITY]) of late-seventh-century Judah seems reasonable, in view of the strong revival which the local cults of this religion (practiced on the "high places" [*see* HIGH PLACE]) enjoyed during the reign of Manasseh (687-642 B.C.). Frenzied revelry, sexual license, and hysterical or "ecstatic" religious phenomena of the type associated with the cult of DIONYSUS were a part of Canaanite religion from the earliest times (*see* UGARIT), as part of the worship of various deities (e.g., Baal; Astarte; ADONIS) related to the fertility cycle. *See also* ASHTORETH; TAMMUZ; ASHERAH.

Bibliography. W. R. Smith, *The Religion of the Semites* (1914), pp. 253 ff; W. F. Albright, *From the Stone Age to Christianity* (1957), pp. 304 ff; 311 ff. J. A. WHARTON

ORIENTATION. The means of fixing direction.

1. Systems of orientation. Several methods of orientation were developed in the long history which preceded the discovery of the compass. Chief among these were: (*a*) basic direction, (*b*) local geographic, (*c*) solar, (*d*) polar orientation. The Hebrews were acquainted with the first three and used them interchangeably. It is impossible to determine which system was the earliest. All three rested ultimately upon a concept of space which conceived of spatial positions, not merely as determining neutral relationships within the universe, but as characterizing the quality of individual spaces.

2. Biblical orientation. The Hebrews divided the world into four parts and described the quarters as "corners of the earth" (כנפות הארץ in Isa. 11:12; γωνίαι in Rev. 7:1; 20:8), or as "four winds" (ארבע רוחות; Ezek. 37:9). Like many other Semitic peoples, the rising sun gave the Hebrews their basic direction. The E was called the "front" (קדם, קדמה, קדים), or the "place of dawning" (מזרח, ἀνατολή). The other directions received their corresponding designation as one faced eastward. The W was the "rear" (אחור; Joel 2:20), the N was the "left" (שמול; Gen. 14:15), and the S was the "right" (ימין; I Sam. 23:24). Directions between the cardinal points seldom appear.

With the exception of the E, the OT used the local geographic designations most frequently. The N was called צפון, from the root צפה, "look out." Most probably this was once the name of the large mountain in Syria, *dshebel 'el-'akra',* later called Mons Casius, which was the seat of the Canaanite god Baal Zaphon (*see* ZAPHON). Frequently the direction of the N has retained traces of a mythical background (cf. Jer. 4:6 ff; Joel 2:20).

The S was called the נגב, which means the "dry country" (*see* NEGEB). Again the term דרום was used, which probably once designated a concrete geographic place before becoming a direction (S Judea; Deut. 33:23; Job 37:17; Ezek. 40:24; etc.). Finally, תימן, located in NW Edom, appeared as the S direction. *See* TEMAN.

The W was called either the "sea" (ים), to designate the Mediterranean, or frequently the "place of the setting sun" (מבוא שמש מערב).

Bibliography. H. Nissen, *Orientation,* vols. I-III (1906-10); K. Tallqvist, "Himmelsgegenden und Winde," *Societas*

Orientalis Fennica, Studia Orientalia, II (1928), 105 ff; O. Eissfeldt, *Baal Zaphon, Zeus Kasios, und der Durchzug der Israeliten durchs Meer* (1932); E. Cassirer, *The Philosophy of Symbolic Forms,* II (1925; English trans., 1955), 83 ff.

B. S. CHILDS

ORION ō rī'ən [LXX *rendering of* MT כסיל]. A constellation of stars. The same term in other contexts has the connotation of "dullness" and "stupidity," not only as intellectual dullness but as impiety (Pss. 49:10—H 49:11; 92:6—H 92:7; 94:8). In three passages (Job 9:9; 38:31; Amos 5:8) it refers to a specific group of stars; in Isa. 13:10 the plural כסיליהם, "their constellations," is used in a more general way.

The LXX is not clear. In Amos 5:8 it attempts no translation, but merely expresses the theological import: "who made and transforms all things." In Job 9:9, followed by the Vulg., the LXX renders "that related to the evening" (therefore, the west). However, in Job 38:31 the LXX has "Orion," where the Vulg. reads "Arcturus." In the plural reference in Isa. 13:10, the MT has כוכבי השמים כסיליהם; the LXX ignores the plural, reading ἀστέρες τοῦ οὐρανοῦ καὶ ὁ 'Ωρείων—i.e., "stars of heaven and Orion." Both the RSV and the KJV in this last usage read "constellations." In this sense, the term refers to no specific astral group, but to the brilliance of two or more constellations, the term being more generally employed.

The versions are helpful: the Targ. and Syr. read "giant." This may properly identify the star; even in modern times, the Arabic name for the constellation, Orion, is *al gebbar,* "the strong one"; the Syriac name is *gabbara,* modern Hebrew *gibbôr,* with the same meaning. Scholars generally agree in this identification, "the strong one," for "Orion."

A mythical allusion lies behind the name "strong one" (גבר), "foolish one" (כסיל), and the notice in Job 38:31 that Orion is bound in cords. Classical mythology represents Orion as a man of great strength who at his death was transferred to the heavens, bound to the sky, and became the constellation Orion. When this myth is adapted to Israel's faith, it is a short step from strength to foolishness. The man who is strong relies upon himself before the Lord; strong as he may be, he is subject to God. The reference of Job 38:31 may be to one who in his foolishness found himself bound by the greater power of God.

This constellation is uniquely appropriate for the myth; the configuration of stars fits the figure. Four bright stars mark the two shoulders and the two legs of what could be a gigantic warrior; a row of three bright stars, midway between the first four, suggests his belt, studded with gems, the cord by which he is confined. Another row of stars, straight down from the center of the belt, may be his sword. The cluster yields the outline of a warrior girded for battle. This makes the identification very likely. Additional support is derived from its proximity to the PLEIADES, with which it is closely associated in the texts.

Note that it is precisely biblical faith which permits derogatory language such as "stupid" concerning the stars. In the religions which surrounded Israel, the stars represented or were powers whose favor must be sought. In utilizing the myth concerning Orion, Israel confessed the sovereignty of its Lord, even over the heavenly luminaries.

Bibliography. E. W. Maunder, *The Astronomy of the Bible* (no date); G. Schiaparelli, *Astronomy in the OT* (1905); G. R. Driver, "Two Astronomical Passages in the OT," *JTS,* (1956), 1-2.

W. BRUEGGEMANN

ORMUZD ôr'mo͝ozd. Alternately: ORMAZD; OHRMAZD. Middle Persian form of AHURAMAZDA.

ORNAMENT. *See* DRESS AND ORNAMENTS.

ORNAN. Alternate form of ARAUNAH.

ORPAH ôr'pə [ערפה, neck, the girl with a full mane(?), *or* rain cloud; *cf.* Akkad. *irpu,* cloud]. One of the characters in the book of Ruth. She and Ruth, both Moabite women, had married Hebrews, sojourners from Bethlehem in Judah. After their husbands died, they set out with their mother-in-law, Naomi, for Bethlehem. When Naomi had told them of the difficulties they would face, and had twice urged them to return to their own people, Orpah yielded. Her dutiful, but more ordinary, obedience contrasts with Ruth's unlimited devotion to Naomi (Ruth 1:4-14).

See also RUTH, BOOK OF. D. HARVEY

ORPHAN. *See* FATHERLESS.

ORTHOSIA ôr thō'zī ə ['Ορθωσίας] (I Macc. 15:37); KJV ORTHOSIAS —əs. A city just N of Tripolis in Phoenicia (Pliny Nat. Hist. V.17); now unidentified, but probably Ard Artuzi, or a place near it. It is mentioned in I Macc. 15:37 as the place to which the Syrian usurper Trypho fled, after his defeat by Antiochus VII Sidetes in the days of Simon Maccabeus.

N. TURNER

OSAIAS ō sā'yəs. KJV Apoc. form of JESHAIAH.

OSEA ō zē'ə. KJV Apoc. form of HOSHEA.

OSEAS ō zē'əs. KJV Apoc. form of HOSEA.

OSEE ō'zē. Douay Version form of HOSEA.

OSHEA ō shē'ə. KJV form of Hoshea in Num. 13:8, 16. The gloss in vs. 16 shows that this name refers to JOSHUA SON OF NUN.

OSIRIS ō sī'rəs. One of the principal gods of the Egyptian pantheon.

Believed by some to have been a deified leader of a prehistoric invasion of nomadic peoples into the Nile Delta from the E, Osiris became one of the most popular and important gods of ancient Egypt. He was the god of vegetation and regeneration—indeed, the most fundamental tenet of his cult was that concerning his death and resurrection. Already in the Pyramid Texts he has become a god of the dead as well, and it is with him that the deceased king is equated. United with APIS under the name Serapis (Osiris-Apis), he attained international recognition during the Greco-Roman period.

In the Brooklyn Museum Collection

12. The Egyptian god Osiris

Figs. OSI 12; EGY 18; ISI 16.

Bibliography. S. A. B. Mercer, *The Religion of Ancient Egypt* (1949), pp. 97-123; J. Černý, *Ancient Egyptian Religion* (1952).

T. O. LAMBDIN

OSNAPPAR ŏs năp′ər [אסנפר] (Ezra 4:10); KJV ASNAPPER ăs—. An Assyrian king said to have brought deported foreign peoples to Samaria; often identified with Ashurbanipal, because among the peoples listed are Elamites and natives of Susa, which was destroyed by this king in *ca.* 640 B.C.

OSPREY ŏs′prĭ [עזניה; LXX ἁλιαίετος, sea-eagle, osprey; Vulg. *haliaeetos;* Targ. (Onq.) עוזיא *or* עזיא, bird of prey, *possibly* black eagle] (Lev. 11:13; Deut. 14:12); KJV OSPRAY. A fairly large fish-eating hawk (*Pandion haliaëtus haliaëtus*), whose anatomy in some respects resembles that of the owls.

The identification of עזניה is uncertain, except that it is in a list of unclean birds, most of which seem to be raptorial. The context would therefore favor a bird of prey of the family Accipitridae. Tristram pointed out that while the osprey was found in Palestine in his time, such a bird, whose food consists entirely of fish, could never have been very common in that area, and he suggested that the word designates the short-toed eagle, also known as the harrier eagle (*Circaëtus gallicus gallicus*), the "most abundant of all the Eagle tribe in Palestine" (Tristram *NHB* 184). Koehler and Bodenheimer favor the Black Vulture (*Aegypius monachus* or *Vultur monachus*), which G. R. Driver also mentions, along with the Bearded Vulture (*Gypaëtus barbatus aureus*).

W. S. MCCULLOUGH

OSSIFRAGE ŏs′ə frĭj [פרס (Lev. 11:13); *cf.* פרס, to break in two, divide]. Alternately: VULTURE (Deut. 14:12). The term (meaning "bone-breaker") used in English to denote (*a*) the lammergeier, or bearded vulture (*Gypaëtus barbatus*); (*b*) the osprey (*Pandion haliaëtus*); (*c*) the giant petrel (*Macronectes giganteus,* formerly *Ossifraga gigantea*), called in some nautical circles "break-bones."

While it is impossible to offer a conclusive identification of פרס (other than that it is an unclean bird mentioned in association with birds of prey), if the word means or suggests "breaker," it would be a very apt term for the lammergeier, which has a fondness for bones and for tortoises, which it smashes open by repeated droppings from the air.

W. S. MCCULLOUGH

OSSUARIES. Small chests, usually limestone boxes, used as receptacles for the bones of the dead after

Courtesy of the Palestine Archaeological Museum, Jerusalem, Jordan

13. A variety of Palestinian ossuaries

the flesh had decayed and the tombs were being prepared for new burials. The term (from Latin *ossuarium,* "for bones") is not a biblical one, although such chests were used in biblical times. Fig. OSS 13.

It is thought that a clay ossuary in the Palestine Archaeological Museum in Jerusalem, fashioned in the form of a miniature house, was used in the Chalcolithic Age.* More common, however, were the rectangular stone chests, of which hundreds have been found in the vicinity of Jerusalem, sometimes in caves and frequently in tombs which were often constructed with small niches (*loculi*) large enough to hold a single ossuary. Dating from the early Roman period in Palestine, they vary in size from *ca.* twenty to thirty inches in length, twelve to twenty inches in width, and ten to sixteen inches in depth. Often inscribed with Hebrew, Aramaic, or Greek words, including personal names, and with rosettes or other decorations, they give evidence of care in the handling of the bones of the dead. Figs. OSS 14, 15.

Bibliography. K. Galling, *Biblisches Reallexikon* (1937), cols. 404-7; M. Burrows, *What Mean These Stones?* (1941), pp. 240,

Courtesy of the Palestine Archaeological Museum, Jerusalem, Jordan

14. A partially restored Palestinian house-shaped ossuary; from Chalcolithic Age (*ca.* 4000-3300 B.C.)

Courtesy of the American Schools of Oriental Research

15. Inscription "Jesus, son of Joseph," from an ossuary of the Roman period

243; C. H. Kraeling, "Christian Burial Urns?" *BA*, IX (1946), 16-20. W. L. REED

OSTRACA ŏs′trə kə [*plural of* ὄστρακον, potsherd; חרש]. Pottery fragments commonly used as writing material, since they were cheaper than papyrus. The term is sometimes loosely used to include flakes of limestone. Inscribed with ink, potsherds were widely used for letters, receipts, school texts, etc. Important finds of ostraca have been made at Samaria and Lachish. *See* WRITING AND WRITING MATERIALS.

Figs. SAM 12; INS 15. R. J. WILLIAMS

OSTRICH [בת־היענה (Lev. 11:16; Deut. 14:15; *elsewhere plural,* בנות יענה; KJV OWL), *possibly* daughter of the greedy one (cf. Syr. *yi'en, ya'nâ,* greedy) *or* daughter of the barren ground (cf. Arab. *wa'na,* white, barren ground); יען (Lam. 4:3, *where* RSV *adopts the* Q *of the* MT, כיענים), *presumably* greedy one *or* desert one; רנן (Job 39:13; KJV PEACOCK), *probably* cry *or* crier]. Any of the order Struthioniformes of the genus Struthio, two-toed, swiftly running, flightless birds, the largest of the birds, now confined to Africa and the Near East, where they live in desertlike districts or areas covered with stunted bushes. The species found in the environs of Arabia is *Struthio camelus.*

Courtesy of the Pierpont Morgan Library, New York

16. A Middle Assyrian seal impression showing an ostrich hunt

It is probable that the Hebrew words cited above designate the ostrich, although G. R. Driver contends (*see bibliography*) that בת־היענה means "owl."

Job 39:13-18 alludes to familiar features and habits of the ostrich, although some of its statements need qualification. Vs. 13 is so obscure that it is quite impossible to say whether originally there was a reference to the beauty of the ostrich plumes. Ostrich eggs are laid in the sand (vss. 14-15), but are apparently neglected only in the daytime when the sun is warm; the cock bird does most of the incubating, particularly at night. The unhatched eggs, placed in the vicinity of the incubated ones, are intended to serve as food for the young; such extra eggs may have led to the view, expressed in Lam. 4:3, that the ostrich was indifferent to its brood. The stupidity of the ostrich (Job 39:17) is most in evidence when it is being hunted and is cornered, and when it often fails to take the evasive action that would save it. But in open terrain it is very wary. Another instance of seeming witlessness is its habit of swallowing all manner of objects of no value nutritionally (cf. the etymology above, "the greedy one"), though this procedure is said to help in the trituration of food. The speed of this bird (vs. 18) is proverbial. Tristram testifies that its maximum stride is from twenty-two to twenty-eight feet, and he confirms Livingstone's calculation of a speed of twenty-six miles an hour.

Although Tristram found ostrich flesh "good and sweet" and its eggs "excellent eating like those of poultry," Israel's law declared this bird to be unclean (Lev. 11:16; Deut. 14:15). Presumably it was thus ranked because of its eating habits. While it is not raptorial, it is omnivorous, and its food includes small mammals, birds, snakes, and lizards, as well as grass, fruit, etc. Most of the other OT references associate this bird with wild creatures and uninhabited areas (Job 30:29; Isa. 13:21; 34:13; 43:20; Jer. 50:39). Its night cry, which Tristram thought to be "like the hoarse lowing of an ox in pain," is referred to in Mic. 1:8.

See also FAUNA § B3.

Fig. OST 16.

Bibliography. G. R. Driver, *PEQ* (April, 1955), pp. 12-13.
W. S. McCullough

OTHNI ŏth'nī [עָתְנִי] (I Chr. 26:7). A Levitic gatekeeper in the temple; a son of Shemaiah.

OTHNIEL ŏth'nĭ əl [עָתְנִיאֵל]. The first deliverer or judge of the Israelites mentioned in the book of Judges (3:7-11). Probably the nephew of Caleb, he became Caleb's son-in-law as his prize for capturing the city Debir (Josh. 15:15-19; Judg. 1:11-15). Othniel's rescue of Israel, from the divinely ordained oppression of its first conqueror, Cushan-rishathaim, was followed by a generation of "rest."

The name Othniel is a compound with "God" ("El") of a root whose meaning is unknown and appears elsewhere in biblical Hebrew only in the proper name Othni.

Othniel was probably the personal name of a traditional ancestor of a tribe related to that of Caleb, although the blood relationship is not clear. While "Othniel the son of Kenaz, Caleb's younger brother" (Judg. 1:13; 3:9; cf. Josh. 15:17, where "younger" is omitted in the MT), can mean that Othniel was either Caleb's son or his nephew, the latter is evidently intended. According to the Chronicler's genealogy Othniel was Caleb's nephew, for he was the son of Kenaz, and his own sons were Hathath and Meonothai (I Chr. 4:13).

Othniel is most clearly a clan or tribal name in the Chronicler's list of the organization of David's army, where one Heldai "the Netophathite, of Othniel," was to serve as supply officer for the twelfth month (I Chr. 27:15). Apparently Othniel was a younger clan, and Caleb an older, of the tribe of Kenaz or Kenizzites. Whereas tradition named the Kenizzites as being originally Edomite (Gen. 36: 11, 15, 42; I Chr. 1:36, 53), in the Chronicler's genealogies and the Joshua-Judges narratives both Caleb and Othniel are clans of the tribe of Judah. Thus Othniel is a S hero.

This fact may in part account for the preservation of the stories of Othniel and their place in the book of Judges. According to one tradition the N hero, Ephraimite Joshua, in his organized conquest had taken Debir (Josh. 10:38-39). While it is possible that Othniel's heroic deed which won him his bride was the occupation and rebuilding of the site after its destruction by Joshua's army, it is likely that this story is to account for the Judean occupancy of a city close to Hebron, a city which already belonged to the Calebites (15:13-14). That Othniel should marry a near relative, his niece or cousin, occasions no surprise (cf. Abraham and Sarah in Gen. 20:12). The dowry given the bride Achsah by her father, "the upper springs and the lower springs," may have sealed the claim of Othnielites to important sources of water supply in the Negeb claimed by Calebites of Hebron. The identification of the site of Debir or Kiriath-sepher with Tell Beit Mirsim is not undisputed.

The story of Othniel's deliverance of Israel from Cushan-rishathaim stands immediately after the Deuteronomic introduction to the heroes of the book (Judg. 2:6–3:6) as prime example of its philosophy of history (*see* Judges, Book of, §§ C1-2). Because of the Lord's anger at their apostasy, the people suffered for eight years under "Cushan of double wickedness." But in response to their cry "the Lord raised up" the deliverer Othniel. After his victory "the land had rest" for a generation, presumably because, until Othniel died, they remained religiously faithful. Othniel is described in terms typical of the judges: he was specially raised up by the Lord; he was a charismatic leader upon whom the Lord's spirit came to meet crises; he "judged Israel"—i.e., presumably rendered case decisions and exercised general oversight; "his hand prevailed over" the oppressor; the result was "rest" for the land. *See* Judge.

The story of Othniel as judge may be the fiction of the Deuteronomic editor to place a Judean hero as first judge, particularly since the other judges were all northerners. There are no details in Othniel's story which have the ring of authenticity or antiquity like those in the stories of Ehud, Deborah, Gideon, etc. There is a mystery about Cushan-rishathaim. Nevertheless, Othniel was probably a historical figure who delivered, not "all Israel," but S Judean clans, from a powerful foreign ruler who swept down from the Upper Euphrates region into Judah via the S end of the Dead Sea (cf. the conquest by the four kings in the days of Abraham in Gen. 14).

Bibliography. L. Desnoyers, *Histoire du peuple hébreu* (1922), I, 131-33; M. Noth, *History of Israel* (1958), pp. 56-59, 76-77, 147-48. *See also* the bibliography under Cushan-rishathaim.
C. F. Kraft

OTHONIAH ŏth'ə nī'ə ['Οθονίας]; KJV OTHONIAS —əs. One of the priests with foreign wives mentioned in I Esd. 9:28. The corresponding name in Ezra 10:27 is Mattaniah (10).

OUCHES [משבצות]. KJV archaism, meaning "settings for precious stones" (Exod. 28:11, 13-14, 25; 39:6, 13, 16, 18; RSV "settings"). The Hebrew word is derived from a verb meaning "to weave," and it probably therefore means a filigree setting. When it is used with זהב, "gold," the RSV reads "settings of gold filigree."
H. G. May

OUTCAST [*various forms related to* נדח, to thrust, push away]. Most often, the Hebrew equivalents of this word are used to describe the driving out of the people of Israel by the successive waves of attack by the Near Eastern empires of Assyria and Babylonia from the eighth through the sixth centuries B.C. It is never used in the English translations to denote the "outcasts of society." *See* Blindness; Fatherless; Leprosy; Poor; Sojourner; Widow.

The Hebrew word in its various forms becomes a kind of *terminus technicus* for the Dispersion of the Jews, seen as the judgment of God upon his people for their unfaithfulness. An important aspect of the OT and later Jewish eschatology is God's ingathering of the "outcasts of Israel" (cf. Ps. 147:2; Isa. 11: 12; 56:8) and their return to Jerusalem.
J. A. Wharton

OVEN [תנור; κλίβανος]. Modern baking ovens used by Palestinian peasants do not differ much from the ovens discovered in the ruins of ancient agglomerations or represented on Egyptian and Assyrian paint-

Courtesy of the Oriental Institute, the University of Chicago

17. A typical Iron Age (*ca.* 1200-300 B.C.) oven, from Megiddo, composed of a large bell-shaped vessel of unbaked clay with numerous potsherds plastered around the outside to retain the heat

ings and reliefs. They consist in a cylindrical structure of burnt clay, two to three feet in diameter, at the bottom of which a fire is built on a floor of pebbles (Fig. OVE 17). Once the oven is adequately heated, the ashes are scooped or swept away, and flat cakes of dough are stuck against the inner wall of the oven, or laid to bake on the pebbles. Modern ovens are often sheltered in small bakehouses, erected in the yard of private houses or grouped together in a corner of the village.

The tower defending the NW angle of Jerusalem in Nehemiah's time was called מגדל התנורים, "Tower of the Ovens" (Neh. 3:11; 12:38), because the commercial bakers of the city had their ovens in this vicinity.

The usual fuel burned in the baking ovens was, and still is, dry grass (cf. Matt. 6:30; Luke 12:28), thorny desert bushes, and cakes of dung kneaded with straw and laid to dry on rocky slopes near the ovens. The reference of Ezek. 4:12 to human dung used for fuel was meant to emphasize the abject condition of the beleaguered population.

See BREAD; BAKING. For industrial ovens, *see* FURNACE; POTTER.

Bibliography. K. Galling, *Biblisches Reallexikon* (1937), cols. 75-78; G. A. Barrois, *Manuel d'Archéologie Biblique,* I (1939), 320-22.

G. A. BARROIS

OVENS, TOWER OF THE [מגדל התנורים] (Neh. 3:11: 12:38); KJV TOWER OF THE FURNACES. A tower in JERUSALEM (*see* § 7*b*) restored under Nehemiah. It defended the NW angle of the city wall, close to the Corner Gate. It was named presumably for baking ovens established in the vicinity. Fig. NEH 13.

G. A. BARROIS

OVERLAY [חפה; טוח; צפה; תפש; רקע]. There are references to overlaying parts of the tabernacle of the Exodus and the temple in Jerusalem with gold, silver, or bronze. Presumably the overlaying consisted of fastening metal of appreciable thickness—more than the attachment of leaf. Many Egyptian obelisks, pillars, and statues were overlaid with gold. According to I Chr. 29:4, David contributed three thousand talents of gold and seven thousand talents of silver, equal to about sixty million dollars, for overlaying the house of God. When Sennacherib demanded three hundred talents of silver and thirty talents of gold, Hezekiah emptied the treasury of silver and provided the gold by stripping the overlay from the doors of the temple and the doorposts (II Kings 18:16).

In the tabernacle gold was used for overlaying the ark and its poles, the table and its poles, boards of the wooden structure, five pillars of acacia, the altar of incense and its poles, four pillars of acacia, and capitals of the pillars. Bronze was used to overlay the altar and its poles; silver was used for some of the capitals (Exod. 25:11–38:28).

In the temple gold was used to overlay the inner sanctuary, the inside of the house, the whole house, the altar belonging to the inner sanctuary, the cherubim, the floor, two doors of the inner sanctuary, the ivory throne, and the porch (I Kings 6:20-32; 10:18; II Chr. 3:4, 10; 9:17), while bronze was used to overlay the doors of the court of the priests (II Chr. 4:9). Overlaying idols is mentioned in Isa. 40:19; Hab. 2:19. In I Kings 3:19 KJV a child is said to have died because his mother "overlaid it." RSV has "lay on," which is better.

See ARCHITECTURE; BRONZE; GOLD; SILVER; TABERNACLE; TEMPLE, JERUSALEM.

O. R. SELLERS

OVERSEER [נצח; פקד, פקדה (KJV "officer"); פקיד (RSV "leader" *in* Neh. 12:42; KJV "officer" *in* Gen. 41:34); KJV שטר (Prov. 6:7; RSV "officer"); KJV ἐπίσκοπος (Acts 20:28; RSV "guardian")]. A term designating several types of leaders or supervisors—e.g., the superintendent or foreman of a labor gang. In Egypt they carried long rods for punishment and were hard taskmasters (Exod. 1:11). The Israelites forgot their oppressive overseers, and under David and Solomon they also employed forced labor (II Sam. 20:24). Overseers were used in building and repairing the temple (II Chr. 2:18; 34:13, 17; LXX ἐπίσκοπος for פקיד). In a better sense, Joseph was an overseer (Gen. 39:4-5) and encouraged Pharoah to appoint other overseers for the land (41:34). The leader of the singers after the return from the Exile is called an overseer in the KJV (Neh. 12:42; RSV "leader"). Nehemiah had overseers with him (Neh. 11:9). Ants work willingly without an overseer (Prov. 6:7 KJV; RSV "officer"). The elders in Ephesus are overseers of the church (Acts 20:28 KJV; RSV "guardian"; *see* STEWARD; BISHOP).

In the titles of fifty-five psalms the word נצח occurs ("choirmaster"; KJV "chief musician").

C. U. WOLF

OWL [כוס (*see bibliography; alternately* LITTLE OWL); קפוז (*see bibliography;* Isa. 34:15; KJV GREAT OWL), *cognates in* Aram., Arab., to jump; KJV בת היענה (RSV OSTRICH), ינשוף (RSV GREAT OWL)]. Any one of a group of birds of prey of the order Strigiformes (the Strigidae family being the commonest), of from small to medium size, mostly of nocturnal habits. There are *ca.* two hundred species.

Undoubtedly owls were known in the biblical world; Tristram testifies that in his time eight varieties were found in Palestine, of which five were quite plentiful. A priori we should therefore expect owls to be mentioned in a list of raptorial birds. There is, however, little or no evidence to support the identification of a particular species of owl with any Hebrew word in the OT. כוס may be the Little Owl (*Athene noctua lilith*), which is the commonest of all the owls which Tristram found in the Holy Land. קפוז may be the diminutive screech or scops owl (*Otus scops*), which abounds around Palestine's ruins and caves; in Isa. 34:15 it is associated with desolated Edom. The barn owl (*Tyto alba*) is said to be "as common in Palestine as in England" (Tristram), but whether it is ever referred to in the OT is uncertain.

Bibliography. On כוס, see J. B. Pritchard, ed., *ANET* (2nd ed., 1955), p. 92, col. 2, line 31. On קפוז, cf. Tristram *NHB* 227-28; C. C. Torrey, *Second Isaiah* (1928), pp. 292-94; G. R. Driver, *PEQ* (May, 1955), p. 136. W. S. McCullough

OX (PERSON) ōks [῞Ωξ; Vulg. *īdox; cf.* עוץ *in* Gen. 22:21] (Jth. 8:1). Descendant of Israel; father of Merari; grandfather of Judith. J. C. Swaim

OX [אלף (*only in plural*); שור, Aram. תור (Ezra 6:9, *etc.*); בקר (*usually collective*); פר, young bull, *cf.* Ugar. *prt*, young cow; Arab. *purār*, young (of sheep, goat, cow); βοῦς, *cf.* Sanskrit *go, gaus,* ox, cow; μόσχος, young shoot, *hence* Calf; ταῦρος (*some assume a Semitic derivation, see* שור *above; others derive from* Sanskrit *sthūra,* strong, *or sthūras,* bull)]. Alternately: BULL (שור; בקר; פר; ταῦρος), KJV BULLOCK; HERD, HERDS (בקר); CALF (μόσχος); OX (μόσχος; Rev. 4:7). A domesticated horned quadruped of the genus *bos,* believed to come from *bos primigenius,* the Wild Ox; especially the adult castrated male of this species. The oxen of biblical Palestine were presumably akin to those of Mesopotamia and Egypt. Figs. OX 18; CAR 15-16; FAM 2.

Courtesy of the Oriental Institute, the University of Chicago

18. The Apadana stairway at Persepolis, showing Babylonian and Syrian tribute-bearers; time of Xerxes (486-465 B.C.); showing use of ox, camel, and horse

1. As a draught animal
2. As food
3. As a sacrificial animal
4. As a form of property
5. Decorative and symbolic uses

1. As a draught animal. Oxen pulled wagons (Num. 7:3; II Sam. 6:6), drew the plow (Deut. 22:10; I Sam. 11:5; I Kings 19:19; Job 1:14; Prov. 14:4; Isa. 30:24; Amos 6:12), and dragged the threshing sled (Deut. 25:4; cf. I Cor. 9:9). They were to be rested on the sabbath (Exod. 23:12; Deut. 5:14) and were subject to the law of firstlings (Exod. 34:19; Lev. 27:26). They usually fed on such grass as was available (Num. 22:4; Job 6:5; 40:15; Ps. 106:20; Dan. 4:25), but they also ate straw, perhaps when pasturage was poor (Isa. 11:7). An ox might be kept in a stable (Luke 13:15). Its dung could serve as fuel for cooking (Ezek. 4:15). A number of regulations pertinent to oxen (goring, injuries, theft, illegal grazing, etc.) are found in Exod. 21:28–22:15—H 22:14.

2. As food. Although the ox was a clean animal and could be eaten (Deut. 14:4), its flesh was not a common article in the diet of the Hebrews. It was only on special occasions that oxen were slaughtered (I Sam. 14:31-34; I Kings 1:19; Prov. 15:17; Isa. 22:13; Matt. 22:4), though royalty and people of importance may have had beef more frequently (I Kings 4:23—H 5:3; Neh. 5:18; Amos 6:4).

3. As a sacrificial animal. The use of oxen as sacrificial victims was well known in the ancient Near East (cf. Acts 14:13), and Israel's offerings of oxen to Yahweh therefore occasion no surprise. From Exod. 20:24 we may conclude that among the Hebrews this practice went back at least as far as the days of earth altars (cf. Lev. 3:1; 9:4; 22:23; Num. 7:88; etc.). *See* Sacrifice and Offerings.

4. As a form of property. The possession of an ox, like that of an ass, was almost the bare minimum for existence (Job 24:3; cf. Exod. 20:17). On the other hand, herds of oxen, sheep, and goats were the mark of wealth and social position (Gen. 12:16; 32:5; II Sam. 12:2; Job 1:3; Eccl. 2:7), and were fair prey for enemies (I Sam. 15:9; 27:9; Job 1:14-15; Jer. 5:17; 49:32).

5. Decorative and symbolic uses. The molten sea of Solomon's temple rested upon the backs of twelve bronze oxen (I Kings 7:25), and the ten bronze lavers had lions, oxen, and cherubim on their panels (vs. 29). Oxen and other animals were often associated with deity in Western Asia, the ox doubtless because of its strength and the bull of the ox as a symbol of fertility (*see* Calf, Golden). In Ezekiel's vision each cherub has four faces, one of which is that of an ox (1:5-10; cf. 10:14). This has influenced Rev. 4:6-11, where each of the creatures surrounding the heavenly throne has only one face, one having that of an "ox" (KJV "calf"). W. S. McCullough

OX-GOAD. *See* Goad.

OXYRHYNCHUS SAYINGS OF JESUS ŏk′sĭ-rĭng′kəs. Four fragments of papyrus and parchment found in the rubbish mounds of Oxyrhynchus and containing several sayings attributed to Jesus.

The ancient site Oxyrhynchus (modern Behnesa), 125 miles S of Cairo and 10 miles W of the Nile, has been since 1897 a treasure chest of ancient texts of all sorts, literary and nonliterary, dating from the first to the ninth century. Eighteen volumes under the title *Oxyrhynchus Papyri* (1897-1941), edited by

Grenfell and Hunt and their successors, have made available to scholarship this amazing welter of materials from the past. Among these finds are four, all small and badly mutilated, containing sayings purporting to be from Jesus.

The first of these, Oxyrhynchus Papyrus 1—so named because it was the first item in the initial volume—was discovered in 1897. It is a fragment of the leaf of a papyrus codex (not a roll); bears the folio symbol 11 on the verso; and contains eight (seven?) sayings, of which all but one are in part decipherable. They are not part of a continuous discourse but rather appear as an unconnected series of separate sayings, each preceded by the expression "Jesus saith." While several of these sayings are distinctly similar to those in the canonical Matthew and Luke, three (2-4) are distinctly different. Two of them, as reconstructed by Evelyn White (*see bibliography*), read: "Jesus saith: If ye fast not from the world, ye shall not find the kingdom of God, and if ye keep not sabbath for the whole week, ye shall not see the Father." "Jesus saith: . . . Lift up the stone and thou shalt then find me; cleave the wood and I am there."

Oxy. P. 654, discovered in 1903, contains five words of Jesus, after a short prologue. It is a very badly preserved fragment of a papyrus roll and contains forty-two lines written on the verso of a survey list of various pieces of land. Since the entire right half of the column is lost, only the first half of each short line is decipherable, while after line 31 the beginnings of each of the remaining lines are increasingly badly marred, with the result that in the last line only two letters are preserved. Despite these extensive lacunae, various editors have attempted valiantly and, at times, perhaps a bit rashly, to fill in the gaps with conjectural restorations. Since conjectural emendation is at best highly subjective, it is not surprising that no two editors agree in their final results. Following the prologue, which Evelyn White restores to read: "These are the life-giving Sayings which Jesus spake who liveth and was seen of the Ten and of Thomas. And He said to them: Whosoever heareth these Sayings shall not taste of death," comes a word similar to one quoted by Clement of Alexandria as standing in the Gospel According to the Hebrews (*see* HEBREWS, GOSPEL ACCORDING TO THE): "Let not him that seeketh cease seeking till he find, and when he findeth he shall marvel, and having marvelled he shall reign, and having reigned he shall rest." Others of the sayings, so far as they can be restored by conjecture, appear to be expanded and reworked versions of canonical words, notably Matt. 7:7; 10:26; Luke 17:20-21, and with no marked doctrinal deviations.

Oxy. P. 655 is a broken leaf of a papyrus roll, apparently quite distinct from 654. The second column is very badly mutilated—only twenty-two letters are preserved—but appears to be a sort of free adaptation of Luke 11:52. The first column concerns the lilies of the field and is strongly reminiscent of Matt. 6:25, 28. It concludes with the surprising statement: "His disciples say unto him, When wilt thou be manifest unto us and when shall we see thee? He saith, When you have put off your raiment and are not ashamed," which is similar to the citation in Clement of Alexandria from the Gospel According to the Egyptians. *See* EGYPTIANS, GOSPEL ACCORDING TO THE.

The fourth fragment (Oxy. P. 840) was discovered in 1905. It is a parchment leaf of a Lilliputian codex, written on both sides and containing forty-five lines in a very tiny hand. E. Preuschen (*see bibliography*) plausibly conjectured that the codex was a sort of

Courtesy of the Egypt Exploration Society

19. Oxyrynchus papyrus with new "sayings of Jesus," belonging to the third century A.D.

amulet which Chrysostom (*Hom. de Statuis* XIX.4) reports women and children were accustomed to wear about their necks to keep off evil spirits. The first seven lines are apparently the conclusion of a speech by Jesus in Jerusalem to his disciples, exhorting them to avoid the example of certain wrongdoers and warning them of the penalties awaiting such in this world and the next.

Then follows an animated conversation between Jesus and a (the?) pharisaic chief priest, named Levi, regarding the proper way to achieve true purity. The priest had chided Jesus for walking with his disciples "in this holy place among these holy vessels," without first bathing and without having had his disciples wash their feet. In answer to Jesus' reply and his query as to Levi's own purity, the latter assures Jesus that he had bathed in the pool of David, descending by one set of stairs into the pool and emerging by the other. Then Jesus (styled in this fragment the Savior) assured him that this sort of bathing in waters "into which, night and day, dogs *and swine* are cast," was useless, was in fact essentially the sort of useless prettying of himself which harlots and flute girls made use of. "But I and my disciples, of whom thou sayest, that we are not washed, have been washed in living waters which came down from God out of heaven." Appraisals of this not uninteresting story have varied widely. Many, following an early criticism of it by E. Schürer (*see bibliography*), not unplausibly regard it as a far from authentic fiction produced by one utterly ignorant of Jewish practices. Jeremias, on the other hand (*see bibliography*), valiantly, but not convincingly, discounts these objections and considers it not unlikely as an accurate portrayal of an actual incident in the life of Jesus. While few have gone so far, many regard 840 and 655 as fragments of non-canonical gospels; but there has been no agreement as to which gospels. Since there seems no way of identifying the source, guesses are at best futile. While 1 and 654 have been commonly regarded as distinct, with the former perhaps a few decades earlier, Evelyn White considers them parts of the same work and with 654 preceding 1. Of course, since 1 is a leaf of a codex and 654 part of a scroll, he does not consider these two fragments parts of the same MS but rather argues that they are parts of two copies of the same collection, which collection he is strongly inclined to identify as the Gospel According to the Hebrews. Because of our so scanty exact information of these long-lost gospels and because of the extremely fragmentary condition of these tiny remains, which makes all restoration open to the danger of subjective slanting, it seems wiser not to attempt such precise identification. That they evidence a clear knowledge of and dependence upon the canonical gospels—not omitting the Gospel of John, as many critics have sought to do—can scarcely be denied. That imagination and the readiness to embroider and expand canonical stories are a more likely source for these novel touches than is "oral tradition" would seem very probable. A date in the third century for all four fragments would seem to be the most likely. Fig. OXY 19.

Bibliography. M. R. James, *The Apocryphal NT* (1924), pp. 25-32, provides a restrained survey of these four fragments from Oxyrhynchus, together with other fragments discovered elsewhere. The classic edition, as mentioned above, is B. P. Grenfell and A. S. Hunt, *Oxyrhynchus Papyri* (1897-1924). In addition, H. G. Evelyn White, *The Sayings of Jesus from Oxyrhynchus* (1920); J. Jeremias, *Unbekannte Jesusworte* (1948), will be found of value to the general reader as well as to the specialist; both provide a wealth of additional bibliographical data. See also: E. Preuschen, "Das neue Evangelienfragment von Oxyrhynchos," *ZNW*, 9 (1908), 1-11; E. Schürer, *TLZ*, 33 (1908), 170 ff. M. S. ENSLIN

OZEM ō'zəm [אצם]. **1.** The sixth son of Jesse; therefore the brother of King David (I Chr. 2:15).

2. A descendant of Judah, and the fourth of the five sons of Jerahmeel (I Chr. 2:25).

OZIAS ō zī'əs. KJV form of UZZI 1 (II Esd. 1:2); UZZIAH 3 (Matt. 1:8-9); UZZIAH 6.

OZIEL ō'zĭ əl ['Οζιήλ; Vulg. *Oziae*]. An ancestor of Judith (Jth. 8:1).

OZNI ŏz'nī [אזני, my hearing(?)] (Num. 26:16); **OZNITES** —nīts. A member of the tribe of Gad, named in the second census taken by Moses in the wilderness. He is the eponymous ancestor of the "family of the Oznites."

OZORA ō zôr'ə. KJV Apoc. form of EZORA.

P. The designation of the so-called Priestly source of the PENTATEUCH. To this source are assigned most of the liturgical, genealogical, legal, and technical materials, connected by a bare minimum of narrative. The Priestly compilation is usually dated after the Captivity, in the sixth or fifth century B.C. *See* DOCUMENTS. D. N. FREEDMAN

PAARAI pā'ə rī [פַּעֲרַי] (II Sam. 23:35). An Arbite who was a member of the Mighty Men of David known as the "Thirty." In the parallel list he is called Naarai the son of Ezbai (I Chr. 11:37). It is possible that the original name was Naarai the Arbite (cf. Josh. 15:52). E. R. DALGLISH

PADDAN-ARAM păd'ən âr'əm [פַּדַּן אֲרָם]; KJV PADAN-ARAM pā'dən —. Alternately: PADDAN păd'ən (Gen. 48:7); KJV PADAN pā'dən. The homeland of the patriarchs (Gen. 25:20; 28:2; cf. 48:7) in N Mesopotamia (now S central Turkey). It included the city of HARAN. In the patriarchal period (which the constantly accumulating evidence tends to place in the TELL EL-AMARNA Age), Paddan-aram had an Aramean population attached to cities, although the citizens frequently owned cattle that grazed on fairly distant ranges. Some communities there, like Ur of the Chaldees (which can no longer be identified with the Sumerian city of Ur), were devoted to foreign trade; and recently published texts exchanged between the Hittites and Ugarit indicate clearly that the Hebrew patriarchs pursued trading interests abroad in Canaan and Egypt.

The language of Paddan-aram was Aramaic (Gen. 31:47), and the members of the patriarchal family who remained there are called Aramean (e.g., Gen. 31:24). C. H. GORDON

PADDLE. KJV translation of יָתֵד, "peg" (RSV STICK) in Deut. 23:13. The instrument, along with (cf. KJV "upon") one's weapons, was to be used to dig a hole for latrine purposes. The word "paddle" is here used in its English dialectic sense to refer to a spadelike digging instrument with a narrow blade. H. G. MAY

PADON pā'dŏn [פָּדוֹן; Apoc. Φαδών] (Ezra 2:44; Neh. 7:41; I Esd. 5:29); KJV Apoc. PHALEAS fə lē'əs. A family of temple servants in the postexilic period. *See* NETHINIM.

PAGANS. The translation of ἔθνος in I Cor. 5:1; 10:20. *See* NATIONS.

PAGIEL pā'gĭ əl [פַּגְעִיאֵל, fortune of God(?), *or* God is entreated(?), *or less probably* God has met (his worshiper)]. Leader of Asher; son of Ochran (Num. 1:13; 2:27; 7:72, 77; 10:26). He was one of twelve tribal leaders or deputies who assisted Moses in taking a census of Israel and in other tasks in the wilderness.

Bibliography. M. Noth, *Die israelitischen Personennamen* (1928), p. 254; W. F. Albright, "Ostracon No. 6043 from Ezion-Geber," *BASOR*, LXXXII (1941), 13. R. F. JOHNSON

PAHATH-MOAB pā'hăth mō'ăb [פַּחַת מוֹאָב, governor of Moab]; KJV Apoc. PHAATH MOAB fā'ăth — in I Esd. 5:11. An officer or ruler in Moab; evidently a Hebrew (cf. II Sam. 8:2, where Judah rules Moab under King David), whose title now designates a family or clan presumably descended from him. The latter is represented among the exiles returned from Babylon (Ezra 2:6; cf. Neh. 7:11; Ezra 8:4; I Esd. 5:11; 8:31), and several members of the clan are listed among those who had married foreign wives in the time of Ezra (Ezra 10:30; absent in I Esd. 9:31). One Hasshub, who aided Nehemiah in repairing the wall of Jerusalem, was of this clan (Neh. 10:14).

Bibliography. L. W. Batten, *Ezra and Nehemiah*, ICC (1913), p. 80. B. T. DAHLBERG

PAHLAVI pä'lə vē'; also, less correctly, PEHLEVI pā'lə vē'. The official language of the Sassanian state (*ca.* A.D. 225-651; *see* PERSIA §§ C2, D6); chronologically and geographically that variety of Middle Iranian which is the continuation of Old Persian (*see* PERSIAN, OLD) and the ancestor of New (or Modern) Persian. Etymologically the name is the regular descendant of the Old Persian word *parθava,* "Parthian."

1. Language. The written language is known from such sources as (*a*) legends on coins, seals, and intaglios; (*b*) inscriptions dating from the third and fourth centuries A.D., some of which possess parallel versions in (Middle) Parthian and Greek; (*c*) fragments of translation of the Psalms from the seventh century A.D.; (*d*) papyri; and (*e*) dipinti discovered in the synagogue in Dura-Europos on the Euphrates, to mention only the most important. The Manichean fragments found in Turfan form another highly important source. *See* MANICHEISM.

The main bulk of Pahlavi language materials is to be found, however, in what has been preserved of Sassanian literature, most of which is of a religious and theological nature (*see* PERSIA § C2). These texts are written in an alphabet of Aramaic origin. This script is ambiguous to the extent that some symbols resemble one another so much that in the cursive script they become identical. In such cases the only way to establish the correct reading is the context. Another difficulty resides in the frequent use of so-called ideograms or heterograms, a system by which for reasons of convenience or otherwise Aramaic words are substituted in the writing for the corresponding Pahlavi terms. There exists adequate evidence to show that in reading the written text only the Pahlavi words were used. The technical term for this system of "translation" by the scribe from Pahlavi into Aramaic and by the reader of the written text from Aramaic into Pahlavi is *uzvārišn,* "understanding, interpretation." Although Aramaic is known to have been widely used during the Achaemenian Empire (521-330 B.C.) for administrative purposes, it is somewhat uncertain to which period the systematic use of the Aramaic "masks" is to be ascribed. In later times Zoroastrian scholars tried to facilitate the often puzzling sacred texts by replacing the Aramaic words by their Pahlavi counterparts in phonetic writing. This kind of "transliterated" text is called *Pāzand* or *Pārsī.*

In spite of the existence of lists in which the Aramaic and Pahlavi words are given side by side, these technical handicaps, together with the lack of reliable text editions and translations, account for slow progress in Pahlavi studies. Caution is, therefore, recommended in using the existing translations, most of which, in addition, are dated.

2. Literature. In all cases where it is at all possible to date the existing Pahlavi books it appears that they were not committed to actual writing until after the Muslim conquest of Iran in the middle of the seventh century. In matter they contain elements from different chronological periods, some as early as pre-Archaemenian times, but molded into the orthodox shape established under the Sassanians.

Of the more important religious-theological books the following deserve to be mentioned: (*a*) the so-called *Bundahishn* or, more correctly, *Zandāgāhīh,* "exposition of information (as provided by the Pahlavi version of the Avesta)," a work on cosmology, written toward the end of the Sassanian period, in which the teachings of the Avesta on the subject were brought together; (*b*) *Dēnkart,* the longest and, perhaps, most important of the Zoroastrian texts, a work of theological and philosophical subject matter including many topics of a miscellaneous nature (history of the Avesta, legendary materials on Zarathushtra), while some passages show evidence for the success of the efforts of Shapur I (A.D. 239/241–70/73) for the promotion of foreign, both Greek and Indian, science and knowledge (astronomy, astrology, medicine, physics, grammar, philosophy, etc.); (*c*) *Shkand-gumānīk vičār,* "doubt-dispelling solution," an apologetic treatise of Zoroastrian doctrines against other religions.

Of a less strictly religious tenet are: (*d*) the so-called *handarz* ("counsel") or *pand-nāmak* ("book of advice") texts, collections of practical wisdom; (*e*) *Shāyast-nē-shāyast,* "(what is) proper (and) improper," a collection of ritual regulations and customs; (*f*) *Artāy Virāf Nāmak,* the "book of Artāy Virāf," an account of Artāy Virāf's journey to the nether world and his description of heaven and hell; (*g*) texts of an apocalyptic nature, such as the *Žāmāsp Nāmak,* the "book of Žāmāsp," containing the prophecies on the end of the age of Zarathushtra as given by the wise minister Žāmāsp; (*h*) *Mādiyān ī hazār dātastān,* the "record of thousand verdicts," dealing with law and jurisprudence.

Of a secular strain are: (*i*) *Draxt ī asūrīk,* the "Assyrian [i.e., Babylonian or palm] tree," a dispute between the palm tree and the goat on the respective qualities and virtues of the two contestants; (*j*) *Husrav ut rētak,* "(king) Husrav and the page," a discussion between the Sassanian king of that name and a page on the luxuries and elegancies of Sassanian court life; (*k*) *Abyātkār ī Zarērān,* the "memorial of Zarēr," an epical story of the dealings of King Vishtāspa (*see* ZARATHUSHTRA) and his general Zarēr with their enemies; (*l*) *Kārnāmak ī Artaxshēr ī Pāpakān,* the "book of the exploits of king Artaxshēr (Ardashīr)," on the epical feats of that king (*see* PERSIA § D6*a*); (*m*) *Shahrastānīhā ī Ērān,* the "cities of Iran," a work of geographical nature.

From this incomplete survey it appears that Sassanian literary activities extended over the fields of religious and secular literature. While attempting an evaluation of its literary value and utilizing this literature for the reconstruction of a picture of Sassanian religion and civilization, it should be kept in mind that only a presumably small portion of a once vast literature has survived.

Bibliography. On coins: F. D. J. Paruck, *Sassanian Coins* (1924). R. Göbl, "Stand und Aufgaben der sasanidischen Numismatik," *La Nouvelle Clio* (1952); "Aufbau der Münzprägung," in F. Altheim and R. Stiehl, *Ein asiatischer Staat,* I (1954), 51-128. On seals: P. Horn and G. Steindorff, *Sassanidische Siegelsteine* (1891). On inscriptions: M. Sprengling, *Third Century Iran* (1953). Translation of the Psalms: K. Barr, "Bruchstücke einer Pehlevi-Übersetzung der Psalmen," *Sitzungsberichte der Preussischen Akademie der Wissenschaften, Philologische-Historische Klasse* (1933), pp. 91-152. On papyri: O. Hansen, "Die mittelpersischen Papyri der Papyrus-sammlung der Staatlichen Museen zu Berlin," *Abhandlungen der Preussischen Akademie der Wissenschaften, Philologische-Historische Klasse* (1937), No. 9. On dipinti: B. Geiger, "The synagogue, the Middle Iranian texts," *The Excavations at Dura-Europos, Final Report,* VIII, pt. I (1956), 283-317.

An introduction to the language of the Pahlavi books is provided by H. S. Nyberg, *Hilfsbuch des Pahlavi,* vols. I-II (1928-31), with chrestomathy and lexicon. On Sassanian literature: J. C. Tavadia, *Die mittelpersische Sprache und Literatur der Zarathustrier* (1956), with bibliographical references for the individual texts. R. C. Zaehner, *The Teachings of the Magi: A Compendium of Zoroastrian Beliefs* (1956), gives up-to-date translations from several of the most important texts, as does the same author's *Zurvan: A Zoroastrian Dilemma* (1955), though the latter deals primarily with heterodox tendencies in Zoroastrianism. H. W. Bailey, *Zoroastrian Problems in the Ninth-Century Books* (1943), considers a number of essential problems connected with the study of the Zoroastrian books. On the term *zand,* see: J.-P. de Menasce, "La conquête de l'iranisme et la récupération des mages hellénisés," *Annuaire de l'École Pratique des Hautes Études* (1956-57).

There is no need to repeat here the literature given in Tavadia's survey (*see above*). In addition the following are of importance: For the *Bundahishn,* W. B. Henning, "An Astronomical Chapter of the Bundahishn," *JRAS* (1942), pp. 229-48. For the *Dēnkart,* J.-P. de Menasce, "Une encyclopédie mazdéenne: le Dénkart," *Bibliothèque de l'École des Hautes Études, Section des Sciences Religieuses,* vol. LXIX (1958). For texts of an apocalyptic nature, H. W. Bailey, "To the Žāmāsp-nāmak," *Bulletin of the School of Oriental Studies,* VI (1930-32), 55-85, 581-600. E. Benveniste, "Une apocalypse pehlevie: le Žāmāsp-nāmak," *RHR,* CV-CVI (1932), 337-80. Work on the Sassanian law code (*mādiyān,* "book, record," rather than the traditional *mātikān;* see W. B. Henning, *JRAS* [1942], p. 241) is still in the beginning; see, e.g.: A. Pagliaro, "Riflessi del diritto publico nel diritto privato dell' età sassanidica," *Archives d'histoire du droit oriental* (1948). For a comparison between Sassanian law and the code of the Christian jurist Išō'bōxt (E. Sachau, *Syrische Rechtsbücher,* vol. III [1914]), see: N. Pigulevskaya, "Transitional Forms of the Slavery System in Iran According to the Syriac Code of Pehlevi Law," *XXIII Orientalist Congress* (1954). For *Draxt ī asūrīk,* see W. B. Henning, "A Pahlavi poem," *Bulletin of the School of Oriental and African Studies,* XIII (1950), 641-48.

M. J. DRESDEN

PAI. Alternate form of PAU.

PAINT. 1. For cosmetic paint, *see* EYE PAINT; COSMETICS §§ 2, 4.

2. Liquid color applied to buildings or articles. The biblical references to paint and painting are comparatively few, perhaps because of the prohibition of image-making in the Decalogue.

In Palestine as early as the Neolithic period walls of houses in Jericho were painted, and in the Chalcolithic period designs and scenes were painted on the walls of houses in Teleilat el-Ghassul. At Megiddo in stratum VIIA (*ca.* 1200 B.C.) the mud-plaster walls of a palace court were painted, and there were traces of design in blue, green, red, yellow, black, and white. In the descriptions of Solomon's temple no painting is mentioned. In the second temple, according to the Mishna (Middoth III.1), a red line was painted around the altar of burnt offering, halfway up, to direct the sprinkling of the blood. According to Jer. 22:14, Jehoiakim decorated his palace by "painting it with vermilion" (משוח בששר). This decoration may have been influenced by the palaces in Egypt and Assyria, which were painted within. In condemning idolatry in Jerusalem, Ezek. 8:10 tells of animals and idols "portrayed" (מחקה; lit., "carved") on the wall of a secret place in the temple. In both Egypt and Assyria animal gods were carved on the walls in bas-relief and painted. Ezek. 23:14 refers to bas-reliefs of Chaldeans "portrayed in vermilion."

The attackers of Nineveh (the Medes and Babylonians) had reddened shields (Nah. 2:3—H 2:4), either painted or, if leather, perhaps dyed.

Painting on pottery, though not mentioned in the Bible, was widely practiced in the Near East. In Palestine the painting of designs and figures on pottery became common in the Early Bronze period; rose to a climax in a bichrome painted decoration with friezes divided into panels, and with bird, fish, tree, and geometric patterns, such as found at Lachish, Megiddo, Tell el-Ajjul, and elsewhere, and belonging to the Late Bronze I period (*ca.* 1500 B.C.); and declined after the Israelite invasion. *See* POTTERY.

In passages on the folly of idolatry the Wisdom of Solomon describes making an image and "smearing it with vermilion" (καταχρίσας μίλτῳ; 13:14; RSV "giving it a coat of red paint"), and an idol spotted with various colors (15:4). In Egypt, where this book originated, most of the statues of gods in wood and softer stones were painted. In a comparison between historiography and housebuilding II Macc. 2:29 refers to painting (ζωγραφεῖν) a house with figures. IV Macc. 17:7 speaks of how moving a painting of the martyrdom of some pious Jews would be, but indicates that such painting (same root as above) would be a transgression against the law of God.

In Tulul Abu el-'Alayiq, a suburb of Jericho, the houses of the rich were painted to imitate marble, as in contemporary Pompeii. Some Galilean synagogues of the third century A.D. and the synagogue of Dura-Europos of the same period were painted with figures, but it is uncertain whether the synagogues which Jesus attended were so decorated. *See* ARCHITECTURE § 3; HOUSE.

Bibliography. B. Meissner, *Babylonien und Assyrien,* I (1920), 234, 278, 325, 329-31. A. Erman and H. Ranke, *Ägypten und ägyptisches Leben im Altertum* (1923), pp. 494, 503-5, 546. W. A. Heurtley, "A Palestinian Vase-Painter of the 16th Century B.C.," *QDAP,* VIII (1939), 21-36. G. Dalman, *Arbeit und Sitte,* V (1937), 88; VII (1942), 61-62. A. Lucas, *Ancient Egyptian Materials and Industries* (3rd ed., 1948), pp. 391-413. A.-G. Barrois, *Manuel d'archéologie biblique,* painting on pottery: I (1939), 407, 411, 416, 424-28, 433-36, 439-40, 443, 447, 508; other painting: I (1939), 488-91; II (1953), 306-7, 466-68. R. J. Forbes, *Studies in Ancient Technology,* III (1955), 202-55. J. L. Kelso, *Excavations at NT Jericho,* AASOR, XXIX-XXX (1955), 45-49.

J. A. THOMPSON

PALACE.

1. Terminology. Though there is no Hebrew or Greek word meaning "palace" in the strict sense, the residence of a sovereign or a high dignitary, words or expressions obviously referring to such edifices are translated "palace" in the English versions. Some words translated "palace" in the KJV are translated otherwise in the RSV, while some words translated "palace" in the RSV are translated otherwise in the KJV.

The word אפדן, of Persian origin (Old Persian *apa-dāna; see* HALL § 4), meaning "armory" or "treasury," means "palace" in Akkadian and Syriac and so is taken in Dan. 11:45 KJV—אהלי אפדנו, "tabernacles of his palace" (RSV "his palatial tents"). ארמון, "high building," is translated "palace" in some passages (e.g., II Chr. 36:19; Isa. 23:13); while in others the KJV has "palace" and the RSV uses other terms, such as "citadel" (I Kings 16:18; II Kings 15:25, where KJV "palace of the king's house" is redundant), "tower" (Ps. 122:7), and "stronghold" (Isa. 34:13; Amos 1:4, 7, 10, 14). בירה, a late word designating an important building or city, is taken as "palace" in I Chr. 29:1, 19. Elsewhere, when it is translated "palace" in the KJV, it is in the RSV "castle" (Neh. 7:2) or "capital" (Ezra 6:2; Neh. 1:1; Esth. 1:2, 5; 2:3, 5; etc.; Dan. 8:2). בית, meaning "house," is translated "palace" in the KJV only in II Chr. 9:11, where בית המלך is "king's palace." Elsewhere the KJV generally translates בית by other words, such as "house," "household," "place." In the RSV where the reference is clearly to the king's house, the translation frequently is "palace" (e.g., I Kings 4:6; II Kings 10:5; II Chr. 2:1), though occasionally the RSV is satisfied with "house" (e.g., Gen. 12:15; Jer. 39:8). ביתן, from the same root, is translated "palace" (Esth. 1:5; 7:7-8). היכל (Assyrian *êkallu;* Ugaritic *hkl;* from Sumerian *e-gal,* "great house") generally means "temple," but in fifteen OT passages (e.g., I Kings 21:1; Isa. 39:7; Dan. 1:4) it is translated "palace." הרמון (Amos 4:3) is "palace" in the KJV, but merely transliterated "Harmon" in the RSV; the meaning is uncertain. טירה (Syriac *ṭiyarâ;* Arabic *ṭiwâr*), "palace" in the KJV, in the RSV is "battlement" (Song of S. 8:9) and "encampment"

(Ezek. 25:4). In the NT αὐλή, primarily meaning "court," is "palace" in Matt. 26:3; Luke 11:21. Where the KJV has "palace" in Matt. 26:58, 69; Mark 14:54, 66, the RSV has "courtyard" and in John 18:15 "court." In Mark 15:16 the KJV has "hall," and the RSV surprisingly "palace." In Phil. 1:13 πραιτώριον is "palace" in the KJV and "praetorian guard" in the RSV.

2. Foreign palaces. There are some biblical references to foreign palaces, such as the houses of Pharaoh (Gen. 12:15), Nebuchadnezzar (Dan. 1:4; 4:4), Belshazzar (Dan. 5:5), Darius (Dan. 6:18), Ahasuerus (Esth. 1:5, 8), Artaxerxes (Ezra 4:14). The commercial and political relations which Israel and Judah had with Mesopotamia and Egypt must have acquainted a number of Hebrews with the palaces of these countries. In Palestine excavations have uncovered foundations of large Bronze Age buildings, as at Tell Beit Mirsim, Lachish, and Ai, so imposing that apparently they were palaces of rulers.

3. Palaces of the Hebrew kings. Excavations at Tell el-Ful, Saul's Gibeah, show strong fortifications, but give little evidence of luxurious living quarters. David's dwelling in Jerusalem must have been imposing for its time; for it was built with cedar by carpenters and masons sent by Hiram king of Tyre, and it housed a considerable number of wives, concubines, servants, children, and guards (II Sam. 5:11-15). Solomon's palace was more elaborate, also built by Hiram's artisans and containing a large amount of cedar hewn in Lebanon. According to I Kings 7:1-12, the "House of the Forest of Lebanon" was a hundred cubits long, fifty cubits wide, and thirty cubits high (*see* HALL § 2).* The royal dwelling quarters were adjacent, and there was a separate house for one of the wives, Pharaoh's daughter. Presumably subsequent kings of Judah occupied Solomon's palace. Both David's and Solomon's palaces seem to have survived, at least in part, the destruction of Jerusalem in 587 B.C. (Neh. 3:25); but so thorough was the destruction by Titus in A.D. 70 and Hadrian in A.D. 135 that no remains of these palaces have been found. During Solomon's reign probably imposing residences were built for some of his local governors. One such building, which may be called a palace, was uncovered at Megiddo. Figs. HOU 32-33; MEG 34.

In Israel, Jeroboam and his successors must have had palaces. Zimri at the end of his seven-day reign in Tirzah died by burning the king's house over him with fire (I Kings 16:18). Zimri's conqueror and successor Omri started the building of a palace on the hill Samaria, where he founded his capital. It seems that the palace was extended by his son Ahab. Excavators have found a large number of ivory inlays from this palace, which doubtless was the "ivory house" built by Ahab (I Kings 22:39) and explains the "houses of ivory" and "beds of ivory" of Amos 3:15; 6:4 (*see* SAMARIA § 2*a*). Ahab also had a second palace in Jezreel (I Kings 21:1). The palace in Samaria, with the city, was destroyed by the army of Sargon II in 722/21 B.C.

4. Hellenistic and Roman period palaces. After the Exile the rulers in Jerusalem had special houses (Neh. 2:8). Jason the high priest, at the instigation

Courtesy of the Israel Office of Information, New York

1. General view showing the three levels of the rock on which Herod's palace was built at Masada

of Antiochus Epiphanes, built a Greek gymnasium "under the citadel," presumably attached to his residence (II Macc. 4:12). The Hasmoneans, after gaining power in Palestine and coming into the high priesthood, had their palace in Jerusalem, near the temple. Simon is said to have repaired "the house" (Ecclus. 50:1).

Herod the Great, on becoming king of the Jews, inaugurated a large program of building. In Jerusalem he erected his magnificent palace in the NW of the city with its three towers: Phasael, Hippicus, and Mariamne (*see* JERUSALEM § 10). At Jericho (Tulul Abu el-ʿAlayiq, a mile W of modern Jericho) he built another palace (Jos. War I.xxi.4), which on his death was burned by his former slave Simon (Jos. Antiq. XVII.x.6). Excavations in 1950-51 indicated the opulence of this, which doubtless was a winter residence. Another palace was at MASADA, on the W cliffs by the Dead Sea, where Herod took refuge in 40 B.C., when the Parthians seized Jerusalem (Fig. PAL 1). An expedition there in 1955 and 1956 showed formidable buildings with an elaborate system of cisterns.

References in the NT (Matt. 26:3, 58, 69; Mark 14:54, 66; John 18:15) make it clear that in Jesus' time the high priest, though there was a Roman governor, had a palace.

For the question of the palace used by Pilate at the trial of Jesus *see* PRAETORIUM.

Bibliography. I. Benzinger, *Hebräische Archäologie* (1927), pp. 31, 100-103, 211-15. *BASOR,* 120 (Dec., 1950), 11-22; 123 (Oct., 1951), 8-17. *IEJ,* vol. 7, no. 1 (1957).

O. R. SELLERS

PALAL pā'lăl [פָּלָל, *possibly* (God) has judged] (Neh. 3:25). One of those aiding Nehemiah in the repair of the Jerusalem wall.

Bibliography. M. Noth, *Die israelitischen Personennamen* (1928), p. 187.

PALANQUIN păl'ən kēn' [אַפִּרְיוֹן, *'appiryôn, possibly from* φορεῖον, litter] (Song of S. 3:9). A canopied couch borne on men's shoulders. Although *'uppiryôn,* found only in Song of S. 3:9, appears to be synonymous with *miṭṭâ* ("bed"; RSV "LITTER") in 3:7, its posts, back, and seat (3:10) point to something like a sedan chair. W. S. MCCULLOUGH

PALEOLITHIC pā'lĭ ə lĭth'ĭk, păl'ĭ—. The earliest stage of culture, characterized by the use of chipped stone implements. *See* PREHISTORY.

PALESTINE, CLIMATE OF păl'ə stīn. Many references in the Bible to phenomena of weather and climate can be understood more clearly in the light of modern meteorological observations and theory. Though the possibility of climatic change must be considered, the basic factors remain the same. Narratives in which weather conditions are important to the story; figures of speech which make use of weather terminology; the distinctions in translation between related terms for cloud, storm, wind, and rain gain interest as they are read against the background of elementary meteorology.

1. Weather and climate
2. Factors in the Palestinian climate
3. The climatic regions
   a. The coastal plains
   b. The W highlands, including Carmel
   c. The Rift Valley
   d. The plateau of Transjordan
   e. The deserts
4. Summer
5. Winter
6. The transitional periods
7. Climatic change
8. Meteorological terminology of the Bible

Bibliography

1. Weather and climate. The climate and weather phenomena of Palestine can be properly described and understood only in a larger meteorological context. By "climate" is meant the characteristic weather of a locality or region over a period of time, including its occasional deviations from the usual pattern. "Weather" is the condition and behavior of the atmosphere as experienced at a particular time and place, with its attendant phenomena of atmospheric pressure and humidity, heat or cold, clear or cloudy skies, wind, precipitation, and visibility. These phenomena are the product of the interaction of three principal factors: (*a*) the warming or cooling of the atmosphere by contact with the earth, or by its own vertical movement; (*b*) the presence in it of water vapor evaporated from large bodies of water, or of fine dust and salt particles picked up by the wind from land and sea; and (*c*) the restless, ceaseless movement of the air in streams and eddies. The horizontal movement of the air manifests itself as wind, and the vertical movement produces clouds and rain.

Changes of climate are measured in millenniums. Weather, on the other hand, particularly in middle latitudes, is subject to frequent and sudden changes. Local weather is profoundly affected by the movement across the surface of the globe of vast air masses, homogeneous in temperature and humidity, which circle slowly—in the Northern Hemisphere in a clockwise direction—round a center of high barometric pressure. An air mass may be cold and moist, cold and dry, warm and moist, or warm and dry, depending on its region of origin. Cold, moist air, e.g., comes to Palestine in winter from the North Atlantic, modified somewhat by its passage across the Mediterranean. Warm, dry air comes from the North African deserts in the van of spring and autumn storms. Where air masses of different characteristics meet (at a "front"), they do not mix, but clash, producing counterclockwise eddies of low pressure. These counterclockwise eddies or "cyclones" are usually accompanied by cloud, wind, and precipitation.

2. Factors in the Palestinian climate. The first factor which contributes to the climate of a particular region is its latitude, since this determines the amount of heat received directly from the sun while the sun is shining, as well as the length of the day and of the seasons. Palestine lies between 31′15″ and 33′15″ N latitude, in the same latitude as the state of Georgia. It is thus on the N margin of the subtropical zone, and, with the shift southward of the zones in winter, it is invaded by the atmospheric disturbances of the temperate zone. Hence it is a land of two seasons—a summer which is sunny, warm, and almost rainless, with moderate, regular winds, and a winter which is mild to cool, and intermittently wet and stormy. The brief transitional periods between summer and winter bring the "former and the latter rains" of the Bible, which are, in fact, but the first and last installments of the winter rains. In these periods, also, the hot, dry winds of the khamsin or sirocco raise the temperature often to its highest point in the year.

The second element to be considered is the effect of the principal currents and eddies of the global atmosphere. In summer the circulation in the E Mediterranean is sluggish, because it is midway between the monsoon low over Southern Asia and high pressure centered in the Atlantic. The steady "Etesian winds" from the NW are part of the monsoon circulation. There are no "frontal" storms, because there is no cold air to clash with the warm; and there are no convection thunderstorms, because the upper air is dry and warm. But, beginning with autumn and continuing more intensely in winter, cold maritime air pushes into the Mediterranean basin from time to time; as this clashes with the tropical air mass, eddies of low pressure are created which travel along the front between the two. The eddies create storms of wind and rain. Ahead of them the air is warm, and behind them it is cold. Sometimes cold, dry air spreading out from the winter high pressure in Central Asia is able to pass the mountain barriers to the N and sweep down over Palestine.

The third factor is the location of the country in relation to large bodies of water and large areas of land. Since the former grow cool or warm more slowly than the latter, the daily and annual range of temperature is much less in maritime than in continental climates. Palestine again is on the margin between the two. Warm, moist air covers the low coast line in summer, and the winter rains come from across the sea. But the rains do not penetrate far inland beyond the barrier of the double range of mountains which lies across their path. To the E, S, and SW are deserts of the subtropical zone, and these too affect the climate of the land. Rainfall decreases from the coast inland, and from N to S. The wilderness of Judea is itself a desert, as is the

Negeb or southland. Indeed, the inhabitants of Palestine live always precariously on the desert's edge, by the grace of God and of the sea. The proximity of the Mediterranean means more than the gift of rain; there is also the dew deposited by the moist air of summer when the land cools at nightfall, and also the sea breeze which mitigates the daytime heat.

The fourth element in climate is regional and local—the nature and covering of the terrain, its elevation and the angle of its slope, the presence or absence of lakes and large rivers, as well as irregularities of contour which modify the general air movement and give rise to local winds. Two physical features of Palestine are important in this connection: the strongly marked lines of relief running N-S, roughly at right angles to most of the rain-bearing storms, and the abrupt changes in altitude and in the nature of the terrain. The result is that striking climatic differences are found within short distances. The annual rainfall at Jerusalem averages 26.1 inches, whereas fifteen miles to the E, near the Dead Sea shore, it is only 3.4 inches, and the mean annual temperature there is 14° F. higher than at Jerusalem. The daily range of temperature is greater in the hills than in the maritime plain, and is greater still in the deep trough of the Rift Valley, because there the daily maximum is so high. The prevailing winds at Jerusalem are close to those of the general circulation, N to NW, but at Gaza they are S, and at Beersheba W. At Ezion-geber, at the head of the Gulf of Aqaba, Solomon's smelters were oriented to take advantage of a natural "chimney effect" which produces a preponderance of steady northerly winds blowing toward the Gulf.

3. The climatic regions. Five regional modifications of climate are found within the narrow confines of the land. If we include the Alpine heights of Hermon, a sixth must be added.

a. The coastal plains. Between the sea and the hilly plateau which forms the backbone of W Palestine is a series of alluvial plains which grow broader and rise higher toward the S. Here the influence of the sea is dominant. The humidity is high, and the daily and annual range of temperature is less than in the hills. Consequently the summer nights are hot, and in winter frost is rare. Rainfall near the shore is heavier than it is a few miles inland, but not so heavy as in the hill country. It also begins earlier in the autumn, and sometimes falls for brief periods with great intensity.

b. The W highlands, including Carmel. The hilly plateau, rising at points to over 3,300 feet, presents a barrier to the westerly winds, except where it is broken by the Plain of Esdraelon and the valleys of lower Galilee. In the extreme N and at Mount Carmel it almost reaches the sea. On the W slopes rainfall increases with height, so that the contours of the rainfall map follow closely those of the elevation. On the E side toward the desert the precipitation falls off sharply in the "rain shadow." It falls off, too, from N to S, from 47 inches annually in upper Galilee to 12 inches below Hebron. The temperature range is greater than in the plains, so that summer nights are not too hot, and the winter is longer and colder. The average minimum in winter at Jerusalem is 44° F., but night frosts are not uncommon, and sometimes there is snow.

c. The Rift Valley. E of the central range the land falls off sharply into the Ghor or Rift Valley. This is well below sea level for most of its length. Here the effects of topography on climate are most marked. Air from the sea which cools and gives precipitation on the W slopes is warmed and dried as it descends into the valley of the Jordan. One can observe this when fine weather clouds moving from the W fade away at the edge of the cliffs, only to re-form where the air currents rise again over the lip of the Transjordan Plateau. The lower Jordan Valley is warm in winter and unbearably hot in summer. At Jericho the normal mean maximum temperature in January is 68° F. A high of 84° F. has been recorded in January, and 114° F. in July. Even at Tiberias the comparable figures are 81° and 115°. The mean annual rainfall at Tiberias is 18 inches; a few miles S, near the river, it is 10 inches; at Jericho, 5½ inches; and at the S end of the Dead Sea, 2 inches. But heavier rains can occur, and in the wet year 1944 the rainfall at Jericho rose to 13 inches.

d. The plateau of Transjordan. Beyond the Rift Valley the plateau is in places higher than the W range; in S Edom it is considerably higher. Hence, in spite of the greater distance from the sea, there is substantial rainfall along the W margin of the plateau, equaling in Gilead and Ammon that of the W highlands opposite. In the dry year 1931-32 there was more rain in the S highlands of Moab than at Bethlehem—which throws light on the story of Ruth. Only a narrow strip of land, however, receives the rain, owing to the proximity of the desert. Between the arable land and the desert is a band of steppe country where evaporation exceeds precipitation, and the temperature range is higher.

e. The deserts. In the lower Rift Valley, in the Negeb or southland, and in the "wilderness of Judea" the surrounding subtropical deserts encroach on Palestine. The deserts are not altogether without rain, but it falls irregularly and is largely lost through evaporation. The rate of evaporation at the S end of the Dead Sea is four times that at Tel Aviv. Such vegetation as exists surrounds the rare springs, or is of a type adapted to depend on dew. The deserts are characterized also by a great daily range of temperature, because of the daytime heating of the land surface and the unhindered loss of this heat at night through radiation. Sometimes the air rises so rapidly above the hot ground in daytime that strong winds and whirling sandstorms or duststorms may result.

4. Summer. The long, rainless summer begins in May or June and lasts until September. Its features are the consistently fine weather, regular winds, daytime heat, and almost complete drought. The average maximum temperature at Tel Aviv in August is 84° F., at Ramle 88°, and at Beisan 99°. This is the "heat of the day," when men sat in their tent doors (Gen. 18:1), and a child in the harvest field might suffer sunstroke (II Kings 4:18-19). The "cool [lit., 'wind'] of the day" (Gen. 3:8) comes when the sea breeze moves in beneath the warm air rising from over the land; it reaches Jerusalem before noon,

Jericho soon afterward, and the Transjordanian Plateau by midafternoon. In summer the sky is mainly clear of clouds except for some fair-weather cumulus and strato-cumulus. In most of the country the cloud cover is less than one tenth of totality in July and August, though there is more cloud over upper Galilee. Sunshine hours may reach 98 per cent of the possible.

Rain is rare in June except in the extreme N, and is almost unheard of in July and August (cf. II Sam. 21:10). There are, however, exceptional cases of "rain in harvest" (Prov. 26:1). The summer drought is not due to any lack of moisture in the air. In fact, absolute humidity in the hill country is double that of winter, and at the coast it is nearly triple. The reason the moisture is not precipitated as rain is that there is no clash of warm and cold air masses causing frontal storms, and the warm air is normally too stable for thunderstorms to be created by convection. The humidity shows itself, however, in abundant dew formation on calm nights when the ground and surface objects cool sufficiently to condense the moisture. Dew forms on five nights out of six on the coastal plains in August and September, and similarly on the seaward slopes of Mount Carmel and the heights of Galilee. It is somewhat less in July, and in other parts of the land, but everywhere dew is important as a mitigation of the drought.

5. Winter. Winter (חרף) is pictured in the Bible as the season of rain (Lev. 26:4; Deut. 11:14; Ezra 10:9, 13; Song of S. 2:11; Isa. 4:6; John 10:23), of cold (Gen. 8:22; Ezra 10:13; Ps. 147:17; Jer. 36:22; Acts 28:2), and of stormy weather (Job. 37:9; Isa. 25:4; Acts 27:12). When the weather turned cold, the well-to-do moved into their "winter houses" (Amos 3:15), and the lazy man made the excuse that it was too cold to begin his fall plowing (Prov. 20:4), after the EARLY RAIN had softened the ground. A second word for winter, סתו, means the "rainy, stormy season" (Song of S. 2:11). Χειμών in the NT means both "winter" and "storm."

Compared with N climates, that of Palestine is not cold in winter. The cold was felt because of its contrast with the heat of daytime (Gen. 31:40) and of summer (Job 6:16-17), and because clothing and shelter were inadequate (Exod. 22:26). The mean temperature at Jerusalem drops only 3° F. in October, but in November it drops 10°, in December 8½°, and in January a further 4½°. There is frost at Jerusalem on an average .7 days in December, 2.5 days in January, and .3 days in February, but seldom on the maritime plain and never in the Jordan Rift. The mean maxima and minima for January (in degrees Fahrenheit) are 64 and 48 at Tel Aviv, 65 and 46 at Gaza, 61 and 47 at Afula in the Plain of Esdraelon, 54 and 42 at Jerusalem, 51 and 40 at Ramallah in the hill country N of Jerusalem, 65 and 50 at Tiberias, and 50 and 40 at an altitude of over 2700 feet in N Galilee. Although February is normally a little milder than January, record low temperatures have occurred in that month—29° at Gaza, 23° at Jerusalem, 18° at Afula, and 14° in upper Galilee.

Certain passages in Job (6:16; 37:9-10; 38:29-30) suggest familiarity with winter conditions more severe than that of Palestine itself, but which might be found on the higher parts of the Arabian Plateau. Snow falls at Jerusalem on only about three days a year on the average, most often in January. Occasionally there is a heavy fall—e.g., 17 inches in December, 1879; 29 inches in February, 1920; and 20 inches in January, 1950 (cf. II Sam. 23:20; I Macc. 13:22). This happens when the polar maritime air of a winter depression is particularly cold and moist. The cold which comes with NE to SE winds, on the other hand, is dry, because it comes across mountains and deserts from its source in Central Asia.

The rainy season is not a time of continuous rain, but of rain alternating with bright periods. Hours of sunshine may be as much as 50 per cent of the possible. Nor are the rains regular in amount or distribution. For the period 1930-49 it rained at Jerusalem on the average three days in October, six in November, nine in December, thirteen in January, twelve in February, eight in March, four in April, and two in May. The comparable figures for Tel Aviv at the coast were three, seven, eleven, fourteen, twelve, eight, three, and one, with .7 day also in September. At Jericho it rained on one day in October, and in the following months four, five, seven, six, four, two, one. The total annual rainfall at Jericho averaged in recent years 5½ inches, compared with 26 inches at Jerusalem, 21 inches at Tel Aviv, and 25 inches at Dan. For the period 1859-1948 Ashbel's rainfall map shows over 31 inches at the highest points in the central and S hill country, at Mount Carmel, N and S of the Jabbok in Transjordan, as well as a steep rise in upper Galilee to 47 inches near Safad. These long-term-average figures, however, conceal the fact that, in addition to considerable variations from year to year, the rainfall between 1875 and 1895 was distinctly greater than it has been since *ca.* 1922.

To the differences in total rainfall in successive years and over longer periods must be added variations in distribution through the rainy season. Sometimes the precipitation is evenly distributed by months, as in the averages of rainy days quoted above. In other years the early rains of autumn may fail almost entirely, as in 1937-38, and yet the total fall be not far below the normal. Rain may be very intense for a brief period; on November 23, 1949, there was an extreme example of this when over 4½ inches, or 17 per cent of the total rain for that year, fell at Haifa in a single hour.

The fact that precipitation is barely sufficient at best, and is not dependable, explains the frequent biblical references to drought and consequent FAMINE (Gen. 41:54; I Kings 17:1; II Kings 8:1; Luke 15:14). In the years 1922-35 the annual rainfall at Jerusalem totaled only 74 per cent of the average over the last century, and several times it fell to *ca.* 50 per cent, though never less than this. The meteorological explanation of these droughts is somewhat as follows: In a winter of average or above-average rainfall the low-pressure systems with their cyclonic storms reach the E Mediterranean about once a week for several weeks in succession. These depressions may have traveled all the way from the Atlantic, but more often they have been formed in the lee of the Alps when a cold, moist wave breaks into the Mediterranean between the Alps and the

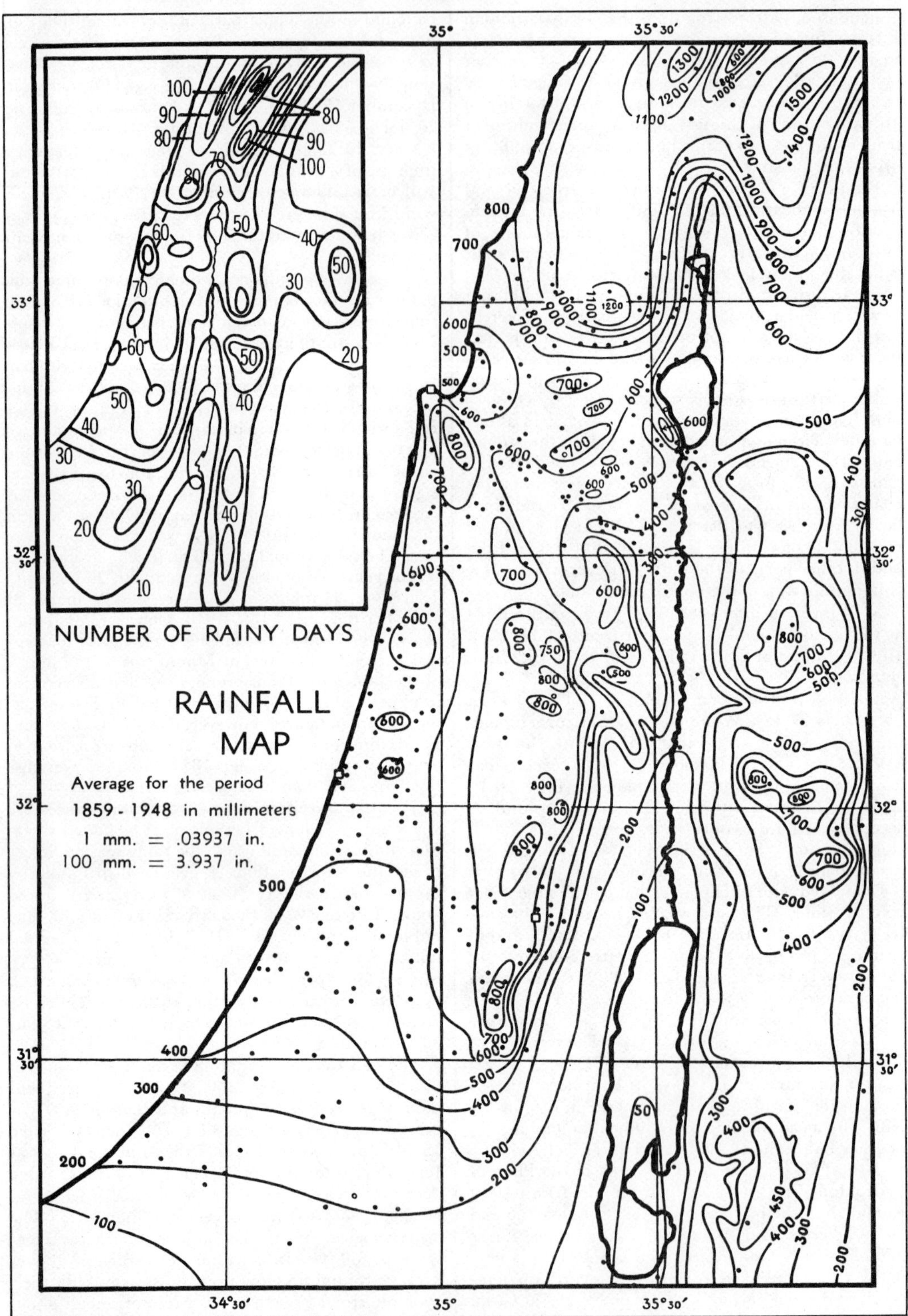

From D. Ashbel, *The Bio-Climatic Atlas of Israel* (Jerusalem, Israel: The Hebrew University)

2. Rainfall map of Palestine, showing number of rainy days, and average for the period 1859-1948

Pyrenees. Sometimes they originate over the Mediterranean itself, when high pressure over Europe sends cold continental air to meet warm continental air from Africa. Should these two high-pressure systems, as sometime happens, become linked at their margins instead of clashing, the resulting ridge of high pressure temporarily blocks the progress eastward of rain-bearing depressions. This, along with the displacement northward of the westerly upper winds in some years, is what brings drought to Palestine.

The dry year 1924-25, when rainfall was only about half the long-term average, succeeded a year when it was more normal. In the dry winter fourteen depressions reached Palestine, only seven of them in the normally rainiest months from December to March, and only five bringing cold, moist air from the Atlantic. The more normal year saw twenty-one depressions, fifteen in the months when resulting rainfall would be heaviest, and eleven bringing Atlantic air. The pattern is clear.

The two-years' drought in Elijah's time, extended in tradition to three years and a half (I Kings 18:1; Luke 4:25), could not have been complete, even though more severe than any recorded in recent times. Its duration, however, is not surprising; from 1929 to 1933 precipitation was only two thirds of normal, and in 1931-33 only 56 per cent of normal. Fig. PAL 2.

6. The transitional periods. There are no spring and autumn seasons, properly speaking, but merely transitional periods marked by characteristic weather. The "former and the latter rain" (Jer. 5:24 KJV; RSV "autumn rain and spring rain") are the first and last showers of the rainy season of winter. After the long, dry summer, "the [rain] clouds return *with* [not *after*] the rain" (Eccl. 12:2), usually in October. About 20 per cent of the annual rainfall comes in October and November at the coast, compared with 11-15 per cent in the hill country. This early rain is especially important to prepare the ground for plowing and seeding; the late showers of April and early May (4-8 per cent of the total) help bring the crops to maturity (cf. Deut. 11:14); hence their name מלקוש, from לקש—"crops sown late." Although, as already noted, total rainfall in modern times has never fallen below about 50 per cent of normal, the early rains (יורה) may be delayed until late November or, like the מלקוש, may fail entirely (Amos. 4:7). If the thermal difference between the warm and cold air masses is not great enough, there may be clouds and wind which promise rain but fail to give it (Prov. 25:14). On the other hand, if the air aloft is cold, the moist air from the sea rises rapidly from over the warm surface of the land, and local hail and thunderstorms may follow. Even in early summer late surges of cold Atlantic air may travel as far E as Palestine and bring "rain in harvest" (Prov. 26:1), though this is rare.

The sirocco or khamsin wind (the "east wind" of the OT) is a disagreeable feature of the months April to early June, and September to November. For periods of three days to a fortnight hot and very dry winds blow from the SE quarter, with a withering effect on men and beasts and vegetation (cf. Jer. 4:11; Jonah 4:8; Luke 12:55). Although the mean maximum daily temperature is highest in August, the record maxima have been recorded in May and June in connection with the sirocco. Even in October a high of 102° F. has been recorded at Jerusalem, and 93° in November. The extreme dryness of the air makes the heat more trying; the wind is parching, and fine dust fills the air. These winds blow when depressions moving eastward along the North African coast, or which are stationary over Abyssinia, draw ahead of them air which has been descending over the Sahara Desert, and which is therefore both hot and dry. Sometimes they blow strongly enough to endanger small craft off the coast, like the "east wind" which shattered the ships of Tarshish (Ps. 48:7—H 48:8).

7. Climatic change. The eroded hills and stony desert areas of Palestine have led many to wonder how this ever could have been regarded as a "land of milk and honey." The question springs to mind: In biblical times, must not the rainfall have been greater than now? Broadly speaking, weather phenomena and climatic conditions as pictured in the Bible correspond with conditions as observed today. Evidences of ancient occupation in regions now arid may indicate only that effective measures were taken in those days to conserve in dams and cisterns what water was available. It may well be that erosion was less advanced than today, since we know that in some areas there were forests where there are none now. Even today the desert regions are not rainless; indeed, they are subject to occasional violent thunderstorms and cloudbursts, which have left their mark in the intricate drainage pattern visible from the air.

We cannot rule out the possibility of climatic fluctuations sufficient to encourage or deter sedentary occupation in marginal lands. Otherwise it is hard to account for Glueck's evidence that S Transjordan was occupied before 2000 B.C., was abandoned until the thirteenth century B.C., then occupied until *ca.* the seventh century, and again abandoned for five hundred years. There are such fluctuations on record in modern times. Since *ca.* 1885 there has been a global warming trend; glaciers have retreated, and the sea level has risen. Rainfall in Florida was 30-40 per cent greater in the decade 1928-37 than it was twenty years earlier, and the mean annual temperature in Illinois rose 3.6° F. From tree rings, varves, and other evidence, climatologists conclude that *ca.* 4000 B.C. the mean temperature in the Northern Hemisphere was 3-4° higher than today, that it declined in undulations until the sixteenth and seventeenth centuries A.D., and now is again showing an upward trend. These global variations in temperature, apparently due to changes in solar radiation, result in advances and retreats of the polar ice, with corresponding shifts in the climatic zones. It is perhaps suggestive that the earliest Neolithic walled town was built in the seventh millennium at Jericho, deep in the Jordan Rift. This would be one of the first places where the returning warmth would make life more comfortable, after the cold, wet climatic period which in this latitude accompanied the last glaciation in Europe.

8. Meteorological terminology of the Bible. If, as seems to be the fact, weather and climate in Palestine are today broadly the same as in biblical times, attention to descriptions and terminology used in the Bible may be of some value for lexicography and exegesis. Although the descriptions often are vague and the use of terms is not always consistent, meanings may be missed through failure to observe the meteorological context. God did not speak to Job from a "whirlwind" or tornado, but from a tempest or gale (סערה). The two commonest Hebrew words for "cloud" are not synonyms, though sometimes they are used loosely; ענן refers to cloud stuff as extended rather than defined, cloud as such, a cloud mass covering the sky, overcast, stratus, mist, fog. It is cloud that covers and hides something, not cloud that gives or might be expected to give rain, which is עב. The latter is not adequately translated "thick cloud," though it usually is thick and dark. עב is a distinct cloud; hence it is pluralized, as ענן is not (with one exception). Usually it is a rain cloud, often a thundercloud, the familiar cumulo-nimbus, towering, dark, and wind-driven.

Hail can fall only from thunderclouds. Joshua's prayer for the sun to stand still *in the context of a hailstorm* (Josh. 10:11-13) was for the sun to remain hidden (cf. Hab. 3:11), so that its blazing heat would not impede pursuit of the enemy (cf. I Sam. 11:11). Again, the "strong east wind" (Exod. 14:19-28) which drove back the shallow waters of the Red Sea could have been a sirocco gale blowing into the NE quadrant of a deep depression over the Libyan Desert, bringing between the Egyptians and the Israelites a cloud (ענן) of sand and dust. With the passing of the depression, the wind would back to NW and drive the water in the opposite direction. The synoptic weather chart of the E Mediterranean for March 15, 1924, illustrates such a phenomenon precisely in the area of the Suez Canal.

Some of the principal terms used of weather phenomena may be distinguished as follows: (*a*) Rain. The general word for the falling of rain and the rain which falls is מטר in the OT and ὑετός in the NT. In Deut. 28:12; Acts 14:17, this is used of the seasonal rains; in Ezra 10:9; Acts 28:2, it is accompanied by winter cold, in I Sam. 12:17 by thunder, and in Exod. 9:34 by hail. In Prov. 28:3 it is "beating rain." The words גשם, βροχή, and ὄμβρος signify a heavy shower or downpour (Gen. 7:11-12; Matt. 7:25; Luke 12:54), especially the "former and latter rains" at the beginning and ending of the rainy season (Amos 4:7; cf. Deut. 11:14; Jas. 5:7). רביבים are spring showers (Ps. 65:10—H 65:11). שעירים may mean the drizzle from wet fogs of autumn (Deut. 32:2). שטף, "sweeping" (Nah. 1:8), and נפץ, "shattering," are epithets descriptive in particular of the rain of a desert storm (cf. Job 38:25).

b) Storm. זרם, χειμών, is a storm of wind and rain (Isa. 28:2; Matt. 16:3), sometimes accompanied by thunder, lightning, and hail (Isa. 30:30). The emphasis of the word is on the storminess which drives men to seek shelter (Job 24:8; Isa. 32:2). In Isa. 25:4 it is a "winter storm" (reading קר for קיר). Χειμών, though not זרם, comes to mean winter, the season of storms (II Tim. 4:21). The "sound of the rushing [KJV 'abundance'] of rain" (קול המון הגשם) is the sound which presages a downpour—either the sound of distant thunder or the noise of the wind (I Kings 18:41; cf. Jer. 10:13). The words סער or סערה, λαῖλαψ, refer to a squall or gale (Amos 1:14; Jonah 1:4), sometimes associated with thunder and rain (Ezek. 13:11), but not necessarily so (Luke 8:23; II Pet. 2:17). סופה also means a gale, with emphasis on the destructiveness of the wind's force. An epithet used of such a destructive wind is שואה, "devastation" (Prov. 1:27). The "scorching" or "harassing" wind (רוח זלעפות; Ps. 11:6) is the hot, dry wind of the sirocco (Gen. 41:6; Hos. 13:15); it may be a violent wind (Job 27:21; Ps. 48:7—H 48:8). The typhonic wind known as "Euroclydon" (KJV) or "the northeaster" (RSV) in Acts 27:14 was an easterly gale which followed a moderate S wind, and hence was probably a sirocco.

c) Wind directions. In Song of S. 4:16; Acts 27:13, the S wind is gentle. In Job 37:17; Luke 12:55, it brings heat. In Zech. 9:14 it is violent and accompanies a desert thunderstorm. "The north wind brings forth rain [גשם]" was a proverbial saying (Prov. 25:23); the situation referred to may have been a surge southward of polar air across the Balkans, as this has been known to result in heavy rains in March. Perhaps this is in mind when Jer. 47:2 pictures storm clouds (lit., "waters") piling up to the N of Palestine (cf. Ezek. 1:4). Paul's ship had to beat its way from Sidon to Crete against the prevailing NW winds before the storm struck (Acts 27:3-8).

d) Fine weather. The "fair weather" (εὐδία) of Matt. 16:2 means "a clear sky." In II Sam. 23:4 we read of a "cloudless morning," and in Exod. 24:10 (cf. Job 37:21) of a clear blue sky. The prolonged fine rainless weather of summer results in the drying up of pools and streams (Job 14:11).

e) Clouds. When air is cooled to its saturation point, the water vapor in it condenses into infinitesimal water droplets, which become visible as cloud. The general word for "cloud" or "mist," as already noted, is ענן. A particular cloud, עב, is composed of ענן (cf. Exod. 19:9; Job 26:8). It veils the sky (Ezek. 30:3), envelops a mountain (Exod. 19:16), covers ground and sea as mist or fog (Job 38:9; Hos. 13:3). The cloud (ענן) which rose or failed to rise from over the tabernacle (Exod. 40:36-37) was either a morning mist or an overcast, threatening sky; in any case, it was not a particular local cloud. The original distinction in Greek between νέφος, cloud in general, and νεφέλη, a particular cloud, is obscured in the LXX and the NT. The rain cloud (עב) may be a towering thundercloud (חזיז; Job 28:26), a נשיא rising above the horizon (Jer. 10:13; cf. I Kings 18:44); or it may be dark, wet-looking nimbostratus (ערפל, "murky cloud") scudding before the wind (I Kings 18:45; cf. II Pet. 2:17). In Isa. 25:5 עב seems to mean fine-weather cumulus giving temporary shade from summer heat. The "dew cloud" of Isa. 18:4 is most likely cirrus (שחק, "dust"; II Sam. 22:12), the highest cloud, thin and dusty in appearance, since dew was believed to descend imperceptibly from heaven (Prov. 3:20; Zech. 8:12).

Bibliography. G. Dalman, *Arbeit und Sitte in Palästina* (1928-33). C. E. P. Brooks, *Climate Through the Ages* (1949). D. Ashbel, *Regional Climatology of Israel* (in Hebrew; 1951); *Bio-Climatic Atlas of Israel* (in Hebrew and English; n.d.). F. K. Hare, *The Restless Atmosphere* (1953). H. Shapley, ed., *Climatic Change* (1933). D. Baly, *The Geography of the Bible* (1957), chs. 4-6. An excellent small popular introduction to meteorology is P. E. Lehr, R. W. Burnett, and H. S. Zim, *Weather* (1957).

R. B. Y. SCOTT

PALESTINE, GEOGRAPHY OF. To put the subject into correct perspective, this needs to be said: Aside from the divine, there are three chief factors in human experience: the earth, the air, and humanity —geography, climate, and society. All three interact.

The earth makes climate, climate makes the earth, and history is made by all three through man's reactions to, and his use of, them.

Since the ancient Hebrews believed that God had made the earth and had chosen one particular portion of it for their home, their concept of God was formed under the influence of its geography, climate, and human relations, all of which were his work. Their "Promised Land" was both a blessing and a challenge (see Judg. 3:1-6). As interpreted by the prophets, the land, the climate, and the peoples about them, who were usually hostile, were all a part of God's plan. These three factors and their own reactions and activities together made their history what it was. The OT is the record of their response, their reactions, and their interpretations of the results.

This article is an attempt to set forth the geographical conditions with which the Hebrews had to deal. The emphasis here is upon description of the land and upon human response to its challenge. *See also* PALESTINE, CLIMATE OF; PALESTINE, GEOLOGY OF; AGRICULTURE; HISTORY; MAN, ETHNIC DIVISIONS OF; etc.

A. Geography defined
B. The area identified
  1. Its general character and history
  2. Designations
  3. Boundaries
C. Climate
D. Geology
E. Land forms: regional studies
  1. The coastal regions
  2. The central mountain range
    a. Galilee
    b. The Great Plain
    c. Samaria
    d. Judea
    e. The Shephelah, or "Lowland"
    f. The wilderness (מדבר, *midhbār*)
    g. The Negeb (נגב, *neghebh*)
  3. The central Rift Valley
    a. The Upper Jordan
    b. The Sea of Galilee
    c. The Arabah
      i. Descriptive terms
      ii. The original valley floor
      iii. Special problems and usages
      iv. NT problems
    d. The Dead Sea and Wadi el-ʽArabah
  4. Transjordan
    a. Its general character
    b. Its main regions
F. Geography and culture
  1. Physical factors in historical problems
    a. Critical methods
    b. Physical changes and differences
    c. Intercultural effects
    d. Climate
      i. Regional differences
      ii. Temperature and health
      iii. Indispensable agricultural factors
    e. Cultural resources
      i. Agriculture
      ii. Pastoral
      iii. Non-agricultural resources
      iv. Industry
      v. Value of indigenous resources
  2. Population
    a. Unsatisfactory data
    b. Probable limits
    c. Settlements and housing
  3. Geography and ideology
    a. Cultural conflicts
    b. Ideological results
Bibliography

A. *GEOGRAPHY DEFINED.* Geography (the description of the earth), as applied to biblical interpretation, involves numerous aspects of a many-sided subject. The word has grown to include a variety of overlapping areas. Physical geography, in particular, includes the description of the terrain; its relief, or orography; its climate and resources; and especially its ecology—i.e., the relations between all organisms and their environment. The real nature of the simple biblical narratives of journeys and military campaigns is not at all clear unless the character of the terrain covered is indicated. The identification of place names of cities, mountains, rivers, springs, etc., with their proper sites is not unimportant, but is rarely discussed in this article. It is left to the notices of the individual places.

The subject of most significance for the interpretation of the biblical text and the understanding of the course of Hebrew history is "human" and "historical" geography—i.e., a people's use of the land and the effect of its various geographical features upon the life, literature, and development of the people. It is expressed in the now familiar phrase, "challenge and response." If, as the Christian believes, this is God's world, man is not "against his environment," but has the task of mastering it and using it (Gen. 1:28).

B. *THE AREA IDENTIFIED.* 1. Its general character and history. Palestine belongs to the part of the Near East that, since the beginning of historical records, has been dominated by Semitic languages. Geographically the area was bounded on the N by the Amanus-Taurus Mountains, on the E by the Zagros range and the Persian Gulf, on the S by the Indian Ocean, and on the W by the Red Sea and the Mediterranean. These boundaries did not protect it but laid it open to immigration and invasion, except on the S, where, in the great Arabian steppe, lay the breeding grounds of the Semitic-speaking peoples themselves, who came to dominate and occupy it as Arabic does today. Since long before the beginning of written records, the prolific nomads of that area had spilled over into the Fertile Crescent, which arches over the steppe from the Red Sea to the Persian Gulf. Lying at the SW tip of the Crescent, with a long shore on the sea, its E border on a limitless steppe, Palestine was open to all the cultural winds that blew. Near the head of the Dead Sea, Palestine had a prehistoric, city culture, based on agriculture, at JERICHO, now the oldest city known (*ca.* 7000 B.C.; *see* ARCHAEOLOGY).

2. Designations. The word "Palestine" is derived from the name of the *Pelishtim* (I Sam. 4:1), one of the tribes of Sea Peoples who, early in the twelfth century, invaded the narrow W coastal plain by the

Mediterranean on their way to conquer and settle in Egypt (*see* PHILISTINES). Defeated by Ramses III *ca.* 1167, they settled on the Maritime Plain. Since they were vigorous and warlike, dominated the Canaanites, and also occupied the most accessible part of the land, strangers gave their name to the whole of the land. Otherwise the land had no distinctive name but was usually reckoned a part of Syria. The word does not appear in the NT. In the OT it is used, not for the whole land, but only for Philistia proper, the S seacoast plain, and only in late poetical passages (Exod. 15:14; Isa. 14:29, 31; Joel 3:4).

The common Hebrew name for the Promised Land (cf. Gen. 12:4-7; Deut. 9:28; etc.) was CANAAN. This is also chiefly the seacoast plain and appears in parallelism with "Philistia" (Exod. 15:14-15; Zeph. 2:5; cf. Num. 13:29; 14:25; but cf. 14:43, 45). Neither term belongs to Transjordan (Num. 32:32; 33:51).

3. Boundaries. Modern usage, which will be followed here, applies the term Palestine to the entire territory allotted to the "twelve tribes," and speaks of W Palestine between the Jordan and the sea, and of E Palestine, or TRANSJORDAN, between the river and the Arabian steppe.

The area specifically included in this study runs from Ras en-Naqura, the ancient Scala Tyrorum, on the coast and the foothills of Mount Hermon on the N, to the "River of Egypt" (Wadi el-'Arish) and the S end of the Dead Sea on the S. However, immediately neighboring lands will often have to be included because of common geographical features, such as continuing rivers, mountains, and plains. Moreover, the Negeb as far as Kadesh-barnea, and even Mount Sinai, on the Wadi el-'Arabah as far as the Gulf of Aqabah, belong to special periods of Hebrew tradition and history.

The familiar biblical phrase "from Dan to Beer-sheba," used of the extent of the land from N to S (Judg. 20:1; I Sam. 3:20), was unsatisfactory to some. A more detailed statement regarding the "land of Canaan in its full extent" appears in Numbers (34:1-12). Here the "entrance of Hamath" is the most northerly point. Unfortunately, neither here nor elsewhere is the phrase's exact meaning discoverable, although it often appears. It can be either the Tripoli-Homs pass S of modern Hama or the narrow gorge between the Jordan Valley and the Beqa' (Coele-Syria) on the W flank of Mount Hermon. In the latter case it is only a little N of the site of ancient Dan. Since no territory N of Dan plays any role in Hebrew history, the latter interpretation is the more reasonable, although it can hardly extend Hebrew territory more than from ten to twenty miles beyond Dan, into a region of gorges and steep mountainsides. In the S, Kadesh-barnea, some forty miles S of Beer-sheba, is included. It is to be noted that in this passage the E border is the Jordan River. In the book of Numbers (32:33-42; 34:13-15), the two tribes and the half-tribe are treated separately, and no attempt is made to mark their borders.

The upshot of a study of various passages puts the effective limits of Hebrew territory in ancient times near Dan in the N and Kadesh-barnea in the S, a distance of 190 or 200 miles in a straight line, or, to include only the really cultivable territory, from Dan to Beer-sheba, a distance of under 150-60 miles. The area W of the Jordan is usually put at a little under 6,000 square miles. Since the Hebrews rarely actually ruled the extensive territories which they claimed, in Syria, Transjordan, and along the coast (*see* TRIBES, TERRITORIES OF), their material basis, even W of the Jordan in ancient times, must be put at very much less.

In the times of the kings, the Hebrew territory E of the Jordan usually ran, at its largest, from the Yarmuk to the Arnon. Since this area rarely played any decisive role in the national history, its records are scanty, and much remains to be done in archaeological research (*see* N. Glueck in *bibliography*). The political allegiance of the various parts of the territory also changed frequently (*see* TRANSJORDAN; MOAB; GILEAD 4). The distance from the Arnon (Wadi Mojib) to Ashteroth-karnaim in Bashan, which covers the territory the Hebrews partially and intermittently occupied, is *ca.* ninety miles N and S. The width of the arable land before the steppe begins varies from twenty-five miles in the S to some sixty miles E of the Sea of Galilee. The habitable area is usually estimated at *ca.* four thousand square miles, making, with W Palestine, a total of ten thousand square miles.

Briefly stated, the N border was Syria, consisting of Tyre and Sidon on the N coast, various cities or districts in the Lebanon and Anti-Lebanon Mountains and the Beqa' on the N, and Aram, or Syria proper, on the NE. All these borders fluctuated. On the E is the Arabian steppe, inhabited from time immemorial by nomadic tribes, but claimed by no settled political administration during early OT times. On the E, SE, and S were the Ammonites, Moabites, Edomites, and later the Nabateans, who, in the fifth or fourth century B.C., settled down along with the Edomites or after them, while the Edomites moved over into the Negeb and occupied the territory of Judah up to beyond Hebron. S of Beer-sheba was the Sinaitic steppe, which had no settled administration, but like the Arabian steppe was the home of nomadic tribes, some allied with Israel (e.g., the Kenites and the Jerahmeelites), some potentially hostile Ishmaelites, Midianites, Amalekites, etc. On the SW were the Red Sea and Egypt, all along the W the Mediterranean, with various Philistine and Canaanite cities usually in control of the coastal region and its ports.

C. *CLIMATE.* A dominant role in cultural history is played by climate. To understand the historical geography of Palestine, it is necessary to bear in mind the outstanding characteristics of the Palestinian climate. Be it noted that: (*a*) Palestine is in the area of the "Mediterranean" climate, with winter rains and summer drought. (*b*) It lies on the N edge of the world-encircling Sahara belt. It may well be said that the Sahara moves in over the land each summer. (*c*) As a result of the remarkable variety in its terrain, within its narrow limits, it has a great variety of individual climatic regions: from seacoast to desert, from subarctic to subtropical (from Mount Hermon, 9,230 feet above sea level, to the surface of the Dead Sea, 1,300 feet below).

d) The SW winds from the Mediterranean bring

storms and torrential rains in winter and coolness in summer. (*e*) At the turn of the two main seasons, in May and September-October, the sirocco (*sharqiyeh*, "east wind") brings burning heat that withers crops, beasts, and men. (*f*) Locusts, mildew, and the pests of both tropical and temperate climates are a constant threat. (*g*) As in all border climates, extremes of all kinds are constantly to be expected; climate is always unusual. *See* § F1*d below*.

See PALESTINE, CLIMATE OF.

D. *GEOLOGY.* The small area of ancient Palestine is divided into an astonishing variety of land forms. A word regarding the geological history of the land (*see* PALESTINE, GEOLOGY OF) is necessary to make their nature clear. The whole Arabian Peninsula, including the Fertile Crescent and a large section of North Africa, originally constituted a single block of the earth's surface. Over most of Palestine, the lowest stratum, lying upon the basic granite, is Nubian sandstone, followed by Cenomanian limestone, Senonian chalk, Senonian chert, and Eocene limestone. These, with basalt, are the chief elements in the earth's crust and its soils. Thrust up repeatedly by pressures from different directions, and sinking again, it gradually broke apart and created the great crack in the earth that, beginning in the Amanus Mountains, becomes the strange Rift Valley at the foot of Mount Hermon, reaches 2,600 feet below sea level in the Dead Sea, and ends in Lake Nyasa in SE Africa—a long ribbon of the earth's crust dropped down to Sheol, as it were.

The rift allowed the whole W section to drop, leaving the corresponding strata on the E side higher and more fully exposed to erosion in pluvial periods. But the W section was more seriously broken and folded as it dropped, and, consequently, its terrain is much rougher than that of E Palestine. Especially W of the Jordan, complex systems of faults and flexures in the limestone strata laid the surface open to deep erosion and, through seeping water, led to the creation of fantastic caves in parts of the land. Only a relief map or carefully taken aerial photographs can give any adequate idea of the tortured terrain of W Palestine. Four types of faults appear: (*a*) the parallel faults of rift valleys; (*b*) single fault lines running N and S; (*c*) transverse (E-W) faults; and (*d*) oblique (or "hinge") faults. There are equally complicated folds, or flexures.

The tremendous seismic disturbances were in some areas accompanied by both ancient and fairly recent volcanic activity, especially in Bashan and the Hauran, which were covered with basalt and where numerous craters and cones are still visible. In Galilee NW and SW of the Lake (*see* CHORAZIN; TIBERIAS; on Nebi Dhahi, the "hill of Moreh," *see* MOREH, HILL OF) and on Mount Carmel basalt is in evidence. Also along the NE side of the Dead Sea and SE of it in Wadi el-Hesa (River Zered) basalt appears. Jebel Shihan (3,470 feet), S of the Arnon, is regarded as an extinct volcano. An extinct volcano is found also in Nebi Dhahi. The hot springs at Tiberias, Tell el-Hammeh, Callirrhoe, and other places in the Rift Valley are further, still visible evidence.

The long and complex geological history of the Near East created four chief geographic divisions within the little country of Palestine, four narrow strips running N and S. A series of cross and hinge faults divided these four again into E-W segments with minor subdivisions. The N sections on both sides of the Jordan Valley are put by Denis Baly into a "zone of greater complexity."

E. *LAND FORMS: REGIONAL STUDIES.* 1. The coastal regions. The area from Ras en-Naqura to the River of Egypt and running back to the foothills of the central mountain range presents no stern and rock-bound coast. The only major break is at the Bay of Acre (Acco), where Mount Carmel juts out to within a short distance of the water. From Beirut S, there was no good harbor according to modern standards, but Acco on its projecting point and Joppa, with its reefs at a distance from the shore, could shelter ancient ships. Reefs projecting from the shore at water level served at some points. Thus Dor, or Dora, near modern Tanturah, was a "port of call." Caesarea Stratonis was made a passable harbor by Herod the Great.* Other cities such as Ashdod, Ashkelon, and Gaza had beaches that could serve in good weather. The mouths of the little rivers that ran into the sea could serve also, but they developed sandbanks from the silt-laden Nile waters. The shore of Palestine was not favorable to traffic by sea. Figs. CAE 1; PAL 3; PAL 4.

Courtesy of Chester C. McCown

3. Site of Caesarea Stratonis from the N. Reefs run out from the point made by the harbor. The city extended back a considerable distance from the harbor.

Courtesy of Chester C. McCown

4. Yellow daisies and red poppies on the edge of the maritime plain near Caesarea

Properly speaking, there are two divisions to the Coastal Plain, one N of Mount Carmel, the other S of it. The former, which never received a name, is narrow. Starting S of Ras en-Naqura, it widens irregularly until, back of the Bay of Acco, it runs behind a spur of the Galilean hills into the Plain of Esdraelon. The bay shore is lined with sand dunes, back of which is marsh. S of the Carmel headland, although the ridge runs SSE, the mountain presents its W face as a low precipice running southward. With the sea it forms a narrow corridor, the Plain

Courtesy of Chester C. McCown

5. Dura harvest in August on the edge of the Philistine plain near Beth-shemesh

of 'Athlit, or Dor, two to four miles wide and twenty-four miles long, before it widens out into the Plain of Sharon and then Philistia. Fig. PAL 5.

Here is a real maritime plain, chiefly alluvium and capable of intense cultivation. The N section, the Plain of Sharon, was marshy, for it was poorly drained by its small, sluggish rivers and was more famous for flowers than for crops. The S portion, the real Philistia, the most extensive level area in all Palestine, was by far the best for agriculture; but the rainfall decreases toward the S, and there are no copious springs or rivers for irrigation. Between Beer-sheba and Gaza real aridity appears.

2. The central mountain range. Actually a continuation of the Amanus-Lebanon range that begins at the NE corner of the Mediterranean Sea in what is now Turkish territory, it ends in the Sinaitic Peninsula. It is a relatively low, but rugged, range. The higher portions throughout are Cenomanian limestone, from the Litani to near Nazareth, from a little S of Beth-shan almost to Beer-sheba, and again in the S steppe. It is bordered by Senonian and Eocene limestone.

a. Galilee. Somewhere in the mountains between the Litani and Ras en-Naqura, Galilee begins. It belongs to Baly's "zone of greater complexity"—i.e., to regions so tortured by faults and flexures that they present a highly complicated geological picture and a most diversified terrain. As Josephus noted, the area is divided transversely into an Upper and a Lower Galilee. Unfortunately neither the statements of Josephus (War III.xxxv-xl[III.i]), nor those of the OT (Josh. 19:27-28), nor again geography and geology, give a clear idea of the N border. As to the W border, since the Israelites were men of the hills, it can be assumed that they lived in the mountains and left the lowlands to the Phoenicians here as Judah did to the Canaanites and the Philistines. Upper Galilee would probably have included most of the cities assigned to Asher and Naphtali (Josh. 19:24-39), except those on the coast, from a line S of the Litani River to Wadi esh-Shaghur. It marks a major fault, a sharp drop and visible scarp, which the road from Acco to Safed follows. It marks a geological border between Upper and Lower Galilee, with which Josephus' border agrees remarkably (Life 187-88[37]; War II.573-74[xix.6]; III.35-40[xii.1]).

Upper Galilee is a deeply fissured and roughly eroded tableland, with high peaks and many wadis. It has its bleak landscapes, but also its fruitful orchards and its pleasant prospects. A relatively heavy rainfall makes it a prosperous land, as mountain regions go. Possibly in the beginning Upper Galilee was heavily covered with real and scrub forest and therefore was slowly settled by the Hebrews. No important cities, either Canaanite or Hebrew, are reported except on its perimeter. This may explain its small role in recorded history.

Lower Galilee stretches from Wadi esh-Shaghur to the S foot of the Nazareth hills and of Mount Tabor and from the Acco Plain to the Jordan River, making it *ca.* sixteen miles N and S and *ca.* twenty miles E and W, *ca.* three hundred square miles in all. It is one of the most attractive and fertile parts of Palestine. With the gentle slopes of its hills covered with olive and fig trees, its open prospects, and the distant views from its rounded mountaintops, it can be rivaled—but not surpassed—only by Samaria. Fig. PAL 6.

Courtesy of Herbert G. May

6. Looking across the N bay of the Gulf of Aqabah toward the modern Israeli city of Eilat

Lower Galilee's historical associations with the life of Jesus, the Jewish-Roman War, and Talmudic Judaism are almost as numerous and are as varied and dramatic as those of Judea. It benefited historically and commercially by abutting on Esdraelon, one of the most important plains in all Palestine. Though it is not a part of the central mountain range, the plain can best be discussed here, since it is central to the whole country both economically and historically.

b. The Great Plain. One of the conspicuous geological and geographical land forms of Palestine is the break-through from the Mediterranean to the Jordan between Galilee and Samaria. A series of oblique (NW-SE) fractures and folds, crossed by minor NE-SW disturbances, created the fault basin and rift valley that are given the conventional names respectively of Esdraelon and Jezreel (*see* JEZREEL 2).* Esdraelon opened out on the NW to the narrow coastal plains running N. Through the low E saddle of Mount Carmel it received the caravans from the S. Through the Jezreel rift valley, it opened the door to the Jordan Valley and the great plains and the Arabian steppe itself on the E. In the Oligocene Period an arm of the sea, which still covered the maritime plains, reached through this gap to form the inland lake that played a major role in the formation of interior Palestine. The fertile valley thus played a most important role in historical times, for it opened the way to invaders and to commerce, and

Courtesy of Chester C. McCown

7. The Valley of Jezreel (Esdraelon), looking NE from the point of Gilboa

it hopelessly divided the richest areas of Israel, Lower Galilee and Samaria. Fig. PAL 7.

c. Samaria. The Mountains of Samaria (*see* SAMARIA 2)* constitute one of the most significant areas in Hebrew history, for here the bulk of the Israelites lived, to form the strong nucleus of Israel's most promising kingdom. Samaria is a land of mountains, but it is distinguished by wide, fertile valleys. Numerous faults and flexures render the geological and geographical pattern most complex. A series of disturbances running obliquely ENE-WSW roughly divide the N and NW section (Manasseh) from the S and SE (Ephraim). The former is quite similar to Lower Galilee, the SE section somewhat like Upper Galilee; but, as a whole, Samaria is much superior in agricultural availability to any other part of Palestine. From the Plain of Sharon and Mount Carmel to the Jordan Valley, it had a most unusual diversity of terrain and climate. Figs. GER 24; EBA 2.

Its borders are impossible to determine precisely. On the N it varied by the width of the "Great Valley," on the S between Mizpah (Tell en-Nasbeh) and Bethel (Beitin). At the largest it would have measured some forty miles E and W, fifty miles N and S, making an area of two thousand square miles or more. The possession of the Great Valley added a very considerable area of high fertility. But it was a nation without defensible borders, even if Galilee be forgotten.

When Omri moved the capital from Tirzah to Samaria's beautiful hill, he kept his capital within Manasseh, but definitely committed his kingdom to a policy, not of isolation, but of communication and commerce with the outside world, for it was surrounded and crossed by easy caravan routes. He played for trade and luxury. But he laid Samaria open to attack and plunder, as the nation learned to its peril.

d. Judea. On the contrary, the "zone of relative simplicity," in which JUDEA lay, was far more prone to isolation and far less attractive economically. There is no geologically marked border between Samaria and Judea, but a gradual increase of barrenness and rocky terrain indicates the change. The much-used route beginning in the Valley of Aijalon and running up past the Beth-horons and Beeroth (el-Bireh) to Bethel and down to Jericho (a bone of contention between the two kingdoms) may serve to mark the approximate border. Geologically regarded, Judea came to an end at the S where a fault seems to run out from the S end of the Dead Sea and down Wadi Ghazzeh to the coast. The central block ended on the E at the W fault of the Jordan Valley, but politically it usually included the valley floor as far as the Jordan River and the Dead Sea. On the W it ended at the shallow valley that divided it from the so-called Shephelah. Only rarely did strong Judean monarchs extend their authority to the coast.

For gracious living, Judea has the least to offer of all the central mountain regions. The distance from Bethel to Beer-sheba is *ca.* fifty miles, the average width not twenty miles, making *ca.* one thousand square miles. The best part for farming is in the S, where the rains dwindle to twelve inches in a year. The predominating Cenomanian limestone makes rich red soil, but erosion has removed much of it from the tortured landscape. Down-faulted basins and valleys are rare. Judea was not an ideal agricultural land. Fig. PAL 8.

Courtesy of Chester C. McCown

8. Qattara, or "Bad Lands," in the lower Jordan Valley

Courtesy of Chester C. McCown

9. The stony mountains of Judea, with Bethlehem lying in the background

Of the main areas of W Palestine, Judea was the most isolated, the least desirable, and the easiest to defend. The Jordan Valley and the "wilderness" on the E, the Negeb on the S, the mountains on the N, and, above all, on the W mountain front a succession of narrow, stony gorges, made it almost inaccessible to any but the most determined attack. The same features sent commerce around it, not through it. Jerusalem was not well placed to become an emporium. Fig. PAL 9.

e. The Shephelah, or "Lowland." The SHEPHELAH, as George Adam Smith long ago pointed out, was not the coastal plain, but the valley and the low range of the hills that run parallel to the fault marking off the mountains of Judah from the plain. It is a band of hard Eocene limestone that begins at the Beth-horon pass and runs southward, with occasional depressions, almost to Beer-sheba. The shallow "moat" between the Shephelah hills and the Cenomanian limestone consists of Senonian chalk, which breaks down into a poor grayish soil, while the hard

Eocene limestone and the equally hard Cenomanian of the mountains weather into a rich red soil that produces excellent cereal grains (*see* PALESTINE, GEOLOGY OF). The Shephelah was a valuable asset both economically and strategically, and the rival powers of the mountains and the plain both coveted it.

f. The wilderness **(מדבר, *midhbār*).** Judea had a unique defense on the E side: its historically noteworthy and very characteristic wilderness (*see* DESERT). It begins within a short distance E of the Mount of Olives and, at this widest point, reaches eighteen miles to the Jordan River. Its W border runs shortly E of the watershed, along the E edge of the Cenomanian limestone that makes Judea. On the N it appears E of Bethel and continues, with many irregularities, to the greater steppe-desert area of the Negeb. Geologically considered, its E border is at the precipitous cliffs formed by the W faults of the Jordan–Dead Sea Valley. Its width runs between ten and fifteen miles; its length is fifty or sixty miles. Figs. PAL 10-11; JUD 32.

The peculiar character of the wilderness is due to three facts: (*a*) it consists of easily eroded Senonian chalk; (*b*) it lies beyond the watershed and receives only the heaviest rains that rush down through its gullies and gorges to scour the soft limestone; and

Courtesy of Chester C. McCown

10. Deir Diwan toward the wilderness

Courtesy of Chester C. McCown

11. Beginnings of Wadi Qelt and the wilderness NE of Jerusalem

(*c*) the extreme folding and breaking of the limestone strata near the great fault promoted excessive erosion, while the rains easily percolated through the chalky limestone to carve it into fantastic caverns. Nowhere does "the grass wither and the flower fade" more rapidly than in such a landscape.

Biblical usage varies with the authors of the books and documents. Names are taken from the nearest tribe, town, or village: e.g., "wilderness of Judah" (Judg. 1:16: "in the Negeb near Arad"; Ps. 63, title); of Engedi (I Sam. 24:1); of Tekoa (II Chr. 20:20); of Maon (I Sam. 23:24-25); of Ziph (I Sam. 23:14-

Courtesy of Chester C. McCown

12. Near 'Ain el-Qudeirat (Hazar-addar) at the S border of Judea

15; 26:2). There are some seventeen different designations. The portion lying SE of Hebron and Ziph and N of Maon is called the *Yeshîmôn* (*see* JESHIMON 1), the "Desolation" (I Sam. 23:24). The descriptive term is applied especially to the SE corner of the area and to the *'Arebhôth Mô'ābh* (Num. 21:20; 23: 28), the desolate area at the head of the Dead Sea (*see* § E3ci *below*). Fig. PAL 12.

Midhbār is not DESERT, but uncultivated "pasture land, steppe," where low, sparse grass grows in spring and where there are occasional springs, wells, and cisterns, with wadis and small, level fields on which in good years wheat or barley may be successfully grown. The Beni-Ta'amirah, many of whom are now "rich" from finding MSS in their caves, have lived there precariously for generations. The area includes land that is totally uncultivable, whether from unevenness, rocks, poor soil, lack of soil, or lack of water.

g. The Negeb **(נגב, *neghebh*).** This is also "wilderness" and so has been partially described. The word, meaning "south country," was given to the land about and S of Beer-sheba. As in the Judean wilderness, there are occasional springs, wells, and pools in the N portions, which had prehistoric settlements and considerable towns in Byzantine times. It cannot be taken as demonstrated that 'Ain Qedeis was the OT Kadesh-barnea; but, with the larger springs, 'Ain Qoseimeh, and 'Ain el-Qudeirat, which are all three within a few miles of one another, a small band of nomads could have maintained themselves. The springs, it will be remembered, are specifically included in the Promised Land (*see* § B2 *above*). S of them the terrain becomes more inhospitable.

The greater part of the Negeb is a plateau 1,500-2,000 feet above sea level with peaks running up to 3,500 feet. It belongs to the same geological block as the N sections but has been subjected to different pressures and climatic conditions. There are three areas—two small, one rather large—of sand dunes SW of Beer-sheba. There is more Eocene limestone and Senonian chalk, much less Cenomanian limestone, than farther N, and the Nubian sandstone has been thrown up into view in some heavily eroded sections. The SW winds that bring rain from the Mediterranean to lands farther N blow to the Negeb from the Sahara over Egypt. The N and S borders of the Negeb are meteorological. The Promised Land and the Negeb may be taken as ending with the three springs. The central mountain range comes to a climax in the wild mountains of the Sinaitic Peninsula, Jebel Musa, *ca.* 7,400 feet, and others up to 8,600 feet.

3. The central Rift Valley. ***a. The Upper Jordan.**** The unique and outstanding geographical feature of Palestine is the Rift Valley that splits it down the center (*see* § D *above*). The parallel faults that form the Rift Valley appear near where the most northerly point of the Promised Land lies and where the River Jordan rises. N, W, and S at the foot of Mount Hermon, springs form small streams that come together near Dan (Tell el-Qadi) and finally in the marsh called Lake Huleh, at 230 feet above sea level (not 7 feet, as some publications still report). In the next ten miles Lake Huleh drops, not 700 feet, as the old accounts reckoned it, but 925 feet, to reach

13. Lake Huleh (known as Lake Semechonitis in NT period), with Mount Hermon in the background

the Sea of Galilee at 695 feet below sea level. The river flows in part through a narrow canyon. In this area the Rift Valley itself varies from some four to eight miles in width. Figs. JOR 26; PAL 13.

b. The Sea of Galilee. This sea is formed by a widening of the Rift Valley connected with cross faults that run into the hills. An overflow of lava from the volcanic area in S Syria gave the lake a hard basalt threshold and, therefore, a practically unvarying level and size (*ca.* seven by thirteen miles). While there is sufficient shore for driving around the lake except at a couple of spots, there is very little arable land. At the left of the mouth of the Jordan is a small marshy plain (el-Bateiha, site of Beth-saida). On the SE shore an attractive little plain spreads out southward. On the W side, the Plain of Gennesaret, an arc of a circle, less than four miles wide and a mile and a half deep, stirred Josephus into ecstasies over its luxuriant fertility (War III.506-21[X.8]). The hot springs just S of Tiberias, on the opposite side of the lake, and by the Yarmuk River a few miles to the E, recall the volcanic activity of the not-too-distant past. They represent a well-known health factor.

c. The Arabah. It has long been recognized that biblical writers called the main section of the Rift Valley, from the Sea of Galilee to the Dead Sea, "*the* Arabah." The term may also designate the extension of the depression S of the Dead Sea, as noted *below* (*see* § *d*).

i. Descriptive terms. The word *'ᵃrābhâh* (ערבה) connotes aridity, as do the words "Arab" and "Arabia." It may be doubted whether the word means "desert" in general, except in poetry, where it often stands (as in Isa. 40:3) in parallelism with *midhbār* ("pasture"). The word *midhbār* is, indeed, applied to the Arabah (II Sam. 15:28). It is to be noted, however, that "Arabah" does not in itself mean "plain." It apparently assumed this connotation only because it is so often applied to areas that are fairly level, just as the word "steppe" does. As a name it is untranslatable, but it suggests aridity and sterility. It is also called the *'ēmeq,* "depression" (Josh. 13:19, 27), and the *biq'â,* "cleft, fissure" (Deut. 34:3); both words are usually translated "valley."

The Arabic words applied to it aptly describe and analyze it. The Rift Valley is called the Ghor, or "depression"—i.e., "gorge." Within the Ghor is the Zor, to which the Hebrew word *gâôn* (גאון), "jungle," corresponds. The words "Zor" and "Gaon" describe the flood plain that the Jordan has created in its meanderings through the valley floor of the Ghor. The Meander in Asia Minor can hardly equal its convolutions. The wealth and luxuriance of the entangled semitropical trees and plants that grow in it probably suggested the Hebrew *gâôn,* which means "pride, excellence, swelling." "Jungle" is a better description (Jer. 12:5; 49:19; 50:4; Zech. 11:3). The Arabic *qattara* and *qattar* describe the clay flats, often carved into remarkable shapes, which are best described as "badlands," or "slime pits." It is a slippery, or dusty, marl impregnated with lime and cannot be cultivated. Anyone caught in it by a shower finds himself trapped, perhaps for days. It is most prominent at both ends of the Dead Sea. Fig. JOR 28.

ii. The original valley floor. This varies greatly in width. Near its center, above Wadi Kufrinjeh, it narrows to some two miles. Above this point it is at its widest where its walls are broken by the break-through of the Great Plain from the W and the Yarmuk River from the E. Here the Zor is negligible, and there is cultivable land on both sides. Below this constriction the Zor widens and deepens. Above, there are many fords, for the Jordan is hardly more than a brook. Below, there are few. Below, the rainfall is too little to be effective and the Jordan too low in its bed to be used. At Jericho the width of the Ghor is *ca.* twelve miles.

Two important rivers feed the Jordan on the E side, the Yarmuk (not named in the Bible) and the Jabbok (Nahr ez-Zerqa).* Indeed, the Jordan flows into the larger Yarmuk. On the W side, the River Jalud (also not named in the Bible) flows in from the rift valley of Jezreel, and the stream of Wadi Far'ah comes down from Samaria; these are both smaller streams. These streams and many a wadi have dug through the valley bed or spread their fans of detritus upon it, with the result that the valley floor offers a very small cultivable area in comparison with its size. To propose a Jordan River Authority in analogy with the Tennessee Valley Authority is to compare a fruit fly to a bumblebee. It

Courtesy of Chester C. McCown

14. The Jabbok (Nahr ez-Zerqa) S of Gerasa

suggests a totally incorrect conception of ancient Palestine and the Arabah. It is equally beside the point to call the Arabah or any part of it a "garden of the LORD" (Gen. 13:10). Fig. PAL 14.

iii. Special problems and usages. Certain special sections with their designations need mention because they have led to wrong interpretations.

The invading Israelites camped in the *'Arebhôth Mô'ābh* while waiting to cross the Jordan (Num. 22:1; 26:3, 63; twelve times in all; elsewhere with modifications). Joshua 13:32 locates them "beyond the Jordan east of Jericho" and puts the *'Arebhôth Yerîḥô* (4:13; 5:10) opposite them. The generally accepted translation, "Plains of Moab" and "Plains of Jericho," is misleading as well as incorrect, for Moab has its real plains on the plateau. Only a circumlocution such as "steppes of Moab in the Arabah" can correctly convey the idea.

Another designation is the "basin of the Jordan" (ככר הירדן, *kikkar hay-yardēn*). In Genesis there are seven occurrences of the word *kikkār,* all clearly referring to some portion of the Jordan Valley that apparently can be seen from a point near Bethel (13:10-12; 19:17, 25, 28-29). The LXX translation is always περίχωρος τοῦ Ἰορδάνου (περιοίκῳ in I Kings 7:33), except where it transliterates. It does not blunder into putting a "plain" around Jerusalem (Neh. 12:28 KJV). Since *kikkār,* like *'arābhâ* (Arabah), does not mean "plain," this term should be displaced by "basin" or "country around" (*see* § E3civ *below*). The term is extended in two passages to a little below the "narrows" in the center of the valley (II Sam. 18:23; I Kings 7:46).

iv. NT problems. Two historical problems of the NT may be briefly mentioned. One grows directly out of that of the *kikkār.* Both Luke (3:3) and Matthew (3:5) use the LXX phrase "all the region about the Jordan" in describing the ministry of John the Baptist. Luke has Jesus going "into all the Jordan basin"; Matthew has "all the Jordan basin" coming to John. Both writers apparently think the "basin" a populous area. Matthew understands the place where John baptized to belong to the wilderness of Judea. (That he preached in one place and baptized in another is absurd, particularly considering the character of the *midhbār* in E Judea.)

That John (and Jesus) may have visited the Qumran community is possible. But Luke's statement (1:80) that John was prepared for his ministry "in the wilderness areas" (ἐν ταῖς ἐρήμοις) does not prove it. The Qumran monastery was only 125 feet above the level of the Dead Sea, and the fords where John would have baptized (to escape the Zor and "badlands" [*see* § E3ci *above*]) are only eight or ten miles away; but this suggests only a possibility.

NT ἔρημος, "empty, uninhabited," which usually represents OT *midhbār,* is equally difficult to translate. In the account of John's ministry and Jesus' baptism it, of course, refers to the *'Arebhôth Mô'ābh.* In Galilee there are no such steppe areas. But there is—and must always have been—much uncultivated land, which served as pasture. When Jesus sought a quiet retreat, or room for the crowds that flocked to him, it was easily found within a short distance.

A careful study of the terrain suggests answers to problems of the journeys of Jesus. Jews in Galilee would naturally take one or another of the routes across the Plain of Esdraelon and through the mountains of Samaria, perhaps past Bethulia. From Capernaum, whence Jesus began his last journey to Jerusalem, the most natural route was down the Jordan Valley. He could easily visit Samaritan villages S of Beth-shan. At the mouth of Wadi Far'ah he would have come to the frontier of Judea. Crossing the Jordan at Adamah, he would have been in Perea, where there were villages at hand near the valley. Crossing the Jordan again, he would arrive at Jericho. That there were multitudes to crowd about Jesus in this brief Perean journey may be doubted (see Mark 10:1).

d. The Dead Sea and Wadi el-'Arabah. From the mouth of the Jordan to the Gulf of Aqabah, the Arabah played a relatively small part in Hebrew history, except that it separated Moab and Judah.* On the E side the cliffs descend almost perpendicularly to the water's edge, except where the Lisan, an irregular peninsula of marl, projects. On the W side in periods of low water, around the beginning of the twentieth century, it was possible to ride or walk all the way from the N to the S end, as it was possible to ford from the Lisan to the W side. S of the Lisan the water is very shallow. The water level seems to have risen a little even in recent years, and the length of the sea (forty-eight miles; width eight miles) has increased very slightly, at the expense of the Sebkha, but now has retreated again.* Practically no water from the W flowed into it. There was a small stream from Wadi Zerqa Ma'in. The River Arnon (Wadi Mojib) discharged much more through its narrow, high-walled gorge. Figs. PAL 15; DEA 6-7; ARN 60.

Courtesy of Chester C. McCown

15. Looking eastward from Beth-shan (Tell el-Hosn) along the River Jalud across the Jordan Valley

In the part of the Rift Valley S of the Dead Sea the ancient Hebrew name for the valley is still preserved as Wadi el-'Arabah. Forbidding as it is, it has not served to divide E and W as the Jordan did. The Edomites, and after them the Nabateans, crossed it regularly with their caravan traffic. They, along with both Judeans and Israelites, exploited the copper and iron ores that were found there. Forests in the mountains on both sides provided charcoal for the fires of the smelters that were located in the valley, where the winds that blow down from the cold of Hermon to the heat of the Red Sea provided the blast furnaces. The potential supplies of ore now apparent are not sufficient for modern industry, but could doubtless give a decided advantage to the ancient kingdom that had possession of the area. Its total length is a little over one hundred miles. The wadi floor rises gradually to reach its highest point over 650 feet above sea level near Jebel er-Rishe, some 40 miles from the Gulf of Aqabah. The total length of the Rift Valley from Mount Hermon to Elath is *ca.* 260 miles.

4. Transjordan. ***a. Its general character.*** While the Transjordan tableland plays a relatively small part in biblical history, it is far from unimportant, and its physical geography is far from uninteresting. It begins on the N with Mount Hermon at 9,230 feet. The land southward lies below 4,500 feet and mainly below 2,500 feet. However, it is a high plateau, rarely falling below 1,500 feet, and that only in the Jordan rift and in a few deep canyons, such as those of the Yarmuk, Jabbok, and Arnon. After the Hauran break-through, the mountains rise again to reach over 5,000 feet in Edom.

The geology of the total area must be briefly summarized before turning to details. From Mount Hermon southward to the Gulf of Aqabah, the basic components of the land are the same as W of the Jordan rift, but erosion has uncovered different strata. There is practically no sand, but lava has covered the territory S to the Yarmuk River and S of the Jebel Druz has gone much farther.

As a result of the downward slope of the strata eastward from their high point by the Rift Valley, erosion has exposed the Nubian red sandstone in great patches from the Arnon River down to the Gulf and has even reached the underlying granite. A large core of Cenomanian limestone forms the mountains of Gilead. But farther S, below 'Amman, it becomes a narrow strip between the sandstone and an even narrower strip of Cenomanian chalk. Beyond that the steppe to the E is Senonian chert that produces an ugly desert landscape, a surface covered with thin, shiny black pebbles. The rich soil produced by Eocene limestone appears only in Edomite territory E of Maan. The most impressive mountain scenery is in the tremendous mass of peaks and gorges of variegated Nubian sandstone on both sides of the Wadi el-'Arabah from Petra to the Gulf.

b. Its main regions. The E section may be divided into seven main regions, which are marked off by physical features: (*a*) The Damascus area and the Bashan Plateau S of it, (*b*) the Hauran area opposite the Accho–Beth-shan break through the W range, (*c*) Gilead, (*d*) Ammon, (*e*) Moab, (*f*) Edom or Seir, and (*g*) "Midian."

Aram, the area about Damascus, is distinguished for its rivers and the brief richness of its green oasis and then by the forbidding blackness of the basalt that spreads from the volcanoes of el-Leja and the Druz Mountains to E Galilee.

Bashan and the Hauran, enriched by the basalt in their soil and watered by the rain clouds that blow through the gap over Esdraelon and N Samaria, could help feed the Roman Empire when peace made commerce possible. The Yarmuk River marks roughly the S border of Bashan and the Hauran and also of the spreading lava.

Gilead, like all the E regions, is difficult to define exactly, on both N and S. In OT times the territory from the Yarmuk to Wadi Hesban was from time to time included in Gilead. National and tribal boundaries were uncertain and fluctuating. But there are physical differences that define certain areas. Eighteen to twenty miles S of the Yarmuk by way of Irbid, the mountains of Gilead appear at three thousand feet above sea level. 'Ajlun is over four thousand feet, Jerash *ca.* two thousand. Between the two elevations, most of the area of Gilead N of the Wadi ez-Zerqa is to be found. Faults bordering an upthrust running NE-SW across the Rift Valley relate it geologically to Judea. It is one of the most delightful regions in all Palestine. Other cities did not have such springs as Jerash, but the hills are, in the main, rounded and tree-covered. There are small valleys with gentle contours, covered with olive trees and grapes. Transjordan grapes are famous as the best in all Palestine. Its rains average about the same as at Jerusalem, *ca.* twenty-four and even twenty-eight inches. The vast Arabian steppes begin some twenty-five to thirty miles E of the Jordan. Fig. PAL 16.

Courtesy of Chester C. McCown

16. A spreading oak and flowering fields in N Gilead

Ammon, from its base at Rabbath-Ammon on the upper Jabbok, attempted to establish itself between Gilead and Moab. It never succeeded until the Exile, when its renegade Jewish commander, Tobiah, established a dynasty at 'Araq el-Emir. The character of the territory from the Jabbok to the Arnon changes gradually, below es-Salt and the Buqei'a more sharply, toward greater aridity and ruggedness, especially on the W side. Trees almost disappear, although small forest areas appear. All down the E side of the rift, rainfall varies with the height of the mountains, but the erosion of the wadis at the NE shoulder of the Dead Sea, of the larger Zerqa Ma'in, Hesban, and the Kerak, not to mention many that are smaller, drove agriculture farther eastward toward the steppe.

Moab, originally between the River Arnon (Wadi Mojib) and the Brook Zered (Wadi Hesa), succeeded in passing northward, not only past the Arnon but past Wadi Hesban, and fixing its name on the Moabite steppes by the Jordan. It had an area where wheat and barley grew well, and there was ample range for sheep, goats, and camels.

Edom occupied Seir, when the Israelites entered Palestine. The area from Wadi Hesa to the Gulf is aridly picturesque beyond description. The original Edomite territory probably ran S for some sixty to seventy-five miles to the Negeb. Near Wadi el-'Arabah the Nubian sandstone, which predominates, was fantastically eroded. Petra is the most famous of its spectacles. Beyond the area the relatively level steppe stretches out endlessly, and the Edomites, as well as the Nabateans who eventually drove them across the Wadi el-'Arabah into the Negeb and S Judea, found it possible to conserve water and cultivate rather extensively. However, the wealth of both peoples came from commerce. The Edomites are of interest to the OT student because of their possible contributions to OT literature (Job; parts of Proverbs?) and to Israel's troubles.

Edom may be said to end at the Negeb, a sharp fault and scarp. Below it lies the Hasma, a wild, barren, but picturesque area of Nubian sandstone mountains lying on and often revealing the basic granite that runs to the Gulf. Here, as well as in S Edom, wild tribes such as the Midianites roamed.

F. *GEOGRAPHY AND CULTURE.* 1. Physical factors in historical problems. *a. Critical methods.* Such was and is Palestine. Any attempt to discover what use the Hebrews made of the Promised Land and the consequent character of their culture must take account of the lapse of time and the accompanying changes within the period of ancient Hebrew history and between that time and ours. Our understanding of their world and their world view is based upon their land as it now is, on what the archaeologist discovers there, and on what the historian finds in all the pertinent ancient documents, including especially the Bible. One must reckon with all the physical and cultural changes that took place in over a thousand years of biblical history and two thousand subsequent years, and with the differences between the ancient and the modern, as well as between the Orient and the Occident. How the ancients lived and what they wrote must be interpreted in the light of their perspectives. The modern traditional perspectives—e.g., medieval and modern art, religious sentiment, and, above all, the modern glamorous, spectacular cinema—must be rejected as totally falsifying the picture.

b. Physical changes and differences. Biblical geography must take account of the physical deterioration due to deforestation and defective agricultural methods, with consequent erosion, impoverishment of the soil, and loss of useful rainfall. The Hebrews from the beginning furthered the process of deforestation (Josh. 17:15-18). The increasing use of stone pillars in the Middle Iron Age indicates its progress. However, mud roofs laid on a base of reeds, bushes, and branches over wooden rafters were still in use in the first century A.D. (Mark 2:4: "They dug up the roof"; Luke 5:19: "through the tiles," introduces Hellenistic custom.)

c. Intercultural effects. As an illustration of the effects of one factor upon another, it is to be noted that deforestation not only promoted erosion of the soil but also gradually deprived the land of fuel. One useful substitute was a little thorn bush that burns fiercely but briefly. Another was the use of cow dung for fuel, which lessened the very meager store of fertilizing material for the fields. This reacted unfavorably in the total economy. Similar interactions will appear *below*.

***d. Climate.* i. Regional differences.** Palestine's climate was, and is, far from unhealthful, partly because it was far from uniform. Following the geographical regions, the land may be roughly divided into six climatic zones: (*a*) the coastal plain and the Plain of Esdraelon; (*b*) the Central Mountain Range and Mount Carmel; (*c*) the Rift Valley and the Valley of Jezreel; (*d*) Transjordan as far as the Hejaz Railway; (*e*) the steppe; (*f*) the desert. The last two are not localized but appear in Transjordan, the Judean wilderness, the Negeb, and Wadi el-'Arabah.

ii. Temperature and health. In the summer the S coast might be unpleasant and the Rift Valley almost unbearable, but the mountains enjoy a strong breeze from the Mediterranean from morning till sundown. In winter snow might fall as far S as Jerusalem, but there is never extreme cold. Within a few hours' walk there is the warmth of the Arabah in winter, the coolness of the mountains in summer.

The variations in climate between valley and mountain, summer and winter, day and night, may not be sufficient to provide the maximum stimulation required by modern industry, but they were eminently suited to an economy where the population could spend most of the year without discomfort out of doors instead of within windowless and unheated stone hovels. It was both a health and an economic factor. Palestine had its diseases (*see* DISEASE), but it was a healthful land. It has always produced a vigorous, enterprising population too large for it to feed.

Within a distance of a hundred miles (Jericho to Mount Hermon) all varieties of climate from subtropical to subarctic, including a large diversity of plants, could be found, and a remarkable variety of standard adaptations to living conditions could be experienced. One reason the Bible is intelligible in nearly all parts of the earth is that it so nearly runs the gamut of the world's climates, land forms, and living conditions.

iii. Indispensable agricultural factors. Temperature is a factor of general importance to human life and health. But for agriculture in a land and culture like that of ancient Palestine, temperature, rainfall, soil, and terrain are all of fundamental importance, and no one of them can be discussed without including the others. Temperature—i.e., insolation, or sunlight—determines evaporation and thus the amount of moisture from rain or irrigation that becomes actually available for plant growth.

Soil, its consistency and chemical composition, determines what will grow and the quantity of water absorbed, as well as the amount that percolates through to subterranean pools and underground channels. Thus soil, with its underlying subsoil and rock, determines the number and value of springs and the height of water tables. Terrain, whether level, sloping, or precipitous, determines runoff and erosion, and creates marsh or well-drained land. And, of course, the composition of the rocks, with other factors, determines the availability and composition of the soil. The nature of the storms that bring rain is an important factor. Unfortunately an arid, border climate has a preponderance of tempestuous downpours that run off rapidly and carry away soil without penetrating it.

e. Cultural resources. In § E *above* an attempt has been made to describe the different regions and their general character as a basis for the development of Hebrew culture. It remains to summarize here the successes and failures of the Hebrews in their use of the Promised Land.

i. Agriculture. The basis of their economy was AGRICULTURE. As already indicated, the choice of Palestine condemned them to hard work and poverty. They had the last area on the narrow point of the Fertile Crescent in which a settled agricultural economy was possible. The geological and geographical reasons for the poverty of Palestine are evident. Low rainfall and aridity (evaporation) due to the sun's heat are combined with lack of level arable land. Of necessity fields were commonly small, and they were covered with lumps of limestone. The stones could be used as walls. But large, half-protruding slabs of underlying limestone strata, the "rocky ground, where it had not much soil" (Mark 4:5), ruin many an acre. Sloping wadis and hillsides had to be terraced with infinite and constantly repeated labor.

Their agricultural methods were of the crudest kind. The little plow drawn by diminutive oxen—both plow and oxen were suited in size to the fields—barely scratched the ground, and common custom probably was to sow the seed broadcast on fallowed ground and then plow it under. The results equaled the labor. After the First World War the average yield of wheat was nine bushels per acre, when, as experiment discovered, forty were possible with modern methods. The ancient Israelites knew nothing of selected seeds, careful fertilization, and deep plowing. Fortunately the limestone itself partially refertilized the fields, or the results would have been worse.

Grain, however, was exported from E Palestine and was also grown successfully, if not abundantly, on the W side. Vineyards and olives gave the most valuable crops. It is generally believed that the destruction of vineyards by alcohol-hating Muslims has contributed to the present low agricultural level of Muslim Palestine. But Palestine never could have become rich and prosperous on its agriculture. It is a miracle that its peasants, after paying taxes to palace and temple, were able to live.

ii. Pastoral. A large proportion of Palestine was condemned by nature to serve as range land for sheep, goats, cattle, and camels. The extent and value of the pastoral side of Hebrew land use is difficult to estimate. We learn of vast flocks and herds owned by Nabal, who was "very rich" (I Sam. 25:2). "Mesha king of Moab, [who] was a sheep breeder," had to pay an enormous annual tribute of lambs and wool to Ahab (II Kings 3:4). Solomon's tables devoured vast quantities of beef, mutton, and venison (I Kings 4:22-23). Every village had its oxen for plowing and its flocks and possibly herds of animals individually owned but shepherded in common by the boys. Feasts and sacrifices must have made great demands upon the nation's pastoral resources (I Kings 8:5, 62-64), but they at least satisfied the hunger of multitudes. Possibly the nomadic tribes in the steppe provided for such needs.

iii. Non-agricultural resources. It might be supposed that FISH from the Mediterranean, the Sea of Galilee, and the River Jordan would play a part in the economic life of the Hebrews. Quite the contrary is true. Their use was well known. But the Hebrews were men of the soil. Partly because they rarely occupied the coast and partly because transport was difficult, we hear little of fish as food. The Sea of Galilee was internationally famous for dried fish in Roman times, and the NT knows the fishermen there. Jerusalem had its "Fish Gate" in the postexilic period. This would intimate that the lack of allusions to commerce in fish and of their common use may have been the want of access to the sea. This was remedied under the Persians.

Along with its limited agricultural resources, Palestine's lack of mineral resources was almost fatal. The value that seems to have been laid and the labor expended on the meager amounts of copper and iron mines found in Wadi el-ʿArabah and N of the Wadi ez-Zerqa near ʿAjlun and Rajib emphasize the dire want of resources in the land. These mines may have assisted in producing the prosperous times of Solomon (I Kings 9:26; cf. 22:48) and of Amaziah and Jotham (II Kings 14:22), but their contributions were irregular.

The only mineral product of which Palestine had enough was limestone (not marble) of various qualities, much of it excellent for building. About the Sea of Galilee and N of the Yarmuk, basalt was widely used, sometimes patterned with limestone. It was widely used also for millstones and grinding bowls. Good clay for pottery was abundant.

iv. Industry. Craftsmen such as were necessary in an agricultural community and also for moderate luxuries are mentioned in the Bible. But for more than ordinary activities they were imported. The skilled hands of Hiram's masons are to be seen in Samaria's walls, as men of foreign training have left their mark on Herod's building. Luxury items, such as ivory carving, evidently came from Syria. Its lack of indigenous materials prevented Palestine from developing industry beyond its internal needs. Industry could not enrich Palestine unless commerce accompanied it.

v. Value of indigenous resources. The Deuteronomist (8:7-10; 11:8-12; 26:9) is often quoted as proving that Palestine was a real "Land of Promise" in biblical times. But his engaging rhetoric goes too far. Doubtless it was much more productive in the seventh century B.C. than in the twentieth century

A.D. But it has physical limitations that are inescapable. For many thousands of years there have been no major changes in climate, only those short and long cycles through which all lands pass. However, there has been one major change. The center of commerce and culture has moved from the E Mediterranean to the Atlantic—on the way to the Pacific perhaps. Eventually, the Jews, perforce, followed commerce and culture.

2. Population. ***a. Unsatisfactory data.*** In the light of the description of Palestine's physical features, what were its human resources? What was the human result of the Hebrews' use of their land? Unfortunately the data on which to base conclusions are extremely scanty. M. Rostovtzeff, who probably knew the Hellenistic world as well as anyone ever has, said that we have "not even an approximate idea of the density of its population." He refused to make a guess. All that is possible is to indicate limits beyond which guesses should not go. Ancient censuses and "vital statistics" in the Bible are incomplete and often implausible. Palestine was never occupied by Hebrews alone, but the proportions of other races to Hebrews, like the density of population itself, is impossible to ascertain.

b. Probable limits. Some helpful suggestions are to be found—e.g., in an estimate of the population of Galilee, made by E. W. G. Masterman in 1909, at 250,000 for 900 square miles, or 277 per square mile. But the survey of Conder and Kitchener in 1875-77, after very careful observation, estimated 312 Galilean villages in an area of 1,341 square miles at 103,000, or 77 per square mile. There could hardly have been such an increase in three decades. The disparity of the figures illustrates the difficulties in making an estimation of the density of population. Masterman's estimate was much too large.

The total population of mandated Palestine in 1919 was set at *ca.* 650,000; in 1939 the non-Jewish population had risen to 927,000 by normal processes, including some immigration. The total of 1,210,000 includes a Jewish increase of over 200,000, which was abnormal. Even earlier, various sections of the country, both Jewish and Arab, were listed as "overcrowded." Many abnormalities since then, perhaps even before, render comparisons of dubious value.

At a venture, all things considered, the minimum population of Palestine may have run between 500,000 and 600,000 during the first millennium B.C.; the maximum, in peaceful and prosperous times, may have been 1,000,000 or more. Late in the sixth century the population of Judea may have been 20,000; a century later, 50,000, according to Albright. In the first century in little Judea and scattered among the Gentiles elsewhere, could there have been as many as 500,000?

c. Settlements and housing. The walled city, the military fortress, the market town, and the agricultural village provided homes for the bulk of the population. There were no isolated farm houses. The nearest approach to such would have been the manorial house surrounded by a "village" of huts for slaves, hired laborers, and hangers-on. Now there are a few such, and then there may have been some. The detached villa appears in Roman-Byzantine times (*see* CITY; HOUSE; VILLAGE). In addition, there have always been Bedouin encampments, as there are now, some more or less permanent, or centered around caves used for storage and shelters from the cold and rains of winter. *See* NOMADISM.

The extent to which caves served as living quarters will always be an unsolved problem. The so-called HORITES were, no doubt, actually Hurrians. That the numerous caves, natural and artificial, in the limestone rock served as dwellings to a lesser or greater degree, depending on economic conditions, cannot be denied, the more so as it is still true. Cave dwellings probably point to poverty rather than overcrowding. In general the level of comfort was extremely low.

3. Geography and ideology. ***a. Cultural conflicts.*** The Hebrews' racial and national history and their total geographical situation imposed upon them a series of cultural and ideological conflicts. There were the conflicts between nomadism and a pastoral-agricultural ideal, between these ideals and commerce.

More than is the case with the great majority of peoples, the history of the Hebrews is the story of cultural conflicts. Their own traditions looked back upon a nomadic or seminomadic life of generations before their half-voluntary servitude to Egypt and its fleshpots. They had formerly enjoyed the freedom of the steppe for long periods; then an escape from the hardships of the steppe into a "land flowing with milk and honey." But the Promised Land proved to be no Garden of Eden. Settled agricultural life in rugged, arid Palestine had its hardships and its servitudes also. There was always the temptation to escape into the license of the steppe, far from royal commissioners and temple and palace taxes. David in his time and Jonathan the Maccabee in his were saved by the wilderness and enabled to fight another day.

Subscription to radical critical views, which see the Hebrews as basically Habiru, or "wandering Arameans"—roving, homeless adventurers of diverse origins, known for nearly two thirds of a millennium before the Conquest as outlaws living on the outskirts of civilization—does not fundamentally alter the historical situation. Their traditions, if not their genes, were impregnated with nostalgic sentimental admiration for the simple life of the steppe as Abraham and his offspring had enjoyed it. Settlement in Palestine involved conflicts, not merely between Yahweh and Baal, but between differing types of culture, between incompatible ideologies. Both mores and morals were involved in the very techniques of agriculture and the practices of the cult.

A self-sufficient agricultural economy was impossible in a land as barren of resources as Palestine. Situated as they were, competition with neighboring nations for resources was inevitable. Political alliances were demanded to preserve independence, and unfortunate consequences followed. In their situation commerce also was inescapable. These contacts with the great cultural area, with the Fertile Crescent and neighboring regions, introduced new ideas, new conceptions of the world, and new conflicts, both economic and ideological.

The conflicts between nomadism and agriculture, and between the Israelite pastoral-agricultural ideal and commerce, do not become explicit as such until the eighth century, when, in Hosea, they are still regarded as primarily a conflict between Baal and Yahweh. They appear as a moral and religious conflict again and again in the Pentateuch. Also as a cultural, religious, and economic conflict they appear in the eighth-century prophets. Amos, Hosea, Isaiah, and Micah make their plea for the poor against the rich, the nobility, and the royalty. Examples can be found scattered throughout Hebrew history: in Nathan's parable of the poor man's lamb, Naboth and his vineyard, the plea of the poor to Nehemiah (II Sam. 12:1-7; I Kings 21:1-19; Neh. 5:1-13). The new priestly "royalty" seem to be the chief offenders.

b. Ideological results. These cultural conflicts, with their moral and religious implications, grew into ideological conflicts of far-reaching significance and historical results, which continue "to this day." Commerce and foreign contacts were regarded as chief causes of city luxury and as also the guilty purveyors to its extravagances. The class conflict between rich and poor, city and country, city sophistication and rural simplicity, becomes also a conflict between assimilation and isolation. Racialism and nationalism are arrayed against universalism and internationalism.

Considering all this pyramid of woes erected on the basis of the abandonment of nomadism, the thoughtful and conscientious Israelite might well conclude that a return to the steppe was the only cure for Israel's woes. The Kenites from the first had refused to live in houses or drink wine, because these were not nomadic customs. Hosea was the first to put into writing this prescription for his people's salvation. (So, at least, Hos. 12:7-10—H 12:8-10 may be interpreted.) Israel had become rich by the trader's false balances and by oppression. Therefore Yahweh would coax her back into the wilderness, yet also give her vineyards (Hos. 2:14-15—H 2:16-17). The idea of a return to nomadism, or at least pastoralism, appears elsewhere (Isa. 7:21-25; Jer. 31:5, 12, 24). Zephaniah sees all Philistia become a pasture for Israel's flocks (2:5-7).

No religion could be more completely materialistic, hedonistic, and this-worldly than that of the Deuteronomist (ch. 38). There was, indeed, as yet no "other world." Obedience to God would bring health, wealth, and happiness. The problem of justice on earth was the prophetic problem, the most trying problem of the psalmists. The only explanation of Israel's failure to rule all nations was that she had sinned against God.

Bibliography. See the recent historical atlases of L. H. Grollenberg; E. G. Kraeling; and G. E. Wright and F. V. Filson; the maps of the Jordan and Israeli governments, which are excellent on topographical data. However, for original work only the *Historical Atlas* of G. A. Smith (rev. ed., 1936) is useful, since only it preserves the traditional names of mounds and ruins. His *Historical Geography of the Holy Land* is still the most interesting, but D. Baly, *Geography of the Bible* (1957), is far superior on climate, terrain, and purely geographical matters, especially in the relation of geology to the morphology of the land. See also N. Glueck, *Explorations in Eastern Palestine,* vols. I–IV (in 5 vols.; 1935-49); *AASOR,* vols. XIV, XV, XVIII–XIX, XXV–XXVIII.

C. C. McCown

PALESTINE, GEOLOGY OF.

A. General physiographic features, stratigraphy, and structure
  1. Physiographic features
  2. State of geologic mapping; quality of outcrops
  3. Stratigraphy
    a. Archaeicum (Archean, Early Pre-Cambrian)
    b. Algonkian (Late Pre-Cambrian or Proterozoic)
    c. Paleozoic
    d. Triassic
    e. Jurassic
    f. Lower Cretaceous
    g. Albian and Aptian (Lowest Upper Cretaceous)
    h. Cenomanian (Lower Upper Cretaceous)
    i. Turonian (Middle Upper Cretaceous)
    j. Senonian (Uppermost Cretaceous)
    k. Eocene (Lower Tertiary)
    l. Upper Tertiary
  4. Structure and tectonics
B. Surface geology: rock outcroppings
  1. The major rocks
  2. Regional survey
    a. The central region
    b. The N region
    c. The S region
Bibliography

A. ***GENERAL PHYSIOGRAPHIC FEATURES, STRATIGRAPHY, AND STRUCTURE*** (Figs. PAL 17-18). **1. Physiographic features.** Cisjordan (present-day Israel and W Jordan) can be conveniently divided into three mountainous regions separated by plains and valleys. The mountainous sections from N to S are: the mountains of Galilee, the mountain ridge of Carmel–Ephraim–Judah, and the mountain ridges of the Negeb. Bordering the mountainous area are the NNE-SSW-oriented plain of the Mediterranean coast in the W and the Jordan–Dead Sea–Arabah valley in the E, the central part of which lies *ca.* 1,300 feet below sea level. The two main separating features are: the WNW-ESE-oriented plain of Jezreel, separating the mountains of Galilee from the Carmel–Ephraim–Judah mountains, and the valley of Beer-sheba–Tell el-Milh (Wadi Bir es-Seba'–Wadi el-Milh), separating the Judean ridge from the mountains of the Negeb. This last dips strongly from E to W, from a level of 1,300 feet above sea level at Ras ez-Zuweira to the Mediterranean coast. The highest peaks in Cisjordan are Jebel Jermaq (3,973 feet) in Upper Galilee and the Ras Raman (3,389 feet) in the central Negeb.

Transjordan (present-day E Jordan) is a fairly homogeneous plateau, bordered on its W side by the steep cliff of the Jordan–Dead Sea–Arabah valley and dipping gently to the E. Its W rim is somewhat higher than the highest tops of Cisjordan.

This outline has left out of account the sharp dissections of the mountains: the highest anticlinal ridges in the central Negeb are eroded and hollowed out into steep-walled round caldrons or canoe-shaped valleys called *makhteshim;* synclines in the Negeb usually appear in topography as elongated depressions; and in the N part of the country, in

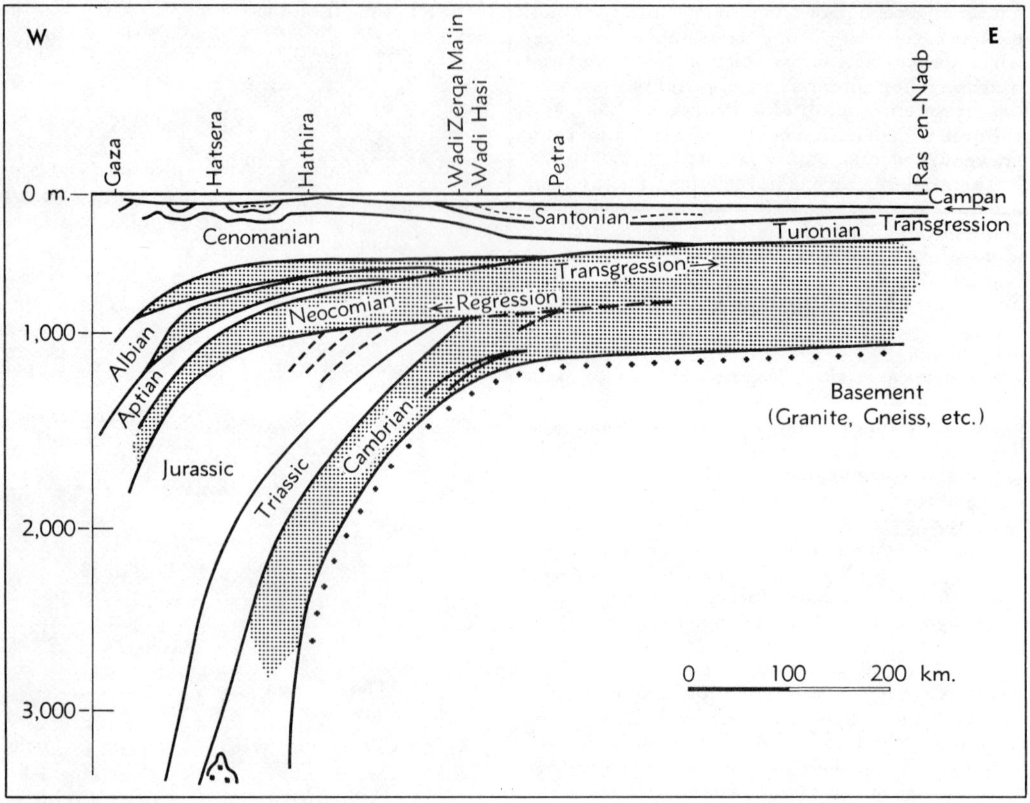

17. Schematic cross-section of geologic strata of Palestine

Galilee, the mountains are dissected by transverse valleys, mostly tectonic trenches such as the Valley Biq'at Beit Netufa.

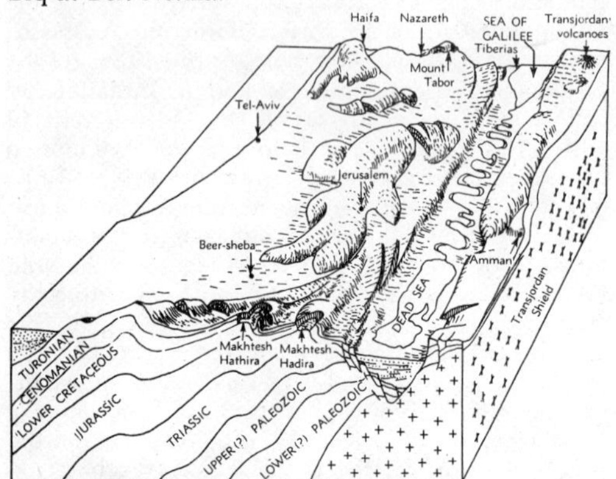

18. Structural block-diagram of Palestine

2. State of geologic mapping: quality of outcrops. The climate of the country ranges from warm Mediterranean to "Sudan-Deccanic" (i.e., comparable with the continental regions of African Sudan or of India), and consequently we may expect ideal outcrops in the dry S part of the country and good to fair outcrops in the N part. With the help of only a moderate amount of field work, we may indeed in the Negeb draw a nearly accurate geologic map from the air photographs. Scrub and agriculture limit the usefulness of air pictures in the N, but carrying out a geologic survey presents serious problems nowhere in the mountains and hills. Geophysical surveys, water holes, and some deep drilling for oil in the soil-covered plains give at least an idea what the alluvials may hide.

The geological maps of the N part of Cisjordan by G. S. Blake (1936) and of the Negeb by S. H. Shaw (1947), both on a 1:250.000 scale, are available. Of Transjordan only generalized maps on a 1:500.000 scale by Blake and one by Quennell are available.

3. Stratigraphy. ***a. Archaeicum*** **(*Archean, Early Pre-Cambrian*).** The outcrops of the oldest rocks are located W and NW of the Gulf of Eilat (Aqabah) in three separate massifs: the massif of Eilat, the massif of Bir Ora, and the massif of Timne. The oldest rocks are gray gneisses and mica schists, occurring some miles S of Eilat. The mica schists are rich in garnet and staurolite. They are intruded by younger gray and red granite and granite porphyry. The still younger dikes cutting through these rocks are so numerous that at some instances the original character of the country rock has been obliterated and changed into a "dike country," the elements of which range through the entire gamut of the alkali-calcium series (i.e., from diabase to quartz porphyry).

b. Algonkian **(*Late Pre-Cambrian or Proterozoic*).** Possibly of Algonkian age are volcanic masses of quartz porphyry and flows with green tuffs, and a series of coarse conglomerates, the matrix of which consists often of a kind of soaking by quartz porphyry.

These Algonkian rocks are cut by still younger Algonkian narrow dikes of quartz porphyry and diabase, which seem to be the last volcanic activity before the basalts and the more acid eruptions in Lower Cretaceous times: from these younger Algonkian rocks up to the base of the Cretaceous, only sedimentary rocks are known.

The Archean and Algonkian rocks are much more extensive in Transjordan than in Cisjordan; outcrops of granite and the like are visible along the E cliff of the Arabah from the S tip of the Dead Sea down to Aqabah. The rocks in general are similar to those of Cisjordan, but a detailed survey is not yet available.

c. Paleozoic. The Pre-Cambrian is covered by arkose sands and conglomerates of probably Lower Cambrian age. In Cisjordan these sands and conglomerates are laid down on a surface of small knolls (hummocks), but in Transjordan similar sediments of the same age were deposited on a flat Pre-Cambrian plain. The small hills of the hummocky topography of the Cisjordan area disappeared as the sediments filled the valleys in between the hills (onlaps).

The older Paleozoic rocks are interbedded shales and dolomites; some poorly preserved fossils are found in the dolomites.

d. Triassic. The Cambrian is covered with variegated and white sands, which in the S Negeb are devoid of any sign of a major transgression older than the Cenomanian: the Triassic transgression seems not to extend farther to the S than the line linking Areif en-Nahgha (N Sinai) with E Ramon. The facies (i.e., the mineral composition, type of bedding, fossils, etc., of a sedimentary formation) of the Triassic is neritic and thin; fossils are mainly Encrinus stems. Myophoria, Pseudoplacunopsis, Germanoautilus, and various Ceratites are embedded in a yellowish-to-gray limestone. The base of the Triassic is sandy and contains bones of Stegocephales. In the Makhtesh of Ramon this series is covered by more than 325 feet of gypsum beds, which seem to be absent farther to the S, but have been encountered in the deep drill holes farther N in the Makhtesh of Hathira and Har Boqer. Triassic is developed in a similar facies in Transjordan (outcrops of Wadi Zerqa Ma'in at the NE corner of the Dead Sea), but farther S, no marine Triassic seems to have been laid down, though A. M. Quennel believes that the purple-colored sandstones of a land and desert facies are of the same age (between Kerak and Aqabah).

e. Jurassic. In the Roman area the gypsum series of the Upper Triassic is slightly uncomformably overlaid by (?) Liassic (Lower Jurassic) limestone, starting with a residual fire clay. The Lower Dogger (Early Middle Jurassic) in this area is sandy, and the Higher Dogger contains a thin layer of red limestone with Trigonia, Rhychionella, etc. No Malm (Upper Jurassic) is known from here or farther to the S. Jurassic seems to be developed in a similar facies as in the Makhtesh of Ramon in the Makhtesh of Areif en-Nagha (N Sinai), but no fossils are known from this region yet. No Jurassic rocks exist in the section of Har Arif, where the Triassic limestones are unconformably overlaid by Neocomian (Lower Cretaceous) sands. Everywhere in the central Negeb and N Sinai the Dogger is cut off unconformably by a dark conglomerate of Lower Cretaceous age, but farther to the N, in the Makhtesh of Hathira, the outcrops at the bottom of the valley start, where the section of the Ramon Makhtesh stops—i.e., at base Malm. Kimmeridge and Portland (i.e., Uppermost Jurassic) are here developed as yellow marls, limestones, coral reefs with brachiopods, Nerinea, etc.

No Jurassic is exposed farther N or NW of Hathira, but Jurassic formations have been pierced by several drill holes carried out by various oil companies. Near Beeri (E of Gaza) and farther N in the Helets oil field the Jurassic is developed as a very thick geosynclinal series of dark shales and highly oölitic and pisolitic limestones. In the N the nearest outcrops of Jurassic age occur in the S Lebanon and Anti-Lebanon. In Mount Hermon this formation consists of a *ca.*-5,000-foot series of dolomites and limestones of Bajocian (Middle Jurassic) to Lower Callovian (Lower Upper Jurassic) age covered by limestone and marl of Upper Callovian to Oxford. The Kimmeridge (Uppermost Jurassic) is again a hard, reefy limestone, covered by the Lower Cretaceous sands.

This very thick section (of W Israel and the Lebanon) is in contrast with the much thinner Jurassic section of Transjordan, which shows a sequence of rocks of fairly the same habitus as at Wadi Ramon: at Wadi Zerqa the Jurassic rocks consist of some Bajocian. Jurassic is not represented in a marine facies. S of the River Zerqa, Jurassic is not recognizable, though some of the sandy land deposits may belong to this formation (according to Quennell).

f. Lower Cretaceous. The sandy, mainly continental, section of the Cambrian to Cenomanian ages in the S part of the Negeb and of Transjordan does not allow a clear stratigraphic separation in formations. The southernmost indisputable contact between Cretaceous on Triassic (or Cretaceous on Jurassic) is exposed in the above-mentioned Makhtesh of Areif en-Nahga, and is marked by the black conglomerate of quartzite pebbles, which are well rounded. The sands covering this conglomerate are of Neocomian age and contain two separate basalt layers, in the Ramon area interbedded by a freshwater chalk with fossil frog bones. The Neocomian is a real blanketing sand—i.e., of very general and fairly uniform distribution—in Israel and surrounding countries, though it thins out considerably to the W and NW: the Lower Cretaceous of the Helets oil wells shows a complete, marine, geosynclinal section with all the members Barremian, Hauterivian, and Valengian represented, in which the sands form only a thin interlayer.

Wherever exposed, the Neocomian sands are variegated, mostly terrestrial, and contain plant remains.

g. Albian and Aptian (Lowest Upper Cretaceous). Albian and Aptian are developed only as some poor marine interbeddings in the sandy land deposits of the Negeb, but the section becomes more complete to the N and NW. In Galilee, e.g., the section is very similar to the sequence in the Lebanon. The Albian is a fossiliferous marl overlaying an oölitic, greenish limestone, the *Zumoffenbank,* which covers the Aptian. The Aptian consists, just as in the Lebanon, of an Orbitolina-bearing marl, covering cliff-forming dense white limestone, resembling in its lithological features the Turonian (called *Mizzi Hilu*). This cliff, called "suicide cliff" by the Israelis, is known among geologists as *Fallaise de Blanche*. This bank rests directly on top of the variegated Neocomian sands below Kibuts Ramim (Manara) in Upper Galilee. Typical fossils of the Albian are, among others, Knemiceras and Heteraster.

h. Cenomanian (Lower Upper Cretaceous). The Cenomanian of central Israel and Galilee can be divided into three units: the lowest part is hard, forms generally steep walls, and consists of well-banked dolomite, as, e.g., exposed along the NW side of Mount Carmel or along the Tel-Aviv–Jerusalem railroad.

The middle section of the Cenomanian consists of much softer chalks, dolomitic chalks, and dolomites generally rich in flint nodules and quartz concretions called in Hebrew *Tappuche eliyahu* ("Elijah's Apples") and in the Lebanon *concrétions de choux fleurs* ("cauliflower concretions").

The upper series of the Cenomanian consists of hard, often reefy dolomite or, rarely, crystalline white limestone, called *Meleke* (such as on Mount Carmel). With the exception of Mount Carmel, the Cenomanian section is in the N rather poor in fossils. The main ammonite is Acanthoceras. In the S and in Transjordan the fauna is much richer: among the ammonites, Neolobites is the most abundant. The most common fossils are Exogyra (various species), Arca, Cardium, Trigonia, Plicatula. However, a lithologic compilation of the various members of the Cenomanian of the S part of the country and of Transjordan has still to be made.

Marked and exceptional features of Cenomanian and Turonian in Mount Carmel are thick interbeddings of soft volcanic tuffs and basalts; marine Cretaceous covers the flanks and tops of the relief of the submarine volcanoes.

In Transjordan, W Galilee, Mount Carmel, and most of the Negeb, the boundary between Cenomanian and Turonian is marked by a yellowish marl rich in ammonites such as Leoniceras, Thomasites, and Vascoceras. These beds alternate in the far S and in Transjordan with banks of gypsum.

i. Turonian (Middle Upper Cretaceous). The "classical" facies of the Turonian throughout the country is a dense, white, well-bedded limestone, called *Mizzi Hilu*. These beds are rich in Nerinea and Actaeonella. In E Galilee the Turonian is represented by bedded dolomite, hardly distinguishable from the underlying Cenomanian dolomites. In W Galilee the *Mizzi Hilu* is underlaid by *Meleke* beds—i.e., white crystalline limestone.

Lithologic compilations of most of the Turonian have still to be carried out.

j. Senonian (Uppermost Cretaceous). Though all the units of the Uppermost Cretaceous (Coniacian, Santonian, Campanian, Maestrichtian, Danian to Paleocene) are represented in Israel, many occasional stratigraphic gaps occur because of Pre-Eocene erosion or absence of sedimentation. As a rule, the section is completest in the present synclines and greatly reduced on top of the anticlines, where shallow marine to terrestrial conditions prevailed. The cause of this irregular condition is that the folding period started at least as early as Turonian.

Coniacian is best developed as an E-W-striking belt crossing the S half of the Negeb and part of Transjordan. It is a beige-to-red-brown marl with friable limestone, containing *Alectrionia dichotoma Barroisiceras* and many other macro-fossils. There are, however, indications that the silicified contact of the Senonian chalks with the Turonian in other parts of the country should also be attributed to the Coniacian. This series passes upward into a hard chalk with reddish bands and stripes, called *Kakule*, probably of Santonian age. Texanites is the most common fossil in these rocks, especially in the N.

The Upper Santonian to Lower Campanian is generally a white, soft chalk, often rich in large Gryphea. This is the lowest unit which shows clearly the above-mentioned facial differences—i.e., the section is most complete in the synclines and reduced on top of the anticlines.

The Campanian contains—especially in the S—many interbeddings of flint layers, alternating in the synclines with chalk beds. These chalk beds are, however, absent on top of the anticlines, and the Campanian may therefore be developed on the anticlines as a nearly pure section of flint beds. The Upper Campanian and Lower Maestrichtian contain in the synclinal facies of the central Negeb phosphatic chalks.

The Upper Maestrichtian consists both in Galilee and in the Negeb of a compact or stratified white chalk, rather poor in macro-fossils, which are mainly small Pectenides and Terebratulina.

The Danian to Paleocene rocks consist of a marl or clay with limonite, marcasite, and pyrite concretions. In the N it is nearly impossible to map this series as a separate unit, as it is mainly covered with the same weathering crust (*nari*) as the under- and overlaying chalks of Senonian and Lower Eocene age; in the dry S, however, the gray color of these marls stands out clearly.

k. Eocene (Lower Tertiary). Wherever developed, the Lower Eocene is a white chalk with some flint, covered with hard limestone beds with flint. It is this flint which forms—together with the waste of the Campanian flint—the gravel deserts or *Hamadas* of the high plateau of Transjordan, the Negeb, and E Sinai. Macro-fossils are rare.

The Middle Eocene lies generally unconformably on the older formations and W of Jerusalem and in W Galilee consists of a white, unstratified chalk. In the rest of the country the Middle Eocene consists of a hard, crystalline, marblelike limestone rich in nummulites.

The Upper Eocene is a white chalk or marl, but the precise distribution is as yet unknown.

l. Upper Tertiary. Sediments of the younger Tertiary covered probably only smaller parts of the country, as irregular uplifts reduced the zones of sedimentation to the coastal area and several more or less isolated basins. The basins were the Bay of Haifa, the Plain of Jezreel, the Tiberias-Beisan Basin, the basin of the S end of the Dead Sea. Marine sediments are mainly limited to the coastal plain. Undoubtable Oligocene to Pliocene beds occur only along this plain. Along its E border the rocks are of littoral facies, such as calcareous sandstones, marine conglomerates, and coral reefs; but boreholes farther to the W revealed more geosynclinal conditions—i.e., thicker sediments; the Mio-Pliocene formations are clay and marl, very thick, and in them gas accumulated on fissures and in sacks; they are called *Sakye* beds. These clays pass eastward into a thin calcareous sandstone (Astian facies) running deeply into the bays of Beer-sheba and Haifa. Still farther eastward the facies becomes still more epicontinental (i.e., a shallow marine sea on a continent), and E and S of Beer-sheba the Pliocene consists mostly of a reddish sand, the *Hosb* series covering inland basins along the Arabah and the W plains of the Negeb.

The cliff of rock salt of Mount Sodom (Jebel Usdum, at the S end of the Dead Sea) and the covering sands and shales are probably Oligocene. Drilling on Mount Sodom revealed an apparent thickness of several thousands of feet of salt; this thickness is only an apparent one, due to intense "salt tectonics" (i.e., complicated folding and flow of salt beds under tectonic forces).

Around Tiberias and Beisan the yellowish marls, covered by gypsum, are probably continental Miocene; the covering pseudo-oölithic limestone is probably Pliocene. In these N basins the formations are interbedded with extensive and thick sheets of basalt lavas, but no Upper Tertiary volcanics are known in the S basins. Upper Pliocene to Lower Pleistocene is probably the clay rich in Melanopsis and Unio S of the Sea of Galilee and the steeply inclined envelope of clays and marls around Mount Sodom. Both series are unconformably overlaid by the Pleistocene *Lisan* marl, a typical *playa* deposit consisting of varved chalks extending far S of the Dead Sea to the Sea of Galilee.

The orange-grove-covered red sands and the calcareous sandstone (*Kurkar*) of the coastal plain are of Pleistocene age.

4. Structure and tectonics. Only epeirogenic movements (i.e., wide uplifts without folding) prevailed from Cambrian to Upper Cretaceous. Indications of earlier folding movements are only slight (the first clear folding started—as has been pointed out—at the end of the Turonian). These epeirogenic movements are expressed as a deepening of the Jurassic sea W of the present Dead Sea, and as a deepening of the Lower Cretaceous sea W of the present mountain border.

The iso-facies lines and lines of general equal sediment thicknesses of the Jurassic and Cretaceous show on a general map a clear "S" shape—i.e., NE-SW in Galilee and Lebanon, N-S from Nablus to Beer-sheba, again NE-SW from Beer-sheba to the S. The deep-sea facies lies always W of the iso-facies and iso-pach lines, and the shallow-sea facies E of them.

It is remarkable that the post-Turonian fold lines curved and adapted themselves largely to this "S" curve: the Lebanon and Anti-Lebanon strike NE-SW, the Judean mountains N-S, the Negeb folds again NE-SW. It looks as if the "waves" of the folding, "rolling" forward from W to E, "broke" against the "shore" of the "S"-curved basement border. The following features make this dynamic interpretation still more appealing:

Most of the folds S of Beer-sheba and N of Damascus are asymmetrical to the E, whereas the N-S-trending middle section consists of more or less symmetrical anticlines.

A second remarkable feature fitting into this concept is the so-called virgation of the fold bundle N of Damascus and S of Beer-sheba, whereas the N-S-striking middle section is tight: between Nablus and Beer-sheba the pressure was most probably at right angles to the border of the basement, whereas in the Lebanon and Negeb the pressure was oblique to it.

A third feature fitting into the same pattern is the presence of a number of more or less E-W-striking strike-slip faults ("transcurrent" faults, or "wrench" faults) N of Haifa and S of Beer-sheba. The sense of movement is "right-hand"—i.e., the N blocks moved always eastward in relation to the blocks S of the fault.

It is conceivable that the *makhteshim* are a feature related to the same couple of forces which caused the just-mentioned faults: They are all located in the very knee or strongest bend of the fold direction—i.e., where an extra rotational folding movement was added to the "normal" folding of the anticlinal ridges. By these E-W-oriented forces, extra domes developed on top of the anticlines, and these domes were later eroded into the steep-walled erosion mortars of *makhteshim*. Some of these domes were split into two parts by movement along one of the E-W-striking strike-slip faults: the N part of the *makhtesh* shifted to the E in relation to the S part (such as in the case of the double Makhtesh of Har Arif).

The style of the folding reflects, not only the thickness of the Lower Mesozoic, but also its facies: The folds are of a wide amplitude where the Jurassic facies is reefy, but elegant and narrow where folds are peeled off (*Abscherung*) from the Jurassic along the plastic Albian clay beds (N of Damascus) and where the total sediment thickness is shallow (central Negeb).

Concurrently with the last folding phase, however, a strong warp has set in since the Mio-Pliocene, not only lifting the mountains upward, but also bending the coastal zone downward: thick marine Pliocene *Sakye* beds lie uncomformably on top of the Cenomanian on some of the buried coastal anticlines. This warp may be partially due to the sinking of the N-S-oriented deep tension-graben of the Jordan–Dead Sea–Arabah area, as it is a well-known fact that the sinking of a graben may result in the uplifting of the bordering blocks. A. J. Vroman

B. *SURFACE GEOLOGY: ROCK OUTCROPPINGS* (Fig. PAL 19). **1. The major rocks.** For an understanding of biblical history the most important Palestinian rocks are:

a) The hard, crystalline rocks of the Archean platform, exposed in the extreme S of Transjordan and W of Eilat.

b) The Nubian sandstone on the E edge of the Arabah, laid down, on and off, during the whole period from the Mid-Cambrian to the early Cretaceous, and justifying, by its copper deposits, the description of Palestine as a land "whose stones are iron, and out of whose hills you can dig copper" (Deut. 8:9).

c) The Cenomanian-Turonian limestones, the major rock of Cisjordan. They provide excellent building stone; Solomon's Quarries in Jerusalem, the reputed source of stone for the first temple, were in the Upper Cenomanian.

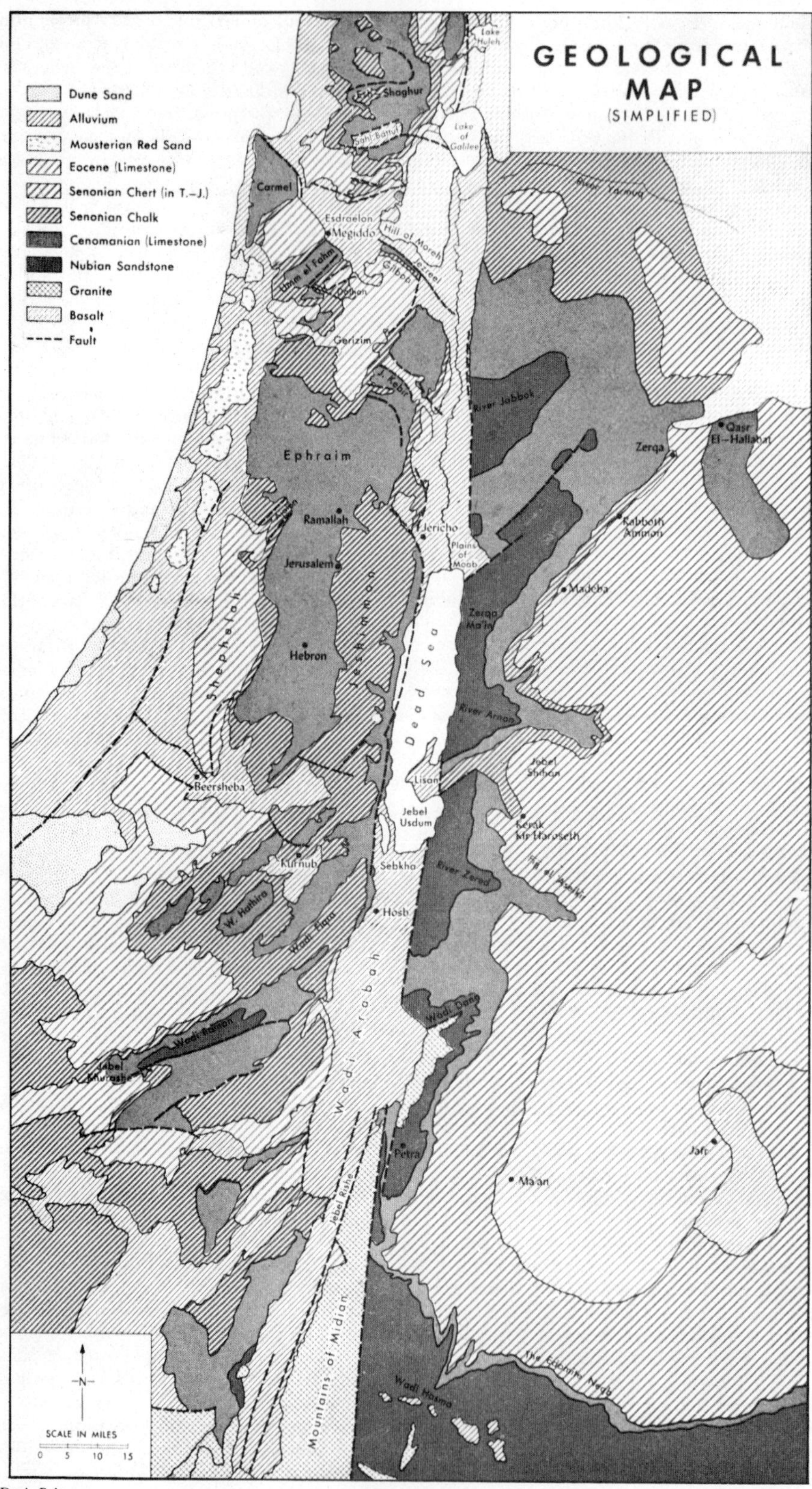

Courtesy of Denis Baly

19. Geological map of Palestine

d) The Senonian chalk, very infertile and useless for building purposes ("chalkstones crushed to pieces" [Isa. 27:9]), but important historically. It is so soft that it always forms a valley, and is easily worn down by the passage of men and animals to a hard surface, undisturbed by rocks. Thus, the Senonian valleys, especially in Cisjordan, formed many of the major roads—e.g., the Megiddo Pass across Carmel.

e) The hard Eocene limestone of the Shephelah, the lower central part of the Carmel spur, central Samaria, and parts of Lower Galilee. Much of E Transjordan is covered by Eocene deposits which, as a result of erosion, have formed the wide flint desert of Ardh es-Suwan W of the Sirhan depression.

f) Post-Eocene deposits. These include the low hills of Pleistocene limestone along the coast N of Jaffa. The merest thread, and no more than 150 feet high, they nevertheless contributed to the marshy conditions of the Sharon Plain by blocking the drainage to the sea, and they provided the strong defenses of Dor (possibly the "Naphoth-dor" of Josh. 11:2; ERV-ASV "heights of Dor"). Also must be included the recent alluvium of the coastal plain and intermontane basins, and the Lisan marls of the Jordan Valley and Dead Sea region, which form the badlands of the Qattara, enclosing the thick jungle of the Jordan.

g) The basalt of E Galilee and Transjordan. In Galilee the Hill of Moreh and the dam blocking the Jordan Valley S of the Huleh Basin are both basaltic. In Transjordan the high Jebel Druze, believed by some to be the "mountain of Bashan" (Ps. 68:15), and Trachonitis to the N of it, both of them regions of refuge, are also of basalt. Further S, in Moab, outflows from the ancient volcano of Jebel Shihan have created the resistant surface layer responsible for the precipitous slopes of the Arnon Canyon.

2. Regional survey. ***a. The central region.*** In the central region, roughly E and W of the Dead Sea, the structure is relatively simple. In Cisjordan the relief is dominated by the broad arch of the Judean upwarp. The greater erosion on the W side has pushed the water parting eastward so that the water-parting route, joining such towns as Jerusalem, Bethlehem, and Hebron, lies E of the real top of the arch. This Judean region is defended on both the E and the W by the Senonian chalk. On the E an unusually wide exposure of this porous, infertile rock has combined with the drought of the E slopes to produce the desolate Jeshimon, or Wilderness of Judea. Where the wadis have cut down through the Senonian to the harder Cenomanian underneath, striking gorges are formed. On the W the Senonian outcrop is narrow, but the valley it creates forms a protective moat the full length of Judea, dividing it from the Eocene limestone hills of the Shephelah, the important battleground between Judah and the Philistines. E of the Dead Sea the strata are notably level, but on the edge of the Rift Valley they have been pulled down in a great plunging monocline, which provided a strong defense for Moab on the W side.

On both N and S the central region is limited by hinge faults cutting in obliquely either from the Dead Sea region or from the N-S fault which outlines Judea on the W. SE of the Dead Sea is the fault valley of the Zered, the ancient frontier between Moab and Edom, and to the NE the cutting back of the plateau edge by a NE-SW fault has produced the enclave known as the Plains of Moab, where the Israelites encamped before crossing the Jordan into the Promised Land (Num. 22:1). On the other side of the Jordan Valley a similar hinge fault, running from Jericho toward the NW, provided the route from Jericho to Bethel, and on the W slope of the Judean Plateau the down-faulted Valley of Ajalon formed the most dangerous point in the Judean defenses, the Ascent of Beth-horon.

b. The N region. In Cisjordan the protective Senonian outcrops on each side of Judea have been terminated by the inward-curving hinge faults, and in Ephraim the Cenomanian limestone, exposed across the whole arch, has produced a high plateau with steep and difficult slopes. N of this again is Manasseh, where, instead of an arch, there is a basin surrounded by Cenomanian limestone hills. On the E is the main continuation of the Ephraimite arch through Jebel Kebir, gradually sinking toward Beth-shan. On the N are the hills of Gilboa overlooking the Valley of Jezreel, and on the W is the Umm el-Fahm upfold, the beginning of the Carmel spur. The center of the basin is filled with Eocene limestone which, being resistant to erosion, stands up as hills or mountains—e.g., Ebal and Gerizim near Shechem. Just inside the rim of the basin are the soft Senonian chalk valleys between the Cenomanian and the Eocene limestone outcrops. These formed the main routes of the region, and were easily accessible because the rim was broken by many faults. Manasseh, therefore, could not be well defended, and had no obvious central site for a capital.

N of the minor rift valley of Esdraelon and Jezreel is Galilee, divided into two parts by the great cross fault of esh-Shaghur, about the latitude of Acco. To the N of this fault is the high Cenomanian plateau of Upper Galilee, and to the S is Lower Galilee with limestone hills divided by down-faulted basins—e.g., Sahl Battuf, the Campus Asochis of the Romans. The "brow of the hill" at Nazareth (Luke 4:29) appears to have been the steep fault overlooking the Esdraelon Plain. The E part of Lower Galilee is largely basalt.

E of the Jordan the dome of Gilead stands opposite Ephraim and Manasseh. The greater part of this is Cenomanian limestone, but in the center the Jabbok Canyon has exposed a wide area of Nubian sandstone, which outcrops also in the down-faulted Beqa'a basin near es-Suweileh. The trend of the dome is NE-SW, and it runs out toward the NE corner of the Dead Sea in the hilly region known as Abarim.

c. The S region. In Cisjordan this is bounded on the N by the alluvium-filled depression of the ancient Beer-sheba–Tel el-Milh gulf. S of this, in the great triangle of the Negeb, is a series of NE-SW-upfolded ridges. Except in the extreme S, they are nowhere very high, and form Cenomanian hills in an otherwise generally Senonian region. Several of them have been broken open to form *makhteshim* (*see* § A1 *above*). The W slopes of the Negeb uplands are mainly Eocene limestone, with considerable areas of dune sand and loess.

E of the Arabah, in the district of Edom, the plateau edge has been pushed up to its greatest height (over 5,500 feet in several places). There is considerable exposure of the Nubian sandstone, fantastically eroded, and here were the copper mines of such places as Punon, probably the place where Moses lifted up the brazen serpent (Num. 21:9). The city of Petra is carved out of these same sandstone cliffs. Almost opposite Petra an upfold, crossing the Arabah diagonally from the SW, has raised the floor of the Rift Valley to 650 feet above sea level in Jebel Rishe. Somewhat S of Petra a great fault cutting ESE brings the plateau to an end in a tremendous scarp which once marked the S frontier of Edom. To the S lies Wadi Hasma, a sandy plain with islands of granite capped by sandstone, some rising well over 5,000 feet in height. The edge of the Arabah is now the huge wedge of the Mountains of Midian, which touch 5,000 feet in places. At the junction of this wedge with the S edge of the plateau is a shattered zone, permitting fairly easy movement from Wadi Hasma into the Arabah.

Bibliography. R. Koeppel, *Palästina, die Landschaft in Karten und Bildern* (1930); F.-M. Abel, *Géographie de la Palestine* (1933-38); G. S. Blake, "Geology, Soils and Minerals," in M. G. Ionides, *Report on the Water Resources of Transjordan and Their Development* (1939); L. Picard, *Structure and Evolution of Palestine* (1943), p. 134; D. Baly, *The Geography of the Bible* (1957), p. 303.

A. D. BALY

PALLET [κράβαττος, κράβατος; Lat. *grabatus*]. A small bed or mattress, light enough to be carried. It was the "poor man's bed," sometimes used as a camp bed (cf. Mark 2:4 ff; John 5:8 ff; Acts 5:15). "Bedridden" in Acts 9:33 is literally "lying on a pallet."

B. H. THROCKMORTON, JR.

PALLU păl'o͞o [פלוא, *from* פלא, be conspicuous; *cf. personal name* פלאיה]; KJV PHALLU făl'— in Gen. 46:9; PALLUITES păl'o͞o īts. Second son of Reuben (Gen. 46:9; Exod. 6:14; I Chr. 5:3); father of Eliab, and head of the Palluites (Num. 26:5, 8).

PALM TREE [תמר, *tāmār, tōmer;* תמרה, *tîmōrâ;* φοίνιξ]. A tree and its fruit (*see* DATES), the *Phoenix dactylifera* L.

JERICHO is frequently referred to as the "city of palms" (Deut. 34:13; Judg. 1:16; 3:13; II Chr. 28:15; cf. Jos. War IV.viii.2-3). Several charred palm logs were found during the excavation of Khirbet Qumran by the Dead Sea. The Essenes, according to Pliny, lived "in the company of palm trees."

There were "seventy palm trees" in Elim, a desert oasis on the route of the Exodus (Exod. 15:27; Num. 33:9). ELATH, at the head of the Gulf of Aqaba on the wilderness route (Deut. 2:8), is believed to have derived its name from its "lofty trees," probably referring to palms (II Kings 14:22; 16:6; also Eloth in I Kings 9:26; II Chr. 8:17; 26:2). They are abundant in Aqaba today.

The palm appears in figurative language in Ps. 92:12: "The righteous flourish like the palm tree"; in Song of S. 7:7-8 as a figure of the stateliness of the bride; in Isa. 9:14 (cf. 19:15) as a symbol of the rulers of Israel; and in Joel 1:12 in an oracle of destruction.

Sacred associations with the palm are found throughout the ancient Near East, especially in glyptic art. It often appears as the TREE OF LIFE on cylinder seals and in other forms of art. The "palm of Deborah" (Judg. 4:5) may have been a sacred tree. The frequent occurrence of the palm tree carved in relief on the walls, doors, doorjambs, and other parts of Solomon's temple (I Kings 6:29, 32, 35; 7:36) and the visionary temple of Ezekiel (Ezek. 40:16, 22, 26, 31, 34, 37; 41:18-20, 25-26) suggests more than mere decorative coincidence. Similar decorations are found on Assyrian temples and royal buildings.

The association of palm fronds with the Feast of Booths (Lev. 23:40; Neh. 8:15) is carried into the decoration of ancient Jewish synagogues by reliefs (a well-preserved one is still at Capernaum) and mosaics. The palm figures prominently on the coins, especially those of Vespasian and Nerva. *See* MONEY, COINS, § 5, nos. 20, 23, 35, 38-42.

Christian traditions and legends refer frequently to the palm tree and its leaf. Palm Sunday received its name from the use of the fronds during Jesus' triumphal entry into Jerusalem, as recorded in John 12:13. In the vision of John of Patmos (Rev. 7:9) the white-robed multitude stands before the throne with palm fronds.

TAMAR appears as a personal name (Gen. 38:6; II Sam. 13:1; 14:27) and as a place name (Ezek. 47:19; 48:28). *See also* TAMIR; HAZAZON-TAMAR; BAAL-TAMAR.

In Jer. 10:5 *k^ethômer miqšâ* is translated by KJV "upright as the palm tree" (ASV "like a palm-tree [mg. 'pillar'] of turned work"); but the parallel passage in Bar. 6:70—G 6:69 makes the original meaning clear: "like scarecrows in a cucumber field" (RSV; *see* CUCUMBER).

See also FLORA § A2*h;* BOOTHS, FEAST OF; TEMPLE, JERUSALEM.

Bibliography. A. J. Wensinck, *Tree and Bird as Cosmological Symbols in Western Asia* (1921); I. Löw, *Die Flora der Juden*, II (1924), 306-62; H. Frankfort, *Cylinder Seals* (1939), Index and plates; H. N. and A. L. Moldenke, *Plants of the Bible* (1952), pp. 169-72.

J. C. TREVER

PALMER WORM. KJV translation of גזם in Joel 1:4 (RSV "cutting locust"); 2:25 (RSV "cutter"); Amos 4:9 (RSV "locust"). *See* LOCUST; FAUNA § F2.

PALSY. The KJV translation of παραλυτικός; παραλελυμένος (the RSV refers to being paralyzed). "Palsy" was a sixteenth-century English corruption of the French *paralysie,* and became the popular designation of various sorts of paralysis. The term occurs only in the NT.

This condition, which usually results from cerebral damage, injury sustained by the spinal column, or disease of the central nervous system, is characterized by a lack of ability to move or to exercise full bodily functions.

Apart from general designations (Matt. 4:24; Acts 8:7), the different forms of what the KJV designates "palsy" probably were paraplegia (Matt. 9:2; Mark 2:3; Luke 5:18), acute ascending (Landry's) paralysis (Luke 7:2), and acute atrophic (infantile) paralysis (Matt. 12:10; Mark 3:1; Luke 6:6). Aeneas (Acts 9:

33) had been paralyzed for eight years, but his particular palsy is uncertain. *See* DISEASE § 4.

R. K. HARRISON

PALTI păl'tī [פלטי]; KJV PHALTI făl'— (I Sam. 25:44. Alternately: PALTIEL păl'tĭ əl [פלטיאל] (II Sam. 3:15); KJV PHALTIEL făl'—. **1.** Son of Raphu; a leader of the tribe of Benjamin. Moses sent him with eleven other spies to survey the land of Canaan in view of the impending Israelite invasion (Num. 13:9).

2. Son of Laish, a native of Gallim in Benjamin. Saul gave his daughter Michal, David's wife, to Palti after David had been proscribed (I Sam. 25:44). Subsequently, however, when Abner had quarreled irreparably with Ishbaal (Ishbosheth), the reigning scion of the house of Saul, at Mahanaim, and had opened negotiations with David to effect a united kingdom, David stipulated that before further steps were taken, his former wife Michal must first be returned. Ishbaal, no doubt at the instance of Abner, took Michal from her grief-torn husband Palti and delivered her to David (II Sam. 3:15-16).

E. R. DALGLISH

PALTIEL păl'tĭ əl [פלטיאל, God is (my) deliverance]; KJV PHALTIEL făl'— in II Sam. 3:15. **1.** A leader of the tribe of Issachar; son of Azzan (Num. 34:26). He was one of those appointed, under the oversight of Eleazar and Joshua, to superintend the distribution of the W Jordanian territory among the ten tribes to be settled in that area of Canaan. The meaning of the name Paltiel and of other names in this account underscores Israel's dependence upon God for the new life in Canaan.

2. Alternate form of PALTI 2.

Bibliography. M. Noth, *Die israelitischen Personennamen* (1928), pp. 38, 156. R. F. JOHNSON

PALTITE, THE păl'tīt [הפלטי]. Descriptive adjective of Helez, one of David's heroes (II Sam. 23:26). It means an inhabitant of BETH-PELET. The parallel passages in I Chr. 11:27; 27:10 read "the Pelonite," which should probably be emended to "the Paltite."

S. COHEN

PAMPHYLIA păm fĭl'ĭ ə [Παμφυλία]. A region on the S coast of Asia Minor bounded on the W by Lycia, on the N by Pisidia, and on the E by Cilicia Tracheia. The area of the Mediterranean on the S was called the Pamphylian Bay or Pamphylian Sea. Pamphylia was *ca.* eighty miles long and up to twenty miles broad. It was, for the most part, a low, moist, fever-laden area; although at some points the Taurus Range, which makes travel to the N difficult, reaches to the sea. The country faced the sea; and although rugged roads did lead N to Phrygia and Lycaonia, its chief contacts with other regions were by water. Chief ports were Attalia and Side; Perga was several miles inland and near the River Cestrus, but was also considered a port (Acts 13:13).

While Greek colonists settled in Pamphylia at least as early as the fifth century B.C. and Jews lived there in the second century B.C. (I Macc. 15:23; see also Acts 2:10), the native element remained dominant; and the population, outside of a few cities, was not highly civilized. Of the chief cities, Perga was a stronghold of the native life and religion; Attalia, founded in the second century B.C. by the Attalid rulers of Pergamum, was more Greek; and Side in the second and first centuries B.C. was wealthy in large part through acting as the slave market for the Cilician pirates (whom Pompey suppressed in 67 B.C.).

Politically Pamphylia was never important. It was successively subject to the Persians, Macedonians, Seleucids, Attalids of Pergamum, and Romans. The history of Pamphylia as a Roman province is complicated and not entirely clear. The Romans usually combined it with neighboring regions, such as Cilicia and Galatia. According to Dio Cassius 60.17, it was combined with Lycia in one province in A.D. 43. Not much later, however, Lycia was separate from Pamphylia, which was then for a time again united with Galatia; but *ca.* 74, under Vespasian, Pamphylia was again joined with Lycia as one province.

Paul with Barnabas visited Pamphylia on his so-called first missionary journey, coming from Paphos on Cyprus and arriving at PERGA. There John Mark left them, either because he was displeased that Paul had supplanted his cousin Barnabas as leader of the party or because the plan to go over the mountain roads to the upland and reach "Antioch of Pisidia" was more than he had agreed to share (Acts 13:13-14). Pamphylia itself was so little Hellenized that it was not a promising field for mission work, and Acts gives no indication that Paul stopped to work there. Perhaps the unhealthy climate led him to hurry to the uplands and escape the fever-haunted coastland, where malaria could have troubled him (cf. Gal. 4:13). On the return journey from Pisidian Antioch, Paul and Barnabas stopped and preached in Perga; nothing is said of any success in this venture. From Perga the missionaries went to the port of Attalia and took ship for Syrian Antioch. Nothing further is said of Pamphylia in the NT, either in the account of Paul's further work in Acts or in I Pet. 1:1, which is directed to a large proportion of Asia Minor but makes no mention of Pamphylia. Christianity was late in gaining strength there. Its real evangelization occurred much later than the apostolic age.

Bibliography. K. Lanckoroński-Brzezie, *Städte Pamphyliens und Pisidiens*, vol. I (1890); *Cambridge Ancient History*, XI (1936), 590-97; A. H. M. Jones, *Cities of the Eastern Roman Provinces* (1937), ch. 5; D. Magie, *Roman Rule in Asia Minor* (1950), pp. 260-66. F. V. FILSON

PAN. *See* POTTERY; VESSELS.

PANEL [מסגרת (KJV BORDER), *from* סגר, close; ספון, *sippûn* (KJV CIEL), *from* ספן, cover]. In Solomon's temple were ten stands (KJV "bases") of bronze (*see* LAVER), four cubits long, four cubits wide, and three cubits high; and each had panels (מסגרות) set in frames (KJV "borders"). On these panels were lions, oxen, and cherubim (I Kings 7:28-29, 31-32, 35-36). Jeremiah in denouncing Shallum (Jehoahaz), son of Josiah, derides him for saying: "I will build myself a great house . . . paneling [ספון, *saphûn*] it with cedar" (Jer. 22:14). The text is uncertain; but "paneling" seems better than KJV "cieled." Haggai (1:4) denounces the people for dwelling in their paneled (ספונים; KJV "cieled") houses while the temple lies in ruins. שחיף (Ezek. 41:16) is translated "paneled" as a conjecture (KJV "cieled").

See also ARCHITECTURE; CEILING. O. R. SELLERS

PANNAG păn'ăg. KJV translation of פנג (Ezek. 27:17), as a place name. The RSV follows three variant MSS, reading פגג, and translates "early figs," as an item in a list of Palestinian exports to Tyre. The ASV mg. suggests "a kind of confection," and this is supported by the Targ. and the Akkadian cognate *pannigu,* a variety of baked goods.

J. F. ROSS

PAPER [χάρτης] (II John 12). Not true paper, but PAPYRUS. *See also* WRITING AND WRITING MATERIALS.

PAPER REED. KJV translation of ערות (Isa. 19:7). The RSV derives the word from the root ערה, "bare," and translates "bare places." Possibly the word has been borrowed from the Egyptian *'r,* "bulrush."

Bibliography. T. W. Thacker, "A Note on ערות," *JTS,* XXXIV (1933), pp. 163-65.

PAPHOS pā'fŏs [Πάφος] (Acts 13:6, 13). A city in the SW part of the island of Cyprus visited by Paul, Barnabas, and John Mark on the first missionary journey. The Pauline city, New Paphos (the modern Baffo), is to be distinguished from the old city of the same name, located *ca.* nine miles to the N. It was the seat of the government of Cyprus during the Roman period (Cicero Fam. XIII.48). Annexed by the Romans in 55 B.C., Cyprus became a senatorial province in 22 B.C., with a governor bearing the title of proconsul, as Acts 13:7 correctly names Sergius Paulus, who received Barnabas and Saul. The seaport, which is situated on a natural harbor immediately E of the rocky tip of the island's SW coast, was first distinguished by the name Πάφος Νέα, New Paphos, from the older city during the Roman period (Ptolemy *Geography* V.13[14].1; Pliny Nat. Hist. V.130); Strabo refers to the earlier city as Old Paphos (Παλαίπαφος; *Geography* XIV.683). According to tradition, the city was founded by a Greek named Agapenor, who settled there with a group of colonists from Arcadia and founded a dynasty. An Assyrian monument preserves a list of ten Cyprian kings of Paphos (IGR III, no. 939), evidently referring to New Paphos, which was the seat of the tiny Greek kingdom known from coins dating to *ca.* 480 B.C.

Courtesy of the Zion Research Library

20. The harbor at Paphos

In the Hellenistic and Roman periods the port became a naval station (Diodorus XX.49.1). In 15 B.C. the honorary title Augusta was bestowed upon the city; later the names Claudia and Flavia were added during Tiberius' reign. In Byzantine times, perhaps because of the damage inflicted by a severe earthquake in the fourth century A.D., the city lost its title as the island's leading city to Constantia, the rebuilt city of Salamis.

Fig. PAP 20.

Bibliography. R. Gunnis, *Historic Cyprus* (1936); Pauly-Wissowa, *Real-Enzyclopädie,* vol. XVIII, no. 3 (1949), cols. 937-64. E. W. SAUNDERS

PAPIAS pā'pĭ əs. A bishop of Hierapolis in Asia Minor, who flourished in the second quarter of the second century; author of a five-volume work, *Interpretation of the Lord's Oracles,* of which only fragments survive in the writings of Irenaeus, Eusebius, and medieval Byzantine exegetes and historians. *See* APOSTOLIC FATHERS.

According to Irenaeus (V.33.3-4), Papias was a hearer of John, the disciple of the Lord, and a comrade of POLYCARP. He was certainly a convinced millenarian, influenced by the author of Revelation; but what "John" he may have known is quite problematic. Philip of Side (*ca.* 430) preserves a tradition from Papias that both James and John, sons of Zebedee, were killed by the Jews.

Eusebius had a poor opinion of Papias' intelligence. His excerpt (Hist. III.39) shows that Papias was an avid collector of oral traditions from the "elders" about the sayings of the apostles and other disciples of Jesus, which he treasured above anything recounted in books. He apparently distinguished two persons named John among the Lord's disciples, the apostle and an "elder John." Eusebius is probably right that Papias had no personal acquaintance with any eyewitnesses of the Lord. But some of the miracles and legends about personages of the apostolic age Papias claims to have received from the daughters of Philip the Evangelist (cf. Acts 21:8-9), after they settled in Hierapolis.

The remarks of Papias about Mark and Matthew, also preserved by Eusebius, have baffled all students of gospel origins, and to date there seems no prospect of a consensus as to their precise meaning or significance. Mark, he said, had not been a hearer or follower of Jesus, but was an interpreter of Peter. After Peter's death, Mark committed to writing what he remembered from Peter's recollections of the Lord—accurately, but not "in order." We do not know what Papias meant by "order." Matthew, said Papias, "put in order" the oracles (or sayings) of the Lord in Aramaic, which "each one interpreted as he was able." Concerning other early Christian writings, Eusebius says only that Papias knew and used I John and I Peter, and that he related a story about a woman accused of many sins which was contained in the Gospel According to the Hebrews.

Bibliography. Most NT introductions and commentaries on Mark and Matthew discuss Papias. For texts and translations, *see* the bibliography under APOSTOLIC FATHERS.

M. H. SHEPHERD, JR.

PAPYRUS pə pī′rəs [גמא, *gōmê*]. A tall, aquatic reed plant, *Cyperus papyrus* L., noted especially for its use for ancient writing material. The papyrus plant, so abundant in ancient lower Egypt, is no longer found there.

Job 8:11 refers to the watery habitat of the papyrus reed (KJV RUSH). In Isa. 18:2 (KJV BULRUSHES) the word means papyrus used for light boats or canoes, commonly employed in ancient Egypt because of the scarcity of timber. In Exod. 2:3 most translations retain "bulrushes" (*see* BULRUSH) for the reeds from which the basket was made for the infant Moses, but doubtless papyrus was meant. The basket was floated among the reeds (*see* REED), along the banks of the Nile. In Isaiah's figure of the transformed wilderness (35:7), grass is to become "reeds (קנה) and rushes (גמא)." Here, too, the papyrus is probably meant to symbolize the abundance of water, though the meaning may be more general.

Papyrus as a writing material (*see* WRITING AND WRITING MATERIALS) was common in Egypt from the early third millennium B.C. (a few fragments from that period are extant) and continued in use well into the first millennium A.D. It was an important item of export from Egypt for many centuries.* In the familiar story of Wen-Amon, five hundred rolls of papyrus were part payment for a shipment of cedars from the ruler of Byblos (the Greek name meant "papyrus stalk" or "pith used for paper"). Figs. EGY 17, 20.

PAPER (the English word is derived from the word "papyrus") was prepared from thin strips of the inner pith of the papyrus stalk laid vertically, with another layer placed horizontally on top. An adhesive was used (Pliny says it was Nile water!) and pressure applied to bond them together into a sheet. After drying, it was polished with shell or stone implements; then the sheets were glued together to form rolls. Fig. ELE 25.

The only specific biblical reference to the paper made from papyrus is in II John 12, where the Greek χάρτης refers to the papyrus roll or sheet used in writing a letter.

The KJV refers to "paper reeds" (papyrus) in Isa. 19:7, following the versions, but the Hebrew (ערות) means "bare places" (so RSV).

To judge from the earliest extant Hebrew MSS which have come from the Qumran caves by the Dead Sea (the fragments date from *ca.* 250 B.C. to A.D. 50), papyrus was not so commonly used there, probably because of the greater abundance and accessibility of leather. Only a small number of papyrus fragments have been found among the thousands of those of leather. Many scholars consider the story in Jer. 36 to imply the use of papyrus for Jeremiah's writing in the late seventh century B.C.

See also FLORA § A11*b;* RUSH.

Bibliography. Pliny Nat. Hist. XIII.68-69 (xxi-xxvii); I. Löw, *Die Flora der Juden,* I:2 (1928), 559-71; H. N. and A. L. Moldenke, *Plants of the Bible* (1952), pp. 92-94; D. Diringer, *The Hand-Produced Book* (1953), pp. 125-69.

J. C. TREVER

***PARABLE** [משל, *from the verb* to be similar, to be comparable; παροιμία, παραβολή]. An extended metaphor, or simile, frequently becoming a brief narrative, generally used by men of biblical times for didactic purposes. Since an allegory is also an extension of a simile and since every metaphor presupposes a simile, confusion between the forms of parable and ALLEGORY has frequently and understandably occurred. The wide range of literary types designated as parables by biblical authors has also contributed to this confusion. The most familiar type of parable is the brief narrative which forcefully illustrates a single idea. During the biblical period Jesus in particular used the parable with skill and artistry.

1. Terminology of parable in the Bible
   a. In biblical Hebrew
   b. In LXX Greek
   c. In NT Greek
2. Use of parable in the OT
3. Use of parable in the Apoc. and the Pseudep.
4. Use of parable in the Synoptic gospels
   a. The parable form
   b. The evangelists' use of Jesus' parables
5. The message of Jesus' parables
Bibliography

1. Terminology of parable in the Bible. In contrast to the infrequent occurrences of the word משל in the OT, the Synoptic evangelists use the word παραβολή forty-eight times (Matthew seventeen times, Mark thirteen times, and Luke eighteen times), and the author of Hebrews uses it twice (Heb. 9:9; 11:19).

a. In biblical Hebrew. With the exception of two occurrences of the word משל (Job 27:1; 29:1), it always involves a comparison, either directly or by implication. Throughout the history of Israel's linguistic developments, however, the word is given varied meanings. Its earliest and continuously dominant significance is a popular saying or PROVERB (cf. I Sam. 10:12; 24:13; Ezek. 12:22-23; 16:44; 18:2-3). Consequently this form has closest affinities with the wisdom literature of the OT, whose authors occasionally give it the meaning of a profound discourse upon a difficult problem (Job 27:1; 29:1; cf. Pss. 49:4; 78:2). As a popular saying the משל frequently expresses derision and contempt (Ezek. 16:44; cf. Deut. 28:37; I Kings 9:7; II Chr. 7:20; Pss. 44:14; 69:11; Jer. 24:9; Ezek. 14:8) and takes the poetic form of a taunt song (Num. 21:27-30; Isa. 14:4; Mic. 2:4; Hab. 2:6). Some OT authors associate the משל with the word חידה, a dark or riddle-like saying (Pss. 49:4; 78:2; Prov. 1:6; Ezek. 17:2; 24:3). Hence משל also signifies an oracular utterance (Num. 23:7, 18; 24:3, 15, 20-21, 23) and in its more developed forms assumes an allegorical character (Ezek. 17:2-3; 24:3-4). In biblical Hebrew, therefore, משל includes popular and proverbial sayings, discourses of sages, taunt songs, and oracles.

b. In LXX Greek. The Greek terms παραβολή and παροιμία are used in the LXX for the word משל when it means a proverbial saying and involves the element of comparison. The greater precision of Greek vocabulary makes possible more exact translations of the varied nuance of משל than the limitations of the Hebrew language afford. For the opening of the lengthy discourses of Job, the LXX translator uses correctly the Greek word for exordium, προοιμίον (Job 27:1; 29:1). Three Greek words are used to convey the various overtones of the derisive meaning of משל: θρύλημα for mockery (Job 17:6), ἀφανισμόν for desolation (I Kings 9:7), and θρῆνος for the taunt song or the dirge (Isa. 14:4; Mic. 2:4). In Num. 21:27 the significance of משל as an oracle was expressed by calling the משלים αἰνιγματσταί.

c. In NT Greek. An analysis of Jesus' use of the parable form for didactic purposes indicates that the evangelists included three varieties of illustrative examples within the single category of the παραβολή. First, there is the narrative parable, which is fully developed without an introductory formula of comparison such as "The kingdom of heaven is like . . ." In these parables the subject is, with four exceptions (the rich fool, the rich man and Lazarus, the publican and the Pharisee, and the good Samaritan), secular, and the story as a whole makes its own point. The second variety is the simple parable, which is introduced by formulas of comparison ("It is like . . . ," or "as" followed by a noun or a verb), by "when," or by a form of command or of question. The third variety is the parabolic saying, which is a brief utterance stating a fact of common human experience to be applied by the listener to some present situation or circumstance (e.g., Matt. 5:14*b*, 15-16; Luke 16:13). The parabolic saying differs from a parable in the absence of a comparative element and from the narrative parable in its brevity. The parabolic saying and the narrative parable, therefore, are extensions of metaphors, while the simple parable is an extension of a simile.

The author of Hebrews uses the word παραβολή in quite a different sense. In Heb. 9:9 the first tabernacle (called the παραβολή) functions as a symbol for the present age, which offers man no means of salvation. The reference to Abraham's recovery of Isaac in Heb. 11:19 points figuratively or parabolically to Christ's resurrection from the dead. The Fourth Evangelist uses the word παροιμία (an alternate translation of משל in the LXX for a proverb and so used in II Pet. 2:22) rather than παραβολή. The word as used by the Fourth Evangelist, however, does not mean a proverb but a hidden or esoteric saying which can be understood only by those who have a clue to its meaning.

2. Use of parable in the OT. Parabolic sayings and parables, which appear less frequently in the literature of the OT as compared with the use made of them by the rabbis and Jesus for instructional purposes, are a popular and familiar form of wisdom teaching. The preferred form of wisdom teaching is the gnomic saying which deals with familiar aspects of human life and conduct in a direct way without attempting to express any tangential or obscure concepts. By quoting several examples of gnomic and parabolic sayings found in the book of Proverbs, it is possible to point out their dissimilarities and the origin of their association. The proverb (10:1):

> A wise son makes a glad father,
> but a foolish son is a sorrow to his mother,

is an illustration of a gnomic saying. Parabolic sayings, which by comparison are rare in the book of Proverbs, may be illustrated by the following quotation (6:7-8):

> Without having any chief,
> officer or ruler,
> she [the ant] prepares her food in summer,
> and gathers her sustenance in harvest.

The difference between this statement and the gnomic utterance is that the former is merely a factual observation, while the latter pronounces a judgment upon a moral or religious issue. The parabolic saying, however, must be placed in juxtaposition (implicitly or explicitly) with a gnomic saying. In the case of the parabolic saying quoted above, the wisdom writer has made clear his didactic purpose by adding an interpretative application (vss. 9-11):

> How long will you lie there, O sluggard?
> When will you arise from your sleep?
> A little sleep, a little slumber,
> a little folding of the hands to rest,
> and poverty will come upon you like a vagabond,
> and want like an armed man.

The purpose of the parabolic saying, then, is the provision of a vivid illustrative example for wisdom teaching and may derive from the tendency toward parallelism in gnomic utterances. To be sure, the characteristics distinguishing a parabolic saying from a gnomic saying tend to blur. However, one may conclude that the parabolic saying is illustrative and dependent upon its association with another statement for clarification of its significance, while the gnomic saying is an independent moral maxim. Even though all parabolic sayings can be expanded into parables and some into narrative parables, wisdom writers generally prefer the briefer parabolic utterances.

In wisdom literature skilful use of the narrative parable is found in Eccl. 9:13-16. The narrative has an introduction: "I have also seen this example of wisdom under the sun, and it seemed great to me" (vs. 13). The author illustrates this idea by the following narrative: "There was a little city with few men in it; and a great king came against it and besieged it, building great siegeworks against it. But there was found in it a poor wise man, and he by his wisdom delivered the city. Yet no one remembered that poor man" (vss. 14-15). The gnomic saying: "But I say that wisdom is better than might, though the poor man's wisdom is despised, and his words are not heeded" (vs. 16), is appended to the story to guarantee a correct interpretation.

Wisdom and prophetic literature tend to use the parabolic saying for a second, though not so prominent, purpose. By associating the word משל (παραβολή) with חידה (αἴνιγμα; cf. Prov. 1:6; Ps. 49:4) and by associating both these words with an oracle concerning God's judgment in the future (Ezek. 17:2-21), the parable begins to have an esoteric significance. While the use of the parable form to conceal knowledge is rare in the OT period, it becomes an important factor for the writers of some pseudepigraphal books of the OT and for the Synoptists.

3. Use of parable in the Apoc. and the Pseudep. Of the apocryphal writers, Sirach continues to use the parabolic saying in the wisdom tradition. In the following quotation (Ecclus. 13:2) the gnomic saying precedes the parabolic utterance:

> Do not lift a weight beyond your strength,
> nor associate with a man mightier and richer than you.
> How can the clay pot associate with the iron kettle?
> The pot will strike against it, and will itself be broken.

(Cf. 9:10; 11:2-3; 11:10*b*-13; 28:11*b*-12.)

In Enoch one finds a pseudepigraphic author using the word "parable" in a sense quite different from that of the wisdom writers, the rabbis, and the Synoptic evangelists. The parable is no longer a truism of common human experience but a vision of future things revealed to one chosen by God to receive knowledge of divine mysteries (Enoch 1–5; 37:5; 38:1; 45:1; 58:1; 68:1). Here observation and deduction have been replaced by revelation, without which the secrets of God would be inaccessible to mankind. Since these parables deal with subjects concerning knowledge of the future state of the wicked and the blessed, of astronomical secrets, of God's judgment of the world, and of the angelic world, they are eschatologically oriented and used to bridge the gap between the earthly and the heavenly and between the present and the future. At first glance such parables appear to have no association with the earlier Hebraic tradition. Their link with the tradition of wisdom and of prophecy, though tenuous, may lie in the parallel references to parable and riddle (or dark saying) in Proverbs (cf. Prov. 1:6), in the exordial significance given to the word "parable" in Job's discourses on the problem of evil (Job 27:1; 29:1; cf. Ps. 49:4-20), and in its oracular significance (cf. Num. 23:7).

4. Use of parable in the Synoptic gospels. Since the gospels are the works of Christian believers and preserve in written form the reminiscences of things said and done by Jesus, elements of the tradition concerning Jesus' activities have been influenced by their faith. Consequently it is necessary to keep in mind the probability that the evangelists have altered the wording of the parables themselves and the contexts within which they were originally spoken. Recognition of this problem requires observation of significant details which indicate the use made by the evangelists of Jesus' parables and the motives for their transformation of them.

a. The parable form. An initial problem concerns the material which can be appropriately classified as parable. The variation of opinion regarding the number of illustrative examples which scholars designate as parables is indicative of the intrinsic difficulties with this literary form. A solution is to eliminate similes and metaphors which some have included within the category of parables. Examples of Jesus' use of metaphor, as reported by the evangelists, are such phrases as the following: "Tell that *fox*" (Luke 13:32; an illustration of the simple metaphor); *"den* of *robbers"* (Matt. 21:13; a double metaphor); *"blind guides, straining out a gnat"* (Matt. 23:24; a compounded metaphor); and "Give, and it will be given to you; *good measure, pressed down, shaken together, running over, will be put into your lap. For the measure you give will be the measure you get back"* (Luke 6:38; an extended metaphor). The expression "Every plant which my heavenly Father has not planted will be rooted up" (Matt. 15:13) illustrates the transition from a metaphor to a parabolic saying, and the statement, "When the unclean spirit has gone out of a man, he passes through waterless places seeking rest, but he finds none . . ." (Matt. 12:43-45), is an example of its transition to a parable. In contrast to the metaphor, the simile involves comparison and contrast—e.g., "that he [Satan] might sift you *like* wheat" (Luke 22:31; a single simile) and "for you [Pharisees] are *like* whitewashed tombs, which outwardly appear beautiful, but within they are full of dead men's bones and all uncleanness" (Matt. 23:27; an extended simile). The comparison of the scribe to the "householder who brings out of his treasure what is new and what is old" (Matt. 13:51) illustrates the transition of a simile to a parable.

What remains of illustrative examples used for didactic purposes may be classified as parabolic sayings, parables, and narrative parables. The parabolic sayings, which are brief statements of fact and were applied by the evangelists in some way to larger contexts, are the utterances concerning the physician (Luke 4:23), the salt (Matt. 5:13), the city built on a hill (Matt. 5:14*b*), the lamp on the stand (Matt. 5:15), the eye as the light of the body (Matt. 6:22-23), serving two masters (Matt. 6:24), the requesting son (Matt. 7:9-10), the tree and the fruit (Matt. 7:17-19), the need of a physician by the sick (Mark 2:17*a*), things old and new (Mark 2:21-22), disciple and teacher (Matt. 10:24-25), manifestation of the hidden (Matt. 10:26-27), the blind leading the blind (Matt. 15:14), the divided kingdom (Matt. 12:25*a*), the divided house (Matt. 12:25*b*), the strong man (Matt. 12:29), children's bread (Matt. 15:26-27), pearls before swine (Matt. 7:6), figs and thistles (Matt. 7:16), adding measure to one's stature (Matt. 6:27), and the eagles and the carcass (Matt. 24:28). The simple form of a parabolic saying is the statement "Physician, heal yourself" (Luke 4:23); the double form, the saying on trees and fruit (Matt. 7:17-19); the conditional form, the blind leading the blind (Matt. 15:14); the extended form, the strong man (Matt. 12:29); and the transitional form from parabolic saying to the parable, the lamp on the stand (Matt. 5:15).

Various introductory formulas of parables relate this variety to the simile. These formulas are: "It is like" (Matt. 11:16; 13:44; 13:47; 7:24-26), "as" (Matt. 25:14; Mark 4:26; Luke 12:58), "when" (Mark 13:28; Luke 12:54; 14:8, 12), the question form (Matt. 24:45; Luke 11:5; 14:28-30, 31; 15:4, 8; 17:7), the conditional form (Matt. 18:12; 24:43), and the command form (Matt. 5:25). While all these parables invariably have an element of comparison, this relationship is not necessarily original with Jesus but may be the result of the evangelists' editorial work. The development of details in some of the parables, such as those in the parables concerning the pounds, the great supper, the ten virgins, the tares, the unmerciful servant, etc., suggests that originally these stories were told as independent narrative parables. In contrast to the parable, the narrative parable has no formula of comparison but is a fully developed and independent story which begins with such phrases as "there was" or "a certain," and is narrated in detail (cf. the parable of the good Samaritan, Luke 10:30-37). The Synoptic evangelists have preserved fourteen narrative parables attributed to Jesus: the good Samaritan (Luke 10:30-37), the rich fool (Luke 12:16-21), the rich man and Lazarus (Luke 16:19-31), the unjust judge (Luke 18:1-8), the Pharisee and the publican (Luke 18:10-14), the sower (Mark 4:1-8), the fig tree (Luke 13:6-9), the great supper (Luke 14:16-24; cf. Matt. 22:1-10), the unjust steward (Luke 16:1-8), the pounds (Luke 19:12-27; cf. Matt. 25:14-30), the wicked husbandman (Mark 12:1-9 and parallels), the two sons (Matt. 21:28-32), and the two debtors (Luke 7:41-43).

b. The evangelists' use of Jesus' parables. From the evangelists' record of Jesus' use of parables for didactic purposes, one is impressed by the vivid and dramatic presentation of ideas through the narration of commonplace incidents. This characteristic of his teaching is heightened by a comparison of his parables with those of the rabbis, who were also skilful in the narration of a good story. However, since the rabbis use the parable form primarily to clarify or to prove a point of the Mosaic law, their parables are usually characterized by scholastic pedantry, rather than vigor and originality. Jesus' parables, on the contrary, support the evangelists' claim that he taught and preached with authoritative power and with creative novelty. Prior to a discussion of the message communicated by Jesus through parables, it is necessary to clarify the process of their adaptation to the gospel record.

A comparison of the details of two stories, the parables of the great supper (Luke 14:16-24) and the wedding feast (Matt. 22:1-14), leads one to conclude that they are undoubtedly alterations of the same parable. This comparison illustrates the treatment of Jesus' parables by the embellishment of details. The Matthean report of the parable changes the setting from a great supper to a wedding feast and the leading characters from a certain man and his servant to a king and his groups of servants. There is one important addition in the Matthean version, without parallel in the Lukan; this addition relates that the king was enraged at the refusal of the first guests and sent his armies to destroy his servants' murderers and to burn their city. The Matthean embellishments reflect developments occurring after A.D. 70: the Jews' rejection of Christian missionary endeavors, the consequent destruction of Jerusalem by Roman conquest, and the attempt to formulate historically God's plan of salvation from the Jews' rejection of their own prophets down to the final judgment day. Such interpretative corrections, which adjust Jesus' parables to the situation of the church, probably were made frequently by the evangelists, but it is not always possible to check them so readily as in this instance.

The variation between the Matthean and Lukan forms of Jesus' statement on going before the judge (Matt. 5:25-26; Luke 12:58-59) illustrates how great an alteration in meaning can occur merely by changing verbal forms. In Luke, the eschatological parable makes the following point: as the man conscious of his guilt, threatened with a lawsuit, seeks reconciliation with his accuser before the court trial, so the man conscious of the coming judgment must seek reconciliation with his God. In the Matthean form, the narrative style has been transformed to the command: "Make friends quickly with your accuser." The context no longer suggests that God, but one's fellow man, is the accuser. The Matthean form, therefore, represents Jesus as saying that one is to act as expediently as possible to avoid a heavy penalty for one's crimes. Since Jesus' ethical teaching urges men to consider seriously their responsibilities toward their fellow men, the Matthean version of the parable is obviously secondary to the Lukan version. The Matthean adaptation of the parable, however, represents a trend within the church, particularly on the part of the First Evangelist, to turn Jesus' parables into hortatory statements.

This trend is further illustrated by the theory concerning the use of parables advanced by Mark (4:10-12) and by his explanation of the parable of the sower (4:13-20). According to Mark, parables are means of concealing the real character and content of Jesus' teaching from the masses and of revealing their hidden meaning to a chosen few. Since Jesus' parables in themselves are generally quite clear and were received by the crowds gladly, Mark's theory is a strange representation of Jesus' use of parables. The evangelist presupposes an esoteric quality of Jesus' teaching which matches his theory of Jesus' secret messiahship. Both theories apparently have their origin in the idea that Jesus is warring against the powers of darkness, to whom he must not betray his powers of insight and of office, lest they take advantage of him and of his powers.

The theory regarding Jesus' use of parables is followed by Mark's explanation of the parable of the sower. By allegorizing the parable, Mark has indicated that he has not understood what a parable is. His allegorization of the parable tends to make the elements of the story significant in themselves. The explanation not only confuses the sets of equations but also changes the main point of the parable. The parable states that as the farmer must expect varying returns from his activity, so God also at the time of judgment. The allegory, on the contrary, stresses the aspects of failure in harvesting and serves, therefore, as a word of warning to all converts to guard against attitudes which will undermine the sincerity of their commitment to Christ. Mark's theory and explanation suggest that parables in themselves are obscure and that the church no longer was aware of their original situation and function.

The individual sayings (Luke 16:9, 10-12, 13) appended to the parable of the unjust steward indicate that a method other than allegorization was used to interpret difficult parables. Allegorization could not have made the unjust steward in his various acts exemplary as a whole. The central point of the parable itself (Luke 16:1-8) is that a steward, being a rogue and faced with a crucial situation, realizes that action is necessary to prevent disastrous consequences. Jesus' own didactic application of the story appears in vs. 8 and is a criticism of many devout people who, when confronted by situations requiring action, do nothing. The first appended saying (vs. 9) interprets the parable to mean that one can find a dwelling in "eternal habitations" by the correct use of "mammon" (presumably by giving alms). The second appended saying (vss. 10-12) attempts to point up the parable in another way. By faithfully discharging small duties that concern mammon, one will be given a greater stewardship over heavenly things. The third saying (vs. 13) turns the parable in quite another direction by calling attention to the irreconcilability of one's allegiance to both God and mammon. By creating such contexts within which the parables are to be understood, the evangelists frequently altered the original meaning and intention of Jesus' parables, which can be recovered only by a careful analytical examination of the parables.

The evangelists' collections of Jesus' parables brought about similar changes, particularly the collection which uses the introductory formula "The kingdom of heaven is like" (Matt. 13:24, 31, 33, 44, 45, 47; cf. Matt. 18:23; 20:1; 22:2; 25:1; Mark 4:26). In the great majority of instances in which it is used, the theme of the parable does not deal with the kingdom as such but more often is concerned with one's attitudes toward the coming of the kingdom of God and relationships toward one's fellow man. Only four parables merit consideration as kingdom parables: certainly the parables of the self-growing seed (Mark 4:26-29) and of buried treasure (Matt. 13:44); and possibly the parables of the mustard seed (Matt. 13: 31-32) and of leaven (Matt. 13:33). The use of the formula is a further indication of the difficulties the early Christians had in trying to explain the meaning of the parables and of the alterations they made in adjusting the parables to the context of their own era.

Analysis of the gospel record and of its preservation of Jesus' parables indicates that the evangelists had available significant parabolic sayings, parables, and narrative parables, which had been transmitted to the Christian community by auditors as separate words of Jesus and which had become detached from their original context and situation. Eventually collections of such remembered words were made. While most of this parabolic material reliably represents Jesus' teaching, it is also necessary to recognize the activity of the Christian community in molding the tradition. There is one parable, the parable of the weeds (Matt. 13:24-30), however, that gives every indication that the First Evangelist created both the parable and its allegorical interpretation. The linguistic and ideological peculiarities of the interpretation are quite clearly Matthean, and the lack of reality in the parable itself suggests that the parable was written with the allegorical interpretation in mind.

One further observation needs to be made regarding the types of situations within which the parabolic material appears in the gospels. On the one hand, the evangelists reported Jesus' use of this material in controversial conversations, which implies that the parable had been and still was a useful instrument in hostile debates. On the other hand, the evangelists also frequently record the appropriateness of the parable for didactic purposes, particularly as a means of instructing the masses who thronged around a new teacher. Jesus dedicated his narrative skill to bringing a new note of hope for the discouraged, the dispossessed, and the outcast.

5. The message of Jesus' parables. Without an analytical study of the gospel record it would be impossible to use the parabolic material for historical purposes. Recognition of the changes brought about by the developing tradition, however, cannot solve the historical problem when crucial clues are missing. For example, the two parabolic sayings about things old and new in Mark 2:21-22 have been handed down without an interpretative application and without a reference to the original situation. In this instance, and in others similar to it, one may suggest possible didactic or polemic purposes for Jesus' use of these illustrative examples. However, no final criterion of his actual meaning has been established: Should the new order *not* be combined with the old lest the old be wasted? Or, should the new order *not* be prevented from creating new expressions of new religious insights? In instances of such parabolic sayings it is wise to admit ignorance regarding the precise significance of the saying, because its original context and function are lost and the utterance itself is insufficient to suggest anything more than possible interpretations.

Jesus and his rabbinic contemporaries use the parable form to clarify the main themes of their religious and ethical teachings. The chief concern of the rabbis is the exposition of the Law. The theme of Jesus' proclamation and teaching, however, is the kingdom of God, with particular stress upon its eschatological significance (Mark 1:15). His treatment of this theme was not that of the apocalyptic visionary who wrote the parables of Enoch (cf. especially Enoch 37–71), but that of the prophets who used the theme regarding the imminent arrival of God's kingdom as an occasion for practical religious preaching and instruction. For the writers of apocalypses, two factors were important: a description of the great drama in which God's sovereignty is to be established, and a calculation of the time of its arrival with full force. Both factors give free reign to vindictiveness and emotionalism. According to the parables which may genuinely have their origin in Jesus' thinking, he is not interested in scheduling future events or in contemplation of the procedures, of transition from the present world order to a new, heavenly type of existence.

Jesus' development of the theme "The kingdom of God is at hand" includes three main aspects. First, the imminence of God's assumption of sovereignty involves a crisis in the life of his people. Man's eternal destiny is about to be decided. Convinced of the inevitability of the imminent coming of judgment, Jesus devotes his life and his message to warning people of the crucial nature of their situation (Luke 12:57-59; 12:16-20; 16:19-31; 14:16-24; 16:1-8; etc.). Second, while Jesus does not minimize the awful fate that will overtake those who wilfully reject participation in the kingdom of God, he stresses, in particular, the eschatological joy of the kingdom's coming for the oppressed and the distressed (especially Luke 15:4-7, 8-10). In parables which illustrate this concept, he reassures those who are "poor in spirit" and who at the same time yearn for the kingdom's coming, by asserting that God will intercede in their behalf. Jesus clearly explains, however, that the initiation of God's beneficent action toward men does not lie in man's attitudes and actions (Luke 17:7-10), but in God's nature (Matt. 20:1-16).

Third, Jesus uses the theme of the imminence of the kingdom to teach men what is specifically required of them that they may prepare themselves for entrance into the kingdom. Preparation requires singleness of devotion toward God as shown in attitudes of repentance, faith, love, and obedience. The sincerity of these attitudes is to be expressed in concrete acts (Matt. 7:15-20). In the parabolic saying on serving two masters, Jesus illustrates what is meant by singleness of devotion. There can be only one fundamental and all-absorbing attachment for man: either God or mammon. While Jesus never defines what is involved in repentance, he describes it vividly in his parables of the prodigal son, and of the publican and the Pharisee. It involves a profound inner experience which is more than a feeling of shame or of insufficiency and is primarily a recognition of the forgiving quality of God's mercy and love never previously recognized. Without making calculations or comparisons, man is drawn by the Father's love and, as a consequence, finds both love and life. The son who was formerly lost and dead is now found and alive. A second attitude which reflects man's singleness of devotion to God is faith. As a dependent child may trust his father to give him things that are needful for his well-being, how much more may he trust in God, who will take care of the needs of his children (Matt. 7:9-11)? Implicit in these parables is man's attitude of love and devotion. A number of parables are dramatic illustrations of the necessity for absolute obedience to the Father's or the Master's will (e.g., Matt. 21:28-30; Luke 19:12-27).

The parables also clarify what obedience means with regard to concrete attitudes and acts toward one's fellow man. As God attempts to break down all barriers of hostility erected by men against him, so man is to reflect this same quality of love and mercy toward his fellow man (Matt. 18:23-35; Luke 10:30-37; and the parabolic sayings in Matt. 5:38-42, which the evangelist has transformed into rules for the Christian community). No boundaries are to limit the expression of constructive and creative good will for the neighbor. While Jesus' parables reveal his creativity in using this literary form, it is even more significant that they present a challenging and enduring religious and ethical outlook. On this subject *see also* TEACHING OF JESUS.

Bibliography. A. T. Cadoux, *The Parables of Jesus* (1931); C. H. Dodd, *The Parables of the Kingdom* (1936); W. O. E. Oesterley, *The Gospel Parables in the Light of Their Jewish Background* (1936); J. Jeremias, *The Parables of Jesus* (trans. S. H. Hooke; 1954). L. MOWRY

PARACLETE păr'ə klēt [παράκλητος]. Transliteration of a Greek word whose basic meaning is "one called to the side of" and which combines this passive sense (thus signifying one who stands by to aid and succor) with active extensions of it, thus denoting one who pleads as an "advocate" (I John 2:1) for someone, and so convinces and convicts, and also one who as a "counselor" (KJV "comforter"; John 14:16, 26; 15:26; 16:7) exhorts, strengthens, and comforts another.

The term is applied to Jesus Christ in I John 2:1. Here it indicates his function as the representative of his people who makes intercession for them with the Father. As "righteous" (cf. the description of the Servant of the Lord in Isa. 53:11), he establishes a right relationship for his people with God, being himself the expiation for their sins. Through Christ the barrier, interposed by sin, between man and God is done away, and fellowship between them is established. Thus Christ is the "advocate" who pleads for men and represents them toward God. His function as "paraclete" is identical with his high-priestly office as expounded by the Letter to the Hebrews (cf. especially Heb. 7:25-28).

In the Fourth Gospel, Jesus promises that in answer to his prayer the Father will give his disciples "another paraclete" ("Counselor"; KJV "Comforter"). This is the Holy Spirit, whose function is thus said, by implication, to be identical with that of Christ, but who is yet distinguished from him. The use of masculine pronouns and adjectives (John 14:16: "another"; 14:26: "he"; 16:13: "he") shows that the Spirit is regarded as fully personal; indeed, the "paraclete" passages of the Fourth Gospel mark the most highly developed thought in the NT in respect of the personality of the Spirit of God. The Paraclete is pre-eminently the revealer of Christ to believers and the witness to him, in various ways, to disciples and to the world. He is the Spirit of truth (John 14:16-17), who is the guide to Christ, who is himself the truth (vs. 6). As the revealer of Christ he takes the place of the physical presence of the incarnate Word, and is in this sense "another paraclete" (vs. 16), being present at the side of Christ's followers. The Spirit will belong to all who are disciples of Christ and keep his commandments, being with them as an indwelling personal presence (vss. 17, 20-24). It is through the Spirit that Christ will be known and manifested, and the presence of Christ through the medium of the Spirit is very closely associated with his return to his disciples in the postresurrection appearances (14:18; 16:16; cf. 20:22).

This connection of the Resurrection with the revelation of Christ through the Paraclete is fundamental to Johannine theology, and is affirmed, explicitly or by implication, throughout the NT. The coming of the indwelling Spirit to Christ's followers is dependent upon, and consequent upon, the completion of the saving work of Christ himself in his death and resurrection, which together signify his exaltation (cf. 7:39). Hence the coming and the work of the Paraclete are spoken of in the future tense throughout, and the promise of the gift of "another Counselor" is fulfilled only when the dead and glorified Christ breathes the indwelling Spirit upon his disciples in a new act of creation (20:22). The coming of the Paraclete is therefore conditional upon the departure of Jesus, the removal of whose physical presence will enable his followers to receive through him the Spirit, who was not present during the earthly ministry of the Lord (7:39).

For the Fourth Gospel, as for Paul, the indwelling of the Spirit is the basic principle of life "in Christ." The union of Christ with the Father is to be extended to the believer through the return of Christ after death, by which are indicated both his postresurrection appearances and his continuing presence through the medium of the Spirit. It is the work of the indwelling Paraclete to reveal Christ—i.e., to enable his followers, individually and corporately, to apprehend the true meaning of Christ's person and understand the significance of his deeds and words. Through the Spirit, Christians will have all that Christ said to them brought to their remembrance (14:26). It is from this standpoint that the Fourth Gospel is written; the author believes that through the work of the Spirit in the church it is possible to know Christ far more fully and adequately than he could be known by those who only saw him in the days of his earthly life. The Paraclete speaks of Christ. Christ is, in fact, the total content of the Paraclete's revelation to believers.

His task is thus to present the glorified Christ to men, and to unfold the meaning of what was once for all enacted by him in the gospel events. He will guide Christians into all the truth; but though he gives fresh understanding, the truth itself has already been revealed, for the truth is Christ (cf. 16:13-15). The Paraclete's witness to Christ reveals his true significance; it vindicates him to the world, convicting the world of sin in rejecting Christ, attesting Christ's vindication by the Father, and manifesting his final condemnation of the devil (16:8-11). This witness is the content of the apostolic testimony. It is the Paraclete who will inspire the preaching of Christ's disciples and enable them to testify to him; and their testimony, which is that of the Paraclete himself, is directly related to martyrdom and the confession of Christ under persecution (15:26–16:4). In the emphasis which it lays on this aspect of the work of the Spirit, the Fourth Gospel echoes a favorite theme of the Synoptists (cf. Mark 13:11; Luke 12:8-12).

See also RESURRECTION IN THE NT; CHRIST; HOLY SPIRIT.

Bibliography. H. B. Swete, *The Holy Spirit in the NT* (1910); C. K. Barrett, "The Holy Spirit in the Fourth Gospel," *JTS*, vol. I (1950); J. G. Davies, "The Primary Meaning of παράκλητος," *JTS*, vol. IV (1953). G. W. H. LAMPE

PARADISE [פרדס; παράδεισος; Old Pers. *pairidaēza*, enclosure *or* wooded park]. A word meaning "park" or "garden" used, in some Jewish circles, to identify the Garden of Eden and the abode of the righteous beyond death which was associated with that garden. The term bears this meaning in its three NT occurrences (Luke 23:43; II Cor. 12:3; Rev. 2:7).

1. The word. "Paradise" was an Old Persian word that achieved international circulation, appearing in Hebrew, Aramaic, and Greek. In Hebrew and Aramaic it was used substantially in its original sense of "park" or "garden," without special religious connotation. It occurs three times in the Hebrew OT (Neh. 2:8; Eccl. 2:5; Song of S. 4:13) and continued to be used in subsequent rabbinic literature (e.g., Sanh. X.6; T.B. Soṭ. 10*a*). Its occurrence in T.B. Ḥag. 14*b* and parallels, as a term for the heavenly Garden of Eden, is exceptional.

In Greek literature παράδεισος appeared with the writings of Xenophon and was adopted by the language in its meaning of "park" or "garden." The Hebrew word for GARDEN was translated in the LXX sometimes by παράδεισος and sometimes by another Greek word κῆπος. However, in Gen. 2–3 παράδεισος was used exclusively and repeatedly for the original Garden of Eden. Presumably because of this identification, some circles in Judaism came to regard παράδεισος as a standard name for that garden —e.g., Philo (but not Josephus). After belief arose in an abode for the righteous beyond death, this abode was identified with the Garden of Eden and the name παράδεισος applied to this further development, as in I Enoch 20:7; Pss. Sol. 14:2; Test. Levi 18:10; Sibylline Fragment 3:48; IV Ezra 3:6; II Enoch 8:1-6; II Bar. 4:2-7; 59:8; repeatedly in the Apocalypse of Moses and the Books of Adam and Eve.

2. The Jewish background. According to traditional Hebrew theology the dead descended to SHEOL, where life was shadowy and distinctions between the good and the evil negligible. *Ca.* 200 B.C. this view was drastically modified by the emergence of belief in the RESURRECTION of the dead, or at least some of the dead (cf. Isa. 26:19; Dan. 12:2-3). While speculation flourished, there was a growing consensus that the abode of the righteous after their resurrection would be the Garden of Eden, or, as some called it, "Paradise." The corresponding place for the wicked was GEHENNA. Frequently the two were paired—e.g., T.B. Soṭ. 22*a:* "Lord of the Universe! Thou hast created the Garden of Eden and Gehenna; Thou hast created the righteous and the wicked"; II Esd. 7:36: "The furnace of Gehenna shall be made manifest, and over against it the Paradise of delight."

But what of the dead between the moment of death and their final resurrection? This question was finding an answer at the beginning of the Christian era. The older view of a Sheol without distinctions was replaced by that of a segregated Sheol in which the righteous were separated from the wicked. Finally the righteous were moved out of Sheol into the Garden of Eden, or Paradise.

At this point "Paradise" was used in three ways. It could refer to (*a*) the original Garden of Eden of Gen. 2–3; (*b*) that garden as the abode of the righteous dead prior to their resurrection; or (*c*) that garden as the eternal home of the righteous. This does not mean that there was more than one Paradise but rather that Paradise had three stages in its history. It fulfilled different functions in different periods. There was a notable lack of agreement as to the geographical location of Paradise during the second and third stages. For some it was on earth, for others in HEAVEN (cf. the "third heaven" of Apoc. Moses 40:2; III Bar. 4:8; II Cor. 12:2-3). For obvious reasons the "tree of life" (Gen. 2:9 ff) acquired particular significance in the descriptions of Paradise as the abode of the righteous dead (cf. Test. Levi 18:10; I Enoch 25:4-5; IV Ezra 8:52; Apoc. Moses 13:2-3; 28:4; Rev. 2:7).

3. The NT passages. The NT passages may be considered in the light of this summary of Jewish thought. In Luke 23:43 Jesus is reported to have said to the penitent thief: "Truly, I say to you, today you will be with me in Paradise." Attempts have been made to transfer the "today" of this saying to the introductory formula—i.e., "Truly, today I say to you . . . ." This would permit harmonization with belief in the DESCENT INTO HADES between Good Friday and Easter (cf. Eph. 4:8 ff[?]; I Pet. 3:19). However, a survey of the many other occurrences of this introductory formula in the gospels suggests that whatever follows the words "Truly, I say to you," is always part of the statement and not of the formula. The reference to ABRAHAM'S BOSOM in Luke 16:22-31 confirms the view that Jesus, or at least Luke, assumed the entrance of the righteous into paradise at death. It has been suggested that if these are even approximately the words of Jesus, they could originally have presupposed an immediate PAROUSIA, in which case the reference could be to the final Paradise. Clearly this cannot be the meaning in the present context.

In II Cor. 12:1-4 Paul relates an experience in which he visited Paradise—in or out of the body—and received a revelation. If, as is probable, vs. 3 parallels vs. 2, then he locates Paradise in the third heaven (*see* § 2 *above*). While describing his experience as a "revelation of the Lord," Paul leaves it uncertain whether he saw the Lord in Paradise or whether the Lord granted the revelation without himself being present. Preponderant NT usage favors the former view. If this is correct, then Paul thought of the righteous dead as already living in Paradise with the Lord. This is in harmony with such passages as II Cor. 5:8; Phil. 1:23, though at an earlier stage Paul apparently assumed the believing dead were not reunited with the Lord until the Parousia. The awesome character of Paul's experience is reminiscent of T.B. Ḥag. 14*b*, in which it is asserted that four rabbis were temporarily translated into Paradise but only one, Rabbi Akiba, returned unharmed.

In Rev. 2:7 the church of Ephesus is encouraged with the words: "To him who conquers I will grant to eat of the tree of life, which is in the paradise of God." Did the writer expect this promise to be fulfilled at death or at the resurrection? The latter is more probable, since the parallels in the other letters of Rev. 2–3 point toward the end of history. Furthermore, eating of the tree of life was traditionally associated with the final deliverance (cf. Rev. 22; Test. Levi 18:10 ff; I Enoch 25:4-5; IV Ezra 8:52; Apoc. Moses 13:2 ff; 28:3-4. However, Revelation explicitly teaches that at least some of the righteous enter a heavenly abode prior to the final resurrection (cf. 6:9-11; 7:9-17), even though the tree of life may be reserved for the postresurrection period.

While only the three passages we have noted use the term "Paradise," there are numerous others which refer to the existence of the righteous beyond death—e.g., Mark 12:18-27 and parallels; Luke 16: 9, 19-31; Rev. 6:9-11; 7:9-17 (*and see below*). It is clear that in the NT, as in the Judaism of the period, beliefs were in transition, and conflicting traditions supplied the language for eschatology—e.g., some NT passages may have presupposed the descent of the righteous to Sheol at death (cf. Matt. 12:40; Acts 2:24-32; I Thess. 4:13-16; Rev. 20:13). Yet the presence of divergent language is evidence not so much of inconsistency as of an awareness that all such language is symbolic and can at best only point in the direction of the final reality. While the details of the future life are not clear, it is characteristic of the Christ-centered NT faith that its confidence in life beyond death is based upon Christ's resurrection and, further, that this future life is most frequently described as life with Christ (John 12:26; 14:2-3, 18 ff; 16:16 ff; Acts 7:59; Rom. 6:8-11; 8:17, 29; 14: 7-9; II Cor. 4:14; 5:8; Phil. 1:21-23; I John 2:28; 3:2; Rev. 7:17; 20:4; 21:23-24; 22:3-5). The dominant NT belief concerning the eschatology of the individual is adequately summarized by Paul's words: "I am sure that neither death, nor life, nor angels, nor principalities, nor things present, nor things to come, nor powers, nor height, nor depth, nor anything else in all creation, will be able to separate us from the love of God in Christ Jesus our Lord" (Rom. 8:38-39).

Bibliography. G. F. Moore, *Judaism*, II (1927), 389 ff; H. L. Strack and P. Billerbeck, *Kommentar zum NT aus Talmud und Midrasch*, IV (1928), 1118 ff; H. Bietenhard, *Die himmlische Welt im Urchristentum und Spätjudentum* (1951), pp. 161 ff.

H. K. MCARTHUR

PARADOX. Biblical forms of paradox are the exaggerated expressions of concepts which, though contrary to fact and often absurd, contain an element of truth. Hence paradoxes are frequently associated with hyperboles and are used primarily by Jesus to communicate the radical and intense seriousness of his outlook. Thereby he sharpens the cutting edge of an idea, whether in debates with opponents or in conversations with men whose lives still lack commitment.

Paradoxical indictments directed against the Pharisees accused them of straining out gnats and swallowing camels (Matt. 23:24) and of seeing specks in their neighbors' eyes while ignoring logs in their own (Matt. 7:3-5). Whether the saying about giving and taking (Mark 4:25) is a part of his polemic caricature of the Pharisees' lack of perspective and inability to differentiate between essentials and nonessentials is difficult to ascertain, because of the varied contexts given to this paradox by the evangelists (Matt. 13:12; 25:29; Luke 8:18; 19:26).

Jesus also uses paradoxical statements to make more bold and incisive the significance to men of the imminent arrival of the kingdom of God. The coming of the kingdom should alter men's duties and vocations. "It is easier for a camel to go through the eye of a needle than for a rich man to enter the kingdom of God" (Mark 10:25) is a thrust at the complacency of the rich. The demands made of those who seek to commit their lives more specifically to the kingdom are expressed in such statements as: "Leave the dead to bury their own dead" (Matt. 8:22). By losing their lives in dedicated service, men find life (Matt. 10:39), and by serving the needs of others they find greatness (Mark 10:43). This paradoxical idea is basic to Paul's religious life, for he found that to be a slave of Christ and to serve his fellow men with love brought a freedom formerly unknown.

L. MOWRY

PARAH pâr'ə [פרה, heifer, young cow]. One of the villages in the inheritance of Benjamin (Josh. 18:23), located some 5½ miles NE of Jerusalem. The site is represented by the modern Khirbet el-Farah near the copious spring 'Ain Farah, from which water is supplied to the Old City of Jerusalem. It is conceivable, also, that here was *Parath* (translated

From *Atlas of the Bible* (Thomas Nelson & Sons Limited)

21. 'Ain Farah, which supplies water for present-day Jerusalem; near the spring is Khirbet el-Farah (Parah).

"Euphrates") of Jer. 13:4-7, at which place the prophet made symbolic use of his waistcloth.

Fig. PAR 21. W. H. Morton

PARALIPOMENON păr'ə lĭ pŏm'ə nŏn. Douay Version form of Chronicles.

PARALYSIS, PARALYTIC. *See* Disease §§ 3-4.

PARAN pâr'ən [פארן]. A wilderness in which the Israelites camped after they left Mount Sinai (Num. 10:11-12), and which they reached after Hazeroth (12:16). Moses sent out spies to explore Canaan from the Wilderness of Paran (13:3); and they returned there, to Kadesh (vs. 26), after completing their task. Deut. 1:22 states that the spies were sent out specifically from Kadesh-barnea, which indicates that the encampment of the Israelites was at Kadesh-barnea, and that this locality was within the territory of the Wilderness of Paran. Since the objective of the spies was the exploration of S Canaan, the Wilderness of Paran must be located in the vicinity of its S border, and W of Edom, and N of the Wilderness of Sinai.

While the itinerary of the Israelites as given in Num. 33 does not mention the Wilderness of Paran —it mentions only the Wilderness of Zin (*see* Zin, Wilderness of), identifying it with Kadesh (Num. 33:36)—the LXX identifies Kadesh with the Wilderness of Paran: "They journeyed from the Wilderness of Sin [the LXX has Σὶν for both Sin, סין, and Zin, צן] and encamped in the Wilderness of Paran (that is, Kadesh)." Such identification is not made anywhere else. The LXX reading also places the Wilderness of Paran after the Wilderness of Sin, which makes the location of Paran more complicated.

The name Paran appears also in several other passages: Gen. 14:6; 21:21; Deut. 33:2; I Sam. 25:1; I Kings 11:18; Hab. 3:3. The Deuteronomy and Habakkuk passages are poetic and deal with the theophany of God. Here Paran is referred to as Mount Paran (הר פארן), and both passages are similar in thought, but not in expressions, to Judg. 5:4-5; Ps. 68:7-8. God of Israel comes forth from his habitation which is variously referred to as Sinai, Seir, Teman, the region of Edom, and Paran (all located in the same general direction from Palestine), to save his people from oppression.

The following four references are pertinent to the location or extent of Paran:

a) In Gen. 14:5-7 the expression "El Paran" (איל פארן) is used in describing the geographical limit of the conquest of Edom by Chedorlaomer and his allies; they conquered "as far as El-paran on the border of the wilderness," and then turned back and came to En-Mishpat, identified with Kadesh. From this description, El Paran must be located in the neighborhood of Seir and Kadesh, "on the border of the wilderness." This wilderness may be the same which is referred to in the journey of the Israelites as the "wilderness of Paran."

b) In Gen. 21:21, Ishmael's dwelling place is called the "wilderness of Paran," which, from the rest of the context, appears to adjoin or extend into the Wilderness of Beersheba and perhaps to reach in the direction of Egypt, whence Hagar obtained a wife for him.

c) According to I Sam. 25:1, after Samuel died, David "rose and went down to the wilderness of Paran." Since the LXX B has Μαάν and the LXX A has Φαράν, the occurrence of "Paran" in the above passage has been questioned, because (*a*) this would place the activity of David too far S, and out of the territory of Judah, and (*b*) the narrative after vs. 1 deals with a man from Maon. In any event, if "Paran" is the correct reading, then the Wilderness of Paran reached into the S part of Judah.

d) I Kings 11:18 contains the narrative of the successful escape of Hadad the Edomite from Joab's slaughter. Hadad and his retinue fled from Edom to Midian, and from there they passed through Paran to Egypt. This would place the location of Paran in the general direction of SW of Edom and W of Midian.

Bibliography. N. Glueck, "Explorations in Eastern Palestine," *AASOR,* XV (1935), 104, 138; XVIII-XIX (1939), 83, 91, 265. W. F. Albright, *Recent Discoveries in Bible Lands* (1955), p. 75. E. G. Kraeling, *Bible Atlas* (1956), pp. 64, 67, 116, 189.

J. L. Mihelic

PARAPET [מעקה, to check] (Deut. 22:8); KJV BATTLEMENT. A railing about a roof to check people from falling. As houses had flat roofs, people might easily be on them. It was prescribed that in building a new House a parapet must be made for the roof so that bloodguilt might not be brought on the house by someone's falling from the roof.

PARBAR pär'bər [פרבר] (I Chr. 26:18). A word referring to a room, or more likely to a section of the courtyard not covered by a roof, on the W side of the temple area, which, from the fifth century on(?), was presumably designated for the waste from sacrifices. With respect to location, it corresponds to the area called בנין, "the building," behind the temple in the vision of Ezekiel (41:12). Although it is not absolutely undisputed, this non-Hebraic word must probably be connected with the plural פרורים in II Kings 23:11. The פרורים there are the roofed-over areas for chariots and horses of Shamash (from the time of Manasseh).

"Parbar" occurs in an Aramaic-Lydian inscription from Sardis as the open anteroom (vestibule?) of a tomb. It is still unclear whether it can be connected with the Babylonian *ê-bar-bar,* Egyptian *pr wr,* or Iranian *frabada.*

Bibliography. J. A. Montgomery, *Kings* (1951); W. Rudolph, *Chronikbücher* (1955). K. Galling

PARCHED GRAIN [קלי, קלוי, קליא, something roasted; Apoc. ἄλφιτον]; KJV PARCHED CORN. A food eaten by all people (Lev. 23:14; Josh. 5:11; I Sam. 17:17; Jth. 10:5), from the harvest worker (Ruth 2:14) to the king (II Sam. 17:28; cf. I Sam. 25:18). It was prepared either by roasting grains of wheat in a pan or simply by holding a small bundle of wheat in the fire.

See also Cereals.

Bibliography. E. Robinson, *Later Biblical Researches in Palestine* (1856), p. 393; W. M. Thomson, *The Land and the Book,* II (1859), p. 510. J. F. Ross

PARCHMENT [περγαμηνή, μεμβράνας] (II Tim. 4:13). A writing material made from the skins of sheep or goats, which gradually supplanted papyrus because of its durability. Eumenes II of Pergamum (197-158 B.C.) is said to have been responsible for its production, hence its name, derived from περγαμηνή, "of Pergamum."

The hair was removed from the skins by soaking them in lime and scraping them; then they were washed, dried, and stretched out on frames, and finally rubbed smooth with fine chalk and pumice stone. Thus parchment differs from leather in not being tanned. A superior quality of parchment known as vellum was made from the skin of calves or kids. *See* Writing and Writing Materials.

The reference to parchments (μεμβράνας) in II Tim. 4:13 is obscure, especially as they are singled out for special mention, and scholars are divided as to their nature. That they were copies of the Greek OT is unlikely. Other suggestions are that they were documents of Roman citizenship, or merely blank sheets of parchment for future use. R. J. Williams

PARENTS [γονεύς]. *See* Children; Family; Father; Mother.

PARK [פרדס, *pardēs, from* Pers. (Avestan) *pairidaēza,* enclosure; *cf.* παράδεισος, paradise, *and possibly* Akkad. *pardīsu,* park] (Eccl. 2:5). Alternately: FOREST (Neh. 2:8); ORCHARD (Song of S. 4:13). A wooded enclosure.

PARLOR. KJV translation of:

a) חדר (I Chr. 28:11; RSV "chamber"), an inner room of the temple.

b) לשכה (I Sam. 9:22; RSV "hall"), a room in which the sacrificial meals were held at the high place.

c) עליה (Judg. 3:20, 23-25; RSV "roof chamber"), a room in Ehud's palace. *See* House.

PARMASHTA pär măsh'tə [פרמשתא] (Esth. 9:9). One of the ten sons of Haman.

Bibliography. On the relevant textual and etymological problems, see L. B. Paton, *Esther,* ICC (1908), pp. 71, 284.

PARMENAS pär'mə nəs [Παρμενᾶς, *perhaps contracted from* Παρμενίδης, steadfast] (Acts 6:5). One of the Seven selected by the church in Jerusalem to assist the apostles.

PARNACH pär'năk [פרנך, Pharnaces(?), *from* Pers.] (Num. 34:25). The father of the Zebulunite leader Elizaphan, who was selected to help superintend the distribution of W Jordanian Canaan among the tribes to occupy that territory.

Bibliography. M. Noth, *Die israelitischen Personennamen* (1928), pp. 8, 64. R. F. Johnson

PAROSH pâr'ŏsh [פרעש, flea; Apoc. Φόρος]; KJV PHAROSH fâr'— in Ezra 8:3; KJV Apoc. PHOROS fôr'əs. The name of two persons in the postexilic era. Earlier the word in its literal sense, translated "flea," was used as a figure of insignificance in I Sam. 24:14; 26:20.

1. Head of a postexilic family (Ezra 2:3; 8:3; 10:25; Neh. 3:25; 7:8; I Esd. 5:9; 8:30; 9:26).

2. A chief who set his seal to the covenant in the time of Ezra (Neh. 10:14). E. R. Achtemeier

PAROUSIA pə rōō'zhĭ ə [παρουσία, presence, *then* arrival *or* coming]. A Greek word transliterated and adopted as a technical term for the future, eschatological coming of Christ (*see* Eschatology). This usage is derived from the sixteen NT occurrences of the term in this sense.

1. The word
2. Hebrew-Jewish background
3. Other relevant terms
4. The NT teaching
  a. In the letters of Paul
  b. In Acts and the Synoptic gospels
  c. In the Johannine literature
  d. In Hebrews
  e. In other NT books
5. Further observations
Bibliography

1. The word. "Parousia" was used in classical and Koine Greek in the general sense of "presence" but also of "arrival" or "coming." It occurs four (five?) times in the LXX with these meanings (Neh. 2:6 [text?]; Jud. 10:18; II Macc. 8:12; 15:21; III Macc. 3:17). Of the twenty-four occurrences in the NT, six are of this type—e.g., I Cor. 16:17: "I rejoice at the coming of Stephanas and Fortunatus and Achaicus" (see also II Cor. 7:6-7; 10:10; Phil. 1:26; 2:12). However, in Hellenistic literature the term was frequently used in connection with the official visit of a ruler or the epiphany of a deity—e.g., Polyb. XVIII.48.4: "that they might not think he was . . . looking forward to the coming of Antiochus"; Diod. IV.3.3: "while the matrons . . . offer sacrifices to the god and celebrate his mysteries and, in general, extol with hymns the presence of Dionysius." From this custom a quasi-technical usage of the term arose which is reflected in the majority (eighteen) of the NT passages. Except for II Thess. 2:9: "the coming of the lawless one" (*see* ANTICHRIST), and possibly II Pet. 1:16 (the first coming?), these passages refer to the coming of Christ at the end of history (cf. Matt. 24: 3, 27, 37, 39; I Cor. 15:23; I Thess. 2:19; 3:13; 4:15; 5:23; II Thess. 2:1, 8; Jas. 5:7-8; II Pet. 3:4, 12 [day of God]; I John 2:28). The eschatological usage may have been created by the Christian community—if Test. Levi 8:15; Test. Judah 22:2 are of Christian origin. (The term does not occur in Philo, and Josephus does not use it eschatologically, though he does use it with reference to divine manifestations—e.g., Antiq. III.v.2). It should be noted that the phrase "SECOND COMING" does not occur until Justin Martyr.

2. Hebrew-Jewish background. The OT people, whose national consciousness was shaped by the "mighty acts" of the Exodus, awaited a further divine deliverance in the future. This expectation is referred to in OT passages describing the DAY OF THE LORD or the "latter days," "that day," etc. During the intertestamental period this many-colored hope was modified by apocalyptic thought (*see* APOCALYPTICISM) and by the increasingly widespread belief in a personal MESSIAH as the agent of God's deliverance. No single pattern of messianic expectation emerged. Some leaders regarded him as the reviver of the Davidic dynasty (e.g., Pss. Sol. 17–18); to others he was the apocalyptic SON OF MAN; still others expected no personal messiah at all. Political, ethical, and apocalyptic ideas mingled in confusing fashion. The common factor was belief in a divine, eschatological intervention to occur at the end of history. While NT faith asserted that in Jesus the Messiah had already come, it awaited his further coming in glory—i.e., the Parousia—and regarded this expectation as the continuation of the OT hope.

3. Other relevant terms. Any study of the parousia concept must include consideration of other NT terms which express the same idea. Thus the OT "day of the Lord" and related phrases reappear in varying NT forms with reference to Christ: "day of the Lord" in I Cor. 1:8 ("day of our Lord Jesus"); 5:5; I Thess. 5:2; II Thess. 2:2; II Pet. 3:10, 12 ("day of God"); "day(s) of the Son of man" in Luke 17:22, 24, 26, 30; "day of Christ (Jesus)" in Phil. 1:6, 10; 2:16; "day" in Acts 17:31; Rom. 2:5 ("day of wrath"); I Thess. 5:4; Heb. 10:25; "in that (those) day(s)" in Matt. 7:22; Mark 13:24; Luke 17:31; John 14:20(?); II Thess. 1:10; II Tim. 1:18; 4:8. (Clearly parallel passages in the Synoptics have not been quoted.) While some of these references do not speak explicitly of Christ, it is clear that his "coming" was part of the expected schedule for that final day.

None of the four occurrences of "revelation" (ἀποκάλυψις) in the LXX is eschatological, though the verb form does occur in such contexts—e.g., Isa. 56:1. However, seven of the eighteen NT occurrences are eschatological. Of these, five refer to the revelation of Christ at the end of history (I Cor. 1:7; II Thess. 1:7; I Pet. 1:7, 13; 4:13; cf. the verb in Luke 17:30; I Pet. 5:1). A similar use is made of the verb "to be manifested" (passive of φανερόω), which occurs four times with reference to Christ's coming (Col. 3:4; I Pet. 5:4; I John 2:28; 3:2). In Hellenistic Greek the related term "epiphany" (ἐπιφάνεια) was used for the manifestations of deities either in person or through their acts (see Diod. IV.3.2-3, where "epiphany" and "parousia" are used interchangeably). This development is reflected in II Macc. 2: 21; 3:24; 5:4; 12:22; 14:15; 15:27; III Macc. 2:9; 5:8, 51—though not in Philo or Josephus. In the NT "epiphany" is used with reference to Christ's earthly life in II Tim. 1:10, but elsewhere it is applied exclusively to his parousia (II Thess. 2:8; I Tim. 6:14; II Tim. 4:1, 8; Tit. 2:13; cf. II Clem. 12:1; 17:4).

It is only natural that the verb "to come" (ἔρχομαι) should be used frequently in eschatological passages, with or without supporting technical terms—e.g., Matt. 10:23; 25:31; Mark 8:38; 13:26; 14:62; Luke 12:40; 18:8; 23:42; John 14:3(?), 18(?); 28(?); 21:22; Acts 1:11; 3:20; I Cor. 4:5; 11:26; Rev. 1:7; 2:5(?), 16(?); 3:11, 20(?); 22:7, 12, 20, to mention only those not previously indicated. Other passages, not easily classified by terminology, are: Matt. 13:41(?); 19:28; Mark 10:37(?); 13:6(?); 14:28(?); Luke 12:8-9; 13: 35(?); 21:36; 22:28 ff; John 16:16 ff(?); I Cor. 16:22; II Cor. 4:14(?); 5:10(?); Eph. 1:10(?), 14(?); 4:30(?); Phil. 3:20-21; 4:5; I Thess. 1:9-10; 4:14, 16; II Tim. 2:11 ff(?); Heb. 9:28; 12:14(?); Jas. 5:9; I Pet. 1:11; 4:5; Jude 21(?), 24(?); Rev. 2:25; 3:3; 19:11–20:10.

Possibly passages referring to the coming of the KINGDOM OF GOD should be included here, since Jesus may have expected the arrival of the kingdom at the Parousia, contrary to the interpretation of scholars who assert that the kingdom arrived during Jesus' ministry. This controversy can only be alluded to here.

4. The NT teaching. In general the NT writers expected an imminent, dramatic, visible return of Christ to usher in the New Age. The work begun in his ministry, death, and resurrection was to culminate in his triumphant parousia. This may be documented by a survey of the major divisions of NT literature.

a. In the letters of Paul. Nearly every letter of the Pauline corpus witnesses to the parousia expectation. I Thessalonians, probably his earliest extant letter, returns repeatedly to this hope. Its centrality for Paul's missionary preaching is indicated in 1:9-10. Other references are: 2:19; 3:13; 4:13–5:10; 5:23. Christians are comforted about their dead, not with the promise that at death they enter into God's presence, but rather with the hope of the Parousia, which is to occur in that generation (4:15, 17). This basic pattern is not changed by subsequent minor modifications: II Thess. 2 lessens the sense of imminence; I Cor. 15 and II Cor. 5 raise questions, by implication, concerning the nature of the body with which Christ is to return; Phil. 1:23 suggests that Paul ceased to be confident he would survive until the Parousia and that he came to believe he would go to be "with Christ" immediately at death. But his basic confidence in the Parousia remained unshaken (cf. Rom. 2:16; 8:18 ff; 13:11; I Cor. 1:7; 4:5; 5:5; 11:26; 15:20-28, 51-57; 16:22; II Cor. 4:14[?]; Phil. 1:6, 10; 2:16; 3:20-21; 4:5; Col. 3:4; II Thess. 1:5-10; 2:1-12).

Explicit parousia references are lacking in Galatians, Philemon, and Ephesians, but only the silence of Ephesians is significant. It may be that the idea is implicit in Eph. 1:10,14, 18, 21; 4:30; 5:5-6; yet eschatology appears to have been eclipsed by ecclesiology. This may be an additional indication of non-Pauline authorship. The Pastorals, though presumably post-Pauline and presenting distinctive terminology, do not vary from the Pauline pattern (cf. I Tim. 6:14; II Tim. 1:18; 2:11 ff[?]; 4:1, 8; Tit. 2:13).

b. In Acts and the Synoptic gospels. Acts and the Synoptics confirm the view that the parousia expectation was vital to the early church and that it originated in the teaching of Jesus. For Acts, see 1:10-11; 3:20; 10:42-43; 17:31. The Synoptics present a more complicated problem, since the words of Jesus have been modified by later interpretations. However, the view that Jesus taught his imminent and essentially apocalyptic parousia is strongly supported by the appearance of such teaching in all strands of the Synoptic tradition (*see* SYNOPTIC PROBLEM): For Mark, see 8:38–9:1; 10:37; 13:6-7, 24 ff; 14:62. For Q, see Luke 12:8 ff, 39 ff; 13:35; 17:20-37; 22:28 ff (L?). For M, see Matt. 10:23; 13:40-41; 19:28(Q?); 25:31. For L, see Luke 12:35-38; 18:8; 21:36; 23:42.

While some of these passages are obviously creations of the early community, the cumulative mass of evidence cannot be ignored. (For divergent views *see* § 5 *below*.) Passages sometimes cited against the view that the Parousia was regarded as imminent are: Mark 2:19-20; 9:1; 13:9 ff, 32-37; 14:9; Matt. 10:17-18; 24:42; 25:13; Luke 12:39 ff; 17:22; I Cor. 11:25.

c. In the Johannine literature. The Johannine literature, taken as a whole, supports this same view of the Parousia, despite significant ambiguities in the gospel. Revelation is explicit (cf. 1–3; 19–22); imminence is stressed particularly in 1:1, 3; 6:10-11; 22:7, 10-12, 20. The new note is found in Rev. 20, where a temporary, messianic kingdom or MILLENNIUM is clearly taught. The present text of John's Gospel contains clear references to an eschatological *day* at the end of history (cf. 5:28-29; 6:39-40, 44, 54; 12:48; 21:22-23). These references indicate that the author presupposed the parousia of Christ, and this view is confirmed by I John 2:28; 3:2. Yet some of the most significant passages in the gospel are ambiguous—e.g., 14:2 ff, 15-31; 15:26; 16:5-11, 16-24. Does the "coming" here referred to mean the resurrection appearances, the gift of the Spirit, the death of believers, or the eschatological parousia? Are passages such as 5:25-27; 11:25 ff intended as substitutes for the eschatological hope, or do they complement it? Is the gospel a unity? On any assumption, the future hope is here balanced by a present possibility which goes beyond Paul's concept of the "first fruits of the Spirit."

d. In Hebrews. Hebrews raises problems similar to those in John's Gospel. The eschatological expectation is explicitly stated and includes the Parousia (cf. 9:28; 10:25). Traces of this same pattern reappear in 1:2; 2:8*b;* 3:7 ff; 4:1 ff; 6:2; 9:26; 10:12-13, 27, 37; 11:40; 12:26 ff; 13:14. Yet the basic interest is in present possibilities. A "new and living way" has been opened into the heavenly sanctuary; it is for the believer to enter "now." (But 10:11-25 ends with an appeal based on the eschatological *day!*) Probably the author took the Parousia seriously, but, with the passing of time, was discovering new possibilities in the already present reality.

e. In other NT books. James in 5:7-9 expresses his confidence in the imminent parousia, though this emphasis is not dominant. The same faith is a more vital part of I Peter, where the thought is conditioned by this expectation (cf. 1:3-21; 4:5–5:11). Though obviously on the defensive, II Peter reaffirms the traditional view (cf. 1:16[?]; 3:1 ff). Even brief Jude has references which probably belong in this category (vss. 6, 21, 24).

It is significant that the only books of the NT without any reference to the Parousia or related events are the single-chaptered II and III John and Philemon, the somewhat longer Galatians, and, possibly, Ephesians. Clearly primitive Christianity was an eschatological faith, though a shift of emphasis is apparent in Ephesians, Hebrews, and John, while II Peter implies a rising skepticism, presumably within the Christian community itself.

5. Further observations. Roman Catholic and conservative Protestant scholars dissent from the general position presented above and insist that the NT writers did not teach an imminent parousia. Thus the Pontifical Biblical Commission in its reply of June 18, 1915, affirmed that even I Thess. 4:15-17 may be interpreted "without in any way involving the assertion that the Parousia was so near that the Apostle counted himself and his readers among the faithful who will be left alive and go to meet Christ." The idea of the Parousia itself is, of course, recognized and accepted by these groups.

Dominant Protestant scholarship assumes that the NT writers regarded the Parousia as imminent, but is divided as to the actual teaching of Jesus in this entire area. A few eliminate the Synoptic parousia passages entirely by a drastic use of the scissors of literary-historical criticism. Some of these scholars suggest that the teaching of Jesus about the coming of the kingdom was transformed by the early community into the parousia concept centering in Jesus himself. Others accept the parousia passages but deny that Jesus identified himself with the SON OF MAN who is referred to in most such passages. (The parousia passages without this ambiguity—e.g., Matt. 7:22-23; 24:3; Mark 10:37; 13:6; Luke 13:35; 22:28 ff—are not impressive, yet it is difficult to believe that Jesus did not identify himself with the Son of man, since all strands of the Synoptic tradition make this identification.) Still other scholars admit that Jesus spoke of his own parousia but deny that he stressed its imminence; they emphasize sayings indicating either a lapse of time or uncertainty as to the time (*see* § 4*b above*). (It may be observed that uncertainty as to the day and hour of one's death is not incompatible with the conviction that it will occur within a generation.) Again, others speak of a number of parousias—e.g., the resurrection appearances, the outpouring of the Spirit, the fall of Jerusalem, the death of the believer, and the end of history. By this device the predictions stressing imminence may be alleged to have found fulfilment at the designated time. While most of these, and other, divergent views merit serious discussion, they can only be listed here.

This article has been concerned with the interpretation of the NT texts in their first-century setting. The theological problem of the reinterpretation of the parousia concept deserves mention by way of conclusion. There are three basic possibilities: the entire eschatological pattern, of which the Parousia is a segment, may be regarded as part of the eternal Word and hence accepted with comparative literalness; the eschatological pattern may be discarded on the grounds that it was the temporal garb in which the eternal gospel appeared; or the eschatological pattern may be translated into other terms. The first of these possibilities has been adopted, with modifications, chiefly by Roman Catholic and conservative Protestant scholarship; the second received the support of the extreme wing of late nineteenth-century and early twentieth-century liberalism; the third has commanded the attention of the various "neo-theologies" of the twentieth century. No single, definite pattern has yet emerged. It may be assumed, however, that the main line of the Christian tradition will interpret the Parousia to mean, at least, that God will bring to perfect completion the work begun through Christ, and that the same Christ who stands at the center of Christian faith will also stand at the final boundary of human experience in time, in space, and in eternity.

Bibliography. A. Schweitzer, *The Mystery of the Kingdom of God* (English trans., 1925); A. Deissmann, *Light from the Ancient East* (rev. ed., 1927), pp. 368 ff; J. H. Moulton and G. Milligan, παρουσία, *The Vocabulary of the Greek Testament* (1930); C. H. Dodd, *The Parables of the Kingdom* (rev. ed., 1936); T. F. Glasson, *The Second Advent* (rev. ed., 1947); P. S. Minear, *Christian Hope and the Second Coming* (1954); O. Cullmann, "The Return of Christ," *The Early Church* (1956), pp. 141 ff; W. G. Kümmel, *Promise and Fulfilment* (1957).

H. K. McArthur

PARSHANDATHA pär shăn′də thə [פרשנדתא] (Esth. 9:7). One of the ten sons of Haman.

Bibliography. On the relevant textual and etymological problems, see L. B. Paton, *Esther,* ICC (1908), pp. 70, 284.

PARSIN. *See* Mene, Mene, Tekel, and Parsin.

PARTHIANS pär′thĭ ənz [Πάρθοι]. An Iranian tribal group. Among those who gathered in Jerusalem for the festival of Pentecost were the Parthians, along with the Medes, Elamites, and others (Acts 2:9-11).

Ca. the middle of the third century B.C. the Parthians claimed independence from the Seleucid rulers of Iran in their homeland, the ancient satrapy of Parthia (Old Persian *Parθava;* Greek Παρθία), to the SE of the Caspian Sea. Their rulers are known as Arsacids after the name of Arsaces, the founder of that dynasty. In the following centuries the Arsacids built an empire which stretched from the Euphrates to the Indus. One of its capitals was Ctesiphon on the Tigris River.

See also Persia, History and Religion of, § D5.

M. J. Dresden

PARTITION, MIDDLE WALL OF (KJV); RSV DIVIDING WALL OF HOSTILITY. In the description of the Herodian temple Josephus (War V.v.2) mentions a stone trellis three cubits high. It contained, he said, at intervals blocks of stone with

Courtesy of the Musées d'Archéologie d'Istanbul

22. Warning-stone from wall around inner courts of Herod's temple

inscriptions in Greek or Latin, by which all strangers were warned against stepping out of the Court of the Gentiles into the inner area (after the time of Antiochus III [Antiq. XII.iii.4] the Jews had the privilege of policing the temple). In 1871, Clermont-Ganneau found such a stone with a Greek inscription to the N of the temple area; in 1935 a fragment was found on the E slope of Haram. The text reads: "No non-Jew may walk through the trellis and the area of demarcation to the sanctuary. Whoever is caught must blame himself that the death penalty is carried out at once."* The statement of Eph. 2:14 that Jesus Christ broke down the "dividing wall of hostility" has been interpreted as a reference to the middle wall of partition in Jerusalem, but it is completely improbable that such an allusion would have been understandable to the Ephesians. Fig. PAR 22.

See also Temple, Jerusalem.

Bibliography. A. Deissmann, *Licht vom Osten* (4th ed., 1923), pp. 62-63; J. H. Iliffe, "The ΘΑΝΑΤΟΣ Inscription from Herod's Temple," *QDAP,* VI (1938), 1-3. K. Galling

PARTRIDGE [קרא, *qôrê* (I Sam. 26:20; Jer. 17:11; *cf.* Judg. 15:19), *possibly onomatopoeic, or* caller, *from* קרא, to call; πέρδιξ, *cf.* πέρδομαι, to break wind]. Any of various game birds of the subfamily *Phasianinae,* mostly of the genera *Alectoris* and *Ammoperdix.* Tristram states that the commonest partridge of Palestine is the chukar (probably *Alectoris graeca werae*), but that other varieties are found (*Alectoris graeca cypriotes, Ammoperdix heyi heyi*). The francolin (*Francolinus francolinus francolinus*), the black partridge of India, is also to be seen and heard in the lowland plains. In addition, Tristram tells of no fewer than four varieties of sand grouse (*Pteroclididae*).

It is conjectural that קרא refers either to the partridge or to one of the other birds mentioned above (*see* Fauna §B6*d*); the partridge conjecture, however, is supported by most of the ancient versions (but not by the LXX at I Sam. 26:20). It is commonly supposed that I Sam. 26:20 reflects the practice of hunting a bird by continuously chasing it; and this, in fact, was how, in Tristram's day, many partridges in Palestine were caught (cf. the use of a partridge as a decoy bird in Ecclus. 11:30). Jer. 17:11 may rest on a popular but erroneous belief that the partridge incubates eggs which she did not lay (cf. the Jewish Midrashic tradition on this point); this belief appears to be a misinterpretation of the fact that the chukar partridge lays two batches of eggs, one for herself and the second for the cock (*cf. bibliography*).

Bibliography. G. R. Driver, *PEQ* (May-Oct., 1955), p. 133.

W. S. McCullough

PARTY [αἵρεσις (Acts 5:17; 15:5; 26:5; Gal. 5:20)]. A word used in references to the Pharisees (Acts 15:5; 23:9; 26:5); the Sadducees (Acts 5:17); and the "circumcision party" (οἱ ἐκ περιτομῆς; Acts 11:2; Gal. 2:12; Tit. 1:10). The word αἵρεσις is translated in other passages by different English words—e.g., "sect" (Acts 24:14), "faction" (I Cor. 11:19), and "heresy" (questionably; II Pet. 2:1).

"Party" is sometimes used without reproach, as, e.g., of the Sadducees in Acts 5:17, and of the Pharisees in Acts 15:5; 26:5. In Gal. 5:20, however, where Paul lists "party spirit" (or, perhaps, "divisions") among the works of the flesh, "party" is a term of reproach.

The term "circumcision party" is used of certain Jewish Christians whose leader was James the Lord's brother, and who criticized Peter for having broken Jewish food laws when he ate with Gentiles. *See* Judaizing.

B. H. Throckmorton, Jr.

PARUAH pə ro͞o'ə [פרוח] (I Kings 4:17). The father of Jehoshaphat, who was one of the twelve commissariat prefects under Solomon with the territory of Issachar as his assigned district.

PARVAIM pär vā'əm [פרוים] (II Chr. 3:6). A region from which came a gold used in the temple of Solomon. According to rabbinic sources (Yom. 21*b;* Shir Hashirim Rabbah to Song of S. 3:10), it was of a reddish hue, and from it was made the vessel used by the high priest to remove the ashes from the altar of burnt offering on the Day of Atonement. Since gold was mined extensively in Arabia in ancient times, Parvaim was probably in that country; the most probable identification is with Sak el-Farwein in Yemama.

S. Cohen

PASACH pā'săk [פסך] (I Chr. 7:33). An Asherite; the first-born of Japhlet's three sons.

PASCHAL LAMB păs'kəl [τὸ πάσχα] (I Cor. 5:7). Paul's designation of Christ in relating the Death of Christ to the Jewish Passover.

PAS-DAMMIM păs dăm'ĭm [פס דמים] (I Chr. 11:13). The scene of one of David's victories. *See* Ephes-dammim.

PASEAH pə sē'ə [פסח, limper; Apoc. Φεσσά, Φισόν, Φασέα]; KJV PHASEAH fə— in Neh. 7:51; PHINEES fĭn'ĭ əs in I Esd. 5:31. A name suggesting, by its original meaning, that those bearing it were in some way lame.

1. A descendant of Judah; the son of Eshton (I Chr. 4:12).

2. Head of a family of temple servants who returned to Judah with Zerubbabel from the Exile (Ezra 2:49—Neh. 7:51; I Esd. 5:31).

3. The father of Joiada, who was one of the wall builders (Neh. 3:6).

E. R. Achtemeier

PASHHUR păsh'ər [פשחור, *perhaps from* פשח, be quiet, *and* סחור, round about (*cf.* Jer. 20:3), *or* Egyp. *Pš Ḥr;* Apoc. Φασσούρ]; KJV Apoc. PHAISUR fā'zər; PHASSARON făs'ə rŏn. **1.** Son of Immer, and chief officer in the Jerusalem temple during the last years of the monarchy. He was probably second only to the high priest and in charge of maintaining order. He beat Jeremiah and threw him in stocks, for which the prophet pronounced his judgment along with that of the nation (Jer. 20:1-6). The play on words in the Hebrew of vs. 3 is absent in the Greek and may show assimilation to vs. 10. This Pashhur may be identical with 2 *below.*

2. The father of Gedaliah, one of the princes during the reign of Zedekiah (Jer. 38:1).

3. Son of Malchiah, and prince under Zedekiah (Jer. 21:1; 38:1). He sought from Jeremiah an oracle of the Lord on the eve of the Babylonian siege and was given a prophecy of doom for the king (21:1 ff). Later he was in the princely audience which heard the prophet's advice to capitulate to the Babylonians (38:1). His descendant was among the priests of the restoration under Nehemiah (Neh. 11:12; cf. I Chr. 9:12).

4. Ancestor of one of the postexilic priestly families mentioned in the list of the returned exiles (Ezra 2:38; Neh. 7:41; I Esd. 5:25). Several of the members were among those who gave up their foreign wives (Ezra 10:22; I Esd. 9:22).

5. One of the priests of the restoration who attended the sealing of the covenant under Nehemiah (Neh. 10:3—H 10:4).

J. M. Ward

PASS [מעבר, מעברה, *from* עבר, cross over]. A passage, ravine, or narrow route through a mountainous region. Although the mountain passes near Megiddo, Shechem, Michmash, and elsewhere in Canaan were prominent features of the land, the pass of Michmash is the only one mentioned by this term in the OT by name (I Sam. 13:23; cf. 14:4, where the same topographical feature is intended, although the Hebrew plural מעברות is used [KJV "passages"]). Isa. 10:29 mentions the same pass (see "Michmash" in vs. 28).

A pass in the hill country might be called an ascent (מעלה) or a descent (מורד), such as the ascent of Beth-horon between the coastal plain and Jerusalem, the ascent of Adummim from the Jordan Valley to the hill country, the ascent of Akrabbim on the S border of Canaan. *See also* the ascent of Gur, of Luhith, and of Heres, the descent of Horonaim, etc.

W. L. Reed

*****PASSION, THE.** A term used in the translation of the phrase μετὰ τὸ παθεῖν αὐτὸν (Acts 1:3), in reference to Jesus' suffering and death. English translations, following Wyclif, are influenced by the Vulg. *post passionem suam,* "after his passion." Goodspeed translates, more literally, "after he had suffered." Prior to the Vulg., the apostolic fathers, especially Ignatius in his Letters, popularized the use of "passion" (πάθος) for the sufferings of Jesus. "Passion" was in common use by the middle of the third century. Subsequently the term acquired no exact definition. It is variously used to refer to the suffering of Jesus, to his crucifixion or death, to the section of the gospel narratives dealing with them, to the musical setting for these events, to the church's observance of the Sunday or the week preceding Holy Week. In general, "the Passion" is best taken in reference to the last two days of Jesus' life, including the Last Supper, the agony in Gethsemane, the arrest, trials, crucifixion, death, and burial.

Among the many NT references to Jesus' sufferings we may distinguish (*a*) those attributed to Jesus and (*b*) those about him. In the "passion sayings" Jesus thrice forecast to his disciples his suffering, death, and resurrection ([*a*] Mark 8:31-32; Matt. 16:21; Luke 9:22; [*b*] Mark 9:31-32; Matt. 17:22-23; Luke 9:43-45; [*c*] Mark 10:32-34; Matt. 20:17-19; Luke 18:31-34). After the Transfiguration he taught that the Son of man must suffer many things (Mark 9:12; Matt. 17:12; cf. Luke 17:25). At the Last Supper he desired the Passover before he suffered (Luke 22:15). His suffering is implied in his words about the bridegroom to be "taken" (Mark 2:20; Matt. 9:15; Luke 5:35); the constraint of a baptism (Luke 12:50); Jerusalem, where prophets perish (Luke 13:33); the slain son (Mark 12:8; Matt. 21:39; Luke 20:15); his body anointed for burial (Mark 14:8; Matt. 26:12). Glimpses of his purposes in the Passion appear in his life as a "ransom for many" (Mark 10:45; Matt. 20:28); his blood of the covenant is "poured out for many" (Mark 14:24; cf. Matt. 26:28: "for the forgiveness of sins"; Luke's longer text, 22:20: "poured out for you"); his necessary suffering is supported from scripture (Luke 24:27, 46); God's will must be done (Mark 14:36; Matt. 26:39; Luke 22:42).

Jesus' disciples, bewildered by his words about suffering, later gained insight from his death and resurrection; and from their faith they added explanations. Paul knew the wonder, the comfort, and the promise of sharing Christ's sufferings (Rom. 8:17; II Cor. 1:5; Phil. 3:10; Col. 1:24). He viewed Christ's resurrection as a sign of Christ's victory over suffering and death. As the believer shared Christ's death, he too arose to newness of life. The sufferings of Jesus appear also in the Letter to the Hebrews and in I Peter. In Hebrews, Jesus was made perfect through suffering (2:10); tested in sufferings, he can help others (2:18); he suffered once in sacrifice (9:26) outside the gate to consecrate people through his blood (13:12). The writer of I Peter claims to be an eyewitness of Jesus' suffering, which was predicted by scripture and rejoicingly shared by his followers (1:11; 4:13; cf. Acts 3:18; 17:3); though Christ's servants suffer unjustly, they must follow "in his steps" (I Pet. 2:21, 23).

The Passion requires some unity of thought and significance beyond a catalogue of NT references. Jesus anticipated his passion and found in it the deep mystery of God's will, in behalf of the sins of "many" (a Semitic expression [Isa. 53:12] for "everyone"). He looked for a kingdom beyond suffering. His first followers found in his passion a revelation of a merciful and forgiving Father. With joy they shared their sufferings in Christ, who was their example. Though he was the Lamb, slain for man's deliverance from sin, he was alive forevermore. The narrative of the Passion became the earliest and most significant nucleus around which the gospel was preached and the four gospels were composed.

Bibliography. On πάσχω, meaning "to suffer death" or "to endure suffering," see W. Michaelis, *TWNT,* V (1954), 910-18. See also: A. Schweitzer, *The Mysticism of Paul the Apostle* (trans. W. Montgomery; 1931), pp. 141-59; V. Taylor, *Jesus and His Sacrifice* (1937); K. Bornhäuser, *Die Leidens- und Auferstehungsgeschichte Jesu* (1947), pp. 11-128; G. S. Duncan, *Jesus, Son of Man* (1947), pp. 151-71; G. Schille, "Das Leiden des Herrn," *ZThK,* 50 (1955), 161-205.

D. M. Beck

PASSION OF PAUL. *See* Paul, Passion of.

PASSION OF PETER. *See* Peter, Passion of.

PASSION OF PETER AND PAUL. *See* Peter and Paul, Passion of.

PASSOVER AND FEAST OF UNLEAVENED BREAD. The first of the three great festivals in Israel's liturgical calendar, commemorating the deliverance from Egypt; observed in the spring.

1. Terminology
2. In the NT era
3. OT references
4. Current interpretations

Bibliography

1. Terminology. "Passover" is used both of the feast as a whole (Exod. 12:48, etc.) and of the sacrifice proper (Exod. 12:11, 27; Deut. 16:2; etc.). The Hebrew term translated "Passover" is פסח, "passing over"—i.e., "sparing" (Lev. 23:5; Num. 28:16; 33:3; Josh. 5:11; etc.). Etymologically, it may be related to the verb פסח, "to limp," referring to a ritual dance (cf. I Kings 18:21, 26). Other Hebrew terms are חג הפסח, "the Feast of the Passover" (Exod. 34:25; Ezek. 45:21) and זבח־פסח הוא ליהוה, "the sacrifice of the Lord's passover" (Exod. 12:11, 27; Num. 28:16).

In the LXX and the NT the term is τό πάσχα (cf. Aramaic פסחא), except in II Chronicles; Jer. 31:8—G 38:8, where φασέκ is used. The term φάσκα is found in Jos. Antiq. V.i.4; XIV.ii.1; XVII.ix.3; War II.i.3.

For "Feast of Unleavened Bread" the Hebrew term is חג המצות, "(the feast of) the unleavened loaves (or cakes)" (Exod. 12:17; 23:15; 34:18; etc.); the LXX and the NT use ἡ ἑορτὴ τῶν ἀζύμων.

In contemporary Judaism the word *Pēsaḥ,* or "Passover," is used to refer to the whole range of observances related to the season. This usage has been customary since *ca.* the second century of the Christian era. The tractate *Pēsaḥîm* (plural of *Pēsaḥ,* probably with reference to the individual sacrificial lambs; cf. II Chr. 35:7) in the Mishna both exemplifies and serves as basis for this custom. The single term serves as the title for all the festivities, including those observances which relate to unleavened bread, to which, indeed, the first three chapters of the tractate are devoted. Josephus refers to the "feast of unleavened bread" as the proper title for the whole; but in two places he adds the clause "which is called Passover," as if to indicate popular usage (Jos. War II.xiv.3; VI.ix.3; Antiq. XVII.ix.3; XX.v.3).

As the employment of the one title, Passover, indicates, the Mishna, like Josephus, treated all the observances as parts of a single integrated feast. This had not always been so. Earlier, in the OT, and into the NT as well, "Passover" and "feast of Unleavened Bread" (Mark 14:1) were both used with reference to the rites. Now one and now the other covered the entire sequence. But basically the Passover referred to the eve of the first day, the fourteenth day of the month (Lev. 23:5, etc.), on which the sacrifice of the Passover lamb took place, while the Feast of Unleavened Bread (Lev. 23:6, etc.) applied to the seven days following. This indicates a recollection that there were two separable units or feasts in the single complex of observances. But this distinction was not carefully kept (cf. Luke 22:7). Because the two observances fell at the same time, and also because Passover proper lasted only a single night, this was almost impossible. E.g., the removal of leaven had to be completed before the slaying of the Passover sacrifice took place (Deut. 16:4; Pes. 1.1-4); so that the Passover meal itself was also a meal of unleavened bread (Exod. 12:8); and the term "Passover" was used for all the festal days (Deut. 16:2-3; Ezek. 45:21-25).

Exod. 23:15, a part of what is probably the oldest extant liturgical calendar of Israel, speaks of the "feast of unleavened bread" (cf. Deut. 16:16). This statement has been pivotal in all research and discussion about the history of Israel's culture. The issue at stake is whether at the time of the framing of this calendar, assigned to the Yahwistic editor and placed in the early period of the monarchy, the Passover sacrifice was a part of the cultus of the community of Israel as a whole, and whether, indeed, it had ever been such. Beginning with Wellhausen, the widely accepted view has been that until the reformation of Josiah, and the Deuteronomic legislation related to it, Passover as distinct from Unleavened Bread was a domestic observance rather than a rite serving as a celebration of Israel's national history. This view interprets II Kings 21–23 to mean that Passover was not nationally celebrated in the monarchic period and questions the historical tenability of the implication that there were such national celebrations in the days of the judges. It also holds that a clause such as Exod. 34:25*b* represents a later interpolation into old accounts. This well-established view of the history of Passover is sharply challenged today, as will be seen below.

Amid all the uncertainty about the history of Passover and Unleavened Bread in Israel there is general agreement on two points: the feast contains two originally separate components; and both of these have a pre-Israelite history, Passover as a nomadic shepherds' rite and Unleavened Bread as a Canaanite agricultural feast. On the latter point scripture itself seems to substantiate this view, at least with respect to Passover. Moses asked the Pharaoh to let the children of Israel go so that they might keep a feast to the Lord in the wilderness (Exod. 5:1; 10:9). The plausible hypothesis derived from these statements is that this "feast" was the pre-Israelite form of Passover, probably a shepherds' festival. Thus Wellhausen made the statement that "the exodus is not the occasion of the festival, but the festival the occasion, if only a pretended one, of the exodus." The subsequent analysis of the history of the forms of the Israelite cultus has confirmed this view that Passover and also Unleavened Bread had a long history as cult forms before being adopted as such by Israel to serve in the celebration of Israel's historic deliverance from Egypt. All accounts of both as pre-Israelite rites must, however, in the nature of the case, be hypothetical reconstructions based on their form in Israel and on our knowledge of analogous observances in ancient Semitic culture.

The following discussion will begin with a brief description of the form and role of Passover in the NT era, especially as reflected in the Mishna. Next it will treat various aspects of the form and meaning of the feast in its earlier history as indicated by OT references to it. The quasi-sacramental role of the rite in the priestly religion will be noted, as well as its memorial function elsewhere. Finally there will be a brief account of the current efforts to give a new description of the history of the feast in Israel and, consequently, of the history of the religion of Israel.

2. In the NT era. Until the destruction of the temple in A.D. 70, Passover was a pilgrim festival. It shared this distinction with Weeks and Booths (*see* WEEKS, FEAST OF; BOOTHS, FEAST OF). In popularity and in the number of pilgrims, coming from all lands of the Diaspora, it was matched only by the latter. A realistic estimate has suggested that as many as 100,000 pilgrims may have come to Jerusalem annually for the feast. The figures cited by Josephus seem fabulous (War II.xiv.3; VI.ix.3); but his indication that disturbances involving the occupying power were likely to occur at the time of the feast is familiar because of similar NT references (Mark 15:6-15, etc.).

In comparison with Booths, Passover was a rather solemn feast. The observances of Passover Eve proper consisted of two parts: the ritual slaughter of the sheep and goats at the temple with the sacrificial sprinkling of the blood against the altar, and the domestic meal and its role of fellowship and historical commemoration. For the host of pilgrims without residence in the city, the procuring of a "room" (Mark 14:15) and the purchase of a sheep for sacrifice were the first important preparations upon arrival. The feast brought a great influx of trade to the sacred city. Wine and spices were needed for the feast; and many who came from abroad brought foreign wares for sale, resulting in a holiday "business rush" (cf. Matt. 21:12). The lamb and the room were procured by the head of a "company" or family groups. The minimum number permitted for a group was ten (Pes. 7.13 ff); often the companies were much larger. Since the entire sheep had to be eaten, its size corresponded to the size of the group. Every member had to eat an amount of the meat as large as an olive. In the case of very large companies, every member first received such a small token portion from the lamb of the sacrifice. Thereafter nonritual roasts were provided for the meal itself.

At the temple all twenty-four divisions of priests were in attendance, though normally there was only one. The first ceremonial action consisted in the removal of leaven. This was done in the morning, and its completion was indicated by the ritual burning of leaven by the priests. Work ceased at noon. The daily afternoon sacrifice at the temple was made an hour earlier than usual (Pes. 5.1). At about 3:00 P.M. the slaughtering of the Passover sacrifices began, announced by a threefold trumpet blast sounded by Levites. While some Levites sang the Hallel, others slew the sacrificial animals and bled them in gold or silver trays held by the priests. Then they flayed and dressed the animals. The priests meanwhile tossed the blood against the great altar and burned the portions of fat on the altar (Pes. 5.5-10). The tossing of the blood was the heart of the sacrificial action; originally it was probably a rite to protect, or substitute for, the first-born. But now it was a means of declaring or releasing the redeeming action of God for his whole people.

The dressed animals, with legs unbroken and head attached to the carcass, each wrapped in its own skin, were returned to the worshipers. Each company went to its house or room. The animal was spitted on a stick of pomegranate wood, with its head and legs folded into the cavity of the rump, and roasted in a portable clay oven.

The meal was served on low tables around which those who partook reclined on cushions (cf. Matt. 26:20), in the manner of a solemn banquet, and all were dressed in festive white. After the blessing the meal opened with a first glass of wine. This was followed by the eating of the lamb with bitter herbs dipped in *harosheth,* a paste of mashed fruits and nuts. Following a second glass of wine a designated "son" of the family asked the ceremonial question: "Why is this night different from all other nights?" This introduced the recital in song and story of the historical redemption of Israel from slavery in Egypt. It continued with the story of the subsequent crises and deliverances of Israel's long history and ended with a prayer for the redemption of the land from the occupying power of Rome. Following this prayer, which was later changed into a prayer for a return to Jerusalem, the formal commemoration was over. Gatherings could continue informally or members of one group could leave to greet those of another, groups having been kept carefully separate up to this point (Pes. 9.10).

With the destruction of the temple, Passover ceased as a sacrificial rite; as a sacred commemoration of God's redemption it has continued. The sacrifice still survives in the dwindling Samaritan community at Nablus, Jordan. This schismatic Jewish group separated from the temple in Jerusalem in *ca.* the fourth century B.C. Its observance of both the sacrifice and the communal meal in all probability preserves forms that antedate those described above. The slaughter is made at the foot of Mount Gerizim, precisely at sunset rather than earlier (Exod. 12:6). Instead of the chanting of psalms, the reading of Exod. 12 accompanies it. The actual communal eating of the sacrifice does not occur until after midnight and is done in great haste (cf. Exod. 12:11, 29). Unleavened cakes are used and bitter herbs. But there is no wine or *choroses.* In many respects the observance corresponds more closely to the scriptural prescriptions, notably those of Exod. 12, than was true of the observance in Jerusalem in the days of Jesus—a reminder, among other things, that, in its three thousand years or more of history as an Israelite observance, Passover has never ceased to change, however imperceptibly. In NT times the agricultural side of the feast, particularly as illustrated in the ceremony of the sheaf (*see below; see also* WEEKS, FEAST OF), seems to have played an insignificant role. It is a facet of the feast which has enjoyed a revival in the state of Israel in recent times.

The destruction of the temple, by eliminating the sacrifice with its sacramental implications, inevitably had the effect of making the celebration mainly a historical memorial of the great acts of God in Israel's past. It became Israel's festival of freedom. Yet it has never ceased to awaken Israel's hope for the future; this is indicated by the parting benediction at the Passover table, centuries old and still used today: "Next year in Jerusalem." And, while Passover is mainly a historical commemoration, its faithful observance is indispensable to the fulfilment of that prayer. The NT, on the other hand, concentrates on the Passover as a sacrifice. Christ is the Lord's true Passover; the redemption set forth in sacramental action, it holds, is historically actualized in the death of Christ.

3. OT references. In discussing Passover and Unleavened Bread on the basis of the relevant OT texts, two general statements must be made at the outset. In the first place, even where it is possible to be relatively certain about the date of the composition of a given literary unit, it is increasingly difficult with real confidence to associate its account of the feasts with that date alone. Current methods of historical criticism have persuasively shown that, notably with reference to cultic practices and traditions, relatively late documents often incorporate much older forms or reinterpret older practices. In the second place, in selecting the texts that have a bearing on the history of Passover, there are a number of references to "feasts" (I Kings 8:2; Isa. 29:1; 30:29; Hos. 2:11; 9:5; 12:9; Amos 5:21; 8:10), most of which have at some time been associated with Passover. This is especially true of Isa. 30:29. However, while it cannot be said that the issue is finally settled, it seems more probable that all these should be related to Booths (*see* BOOTHS, FEAST OF). In any case, an account of the history of Passover cannot be based on them.

The largest block of material in the OT dealing with Passover and Unleavened Bread is found in Exod. 12:1–13:16. It occurs as a part of the narrative of the slaying of the first-born of the Egyptians and of the ensuing departure of the Israelites. The object of the narrators is to associate both observances with the historical deliverance of Israel. They do this by stressing that both were established in Egypt and kept at the very time of the tenth plague and of Israel's departure, on "that night" (Exod. 12:12; cf. I Cor. 11:23) and on "this very day" (Exod. 12:17; 13:3-4).

The composition of most of this section, as we now have it, probably occurred in the Exile or in the post-exilic period. Documentary source criticism traditionally assigned Exod. 12:1-20, 28, 40–13:2, to the priestly writing. 12:24-27; 13:3-16 were considered the work of a Deuteronomic editor. Insofar as the narrative deals with the feast, this left only the brief section 12:21-23 to represent a pre-exilic source (J); and it gives no positive evidence that Passover was a national observance celebrating Israel's history. This account of the literary history has not materially changed. H. G. May has rejected the notion that 12:21-23 must be early because it features a blood rite presumably not practiced in later Israel. He treats the entire unit 12:21-28 as a part of P also, associating it with Lev. 23:4 ff. He feels that 12:1-28 as a whole associates the feast with Jewish life in the Diaspora; "the representation," he says, "is consistently that of a simple, private home celebration with the sacrificial animal a sheep. Not only do the early legislators, Deuteronomy and Ezekiel, ignore these particular blood rites, but they have no place in their ordinances where such a celebration could have been performed" (*JBL*, LV [1936], 72). May's significant effort to tie the entire section more closely to later Jewish practice is matched by the persuasive observation of Kraus that all of it, both J and P, is archaic in quality and harks back to pre-Israelite elements. Both emphases are well founded. By giving both equally serious attention the full import of this section for our understanding of the history of the observances is best realized. I.e., the section seems to illustrate in a remarkable way both the tenacious persistence of the cultic forms and the constant, though sometimes imperceptible, changes of emphasis in the manner of observance of the feast.

Exod. 12 begins by saying that the institution of Passover establishes the month of its observance as the "first month of the year" (vs. 2). Elsewhere this month is known as Abib (Exod. 13:4; 23:15; 34:18; Deut. 16:1), meaning "ears," more specifically barley ears (Exod. 9:31). In all probability Israel's year originally began in the autumn (*cf.* BOOTHS, FEAST OF). With the Babylonian conquest came the adoption of the conqueror's calendar. But this was made palatable by using it as an illustration of Israel's cultic pattern. The Babylonian names of months were not used at first. The month of Passover is called the "first month" rather than Nisan, as later. What is more, it is the first month by virtue of the fact that the feast occurs in it. This reconstruction of the liturgical calendar probably occurred in the Exile and was the work of the priestly school (*cf.* FEASTS AND FASTS).

The precise words used here to describe the rite are: "It is the LORD's passover" (פסח הוא ליהוה; Exod. 12:11, 27). The same form occurs twice elsewhere in closely related passages (Lev. 23:5; Num. 28:16). The distinctive feature of this usage is that there is no verb of action, as in the many passages that say that the Passover is "kept" (Num. 9:2, etc.), "offered" (Deut. 16:2, etc.), "killed" (II Chr. 35:6, etc.), or "eaten" (II Chr. 30:18, etc.). The title seems to refer immediately to the action of God in passing over and smiting the first-born in Egypt (Exod. 12:12) or, on the other hand, in his passing over and sparing the "houses of the people of Israel" (12:27). And, simultaneously, it may well refer to the ritual action by means of which this redemptive and protective work of the Lord is both celebrated and made presently available for Israel. It is characteristic of the priestly strand of the OT to imply this sort of sacramental efficacy for the rites divinely appointed for the maintenance of the covenant (*cf.* ATONEMENT, DAY OF).

In relation to the Passover of the NT period this section disclosed both similarities and differences. There is the same concern for a family arrangement of the feast; though instead of stating that the minimum size of a "family" is ten, it insists that a man must join with "his neighbor" (Exod. 12:4) so that his group may be large enough to consume the lamb. The ordering seems to have been done more in terms of natural family units than by means of the "companies" of the era of the Mishna. Moreover, there is no hint here that Passover was a pilgrim feast, nor even of any common shrine for the several families. As in the time of the NT, the victim must be a male, sheep or goat, and without blemish; in both cases, too, the rite occurs on the fourteenth, though in later accounts one misses the prescription about the selection of the victim on the tenth of the month. There is no explicit reference to priestly or Levitical assistance at the slaughter; the Mishna obviously changes the original meaning of the phrase "the whole assembly of the congregation of Israel" (Exod. 12:6) by treating it as a warrant for the three courses needed to accommodate all for the temple sacrifice (Pes. 5.5). The counsel to kill the lambs "in the evening" is more literally followed in the Samaritan rite; the Hebrew is properly interpreted as dusk and cannot be fully reconciled with the later practice of making the sacrifice in the late afternoon; it also seems probable that, as with the Samaritans, the communal meal was about midnight, rather than in the evening, as was later true in Jerusalem.

The most striking difference between this priestly account and the later practice, however, is that the observance, though obviously sacrificial in character, was entirely a domestic affair. There is no clear reference to a shrine; and, instead of being dashed against an altar, there is the application of "some of the blood" (Exod. 12:7; cf. vs. 22) to the doorposts and lintel of each house in which the celebration occurs. Exod. 12:21-23 parallels vss. 6-7, 12-13, but may represent an older version of the matter. The word translated as "basin" also means "threshold" or "sill." This leads to the very plausible proposal that the slaughter occurred in the doorway of the house and that the blood was a means by which a house entered into a covenant with the Lord and served apotropaically to ward off evil. The directions in vss. 21-23, especially, carry an awesome aspect: the preparation is for a dreadful night; no one "shall go out of the door of his house until the morning"; at sight of the blood the Lord, passing through, will exempt the marked homes and restrain the destroyer. The rite seems to serve both as a sign for the Lord and as a protection against a nocturnal demon. This is not just a simple domestic celebration; it is a most solemn observance. It is generally agreed, too, that this form of Passover incorporated some ancient rite of protection through a blood sign, perhaps originally practiced by shepherd wanderers and employed at a crucial season or in a night of evil.

In vss. 6-7, 12-13, the awesomeness is somewhat reduced; the basin and the hyssop are not mentioned, nor is the destroyer. The setting and motivation, however, are identical: the Lord will pass through Egypt to "smite all the first-born" (vs. 12), or, simply, to "slay the Egyptians" (vs. 23). The Passover is here instituted as a sacrifice by means of which Israel is to escape the tenth plague. The institution is not a commemoration of the escape but an anticipation of it and a means by which it becomes possible. It is the sealing of the covenant between the Lord and Israel by which the people pass into his protection and possession; it is a sign of the divine redemptive action that is about to take place. As words of institution, these verses speak of the first Passover. On this ground later rabbis also explained the fact that the marks of "haste"—loins girded, feet shod, and staff in hand—belonged to the institution and were not to be repeated. The sacramental emphases of the priestly writers, already noted above, are probably mainly responsible for the perpetuation of these accounts of institution.

Exod. 12:24-27 deals with Passover as a commemorative ordinance. There is the command to observe the rite "for ever." And this is illustrated by the prescribed reply to the question of the children: "What do you mean by this service?" (vs. 26). This didactic device corresponds to Deut. 6:20 ff, giving these verses a Deuteronomic cast. It is to be noted, however, that it is used there for the sake of the laws rather than the feasts.

The memorial ordinance also applies to the Feast of Unleavened Bread (12:14-20), which seems to play a secondary role in the section. While the Passover commemorates the slaying of the first-born, Unleavened Bread emphasizes the Exodus itself (vs. 17). The seven-day feast, with its holy assembly on the first and seventh days, corresponds closely to the provisions in Lev. 23. The account is of priestly origins. The statement that on the assembly days, which are days of sabbath rest, there may be prepared only "what every one must eat" (Exod. 12:16) —i.e., unleavened bread—may hint at the practice in the Samaritan observance of consuming all the unleavened bread, as well as the meat, on Passover night, baking additional amounts on the following days.

The importance of keeping the seven-day feast as a memorial of the Exodus is also reinforced by the parenetic device of the answer to the son's question (Exod. 13:9). The entire section, 13:1-16, shows strong Deuteronomic influence. Throughout, it implies that the feast is the occasion for the offering of the first-born. The offering of first fruits began at the Feast of Weeks (*see* WEEKS, FEAST OF) and was completed at Booths. The consecration of the harvest and the harvest season by the waving of the freshly cut sheaf of barley (Lev. 23:9-11) was an aspect of the observance of the Feast of Unleavened Bread, not mentioned here. It reminds us that it was originally an agricultural observance. After the ceremony of the sheaf the new crop could begin to be used for food; but not until the presentation of the leavened loaves at the Feast of Weeks, fifty days later (Lev. 23:17), did the grain harvest end. It seems probable that a special sacredness originally attached to this entire period, marked by the prohibition of leaven. Though the prohibition of leaven in Israel was only for the duration of the seven-day feast, the original pattern seems indicated by the connection between the sheaf of ceremony and the presentation of leaven at Weeks. Apart from the sheaf there were no special sacrifices at this time. Though it later became an individual matter, it is plausible that one original component of Passover was a communal offering or redemption of the first-born by the seminomadic ancestors of Israel. This would help to explain the fact that the greatest plague upon Egypt is the destruction of its first-born and also the institution of the Passover in this connection. The occurrence of the requirement to offer and redeem the first-born in the context of a discussion of the Feast of Unleavened Bread seems to show that this Deuteronomic interpretation of it is deeply influenced by nomadic and Passover traditions.

The far-reaching implications of the account in Exod. 12:1–13:16 can now be summarized. Its strongly sacramental interpretation of the role of the Passover rite points to a predominantly priestly origin. The large measure of agreement between this account of the feast and later practices, especially as recorded in the Mishna, indicates that it had wide influence. The fact that it is given a wholly domestic setting and lacks a temple ceremony—its most important distinction in relation to all other accounts—may point to an exilic origin. The account may represent practices begun or revised in Babylon; that its exilic origin would have made it readily usable by the subsequent Diaspora, as may be stressed, is easy to understand. The adaptation of the feast to a setting that lacked a temple may have involved the revival of some very old forms—e.g., the striking of the blood on the doorposts and lintel that focuses upon the pre-Israelite apotropaic or blood-covenant components reinterpreted in the observance. The offering of the first-born may also have pre-Israelite roots. If, as seems probable, it was in origin a Passover sacrifice, one feels that reference to it here in a predominantly Deuteronomic account of the Feast of Unleavened Bread may indicate that it formed a central factor in the pre-exilic observance of Passover. It likewise seems to bespeak a pre-exilic coalescence of some rites of the two originally separate "feasts."

Among the passages in the OT that were composed later than the section in Exodus discussed above, II Chr. 30; 35 are the most important. The first reports on a Passover attributed to Hezekiah, but on which there is no report in Kings. The account stresses the special themes of the Chronicler: the house of David is divinely chosen, and the temple in Jerusalem is the one true site for worship. As a true king, Hezekiah invited the people of the N to Jerusalem. The report that the feast was kept in the second month (30:2-3, 13), since the priests were unprepared at the proper time, must in all probability be read as a warrant for the later practice of permitting all who were disqualified to observe the feast in the first month to do so a month later (Pes. 9.1-2). Similarly, the statement that the priests and Levites slew the animals and tossed the blood, respectively, because the heads of families were not sanctified, is probably an attempt to explain how these functions had come to be transferred. The date, the sprinkling of the blood, the singing of the Levites, and the participation of those from beyond Judah are all in accord with later practice. The event is described as the greatest in Jerusalem since the days of Solomon (II Chr. 30:26). The description of Josiah's Passover in II Chr. 35 compares closely with that of Hezekiah's. Josiah and the princes distributed the sacrifices for the people. The people are arranged by families and clans (35:4, 12), but one is given the impression that the account of the sacrifice and its distribution (35:13) unsuccessfully combines the prescriptions of P with those of Deut. 16, yielding an unintelligible result. The report in Ezra 6:19 ff, from approximately the same period, seems to correspond closely to the practice of the NT period. What, however, distinguishes all this material that is later than Exod. 12:1–13:16 is the role it assigns to the priests and Levites.

4. Current interpretations. The current debate about the history of the Passover feast relates to the interpretation of the earlier references to it. In II Kings 23:21-23, with respect to the Passover of Josiah, we are told that no such Passover "had been kept since the days of the judges." In the calendar of feasts, in Exod. 23:14-17, it is the Feast of Unleavened Bread, not Passover, that is coupled with those of Harvest and Ingathering, while the reference to Passover in 34:25 is suspect of being an insertion because of its context. From all this Wellhausen concluded that the coalescence of Passover and Unleavened Bread did not occur until the time of Josiah. The agricultural festival of unleavened bread was kept as such as a national Israelite feast, he felt, until the days of Josiah. The section in Deut. 16:1-10 was interpreted as an attempt to abolish the private Passover celebrations and to eliminate the apotropaic rites characteristic of these; therefore, Passover was combined with the national feast in Jerusalem, and, so he felt, the eating of the meal indoors was no longer permitted. The time of the feast was at the new moon of Abib rather than at the full moon as in Exod. 12 and subsequently.

Whereas Wellhausen held that the coalescence of the two facets of the feast in a national observance occurred for the first time under Josiah, furthering their "historification," recent interpreters, notably Joachim Kraus, hold that what Josiah effected was a re-establishment. He argues that Passover, though once a clan rite, was indeed celebrated at a central shrine of Israel in the days of the judges. Moreover, he maintains that the rites of Unleavened Bread entered the Passover observance even before that time; this view can claim some support from the fact that in all biblical records the use of unleavened bread with the Passover sacrifice is stressed.

Kraus's reinterpretation of the matter is predicated upon the well-known and widely accepted thesis that from its beginning Israel was an amphictyonic confederacy of tribes held together by a common religious tradition and a unifying cultus. The entire community would gather at some shrine center annually, or more frequently, to renew the covenant bonds of the confederacy and celebrate the common tradition. At this stage in Israel's history and in this manner, rather than much later, the assimilation of the Canaanite agricultural feasts of Booths and Unleavened Bread occurred, the former at Shiloh, the latter at Gilgal.

Kraus finds the relevant text in Josh. 4:19-23 and, especially, in 5:10-12. The present form of these passages shows the mark of the priestly editor. But Martin Noth, assuming Israel's amphictyonic history, finds that behind their priestly documentary form they contain authentic bits of a "Gilgal tradition." When we read the passage as a tradition of the Passover at Gilgal, we note that it celebrated both the deliverance from Egypt and the inheritance of the Land of Promise as the association of the crossing of the Jordan with the crossing of the Sea indicates. This occurs on the tenth day, the day on which, in Exod. 12:3, the Passover lamb is selected. Moreover, the Feast of Unleavened Bread is treated as a memorial of Israel in the wilderness in a way that complements its agricultural character. It marks the transition from the manna of the desert to the eating of the fruit of the land of Canaan. The institution of the Unleavened Bread rite corresponds to that of Passover in Exod. 12:1-13 in that it precedes the event of the inheritance of the land, of which it is the pledge. The eating of the parched grain, the first food eaten in the Land of Promise, presupposes the waving of the barley sheaf (Lev. 23:14), making the new crop available for food. In the feast, as here delineated, the Unleavened Bread observance is profoundly reoriented, as nowhere else, to celebrate Israel's holy history in terms of one of its great events. However, the form and emphasis strongly reflect the priestly tradition. It must also be pointed out that Kraus's view that this process of integrating Passover and Unleavened Bread by assimilating them to Israel's faith began very early, at Gilgal, depends both on the amphictyonic hypothesis and on the tenability of the results of his tradition criticism. Since the testing of the latter, especially, is far from complete, it is perhaps too early to predict to what extent his conclusions will be vindicated.

Bibliography. J. Wellhausen, *Prolegomena to the History of Israel* (1885), pp. 83-120; G. Beer, *Pascha oder das jüdische Osterfest* (1911); J. Morgenstern, "Two Ancient Israelite Agricultural Festivals," *JQR,* 8 (1917-18), 39 ff; H. G. May, "The Relation of the Passover to the Feast of Unleavened Cakes," *JBL,* LV (1936), 65-82; H. Schauss, *The Jewish Festivals* (1938), pp. 38-84; E. Auerbach, "Die Feste im alten Israel," *Vetus Testamentum,* VIII (1958), 1-18; H.-J. Kraus, "Zur Geschichte des Passah-Massot-Festes im AT," *Evangelische Theologie,* 18 (1958), 47-67. J. C. Rylaarsdam

PASTOR. The translation of ποιμήν (Latin *pastor*) in Eph. 4:11. The word is usually translated "shepherd" (*see* Shepherd [Theological]) and is used of: (*a*) sheepherders, literally or symbolically; (*b*) Christ, as the "good Shepherd"; (*c*) leaders in the church. It is to be noted that only in the Ephesians passage are Christians called "shepherds" or "pastors" (but note John 21:15-17) and that here the term, closely linked with "teachers," apparently designates an office. *See* Ministry. B. H. Throckmorton, Jr.

PASTORAL LETTERS, THE. A common way of referring to I and II Timothy and Titus, three letters of the NT which together form a distinct group within the Pauline letter corpus. The term, first used by Anton in 1753, emphasizes the pastoral and ecclesiastical concerns of the letters, written in the name of Paul as a chief pastor and administrator of churches to two associates.

Although the letters are intended to be private

communications to Paul's associates, they are actually more. Their official character as church documents is revealed by the greetings at the end of each letter; even the most private letter among the three, II Timothy, carries the plural greeting: "Grace be with you [all]" (4:22). The author has one primary concern, the stabilization of the church. He therefore exhorts his associates to enforce obedience to the Christian faith; to take and uphold solid measures with respect to worship, ordination, and the organization of the church; and to combat heresy.

A. Authorship
  1. Ecclesiastical tradition
  2. Internal evidence
    a. Vocabulary
    b. Style
    c. Situation
B. Historical setting and purpose
C. Contents
D. Nature of heresy
E. Marks of ecclesiastical stabilization
  1. Worship and creed
  2. The ministry
F. Theological emphases
Bibliography

A. *AUTHORSHIP.* The question of authorship continues to be a much-debated issue in NT scholarship. Are the letters to be ascribed to the apostle Paul, or are they pseudonymous in character? The issue turns on ecclesiastical tradition and internal evidence.

1. Ecclesiastical tradition. It is only since Irenaeus, who wrote his *Against Heresies* between 181 and 189, that explicit quotations from the Pastorals occur. Irenaeus cites from all thirteen chapters of the Pastorals except the first chapter of Titus. *Ca.* A.D. 190, the Muratorian Canon (*see* CANON OF THE NT) puts them at the end of the Pauline letters, with these words: "Howbeit to Philemon one, to Titus one, and to Timothy two were put in writing from personal inclination and attachment, to be in honour however with the Catholic Church for the ordering of ecclesiastical discipline." Yet it must be observed that the Michigan Beatty Codex of Paul (*ca.* 250; *see* TEXT OF THE NT) in all probability did not contain the Pastorals. Likewise the canon of MARCION did not contain them, and it seems unlikely that Marcion rejected the Pastorals, as Tertullian asserts (Tert. Marcion V.21). The later Marcionite churches seem to have accepted the Pastorals, which is unlikely if Marcion had explicitly rejected them. It is more probable that the Pauline canon known to Marcion did not contain them.

At the end of the second century, then, the evidence is ambiguous. Before that time the Pastorals seem to have been neglected, whereas they became common property of the church after that time. The Apologists are silent about the Pastorals; yet it may be contended that Pauline quotations are, in any case, rare in them. When we come closer to the beginning of the second century, there seems to be evidence of a knowledge of the Pastorals in the Apostolic Fathers, especially in Polycarp. The evidence is:

I Clement 2:7 (A.D. 95) gives the expression "ready for any good work," which seems to be identical with Tit. 3:1 (cf. II Tim. 2:21; 3:17).

Ignatius has some points of contact with the Pastorals, especially in the interpretation of Jesus as "our (common) hope" (Ign. Eph. 2:2; Magn. 11; Trall. 2:2; Phila. 11:2 [cf. I Tim. 1:1]).

Polycarp's Letter to the Philippians has striking parallels with the Pastorals. Polyc. Phil. 4:1 reads: "The beginning of all vices is love of money; knowing therefore that we brought nothing into the world, but neither have we anything to carry out . . . ," and seems to be a reminiscence of I Tim. 6:7, 10. Likewise Polyc. Phil. 9:2: "For neither have they loved the present world," seems a recollection of II Tim. 4:10. Many less certain parallels can be adduced. However, when we notice the language of the Pastorals and its general proximity to the language of the higher Greek Koine, especially to that of the Apostolic Fathers, we must be cautious about arguing on the basis of literary dependence. Especially with respect to Polycarp, various conclusions have been drawn. It has been argued (*a*) that the Pastorals are prior to Polycarp's letter, which is traditionally dated *ca.* 110; (*b*) that the Pastorals are later than Polycarp's letter, the Pastorals quoting Polycarp rather than the reverse; and (*c*) that Polycarp and the author of the Pastorals are the same person. It seems more probable, however, in view of the proverbial character of the quotations, that both authors depend on a common source, which they cite independently.

2. Internal evidence. Vocabulary, style, and the situation which the letters presuppose are the three factors involved here.

a. Vocabulary. It has long been observed that there is a notable difference in the vocabulary of the genuine Pauline letters and the Pastorals. Although the argument from vocabulary in itself cannot be conclusive, it must be seen in conjunction with the other objections raised to Pauline authorship. The most complete study of the vocabulary of the Pastorals was undertaken by P. N. Harrison (*see bibliography*). Its main conclusions are here summarized:

The vocabulary of the Pastorals contains 902 words, of which 54 are proper names. Of the 848 remaining, 306 or more than ⅓ are not found in the ten other Pauline letters. There is an astounding number of *hapax legomena* (words occurring only once) among them: 175 do not occur in the NT at all; 131 words do occur in the Pastorals and other NT books, but not in the Pauline letters. The words, then, which Paul and the Pastorals share are 542. Of these, only 50 can be characterized as exclusively Pauline, since they do not appear in the other books of the NT. And only three of them (ἀφθαρσία; οἰκέω; χρηστότης) occur more than twice in any Pauline letters. These distinctly Pauline phrases were probably taken over literally by the author from the Pauline letters which he had before him.

The striking similarity in vocabulary between the Pastorals and the Apostolic Fathers and Apologists has already been mentioned. Of the total vocabulary of the Pastorals (848), 211 words, while absent from the vocabulary of Paul, are part of the working vocabulary of Christian writers in the second century. Furthermore, the language of the Pastorals is far closer to the popular-philosophical language of the time, as reflected in Epictetus and other Stoic philosophers, than it is to the language of Paul. The non-Pauline vocabulary reflects often the peculiar religiosity of the author. Phrases not used by Paul become prominent in the Pastorals. The author stresses a rationalized Paulinism, wanting to come to terms with an ongoing world in which the church has to find a place for itself. Therefore he uses terms such as: εὐσέβεια ("godliness, piety"); ὑγιαίνουσα διδασκαλία ("orthodoxy, sound teaching"); σώφρων ("sensible"); σεμνός ("respectable"); ὅσιος ("holy, chaste"); παραθήκη ("deposit of faith").

Furthermore, when the author uses Pauline phrases or compounds, he uses them with a different meaning: e.g., δίκαιος ("upright"); πίστις ("*the* body of Christian faith"). Whereas Paul uses for "revelation," ἀποκάλυψις, ἀποκαλύπτω, the Pastorals use "appearing" and "appear" (ἐπιφάνεια; φανερόω).

The use of concepts of mystery-religion and emperor-worship is conspicuous: e.g., σωτήρ; σωτήριος χάρις; μακαρία ἐλπίς; μέγας θεός; φιλανθρωπία. The word "good" (καλός) which Paul employs regularly as substantive is used twenty times as an adjective, often associated with ἔργα, "works."

One is thus led to observe the absence of the terms expressive of Paul's characteristic piety and theology. The place of the Spirit is amazingly reduced. Statistically, the ninety occurrences in Pauline letters are reduced in the Pastorals to six. Three of these are liturgical in character and are citations: I Tim. 3:16; II Tim. 1:14; Tit. 3:5. One (I Tim. 4:1) is a citing of prophecy in conventional language; the last two occur in II Tim. 1:7; 4:22. But the meaning of the Spirit in a christological connotation, as the agent by which the new creature lives, has disappeared. Likewise the characteristic Pauline term σῶμα, so often associated with πνεῦμα, has gone. Furthermore, δικαιοσύνη, as the justifying act of God in Christ, is present only in the liturgical citation of Tit. 3:7; in I Tim. 3:16 the verb δικαιόω is used in a creedal context of Hellenistic origin. And then ἐπίγνωσις τῆς ἀλήθειας has lost its Pauline mystic connotation (Phil. 3:10) and refers to the ethical conduct which is consonant with the truth of the Christian faith.

b. Style. The language of the Pastorals is more akin to a literary Koine similar to Luke, Hebrews, and I Peter than to Paul's use of the popular Koine. One notes also that the dramatic vivacity of Pauline argumentation, with its emotional outbursts, its dialogue form of thought, its introduction of real or imaginary opponents and objections, and the use of metaphor and image, is replaced by a certain heaviness and repetitiousness of style. The proponents of Pauline authorship cannot escape this argument by referring to the quietude of style which would be the result of the apostle's writing in his old age. Nor can they argue that in writing to friends Paul has no need of arguing his case vehemently. Psychological arguments such as these are dangerous to employ, especially when the vocabulary stands so decisively against Pauline authorship.

c. Situation. It seems impossible to fit the situation which the Pastorals describe anywhere in the life of Paul as described in Acts and the Pauline letters. Acts, to be sure, does not report the death of Paul at the end of the book. This silence is probably to be explained, not by the hypothesis that Paul's imprisonment at Rome did not result in his condemnation and death, but by the author's literary purpose. He is setting forth the successful missionary work of the apostle and therefore prefers to end his book with a reference to Paul's "unhindered" work in Rome. To have concluded with the martyrdom of Paul at the hand of the Roman authorities would have been an anticlimax for this early Christian apologist, whose aim is to show the political innocence of the Christian movement. It is evident, however, from Paul's farewell address at Miletus that the author of Acts knew of Paul's death, which he stresses twice (Acts 20:25, 38).

When we consider the Pastorals as one unit, the situation described in them seems to presuppose a release from a prior Roman imprisonment. After Paul's deliverance "from the lion's mouth" (II Tim. 4:17), he was able to continue the proclamation of his message to the Gentiles for several years and in many lands. He traveled in Asia Minor, and from there to Macedonia (I Tim. 1:3); he visited Crete and Epirus, passing a winter in Nicopolis. And prior to his final arrest he was again in Greece (II Tim. 4: 20) and in Asia Minor in Miletus and Troas (vss. 13-20). He may even have traveled to Spain, the "limits of the West," as I Clement indicates (cf. Rom. 15:24; I Clem. 5:7). Yet the evidence of *two* imprisonments is not so clear as we might wish: II Tim. 4:16 does not necessarily mean a release from a first imprisonment, but may refer to a first sitting of a trial at the first imprisonment.

If we do not take the Pastorals as one unit, the personal references may involve separate episodes in the life of Paul and can be more easily accommodated within the framework of the Apostle's career as we can reconstruct it from the other letters and from Acts; but, even so, no consistent picture emerges from the study of the data in any one of the three letters, and it seems likely that the author has created certain settings derived from Acts or legendary materials which would give his letters a more secure Pauline basis. The suggestion that the Pastor has included certain authentic Pauline personalia in his account has been defended and cannot be ruled out. The conclusion to which the great majority of scholars has come is that the Pastoral letters are (at least in their present form) non-Pauline and must be ascribed to a pseudonymous author of the early second century, who invokes the authority of the great Apostle to the Gentiles in order to give his exhortations the necessary apostolic support and weight.

B. ***HISTORICAL SETTING AND PURPOSE.*** Any evaluation of the Pastoral letters must attempt to place them in their historical setting. For it is only when this historical setting is elucidated that we gain an insight into the purpose and importance of the letters.

The apostolic period had passed. And with it the eschatological drive of that period, which saw the world passing away to make place for the glorious return of the Lord Jesus Christ and the establishment of God's visible kingly rule (*see* ESCHATOLOGY OF THE NT). The eschatological hope had been the main drive in the apostolic church. This hope had been stimulated by prophetic-charismatic utterances which strengthened the early churches in their consciousness of being the eschatological communities living in the end-time. The hope had been accompanied by a certain indifference to the world and its culture, since the final judgment over the world was thought to be forthcoming in the immediate future. In the postapostolic church the theme of hope had to be modified. The delay of Christ's glorious PAROUSIA made the church aware of the need to reformulate its attitude toward the world, and of coming to terms with its own existence as having to endure within the world. The hope is modified—not abandoned. The theme becomes that of pilgrimage: What does it mean to be in the world—to continue to live in it, but not to be of it? In the Pastorals this theme of pilgrimage is expressed in the appeal to the confession, to fighting the good fight, to suffering for the faith. Existence within the world involves certain forms of stabilization and organization. The church searches for its self-identity amid the forces of the world. And this search for self-identity is made more urgent by two movements which threaten to dissolve the church.

One of these threats arises within the church and the other from without the church. One is the threat of heresy; the other, that of public opinion and the state. Both threats are related to the struggle of the church to maintain its self-identity in the face of the new historical conditions. Heretics pervert the pilgrimage of the church, and the state desires to destroy the church. In the face of these two movements the church must react. The reaction opened the way for the three canons of the early Catholic church: (*a*) the formation of a creed; (*b*) the formation of a canon, and (*c*) the formation of an ordained clergy. In confrontation with heresy, forms of orthodoxy were being developed. In these early days of transition all these forms were in a flexible state, and it is difficult for the interpreter to get a clear picture of the issues. We must not forget that quite different developments may have taken place in various geographical areas. The development in Asia Minor was probably different from that in Syria; Syria, in turn, differed from Rome and Egypt.

Furthermore, the categories of orthodoxy and heresy were in the process of being formulated. As categories they are confusing, since we have no access to the heretical literature of the time. What seemed "sound doctrine" to our author may well have been marked heretical by his opponents. And how shall we ascertain the opinion of the majority? Does our author represent a minority opinion forcing itself as orthodox upon a majority which considers our author heretical? If, as there is good reason to believe, our author writes in the same era as IGNATIUS, he may have shared the same struggle in carrying through his convictions.

At the same time the church becomes increasingly aware of its relation to society and the state. When the church is identified as a movement different from Judaism, it faces persecution from public opinion and the state. The self-identity of the church became increasingly obvious after the first Neronian persecution (64); and especially after the fall of Jerusalem, which spelled the defeat of the Jewish Christian wing of the church. Apologists for the Christian church became active: the book of the ACTS OF THE APOSTLES is the first apology which emphasizes the political innocence of the church. In the Pastoral letters the self-conscious attitude of the church in relation to the world is reflected in the formulation of an ethic determined to create good will for the church. "Those outside" become an important category. Therefore, we find in these letters the insistence on good works and the avoidance of gossip. The source of the ethic is found in Jewish-Hellenistic ethical LISTS, in commonplace virtues of good behavior and chastity. Indeed, the adaptation of a secular ethic for Christian usage forms an important element of the appeal of the author.

In conclusion then, there are several themes in the Pastorals. They come from the church's search for self-identity. The threat within the church is heresy, and it is met by a search for reliable criteria—i.e., by a trend toward orthodoxy. This trend occurs in the areas of worship, creedal norms, and the ministry. The threats from without the church are met by the effort to Christianize the best secular virtues in the interest of better public relations. But although the church is willing to go a long way toward finding rapport with the world, it knows that it may have to suffer for its convictions. The faithfulness to the confession is the boundary line. Here the church stands firm against the world; here clashes may come, and indeed have come, as the post-Pauline literature of the NT unmistakably indicates.

The Pastorals may be characterized as a manual for the clergy. Their purpose is to strengthen the church in its beleaguered position, and to give it guidance in its search for self-identity. Heretics must be shunned or excommunicated. The clergy must be selected carefully, its authority recognized, and its guidance in forms of worship followed.

The author has adopted the name of Paul because he is convinced that Paul would have addressed the church in the same way, had he been alive. Furthermore, the authority of Paul strengthens his hand and establishes the apostolic tradition in the church. It may well be the case that heretics employed the authority and letters of Paul to prove their points and that the author thus counterattacks.

C. *CONTENTS.* Although the chronological order of the letters is a disputed matter and cannot be solved definitely, the order is probably that of Titus, I Timothy, II Timothy. It may be observed that Titus is addressed to missionary regions, whereas I Timothy concerns itself with established churches. Yet their similarity in content makes it difficult to believe that there would have been a need for Titus if I Timothy had been written first. Whereas Titus and I Timothy are mainly occupied with church order, II Timothy is the most Pauline among the Pastorals. Here we find the largest number of personal references and more personal character than either I Timothy or Titus possesses. II Timothy may be called an "invitation to martyrdom."

The outline of the three letters indicates the emphases of the author. Two themes intermingle and influence each other: (*a*) the disrupting influences of the heretics, and (*b*) efforts toward consolidating the church in opposition to heretics.

Titus

I. Salutation, 1:1-4
II. Church polity against heresy, 1:5-16
  A. Manual for church officers, 1:5-9
  B. Attack upon heresy, 1:10-16
III. Manual for the ordering of the Christian life, 2:1–3:11
  A. Behavior in daily life for the various groups, 2:1-15
  B. Behavior toward non-Christians, 3:1-7
  C. Behavior toward heretics, 3:8-11
IV. Personal notes, 3:12-15

I Timothy

I. Salutation, 1:1-2
II. Attack on the theology of the heretics, 1:3-20
III. Manual for church life, 2:1–3:16
  A. The correct worship, 2:1-15
  B. The correct clergy, 3:1-16
IV. Attack on the ethics of the heretics, 4:1-11
V. Manual for church officers, 4:12–6:2
VI. The danger of the world's riches, 6:3-19
VII. Antiheretical ending, 6:20-21

II Timothy

I. Salutation, 1:1-2
II. Exhortation to courageous witness on the basis of Paul's example, 1:3–2:13
III. Behavior toward heretics, 2:14–4:8
IV. Paul's personal situation, 4:9-18
V. Greetings, 4:19-22

D. *NATURE OF THE HERESY.* The identification of heresy in the post-Pauline period is an exceedingly complex matter. This is primarily due to the fact that no heretical literature from this period has survived which enables us to describe it sufficiently. Moreover, the canonical literature of our period is of such a nature that we cannot draw a clear profile from the antiheretical sections. The church was just beginning to formulate an antiheretical front, and in doing so, it was not interested in a description of heretics or in a debate with them. The heretics are denounced in the most general terms, and all the vices of contemporary society are ascribed to them. Abuse seems to replace debate. Moreover, we must realize that the church was fighting for its existence and could not afford a debate. In this situation it adopted the *mores* of the time and encountered heretics in much the same way as the popular philosophical schools denounced one another. This was often in terms of traditional ethical lists. Notice, e.g., the barrage of vices attributed to the heretics in II Tim. 3:2-5: "Men will be lovers of self, lovers of money, proud, arrogant, abusive, disobedient to their parents, ungrateful, unholy, inhuman, implacable, slanderers, profligates, fierce, haters of good, treacherous, reckless, swollen with conceit, lovers of pleasure rather than lovers of God, holding the form of religion but denying the power of it." This general indictment of the opposition should not be used as a means of identifying it.

In view of these difficulties, two dangers must be avoided. The first one is that of dividing the heretical opposition into several groups or insisting on their Jewish Christian character. The essentially Hellenistic character of the Pastorals and the lack of evidence that the opponents insisted on circumcision or the OT food laws shows that the fight between Judaism and Christianity is over. Notwithstanding a Jewish element in the opposition (I Tim. 1:7; Tit. 1:10, 14; 3:9), we shall see that the nature of the heresy has nothing in common with legalistic Judaism. The second danger is the identification of the opposition with a well-known Gnostic movement of the second century. The extent to which the opposition has formulated a system cannot be ascertained, but it seems a doubtful undertaking to identify the heresies of the Pastorals with any of the elaborate Gnostic systems described by Irenaeus, Hippolytus, or Epiphanius. It has proved to be tempting to identify the heretics with the Marcionite movement, especially because of the similarity in name of a Marcionite tractate, the "Antitheses," with the "contradictions [*antitheses*] of what is falsely called knowledge [*gnosis*]" of I Tim. 6:20.

One should not associate the heretics with the name of a well-known heresiarch, but should determine, if possible, what stage of the early Christian church the Pastorals illuminate for us. GNOSTICISM is not a late offshoot of the Christian gospel. In fact, a Gnostic climate surrounds the NT from its beginning; already Paul had to struggle with Gnostic tendencies in some of his churches (*see* COLOSSIANS, LETTER TO THE). Gnosticism narrates basically the tragic fall of the soul. The soul has fallen from the heavenly world of light and has been imprisoned by the demonic powers which rule over the world. The presupposition of Gnosticism is an absolute dualism in the macrocosmos (heaven-earth) and in the microcosmos (soul-body). Salvation consists of escaping this earth and this body in order that man's inmost being, his divine soul or spirit, may return to its heavenly source. The way of salvation is gnosis, revealed mystical knowledge which is communicated by a divine messenger sent from the heavenly world to redeem his own. All the variations of the Gnostic myths basically tell this story. The complete dualism is accompanied by an ethic which, because the world is evil, demonstrates the superiority and freedom of Gnostic man. This freedom is demonstrated, in different Gnostic circles, in two ways seemingly opposed to each other. One way is that of ethical libertinism, the other of asceticism. Both ways show the indifference of spiritual man to his existence in the world.

The Pastorals give some clear indications of the growth and character of the Gnostic heresy which the author opposes:

a) Asceticism. Asceticism manifests itself in the Gnostics' prohibition of marriage (cf. I Tim. 2:15; 4:3; 5:14; Tit. 2:4) and their abstinence from certain foods (cf. I Tim. 4:3; 5:23; Tit. 1:15). These ascetic features arise from their conviction that creation and procreation are essentially harmful to salvation and that salvation consists in avoiding contact with an evil and corrupt world.

b) Spiritualism. In contrast to their negative view of matter, the Gnostics exalt the soul. They believe it to be a consequence of Jesus' resurrection and ascension to the right hand of God that their own lives in Christ have already been essentially transported to a heavenly existence. In this sense Timothy must "avoid the godless chatter and contradictions of what is falsely called knowledge" (I Tim. 6:20). Part of this pseudo knowledge is the teaching of the heretics that "the resurrection is past already" (II Tim. 2:18).

c) "Myths and endless genealogies" (I Tim. 1:4; cf. 4:7; II Tim. 4:4; Tit. 1:14). This may refer to Gnostic interpretations of OT texts, especially speculation on the genealogies of the Pentateuch with reference to Gnostic aeons and other figures of the PLEROMA, the Gnostic world of the heavens. Yet in the abusive language of the Pastorals, myths may refer, not so much to specific Gnostic myths, as generally to "foolish stories."

d) Jewish elements. The occasional reference to Jewish elements of the heresy (Tit. 1:10: "the circumcision party"; 1:14: "Jewish myths"; 3:9: "quarrels over the law"; cf. I Tim. 1:7) does not exclude, but rather confirms, the Gnostic character of the heresy. The heresy is related to a gnosticizing Judaism, elements of which we meet already in Colossians. In fact, the earliest Gnostic systems arise in the Syrian basin and seem to have been associated with the baptismal movements of that region. The DEAD SEA SCROLLS exhibit Gnosticizing features already, and it is probable that the *minim* (heretics) of rabbinical literature should be thought of as Jewish gnostics, speculating on the names of God and on creation.

e) Libertinism. It is difficult to assert positive marks of libertinism in the Pastorals, since many references to it may simply have been part and parcel of the author's antipolemical arsenal. Yet I Tim. 1:8; II Tim. 3:6 may refer to antinomian practices.

f) Emancipation of women. The appeal of Gnostic teaching to women is evident from II Tim. 3:6-7: "Among them are those who make their way into households and capture weak women, burdened with sins and swayed by various impulses, who will listen to anybody and can never arrive at a knowledge of the truth." This seems quite in line with Irenaeus' testimony to the influence of Gnostics among women (Iren. Her. I.13.3; 23.2; cf. Just. Apol. I.26.3). In this light the Pastor stresses the household duties of women and gives strict rules about the order of widows and commands them to be silent in the church (I Tim. 2:9 ff).

The strength of the heretics is considerable. They are not outsiders but flourish in the midst of the church and seem to have considerable success. "Their talk will eat its way like gangrene" (II Tim. 2:17). The author puts prophecies about the end of time in the mouth of Paul, to let his readers know that what "Paul" prophesied is now a fact. "Now the Spirit expressly says that in later times some will depart from the faith by giving heed to deceitful spirits and doctrines of demons" (I Tim. 4:1). Again: "The time is coming when people will not endure sound teaching, but having itching ears they will accumulate for themselves teachers to suit their own likings, and will turn away from listening to the truth and wander into myths" (II Tim. 4:3-4). The Pastor seems to have changed his strategy toward the heretics or may have hardened his line of attack in the letters. A soft line of approach is suggested in II Tim. 2:24-25, where it is said that the "Lord's servant must not be quarrelsome but kindly to every one, an apt teacher, forbearing, correcting his opponents with gentleness"—presumably in view of the heretics Hymenaeus and Philetus, referred to just prior to this passage (vs. 17). Tit. 1:13; 3:10 suggest a short refutation and a shunning of the "heretical person," whereas in I Tim. 1:19-20 the heretics of II Tim. 2:17; 4:14 have already been "delivered to Satan that they may learn not to blaspheme"—i.e., excommunication has taken place.

E. *MARKS OF ECCLESIASTICAL STABILIZATION.* In the face of these heretical threats the church made serious efforts of consolidation. These efforts are clearly seen in the area of worship and of the ministry.

1. Worship and creed. There is a double movement at work here. The need for a church order is matched by the establishment of an apostolic tradition which will give the church a firm foundation of the true apostolic faith. Regularly we meet in the Pastorals the living tradition on which the church is founded. Traditional formulas are used. Hymnal and creedal fragments are set in the midst of the hortatory emphases of the author (cf. I Tim. 3:16). Such creedal fragments may have been used in the worship service of the church and are often introduced with the formula: "The saying is sure and worthy of full acceptance" (I Tim. 1:15; 4:9). So it happens that most christological statements in the Pastorals are not the creation of the author, but citations from the early church confessions. (This would explain the often primitive features of this Christology.) In I Tim. 2 we find one of the earliest rules for the conduct of worship. This is in harmony with the emphasis on how to behave in church, how to conduct the correct worship. The charismatic gatherings of the primitive church had already been regulated by Paul according to the norm: "God is not a God of confusion but of peace" (I Cor. 14:33). The need for order and form drove the church to apply more rigidly the Jewish pattern of worship, which it had first adopted.

The pattern of the church order is primitive. We can still discern its origin. It is derived from the regulations for family life and the ethical LISTS (Col. 3:18-19; I Pet. 2:13–3:7). These regulations for family life are now applied to the life of the church. The structure of the house of God is built upon that of the family (I Tim. 3:15). This applies to the clergy as well: "He [a bishop] must manage his own household well, keeping his children submissive and respectful in every way; for if a man does not know how to manage his own household, how can be care for God's church?" (vss. 4-5). Similarly, patterns of behavior in the worship service are being formulated (2:1-2).

2. The ministry. The question of an officially ordained MINISTRY became an issue of importance in the post-Pauline church. The continuing existence of the church in the world, the gradual extinction of charismatic leadership, and the intrusion of incorrect interpretations of scripture made the question paramount: Who is the legitimate interpreter of scripture and the faithful guardian of the apostolic teaching? Ultimately the church arrived at a threefold apostolic criterion: an apostolic ministry, an apostolic creed, and an apostolic canon. They were to safeguard the church against arbitrary perversions.

In the Pastorals we see the beginnings of this process. There is concern about requirements for ordination, concern about the offices of bishops, presbyters (*see* ELDER), deacons (*see* DEACON), and widows. Yet we must not imagine the threefold "apostolic" ministry to be present. We are here at a stage in the development of the church in a particular geographical area, where the office of BISHOP is not yet clearly distinct from that of presbyter. Ἐπίσκοπος and πρεσβύτερος occur, but never in conjunction. This is a stage of the ministry similar to that in Acts 20, where ἐπισκοποι and πρεσβύτεροι are synonymous (vss. 17, 28). It is probable that a fusion took place between the terms "elder" and "overseer." The first term refers to the patriarchal structure of extra-Pauline Jewish Christian churches; the second to the Pauline order of overseers-deacons (cf. Phil. 1:1). The Pauline order was probably derived from Hellenistic society, in which the function of ἐπίσκοπος refers to a general title for "office," often that of the finance officer. However, a complete synonymity between ἐπίσκοπος and πρεσβύτερος seems excluded by the fact that ἐπίσκοπος is always spoken of in the singular. This does not necessarily refer to the monepiscopate, since the singular may be a generic singular (cf. I Tim. 5:1: πρεσβύτερος). A stage in the development of the ministry seems reflected in which the bishops are about to emerge out of the presbyterate and assume a position of leadership. The function of the bishop has not yet become pastoral. The office of teaching is still charismatic (II Tim. 2:2), yet the bishop's authority is emerging (I Tim. 3:5), especially in the antiheretical struggle. The situation seems not unlike the one reflected in the DIDACHE (15:1), where the transition from the charismatic pastoral function of prophets and teachers to the regular ministry of the bishops is reflected.

It should be observed that the rite of ordination is in the hand of the "apostles" and presbyters, but is still accompanied by the authority of the charismatic prophet (I Tim. 1:18; 4:14; II Tim. 1:6).

F. *THEOLOGICAL EMPHASES.* The Pastorals have the imprint of second-generation Christianity, in which the spiritual urgency of the apostolic era has made way for efforts of stabilization. A growing institutionalism within and a gradual adjustment to the world outside are signs that the church faces a future in society and must come to terms with that society. A strategy is developing. Unity in obedience to orthodox norms and to church officers who guard over these norms is a defense against opposition without and division within. Good works and intercession for the authorities serve to show that the church is a positive factor in society and not something to be hastily condemned.

The Pastorals can be studied from two different points of view: (*a*) One may compare their theological mood with that of Paul; (*b*) one may view their emphases in the context of their own time.

When we compare the Pastorals with the genuine Pauline letters, we see that although the author wants to write in Paul's name and authority and is familiar with the Pauline letters, the vitality and originality of Pauline religion has been replaced by a conservative religious emphasis. The subjective element of faith, its character as surrender to and trust in the living Lord, who permeates the whole life of church and believer, has undergone a shift to a more propositional, institutionalized emphasis. Faith approximates an acceptance of a creedal formulation, the content of Christian belief. In this light, the emphases on "sound doctrine" (I Tim. 1:10; II Tim. 4:3; Tit. 1:9; 2:1), on "sound speech" (Tit. 2:8; cf. I Tim. 6:3; II Tim. 1:13), on "religion" and "piety," must be seen. Justification by faith is, indeed, expressed in Tit. 3:4-5, but within the context of the Pastorals it has become a traditional phrase without living content. Thus the author can say: "The grace of God has appeared for the salvation of all men, training us to renounce irreligion and worldly passions, and to live sober, upright, and godly lives in this world" (Tit. 2:11-12). Righteousness has become uprightness, and "good works" receive an independent emphasis.

This has consequences for ethics, as well. The antithesis in Paul between faith and the law is not any longer felt. "Now we know that the law is good" (I Tim. 1:8) is indeed a quotation from Paul (Rom. 7:12); yet its Pauline meaning has disappeared, as this sequel shows: "if any one uses it lawfully, understanding this, that the law is not laid down for the just but for the lawless and disobedient." For those who lead a decent life the law is nothing to be feared, the author seems to say. Indeed, a certain rationalism molds Christian faith and ethics. The reasonableness and respectability of Christian faith are stressed. The church takes over the secular virtues of the society around it and Christianizes them. Thus an ethic of humanity, decency, and godliness is introduced. Words rarely found in the Pauline letters show this tendency toward a bourgeois ethic. "Sobriety," a "godly life," a "good conscience," and a "good standing in the community" become essential marks of the Christian. "I desire you to insist on these things, so that those who have believed in God may be careful to apply themselves to good deeds; these are excellent and profitable to men." (Tit. 3:8.)

Yet it would be a misrepresentation merely to compare the Pastorals with Paul. Their importance can be assessed only when we view them in their own setting. One must consider seriously the changed situation of the church. The church must undergo a structural change in its self-understanding. It must come to terms with a continuing existence in the world. And in doing so it must hold fast to its confession, to its basic dissimilarity from the world. At the same time it must combat a perverted Paulinism—the Gnostic interpretation of Paul—in its midst. Therefore, we must not reject too easily the moralistic tone of the Pastorals as merely an expression of the bourgeois ideal of a good, healthy, and sober life. When we understand the issues the church faces, with respect to the dangers both from within and from without, we shall appreciate its attitude. For the heretics in the church belong to a type of introspective religiosity which claims its own esoteric traditions and which spiritualizes religion in such a way as to disregard the material life. The dualism of Gnosticism leads to the conviction that the God of redemption is really not the God of creation, or at least that salvation is for the soul, not for the body. This way of thinking is opposed by the insistence of the church that the apostolic tradition, which affirmed the God of redemption to be the God of creation, be safeguarded. This implies a healthy concreteness of earthly life, an appreciation for the gifts of creation, and the insight that "everything created by God is good, and nothing is to be rejected if it is received with thanksgiving; for then it is consecrated by the word of God and prayer" (I Tim. 4:4-5). Therefore the author insists on marriage, on childbearing, and on the enjoyment of wine. And all this in moderation—"if we have food and clothing, with these we shall be content" (6:8).

Also the author recognizes that if the life of creation is important, so is the life of the community. The tendencies to weld the church into an organized community, and to make it an instrument for the good of society, are important at a time when Gnosticism disrupts the church from within, and when gossip, slander, and the possibility of persecution threaten it from without. Therefore, the church must lead a life which carries its own apology. An ethic of good will must encounter the suspicion of the world. "Remind them to be submissive to rulers and authorities, to be obedient, to be ready for any honest work, to speak evil of no one, to avoid quarreling, to be gentle, and to show perfect courtesy toward all men." (Tit. 3:1-2.) Even so, the author calls men to be loyal to the faith of the church; and as II Timothy shows, this loyalty can mean suffering and martyrdom.

Bibliography. P. N. Harrison, *The Problem of the Pastoral Epistles* (1921); W. Lock, *A Critical and Exegetical Commentary on the Pastoral Epistles* (1924); J. Jeremias, *Die Briefe an Timotheus und Titus* (1935); C. Spicq, *Saint Paul: Les épitres pastorales* (1947); B. S. Easton, *The Pastoral Epistles* (1947); H. von Campenhausen, *Polykarp von Smyrna und die Pastoralbriefe* (1951); M. Dibelius, *Die Pastoralbriefe* (3rd ed. rev. H. Conzelmann, 1955); F. D. Gealy, *IB*, XI (1955), 343-551.

J. C. Beker

PASTURE LANDS [מגרש, common land, common *or* pasture lands]. Open country around the villages, to be used freely in common by the herdsmen and shepherds in the village. These lands are frequently mentioned in the allocating of lands in the Priestly sections of the Pentateuch (Num. 35:7, etc.); Joshua (14:4, etc.); and Ezekiel (45:2, etc.).

C. G. Howie

PATARA păt'ə rə [τὰ Πάταρα] (Acts 21:1). An ancient city of Lycia *ca.* six miles E of the mouth of the Xanthus River. Its good harbor, sea commerce, and trade with the fertile Xanthus Valley made it one of the largest and most prosperous cities of Lycia. It was one of the six largest cities of the Lycian League of twenty-three cities described by Strabo (*Geography* XIV.3.2-3), and as such had three votes in the meetings of the League. The city was said to have been founded by Patarus, son of Apollo. Prominent in the religious life of Patara was the worship of Apollo, called Apollo Patareus. His temple and oracle at Patara were famous. Remains of a theater, baths, walls, etc., can still be seen; the modern village at the site is called Gelemish.

When the Ptolemies controlled Lycia, Ptolemy Philadelphus (285-246 B.C.) enlarged Patara and renamed it Arsinoe, but the new name never came into general use and was soon forgotten. Patara had strong commercial ties with Egypt. The prevailing westerly winds of the Mediterranean made it convenient to cross from Egypt to Lycia and thence sail westward under cover of Asia Minor and various islands.

Paul, on his final journey to Jerusalem, came from Miletus and Cos and Rhodes to Patara, probably on a small coastal vessel. To get to Palestine, he transferred to another ship and sailed directly, on the W and S sides of Cyprus, to reach Tyre (Acts 21:1-3).

So says the usual text. However, in vs. 1, Codex D and some other ancient MS authorities read, not merely "to Patara," but "to Patara and Myra." If this latter reading is correct, it was not at Patara but at MYRA that Paul transferred to a ship sailing directly to Tyre.

Bibliography. A. H. M. Jones, *The Cities of the Eastern Roman Provinces* (1937), pp. 98-102. F. V. FILSON

PATH [ארח, נתיבה, מעגל; ὁδός]. In the typical biblical sense, the course of human life in relationship to God and man. This is seen in the doctrine of the two "ways" or "paths" in the wisdom literature (*see* WISDOM; WAY), which contrasts the "good path," the path of "justice" and "life" (Prov. 2:9, 19; 8:20), with the path of the "wicked," of "sinners" (Prov. 1:15; 4:14). The former is the path of the "righteous" and "wise," while the latter is the path of the harlot and "evil men," the path to SHEOL (Prov. 2:15; 5:5; 7:25).

Other passages speak of the "path of Yahweh" (Ps. 17:5; Isa. 2:3)—i.e., the life which he ordains (Ps. 16:11; Isa. 30:11; Jer. 31:9). Yahweh leads the faithful along paths that are level and straight (Ps. 27:11; Isa. 26:7), not tortuous and fraught with danger, as is the "crooked path" of those under judgment (Lam. 3:9; cf. Job 19:8; Jer. 23:12).

In vivid descriptive language, the "path" may refer to the mysterious thoroughfares of the sea (Ps. 8:8); the route to the "home of darkness" (Job 38:20); the channel of God's anger (Ps. 78:50); or his avenue through the sea for Israel's deliverance (Isa. 43:16; cf. Job 28:7; Ps. 77:19; Hos. 2:6; Joel 2:7-8).

For the NT ὁδός, occasionally "path," *see* WAY.

Bibliography. R. Pfeiffer, *Introduction to the OT* (1948), p. 657. J. A. WHARTON

PATHEUS pə thē′əs. KJV Apoc. form of PETHAHIAH 3 (I Esd. 9:23).

PATHROS păth′rŏs [פתרוס; LXX Παθουρη]. A designation of Upper Egypt.

Hebrew *Pathrôs*, with the gentilic *Pathrûsîm*, is a borrowing from Egyptian *pꜣ-tꜣ-rsy*, "the Southern Land," the exact pronunciation of which is disputed. On the basis of LXX Παθουρη, Assyrian *pa-tu-ri-si*, and Coptic data bearing on the vocalization of the final element as *-rîs*, it would appear that the Hebrew vocalization of the word is incorrect, a form *Peṯhōrîs* or *Peṯhōrēs* being expected.

In Egyptian texts the term *pꜣ-tꜣ-rsy* is used to designate the whole of Egypt above Memphis. To judge from the Assyrian material, in which Esarhaddon refers to himself as the king of *Muṣur, Paturisi*, and *Kûsi* (i.e., of Egypt, the Southern Land, and Cush) and from the same sequence in Isa. 11:11, this would restrict *Muṣur* and Hebrew *Miṣrayim* to Lower and Middle Egypt, leaving *Pathrôs* for the Thebaid. OT *Pathrôs* is further attested in Jer. 44:1; 44:15; Ezek. 29:14, where Pathros is called the original home of the Egyptians; and in Ezek. 30:14. The gentilic *Pathrûsîm* occurs only in the ethnographic lists of Gen. 10:14; I Chr. 1:12.

Bibliography. G. Steindorff, "Die keilschriftliche Wiedergabe ägyptischer Eigennamen," *Beiträge zur Assyriologie*, 1 (1890), 343-44; B. Stricker, "Trois études de phonétique et de morphologie copte," *AO*, 15 (1937), 9. T. O. LAMBDIN

PATHRUSIM pə thrōō′zĭm [פתרסים; LXX Πατροσωνιιμ]. The people of PATHROS, Upper Egypt. The term occurs only in the ethnographic lists of Gen. 10:14; I Chr. 1:12.

PATIENCE [ארך; ὑπομονή; μακροθυμία]. The words "patience," "patient," and "patiently" occur infrequently in the English versions of the OT. "Patience" is found in Prov. 25:15 and "patient" in Job 6:11, where the KJV has, respectively, "long forbearing" and the more literal "prolong my life." Prov. 14:17 RSV has "patient," depending upon the LXX, while the corresponding passage in the KJV has "is hated," based on the Hebrew. Both versions have "patient in spirit" for ארך רוח in Eccl. 7:8, where the meaning seems to be "humble" as opposed to the "lofty in spirit"—i.e., "haughty." The adverb, "patiently," occurs in Pss. 37:7; 40:1, where the emphasis appears to be on waiting persistently for God to act when other help has failed.

So far as the NT is concerned, in the great majority of instances where "patience" occurs in the KJV, the original Greek word is ὑπομονή or the cognate verb; but the RSV prefers to translate this term with STEADFASTNESS, although other synonymous words are also found. Occasionally, however, μακροθυμία is translated "patience" in both versions. In one place, II Tim. 2:24, the KJV has "patient" as a translation for ἀνεξίκακος, which the RSV better renders by "forbearing," since the word means literally "to bear up under pain or evil"; and in I Tim. 3:3 the KJV has "patient" where the RSV has "gentle," which is a better translation for ἐπιεικής.

Trench (*see bibliography*) distinguishes between the use of the two principal terms by asserting that μακροθυμία has to do with persons and ὑπομονή with circumstances. The man who has μακροθυμία, "having to do with injurious persons, does not suffer himself to be provoked by them or to blaze up into anger," but the man who exercises ὑπομονή is the one "who, under a great siege of trials, bears up and does not lose heart or courage . . . . Thus while both graces are ascribed to the saints, only μακροθυμία is an attribute of God." Usually, therefore, "endurance" is a better translation for ὑπομονή than "patience," which in current English seems more to have the connotation of passive resignation, although there is always in the truly religious man a hope and a trust in the power of God to deliver him. Trench again remarks, quoting Ellicott on I Thess. 1:3: "In this noble word, ὑπομονή, there always appears a background of ἀνδρεία . . . . It does not mark merely the *endurance* . . . but . . . the *brave* patience with which the Christian contends against various hindrances, persecutions, and temptations that befall him in his conflict with the inward and outward world." Heb. 12:1-3 provides a good illustration of the use of the word, both in its nominal and its verbal form—we are to run "with perseverance" (δι᾽ ὑπομονῆς) the race that is set before us, looking to Jesus who "endured" (ὑπέμεινεν) the Cross as he had previously "endured" (ὑπομεμενηκότα) such hostility against himself. The RSV sometimes agrees with the KJV in translating ὑπομονή by "patience," but generally it renders the word by "endurance," "steadfastness," "perseverance," or "patient endurance."

See also LONGSUFFERING.

Bibliography. R. C. Trench, *Synonyms of the NT* (1880).

E. J. COOK

PATMOS păt'məs [Πάτμος]. One of the Sporades Islands in the Icarian Sea. It lies *ca.* thirty-seven miles W-SW of Miletus; it is *ca.* ten miles long from N to S; and its greatest width, at the N end, is *ca.* six miles. It consists of rocky, volcanic hills. Such small islands of the Aegean Sea were used as places of political banishment by the Romans (Tac. Ann. 3.68; 4.30; 15.71). The reference to Patmos in Rev. 1:9 seems best explained as such banishment, or as banishment at hard labor. John the Seer states that

Courtesy of Harriet-Louise H. Patterson

23. Panorama of Patmos

he "was on the island called Patmos on account of the word of God and the testimony of Jesus." This hardly means that he was there to preach the gospel or to receive the revelation he is to "write . . . in a book." He is sharing with the persecuted churches "the tribulation and the kingdom and the patient endurance." Cf. Rev. 6:9; 20:4, where "word of God" and "witness" or "testimony" are used in reference to a persecution situation. An ancient Christian tradition, reported, e.g., by Eusebius (Hist. III. 18.1), says that John was banished to Patmos by the Emperor Domitian in A.D. 95, and released eighteen months later when Nerva became emperor (III.20.8-9). The Monastery of Saint John, founded by Christodulos in A.D. 1088, is located near the traditional "cave of the revelation."

See also REVELATION, BOOK OF.

Fig. PAT 23.

Bibliography. V. Guerin, *Description de l'île de Patmos et de l'île de Samos* (1856); G. Hofmann, *Patmos und Rom* (1928).

F. V. FILSON

***PATRIARCHS** [πατριάρχαι; Lat. *patriarchae*]. Forefathers of the Israelite nation. The translation of the two words commonly used by the LXX and the NT to express the concept "patriarchs," πατριάρχαι (singular πατριάρχης) and πατέρες (singular πατήρ), varies in the English version, but they are usually rendered by "patriarchs" (e.g., Acts 2:29; Rom. 9:5), "forefathers" (Jth. 8:25; Rom. 9:10), "fathers of old" (Tob. 4:12), or most frequently "fathers" (Gen. 48:16; Deut. 1:11 [אבות]; so Luke 1:55, 72).

1. Usage
2. The antediluvian patriarchs
3. The postdiluvian patriarchs
   a. The historicity of the patriarchal period
   b. The patriarchs as individuals
4. The religion of the patriarchs

Bibliography

1. Usage. When applied to biblical figures, "patriarch" has both a strict and a loose usage. Specifically the term is limited to the ancestors of Israel presented in Genesis, whether those living before the Flood (the "antediluvian" patriarchs) or after it (the "postdiluvian" patriarchs). Of the latter group Abraham, Isaac, and Jacob are traditionally "the patriarchs" par excellence (IV Macc. 7:19; 16:25; Heb. 7:4), though the twelve sons of Jacob might be added to this inner group (Acts 7:8-9). It is to this inner group of three that the terms "patriarchs" and "patriarchal" most frequently apply.

However, a broader scope is also found, ranging widely across Israel's history. Acts 2:29 calls David a patriarch specifically; I Macc. 2:51-60 lists eleven worthy names from Abraham to Daniel; and the ὕμνοι πατέρων in Ecclus. 44–50; Heb. 11 are even more inclusive.

2. The antediluvian patriarchs. Genesis offers two genealogies of the early fathers who lived before the Flood. The first is from the Yahwist and concentrates on the line of Cain (ch. 4). The second, from the priestly writer, follows the line of Seth (ch. 5). Since both exhibit undeniable similarities of names and order, conclude in Lamech, and purport to trace mankind's growth from Adam to Noah, they probably represent two versions of an original (perhaps Mesopotamian) list. The great length of life spans, which has been variously explained, illustrates the phenomenon, shared by many cultures, of idealizing a golden age in the past by exaggeration.

3. The postdiluvian patriarchs. Previous generations have debated at length two major questions concerning the postdiluvian patriarchs: Is the picture of the period in which the OT sets them historically dependable, and did they actually live?

a. The historicity of the patriarchal period. The wealth of data now available from recent excavations at ancient Near Eastern sites permits a reconstruction of the Middle Bronze Age (*ca.* 2000-1500 B.C.) on a far more extensive and accurate scale than past ages could have hoped. The thousands of tablets from UGARIT; MARI; and NUZI have, almost by themselves, restored this period to its former richness. These texts and the patriarchal narratives in Genesis show such notable parallels in the formation of proper names, linguistic and stylistic expressions, as well as in legal and social customs, as to justify carrying the Abraham, Isaac, and Jacob traditions back to the Middle Bronze era. Although this would not necessarily make Abraham a contemporary of Hammurabi (*ca.* 1728-1686 B.C.), it does equate the age of the Hebrew patriarchs with an unusually brilliant and flourishing Mesopotamian civilization. *See* ASSYRIA AND BABYLONIA § C3; HAMMURABI.

b. The patriarchs as individuals. To the question of whether the Hebrew patriarchs really lived, contemporary scholarship tends to give an affirmative, though not unanimous or unqualified, answer. It recognizes that the Genesis stories are built on ancient oral traditions which have a long, complex history of transmission behind them, and that they came to be valued as much for their theological as for their sociological and historical importance. The narratives were handed down and received, not as the straight history of mere individuals or as general personifications of tribes, but as recollections of real and distinct personalities whose lives continued to shape the character of the nation.

Abraham, Isaac, and Jacob have not turned up in ancient Near Eastern records as either individuals or tribes. But although history has not discovered the individual patriarchs, it has recovered the period into which the personalities seem to fit without distortion.

4. The religion of the patriarchs. The problem of the nature of patriarchal religion is even more complex than the historical problem and has received a less satisfying answer. Nevertheless, the materials which have helped recover the historical background of the Hebrew patriarchs contribute also to the reassessment of their religion and the evaluation of the Genesis traditions.

The patriarchs worshiped a God who appeared to each of them, calling them and promising to be with them, and whom each chose as the patron of his family. He was thus known as "the God of Abraham, the God of Isaac, and the God of Jacob" (Gen. 24:12; 26:24; 28:13; 32:9; cf. 50:24; Exod. 3:6).

This God would bless the patriarch, and through him "all the families of the earth" (Gen. 12:2-3; 18:18; 26:4; 28:14). Specifically the blessing entailed the promise of the land of Canaan and innumerable descendants (12:7; 13:14-17; 15:4, 18; 17:6-8; 22:16-18; 24:7; 26:3; 28:13; 50:24). He who blesses also protects and saves (ch. 19 [Lot]; ch. 21 [Ishmael]; ch. 22 [Isaac]; ch. 28 [Jacob]). He hears the cry of the afflicted (18:20-21; 19:13; 21:15-19 [*see* Ishmael § 1]; 32:9-12) and allows himself to be called by name and petitioned (e.g., 18:22-33).

He is, therefore, a personal God; and it is of his nature to associate himself with persons—both individuals and families—not principally with places. In this he is sharply distinguished from the Canaanite deities. Nevertheless, the places where he chooses to appear are accorded special prominence (Gen. 12:7; 16:13-14; 22:14; 26:23-25; 28:10-22; 32:1-2, 22-32).

The chief cultic means by which this God binds a person to himself is the "covenant relationship." If the worshiper accepts the covenant (Gen. 15:7-21; ch. 17), he must also fulfil the covenant obligations of worship, faithfulness, and morality (18:19; 22:2). *See* Covenant § 3.

Finally, the patriarchal religion of Genesis was so similar in basic type to the Yahwism championed by Moses that Yahweh could be identified as the "God of my/your father" (אלהי אבי[ך]; Exod. 3:6; 15:2; 18:4).

Bibliography. H. G. May, "The God of My Father—A Study of Patriarchal Religion," *JBR*, IX (1941), 155-58; W. F. Albright, *From the Stone Age to Christianity* (2nd ed., 1946), pp. 179-89; J. Muilenburg, "History of the Religion of Israel," *IB*, I (1952), 294-97; G. von Rad, *Das erste Buch Mose* (1952), III, 159-60 and *passim;* A. Alt, "Der Gott der Väter," *Kleine Schriften zur Geschichte des Volkes Israels* (1953), I, 1-78; F. M. T. Böhl, "Das Zeitalter Abrahams," *Opera Minora* (1953), pp. 26-49; J. P. Hyatt, "Yahweh as 'The God of My Father,' " *Vetus Testamentum,* V (1955), 130-36; G. E. Wright, *Biblical Archaeology* (1957), pp. 36-52; M. Noth, *The History of Israel* (1958), pp. 120-26. L. Hicks

PATROBAS păt′rə bəs [Πατροβᾶς, *shortened form of* Πατρόβιος] (Rom. 16:14). A Christian man greeted by Paul.

PATROCLUS pə trō′kləs [Πάτροκλος] (II Macc. 8:9). The father of Nicanor, one of the generals sent to battle Judas Maccabeus.

PATROL (התהלך, to go to and fro). A verb used in Zech. 1:10-11, where the prophet sees horsemen patrolling the earth and reporting to the angel, and the steeds of the four chariots were impatient to get off and patrol the earth (6:7). The figure is that of a military patrol. *See* Zechariah, Book of.

J. A. Sanders

PAU pô, pā′ū [פעו, groaning, bleating] (Gen. 36:39). Alternately: PAI pī, pā′ī [פעי] (I Chr. 1:50). An Edomite city, the home of a King Hadad (Gen. 36:39; read "Hadad" for "Hadar"; cf. I Kings 11:14; I Chr. 1:50, where one should read, with many MSS and several versions, "Pau" for "Pai"). Its location is unknown. V. R. Gold

***PAUL, ACTS OF.** One of the earliest of a long series of romances, commonly styled apocryphal Acts (*see* Acts, Apocryphal), which attempt to provide the information missing in the canonical Acts as to the subsequent doings of the several apostles. This work contains the widely circulated story of Paul and Thecla, the apocryphal correspondence between Paul and Corinth, and the legendary Martyrdom or Passion of Paul.

References to the existence of such a book have long been known, but it was not until the end of the nineteenth century that its original content was determined. Its earliest mention is by Tertullian (*On Baptism* 17), who strongly disapproved of it as encouraging women to preach and baptize, and who records that its author, a presbyter in Asia, had been convicted and removed from his office, although he had confessed that he had written it solely from love for Paul. Among other early fathers who mention the book are Hippolytus, Origen, Eusebius, and Jerome, the latter two reporting that it was rejected in their day. In the Stichometry, now appended to the ninth-century Chronography of Nicephorus, but very probably several centuries earlier, its length is given as 3,600 lines—i.e., 800 lines longer than the canonical Acts. Photius (A.D. 890), who read it along with the four other Acts, with which it had been combined by the Manicheans as a substitute for the canonical Acts, reports that all five were attributed to Leucius, but the nature of the work, as we know it, together with Tertullian's identification of the author, makes probable that it was produced by an orthodox Christian *ca.* A.D. 160-70.

Despite these several references, little of the actual content of this apocryphon was known until recently. In 1904, C. Schmidt published a very defective sixth-century Coptic MS which contained material long known but hitherto as separate writings—viz., the Acts of Paul and Thecla, the correspondence of Paul with the Corinthians, and the Martyrdom of Paul —and argued that these were all parts of the original apocryphon. Subsequent discoveries of two Greek fragments, each but a page in length, and a little later of a substantial eleven-page Greek fragment (A.D. 300) did much to confirm Schmidt's judgment as to the original content of the writing.

As reconstructed from the clues provided by the Coptic MS, the original form seems to have been substantially as follows: In Pisidian Antioch, Paul restores to life the son of Panchares and Phila, but soon is obliged to flee from the city. Then follows the famous episode of Paul and Thecla, preserved complete in several Greek MSS, in Latin, in many oriental versions, and in part in Schmidt's Coptic MS. The abrupt beginning, which had long perplexed critics: "When Paul went up to Iconium after he had fled from Antioch, there journeyed with him Demas and Hermogenes the coppersmith," is now explained. This is not a complete story but only a chapter in a larger work.

Thecla, a Greek girl in Iconium who is of prominent family and is engaged to be married, hears from her window Paul's preaching. Impressed by his insistence on the importance of chastity, she breaks off her engagement, visits Paul in prison, engages in missionary work, miraculously escapes death several times in the arena, and then baptizes herself without ill effects in a great tank of water containing seals. Later she goes to Myra to rejoin Paul, reports to him her baptism, and is sent back by him to Iconium to preach. Finally she departs to Seleucia, "and after she had enlightened many with the word of God, slept a good sleep." In some Greek MSS the tale is still further embellished: At the age of ninety, while living on Mount Calamon, she is visited by lewd fellows who seek to rape her. In answer to prayer the rock opens and, after her entrance, closes upon her. In some of these later additions she goes underground to Rome.

To what extent this legend was produced as a direct correction of Paul's views with regard to women as teachers (I Cor. 14:34; I Tim. 2:12) and his reported counterendorsement of marriage (Tit. 2:4) is perhaps uncertain, although far from unlikely. The romance became very popular, and Thecla became by far the most famous virgin martyr. It is in this little episode that the description of Paul, which has so influenced subsequent ecclesiastical art, is given: "a man little of stature, thin-haired upon the head, crooked in the legs, of good state of body, with eyebrows joining, and nose somewhat hooked, full of grace: for sometimes he appeared like a man, and sometimes he had the face of an angel."

Then follow episodes in Myra (where he heals a man of dropsy, and thereby incurs the wrath of the man's son and heir), in Sidon (where the temple of Apollos in which he was imprisoned suffered collapse), and in an unidentified place where he is condemned to the mines and restores to life a Christian convert, Frontina, who has been flung from the cliff. It is probable that at this point the episode of the lion who caressed him in the Ephesian arena occurred. The story, long known from the *Ecclesiastical History* of Nicephorus, and a natural consequence of Christian curiosity as to how Paul had escaped the wild beasts at Ephesus (I Cor. 15:32), does not occur in the Coptic MS but is found in the lengthy Greek fragment already referred to. In this Greek fragment the lion speaks to Paul, and Paul asks in return if he is not the same lion whom he has earlier baptized. In an Ethiopic MS now in the British Museum, E. J. Goodspeed discovered a story of Paul's baptism of a lion and of its subsequent recognition of him in the Ephesian arena, and not unplausibly conjectured that this was the story which Jerome knew and rejected ("the pure fable of the baptized lion" [*Illustrious Men* 7]).

From Ephesus, Paul goes to Philippi, where, following the Coptic account (the Greek omits mention of a stay in Philippi), he is imprisoned. It is during this imprisonment that he has his later correspondence with Corinth. The Corinthians write him to report that two men, Simon and Cleobius, are overthrowing the faith in Corinth by their insistence that "we must not use the prophets, that God is not almighty, that there shall be no resurrection of the flesh, that man was not made by God, that Christ came not down in the flesh, neither was born of Mary, and that the world is not of God but of the angels." In reply Paul refutes these evil notions in considerable detail and in phrases strongly biblical.

Like the Acts of Paul and Thecla, this section enjoyed wide independent publicity and popularity. Not only did it circulate in Syriac, Latin, and Armenian, but the two letters were regarded as authentic and a part of the Pauline letters in both the Syriac and Armenian churches. In consequence, Paul's reply is commonly styled III Corinthians. In his commentary, now available only in Armenian, Ephraem the Syrian commented on it along with the rest of the Pauline letters. It is also extant in many Armenian MSS and in three Latin ones.

The Coptic text from this point on is very fragmentary and obscure. In the Greek fragment Paul visits Corinth and then embarks for Rome, having baptized the vessel's captain. He meets Jesus walking on the water, is urged by him to continue to Rome, arrives, is saluted by the brethren, is arrested, tried before Nero, beheaded, and later appears to terrify this wicked monarch.

Although the Coptic MS is here incomplete, it contains fragments of the famous Martyrdom, extant as a separate story in two Greek MSS, in an incomplete Latin version, and in Syriac, Coptic, Ethiopic, and Slavonic. It is thus highly probable that this section too was originally a part of the Acts. Like the other parts of the apocryphon, it is a purely legendary expansion of themes from the canonical Acts. Thus Paul restores to life Nero's cupbearer, Patroclus, who has fallen from a high window as he sat listening to Paul. Because of Patroclus' not unnatural subsequent conversion, Nero has Paul arrested and beheaded. As Paul's head is struck off, milk spurts upon the cloak of the soldier. Paul appears to Nero and warns him of the evils soon to befall him.

No sources for this thoroughly orthodox expansion and completion of the life of Paul, so intriguingly incomplete in the book of Acts, need be sought other than a knowledge of the canonical Acts and of the districts of Asia Minor, and a fertile imagination. There seems little reason to question that it was an honest and well-meaning attempt by the unfortunate Asian presbyter to add to the fame of the apostle he so greatly venerated. Despite occasional voices to the contrary, the work appears to have enjoyed wide favor in the early church.

Bibliography. M. R. James, *The Apocryphal NT* (1924), pp. 270-99, contains a readable translation of all this material save the eleven-page Greek fragment later discovered. For a more extensive bibliography, including the work by Schmidt, *see* J. Quasten, *Patrology* (1950), I, 132-33. For a survey of the various types of apocryphal writings, of which these Acts are but one part, *see* APOCRYPHA, NT. M. S. ENSLIN

PAUL, ACTS OF ANDREW AND. *See* ANDREW AND PAUL, ACTS OF.

PAUL, ACTS OF PETER AND. *See* PETER AND PAUL, ACTS OF.

***PAUL, APOCALYPSE OF.** A late but widely circulated apocalypse, which purports to set forth the experiences of Paul when he was "caught up to the third heaven" (II Cor. 12:2-4).

In his *Church History,* Sozomen writes: "The book now circulated as the Apocalypse of Paul the apostle, which none of the ancients ever saw, is commended by most monks; but some contend that this book was found in the reign of which we write [Theodosius]. For they say that by a divine manifestation there was found underground at Tarsus of Cilicia, in Paul's home, a marble chest, and that in it was this book" (VII.19). He continues that when he inquired, an aged priest at Tarsus assured him that no such thing had ever happened in that city and that he had never heard the story.

Augustine is contemptuous of those who had forged a writing full of fables regarding the unutterable words which Paul had heard (*On John,* Tract 38). There seems no reason to question that the book to which he makes reference is the same as that reported by Sozomen and extant in many versions.

In addition to the Greek, copies of which are both few and incomplete, it is preserved in a full Latin text, commonly styled *Visio S. Pauli,* and in several abridged Latin texts from which many popular translations have been made. Besides the Greek and Latin versions it is extant in Syriac, Coptic, and Ethiopic. It is commonly dated in the last years of the fourth century.

It was inevitable that Paul's reference to the "man in Christ" who was snatched up into the third heaven and in paradise "heard things that cannot be told" (II Cor. 12:2-4) should prove fertile seed. Epiphanius (*Heresies* XXXVIII.2) mentions a forgery on this theme by the Cainites styled the "Ascent [*Anabastikon*] of Paul." While this writing—surely not the same as the widespread apocalypse—is commonly said to have vanished without a trace, it is not impossible that the Coptic Apocalypse of Paul, found in 1946 along with many other Gnostic treatises at Chenoboskion in Upper Egypt (*see* APOCRYPHA, NT), may eventually be found to have some connection with the work cited by Epiphanius.

With this intriguing word of Paul as a text and the Apocalypse of Peter (*see* PETER, APOCALYPSE OF) as a model, the present apocalypse was composed. The long section regarding ministering angels and their daily reports to God (7-10) may well have been suggested by the mention of "their angels" in Matt. 18:10. That the "man" referred to by Paul was the apostle himself—the regular (and undoubtedly correct) understanding of early readers—is, of course, the view of the highly imaginative compiler of the present apocryphon.

The writing falls into seven parts: (*a*) the story of the discovery of the book in a marble chest underground at Tarsus by the occupant of Paul's former home; (*b*) the Lord's command to Paul to preach repentance to the children of men, against whom, because of their wickedness, the sun, the moon and stars, the sea, the waters, and the earth were wont to make passionate pleas to God to allow them "to do according to our powers"; (*c*) a lengthy account of the functions and daily reports of the "angel of every people and of every man and woman, which protect and keep them, because man is the image of God"; (*d*) Paul's vision from on high of the representative deaths and subsequent fates of one righteous and one sinful man; (*e*) his first view of paradise, his meeting with Enoch the scribe, the amazing fertility of the place, the city of Christ on Lake Acherusa, the rivers of honey and of milk and of oil, the golden throne, and (a climax) the exceedingly high altar and beside it David, who alone was privileged to act as minstrel before Christ and his Father; (*f*) his tour of hell and his visions of the torments of the damned, of whom (among many other sinners) faithless priests, bishops, deacons, readers, and heretics (who deny such doctrines as the virgin birth, real presence in the Eucharist, and physical resurrection) are especially singled out for hideous torment. This section concludes with Paul's plea to God for mercy for them, and the appearance of the Son of God, who after assuring the tormented of the propriety of their fate, grants them, in part for Paul's sake but chiefly because of his own goodness, a respite of one day and night each week forever, as a sort of weekly anniversary of his own resurrection.

Here the document would seem properly to have ended, but in all our copies there is a seventh section in the form of a second vision of paradise, in which Paul has a personal introduction to and word with such figures as the three patriarchs (Abraham, Isaac, and Jacob), Moses, the three major prophets (Isaiah, Jeremiah, and Ezekiel), Lot, Job, Noah, and Elijah and Elisha. At this point the Greek, Latin, and Syriac texts end, but the Coptic continues with Paul meeting Zacharias, John the Baptist, Abel, and Adam.

At this remove it is pointless to attempt any reconstruction of what has been, not inaptly, styled "so ill-proportioned and inartistic a book"; but the obvious repetition involved in the second tour of paradise, together with the fact that the mitigation of the punishments of the damned on Sunday, due to Paul's entreaty, is the so patent climax, raises a question as to whether the earliest form of this work did not end with this elaboration of Paul's cryptic word in II Cor. 12:2-4.

Bibliography. An English translation, largely following the text of the longer Latin version, is provided by M. R. James, *The Apocryphal NT* (1924), pp. 523-55. A convenient bibliography of some of the studies this apocryphon has inspired may be found in J. Quasten, *Patrology* (1950), I, 148-49.
M. S. ENSLIN

PAUL, PASSION OF. A revision in Latin, attributed to Linus, of the original Martyrdom of Paul, now known to have been a part (although circulated independently) of the Acts of Paul (*see* PAUL, ACTS OF). This later version adds several stories, notably that of the handkerchief given to Paul by Plautilla and returned to her stained with blood by Paul, who appeared to her "with a celestial company"; and a paragraph about Seneca's profound admiration of Paul and his letters and about his reading portions of them to Nero. M. S. ENSLIN

PAUL, PASSION OF PETER AND. *See* PETER AND PAUL, PASSION OF.

PAUL AND SENECA, EPISTLES OF sĕn′ə kə. A series of fourteen Latin letters between Paul and the Roman philosopher Seneca, in which in most intimate fashion each applauds the other. Seneca is deeply impressed by the majesty of Paul's thought and the clear evidence of his divine inspiration, but regrets that the literary form of the letters is not more in keeping with the sublimity of their content.

Since this correspondence was known to Jerome, who says that it was "read by many" (*Illustrious Men* 12), it cannot be later than the fourth century. It was presumably composed in Latin. Many MSS are extant, some as early as the ninth century. The precise reason for its composition—to bring Seneca, long regarded as lacking but little of being a Christian, the more securely into the fold; or to encourage Roman society to read the Pauline letters—is uncertain. While manifestly a crude and trivial forgery, the letters were very influential in establishing Seneca at an early date as a "Christian." The tenth Council of Tours (A.D. 567) invokes his words as though he were a father of the church. In his native Spain, Seneca is represented along with Peter and Paul in the antics of the marionettes as playing a part in the Lord's passion. *See* APOCRYPHA, NT.

Bibliography. An English translation of the letters is printed by M. R. James, *The Apocryphal NT* (1924), pp. 480-84. A useful critical discussion of the letters is to be found as an addendum to J. B. Lightfoot's lengthy essay, "St. Paul and Seneca," at the end of his commentary, *Saint Paul's Epistle to the Philippians*. M. S. ENSLIN

***PAUL THE APOSTLE** pôl [Παῦλος; Lat. *Paulus*, little]; SAUL sôl [Σαῦλος, Σαούλ; שאול] only in Acts. A first-century Jew who from being a persecutor of the followers of Jesus was transformed into the leading missionary of early Christianity. He called himself an "apostle to the Gentiles" (Rom. 11:13) and was the founder of churches in Asia Minor and Greece, carrying on an extensive correspondence with these new churches as he moved about. Paul's extant letters form an important part of the NT, and Acts devotes more than half its contents to his career. He was a pioneer in formulating the doctrines and the ethical implications of the gospel. His influence has persisted across the Christian centuries, and he must be reckoned as second only to his master, Jesus Christ, as a creative personality in Christianity.

- A. The life of Paul
  1. Sources
     - *a.* Paul's letters
     - *b.* The Acts of the Apostles
  2. The events in the life of Paul
     - *a.* Tarsus
     - *b.* Jerusalem
     - *c.* Damascus
     - *d.* Asia Minor and Greece
     - *e.* Jerusalem to Rome
  3. Paul as a person
     - *a.* "Man of conflict"
     - *b.* Man of inward peace
     - *c.* Other traits
- B. Paul's message
  1. Introduction
  2. The power and righteousness of God
     - *a.* God is the author of salvation
     - *b.* The righteousness of God
     - *c.* The power of God as love
  3. Man from the human point of view
  4. Christ the wisdom and power of God
     - *a.* Christ the gospel's center
     - *b.* Who is Paul's Christ?
     - *c.* The origin of Paul's Christology
  5. The word of the Cross
  6. To everyone who has faith
     - *a.* Faith and the law
     - *b.* Faith as the opposite of boasting
     - *c.* Faith as obedience, receptivity
  7. Life through the Spirit
     - *a.* What does Paul mean by the Spirit?
     - *b.* Life in and through the Spirit
     - *c.* The Pauline mysticism
  8. The church is the body of Christ
     - *a.* The meaning of the church
     - *b.* The church is divinely constituted
     - *c.* The church and the eschatological event
     - *d.* The body of Christ
  9. Walking by the Spirit
     - *a.* The nature of Paul's ethics
     - *b.* The Pauline standards of conduct
     - *c.* The Pauline paradox
  10. The Lord is at hand
     - *a.* The importance of eschatology for Paul
     - *b.* Was Paul apocalyptic?
     - *c.* Eschatology and ethics
  11. The permanent significance of Paul
- Bibliography

A. *THE LIFE OF PAUL*. 1. Sources. If we may disregard the Acts of Paul, and other relatively late apocryphal works, Paul is never mentioned in any ancient nonbiblical source. Even Josephus, who might have known and been interested in him, is silent. It is clear that Paul did not sufficiently impress contemporary literary or official circles to gain recognition.

The NT, however, contains a wealth of material on Paul, for we possess not only firsthand sources in Paul's own letters to the churches but also an important and lengthy account of his missionary career by the author of Acts. These two sources are independent of each other. It is generally held among scholars that the author of Acts did not know Paul's letters. The few verbal identities and similarities between Acts and the letters are more likely to be the result of chance agreement of two writers on the same theme than of any dependence of the one on the other, while the striking differences include both

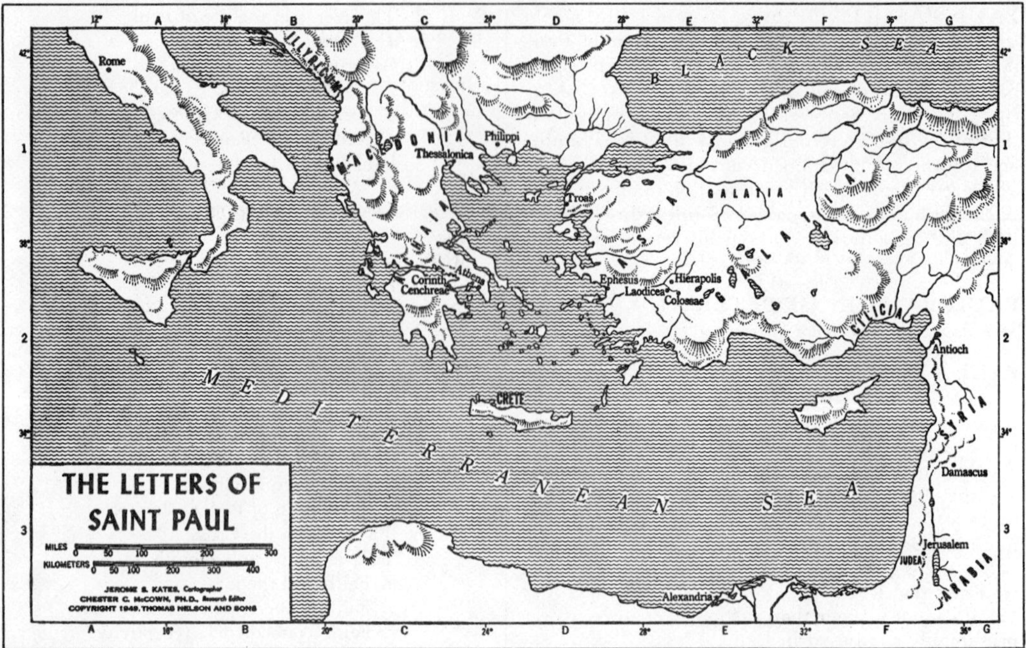

significant omissions and equally significant contradictions. This independence of our sources is both an advantage and a liability. Where they agree, they confirm each other and give us confidence in the reliability of the information or understandings they convey; but when they differ, they confront us with many problems, especially since Acts is prevailingly biographical, while Paul's letters are, of course, only incidentally so. These facts not only work out in major difficulties as regards chronology, but also raise important problems with reference to Paul's career.

a. Paul's letters. The very substantial corpus of extant Pauline letters, out of what may well have been scores now lost, affords a fascinating field of study from the purely literary point of view. It is now generally acknowledged that the Pauline writings in the NT are indeed genuine letters—not, of course, private, "off the record" communications, for they are addressed to the churches and presumably intended for public reading. Even Philemon, the one genuine Pauline letter addressed to an individual, is addressed also to the "church in your house." For our purposes a letter may be defined as a communication, on whatever subject, determined as to its contents by the personal relations existing between writer and reader(s). With some small exceptions, Paul's writings conform to this definition. Even the first eight chapters of Romans, the longest discussion of a single theme (Rom. 1:16-17), have a personal purpose growing out of Paul's plans and hopes with regard to the church at Rome (1:8-15; 15:14-33).

Paul conforms to the general epistolary style of his times, with significant changes due chiefly to the nature of the message he proclaims or to his work as a missionary (*see* LETTER). E.g., the epistolary greeting in the usual Greek letter consisted of the writer's name, the name of the person addressed, and a greeting (χαίρειν). Paul follows this pattern but enlarges it so as to indicate the Christian status of both writer and readers, with such phrases as "an apostle," "the church of God which is at Corinth, . . . sanctified . . . , called to be saints." He also changes "greeting" (χαίρειν) to "grace" (χάρις) and adds the familiar Semitic "peace." He often names one or two persons with himself in the salutation (I Cor. 1:1; II Cor. 1:1; Phil. 1:1; I and II Thess. 1:1), but it is unlikely that this means joint authorship; the letters are often too personal for that (see especially II Corinthians). It means rather a joint greeting. Frequently in a Greek letter a word of praise or thanks or a prayer for the health of the recipient follows the salutation. This too is so characteristic of Paul's letters that the absence of the thanksgiving from Galatians appears to be deliberate and in keeping with the tension under which he writes this letter. Apparently it was Paul's custom to dictate his letters to an amanuensis, who on one occasion identifies himself (Rom. 16:22; cf. references to Paul's writing with his own hand in I Cor. 16:21; II Thess. 3:17; Gal. 6:11; Col. 4:18).

Occasional corrections (e.g., I Cor. 1:16), incomplete sentences (e.g., Rom. 5:12), and a general roughness and vigor of style witness to the extempore character of the compositions. But many passages are carefully and exactly phrased. E.g., I Cor. 13, the "hymn of love," while obviously pertinent to the unlovely divisions at Corinth, does seem to go beyond the immediate requirements of the context; and a great passage such as Phil. 2:5-11 has been thought to be from an early Christian hymn. Perhaps Paul, like an experienced preacher, makes use of passages, here and there, which have been independently composed. It is natural to suppose that extended exegesis of OT materials (cf. Rom. 15:7-12; Gal. 3:10-13; 4:21-31) often first appeared in sermons preached by Paul. And the collocations of exhortations of a general rather than specific nature, which tend to appear near the close of the letters (cf. Rom. 12:9-13; II Cor. 13:11-12; Phil. 4:8-9; and the "household lists" of Col. 3:5–4:6), bear more than a superficial resemblance to what we find in James, I Peter, and Hebrews, and witness to the beginning of a Christian "didache."

What impresses one most of all in the letters is the dominance of Paul's central message about Christ and the salvation that is in and through him. Paul does, indeed, seek to "take every thought captive to obey Christ" (II Cor. 10:5). Every subject he touches —vegetarianism, women's headdress, lawsuits, personal illness, gross immorality, the status of a Christian slave, party strife—is brought into some connection with the "law" of Christ. Quite earnestly and consistently, Paul seeks to bring everything under the one principle of being "in Christ." It is this above everything else—not Paul's literary gifts, which were considerable; not his eloquence, which could leap like a flame at times—which makes his letters of permanent significance.

No autograph of any of Paul's letters is known, and none is apt to turn up. We have only copies of copies many times removed from the originals, and these copies have been edited and collected before forming the considerable part of the NT canon that we know. It is not surprising that the question of authenticity has been raised and discussed for more than a hundred years. Something like a consensus on the major questions has been achieved. Thirteen writings bear the name of Paul (the Letter to the Hebrews does not have Paul's name in the text). Of these the most important for Paul's thought, Romans, I and II Corinthians, and Galatians, are fortunately widely held to be substantially as they came from him. So are Philippians, Philemon, and I Thessalonians. Many scholars would also include Colossians and II Thessalonians, although these are often seriously questioned. Ephesians, while quite Pauline in content, is often held to be by a Paulinist; and the Pastorals, I and II Timothy and Titus, are usually thought to be post-Pauline but to contain perhaps genuine fragments of his letters.

b. The Acts of the Apostles. In Acts we possess another source of major importance for the life and thought of Paul. Since the letters contain a minimum and Acts a maximum of biographical data, we would seem to be in the happy situation of combining Paul's letters and the Acts for a knowledge of his life and his message. This is exactly what has happened across the centuries. The very simplicity and consistency of the record in Acts is impressive as the framework for the letters, which have been fitted in even when some admitted difficulties arose. If we had four Acts of the Apostles, as we have four gospels, the picture might be much less simple and consistent but nearer the truth. While errors may occur in firsthand sources, these are obviously to be preferred to secondary accounts, which must always justify themselves as over against the primary records in every case of difference. It is a mistake in method to assume that a secondary source provides a framework of events into which the primary sources must be made to fit. This is the mistake frequently made with regard to Acts, probably because it is the only source we possess for much of the biographical data we desire. The extraordinary value of Acts must not be allowed to obscure the fact that it is a later and secondary source to be critically examined in comparison with Paul's letters.

The purpose of Acts is to record the expansion of Christianity from Jerusalem to Rome under the inspiration and control of the Holy Spirit (see 1:8, which is indeed a condensed "table of contents" of the book). While Acts is not, therefore, intended as a biography of Paul, his place in it is of unparalleled importance. He is mentioned in 7:58; 8:1; the first account of his conversion comes in 9:1-30 (cf. 22:1-29; 26:1-23); the initial mission as a colleague of Barnabas is described in 11:25-30; 12:25. But beginning with 13:1, the following sixteen chapters are devoted entirely to Paul.* This considerable amount of unique material so important for the career of Paul needs to be critically assessed (*see* ACTS OF THE APOSTLES), but only some of the results of this study can be referred to here. It is widely recognized that Acts and Luke form a two-volume work by one author. Now we can know, from observing the way the Gospel of Luke is related to Mark and Matthew, how our author used his sources and what emphases are characteristic of him. Among these (some of them become clearer and more explicit in Acts) are the dominant role of Jerusalem and the Jerusalem church; the prominence of the Holy Spirit in the motivation, guidance, and discipline of the early church; the mission to the Gentiles acknowledged by all the leaders (even Peter was sent to the Gentiles [15:7]), with amazement but without dissension (cf. 11:18); and the innocence of Christians of any charge of rebellion against Rome, coupled with the constant malice and persecution of the Jews. This last is especially noteworthy, for Pilate three times asserts the innocence of Jesus in the Gospel of Luke, while the magistrates at Philippi, Gallio in Corinth, the Roman captain, Felix, and Festus in Jerusalem regularly attest to Paul's innocence according to Acts. *See* map "The Travels of Paul in the Book of Acts" under ACTS OF THE APOSTLES.

The straightforward narrative of Acts predisposes the reader in its favor. Is it not unwarranted to question so clear and satisfactory an account? Two answers must be given to this question: First, the author is not an eyewitness—at any rate, for most of the events he records (*see* ACTS OF THE APOSTLES for a discussion of the "we" passages)—and he is accordingly dependent on the reliability of his sources. Second, while it can be shown that he introduces his sources without radical re-editing, it can also be shown, in the case of the gospel, that he is quite free to select and arrange material from his sources in such a way as to bring out his own views. Much, perhaps most, of the surplus information of Acts, as compared with the letters, is to be welcomed as adding to our knowledge. When, however, Acts stands in clear contradiction to the letters (*see* § A2 *below*), the student must not be obsessed with the necessity of harmonizing the two; the letters must be accorded primary authority unless they can be shown to be themselves contradictory or otherwise of doubtful validity.

2. The events in the life of Paul. Only occasionally do Paul's letters furnish data for his biography, and while these glimpses are of great value, they do not add up to anything like a life story. We are so accustomed to draw upon Acts and the letters without discrimination that the results of isolating the biographical materials according to sources is somewhat startling; we are dependent on Acts alone for most of our knowledge of Paul's career. That he was born in Tarsus, and was a citizen of Tarsus by birth; that he was named Saul; that he was educated in Jerusalem "at the feet of Gamaliel" (Acts 22:3); that he was present at the stoning of Stephen and was a persecutor of the Jerusalem church; that he made a persecuting trip to Damascus and was converted as he approached this city; that he subsequently engaged in three distinct missionary journeys; that he was arrested in Jerusalem, appealed to Caesar as the right of a Roman citizen, and was sent to Rome for trial—all this we know only from Acts. Paul himself never mentions any one of these items. Of course, Paul's known letters may have been written before the final sea voyage to Rome, but the other data lie certainly within their scope. Probably the best arrangement of the materials on the life of Paul is geographical.

a. Tarsus. According to Acts, Paul says he was "born at Tarsus in Cilicia" (22:3; cf. 21:39), and three times in Acts he is associated with this city (9:11, 30; 11:25). While the letters do not mention Paul's birthplace, there appears to be no reason why they should, just as there appears no reason why the author of Acts should have invented it. Tarsus had a considerable reputation for culture, and, as a Hellenistic city in Cilicia—one of the early fields of Paul's missionary activity (Gal. 1:21)—it would provide the environment for his use of the common Greek speech and perhaps also for some acquaintance with the kind of thinking exposed in the streets and market place by Stoic, Cynic, and other propagandists.

That he received at birth the Jewish name Saul may also be assumed without much question. While he never uses any other name than Paul in the letters, addressed as they were to churches with many Gentiles, he does claim to belong to the "tribe of Benjamin" (Rom. 11:1; Phil. 3:5), and Saul would be an appropriate name. It has been pointed out that the author of Acts shifts from Saul to Paul (13:9) as Paul moves into more Hellenistic territory, and that Semitisms yield in general to a superior type of Greek in the second half of Acts.

The letters also confirm in general that Paul was a Hellenistic Jew, but it is unwarranted to conclude from his birthplace that he would be acquainted in more than a superficial way with Greek philosophy and culture. He insists on the correctness of his Jewish upbringing and on his zeal for Judaism (cf. Rom. 11:1; Gal. 1:14; Phil. 3:5), and we know how ingrown and intense small minorities in a large and alien city can become.

It is generally assumed that Paul came from a family of some wealth and position. That he had a trade of "tentmaker" or "leatherworker" (Acts 18:3) would not be inconsistent with this assumption, since there is reason to believe Paul was a student of the law, and every such student had a trade to live by. The letters do not add to our knowledge here, unless the phrase "We labor, working with our own hands" (I Cor. 4:12), shows a self-consciousness about physical work unnatural in a hand worker. That he was a citizen of Tarsus (Acts 21:39) and of Rome by birth (Acts 22:25-28) has been much discussed, for we do not know precisely what citizenship meant in the first century, and Acts does not tell us how Paul's citizenship had been earned by his forebears. Paul himself does not mention this fact of his citizenship.

b. Jerusalem. Acts tells us of Paul's education at the feet of Gamaliel in Jerusalem (5:34; 22:3), of Paul's presence at the stoning of Stephen (7:58; 8:1; 22:20), of his persecution of the Jerusalem church (9:1), and of his journey from Jerusalem with letters to the synagogues in Damascus "so that if he found any belonging to the Way, men or women, he might bring them bound to Jerusalem" (9:2). Each of these items is known to us from Acts alone, and each raises a difficulty when the letters are considered. It is strange that Paul does not mention Gamaliel, the famous rabbi, when he is asserting his own thorough grounding in Judaism. Furthermore, Paul's rigoristic interpretation of Judaism—especially his statement that failure to keep the whole law brings the legalist under a curse (Gal. 3:10)—disregards the Jewish emphasis on repentance and forgiveness, and is hard to understand if he had indeed sat at the feet of Gamaliel, a teacher of the liberal school of Hillel. Again, we face a difficulty in the account of Paul's persecution of the Jerusalem church. That he had been a persecutor of Christians is unquestioned (I Cor. 15:9; Gal. 1:13). But he is so emphatic in asserting that after his conversion he was "still not known by sight to the churches of Christ in Judea" (Gal. 1:20, 22) that it is difficult, indeed, to suppose that he had been active in persecuting these very churches. The view that Paul was an inconspicuous participant in the Jerusalem persecution is hardly convincing.

c. Damascus. If we had only Paul's own words in Galatians, we would assume that his place of residence at the time of his conversion was Damascus, since he never mentions Tarsus and speaks of not going "*up to* Jerusalem" and of returning "*to* Damascus" (1:17). It is the account in Acts of his education in and his persecuting activity in and out from Jerusalem, together with the conversion experience on the Damascus Road (9:3; 22:6; 26:12), that predisposes us to Jerusalem as his residence. It has been argued that Luke's special interest in Jerusalem and the church there must be set over against Paul's passionate insistence that he was quite independent of that church. Do both overstate the case? It is hardly possible to reconcile the two positions as they are stated. At any rate, both Acts and the letters associate Damascus with Paul's transforming experience.

"Conversion" is a convenient word for Paul's transformation, although Paul himself calls it a revelation (Gal. 1:16), a new creation (II Cor. 5:17), an appearance (I Cor. 15:8). It did mean a radical about-face in his attitude toward the followers of Jesus, on the one hand, and in his estimate of the role of the Jewish law, on the other. There are several implications usually associated with the word "conversion" which are not appropriate in describing Paul's experience. He was not changed from a morally bad to a morally good man nor from an irreligious to a religious man. He had, he insists, always striven to obey the law and in the eyes of men could claim to be "blameless" (Phil. 3:6). If the seventh chapter of Romans is reckoned to be autobiographical, it does not refute this claim, for it was powerlessness to obey the law perfectly, rather than licentiousness or any type of gross immorality, that drove Paul to the verge of despair (Rom. 7:8, 16 ff).

Nor was it a conversion in the sense of a change from one religion to another. Paul never consciously forsook Judaism for "Christianity." The gospel he insisted upon was the proclamation of the age-old plan and purpose of God, which his fellow religionists had so tragically rejected. Paul did assert that the function of the law had been misunderstood, and he endeavored to prove the true relationship of faith and the law from the very history of his own people. To the end he yearned for their redemption and believed that in the providence of God, Israel's temporary rejection of the gospel opened the door to the Gentiles, and that ultimately "all Israel will be saved" (Rom. 11:26). It was dissatisfaction with himself, and so with man as man in isolation from God, which was the background for the central experience that transformed Paul. Various attempts have been made to rationalize the conversion experience in psychological terms. Paul was moved, it is held, by the behavior of Christians under persecution, especially by the behavior of Stephen (whom he never mentions). Their spirit, unbroken and unembittered by persecution, witnessed to an inner peace which he himself longed for. He tried to resolve his own inner conflict by externalizing it and persecuting the Christians, who represented one side of his own inner conflict. This only intensified the struggle, which was resolved by the "vision" on the Damascus Road, for only an external stimulus adequate for reorganizing Paul's inner self could avail. He believed it was an outside life and light and energy that flooded his embattled mind and heart to bring him into a new creative state of being, and he named this power "Christ," "the Spirit (of Christ)"; and his new state he called being "in Christ."

This and other ways of explaining the event are, of course, legitimate, but we must remember that they are almost purely conjectural, since our sources do not so understand it. Paul presents his experience as the act of God, penetrating, indeed, to the innermost core of his being, but inexplicable, humanly speaking, and to be ascribed to the unmerited favor, the grace, of God. Here the three accounts in Acts (9:1-18; 22:1-16; 26:1-18) and the scattered references in the letters are in agreement. They also agree that Paul was not instructed in the truths of Christianity; how he came to know these truths is not told in our sources. A further agreement is in the immediate connection of the "conversion" and the sense of Gentile mission (cf. Acts 9:15; 26:17; Gal. 1:16). In other respects the accounts differ. The three accounts in Acts constitute a pattern and sound like a traditional phrasing of the decisive event. All three reflect a sense of an organized Christian group to which Paul was now joined; all three omit the interior emphasis so unmistakable in the letters; and all three stress the voice, the light, but not the actual vision of Christ, which is central in Paul's own words (cf. I Cor. 9:1; 15:8). Paul refers to his own transforming experience on several occasions (I Cor. 15:8; Gal. 1:15-16; and perhaps II Cor. 4:6), but there is no pattern; indeed, the idea that his own "conversion" could be duplicated by any other man is probably excluded. Paul was not only the latest, but also the last, witness of the risen Christ—there are to be no more. The clear chronological sequence in I Cor. 15:3-8, together with Paul's view that the mark of belonging to Christ is to "have the Spirit of Christ" (Rom. 8:9), would seem to suggest this; and we are probably safe in assuming that he regarded his own unique experience as the authentication of his apostolic standing and mission (Gal. 1:15-16), rather than as a pattern for others. There is no clear statement, either in Acts or in the letters, regarding Paul's knowledge of Jesus' life and teaching and of the teaching of the earliest church and how he came by such knowledge. We must assume that he did know why he persecuted the church and that he did have contacts with the leaders—"those, I say, who were of repute." When he writes of the latter that they "added nothing to me" (Gal. 2:6), he is insisting on the independent validity of his apostolic commission, and the polemical context of the words would not encourage him to admit that he had learned much from these leaders and from other Christians outside the area of controversy.

d. Asia Minor and Greece. Neither the letters nor Acts furnish much data for the early days of Paul's Christian career. The important biographical passage in Gal. 1:11–2:21 is keyed, not to biography as such, but to Paul's vigorous defense of his apostolic commission and its consequences. Acts seems not to know about most of the items in the Galatians passage, and it is difficult to harmonize Acts and Galatians, as we shall see. From ch. 13 on, however, the author of Acts has very detailed sources at his command, including the famous "we" passages generally thought to be extracts from a diary kept by the author or some other companion of Paul (16:10-17; 20:5-15; 21:1-18; 27:1–28:16). The exact limits of these "we" passages are uncertain, since the diary may be quoted beyond the point where the last plural pronoun appears.

Let us sketch rapidly the run of the material in Acts and then face the questions raised by a comparison of Acts with the letters. The "first" missionary journey—Acts does not enumerate but does quite definitely separate the three—is formally initiated at Antioch when Barnabas and Saul are "set apart . . . for the work to which I have called them" (13:2), John (Mark) accompanying them as far as Perga (13:13). They sail to Cyprus, Barnabas' native island, where Salamis at the E and Paphos at the W end are mentioned. Sailing again to the mainland of Asia Minor, they journey in the provinces of Pamphylia, Pisidia, and Lycaonia, the towns of Perga, Antioch, Iconium, Lystra, and Derbe being noted along their way and in reverse order as they retrace their steps. They sail this time from Attalia directly to Antioch in Syria (of course, Seleucia was actually the seaport). Chs. 13–14 tell this story with vivid detail. The contrast between Paul's sermons to Jews at Antioch (13:16-41) and those to Gentiles at Lystra (14:15-17) is noteworthy. Assuming that these sermons were freely composed by the author of Acts, we must admire his skill and the appropriateness of the words he ascribes to Paul. The famous Jerusalem "conference" (15:1-29) account follows, rounding out the scheme of Acts, according to which each journey terminates in Jerusalem (cf. 18:22; 21:15). Both the content and the chronology of this "conference" must be considered later.

The "second" missionary journey (15:36–18:22) begins with changed personnel—Silas (Silvanus) and later Timothy (16:3), instead of Barnabas (15:36-40), are the companions of Paul. After "strengthening the churches" in Syria and Cilicia (15:41), whose founding is only hinted at (Acts 15:23; cf. Gal. 1:21), he revisits Derbe and Lystra. The journey through the enigmatic "region of Phrygia and Galatia" follows, and the divinely guided decision to go to Macedonia—Europe to us but not, of course, to Paul—with the significant planting of new churches at Philippi, Thessalonica, Beroea; the incident at Athens; and the longer and more fruitful stay at Corinth. Ephesus, destined to be a center for future evangelization, was briefly visited, and Paul sailed for Caesarea, "went up and greeted the church" (18:22), and then "went down to Antioch." The graphic style and the highlighting of dramatic incidents, such as the stories of the slave girl and of the jail delivery at Philippi (16:16-40) and Paul's address at Athens (17:22-34), give us the authentic flavor of Paul's mission, although we have only a very general outline of it. The address at Athens,* like that at Lystra (14:15-17), seems very appropriate, whatever is to be made of the inscription "To an unknown god," which has been so much debated. 18:22 marks the close of the "second" journey, but it is strangely worded. Is "the church" at Caesarea or at Jerusalem? Most scholars would answer "Jerusalem," "went up" and "went down" being almost technical phrases in Acts for visits to the religious capital. Does this brief, almost casual sentence really mark the end of an important and separate stage in Paul's mission, or does the author lack information at this point and simply introduce it to conform to the pattern of Paul's missionary journeys as he understands them, each ending at Jerusalem? Fig. ARE 58.

The "third" missionary journey (18:23–21:16) again starts from Antioch and ends in Jerusalem. After another vague reference to the "region of Galatia and Phrygia," where the disciples were strengthened (18:23), and the introduction of Apollos and others who needed and received Christian instruction (18:24–19:7), the rest of the nineteenth chapter is devoted to events at Ephesus, where Paul stayed for two years and three months (cf. 19:8, 10). It is assumed that churches at Colossae, Laodicea, and Hierapolis were founded by Paul's disciples during this period, but Acts only summarizes by reporting "that all the residents of Asia heard the word of the Lord, both Jews and Greeks" (19:10), by noting that Paul's authentic miracles aroused the envy of Jewish exorcists (19:11 ff), and by giving a full account of the riot at Ephesus (19:23-41). A visit to Macedonia and Achaia is given in very condensed form (20:1-6), and then the coastwise trip from Troas to Caesarea, amplified only by the moving words of Paul to the elders from Ephesus who came down to Miletus at Paul's request to hear what was to be his valedictory (20:1–21:16).

Before going on to the account of the final events as recorded in Acts (21:17–28:31), we must consider briefly some of the many questions raised by a comparison of Acts with the Pauline letters. First, we may note that the agreements are quite as numerous and substantial as sources separated by almost a generation in time of writing could be expected to yield, especially if they are independent. It was in the area of Asia Minor and Greece that Paul did his major work, as Acts and the letters agree. The churches addressed in the letters are all mentioned in Acts, with the exception of Rome, which Paul did not found, and possibly the Galatian churches if the "North Galatia" theory is held (*see* GALATIA; GALATIANS, LETTER TO THE). A convincing, if incidental, item is the fact that about three fourths of the fifty or so persons associated with Paul in Acts appear in the letters. Of course, Acts is far from a complete record of Paul's career, in spite of its considerable detail. His residence at Corinth (18:11 [a year and a half]) and at Ephesus (19:8, 10 [two years and three months] or 20:31 [three years]) is summarized only, with striking incidents recorded. Neither Illyricum (Rom. 15:19) nor Arabia (Gal. 1:17) is mentioned, nor is Titus, although he is important in Galatians (2:1 ff) and in II Corinthians (2:13; 7:6, 13-14; 8:6, 16, 23; 12:18). The list of hardships in II Corinthians (11:24 ff) is scantily documented in Acts—of the many items only one beating with rods (16:22-23), one stoning (14:19), and no beatings "at the hands of the Jews" are recorded. Acts does have the escape from Damascus (9:23-25), which Paul appends to his list (II Cor. 11:32-33); the variations between the two accounts observable in the Greek suggest that they are independent of each other.

These differences and others are not serious; they are what we would expect. But the case is other with some basically contradictory material which we must now consider. Paul's letters record three visits to Jerusalem, each quite pointedly characterized as to purpose and result (Rom. 15:25-32; I Cor. 16:4; Gal. 1:18-21; 2:1-10). Acts, on the other hand, records five visits (9:26-27; 11:29-30 [12:25]; 15:1-29; 18:22; 21:15). Not only is the number of visits in question, but it is by no means easy to identify the three letter visits with any three of the Acts visits, so variously are they described as to purpose and outcome. Many scholars hold that the third visit of Acts (15:1-29) is identical with the second in Galatians (2:1-10), arguing that this visit is recorded from two different viewpoints: a private, informal conference vindicating Paul and Barnabas and laying no restriction on them, "only they would have us remember the poor, which very thing I was eager to do" (Gal. 2:10); and a formal, official council resulting in a compromise formula communicated to the churches (Acts). While not all the difficulties are resolved by this view, it should be noted that the account in Galatians is strictly consonant with Paul's thinking and that the Acts account, with its emphasis on the authority of Jerusalem, is in harmony with the viewpoint of that writer. The suggestion that Acts 11:

29-30; 12:25 is to be regarded as the parallel to Gal. 2:1-10—i.e., that the Galatians visit is not the "council visit" of Acts 15—has the advantage of eliminating a visit by Paul to Jerusalem between the two noted in Gal. 1:18; 2:1, but it is something of a tour de force, since the famine visit in Acts 11:29-30; 12:25 simply has no point of contact with the issues raised in Gal. 2:1-10 and is relieved accordingly of any overt contradictions. This solution often discounts Acts 15 as tendentious—James proposes the compromise, and Peter talks like Paul—and suggests that the "decrees" (vss. 28-29) are really later in date than this visit.

The most radical proposal for dealing with the confusion about the visits is to identify the three letter visits with the only three visits in Acts described as having the same purposes—i.e., Gal. 1:18-21 with Acts 9:26-27, both presenting the new convert Paul to the Jerusalem apostles; Gal. 2:1-10 with Acts 15:1-29, both dealing, with whatever differences, with the basic Jewish-Gentile issue; and I Cor. 16:1-4 and Rom. 15:25-32 with Acts 11:29-30; 12:25, both having as a purpose the bearing of an offering to the Jerusalem church. It has also been suggested that Acts has confused the chronology of these three visits. The famine visit in Acts could not have happened at the time there indicated (cf. Gal. 1:18–2:10), and it is cogently argued that the council visit (Acts 15:1-29) should be after, not before, the "second" missionary journey (could 18:22 be the right place for it?) and only a few years before the final visit. This would have the great advantage of eliminating the fourteen to seventeen "silent" years so difficult to fit into the Pauline chronology, since the whole of the "second" journey would be located in this period. It would also explain why the "decrees" do not figure in Paul's letters, as they would come, not in the middle, but toward the end of his active career. Perhaps the nature of our sources is such that no completely satisfactory solution of the visits to Jerusalem, around which the chronology of Paul's active life revolves, is possible. We ought, indeed, to be thankful that the sources are not even more confusing.

Two other issues as between the letters and Acts must be noted: the Jews as persecutors of the Christians, and the collection of funds for the saints of Jerusalem as the ruling motive for the final visit. In Acts the Jews are repeatedly said to be persecutors (9:23-24; 13:45, 50; 14:2, 19; 17:5 ff, 13; 18:6, 12 ff; 20:3; 21:27; 23:12 ff; 24:1-9; 25:7), and when Paul and his companions once gain the ear of the Roman officials, they can count on protection and justice. Paul's letters represent the Jews as rejecting the gospel, to be sure, but they are not conspicuously persecutors. I Thess. 2:15 is almost alone in branding the Jews as active persecutors; elsewhere Paul's sorrow and dismay arise from their failure to respond to the good news, rather than from persistent persecution. Acts may possibly reflect here the hostility which emerged toward the end of the first century when Christianity began to be defined as a separate religion. The Dead Sea Scrolls are adding to our understanding of late Judaism as a much more flexible, less rigid religion than we had supposed. According to Paul's letters, the "contribution for the saints" (Rom. 15:25-29; I Cor. 16:1-4) was quite definitely the major purpose of his final visit to Jerusalem. Acts, too, regards this last visit as important and dangerous, but nowhere reveals any knowledge of "aid for the saints" (Rom. 15:25) which Paul has been collecting for some time past. In Acts the motive for the visit seems to be the fulfilling of a vow (18:18; 21:23-26), and the one reference to an "offering" comes late and is far from clear. The words: "I came to bring my nation alms and offerings" (24:17), would suggest a temple offering rather than gifts from Gentile to Jewish churches. Perhaps the obscurity in Acts is the consequence of the author's thesis that tension between Gentile and Jewish Christians had been early faced and settled harmoniously and that the "offering" could hardly be regarded as the strategic and symbolic act intended to resolve a continuing conflict between the two racial groups.

e. Jerusalem to Rome. Acts is our only source for the events in Jerusalem leading up to Paul's appeal to Caesar and the dramatic record of his journey to Rome (21:17–28:31). Even if Rome is to be regarded as the provenance of the so-called "prison letters"—Philippians, Philemon, Colossians, Ephesians—in contradiction of the currently popular view that Ephesus is their place of origin, they throw almost no light on the Pauline biography.

From Acts we learn of Paul's rescue by the Roman soldiery from the hands of a temple mob, aroused by the rumor that he had brought Gentiles into the inner court, and of the permission granted him to address his accusers—an address which permits the author to insert the second account of Paul's conversion (Acts 21:18–22:21) but which it is difficult to imagine that a Roman officer would allow. Paul's assertion of Roman citizenship saves him from scourging (22:22-29), but he is brought before the Sanhedrin in order that the authorities may be enlightened on the real issues involved (22:30). The turn of the controversy to the question of resurrection must have left them uninformed (23:1-10).

Paul's removal to Caesarea, when the plot to assassinate him was discovered, and his relations with the governor Felix and his Jewish wife, Drusilla, including the charges brought against Paul by the Jews, and his defense, are recorded in Acts 23:12–24:27. The "two years" of 24:27 are usually reckoned as the time of Paul's imprisonment, although the alternative view—i.e., the term of Felix' governorship—remains a possibility.

Chs. 25–26 give the next act in the drama, with Festus, successor to Felix, and Agrippa and Bernice as the actors, and the Jews as the accusers. Given the choice of going up to Jerusalem to stand trial before Festus, Paul appeals to Caesar. He makes his final defense before Agrippa; it consists, in the main, of the third account of his conversion, the three (cf. 9:1 ff; 22:3 ff) serving as a kind of chorus to remind the reader of the motif binding the varied events into an ordered whole.

The voyage and shipwreck have been called among the best sea tales from antiquity (Acts 27–28). Paul is at last at Rome (28:14), but what the closing verses of the book: "He lived there two whole years at his own expense, and welcomed all who came to him, preaching the kingdom of God and teaching about the Lord Jesus Christ quite openly and unhindered" (28:30-31), intend to convey to the reader and why they form the conclusion of Acts—these are as yet unanswered questions. Was Paul released? Was he martyred? And why, in either case, did the author not inform his readers? No answer commanding general assent has yet been given.

For the dating of each letter and its setting in the career of Paul, *see* THESSALONIANS, FIRST LETTER TO THE, and the other Pauline letters. For the chronology, *see* CHRONOLOGY OF THE NT; the articles on the several letters; ACTS OF THE APOSTLES.

3. Paul as a person. Paul was a Jew by race, and he had been a Jew in religion; indeed, he never ceased to think of himself as belonging to God's people (Rom. 11:1 ff) and to yearn for the ultimate inclusion of the Jews in God's gracious purpose (Rom. 9-11). His message was proclaimed in terms familiar to Jews—the law, faith, the promises, the righteousness of God, the Judgment, the Spirit—however unacceptable his presentation of these themes might be to his fellow religionists. Paul was, of course, a Hellenistic Jew, a Jew of the Diaspora, who wrote in Greek, used the Greek translation of the OT, and at points betrays Hellenistic influences. He must be appraised, accordingly, in the light of the mingled Greek and oriental syncretism which was the atmosphere of the first-century Mediterranean world.

Paul was a Christian although he never uses this word. Jew and Greek alike were in his eyes only custodians "until Christ came" (Gal. 3:24), and he felt himself to be "under obligation both to Greeks and to barbarians, . . . to preach the gospel" (Rom. 1:14-15). He quotes no Hellenistic source in his writings, only the OT; and the impact of the larger world around him must be discerned in his ideas, style of writing, and unconscious absorption of the contemporary culture, rather than in direct borrowing. The centrality of Christ is evident on every page of his letters.

When the student has exhausted all the resources at his disposal in appraising Paul as Jew, Hellenist, Christian, Paul himself is still unexplained. Something has been left out—indeed, the most important something. Paul was a unique person. Just as aunts see now the father and now the mother in the child, so we can see now the Jew and now the Hellenist in Paul. But the child is not his mother or his father; he is himself. Paul was emphatically himself. His letters to the churches of Galatia, to Thessalonica, to Corinth or Philippi, are not just the serious communications of a Christian theologian; it is Paul writing, and the unmistakable flavor of his personality pervades them. Perhaps it would have been easier to estimate him if his writings had been less personal, for we get hints, flashes, intimations, of a rich, many-sided, complex character who remains something of an enigma in spite of the unusually revelatory nature of our sources. But just as Paul's thought is clear in its main outlines, however difficult in particular aspects, so his personality is reasonably clear, however complex and baffling certain traits may seem to be.

a. "Man of conflict." Conflict, struggle in the inward man and in outward situations, characterized not only the pre-Christian but also the Christian Paul. He was born into a conflict of cultures. His heritage was strict Judaism (Phil. 3:5 ff), and the Jews were a minority group whose loyalty to the one God made them resist the eclectic, syncretistic temper of the first century. Hardly an ancient writer has a kind word to say about the Jews. We do not know precisely how a Jewish family outside Palestine would react or adjust to Gentile customs, but Paul's lengthy and labored discussion of the dietary laws and the Christian's relation to them in I Cor. 8-10 suggests that he himself had battled long and hard with this problem. Whether Rom. 7 is to be reckoned as autobiographical or as typical, the chapter shows a profound insight into the struggle between the law as an external code and the inward desires and frustrations of an earnest and serious soul.

Paul viewed nature as sharing the struggle between good and evil. The creation, he writes, knows the pain and also the hope of a woman in childbirth (Rom. 8:22 ff). This cosmic struggle will go on until Christ "delivers the kingdom to God the Father after destroying every rule and every authority and power" (I Cor. 15:24). He sees nature as within the framework of the apocalyptic warfare.

Conflict continued to be the very breath of Paul's life as a missionary. If his inner conflict had been resolved "in Christ," Paul was still "in the flesh." His personal situation—indeed, that of all Christians—has often been compared to a war in which the decisive battle has been fought and won but the war lasts on, and exhortation and effort are required even though the victorious outcome is now assured and triumph can be anticipated. Paul was a protagonist defending the gospel against Jews and Jewish Christians, on the one hand, and against libertines and sectarians among the Gentile converts, on the other. Hardly a letter omits entirely this note of struggle, not even so joyous a communication as Philippians.

Paul's argumentative style of thinking and writing also reveals the same characteristic note of conflict. He has the habit of putting things in terms of their opposites: flesh versus spirit, faith versus works, grace versus merit. The question-and-answer method of the rabbis, the Stoic diatribe, the epistolary "I" and "you," or just the native temper of a born debater—all these have been credited with Paul's style. The virtue of this dialectical method is its clarity. We can hardly mistake where Paul stood on the main issues he discusses. The weakness of the method is the tendency to exaggeration, so that very little ground remains for opposing parties to stand together on.

b. Man of inward peace. Paul was indeed a "man of conflict," but he was also a man of inward peace, whose wholeness of outlook and statesmanlike leadership are conspicuous among the early followers of Jesus. He knew an inner center of peace and joy "in Christ." Outward turmoil, external circumstance, whether of plenty or of hunger, abundance or want, did not disturb him. "I can do all things in him who strengthens me" (Phil. 4:12-13). He believed that "in everything God works for good with those who love him" (Rom. 8:28). Whatever scars, whatever memories of his tumultuous life, still plagued him,

Paul knew a radiant oneness and wholeness of life so that nothing "in all creation" is "able to separate us from the love of God in Christ Jesus our Lord" (Rom. 8:39). His dark view of the creature and of the creation is not his final word, for he held that the walls that separate man from man—slave, freeman; Jew, Gentile; male, female—have actually been leveled, and that the entire creation has been unified, healed, redeemed, and reconciled by the revelation of God in Christ. His gospel has behind it and within it a cosmic sweep and sanction. There is for him no such unit as an isolated individual; the tiny person "in Christ" is caught up into a cosmic purpose, and conversely the power and love of God are available for every particular human situation. It is this central conviction that speaks to us through Paul, flowing over all the ancient vocabulary and thought-forms that separate us from him. Paul moves from the particular to the universal, from the temporal to the eternal and vice versa, without effort or strain. "If we live by the Spirit, let us also walk by the Spirit" (Gal. 5:25), is the constant correlation he makes; and to particularize this, he adds: "Let us have no self-conceit, no provoking of one another, no envy of one another" (vs. 26). "Do you not know that the saints will judge the world?" (I Cor. 6:2), he asks the quarreling Corinthians, and then: "If the world is to be judged by you, are you incompetent to try trivial cases?" They expect to sit on the Supreme Court of the universe but cannot qualify as justices of the peace (perhaps Paul did have a sense of humor).

c. Other traits. We possess no reliable evidence about Paul's physical appearance except his own quotation from opponents: "They say, 'His letters are weighty and strong, but his bodily presence is weak, and his speech of no account' " (II Cor. 10:10). The earliest external witness comes from a late second-century collection of legends (*see* PAUL, ACTS OF) to the effect that he was small in stature, baldheaded, bowlegged, of vigorous physique, with meeting eyebrows and a slightly hooked nose, and full of grace. Paul himself writes of a recurrent physical ailment, deliverance from which was not granted him although he prayed three times for it. He came to see that this weakness of the flesh had its lesson for him (II Cor. 12:7-8). All conjectures as to the nature of this affliction—epilepsy, malaria, an eye malady (Gal. 6:11)—must remain conjectures, since we simply do not have enough evidence for a diagnosis. The amazing list of physical hardships endured (II Cor. 11:24-29) witnesses rather to a rugged than to a frail physical constitution. That Paul was by nature a sensitive, proud, quick-tempered man can be abundantly documented from his letters, for he is conscious of his tendency to boast (II Cor. 10:8, 13, 15; 11:1, 16, 21, 30; 12:1), and he glories in the victory faith in Christ assures (Phil. 3:4-14) and in the sublimation made possible by another object of glorying (Gal. 6:11-15). He is capable of sarcasm and irony, although he himself regrets that his opponents have maneuvered him into playing the fool (II Cor. 11:16-21).

Paul had a genius for friendship. The extraordinary list of twenty-seven names in Rom. 16 (whether this chapter was originally addressed to Rome or elsewhere is immaterial at this point), with just the little touches here and there that save the names from being a mere catalogue, is eloquent of his concern for people. He could be magnanimous—this protagonist—even with persons whose motives were questionable (Phil. 1:12-18). He was tenderhearted —this fighter for his own understanding of the gospel—like a "nurse taking care of her children . . . , ready to share with you not only the gospel of God but also our own selves, because you had become very dear to us" (I Thess. 2:7-8). The catalogue of his sufferings reaches its climax, not in some physical agony, but in the words: "Apart from other things, there is the daily pressure upon me of my anxiety for all the churches. Who is weak, and I am not weak? Who is made to fall, and I am not indignant?" (II Cor. 11:28-29).

Although Paul traveled through spectacular country, his letters are wanting in figures from nature in either its humbler or its more majestic aspects. The few nature illustrations he does use (e.g., I Cor. 9:8-10) are not very happy. But when he turns to city life, the arena, the court, the military, he is often effective in analogy, imagery, and figure of speech (I Cor. 3:10-15; 4:9; 9:24-27; etc.).

Had Paul a sense of humor? The writings we possess are so deadly serious in intent that the lighter touch may well have been rigorously excluded, but with all his truly extraordinary gifts as a phrasemaker, the humorous, witty flavor so characteristic of the remembered teaching of Jesus seems not to be native to Paul.

Subject as he was or had been to ecstatic experiences (II Cor. 12:1-4), it is inevitable that Paul's psychic health should be questioned. He had, no doubt, passed through a period of psychical instability, but the amazingly balanced estimate of spiritual gifts in group worship and in relation to ethics contained in I Cor. 12–14 is powerful evidence of the kind of integration Paul had achieved. The impact of his life and work on his own times and ours is also eloquent testimony to his essential sanity.

The most serious charge that can be brought against Paul is that of personal inconsistency. Proclaiming an ethos of love, did he himself deal with his opponents lovingly? Especially in Galatians and in II Cor. 10–13, Paul uses sarcasm, irony, and bitter denunciation, including curses, against those who have attacked him and his gospel. Without attempting to defend him, for he himself is conscious that his words do not represent a very high plane of thinking (II Cor. 11:1), we may point out the considerations necessary for a proper perspective. His language betrays an oriental exuberance foreign to the usual standards of Western speech and writing. These are letters, after all, and they show a spontaneity which more careful editing would perhaps have modified. His opponents, moreover, are not attacking him and his message from outside the Christian movement but from within it. He can endure persecution from "the world" (II Cor. 11:23-33) without any hint of bitterness—indeed, as almost normal Christian experience, the sharing of "his sufferings" (Phil. 3:10)—but when the gospel is attacked directly or indirectly through his own apostleship, he indignantly strikes back. He knows the teaching of Jesus about loving the enemy (Rom. 12: 14; I Cor. 4:12-13) and has lived it out in some of his own personal relationships. Cast out by his fellow Jews, he maintains a moving loyalty to them and is convinced that their rejection of the gospel is only temporary and that, in the providence of God, it has opened the door to Gentiles (Rom. 9–11). But when from within the Christian fellowship leaders play upon the fickleness, the credulity, and the lower nature of his converts to subvert what Paul believes to be the gospel of the love and grace of God in Christ, he meets this challenge with all the force of his aroused emotions and his agile mind. We may argue that Paul was deficient in an understanding of his opponents and less loving in his attitude toward them than he ought to have been, but he does not condemn them out of personal pique. He believes that the gospel itself in all its implications is at stake; he could do nothing less than meet this danger with vigor. That this is more than mere rationalization becomes apparent when we consider how Paul dealt with rivalries between the partisans of genuine Christians leaders. Cephas, Apollos, Paul—who are they? "Servants of Christ and stewards of the mysteries of God" (cf. I Cor. 1:12-13; 4:1-5; Phil. 1:15-18). Rivalry is unthinkable.

B. *PAUL'S MESSAGE.* 1. Introduction. Paul's letters afford us rich firsthand source material for his thinking. Yet as letters they depend on situations and relationships known to the writer and his readers but not always entirely clear to us. The epistolary form of our sources creates another difficulty. The letters do not purport to be systematic presentations of Paul's theology; their content is rather determined by the needs of the readers as Paul conceives those needs. Accordingly the nature of our sources is at once an asset and a liability—an asset because we are able to come at Paul's thinking so directly and in immediate relation to human situations; a liability because we must undertake to organize his thinking without any systematic presentation from his own hand.

The interpreter seeks for a key to open up Paul's thought or, better, some central thesis about which all his thinking may be arranged. Paul's doctrine of God, of Christ, of man; Paul's background, Jewish and Hellenistic; Paul's religious experience; these and other focuses have been proposed as central in his theology. Solid gains in understanding Paul have been achieved by this method, even when a single thesis proves inadequate. We have always to remember, however, that any organization is the work of the interpreter and so must be constantly subjected to the test of our sources. We are not dealing with theological treatises but with firsthand communications addressed by a complex personality to diverse human situations. The interpreter's legitimate urge to establish consistency in the whole range of Paul's thinking must be balanced by his determination to let the sources speak for themselves even when consistency is threatened.

The headings selected for this article do not, of course, escape an imposed arrangement of Paul's thought. The order of topics is determined in part by the run of the thought in Romans. The first eight chapters of Romans constitute the longest and most orderly presentation of a theme in Paul's writings, although important topics such as the nature of Christ in distinction from his work, the Resurrection, and the sacraments are not discussed at any length. Paul is addressing a church which he has neither founded nor visited. He wants to inform them of his own understanding of the gospel of which he is not "ashamed" (1:16), "that we may be mutually encouraged by each other's faith, both yours and mine" (vs. 12). Perhaps he is also clarifying and arranging his own thinking as he contemplates a fresh stage in his missionary career (15:22-29). The wording of the following topics is derived from Paul's own writings; that the topics correspond in part with rubrics of systematic theology is inevitable, since Paul is concerned with fundamental theological issues. It is not to be assumed that Paul always thought in this sequence. He could and did present his message beginning from any one of these points as the epistolary situation required.

2. The power and righteousness of God. Addressing readers who had never heard him expound his message, although they are "God's beloved" (Rom. 1:7) whose "faith is proclaimed in all the world" (vs. 8), Paul begins with these oft-quoted words: "I am not ashamed of the gospel: it is the power of God for salvation. . . . For in it the righteousness of God is revealed" (vss. 16-17). Paul glories in the power (δύναμις) of the gospel. The word and the thought pervade his letters. Christ is the "power of God and the wisdom of God" (I Cor. 1:24). "The word of the cross is . . . the power of God" (vs. 18). He longed to know Christ "and the power of his resurrection" (Phil. 3:10). This power is not an enhancement or release of human energy; it is a divine gift given when a man confesses that his own power is utter weakness: "I can will what is right, but I cannot do it" (Rom. 7:18); "for when I am weak, then I am strong" (II Cor. 12:10); even Christ "was crucified in weakness, but lives by the power of God" (II Cor. 13:4). We must examine Paul's thought about the power of God.

a. God is the author of salvation. In Rom. 1:16-17, Christ is not mentioned, although it is clear from the following chapters that God's saving act is in Christ. Paul's theology has been called Christ-centered, and this is true enough if we remember that the center and the circumference alike depend on God. Writing of the ultimate outcome, he says: "When all things are subjected to him, then the Son himself will also be subjected to him . . . , that God may be everything to every one" (I Cor. 15:28). Or when he speaks of the "new creation" in Christ, he immediately adds: "All this is from God" (II Cor. 5:17-18). God is the ultimate reference for Paul. Not Paul, not Christ, but God alone is the author of salvation. "All things are yours, . . . and you are Christ's; and Christ is God's" (I Cor. 3:21-23).

Paul's God is the God of Judaism. Paul has no new conception of God to propose. He constantly stresses the will and the purpose of God as revealed in his acts and supremely in his new and final act in Christ. God for Paul, as for Judaism, is the living God to be known, as all life is known, through action. Doubtless Paul might have quoted the words ascribed to him in his address at Athens: "In him we live and move and have our being" (Acts 17:28), but they certainly are not characteristic of his own writings. God is the living, active, dynamic source of events, rather than the ground of being or the Absolute beyond empirical knowledge. It is the God who rescued the Hebrews from Egyptian bondage, led them to the Promised Land, and brought them back from exile, who has acted in Christ and will act decisively in the final outcome of human and cosmic history. The gospel is the power of God, and Paul would have been amazed at the charge that monotheism was threatened by his doctrine of Christ. Christ is for Paul the manifest proof on the plains of history of the power of God. He has no other terms in which to present God's act than the familiar OT concepts of justice and mercy. Perhaps most strikingly Jewish is Paul's emphasis on the righteousness of God.

b. The righteousness of God. "In it [i.e., the gospel] the righteousness of God is revealed" (Rom. 1:17). Righteousness is revealed in the gospel to be the kind of power God exercises for salvation. The context of this verse requires the meaning here that God is the source, not the object, of righteousness. Perhaps Paul would not have been disturbed by the grammarian's difficulty in deciding whether the "righteousness of God" is objective or subjective genitive, for although it is obvious here that God's power, not man's, is being proclaimed, yet Paul was so convinced that man must possess or be possessed by this righteousness that the distinction would have seemed oversubtle to him.

Was it Paul's Jewishness, the necessities of his polemic against the law-righteousness of Pharisaism, or something else that led him to single out the word "righteousness"? Obedience to the law was the *sine qua non* of being "right" with God according to Pharisaic teaching. Paul could hardly expound the gospel in relation to Judaism without facing this position squarely. But we will not understand him unless we sense his deep personal hunger for rightness with God beneath all the polemical necessities. Of course, Paul includes in the term "righteousness" the connotation of "goodness" included in ethical monotheism. Of course, there is a genuine forensic factor in his argument, for Paul is keenly aware that man does not and cannot earn the verdict of acquittal before God's judgment seat. Man is offered in God's boundless mercy a status, a relationship with God which he does not deserve. The dominant note, however, is neither exclusively ethical nor exclusively forensic. It is centrally dynamic. States of being such as "goodness" or "acquittal" do not really do justice to Paul's thought. We must consider later what Paul meant by the righteousness of God. Here we need only note that it is God's own righteousness which gives content to his saving act in Christ.

c. The power of God as love. Paul's emphasis on God's righteousness neither excludes nor contradicts in his thinking God's gracious love in his salvation. He can and does write of the love of God (Rom. 5:5, 8; 8:37-39; II Cor. 13:11) and of the grace of God (Rom. 1:5; I Cor. 15:10; Gal. 1:15; 2:9) without using the word "righteousness." He writes also of the fatherhood of God quite in the manner of Jesus—i.e., God *is* the Father, men *become* his sons, for the father-son relationship is neither necessary nor physical as based on the creator-creature status; it is ethical and spiritual, based on God's unmerited choice and man's response in faith (Rom. 8:14-17). God is first of all Father of the Lord Jesus Christ (Rom. 15:6; I Cor. 1:9; II Cor. 1:3). Through Christ, God is the Father of all believers (I Cor. 8:6; II Cor. 1:3; 6:18). They name him Father (II Cor. 1:2; Gal. 1:4; Phil. 1:2; Philem. 3). Yet men are not children of God by nature but by faith (Gal. 3:26), by adoption (Gal. 4:4-7), by the Spirit (Rom. 8:14-17). The variety and richness of Paul's vocabulary when he writes of God and of God's relationship with man confirms our view that Paul is centrally concerned to show that God has acted for the salvation of men and that the gospel is the power of God to this end. "Righteousness," "love," "grace," "fatherhood," can be used almost interchangeably to express the character of the God who acts. It is God's *act* in Christ that reveals his power unto salvation. Righteousness is particularly relevant when Paul explicitly relates his thought to the Judaism he is seeking to reinterpret, but the word "righteousness" is not the only or the inevitable term for the power of God.

3. Man from the human point of view. Having announced the theme of Romans, the "power of God for salvation to every one who has faith" (1:16), Paul follows with a sustained argument to show that all men, Jews and Gentiles alike, are guilty before God, that they are in bondage to sin, and that they are powerless to save themselves by obeying God's law, whether written in the scriptures or in their consciences (1:18–3:20). Man's utter and unexceptionable need of salvation and God's grace and power to save—these are the focuses of Paul's theology. The link between power and need is faith, without which even God's amazing offer of salvation cannot avail. This does not mean that Paul centers his gospel in "experience" as over against "theology." It means, as his letters show, that he is concerned to lift the saving acts of God in Christ and man's response in faith into the "clarity of conscious knowing." He is not engaged in formulating a speculative system, even as he is not content to present salvation as a vague and formless "experience." As we grasp his purpose, which cannot be called exclusively experiential or exclusively theological—being, indeed, the interpenetration and illumination of both—we shall be prepared for certain obscurities, and even contradictions, which more systematic thinking might have avoided.

"From now on, . . . we regard no one from a human point of view" (II Cor. 5:16). The RSV rendering of κατὰ σάρκα is an interpretative, rather than an exact, translation. It has the value of carrying Paul's thought over into contemporary English more adequately, if not perfectly, than the literal "after the flesh." For σάρξ means, not just a phase of man's life such as his desires and passions, but the whole man when he is viewed apart from or in opposition to God. Man so viewed can be saved only by a "new creation," by becoming a "new creature" (vs. 17).

Let us examine further Paul's view of man as isolated from or in opposition to God. Paul accuses the Gentiles of sinful deeds such as idolatry and sensual and antisocial behavior (Rom. 1:18-32). He then brings home to the Jews their own sins, which are even more blameworthy in the light of their privileges (Rom. 2). His indictment might merit the charge that it is never possible to condemn wholesale an entire people. Were there not "good" Gentiles and "good" Jews? Paul would, no doubt, have agreed. His listing of overt sinful acts may be regarded as a description of the symptoms of the disease which afflicts all mankind, even those men who do not exhibit the flagrant symptoms. The human predicament, Paul holds, is deeper than "sins." "Sins" are the fruit of "sin." "All men, both Jews and Greeks, are under the power of sin" (Rom. 3:9). "There is no distinction; since all have sinned and fall short of the glory of God" (Rom. 3:22-23). Man as man is the slave of sin (Rom. 6:17, 20; 7:14); sin is the constant pattern or principle of his life (Rom. 7:25; 8:2).

What is sin? We shall miss Paul's meaning if we equate sin with "badness" defined in terms of an ethical standard or code, although he is convinced that sin bears evil ethical fruit. Sin is falling "short of the glory of God" (Rom. 3:23). It is man's isolation from, his independence of, God, and his pride in his own ability to deal with life on the level of his own wisdom. Paul believes that this self-confidence leads to gross moral evils, but its chief disaster is that men are caught in the toils of their own little selfhood. The ultimate tragedy of existence does not lie in little or larger misdemeanors but in the failure to rise to the creative purpose of God, the "glory of God." Sin is more than an act or an attitude of rebellion against God; it is more than a transgression of God's law; Paul appears to regard sin as an objective condition or status, even when man is not guiltily responsible (Rom. 6:12-14). Indeed, many expressions Paul uses suggest that sin is actually a personal being, an outside, demonic power. Sin "came into the world" (Rom. 5:12), "reigned in death" (5:12), "lies dead" (7:8), "revived" (7:9), "wrought in me all kinds of covetousness," "deceived me and . . . killed me" (7:8, 11; cf. vs. 13), "dwells within me" (7:17, 20), enslaves me (cf. 6:6, 17), pays the "wages of . . . death" (6:23). This is either mythology or vivid rhetorical language. Suggesting the latter is the fact that Paul speaks of the flesh in similar personal terms (cf. Rom. 8:12; Gal. 5:13, 17, 19, 24), and so he does of the world (I Cor. 1:20-21). In any case, Paul is clearly saying that man is caught in the toils of sin beyond his power to extricate himself and that sins —i.e., deeds and attitudes patently evil—spring from sin as the objective condition of man as man, man from the human point of view.

When man becomes conscious of this status, he may be driven to the verge of despair (Rom. 7:24). Yet God created man in his own image (I Cor. 11:7), and one of the benefits of the gospel is "our hope of sharing the glory of God" (Rom. 5:2). Even as the desperate nature of man's plight is brought home to him, he is aware that this sinful condition is alien to his true nature and not part of the creative work of God (Rom. 7:20, 23). The awareness that man is essentially a creature and child of God, though he is actually estranged from him, results in the deep inward cleavage in the self so characteristic of Paul's view of man from the "human point of view."

What of the origin of sin? Paul seldom raises this question, and when he does, his answer is far from clear. The classical passage is Rom. 5:12-21. The terse, closely packed opening sentence: "As sin came into the world through one man and death through sin, and so death spread to all men because all men sinned," is never finished, but few sentences, finished or unfinished, have occasioned more discussion. The "one man" is Adam (vs. 14), whose "transgression" had dire consequences for all humanity. Is Adam regarded as a historical figure (Christ is his counterpart in vss. 15-21), or is he the symbol of a doomed humanity in mystical union with him, just as the redeemed are to be "made alive" in Christ (cf. Rom. 5:17; I Cor. 15:22)? Or did Paul think in such categories as literal over against symbolic? In the verse as it stands, it is death which "spread to all men because all men sinned," and it has been argued that Paul regarded death as inherited from Adam, rather than sin. Each man does his own sinning, it is held, but he is born into a world in which death is the penalty for sin. Yet in this very context Paul writes: "By one man's disobedience many were made sinners" (vs. 19), and: "Sin reigned in death" (vs. 21). He makes no distinction between sin and death as inherited from Adam. We do scant justice to Paul's thought, however, if we fail to note that every statement about the reign of sin and death and about man's helplessness and hopelessness in the grip of sin is set in immediate and vivid contrast to the "reign in life through the one man Jesus Christ" (vs. 17). Paul's impact on successive generations since his time is due in part to the sheer realism with which he faces our human situation and the equally amazing faith that he proclaims in the redeeming, transforming power of God in Christ. We are born into a human situation corrupted by sin, whether the spread of sin is reckoned biologically, sociologically, or psychologically. Yet we are perpetually haunted by the consciousness that we are children of God, made in his image and with the hope of sharing his glory.

How and where does sin lay hold of man? Paul is deeply concerned with this question, and he answers it in many and varied ways. The words "flesh" (σάρξ), "body" (σῶμα), and "soul" (ψυχή) are the chief terms he employs, while the word "spirit" (πνεῦμα; *see* § 7 *below*) is the chief term for the redemptive power which overcomes the power of sin and death.

"Flesh" (*see* FLESH [NT]) as Paul uses the word has many different shades of meaning which only the context can determine. (Translators render the Greek word σάρξ by different English words and phrases such as "worldly," "earthly," etc. This is confusing to the reader who does not know Greek. In the following documentation the Greek word for "flesh," σάρξ, is always present, even when the English translation does not reveal it.) Often, perhaps usually, Paul uses the word "flesh" for the physical or natural man, the tangible stuff of human life (cf. Rom. 1:3; I Cor. 15:39; II Cor. 12:7; Gal. 4:13; Phil. 1:22; Philem. 16). But it is clear that Paul does not limit the use of this word to the instinctual or sensual aspects of man's life. The "works of the flesh" include not only the vices that we call sensual but also "enmity, strife, jealousy, anger, selfishness, dissension, party spirit" (Gal. 5:20). While the flesh is the sphere of imperfection (cf. Rom. 2:28; 6:19; I Cor. 3:1; 15:50; II Cor. 5:16; Gal. 1:16) and so subject to capture by sin, many scholars think that Paul regards the flesh itself as morally neutral. Perhaps in principle he thought of the flesh as neutral but in fact saw it as sinful and, indeed, as the seat of sin. Nevertheless, it is "sin in the flesh" (Rom. 8:3) which is the essentially evil thing. Flesh for Paul may be characterized as the sense-bound, earth-bound, time-bound, self-bound existence of man apart from God and in opposition to his will.

The word "BODY," σῶμα, also has a number of different meanings and shades of meaning for Paul. He can use it for the natural, physical human body (I Cor. 5:3; 12:12; 15:38; I Thess. 5:23). He can also use it of the whole community of Christians in his famous figure of speech (Rom. 12:4-5; I Cor. 12:12-30). But perhaps the characteristic use approaches the meaning of our word "personality," a word not available for Paul. Paul's sustained argument about the spiritual body in I Cor. 15 contains the real clue to his meaning. He cannot conceive of existence after death as bodiless. The spiritual body, however, is not of "flesh and blood" (vs. 50). "Body" for Paul in this context is the principle of individuality, the imperishable mold of the person. The body, so understood, is capable of being glorified, transmuted from the physical to the spiritual (vss. 42-50), and so has a spiritual potential not attributed to the flesh.

The word "SOUL," ψυχή, is perhaps the least important of the three terms for Paul and at the same time the most difficult for the English reader, since the word "soul" carries with it meanings not present for Paul. It is usually defined as the animating, vital principle of the fleshly body. As such Paul can at times use the word to mean "physical," "soulish," "unspiritual," in ways that seem very like his use of "flesh" (cf. I Cor. 2:14; 15:44, 46). But it has a wider significance than the word "flesh," and Paul can use it of full human life, the natural life of earthly men, in contrast to the life endowed with the "gifts of the Spirit of God" which constitute a new creation (I Cor. 2:14). Paul was pioneering in religious psychology, and it is not surprising that he leaves the modern reader somewhat confused as to the precise meanings intended. It seems clear, however, that he intends to say that man by his very nature is open to the onslaught of sin and that sin may capture—indeed, has captured—his whole being.

4. Christ the wisdom and power of God. Paul is proud of the gospel because it is the power of God for salvation (Rom. 1:16). But how is this saving power revealed and made operative for men? Paul answers: "In Christ," who is the "power of God and the wisdom of God" (I Cor. 1:24). Paul's thought may be gathered around three questions: Why did Paul center his gospel in Christ? Who is Paul's Christ? What is the origin of his Christology?

a. Christ the gospel's center. Paul's background, racial and religious, was Jewish, and while Judaism could look for the manifestation of God's sovereignty by God's own acts without reference to an anointed Agent or Messiah (*see* MESSIAH [JEWISH]), yet the coming of Messiah and of the messianic age was characteristic of Judaism. Paul as a Jew was predisposed to look for the coming of Messiah. As a Jew he would look for God's reign to come through deeds rather than by the emergence of new ideas. The structure of Paul's thought required a revelation of God in terms of history. But it was surely the impact of the historic Jesus upon Paul that determined his emphasis and led him to the full and formal ascription: "the Lord Jesus Christ."

If the historic Jesus was determinative for Paul, why did he make so little use of the words and deeds of Jesus in his letters? He centers attention almost exclusively on the death and the Resurrection. Paul does refer to words of Jesus (I Cor. 7:10), and they are authoritative for him. An impressive list of possible allusions to sayings of Jesus can be compiled (*see* § B9*b below*). Perhaps most significant of all is the central place of "love," ἀγάπη (I Cor. 13), in the Pauline ethos and the fact that he understands so clearly the Lord's deeds and words as manifesting God's outreaching love to men who do not deserve it. He can catch this up in one memorable sentence: "While we were yet sinners Christ died for us" (Rom. 5:8). Yet we must not gloss over the fact of the fewness of references to Jesus' life and words. It is due in part to Paul's radical evaluation of human existence apart from God. Outside the divine purpose and power, death spiritual and physical is the final outcome for humanity. The ultimate issue, then, is whether there can be life-through-death. The death and resurrection of Jesus is the answer. More positively put, the messianic role for Paul does not lie in the past; Christ is the living Lord now, and his lordship will be gloriously consummated in the future. This dominates Paul's thinking. The historic Jesus is now caught up in the divine Lord. It may well be that Paul told his converts more about Jesus' words and deeds than the letters reveal, but it is abundantly clear that Christ is now the living Lord for him.

b. Who is Paul's Christ? The risen Lord Jesus Christ is unmistakably a divine being for Paul. The older messianic concept of a divinely anointed and empowered king who would be God's instrument in restoring the kingdom to Israel has little, if any, meaning for him. Jesus Christ was indeed "descended from David according to the flesh," but he was "designated Son of God in power according to the Spirit of holiness by his resurrection from the dead," and the name given him was not "son of David" but "Jesus Christ our Lord" (Rom. 1:3-4). Christians are called of God (Rom. 8:30) and of Christ (Rom. 1:6; I Cor. 7:22) and of both together (Gal. 1:6). Paul's apostolic commission is from God (II Cor. 5:18; Gal. 1:16) and from Christ (Rom. 1:5; II Cor. 5:20; 10:8; 13:10; Phil. 3:12). Revelation is from God (Gal. 1:16) and from Christ (Gal. 1:12). Paul is the servant of God (II Cor. 6:4; I Thess. 3:2) and of Christ (I Cor. 3:5; II Cor. 11:23). Christ is the object of prayer, is seated at the right hand of God, and is Judge. The title "Lord" is freely used, and it is not always possible to be sure whether Paul means God or Christ by it. Paul's freedom in using almost interchangeably the same expressions of God and of Christ raises the inevitable question: Was Christ God for him? The few verses which in some versions seem to identify God and Christ, actually distinguish between them, as the modern translations correctly indicate (cf. Rom. 9:5; II Cor. 4:4, 6; II Thess. 1:12). Two verses in Colossians (1:17; 2:9) are more difficult to harmonize with Paul's usage elsewhere, but Colossians has a different orientation from the other generally accepted letters and reflects a type of controversy not so central in them. Yet even in Colossians (*see* COLOSSIANS, LETTER TO THE) God is "the Father of our Lord Jesus Christ" (1:3). Only the Paulinist author of Titus seems to allow a direct ascription to Christ of the name God (2:13). Over against these scattered verses are the several passages which explicitly distinguish Christ from God and subordinate him to God (Rom. 11:36; I Cor. 3:23; 11:3; Phil. 2:11; I Thess. 1:9). That Paul never thought of his monotheism as compromised by his conception of Christ is spelled out in the full and formal pronouncement of I Cor. 8:4-6: "We know that 'an idol has no real existence,' and that 'there is no God but one.' For although there may be so-called gods in heaven or on earth—as indeed there are many 'gods' and many 'lords'—yet for us there is one God, the Father, from whom are all things and for whom we exist, and one Lord, Jesus Christ, through whom are all things and through whom we exist."

None of the titles Paul uses was invented by him. "Christ," "Son of God," "Lord"—all these were current religious titles in the Jewish and Hellenistic environment. The full and formal "our" or "the Lord Jesus Christ" (Rom. 5:11, 21; 6:23; 7:25; 8:39; I Cor. 1:10; 15:57) and the "grace of our Lord Jesus Christ" (Rom. 16:20; I Cor. 16:23; II Cor. 13:14; Gal. 6:18) sound like accepted forms needing neither explanation nor defense. Paul as a Jew must have known that the word "Christ" was a title (*see* CHRIST), but in most cases he uses it as part of a proper name. Possibly his usage of "Christ Jesus" interchangeably with "Jesus Christ" retains the memory of the title, since strictly proper names were not variable in this fashion. "Christ" as a title has all but disappeared in his letters. Was this because Gentile readers had no background of tradition for the Messiah-Christ title unless and until they had been instructed? Was it made congenial because for Paul and the early Christians, Jesus and Jesus alone was the Christ?

SON OF GOD is a frequent designation in Paul's letters. In its Jewish meaning, "Son" or "my Son" would refer to character and appointment, not to metaphysical relationship. Paul's usage certainly implies more than the Jewish implications, although many scholars question whether he is primarily concerned with metaphysical relationship of the Son to the Father. His presentation at this point, however, would bring the Lord Jesus into the area of Hellenistic thought. "Lord" was perhaps the most significant and characteristic title used by Paul. The exact contemporary religious usage of "Lord" (κύριος) is a complicated area of research. We may only remark that Paul uses "Lord" to designate Christ as a pre-existent, divine being just as he uses the name Jesus to retain the significance of the historic man. The title Lord brought Paul's message within the circle of Hellenistic religious thought as the title Messiah-Christ could not do. Yet Paul was not the founder of a Christ cult in which the Lord Christ paralleled the Lord Serapis or the Lord Mithras. Such a passage as I Cor. 8:4-6 makes such an interpretation impossible. The use of the title Lord no doubt carried with it certain dangers to be guarded against. Paul had, indeed, a "mystery" to proclaim (I Cor. 2:7; 4:1), but it was not to be kept secret but to be broadcast to all who had faith to hear and heed.

Some christological titles do not appear in Paul's letters. "Born of the seed of David," Jesus Christ is "Son of God" and "our Lord," not "son of David" (Rom. 1:3-4). The title Savior (*see* SALVATION, SAVIOR) is not applied to Christ; God is Savior, and the one exception, in Phil. 3:20, immediately adds the familiar "the Lord Jesus Christ." Although Paul never uses the exact title SON OF MAN—it would be a barbarism in Greek—he does make significant use of a related concept, the first Adam and the last Adam, the earthly and the heavenly man (Rom. 5:12-20; I Cor. 15:45-49).

c. The origin of Paul's Christology. When we ask how Christ became the "power of God and the wisdom of God," Paul's answers are not in the form of precise definition but in glowing and vivid figures of speech. The three most important passages are I Cor. 15:20-28 (cf. Rom. 5:12-21); Phil. 2:5-11; Col. 1:13-20. According to Philippians, the "mind . . . in Christ Jesus" was far other than that of the presumptuous and rebellious angels who would have grasped "equality with God." His mind was bent on obedience, on humiliation and self-emptying, that he might despoil death, "even death on a cross," of its doom. And this, writes Paul in bold phrases, turned out to be in accord with the very mind of God, who "has highly exalted him . . . , that . . . every tongue [should] confess that Jesus Christ is Lord, to the glory of God the Father." Here the age-old myth of rebel angels cast out of heaven is daringly replaced by the Son, who in complete obedience to the Father chooses the life of a slave among men and a death on a cross. The outcome is that our humanity is no longer doomed to death as the penalty for sin but has the potential of sharing with Christ in the hope of glory.

Whether from the pen of Paul or of a Paulinist, Col. 1:13-20 only carries into the cosmic realm Paul's thought of Christ as the power and wisdom of God. Here, as the agent of God in creation, the Son is the "first-born of all creation," and "in him all things hold together," since "in him all the fulness of God was pleased to dwell." Although the language here differs in emphasis from the other letters, it is to be noted that this cosmic speculation yields practical consequences (vss. 12-14) and has an ethical outcome, "to lead a life worthy of the Lord, fully pleasing to him, bearing fruit in every good work and increasing in the knowledge of God" (vs. 10). The type of thought in the whole passage reminds us of contemporary thinking in Alexandrian Judaism (*see* PHILO JUDEUS) and in the late WISDOM literature. If this is Paul, he is presenting Christ as the sole MEDIATOR over against some threat of angelic mediators.

In the final key passage (I Cor. 15:20-28) Paul presents the Lord Christ as the head of the new humanity (cf. vs. 22 with Rom. 5:12-21), this time as the victor over sin and death. He will vanquish all rebellious wills, human and demonic, to achieve the final consummation, when God will "be everything to every one" (vs. 28). The framework of this kind of thinking is clearly apocalyptic messianism.

One other christological passage has been much discussed: Rom. 1:1-4. Here the crux is the ambiguous verb in vs. 4. Is it to be rendered "declared to be" (KJV), "installed" (Moffatt), or "designated" (RSV)? In other words, is the Resurrection here presented as the proclamation of a status already existing, or as the assumption of an office not previously possessed, or is the verb designedly ambiguous? The last suggestion seems a bit subtle. Would it not be more likely that Paul was unaware of the theological problem he raises for us? If the verb is translated "installed"—i.e., the assumption of an office not previously held—this might support the adoptionist Christology which passages implying the pre-existence of Christ (II Cor. 8:9; Gal. 4:4; Phil. 2:6-11) would contradict. It has been argued that Paul here represents a transition between a primitive adoptionism (cf. Acts 2:36) and the thoroughgoing pre-existence, incarnation, exaltation, of the Gospel of John and the Letter to the Hebrews. Another way out of the difficulty is to hold that Paul is tactfully beginning his Letter to the Romans by citing *their* Christology, which is not *his*. Paul could be tactful, but hardly at a point like this.

If we ask of Paul, Was your Christ once really a man? he answers: *Was?* He *is* the heavenly man, and "just as we have borne the image of the man of dust, we shall also bear the image of the man of heaven" (I Cor. 15:49). If we ask, How could the exalted Lord be genuinely human? he replies: He "emptied himself, . . . and became obedient unto death, even death on a cross" (Phil. 2:7-8). If we ask, How can a cosmic Christ be conceived as personal or a personal Christ as cosmic? he answers: This is the whole goal of creation, which "waits with eager longing for the revealing of the sons of God" (Rom. 8:19). If we object that Jesus was, after all, but an incident, an episode, in human history, Paul answers that there is no isolated fact hereafter, for "all are yours; and you are Christ's; and Christ is God's" (I Cor. 3:22-23). *See also* CHRIST.

5. The word of the Cross. "The word of the cross is folly to those who are perishing, but to us who are being saved it is the power of God" (I Cor. 1:18). At the outset it is important to remember that to isolate the Cross from the Resurrection is a formal procedure, for just as the Resurrection can have no meaning apart from death, so the death is informed by the Resurrection, even when there is no verbal reference to it in Paul's words. What is everywhere implicit becomes explicit in such a sentence as: "If while we were enemies we were reconciled to God by the death of his Son, much more, now that we are reconciled, shall we be saved by his life" (Rom. 5:10). Was the sequence death-life, or was it life-death? Or was the former the logical, and the latter the experiential, sequence? Surely it was the living Lord Jesus Christ whose impact upon Paul illuminated the Cross and gave it significance. The two events are inseparable, inextricable; and when the one is considered apart from the other, we must remember that their relationship to each other is almost organic.

Why and how is the death of Christ on the cross effective for salvation? No part of Paul's message has been more debated, as he himself anticipated when he said of the Cross that it was a "stumbling block to Jews and folly to Gentiles" (I Cor. 1:23). Paul employs a number of metaphors to communicate what God has done for man's salvation in the death of Christ: It is a redemption, a ransoming, like a slave's release from bondage (Rom. 3:24; I Cor. 1:30). It is a sacrifice adequate for restoring favorable relations with deity (Rom. 3:25; 5:9). It is a victory over demonic powers who are competing for man's soul (Rom. 8:38-39; I Cor. 2:8; 15:25; Col. 2:15). It is the end of the old and the beginning of the new humanity (Rom. 5:12-21; I Cor. 15:20-22). Similarly, the consequences flowing from God's saving act in Christ are presented in richly varied imagery: as acquittal or justification when man is arraigned before the heavenly court (Rom. 3:24; 5:1); as reconciliation replacing the estrangement between God and man (Rom. 5:10-11; II Cor. 5:18-20); as belonging in Christ to the new humanity instead of in Adam to the old (Rom. 5:12-21; I Cor. 15:22; II Cor. 5:17); as sustained by the love of God, from which not even demonic powers can separate (Rom. 8:35-39); and ultimately as salvation, which is already initiated but will be consummated in glory (Rom. 5:2; 8:18).

Yet the Pauline imagery, varied though it is, is far from chaotic. God is always the author of salvation; there is no slightest hint that it is wrested from an unwilling God, even though the nature of sin is such as to involve estrangement, nor is there any suggestion that the death of Christ is the noble sacrifice of a good man over against an unfeeling or hostile world. Paul can exhort his readers to the imitation of Christ (II Cor. 8:9; Phil. 2:5), but always this is imitation of the will and the act of God in Christ (II Cor. 8:5, 16; Phil. 2:9). Furthermore, it is clear that the death of Christ is the way God deals with human sinfulness, universal and unexceptionable (Rom. 3:22-23). For Paul the origin of sin is on the circumference rather than at the center of his thought. He uses in homiletical fashion an analogical argument from Adam's sin (Rom. 5:12-21; I Cor. 15:21), but it is the fact of sin supported by data (Rom. 1:18-32) and by experience (Rom. 7:7-25) and the cure of sin by the creation of a new humanity in Christ which chiefly concern him. And finally, it is clear that the death of Christ reveals the nature and meaning of God's forgiveness. Paul seldom uses the word "FORGIVENESS." Was it too closely associated with the legalism he was opposing? But his favorite words, "grace," "peace," "reconciliation," express the same deep sense of God's forgiving, restoring love. The death of Christ carries the note of the cost of sin and the costly character of God's act in Christ. These are the major notes sounded throughout Paul's letters when he treats of the death and the resurrection of Christ. He is neither obscure nor esoteric in expressing these convictions.

It is when we ask how the death of Christ reveals and makes operative God's saving action—exactly how—that the recurrent discussion of Paul's doctrine of the Atonement arises. Some of the more important passages in which Paul treats this question are the following:

Rom. 3:21-26. Here the three major notes are clearly sounded: God is acting in Christ, "whom God put forward" (vs. 25); his act deals with universal sin—"all have sinned" (vs. 23); and in this act the nature of the divine forgiveness is set forth (vss. 25-26). Two figures of speech are used: redemption—i.e., emancipation from slavery—and sacrifice, an "expiation by his blood" (vs. 25). "Expiation" is to be preferred to "propitiation," not only because the Greek word ἱλαστήριον usually has this meaning in the LXX, but also because it is God himself who "put forward" Christ Jesus to this end. The two figures of speech proclaim that in the death of Christ both the power and the guilt of sin are broken. But does Paul mean to say that the death of Christ exhibits in action God's costly forgiving love, or does he mean that Christ paid the inevitable, inexorable penalty for sin as an atoning sacrifice? In the latter case it is God who acts to propitiate himself. Or does Paul rest back upon the ancient axiom: "Without the shedding of blood there is no forgiveness of sins" (Heb. 9:22), without regard to the subtleties of our modern interpretation?

Rom. 5:8-11. Here again Paul is discussing the death of Christ, but his thought is oriented to the new life issuing from justification by faith (5:1), which is here called "reconciliation." The same three notes are sounded again: it is God who is the actor (vs. 8); his act deals with sin (vs. 8); and it exhibits the nature of God's forgiveness—i.e., there is a wrath of God to be saved from (vs. 9). Two emphases not present in Rom. 3:21-26 appear: the word "RECONCILIATION," found only in the Pauline letters (Rom. 11:15; II Cor. 5:18-20; Eph. 2:16; Col. 1:19-22); and the eschatological reference to salvation (vs. 9). The barrier between God and man—which must be a barrier, in some sense, for God himself—is removed by Christ, who "died for us" as an act of God's love (vs. 8).

Rom. 6:1-11. This important passage relates the death of Christ to still another area of thought. Instead of the language of sacrifice or of reconciliation, the imagery is of the "old self" (vs. 6) and the new, of dying to sin and living to God (vs. 10), of being buried "by baptism into death" and being "raised from the dead [as Christ was]" that "we too might walk in newness of life" (vs. 4). The death of Christ is a death to sin (vs. 10), but the "life he lives he lives to God," and "we believe that we shall also live with him" (vs. 8). The old humanity "in Adam" as contrasted with the new humanity "in Christ" (Rom. 5:12-21) is the background for this thought. The death of Christ, a death to sin, is the end of the old; the Resurrection is the beginning of the new order. By a vivid use of the analogy of baptism—"baptized into his death," "buried . . . with him by baptism into death"—Paul conceives the believer as having died to sin and potentially to be raised to that newness of life characterized as being "alive to God in Christ Jesus" (vs. 11). Again it is God who is the ultimate actor, the death of Christ (and here explicitly the Resurrection) which reveals the nature of God's act, and sin which conditions that redeeming act.

II Cor. 5:14-21. This great passage is reminiscent of Rom. 6:1-11. The same controlling concern with the new life dominates, although the occasion is a very personal one (vss. 11-13). There is the same emphasis on personal appropriation of the death and the Resurrection (vss. 14-15), with an even stronger note of the believer's solidarity with Christ (vs. 14), this time without the analogy of baptism. Once again it is God who is the actor, even more emphatically than before (vss. 18-20); it is the death of Christ which reveals the significance of God's act; and it is sin which is vanquished. The closing verse, 21—one of the many terse, enigmatic Pauline sentences—has been variously interpreted. Does it mean that the sinless Jesus bore the penalty for sin on our behalf, or does it mean that by his incarnation he lived the life of man, a life dominated by sin and death, and so wrought out our salvation in the real world of our human experience? In addition to these more ordered treatments of the death of Christ there are occasional references scattered through Paul's letters (I Cor. 2:8; II Cor. 8:9; Gal. 2:20; 6:14; Phil. 2:8-9).

6. To everyone who has faith. According to Paul the gospel "is the power of God for salvation to every one who has faith" (Rom. 1:16). Faith is man's response to the gospel; it is the gateway to salvation. Paul uses the word "faith" with more than one meaning, but his characteristic use is to be seen in relation to the law. An understanding of his view of the law is essential to an understanding of faith.

a. Faith and the law. By "law" Paul usually means the revelation of God's will in the Scriptures. In a few passages "law" means obligation such as conscience exerts (Rom. 2:14-16), or civil law (Rom. 7:2-3), or even the demand of Christ (Gal. 6:2). Again, without losing the sense of "obligation," "law" can mean principle or pattern (Rom. 8:2). But most frequently Paul means the OT law or the whole OT (Rom. 3:10-19, where passages from the Psalms and the Prophets are regarded as law; I Cor. 14:21, which includes Isa. 28:11-12 as law). Paul draws no explicit distinction between the ritual and the ethical demands of the law; both are law for him as a Jew (Gal. 3:10; 5:3). Nevertheless, an unconscious distinction is apparent. What the conscience of a Gentile demands can hardly be the ritual, but only the ethical, requirements of the law (Rom. 2:14-16), and Paul regularly thinks of the ethical demands when he discusses the permanent validity of the law (Rom. 2:21-29; 13:8-10; Gal. 5:14-23). He deals with the dietary laws in considerable detail, reckoning them as of relative rather than absolute validity (I Cor. 8:1–11:1; Gal. 2:11 ff), and circumcision is spiritualized in a way that would not be satisfactory to a Jew (Rom. 2:28-29). Perhaps the solution of this apparent contradiction lies in recognizing that Paul thinks like a Jew in his view of the law. He is not so much concerned with the content of the commandments as with the fact that they are commandments. Then how are they to be fulfilled? This is the question facing him, and in answering it he undoubtedly, if perhaps unconsciously, shifts the center of gravity from the ritual to the ethical demands, for it is in the area of ethical requirements that the inward struggle goes on (Rom. 7:7-25).

The major difficulty, however, lies in the apparent contradiction between the law as embodying the will of God for men and the law as intimately related to sin and death in Paul's view. He is quite aware of this difficulty and devotes considerable space to its solution. On the one hand, he asserts the validity of the law and his own zeal in upholding it (Rom. 2:13; 3:31; 7:12). The law is to be fulfilled (Rom. 13:8-10; Gal. 5:14); and it brings no charge against those who bear the fruit of the Spirit (Gal. 5:23). On the other hand, "Christ is the end of the law, that every one who has faith may be justified" (Rom. 10: 4); the law brings knowledge of sin (Rom. 3:20; 7:7) and death (Rom. 7:9); it stimulates sinful activity (Rom. 5:20; 7:8) and brings those who "rely on works of the law . . . under a curse" (Gal. 3:10). Not only is this puzzling, but it is also shocking to Paul's Jewish readers, as he well knows it will be. He insists again and again that he is an upholder of the law, that "the law is holy, and the commandment is holy and just and good" (Rom. 7:12), and that the law itself is not sin (Rom. 7:7). He answers the charge of blasphemy in a twofold way: first, the law is the instrument of sin, not sin itself; and second and more important, the function of the law in the divine economy has been misunderstood. It is not the validity of the law, but its misunderstood role, that Paul attacks. The law does not bring a man into right relationship with God, as the classic example of Abraham shows, for faith in his case preceded the very existence of the law (Rom. 4; Gal. 3:6-18). Furthermore, the law is good but powerless as a motivating force, since, on the one hand, it fails to ensure right conduct (Rom. 1:18–2:29), and, on the other hand, zeal in keeping the law only increases one's confidence in his own righteousness and thus defeats the end in view—i.e., the righteousness of God (Rom. 10:3; Phil. 3:4-9).

Law and gospel are thus mutually exclusive as ways to the right relationship with God. Law has the positive function of revealing sin as sin—indeed, of stimulating the activity of sin and showing man that he is in sin's fatal grip, from which only a power not his own can rescue him (Rom. 7:24). Passage after passage (Rom. 3:20; 7:7-25; Gal. 3:21-25) sets forth the role of the law as an instrument in God's gracious providence to reveal to man, to stab him broad awake to the fact, that no effort of his own, however strenuous, will enable him to lift himself by his own bootstraps out of the entangling web of sin, and to show him that every victory apparently won by his own effort is actually a defeat, since it encourages the self-deception that he can save himself. Only a "new creation" like the creative act of the God who made light to shine in darkness (II Cor. 4:6) will restore, redeem, reconcile, and save mankind. But how is man to respond to God's saving act in Christ? Paul's answer is, By the obedience of faith.

b. Faith as the opposite of boasting. Negatively, faith is the absence of all self-confidence, self-assurance, self-satisfaction in human goodness, wisdom, power. While Paul can use the word "faith" to mean "trust" or "intellectual assent" and the like, faith owes its characteristic features to the sharp antithesis: faith versus law. Law—any kind of law—is powerless to set a man right with God, to put him in creative relationship with God. On the contrary, law shows man his powerlessness, incites him to sin, makes sin into guilt, and, in short, closes every avenue to salvation save only the way of faith. The objectivity of law, in other words, cuts through the subjective rationalizing of conduct ("I meant well, however short the deed fell from the intention"). The impact of the law, accordingly, either sets a man at enmity with a God who demands what no man can fulfil, or else it opens up the possibility of a radically different relationship with God from that between a lawgiver and a lawkeeper. This is what Paul means when he writes: "The law was our custodian until Christ came, that we might be justified by faith" (Gal. 3:24).

Lover of paradox as he is, Paul expresses this negative quality of faith by writing about "boasting," "glorying," but now the object has been shifted from man to the gospel which reaches man in his helplessness (Rom. 4:20; I Cor. 1:31; II Cor. 10:17; 12: 9; Gal. 6:14). Paul knows that human boasting is folly, even when he feels that he is forced by his adversaries to indulge in it (II Cor. 10:8, 13; 11:1, 16, 21), and he often sets faith over against it as its radical opposite (Rom. 11:18; I Cor. 1:29; 4:7).

c. Faith as obedience, receptivity. Faith is obedience, surrender, receptivity; it is acceptance with the whole self of the good news that God's saving grace is offered to men in Christ. Paul does not think of faith as a native, human quality progressively clarified as to its object (with the author of Hebrews; cf. Heb. 11:1–12:2), even though he can include the idea of faith as an attitude toward the unseen reality (II Cor. 4:18; 5:7). Faith is the response of the whole man toward the humanly unbelievable love of God in Christ, freely offered to men who do not deserve it. This act Paul calls "obedience," almost interchangeably with "faith" (cf. Rom. 1:5, 8, with 16:19), and its opposite he terms "disobedience" (cf. Rom. 11:30-32 with 10:3, 16), for faith is submission and "heeding" (Rom. 10:16). It is, in other words, the condition for receiving salvation, and not a virtue, an attitude, or an experience. It is the continuous necessity of an act of submission, of receptivity to God's grace in Christ. Thus, of course, faith cannot be regarded as meriting salvation, since it is surrender of the self and one's own estimate of the self. But while faith is the basic response of the whole man to the revelation of God in Christ, it is not the whole of salvation. The Spirit and the fruits of the Spirit issue from the faith that puts man in creative relationship with God.

7. Life through the Spirit. If faith is the human response to God's saving act, the consequence of faith is a "new creation" (II Cor. 5:17; Gal. 6:15). This new life can be characterized as life in and through the Spirit; it can also be described as life in and through Christ, "Spirit" and "Christ" being used interchangeably.

a. What does Paul mean by the Spirit? The antecedents of Paul's concept of the Spirit are clearly Jewish. As in the OT, "Spirit" is predominantly a religious rather than a metaphysical term, standing for the divine presence and power and for man's capacity for receiving it, and not for an invisible essence in man relating him to the rest of creation (*see* SPIRIT; HOLY SPIRIT). Paul knows of the Spirit as a miraculous divine power, a kind of invading energy enabling man to perform more than human deeds. He writes at length about "spiritual gifts" (I Cor. 12–14), quite in the temper of the OT, if with different terminology. In two respects, however, Paul deviates from the OT pattern. First, he relates spiritual gifts, unquestionably personal and individual, to group sanctions, arguing that the variety of gifts is a manifestation of the one Spirit (I Cor. 12:4-11) and that an individual gift, however highly prized, is for the edification of the church (I Cor. 14:18-19), which is itself the product of the Spirit (I Cor. 12:13). Second, the gift of the Spirit is no longer temporary or an *ad hoc* endowment; it is a permanent possession of the believer. He now lives by the Spirit (Gal. 5:25); without the Spirit (of Christ) he does not belong to Christ (Rom. 8:9). He is one of the "spiritual" (Gal. 6:1). Here we meet again the persistent Pauline paradox: the Christian *is*, the Christian *ought to be*. His true life is the life of the Spirit; yet he is exhorted to "walk by the Spirit" (Gal. 5:25; *see* § B9 *below*). That Paul thinks of the Spirit as more than an invading, dynamic energy manifested in spectacular gifts such as speaking with tongues, is evident from expressions such as "led by the Spirit of God" (Rom. 8:14; Gal. 5:18) and setting "the mind on the Spirit" (Rom. 8:6, 27). The Spirit means a direction, a will, for all of life.

Paul can and does use the word to designate the human spirit (I Cor. 7:34; I Thess. 5:23) and as an equivalent of "I" (I Cor. 16:18; II Cor. 2:13; 7:13 [translated in the latter two cases as "mind" in the RSV]; Gal. 6:18; Phil. 4:23; Philem. 25). Perhaps it is unwarranted to say that Paul thinks of the human spirit as having the capacity for receiving the divine Spirit, since he usually thinks of the self as a unified whole, yet there are at least two passages in which the spirit of man appears to be that part or aspect of the self which is open to the divine Spirit. "When we cry, 'Abba! Father!' it is the Spirit himself bearing witness with our spirit that we are children of God" (Rom. 8:15*c*-16)—this passage and especially the analogy in I Cor. 2:10*b*-13 point in that direction. It is clear that the term "spirit" has a Jewish rather than a Hellenistic background in Paul's usage, for it does not so much reflect a dualism as refer to the divinely empowered transformation of the whole person to be a "new creation." It is not clear whether "Spirit" is consistently personal or impersonal for Paul, whether we should use the pronoun "he" in all cases or "it" in some instances. There can be no question of the personal meaning in passages such as Rom. 8:16; I Cor. 2:10-16, but where impersonal expressions such as "pouring out," "sealing," "supplying," are used (Rom. 5:5; II Cor. 1:22; 5:5; Gal. 3:5)—and these are the more numerous—the precise intention is less clear. The answer to this question may lie in another direction. Personal and impersonal conceptions of the Spirit are both found in the OT. Paul's use of both, accordingly, is not surprising. What is significant is his intimate association of "Spirit" and "Christ."

b. Life in and through the Spirit. The new life is life in and through the Spirit. The Spirit is the seal, the guarantee, the first installment, of the new life (Rom. 8:23; II Cor. 1:22; 5:5). We live by the Spirit (Rom. 8:13; Gal. 5:25). The Spirit means "peace and joy" (Rom. 14:17), the freedom of sonship (Rom. 8:14-17; Gal. 4:4-7), hope (Rom. 15:13), and fruit (Gal. 5:22-23). Similarly, the new life is life in Christ and through Christ. The believer has his "life in Christ Jesus" (cf. Rom. 8:1; I Cor. 1:2, 30; Gal. 2:17; Phil. 4:1). "In Christ" are all the goods of the new life: joy (Phil. 3:1; 4:4, 10), the love of God (Rom. 8:39), the peace of God (Rom. 5:1; Phil. 4:7), and freedom (Gal. 2:4). The new life is life in the Spirit and in Christ, both expressed in the same passage: "You are in the Spirit . . . . Christ is in you . . . . Your spirits are alive . . . . Life to your mortal bodies . . . through his Spirit" (Rom. 8:9-11; cf. 8:1; Gal. 5:5-6). Paul also uses the expression "the Spirit of Jesus Christ" (Rom. 8:9; Gal. 4:6; Phil. 1:19), but never "the Spirit of Jesus." He apparently reserves the name Jesus for the historical person. Some scholars think that complete identification of Spirit and Christ is indicated by II Cor. 3:17: "Now the Lord is the Spirit, and where the Spirit of the Lord is, there is freedom," since "Lord" undoubtedly means "Christ" here, as vs. 14 assures. But a study of the context does not warrant this conclusion. The essence of Paul's thought here (3:4-18) is that scripture, which can be rightly interpreted only by the Spirit, is unveiled by the "Spirit of the Lord," which Spirit sets us free from the written code (vs. 6), for we are "changed into his likeness . . . . This comes from the Lord who is the Spirit" (vs. 18). That the Lord (Christ) has the universality and effectiveness of the Spirit is, no doubt, Paul's meaning, but that he is identifying Spirit and Christ in any metaphysical sense is questionable. The whole passage is to be understood from the religious and experiential viewpoint.

c. The Pauline mysticism. We have seen that the new life is described by Paul as life in and through the Spirit and in and through Christ. What does he mean when he writes of being "in Christ" and of Christ "in me"? This is usually called "mysticism," a word with many meanings. It will be well to appraise Paul's thought as positively as possible.

The new life is personal life. While it is true that Paul can use impersonal terms of the Spirit (*see above*) and in Col. 1:15-20, terms which strain, if they do not burst, the bounds of the personal in setting forth the cosmic aspects of Christ's role, these terms are not typically Pauline. The life of the Spirit, the life in Christ, is a definite *way* of living patterned after Jesus. Even the cosmic Lord "emptied himself," and his followers are to "have this mind among yourselves" (Phil. 2:5-11). Love even toward the unlovely is the mark of the new life (I Cor. 13). Paul writes the famous "hymn to love" in a context (I Cor. 12–14) devoted to the discussion of spiritual gifts, and he makes it as explicit as words can that the ultimate and only permanent gift of the Spirit is love expressed in personal relations. Every Pauline letter issues in the same concrete, personal application to specific human situations. This is to be the outcome of life in the Spirit, in Christ. The classic statement of Paul's mysticism is found in Gal. 2:19-20: "I through the law died to the law, that I might live to God. I have been crucified with Christ; it is no longer I who live, but Christ who lives in me; and the life I now live in the flesh I live by faith in the Son of God, who loved me and gave himself for me." This statement shows at once the intimate relationship with Christ and the resultant redirection and reconstitution of the self. The self is neither annihilated nor merged with the divine as a stream is absorbed into the ocean; the "I"-"Thou" relationship is retained, "that I might live to God," and its ultimate purpose realized.

The new life is corporate life. If a passage like Gal. 2:19-20 stresses the individual aspect of the new life, many other passages emphasize the corporate aspect. Life in the Spirit, life in Christ, is life in the new humanity (I Cor. 15:22). Perhaps being "in Adam" is not less "mystical" than being "in Christ," and this corporate consciousness may well be a central aspect of Paul's thought. To be "in Christ" may well mean a complete sharing in the body of Christ, the church (Rom. 12:4; I Cor. 12:12-27). Paul's discussion of baptism (Rom. 6:1-11; Gal. 3:27-29) and of the Lord's Supper (I Cor. 11:23-25) is probably to be understood from the same corporate viewpoint. Paul does, indeed, use language which approaches the terminology of the mystery cults, but the major reference seems to be directed toward the new humanity, the body of Christ.

The new life, then, is personal life in a new realm or a new creation. It is conditioned by faith, which involves a personal response to a definite object, God's gracious act in Christ, and which issues in a new relationship with God through the Spirit. Christ is released from the limitations of the man Jesus and is made contemporary and inward by the Spirit; the Spirit, on the other hand, is given the ethical content and the personal implications inherent in Jesus.

8. The church is the body of Christ. It is generally agreed that Paul's most significant contribution to the concept of the church is his teaching about the "body of Christ." In the two classic passages (Rom. 12:4-5; I Cor. 12:12-30) the word "church," ἐκκλησία, does not appear; it is only in Colossians and Ephesians that the identification is explicit (Eph. 1:22-23; Col. 1:18). The content and context of the extended Corinthian passage on spiritual gifts (I Cor. 14:4-5, 19, 28) make it certain, however, that Paul uses "body" and "church" synonymously. No other NT writing employs the concept of the body, unless it is hinted at in John 2:21. The new life manifests itself most conspicuously in the church and in the personal conduct of the believer. These two, church and ethics, are, indeed, intimately associated (*see* §§ B9*b-c below*), for the Spirit is the unitary source—the lifeblood, so to speak—of the varied spiritual gifts, and the ethical issue of the new life is described as "fruit of the Spirit" (Gal. 5:16-25).

a. The meaning of the church. There are at least two reasons why it is a mistake in method to stress the meaning of the Greek word ἐκκλησία, used by Paul for the new community. First, he can and does use other words, such as "saints" (more than twenty-five times), "brethren" when the reference is to the common faith (about one hundred times), and a variety of other expressions to indicate that the new community constitutes the true Israel of God (Rom. 4:11: "all who believe"; 9:6-8: "children of the promise"; Gal. 3:29; 6:16; Phil. 3:3: "the true circumcision"). Second, the Greek word ἐκκλησία has behind it Aramaic and Hebrew words (*see* CHURCH, IDEA OF), and the linguistic genealogy is by no means clear. Both etymologically and genealogically the background of the Greek word is uncertain, not to speak of the fact that our English word "church" has no relation whatever to the Greek word Paul uses.

It is best to study Paul's usage from the immediate context. His free use of the word we translate "church" indicates that he regards it neither as peculiar to himself nor as in need of definition. This corresponds with the common use of the word in Acts, which purports to give the story of the primitive pre-Pauline community. In Acts and in Paul's letters the word "church" occurs both in the singular and in the plural. Did Paul move from the particular (a church at Corinth) to the several churches, here and there, and so to the universal (the "church of God") by a kind of sociological progression? It is quite widely, and probably correctly, held today that the reverse is true. Paul conceived of the church, not as a new and tiny entity, but as the existing and true Israel, the "church of God which is [i.e., has its local habitation] at Corinth" (I Cor. 1:2). In the same way he can recall that he persecuted "the church of God" or "the church" (I Cor. 15:9; Gal. 1:13; Phil. 3:6) when his Jewish zeal was directed against Christians in a specific locality. This helps us to understand his otherwise extravagant hope and confidence in the struggling little communities so seemingly insignificant over against mighty Rome. The church was the eschatological community. Only so can we understand its existence as the heart of a movement which in its inception, at least, looked for the imminent coming of the kingdom.

It has been argued that there was no room for the church as an institution in the eschatological expectation. But is the church envisaged as an institution in the NT? Certainly not in Paul's writings. The church is the eschatological community; it is a "colony of heaven" (Phil. 3:20 Moffatt). This accounts for the informality and flexibility of its organization and worship, on the one hand, and for the fact that organization stems from the consciousness of the one body with its several members rather than from any sense of the need for a polity, on the other (I Cor. 12:14-30; *see* CHURCH, LIFE AND ORGANIZATION OF THE). Paul's view of the church is seen to be entirely consonant with the Synoptic records, according to which the individual is not so much saved by a unilateral relation to God as by being incorporated into the fellowship of God's people, the kingdom of God. Paul develops his thought along his own distinctive lines, but he is not in conflict with Acts and the Synoptics at this point.

b. The church is divinely constituted. We must unthink our modern sociological approach to the rise of the church, if we are to understand Paul's thinking. He does not think of himself as an organizer or even as a missionary in our modern sense of the word; he is not one who selects strategic centers for propaganda and strategic methods of work. We may well appreciate the statesmanship of Paul in choosing the bases for his operations and the skill with which he discovers and develops prepared groups, ready for his message. But these are quite incidental, almost unconscious aspects of his work. He believes that he is heralding the "message of reconciliation" as an ambassador for Christ (II Cor. 5:19-20), and those who hear and heed are the "saints" (Rom. 1:7; I Cor. 1:2; II Cor. 1:1; Phil. 1:1; Col. 1:2 and often). The saints are the called ones, the separated ones, the holy ones. The word "saint" does have an ethical connotation, but goodness is the implication, not the explication, of sainthood. When Paul writes to the Corinthian or to the Roman Christians as to κλητοῖς ἁγίοις ("called saints"), he does not mean that they are called to *become* saints any more than he means that he himself as a "called apostle" (κλητὸς ἀπόστολος) is called to *become* an apostle. He *is* an apostle because he has been called; they *are* saints by virtue of their calling. Any other understanding makes nonsense of the use of the word "saints" to characterize those Corinthian Christians whose moral deficiences Paul is going to expose in the frankest way. It is just because they are "saints" in the Pauline sense that he can appeal to them to behave as such. When we remember that the word "saint" is never used in the singular in the NT (Phil. 4:21 is an apparent but not a real exception), we become aware of the power of Paul's conception of the church as made up of the saints who have been called by God and who constitute a "colony of heaven."

c. The church and the eschatological event. The modern idea of the church as a means of propaganda for high ends is also foreign to Paul's thinking. To be sure, he urges the Corinthian Christians to "give no offense to Jews or Greeks or to the church of God" (I Cor. 10:32); but to regard the church as a means to an end is not the Pauline thought. He does, indeed, believe that the end of the old world will come with the imminent parousia of Christ (I Cor. 15:23, 51-57; I Thess. 4:16), but this anticipated event has already been manifest with the coming of Christ (Gal. 4:4), so that "the old has passed away, behold, the new has come" (II Cor. 5:17). The church is not so much an agency for promoting desirable causes; it is itself an invasion of the eschaton into time, having already the "first fruits of the Spirit" (Rom. 8:23) as a "guarantee" of things to come (II Cor. 1:22; 5:5) and of "sonship" (Rom. 8:15; Gal. 4:6). Paul makes use of the cosmic imagery of Jewish apocalyptic to prefigure the eschaton (I Cor. 15:51-57; I Thess. 4:13-18), but with his teaching about the new life and the church he has decisively "lifted the eschaton out of the dimension of cosmic occurrence into that of historic events."

d. The body of Christ. With this background we come to a consideration of the church as the body of Christ, an important Pauline concept, consonant, as we shall see, with his total view of the new humanity in Christ. The figure of the body must not be too rigidly interpreted, since Paul himself develops various aspects of it. In I Cor. 12:12-30 after a brief statement to the effect that the body is one, its many members actually demonstrating rather than negating its unity and "so it is with Christ," Paul focuses attention on the vital interrelations in the community of Christians. Each member, however insignificant in himself, is related organically to the body by the "same Spirit," and the differing spiritual gifts are to be understood from the functional viewpoint, for "you are the body of Christ and individually members of it" (vs. 27). In Rom. 12:4-8 the figure is again directed to the same end of unity in diversity. In Colossians, however, a different note is sounded. Here there is no suggestion of rivalry over spiritual gifts; the danger is from those who fail to acknowledge that Christ is the "head of the body, the church" (1:18), and so the "head of all rule and authority" (2:10). That Christ is the head of the church is apparently derived from the cosmic headship of Christ in the universe (Col. 1:15-20), and Christians are not so much thought of as separate parts of one body as they are incorporated into the very person of Christ. The Paulinist Ephesians carries this concept much further, along lines, many think, of Gnostic mythology, although designed to combat it.

Whatever the source of this striking figure of the body of Christ, Paul uses it to emphasize, now in one way and again in another, the unity of the Messiah-Christ and the messianic community. It is thoroughly consonant with the eschatological and the ecclesiological outlook so central in his thought. It is, as indicated above, so closely related to the mysticism of Paul as to constitute an integral part of his thought about being "in Christ." Is this phrase Paul's way of proclaiming that the Christian is "in" the fellowship of believers, "in" the church, and "in" the eschatological community of those who are being saved? At the least, this aspect of his thought must be included in any consideration of his mysticism. But does the complementary "Christ in you" (Rom. 8:10; Gal. 2:20; Col. 1:27) find its explanation so readily in eschatological and ecclesiological terms? Should we not be willing to allow Paul a genuinely mystical idea of the interpenetration of the living Lord with the spirit of the believer, which is not inconsistent with the mysticism of the body and its members?

9. Walking by the Spirit. Paul knows what ecstasy means (II Cor. 12:1-4), and he prizes the spiritual gift of speaking with tongues in its rightful place (I Cor. 14:18-19), but the fruit of the Spirit is a kind of character and conduct consonant with the new life in Christ and quite different from spectacular gifts; it is a matter, not of flying or soaring, but of walking (Gal. 5:25). The importance of ethics in Paul's message is unmistakable. Not only does he commonly close his letters with ethical admonitions and exhortations, but in most instances his doctrinal discussions are conditioned by some ethical problem or interwoven with it. It is the ethical collapse of both Gentile and Jew (Rom. 1:18–2:29) that makes justification by faith alone a necessity. The most significant passages on the sacraments are related to questions of behavior: baptism ought to issue in "newness of life" (Rom. 6:1-14), and we possess the words of the institution of the Lord's Supper only because of the disgraceful conduct of members of the Corinthian church (I Cor. 11:17-34). An important christological passage such as Phil. 2:1-11 and the significant discussion of the church in I Cor. 12:12-30 both appear to owe their presence in the Pauline corpus to the ethical needs of the churches addressed. Whether Rom. 7:7-25 is autobiographical or meant to represent the typical experience of man-under-the-law, or partly both, the ultimate despair (vs. 24) is occasioned by a "commandment" and by man's inability to "do the good" (vs. 19).

Paul's doctrine of salvation is set forth in language which at a number of points reminds us of the mystery cults, but his insistence on morality as the fruit of the Spirit sunders him sharply from these cults. It is unnecessary to look to Stoicism as the source of Paul's ethical emphasis, although he would approve and on occasion appears to have used some Stoic terms (*see* STOICS). The obvious background of Paul's ethical emphasis is Judaism, with its identification of religion and conduct. The ethical monotheism which was Paul's heritage made it quite impossible for him to think of conduct without its source in religion or of religion without its consequence in behavior. Judaism, however, had the law as the standard of conduct, and when Paul displaced law by faith as the basis of right relationship with God, what was to be the new standard? This question troubled both Paul and his readers and must be considered later.

a. The nature of Paul's ethics. Paul was, ethically speaking, a Jew from the beginning to the end of his life, and as a Jew he was the heir of an ethical monotheism he never abandoned and of the law of Moses, which remained valid for him as a guide to conduct although he denied that it was capable of setting a man in right relations with God. Consciously or unconsciously, Paul's ethical center of gravity had shifted from the ritual to the moral commandments of the law, although he made a gesture toward the latter by interpreting them symbolically (Rom. 2:28-29). His respect for the law as a guide to behavior obviates the necessity of providing a new system of ethics for converts to the gospel. Paul conceives the Christian as freed from all external requirements (Gal. 5:1, 13), but this freedom does not mean license (vs. 13); it is freedom to act according to the new life principle (Gal. 5:25). The law of Moses—indeed, all law as an externally binding control—is finished, "for Christ is the end of the law" (Rom. 10:4). This was not, at least in Paul's intention, a charter of moral subjectivity, although some of his converts so interpreted it, creating thereby one of the most difficult problems he had to face. They understood his teaching to mean that every man might now do what was right in his own eyes. Paul meant that the new man in Christ now wants to do from inward compulsion what was formerly imposed from without. This is the new Christian freedom. Henceforth good deeds are to be considered the normal expression of the Spirit-filled life; the Christian is to walk by the Spirit by which he lives (Gal. 5:25). Just as the child learns to walk with many a fall, so Paul believed that the new life in the Christian would mean walking after the pattern of Christ, and falling was not ruled out as a possibility. He found this difficult to explain to his new converts, and he devotes much space in his letters to the ethical implications of the new life.

b. The Pauline standards of conduct. Eager as Paul was to escape from the bondage of all law—for sin used the law as its instrument—and emphatic as he was in insisting that the new life creates its own "fruit" and is untrammeled by external rules, he cannot avoid standards, norms of conduct, if he is to deal concretely with ethical issues as they arise in the Gentile churches. "Walking" (Gal. 5:25) involves putting one foot before the other and doing this in a certain direction. Right conduct is not inevitable, even among the "saints," as Paul knows from experience; it is a matter of decision and of effort. Accordingly, Paul's letters do reveal certain standards of conduct even though he has no system of ethics as such. Chief among these norms are the law of Moses, the words and example of the Lord, and the leadings of the Spirit. Although Paul repudiates the law of Moses—indeed, all law—as the way to justification and shocks his Jewish readers by associating it with sin and death (Rom. 7:7-11), he himself is certain that he has maintained the validity of the law as "holy and just and good" (vs. 12). It is the function of the law which Judaism misrepresents, not its demands. God in Christ has acted so that the "just requirement of the law might be fulfilled in us" (Rom. 8:3-4). The ethical demands remain in force for him, and they are meant to be fulfilled, except that the new man, Spirit-filled, now performs what the law demands from an inward motivation rather than from an outward compulsion. There are a number of passages (Rom. 2:6; II Cor. 5:10; Gal. 6:7; Col. 3:24-25) in which Paul appears to look forward to a judgment according to deeds done "in the body" quite in terms of the Jewish pattern which he has repudiated. The apparent contradiction is to be resolved, not by supposing that Paul has forgotten for the moment his doctrine of the saving grace of God in Christ to be received by faith, but by remembering that the divine grace was a morally creative power, in his view, which made possible all and more than the law required.

The words and example of the Lord are also authoritative as a standard of conduct. While there is little direct quotation, Paul's letters reflect, here and there, the influence of Jesus' teaching (cf. I Thess. 4:8 with Matt. 10:40; Luke 10:16; cf. Gal. 4:17 with Matt. 23:13; Luke 11:52; cf. I Cor. 4:12-13 and Rom. 12:14 with Matt. 5:44; Luke 6:27; cf. I Cor. 5:4 with Matt. 18:20; cf. I Cor. 9:19 with Mark 10:44; cf. I Cor. 13:2 with Matt. 17:20; Mark 11:23; cf. I Cor. 13:3 with Mark 10:21; Luke 12:33; cf. II Cor. 10:1 with Matt. 11:29; cf. Rom. 2:1 and 14:13 with Matt. 7:1; cf. Rom. 14:14 with Matt. 15:11; Mark 7:15; cf. Rom. 16:19 with Matt. 10:16 and many other passages). Three explicit references to Jesus' teaching are: I Cor. 7:10 (cf. Matt. 5:32; Mark 10:11-12); I Cor. 9:14 (cf. Matt. 10:10; Luke 10:7); I Cor. 11:23-25 (cf. Matt. 26:26-29; Mark 14:22-25; Luke 22:15-19). To this should be added Paul's stress on love (ἀγάπη) as the ultimate determinative of conduct. Love is the Pauline ethos, the "way" (I Cor. 12:31) in which all spiritual gifts are to be expressed. I Cor. 13 does not mention Christ, but the context makes it evident that Paul is speaking of the way in which the Spirit (of Christ) issues in conduct. Even when Paul refers to the teaching of Jesus explicitly, the manner of his reference is significant. Jesus' teaching about marriage has, indeed, final authority (I Cor. 7:10), but Paul does not present it as an objective command like the law of Moses. It is rather part of that revelation of the new life in the Spirit, in Christ, which Paul himself shares (7:12, 25). Jesus' saying is not an isolated dictum but an integral part, if the supremely authoritative part, of the total revelation.

It is the Spirit which is the prevailing sanction and norm of Christian conduct. What saves this standard from being vague and indecisive is the role of the Spirit in binding the many into one body (I Cor. 12:12, 27). Because of the Spirit each individual member has an organic relationship (obligation?) to all other members. There can and must be no schism (I Cor. 1:10-13), no self-conceit (Gal. 5:26), no censoriousness, but only a "spirit of gentleness" (Gal. 6:1), for this is the "law of Christ" (vs. 2). This sense of sharing, κοινωνία, produced the Pauline ethic or, at any rate, gave it its distinctive form. This is another reason for the lack of any formal system of ethics, although the list of household duties (*see* HOUSEHOLD DUTIES, LIST OF) in Col. 3:18–4:1 (cf. Eph. 5:21–6:9) is a step in that direction.

c. The Pauline paradox. It is in the realm of ethics that the Pauline paradox is most clearly encountered. The Christian, Paul insists, lives a new life; he is a new creation; yet he must be exhorted and admonished to *be* what he *is*, to act in accordance with his new nature. Perhaps there is no logical solution of this paradox. Paul simply knows that the new life comes from God through Christ and the Spirit as men open their hearts in faith to receive it; he also knows that he must exhort his converts to walk by the Spirit, which is their true life. Of course, salvation for Paul is still an end event, the Christian is still living "in the flesh" (Gal. 2:20), and the battle with sin is still going on even though the decisive victory has been won. Accordingly Paul exhorts and admonishes, for the believer has the seal, the guarantee or down payment, of the Spirit, but the final and complete salvation is still to be expressed in future tenses (Rom. 6:5, 8, 14).

Another unsolved problem, logically speaking, is the basis for obligation in the Pauline ethic. He has abandoned the law, all law, as the means of a right relationship with God and has reinterpreted its role in the economy of salvation. Has Paul also abandoned all objective grounds for obligation? This was the position taken by certain antinomian Christians in the Pauline churches, and Paul is seriously troubled by their plausible arguments (Rom. 3:7-8; 6:1, 15). Our obligation is to God, who in Christ has acted for our salvation, but what is the ground of our obligation to our fellows once the law has ceased to play that role? Paul's answer appears to be, We are bound into one body by the gift of the Spirit, and so our obligation is as members one of another. But here his striking figure of the body is not wholly satisfactory as a logical solution, for the members of the body operate organically and automatically and not from obligation in a moral sense. It is clear, therefore, that in Paul's thought the body is still a metaphorical term and is not meant to be taken literally.

10. The Lord is at hand. The coming of the Lord (*see* PAROUSIA) is but one aspect, although of central significance (I Cor. 15:20-28; I Thess. 4:13-17), in Paul's expectation of events to be realized at the end of history and as its divinely ordained culmination. Eschatology is central rather than peripheral for Paul. He contemplates these end events both in chronological terms as near (Rom. 13:11-12; I Cor. 7:29) and in terms of decisive opportunity and fulfilment (*see* TIME), looking forward, not with foreboding, but with eager joy, to the emancipation from human and cosmic enslavement when "the creation itself will be set free" (Rom. 8:19-23).

a. The importance of eschatology for Paul. How important eschatology was for Paul is to be seen by surveying the scope of his expectations. The most complete statement is I Cor. 15:20-28. There the major notes are sounded, although his terse phrases leave the precise meaning open to conjecture. The destiny of believers, alive and dead, is bound up with the coming of Christ in messianic power (I Thess. 2:19; 4:15; 5:23). He is the "first fruits" of the new humanity. The resurrection of Christ—so the logic of Paul's reasoning runs—means the resurrection of believers, who are members of his body. Just as they have been "in Adam," so they are now "in Christ" (I Cor. 15:22). The rule of Christ is to mean the defeat of all alien powers (vss. 24-26). How long this rule of Christ is to continue is not indicated (contrast Rev. 20:5, 7), but it is to issue in the complete conquest of the enemies of God and in the final consummation when the Son delivers the kingdom to God (vs. 28). Whether the final judgment of all, believers and unbelievers alike, is meant by the words τὸ τέλος (vs. 24; "the end" or "finally"?) is not clear; Paul is here concerned primarily with the destiny of believers, although, no doubt, sharing the view that all will be judged (Rom. 2:6-11; but Rom. 14:10; II Cor. 5:10 refer to the judgment of Christians). Two Thessalonians passages deal with the destiny of Christians who have died before the coming of the Lord, in order to assure the readers that the dead in Christ will share equally with the living at his coming (I Thess. 4:13-18) and to correct their view that "the day of the Lord has come" by an enigmatic presentation of the "man of lawlessness" and of events that must yet occur before the coming of the Lord (II Thess. 2:1-17; *see* THESSALONIANS, SECOND LETTER TO THE).

An integral part of Paul's eschatology is his view of the cosmic conflict between Christ and the invisible, supernatural powers of evil. These "principalities" and "powers" (Rom. 8:38; Col. 1:16) reign over all mankind, bringing sin and death since Adam. But in the Cross they have been defeated (I Cor. 2:8; Col. 1:13; 2:10, 15), for Christ's coming and especially his resurrection marked the turning point in the tide of battle, and the ultimate victory is now assured (I Cor. 15:26-26).

It follows naturally that salvation for Paul is a strictly eschatological event, the climax of God's dealing with men (Rom. 13:11 and often): we have been reconciled to God; we shall be saved (Rom. 5:10). That Paul can speak of salvation as a present reality (Rom. 8:24) is a contradiction in terms but not in reality, for he is emphasizing the fact that ours is, indeed, a saving hope, not contrasting something completed now over against the eschatological climax.

b. Was Paul apocalyptic? Neither Paul's eschatology nor the apocalyptic form it took (*see* APOCALYPTICISM) when he was contemplating the sequence of coming events (I Cor. 15:20-28; I Thess. 4:13-18; II Thess. 2:1-12) can be dismissed as oriental hyperbole or as merely the framework of his thought from which his essential message can be lifted without surgery. These ideas are too deeply embedded in his gospel and too intimately woven into it to be treated as incidental. Yet the question, Was Paul apocalyptic? remains a valid one. He did think in terms of the two ages, the Judgment and the resurrection, the reign of the saints and the coming of the Lord. Apparently he also accepted the intermediate messianic kingdom as preceding the age to come (I Cor. 15:25-28), after the general pattern of Jewish apocalypses (cf. II Bar. 30:1; II Esd. 7:26-30), although this plays an incidental role in his presentation of end events.

But Paul stands over against the apocalypses in important respects. His OT citations and allusions are from the Pentateuch, Isaiah, and the Psalms prevailingly, and he makes almost no use of the apocalyptical parts of the OT. In contrast to the pseudonymity of the apocalypses, Paul's personality is of significance in his writings. While the epistolary character of our sources guarantees this, it remains true that a thoroughgoing apocalyptist would have regarded an apocalypse as alone worth writing. Furthermore, moral values and motives, peripheral in the apocalypses, are central for Paul. The apocalyptic message was primarily one of comfort for the faithful and of condemnation for unbelievers. Paul's eschatology had a different relevance to his ethics (*see* § B10*c below*) than in the Jewish apocalypses. Finally and chiefly, the apocalyptic dualism —this age and the age to come—has been essentially transformed in Paul's thought. There is no longer a sharp boundary between the now and the then, for "all things are yours, whether . . . the present or the future, all are yours" (I Cor. 3:21-22). The dualism is now not simply a matter of time or of space, but it is a warfare between flesh and Spirit. Though the believer is still "in the flesh" (Gal. 2:20), he is also "in the Spirit," and the Spirit dwells in him. The age of the Spirit is yet to come, but the reality of the Spirit's presence is the guarantee of victory and of participation in the kingdom of God (Rom. 14:17). Paul puts this in a striking phrase in I Cor. 10:11: "written down for our instruction, upon whom *the end of the ages has come.*" He believes that he and his readers "stand in the isthmus of time between the ages," or better, he believes that the age to come can be entered from within history. Indeed, Paul has lifted the eschaton out of the "dimension of cosmic into the realm of historic occurrence." Accordingly, while it is correct to say that Paul accepted and employed apocalyptic, it is more accurate to say that he stands above apocalyptic, unconfined by its boundaries. This age of historical time has yet opportunities opening out into the age to come. That age has invaded this in Christ and the Spirit.

c. Eschatology and ethics. Paul's ethical teaching is surprisingly free from an explicit eschatological sanction and motivation. It is, of course, true that all his exhortations to right conduct imply the "new creation" in Christ (II Cor. 5:17), which is to be consummated in salvation as an end event. Behavior, however, is usually the "fruit of the Spirit" (Gal. 5: 22-23). "Love is the fulfilling of the law" (Rom. 13: 8-10), and it is through the Holy Spirit that "God's love has been poured into our hearts" (Rom. 5:5). Paul seeks to work out each ethical problem to the "way" of love (ἀγάπη). In two instances he does make explicit use of the eschatological sanction: In Rom. 13:11-12 he follows the important declaration that "love is the fulfilling of the law" (vs. 10*b*) with the words: "Besides this you know what hour it is . . . For salvation is nearer to us now than when we first believed; the night is far gone, the day is at hand." The imminence of the end is not used to control the content (love) of conduct; it only enforces the relevance of that teaching. The situation in Paul's discussion of marriage in I Cor. 7 is quite different, however. Here, in counseling the unmarried to remain in their present state, Paul explicitly introduces the imminence of the end as the reason for his advice (vss. 26, 29). This is the clearest example of "interim ethic" in the NT. It is to be observed that Paul uses eschatology here, not to invalidate the institution of marriage, but only to show its inadvisability in view of the imminent end.

How thoroughly eschatological Paul's thought is can be tested by considering any one aspect of it. He cannot think of the destiny of the Jewish people, e.g., without evaluating their present rejection of the gospel in terms of the ultimate purpose of God (Rom. 9–11). Salvation, the conduct of the believer, the unceasing battle with the flesh—every aspect of the new life is at once a mingled faith and hope and a definitive assurance of victory. Yet Paul was never obsessed with speculations about the end, else we would have had only an apocalypse from his pen. His letters are replete with admonitions, exhortations, warnings, and encouragements. He is convinced that "the form of this world is passing away" (I Cor. 7: 31), but what saves him from being an apocalyptist is the event of Christ and the gift of the Spirit. Because of these events human history is now conjunct with the age to come. The day is dawning, and the eyes of faith can see its approaching glory. To the Christians at Thessalonica who are tempted to sloth by the imminence of the end, Paul writes a sharp rebuke (II Thess. 3:6-12). The nearness of the end should mean the release, the enhancement, the revitalization, of the whole man to live the new life. What the end means is a new range and significance for life here and now "so that whether we wake or sleep we might live with him" (I Thess. 5:10). Into this temporal, transient age new and lasting powers and values have come. Love, "poured into our hearts through the Holy Spirit," lasts on, even when the form of this world passes away. The church is a "colony of heaven" (Phil. 3:20 Moffatt), and the believer is being changed into the Lord's likeness.

11. The permanent significance of Paul. It is hard to write calmly about Paul. Across the centuries, as during his lifetime, he has been the center of controversy arousing passionate defense and equally passionate opposition. The fact that his letters were preserved and that they were ultimately accepted as scripture is solid evidence of the verdict of the early church. That verdict has never been successfully challenged. It is true, however, that the significance of Paul's message has been quite variously assessed. Sometimes little more of Paul is known today than the well-loved I Cor. 13, together with Rom. 12; Phil. 4:8-9; and other such ethical exhortations. Sometimes one would gather from theological works that Paul only wrote a series of proof texts to support and illustrate the rubrics of systematic theology. Perhaps Paul would write again as he did to the church at Philippi: "What then? Only that in every way, whether in pretense or in truth, Christ is proclaimed; and in that I rejoice" (1:18).

Paul himself acknowledged the marks of human frailty both in his thinking and in his doing. His achievement—or, as he would say, what God wrought through him—is the more impressive because of it. He asked and gave significant answers to the major theological questions which were to recur again and again through the subsequent centuries. But perhaps his most creative contribution was the union in him of the universal and the particular, for he released the universal message of Jesus from Jewish limits, laying the foundation for Gentile Christianity, and at the same time he planted little Christian churches in the strategic centers of the NW Mediterranean world in the firm conviction that they were "colonies of heaven," thus influencing and helping to shape the history of the Western world. Paul was an authentic ambassador for Christ whom nothing "in all creation" could separate from the love of God.

Bibliography. W. M. Ramsey, *St. Paul the Traveller and the Roman Citizen* (1896); H. Weinel, *St. Paul, the Man and His Work* (trans. G. A. Bienemann; 1906); A. Schweitzer, *Paul and His Interpreters* (trans. W. Montgomery; 1912); R. W. Robinson, *The Life of Paul* (1918); C. H. Dodd, *The Meaning of Paul for Today* (1920); G. A. Deissmann, *St. Paul: A Study in Social and Religious History* (trans. W. E. Wilson; 1926); F. J. Foakes-Jackson, *The Life of Saint Paul* (1926); B. W. Bacon, *The Story of Paul* (1927); T. R. Glover, *Paul of Tarsus* (1930); F. C. Porter, *The Mind of Christ in Paul* (1930); A. D. Nock, *St. Paul* (1933); C. A. A. Scott, *St. Paul, the Man and the Teacher* (1936); J. Weiss, *The History of Primitive Christianity* (trans. F. C. Grant *et al.;* 1937), bks. II-III; J. Knox, *Chapters in a Life of Paul* (1950).

A. C. PURDY

PAULUS, SERGIUS sûr'jĭ əs pôl'əs [Σέργιος Παῦλος] (Acts 13:7-12). PROCONSUL of Cyprus when Paul and Barnabas visited the island, *ca.* A.D. 45. By temporarily blinding a magician who was with the proconsul, Saul, "also called Paul" (for the first time in Acts), convinced Sergius Paulus of the truth of the gospel, though it has been suggested that either Luke or Paul "may have mistaken courtesy for conversion."

A certain L. Sergius Paullus was consul for the second time in 168, but inscriptions and literary evidence tell us nothing of an earlier consul of that name. There is, however, an inscription which mentions L. Sergius Paullus as a Curator of the Tiber during the reign of Claudius; this may well be the man mentioned in Acts.

The theory that the apostle changed his name from Saul to Paul in honor of the proconsul, though known to Origen, has little but antiquity to commend it.

Bibliography. F. J. Foakes-Jackson and H. J. Cadbury, *The Beginnings of Christianity,* V (1933), 455-59 (K. Lake), 183-87 (A. D. Nock).

R. M. GRANT

PAVEMENT [מלבן (Jer. 43:9; KJV BRICKKILN), brick mold, pavement of bricks (Akkad. *nalbanu*); מעשה לבנה (Exod. 24:10; KJV PAVED WORK), a construction of tile *or* flagstone (Akkad. *libittu,* tile pavement); רצפה, *from* רצף, fit (stones) together (Akkad. *raṣapu*); KJV מרצפת (II Kings 16:17; RSV "pediment"); λιθόστρωτος]. The pavement of the palace at Susa was made of porphyry, marble, mother-of-pearl, and precious stones (Esth. 1:6). Ezekiel's temple had a pavement around the outer court (Ezek. 40:17-18). Jeremiah hid some stones in the mortar of the palace court at Tahpanhes (Jer. 43:9). In a theophany the pavement under God's feet was made of sapphire (Exod. 24:10; cf. Ezek. 1:26).

Jesus sat on the judgment seat at a place called "The Pavement" (in Hebrew, GABBATHA; John 19:13). It was the courtyard of Pilate's headquarters. It has been identified with the Roman pavement now under the Convent of the Sisters of Zion. The pavement and the underground constructions may belong to the tower of ANTONIA.

See also JERUSALEM § 11; CITY § B2*c*.

C. C. MCCOWN

PAVILION [סכה; KJV סך (Ps. 27:5; RSV "shelter"); *both from* סכך, to weave together]. A shelter or covering. In I Kings 20:12, 16, the word is used in the KJV (RSV "booth") to designate tents of the royal entourage in which Ben-hadad and his aides became drunk at noon before Ben-hadad's decisive defeat at Samaria.

The word is used figuratively in several contexts. In Pss. 27:5 KJV (RSV "shelter"); 31:20 (RSV "covert") it refers to a place where Yahweh hides from evil those who fear him. In Isa. 4:5—H 4:6 it is a protective covering over the restored Jerusalem (KJV "tabernacle"). A "pavilion" is also the concealment of Yahweh in theophanic appearances (Job 36:29; KJV "tabernacle"; cf. KJV "pavilion," RSV CANOPY, in II Sam. 22:12=Ps. 18:11—H 18:12). The object so designated may have been the kind of booth built from boughs used at the Feast of Booths or a tent pavilion, woven from textile material. In Job 36:29; Ps. 18:11=II Sam. 22:12 it is the clouds that are the pavilion, or canopy, of Yahweh.

E. M. GOOD

PE pē (Heb. pā) [פ, *p* (*Pê*)]. The seventeenth letter of the Hebrew ALPHABET as it is placed in the KJV at the head of the seventeenth section of the acrostic psalm, Ps. 119, where each verse of this section of the psalm begins with this letter.

PEACE IN THE OT. The state of wholeness possessed by persons or groups, which may be health, prosperity, security, or the spiritual completeness of covenant. In the OT no particular distinction is made among these categories; military or economic peace is similar to the bodily and spiritual health of the individual.

1. Vocabulary
2. Secular peace
   a. Individual
   b. Communal
3. Religious peace
   a. Peace and righteousness
   b. Peace and covenant
   c. Peace and blessing
   d. Peace and salvation

Bibliography

1. Vocabulary. The most important word, covering the whole range of connotations, is the verb שלם, "to have or be at peace," with its cognate nouns, שלום, "peace"; שלם, "PEACE-OFFERING"; and Aramaic שלם, "peace." A denominative verb from שלום is שלם, "to make or be at peace." The root meaning of שלם seems to be "completeness, wholeness" (cf. Akkadian *šalāmu,* "to be faultless, healthy, complete"), whence come the connotations of "health," "prosperity," "political and spiritual weal." The verb שלה (originally שלו) is "to be at rest" (Job 12:6), and its derivative nouns, שלוה (Dan. 8:25 KJV) and שליו (I Chr. 4:40), are used for "peaceable" or "time of peace" (so Dan. 8:25; 11:21, 23—H 11:24, "without warning"—i.e., at a time when peace seems assured). The *Hiph'il* of נוח, "to rest," is rendered "give peace" in Chronicles, and its cognate noun, מנוחה, appears in I Chr. 22:9 (*see* REST). Other terms translated "peace" are: עשה ברכה (lit. "to make a blessing"; II Kings 18:31; Isa. 36:16); מישרים ("equitable terms"; Dan. 11:6, 17—the latter emended from ישרים); and רגע (Job 21:13; KJV "a moment"). Several verbs are translated "to hold one's peace" (חרש, חשה, דמם; cf. also Neh. 8:11 KJV; Job 29:10 KJV [קול נחבא, "the voice . . . was hushed"]; Zeph. 1:7 KJV [הם, the interjection, "Hush!" formed as if from a verb הסה]), but this means simply "be silent."

2. Secular peace. The distinction between secular and religious peace is made only for analytic purposes. In the OT, peace of any kind is a wholeness determined and given by God. What is here called secular peace is the wholeness of men in their social relations and individual existence.

a. Individual. This peace principally involves health and the good life. It is protection by God's favorable promise (Judg. 18:6) or by someone who cares for one's needs (Judg. 19:20). Restoration to health is restoration to peace (Isa. 38:17; RSV "welfare"). The man who returns in safety from battle has preserved his health and is at peace (Josh. 10:21; I Kings 22:17; II Chr. 19:1; Ps. 55:18—H 55:19); one who is going into danger is therefore wished peace (Exod. 4:18; II Sam. 15:27). The individual's peace is synonymous with his good life, for it involves his healthful sleep (Ps. 4:8—H 4:9), length of life (Prov. 3:2), posterity (Ps. 37:37), and a tranquil death after a full life (Gen. 15:15; Judg. 6:23; II Kings 22:20; II Chr. 34:28; Job 21:13; Jer. 34:5; negatively, I Kings 2:6).

b. Communal. Just as the peace of the individual is his health and safety, the peace of the nation or of the family is its prosperity and security. Peace is often economic prosperity (cf. I Chr. 4:40; 22:9; Pss. 37:11; 147:14; Isa. 54:13; 66:12; Zech. 8:12), and some passages describe it as a state wherein society and nature are harmoniously joined in covenant (Lev. 26:6; Job 5:23-24; Ezek. 34:25; cf. Ps. 72:3). Political security is also peace (II Kings 20:19; Isa. 32:18; Hag. 2:9), but this is negated by the entrance of "sickness" or "wounds" into the society (cf. Jer. 6:14; 8:11; 14:19; Ezek. 13:10, 16), which can be healed only by Yahweh (Isa. 57:19; Jer. 33:6). Peace then comes to attain its connotation as the reverse of strife (cf. Jer. 12:5; Zech. 8:10), when peaceful covenants are entered upon (Gen. 34:21; Josh. 9:15; Obad. 7). It may be simply the absence of war (Judg. 21:13; I Sam. 16:4-5; 29:7; I Kings 2:5; 4:24—H 5:4; Ps. 120:7; Eccl. 3:8; Jer. 14:13; 28:9). On the other hand, peace is frequently the term for the ending of war. It may mean making a treaty or agreement of nonviolence (Deut. 2:26; 20:10-12; Josh. 10:1, 4; 11:19; Judg. 4:17; I Sam. 7:14; I Kings 5:12—H 5:26; 22:24; II Kings 9:17-31; 18:31; Isa. 36:16; Dan. 11:6). It is sometimes military victory (Judg. 8:9; II Sam. 19:24, 30; I Kings 22:27-28; I Chr. 22:18; Isa. 9:7—H 9:6; Jer. 43:12; Mic. 5:5—H 5:4; Zech. 9:10). The royal name in Isaiah's oracle, "Prince of Peace" (שר שלום; Isa. 9:6—H 9:5; *see* MESSIAH [JEWISH]), seems to denote a victorious prince. To make peace may also be to surrender (II Sam. 10:19; I Kings 20:18; I Chr. 19:19; Isa. 27:5; Dan. 11:17).

3. Religious peace. All peace is of God (Isa. 45:7; RSV "weal"), and the condition of peace is the presence of God (Num. 6:26; I Chr. 23:25). It is therefore man's righteousness under the covenant which makes him peaceable.

a. Peace and righteousness. "The effect of righteousness will be peace" (Isa. 32:17), and the two ideas are frequently combined (cf. Pss. 72:7; 85:10—H 85:11; Isa. 48:18; 57:2; 60:17). To be at peace is to be upright (Mal. 2:6), faithful (II Sam. 20:19), an upholder of truth (Esth. 9:30; Zech. 8:19). It is to practice justice (Isa. 59:8; Zech. 8:16). Peace is thus the antithesis of wickedness (Ps. 34:14—H 34:15; Prov. 10:10 [RSV with LXX]; Isa. 48:22). The wholeness of man's life includes his obedience to God. *See* RIGHTEOUSNESS (IN THE OT); JUSTICE.

b. Peace and covenant. Since the COVENANT is the relationship which restores man to wholeness of relationship with God, it may be referred to as a covenant of peace which is everlasting (Ezek. 37:26), which brings man the love of God (Isa. 54:10; *see* LOVE [OT] § 3*b*). For Yahweh to remove his peace is for him to abrogate the covenant (Jer. 16:5). The covenant of peace involves a mutuality of relationship which is absent from the cognate term in Islam (cf., e.g., the infinitive *islam,* "submission," and the participle *muslim,* "one who submits to Allah"; but cf. also Job 25:2). At the same time, the covenantal peace conveys Yahweh's blessing on man (Num. 25:12; Mal. 2:5; in these cases, a blessing on the priestly function).

c. Peace and blessing. The blessing is Yahweh's gift of the wholeness of relationship. It may be applied to strength (Ps. 29:11; negatively, Ezek. 7:25), to pardon for sin (II Kings 5:19), to joy (Isa. 55:12), to the assurance of an answer to prayer (Gen. 41:16

[RSV "favorable answer"]; I Sam. 1:17). The blessing of peace is essential for the integrity of Jerusalem and therefore of Israel's religion (Pss. 122:6-8; 125:5), and with it comes the promise of continued blessing (I Kings 2:33; Ps. 128:6). *See* BLESSEDNESS.

d. Peace and salvation. Because God rules over the fortunes of men, his peace is salvation (Isa. 52:7; Nah. 1:15—H 2:1). Those who trust him (Isa. 26:3), who hope in his salvation (Ps. 119:165), have peace. For the eschatological promise of God is a promise of peace (Ps. 85:8—H 85:9; Isa. 26:12). Indeed, though judgment and trouble may precede the actuality of eschatological peace, Israel knows that her suffering is the "chastisement of our peace" (Isa. 53:5 KJV), the stripes that bring about God's own healing. *See* SALVATION.

Bibliography. J. Pedersen, *Israel, Its Life and Culture,* I (1926), 263-335.

E. M. GOOD

PEACE IN THE NT [εἰρήνη]. In classical Greek the word is used to describe the cessation or absence of hostilities between rival groups. In the NT, however, the word carries a far wider range of meaning. This is partly because it was used in the context of Christian faith and experience, and partly because of the influence of the Hebrew word שלום. This word was represented in the LXX by εἰρήνη, and therefore its meaning dominates the Greek word which translated it. *See* PEACE IN THE OT.

The Hebrew word embraces all that the Greek word normally meant, and much more besides, and in the NT the Greek word has some of the breadth of meaning of its Hebrew counterpart. Perhaps we should recognize this in such passages as Luke 1:79; 2:14; 19:42; Rom. 3:17; etc.

Because of its comprehensiveness of meaning, the Hebrew word came to be used as a common greeting, both on meeting and on parting. This greeting is found on the lips of Jesus, as "Go in peace" (Mark 5:34; Luke 7:50), or "Peace be with you" (John 20:19, 21). It is clear, however, that as he used it, and as he expected his disciples to use it, it was much more than a merely conventional salutation. With the word of peace went the actual bestowal of peace, and if this proffered gift was spurned, the peace returned to him who had offered it (Matt. 10:13; Luke 10:5-6). Paul also incorporates this greeting into the opening sentences of his letters, and other letter writers follow his example (I Pet. 1:2; II John 3; Jude 2; Rev. 1:4).

In these greetings the peace which is offered comes from God (Gal. 1:3; Eph. 1:2; Rev. 1:4). It can, therefore, elsewhere be described as the "peace of God" (Phil. 4:7; Col. 3:15); and God himself is the "God of peace" (Rom. 15:33; II Cor. 13:11; Phil. 4:9; Heb. 13:20), since it is from him that peace comes to man. In John 14:27 it is the gift of Christ.

Within this inclusive significance of the word, derived from the OT, there are, however, in the NT three more precise meanings which can be distinguished:

a) The first follows the usage of classical Greek and indicates peace, as opposed to war or strife. This is found in its ordinary secular sense in Luke 14:32; Acts 12:20. An extension of this meaning occurs in Eph. 2:11-17, where "peace" is the reconciliation which Christ has brought about between Jews and Gentiles, groups normally antagonistic to each other.

In I Cor. 7:15 it refers to "domestic peace" between husband and wife, and in Matt. 10:34; Luke 12:51 to harmonious relationships within the whole family. In the sense of happy personal relationships with others, especially one's fellow Christians, it is set forth as the goal of a Christian man's endeavor (Rom. 14:19; Eph. 4:3; Heb. 12:14; I Pet. 3:11). The cognate verb εἰρηνεύω is also used to exhort Christians to be at peace with one another (Mark 9:50; Rom. 12:18; II Cor. 13:11; I Thess. 5:13). Jesus also speaks his blessing upon the "peacemakers" (εἰρηνοποιοί) in Matt. 5:9 (cf. Col. 1:20).

In I Cor. 14:33 the word εἰρήνη is used, in contrast to "confusion," to mean a proper orderliness in the conduct of church meetings.

b) Since the NT is so greatly concerned with the restoration of right relationships between God and man, it is not surprising to find the word "peace" used to describe this restored relationship. Before his conversion man is "alienated" from God (Eph. 4:18; Col. 1:21), an "enemy" of God (Rom. 5:10; Col. 1:21). In Christ, however, this wrong relationship has been set right. Man has been reconciled to God (II Cor. 5:19; Col. 1:22), and "justified by faith" (Rom. 5:1). Thus he has "peace with God through our Lord Jesus Christ" (Rom. 5:1). God has made peace through the blood of the cross (Col. 1:20). So emphatically is this the work of Christ (Eph. 2:15) that he himself is called "our peace" (vs. 14).

c) In the NT the word may also mean "peace of mind" or serenity. This appears to be a distinctively Christian meaning, since it is not characteristic either of εἰρήνη in classical Greek or of שלום in Hebrew. In consequence some scholars are reluctant to acknowledge its presence even in the NT. There are, however, certain contexts from which it cannot reasonably be excluded—e.g., Rom. 8:6, where the "mind of the Spirit" is described as "life and peace"; 15:13 ("joy and peace in believing"). So too in Gal. 5:22 "peace" as one of the fruits of the Spirit must carry something of this significance. Its association with joy, patience, and self-control requires it (cf. also Rom. 14:17). At Phil. 4:7 we read that "the peace of God . . . will keep your hearts and your minds in Christ Jesus"; and in Col. 3:15 the "peace of Christ" is to "rule in your hearts." The actual mention of "heart" and "mind" as the sphere where peace rules points to this same meaning. Moreover, it is difficult to deny this meaning to John 14:27, since the gift of peace is explicitly offered in contrast to the troubled and fearful hearts of the disciples.

In certain contexts, therefore, "peace" may bear any one of these three distinguishable meanings. It is, however, more than probable that in many cases it is used comprehensively to embrace all three, as, e.g., when one Christian wished for another "peace from God."

C. L. MITTON

PEACE OFFERING. *See* SACRIFICE AND OFFERINGS § C2.

PEACEMAKER. The translation of εἰρηνοποιός (Matt. 5:9). The peacemakers who are "blessed" are not primarily those who spread cheer and good will; but those who create peace where there is hatred, who reconcile where there is separation. These are the "sons of God," who draw upon the peace they have been given by God—the eschatological peace, which is proleptically available—to reunite the estranged. The peace which they offer can only be reconciliation through Christ. The price is high; and to those who will not accept the terms, Christ brings, not peace, but a sword. *See* BEATITUDES.

B. H. THROCKMORTON, JR.

PEACOCK [תכיים (I Kings 10:22); תוכיים (II Chr. 9:21), *probably from* Egyp. *kyw,* a kind of monkey (*see* FAUNA § B2*k*), *but Koehler favors* poultry, *cf.* Vulg. *pavos,* peacocks; KJV רננים (Job 39:13; RSV OSTRICH)]. The male bird of the peafowl, especially of the common species, *pavo cristatus.*

It seems unlikely that the peafowl, a native of India, was introduced into Palestine as early as the age of Solomon. It is more probable that it came into the Mediterranean area only after Achaemenid Persia had established relations with India. The peacock is first mentioned in Greek literature in Aristophanes' *Birds* (102, 268), which was produced in Athens in 414 B.C. Aristotle was familiar with this bird (*History of Animals* 488*b*), as, of course, were the later Romans (e.g., Pliny Nat. Hist. X.22-23).

In I Kings 10:22; II Chr. 9:21 "peacocks" is a very questionable translation of תכיים; "monkeys" is to be preferred. These would be Old World monkeys, doubtless from Africa, and probably of the genus *Cercopithecus. See* APE.

W. S. McCULLOUGH

PEARL [פנין (Job 28:18; KJV RUBY); KJV פנינים (Job 28:18; RSV CRYSTAL); μαργαρίτης]. A dense shelly concretion, formed as an abnormal growth within the shell of mollusks.

"The price of wisdom is above pearls" (Job 28:18). "Pearl" is used in evaluating the kingdom of heaven (Matt. 13:46). It is a simile for religious truth (Matt. 7:6); an ornament not worn by modest women (I Tim. 2:9), of a great harlot (Rev. 17:4), of Babylon (Rev. 18:16). It is an export of Babylon (vs. 12). It is material for the gates of the New Jerusalem (21:21).

See also JEWELS AND PRECIOUS STONES § 2.

W. E. STAPLES

PEASANTRY. A reasonable translation of the obscure word פרזון, found only in the ancient song of Deborah (Judg. 5:7, 11). Related Semitic words indicate "those who dwell in open country, away from walled cities."

PEDAHEL pĕd'ə hĕl [פדהאל, God has delivered] (Num. 34:28). A Naphtalite leader, son of Ammihud. He was one of those appointed, under the oversight of Eleazar and Joshua, to superintend the distribution of the W Jordanian territory among the ten tribes to be settled in that area of Canaan. The meaning of the name Pedahel and of other names in this account underscores Israel's dependence upon God for the new life in Canaan.

Bibliography. M. Noth, *Die israelitischen Personennamen* (1928), pp. 92, 180.

R. F. JOHNSON

PEDAHZUR pĭ dä'zər [פדהצור, (the) rock has ransomed] (Num. 1:10; 2:20; 7:54, 59; 10:23). The father of Gamaliel, who was the leader of Manasseh in the wilderness.

Bibliography. M. Noth, *Die israelitischen Personennamen* (1928), p. 180.

PEDAIAH pĭ dā'yə [פדיהו, פדיה, Y has ransomed; Apoc. Φαδαία]; KJV Apoc. PHALDAIUS făl dā'yəs.

1. The maternal grandfather of King Jehoiakim of Judah (II Kings 23:36); from Rumah.

2. A descendant of King David; named in I Chr. 3:18-19 as the father of Zerubbabel. However, according to Ezra (3:2, 8; 5:2), Nehemiah (12:1), and Haggai (1:1, 12, 14; 2:2, 23), Zerubbabel was the son of Shealtiel, Pedaiah's brother.

3. The father of Joel, from that part of the tribe of Manasseh which lived W of the Jordan in the time of David (I Chr. 27:20).

4. One of those who helped repair the wall of Jerusalem after the Exile (Neh. 3:25; II Esd. 13:25). He was the son of Parosh.

5. One of those who stood at the left hand of Ezra during the reading of the "book of the law of the LORD" before the people (Neh. 8:4; II Esd. 18:4). Pedaiah's position is reminiscent of the seat of honor afforded leading men in the synagogue service of the third and second centuries B.C.

6. A Benjaminite; son of Kolaiah; father of Joed (Neh. 11:7; II Esd. 21:7).

7. A Levite appointed by Nehemiah as a treasurer over the storehouses to distribute the required portions to the Levites serving in the temple (Neh. 13:13; II Esd. 23:13).

E. R. ACHTEMEIER

PEDDLER [καπηλεύων]. In II Cor. 2:17 Paul writes that he was not a "peddler" of God's word. This may imply that he did not receive pay from the churches, or it may mean something quite different. Paul knew Jesus' word that the "laborer deserves his food" (Matt. 10:10; Luke 10:7-8; cf. I Cor. 9:14; I Tim. 5:18); but he may also have known another word of Jesus about giving without pay (Matt. 10:8-9). At Corinth he had apparently not "made use of his right" to remuneration (cf. I Cor. 9:12*b,* 15). So in II Cor. 2:17 Paul may be referring in part to "not receiving pay." But the point is primarily that Paul had not used tricks in his preaching and had not falsified the gospel. The contrast is between "peddling," with which various cheap or dishonest practices might be associated, and preaching out of pure motives and in the knowledge of having been commissioned by God to do so (cf. II Cor. 4:2).

B. H. THROCKMORTON, JR.

PEDESTAL [כן] (I Kings 7:31); KJV BASE. The round foot of a column; elsewhere "base." *See* LAVER; PILLAR.

PEDIMENT [מרצפת] (II Kings 16:17); KJV PAVEMENT. A stone foundation with which Ahaz replaced the bronze oxen which supported the "sea" in the temple, after he had melted them down. *See* SEA, MOLTEN.

PEG, TENT PEG [יתד, יתד אהל]; KJV NAIL. Alternately: PIN; STAKE; STICK. A stick for digging (Deut. 23:13), a peg for hanging articles on a clay wall (Isa. 22:23, 25; Ezek. 15:3), a pin used in loom weaving (Judg. 16:14), or the stake with which a tent was made fast to the ground. Jael extended the hospitality of her tent to Sisera, the fleeing Canaanite commander, and then slew him with a tent peg and mallet (Judg. 4:21-22; 5:26). The term is used as a fitting metaphor to describe Jerusalem made secure and strong by the favor and power of the Lord (Isa. 33:20; 54:2; cf. Ezra 9:8; Zech. 10:4). G. B. Cooke

PEKAH pē'kə [פקח, he has opened (the eyes), *perhaps contraction for* (ו)פקחיה, Yahu has opened (the eyes); Assyrian *Pa-qa-ḫa*]. King of Israel *ca.* 737-732 B.C.; son of Remaliah. Pekah succeeded to the throne after his murder of Pekahiah.

The close similarity between the names of these two successive kings, Pekahiah and Pekah, has led to the suggestion that they were one and the same individual. This is most unlikely. Pekahiah is said to have been the son of Menahem, while Pekah's father was Remaliah. A more plausible hypothesis is that the usurper Pekah, one of Pekahiah's officers, was so eager to ensure his position as king that he deliberately assumed the name of his predecessor. This seems to be borne out by the fact that only in these two biblical names is the root פקח to be found. In this connection Isaiah's practice is to be noted of referring to the king, almost scornfully, it seems, as the "son of Remaliah" (Isa. 7:4-5, 9; 8:6), even when he uses the specific name of his ally, Rezin the king of Syria (cf. a parallel in the reference to the "son of Tabeel" in 7:6).

Pekah is said to have reigned twenty years (II Kings 15:27). But a reign of this duration is impossible. Assyrian sources indicate that Menahem paid tribute to Tiglath-pileser in 738, and that Hoshea became king of Israel in 732. Between these two dates the reigns of Pekahiah and Pekah have to be fitted. If Pekahiah occupied the throne for *ca.* two years, it is clear that Pekah's reign can have lasted no more than six years. Those who seek to defend the general historicity of the text hold that Pekah may have "reigned twenty years" (II Kings 15:27), but not necessarily in Samaria. He seized power in Gilead at the death of Jeroboam II, and maintained it there throughout Menahem's reign. This was the cause of Menahem's constant insecurity until the appearance of Tiglath-pileser III confirmed him on the throne of Israel. Then Pekah capitulated, declared his loyalty to the king, and was given a high military office. When the opportune moment arrived, he murdered his royal master, with Syrian assistance, and became king himself in Samaria.

Apparently the two states of Syria and Israel attempted to force Ahaz of Judah to join them (Isa. 7:2). In view of Ahaz' determination to resist, the allies had their plans ready to conquer the land, dethrone the king, and install the son of Tabeel as king in his stead (vs. 6). But the attempt was unsuccessful. Ahaz appealed for help to Tiglath-pileser, over the strong protestations of Isaiah.

Such an appeal, however, was unnecessary. The provocation of Syria and Israel was such as Tiglath-pileser could not be expected to tolerate. The Assyrian records indicate that in the twelfth year of his reign—i.e., 734—he marched again to the West, especially "against Philistia." For the years 733 and 732 campaigns are listed "against Damascus." In the course of the first campaign Tiglath-pileser attacked N Israel, including Gilead, captured all of Naphtali (Galilee) and Transjordan, and annexed this territory (II Kings 15:29). It is probable that the reference to Argob and Arieh (vs. 25) is to be included here, with a change of reading from "Arieh" to "Havvoth-jair." Both these territories are in Transjordania. In the inscriptions only the "wide land of Naphtali" is specifically named, but II Kings 15:29 gives a broader picture of Tiglath-pileser's conquests. That all these N towns were still in the possession of Israel at this time is an item of considerable interest. Some of them had been taken from Baasha of Israel by Ben-hadad king of Aram (I Kings 15:20). They had subsequently been recovered. Then Tiglath-pileser turned on Syria. Damascus was captured, and the people carried captive to Kir. Rezin was put to death (II Kings 16:9). After his conquest of N Israel, Tiglath-pileser used the method of extensive deportations of the population, whom he settled elsewhere in his empire (15:29*b*). N Israel and Aram were made into Assyrian provinces.

But intrigues still continued in Samaria. According to II Kings 15:30, a conspiracy took place, led by Hoshea son of Elah. Pekah was murdered, and Hoshea took his place on the throne of Samaria. Tiglath-pileser's inscription gives a different picture: "Israel [lit., 'Omri-Land' Bît Ḫumria] . . . all its inhabitants [and] their possessions I led to Assyria. They overthrew their king Pekah [Pa-qa-ḫa] and I placed Hoshea [A-ú-si-'] as king over them. I received from them ten talents of gold, one thousand[?] talents of silver as their [tri]bute and brought them to Assyria." That the entire population of Samaria was deported to Assyria at this time is not historical. Rather is it a piece of boastfulness on the part of the Assyrian king. Further, the inscription makes no mention of a conspiracy in the land in which Pekah was assassinated. This item is almost certainly historical, and its historicity is borne out by the fact that no mention is made of his burial. With the land in the position of a vassal state of Assyria, the revolt led by Hoshea must have been largely a domestic matter, as Hoshea during the first years of his reign continued to acknowledge the overlordship of Assyria.

Bibliography. N. Glueck, "The Third Season of Excavation at Tell el-Kheleifeh," *BASOR,* 79 (1940), 2-18; A. M. Honeyman, "The Evidence for Regnal Names Among the Hebrews," *JBL,* vol. LXVII (1948), pp. 13-25, especially p. 24, note 46; E. R. Thiele, *The Mysterious Numbers of the Hebrew Kings* (1951), pp. 99-135; A. Alt, *Kleine Schriften zur Geschichte des Volkes Israel,* II (1953), 163-87; W. F. Albright, "The Son of Tabeel (Isaiah 7:6)," *BASOR,* 140 (1955), 34-35; J. B. Pritchard, *ANET* (2nd ed., 1955), pp. 283-84; M. Noth, *Geschichte Israels* (3rd ed., 1956), pp. 233 ff.

H. B. MacLean

PEKAHIAH pĕk'ə hī'ə [(ו)פקחיה, Yahu has opened (the eyes)]. King of Israel *ca.* 738-737 B.C.; son and successor of Menahem. Pekahiah was murdered by Pekah.

The uneasy situation which prevailed in Israel

during Menahem's reign continued during his son's brief reign of two years. Rival parties, presumably pro-Assyrian and anti-Assyrian, vied for control of the kingdom. In all probability Pekahiah continued his father's policy and served as a vassal of Assyria.

He was assassinated at the hands of PEKAH son of Remaliah (II Kings 15:25), the king's "captain." The meaning of the Hebrew word שליש used here is not altogether clear. Its root meaning, on the evidence of Hittite pictures, was the third man on a war chariot. But it also had a more general meaning—"adjutant" or "military officer." It may be assumed that Pekah was an army officer in close touch with the king. "Fifty men of the Gileadites" took part in the murder along with Pekah. This probably indicates that Pekah himself was a Gileadite and came from the territory E of the Jordan. If this was so, it seems highly probable that he had the backing of Damascus, more especially as Damascus and Israel acted together in close concert during his reign (II Kings 15:37; 16:5 ff; Isa. 7:1 ff).

Bibliography. E. G. Kraeling, *Aram and Israel* (1918), pp. 115-21. H. B. MacLean

PEKOD pē'kŏd [פקוד; Assyrian Babylonian *Puqûdu*]. A minor Aramean tribe dwelling on the E bank of the Lower Tigris, approximately between modern Kut-el-Amara and the confluence of the Kerkha. Temporary subjection of the Puqûdu (Pekod) is recorded in the annals of the Assyrian kings Tiglath-pileser III (746-727), Sargon II (722-705), and Sennacherib (705-681). Puqûdu (Pekod) appears to have been organized under village sheiks and to have subsisted mainly on agriculture and husbandry. Sargon II forced their surrender by damming the Tupliash River, on which they relied for irrigation water; tribute paid by them consisted of horses, cattle, and sheep; four of their sheiks and the villages or towns in which they resided are mentioned by name in the annals of Sargon II. Pekod appears in Jeremiah's oracle against Babylon (Jer. 50:21); and Ezekiel includes Pekod along with the Babylonians, Chaldeans, Shoa, and Koa among the lovers of Jerusalem who will turn against her (Ezek. 23:23).

T. Jacobsen

PELAIAH pĭ lā'yə [פלאיה, פליה (I Cor. 3:24), Yahu is wonderful; Apoc. Φιαθάς (I Esd. 9:48)]; KJV Apoc. BIATAS bī'ə təs. **1.** Son of Elioenai, among the remote descendants of David (I Chr. 3:24).

2. A Levite who attended Ezra's public reading of the law and helped expound it to the people (Neh. 8:7; 10:10). J. M. Ward

PELALIAH pĕl'ə lī'ə [פלליה, Yahu has interceded (to judge)] (Neh. 11:12). A priest of Ezra's time.

PELATIAH pĕl'ə tī'ə [פלטיה, פלטיהו, Yahu delivers]. **1.** Son of Hananiah, and a remote, obscure descendant of David (I Chr. 3:21).

2. One of the captains, all sons of Ishi, of the Simeonite band that destroyed the Amalekite remnant at Mount Seir during the reign of Hezekiah (I Chr. 4:42).

3. Son of Benaiah, and one of the two Judean princes seen by Ezekiel in a vision of judgment (Ezek. 11:1, 13). Apparently they were in the pro-Egyptian party during the Babylonian siege of Jerusalem, who helped assure the destruction of the city by giving "wicked counsel" of rebellion (vs. 2).

4. One of the "chiefs of the people" who attended the sealing of the covenant under Nehemiah (Neh. 10:22). J. M. Ward

PELEG pē'lĕg [פלג; Φάλεκ]; KJV NT PHALEC fā'lĕk. A son of Eber, and descendant of Shem (Gen. 10:25; 11:16-19; I Chr. 1:19, 25). The name is explained as "division," because in his days the earth was divided—probably a reference to the Tower of Babel story. However, "earth" in this case may be a more limited region and may refer to the fact that in the original table the descendants of Peleg and Joktan were regarded as the two main branches of the Semitic group, the latter containing Arabian peoples and the former those located in Aram and Mesopotamia. In the present text all the descendants of Peleg have been omitted except the line that leads to Abram. Some scholars have regarded the explanation of the name as a later gloss on the genealogy and have suggested other explanations. Among these is the suggestion that, as Peleg can also mean "watercourse," the Peleg peoples were those who lived in a region where there was artificial irrigation by canals; or that the name is derived from the city of Phalga, at the junction of the Euphrates and Chaboras rivers. S. Cohen

PELET pē'lĕt [פלט]. **1.** A Calebite who is included among the sons of Jahdai (I Chr. 2:47).

2. One of the two sons of Azmaveth who were among the disaffected Benjaminite warriors who joined the proscribed band of David at Ziklag (I Chr. 12:3).

PELETH pē'lĕth [פלת, swift(?)]. **1.** A Reubenite; the father of On, who is named as a participant in Korah's rebellion against Moses (Num. 16:1). Since nothing is related about the activity of On, in the rebellion, the name is probably to be removed as a textual corruption. "Peleth" should then be read as "Pallu," who appears elsewhere as a son of Reuben and the father of Eliab (Gen. 46:9; Num. 26:5, 8).

2. A Jerahmeelite; son of Jonathan, whose ancestry is traced in the tribe of Judah (I Chr. 2:33). The Jerahmeelites were probably of Edomite extraction, resident in S Judah.

Bibliography. M. Noth, *Die israelitischen Personennamen* (1928), p. 255. R. F. Johnson

PELETHITES pĕl'ə thīts [פלתי]. A group of foreign mercenaries who are always associated with the Cherethites and with them formed the royal bodyguard under the command of Benaiah in the time of David (II Sam. 8:18; 20:23; I Chr. 18:17). Their origin is, no doubt, to be located among the Peoples of the Sea. Montgomery is of the opinion that "Pelethite" is an obvious equation of "Philistine" (פלשתי), by the absorption of š in t, and that the original pronunciation is represented by the Greek Φελεθθει.

The loyalty of the Pelethites to the crown is illustrated when they accompanied David in his flight from Jerusalem during the rebellion of Absalom (II Sam. 15:18) and by the role they played in arresting the Israelite defection from the house of David in the insurrection of the Benjaminite Sheba (II Sam. 20:7). Moreover, they followed Benaiah when he supported the Solomonic claims to the Davidic throne, and their presence at Solomon's coronation was sufficient reason for the complete fiasco of his rival Adonijah (I Kings 1:38, 44). E. R. DALGLISH

PELIAS pĭ lī'əs. KJV Apoc. form of BEDEIAH.

PELICAN [קאת, *qā'āth, possibly onomatopoeic;* Vulg. *onocrotalus and pellicanus,* pelican *except in* Deut. 14:17 (*mergulus,* diver); LXX πελεκάν, pelican *in* Lev. 11:18; Ps. 102:6—G 101:7; *in* Deut. 14:17 καταράκτης, swooper (*but text of* LXX *in* Deut. 14:15-17 *is different from* Heb., *and* pelican *occurs in vs.* 18); Targ. (Onq.) קתא]. Alternately: HAWK (Isa. 34:11); VULTURE (Ps. 102:6—H 102:7; Zeph. 2:14); KJV CORMORANT (Isa. 34:11; Zeph. 2:14). Any of a family (*Pelecanidae*) of large, web-footed birds distinguished by an enormous bill, with a dilatable pouch attached to the lower mandible. They are found in the vicinity of swamps, estuaries, rivers, and seas; their food is mainly fish.

Courtesy of the Oriental Institute, the University of Chicago

24. Egyptian wall painting from the tomb of the royal scribe Haremhab, showing a trapper with pelicans (fifteenth century B.C.)

Although Tristram records the occasional appearance of the pelican in nineteenth-century Palestine, it is not certain that this bird is designated by any known Hebrew word. If קאת means, as was once supposed, "the vomiter," this rules out the pelican, which does not regurgitate its food for its young. Moreover, קאת in Ps. 102:6—H 102:7; Isa. 34:11; Zeph. 2:14 is associated with the wilderness and with the ruins of Edom and Nineveh, regions in which the pelican would not normally be found. Bodenheimer takes this word as "a night bird" (*see* FAUNA § B5); G. R. Driver (*see bibliography*) as the scops owl.

Fig. PEL 24.

Bibliography. G. R. Driver, *PEQ* (April, 1955), p. 16. W. S. MCCULLOUGH

***PELLA** pĕl'ə. A city of the Decapolis in E Palestine and the seat of a bishopric in the early centuries A.D. Though it is not mentioned in the Bible, it was an important center with a long history. It is mentioned in the Egyptian Execration Texts (1850-1825 B.C.; *ANET* 329) and in the Amarna Letters (*ca.* 1400) under the name Piḥilum (*ANET* 486), the equivalent of the Canaanite form *Pahel.* It appears in the records of Thut-mose III (*ca.* 1490-1436) and Seti I (*ca.* 1318-1301); see *ANET* 243, 253. The stele of Ramses II, dated 1284, gives the details of an interesting little war between Pahel and Hammath on one side and Beth-shal (Beth-shan) and Rehob on the other, in which the Pharaoh was called upon to intervene. Pahel was destroyed before the Israelite conquest, apparently in some such war, and was not rebuilt until Greek colonists settled in the region after the conquest of the country by Alexander the Great (332). They were Macedonians, and the name Pahel recalled that of Pella, the famous capital of Macedonia; accordingly Pella became the official Greek name of the town. It was destroyed by Alexander Janneus in the early part of the first century B.C. but was rebuilt and adorned by Pompey (Jos. Antiq. XIII.xv.4; XIV.iv.4).

When the great revolt against the Romans broke out in A.D. 66, the Christian community of Jerusalem, being warned of the impending destruction of the city, removed to Pella; from that time on, it became an important center of the church, and did not lose its importance after the return of a large part of the community to Jerusalem after 135. The site of ancient Pella is marked by the ruins of Tabaqat Fahil, with the Roman and Byzantine remains mostly in the nearby Khirbet Fahil; it is located on the Wadi Jurm on the E side of the Jordan Valley, *ca.* eight miles SE of Beth-shan on the other side. In addition to Bronze and Iron Age pottery, there are ruins of a Roman theater and many buildings of the Hellenistic and Roman ages, as well as numerous caves of anchorites and sepulchres.

Bibliography. G. Schumacher, *Pella* (1888); J. Richmond, *PEQ* (1934), pp. 18-31; N. Glueck, *AASOR,* XXV-XXVIII (1951), 254-57. S. COHEN

PELONITE, THE pĕl'ə nīt [פלוני, פלני] (I Chr. 11:27, 36; 27:10). A title given to Helez and Ahijah, two of David's Mighty Men who fought with him in his wars against the Philistines and lesser foes. However, in the parallel list in II Sam. 23:26 Helez is called the PALTITE—i.e., a native of Beth-pelet in the Negeb of Judah—and this is undoubtedly his proper designation. Ahijah is probably identical with Eliam in II Sam. 23:34, where he is properly identified as a Gilonite. The text of Chronicles is here recognized by most scholars to be erroneous.

E. R. ACHTEMEIER

PELUSIUM pĭ lo͞o'shĭ əm [Πηλουσιον]. An important fortress town on the extreme NE frontier of Egypt.

The Hebrew name for Pelusium, סין (*Sîn*), is taken directly from the native Egyptian *Sìn,* modern *El-Faramā,* near the mouth of the easternmost branch of the Nile, *ca.* 18½ miles W of the Suez Canal and *ca.* a mile from the Mediterranean. Pelusium is cited in texts of the Old Kingdom for its excellent wine, but because of its strategic location in reference to the Asiatic countries to the N and E it acquired considerable military importance in Late Egyptian times. Thus we find it mentioned in the Annals of Ashurbanipal and in Ezek. 30:15, where it is called the "stronghold of Egypt."

The Greek name Πηλουσιον is perhaps based on a false etymology, wherein the Egyptian name *Sin* is taken to be the homonymous *sin*, "mud," translatable by Greek πηλος. It is possible, however, that it corresponds partly to a religious name which the fortress town had and which is more accurately retained in Coptic *Peremūn*, the source of the modern Arabic name *El-Faramā*.

Bibliography. W. Spiegelberg, "Der ägyptische Name von Pelusium," *Zeitschrift für Ägyptische Sprache und Altertumskunde*, 49 (1911), 81-84; A. H. Gardiner, "The Delta Residence of the Ramessides," *JEA*, 5 (1918), 253-54.

T. O. Lambdin

PEN. The translation of several words in the Bible.

a) The term עט is used either of an iron stylus (Job 19:24; Jer. 17:1) or of a reed pen (Ps. 45:1—H 45:2; Jer. 8:8; cf. 36:18), the end of which was frayed to be used as a brush.

From H. Junker, *Giza;* courtesy of Österreichische Akademie der Wissenschaften, Vienna

25. Scribes with rush pens and palettes, from the tomb of Ka-ni-nesut, son of Snefru, at Gizeh, Fourth Dynasty (2650-2500 B.C.)

b) The pointed, split-reed pen called κάλαμος in the NT (III John 13) was developed only when parchment came into use.

c) The word חרט, rendered "pen" in the KJV, paraphrased as "(common) characters" in the RSV (Isa. 8:1), probably designates a stylus for writing on a tablet; in Exod. 32:4 it denotes a tool for carving the molten calf.

d) For שרד, probably a stylus for marking wood (Isa. 44:13), *see* Pencil.

e) The צפרן, "nail, claw," made of diamond and rendered "point" (Jer. 17:1), may be yet another term for stylus, or may designate the point of the עט; perhaps צפרן should be read in Job 19:24 (for עפרת, "lead").

f) The KJV "pen" for שבט (Judg. 5:14) is a mistranslation, corrected in the RSV to "staff."

See also Writing and Writing Materials.

Fig. PEN 25. R. J. Williams

PENCIL [שרד; LXX παραγραφίς, writing instrument; Vulg. *runcina*, plane] (Isa. 44:13); KJV LINE. An instrument for marking wood; perhaps a type of stylus. *See* Pen; Writing and Writing Materials.

PENDANT. 1. נטיפה ("drop"). A droplike pendant. This item was listed among the materials captured from the Midianites and contributed toward Gideon's ephod (Judg. 8:26; KJV "chain") and among the items of luxury of the women of Jerusalem (Isa. 3:19; KJV "collar"). Pendants were of varied character; some were droplike clusters worn as earrings, while others were worn on chains or cords and suspended from the neck,* as was the case with those mentioned in Judges. They doubtless often had amuletic sig-

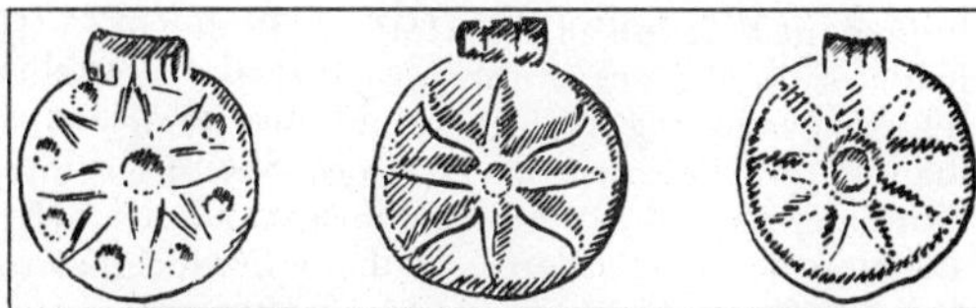

From Kurt Galling, *Biblisches Reallexikon* (Tübingen: J. C. B. Mohr)

26. Gold pendants, from Shechem

Courtesy of the Oriental Institute, the University of Chicago

27. Bone pendants, from Megiddo

nificance, such as some found in the excavations. They were of gold, bronze, bone, iron, faïence, or various kinds of stone. *See* Jewels and Precious Stones. Figs. GOL 35; PEN 26-27.

2. The translation of ענק ("necklace"; cf. Akkadian *unqu*, "ring") in Prov. 1:9 (KJV "chain"), in the phrase "pendants for your neck." This was probably a necklace. Translated "necklace" (KJV "chain") in Song of S. 4:9; "collar" (KJV "chain") in Judg. 8:26. J. M. Myers

PENIEL. Alternate form of Penuel 3.

PENINNAH pĭ nĭn'ə [פננה; Arab. *fainānā*, woman with rich hair(?), *or* coral (branching?)] (I Sam. 1:2, 4). Wife of Elkanah the Ephraimite. She had children, while Hannah, Elkanah's other wife, had none. Hannah, provoked and irritated each year by the fecundity of her rival, was finally "deeply distressed" and besought God for a son (I Sam. 1:6-11).

D. Harvey

PENITENCE. *See* Repentance.

PENKNIFE [תער]. A knife employed for making and repairing reed pens and for cutting papyrus and rolls (Jer. 36:23). The Hebrew term elsewhere refers to a "razor" (Isa. 7:20) or a "sheath" for a sword (II Sam. 20:8). *See* Writing and Writing Materials. R. J. Williams

PENNY. *See* Money, Coins § 3*c*.

***PENTATEUCH** pĕn'tə tōōk, —tūk. The Pentateuch, or Five Books of Moses, constitutes the first and most important division of the Hebrew Bible (OT). It holds pride of place in the Jewish canon, and was regarded as having the highest authority, higher even than the Prophets and the Writings, since it was traditionally thought to be the work of Moses, who alone of the biblical heroes spoke with God face to face (cf. Exod. 33:11; Deut. 34:10-12).

A. Composition
  1. The primary history
  2. G (the underlying source)
  3. J and E
    a. J
    b. E
    c. JE
  4. D and DH
    a. The Deuteronomic Code
    b. The Deuteronomic history
  5. P
B. Form and contents
  1. The beginnings (Genesis)
    a. The primeval story (chs. 1-11)
    b. The patriarchal narratives (chs. 12-50)
  2. The Exodus (Exod. 1-18)
  3. Sinai (Exod. 19:1-Num. 10:10)
  4. The wilderness wanderings (Num. 10:11-36:13)
  5. The epilogue (Deuteronomy)
C. History of Pentateuchal criticism
  1. Documentary hypotheses
  2. Form-critical analysis
  3. Traditio-historical criticism
  4. Synthesis and summary
Bibliography

A. *COMPOSITION.* The Pentateuch itself is the first part of a larger literary complex, which we may designate the "primary history." This comprises the books from Genesis through II Kings, but omits Ruth (which in the Hebrew Bible is to be found among the Writings). The primary history recounts the story of Israel in the context of the total human experience from the beginning (i.e., Creation) to the collapse of the kingdom of Judah and the Babylonian exile. It is to be distinguished from the Chronicler's history (I and II Chronicles-Ezra-Nehemiah), which, while covering the same general subject matter, omits most of the earlier narratives and focuses attention on the kingdom of David and Solomon and their successors. It continues down to the Persian period and the reconstitution of the Jewish community under the leadership of Ezra and Nehemiah. It is apparent from an examination of the two histories that not only do they reflect drastically different points of view, but they are also the products of vastly different periods in Israel's history. The inconclusive endings point toward a date of composition shortly after the events with which the story closes (i.e., before the next significant occurrence). Thus with regard to the primary history it is difficult to suppose that the return from Babylon would not have been mentioned had the primary history been completed subsequent to that momentous event. By contrast the Chronicler's account includes this datum, and brings the narrative down to the reforms of Ezra and Nehemiah (late fifth century B.C.). His story ends at this point somewhat inconclusively, and

Courtesy of the Trustees of the British Museum

28. Reduced facsimile of a page of the ninth-century-A.D. Pentateuch in the British Museum

it is a reasonable inference that the Chronicler's history was compiled about this time, or in any case not later than the early fourth century.

Fig. PEN 28.

1. The primary history. The date of composition of the primary history may be fixed by the final entry in II Kings, itself a footnote to the story of the fall of Jerusalem and the Exile. This note refers to the favor shown the shadow-king Jehoiachin by Evil-merodach the Babylonian emperor, in the year 561 B.C. Since the death of Jehoiachin is hinted at in these verses (II Kings 25:29-30), we may date the work of the editor (R_{PH}) in the decade following. By 550 the primary history in substantially its present form was completed.

The compilation of this sacred history was itself a remarkable achievement. It reflected the determination of the exilic community to remain alive and to retain its identity as the people of God, in spite of a series of catastrophic blows culminating in the loss of king and land, temple and priesthood. Nor could they minimize the significance of the disaster by attributing it to a hostile fate or the changing fortunes of war, or the superiority of alien gods or peoples; rather, it was the deliberate act of judgment by their own God, the covenant God of Israel, who was Lord of heaven and earth and the disposer of the affairs of men. Soberly the exiles reviewed their history in order to discern the meaning of their fate: What had happened between God and his people in the past, from the start? How had they come to their present unhappy state, and what, if anything, might the future hold for them? They could delineate throughout the course of history a consistent pattern of divine grace and favor toward men: a special commitment by God to Abraham and his descendants, fulfilled in the mighty deeds of Exodus and Conquest surrounding the covenant-making mystery of Sinai, wherein God had declared Israel to be his people and they had claimed him as their God. Successive generations saw the unfolding of this relationship of promise and demand, of grace and obligation, of hope and threat, through the tumultuous period of the judges until it reached fruition in the kingdom of David and Solomon. At the same time the unity and cohesion of the nation were flawed by disobedience to the terms of the covenant and defiance of the will of God, so that the state divided under pressure from within, and finally collapsed in ruins from the attacks of foreigners. Thus had a singularly blessed, but persistently sinful, people reaped an inevitable judgment. Nevertheless, the end was not the end. Before and beyond the law of sin and death, there was an unconditional commitment and an eternal relationship of love (cf. Jer. 31:3). The God who had summoned Abraham from the East would call his seed to a new pilgrimage westward. And the God who had saved his people from Pharaoh would deliver them again from bondage. Out of the momentous past, and in view of the present agony, the serious student could read sobering lessons for himself and his people. This history was not only a record of what had happened, but words of life and hope for today and tomorrow.

Here was Israel's legacy to Israel: the remains of the old age and a foundation for the new. Old Israel perished in the furnace of exile, but a new Israel was to emerge. The authoritative guide of postexilic Judaism was the Pentateuch. The division of the primary history into Pentateuch and Former Prophets (Joshua–II Kings) was occasioned by the needs and insights of the postexilic community: the law of Moses and the social and cultic pattern of the wilderness society were to be normative for the Persian province of Judea. It may well have been Ezra who permanently fixed the authority of the Pentateuch in the Jewish community, although the books themselves had long since been written. There can be little doubt of the relative antiquity of the text of the Pentateuch (and the Former Prophets) as compared with the other books of the OT. Not only do we have distinct recensions—e.g., the MT, the LXX, the Samar.—but also a long, traceable history of textual transmission. The *Vorlage* of the LXX text goes back at least to the third century B.C., and almost certainly to the fourth, while the Samar. is almost as old. The MT, on the other hand, may be even older. All three are represented in ancient MSS from Qumran.

If the Pentateuch was a finished product by the fifth century B.C. (probably it was already complete in the sixth century B.C., as part of the primary history), is it possible to trace the earlier history of this great work and the sources which contributed to its compilation? Such questions have exercised the minds of biblical scholars for hundreds of years, and the results of their inquiries have varied considerably. While there is as yet no consensus, and the "assured results" of critical analysis are no longer so sure, certain conclusions may be regarded as highly probable, and others as likely. The documentary hypothesis, commonly associated with the name of Wellhausen, but actually the product of the labor of many eminent OT scholars of the past two hundred years, remains the point of departure for the scientific study of the Pentateuch. The minute source analysis, which was one of the crowning achievements of nineteenth-century biblical criticism, grew out of repeated efforts to deal with the difficulties apparent in the received text. Inconsistencies in content, duplicate or parallel narratives, and significant variations in diction and style militated against the traditional view of the unity of authorship. Obvious anachronisms, and shifts in the historical and geographical perspective, likewise indicated that a Mosaic date for the composition of the Pentateuch was untenable.

In its standard form the documentary hypothesis rested upon arguments of two kinds: those based upon literary and linguistic evidence, which resulted in the division of the Pentateuchal material into various written sources; and those based upon historical evidence for the evolution of religious institutions and ideas in Israel, which produced an analytical description of the interrelationships among the documents, and a chronological arrangement to account for them.

Literary investigation isolated four primary written sources: J, E, D, and P. D was the simplest to identify, since it stands out as a literary unit (i.e., the bulk of the book of Deuteronomy—hence the designation D), with a distinctive style and viewpoint. The separation of P (for "Priestly document") from the remaining narrative material was also a comparatively routine undertaking, and practical unanimity has been achieved by scholars in defining the contents of this work. It consists chiefly of archival and institutional data spread out on an elaborate genealogical framework. What remains is the general narrative, itself manifestly composite. Thus the separation of the two creation stories in Genesis (1–2:4*a;* 2:4*b*–3), and the assignment of the former, with its schematized and formulaic pattern, to P, and the latter to the narrative source (in this case J), is easily seen. On the other hand, the disentanglement of the narrative strands has proved much more difficult. The Joseph story (Gen. 37; 39–50) is clearly composite. In the episode describing the brothers' treachery against Joseph (37:12-36), there are two accounts of what happened, which have been blended into confusion. In one, Joseph was thrown into a pit and left there to die. He was found by Midianites, brought to Egypt, and sold there (vss. 22-24, 28*a* [to "pit"], 28*c*-30, 36; the source is E). In the other, he was sold to a passing band of Ishmaelites (vss. 25-27, 28*b* [to "silver"], 31-35; the source is J). Reuben figures as the intercessor for Joseph in one (E), Judah in the other (J). Only such a separation offers an intelligible account of the episode.

Two principal narrative sources were identified: J (so-called because of its standard use of the name Jehovah [YHWH] for God; it has also been associated with the S kingdom, Judah), and E (because of its use of Elohim for God, though with less consistency beyond the book of Genesis; it has been connected with the N kingdom, Ephraim). The details of the division are not nearly so certain as in the case of D and P; in many passages where J and E have been fused, the analysis is disputed (e.g., Exod. 32–34).

D was the starting point in the determination of the chronological relationships of the sources among themselves and with respect to the history of Israel. D was identified with the law code discovered in the Jerusalem temple in the eighteenth year of Josiah (622 B.C.); its composition has generally been dated in the seventh century. Careful comparison of D with JE, on the one side, and with P, on the other, showed that D was the middle term chronologically. With regard both to narrative and to legal material, D proved to be later than and dependent upon JE; but independent of and prior to P. JE therefore belonged to the monarchic period (tenth to eighth centuries), while P was exilic or later. More precise examination of JE established the priority of J (tenth-ninth century perhaps) over E (ninth-eighth century). This decision was based in part on the opinion that J was more primitive in his theology (i.e., grossly anthropomorphic), more exuberant and naïve in his storytelling. E, on the other hand, was more subtle and sophisticated, and therefore of a later date.

The major conclusions of the documentary hypothesis with regard to source analysis and the relative dating of the documents stand fairly firm. Some of the premises are less certain, particularly the theory of a simple evolutionary development of Israel's religious institutions and ideas. And the details of the analysis are open to question in a number of instances. In addition, important new areas of interest have been opened up in the continuing quest for knowledge about the Pentateuch. *See bibliography.*

A synthesis of what appear to be the soundest insights of scholars who have worked and are now working in the field follows:

2. G (the underlying source). In the beginning was G. This symbol represents the original narrative source (*Grundlage*), which dealt in connected fashion with the principal themes of Israel's early history and prehistory: including the primeval history, patriarchal sagas, the Exodus and wanderings, and presumably the settlement in the Promised Land. G is no longer extant, but what remains of its contents is scattered through the books from Genesis to Joshua. Its outline is still to be found in the Israelite credos (to use the happy expression of G. von Rad) —e.g., Deut. 26:5-10 (cf. Exod. 13:14-16). Josh. 24 preserves a much more detailed account based on the same pattern. G thus constituted the official tradition of "all Israel." It traced the beginnings of the people back to the fathers and their wanderings, and brought the story of hardship and deliverance, wandering and conquest, down to the present circumstance: the confederation of tribes settled in the land chosen and promised to the fathers.

The precise character of G can hardly be determined now; it was composed of older poetic materials, perhaps a sequence of patriarchal sagas, and a continuity dealing with the exodus-conquest cycle. Behind these are the individual stories, legends, etiological tales, cult narratives, the original data which formed the oldest traditions of Israel. G may have been a connected poem or series of poems orally transmitted and recited in whole or in part at the sacred festivals of "all Israel." Or it may have been a prose document derived from such an oral poetic collection. The former would seem more likely for the period of the judges. We conclude that G was a poetic composition, orally transmitted, relating the official story of Israel and its forebears. It is to be dated in the twelfth-eleventh centuries B.C. and finds its cultic locus in the amphictyonic festivals.

3. J and E. J and E, the familiar narrative sources of classic Pentateuchal analysis, are prose compositions derived from G. In the Tetrateuch at least, J and E follow the same basic pattern and order of events, thus presuppose a common source. At the same time they are distinct compositions, with diverging concerns and attitudes, and differ strikingly in numerous details. On the basis of a minute analysis of these sources, so far as they can be extricated from the Hexateuch, scholars have concluded that J has a S orientation, as against E, which is N; that J is concerned with David as king and with his dynasty, while E has marked affinities with and interest in the prophetic movement, especially as it was related to political developments in the N. In general, J has been regarded as a product of the United Monarchy (*ca.* tenth century), E of the N kingdom (*ca.* ninth-eighth centuries). Subsequent editions (e.g., J_2, E_2, etc.) would be dated still later.

The distinctive historical character of Israel's religion made it inevitable that the story would be rewritten repeatedly so as to include the most recent events which were the result of Yahweh's dealings with his people. Unlike pagan myth, which was timeless and self-completing, and which required only to be rehearsed and re-enacted in the cult, Israelite traditions could not finally be contained in this fashion; and re-enactment did not exhaust the historical significance or future possibilities of the tradition. In like manner the pagan epic was a self-enclosed entity describing a distinct era of the past: the age of the heroes and their great deeds. But Israel, even with the "epic" tradition reflected in G, could not simply look back to the glorious past, but was concerned with the continuing actions of God. Even G may have been expanded and revised during the period of the amphictyony.

a. J. While scholarly agreement on the scope of J and E has never been reached, and end points for both have been fixed all the way from the end of Numbers on into Samuel and Kings, it is likely that the end point is determined roughly by the date of the writer. The interpretation herein adheres to the common, if somewhat conservative, view that J dates from the United Monarchy (i.e., tenth century), and that E is northern and is to be dated in the late ninth or early eighth century. This means that both J and E are not simply prose abstracts of G, but rather separate historical accounts based upon G, carrying the story beyond G to their own time. Thus J finds the complete fulfilment of G's promise to the fathers, not in the original settlement under Joshua, but in the conquests and kingdom of David. Without attempting to pin down precisely the J material in Judges and Samuel, one may nevertheless point to the two sources of I Samuel and identify the earlier, pro-monarchy source with J. The transference of the Abrahamic covenant (Gen. 15—originally G) to David and his house (II Sam. 7) is also to be attributed to J. Whether J extends beyond this point is debatable (the so-called court history—II Sam. 9-20; I Kings 1-2—is a separate source); other possibilities for the reign of Solomon are I Kings 4:20-21—H 4:20-5:1: "Judah and Israel were as many as the sand by the sea; they ate and drank and were happy. Solomon ruled over all the kingdoms from the Euphrates to the land of the Philistines and to the border of Egypt; they brought tribute and served Solomon all the days of his life." Subsequent editions of J may well have carried further the story of the fortunes of the house of David and the kingdom of Judah.

b. E. E is more difficult to fix as to date and extent. On the basis of a N provenience and demonstrable interest in the prophetic movement, E may be regarded as a product of the religious enthusiasm stimulated by Elijah and Elisha, and his work may be placed in the age of Jehu and his successors (*ca.* 842-745 B.C.). A clue to the character of E may be found in the evaluation of Jehu's revolution in II Kings 10:28, 30: "Thus Jehu wiped out Baal from Israel. . . . And the LORD said to Jehu, 'Because you have done well in carrying out what is right in my eyes, and have done to the house of Ahab according to all that was in my heart, your sons of the fourth generation shall sit on the throne of Israel.' " This material is embedded in a typically hostile Deuteronomic estimate of the same king (vss. 29, 31) and must therefore derive from a different, and sympathetic, N source. The reference to the descendants of Jehu to the fourth generation would bring us down to Jeroboam II, whose dominion might be regarded more suitably as a fulfilment both of promise and of prophecy. The assertion that Jeroboam's victories were achieved as fulfilment of the word of the prophet (Jonah son of Amittai) is particularly instructive: "He restored the border of Israel from the entrance of Hamath as far as the Sea of the Arabah, according to the word of the LORD, the God of Israel, which he spoke by his servant Jonah the son of Amittai, the prophet" (II Kings 14:25). E reconstructed the story of Israel in the light of the prophetic movement, beginning with Abraham, anachronistically described (by E) as a prophet and similarly identifying Miriam, Deborah(?), Samuel, and other ancient figures by the same term. If we remove the Deuteronomic framework and commentary, what remains of Kings (through II Kings 14, essentially E) is predominantly the story of the prophets and their impact on the history of the N kingdom; for it was the prophets who were the successors to the judges, and the N kingdom that inherited the traditions of the amphictyony and its cult center. Thus E was the defender of the older tradition against the claims of the Davidic dynasty. It may be concluded that E was composed in the eighth century B.C., in the N, and represented an attempt, in the prophetic tradition, to relate the ancient pattern of G to the history of the N kingdom, and to establish the latter's claim to be the true successor and heir of "all Israel."

c. JE. JE is the product of a literary merger. At some time after the completion of J and E as separate entities, they were blended into a continuous narrative by an editor or redactor, R_{JE}. Analysis of the surviving material in the Pentateuch (or Tetrateuch, since J and E are practically nonexistent in Deuteronomy) indicates that the editor used a variety of methods in weaving the narratives together. First, it is clear that the dominant strand is J, which, in fact, formed the basic narrative. E has actually been broken up and inserted piecemeal into the over-all structure of J. On occasion there are parallel accounts (J and E) of the same episode; on occasion one version has been suppressed in favor of the other (where apparently they were practically identical); elsewhere they have been woven together into a single narrative. On the face of it, JE is the work of a S (Judahite or Jerusalemite) editor whose object was to preserve the traditions of the N and to harmonize them with the J narrative to form a single composite history of the people of God. The logical occasion for this work would have been the destruction of Samaria and the collapse of the N kingdom (722-721 B.C.). Its purpose was to win the surviving population of Ephraim to allegiance to the temple in Jerusalem and the Davidic king of Judah. Since this was the announced policy of Hezekiah, according to the account in II Chr. 30:1-31:1, in which a determined effort was made to establish Jerusalem as the center of worship for northerners as well as southerners, we may plausibly connect the compilation of JE with the movement toward religious reunion initiated by Hezekiah. We may date R_{JE} in the early seventh century B.C., and hold that his work included the major part of J, selected material from E, and closed with the reformation of Hezekiah and the attempt to unite "all Israel" in the worship at Jerusalem.

4. D and DH. ***a. The Deuteronomic Code.*** The next major subdivision in the classic analysis of the Pentateuch is D, identified with the document found in the temple in the eighteenth year of Josiah (622 B.C.) and corresponding roughly to the present book of Deuteronomy (perhaps chs. 5-26; 28). Scholars have been divided on the questions of the date of composition and provenience of this document, though there is increasing agreement that D, like E, has N affinities, and that it was composed during the century preceding its discovery. Its nucleus is a legal corpus, preserving many ancient laws and customs derived from the days of the confederation (e.g., the law of holy war), and reflecting the traditions of the cult center at Shechem and its priesthood. In their present form, chs. 5-26; 28 constitute a series of warnings and exhortations uttered by Moses just before his death. A date of composition in the reign of Hezekiah or later is practically required by the emphasis upon centralization of worship in a single sanctuary, presumably the temple at Jerusalem. The tradition of the central sanctuary is very old, going back to the days of the amphictyony, if not to the wilderness wanderings. But the principle of exclusiveness—i.e., the single, central sanctuary—is new. It reflects the circumstances of Hezekiah's time: the fall of the N kingdom and the emergence of the Jerusalem temple as the only "independent" cult center. The temple at Bethel apparently survived, but was under constant attack from the S as heterodox, and had suffered considerable loss of prestige with the fall of Samaria. It was finally wrecked by Josiah (cf. II Kings 23:15 ff). Furthermore, the sermonic addresses anticipate or more probably presuppose the destruction of the N kingdom and the captivity of its inhabitants, thus pointing likewise to a date *ca.* 700. A date in the reign of Manasseh is also possible but less likely, while the idea that D was composed in the reign of Josiah and deliberately planted in the temple in order to be discovered there, may be dismissed as a fantasy.

The principal concern of D is the Horeb (Sinai) covenant, and its significance for the life of Israel. The COVENANT is a guarantee of life to those who obey its stipulations (the Ten Commandments and subsequent legislation), but for those who forget, ignore, or defy its demands, there is certain disaster. Placed in the mouth of Moses, these sermons are not only a reminder of the solemn bond between God and Israel; an explanation of the requirements of the covenant, with its promise of security and threat of destruction; but also a prophetic anticipation of the culmination of Israel's history. For D, Moses is the true prophet (18:15 ff; cf. 34:9-10, which is secondary), who, long before the great prophets of more recent times, foresaw the threatened catastrophe of military invasion and conquest, intensified by that peculiarly inhuman practice of mass deportation. The only hope of Israel, or what survived of it, lay in strict adherence to the covenant obligations beginning with the first commandment, which requires the exclusive worship of Yahweh, and which, on the Deuteronomist's reasoning, restricts worship to the one place which he has chosen for his name.

b. The Deuteronomic history. The effect upon Josiah and Judah of the discovery of D in the temple is familiar to all. The great reformation of the national life and religion is described in detail in II Kings 22: 3-23:25 (cf. II Chr. 34:8-35:19). The so-called Deuteronomic history (DH) probably owes its inspiration and composition to the reformation stimulated by the discovery of D. In a major contribution to the higher criticism of the OT, Martin Noth has identified and isolated the Deuteronomic history as a single work including the books from Deuteronomy through II Kings. Beginning with the Mosaic sermons (to which he has prefixed an introduction, Deut. 1-4), the Deuteronomic historian has traced the Horeb covenant through the history of Israel, interpreting it in the light of the covenant requirements, and evaluating kings and people according to their adherence or defiance of them. He has incorporated much older material practically untouched—e.g., the court history of David (II Sam. 9-20; I Kings 1-2)—while providing for the whole a chronological and theological framework. Thus in the book of Judges he has organized chronologically and classified theologically a heterogeneous group of ancient heroes and the folk tales handed down about them. In the books of Kings he has inserted from the official court records the necessary chronological data of accessions, reigns, deaths, and successions; he has also interspersed a theological commentary grading each king in relation to his good or evil deeds.

According to Noth, the Deuteronomic history was compiled during the Exile (i.e., after the last date in II Kings), but it has been cogently argued by others that the first edition of this work was issued earlier, during the reign of Josiah. It is clear that the description of the Josianic reform in II Kings 22-23 is the climax of this history, while what follows is a melancholy epilogue. Note especially the fulfilment of the prophecy concerning Bethel (from I Kings 13: 1-3) in II Kings 23:15-18, with particular reference to the name of Josiah (which is anticipated in the prophecy), and the conclusion in vs. 25: "Before him there was no king like him, who turned to the LORD with all his heart and with all his soul and with all his might, according to all the law of Moses; nor did any like him arise after him." This, together with the formal summary of his reign in vs. 28, looks like the original ending of the historical work. It is interesting that the notice of his defeat and death at Megiddo follows the summary.

The Deuteronomic historian was inspired by the conviction that Josiah was the long-awaited scion of David who in his work and life would fulfil the ideals of kingship, restore the empire of his illustrious ancestor, and also lead his people to renewal of life in obedience to the terms of the ancient Mosaic covenant. The entire history aims at this conclusion, the happy climax of the biblical story. At the same time the Deuteronomic discourses of Moses and the disastrous experience of the N kingdom served as a warning of another denouement, so that the catastrophe which actually ensued was not entirely unprepared. All along there had been two possibilities. With the tragic death of Josiah, it became clearer which alternative was the more likely. It is probable that the Deuteronomic history originally ended with the successful reformation of Josiah, and was subsequently revised to accord with the somber facts of history (cf. the pathetic attempt at reinterpretation, II Kings 23:26: "Still the LORD did not turn from the fierceness of his great wrath, by which his anger was kindled against Judah, because of all the provocations with which Manasseh had provoked him").

Concerning the scope of DH, the question must be raised whether Deut. 1 actually constitutes the beginning. In other words, does Deut. 1-4 serve simply as an introduction to DH, or is it rather a bridge between the narrative of the Tetrateuch (JE) and DH? When it is remembered that D is explicitly attributed to Moses, then the necessity for placing these addresses in the context of the JE narrative becomes clear. Unless JE (and G) is to be cut off at the end of Numbers plus a few verses on the death of Moses, it is not possible to argue that DH is an entirely independent work. Not only does such a view leave JE in the Tetrateuch a hopeless torso, but it offers no explanation for the beginning of DH in the fortieth year of the wanderings. If in the course of D, Moses actually reviewed the previous sequence of mighty deeds, then we could recognize here an imitation of epic style. But there is specific recapitulation only as far back as the Horeb (Sinai) experience, while the antecedent history is dealt with in the vaguest possible way. In short, JE is assumed, because it was attached. If J and E actually carried the story down into the period of the monarchy, then DH must have used them, as he used the court history, D, and other sources. And if he made use of JE for the post-Mosaic period, he could hardly have dismissed or ignored it in the pre-Mosaic and Mosaic eras.

It is likely, therefore, that DH compiled his history along the same lines as J and E (or JE, which is presumably all that was available to him)—i.e., he began with Genesis and carried the story down to the reign and reformation of Josiah. However, the fulcrum of his account was the major prophetic exhortations of Moses, the new document, D, found in the temple. DH had little or nothing to add to the JE narrative in the Tetrateuch, though there may be traces of his work (so-called D_2, which need not be categorically dismissed). His creative enterprise begins with Deut. 1-4, which constitutes an introduction to the history which follows but also serves as a bridge connecting it with what has gone before. It is clear that DH did not think that Israelite history began with Moses, whatever may be the opinion of scholars since Wellhausen.

We conclude that the Deuteronomic history was originally composed before the fall of Jerusalem, and that it consisted of JE and D, plus other materials of a narrative and archival nature, covering the period from the Creation down to the reign and reformation of Josiah.

5. P. It remains to deal with P, the last of the sources identified in the classic Pentateuchal analysis. It is generally agreed that P was compiled, chiefly from older sources, during the Exile, if not in post-exilic times. P consists mainly of archival data of different kinds: genealogical tables, tribal lists, including a pair of census tabulations, and priestly data and regulations—concerning, e.g., the tabernacle, the priesthood, sacrifices, questions of clean and unclean. Embedded in P, there are also legal prescriptions which form part of the complex legal corpus of the Pentateuch (e.g., the Book of the Covenant and Exod. 34, usually associated with JE; the law code in D; and H, the so-called Holiness Code of Lev. 17–26). The principal questions concerning P are: (*a*) Is P an independent source, or is it merely supplemental to JE in the Hexateuch (or Tetrateuch)? Put another way, is P himself the compiler of the Pentateuch incorporating into the narrative such archival data as seemed desirable? (*b*) What is the extent of P? It is generally agreed that P is to be found in the books through Numbers, and not in Deuteronomy (except for a couple of verses). But what about Joshua?

The two questions are linked, and the answer given to one will influence one's view of the other. It would seem that the meticulous analysis of earlier scholars and their conclusions concerning the nature of P have not been overthrown by more recent advocates. It still appears that the case for P as an independent source is stronger than the case against it. If P was a self-contained entity, what was its character and scope? That P in Exodus–Numbers is primarily concerned to fix in detail the cultic practice of the wilderness encampment and to establish it as a permanent norm for Israel through the unquestioned authority of Moses is clear. Here there is essentially a static treatment of ancient materials, with a concern, not, as in the older sources, for the movement of God in history, but for the original pattern of worship, which is binding forever. The particular historical event has partly given way to the timeless and unchangeable pattern of heavenly things. If P were limited to Exodus–Numbers, then the question of its independent status would not figure seriously, and its incorporation into the narrative as essentially supplementary data would be understandable. But the presence of P in Genesis, where it provides the chronological framework and some narrative details, suggests a broader, at least partly historical, concern. If this is true, and it can hardly be doubted, then we must recognize in P the old *heilsgeschichtliche* pattern of Israelite religion already observable in G, present in the other historical works, and preserved in the festivals which are a principal interest of P. P's interest in the patriarchs, however, requires a corresponding concern with the settlement in the Promised Land. While Moses and the pattern of life and worship in the wilderness are central to P, the prelude in Genesis can only be balanced by the fulfilment in Numbers and Joshua; but it is only in Joshua that the specific expectations of P in the patriarchal narratives are fulfilled. In no way can Moses and the wanderings or even Sinai be regarded as the resolution of patriarchal anticipation. The divine promise can only be realized in the occupation of the land (which is explicitly not Transjordan, and for P does not even include it). Therefore, if P is an independent source, and is found in Genesis, as well as in Exodus–Numbers, then we should expect to find it in Joshua also.

It is probable that P was compiled early in the Exile and was incorporated by the final redactor into the so-called Deuteronomic history (including JE, as already pointed out) shortly after. Apparently R_{PH} added the final reference to Jehoiachin, and this points to the completion of the work in the decade 560-550 B.C. Thus by the middle of the sixth century, the primary history was complete, and has been preserved substantially without change. Subsequent to the completion of this work the Pentateuch was abstracted, and not later than the time of Ezra it was firmly established as the Holy Scripture of Israel.

B. *FORM AND CONTENTS.* The separation of the Pentateuch from the primary history, and its assignment to a unique place of honor and authority in Israel, was a development of the greatest importance. The factors responsible for the division between Deuteronomy and Joshua were neither literary nor historical, but primarily theological; they arose out of the concerns and needs of the exilic community. As we have seen, classic critical scholarship identified the Hexateuch as the basic literary compilation, recognizing the close connection between the occupation of the land described in Joshua and the preceding stories of the Pentateuch. More recent scholarship has identified the Deuteronomic history as a single literary work, thus dividing the primary history at the end of the book of Numbers and connecting Deuteronomy with the following books. It will be seen that neither approach allows for a normal break at the end of Deuteronomy. At the same time, the ultimate sources, oral and documentary, cut across the same dividing line. The conclusion seems inescapable that the isolation of the Pentateuch from the primary history was the last stage in the process, and that it was occasioned by the special interest of the exilic community in the person of Moses and the experience of Israel in the wilderness. A subtle shift in emphasis from the historical pattern of the older sources (e.g., the *heilsgeschichtliche* promise and fulfilment of G, elaborated in J and E, and the theme of covenant and consequence in D and DH) to the more static pattern of P is discernible in the new arrangement. Where the primary history is essentially the record of God's dealings with his people, and their experience together through more than twelve hundred years, the Pentateuch, while retaining a chronological framework and, of course, sharing the same narrative for the first half of this era, nevertheless has its central interest, not in the mighty deeds of God nor in the historical vicissitudes of Israel, but rather in the description of an eternal, perfect, and unchangeable pattern of community life, first and fully revealed at Sinai and successfully achieved by Israel in the wilderness. For the Pentateuch, the desert encampment governed by all the laws, civil and criminal, cultic and dietary, was the first true realization of the anticipations outlined in Genesis, and the embodiment of the kingdom of God. The pattern of the desert constituted the authoritative example and model for the postexilic community. History has been subordinated to revelation, and mighty deeds to eternal words. Essentially what was required of Israel was conformity to the Sinai pattern; in this would be found the guarantee of its survival and the promise of its security. To a considerable extent, the Pentateuch defined and also restricted the future hope of the postexilic community. While Pentateuchal passages could be pressed into service for messianic purposes, such expectations were more at home in the prophetic literature. The themes of a second Moses, a second Exodus, and the perfect realization of the Sinai pattern reflect the shadow cast by the Pentateuch upon all hopes and speculations about the future. Alongside the controlling pattern of community life is the figure of Moses, which dominates the Pentateuch. His life constitutes the frame and thread of the story from the beginning of Exodus to the end of Deuteronomy (to which may be added the traditional view that he was the author of all five books). Not only is he the charismatic hero of the JE narrative, but he is also the prophet "nonpareil" of D, and Israel's sole lawgiver of P. Thus all the sources and strands of the four latter books of the Pentateuch are drawn together around the superhuman figure of Moses (cf. Exod. 34:29-35), while Genesis serves as prologue to the great drama. The chief emphases of the Pentateuch are upon the intricate but ultimate pattern of laws governing the life of the people of God, and the mediator of these laws, Moses, who at the same time receives a full biographical treatment.

1. The beginnings (Genesis). ***a. The primeval story (chs. 1-11).*** Here is provided the universal setting of the *Heilsgeschichte,* which follows. The Mesopotamian orientation of the familiar legends and folk tales is striking, confirming the traditions associating the patriarchs with that region (i.e., Ur, and more particularly Harran). The selection and arrangement of the materials serve to stress certain points essential to the whole narrative. Thus Creation is not only the proper starting point for world and faith history, but stands out starkly as the uniquely divine achievement of the sole God. Both absolute power and ultimate goodness are revealed in the mounting sequence of creative acts, while corollary to divine authority are human dignity and responsibility. Man is not only obliged to obey, but is also answerable for his deeds, from which flow irreversible consequences, as the tragic stories of Adam and Eve, Cain and Abel, show. Alongside the power and authority of the Creator are revealed his righteousness and wrath; but these latter are punctuated by mercy. The flood story, ultimately derived from a widespread myth of great antiquity, is nevertheless the vehicle of profound insight into the nature of God and his ways with men. An angry judgment overwhelms a sinful world; the righteous Noah is spared, and the operation of moral law is confirmed. The aftermath, however, involves the revocation of the divine curse upon the earth (cf. 8:21 with 3:18), and the unilateral commitment to preserve the world from natural catastrophe in spite of, or rather in view of, man's sinfulness. The covenant with Noah, sealed by the sign of the heavenly bow, establishes the basis for the future action of God described in the Bible—an action essentially gracious and kindly, in full recognition of man's failure to discharge his responsibilities and his inability to rectify either his attitudes or his behavior. Already in the primeval history, the basic features of the biblical narrative are present: the power and authority, the righteousness and mercy, of God; man's dignity and inferiority—his responsibility and his defiance; God's commitment in grace to man and man's obligation in love to God.

b. The patriarchal narratives. In the tradition, both literary and liturgical, the patriarchal figures are Abraham, Isaac, and Jacob, but in the Genesis narratives Isaac plays a minor role, while Jacob's son Joseph is the hero of the longest sustained narrative in the book (chs. 37; 39-50). Doubtless in this case the tradition is more conservative, while the Genesis narratives are the end product of a lengthy process of sifting and selection. The material falls conveniently into three sections of approximately equal length: (*a*) Abraham, chs. 12-25; (*b*) Jacob, chs. 25-36; (*c*) Joseph and his brothers, chs. 37-50.

Without analyzing the stories in detail, one may sketch the principal themes. From the biblical point of view, the history of Israel properly begins with the patriarch Abraham, since he was the ancestor from whom Israel traced its origin. At the same time, it is with the appearance of the fathers that we can speak of general historical reliability, though not of history in the proper sense. However the chronological sequence and factuality of the events are to be reconstructed, there can be no doubt of the substantial validity of the account of the fathers in the Middle Bronze Age, and their movements from Harran through Canaan to the Nile Delta.

The main theme of GENESIS is the promise to the fathers. This promise is first made to Abraham, when he is summoned to embark on a new adventure: "Go from your country and your kindred and your father's house to the land that I will show you. And I will make of you a great nation, and I will bless you, and make your name great, so that you will be a blessing. I will bless those who bless you, and him who curses you I will curse; and by you all the families of the earth will bless themselves" (Gen. 12:1-3). It is repeated frequently throughout the book, in almost identical language, both to him and to his descendants. This promise, which is solemnized by oath in a covenant ceremony (cf. Gen. 15:17 ff and the repeated expression: "The land which I swore to give to your fathers," in later sources), represents the unilateral, unconditional commitment of God. It consists of three major points: (*a*) the assurance of a posterity, which has particular relevance to Abraham's childlessness at an advanced age; but it also refers to the innumerable population of the patriarchs' descendants; (*b*) from the uncounted progeny a great nation will emerge in the future; and (*c*) they will possess the Promised Land—i.e., Canaan, specifically as surveyed by Abraham after his separation from Lot (ch. 13).

Posterity, nationhood, and the gift of the land are the different facets of the divine promise; and to these are attached the rather heterogeneous narratives of Genesis. Alongside the divine commitment and corresponding actions are human obligation and response, reflected in the behavior of the patriarchs. These are intertwined in a series of dramatic episodes, which maintain interest, even suspense, though over-all plot development and story movement in the book of Genesis are more illusion than fact. Thus the theme of progeny is stressed in connection with the birth of Isaac (and repeated in connection with Rebekah and Rachel), which requires miraculous intervention by God. Once born, Isaac is the sole heir of the promise; consequently the hope of progeny remains in jeopardy with each threat to the child's life. The masterful story of the sacrifice of Isaac (ch. 22) weaves this theme into the testing of Abraham, by portraying God as the instigator and Abraham as the reluctant instrument of the plot to destroy the child and wreck the promise altogether. When the angel intervenes at the last moment, it is more than Isaac that is saved. On a broader scale, the theme involves the survival of the patriarchs and their families, constantly threatened by the violence of nature and man. In addition there is the delicate problem of maintaining identity in the midst of an alien population whose friendship poses a graver danger (of submersion) than its hostility, which is bad enough. Just to secure and maintain a foothold in Canaan proves beyond their power. In fact, they are almost as far from the Promised Land at the end of Genesis as they were at the beginning—i.e., in Egypt instead of Mesopotamia. Nevertheless, a certain symbolic success was achieved: Abraham, though paying an exorbitant price (cf. ch. 23), was able to secure outright a small plot of ground as a graveyard for his family and himself. So the book closes symbolically with the children of Israel making a pilgrimage to this graveyard in Canaan in order to bury their father, Jacob, who had died in Egypt.

According to the tradition a long interval (400 years) separated the patriarchs from the Exodus and the age of Moses. While the accuracy of the number may be questioned, the efforts of certain scholars to close the gap entirely and bring the patriarchs, and Joseph in particular, down to the Late Bronze Age have not been successful. The patriarchal stories reflect a Middle Bronze (*ca.* 2100-1500 B.C.) orientation and background, while Moses belongs to the end of the Late Bronze Age, specifically the thirteenth century. The sharp break in narrative sequence confirms the validity of the tradition: a new era has begun with the book of EXODUS. The life of Moses, 120 years according to the biblical record, spans the remaining books of the Pentateuch. There is a convenient division into three generations of 40 years each: from birth to banishment; the shepherd in the desert; the deliverer and lawgiver. The Bible, however, passes briefly over the first two phases of Moses' life (chs. 1–2 of Exodus) and concentrates attention upon the third (from ch. 3 on). The biblical materials fall into the following convenient pattern: (*a*) the events surrounding the Exodus from Egypt; (*b*) the experience of Israel at Mount Sinai; (*c*) the wanderings in the wilderness and the conquest of Transjordan; (*d*) Moses' farewell discourses.

2. The Exodus (Exod. 1-18). On the basis of the close association of the exodus tradition with the PASSOVER festival, it has been argued that the narrative (chs. 1–15) actually constituted the liturgy of the Passover. Though the case can hardly be proved for the chapters in their present form, the idea has nevertheless proved fruitful. The story is related in such a way as to emphasize both its unrepeatable historicity and its dramatic character, designed for liturgical re-enactment. It is at once the unique adventure of the generation of slaves in Egypt, and the common experience of all the generations of Israel. The artificial pattern of the material suggests both a long period of transmission and a liturgical setting for its preservation. Whatever relation to a sequence of natural phenomena the plagues may originally have had, they are now immobilized and isolated by stereotyped formulas, and arranged like tenpins or wooden soldiers in the conflict between Moses and Pharaoh for the release of the slaves. In the present form of the narrative, even protagonist and antagonist are puppets acting out the parts already prepared for them. The only independent participant is God himself, and the whole order of events is designed as a pyrotechnic display of divine power and majesty: to show, in short, that God is God, and that Moses and Pharaoh are both his servants, but in different ways. Through the agency of Moses and the obstinacy of Pharaoh, miracle is piled upon miracle until the triumphal climax is reached. In order to achieve this cumulative effect, God finds it necessary not only to encourage Moses and the Israelites, but also to stiffen Pharaoh's resistance, lest he falter and release the slaves too soon.

While the actual course of events is obscured, and the interplay of human factors is distorted by the one-sided presentation of the mighty deeds of God, nevertheless the theological emphasis is valid. Except for the powerful intervention of the almighty God, deliverance of a rabble of slaves from Egypt, the greatest empire in the world, was both impossible and unthinkable. Let no one, Israelite or Egyptian, or anyone else, whether of that time or of any future time, delude himself with the notion that what happened was natural, or explicable in human terms. The decisive, and only truly significant, factor was the hand of God. If not for that, the bravery of a Moses and the loyalty of his followers would have gone for nought. As it is, Moses is characterized more by reluctance than by enthusiasm for the cause, and the people by cowardice rather than by courage. But it is all one. God acts in a series of shattering blows, which reach a climax in the slaying of the first-born and the hasty departure of the Israelites. These two events constitute the occasion of the Passover, and doubtless formed the nucleus of the liturgy. The famous crossing of the Reed Sea caps even this climax, and constitutes the mightiest deed of all. This event is described in a prose account in ch. 14, which is divided, according to most scholars, among J, E, and P. It is also celebrated in the victory song of ch. 15, which may have served Israel as its national anthem and the culmination of the Passover observance. The crossing of the sea marks not only the end of bondage and the beginning of freedom, but also the separation of Israel from the world, and the commencement of its history as the peculiar and distinctive people of God. In the course of the wandering, the process of separation gains sharpness and clarity. Already in the later plagues this tendency was apparent; the plagues afflict only the Egyptians, while the Israelites are spared. In the wilderness the special marks of favor and protection are likewise present: the pillar of cloud and fire, the angel, the miraculous gifts of quail and manna, all identify Israel as uniquely different. The distinguishing characteristic is the relationship with God. It is precisely in the fact that God was with them that their separateness is to be seen (cf. Exod. 33:16). Both people and era were thus marked off by special signs of divine protection. Only the wilderness generation enjoyed the miracles of manna and quail; the pillar and the angel; and, above all, the man Moses, whose shining face reflected the glory of God. While this was a period of testing for all and punishment for many, it was also the uniquely creative and normative experience of Israel, determinative for its whole future history.

3. Sinai (Exod. 19:1-Num. 10:10). The Sinai revelation and the COVENANT of the Ten Words are justly regarded as the crucial event in Israel's religious experience. The compiler of the Pentateuch has underlined the importance of Sinai by making it the scene, and Moses the agent, for the ordering of the whole life of Israel. Practically the whole legislation of Israel, including the prescriptions for the tabernacle, priesthood, feasts, sacrifices and services, as well as the rules of community life, is assigned to the Sinai sojourn. The demands or obligations of the covenant are the principal word of God to Israel, while for Israel the ultimate goal was to achieve in word and deed the pattern of holiness established for it at the beginning of nationhood, and to fulfil by enthusiastic obedience and detailed observance the requirement of the summons of God to be a "kingdom of priests and a holy nation" (Exod. 19:6). It is therefore no accident that the chief efforts of the postexilic community were bent toward reconstituting the Mosaic commonwealth. From the Exile on, community life was governed by the prescriptions of the Pentateuch, as elaborated and interpreted by priest, Levite, and scribe—and later, rabbi—in the extensive body of legal opinion and decision which accumulated over the centuries, and were gathered in the tractates of the Mishna and the Gemara. There has been, therefore, a legal tradition in Israel going back to patriarchal times and continuing down through biblical and postbiblical times to the present. The tenacious conservatism as well as flexible adaptability of biblical law (*see* LAW IN THE OT) can be illustrated amply by comparison between legal procedures recorded in early Mesopotamian codes to which patriarchal legal customs are related, and those described in the Talmud 2,500 years later. The biblical datum constitutes the middle term in the long process of legal transmission and development. Thus in the division of the inheritance among the heirs, the old Mesopotamian practice of assigning a "double portion" to the oldest son is reflected in the patriarchal stories. The same practice is attested in Pentateuchal law, and explained and confirmed in detail by the Talmud.

In this long process the period of the monarchy may be regarded as a legally insignificant interlude. The Pentateuchal legislation, with roots in the patriarchal customs, and its substance derived from the decisions and precedents of the age of the judges, shows little influence of or interest in the monarchy (cf. Deut. 17:14-20, which is the only specific reference to the king in all the legal codes of the Pentateuch, and hardly to be regarded as codified law). That the monarchy powerfully influenced judicial procedure and legal practice may be seen from the frequent allusions in the historical books: e.g., the different judicial reforms instituted by various kings, and the combination of royal decrees affecting the population or some part of it, and royal decisions made in a variety of cases creating precedents with binding force. But of all this, little or nothing has survived in the law. The cultus was doubtless an exception, since the monarchy was the period of the great elaboration of public worship at the temple; such, at least, is the tradition preserved in the Chronicler's history. Even here, however, the sacred customs of the premonarchic age were preserved, embedded in the later ritual of the temple. Furthermore, the repeated purges and reforms of Israel's worship tended to restore the older practice and remove later accretions. Thus the Pentateuchal legislation was the result of a deliberate effort to compile the ancient laws and customs of Israel, even to recover the original pattern given at Sinai and publish it as the work of the architect of the nation, Moses. While the claim is somewhat greater than the fact, we have nevertheless an archaic collection of legal and cultic material reflecting the earliest period of the nation, between Moses and the monarchy. The differences in the legal formulations of the codes of the Pentateuch do not, as a rule, indicate evolution in the pattern of law, but local variation and development. The codes embody the traditions of different shrines.

The events of Sinai were associated in later Judaism with one of the three great religious feasts of early Israel—the Feast of Weeks (Pentecost) or First Fruits. The other phases of the Exodus-Deuteronomy complex are likewise associated with the major festivals: the Exodus with Passover (or Unleavened

Bread), and the wanderings with the Feast of Tabernacles (or Ingathering). Thus the three annual celebrations together reproduced the cycle of Exodus–Sinai–wanderings, which are the very substance of the Pentateuch. Each year Israel relived the most important days of its existence: once again delivered from bondage, created the people of God by covenant rite, and tried and purified by the rigors of the desert sojourn to be fit for the life of the Holy Land promised to the fathers. *See* WEEKS, FEAST OF; PASSOVER AND FEAST OF UNLEAVENED BREAD; BOOTHS, FEAST OF.

Sinai and its covenant are the central theme of the Pentateuch in its present form. For the compiler, Sinai is the main objective of the Exodus, the creation of the covenant community the purpose of the divine deliverance (cf. Exod. 3:12: "When you have brought forth the people out of Egypt, you shall serve God upon this mountain"). It has long been recognized, however, that the Sinai events are intrusive in the pattern of promise and fulfilment of the older narratives, in which the possession of the land is the goal. Thus one would expect the story to proceed from the initial experience of the patriarchs to the oppression in Egypt, the deliverance from bondage, the movement through the wilderness, and the invasion and conquest of the Holy Land (as, in fact, we find it in the confession of faith, Deut. 26:5-9). At this point, the formal establishment of the new state should take place with the ratification of a solemn agreement between God and his people. Such an event is actually recorded in Josh. 24, the historical significance of which has increasingly been recognized. With the reconstruction of this logically cohesive sequence of events, matters ought to rest. But the Shechem celebration is treated as the occasion for renewing and not initiating the covenant. Sinai has entirely replaced it in the latter role, so far as the tradition is concerned. Sinai may come embarrassingly in the middle of the story, but it is no late invention capriciously inserted where it would do the most damage. It is too ancient and important a tradition (in both J and E, and therefore G) to be set aside. While the Sinai events might fit better in a different locale or a different time, the awkwardness of their present position may help to validate the tradition.

The difficulty with Sinai, however, concerns not only questions of geography and history. There is also a conflict in motivation between the basic story of promise and fulfilment and the Sinai covenant. In the former we have the divine commitment to the fathers, which finds its realization in the mighty deeds of deliverance and conquest. These constitute the gracious action of the deity, to be duly acknowledged by a grateful people. But Sinai, with its demands and threats, comes in the middle of this story: after the Exodus, which is the down payment on the original promissory note, but before the obligation is fully discharged through the Conquest. At Sinai the movement of the story is temporarily halted, for the storyteller wishes to re-examine and specify in more formal terms the meaning of the relationship between God and his people. Already in the patriarchal narratives the significance of the divine promise and protection had been assessed in terms of obligation. Gratitude itself is the heaviest of obligations; and the unsolicited gift evokes the most elaborate response. An unconditional commitment actually imposes an unlimited obligation: the stories of Abraham in Gen. 15 (of unilateral divine promise); 22 (of unlimited human obligation) illustrate this inescapable interrelationship. Less dramatically, Jacob likewise recognizes both the privileges and the responsibilities of a junior partnership with El Shaddai (cf. Gen. 28:10-22).

Such stories, however, reflected the indeterminate scope and depth of a personal relationship, and could not define the formal status of a people. Only after definite assurance had been given of God's powerful good will, and independently of the course of predetermined grace, the Sinai interlude occurred, to establish a responsible community and to specify the nature and extent of its obligation to its suzerain. Just as God had previously announced his responsibility for and involvement in the destiny of Israel, so now the cost to Israel of its own responsibility and involvement is revealed. The formulation of the terms is put in negative form to indicate the limits within which the community of God is to conduct its affairs and beyond which it may not go. The commands are binding upon each member of the covenant community, but society as a whole is responsible for their enforcement. Essentially, what is required of Israel is obedience, formally in the sense of subscription to the divine demands, but more than this, conformity to the character and purpose of God. The distinction of Israel is the presence of God in its midst, at once its source and hope of glory and the chief threat to its existence. To ensure that blessing and honor, peace and security, rather than judgment and destruction, are the accompaniments of this intimate relationship, is the purpose of the covenant codes. The object is to attain to the holiness of God: "You shall be holy; for I the LORD your God am holy" (Lev. 19:2; cf. 11:44; 20:7; Exod. 19:6; etc.).

That the whole of Israelite life was involved in covenant regulation was recognized from the start. The original stipulations are summed up in the Ten Words, as tradition attests (*see* TEN COMMANDMENTS). But case and cult law, moral and ethical behavior, social and economic practice, religious observance and festival, are subsumed under the covenant terms, so that the major part of Pentateuchal legislation was regarded as an extension of the Sinai agreement. The Book of the Covenant and its incomplete parallel in Exod. 34 (cf. also the Holiness Code [Lev. 17-26]) represent historically the penetration of the Sinai covenant into the life of the community after the settlement in Canaan. The process of expansion and proliferation is carried on through Leviticus and Numbers, while Deuteronomy is a recapitulation of this process, stemming from a separate (N Israelite) source. The elaboration of the covenant in the detailed regulations associated with the Sinai encampment reflects in an artificial and static way what was nevertheless true in a historical sense. The Pentateuchal legislation grew out of the Sinai covenant. The compiler sees it as a perfect whole originating in a single revelatory event.

While the law unfolds in glacial fashion, emphasizing permanence and immutability, the narrative pursues a different tack. Here the covenant is broken almost as soon as it is made. After suitable protestations and ceremonies, the covenant is ratified through a common meal eaten by the elders in the presence of God (Exod. 24:9-11). Within forty days, the people have rebelled, violated the principal terms of the covenant, and incurred the wrath of the suzerain. The penalties implicit in the covenant are threatened, but disaster is narrowly averted by the intervention of Moses. A second covenant is made, with new tablets to replace the broken ones.

The essential conflict between the two covenant ideas—the one of divine commitment to Israel through the fathers, which is irrevocable, and the other, of demand with the threat of annihilation through Moses—is brought out clearly in the episode of the golden calf. The result is that the promise to the fathers remains unbroken—i.e., Israel survives—but this by no means guarantees blanket protection or exemption from the consequences of the Sinai covenant. At the same time, although the penalties for violation of the Sinai covenant are inescapable and devastating, they nevertheless are subject to the prior and unbreakable divine commitment. So divine and human obligation are intermeshed, but without contingency or dependence upon each other. Each pursues remorselessly the logic of its own character, and together they determine the course and consummation of Israel's history. Israel's defection at Sinai is grievously paid for, but the divine commitment is fulfilled in a renewal of the covenant. A second and a third defection are similarly disastrous for Israel; in fact, the whole generation must perish in the wilderness, but the oath to the fathers is maintained when the next generation makes successful entry into the Promised Land.

The chief practical consequence of the sojourn at Sinai and the solemnizing of the covenant was the construction and dedication of the TABERNACLE. The detailed instructions concerning the tabernacle and its furnishings, and the priesthood who serve in it, were given to Moses by God himself (Exod. 25-31). These are repeated *in extenso* (Exod. 35-40), when the work was actually carried out, perhaps to emphasize the meticulous care with which each detail was accomplished in conformity with the original pattern. While the aniconic character of Israel's religion (i.e., the absence of an image of the deity) militated against a complete identification of the tabernacle with the heavenly abode as in pagan religion, nevertheless the presence of God was localized in the tabernacle (for P in the expression כבוד יהוה "the glory of the LORD"; for D in the expression שם יהוה "the name of the LORD"). The tabernacle was designed to serve a twofold function: to protect the holiness of God from contamination by the people (note the regulations restricting the approach to Mount Sinai and the reasons for them, in Exod. 19); and, on the other hand, to protect the people from an outburst of divine wrath. The priests also perform a double function: to serve the Lord of the tabernacle, according to his needs and wishes; and to mediate his presence to the people, including instruction in, and interpretation of, the divine will. Appropriately in the book of LEVITICUS, the service of the tabernacle is described in detail: the types and purpose of the sacrifices which are central to worship (chs. 1-8), and the responsibilities and prerogatives of the priesthood (chs. 9-15) culminating in the liturgy of the Day of Atonement, later Israel's most solemn observance (ch. 16). Here the high priest, who alone may enter the holy of holies, mediates the mercy of God to his people through the scapegoat ritual. In this fashion the accumulated sins and iniquities of the previous year are removed, and the reconciliation between God and people achieved. *See* SACRIFICES AND OFFERINGS; WORSHIP IN THE OT; ATONEMENT, DAY OF.

The so-called Holiness Code (Lev. 17-26) is a summary catchall of legal prescriptions, cultic regulations, and moral exhortation, which may well have served as a catechism for some sanctuary school, or as a guide for PRIESTS AND LEVITES in their work as teachers of the people.

NUMBERS begins with the final action at Sinai: the dedication of the tabernacle. Only when this elaborate and prolonged ceremony was completed, the last animal sacrificed and the last gift offered, was Israel ready to march.

In its present form the Sinai tradition centers upon the elaboration of covenant obligation, in close association with the construction and dedication of the tabernacle. The tabernacle symbolized the PRESENCE of the holy God in the midst of his people, while the covenant legislation defined the character and duties of a not-yet-holy people. Behind the tabernacle of P, as also behind the different codifications of law, lay a simpler and perhaps historically more valid tradition of the Sinai covenant, and the TENT OF MEETING. This tent was no replica of the heavenly house, but rather the place where God and man met to settle their pertinent business. Central to its function was the ARK OF THE COVENANT, symbol of the legally binding nature of the relationship between God and Israel. The association of ark and tent made legal righteousness rather than cultic HOLINESS the principal concern of the worshiping community (*see* RIGHTEOUSNESS IN THE OT). To render just decisions and carry them out in conformity with covenant regulations was the chief obligation of the community gathered at the ark.

From ark and tent developed the elaborate scheme now preserved in the Pentateuch, but the essential emphases are still discernible: a holy God joined to a holy people, but holiness defined in terms of moral and legal obligation, as well as of cultic and ritual purity.

4. The wilderness wanderings (Num. 10:10-36:13). This section consists of a patchwork of narrative material intermingled with priestly data, which have some apparent or superficial connection with the stories or their personnel. Its purpose is to explain how it happened that Israel, which set out from Sinai for Canaan at the start of the second year after the Exodus (Num. 10:11), managed to end up thirty-eight years later far off course in Transjordan, still trying to make entry into the Promised Land. This state of affairs posed serious problems to the compiler, who made little effort to relate a continuous narrative—e.g., thirty-eight years are passed over in silence. While granting that there are numerous gaps in the story, which is itself strange and improbable, these facts alone suggest that an authentic nucleus of tradition is at the bottom of it. Invention would have produced a smoother account, and would hardly have led Israel by the bizarre route described, to the wrong country.

The gap in the chronology is largely a blank, so the narrative is artificially divided between the events of the second year and those of the fortieth (after 20:1). This awkwardness clearly reflects a firm tradition that the generation which came out of Egypt did not reach the Promised Land, but perished in the wilderness—including specifically the leaders, Moses, Aaron, and Miriam. This contretemps, which seems factual on the face of it, is explained rather elaborately as the result of the mishandling of the report of the spies (chs. 13–14). The mixture of *Realpolitik* and theology may not be convincing, but it doubtless preserves the important truth that an attempted invasion of Canaan from the S failed. It failed so badly, in fact, that a generation passed before Israel could build up strength for another effort, and even then it had to be made from another direction. The avoidance of war with Edom and Moab (here a kind of reciprocal evasion was practiced) tends to confirm the impression of military diffidence, though doubtless other factors, not excluding kinship, played a role. At the same time, the rather aimless wanderings of Israel, during the whole period from the Exodus on, may suggest that the Promised Land was not so fixed an objective as our present sources indicate. It may be that they drifted about until they found a weakness in the settled areas. The conquest of Transjordan was not part of the original plan; according to the biblical account, it resulted from the obstinacy of Og and Sihon, who refused the Israelites passage through their territories.

The impression made by the stories is that of growing strength and consolidation of forces until the Israelites were able to meet the enemy in the field and defeat him. Internal difficulties continued: the aftermath of the spies episode is disastrous, and the revolt of Korah (P) and Dathan and Abiram (JE) threaten the very existence of the community. On the other hand, the Balaam narrative shows Israel in a most favorable light, as this international diviner is unable to resist the persuasive pressure of the God of Israel and prophesies the splendor and power of the new nation to the dismay of his patron and the serious detriment of his own fortune. The oracles of Balaam, like the Song of the Reed Sea, are a potent example of early Hebrew poetry, authentically portraying the Israel of the wilderness wanderings.

With the defeat of Og and Sihon, Israel at last was able to claim possession of a suitable territory. While the settlement in Transjordan was provisional and preliminary, it is on this note that the Tetrateuch closes. The wanderings have come to an end, and Israel is poised for the final adventure.

5. The epilogue (Deuteronomy). Before the invasion of Canaan, there was an interlude: Moses' farewell sermons in the Plains of Moab in the last year of the wanderings, and shortly before his death (*see* DEUTERONOMY). It is this break in the narrative sequence which focuses attention on the special significance of the wilderness experience. For in these addresses Moses recapitulates the desert experience beginning with the revelation at Horeb (Sinai). Particular emphasis is placed upon the covenant and its stipulations. The Ten Words are repeated (in ch. 5); then the sense of the first commandment is explained and elaborated for six additional chapters (6–11), beginning with a restatement of the main theme of the covenant in positive terms: "You shall love the LORD your God with all your heart, and with all your soul, and with all your might" (6:4). There follows (chs. 12–26) a body of legal material similar to the collections in the earlier books of the Pentateuch, but worked out in a special hortatory style. Additional and presumably original features of the covenant pattern are preserved in ch. 27 (blessings and curses); the covenant-renewal ceremony is connected with mounts Ebal and Gerizim, in the vicinity of Shechem (cf. Josh. 24).

Two old poems (Deut. 32–33, both probably dating from the period of the amphictyony or early monarchy) are attached to the book, which closes with the death of Moses. For the Deuteronomist, Moses was a prophet, but more than a prophet: "There has not arisen a prophet since in Israel like Moses, whom the LORD knew face to face" (34:10).

The Pentateuch is a composite presentation of the beginnings of Israel. Genesis, including the Creation and primeval history, even the patriarchal narratives, is preamble. The center of interest is the formation of Israel: Exodus, Sinai, wanderings, and Transjordan are the key words. The story is bounded by the life of Moses, who is the master agent of God's will and the chief architect of Israel. The mighty deeds of God constitute the basic narrative, set in sharp relief by the stupidity and wickedness of Israel. Tabernacle and covenant describe the presence of the holy God in the midst of his chosen people, while the interaction of divine commitment and human obligation defines the area of Israel's experience. The special emphasis of the Deuteronomic sermons, with which the Pentateuch closes, is on the covenant responsibilities of Israel: to obey means life, to disobey death, in the simplest possible terms (cf. Deut. 30:15 in the context of this speech). These words were aimed at a community on the verge of disaster (cf. also Jer. 38:2 ff). The Sinai-Horeb covenant, with its sanctions and penalties, could not be set aside in favor of some more palatable doctrine of election privilege. But the last word even of the Deuteronomist was one of hope. The commitment to Abraham was eternal and irreversible: "For the LORD your God is a merciful God; he will not fail you or destroy you or forget the covenant with your fathers which he swore to them" (Deut. 4:31).

C. *HISTORY OF PENTATEUCHAL CRITICISM.* The systematic, critical investigation of the Pentateuch has been carried on for the past two hundred years. Practically every OT scholar of note has written extensively on the subject, with the result that the pertinent literature is so vast as to defy satisfactory compilation, much less adequate review and evaluation. We must be content with a hasty sketch of the subject.

Scientific Pentateuchal criticism is commonly said to have begun with Jean Astruc, a French Catholic physician, who published his *Conjectures sur les mémoires dont il paroît que Moyse s'est servi, pour com-*

poser le livre de la Genèse, in 1753. Nevertheless, he had precursors, and some of his conclusions about the diversity of sources in Genesis had been anticipated but forgotten. During the hundred years following, the main issues of the literary analysis of the Pentateuch were worked out by a succession of brilliant Continental scholars until the proponents of the "new documentary theory" emerged triumphant. By the last quarter of the nineteenth century, the Reuss-Graf-Kuenen-Wellhausen hypothesis had swept the field, and was widely accepted as the definitive solution to the literary problems of the Pentateuch. In particular, the writings of Julius Wellhausen summed up the scholarly contributions of previous generations and presented the assured results of literary criticism in a compact and decisive fashion, briefly symbolized by the scholarly tetragrammaton JEDP. J and E were narrative sources, dating in the ninth and eighth centuries respectively, while the compilation JE was achieved in the seventh. D was composed in the seventh century, while P was postexilic. The final editing of the Pentateuch took place *ca.* 400 B.C.

Many new developments have occurred since the time of Wellhausen, though it is fair to say that the documentary hypothesis remains the landmark of Pentateuchal criticism, and the foundation for all further research. These developments may be grouped under three classifications: literary analysis, form-critical investigation, and tradition history. While these overlap, and scholars work across the lines of division, they are helpful in indicating the direction of interest and investigation.

1. Documentary hypotheses. Since the Pentateuch is literature and behind its present compilation there are sources (whether clearly defined documents or oral traditions), literary analysis will remain a basic task in Pentateuchal criticism, though other disciplines may be useful and necessary. For many years scholars have been engaged in refining the documentary analysis. It has generally been conceded that none of the major sources is itself a unity.

On the one hand, secondary and supplementary data have been separated from primary source material (thus, e.g., D_S is the Deuteronomic redaction of D, the code found in the temple); on the other, independent sources have been identified within the larger groupings of older analysis. Just as P and E were separated out of the original E source, so J_1 and J_2 were isolated, P_A and P_B, and so on. Because the sigla used to identify separate sources and secondary additions tended to be confused, new letters have appeared in the documentary formulation: L (for J_1, Eissfeldt); K (J. Morgenstern); and S (R. Pfeiffer). As part of the same process of re-examination, two of the older sources have been challenged, E and P. Are these independent documents or supplements and insertions into the basic J narrative?

The net effect of the close investigation of the sources has been to blur the clear lines of the documentary hypothesis. Looked at from one point of view, there are too many documents; thus the fragmentary hypothesis revives. From the opposite viewpoint, there are too few or none at all. As a result, the documents appear to be compilations themselves rather than original compositions, and to reflect a process covering hundreds of years and reaching back into the period of oral tradition with its discrete entities. The increasingly unsatisfactory results of literary analysis (for no new scheme has commanded anything like the support given to the older documentary alignment) have led scholars behind the literary sources into the preliterary origins of the contents of the Pentateuch, and also to a new investigation of the process by which the sources were gathered and preserved, and the Pentateuch compiled.

2. Form-critical analysis. The form-critical analysis of the Pentateuch is associated primarily with the name of Hermann Gunkel, whose monumental commentary on Genesis (1902; 3rd ed., 1910) marked an epoch in OT scholarship (cf. also *Die Urgeschichte und die Patriarchen* [2nd ed., 1921], and Gressmann's *Die Anfänge Israels* [2nd ed., 1922]). Gunkel was mainly concerned with two matters: to classify the biblical materials according to formal characteristics (i.e., the structure or pattern of the unit, rather than its content), and also to determine the *Sitz im Leben* (life situation) reflected by the particular item, out of which it arose, or in which it found its function and place. By close examination of the biblical materials, and comparison with similar literature of the other peoples of the Near East, it was possible to deal with both questions in a highly satisfactory and stimulating way. Some authentic idea of the prehistory of the literature of the Pentateuch could be gained, as well as helpful insights into the nature of Israelite and pre-Israelite patriarchal life. The danger of circular or self-validating reasoning was always present—i.e., to reconstruct a *Sitz im Leben* from the contents of a given piece, and then to interpret the piece on the basis of the supposed *Sitz im Leben.* In addition, while the purely scientific and objective discipline of form-classification has proved extremely useful, inferences concerning historicity and accuracy have been drawn on the basis of such classifications, which are often given tendentious titles—e.g., legend, myth, etc. With the aid of archaeological research, and in the light of the enormous quantities of inscriptional and other data bearing on the life of man in the ancient Near East, it was possible to put Pentateuchal criticism on a much sounder historical foundation than ever before. While the literary interrelationships of the Pentateuchal sources could be dealt with by the tools of literary analysis, and the relative chronology of the sources worked out, the question of the antiquity of the P material, e.g., could only be guessed at, or treated inadequately by the hazardous comparison of the Pentateuch with the historical books. Now it was possible to evaluate the traditions, customs, and nomenclature of the Pentateuch on the basis of contemporary data from the Near East and to show that the date of compilation of a Pentateuchal source did not necessarily bear upon either the antiquity or the accuracy of its contents. As a result of the archaeological revolution there has been a wholesale re-evaluation and redistribution of the Pentateuchal materials, especially those assigned to P. While this does not signify a return to the traditional view of Mosaic authorship or date, it has meant the rehabilitation in appropriate settings of the large mass of data hitherto regarded as mere priestly invention. Used cautiously, the Pentateuch is an invaluable source, not merely for the point of view of its compilers, but for the actual early history of Israel.

Albrecht Alt, following the labors of A. Jirku (*Das weltliche Recht im AT* [1927]), and A. Jepsen (*Untersuchungen zum Bundesbuch* [1927]), established a landmark in the application of the form-critical method to the laws of the Pentateuch in his *Die Ursprünge des Israelitischen Rechts* (1934; now available in Alt's *Kleine Schriften zur Geschichte des Volkes Israel* [1953], vol. I). Alt distinguished formally between casuistic and apodictic laws, the former being characteristic of the jurisprudence of the ancient Near East, while the latter (with the form "Thou shalt not . . .") were peculiarly Israelite in their formulation and belonged to the sphere of sacral usage. Subsequent investigation has followed the lines laid down by Alt, though some of his conclusions have been questioned or modified. It does not seem likely that Israelite case law developed directly from contemporary Canaanite practice, but rather that it evolved indigenously in Israel from older, pre-Israelite patriarchal custom, going back ultimately to Mesopotamian sources. On the other hand, G. E. Mendenhall in *Law and Covenant in Israel and the Ancient Near East* (1955) has suggested that the suzerainty treaty of the second millennium provides an appropriate setting for categorical stipulations such as we have in the apodictic laws in the Pentateuch. Just as the suzerain imposes obligations upon his vassal, so the God of Israel requires obedience to the terms of the covenant (Exod. 19–24). The possible cultic *Sitz im Leben* for the presentation of the Decalogue—i.e., the covenant-renewal festival—had already been described by Sigmund Mowinckel in *Le décalogue* (1927).

Another development of the form-critical approach is to be seen in the works of G. von Rad and M. Noth. Von Rad retains the traditional JEDP pattern but regards the sources as aggregates of tradition accumulated or compiled over centuries. The basic pattern of the Hexateuch is defined by the credo (e.g., Deut. 26:5-9), while it is out of the cult that the Pentateuchal sources and the Pentateuch itself emerge. The sources, beginning with J, reflect the same historical (i.e., *geschichtliche,* or really *heilsgeschichtliche*) pattern, because it antedates them, having already been shaped by the confession of the worshiping community at the (central) sanctuary.

Noth deals similarly with the process of oral tradition which lies behind the documentary sources of the Pentateuch. He identifies a number of major themes, like the promise to the fathers, the deliverance from bondage, the Sinai experience. Around each of these cluster the etiological tales, cult legends, etc., which constitute the original oral materials. In his analysis of the documents, Noth separates Deuteronomy from the rest of the Pentateuch and attaches it to the Deuteronomic history. The other sources, J, E, and P, do not extend beyond Numbers, with the exception of some material at the end of Deuteronomy. On the other hand, there are no traces of the Deuteronomist in the Tetrateuch. Behind J and E, he recognizes a common source G (*Grundlage*). Some of the implications, and difficulties, of Noth's position have been considered above. Whether the Deuteronomic history will succeed the Hexateuch as the basic literary unit of the primary history remains to be seen. It is clear that both cannot survive.

Counterbalancing Noth's restriction of JE to the Tetrateuch is Hölscher's extension of these sources throughout the primary history. For him, J comes down to the division of the monarchy (I Kings 12), while E includes the whole history from Genesis to the end of II Kings. His views have not met with general acceptance. The contrast with Noth is so striking as to provoke the question of the nature of Israelite history writing, and the proper approach to the materials at hand. Eissfeldt has treated both presentations in a short but penetrating critique (*Geschichtsschreibung im AT* [1948]).

3. Traditio-historical criticism. The most radical resistance to the Wellhausen hypothesis has come from the so-called Uppsala school. Its chief representative is Ivan Engnell, who has proposed a new analysis of the Pentateuch, based upon the view that oral tradition played a much larger and longer role in the formation of the Pentateuch than is usually assigned to it. While much of the technical and legal material in the Pentateuch was written down, the narrative traditions were transmitted orally. It is useless, therefore, to try to isolate documentary sources, since these did not exist, and what sources there were had already been fused with one another and the P narrative framework in the preliterary stage. Engnell distinguishes two principal collections of material: the "P-work," which corresponds to the Tetrateuch, and the "D-work," which corresponds to Noth's Deuteronomic history. These works developed independently of each other, and were ultimately written down separately in postexilic times (fifth century). Later they were joined, since the "D-work" begins approximately where the "P-work" leaves off. The P-work centers upon the exodus tradition (Exod. 1–15), which reflects the cultic celebration of the deliverance from Egypt. (Here Engnell follows the lead of J. Pedersen, whose own views of the Pentateuch are highly original and anti-Wellhausenian.) It is around this nucleus that the rest of the material has accumulated in P-circles. By the time the traditions were reduced to writing, they were verbally fixed, so that the MT reflects faithfully the original. This conservative approach to the MT is a welcome shift from the days of free emendation. At the same time, however, the well-known Uppsala disregard for the LXX is less defensible, especially since the Qumran discoveries. A number of Hebrew MSS have been found which preserve a LXX-type text, thus confirming the fact that in the Pentateuch and historical books the LXX was a faithful, almost literal rendering of its *Vorlage*. The existence of distinct scribal recensions of the Pentateuch can only be damaging to the Scandinavian view of the very late compilation of the text.

There can be little doubt that Engnell's general emphasis upon the importance, the tenacity, and the reliability of oral tradition is warranted and commendable. His contention that much ancient material has been preserved faithfully in the text of the Pentateuch is likewise valid, and the idea of continuing circles of "P" and "D" may offer a solution to the problem of the accumulation of traditions. Nevertheless, the sharp distinction between oral and written transmission tends to break down, the more the tenacity and reliability of oral tradition are maintained. There is no reason to doubt that the art of writing, even of narrative and poetic material, was practiced in early Israel, especially after the rise of the monarchy. It is very difficult to suppose that the court history of David was not written down within a comparatively few years of the events described, and so with other narrative materials, particularly those in prose. Moreover, the problems of the Pentateuch are literary, at least to a considerable extent; and one cannot banish them by transferring them from a written to an oral setting. In the future we shall have to reckon more with the oral traditions and their transmission, but hardly less with the written materials and their transmission.

4. Synthesis and summary. A. Weiser in his *Einleitung in das AT* (2nd ed., 1949) attempts a synthesis of the different approaches and methods of dealing with the Pentateuch. Instead of choosing one over another, use can be made of all, since the Pentateuch is more than a collection of traditions, more than a mixture of literary sources. It is closely bound to the cult and faithfully reflects the religious life and experience of the people. Its basic structure and unity come out of the cultic confession, which itself is the affirmation of Israel's historical experience. So Israel's authentic history, focused in the cult, finds expression in the Pentateuch, which is the precipitate of accumulated cultic traditions.

C. R. North, after surveying recent developments in Pentateuchal criticism, summarizes as follows: (*a*) It must now be recognized that the Pentateuch consists of traditions concerning the history of Israel down to the death of Moses, and that they do not have the values of scientific history. This is *Heilsgeschichte*—Israel's confession, its affirmation of what God has done for and to Israel in the world. That it is based upon some nucleus of fact may be granted, but this is not the most important fact about this type of literature. It has its *Sitz im Leben* in the cult; it is first of all a religious document. (*b*) Can the development of Israel's religious ideas be traced in the familiar JEDP arrangement, or are the evolutionist assumptions of the Wellhausen school no longer acceptable now that the simple chronological scheme of documents can no longer be sustained? North believes that some defense can be made both of the documents and the "evolution" of Israelite religion, though hardly with the assurance of the earlier scholars. North's view is judicious, and reflects the evolution of OT scholarship in its grasp of the nature and complexity of the Pentateuchal traditions. Nevertheless, we suggest that the distinction between *geschichtlich* and *historisch* should not be pressed too far in dealing with the Pentateuch. A religion that affirms the mighty deeds of God and attempts to place them in a historical context cannot afford to make nice distinctions between the fact and the affirmation of it. Admittedly what is central is the interpretation of the event, which itself is the confession of faith. But the event is or must be historical. Beneath the layers of tradition there was an event, which may not now be recoverable, though pessimism about the possibility of such recovery is excessive. It is that event (i.e., what actually happened, but theologically interpreted) which faith must affirm, not some imaginative tradition about it.

With regard to the second point, the question of evolution in Israelite religion can be separated from the chronological interrelationship of the sources. One may accept the scholarly dating of the sources without accepting also some evolutionary scheme concerning the religion of Israel: e.g., from polytheism to henotheism to monotheism; or from a tribal to a national to a universal God; or in ethical and moral principles. The arrangement and dating of the contents of the Pentateuch (as distinguished from the documents) will depend, not upon the inner criticism of the sources, but on comparison with objective nonbiblical data from the contemporary Near East.

The Pentateuch is the end product of an incredibly long process of accumulation, transmission, and redaction. Its original traditions go back to dim antiquity (e.g., the traditions behind the flood story must be many thousands of years old), and were transmitted orally for hundreds of years: folk tales, cult legends, etiological stories, and the like, each with its characteristic form, shaped and polished through repeated telling. These were linked into more complex collections, until a connected narrative emerged, built out of the basic pattern of the credo, or confession of faith. These poetic materials were consolidated into the official tradition of the confederation around its sanctuary during the period of the judges (G). Likewise going back to patriarchal times was a legal tradition, around which gathered customs and precedents, and from which emerged the various bodies of law preserved in the Pentateuch. With few exceptions, the mass of the material is premonarchic. Cultic practice is also of great antiquity; and in various collections, the Pentateuch preserves the sacral customs of early Israel. Because of the tenacity and conservatism of religious observance, it is almost impossible to trace development, but in general the Pentateuchal cult legislation reflects the practice of the early monarchy.

Formal classification, oral tradition, cultic setting and function, are important new tools in the struggle to understand the Pentateuch. Even more significant is the mass of archaeological data, which increasingly provides an external, historically reliable check upon the theories imposed upon the Pentateuchal material, and the reconstructions made of them. The Pentateuch apparently consists of essentially authentic data concerning the history of Israel from the time of the patriarchs down to the death of Moses, but including cultic, legal, and other technical data, which in their present form derive from later periods, particularly the amphictyony and the early monarchy. The documents themselves were composed at various times, beginning in the tenth century B.C. and ending in the middle of the sixth, when the whole of the primary history was completed. During the next century the Pentateuch was separated, and officially promulgated as the authoritative word of God for Israel, the only infallible rule of faith and practice.

Bibliography. The most recent presentation of the general subject of Pentateuchal criticism is to be found in O. Eissfeldt, *Einleitung in das AT* (2nd ed., 1956), which has an extensive bibliography. Very worthwhile are: C. R. North, "Pentateuchal Criticism," *The OT and Modern Study* (1951), pp. 48-83, which also includes a useful Bibliography; and H. F. Hahn, *OT in Modern Research* (1954).

General treatments in English: A. Bentzen, *Introduction to the OT* (2nd ed., 1952). R. H. Pfeiffer, *Introduction to the OT* (2nd ed., 1953). The old classic is S. R. Driver, *Introduction to the Literature of the OT* (9th ed., 1913). The most comprehensive publication of the Wellhausen hypothesis, along with a complete history of criticism to that time, is to be found in J. E. Carpenter and G. Harford-Battersby, *The Hexateuch According to the Revised Version* (1900).

Relevant books and articles in other languages: J. Wellhausen, *Prolegomena to the History of Ancient Israel* (trans. J. S. Black and A. Menzies; 1885); *Die Composition des Hexateuchs und der historischen Bücher des ATs* (3rd ed., 1899). J. Pedersen, "Die Auffassung vom AT," *ZAW*, XLIX (1931), 161-81. P. Volz and W. Rudolph, *Der Elohist als Erzähler: Ein Irrweg der Pentateuchkritik?* BZAW, vol. LXIII (1933). G. von Rad, *Die Priesterschrift im Hexateuch*, BWANT, vol. XIII (1934); *Das formgeschichtliche Problem des Hexateuchs*, BWANT, vol. XXVI (1938). W. Rudolph, *Der "Elohist" von Exodus bis Josua*, BZAW, vol. LXVIII (1938). J. Pedersen, *Israel: Its Life and Culture* (trans. A. I. Fausbøll; 1940). G. Hölscher, *Die Anfänge der hebräischen Geschichtsschreibung* (1942). M. Noth, *Überlieferungsgeschichtliche Studien*, vol. I (1943); *Überlieferungsgeschichte des Pentateuch* (1948). G. Hölscher, *Geschichtsschreibung in Israel* (1952). G. von Rad, *Studies in Deuteronomy* (trans. D. Stalker; 1953); *Das erste Buch Mose, Genesis, Das AT Deutsch*, 2/4 (1953). Y. Kaufmann, *The Religion of Israel* (1960).

For an extended and authoritative presentation of the documentary hypothesis, see: S. R. Driver, *Introduction to the Literature of the OT* (9th ed., 1913), pp. 1-159. Cf. also: J. E. Carpenter and G. Harford-Battersby, *The Hexateuch According to the Revised Version* (2 vols.; 1900), I, 1-179. R. H. Pfeiffer, *Introduction to the OT* (2nd ed., 1953), pp. 129-289.

D. N. FREEDMAN

PENTATEUCH, SAMARITAN. *See* SAMARITAN PENTATEUCH.

PENTECOST pĕn'tĭ kôst, —kŏst [πεντηκοστή, fiftieth; *or* ἡ ἡμέρα τῆς πεντηκοστῆς, the fiftieth day]. The Greek term for the Jewish Feast of Weeks (*see* WEEKS, FEAST OF), so named because it fell on the fiftieth day after the ceremony of the barley sheaf during the Passover observances (*see* PASSOVER AND FEAST OF UNLEAVENED BREAD). It marked the beginning of the offering of first fruits. The NT uses the term to refer to the established Jewish feast. But since the gift of the Holy Spirit to the church occurred on the day of Pentecost (Acts 2:1), Christians reinterpreted the meaning of it in terms of this event.

J. C. RYLAARSDAM

PENUEL pĭ nōō'əl, pĕn'yōō əl [פנואל, face of God]. Alternately: PENIEL —nī'—, pĕn'ĭ əl [פניאל] (Gen. 32:30). **1.** A son of Hur and grandson of Judah, mentioned as the "father" (founder) of Gedor (I Chr. 4:4).

2. A Benjaminite, son of Shashak (I Chr. 8:25).

3. A city in E Palestine, situated on the River Jabbok (Nahr ez-Zerqa) above and to the E of Succoth. According to the story told in Gen. 32:24-32, Jacob was returning home from Paddan-aram and was spending the night on the banks of the Jabbok when one (cf. Hos. 12:4: "angel") in the form of a man came and wrestled with him all night, departing in the morning after giving him the name Israel. Thereupon Jacob called the place Peniel, "for I have seen God face to face, yet my life is preserved." Elsewhere, however, the only name given for the town is Penuel.

When Gideon was pursuing the Midianites after he had defeated them in the Valley of Jezreel, he asked the citizens of the town for food and received a rude answer; on his return he avenged this insult by destroying the tower of the city and killing all its male inhabitants (Judg. 8:8-9, 17). Nothing further is heard of the city for two centuries, and it may have been in ruins when Jeroboam I of Israel "built" it (I Kings 12:25); but the term may mean that he enlarged and fortified it. The city is perhaps Pernoual, number fifty-three in Shishak's list of conquered cities; it is mentioned in late Assyrian records as Panili. The site of Penuel is the E of the two mounds Tulul edh-Dhahab (N. Glueck named this Tell edh-Dhahab esh-Sherqi), which contains sherds from the Early Iron period (1200-900 B.C.) and was evidently a strongly fortified place, nearly surrounded by the river and very steep on the E side; it commanded the entrance into the Jordan Valley from the gorge of the Jabbok and was in a fertile district.

Bibliography. S. Merrill, *East of Jordan* (1881), pp. 390-92; N. Glueck, *AASOR*, XVIII-XIX (1939), 232-35.

S. COHEN

PEOPLE OF GOD [עם אלהים; λαὸς τοῦ θεοῦ]; PEOPLE OF THE LORD [עם יהוה]. One of many expressions in the OT which indicate the unique relationship which exists between Yahweh and his people (Num. 11:29; 16:41; Judg. 5:11, 13; I Sam. 2:24; II Sam. 6:21; II Kings 9:6; Zeph. 2:10; cf. Judg. 20:2; II Sam. 14:13); used in the NT in a similar framework (*see below*).

1. In the OT. Israel is Yahweh's "property, possession, inheritance" (Exod. 19:5; Deut. 4:20; 7:6; Mal. 3:17); his "servant" (Ps. 135:14; Isa. 48:20); his "son" (Exod. 4:22-23; Hos. 11:1); his "sheep" (Ps. 95:7); his "holy people" (Deut. 14:2; 28:9; Isa. 62:12). While the term "people of God" appears relatively few times, the use of עם with personal suffixes ("my people," "thy people," "his people") occurs very frequently in this sense (cf. also the "congregation, assembly of the LORD"; Num. 16:3; Deut. 23:2-4; cf. Neh. 13:1).

The term עם יהוה, "people of Yahweh," may have had its origin in the cultic institution of the holy war in the days of the tribal federation before the monarchy, as a designation for the assembly of able-bodied men gathered for defensive warfare (*see* WAR, IDEAS OF) against a common enemy (Judg. 5:11, 13; cf. 20:2). Behind this institution lay the unique COVENANT relationship, according to which the tribes confessed Yahweh as the one who had constituted the people Israel through certain mighty acts in history, and had entered into covenant with them (cf. Deut. 26:5-9; Josh. 24:2-13). Cultic renewal of this covenant, with its obligation of faithfulness to covenant law, seems to have formed the core of ancient Israelite worship. *See* WORSHIP IN THE OT.

Deut. 4 (cf. Exod. 19:4-6; Deut. 7:6-12; 32:8 ff; Ps. 135) expresses the relationship of Yahweh to Israel in the theological terms of the seventh century: Israel is Yahweh's possession (vs. 20) because of his gracious choosing, wrought in love (vs. 37; cf. Deut.

7:6; 14:2; Ps. 135:4), though there is nothing impressive (Deut. 7:7) or virtuous (9:5-6) about Israel which evokes this love. Yahweh remains faithful to his covenant (4:31), while Israel's enjoyment of the covenant promises is conditioned by faithfulness to the obligations (vs. 40).

While the expanding glory of the Davidic-Solomonic empire seemed to epitomize Israel's special relationship to God as the foundation and norm of her existence, the prophets of the ninth through the seventh centuries proclaimed that this relationship placed Israel under judgment; the covenant had been broken through Israel's unfaithfulness, and she was no longer "my people" (Hos. 1:9; cf. Deut. 4:27; Isa. 1:10; Amos 3:2).

Nevertheless, Yahweh's faithfulness remains unchanged (Hos. 2; cf. Deut. 4:31), and a repentant REMNANT might yet expect the restoration of Israel as the people of Yahweh (Hos. 2:23; cf. Jer. 31:31-34; Ezek. 11:16-20). In postexilic prophecy the doctrine of restoration occasionally broke nationalistic bounds to include all nations (Zech. 2:10-12; cf. Isa. 45:18-25; 49:6; 55:4-7), but such universalism was countered by a strong religious particularism, which ultimately became the guiding element in late Judaism.

2. In the NT. Λαὸς τοῦ θεοῦ, "people of God," and related terms may be used to describe the "old Israel" (Heb. 11:25; cf. Matt. 1:21; Luke 1:68; Rom. 11:1-2), but the decisive NT usage identifies the people of God with the church (Rom. 9:25-26; II Cor. 6:14 ff; Tit. 2:14; Heb. 8:10; I Pet. 2:9-10; Rev. 21:3; *see* CHURCH, IDEA OF) grounded upon faith in Jesus Christ. In a similar framework of OT fulfilment, the NT sees the church as the true Israel (Rom. 9:6; I Cor. 10:18; Gal. 6:16), the true seed of Abraham (Gal. 3:29; cf. Rom. 9:7-8), the true circumcision (Phil. 3:3), and the true temple (I Cor. 3:16).

Bibliography. G. von Rad, *Der heilige Krieg im alten Israel* (2nd ed., 1952), pp. 7-14. J. A. WHARTON

PEOPLE OF THE EAST. *See* EAST, PEOPLE OF THE.

PEOPLE OF THE LAND. The literal translation of the עם הארץ, a technical term designating originally the qualified male citizenry of a land. *See* 'AM HA'AREZ.

PEOR pē'ôr [הפעור, the opening. **1.** A mountain in Moab, the last place to which Balak took Balaam that he might curse Israel (Num. 23:27-28). They went "to the top of Peor, that overlooks the desert" (KJV "that looketh toward JESHIMON"), from which the camp of the Israelites in the Plains of Moab was visible (24:2). The location must be near Mount Nebo, but a specific mountain has not been identified. *See* BAAL-PEOR; BETH-PEOR.

2. The god of Mount Peor (*see* 1 *above*); a shortening of the name BAAL-PEOR. The Midianite incident in Num. 25 is referred to Peor (vs. 18). In 31:16, but not elsewhere, it was by the counsel of Balaam that the Midianite women led Israel astray in the matter of Peor. In Josh. 22:17, the sin of the Reubenites, the Gadites, and the half-tribe of Manasseh in building an altar is compared to the sin at Peor.

3. A location in Judah (Josh. 15:59 LXX); modern Khirbet of Faghur, SW of Bethlehem.

E. D. GROHMAN

PERAZIM, MOUNT pĭ rā'zĭm [הר פרצים] (Isa. 28:21). A place in Isaiah's warning message. *See* BAAL-PERAZIM.

PERDITION. A translation of בליעל and of ἀπώλεια.

In the OT the word occurs in II Sam. 22:5 and in the parallel verse in Ps. 18:4. Here the meaning of "perdition" is "death." The psalmist, in referring to the "torrents of perdition" or floods of destruction which assailed and terrified him, is alluding to Sheol and death.

In the NT "perdition" translates ἀπώλεια four out of the eighteen times the Greek word occurs. The Greek word means essentially "destruction, annihilation, ruin," and it is usually translated "destruction." The reference is primarily to eternal destruction—e.g., in Matt. 7:13, where "destruction" is opposed to "life," and in Phil. 1:28, where it is opposed to "salvation." In Rev. 17:8, 11, the reference is not to the destruction of an ordinary mortal, but to the ruin of "the beast," and here the KJV-RSV translation is "perdition." The beast goes to perdition—i.e., he is doomed to destruction; he is not to participate in the new creation.

"Perdition" occurs in two other NT passages, both times in the expression "son of perdition" (John 17:12; II Thess. 2:3). In the gospel passage the "son of perdition" is Judas Iscariot, who alone, of those whom the Father gave the Son, was lost. The "son of perdition" is the son destined for destruction. In the Thessalonians passage the "son of perdition" is the "man of lawlessness" who proclaims himself to be God and must be revealed before the end comes. (*See* ANTICHRIST.) But this man of lawlessness will be destroyed by the Lord Jesus (II Thess. 2:8).

The phrase "son of perdition" refers also to those who perished in the Flood (Jub. 10:3); to Satan (Gospel of Nicodemus XX); and to false prophets (Akhmim Fragment of the Apocalypse of Peter 1.1).

B. H. THROCKMORTON, JR.

PEREA pə rē'ə [Περαία, *from* πέραν τοῦ Ἰορδάνου = עבר הירדן (Isa. 9:1), beyond the Jordan]. The Transjordan district which was part of the kingdom of Herod the Great and after his death in 4 B.C. inherited with Galilee by his son, Herod Antipas; significant as the route of Jesus' last journey to Jerusalem.

1. Location. The district was bounded on the W by the Jordan River and the NE part of the Dead Sea; on the E by the districts of Gerasa, Philadelphia, and Heshbon. The city of Pella, to which the Christian community of Jerusalem fled shortly before the outbreak of the Jewish Revolt in A.D. 66, marked the N boundary; and the Herodian fortress of Machaerus, the scene of the execution of John the Baptist, established the S line against which the Nabatean kingdom pressed (Jos. Antiq. XX.i.1; War III.iii.3). According to Josephus (War IV.vii.3) the capital was Gadara or Gador, the modern Tell Gadur, which is to be distinguished from the city of the same name in the Decapolis. The fortified city of Amathus (Tell

'Ammata) may have served as the N capital above the Jabbok. Glueck's surveys in Transjordan have confirmed the S boundary as running from Machaerus to the top of the W edge of the Moabite Plateau; on the E the boundary consists of a N-S line running somewhat W of MEDEBA, thus correcting Josephus' notation "from Philadelphia to the Jordan" to read "from the Jordan to about one half the way to Philadelphia." Dalman (*see bibliography*) places the N limit as S of Pella near the Wadi Fakaris. One of three main routes from Galilee to Judea led southward through Perea along the Jordan Valley; another followed the valley on the W side of the Jordan via Scythopolis, Koraia, and Jericho; and the third, via Scythopolis, Shechem, and Bethel. According to Matt. 19:1 it was the first of these roads that Jesus and his disciples took, remaining for some time in Jewish Perea.

2. History. In earlier times this territory had been inhabited by the peoples of Gilead, Ammon, and Moab. In early Maccabean times Judas Maccabeus brought relief to an oppressed Jewish minority in the cities of Gilead and transported them for safety to Judea (I Macc. 5:9-54). John Hyrcanus (135-104 B.C.) conquered the important city of Medeba and possibly introduced the policy of forcible conversion to Judaism; this policy then carried on by the ruthless Hasmonean ruler Alexander Janneus (103-76), who in bloody campaigns subdued and Judaized Perea and Galilee. Ragaba in Perea was the scene of Alexander Janneus' death from malaria in 76 B.C. In 57, Gabinius, the proconsul of Syria, made Amathus the capital of one of the five districts of Palestine. During Jesus' time the district of Perea was under the control of Herod Antipas, who rebuilt the city of Betharamphtha, giving it the names Julias and Livias (Jos. Antiq. XVIII.ii.1; *see* BETH-HARAM). At this time the population was predominantly Jewish. The Mishna speaks of Perea as one of the three Jewish provinces (B.B. III.2). In some sense, however, these provinces were regarded as separate districts; Keth. XIII.10 says that a wife (or husband) could not be forced by her partner to move from one to another of these territories. *Ca.* A.D. 44 strife broke out between the Pereans and the Philadelphians over border lines (Jos. Antiq. XIX.ix.2). In the Jewish Rebellion the Jews of Perea joined their brethren all over Palestine in the fatal struggle to throw off the Roman yoke (Jos. War IV.vii.4-6). Under Nero the territory was given to Herod Agrippa II, who ruled until his death in A.D. 100; thereafter, it became part of the Roman province of Syria.

3. In the NT. The name Περαία is found frequently in Josephus, but it occurs nowhere in the NT except in a variant reading of Luke 6:17. Instead the expression "beyond the Jordan" (πέραν τοῦ Ἰορδάνου) is found, a translation of an Aramaic or Hebrew form. In John 1:28, John is said to have been baptizing in the Perean city of BETHANY. Early in Jesus' Galilean ministry crowds followed him from all three of the Jewish provinces (Matt. 4:25; cf. Mark 3:8). According to Matt. 19:1 (note the expression "Judea beyond Jordan") Jesus and his disciples came into this territory after they left Galilee for the last time, perhaps crossing the Jordan at Scythopolis or coming around the E side of the lake and thence descending into the Jordan Valley. Mark 10:1 may be understood to mean that they traveled through Samaria into Judea, crossing into Perea along a Roman road NE of Bethel. It is not known whether Jesus on his way through Perea remained in the valley or went up to the highlands, where he might have passed through such cities as Ragaba, Mahanaim, Gador, Beth Nimrin, and Bethany; but Matthew clearly states that he continued his active ministry of healing and teaching while he remained for some time in this area.

Bibliography. E. Schürer, *History of the Jewish People,* div. 2, vol. I (1885), pp. 2-4 *et passim;* G. Dalman, *Sacred Sites and Ways* (1935), pp. 233-39; F.-M. Abel, *Géographie de la Palestine,* II (1938), 154; N. Glueck, *Explorations in Eastern Palestine,* III, *AASOR,* XVIII-XIX (1939), 140, 143.

E. W. SAUNDERS

PERES pĭr'ĕz [פרס]. Singular of "parsin." *See* MENE, MENE, TEKEL, AND PARSIN.

PERESH pĭr'ĕsh [פרש] (I Chr. 7:16). Son of Machir and his wife Maacah, of Manasseh.

PEREZ pĭr'ĕz [פרץ, breach, bursting forth, *or perhaps* spreading; *cf. place name* פרץ עזה *and* Akkad. *personal name Parṣī;* LXX and NT Φάρες]; KJV OT PHAREZ fâr'— except in I Chr. 27:3; Neh. 11:4, 6; KJV NT PHARES —ĕs; PEREZITES pĭr'ə zīts; KJV PHARZITES fär'—. One of twin sons (the other was Zerah) born to Judah and his daughter-in-law Tamar (Gen. 38:29; I Chr. 2:4; 4:1); the father of Hezron and Hamul (Gen. 46:12; Num. 26:21; I Chr. 2:5); ancestral head of the "family of the Perezites" (Num. 26:20).

The story of his birth (Gen. 38:27-30, with which cf. 19:36-38 and especially 25:21-26) gives the popular etymology of his name, but is more significant for its attempt to account for the pre-eminence of the younger Perez clan over the older clans of Judah. The importance of the Perez group is reflected in the later notices giving the positions occupied by the Judahites in and around Jerusalem (I Chr. 9:4; 27:3; Neh. 11:4-6). But the superiority of Perez must also be linked with the tradition that David descended from this branch (Ruth 4:18-22; Matt. 1:3; Luke 3:33).

The reference to Perez in Ruth 4:12 harks back to Gen. 38, in that both stories concern the institution of Levirate marriage and the blessing of numerous descendants. *See* MARRIAGE § 1*g*. L. HICKS

PEREZ-UZZAH pĭr'ĭz ŭz'ə [פרץ עזה, breach of Uzzah] (II Sam. 6:8). Alternately: PEREZ-UZZA [פרץ עזא] (I Chr. 13:11). The name given to the site, associated with the threshing floor of Nacon (or Chidon; I Chr. 13:11), commemorating the death of UZZAH in connection with David's attempted transport of the ark to Jerusalem (II Sam. 6:8). The designation reflects the belief that Uzzah's death resulted from the breaking forth of the anger of the Lord upon him for his presumptuous touching of the ark.

Although the exact site is unknown, it was W of Jerusalem, along the road leading to that city from Kiriath-jearim. W. H. MORTON

PERFECTION. The classical definition of "perfection" is given by Aristotle (Metaphysics V.16): a thing is perfect (τέλειος) when it "lacks nothing in respect of goodness or excellence" and "cannot be surpassed in its kind." By this definition, taken strictly, perfection is an ideal condition, never actually realized in this imperfect world. But even Aristotle is not concerned with the theoretic ideal of perfection, for he goes on to speak of a flute player and a physician as being perfect when they lack nothing in regard to the form of their peculiar excellence. Ordinarily, in the Bible as elsewhere, the words "perfect" and "perfection" are used of what closely approaches the ideal condition. This is not a misuse, or even a loose use, of language, for in all the languages with which we are now concerned the words which are rendered in English by "perfect" and "perfection" denoted originally something other and less than ideal perfection. In Hebrew, תמים—to take only the most common of a dozen or more words which can be translated by "perfect"—meant "whole, entire, sound." In Greek τέλειος meant "full-grown, mature, having reached the appointed end [τέλος] of its development." In Latin, similarly, *perfectus* meant, to begin with, "thoroughly made or done." Much more often than not, it is in this lower or loose sense that these words are used in the Bible.

Thus in the OT more than half the ninety or so occurrences of תמים refer to the requirement that animals offered in sacrifice must be "unblemished." Wherever the word is used of men or their conduct, "upright" or "blameless" is a better rendering than "perfect" (e.g., Gen. 6:9). Only in five instances, where the reference is to God (Deut. 32:4; II Sam. 22:31=Ps. 18:30; Job 37:16; Ps. 19:7), may "perfect" rightly be used, and in its strictest sense.

In the NT the word τέλειος occurs nineteen times. In two passages (I Cor. 14:20; Heb. 5:14), because of the contrast with "children" or "babes," some word expressing "full growth" or "maturity" is plainly required, and in five other places the same sense is almost certainly intended (I Cor. 2:6; Eph. 4:13; Phil. 3:15; Col. 1:28; 4:12). In most of the remaining twelve instances it is fairly clear that the word is used in the lower sense mentioned above (cf., e.g., Matt. 19:21; Jas. 3:2). Even in Matt. 5:48: "You, therefore, must be perfect, as your heavenly Father is perfect," although the perfection of God is absolute, it is obvious that such absolute perfection cannot be rightly required of men. The parallel in Luke (6:36) is: "Be merciful, even as your Father is merciful," and in the context thus seems to express more exactly the meaning intended. But it is as clearly impossible for men to be merciful as God is merciful as for them to be perfect as God is perfect. In both versions this saying presents an ideal to which the Christian must aspire, not a standard to which he must attain. So understood, it involves no difficulty, at least for our understanding of it.

The verb τελειοῦν, "to make (something) τέλειος," has a wider range of meaning than the adjective itself; it is used of the fulfilling of a prophecy (John 19:28), of the completion of a period of time (Luke 2:43), and of the finishing of a course or task (Acts 20:24). It is used more often in Hebrews (nine times) than in any other NT writing. The gifts and sacrifices prescribed by the law cannot perfect the worshiper (Heb. 9:9; 10:1; cf. 7:19), but Christ "by a single offering . . . has perfected for all time those who are sanctified" (10:14). Clearly this does not mean that they are made morally and spiritually perfect, but that their consecration is complete and final. But the phrase "the spirits of just men made perfect" (12:23) may perhaps indicate that it is only after death that spiritual perfection is attained by those who have been so consecrated on earth (cf. also 11:40). (There may be the same suggestion in Phil. 3:12, where the perfection toward which Paul strives seems to be identified with the "resurrection from the dead" [vs. 11].) The three remaining instances of the word in Hebrews refer to Christ's being made perfect through his sufferings (2:10; 5:9; 7:28). Since, as the Son, Christ had the perfection of God before his incarnation, it is clear that it is only as the Redeemer of men that he could be "made perfect" through sufferings—i.e., made completely adequate and effective as Redeemer (cf. 2:14-18).

The only NT passage in which the word causes real difficulty is Jesus' message to Herod Antipas: "Behold, I cast out demons and perform cures today and tomorrow, and the third day τελειοῦμαι" (Luke 13:32). Here the RSV renders: "I finish my course," but it is very doubtful that the verb by itself can have this sense. It is probably better to take it to mean: "I am (being) made perfect," and admit that the phrase is a gloss, which expresses much the same idea as the three passages in Hebrews just considered.

It is unnecessary to consider the other words derived from τέλειος which occur in the NT—τελείως (I Pet. 1:13; "fully"); τελειότης (Col. 3:14 ["perfect harmony"]; Heb. 6:1 ["maturity"]); τελείωσις (Luke 1:45; Heb. 7:11 ["fulfilment, perfection"]); and τελειωτής (Heb. 12:2). (In this last instance the meaning of the whole phrase depends upon whether πίστις is "*our* faith" [RSV] or faith generally of which Jesus himself was the perfect example.) Nor is it necessary to consider the other words (ἐπιτελοῦν, καταρτίζειν, and the cognate nouns) sometimes rendered in the KJV by "perfect" or "perfection"; in all but two instances the RSV gives a different rendering, and even in those two instances "perfect" must be understood in its loose sense.

J. Y. CAMPBELL

PERFUME. Perfume occupied an important place in the life and worship of the Near East in biblical times.

1. Terminology
2. Perfume trade
   a. Sources of perfume
   b. Routes of transport
   c. Manufacture
3. Containers
4. Secular uses of perfume
   a. As a cosmetic
   b. On clothes and furniture
   c. In wine
   d. Mortuary use
5. Liturgical uses
6. Comparison and figurative references

Bibliography

1. Terminology. Words translated by "perfume" or its derivations are:

a) Forms of the root רקח, *rāqāḥ*, "to prepare perfume or ointment": the participle, רקע, *rôqē^aḥ* (Exod. 30:25, 35; 37:29; Eccl. 10:1; "perfumer"; KJV "apothecary"); and the nouns רקח, *raqqaḥ* (feminine plural, I Sam. 8:13; masculine plural, Neh. 3:8; "perfumers"; KJV "apothecaries"), רקח, *riqqû^aḥ* (Isa. 57: 9; "perfumes"), מרקחת, *mirqaḥath* (II Chr. 16:14; "perfumer's art"; KJV "apothecaries' art"; lit., "perfume mixture," or "spice or ointment mixture"; cf. Exod. 30:25; I Chr. 9:30).

b) קטרת (Prov. 27:9; "perfumes"), usually meaning "incense"; the participle מקטרת, *m^equṭṭereth* (Song of S. 3:6; "perfumed").

c) להריח (Exod. 30:38; "as perfume"; KJV "to smell thereto"; lit., "to make a smell or perfume"; cf. ריח, "scent, fragrance, smell, savor," of garments, nard, ointments, in Gen. 27:27; Song of S. 1:3, 12; 4:11).

d) בשם (Isa. 3:24; "perfume"; KJV "sweet smell"; elsewhere usually rendered "spices" [Exod. 25:6; 35: 28; I Kings 10:2; Ezek. 27:22; etc.]; possibly balsam oil).

e) נוף (Prov. 7:17; "to perfume"; lit., "to sprinkle").

f) בתי הנפש (Isa. 3:20; "perfume boxes"; KJV "tablets"; lit., "soul houses," perhaps a reference to "charms").

For specific perfumes mentioned in the Bible, *see:* ALOES; BALM; BALSAM; BDELLIUM; CAMEL'S THORN; CASSIA; CINNAMON; FRANKINCENSE; GALBANUM; GUM; MYRRH; NARD; ONYCHA; SAFFRON; STACTE; SWEET CANE. *See also* SPICE; INCENSE; OINTMENT.

2. Perfume trade. ***a. Sources of perfume.*** The known sources of the biblical perfumes are: Arabia (bdellium, frankincense, myrrh), India (aloes, nard), Ceylon (cinnamon), Persia (galbanum), Palestine (stacte, saffron), Somaliland (frankincense), and the Red Sea (onycha).

b. Routes of transport. In Bible times Arabia was not only itself the source of many perfumes, but also the land of transit for perfumes from Africa and India. From Arabia caravans took the spices to Babylon or to Mediterranean ports. Gaza was an important terminus for such caravans, and the Sabeans also transported spices to Tyre (Ezek. 27:22). It was to such Arabian spice merchants that Joseph's brothers sold him (Gen. 37:25). I Kings 10:10 records the large quantity of spices which the Queen of Sheba brought to Solomon as a gift. Job, who lived along the route of the perfume caravans, named one of his daughters Keziah—i.e., "cassia" (Job 42:14). In the first century A.D., Rome was a center for spices, as well as for all other merchandise (Rev. 18:13).

c. Manufacture. The first maker of perfume mentioned in the Bible is Bezalel, who prepared the holy anointing oil and the sacred incense (Exod. 37:29), doubtless according to Egyptian methods. Samuel warned that a king would take women (as in Egypt) to be perfume makers (I Sam. 8:13). Perfumers are mentioned in Jerusalem after the return from exile (Neh. 3:8). I Chr. 9:30 indicates that certain priests were responsible for mixing the perfumes for the incense. According to the Mishna (Sheḳ. V.1), the priestly family of Abtinas had this duty. In ancient Egypt the overseer of incense for the Temple of Amon at Thebes was an important personage.

The process of making the perfume varied according to the raw material and the purpose. The raw material could be the hardened sap of a plant (bdellium, frankincense, galbanum, myrrh, stacte), the bark (cinnamon), the flower (saffron), or the root (nard). Onycha was the closing flap of a species of mollusk, called stromb or wing shell. Fresh flowers were squeezed, as women are shown doing on Egyptian reliefs.* Sometimes the raw material was powdered and used in a dry form, like a sachet powder (Song of S. 3:6). The modern method of distilling an essence was not practiced in ancient times. On the making of ointment with oil, *see* OINTMENT § 3. Fig. PER 29.

Imprimerie de l'Institut Français d'Archéologie Orientale

29. Lotus blossoms being gathered, pressed, and the liquid presented to a woman holding a lotus; from Egypt (450-350 B.C.)

An important element in the art of the perfumer was the blending of different scents. In the sacred anointing oil, myrrh, cinnamon, aromatic cane, and cassia were combined (Exod. 30:22-25), as fourteen perfumes were used in an anointing oil for the idols at Edfu in Egypt. The holy incense of the Hebrews originally included four perfumes: stacte, onycha, galbanum, and frankincense (Exod. 30:34-35). In the Herodian temple seven other perfumes were added to the incense: myrrh, cassia, nard, saffron, costus, aromatic cane, and cinnamon (T.B. Ker. 6*a*). The Egyptian incense called kyphi had sixteen ingredients. Exod. 30:33, 38, warns that the formulas of the holy oil and incense were not to be imitated for secular use.

3. Containers. A dry perfume could be kept in a bag (Song of S. 1:13). The luxury-loving women of Isaiah's day carried perfume boxes (Isa. 3:20). The Mishna (Shab. VI.3) forbids women to carry perfume boxes or flasks on the sabbath. The nard ointment with which Mary anointed Jesus was in an alabaster jar (Matt. 26:7). Many ornate perfume containers of alabaster were found in the tomb of Pharaoh Tut-ankh-Amon. *See* ALABASTER.

4. Secular uses of perfume. ***a. As a cosmetic.*** In a hot climate perfume is needed to counteract body odors. Perfume in oil could be used on the head (Matt. 26:7), on the feet (Luke 7:38), on the hands (Song of S. 5:5), or on the body especially after a bath (Ruth 3:3; *see* OINTMENT § 6*a*). In powdered form perfume might be carried in a bag inside the clothes (Song of S. 1:13). The sweetness of breath in Song of S. 7:8 may well be natural, though some suggest the verse implies chewing perfume. Perfume was especially applied by women who wished to be attractive—e.g., Esther (Esth. 2:12) and Judith (Jth. 10:3)—and was much employed by lovers (Song of Solomon and the erotic poetry of Egypt). Its excessive use is associated with a life of pleasure (Wisd. Sol. 2:7).

b. On clothes and furniture. The clothes of the beloved (Song of S. 4:11) and of the king at his wedding (Ps. 45:8—H 45:9) were perfumed. The palanquin of Solomon was fragrant with many perfumes (Song of S. 3:6). The harlot sprinkles her bed with various scents (Prov. 7:17).

c. In wine. Spiced wine is mentioned in Song of S. 8:2. Wine with myrrh was offered to Jesus at the Crucifixion as an anesthetic, but he refused it (Mark 15:23).

d. Mortuary use. According to the Egyptian process, perfumes were undoubtedly employed in the embalming of Jacob (Gen. 50:2-3) and of Joseph (Gen. 50:26). Perfumes were strewn on the bier of King Asa (II Chr. 16:14) and were doubtless burned in the fire at this royal funeral. Nicodemus brought a mixture of myrrh and aloes which was used in wrapping Jesus' body (John 19:39-40). The weight of these spices, a hundred pounds, is not excessive, in light of the fact that five hundred slaves carried the spices used for the funeral of Herod the Great (Jos. Antiq. XVII.viii.3).

5. Liturgical uses. Various perfumes were combined, as indicated above (§ 2*c*) in the holy oil (*see* OINTMENT § 6*a*) and in the sacred INCENSE.

6. Comparisons and figurative references. In the Song of Solomon both the lover (1:13) and the beloved (4:13-14) are metaphorically called perfumes. Wisdom is compared in excellence to various perfumes (Ecclus. 24:15), and the memorial of Josiah is like incense compounded by the perfumer (Ecclus. 49:1). Perfume used as incense is a symbol of the knowledge of Christ (II Cor. 2:14), of the self-sacrifice of Christ (Eph. 5:2), of the offering of the Philippians to Paul (Phil. 4:18), and of the prayers of the saints (Rev. 5:8).

Bibliography. S. Krauss, *Talmudische Archäologie,* I (1910), 237-38, 241-44. A. Erman and H. Ranke, *Aegypten und aegyptisches Leben im Altertum* (1923), pp. 245, 259-61, 287, 611. A. Schmidt, *Drogen und Drogenhandel im Altertum* (1924). B. Meissner, *Babylonien und Assyrien,* I (1920), 242-44, 353, 403, 411-12; II (1925), 82, 84, 239. G. Dalman, *Arbeit und Sitte,* IV (1935), 259-68; V (1937), 266-67, 274, 339. A. Lucas, "Notes on Myrrh and Stacte," *JEA,* XXIII (1937), 27-33; *Ancient Egyptian Materials and Industries* (3rd ed., 1948), pp. 353, 355, 359-64. G. W. Van Beek, "Frankincense and Myrrh in Ancient South Arabia," *JAOS* (1958), pp. 141-52.

J. A. THOMPSON

PERFUMER. *See* PERFUME §§ 1, 3*c*.

*__PERGA__ pûr'gə [Πέργη] (Acts 13:13-14; 14:25). One of the leading cities in ancient Pamphylia, a province on the S coast of Asia Minor.

Perga is located in the Plain of Pamphylia, some eight miles inland from the coast and some five miles W of the ancient River Cestrus (modern Ak Su). This situation had a double advantage: the city was sheltered from coastal attacks and was located on the road from Attalia to Side, still an easy W-E communication in the Pamphylian Plain. A natural rocky hill formed its citadel.

The period of foundation of Perga is uncertain. Its name is pre-Greek, and presumably carried over from prehistoric times. Greek settlers may have occupied the city in the time after the Trojan War, when Pamphylia absorbed groups of Mycenean refugees. Late local dedications name Mopsos and Kalchas as founders of Perga in a clear reference to the colonization by Greeks of the Late Mycenean Diaspora. The dialect of Pamphylia confirms such guesses. At Perga the local goddess, sometimes labeled Artemis, was also referred to as Wanassa Preija, which sounds like a Bronze Age epithet.

The general history of Perga in the Persian period is unknown, and it cannot have been a prominent city at the time. Alexander in 334 B.C. borrowed guides from Perga and came through the city twice, once on his way E from Lycia to Side, and after a detour in E Pamphylia again on his way to Phrygia. In Hellenistic times the city had a Seleucid garrison when Manlius Volso approached Perga in 188 B.C. Its surrender was ordered by Antiochus; and the city, although claimed by Eumenes, seems to have become free after 188.

The coins of Perga begin at this period and continue into the third century A.D. The history of the town is uneventful except for minor local incidents such as the plundering of some temple treasure of Artemis by Verres in 80-79 B.C. Several honorary inscriptions mention the Roman emperors of the first and second centuries A.D. The most outstanding proof of the activity in Roman Perga is its buildings and monuments.

Perga appears as a metropolis on coins issued under the Emperor Tacitus (275-76). In early Byzantine times Perga was the metropolitan bishopric of W Pamphylia, but later on it was eclipsed by Attalia.

Paul and Barnabas on their first missionary journey set out from Paphos and came to Perga (Acts 13:13). Since Attalia is not mentioned as an intermediate port here, it seems possible that their ship sailed up the Cestrus River to a port E of Perga, or perhaps stopped at the mouth of the Cestrus. They traveled from Perga to Pisidian Antioch without delay, but after their return from Antioch they traveled back through Pisidia to Perga, where they preached, this time leaving the country via the harbor of ATTALIA.

The ruins of Perga are relatively well known. The site is near the village of Murtuna some eleven miles E of Antalya. It consists of an acropolis, a walled lower city, and outlying monuments. The acropolis, *ca.* 160 feet high, dominates the town. Its access is from the S. No major buildings have been identified on the citadel, which must have been the point of attraction for the earliest settlers at Perga.

The lower city was at least of Hellenistic origin, but probably of earlier date. Its city walls are Seleucid in appearance. They formed a rough rectangle with a magnificent city gate to the S. Two round towers flanked the entrance into an oval court. This Hellenistic complex was remodeled in the early second century A.D. by a Roman benefactress of the city, Plancia Magna, whose lavish dedications have recently been found.

The Hellenistic city plan presumably was less regular than the Roman remodeling. In the final version, two wide colonnaded streets formed vast crossroads through the town, one leading from the citadel to the S gate and the other connecting the E and W gates. The streets had Ionic colonnades, were over seventy feet wide with channels in the center, and had shops behind the colonnades. E of the chief gate lay a Roman market place with shops on four sides behind Corinthian stoas.

Some of the civic buildings have been identified within the walls—e.g., a palestra and baths. The theater and the stadium are outside the walled lower city. The stadium is built in Roman fashion on ground level, supported on sloping barrel vaults. The theater is built into a natural hill. Its capacity is estimated at twelve thousand spectators, an indication of the attendance at festivals in Roman times.

The cemeteries of Perga are neatly aligned along the streets leaving the S and W gates. Decorated sarcophagi and small mausoleums of the second century A.D. display the talents of Pamphylian sculptors.

The most important monument of Perga, the temple of the city goddess, has not yet been located. The Wanassa Preija or Artemis Pergaia is known from coins as a Hellenized Artemis figure or an idol resembling Artemis of the Ephesians. Her shrine, which had the rights of an asylum, was on a height near the city (Strabo XIV.667). The goddess, whose cult was known in other cities (e.g., Rhodes, Halicarnassus), maintained herself and her festival tenaciously as a survival from time immemorial. Begging priests were associated with her ritual.

Courtesy of William Sanford La Sor

30. View of Perga with stadium in left center

Of Christian remains there are at least four churches: two large basilicas in the lower city seem to date to the fourth century A.D.; and on the citadel there are ruins of two medieval churches.

Fig. PER 30.

Bibliography. K. Lanckoroński, *Städte Pamphyliens und Pisidiens*, I (1890), 33-63; W. Ruge, "Perge," in Pauly-Wissowa, *Real-Enzyclopädie*, XIX (1937), 694-704; A. M. Mansel and A. Akarca, *Excavations and Researches at Perga* (1949); A. M. Mansel, "Bericht über die Ausgrabungen und Untersuchungen in Pamphylien in den Jahren 1946-1955," *Archäologischer Anzeiger* (1956), pp. 99-120.

M. J. Mellink

***PERGAMUM** pûr′gə məm [ἡ Πέργαμος, τὸ Πέργαμον] (Rev. 1:11; 2:12). A city in Mysia, W Asia Minor, famous in Hellenistic times.

1. Location
2. History
   a. Early
   b. Hellenistic
   c. Roman
3. Topography and monuments
4. Biblical references
Bibliography

1. Location. Pergamum is located *ca.* fifteen miles inland from the Aegean Sea, some two miles N of the ancient River Caicus (modern Bakir çay). The Caicus is approximately the border between the ancient districts of Mysia and Lydia. The citadel of Pergamum was built on a hill *ca.* one thousand feet high between two tributaries of the Caicus, the Selinus to the W, the Cetius to the E.

2. History. ***a. Early.*** Pergamum is certainly a prehistoric site, as attested by its pre-Greek name (presumably meaning "citadel," a name also applied to the fortress of Troy) and by Bronze Age finds in the neighborhood. Its contact with Greek colonists began at least as early as the archaic period, but little mention is made of the town until the Hellenistic period. Xenophon and the remnants of his ten thousand occupied it as a prominent town in Mysia (*Anabasis* VII. 8.8). The city issued coins in the fifth century B.C.

b. Hellenistic. The great period of Pergamum began with the successors of Alexander. The city was originally part of the territory seized by Antigonus. After his death in 301 B.C., Lysimachus king of Thrace took control of W Asia Minor. He entrusted Phileterus, an officer, with the charge of Pergamum and a treasure of nine thousand talents put in safekeeping there. This Phileterus revolted and took the side of Seleucus against Lysimachus in 282. After Lysimachus had been killed in battle (281) and his rival Seleucus murdered in Thrace, Pergamum gradually worked its way up from the status of a Seleucid vassal to that of an independent kingdom under the dynasty founded by Phileterus (283-263).

There are three main themes in the Hellenistic history of Pergamum: the struggle against the Galatians, dangerous invaders of Asia Minor since 278 B.C.; the friendship with Rome; and above all, the cultural interests of the kings who made their city into a renowned center of art and learning.

Phileterus was the first Pergamene king to defeat the Galatians in battle. His nephew and successor Eumenes I (263-241) preferred to pay ransom to them; but Attalus I (241-197) gained a great military victory over the barbarians. This triumph was celebrated in the erection of bronze commemorative statue groups in Pergamum and Athens. Another battle was won in 167 by Eumenes II (197-159).

The glorious days of Pergamum began under

Attalus I. He supported the Roman cause against Macedon. Eumenes II continued this policy and sided with the Romans against Antiochus III of Syria. In spite of consistent pro-Roman politics, the importance of Pergamum declined under his successors Attalus II (159-138) and Attalus III (138-133).

Eumenes II's achievements within Pergamum are perhaps the greatest contribution to the splendor of the city. Its library was superseded in size only by that of Alexandria. Cultural patronage remained a dynastic tradition until 133 B.C., when Attalus III bequeathed his kingdom to Rome.

*c. **Roman.*** The outcome of this decision was far from profitable for Pergamum, a city of tremendous wealth accumulated by the Attalids. The treasure of Attalus was sent to Rome, a brief civic war strained the resources, and taxation was high. Opposition to Rome found the Pergamenians willing to follow Mithradates' order to massacre all the Romans in their city in 88 B.C. As a result Pergamum lost its freedom temporarily, but had it restored under Caesar in 47-46.

In the period of the Roman Empire, Pergamum, although not a commercial center, regained its prominence as a prosperous city with a glorious past. Under Augustus a cult of Roma and Augustus was established in the city. Later a temple of Trajan was built on the citadel and one for Caracalla on the theater terrace, making Pergamum "thrice temple-warden" of the emperor cult and an official cult center in the province of Asia.

The city by now had lost some of its cultural treasures, such as the library which had been sent by Antony to Alexandria as a gift to Cleopatra, or the bronze statues of the Galatians, carried off to Rome by order of Nero; but the building of public monuments and shrines continued, especially under the Flavians. Among the famous later intellectuals of Pergamum was the physician Galen, who worked in the city *ca.* A.D. 160.

3. Topography and monuments. Pergamum was easily the most spectacular Hellenistic city of Asia Minor because of its imaginative town-planning. While the lower city to the S of the citadel contained the residential area, the important public buildings, shrines, and palaces were built on terraces artificially created on the mountain slope.

Courtesy of Ahmet Dönmez

31. The Asclepieum theater at Pergamum

One approached the city through the S gate of the Hellenistic city wall and followed a street uphill to the first major complex, the core of which was the rectangular lower market place surrounded by multistoried colonnades. The middle terrace of the citadel grouped three gymnasiums (for the different age groups) on separate levels. Sanctuaries, a small theater, and baths formed part of the upper gymnasium complex.

The most spectacular planning was displayed in the upper citadel terrace. With a vast Hellenistic theater as its center, a radiating array of sacral and royal buildings spread out on the slope which consisted of an inner half-circle of the upper market place, the great altar, the Athena shrine, the temple of Trajan and Hadrian, and an upper crescent of palaces, barracks, and arsenals across the rising street.

The great altar on the upper terrace, with its dramatic sculptural decoration of the battle of gods and giants, is the most important artistic monument preserved at Pergamum. Its specific destination is unknown. It may contain a symbolic reference to the battles against the Galatians and be dedicated to Zeus Soter, the Savior.* The reference to Satan's throne in Rev. 2:13 could hardly refer to this altar, as some would have it, but more probably aims at the emperor cult established in Pergamum. Figs. PER 32; ZEU 2.

Courtesy of the Oriental Institute, the University of Chicago

32. Excavations at Pergamum showing the altar of Zeus

The terrace to the N of the altar, containing the Athena temple set in a colonnaded courtyard, gave entrance to the great library. This complex also was decorated with the bronze statues of the defeated Galatians and many works of art collected by the Attalids.

The lower city S of the walls was expanded in Roman times. A Roman theater, stadium, and amphitheater lay on the W slope, from where a covered street led to the shrine of Asclepius, where Galen worked in the second century A.D.

4. Biblical references. The early church at Pergamum and its struggle against the emperor cult are referred to in Rev. 1:11; 2:12. The setting and circumstances of the early Christian community can be reconstructed from historical evidence, but no specific light has been thrown on the first century A.D. by archaeological exploration. The Roman city with its houses and mosaics lies under the modern town of Bergama. In Byzantine times, when Pergamum was a bishopric, the inhabitants withdrew to the citadel and built a new fortification wall with ancient blocks such as the sculptures of the altar friezes.

Bibliography. *Altertümer von Pergamon,* vols. I-VIII (1885-1930); E. V. Hansen, *The Attalids of Pergamon* (1947); D. Magie, *Roman Rule in Asia Minor* (1950), pp. 1-33.

M. J. MELLINK

PERIDA. *See* PERUDA.

PERIZZITE pĕr′ə zīt [פרזי, *p^{e}rizzî,* dweller of the open country(?)]; KJV Apoc. PHEREZITE fĕr′—, PHERESITE —sīt. One of the population groups encountered by the Israelites in Palestine. The derivation and exact meaning of the term are obscure. Its association with the names of other peoples in population lists suggests that it is an ethnic term, but the occurrence of other nouns apparently derived from the same root suggests that is is an appellative (cf. פרזות, *p^{e}rāzôth,* "unwalled villages," in Esth. 9:19; Ezek. 38:11; Zech. 2:4—H 2:8; and פרזי, *p^{e}rāzî,* "unwalled villages" and "dwellers of the open country," in Deut. 3:5; I Sam. 6:18; Esth. 9:19). Some commentators suggest that *p^{e}rāzî* is the proper form, that "Perizzite" (*p^{e}rizzî*) is a variant, probably incorrectly vocalized, and that the term refers, not to a tribe, but to a class—namely, the inhabitants of peasant villages. On the other hand, the name, apparently in an ethnic sense, occurs frequently as the designation of one of a group of peoples. In the Tell el-Amarna Letters, Tushratta of Mitanni in his correspondence with Amen-hotep IV names one Perizzi as his messenger or envoy. This has raised the suggestion that the name is of Hurrian origin.

The name Perizzite occurs twenty-three times in the OT (also II Esd. 1:21; Jth. 5:16), but always in lists without details to assist in an identification or to fix a specific area which they inhabited. Four times they are named with the Canaanites as the two main population groups in Palestine (Gen. 13:7; 34:30; Judg. 1:4-5). This may be intended to suggest the population of Palestine generally, those living in fortified cities and those living in the unwalled towns or hamlets. Of these four references, the first relates an incident near Bethel, the second apparently in the vicinity of Shechem, and the last two inform us that the Perizzites were in the territory occupied by Judah.

The REPHAIM are once named together with the Perizzites (Josh. 17:15), and this had led some scholars to conclude that they were to be found in Transjordan. But the Rephaim were not restricted to the Transjordan region, and Joshua's suggestion to the Joseph tribes can as well be interpreted as a reference to clearing the forests of the hill country of Ephraim to make room for themselves.

More frequently the Perizzites are summarily named in longer lists, once among ten peoples (Gen. 15:20) but most commonly with five others—namely, the Canaanites (*see* CANAAN); the HITTITES; the AMORITES; the HIVITES; and the Jebusites (*see* JEBUS; Exod. 3:8, 17; 23:23; 33:2; 34:11; Deut. 20:17; Josh. 9:1; 11:3; 12:8; Judg. 3:5). The only other passage of interest is I Kings 9:20 (=II Chr. 8:7), which informs us that Solomon recruited those who remained of the Perizzites (and of other nations) for his forced levy of slaves.

R. F. SCHNELL

PERSECUTION [Lat. *persecutio, from persequor, literal rendering of* διώκω, pursue, *in its secondary sense of* persecute]. Suffering inflicted upon an individual or group for fidelity to a faith, usually with the object of inducing apostasy or of destroying the faith itself by killing its adherents and intimidating prospective converts. Persecution may be inflicted by official authority (civil or religious or both in concert), or by unauthorized activity of hostile individuals or crowds; it may be limited to insult and scorn, but may extend to the loss of civil rights, imprisonment, torture, and death.

A. Persecution in OT times
 1. Persecution of prophets by kings
 2. Persecution of Jews by aliens
B. Persecution in NT times
 1. Persecution of the church by Jewish opponents
 2. Persecution of the church by Roman authorities
  a. Before the Neronian persecution
  b. The Neronian persecution
  c. Persecutions under the Flavian emperors
Bibliography

A. *PERSECUTION IN OT TIMES.* 1. Persecution of prophets by kings. It is consistently presupposed in the NT writings that all the prophets of Israel suffered persecution at the hands of their own people. Thus we read in Stephen's indictment of the nation, addressed to the Sanhedrin: "Which of the prophets did not your fathers persecute? And they killed those who announced beforehand the coming of the Righteous One, whom you have now betrayed and murdered" (Acts 7:52). The killing of Christ and the persecution of his followers were seen as the repetition of a pattern which had been followed over and over again in the national life (Matt. 5:12; 23:34-37; I Thess. 2:14-15). The Hebrew scriptures themselves, however, afford little support for such a sweeping generalization; the case of Micah is expressly cited to the contrary (Jer. 26:17-19); and many of the earlier prophets, for all their boldness, were treated with the greatest respect (e.g., Nathan, Elisha, and Isaiah [II Sam. 12:1-15; II Kings 13:14; Isa. 37:1-2]). The persecution of prophets seems to have been relatively rare, except in times of moral and religious decadence.

In the reign of Ahab, the introduction of the worship of the Tyrian Melkarth through the influence of Jezebel, Ahab's Tyrian queen, seems to have been followed by a persecution of the prophets of Yahweh. Elijah was forced to flee the country, and at one time complained that all the prophets except himself had been slain; Obadiah tells of saving a hundred prophets from the murderous fury of Jezebel by hiding them in caves (I Kings 17:9; 18:13-14; 19:10). In the last years of the kingdom of Judah, Jeremiah was saved from death at the hands of Jehoiakim by the intervention of a powerful protector, but another prophet, who delivered a similar message was executed (Jer. 26:20-24); and a few years later Jeremiah was flung into a dungeon at the insistence of the princes, and was rescued by an Ethiopian eunuch in the service of Zedekiah (Jer. 38). It is possible that Manasseh slaughtered a number of prophets for protesting against his introduction of Assyrian rites into the worship of Judah; we are told that he "shed very much innocent blood, till he had filled Jerusalem from one end to another" (II Kings 21:16); but it is not clear that his victims were killed for their stand on religion.

2. Persecution of Jews by aliens. The sufferings of the Hebrews at the hands of the Egyptians and of the Philistines can hardly be regarded as persecutions, for there is no suggestion that anything more was involved than oppression by foreign masters. The first attempt to force the people of God to renounce their own faith is that which was initiated by Antiochus IV (Epiphanes) of Syria (175-164 B.C.), who drove out the legitimate high priest, profaned the temple by the sacrifice of swine, and sought to compel conformity with the Hellenic worship of Zeus, which he was promoting as part of his policy of Hellenizing his empire. By fostering Greek cultural institutions and especially by promoting the worship of the great gods of Greece among the peoples of his multiracial dominions, he hoped to give them an inward unity which would enable him to hold them in firm possession against the encroachments of Roman imperialism, the growing Parthian menace to the East, and the unceasing conflict with Egypt. Some elements of the Jewish community were fully prepared to co-operate with him (I Macc. 1:11-15, 43, 52); but large numbers suffered death rather than submit to his religious ordinances or fail in the obligations of their own faith (I Macc. 1:44-61). Jewish resistance increased as the pressure of persecution was intensified, until the situation was brought to an end by the successful revolt of the Maccabees. *See* ANTIOCHUS 3; DANIEL; JUDAS 10; MACCABEES.

B. *PERSECUTION IN NT TIMES.* 1. Persecution of the church by Jewish opponents. The early chapters of Acts tell of attempts by the Great Sanhedrin to prohibit public preaching by the apostles (4:17-18); but they were unable to secure obedience to their injunctions, even though they sentenced the apostles to a flogging (5:27-42). The first sustained persecution arose around the Hellenist preacher Stephen, who probably voiced more radical views about the transience of the temple and the law than had the Galilean leaders. He himself was put to death by stoning, the ancient punishment for blasphemy; but it is not entirely clear whether this was a judicial execution or an act of mob violence (7:54–8:1*a*). The ardent young Pharisee Saul—destined to become the great apostle of the Gentiles, Paul—makes his first appearance in Christian history as leader of the stoning party and of the general persecution which followed (Acts 8:1*b*-3). Christian men and women were thrown into prison, and many were driven to seek safety in flight; but the flight led to a wide and significant expansion of the Christian mission. The gospel was brought to Samaria, in disregard of the bitter hostility between Jews and Samaritans (8:4-25); and to Antioch on the Orontes, one of the chief cities of Syria, where the first Gentile converts were made (11:19-26); and the church was launched on its secular task of the evangelization of the world. *See* STEPHEN.

Shortly before the end of his life (A.D. 44), Herod Agrippa I, king in Jerusalem, struck savage blows at the leaders of the church; he executed James the son of Zebedee (and perhaps his brother John with him), and put Peter into prison (Acts 12:1-5). We are told that his action "pleased the Jews" (vs. 3)—an indication that the public generally had become hostile to the Christians, in contrast to the favorable, even protective, attitude of the earliest days (2:47; 4:21; 5:12-16). Peter escaped, by what the church interpreted as a divine intervention made in answer to its prayers (12:6-17); and with the death of Agrippa, the church was able to resume its mission more energetically than ever (vss. 20-24); but the smoldering hostility of the populace remained, carrying a continual menace of renewed violence, held in check by the Roman procurators, to whom the government of Palestine was again entrusted.

We hear nothing more of the situation of the Jerusalem church until the year 62, when James the Lord's brother, long its head, was murdered by a fanatical mob. (The attack on Paul of which we read in Acts 21:27-36 was occasioned by the rumor that he had brought Gentiles beyond the barrier in the temple.) It would appear that the church incurred bitter hatred by its refusal to share in the madness which was soon to come to a climax in the rebellion against Rome. As the legions gathered for the siege of Jerusalem, the Christians departed from the city, scorned by their fellow countrymen as traitors and cowards.

It is indicated in our documents that at some point the decision was made to expel Christians from the synagogues (John 16:2; cf. 9:22 and the note of C. K. Barrett); this was regarded as a more serious punishment than the floggings which were frequently administered to Christians by the rulers of the synagogues.

2. Persecution of the church by the Roman authorities. *a. Before the Neronian persecution.* During the first generation, the church had constantly to contend with popular hostility, but seldom with official police measures; the Roman administrators, as a rule, acted for the protection of the Christians against mob violence. Our only evidence for the period consists of the references in Acts and the Pauline letters. Paul tells us, indeed, that he was beaten with the rods of the lictors three times (against five floggings in synagogues [II Cor. 11:24-25]); but only one of these beatings is recorded in Acts, and there it is said that the magistrates were full of apologies the next morning, as soon as they learned that Paul was a Roman citizen (Acts 16:22-23, 35-40). On the other hand, the proconsul of Achaia refused to take action against him, on complaints made by Jews (Acts 18:12-16); some of the Asiarchs were among his friends at Ephesus, and the town clerk pacified a hostile crowd and threatened them with Roman sanctions (Acts 19:30-41); and a detachment of Roman troops saved Paul from death at the hands of the mob in Jerusalem (Acts 21:27-36). He was not afraid to appeal to Caesar (and the Caesar was Nero!) from an accusation brought against him by his own people (Acts 25:9-12); and he assured the Christians of Rome that "rulers are not a terror to good conduct, but to bad" (Rom. 13:3).

b. The Neronian persecution. The Christian church at Rome suffered inhuman treatment at the command of the Emperor Nero, following the great fire which broken out in July of 64 and ravaged much of the poorer quarters. The populace, which had already come to detest Nero, was persuaded that he had ordered the fire set and had sent his guards to spread it, in order to clear space for his great building schemes. Nothing that he could do had any effect in dissipating these rumors (which were probably untrue); and at last he sought to find a scapegoat. He found it in a "people whom the masses called Christians, who were hated for their vicious crimes" (Tacitus). Some of those who were first arrested "confessed"—probably to the guilt of arson, rather than to the profession of Christianity; Nero, that is to say, procured false confessions, both to facilitate prosecutions and to divert the public anger from himself. Those who confessed implicated others, and "on their testimony a mighty multitude [*ingens multitudo*] was convicted, not so much of arson, as of hatred of the human race" (Tac. Ann. XV.44). Evidently the charge of arson could not be proved, but the general detestation of the Christians provided sufficient excuse for the severest measures against them.

The legal basis of this persecution is not clear. Obviously, some more specific charge than "hatred of the human race" must have been alleged—possibly treason (*maiestas*) or violence (*vis*). It is sometimes held that Nero must have issued a formal decree making the profession of Christianity an offense punishable by death (*Institutum Neronianum de Christianis*); but it is more likely that the action taken was an exercise of police powers (*coercitio*), which would not change the legal position, or have effect in other parts of the Empire. Even if a decree were issued, its validity would cease with Nero's death, for the Senate condemned his memory and nullified all his decrees. The Neronian persecution, then, was fierce but limited to the time and the place. After him as before him, the Christians had to fear mainly the inflamed passions of hostile crowds, fed with slanderous rumors of what went on in their secret gatherings, and often enough fanned by commercial interests (as of the silversmiths at Ephesus).

c. Persecutions under the Flavian emperors. The Julian line of emperors ended with Nero, and the Flavian succession began with Vespasian, who was the final victor in the struggle for power which followed Nero's death. There is no solid evidence that Christians suffered persecution by the Roman state under Vespasian and his two sons, Titus and Domitian. It is possible that some of the victims of the terror under Domitian were Christians, but there is nothing to show that they suffered for their faith.

Our first concrete evidence of measures taken against Christians as Christians, for no other offense than confession of the name, comes from the reign of Trajan (98-117). The correspondence of Ignatius, bishop of Antioch, is generally regarded as having been written on his journey to Rome, as a prisoner, in the anticipation of suffering martyrdom; if it is authentic, it belongs to the time of Trajan. Indisputable evidence of the first importance comes from the province of Bithynia and Pontus, in the correspondence of its governor, Pliny the Younger, with Trajan, in 111-12. Pliny informs Trajan that he has had occasion to deal with Christians, and as he has had no previous experience with such cases, he asks for instructions on how to dispose of them. His inquiries have shown him that they are not, in fact, guilty of the offenses with which they were commonly charged, but only of illegal association for an unauthorized worship. He has nevertheless sentenced them to death, whenever they refused to renounce their faith, on the ground that "stubbornness and unbending obstinacy certainly deserve to be punished." He is prepared to set free any who recant under his threats. (The same pattern is seen in the "Acts" of later martyrdoms, where the Roman officials are reluctant to enforce the law against Christians, and give them every opportunity to escape execution or banishment by denying Christ and offering incense on the altar of the emperor.) Trajan approves Pliny's procedure. Christians are not to be sought out, and anonymous accusations are not to be entertained; but if a charge is laid and proved in proper fashion, punishment must be inflicted, except that a free pardon is to be granted to all who recant and offer sacrifice to the Roman gods (Pliny *Letters* X.96-97).

This rescript defined the legal position and governed the official treatment of Christians for the next hundred years. It was against the law to be a Christian; but in practice, the law was seldom enforced. *See* PETER, FIRST LETTER OF.

Bibliography. L. H. Canfield, *The Early Persecutions of the Christians* (1913); H. Grégoire *et al.*, "Les persécutions dans l'Empire romain," *Mémoires de l'Académie royale de Belgique*, vol. XLVI, no. 1 (1951); A. N. Sherwin-White, "The Early Persecutions and Roman Law Again," *JTS*, N.S. vol. III, no. 2 (Oct., 1952), pp. 199-213; M. Goguel, *The Birth of Christianity* (trans. H. C. Snape; 1953), pt. V: "The Reactions Provoked by the Preaching of the Gospel"; J. Vogt and H. Last, "Christenverfolgungen" (I and II), in *Reallexikon für Antike und Christentum*, vol. II (1954), cols. 1159-1228, with extensive bibliography; M. Moreau, *La persécution dans l'Empire romain* (1956).

F. W. BEARE

PERSEPOLIS pər sĕp'ə lĭs [περσέπολις]. Ancient site in the province of Fārs (Old Persian *pārsa*) in SW Iran, some fifty miles N of the modern city of Shiraz; now known as *Takht-i Jamshīd*, "throne of (the legendary king) Jamshīd." II Macc. 9:2 mentions the unsuccessful attempt of Antiochus IV Epiphanes to plunder the city of Persepolis shortly before his death in 164 B.C.

The extensive building activities which made Persepolis into a city of splendor and magnificence started shortly after the accession to the throne of Darius the Great (521-485) and were continued on

Courtesy of the Oriental Institute, the University of Chicago

33. The E stairway with the gate of Xerxes at the right in the Apadana at Persepolis; begun by Darius (521-486 B.C.) and completed by Xerxes (485-465 B.C.)

Courtesy of the Oriental Institute, the University of Chicago

34. The mammoth stairs of the Apadana at Persepolis

an even larger scale by his son Xerxes (485-465) and his successors. Its glory was forever crippled by the thorough though, perhaps, only partly intentional holocaust lit by the victorious Alexander the Great in 330 B.C. in a gesture of political bravado. Its ruins, however, have offered a fascinating attraction for travelers and archaeologists from the fourteenth century on. In spite of its splendid outlay and facilities Persepolis at no time could compare with SUSA as a political, administrative, or commercial center. Persepolis' role as a recreational resort in the heart of the homeland to which the Achaemenians were naturally attached came virtually to an end after the disaster of 330.

After the descriptions and drawings of the ruins of Persepolis provided by such men as Pietro della Valle (*ca.* 1622), Jean Chardin (1665-75), Cornelis de Bruin (*ca.* 1704), Carsten Niebuhr (*ca.* 1765), William Ouseley (1811-12), E. Flandin and P. Coste (1840-43), F. Stolze and F. C. Andreas (1874 and after), and others, systematic archaeological investigations did not start until Ernst Herzfeld reported on Persepolis and directed excavations under the auspices of the Oriental Institute of the University of Chicago between 1931 and 1934. These excavations were continued by E. F. Schmidt between 1934 and 1939 and after his departure by the Iranian Archaeological Service (A. Godard and M. T. Mustafavi).

Only some of the most important structures, the

Courtesy of the Oriental Institute, the University of Chicago

35. General view of Persepolis: (1) treasury; (2) hall of a hundred columns; (3) restored harem; (4) palace of Xerxes

Courtesy of the Oriental Institute, the University of Chicago

36. The tribute procession on the E stairway of the Apadana, showing Syrians with gold vessels and braces, and a pair of horses

total of which constitutes a model of Achaemenian architecture, can be listed: (*a*) a monumental staircase* leading through (*b*) a gate building (Xerxes *Persepolis a* as translated by R. G. Kent, *Old Persian* [1950], p. 148) to (*c*) a gigantic terrace laid out under Darius the Great; on the terrace which at one time was surrounded by a high wall are found (*d*) the "hall of hundred columns," built under Xerxes (Xerxes *Persepolis b;* Kent, p. 148), (*e*) Xerxes' harem building, (*f*) Xerxes' palace (Xerxes *Persepolis d* 16-17: "This palace [Old Persian *hadiš*] I built"; Kent, p. 149), Darius' palace (Darius *Persepolis a* 6: "This palace [Old Persian *tačara*] I made"; Kent, p. 135), (*g*) the *apadāna* or audience hall, built by Darius and Xerxes, with famous bas-reliefs of the "immortals," the king's special regiment, and of a succession of tributary subjects. Figs. PER 33-34, 35-36; MED 19.

Bibliography. The older publications such as F. C. Andreas and F. Stolze, *Persepolis* (1882); F. Sarre and E. Herzfeld, *Iranische Felsreliefs*, vols. I-II (1910); E. Herzfeld, "Rapport sur l'état actuel des ruines de Persépolis et propositions pour leur conservation," *Archäologische Mitteilungen aus Iran,* vol. I (1929); A. Sami, *Persepolis* (1954), are now all replaced by E. F. Schmidt, *Persepolis,* vols. I-II (1953, 1957). Important archival documents in the Elamite language found in Persepolis were published in G. G. Cameron, *Persepolis treasury tablets* (1948).

M. J. DRESDEN

PERSEUS pûr'sĭ əs [Περσεύς] (I Macc. 8:5). Illegitimate son and successor of Philip III. He is called

37. Coin showing Perseus, king of Macedonia

king of "Kittim," which is loosely applied in I Maccabees to Macedonia; Josephus has the word "Greece." Perseus was defeated by Aemilius Paulus at the Battle of Pydna 168 B.C., after which Macedonia became a Roman province. He was taken captive by the Romans.

Fig. PER 37. S. B. HOENIG

PERSIA, HISTORY AND RELIGION OF [Heb.-Aram. פרס; Περσῶν (*usually*), Περσίδι (Dan. 11:2) *referred to as* Μήδων (II Chr. 36:20) *and reversely* Περσῶν *for* מדי (Isa. 21:2)]; PERSIANS [פרסי (Neh. 12:22), פרסיא (K) *and* פרסאה (Q; Dan. 6:28—H 6:29); Old Pers. *pārsa, used for both* Persia *and* Persians; Elam. *par-sin;* Akkad. *pa-ar-sa;* Πέρσης, Περσία]. The terms "Persia" and "Persians" refer to the empires of various duration and territorial expanse from the Achaemenian until the present Pahlavi dynasty which reigned from capitals in different parts of the Iranian territory. At the initiative of Reza Shah (1925-41) "Persia" was replaced, for purposes of international nomenclature, by "Iran." More recently either name, Persia or Iran, has been officially recognized. It may further be remarked that the designation Iran (derived from Avestan *airyana*, "Aryan," in *airyanəm vaējah*, "the Iranian expanse"; Middle Iranian *'yr'n* ["Ērān"], *'ry'n* ["Aryān"]; New Persian *Īrān*) has been and is used by Western scholars for the area which comprises, besides the territory of the present kingdom of Iran, the regions of Afghanistan, Baluchistan, and W Turkistan.

- A. Biblical references
- B. The land
- C. Languages
  - 1. Old Iranian
    - *a.* Old Persian
    - *b.* Avestan
    - *c.* Aramaic
  - 2. Middle Iranian
  - 3. New Iranian
  - 4. Iranian elements in Aramaic and elsewhere
- D. History
  - 1. Extent
  - 2. Prehistory
  - 3. Achaemenians
    - *a.* History
    - *b.* Organization
    - *c.* The king and his court
    - *d.* The administration of justice
    - *e.* Finance and economic conditions
    - *f.* Foreign relations
  - 4. Alexander and the Seleucids
  - 5. Arsacids (Parthians)
  - 6. Sassanians
    - *a.* History
    - *b.* Religion
- E. Religion
  - 1. The most ancient period
  - 2. Zarathushtra
  - 3. The Achaemenian period
  - 4. The Arsacid period
  - 5. The Sassanian period
- Bibliography

A. *BIBLICAL REFERENCES.* Persia and the Persians, either with or without the Medes and MEDIA, are frequently mentioned in the OT. The Persians are not mentioned in the NT. The Medes (Μῆδοι), however, occur, together with the Parthians and the Elamites, in Acts 2:9.

Ezra 9:9 speaks of the "kings of Persia"; Ezra 6:14 of "Cyrus and Darius and Artaxerxes king of Persia"; and Dan. 8:20 of the "kings of Media and Persia." Dan. 10:13 mentions the "prince of the kingdom of Persia" (cf. vs. 20), and "three more kings . . . in Persia" occurs in Dan. 11:2. References to the "army chiefs of Persia and Media," the "seven princes of Persia and Media," and the "ladies of Persia and Media" are to be found in Esth. 1:3, 14, 18, respectively. Belshazzar's kingdom is going to be "given to the Medes and Persians" (Dan. 5:28).

The following individual Achaemenian rulers are referred to: (*a*) CYRUS as the "king of Persia" (II Chr. 36:22-23; Ezra 1:1-2, 8; 3:7; 4:3, 5; Dan. 10:1) and as "the Persian" (Dan. 6:28—H 6:29); (*b*) DARIUS as the "king of Persia" (Ezra 4:5, 24), as "the Persian" (Neh. 12:22), and as "the Mede" (Dan. 5:31; cf. 6:1, 25; 9:1; 11:1); and (*c*) ARTAXERXES (Ezra 4:7), "king of Persia" (Ezra 7:1). *See* AHASUERUS, perhaps in Esther to be identified with Xerxes.

References to the immutable laws of the Medes and the Persians are to be found in Dan. 6:8, 12, 15—H 6:9, 13, 16 (cf. Esth. 1:19), and the "Book of the Chronicles of the kings of Media and Persia" occurs in Esth. 10:2.

B. *THE LAND.* Iran, in the larger sense, is situated between the Caspian Sea and W Turkistan in the N, the Persian Gulf and the Gulf of Oman in the S, the lower and middle Indus Basin in the SE, and Mesopotamia in the SW. Geologically it forms a part of the highland belt which stretches across Asia from the Bering Strait to the Mediterranean.

In the W a mountain range (Kurdistan Mountains and Zagros Range), which extends from Armenia to the Persian Gulf over a distance of some 1,250 miles with a width of nowhere less than 125 miles, marks the border of the plateau. Through the massif of S Kurdistan leads one of the main routes which connect Mesopotamia and the Iranian Plateau. As such it was used under the Achaemenians, as it appears from the fact that Darius had his largest inscription engraved on the Rock of Behistun* on that route, and later by Alexander the Great and by the Arab armies. The city of ECBATANA, modern Hamadan, is situated at the point where this route enters the plateau. The province of Fars, ancient Pārsa, constitutes the connection between the W and S borders of Iran. Under the Achaemenians its principal city was PERSEPOLIS. At the W feet of the mountains of Fars the plains of Khuzistan are situated in the lower

Courtesy of the Oriental Institute, the University of Chicago

38. The Rock of Behistun

basin of the Karun River. Under the Achaemenians, and later under the Sassanians, the water of this river was used for effective irrigation, as it appears from the importance and splendor of the city of Susa. Fig. PER 38.

The littoral plains along the Persian Gulf and the Gulf of Oman are of little depth, squeezed in as they are between the Mekran Mountains and the sea, and have offered little attraction to potential settlers because of adverse climatic and physico-geographical conditions.

In the NW, Azerbaijan (capital Tabriz), ancient Atropatene (*see* MEDIA), continues the Kurdistan mountain range and at the same time forms the beginning of another range, the Elburz (highest peak Demavend), which stretches eastward along the S coast of the Caspian Sea. The conditions of the intermediate belt between the Elburz Mountains and the plateau was favorable to the foundation of such cities as Qazvin, Rhages (Ray[y]), and Teheran. The two provinces to the S of the Caspian Sea, Gilan in the W and Mazanderan in the center and E, are favored by a mild and humid climate, and they harbor in numerous villages about one fifth of the total population of the country.

In N Khurasan (Khorasan), today the most eastern province of Iran and in the terminology of the Muslim geographers all of E Iran, a series of plains between E-W mountain ranges constitutes a natural way of access between the Elburz and Hindu Kush mountain chains for migrations from Central Asia in a westward direction. The plateau of S Khurasan marks the beginning of the vast desert known as Dasht-i Lut, which occupies the major part of central E Iran. The Helmand River, which originates in the mountains of Afghanistan and ends in a conglomeration of lagoonlike basins, offers what little attraction for sedentary life exists in the area known as Seistan (Sistan), to the SW of Khurasan.

To Iran in the larger sense (*see above*) and, at the present, to part of Afghanistan and the U. S. S. R. belong such areas as Gurgan, at the SW corner of the Caspian Sea; Khwarezmia (Chorasmia, Khwarizm), to the S of the Aral Sea; Sogdiana, in what was later known as Transoxiana, between the Oxus (Amu Darya) and Yaxartes (Syr Darya) rivers, with the cities of Bukhara and Samarkand; Bactria in N Afghanistan; and, farther to the E, the areas around the cities of Khotan, Turfan, and other settlements in the Tarim River basin in Chinese Turkistan.

C. *LANGUAGES.* For the sake of convenience, three stages of development have been assumed for the Iranian language group.

1. Old Iranian (600 B.C.-300 B.C.). ***a. Old Persian.*** The foundation of the Achaemenian Empire (*see* § D3 *below*) raised Old Persian (*see* PERSIAN, OLD), the local speech of SW Iran, to the rank of the official, imperial language, as found in the royal Achaemenian inscriptions. Of the other vernaculars used by local communities within the vast territory of the Empire, next to nothing has been preserved. Of the language of the SCYTHIANS, e.g., only a few vocables are known from Herodotus, and a limited number of Median words have survived as loan words in Old Persian. *See* MEDIA.

b. Avestan. The other known representative of Old Iranian is the language in which AVESTA is composed. In the Avestan writings two different forms of language can be distinguished: (*a*) "Gāthic," the language in which Zarathushtra's preachings are written, and (*b*) "Younger Avestan," the language of the remainder of the Avestan writings. At the moment the available linguistic and other evidence seems to warrant the suggestion of E Iran as the most likely area of origin.

c. Aramaic. It should be mentioned at this point that the existing language diversity within the Achaemenian Empire became the reason for the introduction and use of Aramaic as the common language for purposes of administrative communication. The appropriate name *Reichsaramäisch*, "imperial Aramaic," was coined for it by J. Markwart (*Ungarische Jahrbücher*, vol. VII [1927], p. 91, note 1), and a survey of the available linguistic materials was given by F. Rosenthal (*see bibliography*). One of the immediate results of this practice was the fact that the Aramaic alphabet initiated the inhabitants of the faraway provinces for the first time in the art of writing and subsequently not only served as the basis for most, if not all, of the writing systems used in Iran until the Islamic period, but also became the example of the Kharoshthi script used in NW India.

Besides the Aramaic documents, which form part of the correspondence between the Achaemenian prince Aršām(a), governor of Egypt, perhaps written from Susa to his officials and friends in Egypt (*see bibliography*), the wide spread of the Aramaic language and script is proved by the discovery of Aramaic documents in areas as far apart as Armenia and Georgia in the W and Afghanistan in the E. For the reverse process of Aramaic borrowings from Iranian, *see* § C4 *below*.

2. Middle Iranian (300 B.C.-A.D. 700). Until around the beginning of the twentieth century only one Middle Iranian language, Middle Persian or Pahlavi, was known. Through discoveries in Central Asia (Turfan) and philological research, more materials have been brought to light since then. Today five major forms of Middle Iranian, some of which, in addition, show what may be dialectical or other differences, can be distinguished. Of these, Middle Persian and Parthian belong to the western, and Sogdian, Khwarezmian, and the Saka languages to the eastern, language group.

3. New Iranian (700—). The main representative of this stage is New (or Modern) Persian, the standard language of Persia. The first documents in (New) Persian, written in Arabic script, date from the ninth century A.D. Of other Iranian languages, such as

Kurdish (Persia, Iraq, Turkey), Ossetic (Caucasus), Baluchi (Baluchistan), Pashto (Afghanistan), Wakhi and other languages spoken in the Pamirs, and dialects used in Persia and Russian Azerbaijan, mention can be made by name only.

4. Iranian elements in Aramaic and elsewhere. Reference has already been made to the importance of Aramaic for Iranian studies (*see* § C1*c above*). In not a few cases Aramaic is on the receiving end of the borrowing process. This is not only the case in such well-known words as אספרן, אספרנא, "fast, with speed, speedily, diligently" (Ezra 5:8; 6:8, 12-13; 7:17, 21, 23; Old Iranian **asprnā/usprna;* Avestan *aspərənah,* "completeness"; Manichaean Middle Persian and Parthian *'spwr;* Sogd[ian] *'spwrn;* Khotanese Saka *uspurra,* "complete, entire, thorough"; New Persian *siparī,* "finished"); דת, "law" (Dan. 6:8, 12, 15—H 6:9, 13, 16; Old Persian *dāta* and many other forms until New Persian *dād,* "law, justice"); דתבר, "judge" (Dan. 3:2-3; Pahlavi *d'twbr;* Christian Sogdian *d'ṯbr*); גזבר, "treasurer" (Ezra 1:8; 7:21; cf. [המלך] גנזי, "[the king's] treasuries," in Esth. 3:9; 4:7; Manichaean Middle Persian *gznwr;* Manichaean Parthian *gznbr;* Sogdian *γznβr;* cf. Pahlavi *gnz,* "treasure"; Elamitic *kan-ṣa-iš* [*nu-da-nu*], "treasure [storehouse]"); perhaps also אשרן (Ezra 5:3, 9; and in the Elephantine Papyri) and אופשר (Elephantine Papyri), if respectively from Old Iranian **ācarna* and *upacāra* (cf. New Persian *afzār,* "tool"). Not only words but also idioms are borrowed. E.g., עבד לנפשה, "to make one's own, to appropriate," seems to be a translation of Old Persian (*h*)*uvāipašiyam akuta,* "he made his own, appropriated"; the verb שאל, "to ask," is used (תשתאל, "you will be punished") in the sense of Old Persian *fras-*, with the double meaning of "to ask" and "to punish"; the expression אספרן והדאבגו, "the base sum [for אספרן, *see above*] together with [Old Persian *hadā,* 'with'] the interest" (*'bgw;* Manichaean Parthian *'bg'w,* "increase"), is clearly Iranian.

Iranian loan words are also found in Elamite and Armenian. In the former case the publication of tablets from the Persepolis "treasury" (*see bibliography*) has proved to be of great importance; further discoveries may be expected from the "fortification" tablets, also from Persepolis. In the latter case, a field of longer standing, renewed investigation of the Iranian elements in Armenian is highly desirable.

D. *HISTORY.* 1. Extent. Iran's history, in pre-Islamic times, falls into the following periods, which correspond to the reigning dynasties: (*a*) Medes (*see* MEDIA); (*b*) Achaemenians (middle of the sixth century B.C.–330 B.C.); (*c*) Hellenistic intermezzo (Alexander the Great [330-323]; Seleucids); (*d*) Arsacids or Parthians (middle of the third century B.C.–A.D. 223/224 [or 226/227]); (*e*) Sassanians (223/224 [226/227]-651). In the following discussion the Achaemenians will for obvious reasons be accorded more space than the other periods.

2. Prehistory. Systematic archaeological investigations, conducted at such *tepes* as Hissar, Giyan, Siyalk, and Susa, have shown the existence of a homogeneous culture, with local variations in Iran, from the Hassuna period onward. *See bibliography.*

3. Achaemenians. *a. History.* By the middle of the sixth century B.C., after the downfall of the Assyrian Empire, two great powers, Babylonia and Media, faced each other. In Anshan, a district in Elam, a revolt against the Median king Astyages was started by Cyrus II in 550. (For the events of the next two decades, *see* CYRUS.) The outcome was the establishment of the Achaemenian Empire. The Achaemenians traced their family to its founder, Achaimenes (Old Persian *haxāmaniš*), the father of Teïspes (Τείσπης; Old Persian *čišpiš;* Elamitic *ṣi-iš-pi-iš;* Akkadian *ši-iš-pi-iš*), Cyrus' ancestor. The genealogy of the Achaemenian offers certain difficulties. *See bibliography.*

After his death (529) his son Cambyses II (Old Persian *ka*(*m*)*būjiya;* Elamite *kan-bu-ṣi-ia;* Akkadian *kam-bu-zi-ia;* Greek Καμβύσης) continued his father's work and after careful preparation succeeded in the conquest of Egypt (525) and of the Greek islands of Cyprus and Samos. These and other events are related in colorful detail by Herodotus (III.1-60). Before his death (522) the throne had been forcefully taken by the so-called Pseudo-Smerdis. The Behistun Inscription (Figs. PER 39; INS 10) gives this account:

Courtesy of George C. Cameron, American Schools of Oriental Research and the University of Michigan

39. The Behistun Inscription of Darius, in Old Persian, Elamite, and Akkadian

"A son of Cyrus, Cambyses by name, of our family, he was king here. Of that Cambyses there was a brother, Smerdis [Old Persian *bardiya;* Greek Σμέρδις] by name, having the same mother and the same father as Cambyses. Afterwards, Cambyses slew that Smerdis. When Cambyses slew Smerdis, it did not become known to the people that Smerdis had been slain. Afterwards, Cambyses went to Egypt. . . . There was a man, a Magian [Old Persian *maguš*], Gaumāta by name. . . . He lied to the people thus: 'I am Smerdis, the son of Cyrus, brother of Cambyses.' After that, all the people became rebellious from Cambyses, (and) went over to him, both Persia and Media and the other provinces."[1] The reason for the rapid success of Gaumata, whose reign lasted only six months (from March, 522) may have been general discontent with Cambyses among both the "people" and the nobility.

The Behistun Inscription relates in annalistic form how in a series of bold campaigns Darius, a member of the older branch of the Achaemenian family, succeeded in securing the throne for himself and in restoring the Empire to its former extent and strength. These successes were due to Darius' extraordinary military genius, which showed itself in the skilful

[1] R. G. Kent, *Old Persian* (New Haven, Conn.: American Oriental Society).

combined use of different kinds of armament and in the expert handling of his troops at the right time and place. *See* DARIUS 1. Fig. XER 1.

On the other Achaemenian kings, Xerxes (486-465), Artaxerxes I (465-425), Darius II (423-404), Artaxerxes II (404-359), Artaxerxes III (359-338), and Darius III (336-330), *see* ARTAXERXES; DARIUS; XERXES.

b. Organization. The many peoples which together formed the subjects of the "king of kings" (Old Persian *xšāyaθiyānām xšāyaθiya*) were governed on the basis of a division into some twenty administrative units, known as satrapies (provinces), of the Empire. This system, begun by Cyrus and fully developed by Darius, left to each of the satrapies a relative amount of autonomy under the government of a local administrator or satrap (Old Persian *xšaçapāvan;* Greek σατράπης; Hebrew-Aramaic אחשדרפן [Ezra 8:36; Esth. 3:12; 8:9; 9:3; Dan. 3:2-3, 27; 6:7]). The Old Persian inscriptions give several lists of satrapies, and a list of the revenues from each of the provinces is to be found in Herodotus (III.90-95). Darius (Naqš-i Rustam A Inscription; see R. G. Kent, *Old Persian* [1950], pp. 137-38) lists the following: Media, Elam, Parthia, Aria, Bactria, Sogdiana, Chorasmia, Drangiana, Arachosia, Sattagydia, Gandara, Sind, the *haumavarga* Sakas, the Sakas with pointed caps, Babylonia, Assyria, Arabia, Egypt, Armenia, Cappadocia, Sardis, Ionia, the Sakas across the sea, Skudra, the *petasos*-wearing Ionians, Libyans, Ethiopians, men of Maka, and Carians. In the majority of cases the satraps came from noble families or, sometimes, from the royal family itself. They exercised civil and judiciary authority and controlled the local finances. In foreign policy they enjoyed large autonomy, especially in the frontier provinces. The local armed forces were under the orders of a local military commander. A delegate from the central government and responsible to it, known as "the king's eye" (τὸν σὸν πιστὸν πάντ' ὀφθαλμόν [Aeschylus *Persae* 980, and elsewhere]; "the king's ear(s)," τὰ βασιλέως ὦτα [Xenophon *Cyropaedia* VIII.2.10], also occurs in Aramaic גושכ), checked on the functioning of the local government. Rapid and reliable communication was assured by the royal mail service between Susa and the local centers of administration (cf. Esth. 3:15). Although precise details are lacking, it can be inferred that the individual satraps used a large number of officials of all ranks. In Neh. 5:14-18 a glimpse is caught of the circumstances under which they lived (vs. 15), in contrast with Nehemiah's own understanding of a governor's life (vss. 16-17). The "governor" (פחה; Ezra 5:3, 6; 6:6, 13; Neh. 3:7) "this side the river" refers to the satrap.

c. The king and his court. There is little doubt that both in theory and in practice the form of the Persian state was absolutistic. Contrary to the statement of Curtius (VIII.5.18), the king was probably not considered a divine being. The so-called *xvarənah* (Old Persian *farnah;* Middle Persian *farrah,* regularly represented by the Aramaic ideogram גד[ה] in the Pahlavi books; *see* § E1 *below*), the royal majesty and good fortune of the legitimate king, to which a complete Avestan hymn (Yasht 19) is devoted, was given, however, divine status. In executive, judiciary, military, and possibly also religious matters, the ultimate decision was in the king's hands. His edicts sealed with his ring (Esth. 3:12; 8:8) had force of law (8:8). The "seven counselors" (Ezra 7:14) and the "seven princes of Persia and Media, who saw the king's face, and sat first in the kingdom" (Esth. 1:14), may have been the king's ministers who were under his immediate orders. The heads of the six prominent families, known as *vispati,* held hereditary privileged positions. It has been suggested that the chiliarch—the commander of the "immortals," the ten thousand men of the king's guard—was the most distinguished among the *vispati* and, in later times, also held the rank of great vizier.

A number of details in the nomenclature and function of the members of the bureaucracy remain uncertain. The Aramaic papyri from Egypt shed some light on Persian officials on the subsatrapal, provincial level. An official with the title בעל טעם (Ezra 4:9) seems to have held a high, if not the highest, position in the chancery of the satrap. At the head of the province was the פקיד (Gen. 41:34); among the members of his bureau were the אזדכריא; in his treasury the המרכריא, officials of the treasury (גנזא), or "accountants," were employed. It seems legitimate to use these and similar data, by transferring them from the provincial to the satrapal and to the royal level, for conclusions regarding the functioning of the government in the highest echelons.

d. The administration of justice. On the matter of law and its administration little or no direct Iranian evidence is available. Most of the information is of Greek or other non-Iranian origin. Ezra 7:26 refers to the "law of the king" (דתא די מלכא), and Darius refers to the matter of law in similarly general terms ("These peoples by the grace of Ahura-mazda showed respect for my law"; Behistun Inscription I.23). The attempt of Olmstead (*see bibliography*) to establish a close parallel between Hammurabi's Code and Darius' assumed "Ordinance of Good Regulations" does not seem to carry sufficient persuasive power.

The Aramaic papyri from Egypt give some information concerning the conduct of judicial action. Besides "the judges," "the king's judges," or "judges of the court," the local commander took an active part in the procedure and in an adoption case acted entirely on his own. In another case the commander ordered a special investigation to be carried out by the judges, the תיפתיא (cf. Dan. 3:2), and the גושכיא (lit., "the listeners"; *see* § D3*b above*). It seems likely that, as in the case of the provincial administration and its officials, the judiciary system of the provinces and satrapies was modeled after that of the capital.

The Greek sources give abundant examples of capital and other physical punishment. The form of execution referred to in Old Persian as *uzmayāpatiy kar-,* with regard to some of those who rebelled against Darius, is probably "impalement." Ezra 7:26 mentions "death . . . banishment . . . confiscation of goods . . . imprisonment" for those who "will not obey the law of . . . God and the law of the king."

e. Finance and economic conditions. Among the revenues of the state, taxes or tributes (Old Persian *bāji;* βαζιγραβαν ὅ ἐστι τελώνιον [Isidorus of Charax]) levied from all over the Empire were the most important. Herodotus (III.90-97) gives a list in which the Babylonian silver talents and other tributes to be contributed by each of the satrapies are itemized. Darius set up a uniform tax system, standardized the monetary unit, and introduced uniform weights and measures. As a result industry and commerce in the Empire grew rapidly, banking houses such as the Murashu family from Nippur thrived on the increasing need for ready cash, and new markets were opened by the improvement of the ancient caravan routes. The keen interest taken by the Achaemenian rulers in seafare and foreign commerce is shown by the trips of Democedes of Croton along the coasts of Greece and S Italy, by the exploration of the Indus River by Skylax of Karyanda, and also by the termination of the canal between the Nile and the Red Sea. ("Darius the king says . . . I gave order to dig this canal from the river Nile which flows in Egypt to the sea which goes from Persia. Then this canal was dug . . . and ships went from Egypt . . . to Persia.")[1]

Among human activities agriculture and cattle breeding were considered the most commendable from both the socio-economic and the religious point of view. The existing conditions of climate necessitated large-scale irrigation, and in spite of their scarcity references in both Iranian and Western sources testify to the great importance attached to the proper care of irrigation systems.

The Avestan scriptures contain evidence for a socio-religious division of society into three classes: (*a*) priests (*āθravan*), (*b*) warriors (*raθaēštar*), and (*c*) farmers (*vāstryō fšuyant*), to which in one instance a fourth group, the artisans (*hūitu*), is added. There seems to have existed a political hierarchy, from the smallest unit, that of the family (*nāfa*), to the largest, that of the "land" (*dahyu*).

f. Foreign relations. The Greek settlements along the W coast of Asia Minor which had come under the control of Cyrus and had been organized by Darius into two satrapies revolted against Persian rule under the leadership of Aristagoras of Miletus in 499. In spite of its abundance, the information on the causes of this revolt, which led to the Median Wars, is incomplete. Only the Greek argument, as presented by Herodotus, is available, while Persian inscriptional materials bearing on them are practically nonexistent. In a general way, when dealing with the relations between Persia and the West, it should be kept in mind that in most cases the lack of a proportionate amount of Iranian information to counterbalance the Greek and other Western sources is responsible for what necessarily can be only an imperfect picture.

The history of the Median Wars—two expeditions, both ending, in spite of the most careful military, technical, and political preparations, in utter failure for the Persian armies and fleet (Marathon [490] and, under Xerxes' personal command, Thermopylae [480], where Leonidas and his three hundred Spartans died their heroic death at a place named Kolonos near to the Phocidian wall; Salamis [480] and Plataeae [479])—is too much a part of the Western heritage to justify an attempt at repetition.

As one of the results of the Median Wars a strong impulse was given to the material and cultural development of classical Greek civilization. As another, the Persian rulers continued to keep a finger in the pie of Greek politics (Peloponnesian War). In general it can be said that the range of relations between Persia and Greece is extraordinarily wide and varied.

From the reign of Darius, Greek scientists and artists were employed at the Persian court. Besides explorers like Skylax of Karyanda (*see* § D3*e above*) and Hecataeus of Miletus, Greek physicians enjoyed the particular favor of the Achaemenian kings. The same Democedes who surveyed the coasts of Greece and S Italy (*see* § D3*e above*) was held in high esteem by Darius as his personal physician; Apollonides of Cos and Ctesias practiced at the court. It seems likely that they served as intermediaries for the incorporation of certain data from Indian medicine into the Hippocratic corpus.

Of even greater importance is the subject of the relations between Iranian and Greek philosophical thought. On this much-discussed and complex matter opinions range from those that tend to consider Iranian influence responsible for some of the basic ideas of Greek philosophy to those that minimize this influence. The seemingly attractive parallelism between a passage from the Sassanian text known as *Bundahishn* (*see* PAHLAVI 2) and from the Greek Περὶ Ἑβδομάδων, between the concept of time as found in Pherecydes and in Iran, between the Platonic world of Ideas and the spiritual creation of Zoroastrianism, between the myth of Er (Plato *Republic* 614B ff) and certain passages in Iranian sources—each of these and other, similar parallelisms have to be studied and analyzed separately before a conclusive and comprehensive answer, if any, to the problems they raise can be proposed. *See bibliography.*

For the political influence exercised by Cyrus, Darius, and Artaxerxes I on the fate of the people of Israel, see the articles on these rulers.

Next to these political relations the question of the interdependence of Iranian religion and postexilic Jewish thought and speculation arises. Here, as in the case of Iran and Greece (*see above*), scholars vary in their points of view with regard to problems both of detail and of a more general nature, from those who estimate the influence of Iranian religion on Judaism as decisive to those who are reluctant to admit any such dependence. Such points as that of the growing rank of Satan, if compared with Ahriman's position; of the Two Spirits as found in the Manual of Discipline, if compared with the Gāthic doctrine; of the introduction of abstract entities in Jewish literature, such as the Wisdom of God, the Spirit or the six potencies of God (Philo), if compared with, respectively, *Vohu Manah* (or *Ārmaiti?*), *Spənta Mainyu*, and the six *Aməša Spəntas;* of the Son of God with the Iranian *Gayōmart;* of the doctrine of millennial periods; of the book in which the deeds of men are recorded, the belief in resurrection, the final transformation of the earth—each of these seems to be a case of general analogy, the details of which deserve careful attention, rather than of decisively proven immediate borrowing. (For the Zoroastrian terms, *see* §§ E2, 5, *below.*)

4. Alexander and the Seleucids. Within the short span of a few years between the crossing of the Dardanelles (334) and the sack of Persepolis (331),

[1] R. G. Kent, *Old Persian* (New Haven, Conn.: American Oriental Society).

Alexander succeeded in a series of rapid victories to bring about the end of the existence of the Achaemenian Empire. *See* Darius 3; Alexander 1.

In the first years after his death (June 13, 323) Iran did not attract the immediate attention of the Diadochs, among whom Seleucus emerged as the master of Iran. In 304 Seleucus came to an agreement with the Indian ruler Chandragupta, by which he gave up Afghanistan and other Eastern possessions in return for a corps of Indian war elephants, which enabled him to win a victory over his rival Antigonus in the Battle of Ipsus (301).

The Seleucid Dynasty, which ended in 63 B.C. when Pompey deposed its last ruler, witnessed an increasing diminution of their territory. In spite of the foundation of several Greek Antiochs, Laodiceas, and Seleucias, their grip on Iran constantly loosened. Gradually Media, Armenia, and other areas became independent; the campaigns of Antiochus III and IV in Iran had little or no lasting success; the Jews revolted against Antiochus IV; and the Parthians, in N Iran, started a movement of independence under the leadership of Arsaces.

5. Arsacids (Parthians; middle of the third century B.C.–A.D. 223/224 [226/227]). The tribe of the *Parni*, who invaded and subjected Parthia before the middle of the third century B.C., exchanged their own E Iranian for the indigenous Parthian language. Under the dynasty of the Arsacids (after its ancestor, Arsaces), they conquered most of the rest of Iran and established Ctesiphon, their capital, near Baghdad in Babylonia. It was Mithridates I (*ca.* 171-138/137) who was instrumental in this expansion. Preoccupied by the Indo-Scythian Kushans in E Iran and the threat of nomadic invasions in N Iran, they remained for a long time confined, in the W, by the Euphrates.

The Parthians served as middlemen in the traffic between the Mediterranean and the Far East. At Dura-Europos, on the middle Euphrates, Hellenistic, Semitic, and Iranian cultural influences met. Hellenistic art penetrated via Parthian Iran into Afghanistan and into what is now Pakistan. From Palmyra, in the Syrian Desert, the beginning of the caravan routes from Syria to Iran, Syrian glassware and decorative motifs reached Afghanistan.

After Rome became the master of Syria, it was tempted on several occasions to try to transfer its boundaries beyond the Euphrates. The disastrous results of the attempts made by Crassus (Carrhae [53 B.C.]) and Mark Antony (defeat in Atropatene [36 B.C.]) are well known. Although Trajan succeeded in entering Ctesiphon (A.D. 116), his successor, Hadrian, had to renounce the newly won possessions and was forced to accept once more the traditional Euphrates frontier.

In 40 B.C. the Parthians, who invaded the Roman provinces in the Near East and occupied Syria, were considered by the Jews as their liberators. They put Antigonus, son of Aristobulus, on the throne in Jerusalem. Antigonus reigned for three years (40-37 B.C.), at the end of which Jerusalem was recaptured by Herodes, with the support of Roman troops, and looted. The Parthian rulers gave military support to Jerusalem during the siege by Titus (Jos. War II.520; VI.356); and under Trajan and Hadrian, Jews and Parthians worked together against the Romans. The *Oracles of Hystaspes* seem to reflect some of the expectancy on the part of the Jews of their coming liberation from Roman supremacy through help from Iran (see, e.g., Lactantius *Institutions* VII.15.19; VII. 15.11). *See also* Parthians.

6. Sassanians (223/224 [226/227]–651). ***a. History.*** In the beginning twenties of the third century the rule of the Arsacids came to an end because of the defeat suffered by Ardavān (Artabanus V) at the hands of Ardashīr (the Middle Persian form of Artaxerxes), son of Pāpak and descendant of Sāsān, from the province of Fars, who had previously become master of the city of Istakhr, the capital of that province. The rock reliefs of Naqsh-i Rajab and Naqsh-i Rustam near Persepolis retain the memory of the investiture of Ardashīr by Ahura-mazdā. The decipherment of the inscriptions on the reliefs by Silvestre de Sacy in 1793 ranks among the first major achievements in the systematic study of Iranian antiquities.

Within a period of some fifteen years Ardashir succeeded in rebuilding the power of Iran. By the time of his death his son and successor, Shāpūr I (239 or 241–270 or 273), was in a position to annex part of the Kushan Empire in NW India and N Mesopotamia and Armenia by defeating and capturing the Roman emperor Valerian at Edessa (260); "at Edessa battle with the emperor Valerian took place and by me the emperor Valerian himself . . . was made prisoner," as the *Ka'be-yi Zardušt* Inscription (Persian version, lines 13-14) puts it. In the period between Ardashir and the end of the Sassanian Empire (651), Iran was in close contact with such different civilizations as the Roman and Byzantine empires, China, and India. As a result Indian works were translated into Pahlavi (*Kalila wa Dimnah,* after the Indian fable collection known as *Pañchatantra;* an Indian original is at the origin, through several intermediaries, of the romance of *Barlaam and Josaphat*); Iran used, and exported to the West, Chinese silk and other products; Iranian examples inspired Chinese painting in Central Asia; Greek science, probably through Syriac intermediaries, was incorporated in the Pahlavi scriptures ("Shāpūr . . . collected and incorporated in the Avesta books on medicine, astronomy . . . , which had been scattered in India, Rome and other countries" [*Dēnkart* 412.17-21]); etc.

In political and military terms Sassanian history is a long struggle against Western and Eastern rival powers. In the West the possession of Armenia and adjacent areas was among the main causes of war. On the Eastern front, the more dangerous one in the long run, the Sassanian rulers had to face the ever-present threat of invasions. In the end of the fifth century Kavād paid tribute to the Hephthalites, but this situation was brought to an end by Khosrau I in the beginning of the next century. The latter's reign became the apogee of Sassanian power and civilization.

b. Religion. The religious situation in Sassanian Iran reflects the multiple influences to which the state was subject. Apart from Zoroastrianism (*see* Zarathushtra; *see also* § E5 *below*), the official state religion, an inscription, from the second half of the third century, of Kartīr, the then high priest of the Sassanian church, mentions "Jews, Buddhists, Brahmins,

Nazoreans [(?); *n'cl'y*], Christians, *mktyky*[?] and Manichaeans" (*Ka'be-yi Zardušt,* lines 9-10) as subject to persecution.

Judaism flourished in all of Mesopotamia, and centers of learning could be established where the arts of exegesis and casuistry were fostered, which led to the compilation of the Babylonian Talmud. The Indian religions, Buddhism and Hinduism, recruited the majority of their followers in the E parts of the Empire. Christian communities were founded in Persian territory in the first century A.D. Periods in which a policy of tolerance was displayed by the state alternated with times of violent persecution, the change from one attitude to the other being motivated in not a few cases by political and military considerations. After a critical period of *ca.* half a century the Persian church received the official blessing of the secular authorities in 410, partly because of the dangerous situation on the E frontier. In 468 it became schismatic (Nestorianism) with the approval of the state, which perceived its own advantage in a dogmatic breach between its own Christian subjects and those of the Byzantine emperor. From Iran the Nestorian church spread eastward, and its remaining followers were encountered by Franciscan missionaries (Willem van Ruysbroeck, Giovanni di Piano Carpini) and travelers (Marco Polo) on their trips to the Mongol rulers in the thirteenth century. The numerous Christian fragments in Sogdian (*see* § C2 *above*) testify to the same expansion. For the Manicheans, *see* MANICHEISM.

Partly religious, partly social, motives are behind the movement started by Mazdak (died 524[?]) toward the end of the fifth century.

E. *RELIGION.* 1. The most ancient period. The correspondence in both concepts and names of divinities as found in the Indian Rig Veda and the Iranian Avesta point to a period in which the Indo-Iranian tribal community held common religious beliefs. The earliest document, outside India, in which Indo-Iranian divinities are mentioned is a treaty between the Hittite king Suppiluliumas and Mattiwaza, the ruler of the Hurrian kingdom of Mitanni from the fourteenth century B.C. In it the gods Mitra, Varuna, Indra, and the twin Nāsatya occur; all these are known from the Rig Veda.

Since written documents for this period are absent, it can only be surmised from later evidence that in Iran several Iranian varieties of these Indo-Iranian beliefs existed. In one, or some of these, Ahura-mazdā was given a supreme position. Other divinities, referred to as *yazata,* existed next to him. Animal sacrifice and libations of *haoma,* the Indian *soma,* were common practice. Among the other divinities are Mithra (Indian Mitra), the god of contract; Haoma (Indian Soma), the personification of the intoxicating beverage of that name; Xvarənah, the personification of fortune and royal majesty; (Arədvīsūrā) Anāhitā, goddess of rivers and fertility; Tishtrya, the rain-bringing star Sirius; and the Fravashi, the spirits of the righteous dead and, at the same time, protecting genii.

2. Zarathushtra. In the Gāthā (*see* AVESTA), Zarathushtra's preachings, an ethical dualism, along with a tendency toward monotheism represented by Ahura-mazdā,* is evident. The dualism shows itself

Courtesy of the Oriental Institute, the University of Chicago

40. Ahura-mazdā, the Persians' winged god, on the E doorway of the main room of the Council Hall at Persepolis

in the opposition of *Aša,* "Truth" (Old Persian *arta;* Indic *ṛta*), versus *Drug,* "Falsehood" (Old Persian *drauga*); and of *Spənta Mainyu,* "the Augmentative Spirit," versus *Angra Mainyu,* "the Wicked Spirit" (later *Ahriman*); the latter pair are represented as twin brothers (Yasna 30.3). The relation of Ahura-mazdā and Spənta Mainyu is one of father and son (Yasna 47.3). Next to Spənta Mainyu, Ahura-mazdā is the creator of the six entities: (*a*) *Vohu Manah,* "Good Mind"; (*b*) *Aša,* "Truth"; (*c*) *Xšathra,* "Power, Dominion"; (*d*) *Ārmaiti,* "Devotion"; (*e*) *Haurvatāt,* "Wholeness"; and (*f*) *Amərətāt,* "Immortality"; all six of these together are referred to as the *Aməša Spənta,* "the Augmentative Immortals," and connected with cattle, fire, metal, earth, water, and plants respectively. The notion of monotheism as evidenced by Ahura-mazdā and the Aməša Spənta is coupled with the dualistic notion of truth versus falsehood, and both are integrated by the introduction of the concept of free will. Figs. PER 40; AHU 6.

So far for part of Zarathushtra's ideology. In the Younger Avesta, the documents written in Younger Avestan (*see* AVESTA), there is clearly a considerable admixture of other ingredients. Some of those non-Zarathushtrian components, part of which have counterparts in the Rig Veda (Soma, Mitra) and others of which do not (Xvarənah, Anāhitā), are represented by the divinities already mentioned. The Avestan scriptures, therefore, contain several religious strata. In the process of codification, which may have taken place in the course of the fifth and fourth centuries B.C., most of the subject matter contrary to the teachings of the Gāthā was incorporated, after having been duly legalized by such introductory phrases as: "Thus Ahura-mazdā said to Zarathushtra." The result of the process of integrating opposite religious concepts leaves, nevertheless, a considerable number of patently incompatible elements. In other words, the apparently intentional outcome of the efforts of the priestly diaskeuasts was a corpus of mixed origin and purpose, intended for a likewise composite audience.

One of the important facts in the emergence of the Avesta is that the linguistic structure of the Avestan language points to E Iran and more specifically Khwarezmia (*see* §§ B, C2 *above*), part of which coincided with what in the Avesta is called Airyana Vaējah as its place of origin. When this area politically became part of the Achaemenian Empire under CYRUS a direct connection was established between it and the center of the Empire in SW Iran.

3. The Achaemenian period. The problem of the religion of the Achaemenians is among the most passionately discussed. In the heat of the debate the pendulum has swung to both extremes: those who, taking the identity of Vishtāspa, the father of Darius and the protector and patron of Zarathushtra, for granted, held that the Achaemenian kings were orthodox Zoroastrians; and those who took the opposite view.

In the inscriptions frequent mention is made of Ahura-mazdā and, to a lesser degree, of Drauga (Avestan *drug*) and Arta (Avestan *aša*); Xerxes, *Daiva* Inscription, lines 51-56, reads: "The man who adheres to the law which Ahura-mazdā has established and worships Ahura-mazdā in the proper way in accord with Arta, becomes happy while living and *artāvan* ['blessed'; Avestan *ašavan;* Old Indic *ṛtāvan*] when dead." On the other hand, no reference is made to Spənta Mainyu, Angra Mainyu, the Aməša Spənta, or Zarathushtra. It may, therefore, seem as if part of Zarathushtra's most essential concepts, the cult of Ahura-mazdā (cf. the Aramaic term *mzdyzn,* "worshiper of Mazdā") and the opposition Drauga-Arta, were introduced in SW Iran from the time of Darius onward. This novelty must have run counter to the ideas of the priestly Magi, as it appears from the fact that Darius rebuilt the "places of worship" destroyed by the Magus (Old Persian *maguš*) Gaumāta (*see* DARIUS 1; *see also* § D3*a above*) and killed a large number of other Magi (Herodotus III.79)—an occasion which was since yearly commemorated as the μαγοφονία festival. From then on, the Magi might have been forced to yield to royal pressure and to assign a place, the most prominent perhaps, to Ahura-mazdā in a pantheon which included Mithra, Anāhitā (both mentioned in inscriptions of Artaxerxes II and III), and others. By the time of Artaxerxes I (*see* ARTAXERXES 1) it seems as if the clergy of Airyana Vaējah may have put the Avestan texts together in the form of the mixed religion in which it is now known, under the influence of the fact that "Zoroastrianism" had by then become the official form in SW Iran, where the royal rulers had faltered in their sole allegiance to Ahura-mazdā. The introduction, in 441, of the Zoroastrian calendar, a reform of the Old Persian calendar with Zoroastrian names as, in fact, they occur in the Younger Avesta attached to the names of the months, possibly constitutes an important factor in this process. By then it had also become a matter of further recovering the formerly lost prestige for the Magi to claim ZARATHUSHTRA as their own and to locate his birthplace in Media.

4. The Arsacid period. There is little direct evidence for the form of Zoroastrianism prevalent in Iran during the Arsacid period. If credit is to be given to the Zoroastrian tradition that the Avestan books were collected by a Parthian king Vologesus, which seems to receive confirmation from a statement by MANI in the Coptic *Kephalaia* (*see* bibliography under MANICHEISM), in which it is said that "he [Zarathushtra] did not write any books, but his disciples after his death remembered [his words] and wrote the books which they read today," a continued strong activity of the Zoroastrian clergy under the auspices of the secular rulers is indicated.

A revival of the cult of Mithra in this period is likely, from the immense success of the Mithras cult, from Armenia to Spain and from Libya to Scotland, in the Roman Empire from the middle of the first century B.C. onward. The Roman Mithras is clearly modeled after the Iranian Mithra.

5. The Sassanian period. In the PAHLAVI books, which in matter may be assigned to the sixth century and in actual written form to the period immediately following the Muslim conquest of Persia, the opposition between Ormuzd (the principle of good) and Ahriman (the principle of evil) is fully systematized. The Aməsa Spənta (*Amahraspand*) and the other Zoroastrian divinities have become Ormuzd's created spirits and his willing servants. Both Ormuzd and Ahriman are pure spirits. Their antagonism necessarily will lead to a struggle, which will take twelve thousand years, the equivalent of one cosmic year. Ahriman initiates the hostilities and is temporarily repelled. Taking advantage of his indisposition, Ormuzd fashions creation, which has become necessary to him for use as a weapon with which to meet Ahriman. Man, by his own individual choice between good and evil, sides with Ormuzd ("I belong to Ormuzd, not to Ahriman; I belong to the gods, not to the demons, to the good, not to the wicked; I am a man, not a demon, a creature of Ormuzd, not of Ahriman") by adhering to the principles of good thoughts, words, and deeds (*humat, hūkht, huvaršt*), or with Ahriman. Both Ormuzd and Ahriman have their assistants, the Amahraspands (*Vahuman,* "Good Mind"; *Artvahišt,* "Best Truth"; *Šahrēvar,* "Choice Kingdom"; *Spandarmat,* "Augmentative Devotion," identical with the earth; *Hurdāt,* "Wholeness"; and *Amurdāt,* "Immortality") and gods (*yazatān*), and the demons (*dēv*) respectively. Ahriman, then, returns to the attack, brings death, disease, anger, envy, and other, similar entities into the world and destroys *Gayōmart,* father of the human race and origin of the first human couple (*Mašya* and *Mašyānag*). On the fourth day after individual death the soul of the departed has to face the judgment on the *Činvat* bridge, where his good and evil deeds are weighed so as to determine his ultimate destination—heaven, hell, or the "place of the mixed." In the end, a resurrection (*fraškart*) is brought about by the *Sōšyans* or "savior," which at the same time signifies the final victory of Ormuzd over Ahriman.

It should be pointed out that in Sassanian times, as it appears from passages in the Pahlavi books, a heterodoxy, known as *Zervanism* (from *zurvān,* "time"), which attempted to derive the principles of good and evil from the common principle of "Infinite

Time," existed. *See* bibliography under PAHLAVI.

Bibliography. The most recent survey of the Iranian languages is: K. Hoffman (on Old Iranian), W. B. Henning (on Middle Iranian), H. W. Bailey (on languages of the Sakas), G. Morgenstierne (on New Iranian languages), and W. Lentz (on New Persian), *Iranistik, Erster Abschnitt, Linguistik* in *Handbuch der Orientalistik,* vol. IV, no. 1 (1958). Shorter surveys are: H. W. Bailey, "The Persian Language," in A. J. Arberry, ed., *The Legacy of Persia* (1953), pp. 174-98. G. Redard, "Panorama linguistique de l'Iran," in *Festgabe Emil Abegg* (*Asiatische Studien,* VIII; 1954), pp. 137-48.

References to publications on the Iranian Turfan materials are given by W. Lentz, "Fünfzig Jahre Arbeit an den iranischen Handsschriften der deutschen Turfan-Sammlung" *ZDMG,* CVI (1956), *3-*22. For a Sogdian bibliography, see M. J. Dresden, "Bibliographia sogdiana concisa," in *Jaarbericht No. 8 van het Voor-Aziatisch-Egyptisch Gezelschap Ex Oriente Lux* (1942), pp. 729-34. Major studies on Khwarezmian are: Z. V. Togan, *Islamica,* III (1927), 190-213. Z. V. Togan and W. B. Henning, *ZDMG,* XC (1936), *27-*34. A. Freiman, *Xorezmiyskiy Yazik* (1951). W. B. Henning, "The Structure of the Khwarezmian Verb," *Asia Major,* N.S. V (1955), 43-49; "The Khwarezmian Language," in *Zeki Velidi Togan'a Armağan* (1955), pp. 421-36. A bibliography on the Saka languages is to be found in H. W. Bailey, "Languages of the Saka," in *Iranistik* (1958), p. 154. New Persian and other modern Iranian languages are discussed by W. Lentz and G. Morgenstierne in *Iranistik* (1958), pp. 155-78, 179-221, both with bibliography.

For a survey of the available linguistic materials on Aramaic, see: F. Rosenthal, *Die Aramaistische Forschung* (1939), pp. 24-71. The main collections of Aramaic documents are: A. Cowley, *Aramaic Papyri of the Fifth Century B.C.* (1923). E. G. Kraeling, *The Brooklyn Museum Aramaic Papyri* (1954). G. R. Driver, *Aramaic Documents of the Fifth Century B.C.* (1954; abridged and rev. ed., without facsimiles, 1957). See also: S. Telegdi, "Essai sur la phonétique des emprunts iraniens en araméen talmudique, *JA,* CCXXVI (1935), 177-256. W. Eilers, "Neue aramäische Urkunden aus Ägypten," *Archiv für Orientforschung,* XVII (1954-55), 322-35. Some of the examples quoted are taken from E. Benveniste, "Éléments perses en araméen d'Égypte," *JA,* CCXLII (1954), 297-310. H. Cazelles, "Nouveaux documents araméens en Égypte," *Syria,* XXXII (1955), 75-100. E. Hammershaimb, "Some Observations on the Aramaic Elephantine Papyri," *Vetus Testamentum,* VII (1957), 17-34. On the publication of tablets from the Persepolis "treasury," see: G. G. Cameron, *Persepolis Treasury Tablets* (1948). E. Benveniste drew attention to the importance of the Elamite materials in "Notes sur les tablettes élamites de Persépolis," *JA,* CCLVI (1958), 49-65. The matter of Iranian elements in Armenian was last comprehensively treated by H. Hübschmann, *Armenische Grammatik,* vol. I (1897).

No comprehensive study of the results of archaeological activities in Iran exists. A provisional survey was written by L. v. Berghe, "De stand van de archaeologische opgravingen in Iran," in *Jaarbericht No. 13 van het Vooraziatisch-Egyptisch Genootschap Ex Oriente Lux* (1953-54), pp. 347-93; a more extensive work by the same author has been published under the title *Archéologie de l'Irān ancien* (*Documenta et Monumenta Orientis Antiqui,* vol. VI; 1959). On stratigraphy, see: D. E. McCown, *The Comparative Stratigraphy of Early Iran* (1942); "The Relative Stratigraphy and Chronology of Iran," in R. W. Ehrich, ed., *Relative Chronologies in Old World Archeology* (1954), pp. 36-68.

There exist two comprehensive works on the Achaemenian period, neither of which is quite up to date: A. Christensen, *Die Iranier* (1933), in *Handbuch der Altertumswissenschaft* 3. Abt., 1. Teil, 3. Band, *Kulturgeschichte des Alten Orients* 3. Abschn., 1. Lief. A. T. Olmstead, *History of the Persian Empire* (1948; paperback ed., 1959). Both works are documented. For a discussion of the difficulties of Achaemenian genealogy, see: R. G. Kent, *Old Persian* (1950), pp. 158-59.

Scholars who accept the thesis of a basic Iranian contribution to Greek thought are: W. Eisler, *Weltenmantel und Himmelszelt* (1910). R. Reitzenstein and H. H. Schaeder, *Studien zum antiken Synkretismus* (1926). And, to a lesser degree, J. Bidez, *Eos, ou Platon et l'Orient* (1945). A negative conclusion is reached by: J. Kerschensteiner, *Platon und der Orient* (1945). W. J. W. Koster, *Le mythe de Platon, de Zarathustra et des Chaldéens* (1951). See also: A. Goetze, "Persische Weisheit in griechischem Gewande," *Zeitschrift für Indologie und Iranistik* (1923), pp. 72 ff; and the discussion of this article by J. Duchesne-Guillemin, "Persische Weisheit in griechischem Gewande," *HTR,* XLIX (1956), 115-22.

A positive view with regard to the influence of Iranian religion on Judaism is held by: E. Stave, *Über den Einfluss des Parsismus auf das Judentum* (1898). E. Böklen, *Die Verwandtschaft der jüdisch-christlichen mit der parsischen Eschatologie* (1902). L. Mills, *Zarathuštra, Philo, the Achaemenids and Israel* (1906); *Our own religion in ancient Persia* (1913). E. Meyer, *Ursprung und Anfänge des Christentum,* vol. II (1921). W. Bosset, *Die Religion des Judentums im späthellenischen Zeitalter* (3rd ed., 1926). G. Widengren, "Juifs et Iraniens à l'époque des Parthes," *Supplements to Vetus Testamentum,* IV (1957), 197-240. The opposite view is held by: N. Söderblom, *La vie future d'après le Mazdéisme* (1901). J. H. Moulton, *Early Zoroastrianism* (1913). J. Scheftelowitz, *Die altpersische Religion und das Judentum* (1920).

The literature on Alexander is, of course, very large. The most commendable monograph is, perhaps, W. W. Tarn, *Alexander the Great,* vols. I-II (1948-50). See also the recent survey articles of R. Andreotti, "Il problema di Allesandro Magno nella storiographia dello ultimo decennio," *Historia,* I (1950), 583-600. G. Walser, "Zur neueren Forschung über Alexander den Grossen," *Schweizer Beiträge zur allgemeinen Geschichte,* 14 (1956), 156-89. The Alexander romance is the subject of A. Abel, *Le roman d'Alexandre, légendaire médiéval* (1955). For the Seleucids, see such general works as: M. Rostovtzeff, *The Social and Economic History of the Hellenistic World,* vols. I-III (1940). W. W. Tarn and G. T. Griffith, *Hellenistic Civilization* (3rd ed., 1952). The Eastern Hellenistic world is the subject of: F. Altheim, *Weltgeschichte Asiens im griechischen Zeitalter,* vols. I-II (1947-48).

N. C. Debevoise, *A Political History of Parthia* (1938), discusses the political relations between the Arsacids and Rome. For the relations between Parthians and Jews, see: G. Widengren, "Juifs et Iraniens à l'époque des Parthes," *Supplements to Vetus Testamentum,* IV (1957), 197-240.

The main work on Sassanian history and civilization is A. Christensen, *L'Iran sous les Sassanides* (2nd ed., 1944). See also: F. Altheim and R. Stiehl, *Ein asiatischer Staat, Feudalismus unter den Sasaniden und ihren Nachbarn,* vol. I (1954). O. Widengren, "Recherches sur le féodalisme iranien," *Orientalia Suecana,* 5 (1957), 79-182. On the relations with the Hephthalites, see: G. Widengren, "Xosrau Anašurvan, les Hephthalites et les peuples turcs," *Orientalia Suecana,* 1 (1952), 69-94. On Mazdak, see: O. Klíma, *Mazdak, Geschichte einer sozialen Bewegung im sassanidischen Persien* (1957).

On Christianity in the Sassanian Empire, see: J. Labourt, *Le christianisme dans l'empire perse sous la dynastie sassanide* (1904; 2nd ed., 1914). On Persian martyrs, see: G. Hoffman, "Auszüge aus syrischen Akten persischer Märtyrer," *Abhandlungen für die Kunde des Morgenlandes,* vol. VII, no. 3 (1880).

The literature on Iranian religion is of considerable extent. Not even an attempt at approximate completeness can be made here. In addition to the references given above and in the bibliographies under PAHLAVI; ZARATHUSHTRA; ZOROASTRIANISM, see: G. Widengren's articles "Stand und Aufgaben der iranischen Religionsgeschichte," *Numen,* I (1954), 16-83; II (1955), 47-132 (also available together separately), which present the present status of the subject with the pertinent literature. They deserve particular attention and, at the same time, make repetition unnecessary. An exception may be made for two important contributions on Mithra: M. J. Vermaseren, *Corpus inscriptionum et monumentorum religionis Mithriacae* (1956). I. Gershevitch, *The Avestan Hymn to Mithra* (1959).

M. J. DRESDEN

PERSIAN, OLD. The language of ancient Fars (Greek Persis) in SW Iran (*see* PERSIA, HISTORY AND RELIGION OF, § C1*a*); primarily known through the inscriptions of the Achaemenian kings from Darius the Great (521-486 B.C.) to Artaxerxes III (359-338 B.C.). Old Persian and Avestan, the language of the Zoroastrian scriptures, the AVESTA, are the most ancient representatives attested in writing of the Iranian language group, a member of the Indo-European language family.

The existence of some of the inscriptions had been known to the Western world since the Greeks. European visitors to PERSEPOLIS from the end of the fifteenth century onward gave more or less accurate descriptions of them and copied some passages. Carsten Niebuhr (1733-1815), a Danish-German explorer and traveler, was the first who, while taking advantage of a short stay in Persepolis in 1765, made approximately correct copies of half a dozen inscriptions of Darius and Xerxes. The decipherment of the cuneiform script and the language was initiated by G. F. Grotefend in 1802. It opened the way to the understanding of other languages such as Elamite, Assyrian, Babylonian, and others. *See* ASSYRIA AND BABYLONIA § D.

The most important inscriptions were found in Bisutun (to the NW of Kermanshah), Elvend (near Hamadan), Persepolis, Naqsh-i Rustam (to the NW of Persepolis), Susa, and Suez. The majority is written in three versions: (*a*) Old Persian, (*b*) Elamite, and (*c*) Babylonian.

As to their contents, the inscriptions are official state documents which proudly commemorate for public cognizance and consumption the high exploits of the Achaemenian rulers such as military campaigns and victories, the building of palaces and canals, and the like. Limitation in number and repetitiousness by reason of the contents of the inscriptions impose natural restrictions on the variegation of the vocabulary of the Old Persian language. The usefulness of its vocabulary, however, for comparative Indo-European and Iranian language studies ranks high.

Bibliography. The extensive literature on the subject is aptly summarized by R. G. Kent, *Old Persian, Grammar, Texts, Lexicon* (1950; 2nd rev. ed., 1953), which gives the text of all the inscriptions in transliterated form, accompanied by an English translation. M. J. DRESDEN

PERSIS pûr'sĭs [Περσίς, a Persian woman] (Rom. 16:12). A Christian woman, greeted and praised by Paul. The name is often found in papyri and inscriptions, especially in connection with female slaves.
F. W. GINGRICH

PERSON OF CHRIST. *See* CHRIST.

PERUDA pĭ ro͞o'də [פרודא; Apoc. Φαρειδά, Φερειδά] (Ezra 2:55; I Esd. 5:33; II Esd. 17:57); Apoc. PHADOURA fə do͞or'ə in II Esd. 2:55. Alternately: PERIDA pĭ rī'də [פרידא] (Neh. 7:57). Head of a family of Solomon's servants who returned from the Exile. The name should probably be Perida in all occurrences. E. R. ACHTEMEIER

PERVERSE. The translation of a number of Hebrew words which generally share the meanings "twist," "bend," "be crooked," etc. Most often, it occurs in the WISDOM literature and in deuteronomic sources (*see* DEUTERONOMY). Our term belongs in the context of the unrighteous WAY of the wisdom literature, as opposed to the righteous way, and is characterized by foolishness, sensuality, and disobedience to God's order. In the Deuteronomic framework of blessing and curse (*see* BLESSINGS AND CURSINGS) the word takes on the clear distinction of "twisting" the commandments of God into something different or opposite, through disobedience. The perverse man (cf. perverse speech, mind, way, thing, etc.) is the man who behaves in a manner opposed to the demands of the law of God and the practical wisdom and morality which derive from it.

In the NT the word is used to translate various forms of στρέφω ("to turn, twist"), and reflects the typical OT usage (cf. Matt. 17:17; Luke 9:41; Phil. 2:15; cf. Deut. 32:5).

Bibliography. W. O. E. Oesterley, *The Wisdom of Egypt and the OT* (1927), pp. 75 ff. J. A. WHARTON

PESHITTA pə shē'tə. A Syriac term, meaning "simple," which came to be applied to a Syriac translation of the Bible which lacked the elaborate marginal annotations of the Harclean Syriac version and Paul of Tella's Syriac Hexaplar. *See* VERSIONS, ANCIENT, § 4*b*.

PESTILENCE [דבר; λοιμοί]. A general though quite distinctive designation of scourges of fatal termination sent by God as a punishment, and normally linked with other catastrophic events such as famine or the ravaging of the land. Moses utilized the possible incidence of pestilence as a threat to Pharaoh (Exod. 9:14), while in the Egyptian plague (Exod. 9:3) דבר was devastating MURRAIN.

The rebellious Israelites were frequently confronted with warnings concerning pestilence during the wilderness wanderings (cf. Num. 14:12; Deut. 28:21), and a number of unspecified epidemics actually broke out consequent upon Israelite disobedience (Num. 11:33; 16:46; 25:8). In Num. 14:37 the term מגפה is used in a synonymous sense.

The dedication prayer of Solomon (I Kings 8:37) incorporates a clause for the removal of sundry calamities, including pestilence, when national repentance was evident. In Amos 4:10, "pestilence" is used to describe the plague of Egypt, while in Hab. 3:5 it is one of the heralds of divine judgment. λοιμοί is rendered as "pestilence" and linked with "famine" in the apocalyptic utterance of Matt. 24:7 KJV; Luke 21:11.

While "pestilence" and "plague" are frequently associated with each other in incidence, there appears to have been a distinction made between them in antiquity, and thus there is no real justification for identifying them, as some philologists do. Cholera, typhoid, typhus fever, dysentery, smallpox, and bubonic plague were all scourges of Bible lands to varying degrees. But bubonic outbreaks are generally designated as "plague," while "pestilence" is often associated with sieges, suggesting a contaminated water supply, and hence diseases such as cholera or enteric fever. However, smallpox, bubonic plague, and pneumonic plague may be indicated occasionally. R. K. HARRISON

PESTLE [עֱלִי]. A hand tool used to pound, crush, or rub substances in a MORTAR. Fig. MOR 70.

*__PETER__ pē'tər [Πέτρος]. The name which Jesus gave to the most prominent of his twelve apostles.

1. The names of Peter
2. Home and family
3. Call as disciple and apostle
4. Role among the Twelve
5. "On this rock"
6. Witness to the Resurrection
7. Leadership in and near Jerusalem
8. Wider work
9. Relation to other apostolic leaders
10. Peter in Rome
11. Place of burial
12. Writings ascribed to Peter
13. The message Peter preached
14. Permanent contribution

Bibliography

1. The names of Peter. The NT uses four names to refer to Peter. Least used is the Hebrew name Symeon (שִׁמְעוֹן; Συμεών), which appears only in Acts 15:14 and in most Greek MSS of II Pet. 1:1. The Greek name Simon (Σίμων) occurs much more often: in Matthew, five times; in Mark, six; in Luke, eleven; in John, twenty-two; in Acts, four (all in the Cornelius story); and possibly in II Peter, one (1:1). Nearly twenty times, almost all of them in John, the name Simon is used in the double name Simon Peter. The other two names, Cephas and Peter, are identical in meaning. Both mean "rock." Cephas (Κηφᾶς) is the Greek transliteration of the Aramaic word כֵּפָא, "rock." It occurs in John once, in I Corinthians four times, and in Galatians four times. The Greek word πέτρος has the same meaning (John 1:42). It occurs in Matthew twenty-three times, in Mark nineteen, in Luke seventeen, in John thirty-four, in Acts fifty-six, in Galatians twice, and in I Peter and II Peter once each. Because Greek MSS vary in the name given in some passages, these figures are only approximate, but they show clearly that the name Peter is dominant in NT usage, and that the name Simon, though used often, is much less frequent. The double name Simon Peter and the phrase "Simon called Peter" recall that Simon was the earlier name and the name Peter was given later. The frequency of the name Simon in the gospels and the rare use of Symeon in the NT indicate that the name Simon was not merely a later Greek substitute for Symeon, but that the name Simon was his alternate original name and was in common use during Jesus' ministry. If this is so, it hints at some Greek background for the pre-Christian life of Peter. He was not an Aramaic-speaking Jew who had no touch with the Hellenistic forces in Galilee, but a bilingual Jew who thereby had some providential preparation for later missionary preaching.

2. Home and family. Two gospels refer to the father of Peter. In Matt. 16:17, Jesus calls his leading disciple Simon Bar-Jona—i.e., Simon son of Jonah (although an attempt has been made to interpret it as a descriptive title meaning he was an "extremist"). In John 1:42, according to the probable text, he is called Simon the son of John (Σίμων ὁ υἱὸς Ἰωάννου).

That Peter was married is clear from Matt. 8:14; Mark 1:30; Luke 4:38, which speak of his mother-in-law, whose fever Jesus healed. Later, in the apostolic age, Paul states that Cephas took his wife with him on journeys to various churches (I Cor. 9:5).

The gospels speak often of Peter's brother Andrew. The two brothers were partners in a fishing business on the Sea of Galilee, and Mark 1:29 indicates that they lived together. Just which city on that lake was their home is not entirely clear. According to Mark 1:21, 29, they lived at CAPERNAUM on the NW shore of the lake. John 1:44 says that BETH-SAIDA, the residence of Philip, was the "city of Andrew and Peter." John 12:21 locates this Beth-saida in Galilee. There is no convincing evidence of a Beth-saida W of the Jordan. The only Beth-saida of which we have clear knowledge lay a little E of the Jordan, on the N shore of the Sea of Galilee. Either the Gospel of John is in error in placing Beth-saida in Galilee, since the site of Beth-saida Julias is not in Galilee but in Gaulanitis, or Galilee is here used in a popular sense to indicate the settled region W and N of the Sea of Galilee, in which sense Beth-saida could be considered a city in Galilee. If the Gospel of John is correct in placing the home of Andrew and Peter in Beth-saida, this must refer to the original family home; in the days of Jesus' ministry the home of these brothers was in Capernaum, where in their fishing business they were "partners" (κοινωνοί) of James and John the sons of Zebedee (Luke 5:10).

3. Call as disciple and apostle. All four gospels unite in reporting that Peter became a disciple of Jesus in the very early days of Jesus' ministry. They differ, however, as to the place and circumstances. The Synoptic gospels place the event by the Sea of Galilee. According to Matt. 4:18-22; Mark 1:16-20, Jesus walked along the shore and called first Simon and Andrew, and then James and John, to follow him; he told Simon and Andrew, and presumably the other two also, that they were to "become fishers of men." They promptly left their boats and nets and followed him. Luke 5:1-11 agrees as to the location of the call; this account, however, centers attention on Peter; Andrew strangely is not mentioned, and James and John receive minor attention. A remarkable catch of fish while Jesus was in Peter's boat led Peter to confess his own unworthiness, but Jesus promised him and the sons of Zebedee that thenceforth they would be "catching men." This account reflects what the other Synoptic gospels take for granted—the overawing sense of a mysterious greatness in Jesus. Whatever the exact circumstances of the call, it occurred at the Sea of Galilee, included the two pairs of brothers, and evoked a sense of personal power in Jesus.

The Gospel of John dates Peter's first contact with Jesus earlier, and places it in Judea near the place where John the Baptist was carrying on his ministry (1:35-42). In this account Andrew, and apparently Peter, had come to hear John and had become his disciples. When John pointed to Jesus as the Lamb of God, Andrew and another disciple of John followed Jesus, and Andrew came away from this first encounter convinced that Jesus was the expected Jewish Messiah. He at once reported this discovery to his brother and brought him to Jesus, who promptly announced that Simon was to be called Cephas, which means Peter.

In this account the initial call occurred in the S Jordan Valley (1:28); the first disciple named is Andrew; and the messianic identification of Jesus, ascribed in the Synoptic gospels to Peter as a new insight attained near the end of the Galilean ministry, here occurred on the first day of Jesus' contact with his disciples, and it was made, not by Peter, but by Andrew, before Peter had even seen Jesus. It may be said, and often is said, that this was the preliminary call, while the full and definite call to active and full-time discipleship was given later by the Sea of Galilee. But this leaves a serious problem unexplained: in the Johannine account it was Andrew who first identified Jesus as the Messiah, while the Synoptic gospels assign this act to Peter, and Andrew did so on the first day Jesus met his disciples rather than toward the end of the Galilean ministry. This early connection of Peter and Andrew with John the Baptist is entirely possible, but the dramatic method of the Gospel of John, which emphasizes its witness by giving its full testimony to Jesus from the first chapter on, has apparently led it to place the Messianic identification much too early in the story. The actual call to accompany Jesus as full-time disciples may therefore be dated at the beginning of the Galilean ministry of Jesus.

From the day of the call by the Sea of Galilee, Peter was a full-time disciple, living with his Teacher, learning his Master's message and spirit, and helping him in minor ways. The word "disciple" (μαθητής) means "pupil," "learner." To live as a disciple implied more than classroom instruction; it included continual personal association with the Teacher as an integral part of the learning process. The word "disciple" did not mean the same as the word "apostle" (ἀπόστολος). Yet to be a disciple in the full sense prepared the way for later appointment as apostles. For Jesus called these men to learn from him that they might then "become fishers of men." A mission, a commission to carry forward the work of Jesus, was his purpose in calling Peter to discipleship. So when Jesus later "appointed twelve, to be with him, and to be sent out to preach and have authority to cast out demons" (Mark 3:14-15), he did not do something entirely new. Some such mission was in his mind from the start, though the appointment of twelve made it more specific and fixed the number of men chosen for the immediate task.

When the definite number was fixed and the Twelve chosen, and the plan to send them out through the Galilean cities was formed, these men began to be called apostles (Matt. 10:2; Mark 6:30; Luke 6:13; 9:10). Some scholars have argued that the title APOSTLE came into use only in the apostolic age. But the title was appropriate as soon as a definite mission was planned; the gospels clearly report that the title was used of the Twelve during the lifetime of Jesus; there is no sound reason for denying that Jesus designated these men as his apostles. The wider use of the title "apostle" in the apostolic age shows that the term was not identical in meaning with "the Twelve," but the evidence indicates that the Twelve were called apostles from the time that Jesus sent them out on a preaching and healing mission in Galilee.

Among the Twelve, Peter was included, and he was always named first (Matt. 10:2; Mark 3:16; Luke 6:14; cf. Acts 1:13). Indeed, Matt. 10:2 emphasizes his right to first mention: "first, Simon, who is called Peter." In the Synoptic gospels, he is the first to be called to follow Jesus; he is the first to be named in the lists of the Twelve. To think of the apostles is to think first of Peter.

4. Role among the Twelve. The practice of mentioning Peter first was not due simply to his early call or to his prominence in the apostolic age. Throughout Jesus' ministry Peter was the outstanding member of the Twelve. At times he acted as a vigorous individual quick to take the initiative. This occurred in Matt. 14:28, where Peter volunteered to come to Jesus upon the water, though he became afraid while carrying out his proposal, and also in Matt. 18:21, where he asked Jesus how often he must forgive his brother.

Usually, however, Peter acted or spoke for the group of disciples, and was recognized as the outstanding one of the group. At one time he asked Jesus for whom a parable is intended (Luke 12:41). At Caesarea Philippi he spoke for the disciples in affirming Jesus to be the Messiah (Matt. 16:16; Mark 8:29; Luke 9:20); and when Jesus announced his impending suffering and Peter rebuked him, Jesus' stern rebuke of Peter was not intended for Peter alone, for Jesus' act in looking at the disciples while rebuking Peter shows that he recognized in Peter's words an expression of the mind of the group (Mark 8:33). Peter spoke again for the disciples when, thinking of future rewards, he reminded Jesus of their sacrifice in following him and asked what their reward would be (Matt. 19:27; Mark 10:28; Luke 18:28). On a few occasions a question is ascribed to the disciples in one gospel but to Peter in another (cf. Mark 7:17 with Matt. 15:15; Matt. 21:20 with Mark 11:21).

The prominent role of Peter is reflected where Peter is singled out and the other disciples are mentioned as a group associated with him: "Simon and those who were with him" sought out Jesus when he left Capernaum for prayer (Mark 1:36; but cf. Luke 4:42: "the people"); "Peter and those who were with him" remonstrated with Jesus when he asked who of the crowd had touched him (Luke 8:45, according to a well-attested reading; but other good authorities read only "Peter," and the parallel in Mark 5:31 says "his disciples"); "Peter and those who were with him"—i.e., John and James—were heavy with sleep on the Mount of Transfiguration (Luke 9:32); and the angel at the empty tomb, according to Mark 16:7, instructed the women to "tell his disciples and Peter" (Matt. 28:7 says only: "tell his disciples"). Back of the varying form of these statements is the common knowledge that when the disciples spoke or acted, Peter was normally their spokesman and took the lead.

When an inner circle of the Twelve is mentioned, Peter is always included and is named first. Peter,

James, and John are the most often mentioned inner group: on the occasion of the miraculous catch of fish (Luke 5:10); when Jesus entered the house of Jairus the ruler of the synagogue to raise his daughter from the dead (Mark 5:37; Luke 8:51 names John before James); at the Transfiguration (Matt. 17:1; Mark 9:2; Luke 9:28 names John before James); and in the Garden of Gethsemane, when Jesus went apart to pray (Mark 14:33; Matt. 26:37 says here: "Peter and the two sons of Zebedee"). In Mark 13:3 Andrew is included with these three as asking the time of the destruction of the temple; Matt. 24:3 says that the disciples asked the question, and Luke 21:5 ascribes the question to an unidentified "some." Luke 22:8 says that Jesus sent Peter and John to prepare the Passover; Matt. 26:17 and Mark 14:12 say that "his disciples" asked about the plans, and they (in Matthew) or "two of his disciples" (in Mark) were instructed to make ready.

The prominence of Peter appears in other ways. Jesus went to Peter's house in Capernaum (Matt. 8:14; Mark 1:29; Luke 4:38), and made use of Peter's boat as a vantage point from which to teach (Luke 5:3). It was Peter who made the epoch-making confession that Jesus is the Christ (Matt. 16:16; Mark 8:29; Luke 9:20). Peter was to rally the disciples after Jesus' arrest had scattered them (Luke 22:31-32). Peter's denial of Jesus had its pathos precisely in the fact that Peter was the outstanding disciple who, above all others, should have held fast and encouraged the others (Matt. 26:69-75; Mark 14:66-72; Luke 22:54-62). But he proved of crucial importance as the first witness to the resurrection of Jesus (Luke 24:34; I Cor. 15:5).

The role of Peter in the Gospel of John is not quite the same. Here, too, Peter entered the scene early (John 1:40-42); he uttered for the disciples the stirring confession: "You have the words of eternal life; . . . you are the Holy One of God" (6:68-69); and he was prominent at the Last Supper, in his denial, and at the empty tomb (chs. 13–20). In the appendix he is solemnly charged to carry out a pastoral ministry: "Feed my lambs. . . . Tend my sheep. . . . Feed my sheep" (21:15-19). But the outstanding role of Peter, while not obscured, is somewhat qualified. It was Andrew who first met Jesus and then brought Peter to Jesus (1:40-41). It was Andrew who first discerned that Jesus was the Messiah; he told Peter this central fact (1:41). Between that first meeting with Jesus and the Last Supper this gospel reports no act or word of Peter except the confession of 6:68-69. At the Last Supper and throughout the passion narrative and resurrection account the Beloved Disciple appears with Peter in a prominent role (chs. 13–21). This "Beloved Disciple" had the highest-ranking position, "close to the breast of Jesus" (13:23). To him was entrusted the mother of Jesus (19:26-27). He ran to the tomb when it was reported empty, and was the first to realize what had happened; he "believed" (20:8). He first recognized the risen Lord at the Sea of Tiberias (21:7). He shared the attention with Peter. Whether he was the "other disciple" (18:16) who had access to the court of the high priest and could obtain entrance for Peter is not certain, but here too Peter was not the unchallenged leader of the disciples. Peter is prominent in the Gospel of John, but he does not hold the unrivaled position among the disciples which he does in the Synoptic gospels.

5. "On this rock." Peter's original names were Symeon and Simon, and it appears that during Jesus' ministry he was commonly called Simon. He is known to us, however, through the new name which Jesus gave him. This Aramaic name, transliterated, was Cephas, and its Greek translation, soon to prevail, was Peter. It is not clear when Jesus gave this name to Simon. John 1:42 states that he did so the first time he saw Simon. Since the Gospel of John, for dramatic purposes, seems to date too early the full confession of Jesus as Messiah, it is possible and, indeed, probable that the giving of the new name is likewise dated too early. In Mark 3:16; Luke 6:14 the new name is said to have been given when Jesus chose the Twelve. Matt. 16:18, however, puts the naming at the time when Simon, on behalf of the group of disciples, declared that Jesus was the Messiah. This conflicting evidence of the gospels makes it impossible to be certain just when Jesus gave the new name. We may accept it as fact that he did so at some time during the public ministry. The name Cephas or Peter soon superseded the name Simon, perhaps in part because it was a distinctive name and not so commonly used as Simon, and perhaps even more because the followers of Jesus knew that the name carried significance not only for Peter but also for the life of the church. While the name actually given to Simon by Jesus was Cephas, Aramaic for "Rock," it was natural for this to be expressed in Greek translation as Peter, and just as in the past this disciple had had both a Semitic name, Symeon, and a Greek name, Simon, we may infer that almost at once began the use of the name Peter, Greek for "Rock."

The gospels do not say why Jesus gave Simon the new name of "Rock." It was not simply a description of his character, for he was volatile and impulsive and liable to failure. Nor was it an ironic jest, for the giving of a new name was a solemn and significant act; it had some serious meaning. It may express in part a sense of Peter's potential usefulness and challenge him to live up to his possibilities and his trust. Certainly it indicates that he now has a new role and is responsible for giving strength and steadiness to the group of disciples.

Crucial for the understanding of Peter's role is the interpretation of Matt. 16:17-19. Did Jesus speak these words? Many scholars have denied that he could have done so. They point out that these verses have no parallel in any other gospel, that Jesus throughout his ministry showed no interest in ecclesiastical organization, and that apart from Matt. 18:17 the word "church" does not occur in any other passage in the four gospels. They point out that James the brother of the Lord and Paul the apostle take the leadership of large portions of the church, with no hint that they are under Peter's control.

If we are to understand these verses, we must put aside certain modern preconceptions: (*a*) We must not assume that the word "church" meant to Jesus what it means today. We must not think in terms of advanced organization. We must not think that Jesus had seceded from Judaism and was speaking of an organization completely separate from his ancestral religious home. He was speaking of the group which centered in him and which was the true center of the people of God. Whatever Aramaic word he may have used—it may have been *qah*^{e}*la* or *k*^{e}*nishta*—he meant this loyal people of God rather than an organization. (*b*) We must put aside all thought of successors to Peter. The passage makes no mention of such. Peter is given a basic work to do, and nothing is said of any need or right to convey his authority and role to successors. (*c*) We must avoid the idea of external, automatic, and exclusive authority. In Matt. 18:18 Jesus gives to the entire group of disciples authority like that which in Matt. 16:19 he gives to Peter. Then in Matt. 18:19-20 he promises to give to any two or three of his followers whatever they ask. It is clear to every Christian that this latter promise is spiritually conditioned. A request for what is evil or damaging to others will be denied; no true Christian would want an unworthy request granted. In other words, just as in Matt. 18:19 there are unexpressed spiritual conditions, so the promise of authority to Peter or to the entire group of disciples does not mean that unworthy human leadership or judgments will be sanctioned by God. The writer of the Gospel of Matthew knew this; he reports that, immediately after the apparently unconditional promise of Matt. 16:19, Jesus condemned Peter for being untrue to the mind of Jesus: "Get behind me, Satan" (16:23). (*d*) We must not assume that these verses necessarily belong in the context where we now find them. Form criticism has made it clear that the gospel tradition was preserved at first mainly in the form of separate units; single incidents, sayings, or parables were repeatedly used in the life of the church to serve its needs. Even though a general outline of Jesus' life was preserved, the exact situation in which a saying was spoken by Jesus was often unknown. Our gospel writers therefore had to organize their material in a form more unified than the oral tradition had. And of all the gospel writers, the writer of Matthew is most clearly skilled in organizing sayings of Jesus in large discourses. Matt. 16:17-19 may preserve genuine words of Jesus which are not now within their original historical setting.

If we examine these verses with such cautions in mind, it becomes much more reasonable to say that they were spoken by Jesus. In the first place, they are Semitic in language and thought-world; they must come either from Jesus or from the early Aramaic-speaking wing of the apostolic church. Moreover, the reference to Peter as a rock has a real Jewish tone; a rabbinical saying reports that when God saw Abraham, he said that he had found a rock on which he could build the world (Yalkuth 1.766). It was Peter who was the rock—not merely his faith, though this was included, and not Christ, although Peter would be a rock only through his relation to Christ. It fits Jesus' outlook to say that Peter's understanding of Jesus' role in God's work was God-given. Matt. 16:17 could hardly be from Jesus if, as John 1:41 says, Peter already knew from Andrew, before he ever became Jesus' disciple, that Jesus was the expected Messiah. But if, as seems true, Peter first of the disciples realized and stated the role of Jesus, he had been guided by God to the truth and its expression. In the beginnings of the church Peter was to be the key figure; all its later stages would build upon his pioneer witness and leadership. This church, this people of God, would survive martyrdom and every threat of destruction; its promise of life would be vindicated in the fulfilment of God's purpose, and Peter would make a basic contribution to that ongoing life of God's people. In his crucial pioneer work Peter would have authority; he could not use it selfishly or capriciously, nor exercise it mechanically, but he could speak and act for God insofar as he acted in the spirit of Christ and served the purpose of Christ. There was to be leadership and authority in the church, and Peter would have a crucial role in laying its foundation. The church was not to live in anarchy but in unity and with order adapted to the living situation, and Peter had his basic place in this original development and work of the church.

When later ideas foreign to the mind of Jesus are kept out of the picture, it is clear that Jesus did give to Peter the place of outstanding leadership among his disciples. It may be that these words were not spoken near Caesarea Philippi but toward the end of Jesus' life, and in the course of talks with the disciples about what lay ahead. Certainly these words reflect an important fact: Peter was the outstanding member of the Twelve; he was the one who took the lead, and Jesus parried the attempt of James and John to supersede him (Mark 10:35-37; cf. Matt. 20:20-21); it was to Peter Jesus committed the task of rallying his fellow disciples even after Peter's denial (Luke 22:31-32); and Peter was the founding leader of the apostolic church, as the early chapters of Acts show. Luke 22:31-32 offers a parallel to Matt. 16:17-19 in the essential commission of Peter to take the lead among his fellow disciples. It is a fact of history that Peter was the Rock; he followed Jesus' instruction to "strengthen [his] brethren"; he was the key leader of the earliest years of the church. The later sharing of prominence with James the brother of the Lord and with Paul bars the way to unjustified ideas of hierarchy and apostolic succession, but it does not take from Peter the honor of basic leadership in the crucial days of the church's beginnings.

6. Witness to the Resurrection. The usual Christian view emphasizes Peter's confession of Jesus as Messiah as his unique and basic contribution. There is no reason to minimize the importance of this event, although the necessity Jesus found to rebuke Peter immediately afterward shows that Peter's confession was but a stage on the way to that full understanding and insight needed as the basis for the apostolic church. His denial of Jesus at the time of the trial is further evidence that Peter needed more than he possessed when he first confessed Jesus as Messiah. Peter was not ready to lead the church or to give its basic witness until he could witness to the resurrection of Christ. In fact, there was and could be no church until the resurrection witness became the triumphant climax and interpreting center of the gospel.

It is at this turning point that the leading role of Peter is most clear. In the earliest written report of the resurrection appearances, that of Paul in I Cor. 15:3-8, the first appearance is "to Cephas." Luke 24:34 seems to agree with this; it was to Peter, who had been instructed to "strengthen [his] brethren" (Luke 22:32), that Jesus first appeared. This is not entirely clear in Luke, since it may be thought that Jesus had appeared to the two disciples on the way to Emmaus before he "appeared to Simon." But Luke probably means that the appearance to Peter came first.

The central work of an apostle of Christ, as Peter himself is reported to have said, was to be a "witness to his resurrection" (Acts 1:22). It was fitting for the "first" of the apostles (Matt. 10:2) to be the first to see the risen Christ. He then was ready to do what Jesus had instructed him to do. He then was ready to begin the courageous witness which played so important a role in the apostolic church.

7. Leadership in and near Jerusalem. During the period of approximately fifteen years which is covered by the first twelve chapters of Acts, Peter was the dominant leader of the church. Undoubtedly the other apostles were faithful, but nine of them Acts never mentions as active individual leaders. John the son of Zebedee accompanied Peter to the temple (3:1), was imprisoned with Peter (4:3), and later went to Samaria with him (8:14), but he was a secondary figure who never took the initiative. James his brother was singled out for martyrdom (12:2), and this shows that he had been active in Christian work and so had attracted Herod Agrippa I's attention; but no acts of his career are reported, and he cannot have been the church's dominant leader. Two members of the Seven appear prominently in Christian leadership: Stephen, whose powerful preaching at Jerusalem among Greek-speaking Jews resulted in his martyrdom (6:8–8:1), and Philip, who, when driven from Jerusalem by persecution, preached effectively in Samaria, on the way to Gaza, and in the coastal cities of Palestine (8:4-8, 26-40). It is entirely possible that prior to Stephen's death the Seven played a more prominent role in Jerusalem than the narrative of Acts reports, but it would be wrong to assume that either Stephen or Philip matched the leadership of Peter. Barnabas emerged as an able and sincere leader (4:36-37; 11:22-30; 12:25), but his role was obviously subordinate. By the time of 12:17 James the brother of the Lord, associated with the church from its earliest days (1:14; cf. I Cor. 15:7), had risen to a place of leadership, but during the period of Peter's stay in Jerusalem, James did not hold first rank there. Peter dominated that period.

It was Peter who proposed the selection of a twelfth witness to the Resurrection, to take the place of Judas Iscariot (1:15-22). On Pentecost, Peter seized the opportunity to preach to the assembled pilgrims, and his powerful appeal, which led to the conversion of "three thousand souls," marked him as worthy to carry evangelistic leadership in the church (2:14-41). When Peter and John went "to the temple at the hour of prayer," about 3 P.M., and encountered the lame beggar, Peter spoke the word that gave healing, and so proved powerful not only in preaching but also in the working of miracles; and he again seized the opportunity to speak to his fellow Jews in the outer court of the temple (3:1-26). When he and John were arrested and brought before the Jewish authorities for examination, Peter spoke with "boldness" (4:13), and no threats from the officials intimidated him (4:1-31). When Ananias and his wife, Sapphira, tried to deceive the other Christians by pretending to give the church all their money while really keeping part of it, Peter sensed the danger which hypocrisy brought to the church; he denounced each of the conniving couple in turn, and their death resulted (5:1-11). Peter was undoubtedly active in the healing and preaching which led to the arrest of all the apostles, and in the ensuing rebuke before the Sanhedrin he voiced the apostles' determination to "obey God rather than men," and again gave his witness to Christ (5:12-42).

Up to this time the story centered in Jerusalem, and the Twelve, with Peter in first place, were the center of the life and work of the church. The appointment of the SEVEN calls attention to the Hellenistic portion of the Jerusalem church. It had been present all the time, and its vigorous leadership finally provoked a crisis, and the martyrdom of Stephen led to the scattering of the Hellenistic Jewish group. The Twelve were not driven from Jerusalem (8:1). But just at that point the role of Peter changed. By his Galilean origin he had been given some knowledge of Greek, and he was able to follow the work of Philip at Samaria and bring help to the new Christians there (8:14). Thus by the decision of the Twelve he began an outreaching ministry. As 9:32 says: "Peter went here and there among them all," and this means that he went not only to the Hellenistic Christians and Jews but also to any Aramaic-speaking Christians and Jews that he found. He probably spent most of his time among the Aramaic-speaking population, and his work at Lydda and Joppa may have been with such people (9:32-43), but he could go to the Caesarea home of the centurion Cornelius, who no doubt spoke Greek, and preach the gospel to him and his household and friends (10:1–11:18).

A broadening spirit marks the story at Joppa and especially at Caesarea. At Joppa, Peter stayed with "one Simon, a tanner," whose trade was objectionable by strict Jewish ceremonial law. At Caesarea, Peter was led, somewhat against his inclination and with obvious reluctance, but in response to what he was certain was God's guidance, to speak to uncircumcised Gentiles. He admitted them to baptism without requiring them first to conform to the rites which Judaism required of proselytes. This free spirit, added to the vigor and prominence of Peter's work at Jerusalem, no doubt enraged Jewish leaders so that Herod Agrippa I could see that Peter's arrest would please them (12:3). The increased hostility to Peter indicated that his days of free and active leadership in Jerusalem were at an end, and so, when he was released from prison and had visited the Christians at the home of Mary the mother of John Mark, he indicated that James the brother of the Lord should now lead the Jerusalem church, and "he departed and went to another place" (12:4-17). This marked the end of Peter's dominant leadership in and near Jerusalem. On the one later occasion when he appeared in Jerusalem, at the apostolic conference

(15:1-29), James presided and formulated the decision of the conference.

8. Wider work. The later career of Peter cannot be traced in detail. No connected account of this period of his life exists, and only scanty evidence at best supports traditions about his later work. He "went to another place" (Acts 12:17). This evidently means that he left Jerusalem, and probably implies that he began to work outside Palestine. But it does not say where he did go. Wherever it was, his wife went with him (I Cor. 9:5).

He may have gone to Antioch in Syria. Certainly he later visited the city (Gal. 2:11), and the strong ancient tradition that he was the first bishop at Antioch suggests that even though this tradition as it stands cannot be true, he may have visited the church there at an early date and stayed long enough to have real influence.

He may have gone to Asia Minor. This is not probable at such an early date as Acts 12:17, and even I Pet. 1:1 does not claim he had visited these regions. But even if Peter did not write I Peter, this verse shows that the church thought he had some interest in the greater part of Asia Minor. The case for extensive missionary work by Peter in Asia Minor is weakened by the fact that I Peter contains no indication of personal acquaintance with the areas addressed.

He may have gone to Corinth and neighboring regions. The presence of a Cephas party at Corinth (I Cor. 1:12) may indicate that Peter had been there and won adherents to his point of view. The later tradition, stated by Dionysius, bishop of Corinth, that Peter and Paul had founded the church at Corinth, is obviously a fiction, and at most reflects a knowledge that Peter had at some time been in that city.

Some have thought that he went to Rome. However, there is no evidence that he went to Rome so early. The later tradition that Peter spent twenty-five years at Rome, founding the church there and acting as its first bishop until his martyrdom, is certainly untrustworthy. With the problem of Peter's connection with Rome we shall deal later. We must not exclude work there, but we must not assume that Peter went there directly from Jerusalem at the time of Acts 12:17.

9. Relation to other apostolic leaders. To estimate correctly the role of Peter in the primitive church, we must study carefully his relations with other apostolic leaders of that period. We have seen (§ 7 *above*) that during the period of his dominant leadership at Jerusalem his importance greatly surpassed that of James and John the sons of Zebedee. Stephen was an outstanding leader, and may have had a longer and more influential career of leadership than a first reading of Acts might suggest, but he was not the equal of Peter, and attempts to picture the Jerusalem church as divided into two separate groups, an Aramaic-speaking wing under Peter and a Hellenistic wing in which Stephen was dominant, are unconvincing. The Jerusalem church was not split into two separate denominations, even though there were two groups which had a partially separate life because of language differences. Peter and other Christians (including Barnabas) were able to bridge these differences, and Peter was the outstanding leader of the entire Jerusalem church.

James the brother of the Lord gradually became the dominant leader of the Jerusalem church. Paul reflects an early stage of this process in Gal. 1:18-19; he went to Jerusalem, three years after his conversion, primarily "to visit Cephas," who was then the most important leader there; he mentions James, but not as equal to Peter. By the time of Acts 12:17 James had become more prominent. Peter indicates this by saying: "Tell this to James and to the brethren." During the past few months or years Peter had begun to travel about Palestine, and James had proved an adequate and able leader during his absence. The departure of Peter in Acts 12:17 left the leadership of the Jerusalem church in the hands of James. In Acts 15, at the apostolic conference, though Peter was present, James apparently presided, and he formulated the decision which the conference approved. This indicates that James had an influence that reached far beyond Jerusalem. Paul confirms this dominant position of James; in speaking of his conference with the Jerusalem leaders, he names James first and gives Peter second place (Gal. 2:9).

The continuing dominance of James at Jerusalem and in a wider area is suggested, not only in Acts 21:18, where Paul "went in" to see James on his final visit to Jerusalem, but especially in Gal. 2:12, where "certain men came from James" to Antioch in Syria and so awed Peter and Barnabas that they stopped eating with Gentiles. Even if these men did not have a direct commission from James to act as they did, it remains true that the influence of James was felt outside Palestine, and Peter and Barnabas did not feel able to resist it. These facts imply that Peter was no longer the dominant head of the Jewish Christian portion of the church.

Paul's relation to Peter combined respect with independence. On his first journey to Jerusalem after conversion (Acts 9:26-30; Gal. 1:18-20), Paul's purpose was "to visit Cephas," to establish friendly relations and no doubt to learn more of Jesus. Paul is careful to emphasize, however, that he already had his gospel before he met Peter. He did not place himself under Peter, but continued to work independently (Gal. 1:21-24). The next visit to Jerusalem which Paul reports (Gal. 2:1-10) is probably that described in Acts 15:1-29. These narratives raise many questions, but for our purpose two facts stand out: (*a*) according to both accounts Paul won approval of his essential gospel to the Gentiles, and his future work was not subjected to the control of Peter; (*b*) Paul states as a fact not open to dispute that Peter was an apostle to Jews as Paul was to Gentiles. It had never occurred to Paul that Peter had authority over the entire church. Each had his independent field of work and sphere of leadership. The independence of Paul was illustrated when Peter visited Antioch (Gal. 2:11-14); when Peter submitted to the influence of James, Paul rebuked his vacillating attitude. As Peter's equal, Paul felt justified in condemning Peter for inconsistency in first eating with Gentiles and then refusing to do so.

10. Peter in Rome. Lack of clear early evidence makes it impossible to determine definitely the relation of Peter to the church at Rome. The NT never reports a visit of Peter to that city. Acts tells nothing of such a visit, and the story of Paul's arrival in Rome never suggests that Peter had been there or was there when Paul arrived. Paul's letter to the Roman church gives no hint that this church had any connection with Peter. These facts are at least decisive against any view that Peter spent long years in residence at Rome or was present there when Paul wrote to Rome or arrived there.

I Pet. 5:13, which sends greetings from "Babylon," probably implies that Peter writes from Rome; here, as in the book of Revelation, it seems that Rome is cryptically called Babylon. Even if Peter did not write I Peter, the letter reflects the view that he had been there and so could have written from there. This is the one NT hint of a visit to Rome, for the suggestion that the two witnesses in Rev. 11:3-12 were Peter and Paul, martyred in Rome, is by no means convincing; this passage is usually thought to be a reference to Moses and Elijah. The NT thus does little to indicate the presence of Peter in Rome. John 21:18-19 does predict the future martyrdom of Peter, but does not say where it will occur.

Somewhat stronger evidence comes from I Clem. 5.4, where, in connection with a mention of Paul and his martyrdom, it is said of Peter that he "suffered not one or two but many trials, and having thus given his testimony went to the glorious place which was his due." The context on the whole favors the view that this vague sentence refers to Peter's martyr death and places it at Rome. Ignatius, bishop of Antioch, on his way to Rome and anticipated martyrdom, writes to the Roman church: "I do not order you as did Peter and Paul" (Ign. Rom. 4.3). In the context, this suggests that both apostles had been at Rome, and it can be taken to imply their martyrdom there.

Explicit tradition begins only toward the end of the second century. Dionysius, bishop of Corinth, writing somewhere near A.D. 175, says that Peter and Paul founded both the Roman and the Corinthian churches: "Both planted also in our Corinth, and likewise taught us; and likewise they taught together also in Italy, and were martyred on the same occasion" (Euseb. Hist. II.25.8). Since it is certain that Peter did not collaborate with Paul in founding the church at Corinth, this witness about their work and death at Rome is not above suspicion. At about the same time or a little later, Irenaeus speaks of "Peter and Paul . . . preaching at Rome, and laying the foundations of the Church" (Her. III.1.1). These and other words of Irenaeus are weakened by the fact that Peter and Paul did not found the church at Rome. Tertullian refers to three martyrdoms at Rome: those of Peter, Paul, and John, who was plunged (unhurt) into boiling oil (Presc. Her. 36). Either Clement of Alexandria or some unidentified voice of tradition assigns the writing of I Peter to Rome (Euseb. Hist. II.15.2). Origen reported that Peter "at the last came to Rome and was crucified head-downwards" (Euseb. Hist. III. 1.2). Gaius of Rome refers to the "trophies" (τρόπαια—places of martyrdom or burial or observance of the martyrdom) of Peter and Paul; "if you will go to the Vatican [i.e., the Vatican Hill] or to the Ostian Way you will find the trophies of those who founded this church" (Euseb. Hist. II.25.7). From this time on, the tradition is definite. The witnesses at the end of the second and opening of the third century are strong, although it must be said that every statement cited above contains at least some legendary aspect.

The conclusions that seem indicated by the evidence are: Peter did not found the church at Rome or live long in that city; he was not there when Paul wrote to the Romans or when Paul reached Rome; he probably went to Rome toward the end of his career and had a ministry of limited length there; he probably suffered martyrdom in Rome, as did Paul, but it is much less certain that the two died at the same time.

11. Place of burial. For centuries scholars and churchmen have debated the location of Peter's grave. Denominational and theological interests must be excluded from such a study. To those who accept John 4:21-24 these interests are not involved. The place of burial is a historical and archaeological question. It has received renewed attention in recent years on account of explorations under the Church of St. Peter at the Vatican.

The statement of Gaius of Rome (*see* § 10 *above*) shows that by the beginning of the third century at the latest, a remembrance of Peter took place on the Vatican Hill. Some "trophy" or memorial monument was located there. With this site was connected the death of Peter or his burial or a memorial to recall and honor his martyrdom. On this site the Emperor Constantine built a church in the conviction, it would appear, that Peter was martyred or buried there. The present St. Peter's stands on the same site.

In 1939 alterations were undertaken under the altar area of this church, and when an early pagan cemetery and other important data were found, extensive and systematic explorations were undertaken. In the pagan cemetery were found the ruins of a memorial monument, which may reasonably be identified with the "trophy" or memorial which Gaius mentioned. The area under this memorial had been disturbed centuries ago, so that the early history and use of the site are difficult to determine. The official reports of the explorations claim that the burial place of Peter has been found but do not clearly establish this conclusion.

This may be the actual burial place of Peter. It certainly has been so regarded since the end of the second century or shortly thereafter. For even if the "trophy" of which Gaius speaks was built to locate or recall the martyrdom rather than the place of burial, it was soon taken to mark the place of burial; and it remains possible, or rather probable, that Gaius himself thought it was the place of burial. However, what he thought toward the end of the second century is not decisive proof of what actually happened in the sixties of the first century. More than one question still remains to hinder a final answer to the question where Peter was buried.

Was Peter put to death in the fury of the Neronian persecution, as is widely thought? If so, was it possible for the hunted Christians to identify and recover and bury the body of the martyr? Would they have buried the body in the very neighborhood of Nero's gardens, as the traditional location of the burial would imply? In view of the legendary features (*see* § 10 *above*) concerning Peter's connection with Rome (and Corinth), can we trust fully the tradition about the burial which we first get toward the end of the second century? What of the tradition that Peter was buried on the Appian Way? Is it fully satisfactory to reconcile this tradition with the Vatican burial site by saying that Peter was first buried on the Vatican, then transferred *ca.* A.D. 258 to the Appian Way site, and a few generations later transferred back to the Vatican site? Since this theory about a transfer relies on a hypothetical *correction* of ancient data to complete the theory, can we be content with such evidence?

These questions do not disprove the traditional view that Peter was buried under the spot where the altar of St. Peter's now stands. The tradition may be correct. The burial site could have been remembered in the life of the grateful Roman church. But one fact is clear: the evidence for Peter's martyrdom in Rome is much stronger than that for his place of burial. The evidence is sufficient to establish the possibility that Peter was buried where the memorial monument has been found. Many would say that it establishes the probability; but it certainly does not constitute a decisive demonstration that this is where Peter was buried.

12. Writings ascribed to Peter. Three NT writings have been connected with Peter. The Gospel of Mark, according to a tradition which goes back to Papias (Euseb. Hist. II.39.15), was indebted to the preaching of Peter, but no one claims that Peter wrote this gospel. The opening verse of I Peter (*see* PETER, FIRST LETTER OF) ascribes the writing of this letter to Peter, and there is good ground for accepting this position if we may assume, as 5:12 indicates, that Silvanus phrased the writing as it now stands. It is generally agreed that Petrine authorship cannot be defended for II Peter (*see* PETER, SECOND LETTER OF); it is one of the latest writings of the NT.

In addition to these writings, a number of apocryphal works are ascribed to Peter. These later works, all of which come from the second century or later, include the Preaching of Peter, the Gospel of Peter, the Apocalypse of Peter, and an Epistle of Peter to James connected with the Clementine Homilies. They cannot be trusted for information about the life and thought of Peter. Nor can the apocryphal Acts of Peter, which make no claim to Petrine authorship, be used for writing the life of Peter. (For further information on these apocryphal works *see* the separate titles and APOCRYPHA, NT.) It is clear that the essential contribution of Peter did not lie in the realm of writing but in action.

13. The message Peter preached. It is hard to determine clearly the distinctive message of Peter. We cannot derive it directly from the Gospel of Mark, for while one source of Mark was the preaching of Peter, its material, as form criticism has taught us, came largely from the gospel tradition used by the church; what Peter and other eyewitnesses had told, the church preserved, used, and shaped for its needs in worship, teaching, and daily life. Similarly, we must exercise caution in using I Peter, for even if it goes back to Peter, it still owes something to Silvanus (5:12) and shows linguistic kinship with letters of Paul; so we cannot hold that Peter dictated the letter. Nevertheless, the resurrection hope, the redemption through Christ, the new life in Christ, the church as the people of God, faithfulness under persecution, and steadfast loyalty to God, who judges the wicked and saves the faithful, are themes of I Peter which accord with Peter's mind and work.

Some things about Peter's message can be learned from Paul's letters. Points which stand out are the leading role of Peter in the resurrection witness, his loyalty to his ancestral faith even to the point of breaking with Paul when James pressed its claim upon him, his recognition of Paul's gospel as a valid presentation of the work of Christ, and his willingness to break down narrow Jewish lines and eat with Gentiles when not confused by conservative Jewish pressure. Paul obviously thought that Peter was in fundamental agreement with his universal gospel, and indicates that at Antioch only vacillation kept Peter from siding with Paul; indeed, Peter, by his action prior to the coming of representatives from James, *had* sided with Paul, so that Paul could feel sure that Peter was basically on his side.

Perhaps our best source for understanding the message of Peter is found in the speeches of Peter found in Acts. These have often been regarded as the free composition of the author of Acts, and so of little or no value in determining what Peter preached. It is more likely that Luke used early reports of the preaching of the apostolic leaders and presented its substance largely in his own style. If this is so, we may use Acts 1:16-25; 2:14-40; 4:7-12; 5:29-32; 10:34-43 as giving us, not the exact words of Peter's preaching, but its essential substance. These sermons are not unique in content. Part of the power of Peter was that he preached the basic, common faith of the early church, and took a leading part in shaping its message.

Included in this message which Peter preached, according to Acts, were the importance of the resurrection of Jesus; loyalty to the OT and the heritage from Israel; the fulfilment of God's plan and Israel's history in Christ; the control of history by God; Jesus as Prophet, Messiah, Lord, Suffering Servant, and Judge of all men; the necessity of repentance and faith; the promise of the Holy Spirit to those who believe and are baptized; the outreach of the gospel to "every one whom the Lord our God calls," since God shows no partiality and no man is common or unclean; and the necessity to obey God rather than man. The prominent and clear reference to Jesus as the Suffering Servant occurs in Acts only in 3:13, 26; 4:27, 30, passages particularly connected with Peter; this may have been a special emphasis in Peter's thought and message.

14. Permanent contribution. The significance of Peter is often obscured by disputes over his connection with the papacy. The NT does nothing to link him with a chain of completely authoritative successors, or with a chain of bishops at Rome, and the earliest ancient traditions do not support such ecclesiastical claims. The real contribution of Peter lies elsewhere. Protestants should not belittle that contribution because of exaggerated claims made for a hierarchy on the basis of its supposed dependence on Peter.

The Twelve were responsive followers of Jesus and made advances during the ministry of Jesus largely because Peter was their active and vocal representative. He was the outstanding member of the group. His initial, basic confession of Jesus as the Christ, while weak in its blindness to the role of suffering in Jesus' mission, gave the Twelve a clear basis of loyalty. To Peter, Jesus committed the task of rallying and leading the disciples after his departure. He was the key witness to the resurrection of Jesus, and he was the strong leader of the church in its earliest years. Then, in a way less striking and less far-reaching than Paul, he became a missionary evangelist and led in the preaching of the gospel among the Jews of Palestine, Syria, and still wider areas. While not a great theologian, he took a constructive part in understanding and interpreting the work of Christ and its gift of grace.

In a real sense every later generation of the church rests upon the basic confession, witness, and ministry of Peter. Moreover, he remains a moving example of how a warmhearted, impulsive, gifted, but imperfect man can be won by love, deepened by training, disciplined by hardship, and used by God to be an outstanding instrument of God's purpose until his fruitful ministry ends in the final witness of martyrdom for Christ.

Bibliography. C. Bigg, *The Epistles of St. Peter and St. Jude,* ICC (1901); F. J. Foakes-Jackson, *Peter: Prince of Apostles* (1927); K. G. Goetz, *Petrus als Gründer und Oberhaupt der Kirche* (1927); H. Lietzmann, *Petrus und Paulus in Rom* (2nd ed., 1927); O. Linton, *Das Problem der Urkirche in der neueren Forschung* (1932); J. A. Findlay, *A Portrait of Peter* (1935); M. Goguel, *L'Eglise primitive* (1947), pp. 184-231; E. G. Selwyn, *The First Epistle of St. Peter* (2nd ed., 1947); B. M. Apollonj Ghetti, A. Ferrua, E. Josi, and E. Kirschbaum, *Esplorazioni sotto la Confessione di San Pietro in Vaticano eseguite negli anni 1940-1949* (2 vols.; 1951); O. Cullmann, *Peter: Disciple—Apostle—Martyr* (English trans., 1953); C. Journet, *The Primacy of Peter* (English trans., 1954); J. Lowe, *Saint Peter* (1956); J. Toynbee and J. W. Perkins, *The Shrine of St. Peter* (1957). F. V. FILSON

PETER, ACTS OF. One of a long series of romances, commonly styled apocryphal Acts (*see* ACTS, APOCRYPHAL) devoted largely to Peter's activity in Rome—his contest with Simon Magus, his miracles, and his martyrdom.

Eusebius mentions this writing, along with others attributed to Peter, as unknown in catholic tradition, "for no orthodox writer of the ancient time or of our own has used their testimonies" (Hist. III.3.2). In the Stichometry of Nicephorus its length is given as 2,750 lines, approximately 1,000 more than are now extant. A large section of this writing, which was certainly composed in Greek and probably before A.D. 200, is preserved in a single Latin MS (Vercelli Acts) and contains several episodes: (*a*) the departure of Paul from Rome to Spain in obedience to a vision from heaven; (*b*) the arrival in Rome of Simon Magus, who by his miracles and defamation of Paul causes all but Narcissus and six devout women to fall away from the faith; (*c*) the departure of Peter from Jerusalem, in obedience to a heavenly vision, to combat his old adversary (Acts 8:9-24), his miracles in Rome, his contest with and discomfiture of Simon; (*d*) his martyrdom, in consequence of the wrath of Agrippa and a friend of Caesar because their concubines and wives had been led by Peter's preaching to abstain from intercourse.

The Martyrdom is also preserved separately, in two Greek MSS, in Latin, and in Syriac, Coptic, Armenian, Arabic, Ethiopic, and versions.

In addition to the material in the Vercelli Acts several other episodes, presumably also from the Acts of Peter, are extant. Among these are the story of Peter's paralyzed daughter, momentarily restored to health to prove Peter's power to heal, but subsequently returned to her infirmity to preserve her from Ptolemaeus, who has seen her while bathing. This story, now contained in the Coptic Berlin MS carrying Gnostic writings, was known to Augustine, who mentions it along with the not dissimilar story of the gardener's daughter, now known from the Letter of Titus. *See* TITUS, LETTER OF.

These two stories suggest that the original form of the Acts of Peter may well have carried a more outspoken attack upon marriage and that the lost sections may well have been excised because of their acceptance by the Manicheans. Traces of an ascetic nature—the use of *water* and bread by Paul in the Eucharist celebrated prior to his departure from Rome; the decision against sexual intercourse by those who listened to Peter's preaching—are present in the parts known to us, but the present form of the writing as a whole, perhaps in part because of editing, is far less insistent at this point than is either the Acts of John or the Acts of Paul. *See* JOHN, ACTS OF; PAUL, ACTS OF.

The definitely secondary nature of all the writings of this type—i.e., their purely imaginative expansion and elaboration of the materials preserved in the canonical book of Acts and gospels—is particularly evident in this writing. There is no slightest evidence of tradition which by any stretch of imagination can be considered historical. That anterior to this writing the tradition had arisen connecting Peter with Rome is certain. This writing seeks to explain what led him to go to Rome: the explanation is found in the episode of Peter's first contact with Simon Magus in Samaria. Familiarity with the earlier Acts of John and Acts of Paul has frequently been postulated, and with probability. The reference to Peter's departure from Jerusalem "whereas the twelve years which the Lord Christ had enjoined upon him were fulfilled" (5) is plausibly explained as taken from the Preaching of Peter (*see* PETER, PREACHING OF), which, according to Clement of Alexandria, carried the Lord's command to the apostles: "After twelve years go ye into all the world, lest any say, 'We did not hear.' " These evidences of dependence suggest no earlier date than the beginning of the third century; the total silence regarding Peter as bishop of Rome, on the other hand, makes any date after 200 increasingly unlikely.

Some of the exploits are not without interest—the conversion of the sea captain during a calm, and Peter's descent by a rope to baptize him in the sea; the supernatural gift of speech to the watchdog and to the seven-month-old child to enable them to force Simon to meet Peter; the combat between Simon and Peter and the latter's fall to earth, due to Peter's prayer. But as a whole the document is definitely slow reading and clogged with turgid speeches. In contrast, the story of Peter's martyrdom stands out: Peter's reluctant departure from Rome at the instance of his well-wishers; his meeting with Jesus as the latter approaches Rome; the latter's reply to Peter's "Lord, where are you going?" "I go unto Rome to be crucified"; Peter's return to the city and his death by crucifixion, head downward. But even this narrative is clogged by the labored explanation as to why he wished thus to be crucified.

See also APOCRYPHA, NT.

Bibliography. The extant sections of this writing are found in convenient English translation in M. R. James, *The Apocryphal NT* (1924), pp. 3-36. M. S. ENSLIN

PETER, APOCALYPSE OF. The earliest of the apocalypses attributed to apostles; highly regarded by orthodox Christians in the second century and, although subsequently rejected, reported by Sozomen (*Ecclesiastical History* VII.19) to have been read annually in the fifth century in some churches of Palestine on Good Friday.

The so-called Muratorian Canon lists it after the canonical Revelation of John, but with the warning: "Some of our people will not have it read in the church." Clement of Alexandria appears to have regarded it as canonical and makes several quotations from it. It closes the list of biblical books in the Codex Claromontanus, and its length is there given as 270 lines. In the Stichometry of Nicephorus it is listed as containing 300 lines. Eusebius' statement regarding it (which he joins with the Acts, Gospel, and Preaching of Peter): "We have no knowledge at all in Christian tradition, for no orthodox writer [ἐκκλησιαστικὸς συγγραφεύς] of the ancient time or of our own has used their testimonies" (Hist. III.3.2), is thus scarcely strictly accurate. Jerome (*Illustrious Men* 1), following Eusebius, lists it as uncanonical. Its unmistakable use in later apocrypha, such as the Epistle of the Apostles, Acts of Paul, Acts of Thomas, bk. II of the Sibylline Oracles, and a late Latin homily on the Ten Virgins, all evidence its wide popularity. At an early date it was translated into Ethiopic, a complete text of which was discovered in 1910, and also into Arabic.

In 1886 a substantial Greek fragment of this apocryphon was discovered in a tomb at Akhmim in Upper Egypt, together with a fragment of the Gospel of Peter (*see* PETER, GOSPEL OF). Comparison with the subsequently discovered Armenian suggests that our Greek fragment is from a shortened or condensed form in which the far briefer account of the delights of paradise preceded that of the torments of the damned.

The Greek fragment opens abruptly toward the end of a discourse of the risen Lord. Then at his word the apostles go to the Mount of Olives, where, in answer to the plea that he should show them "one of our righteous brethren that had departed out of the world, that we might see what manner of men they are in their form, and take courage, and encourage also the men that should hear us," they are first afforded a vision of two men "upon whom we were not able to look." The vision is clearly dependent upon the canonical account of the Transfiguration, although with modifications and romantic additions. Then follows a second vision: "And I saw also another place over against that one, very squalid." In the subsequent paragraphs the various torments suffered by sinners are described in full detail, later to be reflected in Dante's *Inferno* and its illustrations by Gustave Doré. One short sample will indicate the nature of the whole: "And some there were there hanging by their tongues; and these were they that blasphemed the way of righteousness, and under them was laid fire flaming and tormenting them. And there was a great lake full of flaming mire, wherein were certain men that turned away from righteousness; and angels, tormentors, were set over them. And there were also others, women, hanged by their hair above that mire which boiled up; and these were they which adorned themselves for adultery."

That this writing, in all likelihood in no small part suggested by the canonical Revelation, and the product of perfervid imagination, aided by Orphic and Pythagorean accounts of the future, is not later than the middle of the second century is universally admitted. That it was earlier than the Gospel of Peter is probable. That the latter made heavy use of it, even incorporating it almost entire, has been urged by M. R. James, who would regard the fragment of this apocalypse discovered at Akhmim actually a second fragment of this expanded gospel.

Among the Gnostic texts discovered in 1946 at Chenoboskion in Upper Egypt there is reported to be a Coptic writing also entitled Apocalypse of Peter. This latter would appear to have been a Gnostic document with nothing in common with the one described herein.

See also APOCRYPHA, NT.

Bibliography. The Greek text and an English translation of both the gospel and the apocalypse, as well as a discussion of their nature, were provided by J. A. Robinson and M. R. James, shortly after their first discovery, in the still useful little volume, *The Gospel According to Peter and the Revelation of Peter* (1892). The text is also translated by James in *The Apocryphal NT* (1924), pp. 505-24. M. S. ENSLIN

PETER, FIRST LETTER OF. One of the so-called CATHOLIC LETTERS in the NT; written by, or in the name of, Peter the apostle to Christians of Pontus, Galatia, Cappadocia, Asia, and Bithynia. The author himself has defined his work in 5:12 as an "exhortation" and as a "declaration" of the true grace of God, in which his readers must firmly stand. These two words are a fair description of the contents, in which dogmatics and ethics, Christian faith and behavior, are interwoven into an indissoluble unity. This characteristic makes it one of the finest and clearest examples of NT teaching. Its main thoughts are very distinct and are repeated with various modifications, although the sequence of the different parts of the letter is not always clear.

See map "I and II Timothy, Titus and I Peter," under PASTORAL LETTERS, THE.

1. Contents
2. Character of the letter
3. Attestation in the early church
4. The readers
5. Date
6. Authorship

7. Origin
8. Main theological ideas
Bibliography

1. Contents. It is impossible to distinguish as clearly as one can in many of Paul's letters between doctrinal and ethical sections. Therefore, it will be better simply to summarize the contents as the letter proceeds.

The salutation (1:1-2), containing the names of the sender and of the recipients, with greetings, is in form like the salutations in Paul's letters and follows the pattern of ancient letter writing generally, with (of course) distinctively Christian notes. There follows (vss. 3-12) a benediction of God for the blessedness given to the Christians in the present time and for eternity. Their living hope is the eternal salvation which will be revealed in the future, but which, in spite of fiery trials, is a certainty through the resurrection of Christ. By love they are bound to Jesus Christ, whom they have not seen, but in whom they believe. The prophets of the OT foretold the sufferings of Christ and his subsequent glory, so important to the Christians. This preaching of the prophets was inspired by Christ's Spirit and was destined for the present generation, which has received the gospel through the messengers sent by the same Spirit.

The writer next points out (1:13–2:3) that this gospel is the Word abiding forever. It has completely changed the lives of his readers, bringing the new birth of eternal life. The foundation of their faith and hope is the precious redemption by Christ's blood. This new life involves a break with their former way of life, and a new obedience to God, Father and just Judge, which expresses itself in holiness and brotherly love. For them, the people of the New Covenant (*see* COVENANT), Christ has become the cornerstone, spoken of in the OT, laid down by God, a sure foundation for the believers, a stumbling block for the unbelievers (2:4-10). The believers are built upon Christ; they have become a holy nation, to which, by the mercy of God, the epithets of the Lord's people in the OT can be applied.

In 2:11–3:7 we have an ethical passage whose unity appears in the thrice-repeated theme of submission (2:13, 18; 3:1; cf. 5:5), in all probability forming part of an early Christian ethical code. This code is headed by some general instruction (2:11-12): the Christians shall not follow worldly lusts, but shall lead a decent life, which ultimately brings the glorification of God. The first submission paragraph (2:13-17) is concerned with subjection under the civil authorities; Christianity means freedom, not revolution; right behavior as servants of God will stop slander. This message is summed up in these commandments: "Honor all men. Love the brotherhood. Fear God. Honor the emperor" (the latter part being a slightly, but interestingly, modified version of Prov. 24:21). The second paragraph (2:18-25) is directed to house slaves, who are directed to give perfect service to their masters, even the harsh ones. Injustice has to be endured in imitation of Jesus Christ, whose saving suffering and trust in God are described with the words of Isa. 53. The third paragraph deals with Christian women, married to unbelieving husbands, whom they must try to win for Christ, not by their outward appearance, but by their chaste and gentle behavior (3:1-6); Sarah of the OT is their example of submission. I Pet. 3:7 is a rule of conduct for Christian men to look upon their wives, not as a means for sexual pleasure, but as "joint heirs of the grace of life," that their contact with God in prayer may be undisturbed.

In 3:8–4:6 the readers are reminded that according to the word of God (Ps. 34:13-17), the way to attain life eternal is to abstain from all unrighteousness. So Christians must live in "unity of spirit," with sympathy, love of the brethren, a tender heart and a humble mind." Their new life may be reviled, because they no longer join in the pleasures of the world (4:4), but this must not cause the Christians to return reviling. They should have a clear conscience, and be able to defend their convictions and to bless their opponents. In all this they must follow the example of Christ, the righteous, who died for the unrighteous and brought salvation, who even preached after his death to the disobedient generation of Noah's time. Just as Noah was saved through the Flood, so now baptism washes away sins and is an "appeal to God for a clear conscience through the resurrection of Christ," who reigns over all powers of the universe. Christ's suffering, which led to glory, meant death to flesh and sin; therefore, Christ's followers should no longer serve earthly passions. For those who are disobedient the judgment is at hand.

The life in this world stands in the light of this coming final judgment (4:7-19). Again the writer urges his readers to mutual love, which passes by the sins of others; they must use their special abilities in the service of the brethren, for God bestowed a large variety of gifts, "in order that in everything God may be glorified." It may be that their way will go through tribulations. These are the refining fire, a test to the Christians. If they are suffering for the name of Christ—and not for ordinary crimes—they will be sharing in Christ's sufferings, which means sharing also in his glory. The final judgment will mean a narrow escape even for the righteous, and sinners will disappear.

There is finally (5:1-11) an exhortation to the elders to be good shepherds, without seeking shameful gain or domination, in order that they may receive the crown of glory, and to the younger members of the congregation to be submissive to the elders. Humility is the great virtue. In all their anxieties they may be sure of God's care. In this difficult time they must be watchful, resisting the wiles of the devil. After a short time of suffering they will be restored by God.

The letter closes (5:12-14) with the name of the writer's assistant, a brief summary, some greetings, and a final blessing.

2. Character of the letter. The outward appearance of this writing is that of an ordinary ancient LETTER, in both its opening and its final section. But what kind of letter? The fact that no direct personal relations between the writer and the readers become manifest points in the direction of a general letter, an open one meant for public circulation (like, e.g., those of Seneca), and not a private one. This letter does not enter into questions raised by a particular community, as Paul's Corinthian letters do, nor does it show close friendship with the recipients as Philippians does. It has more the general tone of an address. On the other hand, it should be noted that its salutation is not that of a "catholic letter" to be read by Christians anywhere in the world. It is not a theological or ethical treatise, but is directed to a special group of persons and deals with a very specific situation. Whatever may be the meaning of "the exiles of the dispersion" (1:1), it is evident that they form a special group in a special part of the world. The instructions given to certain groups (2:13 ff) may form part of a current catechetical pattern; but comparison with other parallel lists, as in Ephesians and Colossians, brings to light that while there are certain obvious similarities, there are also unmistakable divergences: certain items are left out (slaves are mentioned, but not masters; in the marriage section nothing is said about children). Also, in the phrasing certain additions are found, such as the examples of Jesus and of Sarah. The common material has not been taken over automatically, but has been formulated as needs required (the comparison of I Pet. 2:13 ff; Rom. 13:1 ff is also highly instructive, because it shows that Paul has a more personal touch and is less "general" than I Peter). All this points to the conclusion that the letter was conceived with particular persons in view, persons living in a particular situation.

The ascription of a general character to the letter has led some critics to the excision of the opening and closing sections as having been added in a later period to connect this work with the name of Peter. This critical operation is entirely arbitrary; it is unwarranted by MS evidence, and other writings under the name of Peter show a quite different character. Moreover, and most important of all, no feasible explanation can be given why a forger of the second century should have invented the strange address—why these out-of-the-way countries?

In 1911 the German scholar Perdelwitz formulated another theory which was to become of great influence in the course of years. His main point was that there is a clear break between 4:11 and 4:12 (doxology; new address), and that there is a certain amount of repetition before and after the break; the persecutions which the readers have to suffer are spoken of in 4:12 as actual facts, while in 1:6; 3:13 ff they are only a possibility. For these reasons Perdelwitz distinguished two parts: (*a*) 1:3–4:11; (*b*) 1:1-2; 4:12–5:14; the latter being a letter to comfort Christians in time of persecution, while the former part was a homily to newly baptized persons. This idea that the first half of the letter in reality was no letter but a baptismal sermon, following the pattern of a baptismal liturgy, has become influential through commentaries of Windisch-Preisker and F. Beare and the studies of F. L. Cross and Boismard. A number of texts have been adduced either from the NT or from other early Christian literature in which ideas similar to those in I Peter are found in the setting of baptism.

After a detailed examination of the arguments this view was rejected by C. F. D. Moule, on good grounds. It is hard to see where baptism would have taken place within the structure of this letter; the distribution of the various sections according to a supposed liturgy appears forced. Some "parallels" turn out on closer inspection to be merely superficial. Such parallelism as there is cannot be pressed further than to testify of a common Christian vocabulary connected with the conversion from paganism to Christianity, of which baptism was the visible sign. Attention is sometimes called to the thought "regeneration" that occurs here (1:3, 23; 2:1); an allusion to baptism is seen in it (cf. Tit. 3:5); but let it be observed that in I Peter the new birth is connected with the resurrection of Christ (cf. also 3:21) and the word of God in the preached gospel (1:23-25; cf. vs. 12). Not the mere moment of baptism, but the whole process of the transition from paganism to life in Christ with all its implications, stands before the writer's mind.

The division of the letter into two parts is unnecessary. A certain amount of repetition belongs to the style of the writer and can also be found in part 1. He is always moving in the same circle of ideas, but making different applications. There is, then, no reason to take this letter as other than an ordinary letter written to newly converted Christians in certain parts of the ancient world to give them comfort and exhortation (both are implied in the Greek word παρακαλέω) amid imminent dangers, and to testify to the greatness of their faith triumphing over all hardships (see 5:12).

3. Attestation in the early church. Among the so-called Apostolic Fathers there is no unequivocal testimony about this letter in I Clement, Ignatius, Barnabas, Didache, Hermas, and II Clement. Similarities in expressions which have been adduced are not so striking as to prove familiarity; they can easily be accounted for as derived from common Christian teaching. In view of the small body of literature concerned, this argument from silence does not tell very much; and this is the more true because the writings just mentioned belong to varying times and places. It is important to learn that, according to Eusebius, Papias of Hierapolis (Asia Minor, *ca.* 125) used this letter (Euseb. Hist. III.39.17: "The same writer [=Papias] has used testimonies drawn from the former epistle of John, and likewise from that of Peter"). Since, however, Papias' works are lost, it is impossible to know in what form he quoted these testimonies (whether under the actual name of the apostle or anonymously, a phrase or two which made Eusebius think of this letter). The same observation must be made with regard to the group of Asian teachers, called the "presbyters," of whom Eusebius (Hist. III.1.3) reports: "Of this [I Peter] the elders of older time have made frequent use, as a work beyond dispute, in their own treatises."

Papias' contemporary Polycarp of Smyrna was clearly quoting this letter; the express statement of Eusebius (Hist. IV.14.9: "Polycarp in the said writing of his to the Philippians, extant to this day, has employed certain testimonies taken from the former epistle of Peter") is confirmed by the actual letter: Polyc. Phil. 1:3 (=I Pet. 1:8); 2:1 (=1:15, 21); 2:2 (=3:9); 6:3 (=3:13); 7:2 (=4:7); 8:1-2 (=2:22, 24); 10:2 (=2:12). Polycarp, however, does not mention the name of his source, nor does he even give these texts as quotations; they are simply incorporated in the sentences. Striking though this may seem to us,

Polycarp does the same with words of Paul; it was usual in antiquity to leave it to the hearers to recognize such citations. The date of Polycarp's letter is still in dispute (according to many scholars written in 117, according to others 135). But at any rate, one is allowed to say that *ca.* A.D. 125 I Peter was well known by leading churchmen in Asia Minor.

Other traces may be found in the writings of Gnostics like Basilides (*ca.* 125; see Clem. Misc. IV. 12.81) and the Eastern disciple of Valentinus, Theodotion (*ca.* 160; see Clem. *Excerpts from Theodotion* 12:3 [=I Pet. 1:18: "according to the Apostle"]; 12:2 [=I Pet. 1:12: "Peter says"]). Since here again it is difficult to determine in these *Excerpts* what belongs to the terminology of Clement, it is unsafe to rely completely upon this expression. On the other hand, Irenaeus offers a number of references in his *Against Heresies* (*ca.* 180); besides some general quotations, he remarks explicitly (IV.9.2): "Peter says in his epistle"; there follows I Pet. 1:18 (cf. also IV.16.5; V.7.2). Irenaeus lived in Gaul, but he had been born in Asia Minor. There he had known men like Polycarp. A little younger are Tertullian, who (*Scorpiace* 12) quotes I Pet. 2:20-21: "Peter said to the Pontians"; and Clement of Alexandria, who cites I Pet. 3:14 ff as a word of Peter (Clem. Misc. IV.7. 46). This is only one out of a great number of citations. Clement also commented on the letter in his *Outlines* (*Adumbrations*).

From this survey it appears that by 200 this letter was accepted as the work of the apostle Peter by the churches in various countries. It will be noted that the name of MARCION is missing in this list. This is striking, since he was from Pontus (cf. I Pet. 1:1), but his silence about I Peter can be explained by the assumption that he rejected it because of his distrust of Peter the Jew. That he did not know it is less probable. Neither is the letter found in the Muratorian Canon (*ca.* 200; *see* CANON, NT), but the omission may be due to the fragmentary state of this document. The great scholar Origen (died 253) wrote in his exposition of John 5 (see Euseb. Hist. VI.25.8) that "Peter . . . has left one acknowledged epistle, and, it may be, a second also; for it is doubted." This remark shows that in Origen's time our letter formed an undisputed part of the canon. So it continued to do everywhere except for a while in the Syriac church, although it was at last accepted there also, in contrast with II Peter and other Catholic letters. *See* CANON, NT.

From this survey we may conclude that I Peter has good credentials. By its author's name it is first quoted *ca.* 170; but since then it has never been disputed, as Hebrews and other books have been. It is used without citation of name in the first half of the second century; but the fact that the name is missing does not tell against the attribution of the letter to the apostle, in view of literary habits in antiquity. It makes its first appearance, as far as we can see, in Asia Minor, the area to which it had been sent.

From the point of textual criticism this writing does not offer particular features; the text is fairly well preserved. *See* TEXT, NT.

4. The readers. According to the address the letter is sent to the "exiles of the dispersion in Pontus, Galatia, Cappadocia, Asia, and Bithynia" (1:1). The ERV-ASV reads for "exiles" the word "sojourners," which seems to be preferable, although it must be conceded that the exact meaning of the Greek term is difficult to determine. In any case, the readers lived in certain well-defined parts of Asia Minor. These districts are enumerated in a rather strange order, running from NE through the middle to the W and the NW. It is remarkable that the letter is not dispatched to particular churches in this area. On the other hand, it should be observed that its address does not speak about Christians or Christianity in general (though the writer speaks of the "world-wide" movement [5:9]), but of those individuals who bear the Christian name (4:16), called "sojourners of the dispersion," in a clearly marked part of the world.

The word DISPERSION is well known from Jewish history. It was applied to those Jews who lived outside the Holy Land, among the Gentiles. It is supposed by almost all commentators that this was one of the many Jewish words taken over by the early Christians to describe the situation of the new people of God spread in all the world while their homeland was in heaven (cf. Phil. 3:20; Heb. 13:14; Jas. 1:1; etc.). This impression is strengthened by the words of 1:17; 2:11, where the readers are spoken of as living in the situation of aliens. The difficulty of this explanation is that "dispersion" is never used for the Christian church in early Christian literature (Jas. 1:1 is an extremely dark text). It is not very feasible to suggest that it was borrowed from the OT, because there it was always linked with the wrath of God against his disobedient people (which would be in flat contradiction with 1:14: "obedient children").

This word "dispersion," taken in its Jewish sense, has long been one of the main arguments for the opinion that the readers had been Jews by birth and were now converts to Christianity. From inscriptions and literary sources the existence of Jewish communities in these districts is proved. Another argument for this view is the extensive use made by the author of the OT, in both direct quotations and allusions, especially words like 2:9. This long-standing opinion, however, has been definitely abandoned since the beginning of the twentieth century. All students have reached an agreement that the people addressed had come into the church from paganism. Texts like 1:15 ("ignorance"); 1:18 ("the futile ways inherited from your fathers"; "futile" is a favorite word in the OT for "idols"); and especially 4:3 ("Let the time that is past suffice for doing what the Gentiles like to do") are conclusive.

These former pagans have given up their previous way of life and turned to the "living God." This change was experienced as the consequence of God's election and mercy (1:2-3; 2:10). It was a redemption by the blood of Christ (1:18-19). This conversion came about by the preaching of the word of God, announced by the OT prophets and "by those who preached the good news to you" (1:12)—the word which, according to Isa. 40:9, abides forever (1:25), and by which they are regenerated. They were "no people, but now [they] are God's people" (2:10). Although, strictly speaking, belonging to a passage directed to slaves, the words of 2:25 apply to all: "You were straying like sheep, but have now returned to the Shepherd and Guardian of your souls." Christ died to "bring us to God" (3:18); just as Noah was saved through water, they have been saved by baptism (3:21). They belong to a world-wide brotherhood (5:9) which is bound together by mutual love (1:22). This religious change meant a break with their own past (1:18) and with the habits of their environment (4:4). Therefore, they have become "aliens" in this world (2:11). Their present condition is not very happy, because they are slandered and abused (*see* § 5 *below*). Yet their situation is not hopeless or without good prospect. A deep tone of joy rings through this whole letter from beginning to end (cf. 1:3; 5:10). The writer, reminding his readers of the greatness of their new life in Christ, wants also to incite them to firmness in their faith and to behavior in agreement with their Christian calling. Surrounded by suspicion, their lives must be a witness of their religion. *See* § 8 *below*.

Nowhere are we told who was the first preacher of the gospel among them. The author himself does not seem to have any such special claim in this respect, as Paul asserted in Corinth (I Cor. 4:15). Their conversion came as the gift of God, the writer wishes to stress, and not as a deed of men.

5. Date. With other NT writings I Peter shares the lack of a direct indication about its date, as is true of many papyri. One must depend here on inward criteria, the interpretation of which is difficult and opens the way to many guesses. Not even the way to a relative chronology through references in contemporary writings is open.

The address mentions PETER the apostle of Jesus Christ as the author (1:1). If this is correct, the date must fall before 64 or 67, the probable year of Peter's death. But this name is considered fictitious by many scholars (*see* § 6 *below*), for the very reason that, in their view, the situation presupposed here must be later than 64. What was this situation? It is clear that it is very unpleasant. See 1:6-7: "Now for a little while you may have to suffer various trials . . . tested by fire" (cf. also 4:12; 5:9). This uneasy condition is not the consequence of their social status, as in the case of the slaves or the wives (2:18; 3:1 ff), but applies to all. It is not confined to the readers alone, but is shared by all Christians (5:9). The hardship of this ordeal is compared to fire—in the eyes of the writer it is a refining fire, a sharing in the sufferings of Christ; this comparison sufficiently reveals its heavy character. If one tries to ascertain more precisely what kinds of sufferings are involved, one notes at once the recurring references to slander and reviling. The Christians are looked upon as evildoers (2:12); they suffer unjustly (2:20); their good behavior is reviled (3:16-17). The readers are admonished not to "return evil for evil or reviling for reviling" (3:9), but to follow the example of their Master (2:21; 3:18). They must not be punished because of offenses against the civil order: "Let none of you suffer as a murderer, or a thief, or a wrongdoer, or a mischief-maker; yet if one suffers as a Christian, let him not be ashamed" (4:15-16). All this amounts to sufferings because of the new life they lead in Christ (punishments for transgression of the general social code are not considered as "sufferings" in the Christian sense; cf. 2:20; 4:15). Because the Christians do not join their pagan fellow men in wild profligacy (4:4), they have become outcasts.

Since it seems in 4:16 that to bear the name of CHRISTIAN is itself a crime, as it was in the second century according to the apologists, it has often been thought that official persecutions by the state authorities were threatening the Christians at the time of I Peter. On this supposition three possible dates offer themselves: (*a*) if the writer was Peter, it may be the persecution under Nero (64); (*b*) if the Petrine authorship is unlikely on other grounds, it could be that under Domitian (95); (*c*) whereas various parallels between I Peter and the famous letter of Pliny, the governor of Bithynia (cf. I Pet. 1:1) under Trajan, about the prosecutions of Christians in that district (*ca.* 110; Pliny X.96-97), can be detected, many critics have favored this date (e.g., Beare; *see bibliography*). Many pages have been devoted to the discussion of which of these three persecutions is reflected in the letter.

Actually, however, much of this discussion is beside the point, because the presupposition is wrong (*see bibliography* for works by Selwyn and Moule). No state persecution in any period is reflected in the letter. Three facts point to this conclusion: (*a*) In 5:9 it is said that the whole church throughout the world shares in the same sufferings; now, all the persecutions before the third century were more or less local; therefore, the sufferings must have another character. (*b*) In 2:13 ff a very positive relation with the state authorities is implied which is important even if it is part of catechetical instruction; the emperor and the governors are not decried, as in Revelation, and it is supposed that they will praise the Christians as good citizens, since they do good. (*c*) The sufferings all belong to the personal sphere; they are the results of evil feelings and hatred against people who do not follow the general line—i.e., a nonconforming minority who have become the victims of suspicion and slander. All this makes it impossible to look upon the difficult situation of the Christians addressed as if it had been brought about by state measures; it had more the character of a pogrom, which can be nerve-racking and hardly less difficult than open, official persecution. Most certainly it was a fierce trial of the faith. But once we rule out the possibility of identifying these sufferings with some particular persecution, we are left with no direct indication as to the date. The situation reflected in the letter could have happened at any time in the first or second century wherever a Christian group was found.

6. Authorship. The salutation explicitly mentions "Peter, an apostle of Jesus Christ" (1:1). There is no doubt that here the disciple of that name (*see* PETER) is intended. Unfortunately his whereabouts after the COUNCIL OF JERUSALEM and the meeting with Paul in Antioch (Gal. 2:11 ff) are unknown. He made missionary tours in the company of his wife (I Cor. 9:5), but where and how is hidden. This gap in our knowledge involves a period of *ca.* fifteen years! Ignorance makes it impossible to say what kind of relations existed between him and the communities or individuals to whom the letter was sent. It is nowhere claimed that he was their special apostle, and it is not clear, either, what induced him to write this letter except the general desire to fortify their faith. He does not defend his personal work or express his personal affection, as Paul often did.

It is completely obscure why this writing was sent to certain remote areas which, so far as we know, did not play an important part in first-century Christianity. This fact pleads strongly in favor of the authenticity of this salutation, for no reason can be found for the invention of these "sojourners of the dispersion" in, e.g., Pontus and Cappadocia (on the implications of Gal. 2:7, *see* § 7 *below*). In 5:13 the writer mentions his "son Mark," who cannot be other than the evangelist. Papias (Euseb. Hist. III. 39.15) declares that Mark (*see* MARK, JOHN) functioned as the "interpreter of Peter"—an activity which was important for the propagation of the gospel, since Peter as a Galilean fisherman would not have been well versed in Greek. This fact also strengthens the case for Peter as the author. In one text (5:1) the writer claims to be an eyewitness of the Lord's sufferings (other texts, such as 1:8, have not sufficient weight); this also points to a disciple and apostle. All these facts have long been sufficient reasons for accepting the veracity of the salutation and for considering Peter as the author—the more so because the early church (*see* § 3 *above*) did not hesitate to do so.

This view has, however, not passed unchallenged. Many NT scholars, especially in Germany and America—British scholarship was, on the whole, more conservative—discovered great difficulties in the traditional view and therefore considered the letter pseudonymous. In discussing these arguments we may disregard the wrong supposition about the so-called persecutions (*see* § 5 *above*) and the false argument taken from the mention of Silvanus (5:12; *see* SILAS). This prophet and companion of Paul, so ran the latter argument, could not have been in the company of Peter, who was looked upon as the great opponent of Paul. But we know too little about the history of the church in NT times to make such a judgment. The view that the early church was divided as between "parties" of Peter and Paul has been largely discredited. Other arguments deserve more serious attention.

The first of these is the claim that if the writer were the disciple of Jesus, it is unintelligible that he does not refer to words and deeds of his Master except for his death and resurrection. In 5:5-6 he expresses a thought found in Luke 14:11, but he formulates it, not in Jesus' words, but in those of Prov. 3:34. In 2:12 there is a parallel to Matt. 5:16, and in 3:9 a parallel to Matt. 5:39 ff; but in both cases no reference to the Lord appears. Christ's suffering is described with words from Isa. 53, rather than in terms more reminiscent of a disciple's experiences.

In answer to this argument it may be pointed out that the letter is much more concerned with the Cross and the Resurrection, because they created the new situation of grace, than with the earthly career of Jesus. It is the crucified and risen Lord, rather than the teacher of Galilee, who is the prime importance. The drawing of Jesus' sufferings with the words of Isa. 53 is due to the fact that this chapter so clearly sets out the meaning of his sufferings. A pseudonymous writer by the end of the first or the beginning of the second century would have been inclined to lay more stress upon the special relation of Peter with Jesus and would have quoted sayings of Jesus, since the gospels were then already in existence, in order to give his work more authority. In later Petrine stories various incidents of Peter's life are recounted as providing an example; but nothing of the kind is done here. Finally one may ask whether this argument does not start from the false presumption that the apostle would have written as we would expect him to do.

Secondly, it is urged that if the writer were the Jew Peter, he would have stressed obedience to the Mosaic law and other peculiarities of Judaism, whereas the law is actually not mentioned at all and the letter breathes the same atmosphere as those of Paul. The similarity is so great that I Peter is often ascribed to a follower of Paul who missed the deep spiritual insights and toned down the lofty ideas of his master. Typical Pauline expressions like "in Christ" (3:16; 5:10) are used; there are many points of contact and agreement in connection with the work of Christ. A detailed discussion of these points may be found in Selwyn's Commentary; and the upshot of it is that behind this correspondence lies, not Paul merely, but a common pattern of catechetical instruction. With regard to the relation between I Peter and Ephesians, C. L. Mitton (*see bibliography*) does not agree; he finds I Peter dependent upon EPHESIANS. Many other scholars would hold that the relation is not sufficiently close to prove dependence. The common elements can be explained by the fact that there was much "common ground" in the preaching and teaching of the gospel and that the similarity in the situation of the readers of the two letters must be taken into account.

A third argument against the Petrine authorship of this letter is the relative excellence of the Greek. It is not ordinary Koine (*see* GREEK LANGUAGE), but shows preference for a certain literary style. Semitisms or "mistranslations" are absent. It is incredible, some argue, that the Galilean fisherman who used an interpreter and was known as "uneducated" (Acts 4:13) had such a command of the Greek language that he could produce a document like this. This argument would be decisive were it not for 5:12, which reads: "By Silvanus, a faithful brother as I regard him, I have written." From these words it is clear that the author used the services of Silvanus (*see* SILAS), whom, he assures his readers, he considers absolutely trustworthy. What were these services? The word "by" may mean that Silvanus was the messenger who carried the letter; in this case no particular value can be attached to this note. But the "by" can refer to Silvanus' agency as the amanuensis who wrote the actual letter (cf. Dionysius of Corinth in Euseb. Hist. IV.23.11, where the same preposition is used of Clement as the secretary of the Roman church). This explanation is preferable. If Silvanus was merely the bearer of this letter, it would not be necessary to state this so expressly, even before the recapitulation and the greetings. On the other hand, the statement is perfectly intelligible if it was meant to prevent suspicions on the part of the readers of a letter in such perfect Greek from the "barbarian" Peter. To be sure, it was he who gave the general outline and leading thoughts; but it was Silvanus who put them into their proper Greek form.

Fourthly, it is argued that the writer's habit of quoting the OT in ways which point to his using the LXX rather than the MT is peculiar for a Jew in Palestine (*see* SEPTUAGINT; MASORA). But textual criticism of the OT (*see* TEXT, OT)—especially after the DEAD SEA SCROLLS—shows that the MT was one Hebrew text form among others, chosen for its value in the second century A.D., but not the only one. It could be that Peter's Hebrew text was much more akin to the text from which the LXX was made. Besides, a foreigner writing in another language will usually stick to the standard translation for literal quotations and not dare to change it to suit his own text. Finally, if Silvanus really served as an amanuensis, this consideration does not arise at all. Silvanus was a Greek, and his Bible would naturally have been the LXX.

None of these arguments by itself nor all of them taken together amount to proof against the authorship of Peter. On the other hand, it must be said that no proof in favor of it can be derived from a comparison between this letter and the speeches of Peter in Acts (chs. 2–5; 10), since it is yet undecided how far these speeches in Acts reflect the ideas of the author of the ACTS OF THE APOSTLES and how far they are expressions of a common stratum of early Christian teaching. On the whole, it must be said that the view which takes Peter as the author but sees him as using the services of Silvanus offers the most satisfactory explanation of the data of the letter. One small point may be noticed: in 5:14 the author uses "peace" instead of "grace," the usual term in the Pauline letters. This is decidedly more Semitic; does it point to a Jewish writer?

As to the place of writing, it may be pointed out that according to 5:13, "she who is at Babylon who is likewise chosen" sends her greetings together with Mark. The reference is evidently to the church in "Babylon" (*see* BABYLON [NT]). Practically all commentators regard the word as a sobriquet for Rome, as in Revelation; Sibylline Oracles V.143, 152; Apocalypse of Baruch IX.1. This explanation is supported by the fact that the only name of a dwelling place of Peter known to tradition was Rome, and that in the Eastern church nothing is said about a connection between Peter and Babylon (names of other missionaries are mentioned). Reasons for questioning this explanation are that elsewhere the writer never uses the cryptic language of apocalyptic writers; that it is closely linked with the hypothesis of state persecution (*see* § 5 *above*); that the list of countries in 1:1 runs from E to W, and our ignorance about Peter's travels makes it impossible bluntly to declare that a residence in Babylon, with its large Jewish communities (and Peter was the apostle to the circumcised [Gal. 2:9]), is excluded. Until further notice either possibility is still open.

7. Origin. It has been shown (*see* § 4 *above*) that the readers of I Peter were former Gentiles who had been converted to God and now belonged to his people, to which the epithets of Israel as a holy nation are applied (2:9-10). This result was brought about by the death of Christ, who died "that he might bring us to God" (3:18). This expression may seem somewhat pale to modern readers, but it was full of meaning in ancient times. It is a translation of the rabbinic *hiqrib,* which meant "to make proselytes"—i.e., to make pagans full members of the people of God. *See* PROSELYTE.

Careful reading of this letter reveals that this case of proselyte terminology does not stand alone. In various places parallels with expressions used by Philo, Josephus, and the rabbis with regard to the proselytes can be detected. E.g., the salutation contains a very strange "trinitarian" order ("Father . . . Spirit . . . Christ"), and at the end a clear reference to the blood of the covenant (Exod. 24:8)—not improbably an allusion to proselytes' being made members of the people of God. Again, the phrase "to be called from darkness to light," found in I Pet. 2:9 in connection with sayings about the "holy nation" or "God's own people," is also used by Philo in speaking of the transition from paganism to Judaism. Similarly the warning in 4:12: "Do not be surprised at the fiery ordeal . . . ," may be interpreted in the light of the fact that rabbis warned their converts that the Israel which they were joining was oppressed in this world. It was part of proselyte instruction that suffering was the lot of the chosen people.

The same background can be detected in 1:18-19. The usual interpretation finds here the merging of two images: the redemption of a slave and the offering of a lamb. Yet the passage is simple and clear if reference is being made to the sacrifice connected with a conversion. Later rabbinic sources hardly mention this sacrifice for proselytes, because after the destruction of the temple in A.D. 70 this part of the ceremony had gone out of use. For fuller discussion and other examples of proselyte terminology, *see bibliography.*

Perhaps the "sojourners of the dispersion" (*see* § 4 *above*) were the so-called "God-fearers" like Cornelius (Acts 10:2; cf. 13:16, 26; 16:14; 17:17; 18:7), pagans who lived on the fringe of the synagogues, but according to Jewish standards could not become full members, proselytes, and share in the benefits of Israel unless they were baptized, circumcised, and an offering for them was brought. It is interesting to see that in this letter, not the preaching of the only God stands in the center, but the glory and duties of the people of God. The readers must already have had instruction in the OT, since it is so freely used and was so obviously authoritative for them. They are assured by the writer that the sacrifice of Christ is absolutely satisfying; everything has been done "to bring them to God." Therefore, it is said: "Through him [Jesus Christ] you have confidence in God, who raised him from the dead and gave him glory, so that your faith and hope are in God" (1:21). But this membership is beset with dangers which may make these converts waver; therefore, he admonishes them to live according to the standards of God's people in freedom, but as slaves of God (2:16).

If the proposed exegesis of 1:18-19 is sound, it must be concluded that the proselyte offering stood still in force—i.e., the letter was written before A.D. 70. Peter had been specially commissioned for the Christian mission among the Jews (Gal. 2:7). His word as a spokesman of the Jewish part of the church, as the man who had consented to the abolition of the requirement of circumcision for the Gentiles (cf. Acts 10; 15), would carry great weight with these pagans who had been nourished in Judaism. Because this letter is addressed, not to churches as such, but to a special class of individuals who have had relations with the synagogue, Peter can speak even to some living in districts which belonged to Paul's missionary area. When the missionary situation of the middle of the first century, as we see it reflected in Acts, is taken into account (cf. Acts 2:9), this letter fits perfectly well into it. It was written, as the salutation says and the end suggests, by Peter, probably *ca.* A.D. 60.

8. Main theological ideas. The comparison of the ideas in I Peter with certain ideas in Paul's letters brings to light an important fact. They are not mere copies or repetitions, but rank alongside those of the Apostle to the Gentiles. In certain places, as in 1:20; 3:18, the tone of a confession of faith is heard. It has been well pointed out that the primitive kerygma and didache are reflected in the phraseology of this writing. The letter wishes to bring home to its readers what is the "grace" into which they have come by their conversion. This new situation, graphically described as a transition from darkness to light, rests upon God's election, mercy, and calling (1:2; 2:10). It had been announced by the prophets of the OT (1:10 ff), effectuated by Jesus' work, and preached in the gospel. All these things have been prepared from the beginning of the world, but now "at the end of the times" it has been completely revealed in the coming of Jesus Christ (1:20). This is the great turning point, the decisive step in God's salvation of the world. The time of the writer and his readers is the end of times. A strong eschatological note pervades the whole letter; "the end of all things is at hand" (4:7). This implies the final judgment by Him who judges without respect of persons (1:17; 2:23); and this moment of judgment is near by (4:6), just as the salvation is "ready to be revealed in the last time" (1:5). All this makes the teaching and preaching the more earnest. The writer does not give a number of wise proverbs or pious sayings; but since the hour is pressing, all things have come into a decisive stage. Time is hastening to its end; the sufferings which befall the Christians will not last long (1:6; 5:10), because the present world order to which these sufferings belong is quickly passing away.

The foundation of the teaching is Jesus' death and glorification as the risen Lord. By his sacrificial death he took away sins and opened the way to God (1:18; 2:24; 3:18). By his resurrection and entrance into the glory of God (cf. Luke 24:26) his followers are assured that they, sharing in his sufferings, will also share in his glory (4:13; cf. Rom. 8:17; II Tim. 2:12). This coming glory means salvation (1:9), which fills the hearts with joy (1:6). In glowing terms (1:3 ff) the future blessedness is described; but this is still the period of faith and hope (1:21; cf. vss. 3, 9). The saving power of Jesus' work is preached in the world as the good news (1:12, 25). By some it is rejected; they are the disobedient (2:8; 3:1; 4:17) and will receive punishment. But the readers have become "obedient children" (1:14); they believe in Jesus (2:4) and will not be put to shame. They have become new men and women, "regenerated" (1:3, 23; 2:1) by the resurrection of Christ. This new life expresses itself in a new behavior, a readiness for the service of God (1:13 ff) in holiness and brotherly love.

As regards the character of this new life, the author emphasizes two main themes. The former is that of steadfastness in suffering, which is to be expected and which must be firmly borne. But in spite of this emphasis, the outlook of this letter is not gloomy. Belief in Christ means rejoicing "with unutterable and exalted joy" (1:8). "Rejoice in so far as you share Christ's sufferings, that you may also rejoice and be glad when his glory is revealed" (4:13). Christ Jesus is not only the foundation of their salvation, but also the example: "that you should follow in his steps" (2:21; cf. 3:18 ff). Suffering in the flesh means being set free from sins: "Since therefore Christ suffered in the flesh [to take away the sins], arm yourselves with the same thought, for whoever has suffered in the flesh has ceased from sin" (4:1; cf. Rom. 6:7; both reflect a Jewish theological thought). Those who suffer are blessed, because they may be sure of the coming blessing. God himself will give them strength (5:10). Hearts may be fainting, but they must be sober and watchful (1:13; 5:8), full of hope amid the tribulations.

The second theme is that of good behavior (a phrase which occurs in this letter as many times as in the rest of the NT). It recurs after 2:11 in all sections till 4:19. These "good works" are not those of later Judaism, such as special deeds on behalf of the poor, the dead, etc.; nor are they those of the later Christian church, such as fasting, etc.; but they are right attitudes toward all one's fellow men, including even a slave's attitude toward his master (2:18 ff). The excellence of such good works will be praised by the authorities (2:14). They may have missionary power (3:1) and serve to stop slander (2:15); and in the day of judgment it will become manifest that the Christians performed them in the service of God Almighty (2:12). The Christians, redeemed by Jesus Christ, may live as free men, but this freedom is not license, but holiness (1:15; 2:16). Their character expresses itself, on the one hand, in the rejection of former vices toward their neighbors such as malice, guile, insincerity (2:1), and, on the other hand, in true love toward their brethren (1:22) and in tenderness and humble-mindedness (3:8; 5:6). The demand for such life is set before them in the word of God (Ps. 34:12 ff; cf. I Pet. 3:10-12)—and as a general rule, not as an endless code of rules. This righteousness is the essential condition of attaining the goal. And although notwithstanding these good works they may be subject to reviling, they will have a good conscience and can make a defense about the hope that is in them (3:15). So their life and work as disciples of Christ will be a continual glorification of God: "that you may declare the wonderful deeds of him who called you out of darkness into his marvelous light" (2:9). They themselves glorify God, because their sufferings (4:16) and their service (4:11) are for Christ's sake, and at the end even the Gentiles will be won over (2:12). Therefore, they are a holy priesthood which offers spiritual sacrifices (2:5; cf. Rom. 12:1). This offering is not only prayer, but the complete daily service of their lives. They who are called "sojourners of the dispersion," without any rights according to Jewish standards, thus come to be called by the highest names—names reserved for the people of God. Set apart to be God's own people in the highest sense, they live in this world expecting the glorious revelation of the fulness of God's kingdom.

As an element in Christology (*see* CHRIST), this letter has (3:18-19; 4:6) the remarkable teaching of Christ's DESCENT INTO HADES, thus bearing testimony to the all-embracing power of the work of Christ, who now reigns over all powers. In glowing words the writer sets forth the greatness of the Christian faith in Jesus Christ, the Suffering Servant (*see* SERVANT OF THE LORD) and glorified Lord (*see* LORD [CHRIST]); the greatness of the Christian hope amid adversities; the greatness of Christian love. The letter combines in a marvelous way faith and works; it is an exposition of dogmatic truth with attention to its direct impact upon ordinary life. The burning gratitude for all God gave in Jesus Christ will exhibit itself, according to this writer, in a lofty way of life—life to the glory of God.

Bibliography. Commentaries: (*a*) English: C. Biggs (2nd ed., 1902); J. H. A. Hart (1910); J. Moffatt (1928); J. W. C. Wand (1934); E. G. Selwyn (1946); F. W. Beare (1947); A. M. Hunter and E. G. Homrighausen, *IB*, vol. XII (1957). (*b*) German: R. Knopf (7th ed., 1912); G. Wohlenberg (3rd ed., 1923); W. Wrede (4th ed., 1932); F. Hauck (5th ed., 1949); H. Windisch and H. Preisker (3rd ed., 1951). (*c*) French: U. Holzmeister (1937). (*d*) Dutch: S. Greydanus (1929). (*e*) Norwegian: L. Bryn (1949). See also Introductions to the NT by Moffatt, Zahn, Jülicher and Fascher, Feine and Behm, De Zwaan, McNeill and Williams, Wikenhauser, and Michaelis.

Special studies: R. Perdelwitz, *Die Myserienreligionen und das Problems des I. Petrusbriefes* (1911). T. Spörri, *Der Gemeindegedanke im ersten Petrusbrief* (1925). For discussion and examples of proselyte terminology, see W. C. van Unnik, *De Verlossing I Petrus 1:18-19 en het probleem van den eersten Petrusbrief* (1942). B. Reicke, *The Disobedient Spirits and Baptism* (1946). W. Bieder, *Grund und Kraft der Mission nach dem I. Petrusbrief* (1950). On the relation between Ephesians and I Peter, see C. L. Mitton, *The Epistle to the Ephesians* (1951). W. Brandt, "Wandel als Zeugnis nach dem I. Petrusbrief," in W. Foerster, ed., *Verbum Dei manet in aeternum* (1953). F. L. Cross, *I Peter, a Paschal Liturgy* (1954). W. C. van Unnik, "The Teaching of Good Works in I Peter," *NTS*, I (1954), 92-110. E. Lohse, "Paränese und Kerygma im I. Petrusbrief," *ZNW*, XLV (1954), 68-69. C. F. D. Moule, "The Nature and Purpose of I Peter," *NTS*, III (1956), 1-11. E. Boismard, "Une liturgie baptismale dans la *Prima Petri*," *RB*, LXIII (1956), 182-208; LXIV (1957), 161-83.

W. C. VAN UNNIK

PETER, GOSPEL OF. A passion gospel, current in Syria and Egypt in the second half of the second century, purporting to have been written by Peter and evidencing a distinctly Docetic view of the relationship between the divine Christ and the human Jesus, as well as a markedly anti-Jewish bias.

Until the end of the nineteenth century this writing was known to us through the preservation by Eusebius of a portion of a refutation of it by Serapion, bishop of Rhossus. The latter had earlier known that this book was being read by Christians, but, when subsequently informed of its true nature, wrote a tract "Concerning What Is Known of the Gospel of Peter." In the passage preserved by Eusebius (Hist. VI.12), Serapion charges that the writing was composed by the Docetists. Origen also refers to a book by this title, which, he says, with the "book of James" indicates that the brothers of Jesus were the sons of Joseph by a former marriage (*On Matthew* X.17). Theodoret (*Of Heretical Fables* II.2) mentions a book bearing this title as in use by the Nazarenes, "who regard Christ as a righteous man."

In 1886 a considerable fragment of this writing was found in a tomb at Akhmim in Upper Egypt, together with a portion of the Apocalypse of Peter and thirty-two chapters in Greek of the book of Enoch. This fragment, published in 1892, begins abruptly with the words: "But of the Jews no man washed his hands, neither did Herod nor anyone of his judges," recounts the crucifixion of Jesus as due entirely to the hostility of the Jews, and explicitly remarks that the Lord "kept silence, as one feeling no pain," only subsequently to cry out "aloud saying, 'My power, my power, thou hast forsaken me.' And when he had so said, he was taken up." Then follows a description of the descent of two figures from heaven (in the presence of the guards at the tomb) who entered the tomb and brought Jesus out. Their heads reached to heaven, but Jesus "overpassed the heaven." The cross followed the three, and in answer to a query from heaven: "Hast thou preached to them that sleep?" replied: "Yea." After a brief account of the women at the tomb the next morning and their flight in fear, the fragment closes with the intriguing words: "But I, Simon Peter, and Andrew my brother, took our nets and went unto the sea; and there was with us Levi the son of Alphaeus, whom the Lord. . . ."

Dependence upon all four of our canonical gospels (including John 21) is unmistakable, while the words "Then the women were affrighted and fled," suggest that the author's copy of Mark ended with 16:8. The variations from the canonical accounts are all of the nature of interpretation: the transfer of complete responsibility for the tragedy to the malice of the Jews; and the sharp distinction between the superhuman Christ ("my power"), who ascended from the cross, and the earthly Jesus.

To what extent the present fragment represents the original Gospel of Peter it is hard to say. It is clear that it is a complete copy of a fragment, which in turn also began *in medias res*. The present fragment (eighth century) gives no indication of the section referred to by Origen (*see above*); the statement by Theodoret that a "Gospel of Peter" was in use by the Nazarenes, if correct, most certainly does not refer to the present so strongly anti-Jewish writing.

The manifest use of the fourfold gospel would make any date before 125 unlikely; its use in Rhossus, as attested by Serapion, would make any date after 175 impossible. Its use by Justin Martyr, occasionally hazarded on the basis of possible similarities and phraseology, is, at best, far from certain. The most probable date is the third decade of the second century. *See also* APOCRYPHA, NT; PETER, APOCALYPSE OF.

Bibliography. A convenient translation of the fragment is printed by M. R. James, *The Apocryphal NT* (1924), pp. 90-

94, while a working bibliography of studies which this intriguing fragment has occasioned is given by J. Quasten, *Patrology* (1950), I, 114-15. M. S. ENSLIN

PETER, PASSION OF. A late revision in Latin of the Martyrdom of Peter, which stood as the concluding section of the Acts of Peter (*see* PETER, ACTS OF). The Passion of Peter has been attributed to Linus, by tradition Peter's successor as bishop of Rome. This Latin rescript, no earlier than the sixth century, follows largely the traditional Martyrdom, but adds some details. In addition to naming the jailers, it records the somewhat complicated vision which occurred at the time of Peter's crucifixion: "angels standing with crowns of the flowers of roses and lilies, and upon the top of the upright cross Peter standing and receiving a book from Christ, and reading from it the words which he was speaking."

M. S. ENSLIN

PETER, PREACHING OF. An early handbook of mission preaching, attributed to Peter and in keeping with the Lord's command to go into all the world and preach the gospel (Matt. 28:19-20; Acts 1:8).

It is dismissed by Eusebius (Hist. III.3.1-4), together with three other writings ascribed to Peter, with the word: "We have no knowledge at all in catholic tradition, for no orthodox writer [ἐκκλησιαστικὸς συγγραφεύς] of the ancient time or of our own has used these testimonials."

Clement of Alexandria, despite Eusebius, knew it, accepted it as genuine, and made several extended quotations from it, not improbably thereby giving an essential epitome of its contents. The twelve apostles are directed to go into all the world that men should know that there is one God and to declare by faith in Christ that those who hear and believe may be saved (Misc. VI.6). If any of Israel repent so as to believe in God through Christ, they shall be forgiven. After twelve years the apostles are to go to the Gentile world (VI.5). We must not worship God after the manner of the Greeks, with idols and deified animals, nor after the manner of the Jews, who, though they claim alone to know God, do not know him but serve angels and keep days and seasons; rather, we are to worship him in a new way, in accord with the new covenant he has made with us, "for the ways of the Greeks and Jews are old, but we are they that worship him in a new way, in a third generation [race], even Christians." Whatever we do in ignorance God will forgive (VI.6). The grounds of Christian belief are clearly established in the prophets who predicted his coming, death, resurrection, and ascension unto heaven; which prophecies we know are commanded by God, "and without the Scriptures we say nothing" (VI.15).

Thus this little writing—if we may trust Clement's seemingly full epitome—would seem to have been a forerunner of such apologies as those of Aristides and Quadratus, although the assumption, often made, that these latter embody its contents is rash. Origen (*On John* 13:17) repeats a quotation made by Heracleon (*ca.* 180) from this writing, and is noncommittal as to its Petrine authorship. Origen also knew a Teaching of Peter, which contained the word: "I am no bodiless spirit," which Jerome mentions as being found in the Gospel According to the Hebrews (*see* HEBREWS, GOSPEL ACCORDING TO THE). That Origen considered the Preaching and the Teaching the same book, while often assumed, is far from certain. The detailed warning against the worship of animals (including weasels, mice, cats, dogs, and apes), together with Clement's seeming firsthand knowledge of it, would suggest Egypt as a likely source of origin.

There would seem no real reason to identify this little booklet, which apparently had but limited circulation, with the expanded "Preachings of Peter," which bulk so large in the late Clementine fictions known as the *Homilies* and *Recognitions*. *See bibliography.*

See also APOCRYPHA, NT.

Bibliography. Occasionally the identification of the Preaching of Peter and the Preachings of Peter, central to the claims of F. C. Baur and his disciples, has been reasserted, notably by H. J. Schoeps, *Theologie und Geschichte des Judenchristentums* (1949), who contends that the early apocryphon was not only a real source for these romances but also is epitomized in *Recognitions* III.75. M. R. James, *The Apocryphal NT* (1924), pp. 16-19, provides an assembly of possible quotations.

M. S. ENSLIN

PETER, SECOND LETTER OF. A letter said to have been written by the apostle Peter to the church at large in order to combat doubts growing out of the delay of the Parousia. The letter is the latest one of the NT, and its canonicity was long in doubt. Yet it is an important work, on both theological and historical grounds. The theological importance rests on the facts that (*a*) its presence in the canon raises sharply the issues of the "apostolic" authority and unity of the NT canon; (*b*) it has provided the church with a rationale to deal with the delay of the Parousia while retaining a doctrine of the destruction of the world at the time of the Last Judgment. The letter is important for historical reasons because it gives a picture of the period of transition from the primitive church to the early Catholic church of the second century.

1. Authorship, style, and canonicity. It is clear that although the author wants to convey the impression that he is writing a letter (3:1), the epistolary character of his work is not emphasized. Its destination cannot be ascertained, since the letter is truly a Catholic letter—i.e., it is addressed to the church at large: "to those who have obtained a faith of equal standing with ours in [by means of] the righteousness of our God and [of the] Savior Jesus Christ" (1:1). This impression is confirmed by the absence of epistolary marks at the conclusion, which is a doxology to Jesus Christ. (It should be noted that except for II Tim. 4:18 this forms the only clear doxology to Christ in the NT.)

But though the epistolary character is not emphasized, the Petrine authorship is conspicuously and sonorously stressed: "Simon Peter [Συμεών, found elsewhere only in Acts 15:14], a servant and apostle of Jesus Christ" (1:1). The prince of the apostles is the authoritative voice which speaks to the church in this his second letter (3:1)—a clear reference to I Peter—to remind the church of the "predictions of the holy prophets and the commandment of the Lord and Savior through your apostles." He is in a position to write authoritatively, since he has been a witness of Christ's glorification on the "holy mountain" (1:18). And, as if to stress the solidarity of all the apostles, Paul is called his "beloved brother" (3:15). The author has adopted the name of the foremost apostle, Peter, to enhance the authority of his letters—a practice not unknown in the early church. We have evidence of a rich Petrine literature. Fragments of a Gospel of Peter, an Acts of Peter, and an Apocalypse of Peter have survived (*see* PETER, GOSPEL OF; PETER, ACTS OF; PETER, APOCALYPSE OF). II Peter belongs to this class of literature. Both internal and external evidence show with cumulative force the impossibility of ascribing the letter to Peter, the disciple and apostle.

The author addresses Hellenistic-Christian churches which must have been established for some time, since the first generation of Christians has died (3:4). In view of Peter's martyrdom in Rome *ca.* A.D. 64, it is difficult to imagine that at so early a date the situation described in II Peter prevailed.

The only explicit reference to I Peter is to be found in 3:1, where the author refers to II Peter as his second letter. If I Peter is unauthentic and is to be dated in the beginning of the second century A.D., it follows that II Peter is likewise not a product of the apostolic era. If, however, I Peter is authentic, no theory of secretarial aid (*see* PETER, FIRST LETTER OF) can explain the differences in style and thought between I and II Peter.

The author presupposes the collection of the Pauline letters and their Gnostic interpretation (3: 15-16). He may know the fourfold gospel (1:16-17) and seems to attribute canonical value to other writings besides the OT (3:16).

All of the Letter of Jude (*see* JUDE, LETTER OF) is virtually incorporated in II Peter 2. Since Jude is most certainly a post-apostolic writing, the apostolic origin of II Peter can be defended only on the basis that Jude borrowed from II Peter. However, that II Peter is the borrower is evident from the fact that Jude is intelligible without II Peter, while certain sentences of II Peter require a knowledge of Jude in order to be understood—i.e., the reference to "angels" in II Pet. 2:11 is unintelligible without the reference to Michael in Jude 9, and II Pet. 2:17 requires the reference to the stars of Jude 13 in order to make sense. Moreover, the author mixes up Jude's imagery—it is more appropriate for "wandering stars" (Jude 13) to be imprisoned in darkness than for "waterless springs" (II Pet. 2:17). He improves upon Jude's chronology (Jude 2:4-10) in the sequence angels, Flood, Sodom and Gomorrha (cf. Jude 5-7), and overcomes the judgment theme in Jude by emphasizing the rescue of the faithful ones (Noah with seven other persons and Lot), illustrating thereby his parenetic concern for his addressees. The author makes out of the general reference of Jude 17-18: "the predictions of the apostles of our Lord Jesus Christ," a specific one, by adopting the high authority of the apostle Peter (3:1-2). But by the time the author writes, pseudepigraphical references have become suspect. He omits, therefore, the references to the ASSUMPTION OF MOSES and to Enoch (*see* ENOCH, BOOK OF) in Jude 9-10, 14-15. Pseudonymity shines through when the author forgets his own Petrine status and stature in adopting Jude 17 in the awkward Greek of II Pet. 3:2: "that you should remember the predictions of the holy prophets and the commandment of the Lord and Savior through your apostles."

With regard to style and language, it has been said that "II Peter is perhaps the only book of the NT whose language profits from being translated." Clumsy sentence constructions, an artificial Atticism, and a preference for Hellenistic expressions and thought-forms—especially those of the mystery religions—abound. It seems clear that a second-century author is at work here, rather than a Palestinian of the first generation.

A look at the canonical history of II Peter can only confirm its unauthentic nature as this was established by internal criticism. The first explicit reference to II Peter occurs in Origen (A.D. 217-51), and only once. "Peter left one epistle which is acknowledged [*homologoumenen*], but there is also a second one. This one however is doubtful" (Commentary on John 5:3). Before Origen, the letter has not left any sure traces. Neither the Muratorian Canon, Tertullian, nor Cyprian mentions it. Clement of Alexandria does not refer to it in his extant writings, although Eusebius states (Hist. VI.14.1) about Clement's Outlines: "He gave concise explanations of all the canonical scriptures not passing over even the disputed writings such as Jude and the remaining Catholic epistles and the Epistle of Barnabas and the Apocalypse known as Peter's." Not even implicit references in the Apostolic Fathers or Apologists are of such a nature as to establish an acquaintance with II Peter. Eusebius (Hist. III.25.3) pronounces it "disputed, but familiar to the majority." After Origen, it is mentioned in Asia Minor by Firmilian in a letter to Cyprian and also by Methodius; then in the West by Jerome, who registers the doubts of many, yet states: "Peter wrote two epistles which are called Catholic." From the fourth century on (Athanasius, Augustine, and the third Council of Carthage [397]), it is accepted as canonical. In the Syrian church it was excluded generally until the sixth century.

The canonical history of II Peter is the weakest of all the NT books. Its place in the canon must be regarded as the test case, not only for the historical, but also for the theological, validity of a NT canon.

2. Purpose and date. The purpose of the letter is clearly expressed in 3:4, where the author cites his opponents: "Where is the promise of his coming? For ever since the fathers fell asleep, all things have continued as they were from the beginning of creation." To combat this skepticism and to defend the Parousia, with its accompanying judgment, is the sole intent of the author. II Peter, then, is an apology for early Christian eschatology. Although only the last chapter is explicitly devoted to this purpose, the first two chapters cannot be understood unless seen in the light of the parousia discussion.

The theological and historical importance of this letter then can be assessed only if we see it in the context of the situation out of which it arose. Internal and external criticism seem to point to a date around the middle of the second century. The difficulty in understanding the letter against its background lies in the historical obscurity of this period. Several attempts have been made to identify the opponents with names of well-known heresiarchs such as Cerinthus, Marcus, Marcion, etc., and to locate the letter in a specific area of the Roman Empire (*see* JUDE, LETTER OF). An ultimate judgment on these matters is impossible because of the nature of the polemics it carries on, and the pseudonymity of the letter itself. Yet several significant features can be ascertained which would point to a more definite stage within the fluid history of the second-century church in which the letter may have to be located:

a) The style and language of the letter show an indebtedness to the religious language of Hellenistic Roman culture and to an ideology which is in the midst of a "Hellenization of the Christian church." A doctrine of immortality, a submersion into the divinity, is mixed with the traditional Jewish apocalyptic language of the early church.

b) The orthodoxy of the author and the way he appeals to apostolicity and a legitimate ministry point to the postapostolic era in which the church began to formulate criteria of authenticity and legitimacy. Peter, the Twelve, and Paul form the exclusive apostolic authority, and this authority is based on a criterion of apostolicity which is close to that of Acts 1:21 ff. The kerygma is hardened into a sacred history which only the apostles can guarantee and safeguard. The appeal to the "established truth" (1:12) is the apostolic testimony in objective propositional form. Apostolicity, then, is the criterion of truth—not only inasmuch as it safeguards the gospel tradition, but also because it guarantees the correct interpretation of scripture (1:20; 3:5). The canon seems established: the fourfold gospel may be a fact; the collection of the Pauline letters certainly is, also Gnostic interpretations thereof. The apostolic canon must be protected by apostolic authoritative interpretation against false interpretations.

c) The first generation of Christians has died. Heretics are in abundance and have seemingly the majority (πολλοὶ [2:2]) of the church behind them. It is unclear whether they still belong to the church or have already organized themselves in separate groups (2:13). The situation is not dissimilar from that of Jude (*see* JUDE, LETTER OF), while that of I John, where the heretics have definitely been ousted, is not yet present. The letter may actually give a true picture of the confusing state of the church in Asia Minor, just prior to the formulation of definite criteria of orthodoxy. Bauer has shown that the status of "unorthodox" as over against "orthodox" churches may have been unsettled at that time.

d) The Gnostics are, in all probability, closely linked to the Marcionite wing of the movement. The reference to a perverted interpretation of the Pauline corpus may well be seen in this light, and would yield a picture similar to that of the Pastoral letters, where Marcionites seem explicitly mentioned (I Tim. 6:20). The attempt to claim "our beloved brother Paul" for orthodoxy may have been a dire necessity, if we remember the peculiar silence about Paul in general in the second-century church prior to Irenaeus and Hippolytus. This silence was due to the appropriation of Paul by proto-Gnostics and Gnostics (e.g., Marcion and Basilides), who also wrote the first commentaries on the Gospel of John (cf. Heracleon and Ptolemaeus). The kerygma of the Gnostics percolates at times through the abusive language of the author: "freedom" (ἐλευθερία; 2:19); "corruptibility" (φθόρα; 2:19); "gnosis" (cf. the antithesis, ἐπιγνώσις [1:2-3, 8; 2:20; 3:18]); emancipation from the rule of angels (κυριοτης, δόξαι; 2:10)—i.e., the angels and powers which dominate the world of matter (2:10-12). Their pneumatic freedom is interpreted as ethical licentiousness and their teachers as men of greed—which may rest on fact, if we take into account the ethical consequences the Gnostics at times drew from their pneumatic freedom. The contempt for an eschatological future and, in connection with it, for an earthly realization of the kingdom would follow from their interpretation of eschatology. They probably held this in the form of an eschatology realized in their pneumatic existence, an emphasis we find already in the Corinthian letters and in II Tim. 2:18. The stress of the author on perseverance and "gnosis" as ethical discipline, become intelligible in the face of this. These factors, then, point to a date *ca.* 150 and to Asia Minor or Syria as the seedbed of early Gnosticism.

3. Contents. The letter may be outlined around the theme of the promise of the Parousia, as follows:

I. Greeting, 1:1-2
II. Preface: the promises of God (to the apostles?) are great and wonderful, but require a virtuous life, 1:3-11
III. The promise stands sure, 1:12-21
   A. On the basis of the apostolic eyewitness to the glorification of Jesus on the Mountain, vss. 12-18
   B. On the basis of OT prophecy, vss. 19-21
IV. Those who attack the promise are doomed, ch. 2
V. The "apocalypse of Peter": refutation of those who deny and doubt the promise, 3:1-13
VI. Final exhortations, 3:14-18

The greeting (1:1-2) suggests the emphases of the letter: (*a*) apostolic authority; (*b*) the true knowledge of Christ (ἐπιγνώσις) over against the Gnostic opponents who confuse the church with their false knowledge, "gnosis."

The true knowledge of Christ has been communicated to the apostles (1:3-11). The promises form an integral element of it by which we will attain to the divine nature. This seems to be the content of the awkward third verse—difficult in construction and vague in content. The author does not show how the participation in the divine nature is consistent with his apocalyptic outline in 3:1-13 (cf. vs. 13: "According to his promise we wait for new heavens and a new earth in which righteousness dwells"). The change of the personal pronoun in 1:4 should be noticed, for it may indicate that the "we" of the preceding verses refers to an exclusive apostolic privilege (vs. 3), granted by the divine and sinless Jesus (cf. 1:17).

The expectation of new heavens and a new earth clothed with righteousness, which follows Jewish apocalyptic linear-temporal thinking, cannot be easily harmonized with the dualistic Hellenistic antithesis of "divine nature" (θεία φύσις) and the transitory corruptibility (φθόρα) of this world. For this introduces a spatial eschatology of a Philonic-Platonic type. The condition for participation in this divine world is a gnosis which, contrary to the ill-founded speculations of the opponents, is communicated through apostolic authority and exhibits itself, not in esoteric truth, but in outward ethical behavior: a catena of Hellenistic virtues is introduced as the embodiment of the gnosis of Jesus Christ (vss. 5-8). It would seem that in face of the protracted parousia delay and the mocking attacks by the opponents, "Peter" emphasizes self-discipline and perseverance ("self-control" and "steadfastness") within the context of the unity of the church. The unity of the church is threatened and torn apart by opponents from within and without.

The following verses (9 ff) show that vss. 3-11 are reminiscent of the characteristic NT attitude with respect to Christian life between the Resurrection and the return of Christ. It is marked by the dynamic tension of the "already" and the "not yet." This tension is expressed by the dialectic of an imperative based on an indicative. The indicative of God's redemptive act in Christ is complemented by the imperative of ethical action in correspondence with it. "Peter" wants to indicate that church members are in error if they forget the imperative of ethical action (vs. 9 shows that they—i.e., the ones cleansed from their old sins—are the heretics, and not outsiders). But since the call and election of vs. 10 are left vague and seem to refer to the futuristic promises and glory of the kingdom (vss. 3-4)—since, in other words, the indicative is not clearly grounded in a christological present—the theological depth of the indicative-imperative correlation is misunderstood and approximates a new legalism, in which the ethical virtues of vss. 5 ff become an "entrance Torah" (cf. εἴσοδος [vs. 11]) for the kingdom. This conviction is heightened by the doctrine of forgiveness of prebaptismal sins, which, because of the absence of the power of the Holy Spirit in II Peter, effects an ethical rigorism of Judaistic color.

The promise stands secure (1:12-21). There can be no doubt about it. The growing disruption within the church (cf. πολλοὶ [2:2]) is encountered, not by theological debate, but by historical criteria of authenticity which must safeguard the church against dangerous heretical inroads. The author makes it abundantly clear that the apostle Peter was aware of impending heresies (3:3) and that he has left his letter as a testament to the church which must put beyond any doubt the orthodox teaching about the end and the Parousia. The prophetic element of 2:1 shows the utopian view the author has of the pristine purity of the apostolic church. The security of orthodox teaching rests both on the witness of scripture and on that of apostolic ear- and eye-witness. This section (1:12-21) betrays a possible knowledge of the four gospels: the reference to Peter's "exodus" (vs. 15) may refer to John 21; the transfiguration scene to the Synoptic account. It may be that the author is acquainted, not only with the collection of the Pauline letters (3:15-16), but with the fourfold gospel as well, which would indicate a post-Marcionite date for his letter. It is more probable, however, that the author has recourse to a (lost) oral tradition. The author changes his pronoun again to a solemn "we" as in the opening verses: the authority of the Twelve stands behind the message of the church.

The ground for the authority of the Twelve and Peter as their foreman rests in their presence at the transfiguration of Christ. The scene is described as a Hellenistic initiation rite. The mysteries are disclosed: the holy mountain (vs. 18), the initiates (ἐπόπται), the divine majesty (μεγαλειότης; vs. 16), and the metamorphosis of the cult hero (τιμὴν καὶ δόξαν; vs. 17). The importance of the scene for the author is twofold: the transfiguration of Christ is the earthly anticipation of his heavenly glory, and this anticipation makes the coming fulfilment of the Parousia sure, when again Christ will come in heavenly glory, but then publicly manifesting what had been a secret vision to the privileged few on the Mountain. The Transfiguration is an earthly, historical fact, and the author has been a witness to this fact, which was both seen and heard. Just as the voice on the Mountain carried divine authority, so the voice of the one who bears witness to it must be heard with equal deference. Peter, then, witnesses to the resurrection appearance as an objective historical phenomenon which will guarantee the Parousia. The apostolic witness is affirmed by scripture: the messianic promises of the OT have been vindicated by the transfiguration of Christ. In the same manner, the promises contained in the proleptic realization of the heavenly glory on the Mountain will be fulfilled in the final glory of the kingdom. For this reason the prophetic word is "made more secure." An attack on heretical interpretations of the OT follows—possibly alluding to Gnostic interpretations of the creation stories and genealogies of the OT. Just as apostolic authority guarantees the gospel message, so this same apostolic authority guarantees the interpretation of scripture. The principle seems to be: only like knows like. The pneumatic authority of the apostles alone is capable of expounding the pneumatic authority of the OT prophets (cf. I Pet. 1:11).

The attack against an individualistic and speculative interpretation of the OT (1:16-21) forms the introduction to a vehement defamation of the Gnostics (ch. 2). The author has incorporated Jude in this chapter (*see* § 1 *above*) along the following lines: (*a*) general description of heretics (vss. 1-3; cf. Jude 4); (*b*) three OT examples—the fall of the angels, Noah and the Deluge, Lot and Sodom and Gomorrha (vss. 4-9; cf. Jude 5-7); (*c*) sins against the flesh and against authorities (vss. 10-12; cf. Jude 8-10); (*d*) licentiousness (vss. 13-14; cf. Jude 12); (*e*) OT examples (vss. 15-16; cf. Jude 11); (*f*) illustrations from nature (vs. 17; cf. Jude 12*b*); (*g*) spiritual pride (vs. 18; cf. Jude 16*c*).

This section is characteristic of the polemics of the second century: abusive language, in which the opponents are especially blamed for sexual offenses and greed, follows a pattern of heresiological polemics. This general pattern does two things: (*a*) it makes it difficult to draw any conclusions as to the nature of the opposition (*see* JUDE, LETTER OF), and (*b*) it shows the intellectual shallowness of the author. Abuse replaces debate. The successfulness of the Gnostics may have been one of the reasons for this polemical style. Likewise, the close association of idolatry and adultery in early Christian teaching may be responsible for the emphasis on sexual perversity. It is apparent that the author addresses recent converts (vs. 18) who have slipped away or are in the process of doing so, and the reference to *apatai* (ἀπάται, "deceits") may be a pun on the separatist *agapai* (ἀγάπαι, "love feasts") of the heretics.

In 3:1-13 the real purpose of the author becomes plain. The groundwork has been laid for his apology for Christian eschatology. The legitimacy and authority of his witness have been established; the "myths" of the Gnostics have been condemned, together with the persons who fancied them. Their pneumatic freedom has been denounced as slavery to perishable matter (2:19). All this is directed to one goal: to remove the sting out of their biting questions about the Parousia. The author gives his apology a fourfold argument:

a) Just as the earth has once perished (ἀπώλετο; 3:6) by water, so it will in the future be burned up by fire. The Gnostic argument of the essential unchangeability of creation ("All things have continued as they were from the beginning of creation"; vs. 4) is disproved by scripture itself in the deluge story. The author uses here a theory of Stoic and Iranian provenance—i.e., the concept of "world fire," traces of which we find already in Jewish apocalyptic sources (Zech. 1:18; 3:8; Sibylline Oracles IV.172-82; V.155-61) and more rarely in Christian apocalypses (Apocalypse of Peter 5 [*see* PETER, APOCALYPSE OF]; Herm. Vis. 4.3.3). Justin Martyr (Apol. I.20) refers to the twofold origin of the concept as follows: "Both Sybil and Hystaspes [a Persian legendary sage] declared that there will be a destruction of corruptible things by fire. Those who are called Stoic philosophers teach that God himself will be resolved into fire and the universe come into being again by return."

b) God's sense of time is not ours—Ps. 90:4 provides scriptural authority to suspend any restlessness about the delay of the Parousia. The author seems to be unaware that this argument undercuts his own theme. The promise of the kingdom, which brings reward for the "godly" (1:11; 2:9) and swift punishment for heretics (2:1), may give an answer to disappointed expectations about the Parousia, but annuls these expectations in substituting eternal categories for those of time.

c) Furthermore, God does not foreshorten the time of the end, as Jewish and Christian apocalypses have it, but lengthens it, out of his mercy to give everyone opportunity for repentance (cf. I Tim. 2:4).

d) Finally, the author switches back to the early Christian expectation of the suddenness of the end (cf. Mark 13:35; I Thess. 5:2). This switch comes somewhat unexpectedly after the change of time categories in 3:8 and points to the inability of the author to cope with the question of the mockers (vs. 4). The description of cosmic catastrophe which accompanies the "Day of Yahweh" provides the background for the final ethical exhortations. Here Peter calls upon Paul, who had said similar things (Rom. 2:4; Phil. 1:10 ff; I Thess. 3:13), to strengthen the apostolic witness. Notwithstanding false interpretations by Gnostic Paulinists, Peter and Paul guarantee the authenticity and legitimacy of the one apostolic tradition.

Bibliography. J. B. Mayor, *The Epistle of St. Jude and the Second Epistle of St. Peter* (1907); R. Knopf, *Die Briefe Petri und Judae* (1912); J. Moffatt, *The General Epistles James, Peter, and Judas* (1947); H. Windisch and H. Preisker, *Die Katholischen Briefe* (1951); E. Käsemann, "Eine Apologie der urchristlichen Eschatologie," *ZThK,* 49 (1952), 272-96. J. C. BEKER

PETER, SLAVONIC ACTS OF slə vŏn'ĭk. A late and grotesque romance, unfettered by either history or earlier legend, of some of Peter's experiences en route to and in Rome, and culminating in his martyrdom. It is extant only in Slavonic and has no seeming connection with the so-called Leucian Acts of Peter. *See* PETER, ACTS OF.

During his voyage to Rome, made at the insistence of a young child, Peter purchases the child, also now on the ship, from the captain. The child performs many miracles in Rome, both for Peter and for Aravistus, to whom Peter sells him. When Nero arrests Peter, the child appears to rebuke him and withers Cato, Nero's adviser, when Cato cuffs Peter. At that the city is shaken by an earthquake and the dead are raised, only to be restored to their graves by Peter, to await the advent of Michael. Peter is crucified head downward. The child appears again; the nails fall from Peter's head, breast, hands, and knees; Peter forgives his enemies, and the child at long last reveals himself as Jesus.

Bibliography. A précis of this curious work is given by M. R. James, *The Apocryphal NT* (1924), p. 474. A German translation was made by I. Franco and published in *ZNW* (1902). M. S. ENSLIN

PETER AND ANDREW, ACTS OF. A short sequel to the flashy Acts of Andrew and Matthias (*see* ANDREW AND MATTHIAS, ACTS OF), extant in Greek and Slavonic. The identical story, although in still shorter form, is found in Ethiopic in the amorphous Oriental Acts, with Thaddaeus in the role of Andrew.

Andrew is carried by a cloud from the land of the cannibals to the mountain where Peter is preaching and to which Matthias has earlier escaped. Jesus appears—as a child—and bids Peter and Andrew go to the land of the barbarians. This they do. They produce a crop of ripe grain for a hospitable old man, and then come into contact with the hostile Onesiphorus. Peter twice causes a camel to go through the eye of a needle, the second time employing the accessories provided by the still skeptical Onesiphorus: his own needle, swine's flesh, a camel, and a defiled woman upon the camel's back. The doubter is now convinced and is bidden by Peter to attempt the miracle himself. He does; the camel passes through as far as the neck, then stops because Onesiphorus has not been baptized. He is forthwith baptized, together with a thousand other converts, including a now penitent wanton woman, who had earlier been hung up naked by her hair by the city gate in the vain attempt to prevent the men of God from entering. She makes lavish gifts, including her own house for a monastery for virgins. The apostles consecrate a church, ordain clergy, and commit the people to God.

The change in style and emphasis in these later Acts from that in the five principal romances, which earlier had suggested the possibilities of edifying fiction outside the ranges of the canonical Acts, is very evident. No longer is there any emphasis on, or seeming interest in, doctrine. The prayers and exhortations of the apostles, which in the earlier Acts bulked large in the eyes of the authors, are no longer to be found. Instead, we have a welter of wonder stories, seemingly the sole concern and interest of the writers. *See* APOCRYPHA, NT. M. S. ENSLIN

PETER AND PAUL, ACTS OF. A writing extant only in Greek, and, save for the early chapters, essentially the same as the Passion of Peter and Paul (*see* PETER AND PAUL, PASSION OF), commonly ascribed to Marcellus. In this version Paul comes to Rome from the island of Gaudomelete. The Jews in Rome, having heard of his intent, persuade Nero to forbid his landing. While in Sicily, en route to Rome, Paul's friend the shipmaster, who like Paul is bald, is mistaken for Paul; he is beheaded by the local toparchs, and his head is sent to Nero. The description of the voyage to Rome is heavily dependent upon the canonical Acts, although embroidered with other local legends. After Paul's arrival in Rome the account is essentially the same—often in identical language—with the above-mentioned Passion. *See* APOCRYPHA, NT.

Bibliography. The Greek text is printed in Lipsius-Bonnet, *Acta Apostolorum Apocrypha* (1891), I, 178-222.

M. S. ENSLIN

PETER AND PAUL, PASSION OF. A comparatively late and thoroughly orthodox writing, extant in both Latin and Greek, recounting the close relationship and harmony between Peter and Paul, their continued and successful opposition to Simon Magus, and their subsequent martyrdoms. Though it contains earlier material, this work is not to be dated before the fifth century. It is commonly, but without warrant, ascribed to Marcellus.

There is also a quite different writing, having the same title, extant only in Latin. The two apostles, lodging in Rome in the home of a relative of Pontius Pilate, are recommended by their host as competent to reply to Simon Magus' claims to be the Christ. Their death sentence follows, but only the briefest mention of their execution is given. *See also* PETER AND PAUL, ACTS OF; APOCRYPHA, NT.

Bibliography. The full text of both of these writings is available in Lipsius-Bonnet, *Acta Apostolorum Apocrypha* (1891), I, 118-72. M. S. ENSLIN

PETER AND THE TWELVE DISCIPLES, ACTS OF. A Gnostic apocryphon discovered in 1946 at Chenoboskion in Upper Egypt. It apparently has no connection with the Acts of Peter, the Ebionite Acts of the Apostles, or the Manichean Acts of the Twelve Apostles. *See* APOCRYPHA, NT.

M. S. ENSLIN

PETHAHIAH pĕth'ə hī'ə [פתחיה, *perhaps* Yahu opens, *though probably an ethnic name*]. **1.** Ancestor, supposedly of David's time, of one of the postexilic priestly families (I Chr. 24:16).

2. A postexilic Judahite, son of Meshezabel, and adviser to Zerubbabel in matters "concerning the people" (Neh. 11:24).

3. A Levite in Ezra's time who attended the covenant ceremony at the Feast of Tabernacles (Neh. 9:5) and who was among those required by Ezra to put away their foreign wives (Ezra 10:23).

J. M. WARD

PETHOR pē'thôr [פתור; Assyrian-Babylonian *Pitru*]. An ancient city located in Upper Mesopotamia on the Sajur River near its confluence with the Euphrates below Birejik. Pethor figures in biblical tradition as the home of Balaam, who was called in by King Balak of Moab to curse the advancing Israelites (Num. 22:5; Deut. 23:4). It is mentioned in the inscriptions (Obelisk 40, Monolith rev. 36 and 85) of Shalmaneser III (859-824) as located on the other side of the Euphrates on the Sajur River. Besides the name Pitru (Pethor), by which it was known to the Hittites, the city had an Assyrian name, *Ana-Asshur-utīr-aṣbat,* "I settled it again for Asshur," which seems to commemorate the fact that it and the neighboring city of Mutkīnu had earlier been settled by Shalmaneser's predecessor Tiglath-pileser I (1116-1077), had been lost to the Arameans, and were now again settled with Assyrians by Shalmaneser.

T. JACOBSEN

PETHUEL pĭ thōō'əl, pĕth'yōō əl [פתואל] (Joel 1:1). The father of the prophet Joel.

PETRA pē'trə [Πέτρα, rock]. The famous capital of the Nabateans, situated in a valley of the mountains of W Edom, *ca.* sixty miles N of Aqabah. It is reached by ascending the Wadi Musa and passing through a narrow gorge called the Siq, which opens up into a plain *ca.* a thousand yards wide, surrounded by massive cliffs of red and variegated sand-

Courtesy of Denis Baly

41. General view of Petra, showing theater at the left center

Courtesy of Denis Baly

42. General view of a line of tombs known as Umm es-Sanadiq at Petra

stone. This plain contains ruins of temples and houses, as well as a number of structures which are hewn out of the rock, and a Roman basilica and theater, which make it one of the most impressive sites in the Near East. Fig. PET 41-42.

Attempts have been made to identify Petra with the biblical SELA, on the grounds of the identity of the meanings of the names. However, there is no evidence of any Edomite settlement except at the Umm el-Bayyarah fortress, around which the later city grew.* Petra, therefore, is not mentioned in the Bible. It seems to have been built beginning *ca.* the fourth century B.C. and to have lasted through the period of Roman rule, but it fell into ruins after the Mohammedan conquest of the seventh century A.D. Figs. SEL 37-38; HIG 23.

Bibliography. For excellent descriptions and illustrations of the ruins of Petra, see Erskine, *Vanished Cities of Arabia* (1925), pp. 21-71; Robinson, *Sarcophagus of a Vanished Civilization* (1930), pp. 1-171.

S. COHEN

PEULLETHAI pē ŭl'ə thī [פעלתי, recompense (of God)] (I Chr. 26:5). One of the gatekeepers for the sanctuary; a Levite, and son of Obed-edom.

Bibliography. M. Noth, *Die israelitischen Personennamen* (1928), p. 189, note 3.

PHAATH MOAB. KJV Apoc. form of PAHATH-MOAB.

PHACARETH. KJV Apoc. form of POCHERETH-HAZZEBAIM.

PHAISUR. KJV Apoc. alternate form of PASHHUR.

PHALDAIUS. KJV Apoc. form of PEDAIAH.

PHALEAS. KJV Apoc. form of PADON.

PHALEC. KJV NT form of PELEG.

PHALLU. KJV form of PALLU in Gen. 46:9.

PHALTI. KJV form of PALTI in I Sam. 25:44.

PHALTIEL. KJV form of PALTIEL in II Sam. 3:15.

PHANUEL fə nōō'əl, făn'yōō əl [Φανουήλ=פנואל, PENUEL (I Chr. 4:4)] (Luke 2:36). The father of Anna the prophetess.

PHARAKIM făr'ə kĭm [Φαρακέμ(B), Φαρακειμ(A)] (I Esd. 5:31). Head of a family of temple servants who returned from the Exile with Zerubbabel. The name is omitted in the parallels Ezra 2:51; Neh. 7:53.

C. T. FRITSCH

PHARAOH fâr'ō, —ĭ ō [פרעה; LXX Φαραώ; Akkad. *pir'u, pir'ū;* Egyp. *pr-*'', the great house]. In the Bible, a title used as a name, or a title prefixed to a name (as in Pharaoh Hophra), of the king of Egypt.

By 2500 B.C., under the Egyptian Old Kingdom one of the designations of the royal palace was "the Great House." This was a common exponent of authority in titles, such as "Superintendent of the Domain of the Great House." By 1800 B.C. this name for the palace had attracted to itself some of the divine epithets associated with the name of the king, but it was not until 1500, in the Eighteenth Dynasty, that it came to be used as a title for the inhabitant of the palace, the king of Egypt. By the ninth century B.C. it was prefixed to a royal name—e.g., Pharaoh Shishak. Early in the seventh century B.C. it was written in the cartouche, or name ring, regularly reserved for the writing of the royal name. Thus in biblical times it was so effective a substitute for a name that it might be used alone to designate the ruling king.

1. Names of the pharaohs. The names of the pharaohs had meaning. The majority of them can be translated as assertive sentences: e.g., Ramses, "(the sun-god) Ra is the one who begot him"; Amenhotep, "(the god) Amon is satisfied." The first name in time was the personal name, that given a prince at birth. This tends to be a family name. The Eighteenth Dynasty had four kings named Amen-hotep and four named Thut-mose; the Nineteenth Dynasty had two kings named Ramses, and the Twentieth had nine. These names, like those later added, had religious relationship, Amen-hotep to the god Amon, Thut-mose to Thoth, and Ramses to Ra. When the heretic pharaoh changed his religion, he changed his name from Amen-hotep to AKH-EN-ATON, asserting a devotion to the god Aton.

At coronation a king received four additional names asserting religious devotion or purpose. The most important of these four was the prenomen. For Ramses II the prenomen was User-maat-Re, "Strong is the right of Ra," which was rendered in Greek as Ozymandias. The prenomen and the personal name (the nomen) were written within ovals, modernly called cartouches. This isolation of such royal names as Ptolemy and Cleopatra was of help for the first steps in the decipherment of the hieroglyphic system.

2. The pharaoh in the state dogma. Egypt was the first civilization in which widely separated areas were bound together as a nation under a single government. Culturally, Upper Egypt was as different from Middle Egypt as Middle Egypt was from Lower Egypt (the Delta). The economy of Upper Egypt (biblical Pathros) was based upon barley and the cow; the economy of Lower Egypt was more varied in agriculture and was more mercantile. Upper Egypt's religion and political organization were related to African forms, Lower Egypt's to Asiatic and Mediterranean forms. Although all parts of the land were united by a common dependence upon the Nile, the Egyptians were so conscious of internal difference that they called their country the "Two Lands"—i.e., Upper and Lower Egypt.

To bind together such disparate regions, the Egyptians insisted that their ruler was a god. He did not come from any province or town of Egypt; he came from the realm of the gods, carrying the divine function of rule. By the dogma of the state, the entire land, its properties, and its peoples were his by divine right. There was no need to codify law, because the word of the god-king was present to make law. From the beginning of the dynasties he was Horus, the "distant" or "upper" god. By the Fifth Dynasty the dogma asserted that at death he became the god

Osiris, who, though dying, yet lived forever in rule over the dead.

In the course of history various challenges were made to the doctrine that the king was absolute because he was a god. Yet modifications of his absolutism did not essentially alter the assertion of the dogma. As government became more complex, it was no longer possible to govern the nation directly from the palace. An elaborate bureaucracy was constructed, headed by a vizier. Under weak kings, the authority of such an official might be as sweeping and as independent as was the authority of Joseph. The armies in earlier Egypt were raised by a civilian draft, but by biblical times there was a professional army, including foreign mercenaries. Out of army command there might arise such founders of dynasties as Shishak.

The priests of the important gods were also jealous for worldly power. By the Fifth Dynasty it was asserted that the sun-god Ra of On (Heliopolis) was the father of the king, who thus owed filial allegiance to his sire. By 1500 B.C., in the Eighteenth Dynasty, Amon, the "hidden" god of Thebes, compounded with Ra to become Amon-Ra, was the imperial god in Egypt's attempts to control other nations. At least by that time the pharaoh began to seek the oracle of the great gods to sanction the major enterprises of the state. The high priest of Amon-Ra of Karnak became a powerful figure in the nation, taking his place beside the pharaoh, the vizier, and the commander of the army. Perhaps Exod. 7:1 reflects this dependence of the pharaoh upon the oracle of a god, where Moses is made the "god to Pharaoh" and Aaron is the priestly spokesman for that god.

Although state dogma continued to assert the pharaoh's divine and single right to rule, these competitors for political power united to remove the king from immediate contact with the people and the state. In large measure he became the god-symbol of the state, rather than the ruling magistrate. As such, he still had great power, but it was a power which he had to share with others.

3. The biblical concept of pharaoh. This picture of a remote palace figure does not accord very well with the account given in Genesis and Exodus, where the pharaoh takes so paternal an interest in the young slave Joseph or where Moses and Aaron may appeal to the pharaoh as he returns from a morning bath in the river. In defense of the biblical picture it may be claimed that after 1100 B.C. there were pharaohs and pharaohs, some of whom were little more than rulers of city-states. Further, much of the background of the court of pharaoh as suggested in the Bible can be paralleled out of the Egyptian texts.

From the time that Egypt attempted to set up an Asiatic empire, the pharaohs contracted a number of international marriages to cement alliances with friendly nations, and these included wedding an Egyptian princess to an Asiatic, just as Solomon received a daughter of the pharaoh (I Kings 3:1). Victories abroad brought many foreign slaves into Egypt. Some of them became household servants and body servants to the kings and nobles, and thereby rose to positions of trust and responsibility. Although we know no other who gained such sweeping powers as Joseph, the parallel is still valid. Other foreign slaves were placed in charge of the palace herds or temple herds of cattle (like Gen. 47:6), were made mercenary soldiers, or were formed into gangs for the great public works projects (like Exod. 1:11).

The picture of the pharaoh's court, with his counselors, the "wise men and magicians," is also familiar from Egyptian texts. These tell of the constant attendance upon the pharaoh by a body of experienced officials and the summoning of priests who were learned in the magical lore of ancient documents. The interpretation of dreams had its special importance for the pharaohs. Joseph's responsibility for the assessing and collecting of taxes (Gen. 47:13-26) accords with what we know about the duties of the vizier of Egypt. The statement that Joseph exempted the land of the priests from taxation, because the priests enjoyed special privileges accorded by the king, has some general conformance to Egyptian practice. However, the situation is puzzling: certainly at some times in Egyptian history the lands of the priests and of the temples were taxed against their produce, but several of the pharaohs did grant some of the temples special immunity from the draft of forced labor.

The pharaoh who promoted Joseph, the pharaoh of the Oppression, and the pharaoh of the Exodus cannot be satisfactorily identified by name or even by century (*see* Exodus, Book of). For the pharaoh of the Oppression, the task of building the store cities of Pithom and Rameses should point to Ramses II (1290-1224 B.C.), but there are complicating factors when one assumes that his successor Mer-ne-Ptah was the pharaoh of the Exodus. The pharaoh who honored Joseph was, of course, much earlier, but the Egyptian names in the Joseph story, Potiphar, Potiphera, Asenath, and Zaphenath-paneah, are of types which occur late in Egypt, chiefly after 1100. The frank attitude toward the stories about Egypt in Genesis and Exodus is that folk memory had retained the essentials of a great Hebrew experience but had later clothed that memory with some details imperfectly recollected and some circumstantial detail borrowed from later times and conditions.

Bibliography. H. Frankfort, *Kingship and the Gods* (1948); C. J. Gadd, *Ideas of Rule in the Ancient East* (1948); J. A. Wilson, *The Burden of Egypt* (1951). Index under "king."

J. A. Wilson

PHARAOH-HOPHRA. *See* Hophra.

PHARAOH-NEC(H)O. *See* Neco.

PHARATHON; PHARATHONI. Apoc. forms of Pirathon.

PHARES, PHAREZ. KJV forms of Perez.

PHARIRA. KJV Apoc. form of Peruda.

***PHARISEES** fâr′ə sēz [פרושים; φαρισαῖοι]. An influential party among the Jews during intertestamental and NT times.

1. Origin and name
2. Leading characteristics
   a. Legalism and separatism
   b. Observance of ancestral traditions
   c. Pharisaic "modernism"

3. Doctrines and beliefs
   a. History divinely controlled
   b. The resurrection
   c. Angelology
   d. Eschatology
   e. The Messiah
4. The history of Pharisaism
   a. Greek period
   b. Roman period
Bibliography

1. Origin and name. For an understanding of the origins and antecedents of the Pharisees, we must go back to Ezra and beyond—to the pre-exilic institutions of the prophetic guilds and the priesthood.

In the light of the NT picture of Pharisaism, it may seem unnatural to connect the Pharisees with the ancient prophets of Israel; in Christ's day the prophetic demands, the "greater things of the law," were buried beneath a mass of petty Pharisaic regulations. Nevertheless, there is a sense in which the conflict between Pharisees and SADDUCEES, in its origins and much of its later history, was a revival—in new ages and new forms—of the ancient, unresolved conflict and opposition between prophet and priest in Israel.

The seeds of historical Pharisaism were sown during the Exile. Deprived of the temple and its cultus, exiled Israelites had to be content with the dream of its restoration and the reality of the Book of the Law, which they had been able to take with them into exile. During the Exile it was the law which became the center of Jewish religion and supplied the pattern of Jewish life; and it was to remain ever afterward the soul of Judaism. Under the restoration of Ezra and his successors the temple was again to become the focus of national life. The old hierocratic Israel, with the high priest as supreme authority in matters of law and religion, was re-established; but the law did not cease to be the soul of the nation.

There grew up side by side with the temple and its priestly aristocracy a new authority, a body of "lawyers" called scribes or Sopherim (*see* SCRIBE). Torah was still taught and practiced (we must presume from our records) under the aegis of the temple and its restored priesthood; its interpretation and application was still, like the cultus itself, the primary function of the temple hierarchy and their assistants, the Sopherim. Scholars are agreed that it is still the priestly scribe or sage who is glorified in the pages of ECCLESIASTICUS (38:24-39:15), and the guilds or families of Sopherim (I Chr. 2:55) were restricted to the ranks of the priestly families or the Levites (cf. II Chr. 34:13; Neh. 8:7, 13). In this respect the Israel of the restoration stood in the pre-exilic hierocratic tradition: it was a restored priestly hierocracy in which the privileges of interpretation and application of Torah were vested solely in the priestly caste.

But it is doubtful if the realities of the restoration correspond to the blueprint of the exiles' dreams of a new Israel with temple and Torah as its center. The law, not the temple, was the primary factor in postexilic Jewish life; and the stage was set for the next development, when Torah could stand in opposition to temple and be taught and applied among the people by a new class of lay "lawyer," non-priestly doctors of the law, who owed no allegiance to the temple hierarchy and were prepared even to resist its rule and enactments.

It is not known for certain when this revolution within postexilic Judaism took place, but its beginnings are probably to be set at the end of the Persian and the beginning of the Greek period. There may have been lay lawyers in Israel during the Exile itself and at the time of the restoration; the leading figures of the period, perhaps drawn from the Sopherim or *Hakhamim* (sages), and certainly including them, are traditionally referred to as the "Men of the Great Synagogue" (*see* SYNAGOGUE, THE GREAT), the "Men of the Second Temple." The records of Ezra, Nehemiah, and Chronicles present us with the ideal, not the actualities, of the reorganized Judaism of the period. What we certainly can observe is that the chaotic conditions which followed the breakup of the restoration temple and the rule of the Men of the Great Synagogue led to the progressive weakening of the power of the hereditary priesthood. The high-priestly office was discredited in the eyes of the loyal Jewish nation; the Seleucid nominees did not even belong to the hereditary priestly families. For a long period after the invasion of Jewish life by Hellenism, there was a complete moratorium on the temple services. But no foreign power or priestly collaborators could destroy the law, which became the rallying point of Jewish loyalty.

The religious backbone of the Maccabean resistance was provided by an assembly or "synagogue" of scribes, and the HASIDIM, the "pious," or loyalists for the law (I Macc. 7:11-17). Whether these scribes were priestly scribes or lay lawyers or (just as probably) included both, cannot be known for certain. According to one ancient authority, there was a body of priests who seceded from the temple, about the same time as the rise of the Hasidim, in protest against Seleucid Hellenization; these, along with the "synagogue of the scribes," must have formed the spearhead of the popular resistance. The Maccabean family itself was a priestly family. But the revolt came from the Jewish people, and the priestly caste which remained in office betrayed the national cause by making terms with the Syrian conqueror (cf. I Macc. 7:14). They were the forerunners of the Sadducees.

Though the temple services were again restored under Judas Maccabeus (*see* JUDAS 10), the Hasmonean dynasty which he founded represented a new order in Judaism. It became a monarchy with a governing body known as the *Gerousia* or Senate (the predecessor of the SANHEDRIN). The most significant feature of the *Gerousia*—an indication of the revolution that must have taken place in Judaism in the preceding half century—is that lay Sopherim were now admitted as representatives of the people to its councils. When the ancient office of the high priest was revived under the Hasmoneans, it was a revival of the form of hierocracy, when the reality of priestly rule had long since been discarded. The name given the highest authority in the Jewish state is itself eloquent of the inroads made by Hellenism in Jewish life; the *Gerousia* was a Greek institution with laymen as rulers and administrators, of a higher rank than the priesthood, whose office and function was now largely confined to tending the altar.

There can be little doubt that the Pharisaic movement took its rise from among the ranks of these lay lawyers of the Greek period. The Pharisees were, no doubt, the successors of the Hasidim, but only in a very general sense; it must have been a body of lay scribes that formed the core of the emerging Pharisaic party, soon to be strengthened by partisans from the people and eventually to include priests in their numbers. At the beginning and during the early Greek period, such a group or party must also at some stage have successfully challenged the pretensions of the priestly caste to be the sole authorities on Torah, and so rulers of the people. When the Pharisees first emerge in the historical records, they do so, as we shall see, as an already established religious-political party in the Jewish state.

This revolution in postexilic Judaism was not effected without a prolonged and bitter struggle, for the temple was still the national shrine, and the ancient office of temple priest still possessed great prestige and authority. It was a revolution which was never completed, for the struggle for power within the Jewish state between the priestly caste and its adherents (the Sadducees) and the lay element in the state and their followers (the Pharisees) was to continue for the next two centuries. Indeed, this tension between temple and Torah, or rather temple and a lay-interpreted Torah as a new center of power and authority, between Sadducee and Pharisee, is the key to an understanding of much in Jewish life in the two centuries before Christ.

The derivation of the name Pharisee is obscure. A common form of explanation derives the word from Hebrew *parash* (Aramaic *perash*), meaning "one who is separate [*parush, perish*]," but separate from what (or whom) is not clear. Some explain the word as the "seceders" from the priestly interpreters of the law; the lay interpreters at one time "separated" themselves from their clerical colleagues. Alternatively, it has been suggested that the name arose from the "separation" of the Hasidim from the partisans of Judas Maccabeus in 163 B.C. Perhaps these explanations have less to be said in their favor than the meaning of *perushim* as those who, in their meticulous observance of the law and in particular its Levitical observances, "separated themselves" from uncleanness, and especially from the unclean, the "people of the land" (*'am ha'areṣ*). Hebrew *parush* is associated with *qadhosh,* "holy"; thus Sifra on Lev. 11:44-45 comments on the words "You shall . . . be holy; for I am holy": "As I am separate [*parush*], so be ye also separate [*perushim*]." The Pharisees were the "separate" or "holy ones" (cf. the use of ἅγιοι for Christians in the NT). Another explanation takes the noun "Pharisee" to mean "interpreters," since this is one meaning of Hebrew *parash,* "to divide [Scripture]" and so "to interpret." The form of the name (passive) is not, however, what this theory would require. A third type of explanation is that the Greek name is a Grecized form of the Aramaic word פרישיא, meaning "Persian"; "Persians," it is argued, was a nickname applied to the Pharisees by their opponents the Sadducees because of their willingness to introduce foreign (in particular, Iranian) doctrines into Judaism. No single theory can be said to hold the field to the exclusion of any other. The one possibly more generally favored is the meaning "those who are separated" from impurity, the reference being to the legal, and, in particular, ritualistic, separatism of the party.

2. Leading characteristics. ***a. Legalism and separatism.*** The main characteristic of the Pharisees was their legalism or legalistic rigorism. Josephus informs us that the Pharisees were noted for their strict accuracy in their interpretation of the law and their scrupulous adherence to it (War I.v.2; II.viii.14; Life 38; Antiq. XVII.ii.4). It was their "accuracy" in the interpretation of the law which led to the development of the elaborate system of legal traditions, handed down orally "from the Fathers," which came to be regarded as the main characteristic feature of historical Pharisaism (*see* § 2*b below*). The Pharisees were accused by their opponents of building a "fence around the law," and one of the opprobrious epithets applied to them was that of being "builders of the wall"—i.e., builders of a wall around the Torah, fencing it in with the "wall" of Pharisaic tradition, and at the same time excluding non-Pharisaic interpretations (or halakoth)—and non-Pharisees—from the benefits and privileges of a monopolized Torah. *See* HALACHAH.

It was not, however, only their detailed and elaborate system of traditional halakoth which characterized Pharisaism as a living and influential movement in Judaism. What gave this system of Jewish legalism its force and influence was the rigorism of this strictest of Jewish sects in the actual observance of their tradition. It was their scrupulous adherence to their legalistic traditions which created the Pharisaic ethos, and which has given rise to the modern use of the name Pharisee as a self-righteous formalist.

It is this central characteristic of legalistic rigorism which led to and accounts for Pharisaic emphasis on ritual purification and separateness, with regard to both their own persons and their cult furniture or implements (Mark 7:3 and parallels). The Pharisees strove to achieve a perfectionism of purity and purification by the meticulous observance of the ritual requirements of the Levitical code, again as handed down in their traditional halakoth or legalistic observances and ordinances. This also explains their policy of separateness or exclusiveness, especially from the common people, the *'am ha'areṣ*. Just as the priest and the Levite in the gospel parable avoid the wounded Samaritan from fear of ritual contamination, the Pharisee shunned the non-Pharisee as unclean. The closest modern parallel is the caste system in Hinduism. Pharisaic exclusiveness led to a caste-bound society where contact between members of the exclusive sect and the rest of the population was avoided or regulated by a system of elaborate legal precautions designed to minimize or remove ritual uncleanness contracted in the unavoidable intercourse of daily life.

The Pharisees were not the only exclusive and rigoristic sect in Judaism. There were other, even more exclusive sectarians, such as the ESSENES and the Qumran sect (if they are not one and the same group; *see* DEAD SEA SCROLLS), and these at times could out-Pharisee the Pharisees themselves. But it is the Pharisees who came to enjoy this reputation in later times; and the picture of the Pharisees in the gospels as strict legalists, observing all the minutiae of their elaborate legal tradition, including their ritualistic ordinances, is in keeping with all we know about them from other sources. Cf., e.g., their attitude toward the Sabbath or toward the washing of the outside of the cup and the platter (Matt. 23:25).

b. Observance of ancestral traditions. Their second main characteristic, deriving from the fundamentally legalistic character of the movement, was Pharisaic respect for ancestral tradition, the "tradition of the elders" (Matt. 15:2; cf. Mark 7:3, 5). It was in this respect that the Pharisees differed, on principle, from the Sadducees, who followed a more literalist interpretation of Torah.

This bald contrast calls, however, for qualification. The Sadducees, as ecclesiastical and juridical authorities, had also their own developed tradition of halakoth, of laws and ordinances. The Sadducean code of law was also a *traditio* or *paradosis,* based on the Pentateuch. The essential difference from the Pharisaic form of law was that Sadducean law tended to be conservative, static and fixed, incapable of adjusting itself to new conditions. Pharisaic traditional halakoth retained a flexibility capable of adjustment to new situations. Furthermore, as an *oral* tradition (and this was also an essential feature), it remained flexible and adjustable. The result in the end was the growth within Pharisaism of a large body of authoritative tradition which could always be enlarged. It was, of course, also built primarily around the law; but another factor, as we shall now see, contributed enormously to this growing and adaptable system of Pharisaic tradition.

The Pharisaic canon of scripture went far beyond the five books of Moses, to include both the Prophets and the Writings. The Pharisees were prepared to allow their halakoth of the Torah to be influenced by this wider scriptural authority to an extent which the Sadducees, with their narrower views of scripture, were prevented from doing. In this respect, Pharisaism represents a development similar to that of the Qumran sectarians: side by side with their legalism and ritualism went an openness to the new ideas of the prophetic scriptures which challenged and corrected the narrower outlook of the ancient legal code. It was in the circles of the Pharisees (and other sectarians) that the Jewish messianic hope was nourished on the ancient prophetic scriptures, as well as on the Torah.

c. Pharisaic "modernism." So far as the period of their greatest influence is concerned, this openness to new ideas, including ideas from other religions, represents one of the main characteristics of historical Pharisaism. It is for this reason that Josephus speaks of them as "rationalists" (Antiq. XVIII.i.3). They were the progressives in the religion of their day.

This is the important element of truth in some of the older views about the essential character of Pharisaism. A. Geiger (whose views were, in the main, accepted by such older liberals as Graetz, Klausner, and others) tried to show that the Sadducees were the conservative group in postexilic Judaism, attached to the traditional laws and customs; in opposition to them were the Pharisees, a liberal, forward-looking party, corresponding, in both their spirit and their aim, to reform Judaism in its relation to traditional Jewish orthodoxy. Geiger's views were challenged by Wellhausen, who tried to prove that Sadducees and Pharisees represented two divergent attitudes toward the destiny of the Jewish people: the Sadducees were a political party only, closely associated with the HASMONEANS, the priestly caste and the ruling nobility; they stood for Jewish independence and opposition to Syria and Rome. The Pharisees formed a movement which was not essentially political, so long as their religious life was unaffected.

It was a mistake to regard the Pharisees as religious quietists. Both Pharisees and Sadducees were power groups, each striving for ascendancy in the Jewish state; political alignments were formed by both groups with the dominant foreign power. But it is true that the Pharisees were actively concerned with the progress and development of Jewish religion. Studies by Finkelstein have shown that the Pharisees were not only a democratic party, but also a progressive religious movement originally drawn from the people; the Sadducees represented the old priesthood and the landed nobility. The most fundamental differences between the two groups was, however, undoubtedly that the Sadducees stood for the old ways and the *status quo,* eventually becoming in Roman times little more than a civil service or bureaucracy holding the form of the old order together; the Pharisees were the popular democrats, the liberals and the progressives in the Jewish state and society of the two centuries before Christ.

3. Doctrines and beliefs. For the doctrines and beliefs of the Pharisees our main source is again Josephus (War II.viii.4). Josephus' account can, however, be supplemented by Pharisaic writings of the intertestamental period, as well as from the NT and to some extent also from later rabbinical sources. It is not, of course, always certain that an apocryphal or pseudepigraphical writing was written by a Pharisee; Ben Sirach, e.g., has been claimed for both Pharisees and Sadducees, though he was in fact too early to belong to either party (his sympathies were clearly with the old priestly order, and any Pharisaic traits in his work are probably redactional). Fortunately there is no doubt about the Pharisaic authorship of the Psalms of Solomon (*ca.* 60 B.C.), doctrinally one of the most important of the Pharisaic and anti-Sadducean documents of this century, since it supplies our main evidence for the Pharisaic messianic hope. *See* § 3*e below.*

The main account of the Pharisees in Josephus reads:

"Of the two first-named schools, the Pharisees, who are considered the most accurate interpreters of the laws, and hold the position of the leading sect, attribute everything to Fate and to God; they hold that to act rightly or otherwise rests, indeed, for the most part with men, but that in each action Fate co-operates. Every soul, they maintain, is imperishable, but the soul of the good alone passes into another body, while the souls of the wicked suffer eternal punishment.

"The Sadducees, the second of the orders, do away with Fate altogether, and remove God beyond, not merely the commission, but the very sight, of evil. They maintain that man has the free choice of good or evil, and that it rests with each man's will whether he follows the one or the other. As for the persistence of the soul after death, penalties in the underworld, and rewards, they will have none of them.

"The Pharisees are affectionate to each other and cultivate harmonious relations with the community. The Sadducees, on the contrary, are, even among themselves, rather boorish in their behaviour, and in their intercourse with their peers are as rude as to aliens. Such is what I have to say on the Jewish philosophical schools."[1]

We can best summarize by noting the main differences between Pharisees and Sadducees (in each case the Pharisees put forward a positive position which the Sadducees rejected):

a. History divinely controlled. The Pharisees believed that history was divinely controlled and governed by a divine purpose (Josephus gives us this doctrine in Stoic terms). The Sadducees denied it, insisting on the individual's freedom to direct his own life and so history itself.

It is possible that Josephus has to a great extent "Stoicized" Pharisaic doctrine in this connection and that all that lies behind the Pharisaic doctrine of Είμαρμένη (Destiny) is the OT idea of divine providence. It may have been passages such as the following from the Psalms of Solomon (5:6) which gave rise to this conception:

> Man and his portion lie before Thee in the balance;
> He cannot add to, so as to enlarge, what has been prescribed by Thee.[2]

b. The resurrection. The Pharisees believed in resurrection and in a future world where men are rewarded or punished according to their behavior in this one. The Sadducees held fast to the doctrine of Sheol. In this the Sadducees were true Semites; T. W. Manson recalls the derision with which Mohammed's teaching of the resurrection was met in the early stages of his career.

c. Angelology. The Pharisees had a highly developed angelology which the Sadducees rejected. Acts 23:8 is our main authority for this item of Pharisaic belief: "The Sadducees say that there is no resurrection, nor angel, nor spirit; but the Pharisees acknowledge them all."

d. Eschatology. The Pharisees regarded themselves as the true and pious Israel, enjoying a specially close relationship with God (with divine revelations through God's holy angels). To be sure, God's favor was not specially manifest in the sufferings and miseries of the present times of foreign conquest, but there was a good time coming in which the tables would be turned and the glories of David's kingdom restored on earth by a descendant of Davidic line, "the anointed Lord." It was an earthly Paradise which the Pharisees expected; their expectation was this-worldly, not otherworldly, though they appear also to have expected the pious dead to arise to share these earthly glories with them in the messianic age.

e. The Messiah. The classic passage for the Pharisaic doctrine of the Messiah is Pss. Sol. 17:23–18:9 (the book is dated by several references to Pompey's capture of Jerusalem in 63 B.C.). God's Anointed One (or the "Anointed Lord" [Χριστὸς κύριος], the "son of David") is to be raised up by the Lord God as King over Israel.

> Behold, O Lord, and raise up unto them their king, the son of David,
> At the time in the which Thou seest, O God, that he may reign over Israel Thy servant.
>
> . . . .
>
> This (will be) the majesty of the king of Israel whom God knoweth;
> He will raise him up over the house of Israel to correct him.
>
> . . . .
>
> At his rebuke nations shall flee before him,
> And he shall reprove sinners for the thoughts of their heart.[2]

(The "nations" refer to the Gentiles, and by "sinners" the author probably means the Sadducees.)

The Messiah (*see* MESSIAH, JEWISH) was to overthrow the supremacy of the Gentiles, to drive them from Jerusalem and Israel (17:25, 27, 31). But he was also to restore Israel, to set up a kingdom in place of that of the Gentiles and sinners (17:23 ff):

> He shall have the heathen nations to serve him under his yoke;
> And he shall glorify the Lord in a place to be seen of [?] all the earth;
> And he shall purge Jerusalem, making it holy as of old:
> So that nations shall come from the ends of the earth to see his glory.[2]

There are hints at the reassembling of Israel and its tribes (8:27 ff; 17:28 ff; etc.). Jerusalem will be his capital, and the temple worship will be restored (17: 33-35). The Gentiles will be subject to him, bringing him tributes, and they shall be converted to the worship of Israel (17:31-32, 34).

There are certain distinctive features of this picture which exercised a determinative influence on NT Christology.

It is frequently claimed that the title "Christ," "Anointed One" (Χριστός), is here used for the first time of the expected savior of Israel. The OT usage has been usefully summed up by Westcott: "It is not a characteristic title of the promised Saviour in the Old Testament. It is not even specifically applied to Him, unless perhaps in Dan. 9:25 f, a passage of which the interpretation is very doubtful." But the name occurs three times in the Psalms of Solomon (17:36; 18:6, 8). The Messiah was to be the "son of David." We thus return to the conception of the ideal of the restoration of the lineage of David, and of the glories of the Davidic age of the prophecy of Nathan, so prominent in the great prophets (Isa. 9:7; 11:1; 55:3; Jer. 23:5; Ezek. 37:24); Haggai had been the last to point to the lineage of David (2:21-23); Zechariah had emphasized the priestly aspect of the messianic hope (6:11-13). The Maccabean age looked for the return of a "trustworthy prophet"

[1] Reprinted by permission of the publishers and The Loeb Classical Library from Loeb Classical Library Volume: Josephus *Jewish Wars* (Cambridge, Mass.: Harvard University Press, 1927, 1956).

[2] R. H. Charles, ed., *The Apocrypha and Pseudepigrapha of the Old Testament* (Oxford: The Clarendon Press).

(I Macc. 14:41; cf. 4:46); Jeremiah, not David, appears in a dream to Judas Maccabeus (II Macc. 15: 12-16). In Ecclesiasticus (48:10-11) it is Elijah the prophet who is to "restore the tribes of Jacob." Thus, as Ryle and James comment: "The Messianic vocation of the house of David, which since the Captivity had fallen into the background, and under the glorious reign of the first Asmonaean princes had almost been lost to view, reappears in the Pharisaic Psalms."

The Psalms of Solomon are thus the bridge uniting the hope of the ancient prophets, which centered on a restoration of the Davidic kingship, with NT times.

4. The history of Pharisaism. ***a. Greek period.*** It is not until well into the Greek period of Jewish history, during the reign of the Hasmonean ruler John Hyrcanus (135-105 B.C.), that we come upon the first mention, in our primary historical source (the works of Josephus), of the Pharisees and Sadducees (Antiq. XIII.v.9; x.5-7).

There the Pharisees emerge as an already strongly established and powerful religious-political party in the Jewish theocratic state, partisans of an authoritative system of law based on tradition, and opposed to the Sadducean party, with its restricted, literalist appeal to the law of Moses.

"For the present I wish merely to explain that the Pharisees had passed on to the people certain regulations handed down by former generations and not recorded in the Laws of Moses, for which reason they are rejected by the Sadducean group, who hold that only those regulations should be considered valid which were written down (in Scripture), and that those which had been handed down by former generations (lit. by the fathers) need not be observed. And concerning these matters the two parties came to have controversies and serious differences, the Sadducees having the confidence of the wealthy alone but no following among the populace, while the Pharisees have the support of the masses. But of these two schools and of the Essenes a detailed account has been given in the second book of my *Judaica*" (War II.viii.14; Antiq. XIII.x.6).[1]

In this same passage Josephus supplies us with evidence of the power and popularity of Pharisaism in this early period of its history; of its social position (as a democratic movement); and in general of its character as a laymen's party.

He recounts an incident in which the Hasmonean king (Hyrcanus) came into conflict with the Pharisaic party, which he had hitherto supported. The story itself is prefaced by the statement that it was the Pharisees at that time who were, among all the Jews, the most envious of Hyrcanus' success and prosperity; and "so great is their influence with the masses that even when they speak against a king or high priest, they immediately gain credence" (Antiq. XIII.x.5).

Pharisees had been invited by the king to a banquet, in the course of which John Hyrcanus explained that he was anxious to do everything in his power to please God after the manner of the Pharisees; if there was any way in which he erred, he begged them to inform him. The assembled Pharisees expressed their satisfaction, except one, a certain Eleazar, who informed Hyrcanus (in the manner of an ancient prophet) that, if he would be really righteous, he must lay down the office of the high priesthood; at the same time he cast aspersions on Hyrcanus' descent, implying that, as coming from a non-priestly line, he had no right to the title of high priest. The rest of the company were indignant, but their protestations did not help, for the Sadducees managed to persuade the king that Eleazar was, in fact, expressing the real views of the Pharisaic party. John Hyrcanus withdrew his support from the Pharisees and went over to the Sadducean side, abolishing all his earlier decrees in which he had been guided by the Pharisaic legal tradition.

We have to read between the lines of Josephus' narrative to understand the main cause (or causes) for this break between the Pharisees and John Hyrcanus. Josephus tells us that it was out of envy for Hyrcanus' successes; but he reveals the real reason in his statement about the popular influence of the Pharisees being so high that "even when they speak against a king or a high priest," they are believed. It seems probable that it was because Hyrcanus was the first Hasmonean to assume the royal title that the Pharisees broke with him. They may have objected to this as "loyalists" for the law. It may also be argued, however, that it was Hyrcanus' assumption of the high-priestly office to which the Pharisees mainly objected.

Under Hyrcanus' successor, Alexander Janneus, the Pharisaic-Sadducean conflict became even more acute and bitter. The Pharisees returned to power and eventually succeeded in securing the banishment of the king himself from Jerusalem, after inflicting insult and humiliation upon him. The outstanding popular Pharisee at the time was a certain Simon ben Shataḥ. Simon appears to have been a powerful and violent personality. He succeeded in ousting the Hasmonean king and high priest from the leadership of the *Gerousia* and himself assumed the office and duties of its president in place of the exiled king–high priest. The fortunes of the Pharisees were never higher. A Pharisaic layman now held the highest office in the state, if only for a brief period. Simon set about reforming the constitution of the *Gerousia*. He demanded that Alexander should lay down his office as high priest. There is a story that the king was summoned on one occasion to appear before the *Gerousia;* and that when he did appear, Simon forbade him to sit, "for thou standest not before Simon ben Shataḥ but before Him Who spoke and the world was." It is not surprising to read that, when the tide did turn again and Janneus was restored to power, he immediately had eight hundred Pharisees put to death (Antiq. XIII.xiv.2). Simon went into exile.

Josephus tells us that Janneus, presumably toward the end of his reign, advised his wife, Alexandra Salome, to make peace with the Pharisees and to allow herself to be guided by them. Since Alexandra was the sister of the exiled Simon ben Shataḥ, this advice was followed with alacrity. When Janneus died, Alexandra (76-67 B.C.) recalled Simon and other exiled Pharisees, allowed the Pharisaic party a large share in the government, and reintroduced

[1] Reprinted by permission of the publishers and The Loeb Classical Library from Loeb Classical Library Volume: Josephus *Jewish Wars* (Cambridge, Mass.: Harvard University Press, 1927, 1956).

Pharisaic laws and decrees which Hyrcanus had abolished (Antiq. XIII.xvi.1; War I.v.1). The powerful Pharisaic lawyer Simon ruled with almost papal authority, resisting especially the Hellenization which had been allowed to go unhindered under Alexander. He executed eighty "witches" on a single day, thus creating a terrible precedent for subsequent mass murders of Pharisees by Sadducees and Sadducees by Pharisees. (Only one execution on one day had hitherto been permitted by Pharisaic tradition.)

Now securely in power, the Pharisaic party proceeded once again to take a terrible revenge on their Sadducean opponents. The latter sought out the support of Aristobulus, Salome's younger son (the heir apparent was a second Hyrcanus). A deputation pleaded the Sadducean case to the queen, reminding her of their services to her late husband. They not only succeeded in stopping the Pharisaic reign of terror, but also managed to get control of a number of strategic fortresses. There they were joined by Aristobulus, who only waited his mother's death to seize power (Antiq. XIII.xvi.2-3, 5; War. I.v.3-4). On the death of Alexandra (69-63 B.C.), Hyrcanus II was dispossessed by his younger brother Aristobulus (Antiq. XIV.i.2; XV.vi.4; XX.x), and the Sadducees again advanced to power.

This internal struggle between the two parties, however, had momentous consequences for the Jewish people, for both sides appealed to Rome. They met the Roman general Pompey in Damascus, bidding for his support. Soon afterward (*ca.* 63 B.C.) Pompey marched on Jerusalem. This was more than the people or its leaders had bargained for, and they resisted the invasion. Pompey took the temple by storm and entered the Holy of Holies, though he does not appear to have laid sacrilegious hands on the temple treasure. The usual proscriptions followed; leading Sadducees were executed, and Aristobulus and his family were deported to Rome. Hyrcanus was restored, not as king, but as high priest and ethnarch. The outward form of the Jewish state was preserved, but the real power passed to Rome (Antiq. XIV. iii–iv).

The story of the fortunes of the Pharisaic party in Hasmonean times as told by Josephus is a tale mainly of political intrigue, wholesale murder of their Sadducean opponents (who were never slow to retaliate), and traitorous bargaining with powerful outsiders in their ceaseless struggle for power within the state. It was undoubtedly this irreconcilable cleavage between Pharisees and Sadducees within Hasmonean Judaism which eventually led to its downfall, when Rome stepped in and eventually took over the reins of government in Jerusalem.

Yet it was no less certainly in this period that Pharisaism as a religious system reached its heyday; and it was the hour of its eclipse as a political power which saw the production of its greatest literary monuments—writings such as the Psalms of Solomon.

b. Roman period. The second stage in the history of Pharisaism, the Roman period, is a period of declining influence and the gradual decay of what had been for two centuries the living stock of Judaism. As the nation lost its independence, the differences between Pharisees and Sadducees tended to become less and less political and more distinctively religious. It is true they still remained a powerful political factor, especially during the long reign of Herod the Great. During the ethnarchy, under the Romans, of the second Hyrcanus, the Sadducees sought to call Herod to account for his conduct in Galilee, but they only succeeded in demonstrating their own powerlessness. When Herod captured Jerusalem in 37 B.C., he put forty-five of the Sadducean Sanhedrists to death (Antiq. XV.i.2 calls them the leaders of the party of Antigonus; cf. War I.xviii.4; Antiq. XIV. ix.4 speaks of "all the members of the Sanhedrin" except Sameas), and sought further to diminish their power by introducing members of the (nonpriestly) Herod clan among the high-priestly families. When the Sanhedrin was thus purged, however, the leaders of the Pharisees were spared, since they had advised the citizens of Jerusalem to throw open the gates of the city to receive Herod (Antiq. XV.i.1). Although the Pharisees refused to take the oath of allegiance to Herod, the king appears to have resorted to no more drastic measures than a fine (Antiq. XV.x.4; XVII.ii.4). It was because of their influence with the people that Herod went out of his way to respect their religious views; for their part, they simply acquiesced in his rule as a judgment on the people for their sins. Toward the end of Herod's reign their attitude, however, ceased to be one of passive acceptance and became actively hostile. Pharisees conspired with members of Herod's household to secure his overthrow (Antiq. XVII.vi.2); and in 4 B.C. they instigated their pupils to cut down the golden eagle, which the king had erected as a symbol of Roman sovereignty, over the main entrance to the temple. (For this offense the culprits were buried alive [Antiq. XVII.vi.2-4].)

When the Romans, after deposing Archelaus, took over what was virtually the direct rule of the country, internal affairs became the concern of the Sanhedrin under the presidency of the high priest (himself controlled by the Romans). But the struggle for ascendancy and power between the two great parties still continued; the Sadducean aristocracy, though it had been strengthened by the accession to its ranks of members of the Herod family, was still obliged to respect the opinions of the Pharisees on legal matters (Antiq. XVIII.i.4). On two different occasions in the book of Acts (5:34; 23:6) it is Pharisees who prove to be the real leaders of the people, and under Agrippa I (A.D. 41-44), they seem to have had matters much in their own hands. It was on the instigation of the Pharisees that Agrippa put James, the Lord's brother, to death.

Some conception of their numbers and influence in Jesus' time may be formed from the figures given by Josephus, who puts them at the time of Herod the Great above six thousand (Antiq. XVII.ii.4). Josephus is probably here dependent on a contemporary member of Herod's court (Nicholas of Damascus), and likely to be accurately informed. This number applies, no doubt, to full membership of the Pharisaic order only. Various estimates have been made for their total numbers (members and adherents) in the time of Christ. T. W. Manson, following J. Jeremias, estimates a total number of members and adherents at twenty-five thousand, with probably as many as twenty thousand resident in Jerusalem.

There is no reason to doubt that the Pharisees still exercised a powerful influence within the Judaism of our Lord's time. But it is doubtful if they still enjoyed the same popularity with the masses as in the heyday of their political power in the previous centuries. By the first century A.D. (before the fall of Jerusalem) Pharisaism had become a bourgeois rather than a popular movement, a predominantly Jerusalem "city" party. No doubt the Jerusalem Pharisees also had their followers in the country districts, but their attitude to the *'am ha'areṣ* suggests that the gulf between the Pharisees and the peasants who formed the bulk of the population was as great as that between the Sadducees and the small traders in the cities from whom the Pharisees drew their main support.

This loss of influence with the broad masses, especially in the provinces and the countryside, applied to Pharisaic religion no less than to the membership of the sect. Pharisaism is the immediate ancestor of rabbinical (or normative) Judaism, the largely arid religion of the Jews after the fall of Jerusalem and, finally, the Bar Cocheba debacle (A.D. 135). In Jesus' time, no doubt with certain differences, the broad picture of Pharisaism cannot have been so far removed from that of rabbinical Judaism of the post-Jamnia period, the Judaism of the Tannaites. It is a sterile religion of codified tradition, regulating every part of life by a halachah, observing strict separation, and already as entrenched in its own conservatism as that of the Sadducees. Its golden age lay in the second and first centuries B.C., from which its main literary monuments come, and where its important ideals and conceptions are to be found.

Bibliography. A. Geiger, "Sadducäer und Pharisäer," *Urschrift und Übersetzungen der Bibel* (1857). J. Wellhausen, *Die Pharisäer und die Sadducäer: Eine Untersuchung zur inneren jüdischen Geschichte* (1874). J. Lauterbach, "The Sadducees and Pharisees," in *Studies in Jewish Literature, Issued in Honor of Dr. K. Kohler* (1913), pp. 176-98; *Midrash and Mishnah* (1916). L. Ginsberg, *Unbekannte jüdische Sekte* (1922). R. T. Herford, *The Pharisees* (1924). V. Aptowitzer, *Partei-Politik der Hasmonäerzeit im rabbinischen und pseudoepigraphischen Schrifttum* (Alexander Kohut Foundation, Band V; 1927). L. Finkelstein, "The Pharisees: Their Origin and Their Philosophy," *HTR*, vol. XXII, no. 3 (July, 1929); published in two volumes (2nd ed., 1940). J. Lauterbach, "The Pharisees and Their Teachings," *HUCA*, VI (1929), 69. T. W. Manson, *The Servant-Messiah* (1953). MATTHEW BLACK

PHAROSH. KJV form of PAROSH in Ezra 8:3.

PHARPAR fär'pär [פרפר] (II Kings 5:12). A river mentioned together with ABANA as one of the rivers of Damascus. It may be identical with the river now called Nahr el-'A'waj, which flows down from Anti-lebanon in Wadi 'A'waj S of Damascus to disappear in Bahret Hijjane. As to the identification of the river of Pharpar, other suggestions have been set forth. Of these one may particularly deserve mentioning, according to which Pharpar is identical with Nahr Taura, an arm of the river of Barada. It is, of course, difficult to decide which identification may be considered to be correct. The fact that in II Kings 5:12 Pharpar is called one of the rivers of Damascus may be in favor of the view that it is to be identified with Nahr Taura, though a river identical with Nahr el-'A'waj flowing *ca.* ten miles S of Damascus may very well have been said to be one of the rivers of Damascus. In Wadi 'A'waj there were in ancient times important centers of settlement. The mound of Deir Khabiye, SW of Damascus, hides the remains of a town which, particularly in the Old Babylonian period, must have been of considerable importance.

Bibliography. E. Robinson, *Neuere biblische Forschungen* (1857); W. Wright, *Exp.* (1896). A. HALDAR

PHARZITES. KJV form of Perezites. *See* PEREZ.

PHASEAH. KJV form of PASEAH in Neh. 7:51.

PHASELIS fə sē'lĭs [Φάσηλις] (I Macc. 15:23). A city of Asia Minor, situated on a promontory on the coast of Lycia. Possessing three harbors, it was an important trading place in the sixth century B.C., and at that period it was issuing its own coins. It had to cease doing so for a time when the Athenian confederacy gained ascendancy on the coasts of Asia Minor, but from the beginning of the fourth century Phaselis became virtually independent. It probably came under the power of the Ptolemies in the third century, and it seems to have been a member of the Lycian confederacy from *ca.* 168 B.C. On the other hand, it must have been a free city in 138, when the Roman consul Lucius required certain states, expressly including Phaselis, not to fight against the Jews, and to grant them privileges. It would therefore appear that Phaselis held a substantial Jewish colony at that time. In the next century, under the Romans, the city lost its independence. It had become the ideal haven for pirates.

This city is not to be confused with Phasaelis, the town in the Jordan Valley which was founded by Herod the Great in memory of his brother Phasael. N. TURNER

PHASIRON făs'ə rŏn [Φασιρών; Vulg. *Phaseron*] (I Macc. 9:66). Ancestor of some who were struck down by Jonathan near Bethbasi. J. C. SWAIM

PHASSARON. KJV Apoc. alternate form of PASHHUR.

PHEBE. KJV form of PHOEBE.

PHENICE, PHENICIA. KJV forms of PHOENICIA.

PHERESITE; PHEREZITE. KJV Apoc. forms of PERIZZITE.

PHICOL fī'kŏl [פיכל]; KJV PHICHOL. Abimelech's commander-in-chief in contests with Abraham (Gen. 21:22-32 [E]) and Isaac (26:26-31 [J]).

Bibliography. W. F. Albright, "Egypt and the Early History of the Negeb," *JPOS*, IV (1924), 138-39. L. HICKS

PHILADELPHIA fĭl'ə dĕl'fĭ ə [Φιλαδελφία, Φιλαδέλφεια]. **1.** A city in the province of Lydia in W Asia Minor (Rev. 1:11; 3:7).

Philadelphia, modern Alaşehir, is located in one of the river valleys of the ancient country and Roman province of Lydia. Its river, the ancient

Cogamis, is a tributary of the Hermus (modern Gediz) and a natural line of communication from Sardis, the ancient capital of Lydia, to the East. The modern railroad still follows the Hermus and Cogamis valleys, with an important town and station located at Alaşehir.

The city of Philadelphia was built on a plateau on the S side of the Cogamis River, its high ground an extension of the Tmolus Mountain and protected by minor streams flowing to the N. Its strategic location was one of the main reasons for its Hellenistic foundation by Attalus II (Philadelphus; 159-138 B.C.), after whom the city was named. The Pergamene kings needed the communication from Pergamum via Sardis and Philadelphia to the Maeander Valley and the S highway (with the cities of Laodicea and Hierapolis). The country was fertile enough to support the new city, although the region was subject to severe earthquakes (Strabo XII.579; XIII. 628). Many people preferred living in the country to staying in the city, and part of the wealth of Philadelphia was located in villages belonging to the city, as attested for imperial times.

The Hellenistic career of the city seems to have been fairly prosperous. Coinage began in the second century B.C.; Macedonian shields appearing as coin types indicate that some colony of Macedonian veterans was incorporated in the city.

In Roman times the vicissitudes of the city again are mostly reconstructed from numismatic (and some epigraphic) evidence. The disastrous earthquake of A.D. 17 hit Philadelphia as one among many prominent cities of Asia Minor (Tac. Ann. II.47). Tiberius came to its aid, and in gratitude the city assumed the epithet of Neocaesarea. Under Vespasian the title Flavia began to appear on coins; from the time of Caracalla (*ca.* 214) the city was called Neokoros ("temple warden") in connection with the cult of the emperor.

Administratively the city belonged to the district of Sardis, which maintained its status as the leading city of Lydia. The prosperity of Philadelphia was based on agriculture as well as industry, which here, as elsewhere in Lydia, was marked by textile and leather production. Considerable wealth of private citizens is attested, and in the fifth century A.D. the city was nicknamed "little Athens" because of its festivals and pagan cults.

The rise of Christianity in Philadelphia and the early history of its church (Rev. 1:11; 3:7) cannot yet be substantiated by archaeological discoveries.

Courtesy of the Oriental Institute, the University of Chicago

43. General view of ancient Philadelphia in Asia Minor

Courtesy of William Sanford La Sor

44. Roman ruins of Philadelphia (modern Alaşehir), founded by Attalus Philadelphia of Pergamum before 138 B.C.

The subsequent history of the site and the rise of the modern city of Alaşehir have left little visible evidence of its Hellenistic and Roman past.

The glory of Philadelphia as a stronghold of Christianity was, however, renewed in the days of the Seljuk and Ottoman attacks on the Byzantine Empire. Philadelphia maintained itself as an isolated Christian city in conquered territory and withstood two sieges with heroism. When it fell in 1391, it surrendered to the combined forces of Beyazit I and his Greek supporters under Manuel II.

Figs. PHI 43-44.

Bibliography. W. M. Ramsay, *The Letters to the Seven Churches of Asia* (1904), pp. 391-412; D. Magie, *Roman Rule in Asia Minor* (1950), pp. 124-25, 982-83.

2. *See* RABBAH OF THE AMMONITES.

M. J. MELLINK

PHILARCHES fĭ lär′kēz. KJV transliteration of φυλάρχης (RSV COMMANDER) in II Macc. 8:32.

***PHILEMON, LETTER TO** fĭ lē′mən, fī— [Φιλήμων]. A letter written by Paul; now the eighteenth book of the NT canon. As the letter has usually been interpreted, it carries a request that the slave ONESIMUS be restored to the household of his owner, Philemon. Another interpretation of the request, which has been persuasively defended by John Knox, is that the slave be freed for evangelistic work in the Christian community.

1. Authorship
2. Destination

3. Content and purpose
4. Place and time of writing
Bibliography

1. Authorship. Although some few scholars have questioned the authenticity of Philemon, most accept it as genuine. The major ground for question is the close connection of this letter with Colossians, and the fact that the Colossian letter in both content and vocabulary has major differences from the rest of Paul's letters. Such differences can, however, be accounted for by the circumstances under which the letter was written and the purpose it was intended to serve. Once the Colossian letter is mentioned in this connection, the problem created by its close similarity to Ephesians must be considered; and many scholars hold that Ephesians is not from the hand of Paul, but is rather a covering letter written by a to-us-unknown Christian when the corpus of Paul's letters was made up. Even if this view of Ephesians is accepted, however, there is no valid reason for doubting the Pauline authorship of Colossians and Philemon, although some hold that additions were made to Paul's Letter to the Colossians by the author of the Ephesian letter (*see* COLOSSIANS; EPHESIANS). The earliest quotation of the Letter to Philemon is by Origen, who ascribes it to Paul. Marcion and the Muratorian Fragment both include it in their lists of Paul's letters, and all evidence points to its having belonged to the earliest Pauline collections.

2. Destination. The destination of the letter is not so easily settled. Both Goodspeed and Knox believe that the letter now entitled "Philemon" is the original "letter from Laodicea" mentioned by Paul in Col. 4:16: "When this letter has been read among you, have it read also in the church of the Laodiceans; and see that you read also the letter from Laodicea." The grounds for this view are, briefly, the fact that a letter so commended by Paul is not likely to have been lost; the improbability that the letter referred to as being written at the same time as Colossians to the same or a neighboring church is not identical with the letter (i.e., our Philemon) which on other grounds we know was sent at this same time; and most cogently, the fact that the content of the letter and the salutation make it clear that it is actually a church letter, not a personal one, and therefore appropriate for reading in the congregation. Whether Archippus or Philemon was the owner of the slave Onesimus, and whether Archippus lived at Colossae (as Knox believes) or at Laodicea (according to Goodspeed), the burden of the request is the same: that the slave Onesimus be freed.

3. Content and purpose. The purpose and content of the letter are in most major respects free from question. This is an eloquent and graceful appeal for the freedom of a slave, an appeal which gains the reader's appreciation for its tact and skill when the conditions of slave life in the Roman Empire in the first century A.D. are brought to mind. Punishments were severe for runaways, and this slave had not only run away, but had also robbed his master (Philem. 18-19). One of Juvenal's Satires (VI) describes brutal treatment administered as punishment to slaves, and a legal provision of this period prohibits the giving over of slaves to wild beasts without the approval of constituted authorities. Under ordinary circumstances, Onesimus might have been in danger for his life in going back to his master.

But something momentous has happened to him since he ran away. He has come to know that master of souls, Paul, and has become his "child" (Philem. 10) and a helper to him in his imprisonment (vs. 11). Here the pun on the slave's name, Onesimus, which in Greek means "useful," introduces delicately the fact that Paul might have been minded to keep the young man with him in prison instead of sending him back to his master. How skilfully the request for the slave's freedom is put! Paul might have kept him for his own comfort and help in prison. He does not even command the owner to free the culprit, though he might have done so by reason of the authority of his leadership. He makes the request diplomatically, indicating his preference for the consent of the owner, so that the slave's freedom would be a gift of the spirit, and not an act compelled by any outward authority. Then the note of Christian brotherhood is struck. Whether the young man remained with Paul or was freed by his master and taken back into the household, or was freed for evangelistic work, they would all be partners, brothers beloved in the circle of Christian friendship (vss. 15-17). Paul himself, like the good Samaritan in the story, will repay what has been lost to the slave's master. The final touch of tactfulness and skill is the expression of faith in the master on Paul's part that even more will be done for the runaway than is explicitly asked in the letter. The impact of this letter on the reader even twenty centuries later is such as to evoke the question: How could anyone resist such an appeal?

The point of greatest question with respect to the content of the letter is as to whether Paul's request is for the slave's reinstatement in the household of the owner, or for his freedom for evangelistic work. The preposition περὶ in Philem. 10 and the noun διακονία in Col. 4:17 bear the weight of this question. Does the preposition, translated "for" in the RSV: "I appeal to you *for* my child, Onesimus," really mean "in behalf of"? Is the "ministry" that Archippus is called to fulfil a service to the Christian community, a service which we know about through the Letter to Philemon, or does it have to do with his general responsibility, and not specifically with the request in the Letter to Philemon? The evidence, though not conclusive, is strong enough to support the conclusion drawn by Knox that we do know the nature of the service to which Archippus is called and that that service is the freeing of the slave, not just for reinstatement in the owner's household, but for the work of the Christian church. This position gains support from the mention of one Onesimus in the letter of Ignatius of Antioch in the early second century to the Ephesians as the bishop of the church at Ephesus. The same pun on the name Onesimus occurs in the Ignatian letter as occurs in Philemon. If Onesimus was a young man at the time of the writing of Philemon, he would not be too old to be the bishop of Ephesus at the time of Ignatius' writing. There is at least nothing to deny the identification in the available evidence.

Superlatives abound in the discussion of the Letter to Philemon. Knox calls it "one of the most skillful letters ever written"; P. N. Harrison, "a gem unique." Lightfoot speaks of it as "infinitely precious." Even the casual reader experiences a glowing sense of the partnership of the early Christians at opposite ends of the social scale as he reads the restrained eloquence of Paul's appeal to a slave-owner on behalf of a slave. After twenty centuries, the appeal of the letter is not diminished. Reading it today, one knows that this appeal is for the ultimate, the unchanging, the universal and immortal way, the way of gentleness and brotherhood—not for the assertion of authority, but for eliciting the best in the one addressed. It calls to a man and a community for the exercise of Christian love in a situation in which authority would have been the natural way, and in which according to accepted standards of the time cruelty would not have been criticized.

In this connection a word should be said about Paul's attitude toward the institution of slavery. Nowhere in Paul's letters is there a discussion of the institution of slavery. Like the letter of Pliny the Younger to Sabinianus on a similar subject, the Letter to Philemon does not raise the question of the institution of slavery. Nor does the Colossian letter discuss it, where the institution is taken for granted and slaves are enjoined to "obey in everything those who are your earthly masters, not with eyeservice, as men-pleasers but in singleness of heart, fearing the Lord. Whatever your task, work heartily, as serving the Lord and not men" (Col. 3:22-23). This passage suggests that even slavery can be lifted up into the service of God and be dedicated as Christian service. In its very nature, however, slavery is antithetical to the heart of the Christian gospel; but so are political revolution and bloody warfare. Only a bloody revolution could at that time have changed the institution, and Paul chose the method of working for brotherhood within the prevailing social pattern. As many have pointed out, he was sowing the seeds of a more spiritual type of revolution—that of the transformation of relationships.

4. Place and time of writing. Paul was in prison (Philem. 1, 9-10, 13, 23), and the same persons send greetings with his as send them in the Colossian letter. Onesimus is mentioned in the Colossian letter along with Tychicus (Col. 4:9) as the bearer of the letter. The customary assumption has been that these two letters went together from Paul's imprisonment in Rome. Only one other imprisonment is mentioned in the book of Acts—namely, that in Caesarea—and most scholars have seen Rome as the more probable situation of these two alternatives. But recent scholarship has turned to another possibility: Ephesus, a city far more accessible to the runaway slave from Colossae or Laodicea, and quite possibly one of the "far more imprisonments" mentioned by Paul in II Cor. 11:23. Ephesus also provides an acceptable answer to the question as to how Paul could be expecting to visit the churches in the Lycus Valley if he were at a far-distant point, such as either Rome or Caesarea. If he is in Ephesus, the request for a guest room to be prepared for his visit has a more plausible background (Philem. 22). The greatest deterrent to this placing of the letter is that of its necessary connection with Colossians, and the difficulty of giving Colossians a date earlier than the very end of Paul's life. The language and style of Colossians, as well as its theology, differ radically from Paul's earlier letters, and thus the latest possible date is welcomed for it. As has been indicated above, P. N. Harrison solves this difficulty by positing additions to the original Colossian letter by the author of the Letter to the Ephesians. If the Ephesian imprisonment is accepted as the place of the writing, then the date of the Letter to Philemon would be *ca.* A.D. 56. If Rome is held to be the place of writing, then the date would be half a decade later.

Bibliography. Commentaries: J. B. Lightfoot, *St. Paul's Epistles to the Colossians and to Philemon* (1890). E. Lohmeyer, *Die Briefe an die Philipper, an die Kolosser und an Philemon* (1954). J. Knox, Introduction and Exegesis of Philemon, *IB,* vol. XI (1957). C. F. D. Moule, *The Epistles to the Colossians and to Philemon, The Cambridge Greek Testament* (1957).

Special studies: E. J. Goodspeed, *New Solutions to NT Problems* (1927); *The Meaning of Ephesians* (1933). E. R. Goodenough, "Paul and Onesimus," *HTR,* vol. XXII (Oct. 1950). P. N. Harrison, "Onesimus and Philemon," *ATR*, vol. XXXII (Oct., 1950). J. Knox, *Philemon Among the Letters of Paul* (rev. ed., 1959). M. E. LYMAN

PHILETUS fĭ lē'təs, fĭ— [Φίλητος, beloved] (II Tim. 2:17). A Christian who used "profane jargon" (Moffatt)—no doubt, of a Gnostic variety—and thereby could destroy the faith of some believers. Timothy is instructed to avoid such teaching, which included, among other things, a denial of the resurrection of the body.

See also HYMENAEUS. B. H. THROCKMORTON, JR.

PHILIP fĭl'ĭp [Φίλλιππος]. **1.** Philip II, king of Macedonia 359-336 B.C.; father of Alexander the Great (I Macc. 1:1). Under his rule Macedonia rose from an obscure, beleaguered state to become the dominant power in Greek affairs. Following the Battle of Chaeronea (338 B.C.), Philip forced all the Greek states except Sparta to form a Hellenic League and began to marshal their combined strength against Persia. He was assassinated in 336 B.C. shortly before he was ready to send his armies into Asia Minor. His son Alexander, who was then twenty years old, was able to restore order and to hold his father's position. Two years later, in 334 B.C., Alexander began the campaign which overthrew the Persian Empire and extended the power of the Greeks to the "ends of the earth" (I Macc. 1:3; cf. Dan. 8:5-7).

2. Philip V, king of Macedonia 220-179 B.C. He was humiliated by the Romans in 197 B.C. (I Macc. 8:5; cf. Livy 33.7). During the Carthaginian wars, Philip entered into an ineffectual alliance with Hannibal (215 B.C.). In 200, Roman armies invaded his

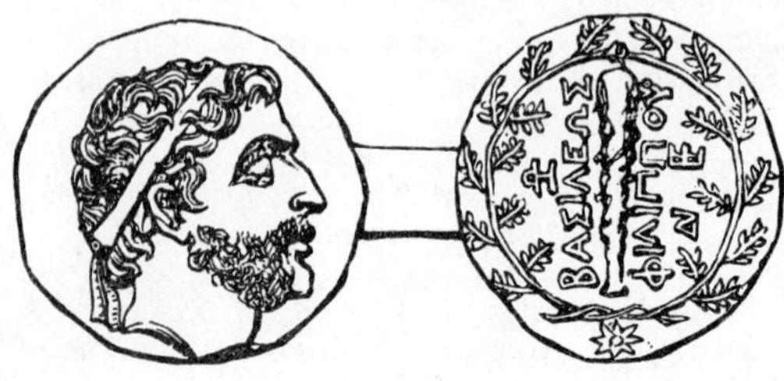

45. A coin showing Philip V of Macedon

kingdom, and after the Battle of Cynocephalae in Thessaly (197), forced him to accept humiliating terms of peace. Macedonia did not become a Roman province until 168 B.C., when Perseus, his eldest son and successor, was defeated and taken prisoner by Aemilius Paulus at the Battle of Pydna. Fig. PHI 45.

3. A Phrygian, appointed governor of Jerusalem and Judea by Antiochus Epiphanes (II Macc. 5:22). He is mentioned only in II Maccabees, where it is said that he was "more barbarous in character" than Antiochus. The appointment was made shortly after Antiochus plundered the Jewish temple, probably in the late summer or fall of 169 B.C. (I Macc. 1:20-24; cf. Dan. 11:25-28), although the reference in II Maccabees places this event one year later. He was active during the period when Antiochus proscribed Judaism and attempted to force Hellenization on the Jewish people (II Macc. 6:11; 8:8).

4. The foster brother and trusted courtier (friend) of Antiochus Epiphanes (I Macc. 6:14-18; II Macc. 9:29; cf. Jos. Antiq. XII.ix.2). Following the death of Antiochus, both he and LYSIAS sought control of the Seleucid state. Philip, who was with Antiochus in Persia at the time of his death, was appointed to serve as regent during the minority of Antiochus V. Lysias, however, seized the regency for himself (I Macc. 6:17) and either executed Philip (Jos. Antiq. XII.ix.7) or forced him to withdraw to Egypt (II Macc. 9:29; cf. I Macc. 6:62-63). The fact that Philip returned from Persia and took temporary possession of the capital city of Antioch may have aided the cause of the Jewish patriots. Lysias was besieging Jerusalem and was about to force its capitulation when word of Philip's presence in Antioch reached him (I Macc. 6:55-56; cf. II Macc. 13:23). Lysias immediately lifted the siege, made a favorable treaty of peace with the Jews, and hastened to Antioch to deal with Philip (I Macc. 6:57-63).

5. Philip the tetrarch, son of Herod the Great and Cleopatra of Jerusalem. From 4 B.C. to 34 A.D., Philip was tetrarch of the sparsely populated area stretching N and E from the Sea of Galilee toward Damascus. The appointment was made by the Emperor Augustus in accordance with the latest will of Herod the Great. The remaining portions of Herod's kingdom fell to Philip's half brothers ARCHELAUS and Herod Antipas (*see* HEROD [FAMILY] § E). According to Josephus (Antiq. XVII.viii.1; xi.4), Philip's tetrarchy included Batanea, TRACHONITIS, Auranitis, Gaulanitis, and Panias. Luke 3:1 indicates that ITURAEA was also included. Effective control of these regions was essential to the Roman state, because they formed a first line of defense against the Nabateans and the Parthians and because strategic lanes of commerce and communication were located here. The population of the area was largely non-Jewish. In this difficult situation Philip not only fulfilled his responsibilities to Rome but ruled with such justice and benevolence that he gained the respect and affection of his subjects (Jos. Antiq. XVIII.iv.6). His capital was located at BETH-SAIDA, on the E shore of the Sea of Galilee. He transformed the village into a city and renamed it Julias in honor of the daughter of Augustus. He also built the pagan city CAESAREA PHILIPPI. After his death (A.D. 34) his tetrarchy became part of the Roman province Syria. Later it was included in the kingdom of Herod Agrippa I (37-44).

Philip the tetrarch should not be confused with the "Philip" who is named as the first husband of HERODIAS in Mark 6:17 (=Matt. 14:3; cf. Luke 3:19). Philip the tetrarch married Herodias' daughter SALOME. The person referred to here is Philip's half brother Herod, the father of Salome and the son of Herod the Great and Mariamne II. It is possible that he also had the name of Philip, but there is no other record of it (cf. Jos. Antiq. XVIII.v.4).

6. Philip the apostle. In the Synoptic gospels Philip is mentioned only in the lists of the apostles (Mark 3:18=Matt. 10:3=Luke 6:14; cf. Acts 1;13). In the Gospel of John he has a larger role. Here he is one of the first to be called (1:43); is instrumental in bringing Nathanael to Jesus (vss. 45-49); and is mentioned personally in connection with the feeding of the five thousand (6:5-7), and in one of Jesus' major discourses (14:8-9). It is particularly noteworthy that he came from BETH-SAIDA (1:44) and that he was singled out as an intermediary by "certain Greeks" who sought contact with Jesus (12:20-23). References to Philip in the second century reflect a tendency to confuse the apostle with Philip the evangelist (*see* 7 *below*). An explicit identification was made by Polycrates, bishop of Antioch (Euseb. Hist. III.31.3), and Clement of Alexandria (Strom. III.6.16). The confusion may have occurred as early as Papias (*ca.* A.D. 140; see Euseb. Hist. III.39.9). Some scholars suspect that the tradition recorded in John reflects a similar confusion. A Gnostic work, the Gospel of Philip, is mentioned by Epiphanius (*Heresies* XXVI.13). Philip also has a prominent place in the Pistis Sophia, a remarkable Gnostic work of the third century.

7. Philip the evangelist (Acts 21:8). This Philip should not be confused with Philip the apostle (6 *above*). He appears first as one of the Greek-speaking Christians set apart to perform certain administrative tasks in the Jerusalem community (Acts 6:5). According to Acts 8:4-5 he was among those who were forced to leave Jerusalem following the martyrdom of Stephen. He fled to Samaria, where he was successful as a missionary (vss. 5-13). SIMON MAGUS is said to have been one of his converts (vs. 13; cf. vss. 20-21). He instructed and baptized a non-Jew (vss. 26-39) and preached in every city from Ashdod to Caesarea on the sea (vs. 40). According to 21:8-9, he and four daughters, who were known as virgin prophetesses, established a residence there. Both Philip and his daughters are remembered in later tradition, particularly by the Montanists (Euseb. Hist. III.31.3-4; V.24). Philip is said to have been bishop of Tralles (Basil *Menol.* I.cxi, in Migne, CXVII, 103).

H. H. PLATZ

PHILIP, ACTS OF. One of several romances, not earlier than the fourth or fifth century, purporting to chronicle the destinies of those apostles who had not been treated in the earlier corpus of apocryphal Acts assembled by the Manicheans. In this later romance, spun out of legend and folklore, but not without interest, attention is paid to the adventures and miracles of Philip and his martyrdom by crucifixion head downward at Hierapolis. In Greek the account is divided into fifteen acts, of which we have the first nine and the martyrdom, which latter, as was true of all this type of writing, circulated separately in several recensions. *See* ACTS, APOCRYPHAL; APOCRYPHA, NT.

Bibliography. The best critical edition of the reconstructed text is still that found in Lipsius-Bonnet, *Acta Apostolorum Apocrypha* (1898), II, 1. A résumé and translation of selected sections is provided by M. R. James, *The Apocryphal NT* (1924), pp. 439-53. See also J. Flamion, *Les trois recensions greques du martyre de l'apôtre Philippe* (1914). M. S. ENSLIN

*__PHILIP, GOSPEL OF.__ A gospel forged "in the name of Philip the holy disciple" and used by the Egyptian Gnostics, according to Epiphanius (*Heresies* XXVI.13). He quotes a few sentences from it, beginning with the words: "The Lord revealed unto me what the soul must say as it goes up into heaven, and how it must answer each of the powers above." Then follows the "answer," including the words: "I have begotten no children unto the ruler"—apparently a password. It evidences a strong asceticism, as well as the popular Gnostic notion that the sparks of the divine, disposed in the world of matter, must be collected and freed from such defiling contact.

In the PISTIS SOPHIA this gospel may be indicated in the statement that it was Philip who wrote down the revelation given by Jesus to his disciples during the years following his resurrection. Clement of Alexandria states that the Marcionites considered Philip an enemy of marriage. These references suggest that the writing was current in the third century, perhaps during the late years of the second. In a MS found in 1946 among other heretical (Gnostic) Coptic books at Chenoboskion in Upper Egypt, it is reported that there is a treatise bearing this title, which may prove to be the work referred to by Epiphanius. *See* APOCRYPHA, NT. M. S. ENSLIN

*__PHILIPPI__ fĭl'ə pī [οἱ Φίλιπποι] (Acts 16:12; 20:6; Phil. 1:1; I Thess. 2:2). A city of MACEDONIA.

Philippi was in E Macedonia in the region bounded by the Strymon River on the W and the Nestos River on the E. The site was *ca.* ten miles inland from the Aegean Sea on a plain enclosed by mountains, the coast range of Symbolon on the S, the advance ranges of the Balkan Highlands on the N, Pangaion on the W, and Orbelos on the E. The acropolis of Philippi was on a spur of the Orbelos massif, and the city lay at its foot. Through the plain and directly through the city ran the chief overland route from Asia to the West, the ancient military and commercial way known in Roman times as the Via Egnatia.

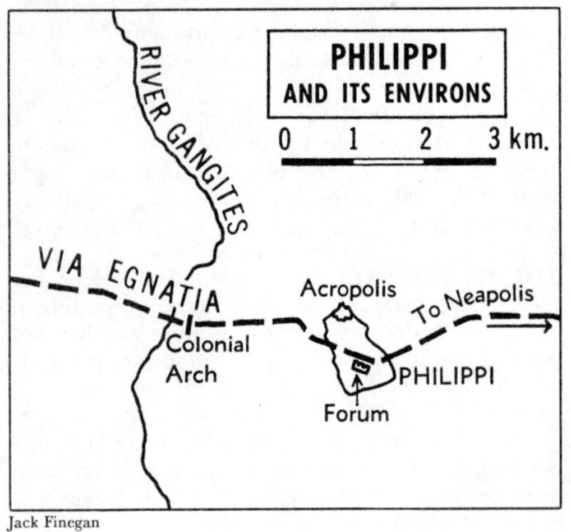

Jack Finegan

According to Diodorus (XVI.iii.7), the site was occupied originally by settlers who came from the offshore island of Thasos, and there is reason for believing that the orator Callistratus, who fled from Athens in 361 B.C., was active in making this settlement. At this time the name of the place was Krenides (αἱ Κρηνίδες), probably with reference to the springs and waters in the vicinity (from κρήνη, "well, spring," plural "water"). In 356 B.C., according to information also provided by Diodorus (XVI. viii.6), Philip II, king of Macedonia (359-336 B.C.), went to Krenides, increased its size with a large number of inhabitants, and changed its name to Philippi, giving it his own name. It was probably also Philip II who built the wall which can still be traced around the city and up over the acropolis, and who constructed the Greek theater, the ruins of which are at the foot of the hill. In 335 B.C., when Alexander the Great marched from Amphipolis toward Thrace, he passed Philippi and Mount Orbelos on his left, as Arrian relates (*Anabasis of Alexander* I.i.5).

In 167 B.C., when Macedonia was divided into four districts (μερίδες) by the Roman consul L. Aemilius Paullus, Philippi fell in the first district, which comprised mainly the area between the Nestos and Strymon rivers; but the honor of being the capital of this district went to Amphipolis.

In 42 B.C., Antony and Octavian defeated Brutus and Cassius in the famous Battle of Philippi, which was fought W of the city near the River Ganga or Gangites. Strabo (VII, fragment 41) says that up to this time Philippi had remained only a small settlement, but was now made larger. By order of Antony some Roman soldiers were settled here, and his legate Q. Paquius Rufus marked out the territory of Philippi as a Roman colony. The title of the colony celebrated the victory just won: Colonia Victrix Philippensium. A dozen years later, in 30 B.C., Octavian dispossessed from their homes in Italy many persons who had sided with Antony, in order to settle his veterans in their communities, and these dispossessed persons were in turn allowed to establish themselves in Philippi and elsewhere (Dio LI.iv. 6). The colony was now refounded with the title Colonia Julia Philippensis; and when in 27 B.C. Octavian received from the Senate the designation Augustus, it was called Colonia Augusta Julia Philippensis.

Excavations were conducted at Philippi by the École Française d'Athènes from 1914 to 1938. The forum of the city lay directly beside the Via Egnatia and was a rectangular area over 300 feet long and 150 feet wide. In the center of the N side was a rectangular podium which must have served as a place for speakers. At the NE and NW corners of the forum rose the symmetrical façades of two large temples. Elsewhere around the forum were other public buildings, including a library, and in addition there were colonnades, porticoes, fountains, and monu-

Courtesy of Harriet-Louise H. Patterson

46. General view of setting of ancient Philippi, showing ruins

Courtesy of Harriet-Louise H. Patterson

47. The theater at Philippi

ments.* The symmetrical arrangement of the forum as uncovered suggests that its major buildings were planned and erected at the same time; and since a temple inscription mentions *divus Antoninus* (died A.D. 161), it is judged that this construction work was not earlier than his successor, Marcus Aurelius (161-80). A few remains were found, however, from the first century A.D., and it is probable that the forum of the Antonine period was built on the place and to some extent after the plan of the more ancient forum, which may have come into existence any time after the founding of the colony. The theater, already mentioned, was rebuilt in Roman style, probably at the same time in the late second century that the main forum buildings were erected.* Fine Roman baths were also constructed, with mosaic pavements dating probably in the middle of the third century A.D. Figs. PHI 46-47.

As revealed in the inscriptions found there and as known from the history of the city, the population of Philippi included Thracians indigenous to the region, Greeks descended from the settlers brought by Callistratus and Philip II, and Romans introduced as colonists by Antony and Octavian. Likewise the religion was composite and included the Thracian god Liber Pater and goddess Bendis; the Greek Athena; the Roman Jupiter, Mars, and the emperor cult; the Anatolian Cybele; and the Egyptian Isis, Serapis, and Harpocrates.

In the text of Acts 16:12 given by Codex Sinaiticus, Codex Alexandrinus, and Codex Ephraemi rescriptus, Philippi is described as the "leading city of the district of Macedonia, and a colony" (πρώτη τῆς μερίδος Μακεδονίας πόλις κολωνία). This is scarcely correct, since, as we have seen, Amphipolis was chosen as capital of the first district, and Thessalonica was the capital of the entire province. Textual variants in Codex Vaticanus and Codex Bezae show that the sentence was not well understood, and it may be conjectured that in its original form it read: πρώτης μερίδος Μακεδονίας πόλις κολωνία. This would then describe Philippi as a "city of the first district of Macedonia, and a colony," which is in precise accordance with its actual status as revealed in the preceding historical sketch.

In Acts 16:13 Paul and his party are described as going "outside the gate to the riverside" (ἔξω τῆς πύλης παρὰ ποταμόν) to find the "place of prayer" (προσευχή) where the Jewish women were assembled to whom the apostle preached. While the gate may have been in the city wall and the place of prayer beside some small stream just outside it, another identification is possible. Over the Via Egnatia, a little more than one mile W of Philippi, was a Roman arch, now ruined; and just beyond this was the river which Appian (*Civil Wars* IV.106) says was called by some Ganga and by others Gangites. The erection of an arch of this sort often accompanied the founding of a colony and was intended to symbolize the dignity and privileges of the city. It could also mark the pomerium, a line enclosing an empty space outside the city wall within which building and burial were prohibited and strange cults were not to be introduced. The Jews may have been required, therefore, to hold their meeting at this distance, and the arch, the simple lines of which indicate a date not later than the first century, may have been the very one beneath which Paul passed.

In connection with Lydia, a "seller of purple goods" (πορφυρόπωλις), a Latin inscription at Philippi is of interest which, with the word [PV]RPVRARI, gives independent testimony to the existence of commerce in purple. Later evidences of Christianity at Philippi include two Latin crosses which may belong from the second to the fourth century; Christian epitaphs, one perhaps as early as the third century; and two large basilicas of the fifth and sixth centuries.

See also NEAPOLIS.

Bibliography. P. Collart, *Philippes, ville de Macédoine, depuis ses origines jusqu'à la fin de l'époque romaine,* École Française d'Athènes, Travaux et Mémoires, fasc. 5 (2 vols.; 1937); J. Schmidt, "Philippoi," *Pauly-Wissowa,* vol. XIX, pt. ii (1938), cols. 2206-44; P. Lemerle, *Philippes et la Macédoine orientale à l'époque chrétienne et byzantine,* Bibliothèque des Écoles Françaises d'Athènes et de Rome, fasc. 158 (2 vols.; 1945); articles in *Bulletin de correspondance hellénique,* École Française d'Athènes.

J. FINEGAN

***PHILIPPIANS, LETTER TO THE** fĭ lĭp'ĭ ənz [Φιλιππήσιοι, *see* PHILIPPI]. A letter written by Paul to the church founded by him in the Macedonian city of Philippi (Acts 16:11-40), his first Christian congregation in Europe; the eleventh book of the NT canon.

Paul is apparently in prison, facing a crisis which may yet issue in death, though as a Christian he dares to hope that he will soon be free to resume his missionary activity and to visit Philippi. Church tradition associates the letter with Rome; but we shall have to consider whether it may not rather have been written from the apostle's imprisonment at Caesarea (Acts 23–26) or from a still earlier imprisonment (not recorded in Acts 19) during his ministry in and around Ephesus.

Of all Paul's letters to churches, Philippians is the most intimately personal. It glows with courage and affectionate concern for his converts. Facing misrepresentation, persecution, and possible martyrdom, he repeatedly proclaims his Christian confidence, and sounds the call to "rejoice."

A. Authorship, canonicity, and text
B. Paul's relations with Philippi
C. Contents and purpose
 1. Salutation and introduction
 2. Reactions to his imprisonment
 3. Appeal for Christian standards and behavior
 4. A statement of plans
 5. Warnings against possible dangers
 6. Closing exhortations
 7. Expression of thanks and conclusion
D. Place and date of writing
 1. Rome
 2. Caesarea
 3. Ephesus
 4. Concluding survey
  a. The silence of Acts
  b. The prospect of martyrdom
E. Doctrine
F. Is the letter a unity?
Bibliography

A. *AUTHORSHIP, CANONICITY, AND TEXT.* This letter was unquestionably written by Paul; in thought and language it bears throughout the impress of his personality. With regard to canonicity (*see* Canon of the NT; Galatians § 6), one may note: Clement of Rome and Ignatius almost certainly show acquaintance with it; it is included in the second-century canons; Irenaeus, Tertullian, and Clement of Alexandria all quote it as Pauline. The textual evidence raises no serious problems.

B. *PAUL'S RELATIONS WITH PHILIPPI.* Acts tells nothing of a Jewish synagogue at Philippi, or of the reactions of Philippian Jews to Paul's preaching. The congregation may have been predominantly Gentile. Acts 16:14-15 (*see* Lydia 1) and Phil. 4:2-3 tell of the active part played by women in its early history; and we know from other sources of the prominent place accorded to women in the social life of Macedonia. The progress to which the letter witnesses had no doubt been furthered by the presence of Luke (indicated by the "we narrative" in Acts 16:10-17, resumed in 20:5) and by a visit subsequently paid by Silas and Timothy (Acts 18:5). The devotion of the Philippians to the Apostle found practical expression in the repeated contributions sent to help him in his missionary work (Phil. 4:10-18). According to Acts, Paul paid them a second and a third visit, both previous to the imprisonments at Caesarea and Rome. Of these the second came when, on the conclusion of his ministry in the province of Asia, he passed through Macedonia on his way to Greece (Acts 20:1-2); and if the letter was written from Ephesus, this would be the visit anticipated in Phil. 2:24. The third visit was an unexpected one in the following spring (Acts 20:6).

C. *CONTENTS AND PURPOSE.* The contents of Philippians show an ordered sequence of thought rather than a systematic arrangement of topics. It has in a special degree the marks of an ordinary "letter": it imparts information; conveys thanks; and expresses good wishes, encouragement, and counsel. But it has also a deeper purpose. In the crisis which has confronted him the Apostle has read a soul-searching lesson which he wishes his beloved Philippians to share with him. It is that the Christian goal can be reached only through humility, self-abnegation, and suffering that does not stop short even of death.

1. Salutation and introduction (1:1-11). The salutation comes from Paul and Timothy—Timothy, with Silas and presumably Luke, had been with the Apostle when the church was founded; and he is with him now, as Silas and Luke are not. But Paul alone is responsible for the letter; he never uses here, as he does in some letters, the first person plural, and he refers objectively to Timothy in 2:19-23. He does not stress his apostolic authority: he and Timothy are "servants of Christ Jesus." Grouped with "the saints" as recipients are bishops and deacons (*see* Bishop; Deacon), presumably in recognition of their assistance in sending help to the Apostle. It is probable that the ministry at Philippi is still at a rudimentary stage, and that the terms used, though on the way to acquiring their later technical use, are still in a measure descriptive of function. The bishops (ἐπίσκοποι; lit., "overseers"), of whom there are several in this one congregation, are no doubt equivalent to presbyters (*see* Elder). The deacons (διάκονοι; lit., "men who serve") would have specific duties of a subordinate kind, including perhaps the charge of finance.

The introduction, longer and more detailed than is usual in Paul's letters, strikes the keynote of "fellowship in service"; and the frequent repetition of the word "all" suggests the Apostle's deep concern for unity. The active partnership of the Philippians "from the first day until now" leads the Apostle to anticipate with confidence their continued progress, and it is significant that he twice points forward to the "day of Christ." *See* § E *below*.

2. Reactions to his imprisonment (1:12-26). Paul proceeds at once to assure the Philippians that his recent experiences (of which they had probably heard with some anxiety) have advanced, rather than hindered, the cause of the gospel. It was now recognized in government circles (*see* § D3 *below*) that his imprisonment arose simply from his loyalty to Christ (apparently his accusers had misrepresented him to the authorities), and many of the local Christians had acquired a new boldness in preaching. Others of them were, unfortunately, dissociating themselves from the Apostle, apparently out of a desire to avoid persecution; but Paul's only reaction (in striking contrast to Gal. 1:7-9, where the truth of the gospel is in question) is to rejoice that Christ is being proclaimed. His joy and confidence in the progress of the gospel will, he asserts, be unaffected by what may happen to him; and in vss. 21-24 he balances the relative advantage of life and death, expressing in the end his firm conviction that he will live, to be of further service to the Philippians and to visit them.

3. Appeal for Christian standards and behavior (1:27–2:18). The Philippians have something to learn from all this. They, too, must contend unitedly for the faith and be ready to suffer for it, as they have seen Paul do at Philippi (Acts 16:19-40) and as they have heard that he is now doing. An appeal for Christian humility in their corporate relationships (in vs. 5 contrast RSV with KJV) is reinforced in a sublime christological passage (2:5-11; *see* § E *below*) depicting the utter self-abnegation of Jesus (even "unto death") and his consequent exaltation. Emphasis is here laid on obedience (i.e., to the divine will); in Christian obedience the Philippians must continue, even in the apostle's absence, to carry on under God the work of salvation, advancing by their lives the cause of the gospel in a heathen environment and keeping in mind the coming of the "day of Christ." As a climax the apostle adds that, if he should be called to consummate by his death the sacrifice which they by their faith are offering in life, he and they will have good cause to congratulate one another.

4. A statement of plans (2:19-30). From this glance at death's lurking shadow Paul turns to write calmly about future plans. In Christian hope and confidence ("in the Lord"; vss. 19, 24) he looks forward to sending Timothy "soon" to Philippi, also to coming "soon" himself. Epaphroditus (whom the Philippians had sent to bring their latest gift to Paul and probably to remain as their missionary-representative on his staff) has been so very ill that he must now return to Philippi—is he perhaps to take the letter with him?

5. Warnings against possible dangers (ch. 3). After a further call to "rejoice" in 3:1, there is an abrupt transition (*see* § F *below*). Paul suddenly launches out into an impassioned tirade against Jewish (possibly Jewish Christian) propagandists. They had perhaps not yet reached Philippi; but the violence of his language is a measure of his sense of the danger as he had experienced it elsewhere (*see* § D4 *below*). Stirred to the depths, he turns from denunciation to recall what Christian faith has meant to him, as true a son of Israel as any of his opponents —he tells of his utter discarding of Jewish privileges, his turning from legalism to faith in Christ, his dying with Christ, his hope of sharing Christ's resurrection. This in turn leads him to issue stern warnings against two retrograde tendencies in the Philippian church. One is a false "perfectionism" (*see* PERFECTION); against this Paul emphasizes, as elsewhere in this letter, the need for progress in the Christian life (vss. 10-15; cf. 1:9-11, 25; 2:12-13). The other tendency is a libertinism which panders to the body, forgetful that the Christian belongs to a heavenly commonwealth and that, after Christ has come from heaven to deliver the body (cf. Eph. 5:23) from the conditions of earth, he is to have like Christ a glorified body (vss. 17-21).

6. Closing exhortations (4:1-9). These warnings completed, the apostle again exhorts his converts to steadfastness, to concord (here he mentions by name two women, and asks his "true yokefellow," who may perhaps be Epaphroditus, to help them), to prayerfulness, and to other virtues, including (4:8) the pursuit of certain ideals that are honored in the pagan ethic.

7. Expression of thanks and conclusion (4:10-23). Paul has purposely kept to the end what he has now to say—does he perhaps write this in his own hand? He thanks the Philippians for their latest gift, received some little time ago with the coming of Epaphroditus (*see* § D3 *below*). He does so with cordiality, but also (for his acceptance of financial help was liable to be misrepresented by his enemies; cf. II Cor. 11:7-12) with a manly independence. Here he introduces two terms (αὐτάρκης [vs. 11] and μεμύημαι [vs. 12]) which, though they had a wider currency, recall Stoic teaching and the language of the mystery religions; and some of his other expressions have parallels in the parable of the lost son (Luke 15:14, 16-17)—had Paul perhaps read Luke's narrative at this point (cf. also 2:18 with Luke 15:6, 9)? The letter then closes with greetings and the benediction.

D. *PLACE AND DATE OF WRITING.* Three possibilities fall to be considered: Rome, Caesarea, and Ephesus.

1. Rome. Church tradition since Chrysostom has maintained that Paul's imprisonment letters (Philippians, Ephesians, Colossians, Philemon) were written from Rome. Critical scholarship has on the whole, until recently, endorsed this position, and has gone on to discuss the place of Philippians within the group—the prevailing opinion being that Philippians, with its threat of death, comes last (Paul's "swan song"), though its literary affinities with Romans have led some scholars to put it first. There are loopholes, however, in the pre-Chrysostom tradition. Origen thought that Philippians, because of its teaching on Christian "perfection," might have come between I and II Corinthians; and the Marcionite Prologues, while dating Philippians and Philemon from Rome, connect Colossians with Ephesus. Chrysostom and his successors in the school of Antioch seem to have had no other authority for connecting Philippians with Rome beyond what seemed to be the evidence of the letter itself (notably 1:13; 4:22), supplemented by their knowledge of the Apostle's trial and death at Rome. This being so, the Roman origin of the letter is essentially a hypothesis, to be weighed in the balance with other hypotheses. Among other arguments against it, we may note that Acts 28 gives a very different picture (admittedly not a complete one) of Paul's position as a prisoner and of the attitude of the local Christians, and that his expectation of proceeding on his release to Philippi (2:24), as also to Colossae (Philem. 22), would imply an abandonment of his hope of advancing from Rome to Spain (Rom. 15:28).

2. Caesarea. First propounded in 1799, the hypothesis that Philippians dates from the Caesarean imprisonment has continued to have a few powerful advocates. But is it likely that at Caesarea death loomed for Paul so threateningly on the near horizon? And why should Paul at Caesarea plan to go soon to Philippi (which he had visited twice recently; Acts 20:1, 3-6) instead of proceeding as soon as possible to Rome?

3. Ephesus. The case for Ephesus (put forward, in a form no longer acceptable, by H. Lisco in 1900) calls for more detailed examination.

The fierce hostility which Paul experienced in

Asia (Acts 20:18-19; I Cor. 15:32; cf. II Cor. 1:8-10) very probably issued in one or more imprisonments (II Cor. 11:23). *See* EPHESUS.

If Paul writes from Ephesus, the visits of Timothy and him to Philippi (2:19-24) have an exact parallel in the Ephesus narrative of Acts 19:21-22, and also (as they expected to go on from Macedonia to Corinth) in I Corinthians (4:17-19; 16:5-11), which was written from Ephesus.

We learn from 2:25-26 that the Philippians, having sent Epaphroditus, had heard with sorrow of his illness, and he in turn had heard of their distress. This indicates three journeys already made; and two journeys are to follow, when Timothy goes to Philippi and returns to report, and thereafter Paul himself hopes to go "soon" (2:19-24). Allowance must, of course, be made for the length of Paul's imprisonment in Rome and for reasonably easy communications between Philippi and the capital city; nevertheless, these frequent comings and goings are much more easily understood if Paul is in Ephesus, which (as we see from Acts 20:6-16) could be reached from Philippi within ten days.

The interval during which the generous Philippians "had no opportunity" to help the apostle (4:10-18) was, if he is writing from Rome, perhaps as much as ten years, and during this time he had visited Philippi twice. The situation becomes much more probable, and Paul's language is redeemed from any suggestion of cynical rebuke, if after assisting the Apostle at Thessalonica and at Corinth the Philippians had now come to his help at his next center, Ephesus, after a comparatively short interval of which part had been spent in revisiting Jerusalem(?), Antioch, and Galatia (Acts 18:21-23).

The terms in 1:13; 4:22, PRAETORIUM and CAESAR'S HOUSEHOLD, have no necessary reference to Rome. Members of Caesar's administrative staff (*domus Caesaris*) were, as we know from inscriptions, to be found at Ephesus, as elsewhere throughout the Empire. The precise meaning of the phrase in 1:13 has been much disputed. In Rome it would refer to the PRAETORIAN GUARD—not "the palace" (KJV). But in the provinces *praetorium* was the name for the governor's headquarters; and here, where the reference is obviously personal, Paul is probably thinking primarily of the judicial authorities, though a more general reference, to include other officials and soldiers of the guard, need not be wholly excluded.

4. Concluding survey. Paul's ministry in Asia was one of the most challenging periods in his missionary career; for by this time certain parties in Judaism were fully determined both to accomplish (if need be) his death and to win back his Gentile churches into the all-embracing fold of the ancient Jewish religion. This, rather than the Roman period, would seem to provide the background for the crisis of Phil. 1:12-26 and the denunciatory outburst of 3:2.

Partly to counter this Judaizing movement, and as a demonstration of the reality of Gentile Christianity, Paul began toward the end of his Ephesian ministry to organize an OFFERING for the needy "saints" in Jerusalem, soliciting contributions from the churches of Galatia, Achaia (Corinth), and Macedonia. The absence of any reference in Philippians to the collection has been urged as an argument against dating Philippians from Ephesus. But an entirely adequate explanation is that Paul, who was indebted to the Philippians for their other gift, preferred to wait till he or one of his deputies could arrive to lay the scheme personally before them. It would appear from I Cor. 16:1 (which does not mention Macedonia) and II Cor. 8:1-5 that the initiation of the collection in Philippi came between I and II Corinthians.

The case for Ephesus is strong; yet doubt may remain till clearer light is seen on certain problems.

a. The silence of Acts. The crisis behind Philippians was obviously serious and prolonged. But the objection that Acts 19 says nothing of it must not be exaggerated, in view of the general purpose and character of the book (*see* ACTS OF THE APOSTLES, *especially* § 5) and the many known gaps in the narrative at this point. The attempt to overcome this objection by supposing that, though written from Ephesus, Philippians refers to an imprisonment at Corinth (Acts 18:12), is gratuitous and unconvincing.

b. The prospect of martyrdom. It is urged that Paul could never have been in danger of a death sentence at Ephesus because as a Roman citizen he could have appealed to Caesar. But as a Christian he might have preferred to accept death, as he accepted flogging (Acts 16:37; II Cor. 11:24). By this time he had come to see clearly that as an apostle he must, like his Lord, be prepared for both persecution and martyrdom (I Cor. 4:9; cf. II Cor. 4:8-12); and he courageously recognizes in Phil. 1:20 that he may honor Christ by death as by life.

Philippians, if written from Ephesus, may be dated in the winter of 54-55. In October, 54, the proconsul of Asia had been murdered (Tac. Ann. XIII.1); and if at such a time Paul's enemies had attempted to secure his condemnation, very little may have stood between him and death. Soon afterward (on his release) he dispatched I Corinthians (Timothy had now left on his mission); and the words in I Cor. 15: 32 about "fighting with beasts at Ephesus" may well recall the crisis behind Philippians. Philemon and Colossians perhaps belong to a period of *libera custodia* in or near Ephesus, after Timothy had returned from Macedonia.

E. *DOCTRINE.* Doctrinal issues affect the question of date. In Philippians doctrine is expressed, as it were, incidentally, in relation to the hard facts of life and of death.

The theological high light is the christological passage in 2:6-11, telling how the humiliation and self-sacrifice of Jesus (the personal name is used) was a prelude under God to exaltation and universal acclamation. Regarded at one time as a sublime piece of theological argument, this passage was used as a basis for the "kenotic" theory of the Atonement, and taken as marking a late stage in Paul's doctrinal development. Against this we must note: (*a*) its setting and purpose are essentially hortatory (cf. II Cor. 8: 9); (*b*) the impressive climax in vss. 9-11 interrupts the logical sequence of the appeal in vss. 4-5, 12-13; and these facts, together with (*c*) its poetical structure, its Semitisms, and certain un-Pauline expressions, suggest that (stripped of a few amplifying phrases) it represents an early Christian hymn (it may be pre-Pauline) expressing Christian doctrine in terms of Christian worship. As commonly interpreted, the hymn would be the earliest known instance of the threefold division of Christ's life into pre-existence, life on earth, and exaltation to heaven. But there is justification (e.g., in the Peshitta rendering) for taking vs. 6 to mean: "He was in the image of God" (i.e., truly man; Gen. 1:26); and the passage may then be read as contrasting the way chosen by Jesus with that followed by Adam (or it may be the fallen angels), whose pursuit of self-glorification had led to downfall. The occurrence in I Corinthians and Romans of this contrast between the first and the second Adam is in line with an Ephesian date for Philippians.

Jesus is depicted in the hymn as the "servant" of Isa. 52:13–53:12; his self-emptying (vs. 7) is not the Incarnation, but the sacrificial outpouring of his life (Isa. 53:12, Hebrew text, not LXX); his obedience (vs. 8; cf. vs. 12) is carried to the extreme length of accepting death; and this unqualified obedience has its fulfilment in his exaltation (cf. Isa. 45:23; 52:13), when he is acclaimed Lord, not of the church merely, but of the universe. The general picture is not the familiar Pauline one of the Messiah, crucified and risen, but that other picture (which has parallels in Hebrews; e.g., 2:9; 12:2) of the Son of Man who was God's "servant" and is now enthroned as Lord. Echoes of the hymn resound in later parts of the letter: life for Paul involves self-abnegation and self-emptying (2:17, 30; 3:7 catch up 2:6-7), and by sharing Christ's sufferings and conforming to his death he trusts he may share Christ's resurrection and glorification (3:10-11, 20-21).

Philippians has many links in its eschatological outlook and teaching with I Corinthians, a letter written near the end of Paul's time in Ephesus. In both he writes (influenced perhaps by the pressure of events) as if the Parousia might not be far off (with Phil. 4:5 cf. *Maranatha* [I Cor. 16:22]; and there are three references in Philippians to the "day of Christ" [1:6, 10; 2:16]). Both letters show that he himself has looked death in the face, and has been thinking deeply about a heavenly or glorified body, the earthly body being "changed" (I Cor. 15:51; Phil. 3:21) to conform to the body of Christ. In line with this teaching is his deep sorrow for those who make their belly their god (3:19); and his brief reference to circumcision in 3:3 probably implies (as in Col. 2:11) that for Christians circumcision involves complete divestment of the "body of flesh."

F. *IS THE LETTER A UNITY?* The abrupt transition to fierce invective at the beginning of ch. 3 has led to the hypothesis that here we have part of a separate letter; and we may note how the call to "rejoice in the Lord" (3:1) is taken up again in 4:4. But the hypothesis is unnecessary and improbable. Where are we to say that this second letter ends? Nothing in the separated parts points to their having originated in different situations (e.g., 3:7-14 has unmistakable links with 2:5-11). It is sufficient to believe that, before turning to those other matters with which he wished to close the letter, Paul recalled that he ought to warn the Philippians of the Judaizing danger. Some critics even postulate a combination of three letters, but without sufficient cause.

It is altogether probable, however, that just as the Philippians communicated from time to time with the Apostle, so also other letters (now lost) passed from him to them, to say nothing of communications made through his deputies. This may have some bearing on the words in 3:1 ("to write the same things"); 3:18 ("of whom I have often told you"), if Paul, writing from Ephesus, had not revisited the church at Philippi since its inception.

Bibliography. Commentaries: J. B. Lightfoot (1890). M. R. Vincent, ICC (1922). J. H. Michael, Moffatt NT Commentary (1928). W. Michaelis, *Theologischer Handkommentar zum NT* (1935). M. Dibélius, *Handbuch zum NT* (1937). P. Bonnard, *Com. du NT* (1950). Lohmeyer, *Meyer's Kommentar* (1953). P. Benoit, *Bible de Jérusalem* (1953).

Introductions to the NT by Moffatt, Goodspeed, Goguel, Feine-Behm, Lake, Michaelis, and McNeile.

Special studies: P. Feine, *Abfassung des Philipperbriefes in Ephesus* (1916). G. S. Duncan, *St. Paul's Ephesian Ministry* (1929); and articles in *ET* (Oct., 1931; March, 1956). W. Michaelis, *Datierung des Philipperbriefes* (1933). Articles in *Bulletin of John Rylands Library, Manchester,* by C. H. Dodd ("The Mind of Paul: Change and Development," Jan., 1934, reprinted in *New Testament Studies,* 1953); and by T. W. Manson (April, 1939).

Important studies of Phil. 2:5-11: E. Lohmeyer, *Kurios Jesus* (1928). E. Käsemann, *ZThK,* XLVII (1950). O. Cullmann, *The Christology of the NT* (1959).

Of recent writers Goodspeed, Dodd, and Beare decide for Rome as the place of origin; Lohmeyer for Caesarea; Feine, Goguel, Dibelius, Michaelis, Bonnard, Benoit, Duncan, favor Ephesus. G. S. DUNCAN

PHILISTINES fĭ lĭs'tĭnz, fĭl'ə stēnz, —stīnz [פלשתים]; PHILISTIA fĭ lĭs'tĭ ə [פלשת]. A people of Aegean origin who occupied the S coast of Palestine and were often at war with the Israelites. Philistia is the name applied to the territory that they occupied.

1. Name and origin
2. Territorial definition
3. Culture and religion
   a. Language
   b. Traits
   c. Political and military organization
   d. Material culture
4. History
   a. From period of expansion to defeat by David (*ca.* 1180-965)
   b. From the time of Solomon to the reign of Ahaz (*ca.* 960-735)
   c. Under Assyrian and Babylonian domination (*ca.* 735-586)

Bibliography

1. Name and origin. The name Philistine is first found in the Egyptian form *prst* as the name of one of the "People of the Sea," who invaded Egypt in the eighth year of Ramses III (*ca.* 1188 B.C.). The Hebrew פלשתי (*pelishtî*) is an ethnic adjective based on the territorial designation פלשת (*pelesheth*). The name occurs in Assyrian sources as both *Pilisti* and *Palastu*. The LXX, when not translating it as "strangers" ('Αλλόφυλοι), usually renders it as Φυλιστιιμ (i.e., Genesis–Joshua). There is no acceptable Semitic etymology for this name, and it is quite probably of Indo-European origin.

According to biblical tradition, the Philistines came originally from CAPHTOR, the Hebrew name for Crete (Jer. 47:4; Amos 9:7; cf. Deut. 2:23). This tradition was accepted by the biblical writers, and it is buttressed by the fact that part of the Philistine coast was called נגב הכרתי, "the Cretan Negeb" (RSV "Negeb of the Cherethites"; I Sam. 30:14), and by the occurrence of Cretans in parallelism with Philistines (Ezek. 25:16; Zeph. 2:5). There is, however, no archaeological indication of the Philistine occupation of Crete. Rather, the Philistines were part of the second wave of the elusive "People of the Sea," who, according to the Egyptian records, attacked Egypt during the reigns of Mer-ne-ptah and Ramses III after having ravaged the Hittite country, the Cilician and N Syrian coast, Carchemish, and Cyprus. Excavations in Anatolia and Syria have shown that many cities—e.g., Ugarit and Khattushash—were destroyed at the end of the Late Bronze Age (*ca.* 1200). Of the "People of the Sea" only the Philistines, who settled along the Palestinian coast, and the Tjeker, who occupied DOR according to the Wen Amon story (*ca.* 1050), can be positively identified. The others, Shekelesh (Siculi?), Denyen (Danaoi; Akkadian *Danuna,* Phoenician *DNNYM?*), Sherden (Sardinian?), and Weshwesh, have only been conjecturally identified. These peoples were displaced from their original homelands as part of the extensive population movements of the latter half of the second millennium B.C. in the E Mediterranean and SE European area. During the fourteenth and thirteenth centuries B.C. they both assimilated the Minoan-Mycenean culture patterns of the Aegean world and seriously disturbed its E part and Asia Minor and Syria.

2. Territorial definition. "Philistia" (in the poetic portions of the OT: Pss. 60:8; 87:4; Isa. 14:29) or the "land of the Philistines" (*passim*) is the name given to that part of the coastal plain of Palestine which lies between Joppa and the Wadi Ghazzeh, *ca.* 6.2 miles S of Gaza (*see* PALESTINE, GEOGRAPHY OF). The Philistine pentapolis consisted of GAZA, ASHKELON, and ASHDOD on the coast; GATH in the W Shephelah; and EKRON *ca.* six miles inland on the same latitude as Jerusalem. The area is very fertile, but there is constant danger of the encroaching sand dunes in the S part of the coast. In Gen. 21:32, 34; Exod. 13:17; 15:14; 23:31 the references to Philistia, the land of the Philistines, and the sea of the Philistines are anachronistic. The Greeks, familiar at first with the coastal area, gradually applied the name Palestine to the whole of the country.

3. Culture and religion. ***a. Language.*** There are no documents in the Philistine language. Various Hebrew words have been given Philistine provenience. But *seren* (only the plural *sᵉrānîm,* "lords," occurs), used of the leaders of the Philistine confederacy, may be equated with a non-Semitic vocable: *seren=turannos* of pre-Hellenic or Asianic origin. Only two Philistine names have possible Asianic connections—Goliath having been compared with Alyattas and Achish with Anchises. The other names are usually Canaanite (e.g., Ahimelek, Sidqa, Mitinti, Hanun). The Philistines, it may be surmised, lost their language soon after coming to Palestine and spoke a Canaanite dialect which gradually gave way to Aramaic. The "language of Ashdod" of Neh. 13:24 referred to such a local dialect.

b. Traits. Beyond the fact that the Philistines were uncircumcised and were, therefore, despised by the Israelites (Judg. 14:3; 15:18; I Sam. 17:26; 18:25),

From H. Gressmann, *Altorientalische Texte und Bilder zum Alten Testament* (Berlin: Walter de Gruyter & Co.)

48. Aristocratic Philistine in festive dress; faïence tile from the palace at Medinet Habu, time of Ramses III (1198-1167 B.C.)

we know of no other culture trait that can be attributed to them. We are almost equally uninformed as to Philistine religion. All their gods known to us have Semitic names. They had temples to Dagon in Gaza and Ashdod (Judg. 16:23; I Sam. 5:1-7), one to Ashtoreth in Ashkelon (Herodotus I.105) and one to Baalzebub in Ekron (II Kings 1:1-16). Some of these temples lasted into the Hellenistic period (cf. I Macc. 10:83; Diodorus Siculus II.4). The Philistines also achieved a reputation as soothsayers (Isa. 2:6).

Fig. PHI 48.

c. Political and military organization. Until their defeat by David, the Philistines lived chiefly in five independent cities ruled by *sᵉrānîm,* "lords." The *sᵉrānîm* acted in council for the common good of the nation and were able to overrule the decision of any individual *seren* (I Sam. 29:1-7). After their defeat, the title *sᵉrānîm* is no longer used, and it is replaced by "king" (Jer. 25:20; Zech. 9:5). In their period of expansion the Philistines were able to muster large, well-armed troops of foot soldiers, archers, and charioteers (I Sam. 13:5; 29:2; 31:3). Elements of the autochthonous population and mercenaries were among their forces (David in I Sam. 27–29; the Rephaim in II Sam. 21:18-22). Both individual combat (Goliath; I Sam. 17:4-10) and shock troops (the "raiders"; I Sam. 13:17-18; 14:15) were used by the Philistines.

d. Material culture. No real excavation has taken place in Philistine territory proper, with only trial excavations at Ashkelon. The excavations at adjacent sites (Tell Jemmeh, Tell Qasileh, 'Ain Shems [Beth-shemesh], Tell Jezer [Gezer], Tell Far'a) have provided some information, but our sources for Philistine material culture are limited. From the scenes depicted at Medinet Habu in Egypt, the wagon, chariot, and ship used by the Philistines are known to us. The Philistine ship is unique, with its curved keel, high stem and bow, and straight mast rising from the middle of the boat. The Philistine warrior is drawn wearing a variety of the Aegean kilt. His helmet is a plumed headdress, with chin straps.* Affinities to this headdress have been noted by many scholars, the most outstanding being the plumed head of the Phaestos Disk. From the OT we learn that Goliath, who engaged in single combat like a Homeric hero, was also armed to the teeth like one (I Sam. 17:5-7). The weapons used by Goliath were undoubtedly made by a Philistine ironsmith. The Philistines had a monopoly on this profession (I Sam. 13:19-22), and smelting furnaces for iron have been found at Tell Qasileh, Tell Jemmeh, and 'Ain Shems. The clearest sign of Philistine presence remains the so-called "Philistine pottery," which is found in abundance from the first decades of the twelfth century B.C. to the late eleventh century B.C. in the plains of Philistia itself, and in adjacent sites of the Negeb (e.g., Tell Far'a) and the Shephelah ('Ain Shems) and in cities occupied by the Philistines during their period of expansion (Dor, Beth-zur, Tell Beit Mirsim, Megiddo, Tell Qasileh, Bethel, Tell en-Nasbeh). It is not a continuation of Mycenean and Cypriote wares found in Late Bronze Age levels in Palestine. It is, rather, a composite imitation in local clay and with local techniques of thirteenth-century Mycenean styles, notably the panel style, and shows strong points of contact with the Mycenean IIIc wares discovered at Enkomi and Sinda on Cyprus and the other sub-Mycenean wares of Cyprus and Rhodes. The chief types are buff-colored craters, beer jugs with spouted strainers, cups and stirrup vases with a white wash or slip on which are painted reddish-purple or black geometrical designs or metope-like panels with stylized swans preening themselves. At some sites anthropoid clay coffins occur in conjunction with "Philistine" pottery. Figs. MAN 6; PHI 49; ART 75; PHI 50; BET 38.

From H. Gressmann, *Altorientalische Texte und Bilder zum Alten Testament* (Berlin: Walter de Gruyter & Co.)

49. Shackled Philistine prisoners; from the palace at Medinet Habu, time of Ramses III (1198-1167 B.C.)

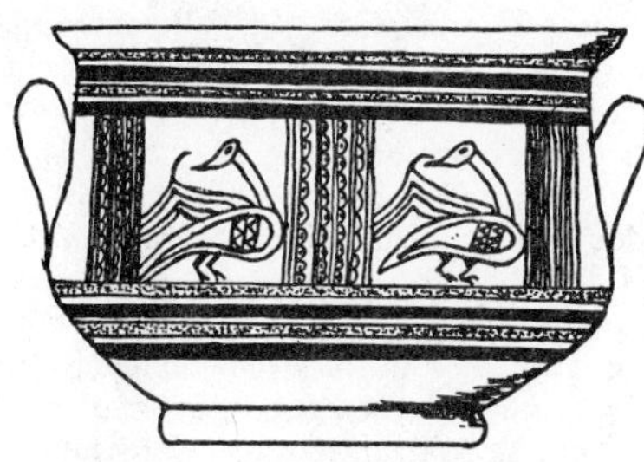

By permission of the Palestine Exploration Fund

50. Philistine decorated pottery, from Gezer

4. History. ***a. From period of expansion to defeat by David*** **(ca.** ***1180-965*****).** Although the references in Gen. 21; 26 may ultimately be based on the presence of an Aegean colony in the Gerar area (*see* CAPHTOR), the use of the term "Philistines" is anachronistic. The Philistines first settled the coast of Palestine after being repulsed from Egypt by Rameses III, together with the other "People of the Sea." Ashkelon, Ashdod, Gath, and Gaza are known from older sources and must have been captured by the Philistines from their Canaanite inhabitants, perhaps with the tacit permission of the Egyptians, who then controlled the area. Ekron may have been a newly founded Philistine city. The excavations at the Philistine-founded Tell Qasileh attest to their building activity during this period. Although they were primarily a warrior overlord class, they came with their families (cf. Medinat Habu reliefs) and imposed themselves upon the autochthonous inhabitants. The tradition concerning Shamgar ben Anath's killing six hundred Philistines may stem from this time (Judg. 3:31). There are no further reports in the OT of any opposition to, or revolts against, the Philistines on the part of the inhabitants of the coastal cities. For the early period of Philistine colonization we must rely on archaeological information, for it is only when they come into conflict with the Israelites that there are literary records concerning them. The expansion of the Philistines into adjacent areas, and their control over them, is demonstrated by the abundance of their pottery found in sites in the Shephelah and the Negeb from *ca.* 1150 on. The ensuing pressure upon the Danites and Judeans is reflected in the Samson saga (Judg. 13–15). The military organization of the Philistines and their superior armaments enabled them, toward the middle of the eleventh century, to encroach upon the Judean hill country. The unsuccessful resistance of the Israelites at Ebenezer (I Sam. 4:1-10) ended in the Philistine destruction of SHILOH and the capture of the ark. Archaeological evidence at Beth-zur, Tell Beit Mirsim, and elsewhere indicates that they also devastated part of W Palestine. They also were able to occupy Gibeah in Benjamin, Beth-shan, and Megiddo. Under the leadership of Samuel, some respite was won from the Philistines (I Sam. 7:7-14). Saul, at the beginning of his reign (*ca.* 1020), was able to remove the Philistine yoke from his people. The resurgence of Philistine power is shown by the Goliath pericope (I Sam. 17) and the account of David's victories over them. However, the acceptance of David and his band as auxiliaries by Achish of Gath and his lack of control over David's movements (I Sam. 27) point up Philistine weakness. They were first able to make deep inroads into Israelite territory after the defeat of Saul at Gilboa* and to re-establish their control over the land and once again control a city as far N as Beth-shan. After David was anointed king over all Israel, they reacted and attacked him in the Valley of Rephaim near Jerusalem, but were defeated by David at Baal-perazim and beaten back to Gezer (II Sam. 5:17-25). For this victory, David was able to use his own well-trained troops and his familiarity with Philistine strategy. The Philistines were reduced to a secondary role. Their hold over the shores of Palestine and Phoenicia was broken, and Phoenician maritime expansion became possible. Fig. GIL 33.

Scraps of various tales current among the Israelites which celebrated these victories and the exploits of various warriors have been preserved (II Sam. 21:15-22; 23:8-19; I Chr. 11:11-21; etc.). David subdued the city of Gath (I Chr. 18:1) and imposed vassalage upon it; Gath supplied him with faithful warriors like Ittai the Gittite (II Sam. 15:18-22; 18:2). From the other independent Philistine cities, mercenary troops joined the ranks of David's personal army, as the CHERETHITES and PELETHITES under the command of Benaiah son of Jehoiada.

After their defeat by well-organized forces, the Philistine drive for expansion ceased. Philistine history was now that of individual cities, rather than that of a people acting in concert. It is quite possible that in the course of their battles with Saul and David, the ruling Philistine military class had been wiped out and strong assimilation with the native Canaanite population had already taken place. Except for Achish of Gath, mentioned in I Kings 2:39-40, who is most probably the same person as the ruler of Gath under whom David served, and Ikausu of Ekron, a contemporary of Ashurbanipal of Assyria, all the following Philistine rulers known to us have Semitic names. The title *sᵉrānîm* was also no longer used for the Philistine rulers. The typically Philistine pottery of Early Iron Age II sites dominated by the Philistines disappears, and the pottery and other artifacts found in Early Iron Age III levels is the same as that found elsewhere in Palestine (e.g., Tell Qasileh, Gezer, Khirbet el-Muqanna' [Ekron?]).* The Philistines were, on the whole, limited now to their pentapolis and the immediate coastal area. Fig. PHI 50.

***b. From the time of Solomon to the reign of Ahaz* (ca. *960-735*).** At the beginning of the reign of Solomon the vassal status of Gath remained unchanged, as the ease of movement of Shimei son of Gera into and out of the city, as well as his retrieval of two slaves from there, attests (I Kings 2:39-40). Egyptian influence in Philistia during the end of the United Monarchy and the early part of the Divided Monarchy may be surmised from the campaign of an unnamed Pharaoh of the Twenty-first Dynasty at Gezer (I Kings 9:16-17) and the use of Sheshonk I (OT Shishak) of Gaza as the starting point of his campaign in Palestine (ca. 917), as reported in his itinerary. Among the cities that Sheshonk captured in this campaign were those near the Philistine border that Rehoboam had fortified (II Chr. 11:5-10; 12:2-4). During the next fifty years there were border battles involving troops of relatively large numbers between the Philistines and Israel at Gibbethon (Tell Malat?) near Gezer, which was held by the Israelites (I Kings 15:27; 16:15-17). During the reign of Jehoshaphat, the Philistines paid tribute to Judah (II Chr. 17:11). During the reign of Jehoram they were able to make incursions into Judahite territory and raid the king's household, carrying off his wives, children, and possessions (II Chr. 21:16-17). From these scant references to the Philistines, it is also clear that Arabian tribes now occupied the territory to the S of Philistia. In a period of Israelite and Judean weakness the city of Gath had been captured by Hazael of Aram during his raid into Judah *ca.* 815 (II Kings 12; 18). The first sure reference to Philistia in Assyrian sources dates from the reign of Adad-Nirari III (810-783), who boasts of having collected tribute from Philistia (Palastu) in his fifth year. Uzziah successfully raided Philistine territory. According to biblical report, he tore down the walls of some cities and set up garrisons of his own (II Chr. 26:6-7). Even though no destruction of the city is reported, except in the enigmatic reference in Amos 6:2, Gath lost its former importance. In the various prophetic condemnations of the Philistines, Gath is not listed (Jer. 25:20; Amos 1:6-8; Zeph. 2:4; Zech. 9:6-7), and in all likelihood Gath came under the rule of Ashdod.

***c. Under Assyrian and Babylonian domination* (ca. *735-586*).** During the reign of Ahaz, the Philistines once again raided Judah and occupied cities in the Shephelah and the Negeb (II Chr. 28:18; cf. Isa. 9:11; 14:28-32). This occupation was short-lived, since both Ashkelon and Gaza were attacked for disloyalty in 734 by Tiglath-pileser III. Mitinti of Ashkelon was replaced. Hanun of Gaza escaped to Egypt, but was finally captured and exiled to Assyria by Sargon II, who stormed Gaza in 720 after Hanun participated in an anti-Assyrian coalition. In 713 Sargon replaced Azuri of Ashdod with his brother, Ahimiti, because of Azuri's failure to pay tribute regularly. The Ashdodeans placed a local usurper, Iamani, on the throne. By forming an alliance including Philistia, Judah, Edom, and Moab, he precipitated an attack in 712 by Sargon, who converted Ashdod temporarily into an Assyrian province (Isa. 20:1). In this campaign Gath, Gibbethon, and Ekron were also raided. Hezekiah invaded Philistia and attacked Gaza (II Kings 18:8) in alliance with Sidqa of Ashkelon and the people of Ekron, who handed over their king, Padi, to him. In 701 Sennacherib invaded S Palestine and captured the cities of Beth-dagon, Joppa, Banai-Barqa, and Azuru and their capital, Ashkelon; deported Sidqa and his family and imposed a new king; punished the patricians of Ekron and restored Padi to his throne and rewarded the faithful kings of Ashdod, Ekron, and Gezer with a strip of Judean territory in the Shephelah. The traditional dislike of the Philistines, reflected in both the Prophets and the Psalms, was intensified by their participating during this period in the Phoenician slave trade (Joel 3:1-8—H 4:1-8). During the reigns of Esarhaddon and Ashurbanipal the kings of Gaza, Ashkelon, Ekron, and Ashdod are listed as loyal vassals of Assyria and supplied troops to the Assyrian army. The constant passage of Assyrian troops through Philistia in the campaigns against Egypt ensured the peace of the area. After the breakdown of Assyrian might, the Philistine cities, particularly Ashdod, were under strong Egyptian pressure (Herodotus II.157); were overrun by the Scythians, who destroyed the temple of Astarte in Ashkelon (Herodotus I.105); and were overrun by the Egyptians under Neco, who conquered Gaza *ca.* 609-608 (Herodotus II.159; cf. Jer. 47:1). The Philistines were allied with Egypt against Nebuchadnezzar of Babylon, as is now clear from the Aramaic letter found at Saqqarah from Adon (of Ashkelon?) to Pharaoh pleading for help and the attack upon Ashkelon in 604 by Nebuchadnezzar. Nebuchadnezzar put out any remaining sparks of Philistine independence. He deported both rulers and people, as the mention of the kings of Gaza and Ashdod and the princes of Ashkelon in the lists published by Unger and Weidner has shown (cf. Jer. 25:20; 47:2-7; Zeph. 2:4-7; Zech. 9:5-6). The later history of the cities Ashdod (Azotus), Ashkelon (Ascalon), and Gaza is that of Phoenician, and then Hellenistic, cities with highly mixed population. Only the territorial name Palestine connected them with their Philistine past.

Bibliography. R. A. S. Macalister, *The Philistines* (1913): although antiquated, it remains the only comprehensive work in English. G. von Rad, "Das Reich Israel und die Philister," *PJB,* 29 (1933), 30-42. O. Eissfeldt, *Philister und Phönizier* (1936). W. A. Heurtley, "The Relationship Between 'Philistine' and Mycenaean Pottery," *Quarterly, Department of Antiquities of Palestine,* V (1936), 90-110. E. F. Weidner, "Jojachin, König von Juda, in babylonischen Keilschrifttexten," *Mélanges syriens offerts a M. René Dussand,* II (1939), 923-35. H. L. Ginsberg, "An Aramaic Contemporary of the Lachish Letters," *BASOR,* 111 (1948), 24-27. W. F. Albright, *The Archaeology of Palestine* (1949), 110-22; "Some Oriental Glosses on the Homeric Problem," *AJA,* 54 (1950), 162-76. A. Malamat, "The Historical Setting of Two Biblical Prophecies on the Nations," *IEJ,* 1 (1950-51), 149-59. J. Bérard, "Philistins et Préhellenes," *Revue Archéologique* (1951), pp. 129-42. J. B. Pritchard, ed., *ANET* (2nd ed., 1955), 262-63, 281-94, 307-8. D. Wiseman, *Chronicles of Chaldean Kings* (1956), pp. 28, 68. A. Malamat, "A New Record of Nebuchadnezzar's Palestinian Campaign," *IEJ,* 6 (1956), 246-56. T. Dothan, "Archaeological Reflections on the Philistine Problem," *Antiquity and Survival,* II (1957), 151-64. H. Tadmor, "The Campaigns of Sargon II of Assur: A Chronological-Historical Study; III, The Campaign to Philistia and the Egyptian Border," *JCS,* XII (1958), 77-100.

J. C. Greenfield

PHILO, BIBLICAL ANTIQUITIES OF. The title of a book by an unknown author which was found in a Latin medieval MS bearing the heading *Libri Philonis Judaei de initio mundi* and was first published together with some genuine treatises of Philo of Alexandria. The author is now generally referred to as Pseudo-Philo. His work contains an abstract of the biblical story from Adam to the death of Saul. Some incidents of the biblical narratives are abridged or completely omitted, while others are considerably elaborated. Occasionally the author furnished quite novel additions to the biblical story. In particular, the period of the judges is treated comparatively more fully than other parts. As the Chronicler, in rewriting Israel's history, besides contributing his own theological scheme, apparently drew on narratives of which no trace has been preserved in other historical books of the OT, so the author of the Biblical Antiquities evidently made use of folklore concerning Israel's past. E.g., he names Kenaz, the father of Othniel (Judg. 3:9), as the first judge in Israel, and reports on many of his activities. He is fond of inserting lengthy speeches, or songs, into his narratives, and though most of these appear to be of his own creation, it is possible that here and there lyrics of older provenance have been preserved by him. In essence, Pseudo-Philo renders the OT story in a midrashic form which it had assumed through repeated retelling for popular edification and instruction, and he reinterprets this story in the light of his own religious experience and theological notions.

The book is important, not only because it preserves old Jewish legends and sheds light on the technique of Hebrew writing from a time before the composition of the Mishna, but also because its production falls approximately in the same period as that of the Synoptic gospels. There are close parallels in thought, expression, and image with various parts of the NT. Though not preserved by Jews, but handed on only by Christian copyists, the work has apparently remained free from interpolations, and is thus a valuable source of information regarding the Jewish world of ideas in the first century.

It is widely assumed that Pseudo-Philo wrote sometime after A.D. 70. This assumption is based on the scarcity of references to temple worship (the contents of Leviticus are, e.g., completely omitted). If the author lived after the destruction of the Second Temple, he found himself in a situation that put special demands on a writer of Israel's history, and he did his best to meet them. One of his oft-repeated affirmations is the indestructibility of Israel. Israel's duty is to trust in God. The world will be destroyed sooner than Israel, for God has not made his covenant and given his instruction in vain. Only by sinning and abandoning God can Israel be defeated; if faithful, they are invincible. On occasion, the writer speaks of Israel almost in terms of pre-existence (IX.3.4). The chosen people's role in God's plan for the world has been ordained before creation: when Israel was not yet, God spoke of her. This privileged status of the nation does not, however, offer any guarantee for salvation to individual Israelites. "Hope not in your fathers, for they will not profit you unless you are found like unto them" (XXXIII.5).

The belief in resurrection (III.10; XI.6) is affirmed. When required of God, the nether world will restore its booty. Angelology is fairly developed; the Biblical Antiquities gives the names of many angels not known from any other source.

There appears to be no messianology of the type known from the NT. The term "messiah" occurs in the book, but invariably in a concrete, historical context. Striking is the expression "the Holy Anointed One of the Lord" (*sanctus christus domini;* LIX.2; the passage refers to David); it has a parallel in the Dead Sea Scrolls, but no connection between these and the Antiquities has as yet been established.

Pseudo-Philo's work possibly covered a wider period than the extant work, which ends with the dying Saul's message to David "not to remember that I hated him nor that I dealt unjustly." In many respects the book may serve as a corrective of misconceptions about Judaism. It reports, e.g., that Job was married to DINAH, Jacob's daughter (also mentioned in the Talmud); this is a significant view, as it implies that Job, a man "blameless and upright, one who feared God, and turned away from evil" (Job 1:1), was not even a Hebrew. This, as well as other passages, shows that the author's elated concept of Israel's election by God stems from a sense of duty, not from presumption or self-assertiveness.

The book is extant only in Latin; we know that all codices go back to the same parent MS, because they contain gaps (ch. XXXVII) in the same places. The Latin translation was made from the Greek, and this in turn was made from Hebrew. In spite of the fact that what we have of the book is only a translation of a translation, the Hebrew rhythm still vibrates through some of the songs and prayers that are recorded. The medieval Hebrew *Chronicle of Yerahmeel,* which contains part of the Pseudo-Philonic story, is a retranslation from Latin into Hebrew.

Bibliography. L. Cohn, "An Apocryphal Work Ascribed to Philo of Alexandria," *JQR,* O.S. 10 (1898). P. Lehmann, *Johannes Sichardus und die von ihm benützten Bibliotheken und Handschriften* (1912). L. Cohn, *Pseudo-Philo und Jerachmeel* (*Festschrift Jakob Guttmann;* 1915). M. R. James, *The Biblical Antiquities of Philo* (1917). P. Riessler, *Altjüdisches Schrifttum ausserhalb der Bibel* (1928). L. Gry, "La date de la fin des temps," *RB,* vol. 48 (1939). G. Kisch, *Pseudo-Philo's Liber Antiquitatum Biblicarum* (1949). A. Spiro, *Samaritans, Tobiads, and Judahites in Pseudo-Philo,* Proceedings of the American Academy for Jewish Research, no. 20 (1951); *Pseudo-Philo's Saul and the Rabbi's Messiah Ben Ephraim,* Proceedings of the American Academy for Jewish Research, no. 21 (1952). O. Eissfeldt, "Zur Kompositionstechnik des Pseudo-Philonischen Liber Antiquitatum Biblicarum," *Interpretationes ad VT pertinentes S. Mowinckel Missae* (1955). G. Vermès, "Deux traditions sur Balaam," *Cahiers Sioniens,* no. 9 (1955).

P. WINTER

PHILO JUDEUS fī'lō jōō dē'əs. A Jew of Alexandria contemporary with Jesus. In the history of philosophy his writings are the first after Aristotle to be more than mere fragments. In the history of Judaism he is the one Jew of his time from outside Palestine whose writings survive *in extenso;* accordingly he stands unique as a source for estimating the impact of Hellenism upon Judaism, though opinion has always been divided as to how far he can be taken to represent the general thinking of Jews in Hellenized centers. Similarly scholars by no means agree upon how much Philo's writings can be used in explaining the rapid Hellenization of Christianity.

1. Life. Little is known of Philo's life except one incident that happened in A.D. 39, at which time he called himself an "old man"; accordingly it is usually supposed that he was born *ca.* 20 B.C. The incident was a great pogrom in Alexandria. The Jews of the city resisted an attempt of Flaccus, the prefect, to force upon them cult images of the mad emperor Gaius (*see* CALIGULA), and the prefect encouraged the Gentile mob to loot and slaughter. To get protection from Gaius himself, a Jewish embassy headed by Philo was sent to Rome. Philo handled the matter so adroitly that at least he did not provoke the emperor to fresh violence, though the solution of the problem was not actually reached until a few months later, when Gaius was murdered and Claudius succeeded him. The story of the pogrom and of Philo's going to Rome is told by him in two treatises, *Against Flaccus* and *Embassy to Gaius.*

To have had such a responsible mission Philo must have been one of the leading Jews of the city, and we learn from Josephus that this was so. His brother, Alexander the Alabarch, had one of the largest fortunes in the Roman world. Many believe that Philo himself spent a considerable part of his life in public administration for Jews. He certainly had a thorough Alexandrian education and wrote a florid but fluent Greek; he moves in Greek history and philosophy with ease. At the same time he felt deeply loyal to Judaism; but as to his Jewish education, while he often agrees with rabbinic interpretations of the law, he often disagrees with them. Agreement cannot automatically be taken to indicate rabbinic influence on his thinking, since interpretations made in Alexandria must often have been regarded with approval by the rabbis. Certainly Philo gives no such evidence of having been acquainted with rabbinic tradition as he does with Hellenism. Even of the Hebrew language he shows no knowledge beyond the interpretation of a few proper names and perhaps a scattering of Hebrew tags. His Bible was the LXX, which he considered verbally inspired, and he never betrays the least sense of its having less authenticity than the Hebrew. He therefore must be considered a loyal Jew—loyal to his people and to their law as written, and as practiced in Alexandria—but one whose formal education was that of a thoughtful Greek.

2. Writings. The extant writings of Philo, when completely published, will occupy at least twelve volumes of the Loeb Edition, but a great many of his treatises we know only by name, and many of those surviving have large gaps in the text. For discussion of Philo's treatises, *see bibliography.*

The first group of writings is made up of apologetic works addressed to Gentiles. The two treatises just mentioned are of this type, as is a larger work, the *Apology for the Jews,* of which a few fragments are preserved in Eusebius. The short treatise *On the Contemplative Life* is thought to have been a part of this *Apology.* The *Contemplative Life* describes the customs of a fascinating group of Jewish ascetics in Egypt which corresponded to the Essenes in Palestine; Philo may well have belonged to the group as a young man. Philo's discussion of the Essenes, a fragment preserved in Eusebius and now much read in connection with the Dead Sea Scrolls, may well have been in the same *Apology.* Another document, apparently intended to introduce the Gentile into the substance of Jewish faith, exists in Philo's *Life of Moses.* In this extended work (in two books) all biblical narratives are told as for people who had never heard them. Philo says that Moses was the ideal hero in four guises: he was the king as the Gentiles themselves described the ideal king, the true priest and prophet, and hence the perfect lawgiver. In such a presentation Gentile and Jewish conceptions obviously blend. The story is faithful to the Bible, but each of the roles is described in terms of Gentile thought. The highest law of the Jews appears to be, not the injunctions written by Moses, but an unwritten law behind the Torah, one basically revealed in the very person of the hero-king himself. Such a conception of the unwritten law presented in a unique person is a Gentile notion that continued on in all theories of absolute kings who were "above all law"—i.e., who were above the law their subjects had to obey; they were themselves the source of law, the vehicle through whom law came to men from God or nature. The biblical presentation of Moses as leading the people out of Egypt, and as going to God and bringing the law to men, was easily explained in this way.

A second division of Philo's works, the *Exposition of the Law,* is made up of a series of related treatises, originally at least nine in number: *On the Creation of the World, On Abraham, On Isaac* (now lost), *On Jacob* (now lost), *On Joseph, On the Decalogue, On the Special Laws* (in four books), *On Virtues, On Rewards and Punishments.* This series again seems addressed to Gentiles, or to Jews so Hellenized that they had a basically Hellenistic point of view. Its purpose is to make a much more systematic alignment of Jewish biblical tradition with Greek thought-ways than did the *Life of Moses.* The *Creation of the World* presents God making a world through the Logos, and is thoroughly aligned with the *Timaeus* of Plato. The Logos was not only the creative agent, but it abides in the world as the law of nature. God made it even more startlingly available, however, in living, personal form, in the great heroes of the Bible—Enos, Enoch, and Noah; Abraham, Isaac, and Jacob—and, as those will understand who have read the *Life of Moses,* in Moses as the greatest of all. These men knew and lived by the law before it had been revealed on Sinai or codified by Moses. We see in such men the true way of life, and they in turn are what Philo called "mystagogues," people who can take a man who attaches himself to them and lead him into an immediate comprehension and apprehension of the law of God in its pure form. This personal manifestation of God's law is explained by Philo in *On Abraham,* and presumably he went to even greater heights in the lost lives of Isaac and Jacob.

The *Decalogue,* however, begins by saying that God also revealed his law to the Jews in verbal form. The highest expression of this is the Decalogue. From these ten laws are derived all other laws, since they are the ten basic principles of all codes of law. So in the four books of the *Special Laws* that follow, Philo goes on to discuss the detailed legislation under these ten heads. *On Virtues,* the next treatise, gives a general summary of Jewish legal principles under the categories of the Greek cardinal virtues. Here again the patriarchs emerge as showing Judaism in its full realization. *On Rewards and Punishments* is a quite prophetic Deuteronomic sermon to show the values of obedience to the code and the disaster of ignoring it.

A third group of Philo's writings also forms a consecutive series of treatises. This series is usually called the *Allegory of the Jewish Law,* in contrast to the *Exposition* series. The *Allegory* consists now of eighteen titles, twenty-one books, but was originally much longer. At least nine treatises are definitely known to be lost, and many of those we have are incomplete. Individually and as a series, they have almost no form at all. In them it is assumed that the basic point of view of the *Exposition* was familiar and accepted, so that while the treatises discuss in general consecutive incidents and passages of Genesis, they begin without explanation with the second chapter of Genesis and stop suddenly with the dreams of Jacob, Joseph, the butler and baker, and Pharaoh.

Scholars have suggested an over-all plan for the *Allegory,* but if Philo ever had a plan at all, it is so repeatedly abandoned for indefinite digression as to be of little help to the reader. Yet this is Philo's major work, and here he presents his thoughts at their richest. The audience now appears to be a group of people with esoteric understanding of the Bible. The patriarchs and the mystic value of the law have been fully accepted, and Philo is only writing for the inspiration of what he calls the "initiates." In this sort of writing, as in Thomas à Kempis' *Imitation of Christ,* plan has little importance. A devotional study, the *Allegory* can usually be read wherever the book opens. One must read it, however, in the spirit of the day in which it was written. The *Allegory* has quite as much arrangement and order as the *Enneads* of Plotinus, or most of the essays of Plutarch. In discussing the *Allegory,* accordingly, as in the writings of Plotinus, we discuss the ideas in it rather than their successive presentation.

Still another series of treatises by Philo is the *Questions and Answers in Genesis and Exodus.* This great work is preserved less satisfactorily than any other series of Philo's writings. We have only a few scattered fragments of it in Greek, and large sections, but only sections, in Armenian. The *Questions* is again commentary, but here in the more midrashic form of verse-by-verse commentary. For almost every verse two interpretations are given, one the "literal," where the words of the text have their story or law explained directly as though for what we should now call "orthodox" Jews, and the other an allegorical or mystical interpretation. The latter is quite in the spirit of the *Allegory.* The *Questions,* in offering both sorts of interpretations, shows how Philo never forgot or abandoned the literal type of Judaism, though he felt that the heights of Judaism rose far beyond that level. In one passage Philo mentions Jews whom the mystic meaning of their religion had led to abandon the literal. He would have nothing to do with them, just as it seems quite likely that he would have joined in stoning Paul for suggesting that the law of the spirit had freed him from the law of the letter. The *Questions* is a monument to Philo's refusal to choose between these two.

Several miscellaneous treatises are preserved. Their titles are *On the Indestructibility of the World* (opening fragment of a larger work), *That Every Virtuous Man Is Free* (with another allusion to the Essenes), *On Providence,* and *Alexander or On the Question Whether Dumb Animals Have the Power of Reason.* It need only be said that they are directly concerned with problems of philosophy, in contrast to the greater series of Philonic writings.

3. Teachings. One can approach the teachings of Philo by trying to understand the central interest or thesis of his writings, or by trying to reconstruct

Philo according to preconceived categories of Judaism or philosophy. From each way of reading him a different Philo will emerge. In beginning with his writings we are here taking the former approach. The alternative approach (*see bibliography*) puts Philo into his proper place in the history of philosophy, where he may be seen as the first writer of the medieval tradition in which the problem was to reconcile reason—that is, Greek logic and traditional science—with the teachings of the Bible. Philo, of course, worked on this problem, but he had other interests than creating a philosophical system. Indeed, to seek a consistency in Philo's thinking seems inappropriate to Philo's own frequent indifference to consistency.

From Philo's short philosophical writings just mentioned, a treatise on his philosophy could well be written. From these, however, a rather eclectic and superficial thinker would emerge. In cosmology he follows Plato and Aristotle against the Stoics, but in discussing "Providence," or the divine control of the universe, he follows Stoic ideas as over against the atomistic tradition of chance. His ethics are predominantly Stoic. In interpreting the Bible, on the contrary, he is concerned to make it a document of mysticism: repeatedly he identifies philosophy with mystical metaphysics, and this much more in the sense of mystic union than mystic theory.

Since by far the greatest part of Philo's writings is devoted to developing this point, it is reasonable to suppose that in him we have a man educated in the philosophic schools to some extent, but one who found his chief satisfaction in the mystical possibilities of incipient Neoplatonism, wherein his own Judaism seemed to find its highest value. In later Platonism the utter contrast between matter and the immaterial had driven men to describe ultimate reality in almost Parmenidean abstraction. To Neoplatonic philosophers the Good of Plato became Being, the One; it represented the center of all existence, the goal of all endeavor. To theists, of course, this would be God—i.e., to theistic pagans, and later to Christians. It was both the abstract and the personal to Philo the Jew. In philosophical formulation Being would be related to the world of experience still in terms of abstraction. In the religious thinking of most men Being as God would relate himself to matter and men in a much more personal way. The Gnostics were soon to describe this relationship in terms of descending pairs of divinities. Philo described the link as a stream or radiation from the One, by which, while not ceasing to be the Absolute, God gave out his nature, his reality. Philo called this stream by various names, most commonly the Logos. It could be thought of as divided into a series of descending abstract manifestations of existence, or as a single abstraction. But when Philo the man of religion spoke, as he more commonly did, he described the stream as manifesting itself in the personal attributes of grace, justice, and mercy. The Logos gave to the world its form, and to men their image of God, their minds; and it led men back to God. Pagans were trying to make the stories of Homer, the myths of Dionysus, Osiris, Adonis, and Mithras, mean such a concern of God for man. To them Philo proudly told the stories of his own God's relations with the patriarchs and the people, and understandably boasted that what the others were looking for, the Jews already had.

Philo had many names for the effluence from God which brought the Unrelated into relations with matter and man, and he used any of these names according as the mood, the text he was expounding, the sex of the person he was praising, made convenient. The stream first manifested itself in the order of the universe, so that it was the natural law of the universe. Like Paul in the first chapter of Romans, Philo said that this order of nature should be a sufficient revelation of divinity for man to grasp it. But actually the manifestation in nature is not enough, and so, we have already seen, it represented itself as Logos in the great patriarchs, as Sophia or Virtue (both feminine words) in their wives. The manifestation in coded law, even the Mosaic code, we saw, was inferior to the revelation in persons. When Paul went on in Romans to explain that the Jewish law is quite inferior to the law of the Spirit manifest in Jesus Christ, he drew inferences that Philo would not have allowed, but he only carried Philo's way of thinking to its natural conclusion in applying it to Christ. Indeed, Paul shows in the fourth chapter of Romans that he was quite aware that the miracle had already been worked in Abraham. The heart of Philo's message is exactly expressed in Rom. 4:13: "The promise to Abraham and his descendants, that they should inherit the world, did not come through the [written] law but through the righteousness of faith." Philo spoke now about Abraham, now Sarah, now Isaac, or others, as the exemplars, but so supremely did Moses represent the law that Philo said he was himself initiated into Moses.

How far we are to suppose Philo meant literally his frequent statements that the true Judaism is the true mystery religion, has caused much recent controversy. If we are to understand Greek words in their ancient usage rather than in modern categories, and if we believe Philo meant what he said, then we may conclude that he found in Judaism an authority for taking to himself, not the persons or rites of pagan mysteries, but their values. Whether or not one follows Philo in using the terms of mystery religions to describe his evaluation of Judaism, it is patent that to him the Jewish Bible revealed the path from matter to the immaterial, the path men of his time were everywhere seeking in mystic rite and philosophy.

The early Christian exegetes—from Clement of Alexandria to Ambrose—found Philo's exposition of the Bible so congenial that they used his works as a basis for much of their exegesis, while the allegories of Justin Martyr are plainly Christian versions of allegories much like those of Philo. It does not appear that the books of Philo himself were used and quoted by any writer of the New Testament; similarly there is no evidence that Philo was himself widely read by the Jews of the Dispersion who put on their graves and synagogues the amazing decorations of the next four centuries. But Philo clearly speaks for a group of Jews whose thinking took much the line of Hellenized Christianity and later Jewish mysticism.

Bibliography. Editions and secondary works are listed in H. L. Goodhart and E. R. Goodenough, "General Bibliography of Philo," in E. R. Goodenough, *The Politics of Philo Judaeus* (1938), pp. 125-321. The treatises are outlined in detail in E. R. Goodenough, *Introduction to Philo Judaeus* (1940); H. Leisegang, "Philon," in Pauly-Wissowa, *Real-Enzyklopädie der klassischen Altertumswissenschaft,* vol. XX, pt. i (1949), pp. 1-50. H. Wolfson, *Philo* (1947), is designed to treat Philo within the context of the history of philosophy. To the editions should be added R. Marcus' translation of the *Questions and Answers to Genesis and Exodus* in two supplementary volumes of the Loeb Edition of Philo (1953).

E. R. GOODENOUGH

PHILOLOGUS fĭ lŏl'ə gəs [Φιλόλογος, talkative, *or* loving learning] (Rom. 16:15). A Christian man greeted by Paul. From the order of names it seems likely that Philologus was the head of a family, Julia being his wife and the others named in the verse their children.

F. W. GINGRICH

PHILOMETOR fĭl'ə mē'tôr [Φιλομήτωρ]. The PTOLEMY whose enthronement is mentioned in II Macc. 4:21.

PHILOSOPHY [φιλοσοφία]. Etymologically, "love of wisdom"; but this word took on the narrower meaning of the systematic treatment of a given subject, or speculation with regard to truth and reality. In the NT both "philosophy" (Col. 2:8) and "philosopher" (Acts 17:18) are used in an unfavorable sense.

In Col. 2:8 the author warns his readers to beware of those who would "kidnap" them by philosophy, to which he links "empty deceit"; for these are "according to human tradition, according to the elemental spirits of the universe, and not according to Christ." The author understands philosophy as contrary to what has been revealed in Christ, and tells the Christians at Colossae to shun it. The author, however, is not referring to all philosophy, but has a specific philosophy in mind, against which he argues at considerable length in this letter. It may have been a form of Gnosticism; but it is characterized by the term "empty deceit" and appears to have represented a christological position which denied the full divinity of Christ. *See* COLOSSIANS.

In Acts, Paul is said to have conversed with some "Epicurean and Stoic philosophers" in Athens. They apparently did not think very highly of Paul's preaching, but they were sufficiently interested in it to take him to the AREOPAGUS and ask him for a fuller statement, which Paul gave (Acts 17:22-31).

A number of philosophies were influential in the speech and thinking of the man in the street in the Hellenistic age—especially Cynicism and Stoicism. But Epicureanism, Platonism, and Neo-Pythagoreanism were other options. *See* GNOSTICISM; EPICUREANS; STOICS.

Bibliography. F. C. Grant, *Hellenistic Religions* (1953).

B. H. THROCKMORTON, JR.

PHINEES. KJV Apoc. form of PASEAH 2; PHINEHAS.

PHINEHAS fĭn'ĭ əs [פינחס, פנחס, the Negro; Egyp. *pə nḥśj;* Apoc. φινεές]; KJV Apoc. PHINEES fĭn'ĭ əs. **1.** In ancient memory a N Israelite of such importance that a site in the hill country of Ephraim (exact location now unknown) was called "Gibeah of Phinehas" (Josh. 24:33 [secondary E]). In this notice the identification of Phinehas as a descendant of AARON and the implication that Phinehas was a N priest (cf. LXX) may be correct. An Aaronite, priestly family called the "sons of Phinehas" was prominent in Babylonia in the time of Zerubbabel and Ezra; members of this family returned from the Exile (Ezra 8:2; I Esd. 5:5; 8:29). Late postexilic tradition identified Phinehas as the third figure in the Aaronite descent of the priesthood. From Aaron, his son Eleazar, his son Phinehas (Exod. 6:25; *see* the work of C. Simpson in the *bibliography* for the view that a P redactor has worked over Josh. 24:33), the Aaronite line was traced through Zadok to Jehozadak and Ezra (I Chr. 6:3-15, 50-53; Ezra 7:1-5). Postexilic narration of four stories (perhaps in each case midrashic expansion) set forth the significance of Phinehas in late tradition concerning the priesthood (*see* PRIESTS AND LEVITES):

a) In the time of Moses when a plague was raging and the people were weeping before the trysting tent, an Israelite came into camp bringing a Midianite woman to his family. Phinehas "the son of Eleazar, son of Aaron the priest," saw this as an intolerable instance of current defection from Yahweh, left the weeping assembly to go after the Israelite into his inner room, and pierced both of them with a spear. Appeased by this act of conviction, Yahweh stopped the plague sent as judgment against syncretism with the Midianites and the religion associated with Peor. For his zealous devotion to Yahweh's honor, Yahweh gave the priesthood to Phinehas and to his descendants: "I give to him my covenant of peace; and it shall be to him, and to his descendants after him, the covenant of a perpetual priesthood, because he was jealous for his God, and made atonement for the people of Israel" (Num. 25:6-18; cf. Ps. 106:30-31; Ecclus. 45:23-24; I Macc. 2:26, 54).

b) When Moses sent an expeditionary force to exterminate the Midianites, he sent Phinehas along either as leader or as priest. Phinehas took with him "the vessels of the sanctuary and the trumpets for the alarm" (Num. 31:6; cf. 10:1-10; II Chr. 13:12).

c) Phinehas was the leader and spokesman of a commission of the ten chiefs of the tribes W of the Jordan which went to the tribes E of the Jordan to charge them with treachery against Yahweh in the building of an altar. The E tribes defended their action as the erection of a witness to both sides of the Jordan and to all generations that they also, the E tribes, served Yahweh and had a "portion in Yahweh" and in Israel. Phinehas expressed the satisfaction of the commission that no part of Israel had acted to bring the wrath of Yahweh upon all Israel. The commission returned to Shiloh, where its report peaceably dispersed the W Israelites who had assembled to fight if necessary (Josh. 22:9-34).

d) When the Israelites inquired of Yahweh whether to fight against their brethren the Benjaminites for condoning the sin of the inhabitants of Gibeah, Phinehas, who ministered before the ark at Bethel, officiated at the inquiry and delivered the favorable oracle (Judg. 20:27-28). A further notice in Chronicles states that at one time Phinehas was superintendent of the gatekeepers (I Chr. 9:20, which established connection between the gatekeepers and one who then or later held the office of chief priest).

Bibliography. Westphal, "Aaron und die Aaroniden," *ZAW,* XXVI (1906), 223-25; M. Noth, *Die israelitischen Personennamen* (1928), p. 63; T. Meek, "Aaronites and Zadokites," *AJSL,* XLV (1929), 165; K. Möhlenbrink, "Die levitischen Überlieferungen des ATs," *ZAW,* LII (1934), 189, 217-19; C. Simpson, *The Early Traditions of Israel* (1948), p. 322; W. Rudolf, *Ezra und Nehemiah,* HAT (1949), pp. 79-81; J. Bright, Exegesis of Joshua, *IB,* II (1953), 659-63; L. Koehler and W. Baumgartner, eds., *Lexicon in Veteris Testamenti Libros* (1953), p. 759; J. Meyers, Exegesis of Judges, *IB,* II (1953), 814-15, 818-19; R. Bowman, Exegesis of Ezra, *IB,* III (1954), 632; W. Rudolf, *Chronikbücher,* HAT (1955), p. 89.

2. One of the two sons of Eli. *See* HOPHNI AND PHINEHAS.

3. Evidently a priest, father of ELEAZAR 5 (Ezra 8:33; I Esd. 8:63). T. M. MAUCH

PHISON. KJV Apoc. form of Pishon. *See* EDEN.

PHLEGON flĕg'ŏn [Φλέγων, burning] (Rom. 16:14). A Christian man greeted by Paul, along with three other men and the Christians associated with them.

F. W. GINGRICH

PHOEBE fē'bĭ [Φοίβη, radiant]. A Christian woman, DEACONESS of the church at Cenchreae, the E seaport of Corinth. Rom. 16 begins with a recommendation for her (vs. 1); many now think that this chapter was not originally part of Romans but was addressed to Ephesus (*see* ROMANS, LETTER TO THE). Phoebe had distinguished herself by the services she had rendered to her church and to Paul himself; the word προστάτις used for her in vs. 2 may be rendered "patroness" as well as "helper." Her freedom to travel may indicate that she was a widow.

There is a growing tendency (but not RSV, Moffatt, et al.) to translate διάκονος "helper," etc., rather than "deaconess," with reference to Phoebe; thus, Paul surely does not mean to call himself a "deacon" in such passages as II Cor. 11:23; Col. 1:23, 25. Nevertheless, informal service of the kind rendered by Phoebe soon became the inspiration for a regular order of deaconesses.

Bibliography. E. J. Goodspeed, *HTR,* 44 (1951), 55-57.

F. W. GINGRICH

PHOENICIA fĭ nĭsh'ə; KJV PHENICIA (Acts 21:2); PHENICE fĭ nī'sĭ [φοινίκη] (Acts 11:19; 15:3); PHOENICIANS fĭ nĭsh'ənz. A country on the E coast of the Mediterranean, N of Palestine.

1. Name
2. Geography
3. History
4. Religion

Bibliography

1. Name. The term "Phoenicia" was first used by the Greeks to refer to the country of the Canaanites, with whom they traded. This contact in trade started early, and already *ca.* 1200 B.C. the terms "Canaanites" and "Phoenicians" were synonymous. This early use of the term has made scholars seek for an Egyptian, or a wider Semitic, background. There is, however, little doubt that we have here a direct translation of the word "Canaan" (כנען), which means "land of purple." The term "Canaan"

From *Atlas of the Bible* (Thomas Nelson & Sons Limited)

51. Bay on the coast of Phoenicia, with the Fortress of Margab on the citadel

Courtesy of Herbert G. May

52. The Dog River (Nahr el-Kelb) in Phoenicia

was first used of whole Syria-Palestine. It may be of Hurrian (Horite) origin, from the word *knağği,* which meant "purple dye." The purple industry was of great importance already in the eighteenth and seventeenth centuries B.C. when the Hurrians entered the country. The Greek word φοίνιξ means "red purple" (wool), and the name φοινίκη is thus a translation of the name Canaan. In course of time, however, the two terms were used for different countries. *See* CANAAN.

Figs. PHO 51-52.

2. Geography. Phoenicia was a long and narrow country along the seacoast, actually only 120-30 miles long. The mountains of Lebanon formed a natural border to the E. The N border was along the River Eleutherus, now Nahr el-Kebir, and the S border was Mount Carmel, where Phoenicia had Israel as its neighbor. Especially along the mountains the coastal plain is very narrow, *ca.* five miles, and the foothills rise rather abruptly. At Juniyeh, N of Beirut, the plain is only a mile broad, and the hills rise up to 2,500 feet close to the coast. A little farther S, *ca.* three miles, the foothills reach the sea, and around the narrow passage here the Phoenicians used to concentrate their defense forces when they were attacked by mighty and powerful armies. Also at the S border, where Carmel slopes steeply to the sea, the passage is a very narrow one.

The land strip between the sea and the mountains is fertile and was already well cultivated in antiquity. The vegetation here was the usual one in the Mediterranean countries, with many evergreen shrubs and plants, flowering quickly in the spring. Wheat and barley were early used, so also onions, garlic, and other vegetables. Trees of many kinds were found, yielding figs, dates, and olives, and the vines produced grapes. The climate is very well suited for the growing of fruit. There is no rain in the summertime, and the sun ripens the fruit perfectly. There were also other trees: pine, oak, mulberry, and beech. On the whole, a large part of the country was forested, as it is not today. Also, the mountain ranges were densely forested. The winter temperature is lower along the mountain slopes, so subtropical palms and shrubs cannot survive there. Instead, hardier kinds of trees were found, first and foremost cedars, pines, and firs. Big forests furnished the famous cedars and other wood valuable for timber. Today only two small, aging forests of cedar are left, consisting of a few hundred trees. Export of cedars was going on in ancient times, as far back as our documents reach. For ancient Egypt the cedars and pines of Lebanon were the only source of wood, and other neighboring countries imported them frequently. It is no wonder, then, that denudation was the final result.

The mountain range of Lebanon is *ca.* 105 miles long, extending from the Nahr el-Kebir in the N to Nahr el-Qasimiyeh, near Tyre, in the S. The highest peaks are snow-capped half the year. The highest one, el-Qurnat el-Sawda', is 11,024 feet above the sea, and also a few others are more than 10,000 feet high. The mountains are almost entirely of limestone, with its distinctive grayish color.

The strip of land along the mountains is so narrow that the people living there had to turn to the sea in order to find a living. The Phoenicians became able seamen, and they were famous in the ancient world for their capacity as sailors and pilots. They took up sea trade and developed it to a degree which was unknown till then. The long, straight coast along the E Mediterranean had few good harbors, among which were Byblos,* Sidon,* Tyre,* and Berytos (Beirut). Here were important industrial and trading centers. The chief product for which Phoenicia was famous was purple dye. As mentioned above, it also gave the country its name. The purple was produced by the large sea snail murex, which is found in the Mediterranean. Two species were used, and there are still large shell mounds in Saida

Courtesy of Arvid L. Kapelrud

53. Gebal (Byblos); ancient site, seen from the Crusader's Castle

(ancient Sidon) and Sur (ancient Tyre). The shells are waste from the purple industry, which brought enormous incomes to the Phoenician cities, but also made them rather unpleasant to live in, as there was a strong smell from the dye and the factories. Purple dye was produced in different shades of color, in a range which went far beyond what we would call purple today. The dyers knew different techniques which helped them to produce the varying shades. Figs. PHO 53; SID 57; TYR 81.

Also other products came from Phoenicia. Weapons were made, and wine. The sand near Sidon and Tyre was well suited for making glass, and Phoenician glassware was famous.

3. History. The history of Phoenicia goes very far back. Documentary evidence, however, is scarce. The history of Phoenicia is the history of its cities. These were rebuilt on the same sites when they were destroyed, and also today there are towns on the ancient sites. This fact makes excavations difficult or even impossible, so they have not been carried out to the extent which could be desirable.

Excavations at Gebal (Byblos) have shown that in late Neolithic times a Mediterranean race was living there.* The people used circular huts and buried their dead in big earthen pots. They represent an archaic civilization which had affinities at Uruk in Sumer and also in Egypt. Of whatever origin this civilization was, it vanished suddenly in the latter half of the fourth millennium B.C. Its place was taken by a new civilization of a characteristically urban type. Walled cities with temples and rectangular houses were built, and new technical inventions were made. New weapons were used, made of a new metal, bronze. These weapons came from the N, and they were introduced by peoples who invaded the country from the mountainous countries in Asia Minor and along the coast. From the E came other invaders. They were Semites, and they also mixed with the former population. It was actually such a blend of different elements which constituted the Phoenician people. Fig. GEB 13.

Already in the fourth millennium Semites invaded Mesopotamia, probably from Arabia. Waves of Semites reached Phoenicia early. In the middle of the third millennium they held a dominating position in N Mesopotamia, Syria, and Lebanon. They were driven back by Sargon I, himself a Semite, but they kept their hold on Syria and Lebanon. Names such as "Lebanon" and "Sidon" are supposed to be of Amorite origin. Up to the nineteenth century B.C. many of the most important cities of Syria and Lebanon were dominated by Amorite princes. The leading classes were also often Amorites. *Ca.* 1700 King Hammurabi of Babylonia, who was himself of Amorite origin, crushed the Amorite kingdom and its capital, Mari.

The following centuries were troubled times in Phoenicia, as they were in most of the Near East. The Hyksos swept through the countries from N to S, finally invading Egypt, ravaging and burning on their way. The main components of the Hyksos hordes were probably Mitannians and Hurrites (Horites), who also for some periods held their sway over Phoenicia at this time.

Egypt had been interested in Phoenicia from a

time which goes very far back in history. Egyptian objects have been found, especially in Byblos, which date back to *ca.* 3000 B.C. Pharaoh Snefru of the Fourth Dynasty, who ruled in the twenty-sixth century, tells in his annals about "bringing 40 ships filled with cedar logs" from Phoenicia. This is a very early indication that trade was going on between Egypt and Phoenicia. The Egyptians needed first and foremost cedars and pines, but also oil, wine, spices, leather, and other products. They tried to get a firm grip on Phoenicia again when the Hyksos had been driven out. Pharaoh Thut-mose III (1490-1435), who was a great warrior, marched toward the N with his army. The Phoenician and Syrian city-states, which did not usually work too well together, forgot their enmity for once and allied against the advancing enemy. Their armies were crushed by Thut-mose at Megiddo in 1479. It was a decisive victory which gave Thut-mose a firm hold on Phoenicia for the rest of his lifetime. But after his death this situation did not last very long. His successors, Amen-hotep III and IV, were weak and unable to hold Phoenicia under control. We can see clearly how it was from the TELL EL-AMARNA correspondence from the fourteenth century. The princes of the Phoenician city-states, with the exception of the kings of Byblos and Tyre, showed no loyalty toward the Egyptian Pharaoh, except in their letters. The letters also reveal that they were not loyal toward one another, all of them trying to get help, equipment, and soldiers for themselves. Much of the trouble was caused by the Amorite prince 'Abdu-Ashirta, whose kingdom was found along the upper Orontes. In the N he had the mighty Hittites as his neighbors, and though he was an Egyptian vassal, like other kings in these regions, his only possibility of expansion was toward the W and the S. He marched into Arka, NE of Tripolis, and further tried to conquer other Phoenician cities. He still feigned loyalty toward Egypt and wrote a letter to Pharaoh Amen-hotep III, beginning thus: "To the King, the Sun, my Lord, thus says 'Abdu-Ashirta, thy slave, the dust of thy feet. At the feet of the King, my Lord, seven times and seven I fall down." This was the usual introduction in letters written by the loyal vassals of Pharaoh, but other letters, especially fifty of them written by King Rib-Addi of Byblos, reveal that 'Abdu-Ashirta was the very leader of the opposition against the Egyptians. Rib-Addi had to leave Byblos because of the threatening danger. He reproached Pharaoh Amen-hotep IV (AKH-EN-ATON): "I have written repeatedly for garrison troops, but they were not given, and the king did not listen to the words of his servant." His pleas did not help him; he had to flee because of 'Abdu-Ashirta's son 'Aziru. 'Aziru also professed loyalty to Egypt and even visited the country, but he was actually in allegiance with the Hittite conqueror of N Syria, King Suppiluliumas. The king of Tyre, Abimilki, remained loyal to Egypt, but in a letter to Amen-hotep IV he indicated that the king of Sidon was constantly writing "to the criminal 'Aziru, the son of 'Abdu-Ashirta, concerning everything that he heard from Egypt."

Phoenicia was pressed from several sides by different peoples in the middle of the second millennium. Rib-Addi, who tried to stem the Amorite pressure, also reported to Amen-hotep IV: "Since thy father returned from Sidon, since that time, the lands have fallen into the hands of the GAZ." Who the SA-GAZ were, is not quite sure, but they seem to have been mercenaries in some of the great armies operating at this time. They were also ravaging on their own. They have been identified with the HABIRU, who were also active in these centuries. The Habiru were groups of warriors, nomads and brigands, who served in several armies—e.g., in the Hittite army under Mursilis I (*ca.* 1600)—and they also raided Phoenicia. They seem to have taken part in an Aramaic wave of invaders who seized Syria in the fourteenth and thirteenth centuries. In the following centuries they mixed also with the Phoenicians.

Egypt had a revival under Ramses II (1290-1224), who invaded Syria and Phoenicia in order to renew his claim on these territories. He met the Hittite army at Kadesh on the Orontes River *ca.* 1287. Ramses claimed a victory, but the Hittites were not beaten. In 1272 Ramses had to sign a non-aggression pact with them, leaving N Syria with the Hittites, while S Syria was to be under the sovereignty of the Pharaoh. Both sovereignties soon became only nominal. Semitic invaders pressed on from the E, and from the W came the Aegeans with rising power and broke into the Hittite Empire. The story of Wen-Amon from *ca.* 1100 is significant. He arrived in Phoenicia as the representative of the Egyptian Pharaoh commissioned to procure timber for a ceremonial barge from the vassal kings. He was met with scorn and contempt.

A new threat had begun to rise in the E. *Ca.* 1100, King Tiglath-pileser I of Assyria reached the Mediterranean coast with his army. He conquered Arvad, but his conquest was only temporary. The Phoenician cities had attained an independent position at this time, with first Sidon and then Tyre dominating. In the following centuries Phoenicia had its golden age. It was then that King Hiram, or AHIRAM (981-947), ruled in Tyre and was the leading sovereign in Phoenicia.* He delivered timber of cedars and cypresses to King Solomon and furnished him with able seamen and pilots. Important were his building of a long breakwater in Tyre and his development of the trade with Cyprus and Spain. Fig. GEB 15.

This development of trade and shipping just at this time most probably had its special background. The Phoenicians were used to the sea, but now they had to build their whole future on sea trade. They were circled in by strong powers which made expansion on land practically impossible—i.e., Arameans, Israelites, Philistines. If some of these peoples were not so great, they were warlike, and the Phoenicians were never that. They fought, even desperately, when it was necessary, but they did not seek war. Instead, their expansion took place along the sea routes which they had explored themselves to a great extent. Trade between Byblos and Egypt was going on already in the third millennium B.C. It may have started overland, with caravans along the coast, but the sea route was soon preferred. Another route went to Cyprus, and farther to Crete and Sicily. A third route went to North Africa and a fourth one to Spain.

The Phoenicians had learned navigation through experience and hard study. They were able to sail by night by using the polestar, and it is supposed that they were the first sailors to do this. They sailed broad ships, with high stern and bow, driven both by sails and by oars. Often there were two or more lines of rowers above one another. With such ships they made nearly incredible trips. Already in the eleventh century B.C. they had settled in the great Mediterranean islands, and in the end of this century they had founded colonies in Cadiz in Spain, then called Gades, and in Utica in North Africa, now Tunis. *Ca.* 850 B.C., settlers from Tyre founded Carthage, a colony which grew to an important city-state. Before this famous colony was founded, the Phoenicians had built Hippo, which also came to play a role in history. Phoenicians sailed the Atlantic and are supposed to have reached Cornwall in England.

The Phoenician colonies in Spain were important for centuries and were used as bases for trade in the W Mediterranean. Malta and Crete were other centers. From the gold mines of Thrace, N of Greece, the Phoenicians drew gold for their goldsmiths. The colony which prospered most was Carthage. While Phoenicia itself was pressed by the Assyrians, Carthage was free to expand and to promote trade along the coast of the Mediterranean and with the islands. This made Carthage one of the strongest powers in these regions, and ultimately it led to conflict with the Roman Empire and the total destruction of the city.

After the raid of Tiglath-pileser, Aramean invaders had entered Phoenicia. They were slowly mixed with the population already found there. The Assyrians, however, did not intend to give up Phoenicia. King Ashurnasirpal II (884-859) marched with his army to the coast of the Mediterranean, and the Phoenician cities did not hesitate to submit. The son of Ashurnasirpal, Shalmaneser III (859-824), had, however, to redo his father's work. He met the army of the Syrian-Phoenician alliance at Qarqar and defeated it in 853 B.C. In spite of the effective military organization built up by these kings, the domination of Assyria over Phoenicia was not too heavy. Some Phoenicians, however, preferred to build their hopes on the new colony at Carthage. The expansion of trade and shipping was not seriously hampered in this century.

The decline began in the eighth century. Tiglath-pileser III (745-727) started to reconquer Syria, and his son Shalmaneser V (727-722) marched into Phoenicia, where only Tyre caused him some trouble. But Phoenicia was too far away from Assyria to be fully controlled, and King Elu-eli of Tyre tried to seize the reins over all Phoenicia and even Cyprus. This was too much to be tolerated, and the Assyrian king Sennacherib (705-681) made a forced march to Lebanon, destroyed the palace of the king, who had fled, and established a new king, Ethba'al of Sidon. His submission was of the kind that was usual in Phoenicia, and in 677 the king of Sidon led a revolt against King Esarhaddon (681-669). This time the patience of the Assyrian king was out, and he destroyed Sidon. The other leading city, Tyre, held its position for a further hundred years. The Assyrian Empire, which reached its peak in the seventh century, was annihilated with the fall of Nineveh in 612. The Babylonians inherited their trouble with Phoenicia. In 587 Nebuchadnezzar marched into Syria with his army, and after a siege of thirteen years his soldiers defeated Tyre in 572. That was a final blow for Phoenicia. It never revived as a nation. The Phoenicians were often heard of after this time, but their expanding power was gone, and their shipping and colonial activity was gradually taken over by other nations.

A change in the status of Phoenicia came when the Persian king CYRUS had conquered Babylon in 539. It was now part of a new empire, and the Persian rulers deliberately gave the Phoenician cities a tolerably independent position. A Persian governor, the satrap, ruled also over these provinces, but they paid no heavy taxes. The Persians needed the Phoenician fleet and used it on several occasions. When Cambyses (530-522) attacked Egypt, he was supported by a Phoenician fleet. This was the case also when Xerxes attacked Greece in the following century. The usefulness of the fleet may have been the reason why the Persians gave the Phoenician cities the right to have local autonomy. For once the city-states were able to forget their rivalry, and in the fourth century they united in a new federation. Originally, Sidon, Tyre, and Arvad took part, and they instituted a meeting place in the N of the country. This place grew into a new city, called Tripolis by the Greeks. The city was functioning as a capital for Phoenicia. Here the delegates from the united cities gathered at annual meetings. About three hundred representatives used to meet. The meetings were headed by the official Persian governor and his officers. The arrogance of the Persians at these meetings was strongly resented by the Phoenicians, especially as they probably had a definite feeling that the power of the Persian Empire was vanishing.

The next step was obvious. A rebellion was started against Artaxerxes III Ochus (358-338), but it came too early. The result was the tragic destruction of SIDON in 351. The Persian Empire broke to pieces under the attacks of Alexander, starting at Issos in 333. Then came the turn of TYRE, which was annihilated. With the two chief Phoenician cities in ruins, the saga of Phoenicia was practically finished. It is true that the cities were rebuilt and populated again, and that they got a new chance to develop under Roman aegis, but as a nation Phoenicia had lost its distinctive stamp. Hellenistic culture became deeply rooted under the Seleucid kings, and Sidon and Tyre were centers of Greek philosophy and literature in the last centuries B.C. Zeno from Citium on Cyprus (333-261) grew up in a Phoenician colony and had as his teacher another Zeno, from Sidon. As founder of the Stoic school of philosophy, Zeno from Citium made a lasting contribution to Hellenistic culture. Some of the poets who described the life of the time were of Phoenician origin, as Antipater of Sidon and Meleager of Gadara.

Pompey conquered Syria and Phoenicia in 64 B.C. The Seleucid rule was in a state of anarchy at that time, but then the Roman proconsuls took over. They were, however, unable to keep Syria and Phoenicia undisturbed in the first decades. The Parthians, who had their capital in Ctesiphon in Mesopotamia, launched several attacks on the new Roman provinces. Octavian put an end to this, after his victory over Antony and Cleopatra at Actium in 31 B.C. That started the long period of Pax Romana, which is so closely connected with the Emperor Augustus—the new title and name which the senate bestowed upon Octavian in 27 B.C. Also Phoenicia prospered under the new conditions. The tributes which were exacted were usually not too high. Roman settlements of well-trained troops were found in Beirut and in Baalbek. New roads were built and postal service instituted. The connections between the different parts of the Empire were good, and this gave the Phoenicians a new chance for their trade and industry. They produced fine glass, and pottery which was often an imitation of Greek ware. Their dye production was still at its height, and so were also their metalwork and their wine. Dates and wheat flour were other export articles. Syria and Phoenicia were densely populated in this time, and because of the extensive trade many were able to live in luxury.

When the first expansion of Christianity began, it spread also to Phoenicia; see Acts 11:19; 15:3; 21:2. In these passages from the NT the term "Phoenicia" is used, but in Acts 21:3 "Syria" is used as a synonym. This indicates that at this time the term "Phoenicia" was used purely geographically, not about a living nation. This was true also in the fourth century A.D., when "Phoenicia" was used as the name of two administrative districts: Phoenicia Prima, comprised mostly of the historical Phoenicia, and Phoenicia Secunda, which had Damascus as capital.

4. Religion. Spiritual culture had early beginnings in Phoenicia. WRITING was introduced here, probably inspired by Egyptian pattern, in the form of pseudo hieroglyphics, as they have been found in Byblos. The ALPHABET came from this part of the world. Phoenician religion has also influenced the religions of the neighboring countries, and features from Phoenician worship have continued to live in other religions. It has been very hard to get knowledge of Phoenician religion, as few documents were handed down to posterity. Some information is found in the OT, and the church historian Eusebius cites an ancient author, Philo of Byblos, who lived at the time of Jesus. This Philo was supposed to have had his information from a rather legendary Phoenician author, called Sanchuniathon, who according to Philo was a priest from Beirut born in the eleventh century B.C. The work of Sanchuniathon was lost, but Philo had translated it into Greek, and his translation was used by Eusebius. Also the work of Philo is lost.

Apart from this source, information is found in the TELL EL-AMARNA letters, on the sarcophagi from Byblos (*see* GEBAL), and especially in the Ras Shamra Texts (*see* UGARIT). Archaeological work in Phoenicia, which has not been too extensive, has given some new material. The Ras Shamra Texts to a certain extent confirm the picture given by Eusebius and Philo. They show that the Phoenician religion, so far as we can speak of it as an entity, was closely connected with what is otherwise known of W Semitic religion. It was a religion which combined the fears and joys of daily life with cultic performances in the many temples. The leading god of the pantheon was El, also called Bull El, a name which very effectively gives the character of this religion. His consort was Asherah (or Athirat), mother-goddess and queen of heavens. The young god who played a great role in Phoenician religion was Baal, who was very popular in Phoenicia, under slightly changing names. Baal was also called the Bull and was an outspoken fertility figure. He was god of rain and thunder, and in the Ras Shamra Texts he is identified with Hadad. On his side was found the warlike fertility goddess Anath. *See* CANAANITES § 6.

Philo of Byblos has complicated narratives about the creation of the world, the gods, and man. It is hard to find out what is originally Phoenician here and what is of Greek (or other) origin. One is therefore on safer ground in adhering to facts coming from more reliable sources.

Worship of Baal was found in most Phoenician cities. Baal was found in many aspects, as Baal-saphon (Lord of the North), Baal-shamim (Lord of Heaven), Baal-lebanon (Lord of Lebanon) and in other variants. Most famous was the Baal of Tyre, Melqart, for whom King Hiram built a temple in the tenth century. In the course of time Melqart also attained a character of maritime deity. Dagan ("Dagon" in I Sam. 5:1-7) had a similar fate, while Resheph was assimilated with Apollo. In Sidon royal names (cf. Eshmun-azar) bear witness to the importance of the god Eshmun (in the fourth century). The ruins of his temple, which have been dug up, do not indicate anything about his cult, but he was in Greek times identified with Asclepius. Eshmun was not alone to dominate the worship of the Sidonians. The goddess Ashtart (Astarte, OT ASHTORETH), with her cult prostitution, was well known also in other countries (I Kings 11:5, 33; II Kings 23:13). It was not only King Solomon who built temples for Ashtart; Eshmunazar also boasts that he built a temple for her in Sidon. His father, King Tabnit, called himself priest of Ashtart. In Gebal (Byblos) it was also Ashtart who was the chief deity, and in Beirut it was Baalat Beirut.

Ashtart was seldom worshiped alone. On her side was often a male deity, in Phoenicia usually known as ADONIS, meaning "Lord." Adonis was a young god who was killed by a wild boar when he was out hunting. Ashtart, who loved him, descended to the nether world to wrest him out of the hands of death. The usual name of this god in the Semitic world was TAMMUZ. Adonis was a vegetation and fertility god who was supposed to die when the summer heat began. He was the chief figure in a comprehensive fertility cult which reached its peak in a great festival. Worship of Adonis took place also at the Adonis River (Nahr Ibrahim), called so because ferruginous earth colored it red a few times in the year. To the believers this was the blood of the god, and a sanctuary was built at the source of the river, at Afqa. People from Byblos and other parts of Phoenicia came there in the summer to the great festival. Lamentations over the dead god took place, and processions were arranged to places connected with his hunt.

Offerings and sacrifices of the Phoenicians were mainly the usual Semitic ones. Human sacrifices played a certain role, especially in ancient times, and they have given the Phoenicians a reputation of cruelty. Philo tells that human sacrifice was instituted by the gods. It was used for Melqart in Tyre and for Baal Ammon in Carthage, and it continued to be in use for centuries (*see* MOLECH). Apart from that, very little is known about the Phoenician cult. The constantly burning fire in the sanctuaries was seen by foreigners as a symbol of the insatiable greed of the Phoenician gods for human sacrifices. Worship also occurred at "high places," where a holy stone, baetulus, was erected. Sometimes a wooden pillar, ASHERAH, was also set up. These witness a popular cult which had close parallels in Syria and Canaan.

Bibliography. W. W. Baudissin, *Adonis und Esmun* (1911); G. Contenau, *La civilisation phénicienne* (1928); A. T. Olmstead, *A History of Syria and Palestine* (1931); O. Eissfeldt, *Ras Schamra und Sanchunjaton* (1939); M. Dunand, *Byblia grammata* (1945); P. K. Hitti, *History of Syria, Including Lebanon and Palestine* (1951); O. Eissfeldt, *Sanchunjaton von Berut und Ilumilku von Ugarit* (1952). A. S. KAPELRUD

PHOENIX fē'nĭks [Φοῖνιξ]. A harbor of Crete (Acts 27:12), located on the S side of the island and W of Fair Havens (vs. 8). Strabo (*Geography* X.4.3) locates the town of Phoenix on the S side of the isthmus or narrower part of Crete, W of the broader middle part of the island. The exact location of the harbor is much discussed, and depends on the meaning of Luke's narrative in Acts 27:8-15. Fair Havens, not a real harbor but an open roadstead or anchorage, three or four miles E of Cape Matala, was not a safe place for a large grain ship with 276 passengers to winter (even if the alternate reading in vs. 37: "seventy-six persons," is original, this was a fairly large ship). The centurion, who had the final decision, disregarded Paul's advice and agreed with the captain and the owner of the ship and decided to try to reach the harbor of Phoenix and winter there. This implies that Phoenix lay farther W and was a safe harbor for a large ship. When a gentle S wind was blowing, the attempt was made. All went well until the ship had passed close to Cape Matala and was crossing the Gulf of Messara. There a "tempestuous wind, called the northeaster, struck down from the land," from the direction of Mount Ida, and drove the ship W-SW in the direction of the island of Cauda and then on W toward Malta.

The safe harbor at modern Loutro fits almost all of the references to ancient Phoenix. It is on the S shore of the isthmus Strabo mentions. It has about the longitude which Ptolemy gives for Phoenix. A peninsula runs out southward, and an arm of it extends E to give a harbor fully protected on the N, W, and S sides. Only one difficulty stands in the way of identifying this harbor of Loutro with the ancient harbor of Phoenix. This is the description of the harbor in Acts 27:12 as βλέποντα κατὰ λίβα καὶ κατὰ χῶρον. λίψ in the LXX means "south," but in the papyri it means "west" and in the Aristotelian system "west-southwest." Χῶρος, according to Pliny, means "west-northwest." The natural meaning of Acts 27:12 would be: "looking toward the southwest and northwest." This suggests that the harbor opened to the W. Three possibilities have been suggested:

a) The harbor now called Phineka, on the W side of the peninsula whose E side has the harbor of Loutro, was actually the objective of the ship's officers. This gives the Greek its natural sense, but Phineka was a poorer harbor and less easy to reach from Fair Havens.

b) Luke, who had never been at Phoenix, mistakenly thought that the good harbor Loutro opened to the W, when it really opened eastward.

c) The Greek, contrary to the usual meaning the words convey, may be translated from the viewpoint of sailors entering the harbor Loutro as "looking toward the southwest and northwest," thus "looking toward" the direction from which the wind comes, rather than the direction in which it blows. Although this interpretation, which would identify the harbor in mind in Acts 27:12 as Loutro, would give a safe and adequate harbor for such a ship, its interpretation of κατά is so unusual that it must be called at best a possible, but by no means certain, solution.

Bibliography. J. Smith, *The Voyage and Shipwreck of St. Paul* (1880), ch. 3 and Appendix II. F. J. Foakes-Jackson and K. Lake, *The Beginnings of Christianity*, IV (1933), 328-31; V (1933), 338-44. F. V. FILSON

PHOROS. KJV Apoc. form of PAROSH.

***PHRYGIA** frĭj'ĭ ə [Φρυγία]. In the period of written ancient history, the name given to a large area of Asia Minor. The origin of the Phrygians has sometimes been sought in Armenia, but it is more generally thought that they came into Asia Minor from Thrace. There are evidences of the early presence of the Phrygians not only in Thrace but also in Macedonia and beyond. At an early date they or related tribes were found in most of Asia Minor, from the Aegean Sea to the Halys River and from Bithynia to the Taurus Mountains; and they appear in Homer's *Iliad* in association with the Trojans, to whom they are related. The Phrygians of the epic period are mentioned as a vigorous, heroic people, but from the time of their subjection by the Persians they were politically submissive and unimportant, and in later ancient times Phrygian names were considered appropriate for slaves.

1. Geographical limits. The limits of Phrygia varied continually, and it is difficult to define its exact limits at any given time. In NW Asia Minor was Hellespontine, or Lesser, Phrygia, lying S of the Hellespont and Propontis and including the Troad. This recalls the Thracian origin of the Phrygians, and their twenty-five years of sea supremacy, of which Diodorus tells (VII.11). Later invaders from Thrace cut off Lesser Phrygia from Greater Phrygia, which occupied W central Asia Minor, and Lesser Phrygia soon ceased to be Phrygian in life and character. Greater Phrygia had several divisions or recognized areas. The NE portion was taken over by the invading GAULS in the third century B.C. Shortly thereafter, in the NW, a section apparently obtained from Bithynia by Attalus I of Pergamum received the name Phrygia Epictetus ("Acquired Phrygia"); its cities include Cotiaion and Dorylеum. This region is wrongly identified with Hellespontine Phrygia by

Adapted from *The Westminster Historical Atlas to the Bible, Revised*, ed. G. Ernest Wright and Floyd V. Filson. © The Westminster Press.

Strabo (*Geography* XII.4.3); in reality it lay S and a little E of Hellespontine Phrygia. Phrygia Paroreia ("along the mountains") was in the SE part of Phrygia; and at the extreme SE part was Phrygia Towards Pisidia (Strabo XII.8.13), in which Antioch Towards Pisidia was located. Iconium also was often called Phrygian by ancient writers, but at times it was regarded as lying in Lycaonia. In Roman times Phrygia included on the SW the region around Cibyra and the Lycus Valley, with the cities Colossae, Hierapolis, and Laodicea.

The Roman provincial administration of Asia Minor divided Greater Phrygia into two parts. The smaller became a portion of the province of GALATIA; it included Antioch Towards Pisidia and (often) Iconium. The much larger part formed part of the province called ASIA.

Another, unofficial division, rarely used, refers to the high tableland of Phrygia as Upper Phrygia and the low portions as Lower Phrygia. At the very end of the third century or early in the fourth century A.D., when the province of Asia was broken up into seven parts, two new provinces were Phrygia Prima (or Pacatiana) on the W and Phrygia Secunda (or Salutaris) to the E.

2. People and culture. The Phrygians as a people were long subject to alien rulers, and their characteristics must have been affected by their continual mingling with other tribes. So it is difficult to say anything trustworthy and definite concerning their life and character. The references to Phrygians in Homer's *Iliad* would suggest vitality in this tribe, but the Phrygians themselves do not seem to have appealed to an earlier golden age of courage and greatness. They were peaceable, submissive, civilized, and responsive to neighboring influences. They were capable in agriculture, in cultivation of the vine, and in commerce. The great trade routes, which started from the Aegean Sea and the Hellespont and ran eastward through central Asia Minor, crossed Phrygian territory and fostered commercial and cultural interchange there. During the Hellenistic and Roman periods the use of the Greek language naturally spread in this region.

The Phrygian religion, while open to outside influence and so to syncretism, showed a marked tendency to emotional and even orgiastic forms of expression, in which exciting music and frenzied dancing played a part. Prominent Phrygian deities were Rhea Cybele, the mother-goddess, and Sabazius, who was connected with the vital and renewing powers of nature and identified with Dionysus. Thus the sensuous fertility cult and intoxicating revels formed part of Phrygian religious life.

The cosmopolitan population of Phrygia included large numbers of Jews. There is definite evidence that their presence was encouraged by the Seleucid rulers. Seleucus Nicator (312-280 B.C.) granted the Jews "citizenship in the cities which he founded in Asia and Lower Syria"; and Antiochus III (223-187 B.C.), to stabilize conditions among the rebellious Lydians and Phrygians, determined to transport "two thousand Jewish families with their effects from Mesopotamia and Babylonia to the fortresses and most important places" in Lydia and Phrygia (Jos. Antiq. XII.iii.1, 4). Josephus cites other incidents which show that Jews continued numerous in Asia Minor under the Romans and had their privileges confirmed (cf. Jos. Antiq. XIV.x-xii; XVI.vi). Cicero, in his Defense of Flaccus (ch. 28), tells that Flaccus took over from Jews in the province of Asia one hundred pounds of gold at Apamea and twenty at

Laodicea—both cities of Phrygia. These sums represented gifts intended for Jerusalem and have been estimated to represent the annual gift (cf. Matt. 17:24) of fifty thousand Jews.

The Jews of this region were known for their laxity in observing their law. The syncretistic tendency so characteristic of Asia Minor had influenced them also. The Talmud contains a saying that the baths and wines of Phrygia had separated the ten tribes from their brethren. The NT evidence agrees with this report. Paul's Letter to the Colossians opposes a false teaching which mingled Jewish and pagan ideas and reflected a Jewish background which had been freely combined with ascetic and speculative features. The readiness with which many Phrygian and Lycaonian Jews of S Galatia accepted Paul's message shows an openness to a new teaching, and their readiness to live in the church with Gentiles and without strictly observing the Mosaic law suggests a background of laxity in ceremonial practice. The fierceness with which the Jewish leaders in this region opposed Paul suggests that they were conscious of a tendency among Jews to drop features of orthodox Jewish observance; in their eyes Paul was one more promoter of a laxity to which Jews in their region were thought to be all too prone (Acts 13:45, 50; 14:2, 19).

3. Christianity in Phrygia. The spread of Christianity in Phrygia in the apostolic age may be discussed in three parts:

a) It is a question what bearing Acts 2:10 has on the subject. Jews from Phrygia, this verse states, were present in Jerusalem at the first Pentecost, and heard Peter preach. Possibly, therefore, Phrygian Jews were among his three thousand converts (vs. 41) and carried the gospel back to Phrygia. But this can never be proved.

b) The travels of Paul in Phrygian Galatia raise difficult problems, and the conclusions reached determine the destination of Paul's Letter to the Galatians (*see* GALATIANS, LETTER TO THE). Paul's route on his first visit is clear. Coming from Pamphylia, he visited two Phrygian cities, Antioch Towards Pisidia and Iconium, and two Lycaonian cities, Lystra and Derbe; then he retraced this route (Acts 13:14–14:24). On his next visit Paul left Syrian Antioch, passed through the Cilician Gates, and reached Derbe and Lystra (15:41–16:1). Then, with Silas and Timothy, he passed through τήν Φρυγίαν καὶ Γαλατικὴν χώραν (16:6), which means either "Phrygia and the Galatian region" or "the Phrygian and Galatian region." In the former translation "Phrygia" is a noun and refers to the region which contained Iconium and Antioch Towards Pisidia; "the Galatian region" was a separate region, that part of the province of Galatia located N of Phrygia and inhabited by the Gauls. According to this view, Paul went into at least part of the region where Pessinus, Ancyra (modern Ankara), and Tavium lay. The latter translation, however, says only that Paul passed through one region, which in traditional usage was part of Phrygia but in Roman provincial organization was in the S part of Galatia. This means the area of Iconium and Antioch Towards Pisidia, and makes no mention of any visit to the Gauls in N Galatia. On his third visit to the Phrygian region Paul apparently again came from Syrian Antioch, reached upland Asia Minor through the Cilician Gates, and passed through in order τὴν Γαλατικὴν χώραν καὶ Φρυγίαν (Acts 18:23). This means either "the Galatian region and Phrygia" or "the region which is both Galatian and Phrygian." The former translation means that Paul first swung N through N Galatia, the home of the Gauls, and then turned SW to go through Phrygia and on to Ephesus (19:1). The latter translation means that Paul, coming from the Cilician Gates, went through S Galatia—i.e., through the region still called Phrygia in popular usage. He thus passed through Iconium and Antioch Towards Pisidia before going on westward to Ephesus. This latter interpretation says nothing of any visit to the Gauls of N Galatia. While a decisive conclusion is not possible, the interpretation of Acts 16:6; 18:23 which finds mention only of visits to the churches of S Galatia is perhaps preferable. In any case, the frequency with which Paul visited the Phrygian region of S Galatia is noteworthy.

c) The history of the churches of the Lycus Valley is a part of the story of Christianity in Phrygia. It must be recalled that in the apostolic age most of Phrygia lay in the province of Asia (Phrygia Asiana). Paul did not himself preach in the Lycus Valley, where Colossae, Hierapolis, and Laodicea lay (Col. 2:1; 4:13). When he came westward from central Asia Minor to Ephesus (Acts 19:1), he either did not come by way of the Lycus Valley or, if he did, he did not stop to preach in these cities. If, as seems probable, the original reading in Col. 1:7 is ὑπὲρ ἡμῶν, "on *our* behalf," it was Epaphras who represented Paul in evangelizing the Lycus Valley and ministering to the churches there (cf. Col. 4:13). Archippus also was a minister at Colossae (vs. 17). Later tradition says that John the Apostle and Philip worked in this area in the decades after Paul's death. The mention of both Asia and Galatia in I Pet. 1:1, written to churches in a time of hardship and threatened wholesale persecution, makes it clear that in the latter part of the first century the churches of Phrygia had to withstand active opposition. The inclusion of Laodicea in the seven churches singled out for special messages in the book of Revelation (3:14) also throws light on conditions in Asian Phrygia toward the end of the first century A.D. The church at Laodicea is described as well-to-do, complacent, spiritually poor, and facing a persecution that could never be withstood by a lukewarm faith.

The second century shows Christianity strong in Phrygia but marked by dissension. Great leaders, such as the bishops Papias and Apollinaris of Hierapolis, arose in this region. Martyrs proved the courage and dedication of the church. But the native Phrygian bent for highly emotional religious life comes to mind when the Montanist movement, with its appeal to visions and the new era of the Spirit, becomes prominent in Phrygia. The third century saw the churches of the region numerically dominant, and the entire population of one city (Eumenea?) was said by Eusebius (Hist. VIII.11.1) to have been Christian. Martyrdoms continued in this century, and under Diocletian (A.D. 301-12) this city was completely destroyed and persecution was strong in the region. With the coming of more peaceful times the church leadership of Phrygia became more in harmony with that of the wider church.

Bibliography. W. M. Ramsay, *The Cities and Bishoprics of Phrygia* (1895-96); *A Historical Commentary on St. Paul's Epistle to the Galatians* (1900), especially sections 5, 9-10. A. H. M. Jones, *Cities of the Eastern Roman Provinces* (1937): see Index.

F. V. FILSON

PHUD. KJV Apoc. form of PUT.

PHURAH. KJV form of PURAH.

PHURIM. KJV Apoc. form of PURIM.

PHUT. KJV alternate form of PUT.

PHUVAH. KJV form of PUVAH in Gen. 46:13.

PHYGELUS fĭ'jə ləs [Φύγελος, a fugitive(?)] (II Tim. 1:15). Someone who, with HERMOGENES and "all who are in Asia," deserted Paul (Asia is here the Roman province occupying the W tip of Asia Minor). The desertion was probably the result of theological differences or of a fear of sharing in Paul's fate in Rome.

B. H. THROCKMORTON, JR.

PHYLACTERIES fĭ lăk'tə rĭz [φυλακτηρία; Aram. תפלין] (Matt. 23:5). Small receptacles, containing some verses of scripture, which were bound on the forehead and arm during prayer. The Greek word meant, before and during NT times, "safeguard," "means of protection," "amulet." It passed to the Vulg. and entered English Bibles through the Genevan Bible of 1557. Jesus is said to accuse the scribes and Pharisees that "they do all their deeds to be seen by men; for they make their phylacteries broad and their fringes long." Jesus thus says that ostentatiousness leads Jewish leaders to wear phylacteries broader and fringes longer than is necessary. He does not condemn the custom of wearing phylacteries, but the spirit that corrupts a custom.

By "phylacteries" Matthew meant the Aramaic plural of the Hebrew word תפלה, "prayer"—the small leather prayer cases. The Mishna (Shebu. 111. 8, 11, etc.) required male Israelites above thirteen years of age to "lay the tephillin" at daily morning prayer. These two cubical leather boxes were worn on the head and on the left arm.

The head phylactery had four small compartments in which the following four passages of scripture were concealed: Exod. 13:1-10, 11-16; Deut. 6:4-9; 11:13-21; though there is some doubt as to the exact order. In these four passages Jews discovered the warrants for the wearing of the phylacteries. The head phylactery also bore two imprints of the Hebrew letter ש—one on the left of the wearer, with the usual three prongs of the Hebrew letter; and the other on the right, with, exceptionally, four prongs, presumably as a reminder concerning the four passages of scripture. The head phylactery was firmly sewn by twelve stitches, one for each of the twelve tribes of Israel, to a firm base of thick leather.

The hand phylactery had but one compartment containing the few scriptures on one parchment.

The phylacteries were held firm by means of long leather straps which passed through flaps. The strap of the head phylactery was tied at the back of the head in a knot shaped like a Hebrew letter ד. Another knot at the end of the strap was formed in the shape of a Hebrew letter י. Thus the three Hebrew letters involved formed the Hebrew word ש ד י, which is "Shaddai"—"Almighty"—one of the names for God in the OT. There are, of course, many other features relating to these phylacteries which cannot be related here. The phylacteries must be placed on the body in a certain order (hand first), in certain exact positions, to the accompaniment of certain prayers and benedictions and of Hos. 2:19. After prayers the phylacteries are removed in the reverse order.

The scriptural basis for the custom is found in the four passages of scripture involved in the custom: Exod. 13:9, 16; Deut. 6:8; 11:18. Exod. 13:1-16 sets forth the ritual for the Feast of Unleavened Bread (vss. 3-10), and for the first-born. Both institutions are to be as a mark on the hand, or a memorial (vs. 10) or a frontlet (vs. 16) between your eyes, memorials of the deliverance from Egypt. The other pair of passages in Deuteronomy prescribes the same procedure as part of a larger praxis. In Deut. 6:8—"as a sign upon your hand, . . . as frontlets between your eyes"—the ordinance refers to the words of the Shema in vss. 4-5. That is the natural interpretation of the phrase "these words" in vs. 6; some commentators suggest that the phrase should mean the Deuteronomic law in general, as elsewhere in chs. 5–11, but the reference to the immediate context is more natural. A more general reference is inevitable in 11:18, where the same command appears but with some verbal changes. The two passages prescribe the perpetual remembrance of these words. It should be

From Milik, *Ten Years of Discovery in the Wilderness of Judaea* (London: SCM Press, 1959; U.S.A.: Alec R. Allenson Inc.)

54. A threefold enlargement of part of a phylactery containing the Shema (Deut. 6:4-9); from Wadi Murabba'at

noted that for the memorial (זכרון) of Exod. 13:9 the other three passages have "frontlets" (טוטפות). The etymology is uncertain, but it is this word which is rendered by "tephillin" in the Targums, which lies behind the "phylacteries" of Matt. 23:5. Perhaps the word טוטפות should be read as a singular noun, טטפת, meaning a "round jewel" (cf. Judg. 8:26; Isa. 3:19; M. Shabb. VI.1.5). So the four basic scriptures above speak of signs, frontlets, memorial, jewels, as figures of the rites and words of scripture. Fig. PHY 54.

The question thus arises whether in fact these signs or frontlets are to be interpreted in a figurative sense. Some interpreters have taken the Exodus passages literally, and the Deuteronomic passages figuratively. In Deut. 11:18 "these words," it is claimed, must embrace at least Deut. 5–11, and so a literal fulfilment of the injunction is impossible. Deut. 11: 18 may be a reiteration of Deut. 6 and thus a preacher's application of a precise custom in a larger context. Cf., e.g., sermons on the "sacrament of success," the "sacrament of failure," etc. These are figurative, but a sacrament itself is an actual ritual. Apart from 11:18, the other three passages must be taken together either figuratively or literally. Some of the expressions in 6:1-9 are possibly figurative, but others are literal. Exod. 13 is mainly composed of ritual injunctions whose literal enactment was intended. It can be argued verse by verse that the weight of both contexts is for a literal interpretation. Apart from the exegesis of the passages, further considerations support the possibility of a literal interpretation:

a) In Exod. 13:9 the word for "memorial" almost always, if not invariably, has a literal reference. Perhaps its appearance in Exod. 13:9 as a synonym for "frontlet" marks the point at which the literal observation of frontlets began.

b) The increasing tendency to ascribe a real cultic objectivity to many of the words and practices of the Psalms, and the increasing readiness to think of so many psalms as pre-exilic, predisposes a more favorable attitude to the literal interpretation of the frontlet injunctions. Of course, this does not mean that the injunction is necessarily Mosaic, but it is possible to think of the literal fulfilment as something previous to the date of the "documents" (JE) of Exod. 13.

c) Then it must be asked, What is the meaning of a "frontlet between the eyes"? This is essentially a meaningless position so far as the wearer himself is concerned. He is called upon to imagine an object in a position in which he cannot see it except in a mirror. The very idea could have arisen only as an adaptation of similar marks on the forehead. The forehead is a favorite place for ritual signs. The mark or sign (*'ôth*) of Cain placed him under special divine protection (Gen. 4:15). Similarly Ezekiel's cross (Ezek. 9:4, 6; cf. Rev. 7:3; 14:1) and other signs (Pss. Sol. 15:10; Rev. 13:16; 14:9) and marks made by cutting the flesh, tattooing, and mourning customs testify to the widespread nature of the custom. If the frontlets are figurative, then they are figurative applications of literal practices, which themselves later were transformed into actual customs. But it is then clear that to wear these frontlets or phylacteries is a memorial duty laid upon the worshiper, but the actual meaning of them served not only to remind other worshipers of these commands, and of God's law in general, but also perhaps to remind God himself of the obedience and presence of the worshiper. The "memorial" aspect could thus be as ancient an aspect of the "blood on the doorposts," the "sign on the hand," and the "frontlets between the eyes" as the magical, superstitious, and apotropaic interpretation of these things.

It is such considerations as the foregoing which must to some extent correct the views inferred from the fact that the Samaritans apparently did not use them. Similarly the Aramaic תפלין suggests a late date, but it does not follow that the admittedly figurative expressions of Prov. 1:9; 3:3; 6:21; 7:3; etc., mean that "frontlets" were still figurative. The frontlets are expressly mentioned in the Letter of Aristeas (vs. 159) as something very old. It has been claimed that they were in use as early as the fourth century B.C. There must have been centuries of growth in the custom, and in all the complex regulations relating to the custom—possibly, too, the democratization of a custom originally limited to cultic officials, for scribes and Pharisees are condemned by Jesus in Matt. 25:3.

It is doubtful if the commands of Exodus and Deuteronomy were intended literally in the first instance, but it is equally doubtful if the literal fulfilment is to be dated as late as the postexilic period. The cultic reappraisal of religion in Israel predisposes an earlier date for the transformation of the command into a custom.

Bibliography. M. Friedländer, *The Jewish Religion* (1891), pp. 331-34; M. L. Rodkinson, *History of Amulets, Charms, and Talismans* (1893): deals mainly with phylacteries; J. H. Greenstone, L. Blau, and E. G. Hirsch, "Phylacteries," *Jewish Encyclopedia,* X (1905), 21-28; H. L. Strack and P. Billerbeck, "Die *Tᵉphillin* oder Gebetsriemen," *Kommentar zum NT aus Talmud und Midrasch,* IV (1928), 250-76; H. Danby, *The Mishnah* (1933): see Index under "Phylacteries," p. 834; K. G. Kuhn, *Phylakterien aus Höhle 4 von Qumran* (1957); J. Vermès, "Pre-Mishnaic Jewish Worship and the Phylacteries from the Dead Sea," *Vetus Testamentum,* IX (1959), 65-72.

G. Henton Davies

PHYLARCH fī'lärk. KJV translation of φυλάρχης, referring to a chief officer of a cavalry regiment or military contingent. In II Macc. 8:32 it probably refers to a "commander" (so RSV) in the army of Timothy, who was slain by Judas, although some interpreters (Moffatt, Grimm, Bévenot) follow the KJV and the Vulg. in reading *phylarches* here as a proper name with the Callisthenes of vs. 33, who met a similar fate. However, the form *phylarches* is never found as a proper name. Abel (*see bibliography*) conjectures that the writer may be citing two representative Jewish enemies who had led in the massacres of the Jews in Gilead (I Macc. 5:13, 39 ff). In Deut. 31:28 LXX; I Esd. 7:8 the word signifies a "tribal leader" of Israel.

Bibliography. F.-M. Abel, *Les livres de Maccabées* (1949), pp. 394-95.

E. W. Saunders

PHYSICIAN [רפא; NT ἰατρός]. Originally, one who tended and repaired wounds; hence a bandager or healer. *See* Medicine.

PI-BESETH pī bē′zĭth [פי־בסת; LXX βουβαστος] (Ezek. 30:17). A city in the Nile Delta; capital of the eighteenth Lower Egyptian nome.

Pi-beseth occurs only once in the Bible, in Ezekiel's prophecy against Egypt, where it is coupled with On (*see* HELIOPOLIS). This city, known in Egyptian as *Pr-B'st.t,* from which come Hebrew *Pî-bheseth* and Greek Βουβαστις, was situated on the right shore of the old Tanite branch of the Nile, SE of present-day Zagazig; the site is presently known as Tell Basta. The ancient name means "house of Bastet" (an Egyptian goddess represented in the late period by the cat). The most complete description of Bubastis which has survived from ancient times is that of Herodotus (II.60.137); information must otherwise be gleaned from its mention in Egyptian texts and from the various monumental remains discovered at the site.

Bubastis is a very ancient city with remains dating well into the Old Kingdom. It was not until very late in its history, however, that it achieved political importance as the capital and chief residence of the Twenty-second, or Libyan (*see* LIBYA), and Twenty-third dynasties, *ca.* 950-750 B.C.

Bibliography. E. Naville, *Bubastis* (1891); B. Porter and R. L. B. Moss, *Topographical Bibliography of Ancient Egyptian Hieroglyphic Texts, Reliefs, and Paintings,* V (1934), 27-35.

T. O. LAMBDIN

PICK [חריץ, *from* חרץ, to cut in] (II Sam. 12:31=I Chr. 20:3); KJV HARROW. A sharp instrument made of iron. According to the RSV rendering, David set the defeated Ammonites to work with saws, iron picks, and iron axes, and made them toil at the brickkilns. It is an old controversy whether the Ammonites were tortured or set to various kinds of hard labor (cf. KJV and RSV). H. F. BECK

PICTURE. The translation of:

a) משכית (Ezek. 8:12; KJV Num. 33:52; Prov. 25:11), probably a carving. *See* FIGURED STONE.

b) דמות (Ezek. 23:15), lit. "likeness," as in Gen. 1:26.

c) שכיה (Isa. 2:16 KJV), more likely, from Egyptian *śk.ty,* a kind of ship (RSV "craft").

H. F. BECK

PIECE (OF MONEY). 1. קשיטה, *qᵉśîṭâ* (Gen. 33:19; Job 42:11; RSV mg. QESITAH), a weight of unknown origin and size.

2. KJV translation of στατήρ (lit., "stater"; Matt. 17:27; RSV SHEKEL). At the time of Augustus the tetradrachma of Athens was called a stater, a name which was also applied to all other silver coins of the same value. Only two of these issues circulated in Palestine at the period of the NT: the tetradrachma of Antiochia and the shekel of Tyre. Jesus offered such a coin as tribute for himself and Peter. Since ancient times it was the duty of each Jew to pay annually a sacred tribute of half a shekel to the temple in Jerusalem. When half-shekels were no longer current, didrachmas took their place, so that the tax was finally simply called "didrachma." But didrachmas, too, were not circulating any more in NT times, so that there remained the alternatives either to substitute two Roman denars or to pay one tetradrachma or one Tyrian shekel for two people. The reference in Matt. 17:27 gives, therefore, a correct statement of the numismatic situation in that period.

See also MONEY, COINS. H. HAMBURGER

PIGEON [גוזל, young bird; יונה, moaning one (*alternately* DOVE), *cf.* אנה, to mourn; περιστερά (*alternately* DOVE)]. Any of a widely distributed subfamily of birds (*Columbinae*) comprising numerous genera. The term "dove" is rather loosely applied to many of the smaller species (*see* DOVE; TURTLEDOVE). Tristram, who found the pigeon tribe very numerous in Palestine, noted that two kinds of rock pigeon lived there throughout the year (cf. Jer. 48:28); a wood pigeon (*Columba palumbus palumbus*), however, was only a winter visitor, and the stock dove (*Columba oenas oenas*) a summer visitor.

The term "pigeon" is usually employed when one of these birds is in a cultic or sacrificial role (cf. "young pigeon" for גוזל in Gen. 15:9). In Leviticus bird offerings of pigeons and turtledoves are recognized as the least costly of all the animal offerings, and we may surmise that they were the commonest. They serve as burnt offerings and as sin offerings (Lev. 1:14; 5:7, 11), and they have a part in the rituals for purifying a woman after childbirth (12:6, 8), for cleansing a healed leper (14:22, 30) and a person cured of a sexual irregularity (15:14, 29). In Num. 6:10 either pigeons or turtledoves are used to purify a Nazirite who has incurred uncleanness. It was in conformity with the Levitical law that Mary made the traditional bird offerings after the birth of Jesus (Luke 2:24). In Jesus' time merchants were permitted to sell pigeons in the temple area for these various purposes (Matt. 21:12; Mark 11:15; John 2:14, 16). The traditional procedures about bird offerings, which were supervised by a special temple official (M. Shek. 5.1), became very complicated in the course of time (see M. Kinnim, where some of the troublesome points are elucidated). The opinion of Rabbi Hisma, quoted in M. Ab. 3.19, was: "The rules about bird offerings and the onset of menstruation—these are the essentials of the *Halakoth.*"

W. S. MCCULLOUGH

PI-HAHIROTH pī′hə hī′rŏth [פי־החירת]. Alternately: HAHIROTH (Num. 33:8). A town in the E Delta near which the Israelites encamped during the initial stages of the Exodus.

In its present form Pi-hahiroth cannot be identified with any known town or city in the E Delta. The only information supplied by the biblical narrative is that Pi-hahiroth lay near BAAL-ZEPHON and Migdol; Num. 33:7 qualifies Pi-hahiroth with the phrase "which is east of Baal-zephon."

The LXX treats this name very strangely: (*a*) in Exod. 14:2, 9, the Hebrew phrases לפני פי החירת and על פי החירת are translated ἀπέναντι τῆς επαύλεως, "opposite the encampment (or unwalled city)," as though the MT had החצרות or the like; (*b*) in Num. 33:7, על פי החירת is rendered by ἐπὶ στόμα Ειρωθ, where פי is not taken as part of the name, but as the Hebrew word פי, "mouth"; (*c*) in Num. 33:8, the MT omits the פי of the name, and the LXX does likewise with ἀπέναντι Ειρωθ, "opposite Eiroth."

The most reasonable of the suggested identifications is that of A. H. Gardiner, who sees in the Hebrew an altered form of Egyptian *Pr-Ḥtḥr,* "the house of Hathor." A *Pr-Ḥtḥr* is mentioned in Pap. Anastasi III.3.3, a report on the Delta residence Pi-Rameses-Miamun, and again in an adoption stela of Nitokris between the cities of Tanis and Bubastis. Both of these references make it clear that this is not the better-known *Pr-Ḥtḥr* of the W Delta. A recently discovered stela of Kamose also names a *Pr-Ḥtḥr* in the N, but the exact location is not clear from the text.

Bibliography. A. Sarasowsky, "Notizen zu einigen biblischen . . . Namen," *ZAW,* 32 (1912), 146-51; A. H. Gardiner, "The Geography of the Exodus," *Recueil d'études égyptologiques dédiées á la mémoire de Jean-François Champollion* (1922), p. 213; H. Gauthier, *Dictionnaire des noms géographiques contenus dans les textes hieroglyphiques* (1925), II, 117; P. Montet, "La stèle du roi Kamose," Académie des Inscriptions et Belle-lettres, *Comptes rendues* (1956), p. 115. T. O. LAMBDIN

*__PILATE, PONTIUS__ pŏn′shəs, —tĭ əs, pī′lət [Πιλᾶτος, Πειλᾶτος]. The Roman PROCURATOR of Judea A.D. 26-36, and hence the judge in the trial and execution of Jesus.

1. Sources
   a. Greco-Roman
   b. Jewish
   c. NT
2. His character
3. The trial of Jesus
   a. Mark
   b. Matthew
   c. Luke-Acts
   d. John
   e. I Tim. 6:13
4. History and legend
   a. NT
   b. Apocryphal writings
   c. Alleged conversion to Christianity

Bibliography

1. Sources. *a. Greco-Roman.* Pilate receives but one mention in Roman sources, and in connection with Jesus. Tacitus (Ann. XV.44) speaks of the execution of Jesus by Pontius Pilate in the reign of Tiberius. Since Tacitus wrote *ca.* 115, and Christian tradition could have supplied this scanty bit of information, we are in effect bereft of sources which are neither Jewish nor Christian.

b. Jewish. Philo, in *Legation to Caius* 38, relates an incident about Pilate and then characterizes him. The incident was the hanging in the palace in Jerusalem of gilded votive shields inscribed with the emperor's name. Pilate was ordered by the emperor to remove the shields. Philo ascribes to Pilate rape, insult, murder, and inhumanity.

Josephus (Antiq. XVIII.iii.1; War II.ix.2) tells of an occasion when Jewish scruples were offended by troops who entered Jerusalem bearing standards with the image of the emperor on them. A crowd gathered outside Pilate's residence in Caesarea in protest; after five days Pilate had them surrounded in the race course by Roman troops, but determined to accede to their wishes rather than run the risk involved in opposing them. On another occasion, Pilate's intention to use funds from the temple treasury for constructing an aqueduct aroused a protest which was silenced by troops with bludgeons (Antiq. XVIII. iii.2; War II.ix.4). A third incident involved the Samaritans. These, led by an impostor, promised to reveal the place of concealment on Mount Gerizim of sacred vessels supposedly stored there since the time of Moses. When the Samaritans armed and gathered at the mountain, troops dispersed them, and thereafter the leading and notable Samaritans were executed. Complaint was made to the Roman legate to Syria, Vitellius, with the result that Pilate was displaced and sent to Rome (Antiq. XVIII.iv.2).

c. NT. In the NT, Jesus is delivered to Pilate after being examined, or tried, before the Sanhedrin. In § 3 *below,* the various accounts are examined in detail. Luke 13:1-5 alludes to Pilate's massacre of Galileans; the account is peculiar to Luke, and is not mentioned in Josephus. Three times in Acts (3:13; 4:27; 13:28) allusion is made to Pilate. No mention is made in the genuine letters of Paul (perhaps mention might have been expected in I Cor. 15:3); a mention is found in I Tim. 6:13.

2. His character. Philo and Josephus unite in attributing dire and evil practices to Pilate, so that a dark character is ascribed to him. Early Christian literature in general accords with this view, but later literature progressively assesses him more favorably. Too little is known of Pilate for any secure characterization of him to be attempted. The circumstance that this procuratorship lasted for ten years is used by some historians as a basis to doubt the Jewish and early Christian disparagement of him, and to see him rather as a skilful and successful administrator.

3. The trial of Jesus. *a. Mark.* Mark 15:1-15 relates that after the night trial the chief priests, elders, and scribes held a morning consultation. They bound Jesus and led him to Pilate. "Pilate asked him, 'Are you the King of the Jews?' And he answered him, 'You have said so.' " After the chief priests accused Jesus of many things, and Jesus made no further answer, "Pilate wondered." In accordance with the custom of releasing a prisoner at the feast, Pilate asked the crowd if he should release the "King of the Jews." The crowd, however, asked him to release an insurrectionist, Barabbas. Pilate asked what he should do with Jesus; the crowd cried out, "Crucify him." When Pilate asked what evil Jesus had done, "they shouted all the more, 'Crucify him.' " Thereupon Pilate, "wishing to satisfy the crowd, released for them Barabbas; and having scourged Jesus, he delivered him to be crucified."

Pilate in Mark appears as a more or less impartial judge, without special interest in or knowledge of Jesus. While the blame for the Crucifixion is put on the Jews, Pilate is not exonerated for his part in the affair. Some commentators have seen in Pilate a submissive weakness; this, however, goes beyond the direct evidence. It is indifference, rather than weakness, which Mark portrays.

b. Matthew. Matt. 27:1-26 recasts Mark's account in a number of minor insignificant details. A somewhat notable addition peculiar to Matthew (27:19) relates that Pilate's wife sent word to him while he was sitting in the judgment seat, saying, "Have nothing to do with that righteous man, for I have suffered much over him today in a dream." A second addition (vss. 24-25) depicts Pilate as washing his hands before the crowd and proclaiming his innocence in Jesus' death. The people answered, "His blood be on us and on our children!"

By these additions Matthew had set under way a process which was to grow: the progressive exoneration of Pilate and the placing of full blame on the Jews.

c. Luke-Acts. Luke 23 is a drastic reworking of Mark; some suppose that Luke uses some source in addition to Mark, but it is more likely that Luke is engaging in free composition than in the use of many sources (*see* LUKE § 5*a*). As Luke relates matters, Jesus is brought before Pilate, and after one question Pilate states that he finds no crime in Jesus. At the charge by the crowd that Jesus was stirring up people from Galilee to Jerusalem, Pilate took advantage of the presence in Jerusalem of Herod Antipas, the tetrarch of Galilee, to send Jesus over to him. Antipas questioned Jesus; his soldiers treated him with contempt and mocked him; he arrayed Jesus in gorgeous apparel and sent him back to Pilate. Luke adds that Antipas and Pilate became friends that day.

Pilate states a second time that he has found no crime in Jesus, nor has Herod Antipas. Again, on the question of releasing Jesus or Barabbas, Pilate states for a third time that he has found no crime in Jesus. Yet on the insistence of the crowd he turns Jesus over to them.

In Matt. 27:28-31; Mark 15:17-19, the indignities heaped on Jesus come from Roman soldiers; Luke has transferred these and attributes them to the soldiers of Herod. This, together with Pilate's triple assertion of Jesus' innocence, and his citation of Antipas' declaration of that innocence, are consistent with recurring motifs in Luke: that Jesus was innocent of any violation of Jewish law or practice; that Jesus, and in Acts, Peter and Paul, were undeviatingly loyal Jews; that Christianity was no threat to Rome, for no difficulties ever arose except through the malevolent interference of Jews, and the like. Therefore, the Crucifixion in Luke did not result from condemnation by any Jewish body (Luke's accounts of the "trial before the Sanhedrin" [22:54-71] omits the charge of blasphemy of Mark 14:64; Matt. 26:65, and the conclusion in the same verses that Jesus deserved death). So dominating are these themes in Luke's account that it is questionable whether the Pilate represented in his account is truly the historical figure, or only a marionette necessary to Luke's tendentiousness.

It is obvious, as many scholars have noted, that the Synoptic gospels take a positive step toward the tendency of the later apocryphal writings to coat a historical kernel with a thick layer of legend.

The reference in Luke 13:1-5 to the slaughter of the Galileans, unknown in Josephus, is occasionally thought to be a confusion on the part of Luke with Josephus' account (*see* § 1*b above*) of the slaughter of Samaritans; but this latter took place after the time of the Crucifixion. It is wiser to admit that Luke's allusion is unknown than to strain to make it conform with the Samaritan item in Josephus.

Luke 3:1 is only a bare mention of Pilate, this in a context in which Luke is fixing his chronology. The three passages in Acts need listing but no special comment.

d. John. John 18:28–19:16 presents significant differences when comparison is made with the Synoptic accounts. Jesus is brought outside the PRAETORIUM (1), and Pilate comes out to them, to decline to receive Jesus and to suggest that the Jews themselves should execute Jesus. They reply that it is illegal for them to put a man to death. Pilate brings Jesus into the Praetorium; there a discussion on kingship takes place, and Pilate asks the question: "What is truth?" Pilates goes out to the people to declare Jesus' innocence. On their persisting in demanding the death of Jesus, Pilate has Jesus scourged, and his soldiers mockingly dress Jesus in royal garb, though with a crown of thorns. Pilate goes out a second time to declare Jesus' innocence, but in vain. Jesus then tells Pilate: "You would have no power over me unless it had been given you from above; therefore he who delivered me to you has the greater sin." Then a third time Pilate sought to release Jesus, but finally turned him over to be crucified. A titulus was written over the cross: "Jesus of Nazareth, the King of the Jews."

This account in John has two important purposes. It goes beyond the Synoptic gospels in exculpating the Romans and blaming the Jews. It also accounts for the circumstance that the divine Christ permitted himself to undergo this fate of crucifixion by asserting that Pilate was only a minor and passive character in the working out of an elaborately worked-out divine scheme. John reflects theology and Jewish-Christian controversy rather than history.

e. I Tim. 6:13. This verse says that Jesus, when he was before Pilate, "made the good confession." It is a bare mention of Pilate.

4. History and legend. ***a. NT.*** Modern scholarly judgment holds Pilate's role as depicted in the NT to be largely legendary. The character studies of him found in earlier scholarly literature are therefore to be dismissed as gratuitous, and are not to be embraced as historically sound. Neither the Christian nor the Jewish depiction of Pilate is historical, but each is a product of varied and varying biases.

"Legendary" implies that a historical kernel has undergone growth and development. The bare fact that Pilate was procurator in Jesus' time, though it lacks direct corroboration, need not be doubted. The active participation of Romans in the Crucifixion is also sound history, for unless it were unmistakably a part of early tradition—and thereby embarrassing to the church, which was eager to attract Romans—it surely would not have been created out of the whole cloth.

There is as much justice in translating I Cor. 11:23: "the Lord Jesus on the night when he was *handed over,*" as in translating: ". . . when he was *betrayed.*" In either case, however, a reminiscence of such a Roman official as Pilate is unquestionably contained in the passage.

Hence, one can conclude that, however legendary are the gospel accounts, the bare fact of Pilate's having a part in the death of Jesus is historical.

b. Apocryphal writings. Certain apocryphal writings increase the legendary both in extent and in tone; more details come to be presented, and also Pilate changes from being regarded neutrally or with some slight hostility and emerges rather as a hero, and even as a Christian. E.g., Eusebius (Hist. II.7) cites unnamed earlier writers to the effect that Pilate committed suicide in the reign of Caligula. The Gospel of Peter suggests that Pilate had withdrawn entirely from the trial proceedings against Jesus, whose condemnation came exclusively from Herod Antipas and Jews. Tertullian (Apol. 21), in depicting Pilate as a Christian at heart (*pro sua conscientia Christianus*), only makes explicit what the Gospel of Peter implies.

A certain work about Pilate is known by various names: the Gospel of Nicodemus, *Gesta Pilati,* and *Acta Pilati.* Justin Martyr (Apol. I.35, 48) speaks of an "Acts under Pontius Pilate." Most scholars see in the Gospel of Nicodemus a work of the fourth or fifth century, and hence Justin, who flourished *ca.* 150, is alluding probably to some work other than Nicodemus.

Tertullian (Apol. 21) speaks of a report from Pilate to the emperor (*see bibliography*). A similar letter exists, the Letter of Pilate to Herod (and also the Letter of Herod to Pilate; these are appended to the Gospel of Nicodemus). It is usually supposed that what Tertullian saw or heard about was an earlier version than these which have survived.

c. Alleged conversion to Christianity. Pilate's wife is unnamed in the NT; in extracanonical literature she acquires the name of Procula or sometimes Procla. The Eastern church beatified her; her date is October 27. The Coptic church honors Pilate and Procla on June 25, making him both a saint and a martyr.

Out of the apocryphal tradition that Pilate's corpse was carried to France, a hill near Vienne bears his name. Seventeenth- and eighteenth-century German writers embellished the apocryphal accounts even further.

Bibliography. A. Stülchen, "Pilatusakten," in E. Hennecke, ed., *Handbuch zu den Neutestamentlichen Apokryphen* (1914), pp. 143-52. Commentaries are ample—e.g., Klostermann on Matthew, Mark, and Luke; Bultmann on John.

Special studies: Two works which deal only passingly with Pilate, but which may be found helpful, are: A. F. Findlay, *Byways in Early Christian Literature* (1923), pp. 105-7; K. L. Schmidt, *Kanonische und apokryphische Evangelien und Apostelgeschichten* (1944), pp. 51-65. A translation of Tert. Apol. 21 (on a report from Pilate to the emperor) is in M. R. James, *The Apocryphal NT* (1924), p. 146. F. Morison, *And Pilate Said* (1924), though pleasant to read, has limited scientific value.

S. SANDMEL

PILATE, ACTS OF. A passion gospel, not earlier than the middle of the fourth century, which in its present form consists of two sections: (*a*) Part I, an account of the trial of Jesus before Pilate and of his crucifixion (chs. 1–11), and the subsequent acts of the Jewish Sanhedrin, which led to positive proofs of his resurrection and ascension (chs. 12–16); (*b*) Part II, an account by two eyewitnesses, who had themselves returned from the land of the dead, of Christ's descent to hell and rescue of those there held captive (chs. 17–29).

Part I is an imaginative amplification of the accounts of the trial, passion, and resurrection of Jesus, heavily dependent upon the four canonical gospels and the early Christian confidence that Pilate must have made an official report. The present account simply heightens the apologetic note, already present in the canonical gospels, that Pilate's act was forced upon him, against his better judgment, by the hostility of the Jews. Many fanciful details are added, at times far from unskilfully. At the trial testimony is given by many witnesses, among whom are twelve men who assert that Joseph and Mary were married and consequently Jesus was not born in fornication. Joseph of Arimathea and Veronica (identified as the woman with the issue of blood) also bear witness. When Jesus enters the Praetorium, not only do Pilate's attendants show him the most elaborate respect, but the imperial standards miraculously bow before him. At the centurion's report of Jesus' death, Pilate shows the deepest contrition. The proof of the Resurrection and the Ascension is guaranteed by three men—a priest, a rabbi, and a Levite—who report that they themselves witnessed his ascent on the mountaintop. A search for the body was undertaken at the insistence of Nicodemus, in keeping with Elisha's demand following the similar departure of Elijah. Of course, no body was found, but the searchers discovered Joseph of Arimathea, who had been imprisoned by the Jews in their rage at his earlier favorable testimony, but who had surprisingly vanished from the locked prison cell, released, as he now assures his audience, supernaturally through the direct action of Jesus himself.

Attempts to date this writing in the second century, on the assumption that it is to it that Justin Martyr refers in his mention of Pilate's report to the emperor, have occasionally been made, but are quite unconvincing. Justin's word (Apol. I.35.9) simply attests the early confidence that Pilate must have made a report of so significant an event. The earliest apparent reference to the book is by Epiphanius (*Heresies* I.1) toward the end of the fourth century. Eusebius does not know it, as his references to a malicious pagan forgery, which he styles "Memoirs of Pilate" and which he describes as "full of every kind of blasphemy against Christ" (Hist. IX.5.1; cf. I.9.3; I.11.9), make clear. Thus A.D. 350 would appear a not unlikely date for its composition. That it was written to provide a Christian counterblast to this pagan forgery, which Eusebius says had been recently produced and introduced into the schools by order of the Emperor Maximin, is a possible, but far from certain, conjecture.

Part II, the *descensus ad inferos,* is the lively and romantic filling out of the early belief: "He went and preached to the spirits in prison" (I Pet. 3:19), which theme, in variously amplified forms, is so common a note in the writings of the early fathers. Here it is worked out with garish detail and elaborate rhetoric. At the insistence of Joseph of Arimathea—the prominence of Joseph in both accounts may well have caused their subsequent union—two sons of Simeon, now living in Arimathea, write out their amazing experience. They had died but now are alive once more and in a position to record their visit to the underworld and what had happened there: the dazzling light which had suddenly blazed out to the delight of the waiting saints; the arrival of Satan in glee to report to Hades his new, august victim; Hades' fear that once again she was to be worsted (as in the case of Lazarus); the arrival of the Lord; his handing of Satan over to the now wrathful Hades; the setting up of the cross and the ascension of Christ and the saints; a quick view of paradise, in which were Enoch, Elijah, and the recently arrived penitent thief. Since the written accounts of both men agreed exactly, the Jews were much disturbed. Nicodemus and Joseph pass on the word to Pilate, and he includes it in the public book of his judgment hall.

Opinions differ as to the relative age of parts I and II, although most would agree that they were not joined until the fifth century. A prologue to the joint work, appearing in many of the MSS, claims that the translator (variously styled Ananias, Aeneas, and Emaus) had discovered the work in Hebrew, as Nicodemus had written it, and had translated it into Greek in the year 425.

This, together with the conspicuous prominence of Nicodemus in the narrative, may account for the title "Gospel of Nicodemus," which the writing regularly has in the Latin tradition after the fourteenth century. Epiphanius had styled it "Acts of Pilate." Many older MSS bear the title "Memorials of Our Lord Jesus Christ Done in the Days of Pontius Pilate." To Pilate is never ascribed the composition of the book, but solely its preservation.

Part I is extant in many Greek MSS, the oldest of which are commonly dated in the twelfth century. A much inferior Greek text containing both Part I and Part II is found in many much later MSS (fifteenth-seventeenth centuries), and is replete with many garish additions. Part I is also extant in Coptic, Syriac, and Armenian. The whole composite work is found in two Latin versions. The older of these is commonly ascribed to the fifth century, and is the form in which it made its widest contacts in the West. It exerted a very wide influence, being regarded in many circles as a fifth witness to the Passion and the Resurrection, and, as such, virtually canonical. It was taken over nearly complete in the *Speculum Historiale,* greatly influenced the passion plays of the fifteenth century, and has left many other impressions both in literature and in art.

In the course of time many appendixes came to be joined. One of them, standing at the end of the Latin version, and inserted in Greek translation into the Acts of Peter and Paul (*see* PETER AND PAUL, ACTS OF) and the (Pseudo-Marcellus) Passion of Peter and Paul (*see* PETER AND PAUL, PASSION OF), is a letter purporting to be from Pilate to Claudius, telling of the trial and reported "lest some other should lie unto thee and thou should'st deem right to believe the false tales of the Jews." *See also* APOCRYPHA, NT.

Bibliography. The appendixes, including various letters purportedly exchanged between Pilate, Tiberius, and Herod; a Latin tradition of Pilate's death, and the sensational story (Greek) of Joseph of Arimathea (totally distinct from the Latin Narrative by Joseph of Arimathea [*see* JOSEPH OF ARIMATHEA, NARRATIVE BY]), in which the thieves play a lively part, may be found, together with the translation of the book itself, in M. R. James, *The Apocryphal NT* (1924), pp. 94-165. A well-selected bibliography of editions and studies is given by J. Quasten, *Patrology* (1950), I, 118.

M. S. ENSLIN

PILDASH pĭl'dăsh [פלדש] (Gen. 22:22). The sixth son of Nahor and Milcah. If a tribal name, the location is unknown but probably to be sought in N Arabia with other Nahorites.

PILGRIMAGE. The KJV translation of מגור (RSV "sojourning"; *see* SOJOURNER) in Gen. 47:9; Exod. 6:4 (cf. "pilgrims" in Heb. 11:13; I Pet. 2:11); also of the RSV in Ps. 119:54.

The purpose of a religious pilgrimage is to visit and worship at the place where a unique manifestation of divine activity has occurred, and may be expected to occur again, or where some particularly sacred memory is preserved. Thus the ancient centers of pilgrimage in Israel were repositories of traditions about their founding (cf. Bethel [Gen. 12:8; 28: 10 ff; 31:13; 35:15]), as well as related historical memories (*see* HIGH PLACE). Although pilgrimage as part of Israel's life and worship (*see* WORSHIP IN THE OT) is never described directly in the OT, various allusions indicate the part pilgrimages must have played.

The basis of Israel's early life as a federation of tribes in Canaan appears to have been those times of assembly, either for the cultic renewal of the COVENANT with Yahweh which bound them together, or for mutual defense in a holy war (*see* WAR, IDEAS OF) under Yahweh's leadership. The covenant festival then became the occasion of a regular pilgrimage, perhaps yearly, to the central sanctuary of the tribal federation where the ark of Yahweh reposed (*see* ARK OF THE COVENANT)—e.g., Shiloh in I Sam. 1:3 ff (cf. 3:3; 4:4; cf. also Judg. 20:26-27, where "before Yahweh" apparently means "in the presence of the ark of the covenant).

M. Noth finds evidence of an ancient regular pilgrimage to Mount Sinai (cf. I Kings 19:8 ff; the basis of his study was a careful analysis of Num. 33: 1-49), while A. Alt has suggested the possibility that Gen. 35:1-7 preserves the tradition of a cultic pilgrimage from Shechem to Bethel. *See* BIBLIOGRAPHY.

During the period of settlement in Canaan, Israel took over many Canaanite elements of worship, including agricultural festivals (*see* FEASTS AND FASTS) and places of worship. The pilgrimage to the local sanctuary for the three major feasts of the seasonal cycle became a fixed element of the calendar (cf. Exod. 23:17; 34:23).

The ancient centers of pilgrimage were undoubtedly the scenes of markets and fairs which accompanied the festivals, as well as meeting places for the hearing of legal processes (cf. I Sam. 7:16; 8: 1-3; Bethel, Gilgal, and Beer-sheba were among the most renowned cultic centers). The liturgies contained in Pss. 15; 24:3-6; Isa. 33:14-16 are patterned after very ancient rites for the pilgrim's entry into the holy precincts. Expressions of the joys of pilgrimage occur in Pss. 27:1-6; 42–43; 84; 122.

The early prophetic voices denounced pilgrimage to the famous shrines and the attendant rites, which had virtually obliterated worship of Yahweh in the old way (Isa. 1:12-13; Jer. 7:2 ff; Amos 4:4-5; 5:5-6,

21 ff). The Deuteronomic reform (*see* DEUTERONOMY) attempted to abolish worship at the pilgrimage centers, making Jerusalem the only legitimate place of worship (II Kings 23:1-25). After the EXILE pilgrimage to Jerusalem became a sacred dream and obligation of faithful Jews in the DISPERSION. The "Songs of Ascent" or "Pilgrim Songs" of Pss. 120–34 may have been used by postexilic pilgrims en route to Jerusalem. The NT records such an annual pilgrimage to Jerusalem for the Passover (*see* PASSOVER AND FEAST OF UNLEAVENED BREAD) in Luke 2:41.

Bibliography. W. Eichrodt, *Theologie des Alten Testaments,* I (1933), 15, 34-35, 194; A. Alt, "Die Wallfahrt von Sichem nach Bethel," *Kleine Schriften zur Geschichte des Volkes Israel,* I (1953), 79 ff; M. Noth, *Geschichte Israels* (2nd ed., 1954), pp. 19, 94, 127, 133.

J. A. WHARTON

PILHA pĭl'hə [פלחא, millstone] (Neh. 10:24—H 10:25); KJV PILEHA pĭl'ə hä. One of the chiefs of the people, signatory to the covenant of Ezra.

Bibliography. M. Noth, *Die israelitischen Personennamen* (1928), p. 126.

***PILLAR** [מצבה, *once* מצב (Judg. 9:6), *from* מצב, to raise, to erect; *also* עמוד, column]. Specifically, the translation of מצבה, borrowed by modern archaeologists and biblical scholars and spelled "massebah" (plural "masseboth"), as a technical expression for a stone monument set up as a memorial or as an object of worship. Unspecifically, however, the word "pillar" is used in the English versions of the Bible to render עמוד, "column," as an element of architecture, or as it may be used in metaphor.

1. As memorial
2. As sacred object
3. In the sense of "column"
4. Archaeological material

Bibliography

1. As memorial. This meaning is clearly attested in the Bible, however infrequently. Jacob set up a pillar ("massebah") upon Rachel's tomb (Gen. 35:20). The monument which Absalom set up for himself in his lifetime is also described as a massebah (II Sam. 18:18). It was erroneously identified with a monument in the Kidron Valley, the so-called Tomb of Absalom, which, however, is certainly not older than the first century B.C. Fig. KID 6.

2. As sacred object. The sacred pillars of Canaanite places of worship (*see* TEMPLES § 2), or of Hebrew shrines influenced by Canaanite practices, and considered as unorthodox from the standpoint of Yahwism, are frequently mentioned in the Bible, in parallelism with the Asherim (singular ASHERAH), or together with miscellaneous cult objects such as graven images, idols, altars, etc. (Exod. 23:24; 34:13; Lev. 26:1; Deut. 7:5; 12:3; 16:22; I Kings 14:23; II Kings 3:2; 10:26-27; 17:10; 18:4; 23:14; II Chr. 14:3; 31:1; Hos. 3:4; 10:1-2; Mic. 5:13). In these passages the KJV translates "images," or "standing images," the latter in contradistinction to "graven images" (*see* IMAGE). For the interpretation of these monuments from the standpoint of the history of Semitic religions, *see* § 4 *below.*

The word מצבה is explained in Gen. 35:14 as מצבת אבן, "pillar of stone" (lit., "erection of stone"). The meaning of the symbol is quite clear: God's presence was revealed to Jacob during his sleep. Now Jacob set up the stone on which he had rested his head as a testimony to God's indwelling in this particular place, the name of which was accordingly called Bethel—i.e., "House of God" (*see* BETHEL; TEMPLES § 3*a*). The pillar (מצב) of the oak by Shechem (Judg. 9:6) may have been originally connected with the cycle of Jacob.

A messianic passage of Isaiah refers to a massebah which shall be erected on the border of Egypt (Isa. 19:19). It is required, for the significance of the prophecy, that this ideal monument signify the lordship of God over foreign nations. In contrast with this passage, Jeremiah announces that the pillars of the sun-god in the land of Egypt, correctly paraphrased by the RSV as the "obelisks of Heliopolis," shall be destroyed (Jer. 43:13). The above references affirm or assume that the massebah is a monument of God's actual presence, and as such a sacred object, or even an object of worship.

The meaning of the twelve pillars set up by Moses, together with an altar (Exod. 24:4), is rather different. The text states explicitly that they stood for the twelve tribes of Israel united in the common worship of Yahweh. The memorial significance of the twelve stones of Gilgal in connection with the politico-religious event of the crossing of the Jordan by the tribes, is emphasized still more strongly (Josh. 4:19-24).

3. In the sense of "column." The Hebrew word עמוד is rendered often, but not consistently, by "pillar" in the sense of "column"—viz., a structural element to support the beams of a roof, terrace, or gallery. Thus, one of the halls of Solomon's palace is called the Hall of Pillars (I Kings 7:6; *see* HALL 2), and the upper rooms of the building known as the HOUSE OF THE FOREST OF LEBANON, rested on rows of pillars dividing the aisles on the ground floor (I Kings 7:3).

In the same manner, the descriptions of the tabernacle of Exodus mention the four pillars of acacia wood, from which hung the veil dividing the holy from the holy of holies, and five similar pillars for the screen at the entrance of the tabernacle (Exod. 26:32, 37). In all these passages the pillars are strictly functional.

The case of the twin pillars of bronze in, or rather at the entrance of, the vestibule of Solomon's temple is rather different (I Kings 7:15-22, 41-42; II Chr. 3:15-17; 4:12-13). The (untechnical) description of these pillars might well apply to structural columns supporting the architrave of the vestibule. It is quite possible that such was the understanding of the Hebrew scribe. Later traditions have adopted this interpretation, as one may surmise from some pillars of Byzantine monuments, especially in the church of the Holy Sepulchre, the sculptured capitals of which were obviously meant as a replica of the capitals of the bronze pillars of the temple on the basis of the biblical description. A few modern archaeologists and biblical scholars still favor the interpretation of the twin pillars as functional elements of the architecture of the temple. Archaeological analogies, however, support better the theory of the twin pillars of bronze having no structural function, but being religious symbols; this is inferred from their names Jachin and Boaz, which were presumably called upon to avert evil influences from the threshold of God. They are certainly not to be interpreted as astral emblems, nor obelisks, nor a substitute for the masseboth of the Canaanite temples, nor phallic symbols. That they may have been used as supports for lamps is possible, but far from conclusively proved. Fig. JAC 3.

The word "pillar," as a translation of the Hebrew עמוד, is freely used by English translators to render miscellaneous biblical metaphors and poetic imagery. An interesting example is that of the Pillar of Cloud and Fire, repeatedly mentioned in the narratives of Exodus and Numbers. Although one text gives a utilitarian interpretation of the phenomenon —viz., to guide the Israelites by day and by night (Exod. 13:21-22)—the other passages are formal in explaining that the pillar of cloud and fire is a visible sign of the presence of God in the midst of his people (Exod. 33:9-10; Num. 12:5; Deut. 31:15). From this standpoint the miraculous pillar plays, on a supernatural level, a function similar to that of Jacob's massebah as a testimony to God's invisible presence. The biblical author, however, avoided the term "massebah," either because he thought that it should be reserved for man-made monuments, or because he shunned bad connotations suggested by the use of masseboth in Canaanite and dissident sanctuaries.

4. Archaeological material. Stone pillars were found in large numbers in the course of excavations, often in their original position. Most of them are functional structures, as, e.g., the rough monoliths dividing the aisles of the stables of Megiddo;* these are too short for the purpose of supporting the roof, and one may suppose that the upper part of the pillars was originally made of brickwork or of wood.

These crude structures contrast with the pilasters built of well-hewn stones, the capitals of which were adorned with volutes akin to the decorative patterns of Canaanite sculpture. Capitals of this type were found in the ruins of public monuments of the period of the monarchies, especially at Megiddo and Samaria. Fig. STA 78.

It is evident that some stone pillars, standing alone* or in rows, could not have any structural purpose; their irregular or rounded tops, and eventually their unequal length, rule out the possibility of their being used as supports of any kind. On the other hand, their association with ruins and archaeological material obviously of a religious nature invites us to regard them as sacred pillars or masseboth. It is not easy, however, to define exactly what their significance was. Some of them are best interpreted as signs of the presence of an invisible deity, as if the virtue of the god dwelt in the stone, which became an object of worship and was eventually anointed with oil or the blood of victims. A short pillar of basalt, erected on an adobe platform in the temple of Mekal at Beth-shan, is most probably one of these,* as also is one of the pillars of the "high place" of Gezer,* of mediocre size, but the surface of which had been smoothed as if by the repeated contact of pious hands. Thus understood, the massebah is the counterpart of the Asherah, a pillar of wood symbolizing the female principle of fertility. The parallelism,

Courtesy of Denis Baly

55. A menhir (sacred pillar?) in the Wadi Wala, E of the Dead Sea

Courtesy of Yigael Yadin: The James A. de Rothschild Expedition at Hazor, The Hebrew University, Jerusalem, Israel

56. Statue and standing stones in Canaanite temple at Hazor (thirteenth century B.C.)

however, ought not to be carried as far as to interpret the massebah as a phallic symbol; this may be true in some, but certainly not in all, instances. Figs. PIL 55; BET 35; TEM 43.

In the case of multiple pillars, such as those of Gezer, it does not seem that all of them were endowed with the same divine character. The hypothesis according to which the so-called high place may have been a mortuary shrine leaves open the question of exactly what the raised stones meant. A likely interpretation is that they stand for living persons or clans united in the worship of the deity embodied in the sacred pillar mentioned above. This may be tentatively illustrated by the discovery, in a Canaanite temple of Hazor (1), of a row of stelae of basalt with rounded tops, and of a statue of the same material representing a male (deity?). One of the stelae bears the engraved design of two hands stretched in a gesture of adoration, beneath the emblem of the sun-god (Fig. PIL 56). The obelisk-shaped stelae in a Middle Bronze Age temple of Byblos may also be regarded as the symbols of clans or cities worshiping in the temple. *See* HIGH PLACE.

Bibliography. J. M. Lagrange, *Études sur les religions sémitiques* (1905), pp. 187-216; E. Dhorme, *La Religion des Hébreux Nomades* (1937), pp. 159-67; K. Galling, *Biblisches Reallexikon* (1937), cols. 368-71; G. A. Barrois, *Manuel d'Archéologie Biblique II* (1953), pp. 346-48, 358-63; Y. Yadin, "Excavations at Hazor," *BA*, XIX (1956), 2-12.

G. A. BARROIS

PILLAR, OAK (PLAIN) OF. *See* OAK OF THE PILLAR.

PILLAR OF FIRE AND OF CLOUD. This composite phrase appears in Exod. 14:24 (J), and there are a number of occurrences of the separate phrases, "pillar of cloud" (Exod. 13:21-22 and six times in JE; cf. Neh. 9:12, 19; Ps. 99:7) and "pillar of fire" (Exod. 13:21-22 [J]; Num. 14:14 [JE]; Neh. 9:12, 19). The pillar thus meets Israel at the edge of the wilderness and continues thereafter with Israel in the desert. The priestly writer, P, also speaks of the theophany of cloud and glory, but never uses the word "pillar" (*see* CLOUD; FIRE; PRESENCE; THEOPHANY). The word עמוד, "pillar," is the term that distinguishes the JE symbol of the divine presence in the wilderness stories. A study of the above passages shows that J represents the pillar as guiding and protecting. The cloud by day and the fire by night advance in front of the Israelites, and so show them their way, giving them a continuous and perpetual guidance (Exod. 13:21-22). In Exod. 14:19*b*, 20*b*, the pillar of cloud moves from before to the rear of Israel, separating the Egyptians from the Israelites, thus protecting and saving the latter. The cloud, but not the pillar, appears again in Exod. 34:5, where it serves to locate, but also to conceal, Yahweh's presence.

In E the representation is thus of a cloud which, without fire, occasionally descends to "stand" at the door of the tent of meeting outside the camp. When this took place, there was converse between Yahweh and Moses. E then depicts the pillar of cloud as a place of revelation. In P there is the further idea of protection. JE and P thus describe in different ways the tabernacling Presence in his varying functions.

It is clear that the word "pillar" calls for explanation as occurring in JE and possibly mainly in J and not in P. The word is used of ordinary smoke (Judg. 20:40), of a silver pillar to a litter (Song of S. 3:10), or of palace pillars (e.g., Judg. 16:25-26, 29; I Kings 7:2-3, 6), and in various figurative expressions (cf. of Jeremiah: Jer. 1:18; of pillars of earth: Job 9:6; Ps. 75:3—H 75:4; of heaven: Job 26:11; and of wisdom's house: Prov. 9:1). Otherwise the word denotes a cultic platform (II Kings 11:14=II Chr. 23:13; II Kings 23:3; *see* PULPIT), or tabernacle or temple pillars (Exod. 27:10-11, 17; Ezek. 42:6), including especially the two bronze pillars in front of the temple (I Kings 7:15). These pillars, Boaz and Jachin, are now known to be fiery cressets, and at time of festival, no doubt, emitted clouds of smoke and flame by day and night. It is probable, then, that the word "pillar" in the JE accounts of the pillar of fire and cloud derives from the cressets of Solomon's temple. If this be the case, the tradition spoke originally of fire and of cloud. Perhaps the whole image is derived from the pillars of Solomon's temple, or from the smoke that rose from the altar of burnt offering, and was borrowed to portray the fact of the Presence in the exodus stories. Yet it may fairly be claimed that there must have been some feature in the traditions to attract the pillar imagery. Thus it has been suggested that there was a brazier burning wood which marked the route, and this custom is well attested in both military and commercial usage. Otherwise some natural phenomena like a cloud or even the cloudy spine of an active volcano must be the explanation. In any case, cloud and fire variously depict the mystery in the life of desert Israel.

See also GLORY; TABERNACLE.

Bibliography. J. Pedersen, *Israel,* III-IV (1940), 728-37. W. J. Phythian-Adams, *The Call of Israel* (1934); *The Fulness of Israel* (1938); *The People and the Presence* (1942).

G. HENTON DAVIES

PILLOW [כביר (I Sam. 19:13, 16), *see below;* כסתות (Ezek. 13:18, 20, KJV), *probably* bands used for magic (*cf.* RSV); מראשות (Gen. 28:11, 18, KJV), the place of the head while sleeping; προσκεφαλαίον (Mark 4:38 KJV; RSV "cushion")]. A word used to refer to various supports for the head.

The Hebrew word used in I Sam. 19:13, 16, כביר, is derived from כבר, probably "to intertwine," and suggests a netted object, in this case woven from goats' hair. On the other hand, כביר may mean a pillow stuffed with goats' hair.

The stone which Jacob used as a pillow (Gen. 28:11) must have been large enough to serve as a cairn (vs. 18).

The KJV translation of Ezek. 13:18, 20, is probably derived from postbiblical Hebrew, where כסת meant "pillow" (cf. Giṭ. 56*a;* Tosef. Bereshith 6.3), and from the LXX, which translated כסת by προσκεφαλαίον (cf. Mark 4:38).

The pillow (RSV "cushion") on which Jesus slept (Mark 4:38) was probably a pad or mat spread in the stern of the boat.

E. M. GOOD

PILOT [חבל, *probably a denominative from* חבל, cord, rope, band—*i.e.*, a rope puller, a sailor (*cf.* רב החבל, chief pilot, *in* Jonah 1:6; RSV CAPTAIN; KJV SHIP MASTER); εὐθύνω (KJV GOVERNOR)]. The pilots referred to in Ezek. 27:8, 27-29, were Phoenicians associated with the maritime trade of Tyre. In Jas. 3:4 the tongue as a member of the body is compared to the small rudder of the great ships directed by the will of the pilot. *See* SHIPS AND SAILING.

H. F. BECK

PILTAI pĭl'tī [פלטי, (God is) deliverance] (Neh. 12:17). A priest and head of the father's house of Moadiah; contemporary of the high priest Joiakim in the postexilic period.

Bibliography. M. Noth, *Die israelitischen Personennamen* (1928), pp. 38, 156.

B. T. DAHLBERG

PIM pĭm [פים, vocalized by some scholars *payim*]. A weight thought by some to be equal to two thirds of a shekel. The word occurs only in I Sam. 13:21 and was not understood until a stone weight with the inscription פים was found. Since then others have come to light and show an average weight of 7.762 grams, *ca.* 2⅔ ounces.

See also WEIGHTS AND MEASURES §§ B4*b*, *d*.

O. R. SELLERS

PIN. A translation of יתד, a wooden or metal peg used in a variety of ways. The RSV uses "pin" only for the stick used in a loom to tighten the weave (Judg. 16:13-14), but the KJV translates "pin" also for a tent (tabernacle) stake (Exod. 27:19; RSV PEG; cf. Judg. 4:21; Isa. 33:20), and for a peg on which objects may hang (Ezek. 15:3; RSV "peg").

See also NAIL; PADDLE.

Fig. PIN 57. W. G. WILLIAMS

Courtesy of the Palestine Archaeological Museum, Jerusalem, Jordan

57. Toggle pins, from Palestine (Middle Bronze II and Late Bronze)

PINE, PINE TREE [ברוש, *b^e^rôš,* Aram. ברות, *b^e^rôth* (Song of S. 1:7), *elsewhere* CYPRESS, FIR (KJV *always* "fir"); תדהר, *tid̲hār* (Isa. 41:19; 60:13; RSV "plane"; *see* FIR); KJV עץ שמן, *'ēṣ šémĕn* (Neh. 8:15; RSV WILD OLIVE); תאשור, *t^e^'aššûr* (Isa. 41:19; 60:13; KJV "box tree"; *cf.* Ezek. 27:6; *see* CYPRESS)]. A tree and its wood, extensively used in building; usually mentioned with the CEDAR.

The identification of the conifers mentioned in the Bible, except for the cedar of Lebanon, is extremely complex, and there is little agreement among Bible scholars and botanists. It is quite possible that the confusion existed also in Bible times, because of the similarity of many of the trees concerned and the lack of botanical interest or knowledge. Thus it seems best to use the broader term "pine" (this would include several species of pines, *Pinus;* firs, *Abies;* and even the cedars, *Cedrus*) for the Hebrew *b^e^rôš*. It seems possible, however, that the *Pinus halepensis* Mill., the common and abundant Aleppo Pine, is often intended. Zohary (*cf.* FLORA § A9*h*) and Löw favor the junipers (*Juniperus excelsa,* Bilb.) because they are more confined to the Lebanons, like the cedar. "Pine" seems the best translation of *'ōren* in Isa. 44:14 (KJV "ash"; RSV emended "cedar") if a tree is meant, though Löw and Zohary (*see* FLORA § A9*i*) identify it with the laurel (*Laurus nobilis* L.; *see* BAY TREE).

The *b^e^rôš* provided the lumber for the floor and the doors of Solomon's temple (I Kings 5:8, 10—H 5:22, 24; 6:15, 34; 9:11; II Chr. 2:8—H 2:7; 3:5). It was used (with cedar) in poetic taunt songs over Assyria and Babylon (II Kings 19:23 [Isa. 37:24]; Isa. 14:8) and over Tyre and Egypt (Ezek. 27:6; 31:8), and in several poetic expressions: of hope (Isa. 41:19; 55:13; 60:13; Hos. 14:8—H 14:9), destruction (Zech. 11:2), and wealth (Song of S. 1:17). The occurrence of *b^e^rôš* in II Sam. 6:5 (cf. KJV and RSV) is obviously a textual error made clear by I Chr. 13:8 and the LXX. In Ps. 104:17, ברושים, *b^e^rôšîm,* should probably read בראשם, *b^e^rō'šām,* "in the tops of them." In Nah. 2:3—H 2:4 the vague הברשים (KJV "fir trees") is taken by most scholars as an error for הפרשים, *happārāšîm,* "chargers" (so RSV).

The occurrence of *b^e^rôšîm* in II Sam. 6:5 (cf. KJV

Courtesy of the Société Botanique de Genève

58. The Aleppo pine (*Pinus halepensis*), growing in Jerusalem

and RSV) is obviously a textual error, made clear by I Chr. 13:8 and the LXX. In Ps. 104:17 ברושים should probably read בראשם, "in the tops of them." In Nah. 2:3—H 2:4 the vague הברשים (KJV "fir trees") is taken by most scholars as an error for הפרשים, "chargers" (so RSV).

Fig. PIN 58.

Bibliography. I. Löw, *Die Flora der Juden,* II (1924), 119-23; III (1924), 33-38. H. N. and A. L. Moldenke, *Plants of the Bible* (1952), pp. 175-77.

J. C. TREVER

PINNACLE [שמשת (KJV WINDOWS), *plural of* שמש, sun; πτερύγιον, a little wing]. The Hebrew word (Isa. 54:12) suggests the part of the buildings which gleams in the sun in the New Jerusalem. The NT word (Matt. 4:5; Luke 4:9) refers to a part of the temple (*see* TEMPLE, JERUSALEM). The Vulg. has *pinna,* "wing," and *pinnaculum,* "little wing"; the Syr. *kenpâ,* "wing."

C. C. MCCOWN

PINON pī'nŏn [פינן; LXX φινων, φινες]. An Edomite clan chief (אלוף פינן); given either as personal ancestor or as designation of the geographical location of the clan (Gen. 36:41; I Chr. 1:52). Doubtlessly identical with the Edomite copper-mining center PUNON.

PIONEER. *See* AUTHOR OF LIFE.

PIPE. *See* MUSICAL INSTRUMENTS.

PIRA. KJV Apoc. form of CHEPHIRAH.

PIRAM pī'rəm [פראם, wild ass(?)] (Josh. 10:3). King of the city-state of Jarmuth SW of Jerusalem. Piram was one of five kings in an Amorite coalition led by the king of Jerusalem, attempting to halt Joshua's invasion of their territory. Piram and his confederates were defeated in battle at Gibeon, captured after the rout, and put to death.

Bibliography. G. E. Wright, "The Literary and Historical Problem of Joshua 10 and Judges 1," *JNES,* V (1946), 105-14.

R. F. JOHNSON

PIRATHON pĭr'ə thŏn [פרעתון]; **PIRATHONITE** —thə nīt [פרעתוני]. Alternately: **PHARATHON** făr'ə thŏn [Φαραθών] (I Macc. 9:50); KJV **PHARATHONI** —thō'nī. A town "in the land of Ephraim, in the hill country of the Amalekites" (Judg. 12:15). A minor judge was buried there. Both Abdon and Benaiah, two of David's heroes, are called Pirathonites (Judg. 12:13, 15; II Sam. 23:30; cf. I Chr. 11:31; 27:14)—i.e., "inhabitants of Pirathon." Judg. 5:14 indicates a connection between the area in which Pirathon was located and the Amalekites, although the Amalekites are usually represented as dwelling in S Canaan.

Pirathon is usually tentatively located at Far'ata, *ca.* five miles SW of Shechem. Some commentators have sought it in the territory of Benjamin rather than Ephraim, on the suppositions that Abdon was from the tribe of Benjamin (I Chr. 8:23, 30; 9:36), and that the city referred to in I Macc. 9:50 and Josephus (Antiq. XIII.i.3; the name here is Pharatho) was located in the territory of Benjamin. In view of the fact that geographical considerations are obscure in the Chronicler's list in chs. 8–9, and the probability that Bacchides fortified cities N as well as S of Jerusalem, the location of Pirathon near Shechem is more probable.

W. L. REED

PISGAH, MOUNT pĭz'gə [הפסגה]. A location in the Abarim Mountains, opposite Jericho.

Four times Pisgah occurs in the phrase "the top [lit., 'head'] of Pisgah" (ראש הפסגה). The Israelite stopping place following Bamoth is the "valley lying in the region of Moab by the top of Pisgah which looks down upon the desert" (Num. 21:20). One of the places to which Balak took Balaam was "to the field of Zophim, to the top of Pisgah" (23:14). Moses was told to "go up to the top of Pisgah" to view the land (Deut. 3:27), and later he "went up from the plains of Moab to Mount Nebo, to the top of Pisgah, which is opposite Jericho" (34:1).

Also four times Pisgah occurs in the phrase "the slopes of Pisgah" (אשדת הפסגה). In territorial descriptions, mention is made of the "sea of the Arabah, the Salt Sea, under the slopes of Pisgah on the east" (Deut. 3:17); of the "Sea of the Arabah, under the slopes of Pisgah" (4:49); of Sihon ruling "to the sea of the Arabah, the Salt Sea, southward to the foot of the slopes of Pisgah" (Josh. 12:3); and of the Reubenite territory including the "slopes of Pisgah" (13:20). The KJV translates the "springs of Pisgah" in Deut. 4:49 and "Ashdoth-pisgah" in the other references.

Some understand Pisgah to be a section of the Abarim Range, of which Mount Nebo is the summit. More attractive, however, is the idea that the "top of Pisgah" refers to a promontory of a particular mountain. A headland, the Ras es-Siyaghah, is slightly lower than the summit of Mount Nebo, and separated from it by a saddle. It would be the ideal location for Moses' viewing the land. If the top of Pisgah is the Ras es-Siyaghah, the valley of Num. 21:20 may be that of the 'Ayun Musa.

For a discussion of the mountain and the surrounding area, *see* NEBO, MOUNT.

E. D. GROHMAN

PISHON pī'shŏn [פישון]; KJV **PHISON** fī'—, **PISON** pī'sŏn. *See* EDEN, GARDEN OF.

PISIDIA pĭ sĭd'ĭ ə [Πισιδία]. A mountainous region in the S central part of Asia Minor. It was bounded on the S by Pamphylia, on the W by Lycia and Caria or Phrygia, on the N by Phrygia, and on the E by Isauria. It extended from E to W *ca.* 120 miles and *ca.* 50 miles from N to S. It lay in the Taurus Mountain Range; the rugged terrain and mountain strongholds made it difficult for invaders to conquer, and its wild and warlike people were slow to yield to the influence of Hellenistic and Roman civilization. However, the mountainous region enclosed fertile valleys and large lakes; and it was known for its forests, for the cultivation of the olive tree and the vine, and for its excellent pasture land. It thus was able to support a considerable population.

In pre-Roman times Pisidia was never really subjugated by other peoples. When the Galatian king Amyntas lost his life in 25 B.C. before carrying out the conquest of Pisidia, the Romans took up the task. The Roman emperor Augustus, to pacify and stabilize the region, made Antioch, located just NE of ancient Pisidia, a Roman colony, and connected it with Roman roads to other garrisoned colonies in the Pisidian area. At the beginning of Roman control of Pisidia, Antioch was considered to be outside Pisidia. Strabo (*Geography* XII.6.4; 8.14) refers to it as "Antioch Towards Pisidia" (Ἀντιόχεια ἡ πρὸς τῇ Πισιδίᾳ or ἡ πρὸς Πισιδίᾳ καλουμένη). Later this Antioch was considered to lie within Pisidia, and so the secondary

Western text of Acts 13:14 calls it "Antioch of Pisidia" (τῆς Πισιδίας). The original text of Acts 13:14 refers to it as "Pisidian Antioch" (Ἀντιόχειαν τὴν Πισιδίαν), which need not mean it lay in Pisidia but can mean that of the many Antiochs it was the one in the region where Pisidia was located.

When the Roman province of GALATIA was formed in 25 B.C., it included not only Galatia proper, but also Pisidia, Lycaonia, and Isauria, and parts of Phrygia and Paphlagonia. Thus when Paul went N from Perga in Pamphylia to Pisidian Antioch (Acts 13:14), and so passed through Pisidia, the latter region was part of the province of Galatia. There is no indication that on this journey or on the return journey (14:24) Paul stopped to preach at any point in Pisidia. The people had resisted Hellenistic culture; there were few Jews in the region to furnish a point of contact with the local population; and Paul, who aimed for prominent centers as bases for his missionary work, probably left Perga with Antioch in mind as his next preaching center. Back of Paul's reference in II Cor. 11:26-27 to "dangers from robbers" and the hardships of travel may lie in part the memory of his two journeys through this mountainous and dangerous Pisidian region. What route he took through Pisidia cannot be determined. Perhaps he went N from Perga and passed along the SE shore of the twin lakes called the Limnai in ancient times; perhaps his route lay a little farther E and passed through Adada, whose ruins are now called Kara Bavlo, which reflects a (late?) tradition that Paul had been there.

In A.D. 74 Vespasian attached the S part of Pisidia to the Roman province Lycia-Pamphylia. The N part of Pisidia remained part of the province of Galatia. Later (under Diocletian?) this Pisidian region of the province of Galatia was separated, somewhat further enlarged, and made the province of Pisidia.

Bibliography. W. M. Ramsay, *Historical Geography of Asia Minor* (1890), especially pp. 387-415; *The Church in the Roman Empire* (1893), ch. 2. A. H. M. Jones, *Cities of the Eastern Roman Provinces* (1937), ch. 5. D. Magie, *Roman Rule in Asia Minor* (1950), pp. 456-67. F. V. FILSON

PISPA pĭs'pə [פספה] (I Chr. 7:38); KJV PISPAH. An Asherite, son of Jether.

PISTACHIO NUTS pĭs tä'shĭ ō, —tăsh'ĭ ō [בטנים, *boṭnîm*] (Gen. 43:11); KJV NUTS. The edible seeds of the *Pistacia vera* L., and perhaps *Pistacia terebinthus* var. *palaestina* (Boiss.) Post. *See* FLORA § A2*f;* NUTS. J. C. TREVER

PISTIS SOPHIA pĭs'tĭs sō fī'ə [πίστις σοφία, faith-wisdom]. A Gnostic treatise recounting the instructions given by Jesus, in the twelfth year after his resurrection, to his disciples concerning sin and salvation, principally in answer to questions propounded by Mary Magdalene and written down by Philip. The work, originally written in Greek, is extant in a fourth-century Coptic MS (Codex Askewanus) now in the British Museum. In its present form it consists of four books, but Book IV (in which there is no mention of Pistis Sophia) is commonly regarded a quite separate work, a few decades earlier than Books I-III, and dealing with matters recounted by Jesus directly after his resurrection. In Books I-III, to be dated in the late third century, Jesus gives instruction about the fate, fall, and eventual redemption of Pistis Sophia, a spiritual being of the world of aeons, who suffers the same fate as that of mankind in general. (For a likely indication of the nature of this aeon, *see* EUGNOSTOS, LETTER OF.) The author of this writing was apparently a Valentinian or Barbelo Gnostic of the Sethian type, of the sort evidenced by the MSS discovered in 1946 at Chenoboskion in Upper Egypt (*see* APOCRYPHA, NT). The writing is one of the comparatively few documents to be preserved which were written by Gnostics themselves, and is thus invaluable as a control for the traditional picture of Gnosticism painted by orthodox fathers bitterly antagonistic and frequently grossly unfair.

The writing contains five of the Odes of Solomon and many references to the two books of Jeu, which latter has been identified by Carl Schmidt with the Mystery of the Great Logos (λόγος κατὰ μυστήριον), now included in the fifth-century Oxford Codex Brucianus.

Bibliography. An English translation, with introduction, notes, and bibliography, is provided by H. R. S. Mead, *Pistis Sophia* (1947). For further bibliography, see J. Quasten, *Patrology* (1950), I, 276. M. S. ENSLIN

PIT [בור]. One of the many designations employed in the OT for the abode of the dead. *See* DEAD, ABODE OF THE.

PITCH. An inflammable viscous mineral substance, a more or less liquid mixture of hydrocarbon. The word is used to translate the following:

a) כפר (cf. Akkadian *kupru,* "pitch, asphalt"), used with a denominative verb in Gen. 6:14: "pitch it with pitch" (RSV "cover it . . . with pitch"). In the Babylonian flood tale Ut-napishtim uses *kupru* and *ittu* (asphalt and pitch) in calking his ark.

b) זפת (cf. Arabic *zift,* "pitch"). In Exod. 2:3 pitch and bitumen are used to calk the basket of bulrushes. In the visitation of Edom, the streams shall be turned into pitch and the land into burning pitch (Isa. 34:9).

See also BITUMEN; SLIME. W. E. STAPLES

PITCHER. The translation of several words in the Bible:

a) גלגל (lit., "wheel"), used in Eccl. 12:6 in a reference to something broken at the spring or fountain. Perhaps the reference is to a water wheel.

b) גביע (KJV "pot"). This word is properly translated "cup." In Jer. 35:5 it is a larger vessel from which wine could be drunk in cups. *See* POTTERY § 3*a*.

c) כד (Gen. 24:14 KJV; Judg. 7:16, 19-20, KJV; RSV properly "jar"). *See* POTTERY § 3*b*.

d) נבלי חרש ("earthen pitcher" in Lam. 4:2 KJV; RSV "earthen pot"). The reference is to a water jar. *See* POTTERY § 3.

e) Κεράμιον (Mark 14:13 KJV; Luke 22:10 KJV; RSV "jar"). This was a water jar. *See* POTTERY § 3*b*.

PITFALL [שבכה (Job. 18:8; KJV SNARE); פחת (Lam. 3:47; KJV "snare"), *lit.*, pit; שוחה (Ps. 119:

85; KJV PIT); σκάνδαλον (Rom. 11:9; KJV STUMBLINGBLOCK)]. A figurative term referring to a hidden or unrecognized danger or error or to an unavoidable hardship into which persons fall.

H. F. BECK

PITHOM pī'thəm [פתם; LXX Π(ε)ιθω]. A city in Egypt which, together with Rameses (*see* RAMESES 4), was built by the Hebrews for the pharaoh of the oppression.

Because the biblical narrative itself does not localize Pithom specifically, all modern attempts to identify the site of this ancient store city of the Egyptian pharaoh must be based on archaeological discoveries, on extrabiblical sources, or on a combination of both. At present only two cities are felt to be serious candidates for this position—namely, Tell el-Ratabah and Tell el-Maskhutah in the Wadi Tumeilat in the E Delta of Egypt. Because the problem of identification is a difficult one and the evidence is not entirely conclusive, let us examine in order such details as are necessary for a correct evaluation of the situation.

Tell el-Maskhutah was excavated in 1883 by Edouard Naville. A survey of the inscriptions found there and of the architectural remains convinced him that this site was definitely that of ancient Pithom. He supported this contention with the following particulars: (*a*) all the toponyms found on the monuments correspond to otherwise attested place names in the eighth Lower Egyptian nome, notably *Ṯkw*(*t*), the civil name of its capital, and *Pr-Tm,* its religious name; (*b*) a Latin inscription found at Tell el-Maskhutah mentions Ero, which is to be equated with Heroonpolis, the Greek name of Pithom; (*c*) the architectural remains are to be interpreted in part as those of a fortress and of store chambers. The preceding points have been stripped of many philological details, whose validity has become questionable with the knowledge gained since their presentation.

There can be little doubt that Hebrew "Pithom" is a transcription of Egyptian *Pr-Tm,* "house [or temple] of the god Tem," which was, indeed, the sacred name of the capital civilly known as *Ṯkw*(*t*). There is, furthermore, sufficient but not abundant evidence which links Tem with an obscure deity Ero or Hero; it is thus most probable, as Naville contends, that Greek ἡρωωνπολις is a rough translation of *Pr-Tm.* Confirmation for this comes from the fact that where the LXX has ἡρωωνπολιν in Gen. 46:28 (*see* GOSHEN), the Bohairic Coptic version reads *Pethōm.* On the basis of these arguments the identity of Pithom, Heroonpolis, and the Latin name Hero is generally conceded as correct.

Sir Alan Gardiner has been the principal opponent of Naville's more crucial stand, that Pithom-Heroonpolis is to be located at Tell el-Maskhutah. His opposition rests on two major points: (*a*) The testimony of hieroglyphic inscriptions from Tell el-Maskhutah shows clearly that the more common name was *Ṯkw*(*t*) and that *Pr-Tm* and *Ṯkw*(*t*) are quite distinct. This point is considerably weakened by the admission that *Ṯkw*(*t*) seems to be a wider term in certain cases. Thus we cannot conclude that *Pr-Tm* was not in *Ṯkw*(*t*), the former designating the town, the latter the region. An alternative is to localize *Ṯkw*(*t*) in Tell el-Maskhutah and to seek *Pr-Tm,* Pithom, elsewhere. More convincing, however, is (*b*) Gardiner's reading of the Latin milestone as stating that Tell el-Maskhutah is nine miles on the way from Ero (Hero) to Clysma (Suez). His positiveness on the latter point forces him to reject Naville's identification of Pithom and Tell el-Maskhutah and to propose the site Tell el-Ratabah, between nine and ten miles to the W, as the correct site.

Naville's very sketchy publication of the results of his excavation at Tell el-Maskhutah actually supply very little information on the ancient city beyond the fact that the oldest monuments found are those of Ramses II. The discovery most often mentioned in connection with Maskhutah is that of the so-called store chambers, a network of rectangular chambers in the foundation of a building. The British Egyptologist T. Eric Peet maintains that these are nothing but samples of a normal foundation architecture attested elsewhere in Egypt at Tanis and Naukratis and cannot be adduced as store chambers in support of the Pithom identification.

Little more is known of Tell el-Ratabah, which Gardiner favors as the site of Pithom. In 1906 Sir Flinders Petrie published the results of his explorations and excavations at Tell el-Ratabah. He found sufficient proof that the site had been occupied as early as the Middle Kingdom, as well as evidence of building operations there on the part of Ramses II and Ramses III, with no mention of material from a later time. It is interesting to note that Petrie identified this site as biblical Rameses, pointing out the appropriate proximity it had to Pithom (Tell el-Maskhutah!) just eight miles away.

The preceding discussion shows clearly that no positive identification of Pithom-Heroonpolis-Hero can be made until a more careful examination of the sites in question is made. Indeed, the placing of Pithom and SUCCOTH in the area of the Wadi Tumeilat rests on certain assumptions concerning the route of the Exodus. *See* EXODUS, ROUTE OF.

Bibliography. E. Naville, *The Store-City of Pithom and the Route of the Exodus,* Egypt Exploration Fund, Memoir No. 1 (3rd ed.; 1888). W. M. F. Petrie, *Hyksos and Israelite Cities,* British School of Archaeology in Egypt, Publication No. 12 (1906), pp. 28-34. A. H. Gardiner, "The Delta Residence of the Ramessides," *JEA,* 5 (1918), 267-69; "The Geography of the Exodus: An Answer to Professor Naville and Others," *JEA,* 10 (1924), 95-96. E. Naville, "The Geography of the Exodus," *JEA,* 10 (1924), 32-36. T. E. Peet, *Egypt and the OT* (1924), pp. 86-88.

T. O. LAMBDIN

PITHON pī'thŏn [פיתן, פיתון] (I Chr. 8:35; 9:41). A Benjaminite descendant of Saul, and son of Micah.

PITY. *See* MERCY.

PLAGUE [נגע, נגף, מכה, מגפה]. Although plague and pestilence are frequently associated as descriptions of a severe epidemic disease, there appear to be good reasons for distinguishing between them. The Hebrew terms מגפה (Num. 14:37; 16:47; etc.), מכה (Lev. 26:21; Num. 11:33; Deut. 28:59), נגף (Num. 16:46; Josh. 22:17), and נגע (Exod. 11:1; I Sam. 6:4) seem in general to be different designations of one central epidemic concept (*see* PESTILENCE). The disease in question might arise under a variety of conditions, but when it did, it was invariably to be interpreted as a divine judgment on sinful and disobedient people. If the above Hebrew terms are synonymous, as seems most probable, the description of the "plague" of I Sam. 5–6 is sufficient to establish a proper diagnosis.

In these narratives the Philistine defeat of Israel and the capture of the ark was followed by a plague of heavy mortality. The sufferers were afflicted with inguinal tumors (I Sam. 5:12); the disease spread rapidly along the lines of human communication, and during the epidemic there were many rodents in evidence (I Sam. 6:5). This description is characteristic of bubonic plague, the dreaded scourge of antiquity, which is conveyed to man by the rat flea and disseminated by droplet infection. It is marked clinically by high fever, glandular swellings (*see* EMERODS), toxemia, and extreme prostration, with a rapid termination. The inguinal lymph buboes have given the disease its standard designation. It is interesting that the Philistine diviners associated the incidence of the outbreak with the presence of rodents. Despite the licentious nature of Moabite worship, the plague of Num. 25:9 was most probably bubonic rather than venereal in nature.

The dramatic destruction of Sennacherib's forces (II Kings 19:35) was attributed by Herodotus (II. 141) to rodents' gnawing the Assyrian bowstrings. The presence of rodents would indicate the possibility of bubonic plague as the material destructive agency. Pneumonic plague, generally found in colder climates; septicemic plague; or cholera would also be equally fatal. Plague was not endemic in ancient Palestine. *See also* MURRAIN. R. K. HARRISON

PLAGUES IN EXODUS. A series of natural disasters which fell upon Egypt and the Egyptians prior to the release of the Israelites from Egyptian bondage (Exod. 7–12). The scourges are understood as mighty works of God in judgment upon Egypt whereby Israel was set free and the power and sole sovereignty of God made manifest. As such they are variously called "plagues" (מגפות; 9:14), "signs" (אותות; 7:3; 8:23—H 8:19; 10:1-2), "wonders" (מופתים; 7:3; 11:9), and "stroke" or "plague" (נגע; 11:1). They are later repeatedly referred to in the liturgical celebration of the Exodus as the marvelous works, the signs and wonders, of Yahweh, who by them set his people free (e.g., Pss. 78:43; 105:27; 135:9; cf. Deut. 4:34; 7:19; 11:3; Jer. 32:21).

1. Historicity. The concentration of miracles in the period of the Exodus, in the work of Elijah and Elisha, and in the ministry of Jesus is the biblical testimony to God's special and powerful activity acknowledged to have occurred during these events. Time and space, however, together with cultural and mental outlook, so separate us from biblical man that it is impossible to re-create completely the actual situations he faced and interpreted. We are left, in the case of MIRACLES, very largely to his understanding that mighty deeds were indeed wrought by God, of which unusual occurrences in nature were signs. With regard to the Exodus "signs," however, it can be stated that they are peculiarly Egyptian in type and that the traditions about them must be assumed to have arisen ultimately among a people which had had unusual experiences in that country.

The first nine plagues have been explained as natural scourges known in historical times to have been troublesome in Egypt, perhaps, indeed, occurring with particular severity at the time of the Exodus between late summer and the following spring (cf. Exod. 9:31, which suggests an early spring date in the tradition of the seventh plague). After the Nile reaches the height of its inundation by August, it is said that the water often becomes a dull red from the presence of minute organisms, and at certain times the water can be worse than at others. This would appear to be the setting, at least, of the first plague (water turned to blood; 7:14 ff). A plague of frogs, generally in September, has a number of historical witnesses, and quantities of dead frogs would easily give rise to the insect pests (gnats and flies), and probably disease for cattle and human beings (third to sixth plagues). Hail, locusts, and severe sandstorms are also known in plague proportions, the last mentioned being the "thick darkness" which is said to have lasted for three days (10:22). The evidence is such, indeed, that a natural basis for the traditions of the plagues must be assumed; the severity of the scourges was interpreted as the "sign" of God's power.

Yet it would be a mistake to assume that the present form of the Exodus plague traditions can be easily or entirely rationalized in the light of the above-mentioned evidence. They were so long transmitted by a worshiping people and so commonly employed in cultic liturgy that they are not related as history for history's sake, but rather as a celebration of God's great victory whereby he is glorified and acknowledged as sole sovereign and savior. Liturgical usage has given form and heightened theological content to the traditions, though in saying this one must beware of the temptation to assume that the cultus invented the traditions that it celebrated and interpreted.

2. Literary history. Literary criticism in its analysis of Exod. 7–12 has separated, probably successfully, at least two plague traditions, one containing seven scourges and the other ten. The first is contained in the older J stratum of the narrative; the second is the completed tradition as it was given its present form by the Jerusalem priesthood (P). Ps. 78 in its review of the exodus events appears to preserve the J list of seven, while Ps. 105 seems to be based on the completed P narrative (*see* Table 1). In the analysis of the sources there has been fairly general agreement in the separation of those sections belonging to P. His contribution to the JE account of the first plague is held to be 7:19-20*a*, 21*b*-22; and to the J narrative of the second plague: 8:5-7, 15*b*—H 8:1-3, 11*b*. The third and sixth plagues belong solely to P: 8:16-19—H 8:12-15; 9:8-12. Finally, his contribution to the tenth and last plague is 11:9-10. It should be noted in this analysis that P provides no independent account of every plague; his work is that of an editor and supplementer of JE. *See* EXODUS, BOOK OF, § 3.

In separating the P source certain characteristics are observed: Whereas in JE, Moses is the chief actor in God's behalf, while Aaron, if he appears at all, is only the silent partner (8:8-9, 12—H 8:4-5, 8; 8:25-26—H 8:21-22; 9:27-29; 10:8-9); in P, on the other

Table 1
A Comparative Study of the Plagues of Egypt

Exod. 7:8-12:30	Literary sources	Ps. 78:43-57	Ps. 105:28-36	Hebrew	Greek	Latin
1. Water to blood	J (7:14-15*a*, 16-17*a*, 17*c*-18, 20*c*-21*a*, 23-25) E (7:15*b*, 17*b*, 20*b*) P (7:19-20*a*, 21*b*-22)	Vs. 44 (1)	Vs. 29 (2)	חפכו דם	αἷμα	*Sanguinem*
2. Frogs	J (8:1-4, 8-15*a*—H 7:26-29; 8:4-11*a*) P (8:5-7, 15*b*—H 8:1-3, 11*b*)	Vs. 45 (3)	Vs. 30 (3)	צפר דעים	βατράχοις	*Ranis*
3. Gnats	P (8:16-19—H 8:12-15)		כנים Vs. 31 (5)	כנם	σκυῖ φες	*Sciniphes*
4. Flies	J (8:20-32—H 8:16-28)	Vs. 45 (2)	ערב Vs. 31 (4)	ערב	κυνόμυιαν	Ps. 78: *coenomyian* Ps. 105: *coenomyia, cinifer* *Muscae*
5. Murrain	J (9:1-7)	Cattle slain by hail and flocks by lightning (6)	No mention of any harm to cattle	דבר	θάνατος	*Pestis*
6. Boils	P (9:8-12)			שׁחין	φλυκτίδες	*Ulcera*
7. Hail	J (9:13-21, 23*b*, 24*b*, 25*b*-34) E (9:22-23*a*, 24*a*, 25*a*, 35)	Vs. 48 (5)	Vs. 32 (6)	ברד	χάλαξα	*Grando*
8. Locusts	J (10:1-11, 13*b*, 14*b*-15*a*, 15*c*-19, 24-26, 28-29) E (10:12-13*a*, 14*a*, 15*b*, 20)	Vs. 46 (4)	Vs. 34 (7)	ארבה	ἀκρίδα	*Locustam*
9. Darkness	E (10:21-23, 27)		Vs. 28 (1)	חשך	σκότος	*Tenebrae*
10. Death of the first-born	J (11:4-8; 12:21-27, 29 ff) E (11:1-3) P (11:9-10; 12:1-20, 28)	Vs. 51 (7)	Vs. 36 (8)			

Note: Literary sources are according to S. R. Driver, *Introduction to the Literature of the OT* (rev. ed., 1913), pp. 24-29. For slight variations in the analysis of E, *see* EXODUS, BOOK OF, § 3.

hand, Aaron is the chief actor. P's typical literary formula is: "Then Yahweh said to Moses, 'Say to Aaron, Stretch out your rod . . . .' Aaron stretched out his hand . . . . The magicians tried by their secret arts . . . . But the Pharaoh's heart was hardened [חזק], and he would not listen to them; as Yahweh said" (an exception is 8:5, though the conclusion in vss. 11-12 remains within the P context; cf. also 11:9-10). For P the events are specifically "signs and wonders," rather than simply plagues, which prove that Moses and Aaron are the legitimate representatives of Yahweh, and which furthermore take the form of a contest between Moses and Aaron, on the one side, and the Egyptian magicians, on the other. The latter are able to duplicate the feats of Moses and Aaron in the first two wonders but later fail and are forced to admit to Pharaoh: "This is the finger of God" (8:19; cf. 9:11). In the P formula no demand for Israel's release is made; the signs are for the glorification of Yahweh. Finally, the hardening of Pharaoh's heart is expressed by the verb "to be strong" (חזק).

In the older JE narrative, on the other hand, there are clear differences in conception and presentation. The basic stratum (J) appears to employ a literary formula somewhat as follows: "Then Yahweh said to Moses, 'Go to Pharaoh and say to him, Thus says Yahweh, Let my people go, that they may serve me. But if you refuse to let them go, behold, I will . . . .' And Yahweh did so . . . . Then Pharaoh called Moses and said, 'Entreat Yahweh to remove . . .' [here usually follow negotiations of varying length]. Then Moses went out from Pharaoh and prayed to Yahweh. And Yahweh did according to the word of Moses and . . . . But Pharaoh hardened [כבד] his heart, and did not let the people go." For the elements of this formula note especially 8:1-4, 8-15*a*—H 7:26-29; 8:4-11*a;* 8:20-32—H 8:16-28; 9:1-7, 13-

35 (some E admixture); 10:1-20 (some E admixture). In addition, the following passages are also considered to belong to J: 7:14-18, 20*c*-21*a*, 23-24 (with E admixture); 10:24-26, 28-29 (originally a part of the eighth or locust plague?); 11:4-8 (a continuation of 10:29; in the original J list the death of the first-born appears to have followed immediately after the locust plague; cf. Ps. 78:46-51, where, however, the locust and hail plagues are reversed); 12:29-32.

In this literary stratum Moses is the central actor; Yahweh sends the plague after Moses announces it, without mention of Aaron or his rod, that "you may know that I am Yahweh" (7:12*a;* 8:22—H 8:18; 10:2) or "that you know that there is no one like Yahweh" (8:10—H 8:6; cf. 9:14); the plague is regularly connected with the stated purpose: "Let my people go, that they may serve me" (7:16; 8:1, 20—H 7:26; 8:16; 9:1, 13; 10:3; cf. 4:23); the plague is removed without human action other than the prayer of Moses, which Pharaoh has requested him to make; and the hardening of Pharaoh's heart is expressed by the verb "to make heavy" (הכבד).

There still remain certain passages, however, which do not fit easily into either the P or the J sections, and these are attributed to E. They appear in a prevailing J context within the accounts of the first, seventh, eighth, and tenth plagues, and provide the sole record of the ninth scourge of darkness (*see* Table 1). In them the most distinctive feature is the use of the rod in bringing on the plague, but it is stretched out by Moses, rather than by Aaron as in P; whereas in J, Moses does not use a rod, and the plague is simply brought on by Yahweh after Moses has announced it. For this feature of the narratives see 7:15*b*, 17*b*, 20*b;* 9:23*a;* 10:13*a* (cf. 4:17, 20*b;* 14:16; 17:5, 9). Only in the case of darkness does Moses stretch forth his hand (without mention of the rod). Furthermore, with regard to the hardening of Pharaoh's heart, the same word is used as in the P formulas (חזק, "to be or make strong" [9:35]; cf. J's use of the word in vs. 34*b*). In two passages, 10:20, 27, it is Yahweh who hardens the heart of Pharaoh (*Piel* of חזק instead of the *Qal*), while P uses the same wording in 9:12; 11:10; 14:8. Finally, it is felt that the E passages describe the Israelites as neighbors of the Egyptians (11:2; 12:35-36), whereas J seems to consider them as living apart in Goshen (8:22—H 8:18; 9:26; cf. Gen. 46:28-34).

It must be admitted, however, that in themselves the passages in question are too fragmentary, and the criteria for distinguishing them too imprecise, to make it entirely certain that a third document (E) is definitely to be distinguished in the plague narratives. It is only when E has been more clearly delineated elsewhere, that one ventures to ascribe to it the passages here that do not fit easily into either J or P. This explains why scholars have differed on what precisely belongs to E in Exod. 7–12, and also why W. Rudolph in his book *Der "Elohist" von Exodus bis Josua* (1938), after minor adjustment of individual passages, can claim that what is left over cannot be from an assumed "E document," but is simply a series of expansions from an unknown source or sources, together with a series of scribal glosses.

Johannes Pedersen appears to deny the whole validity of the documentary hypothesis as a way of solving the differences in language and conception within the plague narratives. To him Exod. 1–15 is the "cult legend of the Passover reflecting the annual re-living of historical events, as it took shape down through the ages" (*Israel,* III-IV [1940], 726; see pp. 728-30).

Pedersen's rejection of the literary-critical method of handling the traditions, however, is more a denial of the presuppositions behind the former use of the method than of the problems with which it attempted to deal. He feels that the evidence is clear in the plague narrative that an assumption of three distinct, independent, parallel documents cannot explain the phenomena. The internal differences and irregularities of the text remain, but they are best explained as additions and alterations made at various times as the material was used in the yearly Passover festival, rather than as a mosaic of fragments cut from parallel tales.

While most scholars accept the main outlines of the documentary hypothesis, this viewpoint, given expression by Pedersen and others, has brought about a new understanding of the so-called "documents." They are not completely independent literary creations, but collections of traditions which long circulated in oral form before reaching literary fixation. While J and E may have been independent before the fall of Israel in 721 B.C., they are so close together in basic respects that they must be presumed to have been derived from a common source—whether oral or written is not known—composed for the common worship of the twelve-tribe league of the period of the judges. Neither E nor P, however, is now known as an independent source; they are both simply supplementations and expansions of J. Such a view would explain the data regarding the plague stories summarized above, enabling one to see how the J list of seven plagues was expanded to ten from other traditions. Without further, external data (which is not now available), however, we have no way of determining historically which list is the original one employed in the Passover celebrations of the premonarchic period.

Bibliography. A. Dillmann, *Exodus und Leviticus* (1880); J. Wellhausen, *Die Composition des Hexateuchs* (3rd ed., 1899); J. E. Carpenter and G. Harford, *The Composition of the Hexateuch* (1902); B. Baensch, *Exodus-Leviticus-Numeri* (1903); S. R. Driver, *Exodus* (rev. ed., 1913); A. H. McNeille, *The Book of Exodus* (3rd ed., 1931); J. Pedersen, "Passahfest und Passahlegende," *ZAW*, II (1934), 161-75; G. Beer, *Exodus* (1939); J. Pedersen, *Israel, Its Life and Culture,* III-IV (1940), 725-37; C. A. Simpson, *Early Traditions of Israel* (1948); J. C. Rylaarsdam, Introduction and Exegesis of Exodus, *IB*, vol. I (1952).

J. L. MIHELIC AND G. E. WRIGHT

PLAIN [בקעה, ככר, מישור, ערבה, עמק (Josh. 17:16; Judg. 1:19; KJV "valley"), אבל (Judg. 11:33 KJV; *see below*), אלון (KJV; *see below*), שפלה (RSV "Shephelah"); τόπου πεδινοῦ (Luke 6:17 KJV; RSV "level place")]. A word used in English translations to designate several slightly differing types of level terrain. *See also* ARABAH; SHEPHELAH; VALLEY; PALESTINE, GEOGRAPHY OF.

The four words which both the KJV and the RSV usually render as "plain" are: בקעה, ככר, מישור, and ערבה. The first refers to a portion of the plain in Babylonia between the Tigris and Euphrates rivers

(Gen. 11:2; Ezek. 3:22-23; 8:4; Dan. 3:1), but also to the plain of ONO, probably the Sharon Plain (cf. Neh. 6:2), and to a plain as contrasted with a rough place (Isa. 40:4). The RSV renders the same word in Amos 1:5 as "Valley" of Aven, and in II Chr. 35:22; Zech. 12:11 "plain" of Megiddo where the KJV has "valley." ככר is used to refer to the level terrain near Jericho (Deut. 34:3), to the area on both sides of the Jordan River (I Kings 7:46; II Chr. 4:17), and possibly to plateaus in the vicinity of Jerusalem (II Sam. 18:23; Neh. 3:22; cf. Neh. 12:28 [RSV "circuit"; KJV "plain country"]). The RSV renders the same word as "valley" of the Jordan (Gen. 13:10; 19:17; etc.) where the KJV has "plain." מישור is frequently used to designate plains, without indicating their specific locations (I Kings 20:23, 25; II Chr. 26:10; Jer. 21:13). The same word is rendered by the RSV as "tableland," which is more descriptive than the "plain" of the KJV, in the phrase: "all the tableland of Medeba as far as Dibon" (Josh. 13:9). ערבה is rendered "plain" when it designates the territory of Moab (Num. 22:1; 26:3; Deut. 34:1; etc.). When the same word refers to the level area near the Dead Sea, the RSV renders it "Arabah" (Deut. 1:1, 7; 2:8; Josh. 3:16; II Kings 14:25; etc.).

The Hebrew words which the KJV renders as "plain" but the RSV in different ways, call for some comment. The word אבל in Judg. 11:33 is understood in the RSV as part of the proper name Abel-keramim. The term אלון is rendered as "oak" or "oaks" when used in connection with such places as Moreh and Mamre (Gen. 12:6; 13:18; 14:13; 18:1; etc.). שפלה, which the KJV renders as "plain" or "low plain," is transliterated in the RSV as "Shephelah" (I Chr. 27:28; II Chr. 9:27; Jer. 17:26; etc.). It will be seen that the RSV uses a variety of descriptive words to render the original terms, and also shows an acquaintance with the geographical features of the terrain involved. W. L. REED

PLANE [מקצעה, *from* קצע, to scrape off, a wood scraper(?)] (Isa. 44:13). A carpenter's instrument; used in connection with the manufacture of a wooden idol.

PLANE TREE [ערמון, *'armôn* (KJV CHESNUT); תדהר, *tiḏhār* (KJV PINE); πλάτανος]. A tree distinguished by its large leaves, shedding bark, and spreading branches. Jacob used branches of this tree as part of his scheme to trick Laban in Haran (Gen. 30:37 J). Ezekiel likens Pharaoh to this tree (and others) in the garden of God (Ezek. 31:8). Wisdom "grew tall . . . like a plane tree" (Ecclus. 24:14).

Identification of this tree with the plane tree (*Plantanus orientalis* L.) is generally accepted on the basis of the LXX and the implications of its use in Gen. 30:37. The KJV use of "chesnut" does not fit the contexts at all. The תדהר (Isa. 41:19; 60:13; KJV PINE) appears in contexts that seem to require a conifer (*see* FIR). One might assume that a conifer was intended for ערמון in Ezek. 31:8 (cf. LXX ἐλάται, "silver fir"), but not necessarily.

See also FLORA § A9*o*.

Bibliography. I. Löw, *Die Flora der Juden*, III (1924), 65-67; H. L. and A. N. Moldenke, *Plants of the Bible* (1952), pp. 180-81. J. C. TREVER

PLANK [לוח, *cf.* Akkad. *lê'u*, tablet; צלע, *cf.* Akkad. *ṣêlu*, rib, side; קרש; שדר; σανίς].

1. Ship's planks. לוח is the term used for the planking (KJV BOARDS) of a Tyrian ship (Ezek. 27:5). In Acts 27:44 σανίς refers to the planks of Paul's vessel. Such ships were doubtless carvel-built, necessitating much calking of the seams. *See* SHIPS AND SAILING.

2. Building planks and boards. Acacia wood supplies the numerous "frames" (KJV "boards"; plural of קרש) used in the tabernacle (Exod. 26:15 ff). Acacia "boards" (plural of לוח) are required for the altar of the tabernacle (Exod. 27:8; 38:7). Cedar and cypress (or juniper) "boards" (plural of צלע) supply paneling and flooring for Solomon's temple (I Kings 6:15 [KJV "plank" in 15*b*], 16). Planks (plural of שדר, KJV "boards") of cedar in the temple ceiling appear in I Kings 6:9, but the meaning of the word is uncertain. The meaning of the phrase "boards of cedar" (plural of לוח) in Song of S. 8:9 in its context is obscure. W. S. MCCULLOUGH

PLANTATION [ממטע, *from* נטע, to plant] (Ezek. 17:7 KJV [RSV BED WHERE IT WAS PLANTED]; Ezek. 34:29 [KJV PLANT]). The place of planting, or the plants themselves (cf. Isa. 5:7; 61:3; Mic. 1:6); not used in the common technical sense of the English term. J. A. WHARTON

PLASTER [שיד, *sîdh;* טוח; גיר; עפר (KJV DUST); *verb* טוח]. From prehistoric times plaster was used in floors and walls, as is shown in JERICHO § 2. After the Israelite invasion, or the beginning of the Iron Age, thick, waterproof plaster was developed for cisterns, basins, and walls. שיד (Arabic *shîd*) means "lime" or "plaster," and the corresponding verb means "boil up," referring to the making of plaster from the lime. In Dan. 5:5 the Aramaic גיר refers to the plaster on the wall, where the mysterious writing appeared (*see* HALL § 5). The Israelites were told upon entering the land to set up stones and plaster them with plaster, שיד (Deut. 27:2, 4).

See also ARCHITECTURE; HOUSE. O. R. SELLERS

PLATE. In the original languages the words for "plate" and "bowl" tend to be the same. One tells by the context which term is the better English equivalent.

The term "plate" is also used in the sense of a "metal sheet." There was an engraved plate of gold on the miter or turban of the high priest (Exod. 28: 36; *see* PRIESTS AND LEVITES). The censers of the rebels (Num. 16:38) were beaten into sheet metal, or "plates," to serve as a covering for the altar.

J. L. KELSO

PLATTER [παροψίς; πίναξ (KJV CHARGER *in* Matt. 14:8, 11)]. The platter that carried the head of John the Baptist (πίναξ; Matt. 14:8, 11) was doubtless made of gold or silver. Those referred to in Matt. 23:25-26 (παροψίς); Luke 11:39 (πίναξ) would more likely have been ceramic than metal. J. L. KELSO

PLEASANT PLANTS [נטעי נעמנים, plantings of the pleasant one(s)]. There is virtual unanimity for the view that this phrase, found in Isa. 17:10, alludes to a sacred garden of ADONIS (cf. Isa. 1:29). It occurs in a context where Israel is addressed in the feminine, as the errant spouse of the Lord (cf. Jer. 2; Hos. 2). The term נעמן (*see* NAAMAN), meaning "pleasant" or "charming," corresponds to the proper name of an Arabic deity; but it is more probable that it is here used as the descriptive title of the annually dying and rising god of the fertility cult, the אדון ("lord") of Phoenicia, known as Ἄδωνις in Greece. The word is in the plural either because it occurs in construct relation with "plantings" or, more probably, because the young god of the fertility cult had many manifestations, each individualized and personified.

Bibliography. H. Gressmann, "Mitteilungen des Herausgebers: 2. Die Ausgrabungen in Bēsān," *ZAW,* 44 (1926), 71-75; W. Baumgartner, "Das Nachleben der Adonisgärten auf Sardinien und im übrigen Mittelmeergebiet," *Schweizerisches Archiv für Volkskunde,* 43 (1946), 122-23.

J. C. RYLAARSDAM

PLEDGE [חבל, עבטיט, ערבון]. A piece of personal property, such as a garment, a ring, or other valuables, which a borrower surrenders to his creditor as a token guaranty for the future repayment of the loan. *See also* DEBT; SURETY.

PLEIADES plē'ə dēz [LXX *rendering of* כימה, group of stars, *from* כום, to accumulate, heap up; *cf.* Arab. *kama* (heaped up), *kumu,* herd, *kumatu* (head); Assyrian *kumtu,* family] (Job 9:9; 38:31; Amos 5:8); KJV SEVEN STARS in Amos 5:8. A cluster or large grouping; several separate members bound together. The Greek "Pleiades," which the LXX renders Πλείαδος (singular in Job 38:31), is of uncertain derivation. It may be from πλέος, "full," in which case it is a correct rendering of the MT; it may be from πλέω, "to sail," thus a star or constellation important for navigation.

The LXX first clearly designated the term as astral, though the LXX was not always certain. While rendering Job 9:9; 38:32 as "Pleiad," it paraphrased in Amos 5:8: ποιῶν πάντα καὶ μετασκευάζων —i.e., "making and transforming all things." The Syr. reads כימה, which is elsewhere attested in that literature with the same identification. The Vulg. is certain only that the usage is astral, offering a different rendering for the three references, "Hyades," "Pleiades," "Arcturus."

Identity of the "cluster" is generally agreed as being the Pleiades; various peoples in their literature have likewise noted this brilliant group, which suggests that it is the most likely to be especially recognized. The KJV hesitates in Amos 5:8, as did the LXX, reading more vaguely "the seven stars." This is, however, in accord with this constellation, which has seven stars. Thus the identification, while not certain, is generally accepted.

If the dubious equation of עיש (in the same verses) with "Pleaides" is accepted (*see* ARCTURUS), the most likely alternative for כימה is that of Canis Major, with its bright star, Sirius. This possibility is unlikely.

Bibliography. E. W. Maunder, *The Astronomy of the Bible* (no date); G. Schiaparelli, *Astronomy in the OT* (1905); G. R. Driver, "Two Astronomical Passages in the OT," *JTS,* 7 (1956), 1-2.

W. BRUEGGEMANN

PLEROMA plĭ rō'mə [πλήρωμα]. A Greek word of considerable importance in a number of biblical passages, meaning generally "fulness." More precise definition involves a number of serious problems.

1. Terminology. Attempts have sometimes been made to argue from a supposed rule about nouns in -μα to the meaning of "pleroma." But it is evident, in fact, that the relation of such nouns to the verbs whose stems they share varies from instance to instance. Κλάσμα, "a fragment," has a relation to κλάω very different from that of ἄντλημα, "a bucket," to ἀντλάω "to draw"; and different from both of these, again, is the abstract noun ἀνταπόδομα, "requital," in its relation to ἀνταποδίδωμι. Moreover, a study of δικαίωμα and δικαίωσις in Rom. 5:16, 18, etc., and indeed a comparison between πλήρωμα itself and πλήρωσις (see Ezek. 32:15; Dan. 10:3θ) inspires no confidence in the rigidity of meaning attaching to particular noun formations. Accordingly, the only reliable means of determining the sense of "pleroma" is by observing its context.

2. Broad distinctions. ***a. Nonspecialized meanings.*** There are clear instances of the use of "pleroma" for "that which fills." The commonest biblical instance of this is the repeated phrase "the earth and its pleroma" (Ps. 24:1—G 23:1; I Cor. 10:26; etc.), which clearly means "the earth and all that fills it." So too it is used, evidently in Mark 2:21, of a "patch" of cloth on a garment to fill up a hole. (The parallel in Matt. 9:16 has been otherwise explained, from as early as the Vulg. *tollit enim plenitudinem eius a vestimento,* but in all probability means the same as the Markan phrase. In the parallel Luke 5:36 the word is not used at all.) Exactly so, again, in Mark 6:43 (cf. 8:20): δώδεκα κοφίνων πληρώματα means "broken pieces *enough to fill* twelve baskets."

There are other places where a meaning such as "sum total" or "completeness" seems best. In Rom. 11:25, τὸ πλήρωμα τῶν ἐθνῶν seems to mean "the full number of the Gentiles" (so RSV); just as in Gal. 4:4 (cf. Eph. 1:10) we have "when the time had fully come," ὅτε δὲ ἦλθεν τὸ πλήρωμα τοῦ χρόνου (cf. Acts 21:26: τὴν ἐκπλήρωσιν τῶν ἡμερῶν). Probably Rom. 15:29: ἐν πληρώματι εὐλογίας χριστοῦ means "with the fullest possible blessing . . . ." Possibly in Rom. 13:10 πλήρωμα νόμου means "the law in summary form," an epitome of the law.

But the phrase in Rom. 13:10 more probably means (so RSV) that "love is the fulfilling of the law"—i.e., to love is to keep the law fully. Similarly, in 11:12 τὸ πλήρωμα αὐτῶν (their—i.e., the Jews'—pleroma) is contrasted with their ἥττημα (i.e., "reduction"), and thus, despite the seeming parallel in vs. 25 (*see above*), is translated "full inclusion" (in contrast to "their failure"). In these instances "pleroma" seems to mean "completion," "fulfilling."

See, for the theological significance of the second and third connotations given above, FULFIL.

b. Special meanings. There are parallels in nonbiblical Greek for all the above meanings of "pleroma." But, in addition, it is claimed that the sense "that which is filled" may also be detected; and it will be well to examine this now, since it is of importance in connection with the special meanings shortly to be examined.

There is no denying that ships are sometimes spoken of as πληρώματα, and it might be argued that this proves that "pleroma" can mean "a vessel," "that which is filled." The passages commonly quoted are Polybius I.49.4 (ἀγνοούντων μὲν τὴν παρουσίαν τῶν πληρωμάτων, "unaware of the arrival of the ships"); Lucian *Ver. Hist.* II.37-38 (several instances—e.g., ἀπὸ δύο πληρωμάτων ἐμάχοντο); and Philo *Quod omn. prob.* 142 (of the Argonauts' ship) and *Life of Moses* II.62 (of Noah's ark). But, whereas this proves beyond all doubt that the word can mean "ship," it does not follow that it means "ship" *because it means* "that which is filled"; it may still mean (primarily) a ship's filling: its cargo (as it certainly sometimes does)—i.e., that which fills the ship; or its full crew (its full "strength" or "complement" of men), exactly as in racing on the river one speaks of the boat itself as "an eight," by transference from its contents of eight oarsmen. Thus "pleroma" is still not proved to mean strictly "that which is filled"; and certain instances from the *Corpus Hermeticum,* which at first sight might seem to come to the rescue, are in fact patient of interpretation along the lines of the meanings previously defined (VI.4: God is πλ τοῦ ἀγαθοῦ—i.e., not filled with good but the totality of good; IX.7; XII.15; XVI.3: all="totality"). The same would seem to be true of some further passages from Philo sometimes cited for the sense "that which is filled"—viz., *On Rewards and Punishments* 65, 109; *On the Special Laws* I.272; *Every Good Man Is Free* 41, 128. Of these, the first is the most plausible, for the phrase γενομένη πλήρωμα ἀρετῶν ἥδε ἡ ψυχή ("this soul, becoming a pleroma of virtues") is supplemented by οὐδὲν ἐν ἑαυτῇ καταλιποῦσα κενόν ("leaving nothing in herself empty," or "leaving no space in herself"). But at most, this is only one instance.

This result, as will be seen, is important when we come to examine the special uses in the NT. These—the really problematic passages, and doctrinally by far the most interesting—are in Colossians and Ephesians and perhaps also John. Before turning to them, it will be well to note two important technical connections of the word outside the NT.

a) After the NT period, "pleroma" is known to have been a technical term in the system of Valentinus (*ca.* 90-160). This was already known in regard to Valentinus' followers, on the evidence of Epiphanius *Heresies* XXXI.10.13; 13.6; Hippolytus *Ref.* VI. 29.5; Iren. Her. I.1.1. More recently, a precious Coptic document (the "Jung codex") has been found containing what may be Valentinus' own utterances, and in it too the word appears. It seems to mean "the upper world," the world which is eternity, stability, completeness, as contrasted with ὑστέρημα, the world of becoming, the world below, the place of incompleteness and emptiness (κένωμα).

b) There is a strain of thought, very much at home in Stoic pantheism, in which the divine is represented as filling, or permeating, the world. An echo of this thought, though without the word "to fill," is caught in Wisd. Sol. 8:1, where wisdom "reaches mightily from one end of the earth to the other," and "orders all things well" (cf. 1:7; Jer. 23:24 [of God's filling heaven and earth]; Eph. 4:10 [of Christ's]). *See also* FULFIL.

With this in mind, we may turn to the passages in Colossians, Ephesians, and John:

a) Col. 1:19: "In him all the fulness of God was pleased to dwell."

b) Col. 2:9: "In him the whole fulness of deity dwells bodily."

c) Eph. 1:22-23: "He has put all things under his feet and has made him the head over all things for the church, which is his body, the fulness of him who fills all in all."

d) Eph. 3:19: ". . . that you may be filled with all the fulness of God."

e) Eph. 4:13: ". . . until we all attain to the unity of the faith and of the knowledge of the Son of God, to mature manhood, to the measure of the stature of the fulness of Christ."

In the Colossians passages, it is reasonable to assume that (*a*) and (*b*) mean the same thing, and that if Paul is indeed borrowing "pleroma" as a technical term from the errors he is attacking, he uses it in the deepest and most spiritual way—"the whole fulness of deity"—comparable in some degree to the use of the early Valentinian document mentioned above. It seems to mean that Christ is, in a unique and complete sense, the incarnation of God himself. Thus it is (Eph. 4:10) that he fills all things. One could hardly have a "higher" Christology. In (*c*) (Eph. 1: 22-23), a variety of interpretations is offered, turning in part on whether the participle πληρουμένου is taken as passive or as middle with an active sense (so RSV "fills"). The following exegeses cover most of the alternatives: (*a*) ". . . the fulfilment of him who all in all is being fulfilled"—i.e., the church is to be the completion of the Christ, who is thus finding fulfilment through it; (*b*) "the fulness of him who all in all is being filled"—i.e., the church is filled (the fulness in this passive sense—but *see above* for the unlikelihood of this) by Christ who, in his turn, is filled by God; (*c*) ". . . the fulness of him who fills all in all"—i.e., the church is either the completion of (as in *a*) or that which is filled by (as in *b*) Christ, who fills everything (cf. Eph. 4:10). (*d*) Construing "the fulness" as in apposition to "the head," we get the sense that God has appointed Christ both to be head of the church and to be God's own full representative (cf. Col. 1:19; 2:9 above). (*e*) Construing as in *d,* but taking τοῦ πληρουμένου as a periphrasis for the universe or for the church: Christ is himself the totality or filling of that which is to be completed or filled (see the Commentaries).

Eph. 3:19 would be better rendered ". . . filled up to all the fulness of God," and should be compared with Col. 2:10: "You have come to fulness of life in him" (ἐστὲ ἐν αὐτῷ πεπληρωμένοι). The thought appears to be that there is a completeness, a maturity of character, ordained by God ("the fulness of God" in this sense) both for each Christian individually and for the church corporately; and this is the goal toward which we press, and for which we pray. On the other hand, there is a sense in which, being already incorporate in Christ, we already have his completeness (Col. 2:10). It is the usual tension between being and becoming: "Become what in fact you are!"

So in Eph. 4:13, "the fulness of Christ" seems most probably to mean that completeness, that maturity of character, which is already realized in Christ both as an individual and as the Body of which Christians are limbs. It is the full stature of that maturity that, by the grace of God, all of us are together to attain. This interpretation of *d* and *e* is not, however, accepted by all. Those who take *c* in the first sense noted above—of the church as that in which Christ is fulfilled—will be disposed to find the same theme here: in *d* the sense will be that the completion of the church will mean that completeness ("pleroma") designed by God to be ultimately attained by Christ; and *e* will, similarly, mean that Christ will find his completeness when all Christians together have reached maturity—i.e., when the church is one and whole.

f) Finally, we must inquire as to the meaning of John 1:16: "And from his fulness have we all received, grace upon grace." If it is right to relate to this John 3:34: "It is not by measure that he gives the Spirit," we may take the meaning to be that Jesus is uniquely filled with God's Spirit (cf. John 1: 14: "full of grace and truth"), and that it is from this fulness that the Christian receives God's gifts. There is no necessity to see an echo of a Gnostic technical term, although, as with Colossians, it is, of course, possible that some such allusion is intended.

3. Conclusions. Thus the evidence as a whole points to the meanings "that which fills" ("the contents"), "sum total," "fulfilment," "completion"; with "sum total" or "completeness" as the best sense in Colossians and Ephesians, with or without the technical overtones of "Gnostic" thought.

Bibliography. J. B. Lightfoot, *Colossians and Philemon* (2nd ed., 1876), excursus; J. A. Robinson, *Ephesians* (1903), excursus; W. L. Knox, *St. Paul and the Church of the Gentiles* (1939), pp. 163 ff; J. Dupont, *Gnosis* (1949), ch. VII; C. L. Mitton, *Ephesians* (1951), pp. 94 ff; R. Bultmann, "Gnosis," *JTS,* N.S.iii, I (1952), pp. 23 ff; J. Munck, *Christus und Israel* (1956), pp. 99 ff; P. Benoit, *RB,* LXIII (1956), 5 ff. See also the edition of the early Gnostic text, *Evangelium Veritatis,* by M. Malinine, H.-C. Puech, and G. Quispel (1956); C. Spicq, *Agapè II* (1959), pp. 221 ff. C. F. D. Moule

PLOW [חרש]. To break up the ground with a plowshare. The unquestionably poor quality of plowshares in biblical times, as today in some parts of the Near East, undoubtedly precluded turning a furrow and permitted little more than scratching the surface to a depth of four or five inches. Hoeing may have taken the place of plowing after a heavy rain and on steep or very stony ground.

Courtesy of Herbert G. May

59. An Arab plowing with an ass and an ox, a practice forbidden in Deut. 22:10

Courtesy of Staatliche Museen, Berlin

60. Relief from tomb of Pa-heri at el-Kab (Eighteenth Dynasty, *ca.* 1550-1350 B.C.), showing Egyptian plow drawn by slaves and guided by a bearded man

The Deuteronomic Code prohibited using an ox and an ass together in plowing (Deut. 22:10). As today, probably various animals were employed to pull the plow: oxen, cows, asses. *See* Coulter.

Figs. PLO 59-60. H. N. Richardson

PLUMB LINE [אנך, *from* Akkad. *anâku,* lead]; PLUMMET [משקלת (II Kings 21:13; Isa. 28:17), *from* שקל, weigh; אבן (Isa. 34:11; KJV STONES), stone; האבן הבדיל (Zech. 4:10), the stone, the tin]. The plumb line was a cord to which was attached a weight of metal, stone, or clay, called a plummet. This device was used in the building of a wall to ensure verticality.

From the Akkadian etymology it would seem that אנך could mean "plummet" as well as "plumb line." The biblical occurrence of the word is in Amos 7:7-8, where the Lord is pictured standing by a wall with a plumb line in his hand. The wall, representing Israel, had been built correctly, but now it was out of line and would be destroyed.

"Line" and "plummet" are used in connection with destruction (II Kings 21:13; Isa. 34:11); "plummet" is used also in happy circumstances (Isa. 28:17).

O. R. Sellers

POCHERETH-HAZZEBAIM pŏk'ə rĕth hăz'ə-bā'əm [פכרת הצבים, binder of gazelles, gazelle-hunter; Apoc. Φακάρεθ-σαβειή] (Ezra 2:57; Neh. 7:59; I Esd. 5:34); KJV POCHERETH OF ZEBAIM zĭ-bā'əm; KJV Apoc. PHACARETH făk'ə rĕth. Head of a postexilic family among the "sons of Solomon's servants." *See* Nethinim. J. M. Ward

POD [κεράτιον] (Luke 15:16); KJV HUSK. Probably the seed vessel of the carob tree (*Caratonia siliqua*), popularly referred to as the locust or acacia. The reference is in the parable of the prodigal son. These sweet pods, often a foot long, were fed to cattle and swine and were eaten by the poor.

H. F. Beck

POET. The translation of ποιητής in Acts 17:28. The literal meaning of the Greek word, "doer," is used elsewhere (Rom. 2:13; Jas. 1:22-23, 25; 4:11).

In Acts 17:28, Paul quotes "some of your poets" —i.e., Greek poets. The Greek text does not indicate whether the words "as even some of your poets have said" refer (*a*) backward to the line "In him we live and move and have our being"; (*b*) forward to the line "For we are indeed his offspring"; or (*c*) to both lines. The RSV chooses the second alternative, as is indicated by the semicolon after the first quotation. But this decision is editorial, and is not necessarily correct.

The RSV does recognize, however, that the line "In him we live and move and have our being" is a quotation. If this is a quotation from the Cretan Epimenides (as the RSV indicates in a footnote, but there are arguments against it), then it is pre-Stoic and does not mean that men live "in" Zeus, but "by the power of" Zeus. (*See* STOICS.) The argument would therefore be that Zeus is not dead, as Cretans who show his tomb believe, but is living because it is by him that we ourselves live. In any case, the line is as easily interpreted Jewishly as it is Stoically.

The second line quoted is from the *Phaenomena* of Aratus, who was born in Cilicia *ca.* 310 B.C. He was a friend of the Stoic Zeno and was influenced by Stoic philosophy. The quotation is taken from the beginning of the *Phaenomena,* the "his" referring to Zeus. It is possible that Aratus used a line written earlier by the poet Cleanthes in his "Hymn to Zeus." There we read: "For we are thy offspring."

It may be that vs. 27*b:* "Yet he is not far from each one of us," is also an allusion to a poem. In any case, it is interesting to note that in this speech Greek poetry is used in preaching to the Greeks in much the same way in which the OT was usually used in the early church's preaching. *See* AREOPAGUS.

B. H. THROCKMORTON, JR.

*__POETRY, HEBREW.__ Poetry comprises one third of the Hebrew Bible—this fact was fully appreciated only within the past two hundred years. The poetry of the OT is unlike classical, European, and even later Jewish poetry. Rhyme is virtually non-existent, and rhythm is flexible, being marked, not by syllabic feet, but by an elusive tonal system supplied by medieval scholars. The fundamental formal feature of canonical poetry is the correspondence of thought in successive half lines, known as parallelism of members. The thought may be repeated, contrasted, or advanced; it may be figurative, stairlike, or inverted. The parallelism may be both within lines and between lines. Meter, insofar as it exists, is a by-product of the paralleled lines. Hebrew is an explosive, staccato, sound-conscious language, and the devices of alliteration, assonance, paronomasia, and onomatopoeia are used to great aesthetic advantage. Division of poems into strophes or stanzas is demonstrable only in a fraction of OT compositions.

Canonical poetry ranges from brief extracts in the Pentateuch and historical books, derived from pre-exilic anthologies, to the spacious poetic tapestries of Isa. 40-66 and Job. Communal mores and practice gave rise to variant poetic genres. Among the distinctive religious types were hymns, laments and confessions, thanksgiving and trust songs, and royal psalms. As poetic expression became disengaged from cultic activity, the forms were employed with greater freedom by prophets, psalmists, and sages. The line between poetry communally shaped and free compositions is one not easily drawn, for the cult was active and important throughout biblical times.

A. Extent
B. History of interpretation
C. Parallelism of members
 1. Internal
  a. Synonymous
  b. Antithetic
  c. Synthetic or formal
  d. Miscellaneous
 2. External
D. Meter
E. Techniques
 1. Alliteration
 2. Assonance
 3. Paronomasia
 4. Onomatopoeia
F. Strophe
G. Genre and situation in life
 1. Poetic fragments
 2. Anthologies
 3. Recurring and nonrecurring types
 4. "Secular" types
 5. "Sacred" types
  a. Hymn
  b. Lament and confession
  c. Thanksgiving and trust song
  d. Royal psalm
 6. Prophetic poetry
 7. Emancipation from types
Bibliography

A. *EXTENT.* Fully one third of the OT text is poetic in form. Psalms, Proverbs, Song of Songs, Lamentations, Obadiah, Micah, Nahum, Habakkuk, and Zephaniah are poetic in their entirety (with the exception of superscriptions). The greater parts of Job, Isaiah, Hosea, Joel, and Amos are poetic, and Jeremiah is about one half poetry. Several books have substantial poetic portions in otherwise prose material: Genesis, Exodus, Numbers, Deuteronomy, Judges, I and II Samuel, Ecclesiastes, Ezekiel, Daniel, and Zechariah. Only seven OT books appear to contain no poetic lines: Leviticus, Ruth, Ezra, Nehemiah, Esther, Haggai, and Malachi. The three segments of the Hebrew canon (Law, Prophets, Writings) contain poetry in successively greater amounts. Poetry, formally analogous to the canonical compositions, appears in the APOCRYPHA; the PSEUDEPIGRAPHA; and the DEAD SEA SCROLLS. Poems Hebraic in style appear in Luke (*see* BENEDICTUS; MAGNIFICAT; NUNC DIMITTIS) and the book of Revelation (e.g., 4:11; 5:9-10; 7:15-17; 11:17-18; 15:3-4; 18; 19:1-8). Much of Jesus' epigrammatic teaching was expressed in the parallelistic structure of Hebrew poetry. On the whole, however, poetry plays a minor role in the NT.

B. *HISTORY OF INTERPRETATION.* Only recently have consistent efforts been made to represent OT poetry by a stichometric format, either in Hebrew or in the versions, English included. It is noteworthy that Qumran fragments of the Song of Moses (Deut. 32) and certain of the Psalms were copied with attention to poetic line. Even at Qumran, however, this practice was an exception. Some of the

Masoretic MSS arranged the text by poetic units, but only in the case of Psalms, Proverbs, and Job. The more intricate system of punctuation used by the Masoretes for these three books also argues for an awareness of poetic form. However, Pentateuchal and prophetic poetry was ignored. While the Masoretic system of marking punctuation has frequently included several poetic lines in one verse, the form was sufficiently sensed that an actual poetic unit was seldom broken up.

The avoidance of serious mishandling of the poetic text is not the same, however, as true understanding of its formal principles. The Greek and Latin versions paid no attention to poetic form, in spite of the vigorous tradition of classical poetry. The Syriac and Aramaic were likewise insensitive to poetic structure. The authorized English versions have only slowly responded to the discovery of poetry in all parts of the Bible. The ERV and ASV printed the poetic books stichometrically, but it remained for the RSV to do the same throughout the Bible. This has been a particularly significant contribution to an understanding of the Prophets.

Comment on Hebrew poetry has appeared sporadically since biblical times. It has been a mixture of false analogy with dissimilar poetry and of occasional though unsustained insight. Philo reported that the Egyptians taught Moses the "lore of metre, rhythm and harmony" (*Life of Moses* I.5). With reference to Exod. 15, Josephus spoke of "Moses himself composing in hexameter verse a song to God" (Antiq. II. xvi.4), of Deut. 32 that "he recited to them [the Israelites] a poem in hexameter verse" (Antiq. IV.viii.44), and of David that "he composed songs and hymns to God in varied meters—some he made in trimeters, and others in pentameters" (Antiq. VII.xii.3). Josephus was the first—though unhappily not the last—to try to construe the poetry of the Hebrew Bible by classical meters. Thus began the long and unfruitful diversion from the path of true advance in Hebrew prosody.

Origen, in a scholion to Ps. 118:1 (LXX), agreed with Josephus that Deut. 32 is a hexameter. He also noted trimetric psalms, as well as tetrametric. Origen insisted, however, that Hebrew verses are different from Greek. His comment is cryptic, but it is possible that he recognized two stichs (or half lines) as the basic poetic unit (*see* § 3 *below*). Eusebius and Jerome continued to employ Greek and Latin metric terms but always with uneasiness, and they made no attempt to define a metric foot in Hebrew verse. Had a living tradition of Hebrew poetry still survived in Palestine in the fourth century, Jerome would have known it; but he gives us no hint of it.

In fact, Jewish tradition is curiously silent about the formal character of biblical verse. There is no recognition of the essential features of poetry by the men of Jamnia (*see* CANON OF THE OT) or the compilers of the Talmud. Yet the presence of the balanced members in successive lines in such intertestamental writings as the Apocalypse of Baruch and IV Ezra shows that poetry "biblical" in style was written as late as the closing of the canon. The *Hodayoth* (Thanksgiving Psalms or Praises) found among the first cache of DEAD SEA SCROLLS, dating from the first or second century B.C., not only imitate biblical phraseology but also have the formal features of canonical poetry.

Some of the medieval commentators (Ibn Ezra, Kimchi, Levi ben Gershom) recognized the reduplication of thought in biblical poetry, and in a few instances they made their interpretations depend upon the form. Yet it was common for Jewish and Christian exegetes to ignore the synonymity of thought in the two halves of a verse by insisting on separate meanings. It is astonishing that the formal structure of ancient Hebrew poetry was transmitted through the centuries generally intact in spite of the lack of poetic format, even though the older forms were no longer employed in contemporary poetry and were, in fact, largely disregarded in biblical exegesis.

In 1753, Bishop Robert Lowth of Oxford published his noted *Lectures on the Sacred Poetry of the Hebrews* (in Latin; English translation, 1815). A second edition in 1763 incorporated the notes of J. D. Michaelis, who had guided the work into a German edition. His *Isaiah: A New Translation with Preliminary Dissertation* (1787) offered a fuller exposition of Hebrew poetic types. It is a tribute to Lowth's work that, in spite of archaisms and florid style, it retains aesthetic freshness and scholarly relevance.

Lowth's insights were manifold. He saw that Hebrew poetry was mainly a matter of sense, to which sound and form were linked rather loosely. Balancing ideas and phrases had priority over strict meter. In fact, he believed that the original meter had been wholly lost, so that he turned sharply away from trying to understand Hebrew verse through classical formulas. Central to his analysis was the recognition of the counterbalancing of verse members, to which he applied the technical term *parallelismus membrorum* ("parallelism of members"). This phenomenon was no mere ornamentation but of the essence of Hebrew poetry, its fundamental formal feature. He attempted to classify the types of parallelism, and with considerable success. Also of great importance was his acknowledgment of poetry throughout the Hebrew Bible; e.g., he devoted five lectures alone to prophetic poetry, and his work on Isaiah gave careful analysis of the verse forms in the book. Our present understanding is an elaboration and enrichment of Lowth's viewpoint.

C. *PARALLELISM OF MEMBERS.* The habit of the Hebrew poet of balancing thought against thought, phrase against phrase, word against word, is the persisting feature of his method of working. It is so pervasive as to be virtually a mode of thought, taken over from ancient Near Eastern literary culture but elaborated with consummate artistry. Non-Semitic examples of parallelism are generally brief excerpts from nursery rhymes, lyrics, ballads. The more sustained instances have significant departures from the Hebrew pattern. The Finnish epic *Kalevala* tends to parallel several lines instead of the normal two-line parallels of the OT. Anglo-Saxon poetry, and especially *Piers Plowman,* employs alliteration and has a fixed number of stresses, whereas alliteration is only a sporadic device in Hebrew poetry and meter is still an indeterminate factor.

1. Internal. A typical Hebrew poem consists of a series of terms that fall into pairs, each set of terms marked off from preceding and following poetic elements by major stops or caesuras (indicated by double diagonals in the examples cited below). Within each of the pairs, the parts are distinguished by a lesser stop (indicated by single diagonals).

The earth is the LORD's and the fulness thereof, /
the world and those who dwell therein; //
for he has founded it upon the seas, /
and established it upon the rivers. //
Who shall ascend the hill of the LORD? /
And who shall stand in his holy place? //
(Ps. 24:1-3.)

It is apparent that lines 2, 4, and 6 introduce no new thought but rather repeat or echo the immediately preceding lines. In their common assertion of God's ownership of the world and its people, lines 1 and 2 are said to be "parallel" or "in parallelism." The parallelism of lines 3 and 4 extends the divine sovereignty over the waters, and that of lines 5 and 6 poses the question of terms of entrance to the temple of God. The greater stops between the basic terms (the world, the waters, temple entry) are clear; as are also the rests within each of the paired terms when the thought repeats, echoes, or doubles back upon itself in parallel development. Thus the primary elements in Hebrew prosody are the half lines that fall into parallel and that, taken together in pairs (or sometimes in threes), create a single thought or image.

One of the perplexities of Hebrew poetry is that the nomenclature for parallelism is poorly developed. Lowth did not employ a scientific terminology to accompany his sharp insight, and the terms since applied have been unsystematized. Critics have created and borrowed phraseology at random, moved mainly by personal preference. Without some recognition of this diverse terminology, it is impossible to understand the most elementary analysis of poetic forms.

The basic unit of poetic composition is the line, which constitutes normally one half (sometimes one third) of the parallelism. It expresses a complete thought and has grammatical and syntactic unity. This unit (represented by each of the lines in Ps. 24:1-3 as printed above) is variously known as the line, stich or stichos (στίχος, "row, line"), hemistich (ἡμιστίχος, "half line"), colon (κῶλον, "part, member"), or verse member. Two (or three) of these elements together form the larger thought-units by which the poem is articulated. The larger unit (represented by each two lines of Ps. 24:1-3) is known as the distich or tristich (two or three stichs), stich (when the half-line components are called hemistichs), bicola or tricola (two or three colons), and verse (Latin *versus*, "line, row"; composed of two or more verse members).

Herein the basic unit will be called "stich" and the larger verse groupings "distich" and "tristich." Of the Greek terms, "stich" has been more often used in prosody than "colon," and it avoids any confusion with the English punctuation mark called "colon." Lowth's verse and verse member have the weakness of possible confusion with the Masoretic verse punctuation and the later verse divisions introduced into Christian Bibles (*see* TEXT, OT). Often the original poetic, the Masoretic, and the English versional versification are identical, but in many instances they are not.

a. Synonymous. Synonymous parallelism states the same thought in successive stichs. This is the simplest and most easily recognized type of parallelism. The three distichs cited from Ps. 24 are all synonymous. The second stich repeats the idea without significant addition or subtraction. The practical consequences for the biblical exegete are considerable. In the first parallelism of Ps. 24, e.g., "earth" and "world" are not two aspects of creation, but two ways of designating the totality of creation. The repetition is entirely aesthetic, sustaining and prolonging the effect by recasting the notion in other words. Likewise, "rivers" and "seas" refer to the same subterranean watery deep on which the Hebrew conceived the dry land to be established, and the "hill of the LORD" is "his holy place," the temple at Zion.

This feature is readily enough grasped, but it is all too quickly lost sight of, especially in passages where the thought or poetic structure is obscure. The citation of Zech. 9:9 in Matt. 21:5 is a well-known example of the strange interpretation that may result from missing the parallel form:

Tell the daughter of Zion,
Behold, your king is coming to you,
humble, and mounted on an ass,
and on a colt, the foal of an ass.

The gospel writer assumes that Jesus called for two asses to carry him into the city, whereas the other three evangelists rightly treat the statement as synonymous parallelism and report only one beast of burden.

Sometimes the synonymous parallelism is complete —i.e., each term in the first stich is matched by a term in the second. To assess properly the completeness of a parallel, the original language must be taken into account, since the English translation must often use more than one word for a Hebrew term. In the following analyses, all English words representing a single Hebrew term are linked by hyphens.

The-forgiver of-all-our-iniquities /
The-healer of-all-our-diseases //
Not-forever does-he-contend /
And-not-perpetually is-he-angry //
Not according-to-our-sins does-he-deal with-us /
And-not according-to-our-iniquities does-he-reward us. //
(Ps. 103:3, 9-10 orig. tr.)

The pattern of complete synonymous parallelism in the first two distichs is:

a . b
a′ . b′

and of the third distich:

a . b . c . d
a′ . b′ . c′ . d′

A majority of synonymous parallelisms, however, are not strictly complete. This is mainly due to a preference for variation, a delight in the manifold possibilities of inverted word order, of contraction or expansion of parallel terms. In some cases poor textual preservation has disrupted originally complete parallelisms, but the instances that can be verified are not numerous, compared with the deliberately contrived variants. Though difficult to classify, the incomplete parallelism supplies Hebrew poetry with a fluency and attractiveness unrivaled by the generally stereotyped repetitions of ancient Near Eastern poetry.

When parallelism is incomplete, it may be either with or without compensation. The latter is illustrated first (bracketed words are supplied for fluency):

Wicked [is] the-heart above-all /
And-corrupt [is] it //
I the-LORD try the-heart /
test the-reins //
(Jer. 17:9-10*a*).

These two prophetic distichs may be conceived schematically as:

a . b . c
a′ . b′

a . b . c . d
c′ . d′

The second stich balances only two terms in the first ("and corrupt" parallels "wicked"; "it" parallels "the heart"), but there is no counterpart to "above all," so that the parallel is synonymous (saying the same thing) but incomplete (not all terms paralleled) and without compensation (lacking any expansion of the terms that are paralleled).

The next line in the Jeremiah passage illustrates incomplete parallelism with compensation:

And-to-give to-a-man according-to-his-way /
according-to-the-fruit of-his-deed //
(Jer. 17:10*b*)

which we may represent as:

a . b . c
c′2

The parallel is incomplete, since "and to give" and "to a man" have no equivalent in the second stich. Compensation is provided, however, by paralleling the one term "according to his way" with two terms in the second stich. The paralleled term is expanded into two terms, prolonging and emphasizing a single idea from the first stich, although the other elements are implicitly carried over into the thought of the corresponding stich.

Often the compensation fills out the second stich so that it has exactly the same number of terms as the first stich.

He-made-known his-ways to-Moses /
to-the-sons of-Israel his-deeds //
(Ps. 103:7)

is understandable as:

a . b . c
c′2 . b′

Compassionate and-gracious is-Yahweh /
Slow to-anger and-abundant-in-mercy //
(vs. 8)

may be sketched as:

a . b . c
a′2 . b′

b. Antithetic. Antithetic parallelism balances the stichs through opposition or contrast of thought. This may simply mean that the second stich recapitulates the thought of the first in negative form:

In a multitude of people is the glory of a king, /
but without people a prince is ruined //
(Prov. 14:28).

More often, however, the antithetic parallel presents a thought in stark and total opposition to that of the opening stich:

For the LORD knows the way of the righteous, /
but the way of the wicked will perish //
(Ps. 1:6).

Wisdom literature, with its stress on the two courses of action open to men, offers many instances of antithetic parallelism:

The poor is disliked even by his neighbor, /
but the rich has many friends //
(Prov. 14:20).

The glory of young men is their strength, /
but the beauty of old men is their gray hair //
(Prov. 20:29).

Like synonymous parallelism, antithetic may be complete or incomplete, with or without compensation.

c. Synthetic or formal. Synthetic parallelism balances stichs in which the second element advances the thought of the first. It has been objected that this can hardly be called parallelism, since the two stichs are parallel only in the sense that a continuous straight line is parallel with its beginning. The justification for regarding this type as a true parallelism is the fact that the two stichs tend to be quantitatively balanced and marked off by sharp breaks in thought and syntax from the distichs before and after. Even where a whole series of synthetic parallelisms occur, the distich pattern is clearly traceable. Although the poet ceases to repeat or contrast his thoughts and, instead, extends or enlarges them, he operates with a pattern of greater and lesser caesuras at recurrent intervals. Parallelism of form exists even though parallelism of thought is not strictly found between stichs. Some scholars have preferred to call this type of parallelism formal or numerical. As long as it is not confused with a fixed metric scheme, it might also be called rhythmical parallelism, since it arranges its periods in rhythm with the stricter synonymous and antithetic parallelisms.

Ps. 14 illustrates the intermixing of synthetic and synonymous parallelisms:

The fool says in his heart, /
"There is no God." //
They are corrupt, they do abominable deeds, /
there is none that does good. //
The LORD looks down from heaven /
upon the children of men, //
to see if there are any that act wisely, /
that seek after God // (vss. 1-2).

The first and third distichs neither repeat nor contrast thought in their component stichs. Instead, the second stich extends or completes the thought in a fashion that could not be guessed from the initial half line. We do not know from the first stich, e.g., what it is that the fool says inwardly, and so the synthetic parallel gives us the content of his musing: "There is no God." Again, Yahweh looks down from his abode, but we do not know the object of his scrutiny until the synthetic parallel advises us that it is mankind. By contrast, the second and fourth distichs fall into the category of synonymous parallelism, since in each case the second stich only embroiders the basic thought, already complete in the first stich.

By placing synthetic parallelisms at strategic points the poet is able to achieve striking effects, as in the coronation psalm of the Israelite king:

Why do the nations conspire, /
  and the peoples plot in vain? //
The kings of the earth set themselves, /
  and the rulers take counsel together, /
  against the LORD and his anointed, saying, //
"Let us burst their bonds asunder, /
  and cast their cords from us." //
He who sits in the heavens laughs; /
  the LORD has them in derision. //
Then he will speak to them in his wrath, /
  and terrify them in his fury, saying, //
"I have set my king /
  on Zion, my holy hill" // (Ps. 2:1-6).

The psalm makes two points: the intense heathen opposition to the king and his firm establishment by Yahweh's decree. Each of these is underscored by a synthetic parallelism that retards the balanced flow of the poem while it adheres to the formal requirement of parallelism. The second parallelism of the poem (which is also a tristich), synthetic in form, stresses the hostility of the nations "against Yahweh and against his anointed." The last parallelism in the quoted excerpt counters the threats of the enemies with the coronation proclamation of Yahweh, also cast in synthetic form:

I have set my king /
  on Zion, my holy hill.

No small part of the effect of the poem results from the momentary imbalance in shifting from simple reduplication of thought to its extension.

d. Miscellaneous. Additional types of parallelism have been classified. They do not rank with the fundamental patterns of synonymous, antithetic, and synthetic; they are more nearly variants or combinations of the basic types.

Emblematic parallelism employs simile or metaphor:

For as the heavens are high above the earth, /
  so great is his steadfast love toward
    those who fear him; //
as far as the east is from the west, /
  so far does he remove our transgressions
    from us. //
As a father pities his children, /
  so the LORD pities those who fear him //
(Ps. 103:11-13).

Like the partridge that gathers a brood which
    she did not hatch, /
  so is he who gets riches but not by right //
(Jer. 17:11*a*).

Stairlike parallelism is the repetition and advance of thought in successive stichs, often involving three or more stichs. It is a combination of synonymous and synthetic parallelism, in which the thought appears to climb or ascend by recapitulation and extension. Each stich starts from the same point but moves beyond the preceding:

Ascribe to the LORD, O heavenly beings, /
  ascribe to the LORD glory and strength. //
Ascribe to the LORD the glory of his name; /
  worship the LORD in holy array //
(Ps. 29:1-2).

O LORD, how many are my foes! /
  Many are rising against me; //
many are saying of me, /
  there is no help for him in God //
(Ps. 3:1-2).

Inverted or chiastic parallelism involves the inversion of words or terms in successive stichs:

Ephraim shall not be jealous of Judah, /
  and Judah shall not harass Ephraim //
(Isa. 11:13*b*).

The way of peace they know not, /
  and there is no justice in their paths //
(Isa. 59:8*a*).

It is evident that this form is actually synonymous parallelism, and generally complete.

2. External. The possibilities of parallelism are greatly multiplied by correspondence between distichs (external parallelism), which supplements the correspondence between stichs (internal parallelism). In the following, two internal synthetic parallelisms also form an external synonymous parallelism:

Hear the word of the LORD, /
  you rulers of Sodom! //
Give ear to the teaching of our God, /
  you people of Gomorrah! //
(Isa. 1:10).

Two internal synonymous parallelisms may form an external antithetic parallelism:

The ox knows its owner, /
  and the ass its master's crib; //
but Israel does not know, /
  my people does not understand //
(Isa. 1:3).

Two internal synonymous parallelisms may produce an external inverted parallelism. In fact, there are more cases of external inversion than of internal.

Make the *heart* of this people fat, /
  and their *ears* heavy, /
  and shut their *eyes;* //
lest they see with their *eyes,* /
  and hear with their *ears,* /
and understand with their *hearts,* //
  and turn and be healed
(Isa. 6:10).

The concluding stich is illustrative of an occasional independent stich (called a monostich by some), which is outside the poetic pattern in emphatic anacrusis.

As employed by the poets of ancient Israel, the possibilities of parallelism are virtually unlimited. It offers an elasticity that evokes endless aesthetic delight, while it avoids complexity and diffuseness through adherence to the principle of balanced stichs. We can be sure that no enjambment or "run-on" lines, typical of Western poetry, will occur in Hebrew poetry. But within the structure of self-sufficient stichs, coupled or tripled, the combinations and varieties are numerous. Few readers of Hebrew poetry will wish or need to analyze the parallelisms of every poem encountered. But the ability to pause occasionally and spell out the precise parallelistic pattern, and to test the theories against complex passages, serves to heighten the sense of enjoyment of form and content. Faithful study of even a limited number of parallelisms will vastly enhance that sixth sense by which the compression and amplification of poetic thought is grasped almost intuitively.

D. *METER.* While parallelism is a genuine and compelling feature of Hebrew poetry, meter is detectable mainly by analogy with other poetry and by implication from the balanced lines. As a result, certain stress patterns can be formulated on the assumption that a stress should be granted to each of the major words in a distich (or tristich). But the metric hypotheses rest upon a combination of inference from parallelism and application of the Masoretic accents, rather than on any intrinsic evidence from biblical Hebrew.

In the Masoretic accentual system, each word, no matter what its length, receives one stress (except for proclitics joined to following words by the "binder" or *maqqēph*). Since, in the average Hebrew word, the accent is on the last syllable, the "meter" tends to be a rising one. Ordinarily a word possesses two or three syllables, and this produces a pattern analogous to the classical iambic foot (a short unstressed and a long stressed syllable) and the anapaestic foot (two shorts unstressed and a long stressed syllable).

The classical analogies are entirely misleading, however, because in Hebrew the number of unstressed syllables allowable between stresses is variable. It appears that between two stressed syllables an unstressed syllable is not absolutely necessary (e.g., in successively accented monosyllables) and that there can be as many as four or five unstressed syllables (about the maximum length of a Hebrew word). It is a matter of debate whether longer words require or permit a second stress. It is also problematic whether on occasion two short terms may receive a single stress, while terms joined by the "binder" may be permitted separate stresses. Where such accentual flexibility existed—or is suspect of existing—the application of rigid classical meters only obscures the true poetry with an imposed and artificial orderliness.

The most common pattern is a six-stress distich which, taking into account the caesura between stichs, is represented as a 3+3 meter. It is the predominant meter in Deutero-Isaiah, Job, and Proverbs. Its parallelisms are largely synonymous and antithetic, with many complete parallelisms. Occasionally the sense requires that a six-stress line be read as a tristich, and thus a 2+2+2 pattern emerges. Less frequent, but not always to be emended as errors, are instances of 4+4 and 2+2, which appear usually as variants of 3 + 3 and 3 + 2 patterns.

Of the unequal or balancing meters, 3+2 is most widespread. It has been dubbed the Qinah or lament meter because it is dominant in Lamentations (*see* LAMENTATIONS, BOOK OF) and in many of the laments appearing in the Psalms and the Prophets. It is doubtless a product of intense emotion, with the second stich breaking short, like a catch in the throat. Yet it cannot be insisted that the emotion was always grief, since the 3+2 rhythm is dominant in some compositions expressing praise and joy (e.g., Ps. 65). A common variant of 3+2 is 2+2, and there are some lines that can be scanned only as 2+3.

While there are poems and strophes within poems where the fundamental meter of 3+3 or 3+2 is undisturbed, a majority of Hebrew poems have lines of mixed metric length. In many cases the meters are so hybrid that it is impossible to locate the fundamental pattern. With the help of the versions some lines may be restored to a more consistent metric pattern. In other cases we can be fairly certain of disorder but cannot restore the original with any sense of confidence. But a large number of these metrically hybrid poems must be accepted as normal Hebrew poetic practice.

All that we know of ancient Near Eastern poetry supports the principle of metrical fluidity. Babylonian poetry has a prevailing 2+2 meter, but is interspersed with lines that can be read only as threes, often to be scanned as 2+2+3. Sometimes a six-stress line seems to require 2+2+2. The ancient Canaanite literature from UGARIT reveals a frequent 3+3 pattern, but there are innumerable variations. Especially noticeable is the tristich, in 3+3+3 or 2+2+2 schemes. In view of its frequency at Ugarit, it cannot be denied that Hebrew poets purposely used tristichs (*see* § C1 *above*). These Canaanite discoveries in particular, dating from the fourteenth century B.C. and in a tongue dialectically related to biblical Hebrew, argue strongly the futility of seeking metrical exactness in the poetry of the OT. Emendation of the text for metrical reasons and without syntactic or versional support, is a dubious practice. Yet there is consistency in Hebrew poetry to the extent that parallel stichs seldom range beyond a variation of one stress in length; thus, e.g., 4+2 or 2+4 rhythms are distinct rarities.

Meter, insofar as it exists in Hebrew poetry, is actually the rhythmical counterpart of parallelism of thought. Rhythm is not due to syllabic quantities but to the less definable instinct of balancing parts whose exact accentual values are not measurable and probably never were. Ordinarily the conceptual or semantic parallelism is matched by numerical or structural parallelism. The stichs tend to be nearly the same length, but this similar fulness of line is not a metric phenomenon any more than balanced masses in painting are metrical. Both parallelism and meter obey an impulse to regular repetition, but in Hebrew poetry regularity of stress is subordinated to regularity of balanced ideas. Thus the tendency to fill out lines with incomplete parallelisms by means of compensation (*see* § C1*a above*) is not metrical (i.e., the necessity of having two three-stress stichs) but rather is due to the desire to oppose word-masses of about the same weight while varying and emphasizing the thought. The concept is closer to a spatial concern with "mass" than to a temporal concern with "stress."

Nevertheless, however Hebrew verse is analyzed, it is impossible to dismiss the persistence of the caesura or stop, both in its sharper form at the end of lines and in its feebler form within lines. The groupings that result from these breaks are essentially thought-units and the word-masses balance, not because of prior metric convictions, but because the poetic thought pulsates in a series of advancing, recapitulating, and contrasting movements. Meter may be reduced to nothing more than a tallying of accents provided by the Masoretes. Parallelism of thought, and corresponding word-mass, is the substance and mode of Hebrew poetic expression.

E. *TECHNIQUES.* Only occasionally does rhyme or near-rhyme appear in Hebrew—e.g., where the same pronominal suffix sound appears at the end of two or more stichs, as in Isa. 41:11-13. Yet the Hebrew tongue has such forcefulness of sound and image that the absence of rhyme is not felt as a loss (*see* HEBREW LANGUAGE). The Hebrew poet had a keen ear for the texture of words and knew how to marshal them to brilliant effect. As a result, the pleasantries and marvels that he contrives with words appear with greater profusion and surprise than if they were confined to the regularity of rhyme.

1. Alliteration. Alliteration is the consonance of sounds at the beginning of words or syllables. The English rendering:

> Pray for the peace of Jerusalem!
> "May they prosper who love you!"

is totally inadequate to express the ringing cadence of the fourfold occurrence of the *sh* and *l* sounds in Ps. 122:6: *shaalû shelôm yerûshālāyim yishlāyû.* Nor does the English of Isa. 1:18-20 do justice to the sixfold *k* (once *ḥ*) and the threefold sibilants in vs. 18, as well as the fivefold *t* (once *ṭ*) in vss. 19-20:

> *'im-yihyû ḥaṭā'êkhem kashshānîm kashshélegh yalbî́nû*
> *'im-ya'dhî́mû khathôlā' kaṣṣémer yihyû*
> *'im-tō'bhû ûshema'tem ṭûbh hā'ấreṣ tō'khḗlû*
> *we'im-temā' anû ûmerîthem.*

2. Assonance. Assonance, the correspondence of sounds in the accented vowels, is especially prominent where pronominal suffixes and verbs recur. In the Isaiah passage (*see* § E1 *above*), the accented *î* (ē) and *e* (ĕ) in vs. 18 (each three times) and *û* (ū) in vss. 19-20 (also three times) reinforce the alliteration. The climactic Servant Song of Isa. 52:13–53:12 draws an impressive contrast between the innocent sufferer and the guilty confessors, a contrast strengthened by the "ōō" sound in the pronominal forms *hû'* for "he" and *nû* for "we." In 53:4-7 the "ōō" sound, with its emission of grief and awe, occurs fifteen times. In the mocking song over the fall of Tyre, Ezekiel describes the fate of the mercantile city as that of a gaily embarked trading vessel that sinks in the deep. The twelvefold repetition of the long *ê* sound (ā) in the accented syllable exhibits disdain and menace (Ezek. 27:27).

3. Paronomasia. Hebrew poets had a penchant for wordplay. The prophets were especially gifted at concentrating a whole message in a single memorable association of terms. Amos beheld a *qâyiṣ* (basket of summer fruit) and was at once reminded that "the *qēṣ* (end) has come upon [the] people Israel" (8:2). Isaiah crowned his Song of the Lord's Vineyard with this mighty summation:

> For the vineyard of the LORD of hosts
> is the house of Israel,
> and the men of Judah
> are his pleasant planting;
> and he looked for justice [*mishpāṭ*],
> but behold, bloodshed [*mishpāḥ*];
> for righteousness [*ṣedhāqâ*],
> but behold, a cry [*ṣe'āqâ*]!
> (Isa. 5:7).

4. Onomatopoeia. Hebrew is rich in words that sound like what they describe, inasmuch as the language is directly denotative of objects and actions. The Hebrews did not mime reality in drama or in art; but they mimed it exquisitely and movingly with lyric poetry. In Ps. 93:4 we can hear in the alliteration of the *m* sound the swelling fullness of the sea, and in the repeated *r* sound the raging of its waves. In *middaharôth daharôth* we hear the "galloping, galloping" of Sisera's battle horses beside the River Kishon (Judg. 5:22). In the guttural and *p* sounds of Isa. 42:14 we catch the gasping and sighing of a woman in birth pangs. Thus a rich plasticity of sound joins with the flexibility of parallelism to assault the reader's eye and ear with sharp impressions and unexpected sensations. The language is wholly alive, so that an abstract-appearing poem is in actuality vibrating with delectability of sound and impact of image.

F. *STROPHE.* The grouping of distichs (or tristichs) into larger units is not demonstrable in most Hebrew poetry. ACROSTIC poetry shows that such arrangement is possible (e.g., Lam. 1; 2; 4 are composed of two-distich strophes or tetrastichs; ch. 3 of three-distich strophes or hexastichs; and Ps. 119 of eight-distich strophes). Yet in most acrostics the true sequence of thought ignores the formal strophic divisions.

Sometimes a refrain appears at reasonably regular intervals. Pss. 42–43 actually form a single composition. The refrain:

> Why are you cast down, O my soul,
> and why are you disquieted within me?
> Hope in God; for I shall again praise him,
> my help and my God,

is employed three times (42:5, 11; 43:5), twice preceded by nine distichs (except for a tristich in 42:8) and once by eight distichs. In Ps. 46 the refrain:

> The LORD of hosts is with us;
> the God of Jacob is our refuge,

appears twice with the cryptic "Selah" (vss. 7, 11). Although "Selah" has sometimes been explained as a strophe divider, its distribution in the Psalms and Hab. 3 will hardly bear this interpretation in more than a small percentage of cases (*see* PSALMS, BOOK OF). The same refrain seems to have dropped out after Ps. 46:3, although "Selah" has remained. The result would be three strophes of about equal length.

A more elaborate refrain appears in Ps. 107:1-32:

> Then they cried to the LORD in their trouble,
> and he delivered them from their distress;
> . . . .
> Let them thank the LORD for his steadfast love,
> for his wonderful works to the sons of men!

into which is inserted a variable description of the nature of his deliverance (from desert wandering, vs. 7; from prison, vs. 14; from sickness, vs. 20; from storm at sea, vss. 29-30). In spite of the intricacy of the refrain, the resulting strophes are exceedingly uneven in length.

In the absence of acrostic or refrain, the symmetrical articulation of the thought sometimes argues strongly for strophic division. Isaiah's Song of the Vineyard (ch. 5) falls naturally into four subdivisions: the beloved's care of his vineyard (vss. 1-2), the rhetorical appeal for judgment between the owner and his vineyard (vss. 3-4), the announcement of the vineyard's destruction (vss. 5-6), and the clinching of the parable through its application to Israel (vss. 7-8). Each subdivision is four distichs in extent, except for the third, which has four distichs and one tristich.

It is often tempting to assume that glosses or dislocations have disturbed a regular strophic order. In Job's final protest to God, the recurrent oath of clearance ("If . . ." in Job 31) supplies a clue to strophic reconstruction, but no regularity is attainable without drastic rearrangement. The attempts of scholars to delete, introduce, and rearrange lines and strophes in the interests of regularity must be judged individually, but wholesale emendation and reshuffling of the text not only have little evidence to go on but also are contradicted by the Ugaritic poetry, with its analogous freedom of form.

G. *GENRE AND SITUATION IN LIFE.* 1. Poetic fragments. Poetry found early expression in ancient Israel. Embedded in the Pentateuch are poetic vignettes that derive from life before the Conquest. The Song of Lamech bespeaks the nomadic vendetta, uncontrolled by the law of equal retaliation:

> Adah and Zillah, hear my cry!
> Wives of Lamech, give ear to my saying.
> For I kill a man because of my wound,
> And a boy because of my injury.
> For Cain has avenged himself sevenfold,
> but Lamech seventy times seven
> (Gen. 4:23-24 orig. tr.).

The Song of Miriam is widely accepted as the authentic response of those who participated in the Exodus:

> Sing to Yahweh, for he is greatly uplifted;
> the horse and its rider he has thrown into the sea
> (Exod. 15:20-21 orig. tr.).

The Song of the Ark consists of two shouts, one to accompany the setting forth of the ark in battle:

> Arise, O Yahweh,
> and may thy enemies be scattered
> and may thy despisers flee before thee!
> (Num. 10:35 orig. tr.).

The other is recited at the ark's return to the camp:

> Return, O Yahweh,
> to the innumerable families of Israel!
> (Num. 10:36 orig. tr.).

The Song of the Well is a ritual accompaniment to the opening of a well, although it may subsequently have been used by drawers of water:

> Spring forth, O well! Sing to it!
> the well dug by princes,
> opened up by the nobility of the people
> with a rod and with staves
> (Num. 21:17-18 orig. tr.).

The curse on Amalek may reflect bitter struggle between two wandering tribes; however, its structure is not unambiguously poetic (Exod. 17:16). Other poetic snatches in the Pentateuch—e.g., Melchizedek's blessing on Abraham (Gen. 14:19-20) and the blessing of Rebekah's brothers (Gen. 24:60)—are doubtless premonarchic. Only the Aaronic benediction (Num. 6:24-26) is probably later than the Monarchy.

2. Anthologies. Two books are referred to by name as the source of certain of the early poems: the Book of the Wars of Yahweh (Num. 21:14; *see* WARS OF THE LORD, BOOK OF) and the Book of Jashar (Josh. 10:13; II Sam. 1:17-27; *see* JASHAR, BOOK OF). Neither collection is now extant, but, since the Book of Jashar included Joshua's charge to the sun and moon (Josh. 10:13) and David's lament over Saul and Jonathan (II Sam. 1:18), it was compiled no earlier than the United Monarchy. It is likely that others of the poems of the Pentateuch and historical books were inserted from the same or similar anthologies. If, as the title implies, the Book of the Wars of Yahweh recited the victories of Israel's God, then the curse of Heshbon (Num. 21:27-30) and the Song of Deborah (Judg. 5) would be natural entries, possibly also the blessing of Jacob (Gen. 49), the oracles of Balaam (Num. 22–24), and the blessing of Moses (Deut. 33). At any rate, there is often a variance between these short poems and their narrative settings. Sometimes the line of poetry seems no more than a fragment, torn out of one context and adapted to another.

3. Recurring and nonrecurring types. Our impression of this early poetry is that it was not the free composition of individuals, a type of belles-lettres, but rather a communal creation. It grew out of the mores and social functions of a community moved to celebration. Back of the anthologies and their components lay the habit of public recital in memory of great events and in observance of recurrent communal experiences. In birth, marriage, and death; in work and merriment; in war and worship; certain forms (*Gattungen*) of poetic expression developed as accompaniments of social activity. The forms seem to have been shaped in settings that would constantly recur. The introduction of specific names and places (e.g., Adah, Zillah, Cain, and Lamech in Gen. 4:23-24) would follow long after the poetic types were in general use (in the case of Lamech's cry, the basic form is a call for blood revenge). The patriarchal and priestly blessings, rich with the Hebraic sense of family continuity and the power of the divine word, were probably liturgical utterances employed far beyond the setting in which they are placed in the OT (Gen. 14:19-20; 27:27-29; 48:15-16; Num. 6:24-26). *See* BLESSINGS AND CURSINGS.

Other compositions are patently connected with singular and unforgettable events. The victory ode of Deborah and Barak over the Canaanites (Judg. 5) and the lament of David over Saul and Jonathan (II Sam. 1:19-27) could not easily be used to celebrate other victories or lament other deaths. The Song of

Deborah nevertheless owes much of its form to ancient Near Eastern victory odes (*see* NAHUM), and David's lament is inextricably bound up with the form of the funeral dirge.

In general the poetry of the OT may be divided into compositions related to continuous communal functions and those shaped for special artistic or historical purposes. The former are virtually undatable, except as they betray conditions of the desert, conquest, monarchy, exile, or restoration. Most of the psalms belong to the former group. The compositions with special purposes offer greater hope of dating, but in many instances, as in the magnificent poetry of Job, the intention was artistic and religious rather than historical, so that no clear dating criteria survive.

The distinction in principle between the general and the concrete, the communal and the individually creative, is not easily applied in practice. But to recognize the strong impress of religio-social patterns upon Hebrew poetry is to have made long strides toward appreciating its concrete power, its adherence to types, and its frequent lack of historical allusion. FORM CRITICISM attempts to classify the types of Hebrew poetry and to describe the settings or life situations in which they developed. We need always to remember that the inherited types, sprung from a deeply rooted communal tradition, controlled even the greatest poets of Israel far more than in classical or European literature.

4. Secular types. The forms of OT poetry are by and large "sacred"—i.e., they are related to religious celebration and involve the God of Israel. But often they have to do with common functions not restricted to formal religious worship, such as war (Josh. 10:12-13; Judg. 5), blood revenge (Gen. 4:23-24), mocking of an enemy (Num. 21:27-30), work (Num. 21:17-18), marriage (Gen. 24:60), and death (II Sam. 1:17-27). In most cases these songs were not repeated in temple worship, and the name of Yahweh is not often included (the chief exception is the Song of Deborah, Judg. 5), but this fact does not remove them totally from the religious sphere. That the interpenetration of secular and sacred was always typical of Israel may be seen in the way prophetic poetry is cast in forms of secular origin: harvest song (Isa. 5:1-7), mocking or taunt song (Isa. 14:1-27; 47), funeral lament (Jer. 9:17-22; Amos 5:2), victory ode (Isa. 63:1-6; Nahum), and litigation (Isa. 45:20-21; Mic. 1:1-7).

5. Sacred types. The poems reserved for formal worship are mainly of the recurring type (*see* § G3 *above*). They are studiously free of proper names, and were preserved in the Psalter because they could be used repeatedly. They should not be understood, however, simply as a collection of hymns for temple singing. There is no evidence that bodies of worshipers sang together. There were choirs and soloists who chanted or sang. Thus many of the psalms are best understood as incidental music, accompanying some act, such as the coronation of the king or sacrifice. Still other psalms seem detached from any cultic act, and are merely imitative of the fixed forms. It is difficult to trace a clear history of the evolution of forms, since psalms composed for the cult passed into general devotional usage and vice versa. Nevertheless, significant strides have been made in isolating some of the primary forms and their communal setting. For fuller exposition of the categories and examples, *see* PSALMS, BOOK OF.

a. Hymn. The hymn is cast in direct address to deity and extols his attributes and works (*see* HYMNS). Generally the hymn seeks no end other than praise and adoration. The hymn form was probably an outgrowth of public FEASTS such as PASSOVER; WEEKS; and TABERNACLES. A special subdivision is the Song of Zion, extolling the beauty and joy of temple worship and probably used as a pilgrim song.

b. Lament and confession. The lament is occasioned by a threat to the worshiper (individual) or the community (collective). For the individual, sickness and unjust accusation, even ostracism, are frequent complaints, and for the community, famine, military defeat, and exile. The plight of the lamenter is catalogued, often in gruesome detail, and God is entreated to speedy action. Frequently the lament closes with an affirmation of confidence that God will hear, and the delivery from crisis is sometimes described in advance. In general these compositions would be used without reference to the religious calendar, whenever catastrophe struck. Certain festivals, however, such as the celebration of the fall of Jerusalem in 586 B.C., encouraged periodic recitation of communal laments. Some laments decry the sin of the suppliant and are virtually confessions or penitential psalms asking only for forgiveness and new life before God (e.g., Pss. 51; 130; *see* CONFESSION).

c. Thanksgiving and trust song. The THANKSGIVING song stands beyond the disaster which provoked the lament. It presupposes salvation from the threat of individual or social annihilation. It is frequently close to the hymn type, but is more precise in its praise, usually naming the original threat and always focusing upon the memory of specific deliverance. The trust song is not related to immediate crisis. It expresses rather the deep confidence of the psalmist in the presence and power of God. The trust song has the same meditative and spiritual quality as the confession.

d. Royal psalm. The royal psalm is more problematic than the other types. It presumably has for its function a ceremony in which the king was participant. Preparation for war (Ps. 20), celebration after victory (Ps. 21), marriage (Ps. 45), and coronation (Pss. 2; 110) are among the occasions presupposed. It is a matter of debate how widely and in what sense this category should be conceived. Was the installation of the Israelite king anything more than a "secular" appointment? Particularly, are the many psalms in which Yahweh is regarded as king to be assigned as royal psalms? Was there a pre-exilic ceremony in which the Israelite king represented Yahweh, either at his coronation or in an annual New Year's festival? (*See* KING; TABERNACLES, FEAST OF.) Interpreters divide sharply. Some regard Yahweh's kingship as a part of the pre-exilic monarchic pattern which was sacrally supported. Others insist that Yahweh's kingship is a postexilic metaphorical usage, developed to express divine sovereignty over the nations after the kingship ceased. It is hardly to be denied, however, that there are some psalms in which the pre-exilic king was protagonist.

The older view that they were used by Maccabean priest-kings (*see* MACCABEES) need not be ruled out, for pre-exilic royal psalms would have been readily revived by the Maccabees, who certainly regarded themselves as the heirs of the old political order of Israel.

6. Prophetic poetry. The prophetic poetry had its roots in the forms of oracular utterance delivered at shrines. In their roles as interpreters of the divine will, priest and prophet were essentially identical in origin (*see* PRIESTS AND LEVITES; PROPHET). Their utterances were brief and simple, in the form of blessings upon the faithful and curses upon the faithless, or in oracular declarations on some specific request. The overriding force of the utterance is its divine sanction. Although the great prophets renounced mechanistic utterance and the severance of word and life, the modes of their speech continued under the formative priestly influence. Both adhered to the binding power of the divine word. The single sanctuary ministry proliferated into the separate work of priest as custodian of a body of law and ritual, and of prophet as the roving conscience of Israel and mouthpiece of God. A third authority appeared in the sage, who was tribal elder or counselor of kings, later scribe and schoolmaster.

What distinguishes the prophetic poetry from priestly and wisdom poetry is its formulation toward specific situations. The prophetic "life situation" was the moment of social, political, and religious crisis when men must decide the destinies of people and nations. Thus the old sanctuary forms take on the character of reproach and admonition. They are charged with fresh urgency and ultimacy. Moreover, the secular forms (*see* § G4 *above*) are appropriated and merged with older priestly modes of speech. The specific situations to which the prophetic poetry speaks are as manifold as the circumstances in which men must choose or reject God's will. Thus, in basic form and technique, prophetic poetry is not markedly distinguishable from other biblical poetry, just as prophetic faith shares with priest and wise man the common belief in the will and purpose of Israel's God as a binding reality by which all of life was to be shaped.

7. Emancipation from types. A later tendency in Israel was the composition of extended poetic works, of which the prophecy of Isa. 40–55 and the book of Job represent the pinnacle of attainment. Characteristic of both poets is the free use of many previously separate forms, secular and sacred. The forms tend to break down and merge in a larger continuity. Isa. 40–55 celebrates the new act of redemption from exile and the salvation of the nations. Job sounds the depths of divine and human righteousness, their harmony and disproportion. Largeness of theme demanded corresponding vastness of literary conception. Deutero-Isaiah makes particular use of the hymn, lament, taunt song, and litigation. The poet of Job is a master with lament, as also of the hymn style, which he expands gloriously in the rhetorical flood of the whirlwind speeches (Job 38–41).

A general thesis about the types of Hebrew poetry can now be formulated: the earliest types were simple (directed to one situation or event) and brief. The mixing of types and a tendency toward greater length began during the Conquest, accelerated under the Monarchy, but reached its climax during and after the Exile. The profoundly stirring events of the nation's fall seem to have spurred poets to a freer and more spacious use of forms, resulting in a style which in Job and Isa. 40–55 approaches epic grandeur. There was a tendency to break down and fuse secular and sacred forms, since all the orders of life came under Yahweh's aegis. In Israel there persisted, nevertheless, a tension between poetry as the instrument of communal feeling and as a contrivance for specific proclamation. Yet it remains problematic, especially in the Psalms, whether specific poems were written by temple personnel for recurrent recital or whether they came out of more private experience that imitated the existing forms and were in turn sometimes used in the cult.

It is clear that the forms were so settled in usage that they largely determined Hebrew poetry in its style. The Hebrews never won the literary independence from Canaan that would have paralleled their astounding religious independence. While the prophets passed far beyond the mass religious response of the Israelite people and summoned them to new heights as the people of Yahweh, they were satisfied to employ the popular and cultic modes of expression. It is the content and not the form that gives prophetic and psalm poetry its power to transcend the historical setting of ancient Israel.

Bibliography. General: T. H. Robinson, *The Poetry of the OT* (1947); "Hebrew Poetic Form: The English Tradition," *Supplements to VT,* I (1953), 128-49.

On early poetry: G. A. Smith, *The Early Poetry of Israel* (1910). A. Causse, *Les plus vieux chants de la Bible* (1926).

On parallelism: R. Lowth, *Lectures on the Sacred Poetry of the Hebrews* (1815); *Isaiah: A New Translation with a Preliminary Dissertation* (1848). G. B. Gray, *The Forms of Hebrew Poetry* (1915). C. F. Burney, *The Poetry of Our Lord* (1925).

On meter: K. Budde, "Das hebräische Klagelied," *ZAW,* II (1882), 1-52. E. Sievers, *Metrische Studien I-III* (1901-7). W. H. Cobb, *A Criticism of Systems of Hebrew Metre* (1905). S. Mowinckel, "Zum Problem der hebräischen Metrik," *Festchrift Alfred Bertholet* (1950), pp. 379-94.

On techniques: E. König, *Stilistik, Rhetorik, Poetik* (1900). O. S. Rankin, "Alliteration in Hebrew Poetry," *JTS,* XXXI (1930), 285-91. J. Muilenburg, "A Study in Hebrew Rhetoric: Repetition and Style," *Supplements to VT,* I (1953), 97-111.

On strophes: D. H. Müller, *Strophenbau und Responsion* (1898). A. Condamin, *Poèmes de la Bible avec une introduction sur la strophe hébraïque* (1933). C. Kraft, *The Strophic Structure of Hebrew Poetry* (1938), "Some Further Observations Concerning the Strophic Structure of Hebrew Poetry," in E. C. Hobbs, ed., *A Stubborn Faith* (1956), pp. 62-89.

On genre: S. Mowinckel, *Psalmenstudien I-IV* (1921-24). H. Gunkel and J. Begrich, *Einleitung in die Psalmen* (1933). A. Bentzen, *Introduction to the OT,* I (1953). O. Eissfeldt, *Einleitung in das AT* (rev. ed., 1956), pp. 61-137.

On Semitic poetry: D. C. Simpson, ed., *The Psalmists,* Essays I, VI, VII (1926). G. D. Young, "Ugaritic Prosody," *JNES,* IX (1950), 124-33. C. Gordon, *Ugaritic Manual* (1955), ch. 13.

N. K. GOTTWALD

POISON. The translation of several terms in the Bible. One general term is found in the OT to refer to poisonous plants: ראש or רוש. The word is most commonly used metaphorically to refer to the sin and corruption of Israel (Deut. 29:18—H 29:17; 32:32; Ps. 69:21—H 69:22; Lam. 3:5, 19 [RSV "bitterness"]; Hos. 10:4; Amos 6:12). Jeremiah (8:14; 9:15

—H 9:14; 23:15) speaks of poisonous water which Yahweh will give the people to drink; this may also be a metaphorical expression, or it may refer to the effects of a severe drought in the land (see Jer. 8:14; ch. 14). The term is also found once in reference to the poison of asps (פתנים [Job 20:16]; *see* Asp).

No other poisonous plant is referred to directly in the OT. The gourds (פקעת) of the son of the prophets which made the prophets ill (II Kings 4:38-41) were probably not poisonous but a strong purgative. *See* Gourds, Wild.

Poisonous reptiles are more frequently mentioned. The venom of various reptiles is designated by the term חמה, a word which also means "heat," "rage," "wrath." The word occurs with the meaning "poison" in Deut. 32:24, 33; Pss. 58:4—H 58:5 (RSV "venom"); 140:3—H 140:4. The poison of arrows is also referred to by the use of this word (Job 6:4; in a metaphorical sense, the arrows of God). In the LXX this word and ראש are commonly translated by θυμός.

Reptiles considered to be poisonous in the OT include the אפעה, Viper (Job 20:16; Isa. 30:6; 59:5); the נחש, snake or Serpent (a term also used to refer to the mythological dragon of the ancient world and perhaps to the crocodile; cf. Gen. 3:1-4; Num. 21:9; Deut. 8:15; Amos 5:19; 9:3; etc.); the עקרב, scorpion (Deut. 8:15; Ezek. 2:6); the עכשוב, horned viper (Ps. 140:3—H 140:4); the פתן, horned snake or asp (Deut. 32:33; Job 20:14, 16; Pss. 58:4—H 58:5; 91:13; Isa. 11:8; Ecclus. 39:30); the צפעוני, צפע, viper or adder (Prov. 23:32; Isa. 11:8; 14:29; 59:5; Jer. 8:17); the שפיפן, horned snake or possibly adder (Gen. 49:17); and the תנין, the sea dragon and also a serpent (Exod. 7:9; Deut. 32:33; Ps. 91:13).

In the NT, the term ἰός appears in Rom. 3:13 (a quotation from Ps. 140:3—H 140:4); Jas. 3:8, in each case translated "poison" (RSV "venom" in Rom. 3:13). The Greek term behind the RSV translation "poisoned their minds" in Acts 14:2 is ἐκάκωσαν (lit., "made their minds evil").

By far the majority of occurrences of "poison" in the Bible are metaphorical, referring to God's judgment of his sinful people, or of rebellious nations, or to the poisonous effects of sin and rebellion against God. The terror of poisonous reptiles, however, was widespread in the ancient world. In characteristic fashion the OT writers relate the existence and effects of poisonous substances to the action of Yahweh in their midst.

Bibliography. I. Löw, *Die Flora der Juden,* vols. I-IV (1924-34); I. Aharoni, "On Some Animals Mentioned in the Bible," *Osiris,* 5 (1938), 461-78. W. J. Harrelson

POLICE [ῥαβδοῦχος] (Acts 16:35, 38); KJV SERGEANTS. Literally, "one who carries a rod—i.e., the *fasces*—as sign of office and authority." The word is translated "policemen" in Goodspeed; "lictors" in Moffatt and generally in modern English, French, and German translations.

The police or lictors were called ῥαβδοῦχοι because they carried *fasces,* a bundle of (birch) rods tied together with a red thong, and from which protruded an axe. The rods might be used for scourging (with such rods we may suppose Paul was scourged in II Cor. 11:25), and the axe (in earlier times) for carrying out the death sentence. When not so used, the *fasces* was the constant symbol of authority. Since city magistrates were not in possession of the right of life and death over citizens, the *fasces* carried by the lictors in Philippi would not contain axes.

All principal Roman magistrates were publicly attended by lictors who carried the *fasces* before them as emblem of their criminal jurisdiction. It was the function of the lictors to execute the sentences pronounced by the magistrates. Accompanying the magistrates, the lictors were similarly garbed: while in the city, a toga; out of it or in triumphal procession, a red coat; at funerals, black dress. Preceding the magistrate, they announced his approach and secured homage.

The number of lictors in any case was determined by the rank of the official. E.g., each consul had six until *ca.* 300 B.C., and thereafter twelve. A dictator had twelve originally, and then twenty-four. Emperors had twelve until Domitian doubled the number. The city magistrate, such as at Philippi, had two. How many lictors were present in Philippi would depend on how many magistrates were there. *See* Magistrate. F. D. Gealy

POLLUTION. *See* Clean and Unclean.

POLLUX pŏl′əks. *See* Twin Brothers.

*__POLYCARP, EPISTLE OF__ pŏl′ĭ kärp. A letter addressed to the church in Philippi by Bishop Polycarp and his presbyters of the church in Smyrna, probably dating not later than the end of Trajan's reign (A.D. 117); one of the documents of the Apostolic Fathers. The letter is first attested by Irenaeus (III. 3.4), who as a young lad had been brought up in Smyrna under Polycarp's ministry.

The original Greek text of the letter is only partially preserved—chs. 1-9 in late Byzantine MSS and ch. 13 in a quotation in Euseb. Hist. III.36.13-15. The rest of the letter (chs. 10–12, part of 13, and 14) is known from an old Latin version that appears to be a trustworthy, literal translation.

The letter had two purposes. One concerned Ignatius, who had passed through Philippi on his way to martyrdom at Rome. Polycarp requested information about his fate, copies of any letters of Ignatius that the Philippian church may have had, to add to those Polycarp had already collected and appended to his letter; and he was also making arrangements, at Ignatius' request, for delegations from the churches of Asia Minor and Macedonia to visit the distraught church of Ignatius in Syria. *See* Ignatius, Epistles of.

The other matter had to do with Polycarp's pastoral advice, requested by the Philippians, about one of the Philippian presbyters, named Valens, and his wife, who had been excommunicated for some dishonesty in financial dealings. Polycarp took the occasion also to offer sharp warnings about the Docetic heresy that denied the reality of Christ's humanity, and to give a number of moralistic and pastoral admonitions customary in such interchurch communications.

The prevalent inference from this letter has been that Polycarp penned it not long after Ignatius left the Middle East and before his final fate as a martyr was sealed. According to Eusebius, Ignatius was martyred in the reign of Trajan. But an exhaustive study of Polycarp's letter by P. N. Harrison in 1936 attempted to demonstrate that only chs. 13–14 were written at so early a time. Chs. 1–12 form a later epistle, written *ca.* 135, and combat specifically the heresy of Marcion. Harrison's thesis has won a wide but by no means universal acceptance.

Apart from its inherent historical value, the Epistle of Polycarp is of particular importance for the wide range of Christian writings quoted or reflected in it. It is utterly without distinction of style, and exhibits no trace of education in Hellenistic culture. It also reveals little use of the OT—Polycarp himself modestly disclaimed any competence in the "Scriptures" (12:1). But it does show a man of constant study and meditation in Christian works; the letter is a veritable mosaic of quotation and allusion. He knew the Synoptic gospels and Acts—though the sayings of Jesus are rather freely cited, probably from memory. His acquaintance with the Pauline letters was intimate; but I Peter was his favorite, for he quotes it no fewer than fourteen times. He also shows knowledge of Hebrews, James, and I and II John; uses I Clement extensively; and even reflects from his short acquaintance with them the letters of Ignatius. Contacts with the Pastoral letters are frequent, but it is impossible to say whether Polycarp quoted them or the Pastorals used Polycarp. (H. F. von Campenhausen has posited the hypothesis that Polycarp himself composed the Pastorals.)

There is no trace of Revelation in his letter and only one possible contact with the Fourth Gospel (cf. 5:2 with John 5:21; 6:39, 44). This circumstance has been a puzzle to modern critics. For Irenaeus repeatedly affirmed, from his boyhood recollections, that Polycarp was personally associated with John, the "disciple of the Lord," and that "apostles in Asia" had appointed him bishop of Smyrna. For Irenaeus, of course, John son of Zebedee, apostle, evangelist, and seer, were all one and the same person. If Polycarp had been a personal disciple of "John" the evangelist or of "John" the seer of Patmos, his single surviving letter exhibits very scant theological influence from either "John" and no knowledge of their principal writings.

Polycarp was burned at the stake in Smyrna in February, 155 (or 156). Eusebius (Hist. IV.15), followed by a few modern critics, dated it to 167, in the reign of Marcus Aurelius. An authentic—and deeply moving—eyewitness account of his martyrdom is extant, in the form of a letter sent by the church in Smyrna to the church in Philomelium. This document is also generally included in editions of the Apostolic Fathers. At the time of his ordeal, Polycarp confessed that he had been a Christian for eighty-six years. The pre-eminent integrity of his character was admitted even by the pagans who condemned him. To his own flock, Polycarp was a saint without peer; and the anniversary of his martyrdom was annually observed as a festival, not only in Smyrna, but also in many other churches. Irenaeus has left record of the effective witness of Polycarp, during his long episcopate, to the orthodox, apostolic faith against the Marcionite and Gnostic heresies—not only in Asia, but also in Rome upon occasion of a visit there in his late years. The perspective of history has not dimmed the glow of Irenaeus' hero-worship, in accounting Polycarp the outstanding single Christian leader of his generation.

Bibliography. Fundamental is J. B. Lightfoot, *The Apostolic Fathers,* pt. II: *S. Ignatius, S. Polycarp,* vol. III (2nd ed., 1889). For other texts, translations, and commentaries, *see* bibliography under APOSTOLIC FATHERS; to which should be added T. Camelot, *Ignace d'Antioche, Lettres* (1951), for this includes the letter and martyrdom. Extensive bibliography may be found in the important work of P. N. Harrison, *Polycarp's Two Epistles to the Philippians* (1936); C. C. Richardson, ed., *Early Christian Fathers* (Library of Christian Classics, I; 1953), pp. 121-58. Cf. H. F. von Campenhausen, *Polykarp von Smyrna und die Pastoralbriefe* (Sitzungsberichte d. Heidelberger Akad. d. Wiss., 1951). M. H. SHEPHERD, JR.

*__POLYCARP, MARTYRDOM OF__ [Μαρτύριον τοῦ ἁγίου Πολυκάρπου Ἐπισκόπου Σμύρνης]. A letter from the church at Smyrna to the church at Philomelium, containing what appears to be, and probably is, a contemporary description of the martyrdom of Polycarp, the bishop of Smyrna in the first half of the second century. The date of the martyrdom itself is usually set in A.D. 155. This document is included in the collection of the APOSTOLIC FATHERS.

See also POLYCARP, EPISTLE OF.

Bibliography. The authenticity of the work is generally acknowledged, but significant questions about large portions of it are raised by H. F. von Campenhausen, *Bearbeitungen und Interpolationen des Polycarpmartyriums* (1957). J. KNOX

POLYGAMY. *See* MARRIAGE § 1*c*.

POLYTHEISM. Worship of a plurality of gods. *See* GOD.

POMEGRANATE [רמון, *rimmôn;* Aram. רומנא, רימונא; Akkad. *armannu;* Arab. *rummân;* ῥοΐσκος]. A small, shrublike tree and its fruit, *Punica granatum* L. The prominence of the pomegranate fruit in early Bible times is indicated by its use in the decorations on the "robe of the EPHOD," on which it is alternated with golden bells (Exod. 28:33-34; 39:24-26; cf. Ecclus. 45:9), and on the capitals of the temple pillars of JACHIN AND BOAZ (I Kings 7:18, 20, 42=II Chr. 3:16; 4:13; cf. II Kings 25:17; Jer. 52:22-23). As a token of the fruitfulness of S Palestine, the spies took pomegranates, figs, and grapes back to Joshua (Num. 13:23), and Moses mentioned them in describing the Promised Land (Deut. 8:8; cf. Num. 20:5). Saul encamped at Gibeah (probably Geba) near a place identified by its pomegranate tree (I Sam. 14:2). Pomegranates are mentioned in describing and praising the bride in Song of S. 4:3, 13; 6:7; and the flower, as a symbol of spring (6:11; 7:12—H 7:13). Wine was made from the juice of the fruit (8:2). Joel (1:12) includes this tree in his picture of devastation from locusts; and Haggai (2:19) includes it with grapes, figs, and olives as an indication of restoration to God's favor. In city names it appears in Num. 33:19-20 (RIMMON-PEREZ); Josh. 15:32 (RIMMON 1; cf. Isa. 10:27); 21:25 (GATH-RIMMON); Neh. 11:29 (EN-RIMMON). The fruit played a prominent part in ancient art and mythology as a symbol of fertility; the tree was even depicted as the TREE OF LIFE.

See also FLORA § A2*i*.

Bibliography. I. Löw, *Die Flora der Juden*, III (1924), 80-113; H. N. and A. L. Moldenke, *The Plants of the Bible* (1952), pp. 189-91.
J. C. TREVER

POMMELS. KJV translation of גלות (RSV BOWLS) in II Chr. 4:12-13; the bowl-shaped portions of the capitals of the temple pillars. The KJV has "bowls" in the parallel passages in I Kings 7:41-42. *See also* CAPITAL; JACHIN AND BOAZ.

D. M. C. ENGLERT

POND. The translation of אגם in Exod. 7:19 and in Exod. 8:5—H 8:1 KJV (RSV POOL), referring to the pools or marshes with (papyrus) reeds in the delta of Egypt. The word is usually rendered "pool." In Isa. 19:10, אגמי נפש (KJV "ponds for fish") has a variant derivation and is to be taken adjectively (RSV "grieved").

PONTIUS PILATE. *See* PILATE.

PONTUS pŏn'təs [Πόντος, sea]. A term used particularly of the Euxine (Black) Sea. It came to be used as the name of the E portion of the strip of country in N Asia Minor which borders on the Euxine Sea. The area extended from the mouth of the Halys River to the SE limits of this sea. To the W of the mouth of the Halys River lay Paphlagonia and then Bithynia. Later most of Paphlagonia was considered part of Pontus.

1. Geography and history. The shore line of Pontus includes fertile plains, which, however, are not deep and are interrupted by northward thrusts of the mountain ranges of the hinterland. These interruptions prevented the construction of continuous roads along the coast, and forced E-W traffic to move either by sea or along inland roads. Two such inland roads through Bithynia and Pontus were developed and were used, especially in Roman times, for troop movements.

The shore country was dotted with Greek colonies and outposts from the seventh century B.C. Sinope and Amisus were outstanding ports. Such ports were strongly Greek in culture and were in continual communication not only with other ports on the Euxine Sea but also with Greece, W Asia Minor, and even more distant regions.

The inland portions of Pontus had a quite different history. These mountainous areas, through which numerous streams cut gorges to make their way down to the Sea, were largely isolated from the Greek ports and had many ties with Armenia and Cappadocia. Prominent among the rivers were the Thermodon, whose region was the traditional home of the Amazons, and the Lycus and Iris, which together formed the largest river in Pontus. Amasia, ancient capital city of Pontus and birthplace of the famous geographer Strabo, lay well inland on the Iris River. The Halys River rises in SE Pontus, flowing SW into Cappadocia, and after turning northward through Galatia, flows NE on the W border of the original limits of Pontus; it is the longest river in Asia Minor. For the most part the inland mountainous areas of Pontus resisted Greek influence.

Pontus had been under famous empires, notably the Hittite and the Persian, before it became an important independent power. *Ca.* 302 B.C., Mithridates founded the kingdom of Pontus, and the dynasty he established ruled this kingdom until 63 B.C. The kingdom attained its widest extent and influence under Mithridates VI Eupator (111-63 B.C.), who ruled the region S of the Euxine Sea from Heraclea in Bithynia on the W to the regions of Colchis and Lesser Armenia on the E. He boldly challenged the advance of Rome in Asia Minor, and only after repeated campaigns, extending through more than two decades, was he finally defeated by Pompey and his rule ended.

The Romans then divided Pontus. The W part of Mithridates' empire, from Heraclea to the Halys River, was joined to the recently formed province of Bithynia; the new province was called Bithynia et Pontus. It later extended E of the Halys and included the important seaport of Amisus. The other parts of Pontus were added to Galatia (Pontus Galaticus) or entrusted to local rulers under Roman control. But conditions in this region changed repeatedly. Pharnaces, son of Mithridates VI, attempted to win back his father's kingdom, but was defeated by Julius Caesar in 47 B.C. In 37 B.C. much of the E coastal region of ancient Pontus was given to Polemon to rule under Roman control, and the dynasty which this puppet king founded continued to rule this region until A.D. 64, when the Romans took over direct rule and included part of it in Galatia (Pontus Polemoniacus) and part in Cappadocia (Pontus Cappadocicus). Under Vespasian, Galatia and Cappadocia were united in one province, which thus included all of Pontus not in the province Bithynia et Pontus. Later, under Trajan, Galatia and Cappadocia were again made separate provinces, and the three parts of Pontus which the united province had included—Pontus Galaticus, Pontus Polemoniacus, and Pontus Cappadocicus—all became parts of the province of Cappadocia. Roads from the Euphrates River region and from E Cilicia ran N through Cappadocia to ports on the Euxine Sea.

Thus in the days of the apostolic church a reference to Pontus might refer to the entire area; or to the W portion, which formed part of the Roman province Bithynia et Pontus; or to the E portion, which was in the kingdom of Polemon. But it would usually mean to people of the Roman Empire that part of Pontus included in the Roman province.

The presence of Jews in Pontus is attested by Philo of Alexandria, who in his *Embassy to Gaius* 36 says that they had spread into every part of Pontus. Among the Jews present in Jerusalem at Pentecost are mentioned those from Pontus (Acts 2:9). While they may have traveled overland from Pontus to Palestine, it is more likely that they took ship from some such Pontic port as Sinope or Amisus, sailed around the W side of Asia Minor, and so reached Palestine. Such contact by sea between Pontus and the Aegean and Mediterranean seas is illustrated by the movements of Aquila, a "native of Pontus," who had migrated to Rome and then with the other Jews there had been expelled by Claudius. He went to Corinth, where Paul met him (Acts 18:2), and later went with Paul to Ephesus and settled there (Acts

18:18-19). If Rom. 16:3 is a portion of a letter to Rome, Aquila was back in Rome when it was written. The movements of Aquila illustrate the mobility of first-century Jews and the seagoing habits of a Jew of Pontus, for it is safe to assume that Aquila traveled by sea.

2. Christianity in Pontus. In I Pet. 1:1 it is clear that there are Christians in Pontus, for, as vs. 2 shows, the "exiles of the dispersion" here addressed are the Christians scattered through the regions of central and N Asia Minor. We cannot say when Christian preachers first brought the gospel to Pontus. It would be bold to conclude that Jews converted at Pentecost at once brought the gospel to the Pontic region (Acts 2:9). When Paul was turned aside from his tentative plan to preach in Bithynia (Acts 16:7), a plan that could easily have included Pontus, he may have learned that there were already Christian preachers at work there. There is no clear evidence, however, that Peter ever preached in Pontus. But when I Peter was written, there had been churches in that region for years. The churches had elders as leaders (I Pet. 5:1), and seem to have been mainly of Gentile membership. They were under criticism and hostile pressure from their fellow countrymen, and faced the threat of an active and thoroughgoing persecution.

Attempts to date this situation yield no decisive conclusion. There is no real evidence that the persecution of Christians by Nero in Rome in 64 led to similar persecution in Asia Minor. The book of Revelation foresees wholesale persecution for the churches of the province of Asia, and this seems to reflect the situation near the end of the reign of Domitian (81-96), but there is no clear link with the situation in Pontus. When Pliny the Younger was sent by Trajan in 113-15 to set in order the deteriorated economic, social, and political conditions of the province of Bithynia (which included the W part of the ancient region of Pontus), he found that Christianity had been established there for at least more than two decades, had achieved an astonishing growth, and had led the pagan population and leaders to active persecution. Pliny, supported by Trajan, barred penalties against former Christians who had given up that faith, but continued the severe measures already in effect against those who refused to renounce their Christian confession. Back of this situation lies a period of intensive and highly fruitful missionary and evangelistic effort throughout the province of Bithynia et Pontus. Such a period of Christian growth means that Christianity must have come to that region several decades before Pliny visited there, and possibly as early as the days of Paul's active ministry.

Numerous facts attest the importance of Pontus in the religious world of the second century A.D. E.g., Aquila of Pontus, a Jew of the time of Hadrian, translated the OT into Greek. The amazing story which Lycian tells of how the impostor Alexander of Abonuteichos (a city of Pontus) founded a new religious cult gives a picture of one aspect of pagan religious life. Marcion, who went to Rome and headed a powerful heretical sect of the church, came from Sinope in Pontus, where his father is reported to have been a bishop.

Bibliography. Pliny the Younger *Letters*, bk. 10, letters 96-97. W. M. Ramsay, *The Church in the Roman Empire* (1893), ch. 10. *Cambridge Ancient History*, vol. IX (1932), chs. 5, 8; vol. XI (1936), pp. 575-80. A. H. M. Jones, *Cities of the Eastern Roman Provinces* (1937), ch. 6. E. G. Selwyn, *The First Epistle of St. Peter* (2nd ed., 1947), pp. 42-63.

F. V. FILSON

POOL. The translation of several terms designating natural or artificial reservoirs supplied by rain and overflow from springs and rivers. These were important sources of water supply for biblical villages, and many can still be seen. *See also* RESERVOIR; WATER WORKS § 4*b*.

The most common term for "pool" is ברכה (II Sam. 2:13; I Kings 22:38; etc.; so also the Siloam Inscription). It is often mentioned in connection with biblical cities (*see below*). Another term, אגם, refers to a pool full of reeds, probably a swamp area (Exod. 7:19; 8:5—H 8:1; Isa. 14:23; *see* POND). The term is rendered variously as "pool" and "pond" in the KJV (Isa. 19:10; 35:7), but always "pool" in the RSV except in Exod. 7:19 ("pond"); Jer. 51:32: "The bulwarks [האגמים; KJV 'reeds'] are burned with fire." There is no indication that אגם was an artificial pool or that it was associated with particular villages or cities. In one passage another term, מקוה, "a gathering," is rendered "pool" (Exod. 7:19). The LXX uses several different words to render the Hebrew terms, but κολυμβήθρα is generally used for ברכה and is also the NT word (John 5:2-7; 9:7).

Among the pools identified with a particular name or place are the ones at Gibeon (II Sam. 2:13), Hebron (II Sam. 4:12), Samaria (I Kings 22:38), Heshbon (Song of S. 7:4—H7:5; KJV "fishpools"), Jerusalem (II Kings 18:17; Isa. 7:3; 36:2), and also at Jerusalem the King's Pool (Neh. 2:14), the Pool of Shelah (Neh. 3:15; KJV "Siloah"), the pool called Beth-zatha (John 5:2; mg. "Bethesda, Bethsaida"), and the Pool of Siloam (John 9:7).

Most of the pools in the vicinity of cities were rock-cut reservoirs ("artificial pools"; Neh. 3:16; cf. Eccl. 2:6), into which rain water drained by means of channels cut in the rock. Pools are mentioned as places of meeting where important events took place (II Sam. 2:13, a battle between the forces of Abner and David; I Kings 22:38, Ahab's chariot washed). The repair and construction of pools was an important measure in preparing a city against siege (II Kings 20:20). According to John 5:2-3, the pool of Beth-zatha in Jerusalem was constructed with five porticoes to which people came with the hope of being healed. A similar tradition of healing is associated with the Pool of Siloam (John 9:7).

Pools are mentioned in a figurative sense to indicate God's power to transform the wilderness (Isa. 41:18), and to suggest the devastation of Nineveh (Nah. 2:8) and the beauty of a maiden's eyes (Song of S. 7:4—H 7:5).

Among the most famous pools still to be seen are those in Hebron, Gibeon, Jerusalem, and the so-called "Pools of Solomon" in the Valley of Urtas near Bethlehem (Fig. WAT 6). Three in number, they are *ca.* two hundred feet in width, and the largest is almost six hundred feet long and fifty feet deep. At least as early as Roman times the pools supplied water to Jerusalem, as attested by sections of aqueducts which remain; and they are still used by people in their vicinity.

See also GIBEON § 1*b;* JERUSALEM §§ 5*b,* 6*c,* 7*b,* 11; SILOAM; SHELAH (POOL OF); BETH-ZATHA.

W. L. REED

***POOR.** One who is destitute of wealth and of material goods, lacking in even the necessities of life. Also, metaphorically, the humble and the meek. In Hebrew many words are used for the poor man and his condition. *See* POVERTY.

אביון occurs more than sixty times in the OT. It is almost always used of the poor in a material sense. These are the needy (Deut. 15:7; 24:14; Ps. 109:16). In Psalms and Proverbs, אביון is often paralleled with עני (Ps. 109:16; cf. Pss. 35:10; 72:12; 109:22; etc.) and דל (Pss. 72:13; 82:4; 113:7; Prov. 14:31; 31:9). Anyone who needs deliverance from material exigencies, evil, or sin is poor and needy in respect to God. God will deliver him from trouble (Pss. 9:18-19; 12:5; 69:33; 86:1; Isa. 25:4; 29:19; 41:17; etc.).

דל and דלה are from the root דלל, "be low, languish," which is related to the Akkadian *dalûlu,* "be weak." The term appears most frequently in the Writings. They are those whose prosperity and social status have been reduced. In this respect they are the opposite of the rich (Exod. 23:3; 30:15; Lev. 14:21; Prov. 22:16; etc.). In physical strength, in psychological ability, they are also impaired and so become helpless (Job 34:28; Ps. 82:3; Jer. 40:7; 52:16; etc.).

חלכה is the "unfortunate one." It appears only in Ps. 10:8, 10, 14. The RSV translates "hapless." The LXX uses both πενήτα and πτωχός here.

חסר and מחסור are also those who are in need and want (Prov. 6:11; 28:22; etc.). These even lack bread enough for food (II Sam. 3:29; Job 30:3), and so are the poverty-stricken (Deut. 28:48; Prov. 21:17; etc.).

מסכן occurs only in Ecclesiastes and seems related to the Akkadian *muškênu,* "beggar." In Eccl. 9:15-16 he is a wise man as well as a beggar. Perhaps, like many teachers, he did not have a trade and was voluntarily poor (*see below*). He is not necessarily from the lowest economic class, because of the contrast to the great king in these passages and in 4:13.

עני and ענו and related terms are basically the "afflicted," the "bowed down." They are oppressed by the rich (Isa. 3:14; Ezek. 18:16-18; Amos 2:7; etc.). They may be the pious who have been afflicted by the wicked (Ps. 10:2; Isa. 14:32; etc.). The words are sometimes used for the "humble" (Num. 12:3; Zech. 9:9).

רוש, ריש, ראש, may be related to the "dispossessed," and so would be derivatives of ירש, "possess." The concept of hunger is involved—e.g., the hungry lions of Ps. 34:10. The second noun appears only in Proverbs (6:11; 10:15; 13:18; etc.).

The Greek πτωχός refers to those who are destitute of material possessions, as opposed to the rich, who have all things in abundance (II Cor. 8:9; Rev. 2:9). Christ dispossessed himself (πτωχεύω) and became a beggar on behalf of man. This verb appears in the LXX for דלל and רוש. Poor men (πτωχός) may be beggars (Matt. 19:21; Luke 14:13), but they still have the gospel preached to them (Matt. 11:5). Figuratively these are people who are destitute of morals or of the Christian ethic (I Cor. 1:26; Gal. 4:9; Rev. 3:17). The poor in spirit, the true humble followers of the Way, are blessed (Matt. 5:3; Luke 6:20).

Πένης is the humble workman from the lowest economic class. He is not a beggar, and πένης should be distinguished from the first Greek word. Πένης is used only in II Cor. 9:9, a quotation from Ps. 112:9. It is used in the LXX for almost all the Hebrew words.

Πενιχρός is closely related to πένης but is used only for the poor widow in Luke 21:2. In the LXX it appears for עני and דל. These words seem to be related to the English word "penury."

In the OT the poor were a special charge of God. He would not forget them (Pss. 9:12; 10:12; etc.). He pities and comforts them (Ps. 34:6; Isa. 49:13; etc.). He cares for them (Job 5:15; Pss. 107:41; 132:15; Jer. 20:13; etc.). God through the Mosaic legislation and the prophetic exhortation seeks social justice for the poor (Deut. 10:17-18; II Sam. 22:28; Isa. 25:4; Amos 2:6; 4:1; etc.). There are many warnings against the oppression of the poor in both the Law and the Prophets (Exod. 23:3; Lev. 19:15; Isa. 1:23; Ezek. 22:7; Mic. 2:2; Mal. 3:5; etc.). The *ger,* or SOJOURNER, was to be likewise protected. Many of the laws concerning the poor are to be found in Lev. 19; 23; Deut. 14–15; 25.

The Hebrew judges were to give to the poor full protection (Exod. 23:3; Deut. 16:19; Ps. 82:3; etc.). Interest was not to be exacted from the poor (Exod. 22:25; Lev. 25:36; Deut. 23:20). The poor were to be allowed to glean in the fields and vineyards (Lev. 19:9-10; 23:22; Deut. 24:19; cf. Ruth). They had first rights to the sabbatical fruits (Exod. 23:11; Lev. 25:6). The TITHE of the third year was for the benefit of the poor and needy (Deut. 14:28-29; 26:14). Poverty should not exclude anyone from the joy of the festival (Deut. 16:11-12; cf. Esth. 9:22). The poor could pluck from the vineyard or grainfield enough to eat (Deut. 23:25; cf. Luke 6:1). They were allowed to present less expensive offerings at the temple (Lev. 12:8; 14:21; 27:8; cf. Luke 2:24). In the Israelite assembly, the poor were not to be ignored.

The poor were expected to remain faithful to the statutes and covenant of God. In humility, they should accept their condition, not because it was foreordained (but cf. I Sam. 2:7), but because God could bring it to good (Prov. 30:8; Ecclus. 11:27). Job is brought low by the permission of God (Job 1:21). Prov. 22:2 does not proclaim God's ordination of a man's economic status but the doctrine of creation: "rich" and "poor" are here used to mean all mankind. God-fearing men will be blessed despite poverty.

The OT king and Messiah were to be solicitous of the poor (Pss. 22:26; 72:4; Prov. 29:14). Jesus had the prophetic concern for the poor (Matt. 19:21; John 13:29; etc.). Mercy was to be shown even to debtors (Luke 7:41). He praised ALMS giving (Mark 12:42-44). A beggar could be saved (Luke 16:22), but Jesus did not come merely to eliminate poverty (Mark 14:7). The gospel was to be preached to the poor (Matt. 11:5; Luke 14:21). Following his example, the early church cared for its poor (Acts 2:45; 4:34; 11:29; Gal. 2:10; I Thess. 3:6; etc.). They were accepted as members of the church (Jas. 2:2).

To pity the poor was meritorious. It brought blessings, for one honors God by honoring the poor (Ps. 41:1; Prov. 14:21, 31; 29:7; etc.). Charity was considered a virtue throughout all biblical history. The demand for charity was based on a remembrance of Israel's bondage (Deut. 15:11; 16:12). It was the duty of the rich to help the poor, of the strong to protect the weak. To Job this is not a duty but a privilege (Job 31:16 ff). Justice and mercy are to be shown to the poor (Ecclus. 7:10).

The terms "meek" and "poor" in some of the Psalms seem to designate a particular religious affiliation in ancient Israel, which began even in pre-exilic times. These apparently are the faithful, God-fearing sons of the Covenant, who formed an inner remnant loyal to the prophetic message. The Psalms of Lament seem especially to allude to this group of oppressed pious Israelites. The Qumran community (*see* DEAD SEA SCROLLS) also seems to have used the term "poor" as a designation for their own group, perhaps reflecting their origin. The term may be a proper name for the early Christians (Rom. 15:26; Gal. 2:10). The Ebionites (*see* EBIONITES, GOSPEL OF) may be the remnants of such a pious Judaic-Christian group.

Bibliography. W. W. von Baudissin, *Die alttestamentliche Religion und die Armen* (1912); I. Abrahams, "Poverty and Wealth," *Studies in Pharisaism and the Gospels,* I (1917), 113-17; A. Causse, *Les "Pauvres" d'Israël* (1922); H. Bolkestein, *Wohltätigkeit und Armenpflege im vorchristlichen Altertum* (1939); A. Kuschke, "Arm und reich im AT . . . ," *ZAW,* 57 (1939), 31-56; P. Humbert, "Le mot biblique *èbyōn,*" *RHPR,* 32 (1952), 1-6; A. Gelin, *Les pauvres de Yahvé* (1953).

C. U. WOLF

POPLAR [לבנה, *líbhnē, from* לבן, white]. A tree whose branches were used by Jacob in Haran, with those from almond and plane trees, in his scheme to increase his flocks more than Laban's (Gen. 30:37). It grew with oaks and terebinths on the hills of Palestine (Hos. 4:13). It was apparently referred to poetically for its firm and easy rootage (Hos. 14:5—H 14:6, with slight emendation).

Identification of the tree has been narrowed to the white poplar, *Populus alba* L., and the storax tree, *Styrax officinalis* L. (cf. Gen. 30:37 ASV mg.; Ecclus. 24:15 KJV [*see* STACTE]), both of which fit the meaning "white" implied in the Hebrew word. The leaves of both are whitish on the under side. The flowers of the latter are also white. Zohary and some other botanists argue strongly for the storax (*see* FLORA § A9*p*), while some biblical scholars and other botanists prefer the poplar. The LXX has "storax" for the Gen. 30:37 passage and "poplar" for Hos. 4:13. The Arabic word *lubna* is used for the storax tree.

Bibliography. I. Löw, *Die Flora der Juden,* III (1924), 388-95; H. N. and A. L. Moldenke, *Plants of the Bible* (1952), pp. 181-83.

J. C. TREVER

PORATHA pō rā'thə [פורתא] (Esth. 9:8). One of the ten sons of Haman.

Bibliography. On the relevant textual and etymological problems, see L. B. Paton, *Esther,* ICC (1908), pp. 70, 284.

PORCH. 1. אולם ("that which is in front"), the entry room of a building (I Kings 7:6; Ezek. 8:16); usually translated "VESTIBULE." *See also* HALL 2.

2. Πυλών ("gateway"), the entrance to a courtyard (Matt. 26:71).

3. KJV translation of מסדרון (Judg. 3:23; RSV "roof chamber"), perhaps a pillared hall, balustrade.

4. KJV translation of προαύλιον (lit., "forecourt"; Mark 14:68; RSV "gateway").

5. KJV translation of στοα (in John 5:2, porticoes of the pool of BETH-ZATHA; in Acts 3:11, RSV SOLOMON'S PORTICO), a roofed colonnade. E. M. GOOD

PORCIUS FESTUS. *See* FESTUS, PORCIUS.

PORCUPINE. *See* HEDGEHOG.

PORPHYRY pôr'fə rĭ [בהט; LXX σμαραγδίτης, Vulg. *smaragdinus, relate to* emerald] (Esth. 1:6); KJV RED . . . MARBLE. A rock of feldspar crystals embedded in a compact dark red or purple groundmass. It is an ingredient in the mosaic pavement in the king's court in Susa (Esth. 1:6).

W. E. STAPLES

PORTENT. *See* SIGN, especially 1, 7.

PORTER. KJV translation of שׁוער (RSV "gatekeeper"; "watchman"); שׁער (RSV "gatekeeper"); תרע (RSV "doorkeeper"); θυρωρός (RSV "doorkeeper" in Mark 13:34; "gatekeeper" in John 10:3). *See* DOORKEEPER; WATCHMAN. For Levitical porters, *see* PRIESTS AND LEVITES § C3.

PORTICO OF SOLOMON. *See* SOLOMON'S PORTICO.

POSIDONIUS pŏs'ĭ dō'nĭ əs [Ποσιδώνιος] (II Macc. 14:19). One of the three men sent by Nicanor with authority to propose and accept a truce from Judas Maccabeus, after Nicanor saw that he could not be victorious because of the course of Judas' troops.

POSSESSION, DEMONIACAL. *See* DEMONIAC.

POST (COURIER). KJV translation of רץ ("runner"). *See* COURIER; *cf.* GUARD; MESSENGER.

POST, DOORPOST [איל (*plural* JAMBS), סף, אמה, מזוזה]. The word איל apparently refers to something strong and means "ram" (*passim*) or "a sturdy tree," "oak" (Isa. 1:29; 57:5). Its only architectural use is with Ezekiel's temple (Ezek. 40:9–41:3). There in 40:14 the reading is doubtful. The KJV, with the Hebrew, reads: "He made also posts of threescore cubits"; if the posts are jambs, the threescore cubits are too many. So the RSV, with the LXX, reads: "He measured also the vestibule, twenty cubits." This involves changing אילים to אולם and ששים to עשרים. The width of these "jambs," measuring from two to six cubits, would indicate that they were not single posts, but composite.

In Isa. 6:4 the plural of אמה (*'ammâ*) may mean "posts" and so is taken by the KJV; in the RSV it is "foundations." The LXX has ὑπέρθυρον, "lintel."

A more common word is מזוזה (*mᵉzûzâ*), the plural of which is translated "side posts," "door posts," or simply "posts" in the KJV and generally "doorposts" in the RSV. The doorposts played an important part in Jewish religious thought. On the Passover eve they and the lintel were sprinkled with blood (Exod. 12: 7, 22-23). At the *mᵉzûzâ* the slave who desired to stay with his master would have his ear pierced (Exod. 21:6). The words of the Shema are to be written on the *mᵉzûzôth* of the house (Deut. 6:9; 11:20). Among orthodox Jews the *mᵉzûzâ* is a scroll containing the sacred words, placed in a cylinder and attached to the doorpost. Following the LXX, in I Kings 7:5 the RSV reads מחזות, "windows," instead of מזוזה.

The plural of סף in the KJV is translated "posts" (II Chr. 3:7; Amos 9:1) and "doorposts" (Ezek. 41: 16); but a better translation is "threshold," as elsewhere in the KJV (Judg. 19:27; Ezek. 40:6) and regularly in the RSV.

See also ARCHITECTURE; DOOR; FOUNDATION; HOUSE. O. R. SELLERS

POT. A term used to translate a wide variety of Hebrew and Greek words. For details, *see* POTTERY. Most ceramic pots of biblical times had metal counterparts. *See* VESSELS.

POTIPHAR pŏt'ə fər [פוטיפר; *more correctly* פוטיפרע, POTIPHERA; *transliteration of* Egyp. *pꜣ-dꜣ-pꜣ-Rꜥ*, he whom Re has given]. The Egyptian officer who purchased Joseph from the Ishmaelites (or Midianites) when he was first brought to Egypt as a slave. Potiphar is credited with recognizing the natural abilities of his slave and putting him "in charge of all that he had." It was the unnamed wife of Potiphar who attempted to seduce the "handsome and good-looking" slave. The general outline of Gen. 39, which deals with the Potiphar-Joseph relationship, is surprisingly similar to the famous Tale of Two Brothers (*see* JOSEPH). In the Egyptian tale the character Anubis can be compared to the biblical Potiphar.

The form of the name Potiphar offers us some additional information and also some difficulty. The theophorous element in the name is that of the god Re, who was the Egyptian sun-god. It is exactly the same name as that of Joseph's father-in-law, the priest of On, POTIPHERA. The names appear in different forms in both Hebrew and English because of an improper omission of the final *'áyin* from the longer form. It is difficult to explain this loss, because the *'áyin* was normally preserved in the Hebrew of the OT in every position. It may be that the shorter form, which developed as a mistake or faulty transcription, was intentionally preserved as Potiphar to distinguish the captain of the guard from the priest who bore a similar name.

The provenience of the name is likewise puzzling. It has been suggested that the Egyptian names in the Joseph story have fallen victim to the natural practice of substituting more familiar and hence more recent names for stranger, archaic ones. In any case it is to be noted that names of this type do not appear in Egypt until the tenth century.

The office which was held by Potiphar also calls for discussion. It is described by the Hebrew words *sārîs* and *śar haṭṭabbāḥîm*. The word *sārîs* normally means "eunuch." The fact that Potiphar was married does not make this interpretation impossible, since the term *sārîs* was extended to cover officials whose duties were similar to those of eunuchs, and finally to any courtier. The translation "officer" is correct, but it is possible to be a little more specific by pointing out that it is applied only to those who are directly related to the king and court—in the case of Isa. 56:3-4 the eunuch is related to the temple.

The title *śar haṭṭabbāḥîm,* which is translated "captain of the guard," is a title also applied to the Babylonian Nebuzaradan, who appears to have held a military post (Jer. 52:14). On the other hand, the position which Potiphar held was connected with the royal prison. It would be difficult to determine the precise nature of this office from such diverse material. As far as is known, there is no exact equivalent in Egyptian sources. O. S. WINTERMUTE

POTIPHERA pə tĭf'ə rə [פוטיפרע; *also written* פוטיפר, POTIPHAR; *transliteration of* Egyp. *pꜣ-dꜣ-pꜣ-Rꜥ*, he whom Re has given] (Gen. 41:45). Joseph's father-in-law. He is described as a priest of On (Heliopolis), which was the center of the cult of the sun-god. A name containing the divine element "Re" would be very appropriate for such a person. Names of this form do not, however, appear in Egypt until *ca.* the tenth century B.C. O. S. WINTERMUTE

POTSHERD pŏt'shûrd [חרש]. Alternately: EARTHEN VESSEL (Prov. 26:23; Isa. 45:9; KJV POTSHERD); KJV STONE (Job 41:30). A piece of broken pottery. Potsherds serve as a symbol of dryness (Ps. 22:15) and as a symbol of utter worthlessness (Isa. 45:9 KJV).

The judgment on Israel is compared to the breaking of a potter's vessel smashed so ruthlessly that from among its fragments no usable sherd can be found (Isa. 30:14).

There was a city gate in the Hinnom Valley called the POTSHERD GATE (Jer. 19:2). This was the place where the potters could throw away their discards outside the city wall. *See* POTTERY.

Job used a potsherd with which to scrape himself as he sat on an ash heap (Job 2:8).

Ezek. 23:34 KJV refers to the sherds of Samaria's cup, which is to be drunk by Jerusalem, but the text is obscure (see RSV).

The armored underparts of the mythological dragon, the Leviathan, are described in Job 41:30 as like sharp potsherds. J. L. KELSO

POTSHERD GATE [שער החרסות, *to be read* שער החרסית, gate of the potsherds] (Jer. 19:2); KJV EAST GATE; ASV GATE HARSITH här'sĭth. A city gate in the SE section of Jerusalem, leading to the Valley of Hinnom and to the Potter's Field (*see* AKELDAMA). Some scholars identify it with the DUNG GATE.

See map under NEHEMIAH. *See also* JERUSALEM § 6*e*. G. A. BARROIS

POTTAGE [נזיד, boiled thing; ἕψημα]. A thick vegetable soup, usually made with LENTILS but also with herbs in general (Gen. 25:34; II Kings 4:39). Occasionally meat was added, and the whole was boiled

(II Kings 4:38); apparently it was red in color (Gen. 25:30). Pottage is mentioned in connection with Jacob's deception of Esau (Gen. 25:29-34), as a dish prepared by Elisha's disciples (II Kings 4:38-41), as a common food (Hag. 2:12), and as a food for reapers (Bel 33).

See also COOKING; VEGETABLES. J. F. ROSS

POTTER'S FIELD. *See* AKELDAMA.

POTTER'S WHEEL [אבנים, *a dual form, perhaps from* אבן, stone]. A circular disc, fitted on a vertical axis, on which it rotates, thus enabling the potter to fashion clay vessels.

Although ubiquitous, the potter's wheel is not mentioned in the NT and only once in the OT (Jer. 18:3). The potter, who fashions vessels at will out of the formless clay, is there compared to the Lord, who directs the destinies of his people (cf. also Isa. 29:1; 45:9; 64:8; Jer. 18:6; Rom. 9:21-22). It is significant that in OT Hebrew the terms for "Creator" and "potter" are expressed by the same word, יוצר. A similar trend of thought may be seen in an Egyptian relief where the god Khnum is shown fashioning man on a potter's wheel.

Courtesy of the Metropolitan Museum of Art

61. Middle figure is a potter turning the wheel; figure at left is tending the kiln; figure to the right is probably sawing a board. From a tomb at Saqqarah.

Courtesy of the Oriental Institute, the University of Chicago

62. An Egyptian limestone figure of a potter, laboring at his wheel, from the Old Kingdom

Archaeological evidence shows that the potter's wheel came into use in Palestine in the third millennium B.C. first in the form of a *tournette*—i.e., consisting of one disc only. Such a *tournette* is represented on an Egyptian relief of 2000 B.C. in a tomb at Benihasan. During the Middle Bronze Age a second disc, or "fly wheel," seems to have been added, as is also implied by the dual form of the Hebrew word. This second wheel, which speeded the turning, was set in motion by the foot. The earliest literary mention of such a wheel is in Ecclus. 38:29:

> So too is the potter sitting at his work
> and turning the wheel [τροχός] with his feet.

Potters' wheels of stone were found in Megiddo, Tell el-'Ajjul, Lachish, and Hazor. But on the whole, they are seldom found in excavations, perhaps because they were often made of perishable material such as wood or clay, although, on the other hand, the Hebrew term points to stone as a material.

Figs. POT 61-62.

Bibliography. P. E. Newberry, *Beni Hasan,* vol. I (1893), pl. XI; W. M. F. Petrie, *Ancient Gaza,* I (1931), 11 and pl. LII, 10; A. Erman, *Religion der Ägypter* (1934), figure on p. 54 (Khnum); O. Tufnell *et al., Lachish,* IV (1938), 91 and pl. 49, 12-13; *BA,* vol. XX, no. 2, p. 43 and fig. 9; A.-G. Barrois, *Manuel d'archéologie biblique,* I (1939), 408-9; R. S. Lamon and G. M. Shipton, Megiddo, vol. I (1939), pl. 114, nos. 1-3; A. Rieth, *Die Entwicklung der Töpferscheibe* (1939); J. Kelso, "The Potter's Technique at Tell Beit Mirsim," *AASOR,* XXI-XXII (1943), 95-97; C. Singer, ed., *A History of Technology,* I (1954), 195-204 (cf. fig. 124 for a potter's wheel from Jericho). I. BEN-DOR

***POTTERY.** A synthetic stone produced by firing clay to a sufficiently high temperature to change its physical characteristics and its chemical composition. Pottery was man's first synthetic creation, and today ceramics is still a major industry even in the most highly civilized countries. Pottery is now commonly thought of as earthenware dishes and other larger vessels, but the term had a much wider usage in antiquity, more akin to our modern word "ceramics."

Pls. XIX-XXIV.

1. The making of pottery in Bible times
2. The history of pottery
3. The ceramic vocabulary used in pottery manufacture
    a. Bowls, cups, cooking pots, and lamps
    b. Jars, pitchers, and juglets
    c. Miscellaneous ware
4. Ceramics in industry
5. Ceramics in Canaanite cult objects
6. Glass and glaze
7. Pottery in the ceremonial law
8. Figurative language derived from ceramics

Bibliography

1. The making of pottery in Bible times. In the Palestine of Bible days pottery was usually made

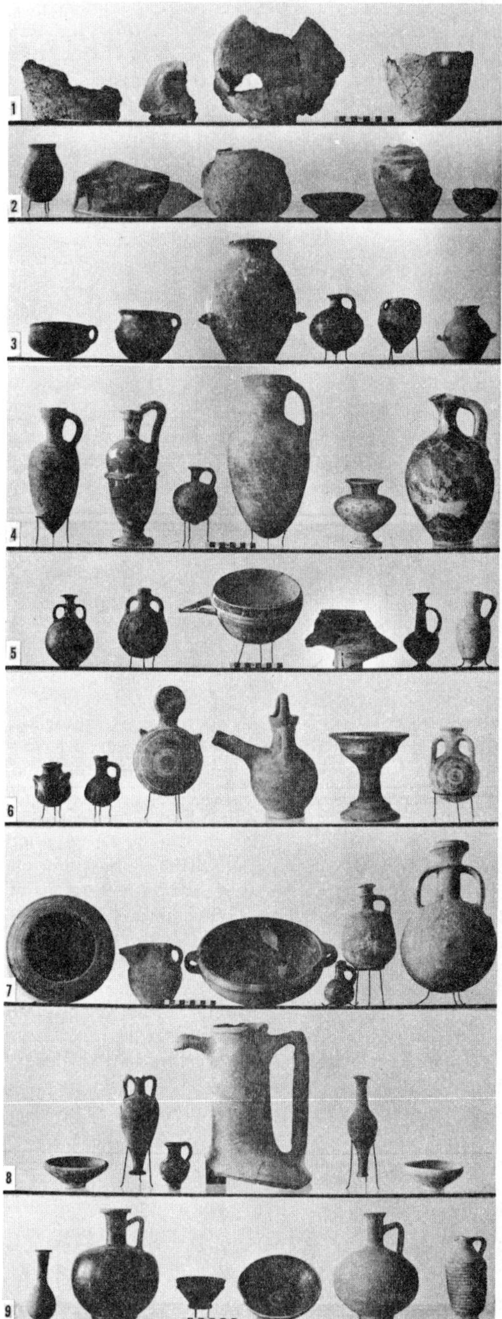

Courtesy of the Palestine Archaeological Museum, Jerusalem, Jordan

63. Representative pottery in the Palestine Archaeological Museum, Jerusalem, Jordan: (1) Neolithic II (*ca.* 5000-4000 B.C.); fragments of large vessels with crude design and coarse texture. (2) Chalcolithic (*ca.* 4000-3000 B.C.); a small jar, fragment of a large jar with ledge handles, two incomplete jars of medium size, and two small bowls; the jar second to right shows two small lug handles. (3) Early Bronze (*ca.* 3000-2100 B.C.); a cup, a pitcher, two button base juglets, and two flat-bottom jars with ledge handles; texture had improved, and the potter's wheel had come into use. (4) Middle Bronze (*ca.* 2100-1550 B.C.); four pitchers, a juglet, and a small carinated bowl with trumpet foot base; the pottery of this age, when the Hyksos influence was predominant, was the best of any period in ancient Palestine. (5) Late Bronze (*ca.* 1550-1200 B.C.); an imported pilgrim flask, a local imitation, an imported "milk bowl" with wishbone handle, a fragment decorated by the "Tell el-'Ajjul painter," a "bilbil," and a small pitcher with round base; in this period the best ware was imported. (6) Iron I (*ca.* 1200-900 B.C.); two juglets, one with lug handles, two types of pilgrim flask, a pitcher with a large spout inside of which is a strainer, and a chalice. (7) Iron II (*ca.* 900-600 B.C.); a hole-mouth jar, a small jar with three handles and a spout, a bowl with ring burnishing, a juglet, a water decanter, and a pilgrim flask. (8) Iron III–Hellenistic (*ca.* 600-300 and 300-63 B.C.); two small bowls (very common in this period), a small amphora, a small pitcher, top of a Rhodian jar, and a spindle bottle. (9) Roman (63 B.C.–A.D. 323); a bottle, two jugs, a pitcher, and two bowls; the left jug and the two bowls are red painted ware; the right jug and the pitcher show ribbing, which developed in this period.

from a good grade of red clay, the commonest of all clays. It was weathered and washed in the potter's yard or near where it was dug. Settling basins, terraced on a hillside, enabled the potter to select various grades of clay. The final step in the preparation of the clay was to mix the proper amount of water with the washed clay by treading until the water had been evenly distributed and until all the air was removed. This treading of the potter's clay required skill (Isa. 41:25), although the treading of clay for sun-dried bricks could be done by anyone (Nah. 3:14).

The true POTTER'S WHEEL was in use during almost all of the Bible period. The potter took a ball of clay and placed it at the center of the wheel, which was then turned rapidly—sometimes by an assistant—while the potter's hands fashioned the clay into the desired vessel. Later, when leather hard, the vessel could be put back on the wheel and turned into more delicate forms, just as we turn wood on a lathe today. The Hebrew term for the potter's wheel, אבנים (Jer. 18:3), was a dual, suggesting that the wheel consisted of two parts—a smaller disk above, on which the vessel was fashioned; and a larger one below, which furnished the necessary momentum. Ecclus. 38:29-30 contains the first reference to the improved potter's wheel. Here the power wheel, which was turned by the foot of the seated potter, was on the same shaft as the thrower's wheel, which was at hand level. If the clay had been well prepared and was of the right plasticity and porosity, it would hold its form well while being thrown on the wheel and afterward while drying, and finally when fired in the kiln. Figs. POT 61-62.

A second method of fashioning clay was to use a press mold (חותם, "seal" [Job 38:14]). The prepared clay was pressed down firmly into an open mold so that all the details of the mold were reproduced in the clay. Astarte plaques of the Canaanite period were made in these press molds, as were most of the lamps of NT times. A third method of fashioning clay was freehand modeling, but this was not much used in Israel except for toys and figurines. Ovens and a few odd vessels were handmade.

The firing of the kiln was a professional's task, for different clays had to be handled differently and various wares had to be fired so as to bring out their required qualities. The firing of the kiln was the ultimate test of the potter's art. The Bible gives us no reference to the potter's firing techniques, for these were trade secrets in antiquity just as they were even in the medieval guilds. In spite of careful firing, however, there was a certain percentage of spoilage. Some of the spoiled vessels were sold, but the rest had to be discarded.

In the field of decoration the Israelites did not use glaze but simply modified the thrown form with slip, painting, burnishing, etc. The best decorated Israelite ware was in the days of the Divided Kingdom. The spiral wheel burnishings used at that time produced narrow bands which alternately absorbed and reflected light, giving a highly decorative pattern (Fig. POT 63, No. 7*c*). In the days of the judges there was some painting, but it was the Canaanite period which preceded it that saw the widest use of painting (Figs. ART 72-73; Pl. XX). The Philistines also used painted decoration, specializing on the swan, the Maltese cross, and the Ionic spiral. Figs. PHI 50; ART 75.

2. The history of pottery. The earliest of all pottery came from Neolithic Jericho, where the evolution of that art can be traced in good detail, and where phenomenal progress was made with that craft (Fig. POT 63, Nos. 1*a-d*). In the early days pottery was hand molded, but at least by Joseph's time—the Hyksos period—throwing on the wheel had replaced it in most communities and for most ceramic products. Fig. POT 64.

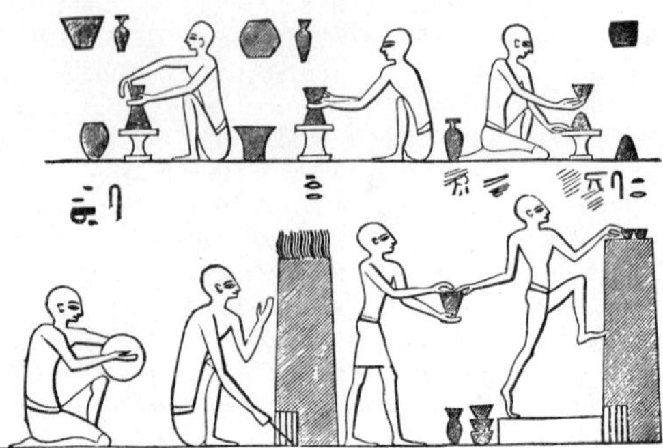

64. Making of pottery in ancient Egypt

In antiquity pottery found many and varied uses. It was the major method of storage, for in those days metal, wood, and sack containers were too expensive. Only baskets were competitors. Pottery revolutionized cooking and improved the general health level. It entered into such unlikely fields as writing materials. Man's earliest tablet was made of wet clay into which a script was imprinted with a stylus (*see* WRITING AND WRITING MATERIALS). A man's signature was made by rolling his signet seal (*see* SEALS AND SCARABS § B2*a*)* into this clay tablet (Gen. 38: 18). In later years large pieces of broken jars often served as an economical form of stationery. At LACHISH they were used for military messages, and at SAMARIA they were used for tax receipts. Pottery jars were the safety deposit vaults of antiquity (Jer. 32: 14; Matt. 13:44). This is the meaning of II Cor. 4:7: "We have this treasure in earthen vessels"—i.e., physical bodies. Pottery was used for the making of children's toys, and in Babylonia the farmer used well-fired pottery sickle edges. Besides creating its own natural clay forms, pottery was also used to reproduce cheap imitations of metalware and stoneware. Fig. SEA 35.

Most of the pottery the archaeologists have found in Palestine is native ware. There was only a minimum of foreign ceramic importation (Fig. POT 63, Nos. 5*c*, *e*), although imitations of foreign ware were often produced in quantity.

Pottery is so indestructible and its styling so distinctive that it furnishes the archaeologist the chief tool by which he can date ancient history. Also, it was so cheap that nobody bothered to remove potsherds, and the ruins of ancient cities contain vast quantities of pottery, which supply plenty of reference data for checking chronology. Anyone who makes his first visit to an archaeologist's dig in Palestine is surprised at the great number of baskets of broken pottery that are unearthed every day. When the use of coins became world wide in the intertestamental period, then the archaeologist had a second and better dating agent. However, even on some late digs, coins are rare, and pottery is therefore still important. *See* ARCHAEOLOGY.

Most of Palestine's pottery was strictly utilitarian, but the term "utilitarian" must not be interpreted as "unartistic," for some of the most common household wares had excellent lines and are worthy of a place in a modern ceramic exhibit. Furthermore, some ware was so artistically designed as to be used for both dry and wet storage, yet without any confusion in design. The most artistic of all pottery forms in Bible times came out of the Hyksos period—the Middle Bronze Age (*ca.* 2000-1500)—which is usually approximated to the time of Joseph (Fig. POT 63, Nos. 4*a-f*). The superior culture of the Euphrates Valley had fled westward to the Mediterranean at that time and left its ceramic impression on Palestine. There was a similar contemporary upsurge in metallurgy. In the Late Bronze Age (*ca.* 1500-1200), which closed about the time of Joshua's conquest, pottery lacked the fine lines of the preceding Hyksos phase, but it still revealed good craftsmanship (Fig. POT 63, Nos. 5*a-b*). New influences in style, however, had come in from different lands, and both new forms and new decorations appeared. There was a special emphasis on painted ware.

Joshua's conquest marked the transition from the Bronze to the Iron Age. In the days of the judges—technically called Iron I—there came a marked deterioration in pottery, not only poorer workmanship but also a considerable diminution in the number of forms made (Fig. POT 63, Nos. 6*a-b*). By David's time, however, there was a quick upspring in craftsmanship, and new forms appeared, along with a heavy emphasis on hand burnishing—a finish which looks something like a light glaze—as decoration. Just as in the Hyksos renascence there had been an upsurge in both ceramics and metallurgy, so in David's day iron came into its own along with improved ceramics. The Divided Kingdom—Iron II—saw a continuation in better wares and more forms as well as the introduction of wheel burnishing (Fig. POT 63, Nos. *7a-f*). Toward the end of that period, however, something entirely new appeared in ceramics. The modern factory techniques, which we use, were created at that time, and mass production appeared. The potter was using assembly-line techniques, standardizing his wares, staggering his sizes, and at times even using trade-marks. The new techniques permitted the use of cheaper clays, cheaper labor, greater volume production, etc.; and yet the quality of the work continued high. The days of Isaiah and Jeremiah witnessed an industrial revolution in various fields, but ceramics seemed to be the most progressive of all. Fig. POT 63, Nos. *7a-f.*

Iron III, *ca.* 550-330 B.C., was roughly contemporaneous with the Persian period. In ceramics there was some modification of the old forms and the introduction of new ones, but nothing so striking as in the preceding period. By the time of Alexander the Great, the international commerce of the Eastern world brought another period of change in native ware and much larger importations of Greek pottery (Fig. POT 63, Nos. *8a-f*). This was the Hellenistic period. By approximately 50 B.C., however, pottery styles had again made sufficient changes to introduce a new ceramic period which we know as Roman (Fig. POT 63, Nos. *9a-d*). This is the pottery of NT times. Fig. POT 63, Nos. *9a-f.*

It is these constant changes in clays, forms, decorations, techniques of manufacture, etc., which enable the archaeologist to date the pottery he finds and thereby to date the cities he excavates. For reference to a popular but scholarly presentation of the various pottery forms as the archaeologist uses them to interpret history, see W. F. Albright, *The Archaeology of Palestine* (1954). For detailed studies and photographs, *see bibliography.*

3. The ceramic vocabulary used in pottery manufacture. The OT makes such wide and exact use of much of the potter's technical vocabulary that an expert ceramist can now re-create a good picture of the OT potter and his wares. The NT, however, presents only a small ceramic vocabulary, and furthermore, only a limited amount of pottery of NT times has been excavated in Palestine.

Clay is hydrated silicate of alumina ($Al_2O_3.2$ $SiO_2.2$ H_2O), mixed with various impurities which may at times constitute half the volume. There is no specific Hebrew term in the OT for a dry clay, so the following common words are pressed into use: עפר, "dust" (Job 10:9); אדמה, "ground" (Gen. 2:19); and ארץ, "ground" (Ps. 12:6—H 12:7; KJV "earth"). טיט is the technical term for a native wet clay which has not yet been reworked by either the potter or the brickmaker. Such a water-borne clay is referred to in Isa. 41:25; Nah. 3:14. חמר (Job 33:6; Isa. 29:16; 41:25; 45:9; 64:7; etc.) is a versatile ceramic term referring to any kind of worked clay. It can be the finest of the clays that are ready for use on the potter's wheel (Jer. 18:3-4), or a poorer grade used to seal wine jars (Job 38:14). The owner's name was imprinted in this clay with a seal (חותם; *see* SEALS AND SCARABS). The poorest grade was made into mud bricks (Nah. 3:14; cf. Gen. 11:3; Exod. 1:14).

After the fired pottery had been removed from the kiln, it was most commonly called כלי חרש, a pottery (RSV "earthen") vessel (Lev. 6:28—H 6:21; 11:33; 14:5, 50; 15:12; Num. 5:17; Jer. 32:14); or כלי יוצר, a potter's vessel (II Sam. 17:28; Ps. 2:9; Jer. 19:11). חרש is the technical term for any kind of fired ware (Prov. 26:23), although in actual usage elsewhere it refers only to potsherds (*see* POTSHERD). The NT uses the noun κεράμιον for "pottery" (Mark 14:13) and the adjectives κεραμικὸς (Rev. 2:27) and ὀστράκινος (II Tim. 2:20). The NT term σκεῦος has something of the all-inclusive meaning of the OT כלי. The Hebrew term יוצר is actually the generic word for any kind of craftsman and can be used of any skilled worker in clay, wood, metal, etc. In practice, however, the OT uses it predominantly for the potter. The corresponding NT term κεραμεὺς (Rom. 9:21), however, is more specific, being reserved exclusively for the craftsman in clay.

The potter worked either alone or with assistants, who were usually apprentices, often his own sons. By the time of the written prophets, however, manufacturing techniques demanded larger potteries for mass production. There was a royal guild (I Chr. 4:23), whose men doubtless made the official government storage jars which bear the inscription "for the king" followed by the name of the county-seat town, such as Hebron (Fig. SEA 35, Nos. 27-29). The king's private estates also had special jars whose handles had the name of the king and his treasurer stamped upon them. Fig. JEH 9.

The potter's house—i.e., his workshop or factory—was not only the building where he fashioned his wares on the wheel and set them aside to dry under proper conditions of evaporation, but where there would also be one or more kilns in his yard and plenty of room to weather the raw clay and purify it. Broken pottery and discards from the kiln were also piled up in the yard. Nearby water was a necessity, and in the city it was often furnished by a cistern on the premises. The Hinnom Valley, S of Jerusalem, was an ideal place for the potters of that city. Jer. 19:2 mentions a Potsherd Gate there. In the winter, water ran in the valley just outside this gate; and in the summer the pool of Siloam was only a short distance away. In the OT the kiln is called תנור (see Neh. 3:11; 12:38, where the Tower of the Ovens seems to refer to pottery kilns; *see* OVENS, TOWER OF THE), although this term is more commonly used to designate the household oven for the baking of bread (Lev. 2:4; 7:9; Hos. 7:4; etc.).

a. Bowls, cups, cooking pots, and lamps. The exact identification of the thirty-four Hebrew and Aramaic terms applied to the pottery vessels of the OT is a difficult task, but the general picture of the most important ware is about as follows: The most common ceramic form found by the archaeologist has been the bowl, and it ran in a great variety of patterns and sizes. The largest of these was the great banquet bowl, which had four handles and was beautifully wheel-burnished. In the Divided Kingdom the average size would be something like sixteen inches for the inside diameter at the rim and about half of that in height. The earlier banquet bowl of Iron I was much taller in proportion to its width and had only two handles. The best of these bowls were hand-burnished. This banquet bowl was also used as a

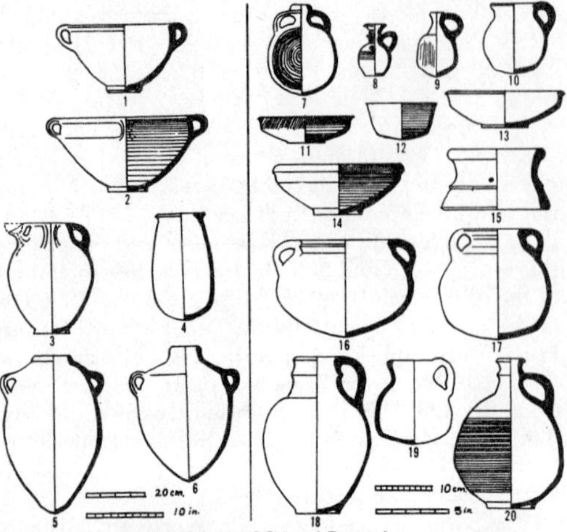

Courtesy of the American Schools of Oriental Research

65. Drawings of typical pottery forms of Israelite times, from Tell Beit Mirsim

crater for mixing wine (Song of S. 7:2—H 7:3). These were termed אגן (Exod. 24:6; Isa. 22:24; Fig. POT 63, No. 2) and ספל (Judg. 5:25; 6:38; Fig. POT 63, No. 1). Jael served Sisera out of the latter (Judg. 5:25). מזרק (Fig. POT 63, No. 2) may have been used for ceramicware (Amos 6:6?), but was certainly more often used of metal bowls (*see* VESSELS § 2). A medium-sized bowl of similar ware and general form, but without handles, was the צלחת (II Kings 21:13; II Chr. 35:13; Prov. 19:24; 26:15; Fig. POT 65, No. 14). The main dish of the meal was eaten from such a bowl. The laziest man alive, the sluggard of Prov. 19:24, was too lazy even to lift his hand out of this dish to feed himself. In the NT, the large dish out of which the meal was eaten was called τρύβλιον and is referred to when Jesus dipped his hand into the dish with Judas (Matt. 26:23). It was a foot or so in diameter and somewhat less than that in height. Παροψὶς, ἡ, of Matt. 23:25 was a smaller side dish for serving dainties. For the basin in which Jesus washed the disciples' feet (John 13:5), *see* BASIN.

A cheaper and smaller unburnished bowl, משארת (Exod. 8:3—H 7:28; 12:34; Deut. 28:5, 17; Fig. POT 65, No. 13), was used in OT times as a bread bowl in which leaven was mixed with flour and the dough allowed to rise (Exod. 12:34). A common size for this bowl was about ten inches wide and three inches deep; larger bowls were needed for larger families. The כיור of Zech. 12:6 was a still smaller bowl (Fig. POT 65, No. 11), which in this instance was used for holding coals. This same term in metalware (see Exod. 30:18; I Sam. 2:14; I Kings 7:38; etc.), however, implied other usages and also larger sizes, and the same was probably true in ceramics. In II Kings 2:20 the צלחית was a smaller bowl for holding salt. *See also* BASIN; BOWL.

Closely related to the last, but of much finer ware, were the סף (Exod. 12:22; Zech. 12:2; etc.; also used for metalware; Fig. POT 65, Nos. 11-12), and the קבעת (Isa. 51:17, 22). They were about the size of our mush bowls and soup plates and were used as serving dishes and wine cups. The סף of Zech. 12:2 was one of the larger wine cups. In Exod. 12:22 it held the blood of the Passover lamb.

The cup shape of today was fairly rare in OT times, except in the days of the Divided Kingdom. The cup with a handle was most commonly used as a dipper. The cup without a handle was more common and, whether it had a wide mouth or a narrow one, was often form-fitted to the hand. The term כוס could be used of both bowls and cups (Fig. POT 65, Nos. 11-12). The cup of the NT was ποτήριον, τὸ (Luke 11:39; Fig. POT 63, Nos. 8*a, f,* 9*c*). It ran from about the size of a small ash tray to that of a large mush dish. The smallest were shallow; the largest ran both deep and shallow. The ware could be native Palestinian or imported Greek or Roman. *See* CUP.

The household oven, תנור (Exod. 8:3; Lev. 2:4), is really an inverted bowl with a missing bottom. It was not thrown on the wheel but was handmade, usually of coiled clay molded into shape. It became pottery only after being used for some time as the oven for baking the family bread. Potsherds were at times inserted into the clay on the outside of the oven, thus giving a higher temperature within the oven. The NT uses κλίβανος for this oven (Luke 12:28). The same shaped oven that was used in Bible times is often used today. *See* OVEN. Fig. OVE 17.

Other modifications of the bowl form were cooking pots. The wide-mouth variety was of shallow depth. In the Divided Kingdom it had two handles, but before that it was handleless. It was called סיר (Fig. POT 65, No. 16). II Kings 4:38 (translated "pot") shows that it came in very large sizes, and such cooking pots have been found by archaeologists. The average one, however, was about a foot in diameter. This form could be used for other purposes, and Ps. 60:8—H 6:10 shows its use as a WASHBASIN. The other major cooking pot, דוד (Job 41:20—H 41:12; Fig. POT 65, No. 17), was a spherical form with only a narrow mouth. It had two small handles. It came in staggered sizes, just like modern pottery, and ran from approximately four to fourteen inches in diameter. It was much more common in the Divided Kingdom than earlier (*see also* BASKET). Closely related to the above in form, but less common in use, was a one-handled cooking pot, פרור (Num. 11:8; Judg. 16:19; Fig. POT 65, No. 19). Manna was cooked in it (Num. 11:8), and Gideon carried broth in it (Judg. 6:19). Mic. 3:3 proves that the קלחת, "caldron," is definitely a cooking pot, but we cannot identify it any more closely unless on the analogy of the similar metal term (I Sam. 2:14), where the reference is to a large-sized cooking pot.

The cooking pot was constantly subject to accident and to the expansion shock of heat and cold. It therefore demanded special skill in manufacture; and in the days of the Divided Kingdom potters often stamped their trade-marks on the handles of the wide-mouth variety. When cooking pots were used for deep-fat frying, they were termed מרחשת (Lev. 2:4-7; "pan"; KJV "frying pan"; see also Lev. 7:9) or משרת (II Sam. 13:9; "pan"; Fig. POT 65, No. 16). When ceramic cooking pots were given a general class name, the term סיר was used (Zech. 14:21; "pot"). NT cooking pots followed something of the OT form but were smaller and of much more delicate ware. The wide-mouth variety now often had a sharp shoulder and the spherical variety a larger mouth. Both used thin, straplike handles. There was also a third form, similar to our casserole. *See* COOKING AND COOKING UTENSILS.

The thin PLATE such as we use today was a difficult ceramic form to manufacture, and it was little used until NT times, when it was made by a new technique. A thick, heavy ceramic plate, however, was used as a griddle (מחבת; Lev. 2:5; 7:9; etc.; cf. the iron griddle of Ezek. 4:3).

The LAMP (נר) of the OT was a member of the bowl family, and the potter threw it as any bowl. While it was still soft, however, he pinched in the rim at one point to make a place for the wick. In early Israelite times it was five to six inches wide and *ca.* two inches or so deep. In the Divided Kingdom, it was much smaller and quite shallow, with a rollover rim. In the intertestamental period the lamp was quite small. The sides of the newly thrown bowl were lapped over one another in such a way that at one end of the lamp there was a large hole into which the oil was poured, and at the other end was a small hole for the wick. Before NT times, however, the lamp had taken on a second form. It was then made in two pieces which were stuck together when they were leather hard. The lower section was an egg-shaped shallow bowl. The upper section covered the lower one except at the center, where a hole was left for filling the lamp. A spout was shaped and added to the bowl. It held the wick. The spout section was handmade; the other pieces were made in a press mold. These lamps were small, often *ca.* three inches in length. None of these lamps gave much light, and if more light was needed, numerous lamps were lighted. In antiquity little work was done at night. The NT "lamp" is λαμπὰς (Matt. 25:1) and λύχνος (Mark 4:21).

b. Jars, pitchers, and juglets. The second basic form in ceramicware was the jar. In this ceramic family height was the major dimension, and the side walls might vary considerably in their pattern, depending upon the material stored in them. The largest storage jar was the נבל (Fig. POT 65, No. 5). It was often used for the storage of wine and derived its name from the earlier wineskin (Jer. 48:11-12). It was a pear-shaped vessel, and during the days of the Divided Kingdom a common size held two baths (*see* BATH) and was *ca.* twenty-five inches in height and sixteen inches in diameter. It had four handles. These are the jars which at times bore the official stamp of the government or even of the king himself, as described in § 3. This jar also came in smaller, two-handle sizes.

In the earliest Israelite history there was a water jar somewhat similar in form to the above but called a כד (Gen. 24:14 ff). In the days of the Divided Kingdom, however, this term was used to describe a distinctly new form of water jar (Fig. POT 63, No. 7*a*). This was a tall, cylindrical form something like an old-fashioned crock but with thinner walls and rounded bottom. A common size approximated thirteen inches in height and seven and a half inches in diameter. It had a fine anti-splash rim (Fig. POT 65, No. 4). This was a multiple-purpose jar, as it also served for the storage of flour (I Kings 17:12) and other dry products. Its mouth was sufficiently wide so that one could take out handfuls of flour, and yet it was small enough to be covered by a lid. Lids, however, are rarely found in the excavations of OT cities. A small bowl, a large potsherd, or a stopper of clay or stone was more likely to be used than a special lid. By NT times, however, the lid had become more common.

The NT term ἄντλημα of John 4:11 (interpreted as something to draw water with) might refer to a PITCHER, a water jar, or a leather BUCKET. However, in the twenty-eighth verse of that chapter ὑδρία ("water jar"; KJV "waterpot") is definitely the jar in which water was carried from the well to the house. Another related term is κεράμιον ὕδατος (Mark 14:13; "jar of water"; KJV "pitcher of water"). The NT water jar ran in various forms and sizes but was usually about twice as high as wide.

Large storage jars were round-bottomed, and therefore, if used in a room with flagstone pavement, they were set in special ring bases, כירים (Lev. 11:35; "stoves"; KJV "ranges for pots"). These bases looked like an old-fashioned spittoon with the bottom missing (Fig. POT 65, No. 15). They also served to hold cooking pots in place over the fire and to concentrate the heat. *See* COOKING AND COOKING UTENSILS.

אסוך ("jar"; KJV "pot"; Fig. POT 65, No. 3) was a special variety of storage jar used exclusively for oil. It was common in the days of the Divided Kingdom and is mentioned in the episode where Elisha replenished the poor widow's supply of oil (II Kings 4:2). This jar had something of an egg shape and stood a little over a foot high. It had three handles and a specially designed spout. The latter was wide-flaring and shallow. It was pierced by only a small hole, thus making it easy to fill small juglets as well as open lamps. Fig. POT 63, No. 7*b*, shows a small jar of this type.

Water pitchers ran in several varieties. The גביע (Fig. POT 65, No. 18) was similar in shape to the common water pitcher of today and averaged about eight to ten inches in height. It could also be used for wine and is mentioned along with wine cups in Jer. 35:5 ("pitchers"; KJV "pots"). The most expensive water decanter was the בקבק (Jer. 19:1, 10; "flask"; KJV "bottle"; Fig. POT 65, No. 20; Fig. POT 63, No. 7*e*). It had a heavy body and a narrow neck with a handle attached to neck and rim. This narrow neck was of utilitarian value, for it aerated the water as it was poured out. The gurgling sound produced by the narrow neck gave the vessel its peculiar name. The water decanter ran in staggered sizes from four to ten inches in height. I Kings 14:3 ("jar"; KJV "cruse") mentions that this jar was also used for carrying strained honey.

The small oil juglets which ran from *ca.* three to six inches in height are very common in all excavations. The exact name is uncertain, but I Kings 17:12 seems to identify them with the צפחת ("cruse"). The corresponding term for this kind of juglet in the parable of the wise and foolish virgins is ἀγγεῖον (Matt. 25:1-13). These NT juglets, unlike the OT ones, tend to be spherical or egg-shaped. The smallest of all juglets, פך (Fig. POT 65, Nos. 8, 9), was the one used for perfume (Fig. POT 63, Nos. 6*b;* 7*d*). Oil, rather than alcohol, was the perfume base in ancient times. I Sam. 10:1 specified this juglet (translated "vial") as the one used by Samuel when anointing Saul. The one used in the anointing of Jehu (II Kings

9:3; "flask"; KJV "box") may possibly have been a Cypro-Phoenician importation, as these were common at that time. The most expensive perfumes throughout all of Bible times came in alabaster jars. This container was still being used in NT times (Matt. 26:7), although glass was fast becoming a competitor.

c. Miscellaneous ware. The צפחת apparently designated two totally unrelated ceramic products, for this term is used not only of small oil juglets but also of the large pilgrim bottle or army canteen (Fig. POT 65, No. 7). It was a two-handled lentoid flask which came into use in Canaanite days and continued on into the early days of the Divided Kingdom (Fig. POT 63, Nos. 5*a-b;* 6*c, f;* 7*f*). The canteen was lightly baked so that there was a little seepage, which tended to cool the water in the canteen. David took Saul's canteen away from the King's head while he slept (I Sam. 26:11-12 "jar"; KJV "cruse"). Those of NT times were very much smaller and were characterized by twisted handles. The מבשלת of "boiling places" of Ezek. 46:23 (RSV "hearths") seems to refer to brick stoves similar to those found in Babylonian temples.

In spite of the low cost of pottery, some of the better pieces were mended. The archaeologist finds where cracked or broken ware had been held in place by rivets or wires which ran through small holes drilled in the pottery. The jar chosen by Jeremiah for his illustrated sermon (Jer. 19) had such a narrow neck that the vessel could never be mended. Even when pottery was broken, it still had a little utilitarian value; the larger sherds from storage jars could be used for jar lids or writing material (*see* § 2 *above*). Also, they were used to carry coals from house to house for starting fire and for dipping up water out of a pool (Isa. 30:14). Job used a potsherd as a strigil (Job 2:8). Finally, potsherds could be ground fine and used in the waterproof plaster of cisterns. Most sherds, however, became a part of the general debris of the house where the pottery had been used. Their finest utilitarian value is to the archaeologist of today. *See* POTSHERD.

4. Ceramics in industry. The most important field for ceramics in industry was metallurgy. The high temperature required for smelting and refining metals made the ceramic crucible a necessity, whether it was large-scale smelting, as at Solomon's refineries at EZION-GEBER, or small-scale refining, as done by the jeweler. Three terms were used for the crucible in the jeweler's art: עליל (Ps. 12:6—H 12:7); כור; and מצרף (Prov. 17:3). כור, however, is the broadest term, for it also refers to the smelter's furnace (Deut. 4:20; Ezek. 22:18-22; the latter passage, however, may refer to the refining of scrap metal or jeweler's sweepings to recover the silver). כבשן by etymology seems to mean a smelting furnace, but the context in the passages in which it appears (Gen. 19:28 ["furnace"]; Exod. 9:8, 10; 19:18 ["kiln"; KJV "furnace"]) suggests a pottery kiln or a charcoal kiln. Perhaps the word had all three usages. Where limestone crucibles were used, these had to be lined with clay. Smelted copper was poured into clay molds. One authority, in commenting on Zech. 11:13, thinks that the Persians used standard-sized clay jars into which they poured molten gold to form bullion.

In the cloth industry cheap spindle whorls, פלך (II Sam. 3:29 ["spindle"; KJV "staff"]; Prov. 31:19 ["spindle"; KJV "distaff"]), were sometimes made of pottery. The loom weights which were used in the weaving of cloth, when this industry was at its peak late in the Divided Kingdom, were almost always made of pottery.

In the toy industry, feeding bottles were made for babies. These bottles were imitations of both animals and birds. The milk was poured into a hole in the back of the animal and then came out a small hole in the animal's mouth. For girls there were small clay dolls and miniature dishes and lamps. For boys there were clay horses and cavalrymen, camels and other animals.

In the building trades of Palestine sun-dried brick was very common, but it is not pottery. If placed in water, it would turn to mud. Fired brick was rare in Palestine but common in Babylonia, where it had to be used in foundations under water. Dan. 3:6 may possibly be a reference to a brick kiln. Glazed tile is referred to in Exod. 24:10, where the translation is literally a "brickwork of sapphire." The palace of Ramses the Great, at Qantir, had featured glazed tile, and he may have been the Pharaoh of the Exodus. Blue was a common color in Egyptian glaze.

5. Ceramics in Canaanite cult objects. The Canaanite cultus was a user of ceramic material. The TERAPHIM or clay figures of Astarte, the Canaanite fertility goddess, were common before Joshua's conquest. They constitute the crux in the episode of the separation of Jacob and Laban, for at that time they had not only religious, but also high legal, significance (Gen. 31:19-55). Baal images were almost exclusively made of metal. The Astartes of the Canaanites were plaques made in a press mold. They were usually thin and smaller than the palm of the hand. The goddess wore the heavy Egyptian wig or the feathered headdress that came down from the N. She often held lotus blossoms in her hands (*see* ASHTORETH). The Astartes of Jezebel's time and later are quite different and look like tiny "snow men" *ca.* four to six inches in height. The body of the goddess was hand-modeled, and her skirts flared out so as to form a solid pedestal. The head was made in a press mold, and the features were often brought out in fine detail. The two units were put together when leather hard. The face was painted red to imitate rouge. There was also a stylized tree holding a lamp in its branches which was used in the household worship of this idol. Pottery rattles, doves, bulls, etc., were also employed in the ritual. Vessels used in the older Canaanite ritual were at times decorated with snakes, another symbol of the goddess. By Jeremiah's time there was a special pottery altar of incense, חמן, used in this and other heathen cults (Jer. 19:13; *see* INCENSE ALTAR). Isa. 65:3 speaks of burning incense upon brick, doubtless brick altars.

6. Glass and glaze. The most difficult field in ancient ceramics was glass and glaze, and both were rare in OT Palestine but not in NT days. In the OT, "glass," זכוכית, is mentioned only once—i.e., in Job 28:17 (KJV "crystal"), where it is as valuable as gold. Egypt was Palestine's major source of glass. In that country glass was a soda-lime silicate, although the properties in its composition differed from those of modern glass. Their formulas produced an opaque glass at low temperature, which made it easy to work the glass into the desired shape. By NT times new techniques were putting glass on the market in ever-increasing quantities. The phrase, rendered literally, "a glassy ὑάλινος sea like crystal" in Rev. 4:6 is an interesting one, for the ideal of the ancient glassmaker was to get the clarity of crystal (see also Rev. 21:21).

Glaze, ספגים (Ugaritic *spsg*), which is a glass coating on pottery, has already been mentioned. The word "glaze" occurred originally in Prov. 26:23 (so RSV), although the phrase "like glaze" has become corrupted to "silver dross" (KJV) through redivision of the consonants. Glazed brick has already been referred to in § 4 *above*. The Greeks were experts on glaze, and by intertestamental times their wares were becoming common among the rich in Palestine. By NT times Roman ware was also imported.

7. Pottery in the ceremonial law. Most vessels used in the ceremonial law were metal, but occasionally a pottery one was specified, as in the law of the cleansing of a leper (Lev. 14:5) and the law concerning jealousy (Num. 5:17). Pottery made ceremonially unclean by dead creeping things was broken (Lev. 11:32-35). More expensive ware was washed rather than destroyed. At the other extreme in the ceremonial law is the great prediction of Zech. 14:20-21. Here the pottery vessels in the temple shall be like the most holy metal ones; and furthermore, even the common household pottery of the inhabitants of Jerusalem and Judah shall be holy unto the Lord.

8. Figurative language derived from ceramics. The most striking of all figurative language that comes from the potter is that of God's molding human personality. The creation story of Gen. 2:7 portrays God as a ceramic sculptor fashioning man just as the toymaker made little children or as the idolmaker fashioned his little statuettes! This figurative language is indeed striking, for it seems to skate on the thinnest of theological ice. There was, of course, one outstanding difference—God breathed into man the breath of life.

The more common figure of God as a ceramist, however, is that of the Master Potter at his wheel fashioning men and nations as the potter fashions his wares. Jer. 18:1-6 is the classic passage. The same theme appears often. There are examples both early and late in Isaiah (29:16; 64:8). Paul picks up the figure in Rom. 9:20-24. The figure of man's frailty is the earthen jar (Lam. 4:2), and the folly of fighting against God is the folly of the potsherd (KJV; RSV "earthen vessel") fighting the potter (Isa. 45:9). At God's command Jeremiah smashed the finest of the water decanters to illustrate the nation's doom (ch. 19). Another ceramic figure for tragedy appears in Lev. 26:26, where ten women must bake bread in only a single oven.

Among the specific pottery vessels most strikingly and commonly used for figurative language are the lamp and the cup. Job speaks of God's lamp shining upon him (Job 29:3). God promised David a lamp forever (II Chr. 21:7). The lamp of the New Jerusalem is the Lamb (Rev. 21:23). Emphasizing the exact extreme of these passages, Prov. 20:20 says that everyone who curses father and mother shall have his lamp put out in blackest darkness. The psalmist speaks of God's Word as a lamp to his feet (Ps. 119:105). For the figurative use of the cup, *see* CUP.

Bibliography. W. F. Albright, "The Excavation of Tell Beit Mirsim, I: The Pottery of the First Three Campaigns," *AASOR*, Vol. XII (1932); "The Excavation of Tell Beit Mirsim, IA: The Bronze Age Pottery of the Fourth Campaign," *AASOR*, vol. XIII (1933). K. Galling, *Biblisches Reallexikon* (1937). J. L. Kelso, "The Ceramic Vocabulary of the OT," *BASOR*, Supplementary Studies, nos. 5-6 (1948). W. F. Albright, *The Archaeology of Palestine* (1954). J. L. Kelso and D. C. Baramki, "Excavations at NT Jericho and Khirbet en-Nitla," *AASOR*, vols. XXIX-XXX (1955).

J. L. KELSO

POUND [μνᾶ (John 12:3; 19:38), λίτρα (Luke 19: 33 ff); KJV מנה (I Kings 10:17; Ezra 2:69; Neh. 7: 71-72; RSV MINA)]. The λίτρα (the same as Latin *libra*) contained twelve ounces and was used both as a weight and as a measure of capacity. In the Lukan version of the "parable of the talents" (Luke 19:11-27) the term "pound" evidently refers to money, as it does in some countries today.

See also WEIGHTS AND MEASURES §§ B4*i*, C4*o*.

O. R. SELLERS

*__POVERTY.__ The condition of having little or no wealth or material possessions. This is a relative condition. Poverty is not the greatest evil in the world, any more than wealth is the greatest good, even though some Talmudic rabbis felt poverty to be almost a curse. There are some expressions in the OT suggesting that life is hardly worth living because of the wretchedness of the poor (Job 24:4-12; Eccl. 4:1-3). To wish someone to become poor is the worst curse (II Sam. 3:29; Ps. 109:9-10). Yet poverty is to be preferred to ill-gotten wealth (Prov. 28:6; Eccl. 4:13-14; etc.). The biblical terms for "poverty" are considered under POOR.

Poverty has many causes. In most instances it is not truly foreordained by God (cf. I Sam. 2:7; Job 1:21). It may be the result of sloth and laziness (Prov. 6:10; 19:15; 24:30; etc.); of drunkenness (Ecclus. 19:1); of sumptuous living (Prov. 21:17; Ecclus. 18:32); of folly and stubbornness (Prov. 13: 18; 28:19; etc.); of oppression and greed (Exod. 1:13; II Sam. 12:1-2; Jer. 22:13; etc.); of calamity, plague, war, disease, fraud, usury, over which the victim has no control (Exod. 10:4-5; Num. 11:4-5; Judg. 10:8; Ps. 105:34; etc.).

Some were poor voluntarily. The Levites may have been voluntarily poor, and in the days of the monarchy they were without land. This may perhaps reflect the religious ideal of NOMADISM. Many prophets and rabbis had no regular income. Jesus became poor for the sake of mankind (II Cor. 8:9; Phil. 2:5-6). The rich young ruler was advised to sell everything (Matt. 19:21 ff). This may not mean that Jesus enjoined voluntary poverty on all his followers, but rather that idolatry of his possessions had to be rooted out of the rich young man. The early church held all things in common (Acts 2:44; 4:32). Similarly, the sectarians of Qumran (*see* DEAD SEA SCROLLS) seem to have practiced voluntary poverty. In Qumran all who entered the sect accepted the state of poverty, but in Christianity it is clearly voluntary and free. So Ananias and Sapphira did not have to give up all (Acts 5:1 ff), but were punished for their deceit.

SLAVERY was preferred by many to poverty. The poor could sell themselves to others (Lev. 25:39 ff). He could sell his minor children (Exod. 21:7 ff; Neh. 5:5). In the Tell el-Amarna Letters, children were sold to provide food for the parents. It is probable that the minor children were sold first before a man sold himself into slavery. This procedure provided the necessities of life and a certain kind of security. In the Jubilee year such voluntary slaves were to be released. It is obvious that security was preferred by some to freedom (Deut. 15:16 ff). Creditors also seized the children of debtors (II Kings 4:1; Amos 2:6). In spite of all this there is evidence throughout the history of the OT and in modern Judaism that children felt an obligation to care for aged and indigent parents.

In the early history of civilization all men lived under conditions we would consider poverty. In the nomadic state there were slaves, but there were few freeborn poor, unless we consider all to have been poor. The bonds of brotherhood and family interdependence averted extremes of poverty unless the whole tribe became destitute. A few, like Abraham, were wealthy (Gen. 12:16). In urban civilization the contrast between economic classes became most noticeable. At the beginning of the Conquest the majority of families were landowners, but it was not long before some became landed barons while others were practically serfs. Some who owned land lost it through calamity, war, or fraud. Craftsmen were seldom wealthy. In the Babylonian captivity all lost their wealth. The farmers who were left behind in Judah lived on the ravished land at a subsistence level. In Babylon a few Israelites became wealthy merchants. The nobles and the priests may have profited by the misfortunes of others. It is possible that "poor" as a sectarian designation may have arisen during this time of crisis. In the return only those who had not profited by their stay in Babylon returned to Palestine. In Hellenistic and Roman times, there were all classes of people in Palestine. In Rome itself most of the Jews were of the poorer class and lived on the wrong side of the Tiber. The early Christian converts apparently came from this group also.

It is possible that at any time in history those who lost their land for any reason would migrate in the hope of meeting better fortune. Some think this is the explanation for the gerim or sojourners (*see* SOJOURNER), rather than that they are citizens of other countries or dispossessed Canaanites. Under such calamity, many preferred to abandon the tribal territory or their native locality and to go elsewhere seeking new opportunity. Hospitality was to be shown to these sojourners at all times. In the third century A.D. a synagogue in Jerusalem had a hospice for housing needy strangers, and the early Christians were always giving shelter to their fellows.

See bibliography under POOR. C. U. WOLF

POWDERS OF THE MERCHANT [אבקת רוכל] (Song of S. 3:6). The litter of Solomon was perfumed with spices and the fragrant "powders of the merchant," perhaps spices pulverized to release their fragrance and peddled by itinerant merchants (cf. Gen. 37:25). J. M. MYERS

POWER. The translation of חיל; כח; עז; גבורה; δύναμις; and ἐξουσία. By its very nature the Hebrew language is concrete and colorful. It made little progress in developing abstract concepts. It expresses ideas of power in a variety of picturesque ways. Greek is far more abstract, tending to consolidate its thought into well-defined ideas; but its words possess great flexibility. Δύναμις, e.g., was used by the LXX translators of the OT into Greek to express no fewer than twenty-six separate Hebrew words and phrases. In the NT it commonly refers to angels or demons (Eph. 1:21; 3:10; 6:12; Col. 1:16; 2:10, 15; I Pet. 3:22; cf. Ign. Eph. 13:1; *Martyrdom of Polycarp* 14:1). In the gospels by metonymy it often means MIRACLE (Matt. 7:22; Luke 10:13), and in Mark 14:62 it even stands as a metonym for God.

1. Powers of nature
2. Labor and industry
3. The human will
4. Political and military power
5. Spiritual power
   a. God
   b. Good and evil spirits
   c. Dragons
   d. Satan

Bibliography

1. Powers of nature. In a scientific and philosophical sense, biblical people did not attain a concept of nature. They had practically no understanding of the natural world. One can read through the Bible without encountering such concepts as forces of gravitation, magnetism, electricity, and atomic energy. There is little understanding of physiology; none whatever of bacteria, infection, etc. Laws of heredity were unknown, although there appears to be some anticipation of these in the idea that sins of the fathers are visited on the children, or, conversely, that children are blessed because of the good character of the parents (Exod. 20:5-6). People of the Bible lived in a prescientific world.

2. Labor and industry. It follows that man had little in the way of implements and machines to aid him in his work, whether for the chores of nomadic life, of agriculture, or of building enterprises. Power had to be supplied by the strength of men and animals. Large projects like Solomon's construction, mining, shipping, etc., of the tenth century B.C. were possible only by the labor of slaves and drafted free men (I Kings 5:13-18; 9:15-22). The most common beasts of burden were the ass and the ox. Camels were used especially for caravans. The horse was not introduced until the time of David and Solomon. The power of wind was exploited by sailing vessels. Fire was used for refining metals and cooking.

3. The human will. Throughout the Bible it is assumed that the will is free. This is expressed in Gen. 1:26 by the idea that man is created in the image of God. This means, not that he is formed in the physical image of God, but that he is like God in a spiritual sense. His intelligence enables him to discern good and evil, and free will makes it possible to choose between right and wrong. So man is responsible for his conduct. His moral character results from his own choice. This is not to say that man possesses unlimited freedom, that he can defy God and defeat his will; but that within his own sphere man is a free and responsible being.

4. Political and military power. Whether in family, tribe, nation, or the world, biblical writers are familiar with the concept of political power, recognizing its importance and validity. It has a religious nature and basis, and is necessary for the life of man. The OT regards the Hebrew nation as a theocracy. Father, chieftain, priest, prophet, or king derives his power from God, and is responsible to him for the way he uses it. The idea of secular political power is unknown to biblical writers.

5. Spiritual power. ***a. God.*** Numerous vestiges of ancient animism and polytheism survive in the Bible, but the faith of those who edited the writings in the form in which they have come down to us was monotheism. God manifests his power, not only by creation, but also by providential control of the world. All power of every kind is derived from God. While he grants autonomy to man and other beings in their respective realms, his own prerogative remains uncompromised.

b. Good and evil spirits. In earlier strata of the biblical documents, the numerous spirits remain anonymous, but they are thought of as servants of God, who, e.g., sends an evil spirit to torment King Saul (I Sam. 16:14). By the end of the OT, in the intertestamental writings, and especially in the NT, evil spirits or demons are called Satan's subjects.

c. Dragons. Several dragons are mentioned in the Bible: the multiple-headed sea serpent Leviathan (Job 3:8; Ps. 74:13-14; Isa. 27:1); Rahab (Job 9:13; 26:12; Ps. 89:10; Isa. 30:7; 51:9), which causes storms at sea; another sea monster and Behemoth, a desert dragon (I Enoch 60:7; II Esd. 6:49); Belial or Beliar (apparently an alternate name for Satan), who is frequent in the Dead Sea Scrolls (CD VI, VIII; 1QS I) and is mentioned in I Cor. 6:15.

d. Satan. But in the NT, on the whole, Satan has become supreme as ruler of evil spirits and evil men and beasts in opposition to God. He was unknown in the earlier strata of the OT. He appears first in I Chr. 21:1 ff; Job 1:6 ff; Zech. 3:1-2. II Sam. 24:1 says it was the Lord who incited David to take a military registration of the people, which was a sin, but the Chronicler says it was Satan. The apparent contradiction results from the more adequate concept of God which was attained in the later period. Late biblical writers held that God and angels, on the one hand, were opposed by Satan and demons on the other—a dualism reminiscent of Zoroastrian theology. But it is not an absolute dualism. Biblical belief holds that God gains the ultimate victory, that good is more powerful than evil.

Bibliography. E. Hatch and H. A. Redpath, *Concordance to the LXX* (1906); F. S. Brown, S. R. Driver, and C. A. Briggs, *Hebrew and English Lexicon of the OT* (1907); M. Burrows, *Outline of Biblical Theology* (1946); W. Bauer, *Greek-English Lexicon of the NT* (1957).

S. V. McCasland

POWER OF KEYS. The power entrusted to Peter by Jesus, saying: "I will give you the keys of the kingdom of heaven, and whatever you bind on earth shall be bound in heaven, and whatever you loose on earth shall be loosed in heaven" (Matt. 16:19). The keys are the symbol of rule and authority entrusted by the real holder, Jesus the Messiah (cf. Rev. 3:7). The power of the keys is thus the power over the whole house of the Lord, and primarily the power to admit into it, which involves also the power to exclude from it. Now, when Jesus himself preaches the gospel and forgives sins (cf. Mark 2:10), he opens to men the doors of the kingdom, while the Pharisees "shut the kingdom of heaven against men" (Matt. 23:13). Jesus does not give his divine power to these "blind guides" but to Peter. It is the power to act as Jesus did—i.e., the power to preach the gospel of grace and judgment, to forgive sins, and thus to gather the new people of God, the church (Matt. 16:18). In fact, the power of the keys does not essentially differ from the power to bind and to loose entrusted to all the apostles (*see* Binding and Loosing). Yet the power of the keys is given to Peter alone, as the church is built on him. Both sayings express his primacy among the Twelve.

P. H. Menoud

PRAETORIAN GUARD prĭ tôr′ĭ ən. The translation of πραιτώριον (KJV PALACE) in Phil. 1:13. This word here almost certainly refers to persons, although in the gospels and Acts it is always a place (*see* Praetorium 1): the official residence or palace of the governor, or the courtyard in which trials were conducted, or the adjoining barracks where the military were housed. In Phil. 1:13 the reference to persons is obvious from the words: "It has become known throughout the whole πραιτώριον and to all the rest." But the question remains: Does the whole "πραιτώριον" refer to the praetorian guard or to the imperial high court? The answer to this question may depend on whether Philippians was written in Rome or in a provincial city such as Caesarea or Ephesus. If in Rome, then the meaning is probably, though not necessarily, the praetorian or imperial (body)guard. "All the rest" is sufficiently vague and inclusive to take in both the menials attached to the barracks and "those of Caesar's household" (Phil. 4:22), even though there is no instance in which "praetorium" is used to mean the emperor's palace in Rome.

If Philippians was written from an imprisonment in a provincial city, 1:13 could refer either (*a*) to the military and "all the rest" of the people attached to the governor's place; or (*b*) more generally, as the KJV translates, to "all the palace," meaning all those who were in any way related to it, whether officials or servants, but without intending to identify them; or (*c*) to the imperial high court, the highest judicial authority. Lohmeyer (*see bibliography*) urges that since it belongs to the martyrology pattern that the martyr present his "witness" in open court before the highest authorities of the heathen world, "praetorium" here must mean the imperial high court. Then "all the rest" would mean those who had no official responsibility for the trial, but made up the audience, such as soldiers, bystanders, or observers of any sort.

Bibliography. See the Notes in M. Dibelius, *An die Philipper* (1913); E. Lohmeyer, *Der Brief an die Philipper* (1953), at 1:13. See also: L. Homo, *Roman Political Institutions* (1929), pp. 241-43, 338; "Praetorians," *Oxford Classical Dictionary* (1949). F. D. GEALY

PRAETORIUM prē tōr'ĭ əm [πραιτώριον, *loan word from* Lat. *praetorium*] (Matt. 27:27 [=Mark 15:16]; John 18:28, 33; 19:9; Acts 23:35); KJV COMMON HALL (Matt. 27:27); HALL OF JUDGMENT (John 18:28); JUDGMENT HALL (John 18:33; 19: 9; Acts 23:35). Alternately: PRAETORIAN GUARD. **1.** Originally, the tent or headquarters of the praetor or general in a Roman camp; then, by extension of meaning, the residence or palace of a provincial governor, whether his title was praetor, proconsul, procurator (John 18:28), or prince (Acts 23:35); and finally, any large country house or villa. In the gospels and in Acts the term always has to do with the governor's official residence, or part of it. In all these six instances the RSV translates "praetorium" (so Moffatt). As transliteration, "praetorium" may be preferred, yet it leaves the word undefined. Does it refer to the governor's residence (Mark 15:16 Goodspeed) or governor's house (John 18:28, 33; 19:9 Amer. Trans.), or Herod's palace (Acts 23:35)? Or should it be taken to mean "barracks" (Matt. 27:27 Amer. Trans.)?

As for Mark 15:16, whether "that is, the praetorium," is a marginal gloss (as some have proposed) or not, and whether αὐλή is to be translated "palace" (RSV) or "courtyard" (Goodspeed, Moffatt), it is not wholly clear whether the text means that the praetorium is the palace or is part of the palace—namely, the barracks. The immediate context in both Matt. 27:27; Mark 15:16, with the presence of "the whole battalion" of soldiers, suggests "barracks" as the chief meaning of "praetorium" here. Since the governor's palace, the open court (atrium) within or before the palace where the judgment seat or bema was set on a mosaic floor or "pavement" (John 19:13) made for the purpose of public hearings, and the barracks were part of the same establishment, "praetorium" seems to have been a term designating either the whole or any part.

In John, in all the references (18:28, 33; 19:9) one "enters into" or "goes out" from the praetorium: Pilate enters the praetorium and brings Jesus out. The inference from 19:1-3 is that the mockery took place within the praetorium. Thus in John, too, "praetorium" seems to cover the governor's residence, barracks, and place of judgment.

"Herod's praetorium" (Acts 23:35) was the palace built by Herod the Great in Caesarea and used as headquarters in Palestine by the Roman procurators. Since there were five cohorts of soldiers stationed in Caesarea, the government premises would be extensive. In stating that Paul was presented personally to the governor, Luke probably suggests that Paul was treated by Felix as a gentleman-prisoner and was regarded as a special "guest" in the "palace," though Paul would probably be put in the appropriate military lockup.

Opinion remains divided whether the praetorium in the gospels is to be located at Herod's palace at the NW corner of the Upper City or in the Tower of Antonia at the NW corner of the outer court of the temple. The normal garrison at Jerusalem consisted of one COHORT, commanded by a tribune (Acts 21:31), and located in the Fortress of Antonia (vss. 31-40). If these were the soldiers involved in the trial and mockery, then the Tower of Antonia would be the temporary residence of Pilate. Also, if Herod was present in Jerusalem at the time, he would be occupying his own palace. As against Antonia, it is urged that Pilate would not have come to Jerusalem without an escort, perhaps another cohort—one of the five in Caesarea—or, if not a cohort, at least a maniple (120 or 60 men). These all could easily have been accommodated in Herod's palace.

2. The military attached to the praetorium; the praetorians, or PRAETORIAN GUARD. In this usage the word could refer to (*a*) the military council in the praetor's tent; (*b*) the imperial high court; or (*c*) the imperial bodyguard.

The imperial high court or supreme court was composed of the emperor or his delegate, the prefect of the praetorian guard, and twenty assessors selected from the Senators. The court functioned both as a council of war and as a council of judgment.

During the last two centuries of the Republic, generals normally had a bodyguard or *cohors praetoria.* When Augustus came to the throne, in 27 B.C., he established his general headquarters, his praetorium, in Italy, and out of the veterans available organized a permanent corps or guard of nine cohorts of a thousand men each. To avoid suspicion of military despotism, only some of the troops were billeted in Rome, the others being stationed either outside the city or in various Italian towns. Because of their attendance on the emperor, the praetorians rated as the *corps d'élite.* They served for sixteen years, received three times the pay of legionaries and, in addition, frequent and large donations. Originally recruited from Italians, shortage of men made it eventually necessary to admit provincials, until under Septimus Severus (146-211) the provincials came to exclude the Italians.

The political importance of the praetorian guard dates from the time of Sejanus, who, appointed sole prefect in A.D. 23, concentrated the cohorts in a single camp just outside the walls of Rome. They now became a permanent threat. On the death of Caligula in 41 they were able promptly to put down the Senate's endeavor to restore the Republic and to proclaim Claudius emperor. Under Trajan (98-117) the whole corps was brought into Rome itself, in the Praetorian Camp on the Viminal. Although the number and the make-up of the cohort shifted during the years, they remained a menace until finally abolished by Constantine.

Bibliography. In addition to the references given in the bibliography under PRAETORIAN GUARD, see the valuable article "Pretoire" by A. Legendre in F. Vigouroux, *Dictionnaire de la Bible,* V (1922), 621-40. F. D. GEALY

PRAISE. A prominent part of man's many-sided response and approach to God through worship. God is essentially the object of man's praise (Deut. 10:21), and thereby the superiority and uniqueness of God in his divine person and activity are set forth. Praise attempts a description of God, but it cannot exhaust God.

Since praise is man's preoccupation with God, it

is inevitable that the Hebrew Bible contains several terms to describe this activity:

a) הלל in the *Pi'el*—i.e., intensive form of the verb. This word is specially familiar in the prime expression of all praise: HALLELUJAH, which means "Praise ye Yah"—i.e., "Praise the LORD." The noun of this root, תהלה, has a wide usage in the OT. It is the title of Ps. 145 and, in the plural, the Hebrew title of the book of Psalms. For some illuminating examples, see Isa. 16:14 ("glory"); Jer. 48:2 ("renown"); 51:41; Hab. 3:3.

b) ידה in the *Hiph'il*, "give thanks, praise." The original connection of the verb with worship is lost (perhaps the gesture of the hand יד); but since the word embodies, in both its verbal and nominal forms, an element of thanksgiving, it is not so purely a word of praise as the first mentioned. The noun תודה means a "thanksgiving hymn," a "thank offering."

c) זמר, probably at first of pruning songs, and then generally of songs of praise. Apart from Judg. 5:3; Isa. 12:5, the verb appears in the Psalms only. The word appears in nominal form as מזמר (LXX ψαλμός). This word occurs in fifty-seven psalm titles in various combinations: of instrumental music and of singing; and זמיר song. *See* MUSIC.

d) שבח (*Pi'el* and *Hithpa'el* only) occurs four times in Psalms and in Ecclesiastes, and its Aramaic form is found in Daniel.

See also such words as ברך, "to bless"; ענה, "to sing antiphonally"; רנן, "shout"; שיר, "sing"; גיל, "rejoice"; etc.

The ideas connected with the activity of praise are perhaps best illustrated by the opening verses of Ps. 113. Here, with one exception, are set forth all the principal aspects or topics of the activity of praise in the OT. "Praise the LORD" sets the theme of the Psalms; but later in vs. 1, and again in vss. 2-3, the object of praise is further defined as the name of the Lord. It is thus clear that the object of praise may be described simply as the Lord, or some attribute such as his name, or some epithet such as "my Strength," "my Redeemer," some metaphorical description such as "rock of our salvation" (95:1; cf. 18:1-3), etc. In 113:1—H 113:2 the second topic is given—"O servants of the LORD"—i.e., those who are to render praise. It may simply be "I," whether this is collectively or personally intended, or "my soul" (103:1; 104:1), "thy saints" (145:10) or "we" or "us," priests (135:19-20), other worshipers in the temple (149:2), the righteous (140:13), the redeemed of the Lord (cf. 107), or the nations (100), all that hath breath (150:6), and all the works of nature (cf. e.g., 19; 89:5; 96:11; 97:1; 98:4, 7-8; etc.), etc. Ps. 113:2*b* gives the third topic of praise, its occasion—when it is to be offered. This verse shows that praise is continuous, for morning, night, New Year's Day, day of victory and even of distress, etc., are all the occasions of praise. Vs. 3*a* likewise gives the place of praise—the fourth topic. Praise must be offered everywhere—from east to west. Praise is thus to be offered in Zion, in Jerusalem, at his holy hill, before the Lord in the sanctuary, upon their beds (63:5-6; 149:5), etc. Ps. 113:4 gives the ground or reason for praise: the Lord is high above all nations. This topic of praise is best pursued by the study of the word "for." The Hebrew word כי, "for," is the clue to the reasons why man must praise God. There is a theology hidden in the כי clauses of the Psalter and of the OT. Sometimes, as in 113:4, the "for" is not expressed, but it is implied, and in 100:3 "know that" is a variant of "because." Altogether "because" is a rewarding study in the OT concept of praise. The one topic of the activity of praise not mentioned in Ps. 113 is the mode of praise. The "how" topic involves sacrifices and offerings, physical activities, instruments, utterance, fasting, meditation, silence, etc. All these six separate topics connected with praise deserve separate studies which would show how natural, spontaneous, and widespread is the Israelite activity of praise. The importance of the Hebrew participial hymns of praise, represented by relative sentences in the English versions—e.g., the relative sentences in 103:3-5; 104:2-4; 113:5-9—and of the doxologies—e.g., 41:13; 72:18-19; 89:52; 106:48; 150; etc.—should not be forgotten.

See also PSALMS, BOOK OF; WORSHIP.

Bibliography. H. Gunkel and J. Begrich, *Einleitung in die Psalmen* (1933), pp. 32-94. P. Humbert, " 'Laetari et exultare' dans le vocabulaire religieux de l'AT," *RHPR*, XXII (1942), 185-214; *La "terou'a"* (1946). A. R. Johnson, "The Psalms," in H. H. Rowley, ed., *The OT and Modern Study* (1951), pp. 162-209. N. H. Snaith, *Hymns of the Temple* (1951). C. Westermann, *Das Loben Gottes in den Psalmen* (1953). A. Barucq, *L'expression de la louange divine et de la prière en Israël et en Egypte* (2 vols.; 1957). G. von Rad, "Der Lobpreis Israels," *Theologie des ATs*, I (1957), 353-67. G. HENTON DAVIES

PRAYER. In the Bible prayer moves from the level of magic to the heights of spiritual communion and identification of will and activity with God. No definition which would cover all the references is possible except in general terms. Prayer is attempted intercourse with God, with or without the mediation of priests or heavenly beings; it is usually, but not necessarily, vocal. It is designed by means of the creation of personal contact to affect the nature and course of the relationship. Its means and ends always depend upon how the nature of God is conceived.

A. Terminology
  1. In the OT
  2. In the NT
B. Prayer in the OT
  1. The sources JE—God and man converse
  2. The monarchic sources—prayer and providence
  3. The eighth-century prophets—the moral requirements of prayer
  4. The Deuteronomic school—prayer as recollection
  5. Jeremiah—prayer as personal meditation
  6. The Exile and after—prayer in Judaism
    a. The P school—development of liturgical prayer
    b. The Psalms and the practice of prayer
  7. The Greek period
    a. Prayer in a troubled world
    b. Prayer in synagogue and sect
    c. Approach to the NT
C. Prayer in the NT
  1. The Synoptic gospels
    a. Jesus at prayer
    b. Jesus' teaching on prayer

   2. Prayer in the early church
      a. Paul
      b. Other NT writers
   3. Hebrews—prayer through Christ's mediation
   4. The Fourth Gospel—prayer as communion
D. The mechanics of prayer
   1. Place
   2. Time
   3. Posture
E. Intercession
F. Unanswered prayer
G. God's initiative in prayer
H. Biblical doctrine of prayer
Bibliography

A. *TERMINOLOGY.* Since prayer can cover petition, entreaty, expostulation, confession, thanksgiving, recollection, praise, adoration, meditation, and intercession (*see* COMMUNION; CONFESSION; PRAISE; REPENT; THANKSGIVING; WORSHIP), the words used are not subject to exactness of use or distribution. This article will deal primarily with petition, intercession, and meditation, and with such other features only as are related to these.

1. In the OT. The most generally used term is the verb פלל, which in the *piel* can mean "to interpose or judge" and in the *hithpael* "to intercede or pray." Its root anciently was connected with slashing oneself as an act of worship (cf. I Kings 18:28; Hos. 7:14). The noun is תפלה, used notably in the titles of psalms. קרא is used of calling on God in praise or invocation of God's name. שאל may be "to request or make a petition" (e.g., Pss. 27:4; 122:6) or "to inquire for an oracle" (e.g., Num. 27:21; Josh. 9:14). The encounter which is a request or an intercession is described by פגע (Jer. 7:16; cf. Isa. 53:12; 59:16). By making the face of another pleasant, one may appease (e.g., Exod. 32:11) or seek a favor (e.g., Ps. 119:58), and here the word is חלה. Men cry out in need, and the verb זעק, "to cry," is used especially in Judges (3:9, etc.; cf. Ps. 22:5); another word for "cry" is רנן (noun רנה), a ringing cry used of both joy and distress (cf. Ps. 17:1; Jer. 31:12; Lam. 2:19). The *hithpael* of חנן, "to incline toward," is used of imploring favor of God, particularly in Solomon's prayer (I Kings 8:33, 47, 59; cf. Ps. 30:8). Less used words are שוע, "to cry for help," and שחר, "to seek."

2. In the NT. The most generally used word (and the most frequent but not uniform LXX translation) is the noun προσευχή, with the middle deponent verb προσεύχομαι, found most often in Luke-Acts (see the Hebrew idiom in Jas. 5:17). It applies particularly to asking of God and is a more religious term than δέησις and δέομαι, which are also found often in Luke-Acts and the LXX, and which mean "a request" and "to ask," but not necessarily of God. (On the absence of these terms from the Fourth Gospel, *see* § C4 *below.*) For "prayer" the Fourth Gospel uses principally the verb αἰτέω, which may be used of asking man or God. It is used with προσεύχομαι in Mark 11:24, and the two are in apposition in Col. 1:9. 'Εντυγχάνω in the sense of "intercede" (cf. פגע) is used of prayer in Rom. 8:27, 34; Heb. 7:25 only, but of a legal petition in Acts 25:24.

B. *PRAYER IN THE OT.* The nature of biblical prayer is best understood in its development through the major sources. The God of the Bible is the God who can be addressed as "thou who hearest prayer" (Ps. 65:2).

1. The sources JE—God and man converse. The oral traditions which reflect the animism and anthropomorphism of primitive Semitic religion, in which God is met with at sacred sites and through the medium of natural objects (*see* ASHERAH; MAGIC; PILLAR; TEREBINTH), are overlaid with the editorial work of the J and E writers, who trace the incipient grace of God manifested in the promise to the patriarchs and the covenant with Israel.

The fundamentals of prayer are found in the meetings with God, often depicted as conversations (in J, Gen. 3:8-19; 4:9-15; 15:1-16; 18:2-5; Exod. 3:1-12; etc.; in E, Gen. 20:3, 6; 28:12-16, etc.; for the meaning of such symbols as J, E, *see* PENTATEUCH). Man may respond to the meeting by erecting a shrine (Gen. 12:7; 13:18), by obedience (12:1-4*a;* 13:14-18), by faith (15:1-16), or verbally by a question or a request (15:2, 8; 18:23; etc.). God shares his intentions with Abraham (Gen. 18:17) and with Moses (Exod. 3, etc.). Moses is very vocal and expostulates with God and frequently asks guidance (Exod. 5:22-23; 32:11-13; Num. 11:1-15, etc.), while Abraham reasons (Gen. 18:22-33) and Jacob bargains (28:20-22 E).

The theophanies may involve an unrecognized visitor (Gen. 18:2, etc.; cf. Judg. 13:6; Heb. 13:2) or, particularly in E, a dream (Gen. 20:3, 6; 28:12-16). From the first, personality is ascribed to God, making the converse possible, though man may not look directly upon him (Exod. 33:18-23 E). Elohim is a god who is moved by prayer, whether verbal or not; in E, God responds to the weeping of a child as though it were a prayer (Gen. 21:16-17) and to the attempted sacrifice of Isaac (22:11-12). The nature of God is indicated by the names ascribed to him—e.g., "Shield" (Gen. 15:1); "Judge of all the earth" (18:25); the "Fear of Isaac" (31:42); the "Mighty One of Jacob, . . . the Shepherd, the Rock of Israel" (49:24, added to J). In Gen. 18:16-33, Abraham appeals to God as Judge, and God responds in character, thereby establishing the true basis of prayer in the first account of intercession.

Recollection of past acts of mercy as a basis for prayer already appears in JE (Gen. 32:9-12; Exod. 32:13); this element was notably to be developed by the D school. The rudimentary seeking of an oracle (e.g., Gen. 25:22) develops nobly into the prayer for guidance (24:12-14). Here prayer is described as "speaking in my heart," indicating that it need not be audible. In the words "Blessed be . . ." (vss. 26-27) Eleazar provides the earliest understanding that to give thanks is to bless God (*see* BLESSINGS AND CURSINGS; THANKSGIVING). By working over a primitive river-night-demon myth in Gen. 32:24-29, 31, the J editors have suggested that prayer is a struggle which may change a man's character and mark him for life. The editors have retained an early description of a tent as a fixed place of prayer where God speaks to Moses "face to face, as a man speaks to his friend" (Exod. 33:7-11). The problem of prayer in the Bible becomes the recovery of this natural and two-way intercourse described by JE when God has later become dreadful, remote, and high exalted.

2. The monarchic sources—prayer and providence. The predominant religious theme is the providence of God, but prayer, as such, plays little part in the earlier strands. God is a God of dread and therefore dangerous (I Sam. 6:19-20; 11:7; II Sam. 6:6-9; *see* FEAR). He hears the cry of his people and acts to save them (I Sam. 9:15-16); but he fails to respond when a taboo is broken (14:36-42; *see* BAN 1). Here prayer relates to determination by lot, a general means of inquiring of God in these sources (e.g., 23:2, 4, 10-12; cf. Acts 1:26; *see* LOTS).

Intercession is illustrated (II Sam. 12:16-18; 24:10, 25), though the later source questions whether intercession is possible (I Sam. 2:25). As intercessor Samuel calls on God to vindicate his judgments (7:5-6, 8-9; 12:16-17, 23; 15:11; on intercession, *see* § E *below*). The result of his concern for Saul is an early reflection of the prophetic emphasis that prayer must result in obedience (15:22-23).

In this source the granting of the people's request for a king brings trouble (8:19-22), so that answered prayer can also be a problem (on unanswered prayer, *see* § F *below*). Hannah's prayer for a son, on the other hand, results in a vow which is confirmed by the dedication of Samuel to the service of the shrine (I Sam. 1:9-28; cf. Jacob's bargain; the nationalistic hymn of ch. 2, a prototype of the Magnificat, has been adapted to this place; prayer and praise are considered one [vs. 1]).

3. The eighth-century prophets—the moral requirements of prayer. The great contribution of the prophets was their clarification of the nature of Yahweh and his demands, necessarily affecting prayer. Amos' God controls nature and history, is righteous, and does not play favorites. Since God is not for Israel apart from Israel's response, and election implies obligation, prayer must consist of something more than ritual and ceremonial (Amos 4:4-5; 5:21-25; cf. Isa. 1:1-11; Hos. 6:6; 8:11-13; 9:4; Mic. 6:6-8; etc.). Calamities are a call to "return to me" (Amos 4:6-11; cf. Isa. 30:15; Hos. 5:15–6:5); and since men must, in any case, meet God (Amos 4:12), they can live only by seeking him (5:4; cf. Deut. 4:29; 6:5-9). But this is synonymous with seeking good (Amos 5:14).

For Hosea the intended intimacy of God and people has been broken by the unfaithfulness of Israel (Hos. 1–3, etc.). Prayer must be a matter of the heart (7:14), and the basis of God's appeal is his past acts (11:1-8; cf. 13:4; Isa. 29:14; Mic. 6:4-5; etc.). The true basis of prayer is recollection (*see* § B4 *below*); and the later passage, Hos. 14:1-2, makes the deduction that to acknowledge God's favor and repent of its abuse is the proper sacrifice; words can express more than sacrifice if they arise from "knowledge" (cf. Deut. 23:21-23; Isa. 29:13-14). Without this, man stands before God as defendant (Isa. 1:18; Mic. 6:1-2).

Isa. 6 is the first clear testimony to individual experience in prayer. Familiar worship is transformed into an ecstatic theophany in which confession leads to cleansing, cleansing to commitment, and commitment to commission. Isaiah's normal worship is transformed into this climax, which foretells the true end of prayer as developed in the NT. The creature before the holy God realizes the wonder of this God's call to service. (The seraph's "Holy, holy, holy," has become the unfailing act of praise in the liturgies of Christendom.) Even when the Lord's face is hidden, such prayer leads to confident waiting (8:17).

4. The Deuteronomic school—prayer as recollection. The basic interest of D is the central sanctuary (Deut. 12:1-14, etc.; *see* JERUSALEM); religious attitude and policy are more important than historical chronicle (see the formula, I Kings 15:3, 11, 26, 31, and throughout). The D legislation does not deal with prayer (true of the law in general except for the prescribed festivals; *see* FEASTS AND FASTS). God is near (Deut. 4:7; cf. 30:11-14), and the very formlessness of God makes prayer more important than ceremony, material aids, or natural phenomena (4:12, 15-19, etc.).

D pre-eminently emphasizes the necessity of recollecting God's mighty acts; the memory is to be stored in the heart to prompt proper prayer (Deut. 4:9, 32-39; 7:18-19; 8:2; etc.; cf. I Kings 8:23-27). Moses' own prayers start with a recollection, or anamnesis, claiming God's previous mercies (e.g., Deut. 9:25-29). The act of thanksgiving in offering first fruits is to be so accompanied (26:5-11).

Prayer is always within the covenant between God and people (4:23, etc.). A God who is terrible and demanding, who has acted mightily and yet is God of covenant and near, will not only brook no competition but also must not be put to the test (6:16; cf. Matt. 4:7). This, however, is not a rubric against seeking a sign as Gideon does (Judg. 6:17-22, 36-40). Israel is to be a holy people (Deut. 7:6; cf. I Pet. 2:9). Biblical prayer cannot be discussed apart from this covenanted relationship.

The D thesis in Judges is that God exposed Israel to their enemies and sent them deliverers when they cried to him (3:7-9; 10:10-16; etc.). This formula of prayer in adversity stands in contrast to the ancient song of praise by Deborah (ch. 5). Solomon's humble prayer at Gibeon is rewarded with more than he asked. His petition comes at the end of a preamble which is a recollection of God's grace (*ḥesedh*), thus supplying a ground for the petition (I Kings 3:3-14). The prayers of Paul and of the Christian liturgies follow just this plan. The "blessing" of Solomon (expanded) and his prayer at the temple dedication begin with a recital of the occasion and provide a prayer phrased in part for the benefit of the congregation (I Kings 8:15-40; cf. Neh. 9).

In spite of God's awesome omnipresence, he can be called on to hear the prayers made in or toward the shrine, always provided that the need for forgiveness is recognized (I Kings 8:30, 39). The response expected (cf. vs. 32) embodies the typical D doctrine of reward and punishment, but there is recognition that the state of the heart is of interest to God (vs. 39). The pre-exilic petitions cover oaths (cf. Matt. 5:33-37), defeat, drought, famine, and plague (vss. 31, 33, 35, 37). God's power to restore physically and spiritually is assumed. The association of prayer and penitence is a permanent insight.

Elijah cries out against the act of an arbitrary God, but when the Lord responds, prayer has become a matter of life and death (I Kings 17:20-22; cf. II Kings 4:32-35). Elijah retires to the mountain to consult God (I Kings 19), and his prayer of commemoration of the God of the fathers prevails over the pagan demonstrations of his opponents (18:26-29, 36-39; *see* § D *below* on modes of prayer). King Hezekiah's prayer to God as creator and god of all the nations, superior to idols, begins with a long exordium followed by a brief petition in which the reason is adapted to the mode of address (II Kings 19:14-19). The proportion of approach to petition and the grounding of prayer in a recollection of God's nature is essentially biblical and contains the seed of the NT teaching and of liturgical practice.

5. Jeremiah—prayer as personal meditation. The D viewpoint is evident in our edition of Jeremiah, but the prophet emerges as the first historical person whose life of personal prayer can be known. God can determine Jeremiah's life in spite of his own reluctance. This introspective knowledge produces what might best be known as his "meditations." They are a form of prayer not strictly praise, confession, or petition, but an intercourse with God in which all these blend. It is the reaction of the sensitive human soul to a God who is both above and near. The first (Jer. 10:23-24) sums up man's situation. He cannot provide from within himself resources for self-direction, yet the felt need for God's guidance is an awesome thing. Prayer seeks the mitigation of God's destroying anger and the tempering of his control (cf. Pss. 103; 139; etc.). Prayer is related to the immediate problems of life (Jer. 11:18-20; 12:1-5). Because Jeremiah is convinced God is righteous, he can debate the problem of the success of the wicked and move beyond the oversimplifications of D, even though he may be challenged to face greater evils (12:5). The hand of God upon him has produced his isolation, yet he must intercede, and God must help him (15:10, 15-18). God assures him that his situation is God's intent (vss. 19-20). Only God can fathom the human mind (heart) and can vindicate the prophet's message by destroying the enemies (17:9-10, 14-18; cf. 18:18-23). Jeremiah's prayer of surrender produces an agonized sense of compulsion (cf. 1:4-8; 20:7-12, 14-18). The way in which God is known is influenced by the situation and also determines the prayer. The D sense of covenant is at war with a growing sense of God's righteous mercy. Prayer is an agonized striving because Jeremiah has no alternative but to commit himself to the Lord. His meditations go far beyond simple petition. From Jeremiah's agonies emerges a sense of the necessity of prayer, though the problems involved call for a deeper exposition and a more radical solution. Only so can the way be opened for a covenant no longer external but graven on the heart (31:31).

6. The Exile and after—prayer in Judaism. With the loss of the temple, gatherings for prayer and reading the Scriptures prepared for the development of the SYNAGOGUE. The poems in Lamentations depict a sorrowful corporate waiting upon God —ch. 5 pleads for remembrance in the hope that the people may be restored. Ezekiel envisions this restoration, and the vision, like Isaiah's, leads to a commission. The prophet's mortal nature is emphasized ("son of man" [Ezek. 2:1, 3, 8; 3:1; etc.]), and the spirit of God begins to play a larger part (3:12, 14; 11:1; etc.; cf. 37:1) but is not as yet directly connected with prayer. Ezekiel prophesies rather than petitions. The vision of a new temple in chs. 40–48 indicates that worship is thought of as essentially corporate, organized under a priesthood. The personal prayers which emerge in other books are therefore the more striking. Festivals and new moons are important, and the new temple is for the circumcised only (44:9). The hope of a new heart and new spirit (11:19; 18:31; etc.) is probably editorial.

Development in prayer awaits a new concept of God, and this new spirit is felt in the second and third portions of Isaiah. God is God alone, incomparable (ch. 40, etc.). Men and nations are insignificant and therefore may receive from such a God strength and endurance (40:30-31). God confronts the nations as Judge, and Israel is revealed as Yahweh's Servant (41:1, 8-10, etc.; *see* SERVANT OF THE LORD). An impassioned cry that God will act is based on God's mighty acts of old (51:9-11). Songs of praise take the form of apostrophes for salvation and the return of the Lord (52:7-10). Abundant pardon is offered to those who will seek the Lord, call on him, forsaking their wicked ways and unrighteous thoughts because God's thoughts are transcendent and his ways incontestable (ch. 55).

The Third Isaiah's "house of prayer for all peoples" (56:7) justifies the postexilic additions to Solomon's prayer (I Kings 8:41-53). A God whose very name is Holy and who dwells high in eternity can also be with the contrite (Isa. 57:15; 66:2; cf. Deut. 4:7). Daily prayer and periodic fasts do not avail unless there are also abstinence from tyranny and the performance of acts of mercy (Isa. 58:2-9). It is possible for Israel to address God as "our Father" after recounting God's suffering with them (63:7–64:1). There is no God like the God "who works for those who wait for him" and comes to meet those who remember him (64:4-5). Though God seems to be absent, he is available, even when not called upon (65:1-5*a*). In the new heaven and earth all flesh shall worship the Lord continually (66:22-23).

There is little attention to prayer in the minor prophets of the period. Jonah in his colloquy with God learns of God's interest even in Israel's enemies (ch. 4). Joel calls for a solemn fast and assembly led by the priests (1:13-14; 2:12-16; cf. Neh. 9:1). Malachi consists chiefly of questions and answers in which prayer has become a sort of formal catechism (1:6-11, etc.). Hab. 1:2-4, 12-13; 2:1-4 in C. L. Taylor's rearrangement (*IB*, VI, 973) is a prayer in which patience is achieved after facing the problem of evil before a holy, immortal God. Zech. 1–8 finds God to be remote and resorts to the mediation of angels.

a. The P school—development of liturgical prayer. In spite of the insistence on the cultus, personal prayer is not ignored by the P editors. Nehemiah is prompted to mourn, fast, and pray for days on end (1:4). His prayer of individual and corporate penitence, reminding God of his promises, is probably a liturgical expansion of a prayer for personal guidance (1:5-11) reinforced by an example of "ejaculatory prayer" when confronted with the need to answer the king (2:4). In the prayers of this period scriptural language is prominent (often Deuteronomic) as interest in liturgical propriety grows. The use of the response AMEN begins to appear (5:13; 8:6; cf. Num. 5:22; I Chr. 16:36; Pss. 41:13; 72:19; 89:52; 106:48). The practice of praying before reading the Law begins (Neh. 8:6). The Levites lead a doxology (9:5; cf. vs. 32) similar to those found in the synagogue service and in the Christian liturgies. The psalm in 9:6-38 is a typical review of God's dealings with Israel leading to confession and a pledge (cf. Lev. 5:5; 16:21; 26:40). Antiphonal singing is used (Ezra 3:11; cf. Pss. 106; 136).

The Chronicler's historical midrash is concerned about the function of the priests with emphasis on liturgical music (cf. I Chr. 16:7-36). He has added a liturgical ending to Solomon's prayer (II Chr. 6:40-42). The repetition of formal phrases in P, which might be criticized in literary works, is appropriate in a liturgical setting and is a mark of the best liturgical prayer at all times.

In the P redaction of the Pentateuch, holiness and separation are emphasized. The absolute God must be approached with scrupulosity, unlike the Yahweh of J or the Elohim of E. Only God's voice is heard. There is concern to tie up religious observances with historic events (e.g., Exod. 12). Emphasis is upon offerings and sacrifice (*see* LEVITICUS), which in themselves become a dramatic form of prayer, and according to the Holiness Code, offerings must be perfect (Lev. 22:17-25). Prayer falls within the setting of observance of the Sabbath as the climax of creation (Gen. 1:1–2:4*a*) and reverence for the sanctuary. A disciplined framework of life, which will assure that God will be with them, gives the people freedom and dignity (Lev. 22:31-33).

b. The Psalms and the practice of prayer. The height of this development is found in the Psalms, which have a liturgical origin and reflect only slightly the emergence of individual piety from corporate devotion. But, although adapted to the corporate "I," many of them are capable of personal use as meditations of prayer and praise. Five bear the title of prayers (*tephillah;* Pss. 17; 86; 90; 102; 142; cf. 72:20), but they are generally mixed expressions of religious relationship with God, moving between praise and confession, trust and petition, imprecation and intercession. Man at prayer can scarcely narrow his expressions of piety to a defined category. (The cry "Hosanna" is, e.g., both an act of homage and a request; Ps. 118:25-26; cf. Mark 11:9; Suk. IV.v). The joy in them testifies to the feelings and personal participation of temple worshipers just as Ps. 119 does to the Torah as a delight and not a burden. Confession of sin is found (e.g., Pss. 32; 51; etc.) but more often confession of trouble (22; 31; 38; etc.). Trust is abundantly documented (23; 46; 62; 84; 90; 91; 103; 121; etc.) and confidence in answer to prayer (e.g., 3:4; 4:1; 6:9; 17:6; 65:2; 138:3), though God sometimes seems afar off or silent (10:1; 13:1-2; 77:5-9; 83:1; 89:46; 109:1; etc.). Prayer, praise, and thanksgiving must arise from a whole and ready heart (108:1; 111:1). The rehearsal of God's acts in history are an integral part of the Psalms as of all biblical prayer after D (e.g., 9:1; 44:1-8; 65:5; 66:5-12; 68:7-18; 77:11-20; 78; 105; 106; 114). Prayer can be equated with incense (141:2), and there are prayers that God will answer prayer (e.g., 20:5; 54:2; 55:1; 61:1; 71:2; 86:6; 130:2; 143:1). Many of the blessings asked are material, but throughout, the important thing is the relationship which can express itself in these bursts of praise and prayerful meditations (63:1-8), many of which seem drawn forth rather than composed.

7. The Greek period. ***a. Prayer in a troubled world.*** The problem for prayer of the distance between God and man is responsible for the book of Job, for the apocalyptic developments (*see* APOCALYPTICISM), and for the idea of Wisdom. In the Prologue to Job the attempt to penetrate the counsels of God finds an Adversary with a limited power to torment men (1:6-12; 2:1-6; cf. Zech. 3:1-2). In the poem a tortured Job seeks to reach God in order to vindicate himself and represents the distress of Israel in this period. On a lower level this is a variety of prayer. He turns to God "in the anguish of my spirit" (7:11) but finds a God who will not let him alone and cannot be answered (7:17-20; 9:14, 32). There is no intermediary (vs. 33; *see* § E *below*), though he proposes a bitter prayer (ch. 10) and suggests a more equal encounter (13:20-27), even if it be after death (14:13-22). The poem passes constantly from debate to appeal to God (e.g., 17:3-5; 30:20-23), but there is no answer (19:7-8). The only advice about prayer is conventional (22:21-30), and Job's problem is that he cannot get at God (23:3-17). In the end awe is substituted for argument and confrontation for complaint, so that Job can only surrender to God (42:5-6). Job learns the wisdom of Eccl. 5:2: "Be not rash with your mouth, nor let your heart be hasty to utter a word before God, for God is in heaven, and you upon earth; therefore let your words be few" (cf. Matt. 6:7-8). This is the basis of all prayer truly aware of the presence of God.

The piety of the period is summed up in Daniel, written for the Maccabean time of trials. Adherence to a life of prayer at all costs is the mark of the true Jew (ch. 3; 6:5, 10), and Daniel is a "man greatly beloved" (10:19). He seeks illumination (2:17-23), by fasting, confession, and prayer (9:3-19; cf. the prayers of Ezra and Nehemiah); and the answer was prepared as soon as he had begun to speak (9:23).

Tobit and his associates are also typical (1:12; cf. 3:1-15; 4:19; 8:5-8, 15-17; 11:14-15). Their didactic prayers are dominated by the act of blessing (thanking) God (cf. 12:6). In addition to the magical substratum, a new feature appears in Raphael, the angel who presents the prayers of the saints (12:15). The prayers of Judith are rationalistic (as are those of Maccabees), with acts of recollection, humiliation, and submission (Jth. 4:9-15; 9:2-14; 16:2-17), and twice Judith prays in the midst of a critical situation (13:4-5, 7). Prayers are provided for Mordecai and Esther (Add. Esth. 13:8-17; 14:3-19) and for King Manasses—a fine example of an act of penitence whose repetitions make the acknowledgment of guilt moving. The Wisdom of Solomon passes back and forth from discourse to prayer and constitutes a rehearsal of God's wisdom in dealing with his people and prays for a share in the same (e.g., 9:13; 15:1-3; 16:15; 19:22). Prayer and sacrifice for the dead are not found in the OT but appear in II Macc. 12:44-45 (though probably not in the prayer of the captives in Bar. 3:1-8). The Song of the Three Children rehearses God's just treatment and turns into a catalogue of praise familiar to liturgical worship as the *Benedictus es domine* and the *Benedicite omnia opera.*

b. Prayer in synagogue and sect. The exact origin of the SYNAGOGUE is unknown, but its relation to the temple service is probably to be traced to the institution known as *Ma'amad,* an association of Israelites attached to each of the twenty-four weekly courses of priests on duty in the temple. Some of the laymen in each course attended the sacrifices; the rest gathered in their own villages at the hours of the temple rites and offered appropriate prayers and read the relevant sections of Torah. There thus came to be elements of the temple ritual in the synagogue services, and after A.D. 70 the rabbis came to hold that prayer was better than sacrifice.

The predominant note of the synagogue services in biblical times was thanksgiving. The basic elements in the service were the Shema framed in benedictions; the reading of Torah with appropriate praises and prayers for enlightenment; the doxologies of the Kaddish, honoring God's name and expecting his kingdom (*see* LORD'S PRAYER); and, centrally, the Tephillah or Amidah, the standing prayers. These consist, on the Sabbath, of six "benedictions," the first three praises and the last three thanksgivings, based on the temple ritual, and between them a benediction-prayer for the Sabbath or festival. On weekdays petition was included between the first and last three benedictions. At first this petition was free or extempore, but it later became fixed, until there developed twelve intervening sections forming the Shemoneh Esreh or "Eighteen Benedictions" (in Babylon, nineteen) which now constitute the Amidah.

The first petitions are personal, asking knowledge, repentance, forgiveness, redemption, healing, and the produce of the earth (years); the last concern the community, for gathering the exiles, for just judgment, for victory over enemies (against the *minnim*), for restoration of Jerusalem and the house of David. These were gradually developed, and some are post-biblical, at least in form. Every petition is, however, an act of praise and ends with a blessing of God. The biblical element of recollection is strong throughout the service. The Psalter and other scriptures are freely drawn on for material, and in this usage the personal pronoun is changed to the plural. Substantial elements of the liturgy, especially the Amidah, can be traced in Ecclus. 36:1-17 and in the Hebrew version of 51:12 (1-16).

The sectarians have left no description of their regular services, but we can see from the Qumran literature (*see* DEAD SEA SCROLLS) that the synagogue combination of praise and edification is characteristic of the Covenanters. The chief emphasis is put on study of Torah (Manual of Discipline and Damascus Document), on purification, and on obedient service. Benedictions are frequent (1QSb) with Amens (e.g., 1QS 1.19; 2.2-4, 10, 18, etc.) and confessions (1.24–2.1; cf. CDC 20.28-29 B). Worship was thought to involve the whole person and his possessions (1QS 1.11, etc.), and the prayer took the place of sacrifice as in the synagogue ("An offering of the lips is accounted as a fragrant offering of righteousness and perfection of way as an acceptable freewill offering" [9.5]; cf. 9.26; 10.6, 8, 14; Hos. 14:2). It was offered at set times (1QS 1.9, 14; 10.5, 10; etc.; CDC 6.18-19). In their worship, rehearsal also had a large place (1QS 1.21-22; CD 13.7-9; 1QM 10.3-10). The spirit and aim of their prayers (the word *tephillah* is used; e.g., 1QH 12.1-4; 16.6; etc.) is reflected in the Manual of Discipline (e.g., 1QS 3.7-9; 4.2-6; 11.12-20) but is more largely documented in the collection of *Hodayôth* or Psalms of Thanksgiving (1QH), where, in spite of much invective against the "sons of Belial" and gloom over the apocalyptic nature of the situation, the note of praise is unmistakable, as is a singular sense of wonder that man can be redeemed to share with the spirits and angelic beings the high calling of God (e.g., 1QH 1.21-26; 3.19-23; 11.3-14 and *passim*).

c. Approach to the NT. Ben Sirach approaches nearer to the attitudes of the NT. He affirms that men may humble themselves before God, because his mercy is equivalent to his majesty (Ecclus. 2:17-18), and men are not, like Job, to seek to justify themselves (7:5). As in Tob. 4:8-11, prayer and alms are associated (e.g., Ecclus. 3:14; 4:10; 12:1-2). Prayer must not be "fainthearted" (7:10) or repetitious (7:14; cf. Eccl. 5:2; Matt. 6:7), and is recommended both for patients and for physicians (38:9, 14; cf. Jas. 5:13-16). Forgiveness in prayer depends upon a forgiving spirit (28:2; cf. Mark 11:25). Craftsmen who cannot become learned may offer their work as their prayer (38:34). God will hear the prayers of the wronged and helpless (35:12-17; cf. Luke 18:1-5). The prayers include petitions for protection from sin and temptation (23:1-6), a national prayer (36:1-17), and a thanksgiving (50:22-24), the last two verses of which are reminiscent of the Kaddish in the synagogue service.

C. *PRAYER IN THE NT.* 1. The Synoptic gospels. The crux of all prayer in the Bible is the prayer of Jesus in Gethsemane, where surrender is yet addressed to God as Father (Mark 14:36).

a. Jesus at prayer. Mark records (editorially) only that Jesus prayed at critical moments. It may be assumed that he joined in synagogue prayer (1:21; 6:2; etc.) and in the customary prayers at home celebrations like the Passover (14:17-26). Mark does not tell us that Jesus prayed at his baptism (1:9-11), though the heavens were opened to him and he heard the voice, nor in the wilderness (1:12), nor at the Transfiguration (9:2). His disciples are criticized for not keeping a fast (2:18; cf. Luke 5:33: "and offer prayers"). Jesus does not call on God for help to heal or to exorcise demons or to raise the dead (e.g., Mark 1:25, 31; 5:41).

Mark tells us that Jesus retired from Capernaum to pray before announcing his preaching tour (1:35-38), that he went alone into the hills to pray after feeding the multitude (6:46; but not 8:10), that he prayed in Gethsemane before his arrest (14:36, 39), and that he prayed on the cross (15:34, in the words of Ps. 22:1). From this we may deduce a custom of prayer in emergencies, before great decisions, and in retirement. We may assume that retreat, especially to the hills, also indicates prayer, as at 3:13 before the appointment of the Twelve, at 6:32 after their mission, and at 9:2 before the Transfiguration.

Mark gives no prayers of Jesus except in Gethsemane (14:36) and from the cross (15:34), though his table blessings are mentioned at 6:41 (cf. 8:6); 14:22-23. Prayer is assumed at 7:34. Mark's emphasis is upon prayer in the critical moments.

Luke is interested in prayer and has edited Mark to supply the impression usually attached to the gospels. He expands Mark 1:10 by "and was praying" (Luke 3:21) and makes the same addition to Mark 3:13 (6:12) and 9:2 (9:28), but not to 6:31 (cf. Luke 9:10), and has no parallel to 6:46. Both Luke and Matthew add that Jesus fasted in the wilderness (Luke 4:2; Matt. 4:2). Luke tells us it was Jesus' *custom* to go to the synagogue on the Sabbath (4:16). He omits from Mark 1:35 that Jesus prayed, perhaps assuming that the lonely place indicates this (4:42), and makes up this deficiency at 6:12 before his version of the Sermon, thus also relating prayer to Jesus' preaching mission. As Mark makes no reference to prayer for power to heal, Luke explains that the power of the Lord was with Jesus (5:17). Luke also adds that Jesus was praying privately at Caesarea Philippi (9:18) but omits the reference to prayer and exorcism in Mark 9:29 and refers instead to the majesty of God (9:43). Unlike Matthew, Luke 11:1 tells us that it was the example of Jesus' own prayers that prompted the LORD'S PRAYER. Luke 22:32 is the only intercession of Jesus except for the Lukan insertion of the prayer from the cross in some readings of 23:34 (omitted by B.D.W.F., sy^s, sa, bo). In place of the prayer from Ps. 22, Luke alone has: "Father, into thy hands I commit my spirit" (23:46).

In the chapters added to the beginning of Luke's Gospel the same interest in prayer is evident (1:13, 46, 67-79; 2:29-32; 2:14—the *Gloria in excelsis* of the liturgies). In Luke's post-Resurrection stories the appearances are associated with eating (24:30, 35, 41-43), indicating an early connection with services of breaking of bread. *See* EUCHARIST.

b. Jesus' teaching on prayer. In Mark there is little teaching on prayer. Certain exorcisms can be performed only by prayer (9:29; some MSS add: "and fasting"); Jesus quotes Isa. 56:7 regarding the temple (Mark 11:17); and 11:25 is virtually parallel to Ecclus. 28:2 in requiring forgiveness before prayer. The assurance that faith will produce an answer (11:24) is connected with removal of the mountain; this passage has connections with the tabernacles eschatology (cf. Zech. 14 in the synagogue). The apocalypse in ch. 13 bids prayer that the crisis come not in winter (vs. 18; cf., for strength to escape, Luke 21:36). Long prayers made as a pretense are condemned (12:40; cf. Luke 20:47). The disciples in Gethsemane are urged to pray against testing (14:38; *see* LORD'S PRAYER).

The teaching comes largely from the discourses common to Matthew and Luke (Q), with major additions from Luke's peculiar material. The pious duties of almsgiving, fasting, and prayer are assumed (Matt. 6:1-18), but none of them must be done for show (vss. 2-6, 16, 18). Prayer is best made in seclusion, without piling up empty phrases, because God knows what we need before he is asked (vss. 5-8). Anxiety is a hindrance to prayer, which should be the expression of the whole person (vss. 22-25) in the service of one Master (vs. 24). Prayer is part of the superrighteousness required of Israel (vs. 32; cf. 5:20, 47) and of the controlling desire for the kingdom, with the gift of which all lesser things are supplied (6:33-34). Yet men are to ask, seek, and knock (7:7-8), for a holy God is more likely to give than even an earthly father (vss. 9-11; "good things"; Luke 11:13: "the Holy Spirit"). Verbal expressions of allegiance do not assure entrance to the kingdom, but only a conforming will (Matt. 7:21; cf. Luke 6:46; 13:25). Yet God is not compelled (cf. Jth. 8:16) but gives only out of unconditioned grace (Matt. 20:1-16). Communion rather than the distraction of business is desired (Luke 10:40-42), and trust rather than seeking for signs (Matt. 16:1-4, etc.).

The LORD'S PRAYER is given a different setting by Matthew and Luke, and the two forms suggest divergent liturgical traditions. In this Jesus supplies a guide for prayer and convenient summary of the prayers required both by Jewish piety and by his own teaching. Corporate in scope, it agrees with the priorities Jesus established and bids prayer for the one object Jesus elsewhere asks men to pray for (Matt. 9:38; Luke 10:2; cf. John 4:35). The only other prayer ascribed to Jesus in Q is the thanksgiving to the Father for the revelation in himself (Matt. 11:25-26; Luke 10:21 adds that Jesus prayed "in the Holy Spirit").

To this teaching Luke has added particular points. The story of the rich farmer seems to warn against self-communion, for the man's soliloquy is interrupted by God (12:13-20). The duty of thanksgiving is sharply illustrated (17:11-19) and exemplified by the Pharisee at prayer in the parable (18:9-14). He represents the best Jewish piety, yet in seeking self-justification (vs. 14*a*) his prayer falls below that of the publican, who makes no claim but throws himself as a sinner on God's mercy (vs. 13; vs. 14*b* is a moralistic addition).

Luke's two parables usually thought to teach importunity may not originally have been so designed. In accord with Jesus' method, Luke 11:5-7 is a question. It would properly expect the answer "No"—i.e., the friend would not answer with a refusal. All the more, will not God respond to urgent need, as the teaching of Jesus above indicates? Vs. 8 is an application (by Luke? "I tell you" often introduces the evangelist's interpretation). The parable teaches that the needy may always resort without hesitation to God.

In Luke 18:1-8 the problem is complicated by the introduction and the appended eschatological application (vss. 1, 7-8). Vs. 1 does not necessarily indicate persistence in the same request apart from the parable (of which it is not a part). Ch. 17 is eschatological, and 18:7-8 deals with the disappointed hope of the persecuted (cf. Zech. 1:12; Rev. 6:9-11). The original function of the parable was to conclude the preceding discourse (17:20-37). Taken alone, the parable also deals with vindication. If vs. 6 is original, the emphasis on the unrighteous character of the judge suggests again an a fortiori interpretation—viz., if a man like this will eventually do justice, how much more, and at the proper time, will

God respond to the situation of the afflicted and persecuted? (Cf. Ecclus. 35:12-17; Rom. 12:19.)

The teaching of Jesus is that God will respond to need expressed in the prayer of faith, particularly when the petitioner seeks primarily the kingdom of God. All that is needful will be added; but, as children ask their father and are not rebuffed for asking, so in close relationship with God to ask as children is expected (cf. Mark 10:15, etc.). The gospels reflect the life of the early church and the basis for its practice of prayer, but this becomes more explicit in the letters.

2. Prayer in the early church. ***a. Paul.*** In Paul we see a Christian at prayer and the Christian practice of prayer in its fulness. In the letters his concern for his people and their problems is lifted up to God. Almost every letter begins and ends with the "grace" (I Thess. 1:1; 5:28; etc.), and all except Galatians and II Corinthians begin with an expression of thanksgiving for his readers and an assurance of constant prayer on their behalf (Rom. 1:8-9; I Cor. 1:4; Phil. 1:3-4; Col. 1:3-5, 9; I Thess. 1:2; 3:9; II Thess. 1:3; 2:13; Philem. 4-6).

Paul not only petitions but also gives thanks, states the ground of a particular request and its aim. His principal prayers are in Rom. 15:5-6, 13; Phil. 1:9-11; Col. 1:9-12; I Thess. 3:11-13; 5:23; II Thess. 1:11-12; 2:16-17; 3:16. The ground of prayer is the new revelation of God in Christ, in whom all the promises of God find their "yes." Hence we can say "Amen" (II Cor. 1:20; *see* AMEN). Prayer is based on the faithfulness of God and of Christ (Rom. 15:5; I Cor. 1:9; I Thess. 5:24; II Thess. 3:3), on Christ's power (Col. 1:11; II Thess. 1:11), and, above all, on the superabundance of God's provision in him (Rom. 10:12; II Cor. 9:8-9; Phil. 4:19). Notably in Paul the Holy Spirit is the motivating power of prayer. The Spirit bears witness with the spirit of man (Rom. 8:16, 27) and causes him to set his mind on the things of the Spirit (vs. 5). Since the Spirit alone knows the mind of God (I Cor. 2:10-12; cf. Rom. 8:27), he can intercede for men, and he actually teaches them to pray (Rom. 8:26-27), interpreting to God their inarticulate sighs according to God's will. Only the Spirit can teach man to say "Lord" (I Cor. 12:3), and it is he who cries in us: "Abba" (Gal. 4:6).

To the God of comfort we pray for comfort (II Cor. 1:3-4), to the God of hope for joy and peace (Rom. 15:13), to the God of peace for peace (II Thess. 3:16). In the nature of God is found the cause of thanksgiving and praise for God's grace and comfort (I Cor. 1:4); for his revelation (Rom. 16:25-27); his inexpressible gift (II Cor. 9:15); and for the fact that in Christ he leads us in triumph (II Cor. 2:14) to the hope of heaven and the inheritance of the saints (Col. 1:5, 12). Paul also gives thanks for his people, for their faith and growth in love and their share in the work of the gospel (Rom. 1:8; I Cor. 1:5, 7; Phil. 1:5; Col. 1:4; I Thess. 1:2; 2:13; II Thess. 1:3-4; Philem. 5).

The objects of Paul's prayers are determined in the same ways. He prays for growth in grace or sanctification of his people (Rom. 15:13; Phil. 1:9-11; Col. 1:9-11; I Thess. 3:12-13; 5:23; II Thess. 1:11; 2:17; 3:5, 16). He both prays and asks prayer for his mission (Rom. 10:1; I Thess. 3:10-11; II Thess. 3:1-2). He prays that Christians may live in harmony (Rom. 15:5) and that the knowledge of the good news may be promoted by Christian witness (Philem. 4). In words probably derived from an early liturgy (in Aramaic) he prays for the Parousia (I Cor. 16:22*b* in Greek; cf. Rev. 22:20*b*).

Paul's prayers, grounded in the faith, have a purpose. He seeks the glory of God and of Christ (Rom. 15:6; Phil. 1:11; II Thess. 1:12); the comfort, hope, and perseverance of his people (Rom. 15:13; I Cor. 1:8; II Cor. 1:4; Col. 1:11; cf. Phil. 1:10). To this end he prays for discernment (Phil. 1:9; Col. 1:9; cf. Eph. 3:18; Jas. 1:5). His aim is a life worthy of Christ (Col. 1:10), in which anxiety will, through prayer, give place to peace (Phil. 4:6-7; cf. I Pet. 5:7) and many will give thanks for the demonstrated effectiveness of prayer (II Cor. 1:11).

By way of method, Paul urges constant prayer and thanksgiving (Col. 4:2; I Thess. 5:17; etc.), for all things (Phil. 4:6), in all circumstances (I Thess. 5:18; cf. Phil. 4:12). He inculcates a joyous spirit (Col. 3:15*b*-17) arising from a mind set on the ascended Lord (Col. 3:1-3). He deals with the use of prayer in worship in I Cor. 11–14 generally. He exhorts the congregation to "maintain the traditions" (11:2), but *agape* is to rule all (ch. 13), and the mind is to share with the spirit (14:15). As in Matt. 6:2-6, the duty of almsgiving is associated with worship (I Cor. 16:1-2; cf. II Cor. 8:1-15, etc.). No clear reference is made to fasting in connection with prayer. (The word is added in a few MSS to I Cor. 7:5; the references in II Cor. 6:5; 11:27 are to enforced hunger.) Paul refers to the liturgical use of "Amen" (I Cor. 14:16; II Cor. 1:20) and probably of the Lord's Prayer (Rom. 8:15; Gal. 4:6). Except for his intercessions, he says little of his own prayers, only to hint at mystical experiences of which he dare not boast (II Cor. 12:1-4) and to invite his people to "strive together" with him in prayer on his behalf (Rom. 15:30).

b. Other NT writers. Ephesians serves as a summation of Paul's teaching, especially in 1:17-23, but with a tendency to merge prayer into exposition (cf. 1:3-10, 15-16; 2:18; 5:4, 19-20; 6:8-19, 24). Eph. 3:14-20 embodies the practice of Paul.

The post-Pauline "Pastorals" mention the varieties of prayer known in the post-apostolic church: supplications, prayers, intercessions, thanksgivings (I Tim. 2:1; cf. 4:4-5), and the duty of prayer for rulers (2:2). Prayer is used by the early church in the practice of unction of the sick (Jas. 5:13-16), including confession (vs. 16; cf. I John 1:8-9). Faith is necessary in prayer (Jas. 1:6), and James also warns that the same tongue cannot properly curse and bless (3:9). Unanswered prayer arises from wrong requests which seek selfish ends (4:3).

The author of Acts has reconstructed the practice of the primitive church and Paul's experience and gives us pictures of the first disciples at prayer in the temple (2:46; 3:1; cf. 22:17), in the Upper Room (1:12-14, 23-26; cf. 2:42; 4:23-31; 12:5), and at home in the "breaking of bread" (2:42, 46). The Holy Spirit comes to a praying church (2:1-4; cf. 4:31). By prayer with the laying on of hands it chooses (1:23-26) and appoints its ministers (6:6; 13:2-3; 14:23) and brings strangers into communion (8:14-17). Prayer is offered for healing the sick and raising the dead (9:40; 28:8). Stephen prays at his martyrdom (7:55, 59-60), Paul and Silas in prison (16:25). The early church's all-night vigil culminating in the breaking of bread is described in 20:7-11. Further glimpses of the importance of prayer are given in 13:2 (with fasting), where it results in the guidance of the Holy Spirit, and in 20:32, 36. Frequently in Acts visions are the means by which God communicates with man (Paul: 9:3-8; 16:9; 22:17; 23:11; 27:23; Ananias: 9:10-16; Cornelius: 10:1-6; cf. vs. 30; Peter: 10:9-20).

The liturgy of the early-second-century church is reflected in Revelation and its mode of worship idealized in heaven (chs. 4–5, possibly owing something also to the Greek theater). It is marked by doxologies and hymns (4:8, 11; 5:9, 12, 13*b;* cf. 11: 15-18; 12:10-12; 15:3-4; 19:1-3). The salutation which begins the book becomes an ascription of praise ending with the Amen (1:4-7; cf. 5:14; 7:12; etc.). In 3:14 Jesus himself is the Amen. "Hallelujah" becomes a liturgical cry (19:4-6). The seer is told to worship God alone, not the angel (19:10; 22:8-9). In the new heaven and earth is no temple (21:22). The prayer *Maranatha* occurs in the Greek, ἔρχου κύριε (22:20; cf. I Cor. 16:22).

3. Hebrews—prayer through Christ's mediation. The prominent development of the basis for prayer occurs when the Letter to the Hebrews (*see* HEBREWS, LETTER TO THE) grounds it firmly in Jesus' experience. Because in obedience he was tried as men are tried, he can mediate our needs; this makes him a unique and definitive high priest (2:18; 4:14-16; 5:7-10; 7:23-28; 10:19-22). The key word is προσέρχομαι, "draw near." Prayer is approaching God in and through Christ (4:16; 7:25; 10:1, 22; 11:6; 12:18, 22). We draw near with confidence, by a new and living way, with a true heart. We draw near, not to the terrifying mount of Moses, but to the heavenly scene dominated by Jesus the mediator of a new covenant, in company with saints and angels (12:18-24). Faith is essential, for to draw near means to believe God exists and that he rewards those who seek him (11:6). The vital thing is to look to Christ, who, as Pioneer and Perfecter of faith, is seated at God's right hand (12:2). No sacrifice is necessary except the sacrifice of praise (13:15; cf. Hos. 14:2), since Christ has offered the one all-sufficient sacrifice (7:27; 9:27-28; 10:10-14).

4. The Fourth Gospel—prayer as communion. The heavenly intercession of Christ as the living core of Christian prayer is made again explicit in the work of the Fourth Evangelist. For John it is essential that the Christian abide in Christ (6:56) by sharing his body and blood, thus experiencing a living union akin to that of vine and branches (15:1-8), within which it is possible to ask what we will and it will be done (vs. 7). This organic union implies unity of will and purpose, with Christ as the basis for prayer (as the branch asks only what it is in the nature of the parent stock to supply). This is otherwise expressed as prayer in Christ's name (14:13-14; 16:23), which is to begin with his ascension (16:23-24). It is not that Christ needs to pray for us but that the Father loves us because of our love for Christ and faith in him (vss. 26-27). The coming of the Paraclete is an answer to Christ's prayer.

In the Fourth Gospel, Jesus has no emergencies in which he prays (cf. § C1*a above* on Mark) but gives thanks over the loaves and fishes (6:11) and lifts his eyes in thanks before raising Lazarus (11: 41). There is no Gethsemane prayer (18:1; cf. 12:27-28) or prayer from the cross, because Jesus' whole ministry has been an act of conformity to God's will (cf. 5:19, 30; 8:29; 18:11; etc.). Neither προσεύχομαι nor δέομαι (or their nouns) is used. The subordination implied is not in keeping with the Johannine picture of Christ who is at one with God and aware of his will, informed with his power. For prayer John uses chiefly the verb αἰτέω, which may be used for asking of anyone and suggests intimacy with God (11:22; 14:13-14; 15:7, 16; 16:23-24, 26; I John 3:22; 5:14-16; cf. Matt. 7:7-11).

Jesus' own life of prayer and concern for his disciples is summed up in one chapter of John (17). The essence of Jesus' prayer is that the oneness between himself and God may be shared by the disciples with him and with one another (vss. 11*b,* 21). In this prayer, rooted in communion, seeking communion, biblical prayer reaches its climax. It is summed up in I John 5:13-15 in the belief, knowledge, and confidence the believer has in Christ, assuring him that in whatever he asks according to the will of the Son of God he is heard and answered.

D. *THE MECHANICS OF PRAYER.* Except for public worship the Bible knows no regulation of time or place and does not prescribe the attitude to be adopted. Jeroboam realized that the time and place of prayer would affect a people's allegiance (I Kings 12:26-33), and set up new altars accordingly. Amos and the D school made such innovations the target of their denunciation.

1. Place. Prayer may be offered in any place, even in prison (Acts 16:25) or on a storm-tossed ship (27:23, 35). D insisted on the Jerusalem sanctuary as the central place of prayer, and Jesus applied to its successor the words of Isa. 56:7: "a house of prayer for all peoples." When men pray apart from Jerusalem, they orient themselves toward it (Dan. 6:10; cf. Ps. 5:7, a prayer used in the Jewish Prayer Book on entering the synagogue). Prayers were proper in the home, particularly at the great Seder of the Passover, for which a place had to be provided even for strangers (κατάλυμα, "guest chamber," or ἀνάγαιον, "upper room" [Mark 14:14-15, etc.; cf. Dan. 6:10; Acts 1:13]). The housetop was a suitable place, probably because one could there withdraw from the household (Acts 10:9; cf. Jth. 8:5, etc.). The solitary place Jesus commended (Matt. 6:6) was hard to find, and he himself sought solitude out of doors in the hills or a secluded grove (Mark 1:35, etc.; Luke 9:28; cf. John 1:48; II Sam. 15:32; I Kings 18:42). In the OT, however, "high places" and groves were associated with the worship of Baalim (e.g., Deut. 12:2; Jer. 17:2; Ezek. 6:13). Formal Jewish prayer required the presence of water for washing (Acts 16:13, 16; cf. Jth. 12:6-8). Withdrawal was essential in critical moments for Moses (Exod. 24:18; Deut. 9:25), Elijah (I Kings 19), John the Baptist (Luke 1:80; etc.), and Paul (Gal. 1:15-17), as well as for Jesus. Elijah was, however, discouraged from seeking God in the manifestations of the past, heard God in his own mind, and was sent back to find answers in the midst of problems. Likewise the Baptist returned to preach at the crossings of Jordan. The Qumran community is an example of mass withdrawal.

2. Time. While the needs of people dictate the time (e.g., Neh. 2:4; cf. Ecclus. 38:34), the preferred occasions coincided with the sacrifices in the temple (Exod. 29:39, etc.; I Chr. 23:30), so that the morning oblation (Pss. 5:3; 59:16; 88:13; Wisd. Sol. 16:28) and that of evening (I Kings 18:36; Ezra 9:5; Ps. 141:2; Dan. 9:21; Jth. 9:1) are the usual times. Three times a day is recognized as appropriate (Ps. 55:17; Dan. 6:10), with the sixth hour (Acts 10:9) and ninth hour (Acts 3:1; 10:3, 30) especially noted. The monastic rule of seven daily offices was often reinforced by Ps. 119:164. Prayer could be offered day and night (Ps. 88:1), all day (Ps. 86:3; cf. Josh. 7:6), or in the night (I Sam. 15:11; Pss. 4:4; 63:6; 119:62; Lam. 2:19)—the night was a favorite time with Jesus (Mark 1:35; cf. 6:46, 48). The prayer in Gethsemane occurred late in the evening (Mark 14:17, 26, 32). Moses and Jesus fasted and prayed for forty days and nights, and David for a week (Exod. 34:28; II Sam. 12:16-23; Luke 4:1-2).

3. Posture. Standing is the normal attitude assumed (Matt. 6:5; Mark 11:25; Luke 18:11; cf. I Sam. 1:26; I Kings 8:22) and is required in the synagogue for the Amidah (Singer, *Daily Prayer Book*, p. 44, based by the Talmud on Ps. 106:30). Kneeling is also described (Ezra 9:5; Ps. 95:6; Dan. 6:10; Luke 22:41; Acts 7:60; added by the Chronicler in I Kings 8:54). Special intensity seems to be characterized by prostration (Num. 16:45; Josh. 7:6; II Sam. 12:16; I Kings 18:42; Ezra 10:1; Jth. 9:1; Mark 14:35). The head may be bowed between the knees or toward the ground in humble thanksgiving (Gen. 24:26; Neh. 8:6) or petition (Exod. 34:8; I Kings 18:42). The tractate Berakoth recommends bending the spine or at least bowing the head to say the Tephillah (IV.iii). Hands were characteristically spread abroad toward heaven (I Kings 8:22; Ezra 9:5; Isa. 1:15; II Macc. 3:20) and lifted up (Pss. 28:2; 63:4; 134:2; 141:2; Lam. 2:19; 3:41; I Tim. 2:8). In penitence or sorrow the eyes may be downcast and the hands used to smite the breast (Luke 18:13; cf. 23:48). Prayer need not be said aloud (Gen. 24:45; I Sam. 1:13; Luke 18:11). It is on occasion accompanied by tears (I Sam. 1:10) or sweat (Luke 22:44) or by tearing both hair and garments (Ezra 9:3, 5). The biblical attitude tends to move away from such frenzy as is described in I Kings 18:26-29.

E. *INTERCESSION* (ἔντευξις). Christ as the ultimate intercessor is the climax of a growing interest in the function of those who pray as mediators. J and E supply the examples of Abraham and Moses (e.g., Gen. 18:22-32; Exod. 5:22-23; 8:8; 32:11-14; etc.), standing between God and man, but as "prophets" rather than as priests (cf. Gen. 20:7). Whether Moses is on the mountain or at the tent of meeting, he stands between people and God as a vital means of communication (Exod. 33:7-10).

David also intercedes (II Sam. 12:16-18; 24:10, 25). The later source at I Sam. 2:25 questions whether there can be intercession for sins against God, although he himself will mediate between men. As offenders men stand alone when they pray and must turn from idols and direct their own hearts to God (7:3). Samuel intercedes for his people because sin is a corporate matter (I Sam. 7:5-6, 8-9). Though he calls on God to vindicate his judgments, he continues his intercessions (12:16-17, 23; cf. 15:11).

It is part of the prophetic function of Amos also to plead for his wayward people in emergencies (Amos 7:1-6). According to D, Moses stood between a disobedient people and an awesome God (Deut. 5:5, 24-27; 9:18; etc.) and persisted through forty days of lying prostrate (9:25-29). Solomon's prayer for himself at Gibeon is as intermediary between God and people (I Kings 3:3-14), and he stands in this position as he dedicates the temple (8:22), as does Hezekiah in presenting the letter before God (II Kings 19:14-19; cf. Isa. 37:14-20). Elijah (I Kings 17:20) and Elisha (II Kings 4:32-33) intercede for a dead child. Jeremiah pleads for a people who rely too much on the covenant before a God who seems to be indifferent (Jer. 14:7-9).

Though Ezekiel as a son of man is called to stand before God, he recognizes that even great intercessors like Moses and Samuel, Noah, Daniel, and Job cannot atone for the failures of a faithless people but only for themselves (Ezek. 14:12-14; cf. Jer. 15:1). Intercession can be full of pangs wrung from the pit of despair (Lam. 3:42-66) yet would not be made without at least an overtone of confidence that God will avenge (vss. 56-58). In Judaism the priests take over the function of the prophet as intercessors (cf. Joel 2:17). Only the high priest can represent the people in the holy of holies (Lev. 16), and the temple is to be the point of intercession for all nations (Isa. 56:7). In the midst of this development Second Isaiah visualizes a new possibility. Israel as the Servant of Yahweh, even if reduced to one obscure soul, might by his vicarious suffering become in himself an act of intercession for his fellows (Isa. 53:12). The danger arises that an hypostatized Wisdom will come to stand between God and man (cf. Prov. 1–3, etc.; Job 28; Ecclus. 24), but this is offset by Job's constant demand for a mediator, a redeemer (*goēl*) even after death to stand between him and a God who will not let him alone (Job 9:33; 19:23-27; cf. 14:13-22; 23:3-17). In Tobit an angel presents the prayers of the saints.

Paul practiced constantly the function of intercession (*see* § C2*a above*), and the Christian church understood it as an obligation (I Tim. 2:1), especially for the sick (Jas. 5:14). According to Luke, Jesus interceded for Peter (22:32) and for his enemies 23:34 in some MSS). Jesus as intercessor, by virtue of his service on earth; his self-offering, and his place in heaven, is primarily set forth by Hebrews (*see* § C3 *above*) as the incarnation of Isaiah's Suffering Servant. Jesus' intercession for his own is presented in the Fourth Gospel (ch. 17) as his last act before his arrest. In this NT understanding of the function of Christ all Christian prayer, of whatever form, becomes intercession as it is presented through him and by him to God. On earth the Holy Spirit is "Paraclete"—i.e., counselor and advocate in prayer.

F. *UNANSWERED PRAYER.* The problem of unanswered prayer receives no formal treatment but is not unknown with the great biblical men of prayer. Moses' petition to see Canaan, based on God's mighty acts, was refused because of God's displeasure with the people for whom Moses was responsible (Deut. 3:23-27). This reflects the D sense of corporate involvement. Saul twice failed to receive an answer, once because a ban had been broken (I Sam. 14:37) and once when in his fear the lack of response drove him to seek a medium (28:5-7). David failed in his prayer for the child of his sin (II Sam. 12:22). (*See* § B6*b above* on unanswered prayer in Pss. 10:1; 13:1; etc.) Failure to recall God's past acts, according to Jer. 2:5-13, prevents a favorable response, and Jeremiah himself receives a question rather than an answer (12:5). Though he believes God to be in the midst of the people who bear his name, the Lord seems to have turned away (14:8-9). Job's failure to reach God might be compared with the figure of the cloud-wrapped God in Lam. 3:43-44, though in Job there is an adversary at work (Job 1:6-12, etc.). For Third Isaiah it is iniquity which has come between man and God (59:1-3; cf. 64:7)—and God in reality works for those who wait for him (64:4) and is ready even for those who do not seek him (65:1). God is not man, to be threatened or wheedled (Jth. 8:16). (On importunity, *see* § C1*b above* on Luke.) The NT answer to the problem is that prayer must be in accord with the will of God (cf. Jas. 4:3), particularly as expressed in Christ. His prayer in Gethsemane was not answered except by the acceptance of his own surrender to God. In the end prayer must be offered only "in his name."

G. *GOD'S INITIATIVE IN PRAYER.* Prayer is not initiated entirely by man but depends ultimately on a prior activity of God. In the JE narratives God takes the initiative in seeking man (e.g., Gen. 3:9, etc.), as does the God envisaged in Jesus' parables (e.g., Luke 15). The Lord hears even the weeping of a child (Gen. 21:16-17) and responds to the condition of the slaves in Egypt (Exod. 3:7-8; not P [cf. 2:23-24]), as later he treats the condition of the poor and the trials of Israel as themselves a prayer (Isa. 41:17; 43:1-7; cf. Ps. 79:10-11). It is the Lord who restores man to himself (Lam. 5:21; Hos. 2:14-15) and seeks out prophets like Amos, Isaiah, Jeremiah and Ezekiel (Amos 7:15; Isa. 6:8; Jer. 1:5; Ezek. 2:1-2). God's offer of refreshment is free and his word effective (Isa. 55:1, 11). Daniel can be answered before his prayer is phrased (Dan. 9:23). In the NT, apart from the interpretation of Christ as God's personal act of initiative (e.g., Rom. 5:8; Eph. 2:1), it is the Spirit of God himself who prompts and gives meaning to prayer (Rom. 8:15*b*-16, 26-27). The Spirit interprets the mind of the God who knows what we need before we ask (Matt. 6:8), and therefore prayer is in itself the discovering of what we really need (cf. Phil. 4:6-7).

H. *BIBLICAL DOCTRINE OF PRAYER.* Prayer in the Bible begins when it is clearly detached and distinguishable from magic, and it ends as a phase of complete communion with God in freely rendered obedience. From a predominant interest in material and worldly things, noticeable even in the Psalms, it rises to heights of self-offering, without ignoring the mundane and practical aspects of life. It becomes a matter of priority, as in the Lord's Prayer.

Biblical prayer has its elements of complaint and expostulation, for it is always one aspect of a close and natural relationship with God amid the stresses and strains of life, but its true basis is in God's acts of revelation—whether of judgment or of mercy. This is the great contribution of the Deuteronomic school. Prayer begins with recollection (anamnesis), proceeds to establish the ground for a request before making it, and states the end for which it is sought. Address and conclusion normally ascribe praise.

The life of Jesus, particularly in the dynamic Christology of the Fourth Gospel, is itself a prayer. He does what he sees the Father do and speaks what he hears the Father say. He knows because his will is to do the Father's will, and this is the way of religious certitude for the believer. Hence Paul prays for love in terms of growth in discernment. A lifelong and whole-person response to the divine reality, a posture of the will oriented toward the divine majesty, is the essence of prayer. Hence prayer in the Bible tends to move more and more toward thanksgiving and praise and consists increasingly in adoration rather than petition, more in contemplation than confession, yet more in the responsive activity of fellowship and not at all in mystical absorption. Jeremiah and the Psalms, Jesus' summary prayer and the hymns of the NT, all testify that prayer is one. The elements usually distinguished are likely to be distorted if held in isolation. For the Christian, Jesus himself is the final act of prayer, and prayer is perfected when the individual and the church are "in Christ."

This over-all understanding gained from the biblical development is of more importance than the piecemeal application of isolated passages, all of which have to be seen in the temporal context and as part of a movement. Matters of time, place, posture, and tone of voice are so various as to supply no rules. Indeed, the biblical teaching implies that the heart oriented toward God will cause the body to act appropriately. The biblical word "draw near," when seen in connection with the fully revealed God, suggests that those who understand what it is to draw near to majestic holiness which is at the same time redeeming mercy will acquit themselves accordingly. If they have nothing to say, they may still be truly at prayer, for in the end it is God who must inform our prayers. This Paul understood when he spoke of the work of the Holy Spirit. It is God who says: "Son of man, stand upon your feet."

Bibliography. Books on biblical prayer are notoriously lacking, especially in English. E. F. von der Goltz, *Das Gebet in der Ältesten Christenheit* (1901); J. E. McFadyen, *The Prayers of the Bible* (1906); J. Doller, *Das Gebet im AT* (1914); Tractate Berakōt (trans. A. Cohen; 1921); I. Rohr, *Das Gebet im NT* (1924); A. Z. Idelsohn, *Jewish Liturgy* (1932); F. Heiler, *Prayer* (1937); N. B. Johnson, *Prayer in the Apoc. and Pseudep.* (*JBL* Monograph II; 1948); E. J. Jay, Origen's *Treatise on Prayer* (1954).

C. W. F. Smith

PRAYER, LORD'S. *See* Lord's Prayer.

PRAYER, PLACE OF [προσευχή, prayer] (Acts 16:13). The Greek word for "prayer" was often used by Hellenistic Jews to denote a synagogue, or a regular place of worship (cf. Jos. Life LIV; Philo *Against Flaccus* 14). This is commonly taken to be the meaning of the word in Acts 16:13, and possibly also in 1:14. But it does not mean necessarily either the existence of a building, or conformity to the Jewish requirement that places of worship be located near streams of water.

Bibliography. See the comments in F. J. Foakes-Jackson and K. Lake, eds., *The Beginnings of Christianity,* IV (1933), 10-11, 191. M. H. SHEPHERD, JR.

PRAYER OF MANASSES. *See* MANASSEH, PRAYER OF.

PREACHER, THE. The customary but doubtful translation of קהלת in Eccl. 1:1.

PREACHING. In NT terms, a public proclamation of this good news: God has accomplished a work of salvation in Jesus Christ and offers a new life to those who believe.

1. Terminology
2. The contents of the preaching
   a. The preaching of Jesus
   b. The apostolic preaching
   c. The preaching of Paul
3. Preaching and teaching

Bibliography

1. Terminology. The most common Greek term for "to preach" is the verb κηρύσσειν (about sixty times in the NT; e.g., Mark 1:14; Acts 10:42; I Cor. 1:23). The chief synonyms are εὐαγγελίζεσθαι ("to evangelize" [RSV "to preach"]; Acts 5:42); ἀναγγέλλειν ("to declare"; Acts 20:27); ἀπαγγέλλειν ("to announce" [RSV "to command"]; Acts 17:30); διαγγέλλειν ("to proclaim"; Luke 9:60); ἐξαγγέλλειν ("to make known" [RSV "to declare"]; I Pet. 2:9); καταγγέλλειν ("to proclaim"; Acts 17:23).

"To preach" means "to make proclamation as a herald." A "herald" (κῆρυξ [RSV "preacher"]; I Tim. 2:7) is a public messenger who lifts up his voice and claims public attention to some definite news he has to announce. Then the Christian preaching (κήρυγμα; I Cor. 1:21) is the public proclamation of the "good news"—i.e., of the gospel—to the non-Christian world. Yet there is a difference between the proclamation of a town crier and the preaching of the gospel. A herald may be more or less indifferent to the news he proclaims. The Christian preacher, on the contrary, is a man who himself has been "laid hold on by Christ Jesus" (Phil. 3:12 ASV) and who personally believes in the good news he announces to others.

The NT writers draw a clear distinction between "to preach" and "preaching" on the one hand and "to teach" (διδάσκειν) and "teaching" (διδαχή) on the other. Preaching is the proclamation of the gospel to men who have not yet heard of it. Teaching is an instruction or exhortation on various aspects of Christian life and thought addressed to a community already established in the faith. The difference between preaching and teaching explains the fact, at first sight astonishing, that the OT writers scarcely use the term "preaching" to describe the mission of the prophets. In fact, their commission was to exhort the elect people to remain faithful to their God. It may well be compared with the charge of the Christian preacher nowadays. These prophets were not bringing news; they asked for a better and stricter obedience to the given law. In two cases only, the terms "preaching" and "to preach" have in the Prophets their early Christian meaning. First, in the book of Jonah (cf. 3:2) the prophet must "preach the preaching" (RSV "proclaim the message") of God to non-Jews—i.e., fulfil a missionary duty. Second, the terms "to evangelize" and "to preach" are used by Isaiah (cf. 61:1-2; Luke 4:18-21) to announce the good news of the eschatological salvation.

2. The contents of the preaching. In the Synoptic gospels we see Jesus "preaching the gospel of God" (Mark 1:14). In the Pauline letters we commonly read of "preaching Christ." In the book of Acts both forms of expression are used. The apostles preach "Jesus" (Acts 17:18) or "Christ" (Acts 8:5), or they preach the "kingdom of God" (Acts 28:31). These variant expressions are by no means opposed to one another. They only mark the development of the message in line with the development of the history of salvation from the days of Jesus to the apostolic age.

a. The preaching of Jesus. By his proclamation that "the time is fulfilled, and the kingdom of God is at hand; repent, and believe in the gospel" (Mark 1:15), Jesus did not simply continue the ministry of John the Baptist. He rather accomplished it, and appeared as that "greater one" the Baptist had announced. The belief in the gospel which Jesus requires is loyalty to him as to the representative of the kingdom, as the King and Messiah. Since the days of Jesus' ministry and later, since Jesus' death and resurrection, the kingdom begins to be realized in Jesus, although it is true that the kingdom itself is still to come. Thus after Jesus' days the kingdom of God is still to be announced. Yet the preaching of the kingdom necessarily becomes likewise the preaching of Jesus or Christ, who has brought the kingdom nearer by his words and mighty works of salvation. *See* KINGDOM OF GOD; GOSPEL.

b. The apostolic preaching. The preaching of the apostles is known by the discourses attributed to Peter in the ACTS OF THE APOSTLES. These are the preaching on the day of Pentecost (Acts 2:14-40), other preachings in Jerusalem (Acts 3:12-26; 5:29-32), and the preaching before Cornelius at Caesarea (Acts 10:34-43). It is now generally admitted that these speeches represent the preaching of the first apostles at an early date. This preaching may be briefly summarized as follows:

God has realized the promises of the OT and brought salvation to his people (Acts 2:16-21, 23; 3:18, 24; 10:43). This has taken place through the ministry, death, and resurrection of Jesus (2:22-24; 3:13-15; 10:37-39). Jesus has been exalted as "Lord and Christ" (2:36). The Holy Spirit in the church is the sign of Christ's present power and glory (2:33; 5:32). Salvation will reach its consummation in the return of Christ to judge the living and the dead (3:21; 10:42). The apostles have been chosen by God as witnesses of the ministry of Jesus and above all of his resurrection (2:32; 3:15; 10:40-41). They address to their hearers an appeal for repentance and offer to the believers forgiveness of sins and the gift of the Holy Spirit (2:38-39; 3:25-26; 5:31; 10:43). In short, the primitive preaching of the apostles is a proclamation of the work of salvation made by God in Christ and a call to believe and be saved.

c. The preaching of Paul. Paul's preaching does not essentially differ from the common preaching, as he himself testifies (I Cor. 15:11). In fact, his speeches reported in the book of Acts (cf. 13:16-41; 14:15-17; 17:22-31) and the references to his missionary preaching given in the letters reveal, besides some minor differences, an important new element. As the apostle to the Gentiles addressing pagan audiences, Paul adds to the preaching of Christ an appeal for faith in the living God who made the heaven and the earth (Acts 14:15; 17:24; I Thess. 1:9).

3. Preaching and teaching. Jesus preached the gospel openly to the crowds, but he reserved his teaching to his disciples, thus revealing to them his most profound thoughts and particularly the mystery of his own person (Mark 8:31-32). Likewise the apostles gave a teaching to those who had accepted the preaching (Acts 2:42; Col. 1:28). The largest part of the NT letters is not preaching but teaching. The teaching develops the fulness of the gospel message in order that the believers may become mature in Christ. E.g., Paul doubtless reports his former oral preaching when he writes: "Do you not know that the unrighteous will not inherit the kingdom of God?" (I Cor. 6:2), but he teaches his converts when he explains what a right Christian life is like (I Cor. 5-6).

Bibliography. C. H. Dodd, *The Apostolic Preaching and Its Development* (new ed., 1944); F. W. Grosheide, "The Pauline Epistles as Kerygma," *Studia Paulina* (1953), pp. 139-45; B. Reicke, "A Synopsis of Early Christian Preaching," *The Root of the Vine* (1953), pp. 138-41; F. V. Filson, *Jesus Christ, the Risen Lord* (1956); K. Goldammer, "Der Kerygma-Begriff in der ältesten christlichen Literatur," *ZNW*, XLVIII (1957), 77-101.

P. H. MENOUD

PREACHING OF PETER. *See* PETER, PREACHING OF.

PRECIOUS STONES. *See* JEWELS AND PRECIOUS STONES.

PREDESTINATION [προορίζειν, to mark out beforehand]. A view of historical events which attributes their cause to a previously established plan or decision of God. Ancient pagan MYTH may be regarded as determinism in that events in the mythical TIME and space are the ground for events and institutions in history. Biblical predestination differs radically from determinism in assigning ultimate religious value to historical events themselves, in assigning their cause to a decision or act of one personal deity rather than to a conflict of opposing wills in the supernatural world, and in assigning ethical and teleological purpose (*see* GRACE) to that decision.

Ancient paganism had long before the time of Moses reached concepts of divinely established patterns of institutions and actions which were, so to speak, predestined to become historical. The OT also very strongly emphasizes divine control over nature and history from creation on, but by specific divine command based upon ethical characteristics of God himself. Though the order of the natural world may thus be regarded as "predestined" (e.g., Gen. 8:20-22; 9:12-16), it is based upon a self-limitation of God himself by COVENANT.

The same is true of one aspect of determinism in the human order. God predetermines, by a deliberate self-limitation in a covenant, certain groups for a specific relationship to him, the seed of Abraham (Gen. 15:12-21; 17:9-14; Deut. 7:6-11), the Davidic Dynasty (II Sam. 23:5), the priestly line (Num. 25:12-13), so that anyone born into this "chosen" lineage is a recipient of this covenant relationship. This predestination of persons appears in another light in prophecy, for Jeremiah (1:5) and Deutero-Isaiah (Isa. 49:1, 5) are formed and set apart for a specific purpose before birth, as a direct act of God entirely apart from lineal descent and covenant traditions.

Predestination of events is also important. Amos proclaims (3:7) that God does nothing without revealing his secret to his servants the prophets, but particularly in Second Isaiah this public proclamation of future events is extremely important. It is the means by which man knows the cause of specific events (Isa. 41:26; 48:3-8; contrast 41:21-24), and consequently must admit the righteousness of God (41:26).

The NT entirely rejected biological lineage as a basis for the relationship to God. The OT predetermination of both persons and events is taken up in the interpretation of Christ as the heir of the OT promises (Gal. 3:16; I Pet. 1:20), destined to suffer (in accordance with the previously proclaimed will of God; Acts 2:23). The NT community also is then predestined to be "conformed to the image of Christ" (Rom. 8:29-30), but no longer in the framework of a biological lineage of elect families; instead, it is a free act of God (as in the case of the prophets), based upon his FOREKNOWLEDGE and love (Eph. 1:5).

G. E. MENDENHALL

PRE-EXISTENCE OF SOULS. The doctrine that souls have an existence prior to and apart from the material body to which they are joined at conception or birth. In John 9:2 the disciples of Jesus ask him: "Rabbi, who sinned, this man or his parents, that he was born blind?" This question presupposes the possibility that the man might have sinned before he was born. Since belief in the pre-existence of souls was widely held in the ancient world, having found its classic expression in the writings of Plato, it has been argued that this passage indicates that the disciples of Jesus shared this belief. The passage more readily supports the view that the evangelist and the readers for whom he wrote his gospel believed the doctrine, although the possibility that the disciples of Jesus also believed it cannot be denied.

Josephus writes that the Essenes believed that the souls of men are immortal, and dwell in the most subtle ether, becoming entangled, as it were, in the prison house of the body, to which they are drawn by a certain natural enticement (Jos. War II.viii.11). We may well think that in this account Josephus has pictured Essene belief much more in terms of Greek thought than the truth would warrant. Nonetheless, the doctrine is clearly taught in the Wisdom of Solomon:

> As a child I was by nature well-endowed,
> and a good soul fell to my lot;
> or rather, being good, I entered an undefiled body
> (8:19-20).

Philo, as well as later rabbinic writers, held to the doctrine of the pre-existence of souls. Origen derived the doctrine from the nature of the soul, and regarded it as the correlative of immortality.

In the OT, man is regarded as a "psychosomatic" whole. The idea of a disembodied spirit, or a soul separated from its body, was not congenial to Jewish thought. And it was not until the Persian and Hellenistic periods that Jewish writers were able to entertain a doctrine of pre-existence of the soul. Even then Jewish speculation on pre-existence was very much conditioned by the limitations of historical existence. Thus Elijah was regarded as Phineas Redivivus, so that when he was taken up into heaven, he was only returning to an existence he had presumably enjoyed prior to being born as Elijah. So also, John the Baptist was regarded as Elijah come again, and Jesus as John Redivivus. This mode of thinking entails the pre-existence of men, but not of disembodied souls. This kind of nondualistic "reincarnationism"-like belief in the resurrection of the body, like Paul's doctrine of "spiritual bodies" (I Cor. 15:42-47), represents an attempt on the part of Judaism within the thought-forms of OT psychology and anthropology to accommodate itself to an Iranian world view of profound ethical dualism to which it was strongly attracted, without capitulating to Greek metaphysical dualism and thus giving up its basic beliefs about the wholeness of man and the goodness of the created world.

Harnack attempted to distinguish between Jewish and Greek conceptions of pre-existence. The first had a religious origin, the second a cosmological and psychological; the first glorifies God, the second the created spirit. For the pre-existence of Christ, *see* CHRIST.

Bibliography. A. von Harnack, *History of Dogma* (1894-99), I, 318-34; R. Moore, "Pre-existence," in J. Hastings, ed., *Encyclopedia of Religion and Ethics* (1919), X, 235-41.

W. R. FARMER

PREFECT [סגן] (Dan. 2:48; 3:2-3, 27; 6:7); KJV GOVERNOR. A person appointed to a position of authority and command. *See* SATRAP.

***PREHISTORY IN THE ANCIENT NEAR EAST.** The stages of society in Egypt, Palestine, Syria, Anatolia, Iraq (Mesopotamia), and Iran down to the period in which written records appear.

1. Stone Ages
2. Chalcolithic Age
   a. Iran
   b. Iraq (Mesopotamia)
   c. Anatolia
   d. Syria
   e. Palestine
   f. Egypt
3. Conclusion
Bibliography

1. Stone Ages. Paleolithic chipped stone implements have been found in various parts of the area, notably Palestine, Anatolia, and the mountainous N and E borders of Iraq. Although the various industries had a basic similarity, differentiated regional cultures already existed. The most important Paleolithic discovery in the Near East was the skeletal material from the Mount Carmel region of a type of early man unknown in Europe and now called *Homo palestinensis*.

The duration of the Paleolithic is a subject of considerable controversy, and absolute dates are best avoided. It was succeeded by a cultural stage often called Neolithic, although the new ground stone implements are less significant culture traits than the domestication of plants and animals, which permitted settled communities; more accurate terms for this age are "Early Food-producing" or "Early Village." Small villages are known in N Iraq,* the Cilician region of Anatolia, Syria, Palestine, and Egypt; some early materials from Iran may also belong to this age. Handmade pottery, which was apparently independently invented in various regions sometime after village settlement began, forms the bulk of the finds. It is usually coarse in fabric but often ornamented with simple linear patterns in incision or paint; a dark ware with burnished surface is especially common in Syria and Cilicia. Chipped flint implements are still very numerous in addition to the newer ground stone types. Toothed flint sickle blades in most sites testify to agricultural activities, and grain itself is occasionally found. A few stamp seals with incised designs suggest an attempt to mark and safeguard private property. Clay figurines, usually crudely modeled, represent animals or human beings; a type of female figurine with strongly emphasized sexual attributes suggests the existence of fertility cults. Much more striking material comes from Jericho—a group of seven human skulls upon which facial contours are modeled in clay and embellished with painted designs and shell-inlaid eyes. The significance of these bizarre objects

Courtesy of the Oriental Institute, the University of Chicago

66. Excavations at Jarmo

is unknown, but some faces show a striking, oddly sophisticated modeling unparalleled in the art of later times. Fig. PRE 66.

Architecture in most areas was confined to simple hut structures of mud or rough stone. Jericho, however, shows an astonishing architectural development even before the invention of pottery, with round or

Comparison of Periods in the Ancient Near East

	EGYPT	PALESTINE	SYRIA	ANATOLIA	IRAQ	IRAN
HISTORIC AGE	Dynasty I	Early Bronze II	Amuq H	Early Bronze II	Early Dynastic	Giyan IV
CHALCOLITHIC PERIOD	Gerzean	Early Bronze I	Amuq G	Early Bronze I		
		Late Chalcolithic (Esdraelon)	Amuq F	Late Chalcolithic	Late Prehistoric	Siyalk IV
	Amratian	Middle Chalcolithic (Ghassulian)	Amuq E	Middle Chalcolithic	Ubaid	Susa I, Siyalk III, Giyan V*c*, and Bakun A
		Early Chalcolithic (Jericho VIII)	Amuq D			
	Badarian		Amuq C	Lower Chalcolithic	Halaf	Siyalk II
NEOLITHIC PERIOD	Tasian and Fayum A		Amuq B	Neolithic		
		Jericho IX	Amuq A		Hassuna	Siyalk I and Bakun B
		Jericho, lower levels			Jarmo	

rectangular brick houses, one somewhat resembling the later Greek megaron. Several successive city walls of heavy stone, one provided with round towers and an elaborate subterranean passage, bear witness to a high degree of civic organization and to a need for protection against large-scale warfare. The other excavated sites in all countries show societies on a simple level of existence, with no indication of complex social, economic, or political organization.

There is little evidence for religious beliefs and practices, but the careful burial of the dead with objects of use or adornment suggests the concept of an afterlife. The anomaly of highly developed Neolithic Jericho* has not been explained, and later phases of that city are in no way more advanced than the rest of the Near East. There are few indications of specific contact between the various regions, but N Syria and Cilicia share a tradition of dark burnished pottery, and similar types of incised and painted decoration on pottery connect N Iraq with Syria. The Fayum A culture of Egypt shows few Near Eastern affinities and is more closely related to African cultures. Figs. JER 14-15.

2. Chalcolithic Age. The succeeding age is generally known as Chalcolithic, a name marking one of its most significant features: the introduction of copper. It supplemented, rather than replaced, stone as material for tools and weapons; even in historic times stone continued to be used. Copper appeared first in very small quantities and not everywhere at the same time, but increased steadily in amount during the course of the period, and metallurgical techniques improved concomitantly. Precious metals were occasionally used for ornaments.

The number of excavated sites is quite large; hence our knowledge of the Chalcolithic cultures is based on a considerable body of evidence. Regional specialization was highly developed, but there was an increasing amount of contact between regions, particularly demonstrable in the spread of pottery styles over wide areas. Whether this contact took the form of commerce, warfare, or migration cannot be stated with certainty; all three may have played a part, but probably commerce, regular or sporadic, was the most important. The necessity of importing copper, stone, and timber into such regions as S Iraq, which lacked all three vital materials, would early stimulate commercial activities, and such raw materials could be paid for in manufactured goods.

Settlements sufficiently large to be called cities are known before the end of the period, especially in S Iraq. Urban life presupposes some form of government beyond family or clan; it may be permissible to extrapolate from later documents and consider the city-state the unit of organization, although the details of administration must escape us. Cults multiplied, numerous and sometimes elaborate temples appeared, and the number and value of burial gifts increased. The general wealth of the communities rose, as witnessed by the many varieties of handsomely decorated pottery, finely carved stone bowls, and elaborate personal ornaments, and by the increasing use of precious and other metals. The growing number and complexity of finds indicates a corresponding growth in specialization of function among the population.

Because of the diversity of the cultures it is advisable to describe the specific developments of the Chalcolithic period in each region separately.

a. Iran. The easternmost region of the Near East is the least known. The relatively few excavated sites are scattered over a wide area: Tepe Siyalk and Tepe Giyan in the central plateau, Susa in the Elamite plain to the SW, and Tal-i-Bakun in the S near the Achaemenid capital Persepolis. None is large enough to be called a city, and architectural remains are confined to simple brick houses.

Elaborately painted pottery was characteristic through most of the Chalcolithic period.* The styles found in Bakun A and Susa I are especially handsome; the Bakun painting shows vigorous, dynamic patterns in bold lines, and the Susa painting is composed with remarkable tectonic skill. Some of these pottery-painting styles traveled westward and

After Pottier, from Frankfort, *Art and Architecture of the Ancient Orient* (Penguin Books Ltd.)

67. Prehistoric vases, from Susa

strongly influenced the pottery of Iraq; and a type of stamp seal with linear design, shared by the two areas, probably also had an Iranian origin. In the time of Siyalk III the Iranian metallurgists had already learned to cast copper (a technical advance of great importance, unknown in contemporaneous sites elsewhere) and were producing copper vessels, as well as small tools and ornaments. Fig. PRE 67.

b. Iraq (Mesopotamia). Through the entire Chalcolithic Age there was a distinct difference between the cultures of N Iraq (Assyria) and S Iraq (Babylonia). Settlement began earlier in the N, probably because alluvial Babylonia was too marshy for habitation. The Halaf culture, an indigenous development out of the Neolithic Hassuna stage but technically much advanced, was confined to Assyria.

The potters now produced lustrous painted pottery, with some very fine pieces in brilliant polychromy, notably plates with balanced, tectonic, static geometric designs. This pottery style was spread over a considerable area, from Lake Van in the Armenian mountains S almost to Baghdad and from the Tigris W to the Mediterranean coast. Stamp seals, often similar in shape and design to the Iranian ones, indicate some concept of private property. A number of stone bowls with angular profiles show considerable proficiency on the part of the stonecutters, which is corroborated by beads and amulets well worked in brittle obsidian. Clay figurines continue types known from Neolithic times, but new to the Halaf period is a squatting woman portrayed in the act of childbirth.

Fragments of mud brick houses are known throughout the area. Less common but of greater architectural interest are circular brick or stone buildings called tholoi, often with rectangular dromoi attached; one tholos retained part of the springing of a dome, the earliest instance known. The use of the tholoi is unknown, save that they were not tombs, but they were built with care and were probably public buildings of some sort, possibly shrines.

Before the end of the Halaf culture in the N the earliest Ubaid culture began in Babylonia, and later a variant succeeded Halaf in the N. In both areas painted pottery was characteristic, in a style differing markedly from Halaf and almost certainly originating under influence from Iran. The linear designs and shapes were, on the whole, simpler than those of Halaf pottery; polychromy and lustrous paint were lacking. Figurines, stone vessels, and seals continued; the S had a peculiar type of figurine with human body and monstrous reptilian head (possibly representing a deity), and the N now began a considerable development of seal design, utilizing animal and human figures for the first time. Little metal has been found in Halaf and Ubaid levels, certainly in part because of the inclement climate, which makes preservation difficult.

The most important feature of the Ubaid culture is the appearance of monumental architecture, chiefly temples built of mud brick in a tripartite plan with a long central cella and a row of smaller rooms on either side. Indicative of cultic development and complexity, these temples are the earliest instances of the plan which became standard for Mesopotamian temples for centuries. A temenos with three such temples grouped around a court is the most ambitious piece of city planning known from this age.

In the Late Prehistoric Age the N and the S diverged almost completely, and there was little contact between them, the S now becoming the cultural leader in all respects. Irrigation methods begun in Babylonia at this time permitted agriculture well away from the vicinity of the rivers. In consequence the population increased; many new settlements were founded in this age and older ones grew markedly, some becoming real cities. Relations between these towns must have attained some organized form, since co-operative effort was necessary to build and maintain the irrigation canals. Such regularization also fostered commerce, and Mesopotamian products are dispersed all across Western Asia to the Syrian coast and even to Egypt. This suggests extensive foreign relations, but, inexplicably, there is no evidence of reciprocal trade.

Temple architecture became very impressive, and the buildings increased in size and ornamentation. Some were placed on terraces, and the flat terrace was probably the precursor of the step tower or *ziggurat,* which characterized Mesopotamian architecture in later times. Secular architecture is less well known, and no monumental public buildings other than temples have been found; fortifications of any kind are unknown. Metal became increasingly common, and metallurgical technique—especially in casting—was highly developed. Stonecutting made equal progress, and the high development of glyptic is especially noteworthy; a new form of seal was the cylinder with design on the circumference, and this is the form used throughout historic times. Monumental sculpture both in relief and in the round made its appearance just at the end of the prehistoric era. Through most of this period the pottery was unpainted and had clearly ceased to be regarded as a medium of art, but technically it was of excellent quality, and the use of the foot-turned potter's wheel allowed considerable expansion in the repertoire of shapes. Certainly the great achievement of this age was the invention of writing. Clay tablets impressed with a cut reed in semipictographic script contain temple records, the beginning of the long, well-documented course of Mesopotamian history.

c. Anatolia. Chalcolithic sites are rare, but a few are known in the high central plateau and others in the Cilician plain. Anatolia did not reach a level of culture at all comparable to that of Mesopotamia; it lacked writing, monumental sculpture, highly developed metallurgy, fine glyptic, and elaborate temple complexes. But here too there is some evidence of more advanced organization of towns. The hitherto undefended Cilician site of Mersin became a military fortress with a city wall of mud brick on a high stone foundation, a series of barracks for soldiers, and a large house thought to be the commander's residence. Dark burnished pottery resembling the Neolithic fabrics has been found in several sites, but light ware with simple painted linear designs is also known. Copper is restricted to such small objects as pins.

d. Syria. Chalcolithic remains are best represented in the Amuq (the plain of Antioch), and the sequence there can be used as a standard for the country. Phase C contains Halaf-style pottery imported from Iraq and then imitated locally, Phase D develops a local polychrome style, and Phase E imports Ubaid-type painted ware from Iraq. Copper occurs rarely and only in small objects. Phases F and G do not show as high a cultural level as the approximately contemporaneous Mesopotamian Late Prehistoric Age, but technical advances include the potter's wheel and improved metallurgy. As far as is known, there were no large cities or elaborate fortifications.

e. Palestine. The Chalcolithic towns were less spectacular than Neolithic Jericho. Numerous private houses, well built of mud brick on stone foundations, are known; at Ghassul some bear mural paintings, too fragmentary for adequate interpretation but often complex and well designed. In the phase called "Early Bronze I" (better considered as terminal Chalcolithic) Jericho again had a city wall, this time of mud brick and less impressive than the Neolithic wall. A very large triple circumvallation surrounds the site of Ai near Jerusalem. Temples or shrines appear in this late phase but are simple one-roomed structures not at all comparable with the striking religious architecture of contemporary Mesopotamia.

Pottery might bear simple painted geometric patterns, but there were no elaborate styles; in the Late Chalcolithic phase a fine gray burnished ware with characteristic shapes appeared. Copper became steadily more common through the period, especially for weapons; but stone was still in common use, and different styles of flintworking form one of the criteria for distinguishing phases.

f. Egypt. Egypt remained outside the sphere of Western Asia, on the whole, and developed its own very distinctive culture. Our information comes almost exclusively from graves—fortunately, well furnished—so we lack knowledge of architecture. The various phases named for type sites are distinct but form a clear developmental sequence leading into the historic Egyptian culture.

The earlier pottery was dark, often of a fine thin fabric with a rippled surface; forms were chiefly rounded and baggy. Light ware began in the Gerzean phase, as did painted design; since both features appeared contemporaneously with a type of wavy handle known to be of Palestinian origin, it is probable that the new style in general came from Palestine. The Egyptian painted decoration, however, was unlike any Asiatic style, with very free and untectonic organization and a fondness for representational design. Ivory was in common use and stonecutting an important industry, judging from the numerous very fine stone vessels. Human figurines were predominantly female, often with the exaggerated sexual characteristics which suggest a fertility aspect. Copper was used in steadily increasing amounts, but metallurgy was not so highly developed as in Mesopotamia. Relief sculpture began near the end of the period, adorning utilitarian objects, in several instances with subjects which may have a commemorative, historical significance.

Religion is known only from the burial customs, where the careful disposition of the dead with a plenitude of objects implies a mortuary cult beyond anything known in Asia. To the end of the prehistoric period there is no trace of the pre-eminence of a single leader, so it seems clear that the characteristic Egyptian concept of the divine king had not yet been developed.

3. Conclusion. Thus the stage was set for the beginning of the historic age. It is clear that the brilliant crystallization of Mesopotamian culture at the end of the prehistoric age was unmatched elsewhere in the Near East; but an equally brilliant phase occurred in Egypt at the very beginning of the dynastic period, again bringing with it writing, monumental art, and complex social organization. These two countries were and remained the great focuses of civilization until the Greek Classical Age shifted the focus to Europe.

Bibliography. D. E. McCown, *The Comparative Stratigraphy of Early Iran* (1942); "The Material Culture of Early Iran," *Journal of Near Eastern Studies,* I (1942), 424-49. W. F. Albright, *The Archaeology of Palestine* (1949). A. Perkins, *The Comparative Archeology of Early Mesopotamia* (1949). H. Frankfort, *The Birth of Civilization in the Near East* (1950). R. J. and L. Braidwood, "The Earliest Village Communities in Southwestern Asia," *Journal of World History,* I (1953), 278-310. S. Lloyd, *Early Anatolia* (1956). A. PERKINS

PREPARATION DAY [(ἡ)Παρασκευή, preparation, provisioning] (cf. Matt. 27:62; Mark 15:42; Luke 23:54; John 19:14, 31). The day preceding the sabbath.

The strict sabbath observance in Judaism demanded great foresight. Food was prepared, business affairs were suspended, and people retired. To avoid all risk of infraction, observance began well before the sunset with which sabbath actually commenced (Jos. Antiq. XVI.vi.2; Jth. 8:6). All of Friday gradually became a Day of Preparation. Through Jewish and Christian influences, Παρασκευή became, and has remained, the proper name for this day in Greek.

In the gospels the Crucifixion occurs on a Day of Preparation. The Synoptists describe it as the day before the sabbath (Mark 15:42; cf. Luke 23:54). They equate the Last Supper with the Jewish Passover meal of the night before (Matt. 26:17; Mark 14:12; Luke 22:7 ff), which would make it fall on the first full day of the Feast of Unleavened Bread. The Fourth Gospel, however, does not identify the Last Supper as the Passover (13:1 ff). And John 19:14 describes the Crucifixion as on the "day of Preparation for the Passover." The day preceding Passover, known as Passover Eve, was, indeed, a day of intense preparation (cf. M. Pes. 1-4). Moreover, the curious reference to "that sabbath" (John 19:31) could refer to the first day of the Feast of Unleavened Bread. Except for the Sadducees, first-century Jews identified that day of holy convocation (Lev. 23:7) as "the sabbath" (vs. 11), on the basis of which the date for the Feast of Weeks (*see* WEEKS, FEAST OF) was computed. Therefore, if the connection of the Last Supper with the Passover can be treated as a secondary development, the references to Preparation are quite reconcilable. J. C. RYLAARSDAM

PRESBYTER prĕs'bĭ tər [πρεσβύτερος, older man]; PRESBYTERY prĕs'bĭ tĕr'ĭ [πρεσβυτέριον]. Literally, "older man," in contrast to "younger man" (cf. Luke 15:25; Acts 2:17 [quoting Joel 2:28—H 3:1]; I Pet. 5:5); also, a notable man of a past generation (Matt. 15:2; Mark 7:3, 5; Heb. 11:2); but usually, in a technical sense, either a member of the Jewish SANHEDRIN or a leader in a Christian church (*see* ELDER IN THE NT; MINISTRY). The word πρεσβυτέριον for a council or assembly of elders ("presbytery") is used of the Jewish Sanhedrin (Luke 22:66; Acts 22:5), and once of Christian elders (I Tim. 4:14). M. H. SHEPHERD, JR.

PRESENCE, BREAD OF THE. *See* BREAD OF THE PRESENCE.

***PRESENCE OF GOD.** It is strange that until recently the modern movement in biblical study has largely neglected the image and genuinely Israelite mythology of the presence of God in the Bible. The importance of the idea is being increasingly recognized. The terminology centers in both testaments in such concepts as face, glory, name, tabernacle, etc., and in the prepositions "before" (lit., "to or in the face of"), "in the midst of," "with." The verb שכן, "to dwell," and its derivatives are also central. The material relating to the conception may be resolved into various divisions.

There are formulas of good will and blessing. Such sentences as "God is with you in all that you do" (Gen. 21:22), and the frequent "The LORD was with him" (e.g., 39:3), are simply the recognition of good fortune interpreted as the evidence of divine blessing. In the future tense such sentences are the promise of this same good fortune (e.g., Exod. 3:12; Josh. 1:5, 9).

There are also a number of visitation and theophany passages, in which through a variety of manifestations, dreams, visions, oracles of visitation, etc. —i.e., visions and auditions—the God of Israel visits individuals, his people and the nations around Israel. None of this temporary visitation or theophanic material properly belongs to the present theme.

Likewise the biblical material relating to the omnipresence of God does not rightly belong here (e.g., Ps. 139; Jer. 23:23-24; Amos 9:2-5; John 4:19-24), for this is the doctrine of the universal presence of God always and everywhere present to the believer.

The separation of the material belonging to the divisions noted above, then, discloses various passages and ideas relevant to the presence theme which are further distinguished by the idea of "dwelling among." It is this characteristic of "abiding" or "dwelling" in the activity or place of the God of Israel that has given rise to the term "tabernacling presence," and it is this conception of the tabernacling presence which constitutes the heart of the biblical portrayal of the theme. (It is to Phythian-Adams that we owe this phrase and the rekindling of interest in this theme.)

Exodus is one of the books of this presence idea. In the first place it shares with the rest of the Pentateuch three conceptions of the presence as manifested in the cloud. The presence in the cloud in J precedes and guides Israel (Exod. 13:21-22; 14:19*b;* Num. 14: 14*b;* Deut. 1:33; etc.), but in E the cloud of the presence occasionally descends to stand by the door to the tent of meeting for purposes of revelation (Exod. 33:9; Num. 11:25; etc.), and in P the cloud covers and protects the stationary tent of meeting. It is the P account of the cloud which most closely resembles the tabernacling presence.

But the cloud is only one of the images of the presence in Exodus. Yahweh dwells in the heavens but manifests himself on earth in many places; yet there is one place where he lodges. In Exodus this place is Sinai-Horeb. Thither the people come as to Yahweh himself (19:4; 24:1-2, 9-11), and to leave the mount without Yahweh requires that they strip themselves of their festive ornaments (33:6). Since Yahweh will not go with Israel from Sinai, the tent of meeting and presumably the ark (so Deuteronomy) are provided, and these constitute an ersatz shrine, a traveling sanctuary of the presence, a substitute presence. This substitute presence is also linked with an angel, "for my name is in him" (23:20-21; 33:14), and the angel's name-bearing, guiding, and possibly military qualities point to the ark (cf. Num. 10:35-36; I Sam. 4; II Sam. 6:2), though some have claimed a reference to Moses' father-in-law. The holy of holies of Exodus is certainly the vision of the elders in Exod. 24:9-11, and especially Moses' vision of Yahweh as he passed by (33:17-23; 34:6-7). The claim that Moses alone spoke face to face with God (Num. 12:8; Deut. 34:10) is here qualified that Moses saw only God's back. The laws of Exodus are likewise controlled by the presence theme, whether the "name" presence of Exod. 20:24, or the dwelling, "glory" presence of 25:8; 29:42-46; 40:34-38.

Even if the images of the presence in Exodus reveal traits and ideas current later in N Israel and in Jerusalem, there is a basis of fact and faith in the tradition which would suggest that the idea of the presence is original to the desert period of Israel's religion, and, therefore, presumably, is part, and the central part, of Moses' ministry to the Israel of the desert. Certainly his associates challenged Moses on this very point at Massah (Exod. 17:7; cf. Deut. 6:16; 9:22; 33:8; Ps. 95:8; cf. Ps. 81:7), and whether the incident is pre-Sinai or post- (Num. 20) does not affect the argument. It is possible to explain the presence material in Exodus in many ways, but the core is certainly Mosaic and represents the uniqueness and originality of Israel (Exod. 33:16).

Certainly in and after Exodus the presence is bound with the sanctuary. First with the ark as a traveling sanctuary, and with the accompanying tent of meeting, and then with the several shrines which served as the home of the ark and the tent, as Shechem, Shiloh, and eventually Jerusalem (I Kings 8:12-13). It has been shown that this sanctuary-presence is represented by the Deuteronomic theologoumenon of the tabernacling name, and by the glory image of the Levitical and Jerusalem priesthood; and the rise of two different portrayals of the presence—i.e., name and glory—suggests a basic root idea, prior to both and from which both had developed.

The same is true of the ideas of the ark and of the tent of meeting, for if at times they appear together, there are other occasions when they appear apart and are separately mentioned. But together or apart they witness to the master theme. The material of the presence theme is so complex, and the media of manifestation so varied, that attempts to trace various stages in the development of the doctrine have not been successful. Rather than assume and portray a unilinear sequence, it is preferable to suppose a variegated pattern of presence imagery in ancient Israel. In the same way no single explanation of the tabernacling-presence theme adequately expounds all the media of portrayal, for the presence may be described in reference to Yahweh in terms of synecdoche—i.e., *pars pro toto;* identity; extension of the personality; and the value of Yahweh without his identity, a curious kind of presence-in-absence (Exod. 32:33; Ezek. 10–11; 43), etc.

The prophets undoubtedly, if indirectly, witness to the tabernacling presence, in such references as: Isa. 6:1-5; 8:18; 30:27-29; 31:9; Jer. 7:12-15; 8:19; 14:9; 23:23, 39; Ezek. 8:6; Hos. 5:15; 11:9, 11; Amos 1:2; 5:14; Mic. 1:2-3; 3:11; 6:6; etc. Their testimony to the place of the presence is corroborated by their portrayal of the renewal of the presence in the new Israel that is to be. This eschatological presence may be studied in such passages as: Isa. 12:6; Ezek. 11:16; 37:26-28; 43:1-7; 44:1-2; 48:35; Joel 3:17, 21; Mic. 4:7; Zeph. 3:15, 17; Zech. 2:10-11; 8:3, 23; Mal. 3:1. Alike then in history, cult, and eschatological promise, the presence is clearly central to the faith and hope of Israel.

Yet the promise of the eschatological presence contrasts with that aspect of the Jewish portrayal of the presence—i.e., the Shekinah—according to which the tabernacling presence, the Shekinah, was absent from the second temple. The classical literature of the Jews shows that they still wait for the return of the Shekinah, or of the word, *memra,* or of the spirit.

In the NT it is, of course, Jesus Christ who is the spiritual, personal, incarnate, and beheld heir and fulfilment of the tabernacling presence and of the Shekinah. The Incarnation is thus a new and final dimension of the theme. In his birth and baptism, his ministry and miracle, his teaching and transfiguration, and in his passion and resurrection, they beheld the glory of the divine presence. Phythian-Adams (*see bibliography*) coins the word "naomorphism," under which he treats of atonement, sanctification, incorporation, etc., in the NT, and relates the tabernacling presence to Christ, the believer, and the church. Unfortunately his stimulating discussion is marred by several errors, such as the false distinction concerning the mode of the presence, which, he claims, was only "among" men in Israel, but "in" Christians in the NT. The incarnate presence is, of course, the center of all the NT and governs all the aspects of life, thought, and institution which spring from it—aspects which must be studied under the main branches of NT theology.

It must suffice here to mention various problems which arise in the NT concerning the presence. The problem of the presence is most acute in the cry of dereliction on the cross (Matt. 27:46; Mark 15:34), and may only be understood, let alone solved, in the light of the OT categories of the presence. Then there is also the presence-absence theme, where Christ speaks of the necessity and desirability of his departure from the disciples (e.g., John 13:1, 33; 14:1-7; 16:7, 28) but promises also his abiding presence (e.g., Matt. 28:20); this paradox is also seen in the vision of Christ at the right hand of the majesty on high and in the experience of Christ in the heart and life of the Christian believer, a paradox which is doubtless resolved in the theology of the church in the advent of the Holy Spirit, but which also receives its final illumination in Rev. 21:22-24.

See also PRAISE; PSALMS, BOOK OF; WORSHIP IN THE OT.

Bibliography. E. G. Gulin, "Das Antlitz Jahwes im AT," *Annales Academiae Scientiarum Fennicae,* Series B, vol. XVII, no. 3 (1923). J. Daniélou, *Le signe du temple ou de la présence de Dieu* (1942). G. H. Davies, "The Presence of God in Israel," in E. A. Payne, ed., *Studies in History and Religion* (1942), pp. 11-29. W. J. Phythian-Adams, *The People and the Presence* (1942). L. H. Brockington, "The Presence of God, a Study of the Use of the Term 'Glory of Yahweh,' " *ET,* LVII (Oct., 1945), 21-25; "Presence," in A. Richardson, ed., *A Theological Word Book of the Bible* (1950), pp. 172-76. A. R. George, *Communion with God in the NT* (1953). H. J. Franken, *The Mystical Communion with JHWH in the Book of Psalms* (1954). Y. M. J. Congar, *Le mystère du temple* (1958).

G. HENTON DAVIES

PRESIDENT [Aram. סרך, *possibly a loan word from a Persian title*]. An appointed governor or chief in the Persian kingdom. Daniel was one of three presidents who were appointed by Darius over the 120 satraps. The envy of the satraps and the other presidents led to the decree which put Daniel in the lions' den (Dan. 6:2 ff).

C. U. WOLF

PRESUMPTION. *See* PRIDE.

PRIDE. At least six Hebrew roots contain the idea of pride, and almost all of them share the meaning "to lift up," "to be high" (e.g., גאה, גבה, רום). The English translations express the idea in various contexts by such words as "arrogance," "loftiness," "presumption," "boasting" (cf. also "proud," "proudly," and similar forms). The NT has a similar range of equivalents including ἀλαζονεία, δόξα, καυχάομαι and related words, and ὑπερηφανία.

Although there are occasional passages in the OT and NT which seem to accept various forms of natural pride (cf. Job 28:8; Prov. 16:31; I Cor. 11:15; *see* GLORY), the distinctive biblical thrust is overwhelmingly against human presumption and self-glorification—on the level of warnings against boasting of more than one can accomplish (I Kings 20:11; Prov. 25:14), or that of condemnation of the proud and commendation of the humble (Pss. 18:27; 101:5-6; Prov. 15:25), or of advice against pride on the basis of the logic of practical WISDOM (Prov. 11:2; 16:18-19; Eccl. 7:8).

More importantly, certain OT passages point toward pride as the virtual ground of sin: classically in Isa. 2:6-22 and echoed in Zeph. 3:11-13 (cf. also Ezek. 16:49 ff; Amos 6:8; cf. I John 2:16). The imagery of Ezek. 28 reflects a mythological tradition of a kind of FALL, apparently based upon pride and jealousy (cf. Gen. 3, where pride as such does not emerge as the origin of sin; cf. also Gen. 11; Ezek. 31). Yahweh in his wrath destroys the proud nations (Isa. 10:12-19; Jer. 50:29-32; Obad. 2-4; Zeph. 2:8–3:20; Zech. 9:6), as well as the arrogant man (II Chr. 26:16; 32:25; Isa. 10:12; Dan. 5:20; cf. Job 22:29; Pss. 22:29; 94:2-7; Prov. 15:25). Thus pride and boastfulness characterize the "wicked" in the Psalms and wisdom literature (Pss. 5:5; 12:3; 49:6; 75:4; Prov. 8:13; 15:25; 21:4; cf. Job 35:12).

Yahweh alone is glorious and exalted (Isa. 2:11-17), and he achieves, by his ultimate victory over the proud, the establishment of the POOR and of a humble REMNANT (Isa. 3:14-15; Zeph. 3:12). Thus the tangible landmarks of pride in the land (including the temple itself) must be destroyed (Lam. 2:4, 7; Ezek. 24:21), in order that Israel's new age of humble obedience may come, bringing with it a proper pride in the fruits of Yahweh's redemptive acts (Isa. 4:2). This abasement of the proud and exaltation of the humble is most clearly expressed in the relatively late hymn (I Sam. 2:1-10) which is the pattern for the MAGNIFICAT (Luke 1:46-55; cf. Phil. 2:8-11). Thus Israel's only proper boast is in the righteous deeds of Yahweh (Pss. 20:7; 34:2; Jer. 9:23-24; 13:15-16; cf. Deut. 10:21; Zech. 10:12). *See* PRAISE.

While false pride is equally condemned in the NT (Mark 7:22; Rom. 1:30; Jas. 3:5, 14; 4:16), the distinctive forms are spiritual pride (Luke 18:9; Rom. 2:23; 11:20; Eph. 2:9) and its opposite, boasting in the redemptive work of God in Jesus Christ (I Cor. 1:29-31; Gal. 6:14; Phil. 3:3; cf. Heb. 3:6). Paul rejects self-commendation (II Cor. 3:1; 5:12; 10:8) because every human boast has been destroyed in Jesus Christ (I Cor. 1:25-30; cf. Jer. 9:23-24), but he is able to boast of his ministry (II Cor. 4:1-6; 6:3-10), his suffering and weakness (II Cor. 11:23-30; 12:9), and his congregations (II Cor. 7:14; 8:24; 9:2-3), because, in different ways, "Jesus Christ as Lord" (II Cor. 4:5) is the content of them all, and God himself is at work in them (I Cor. 15:10; cf. 3:5 ff, 21-23).

Bibliography. A. Richardson, *A Theological Word Book of the Bible* (1951), p. 176.

J. A. WHARTON

***PRIESTS AND LEVITES.** The priesthood in biblical thought represents Israel's union with God. Under the Mosaic covenant the whole nation is to be a "kingdom of priests" and hence a holy people (Exod. 19:6; Lev. 11:44 ff; Num. 15:40). The sanctity required of the people for the service of God is symbolized in the priesthood, which therefore becomes the mediator of the covenant.

In the second temple there is a threefold hierarchy of cultic officials—high priest, priest, and Levite. These are three distinct orders, each having its own distinctive functions and privileges. Their origin and development, together with the relationship of priests and Levites, constitute one of the major problems of OT scholarship. The traditional view regards this hierarchy as having been instituted by Moses during the wilderness wanderings and as persisting virtually unchanged throughout the history of Israel. The Graf-Kuenen-Wellhausen school of criticism, however, sees it as a distinctively postexilic institution whose origin is obscure but whose development can be clearly traced through several well-marked stages. This view, which has been widely held, is now seen to be an oversimplification of the problem. It is therefore being attacked at many points, but there is as yet no alternative view generally acceptable.

A. Terminology
  1. In biblical Hebrew
  2. In LXX and NT Greek
B. Theological significance of the Levitical priesthood
  1. Representative character
  2. The threefold hierarchy
  3. Function
C. The postexilic cultus
  1. The high priest
  2. Priests
  3. Levites
D. Origin and development
  1. The traditional view
  2. The critical reconstruction
    a. The early period
    b. The monarchy
    c. Deuteronomy and Josiah's reform
    d. Ezekiel
    e. The restoration
    f. The Chronicler
E. Reconsiderations
  1. The high priest
  2. Priests and Levites
  3. The date and historical value of P
Bibliography

A. *TERMINOLOGY.* The word "priest," either alone or qualified by "chief" or "high," occurs over seven hundred times in the OT and over eighty times in the NT. The term "Levite" is less frequent; it occurs some eighty times in the OT and only three times in the NT.

1. In biblical Hebrew. The usual Hebrew term for "priest" is כהן (*kôhēn*), which is found also, with the same meaning, in Phoenician inscriptions. It appears in an Aramaized form (*kāhēn*) eight times in Ezra. The regular Aramaic term כמר occurs (probably as a loan word) three or perhaps four times in biblical Hebrew, but its use is restricted to idolatrous priests (II Kings 23:5; Hos. 10:5; Zeph. 1:4; and possibly Hos. 4:4, emending כמרין or ככמר). The use of כהן, however, is not limited to the priests of Yahweh. It is used also of Egyptian priests (Gen. 41:45, 50; 46:20; 47:26), Philistine priests (I Sam. 6:2), priests of Dagon (I Sam. 5:5), priests of Baal (II Kings 10:19), priests of Chemosh (Jer. 48:7), and priests of the Baalim and Asherim (II Chr. 34:5).

The corresponding Arabic word is *kâhin,* meaning a seer or soothsayer, and it has been suggested that this was the original sense of the Hebrew term. There is evidence, however, that כהן is a specifically Canaanite term and *kâhin* a loan word which has acquired a divergent sense. The Hebrew noun כהן is derived from the verb *kāhan,* which appears to have the same meaning as *kûn* (כון), "to stand." The priest is therefore one who stands before God as his servant or minister.

The Hebrew term for "Levite" is לוי, denoting a descendant of Levi (*see* LEVI 1), the third son of Jacob by Leah, from which name the word may be a gentilic. In Num. 18:2, 4, however, there is a play upon words between לוי and the verb לוה, meaning "to attach" or "to be joined": the tribe of Levi is to be joined to Aaron. Some have maintained that this wordplay is an indication of the true etymology of the term. The word "Levite," it is said, is not an indication of genealogy but signifies "one who attaches himself." The Levites are therefore regarded, on this view, as being originally either foreigners who joined the Israelites in the exodus period or Hebrew cultic attendants who acted as an escort to the ark or were attached to some local sanctuary. Others have linked the etymology of "Levite" with that of the South Arabian cultic officials who are called by the term *lawi'a* (feminine *lawi'at*) in the Minean inscriptions, which have been variously dated between 1500 B.C. and 700 B.C. On the earlier dating it may be argued that "Levite" was originally a cultic term borrowed by the Israelites from the Mineans. On the other hand, a late date would involve the possibility of the Minean term *lawi'a* being borrowed from an Israelite tribal name which was associated with cultic functions. In each case it would be necessary to establish, or assume, the etymological identity of the terms.

Any theory that the Levites were an "artificial tribe" of professional cultic officials must reckon with the early biblical testimony that Levi was one of the original tribes of Israel which had engaged in warrior activities before being set apart for cultic functions (Gen. 34:25-30; 49:5). There is no good reason for doubting that this tradition is sound, and the reference to Levi in the Blessing of Moses (Deut. 33: 8 ff) would seem to imply that the official term had its origin in a tribal name.

2. In LXX and NT Greek. The Hebrew word כהן is rendered in the LXX by the Greek ἱερεύς, which is the common Greek term for "priest." The same term is used exclusively throughout the NT.

In both the LXX and the NT the Hebrew לוי appears in its Greek form, Λευίτης or Λευείτης.

B. *THEOLOGICAL SIGNIFICANCE OF THE LEVITICAL PRIESTHOOD.* Priesthood and COVENANT are closely related in biblical thought. As the covenant people of God, Israel is to be a kingdom of priests and a holy nation (Exod. 19:5-6; cf. Isa. 61:6). Keeping the covenant, therefore, implies the consecration of the nation. Because God is holy, the people that is to be his own possession must also be holy (Lev. 11:44 ff; Num. 15:40). Since, moreover, the covenant is made with the whole nation, the existence of an official priesthood does not exclude the rest of the people from their special relationship with God.

1. Representative character. The Levitical priesthood has therefore a representative character: it embodies the duty, as well as the honor and privileges, of the whole nation as the covenant people of God. Corporate responsibility must of necessity be delegated to representative persons, who discharge it on behalf of the community as a whole. Hence in public and national worship the priests act as the representatives of the people.

But the priesthood was necessary not only for practical reasons; underlying it is a great moral and spiritual principle. Likeness to God in character and purpose is essential for those who would serve him. But this likeness was lacking in the people as a whole: the "holy nation" possessed only a very imperfect holiness. The state of sanctity and purity, however, which is necessary for the service of God was symbolized, if not always realized, in the Levitical priesthood. The result was twofold: first, the true requirements of serving God were continually kept before the eyes of his covenant people; and second, the covenant relationship with God was vicariously maintained by the priesthood on behalf of the nation as a whole.

2. The threefold hierarchy. The representative sanctity of the priesthood is expressed in the threefold hierarchy. The lowest grade consists of the Levites, who are set apart for the service of the sanctuary. They represent the people of Israel as substitutes for the first-born sons, who belong by right to God (Num. 3:12-13, 41, 45; 8:14-17; cf. Exod. 13:2, 12-13; 22:29; 34:19-20; Lev. 27:26; Num. 18:15; Deut. 15:19). Above them are the sons of Aaron, who are consecrated for the specific office of priest. They alone may represent the nation in the sacrificial ministrations of the altar. And the hierarchy culminates in the high priest, in whom the vicarious sanctity of the priesthood is gathered up. By bearing the names of the twelve tribes of Israel on his breastplate when he goes into the sanctuary, he represents the people as a whole (Exod. 28:29). He alone can enter the holy of holies—and that only once a year—to make ATONEMENT for the nation's sin. In Zechariah's vision the phrase "The LORD . . . has chosen Jerusalem" (Zech. 3:2) implies that Joshua as high priest is the representative of Jerusalem and hence of the whole Jewish community.

3. Function. The essential function of the Levitical priesthood is therefore to assure, maintain, and constantly re-establish the holiness of the elect people of God (cf. Exod. 28:38; Lev. 10:17; Num. 18:1). Through the covenant with Levi, the priesthood becomes the mediator of the covenant with Israel (Mal. 2:4 ff; cf. Num. 18:19; Jer. 33:20-26). Hence it is through the priesthood that a purified and sanctified Israel is able to serve God and receives his blessing (cf. Zech. 3:1-5).

The Levitical priesthood, along with the sacrificial system which it maintains, finds its culmination and fulfilment in Christ. He is the great High Priest, one with the Father through his eternal sonship (Heb. 1), yet by his Incarnation identified with men (Heb. 2:14-18; 4:15; 5:1-2, 8-10). Hence he is the perfect Mediator of the New Covenant (Heb. 7:23-28; 8:6-13; 9:15), who has once for all made atonement for sin (Heb. 9:11-28; 10:11-18) and opened for men a new and living way into the presence of God (Heb. 10:19-25).

C. *THE POSTEXILIC CULTUS.* The postexilic literature of the OT gives a clear picture of the organization of the priesthood in the second temple. Here alone have we explicit and unequivocal evidence of the existence of a threefold hierarchy of cultic officials. Each order is separate and distinct, with clearly defined duties and privileges.

1. The high priest. At the head of the hierarchy is the high priest, who occupies a position of increasing splendor and power. The restored community of Judah was more a church than a state. No longer a monarchy, it became a hierocracy. The high priest, therefore, acquired much of the dignity that had formerly belonged to the king. In 520 B.C. we find the high priest Joshua and the Davidic governor Zerubbabel placed side by side as equals (Hag. 1:1, 12, 14; 2:2, 4). Together they begin the rebuilding of the temple (Ezra 3:1 ff; Hag. 1–2), and they are to share the rule of the community as the "two anointed" (Zech. 4:14; 6:9-15); but in the temple the high priest is to reign (Zech. 3:6-7). When this double rule comes to an end with the disappearance of the house of David, the high priest becomes the undisputed head of the Jewish state, supreme in the civil as in the ecclesiastical realm. The most outstanding of these high-priest princes is Simon the Just, "the leader of his brethren and the pride of his people" (Ecclus. 50:1-21). In the second century B.C. the high priest presides over a γερουσία or "senate" composed of priests, scribes, and the heads of families (I Macc. 12:6; II Macc. 4:44; 11:27)—the early form of the SANHEDRIN.

The power and influence of the high priesthood is such that during the Greek period it became a prize sought after by unscrupulous men. In 174 B.C., Jason ousted his brother Onias and bought the office for himself by a substantial increase in the tribute (II Macc. 4:7-10; cf. vss. 18-20). Three years later he was outbidden, and therefore displaced, by Menelaus (vss. 23-26), who endeavored to secure his position by the murder of Onias after the latter had publicly exposed him (vss. 33-35). In the time of the Maccabees, however, the high priesthood regained its former honor and glory, which reached its climax when Judea enjoyed a short-lived independence under the rule of the Hasmoneans. *See* HASMONEAN.

The high priest traced his descent from Eleazar the son of Aaron; the office was normally hereditary and conferred for life (Num. 3:32; 25:11 ff; 35:25, 28; Neh. 12:10-11). He was consecrated with an elaborate ceremonial consisting of lustration, vesting in his robes of office, anointing with oil, and sacrificial rites in which the blood of the ram of ordination was applied to the tip of the high priest's right ear, the thumb of his right hand, and the great toe of his right foot. These installation ceremonies lasted for seven days (Exod. 29:1-37; Lev. 8:5-35).

The distinctive high-priestly VESTMENTS consisted of a blue woven robe on the hem of which hung golden bells alternating with blue, purple, and scarlet pomegranates; an EPHOD of blue, purple, and scarlet material and fine linen interwoven with threads of gold, with each of its two shoulder clasps carrying a precious stone engraved with the names of six of the twelve tribes of Israel; a square breastplate or BREASTPIECE of the same materials as the ephod, to which it was attached, but having four rows of three precious stones each, on which were inscribed the names of the twelve tribes and formed like a pouch so as to contain the ancient sacred lots URIM AND THUMMIM; and finally a linen turban, to which was attached a golden crown, or plate, inscribed "Holy to Yahweh" (Exod. 28:4-39; 39:1-31; Lev. 8:7-9). These vestments symbolize the mediatory office of the high priest, the colored materials, gold, and precious stones representing the glory of God and the breastplate, or breastpiece, inscribed with the names of the twelve tribes representing Israel as a whole. When, however, the high priest enters the holy of holies on the Day of Atonement (*see* ATONEMENT, DAY OF), he lays aside his ceremonial robes and wears only linen garments—coat or tunic, breeches, girdle, and turban (Lev. 16:4, 23, 32).

The ceremonies of the annual Day of Atonement are the most important of the high priest's duties. Only he may enter the holy of holies and sprinkle the MERCY SEAT with the blood of the sin offerings for himself and his house and for the people (Lev. 16:1-25). He must also make atonement both for himself and for the people as a whole by sprinkling the blood of other sin offerings before the sanctuary veil and applying it to the horns of the altar (Lev. 4:3-21; cf. 9:8 ff). It would seem that the high priest is expected to share in the general duties of the priesthood (Exod. 27:21) and to offer a daily meal offering (Lev. 6:19-22, where "on the day when he is anointed" is generally regarded as a later interpolation).

Because he is the spiritual head of Israel, a greater degree of ceremonial purity is required of the high priest than of ordinary priests. According to the HOLINESS CODE, he shall not defile himself by contact with any dead body, even that of his father or mother; neither shall he let his hair grow long or rend his clothes as a sign of mourning. He may not marry a widow, as may other priests, but only a virgin of his own people (Lev. 21:10-15). For the same reason special gravity attaches to any sin committed by the high priest. It brings guilt on the people and must be expiated by a specially prescribed sin offering (Lev. 4:3-12). The supreme importance of the high priest in the life of the community is seen in the fact that his death marks an epoch: the manslayer is then released from the city of refuge (Num. 35:25, 28, 32).

2. Priests. Associated with the high priest are the ordinary priests, who are the cultic specialists. They are restricted to the Levitical house of Aaron (Exod. 28:1, 41; 29:9; Lev. 1:5, 7-8, 11; Num. 3:10; 18:7) and must be free from physical defects (Lev. 21:16-23). In its final organization the priesthood was divided into twenty-four priestly families, which attended the temple in turn. Each of these divisions, or "courses," was on duty for a week, beginning with the sabbath, except at the great annual festivals when they all officiated together. Sixteen families traced their descent through Zadok to Eleazar, and eight to Aaron's other son, Ithamar (I Chr. 24:1-19). Priests were consecrated by ceremonies similar to those used for the consecration of the high priest, although less elaborate (Exod. 29:1-37; Lev. 8:5-35); and only the high priest was anointed (Lev. 21:10). The priestly vestments were a tunic, breeches, and turban, all of white linen (שש), with a white linen girdle embroidered with blue, purple, and scarlet (Exod. 28:40, 42; 29:8-9; 39:27-29; Lev. 8:13).

The chief functions of the postexilic priesthood are the care of the vessels of the sanctuary and the sacrificial duties of the altar: only the priest may sacrifice (Num. 18:5, 7). But the priesthood also retains its ancient prerogative of giving תורה—i.e., instruction in the ways and requirements of God (Mal. 2:6-7; cf. Jer. 18:18). As the custodian of sacred tradition, the priest had always been the authority par excellence in all matters relating to the law. He, no less than the prophet, was a medium of revelation. But whereas the revelatory experience of the prophet was personal and direct, that of the priest was collective and mediated, either through divination or through his training in the accumulated knowledge of the past. When, however, in postexilic times the written word supersedes oral tradition and the Jews become the people of a book, ethical teaching passes increasingly into the hands of a new class of teachers, the scribes (*see* SCRIBE), and the emphasis of priestly instruction comes to be in the cultic sphere (Lev. 10:10-11; cf. Hag. 2:10-13).

Again, the priests are the custodians of medical lore and so play an important part in safeguarding the health of the community (Lev. 13–15). They retain their traditional role of administrators of justice (Deut. 17:8-9; 21:5; II Chr. 19:8-11; Ezek. 44:24), carrying out trial by ordeal of a woman accused of adultery (Num. 5:11-31), reconsecrating a Nazirite who has been defiled (Num. 6:1-21), and determining valuation in connection with vows (Lev. 27:8-25). A seal impression from Jericho which has been dated in the fifth century B.C. (for particulars *see bibliography*) provides fresh evidence that the fiscal administration of Judah after the Exile was concentrated in the hands of the temple authorities (Ezra 8:33-34). Finally, it is the priests who are responsible for blowing the trumpets which summon the people for war or for the keeping of a feast (Num. 10:1-10; cf. 31:6), and they alone may bless in the name of God (Num. 6:22-27).

Since the tribe of Levi had no particular territory assigned to it, the priests are entitled to live on certain specified parts of the offerings which the people bring to God (Num. 18:20; Deut. 10:9; 18:1-2). As in earlier times (cf. I Kings 2:26; Jer. 32:6 ff; Amos 7:17), individuals may possess landed property; indeed, some provision of houses and land is made for the priests in Jerusalem and the surrounding district (Neh. 11:3, 21; cf. I Chr. 9:2), and thirteen of the forty-eight LEVITICAL CITIES are assigned to them (Josh. 21:4, 13-19). But they depend chiefly upon the offerings of the people for their support. This revenue is derived from three main sources. First, a substantial part of it consists of the first fruits of the field and the first-born of animals, together with the redemption money which had to be paid for first-born sons and for the firstlings of unclean beasts (Exod. 13:12-13; Num. 18:12-19). Secondly, they receive specified sacrificial dues: the bread of the Presence (Lev. 24:5-9); almost all of the cereal offerings (Lev. 2:3, 10; 6:16; 10:12-13; Num. 18:9) and of the sin offerings (Lev. 5:13; 6:26; Num. 18:9); the breast and thigh—the choicest portions—of the peace offerings (Exod. 29:26-28; Lev. 7:30-34; 10:14-15; Num. 18:11); and the skin of the burnt offerings (Lev. 7:8). Thirdly, from the Levites they receive a tenth of the people's tithe (Num. 18:26-28).

The symbolical sanctity of the priesthood finds expression in the requirement that the priest shall be free from physical defects (Lev. 21:24 ff), in the purificatory rites of his consecration (Exod. 29:1 ff; Lev. 8:5 ff), his lustrations before officiating in the sanctuary or at the altar (Exod. 30:19 ff; 40:31 ff), and his robes of white linen (Exod. 39:27-29). He must conform to regulations for ceremonial purity similar to, although less stringent than, those applicable to the high priest. Thus, he may not defile himself by contact with a dead body, except that of a near blood relation; he may not as a sign of mourning shave his head or the edges of his beard, or cut his flesh; he may not marry an impure or divorced woman. The daughter of a priest who profanes his sacred office by prostitution is to be burned (Lev. 21:1-9). Any violation of this priestly sanctity must be expiated by the high priest and the whole priesthood together (Num. 18:1).

3. Levites. The third order of the hierarchy is that of the Levites. They are subordinate cultic officials, the *clerici minores*, who have charge of the lower duties of the sanctuary (Num. 1:50; 3:28, 32; 8:15; 31:30, 47; I Chr. 23:25-32). Levites are installed by a ceremony consisting of lustration, shaving the body, sacrifice, the laying on of hands, and solemn presentation to God (Num. 8:5-13). Their function is to assist the priests and serve the congregation (Num. 1:50; 3:6, 8; 16:9; 18:2; I Chr. 23:28, 32; Ezra 3:8-9). They are responsible for the care of the courts and chambers of the sanctuary, the cleansing of the sacred vessels, the preparation of the cereal offerings, and the service of praise (I Chr. 23:28-32). Some are mentioned particularly as being porters or gatekeepers (I Chr. 9:19; 26:1, 19; II Chr. 8:14), some as treasurers (I Chr. 26:20), and some as choristers and musicians (Ezra 3:10; Neh. 12:27; cf. I Chr. 6:31-32; 16:4-5, 7; 25:1-8; II Chr. 8:14); although on other occasions singers and porters are listed separately as distinct from the Levites (Ezra 2:40-42; 10:23; Neh. 7:43-45, 73; 12:47). The Levites have also a teaching function as interpreters of the law (Neh. 8:7, 9; cf. II Chr. 17:7-9; 35:3), but this eventually passes into the hands of the scribes (*see*

SCRIBE). Levites assist the priests in the administration of justice (I Chr. 23:4; 26:29; II Chr. 19:8-11) and in the charge of the treasury (Ezra 8:33-34; cf. I Chr. 26:20 ff).

Numerically the Levites appear to have been a much smaller body in the second temple than were the priests. The lists of returned exiles mention 4,289 priests but only 74 Levites (Ezra 2:36-40; Neh. 7:39-43). Even if the 148 singers and 138 porters (Neh. 7:43-45; cf. Ezra 2:41-42 [128 singers and 139 porters]) are to be included in the Levitical order, this would bring their numbers to only 360. There are, however, a further 392 "temple servants" and "sons of Solomon's servants" (Ezra 2:58; Neh. 7:60). Originally these were foreigners who were responsible for the menial work of the temple. As the name of the "temple servants" (NETHINIM) indicates, they were "given" as assistants to the Levites (Ezra 8:20), just as the latter were "given" (נתונים) to assist the priests (Num. 3:9; 8:19). But they seem later to have been included, along with the temple singers and porters, in the Levitical order. *See* § D2*e below.*

The period of service of the Levites seems to have varied. In Num. 4 it is from thirty to fifty years old. Num. 8:23-26 says from twenty-five years old and upward, but stipulates that from the age of fifty years they shall withdraw from their service and only assist their fellow Levites. The initial age is lowered still further in I Chr. 23:24, where they are said to serve from twenty years old and upward, with no set retirement age.

Provision for their subsistence is made by the people's tithe, to which they are entitled (Lev. 27:32-33; Num. 18:21, 24 ff), but a tenth of this must be given to the priests (Num. 18:26-28). As the tribe of Levi possessed no territory of its own, forty-eight cities, with surrounding pasture lands, are given, according to the priestly writer, to the Levites (Num. 35:1-8; cf. Lev. 25:32-34; Josh. 21:1-41). Thirteen of these, however, are assigned to the Aaronic priests (Josh. 21:4, 13-19). There is no convincing reason for regarding these references to the LEVITICAL CITIES as essentially utopian in character, as did critics of the Wellhausen school. It is noteworthy that the Levitical cities are not confined to the ideal borders of the land of Israel (Num. 34:1-12), as is the territory of the Levites according to the ideal program of Ezekiel (Ezek. 47:13-20), but are scattered on both sides of the Jordan and over all the areas where the children of Israel actually settled. On the other hand, they cannot have been inhabited exclusively by Levites in the early restoration period but seem rather to have been cities which contained some Levitical families.

Like the priests, the Levites of the second temple served in courses and only came to the sanctuary at their appointed times (I Chr. 24:31; 28:13, 21; II Chr. 8:14; Neh. 13:30). Their symbolic sanctity is expressed in the purificatory rites by which they are dedicated (Num. 8:5-13). Although there is no biblical reference to any particular robes of office for the Levites, Josephus says that the Levitical singers gained from Agrippa II the privilege of wearing priestly linen robes (Antiq. XX.ix.6). Levites, like priests, must make expiation for any violation of their sanctity (Num. 18:23).

D. *ORIGIN AND DEVELOPMENT.* In no other field of OT scholarship do the conclusions of modern critical study stand in such marked contrast to the traditional view. The line of approach pioneered by Graf, Kuenen, and Wellhausen led to a thoroughgoing reconstruction of the history of the Hebrew priesthood and a revolutionary change of view in regard to the relationship of priests and Levites. But the problem of their origin and development is far from being solved, as differences of view among critical scholars clearly indicate. Indeed, the weaknesses of the Graf-Wellhausen theory, which are becoming increasingly apparent, call for far-reaching modifications of the generally accepted critical reconstruction.

1. The traditional view. Before the rise of historical criticism it was assumed that the account of the priestly writer, which forms the narrative framework of the Pentateuch, was to be taken at its face value as an accurate historical record of the institution of the Levitical priesthood in the wilderness and its subsequent place and function in the life of Israel. According to this account, the Hebrew priesthood originates with Moses, who is assigned by the unanimous voice of tradition to the tribe of Levi. Acting on divine instructions (Exod. 28:1), Moses consecrates his brother Aaron and Aaron's sons as priests. In the ceremonies of consecration, which last for a week, Moses himself temporarily discharges the functions of a priest (Exod. 29:35-36; Lev. 8:15-29, 35; cf. Lev. 1:3 ff; 4:4 ff). But on the eighth day, when the installation is complete, Aaron and his sons undertake the sacrificial duties, thus becoming the first accredited Israelite priests (Lev. 9). The priesthood is invested exclusively in them and in their descendants; all others are barred from the service of the altar on pain of death (Exod. 28:1, 43; Num. 3:10; cf. Num. 16:40; 18:1, 7).

A distinction is made, however, between Aaron and his sons. He occupies a unique position as the only fully accredited priest. He is the anointed priest (Exod. 29:7; Lev. 8:12; cf. Lev. 4:3, 5, 16; 6:22—H 6:15; Num. 35:25), distinguished by special robes of office (Exod. 28:4, 6-39; Lev. 8:7-9). At his death these, along with the office which they symbolize, are transferred to Eleazar his son (Num. 20:25-28). There is thus from the very beginning a "priest who is chief among his brethren" (Lev. 21:10), the "high priest," whose death marks an epoch (Num. 35:28).

Aaron was by descent a Levite. Hence the Israelite priesthood which was invested in him and in his descendants was exclusively Levitical: all legitimate priests were Levites. But, according to the priestly writer, it was only after the consecration of Aaron and his sons to the priesthood that the remainder of the tribe of Levi was separated, as substitutes for the first-born, to assist them in the duties of the sanctuary (Num. 3:5 ff; cf. 8:5-22; 18:2-6). The Levites are divided into three groups according to their descent from the three sons of Levi—Gershon, Kohath, and Merari; special duties are assigned to each group (Num. 3:14-38).

After the rebellion of Korah (Num. 16), in which a group of Levites attempt to gain admittance to the priesthood (vss. 8-10), the divine choice of Aaron and his family is vindicated in the destruction of the rebels (vss. 25-35) and the acceptance of Aaron's expiation (vss. 46-50). It is then confirmed by the sign of the sprouting rod (17:1-10), and the respective positions of priests and Levites are once again defined (18:1-7).

The traditional view of the history of the Levitical priesthood is thus quite simple. According to it the threefold hierarchy of high priest, priests, and Levites goes back to the institution of the priesthood by Moses in the wilderness. All the essential elements of the postexilic cultus are there from the beginning. And these three clearly defined orders of cultic officials persist, with only small modifications, throughout the entire history of Israel.

2. The critical reconstruction. A closer examination of the relevant literature has led OT scholars to conclude that the history of the priesthood, far from being simple, as the traditional view holds, is in fact highly complex. While Hebrew tradition is unanimous in affirming the Mosaic and Aaronic origin of the Levitical priesthood, there is evidence in the older literature that the priesthood was not limited to Levites in the early period. It was, however, narrowed down to Levites by the end of the seventh century B.C. (*see* DEUTERONOMY) and during the next two centuries further restricted to a group within the body of Levites. But the Priestly Code (*see* PENTATEUCH) maintains a distinction between priests and Levites from the first.

a. The early period. The tradition that the Hebrew priesthood originated with Moses and Aaron finds support in the fact that only foreign priests are mentioned in the book of Genesis and the early chapters of Exodus—viz., Melchizedek (Gen. 14:18), Egyptian priests (Gen. 41:45; 46:20; 47:22, 26), and the Midianite priest Jethro (Exod. 2:16; 3:1; 18:1). The only mention of Hebrew priests before the giving of the law at Sinai is in two allusions in the J account of Exod. 19: "Let the priests who come near to Yahweh consecrate themselves" (vs. 22), and: "Do not let the priests and the people break through to come up to Yahweh" (vs. 24). This would appear to imply that the J tradition recognized the existence of a Hebrew priesthood prior to Moses. On the other hand, the J (or possibly JE) narrative of Exod. 32:25-29 has been taken to imply that the Levites were given the regular priesthood as a reward for their faithfulness and zeal in executing the wrath of Yahweh after the apostasy in the matter of the golden calf (vs. 29).

In the early period the priest was not just concerned with sacrifice; he was an organ of revelation and as such gave direction and guidance in the ordinary affairs of life. Indeed, the teaching function of the priesthood seems to have taken precedence over the sacrificial. In the Blessing of Moses (Deut. 33), which belongs in its present form either to the late tenth or early eighth century B.C., both are mentioned (vss. 8-10), but teaching comes first:

> They shall teach Jacob thy ordinances [משפטים]
> and Israel thy law [תורה] (vs. 10).

As the successor of Moses, the priest gave oracular direction. This was given in two ways—through the sacred lot, URIM AND THUMMIM (vs. 8), and by reference to a legal code embodying both the revealed will of Yahweh and the accumulated experience of the past. Through his knowledge of this code the priest could lay down משפטים, rules of action, and give תורה, instruction in the revealed will of God (Lev. 10:10-11; Deut. 33:10; cf. II Kings 17:27-28; II Chr. 15:3; 17:7-9; Jer. 18:18; Ezek. 7:26; Mic. 3:11). The priesthood was thus the custodian of past revelation and legal precedent before any written word was available for the guidance of the people of God. Hence the priest was both the teacher and the administrator of justice (cf. Deut. 17:8-9; 21:5). He was the spokesman of God before the people, as well as the representative of the people before God.

Sacrifice was not the exclusive prerogative of the priest in early times. In the ancient patriarchal tradition it was associated with Cain and Abel (Gen. 4:4), Noah (Gen. 8:20), Abraham (Gen. 12:7-8; 13:4, 18; 15:9), Isaac (Gen. 26:25), and Jacob (Gen. 35:3, 7). Similarly, until the building of the temple, and even after, we find priestly functions discharged by the head of a household (Judg. 13:19; cf. Job 1:5; the killing of the pascal lamb by the father is a relic of his ancient priestly prerogative), a judge (Judg. 6:19 ff, 25-26, 28; I Sam. 7:9; cf. I Sam. 9:12-13; 16:5), a prophet (I Kings 18:30 ff; cf. 19:10), a king (II Sam. 6:17; I Kings 8:22, 54 ff). The priests, it seems, were associated with particular shrines where they gave oracles and officiated at public sacrifices at which a definite ritual was required (Judg. 20:18, 27; I Sam. 1:3 ff; cf. 21:1 ff; 22:9-11, 19).

The priesthood in this early period was not in practice exclusively Levitical; but the priest who was a Levite was preferred to a non-Levitical priest. Thus, in the time of the judges, Micah first appointed one of his own sons as the priest of his private shrine (Judg. 17:5). But he replaced him by a Levite when the opportunity arose (Judg. 17:7-13). In the early monarchy also we find references to non-Levitical priests existing side by side with the accredited Levitical order (*see* § D2*b below*). There are, however, in the judges period two official Levitical priestly families—the priesthood of Dan, established by Micah's Levite, Jonathan, the grandson of Moses (Judg. 18:1-4, 14-20, 30; cf. I Chr. 23:14-15); and the priesthood of Shiloh, held by Eli and his family, who belonged to the house of Ithamar, the fourth son of Aaron (I Sam. 1–4; cf. I Sam. 22:20; II Sam. 8:17 [emend "Abiathar, son of Ahimelech"]; I Kings 2:27; I Chr. 24:3). It is possible that persons, and perhaps families, who were not Levitical by descent were incorporated into the priestly tribe of Levi (cf. Deut. 33:8-9). This seems to have happened in the case of Samuel. Although an Ephraimite by descent (I Sam. 1:1 ff), he ministers in the sanctuary and wears the priestly ephod (I Sam. 1:27-28; 2:11, 18; 3:1); and the Chronicler regards him as a Levite (I Chr. 6:16-28).

b. The monarchy. In the monarchy the priesthood settles increasingly into families. The Mosaic priesthood of Dan continued until the end of the N kingdom in 721 B.C. After the victory of the Philistines and the capture of the ark (I Sam. 4:10-11), the house of Eli apparently moved from Shiloh to Nob, where they were massacred by Saul (21:1-9; 22:9-19). Only Abiathar escaped (22:20). During the reign of David he officiated at Jerusalem in association with Zadok (II Sam. 8:17; 15:24-29, 35; 19:11), but because of his support of Adonijah (I Kings 1:5-8) he was deposed by Solomon (2:26-27), who put Zadok in his place (2:35). Thus the house of Zadok replaced the house of Eli as the most prominent priestly family, and the Zadokite priesthood continued in Jerusalem until the destruction of the temple in 586 B.C. (II Chr. 6:8—H 5:34). Zadok's descent is not mentioned in the early literature. It has been suggested that he may have been the former Jebusite king of Jerusalem, or a member of the Jebusite royal priesthood, who was incorporated into the Levitical order after David's conquest of the city. But it is extremely unlikely that a priest of the Jebusite cultus would have been admitted to the priesthood of Yahweh in David's reign. II Sam. 15:24 seems to imply that Zadok was the head of a company of Levites, and the Chronicler traces his descent to Eleazar the third son of Aaron (I Chr. 6:3-12, 50-53; 24:3).

The outstanding example of a non-Levitical priesthood during the monarchy is that instituted by Jeroboam in the N kingdom. The writer of I Kings states explicitly—and not without disapproval—that Jeroboam not only "appointed priests from among all the people, who were not of the Levites" (I Kings 12:31), but "any who would, he consecrated to be priests of the high places" (13:33).

There are three other references to priests outside the Levitical order. First, the list of David's chief officers, which includes the priests Zadok and Abiathar (II Sam. 8:17; read "Abiathar the son of Ahimelech"), ends with the statement: "and David's sons were priests" (vs. 18). Second, we read of Ira the Jairite's being priest to David (II Sam. 20:26). And third, in the list of Solomon's high officials it is said that Zabud the son of Nathan was priest and king's friend (I Kings 4:5). These three references, however, present a difficulty, since the names of regular accredited priests, Zadok and Abiathar, also appear among the court officials of both David and Solomon. In the case of Ira, if "Jairite" be emended, as has been suggested, to "Jattirite" (i.e., "belonging to the priestly city of JATTIR"), it is possible that he may have been a Levite. With regard to David's sons and Zabud, the word כהן, "priest," may denote a "domestic chaplain," or it may have been used as a mere court title as is "king's friend," although elsewhere in early documents it is used exclusively of priests. Some would emend כהן in each of these references to סכן, "steward" or "administrator" (cf. Isa. 22:15). It is noteworthy that the Chronicler alters the reference to David's sons from כהן to הראשנים ליד המלך, the "chief officials in the service of the king"; and the LXX, while rendering כהן by ἱερεύς in II Sam. 20:25, substitutes αὐλάρχαι, "princes," in II Sam. 8:18 and omits "priest" in I Kings 4:5.

The king himself appears to have exercised priestly functions at great national religious festivals, at least during the early years of the monarchy. Saul, in the absence of Samuel, offers the burnt offering and peace offerings at Gilgal, but is reproved by Samuel for doing so (I Sam. 13:8-13). David, however, not only supervises the removal of the ark from the house of Obed-edom to Jerusalem (II Sam. 6:12-19) but also wears the priestly ephod (vs. 14), offers sacrifices (vss. 13, 17), and blesses the people in the name of God (vs. 18). Similarly, at the dedication of the temple it is Solomon who appears as the leader of the cultus, standing before the altar to offer the prayer of dedication (I Kings 8:22-53), sacrificing sheep and oxen (vss. 5, 62-63), offering the burnt offering and the cereal offering (vs. 64), and blessing the assembly of Israel (vss. 14 ff, 54 ff), while the priests and Levites merely bring up the ark and the sacred vessels into the holy place (vss. 4, 6 ff). Afterward Solomon offers burnt offerings, peace offerings, and incense three times a year (I Kings 9:25). Jeroboam also, after instituting an official non-Levitical priesthood in the N kingdom, himself offers sacrifices and burns incense (12:32-33). Even as late as the eighth century B.C. the king can exercise the prerogatives of the priesthood. Ahaz instructs the priest Urijah to build at Jerusalem a replica of the altar at Damascus, but he himself offers sacrifice upon it and manipulates the blood of the offering (II Kings 16:10:13).

Hebrew kingship is therefore sacral: the king is a priest-king, the mediator between God and his people. If, as some maintain, Ps. 110 is an oracle for the installation of the king, it would seem that his priestly prerogative is associated with a claim to be regarded as the successor of MELCHIZEDEK, the ancient priest-king of Jerusalem (Ps. 110:4; cf. Gen. 14:18). The Chronicler, however, regards an attempt by Uzziah to burn incense in the temple as a flagrant encroachment on the rights of the priesthood, for which the king was punished by being stricken with leprosy (II Chr. 26:16-20).

c. Deuteronomy and Josiah's reform. The reform of JOSIAH in 621 B.C., putting an end to the high places and centralizing worship at Jerusalem, is a turning point in Hebrew history and religion (see II Kings 23:1-24). The Book of the Law upon which it is based (22:8-13; 23:1-3) is generally regarded as an early edition of DEUTERONOMY. Sacrifice is now the prerogative of the priesthood, since it may only be offered at the Jerusalem sanctuary (Deut. 12:5-7, 11, 13-14), and the priests are all "sons of Levi" (10:8; 18:1; 21:5; 33:8). This does not necessarily imply that every priest is an actual lineal descendant of the ancient house of Levi. It may well be that the Levitical priesthood, like other hereditary guilds, was able to exercise the right of adoption and incorporate persons who were not Levitical by descent (*see* § D2*a above*). It is generally maintained that in the Deuteronomic Code "priest" and "Levite" are synonymous terms: not only are all priests Levites, but also all Levites are priests, no distinction being made (see Deut. 10:8; 18:1; 21:5; 33:8 ff). This, however, is by no means certain; the passages cited do not necessarily bear this meaning. *See* § E2 *below*.

Prior to Josiah's reform, the priesthood, although not numerous, was widely distributed. We do, indeed, find over eighty priests at Nob—called the city of the priests—in the early monarchy (I Sam. 22:18-19) and another priestly community in Josiah's time at Anathoth (Jer. 1:1; cf. I Kings 2:26). But in general every town appears to have had its local sanctuary, or high place, with at least one Levitical priest in attendance (cf. Deut. 18:6). This official Levitical priesthood had no territorial possessions (Deut. 18:1), and Deuteronomy does not mention a Levitical tithe but commends the Levite, along with the sojourner, the fatherless, and the widow, to the charity of the community in which he dwells (Deut. 14:27-29; 16: 11, 14; 26:12; cf. Judg. 17:7-8; I Sam. 2:36). The abolition of the local sanctuaries meant, therefore, the loss of their revenues for these "country clergy," who would henceforth be unemployed. Josiah brought them all to Jerusalem, and he seems to have intended that they should share in the full duties of the Jerusalem priesthood at the temple, in accordance with the provisions (if they be so interpreted) of the Deuteronomic Code (II Kings 23:8; cf. Deut. 18: 6-8, but this assumes that "Levite" = "priest"). In fact, however, the priests of the high places did not officiate at the Jerusalem altar—no doubt, because of the opposition of the Jerusalem priests—although they received their share of the perquisites (II Kings 23:9).

It is possible that "all the priests . . . of the cities of Judah" (II Kings 23:8) included others besides the "idolatrous priests" of the high places (vs. 5). If so, the account may be taken to imply that Josiah separated the priests of the high places from other provincial priests, who had not taken part in idolatrous practices at the local sanctuaries, and that only the former were deposed (vs. 5), and therefore prohibited from ministering at the altar in Jerusalem (vs. 9), while the latter were admitted to the full privileges of the Jerusalem priesthood. In that case, Ezekiel's reference to the Levites who went astray after their idols (Ezek. 44:10) may refer only to the idolatrous priests of the high places, whom Josiah deposed, and not, as is generally held, to the provincial priests as a whole. *See* § D2*d below*.

d. Ezekiel. The EXILE is the great watershed of Hebrew religion: it marks the boundary between two periods. Whether or not all Levites were priests in pre-exilic days, as is generally maintained, the priesthood was certainly narrowed down to Levites by the latter part of the seventh century B.C. By then, at least, all priests were Levites. In postexilic times, however, we find the priesthood definitely restricted to a particular section of the Levites—those who are of Aaronic descent. Between these two periods, the pre-exilic and postexilic, stands EZEKIEL. He is transitional, supplying, it is generally believed, the link between the cultic organization of the seventh century B.C. and that of the second temple.

Ezekiel's vision of a new temple (Ezek. 40–44) is a symbolic representation of Yahweh dwelling in holiness in the midst of his people, which is the fundamental idea in the prophet's conception of the future theocracy. His basic principle is holiness through separation. This finds expression both in his plan of the new temple and in his scheme for a drastic reorganization of the priesthood (44:5-16). Indeed, the latter is a corollary of the former. Since the place of Yahweh's presence is protected from ceremonial defilement by being surrounded with areas of graded sanctity, it follows that different degrees of ceremonial purity must be demanded of those who minister in different parts of the temple, access to the most sacred places being restricted to those possessing a greater degree of holiness.

Ezekiel's scheme first of all demands the complete exclusion from the service of the temple of uncircumcised foreigners (Ezek. 44:6-9). There are the NETHINIM and "sons of Solomon's servants," who performed the menial tasks of the temple. They appear to have been originally captives taken in war who were given to the Levites as temple slaves (Num. 31:28-30, 40-41, 47; Josh. 9:23, 27; cf. Ezra 8:20). Their place is to be taken by the Levites who had gone astray after their idols (Ezek. 44:9-14). Because of their apostasy these Levites are to be degraded from the priesthood and no longer allowed to minister at the altar (vss. 12-13). The most they are permitted to do is to slay the burnt offering and the sacrifice for the people (vs. 11). The actual service of the altar is to be restricted to the Zadokite priests of Jerusalem who had remained faithful when Israel went astray (vss. 15-16).

Ezekiel thus makes a clear distinction between two orders of cultic officials—the Zadokite priests and the non-Zadokite Levites. But it is not clear who exactly the latter were, beyond the fact that they had previously been priests who engaged in idolatrous practices, for which they were to be deposed from the priesthood and assigned only menial tasks. It has been widely held that these non-Zadokite Levites are to be identified as the priests of the high places which Josiah had abolished. Although admitted to the temple staff, the provincial priests had been debarred by the Jerusalem priesthood from approaching the altar. This anomalous practice, it is said, now becomes a matter of principle and receives legal sanction in Ezekiel's scheme. As we have seen, however (*see* § D2*c above*), it may well be that Josiah did not depose all the provincial priests but only those who had been involved in idolatry at the high places, and it is to such—and not necessarily to the entire provincial priesthood—that Ezekiel refers. He does not say that the whole body of Levites is to be degraded but speaks only of Levites who had gone astray after idols.

This identification of Ezekiel's idolatrous Levites with priests of the Judean local sanctuaries is not, however, so convincing as it at first appears. Indeed, it is difficult to reconcile it with the prophet's general picture of Judah. Ezekiel demands the degradation of these Levites because they have been involved in some national apostasy (Ezek. 44:10), and he restricts the service of the altar to the Zadokite priests because in this national apostasy they alone have remained faithful to Yahweh (vss. 15 ff). But it cannot be the apostasy of Judah to which Ezekiel refers, for in this the Zadokite priesthood was most certainly involved, as his earlier references to idolatrous practices in the temple imply (5:11; 8:6-17). If idolatry excluded the priests of the Judean high places from the Jerusalem altar, it must also exclude the Zadokite priesthood of the temple who were equally guilty of it.

There was, however, an act of national apostasy in which the Zadokite priests of Jerusalem were not involved—namely, the calf-worship which Jeroboam I had instituted in the N kingdom (I Kings 12:28-32). It may well be, therefore, that Ezekiel's polemic is directed, not against the dispossessed priests of the Judean high places, but against the priests who had taken part in this idolatrous worship in N Israel.

e. The restoration. The decree of Cyrus in 538 B.C. (Ezra 1:1-4) marks the end of the Babylonian exile and the beginning of the restored Jewish community. Those who returned to Jerusalem set about establishing once more the traditional cultus (3:1-6). The restoration of the cultus meant the restoration of the priesthood, and this involved the acceptance of some principle of unification. Ezekiel's scheme for restricting the priesthood to the Zadokites, however, was not carried out in the organization of the second temple. The priesthood was indeed restricted to one section of the Levites, but the restriction was on a wider basis than mere Zadokite descent.

A clear distinction between priests and Levites is made in the lists of the first returning exiles (Ezra 2:36-42; Neh. 7:39-43; 12:1 ff; cf. Ezra 3:10) and of those who were associated with Nehemiah (Neh. 10:28; 11:3, 10-18) and Ezra (Ezra 7:7, 13; 8:15 ff, 30; 9:1). But representatives of two priestly families accompanied Ezra (Ezra 8:2)—the family of Gershom, descended through Phinehas from Zadok, and the family of Daniel, belonging to the house of Ithamar. Both traced their descent to Aaron, and Aaronic—not Zadokite—descent was in fact the criterion of the priesthood in the restored Jewish community. It is noteworthy that in the postexilic literature the priests are consistently referred to as the house of Aaron or the sons of Aaron (I Chr. 15:4; 23:28, 32; Pss. 115:10, 12; 118:3; 135:19; Tob. 1:6; Ecclus. 45:6-24; 50:13, 16; I Macc. 7:14; cf. Heb. 5:4; 7:11).

This is in accordance with the priestly document which gives the fullest information that we have about the priesthood (*see* § C *above*). The priestly writer is generally assigned to the sixth or fifth century B.C. in the critical scheme. For him the distinction between priests and Levites is absolute (Num. 18:2-7; cf. Lev. 8). He regards the priesthood as vested by divine institution in the house of Aaron (Exod. 28:1, 43; Num. 3:10; 8:1, 7) and recounts the story of the rebellion of Korah in the wilderness as a warning to the non-Aaronic Levites not to attempt to usurp the prerogatives of the Aaronic priests (Num. 16:8-10, 40). It is the Priestly Code, therefore, and not the scheme of Ezekiel, which provides the pattern for the restored Jerusalem priesthood. All who claimed to belong to the priesthood were required to prove their descent, and only those who could show their (presumably Aaronic) succession were admitted (Ezra 2:61-63; Neh. 7:63-65).

The reasons for the rejection of Ezekiel's scheme and the restriction of the postexilic priesthood to those of Aaronic rather than merely Zadokite descent are obscure. If, as is generally held, the priestly document is later than Ezekiel, it would seem to represent an accommodation of Ezekiel's ideal to the actual situation with which the priestly writer was faced. As to what this situation really was, we have no precise information; it must be reconstructed on the basis of the slender evidence that we possess.

There are several possibilities. It has been suggested that there was, in fact, no substantial difference between Ezekiel's scheme and that of the priestly writer which was put into operation. The only difference, it is claimed, was one of nomenclature, the Zadokites of Ezekiel and the Aaronites of the Priestly Code being one and the same Levitical group. This view implies either that Ezekiel uses "sons of Zadok" as a general term which includes other priestly families, such as the priests of Anathoth, who had at some time ministered at Jerusalem, or that the title "sons of Aaron" was used by the Zadokite priesthood after the Exile to enhance their prestige. This, however, is highly improbable, since the Aaronic houses of both Zadok and Ithamar are mentioned separately in Ezra (8:2) and later by the Chronicler (I Chr. 24:3-4; cf. 6:8).

Another view is that after the Zadokite priests of Jerusalem had gone into exile, the people who remained in the city appealed to the Aaronite priesthood at Bethel, only eleven miles distant, to maintain the cultus at Jerusalem. As a result Aaronite priests migrated from Bethel, and possibly also from other N shrines, to Jerusalem. When, therefore, the Zadokites returned from Babylon, they were unable to regain their ancient monopoly and hence had to come to terms with the Aaronites already in possession. The Zadokites, however, were eventually able to assert their supremacy at Jerusalem, with the result that the leading Aaronites returned to the N, where they instigated the Samaritan Schism (*see* SAMARITANS). Thus the Zadokites—later known as SADDUCEES—regained possession of the Jerusalem priesthood but retained the honorable Aaronic name. Joshua, who was high priest in the time of Zerubbabel (Ezra 3:2 ff), is said to have been the first of the Aaronic priests from the N to minister at Jerusalem during the Exile; Zech. 3 is the account of an abortive attempt on the part of the returned Zadokites to oust him. The tracing of Joshua's descent to the pre-exilic Zadokite priests (I Chr. 6:12-15—H 5:38-41; cf. Hag. 1:1) is regarded as a late genealogical fiction.

This theory is based upon mere supposition and not only lacks evidential support but also does violence to the only existing evidence. It may well be, as others have argued, that the place of the exiled Zadokite priesthood of Jerusalem was taken by Aaronite priests who had once been associated with the provincial shrines, not of the N, but of Judah. We have no reason to doubt that Joshua was one of the priests who returned with Zerubbabel (Ezra 2:2, 36) and that he was of Zadokite descent. In that case we may see in Zech. 3 the vindication of Joshua and his fellow Zadokites against the charge of the Aaronites at Jerusalem that the exiled priests were unclean by reason of their contact with heathenism and hence disqualified from officiating at the altar.

Any reconstruction of the situation can only be tentative. The only definite facts are these: (*a*) There were priests officiating at the ruined temple in Jerusalem during the Exile. Their presence is implied by the account of eighty men from Shechem, Shiloh, and Samaria bringing offerings to the temple (Jer. 41:4 ff), and priests are mentioned in Lam. 1, which appears to have been written in Jerusalem in the early exilic period (see vs. 4). (*b*) Aaronic priests of the house of Abiathar, who was deposed from his office at the temple by Solomon, lived at Anathoth, only 2¼ miles N of Jerusalem, and at least one of these—namely, Jeremiah—was allowed to remain in Judah (Jer. 39:11-14; 40:2-6). (*c*) Aaronic priests of the line of Ithamar, from whom Abiathar was descended, are mentioned along with the Zadokites in the lists of returning exiles (Ezra 8:2). (*d*) As we have seen, in the postexilic literature the priests are referred to as the house, or the sons, of Aaron.

It seems highly probable, therefore, that the postexilic extension of the priesthood to the Aaronites as a whole resulted from two related factors. First, as we have seen, there was the established practice in Palestine, such evidence as we have pointing to the maintenance of the cultus at Jerusalem during the Exile by non-Zadokite priests. But secondly, there is evidence that conditions at Jerusalem were not unknown to the exiles in Babylon, and the mention in Ezra 8:2 of non-Zadokite as well as Zadokite priests would seem to indicate some agreement reached among the exiles before the actual return. This is supported by the number of priests said to have returned under the decree of Cyrus in 538 B.C. It seems unlikely that the 4,289 priests who came back with Zerubbabel (Ezra 2:36-39; Neh. 7:39-42) were all descended from the captive Zadokites. And the small number of Levites who returned—only 74 (Ezra 2:40; Neh. 7:43)—may indicate that those of Aaronite descent had been admitted to the priesthood. Many of the rest seem to have been reluctant to leave Babylon (cf. Ezra 8:15-20).

Four other groups of temple personnel, besides priests and Levites, are mentioned in the lists of returning exiles—viz., singers, gatekeepers or porters, temple servants (NETHINIM), and sons of Solomon's servants (Ezra 2:41-58; cf. 7:24; Neh. 7:44-60). The singers and gatekeepers either were of Levitical descent or later became incorporated into the Levitical order, since they are referred to as Levites by the Chronicler (I Chr. 6:16-48; 9:26, 33; 16:4-7; II Chr. 8:14). The temple servants and sons of Solomon's servants, however, were of foreign origin, being descended from captives of war who had been given as assistants to the Levites (Ezra 8:20). It was to the presence of such *uncircumcised* foreigners in the temple that Ezekiel objected (Ezek. 44:6-9). But in the time of Nehemiah the temple servants, along with the priests, the Levites, the gatekeepers, and the singers, enter into a covenant "to walk in God's law" and pledge themselves not to intermarry with foreigners (Neh. 10:28-30—H 10:29-31); and Ezra includes them with the Levites as "ministers for the house of our God" (Ezra 8:15-20). This would seem to imply that Ezekiel's uncircumcised foreigners, or their descendants, had during the Exile become proselytes by submitting to the rite of circumcision and were thus accepted as full members of the Jewish community at the return. Although the number of temple servants who returned from Babylon was far greater than the number of Levites (Ezra 2:40-58; 8:18-20), by the time of the Chronicler (*ca.* 300 B.C.) the temple servants as a separate group seem to have disappeared, since the only time they are mentioned is in connection with the early restored community (I Chr. 9:2). It appears, therefore, either that their functions were taken over by the Levites, or, more probably, that they were eventually incorporated into the Levitical order.

There is a noticeable change of emphasis in the functions of the priesthood in the restored Jewish community. Moral teaching is no longer regarded as one of the chief duties of the priest; he is now associated almost exclusively with the cultus. It is, indeed, laid down in the priestly document that the priest shall give instruction in both ceremonial and moral matters (Lev. 10:10-11), but the former is given priority of place, and the only priestly teaching mentioned in the postexilic literature is concerned with ceremonial uncleanness (Hag. 2:10-13). It is part of Malachi's complaint against the priests of his time that they have failed to give the moral instruction for which they are responsible (Mal. 2:7-8). Significantly enough, the priesthood no longer possesses the sacred lots URIM AND THUMMIM, although their restoration is anticipated (Ezra 2:63). At Ezra's promulgation of the law, it is the Levites who instruct the people (Neh. 8:7), and in general the ancient teaching function of the priesthood seems to have been exercised more by the Levites than by the priests in the second temple.

The high priest has been generally regarded by critics of the Wellhausen school as a purely postexilic figure. Since there is no mention of a high priest in Ezekiel's scheme, it has been argued that his office was unknown to Ezekiel and was not therefore in existence before the Exile. Hence Hag. 1:1 is commonly regarded as the first mention of a high priest and Joshua as the first holder of the office; references to the office in the earlier literature are viewed as later interpolations. The description of the high-priestly functions of Aaron, his installation, and his robes of office given in the priestly document is said to be a reading back by the priestly writer of the high priesthood as he knew it in postexilic times. The extent, however, to which the actual high priest of the second temple corresponded to the priestly writer's description has been a matter of debate.

This view now appears to be an oversimplification which does not do justice to the biblical data, and there is need for a reconsideration of the available evidence (*see further* § E *below*). But one thing is clear. Whether or not the name or the office of high priest was known in earlier times, the postexilic high priest occupied a unique position—a position different in degree, if not in kind, from that of any priest in pre-exilic days.

f. The Chronicler. Chronicles has been called both a sequel and a supplement to the Priestly Code. Not only does it continue the history, begun by the priestly writer, to the time of Nehemiah; it enables us to see something of the development of the institutions of Judaism two centuries after the return from Babylon. The preceding period (*ca.* 550-300 B.C.) is transitional. From *ca.* 300 B.C. the practice of the postexilic community fulfils the requirements of Ezekiel and the Priestly Code—the temple personnel consists entirely of priests and Levites. This is the situation portrayed by the Chronicler. The separate groups of singers, gatekeepers, temple servants, and sons of Solomon's servants have disappeared. The first two classes are now given Levitical status (I Chr. 6:16-48; 9:26, 33; 16:4-7; 23:5; II Chr. 8:14), and we may infer that the two groups of temple servants, whose ancestors had become proselyte members of the Jewish community, were finally incorporated into the Levitical order.

The Chronicler gives special prominence to the Levites and emphasizes their high status and the importance of their functions, particularly in connection with the ARK OF THE COVENANT. No one but the Levites may carry the ark (I Chr. 15:2). It was because this requirement was neglected that David's first attempt to bring the sacred symbol to Jerusalem ended in tragedy (I Chr. 15:13). Special care was taken, therefore, to assign this duty to the Levites when the ark was finally brought to Jerusalem (I Chr. 15:11-15), and certain of them were appointed to minister before it (I Chr. 16:4 ff, 37). It was the Levites who carried the ark into Solomon's temple (II Chr. 5:4) and bore it back there at Josiah's reform (II Chr. 35:3). Their function of offering praise to God is stressed (I Chr. 6:31-32; 9:33; 16:4-37; 23:30; II Chr. 8:14; 29:30), as is also their teaching function (II Chr. 17:7-9; 35:3). They assist in the administration of justice (I Chr. 23:4; 26:29; II Chr. 19:8-11). The sanctuary and its holy vessels are in their care (I Chr. 23:28), and the Chronicler points out that at Hezekiah's cleansing of the temple the priests who had sanctified themselves were too few to cope with the number of sacrifices, so the Levites assisted them in flaying the burnt offerings, "for the Levites were more upright in heart than the priests in sanctifying themselves" (II Chr. 29:34).

Although, however, the Chronicler emphasizes the prestige of the Levites, he does not, as some have maintained, do this at the expense of the specific rights of the priesthood. Only the Aaronic priest may burn incense, and not even the king may usurp the priestly prerogative (II Chr. 26:16-20; cf. Exod. 30:1-10; Num. 16:40; 18:7). The organization of the priesthood had now reached its final form. This consisted of twenty-four courses, each of which came up to the temple in turn for its appointed period of duty. The families of sixteen courses traced their descent to Eleazar, and those of the remaining eight to Ithamar (I Chr. 24:1-4, 19).

It seems that in the time of the Chronicler the temporal as well as the spiritual authority of the high priest was firmly established in the Jewish community. He is called, not only כהן הראש, the "head, or chief, priest" (II Chr. 19:11), and הכהן הגדול, "the great priest" (II Chr. 34:9), but also נגיד בית האלהים, "prince of the house of God" (I Chr. 9:11). The Chronicler draws attention to the authority exercised by former high priests. Azariah drove King Uzziah out of the temple for attempting to usurp the functions of the priesthood (II Chr. 26:16-20). Jehoiada put an end to the reign of Queen Athaliah, crowned Joash, and remained to the end of his life the power behind the throne (II Chr. 23–24). In the judicial tribunal set up at Jerusalem by Jehoshaphat, the presidency was shared by the high priest and the governor of the house of Judah (II Chr. 19:8-11). It has been suggested that we may see in this latter reference a reflection of the high priest's presiding over an early form of the Sanhedrin in the Chronicler's time.

E. *RECONSIDERATIONS.* The critical reconstruction of the history of the Levitical priesthood is closely linked with the Graf-Wellhausen literary analysis of the PENTATEUCH into four chronologically successive documentary sources—J, E, D (Deuteronomy), and P (the priestly document). This documentary hypothesis, almost universally accepted in the first two decades of the twentieth century, has been repeatedly challenged, especially by Scandinavian scholars. While, therefore, it is still generally held in some form, it is undergoing considerable modification; and this is true also of the historical reconstruction with which it is allied. The evolutionary presuppositions of the Wellhausen school resulted in an oversimplification of the religious development in Israel. It was assumed that primitive ideas must be early and more advanced conceptions late. Hence the attempt was made to fit the biblical data into an evolutionary mold.

The fallacy of this attempt is now widely recognized, but there is need for a more searching examination of the underlying assumptions of the critical reconstruction than has yet been made. All that is attempted here is to indicate some of the lines along which such an examination should proceed.

1. The high priest. On closer examination, the theory of the Wellhausen school that the high priesthood was nonexistent before the Exile proves to be untenable. It is, indeed, no more than a conjecture which does violence to the biblical evidence in the interests of a theory of development.

In the early postexilic books of Haggai and Zechariah, Joshua the high priest occupies a position of equal authority to that of the Davidic governor Zerubbabel, with whom he shares the rule of the restored Jewish community (Hag. 1:1, 12, 14; 2:2, 4; cf. Ezra 3:2). They are the two anointed ones (Zech. 4:14), the joint heads of state between whom there is to be peaceful understanding (Zech. 6:9-13; cf. 3:7). Now it is quite inconceivable that such an office as that held by Joshua was created *de novo* in the half century between Ezekiel (572 B.C.) and the second return (520 B.C.). There is no indication whatever that it was regarded as a new office; rather, the allusions to it imply a well-established institution.

Much has been made of the fact that the high priesthood is not mentioned by Ezekiel and appears to have had no place in his vision of a new temple and his scheme for reorganizing the priesthood (Ezek. 40–44). But an argument from silence can never be conclusive and must, indeed, always be used with great caution. The fact that an institution is not mentioned does not necessarily mean that it is unknown; it may equally well imply that it is so well established that it can be taken for granted. It cannot be argued from Ezekiel's silence regarding the king that kingship was nonexistent in Israel up to his time. The postexilic dating of the Priestly Code, in which the high priest has a clearly defined place, rests to a large extent upon the Wellhausen hypothesis that the legislation of Leviticus is based upon Ezek. 40–48. That there is a close relationship between the two cannot be denied, but there is no little evidence which points to the opposite conclusion—viz., that Ezekiel himself was familiar with the legislation of the Priestly Code, which must in that case have been already in existence in his time. There is, indeed, little to support the conjecture that Ezekiel's scheme provides the pattern for the priestly legislation; it seems much more likely that his vision is to be understood as an ideal picture of a theocracy in which ancient institutions are freely modified.

There is one particular section of the Priestly

Code with which Ezekiel was unquestionably acquainted, and this is the Law of Holiness (*see* Holiness Code), contained in Lev. 17-26. Not only is this prior to Ezekiel, but it also is generally regarded as being a codification based on pre-exilic practice. And it is here that we find regulations concerning the ceremonial purity of the high priest—the "priest who is chief among his brethren, upon whose head the anointing oil is poured, and who has been consecrated to wear the garments" (Lev. 21:10-15).

In the Priestly Code generally the references to the high priest are not of such a nature as to suggest that the office was new. On the contrary, they imply that the high priest is a familiar figure. It is noteworthy that he is usually referred to simply as "the priest"; the title "high priest" (הכהן הגדול) occurs only three times (Lev. 21:10; Num. 35:25, 28). This is scarcely what we should expect if the high priesthood were an innovation. It is, however, entirely in line with pre-exilic usage.

There are many indications of gradations of rank in the priesthood during the monarchy and even earlier. Eli takes precedence over his sons at Shiloh (I Sam. 1-3); Ahimelech is the head of a priestly community at Nob (I Sam. 22:11-20); Zephaniah is called the "second priest" (II Kings 25:18; Jer. 52:24); and "senior priests" are mentioned in the days of Hezekiah (II Kings 19:2; Isa. 37:2) and Jeremiah (Jer. 19:1). In Solomon's temple there appears to have been a college of priests, at the head of which was one who is generally referred to as "the priest"—e.g., Zadok (I Kings 2:35), Jehoiada (II Kings 11:9; 12:7, 9; cf. Jer. 29:25 ff), Uriah (II Kings 16:10-11, 15-16; cf. Isa. 8:2), Hilkiah (II Kings 22:10, 12, 14). But Jehoiada (II Kings 12:10—H 12:11) and Hilkiah (II Kings 22:4, 8; 23:4; cf. II Chr. 34:9) are also given the title "high priest" (הכהן הגדול), and Seraiah (II Kings 25:18) is called "head" or "chief priest" (כהן הראש; cf. Ezra 7:5).

This is precisely the same phraseology and usage we find in the Priestly Code, and the logical implication is that it is the same office referred to in each case. It is noteworthy that the title "high priest" (הכהן הגדול) occurs four times in the book of Kings, as against only three times in the Priestly Code (Lev. 21:10; Num. 35:25, 28). The references in Kings are supported by the parallel passages in the book of Chronicles and by the LXX; and there is no valid reason for dismissing them as interpolations of a postexilic editor. The book of Kings, together with the Law of Holiness, thus provides strong evidence for the antiquity of the high priesthood, and this finds support in the usage of the Priestly Code. With the disappearance of the Davidic line, it was inevitable that the postexilic high priest should acquire much of the power and prestige which formerly belonged to the king. But what we see in the restored Jewish community is the development of an ancient institution and not the emergence of something entirely new.

2. Priests and Levites. One of the cardinal doctrines of the Wellhausen school is that the distinction between priests and Levites, which is prominent in the Priestly Code, was unknown before the Exile. In the seventh and sixth centuries B.C., it is maintained, not only were all priests Levites, but all Levites were priests. It has, indeed, become an axiom of OT criticism that Deuteronomy does not distinguish between them. The distinction, it is said, begins with Ezekiel's degradation of the idolatrous priests to the rank of temple servants (Ezek. 44:4 ff). This theory is basic in the modern critical reconstruction of the origin and development of the priesthood, but it is extremely vulnerable. It rests ultimately upon certain assumptions which need to be re-examined.

In the first place, it assumes that Ezekiel knows of no other temple servants apart from the foreigners, whose presence he condemns, and the degraded priests, who take their place in his scheme. While, however, he is concerned particularly with these, his reorganization does not preclude the existence of a Levitical order whose proper function was the subordinate service of the temple, from which they appear to have been almost ousted by the foreigners. Indeed, his condemnation of this practice as a violation of God's covenant (Ezek. 44:6-8) would seem to imply the existence of lawful keepers of the charge of the sanctuary (cf. Num. 18:3-4). Ezekiel himself, in fact, appears to be already familiar with two recognized grades of Levitical cultic officials—the keepers of the charge of the house and the keepers of the charge of the altar (Ezek. 40:45-46; cf. 48:13). All that his scheme proposes is that the idolatrous priests should be degraded to the lower rank of service (44:10-11, 14) while the faithful Zadokites approach the table of Yahweh (vs. 16)—i.e., have charge of the altar (40:46). Ezekiel's silence regarding Levites other than the degraded priests in his scheme no more proves that such were nonexistent than does the silence of Haggai and Zechariah half a century later. Neither of these prophets of the restoration mentions the Levites at all, but we know from Ezra and Nehemiah that they were present along with the priests. Here, indeed, the distinction between the two groups appears as something of long standing, and it is incredible that it should have originated only fifty years earlier.

Another assumption of this theory is that in Deuteronomy "priest" and "Levite" are synonymous terms—all priests are Levites and all Levites are priests, or potential priests. Closer examination, however, shows that this assumption also is unwarranted. There is not in Deuteronomy, it must be admitted, anything like the clear-cut distinction between priests and Levites that we find in the Priestly Code. But the distinction is there, and indications are not lacking that it is presupposed throughout the book.

In discussing the phraseology of Deuteronomy it must be remembered that its emphasis is upon the tribe of Levi as the tribe which had been set apart for the ministry of the sanctuary and to which the priesthood was restricted. Hence the characteristic Deuteronomic phrase "the Levitical priests." Priests, however, are in fact distinguished from Levites. Five times they are called "the Levitical priests" (Deut. 17:9, 18; 18:1; 24:8; 27:9), twice "the priests the sons of Levi" (Deut. 21:5; 31:9); and on seven occasions they are simply referred to as "the priests" (Deut. 17:12; 18:3 [twice]; 19:17; 20:2; 26:3-4). Levites (including references to the tribe of Levi) are mentioned some fourteen times. That this is a real distinction is clear from the legislation of Deut. 18, which distinguishes between the provision made for the priest ministering at the sanctuary (vss. 3-5) and that available for the unattached Levite in company with the serving Levites (vss. 6-8). There is nothing to warrant the assumption that the provincial Levite who comes to Jerusalem may exercise priestly functions in the sanctuary.

The first verse of Deut. 18 is an introduction to these two provisions. It does not, as is claimed, equate "the Levitical priests" with "all the tribe of Levi." It is rather an example of a mode of expression characteristic of Deuteronomy—the expansion of a statement by the addition of a phrase which enlarges its meaning (cf. Deut. 12:7, 12, 18; 15:11)—and has therefore the sense "the Levitical priests, indeed all the tribe of Levi." Against this it has been maintained that the terms used in vs. 7 to describe the service of the Levite—viz., to "minister in the name of Yahweh," to "stand . . . before Yahweh"—are those used of the duties of the priest. The verb "minister" (שרת), however, is used for the service of the Levite as well as for that of the priest (e.g., Num. 1:50; 8:26; I Chr. 15:2; 16:4, 37). And so is the phrase "to stand before Yahweh" (e.g., I Chr. 23:30; II Chr. 29:11; cf. 35:5), which is also used of Israel (e.g., Lev. 9:5; Deut. 4:10; 19:17).

A further indication of the implicit distinction between priests and Levites in Deuteronomy is to be found in the reference to the setting apart of Eleazar the son of Aaron to the priesthood and the subsequent separation of the whole tribe of Levi (Deut. 10:6-8), as recorded in the priestly document (cf. Num. 3:1-10).

In actual fact the term "Levite" is not used anywhere in the OT as the exact equivalent of "priest." Even in the period of the judges the Levite who settles with Micah is not at first regarded as a priest. He becomes Micah's priest, not merely because he is a Levite, but by virtue of the ceremony of "filling the hand" by which he is installed in the priest's office as Micah's son had previously been installed (Judg. 17:5-13).

3. The date and historical value of P. As Wellhausen himself admitted, the position of the Levites is the Achilles heel of the Priestly Code. If it be conceded that the distinction between priests and Levites did not originate with Ezekiel but goes back to pre-exilic times, one of the main arguments for the late date of the Priestly Code becomes invalid. And if, in addition, there should be evidence which points to a pre-exilic date for the Priestly Code, the question of its historical value would call for re-examination.

It has long been recognized that the Priestly Code preserves much early material and usage, as many of its ritual laws are of ancient origin. There has been an increasing recognition of this fact during recent years, and it is now considered legitimate to use data from that source, with due precautions, as evidence for the ritual practices of the early monarchy. It is generally conceded, e.g., that the ritual of the Day of Atonement was of very ancient origin. Indeed, some of the regulations of the Priestly Code appear to have been observed more rigidly in the early period than in later times—e.g., the rule of Lev. 21:12 forbidding the high priest to leave the precincts of the sanctuary is kept by Eli, who lives in the temple at Shiloh and awaits the news of the ark, not in the city where it is first told, but at the sanctuary gate to which the messenger subsequently comes (I Sam. 4:12-14). But in the seventh century B.C., Hilkiah leaves the temple to consult the prophetess Huldah, who lives in the city (II Kings 22:14).

There are, however, indications that the Priestly Code itself was in existence before the Exile. Its affinities with Ezekiel, when examined in relation to the differences between the two, suggest an acquaintance on the part of Ezekiel with the Priestly Code rather than, as is usually maintained, a dependence of the priestly writer upon Ezekiel. Ezekiel's law is more systematic than that of the Priestly Code, and his arrangements for housing the temple personnel close to the sanctuary, rather than in distant Levitical cities, more applicable in the restored community. The widely distributed Levitical cities of the priestly document, some of which were ancient sanctuaries, recall the conditions of pre-exilic times. Again, the sacrificial law of the Priestly Code, according to which the lay offerer kills, flays, and cuts up the sacrificial animal (Lev. 1:5-6, 11-12; cf. Exod. 12:6), represents the early custom, whereas in the legislation of Ezekiel it is the Levites who kill the animal (Ezek. 44:11)—a practice evidently familiar to the Chronicler (II Chr. 35:6, 10-11; cf. 30:16 ff).

If the existence of a separate order of Levites in pre-exilic times be admitted, it becomes apparent that the cultic personnel of the Priestly Code is that of the old temple rather than that of the return from Babylon. The priestly writer appears to know of only priests and Levites and makes no mention of the other classes which appear in the lists of Ezra and Nehemiah—singers, gatekeepers, temple servants (Nethinim), and sons of Solomon's servants (Ezra 2:41-58; cf. 7:24; Neh. 7:44-60). This is admittedly an argument from silence and must therefore be used with caution; but we should expect some regard to be shown to the special conditions of the early restoration period if, as is maintained by the Wellhausen school, it is with the ritual of the second temple that the priestly writer is concerned. On the other hand, the Priestly Code is acquainted with another class, which was nonexistent in postexilic times—the "ministering women" (Exod. 38:8) mentioned in connection with the Shiloh temple (I Sam. 2:22) and who may have later degenerated into the cult prostitutes ejected from the Jerusalem temple by Josiah (II Kings 23:7).

We can now carry the argument a stage further. Not only are there clear indications that the Priestly Code is pre-exilic; there is also evidence that it is pre-Deuteronomic. Once the implicit distinction between priests and Levites in Deuteronomy is recognized, the significance of the affinities between Deuteronomy and the priestly legislation becomes apparent. The most obvious and striking instance of a relationship between the two codes is seen in the regulations concerning clean and unclean animals in Deut. 14:3-20, which are to a large extent verbally identical with those of Lev. 11:2-23. Peculiarities of style link this passage with the Priestly Code rather than with Deuteronomy, thus indicating the priority of the former. Similarly, we find in Deut. 24:8-9 a reference to the priestly law concerning leprosy in Lev. 13–14 and an allusion to the account of Miriam's leprosy in Num. 12:1-10. The priestly legislation is frequently presupposed when it is not explicitly referred to—e.g., the permission given to kill and eat flesh at home in Deut. 12:15-16, 20-24, presupposes the more stringent law of Lev. 17:1-6, which it modifies; the law of release in Deut. 15:1 ff has in mind the sabbatical year of Lev. 25:2 ff; the regulations for the centralized celebration of the Passover in Deut. 16:1-8 presuppose and modify the domestic Passover law of Exod. 12:1-20.

A significant feature of these references of Deuteronomy, explicit and implicit, to the Priestly Code is that, taken as a whole, they cover a considerable extent of the priestly legislation (e.g., Exod. 12; Lev. 11; 13–15; 17–19; Num. 18). And while there are indications of the dependence of Deuteronomy upon the Priestly Code, there is no evidence of any acquaintance of the priestly writer with Deuteronomy. Hence the priority of the Priestly Code is clearly implied.

Such a conclusion, if it be maintained, has far-reaching consequences for the study of the Levitical priesthood. If an early date for the Priestly Code be accepted, it must necessitate a complete re-evaluation of its evidence. At least it could no longer be maintained that the priestly writer has read back the organization of the second temple into early times. Indeed, it may well be that the priestly source will prove to be of far greater historical value than many have been disposed to admit.

Bibliography. J. H. Kurtz, *Sacrificial Worship of the OT* (English trans.; 1863), gives the traditional view. A. Eidersheim, "The Officiating Priesthood," *The Temple, Its Ministry and Services* (1874), pp. 58-78. A. Kuenen, *The Religion of Israel*, II (English trans.; 1873-75), 202-307. S. I. Curtiss, *The Levitical Priests* (1877), is a reply to Kuenen. H. Oort, "De Aäronieden," *TT*, XVIII (1884), 289-335. G. W. W. Baudissin, *Die Geschichte des alttestamentlichen Priestertums untersucht* (1889). H. Vogelstein, *Der Kampf zwischen Priestern und Leviten seit den Tagen Ezechiels* (1889). H. Schultz, "The Priesthood," *OT Theology*, I (English trans.; 1892), 197-202. W. R. Smith, "The Deuteronomic Code and the Levitical Law," *The OT in the Jewish Church* (2nd ed., 1892), pp. 358-63. T. K. Cheyne, "The Priesthood of David's Sons," *Exp.*, Fifth Series, vol. IX (1899), pp. 453-57. A. Van Hoonacker, *Le sacerdoce lévitique dans la loi et dans l'histoire des Hébreux* (1899). J. Wellhausen, "Die Priester und Leviten," and "Die Ausstattung des Klerus," chs. 4–5 in *Prolegomena zur Geschichte Israels* (1899; 1st ed., *Geschichte Israels* [1878], pp. 123-74; English trans., *Prolegomena to the History of Israel*). W. R. Smith and A. Bertholet, "Priest," *EB*, vol. III (1902), cols. 3837-47. C. F. Burney, *Outlines of OT Theology* (1903), pp. 81-85. A. B. Davidson, "The Priest," *The Theology of the OT* (1904), pp. 306-11, deals admirably with the theological significance of the Levitical priesthood. R. H. Kennett, "The Origin of the Aaronite Priesthood," *JTS*, VI (1905), 161-86. J. Orr, "The Aaronic Priesthood and the Levites," and "The Priestly Writing. I: The Code," *The Problem of the OT* (1906), present a scholarly defense of the traditional view. B. D. Eerdmans, *Alttestamentliche Studien, IV: Leviticus* (1908-12). H. P. Smith, "Priest, Priesthood (Hebrew)," in J. Hastings, ed., *Encyclopedia of Religion and Ethics*, X (1918), 307-11. G. B. Gray, "The Hebrew Priesthood: Its Origin, History, and Functions," *Sacrifice in the OT* (1925), pp. 179-270, is the most comprehensive study of the Hebrew priesthood in English. A. C. Welch, "The Priesthood," and "The Priests and the Levites," *Post-Exilic Judaism* (1935), pp. 172-84, 217-41; *Prophet and Priest in Old Israel* (1936). N. H. Snaith, "The Priesthood and the Temple," in T. W. Manson, ed., *A Companion to the Bible* (1939), pp. 418-33. J. Pedersen, "The Priest," *Israel, Its Life and Culture*, III–IV (English trans.; 1940), 150-97. A. R. Johnson, *The Cultic Prophet in Ancient Israel* (1944), pp. 6-11. B. D. Eerdmans, "Cult and Law in the Temple of Jerusalem," *The Religion of Israel* (1947), pp. 67-74. G. C. Aalders, "Priests and Levites," *A Short Introduction to the Pentateuch* (1949), pp. 66-71, gives a criticism of the Wellhausen theory. C. R. North, "Sacrifice, III," in A. Richardson, ed., *A Theological Word Book of the Bible* (1950), pp. 210-11. N. Avigad, "A New Class of 'Yehud' Stamps," *Bulletin of the Israel Exploration Society*, vol. XXII, nos. 1-2 (1958), pp. 3-10, supplies fresh evidence of the fiscal responsibilities of the postexilic priesthood. E. Jacob, "The Priest," *Theology of the OT* (English trans.; 1958), pp. 246-50. G. Pidoux, "Priesthood, OT," in J.-J. von Allmen, ed., *Vocabulary of the Bible* (English trans.; 1958), pp. 337-40. T. C. Vriezen, "The Priests," *An Outline of OT Theology* (English trans.; 1958), pp. 263-66. T. F. Torrance, "Consecration and Ordination," *Scottish Journal of Theology*, XI (1958), 225-52.

R. Abba

PRIESTS IN THE NT. The Greek words for "priest" and its cognate, "high priest" (ἱερεύς, ἀρχιερεύς), are used in the gospels and Acts, with but one exception, always with reference to Jewish priests (*see* Priests and Levites). The single exception occurs in Acts 14:13, where the term "priest" refers to a pagan functionary of the cult of Zeus at Lystra in Asia Minor. (The claim of a certain Sceva [Acts 19:14] to be a Jewish high priest was undoubtedly fraudulent.)

In Judaism, priesthood was hereditary in the tribe of Levi. A Jewish priest was born, not made. Among the pagan cults of the Mediterranean world, some priesthoods were hereditary; others were voluntary vocations, or associated, in respect to some of their duties, with the civil magistracy. A persistent tradition invested kings and monarchs with priestly prerogatives. The dignity, emoluments, and responsibilities of pagan priests were extremely varied, depending upon whether the cult they served was official and state-supported, or was a voluntary religious association, and whether the shrine or oracle where they ministered was famous or insignificant.

The essential concept underlying priesthood in the ancient world, among both Jews and Gentiles, was that of mediatorship between the divine and human, by virtue of the priest's superior knowledge of, or power of communication with, the supernatural. The priest was the director, if not the actual performer, of sacrifices offered to deity; the dispenser and interpreter of oracular messages and auguries from the divine realm; and thereby a channel of weal or woe according to the divine pleasure.

The antagonism of Christians to all pagan priesthoods was, of course, a legacy from the Jewish contempt for everything associated with idolatry. But the bitterness between the early Christians and the Jewish priesthood itself is also marked in the gospels and Acts. It reflects not only the opposition of the Jewish priests in general to the person and mission of Jesus, especially the priestly party of Sadducees, but, more than that, the actual persecution of Jesus and his followers by the high priests and their associates. The rejection by the Sadducean priesthood of any doctrine of resurrection served to exacerbate its antagonism to the preaching of the early apostles and evangelists. Yet in one place the book of Acts (6:7) testifies to the conversion of a number of Jewish priests to the Christian faith.

It is likely that many of the humbler priests of Judaism were not in sympathy with the policies or personages of the "chief priests" of the hierarchy. Among such must be counted no less a figure than John the Baptist, himself of priestly lineage, who roundly denounced the Sadducees, with others, who came to hear his preaching (cf. Matt. 3:7). The documents of the Essene sect of Khirbet Qumran confirm the statements of Philo and Josephus that the Essenes rejected all animal sacrifices in the temple, and they reveal a deep-seated antagonism to the official priesthood that controlled the temple. Yet in their own corporate life priests were highly esteemed and given a leading role in their sectarian fellowships.

Neither Jesus nor his orthodox Jewish disciples were so radical as to repudiate either the priesthood or the sacrificial system of the temple, for they accepted these institutions as God-given in the law. Whatever Jesus may have thought about the character of individual members of the priesthood, he was loyal to the system. His attitude is indicated in the healing of the lepers (Mark 1:44 and parallels; Luke 17:14), where he directed them to show themselves to the priests for the customary offerings and ceremonies of purification.

The process of separation of the church from all association with the priestly and sacrificial institutions of Judaism began at a very early time, however —even before the decision of the apostolic council to relieve Gentile converts of any obligation to observe the law (Acts 15:28-29; Gal. 2:1-9). It is already indicated in the attitudes taken by Stephen (Acts 6:11 ff; 7:37 ff). After the destruction of the temple in A.D. 70, the Jewish Christians themselves developed a sharp polemic against sacrifices, and exalted the prophetic as against the priestly traditions of the OT (cf. Matt. 9:13; 12:7; Pseudo-Clementine *Homilies* III.45; *Recognitions* I.36, 39).

Christianity made a positive and creative development of the concept of priesthood, however, in its transferal to Christ himself of the role of perfect and great High Priest. The doctrine is elaborated in greatest detail in the Letter to the Hebrews (*see* HEBREWS, LETTER TO THE). In this work, the person of Christ, presented as unblemished, sacrificial Victim and sinless High Priest, is exalted as the consummation of the OT cultus, bringing it to a definitive end in history, and establishing a once-for-all, eternal mediatorship between God and man. The authority, honor, and effect of Christ's priesthood make it disannul and supplant forever the Aaronic priesthood of the Old Covenant, and it finds its type and pattern in the legendary figure of Melchizedek (Gen. 15:18; Ps. 110:4), who "is without father or mother or genealogy, and has neither beginning of days nor end of life" (Heb. 7:3).

This full-rounded theology of Christ's priesthood was not an original creation of the mind of the author of Hebrews, nor peculiar to his outlook, though he alone among NT writers actually applied the title of priest to Christ. The conception is rooted in Christ's own interpretation of his atoning mission as a "ransom for many" (Mark 10:45 and parallels), and more especially in his words of a new covenant sacrifice associated with the bread and the cup of the LAST SUPPER. In Paul's letters the sacrificial character of Christ's death is clearly marked—whether related to the Passover (I Cor. 5:8), the expiation of the Day of Atonement (Rom. 3:25), or the sin offering (Rom. 8:3). Likewise in Paul one finds the doctrine of Christ's mediatorship (Gal. 3:20), and his reconciliation of God and man (II Cor. 5:19; Col. 1:20-21; cf. Eph. 2:16). Similar ideas are found in I Pet. 1:2, 18-19; 2:24; 3:18; and the theme of Christ's ransom and expiation for sin is one of the threads that link together all the Johannine writings: John 1:29; I John 1:7; 2:2; 4:10; Rev. 1:5; 5:9; 7:14; 12:11.

A corollary of the doctrine of the priesthood of Christ is the NT application of "priesthood" to the whole company of the faithful in the church. As the church is made one with its Lord, by the indwelling presence in its members of his Spirit, and by sacramental union and communion with him in baptism and Eucharist, so the church shares in the dignity and prerogatives of its Lord. I Pet. 2:5, 9, speaks of the church: "Like living stones be yourselves built into a spiritual house, to be a holy priesthood, to offer spiritual sacrifices acceptable to God through Jesus Christ," and: "You are a chosen race, a royal priesthood, a holy nation, God's own people." The theme is accented also in several passages of Revelation: Christ has "made us a kingdom, priests to his God and Father" (1:6); the Lamb in heaven has made the redeemed a "kingdom and priests to our God" (5:10); they who share in the resurrection "shall be priests of God and of Christ" (20:6). Such expressions as these were a natural outcome of the typological application to the church of the promises made to the people of the Old Covenant: "You shall be to me a kingdom of priests and a holy nation" (Exod. 19:6).

> You shall be called the priests of the LORD,
> men shall speak of you as the ministers of our God
> (Isa. 61:6).

The same thought is suggested in Ps. 132:9, 16, a royal and messianic psalm of David and his posterity.

In no instance, however, does any NT writer ascribe the title of priest to any individual member or order of ministry in the church (*see* MINISTRY, CHRISTIAN). Yet the development of this usage was probably inevitable. I Clem. 40-44, written A.D. 95-96, employs the threefold hierarchy of high priest, priests, and Levites, as an analogous type of the Christian ministry, and uses sacrificial terms to describe the "liturgy" of Christian bishops and elders.

The Didache orders its Christian communities to give first fruits of their produce to the prophets who ministered to them, "for they are your high priests" (13.3). The Didachist also speaks of the Eucharist as a "sacrifice" and applies to the sacrament the prophecy of Mal. 1:11 concerning the pure offering among the nations. This exegesis of Malachi became a commonplace in Christian apologetic of the second century.

These trends were perhaps but one step beyond the metaphor Paul uses to denote his own work of evangelization as a "priestly service" in order that the sacrificial offering of the Gentiles might be acceptable (Rom. 15:16).

Heb. 13:15-16; I Pet. 2:5 speak of Christian worship and service in sacrificial terms (cf. also Rom. 12:1; Phil. 4:18). Even so, the primitive prejudice against sacerdotal terms as specifically applicable to the ministry of the church lingered throughout the second century. The first Christian writers to use the words "priest" and "high priest" of the church's ministers were Tertullian (*On Baptism* 17) and Hippolytus (Preface to *Refutation of All Heresies*).

Bibliography. In addition to the standard commentaries on the Letter to the Hebrews, see especially: J. B. Lightfoot, "The Christian Ministry," *St. Paul's Epistle to the Philippians* (1898), pp. 244-69. R. C. Moberly, *Ministerial Priesthood* (1898), pp. 220-82. E. G. Selwyn, *The First Epistle of St. Peter* (1949), pp. 291-98. R. Bultmann, *Theology of the NT*, I (1951), 114-16, 151-52; II (1955), 100-101, 110.

M. H. SHEPHERD, JR.

PRINCE. The translation or possible translation of a number of words designating a ruler; one who has high authority or is pre-eminent in a class or sphere of influence. The Bible does not use the word in the limited sense of the direct male heir of a monarch, as in Western practice. In fact, "sons of the king" are quite distinct from the "princes" in Israel (Zeph. 1:8), except when a king's son has become pre-eminent by some other cause than his heredity. An exception seems to be Abijah, who was made "chief prince" (נגיד) by his father (II Chr. 11:22). The wives of Solomon are called "princesses" (I Kings 11:3; cf. Lam. 1:1).

A נגיד ("prince," "ruler," "commander") is a "leader" who is pre-eminent. This term is used for kings (I Sam. 13:14; I Kings 1:35; II Kings 20:5; etc.), and military officers or captains and generals are so designated (I Chr. 12:27; 13:1; II Chr. 32:31; etc.). Such a leader may also be the "chief" of the tribe (II Chr. 19:11) or temple (cf. II Chr. 31:13; Jer. 20:1). *See* GOVERNOR.

The word נדיב designates a man of noble birth or breeding, a chief, one who is worthy of honor. It is translated "prince" in most passages (I Sam. 2:8; Job 12:21; Ps. 107:40; etc.), but cf. Prov. 17:26; 19:6; Isa. 32:8. The root suggests willingness and freedom of choice (cf. Ps. 51:12) and is characteristic of the poetic books. *See* NOBLE.

A נשיא is one who is lifted up. The leaders in Shechem (Gen. 34:2) and in Midian (Num. 25:18) are called this. Abraham is called נשיא by the Hittites (Gen. 23:6 [LXX "king"]). Tribal leaders or chiefs in Israel (Exod. 16:22 ["leader"]; Lev. 4:22 ["ruler"]; etc.) and of Ishmael (Gen. 17:20) are also so designated. This word suggests a parallel to the modern "sheik." Ezekiel has a preference for the term נשיא, since in his day the kings of Israel and Judah were insignificant. Simon Maccabee re-established this title in Israel. The LXX usually uses ἄρχων.

The term שר (cf. Akkadian *šarru*, "king") is the most popular word for "ruler" or "leader" in any capacity. It is often translated "prince." When it refers to an army officer, however, "commander" or "captain" is used (I Kings 16:9; I Chr. 13:1; II Chr. 18:30; etc.). The angels are the "princes" of God's host (Dan. 12:1; cf. Josh. 5:15). The prefect of a city or province is designated with this familiar title (I Kings 20:15 ["governor"]; Jer. 34:19; etc.). *See* SATRAP.

Many other Hebrew words, variously translated, are used infrequently in the OT for the concept "prince": רב (Jer. 39:13; 41:1); שליש (Ezek. 23:15); סגנים (Isa. 41:25; *see* DEPUTY); נסיך (Josh. 13:3; *see* DUKE); אחשדרפניא (Dan. 3:2-3; 6:1-2; "satrap" is a Persian loan word); קצין (Prov. 25:15; Mic. 3:1); רזון (Prov. 14:28; 31:4; Isa. 40:23). In Job 12:19 the KJV translates כהן "prince," but the correct meaning is "priest."

The king himself is considered a prince in the OT (Saul [נגיד; I Sam. 9:16; etc.]; Solomon [נשיא; I Kings 11:34; "ruler"]; Jeroboam [נגיד; I Kings 14:7; "leader"]; the leaders of the world [נדיב; Ps. 47:9]; Zedekiah [נשיא; Ezek. 7:27, etc.]).

In the NT, ἀρχηγός may be translated "prince." In two passages it is used to designate the leader who goes before and blazes a trail like a pioneer (Acts 5:31; "leader"; KJV "prince"); he sets an example or starts a precedent (Heb. 12:2; "pioneer"; KJV "author"). In the NT this term is reserved for Christ.

The ἄρχων is a commander or ruler in any nation ("prince" in Mark 3:22; cf. Matt. 20:25 ["ruler"; KJV "prince"]; Acts 7:35; etc.). This word is also used for the members of the SANHEDRIN (Luke 23:13). The ruler of the SYNAGOGUE who has charge of the reading is so designated (Luke 8:41).

For ἡγεμών, which refers to the Roman legate, procurator, or proconsul, the governor, the KJV translates "prince" in Matt. 2:6. In this quotation from Mic. 5:2, the KJV confuses "clan" with "prince," perhaps because of the influence of the latter half of the verse.

The MESSIAH is Prince of Peace (Isa. 9:6), Prince of princes (Dan. 8:25; cf. 9:25 [the high priest or the Messiah]), prince (RSV "ruler") of kings (Rev. 1:5), prince (RSV "author") of life (Acts 3:15), and prince (RSV "pioneer") of salvation (Heb. 2:10).

BEELZEBUB is the prince of demons (Mark 3:22; Luke 11:15), and the leader of the unbelievers and rebellious people of the world (John 12:31; 16:11; etc.).

C. U. WOLF

PRINCIPALITY. A term used in the plural form (αἱ ἀρχαί), referring to the organized cosmological powers of angels, in Rom. 8:38 (*see* ANGEL). As the connection with the specifically named "angels" shows, a "principality" is thought of as an extra group of spirits which may interfere and hinder the salvation in Christ. The underlying pattern is mythological and not entirely clear. For similar lists see Eph. 1:21; Col. 1:16. Paul's idea is obvious: No power in the world can destroy God's love; it is greater than and superior to all demonic forces.

Bibliography. W. Sandy and A. C. Headlam, *The Epistle to the Romans* (1902), p. 222; O. Michel, *Der Brief an die Römer* (1955), p. 189.

E. DINKLER

PRISCA, PRISCILLA. *See* AQUILA.

PRISON. As a legal punishment imprisonment is not found in ancient law, and does not appear in the Bible until the Persian period (Ezra 7:26; אסורין, lit., "bonds"). משמר, "place of custody" (Lev. 24:12;

Num. 15:34), refers to a temporary confinement under guard pending clarification of a case. Under the monarchy persons regarded as dangerous to public order or hostile to the state were put into a בית כלא, "prison" (I Kings 22:27; synonyms: בית אסור [Jer. 37:15]; בית מהפכת [II Chr. 16:10; *see* STOCKS]), for which a private house might serve (Jer. 37:15). Confinement might be aggravated by detention in a בית הבור—a pitlike underground dungeon (Jer. 37:16; cf. Isa. 24:22)—and meager rations (I Kings 22:27). Less severe was detention in a palace area called the "court of the guard," which did not cut off the prisoner from contact with the outside (Jer. 32:2; 33:1). Casting Jeremiah into a cistern in this court (38:6) seems to have been a device to kill him without bloodshed. With מסגר, "prison" (Ps. 142:7—H 142:8; Isa. 24:22; 42:7), cf. Aramaic מסגרת (plural), "royal prisons" (Panammu Inscription, lines 4, 8).

The following non-Israelite prisons are also mentioned: an Egyptian בית הסהר for royal prisoners, located in the house of the captain of the guard (Gen. 39:20; 40:3; also called משמר [40:4] and בור [40:15; 41:14]); an Assyrian בית כלא in which the rebellious king Hoshea was confined (II Kings 17:4); a Babylonian one in which Jehoiachin was held, clothed in "prison garments" (II Kings 25:27, 29); and a Babylonian בית הפקדת, "guard house," where Zedekiah was kept in fetters till his death (Jer. 52:11). Also kept in chains in a Philistine prison (בית אסירים) was the captive Samson, who was made to labor grinding at a mill (Judg. 16:21).

Confinement to a specific city is found twice: Solomon confines Shimei ben Gera to Jerusalem on pain of death if he leaves (I Kings 2:36-37); the accidental homicide is confined to the CITY OF REFUGE until the death of the high priest (Num. 35:25-28), and his life is forfeit to the avenger if he leaves. Both cases involve persons who, although they have committed a guilty act (for the accidental homicide, *see* BLOODGUILT), are saved from the death penalty, the one by royal, the other by divine, grace. The city of their confinement has at once the attributes of a prison and of an asylum.

Jewish prisons mentioned in the NT serve for the detention under custody of persons awaiting trial or execution (δεσμωτήριον [Acts 5:21, 23]; τήρησις [4:3; 5:18]; φυλακή [Matt. 5:25]). Imprisonment as a punishment was also known (Acts 22:19; cf. Jos. Antiq. XIII.x.6; M. Sanh. 9.3, 5). Roman authorities were empowered to imprison as a coercive measure (φυλακή; Matt. 18:30; cf. 5:25) and as punishment for minor disorders (δεσμωτήριον [Matt. 11:2; Acts 16:26]; φυλακή [Matt. 14:10]). The *carcer* was made up of several cells (οἴκημα; Acts 12:7), of which the interior (εσωτέρα φυλακή; 16:24), being without light, were the worst. Incarceration was so often accompanied by chaining (cf. 16:26) that *publica vincula* was a synonym for *carcer*. M. GREENBERG

PRISON GATE. *See* GUARD, GATE OF THE.

PRIZE [βραβεῖον]. One detail of the foot-race imagery which Paul borrows from the stadium or the arena to illustrate the Christian life (I Cor. 9:24; Phil. 3:14; cf. Gal. 2:2). The word is directly related to the verb "rule" (βραβεύω) in Col. 3:15, the verb "rule out, disqualify" (καταβραβεύω), in Col. 2:18, and the noun "umpire" (βραβεύς, βραβεύτης).

In I Cor. 9:24, "prize" (βραβεῖον) is used literally in the full picture of the foot race. Its figurative use in Phil. 3:14 has to be inferred. Paul says: "I press on toward the goal for the prize." The "goal" (σκοπόν) is not the prize, but as the end of the race it is assumed in the prize. Some commentators consider the "upward calling" (τῆς ἄνω κλήσεως) as a genitive of apposition with "prize" and therefore the content of the prize—namely, the heavenly destination. More probably the genitive is subjective, and the "divine call" means that God has called Paul to this destination and prize (I Thess. 2:12). The phrase thus fits in with the idea of appropriation in Phil. 3:12*b* (cf. Eph. 1:18: "the hope to which he has called you"; 4:4).

In the context (Phil. 3:8-11) Paul has rejected all pride in birth, religious standing, and attainment, and he concentrates on his true goals: to gain Christ, to be found in him, to have standing with God on the basis of faith, to know him, to have the power of his resurrection, to share his sufferings, to attain the resurrection from the dead. It is for all this that Paul has been "laid hold on, appropriated," and this is the hope of his calling; this is the prize in the race to which God has called him.

The figure of the foot race should not be pressed as though Paul meant to say that his effort and his success in surpassing other men will bring the possession of the prize. Yet there is implicit here a strenuous concentration.

Bibliography. Ante-Nicene Fathers: Tatian *Address to the Greeks* 33.4. Apostolic Fathers: I Clem. 5.5, where Paul receives the "reward of endurance." J. H. Moulton and G. Milligan, *The Vocabulary of the Greek Testament Illustrated from the Papyri and Other Non-literary Sources* (1914-29). W. F. Arndt and F. W. Gingrich, *A Greek-English Lexicon of the NT and Other Early Christian Literature,* trans. from W. Bauer, *Griechisch-Deutsches Wörterbuch zu den Schriften des Neuen Testaments* (1957). P. E. DAVIES

PROCHORUS prŏk′ə rəs [Πρόχορος] (Acts 6:5). One of the seven "Hellenists" chosen to perform certain administrative tasks in the Jerusalem community. Nothing further is heard of him in the NT, but tradition associates him with the apostle John. Prochorus appears in Byzantine art as the amanuensis to whom John dictated the Fourth Gospel, and in the latter half of the fifth century a Life of John was written under his name.

See also SEVEN, THE. H. H. PLATZ

PROCHORUS, ACTS OF JOHN BY. *See* JOHN, ACTS OF, BY PROCHORUS.

PROCONSUL. In the Roman Empire the civil and military administration of the provinces was carried on by senators *pro consule,* "for the consul" or chief magistrate. The proconsul was himself an ex-consul and usually held office for one year, *ca.* seventeen years after his consulship. His actions were subject to review by the Senate. In the NT we read of two proconsuls: GALLIO, proconsul of Achaea; Sergius Paulus (*see* PAULUS), proconsul of Cyprus.

R. M. GRANT

PROCURATOR prŏk'yə rā'tər. Financial and, later, military official responsible to the Roman emperor and representing him, sometimes at Rome, sometimes in the provinces. Under Augustus a larger share in the civil service was given to members of the equestrian order, and they were entrusted with such offices as the prefectures of Egypt, of the police, of the Roman grain supply, and of the praetorian guard. There were also civil servants called procurators; in the reigns of Augustus and Tiberius these were occupied chiefly with government revenues. At a later date the emperor's representatives in military affairs were also called procurators. It is a question whether Pontius Pilate and other early Roman military governors should be called procurators; Tacitus (Ann. XV.44) may be using later terminology when he gives Pilate this title.

Whatever the title may have been, three such administrators in Palestine are mentioned in the NT; Pontius Pilate, Antonius Felix, and Porcius Festus (*see* PILATE; FELIX; FESTUS). In the period before 66 we know the names of the following "procurators": Coponius (*ca.* 6-9), M. Ambibulus (*ca.* 9-12), Annius Rufus (*ca.* 12-15), Valerius Gratus (15-26), Pontius Pilatus (26-36), Marcellus (36-37), Marullus (37?), C. Cuspius Fadus (*ca.* 44-46), Tiberius Julius Alexander (*ca.* 46-48), Ventidius Cumanus (48-52), Antonius Felix (*ca.* 52-58), Porcius Festus (*ca.* 58-62), Albinus (62-64), and Gessius Florus (64-66). Most of them issued local coinage, of which a good many examples survive. It was their duty to keep the area quiet, and Josephus tells us that Coponius could inflict the death penalty; it is not clear whether or not this statement means that the right of inflicting it was withdrawn from Jewish authorities. In pacifying Palestine the procurators avoided placing human or animal figures on their coins, but the Roman religious symbols used by Pilate can hardly have been regarded as conciliatory.

Bibliography. A. N. Sherwin-White, "Procurator Augusti," *Papers of the British School at Rome,* XV (1939), 11-26; G. H. Stevenson, *Roman Provincial Administration* (1939); A. Reifenberg, *Ancient Jewish Coins* (2nd ed., 1947); E. Stauffer, *Christ and the Caesars* (trans. R. G. Smith; 1955).

R. M. GRANT

PRODIGAL SON. A narrative PARABLE of Jesus (Luke 15:11-32) vividly and dramatically describing repentance. Sincere confession of sins (vs. 18) and return to the Father are essential and concrete expressions of the son's desire for renewal of life and love. L. MOWRY

PROFANE [חלל, unloose, set free; חנף, be polluted (Mic. 4:11); *Pi'el of* נכר, treat as foreign (Jer. 19:4); תפש, seize (Prov. 30:9); LXX *and* NT βεβηλόω]. To treat a holy person, place, or institution as if it were not holy (Lev. 19:8; Ezek. 36:20-23; I Tim. 1:9)—i.e., as if it were COMMON.

Any sacred institution of Israel—the sanctuary (Lev. 21:12; Acts 24:6), the altar (Exod. 20:25), the sacrifices (Lev. 22:15), the priests and their families (Lev. 21:4), the sabbath (Isa. 56:6), the covenant (Mal. 2:10), the kingship (Ps. 89:39—H 89:40; "defiled")—could be profaned by disregard of the divinely given laws governing the institution. The most drastic profanation was to bring a holy thing into contact with uncleanness (*see* CLEAN AND UNCLEAN). Hence, "profane" shades over into "defile," "pollute," and the KJV often translates חלל in this way. Since the holy God commands his people to be holy, profanation in Israel is really an assault on the holiness of God, a profanation of his holy name (Lev. 21:6; Ezek. 22:26; Amos 2:7). Idolatry (Ezek. 20:39), child sacrifice (Lev. 18:21), and social immorality (Lev. 19:11-12) were particularly offensive, and profanation "of the name" was punished by loss of holiness (Ezek. 24:21), by foreign conquest (Ezek. 7:24), and ultimately by death (Num. 18:32).

L. E. TOOMBS

PROFANITY. *See* OATH.

*__PROMISE. 1. In the OT.__ The concept of promise is prominent in the OT, since God's word to Israel is considered the very source, support, and destiny of this people. In spite of its importance, however, there is in the OT no single, distinctive term used to convey the basic concept, comparable to ἐπαγγέλεσθαι in the NT. To be sure, the LXX uses the noun ἐπαγγελία half a dozen times to indicate the assurance given by one man to another. The verb ἐπαγγέλεσθαι occurs more frequently, but in only two cases does it refer to God's covenant promise (II Macc. 2:18; III Macc. 2:10). The OT employs quite ordinary words to refer to the pivotal promises of God. Of these the most important are דבר (LXX λαλεῖν; "to speak"); אמר (LXX λέγειν; "to say"); and שבע (LXX ὀμνύειν; "to swear"). When God is the subject of these verbs, and when his chosen people or their leaders are the recipients of his message, then the translator rightly gives to them the sense of a binding promise or oath, for it was axiomatic to OT writers that God is absolutely faithful to every word he speaks.

Pre-eminent among OT promises is that which God gave to Abraham. He swore to this patriarch that he would give to him a son and would make of him a mighty nation, so that all the nations of the earth should bless themselves by him (Gen. 18:19; 21:1; 22:15-18; 26:1-5; Deut. 1:11; I Chr. 16:16). This promise is directly linked to God's later call of Moses to lead his people from Egypt toward the Promised Land (Gen. 50:22-25; Exod. 3:17; 12:25; 32:13; Num. 10:29; 14:16-17; Deut. 6:3-23; 9:3-5, 28; 15:6; 19:8; 26:3-18; 29:13). Declared to all the people at Horeb, and affirmed by them as their charter, this promise guided them throughout their weary pilgrimage, providing the source of their endurance and the object of their rebellions. As celebrated in song and saga, this promise to Abraham and Moses was proof of God's steadfast love, his readiness to forgive, and his determination to bring them to a good end (Num. 14:13-25). After they were settled in the Land of Promise, their history received its continuity through this same promise.

The assurances given to David were both a fulfilment of earlier pledges and steps toward their fulfilment (II Sam. 3:18; 7:18-29). God's one word continued to cover his dealings with "a thousand generations" (Ps. 105:7-11). To each of David's successors, God gave specific pledges covering the duty and destiny of each, but each pledge was oriented toward the initial vow to the patriarchs and toward all the generations yet to come (e.g., the promises given to Solomon: I Kings 2:24; 5:12; 8:15-25; 9:5; II Chr. 1:9; 6:4-20).

Discontent with God's promise was the root sin of Israel (Ps. 106:24); confidence in it was the essence of HOPE (Pss. 18:30; 119:38, 41, 50, 76, 82, 116). Reliance on the promise sustained the individual in his daily obedience to the law. *See* LAW (IN THE OT).

The promise had implications for contemporary decisions by national leaders, and it was part of the prophets' task to make these implications clear. The "word of the Lord" which they declared was a living expression of God's promises (Isa. 14:24; 38:7; 45:20-23; 62:8; Jer. 11:1-8; 22:5-9; 29:10-14). Confidence in God's mercy and power meant for them the expectation of coming salvation in the midst of disaster or of imminent doom in the midst of prosperity, for destiny was determined, not by external probabilities, but by God's covenant pledge (Jer. 32:36-44; 33:14-26; 44:26-30; Ezek. 16:6-22; Amos 4:1-3; 6:4-8; 8:7-8; Mic. 7:18-20; Hag. 2:1-9). The prophets recognized in man a creature who makes and breaks promises; but in the God of Israel they recognized One who guides the whole of human history in accordance with a promise which he has made and will not break.

2. In the NT. The words used for "promise" in the NT are: ἐπαγγέλομαι, ἐπαγγελία, and ἐπάγγελμα. With few exceptions (e.g., Acts 23:21) "promise" in the NT refers to God's pledge given freely to his people (*see* CHURCH, IDEA OF) as the basis of their covenant relationship, as its initiation and consummation. It represents a complex of ideas in which the following may be distinguished: (*a*) the purpose and power of the promise-maker; (*b*) the response of the recipients; (*c*) the act of giving the promise; (*d*) the conditions characterizing gift and reception; (*e*) the effects in the life of the covenant people; (*f*) the mediator who is instrumental in enacting the covenant; and (*g*) the shape of the consummation assured. The conception of these factors varies in idiom and accent, and this variation may be noted in four sets of writings: Paul's letters, Hebrews, Luke-Acts, and the Catholic letters.

a. In Paul's letters. Although Paul is aware of multiple promises which belong to Israel (Rom. 9:4), he thinks of the promise to ABRAHAM as the decisive one which includes all others. God is absolutely faithful to this promise and has full power to accomplish it. In rejecting it, the people of the COVENANT do not destroy the promise but underscore its validity and God's eternal vigilance to maintain it. In fact, the word of promise begets those who are "children of the promise" (Rom. 9:8-9). By his promise God brings into being what has not been, creating a people who have been nothing (Rom. 4:17). In blessing Abraham, God included in that blessing all his descendants and heirs, whether Jew or Gentile. In a singular sense, Jesus Christ is Abraham's seed (Gal. 3:16), but in him are incorporated all Abraham's sons (Gal. 3:29). All who live by faith in the promise are the sons to whom the promise is given, because it is the promise by which they are begotten and sustained. For them, the fulness of time is measured by God's activity in fulfilling his promise (Gal. 4:4).

God's act in giving the promise is a supreme example of unmerited mercy. The gratitude with which his people receive the promise, therefore, becomes a matter of prime importance. God's grace is intended to produce faith (Gal. 3:14), and this faith can and must rely solely upon the promise itself (Rom. 4:20-21). If men assume that the promise depends upon the law, they nullify grace and empty faith of its significance (Rom. 4:13-14). If they limit the range of the promise to those who merit it, to a circle narrower than God's intention, they no longer live by the promise (Rom. 4:16). Where the covenant promise produces FAITH, there too it communicates God's righteousness (*see* RIGHTEOUSNESS IN THE NT), the marks of which include "hope against hope," total trust, unswerving patience, steady endurance. The character of the promise is indicated by these correlative terms: "faith," "grace," "righteousness," "hope," "life," "patience," "sonship."

Paul's understanding of the promise centers in the figure of Jesus Christ. It is in him that all God's promises are affirmed as true (II Cor. 1:20). It is in him that all who believe become sons of Abraham and heirs of God. Through him as a servant of Israel, God confirms his promises to the patriarchs by bringing Gentiles within the covenant (Rom. 15:8). Those who have been "strangers to the covenants of promise" now become its heirs in Christ (Eph. 2:12; 3:6). The guarantor of this transition is the Holy Spirit (Gal. 3:14). The Spirit of promise (Eph. 1:13) begets new sons, and fulfils in them the promise of the SPIRIT. Born of the Spirit, men become free citizens of the heavenly Jerusalem. God's promise thus stands at the beginning of their existence as heirs; it also points to the end of their existence in the inheritance. The Spirit guarantees this inheritance "until we acquire possession of it" (Eph. 1:14).

Paul does not try to describe in detail the full substance of this future "possession." It will include the "inheritance of the world" (Rom. 4:13), "life from the dead," the inclusion of all Israel and of many nations within the family of faith. But Paul sees these promises as realities being fulfilled among the covenant community, where God lives and moves, and where he makes himself known as their father and makes them known as his sons (II Cor. 6:16–7:1).

In the deutero-Pauline letters, thought regarding the promise becomes more stereotyped and formalistic. Here the promise is pretemporal in origin; it is manifested at the times which God orders; it is communicated by preaching; it is consummated in the coming Day. Here its essence is defined simply as eternal life (I Tim. 4:8; II Tim. 1:1; Tit. 1:2).

b. In the Letter to the Hebrews. The book of Hebrews speaks throughout, as does Paul, of God's promise as the ground of the unique covenant relationship (6:17). As in Paul's letters, the understanding of the promise centers in the work of Christ (9:15). For both writers this category covers the whole of God's redemptive work, the whole course of his people's history from beginning to end (11:33, 39). The promise discloses the steady, inexorable intention of God and thereby releases the faithful patience and the enduring hope of his Son and sons.

A different accent appears in the distinction between the new and the old covenants, which rests upon a distinction between the new and the old promise (8:6; 9:15). God's gift of the new promise in Christ is related typologically to his gift of the promise to Abraham and Moses. These events are related to each other through God's purpose. The two events are comparable and contrasting. The new continues and completes the old, and is superior to it. The promise in Christ is comprehended within the promise to Abraham, but only in Christ is the promise to Abraham accomplished (11:39-40).

Hebrews notes the difference between receiving the promise and receiving what is promised. In receiving the promise, recipients are declared heirs; in receiving what was promised, they obtain their inheritance. In between lies their life as pilgrims (11:1–12:4). The gift and receipt of the promise marks a decisive change. It creates the "now," the "today," which gives to every decision its immediate and ultimate significance. "Today" is seen as the strategic time of opportunity and demand created by God's promise.

Jesus as the mediator of new promises gives to this "now" an awesome decisiveness. His sacrificial obedience, his mediatorial blood (9:15), makes accessible the eternal REST, the heavenly city, the kingdom which cannot be shaken (*see* KINGDOM OF GOD). The promise is as near and as distant as its mediator. To receive his promise is to inherit life today. By faithful pilgrimage the reality of what is promised becomes visible in its final mystery. The promised inheritance thus becomes at once a future certainty, an immediate access to God's throne, and an active participation in a kingdom which cannot be shaken. The promise is at once the initiation and the consummation of God's work among his people, in whom are included all who respond in faith and endurance. In Hebrews, as in Paul, we have a complex configuration of categories: promise, rest, covenant, HOPE, faith, kingdom, endurance, indestructible life.

c. In Luke-Acts. Of the ten occurrences of "promise" in Luke-Acts, only one is without special significance (Acts 23:21). All others are in direct discourse, in which the speaker is either Jesus Christ or one of his apostles. In all of these the Maker and the Keeper of the promise is God. All appear in the context of the family—i.e., the stress falls either upon God's gift as father to his sons, or upon the fulfilment among the sons of God's promise to the fathers. Promise thus receives a familial tone and binds together many generations.

Interest in the promise centers in the work of the risen Lord (Luke 24:49; Acts 1:4; 2:33). It is he who sends the "father's promise" upon the apostles. They are not to serve as apostolic witnesses until this promise descends (Luke 24:49). The coming of the promise is inseparable from their being clothed with heavenly power with which to serve as witnesses, just as Jesus began his power-laden work at the descent of the dove. The coming of the promise on them—as on him—is directly co-ordinated with (*a*) their response to the preaching of repentance and (*b*) their empowerment for preaching repentance to all nations (Gentiles). By conveying the power for preaching, the promise produces repentance and forgiveness, and this power covers the spread of the gospel from Jerusalem "to all the Gentiles." Apostolic preaching differs from that of John the Baptist in that apostles are baptized, and baptize, with the Holy Spirit (Acts 1:5). At PENTECOST "what is seen and heard" is due to the actualized power of the promise, which comes simultaneously from the exalted Lord and from the Father. The Holy Spirit is not only what has been promised; he is the promise itself (Acts 2:33). Luke explicitly distinguishes the coming of the promise from the restoration of the kingdom to Israel (Acts 1:7-8).

The apostles call men to repentance with the assurance that those who respond will receive the Holy Spirit as a gift. This is the promise "to you and to your children and to all that are far off, every one whom the Lord our God calls" (2:39). To receive the promise is to be saved from this crooked generation (2:41). Stephen (7:5, 17) makes it clear that the promise realized in Christ is linked to God's promise to Abraham and to his seed, a promise made before the birth of Isaac and before the Egyptian slavery. The fulfilment of the promise to Abraham through Moses is a type of fulfilment of the promise to Moses through Jesus. Christ is also a fulfilment of the promise to David. The resurrection of Christ with the gift of the Holy Spirit brings to men salvation in forgiveness (13:22, 32). The Scriptures had pointed toward justification. Now the justification (accomplished in the Resurrection) has been granted (26:6). Luke stresses two things: (*a*) the promise made to the fathers is now fulfilled for their sons; (*b*) Israel's rejection of the promise, analogous to many earlier rejections, does not nullify the promise itself. It remains the substance of Israel's hope and the ground of existence for God's people. The character of Luke's conception of promise is indicated by the following terms: "resurrection," "Holy Spirit," "power," "the name," "preaching," "witnesses," "repentance," "BAPTISM," "forgiveness," "fathers," and "sons."

d. In the Catholic letters. In II Peter the word "promise" is more closely identical with the expected return of Christ. Antagonists scoff at the promise of his coming, but the faithful wait patiently for it, knowing that God's delay is for good reason. The desire for evident signs is an index of men's bondage to corruption. The substance of God's promise is the return of Christ, the great Day of Judgment, the new heaven and earth wherein righteousness dwells. But this expectation is directly related to the present participation in the divine nature (1:4).

In James the substance of promise is the crown of life which awaits the endurance and love of believers (1:12). Blessedness is identified with the inheritance of God's kingdom (2:5).

In I John, what God has promised is eternal life, and this life is described as mutual indwelling. As the word of life abides in men, they "abide in the Son and in the Father" (2:24). The promise is the life which "was made manifest," which is proclaimed, and which constitutes fellowship in and with God (1:1-4).

Bibliography. L. Goppelt, *Typos* (1939). P. S. Minear, *Kingdom and Power* (1950), pp. 115-62; *Christian Hope* (1954). E. Stauffer, *NT Theology* (trans. J. Marsh; 1955), pp. 94-101.

P. S. Minear

*__PROPHET, PROPHETISM.__ With some justification the person of the prophet and his function in the history of Israel have been accorded a role of unparalleled significance in the literature and tradition both of Judaism and of Christianity. Broadly but legitimately defined, prophetism begins with the historical Moses and continues without critical interruption to appear in the persons of a distinguished succession through both testaments of the Bible. For prophetism may legitimately be defined as that understanding of history which accepts meaning only in terms of divine concern, divine purpose, divine participation. Indeed, by this definition, the vast bulk of biblical record is produced by prophets or at least reflects an unmistakably prophetic understanding of history.

More narrowly defined, and also quite legitimately, prophetism is peculiarly the function of a concentrated succession of men—notably Amos, Hosea, Isaiah, Micah, Jeremiah, Ezekiel, Second Isaiah—appearing in a brief span of about two centuries, preceded by a hundred years or more and even anticipated by the marvelously vigorous prophet Elijah, and followed and at once recalled by a fading succession of lesser lights. To assess the influence on biblical record of this epoch of concentrated prophetism is, of course, impossible, but one may well wonder whether any significant block of biblical tradition has passed through the hands of editors standing in and after that prophetic epoch totally unmodified or in interpretation unaltered.

The broader definition is presupposed in the arrangement of the Hebrew canon of scripture (*see* Canon of the OT), where, between the first division of the Law and the third division of the Writings, the central category of the Prophets is placed. In the appearance of Joshua, Judges, and the books of Samuel and Kings under the heading "Former Prophets" and, as "Latter Prophets," Isaiah, Jeremiah, Ezekiel, and the twelve prophets from Hosea to Malachi (the last twelve writings of the OT canon in the Protestant tradition), recognition is apparently given to the marked influence of the prophetic mind and faith upon the historical writings of Joshua–II Kings. *See bibliography.*

- A. Terminology
  1. In biblical Hebrew
  2. In Greek
- B. Major and often controverted relationships of the prophet
  1. To the seer
  2. To contagious (ecstatic) prophetism
  3. To the cult prophet
  4. To the cultus
  5. To the book
- C. Pre-Amos prophetism
  1. The essence of prophetism: Address to history
  2. Premonarchic "prophets"
  3. The Yahwist as prophet
  4. Prophets to kings
     - *a.* Their relationship to contemporary institutional prophetism and to subsequent classical prophetism
     - *b.* Their relationship to king and Word
- D. The content of faith of classical prophetism
  1. "Thus says Yahweh": Word and symbol
  2. "Out of Egypt I called my son": Election and covenant
  3. "They went from me": Rebellion
  4. "They shall return to Egypt": Judgment
  5. "How can I give you up?": Compassion
  6. "I will return them to their homes": Redemption
  7. "A light to the nations": Consummation
- Bibliography

A. *TERMINOLOGY.* The Hebrew word for "prophet" is a common noun appearing more than three hundred times in the OT. It is applied to a remarkable range of characters appearing from Genesis (20:7) to Malachi (4:5), and to surprisingly disparate personalities from an Aaron (Exod. 7:1) to an Elijah (I Kings 17–19; 21), from the "true" to the "false" (e.g., I Kings 22), from the relatively primitive (e.g., I Sam. 10) to the relatively sophisticated (the Isaiahs, e.g.), from the highly visionary (see Ezek. 1–2) to the concretely ethical (Amos; or Nathan in II Sam. 12; or Elijah in I Kings 21), from the seemingly objective perspective (of an Amos, e.g.) to the intensely participating attitude (of a Jeremiah). And this is only to suggest the breadth of range of application of the term in the OT.

In the NT the term appears commonly in references to the prophets of the OT, and predominantly in Matthew and Luke-Acts. Both Jesus (Matt. 21:11; cf. Matt. 13:57; Mark 6:4; Luke 4:24) and John the Baptist (Matt. 11:7 ff and parallels) are regarded as prophets; Paul understands the continuation of the essential function in the life of the church (I Cor. 12; 14); Judas and Silas, e.g., are subsequently interpreted in this role (Acts 15:32); while the early Christian community at Antioch knows the presence of "prophets and teachers" (Acts 13:1). The NT prophet is in essential function like that of the OT: he conveys to them who will believe the divinely imparted meaning of history (cf. Acts 21:10). But signs of degeneration are suggested in Paul's implicit condemnation of extreme manifestations of prophecy (I Cor. 13); and it would appear that the role of prophet in the NT was in some expressions precisely what it was in its extreme ecstatic form in the OT.

1. In biblical Hebrew. The Hebrew term for "prophet," the only term appropriately so translated, is נביא. I Sam. 9:9 (itself of disputed date) recalls the fact that "he who is now called a prophet [נביא] was formerly called a seer [ראה]." The LXX, apparently presupposing a slightly different text, conveys the sense that the term "seer" was in the past simply a common, popular name for "prophet." The fact remains that one term is normative in the OT, and only one; and further, unfortunately, that all arguments of meaning etymologically derived are inconclusive. We simply do not know and cannot now determine the original meaning of the root. Two verb forms frequently appear (*pi'el* and *hithpa'el*), unquestionably derived from the noun, however; and both convey the meaning "to play the נביא role"—i.e., "to act the נביא part." It is a good, and now widely held, hypothesis that the lost Hebrew root is related to cognate Akkadian and Arabic words meaning "to call" or "to announce." Shall we then take the etymology, itself hypothetical, however plausible, in an active sense and understand the underlying meaning of the noun as "an announcer," or "the one who announces" the purpose and activity of God? Or is the passive sense primary? Is the prophet the recipient of the announcement of God? Is he then one who is called?

And even if we were certain of the original meaning of the root underlying the Hebrew noun as commonly used in the OT, could we take this as conclusive evidence of the basic understanding of the prophet in the middle centuries of the first millennium B.C.? Common words in long usage characteristically are etymologically difficult; and they carry with them a significant history which is at least as important as the etymology, even when the etymology can be reconstructed. The history of the word "prophet" is of the essence here. It is necessary that we see the prophet as he appeared and functioned in the community of ancient Israel.

2. In Greek. *See* PROPHET IN THE NT.

B. *MAJOR AND OFTEN CONTROVERTED RELATIONSHIPS OF THE PROPHET.* Apart from etymological considerations, which, as we have seen, are ultimately inconclusive, what is to be said of the OT prophet as he appears as person, even professional person, in the life and times of ancient Israel? What are his significant connections, associations, relationships, within the institutional complexes of Israelite society? What are for us the most instructive, if debated, areas in the prophets' relationships?

1. To the seer. The Hebrew terms חזה and ראה are both properly translated "seer," and both appear in contexts suggesting some parallel in function with the prophet. Outside Chronicles, which is relatively late and where, in any case, no significant occurrence of the terms appears, the first term for "seer" appears six times; the second, seven. In II Sam. 24:11 (of uncertain date, but not conventionally assigned to the A or early source in Samuel) "the prophet Gad" is "David's seer." In II Kings 17:13 it is the role of prophet and seer alike to warn Israel and Judah. In Isa. 29:10 the role is not identical, but the characteristic poetic parallelism of members puts prophet and seer again in the same essential function:

> The LORD has poured out upon you
> a spirit of deep sleep,
> and has closed your eyes, the prophets,
> and covered your heads, the seers.

In the same way, Mic. 3:7 couples seers and diviners (קסמים):

> The seers shall be disgraced,
> and the diviners put to shame.

The fifth occurrence of חזה, "seer," is in Amos 7:12, in the context of the narrative of the prophet's encounter with Amaziah, the priest of Bethel. Here, too, the effect is a near-equating of seer and prophet, since we read: "Amaziah said to Amos, 'O seer, go, flee away to the land of Judah, and eat bread there, and prophesy there." The verb תנבא is the common denominative form (probably) from נביא; and it is the clear inference of the verse that it is the appropriate function of the seer to act the part of the prophet. Whatever else is involved in Amos' response in vs. 14, it is clear that he means to repudiate Amaziah's implicit charge of professionalism, the strong insinuation that Amos has mouthed merely the "party line" of the seers and prophets.

In all these occurrences of חזה, with the single exception of Mic. 3:7, "seer" and "prophet" are, while not quite synonymous terms, descriptive of very similar functions.

The second term for "seer" (ראה) appears in Isa. 30:9-10 in parallelism with the first (חזה):

> They are a rebellious people,
> . . . .
> who say to the seers [ראים],
> "See not!"
> and to the seers [חזים],
> "*See* not for us [לא תחזו־לנו]
> that which is right;
> *speak* [דברו־לנו] to us smooth things,
> see [חזו] illusions!"

If there existed any significant distinction between the two terms for "seer," it is nowhere apparent in the OT; and this one passage in which both terms appear clearly equates the two designations of the seer.

If, now, we recall the statement of I Sam. 9:9 (*see* § A1 *above*) that "he who is now called a prophet [נביא] was formerly called a seer [ראה]," we are justified, in view of evidence thus far considered, in concluding that prophet and seer, by either designation, were understood as exercising in common the function of "seeing"—i.e., apprehending that which is not normally accessible, and "speaking forth," proclaiming, that which is thus seen and apprehended. The RSV renders Isa. 30:10, not in the language of rigid translation, which is obviously impossible, but in sympathetic and accurate interpretation:

> They are a rebellious people,
> . . . .
> who say to the seers, "See not";
> and to the prophets, "Prophesy not to us what is right;
> speak to us smooth things,
> prophesy illusions."

The seer-prophet apprehends, not necessarily that which is smooth, but emphatically that which is right. His function, prophetism, is never reception alone, but reception-articulation: to see is to prophesy!

It may be that the "office" of seer was chronologically prior to that of prophet as an indigenous institution in Israel. The designation of Samuel as "seer" (ראה) in the presumably relatively old narrative of I Sam. 9 (in the stream of literary criticism virtually unanimously ascribed to the "A" or early source in Samuel) would suggest this. The institution of Israelite prophetism, qua institution, was an appropriation —ultimately phenomenally modified, to be sure, but still an appropriation—transacted on the ground of Canaan; and it did not clearly emerge—again qua institution—until the tenth century at the earliest. As we shall see, that which responsibly wrought the vast modification of the institution of prophetism, as in time it passed from Canaanite to Israelite form, was present from the beginnings of Israel's existence; this is simply to say that something significant of the essence of established Israelite prophetism was present, clearly, from the Mosaic era and not impossibly also from the time of the patriarchs, although the latter cannot be determined.

But granting the possibility or even probability of the prior establishment of the seer in Israel, our biblical references strongly suggest more than a relationship of parent-child—and at once less. More, because the evidence we have just surveyed points to a continuing coexistence of seer and prophet, and constitutes contemporaneous estimates easily and naturally equating the two. Less, because Israelite prophetism, if "biologically" indebted to the institution of seer, is also in unmistakable descent from a prophetism, whatever its origin and distribution, already present in the Canaan occupied by the Israelites.

2. To contagious (ecstatic) prophetism. Prophetism in its Canaanite expression first appears in the OT in that relatively old narrative of I Sam. 9:1–10:16. In the hope of locating his father's lost asses, Saul and his servant have consulted the seer Samuel, who has not only reassured them on the score of the animals but has also anointed Saul "to be prince over his people Israel" (10:1). As sign and token of the validity of the performance, Saul is informed in advance of what is to take place; and precisely in fulfilment, "When they came to Gibeah, behold, a band of prophets met him; and the spirit of God [רוח אלהים] came mightily upon him, and he prophesied among them. And when all who knew him before saw how he prophesied with the prophets, the people said to one another, 'What has come over the son of Kish? Is Saul also among the prophets?' . . . Therefore it became a proverb, 'Is Saul also among the prophets?' " (10:10-12).

I Sam. 19:18-24 repeats the proverb in a more dramatic setting, with marked emphasis upon the highly contagious nature of the seizure and with an elaboration of its manifestation. Saul, in pursuit of the now outlawed David, who has found refuge with Samuel, sends a company to take David. "And when they saw the company of the prophets prophesying, and Samuel standing as head over them, the Spirit of God [רוח אלהים again] came upon the messengers of Saul, and they also prophesied" (vs. 20). Two subsequent companies are dispatched, and both remain, seized by the same contagion. Now Saul comes, "and the Spirit of God [the same Hebrew phrase] came upon him also, and as he went he prophesied [ויתנבא], until he came to Naioth in Ramah. And he too stripped off his clothes, and he too prophesied before Samuel, and lay naked all that day and all that night. Hence it is said, 'Is Saul also among the prophets?' " (vss. 23-24).

The relationship between these two narratives in I Sam. 10; 19 is uncertain. Critical-literary orthodoxy sees the second as a duplicate, later, and therefore unauthentic explanation of the proverb. For our purposes, this question is irrelevant. Both passages may be taken, regardless of relationship and date, as valid commentary on the phenomenon of Canaanite prophetism. This is patently a radically different office from that of the seer. Not now, certainly not yet, could one equate seer and prophet in Israel. If, as an actual item of pragmatic history, Samuel functioned both as seer (I Sam. 9–10) and as ecstatic prophet (I Sam. 19), the roles remained dual—they were in no sense interdependent. They are yet of very different stuff: the seer appears as an office in Israel long familiar and thoroughly at home, quite conceivably dating from pre-Canaan times; but this earliest reference to contagious prophecy conveys the atmosphere of the alien. Israel is not at home with it, and a solidly identified, unmistakable Israelite, this son of Kish, graces it strangely indeed: "Is Saul also among the prophets?" This institution is not yet appropriated, or, if in process of appropriation, not yet domiciled and certainly not yet integrated and adapted into the pattern of familiar Israelite existence.

What, here, is the content of the noun "prophet" and the verb "prophesy"? The phenomenon is induced. Samuel says to Saul: "You will meet a band of prophets coming down from the high place with harp, tambourine, flute, and lyre before them, prophesying" (I Sam. 10:5). It produces apparently a total transformation in personality: "You shall prophesy with them and be turned into another man" (vs. 6). It is created and sustained as a group phenomenon capable of being spread by contagion. And it is popularly interpreted as indicative of seizure by the Deity, in which regard the prevailing but not exclusive (10:6 reads "Spirit of Yahweh") divine name employed is the weak and colorless *Elohim*. This is, in any case, a different kind of seizure from the charisma, the more or less permanent endowment of a chosen person by the Spirit of Yahweh (e.g., I Sam. 16:13-14), a phenomenon which again belongs centrally to Israel and Yahwism.

The brilliant description of the frantic performance of the prophets of Baal on Carmel gives further definition to the phenomenon of prophesying. The contest between the prophets of Baal and the prophet of Yahweh (Elijah) is under way, and Baal's prophets have induced the seizure and are sustaining it in an effort to evoke a tangible response from their deity. Crying: "O Baal, answer us!" they perform a kind of limping dance, apparently; and as Elijah taunts them, their wild performance reaches its emotionally uncontrolled peak, when they "cut themselves *after their custom* with swords and lances, until the blood gushed out upon them" (I Kings 18:28). Noon, Baal's best and strongest hour, passes; but the prophets of Baal (note the language of the text) "continue to prophesy" (vs. 29). The RSV again gives, properly, a translation-interpretation: "They raved on." The verb must be paraphrased in any language which defines prophetism as one of the higher levels of revelation. But precisely so we are eloquently informed on the content of this original, alien, Canaanite phenomenon of prophet and prophetism. This is the prophet. This is his prophecy. This is to prophesy!

Now, if this is a far remove from the content of "seer" and "seeing" as briefly surveyed above, it is at least an equally far remove from the prophet and the prophetism exemplified even in an Ezekiel, to say nothing of an Isaiah! Whatever may be the ultimate judgment (if, indeed, such judgment is ever attained) with respect to the factor of "ecstasy" in the great prophets of Israel, it cannot legitimately be argued that their prophetism is in continuum with and perpetuates the phenomenon of Canaanite prophetism. Where is any significant biblical evidence that OT prophetism was predominantly manifested in a temporary and artificially induced state; that it was productive of a totally transformed personality; that it was a group-created and -sustained, and, as such, highly contagious condition induced by violent seizure by the Deity and involving the absolute suspension of rationality?

Early and late it has, of course, been so argued. The interpretation of OT prophetism as an essentially ecstatic phenomenon, differing not at all in this respect from the ecstatic prophetism characteristic of the ancient Near and Middle East, continues to be advocated especially by those who are persuaded of prevailing ancient Eastern institutional uniformity.

It is impossible to cover even superficially the broad scope and variation in interpretation of the relationship between the great OT prophets and the phenomenon of contagious prophecy. No evidence appears to justify the essential identity advocated by some. If the very term "ecstasy" is applied at all to the giant figures in the succession from Amos to Second Isaiah, we would want to insist on a distinction between ecstasy of the absorption type and that of the concentration type, and a very clear further distinction between the circumspective religion of the prophets and the more common ancient Eastern type of introspective, mystical piety. *Unio mystica* is quite alien to Israel. Let us admit of the ecstatic element in the OT prophet only and specifically in the sense of a profound concentration resulting in the suspension of normal consciousness and the total, if brief, interruption of normal sense perception.

Form-critical studies in the Prophets further enlighten the question of the nature and extent of the ecstatic factor in prophetism. The identification and analysis of a characteristic prophetic form of utterance (German *Gattung*) defines at once the content of that which is the product of "ecstatic" concentration and the nature, the extent, and the significance of the unmistakably nonecstatic, the role of the prophet's normally functioning senses. FORM CRITICISM points out a characteristic prophetic utterance in two intimately related parts: (*a*) the speech of invective (German *Scheltrede*), often extended and eloquent, commonly passionate and bitter, and always portraying, although in different ways, the mind and disposition and personality of the prophet, the *man* the prophet; (*b*) the second part, immediately following, consisting of the word of judgment (German *Drohwort;* "threat" is not quite adequate; perhaps "contingent judgment"), brief, pointed, powerful, devastating, sometimes terrifyingly impersonal, and characteristically devoid of personal-human animus. These repeatedly conjoined parts—the prophet's free invective as extended prelude to the fearfully compact pronouncement of divine judgment—constitute a basic pattern of prophetic speech.

This pattern can be abundantly illustrated, but perhaps nowhere more clearly than in Isaiah. Consider, e.g., the familiar prophetic outburst that begins: "Ah, Assyria, the rod of my wrath!" (10:5). The invective is here remarkably extended and continues with eloquent vigor through vs. 15. All this is the prophet's own utterance, and it would be absurd to contend that this (vss. 5-15) is the product of a supranormal psychological experience, the articulation of ecstatic reception. Here one witnesses a deftly balanced interplay of intellect and emotion and both not merely controlled but highly disciplined, responsive, obedient. The range in verbal mode testifies both to the vast breadth of prophetic sensitivities and to the high order of prophetic intelligence. Here one is confronted by responses at once brilliant and intuitive from the following successive perspectives: Yahweh, initiating Covenanter with David-Zion-Judah (vss. 5-6); an astute political observer who does not question the Lordship of Yahweh in history (vs. 7); a personified Assyria, with artful dramatic identification (vss. 8-11); the same faith-political position again, in central castigation of pride (vs. 12; this is a central theme of Isaiah); Assyria again, characterized in her own words and prophetically condemned in highly deft verbal form:

> My hand has found like a nest
> the wealth of the peoples;
> . . . .
> and there was none that moved a wing
> or opened the mouth, or chirped
> (vss. 13-14).

So to a conclusion in the full power of the prophet's own devastating sarcasm:

> Shall the ax vaunt itself over him who hews with it,
> or the saw magnify itself against him who wields it?
> (vs. 15).

By what possible definition of ecstasy can the skilfully combined elements of articulation in this speech be claimed?

But this is not to say that ecstasy in the sense of supranormal concentration plays no role. All this, in now conventional form-critical analysis, is a part of, a prelude to, and called forth by, the word of judgment, the *Drohwort* (vs. 16), which may very well have come to the prophet in ecstasy. The prophet's own speech of invective represents his considered application, timing, and interpretation of the Word of Yahweh (דבר יהוה), which he hears, or sees, or, involving all the senses directed totally inward, perceives. And psychologically, of course, this is the most important part of the prophetic utterance.

In the relationship between these two primary and inseparable parts of prophetic preaching the controversy over the role and nature of ecstasy is resolved. The prophet receives, possibly and even probably in ecstatic concentration, the actual *dābhār,* the real Word of Yahweh; and here we are confronted by a significant aspect of the phenomenon of revelation. But the Word thus received is not always precisely intelligible in a process of recall which requires its appropriation and integration in the rational mode; and the prophet, in consequence, feels himself called upon by means of the speech of invective to interpret and direct, to point and apply, the word of judgment, the revealed Word of Yahweh. And this he does, in most glaring contrast to the probable ecstatic state of the Word's reception, in a process of deliberation. The compact and certainly, on occasion, enigmatic divine Word is mulled over, reflected upon, wrestled with; and this process, involving the full range of the prophet's best rational powers, becomes his prophetic work, his ministerial task, his professional exercise. It is his own obligation to determine how, in what context, when and to whom, and in what way most effectively, this word of judgment is to be delivered. To this end he composes the speech of invective and places it immediately before the received word, characteristically marking the transition with some such particle as לכן, as in Isa. 10:16:

> Therefore the Lord, Yahweh of hosts,
> will send wasting sickness among his stout warriors,
> and under his glory a burning will be kindled,
> like the burning of fire.

The conventional literary-critical judgment may well be correct in assigning vss. 17-19 to secondary status; but its standard conclusions on vs. 16—that it is fragmentary, a corrupt text, distorted in transmission, etc.—are in fundamental error, resulting from failure to recognize what is suggested in the form-critical analysis of the prophetic utterance as *Scheltrede* and *Drohwort,* the deliberated and composed invective called forth by the received Word, the divine threat or judgment.

This smaller unit, vs. 16, toward which the whole passage is pointed (see *IB,* V, 240), is the reproduction—insofar as such is capable of reproduction—of the word received in prophetic concentration/ecstasy. It differs radically in verbal temperament from the speech of invective. What is perceived—is it heard, or seen, or must we say simply that it is sensed?—is a wasting sickness among warriors and a burning fire beneath a prideful magnificence. Whose warriors? Whose pride? Why is this so? How and when, and to what purpose, shall it be proclaimed? If the wasting and the burning, the sickness and the fire, are undefined certainties out of ecstasy, it is the prophet's hard task by sweat and tears to define the symbols of vision/audition and to determine and declare their meaning. This is not to exclude inspiration and revelation from the task, but this part of the prophetic function, the speech of invective, certainly does not have its origin in any kind of ecstasy.

The OT prophet no doubt underwent what not only we, but also his own generation, would see as outside the limits of normal experience. Perhaps in none of the great prophets was there a total absence of the supranormal psychological manifestation. But both form and content of OT prophetism stand in restraint of persistent tendencies to overstress the ecstatic element in the prophet.

3. To the cult prophet. The question persistently under debate is not whether there existed in ancient Israel associations of prophets. Groups or guilds of prophets are positively attested over the whole range of the history of the kingdoms from the time of Saul in the eleventh century B.C. until the fall of Jerusalem in the early sixth century B.C. (*see* PROPHETS, SONS OF). Nor is the question whether these associated professional prophets were related to the cultus and/or the court, and regularly discharged certain cultic professional functions. There is no reason to doubt that functionaries known as prophets were cultically institutionalized precisely as were the priests and other sanctuary personnel; nor is there any sufficient ground for rejecting the view that such prophets were attached to the temple in Jerusalem and that sometime before the time of the Chronicler (fourth or third century B.C.) the temple prophets became temple singers and merged with the other Levitical orders.

The function of OT prophetism in association with the cultus as institutionalized at sanctuary or court is not in question. The real question has to do with the extent of this association and the possibility that we actually have traces in the canonical OT of the work of such cultic נביאים. Despite excessive claims from some quarters, this possibility has been firmly established in the essentially form-critical studies of a number of scholars. *See bibliography.*

The real question has further to do with the possibility that the great prophets of the OT lived out their careers in such associations and were, in fact, themselves such associated cult functionaries. This aspect of the question of the relationship of the great OT prophets to cult prophetism remains complex, difficult of definition, and thoroughly vexed. We must reject extreme positions which seek to clarify all possible uncertainties in OT prophetism by analogy with associations of cultic personnel in ancient Mesopotamia, the broader West Semitic area, and Arabia. This basic assumption of a uniform religious phenomenology over the ancient East leads ultimately to the conclusion that the great prophets, without exception, are to be interpreted essentially and dominantly in terms of the common category of cult personnel. Not only Jeremiah and Ezekiel (whose possible official relationship to the temple has long been recognized in the fact that both were priests before they were prophets), but also Amos and Isaiah, are in this extreme position alleged to show complete identity with earlier cult prophets.

It is in order now to refer again to Amos 7:14 and to repeat in the present connection a comment already made with reference to contagious prophecy. In denying that he is (or "was") a prophet, Amos could also be rejecting any identification with cult prophetism as it may have been known, as it may have existed, at the Bethel sanctuary over which Amaziah presided.

In any case the interpretation of the great prophets as in no significant way different from the type of cult functionary widely present among the ancient Semites has been considerably stimulated by studies of cult festivals over the ancient Near East and, more than this, efforts to reconstruct from environmental analogy and form-critical analysis of OT texts, especially in the Psalms, Israel's celebration of the New Year and the Enthronement Day of the sacral king—the king in the role of Yahweh. The call of the prophet Isaiah (Isa. 6) has been analyzed in such a way as to make of the prophet a cult functionary whose call experience can be understood only in the terms and images of the annual festival of the enthronement of the sacral king, centering in the Jerusalem temple. In this view a basic cultic mode of thought is seen, common to the ancient Near Eastern culture, and Isaiah becomes one with the cult prophet, his words reflecting living cultic conditions, the core of which is the institution of sacral kingship.

The mass of alleged evidence in support of such identity is impressive, but its structure, upon examination, appears certainly at points to be rather insubstantial. Simpler interpretations of Isaiah's call are more natural. Further reservations appear when we look closely at another item of support for the thesis that the great prophets were merely cult prophets. It is adduced from the statement in Jer. 29:26 that the associations of כהנים ("priests") and נביאים ("prophets") were organized under a common leader entitled כהן, and the conclusion is regarded as axiomatic that the classical נביא too was a cult functionary. It is also presumably inferentially axiomatic that Jeremiah is to be professionally identified simply as one of the associated cult prophets.

The passage in question follows hard upon what is represented as an extended letter from Jeremiah (29:1-23) to persons exiled from Jerusalem in 597 B.C., a decade before the fall of the city. It purports to be the words of one Shemaiah, prominent among the exiles in Babylonia, addressed chiefly to Zephaniah, who is the senior priest, apparently, in charge of the temple priests in Jerusalem: " 'Yahweh has made you priest . . . , to have charge in the house of Yahweh over every madman who prophesies, to put him in the stocks and collar. Now why have you not rebuked Jeremiah of Anathoth who is prophesying to you? For he has sent to us in Babylon, saying, "Your exile will be long; build houses and live in them, and plant gardens and eat their produce." ' Zephaniah the priest read this letter in the hearing of Jeremiah the prophet. Then the word of Yahweh came to Jeremiah" (29:26-30). This has been seriously submitted as one of the weightiest pieces of evidence of identity of Jeremiah and the prophesying attendants on the cultus. But the passage does not even establish the cultic institution of prophetism (which may well have existed, to be sure, but which is certainly not necessarily referred to here), to say nothing of Jeremiah's integral relationship thereto! On the contrary, this passage would much rather appear to be designed as precisely a repudiation of identity between Jeremiah and any prophesying madmen, whether occasional ecstatic orators in the temple area or attached personnel—a possible distinction in no wise indicated in the passage. The powerful thrust of the passage, executed in devastating rebuke and at the expense of Shemaiah, is precisely the polarity between "prophesying" prophets and *the* prophet, between madness and "the Word of Yahweh."

We must reject, then, the view equating and identifying Yahwistic prophetism exemplified in the great OT prophets and that widespread prophetism of the cultic association. A line of crucial and emphatic distinction between the two appears in a study of late-eighteenth-century B.C. texts from Mari on the Upper Euphrates in which prophetlike persons appear a thousand years before the canonical OT prophets, persons much more closely resembling the continuing phenomenon of cult prophetism than Yahwistic prophetism. But even if we assume a historical connection between the messenger of God in the Mari Texts and the prophet of the OT, there is a clear difference in the content of the divine message. At Mari, it deals with cult and political matters of very limited importance. The biblical prophetic literature deals with the great contemporary events in the world as part of a process willed, and in its outcome determined, by God. In sharpest contrast to the prophetic phenomenon at Mari, the great prophets of the OT always speak in the name of Yahweh, whose will all powers of history serve.

And this appears to be an appropriate description of the contemporary contrast between the great prophet and the cult prophet—a striking and profound contrast in the content of prophetism. This does not preclude the possibility even of affiliation of some of the great prophets with cultic associations of prophets, much less the existence of such associations; but if such affiliation existed, it would nevertheless be wrong to assess and evaluate any of the "name" Yahweh prophets of the OT in terms of simple identity with the conventional cult prophet.

4. To the cultus. We cannot, on the other hand, go back to the opposite extreme, to the old view of the great prophets as grandly isolated figures having absolutely nothing to do either with a now divinely repudiated cultus or with any of the fundamentally apostate professional personnel of religion.

Scholarship of a preceding generation commonly characterized classical OT prophetism as strongly and predominantly anticultic; and in support of this interpretation, passages from Amos 5; Isa. 1 were frequently cited.

I hate, I repudiate [RSV "depise"] your feasts,
and I take no delight in your solemn assemblies.
Even though you offer me your burnt offerings and cereal offerings,
I will not accept them;
and the peace offerings of your fatted beasts
will I ignore [RSV "I will not look upon"].
Take away from me the noise of your songs;
to the melody of your harps I will not listen.
But let justice roll along [from גלל; RSV "roll down"] like waters,
and righteousness like an everflowing stream.
(Amos 5:21-24.)

What to me is the multitude of your sacrifices?
says Yahweh;
I have had enough of burnt offerings of rams
and the fat of fed beasts;
I do not delight in the blood of bulls,
or of lambs, or of he-goats.
When you come to appear before me,
who requires of you
this trampling of my courts? (Isa. 1:11-12.)

Your new moons and your appointed feasts
my soul hates.

. . . .

When you spread forth your hands,
I will hide my eyes from you.

. . . .

Wash yourselves; make yourselves clean;
remove the evil of your doings
from before my eyes;
Cease to do evil,
learn to do good. (Isa. 1:14-17.)

These lines have been repeatedly seized upon, with, by and large, the support of critical scholarship, as signifying the unqualified and categorical prophetic repudiation of the institutionalized expression of the religion of ancient Israel; as indicating the positive concern of Amos and Isaiah, imputed also to all the other great prophets, to cut out as a vile malignancy the totality of Israel's cultus. For many interpreters the prophets became the giant protagonists of the Ethical and the brilliant antagonists of any and all institutional religion. In this unfortunate and misconceived enthusiasm, the prophets were not only de-institutionalized, but de-theologized as well—Yahweh was reduced to the Ethical Incentive and the prophets themselves to social strategists—of course, endowed with genius power.

In more recent years scholarly convention has changed, although it is sadly apparent that the ethical culturalists, the anti-institutionalists, and all the other pro-neighbor-anti-God, pro-religion-anti-cult sentimentalists are either unaware of this or indifferent. The now prevailing and almost orthodox critical convention looks in broader and more realistic perspective at the whole structure of Israel's life and history. Expressions of prophetic impatience with or even intolerance of the cultus are seen now as castigation, not of cult qua cult, not of cultic practice per se, but of the cultus in its present guise—the even enthusiastic performance and perpetuation of formalized, regularized, prescribed outward acts of piety unsupported by the qualities of justice and righteousness revealed as at once the character and demand of the very Yahweh upon whom the whole cultus centers. The key to such an interpretation is seen in Isa. 1:13, deliberately omitted in the longer quotation from Isa. 1 above:

> Bring no more vain offerings;
> incense is an abomination to me.
> New moon and sabbath and the calling of assemblies—
> I cannot endure iniquity *and* solemn assembly.

The fault does not lie in the form itself; but the form becomes heinous when it is perpetuated in an existence whose total structure flatly contradicts that which is symbolized in the form!

In the broad perspective of the history of Israel and the role of prophetism, it becomes exceedingly difficult, if not impossible, to maintain an anti-cult and therefore anti-institutional prophetism in Israel. For the cult was from the beginning the tangible expression of the faith of Israel. From the beginning Israel could be Israel only cultically. Israel's understanding of her own divine creation in the exodus event was very early culticized in the Passover. She interpreted her prehistory, as seen in the persons of the patriarchs, in cultic form and continued to appropriate that prehistory cultically in the institution of circumcision. And in Israel's (or a crucial segment of Israel's) understanding of the David-Zion covenant, it was essential to celebrate and renew the meaning of this covenant in the great autumnal festival of New Year and Enthronement in the temple in Jerusalem. The cultus embodied the faith of Israel: it was the rehearsal of God's mighty deeds—and therefore his self-disclosures—of the past; it was, as appropriation of the past, also the dramatic conveyance of meaning in the present; and bringing past and present into the immediate continuum of identity, it appropriated in anticipation the future of the people of God and the history of God.

The cult of the contemporary Christian church is, no doubt, as justifiably castigated as that of ancient Israel. As Christmas and Easter are commonly celebrated by perhaps the majority of celebrants, any latter-day "prophet" might be constrained to cry out: "Thus says the Lord, 'I hate, I repudiate your feasts.' " But it is perfectly clear that the articulation and, indeed, the very preservation of Christian faith requires the cultic enactment of birth and death and resurrection—this appropriation of the past for the present and the consequent faithful union of time in hope and confidence in the future.

Yahwistic prophetism almost certainly remained in close rapport with the cultus. The relationship, indeed, was one of mutual indebtedness. It is obvious that the prophets were familiar with the ritual and meaning of the cultus; that they sometimes spoke in language borrowed from it; that they even quoted directly from its rituals, prayers, and liturgies; and that the role and meaning of the cultus was itself in turn influenced by prophetic interpretation. But it does not at all necessarily follow that the great OT prophet was a "cult" or "guild" prophet, a member of an "association" of cult prophets officially and professionally related to the cultic institution in manner and degree comparable to the priest.

And here it is to be observed that prophet and priest were not so positively, consistently, and inimically opposed as has sometimes been assumed. It is significant that the two figures most highly ranked in the traditions of Judaism, Moses and Elijah, are both remembered and recorded in the dual role of prophet-priest (Moses was a Levite [Exod. 2:1]; Elijah conducted sacrifice [I Kings 18:32 ff]). And at the lower end of the chronological scale, to mention only the most prominent possibilities in the classification of dual functionaries, one thinks of Jeremiah and Ezekiel, both of whom came out of priestly background (Jer. 1:1; Ezek. 1:3) and exhibit a prophetism patently extending, in some significant regards, the ancient dual form. There can be little doubt, in any case, that as a rule the representatives of Yahwistic prophetism saw themselves as essentially allied to the priesthood, as colleagues in a fundamentally common task—whether or not the priests would always accept the prophetic definition of alliance. And this recognition further defines and underscores the relationship of concern of the prophet to the cultus.

Form-critical studies have further confirmed the prophets' cultic orientation. Several shorter prophetic writings (among them Habakkuk, Nahum, and Joel; *see bibliography*) have been interpreted as virtually totally or in significant part produced out of cultic influence, in the liturgical style of the cult ritual. Elsewhere throughout the recorded prophetic utterances, there appear strong suggestions of conscious or unconscious adaptation of cultic ritual.

To entertain reservations as to the great prophets' membership in the guilds of professional cult prophets is in no sense at all, then, to cut the prophet off from influential and productive interrelationship in the cult. So far from repudiating the cultus, the prophet as exemplified in Second Isaiah can and does appropriate the liturgy known and in common use in the daily round of cultic exercise and, again in the case of Second Isaiah, make frequent appeal to familiar lines in the common ritual in the repeated words: "Have you not known? Have you not heard?" (Isa. 40:21, 28). The prophet must not be removed from his own original environment, his own broadly contemporaneous setting.

5. To the book. The interpretation prevailing in a past generation of the great OT prophet, the "name" prophet, as a grandly isolated figure has been attacked and largely routed from yet another quarter. Well into the twentieth century the most common designation, perhaps, of the great prophets was the term "writing prophets," used to distinguish OT prophets with "book" from those without. Elijah was a prophet. Amos was a writing prophet. It was taken for granted that writings bearing prophetic names contained for the most part the actual, written words of the prophet. Or, to say the same thing and make the same distinction, the "writing" prophets were "literary" prophets—they habitually addressed themselves, pen in hand, as it were, to the blank scroll; following an address—e.g., Amos' speech at Bethel—they carefully cast the utterance into written form themselves, being "literary" men; or, years later, they looked back on an event or experience or speech—e.g., Isaiah upon his call (ch. 6)—and "put it down on paper," so to speak, themselves "reducing" the remembered episode to writing. This firm assumption that the books of the prophets were, by and large, hand written by the great prophets themselves from the eighth to the sixth centuries (Amos–Second Isaiah) may be seen in interpretations of the prophets otherwise representing remarkably different perspectives.

As OT scholarship turned into the second half of the twentieth century, the earlier easy assumption of the literary activity of the "book" prophets gave way before an increasing emphasis—certainly exaggerated from some quarters—on the role of oral composition and transmission and the relationship of at least some of these prophets to circles of disciples. In a pattern demonstrated in vast variety over the whole of the ancient Near East, the great prophet played the role of master among a number of more or less formally organized disciples; and responsibility for the original, basic (oral) form of the present prophetic writings came to be fixed upon these disciples, who cherished, preserved, and "edited" the utterances of the master orally, not only during the prophet's lifetime but also for an extended period after his death. The present, written form of prophetic speech may be analyzed, assessed, and interpreted only in consideration of its significant history as oral formalization and entity.

Form criticism has contributed to this emphasis upon the role of oral tradition simply by demonstrating that much of profoundest meaning in the OT is related directly or indirectly to a continuing cultic activity which was largely sustained by the mouth and memory of successive generations of participants. Form criticism shatters the common assumption in the "literate" West that books and documents are created only by writers: the OT, form-critically regarded, is much more the creation of speaking worshipers and remembering worshipers, where the past is orally appropriated in the present and where the community, past, present, and future, is centrally oriented in a common cultus. In highlighting the real context in Israel's actual historical existence giving rise originally to the type of passage, or the passage itself, form criticism confronts us repeatedly with the fact that in the ancient East the role of written transmission, while significantly existent, remained sometimes and for long periods of time subordinate to that of oral transmission.

Studies in comparative culture in the ancient Near East, especially among Scandinavian scholars, have given further emphasis, sometimes in exaggerated form, to the place of oral tradition. One is hardly justified in saying that the written OT is a creation of the postexilic Jewish community and that of what existed earlier only a small part was in fixed written form. This is certainly to go too far. For a number of reasons which we cannot explore here, we should have to see the writing of tradition in Israel in impressive proportion from the tenth century B.C.; but we should at the same time insist on the continuing interrelationship between parallel written and oral formulation and transmission of material; and in the case of certain types—including the utterances of the great prophets—the dominant but not exclusive oral organization and preservation of the material down to the Exile.

Apparently there exists no real question that at least some of the "book" prophets lived and taught and proclaimed a message in the company of disciples. Nor can the function of oral transmission among and by these disciples be eliminated in the history of the organization and preservation of prophetic utterance in the OT. The question has simply to do with the evaluation of that which is received. To what extent may we claim to find, e.g., Isaiah in what is now recorded in the book of Isaiah; to what extent is the content of the prophetic book the product of the machinery of transmission? And this is in fundamental fact to ask the question, What is the relationship between the "book" prophet and the book; between the prophet and his disciples; between the disciples and the book? Have we been wrong for well over two thousand years, now, in assuming that the book of Amos or Jeremiah reflects the mind, personality, and utterance of a prophet Amos, a prophet Jeremiah? Shall we say with certain scholars that OT scholarship can never regain the *ipsissima verba* of OT personalities; or that any hard and fast distinction between what comes from the prophet himself and what had its origin in subsequent tradition is no longer possible?

Surely wrong is that picture of the great prophet as an absolutely solitary figure who is, himself alone, his own community and his own, only scribe. Probably wrong too is the assumption that the form in which we now receive the words of the prophets is with any consistency precisely the form in which it was initially cast by the prophet's own hand. But on the other hand, the evidence hardly justifies the conclusion that no prophet ever wrote anything himself; that we cannot make contact with and define an individual prophet because what is represented as his is in its indistinguishable entirety a traditio-historical creation, the product of decades and even centuries of a fluid, oral process.

In the case of the prophet Isaiah there is the strongest evidence both that the prophet himself wrote, and that on occasion he committed his message for subsequent delivery in oral form to a circle of disciples. In Isa. 8:1 we read: "Yahweh said to me, 'Take a large tablet and write upon it in common characters, "Belonging to Maher-shalal-hash-baz"'" And in Isa. 30:8:

> And now, go, write it before them on a tablet,
> and inscribe it in a book,
> that it may be for the time to come
> as a witness for ever.

Further support is inferential: it is most improbable—it is, in fact, inconceivable—that Isaiah was illiterate, whether or not, as has often been surmised, he was a member of the royalty of Jerusalem.

That there was also oral communication, transmission, and preservation of the words of Isaiah through a circle of disciples is made explicit in the text and almost certainly confirmed in Second Isaiah. Isa. 8:16-17 reads: "Bind up the testimony, seal the teaching among my disciples [בלמדי]. I will wait for Yahweh, who is hiding his face from the house of Jacob, and I will hope in him." The message thus sealed among Isaiah's disciples—the message, probably, of ultimate redemption—may well be intentionally identified as such and brought forth publicly some two centuries later by Second Isaiah, who probably means also to identify himself as a participant and member in that (continuing) discipleship to Isaiah of Jerusalem.

> The Lord Yahweh has given me
> the tongue of those who are taught [disciples; למודים],
> that I may know how to sustain with a word
> him that is weary.
> Morning by morning he wakens,
> he wakens my ear
> to hear as those who are taught [למודים].
> (Isa. 50:4.)

We need have no hesitation in endorsing the interpretation of these words of Second Isaiah as the prophet's wish to make it clear that he, a child of a later age, numbered himself with the disciples of Isaiah and wished to be numbered with them.

Indirect support for a circle of discipleship to Isaiah is given by the very nature of the book of Isaiah, the remarkable unity pervading its various major sections (including not only chs. 40–55, but also 56–66; 24–27) and, within chs. 1–39, the continuing debate as to the "authenticity" of numbers of passages, chapters, and sections. In view of the patent representation of a span of centuries within the present writing of the book of Isaiah, one wonders if the book in its present form does not constitute an effective testimony to a long-continuing discipleship to the prophet.

Isaiah's influence is, of course, widely felt in the OT outside the book of Isaiah. Subsequent prophets commonly betray Isaianic influence, resulting from a knowledge of Isaiah or "the Isaianic" as recorded in writing or in the living discipleship or both. The little book of Micah is especially interesting testimony. If chs. 1–3 (with the possible exception of 2:12-13) may with some confidence be assigned to the prophet Micah (either himself writing or as recorded by his own disciples), we sense in the two sections that follow, chs. 4–5; 6–7, a strong affinity with Isaiah and the circle of his disciples:

> But you, O Bethlehem Ephrathah,
> who are little to be among the clans of Judah [the reference is to the David-Zion covenant, characteristic of Isaiah],
> from you shall come forth for me
> one who is to be ruler in Israel,
> whose origin is from of old,
> from ancient days.
> Therefore he [Yahweh] shall give them [Judah] up until the time
> when she who is in travail has brought forth.
> . . . .
> And he shall stand and feed his flock in the strength of Yahweh,
> in the majesty of the name of Yahweh his God
> (Mic. 5:2-4; cf. Isa. 9; 11; 40:11).

> But as for me [Micah? Or a prophet from the Isaiah circle?],
> I will look to Yahweh,
> I will wait for the God of my salvation
> (Mic. 7:7; cf. Isa. 8:17).

We note also the eloquent anti-Assyrianism so strongly reminiscent even in expression (see Mic. 5:10 ff) of the Isaianic circle. If some of this material is from Micah, or if it fairly represents what was in fact the prophetic mind of Micah, we should have to deduce a relationship, direct or indirect, between Isaiah and Micah; and we should be justified in speculating that Micah was at least known to that circle and that he, too, held in faith the prophetic expectation of redemption beyond judgment.

The affinity between the book of Micah and the Isaiah circle is further marked by the presence of an oracle, the so-called "floating oracle," common to both books. In the context of the present discussion one would hazard the guess that it is not from Micah; that it may originate with Isaiah; that in testimony to its living oracular form, it appears in Mic. 4:1-3 in a form longer than that in Isa. 2:2-4; and that it is one more item in support and clarification of the phenomenon of prophetic discipleship and the joint role, in transmission of the content of prophetism, of the oracular and the written.

To the question of the relationship of the great prophet to the formation, transmission, and preservation of the content of his prophetic utterances, we repudiate any "either-or" answer. It may be that in this regard a distinction is to be maintained between two types of canonical prophetism, the liturgical and the so-called *diwan* type: the former, strongly influenced by established and probably recorded liturgy, represented in such books as Nahum, Habakkuk, Joel, and Second Isaiah, produced by writers and experiencing a predominantly written tradition from the very beginning; the latter, seen in prophets like Amos and Isaiah of Jerusalem, coming down out of a process of transmission largely oral.

Or, possibly, the important distinction is not so much typological as simply chronological; i.e., the role of oral transmission may well have been more prominent in the case of an Amos or an Isaiah because they were farther removed from the cataclysmic events of the sixth century. Whatever the actual circumstances of transmission of the various components of OT prophetism, it is essential to recognize the parallel role—at least as important; not necessarily less accurate, less authentic; and certainly, down to the sixth century, the more widely communicative—of oral formulation and transmission of the prophetic utterance. Even that which the prophet himself recorded with his own hand or directly through a disciple continued orally alive and was far more frequently communicated from tongue to ear than from scroll to eye; and certainly much (proportions here are and will remain absolutely indeterminable) of the great prophet's preaching and teaching achieved written form only after sustained oral life among the disciples of the prophets.

C. *PRE-AMOS PROPHETISM.* In distinguishing an essential prophetism present in ancient Israel long before the rise and development of the classical prophetic movement of the eighth and following centuries, we assume a core tradition of Yahwism maintained in an unbroken but fluid continuum from Moses to Malachi, and the expression of the centrally and characteristically prophetic bent of mind long in advance of and in necessary preparation for the emergence of classical prophetism. By this is meant precisely that the classical prophet, albeit proclaiming the new, was debtor, and certainly conscious debtor, to a core tradition already long established; also, that we shall of necessity, and with all propriety, define the essentially prophetic quality in pre-Amos Israel by the standards of classical prophetism. Further, no history, and perhaps least of all biblical history, may be appropriated in sterile chronological fashion: the past of a people, or any aspect of that people's past, must be interpreted in the light of what that past becomes. Not that we have or will necessarily ever have full knowledge of and total familiarity with the phenomenon of classical OT prophetism; but that the emergence of the form of prophetism may be addressed, apprehended, and assessed only against what we may know rationally and intuitively, of the matured phenomenon.

1. The essence of prophetism: Address to history. OT prophetism may always be—certainly it has been and is now—a subject of vigorous debate in interpretation, but on one point there is no possibility of dispute. The prophetic (be it invective or judgment, assurance or promise, cry of anguish or confession, symbolic act or relationship, or whatever), the characteristically prophetic phenomenon, always presupposes (consciously or unconsciously, made explicit or taken for granted, immediately relevant or only of indirect ultimate pertinence) the decisive impingement of Yahweh upon history. Where this sense of effective relationship of Yahweh to history is absent, prophetism is also absent. Where this is not only present but fundamentally present, where without this sense of the interrelatedness of history and deity the utterance or the situation or the personality or the relationship or whatever would be radically altered—there is prophetism.

2. Premonarchic "prophets." Down to the eighth century, the term "prophet" appears linked to the names of a considerable number of persons. Five prominent names from premonarchic times are associated by tradition with the title: Abraham (Gen. 20:7), Aaron (Exod. 7:1), Miriam and Deborah (both נביאה; Exod. 15:20; Judg. 4:4), and Moses (Deut. 18:18; 34:10; cf. Num. 11:26-29; 12:5-8). The term was hardly then in use—the opinion has already been hazarded above that it came to be applied to an individual prophet, in the classical sense of the term, sometime after Elijah's day; and it is strongly probable that these references reflect a time not earlier than the latter part of the ninth century. It is nevertheless interesting and instructive that these five are awarded the title. The patriarchal saga tends noticeably to impute to Abraham a sense of divinely ordained history, which in Israel could only be post-Exodus. A man who, as remembered in tradition, can in faith (Gen. 15:6) accept the divine promises detailed in Gen. 12:1-3, 7; a man who, in that same tradition, not only stands in awareness of Yahweh's radically purposive impingement on history but also understands himself in an absolutely central role therein—such a man profoundly deserves the ascription "prophet."

Aaron's case is less significant but also instructive: "And Yahweh said to Moses, 'See, I make you as God to Pharaoh; and Aaron your brother shall be your prophet' " (Exod. 7:1 [P]). Again the linking by later tradition of the name with the title presupposes the understanding of prophetism in fundamental terms of Yahweh's effective, effectual relationship to history; and it further conveys the definition of "prophet" as one who articulates the nature and meaning of the divine impingement from a remarkably intimate and knowledgeable position. This interpretation is confirmed and elaborated in Exod. 4:14 ff (E) when Yahweh responds with some heat to Moses' protest, only one of a series, that he is no speaker: "Is there not Aaron . . . ? I know that he can speak well . . . . And you shall speak to him and put the words in his mouth . . . . He shall speak for you to the people; and he shall be a mouth for you, and you shall be to him as God."

To Miriam tradition ascribes, correctly or incorrectly, the composition of the two lines which with brilliant economy convey the whole prophetic theology of the Exodus:

> Sing to Yahweh, for he has triumphed gloriously;
> The horse and his rider he has thrown into the sea.

Comparably and equally appropriately, tradition names Deborah a prophetess. If the song of Judg. 5 is hers, or if it conveys Deborah's essential interpretation of that victory, which is by no means impossible, then this is a case in which pragmatic history would confirm the relatively late bestowal of the title. Miriam and Deborah both are represented in celebration of what Yahweh is doing in concrete relationship to the historical existence of Israel.

In the case of Moses, it is significant that J does not anywhere apply the term "prophet" to him; and in this connection it is necessary to affirm the integrity of J as a documentary entity, the work—almost certainly written—of an individual, and dating probably from the tenth century. Adequate grounds never have existed for the repudiation of D and P as sources; and E continues to require symbolization, whether or not it ever existed originally as a separate and roughly parallel narrative source to J, or simply that Hexateuchal material later than J and earlier than D or P.

The term "prophet" is not applied by J to Moses because it was not so employed in the Yahwist's day. But it is another matter in E, which reflects that century between 850 and 750 B.C. It is of the highest probability that the entire E source stems from early prophetic circles. And here all the E material about Moses bears the marks of E's fundamental conviction about him, stated in Deut. 34:10-12: "There has not arisen a prophet since in Israel like Moses, whom Yahweh knew face to face, none like him for all the signs and the wonders which Yahweh sent him to do in the land of Egypt . . . , and for all the mighty power and all the great and terrible deeds which Moses wrought in the sight of all Israel." The prophetism which Moses represents is of a special sort; he is the performing prophet, actively intervening in events. In this Moses towers above all other prophets (Num. 12:7-8). If mediation and the intercessory are here (Exod. 18:19; 32:11-13; Num. 12:11), these qualities are heightened, augmented, in the extreme: in order to save Israel, Moses is prepared to become anathema for the people (Exod. 32:32; cf. Rom. 9:3).

In the Deuteronomic perspective Moses is the model, the ideal, prophet. In Deut. 18:18, he reports what Yahweh has told him: "I will raise up for them a prophet like you from among their brethren; and I will put my words in his mouth, and he shall speak to them all that I command him." A change has occurred in the century or two separating E and D: in the seventh century, emphasis has passed from the prophet's deed to the prophet's word. But while the role of the prophet as reflected in the ascription of the title to Moses is altered, the central character of prophetism is the same—concern with, and the demonstration of, the critical impingement of divine life upon human history.

All this is retrojection. In identifying Moses as a prophet, E and D inform us not so much about Moses as about the best expectations for the prophet in, respectively, the early eighth, perhaps, and the middle seventh centuries. We may surmise if we will—indeed, it was on this note that the discussion began—that the historical Moses appropriately heads the list of OT prophets, as we have here essentially and broadly defined the function; and that E and D were not wrong in making the identification. But for our purposes the great question of the "historical Moses" must be considered of secondary importance. The real issue is to comprehend the true nature and function of prophetism in ancient Israel. The impression of Moses which is ours from the biblical narrative is already prophetically interpreted (even in the Yahwist; since we shall presently see the Yahwist himself as an early historical figure in the total movement of prophetism); this is a Moses who lived in prophetic experience in Israel, not as a figure of the past, but as the first of a line of prophets who in the present are continuing to bring Israel up from Egypt into existence under God.

The primary effort to recover an exclusively pragmatic historical past in ancient Israel is always doomed; and more than that, it is, as effort, in error. The time span between the given "present" and the appropriated past varies widely, from the relatively narrow gap between David and the account of II Sam. 9–20 plus I Kings 1–2 to the re-creation of Moses in the Deuteronomic corpus, and, still later, the Priestly writing. But we have in the OT no past which has not already been appropriated in the present, and so appropriated as to *be* in the present, to *live* in the present. If the "historical Moses" is irrecoverable for this reason, so is the "historical Exodus"—it *was* past, but it now *is*. The event lives in faith. It has been culticized. As such, it is, psychologically speaking, not so much (if at all) merely memorialized as re-experienced—created and lived again. Moses and the Exodus and all the orally recorded past in the OT are received by us in a form of utterly penetrating and consistent "isness"; and there exists, therefore, no way under heaven to apprehend the now totally silent and absent "wasness." Prophetism is to confront man with God-in-history—it is timelessly the bringing of Israel, always now, up from Egypt into existence under God! So *is* Moses a prophet.

3. The Yahwist as prophet. This is something else. As an entity so termed we predicate a man, an individual. We presume further to place him within rather narrow limits of time, considering the relative antiquity of his epoch—i.e., before the death of Solomon and, at the earliest, the final years of David's reign. We predicate, in addition, a historian; no mere chronicler of the past, but one who addresses and is overwhelmingly addressed by the present; who is impressed with what is for him the indelible meaning of the present; who comprehends this meaning as form, the existent form of Israel; and who, in order to articulate this form, spontaneously expands its meaning into a past already present and, in rare, involuntary bursts, into a future equally present but relatively imperceptible.

The Yahwist is known to us, not as one who like Moses is appropriated from the past, but as himself an appropriator of the past. His work, which constitutes the basic structure of the Hexateuch, is all we know of him; and it is a creative production whose creativity inheres, not in verbal, but in structural composition: by and large he reproduces what has already earlier been produced, and achieves by inspired selection, juxtaposition, and broadly conceived arrangement of varied existent stuff an artistically and theologically unified "history"—an astonishingly coherent and brilliant definition of the essential form of Israel apprehended in a continuum of meaning from the present to the past and back again. If the irrecoverable and undefinable but certainly historical thirteenth-century Moses was among the prophets, as his easy appropriation thereto would lead us to suspect, he is followed (and who is to say how many of these may in fact have come between?) by this nameless, unappropriated appropriator known to us, significantly, by the divine name ("the Yahwist," from "Yahweh"), this tenth-century proclaimer of Yahweh's critical impingement upon history, this prophetic delineator of Israel's form and meaning in terms of emergence from Egypt into existence under God.

Regarded for the prophetic quality, the Yahwist and, to hazard again the unhazardable, Moses the artifact are both confronted by an impingement of the divine life upon history which ruthlessly frustrates any exclusive concentration upon the life of Israel. It is surely wrong to argue, as some do, that Hellenism created the idea of ecumenical history. The Greek language and Hellenistic culture provided the term and a specialized and formalized content; but ecumenicity inheres, if in quietness and subtlety, in the Decalogue and later receives its first emphatic description of meaning—long before the origin of the mere term—in the Yahwist's work, which proclaims in range from whisper to shout the central thesis of Yahweh's impingement on Israel, to be sure, but also —such is the historical form of Israel and its dependent meaning—upon the world, the whole household of God. The primeval history (the Yahwist's material in Gen. 2-11) and its structural relationship to the story of Abraham and all that follows proclaims the Yahwist's astonishingly sweeping ecumenical perspective.

His place in that tradition of a broadly defined Israelite prophetism, then, is sure and even essential; for acknowledgment of the Yahwist renders fully credible and the more comprehensible the roles in prophetism of Samuel, Nathan, and Elijah, as well as those of the classical prophets from Amos to Second Isaiah.

4. Prophets to kings. Six particularly important prophetic figures appear from the eleventh to the ninth centuries—Samuel, Nathan, Ahijah in the tenth century; Elijah, Micaiah, and Elisha in the ninth. To all of them the term "prophet" is applied.

a. Their relationship to contemporary institutional prophetism and to subsequent classical prophetism. The institution of prophetism as a group phenomenon in Israel apparently has its origin immediately before and during the creation of monarchy; and the first application of the term נביא, "prophet," was no doubt to members of such groups (I Sam. 10). If I Sam. 19:18-24 is authentic in suggesting Samuel's integral relationship to such a group, Samuel may have been contemporaneously known as a prophet. But this is uncertain. With rare exception he is represented as a singular figure, functioning in the fashion of a judge or priest or seer; and when a narrator tells us in I Sam. 9:9 that although Samuel was known as a seer then, we should now (in the narrator's somewhat later time) call him a prophet, we assume that Samuel was never primarily identified with the early Israelite institution of group prophecy and was not commonly, if at all, so termed by his contemporaries. This interpretation runs counter to the oftentimes prevailing view of a Samuel who is what he is predominantly as a result of his membership in the associated prophetism of the day. There can be no doubt, of course, that Samuel was in accord with the radical political implications of their fierce loyalty to Yahweh; that he was allied with them in setting up the monarchy; and that there was mutual influence between Samuel and the emerging prophetic institution. But the whole Samuel cannot thus be explained and/or dismissed.

David brought the institution into the court, on how large a scale we do not know. If Nathan also consistently appears in a purely singular role, his official status and title, prophet, is derived from a prophetism thus institutionalized and perhaps in the court initially only in the person of Nathan. The regularity and varying contexts of the designation "Nathan the prophet" suggest an official title, as does the repeated coupling of the phrase with other officially titled persons in I Kings 1.

Ahijah (called a prophet in I Kings 11:29; 14:2, 18) was commonly known as Ahijah the Shilonite (I Kings 11:29; 12:15; II Chr. 9:29; 10:15; cf. also I Kings 14:4). We do not question the appropriateness of the term as applied to him, but, on the example of Samuel and Nathan, we suspect that if he was called a prophet by his contemporaries, it was, again, because of regularized status as a professional, in this case presumably membership in an association of prophets at or near Shiloh.

In the comparable case of Elijah, the evidence is strongly against his having been in his own day commonly termed a prophet, and we suspect the same of Ahijah. Neither prophet, it seems, was identified with any form of professional prophetic organization, and neither was consequently so termed. In the Elijah texts (I Kings 17-19; 21; II Kings 1-2) the name Elijah occurs alone except in I Kings 17:1; 21:17 (vs. 28 is certainly secondary); II Kings 1:3, 8 (which is also from later narrators than the original, basic story of I Kings 17-19; 21). In all these it is "Elijah the Tishbite," as in the preceding century it was "Ahijah the Shilonite." In I Kings 18:36 only, "Elijah the prophet" occurs, and with most commentators "the prophet" should be omitted. In I Kings 18:22: "Elijah said to the people, 'I, even I only, am left a prophet of Yahweh; but Baal's prophets are four hundred and fifty men.' " In I Kings 19:14 (also vs. 10, but by error from vs. 14) Elijah bitterly protests that "the people of Israel have . . . slain thy prophets with the sword; and I, even I only, am left; and they seek my life, to take it away." The narrator understands that Elijah assumes professional status when so precisely cast in opposition to the group-functioning prophets of Baal; and that sympathetic identification is appropriate when the banded Yahweh prophets are under harassment from the vigorous proponents of Baal. The statement in the commission to Elijah that "Elisha . . . you shall anoint to be prophet in your place" (I Kings 19:16) is itself, and in full context, saturated with problems and certainly late.

The epoch which Elijah shared with Ahab and Jezebel, the second quarter of the ninth century, had its prophets, so designated, in profusion, adherents both of Baal and of Yahweh (I Kings 18; 20; 22), and in professional group association both with sanctuary and with court. The term "prophet" probably referred to these in its common and primary connotation and was therefore only later applied to Elijah in an age when the definition of the word had been modified and broadened to include the singular, classical prophet.

In the case of two other ninth-century prophets, Micaiah (I Kings 22) and Elisha (II Kings 2-9; 13), there is no reason to doubt that they were so designated by their contemporaries, since both appear—if in exceptional roles—in association with group prophetism: Micaiah with Ahab's official court prophets, and Elisha with the probably cult-related "sons of the prophets" at Bethel (II Kings 2:3),

Jericho (II Kings 2:5), and Gilgal (II Kings 4:38; cf. 6:1). These "sons of the prophets" (first appearing in Elijah's day in I Kings 20:35) are in direct descent from the phenomenon of the "band of prophets" encountered more than a century earlier in the Saul narratives (I Sam. 10:5, 10) and are no doubt closely related to varied forms of the practice of group prophetism occurring without interruption between.

Samuel was Samuel, or the Seer; Ahijah was probably simply Ahijah, or the Shilonite; and Elijah was Elijah, or the Tishbite—prophets in truth they were, as subsequently seen from the vantage point of the matured form of classical prophetism, but hardly so conventionally identified in their own day. Nathan, Micaiah, and Elisha on the other hand—certainly also prophets in the later sense—were contemporaneously known as prophets, since to be a prophet was to exist in professional association and relationship.

It is only so that the categorical protest of an Amos can be understood. Amos in the middle of the eighth century reflects the common definition of "prophet" as denoting professional association, down to this time deemed necessarily neither bad nor good. Group prophetism has thus far been both of Yahweh and of Baal; and as of Yahweh, neutral as associated with Saul, "good" as associated with Obadiah (I Kings 18:13; cf. 19:14) and Elisha, and on the whole "bad" as contrasted with one of their own number, Micaiah, in relationship to Ahab's court (I Kings 22). "Amaziah said to Amos, 'O seer, go, flee away to the land of Judah, and eat bread there, and prophesy there; but never again prophesy at Bethel. . . .' Then Amos answered Amaziah, לא־נביא אנכי ולא בן־נביא אנכי [i.e., 'I am not a prophet, and I am not a son-of-a-prophet']." It is, of course, possible to translate "was" rather than "am." Grammatically it may even be equally possible, as some have insisted. But contextually, it does not appear to be at all natural, despite valiant efforts to make it appear so. Amos denies, not necessarily in heat, and certainly not in necessary repudiation of the institution of prophetism, that he himself represents what Amaziah has just imputed to him. He has had no contact with the professional, associated prophets: "Yahweh took me from following the flock, and Yahweh said to me, 'Go, prophesy to my people Israel' " (Amos 7:15). His action here at Bethel is inspired out of this personal confrontation with Yahweh, not in any group apprehension. Not that institutional prophetism may not and does not have this valid, authentic apprehension; nor that Amos is unwilling to be cast in a prophetic role (Amos 3:3-8 indicates the contrary!); but simply and exclusively that the group phenomenon happens not to be his origin, as charged by Amaziah.

Evidently a change in the content of the term "prophet" occurs with Amos, and men of prophetic temperament and function but without professional affiliation who preceded him came only after him to be called by this term. With Amos, and no doubt in retrospective regard of earlier prophets similarly confronted by the "word of Yahweh" (especially Samuel, Nathan, Elijah, and Micaiah), the term and office of "prophet" was expanded to include him who without benefit of group stimulation heard the Word of Yahweh and who, knowing that the Lord Yahweh had spoken, could but prophesy (see again Amos 3:8).

b. Their relationship to king and Word. If these remarkable prophetic figures from the tenth and ninth centuries instruct us in the historical delimitation of the term "prophet," they inform us in other significant ways of the emergent form of classical prophetism. Although they differ radically from one another and appear in widely varied contexts, in two regards these early prophets bear the sure evidence of a prophetic continuum from premonarchic times and possibly even from the age of Moses to the decay and collapse of monarchy in Israel and on into the days of Jewish reconstruction. These prophets from Samuel to Elisha brilliantly testify to their place in the roster of prophets in their address to history, their passionate conviction that Yahweh's existence impinges with radical effect upon the political institution. Samuel, Nathan, Ahijah, Elijah, Micaiah, and Elisha—all, without exception—are intimately related to the life of the state, are crucially involved in the most decisive crises of history, and are in psychologically naked contact with the king—that symbol in Israel embracing the absolute totality of the being of a people.

This is the first regard. The second consistently prophetic quality appearing in this pre-Amos succession of prophets and setting them decisively apart from the prevailing institutionalized forms of prophetism is their relationship and responsibility to the דבר יהוה, the Word of Yahweh, their response to it and proclamation of it. In all these (it is weakest, to be sure, in Elisha) the address to history takes its content from the Word, and the divine impingement upon history is made articulate and interpreted by the same Word. The Word may not yet be as clearly and intentionally defined as the entity, the effective, effecting, efficacious singularity which it is articulately apprehended to be by the sixth century:

> For as the rain and the snow come down from heaven,
> and return not thither but water the earth,
> making it bring forth and sprout,
> giving seed to the sower and bread to the eater,
> so shall my word be that goes forth from my mouth;
> it shall not return to me empty,
> but it shall accomplish that which I purpose,
> and prosper in the thing for which I sent it
> (Isa. 55:10-11).

But at the same time one must insist that this definition of the concept of the Word is possible only as the result of an extended period during which it was essentially, if increasingly, so understood. The first OT use of the דבר יהוה, the "Word of Yahweh," as an effecting instrumental entity appears in Gen. 15:1, 4, where, in all probability, the E material is first employed. More pointedly, this concept of the דבר יהוה is expressed in terms strikingly anticipatory of Second Isaiah, and in present form also from the E material, in the Balaam oracle of Num. 23:19:

> God is not man, that he should lie,
> or a son of man, that he should repent.
> Has he said, and will he not do it?
> Or has he spoken, and will he not fulfil it?

The sense of the divine word as accomplishing its own content is further emphasized in the next verse (unless one takes the LXX reading in part *b*, which has "Balaam," not "Yahweh," as subject; see *IB*, II, 257):

> Behold, I received a command to bless:
> he has blessed, and I cannot revoke it.

Both these passages seem to reflect Israelite prophetism no later than the ninth century; and it is not at all impossible that the Balaam oracle rests upon a substantial original form even several centuries earlier. In any case, there is no justifiable reason for questioning the central function of the Word in the succession of prophets beginning with Samuel and Nathan.

Samuel appears in the narratives which bridge the epoch of the judges and the time of the established monarchy. The present narrative structure in the books of Samuel appears to be the result of combining multiple and, at points, radically differing strata of tradition (see *IB*, II, 855-75); but despite striking ambiguities in the portrayal of Samuel, the stories about him present in two crucial regards a unified impression: he played the most instrumental single role in the ascendancy and demise of Saul as first king in Israel; and, more than any other man, Samuel bears responsibility for the inauguration of David and the Davidic dynasty. When Moses is interpreted as a performing prophet—as a prophet whose primary medium is not utterance, but action—we wonder if the typological characterization is not, at least in part, dependent upon the figure of Samuel. In any case, even when allowances are made for heightening and expansion inherent in the nature of the tradition, even with the admission of an ultimately irrecoverable "photographic" image, Samuel and Moses are in a unique class as performers on behalf of Yahweh. One stands in awe when regarding what must have been their extreme output of energy; the one is instrumental in the creation of a people, a nation; the other in the establishment of a political state.

Like Moses, Samuel is an appropriated figure. His revolutionary historical performance is also recorded for its "isness," the living effects of Samuel's existence in the continuing present. No doubt at all that earlier and later strata of tradition are now combined in the single account and that one traditional opinion assesses present monarchy as in divine intent beneficent, another as negative divine judgment already taking effect: it is unmistakable that this conflict in interpretation has been imposed upon the traditional portrayal of Samuel. Equally clearly—it could not have been otherwise—the image of a prophetic form emergent in the century or two following Samuel has inevitably been retrojected upon Samuel in the course of a continuingly fluid process of transmission (especially conspicuous in I Sam. 1–3; 7). It should nevertheless be maintained (and for Moses as well) that while the image is in no sense photographic, while any actual and precise "vital statistics" are irredeemable, a portrait remains. The artist, tradition, has quite properly been involved in the creation of image, exercising an appropriate interpretive function—but tradition has produced the portrait working originally from a life model, from a living presence.

It is tradition, no doubt, that ascribes to the person of Samuel a relationship to "the Word of Yahweh" as that Word was only subsequently emergent (e.g., I Sam. 1:23; 3:1, 7, 21). But this is to use a more refined and deeply connotative language to describe a phenomenon pragmatically existent in Samuel and, in tradition's nature and course, indescribable in any other terms. There can be no doubt that Samuel was Samuel because of the Word of Yahweh and that the interpretive artistry of tradition has at areas in the portrait coincided with what would be the photograph, as, e.g., when Samuel says to Saul: "Tell the servant to pass on before us, and when he has passed on stop here yourself for a while, that I may make known to you the word of God [דבר אלהים]" (I Sam. 9:27). We further take tradition's interpretation to be absolutely sound—i.e., we take the portrait as essentially true—when it ascribes to Samuel that which in essence if not in form, in content if not in vocabulary (but see I Sam. 15:10), could have been revealed to the prophet only through the medium of the Word:

> Has Yahweh as great delight in burnt offerings . . .
> as in obeying the voice of Yahweh?
> Behold, to obey is better than sacrifice,
> and to hearken than the fat of rams
> (I Sam. 15:22).

These words are thrown at Israel's first king, Saul, who becomes King Saul at the instigation of the same Word through the same prophet. The prophet continues, prophet to king, defining another decisive turning point of history, again in content if not in vocabulary revealed in the Word-to-the-prophet:

> Because you have rejected the word of Yahweh,
> he has also rejected you from being king
> (I Sam. 15:23).

If we have doubts, then, of the precise vocabulary, or if we question the use of this stylized phrase "the Word of Yahweh" with this specific implicit content before, at the earliest, the time of Elijah (in connection with whom, we suspect, the heretofore relatively informal phrase became formalized), we do not question the functioning of the Word in the life and time of Samuel, and his essential awareness of its entity and nature. In Samuel the effective juxtaposition of the life of Yahweh upon the course of history begins to come to human consciousness and articulation in the form of the Word of Yahweh to the prophet.

Nathan appears in Samuel and Kings in only three scenes, but each time in immediate relationship to King David. In II Sam. 7 he responds to the King's expressed desire to build an appropriate "house" for the ark of God (cf. I Chr. 17, the only one of the three scenes reproduced by the Chronicler; see also the Chronicler's reference to the "book of Nathan" in I Chr. 29:29; II Chr. 9:29). In II Sam. 12 he confronts David with the King's heinous performance in the Bathsheba affair, and pronounces Yahweh's judgment on king and kingdom. Finally, Nathan appears in that crowded scene of David's last recorded official day, I Kings 1, to play a decisive role in Solomon's (as opposed to Adonijah's) accession.

In the present form of the narrative the Word of Yahweh is prominently featured in the first two scenes, no doubt bearing, as in the case of the Samuel stories, the sense of a definition only later fully crystallized. The Word is equally crucial in the third scene by its very absence. In the first scene, the Word countermands the first affirmative response of Nathan to David (II Sam. 7:4 ff). It is entirely at the inspiration and direction of the Word that the prophet lays devastatingly bare David's double violation of the Decalogue; and it is the content of the Word which he then pronounces in judgment ("Thus says Yahweh!" II Sam. 12:7, 11). Where the Word is so indispensably cast in the first two scenes, it can be no accident of the text that there is not even a suggestion of Nathan's acting as the instrument of the Word in the third scene: as in the opening of scene 1 (II Sam. 7:1-3), the recorders of the drama, at least, understand here a Nathan again acting on his own. In I Kings 1–2 (a continuation of that incomparable narrative of II Sam. 9–20) the failure to affirm Solomon's accession by the Word must constitute at least an editorial indictment of Solomon and the conspiracy which made him king. The intentional silence with reference to the Word testifies further to the sharpening entity of the Word in the tenth century (II Sam. 9–20; I Kings 1–2 can hardly be later).

Still in the tenth century, it is king and Word brought into radically effective concord through the prophetic function of Ahijah the Shilonite (I Kings 11:29 ff; 12:15). Another of OT history's most decisive and consequential events, the secession of the N tribes and the establishment of two political states in the place of one, is instigated by the Word through the prophet Ahijah to the king-to-be, Jeroboam I. *Ca.* a century later, another king-to-be, this time Jehu, is confronted by the Word (II Kings 9:6). Elisha and his "young man, the prophet," act upon and pronounce what is represented as the Word with, again, radically effective results. In view of Jehu's subsequent reprehensible behavior and classical prophetism's ultimate repudiation of any true relationship between Jehu and the Word (Hos. 1:4), one would judge either that this word was not the Word or that Jehu viciously appropriated the divine Word in Elisha to his own brutal ambitions. The first alternative is perhaps editorially entertained: Elisha is, like Nathan in II Sam. 7:1-3, represented as acting on his own in dispatching one of the prophets to Jehu (II Kings 9:1).

The imposition of Word upon king is sharply attested again in that brilliant scene immediately preceding the death of Ahab in the middle of the ninth century (I Kings 22). The Word through Micaiah works its radical historical effects, and another prophet is instrumental in the efficacious juxtaposition of divine life and will upon human events.

King and Word are brought into most moving conflict in the collision of Ahab and Elijah earlier in the second quarter of the ninth century. The Word to David through Nathan involved the dual indictment for adultery and murder; to Ahab through Elijah, it is murder and theft: "Have you killed, and also taken possession?" But in Elijah the Word becomes more consciously an instrumental entity; and for the first time (in the narratives of I Kings 17–19; 21) we suspect a contemporaneous apprehension of the Word by a prophet that is in substance the Word of classical prophetism.

Note first the relative frequency and consistency of the term "the Word" (of Yahweh) in the Elijah narratives: I Kings 17:2, 5, 8, 16, 24; 18:1 (31, 36, secondary?); 19:9 (the notice is, of course, premature, copied from 19:14, where, however, we should certainly read, not: "He said," but, as in 19:9: "The Word of Yahweh came"); 21:17 (28 secondary?). Note also that, as in the records of later classical prophetism, the Word here conveys the sense of a formula, a known formula, the content and nature and potency of which are widely familiar now. Note further that the Word is associated not only with the king but with the people as well. It creates (I Kings 17) and terminates (ch. 18) the drought, a judgment upon people as well as king. It is surely instrumental in the prophet's indictment of the Carmel assembly (I Kings 18:20-21): "How long will you go limping with two different opinions?" (cf. Elijah's lament in 19:14 that the people of Israel have forsaken Yahweh). And it is, of course, the Word which sends the prophet back from Horeb (I Kings 19:15 ff), not in the role of palace prophet to the king and queen, but to minister again to the nation, in the good company of multitudes still faithful to Yahweh.

In the manner of the Word to Samuel (I Sam. 15) and Nathan (II Sam. 12), the instrumental Word is applied through Elijah in judgment of the king (I Kings 19:17 ff). Elijah belongs to the company of preclassical prophets from Samuel to Elisha. But at the same time and more than any other in the company, he anticipates in two regards that succession of prophets beginning with Amos to which he is in a peculiar way the forerunner. Elijah alone of all prophets properly belongs to both groups. In Elijah the Word has attained substantially full prophetic definition and form. Through him the Word finds its mature prophetic expression and application, not merely or even principally to the king, but to the nation, the whole people of the covenant. Yahweh's Word impinges now decisively upon the history of Israel with such force as implicitly to involve all history, or upon the royal house with such intensity as to judge all men. Jesus condenses the OT prophetic ethic (quoting from Deuteronomy and Leviticus) when he declares that "all the law and the prophets" depend upon love of God and love of neighbor (Matt. 22:35-40; cf. Mark 12:28-31). But in reality he reaches ultimately back to Elijah, in whom for the first time in biblical record these two propositions find impassioned, if implicit, expression in a single life. The divine life confronts, is involved in, decisively qualifies, the life of history. To repudiate it ("The people of Israel have forsaken thy covenant"), to delimit it or run in the face of it ("Have you killed, and also taken possession?"), to attempt to compromise with it ("How long will you go limping with two different opinions?"), is not mere folly, but unqualified disaster, the loss of meaning and fulfilment, the imposition of chaos and death. In the passionate intensity of Elijah all men and all history are implicitly embraced. It remains the task and function of classical prophetism to make concrete the decisive involvement of Yahweh in existence.

D. *THE CONTENT OF FAITH OF CLASSICAL PROPHETISM.* In that succession of prophets beginning about a century after Elijah there is that which is distinctly new. There is the new that is external, the emergence out of pragmatic history, out of the actual course of real events, of that which earlier was not, and could not have been anticipated. This is the new of the new page in history, the new of the new epoch—created out of the old, surely, but materializing as one of an inconceivably broad range of inconceivable possibilities. In Israel in the eighth century it was anew charged with tragedy.

There is, of course, also the internal new, but inseparable from the external. For the classical prophets, Israel's historical existence, first brought into being out of Egypt, is seen now to be turning back again into that same essential abyss, that same chaos, that same unendurable meaninglessness. For those of the prophetic disposition from Moses to Elijah and Elisha, Egypt lay only behind. Now, for that same prophetic intuition, it was both before and behind. Out of an Egyptian existence formless and void Yahweh had created for Israel a life relatively formed and ordered; and, at least in the popular mind, this definition of an existence in reality sometimes highly tenuous was nevertheless justification enough, meaning enough, for historical consciousness. In Israel's core of Yahweh loyalists the meaning of the present was, of course, never so superficially determined, but was rather appraised in terms of Yahweh's participation in Israel's past, his impingement upon the present, and his ultimate purpose in the future. But until the eighth century the future, while uncertain and often highly insecure, could be seen as in continuum with the present, as holding in prospect essentially more of the same. In such a state of suspended existence, as it were, the question of meaning out of the past and purpose in the future was no doubt kept alive in the preclassical circles of prophetism; but that same question was impossible of meaningful imposition upon the popular mind, and even in prophetic thought it was apparently easily capable of containment. Of the three promises to Abraham—nation, land, and universal blessing (Gen. 12:1-3, 7)—the third clearly proved to be the most difficult to sustain in faith.

The new, both of the external history and of the related internal prophetic mind of classical prophetism, was initially produced, beginning in the middle of the eighth century, simply by the aggressive ambition of Assyria, backed, for the first time in several centuries, with leadership and power to implement it. Tiglath-pileser III assumed the throne of Assyria in 745 B.C., as the first of an uninterrupted series of great soldiers on the throne of Assyria. He and his immediate successors quickly brought the Neo-Assyrian Empire to the peak of its power and created a political-military institution which for the first time united almost the whole of the ancient Orient under Assyrian rule. Indeed, within a single decade of the accession of Tiglath-pileser all the oriental world that he wanted was clearly his, either in fact or in potential. By 721, when the N kingdom of Israel fell to Assyria, any hopes of political existence independent of Assyria were simply fatuous. From Tiglath-pileser's days (745-727), through the successive reigns of Shalmaneser V (727-722), Sargon II (to 705), Sennacherib (to 691), and Esarhaddon (to 669), Assyria's position of world domination was beyond serious challenge.

If the succeeding reign of Ashurbanipal (669-632)—unlike his predecessors a patron, not of the art of war, but of literature—was the beginning of the undoing of Assyrian world rule; if Assyria succumbed to the vicious powers of the Chaldeans out of Babylon, the Medes out of the mountains of Iran, and the bands of Umman-manda (apparently Scythians) from the steppes of Russia; if the long death agony of Assyria was finally ended in decisive battles of 612 and 610 B.C.—this provided at best only a brief respite, not any fundamental departure, from surviving Israel's (Judah's) untenable position. For now Assyria's position in the world was simply appropriated by Neo-Babylonian power. The political center of the ancient Near East was moved from Nineveh to Babylon. The sentence of political death—that persistent, profoundly unpopular theme in the proclamation of the classical prophets, with its concomitant anguished promise of destruction and exile, of the chaos of the formless and the meaningless, of symbolic descent again into Egypt—was now imposed in the first two decades of the sixth century by Nebuchadnezzar. The cycle was complete. Israel once more became without form and void. She was once more swallowed up in the chaos of captivity. Having gone from uncreation to creation, she was now relegated again to the uncreated.

Classical prophetism rises, then, first in the consciousness that Israel now stands between Egypts, that what she was she will be again. Heretofore in Israelite Yahwism the meaning of the present was taken primarily from the understanding and interpretation of the past, as, e.g., in the ancient cultic confession of faith recorded in Deuteronomy 6:20 ff, and employed (as the here somewhat free translation of the RSV properly renders: "What is the *meaning* of the testimonies . . . ?" [vs. 20]) precisely to answer the question of the meaning of the present: "We were Pharaoh's slaves in Egypt; and the LORD brought us out of Egypt with a mighty hand . . . , that he might bring us in and give us the land which he swore to give to our fathers." The present relatively ordered existence is the creation of God out of former disorder and is to be understood and accepted as his creative gift in fulfilment of his free promise to the patriarchs. The confession addresses the future, if at all, only implicitly: in quality the future is of a piece with the present; "now" embraces tomorrow and tomorrow—in all of which appropriate response to the confessional knowledge of meaning in history is faithful participation in the Yahweh cultus. Such is the sense of Deut. 6:24 (cf. 26:10, the similarly interpretive conclusion of a closely comparable cultic confession in 26:5-9): "The Lord commanded us to do all these statutes, to fear the LORD our God, for our good always, that he might preserve us alive, as at this day."

The preclassical prophet understands the past and present chiefly in terms of Yahweh's positive action on behalf of Israel. He addresses the future, if at all, in the confident expectation that it will be in predictable conformity with the past. The prophets from Amos on are forced to reinterpret the meaning of the present in terms of an immediate future to be charged with tragedy—but a tragedy no less the result of divine action than the great formative event of redemption from Egypt. For the classical prophet the two-member scheme, Out of Egypt–Into This Land, has now become a three-member scheme, Out of Egypt–Into This Land–Into Egypt Again.

Yahweh, who redeemed the nation for his own purposes, will now for the same essential purposes commit the nation to its preredeemed status of chaos and meaninglessness. Why? What lies beyond the second Egypt? Is there a fourth and final member to be added to the three-member scheme? What does this mean? How does this qualify the nature of existence under God in the very present time? These were questions consciously and unconsciously addressed by the classical prophets, questions the answers to which are conditioned and shaped by the great prophets' understanding of a number of concepts, notably: (*a*) Word and symbol, (*b*) election and covenant, (*c*) rebellion and (*d*) judgment, (*e*) compassion and (*f*) redemption, and finally, (*g*) consummation. Five of these appear in remarkably eloquent and integrated form in the eleventh chapter of Hosea (which, whether from the prophet Hosea or not, is a fully characteristic expression of the mind and faith of classical prophetism). The first, Word and symbol, is everywhere prominent in the prophetic canon. The seventh and last appears most prominently in the collection of prophetic utterances now under the name of Isaiah, and especially in the block of chapters conventionally assigned to the so-called Second Isaiah, chs. 40–55.

1. "Thus says Yahweh": Word and symbol. For the nature and significance of the Word of Yahweh in its role in pre-Amos prophetism, *see* § C4*b above*. The concept obviously underlying the use of the Word in the Elijah narratives suggests that by the eighth century the prophetic understanding of the Word was matured and substantially established. As we have seen, it was regarded as an entity containing and releasing divine power to accomplish itself—i.e., to perform or bring to pass its content. The Word of Yahweh was, emphatically, dynamic.

In the classical prophets it appears in a new relationship with the prophet himself, and the prophet's call, his sense of vocational commitment. To a greater or lesser degree in all the great classical prophets one observes the phenomenon of the psychology of captivity, a self-consciousness in vocation characterized by feelings of having been overpowered by the Word of Yahweh. Amos 3:8 has been cited:

> The lion has roared;
>   who will not fear?
> The Lord God [אדני יהוה] has spoken;
>   who can but prophesy?

It is the same instrumental Word, exercising the power of seizure over the same prophet, in 7:15: "The LORD took me from following the flock, and the LORD said to me, 'Go, prophesy to my people Israel.' "

The role of the Word of Yahweh is essentially the same in the remarkable call narratives of Isaiah (ch. 6), Jeremiah (ch. 1), and Ezekiel (chs. 1–2); but the sense of professional bondage to the Word is everywhere apparent in the prophetic canon and appears most eloquently and movingly in the so-called Confessions of Jeremiah—not always explicitly, to be sure, but quite unmistakably. In one of the most intense of these outbursts, the sharp entity of the Word of Yahweh and its commanding power over the prophet is thus expressed:

> The word of Yahweh has become for me
>   a reproach and derision all day long.
> If I say, "I will not mention him,
>   or speak any more in his name,"
> there is in my heart as it were a burning fire
>   shut up in my bones,
> and I am weary with holding it in,
>   and I cannot (Jer. 20:8*b*-9).

The prophetic sense of the entity and power of the Word explains in great part the concentrated emotional character of the prophets and their sometimes deep anguish in proclaiming the negative message, the pronouncement of doom upon the life of the political state. If the prophets suffer in their role, it is not merely the result of a natural distaste for uttering what is unpleasant to their hearers. Rather, the prophetic anguish is the product of the prophets' inevitable sense of participation in and consequently responsibility for the negative Word. To speak in the name of Yahweh and under the formula "Thus says Yahweh!" of the approaching catastrophe is, in the prophetic psychology, to take a positive hand in the destructive event—to release, in the very proclamation of doom, the power to produce the debacle. If this negative Word uttered by the prophet always carries within itself a certain aspect of contingency—destruction is predicated on the present faithless and rebellious structure of the total life of the covenant people—so much more intense, desperate, anguished, is the prophetic call to repentance.

What is true of the Word is true also of the symbolic act of the prophet. Indeed, the devices of symbolism employed by the prophet—e.g., Hosea's and Isaiah's symbolic naming of children (Hos. 1; Isa. 7–8), and the singular and even sometimes weird dramatizations of Jeremiah and even more Ezekiel—are simply graphic, pictorial extensions of the Word, possessing both for the prophet and for his observer-hearer a quality of realism probably unfathomable psychologically to the Western mind. We have said that when the prophet speaks that which he represents to be the Word of God, it is to him emphatically the Word of God and absolutely no kind of courteous condescension to conventional piety, no variety of innocent lie thoroughly stylized to mean in fact the word of man. In the prophetic psyche this Word is initiated by God. It is impellingly dynamic. It breaks through human life, human time, and into human history. And in doing so, it possesses and releases its own power, with or without the consent and/or approval of the human instrument through whom the Word is proclaimed. Observe in the OT that even the word of a man, solemnly spoken under certain more or less formalized circumstances—e.g., in curse or blessing (cf. the Balaam episodes [Num. 22–25]; the Blessing of Isaac [Gen. 27])—cannot be retracted or set aside: once spoken, the power inhering even in the human word is released beyond recall. How much more so with the Word of Yahweh in the mouth of the prophet!

The symbolic act or performance of the prophet was regarded in ancient Israel and especially in the prophets' own understanding as, then, an even more intense and efficacious phenomenon than the spoken Word. These sometimes strange and always dramatic actions of the prophets, charged with dire symbolic meaning, are never merely symbols. The dramatized Word, even more than the uttered Word, is deemed to be charged with the power of performance.

Now if, in addition to all this, we recall another (from our point of view) psychological phenomenon in ancient Israel, the normative sense of corporate personality among the people of Israel (and the East in general, as over against the West), we are in a position to understand as fully as is possible the personality of a Jeremiah or an Ezekiel. In Word and symbol they become in a sense executioners acting at the command, with the authority, and under the power of Yahweh. But in their sense of corporate personality, their understanding of community life in terms of the one identified with the many and the many caught up and embodied in the one, these prophets become in effect their own executioners: In the destructive Word and symbol directed at the people they are themselves, in profoundly realistic psychological meaning, destroyed!

From this sense, none of the great classical prophets is totally free. We shall look presently in another connection at Amos, sometimes misinterpreted as one who objectifies the nation, psychologically extricating himself therefrom. Ezekiel, too, has been not uncommonly charged with the successful suppression of any instincts of a participating, identifying compassion. That Ezekiel appears in pronounced contrast with Jeremiah in this respect is certain; but it may well be that we understand Ezekiel only when we recognize that the intensity and frequency of his destructive symbolisms must have made a self-induced and deliberate callousness imperative. Not that Ezekiel succeeded in this endeavor with consistency, as witness, e.g., 9:8; 11:13; 36:25-32.

The prophetic understanding of the efficacious, dynamic Word and symbol may be and probably is an item of survival out of primitive magic. Much in the OT is derived out of the pagan, the crude, the superstitious, and refined and re-created in the Yahweh faith of Israel. If the prophetic use of symbol represents a survival of sympathetic—i.e., mimetic—magic, the transformation is striking. Magic is coercive of the unseen powers. But the prophet is overwhelmed by the sense of Yahweh's coerciveness; and the prophetic symbol, so far from aiming at control of the deity, is inspired, performed, and interpreted at the behest of the Word of Yahweh and to bring to pass the judgment and will of Yahweh in Israel and the world.

2. "Out of Egypt I called my son": Election and covenant. The notion of Israel as a chosen people elected by Yahweh for special reasons and for a particular purpose is by no means peculiar to the classical prophets. ELECTION is primarily expressed in the OT by the verb בחר, "to choose"—such is the sense of the term—one object freely from among multiple possibilities; but the idea of election is positively conveyed in varying qualities in terms of the call (קרא), of belonging (קנה), of separation (הבדיל), of setting apart (הקדיש), and of knowing (ידע).

The actual term for COVENANT, ברית, appears rarely if at all in the classical, pre-exilic prophets (since the few occurrences of the term have all been regarded as unauthentic). The proposal that the term itself is essentially of postexilic origin in Israel is hardly tenable. It may be that the word "covenant" was deliberately avoided by the great prophets because of its widespread popular misunderstanding—that interpretation which made of the concept of covenant the food of a narrow, prideful, exclusive nationalism. But if the term is rare or even nonexistent in the great classical prophets, the notion of covenant is unmistakably and persistently present: covenant as the working extension and implementation of election, the formal and continual application of what is implicit in election—namely, the concrete responsibilities assumed by the Elector and the obligations of the electee freely undertaken in response. Election with reference to Israel is perpetuated and realized in covenant. Covenant is in the OT the working contract between unequal parties, instigated, initiated, by the senior partner in the act of election. We are justified, then, in speaking of election and covenant in the manner "election/covenant."

This condition of having been chosen and of continuing to exist in a state of chosenness is, of course, given expression in the Prophets in a variety of analogies. The relationship of Yahweh to Israel is expressed in the image of father/son (e.g., in addition to Hos. 11; Isa. 1:2), owner/vineyard (Isa. 5; 27), shepherd/flock (especially Isa. 40:11), potter/clay (so Jer. 18; see also Isa. 29:16; 64:8—H 64:7), and of course predominantly, husband/wife (Isa. 50:1; 54:5; 62:4-5; Jer. 2:1-7; 3:11-22; Ezek. 16; 23; Hosea, as the fundamental thesis).

In classical prophetism the interpretation of Israel's existence is everywhere dependent upon the concept of election/covenant. The meaning of Israel's historical life, past, present, and future, is prophetically apprehended and proclaimed upon what is deemed to be this absolutely fundamental reality. If the prophets speak, as they do, with fierce eloquence on behalf of justice and righteousness in the social and economic life of their people, it represents no general, abstract morality, no goodness-for-goodness'-sake ideology, but specifically and pointedly an election/covenant ethic. The sense of the prophetic ethic and morality is always something like this: You shall refrain from this practice, or you shall do thus-and-so, because I am Yahweh who brought you up out of Egypt (election), and you are a people voluntarily committed in return to the performance of my just and righteous will (covenant). The motivation of the prophetic ethic is election. The nature of that ethic is determined by the covenant.

So it is, emphatically, in what now follows under the headings rebellion, judgment, compassion, redemption, consummation. As the prophet addresses himself with intense concentration to his own generation in his own land, he indicts on behalf of the Deity; proclaims God's negative response; identifies his own and God's anguish, and effects its resolution with the declaration of the love of God for Israel; moves to the proclamation of the nation's fulfilment and finally beyond to her completion of universal mission—in the immutable election/covenant context.

3. "They went from me": Rebellion. It is important to observe that the prophetic castigation embraces, if apparently sometimes incidentally, not simply Israelite man, but man. One thinks in this connection, not only of direct indictment in prophetic discourse (e.g., Isa. 10:5 ff; Amos 1–2), but also of the collection and arrangement of oracles against foreign nations going on in prophetic circles and resulting in such blocks of material in the prophetic canon as Isa. 13–23; Jer. 46–51; Ezek. 25–32. In the prophetic faith, if not always in specific articulation, all men and all nations are in rebellion against God, denying in multiple ways the appropriate terms of human existence under the rule of the actively righteous Yahweh.

But for the prophet, Israel stands immovable, inextricable, as the very hub of human existence and as the precise nucleus of the vast area of God's concern. She is the electee of God, the covenanter with him. She, and in a profound sense she only, is the wife; or the clay; or the flock; or the vineyard; or the son of God the husband, potter, shepherd, landowner, or father. Prophetism as a whole cannot mean to exclude non-Israelites from the same essential relationships:

"Are you not like the Ethiopians to me,
  O people of Israel?" says the LORD.
"Did I not bring up Israel from the land of Egypt,
  and the Philistines from Caphtor and the Syrians from Kir?"
(Amos 9:7.)

"In that day Israel will be the third with Egypt and Assyria, a blessing in the midst of the earth, whom the LORD of hosts has blessed, saying, 'Blessed be Egypt my people, and Assyria the work of my hands, and Israel my heritage.' " (Isa. 19:24—perhaps, and probably, not from Isaiah of Jerusalem; perhaps and probably relatively late; but in any case, of the very essence of the prophetic.)

But the prophet does assume a different quality in the God-Israel relationship from the God-nations relationship. There is an intensity and intimacy (and ultimately a purpose and mission) uniquely present here which leads an Amos (and in effect all exponents of classical prophetism) to cry in Yahweh's name:

You only have I known
  of all the families of the earth;
therefore I will punish you
  for all your iniquities (3:2).

Israel's rebellion against God is shared by that of all peoples, to be sure; but hers is uniquely and totally conditioned by the quality of her relationship to God and is in consequence the more heinous.

Her rebellion against Yahweh is grossly, flagrantly displayed in the totality of her life. The whole head is sick and the whole heart faint. The alienation is wilful and complete. Israel is utterly estranged (Isa. 1:4-5). The extended and most bitter indictments in the three largest prophetic collections (see especially Isa. 1:2-18; 2:6-17; 9:8-11; 29:13-16; 30:8-17; Jer. 2:4-13; 5:20-31; 7:8-11; Ezek. 16), as well as the sweepingly eloquent, often ferocious, denunciations in Amos, Hosea, and Micah and (at the lower end of the chronological scale of classical prophetism) the later Isaiahs (see, e.g., Isa. 59:1-15), make it clear that (to use our categories, not theirs) no distinction existed for the prophet between the rebelliousness expressed in social-economic-political malpractice on the one hand and cultic-religious-theological deviation on the other. And (again to use our rubrics, which inevitably impose a kind and degree of organization quite foreign to prophetism itself) the totality of Israel's rebelliousness is, in the prophetic understanding, the shocking betrayal of Israel's pride and arrogance—seen all the more reprehensibly against such relationships as father/son, owner/vineyard, and husband/wife:

Sons have I reared and brought up,
  but they have rebelled against me
(Isa. 1:2).

What more was there to do for my vineyard,
  that I have not done in it?
When I looked for it to yield grapes,
  why did it yield vile-smelling [RSV "wild"] grapes?
(Isa. 5:4).

I remember the devotion [חסד] of your youth,
  your love as a bride.
. . . .
And I brought you into a plentiful land
  to enjoy its fruits and its good things.
But when you came in you defiled my land,
  and made my heritage an abomination
(Jer. 2:2, 7).

"I plighted my troth to you . . . . But you trusted in your beauty, and played the harlot" (Ezek. 16:8, 15).

Israel's rebelliousness is infidelity; her infidelity, pride. And the rebellion against God that is human pride is ultimately in prophetism castigated in all men; for Israelite prophetism knows, if Israel forgets, that Israel's rotten, unholy pride, productive only of a sickness unto death, is fully shared, by all men!

4. "They shall return to Egypt": Judgment. In Hebrew "to judge" (שפט) and its derivatives convey considerably more than corresponding English terms. The act of judging is one in which wrong is righted either by punishment of the aggressor or by restitution to the victim, or by both. In the OT the underprivileged are to be "judged" (e.g., Isa. 1:17:

Defend the fatherless,
  plead for the widow)

as well as wilful offenders. Judgment, then, is the realization of justice.

In the introduction to this section (§ D) we marked the sense of impending negative judgment upon Israel as a formative characteristic of classical prophetism. The prophets of the eighth–sixth centuries are all predominantly oriented in catastrophe—either the fall of the N kingdom in 722 or the end of the surviving S state in 587—whether they stand before or after the envisaged tragedy. And unequivocally for them this temporal-historical-political event is divine judgment, the creation and establishment of justice, the rebalancing of the scales between Yahweh and Israel. The judge, the performer of the act of judgment, is Yahweh himself. The object of the judgment is Israel. The act of judgment—political death, a figurative return to Egypt. If this is an experience of unqualified catastrophe for Israel; if it is, as has been said, a return to an existence formless and meaningless; it nevertheless has its own kind of order and meaning. It rights the wrong; and more, much more, it provides the now rectified context for a resumption of the relationship between Yahweh and Israel which obtained after the first Egypt and before the conditions responsible for the threat and execution of the second.

Judgment is right. It is of Yahweh. And he still rules.

The prophets, from Amos and Isaiah before the events to the subsequent Isaiahs and other prophets after the final catastrophe, proclaim the judgment with staggering power and in stunning language. If they entertain personal hopes that it may be averted (as they do) or that it will work for good in an Israel that loves God (as emphatically they do), this affects not at all the uncompromised character of the negative proclamation.

Thus says the Holy One of Israel,
"Because you despise this word,
and trust [sic] in oppression and perverseness,
and rely on them;
therefore this iniquity shall be to you
like a break in a high wall . . . ,
. . . .
which is smashed so ruthlessly
that among its fragments not a sherd is found
with which to take fire from the hearth,
or to dip up water out of the cistern"
(Isa. 30:12-14);

but see the full chapter; and cf. the equally unequivocal statement of judgment in 22:14.

The character of the judgment is conditioned by the character of Israel's rebellion. The totality of the judgment is the appropriate and necessary rectifying of the nation's totally wilful, arrogant rejection of Yahweh.

Thou hast smitten them,
but they felt no anguish;
thou hast consumed them,
but they refused to take correction.
They have made their faces harder than rock;
they have refused to repent.
. . . .
They have spoken falsely of Yahweh,
and have said, "He will do nothing" [לא־הוא].
. . . .
Therefore thus says Yahweh, the God of hosts:
"Because they have spoken this word,
behold, I am making my words in your mouth a fire,
and this people wood, and the fire shall devour them."
(Jer. 5:3, 12, 14, but see the full section, vss.1-17.)

For all their own invective, the prophets are misunderstood if their proclamation of judgment against Israel is interpreted as an arbitrary or vindictive action of Yahweh. They want to make it plain (they are demonstrably often hard put to it to do so, because of the intensity of their own feelings and emotions) that it is judgment in the full sense—justice, the setting right of the woefully wrong; and they do make this plain in their not uncommon joining of the issue between Yahweh and Israel in terms unmistakably drawn from current Israelite judicial practice (cf. Isa. 1:2, 18 ff; 3:13; Hos. 4:1; Amos 3:1; Mic. 6:1 ff). God accuses, he renders the verdict, and he is himself responsible for the execution of judgment against Israel.

In other passages (cf. Jer. 1:15 ff; Joel 3:2 ff—H 4:2 ff; Amos 1:3 ff; Mic. 1:2-4; Zeph. 3:8) the judicial setting is convoked, not against Israel, but against the nations. *See* § D7 *below.*

5. "How can I give you up?" Compassion. One may strongly doubt that any of the classical prophets pronounced a divine verdict of unconditioned doom. Amos has often been so understood; and others of the prophets have been made out to be proclaimers exclusively of the negative aspects of divine judgment by resort to a literary criticism which neatly attributes to other sources the prophetic word of God's compassion. Now, obviously, much more originated with an Amos than what is brought down to us as prophetic utterance under his name in the canon; and even in what we have, there is reflected the unmistakable attribution to Yahweh of the prophet's own sense of compassion—the thought expressed repeatedly in the phrase "Yet you did not return to me," that the very catastrophe which Yahweh visits upon his people is itself an expression of his love and faithfulness, since in the negative action he seeks to bring about a reconciliation with prideful, rebellious Israel (Amos 4:6-11).

The mood and language, the faith, hope, and love of the classical prophets as a whole, testify in eloquent passion that rebellion and judgment in the context of election/covenant at once call forth compassion and redemption. The Hebrew terms—noun, verb, and adjective—denoting "compassion" (from a root רחם, of dubious original meaning) appear not uncommonly through the prophetic books and sometimes in conjunction with the root denoting "love" [אהב]; but the unique quality of Yahweh's compassion is best expressed by the prophetic language in the term *ḥésedh* (חסד).

Ḥésedh is necessarily subject to several different English renderings, according to context: "mercy" (a relatively infrequent sense, although so commonly rendered in the LXX), "kindness," "devotion," "faithfulness," "grace." It is, of course, a term descriptively qualifying relationship—man/man or God/man. Its fundamental root sense conveys the quality of sustaining strength, strength in duration, and it is commonly in the OT an attribute of covenant, either God/Israel or such family "covenantal" relationships as husband/wife or father/son. *Ḥésedh* is the strength of faithfulness which constitutes the very life of the relationship, a central quality of the word perhaps best illustrated in the marriage covenant as this figure is used by Hosea, where the ghastly double rupture, of marriage and of covenant, is in prophetic consciousness a *fait accompli,* and the analogy is applied from the personal to the national as the prophet speaks for Yahweh: "In that day, says Yahweh, . . . I will betroth you to me for ever; I will betroth you to me in righteousness [צדק] and in justice [משפט], in steadfast love [חסד], and in compassion [רחמים; RSV 'mercy'] . . . , in faithfulness [אמונה]; and you shall know [וידעת] Yahweh" (Hos. 2:16-20—H 2:18-22).

In the prophetic use of the term (notably in Hosea, Jeremiah, and Second Isaiah), if not indeed elsewhere in the OT, *ḥésedh* quite escapes the confines of covenant; or perhaps it would be better to say that as a quality of covenant it is chiefly responsible for a transformation in the concept of covenant. That covenant of which *ḥésedh* is a part becomes in the exercise of *ḥésedh* something vastly more than that pedestrian covenant which it was in its inception. Look again at the passage just quoted, and its context. The covenant here, both the man/woman and the God/people covenant, is ended, terminated. As covenants go, this one is finished with a rupture of incredible violence and proportion. But *ḥésedh* becomes operative in this covenant to such a transforming degree that what was covenant-with-*ḥésedh* now becomes *ḥésedh*-with-covenant. Covenant it still is, but utterly transformed by compassion that is *ḥésedh*.

The same essential expansion of *ḥésedh* beyond the limits of covenant is to be seen also in Jeremiah and Second Isaiah.

> Return, faithless Israel,
> says the LORD.
> I will not look on you in anger,
> for I am *ḥāsîdh* [adjectival form of
> *ḥésedh;* RSV 'merciful'],
> says the LORD;
> I will not be angry for ever.
> (Jer. 3:12.)

In Hosea (11:8 ff) the divine compassion which converts the judgment and reconstitutes the covenant is expressed in the Deity's cry:

> How can I give you up, O Ephraim!
> How can I hand you over, O Israel!
> . . . .
> For I am God and not man,
> the Holy One in your midst.

In Jeremiah it is: "For I am *ḥāsîdh!*"—this is the quality of my judgment and my covenant! And in Second Isaiah the transforming development is completed:

> For a brief moment I forsook you,
> but with great compassion [from רחם] I will gather you.
> In overflowing wrath for a moment
> I hid my face from you,
> but with everlasting *ḥésedh* [חסד עולם] I will
> have compasion on you [again, from רחם]
> (Isa. 54:7-8).

As the poetic parallelism makes clear, the character of Yahweh's compassion is the *ḥésedh* character—the steady, enduring strength of fidelity, devotion, and commitment which partakes of the quality of grace precisely because it is more than the convention of covenant can appropriately command, because it is greater than the relationship which first produced it, and because it is able, in breaking out of the relationship, to re-create the very relationship in transformed dimensions. If *ḥésedh* begins in the structure of covenant, it ends with covenant as its own renewed creation.

> For the mountains may depart
> and the hills be removed,
> but my *ḥésedh* shall not depart from you,
> and my covenant of peace shall not be removed,
> says the LORD, who has compassion on you.
> (Isa. 54:10.)

It is unnecessary to add that compassion of this sort is inseparably related to love, that *ḥésedh* compounded of grace is itself rooted and sustained in the love of God, as it is so precisely put in Jeremiah 31:3:

> I have loved you with an everlasting love;
> therefore I have continued my *ḥésedh* to you.

6. "I will return them to their homes": Redemption. We are speaking of prophetism, the achievement not of any one prophet but of that unique movement of prophetism spectacularly witnessed in concentrated power in the eighth–sixth centuries but developing from the time of Israel's birth as a people out of Egypt and continuing to find essential, if sometimes dependent, expression in the final six or seven centuries of biblical time. This prophetism, which found its very being in the efficacious Word of Yahweh and could comprehend Israel's (and all men's!) appallingly arrogant and tragically groundless posturing, and in particular consequence in Israel's case persuaded of cataclysmic but rectifying historical judgment; this prophetism equally unshakable in faith in the efficacious quality of divine compassion and *ḥésedh* and in certainty of the unimpedible fulfilment of divine purpose behind Word, election, and covenant—such a prophetism comes inevitably to the affirmation of Israel's historical redemption, even before the historical imposition of judgment.

In doing so, prophetism reveals the magnificent, full body of its faith; but it also betrays, perhaps, the always attendant measure of its unfaith, since by and large the prophets are quite unable to envisage any ultimate establishment of divine sovereignty apart from the re-created and resubstantiated historical Israel. The prophets do not, of course, allow this as a point of pride. That Israel remains a part of Yahweh's redemptive purpose, not out of any divine necessity, but purely because Yahweh so wills it, is emphatically expressed both in Ezekiel (36:22-25, 32) and in Second Isaiah (Isa. 48:11) in the insistent explanation of Israel's redemption in the divine phrase: "For my own sake I do it!" Furthermore, if prophetism is regarded in consistent fact as movement, then we should have to say that faith is the victor over unfaith even in this regard, since it is through and still within the prophetic movement that Israel herself is seen to be ultimately expendable on behalf of the cause of the knowledge and reign of God.

Prophetism, which fairly exploded into full, vocal, self-conscious maturity in the historical era of Israel's existence "between Egypt," had added a third member to the older two-member scheme: Out-of-Egypt, Into-This-Land, and now, in the consciousness of impending divine judgment, Back-to-Egypt. But this was, of course, not the end. In the mind and faith of prophetism this would have been impossible. And so a fourth member in the meaningful scheme of Israel's history was added—a second act of divine redemption from chaos, redemption by return again to the land, redemption by the reconstitution of the people Israel.

It is difficult to deny the addition, not only of the third negative member, but also of the fourth positive element to the scheme as the work of prophetism in the eighth century. It is difficult and probably impossible to separate them. If the first Isaiah was convinced, as in faith he was, of the destruction of his people, he was also and at once persuaded of God's compassionate purpose in judgment-justice, of a judgment-justice never centrally punitive in intention and quality but always itself redemptive in divine conception and function. If judgment is wrath, it is purposive wrath, not vindictive wrath. Judgment is never an end in itself, but that dire necessity which makes redemption possible.

I will turn my hand against you
and will smelt away your dross as with lye
and remove all your alloy. (Isa. 1:25.)

And precisely so we correctly understand that the prophetic declaration of a surviving REMNANT beyond the coming catastrophe (as most notably in Isaiah's symbolic naming of a son "A Remnant Shall Return" [שאר ישוב; Isa. 7:1 ff]) is, if pointed to Yahweh's negative action against Israel, also positive in its import; and it is all the more positive when we recall Israel's habitual identification of one and many, her sense of total participation as people in that which was in reality experienced by others of her number (e.g., "We were Pharaoh's slaves in Egypt," that ancient cultic phrase of Deut. 6:21), whether the others were one, a few, or many, and whether in the past, present, or future. In the faith of Israel the glorious survival and reconstruction of a remnant is Israel's glory and Israel's re-establishment.

The understanding of historical judgment as positive in divine purpose had, perhaps earlier, appeared in Amos (4:6-11, already cited in another connection); but, still in the eighth century, it is most warmly expounded in Hosea (especially 2:14-23; 5:15; 7:13, 15; 11:11). It is a pervasive, if often only implicit, element in the utterances of Jeremiah and makes possible that stunning articulation of a new and/or renewed covenant with Israel "after those days" of judgment: "I will put my law within them, and I will write it upon their hearts; and I will be their God, and they shall be my people. And no longer shall each man teach his neighbor and each his brother, saying, 'Know the LORD' [דעו את־יהוה], for they shall all know me, from the least of them to the greatest, says Yahweh; for I will forgive their iniquity, and I will remember their sin no more" (Jer. 31:33-34).

In Ezekiel that redemption purposed in the very judgment—the reconstitution, rebirth, re-creation, of Israel inherent in the prophetic understanding of Israel's anguished demise—is given singularly vivid expression in the description of the prophet's vision of the valley of death, Israel's vast open grave exposing the bare skeletons of the house of Israel. In this scene of dry death Yahweh commands the prophet: "Prophesy [i.e., speak as prophet, speak prophetically; הנבא] . . . and say . . . , O dry bones, hear the word of Yahweh" (37:4). "So I prophesied as he commanded me, . . . and they lived . . . . Then he said to me, 'Son of man, these bones are the whole house of Israel. Behold, they say, "Our bones are dried up, and our hope is lost; we are clean cut off." Therefore prophesy [as above], and say to them, Thus says the Lord Yahweh: Behold, I will open your graves, and raise you from your graves, O my people; and I will bring you home into the land of Israel. . . . And I will put my Spirit within you, and you shall live, and I will place you in your own land; then you shall know that I, Yahweh, have spoken, and I have done it, says Yahweh." (Vss. 10-14.)

We need not wonder that the form of prophetic utterance as finally solidified and handed down to us seldom, if ever, presents the single, unmitigated word of doom. The very positive ending of Amos, e.g. (9:8*b* ff, following immediately upon the statement of unqualified doom), may or may not be true to that particular context of that particular prophet; but the ending of Amos is certainly and profoundly true to the structure of prophetism.

So it is, finally, on the very eve of the actual episode of Israel's second historical redemption, fraught with such incredibly high prophetic hopes yet doomed in prophetism to such abysmal frustration and disappointment, that the so-called Second Isaiah, now believing this second exodus (as earlier had been believed in high hopes about the first) to signal the fulfilment, the realization of the Word of Yahweh to the elect, covenanted Israel, speaks words moving and profound in consolation, but words, literally taken, only very briefly and highly approximately validated in the actual history of Israel's second redemption (see, e.g., Isa. 40; 44:21 ff; 49:8-13). In a lyrical, soaring projection of faith which summons the act of creation and the dramatic first exodus into the single moment of time occupied by the second exodus, the prophet cries:

Awake, awake, put on strength,
O arm of Yahweh;
awake as in the days of old,
the generations of long ago.
Was it not thou that didst cut Rahab in pieces,
that didst pierce the dragon? (51:9).

This refers to the old mythological language of creation and recalls the creation of order and meaning by the destruction of Chaos (Rahab, the dragon), concepts still latent in the verbal form though hardly in the interpreted content of Gen. 1.

Was it not thou that didst dry up the sea,
the waters of the great deep;
that didst make the depths of the sea a way
for the redeemed to pass over? (vs. 10.)

In the same breath, as it were, and with the same overwhelming sense of contemporaneity, the prophet brings into the present moment of time the past event of the Exodus from Egypt. With absolutely no encumbering sense of disparity in time, he introduces with an equal sense of immediacy that which is about to be Israel's second redemption:

The ransomed of the LORD shall return,
and come with singing to Zion;
everlasting joy shall be upon their heads;
they shall obtain joy and gladness,
and sorrow and sighing shall flee away
(vs. 11).

Faith in such a measure of passion and proclaimed in such rapture cannot, of course, finally be contained in any concept merely of Israel's historical redemption. Prophetism produces a theology out of a process of meditation on history and the meaning of history; and if prophetism is capable, as here, of a theology that takes wings to soar out of the plane of pedestrian history when its meditation is focused on what Yahweh has done in the Creation and the Exodus, it is always brought back again sharply to the realities of a flatly frustrating historical existence. It is the tension between the alternating experiences of flight and the grim march which produces inevitably a prophetic eschatology.

7. A light to the nations: Consummation. From any point of view other than that of faith—and faith, indeed, in its ultimate projection—prophetic affirmations pointing, if not beyond history, at least to a history radically transformed, are unthinkable. But if Israelite prophetism is, from our perspectives, singularly nonlogical, it is not nonreasonable: it adheres to its own reasonableness. If the face of existence appears to be, with only intermittent relief, as hard and as featureless as the rock, it remains an existence Yahweh-given and (surely as we know who were once Pharaoh's slaves in Egypt, to whom it was given, with David, to build Zion) Yahweh-ruled. What it appears to be, then, it only appears to be; or what it appears to be, it will be only in limited duration. The totality of existence is Yahweh's, and his countenance is neither featureless nor hard (we know him to be in the very midst of this grim history "gracious and merciful, slow to anger, and abounding in *ḥésedh*" [Joel 2:13; cf. Jonah 4:2]). Moreover, Yahweh has spoken the word that in Abraham/Israel all the nations of the earth shall be blessed (Gen. 12:3); and his Word cannot but accomplish that purpose to which he sends it (Isa. 55:11).

And so, again and emphatically, we observe that the concept of Israel's historical redemption could not ultimately contain the prophetic faith or answer the questions of prophetism about the meaning of Israel's existence. Prophetism as movement was compelled to abandon any and all notions—even its own —of divine purpose fulfilled in terms limited to Israel. It may even be that where the terms are of Israel's redemption, the intent expressed in intensity of feeling, conviction, and emotion, is universal. This is true of Isa. 51:9-11, just quoted. It is equally true of such passages—in form of Israel, in disposition and intention of all men—as Hos. 2:18-23; Jer. 23:5-6 (and to a lesser degree, perhaps, Jer. 29:10-14; 31:4-5); and emphatically, Isa. 9:2-7—H 9:1-6. The idea of a coming DAY OF THE LORD as somehow Israel's day of justification, fulfilment, and aggrandizement was violently exploded. Some prophets appear to identify the Day as the actual, historical judgment/catastrophe of 722 or 587 (e.g., Amos 5:18-20), while others make it the symbol of the final, universal judgment (e.g., Joel 2:30-31; Zech. 1:14-16); and within the movement of prophetism it becomes that Day when Yahweh "will become king over all the earth," when "Yahweh will be one and his name one" (Zech. 14:5-9).

This is not to deny that even here prophetism has its continuing ambiguities. The structure of faith as apprehended even by the prophets themselves was hardly without its "logical contradictions." But the projection in faith of a final consummation of all that is implicit in prophetism's high affirmations is variously and eloquently articulated; and such raptured extensions of prophetic faith lay every just claim to represent the ultimate words of prophetism.

It seems appropriate, then, to let prophetism now speak, through the remarkable tradition of the Isaiahs, its own concluding lines. One does not need to be able to delineate between terms of realism and terms of symbol, since the distinction is uncritical in prophetism's faith in consummation. Furthermore, we are not concerned with the "source" of these declarations, since all come unmistakably out of Israelite prophetism.

See and hear first the prophetic expectation, the vision of consummation, to be effected through the SERVANT OF THE LORD, even though we probably cannot know the precise identity of the Servant in prophetic understanding—Israel personified; or the remnant of Israel; or one, someone, out of Israel; or, in differing contexts, differing identities.

> And now Yahweh says,
> who formed me from the womb to be his servant,
> . . . .
> "It is too light a thing that you should be my servant
> to raise up the tribes of Jacob
> and to restore the preserved of Israel;
> I will give you as a light to the nations,
> that my salvation may reach to the end of the earth."
> (Isa. 49:5-6.)

Whatever the form of the next passage, and the identity of both the servant and the speaker, the intention of consummation is unambiguous, and all the more so if it is the nations who speak:

> Surely he [the servant] has borne our griefs
> and carried our sorrows;
> yet we esteemed him stricken,
> smitten by God, and afflicted.
> But he was wounded for our transgressions,
> he was bruised for our iniquities;
> upon him was the chastisement that made us whole,
> and with his stripes we are healed (Isa. 53:4-5).

Especially in the light of the next verse, there can be no wonder that in Christian perspective, prophetism here attains the absolutely ultimate projection of its faith:

> All we like sheep have gone astray;
> we have turned every one to his own way;
> and Yahweh has laid on him
> the iniquity of us all.

In Isa. 11:1 ff, "a shoot from the stump of Jesse" will be totally endowed with the Spirit of Yahweh:

> He shall not judge by what his eyes see,
> or decide by what his ears hear;
> but with righteousness he shall judge the poor,
> and decide with equity for the meek of the earth.

And the vision moves with tender perceptiveness to lower orders of creation, among whom the peace of righteous rule is also attested (11:6 ff), with these lines in climactic description of the consummation:

> They shall not hurt or destroy
> in all my holy mountain;
> for the earth shall be full of the knowledge of Yahweh
> as the waters cover the sea.

Read and hear, finally, those incomparable lines referred to as the Floating Oracle because they appear in both Isaiah (2:2-4) and Micah (4:1-3):

> It shall come to pass in the latter days
> that the mountain of the house of Yahweh
> shall be established as the highest of the mountains,
> and shall be raised above the hills;
> and all the nations shall flow to it,
> and many peoples shall come, and say:
> "Come, let us go up to the mountain of Yahweh,
> to the house of the God of Jacob;
> that he may teach us his ways
> and that we may walk in his paths."
> For out of Zion shall go forth the law,
> and the word of Yahweh from Jerusalem.

He shall judge between the nations,
and shall decide for many peoples;
and they shall beat their swords into plowshares,
and their spears into pruning hooks;
nation shall not lift up sword against nation,
neither shall they learn war any more
(Isa. 2:2-4).

The book of Micah, quite possibly out of the same Isaianic circle of prophetism, adds these last lines, words suggesting again the power, the faith, and the ultimate expectation of Israelite prophetism:

They shall sit every man under his vine and under his fig tree,
and none shall make them afraid;
for the mouth of Yahweh of hosts has spoken (Mic. 4:4).

Bibliography. G. Hölscher, *Die Propheten* (1914). E. Troeltsch, "Glaube und Ethos der Hebräischen Propheten," *Gesammelte Schriften* (1925), IV, 36-64. K. Galling, *Die Erwählungstraditionen Israels* (1928). G. von Rad, "Die falschen Propheten," *ZAW*, N.S. 10 (1933), pp. 109-20. A. Jepsen, *Nabi* (1934). H. S. Nyberg, *Studien zum Hoseabuche* (1935). K. Elliger, "Prophet und Politik," *ZAW*, N.S. 12 (1935), pp. 3-22; N.S. 14 (1937), pp. 291-95. A. Guillaume, *Prophecy and Divination* (1938), especially pp. 107-83. N. Porteous, "Prophecy," in H. W. Robinson, ed., *Record and Revelation* (1938). I. Engnell, *The Call of Isaiah* (1949). J. Pedersen, *Israel: Its Life and Culture*, especially III-IV (1940), 107-49. H. W. Robinson, "Hebrew Sacrifice and Prophetic Symbolism," *JTS*, 43 (1942), 171 ff. A. R. Johnson, *The Cultic Prophet in Ancient Israel* (1944). A. Haldar, *Associations of Cult Prophets Among the Ancient Semites* (1945). S. Mowinckel, *Prophecy and Tradition* (1946). H. W. Robinson, *Inspiration and Revelation in the OT* (1946), especially pp. 123-98. J. P. Hyatt, *Prophetic Religion* (1947). G. Widengren, *Literary and Psychological Aspects of the Hebrew Prophets* (1948). M. Buber, *The Prophetic Faith* (1949). J. Hempel, *Worte der Propheten* (1949), especially pp. 83-189. C. Lindhagen, *The Servant Motif in the OT* (1950). H. H. Rowley, ed., *Studies in OT Prophecy* (1950), especially essays by G. H. Davies, pp. 37 ff; C. R. North, pp. 111 ff; N. W. Porteous, pp. 143 ff. O. Eissfeldt, "The Prophetic Literature," in H. H. Rowley, ed., *The OT and Modern Study* (1951). H. H. Rowley, *The Servant of Yahweh* (1952), especially pp. 89-128. M. Weber, *Ancient Judaism* (1952). E. Nielsen, *Oral Tradition* (1954), no. 11 in the series *Studies in Biblical Theology*. A. R. Johnson, *Sacral Kingship in Ancient Israel* (1955). E. Voegelin, *Israel and Revelation* (1956), especially pp. 111-84, 428-515. H. Ringgren, *The Messiah in the OT* (1957). S. Mowinckel, *He That Cometh* (1958).

B. D. Napier

***PROPHET IN THE NT.** Long before the time of Jesus prophecy had ceased to appear in Israel (Ps. 74:9; I Macc. 4:46; 9:27; 14:41), although a special form of it continued to flourish in the writing of apocalyptic visions. The Jews, however, fully expected its revival in the coming age of the Messiah (cf. Joel 2:28-29; Zech. 13:4-6; Mal. 4:5-6; Test. Levi 8:14; Test. Benj. 9:2). It is in the light of this expectation that one must understand the claim, recorded by Josephus (War I.ii.8), that John Hyrcanus had the "gift of prophecy." Josephus also states that such messianic pretenders as Theudas (Antiq. XX. v.1; cf. Acts 5:36) and "the Egyptian" (Antiq. XX. viii.6; War II.xiii.5; cf. Acts 21:38) claimed that they were prophets.

Among the pious Jews who, eagerly looking to the redemption of God's people, nurtured these hopes of prophetic renewal, are to be included the Essenes (*see also* Dead Sea Scrolls). It is doubtless in this context that the references to prophecy in the infancy narratives of Luke 1–2 must be interpreted: Zechariah "prophesied" (1:67); Simeon was subject to revelation by the Holy Spirit (2:25-27); and Anna was a "prophetess" (2:36).

It was the preaching of John the Baptist, however —the "prophet of the Most High" (Luke 1:76)— that excited the Jews with an awareness of the return of authentic prophecy. Not only was he widely held by the people to be a prophet, even to be Elijah returned to earth (Matt. 14:5; 21:26; Mark 6:15; 11:32; Luke 9:8; 20:6); but Jesus himself paid tribute to John as a prophet (Matt. 11:9-15; Luke 7: 24-28), and on one occasion exploited the Baptist's popularity as a prophet to silence his enemies (Matt. 21:25-27; Mark 11:29-33; Luke 20:3-8).

Similarly, Jesus was acclaimed as a prophet, both by the nature of his preaching and teaching and by the miracles that he performed (Matt. 16:14; 21:11, 46; Mark 8:28; Luke 7:16, 39; 9:19; 24:19; John 4:19; 9:17). Occasionally he referred to himself in the same way, as in his sermon at Nazareth (Matt. 13:57; Mark 6:4; Luke 4:24; cf. John 4:44) and his lament over Jerusalem (Matt. 23:37; Luke 13:33-34). The Fourth Gospel employs the title of Jesus as "the prophet" virtually as a synonym for "Messiah" (cf. 1:21, 25; 6:14; 7:40). And the book of Acts refers to him, with much the same meaning, in the foretelling of Deut. 18:15, 18, of the coming of a Prophet like unto Moses (Acts 3:22-26; cf. 7:37). This messianic interpretation of the Deuteronomic passage seems to have been original to the church; it is not known in contemporary rabbinic exegesis.

From its inception, prophesying was a characteristic mark of primitive Christianity—interpreted, as in Acts 2:14 ff, as an evident fulfilment of the promises of the OT that it would revive in the last days. The gift of prophecy was not, however, a possession of all Christians, but a peculiar spiritual endowment ("charism") of a select number, whether of men or of women. The author of Acts preserves the names of a few—Agabus (11:27; 21:10) and Judas and Silas (15:32), who originally belonged to the Jerusalem church; and the four daughters of Philip, one of the Seven (21:9). He also speaks of prophets among the earliest leaders of the church in Antioch (13:1), and, in a peculiar reference, he tells of twelve disciples at Ephesus who prophesied immediately after their baptism by Paul (19:6). The author of Acts appears to have been mainly interested in the predictive features of the prophets' activities, and the outward manifestations of their behavior. It is not altogether clear that he distinguished, as did Paul, the gift of "speaking in tongues" from the prophetic charism.

For Paul, prophecy was one of God's greatest gifts to his church for edification (see especially the whole discussion in I Cor. 14), and he ranked the prophet second only to an apostle in honor and importance (I Cor. 12:28-29). By "prophecy," Paul understands intelligible preaching that builds up the church in faith (cf. Rom. 12:6), explains mysteries, and imparts knowledge ("gnosis"; cf. I Cor. 13:2). In I Pet. 1:10, the prophet's concern is the searching of the Scriptures for the testimonia of Christ. So in Rev. 19:10, witness to Jesus is the "spirit of prophecy." The entire book of Revelation is a classic example of Christian prophecy (cf. 1:3; 22:7, 10, 18-19). Though cast in an apocalyptic form, it is the proclamation of a man "in the Spirit" who expounds from the imagery of the OT the new revelation of God's victory in Christ and in those who belong to Christ.

Prophecy continued to exert a potent influence in the church throughout the postapostolic period. Not only does the issuance of the Revelation to John testify to this. Also, at Rome, a prophet named Hermas imparted persuasively his visions that taught a second repentance after baptism. Though his utterances were subject to the controlling oversight of the hierarchy, his book of prophecies, the Shepherd, was received in many churches with a quasi-canonical authority (*see* HERMAS, SHEPHERD OF). Ignatius has left us an example of his own Spirit-inspired utterance about the ministry in his Letter to the Philadelphians (ch. 7); and the church of Smyrna described their martyred leader, Polycarp, as an "apostolic and prophetic teacher and bishop of the Catholic Church" (Martyrdom of Polycarp 16.2). The Pastoral letters relate the leadership of "Timothy" in the church to gifts given him by prophecy (I Tim. 1:18; 4:14).

Nevertheless, the ministry of prophets exhibited a noticeable decline in effectiveness in the post-apostolic age. Already, in the deutero-Pauline Letter to the Ephesians, there is evident a tendency to look back upon the prophets, as upon the apostles, as belonging to a past generation of founders of the church (cf. 2:20; 3:5; 4:11). Warnings against false prophets—signs of the coming of Antichrist—occur in the Synoptic traditions of Jesus' teaching (Matt. 7:15; 24:11, 24; Mark 13:22), and in the Johannine writings (I John 4:1; Rev. 16:13; 19:20; 20:10). The seer of Patmos singled out one such personage, in the church at Thyatira, a prophetess to whom he gave the distasteful appellation of "Jezebel" (Rev. 2:20).

The DIDACHE, a document of the early years of the second century, discusses at some length the problem of false prophets (11-13), and provides simple tests for sifting true prophets who visit Christian communities from those who are spurious. But the Didachist has in mind, not so much unorthodox prophets, as charlatans of the profession, who impose upon the hospitality of unwary churches. The "new prophecy" of the Montanist movement of the latter half of the century did much to discredit the ministry of prophets in the eyes of the orthodox church leaders, not only because of the exaggerated claims of its proponents, but in large measure because it was not amenable to the discipline of the church's ordained hierarchy.

Bibliography. A. von Harnack, *The Expansion of Christianity in the First Three Centuries,* I (1904), 398-461; E. Fascher, ΠΡΟΦΗΤΗΣ, *Eine sprach- und religionsgeschichtliche Untersuchung* (1927); P. E. Davies, "Jesus and the Role of the Prophet," *JBL,* LXIV (1945), 214-54; H. A. Guy, *NT Prophecy, Its Origin and Significance* (1947); F. W. Young, "Jesus the Prophet: A Re-examination," *JBL,* LXVIII (1949), 285-99; H. Greeven, "Propheten, Lehrer, Vorsteher bei Paulus," *ZNW,* XLIV (1952/53), 3-15; M. Barnett, *The Living Flame* (1953). *See also* bibliography under MINISTRY, CHRISTIAN.

M. H. SHEPHERD, JR.

PROPHETESS [נביאה, *from masculine* נביא, PROPHET; προφῆτις, *from masculine* προφήτης, *from* πρόφημι, to speak before, openly]. A female interpreter speaking for the deity; or the wife of a prophet (cf. "duke" and "duchess").

In the OT the term is applied to Miriam, the sister of Moses (Exod. 15:20); Deborah (Judg. 4:4)—in both instances seen by many scholars as a relatively late ascription; to Huldah, a contemporary of Jeremiah and a functioning woman prophet (II Kings 22:14); to Noadiah, an adversary of Nehemiah and presumably also a professional (Neh. 6:14); and by Isaiah to his wife (Isa. 8:3).

In the NT the term is used of Anna (Luke 2:36) and of one Jezebel (Rev. 2:20). B. D. NAPIER

PROPITIATION. A means of placating or pacifying displeasure due to an offense; hence an atoning action directed toward God.

1. Terminology
   a. In biblical Hebrew
   b. In LXX Greek
   c. In NT Greek
2. In the OT
   a. In human relationships
   b. Propitiation and sacrifice
3. In the NT

Bibliography

1. Terminology. The word "propitiation" is the KJV form of "EXPIATION" in Rom. 3:25 (ἱλαστήριον); I John 2:2; 4:10 (ἱλασμός). The sense of the word, however, is found in several other passages. *See below.*

a. In biblical Hebrew. Although the word "propitiation" does not occur in any of the English versions of the OT, the idea is expressed three times by the Hebrew verb חלה, a *Piel* form followed by פנים, "face." Its literal meaning is "to make the face (of someone) sweet or pleasant," hence "to appease"; its more general sense, however, is "to entreat the favor (of someone)." Also, the verb כפר, besides its regular sense of "EXPIATION," twice has the meaning "propitiation" in reference to a human object.

b. In LXX Greek. On the three occasions when חלה means "propitiation," it is rendered in the LXX by the Greek verb ἐξιλάσκεσθαι, which also regularly translates כפר. In classical and Hellenistic Greek ἱλάσκεσθαι and its intensive compound ἐξιλάσκεσθαι mean "to propitiate," but ἐξιλάσκεσθαι has also a rare secondary meaning of "to expiate" (see Plato *Laws* 862*c;* Ditt. *Syll.*[3] 1042). In the LXX, however, words of the ἱλάσκεσθαι class acquire as their primary meaning the sense of "expiation" through their regular use in translating כפר and its derivatives. The use of ἐξιλάσκεσθαι in the LXX to express "propitiation" is therefore rare and exceptional.

c. In NT Greek. The Greek terms which are translated "propitiation" in the KJV are ἱλασμός and ἱλαστήριον. Their meaning in the NT, however, is derived from their use in the LXX, where they have the general sense of "expiation" and do not as religious terms bear the meaning of "propitiating God."

2. In the OT. The idea of propitiation is not prominent in the OT. The word as a religious term expresses pagan conceptions of appeasing the Deity and is inappropriate to the religion of Israel.

a. In human relationships. The Hebrew verb כפר has the meaning of "to propitiate" only when man is the subject and it is used with reference to a human object—e.g., Jacob propitiates° ("appeases") Esau with a present (lit., "covers his face" or "wipes clean his face" blackened by displeasure; Gen. 32:20); a wise man will propitiate (RSV "appease"; KJV "pacify") a king's wrath (Prov. 16:14). The verb חלה, when used of human relationships, has the sense of entreating a favor rather than appeasing anger (Job 11:19; Ps. 45:12—H 45:13; Prov. 19:6).

b. Propitiation and sacrifice. Some have regarded Hebrew SACRIFICE as essentially a piacular gift by which the wrath of God is appeased. This view has claimed support from, e.g., David's reaction to the idea that God might have prompted Saul to harass him: "May he [God] accept an offering" (lit., "Let him smell an offering"; I Sam. 26:19; cf. Gen. 8:21; Exod. 29:25). But the only clear instance of such a propitiatory conception of sacrifice is Mesha's offering of his son to Chemosh (II Kings 3:27); and this was the act of a pagan king. In Israel the burnt offering is not necessarily a propitiatory gift, as has been maintained; it is more probably an expression of devotion to God. And David's words may well refer to the normal expiation through sacrifice of some inadvertent sin.

In general, at least, OT sacrifices are not propitiatory but expiatory. God is frequently the subject, but never the object, of the key cultic term כפר: it is used of God's expiating (i.e., "covering" or "erasing") man's sin, but never in the sense of man's propitiating God. This is in line with the prophetic teaching that God's favor cannot be bought. The three occasions when the verb חלה in the sense of "propitiate" is used with reference to God (Zech. 7:2; 8:22; Mal. 1:9) are exceptional and apparently deliberate. Its use in Zech. 7:2; Mal. 1:9 is distinctly contemptuous —i.e., Yahweh is not to be "propitiated." And in Zech. 8:22 it is pagan peoples who come to "propitiate" him.

3. In the NT. Nowhere in the NT does the idea of propitiation occur. When the term appears in the KJV, it renders one of the derivatives of ἱλάσκεσθαι. The LXX translators, however, generally use the words of the ἱλάσκεσθαι class to express the divine removal of guilt or defilement and clearly regard their pagan meaning of propitiating the Deity as inappropiate to the religion of Israel. Since, therefore, this LXX usage is determinative for the NT writers, the use of the word "propitiation" in the KJV is erroneous and misleading. In each case "propitiation" should be substituted, as in the RSV, by "EXPIATION." There is no idea in the NT of the wrath of God being propitiated by the sacrifice of Christ. It is God in Christ who reconciles the world to himself (II Cor. 5:19).

Bibliography. G. B. Gray, "Sacrifice, Propitiation, and Expiation," *Sacrifice in the OT* (1925), pp. 55-95. C. H. Dodd, "Atonement," *The Bible and the Greeks* (1935), pp. 82-95, provides an exhaustive study of the LXX use of words of the ἱλάσκεσθαι class as translating כפר and its derivatives. V. Taylor, "Sacrifice," *Jesus and His Sacrifice* (1937), pp. 49-53. A. G. Hebert, "Atone, Atonement," in A. Richardson, ed., *A Theological Word Book of the Bible* (1950), pp. 25-26. R. Abba, "Sacrifice," *The Nature and Authority of the Bible* (1958), pp. 230-33.

R. ABBA

PROSELYTE [προσήλυτος, newcomer, visitor]. The usual LXX rendering of the Hebrew term גר, *gēr*, which designated a person associated with a community not his own. The גר in the OT is one who through some misfortune, such as war (II Sam. 4:3; Isa. 16:4), famine (Ruth 1:1), plague, or bloodguilt, has had to leave his home and kindred and take refuge with a foreign people. The term גר is usually rendered "stranger," but also "alien" and "SOJOURNER." In the Mishna, however, גר designates a convert to Judaism, and in the NT προσήλυτος has the same meaning. The OT meaning of the terms is thus sharply distinguished from the NT and rabbinic usage. The change in the meaning of the term גר from "immigrant" to "convert" is connected with one of the most significant developments in the history of Judaism and the prehistory of Christianity.

1. The original sense of the term גר
2. The LXX renderings of the term
3. Background of the term's evolution
   a. Monotheism and universalism
   b. The effects of exile and dispersion
   c. The Maccabean and Hasmonean periods
4. Proselytism in the Roman period
   a. Propaganda and apologetic
   b. Anti-Jewish reaction
   c. Philo and Josephus on proselytes
5. Successes of Jewish propaganda
   a. The preponderance of women converts
   b. The God-fearers
   c. Paul and the uncircumcised
6. Rabbinic attitudes toward proselytes
   a. Proselyte baptism
   b. Circumcision
   c. Status of the convert
7. The decline of Jewish proselytizing
8. Christianity's debt to Jewish proselytizing
Bibliography

1. The original sense of the term גר. The term גר in the OT designates an alien or immigrant in the process of becoming assimilated. In primitive Semitic society all rights were based on blood relation, but a relationship like consanguinity could be artificially contrived. A displaced person without kin to defend him might gain protection by attaching himself as a client to a chieftain or a clan. The practice harks back to nomadic life of the desert, where lawlessness was tempered by the code of hospitality. A guest or fugitive having entered the tent, or touched the tent rope of his host, was inviolable. The honor of the chieftain and the clan was the only sanction to this obligation, since the stranger had no other appeal. Violation of the duty of hospitality was a heinous crime. Ordinarily the bond between host and guest was only temporary, but more permanent sanctuary might be had, and when granted by one member of the clan, it obligated the entire clan.

Such an agreement might be confirmed by a covenant oath at the shrine of a god. Abraham and Isaac became sojourners in the region of Gerar by covenant oaths with Abimelech at Beer-sheba (Gen. 21:32; 26:28). The god in whose name the oath was taken became the patron and protector of the client who, although he might not relinquish his old religion, still had to acknowledge some degree of allegiance to the protecting deity. Foreigners who lived among the Israelites were anxious to learn the law of the god of the land and to serve him for their own security (II Kings 17:26-28). The Egyptianess Hagar (Gen. 16:7-13), Abraham's Damascene steward (Gen. 24: 2), the Canaanitess Rahab (Josh. 2:11), the Gibeonites (Josh. 9), the Gittites Obed-edom and Ittai (II Sam. 6:10-11; 15:19-22), Uriah the Hittite (II Sam. 11:11), the widow of Zarephath (I Kings 17:12), are represented as worshiping Yahweh.

Since political and religious rights were inseparable, the client could not be admitted to full rights in the host's tribe apart from participation in the cult. Thus the immigrant would tend to become an adherent of his patron's cult. Often the client was a refugee, cut off from the worship of the god or gods of his native land, as David among the Philistines was driven to serve other gods (I Sam. 26:19).

A fugitive who found asylum at a shrine would naturally take the god of the sanctuary as his patron deity and, to ensure security, might attach himself to the cult site as permanent personnel. The Gibeonites were allowed to live among the Israelites as menials in the cult service, "hewers of wood and drawers of water for the congregation and for the altar of the LORD" (Josh. 9:27). The Levites who assisted in the temple service (Num. 3:5 ff) but were not allowed to enter the sanctuary and look upon the holy things (4:20) were a displaced group who managed to achieve and retain status and security as menials in the cult service. In Ezek. 44:7-9 there is a bitter protest against the admission of foreigners, uncircumcised in heart and flesh, into the sanctuary, and especially against their employment in the care of some of the sacred cult objects. A Phoenician inscription (CIS no. 86) indicates that גרים comprised a distinct class of temple personnel and received a stipend.

Besides the relatively small number of immigrants who found a lowly place in the service of the cult, there were numerous other non-Israelites in the land. From the earliest times diverse elements had joined themselves to the Israelites (Exod. 12:38). In the preexilic period considerable numbers of foreigners were found among the Israelites. According to the Chronicler, Solomon took a census of all the aliens (גרים) who were in the land, following the census which his father, David, had taken—which, apparently, had not listed aliens separately—and he found their numbers to be 153,600 (II Chr. 2:17). More than half this group he assigned to the *corvée*. The bulk of these aliens probably consisted of descendants of the Canaanites, and their status was analogous to that of the περίοικοι of the Peloponnesus, who were granted freedom and property rights but had not the full rights of patricians. This sizable body of second-class citizens occupied a position between that of the free-born Israelite and the slave.

The גר is often mentioned along with the poor, widows, and orphans (Lev. 19:10; 23:22; Deut. 24: 19), with whom he shared the triennial tithe (Deut. 14:29). He might become wealthy (Lev. 25:47), but this was rare (Deut. 28:43-44). His usual livelihood was as a worker for wages (Lev. 22:10; 25:6, 40). The Israelite is forbidden to oppress him or withhold his wages (Deut. 24:14; 27:19; Ezek. 22:29).

Israel is enjoined to remember that they were once sojourners in Egypt (Exod. 22:21; 23:9) and ought, therefore, to treat the sojourner in their midst as an equal and love him as themselves (Lev. 19:34; Deut. 10:18-19). Such expressions of concern for the גר in writings otherwise so hostile to the foreigner (cf. Exod. 17:16; Deut. 23:4-7; 25:19) indicate that the גר was so closely assimilated to the Israelite that differences had virtually disappeared. The FOREIGNER was apparently regarded as a transient, while the גר was accepted as a semipermanent or permanent resident, partly or wholly accepted in the community of Israel. From this situation it is easy to see how the word גר came to denote a religious convert.

2. The LXX renderings of the term. The word προσήλυτος is used some seventy-eight times in the LXX as the translation of the Hebrew גר and is not used to translate any other word. The term προσήλυτος is not used by classical writers and was evidently borrowed from colloquial speech by the translators of the LXX. The classical Greek equivalent of Hebrew גר in the sense of "newcomer," "visitor," ἔπηλυς or ἐπηλύτης (*advena*), is not used as a translation of גר in the LXX; the form ἐπήλυτος occurs in Job 20:26, as a mistaken rendering of שריד, "escapee," and the passage has nothing to do with immigrants or converts. The classical term for "resident alien," μέτοικος (*incola*), occurs in Jer. 20:3, but here the Hebrew was thoroughly misapprehended—מגור, "terror," was mistaken for גר. Instead of the regular rendering προσήλυτος, the LXX sometimes uses ξένος, "stranger," but more often πάροικος, which is virtually a synonym of the classical μέτοικος. The use of πάροικος is found in passages where the term προσήλυτος in a sense approaching the meaning "religious convert" would be particularly inappropriate, as when the Israelites are spoken of as גרים in a foreign land (Gen. 15:13; 23:4; Exod. 2:22; 18:3), the pious man as a גר on earth (I Chr. 29:15; Pss. 39:12; 119:19), or the Lord as a stranger and wayfarer in the land of Israel (Jer. 14:8). In Deut. 14:21, where the law discriminates against the גר, the LXX renders πάροικος. The ill-fated Amalekite who claimed to have dispatched the wounded Saul (II Sam. 1:13) is also designated a πάροικος. Elsewhere, however, in similar contexts, when the Israelites are called גרים in a foreign land, in Egypt (Exod. 22:21; 23:9; Lev. 19:34; Deut. 10:19), or in the Promised Land (Lev. 25:23), the rendering is προσήλυτοι. In Exod. 12:19; Isa. 14:1; and in Aquila's version of Lev. 19:34, the Aramaic form of גר, גיורא, is retained in Greek transcription, γειώρας. The reason for this is not altogether clear, though it may be an indication that the translator understood the word to have special significance in these passages, perhaps approaching the sense of "religious convert."

It has been noted that the LXX renderings of גר differ somewhat in the three main strata of the Hexateuch. In JE the rendering is always πάροικος in the sense of "immigrant," while in D the rendering προσήλυτος has the sense of "resident alien" and in HP sometimes approaches the sense of "religious convert." While this is, of course, no evidence that the translators were aware of the different literary strata, it may be a slight indication that they knew the word גר had a history and that its meaning had changed or was in the process of changing. Apart from this bit of evidence, which could scarcely be termed unequivocal, there is no clear difference in the meaning of the term προσήλυτος in earlier or later parts of the LXX. The word occurs in the Apoc. only in Codex Sinaiticus of Tob. 1:18, with reference to Deut. 14:29; 26:12.

3. Background of the term's evolution. The change of meaning which the terms גר and προσήλυτος underwent reflects the missionary spirit which developed in Judaism in the postexilic period, increased in intensity in the Hellenistic and Roman periods, and died out after the rise of Christianity.

From the latter part of the eighth century B.C. onward, increasing numbers of Israelites came to live outside the borders of Palestine. The Assyrian conqueror scattered a large part of the N tribes in various countries of the Empire (II Kings 17:6), and the Babylonian deportations carried many Judeans away. The Dispersion was effected, not only by exile and deportation, but also by the trade and commerce which Solomon initiated (I Kings 9:26; 10:28). In the fifth century there was a colony of Jewish military mercenaries at Elephantine in Egypt with their own temple of Yahweh, and Jews were scattered throughout the rest of the provinces of the Persian Empire (Esth. 3:8). The exilic and postexilic writers speak often of gathering the dispersed of Israel and Judah from the four corners of the earth, from Egypt, Assyria, Ethiopia, Libya, and the Mediterranean islands (I Chr. 16:35; Ps. 106:47; Isa. 11:12; 43:5-6; 54:7; 56:8; Jer. 23:3; 29:14; 31:8, 10; 32:37; Ezek. 11:17; 20:34, 41; 28:25; 34:13; 36:24; Zeph. 3:10; Zech. 10:10).

a. Monotheism and universalism. The Jews carried with them into the foreign lands their monotheistic faith. The triumph of monotheism tended to transform Judaism from a nationalistic to a universalistic religion, for the inevitable corollary of ethical monotheism is the doctrine of the universal brotherhood of man. The Second Isaiah stressed the idea that Israel's mission was to bring other peoples to the worship of the true God. In many passages of the postexilic portions of the OT, the hope and assurance is expressed that the heathen will sooner or later see the error of their way and turn from their idolatry to the worship of the God of Israel (Isa. 2:2-4; 19:18-25; 44:5; 45:23; 65:16; Jer. 3:17; 4:2; 12:16; Zeph. 3:9; Zech. 8:20-23; 9:7; 14:16-19). The bold aspiration of these passages is tempered with eschatological and apocalyptic elements, and there is no indication that Israel by her own efforts will effect the mass conversions; still it is envisaged that, pending the ultimate conversion of the heathen, individuals and groups may be attracted and won over to the religion of Israel. Solomon in his prayer of dedication of the temple is represented as beseeching the Lord to hear the prayer of the foreigner who comes to pray in his temple, so that all the peoples of the earth may come to know and worship the Lord as does Israel (I Kings 8:41-43). It is difficult to determine the date of this passage, but it breathes the universalist and missionary spirit of the Second Isaiah and stands in sharp contrast to the attitude of Ezek. 44:7-9.

The story of Naaman the Syrian presents an instance of partial conversion of a nonresident foreigner to the worship of the God of Israel. The difficulties which Naaman faced in the attempt to worship the God of Israel in a foreign land in the temple of a heathen god are vividly pointed up (II Kings 5:15-19), and in the nature of the case his devotion to Yahweh could hardly be expected to endure. Israel's God was still too much bound to the soil of the tiny land. Still, Naaman's experience was a step toward the achievement of the condition affirmed in the last book of the prophetic canon: "From the rising of the sun to its setting my name is great among the nations, and in every place incense is offered to my name, and a pure offering; for my name is great among the nations, says the LORD of hosts" (Mal. 1:11).

There is considerable evidence that in the postexilic period many foreigners were attracted to the religion of the Jews and were assimilated to it in varying degrees. Intermarriage, then as ever, was the most effective mode of blending ideas as well as genes. Among those who returned from the Babylonian exile, marriage with foreigners had proceeded at such a rate as to alarm the leaders of the restored community and move them to launch a vigorous and drastic campaign to combat and undo (Ezra 9–10; Neh. 13) what they considered a great evil and treason to their God.

Elements of nationalism and pseudoracism were inextricably mixed with religious concerns in the minds of the reformers, who feared contamination and assimilation in both areas. It is patent, in the nature of the case, that not everyone agreed with the ideology and policies of the reformers. The book of Ruth is generally regarded as a protest against the militant particularism of Ezra, Nehemiah, and their cohorts. The poignant story of a destitute foreign-born widow, who became the grandmother of Israel's greatest king, carries with it an implicit defense of intermarriage and a plea for tolerance more eloquent than argumentation. A Moabite woman's assumption of full religious obligations in Israel mocks the discrimination that would exclude her kind to the tenth generation (Deut. 23:3) or forever (Neh. 13:1). National and religious elements are here combined: "Your people shall be my people, and your God my God" (Ruth 1:16). Here we encounter for the first time a form of the expression "to take refuge under the wings of the Lord," which later became almost a technical term for conversion to Judaism. The parable of Jonah also is a caricature of particularism and a sort of manifesto of the foreign mission of Judaism.

In Isa. 56:1-8, we have a passage of considerable interest and import for the history of Jewish attitudes toward the foreigner and his acceptance as a convert. Here the foreigner "who has joined himself to the LORD" is assured that the Lord will not separate him from his (the Lord's) people. Apparently there were a considerable number of foreign adherents to the religion of Israel who were nevertheless victims of discrimination, on the ground of their foreign origin. Their partial conversion is implied by their characterization as those

> who join themselves to the LORD,
> to minister to him, to love the name of the LORD,
> and to be his servants.

Theirs is the assurance that all those who keep the sabbath and hold fast to the Lord's covenant will have a place in his worship on his holy mountain, and their sacrifices will be acceptable on the altar of him whose house is to be a house of prayer for all peoples. The eunuch, too, who by the law was to be excluded from the Lord's community (Deut. 23:1), is promised a memorial better than progeny as a reward for his fidelity to the Lord. The date of this passage, one of the noblest expressions of universalism in the OT, is also difficult to determine. The emphasis on the sabbath agrees with part of the concerns of Nehemiah (Neh. 13:15-22; cf. Jer. 17:19-27), and the defense of the foreign worshiper seems likely to have been called forth by attacks on him such as may have occurred under the influence of Ezra and Nehemiah, but there is otherwise nothing specific by which to date the passage.

While nothing is said here of circumcision, the indirect characterization of these foreigners as those who hold fast the covenant may be taken to mean either that they had been circumcised, or that the author of this passage did not consider the rite requisite. The foreigners whose presence in the temple and participation in the service are denounced as sacrilege in Ezek. 44:7-8 are specifically alleged to be uncircumcised both in heart and in flesh. The juxtaposition of these passages, Isa. 56:1-8; Ezek. 44:7-8, reflects the conflicting attitudes toward the foreigner and possibly the issue of circumcision that we meet in the NT and in rabbinic literature.

b. The effects of exile and dispersion. Since the sixth century B.C. there has been no period when the greater part of the Jewish people was concentrated in Palestine. As one political disaster followed another, the Dispersion increased both numerically and spatially. After the murder of Gedaliah, the governor whom Nebuchadnezzar had appointed over Judah, Johanan the son of Kareah took "the remnant of Judah who had returned to live in the land of Judah from all the nations to which they had been driven" and, with the unwilling prophet Jeremiah, fled to Tahpanhes, or Daphnae, in the Delta of Egypt. Here was one of two large camps of Greek mercenaries, and here must have begun the exchange of ideas between Jews and Greeks which led to such interesting developments later in Alexandria. The impact of the Jewish refugees at Daphnae is attested to this day by the ruins of one of the camp buildings which is called *qaṣr bint el-yehudi*, the "castle of the Jew's daughter." The citizens of Jericho who objected to the depredations of Artaxerxes III were deported to distant Hyrcania on the Caspian Sea.

The natural process of cultural syncretism, of course, had its effects on the uprooted Jew. Josephus (Apion I.xxii) quotes Clearchus the pupil of Aristotle to the effect that the philosopher encountered in Asia Minor a Jew who had become a Greek both in language and in soul and was able to converse with the philosophers and impart more information than he received, yet observed a remarkable rigor in his diet and a continent way of life. Alexander the Great established a Jewish colony in Alexandria in Egypt.

The protracted conflict of the Ptolemies and the Seleucids, which swept back and forth across Palestine, caused more Jews to seek asylum in less turbulent environs. Josephus relates that Onias (III or IV), the son of Simon, one of the Jewish high priests, fled from Antiochus the king of Syria, when he made war with the Jews, and took refuge with Ptolemy in Egypt and there built a temple in the district of Heliopolis in the city of Leontopolis (Tell al-Yahudiah). Many Jews settled in the vicinity of this temple, and the district was called Onion (Wars VII.x.2). This event is related to the prophecy in Isa. 19:18-21, which may be *ex eventu*, or, as Josephus says (Antiq. XIII. iii.1), was invoked in support of the project. This Jewish temple, the House of Onias, is mentioned in the Mishna (Men. XIII.10) and in the Babylonian Talmud (Men. 109*b*, Meg. 10*a*). Like the older colony at Elephantine, this Jewish community influenced the Egyptians and in turn was influenced by them.

The impact of Hellenism on the Jew, both in Palestine and in the Diaspora, was much greater than Judaism's impact on the Greek, and particularly so in the Diaspora. There is no way of knowing how many Jews were drawn into the main stream of Hellenistic paganism and let their ancestral religion lapse, or remained only nominally Jews, but the number must have been considerable. There are numerous examples of syncretism and apostasy, but a couple of cases will serve to point out the dire effects of this tendency. Tiberius Alexander, a nephew of Philo, forsook his ancestral religion and rose to be procurator of Judea for two years, A.D. 46-48, during which time he slaughtered fifty thousand Jews (Jos. Wars. II.xviii.7-8). He later took part in the destruction of Judea and Jerusalem as a general of the Roman army (War V.i.6). Antiochus the Apostate, son of the leader of the Jewish congregation of Antioch in Syria, charged the Jewish community with plotting to burn the city, and when a great fire did occur, he blamed the Jews. He sacrificed to idols, tried to force others to do the same, and stirred up bloody riots against his own people (Jos. War VII.ii. 3). These cases are extreme, but they indicate how far assimilation and apostasy could and did go among some of the Diaspora Jews. The researches of Goodenough in the pagan symbolism adopted by Jews in the Hellenistic and Roman periods show that the degree of syncretism was much greater than previously thought.

c. The Maccabean and Hasmonean periods. In Palestine itself the military and political successes of the Maccabees revived Jewish nationalist pride and may have enhanced somewhat Jewish prestige in the Diaspora. John Hyrcanus and his successors attempted to create a new Jewish empire. John conquered the Edomites and forced Judaism on them (Jos. Antiq. XIII.ix.1), and his son Aristobulus similarly dealt with Galilee, whose population consisted of remnants of the Canaanites and Israelites, Arameans, Itureans (from the Lebanons), and Greeks (Jos. Antiq. XIII.xi.3). Because of its mixed population, Galilee was long known as "Galilee of the nations" (Isa. 9:1), and the Judeans held Galileans in contempt as a mongrel lot (John 1:46; 7:52). Alexander Janneus massacred the Moabites of Pella who refused to convert to Judaism (Jos. Antiq. XIII.xv.4). This policy of enforced conversion was motivated more by political considerations than by religious or missionary zeal. The concern was for cultural uniformity in the interest of political conformity, very much like the policy of Antiochus Epiphanes. During the war with Rome, Metilius, the Roman commander of a garrison in Jerusalem, saved his life by offering to turn Jew and be circumcised (Jos. War II.xvii.10). The people of Sepphoris would have forced two noble refugees from Trachonitis to be circumcised, if Josephus had not intervened (Jos. Life XXIII). Both these cases, however, occurred in the hysteria of war and cannot be regarded as normal. The rabbis never approved of forced conversions, and in Pharisaic law (Yeb. 48*b*) even a slave could not be forcibly converted.

The success of Jewish proselytism in the Hellenistic period is attested by many sources. The book of Tobit, which is perhaps pre-Maccabean, says that Tobit, whenever he visited Jerusalem, used to contribute to the support of orphans, widows, and proselytes (Tob. 1:8 Codex Sinaiticus). In the book of Judith, probably to be dated in the Maccabean period, the friendly Ammonite Achior was circumcised and converted when the Jews were victorious (Jth. 14:10).

In the book of Esther, which probably dates from the Maccabean period, we meet for the first time a specific term for conversion, or, perhaps, feigned conversion, to Judaism. After Mordecai had eliminated Haman and obtained a royal decree allowing the Jews to avenge themselves on their enemies, it is said (8:17) that many of the peoples of the land "became Jews" (KJV; Amer. Trans.), or "declared themselves Jews" (RSV). The verbal form here used may indicate either a genuine or a pretended conversion, and in view of the element of fear in the situation, it seems likely that the conversion was more feigned than real. The rabbis understood the "Esther proselyte" and the "lion proselyte" (II Kings 17:25) as false converts. The term מתיהדים is unique in the OT and rarely used in later Hebrew. The use of a special term for real or pretended conversion to Judaism, in spite of the unhistorical character of the story of Esther, is an indication that the practice was common enough to need a term to describe it. The mere profession of Judaism would not be considered conversion, and the LXX makes the matter decisive by adding that they underwent circumcision. Esth. 9:27 indicates that new adherents, present and future, are expected to observe the festival of Purim. The term used to designate the new adherents is the same applied to the foreigners who join themselves to the Lord (Isa. 56:3, 6), except that in Esther it is the Jewish people to whom they adhere, rather than the God of Israel, who finds no mention in the book.

The upsurge of nationalist zeal under the Hasmonean rulers did not check the development of the ideal of universalism implicit in the ethical monotheism of Judaism, which ideal was already well established and widely disseminated. The political ambitions of the Hasmoneans did not have the full support of the devoutly religious Jews (*see* HASIDIM; HASIDEANS) who had borne the brunt of the Syrian persecution and the war of liberation. Their concern was solely for loyalty to God, and they were indifferent or even hostile to the princely ambitions for national aggrandizement. Moreover, the Jews of the Diaspora were not directly involved in the Maccabean conflict, and the petty triumphs of the Hasmonean princes did not change the fact that Jews in the Gentile world had to make their way and win friends and adherents by peaceful means.

The family and descendants of Herod, himself an Edomite convert, insisted on conversion for those with whom they intermarried. The politically advantageous marriage of Herod's sister Salome with Sylleus of Arabia was prevented by Sylleus' unwillingness to convert to Judaism (Jos. Antiq. XVI.vii.6). Similarly, Epiphanius, son of Antiochus, refused to come over to Judaism in order to marry Drusilla, the sister of Agrippa II. Drusilla married Azizus of Emesa on his consent to be circumcised, and her more notorious sister, Bernice, married Polemo the king of Cilicia on the same condition. Polemo forsook the Jewish religion when Berenice left him (Jos. Antiq. XX.vii.3). This insistence on conversion was a tradition of the dynasty probably based more on political considerations than on religious fervor.

4. Proselytism in the Roman period. As early as the second century B.C., there were Jewish residents in Rome, possibly those who came in the train of the embassy which Simon the Maccabee sent to Rome. From the first the Jews in Rome exhibited such an aggressive spirit of proselytism that they were charged with seeking to infect the Romans with their cult, and the government expelled the chief propagandists from the city in 139 B.C. In the early decades of the first century B.C., considerable numbers of Jews were in Rome and other cities of Italy, as well as in the farthest reaches of the Empire. Josephus (Antiq. XIV.vii.2) quotes Strabo, *ca.* 85 B.C., to the effect that Jews were settled in all cities and that it was hard to find a place in the habitable world where there was not a Jewish community. In Egypt and Cyrene they were especially numerous and prosperous, and a large part of the non-Jewish population imitated the Jewish way of life. There were Jewish quarters in the various cities; the major part of Alexandria was allotted to them, and they were allowed a measure of self-rule and had their own courts for disputes among themselves. In 63 B.C., Pompey carried numerous Jewish captives to Rome for his victory procession. These were sold into slavery, and many later gained their freedom and as FREEDMEN or libertines became Roman citizens.

a. Propaganda and apologetic. The dispersion of Jews throughout the Mediterranean world put them everywhere in the position of a defensive minority and stimulated their self-consciousness as Jews. The Greek curiosity was naturally piqued by the strange customs of the Jews. The Diaspora Jews kept the sabbath, observed the festivals, practiced circumcision, and observed the dietary laws, especially the swine taboo. Juvenal (*Satires* VI.160; XIV.98) says they saw no difference between eating swine and eating human flesh. They preserved a strong attachment to Jerusalem and to the temple. All over the world Jews paid a half shekel a year to the temple (Philo *The Special Laws* I.78) and made pilgrimages to Jerusalem. Some of the Jewish rites and customs seemed bizarre and morose, and yet wide circles of pagan society were fascinated by them. But the great appeal was made by Jewish morals based on ethical monotheism. Many a questing Greek, who no longer believed in the gods or in the doctrines of the philosophers, could find satisfaction and inner peace in Judaism's doctrine of one omnipotent God, creator of heaven and earth, invisible and transcendent, who cannot be represented by any image man may make, whose providence extends to all, who demands a life of virtue and rewards and punishes beyond this life. No other religion had such exalted doctrine. There were still other attractive features; for those inclined to asceticism, there were rigorous rules for fasting, and for those who yearned for release from sin there were taboos and rites for ceremonial cleanliness. The theology and the ethics of Judaism stimulated the Greek interest in ideas. The cosmopolitan spirit and tolerant attitude of the Greeks encouraged the Jews to emphasize the universalistic aspects of their religion and to disregard or explain away such features of their law and customs as seemed difficult or absurd to the Greek mind. In theory, no part of the law was invalid, but in practice much of it was ignored. Many of the injunctions could not well apply in the Diaspora.

The Diaspora Jew was keenly aware of his religious superiority. He fancied himself "a guide to the blind, a light to those who are in darkness, a corrector of the foolish, a teacher of children, having in the law the embodiment of knowledge and truth" (Rom. 2:19-20). An extensive and vigorous propaganda for Judaism was developed in the cities where there were large Jewish minorities, especially in Alexandria. The translation of the Hebrew scriptures into Greek for the benefit of Jews who no longer understood Hebrew became also a vehicle for spreading knowledge of Judaism among the Gentiles. From the early stages of the Diaspora, the synagogues were open to all, and the Gentiles heard the readings and discourses in Greek. "For from early generations Moses has had in every city those who preach him, for he is read every sabbath in the synagogues" (Acts 15:21). Zealous Jews created a whole literature in Greek. They reworked biblical materials and published books under pagan pseudonyms for propaganda purposes. Remnants of what must have been an extensive literature of this sort have been preserved. Most important is the so-called Sibylline Oracles, which in its present form has been reworked by Christians, but which contains original Jewish sections in which idolatry is denounced and monotheism advocated. The Letter of Aristeas and the poem of pseudo-Phocylides are other works intended to promote Judaism. The Wisdom of Solomon, a composite work produced between the second century B.C. and the first half of the first Christian century, is an unexcelled document of religious propaganda, a compound of Judaism and Hellenism, directed at the devout Greeks whose souls found no rest in paganism. The interpolated "treatise against idolatry," chs. 13–15, expresses the conviction that idolatry is a late aberration which must soon pass away (14:12-14). Through the Jews the "imperishable light of the law" is to be given to the world (18:4). Aristobulus the Jewish philosopher, in the middle of the second century B.C., wrote with the aim of reconciling Greek philosophy and Jewish religion. A great part of the writings of Philo of Alexandria are expressly intended to recommend Judaism to the respect and even the acceptance of the Greeks. Like Aristobulus the philosopher, Philo tried to show that the Greek philosophers drew from Moses and that everything good in Greek philosophy had already been better taught by Moses. Josephus in Roman exile during the latter part of his life devoted his energies to apologetic writing on behalf of Judaism.

The convert, of course, stood in need of instruction both before and after his admission to the new religion. Some passages of the OT, notably Pss. 15; 24:3 ff; 34:13-15; Isa. 33:14-16, seem well suited for catechetical instruction, and may have been so used. That there were manuals for the instruction of converts is highly probable. Harnack suggested that we have such a manual in parts of the Didache, or Teachings of the Twelve Apostles (1.1-3*a;* 2.2–5.2; and fragments of chs. 8; 13). These sections, largely ethical in content, are called the "Two Ways" and constitute the basis of the larger Christian work. Jewish features and rabbinic parallels, however, appear in the admittedly Christian sections of the work, as well as in the sections that have been thought to be of Jewish origin. Even if the Two Ways is not the remnant of a Jewish manual for converts, it is altogether likely that such manuals were in use.

b. Anti-Jewish reaction. The Jews were not accorded wholehearted acceptance and approval everywhere. Already in the fifth century B.C., the colony at Elephantine had its temple destroyed. The attempt to resist assimilation by self-isolation aroused suspicion and animosity. The social isolation of the Jews was by no means complete. Ovid (*Art of Love* I.75) mentions that Roman gentlemen often went to the synagogues in quest of amorous adventures, which they presumably found on occasion. Tacitus complained that the Jews "keep themselves and show mercy to their kinsmen, but toward every one else they bear a malignant hatred" (*History* V.5) and similarly Juvenal (*Satires* XIV.103-4) charged that "they show the way only to their fellow believers, and only the circumcised do they lead to the desired fountain." Their refusal to participate in the worship of the pagan gods was interpreted as a lack of community spirit and proper piety. The religion of the Jews did not win the respect of the literati in particular. Horace (*Satires* I.5) thought the God of the Jews a "melancholic" one, while to Cicero the Jews' religion was "barbaric superstition" (*Against Flaccus* 28). Tacitus was baffled by the absence of representations of the gods in their synagogues (*History* V.5). Juvenal thought they worshiped the clouds and sky (*Satires* XIV.97). Deliberate defamation of the Jews, begun by the Egyptian priest Manetho in the third century B.C., was carried on by Lysimachus, Chaeremon, and Apion, by Tacitus and the Roman satirists. Tacitus claimed that the Jews worshiped an ass's head in the temple at Jerusalem; that they abstained from flesh of the swine because this animal often suffers from the scab, which disease the Jews had in Egypt and for which they were expelled (*History* V.3-4). Juvenal ridiculed the swine taboo (*Satires* VI.160; XIV.98) and regarded the sabbath as simply an excuse for laziness (*Satires* XIV.105-6). Apion circulated the tale that the Jews annually captured a Greek, fattened him, and then sacrificed him and ate his guts, swearing always to hate Greeks (Apion II.8). Against such calumnies the Jews wrote apologies, such as Josephus' work *Against Apion.* The charge that the Jews were a late, upstart people was answered by quoting the ancient writers who mentioned them. The charge that Jews had contributed nothing to civilization brought forth the counterclaim that almost everything of value in civilization derived from Moses. The Greek poets and philosophers were quoted to show that they too share something of the exalted concept of God with the Jews. The accusation that the Jews were hostile to strangers was answered by pointing out the humane features of the Mosaic law in respect to foreigners. This latter point was stressed particularly by Philo.

Despite the efforts of apologists and propagandists, anti-Jewish sentiments sometimes erupted into violence. Ptolemy VII tried to punish the Jews of Alexandria for their support of Cleopatra by herding them together to be trampled by inebriated elephants, but the attempt was abortive (Jos. Apion II.v). In A.D. 38 there was a government-sponsored persecution of Jews in Alexandria; synagogues were attacked and pictures of Caligula set up in them (Philo *Against Flaccus; Legation to Caius*). Anti-Jewish violence broke out in Syria during the Jewish Revolt, and ten thousand Jews' throats were cut in Damascus in the space of one hour (Jos. War II.xx.2; VII.viii.7).

*c. **Philo and Josephus on proselytes.*** Philo Judeus was himself a thorough blend of both Jew and Greek. To him Greek was "our language," and the non-Greek-speaking Jews were "barbarians." His own knowledge of Hebrew, if any, was very meager, though he was apparently acquainted with the terminology and interpretation of the oral law. Plato to him was almost on the same level with Moses. Like a pagan he even referred to the stars as "visible gods." Still his loyalty and zeal for Judaism were all-consuming. For the disloyal and apostate Jew he had no sympathy, and he fought against these "sons of Cain," who forsook Jewish ways and regarded them only as figurative acts which were not binding on those who understood their hidden meaning (*On the Posterity of Cain* 35-40; *On Penitence* 180-86; *The Life of Moses* I.6; *On Abraham* 80-94). Philo's purpose, however, was not only to edify his fellow Jews, but also to win friends and adherents among the Gentiles. Since Israel was no longer a political entity, but a religious community whose special relationship to God depended, not on blood and soil, but on fidelity to his will, it was deemed necessary to interpret Jewish life in religious rather than national terms. There was an inescapable responsibility to bring others to the worship of the true God within the Mosaic polity. Accordingly, Philo stressed the universal aspect of Judaism and its moral and humane character. The Mosaic teachings and the purity of Jewish family life were contrasted with the views of the Greek poets and the pagan immorality of Alexandria. The superiority of the Jewish religion commanded the respect of the heathen, and many of them observed the Jewish sabbath and the Day of Atonement (*Life of Moses* II.4). Conversions to Judaism were apparently not infrequent in Alexandria, for Philo refers often to converts and praises them for their courage and zeal and for the radical transformation of their lives.

It was no easy thing for the pagan to forsake polytheism and adopt an entirely new way of life, for the pagan became a Jew only by a violent and complete break with his past. According to Tacitus (Hist. V.5), proselytes learned to despise the gods, cast off the fatherland, and hold parents, brothers, and children in contempt. In Philo's view, however, such alienation from polytheism was a change to a better order, a beautiful migration. These fugitives to God, suppliants who changed to the polity of the Jews, who spurned idle fables and embraced truth in its purity, are praised for their wisdom and virtue. There should be no discrimination against them in Jewish society, but they are to be accepted into the Mosaic polity on equal terms with born Jews. More than that, they are to be shown special consideration, friendship, and love, on the basis of Lev. 19:34. The convert is thus equal, or even superior, to the born Jew, for true nobility is a matter of the heart, rather than of birth. The born Jew does not obtain the approval of God by his birth, but by his loyalty to his God-loving heritage. The convert gains God's approval because he makes the passage to piety (*The Special Laws* I.9.51-52).

Apart from full membership in the Mosaic polity, Philo gave recognition to intermediate classes who are neither born Jews nor full converts. The "alien," ἀλλογενής or ἀλλότριος (the LXX terms for בן־נכר or נכרי), had little part in the scheme of things. For the LXX term πάροικος, which usually renders the Hebrew תושׁב, Philo uses the Athenian term μέτοικος. By this term he apparently designates the half heathen, who were allowed to live with limited rights among the Jews in Palestine (Lev. 22:10; 25:47; Ps. 39:12—H 39:13). In Tannaitic law the equivalent of the LXX πάροικος is גר תושב, who, though uncircumcised, is not a complete heathen but one who has abandoned idolatry and observes the minimum ethic of the Noachian laws ('A.Z. 64*b*), which are: (*a*) to establish courts of justice; (*b*) not to worship idols; (*c*) not to blaspheme; (*d*) not to commit adultery; (*e*) not to murder; (*f*) not to steal; (*g*) not to eat flesh from a living animal (Tosef. 'A.Z. VIII[IX].4-6). The LXX term προσήλυτος Philo understood in the sense of "convert," although there is no warrant in the LXX usage for this understanding. He must have had in mind the Tannaitic use of the term גר in the sense of "convert." Philo, however, for his part, used the term ἐπήλυτης rather than προσήλυτος to designate the convert. The rabbis distinguished the full convert, גר צדק, and the partial adherent, גר תושב, or "resident alien," who accepted monotheism and the Jewish ethic but not the ritual. His ritualistic behavior was uncontrolled, and he had no formal relation to the congregation. The true convert, גר צדק, or גר ברית, "covenant convert," assumed full ritual duties, including circumcision, and was received into full membership in the community and his descendants became fully qualified Jews in the third generation. It seems that Philo at times fluctuates in his notion of the proselyte as the circumcised, full convert and as the uncircumcised, partial adherent—i.e., between what the rabbis called the גר צדק and the גר תושב. In commenting on Lev. 19:34: "You were strangers [גרים/προσήλυτοι] in the land of Egypt," he says in effect that "proselyte" may mean "foreigner" in both the literal and the religious sense and that the Jews were proselytes in Egypt in both senses, because they lived in a strange land and they were uncircumcised. By the same token the pagan who has rejected polytheism but remains uncircumcised is a proselyte in the same sense as were the Israelites in Egypt. This may suggest that circumcision was not required of the proselyte and that the term could designate the uncircumcised half-convert. But the opposite implication is perhaps the more likely, that the concern over noncircumcision indicates that only the circumcised were recognized as proselytes, or true converts, as with the rabbis.

Josephus, for his part, does not use the term προσήλυτος, but he variously describes converts as those who change their course of life and embrace the Jewish customs, who are taught to worship God according to the Jewish religion (Antiq. XX.ii.1, 3), whom the Jews had made a part of themselves (War VII.iii.3). Similar terms are used of the forced conversions of the Idumeans who submitted to the use of circumcision and the rest of the Jewish ways of living and thereafter became no other than Jews (Antiq. XIII.ix.1). Judaism to Josephus was thus not merely a matter of race, but admitted all who had a mind to observe the Mosaic laws and live as Jews (Apion II.xxix).

5. Successes of Jewish propaganda. The vigor and success of Jewish missionary efforts is attested in many sources. The Sibylline Oracles III.195 (*ca.* 140 B.C.) affirm that "the Jews were for all mortal men the guides to [the way of] life," and say of Judea (III.271): "Every land shall be full of thee and every sea." Roman poets and historians refer, usually with animus, to the ubiquity of the Jews and their sympathizers and adherents. Horace (*Satires* I.4.142) threatens the hater of poetry that "like the Jews, we will force you to come over to our numerous party." Horace himself had a friend who observed Jewish customs (*Satires* I.9, 68-72). Seneca (cited by Augustine *The City of God* IV.11) and Dio Cassius (XXXVII.7) also bear witness to the increase of adherents to Judaism. Juvenal (*Satires* XIV.96-104) lashes out at those who learn to practice and revere the Jewish law. The father would begin by observing the sabbath and the food taboos and worshiping the God of heaven, and the son would go all the way and be circumcised.

Before the rise of Christianity, Judaism had won numerous sympathizers, adherents, and even full converts in all parts of the Roman world. Agrippa I in his letter to Gaius Caligula (Philo *The Embassy to Gaius* XXXVI.281-82) mentions Jewish colonies in Egypt, Syria, Phoenicia, Asia Minor, and the Greek islands and asserts that not only are the continents full of Jewish colonies, but also the best-known islands, to say nothing of the countries beyond the Euphrates. Jews, he says, have settled wherever there is any advantage of soil or climate. Josephus speaks with pride of the large number of foreigners who were in some measure converted to Judaism (Antiq. XIC.vii.2; Apion II.xxix). Many Greeks, he says (War VII.ii.3), were made converts in Antioch, and many of the women of Damascus were inclined to Judaism (War II.xx.2). There was, he claimed (Apion II.xl), no city where the sabbath rest and other Jewish usages were not widely observed and Jewish virtues emulated.

a. The preponderance of women converts. Women appear to have predominated among the converts and near converts. The Roman noblewoman Fulvia, wife of the senator Saturninus, embraced the Jewish religion, but when she was defrauded by four unscrupulous Jews who solicited gifts from her on the pretext that the money would be sent to the temple in Jerusalem, Tiberius, at the instigation of his counselor Sejanus, banished the Jews from Rome, A.D. 19 (Jos. Antiq. XVIII.iii.5). This episode is corroborated by Tacitus (Ann. II.85). The size of the Roman Jewish community at that time may be judged by the fact that four thousand Jews capable of bearing arms were deported to Sardinia. In A.D. 31, Sejanus was removed from office, and the Jews returned to Rome. The Emperor Claudius began his reign (A.D. 41) with an edict of toleration for the Jews. Josephus mentions also Poppea Sabina, Nero's mistress and second wife, as a religious woman who acted favorably toward Jews (Life III; Antiq. XX. viii.11), but it is doubtful that she was actually a convert. Titus Flavius Clemens and his wife, Flavia Domitilla, cousins of the emperors Titus and Domitian, embraced Judaism, as a result of a visit to Rome of a deputation of distinguished rabbis, headed by Gamaliel II.

The special susceptibility of women to Jewish proselytizing, apart from the general feminine tendency to religiosity, was doubtless due in large part to the fact that circumcision, which has always been the chief impediment for the male prospective convert, was not required of women. The conversion of the royal family of Adiabene through the queen mother, Helena, was one of the signal successes of Jewish missionary endeavor and shows the vitality of Babylonian Judaism. Josephus gives us a rather full account of the affair (Antiq. XX.ii). The king, Izates, had great difficulty deciding whether to be circumcised. His Jewish mentors gave contradictory advice. Hananiah opined that it was possible to worship God without being circumcised and that the worship of God was of a superior nature to circumcision. Eleazar from Galilee insisted on circumcision. Even though the queen mother was opposed, Izates took the advice of Eleazar and submitted himself to the rite. The Adiabenians remained loyal to Judaism even in the days of the Jewish Revolt, when descendants of the royal house fought with the Jews against the Romans (Jos. War II.xix.2).

b. The God-fearers. For every pagan who became a true convert to Judaism by accepting the full ritual requirements, there were many more who accepted the theological and ethical teachings of Judaism, attended the synagogue, and observed many of the Jewish ceremonies, but could not admit the validity or necessity of the strange and painful surgical rite. Though there were Jews who were inclined to waive this onerous requirement, the majority position remained firm on this point. Thus many remained on the outside as only partial converts. These quasi-converts are referred to in the literature of the first Christian century as "those who fear/worship God" (οἱ φοβούμενοι/σεβόμενοι τὸν Θεόν). The origin of this expression is doubtless to be found in the Hebrew term יראי יהוה, which occurs frequently in the OT, particularly in the Psalter. Some have taken the expression in certain passages of the Psalms to refer to converts or near converts, as does its Greek equivalent in the NT. This has been suggested particularly for Pss. 115:11, 13; 118:4; 135:20, where the expression stands in parallelism with "(the house of) Israel," "the house of Aaron," and "the house of Levi." The problem, however, is whether the parallelism is synonymous or antithetical, whether "those that fear the LORD" are a separate category from the priests, Levites, and lay Israelites, or whether the term is simply a collective designation for pious Israelites in general. In keeping with the legal injunctions to fear the Lord (Lev. 19:14, 32; 25:17; Deut. 6:2, 13, 24; 10:12, 20), the expression became a standard designation for pious Israelites, as in Pss. 15:4; 22:23, 25; 25:12, 14; 31:19; 60:4; Mal. 3:16; 4:2; Ecclus. 2:7-17; 6:16-17; 34:13-15; Pss. Sol. 2:37; 3:16; 4:26, and there is nothing to indicate that this is not also the case in Pss. 115:11, 13; 118:4; 135:20.

Some scholars have understood the terms "God-fearer" and "proselyte" as synonymous, largely on the basis of Acts 13:16, 26, 43. Paul addresses his hearers in the synagogue of Antioch in Pisidia as "men of Israel, and you that fear God" (vs. 16), and again as "brethren, sons of the family of Abraham, and those among you that fear God" (vs. 26), while in vs. 43 the same hearers are called "Jews and devout converts" (KJV "proselytes"). This might appear a neat case for the synonymy of "God-fearer" and "proselyte," but it may be simply a textual error or a loose use of the term "proselyte." That the term φοβούμενος/σεβόμενος τὸν Θεόν does not designate a proselyte in the sense of a true convert is made clear by the fact that Paul at Corinth carried out his threat to leave the Jews and go to the Gentiles by going to the house of Titius Justus, who is called a "worshiper [σεβόμενος] of God" (Acts 18:7), although he was obviously a Gentile and uncircumcised. The uncircumcised God-fearers were brothers to Paul, who set aside all ritual impediments, but they were not regarded as full Jews, or in any sense sons of Abraham, by Jewish religious authorities. According to the strict view, one who rejected a single word of the law was not to be admitted as a proselyte (Mekhilta de Rabbi Simeon ben Yohai on Exod. 12:49; Siphra, Qedoshim VIII). One could not accept the whole law apart from circumcision, and this final rite obligated him to keep it all (Gal. 5:3). The distinction between God-fearers and true proselytes is shown in a Tannaitic comment on Isa. 44:5 which identifies the one who calls himself by the name of Jacob as the true proselyte, and the one who surnames himself by the name of Israel as the fearer of heaven—i.e., of God (Mekhilta, Mishpatim, Tractate Neziqin XVIII, Midrash Numbers Rabbah VIII.2). There is a story of a Roman senator, a God-fearing man, who committed suicide in order to nullify an anti-Jewish decree. He was circumcised shortly before his death; thus he was clearly a God-fearer before he was circumcised (Midrash Deuteronomy Rabbah II.24). Cornelius the centurion of the Italian cohort was clearly an uncircumcised foreigner, with whom proper Jews could not associate (Acts 10:28; 11:3), but the phrase φοβούμενος τὸν Θεόν is applied to him (Acts 10:2, 22). The centurion of Capernaum who loved the Jewish nation and built the local synagogue is not termed a God-fearer, though he certainly must have been in this category (Luke 7:2-10). This centurion's protestation of his own unworthiness expressed the deference of the non-Jew to the Jew in religious matters. Jesus' statement that he had not found so great a faith even in Israel shows that the centurion was not a true proselyte, for the full convert was a part of Israel. In Acts 2:10 the expression "both Jews and proselytes" does not necessarily imply that the proselytes were not also Jews; the probable meaning is that the mixed multitude from all over the world included both born Jews and converts to Judaism. It almost certainly also included numerous devout persons who were not full converts. The many devout Greeks whom Paul persuaded in the synagogue at Thessalonica (Acts 17:4) and the devout persons with whom he argued in the synagogue at Athens (vs. 17) were the same sort of people as those who are elsewhere called "those that fear/worship God" and who in Acts 14:1 are called simply Greeks. They were Gentiles, Greeks, Romans, Syrians, etc., who embraced or were inclined to the monotheistic faith and ethic of Judaism, who admired and even observed some of the Jewish customs such as the sabbath rest, the kindling of lights before the sabbath (in keeping with Exod. 35:3), and some of the food taboos, and who made contributions to charity (Philo *Life of Moses* II.2; Jos. Antiq. XIV. vii.2; Apion II.xl). They visited the synagogues, and read and listened to the reading and expounding of the Scriptures in Greek. They were drawing near to Judaism, but they were not full Jews. Some of them doubtless went on to become full Jews, or their descendants may have, but most continued in an intermediate state between pagans and Jews, chiefly because of the requirement of circumcision. As for the devout women of Antioch (Acts 13:50) and Lydia of Thyatira, "who was a worshiper of God" (Acts 16:14), it is difficult to assay the degree of their attachment to Judaism, but, since the issue of circumcision did not affect them directly, the difference in their religious life and that of their Jewish neighbors was perhaps negligible.

c. Paul and the uncircumcised. The Christian congregation at Jerusalem, under the influence of the circumcision party, inclined to the traditional treatment of the uncircumcised. They formulated a minimum ethic for Gentile adherents and conveyed it to the community in Antioch (Acts 15:20-29; 21:25). Some of the pagan practices most offensive to Jews were prohibited—unchastity, use of food sacrificed to idols, the eating of blood or anything strangled (cf. Lev. 17:10–18:30; Zech. 9:7). These prohibitions were similar to those imposed on the resident alien (גר תושב) in the Talmud as a sort of *modus vivendi* between Jews and Gentiles, but neither satisfied the demands of strict Judaism. The proper Jew could not associate with even the best of God-fearing Gentiles, as shown by the story of Cornelius. The issue of circumcision remained a live one for some time. A division of the mission field between Peter and Paul, the one to the circumcised, the other to the uncircumcised, failed to solve the problem (Gal. 2:3-10). The Holy Spirit poured out on the Gentiles convinced the circumcised with Peter at Caesarea that there was no ground for denying baptism and equality to

Gentiles so possessed (Acts 10:44-48). Peter, under the influence of the circumcision party, later reversed his stand and was taken to task by Paul at Antioch (Gal. 2:11-21). Peter apparently again acceded to Paul's view after the death of James. Paul refused to circumcise Titus, even though his presence at the council in Jerusalem offended the Judaizers (Gal. 2: 3-5), but Timothy, whose mother was Jewish and his father Greek, he circumcised so as to make him acceptable to the Jews in Asia Minor (Acts 16:1-4). When the report was spread in Jerusalem that Paul had been preaching to Jews that they need not circumcise their children or observe the ceremonial law, James and the elders advised him to go to the temple and show that he himself was an observing Jew (Acts 21:21-24). The false rumor that Paul had taken the uncircumcised Trophimus into the temple provoked the mob attack which led to his arrest (Acts 21:29-36). Paul was vexed with the issue of circumcision throughout his ministry, but his clearest and best answer is given in Gal. 5:6, that "in Christ Jesus neither circumcision nor uncircumcision is of any avail, but [only] faith working through love."

6. Rabbinic attitudes toward proselytes. Among the rabbis there were conflicting attitudes toward proselytes and proselytism, as on virtually every other question. There were those who considered it meritorious and God-pleasing to bring a proselyte under the wings of the divine Presence. "Every one who brings a proselyte near, it is as though he had created him" (Midrash Genesis Rabbah LXXXIV.4). It was ideal for one to make a proselyte a year (Midrash Genesis Rabbah XXVIII). There is a parable (Midrash Numbers Rabbah VIII.1-2), similar in spirit to the NT parable of the lost sheep, which shows how God loves the proselyte and admonishes Israel also to love (Deut. 10:19) and not oppress him (Lev. 19: 33-34). Hillel, the outstanding liberal of his day, was especially eager to receive proselytes (Shab. 31*a*) and accordingly inclined to make the requirements easy for them, while his stricter colleague, Shammai, insisted that the prospective proselyte's motives be vigorously tested. After instruction by a scribe, the candidate was subjected to a triple induction; he was circumcised, and when the wound was healed, he was immersed, in accordance with the law which required a ritual bath in all cases of impurity (Lev. 11–15; Num. 19); and then, when the temple stood, there was a sacrifice.

a. Proselyte baptism. It has been argued that there was no proselyte baptism before the destruction of the temple, and it is true that there is no early mention of the rite, but there is general agreement among scholars that it was a part of the reception of proselytes from the beginning. Some such rite would be especially needed for the reception of female proselytes, since it is not likely that they were admitted simply by affirmation. The importance of the ritual bath is indicated by the view that it alone may suffice, apart from circumcision (Yeb. 46). The baptismal rite was singularly appropriate, for it symbolized a radical change of status, an entry into a wholly new life. In token of his conversion, the convert assumed a new name. If the convert's spouse was not also converted, the marriage was considered invalid. Children born before the conversion were not heirs, and, if there were no children after conversion, the community inherited. Many of the proselytes displayed the typical zeal of the convert and even outdid their mentors. Jesus' stricture against the Pharisees, that they traversed sea and land to make a single proselyte, and then made him twice as much a child of Gehenna as themselves (Matt. 23:15), has reference to the Pharisaic obsession with ritual purity, which they impressed with double force on the proselyte. The Pharisaic zeal for proselytizing was accompanied by a rigid segregation of the ritually impure. Proselytes zealous in their observance of the ceremonial laws were a special joy to the rabbis. Some of Israel's eminent scholars were said to be proselytes, or descendants of proselytes. Shemaiah and Abtalion, predecessors of Hillel and Shammai, were reputed to be descended from Assyrian proselytes. Both Akiba and his disciple Meir were thought to be descended from proselytes. The translators Aquila and Theodotion were proselytes.

b. Circumcision. On the issue of circumcision for the convert, the rabbinic authorities were not of one mind. Rabbi Eliezer ben Hyrcanus considered circumcision the main act of conversion, but Rabbi Joshua declared baptism sufficient (Yeb. 46*a*). There are many sayings which reflect a liberal view in this regard. "The righteous among the Gentiles will have a portion in the world to come" (Tosef. Sanh. 13.2). "He who rejects idolatry acknowledges the whole Law" (Ḳid. 40*a*). Rabbi Yohanan (second-third century A.D.), the founder of the Academy of Tiberias, said: "Anyone who repudiates idolatry is called a Jew" (Meg. 13*a*). In general, however, the rabbis of the second-third century had a rather unsympathetic attitude toward the half convert. Rabbi Simeon ben Eleazar in the latter part of the second century averred that half converts were accepted only when the Jubilee was in existence ('Arak. 29*a*). This attitude doubtless reflects a reaction against Christianity's waiver of all prerequisites. It is likely that half converts were wholeheartedly accepted in the pre-Christian period.

c. Status of the convert. The convert, then as now, was often in an awkward position, subject to ambivalent and contradictory attitudes. Though in theory he was now an equal with born Jews, in fact he was not always so treated. The Palestinian scribes tended to be stricter than the written law, which gave the גר, after circumcision, equal rights with the native Israelite (Exod. 12:48; Num. 9:14). While the old ties were severed, the new were not yet firm. Many Jews, both in Palestine and in the Diaspora, were not willing to place their claim to superiority entirely on religious grounds, apart from descent from Abraham. They expected the convert to embrace their religion and bolster them as a national, or religio-political, entity, not only to propagate the true faith, but also to promote the cause of Jewish nationalism. True religion was inextricably bound up with the ideal of the chosen people (cf. Matt. 3:9). The proselyte could not properly claim Abraham as father. It was not permitted him to refer to the Deity as "God of our fathers," the proper formula for him being "God of the fathers of Israel" (Bik. I.4). This restriction, however, was later abrogated, and it was forbidden to remind the proselyte of his origin. Some limitations were placed on the rights of proselytes in regard to marriage. A priest could not marry a proselyte, but he could marry the daughter of a proselyte, provided one of her parents was born a Jew. The prohibition of intermarriage with an Ammonite or Moabite (Deut. 23:3), to the tenth generation, was in time relaxed. Rabbi Yohanan declared the daughter of an Ammonite proselyte eligible to marry a priest (Yeb. 77*a*). The children of proselytes became full Jews by marriage with a Jew.

7. The decline of Jewish proselytizing. Opposition to proselytes and to proselytizing, which finds expression in the Talmud, is probably to be attributed to the intensified antiforeign feelings generated during the rebellions against Rome, the destruction of Jerusalem, and the rise of Christianity. The sayings of the Tannaim and Amoraim date from the second-fourth centuries, but they reflect conditions and attitudes that obtained already in the first century. Even in ordinary times, there must have been a fairly high rate of defection among converts and near converts. In times of stress the new recruit could be expected to falter ('A.Z. 3*b*). The Talmud mentions proselytes who reverted to their previous error ('A.Z. 41*a;* Giṭ. 45*b*), and there was always the fear that such might happen (Mishna and Tosef. Dem. VI.10; Ḳid. 17*b;* 'A.Z. 64*a*). It was a cause of complaint that proselytes were often improperly schooled in the intricacies of the ceremonial laws (M. Nid. VII.3). There was peril to the religion in the marriage of an Israelite girl and a proselyte (Yeb. 47*b*). The proselyte allegedly had a strong inclination to evil, and the Torah, according to Rabbi Eleazer the Great, gave warnings against him in some thirty-six or forty-six places (B.M. 59*b*). It was charged that "evil comes on those who receive proselytes" (Yeb. 109*b*), even that proselytes because of sexual improprieties were to blame for delaying the (advent of the) Messiah. Proselytes came to be regarded as a disease, a scab on the body politic (Yeb. 47*b,* 109*b;* Ḳid. 70*b;* Nid. 13*b*), with an ironic wordplay on Isa. 14:1: "[They] will cleave to the house of Jacob."

After the second ill-starred revolt, when many proselytes became turncoats, Judaism's missionary ardor was considerably weakened and even converted to fear and hostility toward the proselyte. The Roman emperors intervened, because circumcision, viewed as equivalent to castration, disqualified one for office, and could not be tolerated. An absolute ban on circumcision was relaxed for Jews, but conversion to Judaism was forbidden under Domitian, Hadrian, Antonius Pius, and Septimus Severus. The rabbis sometimes denounced the would-be convert to authorities.

Though the Jew was doubly disqualified, by circumcision and inability to participate in the state-cult, Judaism was recognized as a legal cult, and Jews exploited this advantage over Christians, who were not exempt from emperor-worship. Christians blamed Jews as instigators of the Roman persecutions, and the mounting tension and animosity is reflected in the anti-Jewish bias of early Christian writers. The conflict with Rome and competition with its offspring Christianity proved too much for Judaism. Jewish missionary zeal diminished, and Jews increasingly withdrew into self-segregating communities. Jewish proselytizing, however, did not cease entirely, even in the Roman Empire, in spite of the restrictions: the laws remained on the books, but were often ignored.

Beyond the reaches of the Roman Empire, Jewish proselytism retained some of its vigor and succeeded in the conversion of some Arab tribes in the region of Medina, the Himyaritic princes, and the Chazars in the Crimea.

8. Christianity's debt to Jewish proselytizing. Judaism's propaganda assault on polytheism and idolatry and its proselytizing activities prepared the way for the phenomenal successes of Christianity. Judaism attained only limited success, because of its insistence on circumcision and full acceptance of the law. When Paul nullified the ritual laws and made baptism sufficient, without circumcision, the God-seekers and God-fearers welcomed the new faith. Christianity, in proclaiming a universal faith not restricted to any people or nation or set of rules, fulfilled the purpose for which God had scattered Israel among the nations.

Bibliography. Books and monographs: E. Schuerer, *The History of the Jewish People in the Time of Jesus Christ* (1885-90); A. Bertholet, *Die Stellung der Israeliten und der Juden zu den Fremden* (1896); F. Stähelin, *Der Antisemitismus des Altertums* (1905); J. Juster, *Les Juifs dans l'empire romain,* I (1914), 253-88; W. Bousset, *Die Religion des Judentums im späthellenistischen Zeitalter* (1926); A. Causse, *Les dispersés d'Israël* (1929); S. Bialoblocki, *Die Beziehungen des Judenthums zu Proselyten und Proselytentum* (1930); F. M. Derwachter, *Preparing the Way for Paul: The Proselyte Movement in Later Judaism* (1930); G. F. Moore, *Judaism in the First Centuries of the Christian Era* (1927-30); S. H. Hook, "The Way of the Initiate," in W. O. E. Oesterley, ed., *Judaism and Christianity,* I (1937), 213-33; B. J. Bamberger, *Proselytism in the Talmudic Period* (1939); W. G. Braude, *Jewish Proselytizing in the First Five Centuries* (1940); J. Klausner, *From Jesus to Paul* (1944); M. Simon, *Verus Israel* (1948); P. Dalbert, *Die Theologie der hellenistisch-jüdischen Missionsliteratur unter Ausschluss von Philo und Josephus* (1954); S. Baron, *A Social and Religious History of the Jews* (2nd ed., 1951-57).

Articles: M. Guttman, "The Term 'Foreigner' I (נכרי) Historically Considered," *HUCA,* 3 (1926), 1-20; T. J. Meek, "The Translation of GÊR in the Hexateuch and Its Bearing on the Documentary Hypothesis," *JBL,* 49 (1930), 172-80; J. Starr, "The Unjewish Character of the Markan Account of John the Baptist," *JBL,* 51 (1932), 227-37; L. Finkelstein, "The Institution of Baptism for Proselytes," *JBL,* 52 (1933), 203-21; S. Zeitlin, "A Note on Baptism for Proselytes," *JBL,* 52 (1933), 78-79; H. H. Rowley, "Jewish Proselyte Baptism and the Baptism of John," *HUCA,* 15 (1940), 313-34; J. Hempel, "Die Wurzeln des Missionswillen im Glauben des AT," *ZAW,* 66 (1954), 244-72; N. L. Levison, "The Proselyte in Biblical and Early Post Biblical Times," *Scottish Journal of Theology,* 10 (1957), 45-56.

M. H. POPE

PROSTITUTION. A term connoting the practices and activities which involve intercourse with harlots or prostitutes. Several words identify persons who act in this capacity. The context in which these words appear in the sources indicates whether such a person is a common harlot or a sacred prostitute, male or female, attached to and functioning on behalf of a shrine.

1. Definition and terminology
2. The common harlot
   a. Her status in the community
   b. The hire of a harlot

c. The distinguishing marks of a harlot
d. Her practice of her trade
e. The control of harlotry (prostitution)
3. The cult prostitute
a. The role of the sacred prostitute in the fertility cult
b. The male prostitute
c. The female prostitute
4. The biblical attack upon cult prostitution
Bibliography

1. Definition and terminology. "Prostitution" is a term signifying sexual intercourse from which ensues no binding or enduring relationship. It is usually indiscriminate in nature. The purpose of the practice of prostitution, as far as the prostitute is concerned, is not primarily sexual passion or the desire for children. It may be either mercenary or religious (*see* § 2*b below*). The most common term in the OT is זונה, translated "one who is a harlot" or "one who commits fornication." It applies to both kinds of prostitution, the secular and the cultic, and appears often in figurative form. Another word, קדשה, whose root meaning is "apart," "holy" (Babylonian *qadishtu*), is used of the religious prostitute. Related to this feminine form is the masculine word, קדש, which also is translated "cult prostitute." Another term, נתינים, perhaps "dedicated ones," is associated with cult prostitution by some scholars. The NT term πόρνη is used in Matt. 21:31; Luke 15:30; I Cor. 6:13.

2. The common harlot. The common harlot—i.e., the woman who offers her body to men for hire—appeared at an early period in Israel's life and continued to practice her trade throughout biblical history. She was less conspicuous, however, than her sister, the cult prostitute, although her social function was well established and generally recognized.

a. Her status in the community. In a number of biblical allusions to the secular harlot or prostitute, she is evidently accepted as a part of the community, without objection or condemnation. Tamar temporarily served as a harlot to achieve her ends (Gen. 38:14-15) and thus became pregnant by having intercourse with Judah. The subsequent anger of Judah, her father-in-law, was not provoked because of her playing the harlot so much as because she was his daughter-in-law and had caused him to commit incest unknowingly (Lev. 18:15). Rahab the harlot had her special place in the traditions of Israel because she had befriended the Hebrew spies when they came to Jericho (Josh. 2:4-16; cf. Heb. 11:31).

Other passages, however, suggest a different attitude toward harlotry. E.g., the sons of Jacob killed Hamor and his son Shechem, justifying their act by saying: "Should he treat our sister as a harlot?" (Gen. 34:31). As punishment for his treatment of the prophet Amos, Amaziah's wife was to become a harlot (Amos 7:17). Harlots were classed with tax collectors in the first century, when the latter were anathema to the Jews (Matt. 21:32). According to the doctrine of Paul, the body of a Christian belongs to Christ, and it should not be joined to that of a prostitute (I Cor. 6:15-16). *See* § 1*e below.*

b. The hire of a harlot. The wages of harlotry may not be used to pay vows in the temple (Deut. 23:18). The precise nature of these wages is not indicated. The term "hire" is doubtless drawn from the practice of paying a prostitute for her services, although it is applied here primarily to sacred prostitution. Both grain and wine are offered in payment (Hos. 9:2).

c. The distinguishing marks of a harlot. When Tamar wished to enact the role of a harlot, she put on a veil, "wrapping herself up," and sat in a public place (Gen. 38:14). However, in the ancient world the veil signified that a woman belonged to a man as wife or daughter. The Assyrian Code of laws required the secular prostitute to be unveiled, as a matter of fact. The sacred prostitute was commonly veiled, on the other hand. Jeremiah declared that Israel has a harlot's brow (3:3). This is vague, but it opens the possibility that the harlot was distinguished by a special mark on her brow or a special arrangement of her hair or head ornaments.

d. Her practice of her trade. She attracted customers by waiting in a public place (Gen. 38:14). The common harlot might function as an innkeeper, to whom travelers came for food, lodging, and sexual satisfaction. She exploited her beauty by putting on gay garments and fine ornaments (Ezek. 16:10 ff). She might use persuasive language, describing her couch, its coverings, and sensuous perfume, persuading her prospect with "her smooth talk" (Prov. 7:16 ff). Her skill may have included the singing of songs. At any rate, men were advised not to associate with women singers (Ecclus. 9:4). Isaiah may have had in mind harlots of Jerusalem when he wrote of women who

> walk with outstretched necks,
> glancing wantonly with their eyes,
> mincing along as they go,
> tinkling with their feet (3:16).

Perhaps the common prostitute originally served as a votary of some sanctuary and gave her earnings for the promotion of its program. This might be a temporary relationship, abandoned for the sake of public prostitution (see Gen. 38:21).

e. The control of harlotry (prostitution). While harlotry of the secular type was at times unrebuked, at other times it came under severe condemnation or strict control by law. The priestly law of Lev. 21:9 provides that a priest's daughter who acts as a harlot is to be burned to death. A priest must not marry a harlot (vs. 7); and Israelites are prohibited from allowing their daughters to become harlots (19:29). If a girl has been found to be guilty of harlotry, she is to be stoned to death (Deut. 22:21). While these miscellaneous laws do not reflect consistent practice, they indicate a tendency to restrict or to eliminate the practice as far as Israelite girls were concerned.

3. The cult prostitute. The practice of cult prostitution was far more serious in the view of biblical writers than common harlotry. It symbolized to them an abominable form of idolatry which could not be tolerated.

a. The role of the sacred prostitute in the fertility cult. The prostitute who was an official of the cult in ancient Palestine and nearby lands of biblical times exercised an important function. This religion was predicated upon the belief that the processes of nature were controlled by the relations between gods and goddesses. Projecting their understanding of their own sexual activities, the worshipers of these deities, through the use of imitative magic, engaged in sexual intercourse with devotees of the shrine, in the belief that this would encourage the gods and goddesses to do likewise. Only by sexual relations among the deities could man's desire for increase in herds and fields, as well as in his own family, be realized. In Palestine the gods Baal and Asherah were especially prominent (*see* BAAL; ASHERAH; FERTILITY CULTS). These competed with Yahweh the God of Israel and, in some cases, may have produced hybrid Yahweh-Baal cults. Attached to the shrines of these cults were priests as well as prostitutes, both male and female. Their chief service was sexual in nature—the offering of their bodies for ritual purposes. It has been conjectured that cult children were the "orphans" for whom special concern is manifested in the Bible (*see* FATHERLESS). The frequent occurrence of allusions to this cult and to its ritual demonstrates its importance (I Sam. 2:22; II Kings 23:7, 14; II Chr. 15:16; Ezek. 8:14; Hos. 4:13). The Israelites have engaged in sexual intercourse with cult prostitutes so extensively that one prophet inquires:

> Lift up your eyes to the bare heights, and see!
> Where have you not been lain with?
> (Jer. 3:2).

So flourishing was this cult that another prophet (*see* HOSEA) took a drastic step to oppose it—actual marriage with one of its prostitutes. *See* § 4 *below*.

b. The male prostitute. The word for "male prostitute," קדש, based on the root "holy," "separate," appears in a passage that describes the building of high places, pillars, and Asherim "on every high hill and under every green tree; and there were also male cult prostitutes in the land" (I Kings 14:23-24). However, in the next chapter there is a statement to the effect that King Asa "put away the male cult prostitutes out of the land" (15:12). Another king exterminated the "remnant of the male cult prostitutes" (22:46). Apart from the bare allusion to these, always in connection with actual or implied condemnation, the Bible tells us nothing about their function. This must be inferred from the word that identifies them and from usage in ancient nonbiblical lands.

It is clear that they served the needs of the sanctuary. They were associated with the goddess Asherah (Ishtar) and doubtless her counterpart Tammuz or Baal. The word מאהב, "lover" (Jer. 22:20, 22; 30:14; Ezek. 16:37 ff; 23:9; Hos. 2:7 ff; Zech. 13:6), has likewise been held to have a connection with the male prostitute attached to the cult. Another term, sometimes taken to identify male prostitutes, is נתינים, "temple servants." It appears only in the composite work Chronicles-Ezra-Nehemiah (see I Chr. 9:2; Ezra 7:24).

See also SODOMITE.

c. The female prostitute. The law of Deuteronomy prohibits the practice of cult prostitution by the daughters of Israel and likewise by the sons (Deut. 23:17). This law may reveal the non-Israelite origin of this institution, associated as it was with the Canaanite and Babylonian fertility cult.

The word זונה is also used for "sacred prostitute," although it appears with the meaning "(common) harlot," as already shown. The root is frequently used as a verb meaning "to have relations with foreign gods." This leads to the conclusion that the זונה may have been connected with the Canaanite cult in Palestine, even though the word refers also to the common harlot. The זונה as a prostitute common to baalism may be distinguished from קדשה, which possibly derives from non-Palestinian cults, in the view of some scholars. Conversely, others suggest that the institution symbolized by קדשה was indigenous and that represented by the word זונה was foreign.

4. The biblical attack upon cult prostitution. The meagerness of the data regarding the practice of cult prostitution is in contrast to the considerable amount of material of a denunciatory nature. Israel's memory of her peculiar covenant relation to her God was kept alive by the pleas of the prophets and the teachings of her priests. This sense of election and a tradition of seminomadic desert existence caused a revulsion against the agricultural-pastoral nature cults encountered in Palestine.

The radical reform described in II Kings 23 is an example of the strong reaction against cult prostitution. The temple was purged of the "vessels made for Baal, for Asherah, and for all the host of heaven" (vs. 4); the Asherah (image of the fertility goddess) was taken to the brook Kidron and burned (vs. 6). The houses of the cult prostitutes were broken down (vs. 7). With anger and contempt the prophets describe the harlotrous behavior of the people. In going after the Baals, Israel is like a "restive young camel" in heat or like a "wild ass . . . sniffing the wind! Who can restrain her lust?" says the Lord God (Jer. 2:23-24). Israel's hideous idolatry involves gross sexual indecencies and human sacrifice (Ezek. 23:37); harlotrous Israel acts like the sacred prostitute who bathes herself, paints her eyes, and sits on a couch near an altar, holding oil and incense—and waiting for worshipers to come to her (vss. 40-41). For this she shall drink a "cup of horror and desolation" (vs. 33).

The love of fickle Israel is like a morning cloud; therefore, she will be destroyed and the calf of Samaria (bull-worship) broken to pieces (Hos. 6:4; 8:6*b*). The reference here is to the use in Samaria of the sacred bull ("Ephraim" comes from a root meaning "bull" in the dual form and may suggest the bull and the heifer). The prophet condemns them for cultic wailing upon their beds and for self-mutilation, which the cult requires (7:14). So they shall be destroyed.

The Bible's attack which uses the language of harlotry is strongly directed toward that inner harlotry of the spirit of Israel which amounts to a rejection of her Redeemer and the Lord. "Playing the harlot" is the favorite term for this kind of faithlessness (Num. 25:1-2; Judg. 2:13, 17; 8:27, 33; Jer. 3:6). The wanton, harlotrous heart of Israel is described (Ezek. 6:9) as the reason for the judgment that is coming; the people are possessed by the spirit of harlotry (Hos. 4:12). Under the control of this spirit the land is filled with evildoers, robbers, and murderers (6:8-10). The Bible's graphic characterization of Israel as harlotrous, and of neighboring nations and communities as well, involves the use of the figure of personification (Isa. 23:16; Ezek. 16; 23; Nah. 3:4). Babylon is called the mother of harlots, who will be made naked and desolate, and then burned with fire (Rev. 17:5, 16). Here the biblical figure is made to represent the total wickedness of a great city, where by "Babylon" the city of Rome is probably meant.

Bibliography. D. G. Lyon, "The Consecrated Women of the Hammurabi Code," *Studies in the History of Religions* (1912), pp. 341-60; R. A. S. Macalister, *Gezer II* (1912); D. Luckenbill, "The Temple Women of the Code of Hammurabi," *AJSL,* XXXIV (1917), 1-12; W. C. Graham and H. G. May, *Culture and Conscience: An Archaeological Study of the New Religious Past in Ancient Palestine* (1936); B. A. Brooks, "Fertility Cult Functionaries in the OT," *JBL,* LX (1941), 227-53; W. F. Albright, *Archaeology and the Religion of Israel* (1942), pp. 84-94, 115; H. Licht, *Sexual Life of the Ancient Greeks* (1952); D. Barthélemy and J. T. Milik, *Qumran Cave I, Discoveries in the Judaean Desert,* vol. I (1955); H. G. May, "The Fertility Cult in Hosea," *AJSL,* XLVIII (1931-32), 73-98.

See also the bibliographies under SEX; MARRIAGE; WOMAN.

O. J. BAAB

PROTEVANGELIUM OF JAMES. *See* JAMES, PROTEVANGELIUM OF.

PROTO-LUKE. A hypothetical source of the Gospel of Luke. *See* LUKE, GOSPEL OF; SYNOPTIC PROBLEM.

PROVENDER [מספוא; בלל, בליל]. Grains and grasses used for feeding domestic animals. Typical provender, or FODDER, was prepared from chopped straw and chaff, grasses such as *sorghum saccharatum,* and grains such as barley, millet, or one of several species of single-grain wheat. The בליל of Isa. 30:24 may suggest a kind of forage fermented by soaking.

Bibliography. G. Dalman, *Arbeit und Sitte,* I/2 (1928), 334-36; II (1932), 166-67. H. N. and A. L. Moldenke, *Plants of the Bible* (1952), pp. 112, 166, 232.

J. A. WHARTON

PROVERB prŏv′ərb. A saying, usually giving brief, but sometimes extended, and colorful expression to a commonly observed fact or bit of homely wisdom; a sentence or discourse such as those which are assembled in the biblical book of PROVERBS and appear otherwise in the Bible and the Apoc., but especially in the WISDOM literature there.

1. Terminology
2. Form of proverb
   a. The primitive form
   b. The art form
   c. The discourse
   d. The taunt
3. Significance
   a. Capsulated wisdom
   b. The slogan

Bibliography

1. Terminology. The Hebrew noun is משל, *māshāl,* from a verb which means "to be like or to compare." With few exceptions, in the LXX the Greek term for proverb is παραβολή. Although παροιμία occurs in the LXX to the canonical books only in Prov. 1:1, it has, because of its occurrence there (in the plural form παροιμίαι) become the Greek name of the book of Proverbs. It appears also in Ecclus. 6:35; 47:17. Also in the NT the common Greek term is παραβολή (Matt. 15:15; Luke 4:23; cf. Matt. 13:13; Mark 4:11; Luke 8:10), but παροιμία occurs in John 10:6; 16:25, 29; II Pet. 2:22. The Hebrew noun and the Greek terms designate longer compositions, as well as pithy sayings, and sometimes mean "byword" or "taunt song."

2. Form of proverb. The biblical data present the proverb in a simpler form and in more complex forms. The simpler, though more primitive, is not necessarily the oldest. The art forms had probably developed already in prebiblical times along with the simple form, which is primitive in the sense of popular, nonliterary.

a. The primitive form. There are several biblical examples of popular proverbs—which no one composed but everyone repeated—perhaps more examples than are readily recognized. "Like mother, like daughter," in Ezek. 16:44 is called a proverb. So, too, is the observation: "The fathers have eaten sour grapes, and the children's teeth are set on edge" (Ezek. 18:2; found also in Jer. 31:29). It is not characteristic of a proverb that it should be topical, but it is, of course, ready at hand for quotation when circumstances warrant. So Ezekiel could with some right (because "the shoe fit") consider his own prophetic word the butt of the proverb current in his time: "The days grow long, and every vision comes to naught" (Ezek. 12:22). Jesus behaved similarly when he said: "Doubtless you will quote to me this proverb, 'Physician, heal yourself' " (Luke 4:23). Anonymous ancient proverbialists observed: "Out of the wicked comes forth wickedness," and left their truism for David to use in his denial of evil intent against Saul (I Sam. 24:13—H 24:14; Isa. 32:6 begins with a comparable proverb, and cf. Judg. 8:21).

The circumstances surrounding the origin of a proverb are characteristically hazy, and certain biblical narratives may, in fact, owe their existence to someone's guess at the source of a current proverb. Two divergent tales now record the origin of the proverbial exclamation: "Is Saul also among the prophets?" (I Sam. 10:11-12; 19:24)—which duplication merely shows that no one really knew its source. Indeed, the question may quite as well have been prompted by Saul's chronic madness (I Sam. 18:10), which was not unlike the prophet's trance. The response in I Sam. 10:12: "And who is their father?" may well mean: Saul is, indeed, the maddest of them all—a proverb which answered to a proverb.

The first time it is asked: "Is Saul also among the prophets?" the question is expressly called a proverb; the second time it is introduced by the words: "Hence it is said." How many undesignated proverbs are quoted in biblical literature is anyone's guess. "Therefore it is said" (Gen. 10:9) similarly introduces a proverb without so naming it: "Like Nimrod a mighty hunter before the LORD." Doubtless many sayings were adopted for their present context out of a fund of folk wisdom and seemed the more effective by very reason of their familiarity—clichés have not always been disreputable. Such adopted proverbs may include I Kings 20:11: "Let not him that girds on his armor boast himself as he that puts it off"; Jer. 23:28: "What has straw in common with wheat?" and Isa. 22:13:

> Let us eat and drink,
> for tomorrow we die.

That the last of these sayings is not in its original context is clear; the jubilant lords of Jerusalem were thinking of nothing like death on the morrow. (The same proverb is quoted in I Cor. 15:32 and modified in Eccl. 8:15.)

In form these "primitive" proverbs are characterized by an economy of words, more readily noted in Hebrew than in translation. They are prose with no evidence of conscious artistry but with fresh simplicity and directness.

b. The art form. Preponderantly, biblical proverbs are poetic in form. Commonly in the wisdom literature the proverb is a single balanced line made up of two parallel cola, which may be synonymous:

> A hoary head is a crown of glory;
> it is gained in a righteous life
> (Prov. 16:31),

or antithetic:

> The wicked flee when no one pursues,
> but the righteous are bold as a lion
> (Prov. 28:1),

or synthetic:

> Like a dog that returns to his vomit
> is a fool that repeats his folly
> (Prov. 26:11).

One such poetic proverb in the NT resembles this last example but has the form of synonymous parallelism:

> The dog turns back to his own vomit,
> and the sow is washed only to wallow in
> the mire (II Pet. 2:22).

In this final pair of proverbs (Prov. 26:11; II Pet. 2:22) the one saying of the simpler type is expanded, now one way and now another, to produce the two proverbs in poetic form. Examples of this phenomenon are numerous; cf. Prov. 10:2 with 11:4 or Prov. 10:6 with 10:11; or with Prov. 26:27 cf. both Eccl. 10:8 and Ecclus. 27:26. Evidence of this procedure suggests that the production of proverbs of this more artistic form was a conscious literary activity of the sages in wisdom circles (cf. Prov. 1:5-6, where the proverb is listed along with the "words of the wise," and Ecclus. 18:28-29).

As an art form the proverb shows considerable variety. The balanced line sometimes involves an a fortiori argument:

> All a poor man's brothers hate him;
> how much more do his friends go far from
> him! (Prov. 19:7).

Frequently it is built upon a comparison:

> Like a lame man's legs, which hang useless,
> is a proverb in the mouth of fools
> (Prov. 26:7; see also vs. 11).

But proverbs are not limited to the single balanced line; longer compositions occur as well. A series of single-line proverbs dealing with one theme (e.g., the series on fools in Prov. 26:1-12) is not a new form; it is merely a collection. But there are others. A popular, more extended art form is the "numbers" proverb:

> Three things are stately in their tread;
> four are stately in their stride:
> the lion, . . .
> the strutting cock, the he-goat,
> and a king striding before his
> people (Prov. 30:29-31).

c. The discourse. Another form, the discourse or exposition, includes such more extensive literary products as the warning against the "loose woman" in the seventh chapter of Proverbs, Wisdom's invitation in the eighth, and the acrostic poem in praise of the "good wife" in 31:10-31. To call any of these compositions a proverb may seem somewhat to stretch the meaning of the word, and yet the Hebrew term *māshāl* not infrequently designates just such a longer utterance. Ezekiel complains that people chide him as one given to preachments (a "maker of allegories," *m^e^mashshēl m^e^shālîm;* Ezek. 20:49—H 21:5). Also, elsewhere prophetic discourses are called *m^e^shālîm,* as in: "And Balaam took up his discourse" (*māshāl*—seven times in Num. 23–24; cf. Isa. 14:4; Ecclus. 44:5; Enoch 1:2-3; 37:5, for which *see* PARABLE § 3). But more nearly related in content to the discourses in Proverbs are those so termed in Job 27:1; 29:1, and such didactic psalms as Pss. 49; 78 (cf. 49:4—H 49:5; 78:2, where the psalmist uses the term *māshāl*).

Ezekiel's critics may have had a special reason for choosing the word *māshāl* to describe his discourses. The related Hebrew verb in the causative stem means "to compare" (Isa. 46:5), in the *niph'al* "to be like" (Isa. 14:10), and the noun may quite properly describe any of the various poetic figures. Ezekiel's *m^e^shālîm* in 17:2; 20:49—H 21:5; 24:3 are allegories; the balanced-line proverb is often a simile or comparison (as *above*); the *māshāl* in Ps. 49:4—H 49:5; 78:2; Prov. 1:6, is mentioned along with the "riddle," in the last of these passages also along with the "figure." Among Solomon's accomplishments were his making of proverbs and "songs" and his speaking "of trees" and "of beasts" (I Kings 4:33—H 5:13), which last accomplishment may be not the teaching of natural science but the art of composing the FABLE. Yet, though the *māshāl* is often, and probably according to its root meaning, a comparison, it is also more broadly a brief or extended poetic composition, like Balaam's utterances, the discourses in Proverbs and Job, and the didactic psalms.

d. The taunt. The term *māshāl* has another special meaning as the equivalent of the English "byword," and it further designates a mocking taunt song directed against a foe. So, in Deut. 28:37: "You shall become a horror, a proverb [*māshāl*], and a byword, among all the peoples," or in Jer. 24:9: "I will make them a horror to all the kingdoms of the earth, to be a reproach, a byword [*māshāl*], a taunt, and a curse in all the places where I shall drive them." This combination of terms occurs frequently in the Bible and the Apoc. (cf. Tob. 3:4, also Wisd. Sol. 5:3: "a byword of reproach"). The word "curse" in the Jeremiah passage is the key to the understanding of this usage. Just as persons may become "proverbial" as eminently blessed, so that future generations will make reference to them in blessing and say, e.g.: "God make you as Ephraim and as Manasseh" (Gen. 48:20; cf. 12:3), even so calamity can make such a horrible example of persons that to be likened to them is to be called accursed indeed (Isa. 65:15). To be a *māshāl* of this sort is to be the proverbial object of scorn or derision. Also in this use of the term the root meaning "compare" may be involved.

Related is its use to designate a song of derision. So in Isa. 14:4: "You will take up this taunt [*māshāl*] against the king of Babylon," or Mic. 2:4: "In that day they shall take up a taunt song against you" (see also Hab. 2:6). The biblical examples are almost all of anticipatory derision; the events which will warrant the taunts have not yet occurred. But so lively in biblical society was the belief in the effective power of the word that the taunt song was alone itself a weapon. "Ballad singers" is probably not the best translation of *môsh^elîm* in Num. 21:27, for what follows is, at least in part, a gloating over a defeated Amorite or Moabite kingdom, or both. Though it hardly agrees with the narrower meaning of the English word "proverb," this type of literature too—the taunt song—comes within the compass of the corresponding biblical term. *See also* IRONY AND SATIRE.

3. Significance. The proverb, then, is not one form but several. Nevertheless, what is commonly meant is a single short saying of type *a* or *b* (*above*), the "primitive form" or the "art form." The significance of this kind of proverb is twofold: it is capsulated wisdom or a slogan.

a. Capsulated wisdom. With the passing of the generations the race accumulates a certain amount of experience, some of which it wraps up in the small packages known as proverbs. These formulated observations, often pungent, salty, sometimes ironic, are a currency useful in the exchange of ideas and particularly effective for indoctrinating the young with tested truths (I Sam. 24:13—H 24:14; II Sam. 20:18 suggest the antiquity of some proverbs). Apparently intelligence was requisite, not for the coining of proverbs only, as is obvious, but for understanding them as well. They had, indeed, a riddle-like quality, and contained comparisons, figures, and allusions. But if they were currency, they were generally known, and this implies that they were cultivated and propagated, in wisdom circles, in schools for the youth. *See* PROVERBS, BOOK OF, § 10.

b. The slogan. Occasionally as a compliment (Nimrod; or the village Abel [II Sam. 20:18]), but more usually in name-calling (Saul among the prophets; the city Heshbon [Num. 21:27]), reference is made to a proverbial figure out of the past or to a timeless phenomenon of common experience ("The fool speaks folly" [Isa. 32:6]; "Out of the wicked comes forth wickedness" [I Sam. 24:13—H 24:14]). Then as now, but then with more presumed effect and greater expectation, one could reward or damn with a slogan.

Bibliography. W. A. L. Elmslie, *Studies in Life from Jewish Proverbs* (n.d.); O. Eissfeldt, *Der Maschal im AT, BZAW*, XXIV (1913); A. H. Godbey, "The Hebrew Mašal," *AJSL*, XXXIX (1922-23), 89-108; A. S. Herbert, "The 'Parable' Māšāl in the OT," *Scottish Journal of Theology*, 7 (1954), 180-96; A. R. Johnson, משל, *Supplements to Vetus Testamentum*, III (1955), 162-69; O. Eissfeldt, *Einleitung in das AT* (1956), pp. 73-76, 94-100, 106-9.

S. H. BLANK

*__PROVERBS, BOOK OF.__ The twentieth book in the OT canon according to the order adopted by the RSV. It is one of the books in the category of wisdom literature. Attributed (as a courtesy) to King Solomon, it was compiled and for the most part probably also composed during the fifth and fourth pre-Christian centuries by the masters who taught in academies for young men of the "better" families. Although the book was written wholly under the influence of the dogma of divine retribution, it contains much of worldly wisdom. Proverbs is a store of human experience condensed into adages and ancient wisdom attractively garbed. Its purpose was to guide men into ways of profitable living. Although it does not reach peaks of inspiration, Proverbs is a good book.

1. Name
2. Position
3. Nature
4. Language, text, and Greek translation
5. Canon
6. Contents and parts
7. Literary forms
8. Foreign literary influences
9. Authorship
10. Purpose of the book
11. Date
12. Values
Bibliography

1. Name. Like a modern book the book of Proverbs has a title page complete with title and author's name and "degrees": "The proverbs of Solomon, son of David, king of Israel"; and it has a somewhat longer than usual subtitle, which begins: "That men may know wisdom" (1:1-6). Accordingly the book is known as "Proverbs"—in Hebrew משלי שלמה, *mishlê sh^elōmôh*, "proverbs of Solomon"; in the LXX παροιμίαι, "proverbs." The five-line subtitle is both statement of purpose and advertisement. The title page correctly describes the book as maxims offered for the propagation of wisdom. Only the propriety of ascribing the work to Solomon is questionable, as a more detailed analysis of the contents reveals.

2. Position. The book of Proverbs is included among the Kethubhim, "Writings" or Hagiographa. In rabbinic tradition it follows Psalms and Job (*B.B.* 14*b*) or possibly comes between them (implied in *Ber.* 57*b*)—so in the English version of the Jewish Publication Society. The KJV-RSV order (Job, Psalms, Proverbs) may be a presumed chronological arrangement deriving ultimately from rabbinic traditions which assign the three books to Moses, David, and Hezekiah respectively (*B.B.* 14*b*-15*a*). The order in the LXX (Psalms, Proverbs, Ecclesiastes, the Song of Songs, Job) groups together the three books attributed to Solomon—Proverbs, Ecclesiastes, and the Song of Songs.

3. Nature. The book of Proverbs belongs to the general class of WISDOM literature. It shares this class with the biblical books of JOB and ECCLESIASTES, certain PSALMS (e.g., Pss. 1; 34; 49; 73; 92;

127; 128) and the apocryphal books ECCLESIASTICUS and WISDOM OF SOLOMON. The wisdom literature is a type apart—unlike the prophetic, legal, or devotional literature or historical writings in the Bible. It was cultivated by the חכם ("sage"), and served an educational purpose. The book of Proverbs is the prime example of such a repository of wisdom and source book for rules of good and profitable behavior.

4. Language, text, and Greek translation. Classical Hebrew is the original language of Proverbs, and the text for the most part is clear. Occasionally obscurity or a false note suggests that the wording has suffered a change. The Greek version differs considerably, with omissions, additions, variants, and a different order among the parts. The parts of the Hebrew chs. 30:1-31:9, e.g., are distributed in the LXX, with 31:1-10 after H 24:22, and 30:11-31:9 after H 24:34. The differences not only testify to mistakes or misunderstandings on the part of the scribes and translators, but more significantly they also give evidence that the text of Proverbs was still somewhat fluid when this translation was made. Neither the editorial activity nor the creative process was complete; whole sections could yet be shifted about, and new proverbs could still be phrased and added to the translation and to the Hebrew original.

5. Canon. According to the Mishna (Yadayim III.5) the holiness—i.e., canonicity—of Ecclesiastes and the Song of Songs was still a subject of controversy at the end of the first Christian century. Shab. 30*b* associates Proverbs, the third of the "Solomonic" books, with this late controversy. In the Talmudic passage in connection with the discussion on the propriety of Ecclesiastes an authority cites the observation that Proverbs, as well, contains contradictory verses (e.g., Prov. 26:4, 5). According to the first chapter of Aboth d'Rabbi Nathan near the beginning, Proverbs is listed along with Ecclesiastes and the Song of Songs as books in which mere sayings occur, not derived from scripture. Though the "Solomonic" books were suspect (probably because they were not really considered old), it may well have been their attribution to Solomon that helped them eventually to a place in the canon. *See* CANON OF THE OT.

6. Contents and parts. Even a cursory reading suggests that the book is composite—not the product of a single author, of Solomon or of any other one sage. Several of the different parts, in fact, have their own titles. Such titles occur at the beginning of the tenth chapter: "The proverbs of Solomon," and the twenty-fifth chapter: "These also are proverbs of Solomon which the men of Hezekiah king of Judah copied." Chs. 30 and 31 begin respectively with the titles: "The words of Agur son of Jakeh of Massa," and "The words of Lemuel, king of Massa, which his mother taught him." The statement "These also are sayings of the wise" occurs in 24:23, and the word "also" here suggests that the title "sayings of the wise" has appeared in the book before. It is probably to be found in 22:17, where it is concealed now by a change in the original order of the words.

Other, internal evidence supports the evidence of the headings. The poem on the "good wife," 31:10-31, is a self-limiting unit, being an alphabetic acrostic. The sayings of the wise which have their beginning in 22:17 cannot go on indefinitely, since their author specifies: "Have I not written for you thirty sayings . . . ?" (22:20; for this translation *see* § 8 *below*). Just how the "thirty" are to be counted is not certain, but with 23:15 the style changes, and the relationship with the thirty sayings of Amen-em-opet also ceases at this point, so that 23:15-24:22 is to be regarded as an independent composition.

The presence of a variety of literary forms (discourses, balanced lines, couplets, similes, numbers proverbs, an acrostic; *see* § 7 *below*) adds to the impression that the book is composite. Against the supposition of single authorship stands also the fact that sayings are repeated both within the single parts and from part to part. Cf., among others, 18:8; 19:24; 20:16; 21:9; 22:3 in the first collection of "proverbs of Solomon" with 26:22; 26:15; 27:13; 25:24; 27:12 in the second. Unless he worked without method, a single writer or collector is not likely to have included so many duplicates.

The evidence permits the conclusion that the book of Proverbs is a symposium, a compilation of originally independent, though kindred, collections of maxims, observations, and discourses. The following larger literary units may be distinguished:

I. Title page with advertisement and motto 1:1-7
II. Discourses and cautions, 1:8-9:18
III. "Proverbs of Solomon," first collection, 10:1-22:16
IV. "Sayings of the wise," first collection, 22:17-23:14
V. More discourses and cautions, 23:15-24:22
VI. "Sayings of the wise," second collection, 24:23-34
VII. "Proverbs of Solomon," second collection ("which the men of Hezekiah . . . copied"), 25:1-29:27
VIII. "The words of Agur," ch. 30
IX. "The words of Lemuel," 31:1-9
X. The good wife, 31:10-31

7. Literary forms. The several collections that make up the book contain examples of different literary forms. In sections III and VII, the two collections called "proverbs of Solomon," with rare exceptions the proverb is a single balanced line, each proverb a unit in itself and, except for the general uniformity of matter, wholly independent of its neighbors. Some proverbs clustered in 12:17-23 concern speech, and others in 16:10-15 concern kings, but such groupings are rare, and the single, detached proverb is the rule.

The one-line proverb exhibits parallelism—its halves are balanced in antithesis or synonymity, varied occasionally with a line in synthetic parallelism. In chs. 10-15; 28-29, the antithetic form heavily predominates; but beginning with the sixteenth chapter, the synonymous form is strongly favored. Approximately half the proverbs in chs. 25-26 are graphic similes, one of the more popular forms of synthetic parallelism. The comparison in 26:17 may serve as an example:

> He who meddles in a quarrel not his own
> is like one who takes a passing dog by the ears.

Other common variants of this type of parallelism are the "better . . . than" form—e.g., 25:24:

> It is better to live in a corner of the housetop
> than in a house shared with a contentious woman
> (cf. 15:16, 17; 19:1);

and the "how much more" or "how much less" comparison—e.g., 21:27:

> The sacrifice of the wicked is an abomination;
> how much more when he brings it with evil intent
> (cf. 11:31; 17:7).

The impression that all these one-line proverbs make is not that of primitive folk sayings but of maxims phrased with conscious art, some possibly expansions in poetic form of originally simpler popular proverbs. *See* PROVERB § 2*b*.

Slightly longer are the units which make up IV, V, and VI (22:17-24:34). These are often couplets, units of two balanced lines—e.g., 24:19-20:

> Fret not yourself because of evildoers,
> and be not envious of the wicked;
> for the evil man has no future;
> the lamp of the wicked will be put out.

The bulk of these parts, IV, V, and VI, is made up of couplets and somewhat longer units, such extended proverbs as the three-line caution to eat lightly as the guest of a stingy man (23:6-8) or the yet longer cautionary accounts of the fate of the sluggard and the woes of the heavy drinker (24:30-34; 23:29-35). These extended proverbs are wholly missing in III and very rare in VII; the small discourse promoting the cattle business (27:23-27) is distinctly exceptional there. But in I and II (chs. 1-9) the discourse is the rule, each discourse a connected composition phrased in balanced lines. Notable among the discourses in Proverbs are wisdom's two appeals (1:20-33; ch. 8). The warning against the "loose woman" in II (ch. 5) is matched at the end of the book by X (31:10-31), a poem celebrating the "good wife."

The numbers proverb, possibly related to the RIDDLE, occurs in 6:16-19 and as a regular feature in VIII—e.g., 30:15*b*-16:

> Three things are never satisfied;
> four never say, "Enough":
> Sheol, the barren womb,
> the earth ever thirsty for water,
> and the fire which never says, "Enough."

The presence of this variety of literary forms suggests diversity of origin and strongly supports the view that the book of Proverbs is composite.

8. Foreign literary influences. The evidence of foreign literary influence on parts of Proverbs lends further support to this view. There is hardly any doubt that IV (22:17-23:14) depends upon the "thirty chapters" of the Egyptian Amen-em-opet. The parallels are striking, and reading them, one experiences a growing certainty that the two sets of instructions for prudent living did not arise independently in their separate cultures. There is no topical arrangement in either composition, and the different order in which the maxims appear in the two sets does not conceal the relationship between them. The contacts are too close and too many for coincidence to explain away, even if combined with similarity of purpose. A variation such as that in 23:4-5 only strengthens the impression of borrowing. The Proverbs text urges:

> Do not toil to acquire wealth;
> be wise enough to desist.
> When your eyes light upon it, it is gone;
> for suddenly it takes to itself wings,
> flying like an eagle toward heaven.

The "eagle" in the Bible text is only a most natural substitute for the bird indigenous to the Egyptian model, according to which the riches take flight to the heavens, having got themselves wings like "geese" (in Amen-em-opet's seventh chapter). The Egyptian "goose" naturally became a Palestinian "eagle." Without the Egyptian parallel, Prov. 22:20 would not be understood. The KJV: "Have not I written to thee *excellent things* . . . ?" is one of many wrong guesses at the meaning of the Hebrew word שלשום, margin שלישים, made before the Egyptian kinship was noted. Once it was observed that Amen-em-opet set forth his paternal instructions in "thirty chapters" (see his thirtieth chapter), it became apparent that the proper pronunciation of the Hebrew word is שלושים, "thirty"; thus the RSV: "Have I not written for you thirty sayings . . . ?" So the Egyptian is a key for the Hebrew. The author of Prov. 22:17-23:14 did not undertake to furnish a Hebrew translation of the Egyptian model; he used it freely or in some derivative form, but in one form or another he surely used it.

Somewhat less obvious are other presumed external influences upon Proverbs. The contacts with the late Syriac and the older but fragmentary Aramaic texts of the Proverbs of Ahikar are far less concentrated and somewhat less convincingly alike. Traces also are not lacking of early Canaanite thought and vocabulary.

In other words, Israel was no cultural island, and the book of Proverbs did not grow in a vacuum.

9. Authorship. It is not necessary to take seriously the attribution of Proverbs to Solomon in 1:1; 10:1; 25:1. The attribution is the result of a convention by which famous men were honored in Israel. The ascription of a book to a great man of the past was both a tribute to him and a claim upon the prestige which his name might lend to the book. New laws were written and Moses was given the credit; new songs were sung and David was hailed as their source. This convention was observed particularly in the late pre-Christian centuries, the time of such pseudonymous writings as Daniel, Baruch, Enoch, and the Testaments of the Twelve Patriarchs. The canonical Proverbs of Solomon need have no more claim to genuine Solomonic authorship than the apocryphal Wisdom of Solomon.

Accordingly, the question of the Solomonic authorship of Proverbs may be considered without prejudgment. The biblical traditions of Solomon's wisdom in I Kings 3-4; 10 might seem to favor the attribution. Some statements there appear particularly weighty: "Solomon's wisdom surpassed the wisdom of all the people of the east, and all the wisdom of Egypt. . . . His fame was in all the nations round about. He also uttered three thousand proverbs. . . . He spoke of trees; . . . also of beasts, and of birds, and of reptiles, and of fish" (4:30-34—H 5:10-14). The only trouble is that these statements in the book of Kings and the other traditions concerning the wisdom of Solomon are probably of one piece with the ascription to him of Proverbs, Ecclesiastes, the Song of Songs, and the Wisdom of Solomon—all expressions of the one tendency to build up the glory that was Solomon. Was there ever such splendor as his new-built Jerusalem, and was the capital under his patronage not also a center of cosmopolitan culture beyond compare?

"Where there is smoke," according to a non-scriptural proverb, "there is fire"; and so, after all, Solomon may have been the author of some of the proverbs. The possibility cannot be denied, and recent scholarly opinion inclines to the view that Solomon at least cultivated the proverbial art and was responsible for the kernel of the book ascribed to him. Admitting the possibility, one yet observes that teachers in schools for young gentlemen would doubtless produce just such literature as Proverbs, composing, collecting, and editing wise sayings and admonitory discourses; and that professional "wise men" of this description are a much more likely source for such a book than any busy monarch. Possible though it is that unidentifiable proverbs within the book go back to Solomon's time, the probability is greater that the wisdom teachers themselves composed most of the "Solomonic" proverbs. The purpose the book was designed to serve reveals, not indeed the names, but the nature of its authors.

10. Purpose of the book. Along with other wisdom literature, Proverbs was designed as a school book for the instruction of young men. It is instruction intended for young men and not for children, as the caution against the loose woman must indicate. Incidentally, too, it is young men and not young women who here receive instruction; though women are mentioned, it is usually not for praise (one's mother, of course, and the "good wife" in ch. 31 are exceptions), and the teachings are not for the edification of women. Furthermore, Proverbs addresses itself to only a segment of the young male population. It has concern for youths in the upper-class families. Only the sons of gentry could afford most of the follies which Proverbs deprecates, or find the opportunity to display many of the virtues which it commends, or find the leisure to attend the schools where wisdom was cultivated. Only the well-to-do are likely to hold that, as Proverbs assumes, success is a well-deserved reward. The social background and philosophy of the book are decidedly upper-class. *See bibliography.*

To the young men, then, of the "better" families, Proverbs offers instruction. Much of the first nine chapters (I and II) is an invitation to learning. "Son" in Proverbs is probably both literal and a conventional term; the father (4:3-4) and occasionally the mother (cf. 31:1) seem to offer parental counsel, but "sons" in the plural (as in 7:24) and the "sons" whom "Dame Wisdom" addresses in ch. 8 (cf. vs. 32) are sons in name only, and normally it is the schoolmaster who serves as "father." Wisdom, indeed, offers her wares in public "on the heights . . . , in the paths . . . , beside the gates . . . , at the entrance of the portals" (8:2-3), but wisdom also has a house (9:1), and she invites the unlearned to enter. And so, although Proverbs has no more specific word for "schoolhouse" (no such term as the *bêth midhrash* or "house of instruction" of Ecclus. 51:23), it is not hazardous to assume, for the time when the book of Proverbs was taking form, the existence of academies where the sons of patricians studied the ways of success. The book of Proverbs could have served as text in such an academy. Now, if this was its social role, the masters in the schools, the wise men of the academies, who used it as an aid to instruction, themselves probably shaped it and formed it for their purpose.

11. Date. The question of the date of Proverbs is complicated. Both because of the variety of literary forms which it presents and because of the diverse sources upon which its several parts have drawn (*see* §§ 7-8 *above*), it has appeared probable that the book is composite. If so, the question of date becomes a threefold question: (*a*) How old are the oldest materials which the schoolmen used who wrote its several parts? (*b*) What was the period of the schoolmen's activity? (*c*) When did someone finally put the parts together and provide them with a title page?

First, as to the oldest sources: The Canaanite material, possibly scattered here and there, and the "thirty chapters" of the Egyptian Amen-em-opet clearly concentrated in IV, may go back to the second millennium B.C. If the authors or compilers of the "Solomonic" parts of Proverbs (III and VII) really had at their disposal any matter recorded in Solomon's time (which is highly doubtful), this unidentifiable source material comes from the tenth pre-Christian century. Though it is doubtful that any of the proverbs goes back to Solomon's time, the editorial note in 25:1 to the effect that "the men of Hezekiah . . . copied" the following collection of proverbs of Solomon is fairly good evidence that some parts of this latter collection (VII) are pre-exilic. At any rate, the editor here reveals his belief that he has some matter before him with a long tradition. Agur and Lemuel, at the beginning of VIII and IX, being names of unknown personages, are of no help at all. If the supposition is correct (*see* § 7 *above*) that proverbs in art form are sometimes expanded primitive folk sayings, there is no telling how ancient these sayings may be.

As to when the process of collecting, copying, adapting, expanding, the earlier material began, the headings of IV and VI may offer a clue. The editor identified certain collections with Solomon directly or with Solomon by way of Hezekiah; others he knew to be foreign, and he associated them with Agur and Lemuel; but he referred to IV and VI as "sayings of the wise." Speaking so, he may have thought of persons like himself—wise men, teachers, older contemporaries, but recently engaged in collecting, copying, adapting, expanding, even in creating, literature of wisdom.

One may suspect further that the last stage in the growth of the book created the "title page" (I) and the discourses and cautions (II), which seem to know of a body of wisdom (the remainder of the book) and to commend it to the attention of youth.

The date of the later stages, when in fact the book was taking shape, will then be the time when the wise men taught in Israel. Although wise men (and women) were known in Israel since the days of the judges, it appears to be only in the postexilic period that they functioned as teachers in academies for youth. *See* WISDOM § 1; EDUCATION.

Proverbs was certainly complete with title page before the time of Ben Sirach (*ca.* 190 B.C.), who alludes in 47:17 to Prov. 1:6, and who develops further certain thoughts and trends evident in Proverbs.

The place of wisdom in the development of biblical thought, particularly as concerns attention to the individual man and the orthodoxy of retribution, the place also of Proverbs within the wisdom literature, would suggest the fifth or fourth century as the time when the book was taking shape. *See* ECCLESIASTES § 5.

12. Values. The book of Proverbs is not the highest height to which in the Bible the human spirit soars. It is neither profound nor dramatic. It is a manual of prudence, a guide to right living.

Some themes are notably absent. Unlike the Law, Proverbs says next to nothing about worship, sacrificial or otherwise—except for the few neutral (7:14; 17:1) or mildly negative (15:8*a;* 21:3, 27) allusions to sacrifice there are only 15:8*b,* 29; 28:9, which express divine approval of the prayers of good men, and 3:9, which commends the payment of dues to the temple. Unlike the narrative sources and historical writings, Proverbs alludes not at all to Israel's past or its popular heroes (other than Solomon and Hezekiah in the subtitles); it speaks not of folkways but of human nature. Unlike the books of the prophets, Proverbs has nothing to say of the nation's fate, of catastrophe, or of destined glory. Unlike apocalypse, it knows nothing of personal immortality or resurrection; it is wholly this-worldly. And there is nothing devotional about proverbial literature; only in 30:7-9 and possibly 30:1*b* is God addressed as he is in the Psalms. All these themes lie without the province of this book and, for that matter, mostly outside the province of wisdom literature in general (some of the "wisdom psalms" form an exception).

Prudent and moral behavior is the concern of Proverbs; it is a "how-to" book. The skill it teaches is how to please God and live sensibly and well. Virtue is not commended for its own sake; it is related to the will of God, and it leads to success.

The book of Proverbs is a moral book and a fund of wisdom, neither priestly nor prophetic, but human wisdom, the fruit of human experience—its distinction: that it relates sensible living inextricably with walking humbly. The fear of the Lord is the beginning of wisdom. *See* WISDOM § 3.

Bibliography. D. G. Wildeboer, *Die Sprüche,* in *KHC* (1897); G. C. Martin, *Proverbs, Ecclesiastes and Song of Songs,* in *New Century Bible* (1908); C. H. Toy, *Proverbs,* ICC (1916); P. Volz, *Hiob u. Weisheit,* in *Die Schriften des AT* (1921), pp. 96-111; W. O. E. Oesterley, *Proverbs,* WC (1929); B. Gemser, *Sprüche Salomos,* in *HAT* (1937); R. Pfeiffer, *Introduction to the OT* (1941), pp. 645-59. A. Cohen, *Proverbs,* in *Soncino Books of the Bible* (1945); C. T. Fritsch, *IB,* IV (1955), 767-957.

Special articles: W. A. L. Elmslie, *Studies in Life from Jewish Proverbs* (n.d.); F. James, "Some Aspects of the Religion of Proverbs," *JBL,* LI (1932), 31-39; R. Gordis, "The Social Background of Wisdom Literature," *HUCA,* XVIII (1943-44), 77-118; C. I. K. Story, "The Book of Proverbs and Northwest Semitic Literature," *JBL,* LXIV (1945), 319-37; W. F. Albright, "Some Canaanite-Phoenician Sources of Hebrew Wisdom," in Supplement III to *VT* (1955); J. B. Pritchard, ed., "Didactic and Wisdom Literature," *ANET* (2nd ed., 1955), pp. 405-52; R. B. Y. Scott, "Solomon and the Beginnings of Wisdom in Israel," in Supplement III to *VT* (1955).

See also bibliography under PROVERB; WISDOM.

S. H. BLANK

PROVIDENCE. A translation of πρόνοια in Wisd. Sol. 14:3; 17:2; Acts 24:2 (RSV "provision"). Cf. the verb προνοέω, which occurs in the Greek OT eleven times and in the NT twice. Of these thirteen occurrences of the verb, however, all relate (as does the noun in the NT) to human vision or provision except Wisd. Sol. 6:7, where God, the sovereign Lord of all, is spoken of as "taking thought" for all alike, both small and great. The Latin word *providentia* (lit., "foresight") corresponds exactly to a Greek noun from προβλέπω or προοράω. But no such noun occurs in the Greek Bible, although the verbs are used.

For the purposes of this discussion, the verb προνοέω and the noun πρόνοια in their human application, meaning "provide," "provision," are unimportant (cf. II Macc. 4:6 [RSV "attention"]; Acts 24:2; Rom. 13:14). But in the Greek OT, πρόνοια is also used, in a manner familiar in Hellenistic writers of the time, in connection with, and almost as a synonym for, God, exactly as "Providence" may be used in English. In Wisd. Sol. 14:3 it is attributed to God, in an address to him as Father. In Wisd. Sol. 17:2 "eternal providence" is used virtually as a synonym for "God"; and in IV Macc. 13:19; 17:22 "the divine providence" is similarly used, while in IV Macc. 9:24 "our just ancestral providence" (ἡ δικαία καὶ πάτριος ἡμῶν πρόνοια) is a variant of the same. In III Macc. 4:21; 5:30, it is used with a genitive following, as an attribute of God.

"The divine providence" was a common enough periphrasis for "God" in Greek writers; and Philo wrote a whole treatise περὶ προνοίας, according to Euseb. Hist. II.18.6; *Preparation for the Gospel* VII. 20.9; VIII.13.7. But whereas in the non-Jewish writers it tended to be cosmic and impersonal (see Seneca *On Kindness* VI.23.5: "Nature conceived us in thought before she made us"; Cicero *On the Nature of the Gods* II, especially §§ 58, 73, where the Greek word πρόνοια itself is cited), for the Hebrew thinker it needed to be closely associated with the plan and election of a personal God. Indeed, the appropriation of it by pagan philosophers and moralists may be part of the explanation of the rarity of its biblical occurrences, and of the preference in the Bible for other terms discussed in the relevant articles alluded to *below.* The Greek words which are closely related to the idea of a fixed, impersonal destiny, εἱμαρμένη and μοῖρα, are naturally absent from the Greek Bible; and τύχη, "fortune," occurs only at Gen. 30:11 (play on the name "Gad"); Isa. 65:11 (castigation of a pagan cult); II Macc. 7:37 (variant ψυχή).

See ELECTION; FOREKNOWLEDGE; PREDESTINATION; VOCATION; GOD, OT; GOD, NT (especially § 7); LOVE.

Bibliography. M. Pohlenz, *Die Stoa* (1948), *passim.*

C. F. D. MOULE

*__PROVINCE.__ An administrative term originally designating a sphere of action or duty exercised by an appointed magistrate over a conquered territory; later used of the geographical district itself.

1. In the OT. The word מדינה, translated "district" (RSV) or "province" (KJV), denoted the divisions of Israel under governors during the time of Ahab (I Kings 20:14 ff); and later, Babylonian and Persian administrative districts (cf. Esther, *passim;* Lam. 1:1; Ezek. 19:8; Dan. 8:2). Once in the LXX (Esth. 4:11) it is translated ἐπαρχεία (*see* § 2 *below*); elsewhere χώρα is used (e.g., regularly in I Maccabees).

2. In the NT. Administrative divisions of the Roman Empire were termed ἐπαρχεῖαι. So in Acts 23:34 the procurator Felix asked Paul to what province (ἐπαρχεία) he belonged. In Acts 25:1, ἐπαρχεία may signify the office into which the new procurator Festus entered, as the variant reading ἡ ἐπάρχειος suggests. In the Republic the overseas provinces were assigned by lot to magistrates who were amenable to the Senate for their administration of military and civil affairs under the terms of the local *lex provinciae,* which had been drawn up for each at the time of its annexation to the Roman state. The Senate determined annually the provinces to be governed by those of consular status and those of praetorian rank.

In 27 B.C., Augustus assigned certain provinces, which he had previously administered directly through his legates, to the Senate, and reserved for direct imperial control others which were more difficult to manage, chiefly those on the frontiers. In the senatorial provinces ex-consuls or ex-praetors, serving under the common title of PROCONSUL, held office normally for only a year. Acts 13:7 is technically correct in designating Sergius Paulus a proconsul, since Cyprus had been a senatorial province since 22 B.C. These governors had small garrisons of auxiliaries for maintaining and preserving order; legions were stationed only in the imperial provinces, with the exception of Africa, which had a legionary force and a prefectus governor. They held supreme authority in military and judicial administration. In both types of province, financial administration was delegated to equestrian procurators (*see* PROCURATOR), who usually worked through local authorities in raising levies for the state. In senatorial provinces the procurator was an assistant to the questor.

In provinces like Syria, which were directly supervised by the emperor, governors were chosen from among those who had formerly held consular or praetorian office, and bore the title *legatus Augusti propraetore.* They differed from the proconsuls of the senatorial provinces in the extensive military authority they exercised and in the indefinite term of office they enjoyed, subject to the emperor's pleasure. A special form of provincial administration was demanded by those districts of rugged terrain or of a rude and undeveloped culture. Judea and later Palestine, Mauretania, Thrace, and Egypt furnish examples of this third type of imperial province, governed by an imperial procurator (ἐπίτροπος) of equestrian rank and responsible in part to the neighboring *legatus.* Thus under a special commission the Syrian legate Vitellius intervened in Judea to depose Pontius Pilate in A.D. 36 (Jos. Antiq. XVIII. iv.2). After the death of Herod Agrippa II, *ca.* 100, Palestine was fully incorporated into Syria.

In the first century the administration of the provinces was orderly and just. The system of taxation was standardized and considerable local autonomy was permitted, before an increasingly bureaucratic government sharply curtailed municipal government.

3. Principal Roman provinces. The following provinces are of special interest to students of the NT. They are listed in the order of their admission to the Empire:

a) Senatorial provinces: Macedonia (146 B.C.); Achaea (146 B.C.); Asia (133 B.C.); Crete and Cyrenaica (74 B.C.); Bithynia (74 B.C., with Pontus added in 64 B.C.); Cyprus (22 B.C., but annexed in 55 B.C.).

b) Imperial provinces: Pamphylia (101 B.C., added to Lycia in A.D. 43); Cilicia (67 B.C., joined to Syria in 22 B.C.–A.D. 74); Syria (64 B.C.); Egypt (31 B.C.); Illyricum (27 B.C., imperial after 11 B.C.); Galatia (25 B.C.); Judea (A.D. 6); Cappadocia (A.D. 17); Lycia and Pamphylia (A.D. 43).

Bibliography. J. Marquardt, *Römische Staatsverwaltung* (1881); E. Schürer, *History of the Jewish People,* vol. I, bk. 1 (1902), p. 327; A. H. M. Jones, *The Cities of the Eastern Roman Provinces* (1937); G. H. Stevenson, *Roman Provincial Administration* (1939); D. Magie, *Roman Rule in Asia Minor* (2 vols.; 1950); W. Förster, *Das römische Weltreich zur Zeit des NT* (2 vols.; 1956).
E. W. SAUNDERS

PRUDENCE. *See* DISCRETION.

PRUNING HOOK [מזמרה, *from* זמר, to prune]. A blade attached to a handle, used for removing superfluous twigs. Usually vines in Bible lands grow along the ground; and after the clusters of grapes have formed, the vines are propped up on sticks or piles of stones. For pruning, only a sharp knife would be required (Isa. 18:5; cf. Song of S. 2:15). In Mic. 4:4 "under his vine" may imply a trellis. The familiar references to beating spears into pruning hooks (Isa. 2:4; Mic. 4:3; cf. Joel 3:10) might indicate a long handle and so suggest trellising.

An iron head made like a heavy sickle and to be attached to a handle was found at Tell Jemmeh and dated by the excavator *ca.* 800 B.C. To reforge a spear point into a pruning knife, as to make of a sword a point for a PLOW, is plausible and technologically possible. Fig. PRU 68.

Bibliography. F. Petrie, *Gerar* (1928), p. 15, pl. xxvii, 7.
P. L. GARBER

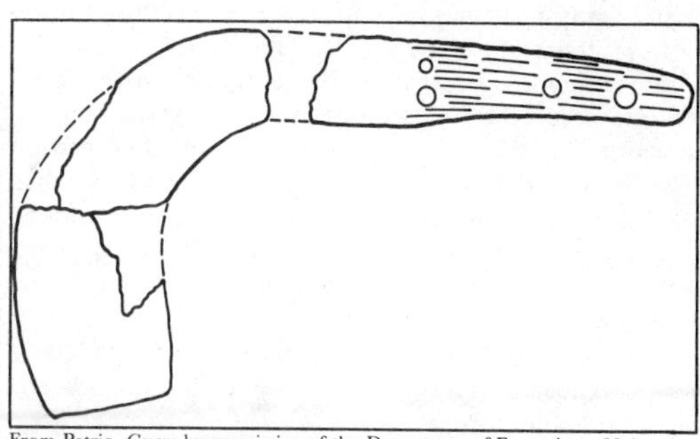

From Petrie, *Gerar;* by permission of the Department of Egyptology, University College, London

68. Iron pruning hook(?), from Tell Jemmeh

PSALM HEADINGS, MUSICAL. *See* Music.

PSALMODY. *See* Music.

***PSALMS, BOOK OF** sämz [תהלים]. The first book of the third group of books, the "Writings," in the MT. It is believed to be the most important book among the Writings, and according to Luke (24:44) was quoted as such by Jesus himself. Luke also believes that words contained in the book of Psalms are fulfilled in the life of Jesus, and his disciples had to obey orders given in it (Luke 20:41-44; Acts 1:20; 13:33).

- A. Origin and divisions
  - 1. Superscriptions
  - 2. Former collections
  - 3. Date
  - 4. Text
- B. Poetic forms
  - 1. Verses and strophes
    - *a.* The smallest units and parallelism
    - *b.* Stanzas
    - *c.* Meter
  - 2. Cultic types
    - *a.* N Israelite poems
    - *b.* Royal psalms
    - *c.* Hymns
    - *d.* Thanksgiving songs
    - *e.* Laments
  - 3. Pedagogic types
- C. The religion and piety of the psalms
  - 1. Yahweh's deeds
    - *a.* Relation to the Pentateuch
    - *b.* Yahweh the mighty God of Israel
    - *c.* Yahweh's morality
  - 2. Yahweh's commandments
    - *a.* Content
    - *b.* Character
- Bibliography

A. *ORIGIN AND DIVISIONS.* Probably the first Christian congregations, even in Greece and Asia Minor, sang hymns from the Psalter in their public services—of course, in Greek translation (I Cor. 14:15; Eph. 5:19; Col. 3:16). Psalms were sung also for private religious edification (Jas. 5:13). This practice follows the example given by the services in the Jerusalem temple, where the Levites sang every week Pss. 24; 48; 82; 94; 81; 93; 92, and where Pss. 113–18 (*see* Hallel) formed a part of the liturgy of the great annual Feasts. The use of at least some psalms in the temple service already in the fourth century B.C. is attested by I Chr. 16:8 ff (*see* Doxology), which refers to David's receiving the ark in the tabernacle erected by him; some scholars today try to combine Pss. 24:7 ff; 76 with this event. The tradition of the temple was probably followed by the synagogues, where the Psalter was used for singing and praying but never for the "lessons," which were strictly confined to the Law and sections taken from the books of the Prophets.

1. Superscriptions. The superscriptions of seventy-three psalms contain David's name in the form לדוד. Its exact meaning ("from David," "concerning David" [like *lb'l*, "concerning Ba'al," in Ras Shamra]) still remains to be determined exactly, as is the case with apparently musical terms like נחילות ("flutes"?) in Ps. 5; גתית in Pss. 8; 81; 84; or the "hind of the dawn" in Ps. 22. The main difficulty consists in the fact that even the Greek translators of the second century B.C. (the LXX) did not understand them, as shown by their rendering εἰς τὸ τέλος for למנצח, probably "To the choirmaster." They tried to combine words unknown to them with other terms—e.g., גתית with גת, "wine press" (e.g., Judg. 6:11; Lam. 1:15); or נחילות with נחלה, "inherited property" (Ps. 8: ὑπὲρ τῶν ληνῶν; Ps. 5: ὑπὲρ τῆς κληρονομούσης; *see* Music.

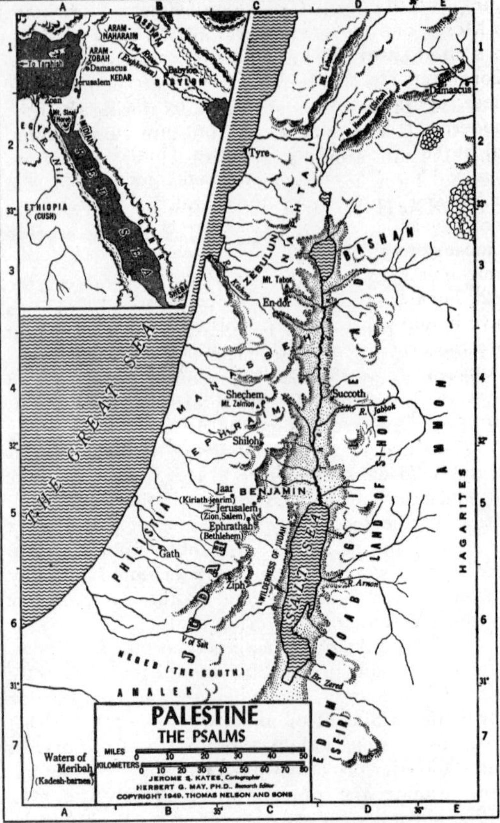

Much clearer are some allusions to certain events in David's life—e.g., to Absalom's rebellion (Ps. 3), the end of the persecution by Saul (18), or the visit by Nathan (51). Some of them follow a tradition which is not preserved in the OT as we have it or another form than that of Samuel. The Philistine king before whom David feigned madness bears the name of Achish in I Sam. 21:10 ff; of Abimelech in Ps. 34; and in the same story in I Samuel, David came to Gath on his own initiative and was not captured by the Philistines as in Ps. 56.

The superscriptions referring to Asaph (Pss. 50; 75–83; cf. I Chr. 6:39; 15:17) and to Heman and Ethan the Ezrahites (Pss. 88–89), who are not mentioned in the books of Samuel, reflect the intention to connect the Levitical guilds whose heads they should have been with the time of David (cf. I Chr. 6:33, 44). Pss. 72; 127 are associated with Solomon, and in the same manner Pss. 39; 62; 77 connect the name of Jeduthun with a choir of his time (cf. II

Chr. 5:12). The superscription of Ps. 90 refers even to Moses, and those of Pss. 42; 44–49; 84–85; 87–88 to a choir instituted by Levi's legendary grandson Korah (cf. II Chr. 20:19). The historical value of these superscriptions is contested by the majority of modern scholars, who believe that they reflect musical life in the fourth century B.C. Dual superscriptions are found in Pss. 39; 62 (David; Jeduthun); and in Ps. 77 (Asaph; Jeduthun), and this fact casts a doubt over their validity. But there is a trend toward a more conservative outlook, revealed especially in some articles by Eissfeldt. *See bibliography.*

2. Former collections. The book of Psalms as we have it contains 150 units. This figure was fixed before the origin of the LXX, whose 151th psalm is counted "outside the number" (ἔξωθεν ἀριθμοῦ). But there is no uniformity in the division of the single canticles. Pss. 9–10 are wrongly counted as two in the MT, rightly as one unit in the LXX. The following equations may be made:

MT		LXX
114–15	=	113
116:1-9	=	114
116:10-19	=	115
117–46	=	116–45
147:1-11	=	146
147:12-20	=	147
148–50	=	148–50

The Vulg. follows the LXX, its Psalter being, not Jerome's *Psalterium juxta Hebraeos,* but an older translation made by him from the LXX, also using perhaps Origen's Hexapla. Neither the MT nor the LXX recognized that Pss. 42–43 were originally one prayer, as clearly shown by the refrain 42:6, 11; 43:5.

These 150 psalms are divided into five books by doxologies (perhaps after the analogous partition of the Pentateuch): 1–41; 42–72; 73–89; 90–106; 107–50. Their limits fall sometimes together with the end of ancient smaller collections. So Pss. 3–41 are bound together by the לדוד and by the use of "Yahweh" as the name by which God is invoked.

The second collection prefers the designation "Elohim" for God (cf. the doublet Ps. 14=Ps. 53). It contains six psalms connected with the "sons of Korah" (44–49), twenty again with David (51–70), and an appendix to this Elohistic David psalter: Ps. 72, introduced by לשלמה, "from[?] Solomon." Ps. 50, now an Asaph psalm, may have been originally a Korah psalm. Pss. 42–43; 71, songs of a man persecuted (in his old age) by his enemies, are without superscription. They may belong together and have their origin in the Diaspora outside the city of the sanctuary (42:5, 7; 43:3-4). For this reason they did not belong to any Jerusalem collection, and they became the framework of 42–70 before Ps. 72 was appended.

The third book is in its main part Elohistic too. It contains the Asaph collection (73–83), four Korah psalms (84–85; 87–88) and one David psalm (86) left aside by the former collections, and a hymn of Ethan (89). Pss. 84-89, which are Yahwistic, were appended to the Asaph collection after its Elohistic redaction.

The division between the fourth and the fifth books is purely artificial, as may be seen by a comparison of Ps. 106 with Ps. 107. The fourth book starts with the prayer of Moses, the man of God (Ps. 90), and embraces: (*a*) canticles with various titles, mostly of hymnal character and celebrating Yahweh's kingship (93 [95–96]; 97 [98]; 99); (*b*) Davidic psalms (101; 103; 108–10; 138–45); (*c*) Hallelujah psalms (104–6; 111–12; 146–50); (*d*) Hallel (113–18; *see* HALLEL); (*e*) songs of ascent (120–34, from which 122; 124; 131; 133 are again Davidic; *see* ASCENT, SONG OF).

The other psalms show no certain principles of ordering. Even from this rapid survey it may be seen that books IV-V are not the work of a single redactor but result from a slow growing together of smaller collections with single songs. It may be that an older book of Psalms contained Pss. 3–110, with Ps. 2 as an introductory counterpart to 110, as Ps. 1 forms the later Introit to the whole collection.

3. Date. The fixing of the age of these smaller collections and of the Psalter itself depends on their interpretation, especially of the songs mentioning the king. Are they testimonials of the pre-exilic monarchies of Judah and Israel or of the Maccabean kingship after 105 B.C.? Do the songs celebrating Yahweh's ascension to his heavenly throne contain the liturgy of a pre-exilic feast, or are they dependent on Deutero-Isaiah? The stylistic difference between the canonical psalms and the hymns discovered in Qumran leaves no doubt that there are surely no Maccabean songs in our Psalter. The quotation of Ps. 79:2-3 as an older song in I Macc. 7:17 seems fully attested. *Ca.* 100 B.C. the book of Psalms belonged to the Scriptures and was no longer open for insertions. The fact that the LXX has the same order and number of psalms with their superscriptions and doxologies (in spite of the differences in 9–10; 114–16; 147) shows clearly that the actual collection was finished between the division of the Pentateuch into five books (which took place before the Samaritan schism) and the Greek translation—i.e., in no case later than the end of the third century B.C. To these external and internal reasons should be added the most pertinent one: the lack of Greek influence upon the theology of the psalms which is to be found in Ecclesiastes and Ecclesiasticus.

This dating of the collection means, of course, nothing against a much earlier dating of its smaller units and of the single psalms. They may reflect much earlier stages of Israelite religious and cultic poetry. This is true even if there are in some of them late (Aramaic) expressions belonging to the time when Aramaic was the official language in the Persian Empire and used by the Jews, not only in Elephantine but also in Palestine, as the Aramaic portions in Ezra and Daniel attest. In liturgical texts (also in our Christian prayer books) there is a double tendency: on the one side to preserve or even to reuse archaic ("sacred") expressions, and on the other side to modernize the language of the holy text—e.g., for pedagogical aims.

The artificial uniformity of orthography and morphology which exists throughout the whole OT and no less in the Qumran texts—e.g., 1QIs[a] or (for the psalms) 1Q 10–12; 16, and by this way attested already in the first or even the second century B.C.—makes it impossible to discern by their language, their grammatical forms, ancient songs like that of Deborah (Judg. 5; twelfth century) from the latest texts—e.g., the Hebrew parts of Daniel (second century). The differences between the Qumran fragments and the best recensions of the MT as printed by Kittel or Snaith are not greater than those between this text and variants collected by Kennicott and De Rossi—e.g., the *scriptio plena* or *defectiva* of עותני or עותוני and בפקדיך or בפקודיך in Ps. 119:78, the former spellings being those of 1Q 11.

This uniformity is also a very serious obstacle to all metrical researches. The history of the psalm poetry in Israel has to be written by interior criteria and by comparison with the religious poetry in the surrounding countries, including the texts from Ras Shamra, and not on the basis of linguistic arguments. Beside these foreign texts it will be useful to compare the poetical intercalations in the prose books of the OT, the Deborah song, or the dirges of David over Saul and Jonathan or Abner (II Sam. 1:19 ff; 3:33 ff), and to look at the liturgical pieces in the books of the Prophets—e.g., Amos 5:2 or Hos. 6:1-8; 14:2-9; Jer. 14:1–15:4. The book of Lamentations, the *Hôdhayôth* from Qumran, the canticles in Luke 1, and the five psalms transmitted only in Syr. are other examples which should not be neglected. They show without doubt that the main types of psalms in the Psalter are pre-exilic and that even the younger poems contained in it are much older than the Hymns from Qumran, which use the phraseology, the imagery, and the leading ideas of the book of Psalms freely or in the form of quotations. Theodor H. Gaster, in *The Dead Sea Scriptures in English Translation,* counts fifty-seven such cases, of which one example is the following (1QH 8.28 ff):

> Grievous was my pain [cf. Isa. 17:11], and could not be stayed.
> [My soul was overw]helmed [Ps. 42:7; 13:5],
> like them that go down to Sheol,
> and my spirit was sunken low amid the dead [Ps. 77:7 combined with 88:6].
> My life had reached the Pit [Ps. 88:4],
> and my soul waxed faint [Ps. 107:5; Jonah 2:8] day and night without rest.[1]

4. Text. The Hebrew text of the Psalms is generally not so faulty as was once believed. Of course, there are many corruptions and alterations, as shown by the irregularities in the acrostic arrangement in Pss. 9–10 or by the differences between texts which are twice delivered (Pss. 14/53; Ps. 18/II Sam. 22). Such alterations may have theological reasons. So the desire of the pious to "see God" was changed into "to be seen [to appear] before God" (e.g., Ps. 42:2). They may be even older than the forming of the Psalter: see, e.g., the invocation of God as "Elohim" instead of "Yahweh" in the second, major part of the third book. In Pss. 42–43 the refrain should be:

> Hope in Yahweh; for I shall again praise him,
> my help and my God;

and 43:4 should read:

> Then I will go to the altar of Yahweh,
> to the God of my exceeding joy;
> and I will praise thee with the lyre,
> O Yahweh, my God.

The name of Yahweh is indispensable in such admonitions and vows which are addressed to this special God, with whom the pious is connected by the deeds in the history of his people. So, too, 44:1 should read:

> We have heard with our ears, O Yahweh,
> our fathers have told us,
> what deeds thou didst perform in their days,
> in the days of old.

Besides these older alterations there is perhaps at least one very late one, representing anti-Christian polemics. In 22:16, "like a lion" (accusative?), כארי, is possibly a change for an ancient "they have pierced," כארו. The scribes wanted possibly to prevent the use of the verse in the messianic interpretation of the church (cf. John 20:25, 27). "They have pierced" is the better reading. Like Luther, the KJV, the RSV, and the Spanish Sagrada Biblia (1953), the Latin version introduced in 1945 by Pope Pius XII into the daily prayer of the Roman Catholic clergy accepts the *foderunt* of ancient versions including Jerome. But the possibility remains that we have before us, not a voluntary change, but an involuntary scribal error, the letters ו and י being very similar, as seen, e.g., from 1QIs[a].

But in spite of such indisputable alterations, and the possibility of errors on occasion of the transcription from the older into the so-called square script and of modernizations of orthography, the commentaries now—not only the Roman Catholic ones!—are more conservative in the treatment of the text than those *ca.* 1900-25. And a comparison of the MT with the text of the LXX and the secondary translations depending on it, especially Jerome's *Psalterium Gallicanum* (and *Romanum*), or with the Syr. text, shows that uncertainties affecting the religious sense or value are rare. There must have been in the temple and later in the synagogue a strong tradition of liturgy and prayer, preserving the text from greater mistakes, and this living tradition was never interrupted for Judaism in its totality.

B. *POETIC FORMS.* 1. Verses and strophes. *a. The smallest units and parallelism.* The smallest unit of Hebrew poetry and psalmody is the line ("verse"), divided into two half lines ("half verses") offering the same or nearly the same content, the so-called *parallelismus membrorum,* so well known since Lowth's epoch-making work of 1753. This construction is used in the quotations of earlier proverbs or poems in the historical books. We read in Gen. 4:23:

> Adah and Zillah, hear my voice;
> you wives of Lamech, hearken to what I say:
> I have slain a man for wounding me,
> a young man for striking me.

Here "Adah and Zillah" is parallel to "you wives of Lamech"; "hear" to "hearken"; "my voice" to "to what I say"; "I have slain" has no parallel; "a man" is parallel to "a young man"; "for wounding" to "for striking"; and "me" to "me." The pattern is: $a+b+c//a'+b'+c'$; and $a+b+c+d//b'+c'+d$. As may be seen by this example, the parallel members of the line may be either identical ("me") or at

[1] From the book *The Dead Sea Scriptures* by T. H. Gaster; copyright © 1956 by Theodor H. Gaster, reprinted by permission of Doubleday & Company, Inc., and Martin Secker & Warburg Ltd., London.

least synonymous (all other examples); but the continuation of the same text shows a third form—antithesis:

If Cain is avenged sevenfold,
truly Lamech seventy-sevenfold.

"Cain" here is opposite to "Lamech," and "sevenfold" to "seventy-sevenfold."

The following ancient example shows another variation:

Spring up, O well!—Sing to it!—
The well which the princes dug,
which the nobles of the people delved,
with the scepter and with their staves
(Num. 21:17-18).

Here "which the princes" is parallel to "which the nobles of the people"; "dug" to "delved"; "scepter" to "staves"; but the theme, "Spring up, O well!—Sing to it!" remains outside the parallelism (so-called "synthetic" or "incomplete" parallelism; a+b+c+d//b'+c'+d').

The same form is to be found in Num. 21:27:

Come to Heshbon, let it be built,
let the city of Sihon be established.
For fire went forth from Heshbon,
flame from the city of Sihon.

Here too, as in 21:17 ("Spring up, O well!—Sing to it!"), it is an imperative ("Come") which remains outside the parallelism (a+b+c//b'+c'; and d+b//d'+c'). The reason is easily recognized: The poetic form of parallelism belongs more to lyricism than to appeal, to description than to commandment. It allows, and even facilitates, the painting of a situation, but retards the flow of an action. By way of these combinations of three or five half lines from which two or four are parallels and one outside the parallelism, the shortest strophes ("stanzas") are formed.

These simplest forms are frequently used in the psalms. For the identity of members, note Ps. 29:1-2:

Ascribe to the LORD, O heavenly beings,
ascribe to the LORD glory and strength (a+b//a+c).
Ascribe to the LORD the glory of his name;
worship the LORD in holy array (a+c'+d//a'+e).

For synonymous parallelism, note Ps. 19:1-2:

The heavens are telling the glory of God
and the firmament proclaims his handiwork.
Day to day pours forth speech,
and night to night declares knowledge
(a+b+c//a'+b'+c'; and d+e+f//d'+e'+f').

Antithetic parallelism is to be found, e.g., in one of the royal psalms (20:7-8):

Some boast of chariots, and some of horses;
but [Hebrew "and"] we boast of the name of the LORD our God.
They will collapse and fall;
but [Hebrew "and"] we shall rise and stand upright
(a+b+a+c//a'+b'; and d+e//d'+e').

The same psalm which showed the synonymous provides also an example of incomplete parallelism, the first line of a couplet remaining outside (19:4-5):

In them he has set a tent for the sun,
which comes forth like a bridegroom leaving his chamber,
and like a strong man runs its course with joy
(a+b+c//b'+c'+d).

Another example is from Ps. 30:1:

I will extol thee, O LORD, for thou hast drawn me up,
and hast not let my foes rejoice over me.

The pattern here is a+b+c//b'+c', the member "a" being, not an imperative as in Num. 21:17, but a self-exhortation. These forms are preserved also in the canticles in Luke 1:

a) Synonymous (vs. 46):

My soul magnifies the Lord,
and my spirit rejoices in God my Savior
(a+b+c//a'+b'+c'+d).

b) Antithetic (vss. 52-53):

He has put down the mighty from their thrones,
and exalted those of low degree;
He has filled the hungry with good things,
and the rich he has sent empty away
(a+b+c//a'+b'; and d+e+f//e'+d'+f').

c) Incomplete (vss. 70-72):

As he spoke by the mouth of his holy prophets from of old,
That we should be saved from our enemies,
and from the hand of all who hate us;
to perform the mercy promised to our fathers,
and to remember his holy covenant.

In this third example, the first line, A has no parallelism; lines 2-5 are arranged a+b+c//a'+b'; and d+e+f//e'+f'.

The same forms may be seen in the Qumran hymns (Gaster translation):

a) Synonymous (3.19-20):

I, that am molded of clay,
what am I?
I, that am kneaded with water,
what is my worth?[1]
(a+b+c//a'+b'+c').

b) Antithetic (2.28):

Yet, while my head was dissolving like water,
my soul held firm to Thy covenant[1]
(a+b//a'+b'+c).

c) Incomplete (2.20-21):

I give thanks unto Thee, O Lord,
For Thou hast put my soul in the bundle of life
and hedged me against all the snares of corruption[1]
(A+[a+b+c]//[a'+b'+c']).

In the incomplete parallelism another line than the first—e.g., the third—may be without corresponding member. In Luke 1:31, Gabriel's announcement:

Behold, you will conceive in your womb
and bear a son,
And you shall call his name Jesus,

runs after the model of Gen. 16:11:

Behold, you are with child,
and shall bear a son;
You shall call his name Ishmael
(a+b//a'+b'+A);

and in 1QH 2.22-23 (Gaster translation):

But they—a league of Falsehood,
a congregation of Belial—
They knew not that through Thee I would stand.

[1] From the book *The Dead Sea Scriptures* by T. H. Gaster; copyright © 1956 by Theodor H. Gaster, reprinted by permission of Doubleday & Company, Inc., and Martin Secker & Warburg Ltd., London.

For Thou in Thy mercy dost save my life;
For by Thee are my footsteps guided[1]
([a//a']+[b+c+d//c'+d']+A).

Even these simplest forms have behind them a history in the old oriental literature long before the OT. Some examples taken from the texts from Ras Shamra by Gordon in his *Ugaritic Manual* (1955) are:

He judges the case of the widow
adjudicates the cause of the fatherless.
Eat bread from the tables,
drink wine from the jars[2]
(a+b+c//a'+b'+c').

How can it be said:
Krt is Il's son,
the scion of Lṭpn we Qdš;
Or do gods die
nor Lṭpn's scion live?[2]
(A+[a+b+c//c'+d']+[d+e//d'+e']).

Like the heart of the cow toward her calf,
like the heart of the ewe toward her lamb,
So is the heart of 'Anat after Ba'l[2]
([a+b+c//a'+b'+c']+A),

and the same form in a Tell el-Amarna letter (Knudz. 264, 15 ff):

If we ascend to the heavens
if we descend to the netherworld,
Our head stays in your hands
([a+b//a'+b']+A).

Another similarity between the OT poetry and the Ras Shamra Texts is seen when the second halves of two lines are parallel and the first halves identical, or vice versa. So it is in Isa. 15:1 MT:

Because in a night is laid down
Ar Moab is undone
Because in a night is laid down
Qir Moab is undone;

or in Ps. 136:1-3:

O give thanks to the LORD, for he is good,
for his steadfast love endures for ever.
O give thanks to the God of gods,
for his steadfast love endures for ever.
O give thanks to the Lord of lords,
for his steadfast love endures for ever;

and in Ras Shamra:

They shake each other like gmr-animals,
Môt is strong, Ba'l is strong;
They gore like buffaloes,
Môt is strong, Ba'l is strong;
They bite like serpents,
Môt is strong, Ba'l is strong;
They kick like Ism-animals,
Môt is down, Ba'l is down![2]

b. Stanzas. These smallest units do not stay unrelated side by side; they start to become combined in a strophic order into stanzas. In some psalms they are visible already by their acrostic arrangement (9–10; 25; 34; 37; 111–12; 119; 145). The stanzas so formed contain from two (Lam. 4) to eight (Ps. 119) lines, all lines within the stanza starting with the same letter or only every first line of the stanza starting with the next letter of the alphabet. For more detailed discussion of this primarily mnemotechnical principle, *see* § B3 *below*.

In other cases some stylistic features or the sense leave no doubt about the stanzas intended by the author—e.g., in two of the best-known psalms: In 121 the beginning of vss. 3, 5, 7, with "He," "The LORD," and "The LORD" shows clearly four stanzas with two lines each, every line being divided into two half lines or three third lines. In Ps. 126 the imperative "restore" (שׁוּבָה), reiterating the stem of the infinitive, "When . . . restored" (בְּשׁוּב), divides the poem into two stanzas with four lines each of the same length as those in 121.

In spite of such clear cases—which could be multiplied—one must confess that there is no certain leading strophic principle in the book of Psalms. Certain questions arise, such as: Should Ps. 20 be divided into two stanzas with five lines each (1-5*a*, 6-9), or into two stanzas with four lines (1-4, 6-8) with one closing line outside the stanza (5*a* and 9) as is the case in Ps. 21—twice two stanzas with two lines each (1, 2-3, 4-5, 6; and 8, 9*a*-9*b*, 10-11, 12) and two independent lines (7 and 13)? And what is the matter with 20:6*b* and 21:9, a very corrupt verse? Even where a psalm is clearly divided by a refrain, the stanzas are sometimes not completely regular in the MT. In Pss. 42–43, vs. 42:8 is too long, and the third stanza (Ps. 43) lacks one line. In Ps. 46, in which the refrain has to be repeated after vs. 4, the third stanza is too long; perhaps vs. 9*b* should be deleted? These examples show that we have to be very careful to change the text in order to get regular stanzas. The regularity of the stanzas is not a ruling principle in the text as we have it, and we do not know if it ever was. It may be that in the service of the temple the music done by the instruments (cf., e.g., Ps. 68: 25 or 150:3-5) secured the regularity of the stanzas by interludes, from which the still unexplained "Selah" (*see* MUSIC) may be a rest.

c. Meter. The same care has to be observed in all questions of meter. The half lines in which the verses are, as we have seen, generally divided have in the majority of cases the same number of words susceptible to bear a full tune—e.g., Ps. 24:1-2:

The earth is the LORD's and the fullness thereof (3 Hebrew words),
the world and those who dwell therein (3);
for he has founded it upon the seas (3),
and established it upon the rivers (3).

In other cases the second half line is shorter than the first—e.g., in Ps. 130:2, 4:

Let thy ears be attentive (3 Hebrew words)
to the voice of my supplications (2)!
. . . .
But there is forgiveness with thee (3),
that thou mayest be feared (2).

Perhaps in vss. 2-3 *'adhônāy* ("Lord"), repeating the preceding "Yahweh" ("LORD"), should be deleted, so the lines would parallel those given before:

Out of the depths I cry to thee, O LORD (3 Hebrew words)!
. . . hear my voice (2)!
If Thou, O LORD, shouldst mark iniquities (3),
. . . who could stand (2)?

The book of Lamentations is completely composed of these so-called "lamentation"—or better, "dirge"—

[1] From the book *The Dead Sea Scriptures* by T. H. Gaster; copyright © 1956 by Theodor H. Gaster, reprinted by permission of Doubleday & Company, Inc., and Martin Secker & Warburg Ltd., London.
[2] From *Ugaritic Manual* by C. H. Gordon; reprinted by permission of the author and the Pontifical Biblical Institute, Rome.

verses (Hebrew *qînâ*). Besides the division into half lines, the division into third lines—e.g., in Ps. 121: 3-5—has been mentioned:

He will not let your foot be moved (3 Hebrew words),
he who keeps you will not slumber (3).
Behold, he who keeps Israel (2)
will neither slumber (2) nor sleep (2).
The LORD is your keeper (2);
the LORD is your shade (2)
on your right hand (2).

More seldom are verses with 4+4 or 4+3 words.

But there is no unanimity among scholars about the metrical system transforming words into metrical beats. Is the Qinah, as Hölscher and Mowinckel think, to be read with 4+4 beats, or, with Sievers and the scholars following him, with 3+2? And is the verse with 3+3 words really to be read with 3+3 beats or with 4+4? The answer depends on another question: Do we have before us an alternating system of stressed and unstressed syllables (with the possibility of neglecting the unstressed) or a system in which the words have their regular accent and in which only these accents are to be counted? So Lam. 1:2 could be read either:

(4) איכה ישבה בדד
(3) העיר רבתי עם

or:

(3) איכה ישבה בדד
(2) העיר רבתי עם

or, taking איכה as an anacrusis outside the verse:

איכה
(3) ישבה בדד העיר
(2) רבתי עם

If we take the second system (Sievers) for granted, the 3+3 alternating with 2+2+2 would be the most frequent one. But both systems, like all others, suffer from the great difficulty that we know so little about Hebrew grammar and pronunciation in older times. The system of the MT is an artificial one coming from the tenth century A.D.! The rests of the second column of Origen's Hexapla giving the Hebrew text in Greek letters as it was pronounced in his time, some older forms of the pronominal endings preserved in 1QIs[a] and some other Qumran texts and going together with the Samaritan pronunciation (not with the written Samar. text), and the researches of Kahle and his pupils have shown that the grammar of the Hebrew spoken in pre-Christian times is still to be reconstructed. For this reason changes in the Hebrew text on account of the meter are tolerable only in some exceptional cases, when the metrical irregularity is confirmed by reasons of the sense or of parallelism, and only with the greatest caution.

2. Cultic types. These simplest forms and their stanzas are the basis of the highly developed cultic types in the service of Yahweh in the Israelite sanctuaries.

a. N Israelite poems. There are, first, some psalms which probably belong to the N kingdom. No marriage is known between a Judean king and a princess of Tyre (Ps. 45) but between Ahab and Jezebel (I Kings 16:31). Only "Jacob and Joseph" are mentioned in Ps. 77:15; 81:4-5, only N tribes in Ps. 80:1-2, or the mountains in the N of Israel's territory in Ps. 133 (cf. 29:6). So the catastrophe contrasted with Yahweh's powerful epiphany at the Red Sea in the days of old is probably the Assyrian invasion in 734.

N Israelite poetry is also attested by its influence on the book of Hosea, first of all by the great liturgy quoted in 14:2 ff, with its combination of confession of sins, the vow to trust in the future only in Yahweh's help, and Yahweh's favorable answer in the forms of the old Palestinian fertility cult—in contrast with a repulse, as in Hos. 6:1 ff or in the analogous Judean liturgy in Jer. 14:2–15:4.

These N Israelite songs are a very valuable help for the dating of psalms in general, for they let us see forms living in the eighth century B.C. It is a pity there are not more, that the big majority of psalms comes from the S kingdom, from the Jerusalem temple. The reason for this is not only the fact that the kingdom of Judah stayed one century and a half longer than that of Israel, but also that Jerusalem as the sanctuary of the ark was, even before the Deuteronomic centralization of the cult, a kind of common shrine for the tribes united in Yahweh's covenant. So Jerusalem preserved (after the destruction of Silo) in a higher degree than, e.g., Sichem, the traditions from the amphictyonic time and later. By the transfer of the ark into David's capital these amphictyonic traditions, including the manners and the texts of the older poetry, were introduced in this shrine, to the detriment of the northern sanctuaries.

b. Royal psalms. The Jerusalem sanctuary, being the royal shrine from the beginning of its Israelite history, is the place in which the royal psalms (2; 18; 20; 21; 72; 101; 110; 132; 144:1-11 according to Eissfeldt) were sung; in which the king sacrificed his offerings, asked for an oracle and received it, and renewed on regular or exceptional occasions the covenant between Yahweh, himself, and his people (II Kings 11:17 ff; 23:3 ff) on the basis of sacred traditions and precepts preserved orally or in written form among the priests.

These royal psalms are prayers of the king assuring that he observes the ordinances of his God in judgment by punishing the bad members of his people and assembling the pious in his service (Ps. 101). They are prayers for the king asking that Yahweh may hear his voice; look at his perfect offerings (20: 2-6); and let the time of his reign be a period of peace, well-being, and good harvest, but also a period of justice for the poor and of a constant fear of his God (72). They praise Yahweh for what he has done and will do for the king who rejoices in his strength (21:1). He trusts in Yahweh and in the steadfast love of the Most High, the Elyon, the old pre-Israelite God of Jerusalem who was, since David, identified with the national god (110; cf. 91:1). The royal psalms give good oracles to the king (2:6 ff; 20:7 ff; 100:1, 4), declaring that the king is adopted by Yahweh on the day of his enthronement to be his son (2:7 ff). For this reason the great political crisis during which this special psalm is written will be finished soon. The best the kings of the nations incorporated into the Davidic empire may do is to renounce all undertaking of liberation (2:1 ff). These hopes and traits are the root of the later, "messianic" expectations, the desire for him "that cometh," the great king at the end days, the "eschatological" king.

This transformation of the hopes confessed in the royal psalms makes explicable the astonishing fact that they survived the catastrophe of the Judean monarchy in 587. Like other psalms which were not forgotten by the prisoners in Babylonia (Ps. 137), where they deeply influenced the language and the faith of Deutero-Isaiah, they were reintroduced into the temple service after 516.

*c. **Hymns.*** What is promised at the end of the royal psalm 20, the praise of God, is the content of the hymns (תהלים) celebrating Yahweh's overwhelming greatness and power he has shown in the creation of the world and in Israel's history. The hymns start with an introduction, for which the cultic shout "HALLELUJAH" seems too simple. This introduction admonishes the priests staying day and night in the temple (Pss. 134–35), the choir of choirs (135:19-20), or the whole congregation to sing his glory, accompanied by the instruments of the temple band:

> Praise the LORD!
> Praise God in his sanctuary;
> praise him in his mighty firmament!
> Praise him for his mighty deeds;
> praise him according to his exceeding greatness!
> Praise him with trumpet sound;
> praise him with lute and harp!
> Praise him with timbrel and dance;
> praise him with strings and pipe!
> Praise him with sounding cymbals;
> praise him with loud clashing cymbals!
> Let everything that breathes praise the LORD!
> Praise the LORD! (Ps. 150; cf. 98:5).

Israelite music was, as we know from Assyrian sources, famous throughout the old oriental world. Besides these temple officials other groups, apparently of laymen including proselytes, were called to the same service (Ps. 107); we do not know when this custom arose. Instead of the exhortation in the imperative, there may be a self-exhortation in the cohortative, either in the plural (e.g., Ps. 95:1) or in the singular (e.g., Ps. 108:2). This single singer may be the leader of the choir or even the choir itself personified. He may be the dancer in the night of the festival (cf. Isa. 30:29) or a dancer like Miriam the prophetess leading her women as she sings her imperative:

> Sing to the LORD, for he has triumphed gloriously;
> the horse and his rider he has thrown into the sea
> (Exod. 15:21).

The age of the hymn as a cultic form is attested by the fact that it is used in a purely literary manner already in the northern psalm 29 (cf. the mentioning of Lebanon and Sirion in vs. 6). The greatness of Yahweh the god of the thunderstorm (cf. Exod. 19:16; I Kings 19:12) shall be celebrated by the "sons of gods" (Ps. 29:1).

Another literary use of the form of the hymn is to be found when the poet addresses his own soul as the choir praising the mercy and glory of his god (Pss. 103; 146) or as the one who adores (in the second person) his majesty (Ps. 104). Again we do not know when this development of the form took place, but it seems that we have before us a late development. Ps. 103 is a polemic against the doctrine of Yahweh's retribution of all sins, as are the books of Job and Ecclesiastes, but not in the negative attitude of these works. For Ps. 103 the best we can say of God is that

> He does not deal with us according to our sins,
> nor requite us according to our iniquities
> (vs. 10).

The poet is the most heterodox in the OT, and he seems to depend on Deutero-Isaiah (cf. vss. 15-16 with Isa. 40:6-7). Ps. 146 seems to reflect the influence of didactic wisdom (vss. 3 ff), as Ps. 104 does—in spite of the indirect influence of the famous Aton hymn from Tell el-Amarna with the creation story in Gen. 1 (P document).

The introduction of the hymn is generally followed by what Gunkel called the "corpus" of the hymn, saying for what reason Yahweh should be celebrated. It usually begins with "because" (כי), "who" (אשר; e.g., Ps. 16:7), or with the participle preceded by the article (e.g., Ps. 103:3 ff). Sometimes the corpus is distributed between two choirs, one chanting the single deeds of God and the other repeating the general theme: "for his steadfast love endures for ever" (cf. Ps. 118:1 ff), thus using a very ancient form of old oriental poetry. *See* § B1*a above.*

Yahweh is the great god who is king forever (Ps. 29:10) above all other gods (95:3; 96:4), who manifested and manifests his power in the creation of the world and in the wonders of nature and of the history of Israel. The celebration of the overwhelming strength of a god shown by the Creation is a theme frequently used in foreign psalms. In an account of his victory over the chaos monster the gods proclaim Marduk to be their king. The creator is greater than all other gods, and they have to adore him who would be able to destroy what he has made (cf. Ps. 97:7; Heb. 1:6). Opposite this connection between Israelite hymns and foreign poetry, history as the realm of Yahweh's power is a theme which is specifically Israelitic. Yahweh is primarily the God of history, of the history of his people as well in the prophetical faith as of the history of the other nations connected with Israel (e.g., Amos 9:7) and of the world. And history not only attests his power but even more his "justice" and morality, especially his love for his people, the trustworthiness of his oath and of his promises, his forgiveness in the present time and in the future as well in the past. With these ideas he proclaims, the poet of Ps. 103:6 ff is not a heretic!

The end of the hymn returns sometimes to the forms of the introduction (cf. with the imperative, Ps. 136:26; for the poet's appeal to his own soul, Ps. 103:22), occasionally with stylistic variations not affecting the sense—e.g., Ps. 106:1, 48:

> O give thanks to the LORD, for he is good;
> for his steadfast love endures for ever!
> . . . .
> Blessed be the LORD, the God of Israel,
> from everlasting to everlasting!
> And let all the people say, "Amen!"
> Praise the LORD!

As seen already by this example, the closing verses are the right occasion to turn the ideas of the singer toward the future, not only the immediate future but also that remote time, the end of the world. When the power of Yahweh in the Creation is celebrated, then the association with the *eschaton,* in which this deed will be renewed, is quite natural. The so-called eschatological hymns, the "new song" of Ps. 149:1 (cf. Isa. 42:10), may describe in the manner of some prophetic utterances the future event as already done in the prophetic perfect (e.g., Ps. 98:1-3, 9*a* [perfect], 9*b* [imperfect], as in Isa. 9:5-6*a,* 6*b*). This use of tenses is the reason for the difficulty in interpreting a special form of the hymn: the enthronement psalms, which celebrate the kingdom of Yahweh by the words which the RSV translates by "The LORD reigns" (93:1; 97:1; 99:1; cf. 47:9; 96:10; יהוה מלך [perfect]) and which are not to be separated from the shout of the other gods proclaiming Marduk their king (*see above*). But what is their exact sense? Do they mean that in the moment in which they are sung, Yahweh becomes king? So Mowinckel interprets them as a part of the liturgy of the Enthronement Feast, which was, according to him, the New Year's Feast. Every civil new year is virtually the day of the new creation. The god who became king by this deed ascends again to the throne when he enters in the great procession into his sanctuary.

Opposite to this interpretation, more recent research, especially that of Kraus, tries to show that there was in a pre-exilic time in Jerusalem a feast in which the election of David as king and of Zion as the shrine and dwelling place of Yahweh was celebrated, but that the proclamation of Yahweh to be king is younger, that it came up under the influence of Deutero-Isaiah and is to be understood as an eschatological hope whose fulfilment started on the day of the liberation from the Exile. This thesis seems to overestimate the importance of the end of the Exile for the Israelitic faith. There was only a small group of the offspring of the deportees who returned to Palestine, and those who lived there were not glad to see them come back; and the religious enthusiasm was so small that the postexilic prophets have to blame the neglect of Yahweh's cult and ordinances. Neither Ezra nor Nehemiah as a true servitor of the Persian king shows anything like a faith in a kingdom of Yahweh present in their time. It is likely that, indeed, in pre-exilic times Yahweh was greeted on New Year's Day as the king who renewed his dominion by re-creating the world. There is in this proclamation a confession against the great monarchies of the East and their religion. Neither Marduk nor Assur, but Yahweh, became king and is now king and will be king when all other powers vanish. יהוה מלך has to be translated: "Yahweh became king [in the first creation], he becomes king [now in his enthronement on New Year's Day, the day of the world renewed by him], and he will become king [at the day of the eschatological 'second' creation]." Creation and eschatology are not ideas excluding each other but the two sides of the same reality, the kingdom of God!

It may be that after the Babylonian model the creation myth was celebrated in the cult not only by songs but also by dramatic performances, in which a priest (or the king?) in the masque of the god had to overwhelm another in the masque of the dragon. The hymns celebrate the God who is present in the midst of the congregation, and even Jesus ben Sirach shows that the sons of Aaron, the singers, the musicians, and the laymen praised the great god when Simon the high priest, adorned with the holy garments, came down from the altar to bless the congregation (Ecclus. 50:22).

d. Thanksgiving songs. The hymns are such powerful poetry that another form of song celebrating Yahweh's deeds in the midst of his people, the song of thanksgiving by the nation in parallelism with the song of thanksgiving by the individual, was not so highly developed. The overwhelming influence of the hymns upon these thanksgiving songs is to be seen in the imperative in the beginning as well in the כי, the אשר, or the participle leading from the introduction to the corpus.

The corpus itself contains the narrative of a deed of God, not in Creation or in history in general, but in the recent past of Israel or in the private life of the singer. Both types appear side by side in Ps. 66 (vss. 8-9, 16-19):

> Bless our God, O peoples,
> let the sound of his praise be heard,
> who [participle] has kept us among the living,
> and has not let our feet slip.
> . . . .
> Come and hear, all you who fear God,
> and I will tell what he has done for me.
> I cried aloud to him,
> and he was extolled with my tongue.
> If I had cherished iniquity in my heart,
> the Lord would not have listened.
> But truly God has listened;
> he has given heed to the voice of my prayer.

The help for the people may not have been complete. Some enemies are still so powerful that the second half of such a psalm must be of an imprecatory type (129:1-2, 5):

> "Sorely have they afflicted me from my youth,"
> let Israel now say—
> "Sorely have they afflicted me from my youth,
> yet they have not prevailed against me."
> . . . .
> May all who hate Zion
> be put to shame and turned backward!

Much more developed than these national thanksgivings is the thanksgiving song by the individual. The term "thanksgiving" has been variously interpreted. Westermann (*see bibliography*) would prefer to speak of "praise of God" (*Lob Gottes*), and Mand (*see bibliography*) of "confession" (*Bekenntnis*). These differences show that no modern term in any European language corresponds exactly with an old oriental one—in this case the Hebrew ידה (*Hiph'il* הודה). There is no thanksgiving without praising God for what he did and without confessing in public his greatness or uniqueness. And there is no such confession or such praise without the element of personal experience.

In the Thanksgiving Hymns from Qumran, as in the Psalms of the OT, thanks are given to the God who helped in the days of distress, who forgave (e.g., Ps. 32:5 ff), who sent his word of grace. The distress may have been an illness which brought the pious to the limits of the nether world (Ps. 30:3; cf. 71:20; 116:3), to the depth of the sea (Jonah 2:3), so that he despaired (Isa. 38:11) and left all hope of returning to the temple of his God. The distress may have consisted in persecution by enemies who were stronger than the poet, whom they hated (e.g., Pss. 18:17; 41:7) even though one of them had been his friend (41:9). While the poet is a true worshiper of Yahweh, representing in some degree his congregation, his enemies are at the same time the foes of his God (92:9), who are to be overwhelmed by him. Who are these foes? There is no unanimous answer to this question. Mowinckel has tried to demonstrate that they were sorcerers producing the illness and misfortune of the poet by all means of ancient magic powers. Birkeland has said they are political adversaries of the king. The decision must be postponed until we have examined the "laments," in which they play a bigger role. But already it may be said that the thanksgiving psalms of the individual were originally not sung by the common members of the congregation but by its representative—i.e., the king. They became every member's canticles by the way of democratization. The mentioning of "all kings of the earth" (Ps. 138:4), the central role which the poet is playing in the cult (118:19 ff), and the richness of his sacrifices (116:15 ff) and the importance of his recovering for the whole world now and in the future (22:28 ff) show indeed clearly that the singer was originally not a private man but a leading personality. When the messengers of Merodach-baladan came to congratulate Hezekiah for his recovering, he should have celebrated in their presence a festivity in honor of his god instead of letting them see his treasure house (II Kings 20:12 ff).

But it is perhaps not unreasonable to think that there is not only one single explanation of the thanksgiving. The evildoers against the king may have been men of a magic power who feared to enter into an open opposition and preferred to kill him secretly and unseen. In contrast to their secret trials, the thanksgiving was a public ceremony, celebrated in the temple, with the pious attending. It was accompanied by sacrifices and other cultic actions such as the elevation of the cup of salvation (Ps. 116:12-13), and it was followed by a big meal to which the poor of the congregation (Ps. 22:26; cf. Deut. 12:12, 18) were invited (Ps. 66:13 ff). When they ate and drank, they too honored the God who by his grace saved the rich, who were feeding them, from illness and distress and death (22:26-29—H 22:27-30).

The main thing in these songs is the proclamation of the name of the God who helped (116:13). Not Baal-zebub, the god of Ekron to whom Ahaziah sent messengers in his illness (II Kings 1:2) in order to get his oracle, nor any other of the healing gods or goddesses in Israel's world, but Yahweh alone is to be recognized as saving lord over life and death. He heard the voice crying to him.

The supplications of the prayer spoken on the day of need are now quoted (Ps. 30:9-10—H 30:10-11) and the vows fulfilled. The speaker remembers the dreadful situation from which he has been saved and describes it with living pictures of oriental fancy, in order to enhance the greatness of his god, who is stronger than all dangers. Yahweh is the god of life, saving from death because he himself is never dying. The contrast between the danger that was and the new life which is now given is the best demonstration of his eternal power.

Similarly, the Qumran *Hôdhayôth* thank and praise their god for having delivered the pious—was he the Teacher of Righteousness himself?—from Belial and his followers who persecuted him. His God has proved himself to be the "Prince of the angels, the king of all that are in glory, the Lord of every spirit and the Ruler of every deed" (X.8). And he did so in spite of all iniquities in the poet's life, in order to be, not only feared (Ps. 130:4), but also glorified for his grace.

e. Laments. One means to reach this aim is to quote (*see above*) in the frame of the thanksgiving psalm the lament, which also has two forms: lament of the people and lament of the private member of the congregation. The two forms have, of course, much in common. For both it is again of the first importance to say exactly who is the god whom they implore. So they start with Yahweh's name (e.g., Pss. 3:1; 5:1; 10:1), and they reinforce this invocation by some attributes showing the reasons why the pious addresses him and no other god: "Shepherd of Israel" (80:1; cf. Jer. 14:8); "God of our salvation" (Ps. 79:9); "Yahweh my [king and my] God" (5:2; 7:1); "Yahweh . . . my rock and my fortress, my stronghold and my deliverer" (144:2); or—leading from the field of power to that of morality—"God of my right" (4:1).

This majestic God is not to be addressed without preparation by fasting (e.g., 69:10), by wearing sackcloth (30:11—H 30:12), and not with empty hands (cf. Exod. 23:15; 34:20). But even when Israel's burnt offerings are continually before Yahweh (Ps. 50:8), who is never hungry and who never eats the flesh of bulls or drinks the blood of goats (vs. 13), because

every beast of the forest is mine,
the cattle on a thousand hills
(vs. 10),

nevertheless they are nothing when his statutes are only recited and not followed, when the covenant is only on the people's lips and not observed in social life between brethren (vss. 16 ff). The right sacrifice to be vowed is Yahweh's thankful glorification and the teaching of sinners and transgressors that they may return to their God (Pss. 50:23; 51:13).

The influence of the prophetic faith is clearly to be seen in this attitude, which seemed too heterodox to an addendum made during the Exile: When the temple was restored, then Yahweh would get again sacrifices and enjoy them (Ps. 51:18-19)! But it is astonishing to see that later psalms of this type which even some very conservative scholars believe to be Maccabean (Pss. 44; 74; 79; 83) do not mention sacrifices. The general arguments against this dating of any psalm are reinforced for this special group by the fact that precisely a verse taken from one of them is the one quoted in I Macc. 7:17. There is no sure influence of the Samaritan schism or of Trito-Isaiah in any of them, and it is likely that the destructions mentioned in them may be associated with the catastrophe of Jerusalem in 485 B.C., which J. Morgenstern reconstructs with verisimilitude (*see bibliography*). Ps. 44:12 seems to be a polemic against Isa. 52:3, and will as such be explained best in a time in which the idea of Yahweh's selling Israel for a small price or for nothing was still living among the people. If this hypothesis is believed to be too audacious, then the time between Nehemiah and Alexander the Great, about which there is a great lack of knowledge of events, would be the period of these psalms.

But however this special problem may be solved it is to be seen that for these psalms sacrifices are no more the indispensable condition for a lament which Yahweh will listen to, nor is the temple the only place in which they may be prayed. They may be spoken at any time, day or night, at home on the bed or the couch (Ps. 6:6), in the desert, in prison, during a storm on the sea (Ps. 107:4, 10, 23). They are not confined to the man himself who is in trouble, but they may pray for a friend who is ill (35:13-14). Their aim is, of course, liberation from the cruelties of this life, health, strength, freedom from persecution by enemies, grace of his God and return to his sanctuary, but never (except perhaps the two uncertain cases in Pss. 49:15; 73:24) salvation after death. Opposite to such a "Christian" prayer, the poets of the laments know that death means separation from the God of life, that after death there is no more any possibility to praise him (Ps. 6:5; 30:9; 88:11; 115:17), and even this fact is the strongest argument to convince Yahweh of the necessity to help now and quickly. He is the God who wants to be glorified! The honor of his name will not tolerate the blasphemous question: "Where is their [your] God?" (79:10; 42:3; 115:2). It is his pride which is in an intolerable manner violated when heathenish nations destroy his temple and introduce into his holy place their idols (74:3 ff), and which will be restored when the prayer brought before him is answered. For this reason it belongs to the style of the laments not only to describe (as it is done retrospectively in the thanksgiving songs) the actual need as terrible as possible in order to enhance God's pity, but also to commemorate before him the iniquity and the wickedness of the enemies by the strongest expressions: Evildoers speak lies; they are bloodthirsty and deceitful (Ps. 5:6). Like a lion they rend the pious (7:2), and the deepest reason for such an attitude is their lack of faith in Yahweh:

For the wicked boasts of the desires of his heart,
  and the man greedy for gain curses and renounces the
    LORD.
In the pride of his countenance the wicked does not seek him;
  all his thoughts are, "There is no God" (10:3-4).

It is Yahweh's own "profit" to help, and perhaps in the last moment in which help is possible (Ps. 30:9-10). Preparing his sacrifice and watching for God's answer (Ps. 5:3), the pious prays that God may let the evildoers bear their guilt:

For there is no truth in their mouth;
  their heart is destruction,
their throat is an open sepulchre,
  they flatter with their tongue (5:9).

And the pious will be satisfied if only now, in the cultic performance of his sacrifice, Yahweh will give him a favorable oracle. Yahweh fulfils what he promises!

The effect of such an utterance by God is to be seen in the actual change from complaint to a great joy—e.g., in Ps. 22 between vss. 19-21 and 22-24:

But thou, O LORD, be not far off!
  O thou my help, hasten to my aid!
Deliver my soul from the sword,
  my life from the power of the dog!
Save me from the mouth of the lion,
  my afflicted soul from the horns of the wild oxen!

I will tell of thy name to my brethren;
  in the midst of the congregation I will praise thee:
You who fear the LORD, praise him!
  all you sons of Jacob, glorify him,
  and stand in awe of him, all you sons of Israel!
For he has not despised or abhorred
  the affliction of the afflicted;
and he has not hid his face from him,
  but has heard, when he cried to him.

Some liturgies preserved in the books of the Prophets deliver such answers of God, which may be favorable (Hos. 14:5) or negative. Then the congregation starts again, and again hoping to impress Yahweh by the repetition and the increasing earnestness of the supplication until he sends them out of his temple into death, sword, hunger, and prison (Jer. 14:1 ff).

We find the same construction of the liturgy in one of the royal psalms, Ps. 20. The prayer for the king, spoken by a priest or a prophet, is answered by God with an oracle which is not cited but is clearly to be seen by the change between vss. 6 and 8—H 7 and 9:

Now I know that Yahweh will help his anointed;
  he will answer him from his holy heaven
  with mighty victories by his right hand.
Some boast of chariots, and some of horses;
  but we boast of the name of the LORD our God.
They will collapse and fall;
  but we shall rise and stand upright.

In spite of this knowledge, the psalmist returns to the petition:

Give victory to the king, O LORD;
answer us when we call
(vs. 9—H 10).

The fact that in these two psalms the oracle is not quoted has a clear reason: the Psalter as we have it is the hymnbook in the hand of the congregation, and not a liturgical handbook or cultic rule for the hand of the priest. In contrast to our Christian liturgies in which, e.g., the word of forgiveness after the confession of sins is as sure as the "Amen in the church," neither the priest nor the congregation in ancient times knew what would be the answer given by an inspired word or by means of signs taken from the liver or other intestines of the animal sacrificed.

But there is one occasion on which the oracle had its firm liturgical form, the day of the ascension of the new king to the throne of his fathers. The priest says:

I have set my king
  on Zion, my holy hill.
. . . .
You are my son,
  today I have begotten you
    (Ps. 2:6-7).

Sit at my right hand,
  till I make your enemies your footstool.
. . . .
You are a priest for ever
  after the order of Melchizedek
    (Ps. 110:1, 4).

So, as the king of Mari is informed by a letter about the sayings of one of his gods, the Judean king has to believe in the truth of what is now proclaimed about future victories (Ps. 21:3 ff), of a just dominion of his so long as the sun and the moon endure throughout all generations from sea to sea and from the River to the ends of the earth (Ps. 72:5 ff). The language and the imagery of these psalms, their promises of world dominion and everlasting life, is that of the old oriental kingship ideology, which did not arise in a small land but in the great empires. The king is nearer to God than any one of the singers of the psalms. So they quote the prayers of the king, which are stronger than theirs. They remember the oath Yahweh has sworn to David, on which their confidence in Yahweh's help is founded. It was sworn without any condition to the anointed, who is at the same time his son and his priest (Ps. 110:4; cf. 2:7), or—showing the sorry experiences of a history full of blows—in a conditioned form for the dynasty but without conditions for Zion. Cf.:

> This is my resting place for ever;
> here I will dwell, for I have desired it.
> I will abundantly bless her provisions;
> I will satisfy her poor with bread.
> Her priests I will clothe with salvation,
> and her saints will shout for joy.
> There I will make a horn to sprout for David;
> I have prepared a lamp for my anointed.
> His enemies I will clothe with shame,
> but upon himself his crown will shed its luster
> (132:14-18).

> One of the sons of your [David's] body
> I will set on your throne.
> If your sons keep my covenant
> and my testimonies which I shall teach them,
> their sons also for ever
> shall sit upon your throne (vss. 11-12).

Then the best the enemies can do is to renounce their plan to burst Israel's bonds asunder and to cast their cords from them, that Yahweh may not laugh and terrify them in his wrath (Ps. 2:3-4). So the role played by the oracle and the prophetic voice in these royal laments show without doubt that they are pre-exilic. They belong to a time in which oracle and prophetism were living in the cult (contrast I Macc. 4:46; 9:27).

Conditions for the laments of the layman to be heard by Yahweh are analogous. The poet may be guilty of having acted against the commandments of his God. There may be wrong in his hands; he may have requited his friend with evil and plundered his enemy without cause (Ps. 7:3-4). There may be hidden transgressions which he does not want to confess (32:3-5). The wrath of his God is then rightful and just. Only the appeal to Yahweh's grace and the humble confession are the means of salvation from a situation in which the "pious" would be groaning all day long. But in other cases he may be accused and persecuted by his enemies without cause. Then Yahweh is obliged by his justice to demonstrate his innocence by helping him. This may be done in an ordeal in which God frees him from all suspicions. These "prayers of the accused" are a part of the ritual, not only in Jerusalem but also in Elephantine (Pap. Sachau 27; *see* ELEPHANTINE PAPYRI), and it is possible that confidence in Yahweh, who leads the pious through the dark valley, prepares a table for him in the presence of his enemies, and allows him to come back to his house as long as he lives (Ps. 23), is to be explained by this custom. Only a man

> who walks blamelessly, and does what is right,
> and speaks truth from his heart;
> who does not slander with his tongue,
> and does no evil to his friend,
> nor takes up a reproach against his neighbor;
> in whose eyes a reprobate is despised,
> but who honors those who fear the LORD;
> who swears to his own hurt and does not change;
> who does not put out his money at interest,
> and does not take a bribe against the innocent
> (15:2-5),

is allowed to sojourn in Yahweh's tent and to dwell on his holy hill. He has to attest his being free from all such guilts before entering the temple's gates (24:3 ff; cf. Isa. 33:14 ff). When there are serious doubts, some proofs like those of the accused wife in Num. 5 may be imposed upon him. The justice of his God and of his knowledge (cf. Ps. 139) is his hope in such a case.

But what is the matter with this justice in the cases in which the poet feels himself, in all sincerity, to be not guilty? Is God's wrath really against him without reason? The singer knows that he did not sit with the false or consort with dissemblers. He washes his hands in innocence and goes round the altar of his God, whose habitations he loves like the place where his glory dwells (26:4-8). The problem arises which was so crucial for the poet of Ps. 73 and for the book of Job: May God prove him! He will find his integrity! This appeal is the greatest contrast against the confession of sins. Both confessions are forms of the lament: the confession of sins and the confession of innocence; and both feelings are those of their singers: the feeling of being a transgressor and the feeling of being just, perhaps not in the sense of an absolute purity—there may be hidden sins (Ps. 19:12) or sins he committed as a youngster (25:7; cf. Job 13:26) and for which he is not fully responsible. But in comparison with the wickedness of his enemies, which he paints in vivid colors, he is righteous before the righteous God who tries the minds and the hearts (Ps. 7:9). Or are his troubles the result of a lack of power of his God? There is in the laments no mention of other gods who may have more power than Yahweh, but it may be that the enemies possess magic qualities and formulas which cause the unlucky situation of the poet. The best example is to be found in Ps. 58:4-9, where the descriptions of the foes and of God's intervention both contain elements of sorcery:

> They [the wicked] have venom like the venom of a serpent,
> like the deaf adder that stops its ear,
> so that it does not hear the voice of charmers
> or of the cunning enchanter.
> O God, break the teeth in their mouths;
> tear out the fangs of the young lions, O LORD!
> Let them vanish like water that runs away;
> like grass let them be trodden down and wither.
> Let them be like the snail which dissolves into slime,
> like the untimely birth that never sees the sun.
> Sooner than their [Syr.] pots can feel the heat of thorns,
> whether green or ablaze, may he sweep them away!

The curse which the wicked likes may "soak into his body like water, like oil into his bones" (Ps. 109:17 ff).

The question which was not answered definitively in § B2*d above* is now to be cleared. The enemies of the king and of the private member of the congregation were at first—besides their political importance for the king and the nation—men of magic power, but during the history of Israelite psalmody the Israelite faith in Yahweh the mighty God overcame the fear of such formulas and doings, which are recognizable only in some texts attesting an early "religious" feeling. This development had the effect of concentrating the inner difficulties of the pious in need, feeling himself not guilty, in the question of Yahweh's justice and not in the question of his power. Yahweh is able to help, and if he does not liberate the singer from his troubles, then he is not just!

As has been shown, the thanksgiving psalms and the laments have many parallels in their structure. *See* Table 1.

Table 1

Thanksgivings	Laments
a) Invocation of Yahweh's name	Invocation of Yahweh's name
b) Description of former need	Description of present need
c) Quotation of former prayer	Prayer for help and deliverance
d) Assurance that a former vow was fulfilled	Statement of a vow to be fulfilled now
e) Constatation that a former oracle was fulfilled by Yahweh	God's oracle in reply, not cited but obvious in effect
f) Thanksgiving again	Public confession of the help given by Yahweh

3. Pedagogic types. The cultic types among the psalms which try to influence God have, nevertheless, at the same time frequently a pedagogic value or even a pedagogic intention trying to influence men—the layman, and especially the younger generation (78:5-6)—in order that they should not be like their fathers.

The liturgies which list the qualifications of those allowed to enter the sanctuary regulate the daily life of the congregation's members. They hinder them from changing an oath sworn to the pious' hurt, from taking interest or bribe against the innocent (15:4-5), or from lifting up their souls to what is false (24:4).

In the context or at the end of the lamentations or the thanksgiving songs, the blessings for the faithful and the curses against their enemies depict the man who acts according to Yahweh's will and stimulate the listeners to act as he demands:

> Blessed is the man who makes
> the LORD his trust,
> who does not turn to the proud,
> to those who go astray after false gods!
> (40:4).

The cultic root of such "teachings" is confirmed (91:1, 14-16) by the combination of the promises given to a man who

> dwells in the shelter of the Most High,
> who abides in the shadow of the Almighty,

that he will be spared from all misfortune and protected in all dangers with an oracle given to him:

> Because he cleaves to me in love, I will deliver him;
> I will protect him, because he knows my name.
> When he calls to me, I will answer him;
> I will be with him in trouble,
> I will rescue him and honor him.
> With long life I will satisfy him,
> and show him my salvation.

Such blessings are given outside these special liturgies in the form of religious admonitions, introduced, not by the cultic ברוך ("blessed"), but by the wisdom expression אשרי (e.g., Ps. 1:1), which should perhaps better be translated by "happy, lucky." They may be combined with the Hallelujah at the beginning of a psalm and with the description of the wicked's misfortune at its end (Ps. 112) or with the wish for whole Israel's peace (Ps. 128). They may derive from the custom of proclaiming Yahweh's ordinances every seventh year at the great assembly of the tribal league (Deut. 31:10 ff). They are influenced by the wisdom literature and its teachings.

To the methods used in those schools of the wise men belongs the alphabetical order of their sayings, and this manner is also to be found in the pedagogic psalms. Every line starts with a consecutive letter of the alphabet in Ps. 112, after the opening Hallelujah:

> *A*greeable to the LORD is the man who fears him,
> *B*eloved is he who greatly delights in his commandments!
> *C*ertainly his descendants will be mighty in the land;
> *D*ignitaries who will be blessed.

Cf. every second double line in Ps. 37:

> *A*gree not to fret yourself because of the wicked,
> be not envious of wrongdoers!
>
> . . . .
>
> *B*e confident in the LORD, and do good;
> so you will dwell in the land, and enjoy security.
>
> . . . .
>
> *C*ommit your way to the LORD;
> trust in him, and he will act.
>
> . . . .
>
> *D*o not worry about the LORD's deeds, but wait patiently for him.

The most complicated form is that of Ps. 119; within the stanzas of eight lines every line starts with the same letter:

> *A*greeable before the LORD are the blameless,
> who walk in the law of the LORD!
> *A*greeable before the LORD are those who keep his testimonies,
> who seek him with the whole heart.
> *A*ll men walking in his ways
> do nothing wrong!
> *A*dmonition came from thee
> to be kept diligently.
> *A*ssist me that all my ways may be steadfast
> in keeping thy statutes!
> *A*lone at all thy commandments will I fix my eyes
> not to become ashamed.
> *A*ccept my thanks from an upright heart,
> when I learn thy righteous ordinances.
> *A*fter thy statutes will I walk observing them.
> O forsake me not utterly!

According to what has been said about the pedagogic intentions within the liturgies, is it not astonishing to find this mnemotechnic manner also in Pss. 9–10; 34; 111; 145; and in Lam. 1–4?

Again as in the wisdom literature, some humorous formulations are used in the pedagogic psalms to impress the young man that he may keep his way pure (119:9). The wicked is depicted as a ridiculous being at whom the Lord laughs (in spite of the danger he means for the pious and his fate)! He may gnash his teeth at the righteous against whom he plots, but he will gnash them again when the horn of the righteous is exalted in honor and when he himself melts away (37:2; 112:10). The heart of the godless is gross like fat (119:70), and their eyes swell out with fatness (73:7) when

> they set their mouths against the heavens,
> and their tongue struts through the earth
> (vs. 9).

Nevertheless, their sword shall enter their own heart (37:15), and they will disappear like a dream and a phantom when one awakens (73:20). In opposition to this diminutive picture of the wicked, the love of the godly for their God and his word is perhaps a little bit exaggerated when described as better than thousands of gold and silver pieces (119:72), above gold and fine gold (vs. 127), and sweeter than honey to his mouth (vs. 103).

But it must be said that such humorous pictures are much rarer in the Psalms than in the Proverbs within the wisdom literature. The feeling of remaining in the presence of God increases the earnestness of the style, especially because a part of these pedagogic psalms participates in the great crisis of the Hebrew wisdom. Life does not run on one single line, as it is believed by the teaching of Yahweh's just retribution, according to which the man whose delight is in Yahweh's law will prosper in all that he does (Ps. 1:3). It may be that for a moment or even for a longer time the pious has to become like a wineskin in the smoke (119:83). Of course, he may hope that this situation will not endure, that the end of the godly will be peace for himself and his posterity (37:37; 94:15); and so long as this outlook prevails, the crisis does not affect too deeply a faith which does not yet reflect upon the deeper problem of the importance of even a temporary lack of God's justice (*see* § C1*c below*), or which consoles one by the belief in God's pedagogic reasons for leading him through calamities to a better insight into his own sinfulness (32:3 ff). Even when the wicked is rich until his death, there is a consolation that

> When he dies he will carry nothing away;
> his glory will not go down after him.
> . . . .
> He will go to the generation of his fathers
> who will never more see the light.
> Man cannot abide in his pomp,
> he is like the beasts that perish
> (49:17, 19).

But do not the wise and the pious share in the same fate?

> Truly no man can ransom himself,
> or give to God the price of his life,
> For the ransom of his life is costly,
> and can never suffice,
> That he should continue to live on for ever,
> and never see the Pit.
> Yea, he shall see that even the wise die,
> the fool and the stupid alike must perish
> and leave their wealth to others
> (49:7-10).

Is there really any hope that only those who have foolish confidence will be

> Like sheep . . . appointed for Sheol;
> Death shall be their shepherd
> (vs. 14),

and that the pious may be sure that

> God will ransom my soul from the power of Sheol,
> for he will receive me (vs. 15)?

The crisis of faith rising from the good luck of the godless is so strong that the pious has to confess:

> When my soul was embittered,
> when I was pricked in heart,
> I was stupid and ignorant,
> I was like a beast toward thee
> (73:21).

Even the hope of being received afterward (to glory), which Ps. 73:24 seems to share with Ps. 49:15, would not be strong enough to overwhelm the crisis if there were not the personal experience of being held here and now by God's hand, of being guided by his counsel, of being allowed to be continually with him, besides whom the pious does not desire anything (*see* § C1*c below*). Such experiences of being lost outside God's presence but saved when he is near are too earnest to be described in humorous terms. They have their own language and style and cannot express themselves in the terms used and taught in the schools.

C. *THE RELIGION AND PIETY OF THE PSALMS.* 1. Yahweh's deeds. Some leading moments of the religion and piety of the Psalms have already been described with their forms and types, the forms being to a great extent governed by the content. Faith in the greatness and the uniqueness of Yahweh found its adequate expression in hymns celebrating his adoration, not only by his people but also by the divine beings. The joyful experience of Yahweh's help in the personal life of the singer is reflected by the style of the thanksgiving songs, especially when it is seen against the dark background of the complaints in the laments and the confessions of sin. It is necessary to deal with some special problems given by the description of Yahweh's deeds in the frame of these forms.

a. Relation to the Pentateuch. Yahweh's deeds are believed, in the first place, to be his actions in the history of Israel, as they are rehearsed in the old narratives as well as in the cultic rememberings—e.g., in Deut. 26:3, 5-9. Yahweh acted in the promises given to Abraham and to the fathers (Ps. 105:8 ff; cf. 47:9), in the liberation from Egypt (105:37 ff=106:8 ff), in the entrance into Canaan (136:21 ff; cf. 78:5 ff), and finally in the foundation and preservation of the Davidic kingdom (78:70). These great steps in what is frequently called the "history of salvation" (*Heilsgeschichte*) are celebrated with joy and thanksgiving. They are the fundamentals of faith in Yahweh's fidelity to his word, his people, and the king. The cultic confessions which remember them at the great festivals, and which are repeated whenever the son asks his father about the reason of some rites (Exod. 12:26; Deut. 6:20 ff), stand at the root of the great narrative sources within the Pentateuch and of the religious lyrics within the Psalter so far as it describes the past.

It is not easy to say whether one of the Pentateuchal sources or the Pentateuch in its totality was used in the Psalms, or if there have been independent traditions and creeds underlying its confessions. The problem arises, e.g., for Ps. 78, by the difference between its sequence of the miracles in Egypt and the wilderness and that told in the Pentateuch, or when it reports the strongest and the picked men to be laid down, whereas Num. 11:33 mentions only a very great plague by which the people was smitten in Kibroth-hattaavah. Unfortunately the text in Ps. 78:9 is so poorly preserved that we cannot say exactly what event is meant.

Another reason for the same problem is the big difference of weight given to single personalities in the Pentateuch and in our Psalms. Abraham is mentioned in only two psalms (47; 105); but Jacob is used as the name of the people in its totality, not only in the "Northern" (*see* § B2*a above*), but also in clearly Judean or at least "neutral," contexts. Under the influence of the *parallelismus membrorum* he appears side by side with "Israel," according to Gen. 32:29 (J), in Pss. 14:7 = 53:6; 22:23; 78:5, 21, 71; 105:23; 135:4. Without this special reason we find "Jacob" in the name of God the "Mighty One of Jacob" (132:2, 5; cf. 59:13), in connection with the salvation of the land (85:2) and even with the election of Zion (87:2; cf. 99:4). As the name of the patriarch, Jacob is quoted, together with Abraham and Isaac, in Ps. 105, the only mention of Isaac at all (vs. 9). Perhaps even more perplexing is the fact that Moses is mentioned in only four psalms (besides the superscription of Ps. 90): as the leader (and the miracle doer) in 77:20; 105:26; as the receiver of the revelation in 103:7; as a priest in 99:6; and as the responsible one in the wilderness in 106:23, 32. Together with him, Aaron is mentioned as the people's leader in 77:20; 105:26; and as a priest in 99:6; and without connection with his brother, as the ancestor of the acting priests in 115:10, 12; 118:3; 135:19. From these facts it is not astonishing that Horeb is quoted only once (106:19; the golden calf) and Sinai also only once (in 68:17 and in the badly preserved 68:8, in which there is perhaps also a reference to the time of the judges besides the only clear one in Ps. 83:9 side by side with the mentioning of the Assyrians in vs. 8).

Among these psalms, the heterodox Ps. 103 and Ps. 105, which speaks of the three patriarchs as "Anointed" and prophets (cf. Abraham in Gen. 20:7 E) and describes as the aim of Yahweh's deeds the observance of his statutes and laws (vs. 45), are late. Ps. 106 depends on the Deuteronomistic description of the history of the people as the history of Israel's sins. It is related, together with the wisdom Ps. 78 (the end of which is lost), to Neh. 9:5 ff, which combines in the same manner as the P document and as Ps. 136 the creation of the world with the election of Abraham.

The complete absence of Noah, of Joshua, of any of the judges (with the exception of Samuel in 99:6), of Elijah or Elisha, and the mention of Saul and Solomon only in the secondary superscriptions of Pss. 52; 57; 59; 72; 127, seem to indicate that there was an older cultic pattern of the historical tradition which was superseded by the Pentateuch only in exilic times, when the cult and its living traditions were interrupted. It would therefore be preferable to see in Ps. 106:47 an allusion to the dispersion of the sixth, and not of the eighth century. Whether these older cultic traditions were preserved orally or transmitted in written form is not to be shown. What is important is the demonstration of the cultic roots of the description of Yahweh's deeds in Israel's history so far as the Psalms are concerned. These cultic roots are also the reason why in postexilic times the psalms depending on them entered into the liturgy of the second temple, as is to be seen from I Chr. 16.

b. Yahweh the mighty God of Israel. By his deeds in Israel's history Yahweh has demonstrated himself as the mighty God who is worthy to be identified with the Most High (the *'ēl 'elyôn*) and the Almighty (the *'ēl shadday;* Ps. 91:1; *see* § B3 *above;* cf. Ps. 83:18), to judge the "sons of the Most High" in the divine council in the midst of the gods (82:1). The difference between him and the supreme God, the El, of Ugarit or even of the Mkl Stele from Beisan, is the fact that he does not grow older and weaker but remains "Yahweh," the strong, active, living God. His force is not to be seen in his sexual life, as is the case with El or with Zeus—Yahweh has no female counterpart, nor does he have intercourse with the cow!—but in his overwhelming "political" and "military" power assuring his victory over all enemies. Even the kings and the rulers of the earth are for him not more than laughable adversaries to be terrified when he speaks to them in his fury (2:2 ff), just as the waters were afraid and trembled when they saw him (77:16).

With the increasing power of Israel's enemies, Yahweh's own power had to increase from the modest horizon of the Syrian struggles to the universalistic outlook necessitated by the wars against the world-wide Assyrian Empire and its successors, the Neo-Babylonian and the Persian. But no less than from the arms blessed or destroyed by her God, Israel like all other people depended upon the fertility of her fields and pastures, which are watered by the river of God and so provided with grain (65:9 ff; 107:33 ff). History and nature are not to be separated; the lord of both has to be the same, Yahweh the One (as Deut. 6:4 formulates this creed). But in spite of all jubilations in the hymns, the songs of Yahweh's ascension to the heavenly throne, and all comforting promises given to the king in the royal psalms, the majority of the texts preserved in the Psalter as we have it show clearly how difficult it was for Israel to gain and to retain such faith. Her history was mainly the history of disasters and great needs. The Philistines and the Midianites, the Syrians of Damascus and the Assyrians, the Babylonians and the Egyptians, from Sishak to Neco, plundered the land, not to forget the intra-Israelitic rivalries among the single tribes and between the two kingdoms after Solomon's death. It seems to be a rule in history, which was proved to be true in Israel too, that wars between brethren are the most cruel and bloody of all, especially when political hostility and religious hatred are combined.

The lack of prayers against Judah or Ephraim shows that the faith in Yahweh as the God of Israel, with whom as with the federation of the twelve tribes he made his covenant—with Israel as an indissoluble unit created by his will—was stronger and more alive than any particularistic tendency or tribal ideology. There were Judean prophetic utterances against the N kingdom and its holy places (e.g., I Kings 13:11 ff), and surely there must have existed hymns celebrating victories of the one particular state over the other, but they were left beside by the congregation of the second temple when they formed the Psalter. Even the election of Judah against Joseph is a part of Israel's election; and the sin of the sanctuaries of Bethel and Dan, the golden calf, is confessed as a sin of the nation in its totality (Pss. 78: 67 ff; 106:19). So strong was that which Galling called the "great-Israelitic ideology," the faith of the belonging together of Yahweh and his whole people, that the great crisis of Israel's faith did not come from a struggle of Yahweh against Yahweh in the wars of the Divided Kingdom but from outside, from the impious scoffing at Yahweh by the nations and their Israelite followers, from the "heathen" that do not know him or call on his name (74:22; 79:6).

The destruction of the temple and all the other calamities combined with it are in such sharp contrast with the former actions of God's power in his victories over the chaotic monsters (74:14); the miracles in Egypt, at the Red Sea, and in the wilderness; the election of David, that the question, Why? arose and required an answer. Does Yahweh sleep (44:23)? Did he sell his people like a careless merchant for no high price (44:12)? Did he forget the hapless (10:10; cf. 42:10; 74:19), their afflictions and oppressions (44: 24), and the clamor of his foes (74:23)? We know from I Kings 18:27 such mocking questions, which now became a temptation for the pious too! The former proofs of the strength of Yahweh's hand were so great that there should be no doubt: If he was willing to help, he could save his people (Ps. 77:11 ff)!

c. Yahweh's morality. For this reason the question of Why? ceases to be a question of might and becomes a problem of morals. It may be—and surely it is mostly the case!—that Israel had committed sins against Yahweh's statutes and laws. Then the punishment would be all right, and the only question would be if it was wise for God to act so severely, to show his "holiness" by such outstanding plagues. His own honor will be endangered throughout the world when the foes are able to scoff at him, asking: "Where is your God?" (Pss. 42:3, 10; 79:10; 115:2). And this problem has quite another side: God's "justice" is not only a formal one by which he punishes the rascal and gives his blessing to the "good," but it has a wider content. It is the honor of the kings, and no less of the gods, in the old oriental world (*see* ETHICS IN THE OT § B2*a*) to be gracious toward the needy, not to forget the poor forever, not to leave the downtrodden to be put to shame (74:19, 21). So it would be the god's honor to be immutable in steadfast love, not to permit himself to become overwhelmed by anger, not to forget his promises, and not to change his hand (77:8 ff). The tension which appears here between a "holiness" in the sense of strict "justice" or in the sense of "grace," as reflected in the double sense of the Hebrew term צדקה, is aggravated in Israel by the faith in the covenant imposing upon Yahweh duty to be רחום וחנון, "gracious and merciful." The bigger his might, the greater his moral obligations toward his people!

The question, How long? (e.g., 4:2; 6:3; 13:1-2) adumbrates the earnestness of the problem and is at the same time the best proof that the religious thinking of the Psalms is a practical, and not a dogmatic or philosophical, one. A temporary moral weakness is in no lower degree "immoral" than a perpetual one, especially on account of the shortness of man's life (89:47 ff), and because the promises contained the assurance that when the sons of David forsook his law, even then the Davidic covenant would remain valid:

> I will punish their transgression with the rod
> and their iniquity with scourges;
> but I will not remove from him my steadfast love,
> or be false to my faithfulness.
> I will not violate my covenant,
> or alter the word that went forth from my lips
> (89:32-34).

And the greatest doubts arose when the people did not feel its sinfulness but had to complain of injustice to God:

> All this has come upon us,
> though we have not forgotten thee,
> or been false to thy covenant.
> Our heart has not turned back,
> nor have our steps departed from thy way,
> that thou shouldst have broken us in the place of jackals,
> and covered us with deep darkness.
> . . . .
> Nay, for thy sake we are slain all the day long,
> and accounted as sheep for the slaughter
> (44:17-19, 22).

But in spite of all these doubts the spiritual miracle happened, that two main points, both vital and fundamental for the piety of the Psalms, remained unshaken: it is *Yahweh* who acts in the calamities of the present time as *he* acted in the great event in the past; and by this faith the hope did not fail that the future deeds of the God of the covenant will return to his first grace and morality. Then the gladness which came forth when he restored the fortunes of Zion (126:1) will rise again when he hearkens to the prayer:

> Restore our fortunes, O LORD,
> like the water-courses in the Negeb!
> May those who sow in tears
> reap with shouts of joy!
> He that goes forth weeping,
> bearing the seed for sowing,
> shall come home with shouts of joy,
> bringing his sheaves with him
> (vss. 4-6).

Or is this psalm to be interpreted as an eschatological song, anticipating the everlasting joy in the reign to come, which will be the greatest of Yahweh's deeds? Only when this faith that Yahweh is acting in calamities is neglected and the enemies themselves in the foreground of the consciousness of the singer, may his hate, springing from all his anxieties and needs, lead him to provoke the future actions of his God and to give them the "right" direction by cursing his foes, as in the imprecatory second half of Ps. 129 (*see* § B2*d above*) or in Ps. 109 (which no Christian may use in prayer if he understands Luke 23:34).

The same problem arises for individual experiences, especially in the laments (*see* § B2*e above*). As it is Yahweh who made Israel a byword among the nations, a laughingstock among the peoples (44:14), so it is he whose hand was heavy for day and night upon the poet of Ps. 32:4. His liberation from the temptation to become untrue to the generation of Yahweh's children (73:15) may be—as in Ps. 32—caused by a deeper insight into his own sinfulness, but much more important than psychological developments or any "theological" reflection is the personal experience of a deed of Yahweh making an end to the scoffing ones (cf. 91:8), and his even greater deed in the personal life by which he held and holds the pious right hand. *See* § B3 *above.*

2. Yahweh's commandments. ***a. Content.*** Among the deeds of Yahweh one of the most important is his giving statutes and commandments to his people (on Sinai). To understand the religious attitude of the Psalms toward them, we have to free ourselves completely from the Pauline critique of the law. For the psalmists these statutes and commandments are given, not to push men into deeper covetousness, but to be fulfilled in order that the man who is obedient to them may become revived, wise, rejoiced, and enlightened (Ps. 19:7 ff). The faith of Deut. 4:8—according to which the greatness of Israel is based on the fact that they have such righteous laws—is the root of such jubilations and of the reiterated confessions of the poets that they will—wiser than their foes (Ps. 119:98)—learn them, teach them, and fulfil them.

And what is their content? Of course, they are the frame within which the Israelite service in the sanctuaries was performed. There is no old oriental cult in which place, time, and manner of worship are not regulated by divine ordinances. Man's liberty to create a cult as he likes is quite modern and completely foreign to the Eastern mind in ancient times. The god asks for certain animals to be sacrificed and forbids others. He wants to get the firstlings from the flock and orders the first-born son and the first-born of the most important animal to be redeemed (Exod. 13:13). Having this in mind, it is astonishing to us that never in the Psalms are such cultic statutes mentioned, either in the confessions of sin, in the pedagogic sentences, or in the declarations of innocence. In the Qumran Hymns, the songs of a sect which separated itself from the temple service, such silence is quite natural, but not in poems sung and recited at the festivals and sacrifices in the temple! Some of the psalmists, probably under the influence of the pre-exilic prophets (e.g., Pss. 40:6 ff; 50:7 ff), deny that the cultic regulations were given by Yahweh. Such abrogation may be corrected later, as in Ps. 51:15 ff by the exilic addition in 51:18-19. But these polemics underline only the importance of the problem of how the lack of positive utterances about divinely ordered rites is to be explained, and show in any case that the Israelite religion as it is reflected by the Psalms was statutory (legal) but not ritualistic.

The first reason for the absence of cultic regulations may be stylistic. The confessions are of a purely "formal" character in order to be appropriate in all circumstances. So they describe no single misdeeds but use intentionally the widest terms:

> I confess my iniquity,
> I am sorry for my sin
> (38:18).

> O God, thou knowest my folly;
> the wrongs I have done are not hidden from thee
> (69:5).

Where this formalism is left, as in the enumeration of the conditions under which the pilgrim may enter the temple, the special ordinances quoted in Pss. 15; 24 are ethical and not ritualistic (*see* § B2*e above*). The same is true of the formal character of the vows recited in the Psalms, with the sole exception of Ps. 66:13 ff, which tells of the fatlings, rams, goats, and bulls to be sacrificed. And here, too, no divine law is quoted according to which this great gift will be brought, and the impression prevails that we have to do with an exaggeration far beyond any statute. In all other cases it is only said that the vows shall and will be fulfilled, but nothing more is told of their content:

> I will lift up the cup of salvation
> and call on the name of the LORD,
> I will pay my vows to the LORD
> in the presence of all his people
> (116:13-14).

Even the words accompanying the gifts are not given. They may be reconstructed from Deut. 26:3 (*see* § C1*a above*) or from the legendary vow of David, which was out of any possibility of repetition by anyone else:

> I will not enter my house
> or get into my bed;
> I will not give sleep to my eyes
> or slumber to my eyelids,
> Until I find a place for the LORD,
> a dwelling place for the Mighty One of Jacob
> (132:3-5).

The best fulfilment of any vow is in the desire to call upon Yahweh in the day of trouble and to bring thanksgiving as his sacrifices (50:14-15).

A second reason for the lack of cultic regulations in the Psalms may be the historical fact shown by the above-mentioned appendix of Ps. 51:

> Do good to Zion in thy good pleasure;
> rebuild the walls of Jerusalem,
> Then wilt thou delight in right sacrifices,
> in burnt offerings and whole burnt offerings;
> then bulls will be offered on thy altar.

The deepest feeling of sinfulness was living after the fall of Jerusalem in 587, in the time of the Exile, in which sacrifices were not possible and could not be vowed either in Babylonia or in Palestine. Unfortunately the hymns of the Jewish colony of Elephantine, whose temple stood probably in this time, have not been found among the Papyri. It may be that the sacred formula by which the pious is able to protect himself against all earthly and demoniacal dangers by using the holy triple name ("Yahweh, Most High,

Almighty"; *see* § B3*a above;* Ps. 91) belongs to this time (as 'el Shadday is the patriarchal name of a God in the P document), and shall replace the sacrifices and other rites which could not be performed.

But there is a third reason going deeper than these two; the feeling of sinful men is not bound to single misdeeds, but finds its cause in a weakness in the character of Israel (cf. 94:8) and in the essence of man. The root of all single sins of Israel in her long and bad history is the fact that they forgot in their stupidity all the wonders of their God. The root of the sin of the pious is the fact that he has to confess:

> I know my transgressions,
> and my sin is ever before me.
> Against thee, thee only, have I sinned,
> and done that which is evil in thy sight,
> so that thou art justified in thy sentence
> and blameless in thy judgment.
> Behold, I was brought forth in iniquity,
> and in sin did my mother conceive me
> (51:3-5).

Only a deed of Yahweh, washing him and purging him with hyssop, is able to change these conditions, and not any human sacrifice, even if it were ordered by God with the force of atonement:

> Create in me a clean heart, O God,
> and put a new and right spirit within me.
> Cast me not away from thy presence,
> and take not thy holy Spirit from me.
> Restore to me the joy of thy salvation,
> and uphold me with a willing spirit
> (vss. 10-12).

b. Character. The deeds of Yahweh the God of Israel in the personal life of the psalmists do not lead to the dissolution of a congregation which had been tied together by the covenant. They do not include the rise of "humanitarian" religion or piety outside the limits of Israel. The psalmists know of men "fearing the LORD"—i.e., proselytes who join the house of Israel, the house of Aaron, and the Levites in the hymns celebrating Yahweh's greatness (135:19-20) and who share in his blessings with the houses of Israel and Aaron (115:12-13). But both these psalms show that such "fear" is connected with the negation of the gods of the heathen, and in Ps. 135 also with the tradition of Yahweh's victories over the foreign kings and of his giving the land to his people. Indeed, his law is appointed in Israel like the testimony of his works he established in Jacob (78:5). Even where its "social" content corresponds to the ideal picture of the old oriental king and became by democratization the ideal picture of every "just" member of the congregation, its root is not a "natural law" but the revelation of Israel's God.

The same is true of the cultic observances, even where they depend on the regulations of the pre-Israelite Canaanite service. In Israel they have their importance, not by reflection on their practical usefulness—e.g., upon hygienic reasons for the washing of hands or clothes or for circumcision. They are to be fulfilled because they are given by Yahweh, and for this reason they are all of equal weight.

As in the cultic psalms the laws of sacrifices and rites are not explicitly quoted, so no preponderance is given even to the commandments of the Decalogue, including the sabbath (except in the secondary superscription of Ps. 92). To kill the just, the orphans, or the poor—such a killing is the sign of a rascal (37:32; 94:6; 109:16), not a simple violation of the fifth commandment. The laws of Yahweh are an inner unit! A congregation living in the religion of the Psalms, as in a part of their sacred scripture, had to feel that the liberty of Jesus toward the sabbath and ritual purity, his differentiation between more and less important commandments, was a danger for the congregation. But in other parts of their content the Psalms prepared the way for him. Not only by their "messianic" utterances, which the Christian faith saw from the beginning (and sees) fulfilled in Jesus' life, death, and resurrection, but also in the inherence of God's deeds and his comforting, preserving, and saving nearness in the soul of the pious, this inner "epiphany" within man's mind, and no less in the experience of his forgiveness and cleansing grace by his most "godly" deed.

In the light of this faith, it is not hard to understand the importance the Psalms had gained already in earliest Christianity, as shown by the frequency of quotations taken from this book in the NT. This position of importance has continued through the ages, not only in private devotion but also in the official daily prayer of the clergy and in the monasteries as in the services, especially the matins, the vespers, and the complines at night since the beginning of the Middle Ages and even before. In some branches of the Reformed churches only the Psalms are sung, frequently in the forms of national poetry—e.g., in the "translations" by Beza for French Protestantism—with its richness of melodies, and they deeply influenced too the religious poetry in the Lutheran and Anglican countries and churches. In them the only God is revealed in a masterly aesthetic form through the greatness, the earnestness, and the goodness of his majestic acts; and the soul of the pious is at the same time and in the same manner revealed in his faith, his anxieties, his sinfulness, and his thanks for God's presence as his sole but sure salvation. "Here you look into the heart of all saints" (Luther).

Bibliography. See bibliographies in: W. S. McCullough, *IB,* IV (1955), 17; J. J. Stamm, *Theol. Rundschau,* 23 (1955), 1-68. See also: G. Bernini, *Le Preghiere Penitenziali del Salterio* (1953); C. Westermann, *Das Loben Gottes in den Psalmen* (1953); H. J. Franken, *The Mystical Communion with JHWH in the Book of Psalms* (1954); H. Birkeland, *The Evildoers in the Psalms* (1955); T. A. Marazuela, *Sefarad,* 15 (1955), 395-419; S. Mowinckel, "Psalm Criticism Between 1900 and 1935," *Vetus Testamentum,* 5 (1955), 13-33; M. Tsevat, *A Study of the Language of the Biblical Psalms* (1955); A. Weiser, *Die Psalmen* (4th ed., 1955); J. H. Marks, *Der textkritische Wert des Psalterium Hieronymi juxta Hebraeos* (1956); P. J. N. Smal, *Die Universalismen in die Psalms* (1956); J. W. Wevers, "A Study of the Form Criticism of Traditional Complaint Psalms," *VT,* 6 (1956), 80-96; F. Mand, *ZAW,* 70 (1958), 185 ff; P. Drijvers, *Les Psaumes* (1958); H. J. Kraus, *Psalmen* (1958—); G. W. Ahlström, *Psalm 89, eine Liturgie aus dem Ritual des leidenden Königs* (1959); H. D. Preuss, "Die Psalmenüberschriften in Targum und Midrasch," *ZAW* (1959), pp. 44-54; R. B. Y. Scott, *The Psalms As Christian Praise* (1959).

J. HEMPEL

PSALMS OF SOLOMON sŏl'ə mən [Ψαλμοὶ Σολομῶντος]. A collection of eighteen extrabiblical psalms extant in Greek and Syriac. (Textual references herein are cited according to the verse numeration of De la Cerda, Ryle and James, and Swete.)

The title may have been chosen to distinguish these poems from the canonical Psalms, which were, for the most part, traditionally ascribed to David. The contents of the Psalms of Solomon are unrelated to King Solomon. For centuries almost forgotten, the work has since the early nineteenth century tended to gain increasing attention, though not unanimous favor. The collection of psalms has been called "a genuine pearl among the trash of apocryphal [=pseudepigraphic] writings," and "feeble imitations, insipid and poetically poor productions."

1. Language and date. Against an earlier view that the psalms were composed in Egypt in Greek, it is now generally held that they were written in Hebrew in Judea, and subsequently—probably before A.D. 70—translated into Greek. Some scholars argue that the Syriac version was made from the Greek translation; others, that it was based on the original Hebrew, possibly with the Greek serving as a subsidiary source. The Hebrew original is lost. Though apparently the work of several authors, the psalms are fairly uniform in style; the differences are chiefly due to differences of content. The authors evidently belonged to a group closely linked by common religious aspirations and political experience.

Modeled on the canonical Psalter, the psalms largely follow conventional themes: mournful and hopeful, didactic and hymnic, decrying men's injustice, imploring God's deliverance, threatening punishment for sinners, and promising reward for the righteous. Technical notes for musical settings (εἰς νῖκος [8:1]; διάψαλμα [17:31; 18:10]), the same as in the biblical Psalter, indicate that these psalms were sung in synagogal services.

They were composed at a time when Israel had suffered internal and external calamities, and the authors were disturbed by increasing impiety in the land and by outward threats to the people's freedom. There is a deep rift within Israel between "men-pleasers," who are reproached for multifarious sins —hypocrisy, graft, sensuality, etc.—and "God-fearers," variously called "the pious," "the righteous," "the poor." The authors voice the feelings and hopes of the pious, who are incensed by the secularization of the regime, the rapaciousness of the priesthood, general disregard for religious and civil law, and the involvement of the Jewish nation in world politics which resulted in foreign invasion. Most scholars (Movers was the first) accept the identification of the invader whose trespasses and punishment are mentioned in 2:2, 6, 30-33; 8:16-24 with Pompey, and accordingly date this work in the years 70-40 B.C. (Eissfeldt prefers 63-30); as to the reference in 17:9, 13-16, to the rising up of a "man that was alien to our race," certain scholars hold that it applies to Herod the Great. It has also been suggested that these passages might be a later interpolation. Earlier dates have also been argued for.

Usually the sentiments in the psalms are taken to express Pharisaic animadversion to Sadducean dominance. Some of the reproaches leveled against the sinners—such as insatiable covetousness or harlotry that does not stop at incestuous relations—were conventional at the time, and any religious party might have accused its opponents of these crimes. Other remonstrations are more definite: the allegation concerning the appropriation of consecrated offerings (1:8; 2:3; 8:12-13, 26) suggests that those against whom the charge is made actually had part in the administration of sacred offices, and thus belonged to the priestly Sadducean aristocracy.

2. Teaching. Indignant at the arrogance of the conqueror who profaned the temple (2:20), the psalmist is harsher on his own compatriots than on the Gentile invader. "Their transgressions went beyond those of the heathen" (1:8; cf. 2:11; 8:14; 17:17). As in the DEAD SEA SCROLLS the Kittim will be the executors of God's judgment upon individual Jews for their misdeeds, so in the Psalms of Solomon the conquest of the Holy City is God's punishment for the nation's impiety. This, however, need not be taken as an indication that the work originated within the same group as the Scrolls and cognate literature. The psalmist's attitude toward the foreign conqueror is actually not different from that of the prophets of the OT to Assyrians and Babylonians who, though evildoers themselves, are the instrument of God's punishment of Israel's transgressions. A decisive difference between the DSS and the Psalms of Solomon lies in the fact that the psalmist expects deliverance through the medium of a king-messiah, whereas in the Scrolls (at least the earlier ones) the paramount role is assigned to a priest-messiah. While the ethical dualism of the Scrolls occasionally comes close to a belief in predetermination (1QS 3.14–4.25, 11.10-14, to name significant instances), the Psalms expound in a more definite manner man's freedom of choice between good and evil. There remains an unresolved conflict within the psalmist's conception of God's ultimate causation and man's personal moral responsibility: man himself can add nothing to the world that is not encompassed in God's sovereign purpose (5:6), yet it is within his power to do what is right or what is wrong (9:7).

When God visits the earth, a day of redemption will dawn for the just, and a day of retribution for the unjust. The just shall rise to eternal life and joy; the wicked will be destroyed unless they have confessed their sins. When men acknowledge their faults, their souls are cleansed and they become new creatures. The fate of unrepentant sinners is in doubt. They will not be remembered when the righteous are visited—

> Sinners shall be taken away into destruction,
> and their memorial shall be found no more
> (13:10; cf. 3:13-14; 9:9).

Though far from consistent or systematic, the tenor of some passages is such as to suggest that sinners will have no part in the world to come (cf. Yehudah ben Bathyra: "They will neither revive nor be judged" [T.B. Sanh. 108*a*]), but there is no explicit declaration to this effect; other passages indicate that sinners, after death, will suffer (14:6; 15:11, 15*b*).

Though Israel's special role in the divine economy is never lost sight of, there is an approach to a universalistic position. Particularistic tendencies run side by side with universalistic ones. God is not exclusively concerned with Israel; his justice extends to every part of the world; he will have mercy upon all who revere him (2:34-37; 5:17; 8:27, 29; 9:14; 18:3). Against this, we have the statement that in the messianic age πάροικοι and ἀλλογενεῖς will not be allowed to live in the Holy Land (17:31; contrast Exod. 22:21; 23:9; Lev. 19:33; Deut. 10:19; Isa. 14:1; Jer. 7:6; Ezek. 47:22-23; Zech. 7:10; Mal. 3:5; and other injunctions by the prophets). Such exclusiveness needs to be considered in the light of the historical conditions: Palestine was dotted with towns and settlements of non-Jewish inhabitants. When a conflict arose between the Jews and a foreign power, pagan colonists more often than not took sides against the Jews and became—from Antiochus IV to Hadrian—willing tools of foreign intervention. Their presence was therefore resented. It is the liberation of Israel from entanglement in non-Jewish affairs that the psalmist prays for, in the expectation that thereby the Jews will devote their lives to God's service, and his aversion to alien residents in the land of Israel needs to be understood with these circumstances in mind. Be that as it may, the final step toward universalism is not taken; in fact, the psalms remain more stringent in their insistence on Jewish particularism than many of the prophets of the OT.

3. Importance. The Psalms of Solomon are an important source of information concerning Jewish beliefs in NT times. Composed within less than a century from the lifetime of Jesus, they evince tendencies and tensions in thought and life of the Jewish people which illuminate the background of the gospel story. Particularly pertinent in this connection are Pss. Sol. 17–18, the former expressing messianic expectations and describing the Messiah's rule over Jews and Gentiles.

It is instructive to compare the psalmist's ideals with those expressed in I Macc. 14:4-15. There is a marked difference between the presentation of society in the panegyric hymn on Simon the Hasmonean and that in Pss. Sol. 17. In the former case a well-regulated society is described whose members enjoy peace and security and follow their occupations in an orderly fashion. In the psalm the aspirations are more sublime. A community is envisaged that also finds fulfilment "in this world," and yet there is an emphasis on a sanctified life directed exclusively toward God and devoted entirely to his service. Dissatisfaction with existing affairs has become deeper; hopes and aspirations have risen higher.

The psalmist prays for the coming of a messiah who will be David's descendant—a reflection of disillusion with Hasmonean rule—and outlines his conception of the Messiah's government. Jewish eschatology is both older and wider than Jewish messianism. In the OT the term "messiah" implies no more than a legitimately appointed holder of high office (i.e., king or high priest). When, as a result of historical events, the Jews no longer had any representative ruler of their own, the concrete term "messiah," previously applied to historical individuals of the past or present, came to signify the embodiment of political-religious hopes—now transferred to the ruler of Israel in a glorious future. The Messiah in Pss. Sol. 17 is thus the symbol of ideal kingship. The time of the Messiah's appearance is known to God alone; he is God's viceregent on earth, for Israel is God's kingdom (cf. Exod. 19:6). God is King (Pss. Sol. 2:34, 36; 17:1-4, 38, 51), and he is the Messiah's hope. Established by God, the Messiah is no supernatural Being, but is man in all human dignity and perfection. Sinless himself, he will gather together a holy people whom he will lead in righteousness. The Messiah will eject sinful Jews from their inheritance; he will make Jerusalem holy as of old. The children of Israel will return from the Dispersion, and no lawlessness shall be in their midst (17:26-36; cf. Test. Judah 24:1-6; Sibylline Oracles 3:573-85, 652-55, 702-18; 5:260-85). Under the Messiah's rule, men will be sons of God, their riches wisdom and gladness (17:30, 40; 18:7-10).

Apart from messianic expectation there are many expressions in the Psalms of Solomon that have their parallels in the NT. Holy men of God are likened to lambs amid the profane (8:28). God corrects the righteous, the "son of his love," as a "first-born" (13:8; cf. II Sam. 7:14); his chastening discipline is upon Israel as upon his "only begotten son" (18:4; cf. IV Ezra 6:58). Passages like these, with their characteristic terminology, provide examples of the way in which the attributes of Israel as a whole came to be transferred to one person, the one in whom all that Israel is and stands for will find valid realization, the one true representative of the nation—the Messiah.

Bibliography. F. K. Movers, "Apokryphen-Literatur," in H. J. Wetzer and B. Welte, *Kirchen-Lexikon* (1847). A. Hilgenfeld, *Messias Judaeorum* (1869); "Die Psalmen Salomos," *Zeitschrift für wissenschaftliche Theologie,* vol. 14 (1871). E. E. Geiger, *Der Psalter Salomos* (1871). M. Vernes, *Histoire des idées messianiques* (1874), pp. 121-39. J. Wellhausen, *Die Pharisäer und die Sadducäer* (1874). H. E. Ryle and M. R. James, ΨΣ (1891). O. v. Gebhardt, ΨΣ (1895). F. Perles, "Zur Erklärung der Psalmen Salomos," *OLZ,* vol. 5 (1902), cols. 269-82, 335-42, 365-72. J. Viteau and F. Martin, *Les psaumes de Salomon* (1911). R. Harris and A. Mingana, *The Odes and Psalms of Solomon* (1916-20). E. Meyer, *Ursprung und Anfänge des Christentums* (1921), vol. II, pp. 315-19. M. J. Lagrange, *Le Judaïsme avant Jésus-Christ* (1931), pp. 149-63. K. G. Kuhn, *Die älteste Textgestalt der Psalmen Salomos* (1937). J. Begrich, "Der Text der Psalmen Salomos," *ZNW,* vol. 38 (1939). F.-M. Abel, "La siège de Jérusalem par Pompée," *RB,* vol. 54 (1947). O. Eissfeldt, *Einleitung in das AT* (2nd ed., 1956), pp. 754-58. S. Mowinckel, *He That Cometh* (1956), pp. 280-321.

P. Winter

PSALTER sôl'tər [ψαλτήριον; Lat. *psalterium*]. The book of Psalms.

PSALTERY (NEBHEL). *See* Musical Instruments.

*__PSEUDEPIGRAPHA__ sōō'də pĭg'rə fə. A large group of Jewish writings outside the OT canon and the Apocrypha, which were composed originally in Hebrew, Aramaic, and Greek between 200 B.C. and A.D. 200. They include, in the main, apocalypses, legendary histories, collections of psalms, and wisdom works. Because certain of these works are attributed to Adam, Enoch, Moses, Isaiah, and other great OT characters, the term "pseudepigrapha," which refers to works written under a fictitious name, became applied in Protestant circles to this whole body of literature. The Roman church, in accordance with ancient Christian usage, has generally called these works Apocrypha.

1. Meaning of the term
2. The outside books
3. Use in the early church

4. Character of the outside books
Bibliography

1. Meaning of the term. The term "pseudepigrapha" is clumsy and misleading, and should be discarded as a designation for this literature. Not all these writings are pseudonymous. Many are anonymous. Besides, pseudonymous works are found among the canonical books of scripture (e.g., Daniel, Song of Songs), as well as in the Apoc. (e.g., I and II Esdras, Wisdom of Solomon, Prayer of Manasseh). Then, too, the word "pseudepigrapha," even when correctly applied, unduly emphasizes a feature of the books which is of minor importance.

In his great English edition of the Apoc. and Pseudep., R. H. Charles not only listed the apocryphal work II Esdras among the pseudepigraphical books, but he also added three works to the standard list of the latter group: Pirke Aboth, Story of Aḥiḳar, and Fragments of a Zadokite Work. C. C. Torrey, on the other hand, in *The Apocryphal Literature: A Brief Introduction,* has omitted the three works which were added by Charles, but includes two other documents, Lives of the Prophets and Testament of Job. There is therefore no recognized limit to the number of works included in the Pseudep. Morever, many similar writings have been lost. Some of these are mentioned in patristic literature (*see bibliography*), and some are coming to light for the first time in the MS material from Qumran.

Torrey, already in 1945, abandoned the term "pseudepigrapha" in his Introduction and used the term "apocrypha" to designate all the extracanonical writings. This corresponds to the convenient rabbinical designation of writings not included in the canon: the "outside books." Following Torrey, R. H. Pfeiffer (*see bibliography*) rejects the artificial classification of the extracanonical writings into Apoc. and Pseudep. and discusses them according to their date, original language, subject, and style. Moreover, the intertestamental works discovered at Qumran cannot be classified accurately under the traditional title of "pseudepigraph" in the technical, Protestant sense of the term. Some of these works are not pseudonymous, and many of them are not found in the original lists of Pseudep. made by scholars in the early days of Protestantism. There are, therefore, important reasons why the term "pseudepigrapha" should be discarded and a more adequate and accurate designation used in its place. Either the term "apocrypha" (with Torrey) or "outside books" (Jewish) could be used to designate these works.

2. The outside books. Since there is no recognized order in the arrangement of the outside books, they are classified herein as either Palestinian (originally written in Hebrew or Aramaic) or Alexandrian (originally written in Greek). For a detailed discussion of each book, *see bibliography.*

The newly discovered intertestamental works from Qumran are listed separately. For details of their publication, *see bibliography.*

I. Palestinian outside books
   A. Testaments of the Twelve Patriarchs
   B. Psalms of Solomon
   C. Lives of the Prophets, written originally in Hebrew during the first century A.D.; a biographical catalogue of the Hebrew prophets which includes much legendary material. To the biographies of the canonical prophets are added those of Nathan, Ahijah of Shiloh (I Kings 14:1-18), Joed (Neh. 11:7), Azariah (II Chr. 15:1-15), Zechariah son of Jehoiada (II Chr. 24:20-22), Elijah, and Elisha.
   D. Jubilees
   E. Testament of Job, an Aramaic midrash on the canonical book of Job; written in the first century B.C. The writer embellishes the biblical story with many fanciful tales, injecting teachings here and there which are characteristic of the Hasidim.
   F. Enoch (*see* Enoch, Book of)
   G. Martyrdom of Isaiah. According to Charles and Pfeiffer, this is a legendary Jewish work of the first century B.C. which became incorporated into a larger Christian work, entitled Ascension of Isaiah. It was probably written originally in Aramaic. Torrey believes that the Ascension was entirely a Christian work. In the Martyrdom we learn that Manasseh had Isaiah sawed apart with a wood saw.
   H. Paralipomena of Jeremiah, written originally probably in Aramaic during the first century A.D. This contains the "remaining acts and words" of Jeremiah, which are of a legendary character. The last chapter of this work is apparently of Christian origin.
   I. Life of Adam and Eve, incorrectly called Apocalypse of Moses by the editor of the Greek text. It is a haggadic piece of literature, written originally in Aramaic in the first century A.D., which adds much legendary material to the biblical account of the life of Adam and Eve.
   J. Assumption of Moses
   K. Apocalypse of Baruch
II. Alexandrian outside books
   A. Aristeas
   B. Sibylline Oracles, a group of fifteen books, written in Greek over a period of more than six hundred years by both Jews and Christians in imitation of the famous Sibylline Oracles of the Greco-Roman world. Books III, IV, and V are of Jewish origin. They contain many disconnected oracles about the last days. The rest of the books —IX, X, and XV are lost—are from Christian hands.
   C. III Maccabees, written in Greek sometime toward the end of the first century B.C. This is the story of a Jewish triumph over the forces of a foreign king. It has nothing to do with the Maccabees, but it was so called in church lists because it described conditions similar to those in the days of the Maccabean Revolt.
   D. IV Maccabees, a kind of philosophical treatise written in Greek by an orthodox Jew who was influenced by the Hellenistic culture of his day

E. Slavonic Book of Enoch, or II Enoch, or Book of the Secrets of Enoch, an apocalyptic work written in Greek at Alexandria during the first century A.D. It is known only in a Slavonic version. It describes Enoch's ascension through the seven heavens and the revelations made to him at the command of God.

F. Greek Apocalypse of Baruch, or III Baruch, preserved in a Greek, as well as a Slavonic, MS. Both MSS are condensations of the original work, which was written in Greek in the second century A.D. This Jewish work was later extensively revised by a Christian editor.

III. Outside books discovered at Qumran. These works were found among the MSS discovered at Qumran in 1947 and the years immediately following. A few of them, from Caves I and XI, were still rolled up in scroll form, but the great majority of them are in fragmentary condition, and are slowly being put together in the Palestine Museum in Jerusalem, Jordan. They consist of known, as well as unknown, works, written in Hebrew and Aramaic during the intertestamental period. The following list includes items which have been noted in various publications up to the fall of 1957. *See* DEAD SEA SCROLLS.

A. Known outside books from Qumran

1. Jubilees. Five MSS of this work have been identified, one on papyrus. The language is Hebrew. The chapters, partially preserved, are: 1–2; 21–23; 32–40.
2. Enoch. This work is represented by eight MSS, all in Aramaic, which correspond in general to pts. I, III, IV, and V of the book of Enoch.
3. Damascus Document. Several fragments of this work have turned up in Caves IV and VI. They differ quite extensively from the Cairo Genizah Text, discovered in 1896 and translated by Charles (*see bibliography*).
4. Testament of Levi, represented by several Aramaic fragments from Caves I and IV. This work appears to be the source of the Testament of Levi in the TESTAMENT OF THE TWELVE PATRIARCHS. *See bibliography*.

B. Unknown outside books from Qumran

1. Apocryphon of Genesis, a collection of stories, written in Aramaic, relating to the book of Genesis
2. Pseudo-Jeremianic work, contained in five or six MSS, which are not textually identical with any of the Jeremiah-Baruch literature known to us, although there are points of agreement
3. Apocalyptic works
   a. War Scroll (1QM), the description of a battle, probably apocalyptic, between the Children of Light and the Children of Darkness
   b. Description of the New Jerusalem. Numerous fragments of this Aramaic work have been found in several caves at Qumran.
   c. Liturgy of Three Tongues of Fire. Several fragments of this liturgical-apocalyptic work have been discovered in Caves I and IV at Qumran.
   d. Book of Mysteries, so called because of the frequent occurrence of the word *raz*, "secret, mystery." This work is represented by several fragments from Caves I and IV. It deals with the final consummation, which is believed to be near at hand.
   e. Collections of messianic passages from the OT, some with commentary, some without
4. Hymnic works
   a. *Hodayoth* (1QH), a group of thanksgiving hymns written in the style of the canonical Psalms
   b. Psalms of Joshua, a pseudepigraphical work
5. Peshers, or commentaries, a type of literature peculiar to the Qumran community. Fragments of commentaries on Isaiah (three different commentaries on this book have been found so far), Hosea, Micah, Nahum, and Psalms have been discovered at Qumran, as well as an entire commentary on Habakkuk from Cave I.

Besides the works here noted from Qumran, there are MSS written in cryptic scripts whose contents are quite similar to the sectarian documents just described. There are also countless fragments of unknown works on liturgical and legal matters, wisdom, the calendar, etc. Caves still to be discovered will doubtless yield more material of this kind.

3. Use in the early church. The large number of Jewish outside books attests to their wide use and great popularity. The author of II Esdras, e.g., tells us that there were seventy "hidden" or secret books which were to be set apart from the twenty-four canonical books of the Hebrew OT (14:46), and other traditions note even greater numbers of these works. These "hidden" books were obviously the apocalypses which contained esoteric teachings about the last things. These works, however, were banned by the rabbis at the Council of Jamnia (A.D. 90), for several reasons. The fall of Jerusalem in 70, e.g., made their apocalyptic messages meaningless and futile. But more important still, the Christians had appropriated many of these works and had recast them in such a way as to fit into their own views about the last things. It became imperative, therefore, for Jewish leaders to warn their people against these heretical writings.

In the early days of the Christian church the outside books were as popular among the Christians as they were among the Jews. The influence of this literature upon the NT writers is a well-known fact. Just to cite the examples and discuss them would take a whole book in itself. I Enoch, e.g., according to Charles, "has had more influence on the NT than has any other apocryphal or pseudepigraphical work." It is the only book from this entire literature which is directly quoted from by a NT writer. Jude 14-15 cites I Enoch 1:9. The great commandment given by Jesus: "You shall love the Lord your God . . . , and your neighbor as yourself" (Luke 10:27; cf. Matt. 22:37-39; Mark 12:29-31), is already found in Test. Iss. 5:2; Test. Dan 5:3, though stated less emphatically. And the reference in Jude 9 to the dispute of Michael, the archangel, with the devil about the body of Moses is a direct allusion to the apocalyptic writing Assumption of Moses.

Unlike the more favored outside books, known as the Apoc., the great bulk of these writings, later called the Pseudep., never got into the Greek and Latin MSS of the early church, and so the problem of their canonicity never arose in the main stream of Christianity. Many of these works, however, were preserved in the various branches of the oriental churches, and so they have come down to us in such languages as Syriac, Ethiopic, Coptic, Georgian, Armenian, Slavonic, etc.

4. Character of the outside books. The Jewish outside books were, for the most part, written in conscious imitation of the Hebrew canonical books. The influence of the historical books of the OT upon Judith, Jubilees, Testaments of the Twelve Patriarchs, and others; of Proverbs on Ecclesiasticus and the wisdom works from Qumran; and of the Psalter on Psalms of Solomon and the *Hodayoth* from Qumran is clearly recognizable. The canonical book of Daniel, written *ca.* 170 B.C., served as the model for the large number of apocalyptic works that were composed in the three centuries following the Maccabean Revolt. This new type of literature, born out of the fires of persecution, was one of the main features of Judaism in the intertestamental period.

Although apocalypticism had its roots in the OT —e.g., Ezek. 38–39; Joel; Zech. 9–14—it came to full bloom during the difficult days of the Maccabean Revolt. It was a kind of theodicy which tried to justify the ways of a righteous God to men who were undergoing terrible persecution. It presented a theological view of history which would sustain the Jews in their times of trouble. Since victory over God's enemies could not be achieved on the field of battle, as in the days of the OT, the apocalyptist taught that the battle had to be joined in the spiritual realm. Loyalty and devotion to God and his laws, disciplined lives, and moral purity were the most effective weapons, therefore, against the powers of evil. This world was despaired of by the apocalyptist, and only God's direct intervention in history could save the saints of the Most High. God's eternal purpose would ultimately be realized, in spite of the attempts of wicked men to hinder it. Therefore, ultimate victory belonged to God's saints, no matter how dark the present situation might be. The figure of the Messiah played an ever more important role in this great drama of the last days, and many ideas and images relating to the Judgment Day and the future state of bliss which are familiar to the Christian derive from this literature. One of the most important of these is the doctrine of the resurrection of the body, which was originated with APOCALYPTICISM.

The value of these outside books for both Jew and Christian is immeasurable. Judaism, however, for reasons already noted, has neglected these works for the most part, and Christian scholars, until comparatively recent times, have regarded them as peripheral and unimportant for biblical studies. In the English-speaking world the first real interest in this field was generated by the appearance of Charles's monumental two-volume work in 1913, with its introduction to, and translation of, virtually all of the then known noncanonical Jewish writings. Further impetus was given to scholarly research in this field when the Society for Promoting Christian Knowledge inaugurated in 1917 a series of publications known as the "Translations of Early Documents," edited by G. H. Box and W. O. E. Oesterley. The excellent works of scholars like E. J. Goodspeed, C. C. Torrey, and R. H. Pfeiffer have thrown much new light on the intertestamental period and its literature. It is almost certain that the MS discoveries at Qumran will arouse new interest in this important period of Jewish history.

No one can understand the religious development of later Judaism or the background of the NT without studying the Jewish outside books. They serve as a bridge between the Old and New Testaments, supplementing much that is found in the Hebrew scriptures, and heralding new ideas which appear in the NT records. The great need in this important area of biblical studies is a new edition of the Jewish outside books. Much new material has been discovered in this field since the days of Charles's great work; scholarly research into the textual, linguistic, and historical problems of this literature has produced many new insights and conclusions. Here is an area of common interest where both Jewish and Christian scholars can work together to produce a much-needed critical edition of the books which are such an integral part of both of their religious traditions.

Bibliography. The text and Introductions: R. H. Charles, ed., *The Apoc. and Pseudep. of the OT in English* (2 vols.; 1913); *Religious Development Between the Old and the New Testaments* (1914). C. C. Torrey, *The Apocryphal Literature: A Brief Introduction* (1945). The most recent authoritative work on the history and literature of the intertestamental period is R. H. Pfeiffer, *History of NT Times, with an Introduction to the Apoc.* (1949). For discussion of individual outside books, see R. H. Pfeiffer, "The Literature and Religion of the Pseudep.," *IB,* I (1952), 421-36.

Special studies: For Charles's translation of the Cairo Genizah Text, see *The Apoc. and Pseudep. of the OT in English* (1913), II 785-834. For references to certain outside books in patristic literature, see M. R. James, *The Lost Apocrypha of the OT: Their Titles and Fragments* (1920). H. H. Rowley, *The Relevance of Apocalyptic* (rev. ed., 1946). N. B. Johnson, *Prayer in the Apoc. and Pseudep.: A Study of the Jewish Concept of God* (1948).

Publication of the outside books from Qumran: M. Burrows, ed., *The Dead Sea Scrolls of St. Mark's Monastery* (1950): the Habakkuk Commentary. D. Barthélemy, J. T. Milik, *et al., Discoveries in the Judaean Desert* (1955): fragments of the Liturgy of Three Tongues of Fire, pp. 130-32; fragments from the Book of Mysteries, pp. 102-7; fragments of the Description of the New Jerusalem, pp. 134-35 (cf. M. Baillet, "Fragments araméen de Qumran 2. Description de la Jérusalem Nouvelle," *RB,* 62 [1955], 222-45). On the Testament of Levi and the Qumran fragments of it, cf. R. H. Charles, *The Apoc. and Pseudep. of the OT in English* (1913), II, 364-67; J. T. Milik,

"Le Testament de Lévi en araméen; Fragment de la grotte 4 de Qumran," *RB,* 62 (1955), 398-406; D. Barthélemy *et al., op. cit.,* pp. 87-91. E. L. Sukenik, ed., *The Dead Sea Scrolls of the Hebrew University* (1955): the War Scroll; the *Hodayoth.* J. M. Allegro, "Further Messianic References in Qumran Literature," *JBL,* 75 (1956), 174-87: the collections of messianic passages from the OT. N. Avigad and Y. Yadin, *A Genesis Apocryphon: A Scroll from the Wilderness of Judaea* (Hebrew and English; 1956): certain chapters of the Genesis Apocryphon. C. T. FRITSCH

PSEUDO-MATTHEW, GOSPEL OF sōō'dō măth'ū. A Latin infancy gospel, often styled *Liber de Infantia,* which in its present form is no earlier than the eighth century—it was utilized by Hrosvita, abbess of Gandersheim, for her poems in the tenth century—but most of the material of which is far earlier. The earliest MSS are of the eleventh century.

It is in no sense an original work but is the substantial rescript of the Protevangelium of James and the Gospel of Thomas (*see* JAMES, PROTEVANGELIUM OF; THOMAS, GOSPEL OF), with many omissions, amplifications, and distinct additions. Chs. 1-17 reproduce the Protevangelium, with some alterations. Mary is fourteen at the time of her betrothal; from the days of Solomon there have always been virgins brought up in the temple and married when of age. Abiathar the priest seeks to obtain Mary as the bride for his son. There is no account of the supernatural suspension of all motion at the time of Jesus' birth, as in the Protevangelium, nor any mention of Zechariah or John the Baptist. Chs. 18-24 are concerned with the flight to Egypt and the sojourn there, with tales of the adoring lions and leopards, the bowing palm tree, and the fall of the idols in the temple of the city of Sotinen at the entrance of Mary and the child. The source of this material can only be conjectured. Chs. 25-42 reproduce the Gospel of Thomas, but with some changes. Instead of Joseph's seizing Jesus by the ear and wringing it soundly when the latter has caused a boy to drop dead, as the story is told in the Gospel of Thomas, in this version Jesus lifts the boy by his ear and restores him to life. Several additional stories are given: Jesus at the age of eight goes along the road to Jericho; enters a cave in which there are much-dreaded lions; is fondled by them and accompanied by them across the Jordan, which is miraculously parted; blesses the lions; and is bidden farewell by them. The family eventually moves to Capernaum, and Jesus restores to life a rich man named Joseph. The writing ends with a statement regarding the awe in which all Jesus' relatives regarded him and the statement that whenever he slept, be it night or day, the light of God shone upon him.

This gospel, while in no sense original, attained a great fame in the Middle Ages and was the medium through which the far earlier stories made their substantial contribution to later legend and ecclesiastical art. Most of the extant MSS carry letters, presumably composed by the unknown compiler to ensure its favorable reception, from two bishops, Cromatius and Heliodorus, to Jerome, imploring him to translate this book which they had found, and Jerome's reply, in which he styles it a secret composition by Matthew in Hebrew, never before translated but which he (Jerome) has now translated to combat a book published by the disciples of the Manicheans and condemned by a church synod.

See also APOCRYPHA, NT.

Bibliography. An English translation is printed in the *Ante-Nicene Christian Library* (1867-72), XVI, 16-52. For a full analysis and résumé of contents, see M. R. James, *The Apocryphal NT* (1924), pp. 70-79. M. S. ENSLIN

PSEUDO-MELITO, NARRATIVE OF. *See* MELITO, PSEUDO-, NARRATIVE OF.

PTOLEMAIS tŏl'ə mā'ĭs [Πτολεμαΐς]. A city in N Palestine, identical with ACCO.

PTOLEMY tŏl'ə mī [תלמי; Πτολεμαῖος]. Primarily, the title peculiar to a dynasty of Hellenistic kings ruling in Egypt 323-30 B.C. They were regarded as pharaohs by the natives, and were the sole source of law in Egypt.

1. Ptolemy I, called Soter (Saviour). Founder of the Ptolemaic dynasty; son of Lagos. He was satrap of Egypt (323-305) and king (305-283). At the time of his death, he had well organized the country for his heirs.

As one of the Diadochi prominent in Alexander the Great's campaigns, he succeeded him. He is reputed to have written a history of Alexander's campaigns. Ptolemy I took possession of Phoenicia and Palestine three times, but on each occasion had to surrender the land. He entered Jerusalem in 320 on the sabbath, since the Jews showed no resistance. Though he annexed Judea to Egypt, he had to return to his own land when Antigonus, the Seleucid master of Asia, approached. Under his rule many Jews came to Alexandria as prisoners of war (320 B.C.) or as immigrants and were employed as mercenaries (Letter of Aristeas 12 ff).

In 312 Ptolemy, defeating Demetrius, son of Antigonus, again occupied the land but had to evacuate Coele-Syria a year later. A pact was then concluded between them. In 302 Ptolemy invaded Palestine a third time, but in 301 Syria fell to Seleucus. Ptolemy maintained that Judea belonged to him because of the earlier pact. In 301 Ptolemy occupied Palestine for the fourth time, but the question of control of Judea was a standing problem between the Seleucid and Ptolemaic dynasties for generations. After the Battle of Ipsus (301), they acquired Coele-Syria and promoted Hellenism. Jews were of great influence in the Empire. The last queen of the dynasty was the famed Cleopatra, who quarreled with Herod and seized Jericho. Polybius 5.86 points out that the peo-

69. A coin of Ptolemy I

ple of Coele-Syria were always more attached to the Ptolemies than to the Seleucids. The friendly disposition of the Ptolemies to the Jews may be seen in the narrative in Jos. Apion II.iv.5. Tac. Hist. 4.83 relates that Ptolemy brought the statue of Serapis from Pontus to Alexandria, introducing the cult there.

Fig. PTO 69.

Bibliography. S. Zeitlin, *History of the Second Jewish Commonwealth* (1933), Prolegomena, pp. 6 ff; R. H. Pfeiffer, *History of NT Times* (1949), pp. 105, 153; V. A. Tcherikover and A. Fuks, *Corpus Papyrorum Judaicarum,* I (1957), 1-48 (Prolegomena, the Ptolemaic Period, 323-30 B.C.).

2. Ptolemy II, Philadelphus (a surname applied to his sister-wife, Arsinoë, but used to distinguish him). He ruled 283-247 B.C. In his regime the material and literary splendor of the Alexandrian court was enhanced, and he is recognized as a great enthusiast for Hellenistic culture. The Zenon Papyri demonstrate the enormous trade relations and economic conditions of this period.

He was successful in establishing the rule of the Ptolemies over Phoenicia and Judea for a long period. He refounded the city of Philadelphia, after his name, on the site of the biblical "Rabbah of the Ammonites," and brought Hellenization to it. The biblical city of Acre, too, received the name Ptolemaïs in his day, and he founded Philoteria on the Lake of Gennesaret. Under his rule (though some scholars do not recognize this as historical) the Pentateuch was translated into Greek; this version is known as the SEPTUAGINT. The details of this act are narrated in the Letter of ARISTEAS and in the Talmud Meg. 9*a*. The translation may have been called forth by the literary interests of Ptolemy Philadelphus and also by the needs of the Jews in Alexandria who wished to preserve knowledge of their Torah through translation into their spoken language in Egypt.

Ptolemy II is known as a promoter of science; and, according to the Letter of Aristeas, he evinced admiration for the Jewish law. He released many Jewish prisoners of war, and they established themselves

70. A coin of Ptolemy II and his daughter Berenice

in various occupations and set up communities. He gave his daughter Berenice in marriage to the Seleucid king Antiochus II (see Dan. 11:6).

Fig. PTO 70.

Bibliography. M. I. Rostovtsev, *Social and Economic History of the Hellenistic World* (1941), p. 350; R. H. Pfeiffer, *History of NT Times* (1949), p. 224; M. Hadas, *Letter of Aristeas* (1951), Introduction.

3. Ptolemy III, Euergetes (ruled [247] 245-221). Ptolemy, not unlike his forebears, struggled with the Seleucid kingdom. He invaded Coele-Syria to avenge the murder of his sister Berenice; but despite his initial success, Seleucus II defeated him in 242, although Ptolemy retained Judea under a pact made with the victor. (See Dan. 11:7-9 for allusion to these events.) It was at this time that Onias II, the high priest of Judea, refused to pay the tribute to Ptolemy, who thereupon threatened seizure of the country. But Joseph ben Tobias, who became the tax collector, saved the situation for the Ptolemies. *See* ONIAS.

Greek inscriptions from the time of Ptolemy III show evidence of the existence of *proseuchai* (synagogues of Jews) in different settlements, as at Leontopolis, in this regime. Jos. Apion II.v records that he offered sacrifices at Jerusalem.

71. A coin showing Ptolemy III

According to Justin 29.1, Ptolemy III was murdered by his son Ptolemy IV, ironically called Philopator, "father-loving."

Fig. PTO 71.

Bibliography. R. H. Pfeiffer, *History of NT Times* (1949), p. 179.

4. Ptolemy IV, Philopator (221-203). The decline of the Ptolemaic kingdom began in his reign. In 220 Antiochus III of Syria invaded Coele-Syria, but in 217 the Egyptians crushed the army of Antiochus III at Raphia. (There is a reference to these events in Dan. 11:11-12.) Ptolemy, after this victory, came to Jerusalem and wished to enter the temple, considering everything as his realm and believing that he could not be denied admission. He had no mercenary motives. He was prevented, however, and, as related in II Maccabees, was smitten by divine agents. Returning to Egypt, he vented his anger upon the Jews, and issued an edict to punish them and reduce them to slavery. III Maccabees speaks of Ptolemy IV as ordering the Jews to be trampled by elephants, but they were miraculously saved. Historically, however, this may refer to Ptolemy VII (Physcon).

Though the stories of Philopator in III Maccabees

72. A coin of Ptolemy IV

and of Heliodorus in II Maccabees concerning the incidents of entry into the temple seem identical, there are distinct differences. Philopator thought that as king he could enter anywhere, whereas Heliodorus came primarily to confiscate the money of the temple.

Fig. PTO 72.

Bibliography. R. H. Pfeiffer, *History of NT Times* (1949), p. 203; M. Hadas, *The Third Book of Maccabees* (1953), pp. 11, 16 (note 26), 30; S. Tedesche and S. Zeitlin, *The Second Book of Maccabees* (1954), pp. 70, 122 (note 12); V. A. Tcherikover and A. Fuks, *Corpus Papyrorum Judaicorum,* I (1957), 68.

5. Ptolemy V, Epiphanes (203-181). In 199 Antiochus III invaded Coele-Syria for the third time (previously it was in 220). He then won a decisive victory over the Egyptian army, and Judea reverted to Syria. A treaty was enacted betwen Antiochus III and Ptolemy in 192, and Cleopatra, daughter of Antiochus, was married to Ptolemy V. (Dan. 11:13-18 refers to these events.) But this treaty was ineffective, and Cleopatra died in 173. The political situation in Judea was influenced by these internal

73. A coin of Ptolemy V

conflicts in foreign policy. Ptolemy was favored by Hyrcanus the tax collector, whereas the sons of Tobias turned toward Syria.

Fig. PTO 73.

Bibliography. S. Tedesche and S. Zeitlin, *The First Book of Maccabees* (1950), p. 7.

6. Ptolemy VI, Philometor (180-146). As an ambitious ruler, he donned two crowns—that of Egypt and that of Asia—and made an alliance with Rome (I Macc. 2:11). Though he ruled in Egypt, he was able to interfere in Syrian affairs, supporting Alexander Balas against Demetrius in 153 B.C. for king. In 150 Ptolemy VI gave his daughter Cleopatra in marriage to Alexander Balas (Jonathan the high priest was present by invitation of Alexander Balas). Later Ptolemy took Cleopatra back and gave her to Demetrius II, the rival king. Ptolemy attacked Alexander Balas on the Plains of Antioch. The latter fled to Arabia and was killed there. But Ptolemy, too, died of the wounds of the battle (I Macc. 11:18).

Concerning the above records there are conflicting notions:

a) I Macc. 11:1-13 points out that Ptolemy, though he seemed to help his son-in-law Alexander Balas against Demetrius, in reality sought to betray him.

Eventually Ptolemy crowned himself king of Asia in Antioch.

b) Josephus (Antiq. XII.iv.5-7) claims that Ptolemy made an alliance with Demetrius, knowing of Alexander Balas.

Josephus also claims that Ptolemy did not want to offend the Romans and, not being ambitious, did not seek to become king of Asia and Egypt.

Ptolemy and his consort committed the care of the entire kingdom to the hands of the Jews. Two Jewish generals, Onias and Dositheus, had command of the whole army. He released Onias IV (son of Onias III) in the time of Antiochus V Eupator (164-162 B.C.) and placed at his disposal an area in Leontopolis in the province of Heliopolis to build a Jewish sanctuary after the model of the Jerusalem temple. This was known as the Temple of Onias. *See* ONIAS 3.

A work by one Aristobulus, as preserved in fragments by Eusebius, was written for and dedicated to King Philometor. This work is an explanation of

74. A coin of Ptolemy VI

the Mosaic laws and is addressed to heathen readers to show that the Peripatetic philosophy was dependent upon the law of Moses.

Fig. PTO 74.

Bibliography. R. H. Pfeiffer, *History of NT Times* (1949), p. 17. S. Tedesche and S. Zeitlin, *The First Book of Maccabees* (1950), pp. 56-57, 185; *The Second Book of Maccabees* (1954), p. 103. V. A. Tcherikover and A. Fuks, *Corpus Papyrorum Judaicarum,* I (1957), 20 ff.

7. Ptolemy VIII, Euergetes II, called Physcon ("fat paunch") because of his appearance; younger brother of Ptolemy VI. Ptolemy VII shared the throne with his brother, Ptolemy VI Philometor, in the years 170-164, and he reigned alone from 145 to 117. Yet he reckoned the years of his reign from 170.

In the days of John Hyrcanus (135-105) the Syrian Empire was very much weakened. Ptolemy VII set up Alexander Zabinus against Demetrius II and was successful for a number of years. He showed great hostility to the Jews as a result of their political partisanship. Jos. Apion II.v tells that after the death of Ptolemy VI, Ptolemy VII tried to supplant Cleopatra, the widow of Ptolemy VI, and set aside the army, which was under the rule of the Jewish general Onias. Marching against Onias, he had the Alexandrian Jews put in arenas. But the Jews were miraculously saved and consequently celebrated the day as an annual festival. The letter in the first chapter of II Maccabees, stressing that God would not forsake them though they lived outside Judea, was also written in the time of Ptolemy Physcon, who was antagonistic to the Jews.

The Jewish Sybilline Oracles (written *ca.* 140 B.C.) in the reign of Ptolemy VII make reference in vs. 608 to the king.

A change occurred after Ptolemy married his chief enemy, Cleopatra. He began to show favor to the Jews, granting them many rights in Alexandria.

Bibliography. R. H. Pfeiffer, *History of NT Times* (1949), p. 203; M. Hadas, *The Third Book of Maccabees* (1953), p. 11;

S. Tedesche and S. Zeitlin, *The Second Book of Maccabees* (1954), p. 101; V. A. Tcherikover and A. Fuks, *Corpus Papyrorum Judicarum,* I (1957), 23.

8. Ptolemy IX, Lathyrus, coregent with his mother, Cleopatra (116-107). Ptolemy Lathyrus had supplied Egyptian troops to aid Antiochus Cyzacenis of Syria to attack the Jews. But they were unsuccessful, and Samaria fell to Hyrcanus and his sons. This occurred *ca.* 107. Cleopatra was so enraged because Lathyrus had aided Antiochus that she almost drove him from the government (Jos. Antiq. XIII.x.2 ff).

A few years later, when Alexander Janneus besieged Ptolemaïs, the inhabitants sought aid from Lathyrus, who, having been driven from the throne by his mother, was now ruling in Cyprus. But Alexander Janneus called upon Cleopatra when Lathyrus attacked. Lathyrus then tried to gain Egypt but was unsuccessful. His mother retained the Egyptian power. When she sought to annex Judea, her Jewish general Ananios induced her not to do so but rather to make a treaty with Alexander Janneus. Thus, despite reverses, Alexander kept power over his land.

Bibliography. R. H. Pfeiffer, *History of NT Times* (1949), p. 21.

9. Ptolemy XIII, Auletes. He was driven out by popular revolt in 56 B.C. Gabinius was instructed by Pompey to help reinstate him. Suspending his operation against the Parthians, Gabinius was successful, aided by the Jews (Antiq. XIV.vi.2).

In the fourth year of his reign the Greek text of the book of Esther was introduced (*ca.* 78 B.C.) into Egypt.

Bibliography. M. Hadas, *The Third Book of Maccabees* (1953), p. 8; V. A. Tcherikover and A. Fuks, *Corpus Papyrorum Judaicarum,* I (1957), 46 (note 119).

There were other persons, not of the Egyptian dynasty, known as Ptolemy:

10. Ptolemy Mennaeus, king of Chalchis on the Lebanon (85-40). Before the arrival of Pompey the Itureans recognized Ptolemy as their head. He was friendly to the Jews. In 49 Ptolemy took under his personal care the children of the Judean king Aristobulus II, who had been murdered by Pompey. Later, in 42, in the time of Cassius, Antigonus, with the aid of Ptolemy, sought to obtain sovereignty of Palestine but was frustrated by Herod. Ptolemy died during the Roman-Parthian War (40 B.C.; Jos. Antiq. XIV.vii.4; War I.92).

11. A Son of Antony and Cleopatra. He obtained Syria as his realm *ca.* 33 B.C. (Plutarch *Antonius* 54).

12. Son of Abubus; son-in-law of Simon the Hasmonean; military commander of Jerusalem. Having ambitions to rule, he plotted against Simon and murdered him and his sons at a feast at Dok, a stronghold near Jericho. John Hyrcanus, however, escaped and besieged him, revenging the murder of his parents and two brothers (I Macc. 16:11).

13. Macron, son of Dorymenes; governor of Cyprus in the time of Ptolemy VI Philometor. But he abandoned King Ptolemy and went to Antiochus IV Epiphanes. Macron was one of the three generals (together with Nicanor and Gorgias) sent by Lysias against the Judeans. He was responsible for the execution of the embassy, sent by the *gerousia* to the king, charging Menelaus for acts of his brother, Lysimachus. Macron was friendly to the Jews. Lysias considered him a traitor because of his pro-Jewish policy. Being disgraced, he drank poison (I Macc. 3:38-41; II Macc. 10:10-13).

Bibliography. R. H. Pfeiffer, *History of NT Times* (1949), p. 14. S. Tedesche and S. Zeitlin, *The First Book of Maccabees* (1950), p. 95; *The Second Book of Maccabees* (1954), pp. 170, 191.

14. Son of Dositheus; a priest and Levite who brought the Letter of Purim (Add. Esth. 11:1) into Alexandria *ca.* 114-113 B.C. Its purpose may have been to aid Hasmonean propaganda in Egypt. *See,* however, 9 *above.*

Bibliography. V. A. Tcherikover and A. Fuks, *Corpus Papyrorum Judaicarum,* I (1957), 46 (note 119).

15. There were several Ptolemies in Herod's time who are recognized as Hellenic counselors:

a) A brother of Nicolas of Damascus was a trusted friend of Herod.

b) Another Ptolemy was head of the finance department and had Herod's signet ring. After Herod's death, one Ptolemy aided Antipas, and the other, with the power of his signet ring, read Herod's will and supported Archelaus (Antiq. XVII.ix.5).

c) A Ptolemy is recorded as the author of a biography on Herod.

d) Another Ptolemy is often identified as the grammarian Ptolemy of Ascalon. Another writer, mentioned by Clemens, is Ptolemy of Mendesius.

Bibliography. E. Schürer, *The Jewish People in the Time of Jesus Christ* (1891), II-III, 260. V. Tcherikover, *Hellenistic Civilization and the Jews* (1959). S. B. HOENIG

PUA. KJV form of PUVAH in Num. 26:23.

PUAH pū'ə [פּוּעָה, *see below*] (Exod. 1:15). **1.** One of the two Hebrew midwives (*see also* SHIPHRAH) ordered by the king of Egypt to kill all male children (*see* MIDWIFE). The name is most probably to be derived from Ugaritic *pġt,* "girl." Later Jewish legends identify Puah with MIRIAM.

Bibliography. L. Ginzberg, *Legends of the Jews,* II (1910), 251; W. F. Albright, "Northwest-Semitic Names in a List of Egyptian Slaves," *JAOS,* LXXIV (1954), 229 and note 50. J. F. ROSS

2. Alternate form of PUVAH.

PUBLICAN. KJV translation of τελώνης (RSV TAX COLLECTOR).

PUBLIUS pŭb'lĭ əs [Πόπλιος; Lat. *Publius*] (Acts 28:7-8). Probably the highest Roman official on the island of Malta on which Paul and his fellow prisoners were shipwrecked on their way to Rome. It is possible, however, that the word designates the island's chief native officer, or even that it refers to any office that was non-Roman in origin.

Publius entertained Paul and his companions in his home for three days. Jerome records a tradition that he was martyred (*On Illustrious Men* XIX). B. H. THROCKMORTON, JR.

PUDENS pū'dĕnz [Πούδης; Lat. *Pudens*] (II Tim. 4:21). A Christian in the church of Rome who is mentioned as sending greetings to Timothy.

Some have identified him as the Pudens who was a friend of the Latin poet Martial (cf. his *Epigrams* I.32; IV.13, 29; V.48; VI.58; VII.11, 97). This

Pudens was a soldier whose wife, CLAUDIA, is described as of British birth. An ancient tradition held that what had been the baths of Pudens' son, Novatus, were dedicated *ca.* the middle of the second century as a Christian church. Pudens is commemorated in the Byzantine church on April 14, and in the Roman on May 19. B. H. THROCKMORTON, JR.

PUHITES. KJV form of PUTHITES.

PUL pōōl [פּוּל]. **1.** The name under which TIGLATH-PILESER III (745-727 B.C.) ruled as king of Babylon 729-727 (II Kings 15:19; I Chr. 5:26). The meaning of this Assyrian name, rarely attested in late Assyrian documents, remains obscure. Tiglath-pileser III's son SHALMANESER V ruled in Babylon under the name Ululai ("born in the month of Elulu"). No document is dated with the name of Pul; only the Babylonian King List A, Jos. Antiq. IX.xiv.2, and the Ptolemaic Canon mention him. A. L. OPPENHEIM

2. KJV translation in Isa. 66:19 (LXX φουδ); probably an error for PUT (so RSV).

PULPIT [מִגְדָּל, *in phrase* מִגְדַּל עֵץ, tower of wood; LXX ἐπὶ βήματος ξυλίνου; Vulg. *super gradum ligneum*] (Neh. 8:4; cf. 9:4). A raised wooden platform reached by steps (cf. that in the Pnyx at Athens for orations). The purpose of the pulpit—i.e., reading of the law and prayer—brings to mind the copper כיור of II Chr. 6:12-13, a portable platform for royal prayers. Cf. also II Kings 23:2-3, where Josiah read the law by, or possibly on (so AJV), the pillar (cf. Deut. 17:18-19; II Kings 11:14). Acts 2:14 might suggest an elevated position, if not a pulpit.

Bibliography. O. E. Ravn, "Der Turm zu Babel," *ZDMG,* XCI (1937), 352-72. G. HENTON DAVIES

PULSE. KJV translation of זֵרְעֹ[נ]ִים in Dan. 1:12, 16 (RSV VEGETABLES). Daniel and his companions refuse to defile themselves with the king's rich food and wine; they ask for and receive vegetables and water. The Hebrew word means "things sown," and thus includes more than legumes (cf. II Sam. 17:28 KJV; cf. also Tob. 1:11; Jth. 12:2; I Macc. 1:62-63; II Macc. 5:27 for the refusal of unclean food). J. F. ROSS

PUNISHMENTS. *See* CRIMES AND PUNISHMENTS.

PUNITES pū'nīts [פּוּנִי] (Num. 26:23). The name given to the descendants of Puvah of Issachar. According to MS evidence, however, the text probably should read "Puvanites" or "Puvites."

PUNON pū'nŏn [פּוּנֹן]. An important mining center in Edom, and possibly the home of one of the chiefs of Edom (Gen. 36:41, where one might read Punon for PINON). Punon, modern Feinan, is a large, abundantly watered site on the E side of the Arabah, 5¼ miles S-SE of Khirbet en-Nahas and 4⅓ miles S-SE of Khirbet Nqeib Aseimer, both large copper smelting sites. It is located at the junction of the Wadi el-Gheweir and Wadi esh-Sheqer, with extensive building on both sides of the wadis as well as heaps of copper slag from the large smelting operations using ore from local and more distant sources, such as Umm el-ʻAmad, two miles SW of Feinan.

The first period of occupation was from *ca.* 2200 to 1800, when copper was presumably first smelted here, with the trade route to Egypt used to transport refined copper ore to market. When Israel camped at Punon in the latter part of the thirteenth century (Num. 33:42-43), the city was just recovering from a half-millennium of no established occupation. *Ca.* 700 or possibly later, Punon was again abandoned. The mining and smelting operations were taken up by the Nabateans and continued through the Roman (probably), Byzantine, and medieval Arabic periods, during which time Punon prospered, especially during the last two periods.

Eusebius reports that Christians were forced to work in the copper mines and smelters at Punon (Φινών, Φαινών), continuing a tradition of forced labor in these occupations from earlier days. A Christian basilica and monastery were built during the Byzantine period. In the monastery ruins an inscription bearing the name of Bishop Theodore (587-88) was found.

Bibliography. N. Glueck, *Explorations in Eastern Palestine,* II, *AASOR,* 15 (1934-35), 32-35; F.-M. Abel, *Géographie de la Palestine,* II (1938), 410-11. V. R. GOLD

PUR. *See* PURIM.

PURAH pyōōr'ə [פֻּרָה] (Judg. 7:10-11); KJV PHURAH fyōōr'ə. The servant who accompanied Gideon in a nocturnal reconnaissance of the enemy camp of the Midianites.

PURIFICATION [טָהֳרָה; KJV חַטָּאָה, תַּמְרוּק; ἁγνισμός, καθαρισμός (KJV *alternately* PURIFYING; PURGE)]; PURIFY [ברר (KJV BE CLEAN), חטא (*alternately* CLEANSE), טהר (KJV *alternately* BE CLEAN); ἁγνίζω, βαπτίζω (KJV WASH; *usually* BAPTIZE), καθαρίζω (KJV *alternately* PURGE)]. The act of ritual cleansing. *See* CLEAN AND UNCLEAN. L. E. TOOMBS

PURIM pōōr'ĭm, pyōōr'ĭm [פּוּרִים, lots]; KJV Apoc. PHURIM fyōōr'ĭm. Singular: PUR [פּוּר, lot] (Esth. 3:7; 9:24, 26, 28-29, 31-32). A Jewish festival on Adar 14-15, celebrating the Jews' deliverance from Haman by Esther and Mordecai.

Purim is not prescribed in the law. In all probability it developed among the Diaspora in Persia. Its nonreligious character, its name, and the names of the characters in the story of Esther all point to the conclusion that its ultimate origins are non-Jewish. Perhaps under the impact of the Maccabean triumph, Jews historicized the drama.

1. The name. "Pur" is a foreign term. Esth. 3:7; 9:24 interpret it as meaning "lot." This etymology is supported by the Babylonian word *pūrū,* used of the casting of lots to obtain oracles, especially as an aspect of the New Year's Festival. "Purim" is the term with a Hebrew plural ending and refers to the festal days. In the LXX and in Jos. Antiq. XI.vi.13 the terms φρουραι and φρουραια designate "Purim." In Greek they do not mean "lot," to which, indeed, Josephus omits all reference. It is possible to treat them as transliterations of the Aramaic פרוריא from the root פרר, "to destroy."

They have also been treated as Greek words meaning "guardians." The Lucianic text has φουρδαια. Finally, II Macc. 15:36 refers to the feast as ἡ Μαρδοχαική ἡμέρα, "the Mordecaian [or Mardukian?] day" (RSV "Mordecai's day").

2. Origin. It is impossible to speak with complete certainty about the early history of Purim in Judaism, let alone its probable pre-Jewish antecedents. There is no evidence for a critical persecution of Jews in the Persian Diaspora. The book of Esther is confused about the Persian royal chronology and in error about court customs. This leads some to conclude that Purim began in Palestine, and that its characters are masks for the leaders of the Seleucid-Maccabean struggle. This is improbable. The Maccabean triumph was celebrated on Adar 13, Nicanor Day; and the first evidence for Purim in Palestine comes a full century later.

The names in the Purim drama seem to point to a mythological legend about the triumph of Babylonian deities. The names of the gods shine through —e.g., Mordecai-Marduk, Esther-Ishtar. But the Greek title, the date, and the character of Purim hint at connections with *Farwardigan,* the Persian feast of the dead, celebrated in the early Persian era from Adar 11-15. The Greek term for *Farwardigan,* φουρδιγαν, may bear on the Lucianic text. The feast honored the spirits of the dead as "guardians," and there was a common meal to which rich and poor were invited. In its non-Jewish sources Purim may well be a composite. First celebrated by Diaspora Jews, its assimilation to Jewish history perhaps occurred in Palestine. Eventually it crowded out Nicanor Day.

3. Character. Throughout Purim has been a gay and noisy feast. Mourning is forbidden. A festal meal lasting late into the night of Adar 14 is featured. The Talmud tells celebrants to drink until they can no longer distinguish between "Cursed be Haman" and "Blessed be Mordecai." The dramatization of Purim events has a long history, with the injection of elements of the Italian carnival in later centuries.

Bibliography. O. Eissfeldt, *Einleitung in das AT* (1934), pp. 560-65; H. Schauss, *The Jewish Festivals* (1938), pp. 237-71, describes the role of Purim in Jewish life; J. Lewy, "The Feast of the Fourteenth Day of Adar," *HUCA,* XIV (1939), 27-51, gives complete philological analysis of names and stresses *Farwardigan* connections; M. Haller, *Die fünf Megilloth,* HAT, 18 (1940), 114-17, stresses mythological antecedents.

J. C. Rylaarsdam

PURPLE [ארגמן, תולע, תכלת; πορφύρα; Sumer. SÌG-ZA-GIN-DIR; Akkad. *argamannu;* Lat. *purpura*]. The most valued of ancient dyes, encompassing various shades within the red-purple range. It was obtained from Mediterranean mollusks of the Gastropoda class and used primarily for coloring woven materials and cloths. The purple industry developed early in the Mediterranean area and reached its greatest heights in the classical period. Legend has associated the discovery of purple with both Crete and Phoenicia, where the color was highly prized in antiquity. The name Canaan ("land of the purple") was derived from the dye; and the name Phoenicia comes from the Greek φοινός, meaning "red purple." Wool dyed "purple" was available in Ugarit *ca.* 1500 B.C. and later was used for the tribute of kings. For a considerable time the Phoenicians monopolized the industry, although the dye was obtainable elsewhere (Ezek. 27:7).

The primary source of the dye was the secretion produced by the hypobranchial gland of the mollusk, and the shade desired was achieved by using different species of mollusks, altering their ratio, adding other ingredients such as Kermes, and varying air- and light-exposure time in the process. The famous Tyrian purple was produced by "double-dyeing." Descriptions of the mollusks and the dyeing process have been given by Pliny and Vitruvius; however, their information is not precise, and the hues they knew have not been satisfactorily identified. In general, a darker color was considered superior to a light shade; according to Pliny, a color like congealed blood was most sought after. Deposits of *Murex brandaris* and *Murex trunculus,* the most important of the mollusks used in the purple industry, have been found in dyeing beds on Mediterranean coasts. The dyeing agent in *Murex brandaris,* 6-6′ dibromoindigo, isolated by Friedländer, was the chief constituent in Tyrian purple, and dyeings with it alone are of a dull red-violet shade. *Murex trunculus* contains the same compound plus a small amount of a blue-violet product.

Doubtless the Hebrews had to import their purple goods (Ezek. 27:16, 27). Purple was used, generally in combination with blue and scarlet and linen, in the tabernacle furnishings (Exod. 26:1, 31; etc.) and the clothing of the priests (Exod. 28:4-6; 39:1, 28-29; cf. 1QM 7.11, where purple is prominent in the battle dress of the Qumran priests). Solomon found it necessary to obtain skilled help from Tyre, center of the Phoenician purple industry, to handle the purple and other materials employed in the building of the temple (II Chr. 2:7, 14; 3:14). He is also said to have built a chariot with a purple seat (Song of S. 3:10). Cords of purple and linen are found in the palace of Ahasuerus (Esth. 1:6), and flowing locks are compared to purple (Song of S. 7:5). Idols were clothed in blue and purple (Jer. 10:9), and Prov. 31:22 says a good wife's dress was purple and fine linen.

Great value was placed on purple by the Hebrews, and purple garments were considered a sign of distinction, royalty, and wealth. Midianite kings wore purple (Judg. 8:26), and Mordecai was rewarded with a mantle of purple (Esth. 8:15). Judas Maccabeus was amazed that the powerful Romans did not wear purple (I Macc. 8:1, 14), and he took purple and blue cloth in booty from Gorgias (4:23). When Alexander appointed Jonathan high priest, he gave him a purple robe (10:20; cf. 11:58), and Andronicus was stripped of his purple robe for slaying Onias (II Macc. 4:38). Part of Daniel's reward was said to be purple apparel (Dan. 5:7, etc.)

תולע is once translated "purple," referring to those "brought up in purple"—i.e., in luxury (Lam. 4:5; KJV "scarlet"); and תכלת is translated "purple" alluding to the dress of Assyrian nobles (Ezek. 23:6; *see* Blue).

References to purple (πορφύρα) in the NT suggest its economic importance and symbolic character. Lydia was a dealer in purple goods in Thyatira (Acts 16:14). Purple clothing denoted wealth (Luke 16:19);

and Jesus was dressed in purple, mocking his claim to be king of the Jews (Mark 15:17, 20; John 19:2, 5). The purple and scarlet dress of the harlot Babylon (Rev. 17:4) symbolized imperial rank. Rome, represented as having once worn purple before her fall (18:16), was mourned by merchants who could no longer buy her purple (vs. 11).

Many inscriptions and various historical references outside the NT testify to the wide extent of the industry in the Mediterranean and the significance of wearing the purple. *See also* COLORS.

Bibliography. Pliny Nat. Hist. IX.36-40, 125-42; V.19; XXI. 45. G. Perrot and C. Chipiez, *History of Art in Phoenicia and Its Dependencies,* II (1885), 423-26. L. Friedländer, "Über den Farbstoff des antiken Purpurs aus murex brandaris," *Berichte der Deutschen Chemischen Gesellschaft,* vol. 42 (1909), pt. 1, pp. 765-70. F. Thureau, "Un comptoir de laine pourpre à Ugarit," *Syria,* 15 (1934), 137-46. J. R. Partington, *Origins and Development of Applied Chemistry* (1935), pp. 458-64, 522-23. F. Mayer and A. H. Cook, *The Chemistry of Natural Coloring Matters* (1943), p. 317. R. J. Forbes, *Studies in Ancient Technology,* IV (1956), 108-21. C. L. WICKWIRE

PURPOSE. In the strict sense, a deliberately conceived plan proposed for action or executed in it.

1. In the OT. Three representative Hebrew words are: (*a*) מחשבה ("thought," "plan," or "device"). Often when this word is translated "thought," the translation "plan" or "purpose" would give better sense (e.g., Isa. 55:7; 59:7). Men can plan, but not without God's knowing (Isa. 66:18). This reveals a deep paradoxical difference between God and man, for man can plan purposes contrary to God, and, in the short run, carry them through. This is clearly expressed in Jer. 18:11-12. Yet it is only God's purpose that can triumph in the end (Prov. 16:3; 19:21). God's purposes are certain and sure in a way that man's are not.

b) יעץ. This word is used for all kinds of advice given and taken, considered and acted on, in human life, in peace and war, in public and private. It has particular theological significance when it is used of God's counsel, plan, or purpose. It is used in Ps. 33: 10-11 to repeat the point made in Prov. 19:21. God's counsels or purposes are ineluctable, whether against Egypt (Isa. 19:17) or Assyria (Isa. 14:26). Nor are his plans the products of emergency thinking; they are "formed of old, faithful and sure" (Isa. 25:1; cf. 46:10-11). They dispose of the destinies of nations; but they are also the guiding and ruling principle for the believer throughout his earthly life (Ps. 73:24). God reveals his purposes to his "servants and messengers," and when they proclaim them, he fulfils them (Isa. 44:26). As Isa. 5:19 indicates, to doubt that God has a purpose, and that it is effectual, is tantamount to denying his existence. God's existence cannot be separated from his victorious purpose.

c) סוד. This word denotes an intimate circle of friends where confidences can be safely exchanged, or an assembly where decisions are made. While there is frank recognition that it is wrong to betray secrets by talebearing (Prov. 11:13) or gossip (Prov. 20:19), the prophets use this word for the source of their overwhelming constraint to speak. Amos (3:7) tells of the "secret" which God reveals to his prophets, and, more daringly still, Jeremiah likens prophetic inspiration to standing in the divine council where God's plans are formulated (Jer. 23:18, 22). But such intimacy with God is not the exclusive prerogative of the prophet, for the psalmist claims the "friendship" (סוד) of God for those who fear him (Ps. 25:14), and Prov. 3:32 puts it that "the upright are in [God's] confidence [סוד]."

The OT does not use the words for "purpose" to refer to the divine salvation as such, but it does sometimes link particular "plans" with the "mighty acts" of salvation (Mic. 6:5) or speak of a general purpose of good (Zech. 8:15). But Israel came to see God's saving purpose throughout history, reaching backward in time to creation itself, and outward to the whole world of men.

2. In the NT. Many OT features are repeated, though now centered in Jesus Christ.

a. Purpose as will. The words expressing purpose (such as βουλή, θέλω) often merit no stronger translation than "wish" or "desire," but sometimes a firmer rendering seems called for, as, e.g., in Mark 3:13; I Tim. 2:4; II Pet. 3:9. As in the OT, men are able to have their own purposes (Acts 15:37) and even pursue them, in the short run, against God (Luke 7:30; Acts 5:38). But in the end God's will is irresistible (Rom. 9:19). In Rom. 8:28; Eph. 1:1; 3: 11, God's purpose (πρόθεσις) is his eternal will and plan. The tension between human and divine purposes is reflected even in the life of Jesus Christ, and has its climax in the prayer in Gethsemane: "Remove this cup from me; yet not what I will, but what thou wilt" (Mark 14:36). *See* WILL OF GOD.

b. Purpose as revelation. God's purpose, aforetime a secret or "mystery," is now disclosed in and by the life and work of Jesus Christ, and publicly proclaimed in the preaching of the gospel (Rom. 16:25-26; I Cor. 2:7; Col. 1:26). It appears as a purpose of salvation for all men (I Tim. 2:4; II Pet. 3:9), and is, as it always was, unchangeable (Heb. 6:17), having its origin in God "before the foundation of the world" (Matt. 25:34; John 17:24; Eph. 1:4; II Tim. 1:9), and controlling every part of human history (cf. Acts 13:27). It has absorbed man's iniquities (Acts 4:28), even the greatest iniquity of the Cross (I Pet. 1:20). It will continue through the coming ages (Eph. 2:7) and find its consummation in a universal summing up in Christ (Eph. 1:10).

c. Purpose as grace. God's universal saving purpose is the proper environment and motivation of the Christian man. But though he knows and purposes this, his sinfulness frustrates him. "I do not do what I want, but I do the very thing I hate. . . . I can will what is right, but I cannot do it" (Rom. 7: 14-18). Paul goes on in Rom. 8 to show that it is God's gift of the Spirit that overcomes even this fatal weakness (vs. 26), and the Spirit is but the "guarantee of our inheritance until we acquire possession of it" (Eph. 1:14). Thus our final salvation, like the guarantee given for it now, is not awarded on our merits (II Tim. 1:9; cf. Jas. 1:18), but is the sheer gift of God. Man's ability to will God's purpose, his ability to fulfil it in this life, together with his final possession of full salvation, is the work of God. "God is at work in you, both to will and to work for his good pleasure" (Phil. 2:13). "It is your Father's good pleasure to give you the kingdom" (Luke 12:32).

J. MARSH

PURSE. No materials for purses are given in the Bible, but from later sources it appears that they were woven in some cases with a netlike effect, of cotton or of rushes. Others were made of leather. All types of purses were baglike, drawn together at the neck with leather straps or strong cords of other material. This is why the same word could be used for weight bags.

1. כיס. Used to designate a common treasury of those banded together in a common cause (Prov. 1:14); a receptacle for gold (Isa. 46:6); or, in a more general sense, expense (Ecclus. 18:32 and in Palmyrene inscriptions of the third century A.D.). *See also* BAG 2.

2. KJV translation of ζώνη (RSV "belt") in Matt. 10:9. *See* BELT 5.

3. Βαλλάντιον. Used in the sense of "money" (Luke 10:4; 22:35-36) and in the figurative sense of "receptacle for the heavenly treasures" (Luke 12:33; KJV "bag"). J. M. MYERS

PURSLANE pûrs'lĭn [חלמות, *ḥallāmûth*]. A mucilaginous plant, today identified with *Portulaca oleracea* L. The word appears only in Job 6:6 in a figure implying repulsive FOOD, symbolic of Job's intolerable vexation. The KJV translates *rîr ḥallāmûth* "white of an egg" (following the Targ.); the RSV, "slime of the purslane." Löw, following the Syr., identifies it with *Anchusa officinalis* L. ("bugloss" or "oxtongue").

Bibliography. I. Löw, *Die Flora der Juden*, vol. I, pt. 2 (1926), pp. 292-96. J. C. TREVER

PUT pŏŏt [פוט; LXX φουδ, φουτ]. A geographical designation, probably of a part of Libya; also named as a son of Ham.

In the ethnographical portions of Genesis and I Chronicles, Put is named with Cush, Egypt, and Canaan as a son of Ham (Gen. 10:6; I Chr. 1:8). While both texts proceed to recount the further progeny of Cush (probably not Ethiopia in this context), Egypt, and Canaan, there is no further mention of Put; it is possible that Put has dropped out of the text in these subsequent verses, and that some of the names associated with Egypt may properly belong to it. Among the Prophets, Put is mentioned in various contexts. Jeremiah speaks of the "men of Ethiopia and Put who handle the shield, men of Lud, skilled in handling the bow," in his prophecy concerning the conquest of Egypt by Nebuchadrezzar (Jer. 46:9). Ezekiel names Put in three separate prophecies: (*a*) against Tyre, where Persia, Lud, and Put are numbered among her armies (Ezek. 27:10); (*b*) against Egypt, where Ethiopia, Put, Lud, Arabia, and Cub occur together (30:5); (*c*) against Gog, where Persia, Cush, and Put are named as auxiliaries (38:5). From the passages cited thus far, little positive information about Put can be obtained except that an African location, along with Ethiopia, Egypt, and Lud, is suggested. The LXX renderings of this name vary considerably. In Genesis and I Chronicles the name is merely transliterated, but in all the passages cited above except Ezek. 30:5 Put is translated by "Libyans." A seventh occurrence in Nah. 3:9 offers textual difficulties: the LXX has καὶ οὐκ ἔστιν πέρας τῆς φυγῆς, "and there is no end of the flight," where *PWṬ* is read as a noun meaning "flight," fancifully connected by some commentators with Coptic *pōt*, "to flee," but more likely presupposing some form of the Hebrew root *PLṬ*. Here again, however, it occurs in the close proximity of Ethiopians and Libyans. Finally, in Isa. 66:19, we read of a land *PWL* along with Tarshish and Lud; because the LXX reads *Phoud*, the majority of scholars emend *PWL* to *PWṬ*.

As may be seen from the above summary of occurrences, the only clear identification of Put which emerges is one with Libya or possibly some neighboring area. Support for this identification is found in several Old Persian inscriptions. In inscriptions of Darius at Naqsh-i-Rustam and of Xerxes at Persepolis we find a region *Putāyā* mentioned, once in association with Ethiopia and once with the Carians and the Ethiopians, as a province of the Persian Empire. Because *Putāyā* of the Persian inscriptions is almost universally identified with Libya, which would otherwise be missing from the province lists, and because Put of the MT is often translated in the LXX by "Libyans," it is only reasonable to assume the identity of the two. The Babylonian form of the name, occurring in translations of the above texts and without the terminal gentilic *-yā* of the Persian, is *pu-ú-ṭu* or *pu-ú-ṭa*, whose spelling with the velarized *ṭ* instead of a regular *t* corresponds exactly to the spelling with ט in Hebrew. In a fragmentary inscription of Nebuchadrezzar referring to the Egyptian campaign of his thirty-seventh year there is a clear reference to a city *Pu-ṭu-ya-a-man*—i.e., Puṭu of Yawan (the Ionians)—which favors a more specific identification of Put with Cyrene.

Insufficient evidence precludes certainty, but few cogent objections could be raised against the equation of Put and Libya. The fact that Lubim and Lehabim also probably refer to Libya offers no special difficulty, since we do not know specifically what geographical entities are to be associated with each of these names. See further the geographical names Anamim and Casluhim, also possibly referring to the same general area.

Note that the older identification of Put with the land of Punt, so well known from the ancient Egyptian inscriptions, must now be dropped. Even without the compelling evidence listed above, the old equation with Punt was objectionable on both philological and historico-geographical grounds.

Bibliography. G. G. Cameron, "Darius, Egypt, and the Lands Beyond the Sea," *JNES*, II (1943), 308; J. Pritchard, ed., *ANET* (2nd ed., 1955), p. 308; D. J. Wiseman, *Chronicles of the Chaldean Kings* (1956), pp. 30, 94, pl. XXI. For a recent summary of material on Punt, see F. W. von Bissing, "Pyene (Punt) und die Seefahrten der Ägypter," *WO*, 3 (1948), 146-57. T. O. LAMBDIN

PUTEOLI pū tē'ə lī [οἱ Ποτίολοι] (Acts 28:13). A city on the Bay of Naples where Paul landed on the way to Rome; the modern Pozzuoli.

According to Stephen of Byzantium (Ποτίολοι, in *De Urbibus*, ed. W. Xylander [1568], col. 240), Puteoli was a foundation of the Samians—i.e., colonists from the Greek island of Samos. Strabo (V.245) says that in early times it was only a port town of the Cumaeans, the town of Cumae being the oldest of all the Greek colonies in Italy and Sicily

(V.243). Puteoli may have been founded in the sixth century B.C., and both of the authorities just cited give its earlier name as Dicaearchia. In 215 B.C., when Hannibal was invading Italy, the Romans put a garrison there (Livy XXIV.vii.10), and the name of the place was changed to Puteoli. In this connection Strabo (V.245) reports two possible derivations of the name, either from Latin *putei,* referring to the wells found there, or from *puteo,* referring to the foul and sulphurous smells of the district. Puteoli became a Roman colony in 194 B.C., when three hundred Roman citizens were settled there (Livy XXXIV. xlv.1), and it continued to rank as a colony under Augustus (*Corpus Inscriptionum Latinarum* VIII.7959) and Nero (Tac. Ann. XIV.27).

Puteoli was in a region where sulphur was exported (Pliny XXXV.174), and was known for the work of its artisans in metal, who manufactured iron objects of every description, from military armor to farm implements (Diodorus V.13), and also for the wide influence of its bankers, one of whom—Cluvius—made loans to at least five communities in Asia Minor (Cicero *To His Friends* XIII.56). Furthermore, at least from the time of Augustus on, Puteoli was the most important harbor in Italy, only losing this position after Trajan prepared an adequate harbor at Ostia. Strabo (V.245) explains that with a mortar mixed of lime and volcanic ash (now known from its place of origin as *pozzuolana*) it was possible to construct very strong jetties at Puteoli, and thus to make the wide-open shores curve into bays so that the largest merchant vessels could moor there in safety. Thus the Alexandrian grain ships came to Puteoli, and travelers from the E and S landed there en route to Rome. Seneca (*Epistle* 77) tells how the inhabitants of Puteoli watched eagerly for the Alexandrian ships to approach, ships of the very type Paul was on (Acts 27:6); and Suetonius (*Titus* V.3) records that Titus, just like Paul, having first put in at Rhegium, disembarked at Puteoli when he was hastening to Rome after the destruction of Jerusalem.

Ruins of ancient Puteoli include the market hall (*macellum*), commonly known as the Serapeum, since a statue of Serapis was found there; the temple of Augustus, built according to inscriptions by L. Calpurnius (*Corpus Inscriptionum Latinarum* X.1613-14), and later replaced by the cathedral of San Proculo; the older amphitheater, probably that where Nero gave a gladiatorial exhibition (A.D. 66) for Tiridates, king of Armenia (Dio LXII.iii.1), a structure which could have been seen by Paul; and the later amphitheater, dated by an inscription (*Corpus Inscriptionum Latinarum* X.1789) in the time when Puteoli was a Flavian colony—i.e., not earlier than Vespasian—and still well preserved.

Since Paul stayed seven days with the "brethren" at Puteoli (Acts 28:14), there were already Christians there, but the origin of the Christian community is unknown. The arrival of Peter by ship from Caesarea, after the departure of Paul for Spain, is narrated in the Acts of Peter (*Actus Vercellenses* 6, in M. R. James, *The Apocryphal NT*), but the source is legendary.

Bibliography. C. Dubois, *Pouzzoles antique (histoire et topographie)* (1907); H. Leclercq, "Pouzzoles et Cumes," *Dictionnaire d'archéologie chrétienne et de liturgie,* vol. XIV, pt. ii (1948), cols. 1673-87. J. FINEGAN

PUTHITES pū'thīts [פּוּתִי] (I Chr. 2:53); KJV PUHITES —hīts. A family of Judahites from Kiriath-jearim on the N border of Judah.

PUTIEL pū'tĭ əl [פּוּטִיאֵל, he whom God gives] (Exod. 6:25). Father-in-law of Aaron's son Eleazar, and grandfather of Phinehas. Putiel is a name partly of Egyptian derivation, as is the case with other names in the tribe of Levi.

Bibliography. M. Noth, *Die israelitischen Personennamen* (1928), p. 63. R. F. JOHNSON

PUVAH pū'və [פֻּוָּה]; KJV PHUVAH fū'və in Gen. 46:13; PUA pū'ə in Num. 26:23. Alternately: PUAH pū'ə [פּוּעָה] (Judg. 10:1; I Chr. 7:1). The second son of Issachar. Puvah went with Jacob into Egypt and became the head of a family there. In Genesis, Numbers, and I Chronicles he is regarded as the brother of Tola; in Judges he is Tola's father.

E. R. ACHTEMEIER

PYGARG pī'gärg. KJV translation of דִּישֹׁן (Deut. 14:5; RSV IBEX), from the LXX πύγαργος. The pygarg is a white-rumped antelope (Herodotus IV. 192), a description appropriate to the *Addax nasomaculatus* of North Africa and Arabia. *See* FAUNA § A2*f.* Cf. Tristram, *NHB* 126-27.

W. S. McCULLOUGH

PYRE [מְדוּרָה] (Isa. 30:33); KJV PILE. A circular pile of wood for human sacrifice. In this passage there is obvious reference to MOLOCH-worship at TOPHET in the Valley of Hinnom (cf. Ezek. 24:9).

See also GEHENNA.

PYRRHUS pĭr'əs [Πύρρος, fiery red, *from* πῦρ, fire] (Acts 20:4; cf. KJV). The father of Sopater, a companion of Paul.

PYTHON [ὁ πύθων, *similar to* אוֹב]. A divining spirit. "Python" is not used in the Bible, but the Greek word occurs in Acts 16:16: "We were met by a slave girl who had a spirit of divination [πνεῦμα πύθωνα]."

According to Greek belief the Python was first the dragon which guarded the oracle at Delphi. It was slain by Apollo when he took over the oracle. Then the dragon spirit inspired the priestess of the shrine, who delivered revelations. Later the spirit was thought of as a divining or soothsaying spirit which anybody might possess, associated especially with what we would call ventriloquism.

Acts 16:16-26 reports that this spirit bore true testimony to Paul and his companions. Apparently the author attaches importance to this testimony of a pagan spirit to the Christian gospel. After the slave had followed Paul for some days with her testimony, he took pity on her and cast out the spirit.

This is an authentic story of a mental illness understood according to the ancient concept of demon possession, probably the psychosis of hysteria, another example of which is found in Mark 1:23-26.

Bibliography. S. V. McCasland, *By the Finger of God* (1951), pp. 42-44; W. Bauer, *Greek-English Lexicon to the NT* (1957), p. 736, πύθων, cites the literature. S. V. McCASLAND

*Q [*from* Ger. *Quelle,* source]. A symbol used to designate the hypothetical source of the (largely) discourse material common to Matthew and Luke and not found in Mark. Other names given this source are: "double tradition," "sayings source," Redenquelle, LOGIA. It constitutes the second document in the two-document hypothesis of gospel origins, the other document being Mark. Not all scholars have accepted the existence of Q as a single document; some find it more plausible to account for the common non-Markan material in Matthew and Luke in other ways. *See* SYNOPTIC PROBLEM.

There is widespread agreement among scholars that this source is represented mainly, if not entirely, by the parallel non-Markan material in Matthew and Luke; that it contained little narrative and no passion story; that it was composed largely of detached sayings of Jesus such as in the Sermon on the Mount (*see* L for contrast); and that its order is better preserved by Luke than by Matthew. Opinions differ widely over its exact reconstruction, its original wording, its use by Mark, and the possible strands of material which may have been amalgamated within it. Despite these disagreements, Q is regarded as an extremely valuable witness to the historical Jesus. Originating *ca.* A.D. 50, perhaps in Antioch, it takes us back to within twenty years of Jesus' death.

D. T. ROWLINGSON

***QERE** kə rā′ [קרי, that which is to be read]. The scribes were prohibited to alter the authoritative consonants of the text (*see* KETHIBH); and where their oral tradition or their own interpretation diverged, it was entered in the margin by means of the *Qere.* It is estimated that there are more than 1,300 such marginal notes in the MT, and they have been partially assembled in Masoroth.

See also TEXT, OT, § A3*a*.

Bibliography. C. D. Ginsburg, *Introduction to the Massoretico-Critical Edition of the Hebrew Bible* (1897), pp. 183-86.

B. J. ROBERTS

QESITAH kĭ sē′tə [קשׂיטה]. An old weight of unknown origin, mentioned in Gen. 33:19; Josh. 24:32; Job 42:11, where both the RSV and the KJV translate "piece of money." The LXX translates ἀμνός or αμνάς, "lamb." *See* WEIGHTS AND MEASURES § B4*g*.

O. R. SELLERS

QOHELETH. Alternate spelling of Koheleth, the Hebrew title of the biblical book of ECCLESIASTES.

QUAIL [שׂלו; *cf.* Arab. *salway,* Syr. *salway,* Jewish Aram. סלוי; ὀρτυγομήτρα (Wisd. Sol. 16:2; 19:12), a bird migrating with quail (Aristotle *History of Animals* VIII.597*b*)]. Any of a genus (*Coturnix*) of various small gallinaceous birds of the subfamily *Phasianinae* (comprising quails, partridges, and pheasants).

שׂלו is referred to in the OT and in the Wisdom of Solomon only in connection with its provision as food at the time of the Exodus. While various opinions about its identity have been held, it is now generally agreed that the Hebrew word signifies the quail (cf. Ps. 78:27). It is to be noted, however, that the LXX uses ὀρτυγομήτρα, not ὄρτυξ ("quail"). According to the tradition, twice after the departure of the Hebrews from Egypt, large numbers of these birds descended on Israel's camp, thus furnishing the people with additional food (Tristram says that quail "is considered the most delicate eating of all game"). The coming of the quails was interpreted as providential; the birds seemed to be directed to the Hebrew tents by a beneficent God.

Quails in the Mediterranean area winter in Africa and migrate northward in vast flocks in the spring (Tristram *NHB* 229-33). This is an exhausting flight and is done in stages. When the birds alight to refresh themselves, they are easily caught. Presumably it was a cloud of migrating quails that came down on the Hebrew encampment. On quails' flying with the wind (Num. 11:31), see Aristotle *History of Animals* VIII.597*b;* on the spreading out of quails to dry in the sun (Num. 11:32), cf. the Egyptian practice cited by Herodotus (II.77).

Fig. FAU 7.

W. S. MCCULLOUGH

QUARRY. 1. An excavation from which stone is cut for building purposes. This noun is used to translate מסע in I Kings 6:7 (KJV translates "at the quarry" by "before it was brought thither"), referring to the source of stones in the temple; and מקבת בור in Isa. 51:1 (KJV "hole of the pit"). The KJV uses "quarries" in Judg. 3:19, 26, to translate פסילים, "sculptured stones." Many commentators believe that השברים in Josh. 7:5 should be translated as "quarry" instead of as the place name SHEBARIM.

Many sites in Palestine preserve evidence of quarrying.* Rock was sometimes cut from the surface, as on the N slopes of Lachish. Sometimes other digging, such as of tombs or cisterns, was done with quarrying methods and the stones used for building. But many cuts were made purely for quarried stone, and unfinished blocks still in them are evidence of their use. The so-called "Solomon's Quarries" is an example. N of Jerusalem in biblical times, it now lies under a section of the walled city E of the Damascus gate. Its great size, *ca.* 325 by 650 feet, suggests that it was a state undertaking, though not likely as early as Solomon. Fig. QUA 1.

2. A verb meaning "to cut stone for building purposes"; used to translate the *Hiph'il* of נסע (I Kings

Courtesy of the Palestine Archaeological Museum, Jerusalem, Jordan

1. Unfinished monolith column in Mahneh Yehudah Quarta, Jerusalem

5:17—H 5:31 [KJV "bring"]; Eccl. 10:9 [KJV "remove"]), and חצב (II Kings 12:12—H 12:13; 22:6; II Chr. 2:2, 18—H 2:1, 17; KJV "hew").

Methods of quarrying are illustrated at Samaria, where unfinished stones were found on a quarry bed dating from the OT period. The stone used was easily worked, soft-quality limestone, which hardens with exposure to the air. The rough blocks were cut loose by cutting deep channels on four sides and then prying, or inserting wooden wedges and swelling them with water, or by splitting along a natural cleavage line with a sharp blow. The channels, just wide enough to let the workman's arm and tool in, were cut with short-handled, narrow-bladed, iron picks, swung apparently with circular, fanlike strokes. The same technique was used for a large shaft—*ca.* twenty-seven feet long and three feet in diameter—found partially cut out in the Jewish quarter of Jerusalem in 1934. Its dimensions suggest that it might have been for the cloisters in Herod's temple.

Such stones, roughly finished in the quarry, were dressed more particularly at the building site, as piles of stone chips by the stairs of the palace at Lachish and around the citadel in Jerusalem would indicate. I Kings 6:7, however, states that stones for the temple were completely finished in the quarry, so that no "tool of iron was heard in the temple."

In the Roman period stones of five to ten tons were not uncommon, and the problem of moving them from quarry to building site almost defies imagination. Presumably rollers or sledges and earth ramps were used. Large stones in the Herodian citadel tower in Jerusalem have square slots cut in them, *ca.* eight inches square, which may have been for ropes or levers for pulling or prying them.

Bibliography. G. A. Reisner, C. S. Fisher, and D. G. Lyon, *Harvard Excavations at Samaria,* I (1924), 37-38, 96 ff; C. N. Johns, "Excavations at the Citadel, Jerusalem," *PEQ* (1940); O. Tufnell, *Lachish III: The Iron Age* (1953), pp. 38, 161-62, 178-79, 246. S. V. FAWCETT

QUART. The translation of χοῖνιξ (a dry measure slightly less than a quart) in Rev. 6:6 (KJV MEASURE). *See* WEIGHTS AND MEASURES § C4*o*.

QUARTER, SECOND. *See* SECOND QUARTER.

QUARTERMASTER [שׂרמנוחה] (Jer. 51:59); KJV QUIET PRINCE. An officer in charge of rations, supplies, etc., for the troops, and possibly custodian of tribute. The KJV translation is inappropriate for the position of Seraiah. A slight orthographic change or metathesis could make this into "prince of the camp." But only a slight change of vowels, as suggested by the versions, makes this "prince of tribute," and so preferably "quartermaster."

See also PRINCE. C. U. WOLF

QUARTUS kwôr′təs [Κούαρτος; Lat. *Quartus,* fourth] (Rom. 16:23). A Christian man who sends a greeting through Paul. He is also mentioned in the subscription to I Corinthians in the Textus Receptus.

F. W. GINGRICH

QUATERNION kwə tûr′nĭ ən. KJV translation of τετράδιον (RSV SQUAD).

QUEEN [מלכה (Esth. 1:9), גבירה (I Kings 15:13), שגל (Neh. 2:6); Aram. מלכתא (Dan. 5:10); βασίλισσα]. A feminine ruling sovereign or the consort, widow, or mother of a monarch.

1. Queen regnant. The queens who ruled as sovereigns of a nation were not unknown in the ancient Near East. The Bible reports two non-Israelite queens, the queen of Sheba (*see* SHEBA, QUEEN OF; I Kings 10; II Chr. 9) and the CANDACE of the Ethiopians (Acts 8:27). The Hebrews had no legitimate ruling queen, except ATHALIAH, who seized the throne after the death of her son, Ahaziah (II Kings 11:1). She misused her influence as queen dowager and queen mother to usurp the power of the throne for seven years (vs. 4). The case of Hatshepset of Egypt (*ca.* 1500 B.C.) might serve as an extrabiblical parallel. Both queens attained the supreme power by illegal seizure.

2. Queen consort. It appears that the queen, as the wife of the ruling sovereign, had no unique official status, either in Israel or in Judah. In Persia, the queens Vashti (Esth. 1:9) and Esther were required to show absolute obedience to their husband (1:13-22), in spite of their being crowned (2:17); and, similarly, Bathsheba bowed and did obeisance to David (I Kings 1:16, 31). However, as the exception to the rule, Saul's daughter Michal mocked and defied her royal husband, David, without penalty (II Sam. 6:20-23). The place of the queen was the place of honor at the right of the king (Ps. 45:9—H 45:10). In the N kingdom, at least, Queen Jezebel had influence enough to threaten the life of Elijah (I Kings 19:1-3) and to plot the stoning of Naboth (21:5-16). Marriages such as that of David and Maacah, the daughter of Talmai, king of Geshur (II Sam. 3:3); Solomon and the Pharaoh's daughter (I Kings 3:1); Ahab and Jezebel, the daughter of Ethbaal of Tyre (I Kings 16:31); and Jehoram of Judah and Athaliah of Israel (II Kings 8:25-27) served, certainly, as tokens of peaceful diplomatic relationships and alliances between the powers involved. The personal influence of a queen probably depended, in large measure, on the political weight—or lack of weight—of her kin. Besides the queen, there were also royal consorts of lesser importance who were indiscriminately called queens (Song of S. 6:8-9). These royal wives, or "princesses," had a status slightly higher than that of a concubine (I Kings 11:3; cf. Song of S. 6:8-9).

3. Queen mother. If the role of the queen consort was not too significant, the role played by the queen mother was more important. The influence of the mother of the ruling king was great in Egypt, Mesopotamia, and in the Hittite Empire. The queen mother had an official status in Judah, as is shown by the incident in which Asa of Judah removed Maacah, his mother, as queen mother because of her cultic offenses (I Kings 15:13). The queen mother was greeted by the king with signs of honor. Solomon rose and bowed before Bathsheba, the queen mother, and a throne was placed for her at the right side of the king (I Kings 2:19). The queen mother probably had a crown (Jer. 13:18). She is repeatedly mentioned together with the king (Jer. 13:18; 22:26; 29:2). The importance of the queen mother in Judah might be illustrated also with the fact that the names of most of the Judean queen mothers are preserved in the biblical account (e.g., I Kings 14:21; 15:2, 10; etc.). Athaliah's ability to usurp the Judean throne and to keep it for seven years after the Omri dynasty, her paternal family, was massacred in Israel (II Kings 11:1-3) is additional proof of the considerable power and influence of the queen mother.

The status of the queen mother in the N kingdom was not of less importance than it was in Judah. In the time of Jehu's revolt, the visiting kinsmen of Ahaziah went to visit "the royal princes and the sons of the queen mother" (II Kings 10:13). That the names of only two queen mothers, Zeruah (I Kings 11:26) and Jezebel, were preserved does not mean that the queen mother had no influence in Israel (cf. II Kings 9:22); this fact can be explained by the unfavorable attitude toward the N kingdom of the Deuteronomic editor of the books of Kings.

The NT references to queens do not shed any additional light upon the status or office of the queen (Matt. 12:42; Luke 11:31; etc.).

Bibliography. J. Pedersen, *Israel, Its Life and Culture,* III-IV (1940), 71-72.

S. Szikszai

QUEEN OF HEAVEN. The object of worship, particularly by women, in Judah in the time of Jeremiah; cakes (כונים), possibly shaped as figurines, were offered to her with libations (Jer. 7:18; 44:17-19, 25). Jeremiah censures the Jewish refugees in Egypt after the fall of Jerusalem for burning incense and offering libation to the queen of heaven. From the second reference this cult seems to have been designed to secure material welfare. From these two isolated references, however, it is not possible to determine with certainty the object of worship, the more so because of variant readings. The MT מלכת is an unusual form of מלכה, the normal word for "queen," and certain MSS read מלאכת ("handiwork," "the heavenly handiwork"), meaning presumably the stars; this was understood by the LXX translators in Jer. 7:18, where "the heavenly host" (τῇ στρατιᾷ τοῦ οὐρανου) is read, supported by the Targ., which reads "the star(s) of heaven" (כוכבת שמיא). If "the queen of heaven" is to be read—which seems more probable—the reference might be to Ishtar, the goddess of love and fertility, who was identified with the Venus Star and is actually entitled "Mistress of Heaven" in the Amarna tablets. The difficulty is that the Venus Star was regarded in Palestine as a male deity (*see* Day Star), though the cult of the goddess Ishtar may have been introduced from Mesopotamia under Manasseh. It is possible that Astarte, or Ashtoreth, the Canaanite fertility-goddess, whose cult was well established in Palestine, had preserved more traces of her astral character as the female counterpart of Athtar than the evidence of the OT or the Ras Shamra texts indicates. The title "Queen of Heaven" is applied in an Egyptian inscription from the Nineteenth Dynasty at Beth-shan to "Antit," the Canaanite fertility-goddess Anat, who is termed "Queen of Heaven and Mistress of the Gods." This is the most active goddess in the Ras Shamra Texts, but in Palestine her functions seem to have been taken over largely by Ashtoreth.

Bibliography. S. A. Cook, *The Religion of Ancient Palestine in the Light of Archaeology* (1930), pp. 104-8, 143; A. Rowe, *The Topography and History of Beth-shan* (1930), pp. 32-33.

J. Gray

QUEEN OF SHEBA. *See* Sheba, Queen of.

QUICK, QUICKEN [חי, מחיה = ζῆν; חיה = (συ)-ζωοποιεῖν]. Archaic KJV expressions for (RSV) "alive, living"; "revive, give life, make alive" (*see* Life). In the phrase "judge of the quick and the dead," the "quick" are those still alive at the Parousia (cf. I Thess. 4:15-17). For "quicken" used of God's resurrecting action at Easter, in the Christian life, and at the eschatological consummation, *see* Resurrection in the NT; Regeneration.

J. M. Robinson

QUINTUS MEMMIUS. *See* Memmius, Quintus.

QUIRINIUS kwĭ rĭn'ĭ əs [Κυρήνιος] (Luke 2:2); KJV CYRENIUS sī rē'nĭ əs. The Roman governor of Syria, a census by whom is given as the date of the Nativity of Jesus. A census taken under Quirinius is known from Josephus, but it clashes both in date and in scope with the meager data provided in Luke, and out of this clash there has emerged an old and oft-debated problem in gospel study.

- A. Career
- B. The narrative in Luke 2:1-3
  - 1. The difficulties
    - *a.* The date of the census
    - *b.* The scope of the census
    - *c.* The place of Jesus' birth
    - *d.* The "first" census
  - 2. Proposed solutions
    - *a.* The harmonization
    - *b.* The vindication of Luke
    - *c.* The rejection of Luke
    - *d.* The *Tendenz* in Luke
- Bibliography

A. ***CAREER.*** P. Sulpicius Quirinius was elected consul of Rome in 12 B.C. He was sent to lead an expedition against rebel mountaineers (the Homodenses) in Alecia, and for his successes received at Rome the honor of a triumph. In A.D. 2 he accompanied Gaius Caesar eastward as his tutor. Appointed legate of Syria in 6, he held the position for several years. He died in 21 in Rome; the Emperor Tiberius, despite Quirinius' unpopularity, provided a public funeral (Tac. Ann. 3.21, 48).

B. ***THE NARRATIVE IN LUKE 2:1-3.*** **1. The difficulties.** ***a. The date of the census.*** Luke early in his narrative (1:5) has allocated the nativity events to the "days of Herod the King."

The continuing narrative (2:1-2) relates that "in those days a decree went out from Caesar Augustus that all the world should be enrolled. This was the first enrollment when Quirinius was governor of Syria."

Herod died in 4 B.C. His son Archelaus was deposed in A.D. 6, and Judea was governed thereafter by a series of procurators (among them Pontius Pilate, 26-36; see Luke 3:1). Josephus (Antiq. XVII.xiii.5; XVIII.i.1) relates that on the deposition of Archelaus, a census (enrollment) for tax purposes took place in Judea, a procedure understandable as a consequence of the shift in authority. If Luke and Josephus are narrating the same event, then the date according to Luke was 4 B.C.; according to Josephus it was A.D. 6 or 7.

b. The scope of the census. The account in Josephus limits the census to Palestine; Luke has stated that "*all the world* should be enrolled." No information is available anywhere about a world-wide census, and certainly not about this particular one.

Luke 2:3 reads: "And all went to be enrolled, each to his own city." While evidence exists that a return to one's native residence for purpose of tax enrollment was required in a limited area (see Pap. London 904, vol. III, p. 124, cited in Creed, *The Gospel According to Luke,* p. 33), the chaos and confusion which could result if "all the world" returned to their native homes scarcely suggests that such a universal requirement would ever be made, let alone enforced. (Harmonizers take the "all" of 2:3 to be limited to residents of Syria.)

Moreover, if a universal census was decreed in the time of Herod, why is Josephus completely silent on it?

c. The place of Jesus' birth. In Luke's context, the census is used for two purposes: it seeks, passingly, to establish the date; primarily, however, it gives the reason for the birth in Bethlehem of the baby previously conceived in Galilee (see 1:24). I.e., had the census not required Joseph and Mary to journey to Bethlehem, Jesus would have been born in Galilee.

Neither Mark nor John states that Jesus was born in Bethlehem. Mark 6:1 supposes, or at least implies, that Jesus was born in Nazareth; John 7:41-43 similarly seems to fix Nazareth, not Bethlehem, as the birthplace. Many scholars reject the birth in Bethlehem as unhistoric, citing their basis in part as the difficulties arising from the "census of Quirinius."

d. The "first" census. Finally, the words translated "This was the first enrollment when Quirinius was governor of Syria," have been translated differently. One proposal reads: "This census was the first of those which took place under Quirinius"; a second reads: "This was the census which took place before Quirinius was governor." If under Quirinius one and only one census enrollment took place, then Luke and Josephus are irreconcilable. If, though, more than one census took place, then reconciliation becomes possible.

2. Proposed solutions. ***a. The harmonization.*** The diverse translations just cited are efforts to reconcile Luke and Josephus. It has been noted that Acts 5:37 reveals that Luke knew of the A.D. 6 census, and therefore he alludes to an earlier, and first census, in 4 B.C. McKinnon, relying largely on the views of Ramsay (especially *The Bearing of Recent Discovery on the Trustworthiness of the NT*, pp. 238-39), considers neither the problem raised by "all the world" nor the unfeasibility of a general movement to native cities of all residents of the Empire.

b. The vindication of Luke. Ramsay escaped from the difficulty by a series of steps. First, Tertullian (Marcion IV.19) dated the Nativity under Saturninus, the legate from 9-6 B.C.; second, he believed that Quirinius was at that time associated with Saturninus; hence, Ramsay assigned the Nativity to 8 B.C. and took literally the world-wide census for that time suggested by Luke and of which no reflection is found at all in Josephus. Ramsay had ample predecessors (and still has followers) whose bent is to suppose that since Luke must be right, the inherent difficulties are no more than arguments based only on the silence of Josephus. Schürer (*A History of the Jewish People in the Time of Jesus Christ*) speaks of two different courses: either to discover "in Josephus traces of a Roman census in the time of Herod," or to deny "that the silence of Josephus proves anything." His discussion will persuade the persuadable that there are no traces at all of a census under Herod, and that "in this case the argument [from silence] is of some importance. In regard to no other period is Josephus as well informed, in regard to none is his narrative so full, as in regard to the last years of Herod."

c. The rejection of Luke. The solution of the problem, though inevitably unpalatable to many, consists in recognizing with Creed that "Luke's history is not always dependable. There can be little doubt that in his account of Gamaliel's speech in Acts V he has wrongly dated the rising of Theudas . . . . It is not unreasonable to suspect a similar error here."

d. The* Tendenz *in Luke. It is likely, however, that we deal not alone with a minor inaccuracy, for which a tentative explanation was offered, two generations ago—that of a faulty use of Josephus (Krenkel, *Lukas und Josephus*). More probable than faulty use was an indifference to historical exactness which characterized Luke, for whom history was a fine art, not the modern precise science.

Luke assumed, with Matthew, that the Messiah must have been born in Bethlehem. Whereas Matthew seems to take Bethlehem as the home of Jesus, for Luke, Nazareth is the home. The purpose of Luke's narrative is "to bring Joseph of the house of David to the city of David for the birth of the Messiah."

The setting aside of the accuracy of the census of Quirinius necessarily sets aside the birth in Bethlehem.

It is not known precisely where or when Jesus was born. *See* JESUS CHRIST § C.

Bibliography. E. Schürer, *A History of the Jewish People in the Time of Jesus Christ* (English trans., 1891), div. 1, vol. I, pp. 105-43; C. Guignebert, *Jesus* (English trans., 1935), pp. 96-104; J. M. Creed, *The Gospel According to St. Luke* (1942), pp. 28-32.

S. SANDMEL

QUIVER [אשפה, *cf.* Ugar. *uṯpt*, Akkad. *išpatu;* תלי, *from root* to hang, suspend (Gen. 27:3), LXX φαρέτρα, *cf.* Aram. תלי *attested only once* (A. E. Cowley, *Aramaic Papyri . . .*, no. 30, line 8), *seemingly in general sense of* weapons]. A container for carrying arrows. The quiver was usually made of leather, ornamented with metal or paint, and hung over the shoulder. In the Annals of Ashurbanipal the goddess Ishtar of Arbela appeared in a dream "with quivers hung [*tullāta išpāti*] to the right and the left," but mortals could use but one.

In the Bible "quiver" is usually used metaphorically: in Ps. 127:5, of the family circle; in Isa. 49:2, of the Servant as contained in God's quiver; and in Lam. 3:13, of chastisement. Elsewhere it is simply part of military equipment. Fig. ELA 23.

J. W. WEVERS

***QUMRAN, KHIRBET** kĭr'bĕt kŏŏm'rän. The ruins of an Essene monastery which was the center of the community of the DEAD SEA SCROLLS. Khirbet Qumran is situated at the W coast of the Dead Sea, 8½ miles S of Jericho. *See* SALT, CITY OF.

QUOTATIONS. Explicit direct quotations occur very rarely in the OT but comparatively frequently in the NT.

1. In the OT. The sparse direct quotations are from earlier books that have perished. Twice the Book of Jashar is directly quoted (Josh. 10:12*b*, 13*b;* II Sam. 1:19-27; *see* JASHAR, BOOK OF). The "Book of Song," quoted according to the LXX in I Kings 8:53*a*, may be the same book from which I Kings 8:12-13 was taken. For a geographical detail Num. 21:14-15 directly cites an incomplete sentence from a "Book of the Wars of Yahweh" (*see* WARS OF THE LORD, BOOK OF); possibly the "Song of the Well" (vss. 17-18) came from the same book.

Explicit but indirect quotations abound in I and II Kings from two lost works referred to as the Books of the Chronicles of the Kings—one of Israel and the other of Judah (*see* BOOKS REFERRED TO). The canonical accounts of the several reigns are probably condensations of the appropriate passages of these Chronicles. I and II Chronicles often profess to quote indirectly a book with many different names; perhaps its real name was "Commentary on the Book of the Kings" (II Chr. 24:27), but whether this book was real or a fiction is a moot question.

Tacit quotation is obvious in the case of the long-recognized Memoirs of Nehemiah (*see* EZRA AND NEHEMIAH, BOOKS OF); the "official" documents in Ezra-Nehemiah are less certainly quoted. Tacit quotation from OT book to OT book is clear in the verbatim and quasi-verbatim repetition of large blocks from Samuel and Kings in Chronicles and from earlier codifications of law in later ones. The many poetic passages in a prose setting should probably be regarded, not as quoted, but as simply here recorded (to our eyes, for the first time, but it makes little difference whether someone may also earlier have written them down). Between the OT and the literatures of Mesopotamia and Egypt, of Canaan (Ras Shamra), and even of Greece, there are many points of contact, in subject matter, expression, and outlook. There may even be some literary indebtedness, but this does not seem to involve actual quotation. Law and proverbial wisdom, myths and philosophies, respect neither political nor cultural boundaries.

2. In the NT. The situation here is greatly altered by the existence of scripture, what we know as the OT, which is explicitly quoted some 150 times and tacitly quoted some 1,100 additional times. In general, the purpose of quoting the OT is to secure confirmation of some NT statement by an authority respected by Jews, Christians, and God-fearing Gentiles, but the OT is also occasionally quoted against itself (Mark 10:2-9) or criticized (Matt. 5:38-39) or polemically interpreted contrary to some other interpretation (Mark 9:12; I Cor. 9:9). What is thereby confirmed may be a matter of conduct (Mark 2:25), a general principle (Matt. 15:8-9), or a theological insight (Rom. 3:10-18). Very often in Matthew, a few times in John, and sporadically elsewhere, an event is set forth as divinely willed by appeal to an OT passage which predicts it or can be made to predict it. But there are also many references to the OT involving quotation without argumentative intent—comparisons like Matt. 12:40; I Cor. 10:7—and still more cases where OT allusions are either reflections of the common culture out of which the NT writers come or literary adornments from the normative literature recognized by those to whom the NT writings were addressed (particularly common in Paul, Acts, Revelation).

By and large, the OT is quoted according to the LXX, the language rarely reflecting any knowledge of the Hebrew text. The chief exception to this generalization is the group of forty-three quotations in Matthew which are peculiar to it (not Synoptic). Of this group only eleven agree with some MS of the LXX; the thirty-two others differ from the LXX and all known Greek versions, usually by being closer to the Hebrew text. The compiler of Matthew (or the tradition behind him) must have used either the Hebrew directly or a Greek version lost to us.

The only passage from noncanonical Jewish literature explicitly adduced in the NT, though not verbatim, is I Enoch 1:9 in Jude 14, but there are a score of echoes from and allusions to such books. Pagan writers quoted, though without acknowledgment, are Aratus of Tarsus (Acts 17:28), Menander (I Cor. 15:33), and Epimenides (Tit. 1:12). Gentile literary forms, but not actual quotations, are present in the lists of household duties, the catalogues of virtues and vices in Paul (*see* LISTS, ETHICAL), and in the mannerisms of the Stoic diatribe frequently present in the Pauline letters. Paul occasionally alludes to a letter received by him (I Cor. 7:1, etc.) in such a way as to allow some inference as to its contents. I Cor. 6:12; 8:1 are regarded by some as direct quotations; II Cor. 10 probably contains some direct quotations, perhaps twisted by Paul's irony.

There is no explicit quoting of one NT book by another, but there is considerable factual "quoting," if one may so designate the more exact of the duplications of Markan pericopes in Matthew and Luke, the use of Jude by II Peter, and the somewhat less apparent use of Colossians in Ephesians. Like the poetic enclaves of the OT, the NT has its hymnic enclaves, which, when recognized, aid the scholar to go a step behind the written document, which may not be literally quoting but only bringing hitherto unwritten hymnody to book. Various scholars see the following passages as belonging to this class: I Cor. 13; Eph. 5:14; Phil. 2:6-11; Col. 1:15-18; I Tim. 3:16; and the various fragments of heavenly liturgy scattered through Revelation. If tradition, though impersonal and unwritten, can rightly be said to be "quoted," this is twice explicitly done by Paul (I Cor. 11:23; 15:3) and implicitly often, especially in his parenetic passages; and it is constantly done in the five narrative books of the NT. K. GROBEL

THE OLD TESTAMENT

Genesis
Exodus
Leviticus
Numbers
Deuteronomy
Joshua
Judges
Ruth
I and II Samuel
I and II Kings
I and II Chronicles
Ezra
Nehemiah
Esther
Job
Psalms
Proverbs
Ecclesiastes
Song of Solomon
Isaiah
Jeremiah
Lamentations
Ezekiel
Daniel
Hosea
Joel
Amos
Obadiah
Jonah
Micah
Nahum
Habakkuk
Zephaniah
Haggai
Zechariah
Malachi

THE APOCRYPHA

I and II Esdras
Tobit
Judith
Additions to Esther
Wisdom of Solomon
Ecclesiasticus (Wisdom of Jesus the Son of Sirach)
Baruch
Letter of Jeremiah
Prayer of Azariah
Song of the Three Young Men
Susanna
Bel and the Dragon
Prayer of Manasseh
I and II Maccabees